TEACHER'S EDITION

Houghton
Mifflin
Harcourt

collections

GRADE 11

Program Consultants:

Kylene Beers

Martha Hougen

Carol Jago

William L. McBride

Erik Palmer

Lydia Stack

A&E   HISTORY   bio.

Cover, Title Page Photo Credits: © Michel Leynaud/Corbis

Printed in the U.S.A.

ISBN 978-0-544-08714-9

4 5 6 7 8 9 10   0868   22 21 20 19 18 17 16 15 14

4500467581   B C D E F G

Houghton
Mifflin
Harcourt

collections

Teacher's Edition Table of Contents

Kylene Beers Nationally known lecturer and author on reading and literacy; 2011 recipient of the Conference on English Leadership Exemplary Leader Award; coauthor of *Notice and Note: Strategies for Close Reading*; former president of the National Council of Teachers of English. Dr. Beers is the nationally known author of *When Kids Can't Read: What Teachers Can Do* and coeditor of *Adolescent Literacy: Turning Promise into Practice*, as well as articles in the *Journal of Adolescent and Adult Literacy*. Former editor of *Voices from the Middle*, she is the 2001 recipient of NCTE's Richard W. Halley Award, given for outstanding contributions to middle-school literacy. She recently served as Senior Reading Researcher at the Comer School Development Program at Yale University as well as Senior Reading Advisor to Secondary Schools for the Reading and Writing Project at Teachers College.

Martha Hougen National consultant, presenter, researcher, and author. Areas of expertise include differentiating instruction for students with learning difficulties, including those with learning disabilities and dyslexia; and teacher and leader preparation improvement. Dr. Hougen has taught at the middle school through graduate levels. Recently her focus has been on working with teacher educators to enhance teacher and leader preparation to better meet the needs of all students. Currently she is working with the University of Florida at the Collaboration for Effective Educator Development, Accountability, and Reform Center (CEEDAR Center) to improve the achievement of students with disabilities by reforming teacher and leader licensure, evaluation, and preparation. She has led similar efforts in Texas with the Higher Education Collaborative and the College & Career Readiness Initiative Faculty Collaboratives. In addition to peer-reviewed articles, curricular documents, and presentations, Dr. Hougen has published two college textbooks: *The Fundamentals of Literacy Assessment and Instruction Pre-K–6* (2012) and *The Fundamentals of Literacy Assessment and Instruction 6–12* (2014).

Carol Jago Teacher of English with 32 years of experience at Santa Monica High School in California; author and nationally known lecturer; and former president of the National Council of Teachers of English. Currently serves as Associate Director of the California Reading and Literature Project at UCLA. With expertise in standards assessment and secondary education, Ms. Jago is the author of numerous books on education, including *With Rigor for All* and *Papers, Papers, Papers*, and is active with the California Association of Teachers of English, editing its scholarly journal *California English* since 1996. Ms. Jago also served on the planning committee for the 2009 NAEP Framework and the 2011 NAEP Writing Framework.

William L. McBride Curriculum specialist. Dr. McBride is a nationally known speaker, educator, and author who now trains teachers in instructional methodologies. He is coauthor of *What's Happening?*, an innovative, high-interest text for middle-grade readers and author of *If They Can Argue Well, They Can Write Well*. A former reading specialist, English teacher, and social studies teacher, he holds a master's degree in reading and a doctorate in curriculum and instruction from the University of North Carolina at Chapel Hill. Dr. McBride has contributed to the development of textbook series in language arts, social studies, science, and vocabulary. He is also known for his novel *Entertaining an Elephant*, which tells the story of a veteran teacher who becomes reinspired with both his profession and his life.

Erik Palmer Veteran teacher and education consultant based in Denver, Colorado. Author of *Well Spoken: Teaching Speaking to All Students* and *Digitally Speaking: How to Improve Student Presentations*. His areas of focus include improving oral communication, promoting technology in classroom presentations, and updating instruction through the use of digital tools. He holds a bachelor's degree from Oberlin College and a master's degree in curriculum and instruction from the University of Colorado.

Lydia Stack Internationally known teacher educator and author. She is involved in a Stanford University project to support English Language Learners, *Understanding Language*. The goal of this project is to enrich academic content and language instruction for English Language Learners (ELLs) in grades K-12 by making explicit the language and literacy skills necessary to meet the Common Core State Standards (CCSS) and Next Generation Science Standards. Her teaching experience includes twenty-five years as an elementary and high school ESL teacher, and she is a past president of Teachers of English to Speakers of Other Languages (TESOL). Her awards include the TESOL James E. Alatis Award and the San Francisco STAR Teacher Award. Her publications include *On Our Way to English, Visions: Language, Literature, Content,* and *American Themes,* a literature anthology for high school students in the ACCESS program of the U.S. State Department's Office of English Language Programs.

Additional thanks to the following Program Reviewers:

Rosemary Asquino
Sylvia B. Bennett
Yvonne Bradley
Leslie Brown
Haley Carroll
Caitlin Chalmers
Emily Colley-King
Stacy Collins
Denise DeBonis
Courtney Dickerson
Sarah Easley
Phyllis J. Everette
Peter J. Foy Sr.

Carol M. Gibby
Angie Gill
Mary K. Goff
Saira Haas
Lisa M. Janeway
Robert V. Kidd Jr.
Kim Lilley
John C. Lowe
Taryn Curtis MacGee
Meredith S. Maddox
Cynthia Martin
Kelli M. McDonough
Megan Pankiewicz

Linda Beck Pieplow
Molly Pieplow
Mary-Sarah Proctor
Jessica A. Stith
Peter Swartley
Pamela Thomas
Linda A. Tobias
Rachel Ukleja
Lauren Vint
Heather Lynn York
Leigh Ann Zerr

FLEXIBILITY

Blended classroom?   Flipped?   Traditional approach?

Collections offers maximum **flexibility** for planning instruction.

Teacher Dashboard

Log onto the Teacher Dashboard and *my*SmartPlanner. Use these **versatile** and fully **searchable** tools to **customize** lessons that engage students and achieve your instructional goals.

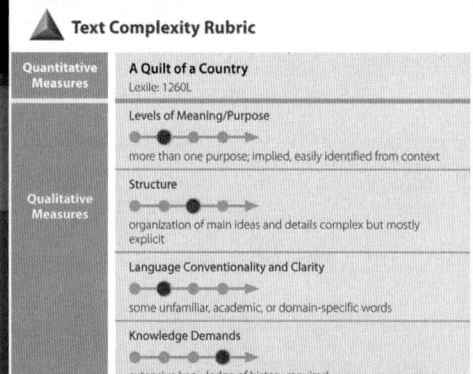

Text Complexity Rubric

Quantitative Measures	**A Quilt of a Country** Lexile: 1260L
Qualitative Measures	**Levels of Meaning/Purpose** more than one purpose; implied, easily identified from context
	Structure organization of main ideas and details complex but mostly explicit
	Language Conventionality and Clarity some unfamiliar, academic, or domain-specific words
	Knowledge Demands extensive knowledge of history required

Text Complexity Rubrics

help you identify dimensions of complex text.

COLLECTION 1 INSTRUCTIONAL OVERVIEW

PLAN

Collection 1 Lessons	Key Learning Objective	Performance Task	Vocabulary Strategy	Language and Style	Student Instructional Support	CLOSE READER Selection
ANCHOR TEXT EXEMPLAR Argument by Anna Quindlen "A Quilt of a Country," p. 3 A Lexile 1260L	The student will be able to... analyze and evaluate an author's claim and delineate and evaluate an argument	Writing Activity: Argument	Patterns of Word Changes	Noun Clauses	**Scaffolding for ELL Students:** Understand Cultural References **When Students Struggle:** Summarize	Blog by Eboo Patel "Making the Future Better, Together" p. 10b Lexile 1170L
ANCHOR TEXT Short Story by Nadine Gordimer "Once Upon a Time," p. 11 A Lexile 1390L	The student will be able to... analyze author's choices concerning text structure; determine and support inferences about the theme; and cite text evidence to support analysis of the text	Speaking Activity: Fairy Tale	Words from Latin	Prepositional Phrases	**Scaffolding for ELL Students:** Analyze Language **When Students Struggle:** • Theme • Words from Latin **To Challenge Students:** Write from Author's Perspective	Short Story by Lisa Fugard "Night Calls" p. 20b Lexile 1110L
Essay by Kimberly M. Blaeser "Rituals of Memory," p. 21A Lexile 1380L	The student will be able to... determine a central idea and analyze its development over the course of a text	Speaking Activity: Discussion	Denotations and Connotations		**Scaffolding for ELL Students:** Analyze Language **When Students Struggle:** Main Idea and Supporting Details	
EXEMPLAR Speech by Abraham Lincoln The Gettysburg Address, p. 27A Lexile 1170L	The student will be able to... analyze an author's purpose and the use of rhetorical devices in a seminal U.S. document	Speaking Activity: Presentation	Multiple-Meaning Words	Parallel Structure	**Scaffolding for ELL Students:** Analyze Language **When Students Struggle:** Comprehension **To Challenge Students:** Compare Speeches	Speech by Bill Clinton Oklahoma Bombing Memorial Address, p. 32b Lexile 1060L
Photo Essay "Views of the Wall," p. 33A Poem by Alberto Ríos "The Vietnam Wall" p. 33A	The student will be able to... analyze the representation of a subject in two different mediums	Media Activity: Reflection			**Scaffolding for ELL Students:** Build Background **When Students Struggle:** Compare Text and Photo	

COLLECTION 1 DIGITAL OVERVIEW

*my*SmartPlanner | eBook | *my*Notebook | *my*WriteSmart | fyi

For Systematic Coverage of and Speaking & Listening S

Collection 1 Lessons	Media	Teach and Practice		Assess	
Student Edition | eBook	Video Links	**Close Reading and Evidence Tracking**		**Performance Task**	Online Assessment
ANCHOR TEXT Argument by Anna Quindlen "A Quilt of a Country"	Audio "A Quilt of a Country"	**Close Read Screencasts** • Modeled Discussion 1 (lines 22–28) • Modeled Discussion 2 (lines 72–79) • Close Read application pdf (lines 94–103)	**Strategies for Annotation** • Delineate and Evaluate an Argument • Patterns of Word Change	Writing Activity: Argument	Selection Test
CLOSE READER Blog by Eboo Patel "Making the Future Better, Together"	Audio "Making the Future Better, Together"				
ANCHOR TEXT Short Story by Nadine Gordimer "Once Upon a Time"	Audio "Once Upon a Time"	**Close Read Screencasts** • Modeled Discussion 1 (lines 1–10) • Modeled Discussion 2 (lines 121–130) • Close Read application pdf (lines 181–188)	**Strategies for Annotation** • Analyze Author's Choices: Text Structure	Speaking Activity: Fairy Tale	Selection Test
CLOSE READER Short Story by Lisa Fugard "Night Calls"	Audio "Night Calls"				
Essay by Kimberly M. Blaeser "Rituals of Memory"	Audio from "Rituals of Memory"		**Strategies for Annotation** • Determine Central Idea • Denotation and Connotation	Speaking Activity: Discussion	Selection Test
Speech by Abraham Lincoln The Gettysburg Address	Video HISTORY® The Gettysburg Address: A New Declaration of Independence Audio The Gettysburg Address		**Strategies for Annotation** • Analyze Seminal U.S. Documents	Speaking Activity: Presentation	Selection Test
CLOSE READER Speech by Bill Clinton Oklahoma Bombing Memorial Address	Audio Oklahoma Bombing Memorial Address				
Photo Essay "Views of the Wall" Poem by Alberto Ríos "The Vietnam Wall"	Photo Essay "Views of the Wall" Video HISTORY® Remembering Fallen Friends Audio "The Vietnam Wall"		**Strategies for Annotation** • Analyze Representations in Different Mediums	Media Activity: Reflection	Selection Test
Collection 1 Performance Tasks: A Present a Speech B Write an Analytical Essay	fyi hmhfyi.com	**Interactive Lessons** A Writing Arguments A Giving a Presentation	B Writing Informative Texts B Using Textual Evidence	A Present a Speech B Write an Analytical Essay	Collection Test

Print planning

pages show the integrated Table of Contents and all assets in the **Student Edition** and the **Close Reader.**

ENGAGEMENT

Digital natives?   Media enthusiasts?   Writers?

Collections engages learners with today's digital tools.

Voices and images

from **A&E®, bio.®,** and **HISTORY®** transport students to different times and places.

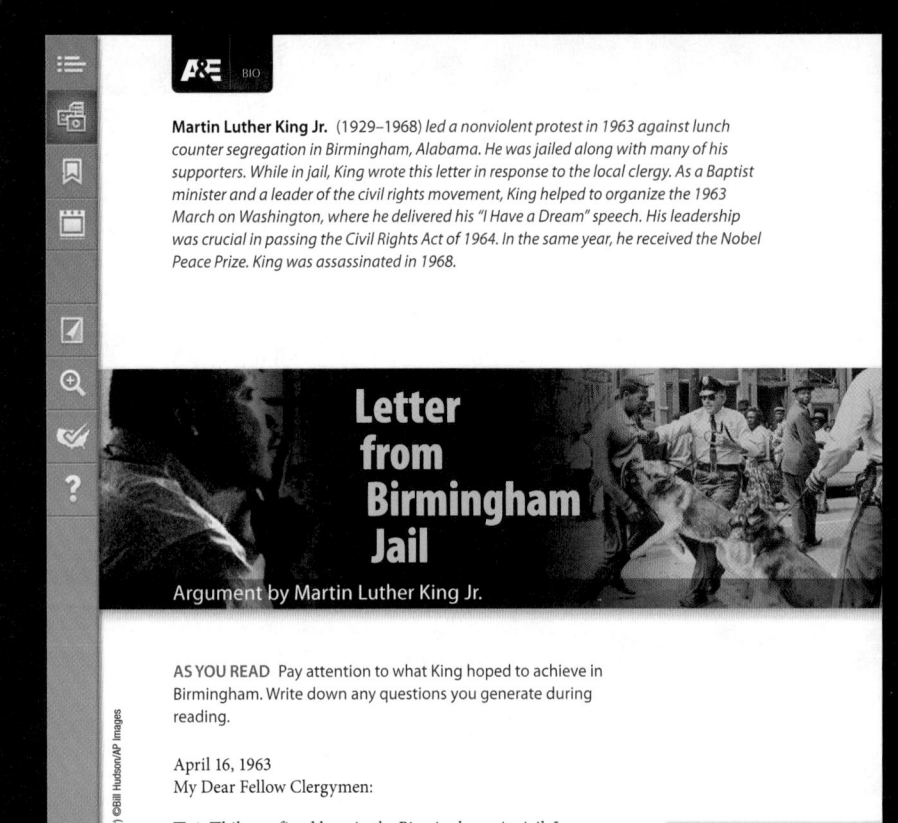

A&E | BIO

Martin Luther King Jr. (1929–1968) *led a nonviolent protest in 1963 against lunch counter segregation in Birmingham, Alabama. He was jailed along with many of his supporters. While in jail, King wrote this letter in response to the local clergy. As a Baptist minister and a leader of the civil rights movement, King helped to organize the 1963 March on Washington, where he delivered his "I Have a Dream" speech. His leadership was crucial in passing the Civil Rights Act of 1964. In the same year, he received the Nobel Peace Prize. King was assassinated in 1968.*

Letter from Birmingham Jail

Argument by Martin Luther King Jr.

AS YOU READ Pay attention to what King hoped to achieve in Birmingham. Write down any questions you generate during reading.

April 16, 1963
My Dear Fellow Clergymen:

While confined here in the Birmingham city jail, I came across your recent statement calling my present activities "unwise and untimely." Seldom do I pause to answer criticism of my work and ideas. If I sought to answer all the criticisms that cross my desk, my secretaries would have little time for anything other than such correspondence in the course of the day, and I would have no time for constructive work. But since I feel that you are men of genuine good will and that your criticisms are sincerely set forth, I want to try to answer your statement in what I hope will be patient and reasonable terms.

I think I should indicate why I am here in Birmingham, since you have been influenced by the view which argues against "outsiders coming in." I have the honor of serving as president of the Southern Christian Leadership Conference, an organization

Letter from Birmingham Jail **319**

Online Tools

allow students to annotate critical passages for discussion and writing, by using **highlighting, underlining,** and **notes.**

Student Note ✕

King characterizes his critics as "men of good-will" to suggest that an understanding can be reached with them.

✔ **Save to Notebook**   (Delete) (Save)

***my*Notebook**

stores students' annotations and notes for use in **Performance Tasks.**

*my*Notebook

King characterizes his critics as "men of good-will" to suggest that an understanding can be reached with them.

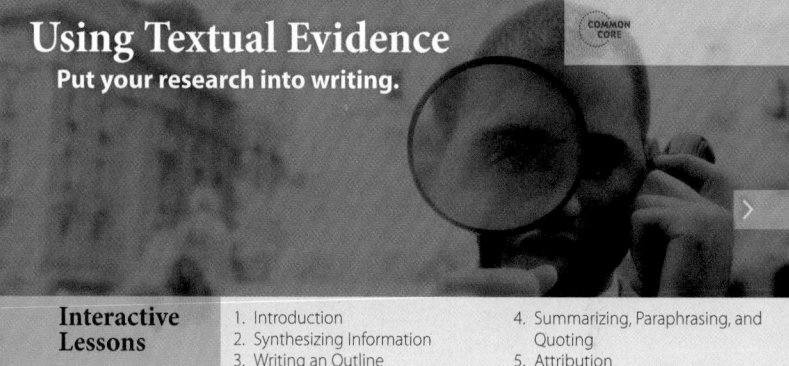

Using Textual Evidence
Put your research into writing.

COMMON CORE

Interactive Lessons

1. Introduction
2. Synthesizing Information
3. Writing an Outline
4. Summarizing, Paraphrasing, and Quoting
5. Attribution

Available in Your eBook

Informational text

on **fyi** is linked to each collection topic and is **curated** and **updated** monthly.

Digital Collections

for **writing, speaking,** and **listening** provide opportunities for in-depth instruction and practice in key 21st-century skills.

Available in Your eBook

Media Lessons

prompt students to read **news reports, literary adaptations, ads,** and **websites** as complex texts.

Close reading strategies?   Conversations about text?

Collections prepares students for rigorous expectations.

Background *The Hmong (hmông) are an ethnic group from southern China, Laos, Vietnam, and Thailand. In the 1970s, war and conflict caused many of the Hmong people in Laos to flee to refugee camps in Thailand. Author* **Kao Kalia Yang** *(b. 1980) was born in one of these camps. She moved with her family, including her older sister Dawb, to Minnesota in 1987. Four other siblings were born in the United States, where all the Yang children received their educations.*

from
The Latehomecomer

Memoir by Kao Kalia Yang

SETTING A PURPOSE As you read, notice the challenges and the opportunities that life in a new country presents Kao Kalia Yang and her family. How does Yang react to her situation?

We had been in America for almost ten years. I was nearly fifteen, and Dawb had just gotten her driver's license. The children were growing up. We needed a new home—the apartment was too small. There was hardly room to breathe when the scent of jasmine rice and fish steamed with ginger mingled heavily with the scent of freshly baked pepperoni pizza—Dawb's favorite food. We had been looking for a new house for nearly six months.

10   It was in a poor neighborhood with houses that were ready to collapse—wooden planks fallin[...] away, sloping porches—and huge, old tr[...] realty sign in the front yard, a small pat[...] of the white house. It was one story, wit[...] and a single wide window framed by bla[...] black door. There was a short driveway

Anchor Texts
drive each collection and have related selections in the **Close Reader.**

Close Reading Screencasts
provide **modeled conversations** about text at point of use in your **eBook.**

I was feeling a strong push to reinvent myself. Without my realizing, by the time high school began, I had a feeling in the pit of my stomach that I had been on simmer for too long. I wanted to bubble over the top and douse the confusing fire that burned in my belly. Or else I wanted to turn the stove off. I wanted to sit cool on the burners of life, lid on, and steady. I was ready for change, but there was so little in my life that I could adjust. So life took a blurry seat.

These images give the impression the narrator is uncomfortable.

(c) ©Houghton Mifflin Harcourt; (tr) ©Der Yang

Background *A member of the Standing Rock Sioux,* **Susan Power** *was born in 1961 and grew up in Chicago. She spent her childhood listening to her mother tell stories about their American Indian heritage. These stories later served as inspiration for Power's writing. As a young girl, Power made frequent visits with her mother to local museums—trips that inspired her memoir "Museum Indians."*

Museum Indians

Memoir by Susan Power

Close Reader

allows students to apply standards and practice close reading strategies in a consumable **print** or **digital** format.

CLOSE READ
Notes

1. **READ ▶** As you read lines 1–16, begin to cite text evidence.
   - Underline a metaphor in the first paragraph that describes the mother's braid.
   - Underline a metaphor in the second paragraph that describes the mother's braid differently.
   - In the margin, note the adjectives the narrator uses to describe the braid.

A snake coils in my mother's dresser drawer; it is thick and black, glossy as sequins. My mother cut her hair several years ago, before I was born, but she kept one heavy braid. It is the <u>three-foot snake</u> I lift from its nest and handle as if it were alive.

thick
black
glossy

"Mom, why did you cut your hair?" I ask. I am a little girl lifting a <u>sleek black river</u> into the light that streams through the kitchen window. Mom turns to me.

"It gave me headaches. Now put that away and wash your hands for lunch."

10 "You won't cut *my* hair, will you?" I'm sure this is a whim

"No, just a little trim now and then to even the e

I return the dark snake to its nest amon

arranging it so that its thin tail hide

© Houghton Mifflin Harcourt Publishing Company • Image Credits: ©Sophie Bassouls/Sygma/Corbis;
© Werner Forman/Universal Images Group/Getty Images

Image Credits: ©dboystudio/Shutterstock

SUCCESS

Collections scaffolds assessment demands in the classroom.

Performance Tasks
create opportunities for students to respond **analytically** and **creatively** to complex texts.

_my_WriteSmart
provides a **collaborative** tool to revise and edit **Performance Tasks** with peers and teachers.

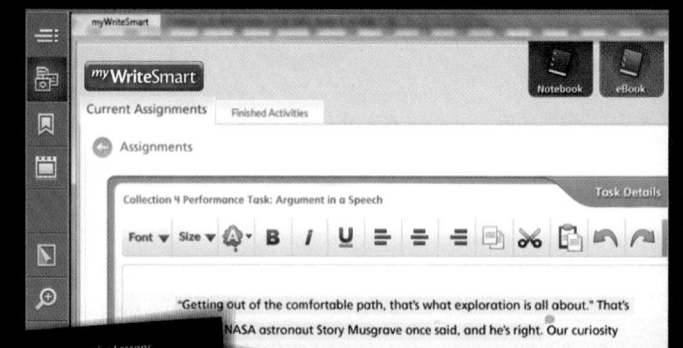

Common Core Assessment

print and **online** resources provide instruction in three steps: **Analyze the Model, Practice the Task,** and **Perform the Task.**

STEP 2 PRACTICE THE TASK

Should a business have the right to ban teenagers?

You will read:

▶ A NEWSPAPER AD
Munchy's Promise

▶ A BUSINESS ANALYSIS
Munchy's Patrons in July–October

▶ A STUDENT BLOG
Munchy's Bans Students!

▶ A NEWSPAPER EDITORIAL
A Smart Idea Can Save a Business

You will write:

▶ AN ARGUMENTATIVE ESSAY
Should a business have the right to ban teenagers?

Unit 1: Argumentative Essay **9**

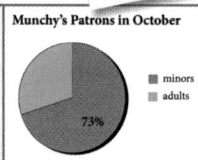

Mr. Jones,
Here is the analysis of
July vs. October data.
Your Accountant,
Hector Ramirez, CPA

Munchy's Patrons in October

- ■ minors
- ■ adults

73%

Monthly Sales

- ■ minors
- ■ adults

September   October

...hart.
...wn in the graph?
...wo forms of data.

Unit 1: Argumentative Essay **11**

...y studies on sleep deprivation have
...nly thing that might improve. An
...ositively affect a student's mood
...says that when he was in school,
...nd were better rested. With
...thers and students would get along

...agers should take affirmative
...otherwise adjust to the reality of
...m to research done in the 1990s,
...nd wake patterns in adolescents
...xperts talked, and California
...stened. She introduced House
... the "ZZZ's to A's Act," to
...earlier than 8:30 A.M.

...g again. It's 7:00 A.M. You say to
...d I've got plenty of time to get
...e a huge difference in your mood

You use an effective transition to create cohesion and signal the introduction of another reason. Your language is formal and non-combative. You remain focused on your purpose.

You anticipated and addressed an opposing claim that is likely to occur to your audience. Your answer to the opposing claim is well-supported with valid evidence.

Smooth flow from beginning to end. Clear conclusion restates your claim. Your evidence is convincing. Excellent use of conventions of English. Good job!

...ool should start later? If so, which data was the most

Unit 1: Argumentative Essay **7**

Graphics

enhance instruction, making **Common Core Assessment** unique and effective.

 **Common Core Enrichment App**

provides instant feedback for **close reading practice** with appeal for today's students.

COLLECTION 1
Coming to America

Collection Overviews

Each collection suggests different starting points and provides overviews of digital resources and instructional topics for selections.

COLLECTION PERFORMANCE TASK

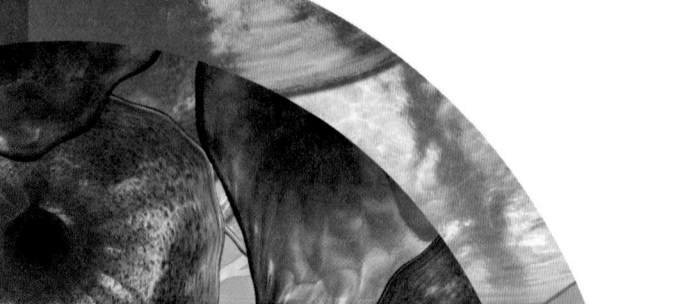

Image Credits: ©Dee Dee Yelverton/Flickr/Getty Images

Annotated Student Edition Table of Contents

Topical Organization

Each collection reflects an engaging topic that connects selections for discussion and analysis, so students can explore several dimensions of the topic.

COMMON CORE

COLLECTION **1**

Coming to America

Close Reader

KEY LEARNING OBJECTIVES
Cite text evidence.
Determine central ideas.
Determine themes.
Support inferences.
Determine meaning of words/phrases.
Analyze language.
Analyze story structure.
Understand point of view and irony.
Analyze and evaluate an argument.
Determine author's purpose.
Analyze drama interpretations.
Analyze foundational texts.

Image Credits: ©Dee Dee Yelverton/Flickr/Getty Images

eBook *Explore It!*

 Video Links  **eBook** *Read On!* Novel list and additional selections 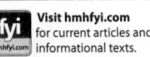 **Visit hmhfyi.com** for current articles and informational texts.

Common Core State Standards

Each collection addresses a range of **Common Core State Standards**, ensuring coverage of the Reading Literature and Reading Informational Texts standards.

Close Reader

The **Close Reader** provides selections related to the collection topic for additional practice and application of close reading skills and annotation strategies.

COLLECTION **2**
Building a Democracy

COLLECTION PERFORMANCE TASK

Student Edition + Close Reader

In each collection, the collection topic is explored in both the **Student Edition** and **Close Reader** selections. This page shows how the two components are integrated.

Image Credits: ©Volanthevist/Flickr/Getty Images

Annotated Student Edition Table of Contents

Anchor Texts

Complex and challenging, the anchor texts provide a cornerstone for exploring the collection topic, while also being integral to the Collection Performance Task.

Variety of Genres

Both the Student Edition and the Close Reader include a variety of genres of literary and informational texts and media.

COMMON CORE

COLLECTION 2

Building a Democracy

KEY LEARNING OBJECTIVES

Analyze and compare themes and topics.
Analyze ideas and sequence.
Analyze language.
Understand a key term.
Analyze style.
Analyze structure.

Analyze and evaluate an argument.
Analyze point of view.
Analyze a video.
Evaluate constitutional principles.
Analyze foundational documents.

Close Reader

Image Credits: ©Volanthevist/Flickr/Getty Images

eBook *Explore It!*

▶ Video Links

eBook *Read On!*
Novel list and additional selections

fyi Visit hmhfyi.com for current articles and informational texts.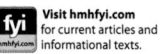

Collection Performance Tasks

One or two Collection Performance Tasks present a cumulative task in which students draw on their reading and analysis of the collection's selections, as well as additional research.

The Individual and Society

INTEGRATED PROGRAM CONTENTS

Focus on Authors

The **Student Edition** and the **Close Reader** complement one another by providing selections by a particular author.

Image Credits: ©Max Oppenheim/Stone/Getty Images

Annotated Student Edition Table of Contents

Compare Texts

To enrich the analysis and discussion of each text, students compare and contrast selections, exploring elements such as authors' choices, themes, and the structure of arguments.

COMMON CORE

COLLECTION **3**

The Individual and Society

KEY LEARNING OBJECTIVES
Cite text evidence.
Summarize.
Determine central ideas.
Determine themes.
Analyze ideas and events.
Analyze language.
Interpret symbols.
Analyze structure.
Analyze structure and mood.
Determine author's purpose.
Evaluate purpose and style.

Close Reader

eBook *Explore It!*

▶ **Video Links**

 **eBook** *Read On!* Novel list and additional selections

 **Visit hmhfyi.com** for current articles and informational texts.

Image Credits: ©Max Oppenheim/Stone/Getty Images

Complex Texts

With rich themes, distinctive language, stylistic elements, and high knowledge demands, complex texts from all genres challenge students to grow as readers and thinkers.

eBook

The eBook, both Student Edition and Teacher's Edition, is your entryway to a full complement of digital resources.

INTEGRATED PROGRAM CONTENTS

Informational Texts

Through a range of informational texts—including speeches, essays, and seminal United States documents—students analyze high-complexity texts.

Annotated Student Edition Table of Contents

Media Analysis
Lessons based on media provide opportunities for students to apply analysis and techniques of close reading to other kinds of texts.

COMMON CORE

KEY LEARNING OBJECTIVES
Cite text evidence.
Analyze ideas and events.
Analyze language.
Analyze structure.

Analyze author's point of view.
Analyze author's purpose.
Integrate and evaluate information.
Evaluate seminal texts.

Image Credits: ©Bettmann/Corbis

eBook *Explore It!*

▶ Video Links   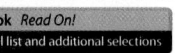 **eBook** *Read On!* Novel list and additional selections 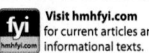 **Visit hmhfyi.com** for current articles and informational texts.

Digital Resources
From video links to additional selections and informational texts, a range of digital resources in the eBook complement and enrich students' reading.

Historical Background

In grade 11, each collection begins with a historical background and timeline to set a context for the selections in the collection.

COLLECTION PERFORMANCE TASK

Image Credits: ©Nick Norman/National Geographic/Getty Images

Annotated Student Edition Table of Contents

Compare Text and Media

To underscore that textual analysis applies to media as well as print, a rich variety of media is compared to other texts for close reading and analysis.

KEY LEARNING OBJECTIVES
Cite text evidence.
Analyze technical terms.
Interpret symbols.
Analyze structure.
Analyze author's choices.
Analyze irony and point of view.
Determine author's purpose.
Determine author's point of view.
Evaluate use of satire.
Integrate and evaluate information.

Image Credits: ©Nick Norman/National Geographic/Getty Images

eBook *Explore It!*

▶ Video Links  **eBook** *Read On!* Novel list and additional selections   **fyi** Visit hmhfyi.com for current articles and informational texts.

Text-Dependent Questions

Both the Student Edition and the Close Reader include text-dependent questions that require students to re-enter the text and cite text evidence to support their claims.

HISTORY® and A&E®

Adding the images and voices that make selections and historical periods come alive, these video assets are available at point of use in the eBook.

INTEGRATED PROGRAM CONTENTS

COLLECTION PERFORMANCE TASKS

Canonical and Contemporary Texts

From the great writers of the twentieth century to contemporary masters, students encounter a range of literature. Canonical texts help to provide a context for more recent selections.

Image Credits: ©Bek Shakirov/Images.com/Corbis

Annotated Student Edition Table of Contents

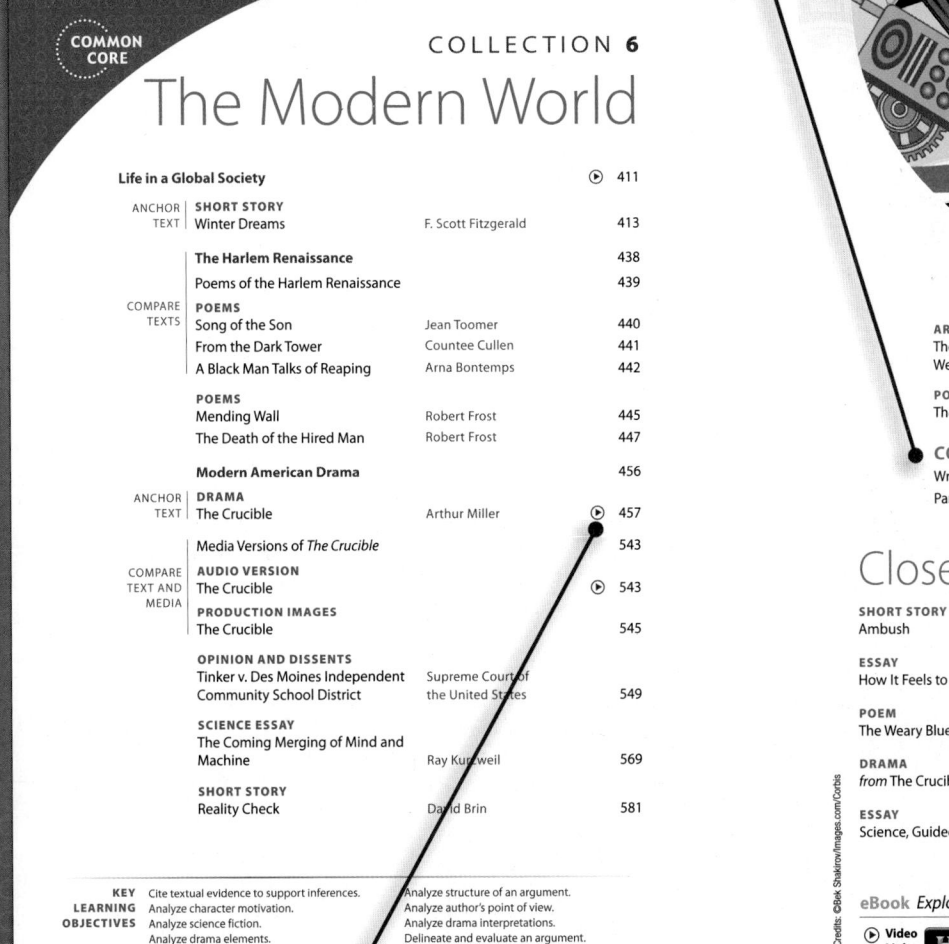

COMMON CORE

COLLECTION 6
The Modern World

KEY LEARNING OBJECTIVES
Cite textual evidence to support inferences.
Analyze character motivation.
Analyze science fiction.
Analyze drama elements.
Analyze language.
Analyze structure.
Analyze structure of an argument.
Analyze author's point of view.
Analyze drama interpretations.
Delineate and evaluate an argument.
Analyze foundational works.

eBook *Explore It!*

▶ **Video Links** | **eBook** *Read On!* Novel list and additional selections | **fyi** Visit hmhfyi.com for current articles and informational texts.

Image Credits: ©Bek Shakirov/Images.com/Corbis

Student Resources

Information, Please

When students have questions, they can turn to Student Resources for answers. This section includes information about performance tasks; the nature of argument; vocabulary and spelling; and grammar, usage, and mechanics.

Word Knowledge

The Glossaries provide definitions for selection, academic, and domain-specific vocabulary, conveniently compiled in a single location.

Connecting to Your World

Every time you read something, view something, write to someone, or react to what you've read or seen, you're participating in a world of ideas. You do this every day, inside the classroom and out. These skills will serve you not only at home and at school, but eventually (if you can think that far ahead!), in your career.

The digital tools in this program will tap into the skills you already use and help you sharpen those skills for the future.

Start your exploration at my.hrw.com

Start with the Dashboard

Get one-stop access to the complete digital program for *Collections,* as well as management and assessment tools.

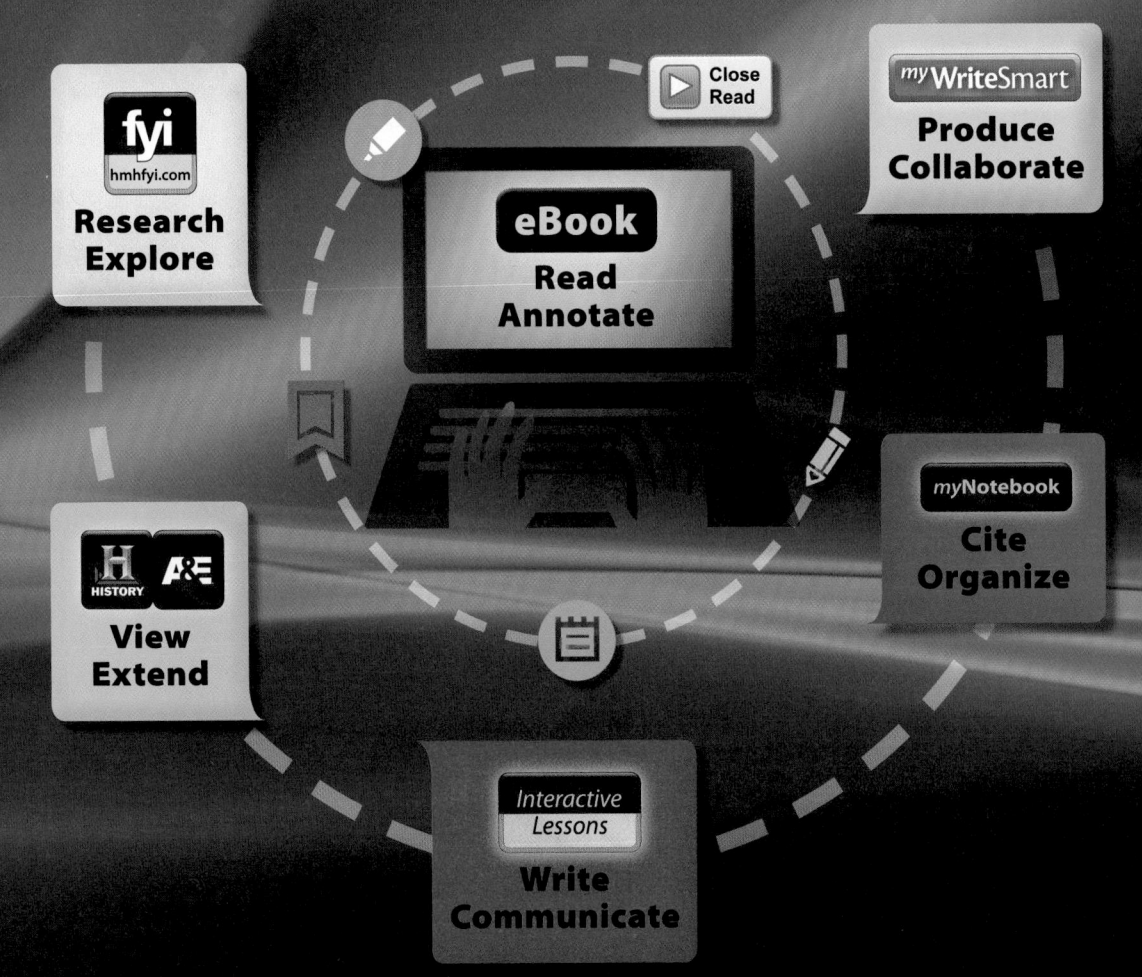

fyi
hmhfyi.com
**Research
Explore**

Close
Read

*my***WriteSmart**
**Produce
Collaborate**

eBook
**Read
Annotate**

*my*Notebook
**Cite
Organize**

HISTORY A&E
**View
Extend**

*Interactive
Lessons*
**Write
Communicate**

COMMON
CORE

DIGITAL COLLECTIONS

Writing and
Speaking & Listening

Comprehensive Standards Coverage

Twelve digital collections provide thorough coverage of all Writing and Speaking and Listening Common Core State Standards.

Communication in today's world requires quite a variety of skills. To express yourself and win people over, you have to be able to write for print, for online media, and for spoken presentations. To collaborate, you have to work with people who might be sitting right next to you or at the other end of an Internet connection.

Available Only in Your eBook

Interactive Lessons

The interactive lessons in these collections will help you master the skills needed to become an expert communicator.

What Does a Strong Argument Look Like?

Read this argument and answer the questions about how the writer states and supports his position.

Tip

Pitching Perfect Pitch
by José Alvarez

Did you know that when you are listening to your favorite vocalist, you might be hearing a computer-generated pitch? Many record companies use pitch-correction software to ensure that their performers are pitch-perfect. While perfectionism is an admirable goal, there is a fine line between using technology to enhance music and using it to make performers into something they're not. Whether recording in the studio or playing a live performance, musicians should not use pitch-correction software. ●

Music production has become a digital experience. Producers use software to cut and paste pieces of music together, just like you cut and paste words together in your word-processing software. ○ When editing these different things together digitally, slight imperfections can occur where the pieces are joined. Enter the correction software. What began as a method to streamline the digital editing process has turned into an almost industry-wide standard of altering a musician"s work. "Think of it like plastic surgery," says a Grammy-winning recording engineer.

What is the writer's position, or **claim**, on the use of pitch-correction software?

- ☐ Musicians should learn to live with their imperfections.
- ☑ Musicians should never use the software.
- ☐ Musicians should use the software to enhance live performances only.

xx   Grade 11

Writing Arguments
Master the art of proving your point.

COMMON CORE W 1, W 10

Interactive Lessons

1. Introduction
2. What Is a Claim?
3. Support: Reasons and Evidence
4. Building Effective Support
5. Creating a Coherent Argument
6. Persuasive Techniques
7. Formal Style
8. Concluding Your Argument

Student-Directed Lessons

Though primarily intended for individual student use, these interactive lessons also offer opportunities for whole-class and small-group instruction and practice.

Writing Informative Texts
Shed light on complex ideas and topics.

COMMON CORE W 2, W 10

Interactive Lessons

1. Introduction
2. Developing a Topic
3. Organizing Ideas
4. Introductions and Conclusions
5. Elaboration
6. Using Graphics and Multimedia
7. Precise Language and Vocabulary
8. Formal Style

Writing Narratives
A good storyteller can always capture an audience.

COMMON CORE W 3, W 10

Interactive Lessons

1. Introduction
2. Narrative Context
3. Point of View and Characters
4. Narrative Structure
5. Narrative Techniques
6. The Language of Narrative

DIGITAL COLLECTIONS

Teacher Support

Each collection in your teacher eBook includes

- support for English language learners and less-proficient writers
- instructional and management tips for every screen
- a rubric
- additional writing applications

Writing as a Process

COMMON CORE W 4, W 5, W 10

Get from the first twinkle of an idea to a sparkling final draft.

Interactive Lessons

1. Introduction
2. Task, Purpose, and Audience
3. Planning and Drafting
4. Revising and Editing
5. Trying a New Approach

Producing and Publishing with Technology

COMMON CORE W 6

Learn how to write for an online audience.

Interactive Lessons

1. Introduction
2. Writing for the Internet
3. Interacting with Your Online Audience
4. Using Technology to Collaborate

Conducting Research

COMMON CORE W 6, W 7, W 8

There's a world of information out there. How do you find it?

Interactive Lessons

1. Introduction
2. Starting Your Research
3. Types of Sources
4. Using the Library for Research
5. Conducting Field Research
6. Using the Internet for Research
7. Taking Notes
8. Refocusing Your Inquiry

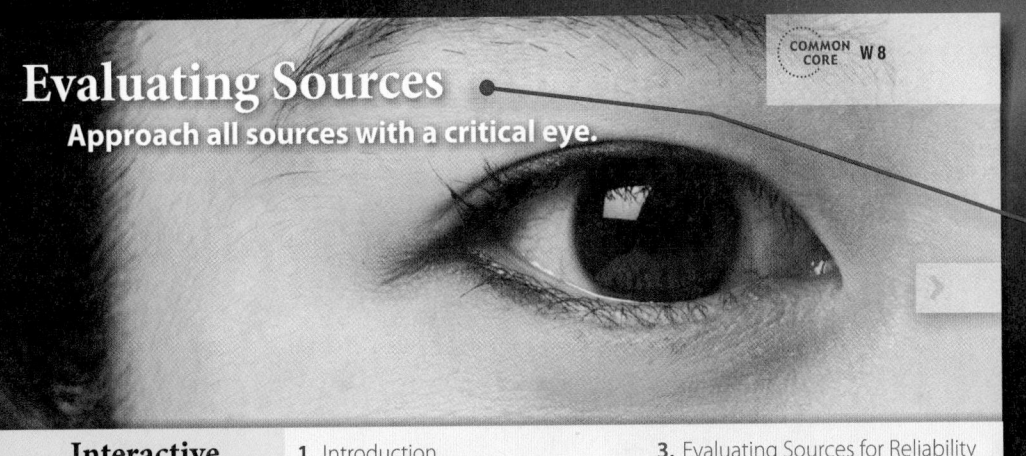

Evaluating Sources

Approach all sources with a critical eye.

COMMON CORE W 8

| Interactive Lessons | **1.** Introduction | **3.** Evaluating Sources for Reliability |
| | **2.** Evaluating Sources for Usefulness | |

Using Textual Evidence

Put your research into writing.

COMMON CORE W 7, W 8, W 9

Interactive Lessons	**1.** Introduction	**4.** Summarizing, Paraphrasing, and Quoting
	2. Synthesizing Information	**5.** Attribution
	3. Writing an Outline	

Participating in Collaborative Discussions

COMMON CORE SL 1

There's power in putting your heads together.

Interactive Lessons	**1.** Introduction	**4.** Speaking Constructively
	2. Preparing for Discussion	**5.** Listening and Responding
	3. Establishing and Following Procedure	**6.** Wrapping Up Your Discussion

Analyzing and Evaluating Presentations

COMMON CORE SL 2, SL 3, SL 6

Is there substance behind the style?

Interactive Lessons	**1.** Introduction	**4.** Tracing a Speaker's Argument
	2. Analyzing a Presentation	**5.** Rhetoric and Delivery
	3. Evaluating a Speaker's Reliability	**6.** Synthesizing Media Sources

Assessments in *my*WriteSmart

Test students' mastery of the standards covered in each digital collection by assigning the accompanying assessment in *my*WriteSmart.

Giving a Presentation

COMMON CORE SL 4, SL 6

Learn how to talk to a roomful of people.

Interactive Lessons	**1.** Introduction	**3.** The Content of Your Presentation
	2. Knowing Your Audience	**4.** Style in Presentation
		5. Delivering Your Presentation

Using Media in a Presentation

COMMON CORE SL 5

If a picture is worth a thousand words, just think what you can do with a video.

| **Interactive Lessons** | **1.** Introduction | **3.** Using Presentation Software |
| | **2.** Types of Media: Audio, Video, and Images | **4.** Practicing Your Presentation |

| eBook | *my*Notebook | fyi hmhfyi.com | *my*WriteSmart |

Supporting Close Reading, Research, and Writing

Understanding complex texts is hard work, even for experienced readers. It often takes multiple close readings to understand and write about an author's choices and meanings. The dynamic digital tools in this program will give you opportunities to learn and practice this critical skill of close reading—and help you integrate the text evidence you find into your writing.

Integrated Digital Suite

The digital resources and tools in *Collections* are designed to support students in grappling with complex text and formulating interpretations from text evidence.

▶ Close Read

Learn How to Do a Close Read

An effective close read is all about the details; you have to examine the language and ideas a writer includes. See how it's done by accessing the **Close Read Screencasts** in your eBook. Hear modeled conversations about anchor texts.

Close Read Screencasts

For each anchor text, students can access modeled conversations in which readers analyze and annotate key passages.

of the birds, how they soared and glided overhead. He pointed out the slow, graceful sweep of their wings as they beat the air steadily, without fluttering. Soon Icarus was sure that he, too, could fly and, raising his arms up and down, skirted over the white sand and even out over the waves, letting his feet touch the snowy foam as the water thundered and broke over the sharp rocks. Daedalus watched him proudly but

Soon Icarus was sure that he, too, could fly and, raising his arms up and down, skirted over the white sand and even out over the waves, letting his feet touch the snowy foam as the water thundered and broke over the sharp rocks.

There might be a sense of danger here.

Daedalus watched him proudly but with misgivings. He called Icarus to his side and, putting his arm round the boy's shoulders, said, 'Icarus, my son, we are about to make our flight. No human being has ever traveled through the air before, and I want you to listen carefully to my instructions.

Annotate the Texts

Practice close reading by utilizing the powerful annotation tools in your eBook. Mark up key ideas and observations using highlighters and sticky notes.

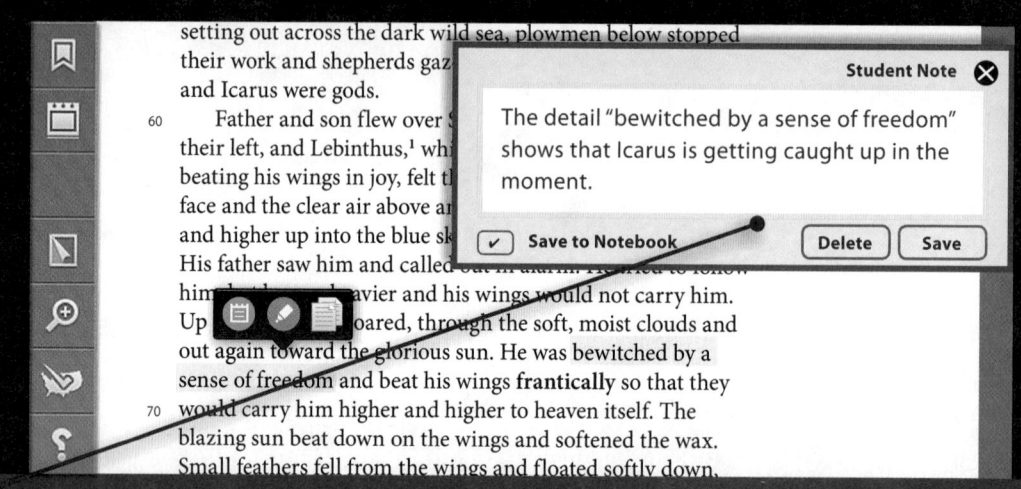

Digital Tools for Close Reading

Annotation tools allow students to note central ideas and details about an author's craft. Students can save their annotations to *my*Notebook, tagging them to particular performance tasks.

Collect Text Evidence

Save your annotations to your notebook. Gathering and organizing this text evidence will help you complete performance tasks and other writing assignments.

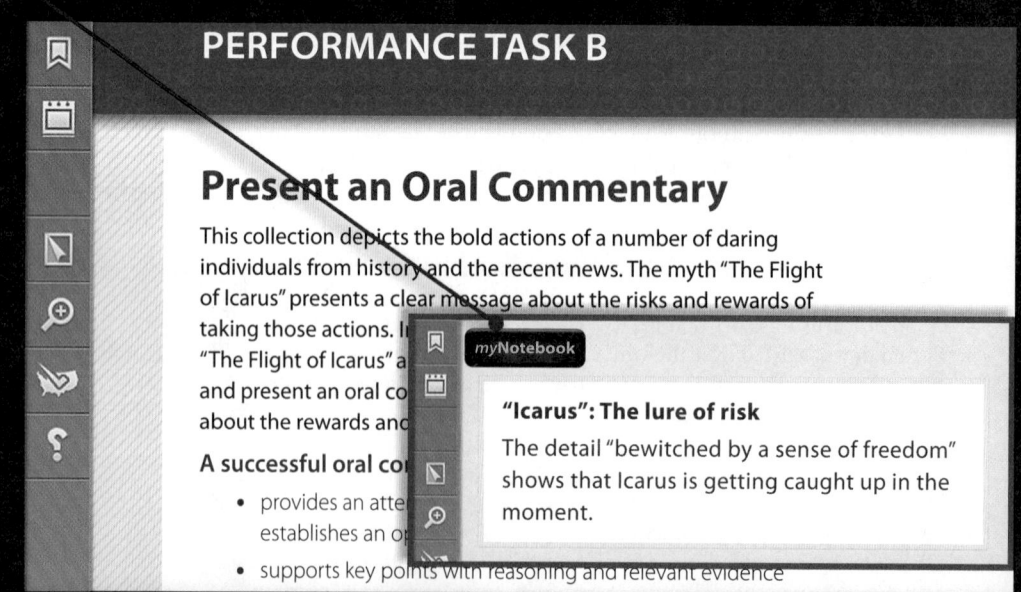

hmhfyi.com

Find More Text Evidence on the Web

Tap into the *FYI* website for links to high-interest informational texts about collection topics. Capture text evidence from any Web source by including it in your notebook.

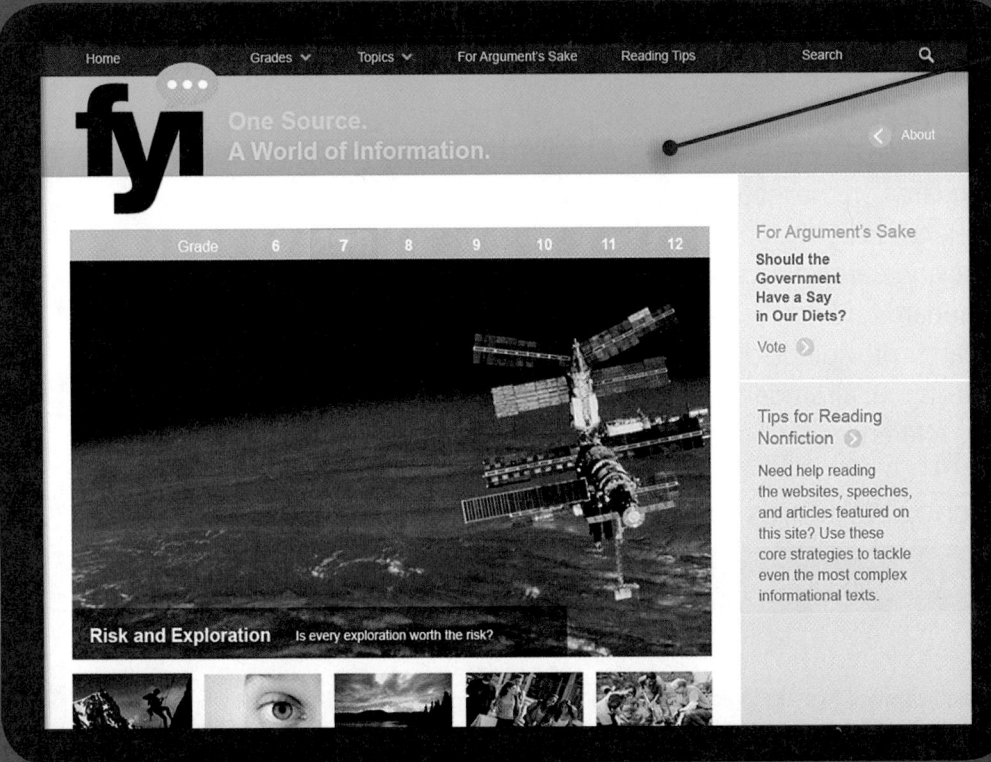

High-Interest Informational Text

Updated monthly, *FYI* features links to reputable sources of informational text.

myWriteSmart

Integrate Text Evidence into Your Writing

Use the evidence you've gathered to formulate interpretations, draw conclusions, and offer insights. Integrate the best of your text evidence into your writing.

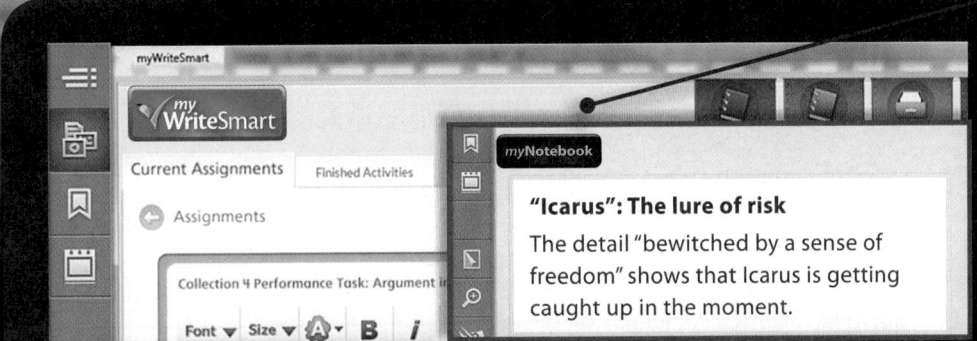

Tools for Writing

Assign and manage performance tasks in *my*WriteSmart. Students can use the annotations they've gathered and tools for writing and collaboration to complete each task.

COMMON CORE

Correlation of *Collections*, Grade 11, to the English Language Arts Common Core State Standards

The grades 11–12 standards on the following pages define what students should understand and be able to do by the end of each grade. They correspond by number to the College and Career Readiness (CCR) anchor standards below. The CCR and grade-specific standards are necessary complements—the former providing broad standards, the latter providing additional specificity—that together define the skills and understandings that all students must demonstrate. In the following pages, Teacher's Edition page references are boldfaced.

College and Career Readiness Anchor Standards for Reading

Common Core State Standards
KEY IDEAS AND DETAILS
1. Read closely to determine what the text says explicitly and to make logical inferences from it; cite specific textual evidence when writing or speaking to support conclusions drawn from the text.
2. Determine central ideas or themes of a text and analyze their development; summarize the key supporting details and ideas.
3. Analyze how and why individuals, events, and ideas develop and interact over the course of a text.
CRAFT AND STRUCTURE
4. Interpret words and phrases as they are used in a text, including determining technical, connotative, and figurative meanings, and analyze how specific word choices shape meaning or tone.
5. Analyze the structure of texts, including how specific sentences, paragraphs, and larger portions of the text (e.g., a section, chapter, scene, or stanza) relate to each other and the whole.
6. Assess how point of view or purpose shapes the content and style of a text.
INTEGRATION OF KNOWLEDGE AND IDEAS
7. Integrate and evaluate content presented in diverse formats and media, including visually and quantitatively as well as in words.
8. Delineate and evaluate the argument and specific claims in a text, including the validity of the reasoning as well as the relevance and sufficiency of the evidence.
9. Analyze how two or more texts address similar themes or topics in order to build knowledge or to compare the approaches the authors take.
RANGE OF READING AND LEVEL OF COMPLEXITY
10. Read and comprehend complex literary and informational texts independently and proficiently.

Reading Standards for Literature, Grades 11–12 Students

Standard	Where Taught

KEY IDEAS AND DETAILS

RL 1
Cite strong and thorough textual evidence to support analysis of what the text says explicitly as well as inferences drawn from the text, including determining where the text leaves matters uncertain.

INSTRUCTION
Student Edition/**Teacher's Edition:**
39, 40, 41, 42, 43, 44, 45, 46, 47, 48, 49, 50, 51, 52, 53, 54, 55, 56, 57, 58, 59, 60, 62, 64, 65, 67, 68, 69, **69, 70a,** 100, **100, 102a,** 159, 160, 161, **162,** 164, **164, 248a, 413, 414, 415, 416, 419, 420, 421, 424, 425, 426, 427,** 434, **434, 437a, 437b, 581, 582, 583,** 584, **584, 586a, 600b**

APPLICATION
Student Edition/**Teacher's Edition:**
37–68, **37–68, 70a,** 97–99, **97–99, 102a,** 152, **152,** 153, **153,** 155, **155,** 159–163, **159–163,** 178, **178,** 201, **201,** 203, **203, 248a,** 331, **331,** 332, **332,** 333, **333,** 334, **334,** 337, **337,** 338, **338,** 339, **339,** 340, **340,** 341, **341,** 413–433, **413–433, 437a, 437b,** 546, **546,** 581–583, **581–583, 586a, 600b**

Close Reader/**Teacher's Edition:**
19–20, **102b–102e,** 37–40, **186b–186e,** 73–82, **350b–350i,** 91–104, **400b–400k,** 105–108, **404b–404e,** 111–114, **437c–437f,** 121–122, **444b, 444f–444g,** 123–144, **542b–542o**

ASSESSMENT
Student Edition/**Teacher's Edition:**
70, **70,** 75, **75,** 76, **76,** 158, **158,** 165, **165,** 185, **185,** 205, **205,** 357, **357,** 372, **372,** 399, **399,** 404, **404,** 435, **435,** 526, **526,** 541, **541,** 548, **548,** 585, **585,** 600, **600,** 601–604, **601–604**

RL 2
Determine two or more themes or central ideas of text and analyze their development over the course of the text, including how they interact and build on one another to produce a complex account; provide an objective summary of the text.

INSTRUCTION
Student Edition/**Teacher's Edition:**
77, 78, 80, 81, 82, 84, **84, 86a,** 97, 98, 99, 100, **100,** 179, 180, 181, 183, 184, **184, 199, 200,** 203, 204, **204, 206a,** 234, **234,** 235, 236, 237, 239, 240, 242, 243, 244, 247, **247, 249, 250, 251, 252, 253, 254, 255, 256, 257, 258, 259, 260, 261, 262,** 263, **263, 266b, 318, 319,** 321, **321, 322b, 331, 332, 333, 334, 335, 336, 337, 338, 339, 340, 342, 343, 344, 345, 346,** 347, **347, 350a, 404a, 437b**

APPLICATION
Student Edition/**Teacher's Edition:**
77–83, **77–83, 86a,** 97–99, **97–99,** 152, **152,** 153, **153,** 154, **154,** 155, **155,** 177–183, **177–183,** 199–203, **199–203, 206a,** 235–246, **235–246,** 249–262, **249–262, 266b,** 317–320, **317–320, 322b,** 331–346, **331–346, 350a,** 395–397, **395–397, 404a,** 405–408, **405–408,** 413–433, **413–433,** 439–442, **439–442, 437b**

Close Reader/**Teacher's Edition:**
19–20, **102b–102e,** 37–40, **186b–186e,** 73–82, **350b–350i,** 91–104, **400b–400k**

ASSESSMENT
Student Edition/**Teacher's Edition:**
85, **85,** 101, **101,** 158, **158,** 185, **185,** 205, **205,** 247, **247,** 263, **263,** 266, **266,** 267–270, **267–270,** 322, **322,** 348, **348,** 357, **357,** 399, **399,** 435, **435,** 444, **444,** 541, **541,** 585, **585,** 600, **600**

CORRELATION

Standard	Where Taught
RL 3 Analyze the impact of the author's choices regarding how to develop and relate elements of a story or drama (e.g., where a story is set, how the action is ordered, how the characters are introduced and developed).	**INSTRUCTION** Student Edition/**Teacher's Edition:** **77, 79, 80, 81,** 84, **84, 249, 250, 251, 252, 253, 254, 255, 256, 257, 258, 259, 260, 261, 262,** 263, **263, 266b, 352, 354, 355,** 356, **356, 413, 414, 415, 416, 417, 418, 419, 421, 422, 423, 426, 429, 430, 431, 432, 433,** 434, **434, 437a, 456,** 456, **458, 459, 460, 461, 462, 463, 464, 465, 466, 467, 468, 469, 470, 471, 472, 473, 474, 475, 476, 477, 478, 479, 480, 481, 482, 483, 484, 485,** 486, **486, 487, 488, 489, 490, 491, 492, 493, 494, 495, 496, 497, 498, 499, 500, 501, 502, 503,** 504, **504, 505, 506, 507, 508, 509, 510, 511, 512, 513, 514, 515, 516, 517, 518, 519, 520, 521, 522, 523, 524, 525,** 526, **526, 527, 528, 529, 530, 531, 532, 533, 534, 535,** 540, **540, 542a, 581,** 584, **584, 586a** **APPLICATION** Student Edition/**Teacher's Edition:** 77–83, **77–83,** 181, **181,** 236, **236,** 238, **238,** 239, **239,** 240, **240,** 241, **241,** 243, **243,** 245, **245,** 246, **246,** 249–262, **249–262,** 336, **336,** 338, **338,** 339, **339,** 340, **340,** 341, **341,** 342, **342,** 344, **344,** 346, **346,** 351–355, **351–355,** 395–397, **395–397,** 413–433, **413–433,** 445–452, **445–452,** 457–539, **457–539, 542a,** 581–583, **581–583, 586a** Close Reader/**Teacher's Edition:** 73–82, **350b–350i,** 91–104, **400b–400k,** 111–114, **437c–437f,** 123–144, **542b–542o** **ASSESSMENT** Student Edition/**Teacher's Edition:** 76, **76,** 85, **85,** 101, **101, 178,** 247, **247,** 263, **263,** 266, **266,** 348, **348,** 357, **357,** 399, **399,** 435, **435,** 454, **454,** 504, **504,** 526, **526,** 541, **541,** 585, **585,** 601–604, **601–604,** 605–608, **605–608**
CRAFT AND STRUCTURE	
RL 4 Determine the meaning of words and phrases as they are used in the text, including figurative and connotative meanings; analyze the impact of specific word choices on meaning and tone, including words with multiple meanings or language that is particularly fresh, engaging, or beautiful. (Include Shakespeare as well as other authors.)	**INSTRUCTION** Student Edition/**Teacher's Edition:** **39, 40, 41, 42, 43, 44, 45, 46, 47, 49, 50, 53, 54, 55, 56, 57, 58, 59, 60, 61, 62, 63, 65, 66, 67, 69, 69, 70a, 97, 98, 99,** 100, **100, 158a, 200, 201, 202, 203,** 204, **204, 245, 318, 319,** 321, **321, 322b,** 350, **350, 352, 354, 355,** 356, **356, 401, 402, 403,** 404, **404, 427, 428,** 438, **438, 439, 440, 441, 442,** 443, **443, 444a, 446, 447, 448, 449, 450, 451, 452,** 453, **453, 455a, 582, 583, 597, 598,** 599, **599, 600a, 600b** **APPLICATION** Student Edition/**Teacher's Edition:** 37–68, **37–68, 70a,** 97–99, **97–99,** 152, **152,** 153, **153,** 156, **156, 158a,** 180, **180,** 182, **182,** 183, **183,** 199–203, **199–203, 322b,** 351–355, **351–355,** 401–403, **401–403,** 439–442, **439–442, 444a,** 445–452, **445–452, 455a,** 597–598, **597–598, 600a, 600b** Close Reader/**Teacher's Edition:** 19–20, **102b–102e,** 37–40, **186b–186e,** 105–108, **404b–404e,** 111–114, **437c–437f,** 121–122, **444b, 444f–444g** **ASSESSMENT** Student Edition/**Teacher's Edition:** 70, **70,** 76, **76,** 158, **158,** 185, **185,** 205, **205,** 322, **322,** 404, **404,** 444, **444,** 454, **454,** 541, **541,** 585, **585,** 600, **600**

Standard	Where Taught

RL 5
Analyze how an author's choices concerning how to structure specific parts of a text (e.g., the choice of where to begin or end a story, the choice to provide a comedic or tragic resolution) contribute to its overall structure and meaning as well as its aesthetic impact.

INSTRUCTION
Student Edition/**Teacher's Edition:**
43, 77, 79, 80, 81, 83, 84, **84, 155, 156, 159, 160, 161, 162, 163,** 164, **164, 166a, 178, 179, 180, 181, 182, 183,** 184, **184, 234, 234, 236, 238, 239, 240, 241, 243, 245, 246,** 247, **247, 248a, 249, 250, 251, 252, 253, 254, 255, 256, 257, 258, 259, 260, 261, 262,** 263, **263, 266b, 317, 318, 319, 320,** 321, **321, 322a, 331, 332, 333, 334, 335, 336, 337, 342, 343, 344, 345, 346,** 347, **347, 350a, 395, 400a, 401, 402, 403, 404, 404, 404a, 437a, 446, 447, 448, 449, 451, 452,** 453, **453, 455a,** 456, **456, 458, 459, 460, 461, 462, 463, 464, 465, 466, 467, 468, 469, 470, 471, 472, 473, 474, 475, 476, 477, 478, 479, 480, 481, 482, 483, 484, 485,** 486, **486, 487, 488, 489, 490, 491, 492, 493, 494, 495, 496, 497, 498, 499, 500, 501, 502, 503,** 504, **504, 505, 506, 507, 508, 509, 510, 511, 512, 513, 514, 515, 516, 517, 518, 519, 520, 521, 522, 523, 524, 525, 527, 528, 529, 530, 531, 532, 533, 534, 535,** 540, **540, 542a, 581, 586a, 600b**

APPLICATION
Student Edition/**Teacher's Edition:**
77–83, **77–83,** 159–163, **159–163, 166a,** 177–183, **177–183,** 235–246, **235–246, 248a,** 249–262, **249–262, 266b,** 317–320, **317–320, 322a,** 331–346, **331–346, 350a, 400a,** 401–403, **401–403, 404a,** 416, **416,** 417, **417,** 418, **418,** 420, **420,** 423, **423,** 426, **426,** 430, **430,** 431, **431, 437a,** 439–442, **439–442,** 445–452, **445–452, 455a,** 457–539, **457–539, 542a, 586a, 600b**

Close Reader/**Teacher's Edition:**
37–40, **186b–186e,** 73–82, **350b–350i,** 105–108, **404b–404e,** 121–122, **444b, 444f–444g**

ASSESSMENT
Student Edition/**Teacher's Edition:**
85, **85,** 101, **101,** 158, **158,** 165, **165,** 185, **185,** 247, **247,** 263, **263,** 266, **266,** 267–270, **267–270,** 322, **322,** 348, **348,** 372, **372,** 399, **399,** 404, **404,** 405–408, **405–408,** 444, **444,** 454, **454,** 486, **486,** 504, **504,** 526, **526,** 585, **585,** 600, **600,** 605–608, **605–608**

RL 6
Analyze a case in which grasping point of view requires distinguishing what is directly stated in a text from what is really meant (e.g., satire, sarcasm, irony, or understatement).

INSTRUCTION
Student Edition/**Teacher's Edition:**
82, 86a, 159, 161, 162, 163, 164, **164, 186a, 248a, 322a, 350a, 352, 353, 354,** 356, **356,** 372, **372, 395, 396, 397,** 398, **398, 400a**

APPLICATION
Student Edition/**Teacher's Edition:**
86a, 159–163, **159–163, 186a,** 201, **201, 248a, 322a,** 333, **333,** 334, **334,** 339, **339,** 351–355, **351–355, 350a,** 395–397, **395–397, 400a**

Close Reader/**Teacher's Edition:**
91–104, **400b–400k**

ASSESSMENT
Student Edition/**Teacher's Edition:**
85, **85,** 101, **101,** 165, **165,** 205, **205,** 357, **357,** 372, **372,** 399, **399,** 404, **404,** 541, **541,** 585, **585**

Standard	Where Taught
INTEGRATION OF KNOWLEGE AND IDEAS	
RL 7 Analyze multiple interpretations of a story, drama, or poem (e.g., recorded or live production of a play or recorded novel or poetry), evaluating how each version interprets the source text. (Include at least one play by Shakespeare as well as one play by an American dramatist.)	**INSTRUCTION** Student Edition/**Teacher's Edition:** **71**, 72, **72, 73, 74**, 75, **75, 76a, 543**, 544, **544, 545, 546**, 547, **547**, 548, **548, 548a** **APPLICATION** Student Edition/**Teacher's Edition:** 71, **71**, 73–74, **73–74, 76a**, 543, **543**, 545–546, **545–546, 548a** **ASSESSMENT** Student Edition/**Teacher's Edition:** 72, **72**, 75, **75**, 76, **76**, 544, **544**, 547, **547**, 548, **548**
RL 8 (Not applicable to literature)	N/A
RL 9 Demonstrate knowledge of eighteenth-, nineteenth- and early twentieth-century foundational works of American literature, including how two or more texts from the same period treat similar themes or topics.	**INSTRUCTION** Student Edition/**Teacher's Edition:** **152, 154, 155, 156**, 157, **157, 158a**, 234, **234**, 266, **266**, 438, **438, 439, 440, 441, 442**, 443, **443, 444a, 455a** **APPLICATION** Student Edition/**Teacher's Edition:** 151–156, **151–156, 158a**, 235–262, **235–263**, 439–442, **439–442, 444a, 455a** Close Reader/**Teacher's Edition:** 121–122, **444b, 444f–444g** **ASSESSMENT** Student Edition/**Teacher's Edition:** 158, **158**, 205, **205**, 266, **266**, 444, **444**
RANGE OF READING AND LEVEL OF TEXT COMPLEXITY	
RL 10 By the end of grade 11, read and comprehend literature, including stories, dramas, and poems, in the grades 11–CCR text complexity band proficiently, with scaffolding as needed at the high end of the range.	**INSTRUCTION/APPLICATION** Student Edition/**Teacher's Edition:** 37–68, **37A, 37–68**, 109–110, **109A, 109–110, 110a**, 175–176, **175A, 175–176**, 235–246, **235A, 235–246**, 277–278, **277A, 277–278**, 317–320, **317A, 317–320**, 329–330, **329A, 329–330**, 352–355, **352A, 352–355**, 411–412, **411A, 411–412**, 457–539, **457A, 457–539**, 597–598, **597A, 597–598** Close Reader/**Teacher's Edition:** 19–20, **102b–102e**, 37–40, **186b–186e**, 73–82, **350b–350i**, 105–108, **404b–404e**, 123–144, **542b–542o**

Reading Standards for Informational Text, Grades 11–12 Students

Standard	Where Taught
KEY IDEAS AND DETAILS	

RI 1
Cite strong and thorough textual evidence to support analysis of what the text says explicitly as well as inferences drawn from the text, including determining where the text leaves matters uncertain.

INSTRUCTION
Student Edition/**Teacher's Edition:**
4a, 16, 23, 24, 25, 26, 27, 28, 29, 30, 31, 32, **32, 35a, 130, 131, 132, 134,** 137, **137, 556, 557, 558, 561, 568a, 590, 592, 593, 596a**

APPLICATION
Student Edition/**Teacher's Edition:**
4a, 23–31, **23–31, 35a,** 129–136, **129–136,** 187, **187,** 188, **188,** 191, **191,** 289, **289,** 374, **374,** 376, **376,** 386, **386,** 390, **390,** 391, **391,** 392, **392,** 549–564, **549–564, 568a, 596a**

Close Reader/**Teacher's Edition**
3–10, **22b–22g,** 11–18, **96b–96g,** 23–26, **128b–128e,** 27–28, **140b–140e,** 29–34, **150b–150g,** 41–46, **220b–220g,** 47–54, **233c–233h,** 57–60, **284b–284e,** 61–64, **300b–300e,** 65–70, **314b–314g,** 83–90, **372b–372g,** 115–120, **444b–444f,** 145–150, **580b–580g**

ASSESSMENT
Student Edition/**Teacher's Edition:**
20, **20,** 33, **33,** 94, **94,** 118, **118,** 128, **128,** 138, **138,** 148, **148,** 196, **196,** 218, **218,** 231, **231,** 282, **282,** 299, **299,** 370, **370,** 372, **372,** 380, **380,** 566, **566**

RI 2
Determine two or more central ideas of a text and analyze their development over the course of the text, including how they interact and build on one another to provide a complex analysis; provide an objective summary of the text.

INSTRUCTION
Student Edition/**Teacher's Edition:**
3–4, **3–4, 5, 7, 8, 11, 12, 13, 17, 18,** 19, **19, 22a, 207, 210, 211, 212, 214, 216,** 217, **217, 220a,** 231, **231, 279, 280,** 281, **281, 284a, 294a, 372a, 374, 378,** 379, **379, 588, 589, 591, 592, 594, 594**

APPLICATION
Student Edition/**Teacher's Edition:**
5–18, **5–18, 22a,** 207–216, **207–216, 220a,** 279–280, **279–280, 284a, 294a, 372a,** 373–378, **373–378, 382a,** 386, **386,** 550, **550,** 587–593, **587–593**

Close Reader/**Teacher's Edition:**
3–10, **22b–22g,** 11–18, **96b–96g,** 27–28, **140b–140e,** 29–34, **150b–150g,** 41–46, **220b–220g,** 47–54, **233c–233h,** 57–60, **284b–284e,** 61–64, **300b–300e,** 83–90, **372b–372g,** 145–150, **580b–580g**

ASSESSMENT
Student Edition/**Teacher's Edition:**
20, **20,** 33, **33,** 94, **94,** 103–106, **103–106,** 218, **218,** 282, **282,** 323–326, **323–326,** 380, **380,** 594, **594**

Standard	Where Taught
RI 3 Analyze a complex set of ideas or sequence of events and explain how specific individuals, ideas, or events interact and develop over the course of the text.	**INSTRUCTION** Student Edition/**Teacher's Edition:** **141, 143, 144, 145,** 147, **147, 150a, 168a,** 175–176, **175–176, 187, 188, 190, 193,** 195, **195,** 230, **230, 233a,** 277–278, **277–278, 278a, 296, 300a, 301, 302, 303, 304, 305, 306, 307, 308, 309, 310,** 311, **311,** 329–330, **329–330,** 411–412, **411–412** **APPLICATION** Student Edition/**Teacher's Edition:** 141–146, **141–146, 150a, 168a,** 187–194, **187–194,** 221–229, **221–229, 233a, 278a,** 296, **296, 300a,** 301–310, **301–310** Close Reader/**Teacher's Edition:** 65–70, **314b–314g** **ASSESSMENT** Student Edition/**Teacher's Edition:** 148, **148,** 168, **168,** 196, **196,** 218, **218,** 231, **231,** 271–274, **271–274,** 312, **312,** 231, **231,** 316, **316,** 579, **579**
CRAFT AND STRUCTURE	
RI 4 Determine the meaning of words and phrases as they are used in a text, including figurative, connotative, and technical meanings; analyze how an author uses and refines the meaning of a key term or terms over the course of a text (e.g., how Madison defines *faction* in *Federalist* No. 10).	**INSTRUCTION** Student Edition/**Teacher's Edition:** **23, 25, 26, 27, 28, 29, 30,** 32, **32, 128a, 129, 130, 131, 133, 135,** 137, **137,** 175–176, **175–176, 287, 288, 289,** 291, **291, 294a, 301, 304, 306, 307, 359, 361, 362, 363, 364, 365, 366,** 369, **369, 374, 375, 376, 377, 382a,** 567, **567** **APPLICATION** Student Edition/**Teacher's Edition:** 5, **5,** 6, **6,** 8, **8,** 11, **11,** 14, **14,** 15, **15,** 16, **16,** 23–31, **23–31, 128a,** 129–136, **129–136,** 144, **144,** 146, **146,** 285–290, **285–290, 294a,** 301–310, **301–310,** 359–368, **359–368,** 373–378, **373–378, 382a,** 549–564, **549–564,** 569–577, **569–577** Close Reader/**Teacher's Edition:** 83–90, **372b–372g,** 115–120, **444b–444f** **ASSESSMENT** Student Edition/**Teacher's Edition:** 33, **33,** 94, **94,** 138, **138,** 292, **292,** 312, **312,** 370, **370,** 380, **380,** 566, **566,** 579, **579**

Standard	Where Taught

RI 5
Analyze and evaluate the effectiveness of the structure an author uses in his or her exposition or argument, including whether the structure makes points clear, convincing, and engaging.

INSTRUCTION
Student Edition/**Teacher's Edition:**
9, 19, **19, 87, 88, 89, 90, 91, 92**, 93, **93, 121, 122, 123, 124**, 125, **125, 141, 142, 143, 145**, 147, **147, 150a, 220a**, 230, **230, 233a, 284a, 588, 589, 591, 592**, 594, **594**, R16–R22

APPLICATION
Student Edition/**Teacher's Edition:**
5–18, **5–18**, 87–92, **87–92**, 121–124, **121–124**, 141–146, **141–146, 150a**, 187–194, **187–194, 220a, 233a, 284a**, 587–593, **587–593**, R16–R22, **R20, R21, R22**

Close Reader/**Teacher's Edition:**
11–18, **96b–96g**, 23–26, **128b–128e**, 47–54, **233c–233h**, 145–150, **580b–580g**

ASSESSMENT
Student Edition/**Teacher's Edition:**
20, **20**, 94, **94**, 103–106, **103–106**, 118, **118**, 126, **126**, 148, **148**, 169–172, **169–172**, 231, **231**, 271–274, **271–274**, 372, **372**, 394, **394**, 579, **579**, 594, **594**

RI 6
Determine an author's point of view or purpose in a text in which the rhetoric is particularly effective, analyzing how style and content contribute to the power, persuasiveness, or beauty of the text.

INSTRUCTION
Student Edition/**Teacher's Edition:**
7, 23, 24, 25, 26, 27, 28, 29, 30, 31, 32, **32, 35a, 87, 88, 89, 91, 92**, 93, **93, 96a, 112, 113, 115, 116**, 117, **117, 140a, 187, 189, 190, 192, 193, 194**, 195, **195, 198a, 207, 208, 209, 210, 211, 212, 213, 214, 215, 216**, 217, **217, 285, 286, 287, 288, 290**, 291, **291, 294a, 295, 296, 297**, 298, **298, 300a, 301, 302, 303, 304, 305, 306, 307, 308, 309, 310**, 311, **311, 314a, 316a, 359, 360, 361, 362, 363, 364, 365, 366, 367, 368, 369, 369**, 372, **372, 372a, 373, 374, 376, 378**, 379, **379, 382a, 384, 388, 569, 570, 571, 572, 573, 574, 575, 576, 577**, 578, **578, 580a, 587, 596a**, R16–R22

APPLICATION
Student Edition/**Teacher's Edition:**
7, **7**, 12, **12**, 14, **14**, 23–31, **23–31, 35a**, 87–92, **87–92, 96a**, 111–116, **111–116, 140a**, 187–194, **187–194, 198a**, 207–216, **207–216**, 285–290, **285–290, 294a**, 295–297, **295–297, 300a**, 301–310, **301–310, 314a, 316a**, 359–368, **359–368, 372a**, 373–378, **373–378, 382a**, 383–388, **383–388**, 569–577, **569–577, 580a, 596a**, R16–R22, **R17, R19, R20, R21, R22**

Close Reader/**Teacher's Edition:**
3–10, **22b–22g**, 11–18, **96b–96g**, 47–54, **233c–233h**, 61–64, **300b–300e**, 65–70, **314b–314g**, 83–90, **372b–372g**, 145–150, **580b–580g**

ASSESSMENT
Student Edition/**Teacher's Edition:**
33, **33**, 94, **94**, 118, **118**, 169–172, **169–172**, 196, **196**, 218, **218**, 292, **292**, 299, **299**, 312, **312**, 370, **370**, 372, **372**, 380, **380**, 394, **394**, 579, **579**, 594, **594**

Standard	Where Taught

INTEGRATION OF KNOWLEDGE AND IDEAS

RI 7
Integrate and evaluate multiple sources of information presented in different media or formats (e.g., visually, quantitatively) as well as in words in order to address a question or solve a problem.

INSTRUCTION
Student Edition/**Teacher's Edition:**
3–4, **3–4, 4a, 10,** 109–110, **109–110,** 175–176, **175–176,** 277–278, **277–278, 315,** 316, **316, 316a,** 329–330, **329–330, 383, 385, 386, 387, 389, 390, 391, 392,** 393, **393, 394a,** 411–412, **411–412**

APPLICATION
Student Edition/**Teacher's Edition:**
4a, 167, **167,** 315, **315, 316a,** 383–388, **383–388, 394a,** 572, **572**

ASSESSMENT
Student Edition/**Teacher's Edition:**
316, **316,** 394, **394**

RI 8
Delineate and evaluate the reasoning in seminal U.S. texts, including the application of constitutional principles and use of legal reasoning (e.g., in U.S. Supreme Court majority opinions and dissents) and the premises, purposes, and arguments in works of public advocacy (e.g., *The Federalist,* presidential addresses.)

INSTRUCTION
Student Edition/**Teacher's Edition:**
121, 122, 123, 124, 125, **125, 128a, 130, 131, 132, 133, 134, 135,** 137, **137, 140a, 279, 280,** 281, **281, 284a, 294a, 549, 550, 551, 552, 553, 554, 555, 556, 557, 558, 559, 560, 561, 562, 563, 564,** 565, **565, 568a**

APPLICATION
Student Edition/**Teacher's Edition:**
121–124, **121–124, 128a,** 129–136, **129–136, 140a,** 279–280, **279–280, 284a,** 285–290, **285–290,** 549–564, **549–564, 568a**

Close Reader/**Teacher's Edition:**
27–28, **140b–140e,** 57–60, **284b–284e**

ASSESSMENT
Student Edition/**Teacher's Edition:**
126, **126,** 138, **138,** 169–172, **169–172,** 282, **282,** 292, **292,** 323–326, **323–326,** 566, **566**

Standard	Where Taught
RI 9 Analyze seventeenth-, eighteenth-, and nineteenth-century foundational U.S. documents of historical and literary significance (including The Declaration of Independence, the Preamble to the Constitution, the Bill of Rights, and Lincoln's Second Inaugural Address) for their themes, purposes, and rhetorical features. ·	**INSTRUCTION** Student Edition/**Teacher's Edition:** 5, 7, 8, 11, 12, 13, 14, 15, 16, 18, 19, **19, 112, 113, 114, 115, 116,** 117, **117,** 120, **120, 121, 122, 123, 124,** 125, **125,** 127, **127,** 128, **128, 167,** 168, **168, 168a,** 277–278, **277–278, 278a, 279, 280,** 281, **281, 284a, 295, 296, 297,** 298, **298, 300a** **APPLICATION** Student Edition/**Teacher's Edition:** 5–18, **5–18,** 111–116, **111–116,** 121–124, **121–124,** 167, **167, 168a, 278a,** 279–280, **279–280, 284a,** 295–297, **295–297, 300a** Close Reader/**Teacher's Edition:** 3–10, **22b–22g,** 23–26, **128b–128e,** 57–60, **284b–284e** **ASSESSMENT** Student Edition/**Teacher's Edition:** 20, **20,** 103–106, **103–106,** 118, **118,** 126, **126,** 168, **168,** 169–172, **169–172,** 282, **282,** 299, **299,** 316, **316,** 323–326, **323–326**
RANGE OF READING AND LEVEL OF TEXT COMPLEXITY	
RI 10 By the end of grade 11, read and comprehend literary nonfiction in the grades 11–CCR text complexity band proficiently, with scaffolding as needed at the high end of the range.	**INSTRUCTION/APPLICATION** Student Edition/**Teacher's Edition:** 3–4, **3A, 3–4,** 5–18, **5A, 5–18,** 23–31, **23A, 23–31,** 34, **34,** 109–110, **109A, 109–110, 110a,** 129–136, **129A, 129–136,** 141–146, **141A, 141–146,** 175–176, **175A, 175–176,** 207–216, **207A, 207–216,** 277–278, **277A, 277–278,** 329–330, **329A, 329–330,** 359–368, **359A, 359–368,** 411–412, **411A, 411–412** Close Reader/**Teacher's Edition:** 3–10, **22b–22g,** 23–26, **128b–128e,** 27–28, **140b–140e,** 29–34, **150b–150g,** 61–64, **300b–300e,** 145–150, **580b–580g**

College and Career Readiness Anchor Standards for Writing

Common Core State Standards

TEXT TYPES AND PURPOSES

1. Write arguments to support claims in an analysis of substantive topics or texts, using valid reasoning and relevant and sufficient evidence.

2. Write informative/explanatory texts to examine and convey complex ideas and information clearly and accurately through the effective selection, organization, and analysis of content.

3. Write narratives to develop real or imagined experiences or events using effective technique, well-chosen details, and well-structured event sequences.

PRODUCTION AND DISTRIBUTION OF WRITING

4. Produce clear and coherent writing in which the development, organization, and style are appropriate to task, purpose, and audience.

5. Develop and strengthen writing as needed by planning, revising, editing, rewriting, or trying a new approach.

6. Use technology, including the Internet, to produce and publish writing and to interact and collaborate with others.

RESEARCH TO BUILD AND PRESENT KNOWLEDGE

7. Conduct short as well as more sustained research projects based on focused questions, demonstrating understanding of the subject under investigation.

8. Gather relevant information from multiple print and digital sources, assess the credibility and accuracy of each source, and integrate the information while avoiding plagiarism.

9. Draw evidence from literary or informational texts to support analysis, reflection, and research.

RANGE OF WRITING

10. Write routinely over extended time frames (time for research, reflection, and revision) and shorter time frames (a single sitting or a day or two) for a range of tasks, purposes, and audiences.

Writing Standards, Grades 11–12 Students

Standard	Where Taught
TEXT TYPES AND PURPOSES	

Standard	Where Taught
W 1 Write arguments to support claims in an analysis of substantive topics or texts, using valid reasoning and relevant and sufficient evidence.	**INSTRUCTION/APPLICATION** **Digital Collections/Lessons** Writing Arguments • Introduction • What Is a Claim? • Support: Reasons and Evidence • Building Effective Support • Creating a Coherent Argument • Persuasive Techniques • Formal Style • Concluding Your Argument Student Edition/**Teacher's Edition:** 103–106, **103–106, 158a, 198a,** 271–274, **271–274,** 323–326, **323–326, 600a,** 601–604, **601–604,** R2–R3 **ASSESSMENT** Student Edition/**Teacher's Edition:** 103–106, **103–106,** 271–274, **271–274,** 323–326, **323–326,** 601–604, **601–604**
a. Introduce precise, knowledgeable claim(s), establish the significance of the claim(s), distinguish the claim(s) from alternate or opposing claims, and create an organization that logically sequences claim(s), counterclaims, reasons, and evidence.	**INSTRUCTION/APPLICATION** **Digital Collections/Lessons:** Writing Arguments • What Is a Claim? • Creating a Coherent Argument Student Edition/**Teacher's Edition** 103–106, **103–106,** 323–326, **323–326,** 601–604, **601–604,** R2–R3 **ASSESSMENT** Student Edition/**Teacher's Edition:** 103–106, **103–106,** 323–326, **323–326,** 601–604, **601–604**
b. Develop claim(s) and counterclaims fairly and thoroughly, supplying the most relevant evidence for each while pointing out the strengths and limitations of both in a manner that anticipates the audience's knowledge level, concerns, values, and possible biases.	**INSTRUCTION/APPLICATION** **Digital Collections/Lessons:** Writing Arguments • Support: Reasons and Evidence • Building Effective Support Student Edition/**Teacher's Edition:** 103–106, **103–106,** 323–326, **323–326,** 601–604, **601–604,** R2–R3 **ASSESSMENT** Student Edition/**Teacher's Edition:** 103–106, **103–106,** 323–326, **323–326,** 601–604, **601–604**

Standard	Where Taught
c. Use words, phrases, and clauses as well as varied syntax to link the major sections of the text, create cohesion, and clarify the relationships between claim(s) and reasons, between reasons and evidence, and between claim(s) and counterclaims.	**INSTRUCTION/APPLICATION** **Digital Collections/Lessons:** Writing Arguments • Creating a Coherent Argument Student Edition/**Teacher's Edition:** 103–106, **103–106,** 323–326, **323–326,** 601–604, **601–604,** R2–R3 **ASSESSMENT** Student Edition/**Teacher's Edition:** 103–106, **103–106,** 323–326, **323–326,** 601–604, **601–604**
d. Establish and maintain a formal style and objective tone while attending to the norms and conventions of the discipline in which they are writing.	**INSTRUCTION/APPLICATION** **Digital Collections/Lessons:** Writing Arguments • Formal Style Student Edition/**Teacher's Edition:** 103–106, **103–106,** 323–326, **323–326,** 601–604, **601–604,** R2–R3 **ASSESSMENT** Student Edition/**Teacher's Edition:** 20, **20,** 103–106, **103–106,** 323–326, **323–326,** 601–604, **601–604**
e. Provide a concluding statement or section that follows from and supports the argument presented.	**INSTRUCTION/APPLICATION** **Digital Collections/Lessons:** Writing Arguments • Concluding Your Argument Student Edition/**Teacher's Edition:** 103–106, **103–106,** 323–326, **323–326,** 601–604, **601–604,** R2–R3 **ASSESSMENT** Student Edition/**Teacher's Edition:** 103–106, **103–106,** 323–326, **323–326,** 601–604, **601–604**

Standard	Where Taught
W 2 Write informative/explanatory texts to examine and convey complex ideas, concepts, and information clearly and accurately through the effective selection, organization, and analysis of content.	**INSTRUCTION/APPLICATION** **Digital Collections/Lessons:** Writing Informative Texts • Introduction • Developing a Topic • Organizing Ideas • Introductions and Conclusions • Elaboration • Using Graphics and Multimedia • Precise Language and Vocabulary • Formal Style Using Textual Evidence • Writing an Outline Student Edition/**Teacher's Edition:** 169–172, **169–172**, 271–274, **271–274**, 357, **357**, 405–408, **405–408**, 542a, 568a, R4–R5, R8–R11 **ASSESSMENT** Student Edition/**Teacher's Edition:** 70, **70**, 128, **128**, 148, **148**, 169–172, **169–172**, 218, **218**, 231, **231**, 271–274, **271–274**, 299, **299**, 357, **357**, 394, **394**, 405–408, **405–408**, 526, **526**, 541, **541**
a. Introduce a topic; organize complex ideas, concepts, and information so that each new element builds on that which precedes it to create a unified whole; include formatting (e.g., headings), graphics (e.g., figures, tables), and multimedia when useful to aiding comprehension.	**INSTRUCTION/APPLICATION** **Digital Collections/Lessons:** Writing Informative Texts • Developing a Topic • Organizing Ideas • Introductions and Conclusions • Using Graphics and Multimedia Student Edition/**Teacher's Edition:** 169–172, **169–172**, 405–408, **405–408**, 596a, R4–R5, R8–R11 **ASSESSMENT** Student Edition/**Teacher's Edition:** 126, **126**, 169–172, **169–172**, 405–408, **405–408**
b. Develop the topic thoroughly by selecting the most significant and relevant facts, extended definitions, concrete details, quotations, or other information and examples appropriate to the audience's knowledge of the topic.	**INSTRUCTION/APPLICATION** **Digital Collections/Lessons:** Writing Informative Texts • Elaboration Student Edition/**Teacher's Edition:** 169–172, **169–172**, 322, **322**, 405–408, **405–408**, 596b, R4–R5, R8–R11 **ASSESSMENT** Student Edition/**Teacher's Edition:** 70, **70**, 72, **72**, 94, **94**, 126, **126**, 169–172, **169–172**, 322, **322**, 405–408, **405–408**, 594, **594**, 596, **596**

Standard	Where Taught
c. Use appropriate and varied transitions and syntax to link the major sections of the text, create cohesion, and clarify the relationships among complex ideas and concepts.	**INSTRUCTION/APPLICATION** **Digital Collections/Lessons:** Writing Informative Texts • Organizing Ideas Student Edition/**Teacher's Edition:** 169–172, **169–172,** 405–408, **405–408,** R4–5, R8–R11 **ASSESSMENT** Student Edition/**Teacher's Edition:** 169–172, **169–172,** 405–408, **405–408**
d. Use precise language, domain-specific vocabulary, and techniques such as metaphor, simile, and analogy to manage the complexity of the topic.	**INSTRUCTION/APPLICATION** **Digital Collections/Lessons:** Writing Informative Texts • Precise Language and Vocabulary Student Edition/**Teacher's Edition:** 169–172, **169–172,** 405–408, **405–408,** R4–R5, R8–R11 **ASSESSMENT** Student Edition/**Teacher's Edition:** 169–172, **169–172,** 405–408, **405–408**
e. Establish and maintain a formal style and objective tone while attending to the norms and conventions of the discipline in which they are writing.	**INSTRUCTION/APPLICATION** **Digital Collections/Lessons:** Writing Informative Texts • Formal Style Student Edition/**Teacher's Edition:** 169–172, **169–172,** 405–408, **405–408,** R4–R5, R8–R11 **ASSESSMENT** Student Edition/**Teacher's Edition:** 169–172, **169–172,** 405–408, **405–408**
f. Provide a concluding statement or section that follows from and supports the information or explanation presented (e.g., articulating implications or the significance of the topic).	**INSTRUCTION/APPLICATION** **Digital Collections/Lessons:** Writing Informative Texts • Introductions and Conclusions Student Edition/**Teacher's Edition:** 169–172, **169–172,** 405–408, **405–408,** R4–R5, R8–R11 **ASSESSMENT** Student Edition/**Teacher's Edition:** 169–172, **169–172,** 405–408, **405–408**

Standard	Where Taught
W 3 Write narratives to develop real or imagined experiences or events using effective technique, well-chosen details, and well-structured event sequences.	**INSTRUCTION/APPLICATION** **Digital Collections/Lessons:** Writing Narratives • Introductions • Narrative Context • Point of View and Characters • Narrative Structure • Narrative Techniques • The Language of Narrative Student Edition/**Teacher's Edition:** **266a,** 267–270, **267–270,** R6–R7 **ASSESSMENT** Student Edition/**Teacher's Edition:** 267–270, **267–270,** 348, **348,** 370, **370**
a. Engage and orient the reader by setting out a problem, situation, or observation and its significance, establishing one or multiple point(s) of view, and introducing a narrator and/or characters; create a smooth progression of experiences or events.	**INSTRUCTION/APPLICATION** **Digital Collections/Lessons:** Writing Narratives • Narrative Context • Point of View and Characters • Narrative Structure Student Edition/**Teacher's Edition:** 267–270, **267–270,** R6–R7 **ASSESSMENT** Student Edition/**Teacher's Edition:** 267–270, **267–270,** 435, **435**
b. Use narrative techniques, such as dialogue, pacing, description, reflection, and multiple plot lines, to develop experiences, events, and/or characters.	**INSTRUCTION/APPLICATION** **Digital Collections/Lessons:** Writing Narratives • Narrative Structure • Narrative Techniques • The Language of Narrative Student Edition/**Teacher's Edition:** 267–270, **267–270,** R6–R7 **ASSESSMENT** Student Edition/**Teacher's Edition:** 267–270, **267–270**

Standard	Where Taught
c. Use a variety of techniques to sequence events so that they build on one another to create a coherent whole and build toward a particular tone and outcome (e.g., a sense of mystery, suspense, growth, or resolution).	**INSTRUCTION/APPLICATION** **Digital Collections/Lessons:** Writing Narratives • The Language of Narrative Student Edition/**Teacher's Edition:** 267–270, **267–270,** R6–R7 **ASSESSMENT** Student Edition/**Teacher's Edition:** 20, **20,** 267–270, **267–270**
d. Use precise words and phrases, telling details, and sensory language to convey a vivid picture of the experiences, events, setting, and/or characters.	**INSTRUCTION/APPLICATION** **Digital Collections/Lessons:** Writing Narratives • The Language of Narrative Student Edition/**Teacher's Edition:** 267–270, **267–270,** R6–R7 **ASSESSMENT** Student Edition/**Teacher's Edition:** 20, **20,** 267–270, **267–270,** 404, **404**
e. Provide a conclusion that follows from and reflects on what is experienced, observed, or resolved over the course of the narrative.	**INSTRUCTION/APPLICATION** **Digital Collections/Lessons:** Writing Narratives • Narrative Structure Student Edition/**Teacher's Edition:** 267–270, **267–270,** R6–R7 **ASSESSMENT** Student Edition/**Teacher's Edition:** 267–270, **267–270,** 437, **437**

Standard	Where Taught

PRODUCTION AND DISTRIBUTION OF WRITING

W 4
Produce clear and coherent writing in which the development, organization, and style are appropriate to task, purpose, and audience. (Grade-specific expectations for writing types are defined in Standards 1–3 above.)

INSTRUCTION/APPLICATION
Digital Collections/Lessons:
Writing as a Process
- Task, Purpose, and Audience

Student Edition/**Teacher's Edition:**
169–172, **169–172,** 267–270, **267–270,** 357, **357,** 601–604, **601–604**

ASSESSMENT
Student Edition/**Teacher's Edition:**
72, **72,** 75, **75,** 169–172, **169–172,** 205, **205,** 267–270, **267–270,** 292, **292,** 357, **357,** 370, **370,** 526, **526,** 541, **541,** 547, **547,** 548, **548,** 601–604, **601–604**

W 5
Develop and strengthen writing as needed by planning, revising, editing, rewriting, or trying a new approach, focusing on addressing what is most significant for a specific purpose and audience. (Editing for conventions should demonstrate command of Language standards 1–3 up to and including grades 11–12.)

INSTRUCTION/APPLICATION
Digital Collections/Lessons:
Writing as a Process
- Introduction
- Task, Purpose, and Audience
- Planning and Drafting
- Revising and Editing
- Trying a New Approach

Student Edition/**Teacher's Edition:**
267–270, **267–270,** 601–604, **601–604**

ASSESSMENT
Student Edition/**Teacher's Edition:**
166, **166,** 267–270, **267–270,** 348, **348,** 601–604, **601–604**

W 6
Use technology, including the Internet, to produce, publish, and update individual or shared writing products in response to ongoing feedback, including new arguments or information.

INSTRUCTION/APPLICATION
Digital Collections/Lessons:
Producing and Publishing with Technology
- Introduction
- Writing for the Internet
- Interacting with Your Online Audience
- Using Technology to Collaborate

Student Edition/**Teacher's Edition:**
169–172, **169–172,** 267–270, **267–270,** 271–274, **271–274,** 323–326, **323–326,** 405–408, **405–408,** 601–604, **601–604,** 605–608, **605–608**

ASSESSMENT
Student Edition/**Teacher's Edition:**
168, **168,** 169–172, **169–172,** 267–270, **267–270,** 271–274, **271–274,** 323–326, **323–326,** 405–408, **405–408,** 601–604, **601–604,** 605–608, **605–608**

CORRELATION

Standard	Where Taught

RESEARCH TO BUILD AND PRESENT KNOWLEDGE

W 7
Conduct short as well as more sustained research projects to answer a question (including a self-generated question) or solve a problem; narrow or broaden the inquiry when appropriate; synthesize multiple sources on the subject, demonstrating understanding of the subject under investigation.

INSTRUCTION/APPLICATION
Digital Collections/Lessons:
Conducting Research
- Introduction
- Starting Your Research
- Refocusing Your Inquiry

Using Textual Evidence
- Synthesizing Information

Student Edition/**Teacher's Edition:**
102a, 166a, 233a, 266a, 322b, 394a, 542a, 568a, 601–604, **601–604,** R8–R11

ASSESSMENT
Student Edition/**Teacher's Edition:**
126, **126,** 165, **165,** 231, **231,** 312, **312,** 394, **394,** 504, **504,** 579, **579,** 594, **594,** 601–604, **601–604**

W 8
Gather relevant information from multiple authoritative print and digital sources, using advanced searches effectively; assess the strengths and limitations of each source in terms of the task, purpose, and audience; integrate information into the text selectively to maintain the flow of ideas, avoiding plagiarism and overreliance on any one source and following a standard format for citation.

INSTRUCTION/APPLICATION
Digital Collections/Lessons:
Conducting Research
- Types of Sources
- Using the Library for Research
- Using the Internet for Research

Evaluating Sources
- Introduction
- Evaluating Sources for Usefulness
- Evaluating Sources for Reliability

Using Textual Evidence
- Summarizing, Paraphrasing, and Quoting
- Attribution

Student Edition/**Teacher's Edition:**
266a, 314a, 322b, 394a, 542a, 601–604, **601–604,** R8–R11

ASSESSMENT
Student Edition/**Teacher's Edition:**
126, **126,** 394, **394,** 504, **504,** 579, **579,** 601–604, **601–604**

Standard	Where Taught
W 9 Draw evidence from literary or informational texts to support analysis, reflection, and research.	**INSTRUCTION/APPLICATION** **Digital Collections/Lessons:** Writing Informative Texts • Elaboration Conducting Research • Taking Notes Using Textual Evidence • Introduction • Synthesizing Information • Summarizing, Paraphrasing, and Quoting Student Edition/**Teacher's Edition:** 103–106, **103–106, 158a,** 169–172, **169–172,** 271–274, **271–274,** 323–326, **323–326, 394a,** 601–604, **601–604** **ASSESSMENT** Student Edition/**Teacher's Edition:** 103–106, **103–106,** 169–172, **169–172,** 271–274, **271–274,** 323–326, **323–326,** 601–604, **601–604**
a. Apply *grades 11–12 Reading Standards* to literature (e.g., "Demonstrate knowledge of eighteenth-, nineteenth- and early-twentieth-century foundational works of American literature, including how two or more texts from the same period treat similar themes or topics").	**INSTRUCTION/APPLICATION** Student Edition/**Teacher's Edition:** 267–270, **267–270,** 271–274, **271–274,** 323–326, **323–326,** 405–408, **405–408,** 601–604, **601–604** **ASSESSMENT** Student Edition/**Teacher's Edition:** 165, **165,** 266, **266,** 267–270, **267–270,** 271–274, **271–274,** 323–326, **323–326,** 405–408, **405–408,** 601–604, **601–604**
b. Apply *grades 11–12 Reading Standards* to literary nonfiction (e.g., "Delineate and evaluate the reasoning in seminal U.S. texts, including the application of constitutional principles and use of legal reasoning [e.g., in U.S. Supreme Court Case majority opinions and dissents) and the premises, purposes, and arguments in works of public advocacy (e.g., *The Federalist,* presidential addresses]").	**INSTRUCTION/APPLICATION** Student Edition/**Teacher's Edition:** 267–270, **267–270,** 271–274, **271–274,** 323–326, **323–326,** 405–408, **405–408,** 601–604, **601–604** **ASSESSMENT** Student Edition/**Teacher's Edition:** 267–270, **267–270,** 271–274, **271–274,** 323–326, **323–326,** 405–408, **405–408,** 601–604, **601–604**

Standard	Where Taught
RANGE OF WRITING	
W 10 Write routinely over extended time frames (time for research, reflection, and revision) and shorter time frames (a single sitting or a day or two) for a range of tasks, purposes, and audiences.	**INSTRUCTION/APPLICATION** **Digital Collections/Lessons:** Writing as a Process • Task, Purpose, and Audience Writing Arguments Writing Informative Texts Writing Narratives Using Textual Evidence Student Edition/**Teacher's Edition:** 103–106, **103–106**, 169–172 **169–172**, 267–270, **267–270**, 323–326, **323–326**, 405–408, **405–408**, 600, **600**, 601–604, **601–604** **ASSESSMENT** Student Edition/**Teacher's Edition:** 103–106, **103–106**, 165, **165**, 169–172, **169–172**, 267–270, **267–270**, 323–326, **323–326**, 405–408, **405–408**, 600, **600**, 601–604, **601–604**

College and Career Readiness Anchor Standards for Speaking and Listening

Common Core State Standards

COMPREHENSION AND COLLABORATION

1. Prepare for and participate effectively in a range of conversations and collaborations with diverse partners, building on others' ideas and expressing their own clearly and persuasively.

2. Integrate and evaluate information presented in diverse media and formats, including visually, quantitatively, and orally.

3. Evaluate a speaker's point of view, reasoning, and use of evidence and rhetoric.

PRESENTATION OF KNOWLEDGE AND IDEAS

4. Present information, findings, and supporting evidence such that listeners can follow the line of reasoning and the organization, development, and style are appropriate to task, purpose, and audience.

5. Make strategic use of digital media and visual displays of data to express information and enhance understanding of presentations.

6. Adapt speech to a variety of contexts and communicative tasks, demonstrating command of formal English when indicated or appropriate.

Speaking and Listening Standards, Grades 11–12 Students

Standard	Where Taught
COMPREHENSION AND COLLABORATION	

SL 1
Initiate and participate effectively in a range of collaborative discussions (one-on-one, in groups, and teacher-led) with diverse partners on *grades 11–12 topics, texts, and issues,* building on others' ideas and expressing their own clearly and persuasively.

INSTRUCTION/APPLICATION
Digital Collections/Lessons:
Participating in Collaborative Discussions
- Introduction
- Preparing for Discussion
- Establishing and Following Procedure
- Speaking Constructively
- Listening and Responding
- Wrapping Up Your Discussion

Student Edition/**Teacher's Edition:**
18, **18**, 31, **31**, **35a**, 68, **68**, 71, **71**, 74, **74**, 83, **83**, 92, **92**, 99, **99**, 116, **116**, 124, **124**, 136, **136**, 146, **146**, 156, **156**, 163, **163**, 167, **167**, **168a**, 169–172, **169–172**, 183, **183**, 194, **194**, 203, **203**, 229, **229**, 246, **246**, **248a**, 262, **262**, **266b**, 271–274, **271–274**, 280, **280**, 290, **290**, 297, **297**, 310, **310**, 315, **315**, 346, **346**, 355, **355**, 368, **368**, 378, **378**, 388, **388**, 390, **390**, 391, **391**, 392, **392**, 397, **397**, 403, **403**, 433, **433**, 442, **442**, 452, **452**, 485, **485**, 503, **503**, 525, **525**, 539, **539**, 543, **543**, 546, **546**, 564, **564**, 577, **577**, **580a**, 583, **583**, 593, **593**, 598, **598**, 605–608, **605–608**, R12–R13, R14–R15

Close Reader/**Teacher's Edition:**
220b–220g, 580b–580g

ASSESSMENT
76, **76**, 158, **158**, 169–172, **169–172**, 247, **247**, 263, **263**, 271–274, **271–274**, 316, **316**, 605–608, **605–608**

---

a. Come to discussions prepared, having read and researched material under study; explicitly draw on that preparation by referring to evidence from texts and other research on the topic or issue to stimulate a thoughtful, well-reasoned exchange of ideas.

INSTRUCTION/APPLICATION
Digital Collections/Lessons:
Participating in Collaborative Discussions
- Preparing for Discussion
- Speaking Constructively

Student Edition/**Teacher's Edition:**
18, **18**, 31, **31**, **35a**, 68, **68**, 71, **71**, 74, **74**, 83, **83**, 92, **92**, 99, **99**, 116, **116**, 124, **124**, 136, **136**, 146, **146**, 156, **156**, 163, **163**, 183, **183**, 194, **194**, 203, **203**, 229, **229**, 246, **246**, 262, **262**, 271–274, **271–274**, 282, **282**, 290, **290**, 297, **297**, 310, **310**, 346, **346**, 355, **355**, 368, **368**, 378, **378**, 391, **391**, 397, **397**, 403, **403**, 433, **433**, 442, **442**, 485, **485**, 503, **503**, 525, **525**, 539, **539**, 546, 564, **564**, 577, **577**, 583, **583**, 593, **593**, 598, **598**, 605–608, **605–608**, R12–R13, R14–R15

Close Reader/**Teacher's Edition:**
220b–220g, 580b–580g

ASSESSMENT
Student Edition/**Teacher's Edition:**
165, **165**, 196, **196**, 265, **265**, 271–274, **271–274**, 282, **282**, 312, **312**, 399, **399**, 486, **486**, 605–608, **605–608**

Standard	Where Taught
b. Work with peers to set rules for collegial discussions and decision-making, set clear goals and deadlines, and establish individual roles as needed.	**INSTRUCTION/APPLICATION** **Digital Collections/Lessons:** Participating in Collaborative Discussions • Establishing and Following Procedure Student Edition/**Teacher's Edition:** **35a**, 138, **138**, 271–274, **271–274**, 292, **292**, 605–608, **605–608**, R12–R13, R14–R15 Close Reader/**Teacher's Edition:** **220b–220g, 580b–580g** **ASSESSMENT** Student Edition/**Teacher's Edition:** 138, **138**, 271–274, **271–274**, 292, **292**, 605–608, **605–608**
c. Propel conversations by posing and responding to questions that probe reasoning and evidence; ensure a hearing for a full range of positions on a topic or issue; clarify, verify, or challenge ideas and conclusions; and promote divergent and creative perspectives.	**INSTRUCTION/APPLICATION** **Digital Collections/Lessons:** Participating in Collaborative Discussions • Speaking Constructively • Listening and Responding Student Edition/**Teacher's Edition:** **35a**, 138, **138**, 196, **196**, 271–274, **271–274**, 282, **282**, 605–608, **605–608**, R12–R13, R14–R15 **ASSESSMENT** Student Edition/**Teacher's Edition:** 138, **138**, 196, **196**, 271–274, **271–274**, 282, **282**, 605–608, **605–608**
d. Respond thoughtfully to diverse perspectives; synthesize comments, claims, and evidence made on all sides of an issue; resolve contradictions when possible; and determine what additional information or research is required to deepen the investigation or complete the task.	**INSTRUCTION/APPLICATION** **Digital Collections/Lessons:** Participating in Collaborative Discussions • Listening and Responding • Wrapping Up Your Discussion Student Edition/**Teacher's Edition:** **35a**, 271–274, **271–274**, 292, **292**, 605–608, **605–608**, R12–R13, R14–R15 Close Reader/**Teacher's Edition:** **220b–220g, 580b–580g** **ASSESSMENT** 271–274, **271–274**, 292, **292**, 605–608, **605–608**

Standard	Where Taught
SL 2 Integrate multiple sources of information presented in diverse formats and media (e.g., visually, quantitatively, orally) in order to make informed decisions and solve problems, evaluating the credibility and accuracy of each source and noting any discrepancies among the data.	**INSTRUCTION/APPLICATION** **Digital Collections/Lessons:** Analyzing and Evaluating Presentations • Introduction • Evaluating a Speaker's Reliability • Synthesizing Media Sources Student Edition/**Teacher's Edition:** **102a,** 316, **316,** 380, **380,** R14–R15 **ASSESSMENT** Student Edition/**Teacher's Edition:** 316, **316,** 380, **380**
ELACC11-12SL3 Evaluate a speaker's point of view, reasoning, and use of evidence and rhetoric, assessing the stance, premises, links among ideas, word choice, points of emphasis, and tone used.	**INSTRUCTION/APPLICATION** **Digital Collections/Lessons:** Analyzing and Evaluating Presentations • Tracing a Speaker's Argument • Rhetoric and Delivery Student Edition/**Teacher's Edition:** 165, **165, 248a,** 271–274, **271–274,** 312, **312,** 316, **316,** 372, **372,** 566, **566,** 605–608, **605–608,** R14–R15 **ASSESSMENT** Student Edition/**Teacher's Edition:** 165, **165,** 271–274, **271–274,** 312, **312,** 316, **316,** 372, **372,** 566, **566,** 605–608, **605–608**

Standard	Where Taught

PRESENTATION OF KNOWLEDGE AND IDEAS

SL 4
Present information, findings, and supporting evidence, conveying a clear and distinct perspective, such that listeners can follow the line of reasoning, alternative or opposing perspectives are addressed, and the organization, development, substance, and style are appropriate to purpose, audience, and a range of formal and informal tasks.

INSTRUCTION/APPLICATION
Digital Collections/Lessons:
Giving a Presentation
- Introduction
- Knowing Your Audience
- The Content of Your Presentation
- Style in Presentation

Student Edition/**Teacher's Edition:**
185, **185,** 271–274, **271–274, 314a,** 323–326, **323–326,** 372, **372,** 504, **504,** 566, **566,** 605–608, **605–608**

ASSESSMENT
Student Edition/**Teacher's Edition:**
185, **185,** 271–274, **271–274,** 323–326, **323–326,** 372, **372,** 504, **504,** 566, **566,** 605–608, **605–608**

SL 5
Make strategic use of digital media (e.g., textual, graphical, audio, visual, and interactive elements) in presentations to enhance understanding of findings, reasoning, and evidence and to add interest.

INSTRUCTION/APPLICATION
Digital Collections/Lessons:
Using Media in a Presentation
- Introduction
- Types of Media: Audio, Video, and Images
- Using Presentation Software
- Building and Practicing Your Presentation

Student Edition/**Teacher's Edition:**
314a, 585, **585,** 594, **594**

ASSESSMENT
Student Edition/**Teacher's Edition:**
585, **585,** 594, **594**

SL 6
Adapt speech to a variety of contexts and tasks, demonstrating a command of formal English when indicated or appropriate. (See grades 11–12 Language standards 1 and 3 for specific expectations.)

INSTRUCTION/APPLICATION
Digital Collections/Lessons:
Participating in Collaborative Discussions
- Speaking Constructively

Giving a Presentation
- Style in Presentation

Student Edition/**Teacher's Edition:**
185, **185,** 271–274, **271–274,** 380, **380,** 605–608, **605–608**

ASSESSMENT
Student Edition/**Teacher's Edition:**
185, **185,** 271–274, **271–274,** 380, **380,** 605–608, **605–608**

College and Career Readiness Anchor Standards for Language

Common Core State Standards

CONVENTIONS OF STANDARD ENGLISH

1. Demonstrate command of the conventions of standard English grammar and usage when writing or speaking.

2. Demonstrate command of the conventions of standard English capitalization, punctuation, and spelling when writing.

KNOWLEDGE OF LANGUAGE

3. Apply knowledge of language to understand how language functions in different contexts, to make effective choices for meaning or style, and to comprehend more fully when reading or listening.

VOCABULARY ACQUISITION AND USE

4. Determine or clarify the meaning of unknown and multiple-meaning words and phrases by using context clues, analyzing meaningful word parts, and consulting general and specialized reference materials, as appropriate.

5. Demonstrate understanding of figurative language, word relationships, and nuances in word meanings.

6. Acquire and use accurately a range of general academic and domain-specific words and phrases sufficient for reading, writing, speaking, and listening at the college and career readiness level; demonstrate independence in gathering vocabulary knowledge when considering a word or phrase important to comprehension or expression.

Language Standards, Grades 11–12 Students

Standard	Where Taught
CONVENTIONS OF STANDARD ENGLISH	
L 1 Demonstrate command of the conventions of standard English grammar and usage when writing or speaking.	**INSTRUCTION/APPLICATION** Student Edition/**Teacher's Edition:** **6**, 16, **16**, 21, **21**, 105, **105**, 106, **106**, 172, **172**, 326, **326**, 408, **408**, 604, **604**, R23–R48, **R31, R33, R35, R38, R42, R45, R47**
a. Apply the understanding that usage is a matter of convention, can change over time, and is sometimes contested.	**INSTRUCTION/APPLICATION** Student Edition/**Teacher's Edition:** 21, **21**, 121, **121**, 153, **153**, 580, **580**, R52–R53, R55–R56, R59–R60
b. Resolve issues of complex or contested usage, consulting references (e.g., *Merriam-Webster's Dictionary of English Usage, Garner's Modern American English*) as needed.	**INSTRUCTION/APPLICATION** Student Edition/**Teacher's Edition:** 21, **21**, 580, **580**, R51–52, R55–56, R59–R60
L 2 Demonstrate command of the conventions of standard English capitalization, punctuation, and spelling when writing.	**INSTRUCTION/APPLICATION** Student Edition/**Teacher's Edition:** 96, **96**, 106, **106**, 172, **172**, 283, **283**, 371, **371**, 408, **408**, 604, **604**, R23, R26–R28, R29
a. Observe hyphenation conventions.	**INSTRUCTION/APPLICATION** Student Edition/**Teacher's Edition:** 150, **150**, R27, R30, R58
b. Spell correctly.	**INSTRUCTION/APPLICATION** Student Edition/**Teacher's Edition:** 106, **106**, 172, **172**, 270, **270**, 408, **408**, 604, **604**, R49, R56–R60

Standard	Where Taught

KNOWLEDGE OF LANGUAGE

L 3
Apply knowledge of language to understand how language functions in different contexts, to make effective choices for meaning or style, and to comprehend more fully when reading or listening.

INSTRUCTION/APPLICATION
Student Edition/**Teacher's Edition:**
200, **203**, 205, **205**, **206a**, 596, **596**, R23–R48, **R45**, **R47**

a. Vary syntax for effect, consulting references (e.g., Tufte's *Artful Sentences*) for guidance as needed; apply an understanding of syntax to the study of complex texts when reading.

INSTRUCTION/APPLICATION
Student Edition/**Teacher's Edition:**
22, **22**, 35, **35**, 96, **96**, 102, **102**, **112**, **113**, **115**, **116**, 117, **117**, 120, **120**, 127, **127**, 140, **140**, 166, **166**, 186, **186**, **188**, **189**, **191**, **192**, 198, **198**, **208**, 220, **220**, 233, **233**, 265, **265**, 284, **284**, **285**, 294, **294**, 314, **314**, 350, **350**, 371, **371**, 382, **382**, 437, **437**, 455, **455**, **528**, 542, **542**, 568, **568**, R2, R3, R8–R11

VOCABULARY ACQUISITION AND USE

L 4
Determine or clarify the meaning of unknown and multiple-meaning words and phrases based on *grades 11–12 reading and content*, choosing flexibly from a range of strategies.

INSTRUCTION/APPLICATION
Student Edition/**Teacher's Edition:**
22a, 86, **86**, 95, **95**, 204, **204**, 206, **206**, 219, **219**, 231, **231**, 232, **232**, 264, **264**, 293, **293**, 300, **300**, 312, **312**, 313, **313**, 358, **358**, 580, **580**, 595, **595**, R23–R25, R30–R48, R49–R50, R50–R52

a. Use context (e.g., the overall meaning of a sentence, paragraph, or text; a word's position or function in a sentence) as a clue to the meaning of a word or phrase.

INSTRUCTION/APPLICATION
Student Edition/**Teacher's Edition:**
86, **86**, 95, **95**, **201**, 202, **202**, **203**, 204, **204**, 219, **219**, 231, **231**, 264, **264**, 312, **312**, **586a**, R30–R48, R49–R50

b. Identify and correctly use patterns of word changes that indicate different meanings or parts of speech (e.g., *conceive, conception, conceivable*).

INSTRUCTION/APPLICATION
Student Edition/**Teacher's Edition:**
95, **95**, 197, **197**, 206, **206**, 232, **232**, 300, **300**, 358, **358**, 580, **580**, 595, **595**, R23–R25, R30–R38, R50–R52

c. Consult general and specialized reference materials (e.g., dictionaries, glossaries, thesauruses), both print and digital, to find the pronunciation of a word or determine or clarify its precise meaning, its part of speech, or its etymology, or its standard usage.

INSTRUCTION/APPLICATION
Student Edition/**Teacher's Edition:**
34, **34**, 119, **119**, 149, **149**, 283, **283**, 293, **293**, 349, **349**, 358, **358**, 381, **381**, 436, **436**, 567, **567**, 580, **580**, 586, **586**, R50–R52, **R50**, **R51**, **R52**

Standard	Where Taught
d. Verify the preliminary determination of the meaning of a word or phrase (e.g., by checking the inferred meaning in context or in a dictionary).	**INSTRUCTION/APPLICATION** Student Edition/**Teacher's Edition:** 86, **86**, 149, **149**, 197, **197**, 219, **219**, 264, **264**, 293, **293**, 313, **313**, R55, R56
L 5 Demonstrate understanding of figurative language, word relationships, and nuances in word meanings.	**INSTRUCTION/APPLICATION** Student Edition/**Teacher's Edition:** 139, **139**, 184, **184**, 204, **204**, 205, **205**, 217, **217**, 218, **218**, 248, **248**, 381, **381**, 404, **404**, 599, **599**, 600, **600**, R49–R50, R53–R54
a. Interpret figures of speech (e.g., hyperbole, paradox) in context and analyze their role in the text.	**INSTRUCTION/APPLICATION** Student Edition/**Teacher's Edition:** **96a, 179,** 184, **184, 186a, 200, 201,** 202, **202,** 204, **204,** 205, **205, 207, 210, 211, 212, 216,** 217, **217,** 218, **218, 220a, 382a,** 404, **404,** 599, **599**
b. Analyze nuances in the meaning of words with similar denotations.	**INSTRUCTION/APPLICATION** Student Edition/**Teacher's Edition:** 139, **139, 241,** 248, **248,** 381, **381, 600a, 600b**
L 6 Acquire and use accurately general academic and domain-specific words and phrases, sufficient for reading, writing, speaking, and listening at the college and career readiness level; demonstrate independence in gathering vocabulary knowledge when considering a word or phrase important to comprehension or expression.	**INSTRUCTION/APPLICATION** Student Edition/**Teacher's Edition:** 2, **2, 9, 13, 24,** 34, **34, 40, 78, 88, 92, 98,** 103, **103,** 108, **108, 113,** 119, **119, 124, 130, 142, 152, 160,** 170, **170, 174, 179, 188, 193, 208, 211, 236,** 268, **268,** 271, **271,** 276, **276, 286, 296, 318,** 324, **324,** 328, **328, 333, 344, 361, 374, 396,** 406, **406,** 410, **410, 439, 545,** 567, **567,** 570, **570, 586a,** 602, **602,** 606, **606,** R49–R53, R55, R56

Navigating Complex Texts

By Carol Jago

Reading complex literature and nonfiction doesn't need to be painful.

But to enjoy great poetry and prose you are going to have to do more than skim and scan. You will need to develop the habit of paying attention to the particular words on the page closely, systematically, even lovingly. Just because a text isn't easy doesn't mean there is something wrong with it or something wrong with you. Understanding complex text takes effort and focused attention. Do you sometimes wish writers would just say what they have to say more simply or with fewer words? I assure you that writers don't use long sentences and unfamiliar words to annoy their readers or make readers feel dumb. They employ complex syntax and rich language because they have complex ideas about complex issues that they want to communicate. Simple language and structures just aren't up to the task.

Excellent literature and nonfiction—the kind you will be reading over the course of the year—challenge readers in many ways. Sometimes the background of a story or the content of an essay is so unfamiliar that it can be difficult to understand why characters are behaving as they do or to follow the argument a writer is making. By persevering—reading like a detective and following clues in the text—you will find that your store of background knowledge grows. As a result, the next time you read about this subject, the text won't seem nearly as hard. Navigating a terrain you have been over once before never seems quite as rugged the second time through. The more you read, the better reader you become.

Good readers aren't scared off by challenging text. When the going gets rough, they know what to do. Let's take vocabulary, a common measure of text complexity, as an example. Learning new words is the business of a lifetime. Rather than shutting down when you meet a word you don't know, take a moment to think about the word. Is any part of the word familiar to you? Is there something in the context of the sentence or paragraph that can help you figure out its meaning? Is there someone or something that can provide you with a definition? When we read literature or nonfiction from a time period other than our own, the text is often full of words we don't know.

Each time you meet those words in succeeding readings you will be adding to your understanding of the word and its use. Your brain is a natural word-learning machine. The more you feed it complex text, the larger vocabulary you'll have and as a result, the easier navigating the next book will be.

Have you ever been reading a long, complicated sentence and discovered that by the time you reached the end you had forgotten the beginning? Unlike the sentences we speak or dash off in a note to a friend, complex text is often full of sentences that are not only lengthy but also constructed in intricate ways. Such sentences require readers to slow down and figure out how phrases relate to one another as well as who is doing what to whom. Remember, rereading isn't cheating. It is exactly what experienced readers know to do when they meet dense text on the page. On the pages that follow you will find stories and articles that challenge you at a sentence level. Don't be intimidated. By paying careful attention to how those sentences are constructed, you will see their meanings unfold before your eyes.

Another way text can be complex is in terms of the density of ideas. Sometimes a writer piles on so much information that you find even if your eyes continue to move down the page, your brain has stopped taking in anything. At times like this, turning to a peer and discussing particular lines or concepts can help you pay closer attention and begin to unpack the text. Sharing questions and ideas, exploring a difficult passage together, makes it possible to tease out the meaning of even the most difficult text.

> **"Your brain is a natural word-learning machine. The more you feed it complex text, the larger vocabulary you'll have."**

Poetry is by its nature particularly dense and for that reason poses particular challenges for casual readers. Don't ever assume that once through a poem is enough. Often, seemingly simple poems in terms of word choice and length—for example an Emily Dickinson, Mary Oliver, or W.H. Auden poem—express extremely complex feelings and insights. Poets also often make reference to mythological and Biblical allusions which contemporary readers are not always familiar with. Skipping over such references robs your reading of the richness the poet intended. Look up that bird. Check out the note on the page. Ask your teacher.

You will notice a range of complexity within each collection of readings. This spectrum reflects the range of texts that surround us: some easy, some hard, some seemingly easy but hard, some seemingly hard but easy. Navigating this sea of texts should stretch you as a reader and a thinker. How could it be otherwise when your journey is in the realms of gold? Please accept this invitation to an intellectual voyage I think you will enjoy.

Understanding the Common Core State Standards

What are the English Language Arts Common Core State Standards?

The Common Core State Standards for English Language Arts indicate what you should know and be able to do by the end of your grade level. These understandings and skills will help you be better prepared for future classes, college courses, and a career. For this reason, the standards for each strand in English Language Arts (such as reading informational text or writing) directly relate to the College and Career Readiness Anchor Standards for each strand. The Anchor Standards broadly outline the understandings and skills you should master by the end of high school so that you are well-prepared for college or for a career.

How do I learn the English Language Arts Common Core State Standards?

Your textbook is closely aligned to the English Language Arts Common Core State Standards. Every time you learn a concept or practice a skill, you are working on mastery of one of the standards. Each collection, each selection, and each performance task in your textbook connects to one or more of the standards for English Language Arts listed on the following pages.

The English Language Arts Common Core State Standards are divided into five strands: Reading Literature, Reading Informational Text, Writing, Speaking and Listening, and Language.

©sveltkd/The Agency Collection/Getty Images

Strand	What It Means to You
Reading Literature (RL)	This strand concerns the literary texts you will read at this grade level: stories, drama, and poetry. The Common Core State Standards stress that you should read a range of texts of increasing complexity as you progress through high school.
Reading Informational Text (RI)	Informational text includes a broad range of literary nonfiction, including exposition, argument, and functional text, in such genres as personal essays, speeches, opinion pieces, memoirs, and historical and technical accounts. The Common Core State Standards stress that you will read a range of informational texts of increasing complexity as you progress from grade to grade.
Writing (W)	The Writing strand focuses on your generating three types of texts—arguments, informative or explanatory texts, and narratives—while using the writing process and technology to develop and share your writing. The Common Core State Standards also emphasize research and specify that you should write routinely for both short and extended time frames.
Speaking and Listening (SL)	The Common Core State Standards focus on comprehending information presented in a variety of media and formats, on participating in collaborative discussions, and on presenting knowledge and ideas clearly.
Language (L)	The standards in the Language strand address the conventions of standard English grammar, usage, and mechanics; knowledge of language; and vocabulary acquisition and use.

Common Core Code Decoder

The codes you find on the pages of your textbook identify the specific knowledge or skill for the standard addressed in the text.

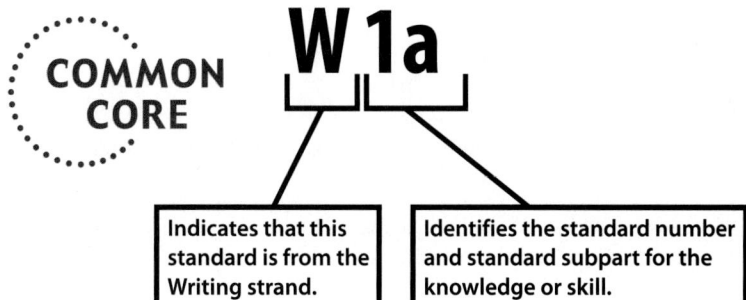

Indicates that this standard is from the Writing strand.	Identifies the standard number and standard subpart for the knowledge or skill.

English Language Arts
Common Core State Standards

Listed below are the English Language Arts Common Core State Standards that you are required to master by the end of grade 11. We have provided a summary of the concepts you will learn on your way to mastering each standard. The CCR anchor standards and high school grade-specific standards for each strand work together to define college and career readiness expectations—the former providing broad standards, the latter providing additional specificity.

College and Career Readiness Anchor Standards for Reading

Common Core State Standards

KEY IDEAS AND DETAILS

1. Read closely to determine what the text says explicitly and to make logical inferences from it; cite specific textual evidence when writing or speaking to support conclusions drawn from the text.

2. Determine central ideas or themes of a text and analyze their development; summarize the key supporting details and ideas.

3. Analyze how and why individuals, events, and ideas develop and interact over the course of a text.

CRAFT AND STRUCTURE

4. Interpret words and phrases as they are used in a text, including determining technical, connotative, and figurative meanings, and analyze how specific word choices shape meaning or tone.

5. Analyze the structure of texts, including how specific sentences, paragraphs, and larger portions of the text (e.g., a section, chapter, scene, or stanza) relate to each other and the whole.

6. Assess how point of view or purpose shapes the content and style of a text.

INTEGRATION OF KNOWLEDGE AND IDEAS

7. Integrate and evaluate content presented in diverse formats and media, including visually and quantitatively, as well as in words.

8. Delineate and evaluate the argument and specific claims in a text, including the validity of the reasoning as well as the relevance and sufficiency of the evidence.

9. Analyze how two or more texts address similar themes or topics in order to build knowledge or to compare the approaches the authors take.

RANGE OF READING AND LEVEL OF TEXT COMPLEXITY

10. Read and comprehend complex literary and informational texts independently and proficiently.

Reading Standards for Literature, Grades 11–12 Students

The College and Career Readiness Anchor Standards for Reading apply to both literature and informational text.

Common Core State Standards	What It Means to You
KEY IDEAS AND DETAILS	
1. Cite strong and thorough textual evidence to support analysis of what the text says explicitly as well as inferences drawn from the text, including determining where the text leaves matters uncertain.	You will use strong evidence from a text to support your analysis of its central ideas—both those that are stated directly and those that are suggested—and to show where the text leaves matters uncertain.
2. Determine two or more themes or central ideas of a text and analyze their development over the course of the text, including how they interact and build on one another to produce a complex account; provide an objective summary of the text.	You will analyze the development of at least two of a text's key ideas and themes by showing how they progress and interact throughout the text. You will also summarize the text as a whole without adding your own ideas or opinions.
3. Analyze the impact of the author's choices regarding how to develop and relate elements of a story or drama (e.g., where a story is set, how the action is ordered, how the characters are introduced and developed).	You will analyze the author's choices related to setting, plot structure, and characterization in a story or drama.
CRAFT AND STRUCTURE	
4. Determine the meaning of words and phrases as they are used in the text, including figurative and connotative meanings; analyze the impact of specific word choices on meaning and tone, including words with multiple meanings or language that is particularly fresh, engaging, or beautiful. (Include Shakespeare as well as other authors.)	You will analyze specific words and phrases in the text to determine both their figurative and connotative meanings, as well as how they contribute to the text's tone and meaning as a whole. You will also consider multiple-meaning words and vivid language.
5. Analyze how an author's choices concerning how to structure specific parts of a text (e.g., the choice of where to begin or end a story, the choice to provide a comedic or tragic resolution) contribute to its overall structure and meaning as well as its aesthetic impact.	You will analyze the ways in which the author has chosen to structure and order the text and determine how those choices shape the text's meaning and affect the reader.
6. Analyze a case in which grasping a point of view requires distinguishing what is directly stated in a text from what is really meant (e.g., satire, sarcasm, irony, or understatement).	You will understand a point of view in which what is really meant is different from what is said or stated.

Common Core State Standards	What It Means to You
INTEGRATION OF KNOWLEDGE AND IDEAS	
7. Analyze multiple interpretations of a story, drama, or poem (e.g., recorded or live production of a play or recorded novel or poetry), evaluating how each version interprets the source text. (Include at least one play by Shakespeare and one play by an American dramatist.)	You will compare and contrast multiple interpretations of a story, drama, or poem, and analyze how each draws from and uses the source text.
8. (Not applicable to literature)	
9. Demonstrate knowledge of eighteenth-, nineteenth- and early-twentieth-century foundational works of American literature, including how two or more texts from the same period treat similar themes or topics.	You will analyze, compare, and contrast important eighteenth-, nineteenth-, and early-twentieth-century works of American literature.
RANGE OF READING AND LEVEL OF TEXT COMPLEXITY	
10. By the end of grade 11, read and comprehend literature, including stories, dramas, and poems, in the grades 11–CCR text complexity band proficiently, with scaffolding as needed at the high end of the range.	11. You will read and understand grade-level appropriate literary texts by the end of grade 11.

Reading Standards for Informational Text, Grades 11–12 Students

Common Core State Standards	What It Means to You
KEY IDEAS AND DETAILS	
1. Cite strong and thorough textual evidence to support analysis of what the text says explicitly as well as inferences drawn from the text, including determining where the text leaves matters uncertain.	You will use details and information from the text to support your analysis of its central ideas—both those that are stated directly and those that are suggested—and to show where the text leaves matters uncertain.
2. Determine two or more central ideas of a text and analyze their development over the course of the text, including how they interact and build on one another to provide a complex analysis; provide an objective summary of the text.	You will analyze the development of at least two of a text's key ideas by showing how they progress and interact throughout the text. You will also summarize the text as a whole without adding your own ideas or opinions.

Common Core State Standards	What It Means to You
3. Analyze a complex set of ideas or sequence of events and explain how specific individuals, ideas, or events interact and develop over the course of the text.	You will analyze the specific interactions among a set of ideas, individuals, or a sequence of events in a text.

CRAFT AND STRUCTURE

4. Determine the meaning of words and phrases as they are used in a text, including figurative, connotative, and technical meanings; analyze how an author uses and refines the meaning of a key term or terms over the course of a text (e.g., how Madison defines *faction* in *Federalist* No. 10).	You will analyze specific words and phrases in the text to determine their figurative, connotative, and technical meanings, as well as to uncover how an author uses them throughout a text.
5. Analyze and evaluate the effectiveness of the structure an author uses in his or her exposition or argument, including whether the structure makes points clear, convincing, and engaging.	You will examine a text's structure and evaluate whether it makes the author's claims clear, convincing, and interesting.
6. Determine an author's point of view or purpose in a text in which the rhetoric is particularly effective, analyzing how style and content contribute to the power, persuasiveness, or beauty of the text.	You will understand the author's purpose and perspective on a topic and analyze how the author uses language to affect the reader.

INTEGRATION OF KNOWLEDGE AND IDEAS

7. Integrate and evaluate multiple sources of information presented in different media or formats (e.g., visually, quantitatively) as well as in words in order to address a question or solve a problem.	You will integrate multiple and varied sources of information to address a question or solve a problem.
8. Delineate and evaluate the reasoning in seminal U.S. texts, including the application of constitutional principles and use of legal reasoning (e.g., in U.S. Supreme Court majority opinions and dissents) and the premises, purposes, and arguments in works of public advocacy (e.g., *The Federalist*, presidential addresses).	You will analyze the reasoning and underlying principles of important historical U.S. texts for their support of the principles of democracy.

Common Core State Standards	What It Means to You
9. Analyze seventeenth-, eighteenth-, and nineteenth-century foundational U.S. documents of historical and literary significance (including The Declaration of Independence, the Preamble to the Constitution, the Bill of Rights, and Lincoln's Second Inaugural Address) for their themes, purposes, and rhetorical features.	You will read and analyze important eighteenth-, nineteenth-, and early-twentieth-century documents pertaining to American history to determine their themes, purposes, and use of language.

RANGE OF READING AND LEVEL OF TEXT COMPLEXITY

Common Core State Standards	What It Means to You
10. By the end of grade 11, read and comprehend literary nonfiction in the grades 11–CCR text complexity band proficiently, with scaffolding as needed at the high end of the range.	You will demonstrate the ability to read and understand grade-level appropriate literary nonfiction texts by the end of grade 11.

College and Career Readiness Anchor Standards for Writing

Common Core State Standards

TEXT TYPES AND PURPOSES

1. Write arguments to support claims in an analysis of substantive topics or texts, using valid reasoning and relevant and sufficient evidence.

2. Write informative/explanatory texts to examine and convey complex ideas and information clearly and accurately through the effective selection, organization, and analysis of content.

3. Write narratives to develop real or imagined experiences or events using effective technique, well-chosen details, and well-structured event sequences.

PRODUCTION AND DISTRIBUTION OF WRITING

4. Produce clear and coherent writing in which the development, organization, and style are appropriate to task, purpose, and audience.

5. Develop and strengthen writing as needed by planning, revising, editing, rewriting, or trying a new approach.

6. Use technology, including the Internet, to produce and publish writing and to interact and collaborate with others.

RESEARCH TO BUILD AND PRESENT KNOWLEDGE

7. Conduct short as well as more sustained research projects based on focused questions, demonstrating understanding of the subject under investigation.

8. Gather relevant information from multiple print and digital sources, assess the credibility and accuracy of each source, and integrate the information while avoiding plagiarism.

Common Core State Standards

9. Draw evidence from literary or informational texts to support analysis, reflection, and research.

RANGE OF WRITING

10. Write routinely over extended time frames (time for research, reflection, and revision) and shorter time frames (a single sitting or a day or two) for a range of tasks, purposes, and audiences.

Writing Standards, Grades 11–12 Students

Common Core State Standards	What It Means to You

TEXT TYPES AND PURPOSES

Common Core State Standards	What It Means to You
1. Write arguments to support claims in an analysis of substantive topics or texts, using valid reasoning and relevant and sufficient evidence.	You will write and develop arguments with strong evidence and valid reasoning that include
a. Introduce precise, knowledgeable claim(s), establish the significance of the claim(s), distinguish the claim(s) from alternate or opposing claims, and create an organization that logically sequences claim(s), counterclaims, reasons, and evidence.	a. a clear organization of precise claims and counterclaims
b. Develop claim(s) and counterclaims fairly and thoroughly, supplying the most relevant evidence for each while pointing out the strengths and limitations of both in a manner that anticipates the audience's knowledge level, concerns, values, and possible biases.	b. relevant and unbiased support for claims that incorporates audience considerations
c. Use words, phrases, and clauses as well as varied syntax to link the major sections of the text, create cohesion, and clarify the relationships between claim(s) and reasons, between reasons and evidence, and between claim(s) and counterclaims.	c. use of transitional words, phrases, and clauses and varied sentence structures to link information and clarify relationships
d. Establish and maintain a formal style and objective tone while attending to the norms and conventions of the discipline in which they are writing.	d. a tone and style that is appropriate and that adheres to the conventions, or expectations, of the discipline
e. Provide a concluding statement or section that follows from and supports the argument presented.	e. a strong concluding statement or section that summarizes the evidence presented

Common Core State Standards	What It Means to You
TEXT TYPES AND PURPOSES	
2. Write informative/explanatory texts to examine and convey complex ideas, concepts, and information clearly and accurately through the effective selection, organization, and analysis of content.	You will write clear, well-organized, and thoughtful informative and explanatory texts with
a. Introduce a topic; organize complex ideas, concepts, and information so that each new element builds on that which precedes it to create a unified whole; include formatting (e.g., headings), graphics (e.g., figures, tables), and multimedia when useful to aiding comprehension.	**a.** a clear introduction and an organization that builds on each successive idea, including formats, headings, graphic organizers (when appropriate), and multimedia
b. Develop the topic thoroughly by selecting the most significant and relevant facts, extended definitions, concrete details, quotations, or other information and examples appropriate to the audience's knowledge of the topic.	**b.** a sufficient variety of support and background information
c. Use appropriate and varied transitions and syntax to link the major sections of the text, create cohesion, and clarify the relationships among complex ideas and concepts.	**c.** appropriate and varied transitions and sentence structures
d. Use precise language, domain-specific vocabulary, and techniques such as metaphor, simile, and analogy to manage the complexity of the topic.	**d.** precise language, relevant vocabulary, and the use of comparisons to express complex ideas
e. Establish and maintain a formal style and objective tone while attending to the norms and conventions of the discipline in which they are writing.	**e.** an appropriate tone and style that adheres to the conventions, or expectations, of the discipline
f. Provide a concluding statement or section that follows from and supports the information or explanation presented (e.g., articulating implications or the significance of the topic).	**f.** a strong concluding statement or section that logically relates to the information presented in the text and that restates the importance or relevance of the topic

Common Core State Standards	What It Means to You

TEXT TYPES AND PURPOSES

3. Write narratives to develop real or imagined experiences or events using effective technique, well-chosen details, and well-structured event sequences.

   a. Engage and orient the reader by setting out a problem, situation, or observation and its significance, establishing one or multiple point(s) of view, and introducing a narrator and/or characters; create a smooth progression of experiences or events.

   b. Use narrative techniques, such as dialogue, pacing, description, reflection, and multiple plot lines, to develop experiences, events, and/or characters.

   c. Use a variety of techniques to sequence events so that they build on one another to create a coherent whole and build toward a particular tone and outcome (e.g., a sense of mystery, suspense, growth, or resolution).

   d. Use precise words and phrases, telling details, and sensory language to convey a vivid picture of the experiences, events, setting, and/or characters.

   e. Provide a conclusion that follows from and reflects on what is experienced, observed, or resolved over the course of the narrative.

You will write clear, well-structured, detailed narrative texts that

   a. draw your readers in with a clear topic, well-developed point(s) of view, a well-developed narrator and characters, and an interesting progression of events or ideas

   b. use a range of literary techniques to develop and expand on events and/or characters

   c. have a coherent sequence and structure that create the appropriate tone and ending for readers

   d. use precise words, sensory details, and language in order to keep readers interested

   e. have a strong and logical conclusion that reflects on the topic

PRODUCTION AND DISTRIBUTION OF WRITING

4. Produce clear and coherent writing in which the development, organization, and style are appropriate to task, purpose, and audience.

You will produce writing that is appropriate to the task, purpose, and audience for whom you are writing.

5. Develop and strengthen writing as needed by planning, revising, editing, rewriting, or trying a new approach, focusing on addressing what is most significant for a specific purpose and audience.

You will revise and refine your writing, using a variety of strategies, to address what is most important for your purpose and audience.

Common Core State Standards	What It Means to You
6. Use technology, including the Internet, to produce, publish, and update individual or shared writing products in response to ongoing feedback, including new arguments or information.	You will use technology to share your writing, provide links to other relevant information, and to update your information as needed.

RESEARCH TO BUILD AND PRESENT KNOWLEDGE

Common Core State Standards	What It Means to You
7. Conduct short as well as more sustained research projects to answer a question (including a self-generated question) or solve a problem; narrow or broaden the inquiry when appropriate; synthesize multiple sources on the subject, demonstrating understanding of the subject under investigation.	You will engage in short and more complex research tasks that include answering a question or solving a problem by using multiple sources. Your understanding of the subject will be evident in the product you develop.
8. Gather relevant information from multiple authoritative print and digital sources, using advanced searches effectively; assess the strengths and limitations of each source in terms of the task, purpose, and audience; integrate information into the text selectively to maintain the flow of ideas, avoiding plagiarism and overreliance on any one source and following a standard format for citation.	You will effectively conduct searches to gather information from a variety of print and digital sources and will evaluate each source in terms of the goal of your research. You will appropriately cite your sources of information and will follow a standard format for citation, such as the MLA or APA guidelines.

Common Core State Standards	What It Means to You

RESEARCH TO BUILD AND PRESENT KNOWLEDGE

9. Draw evidence from literary or informational texts to support analysis, reflection, and research.	You will paraphrase, summarize, quote, and cite primary and secondary sources, using both literary and informational texts, to support your analysis, reflection, and research, for purposes including
a. Apply *grades 11–12 Reading standards* to literature (e.g., "Demonstrate knowledge of eighteenth-, nineteenth- and early-twentieth-century foundational works of American literature, including how two or more texts from the same period treat similar themes or topics").	a. written analysis of themes, author's choices, or point of view in American literature
b. Apply *grades 11–12 Reading standards* to literary nonfiction (e.g., "Delineate and evaluate the reasoning in seminal U.S. texts, including the application of constitutional principles and use of legal reasoning [e.g., in U.S. Supreme Court Case majority opinions and dissents] and the premises, purposes, and arguments in works of public advocacy [e.g., *The Federalist*, presidential addresses]").	b. written analysis of central ideas, text structure, word choice, point of view, or reasoning in American literary nonfiction

RANGE OF WRITING

10. Write routinely over extended time frames (time for research, reflection, and revision) and shorter time frames (a single sitting or a day or two) for a range of tasks, purposes, and audiences.	You will write a variety of texts for different purposes and audiences over both short and extended periods of time.

College and Career Readiness Anchor Standards for Speaking and Listening

Common Core State Standards

COMPREHENSION AND COLLABORATION

1. Prepare for and participate effectively in a range of conversations and collaborations with diverse partners, building on others' ideas and expressing their own clearly and persuasively.

2. Integrate and evaluate information presented in diverse media and formats, including visually, quantitatively, and orally.

3. Evaluate a speaker's point of view, reasoning, and use of evidence and rhetoric.

Common Core State Standards

PRESENTATION OF KNOWLEDGE AND IDEAS

4. Present information, findings, and supporting evidence such that listeners can follow the line of reasoning and the organization, development, and style are appropriate to task, purpose, and audience.

5. Make strategic use of digital media and visual displays of data to express information and enhance understanding of presentations.

6. Adapt speech to a variety of contexts and communicative tasks, demonstrating command of formal English when indicated or appropriate.

Speaking and Listening Standards, Grades 11–12 Students

Common Core State Standards	What It Means to You
COMPREHENSION AND COLLABORATION	
1. Initiate and participate effectively in a range of collaborative discussions (one-on-one, in groups, and teacher-led) with diverse partners on grades 11–12 topics, texts, and issues, building on others' ideas and expressing their own clearly and persuasively.	You will actively participate in a variety of discussions in which you
a. Come to discussions prepared, having read and researched material under study; explicitly draw on that preparation by referring to evidence from texts and other research on the topic or issue to stimulate a thoughtful, well-reasoned exchange of ideas.	a. have read any relevant material beforehand and have come to the discussion prepared with background research
b. Work with peers to promote civil, democratic discussions and decision-making, set clear goals and deadlines, and establish individual roles as needed.	b. work with others to establish goals, processes, and roles within the group in order to have reasonable discussions
c. Propel conversations by posing and responding to questions that probe reasoning and evidence; ensure a hearing for a full range of positions on a topic or issue; clarify, verify, or challenge ideas and conclusions; and promote divergent and creative perspectives.	c. ask and respond to questions, encourage a range of positions, and relate the current topic to other relevant information and perspectives
d. Respond thoughtfully to diverse perspectives; synthesize comments, claims, and evidence made on all sides of an issue; resolve contradictions when possible; and determine what additional information or research is required to deepen the investigation or complete the task.	d. respond to different perspectives, summarize points of agreement or disagreement when needed, help to resolve unclear points, and set out a plan for additional research as needed

Common Core State Standards	What It Means to You
2. Integrate multiple sources of information presented in diverse formats and media (e.g., visually, quantitatively, orally) in order to make informed decisions and solve problems, evaluating the credibility and accuracy of each source and noting any discrepancies among the data.	You will integrate multiple and varied sources of information, assessing the credibility and accuracy of each source to aid the group-discussion process.
3. Evaluate a speaker's point of view, reasoning, and use of evidence and rhetoric, assessing the stance, premises, links among ideas, word choice, points of emphasis, and tone used.	You will evaluate a speaker's argument and analyze the nature of the speaker's reasoning or evidence.

PRESENTATION OF KNOWLEDGE AND IDEAS

Common Core State Standards	What It Means to You
4. Present information, findings, and supporting evidence, conveying a clear and distinct perspective, such that listeners can follow the line of reasoning, alternative or opposing perspectives are addressed, and the organization, development, substance, and style are appropriate to purpose, audience, and a range of formal and informal tasks.	You will organize and present information, evidence, and your perspective to your listeners in a logical sequence and style that are appropriate to your task, purpose, and audience.
5. Make strategic use of digital media (e.g., textual, graphical, audio, visual, and interactive elements) in presentations to enhance understanding of findings, reasoning, and evidence and to add interest.	You will use digital media to enhance understanding and to add interest to your presentations.
6. Adapt speech to a variety of contexts and tasks, demonstrating a command of formal English when indicated or appropriate.	You will adapt the formality of your speech appropriately, depending on its context and purpose.

College and Career Readiness Anchor Standards for Language

Common Core State Standards

CONVENTIONS OF STANDARD ENGLISH

Common Core State Standards
1. Demonstrate command of the conventions of standard English grammar and usage when writing or speaking.
2. Demonstrate command of the conventions of standard English capitalization, punctuation, and spelling when writing.

Common Core State Standards

KNOWLEDGE OF LANGUAGE

3. Apply knowledge of language to understand how language functions in different contexts, to make effective choices for meaning or style, and to comprehend more fully when reading or listening.

VOCABULARY ACQUISITION AND USE

4. Determine or clarify the meaning of unknown and multiple-meaning words and phrases by using context clues, analyzing meaningful word parts, and consulting general and specialized reference materials, as appropriate.

5. Demonstrate understanding of word relationships and nuances in word meanings.

6. Acquire and use accurately a range of general academic and domain-specific words and phrases sufficient for reading, writing, speaking, and listening at the college and career readiness level; demonstrate independence in gathering vocabulary knowledge when considering a word or phrase important to comprehension or expression.

Language Standards, Grades 11–12 Students

Common Core State Standards	What It Means to You
CONVENTIONS OF STANDARD ENGLISH	

1. Demonstrate command of the conventions of standard English grammar and usage when writing or speaking.
  a. Apply the understanding that usage is a matter of convention, can change over time, and is sometimes contested.
  b. Resolve issues of complex or contested usage, consulting references (e.g., *Merriam-Webster's Dictionary of English Usage, Garner's Modern American Usage*) as needed.
	You will correctly use the conventions of English grammar and usage, including
	
	  a. demonstrating that usage follows accepted standards and can change or be contested
	
	  b. using references to resolve disagreements or uncertainty about usage

2. Demonstrate command of the conventions of standard English capitalization, punctuation, and spelling when writing.
  a. Observe hyphenation conventions.
  b. Spell correctly.
	You will correctly use the conventions of standard English capitalization, punctuation, and spelling, including
	  a. hyphens
	  b. spelling

Common Core State Standards	What It Means to You
KNOWLEDGE OF LANGUAGE	

3. Apply knowledge of language to understand how language functions in different contexts, to make effective choices for meaning or style, and to comprehend more fully when reading or listening.
  a. Vary syntax for effect, consulting references (e.g., Tufte's *Artful Sentences*) for guidance as needed; apply an understanding of syntax to the study of complex texts when reading.
	You will apply your knowledge of language in different contexts to guide choices in your own writing and speaking by
	
	  a. using appropriate references for guidance to vary your syntax and to understand syntax in complex texts

VOCABULARY ACQUISITION AND USE	

4. Determine or clarify the meaning of unknown and multiple-meaning words and phrases based on grades 11–12 reading and content, choosing flexibly from a range of strategies.
  a. Use context (e.g., the overall meaning of a sentence, paragraph, or text; a word's position or function in a sentence) as a clue to the meaning of a word or phrase.
  b. Identify and correctly use patterns of word changes that indicate different meanings or parts of speech (e.g., *conceive, conception, conceivable*).
  c. Consult general and specialized reference materials (e.g., dictionaries, glossaries, thesauruses), both print and digital, to find the pronunciation of a word or determine or clarify its precise meaning, its part of speech, its etymology, or its standard usage.
  d. Verify the preliminary determination of the meaning of a word or phrase (e.g., by checking the inferred meaning in context or in a dictionary).
	You will understand the meaning of grade-level appropriate words and phrases by
	
	  a. using context clues
	
	  b. applying various forms of words according to meaning or part of speech
	
	  c. using reference materials to determine and clarify word meaning, part of speech, etymology, and standard usage
	
	  d. inferring and verifying the meanings of words in context

Common Core State Standards	What It Means to You
VOCABULARY ACQUISITION AND USE	

5. Demonstrate understanding of figurative language, word relationships, and nuances in word meanings.
  a. Interpret figures of speech (e.g., hyperbole, paradox) in context and analyze their role in the text.
  b. Analyze nuances in the meaning of words with similar denotations.
	You will understand figurative language, word relationships, and slight differences in word meanings by
	  a. interpreting figures of speech in context
	
	  b. analyzing slight differences in the meanings of similar words

6. Acquire and use accurately general academic and domain-specific words and phrases, sufficient for reading, writing, speaking, and listening at the college and career readiness level; demonstrate independence in gathering vocabulary knowledge when considering a word or phrase important to comprehension or expression.	You will develop and use a range of vocabulary at the college and career readiness level and will demonstrate that you can successfully acquire new vocabulary independently.

Coming to America

❝ [In America] individuals of all nations are melted into a new race ... whose labors ... will one day cause great changes in the world. ❞

— Michel-Guillaume Jean de Crèvecoeur

PLAN

CONNECTING WORD AND IMAGE

ASK STUDENTS to discuss how the collection opener image and the collection quotation work together to create a connection.

PERFORMANCE TASK PREVIEW

Point out to students that they will complete a performance task at the end of the collection. The performance task will require them to further analyze the selections in the collection and to synthesize ideas about these analyses. They will present their findings in a variety of products.

ACADEMIC VOCABULARY

View It!

Professional Development Podcast:

Academic Vocabulary

Students can acquire facility with the academic vocabulary words through frequent, repeated exposure as they analyze and discuss the selections in the collection. Academic vocabulary can be used in the following instructional contexts. This will enable students to incorporate the academic vocabulary words into their working vocabulary.

- Collaborative Discussion at the end of each selection
- Analyzing the Text questions for each selection
- Selection-level Performance Task
- Vocabulary instruction (for Critical Vocabulary and/or for Vocabulary Strategy)
- Language and Style
- End-of-collection Performance Task for all selections in the collection

ASK STUDENTS to review the academic vocabulary word list for this collection. You may wish to pronounce each word aloud, so students hear the correct pronunciation. Then, discuss the definitions and the related forms for each word. Remind students that they will encounter these five academic vocabulary words throughout the collection.

Coming to America

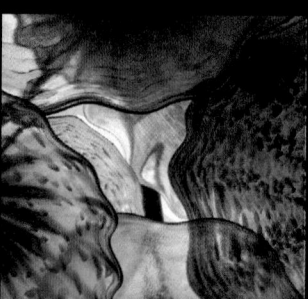

In this collection, you will explore how America has always been a land shaped by immigrants.

hmhfyi.com

COLLECTION

PERFORMANCE TASK Preview

At the end of this collection, you will have the opportunity to complete a task:

- Write an argument about why people come to America or what significant changes occur when they do.

ACADEMIC VOCABULARY

Study the words and their definitions in the chart below. You will use these words as you discuss and write about the texts in this collection.

Word	Definition	Related Forms
adapt (ə-dăpt´) *v.*	to make something suitable for a particular situation; to adjust to an environment	adaptable, adaptability, adaptation
coherent (kō-hîr´ənt) *adj.*	holding together in an orderly, logical, or consistent way	cohere, coherence, coherently, cohesive
device (dĭ-vīs´) *n.*	a literary technique used to achieve a certain effect; something made for a specific purpose	devise
displace (dĭs-plās´) *v.*	to move or force from one place or position to another	displaceable, displacement
dynamic (dī-năm´ĭk) *adj.*	characterized by change, movement, or activity	dynamics, dynamically, dynamism, dynamo

Image Credits: ©Dee Yaverian/Flickr/Getty Images

2

USING THE COLLECTION YOUR WAY

Use the following information, along with the charts on the following pages, to help you decide how you want to introduce the collection. Based on your teaching style, your students' interests, or your instructional goals, you may want to structure the collection in various ways. You may choose different entry points each time you teach the collection.

"I love teaching traditional literature."

In this play from the early 17th century, **William Shakespeare** presents a dark comedy that explores themes such as power, betrayal, justice, and forgiveness, and includes magic as a motif.

---

from **The Tempest**

Drama by William Shakespeare

William Shakespeare *(1564–1616) was born in 1564 in Stratford-upon-Avon, a market town in central England. His father was a prosperous tradesman. Shakespeare probably attended Stratford's grammar school, where he would have studied Latin and read classical authors. In 1582 he married Anne Hathaway. The next year she gave birth to a daughter, Susanna. Their twins Hamnet and Judith followed in 1585. Sometime during the next seven years, Shakespeare found work in London as an actor; he also began to write plays. His early success aroused the envy of Robert Greene, who in 1592 described him as "an upstart crow." In 1594 Shakespeare joined the Lord Chamberlain's Men, which became the most prestigious theater company in London. Shakespeare soon grew affluent from his share in the company's profits.*

The Height of His Career *Shakespeare's rhetorical gifts and poetic power, as well as his profound psychological insight, would have allowed him to become a great writer in any age. To please the varied tastes of Elizabethan audiences, he mastered all forms of drama. In the 1590s, he focused on comedies and English history plays, such as A Midsummer Night's Dream and Henry IV. Between 1600 and 1607, he wrote his greatest tragedies, including Hamlet, Macbeth, and King Lear. The final phase of his career saw the creation of the darker comedies, such as A Winter's Tale and The Tempest.*

His Legacy *Shakespeare died in Stratford in 1616. At the time, some of his plays existed in cheap, often very flawed editions; others had never appeared in print. In 1623, two theater colleagues published a collected edition of his plays known as the First Folio, which ensured the survival of his work. Ben Jonson, a rival playwright, wrote an introduction for the volume in which he declared that Shakespeare "was not of an age, but for all time." Four centuries after Shakespeare's death, his plays continue to be performed around the world.*

The Tempest   **37**

Background *Vasco Núñez de Balboa (1475–1519) was a Spanish explorer and conquistador who first came to the Americas in 1500 as part of a voyage exploring the coast of present-day Colombia. He is most remembered for being the first European to view the Pacific Ocean in 1513. This event and other facts of Balboa's life form the basis for Sabina Murray's story, published in her book Tales of the New World (2011). Murray lives in western Massachusetts, where she is on the Creative Writing faculty at the University of Massachusetts Amherst.*

Balboa

Short Story by Sabina Murray

AS YOU READ Pay special attention to descriptions of Balboa's relations with the Indians and the Spaniards. Write down any questions you generate during reading.

Vasco Núñez de Balboa ascends the mountain alone. His one thousand Indians and two hundred Spaniards wait at the foot of the mountain, as if they are the Israelites and Balboa alone is off to speak with God. Balboa knows that from this peak he will be able to see the western water, what he has already decided to name the South Sea. He takes a musket with him. The Spaniards have been warned that if they follow, he will use it, because discovery is a tricky matter and he wants no competition. The day is September 25, 1513.

Balboa ascends slowly. His musket is heavy and he would have gladly left it down below, but he doesn't trust his countrymen any more than he trusts the sullen Indians. So he bears the weight. But the musket is nothing. He is dragging the mantle[1] of civilization up the pristine slopes, over the mud, over the leaves that cast as much shade as a parasol[2] but with none of the charm.

pristine *(prĭs'tēn') adj.* pure or unspoiled.

[1] **mantle:** a cloak or robe worn by royalty.
[2] **parasol:** light umbrella.

Balboa   **77**

"I like to connect literature to history."

This short story presents a fictional version of Balboa—a real Spanish explorer who came to the Americas in 1500—imagining his relations with other Spaniards and his interactions with Indians in the New World.

"I want to challenge my students to the utmost."

In this essay, **Richard Rodriguez** uses anecdotes to make an argument that discusses race and ethnicity in relation to the concepts of immigration, assimilation, culture, and identity.

Richard Rodriguez *is the son of Mexican immigrants and was born in San Francisco in 1944. When he started school, his teachers asked his parents to speak more English at home, and Ricardo became Richard. He planned on an academic career but never completed his Ph.D. dissertation, deciding to write as a journalist and essayist. In the first volume of his autobiography Hunger of Memory (1982), Rodriguez describes his assimilation into the majority culture. This 2003 essay followed publication of another volume of memoir, Brown: The Last Discovery of America, which explores the issue of race.*

"Blaxicans" and Other Reinvented Americans

Argument by Richard Rodriguez

AS YOU READ Look for clues that reveal Rodriguez's attitudes toward race and ethnicity as they relate to personal identity.

There is something unsettling about immigrants because…well, because they chatter incomprehensibly, and they get in everyone's way. Immigrants seem to be bent on undoing America. Just when Americans think we know who we are—we are Protestants, culled from Western Europe, are we not?—then new immigrants appear from Southern Europe or from Eastern Europe. We—we who are already here—we don't know exactly what the latest comers will mean to our community. How will they fit in with us? Thus we—we who were here first—we begin to question our own identity.

After a generation or two, the grandchildren or the great-grandchildren of immigrants to the United States and the grandchildren of those who tried to keep immigrants out of the United States will romanticize the immigrant, will begin to see the immigrant as the figure who teaches us most about what it means to be an American. The immigrant, in mythic terms, travels from the outermost rind of America to the very center of American mythology. None of this, of course, can we admit to the Vietnamese immigrant who served us our breakfast at the hotel this morning. In another 40 years, we will be prepared to say to the Vietnamese immigrant that he,

cull *(kŭl) v.* to take from a large quantity.

"Blaxicans" and Other Reinvented Americans   **87**

mySmartPlanner | **eBook** | **myNotebook** |  **myWriteSmart** | **fyi** hmhfyi.com

Collection 1 Lessons	Media	Teach and Practice	
Student Edition | eBook	▶ **Video Links** 🅷 HISTORY A&E	**Close Reading and Evidence Tracking**	
ANCHOR TEXT — **Historical Account by William Bradford** from *Of Plymouth Plantation*	🔊 **Audio** from *Of Plymouth Plantation* ▶ **Video HISTORY®** *The Mayflower*	**Close Read Screencasts** • Modeled Discussion 1 (lines 47–56) • Modeled Discussion 2 (lines 178–185) • Close Read application pdf (lines 323–345)	**Strategies for Annotation** • Determine Central Ideas • Archaic Vocabulary
CLOSE READER — **Historical Narrative by John Smith** from *The General History of Virginia*	🔊 **Audio** from *The General History of Virginia*		
History Writing by Charles Mann "Coming of Age in the Dawnland"	🔊 **Audio** "Coming of Age in the Dawnland" ▶ **Video HISTORY** *The Aztecs*		**Strategies for Annotation** • Determine the Meaning of Words and Phrases • Specialized Vocabulary
Drama by William Shakespeare from *The Tempest*	🔊 **Audio** from *The Tempest* ▶ **Video BIO®** *Biography: William Shakespeare*		**Strategies for Annotation** • Analyze Language
Film Version by BBC Shakespeare *The Tempest* (1980)	▶ **Video** *The Tempest* (1980)		
Production Images from Film Version *The Tempest* (2010)			
Short Story by Sabina Murray "Balboa"	🔊 **Audio** "Balboa"		**Strategies for Annotation** • Analyze Structure • Determine Themes • Context Clues
Argument by Richard Rodriguez "'Blaxicans' and Other Reinvented Americans"	🔊 **Audio** "'Blaxicans' and Other Reinvented Americans"		**Strategies for Annotation** • Analyze and Evaluate Structure: Arguments • The Latin Prefix *circum-*
CLOSE READER — **Essay by Amy Tan** "Mother Tongue"	🔊 **Audio** "Mother Tongue"		
Poem by Joy Harjo "New Orleans"	🔊 **Audio** "New Orleans"		**Strategies for Annotation** • Determine Themes
CLOSE READER — **Poem by Sherman Alexie** "Indian Boy Love Song (#2)"	🔊 **Audio** "Indian Boy Love Song (#2)"		
Collection 1 Performance Task: Write an Argument	fyi hmhfyi.com **hmhfyi.com**	**Interactive Lessons** Writing Arguments Using Textual Evidence	

	For Systematic Coverage of Writing and Speaking & Listening Standards	Interactive Lessons Writing as a Process Participating in Collaborative Discussions	Lesson Assessments Writing as a Process Participating in Collaborative Discussions

Assess		Extend	Reteach
Performance Task	Online Assessment	Teacher eBook	Teacher eBook
Writing Activity: Journal Entry and Letter	Selection Test	**Support Inferences: Draw Conclusions**	**Archaic Language > Level Up Tutorial >** Paraphrasing
Writing Activity: Argument	Selection Test	**Participate in Collaborative Discussions > Interactive Whiteboard Lesson >** Types of Elaboration	**Analyze Author's Purpose > Interactive Lesson >** Specialized Vocabulary
Writing Activity: Essay	Selection Test	**Support Inferences: Draw Conclusions**	**Analyze Language > Level Up Tutorial >** Making Inferences About Characters
Writing Activity: Review Speaking Activity: Debate	Selection Test	**Analyze Interpretations of Drama**	**Analyzing the Media and Text > Level Up Tutorial >** Types of Drama
Writing Activity: Captions Speaking Activity: Debate	Selection Test	**Analyze Interpretations of Drama**	**Analyzing the Media and Text > Level Up Tutorial >** Types of Drama
Writing Activity: Dramatic Monologue	Selection Test	**Determine Author's Purpose and Perspective**	**Determine Themes > Level Up Tutorial >** Making Inferences About Characters
Writing Activity: Evaluation	Selection Test	**Analyze Nuances in the Meaning of Words**	**Determine Author's Purpose: Irony**
Speaking Activity	Selection Test	**Doing Research on the Web > Interactive Whiteboard Lesson >** Search Strategies	**Cite Textual Evidence > Level Up Tutorial >** Citing Textual Evidence
Write an Argument	Collection Test		

COLLECTION 1 INSTRUCTIONAL OVERVIEW

Collection 1 Lessons	Key Learning Objective	Performance Task
ANCHOR TEXT **Historical Account by William Bradford** **Lexile 1440** from *Of Plymouth Plantation,* p. 5A	**The student will be able to...** identify and analyze the central ideas of a foundational text	Writing Activity: Journal Entry and Letter
History Writing by Charles Mann **Lexile 1290** "Coming of Age in the Dawnland," p. 23A	**The student will be able to...** determine the author's purpose for writing	Writing Activity: Argument
Drama by William Shakespeare from *The Tempest,* p. 37A	**The student will be able to...** cite effective textual evidence to support an argument	Writing Activity: Essay
Film Version by BBC Shakespeare *The Tempest* (1980), p. 71A	**The student will be able to...** analyze an interpretation of a drama	Writing Activity: Review Speaking Activity: Debate
Production Images from Film Version *The Tempest* (2010), p. 73A	**The student will be able to...** analyze an interpretation of a drama	Writing Activity: Captions Speaking Activity: Debate
Short Story by Sabina Murray **Lexile 920** "Balboa," p. 77A	**The student will be able to...** determine themes and analyze structure	Writing Activity: Dramatic Monologue
Argument by Richard Rodriguez **Lexile 1040** "'Blaxicans' and Other Reinvented Americans," p. 87A	**The student will be able to...** trace and evaluate an argument	Writing Activity: Evaluation
Poem by Joy Harjo "New Orleans," p. 97A	**The student will be able to...** determine a theme of the poem	Speaking Activity

Collection 1 Performance Task:
Write an Argument

Vocabulary Strategy	Language and Style	Student Instructional Support	CLOSE READER Selection
Archaic Vocabulary	Active and Passive Voice	**Scaffolding for ELL Students:** 6, 10, 14, 16 **When Students Struggle:** 8, 12, 18 **To Challenge Students:** Challenge Central Ideas	Historical Narrative by John Smith from *The General History of Virginia*, p. 22b **Lexile 1680**
Specialized Vocabulary	Dependent (or Subordinate) Clauses	**Scaffolding for ELL Students:** 23, 26, 28, 29 **When Students Struggle:** 25, 27, 30	
		Scaffolding for ELL Students: 39, 42, 48, 50, 54, 55, 60, 66 **When Students Struggle:** 41, 46, 52, 56, 58, 61, 64, 67 **To Challenge Students:** 45, 49, 51, 59, 62	
		Scaffolding for ELL Students: Analyze Interpretations of a Drama	
		Scaffolding for ELL Students: • Analyze Interpretations of a Drama • Language Support	
Context Clues		**Scaffolding for ELL Students:** Language: Verb Tenses **When Students Struggle:** Inferring Character Traits **To Challenge Students:** Analyze Characters	
The Latin Prefix *circum-*	Using Colons Effectively	**Scaffolding for ELL Students:** • Verbal Irony • Recognizing Word Roots **When Students Struggle:** Use Context Clues	Essay by Amy Tan "Mother Tongue," p. 96b **Lexile 1120**
	Syntax in Poetry	**Scaffolding for ELL Students:** Analyze Language **When Students Struggle:** Paraphrasing	Poem by Sherman Alexie "Indian Boy Love Song (#2)," p. 102b

*my*SmartPlanner   Create lesson plans and access resources online.

Exploration and Settlement

Collection 1 Historical Introduction

Why This Text?

Students often encounter literary and informational texts that assume that the reader has some knowledge of key historical events, facts, ideas, and issues. The historical introduction to Collection 1 presents information about the period from 1400 to 1700, when the United States was being explored and settled by Europeans.

Key Learning Objective: The student will be able to analyze the selections in the collection in terms of a historical context.

COMMON CORE Common Core Standards

RI 3 Analyze a complex sequence of events and explain how individuals, ideas, or events interact.

RI 7 Integrate and evaluate sources of information presented in different formats.

RI 10 Read and comprehend literary nonfiction in the grades 11-CCR text complexity band.

▲ Text Complexity Rubric

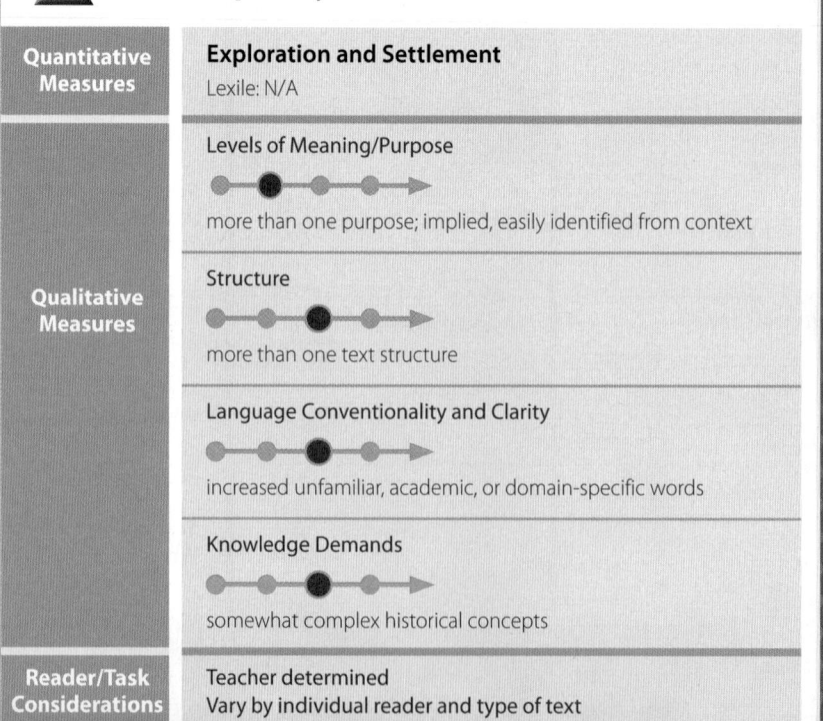

Quantitative Measures	**Exploration and Settlement** Lexile: N/A
Qualitative Measures	**Levels of Meaning/Purpose** more than one purpose; implied, easily identified from context **Structure** more than one text structure **Language Conventionality and Clarity** increased unfamiliar, academic, or domain-specific words **Knowledge Demands** somewhat complex historical concepts
Reader/Task Considerations	Teacher determined Vary by individual reader and type of text

TEACH

For more context and historical background, students can view the video "The Lost Colony of Roanoke" in their eBooks.

Exploration and Settlement Tell students that this section establishes the historical context for the selections in this collection. It presents a brief overview of early European contact with the native peoples living in North America, of the first English settlements, and of the explorations by Spain and France. The section ends with a discussion of early American literature and its influences on contemporary literature.

European Contact with North America

COMMON CORE RI 3, RI 7, RI 10

Sailing under the Spanish flag, Italian navigator Christopher Columbus was once credited with "discovering" America, although he actually made landfall at an island in the Caribbean. The Vikings also preceded Columbus by visiting North America five centuries earlier. Remind students that millions of people lived in the Americas on the eve of the arrival of the Europeans—as many as lived in Europe at the time. The influx of Europeans significantly affected these native cultures.

English Settlements

Remind students that religion was the most influential cultural force of the period. Puritan values and beliefs directed every aspect of the early colonists' lives. They saw human struggle with sin as a daily mission and believed, above all else, that the Bible would help them through the torments of human weakness. Although they felt that humans were essentially sinful, they believed that some, the "elect," would be spared from eternal punishment by God's grace. The thriving settlements and the financial success that grew from the Puritan values of thrift, hard work, and responsibility were thought to be a mark of God's approval. Puritanism had a dark side as well, however. Puritans tended to be inflexible in their religious faith and intolerant of other viewpoints.

 VIDEO

Exploration and Settlement

COMMON CORE RI 3, RI 7, RI 10

Although the Portuguese ushered in the age of European exploration in the early 1400s, Spain, England, and France were the countries that explored and settled most of the Americas. These Europeans encountered a rich variety of native cultures in the New World, creating a mixture of cultures that has shaped American history.

EUROPEAN CONTACT WITH NORTH AMERICA Christopher Columbus's voyage to the Caribbean in 1492 marked the beginning of contact between Europeans and Native Americans. Soon, explorers, fishermen, and traders began making contact from Canada down through South America. When the Europeans first arrived, millions of Native Americans were living on the land, in small villages and in large cities such as the Aztec capital of Tenochtitlán, the site of present-day Mexico City. People had been living in the Americas for many thousands of years, adapting to its diverse environments. At first, Native Americans were generally helpful to the Europeans. Before long, however, it became clear that the newcomers intended to take control of their land. And the firearms were not their most dangerous weapons: the settlers brought new diseases that killed millions.

ENGLISH SETTLEMENTS Although the English were not the first Europeans to explore or colonize North America, their settlements along the Eastern seaboard became the thirteen colonies that later formed the United States. England relied on private trading companies to establish a presence in North America. One of these groups, the Virginia Company, established the first permanent English settlement in Jamestown, Virginia, in 1607. Those who settled in New England were Puritans, Protestant reformers who wanted to "purify" the Church of England. Their efforts met with little success, and some Puritans wanted to separate completely from the English Church. Among them was William Bradford, who helped organize the voyage of the *Mayflower*, bringing nearly a hundred people to Massachusetts in 1620. John Winthrop brought others to Boston in 1630 to set up what he called "a City upon a Hill," a godly society that would be an ideal for others to follow. The Puritans' religious beliefs influenced all aspects of their lives, and the values of hard work, thrift, and responsibility led to thriving settlements and financial success.

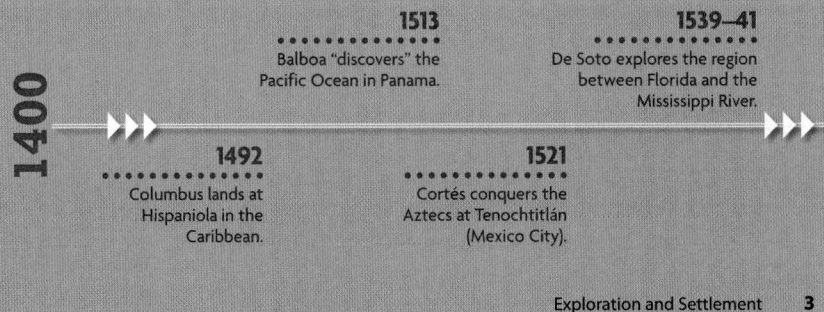

1400

1513 Balboa "discovers" the Pacific Ocean in Panama.

1539–41 De Soto explores the region between Florida and the Mississippi River.

1492 Columbus lands at Hispaniola in the Caribbean.

1521 Cortés conquers the Aztecs at Tenochtitlán (Mexico City).

Exploration and Settlement **3**

SCAFFOLDING FOR ELL STUDENTS

Timeline Review the timeline with students, pausing to discuss each event from 1400 to 1700, the time period covered in this historical introduction.

ASK STUDENTS to discuss in small groups the roles that Spain, England, and France played in this period of exploration and settlement. Then ask each group to summarize their discussion for the class.

Spain and France in North America

Remind students that the Spanish conquered and controlled a vast empire that extended from Central America to California to the southeastern part of the United States. Dominican and Franciscan friars often accompanied the conquistadores, to convert the Native Americans to Christianity and to urge their humane treatment. The missions that they established still stand, for example in California and Texas. The Spanish influence on America continues to the present day. Hispanics are an integral part of American culture and society.

France also sent expeditions to explore the vast lands of North America in the seventeenth century. French explorers, such as Samuel de Champlain, Jacques Marquette, and Pierre-Esprit Radisson, traveled throughout Canada and the central United States and eventually traveled the length of the Mississippi River. Remind students that the French had fewer permanent settlements and so did not influence the United States the way the Spanish did. The French presence in Canada remains, however, notably in French-speaking Quebec.

Early American Literature

Remind students of the richness of the Native American oral tradition, which includes creation stories about the universe and how humans came into being, legendary histories that trace the migrations of a people and the deeds of great leaders, fairy tales, lyrics, chants, children's songs, healing songs, and dream visions. Note that some groups lost as many as 90 percent of their people to disease and conquest. The surviving works show the common themes in the spoken literature, including a reverence for nature and the worship of many gods.

Point out that contemporary writers continue to draw on this oral tradition. The historical events of this period also provide a basis for history writing, historical fiction, and arguments about the nature of contemporary American society that students will read in this collection.

SPAIN AND FRANCE IN NORTH AMERICA The territory of New Spain covered all the land under Spanish control north of the Isthmus of Panama and included territory in what became the southeastern and southwestern United States, including California. The Spanish wanted to gain glory and riches in the New World and to convert the natives to Christianity. Spanish settlements were strongest in central Mexico, where the government was located. However, the Spanish also established settlements at St. Augustine, Santa Fe, and the Caribbean, as well as a large number of missions and forts throughout the frontier regions of North America. Spanish language and culture has had a lasting impact in the region. But the Spanish desire to exploit the riches of their territories through mining and ranching led to forced labor and many other abuses of Native Americans.

After early fishing expeditions beginning in the 1520s, France established settlements along the St. Lawrence River in eastern Canada in the early 1600s. French settlers were far fewer than English or Spanish settlers in the Americas. Many of the French who came were trappers and fur traders. In 1673, French explorers and missionaries became the first Europeans to explore the upper Mississippi River. In 1682, the French explored all the way down to the Gulf of Mexico, claiming the entire river valley for King Louis XIV and naming it Louisiana. Because the French had fewer permanent settlers, they were less likely to come into conflict with Native Americans than the Spanish or English were.

EARLY AMERICAN LITERATURE Although few Native American cultures employed written language, all possessed strong oral cultures and a rich tradition of storytelling. Histories, myths, and legends had been passed down for thousands of years, but many of them were lost as people died from European disease and conquest. Some of these old stories have survived, and contemporary Native American writers, like Joy Harjo, often weave them into their writing. Much of what we know about Native American societies comes from the observations of Europeans, who recorded their experiences in America in diaries, letters, and reports back home, beginning with the journals of Christopher Columbus. William Bradford's *Of Plymouth Plantation* records the early years of the Plymouth colony and its relations with the Indians. Bradford and other Puritan writers were motivated by their beliefs about their role in God's plan. Their writings included historical narratives, sermons, and poems written in a generally plain style.

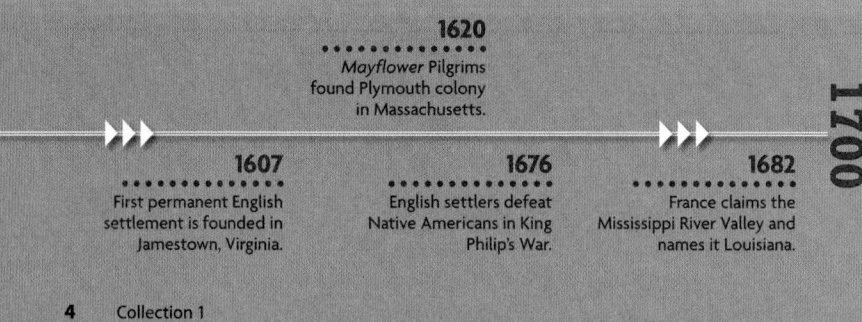

1620
Mayflower Pilgrims found Plymouth colony in Massachusetts.

1607
First permanent English settlement is founded in Jamestown, Virginia.

1676
English settlers defeat Native Americans in King Philip's War.

1682
France claims the Mississippi River Valley and names it Louisiana.

1700

4   Collection 1

WHEN STUDENTS STRUGGLE . . .

Historical Sequence Some students may experience difficulty keeping straight the facts, the events, and the issues presented in the historical background essays that begin each collection.

ASK STUDENTS to take notes for each historical introduction. They can keep these notes on paper or in *my*Notebook in the eBook. As they work through each collection, they can add notes that will provide an overview of the historical periods in the text. They can also refer to their notes as they have questions about the historical setting for some selections in each collection.

Analyze Accounts in Different Mediums

COMMON CORE
RI 7

TEACH

Remind students that nonfiction content can be presented to an audience in a variety of different ways. Each format has its own strengths and weaknesses when helping an audience comprehend information. Sometimes an author might use multiple mediums when presenting similar information to give the audience a more complete understanding of a topic.

Note that in this historical background essay the author included a timeline to organize and present information about specific significant dates being discussed. Also note that some dates that appear in running text do not appear on the timeline, and vice versa. Model how to compare and contrast the effectiveness of each format and discuss why the author might have mentioned some dates in running text and called out others in the actual timeline.

- First, examine how dates can be presented in running text. Reread the first sentence of the second paragraph on page 3. Discuss how this sentence explains why the date is important and serves as an introduction to a section talking about the topic of what happened as Europeans began to make contact with North American people. Then examine the series of dates mentioned in the second paragraph on page 4. Discuss how they help the reader understand the pattern of settlement in one particular place over time.
- Next, read the series of dates listed on the timeline on page 3. Point out features of their format (large date, callout sentence full of detailed information, events listed in sequential order from left to right) and talk about how this format makes it easier to focus on each individual event and to compare one event to another. Compare the presentation of the 1492 date here to its mention in the running text above, noting that this mention of the date offers more specific details about the event—providing the reader with the exact name of the landing place, Hispaniola—but does not address its larger significance in history.

PRACTICE AND APPLY

Have small groups work together to review examples of dates mentioned in running text, to identify which dates are also mentioned on the timeline and which are not, and to discuss how each format (running text and timeline) presents information differently.

Analyze Author's Order: Sequence of Events

COMMON CORE
RI 3

TEACH

Review how, when writing about historical events, an author can structure a text by describing each event in sequential order. Time-order words and phrases help readers follow this sequence of events and understand what happened first, next, and last.

Reread the second paragraph on page 3. Point out time-order words and phrases that the author used to place the events in sequence, such as *soon, first, at first,* and *before long.* Note that in the middle of this paragraph the author describes one event that had been going on since before the first event mentioned in the paragraph, and highlight the words that tell the reader this: "People *had been living* in the Americas *for many thousands of years.*" Then work with students to summarize the events of this paragraph in order:

- First, people lived in the Americas for thousands of years.
- Then, Christopher Columbus voyaged to the Caribbean.
- Next, explorers, fishermen, and traders from Europe began visiting all along the coast of the Americas.
- The Native Americans began by being friendly to the Europeans.
- Finally, it became clear that the Europeans posed a threat to the Native Americans and might take their lands. The Europeans also unwittingly spread diseases that killed many Native Americans.

Work with students to examine other passages from this historical background essay to identify other examples of helpful time-order words that establish the sequence of events, and to summarize other events in order.

Finish by talking about how a timeline can also help an author present information in a clear sequence.

CLOSE READING APPLICATION

Have students work independently to read another example of nonfiction text in which an author structures a series of events sequentially.

mySmartPlanner Create lesson plans and access resources online.

 **ANCHOR TEXT** *from* **Of Plymouth Plantation**

Historical Account by William Bradford

Why This Text?

Students usually learn early U.S. history from textbooks written hundreds of years after the events occurred. Instead, this lesson explores a first-hand account by William Bradford, who helped establish and lead Plymouth, England's second successful settlement in North America.

Key Learning Objective: The student will be able to identify and analyze the central ideas of a foundational text.

For additional practice:

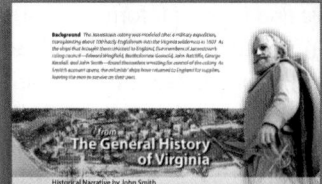

Close Reader selection
from The General History of Virginia
Historical Account by John Smith

COMMON CORE Common Core Standards

RI 1 Cite textual evidence.
RI 2 Determine central ideas of a text.
RI 3 Analyze a set of ideas or sequence of events.
RI 4 Determine the meaning of words and phrases.
RI 5 Analyze and evaluate structure.
RI 6 Determine an author's point of view or purpose.
RI 7 Integrate and evaluate multiple sources of information.
RI 9 Analyze foundational U.S. documents.
W 3c Use techniques to sequence events so that they create a coherent whole.
L 1 Demonstrate command of the conventions of standard English grammar and usage.
L 3a Vary syntax for effect, consulting references.
L 4 Determine or clarify the meaning of unknown and multiple-meaning words and phrases.

▲ Text Complexity Rubric

Quantitative Measures	**Of Plymouth Plantation** Lexile: 1440L
Qualitative Measures	**Levels of Meaning/Purpose** ●—●—●—**●**—→ multiple levels of complex meaning
	Structure ●—●—**●**—●—→ more than one text structure
	Language Conventionality and Clarity ●—●—●—**●**—→ archaic, unfamiliar language
	Knowledge Demands ●—●—**●**—●—→ specialized knowledge required
Reader/Task Considerations	Teacher determined Vary by individual reader and type of text

TEACH

CLOSE READ

For more context and historical background, students can view the video "The Mayflower" in their eBooks.

Background Point out that while Bradford never published his narrative, he did intend for it to be read by future generations, noting in Chapter 6 that he wrote the account so "that their children may see with what difficulties their fathers wrestled in going through these things in their first beginnings, and how God brought them along not withstanding all their weaknesses and infirmities."

AS YOU READ Direct students to use the As You Read note to focus their reading. Instruct them to write down any questions generated by their reading.

Analyze Foundational Texts (LINES 1–5)

COMMON CORE RI 4, RI 9

Explain to students that this passage was written more than 300 years ago. Readers may find Bradford's writing to be **archaic**, or outdated. One feature of **archaic** writing is long, complicated sentences.

A **ASK STUDENTS** to reread the first sentence and **paraphrase**, or state in their own words, what Bradford is trying to communicate. *(The Pilgrims, all on one ship, traveled for many days, and many suffered seasickness.)*

Determine Central Ideas (LINES 6–18)

COMMON CORE RI 2

Remind students that authors do not usually state **central ideas**, or **themes**, directly. Instead, readers must infer the central idea from the details that are included. By identifying and analyzing **themes**, readers can better understand the author's intentions, or **purpose**.

B **CITE TEXT EVIDENCE** Have students read lines 6–18 and use text evidence to identify Bradford's central idea, or theme. *(The central idea is God punishes those who do wrong. Bradford believes that the "proud and very profane" young man's death is "the just hand of God.")*

CRITICAL VOCABULARY

divers: Bradford describes the Mayflower's voyage after it set sail again.

ASK STUDENTS how divers days of prosperous winds would affect the ship's voyage. *(Several days of prosperous winds would move the ship quickly.)*

Background *Born in England in 1590,* **William Bradford** *became involved in the Protestant Reformation while still a boy. He joined the Puritans, reformers who wanted to purify the Church of England and eventually separate from it. With other Puritans, he migrated to Holland in search of religious freedom. He helped organize the journey on the Mayflower in 1620 that brought about 100 people—half of them his fellow "Pilgrims"—to the New World. His* History of Plymouth Plantation, 1620–1647 *describes this journey and provides a glimpse of the settlers' life in what became New England.*

from
Of Plymouth Plantation

Historical Account by William Bradford

AS YOU READ Pay attention to how Bradford describes the settlers' first encounters with Native Americans.

CHAPTER IX

Of their Voyage, and how they Passed the Sea; and of their Safe Arrival at Cape Cod

A *September 6* These troubles[1] being blown over, and now all being compact together in one ship, they put to sea again with a prosperous wind, which continued **divers** days together, which was some encouragement unto them; yet, according to the usual manner, many were afflicted with seasickness. And I may not omit here a special work of God's providence. There was a proud and very profane young man, one of the seamen, of a lusty,[2] able body, which made him the more haughty; he would always be condemning the poor people in their sickness and cursing them daily with grievous execrations;[3]
10 and did not let to tell them that he hoped to help to cast half of them

divers
(dī′vərz) *adj.*
numerous.

B

---

[1] **troubles:** the transfer of passengers to the Mayflower after one of the other ships became unseaworthy.
[2] **lusty:** energetic; robust.
[3] **execrations:** angry words; curses.

Close Read Screencasts 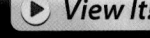 ▶ View It!

Modeled Discussions

Have students click the *Close Read* icons in their eBooks to access two screencasts in which readers discuss and annotate the following key passages:

- John Howland's rescue (lines 47–56)
- special providence of God (lines 178–185)

As a class, view and discuss at least one of these videos. Then have students pair up to do an independent close read of an additional passage—the Starving Time (lines 323–345).

TEACH

CLOSE READ

Understand Usage L 1

(LINES 19–24)

Tell students verbs have either an **active voice** or **passive voice**. If the subject performs the action, the verb is in the **active voice**. If the subject receives the action, the verb is in the **passive voice**.

Have students read lines 19–24 and note which verbs are in the active voice and which are in the passive voice. *(All of them are in the passive voice.)*

C **ASK STUDENTS** how this use of the passive voice affects the meaning of the lines. *(It is unclear who or what is performing the action, which gives the sense that these events are destined to occur.)*

Analyze Key Terms  RI 4

(LINES 29–33)

Explain to students that English usage and vocabulary have changed a great deal over time and that Bradford's account includes many **archaic** words and phrases, that is, words and phrases that are no longer commonly used. Tell students that when they encounter archaic language, it might help them to replace archaic words with current vocabulary. For instance, students could replace the archaic word "fain" with the current word "willingly."

D **ASK STUDENTS** to identify other substitutions that might make the sentence's meaning easier to understand. *("unwilling" might be substituted for "loath")*

CRITICAL VOCABULARY

sundry: The Pilgrims encountered more than one storm during their Atlantic crossing.

ASK STUDENTS to explain whether "sundry storms" could mean 5 storms, 50 storms, or 500 storms. *(Sundry storms could mean 5 storms, but not 50 or 500.)*

---

overboard before they came to their journey's end, and to make merry with what they had; and if he were by any gently reproved,[4] he would curse and swear most bitterly. But it pleased God before they came half seas over, to smite this young man with a grievous disease, of which he died in a desperate manner, and so was himself the first that was thrown overboard. Thus his curses light on his own head, and it was an astonishment to all his fellows for they noted it to be the just hand of God upon him. **B**

After they had enjoyed fair winds and weather for a season, they
20 were encountered many times with cross winds and met with many fierce storms with which the ship was shroudly[5] shaken, and her upper works made very leaky; and one of the main beams in the midships was bowed and cracked, which put them in some fear that the ship could not be able to perform the voyage. So some of the chief of the company, perceiving the mariners to fear the sufficiency of the ship as appeared by their mutterings, they entered into serious consultation with the master and other officers of the ship, to consider in time of the danger, and rather to return than to cast themselves into a desperate and inevitable peril. And truly there was great distraction
30 and difference of opinion amongst the mariners themselves; fain[6] would they do what could be done for their wages' sake (being now near half the seas over) and on the other hand they were loath[7] to hazard their lives too desperately. But in examining of all opinions, the master and others affirmed they knew the ship to be strong and firm under water; and for the buckling of the main beam, there was a great iron screw the passengers brought out of Holland, which would raise the beam into his place; the which being done, the carpenter and master affirmed that with a post put under it, set firm in the lower deck and otherways bound, he would make it sufficient. And as for the
40 decks and upper works, they would caulk them as well as they could, and though with the working of the ship they would not long keep staunch,[8] yet there would otherwise be no great danger, if they did not overpress her with sails. So they committed themselves to the will of God and resolved to proceed.

In **sundry** of these storms the winds were so fierce and the seas so high, as they could not bear a knot of sail, but were forced to hull[9] for divers days together. And in one of them, as they thus lay at hull in a mighty storm, a lusty young man called John Howland, coming upon some occasion above the gratings was, with a seele[10] of the ship,
50 thrown into sea; but it pleased God that he caught hold of the topsail

C

D

sundry
(sŭnʹdrē) *adj.* various or assorted.

E

---

[4] **reproved:** reprimanded.
[5] **shroudly:** shrewdly, used here in its archaic sense of "wickedly."
[6] **fain:** archaic for "gladly."
[7] **loath:** reluctant.
[8] **staunch:** watertight.
[9] **hull:** to float without using the sails.
[10] **seele:** sudden lurch to one side.

6 Collection 1

SCAFFOLDING FOR ELL STUDENTS

Reading Support Guide students in using a strategy to better understand complex sentence structures. Using a whiteboard, project the sentence on lines 33–39. Invite volunteers to do the following to them:

- Change the semicolons to periods.
- Capitalize the first words of the new sentences.
- Underline all of the subjects.
- Highlight all of the verbs.

ASK STUDENTS what other strategies they could use to better understand complex sentence structure. *(paraphrasing, or rewording, the sentence)*

halyards[11] which hung overboard and ran out at length. Yet he held his hold (though he was sundry fathoms under water) till he was hauled up by the same rope to the brim of the water, and then with a boat hook and other means got into the ship again and his life saved. And though he was something ill with it, yet he lived many years after and became a profitable member both in church and commonwealth. In all this voyage there died but one of the passengers, which was William Butten, a youth, servant to Samuel Fuller, when they drew near the coast.

60   But to omit other things (that I may be brief) after long beating at sea they fell with that land which is called Cape Cod;[12] the which being made and certainly known to be it, they were not a little joyful. After some deliberation had amongst themselves and with the master of the ship, they tacked about and resolved to stand for the southward (the wind and weather being fair) to find some place about Hudson's River[13] for their habitation. But after they had sailed that course about

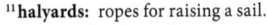

[11] **halyards:** ropes for raising a sail.
[12] **Cape Cod:** They sighted Cape Cod in present-day Massachusetts at daybreak on November 9, 1620.
[13] **Hudson's River:** They were trying to reach Manhattan Island. Henry Hudson had made his voyage in 1609 and had claimed the area for the Dutch, but the English did not recognize the Dutch claim.

Of Plymouth Plantation   7

Determine Central Ideas (LINES 47–56)

COMMON CORE RI 2

Inform students that although William Bradford witnessed first-hand the events of the Mayflower's 1620 voyage, he did not write about them until years later. When he did write his account, he chose to relate anecdotes and details that support his central ideas.

Ⓔ **CITE TEXT EVIDENCE** Have students read lines 47-56 and use text evidence to determine the central idea of these lines. *(Bradford tells the story of a man who was washed overboard during "a mighty storm," but "it pleased God that he caught hold of the topsail halyards." The man went on to become a "profitable member" of the community. The central idea of these lines is that God can save whom he chooses.)*

Analyze Foundational Texts (LINES 60–62)

COMMON CORE RI 6, RI 9

Explain to students that an author's purpose is his reason for writing a particular text. For instance, an author might write to inform, to persuade, to express beliefs and feelings, or to entertain. Have students read lines 60–62.

Ⓕ **ASK STUDENTS** to analyze these lines for clues to the author's purpose. What do these lines reveal about Bradford's purpose? *(In these lines, Bradford explains that he is leaving some parts of the story out of this account in order to be brief, or to get to the point. This shows that Bradford is considering his audience in order to achieve a particular purpose.)*

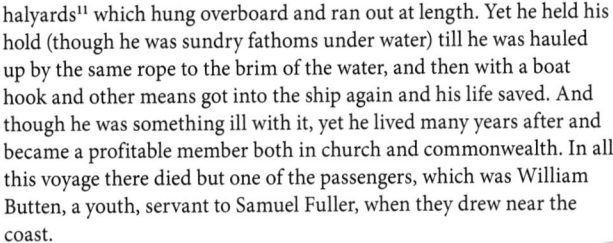

But in examining of all opinions, the master and others affirmed they knew the ship to be strong and firm under water. And for the buckling of the main beam, there was a great iron screw the passengers brought out of Holland, which would raise the beam into his place. The which being done, the carpenter and master affirmed that with a post put under it, set firm in the lower deck and otherways bound, he would make it sufficient.

CLOSE READ

Analyze Foundational Texts (LINES 78–109)

COMMON CORE RI 2, RI 4, RI 9

Explain to students that **rhetorical features** are techniques writers use to communicate ideas and support their **purpose**. One **rhetorical feature** Bradford uses is an **allusion**. An **allusion** is a reference to a person, place, or event that the author expects will be familiar to readers.

(G) ASK STUDENTS to identify the three **allusions** Bradford uses in these two paragraphs (lines 78–109). *(The first is to Seneca, the second is to the Apostle, and the third is to Pisgah.)* Ask students if they are familiar with any of these three **allusions**. If not, explain to them that Seneca was a Roman philosopher and teacher who once wrote about how he hated traveling by ship because of seasickness. "The Apostle" is an **allusion** to early Christian missionary Paul who, when shipwrecked, was met by "barbarians" who provided him food and shelter. Pisgah is an **allusion** to the summit from which Moses could see the "promised land."

ASK STUDENTS how these three **allusions** support Bradford's **central idea** that the Pilgrims endured a difficult journey into an unknown wilderness. *(The allusions emphasize the extreme difficulty of the Pilgrims' journey—the Mayflower voyage was even worse than Seneca's; the Pilgrims were met with arrows, not food and shelter, like the apostle Paul; and the Pilgrims couldn't even see if they were close to their "promised land.")*

CRITICAL VOCABULARY

succour: When the Pilgrims arrived at Cape Cod there was no one there to welcome them.

ASK STUDENTS to list some of the items William Bradford considers *succour*. *(Lines 85–90: "Being thus passed the vast ocean, and a sea of troubles before in their preparation (as may be remembered by that which went before), they had now no **friends** to welcome them nor **inns** to **entertain** or **refresh** their weatherbeaten bodies; no **houses** or much less **towns** to repair to, to seek for succour.")*

---

half the day, they fell amongst dangerous shoals and roaring breakers, and they were so far entangled therewith as they conceived themselves in great danger; and the wind shrinking upon them withal, they

70 resolved to bear up again for the Cape and thought themselves happy to get out of those dangers before night overtook them, as by God's good providence they did. And the next day they got into the Cape Harbor[14] where they rid in safety....

Being thus arrived in a good harbor, and brought safe to land, they fell upon their knees and blessed the God of Heaven who had brought them over the vast and furious ocean, and delivered them from all the perils and miseries thereof, again to set their feet on the firm and stable earth, their proper element. And no marvel if they were thus joyful, seeing wise Seneca was so affected with sailing a few miles on

80 the coast of his own Italy, as he affirmed, that he had rather remain twenty years on his way by land than pass by sea to any place in a short time, so tedious and dreadful was the same unto him.

But here I cannot but stay and make a pause, and stand half amazed at this poor people's present condition; and so I think will the reader, too, when he well considers the same. Being thus passed the vast ocean, and a sea of troubles before in their preparation (as may be remembered by that which went before), they had now no friends to welcome them nor inns to entertain or refresh their weatherbeaten bodies; no houses or much less towns to repair to, to

90 seek for **succour**. It is recorded in Scripture[15] as a mercy to the Apostle and his shipwrecked company, that the barbarians showed them no small kindness in refreshing them, but these savage barbarians, when they met with them (as after will appear) were readier to fill their sides full of arrows than otherwise. And for the season it was winter, and they that know the winters of that country know them to be sharp and violent, and subject to cruel and fierce storms, dangerous to travel to known places, much more to search an unknown coast. Besides, what could they see but a hideous and desolate wilderness, full of wild beasts and wild men—and what multitudes there might be of

100 them they knew not. Neither could they, as it were, go up to the top of Pisgah[16] to view from this wilderness a more goodly country to feed their hopes; for which way soever they turned their eyes (save upward to the heavens) they could have little solace or content in respect of any outward objects. For summer being done, all things stand upon them with a weatherbeaten face, and the whole country, full of woods and thickets, represented a wild and savage hue. If they looked behind them, there was the mighty ocean which they had passed and was now as a main bar and gulf to separate them from all the civil parts of the world. . . .

succour
(sŭk´ər) *n.* help and comfort.

---

[14] **Cape Harbor:** now called Provincetown Harbor.
[15] **Scripture:** In the Acts of the Apostles (Chapter 28), shipwrecked Christians were helped by the "barbarous people" of Malta.
[16] **Pisgah:** mountain from which Moses first viewed the Promised Land.

WHEN STUDENTS STRUGGLE . . .

Paraphrasing large paragraphs is similar to rewording long sentences. Display lines 83-109 from the final paragraph of Chapter IX on the board or on a device. Invite students to mark up the text:

- Divide the paragraph into eight sentences.
- Turn the semicolons into periods.
- Capitalize the beginning of the new sentences.
- Divide the sentences further, if needed.
- Reword each sentence, trying to understand its main idea.

CHAPTER X

Showing How they Sought out a place of Habitation; and What Befell them Thereabout

110 Being thus arrived at Cape Cod the 11th of November, and necessity calling them to look out a place for habitation (as well as the master's and mariners' importunity[17]); they having brought a large shallop[18] with them out of England, stowed in quarters in the ship, they now got her out and set their carpenters to work to trim her up; but being much bruised and shattered in the ship with foul weather, they saw she would be long in mending. Whereupon a few of them **tendered** themselves to go by land and discover those nearest places, whilst the shallop was in mending; and the rather because as they went into that harbor there seemed to be an opening some two or three
120 leagues off, which the master judged to be a river. It was conceived there might be some danger in the attempt, yet seeing them resolute[19], they were permitted to go, being sixteen of them well armed under the conduct of Captain Standish, having such instructions given them as was thought meet.[20]

They set forth the 15th of November; and when they had marched about the space of a mile by the seaside, they espied[21] five or six persons with a dog coming towards them, who were savages; but they fled from them and ran up into the woods, and the English followed them, partly to see if they could speak with them, and partly
130 to discover if there might not be more of them lying in ambush. But the Indians seeing themselves thus followed, they again forsook[22] the woods and ran away on the sands as hard as they could, so as they could not come near them but followed them by the track of their feet sundry miles and saw that they had come the same way. So, night coming on, they made their **rendezvous** and set out their **sentinels**, and rested in quiet that night; and the next morning followed their track till they had headed a great creek and so left the sands, and turned another way into the woods. But they still followed them by guess, hoping to find their dwellings; but they soon lost both them and
140 themselves, falling into such thickets as were ready to tear their clothes and armor in pieces; but were most distressed for want of drink. But at length they found water and refreshed themselves, being the first New England water they drunk of, and was now in great thirst as pleasant unto them as wine or beer had been in foretimes.

tender
(tĕn′dər) *v.* to offer or present.

rendezvous
(rän′dā-vōō′) *n.* meeting place.

sentinel
(sĕn′tə-nəl) *n.* a lookout person or guard.

---

[17] **importunity:** urgent demand.
[18] **shallop:** a heavy sailboat with two masts.
[19] **resolute:** determined.
[20] **meet:** appropriate.
[21] **espied:** saw for a brief moment; glimpsed.
[22] **forsook:** left or abandoned.

Of Plymouth Plantation   **9**

Analyze and Evaluate Structure (LINES 110–116)

COMMON CORE   RI 5

Explain to students that one feature of Bradford's **archaic language** is the inclusion of several ideas in one sentence. Each of these ideas is contained in a **clause**. Clauses are often marked with commas, semicolons, or parentheses.

(H) ASK STUDENTS to reread lines 110–116 and then to suggest how this lengthy sentence might be rewritten in a more modern way. *(Accept any response punctuated correctly and retaining the text's original meaning.)*

CRITICAL VOCABULARY

tendered: Some of the Pilgrims wanted to explore Cape Cod while the shallop was being repaired.

ASK STUDENTS to explain whether the scouts offered to leave the Mayflower, or were forced to leave. *(A few of the men officially requested to make landfall and explore the area.)*

rendezvous: When night came, the Pilgrims set up their camp.

ASK STUDENTS to explain why the Pilgrims met at nightfall. *(The Pilgrims gathered to set up camp and sleep.)*

sentinels: After meeting at their rendezvous point, some scouts were sent to watch over the camp through the night.

ASK STUDENTS whether the Pilgrims were afraid for their safety while sleeping. *(The scouts posted guards to keep watch through the night.)*

APPLYING ACADEMIC VOCABULARY

adapt	coherent

As you discuss *Of Plymouth Plantation's* Chapter IX, incorporate the following Collection 1 academic vocabulary words: *adapt* and *coherent*. To help students understand the culture of the Separatists, ask them to explain how the Separatists **adapt** to the environment around them. As you evaluate the effectiveness of the Separatists' actions, ask students how the group remains **coherent** in the face of uncertainty.

Integrate Multiple Sources of Information

COMMON CORE **RI 7**

Point out to students that historical accounts often include sources of information presented in different media and formats, such as illustrations, charts, and maps. Explain that these sources of information often explain, elaborate on, or illuminate the text. Have students examine the map. Tell them to read the title, the labels, and the place names. Direct students' attention to the legend at the top. Tell them that the **legend** of a map tells what its symbols stand for. For instance, in this map, different routes are represented by different styles of line. The legend also shows the map's scale.

ASK STUDENTS to make connections between the map and the text *Of Plymouth Plantation*. What places, events, and journeys described in the text are also shown on the map? *(Connections include Cape Cod, the route of the Mayflower, the landing place of the Mayflower, and the first encounter with the Indians.)*

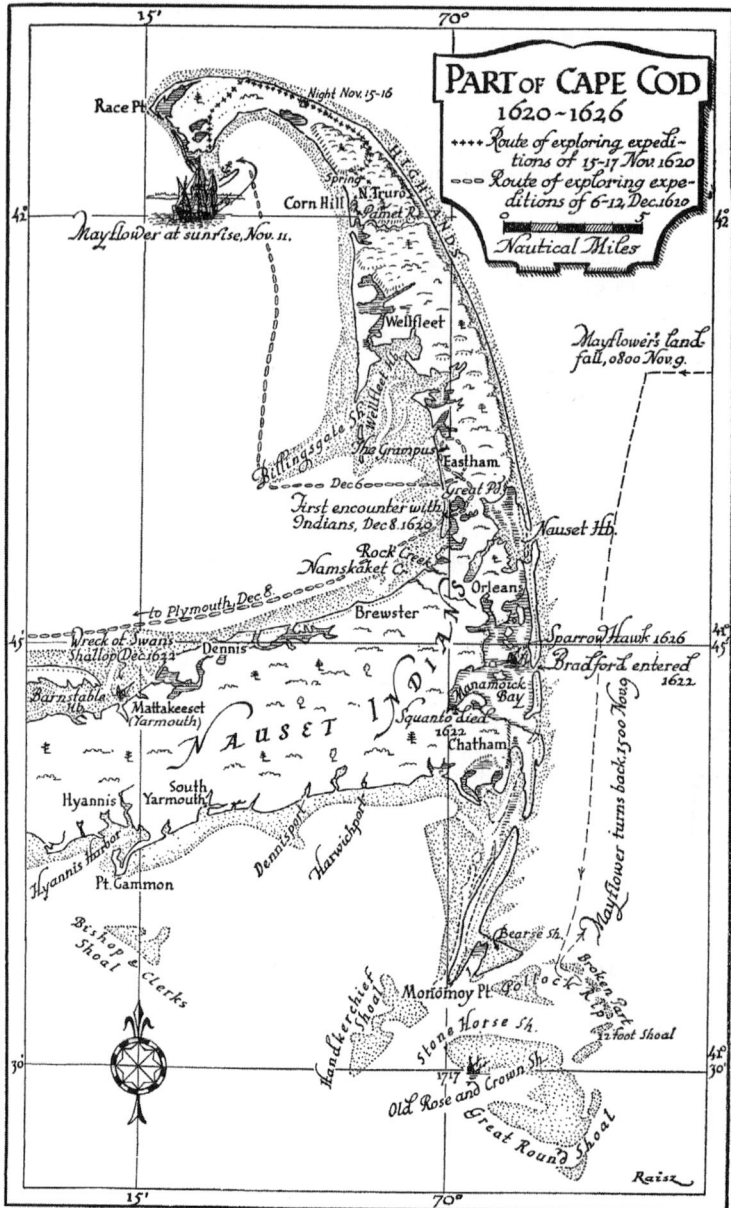

SCAFFOLDING FOR ELL STUDENTS

Analyze Language Explain that **pronouns** are words that are used to replace **nouns**. Bradford uses the pronouns "they" and "their" often throughout his text.

Use a whiteboard to project lines 173–177. Invite volunteers to mark it up.

- Highlight the pronouns *they* and *their*.
- Replace the highlighted pronouns with their referents for easier comprehension.

Afterwards they directed their course to come to the other shore, for they knew it was a neck of land they were to cross over, and so at length got to the seaside and marched to this supposed river, and by the way found a pond of clear, fresh water, and shortly after a good quantity of clear ground where the Indians had formerly set corn, and

150 some of their graves. And proceeding further they saw new stubble where corn had been set the same year; also they found where lately a house had been, where some planks and a great kettle was remaining, and heaps of sand newly paddled with their hands. Which, they digging up, found in them divers fair Indian baskets filled with corn, and some in ears, fair and good, of divers colours, which seemed to them a very goodly sight (having never seen any such before). This was near the place of that supposed river they came to seek, unto which they went and found it to open itself into two arms with a high cliff of sand in the entrance but more like to be creeks of salt water than any

160 fresh, for aught they saw; and that there was good harborage for their shallop, leaving it further to be discovered by their shallop, when she was ready. So, their time limited them being expired, they returned to the ship lest they should be in fear of their safety; and took with them part of the corn and buried up the rest. And so, like the men from Eshcol, carried with them of the fruits of the land and showed their brethren;[23] of which, and their return, they were marvelously glad and their hearts encouraged.

After this, the shallop being got ready, they set out again for the better discovery of this place, and the master of the ship desired to go

170 himself. So there went some thirty men but found it to be no harbor for ships but only for boats. There was also found two of their houses covered with mats, and sundry of their implements in them, but the people were run away and could not be seen. Also there was found more of their corn and of their beans of various colours; the corn and beans they brought away, purposing to give them full satisfaction when they should meet with any of them, as, about some six months afterward they did, to their good content.

And here is to be noted a special providence of God, and a great mercy to this poor people, that here they got seed to plant them corn

180 the next year, or else they might have starved, for they had none nor any likelihood to get any till the season had been past, as the sequel did manifest. Neither is it likely they had had this, if the first voyage had not been made, for the ground was now all covered with snow and hard frozen; but the Lord is never wanting unto His in their greatest needs; let His holy name have all the praise.

The month of November being spent in these affairs, and much foul weather falling in, the 6th of December they sent out their shallop again with ten of their principal men and some seamen, upon

---

[23] **Eshcol . . . their brethren:** In the biblical book of Numbers (Chapter 13), Moses sends spies to explore the Promised Land. They return from the Valley of Eshcol with grapes and other fruit.

CLOSE READ

Analyze Foundational Texts (LINES 164–168)   COMMON CORE RI 4, RI 9

Remind students that an **allusion** is a reference to a person, place, or event that the author expects will be familiar to readers. Have students read lines 164–168. Tell them these lines contain a reference to a Bible story about the Hebrew's passage to "the promised land." As Moses led his people through the wilderness, he sent twelve people to scout ahead. These scouts returned with fruits from Eshcol.

I ASK STUDENTS how the story alluded to here relates to the Pilgrims' experience. *(The Pilgrims saw themselves as traveling to "the promised land." Like Moses' scouts to Eshcol, the Pilgrims' landing party returned with "fruits" from the land.)*

Determine Central Ideas (LINES 178–185)   COMMON CORE RI 2

Explain to students that Bradford wanted to communicate to readers certain ideas, or **themes,** that he considered important.

J ASK STUDENTS to reread lines 178–185 and identify the **theme** that the author wants to convey. *(The Pilgrims believed God's "providence" would supply them with all of their physical and spiritual needs.)* How is does the abandoned corn relate to God's "providence"? *(It provided the Pilgrims the seed they needed to plant crops the following year. Without it "they might have starved.")*

Also there was found more of their (the Indians') corn and of their (the Indians') beans of various colours; the corn and beans they (the Pilgrims) brought away, purposing to give them (the Indians) full satisfaction when they (the Pilgrims) should meet with any of them (the Indians) as, about some six months afterward they (the Pilgrims) did, to their good content.

Analyzing Purpose

COMMON CORE RI 6

(LINES 186–207)

Explain to students that authors often have more than one **purpose**, or intention, when they write a text. When that **purpose** is not clearly stated, readers can **infer** it by looking for clues within the text.

 **ASK STUDENTS** to read lines 186–207 and find words or phrases that describe places, events, or people. *(foul weather, weather was very cold, the savages, fishes dead on the sand.)* What kind of feeling do these descriptions convey? *(This is a hard, cold land full of savages and death.)* Using these clues, what might you infer about Bradford's purpose? *(He wanted readers to understand the hardships the Pilgrims faced when they arrived.)*

Analyze Foundational Text (LINES 110–224)

COMMON CORE RI 2, RI 9

Inform students that a **foundational text** is a document considered important in U.S. history. Readers can better understand the central idea of Bradford's account by analyzing **repetition**—the repetition of a word, phrase, or idea.

CITE TEXT EVIDENCE Have students skim Chapter X thus far (lines 110–224) and find evidence of repetition in the events Bradford describes. *(a few of them tendered themselves to go by land and discover those nearest places [lines 116–117]; they directed their course to come to the other shore [line 145]; they sent out their shallop again (lines 187–188); they ranged up and down all that day [line 208])*

What kind of events does Bradford's writing focus on? *(The author focuses on exploration and discovery.)*

CRITICAL VOCABULARY

circulate: The scouts and seamen wanted to explore the area around Cape Cod Bay.

ASK STUDENTS to explain whether the Pilgrims intended to continue traveling west in a straight line, or circle around the area and return to the Mayflower. *(The Pilgrims planned to circle around the area and return to the ship.)*

---

further discovery, intending to **circulate** that deep bay of Cape Cod.
190   The weather was very cold and it froze so hard as the spray of the sea lighting on their coats, they were as if they had been glazed. Yet that night betimes they got down into the bottom of the bay, and as they drew near the shore they saw some ten or twelve Indians very busy about something. They landed about a league or two from them, and had much ado to put ashore anywhere—it lay so full of flats. Being landed, it grew late and they made themselves a barricado[24] with logs and boughs as well as they could in the time, and set out their sentinel and betook them to rest, and saw the smoke of the fire the savages made that night. When morning was come they divided
200   their company, some to coast along the shore in the boat, and the rest marched through the woods to see the land, if any fit place might be for their dwelling. They came also to the place where they saw the Indians the night before, and found they had been cutting up a great fish like a grampus,[25] being some two inches thick of fat like a hog, some pieces whereof they had left by the way. And the shallop found two more of these fishes dead on the sands, a thing usual after storms in that place, by reason of the great flats of sand that lie off.

So they ranged up and down all that day, but found no people, nor any place they liked. When the sun grew low, they hasted out of
210   the woods to meet with their shallop, to whom they made signs to come to them into a creek hard by, the which they did at high water; of which they were very glad, for they had not seen each other all that day since the morning. So they made them a barricado as usually they did every night, with logs, stakes and thick pine boughs, the height of a man, leaving it open to leeward, partly to shelter them from the cold and wind (making their fire in the middle and lying round about it) and partly to defend them from any sudden assaults of the savages, if they should surround them; so being very weary, they betook them to rest. But about midnight they heard a hideous and great cry, and
220   their sentinel called "Arm! arm!" So they bestirred them and stood to their arms and shot off a couple of muskets, and then the noise ceased. They concluded it was a company of wolves or such like wild beasts, for one of the seamen told them he had often heard such a noise in Newfoundland.

So they rested till about five of the clock in the morning; for the tide, and their purpose to go from thence, made them be stirring betimes. So after prayer they prepared for breakfast, and it being day dawning it was thought best to be carrying things down to the boat. But some said it was not best to carry the arms down, others said they
230   would be the readier, for they had lapped them up in their coats from the dew; but some three or four would not carry theirs till they went

circulate
(sûr´kyə-lāt´) *v.*
to move or travel around or in a circular path.

---

[24]**barricado:** a structure quickly assembled to keep enemies out; archaic form of "barricade."
[25]**grampus:** dolphin.

WHEN STUDENTS STRUGGLE . . .

Tell students that creating a graphic organizer can sometimes help them to understand a passage of a difficult text. Ask students to read the paragraph beginning on line 186 (lines 186–207) and as they are reading, make a list of the events. It can start with "1. Pilgrims send people to explore the bay. 2. The weather was very cold." Then have students work either independently or in pairs to create a timeline of the events in this paragraph. If students find this technique helpful, they can use it to help them understand other passages of the account.

themselves. Yet as it fell out, the water being not high enough, they laid them down on the bank side and came up to breakfast.

But presently, all on the sudden, they heard a great and strange cry, which they knew to be the same voices they heard in the night, though they varied their notes; and one of their company being abroad came running in and cried, "Men, Indians! Indians!" And withal,[26] their arrows came flying amongst them. Their men ran with all speed to recover their arms, as by the good providence of God they did.

240 In the meantime, of those that were there ready, two muskets were discharged at them, and two more stood ready in the entrance of their rendezvous but were commanded not to shoot till they could take full aim at them. And the other two charged again with all speed, for there were only four had arms there, and defended the barricado, which was first assaulted. The cry of the Indians was dreadful, especially when they saw their men run out of the rendezvous toward the shallop to recover their arms, the Indians wheeling about upon them. But some running out with coats of mail on, and cutlasses in their hands, they soon got their arms and let fly amongst them and quickly stopped

250 their violence. Yet there was a lusty man, and no less valiant, stood behind a tree within half a musket shot, and let his arrows fly at them; he was seen [to] shoot three arrows, which were all avoided. He stood three shots of a musket, till one taking full aim at him and made the bark or splinters of the tree fly about his ears, after which he gave an extraordinary shriek and away they went, all of them. They left some to keep the shallop and followed them about a quarter of a mile and shouted once or twice, and shot off two or three pieces, and so returned. This they did that they might conceive that they were not afraid of them or any way discouraged.

260 Thus it pleased God to vanquish their enemies and give them deliverance; and by His special providence so to dispose that not any one of them were either hurt or hit, though their arrows came close by them and on every side [of] them; and sundry of their coats, which hung up in the barricado, were shot through and through. Afterwards they gave God solemn thanks and praise for their deliverance, and gathered up a bundle of their arrows and sent them into England afterward by the master of the ship, and called that place the First Encounter.

[26]**withal:** immediately after that.

TEACH

CLOSE READ

Analyzing Foundational Texts (LINES 234–259)

COMMON CORE RI 9

Remind students that a **foundational text** is a document considered important in U.S. history. Bradford's work provides a rare first-hand account of experiences from the early seventeenth century. But it doesn't include every event, just those Bradford found important.

M ASK STUDENTS to summarize lines 234–259. How has the action, or pace, changed in this paragraph? *(The Pilgrims' slow exploration is interrupted by an attack that is recounted at a fast pace.)* What can readers infer about Bradford's **purpose** from this paragraph? *(The pacing of the narrative gives readers a sense of excitement and fear. Bradford must have wanted readers to understand the terror of these events.)*

Determine Central Ideas (LINES 260–268)

COMMON CORE RI 2

Tell students that the Pilgrims believed they were chosen by God to fulfill a holy mission.

N CITE TEXT EVIDENCE Have students read the final paragraph of Chapter X (lines 260–268). Then, ask students to cite text evidence that suggests that Bradford saw the Pilgrims as having been chosen by God. *("it pleased God to vanquish their enemies," "His special providence," and "they gave God solemn thanks and praise for their deliverance")*

APPLYING ACADEMIC VOCABULARY

dynamic	device

As you discuss *Of Plymouth Plantation*, incorporate the following Collection 1 academic vocabulary words: *dynamic* and *device*. Explain to students that a **dynamic** narrative is characterized by sudden changes in pace or action. Ask students to explain how the narrative becomes more **dynamic** starting in line 234. *(The pace quickens as the Indians invade the camp where the Pilgrims are peacefully beginning their morning meal.)* Shifting from a static, or slow, narrative to a **dynamic** one is a literary **device**, or technique, that authors can use to communicate a **central idea**. What purpose does shifting to a **dynamic** narrative serve? *(to portray the attackers as disruptive and uncivilized barbarians)*

Analyze Foundational Texts (Introduction to the Second Book)

COMMON CORE RI 5, RI 6, RI 9

Discuss with students the form of William Bradford's work thus far. How would you describe the structure of chapters IX and X? *(a retelling of events in chronological order, similar to a journal, diary, or memoir)*

O ASK STUDENTS to read the paragraph that introduces the Second Book. What is the **purpose** of this paragraph? *(It signals a change in format to what Bradford calls "annals.")* Annals are a record of historical events. How does this differ from the previous format? *(The previous books recorded events both big and small. Annals focus only on the most significant items.)*

Analyze Language

COMMON CORE RI 4

(LINES 285–307)

Explain to students that **diction** is a writer's choice of words. Diction can be formal or informal, common or technical. Have students read carefully through the Mayflower Compact (lines 285-307), paying close attention to its **diction**.

P ASK STUDENTS how the diction of the Mayflower Compact differs from the diction in previous sections of *Of Plymouth Plantation*. Have them provide textual evidence to support their conclusions. *(The diction of the Mayflower Compact is legalistic and even more formal, with titles like "our dread Sovereign," and "Defender of the Faith" and words and phrases like "furtherance of the ends aforesaid" and "by virtue hereof to enact, constitute and frame such just and equal Laws.")*

CRITICAL VOCABULARY

patent: Before leaving England, the Pilgrims received legal permission from the king to settle in the "Northern Parts of Virginia" *(now the Hudson Bay area)*. **ASK STUDENTS** to explain why settlers would need permission from the king to form a colony in Virginia. *(Previous English explorers had claimed Virginia for the king. In England, the king was considered Virginia's legal owner.)*

THE SECOND BOOK

270   The rest of this history (if God give me life and opportunity) I shall, for brevity's sake, handle by way of annals, noting only the heads of principal things, and passages as they fell in order of time, and may seem to be profitable to know or to make use of. And this may be as the Second Book.

CHAPTER XI

The Remainder of Anno 1620

[The Mayflower Compact]

I shall a little return back, and begin with a combination made by them before they came ashore; being the first foundation of their government in this place. Occasioned partly by the discontented and mutinous[27] speeches that some of the strangers amongst them had let fall from them in the ship: That when they came ashore they would use their own liberty, for none had power to command them, the
280   **patent** they had being for Virginia and not for New England, which belonged to another government, with which the Virginia Company had nothing to do. And partly that such an act by them done, this their condition considered, might be as firm as any patent, and in some respects more sure.

> The form was as followeth:
> In the Name of God, Amen.

We whose names are underwritten, the loyal subjects of our dread Sovereign Lord King James, by the Grace of God of Great Britain, France, and Ireland King, Defender of the
290   Faith, etc.

Having undertaken, for the Glory of God and advancement of the Christian Faith and Honour of our King and Country, a Voyage to plant the First Colony in the Northern Parts of Virginia, do by these presents solemnly and mutually in the presence of God and one of another, Covenant and Combine ourselves together into a Civil Body Politic, for our better ordering and preservation and furtherance of the ends aforesaid; and by virtue hereof to enact, constitute and frame such just and equal Laws, Ordinances, Acts, Constitutions and Offices, from time
300   to time, as shall be thought most meet and convenient for the general good of the Colony, unto which we promise all due submission and obedience. In witness whereof we have hereunder subscribed our names at Cape Cod, the 11th of

patent
(păt´nt) *n.* an official document granting ownership.

---

[27]**mutinous:** rebellious.

SCAFFOLDING FOR ELL STUDENTS

Analyze Language Explain to students that a compact is an agreement and that the Mayflower Compact was an agreement between the men of the community to work together for the good of the group. Then read the compact aloud to students, stopping after each clause to answer questions.

November, in the year of the reign of our Sovereign Lord King James, of England, France and Ireland the eighteenth, and of Scotland the fifty-fourth. Anno Domini 1620.

After this they chose, or rather confirmed, Mr. John Carver (a man godly and well approved amongst them) their Governor for that
310 year. And after they had provided a place for their goods, or common store (which were long in unlading for want of boats, foulness of the winter weather and sickness of divers) and begun some small cottages for their habitation; as time would admit, they met and consulted of laws and orders, both for their civil and military government as the necessity of their condition did require, still adding thereunto as urgent occasion in several times, and as cases did require.

> " When they came ashore they would use their own liberty, for none had power to command them. "

In these hard and difficult beginnings they found some discontents and murmurings arise amongst some, and mutinous speeches and carriages in other; but they were soon quelled and
320 overcome by the wisdom, patience, and just and equal carriage of things, by the Governor and better part, which clave faithfully together in the main.

[The Starving Time]

But that which was most sad and lamentable was, that in two or three months' time half of their company died, especially in January and February, being the depth of winter, and wanting houses and other comforts; being infected with the scurvy[28] and other diseases which this long voyage and their inaccommodate condition had brought upon them. So as there died some times two or three of a day in the foresaid time, that of 100 and odd persons, scarce fifty

---
[28]**scurvy:** a disease caused by a lack of vitamin C in the diet.

TO CHALLENGE STUDENTS . . .

Challenge Central Ideas Direct students to lines 323–330. Ask students to read this passage and discuss what happened to the Pilgrims during their first winter on Cape Cod. How many settlers died? *(approximately 50 people)* What caused these deaths? *(exposure to cold temperatures, lack of housing, scurvy and other diseases)* How does this relate to Bradford's **central ideas** of "Providence" and "finding a promised land"? Challenge students to work in a small group to find textual evidence in these lines and elsewhere in *Of Plymouth Plantation* that contradicts Bradford's central ideas about Providence.

CLOSE READ

Analyze Foundational Texts (LINES 308–316)

COMMON CORE RI 9

Remind students that although William Bradford witnessed first-hand the events of the Mayflower's 1620 voyage, he did not write about them until years later.

Q CITE TEXT EVIDENCE Have students read lines 308–316. Then ask students to cite evidence for when the Mayflower Compact was signed. *(lines 304–307, November 11, 1620).* Ask students to skim Chapter X looking specifically for relevant dates. *(line 304, November 11)* How does this brief summary of events (lines 308–316) compare to those listed in Chapter X? *(Chapter X does not mention John Carver, the building of cottages, or the formation of civil and military government. It doesn't even mention the Mayflower Compact.)*

Analyze Key Terms
(LINES 317–322)

COMMON CORE RI 4

Explain to students that English usage and vocabulary have changed a great deal over time and that one strategy they can use when confronted with archaic vocabulary is to replace archaic words with their more current equivalents.

R ASK STUDENTS to read lines 317–322 and identify phrases that are unfamiliar or appear out of context. Use surrounding words, and if necessary a dictionary, to find the meaning of the unfamiliar phrases. For example, ask students to identify a synonym for the phrase "discontents and murmurings." *("complaining")* Are there other substitutions that might make the sentence's meaning clearer? *("...they were soon **quieted** and overcome by the wisdom, patience, and just and equal **attitude** of things, by the Governor and better part **of the settlers**, which **stuck** faithfully together for the most part.")*

TEACH

CLOSE READ

Language and Style
 COMMON CORE L 1

(LINES 330–335)

Remind students that verbs have either an **active voice** or **passive voice**. If the subject performs the action, the verb is in the **active voice**. If the subject receives the action, the verb is in the **passive voice**.

S **ASK STUDENTS** to read the sentence (lines 330–335) and note the active and passive verbs. How does the sentence change as it progresses? (*The sentence starts with a passive verb, "there was," and moves to a list of active verbs, "spared," "fetched," "made," etc.*) How does this use of the active and passive voice affect meaning? (*The passive voice suggests the healthy Pilgrims were acted upon by God to remain healthy. The active verbs make clear the great lengths that were taken to care for the sick.*)

Analyze Foundational Texts
 COMMON CORE RI 1, RI 9

(LINES 330–339)

Remind students that *Of Plymouth Plantation* is a **primary source** that can be used to learn about the Pilgrims at this time in history. In lines 330–339, Bradford holds up several colonists as examples of virtue. Based on these lines what characteristics did colonists value? (*self-sacrifice, compassion, endurance*)

T **CITE TEXT EVIDENCE** Have students cite text evidence to support their inferences about the characteristics colonists valued. How might celebrating the characteristics in this account influence Bradford's readers? (*Later generations would emulate Pilgrim values.*)

Analyze Language
 COMMON CORE RI 4

(LINES 346–349)

Remind students that **diction** refers to the words an author chooses to use. **Diction** is often a clue to the **author's purpose**. Have students read lines 346–349, paying close attention to **diction**.

U **ASK STUDENTS** why Bradford might have chosen to use phrases like "skulking about" and "stole away"? (*These phrases label the Native Americans as thieves.*)

---

330 remained. And of these, in the time of most distress, there was but six or seven sound persons who to their great commendations, be it spoken, spared no pains night nor day, but with abundance of toil and hazard of their own health, fetched them wood, made them fires, dressed them meat, made their beds, washed their loathsome[29] clothes, clothed and unclothed them. In a word, did all the homely and necessary offices for them which dainty and queasy stomachs cannot endure to hear named; and all this willingly and cheerfully, without any grudging in the least, showing herein their true love unto their friends and brethren; a rare example and worthy to be remembered.

340 Two of these seven were Mr. William Brewster, their reverend Elder, and Myles Standish, their Captain and military commander, unto whom myself and many others were much beholden in our low and sick condition. And yet the Lord so upheld these persons as in this general calamity they were not at all infected either with sickness or lameness. . . .

[Indian Relations]

All this while the Indians came skulking about them, and would sometimes show themselves aloof off, but when any approached near them, they would run away; and once they stole away their tools where they had been at work and were gone to dinner. But about

350 the 16th of March, a certain Indian came boldly amongst them and spoke to them in broken English, which they could well understand but marveled at it. At length they understood by discourse with him, that he was not of these parts, but belonged to the eastern parts where some English ships came to fish, with whom he was acquainted and could name sundry of them by their names, amongst whom he had got his language. He became profitable to them in acquainting them with many things concerning the state of the country in the east parts where he lived, which was afterwards profitable unto them; as also of the people here, of their names, number and strength, of their

360 situation and distance from this place, and who was chief amongst them. His name was Samoset. He told them also of another Indian whose name was Squanto, a native of this place, who had been in England and could speak better English than himself.

Being, after some time of entertainment and gifts dismissed, a while after he came again, and five more with him, and they brought again all the tools that were stolen away before, and made way for the coming of their great Sachem,[30] called Massasoit. Who, about four or five days after, came with the chief of his friends and other attendance, with the aforesaid Squanto. With whom, after friendly entertainment

370 and some gifts given him, they made a peace with him (which hath now continued this 24 years) in these terms:

---

[29] **loathsome:** offensive or disgusting.
[30] **Sachem:** chief.

16 Collection 1

SCAFFOLDING FOR ELL STUDENTS

Vocabulary Strategy Explain that **archaic** English sometimes uses words that are unfamiliar even to modern English speakers. Other times, words may be used differently.

ASK STUDENTS to read lines 352–356 (the sentence starting "At length they understood…"). Display the text on a whiteboard or other device. Invite students to underline unfamiliar words or words that appear to be used out of context. Encourage them to look at nearby words to help determine the underlined word's meaning. If the meaning still remains unclear, have students look up the words in a dictionary. Replace the underlined words with more easily understood words.

1. That neither he nor any of his should injure or do hurt to any of their people.
2. That if any of his did hurt to any of theirs, he should send the offender, that they might punish him.
3. That if anything were taken away from any of theirs, he should cause it to be restored; and they should do the like to his.
4. If any did unjustly war against him, they would aid him; if any did war against them, he should aid them.
5. He should send to his neighbours confederates[31] to certify them of this, that they might not wrong them, but might be likewise comprised in the conditions of peace.
6. That when their men came to them, they should leave their bows and arrows behind them.

380

---

[31] **confederates:** allies; persons who share a common purpose.

TEACH

CLOSE READ

Determine Central Ideas
COMMON CORE RI 2
(LINES 372–385)

Remind students that they can **paraphrase** text by restating it in their own words to help them determine the text's **central ideas**.

V **ASK STUDENTS** to **paraphrase** the treaty between Massasoit and the Pilgrims (lines 372–385) and determine its **central ideas**. *(Its central idea is that the Massasoit and the Pilgrims can peacefully coexist.)*

Summarize Text

(LINES 388–395)

COMMON CORE RI 2, RI 9

Remind students that when the Pilgrims first encountered Squanto, he already spoke English.

Ⓦ **ASK STUDENTS** to read lines 388–395 and summarize Squanto's life before the Pilgrims' arrival.

COLLABORATIVE DISCUSSION Have students form pairs to discuss and identify passages from the text concerning the relationship between the English and the Native Americans throughout Bradford's account. Then have students use that evidence to draw conclusions about how the relationship changed.

ASK STUDENTS to share any questions they generated in the course of reading and discussing the selection.

After these things he returned to his place called Sowams, some 40 miles from this place, but Squanto continued with them and was their interpreter and was a special instrument sent of God for their good beyond their expectation. He directed them how to set their
390 corn, where to take fish, and to procure other commodities, and was also their pilot to bring them to unknown places for their profit, and never left them till he died. He was a native of this place, and scarce any left alive besides himself. He was carried away with divers others by one Hunt, a master of a ship, who thought to sell them for slaves in Spain. But he got away for England and was entertained by a merchant in London, and employed to Newfoundland and other parts, and lastly brought hither into these parts by one Mr. Dermer, a gentleman employed by Sir Ferdinando Gorges and others for discovery and other designs in these parts. . . .

[First Thanksgiving]

400 They began now to gather in the small harvest they had, and to fit up their houses and dwellings against winter, being all well recovered in health and strength and had all things in good plenty. For as some were thus employed in affairs abroad, others were exercised in fishing, about cod and bass and other fish, of which they took good store, of which every family had their portion. All the summer there was no want; and now began to come in store of fowl, as winter approached, of which this place did abound when they came first (but afterward decreased by degrees). And besides waterfowl there was great store of wild turkeys, of which they took many, besides venison, etc. Besides
410 they had about a peck a meal a week to a person, or now since harvest, Indian corn to that proportion. Which made many afterwards write so largely of their plenty here to their friends in England, which were not feigned but true reports.[32]

---

[32] **reports:** Although the specific day of the Plymouth colonists' first Thanksgiving is not known, it occurred in the fall of 1621. For three days, Massasoit and almost a hundred of his men joined the Pilgrims for feasts and games.

COLLABORATIVE DISCUSSION How did the relationship between the English and the Native Americans change over time? With a partner, discuss how the relationships evolved and why they developed as they did. Cite specific textual evidence from the narrative to support your ideas.

WHEN STUDENTS STRUGGLE . . .

Ask students to think about the excerpt they just read. What were the highlights? What did they find confusing? Explain to the students that understanding a lengthy text written hundreds of years ago can be challenging for many readers. Help them organize their thoughts with an outline. Use the following example to guide them.

> I Chapter IX
>   **a.** Mayflower voyage
>   i Sailor's death

Determine Central Ideas

 COMMON CORE RI 2, RI 5

The main or **central ideas** of a text are the most important ideas that the author communicates. Sometimes an author states a central idea directly in the introduction or conclusion to a text. Often, however, the central ideas are implied. In that case, readers must look at the details the author presents and **infer,** or draw logical conclusions about, the central ideas based on those details. Important details should be closely related to the central ideas and provide support for them. Headings can also provide clues to the central ideas because they hint at the topic of each section of text.

In understanding a long, complex text like *Of Plymouth Plantation*, it is often helpful to **paraphrase** by restating the text in your own words. Determining the central idea of each paragraph or section of the text will then allow you to write an objective summary that conveys the central ideas of the text as a whole.

Analyze Foundational Texts: Historical Accounts

COMMON CORE RI 9

Of Plymouth Plantation is a **historical account**—it tells a true story about events that happened in the past. The events are told mainly in chronological order, or the order in which they happened. The text is also a **primary source,** because the author, William Bradford, observed the events personally. Bradford's vivid details and chronological structure give readers the sense that they are experiencing events right along with the Plymouth settlers.

Bradford's narrative is a **foundational text** because of its great significance in U.S. history. It provides a rare first-hand account of experiences from the early seventeenth century, when Europeans were establishing some of their first permanent settlements in North America. You can better understand Bradford's account by looking at the following elements.

Purposes	Themes	Rhetorical Features
Purpose is the reason why an author writes a particular text. The purpose might be to inform, to entertain, to express one's beliefs or feelings, or to persuade. Many texts have more than one of these purposes. In order to craft a text that will achieve a particular purpose, an author must consider his or her audience, or the people who will read the work.	A **theme** is a central idea or message about life that the author wants to communicate. To identify themes in *Of Plymouth Plantation,* think about the details that Bradford chooses to include. What impression of the settlers and their activities do these details create? Also look for ideas that are emphasized or repeated.	**Rhetorical features** include all the methods a writer uses to communicate ideas to readers. Literary devices such as **repetition** (repeating a word, phrase, or idea) and allusions are examples of rhetorical features. An **allusion** is a reference to something that the author expects will be familiar to readers, for example, the Bible for Bradford's audience.

Of Plymouth Plantation **19**

CLOSE READ

Determine Central Ideas  COMMON CORE RI 2, RI 5

Point out that students can use the descriptions of each chapter provided by Bradford to help them identify the chapter's central events and ideas. Use these descriptions as a springboard for discussion of the central idea of each section. For instance, read Bradford's description of Chapter IX *(Of their Voyage, and how they Passed the Sea; and of their Safe Arrival at Cape Cod)* and lead students in a discussion of whether this is an accurate summary of the central ideas of that chapter. What would students add or delete from Bradford's description? Follow the same process for each chapter and its description.

Analyze Foundational Texts: Historical Narratives  COMMON CORE RI 9

Explain to students that *Of Plymouth Plantation* has great historical significance because it offers one of the few and most complete first-hand accounts of the Pilgrims and their colony. Ask students what they can infer about Bradford's purpose in writing this account. What rhetorical features and themes support his purpose? *(It can be inferred that Bradford wrote* Of Plymouth Plantation *to educate future settlers about the hardships endured to reach what he considered the "promised land" and document historical events. He compares the Pilgrims to God's chosen people. He also references "God's providence" throughout the text and makes several allusions to Biblical stories about difficult voyages.)*

Strategies for Annotation 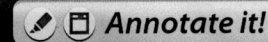 Annotate it!

Determine Central Ideas  COMMON CORE RI 2

Have students use their eBook annotation tools to analyze the text. Ask them to do the following:

- Highlight in yellow the word *God*.
- Highlight in green words with positive connotations or meanings.
- Underline words with negative connotations or meanings.
- Read annotated passages, note word choices that support ideas.
- On a note, record any words or phrases that do not seem to support his central ideas.

Being thus arrived in a good harbor, and brought safe to land, they fell upon their knees and blessed the God of Heaven who had brought them over the vast and furious ocean, and delivered them from all the perils and miseries thereof, again to set their feet on the firm and stable earth, their proper element.

Of Plymouth Plantation **19**

PRACTICE & APPLY

Analyzing the Text COMMON CORE RI 1, RI 2, RI 5, RI 9

Possible answers:

1. *Bradford's central idea is that the Pilgrims endured a difficult voyage into an uncivilized wilderness. They were met with arrows and not food and shelter. They didn't even have evidence that they were close to their "promised land."*

2. *In lines 90–95, Bradford alludes to the apostle Paul who helped spread Christianity. In lines 164–167, he alludes to Moses' search for the "promised land." Both allusions support Bradford's purpose in linking the Pilgrims' voyage to missions from God.*

3. *Squanto was kidnapped and taken to Spain as a slave. Perhaps other Native Americans had heard of or experienced such raids and fled from the Pilgrims for fear of their lives.*

4. *The structure changes from a retelling of events in chronological order to shorter summaries of specific events. The change draws attention to these events. It also focuses the text on what Bradford considers important.*

5. *The compact says the Pilgrims—who traveled for God, king, and country to establish a colony in the "Northern Parts of Virginia"— promised to create and obey a local government. Its diction and imagery suggest formality, legality, and authority.*

6. *Pilgrims and Native Americans should not hurt each other or steal property. If they do, they will be punished. The two groups will defend each other in times of "unjust" war. When Native Americans visit the Pilgrims, they must come unarmed. Except for the last item (lines 380-381), the treaty is fair.*

7. *The Pilgrims believed they were chosen by God to find a "promised land," and that God would provide everything they need. Evidence of this can be found in lines 83–109, 178–185, and 260–268.*

8. *Bradford's central idea was that God provides everything, even when faced with uncertainty and death. His purpose was to educate future settlers about the Pilgrims' sacrifices and assure them that their goals were righteous.*

 eBook *Annotate It!*

Analyzing the Text COMMON CORE RI 1, RI 2, RI 5, RI 9, W 3d

Cite Text Evidence Support your responses with evidence from the selection.

1. **Summarize** Review the last paragraph of Chapter IX (lines 83–109). What is the central idea that Bradford communicates in this paragraph?

2. **Cite Evidence** Locate and analyze two examples of Bradford's use of allusions to the Bible and of references to God's intervention in events. What purpose might these devices serve in his account?

3. **Connect** How might Squanto's experiences with the English (lines 389–399) relate to the Pilgrims' first encounter with the Indians (lines 125–144)? What do the details in these passages tell you about the ways in which early European settlers and Indians made contact with one another?

4. **Analyze** In what way does Bradford change the structure of his narrative at the beginning of Chapter XI? Why might he have chosen to make this change? What effect does this change have on the narrative?

5. **Analyze** What does the Mayflower Compact explicitly say? What does it suggest through its careful **diction,** or word choice, and use of imagery?

6. **Evaluate** Paraphrase the terms of the treaty between Massasoit and the Pilgrims (lines 372–385). Then evaluate whether the treaty is equally fair to both sides.

7. **Analyze** Which beliefs most contributed to the colonists' willingness to face hardships together? What passages best reveal those beliefs?

8. **Synthesize** What is the overall central idea of Bradford's account? How does this reflect his purpose in writing it?

PERFORMANCE TASK

Writing Activity: Journal Entry and Letter Bradford's account describes how the Pilgrims adapted to life in New England. Explore that experience in two brief writing tasks.

1. Choose one event that Bradford describes and write a journal entry in the character of one of the other English participants in the event. Consider how a personal journal might be different from Bradford's narrative written for publication.

2. In the character of one of the Pilgrims who survived the first year in New England, write a letter to someone back in England describing your current situation and how it has improved.

Base both pieces of writing on details from the text to create a coherent narrative. As much as possible, mirror the seventeenth-century style that Bradford uses.

Assign this performance task.

PERFORMANCE TASK COMMON CORE W 3c, W 3d

Writing Activity Point out to students that they will be writing from the point of view of one of the Pilgrims and should use the first-person point of view in their narratives. Consequently, they will use the pronoun "I." Invite students to include as many specific, concrete details as possible about what they see, hear, smell, and feel. For students who have chosen to write a letter, suggest that they identify the person to whom they will be writing the letter.

Critical Vocabulary

divers	sundry	succour	tender
rendezvous	sentinel	circulate	patent

Practice and Apply Choose the alternative in each sentence that best relates to the Critical Vocabulary word and explain your choice.

1. If you and your friends have **divers** opinions about what to eat, is it easy or difficult to choose a restaurant?

2. If someone offered you **succour,** would you be angry or grateful?

3. If you **tender** your resignation, do you quit your job or are you fired?

4. Would **sundry** pairs of shoes be all the same or different?

5. Is a **rendezvous** more like a plan to go with friends to a specific movie or an accidental meeting with them at the mall?

6. Are **sentinels** more like security guards or construction workers?

7. If you **circulate** a lake in a boat, do you travel along the shore or across the middle?

8. Did the *Mayflower* passengers' **patent** decide where they would live or what they would eat?

Vocabulary Strategy: Archaic Vocabulary

Of Plymouth Plantation contains many examples of **archaic vocabulary**—words that are no longer commonly used. The Critical Vocabulary word *divers,* for example, was common until the end of the 17th century but has now been almost completely replaced by *diverse.* English usage and vocabulary have changed a great deal over time. Here are some strategies you can use to help understand archaic vocabulary.

- Notice if the word is similar to a current, familiar word and try substituting the current word to make a meaningful sentence.
- Use context clues as much as possible when reading a selection that contains archaic vocabulary. Don't stop at every unfamiliar word, but read on to see if you can understand the whole sentence or paragraph.
- Look up archaic words in a dictionary. Many dictionaries include notes for archaic words or for archaic meanings of familiar words; this information is often at the end of an entry and is labeled with the word *archaic* or *obsolete.*

Practice and Apply Use the strategies to determine the meaning of the following archaic vocabulary from *Of Plymouth Plantation.*

1. foretimes (line 144)
2. betimes (line 192)
3. betook (line 198)
4. bestirred (line 220)
5. clave (line 321)

PRACTICE & APPLY

Critical Vocabulary

***Answers: 1.** difficult; divers means "numerous"* **2.** *grateful; succour means "help"* **3.** *quit; tender means "offer"* **4.** *different; sundry means "various"* **5.** *plan; a rendezvous is a meeting place* **6.** *security guards; a sentinel is a guard* **7.** *along the shore; to circulate means to move in a circular path* **8.** *live; the patent granted ownership of the land*

Vocabulary Strategy: Archaic Vocabulary

1. *foretimes*
   - Sounds similar to "before times"
   - Context clues: the water was "as pleasant as ... wine or beer had been"
   - The past

2. *betimes*
   - Sounds similar to "times"
   - Context clues: "that night betimes they got down into the bottom of the bay"
   - Soon

3. *betook*
   - Sounds similar to "took"
   - Context clues: "set out their sentinel and betook them to rest"
   - To cause to go

4. *bestirred*
   - Sounds similar to "stir"
   - Context clues: "stood to their arms"
   - Get going

5. *clave*
   - Sounds similar to "cleave"
   - Context clues: "which clave faithfully together"
   - To cling

Strategies for Annotation  Annotate it!

Archaic Vocabulary

Have students locate the sentences containing *foretimes, betimes, betook, bestirred,* and *clave.* Encourage them to use their eBook annotation tools to do the following:

- Highlight each vocabulary word.
- Reread the surrounding sentences, looking for clues to the word's meaning. Underline any clues you find, such as examples, synonyms, or antonyms.
- Review your annotations and try to infer the word's meaning.

> and took out their sentinel and betook them to rest

PRACTICE & APPLY

Language Conventions: Active and Passive Voice

 COMMON CORE L 3a

Explain to students that the examples in the chart are just a few of the reasons why an author may choose to use the passive voice. For instance, the passive voice can also be used to obfuscate, as a means of avoiding naming the subject who performed the action. *(The car was driven into a mailbox!)*

Ask students for other reasons they might use the passive voice. Why is it often better to use the active voice in writing? *(The passive voice can be awkward and less engaging.)*

 Assess It!

Online Selection Test
- Download an editable ExamView bank.
- Assign and manage this test online.

Language and Style: Active and Passive Voice

 COMMON CORE L 3a

The **voice** of a verb tells whether its subject performs or receives the verb's action. If the subject performs the action, the verb is in the **active voice:** *Liam mailed the letter.* If the subject receives the action, the verb is in the **passive voice:** *The letter was mailed.* In Bradford's writing, the Pilgrims or the Indians are most often active subjects who perform the action. Sometimes, however, the subject of a sentence or clause receives the action.

Consider this example from the narrative.

> But it pleased God before they came half seas over, to smite this young man with a grievous disease, of which he died in a desperate manner, and so was himself the first that was thrown overboard. (lines 13–16)

Note how Bradford combines the active and passive voice in this sentence. Almost all of the clauses in this complex sentence are in the active voice ("it pleased God . . . to smite," "they came half seas over," and "he died"). In the final clause, however, Bradford switches to the passive voice: "[he] was himself the first that *was thrown* overboard." Bradford's style choice obscures who or what exactly throws the "profane young man" overboard.

Although it's fairly clear from context that his fellow passengers threw the body overboard, shifting to the passive voice has two effects. First, following right after a description of God's wrath, it suggests that God is ultimately responsible. Second, it allows Bradford to downplay the idea of formerly-abused passengers tossing the man's body into the open ocean. Choosing the active or passive voice, therefore, is a matter of deciding what you want to emphasize as a writer: Do you want to stress who did something? Or do you want, instead, to focus on the fact that something happened?

This chart shows some reasons you may choose to use the passive voice.

Reason	Example
To emphasize the receiver of an action	The president was elected by a small margin.
When the doer is unknown	The windows were broken last night.
When the doer is unimportant	Smoking was banned.

Practice and Apply Return to the journal entry and letter you wrote in response to this selection's Performance Task and review them to see how often you have used the active and passive voices. Check each instance of the passive voice and see if it is better to rewrite the sentence in the active voice. Choose two examples of active voice and rewrite those sentences in passive voice to compare the strength and clarity of writing in each voice.

Support Inference: Draw Conclusions

COMMON CORE

RI 2

TEACH

The central ideas of a text are the most important ideas the author communicates. Sometimes these ideas are stated directly. Often, however, the ideas are implied. In that case, readers must look at the details the author presents. From these details, readers can **infer**, or **draw logical conclusions** about, the text's central ideas.

The details often include **rhetorical features**, which are techniques authors use to communicate their ideas. Provide students with the following definitions of rhetorical features found in *Of Plymouth Plantation*:

- **Allusion** is a reference to a person, place, event, or other literary work the author expects will be familiar to readers. Often, the author hopes to connect his idea to what is referenced.
- **Repetition** is the use of the same word or phrase more than once. It is often used to emphasize and call attention to specific ideas.

PRACTICE AND APPLY

Display lines 97–104 of the text on the board or on a device. Ask students if they are familiar with the word "Pisgah." This is an **allusion** to a Biblical story. *(In the Bible, God commands Moses to climb Mount Pisgah and view the "Promised Land.")* Ask students if they are familiar with the Biblical story of the Hebrews' exodus from Egypt. *(God sends Moses to Egypt to free the Hebrews from slavery and lead them across a wilderness to the "Promised Land.")* Is this an allusion that the Pilgrims would easily understand? *(Yes, Pilgrims would be very familiar with the Bible.)* What conclusions can you draw about Bradford's central idea here, based on these allusions? *(Bradford wants to emphasize the dire straits the Pilgrims found themselves in, and perhaps evoke pity on the part of the reader.)*

Display lines 386–399. Have volunteers point out a word that is repeated. *("Place" appears four times in this paragraph.)* What other references to location can students find in this paragraph? *(Sowams, Spain, England, London, Newfoundland, these parts)* How does Squanto's tale relate to that of the Pilgrims and their search for a "promised land"? *(Squanto was taken far from home; this might have made him compassionate towards the Pilgrims.)* Why would Bradford wish to include this story in his narrative? *(He wants to show that the Pilgrims' fortunes are improving, and that they are perhaps closer to reaching the "Promised Land.")*

Archaic Language

COMMON CORE

L 4

RETEACH

The English language has changed since *Of Plymouth Plantation* was written more than 300 years ago. Modern readers consider William Bradford's style and vocabulary to be **archaic**, or outdated, and often challenging. Here are three strategies students should use to understand **archaic language**:

- Divide long sentences into smaller parts. Punctuation such as commas and semicolons, often mark where sentences can be split.
- Identify the subject and verb. Knowing what is happening and who is doing it in a sentence can unlock its meaning.
- Paraphrase, or restate, challenging passages. Find synonyms for unknown words.

LEVEL UP TUTORIALS Assign the following *Level Up* tutorial: **Paraphrasing**

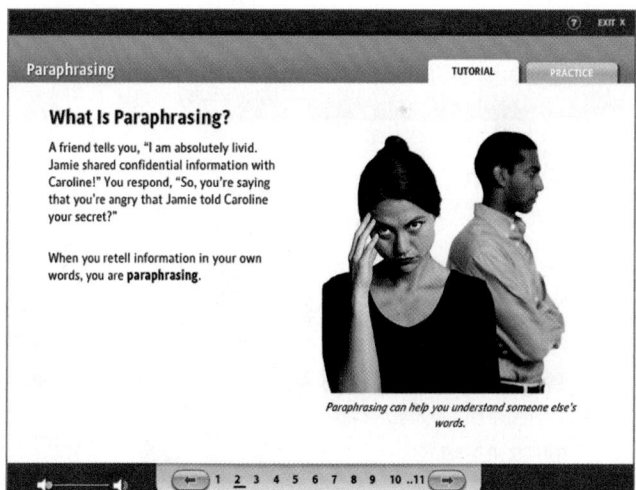

CLOSE READING APPLICATION

Students can apply the skill to other texts they find challenging. Have them work independently to find and read a trade journal, corporate annual report, scientific paper, or other specialized publication. Ask: What is the purpose of this text? What evidence in this text supports that purpose?

from The General History of Virginia

Historical Narrative by John Smith

Why This Text

This excerpt from "The General History of Virginia" provides an opportunity to analyze a historical narrative, a primary source with great significance in U.S. history. Students sometimes find it difficult to read older texts. They may also find it difficult to determine the author's purpose for writing. With the help of the close-reading questions, students will support their conclusions about the central ideas with strong and thorough textual evidence. This close reading will lead students to determine the central ideas of "The General History of Virginia."

Background Have students read the background and the information about the author. John Smith is well known as an American hero who was quick to boast about his accomplishments. Fact is often difficult to separate from fiction in his writing. Introduce the selection by explaining that the colonists were delivered to Virginia as employees of the *Virginia Company* with the purpose of profiting the company. The ships that brought the colonists returned to England, leaving the colonists to fend for themselves.

AS YOU READ Ask students to pay attention to clues that reveal Smith's central ideas and overall purpose. Remind them that this is an autobiography, and ask, "How does Smith present himself?"

Common Core Support

- cite strong and thorough textual evidence
- determine the central ideas of a text
- determine an author's purpose in a text
- analyze seventeenth-century foundational U.S. documents of historical and literary significance

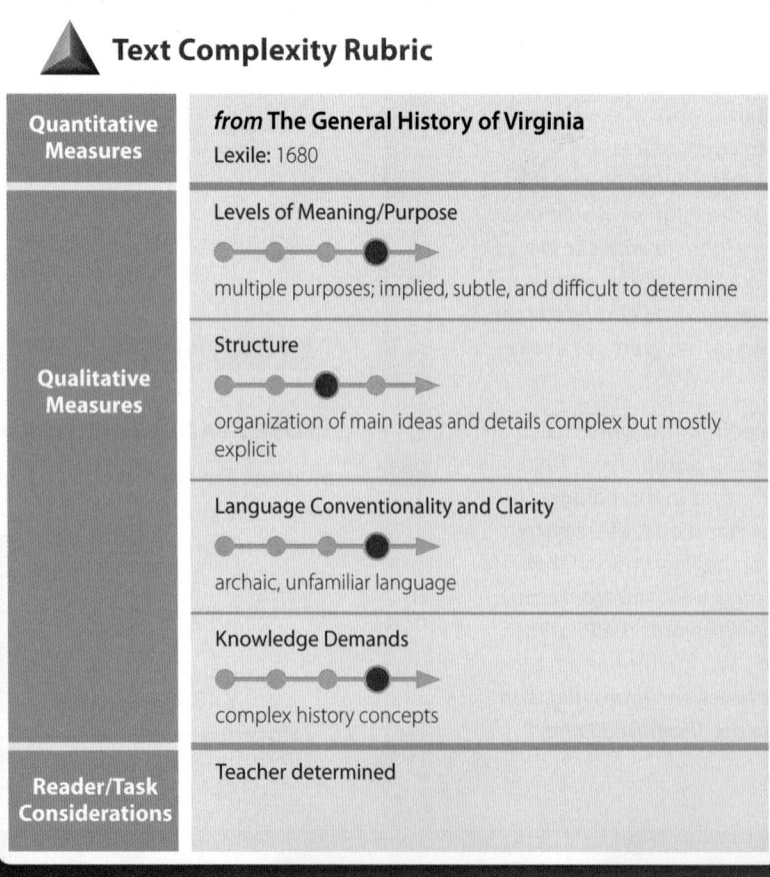

Text Complexity Rubric

Quantitative Measures

from **The General History of Virginia**
Lexile: 1680

Qualitative Measures

Levels of Meaning/Purpose

multiple purposes; implied, subtle, and difficult to determine

Structure

organization of main ideas and details complex but mostly explicit

Language Conventionality and Clarity

archaic, unfamiliar language

Knowledge Demands

complex history concepts

Reader/Task Considerations

Teacher determined

Strategies for CLOSE READING

Determine Central Ideas

Students should read this text carefully all the way through. Close-reading questions at the bottom of the page will help them focus on a thorough analysis of the text. As they read, students should jot down comments or questions about the text in the side margins.

WHEN STUDENTS STRUGGLE . . .

To help students determine the central ideas of the text, have them work in a small group to fill out a chart, such as the one shown below, as they analyze the text.

CITE TEXT EVIDENCE For practice in determining the central ideas of this excerpt from "The General History of Virginia," ask students to cite four important details from which they will determine two central ideas and one purpose. In filling out this chart, they should work from the bottom to the top.

> **Smith's Purpose:** *Smith tells the story of a colony saved by a single exceptional person—himself.*

> **Central Idea:** *Smith was the one person responsible for overcoming the arduous and dangerous conditions at Jamestown.*

> **Central Idea:** *Smith accepts no blame for charges brought against him, and draws attention to his leadership and courage.*

Detail: "such extreme weakness and sickness oppressed us"	**Detail:** the President "committed the managing of all things" to Smith	**Detail:** Smith was "always bearing the greatest task for his own share"	**Detail:** Smith faced hundreds of "grim courtiers" and Powhatan "more like a devil"

Background *The Jamestown colony was modeled after a military expedition, transplanting about 100 hardy Englishmen into the Virginia wilderness in 1607. As the ships that brought them returned to England, five members of Jamestown's ruling council—Edward Wingfield, Bartholomew Gosnold, John Ratcliffe, George Kendall, and John Smith—found themselves wrestling for control of the colony. As Smith's account opens, the colonists' ships have returned to England for supplies, leaving the men to survive on their own.*

from
The General History of Virginia

Historical Narrative by John Smith

CLOSE READ
Notes

1. **READ ▶** As you read lines 1–17, begin to collect and cite text evidence.
   - Circle the main problem described in the first paragraph.
   - Underline phrases that describe Wingfield's behavior.

The Struggle for Jamestown

(A) Being thus left to our fortunes, it fortuned that within ten days scarce ten amongst us could either go or well stand, such extreme weakness and sickness oppressed us. And thereat none need marvel if they consider the cause and reason which was this: While the ships stayed, our allowance was somewhat bettered by a daily proportion of biscuit which the sailors would **pilfer** to sell, give, or exchange with us for money, sassafras, furs, or love. But when they departed, there remained neither tavern, beer-house, nor place of relief but the common kettle.[1] Had we been as free from all sins as [we were free from] gluttony and drunkenness we might have been canonized for saints,

(B) 10 but our President [Edward Wingfield] would never have been admitted [to sainthood] for engrossing to his private,[2] oatmeal, sack,[3] oil, aqua vitae,[4] beef,

pilfer: *steal articles of small value*

---
[1] **common kettle:** food that was available to everyone.
[2] **engrossing to his private:** taking for his private use.
[3] **sack:** wine.
[4] **aqua vitae:** brandy.

3

1. **READ AND CITE TEXT EVIDENCE** Point out that Smith describes challenges faced by the colonists.

   (A) ASK STUDENTS to cite evidence that the colony faces both physical and interpersonal challenges. *Students should cite lines 1–3 as evidence of physical challenges, and lines 10–12 as evidence of a problem with Wingfield's behavior.*

   Critical Vocabulary: pilfer (line 6) Have students share their definitions of *pilfer*. Ask students to explain the exchange between the sailors and the colonists in their own words, and to use *pilfer* in their explanation.

CLOSE READ
Notes

Wingfield kept food and drink for himself; most other food was rotten.

Smith probably refers to himself in the third person to make his account more believable.

industry:
hard work; diligence

eggs, or what not but the kettle; that indeed he allowed equally to be distributed, and that was half a pint of wheat and as much barley boiled with water for a man a day, and this, having fried some twenty-six weeks in the ship's hold, contained as many worms as grains so that we might truly call it rather so much bran than corn; our drink was water, our lodgings castles in the air.

With this lodging and diet, our extreme toil in bearing and planting palisades[5] so strained and bruised us and our continual labor in the extremity

20   of the heat had so weakened us, as were cause sufficient to have made us as miserable in our native country or any other place in the world.

From May to September, those that escaped lived upon sturgeon and sea crabs. Fifty in this time we buried; the rest seeing the President's projects to escape these miseries in our pinnace[6] by flight (who all this time had neither felt want nor sickness) so moved our dead spirits as we deposed him and established Ratcliffe in his place (Gosnold being dead), Kendall deposed. Smith newly recovered, Martin and Ratcliffe were by his care preserved and relieved, and the most of the soldiers recovered with the skillful diligence of Master Thomas Wotton our surgeon general.

30   But now was all our provisions spent, the sturgeon gone, all helps abandoned, each hour expecting the fury of the savages, when God, the patron of all good endeavors, in that desperate extremity so changed the hearts of the savages that they brought such plenty of their fruits and provision as no man wanted.

The new President [Ratcliffe] and Martin, being little beloved, of weak judgment in dangers, and less **industry** in peace, committed the managing of all things abroad to Captain Smith, who, by his own example, good words, and fair promises, set some to mow, others to bind thatch, some to build houses, others to thatch them, himself always bearing the greatest task for his own

40   share, so that in short time he provided most of them lodgings, neglecting any for himself. . . .

---

[5] **palisades:** walls made of tall, pointed wooden stakes.
[6] **pinnace:** a small sailing ship.

---

2. ◀ REREAD Reread lines 1–17. In the side margin, explain the central idea of this paragraph.

3. READ ▶ Read lines 18–41. Underline text where Smith refers to himself.

4. ◀ REREAD Reread lines 30–41. In the margin, explain why you think Smith refers to himself in the third person.

4

CLOSE READ
Notes

> *But now was all our provisions spent, the sturgeon gone, all helps abandoned, each hour expecting the fury of the savages . . .*

A Surprise Attack

Smith, perceiving (notwithstanding their late misery) not any regarded but from hand to mouth, (the company being well recovered) caused the pinnace to be provided with things fitting to get provision for the year following, but in the **interim** he made three or four journeys and discovered the people of Chickahominy,[7] yet what he carefully provided the rest carelessly spent.

Wingfield and Kendall, living in disgrace strengthened themselves with the sailors and other confederates to regain their former credit and authority,

50   or at least such means aboard the pinnace (being fitted to sail as Smith had appointed for trade), to alter her course and to go for England.

Smith, unexpectedly returning, had the plot discovered to him, much trouble he had to prevent it, till with the store of saker[8] and musket shot he forced them [to] stay or sink in the river: which action cost the life of Captain Kendall.[9]

These brawls are so disgustful, as some will say they are better forgotten, yet all men of good judgment will conclude it were better their **baseness** should be manifest to the world, than the business bear the scorn and shame of their excused disorders.

interim:
period in between

baseness:
lack of honor or morality

---

[7] **Chickahominy:** a river in Virginia.
[8] **saker:** canon shot.
[9] **Captain Kendall:** Kendall was executed for mutiny in 1607.

---

5. READ ▶ As you read lines 42–62, continue to cite textual evidence. Paraphrase Wingfield and Kendall's plan in the margin on the next page. Explain what Smith does upon hearing about it.

5

---

2. REREAD AND CITE TEXT EVIDENCE

Ⓑ **ASK STUDENTS** to cite evidence that supports their explanations. *Lines 10–16 show that President Wingfield kept the good food and drink for himself and left rotten food for others to eat.*

3. READ AND CITE TEXT EVIDENCE

Ⓒ **ASK STUDENTS** to cite text evidence showing how Smith refers to himself. *Students should cite "Smith" in line 26, and "Captain Smith" in line 37.*

4. REREAD AND CITE TEXT EVIDENCE

Ⓓ **ASK STUDENTS** what impression Smith would give if he had written lines 35–41 referring to himself in the first person. *He would sound self-opinionated and boastful.*

Critical Vocabulary: industry (line 36) Have students share their definitions of *industry,* and explain how it is used here.

5. READ AND CITE TEXT EVIDENCE

Ⓔ **ASK STUDENTS** to cite textual evidence to support their paraphrase of Wingfield and Kendall's plan and Smith's intervention. *Students should cite text from lines 48–55.*

Critical Vocabulary: interim (line 45) Ask students to share definitions of *interim*. Ask them to paraphrase lines 44–47, using *interim* in context.

Critical Vocabulary: baseness (line 57) Ask students to share definitions of *baseness*. Then ask students to infer a reason that Smith would choose this word. *Students might say that Smith is disparaging Wingfield and Kendall to justify the actions he took that led to Kendall's death.*

FOR ELL STUDENTS Clarify the meaning of the preposition *notwithstanding*, which in this context means "in spite of."

Wingfield and Kendall plan to take over the ship and sail back to England. Smith puts an end to the plot, causing the death of Captain Kendall.

The Council accuses Smith of making little progress in finding the head of the Chickahominy river.

60 The President and Captain Archer[10] not long after intended also to have abandoned the country, which project also was curbed and suppressed by Smith.

The Spaniard never more greedily desired gold than he [Smith] victual,[11] nor his soldiers more to abandon the country than he to keep it. But [he found] plenty of corn in the river of Chickahominy, where hundreds of savages in divers places stood with baskets expecting his coming. And now the winter approaching, the rivers became so covered with swans, geese, ducks, and cranes that we daily feasted with good bread, Virginia peas, pumpkins, and putchamins,[12] fish, fowl, and divers sort of wild beasts as fast as we could eat

70 them, so that none of our tuftaffety humorists[13] desired to go for England.

(G)
(H) But our comedies never endured long without a tragedy, some idle exceptions being muttered against Captain Smith for not discovering the head of Chickahominy river and [he being] taxed by the Council to be too slow in so worthy an attempt. The next voyage he proceeded so far that with much labor by cutting of trees asunder he made his passage, but when his barge could pass no farther, he left her in a broad bay of danger of shot, commanding none should go ashore till his return, himself with two English and two savages went up higher in a canoe, but he was not long absent but his men went ashore, whose want of government gave both occasion and opportunity to the savages

80 to surprise one George Cassen whom they slew and much failed not to have cut off the boat and all the rest.

Smith little dreaming of that accident, being got to the marshes at the river's head twenty miles in the desert,[14] had his two men [Robinson and Emry] slain (as is supposed) sleeping by the canoe, while himself by fowling[15] sought

[10] **Captain Archer:** Gabriel Archer had abandoned the colony and then returned. He did not support Smith.
[11] **victual:** food.
[12] **putchamins:** persimmons.
[13] **tuftaffety humorists:** unreliable lace-wearers.
[14] **desert:** wilderness.
[15] **fowling:** hunting for birds.

6. ◀ REREAD AND DISCUSS Reread lines 42–62. With a small group, discuss the extent to which Smith's account seems credible. To what extent is this a factual narrative?

7. READ ▶ As you read lines 63–89, continue to cite textual evidence.
- Underline the details that make Smith seem like a hero.
- In the margin, explain the Council's complaint against Smith (lines 71–74).

6

---

them victual, who finding he was beset with 200 savages, two of them he slew, still defending himself with the aid of the savage his guide, whom he bound to his arms with his garters[16] and used him as a buckler,[17] yet he was shot in his thigh a little, and had many arrows that stuck in his clothes but no great hurt, till at last they took him prisoner. . . .

At Powhatan's Court

90 At last they brought him to Werowocomoco, where was Powhatan, their Emperor. Here more than two hundred of those grim courtiers stood wondering at him, as [if] he had been a monster, till Powhatan and his train had put themselves in their greatest braveries.[18] Before a fire upon a seat like a bedstead, he sat covered with a great robe made of raccoon skins and all the tails hanging by. On either hand did sit a young wench of sixteen or eighteen years and along on each side [of] the house, two rows of men and behind them as many women, with all their heads and shoulders painted red, many of their heads bedecked with the white down of birds, but every one with something, and a great chain of white beads around their necks.

[16] **garters:** shirtlaces.
[17] **buckler:** shield.
[18] **braveries:** clothes.

8. ◀ REREAD Reread lines 63–89. What explanations does Smith give for the loss of men, and his own capture? Why does he include these explanations? Support your answer with textual evidence.

He blames the Council for pushing him too hard. He blames the colonists who did not obey him. He blames two colonists who fell asleep in the canoe while he was getting food. Finally, he blames being outnumbered 200 to 1 by so-called "savages." He wants to show that it is not his fault that members of his party died and that he was captured. He is trying to remain blameless of all wrongdoing.

9. READ ▶ As you read lines 90–135, continue to cite textual evidence.
- Underline language Smith uses to describe Powhatan.
- In the margin, explain what happens in lines 100–112.

7

---

6. REREAD AND DISCUSS USING TEXT EVIDENCE

(F) **ASK STUDENTS** to cite specific textual evidence to support their conclusion about the degree to which Smith's account seems credible. *Students may cite evidence that shows that Smith takes credit for saving the colony and foiling plots of those who try to escape. They can cite lines 46–47 and lines 61–62.*

7. READ AND CITE TEXT EVIDENCE

(G) **ASK STUDENTS** to give the actual words in the text that Smith uses to describe the Council's claims against him. *Smith writes that he was charged for "not discovering the head of Chickahominy river" and for being "too slow in so worthy an attempt."*

8. REREAD AND CITE TEXT EVIDENCE

(H) **ASK STUDENTS** to read their answers to a partner, discuss the explanations Smith gives for the loss of men and his own capture, and revise their answers. *Students should cite evidence from lines 73–75 to show that Smith blames the Council for pushing him too hard, lines 83–84 to show that Smith blames his men for sleeping, and lines 85–89 to show that Smith blames the 200 savages for the losses incurred on his journey.*

9. READ AND CITE TEXT EVIDENCE

(I) **ASK STUDENTS** to cite text evidence to support their explanations of what happens in lines 100–112. *Students should cite evidence that shows that Smith was brought before the King (line 100), was about to be executed (lines 106–107), and was saved by Pocahontas (lines 107–109).*

Smith was brought before the King, and was about to be executed. Pocahontas, the King's daughter, intervened and the King lets him live.

mollified:
soothed; calmed

I 100   At his entrance before the King, all the people gave a great shout. The Queen of Appomattoc[19] was appointed to bring him water to wash his hands, and another brought him a bunch of feathers, instead of a towel, to dry them; having feasted him after their best barbarous manner they could, a long consultation was held, but the conclusion was, two great stones were brought before Powhatan; then as many as could, laid hands on him, dragged him to them, and thereon laid his head and being ready with their clubs to beat out his brains, Pocahontas, the King's dearest daughter, when no entreaty could prevail, got his head in her arms and laid her own upon his to save him from death, whereat the Emperor was contended he should live to make him
110   hatchets, and her bells, beads, and copper, for they thought him as well of all occupations as themselves. For the King himself will make his own robes, shoes, bows, arrows, pots; plant, hunt, or do anything so well as the rest.

J   Two days after, Powhatan, having disguised himself in the most fearfulest manner he could, caused Captain Smith to be brought forth to a great house in the woods and there upon a mat by the fire to be left alone. Not long after, from behind a mat that divided the house, was made the most dolefulest noise he

L   ever heard; then Powhatan more like a devil than a man, with some two hundred more as black as himself, came unto him and told him now that they were friends, and presently he should go to Jamestown to send him two great
120   guns and a grindstone for which he would give him the country of Capahowasic and forever esteem him as his son Nantaquoud.

  So to Jamestown with twelve guides Powhatan sent him. That night they quartered in the woods, he still expecting (as he had done all this long time of his imprisonment) every hour to be put to one death or other, for all their feasting. But almighty God (by His divine providence) had **mollified** the hearts of those stern barbarians with compassion. The next morning betimes they came to the fort, where Smith having used the savages with what kindness he could, he showed Rawhunt, Powhatan's trusty servant, two demi-culverins[20] and a millstone to carry [to] Powhatan; they found them somewhat too heavy,
130   but when they did see him discharge them, being loaded with stones, among the boughs of a great tree loaded with icicles, the ice and branches came so tumbling down that the poor savages ran away half dead with fear. But at last we regained some conference with them and gave them such toys and sent to Powhatan, his women, and children such presents as gave them in general full content.

[19] **Appomattoc:** a nearby village.
[20] **demi-culverins:** large cannons.

Pocahontas appeals to Powhatan to spare John Smith.

K   Now in Jamestown they were all combustion, the strongest preparing once more to run away with the pinnace; which, with the hazard of his life, with saker falcon and musket shot, Smith forced now the third time to stay or sink.
140   Some, no better than they should be, had plotted with the President the next day to have him put to death by the Levitical law,[21] for the lives of Robinson and Emry; pretending the fault was his that had led them to their ends; but he quickly took such order with such lawyers that he laid them by the heels[22] till he sent some of them prisoners for England.

[21] **Levitical law:** laws, ascribed to Moses, from the Book of Leviticus in the Old Testament.
[22] **laid them by the heels:** put them in prison.

10. ◀ **REREAD AND DISCUSS** Reread lines 90–135. With a small group, discuss why Smith included an account of his time with Powhatan.

11. **READ** ▶ As you read lines 136–154, continue to cite textual evidence.
  • Underline language that hints at Smith's attitude towards the "strongest" in Jamestown.
  • In the margin, explain how Pocahontas again helped Smith.

8

9

Critical Vocabulary: mollified (line 125) Have students explain the meaning of *mollified* as it is used here. Ask them to explain the significance of lines 122–126 using the word *mollified*.

FOR ELL STUDENTS Review the use of the suffix *-est* for superlatives. Point out the words *fearfulest* and *dolefulest* on this page. Ask students to provide the base word for each, *fearful* and *doleful*, and then guess what meaning the word takes with the suffix *-est*. You may have volunteers give examples of other words with the suffix *-est*.

10. **REREAD AND DISCUSS USING TEXT EVIDENCE**

J **ASK STUDENTS** to cite textual evidence to support their conclusions about why Smith included an account of his time with Powhatan. *Students should cite evidence showing that Smith characterizes the Native Americans as "fearful" (line 113), and inhuman (line 117, "like a devil"; line 127, "the savages") and characterizes himself as a hero with God on his side (lines 125–126).*

11. **READ AND CITE TEXT EVIDENCE**

K **ASK STUDENTS** to infer Smith's attitude towards the "strongest" using text they underlined as evidence. *Students should cite lines 136–137 to show that Smith has contempt for the leaders who repeatedly attempt to leave with the colony's ship. They should cite text from lines 140–142 to show that Smith claims to be falsely accused of causing the deaths of Robinson and Emry.*

CLOSE READ
Notes

Pocahontas
brings food to
Smith and his
men.

Now every once in four or five days, Pocahontas with her attendants brought him so much provision that saved many of their lives, that else for all this had starved with hunger.

His relation of the plenty he had seen, especially at Werowocomoco, and of the state and bounty of Powhatan (which till that time was unknown), so
150 revived their dead spirits (especially the love of Pocahontas) as all men's fear was abandoned.

Thus you may see what difficulties still crossed any good endeavor; and the good success of the business being thus oft brought to the very period of destruction; yet you see by what strange means God hath still delivered it.

12. ◀ **REREAD AND DISCUSS** Reread lines 90–154. With a small group, discuss your ideas about how Europeans of the time viewed Native Americans. To whom does Smith attribute his survival? Support your answer with explicit textual evidence.

SHORT RESPONSE

Cite Text Evidence What are the central ideas of Smith's text, and what is the purpose of his account? **Cite evidence** from the text in your response.

Smith presents details of the arduous and dangerous conditions at
Jamestown; he also promotes himself as the one person responsible
for overcoming each event that might have brought ruin to the
colony. He writes that the President "committed the managing of all
things" to Smith, who was "always bearing the greatest task for his
own share." He defends himself against charges, accepting no blame,
and goes on to explain how courageous he was in the face of
hundreds of "grim courtiers" and Powhatan himself, "more like a
devil." Smith tells the story of a colony saved by a single exceptional
person—himself.

10

---

12. ⬭ **REREAD AND DISCUSS USING TEXT EVIDENCE**

Ⓛ **ASK STUDENTS** to cite explicit textual evidence to support their conclusions about how Europeans of the time viewed Native Americans. *Students should cite evidence that shows that Europeans had a negative view of Native Americans, as evidenced in line 117 "like a devil" and line 127 "the savages." They should point out that Smith credits "God" (line 154) with saving the colony despite all the evidence that points to Native Americans having saved the lives of the colonists (lines 145–151).*

SHORT RESPONSE

Cite Text Evidence Students should:

- explain the central idea that life in Jamestown was difficult and dangerous.
- analyze the central idea that Smith defended himself against charges brought against him.
- infer Smith's purpose—to tell a story in which he is the heroic savior of the colony.

TO CHALLENGE STUDENTS . . .

To give students more background for this selection, have them research John Smith and the Jamestown colony online.

ASK STUDENTS to share the results of their research with the class. Encourage students to research Smith's credibility as an author. How do historians regard his account today?

DIG DEEPER

With the class, return to Question 6, Reread and Discuss. Have students share the results of their discussions.

ASK STUDENTS whether they were satisfied with the outcome of their small-group discussions. Have each group share their conclusions about the extent to which Smith's account seems credible, and the extent to which this is a factual narrative. What textual evidence did students find to support their conclusions?

- Guide each group to share whether they came to a unanimous conclusion about the degree to which Smith seems credible and the narrative seems factual. If not, have groups share the variety of conclusions that emerged from their discussion.
- Ask groups to share the textual evidence that seemed the most compelling. Discuss evidence that Smith is credible and that he is not credible.
- After groups have shared the results of their discussion, ask whether another group shared any ideas they wish they had thought of.

ASK STUDENTS to return to their Short Response answer and revise it based on the class discussion.

mySmartPlanner   Create lesson plans and access resources online.

Coming of Age in the Dawnland

History Writing by Charles Mann

Why This Text?

Charles Mann's *1491*, including "Coming of Age in the Dawnland," provides new information about the civilizations of the Americas before Columbus arrived in 1492. Students will understand the enormous changes brought about by European exploration, settlement, and conquest.

> ▶ **View It!**
>
> Professional Development Podcast:
> **Informational Text**

Key Learning Objective: The student will be able to determine the author's purpose for writing.

COMMON CORE Common Core Standards

RI 1 Cite textual evidence.

RI 2 Determine central ideas of a text.

RI 4 Determine the meaning of words and phrases.

RI 6 Determine an author's point of view or purpose.

RI 10 Read and comprehend literary nonfiction.

W 1 Write arguments.

SL 1a Come to discussions prepared; refer to evidence from text to stimulate ideas.

SL 1b Work with peers to promote discussions and decision-making, set clear goals and deadlines, and establish individual roles as needed.

SL 1c Propel conversations with questions that probe reasoning and evidence.

SL 1d Respond thoughtfully to diverse perspectives; synthesize comments, claims, and evidence; and determine needed additional information.

L 3a Vary syntax for effect; apply an understanding of syntax.

L 4c Consult reference materials.

L 6 Acquire and use accurately general academic and domain-specific words and phrases.

▲ Text Complexity Rubric

Quantitative Measures	**Coming of Age in the Dawnland** Lexile: 1290L

Qualitative Measures

Levels of Meaning/Purpose

multiple purposes; implied, subtle, and difficult to determine

Structure

organization of main ideas and details complex but mostly explicit; may exhibit disciplinary traits

Language Conventionality and Clarity

increased unfamiliar, academic, or domain-specific words

Knowledge Demands

complex historical concepts

Reader/Task Considerations	Teacher determined Vary by individual reader and type of text

CLOSE READ

For more context and historical background, students can view the video "The Aztecs" in their eBooks.

Background Have students read the background information. The selection *Of Plymouth Plantation* was written over a century later than the period discussed in this excerpt from Mann's book. Suggest that students keep Bradford's descriptions of Native Americans in mind as they read this excerpt. How do the two descriptions vary?

AS YOU READ Direct students to use the As You Read instructions to focus their reading. Have students write down any questions they generate during reading.

Determine Author's Purpose (LINES 1–13)

COMMON CORE RI 1, RI 6

Explain to students that an author's **purpose** is his reason for writing—to inform or to persuade. Sometimes readers must infer purpose from the details chosen for inclusion, and the **tone**—his attitude toward his topic.

(A) ASK STUDENTS to read the first paragraph and the beginning of the second paragraph to analyze Mann's tone. Have them brainstorm words that describe the tone of the piece so far. *(funny, friendly, erudite)*

Determine the Meaning of Words and Phrases (LINES 5–10)

COMMON CORE RI 1, RI 4

Remind students to look for **figurative language,** such as **similes,** throughout the selection.

(B) ASK STUDENTS to find one comparison in lines 5–10. *(The author compares Tisquantum's name to a person today being called Wrath of God.)* What is the purpose of this comparison? *(to show that Tisquantum's name was intended to express a strong, unusual message)*

CRITICAL VOCABULARY

project: In line 10, Mann explains that Tisquantum is trying to make an impression on the Pilgrims.

ASK STUDENTS what kind of impression is Tisquantum trying to make? *(The meaning of his name indicates he's trying to project an image of anger and power.)* How well does his attempt to project an image succeed, based on the Pilgrims' interpretation of his actions? *(It fails because he is known as the "friendly Indian".)*

Background *In his 2005 book,* 1491: New Revelations of the Americas Before Columbus, *science journalist* **Charles C. Mann** *reviews and synthesizes the work of recent scholars who have studied early Native American societies. Christopher Columbus's voyage to the Caribbean in 1492 marked the beginning of contact between native people in the Americas and Europeans. By 1620, Native Americans in coastal New England had been trading on a limited basis with Europeans for about a hundred years. The man named Tisquantum in this excerpt from Mann's book is the person whom William Bradford called Squanto.*

Coming of Age in the Dawnland
from 1491

History Writing by Charles C. Mann

AS YOU READ Notice how Mann's descriptions or explanations of Native American life compare with your prior knowledge of the subject.

Consider Tisquantum, the "friendly Indian" of the textbook. More than likely Tisquantum was not the name he was given at birth. In that part of the Northeast, *tisquantum* referred to rage, especially the rage of *manitou*, the world-suffusing spiritual power at the heart of coastal Indians' religious beliefs. When Tisquantum approached the Pilgrims and identified himself by that sobriquet,[1] it was as if he had stuck out his hand and said, Hello, I'm the Wrath of God. No one would lightly adopt such a name in contemporary Western society. Neither would anyone in seventeenth-century indigenous society.

10 Tisquantum was trying to **project** something.

Tisquantum was not an Indian. True, he belonged to that category of people whose ancestors had inhabited the Western Hemisphere for thousands of years. And it is true that I refer to him as an Indian, because the label is useful shorthand; so would his descendants, and for much the same reason. But "Indian" was not a category that Tisquantum himself would have recognized, any more than the

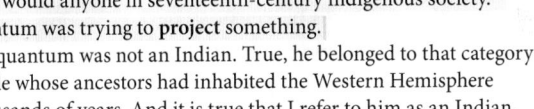
project
(prə-jĕkt´) *v.* to communicate or put forth.

Image Credits: ©haaghun/Flickr/Getty Images

---

[1] **sobriquet** (sō´brĭ-kā´): nickname.

SCAFFOLDING FOR ELL STUDENTS

Determine Author's Purpose Help students build background knowledge about the first Thanksgiving to help them understand why the author has chosen to write about Tisquantum, or Squanto, and why he calls Tisquantum "the 'friendly Indian' of the textbook."

ASK STUDENTS to brainstorm places where they could find more information about Tisquantum's connection to Thanksgiving. *(an American history textbook, an encyclopedia, a website about the first Thanksgiving, the previous selection in this textbook)*

CLOSE READ

Determine Author's Purpose

COMMON CORE RI 1, RI 6

(LINES 15–23)

Tell students that when Mann wrote *1491*, he had to keep his audience in mind, as do all effective writers. A writer can select specific language and ideas that will appeal to his audience in order to achieve a specific **purpose**, or goal.

C ASK STUDENTS which of the following terms in lines 15–23 are commonly used today: Indians, Western Hemisphereans, Norumbega, New England. *(Indians, New England)* Why might the author include terms that would be both familiar and unfamiliar to his audience? *(to help readers understand that the names for places and peoples change depending upon who is doing the naming, to show the change that has happened over time)*

Determine Author's Purpose (LINES 15–23)

COMMON CORE RI 1, RI 6

Tell students that an author achieves his purpose by choosing which information to include in his writing. By including information about how Tisquantum perceived himself and his world, the author helps the reader understand and empathize with Tisquantum.

D CITE TEXT EVIDENCE Have students reread lines 15 to 23 and cite the lines that tell how Tisquantum saw himself. *(Lines 21 and 22 state that Tisquantun "regarded himself first and foremost as a citizen of Patuxet.")*

CRITICAL VOCABULARY

settlement: In lines 22–23, Mann explains that Tisquantum lived in the community of Patuxet, in what is today Massachusetts.

ASK STUDENTS to recall where European groups built settlements in North America. *(The English built settlements in New England and Virginia. The Dutch built settlements in what is today New York. The Spanish built settlements in today's Florida.)*

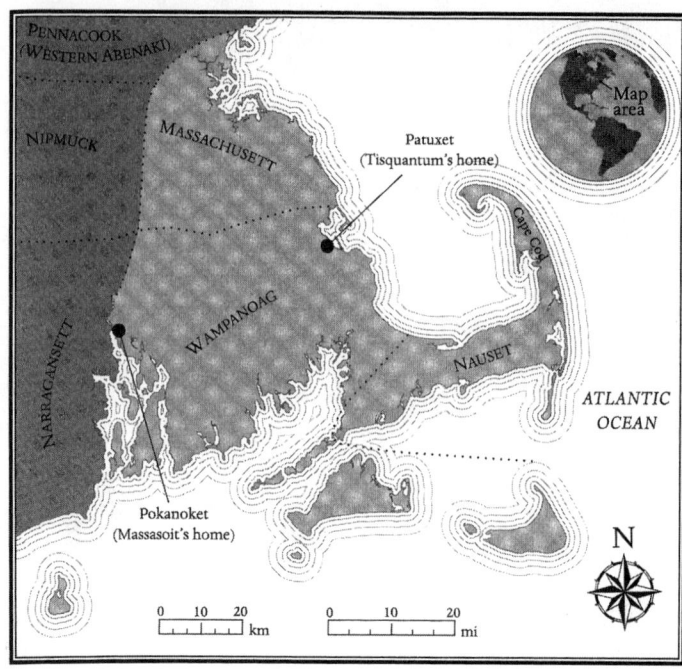

MASSACHUSETT ALLIANCE, 1600 A.D.

 **C** inhabitants of the same area today would call themselves "Western Hemisphereans." Still less would Tisquantum have claimed to belong to "Norumbega," the label by which most Europeans then
20 referred to New England. ("New England" was coined only in 1616.) As Tisquantum's later history made clear, he regarded himself first and foremost as a citizen of Patuxet, a shoreline **settlement** halfway between what is now Boston and the beginning of Cape Cod. **D**

Patuxet was one of the dozen or so settlements in what is now eastern Massachusetts and Rhode Island that comprised[2] the Wampanoag confederation. In turn, the Wampanoag were part of a tripartite alliance with two other confederations: the Nauset, which comprised some thirty groups on Cape Cod; and the Massachusett, several dozen villages clustered around Massachusetts Bay. All of these
30 people spoke variants of Massachusett, a member of the Algonquian language family, the biggest in eastern North America at the time.

settlement
(sĕtʹl-mənt) *n.* a small community in a sparsely populated area.

---

[2] **comprised:** made up of.

APPLYING ACADEMIC VOCABULARY

adapt	dynamic

As you discuss "Coming of Age in the Dawnland," incorporate the following Collection 1 academic vocabulary words: *adapt* and *dynamic*. To help students understand Mann's view of the Indians, ask them to explain how the Indians **adapted** to their environment. Then ask students to find evidence that the Indians' culture and lifestyle was **dynamic.**

(Massachusett thus was the name both of a language and of one of the groups that spoke it.) In Massachusett, the name for the New England shore was the Dawnland, the place where the sun rose. The inhabitants of the Dawnland were the People of the First Light.

Ten thousand years ago, when Indians in Mesoamerica and Peru were inventing agriculture and coalescing into villages, New England was barely inhabited, for the excellent reason that it had been covered until relatively recently by an ice sheet a mile thick. People
40 slowly moved in, though the area long remained cold and uninviting, especially along the coastline. Because rising sea levels continually flooded the shore, marshy Cape Cod did not fully lock into its contemporary configuration until about 1000 B.C. By that time the Dawnland had evolved into something more attractive: an ecological crazy quilt of wet maple forests, shellfish-studded tidal estuaries,[3] thick highland woods, mossy bogs full of cranberries and orchids, fractally[4] complex snarls of sandbars and beachfront, and fire-swept stands of pitch pine—"tremendous variety even within the compass of a few miles," as the ecological historian William Cronon put it.

50 In the absence of written records, researchers have developed techniques for teasing out evidence of the past. Among them is "glottochronology," the attempt to estimate how long ago two languages separated from a common ancestor by evaluating their degree of **divergence** on a list of key words. In the 1970s and 1980s linguists applied glottochronological techniques to the Algonquian dictionaries compiled by early colonists. However tentatively, the results indicated that the various Algonquian languages in New England all date back to a common ancestor that appeared in the Northeast a few centuries before Christ.

60 The ancestral language may derive from what is known as the Hopewell culture. Around two thousand years ago, Hopewell jumped into prominence from its bases in the Midwest, establishing a trade network that covered most of North America. The Hopewell culture introduced monumental earthworks and, possibly, agriculture to the rest of the cold North. Hopewell villages, unlike their more egalitarian[5] neighbors, were stratified,[6] with powerful, priestly rulers commanding a mass of commoners. Archaeologists have found no evidence of large-scale warfare at this time, and thus suggest that Hopewell probably did not achieve its dominance by conquest.
70 Instead, one can speculate, the vehicle for transformation may have been Hopewell religion, with its intoxicatingly elaborate funeral rites. If so, the adoption of Algonquian in the Northeast would mark an era

divergence
(dĭ-vûr′jəns) *n.*
a difference or variation.

---

[3] **estuaries:** tidal inlets.
[4] **fractally:** with an infinitely repeating pattern of geometric shapes.
[5] **egalitarian:** based on the principal of equality.
[6] **stratified:** arranged in layers.

WHEN STUDENTS STRUGGLE...

The author uses many technical terms that may seem daunting to students. Help them by reminding them to use the techniques they have learned to determine the meanings of unfamiliar words. Techniques include reviewing general and specific context clues and footnotes, and using glossaries and dictionaries.

ASK STUDENTS to use these vocabulary techniques to determine the meanings of these words from the passage: *estuaries, glottochronology, linguist. (The definition of* estuaries *can be determined by using the footnoted definition on this page; the definition of* glottochronology *can be determined from a restatement clue; the definition of* linguist *can be determined from general context.)*

CLOSE READ

Determine the Meaning of Words and Phrases

COMMON CORE RI 1, RI 4

(LINES 50–60)

Inform students that Mann uses evidence from various specialized fields of study, such as anthropology and archaeology. Sometimes this evidence includes technical terms related to those fields.

E **ASK STUDENTS** to find the term "ancestral language" in line 60. Based on the context of the previous paragraph, have them define the term. (*An ancestral language is the original language from which various other related languages descended.*)

CRITICAL VOCABULARY

divergence: In line 54, Mann identifies the development of differences in key words as a tool to estimate when languages broke off from their shared source.

ASK STUDENTS to infer how divergences in language might affect a group of people. (*The group could start to split, since members would not be able to communicate easily with one another.*)

Determine Author's Purpose (LINES 60–71)

COMMON CORE RI 1, RI 6

Tell students that writers use elements of **style**, such as word choice, to support their purpose.

F **CITE TEXT EVIDENCE** Have students analyze lines 60–71 to determine how the author likely wants to portray the Hopewell culture and cite textual evidence to support their analysis. (*The author's use of words and phrases like "stratified," "powerful," "commanding," "mass of commoners," "dominance," and "intoxicatingly elaborate" suggest that he wants to portray the Hopewell culture as strong, sophisticated, and compelling.*)

ferment: In line 73, Mann compares the tumult and push for conversion emerging from the Hopewell religion to the rise of Islam in the Middle East.

ASK STUDENTS to identify other periods of religious ferment in history. *(the spread of Buddhism, the development and spread of Christianity, the Protestant Reformation)*

Determine Author's Purpose (LINES 78–115)

COMMON CORE RI 1, RI 6

Tell students that analyzing the facts, examples, and ideas an author includes can help them infer the author's purpose.

 ASK STUDENTS to speculate about why Mann chooses to discuss many different Native American groups. *(Mann wants to show the complexity and variety of Native American civilization in pre-Columbian America.)*

Determine the Meaning of Words and Phrases

COMMON CORE RI 1, RI 4

(LINES 89 and 98–99)

Point out to students that Mann's writing about history is so engaging, partly because of his use of vivid figurative language to communicate meaning.

H ASK STUDENTS to interpret the metaphor that Mann uses on line 89 ("constellations of suburban hamlets and hunting camps") and the simile he uses in lines 98–99 ("like affluent snowbirds alternating between Manhattan and Miami"). Students should explain what is being compared and what effect the comparison has on their understanding of the topic. *(The metaphor compares the settlements to stars in a constellation. This makes the settlements seem artful in their arrangement. The metaphor compares the Native Americans to rich people who have winter homes in warm places. This helps the reader see them as similar to people today and as prosperous.)*

---

of spiritual **ferment** and heady conversion, much like the time when Islam rose and spread Arabic throughout the Middle East.

Hopewell itself declined around 400 A.D. But its trade network remained intact. Shell beads from Florida, obsidian from the Rocky Mountains, and mica from Tennessee found their way to the Northeast. Borrowing technology and ideas from the Midwest, the nomadic peoples of New England transformed their societies. By the end of the first millennium A.D., agriculture was spreading rapidly and 80 the region was becoming an unusual patchwork of communities, each with its preferred terrain, way of subsistence, and cultural style.

Scattered about the many lakes, ponds, and swamps of the cold uplands were small, mobile groups of hunters and gatherers—"collectors," as researchers sometimes call them. Most had recently adopted agriculture or were soon to do so, but it was still a secondary source of food, a supplement to the wild products of the land. New England's major river valleys, by contrast, held large, permanent villages, many nestled in constellations of suburban hamlets and 90 hunting camps. Because extensive fields of maize, beans, and squash surrounded every home, these settlements sprawled along the Connecticut, Charles, and other river valleys for miles, one town bumping up against the other. Along the coast, where Tisquantum and Massasoit lived, villages often were smaller and looser, though no less permanent.

Unlike the upland hunters, the Indians on the rivers and coastline did not roam the land; instead, most seem to have moved between a summer place and a winter place, like affluent snowbirds alternating between Manhattan and Miami. The distances were smaller, of course; 100 shoreline families would move a fifteen-minute walk inland, to avoid direct exposure to winter storms and tides. Each village had its own distinct mix of farming and foraging—this one here, adjacent to a rich oyster bed, might plant maize purely for variety, whereas that one there, just a few miles away, might subsist almost entirely on its harvest, filling great underground storage pits each fall. Although these settlements were permanent, winter and summer alike, they often were not tightly knit entities, with houses and fields in carefully demarcated[7] clusters. Instead people spread themselves through estuaries, sometimes grouping into neighborhoods, sometimes with 110 each family on its own, its maize ground proudly separate. Each community was constantly "joining and splitting like quicksilver[8] in a fluid pattern within its bounds," wrote Kathleen J. Bragdon, an anthropologist at the College of William and Mary—a type of settlement, she remarked, with "no name in the archaeological or anthropological literature."

---

[7] **demarcated:** defined with boundaries.
[8] **quicksilver:** mercury, a liquid metal.

ferment
(fûr´mĕnt´) *n.* a state of violent, unpredictable change.

SCAFFOLDING FOR ELL STUDENTS

Determine the Meaning of Words and Phrases Tell students that the word "snowbirds" (line 98) is an **idiom**, or figure of speech whose meaning is different from its literal meaning.

ASK STUDENTS what words or phrases in the sentence give clues to the meaning of the word? *(moved between a summer place and a winter place, affluent, alternating between Manhattan and Miami)* Then ask: What does the word mean? *(people who spend summers in areas with harsh winter climates and winters in places with warmer, milder climates, like some migrating birds)*

> **Around two thousand years ago,** Hopewell jumped into prominence . . . establishing a trade network that covered most of North America. **"**

In the Wampanoag confederation, one of these quicksilver communities was Patuxet, where Tisquantum was born at the end of the sixteenth century.

Tucked into the great sweep of Cape Cod Bay, Patuxet sat on a low
120 rise above a small harbor, jigsawed by sandbars and shallow enough that children could walk from the beach hundreds of yards into the water before the waves went above their heads. To the west, maize hills marched across the sandy hillocks[9] in parallel rows. Beyond the fields, a mile or more away from the sea, rose a forest of oak, chestnut, and hickory, open and park-like, the underbrush kept down by expert annual burning. "Pleasant of air and prospect," as one English visitor described the area, Patuxet had "much plenty both of fish and fowl every day in the year." Runs of spawning Atlantic salmon, shortnose sturgeon, striped bass, and American shad annually filled the harbor.
130 But the most important fish harvest came in late spring, when the herring-like alewives swarmed the fast, shallow stream that cut through the village. So numerous were the fish, and so driven, that when mischievous boys walled off the stream with stones the alewives would leap the barrier—silver bodies gleaming in the sun—and proceed upstream.

Tisquantum's childhood *wetu* (home) was formed from arched poles lashed together into a dome that was covered in winter by tightly woven rush mats and in summer by thin sheets of chestnut bark. A fire burned constantly in the center, the smoke venting through
140 a hole in the center of the roof. English visitors did not find this arrangement peculiar; chimneys were just coming into use in Britain, and most homes there, including those of the wealthy, were still heated

---
[9] **hillocks:** small hills.

Coming of Age in the Dawnland   **27**

Determine Author's Purpose (LINES 119–135)

COMMON CORE RI 1, RI 6

Tell students that **imagery**—words and phrases that appeal to the senses—is an important part of an author's style and that positive or negative imagery can help support an author's purpose.

CITE TEXT EVIDENCE Ask students to cite images in lines 119–135 that depict Patuxet in either a positive or negative light. *(Possible responses for positive imagery: the visual image of Patuxet overlooking a harbor and surrounded by "park-like" fields and forests; the image of fish so plentiful and determined that they jumped out of the water "silver bodies gleaming in the sun")* Ask how these images make Patuxet sound. Do they depict a positive or negative image of life in this Native American community? *(The images depict life in Patuxet as positive—beautiful, prosperous, and comfortable.)*

Determine the Meaning of Words and Phrases

COMMON CORE RI 1, RI 4

(LINES 136–138)

Remind students that Mann uses technical terms from various specialized fields of study, as well as from the Indians' language.

ASK STUDENTS to identify the Indian word for "home" introduced in line 136. *(wetu)* Ask students why Mann might choose to use this word rather than "home" or "house." *(It describes the particular kind of home where Tisquantum lived and gives readers a glimpse of his language and life.)*

WHEN STUDENTS STRUGGLE . . .

Point out to students that Mann's use of very specific nouns enlivens his writing; however, this use of very specific words means that some of the vocabulary he uses may be unfamiliar. Guide students to use context clues to identify six names of specific types of fish. *(salmon, short-nosed sturgeon, striped bass, American shad, herring, alewives)*

ASK STUDENTS why the author might have used these specific names instead of just using the word "fish." *(It shows how plentiful the fish were, and it creates a more vivid picture in the reader's mind.)*

CLOSE READ

Determine Author's Purpose (LINES 143–149)

COMMON CORE RI 1, RI 6

Inform students that the type of evidence an author uses can help them **infer** the author's purpose, or reason for writing.

K **ASK STUDENTS** to identify the kind of evidence Mann uses in lines 143–149. *(He uses primary source quotations from an English colonist.)* Discuss how this evidence supports Mann's argument about the wetu and the Indians who lived there. *(It shows that the wetu was a sophisticated home that compared favorably to English houses of that time.)*

Determine the Meaning of Words and Phrases

COMMON CORE RI 1, RI 4

(LINES 157–167)

Remind students that words' **connotations**, or associated feelings, help convey meaning.

L **CITE TEXT EVIDENCE** Ask students to find words and phrases related to food in lines 157–167 that have positive connotations. *(simmering, cheerful thuds, sweet, toothsome, hearty, nourishing)* Discuss the impact of these connotations on the description of the Native Americans' food. *(They make the food sound appealing, plentiful, and tasty.)*

 **K** by fires beneath central roof holes. Nor did the English regard the Dawnland *wetu* as primitive; its multiple layers of mats, which trapped insulating layers of air, were "warmer than our English houses," sighed the colonist William Wood. The *wetu* was less leaky than the typical English wattle-and-daub house, too. Wood did not conceal his admiration for the way Indian mats "deny entrance to any drop of rain, though it come both fierce and long."

150   Around the edge of the house were low beds, sometimes wide enough for a whole family to sprawl on them together; usually raised about a foot from the floor, platform-style; and always piled with mats and furs. Going to sleep in the firelight, young Tisquantum would have stared up at the diddering[10] shadows of the hemp bags and bark boxes hanging from the rafters. Voices would skirl[11] up in the darkness: one person singing a lullaby, then another person, until everyone was asleep. In the morning, when he woke, big, egg-shaped pots of corn-and-bean mash would be on the fire, simmering with meat, vegetables, or dried fish to make a slow-cooked dinner

160   stew. Outside the *wetu* he would hear the cheerful thuds of the large mortars and pestles[12] in which women crushed dried maize into *nokake*, a flour-like powder "so sweet, toothsome, and hearty," colonist **L** Gookin wrote, "that an Indian will travel many days with no other but this meal." Although Europeans bemoaned the lack of salt in Indian cuisine, they thought it nourishing. According to one modern

---

[10]**diddering:** trembling.

[11]**skirl:** make a high-pitched sound, like bagpipes.

[12]**mortars and pestles:** bowl-shaped containers and blunt tools for grinding and crushing.

28   Collection 1

SCAFFOLDING FOR ELL STUDENTS

Understanding the Conditional Form of Verbs Point out that in the first full paragraph on this page, Mann sometimes uses the conditional forms of verbs. Use a whiteboard to project lines 153–164. Invite volunteers to mark it up.

- Have students underline verb forms that include the word *would*. *(would have stared, mash would be on the fire,* and *he would hear)*

- Tell students that here Mann is using the conditional forms of verbs to indicate that what he is describing is hypothetical, or imagined, rather than factual. Mann does not know for certain that Tisquantum woke to "cheerful thuds." Rather, he speculates that this is likely.

reconstruction, Dawnland diets at the time averaged about 2,500  calories a day, better than those usual in famine-racked Europe.

Pilgrim writers universally reported that Wampanoag families were close and loving—more so than English families, some thought.
170 Europeans in those days tended to view children as moving straight from infancy to adulthood around the age of seven, and often thereupon sent them out to work. Indian parents, by contrast, regarded the years before puberty as a time of playful development, and kept their offspring close by until marriage. (Jarringly, to the contemporary eye, some Pilgrims interpreted this as sparing the rod.) Boys like Tisquantum explored the countryside, swam in the ponds at the south end of the harbor, and played a kind of soccer with a small leather ball; in the summer and fall they camped out in huts in the fields, weeding the maize and chasing away birds. Archery practice began at age two.
180 By adolescence boys would make a game of shooting at each other and dodging the arrows.

The primary goal of Dawnland education was molding character. Men and women were expected to be brave, hardy, honest, and uncomplaining. Chatterboxes and gossips were frowned upon. "He that speaks seldom and opportunely, being as good as his word, is the only man they love," Wood explained. Character formation began early, with family games of tossing naked children into the snow. (They were pulled out quickly and placed next to the fire, in a practice reminiscent of Scandinavian saunas.) When Indian boys came of age,
190 they spent an entire winter alone in the forest, equipped only with a bow, a hatchet, and a knife. These methods worked, the awed Wood reported. "Beat them, whip them, pinch them, punch them, if [the Indians] resolve not to flinch for it, they will not."

Tisquantum's **regimen** was probably tougher than that of his friends, according to Salisbury, the Smith College historian, for it seems that he was selected to become a *pniese*, a kind of counselor-bodyguard to the sachem. To master the art of ignoring pain, future *pniese* had to subject themselves to such miserable experiences as running barelegged through brambles. And they fasted often, to
200 learn self-discipline. After spending their winter in the woods, *pniese* candidates came back to an additional test: drinking bitter gentian juice until they vomited, repeating this bulimic process over and over until, near fainting, they threw up blood.

Patuxet, like its neighboring settlements, was governed by a sachem, who upheld the law, negotiated treaties, controlled foreign contacts, collected tribute, declared war, provided for widows and orphans, and allocated farmland when there were disputes over it. (Dawnlanders lived in a loose scatter, but they knew which family could use which land— "very exact and punctuall," Roger Williams,
210 founder of Rhode Island colony, called Indian care for property lines.)

regimen
(rĕj´ə-mən) *n.* a system or organized routine of behavior.

SCAFFOLDING FOR ELL STUDENTS

Determine the Meaning of Words and Phrases

- Ask students to highlight the adjectives lines 183–184 that describe ideal personal qualities for the Dawnland people. *(brave, hardy, honest, and uncomplaining)*
- Have students work in pairs or small groups to create their own list of adjectives that describe ideal qualities for a person living in the United States. Then, have students compare the two sets of adjectives.

[They] were expected to be brave, hardy, honest, and uncomplaining.

CLOSE READ

Determine Author's Purpose (LINES 182–193)

COMMON CORE RI 1, RI 6

Remind students that the evidence an author chooses to include in an informational text can help them **infer** the author's purpose, or reason for writing.

CITE TEXT EVIDENCE Ask students to cite details Mann uses in lines 182–193 to explain the goals of Dawnland education. *(Mann cites the characteristics the people valued, gives examples of how younger and older children were trained, and quotes an English observer's view of the results of that education.)* How do these details make Dawnland education sound? *(rigorous, but effective)* How might this support the author's purpose? *(The author seems to be trying to show that pre-Columbian society in America was sophisticated and vibrant. Including details about their effective educational system suggests a high level of sophistication.)*

CRITICAL VOCABULARY

regimen: In line 194, Mann describes the program of education and training that Tisquantum may have followed to become a *pniese*.

ASK STUDENTS to describe the training regimen of an elite athlete. *(Elite athletes must spend time practicing their own sport, as well as doing general physical and strength training. They may also have to follow a special diet to have adequate nutrition.)*

Determine the Meaning of Words and Phrases

COMMON CORE RI 1, RI 4

(LINES 204–212)

Remind students that they can use context clues to unlock the meaning of unfamiliar technical or specialized terms.

ASK STUDENTS to locate the word "sachem" as many times as it occurs in lines 204–212. *(lines 205, 211)* Based on context clues in this paragraph, what is a "sachem"? *(a leader or ruler of Native American communities in the Dawnland)*

CLOSE READ

Most of the time, the Patuxet sachem owed fealty[13] to the great sachem in the Wampanoag village to the southwest, and through him to the sachems of the allied confederations of the Nauset in Cape Cod and the Massachusett around Boston. Meanwhile, the Wampanoag were rivals and enemies of the Narragansett and Pequots to the west and the many groups of Abenaki to the north. As a practical matter, sachems had to gain the consent of their people, who could easily move away and join another sachemship. Analogously, the great sachems had to please or bully the lesser, lest by the **defection** of small communities
220 they lose stature.

defection
(dĭ-fĕkt´shŭn) *n.* the abandonment of one social or political group in favor of another.

CRITICAL VOCABULARY

defection: In line 219, Mann discusses why and how the most important sachems had to retain the loyalty of lesser sachems and smaller communities.

ASK STUDENTS to explain how members' defections would damage an alliance. *(If some members defected, the alliance would have fewer members and become weaker.)*

> ❝ Pilgrim writers universally reported that Wampanoag families were close and loving— more so than English families, some thought. ❞

Determine Author's Purpose (LINES 230–233)

COMMON CORE · RI 1, RI 6

Remind students that the evidence an author uses, such as primary source quotations or quotations from experts in relevant fields, can help them **infer** the author's purpose, or reason for writing.

O **ASK STUDENTS** to identify the kind of evidence Mann cites in lines 230–233. *(a quotation from an expert archaeologist and ethnohistorian)* Ask students to describe the effect of this quotation. *(It provides a voice of authority to support and add depth to the other information in the paragraph.)*

Sixteenth-century New England housed 100,000 people or more, a figure that was slowly increasing. Most of those people lived in shoreline communities, where rising numbers were beginning to change agriculture from an option to a necessity. These bigger settlements required more centralized administration; natural resources like good land and spawning streams, though not scarce, now needed to be managed. In consequence, boundaries between groups were becoming more formal. Sachems, given more power and more to defend, pushed against each other harder. Political tensions
230 were constant. Coastal and riverine New England, according to the archaeologist and ethnohistorian Peter Thomas, was "an ever-changing collage of personalities, alliances, plots, raids and encounters which involved every Indian [settlement]."

---
[13] **fealty:** obedient loyalty.

Determine the Meaning of Words and Phrases

COMMON CORE · RI 1, RI 4

(LINES 234–236)

Remind students that they can use vocabulary strategies they have learned to find the meanings of unfamiliar technical terms.

P **ASK STUDENTS** what strategy they could use to determine the meaning of the term *casus belli*. *(Students could use the footnote at the bottom of the page to determining that the term means "cause for war.")*

WHEN STUDENTS STRUGGLE . . .

To guide students' comprehension of the political situation in sixteenth-century New England, have students work in pairs to complete cause-and-effect graphic organizers. Remind students to look for clues to cause and effect such as signal words (*in consequence,* line 227) and sequence—the cause often comes before the effect.

Depending on your students' needs, you may wish to provide extra support by starting them off with either the cause or effect for each chart.

P Armed conflict was frequent but brief and mild by European standards. The *casus belli*[14] was usually the desire to avenge an insult or gain status, not the wish for conquest. Most battles consisted of lightning guerrilla raids by ad hoc companies in the forest: flash of black-and-yellow-striped bows behind trees, hiss and whip of stone-tipped arrows through the air, eruption of angry cries. Attackers
240 slipped away as soon as retribution had been exacted. Losers quickly conceded their loss of status. Doing otherwise would have been like failing to resign after losing a major piece in a chess tournament—a social irritant, a waste of time and resources. Women and children were rarely killed, though they were sometimes abducted and forced to join the winning group. Captured men were often tortured (they were admired, though not necessarily spared, if they endured the pain **stoically**). Now and then, as a sign of victory, slain foes were scalped, much as British skirmishes with the Irish sometimes finished with a parade of Irish heads on pikes. In especially large clashes, adversaries
250 might meet in the open, as in European battlefields, though the results, Roger Williams noted, were "farre less bloudy, and devouring then the cruell Warres of Europe." Nevertheless, by Tisquantum's time defensive palisades[15] were increasingly common, especially in the river valleys.

Inside the settlement was a world of warmth, family, and familiar custom. But the world outside, as Thomas put it, was "a maze of confusing actions and individuals fighting to maintain an existence in the shadow of change." **Q**

And that was before the Europeans showed up.

stoically
(stōʹĭk-lē) *adv.*
without showing
emotion or feeling.

---

[14] *casus belli* (kāʹsəs bĕlʹī): Latin: cause for war.
[15] **defensive palisades:** fortified walls of tall stakes.

COLLABORATIVE DISCUSSION With a partner, discuss two interesting or unexpected details from Mann's description of pre-Columbian Native America. Explain why they were surprising, citing specific passages in your discussion.

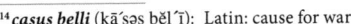

Cause:		Effect:
Growing settlements need more management.	▶	Boundaries between groups were becoming more formal and sachems gained more power.

Cause:		Effect:
Sachems gained more power and had more to defend.	▶	Conflict between different groups increased.

CLOSE READ

> **CRITICAL VOCABULARY**
>
> **stoically**: In line 247, Mann discusses the kinds of behavior the Indians valued, especially in the face of pain and hardship.
>
> **ASK STUDENTS** to explain why the Indians might admire someone who endured torture stoically. *(Students may say that Indians themselves generally acted stoically by not showing emotion, so they would admire this quality in other peoples.)*

Determine Author's Purpose (LINES 255–259)

COMMON CORE RI 1, RI 6

Tell students that an author may review or emphasize his main point at the end of a piece of writing. This conclusion can help readers **infer** the author's goal, or reason for writing the piece.

Q ASK STUDENTS to read the last two paragraphs and summarize their main idea. *(Before Europeans arrived, Tisquantum's settlement was peaceful and prosperous inside, but the larger Native American society was tumultuous and challenging.)* Invite students to make an inference about the author's purpose in writing this chapter. *(to show what life was like in the Dawnland and to describe how complex it was even before Europeans began to settle there)*

COLLABORATIVE DISCUSSION Have students pair up and discuss specific details they found surprising. Why were they surprising? From what other sources of information have students gotten their information about Native Americans? Which sources are most reliable?

ASK STUDENTS to share any questions they generated in the course of reading and discussing the selection.

TEACH

Determine the Meaning of Words and Phrases

Make sure students understand the terms. Have students find examples of technical terms, figurative language, and words with strong connotations from the selection. Then have students identify which kind of language each example represents. Discuss why the author may have chosen to use these kinds of language and how each one adds meaning to the selection.

Determine Author's Purpose

To help students analyze an author's purpose, give them these additional questions and tips.

- What is the title? Does it give a clue to the author's purpose?

- Are there any text features, such as headings, boldface type, or graphic aids that give clues to the author's purpose?

- What types of information are included and what purpose does this suggest? For instance, a text that includes facts and statistics, specific examples, or steps in a process is probably written to inform or explain something, while a text that includes statements of opinion, supporting evidence, and appeals to the emotions is probably written to persuade. Point out to students that sometimes an author wants to inform *and* persuade.

Determine the Meaning of Words and Phrases

To understand a sophisticated text like "Coming of Age in the Dawnland," you must determine the meanings of words and phrases as the author uses them. These meanings may be literal or nonliteral. The chart provides some examples.

Technical Terms	Figurative Language	Connotations
Mann draws on evidence from a variety of social scientists, and some of the language he uses comes from those specialized fields of study. Examples include *tidal estuaries* and *glottochronology*. Mann defines some of these terms in the text; others you must look up in footnotes or in a dictionary.	**Figurative language** uses words in a nonliteral way to make fresh, interesting comparisons. A **simile,** for example, compares two things using the word *like* or *as*. Mann says an Indian failing to acknowledge a loss in a fight was "like failing to resign after losing a major piece in a chess tournament." This simile helps readers understand an unfamiliar topic by comparing it to something familiar.	To convey subtle shades of meaning, authors choose words with particular **connotations,** or associated feelings. For example, describing bedtime for a Native American family, Mann uses the words *firelight* and *lullaby*. These words have pleasant, homey connotations that help readers connect with the lives of Tisquantum's people.

Determine Author's Purpose

Purpose is the reason why an author writes a particular piece. The author might seek to inform readers, to entertain them, or to persuade them to agree with his or her point of view. An author's purpose is not usually stated in the text. Instead, readers must **infer** the purpose, or draw a logical conclusion based on strong evidence in the text.

No matter what the purpose, an effective piece of writing must have an appealing **style.** Elements of style include word choice, **tone** (the writer's attitude toward the topic), and **imagery** (words and phrases that appeal to readers' senses). Well-chosen content—the facts and ideas that the author includes—also contribute to a powerful text. Use these questions to help you analyze "Coming of Age in the Dawnland" and determine the author's purpose:

- Think about what the text says explicitly. What ideas does the author state directly, and what facts and examples does he include?

- Analyze the author's style. What words and images do you find especially powerful? What tone does his writing convey?

- Based on your analysis, what can you infer is Mann's purpose in this excerpt?

Strategies for Annotation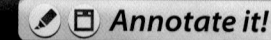

Determine the Meaning of Words and Phrases

Share these strategies for guided or independent analysis:

- In yellow, highlight the two things being compared in a simile. Highlight the connecting word ("like" or "as") in blue.

- Look for clues in the text or footnotes to a word's meaning. Highlight these clues in pink.

- On a note, record words that have strong connotations. Write down the feelings associated with these words.

Each community was constantly "joining and splitting like quicksilver in a fluid pattern within its bounds," wrote Kathleen J. Bragdon, an anthropologist at the College of William and Mary—a type of settlement, she remarked, with "no name in the archaeological or anthropological literature."

[8] **quicksilver:** mercury, a liquid metal.

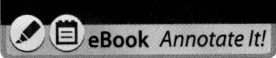 **eBook** *Annotate It!*

Analyzing the Text

Cite Text Evidence   Support your responses with evidence from the selection.

1. **Infer** In lines 87–90, Mann writes that "New England's major river valleys ... held large, permanent villages, many nestled in constellations of suburban hamlets and hunting camps." What words in this sentence have strong connotations? How might these feelings affect readers' impression of Native American life in this time and place?

2. **Analyze** Note the sensory details that Mann uses to describe life in Patuxet at the end of the sixteenth century (lines 119–135). What impression of the community does this imagery create for readers?

3. **Cite Evidence** Mann includes evidence from primary sources written by Europeans in the seventeenth century. Identify examples of this evidence and explain what it reveals about these Europeans' opinions of Native American life.

4. **Analyze** Locate at least three examples of scholarly experts that Mann quotes in his writing. Why does he include this content?

5. **Analyze** Mann says the coastal Indians who moved inland in the winter were "like affluent snowbirds alternating between Manhattan and Miami." What purpose might he want to achieve with this simile comparing the Indians to a group of modern Americans?

6. **Draw Conclusions** What is the central idea about Native American societies in the Dawnland that Mann communicates in this excerpt?

7. **Cite Evidence** What evidence does Mann provide to support the idea that Indians in sixteenth-century New England lived in a dynamic world?

8. **Synthesize** What do you think was Mann's overall purpose for writing this text? Cite reasons and evidence for your answer.

 *my* **WriteSmart**

PERFORMANCE TASK

Writing Activity: Argument This selection presents Mann's view of Indian societies in New England. Evaluate how successfully he achieves his purpose by writing a brief argument.

- Write a statement that summarizes Mann's purpose for writing.
- Decide whether you think he succeeded or failed in achieving that purpose. Are the style and content of his writing strong and persuasive? Your position on that question is the claim of your argument.
- If you think Mann achieved his purpose, cite evidence that supports that claim. If you think he failed, provide reasons for your opinion.
- Present your reasons and evidence in a logical order.

Coming of Age in the Dawnland   **33**

PRACTICE & APPLY

Analyzing the Text

Possible answers:

1. *The words* permanent, nestled, *and* suburban *have strong connotations. Readers might get a positive impression about the sophistication and development of Native American life in this time and place.*

2. *This imagery creates an impression of a happy, quiet, and prosperous community.*

3. *In lines 126–128, "one English visitor" described the area as "Pleasant of air and prospect" and having "much plenty both of fish and fowl every day in the year." These and other examples reveal the Europeans' admiration for Native Americans and their lifestyles.*

4. *Mann quotes scholarly experts in lines 48–49, 111–115, and 231–233. He includes this evidence to strongly support his assertions about Native American life.*

5. *He might want to use this simile to make the Indians' lifestyle seem more familiar and understandable to modern readers.*

6. *The central idea about Native American societies in the Dawnland in this excerpt is that they were highly developed, sophisticated civilizations—especially compared to contemporary European communities.*

7. *Mann provides the evidence of the changing Algonquian languages, the movement of families into and within communities, and communities' ability to choose a sachem to support the idea that Indians in sixteenth-century New England lived in a dynamic world.*

8. *I think Mann's purpose for writing this text is to give readers a more complex view of Indian life in New England before European settlement. Mann explains the Indians' lifestyle, shows ways in which they were like modern Americans, and compares their achievements favorably with those of Europeans at the same time.*

Assign this performance task.  *my* **WriteSmart**

PERFORMANCE TASK

Writing Activity Have students reread the selection. Direct them to take notes on evidence that supports their claim about Mann's success or failure in achieving his purpose. Suggest that students also note evidence against their claim and consider how to respond to this opposing evidence. Once they have finished their notes, suggest that students organize evidence into groups, such as "content Mann chose to include," "tone," and "imagery." Students should then decide on a logical organization for their paragraphs. Encourage students to create an outline or use another type of graphic organizer to order their ideas.

PRACTICE & APPLY

Critical Vocabulary

COMMON CORE RI 10, L 4c, L 6

Answers: 1. *An Indian who acted* stoically *during torture hoped to* project *an image of bravery and indifference to pain.* **2.** *A sachem might be concerned about the* defection *of a small* settlement *because he would no longer have the loyalty of its residents.* **3.** *A time of religious* ferment *might cause a* divergence *of beliefs because religious agitation and change could cause some people to change their beliefs.* **4.** *Young Indians had to endure their training* regimen stoically *because the program of learning to be an adult included many difficult tasks, and the community valued those who could endure difficulties in silence.*

Vocabulary Strategy: Specialized Vocabulary

1. *Anthropology: the study of human beings and their communities; archaeology: the study of material remains from the past; ecology: the study of the environments where different forms of life live*

2. *Sample answers include: compass (ecology, meaning: area); glottochronology (anthropology, meaning: the attempt to estimate how long ago two languages separated from a common ancestor by evaluating their degree of divergence on a list of key words); earthworks (archaeology, meaning: a structure or work of art built of earth); custom (anthropology; a practice of a certain place or culture)*

Critical Vocabulary

COMMON CORE RI 10, L 4c, L 6

project	settlement	divergence	ferment
regimen	defection	stoically	

Practice and Apply Use a complete sentence to answer each question and demonstrate that you understand the meaning of each Critical Vocabulary word.

1. When an Indian acted **stoically** during torture, what image did he hope to **project**?

2. Why would a sachem be concerned about the **defection** of a small **settlement**?

3. How might a time of religious **ferment** cause a **divergence** of beliefs?

4. Why did young Indians have to endure their training **regimen stoically**?

Vocabulary Strategy: Specialized Vocabulary

Mann uses evidence from several different fields to support his ideas. He cites an ecological historian, an archaeologist and ethnohistorian, and an anthropologist. Many of the words he uses are examples of **specialized vocabulary,** or words that are related to a particular field of study. For example, the Critical Vocabulary word *settlement* is used in a specialized sense of "a place where people live, especially in an area where few people have lived before." This is an example of a specialized meaning for a word that you might already be familar with. The following strategies can help you determine the meaning of specialized vocabulary.

- Look it up! If a complex text is about a specialized topic that you are unfamilar with (for example, vulcanology, the study of volcanos), you should *expect* to see specialized vocabulary that you will need to look up.
- Try to guess the meaning. Use context clues, including the word's part of speech and its use in the sentence, to help determine the meaning. Very often specialized vocabulary will helpfully be defined in the text for readers.
- For very technical words, use specialized reference works, such as an atlas or the glossary in a book on a specialized topic, to get more specific information.

Practice and Apply Work with a partner to complete the following activities.

1. Using prior knowledge and context clues from Mann's writing, identify the subject of each of these fields of study: anthropology, archaeology, and ecology. Check your answers by looking up these words in a dictionary or other reference work.

2. Now that you have a clearer idea of these fields of study, begin to identify and classify some of the specialized vocabulary that appears in this text. You might focus first on the passages where Mann quotes various experts. Determine which words are examples of specialized vocabulary and then classify each word according to the list of fields in step 1. Lastly, prepare a definition for each word, consulting appropriate reference materials. Try to get at least three words for each field.

Strategies for Annotation 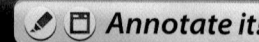 Annotate it!

Specialized Vocabulary

COMMON CORE RI 10, L 4c, L 6

Sometimes specialized vocabulary is defined within the text, or context clues give hints to specialized words' meaning. Have students locate the sentences that include the words *estuaries, glottochronology,* and *stratified.* Encourage them to use their eBook annotation tools to do the following.

- Highlight the specialized vocabulary word in yellow.
- Highlight its definition, if provided, in green.
- Highlight other clues to its meaning, if any, in blue.
- Check the meaning in a dictionary.

In the absence of written records, researchers have developed techniques for teasing out evidence of the past. Among them is "glottochronology," the attempt to estimate how long ago two languages separated from a common ancestor by evaluating their degree of divergence on a list of key words.

Language and Style:
Dependent (or Subordinate) Clauses

All **clauses** contain a subject and a verb. A **dependent** or **subordinate clause** is not able to stand alone as a sentence but depends on or is subordinate to an independent clause. Using dependent clauses skillfully allows Charles Mann to vary the **syntax** or pattern of his sentences.

Consider these examples from "Coming of Age in the Dawnland."

> **And it is true that I refer to him as an Indian, because the label is useful shorthand. . . .**

> **Although Europeans bemoaned the lack of salt in Indian cuisine, they thought it nourishing.**

In each of these complex sentences, the dependent clause begins with a **subordinating conjunction** (*because* and *although*). The conjunction reveals a relationship between the two clauses. The word *because*, for example, indicates a cause-and-effect relationship between two factors. *Although* indicates a concession or exception to the point that Mann makes. Using subordinating conjunctions allows Mann to make nuanced and detailed arguments appropriate for his topic. From a style perspective, it allows him to create a varied rhythm in his prose, making it more engaging and easier to read.

This chart shows some common subordinating conjunctions and the relationships they signal.

Type of Relationship	Subordinating Conjunctions
Causal (i.e., Making Something Happen)	because, since
Concession/Contrast	although, as, as much as, than, though, while
Place	where, wherever
Purpose	in order that, so that, that
Time	after, as, as long as, as soon as, before, since, until, when, whenever, while

Practice and Apply Look back at the argument you wrote in response to this selection's Performance Task. Revise it by combining some simple sentences into complex sentences. Use appropriate subordinating conjunctions to show the relationships between ideas. Vary the placement of dependent clauses at the beginning, the middle, and the end of sentences to create varied sentence structure and a smooth, flowing rhythm.

Language and Style:
Dependent (or Subordinate) Clauses

Make sure students are adding subordinating conjunctions to their sentences correctly. Invite volunteers to share their original and revised sentences with the class.

 **Assess It!**

Online Selection Test
- Download an editable ExamView bank.
- Assign and manage this test online.

INTERACTIVE WHITEBOARD LESSON

Participate in Collaborative Discussions

COMMON CORE
SL 1a-d

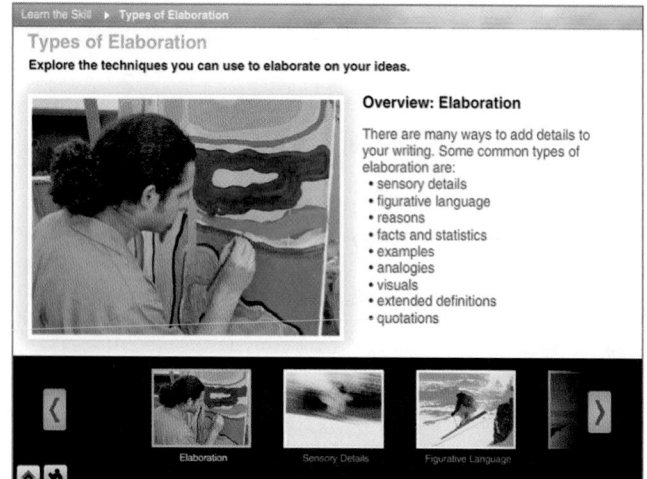

Learn the Skill ▸ Types of Elaboration

Types of Elaboration

Explore the techniques you can use to elaborate on your ideas.

Overview: Elaboration

There are many ways to add details to your writing. Some common types of elaboration are:
- sensory details
- figurative language
- reasons
- facts and statistics
- examples
- analogies
- visuals
- extended definitions
- quotations

Elaboration   Sensory Details   Figurative Language

TEACH

After students write their arguments for the Performance Task, review the steps for sharing their work within the context of a collaborative discussion:

- **Step 1: Come to discussions prepared** Review your own claims and reasons, and make sure you can cite evidence from the text to support your arguments.
- **Step 2: Promote civil, democratic discussions** Decide within your group what you want to accomplish and in what time frame, and make sure that everyone has a chance to present his or her own ideas, as well as respond to others'.
- **Step 3: Respond to questions and challenge ideas** Ask questions that clarify, verify, or challenge reasoning and conclusions. Respond constructively, exploring multiple aspects of a topic.
- **Step 4: Synthesize comments and resolve contradictions** Sum up the various arguments and resolutions, and identify where additional work is needed to finalize the assignment.

COLLABORATIVE DISCUSSSION

Direct students to work in groups to check each other's reasons and evidence. Students should make sure the reasons and evidence provide strong support for the claim and are presented in the most effective order. Group members may make suggestions to help strengthen each other's arguments.

Analyze Author's Purpose

COMMON CORE
RI 1, RI 6

RETEACH

Review the terms *purpose, style, tone,* and *imagery*. Then give several examples of kinds of writing, such as a novel, a newspaper editorial, and a personal e-mail.

- Ask students to identify the **purpose** of each kind of writing. (*Sample Answers: The novel's purpose is to entertain readers. The purpose of the newspaper editorial is to persuade readers. The purpose of a personal e-mail is to stay in touch with a friend or family member.*)
- Point out that the **style** of a piece of writing can help support the author's purpose. Ask students what styles would be appropriate for the various kinds of writing, based on the purposes they already identified. (*Sample Answers: A novel might have a humorous, fast-paced, or lyrical style. A newspaper editorial would have a formal style. A personal e-mail would have an informal style.*)
- Remind students that word choice, **tone**, and **imagery** are all elements of style. Ask how one or more of these elements would contribute to the style and purpose of each kind of writing previously discussed. (*Sample Answers: A novel might use vivid imagery to create a strong style and keep readers interested. A newspaper editorial might use an authoritative tone to persuade readers. A personal e-mail might have a friendly tone, and its informal style could include the use of slang or abbreviations.*)

CLOSE READING APPLICATION

Students can apply the skill to a current magazine or newspaper article or editorial. Have them work independently to identify the author's purpose and describe the style of the piece. Ask: Does the author achieve his or her purpose? In what ways do the writer's tone, word choice, and imagery help achieve the purpose? Would a different tone or different imagery make the article or editorial more effective?

INTERACTIVE LESSON Have students complete the tutorials in this lesson: **Specialized Vocabulary**

mySmartPlanner Create lesson plans and access resources online.

from The Tempest

Drama by William Shakespeare

Why This Text?

Shakespeare's plays, including *The Tempest*, continue to be performed in theaters and adapted for film and television. They are an important part of the literary heritage of the English-speaking world. In particular, *The Tempest* reflects the events that were happening when the play was written: the arrival of English colonists in what would become North America, and their encounters with its inhabitants.

Key Learning Objective: The student will be able to cite effective textual evidence to support an argument.

Common Core Standards

RL 1 Cite textual evidence.
RL 4 Determine figurative and connotative meanings; analyze the impact of specific word choices.
W 2 Write informative/explanatory texts.
W 2b Develop the topic thoroughly.

Text Complexity Rubric

Quantitative Measures	**from *The Tempest*** Lexile: N/A

Levels of Meaning/Purpose

multiple levels of complex meaning

Structure

somewhat complex poetic structure

Qualitative Measures

Language Conventionality and Clarity

archaic, unfamiliar language

Knowledge Demands

increased amount of cultural and literary knowledge useful

Reader/Task Considerations

Teacher determined
Vary by individual reader and type of text

Background Have students read the information about Shakespeare. Tell students that during his lifetime, the first permanent European settlements were being founded in America. In 1607, just four years before Shakespeare completed *The Tempest*, a group of English colonists established Jamestown in what is now Virginia. These settlers forged a life for themselves in America that was completely foreign to what they had known in their home countries. In fact, so extraordinarily were their experiences that the earliest American writers concentrated mainly on describing and trying to make sense of their challenging new environment and the unfamiliar people with whom they shared it. In diaries, letters, and reports back home, they recorded a historical turning point: when the world of the Europeans first intersected with that of the Native Americans. The setting and events of *The Tempest* may have been inspired by the experiences of these early colonists.

Introduction to *The Tempest*

O, brave new world, That has such people in 't!

—*The Tempest* (Act V, Scene 1)

Shakespeare's World Shakespeare's world was Elizabethan England. Named after Queen Elizabeth I, who ruled from 1558–1603, this dynamic era was a time of enormous change in the arts, in social order, and in international affairs. England became a commercial and naval power as explorers such as Sir Francis Drake and Sir Walter Raleigh helped expand England's territories all the way to the Americas. The establishment of the first successful colony at Jamestown, Virginia, in 1607 marked the beginning of a process that ultimately brought thousands of people from England to North America, inspired by dreams of commercial gain or of religious liberty in the New World.

Sources for *The Tempest* Shakespeare wove this growing interest in the New World into *The Tempest* (1611). In fact, real events of the time may have influenced the play's plot. The play opens with a storm that causes a shipwreck, stranding a group of noblemen on an unfamiliar island. In 1609 a fleet of ships financed by the Virginia Company set sail for Jamestown with hundreds of colonists on board. Shakespeare knew the company's leaders and likely read the vividly detailed reports of this event that circulated in 1610. During a violent storm off the Bermudas, one of the company's ships, the *Sea Venture,* was separated from the fleet. While the other ships reached Jamestown within a few weeks, the *Sea Venture* was assumed to be lost at sea. A year later, however, its passengers arrived in Jamestown on two small ships that they had built after being shipwrecked in Bermuda.

Another possible source for elements of *The Tempest* is Michel de Montaigne's 1603 essay "Of Cannibals," which focuses on Europe's problematic perception of the New World's "barbaric" native populations and their customs. Similarly, Shakespeare may have created the character of Caliban, a half-man, half-beast, to comment on British colonialism and slavery in the Americas and elsewhere. Scholars speculate that Caliban—whose name is basically an anagram, or rearrangement of the letters in the word *cannibal*—reveals the degree to which England viewed various native groups as uncivilized or less than human.

CLOSE READ

For more context and historical background, students can view the video "Biography: William Shakespeare" in their eBooks.

Background Have students read the information about Shakespeare. Tell students that during his lifetime, the first permanent European settlements were being founded in America. In 1607, just four years before Shakespeare completed *The Tempest*, a group of English colonists established Jamestown in what is now Virginia. These settlers forged a life for themselves in America that was completely foreign to what they had known in their home countries. In fact, so extraordinary were their experiences that the earliest American writers concentrated mainly on describing and trying to make sense of their challenging new environment and the unfamiliar people with whom they shared it. In diaries, letters, and reports back home, they recorded a historical turning point: when the world of the Europeans first intersected with that of the Native Americans. The setting and events of *The Tempest* may have been inspired by the experiences of these early colonists.

A|E BIO

from The Tempest

Drama by William Shakespeare

William Shakespeare *(1564–1616) was born in 1564 in Stratford-upon-Avon, a market town in central England. His father was a prosperous tradesman. Shakespeare probably attended Stratford's grammar school, where he would have studied Latin and read classical authors. In 1582 he married Anne Hathaway. The next year she gave birth to a daughter, Susanna. Their twins Hamnet and Judith followed in 1585. Sometime during the next seven years, Shakespeare found work in London as an actor; he also began to write plays. His early success aroused the envy of Robert Greene, who in 1592 described him as "an upstart crow." In 1594 Shakespeare joined the Lord Chamberlain's Men, which became the most prestigious theater company in London. Shakespeare soon grew affluent from his share in the company's profits.*

The Height of His Career *Shakespeare's rhetorical gifts and poetic power, as well as his profound psychological insight, would have allowed him to become a great writer in any age. To please the varied tastes of Elizabethan audiences, he mastered all forms of drama. In the 1590s, he focused on comedies and English history plays, such as* A Midsummer Night's Dream *and* Henry IV. *Between 1600 and 1607, he wrote his greatest tragedies, including* Hamlet, Macbeth, *and* King Lear. *The final phase of his career saw the creation of the darker comedies, such as* A Winter's Tale *and* The Tempest.

His Legacy *Shakespeare died in Stratford in 1616. At the time, some of his plays existed in cheap, often very flawed editions; others had never appeared in print. In 1623, two theater colleagues published a collected edition of his plays known as the First Folio, which ensured the survival of his work. Ben Jonson, a rival playwright, wrote an introduction for the volume in which he declared that Shakespeare "was not of an age, but for all time." Four centuries after Shakespeare's death, his plays continue to be performed around the world.*

Background In order to help students understand the characters and their relation to one another, give them the following information about the world of Shakespeare's play.

- **Milan** was a large northern Italian city and the capital of the duchy of Milan. A duchy was an independent territory ruled by a duke or duchess. [http://www.austinlibrary.com:2241/eb/article-10353]

- **Naples** was a large southern Italian city on the Mediterranean coast and center of an independent kingdom. In the fifteenth century Milan and Naples were rivals for power. [http://www.austinlibrary.com:2241/eb/article-6585]

- **The Mediterranean** is the sea that surrounds the Italian peninsula.

The Scene: A barren island in the Mediterranean Sea

CHARACTERS

(IN ACT I, AND ACT II, SCENE 1)

Prospero, the former duke of Milan, now a magician on a Mediterranean island

Miranda, Prospero's daughter

Ariel, a spirit, servant to Prospero

Caliban, an inhabitant of the island, servant to Prospero

Ferdinand, prince of Naples

Alonso, king of Naples

Antonio, duke of Milan and Prospero's brother

Sebastian, Alonso's brother

Gonzalo, councillor to Alonso and friend to Prospero

Courtiers in attendance on Alonso:

Adrian

Francisco

Shipmaster

Boatswain

Mariners

AS YOU READ Look for passages that relate to the experience of coming to a new land with unfamiliar sights and people. Write down any questions you generate during reading.

Act I

Scene 1

[*A tempestuous noise of thunder and lightning heard. Enter a* Shipmaster *and a* Boatswain.]

Master. Boatswain!

Boatswain. Here, master. What cheer?

Master. Good, speak to th' mariners. Fall to 't yarely or we run ourselves aground. Bestir, bestir!

[*He exits.*]

[*Enter* Mariners.]

5 **Boatswain.** Heigh, my hearts! Cheerly, cheerly, my hearts! Yare, yare! Take in the topsail. Tend to th' Master's whistle.—Blow till thou burst thy wind, if room enough!

[*Enter Alonso, Sebastian, Antonio, Ferdinand, Gonzalo, and others.*]

Alonso. Good boatswain, have care. Where's the
10 Master? Play the men.

Boatswain. I pray now, keep below.

Antonio. Where is the Master, boatswain?

Boatswain. Do you not hear him? You mar our labor. Keep your cabins. You do assist the storm.

15 **Gonzalo.** Nay, good, be patient.

Boatswain. When the sea is. Hence! What cares these roarers for the name of king? To cabin! Silence! Trouble us not.

Gonzalo. Good, yet remember whom thou hast aboard.

20 **Boatswain.** None that I more love than myself. You are a councillor; if you can command these elements to silence, and work the peace of the

1 **Boatswain:** a low-ranking ship's officer (pronounced "bosun")

2 **What cheer?:** How goes it with you?

3 **Good:** good fellow; **Fall to 't yarely:** proceed quickly.

4 **Bestir:** get moving.

5 **hearts:** hearties; **Cheerly:** heartily.

6 **Tend:** pay attention.

7–8 **Blow . . . enough:** The storm can blow its hardest as long as we have enough room to sail safely.

10 **Play the men:** Act like men.

16–17 **What cares . . . king?:** What do these roaring waves care about a king's rank?

21 **councillor:** adviser or member of the king's council.

The Tempest: Act I, Scene 1 **39**

SCAFFOLDING FOR ELL STUDENTS

Understand Archaic Language Explain to students that the English language of Shakespeare's time, including some pronouns and verb forms, was quite different from modern English. Tell students that for *you* and *your*, people said *thou* and *thy*, and that the verb forms used with *thou* ended in *-st*. Write "Blow till thou burst thy wind, if room enough!" from lines 7–8 on the board. Underline *thou burst* and tell students that it means "you burst." Then underline *thy wind* and tell students that it means "your breath."

ASK STUDENTS to find another use of *thou* plus a verb on the page and to tell what it means. *(line 19, you have)*

AS YOU READ Direct students to use the As You Read instructions to focus their reading. Remind students to write down any questions they generate as they read.

Support Inferences: Draw Conclusions (LINES 9–19)  COMMON CORE RL1

Explain to students that, unlike a novel, a drama does not usually give readers access to a character's private thoughts. Instead, the reader must make inferences about characters based on what they say, how they say it, and what they do.

Ⓐ CITE TEXT EVIDENCE Have students read the exchange between the boatswain and passengers in lines 9–19. Ask them to infer how the boatswain feels about his passengers and explain how they can tell. *(The boatswain is angry and exasperated. Twice he impatiently asks his passengers to stay in their cabins, he says that he will be paitent when the sea is patient, and he says the waves don't care about rank.)* Then ask students what they can infer about the characters of Alonso, Antonio, and Gonzalo and what evidence they have for their inferences. *(Alonso, Antonio, and Gonzalo are self-important. They insist on bothering the boatswain when he is trying to save the ship from a storm and tell him to remember what important people he has on board.)*

Analyze Language 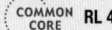 COMMON CORE RL 4

(LINES 16–17)

Explain to students that writers sometimes speak of nonhuman things as though they had human thoughts and feelings. Tell them that this type of figurative language is called **personification**.

Ⓑ ASK STUDENTS what is personified in lines and what impact this personification has. *(The "roarers," or waves, are personified as not caring "for the name of the king." The impact of this personification is to emphasize the ridiculousness of Alonso, Antonio, and Gonzalo in insisting on the perquisites of rank during a storm as though the sea were bound to respect titles of nobility.)*

TEACH

CLOSE READ

Support Inferences: Draw Conclusions (LINES 51–54)  COMMON CORE RL 1

Playwrights do not often directly state what is happening; instead, they expect the reader to infer the events of the play from the dialogue, action, and other details.

C CITE TEXT EVIDENCE Have students read lines 51–54 and infer what is happening. Then ask them to provide evidence for their inference. *(The mariners have given up trying to save the ship, and the ship is beginning to sink. The mariners are wet, which indicates that water is coming into the ship. They exclaim "All lost!" and go to pray in order to prepare for death. Gonzalo says that the king and prince are also praying and goes to join them because they are all going to drown.)*

Analyze Language (LINE 52) COMMON CORE RL 4

Tell students that Shakespeare is known for his use of figurative language, which sometimes makes his writing difficult to understand. Explain that when students come across lines that don't make literal sense, they should look for a figurative meaning.

D ASK STUDENTS to read and determine the meaning of line 52. Have them explain their reasoning process. *(The boatswain asks whether their mouths must be cold. The only reason for a person's mouth to be cold is if they are dead, so the boatswain is asking whether they must all die.)* Finally, ask what impact this language has on the reader. *(It makes the prospect of the characters' deaths seem more real and terrifying.)*

---

present, we will not hand a rope more. Use your authority. If you cannot, give thanks you have lived
25 so long, and make yourself ready in your cabin for the mischance of the hour, if it so hap.—Cheerly, good hearts!—Out of our way, I say!

[*He exits.*]

Gonzalo. I have great comfort from this fellow. Methinks he hath no drowning mark upon him.
30 His complexion is perfect gallows. Stand fast, good Fate, to his hanging. Make the rope of his destiny our cable, for our own doth little advantage. If he be not born to be hanged, our case is miserable.

[*He exits with* Alonso, Sebastian, *and the other courtiers.*]

[*Enter* Boatswain.]

Boatswain. Down with the topmast! Yare! Lower,
35 lower! Bring her to try wi' th' main course. [*a cry within*] A plague upon this howling! They are louder than the weather or our office.

[*Enter* Sebastian, Antonio, *and* Gonzalo.]

Yet again? What do you here? Shall we give o'er and drown? Have you a mind to sink?

40 **Sebastian.** A pox o' your throat, you bawling, blasphemous, incharitable dog!

Boatswain. Work you, then.

Antonio. Hang, cur, hang, you whoreson, insolent noisemaker! We are less afraid to be drowned than
45 thou art.

Gonzalo. I'll warrant him for drowning, though the ship were no stronger than a nutshell and as leaky as an unstanched wench.

Boatswain. Lay her ahold, ahold! Set her two courses.
50 Off to sea again! Lay her off!

[*Enter more* Mariners, *wet.*]

C **Mariners.** All lost! To prayers, to prayers! All lost!

[*Mariners exit.*]

Boatswain. What, must our mouths be cold? **D**

Gonzalo. The King and Prince at prayers. Let's assist them, for our case is as theirs.

55 **Sebastian.** I am out of patience.

21–23 command . . . present: quiet the wind and waves and establish order.

23 hand: handle.

26 mischance of the hour: impending disaster; **hap:** happen.

29–30 An allusion to the proverb "He that is born to be hanged shall never be drowned."

32 cable: anchor cable; **doth little advantage:** is of little use.

35 Bring . . . course: Use the mainsail to bring the ship close to the wind (keep it away from the island by sailing at an angle into the wind).

36–37 They are . . . office: The passengers make more noise than the storm and us as we work.

38 give o'er: give up.

40 A pox o': a curse on.

46 warrant him for: guarantee him against; **though:** even if.

48 unstanched wench: unclean or immoral woman.

49 Lay . . . courses: Keep the ship close to the wind. Set the foresail and mainsail.

40 Collection 1

APPLYING ACADEMIC VOCABULARY

| coherent | dynamic |

As you discuss *The Tempest*, incorporate the following Collection 1 academic vocabulary words: *coherent* and *dynamic*. As the play progresses, have students evaluate the play's plot by asking whether it is **coherent**. Have students keep track of the development of the situations and characters by asking whether they are **dynamic** and, if so, in what way.

Image Credits: (c) ©Liliya Kulianionak/Shutterstock; (b) ©Iouri Tcheka/Shutterstock; (tl) ©Kailash K Son/Shutterstock

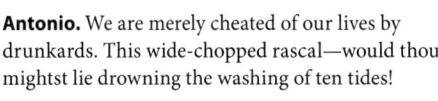

Antonio. We are merely cheated of our lives by drunkards. This wide-chopped rascal—would thou mightst lie drowning the washing of ten tides!

[Boatswain *exits.*]

Gonzalo. He'll be hanged yet, though every drop of
60 water swear against it and gape at wid'st to glut him.

[*A confused noise within:* "Mercy on us!"—"We split, we split!"—"Farewell, my wife and children!"—"Farewell, brother!"—"We split, we split, we split!"]

Antonio. Let's all sink wi' th' King.

Sebastian. Let's take leave of him.

[*He exits with* Antonio.]

Gonzalo. Now would I give a thousand furlongs of sea
for an acre of barren ground: long heath, brown
65 furze, anything. The wills above be done, but I
would fain die a dry death.

[*He exits.*]

56 merely: utterly.

57 wide-chopped: bigmouthed.

57–58 Antonio exaggerates the traditional punishment for pirates, which was to hang them at the shore and leave their corpses until three tides had washed over them.

60 gape . . . him: open wide to swallow him.

64 heath: heather.

65 furze: a shrub.

66 fain: willingly.

The Tempest: Act I, Scene 1   **41**

WHEN STUDENTS STRUGGLE . . .

Help students develop confidence with Shakespeare's verse by reading aloud lines 34–36. *(Down with the topmast! Yare! Lower, lower! Bring her to try wi' th' main course. A plague upon this howling! They are louder than the weather or our office.)* Analyze the passage with the class, encouraging students to define unfamiliar words and expressions. Then have students practice reading the passage expressively in mixed-ability groups.

Support Inferences: Draw Conclusions (LINES 56–66)

 COMMON CORE RL 1

Remind students that in drama as in real life extreme situations tend to reveal a character's most basic traits and values. By noting how the characters react to the ship's sinking, readers can infer more about them.

E CITE TEXT EVIDENCE Have students read this page and infer how Gonzalo differs from his companions. Ask them to give evidence to support their inferences. *(Antonio first reacts to the disaster with anger. His next thought is for his duty to the king, and Sebastian agrees. Gonzalo, on the other hand, continues with his humorous patter about the boatswain being destined to die by hanging rather than drowning. Instead of rushing to be with the king, Gonzalo calmly laments his fate. From this evidence, it seems that Gonzalo is less invested in his identity as the king's companion, and that he is able to keep more perspective on what is happening than are Antonio and Sebastian.)*

Analyze Language

 COMMON CORE RL 4

(LINES 63–66)

Explain that Shakespeare—known as a great dramatic poet—wrote this first scene entirely in prose, but that effective prose often utilizes the same sound devices as poetry, including:

- **alliteration:** the repetition of initial consonants
- **assonance:** the repetition of vowel sounds

F CITE TEXT EVIDENCE Have students read Gonzalo's speech (lines 63–66). Ask them to cite instances of alliteration and assonance. *(Now, thousand, ground, and brown in sentence 1 are examples of assonance. Furlongs and furze include both alliteration and assonance. Sentence 2 includes alliteration in the d sounds of done, die, and dry death.)* Then ask students what effect the use of alliteration and assonance have on the reader. *(The use of alliteration and assonance give the speech a poetic feel and change the mood of the play from active to reflective.)*

Support Inferences: Draw Conclusions (ACT 1, SCENE 2, LINES 1–24)

COMMON CORE RL 1

Remind students that in order to understand the plot and characters in a drama, they must make inferences based on what the characters say and do. Have a class discussion about what it would be like if a playwright directly stated what was happening and what the characters were like. *(It wouldn't be very interesting because there would be nothing for the reader to discover, and there would probably be fewer surprises.)*

G **CITE TEXT EVIDENCE** Have students reread lines 1–24. Ask them what they learn about the shipwreck and about Prospero, and what text evidence helped them to make these inferences. *(Prospero caused the storm that wrecked the ship. He is a magician. In line 1, Miranda wonders whether Prospero "Put the wild waters in this roar" by his "arts," and in line 24, Prospero asks Miranda to take off his "magic garment.")*

Analyze Language (LINES 1–5)

COMMON CORE RL 4

Lead students to notice that Shakespeare is now writing poetry. Explain that Shakespeare often wrote dialogue in **iambic pentameter**, a meter consisting of five units, or feet, each containing an unstressed syllable followed by a stressed syllable. Tell students that poetry written in unrhymed iambic pentameter is known as **blank verse**. Point out that while Shakespeare used this poetic form as a guide, his lines are rarely perfect examples of blank verse.

H **ASK STUDENTS** Have students read lines 1–5. Point out that only one line in this passage is written in perfect iambic pentameter. Ask them to identify that line. *(line 3: The sky, it seems, would pour down stinking pitch).* Then ask a volunteer to read the line aloud.

Scene 2

[*Enter* Prospero *and* Miranda.]

G **Miranda.** If by your art, my dearest father, you have **H**
Put the wild waters in this roar, allay them.
The sky, it seems, would pour down stinking pitch,
But that the sea, mounting to th' welkin's cheek,
5   Dashes the fire out. O, I have suffered
With those that I saw suffer! A brave vessel,
Who had, no doubt, some noble creature in her,
Dashed all to pieces. O, the cry did knock
Against my very heart! Poor souls, they perished.
10 Had I been any god of power, I would
Have sunk the sea within the earth or ere
It should the good ship so have swallowed, and
The fraughting souls within her.

    Prospero.   Be collected.
No more amazement. Tell your piteous heart
15 There's no harm done.

    Miranda.   O, woe the day!

    Prospero.   No harm.
I have done nothing but in care of thee,
Of thee, my dear one, thee, my daughter, who
Art ignorant of what thou art, naught knowing
Of whence I am, nor that I am more better
20 Than Prospero, master of a full poor cell,
And thy no greater father.

    Miranda.   More to know
Did never meddle with my thoughts.

    Prospero.   'Tis time
I should inform thee farther. Lend thy hand
And pluck my magic garment from me.

    [*putting aside his cloak*]

                            So,
25 Lie there, my art.—Wipe thou thine eyes. Have
    comfort.
The direful spectacle of the wrack, which touched
The very virtue of compassion in thee,
I have with such provision in mine art
So safely ordered that there is no soul—
30 No, not so much perdition as an hair,
Betid to any creature in the vessel
Which thou heard'st cry, which thou saw'st sink.

1 **art:** magic, skill.

3 **pitch:** a tarlike substance used for waterproofing ships.

4 **welkin's:** sky's.

6 **brave:** fine.

11 **or ere:** before.

13 **fraughting souls:** passengers.

14 **amazement:** bewilderment; **piteous:** compassionate.

18 **naught knowing:** knowing nothing.

19 **whence I am:** where I come from; **more better:** of higher rank.

20 **full poor cell:** very humble dwelling.

22 **meddle with:** enter.

26 **direful spectacle:** terrible display.

27 **virtue:** essence.

28 **provision:** foresight.

30 **perdition:** loss.

31 **Betid:** happened.

42 Collection 1

SCAFFOLDING FOR ELL STUDENTS

Understand Verb Tenses Explain to students that not all of the actions described on this page actually take place. Tell them that some of Miranda's lines instead tell what would happen if things were different. Remind students that the conditional tense is used to describe situations or events that could exist in the future if circumstances were different. The conditional tense of the verb *to be* often follows the word *if* and takes the forms *would* and *were*.

Sit down,
For thou must now know farther.

[They sit.]

Miranda.   You have often
Begun to tell me what I am, but stopped
35 And left me to a bootless inquisition,
Concluding "Stay. Not yet."

Prospero.   The hour's now come.
The very minute bids thee ope thine ear.
Obey, and be attentive. Canst thou remember
A time before we came unto this cell?
40 I do not think thou canst, for then thou wast not
Out three years old.

Miranda.   Certainly, sir, I can.

Prospero. By what? By any other house or person?
Of anything the image tell me that
Hath kept with thy remembrance.

Miranda.   ʼTis far off
45 And rather like a dream than an assurance
That my remembrance warrants. Had I not
Four or five women once that tended me?

Prospero. Thou hadst, and more, Miranda. But how is it
That this lives in thy mind? What seest thou else
50 In the dark backward and abysm of time?
If thou rememb'rest aught ere thou cam'st here,
How thou cam'st here thou mayst.

Miranda.   But that I do not.

Prospero. Twelve year since, Miranda, twelve year since,
Thy father was the Duke of Milan and
55 A prince of power.

Miranda.   Sir, are not you my father?

Prospero. Thy mother was a piece of virtue, and
She said thou wast my daughter. And thy father
Was Duke of Milan, and his only heir
And princess no worse issued.

Miranda.   O, the heavens!
60 What foul play had we that we came from thence?
Or blessèd was 't we did?

Prospero.   Both, both, my girl.
By foul play, as thou sayst, were we heaved thence,
But blessedly holp hither.

35 bootless inquisition: useless inquiry.

37 ope: open.

41 Out: fully.

43 Of anything . . . me: describe to me anything.

45–46 an assurance . . . warrants: a certainty that my memory guarantees to be true.

50 backward: past; **abysm:** abyss.

51 aught ere: anything before.

53 Twelve year since: twelve years ago.

56 piece of virtue: model of chastity.

59 no worse issued: no less nobly born.

63 holp hither: helped here.

The Tempest: Act I, Scene 2   **43**

CLOSE READ

Analyze Language (LINE 36)    COMMON CORE RL 4, RL 5

Explain that English poets frequently employed blank verse for drama or narrative poetry because its rhythm approximates the natural rhythm of the spoken English language. Point out that Shakespeare's poetic dialogue is intended to be read naturally and expressively, like real speech. Draw students' attention to Miranda's part of line 36 ("Stay. Not yet.") Point out that this is not a full line of iambic pentameter and that Prospero's words complete Miranda's unfinished line immediately before. Read all of line 35 aloud to students.

CITE TEXT EVIDENCE Have students find other examples of lines shared between the speakers. *(Lines 33, 41, 44, 52, 55, 59, 61, and 63 are also broken up in this way.)* Then ask students to discuss the impact on the reader of these shared lines. *(The shared lines make the dialogue seem more like natural speech.)*

Support Inferences: Draw Conclusions (LINES 54–59)    COMMON CORE RL 1

Point out that Prospero uses indirect, riddling language to tell his daughter their history. The reader must make inferences to determine what information is being given.

ASK STUDENTS to reread the exchange between Prospero and Miranda in lines 54–59. Then ask what they learn in these lines about Prospero and Miranda and on what evidence they base their inferences. *(Prospero was the Duke of Milan and Miranda was a princess. Prospero says that Miranda's father was the Duke of Milan. When Miranda asks whether Prospero is her father, he says that Miranda's mother said he was, and that Miranda's father was a duke and Miranda was a princess. Since Miranda's mother was virtuous, it is true that Prospero is Miranda's father. Since Miranda's father was a duke and Prospero is Miranda's father, it follows that Prospero was a duke and Miranda was a princess.)*

Have students work together to find two conditional sentences on this page and tell what event each describes and on what condition the event depends. *(First sentence: "The sky, it seems, would pour down stinking pitch, / But that the sea, mounting to th' welkin's cheek, / Dashes the fire out." The event described is the sky raining down pitch, and the condition is if the sea did not put out the fire. Second sentence: "Had I been any god of power, I would / Have sunk the sea within the earth or ere / It should the good ship so have swallowed, and / The fraughting souls within her." The event described is Miranda making the sea sink into the earth so it won't destroy the ship, and the condition is if Miranda were a powerful god.)*

Analyze Language

COMMON CORE **RL 4**

(LINES 85–87)

Remind students that **figurative language**—language that uses words in nonliteral ways—is an important element of poetry. Figurative language often compares two unlike things, inviting the reader to look at a person or object with fresh eyes. A **metaphor** is a **figure of speech** that compares two dissimilar things without using the words *like* or *as*.

🅚 **CITE TEXT EVIDENCE** Have students find a vivid metaphor on page 44 concerning Prospero and his brother Antonio. Ask students to what Prospero compares Antonio and himself and what effect the metaphor has on the reader. *(In lines 85–87 Prospero compares his brother to ivy and himself to the tree on which the ivy is climbing, both hiding and feeding on it. The metaphor helps the reader imagine Antonio as a damaging parasite with an attractive outward appearance.)*

Support Inferences: Draw Conclusions (LINES 79–105)

COMMON CORE **RL 1**

Explain to students that characters in dramas may not always be reliable narrators of events. Call their attention to Prospero's account of Antonio's treachery. As a class, discuss what reasons Prospero might have for emphasizing Antonio's guilt. *(to avoid thinking about his own responsibility in giving up his power, or examining his own desire to dominate and control others)*

🅛 **CITE TEXT EVIDENCE** Have students review Prospero's explanation of events in lines 79–105. Ask students what they can infer about Prospero's role in Antonio's rise to power and on what evidence they base their inferences. *(Evidence in lines 79–84 indicates that Prospero left all the work of governing to Antonio. Prospero confirms this in lines 89–90, when he says that he neglected "worldly ends," and he says in lines 96 and 97 that his trust of Antonio had no bounds. By leaving all the work of government to Antonio and paying no attention to affairs of state, Prospero made it easy for Antonio to take over.)*

Miranda.   O, my heart bleeds
To think o' th' teen that I have turned you to,
65   Which is from my remembrance. Please you, farther.

Prospero. My brother and thy uncle, called Antonio—
I pray thee, mark me—that a brother should
Be so perfidious!—he whom next thyself
Of all the world I loved, and to him put
70   The manage of my state, as at that time
Through all the signories it was the first,
And Prospero the prime duke, being so reputed
In dignity, and for the liberal arts
Without a parallel. Those being all my study,
75   The government I cast upon my brother
And to my state grew stranger, being transported
And rapt in secret studies. Thy false uncle—
Dost thou attend me?

Miranda.   Sir, most heedfully.

 **Prospero.** Being once perfected how to grant suits,
80   How to deny them, who t' advance, and who
To trash for overtopping, new created
The creatures that were mine, I say, or changed 'em,
Or else new formed 'em, having both the key
Of officer and office, set all hearts i' th' state
85   To what tune pleased his ear, that now he was   🅚
The ivy which had hid my princely trunk
And sucked my verdure out on 't. Thou attend'st not.

Miranda. O, good sir, I do.

Prospero.   I pray thee, mark me.
I, thus neglecting worldly ends, all dedicated
90   To closeness and the bettering of my mind
With that which, but by being so retired,
O'erprized all popular rate, in my false brother
Awaked an evil nature, and my trust,
Like a good parent, did beget of him
95   A falsehood in its contrary as great
As my trust was, which had indeed no limit,
A confidence sans bound. He being thus lorded,
Not only with what my revenue yielded
But what my power might else exact, like one
100   Who, having into truth by telling of it,
Made such a sinner of his memory
To credit his own lie, he did believe
He was indeed the Duke, out o' th' substitution
And executing th' outward face of royalty

64 o' th' teen: of the trouble.

65 from: absent from.

68 perfidious: treacherous; **next:** next to.

71 signories: lordships; **first:** foremost.

72 prime: most important.

77 rapt: engrossed.

79 Being once perfected: having mastered; **suits:** petitions.

81 trash: restrain; **overtopping:** exceeding their authority.

82–83 or changed . . . formed 'em: either changed their allegiance or created new officials.

85 that: so that.

87 verdure: sap; vitality.

90 closeness: privacy.

91–92 but by . . . rate: was more valuable than the public could appreciate merely because it was so secluded.

94 did beget of him: produced in him.

97 sans bound: without limit.

105 With all prerogative. Hence, his ambition growing—
Dost thou hear?

Miranda. Your tale, sir, would cure deafness.

Prospero. To have no screen between this part he played
And him he played it for, he needs will be
110 Absolute Milan. Me, poor man, my library
Was dukedom large enough. Of temporal royalties
He thinks me now incapable; confederates,
So dry he was for sway, wi' th' King of Naples
To give him annual tribute, do him homage,
115 Subject his coronet to his crown, and bend
The dukedom, yet unbowed—alas, poor Milan!—
To most ignoble stooping.

Miranda.   O, the heavens!

Prospero. Mark his condition and th' event. Then tell me
If this might be a brother.

Miranda.   I should sin
120 To think but nobly of my grandmother.
Good wombs have borne bad sons.

Prospero.   Now the condition.
This King of Naples, being an enemy
To me inveterate, hearkens my brother's suit,
Which was that he, in lieu o' th' premises
125 Of homage and I know not how much tribute,
Should presently extirpate me and mine
Out of the dukedom, and confer fair Milan,
With all the honors, on my brother; whereon,
A treacherous army levied, one midnight
130 Fated to th' purpose did Antonio open
The gates of Milan, and i' th' dead of darkness
The ministers for th' purpose hurried thence
Me and thy crying self.

Miranda.   Alack, for pity!
I, not rememb'ring how I cried out then,
135 Will cry it o'er again. It is a hint
That wrings mine eyes to 't.

Prospero.   Hear a little further,
And then I'll bring thee to the present business
Which now 's upon 's, without the which this story
Were most impertinent.

Miranda.   Wherefore did they not
140 That hour destroy us?

108–110 To have ... Milan: To have no barrier between himself and his role, he must become the duke of Milan without any restrictions.

110 Me: for me.

111 temporal royalties: worldly powers.

112–117 confederates ... stooping: Antonio was so thirsty for power that he formed an alliance with the king of Naples, agreeing to make annual payments, to declare his obedience, and to turn Milan into a subject state.

123 hearkens ... suit: listens to my brother's proposal.

124–128 in lieu ... brother: In return for Antonio's agreement to pay homage and tribute, the king of Naples was to immediately remove Prospero and his family from Milan and give the dukedom to Antonio.

132 ministers: agents

135 hint: occasion.

139 impertinent: irrelevant; **Wherefore:** why.

Analyze Language
COMMON CORE RL 4
(LINES 108–133)

Remind students that one way in which writers and speakers persuade their audience is the use of words with strong connotations—associated ideas or feelings. Draw students' attention to lines 118 and 119. Discuss whether Prospero is giving an objective account or trying to persuade Miranda of her uncle's evil nature.

M ASK STUDENTS to read lines 108–133 and list adjectives with strong connotations used by Prospero. Then as a class make lists of adjectives with positive connotations and adjectives with negative connotations. Ask volunteers to describe the connotations of both lists. What effect does Propsero hope to produce on Miranda with his choice of words? Does he succeed in persuading her of his point of view? (Positive: poor, lines 110 and 116; unbowed, line 116; fair, line 127. Negative: ignoble, line 117; treacherous, line 129. The positive words have connotations of innocence, pride, and loftiness, while the negative words have connotations of baseness and evil.)

Support Inferences: Draw Conclusions
COMMON CORE RL 1
(LINES 110–112)

Point out to students that this page continues Prospero's explanation of how he lost his dukedom. As on the previous page, Prospero sometimes says more than he means to express and allows the reader to infer something about Antonio's point of view.

N CITE EVIDENCE Have students look for evidence of Antonio's point of view. Then ask students what they can infer from this evidence about Antonio's possible reason for taking over Milan. (In lines 111–112, Prospero says that Antonio thinks that Prospero is no longer able to rule his kingdom. From this and from Prospero's statement that Antonio wanted "To have no screen between this part he played / And him he played it for" it is possible to infer that Antonio may have taken over Milan because he felt his brother was incapable of ruling it and because he felt that if he was doing the work, he should get the title.)

TO CHALLENGE STUDENTS ...

Analyze Word Choice Discuss with students Prospero's purpose in telling Miranda about how he lost the duchy of Milan. Guide students to understand that Prospero wants to convince Miranda that he has been the victim of a terrible injustice. Have students reread lines 66–133, paying close attention to Prospero's choice of words.

ASK STUDENTS to work in pairs to choose one of Prospero's speeches and locate the words within it that have the greatest emotional impact. Then have pairs replace these words with more neutral synonyms. Have a volunteer from each pair read the rewritten speech to the class.

Analyze Language

 COMMON CORE RL 4

(LINES 145–152)

Remind students that **personification** is a form of figurative language in which writers attribute human feelings or thoughts to nonhuman things. Point out that personification is actually a type of metaphor that compares something nonhuman to a person.

O ASK STUDENTS Ask students to closely read Prospero's description of being put out to sea (lines 145–152). Ask them to find an example of personification in this passage. (*In lines 150–152 Prospero speaks of the winds showing pity, sighing, and loving.*) Then ask students what is ironic about the winds' pity. (*In sighing—or blowing—the winds blow Prospero's boat out to sea.*)

Support Inferences: Draw Conclusions (LINES 161–170)

 COMMON CORE RL 1

Review with students Prospero's description of Gonzalo's kindness to the castaways (lines 161–170). Explain that Gonzalo is a Neapolitan, meaning that he is from Naples, an enemy of Prospero's duchy of Milan. Remind students that they have already met Gonzalo in Scene 1. Discuss points of similarity between the Gonzalo they have met and the man that Prospero describes. (*Gonzalo appears patient, humorous, and even-tempered. He is the sort of man who could be kind to the exiles.*)

P CITE TEXT EVIDENCE Ask students to look for evidence on which to base an inference about how Gonzalo felt about Antonio's treatment of Prospero and Miranda. (*Gonzalo gives Prospero and Miranda food, water, clothing, and other supplies. He even gives Prospero his favorite books. This kindness indicates that Gonzalo feels that Antonio's treatment of Prospero and Miranda is harsh.*)

Prospero.   Well demanded, wench.
My tale provokes that question. Dear, they durst not,
So dear the love my people bore me, nor set
A mark so bloody on the business, but
With colors fairer painted their foul ends.
145 In few, they hurried us aboard a bark,
Bore us some leagues to sea, where they prepared
A rotten carcass of a butt, not rigged,
Nor tackle, sail, nor mast; the very rats
Instinctively have quit it. There they hoist us
150 To cry to th' sea that roared to us, to sigh
To th' winds, whose pity, sighing back again,
Did us but loving wrong.

Miranda.   Alack, what trouble
Was I then to you!

Prospero.   O, a cherubin
Thou wast that did preserve me. Thou didst smile,
155 Infusèd with a fortitude from heaven,
When I have decked the sea with drops full salt,
Under my burden groaned, which raised in me
An undergoing stomach to bear up
Against what should ensue.

160 **Miranda.** How came we ashore?

Prospero. By providence divine.
Some food we had, and some fresh water, that
A noble Neapolitan, Gonzalo,
Out of his charity, who being then appointed
165 Master of this design, did give us, with
Rich garments, linens, stuffs, and necessaries,
Which since have steaded much. So, of his gentleness,
Knowing I loved my books, he furnished me
From mine own library with volumes that
170 I prize above my dukedom.

Miranda.   Would I might
But ever see that man.

Prospero [*standing*]. Now I arise.
Sit still, and hear the last of our sea-sorrow.
Here in this island we arrived, and here
Have I, thy schoolmaster, made thee more profit
175 Than other princes can, that have more time
For vainer hours and tutors not so careful.

Miranda. Heavens thank you for 't. And now I pray
  you, sir—

141 durst: dared.

145 few: brief; **bark:** ship.

147 butt: barrel or tub.

148 Nor...nor: having neither...nor.

151–152 sighing back...wrong: the wind's sympathetic sighing wronged us by blowing the boat out to sea.

156 decked: adorned.

157–158 which raised...bear up: your smiling gave me the courage to endure.

166 stuffs: materials.

167 have steaded much: have been very useful; **gentleness:** nobility.

174 made thee more profit: made you profit more.

175 princes: royal children.

WHEN STUDENTS STRUGGLE...

Help students understand the sequence of events in Prospero's history by creating an outline. Have small groups of students write brief statements of fact about the story on separate note cards. Have each group work together to number the cards in the sequence in which the events took place. Finally, have a volunteer from each group read that group's cards aloud in the correct sequence. Encourage readers to supply extra details for each fact in their outline. Help clarify information where necessary.

For still 'tis beating in my mind—your reason
For raising this sea storm?

Prospero.   Know thus far forth:
180 By accident most strange, bountiful Fortune,
Now my dear lady, hath mine enemies
Brought to this shore; and by my prescience
I find my zenith doth depend upon
A most auspicious star, whose influence
185 If now I court not, but omit, my fortunes
Will ever after droop. Here cease more questions.
Thou art inclined to sleep. 'Tis a good dullness,
And give it way. I know thou canst not choose.

[Miranda *falls asleep.* Prospero *puts on his cloak.*]

Come away, servant, come. I am ready now.
190 Approach, my Ariel. Come.

[*Enter Ariel.*]

Ariel. All hail, great master! Grave sir, hail! I come
To answer thy best pleasure. Be 't to fly,
To swim, to dive into the fire, to ride
On the curled clouds, to thy strong bidding task
195 Ariel and all his quality.

Prospero.   Hast thou, spirit,
Performed to point the tempest that I bade thee?

Ariel. To every article.
I boarded the King's ship; now on the beak,
Now in the waist, the deck, in every cabin,
200 I flamed amazement. Sometimes I'd divide
And burn in many places. On the topmast,
The yards, and bowsprit would I flame distinctly,
Then meet and join. Jove's lightning, the precursors
O' th' dreadful thunderclaps, more momentary
205 And sight-outrunning were not. The fire and cracks
Of sulfurous roaring the most mighty Neptune
Seem to besiege and make his bold waves tremble,
Yea, his dread trident shake.

Prospero.   My brave spirit!
Who was so firm, so constant, that this coil
210 Would not infect his reason?

Ariel.   Not a soul
But felt a fever of the mad, and played
Some tricks of desperation. All but mariners
Plunged in the foaming brine and quit the vessel,
Then all afire with me. The King's son, Ferdinand,
215 With hair up-staring—then like reeds, not hair—

181 Now my dear lady: now on my side. (Fortune was often personified as a fickle woman.)

183 my zenith: the high point of my fortunes.

185 omit: fail to take advantage of.

187 dullness: drowsiness.

195 quality: abilities or fellow spirits.

196 to point: in exact detail.

199 waist: middle part of a ship.

200 flamed amazement: Ariel's antics simulated St. Elmo's fire, which can occur on ships during electrical storms.

205 sight-outrunning: quicker than the eye.

206–208 Neptune: god of the sea (who carries a **trident,** or three-pronged spear).

209 coil: turmoil.

211 of the mad: such as madmen feel.

212 tricks of desperation: desperate actions.

215 up-staring: standing on end.

The Tempest: Act I, Scene 2 **47**

CLOSE READ

Support Inferences: Draw Conclusions (LINES 191–215)

 COMMON CORE RL 1

Point out to students that a new character, Ariel, is introduced in these lines. Prospero calls this character his servant.

Q CITE EVIDENCE Have students review lines 191–215 for evidence that will help them make inferences about Ariel's character. Ask them to state their inferences and their evidence. *(In lines 192–195, Ariel offers to do a number of things for Prospero, most of which are impossible for human beings. In lines 198–208, Ariel tells how he caused lightning to appear on the ship. Finally, in line 208, Prospero calls him a "spirit." From this evidence, one can infer that Ariel is a supernatural being.)*

Analyze Language

COMMON CORE RL 4

(LINES 191–192)

Point out that a skilled writer can use sound devices to supplement and support the literal meaning of words. Invite individuals to read aloud Ariel's opening greeting to Prospero (lines 191–192).

R ASK STUDENTS what sound device Shakespeare uses in Ariel's greeting. How does this contribute to the effect of the lines? *(Shakespeare uses assonance, repeating the long "a" sound four times in the first line: great, grave, and hail twice. This long vowel lengthens the line when it is spoken, giving it a prayerful, musical quality that stresses Prospero's importance.)*

1. Prospero retires from politics to study.

2. Antonio governs in Prospero's place.

3. Antonio forms an alliance with Naples.

4. King of Naples throws Prospero out.

5. Gonzalo gives Prospero and Miranda supplies.

6. Prospero and Miranda land on the island.

CLOSE READ

Support Inferences: Draw Conclusions (LINES 217–241)  COMMON CORE RL 1

Explain that revenge was a popular theme among dramatists in Shakespeare's day. Discuss with students Prospero's motivation for revenge.

S **CITE EVIDENCE** Have students review the exchange between Prospero and Ariel in lines 217–241. Ask them to infer Prospero's purpose in having Ariel simulate a storm and give evidence for their inferences. *(From the concern Prospero expresses for the safety of those on the ship, one can infer that he did not intend to drown them. In lines 222 and 223, Ariel tells Prospero that he has deposited the passengers on different parts of the island, and in line 240 Prospero says that Ariel has done as he had asked. One can infer from this information that it was Prospero's purpose to bring the passengers to the island.)*

Was the first man that leaped; cried "Hell is empty,
And all the devils are here."

Prospero. Why, that's my spirit!
But was not this nigh shore?

> 218 **nigh:** near.

Ariel. Close by, my master.

Prospero. But are they, Ariel, safe?

Ariel. Not a hair perished.
220 On their sustaining garments not a blemish,
But fresher than before; and, as thou bad'st me,
In troops I have dispersed them 'bout the isle.
The King's son have I landed by himself,
Whom I left cooling of the air with sighs
225 In an odd angle of the isle, and sitting,
His arms in this sad knot.

> 220 **sustaining garments:** garments that helped them float.
>
> 221 **bad'st:** commanded.
>
> 222 **troops:** groups.
>
> 225 **odd angle:** out-of-the-way corner.

[*He folds his arms.*]

Prospero. Of the King's ship,
The mariners say how thou hast disposed,
And all the rest o' th' fleet.

Ariel. Safely in harbor
Is the King's ship. In the deep nook, where once
230 Thou called'st me up at midnight to fetch dew
From the still-vexed Bermoothes, there she's hid;
The mariners all under hatches stowed,
Who, with a charm joined to their suffered labor,
I have left asleep. And for the rest o' th' fleet,
235 Which I dispersed, they all have met again
And are upon the Mediterranean float,
Bound sadly home for Naples,
Supposing that they saw the King's ship wracked
And his great person perish.

> 231 **still-vexed Bermoothes:** always stormy Bermudas.
>
> 233 **with a . . . labor:** under the combined effects of my spell and their exhaustion.
>
> 236 **float:** sea.

Prospero. Ariel, thy charge
240 Exactly is performed. But there's more work.
What is the time o' th' day?

Ariel. Past the mid season.

> 241 **mid season:** noon.

Prospero. At least two glasses. The time 'twixt six
and now
Must by us both be spent most preciously.

> 242 **two glasses:** two o'clock (two hourglasses past noon).

Ariel. Is there more toil? Since thou dost give me pains,
245 Let me remember thee what thou hast promised,
Which is not yet performed me.

> 244 **pains:** tasks.
>
> 245 **remember:** remind.

Prospero. How now? Moody?
What is 't thou canst demand?

SCAFFOLDING FOR ELL STUDENTS

Understand Contractions Explain to students that in order to make his language sound more like ordinary conversation, Shakespeare sometimes uses **contractions**. A contraction is a word from which one or more letters have been left out and replaced with an apostrophe. Ask students to think of familiar contractions, such as *don't* and *that's*.

ASK STUDENTS to reread the page to look for unfamiliar contractions. Have them work in small groups to restore the left-out letters to the words. Provide help as needed. *(bad'st, line 221: badest; 'bout, line 222: about; o' th', lines 228, 234, and 241: of the; called'st, line 230: calledest; 'twixt, line 242: betwixt)*

Ariel.   My liberty.

Prospero. Before the time be out? No more.

Ariel.   I prithee,
Remember I have done thee worthy service,
250 Told thee no lies, made no mistakings, served
Without or grudge or grumblings. Thou did promise
To bate me a full year.

Prospero.   Dost thou forget
From what a torment I did free thee?

Ariel.   No.

Prospero. Thou dost, and think'st it much to tread
    the ooze
255 Of the salt deep,
To run upon the sharp wind of the north,
To do me business in the veins o'th'earth
When it is baked with frost.

Ariel.   I do not, sir.

Prospero. Thou liest, malignant thing. Hast thou forgot
260 The foul witch Sycorax, who with age and envy
Was grown into a hoop? Hast thou forgot her?

Ariel. No, sir.

Prospero. Thou hast. Where was she born? Speak.
    Tell me.

Ariel. Sir, in Argier.

Prospero.   O, was she so? I must
265 Once in a month recount what thou hast been,
Which thou forget'st. This damned witch Sycorax,
For mischiefs manifold, and sorceries terrible
To enter human hearing, from Argier,
Thou know'st, was banished. For one thing she did
270 They would not take her life. Is not this true?

Ariel. Ay, sir.

Prospero. This blue-eyed hag was hither brought
    with child
And here was left by th' sailors. Thou, my slave,
As thou report'st thyself, was then her servant,
275 And for thou wast a spirit too delicate
To act her earthy and abhorred commands,
Refusing her grand hests, she did confine thee,
By help of her more potent ministers
And in her most unmitigable rage,
280 Into a cloven pine, within which rift

248 prithee: beg of you.

251 or . . . or: either . . . or.

252 bate me: deduct from the time of my service.

257 veins o'th' earth: mineral veins or underground streams.

258 baked: hardened.

261 grown into a hoop: bent over.

264 Argier: Algiers.

269–272 Sycorax was exiled rather than killed, probably because she was pregnant (blue eyelids were thought to be a sign of pregnancy).

275 for: because.

277 hests: commands.

278 ministers: agents.

The Tempest: Act I, Scene 2   **49**

Support Inferences: Draw Conclusions (LINES 253–280)

Discuss with students the impression they had of Prospero's relationship with Ariel before they read this section. (*Prospero seemed quite pleased with Ariel, and Ariel seemed happy to carry out his orders.*)

CITE EVIDENCE Ask students to describe Prospero's relationship with Ariel as revealed in this passage, citing evidence for their inferences. (*From lines 253–254, we can infer that Ariel serves Prospero in exchange for Prospero having rescued him. From Ariel's request for his liberty, we can infer that Ariel no longer wants to serve Prospero. From Prospero's insulting language in line 259 [malignant thing] and line 273 [my slave] as well as his sarcasm in lines 264–267, one can infer that Prospero doesn't respect Ariel, but merely wishes to control him for Prospero's own gain.*)

Analyze Language (LINES 259–270)

Draw students' attention to the questions Prospero asks Ariel in lines 259–261, 263, and 270. Discuss with students Prospero's reason for asking these questions and lead them to conclude that they are all rhetorical questions—questions to which Prospero already knows the answer.

ASK STUDENTS what impact Prospero's rhetorical questions have on Ariel and on the reader's impression of Prospero. (*The questions and Prospero's recounting of Ariel's time with Sycorax cause Ariel to lose hope of regaining his freedom. To the reader, the questions make Prospero seem like a pompous bully.*)

TO CHALLENGE STUDENTS . . .

Determine Author's Purpose Discuss with students that a single scene of a play may accomplish a variety of purposes, such as introducing and developing characters, furthering the action, and giving background information to the reader.

ASK STUDENTS to reread lines 253–280 and read lines 281–287. Have them work in small groups to identify two purposes accomplished by these lines. (*to give the reader information about Prospero and Ariel's relationship, to develop Prospero's character by revealing how he obtained and keeps power over Ariel, to introduce Caliban*) Have each group report its findings.

Analyze Language COMMON CORE RL 4

(LINES 285–286)

Draw students' attention to Prospero's description of Caliban (lines 285–286). Then remind them that metaphors compare two things by speaking of one as though it were the other. Ask students what the word *whelp* means, and lead them to understand that it means "a puppy."

V **ASK STUDENTS** to what Prospero compares Caliban and what the metaphor reveals about Prospero's attitude to Caliban. *(Prospero compares Caliban to a dog by saying his mother "littered" him and calling him a "whelp." This metaphor reveals that Prospero considers Caliban less than human.)*

Support Inferences: Draw Conclusions COMMON CORE RL 1

(LINES 305–311)

Remind students of how Prospero put Miranda to sleep in lines 187–188 on page 47. Then direct students to lines 309–310, in which Prospero wakes Miranda up.

W **CITE TEXT EVIDENCE** Have students reread lines 305–311 and infer why Prospero chose this moment to wake Miranda. Ask them to give evidence to support their inference. *(Prospero woke Miranda because he has finished talking with Ariel and Ariel has left the stage [stage direction between lines 8 and 9] and because he has commanded Ariel to be invisible to everyone but him [lines 306–307], so if he returns Miranda won't be able to see him.)*

Imprisoned thou didst painfully remain
A dozen years; within which space she died
And left thee there, where thou didst vent thy groans
As fast as mill wheels strike. Then was this island
V 285 (Save for the son that she did litter here,
A freckled whelp, hag-born) not honored with
A human shape.

    Ariel.   Yes, Caliban, her son.

    Prospero. Dull thing, I say so; he, that Caliban
Whom now I keep in service. Thou best know'st
290 What torment I did find thee in. Thy groans
Did make wolves howl, and penetrate the breasts
Of ever-angry bears. It was a torment
To lay upon the damned, which Sycorax
Could not again undo. It was mine art,
295 When I arrived and heard thee, that made gape
The pine and let thee out.

    Ariel.   I thank thee, master.

    Prospero. If thou more murmur'st, I will rend an oak
And peg thee in his knotty entrails till
Thou hast howled away twelve winters.

    Ariel.   Pardon, master.
300 I will be correspondent to command
And do my spriting gently.

    Prospero. Do so, and after two days
I will discharge thee.

    Ariel.   That's my noble master.
What shall I do? Say, what? What shall I do?

W 305 **Prospero.** Go make thyself like a nymph o' th' sea.
    Be subject
To no sight but thine and mine, invisible
To every eyeball else. Go, take this shape,
And hither come in 't. Go, hence with diligence!

[Ariel *exits*.]

Awake, dear heart, awake. Thou hast slept well.
310 Awake.

[Miranda *wakes*.]

    Miranda. The strangeness of your story put
Heaviness in me.

    Prospero.   Shake it off. Come on,
We'll visit Caliban, my slave, who never
Yields us kind answer.

284 as mill wheels strike: as the blades of mill wheels strike the water.

285 litter: give birth to.

291 penetrate the breasts: arouse the sympathy.

300 correspondent: obedient.

301 spriting: spiriting; **gently:** willingly.

311 Heaviness: drowsiness.

SCAFFOLDING FOR ELL STUDENTS

Determine Pronoun Referents Explain to students that because plays are written to be acted in front of an audience, the written play does not always make pronoun referents clear. While the audience can see whom the actor is addressing, the reader cannot and must sometimes make inferences based on clues in the text.

ASK STUDENTS to reread lines 305–311. Then ask students to find clues that let them know whom Prospero is addressing. *(Ariel has left the stage, so he cannot be addressing Ariel. He calls the person "dear heart," and the only person dear to Prospero is his daughter Miranda.)* Lead students to understand that Prospero is addressing Miranda.

CLOSE READ

(X)

Miranda [*rising*].   'Tis a villain, sir,
I do not love to look on.

Prospero.   But, as 'tis,
315 We cannot miss him. He does make our fire,
Fetch in our wood, and serves in offices
That profit us.—What ho, slave, Caliban!
Thou earth, thou, speak!

Caliban [*within*].   There's wood enough within.

Prospero. Come forth, I say. There's other business
    for thee.
320 Come, thou tortoise. When?

[*Enter Ariel like a water nymph.*]

Fine apparition! My quaint Ariel,
Hark in thine ear.

[*He whispers to Ariel.*]

Ariel.   My lord, it shall be done.

[*He exits.*]

315 miss: do without.

316 serves in offices:
performs duties.

321 quaint: ingenious;
elegant.

The Tempest: Act I, Scene 2   **51**

Support Inferences: Draw Conclusions

COMMON CORE **RL 1**

(LINES 313–318)

Discuss with students the use of suspense in drama. Point out the stage direction on line 318, and make sure students understand that it means that Caliban is answering from offstage. Remind students that Prospero compared Caliban to a dog on the previous page.

(X) CITE TEXT EVIDENCE Have students review lines 313–318. Ask them what they can infer about Caliban's appearance, and on what evidence they base their inference. *(Based on the fact that Miranda says in lines 313–314 she doesn't like to look at him and that in line 318 Prospero calls him "earth," or dirt, one can infer that Caliban is horrible to see.)* Then ask why Shakespeare might have chosen not to reveal Caliban yet. *(He wanted to build suspense about what Caliban looks like and whether he matches Prospero and Miranda's descriptions.)*

TO CHALLENGE STUDENTS…

Evaluate Writer's Craft Have students discuss Shakespeare's choice of words and phrases and their impact on meaning and tone.

ASK STUDENTS to read lines 281–296. In small groups discuss how Shakespeare introduces a new character, what the audience learns about him, and the effectiveness of this method of introduction. Remind students to cite text evidence to support their responses. Have each group present a summary of their analyses to the class. *(Shakespeare introduces Caliban through dialogue. The audience learns that Sycorax "littered" [gave birth to] a son who is described as "a dull thing" and "a freckled whelp." These negative descriptions show Prospero's disrespect for this character.)*

TEACH

CLOSE READ

Analyze Language

 COMMON CORE RL 4

(LINES 325–328)

Review with students Shakespeare's use of blank verse. Remind them that a perfect line of iambic pentameter has ten syllables and five metrical feet, each foot consisting of an unstressed syllable followed by a stressed syllable.

Y CITE EVIDENCE Have students reread Caliban's curse on Prospero (lines 325–328). Invite volunteers to read the four lines aloud. Ask students to analyze this passage, identifying any lines written in perfect iambic pentameter and explaining why other lines do not meet the definition. *(Lines 325 and 326 fit the description of iambic pentameter perfectly. Line 327 has ten syllables, but the first word, Drop, must be accented, making the rhythm uneven. Line 328 has only six syllables containing three iambic feet.)*

Support Inferences: Draw Conclusions

 COMMON CORE RL 1

(LINES 334–355)

Review with students the fierce argument that boils up here between Prospero and Caliban. Point out that each character tells something about an earlier, happier relationship between the two.

Z CITE EVIDENCE Ask students to make inferences about why the relationship between Prospero and Caliban might have changed. Have them provide evidence to support their inferences. *(In lines 334–348 Caliban says that when Prospero first came to the island, he treated him well, and he told Prospero all about the island. Then Prospero made Caliban a slave. From this evidence, one can infer that Prospero was only kind to Caliban to find out what he needed to know about the island. In lines 351–352, Prospero says that he treated Caliban well, and Caliban repaid him by assaulting Miranda. Moreover, in lines 353–355, Caliban admits assaulting Miranda by expressing regret that Prospero stopped him. From this evidence, one can infer that the reason for the change in the relationship was Caliban's assault.)*

Prospero [*to* Caliban]. Thou poisonous slave, got by the
    devil himself
Upon thy wicked dam, come forth!

[*Enter* Caliban.]

325 **Caliban.** As wicked dew as e'er my mother brushed
With raven's feather from unwholesome fen
Drop on you both. A southwest blow on you
And blister you all o'er.

Prospero. For this, be sure, tonight thou shalt have
    cramps,
330 Side-stitches that shall pen thy breath up. Urchins
Shall forth at vast of night that they may work
All exercise on thee. Thou shalt be pinched
As thick as honeycomb, each pinch more stinging
Than bees that made 'em.

Caliban.   I must eat my dinner.
335 This island's mine by Sycorax, my mother,
Which thou tak'st from me. When thou cam'st first,
Thou strok'st me and made much of me, wouldst
    give me
Water with berries in 't, and teach me how
To name the bigger light and how the less,
340 That burn by day and night. And then I loved thee,
And showed thee all the qualities o' th' isle,
The fresh springs, brine pits, barren place and fertile.
Cursed be I that did so! All the charms
Of Sycorax, toads, beetles, bats, light on you,
345 For I am all the subjects that you have,
Which first was mine own king; and here you sty me
In this hard rock, whiles you do keep from me
The rest o' th' island.

Prospero.   Thou most lying slave,
Whom stripes may move, not kindness, I have
    used thee,
350 Filth as thou art, with humane care, and lodged thee
In mine own cell, till thou didst seek to violate
The honor of my child.

Caliban. O ho, O ho! Would 't had been done!
Thou didst prevent me. I had peopled else
355 This isle with Calibans.

Miranda.   Abhorrèd slave,
Which any print of goodness wilt not take,
Being capable of all ill! I pitied thee,
Took pains to make thee speak, taught thee each hour

323 got: fathered.

324 dam: mother.

326 fen: bog.

327 southwest: Winds from the southwest were considered unhealthy.

330 Urchins: hedgehogs or goblins.

331 forth at vast: go forth during the long stretch.

332–333 Thou shalt ... honeycomb: The pinches on your body will be as dense as the cells in a honeycomb.

337 strok'st: stroked.

339 bigger light: the sun; **the less:** the moon.

343 charms: spells.

346 sty me: pen me up like a pig.

349 stripes: lashes; **used:** treated.

354 I had peopled else: otherwise I would have populated.

356 Which any ... take: upon whom goodness cannot make any impression.

357 capable of all ill: inclined to every evil.

52 Collection 1

WHEN STUDENTS STRUGGLE . . .

Help students understand the contrast between the symbolic nature of Prospero's two slaves. Use a Venn diagram, like the one on the opposite page, to record the similarities and differences between these two beings. When the diagram is complete, ask students what Ariel and Caliban have in common *(both are enslaved but desire their freedom; both fear Prospero)* and how they differ from each other *(Ariel is an airy and beautiful spirit, while Caliban is earthbound and ugly)*. Why does Shakespeare decide to make Prospero's slaves so different? *(to show that Prospero has power over the forces of the air and of the earth)*

One thing or other. When thou didst not, savage,
360 Know thine own meaning, but wouldst gabble like
A thing most brutish, I endowed thy purposes
With words that made them known. But thy vile race,
Though thou didst learn, had that in 't which
      good natures
Could not abide to be with. Therefore wast thou
365 Deservedly confined into this rock,
Who hadst deserved more than a prison.

   Caliban. You taught me language, and my profit on 't
Is I know how to curse. The red plague rid you
For learning me your language!

   Prospero.   Hagseed, hence!
370 Fetch us in fuel; and be quick, thou 'rt best,
To answer other business. Shrugg'st thou, malice?
If thou neglect'st or dost unwillingly
What I command, I'll rack thee with old cramps,
Fill all thy bones with aches, make thee roar
375 That beasts shall tremble at thy din.

   Caliban.   No, pray thee.
[aside] I must obey. His art is of such power
It would control my dam's god, Setebos,
And make a vassal of him.

   Prospero.   So, slave, hence.

[Caliban exits.]

[Enter Ferdinand; and Ariel, invisible, playing and singing.]

[song]

   Ariel.
      Come unto these yellow sands,
380   *And then take hands.*
      Curtsied when you have, and kissed
            The wild waves whist.
      Foot it featly here and there,
            And sweet sprites bear
385   *The burden. Hark, hark!*
      [burden dispersedly, within:] *Bow-wow.*
            The watchdogs bark.
      [burden dispersedly, within:] *Bow-wow.*
            Hark, hark! I hear
390   *The strain of strutting chanticleer*
            Cry cock-a-diddle-dow.

   Ferdinand. Where should this music be? I' th' air, or
th' earth?
It sounds no more; and sure it waits upon

---

362 race: natural disposition.

368 red plague: plague that causes red sores; **rid:** destroy.

369 Hagseed: witch's offspring.

371 answer other business: perform other tasks.

373 rack . . . cramps: torture you with the cramps of old people.

377 Setebos: a god that was worshiped in Patagonia, a region of South America.

378 vassal: servant or slave.

382 whist: into silence.

383 Foot it featly: dance nimbly.

384–385 bear . . . burden: sing the refrain.

390 strain: tune; **chanticleer:** a rooster.

393 waits: attends.

The Tempest: Act I, Scene 2   **53**

CLOSE READ

Support Inferences: Draw Conclusions

COMMON CORE **RL 1**

(LINES 359–366)

Discuss with students whether they think Prospero and Miranda treat Caliban fairly. Does he deserve to be a slave restricted to a small area of land?

 **CITE EVIDENCE** Have students reread lines 359–366 and make an inference, supported by evidence, about what Miranda believes is the reason for Caliban's bad behavior. *(Miranda believes that Caliban is evil because he has an evil nature. She claims that Caliban's "vile race," or nature, is such that good people cannot bear to be near him.)*

Analyze Language

COMMON CORE **RL 4**

(LINES 379–382)

Point out that Ariel arrives singing a song that is written in a form of poetry different from the main dialogue. These lines are not in blank verse. The lines are shorter and the end words rhyme in pairs *(sands/hands; kissed/whist)*. Explain that the rhythm differs too. Some of the feet, or metrical units, are the opposite of iambic feet. They consist of a stressed syllable followed by an unstressed one. This type of foot is called a **trochee**.

B2 **ASK STUDENTS** to make a metric analysis of lines 379–382. What is the metric unit, or foot, of each line, and how many feet does each line contain? *(Lines 379 and 381 both have a trochaic rhythm with three feet in each line. The last trochee of each line, however, is incomplete, ending in accented syllables. Lines 380 and 382 each contain two iambic feet.)*

Ariel
helps Prospero, performs magic, cheerful and airy

Prospero's slave, lived on island before Prospero, fears Prospero's powers, wants freedom

Caliban
hates Prospero, no magic powers, angry and earthbound

TEACH

CLOSE READ

Analyze Language

COMMON CORE **RL 4**

(LINES 401–409)

Tell students that Ariel's "Full fathom five" song (lines 401–409) is a good example of the sound devices that Shakespeare uses.

 **ASK STUDENTS** to identify the types and examples of sound devices in the song. *(Alliteration: in line 401, "full fathom five thy father"; in line 405, "suffer a sea"; in line 409, "Hark, now I hear." Assonance: in line 401, "five thy father lies"; in line 407, "nymphs hourly ring." Onomatopoeia: in lines 408 and 409, "Ding dong.")* What is the effect of these sound devices? *(They add a musical quality to the song; alliteration of the "f" and "s" sounds call up the flow and sound of the sea; "Ding dong" bell reminds us of death.*

Support Inferences: Draw Conclusions

COMMON CORE **RL 1**

(LINES 421–425)

Remind students that Ariel is acting under Prospero's orders. Review with students what they know about Prospero's story of the loss of his country; his feelings for his brother, Antonio; and who Ferdinand is (son of Alonso, king of Naples, helped unsurp Prospero's position as duke of Milan).

D2 **CITE EVIDENCE** Have students reread lines 422–425. Ask them to look for evidence of what Prospero plans and infer what that plan involves. *(In lines 422–423, Miranda says that Ferdinand is so noble that he must be divine. Clearly she finds him attractive. When Prospero hears her, he says to himself that things are going as he planned. One can infer that Prospero had Ariel lead Ferdinand to them so that he and Miranda will fall in love, eventually making Miranda a queen and helping Prospero gain power over his brother.)*

Some god o' th' island. Sitting on a bank,
395   Weeping again the King my father's wrack,
This music crept by me upon the waters,
Allaying both their fury and my passion
With its sweet air. Thence I have followed it,
Or it hath drawn me rather. But 'tis gone.
400   No, it begins again.

[*song*]

Ariel.
   Full fathom five thy father lies.
      Of his bones are coral made.
   Those are pearls that were his eyes.
      Nothing of him that doth fade
405   *But doth suffer a sea change*
   Into something rich and strange.
   Sea nymphs hourly ring his knell.
[*burden, within:*] *Ding dong.*
   Hark, now I hear them: ding dong bell.

410   **Ferdinand.** The ditty does remember my drowned
      father.
This is no mortal business, nor no sound
That the earth owes. I hear it now above me.

Prospero [*to* Miranda]. The fringèd curtains of thine
      eye advance
And say what thou seest yond.

Miranda.   What is 't? A spirit?
415   Lord, how it looks about! Believe me, sir,
It carries a brave form. But 'tis a spirit.

Prospero. No, wench, it eats and sleeps and hath
      such senses
As we have, such. This gallant which thou seest
Was in the wrack; and, but he's something stained
420   With grief—that's beauty's canker—thou might'st
      call him
A goodly person. He hath lost his fellows
And strays about to find 'em.

Miranda.   I might call him
A thing divine, for nothing natural
I ever saw so noble.

Prospero [*aside*].   It goes on, I see,
425   As my soul prompts it. [*to* Ariel] Spirit, fine spirit,
      I'll free thee
Within two days for this.

397 passion: sorrow; suffering.

398 air: melody

401 Full fathom five: fully five fathoms (30 feet) deep.

407 knell: funeral bell.

410 ditty: song.

411 mortal: human.

412 owes: owns.

413 fringèd curtains: eyelids; **advance:** raise.

416 brave form: splendid appearance.

418 gallant: fine gentleman.

419 but: except that; **something:** somewhat.

420 canker: infection; spreading sore.

424 It goes on: my plan proceeds.

54   Collection 1

SCAFFOLDING FOR ELL STUDENTS

Understand Word Associations Point out to students the word *gallant* in line 418. Explain that today *gallant* is ordinarily used as an adjective. Have a volunteer look up the adjective *gallant* in the dictionary and tell the class its main meanings. *(splendid or stylish, brave, courteous)*

ASK STUDENTS to work in a group to make up one sentence for each of the main meanings of *gallant*. *(The musician looked gallant in a purple cravat. The gallant firefighter jumped into the flames. Peter is gallant: he always insists that ladies go first.)*

54   Collection 1

Ferdinand [*seeing* Miranda]. Most sure, the goddess
On whom these airs attend!—Vouchsafe my prayer
May know if you remain upon this island,
And that you will some good instruction give
430 How I may bear me here. My prime request,
Which I do last pronounce, is—O you wonder!—
If you be maid or no.

　　Miranda. 　　　　　No wonder, sir,
But certainly a maid.

　　Ferdinand. 　　　　My language! Heavens!
I am the best of them that speak this speech,
435 Were I but where 'tis spoken.

　　Prospero. 　　　　　How? The best?
What wert thou if the King of Naples heard thee?

　　Ferdinand. A single thing, as I am now, that wonders
To hear thee speak of Naples. He does hear me,
And that he does I weep. Myself am Naples,
440 Who with mine eyes, never since at ebb, beheld
The King my father wracked.

　　Miranda. 　　　　　　Alack, for mercy!

　　Ferdinand. Yes, faith, and all his lords, the Duke
　　of Milan
And his brave son being twain.

　　Prospero [*aside*]. 　　　　The Duke of Milan
And his more braver daughter could control thee,
445 If now 'twere fit to do 't. At the first sight
They have changed eyes.—Delicate Ariel,
I'll set thee free for this. [*to* Ferdinand] A word,
　　good sir.
I fear you have done yourself some wrong. A word.

　　Miranda. Why speaks my father so ungently? This
450 Is the third man that e'er I saw, the first
That e'er I sighed for. Pity move my father
To be inclined my way.

　　Ferdinand. 　　　　O, if a virgin,
And your affection not gone forth, I'll make you
The Queen of Naples.

　　Prospero. 　　　　Soft, sir, one word more.
455 [*aside*] They are both in either's powers. But this
　　swift business
I must uneasy make, lest too light winning
Make the prize light. [*to* Ferdinand] One word
　　more. I charge thee

427 **Vouchsafe:** grant.

428 **May know:** that
I may know; **remain:**
dwell.

430 **bear me:** conduct
myself.

432 **maid:** a girl
(as opposed to a
supernatural being).

434 **the best:** highest
in rank.

437 **a single thing:** one
and the same.

438 **Naples:** king of
Naples.

440 **at ebb:** dry.

443 **twain:** two.

444 **control:** refute.

446 **changed eyes:**
exchanged loving looks.

448 **done yourself
some wrong:** spoken
in error.

453 **your affection not
gone forth:** not already
in love with someone
else.

454 **Soft:** wait a minute.

455 **either's:** each
other's.

456 **uneasy:** difficult;
light: easy.

457 **light:** cheap.

The Tempest: Act I, Scene 2　**55**

Analyze Language

COMMON CORE RL 4

(LINES 439–441)

Explain that Shakespeare's use of figurative language
is sometimes very subtle. Simply using a verb usually
associated with another situation can set up a
comparison between unlike things.

E2 **ASK STUDENTS** the usual meaning of the word
ebb and in what situation it is most often used.
*(The word ebb means "to move away from the land"
and is most often used to describe the ocean tide going
out.)* Then ask students what two things are being
compared in these lines. *(the sea and Ferdinand's
eyes)* Finally, ask students to explain what Ferdinand's
statement means. *(Ferdinand says that since he saw his
father drowned, he hasn't been able to stop crying. His
eyes have been "never since at ebb," meaning the tide of
tears has always been flowing.)*

Support Inferences:
Draw Conclusions

COMMON CORE RL 1

(LINES 443–457)

Remind students of the inferences about Prospero's
plan they made on the previous page.

F2 **CITE EVIDENCE** Have students reread lines
443–457 to find evidence that supports their previous
inferences about Prospero's plan: that Prospero had
Ariel lead Ferdinand to them so that he and Miranda
would fall in love, eventually making Miranda a
queen and helping Prospero gain power over his
brother. *(In an aside—lines 445–447—Prospero notices
that Miranda and Ferdinand are gazing at each other
lovingly. He promises Ariel his freedom for arranging the
meeting. In another aside—lines 455–457—Prospero
says that the relationship is going too smoothly. He
states that he plans to introduce a few difficulties to
increase the attraction.)*

SCAFFOLDING FOR ELL STUDENTS

Determine Pronoun Referents Explain to students that when a pronoun
referent is unclear, it may be necessary to go back a few lines to find the
noun to which the pronoun refers.

ASK STUDENTS to read lines 438–439 and determine who is meant by "He."
(the King of Naples who his son Ferdinand believes is dead)

Analyze Language
COMMON CORE RL 4

(LINES 462–464)

Have students read lines 462–464. Point out that Miranda is using an extended metaphor in her defense of Ferdinand. Explain that Shakespeare uses *ill* in this passage to mean *bad*.

G2 ASK STUDENTS to analyze the metaphor. To what is Miranda comparing Ferdinand? *(a temple)* Ask students to paraphrase her argument. *(Anything so beautiful cannot be entirely bad.)*

Support Inferences: Draw Conclusions
COMMON CORE RL 1

(LINES 471–473)

Point out to students Miranda's reaction to Prospero's threats against Ferdinand and Ferdinand's response in lines 471–473. Discuss whether this reaction to seeing a stranger draw a sword against her father seems reasonable.

H2 CITE TEXT EVIDENCE Have students make an inference about Miranda's knowledge of her father based on the evidence in these lines. Tell them to explain how they came to their conclusions. *(Because Miranda is afraid for Ferdinand and not for her father, one can infer that Miranda understands her father's magical powers and his willingness to use them to harm others.)*

That thou attend me. Thou dost here usurp
The name thou ow'st not, and hast put thyself
460   Upon this island as a spy, to win it
From me, the lord on 't.

Ferdinand.   No, as I am a man!

 **Miranda.** There's nothing ill can dwell in such a temple.
If the ill spirit have so fair a house,
Good things will strive to dwell with 't.

Prospero [*to* Ferdinand].   Follow me.
465   [*to* Miranda] Speak not you for him. He's a traitor.
      [*to* Ferdinand] Come,
I'll manacle thy neck and feet together.
Sea water shalt thou drink. Thy food shall be
The fresh-brook mussels, withered roots, and husks
Wherein the acorn cradled. Follow.

Ferdinand.   No,
470   I will resist such entertainment till
Mine enemy has more power.

[*He draws, and is charmed from moving.*]

Miranda.   O dear father,
Make not too rash a trial of him, for
He's gentle and not fearful.

Prospero.   What, I say,
My foot my tutor?—Put thy sword up, traitor,
475   Who mak'st a show, but dar'st not strike, thy conscience
Is so possessed with guilt. Come from thy ward,
For I can here disarm thee with this stick
And make thy weapon drop.

Miranda.   Beseech you, father—

Prospero. Hence! Hang not on my garments.

Miranda.   Sir, have pity.
480   I'll be his surety.

Prospero.   Silence! One word more
Shall make me chide thee, if not hate thee. What,
An advocate for an impostor? Hush.
Thou think'st there is no more such shapes as he,
Having seen but him and Caliban. Foolish wench,
485   To th' most of men this is a Caliban,
And they to him are angels.

458–459 Thou dost . . . not: You are unlawfully claiming the title of king, which is not rightly yours.

462 such a temple: Ferdinand's handsome exterior.

468 fresh-brook mussels: freshwater mussels (which are inedible).

470 entertainment: treatment.

Stage direction— *charmed from moving:* put under a spell that immobilizes him.

472 rash a trial: strong a test.

473 gentle: noble.

474 My foot my tutor: Should I let my inferior (Miranda) teach me how to act?

476 ward: fencer's defensive posture.

477 stick: magician's staff.

480 his surety: responsible for him.

485 To: compared to.

WHEN STUDENTS STRUGGLE . . .

Direct students to lines 462–464. Ask students to reread this passage and to paraphrase it in their own words. *(There isn't any evil that could exist within such a handsome man. If the devil's house were as beautiful, then good things would want to live in it.)* Then ask students to discuss what the passage reveals about Miranda's character. *(The passage shows that she is young and inexperienced in love, and thus she is a bit naive.)*

Miranda.   My affections
Are then most humble. I have no ambition
To see a goodlier man.

Prospero [*to* Ferdinand]. Come on, obey.
Thy nerves are in their infancy again
490   And have no vigor in them.

Ferdinand.   So they are.
My spirits, as in a dream, are all bound up.
My father's loss, the weakness which I feel,
The wrack of all my friends, nor this man's threats
To whom I am subdued, are but light to me,
495   Might I but through my prison once a day
Behold this maid. All corners else o' th' earth
Let liberty make use of. Space enough
Have I in such a prison.

Prospero [*aside*].   It works.—Come on.—
Thou hast done well, fine Ariel.—Follow me.
500   [*to* Ariel] Hark what thou else shalt do me.

Miranda [*to* Ferdinand].   Be of comfort.
My father's of a better nature, sir,
Than he appears by speech. This is unwonted
Which now came from him.

Prospero [*to* Ariel].   Thou shalt be as free
As mountain winds; but then exactly do
505   All points of my command.

Ariel.   To th' syllable.

Prospero [*to* Ferdinand]. Come follow. [*to* Miranda]
   Speak not for him.

[*They exit.*]

**489   Thy nerves ...
again:** your sinews are
like those of a baby.

494   but light: of little
importance.

496   All corners else: all
other places.

502   unwonted:
unusual.

504   then: if that is to
occur.

CLOSE READ

Support Inferences: Draw Conclusions

COMMON CORE   RL 1

(LINES 486–500)

Remind students of the inferences they have made so far about Prospero's plan.

CITE EVIDENCE Have students read lines 486–500. Ask them whether Prospero is pleased with the way his plan is progressing and how they can tell. *(Prospero is pleased with his progress. In line 498 he says "It works" in an aside, and in line 499 he again congratulates Ariel for his efforts.)*

Analyze Language

COMMON CORE   RL 4

(LINES 496–497)

Remind students that personification is a type of figurative language in which something nonhuman is spoken of as though it were a person.

ASK STUDENTS to find an instance of personification on this page, explain what is being spoken of as though it were human, and paraphrase it. *(In lines 496–497, Ferdinand personifies the abstract concept of liberty. He says that liberty can wander over all the other parts of the earth.)*

Support Inferences: Draw Conclusions

COMMON CORE RL 1

(FROM "ENTER" –LINE 9)

Explain to students that this act begins with a change of scene. It opens on the other shipwrecked passengers who have landed on another part of the island. Point out that Ferdinand, the king's son, is not among the characters who enter.

 ASK STUDENTS to make an inference about the reason for the king's sadness based on what they know from Act One and what they can infer from Ferdinand's absence. *(The king is grieving because he believes that his son has drowned.)*

Analyze Language

COMMON CORE RL 4

(LINES 10–14)

Point out that Sebastian and Antonio effectively employ figurative language in their mockery of Gonzalo.

 CITE EVIDENCE Have students read lines 10–14. Ask them to identify a simile and a metaphor. *(Simile: Gonzalo's comfort is compared to cold porridge in lines 10–11. Metaphor: Sebastian compares Gonzalo's wit to a watch in lines 13–14.)* Then ask students to explain the meaning of these figures of speech. *(Alonso is rejecting Gonzalo's comforting words the way he might reject cold porridge—a very unappetizing dish. Sebastian suggests that Gonzalo needs time to prepare his next remark, as if his wit were a watch he had to wind up. The suggestion is that Gonzalo's mind works slowly.)*

Act II

Scene 1

[*Enter* Alonso, Sebastian, Antonio, Gonzalo, Adrian, Francisco, *and others.*]

Gonzalo [*to* Alonso]. Beseech you, sir, be merry. You
   have cause—
So have we all—of joy, for our escape
Is much beyond our loss. Our hint of woe
Is common; every day some sailor's wife,
5 The masters of some merchant, and the merchant
Have just our theme of woe. But for the miracle—
I mean our preservation—few in millions
Can speak like us. Then wisely, good sir, weigh
Our sorrow with our comfort.

Alonso.   Prithee, peace.

10 **Sebastian** [*aside to* Antonio]. He receives comfort like
cold porridge.

Antonio. The visitor will not give him o'er so.

Sebastian. Look, he's winding up the watch of his wit.
By and by it will strike.

15 **Gonzalo** [*to* Alonso]. Sir—

Sebastian. One. Tell.

Gonzalo. When every grief is entertained that's offered,
comes to th' entertainer—

Sebastian. A dollar.

20 **Gonzalo.** Dolor comes to him indeed. You have spoken
truer than you purposed.

Sebastian. You have taken it wiselier than I meant
you should.

Gonzalo [*to* Alonso]. Therefore, my lord—

25 **Antonio.** Fie, what a spendthrift is he of his tongue.

Alonso [*to* Gonzalo]. I prithee, spare.

Gonzalo. Well, I have done. But yet—

Sebastian [*aside to* Antonio]. He will be talking.

Antonio [*aside to* Sebastian]. Which, of he or Adrian,
30 for a good wager, first begins to crow?

Sebastian. The old cock.

3 beyond: greater than; **hint:** occasion.

6 just: exactly

11 cold porridge: pease porridge (a pun on Alonso's cry for "peace").

12 visitor: a person responsible for comforting the sick in their homes; **give him o'er so:** abandon him.

16 One: It has struck one; **Tell:** Keep count.

17 entertained: held in the mind.

18 entertainer: person who holds the grief.

19 A dollar: a pun on the meaning of entertainer as "someone who is paid to amuse others."

20 Dolor: sorrow. This is a play on the word *dollar* in line 19.

26 spare: spare your words.

WHEN STUDENTS STRUGGLE . . .

Use the scene on this page to give students practice in reading dialogue. Ask volunteers to play the parts of Gonzalo, Alonso, Sebastian, and Antonio. Have another volunteer act as the director. As a class, discuss each character. What is his body position? What kinds of gestures does he use? How does he speak? Have students read the scene once. Then give the director a few moments to give feedback to the actors. Finally, have the actors try reading the scene again.

Antonio. The cockerel.

Sebastian. Done. The wager?

Antonio. A laughter.

35 **Sebastian.** A match!

Adrian. Though this island seem to be desert—

Antonio. Ha, ha, ha.

Sebastian. So. You're paid.

Adrian. Uninhabitable and almost inaccessible—

40 **Sebastian.** Yet—

Adrian. Yet—

Antonio. He could not miss 't.

Adrian. It must needs be of subtle, tender, and delicate temperance.

45 **Antonio.** Temperance was a delicate wench.

Sebastian. Ay, and a subtle, as he most learnedly delivered.

Adrian. The air breathes upon us here most sweetly.

Sebastian. As if it had lungs, and rotten ones.

50 **Antonio.** Or as 'twere perfumed by a fen.

Gonzalo. Here is everything advantageous to life.

Antonio. True, save means to live.

Sebastian. Of that there's none, or little.

Gonzalo. How lush and lusty the grass looks! How
55 green!

Antonio. The ground indeed is tawny.

Sebastian. With an eye of green in 't.

Antonio. He misses not much.

Sebastian. No, he doth but mistake the truth totally.

60 **Gonzalo.** But the rarity of it is, which is indeed almost beyond credit—

Sebastian. As many vouched rarities are.

Gonzalo. That our garments, being, as they were, drenched in the sea, hold notwithstanding their
65 freshness and gloss, being rather new-dyed than stained with salt water.

30–32 first begins to crow: will speak first. (Sebastian and Antonio allude to the proverbial saying "The young cock (**cockerel**) crows as he the old hears.")

34 A laughter: Antonio alludes to the saying "He laughs that wins."

36 desert: deserted

44 Temperance: climate (also a woman's name, which inspires Antonio's punning response).

52 save: except for.

54 lush and lusty: abundant and vigorous.

56 tawny: yellowish-brown (parched by the sun).

57 eye: tinge.

60 rarity: exceptional quality.

62 vouched rarities: alleged wonders.

TO CHALLENGE STUDENTS . . .

Understand Tone Ask students to describe the tone of each set of characters. *(Adrian and Gonzalo's tone is earnest, while Antonio and Sebastian's tone is sarcastic.)* Then have each student write two additional lines of dialogue, one from either Adrian or Gonzalo describing the island, and one from either Antonio or Sebastian countering the previous line. Direct students to pay special attention to the tone of each character. Then invite students to read their additional lines to the class.

TEACH

Analyze Language COMMON CORE RL 4
(LINES 48–50)

Explain to students that this scene is intended to be humorous. Help them appreciate the richness of Shakespeare's wit by looking closely at the exchange in lines 48–50.

CITE EVIDENCE Have students find an example of personification and explain how its meaning alters as it is taken up by different characters. *(Adrian uses personification in line 48 when he speaks of the air breathing sweetly on them as though it were a person. Sebastian picks up the personification and gives it a negative twist by suggesting that the air is like a person with rotten lungs, a cause of bad breath. Antonio adds ironically that the air is like a person "perfumed" by a fen, or swamp.)*

Support Inferences: COMMON CORE RL 1
Draw Conclusions (LINES 39–59)

Draw students' attention to the starkly contrasting views expressed by Gonzalo and Adrian on the one hand, and by Sebastian and Antonio on the other. Invite volunteers to read the passage from lines 51–59. Point out the rosy optimism of Gonzalo and Adrian and the dark cynicism of Sebastian and Antonio.

CITE EVIDENCE Have students reread lines 39–59 and make an inference about Shakespeare's reason for including this dialogue. Ask them to give evidence to support their inference. *(Shakespeare included this dialogue to reveal something about the characters of Gonzalo and Adrian on the one hand and Sebastian and Antonio on the other. In lines 43–44, Adrian's description of the island is so flowery and idealized that it is clear it cannot be accurate. On the other hand, Sebastian's claim in line 49 that the air smells like the breath of someone with rotten lungs is just as ridiculously exaggerated. Shakespeare is poking fun at both sets of characters.)*

Support Inferences: Draw Conclusions (LINES 70–75)

COMMON CORE RL 1

Point out Sebastian's comment in lines 74–75. Remind students of his sarcasm and mockery of Gonzalo, and discuss with students whether this comment seems to be in character.

02 **CITE EVIDENCE** Ask students to infer the tone of Sebastian's comment and tell on what evidence they based their inference. Then have them tell what they think Sebastian's comment means. *(The tone of the comment is ironic. Readers know that the party does not "prosper well" on their return from the wedding, since they have been shipwrecked and believe Prince Ferdinand to be drowned. Therefore we can also infer that the marriage was not sweet. Sebastian means to say that the wedding was unfortunate and their return has been a disaster.)*

Analyze Language: Allusions (LINES 78–92)

COMMON CORE RL 4

Explain to students that the mention of Dido (lines 78–85) is an **allusion** to Virgil's *The Aeneid*. Shakespeare frequently used allusions — references to people, places, events, or objects— with which his readers would be familiar. Point out that Shakespearean allusions are sometimes difficult for modern readers to decode because the subjects are no longer familiar.

P2 **ASK STUDENTS** to read lines 89–92. What is the allusion in these lines? *(Line 89 refers to Widow Dido, whose word is more powerful than Amphion, the bard in Greek mythology who raised the walls of Thebes by playing his harp.)* Why is the allusion to Amphion's harp included? *(Line 90 suggests that the harp could build city walls and houses.)*

Antonio. If but one of his pockets could speak, would it not say he lies?

Sebastian. Ay, or very falsely pocket up his report.

69 **pocket up:** conceal; suppress.

70 **Gonzalo.** Methinks our garments are now as fresh as when we put them on first in Afric, at the marriage of the King's fair daughter Claribel to the King of Tunis.

71 **Afric:** Africa.

75 **Sebastian.** 'Twas a sweet marriage, and we prosper well in our return.

Adrian. Tunis was never graced before with such a paragon to their queen.

77 **to:** for.

Gonzalo. Not since widow Dido's time.

78 **Dido:** a queen of Carthage who, in Virgil's *Aeneid*, commits suicide after Aeneas abandons her.

80 **Antonio.** Widow? A pox o' that! How came that "widow" in? Widow Dido!

Sebastian. What if he had said "widower Aeneas" too? Good Lord, how you take it!

Adrian [*to* Gonzalo]. "Widow Dido," said you? You make me study of that. She was of Carthage, not
85 of Tunis.

84 **study of:** think about.

Gonzalo. This Tunis, sir, was Carthage.

86 Tunis was built near the site of Carthage.

Adrian. Carthage?

Gonzalo. I assure you, Carthage.

Antonio. His word is more than the miraculous harp.

89 **miraculous harp:** In Greek mythology, Amphion used his harp to raise a wall around Thebes. (Antonio suggests that Gonzalo has surpassed this feat by raising an entire city.)

90 **Sebastian.** He hath raised the wall, and houses too.

Antonio. What impossible matter will he make easy next?

Sebastian. I think he will carry this island home in his pocket and give it his son for an apple.

95 **Antonio.** And sowing the kernels of it in the sea, bring forth more islands.

95 **kernels:** seeds.

Gonzalo. Ay.

Antonio. Why, in good time.

97 **Ay:** probably an affirmation of his earlier statement that Tunis was Carthage.

Gonzalo [*to* Alonso]. Sir, we were talking that our
100 garments seem now as fresh as when we were at Tunis at the marriage of your daughter, who is now queen.

Antonio. And the rarest that e'er came there.

Sebastian. Bate, I beseech you, widow Dido.

104 **Bate:** except for.

105 **Antonio.** O, widow Dido? Ay, widow Dido.

SCAFFOLDING FOR ELL STUDENTS

Understand Contractions Ask students to look at line 103 on this page. Invite a volunteer to read the line aloud. Write the word *e'er* on the board. Remind students that contractions are words from which a letter has been omitted and replaced with a comma. Have students use context clues to guess what letter has been left out of *e'er*. (*v*)

ASK STUDENTS to look at the following Shakespearean contractions and figure out their meanings by identifying the missing letter or letters: 'tis (*it is*), o'er (*over*), gi' (*give*), ne'er (*never*), i' (*in*), o'(*on* or *of*), e'en (*even*). Encourage students to look out for contractions as they read.

Gonzalo [*to* Alonso]. Is not, sir, my doublet as fresh as the first day I wore it? I mean, in a sort.

Antonio. That "sort" was well fished for.

Gonzalo [*to* Alonso]. When I wore it at your daughter's
110 marriage.

Alonso. You cram these words into mine ears against
The stomach of my sense. Would I had never
Married my daughter there, for coming thence
My son is lost, and, in my rate, she too,
115 Who is so far from Italy removed
I ne'er again shall see her.— O, thou mine heir
Of Naples and of Milan, what strange fish
Hath made his meal on thee?

Francisco. Sir, he may live.
I saw him beat the surges under him
120 And ride upon their backs. He trod the water,
Whose enmity he flung aside, and breasted
The surge most swoll'n that met him. His bold head
'Bove the contentious waves he kept, and oared
Himself with his good arms in lusty stroke
125 To th' shore, that o'er his wave-worn basis bowed,
As stooping to relieve him. I not doubt
He came alive to land.

Alonso. No, no, he's gone.

Sebastian. Sir, you may thank yourself for this great loss,
That would not bless our Europe with your daughter,
130 But rather lose her to an African,
Where she at least is banished from your eye,
Who hath cause to wet the grief on 't.

Alonso. Prithee, peace.

Sebastian. You were kneeled to and importuned
otherwise
By all of us; and the fair soul herself
135 Weighed between loathness and obedience at
Which end o' th' beam should bow. We have lost
your son,
I fear, forever. Milan and Naples have
More widows in them of this business' making
Than we bring men to comfort them.
140 The fault's your own.

Alonso. So is the dear'st o' th' loss.

Gonzalo. My lord Sebastian,
The truth you speak doth lack some gentleness

107 in a sort: to some extent.

108 sort: lot (in the game of drawing lots).

111–112 against . . . sense: although I am in no mood to hear them.

114 rate: estimation.

119 surges: waves.

124 lusty: vigorous.

125–126 that o'er . . . him: The cliff at the shoreline, eroded at its base by waves, seemed as if it were stooping over to help Ferdinand.

132 Who . . . on 't: you who have reason to weep over the sorrow of it.

133 importuned otherwise: begged to change your decision.

134–136 the fair . . . bow: Claribel weighed on a scale (**beam**) her distaste (**loathness**) for the marriage against her wish to obey her father.

140 dear'st: most costly.

CLOSE READ

Analyze Language

COMMON CORE RL 4

(LINES 106–118)

Draw students' attention to the change from prose to iambic pentameter at line 111. Point out that since the beginning of Act II, most of the dialogue has been in prose.

Q2 ASK STUDENTS what they notice about the subject matter of the prose in lines 106–110 in contrast to the poetry that follows. *(The prose dialogue is comic and superficial. In line 111 Alonso finally speaks seriously about his grief.)* Invite students to generalize about Shakespeare's use of prose and poetry. From what they have read so far, why might Shakespeare choose to write in one style or the other? *(Act I, Scene 2 involves a serious subject: Prospero's long poetic explanation to Miranda of their exile to the island. Act II begins with rapid dialogue in prose involving word play, crude jokes, and sarcasm. At line 111, the topic suddenly changes and the style changes again to poetry. Shakespeare used poetry for more elevated subjects; he found the prose of ordinary speech more appropriate for lighter topics.)*

WHEN STUDENTS STRUGGLE . . .

Help students practice reading Shakespeare aloud by echo reading Alonso's speech in lines 111–188. Read a line aloud and have students echo you. When you have read the entire speech, reread it chorally. Lead the class in reading the speech aloud together.

Analyze Language   COMMON CORE RL 4

(LINES 143–144)

Draw students' attention to lines 143–144. Go back and read aloud Gonzalo's entire speech beginning on the previous page, pointing out Gonzalo's extreme understatement in saying that Sebastian speech lacks "some gentleness."

 **ASK STUDENTS** what comparison is being made in the metaphor in lines 143 and 144. *(The metaphor compares Sebastian's speech to a doctor rubbing a sore instead of bandaging it. The metaphor means that Sebastian is making the king's grief worse, not better.)*

Support Inferences: Draw Conclusions   COMMON CORE RL 1

(LINES 152–169)

Read with students Gonzalo's vision of ruling the island. Discuss with students whether they believe that Gonzalo is serious about what he proposes.

CITE EVIDENCE Ask students what they can infer about Gonzalo's character from this speech. Have them give evidence for their inferences. *(Gonzalo is an idealist. He describes an ideal place where there is no authority, no work, and no conflict. The fact that his ideas run together without being separated into sentences indicates that he is carried away by his vision.)*

And time to speak it in. You rub the sore
When you should bring the plaster.

Sebastian.   Very well.

145 **Antonio.** And most chirurgeonly.

Gonzalo [*to* Alonso]. It is foul weather in us all, good sir,
When you are cloudy.

Sebastian.   Foul weather?

Antonio.   Very foul.

Gonzalo. Had I plantation of this isle, my lord—

Antonio. He'd sow 't with nettle seed.

Sebastian.   Or docks, or mallows.

150 **Gonzalo.** And were the King on 't, what would I do?

Sebastian. Scape being drunk, for want of wine.

Gonzalo. I' th' commonwealth I would by contraries
Execute all things, for no kind of traffic
Would I admit; no name of magistrate;

155 Letters should not be known; riches, poverty,
And use of service, none; contract, succession,
Bourn, bound of land, tilth, vineyard, none;
No use of metal, corn, or wine, or oil;
No occupation; all men idle, all,

160 And women too, but innocent and pure;
No sovereignty—

Sebastian.   Yet he would be king on 't.

Antonio. The latter end of his commonwealth forgets
the beginning.

Gonzalo. All things in common nature should produce

165 Without sweat or endeavor; treason, felony,
Sword, pike, knife, gun, or need of any engine
Would I not have; but nature should bring forth
Of its own kind all foison, all abundance,
To feed my innocent people.

170 **Sebastian.** No marrying 'mong his subjects?

Antonio. None, man, all idle: whores and knaves.

Gonzalo. I would with such perfection govern, sir,
T' excel the Golden Age.

Sebastian.   'Save his Majesty!

Antonio. Long live Gonzalo!

Gonzalo.   And do you mark me, sir?

144 plaster: a medicinal paste applied to the body.

145 chirurgeonly: like a surgeon.

148 Had I plantation: if I were responsible for colonizing. (Antonio's response plays with the meaning "planting.")

149 nettle seed . . . docks . . . mallows: types of weeds.

152–153 by contraries . . . things: carry out everything in a manner opposite to what is customary.

153 traffic: commerce.

155 Letters: writing learning.

156 use of service: employment of servants; **succession:** inheritance.

157 Bourn: boundary; **tilth:** cultivation of land.

158 corn: grain.

164 in common: for communal use.

166 engine: weapon.

168 foison: plenty.

173 'Save: God save.

TO CHALLENGE STUDENTS . . .

Examine Author's Purpose Tell students that when Shakespeare wrote *The Tempest*, English colonists had just begun to arrive in what would become North America. The play is thought by some to be a commentary on colonialism, or the establishment , maintenance, and expansion of colonies in one territory by people from another territory.

ASK STUDENTS to have a group discussion about how they think Gonzalo's vision for the island might reflect Shakespeare's opinion of European colonialism. Ask students to cite text evidence to support their reasoning. *(Shakespeare does not agree with Gonzalo; Gonzalo's description of life on the island is so far-fetched that Shakespeare must to be making fun of it.)*

175 **Alonso.** Prithee, no more. Thou dost talk nothing to me.

Gonzalo. I do well believe your Highness, and did it to minister occasion to these gentlemen, who are of such sensible and nimble lungs that they always use to laugh at nothing.

180 **Antonio.** 'Twas you we laughed at.

Gonzalo. Who in this kind of merry fooling am nothing to you. So you may continue, and laugh at nothing still.

Antonio. What a blow was there given!

185 **Sebastian.** An it had not fallen flatlong.

Gonzalo. You are gentlemen of brave mettle. You would lift the moon out of her sphere if she would continue in it five weeks without changing.

[*Enter* Ariel, *invisible, playing solemn music.*]

Sebastian. We would so, and then go a-batfowling.

190 **Antonio** [*to* Gonzalo]. Nay, good my lord, be not angry.

177 minister occasion: provide an opportunity.

178 sensible: sensitive; **use:** are accustomed.

185 An it ... flatlong: if it had not been given with the flat of the sword (rather than the edge).

186 mettle: temperament.

187 sphere: orbit.

189 a-batfowling: hunting birds at night with a stick (Sebastian proposes using the moon for a lantern).

The Tempest: Act II, Scene 1 **63**

Analyze Language

COMMON CORE RL 4

(LINES 184–185)

Discuss with students Antonio and Sebastian's use of language. Do they usually speak literally and sincerely? Lead students to conclude that they usually make jokes using figurative language.

T2 CITE EVIDENCE Have students reread lines 184–185. Ask them what sort of figurative language is being used, what two things are being compared, and what each character means. (*Antonio and Sebastian use a metaphor that compares Gonzalo's attempt to turn their wit back on them to the blow of a sword in battle. Antonio speaks ironically and means to say that Gonzalo's attempt was not a "mighty blow" at all, but a feeble one. Sebastian follows up to say that Gonzalo's attempt at wit has "fallen flatlong," or failed to hurt them.*)

Support Inferences: Draw Conclusions

COMMON CORE **RL 1**

(LINES 191–209)

Point out that Ariel entered the scene just before line 189 on the previous page. Remind students that Ariel is still acting under Prospero's orders.

U2 CITE EVIDENCE Have students reread lines 191–209 and make an inference about why Alonso and Gonzalo are sleepy, and Antonio and Sebastian are wide awake. Ask them to provide evidence from the text to support their inference. (*Ariel, acting under Prospero's orders, made Alonso and Gonzalo irresistibly sleepy and Antonio and Sebastian alert. Evidence that this sleepiness and wakefulness is not natural is given in line 203, in which Sebastian calls the sleepiness "strange;" lines 204–205, in which Sebastian points out that if it were the climate that made the others sleepy, it also should have affected him and Antonio; and lines 207–209, in which Antonio describes the suddenness with which he became alert.*)

Support Inferences: Draw Conclusions

COMMON CORE **RL 1**

(LINES 212–220)

Discuss with students whether Sebastian really believes that Antonio is talking in his sleep and ask them to cite text evidence to support their responses.

V2 CITE EVIDENCE Ask students to infer why Sebastian suggests that Antonio is talking in his sleep and support their inferences with text evidence. (*Sebastian is afraid to hear what Antonio is saying, but he doesn't want him to stop talking. In lines 212–214, Antonio says that this is Sebastian's chance to become king. He is suggesting that they murder Sebastian's brother, who is sleeping before them. Sebastian is both attracted and repulsed by Antonio's suggestion, so for the moment he prefers to pretend that Antonio is asleep.*)

U2 **Gonzalo.** No, I warrant you, I will not adventure my discretion so weakly. Will you laugh me asleep? For I am very heavy.

Antonio. Go sleep, and hear us.

[*All sink down asleep except* Alonso, Antonio, *and* Sebastian.]

195 **Alonso.** What, all so soon asleep? I wish mine eyes
Would, with themselves, shut up my thoughts. I find
They are inclined to do so.

Sebastian.   Please you, sir,
Do not omit the heavy offer of it.
It seldom visits sorrow; when it doth,
200 It is a comforter.

Antonio.   We two, my lord,
Will guard your person while you take your rest,
And watch your safety.

Alonso.   Thank you. Wondrous heavy.

[Alonso *sleeps.* Ariel *exits.*]

Sebastian. What a strange drowsiness possesses them!

Antonio. It is the quality o' th' climate.

Sebastian.   Why
205 Doth it not then our eyelids sink? I find
Not myself disposed to sleep.

Antonio. Nor I. My spirits are nimble.
They fell together all, as by consent.
They dropped as by a thunderstroke. What might,
210 Worthy Sebastian, O, what might—? No more.
And yet methinks I see it in thy face
What thou shouldst be. Th'occasion speaks thee, and
My strong imagination sees a crown
Dropping upon thy head.

V2

Sebastian.   What, art thou waking?

215 **Antonio.** Do you not hear me speak?

Sebastian.   I do, and surely
It is a sleepy language, and thou speak'st
Out of thy sleep. What is it thou didst say?
This is a strange repose, to be asleep
With eyes wide open—standing, speaking, moving—
220 And yet so fast asleep.

Antonio.   Noble Sebastian,
Thou let'st thy fortune sleep, die rather, wink'st
Whiles thou art waking.

191–192 adventure . . . weakly: risk my reputation by behaving so weakly.

193 heavy: sleepy.

198 omit: neglect.

208 consent: agreement.

212 Th'occasion speaks thee: the opportunity calls out to you.

214 waking: awake.

221 wink'st: you close your eyes.

64   Collection 1

WHEN STUDENTS STRUGGLE . . .

Help students understand the complicated plotting that concludes Act II, Scene 1 by having them fill out a T chart for Antonio and Sebastian. Discuss with students what they know of these two characters from their behavior and from details in Act I, Scene 1 (up to line 152). Then have pairs of students work on their charts, adding to them as they read. Invite student pairs to share their notes, creating a master chart on the board.

Sebastian. Thou dost snore distinctly.
There's meaning in thy snores.

Antonio. I am more serious than my custom. You
225 Must be so too, if heed me; which to do
Trebles thee o'er.

Sebastian. Well, I am standing water.

Antonio. I'll teach you how to flow.

Sebastian. Do so. To ebb
Hereditary sloth instructs me.

Antonio. O,
If you but knew how you the purpose cherish
230 Whiles thus you mock it, how in stripping it
You more invest it. Ebbing men indeed
Most often do so near the bottom run
By their own fear or sloth.

Sebastian. Prithee, say on.
The setting of thine eye and cheek proclaim
235 A matter from thee, and a birth indeed
Which throes thee much to yield.

Antonio. Thus, sir:
Although this lord of weak remembrance—this,
Who shall be of as little memory
When he is earthed—hath here almost persuaded—
240 For he's a spirit of persuasion, only
Professes to persuade—the King his son's alive,
'Tis as impossible that he's undrowned
As he that sleeps here swims.

Sebastian. I have no hope
That he's undrowned.

Antonio. O, out of that no hope
245 What great hope have you! No hope that way is
Another way so high a hope that even
Ambition cannot pierce a wink beyond,
But doubt discovery there. Will you grant with me
That Ferdinand is drowned?

Sebastian. He's gone.

Antonio. Then tell me,
250 Who's the next heir of Naples?

Sebastian. Claribel.

Antonio. She that is Queen of Tunis; she that dwells
Ten leagues beyond man's life; she that from Naples
Can have no note, unless the sun were post—

222 distinctly: in a way that can be understood.

225 if heed me: if you pay attention to me.

226 Trebles thee o'er: makes you three times as great.

227–228 To ebb ... me: My natural laziness (**hereditary sloth**) makes me pull back.

229 the purpose cherish: encourage (**nourish**) your intention (**the purpose**).

231 invest it: clothe it.

234 setting: fixed expression.

235 A matter: something important.

236 throes thee much to yield: causes you great pain to give forth.

238 of as little memory: as quickly forgotten.

239 earthed: buried.

240–241 only ... persuade: his only profession is to persuade.

245 that way: of Ferdinand's being alive.

247–248 cannot pierce ... there: cannot set its sight on any higher goal

252 beyond man's life: farther than one could travel in a lifetime.

253 note: information; **post:** the messenger.

The Tempest: Act II, Scene 1   **65**

Antonio	Sebastian
Prospero's brother	brother of the King of Naples
made an alliance with the King of Naples	Antonio's friend
kicked his brother out of Milan	sarcastic
always mocking Gonzalo	always mocking Gonzalo

Analyze Language

COMMON CORE RL 4

(LINES 227–233)

Remind students that an extended metaphor is a type of figurative language in which one thing is spoken of as though it were another in more than one line or sentence. Discuss with students why Sebastian and Antonio might prefer to converse in metaphor. *(They do not want to say what they mean to do directly.)*

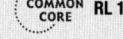 **ASK STUDENTS** to interpret the extended metaphor in lines 227–233. *(Sebastian says that he is like water without a current, moving in no direction. He has not made up his mind and is open to suggestion. Antonio replies that he will persuade him to go forward with their plan. Sebastian asks him to do so, because his natural laziness makes him pull back from the plan like water pulling back from shore. Antonio says that men who are afraid to act end up at the bottom of the heap.)*

Support Inferences: Draw Conclusions

COMMON CORE RL 1

(LINES 244–249)

Discuss with students whether they think Antonio will persuade Sebastian to murder his brother.

X2 ASK STUDENTS Have students reread lines 244–249. Ask them to make an inference about whether Sebastian is seriously considering Antonio's plan and support it with evidence from the text. *(Yes, Sebastian is considering killing Alonso. In lines 242–243, he says of Ferdinand, "I have no hope / That he's undrowned." If Sebastian did not want to be king, he would have no reason to hope that Ferdinand, the heir to the throne, was dead.)*

Analyze Language

COMMON CORE **RL 4**

(LINES 264–266, 288–293)

Draw students' attention to the ideas of sleeping and waking on this page. Remind students that it was after Ariel's appearance that Alonso and Gonzalo became sleepy and Antonio and Sebastian felt wide awake.

Y2 CITE EVIDENCE Ask students what Antonio means when he says "let Sebastian wake" in line 266? Why might he choose this metaphor? Encourage students to support their views with evidence from the text. *(From the fact that they are discussing the viability of Claribel's claim to the throne of Naples, one can infer that Antonio means that Sebastian should become king. By comparing Sebastian's becoming king with waking up, he makes it seems like a natural and inevitable occurrence.)*

Z2 CITE EVIDENCE Ask students to infer with what Antonio is comparing sleep in lines 288–293 and cite evidence to support their inference. Then have them explain why Antonio would choose this metaphor. *(Antonio is comparing sleep with death. He makes this comparison explicit in line 288 when he says that being dead is "that which now he's like," or being asleep. By using this metaphor, Antonio hopes to persuade Sebastian that killing Alonso and Gonzalo is no worse than making their sleep last forever.)*

The man i' th' moon's too slow—till newborn chins
255 Be rough and razorable; she that from whom
We all were sea-swallowed, though some cast again,
And by that destiny to perform an act
Whereof what's past is prologue, what to come
In yours and my discharge.

260 **Sebastian.** What stuff is this? How say you?
'Tis true my brother's daughter's Queen of Tunis,
So is she heir of Naples, 'twixt which regions
There is some space.

Antonio. A space whose ev'ry cubit
Seems to cry out "How shall that Claribel
265 Measure us back to Naples? Keep in Tunis
And let Sebastian wake." Say this were death
That now hath seized them, why, they were no worse
Than now they are. There be that can rule Naples
As well as he that sleeps, lords that can prate
270 As amply and unnecessarily
As this Gonzalo. I myself could make
A chough of as deep chat. O, that you bore
The mind that I do, what a sleep were this
For your advancement! Do you understand me?

275 **Sebastian.** Methinks I do.

Antonio. And how does your content
Tender your own good fortune?

Sebastian. I remember
You did supplant your brother Prospero.

Antonio. True,
And look how well my garments sit upon me,
Much feater than before. My brother's servants
280 Were then my fellows; now they are my men.

Sebastian. But, for your conscience?

Antonio. Ay, sir, where lies that? If 'twere a kibe,
'Twould put me to my slipper, but I feel not
This deity in my bosom. Twenty consciences
285 That stand 'twixt me and Milan, candied be they
And melt ere they molest! Here lies your brother,
No better than the earth he lies upon.
If he were that which now he's like—that's dead—
Whom I with this obedient steel, three inches of it,
290 Can lay to bed forever; whiles you, doing thus,
To the perpetual wink for aye might put
This ancient morsel, this Sir Prudence, who
Should not upbraid our course. For all the rest,

255 from: coming from.

256 cast again: cast into new roles.

259 discharge: performance.

263 cubit: an ancient unit of measure varying from 17 to 22 inches.

265 Measure us: travel over our length; **Keep:** stay.

268 that: those who.

269 prate: babble.

271–272 make … chat: train a jackdaw (a bird related to the crow) to speak as profoundly.

275–276 how does … Tender: what do you think of.

279 feater: more suitably.

282–283 If 'twere … slipper: if it were a sore on my heel, it would force me to wear slippers.

285 candied: covered with frost; frozen.

289 steel: sword.

291 To the … put: might put to sleep forever.

66 Collection 1

SCAFFOLDING FOR ELL STUDENTS

Distinguish Possessives from Contractions Have students read Sebastian's remark in line 261, "'Tis true my brother's daughter's Queen of Tunis." Remind students that in English apostrophes are used both in contractions to indicate a missing letter and to form the possessive.

ASK STUDENTS to work in pairs to rewrite line 261, adding the missing letters to any contractions ('Tis becomes "It is") and leaving any possessives as they are written (brother's). (It is true my brother's daughter is Queen of Tunis.)

They'll take suggestion as a cat laps milk.
295 They'll tell the clock to any business that
We say befits the hour.

Sebastian.   Thy case, dear friend,
Shall be my precedent: as thou got'st Milan,
I'll come by Naples. Draw thy sword. One stroke
Shall free thee from the tribute which thou payest,
300 And I the King shall love thee.

Antonio.   Draw together,
And when I rear my hand, do you the like
To fall it on Gonzalo.

[*They draw their swords.*]

Sebastian.   O, but one word.

[*They talk apart.*]

[*Enter* Ariel, *invisible, with music and song.*]

Ariel [*to the sleeping* Gonzalo]. My master through his
    art foresees the danger
That you, his friend, are in, and sends me forth—
305 For else his project dies—to keep them living.

[*sings in Gonzalo's ear:*]

> While you here do snoring lie,
> Open-eyed conspiracy
>   His time doth take.
> If of life you keep a care,
310 Shake off slumber and beware.
>   Awake, awake!

Antonio [*to* Sebastian]. Then let us both be sudden.

Gonzalo [*waking*]. Now, good angels preserve the King!

[*He wakes* Alonso.]

Alonso [*to* Sebastian]. Why, how now, ho! Awake? Why
    are you drawn?
315 Wherefore this ghastly looking?

Gonzalo [*to* Sebastian].   What's the matter?

Sebastian. Whiles we stood here securing your repose,
Even now, we heard a hollow burst of bellowing
Like bulls, or rather lions. Did 't not wake you?
It struck mine ear most terribly.

Alonso.   I heard nothing.

294 take suggestion: accept temptation.

295–296 tell the… hour: agree to anything that we say is appropriate.

305 else: otherwise; **them:** Gonzalo and Alonso.

308 His time: its opportunity.

314 Why are you drawn?: Why have you drawn your weapons?

315 Wherefore: why; **ghastly:** fearful.

316 securing your repose: guarding you while you slept.

The Tempest: Act II, Scene 1   **67**

CLOSE READ

Support Inferences: Draw Conclusions

COMMON CORE   RL 1

(LINES 297–300)

Remind students of what they learned in Prospero's narrative about how he lost his duchy: that Antonio made an alliance with the king of Naples (Alonso) in which the king made him Duke of Milan in exchange for tribute. Discuss with students Antonio's possible motives for wanting Sebastian to become King of Naples.

A3 **CITE TEXT EVIDENCE** Have students reread Sebastian's statement in lines 297–300. Ask them what evidence they can find about Antonio's motives and what they can infer from that evidence. *(In lines 298–299, Sebastian says that if Antonio kills Alonso and Sebastian becomes king, he will free Antonio from the requirement of paying tribute to Naples. One can infer that Antonio hatched this plot to get out of paying tribute.)*

Analyze Language

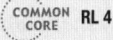 COMMON CORE   RL 4

(LINES 316–319)

Discuss with students Sebastian and Antonio's situation in having Gonzalo and Alonso wake up to find them with their swords drawn.

B3 **ASK STUDENTS** to identify the type of sound device used in lines 317–318 and analyze its dramatic effect. *(The type of sound device used is alliteration. The repeated "b" sound suggests stuttering and has the effect of illustrating Sebastian's surprise and confusion.)*

WHEN STUDENTS STRUGGLE...

Direct students to lines 302–305. Ask students to reread this passage and to discuss what they can infer about Prospero's plan and what evidence they have for their inference. *(Prospero does not intend for Alonso, the King of Naples, to be killed, or for Sebastian to become king. The evidence for this is that Ariel, who acts under Prospero's orders, wakes Alonso and Gonzalo before Antonio and Sebastian can strike, and that in line 305 Ariel says that if Alonso and Gonzalo die, Prospero's project, or plan, also dies.)*

Support Inferences: Draw Conclusions

 RL 1, RL 4

(LINES 324–329)

Review with students the explanation given by Sebastian and Antonio of why they have drawn their swords and discuss the fact that Gonzalo appears to believe this lie.

 CITE EVIDENCE Have students reread lines 324–329 and look for evidence that allows them to infer why Gonzalo found the lie believable. Ask them to state the evidence and explain their inference. *(Gonzalo says he heard a strange humming. The reader knows that this sound was made by Ariel singing into his ear, but Gonzalo mistakes it for the sound of the wild beast that Sebastian and Antonio claim to have heard.)*

COLLABORATIVE DISCUSSION Have students pair up and discuss specific passages in the play, what aspects of these passages they found interesting, and whether they think the passages reflect the experiences of explorers in America. Invite students to share the passages they chose with the class.

ASK STUDENTS to share any questions they generated in the course of reading and discussing the selection.

---

320 **Antonio.** O, 'twas a din to fright a monster's ear,
To make an earthquake. Sure, it was the roar
Of a whole herd of lions.

Alonso. Heard you this, Gonzalo?

Gonzalo. Upon mine honor, sir, I heard a humming,
325 And that a strange one too, which did awake me.
I shaked you, sir, and cried. As mine eyes opened,
I saw their weapons drawn. There was a noise,
That's verily. 'Tis best we stand upon our guard,
Or that we quit this place. Let's draw our weapons.

330 **Alonso.** Lead off this ground, and let's make further search
For my poor son.

Gonzalo. Heavens keep him from these beasts,
For he is, sure, i' th' island.

Alonso. Lead away.

Ariel [*aside*]. Prospero my lord shall know what I have done.
So, king, go safely on to seek thy son.

[*They exit.*]

326 cried: cried out.

328 verily: indeed true.

COLLABORATIVE DISCUSSION Which passages about coming to a new land were most interesting to you? Discuss this question with a partner, citing specific textual evidence from the play. Explain why the passages drew your interest and whether you think they reflect the actual experience of explorers who came to the Americas.

Support Inferences: Draw Conclusions

 **COMMON CORE** RL 1

To understand any work of literature, you must analyze what the text says explicitly or directly. You must also make **inferences,** or logical assumptions, based on details in the text. This chart shows how textual evidence from *The Tempest* could be used to draw conclusions about Prospero's character.

Textual Evidence	Analysis
"Thou art inclined to sleep. 'Tis a good dullness, / And give it way. I know thou canst not choose. [Miranda *falls asleep* . . .]" (I, ii, 187–188)	Prospero tells Miranda she is tired and cannot choose to stay awake; she immediately falls asleep. Readers can infer that Prospero has magical powers and has made his daughter sleep so that he can speak privately with Ariel.
"It was mine art, / When I arrived and heard thee, that made gape / The pine and let thee out." (I, ii, 294–296)	Prospero tells the story of how he freed Ariel from an enchantment. He directly refers to his magic ("mine art"), so the audience knows that he is a powerful magician.

Analyze Language

 **COMMON CORE** RL 4

Shakespeare wrote his plays mainly in the poetic form of **blank verse,** unrhymed poetry with the **meter** of iambic pentameter. This meter has five feet or units per line; each unit contains two syllables, the first unstressed and the second stressed. Iambic pentameter is suitable for drama because its rhythm is similar to ordinary spoken English. Here is an example of a line in iambic pentameter from *The Tempest.*

> ˘ ´ ˘ ´ ˘ ˘ ´ ˘ ´ ˘ ´
> The sky, it seems, would pour down stinking pitch, (I, ii, 3)

This line shows the richness of Shakespeare's language. With just a few words, he creates a powerful image to describe a dark and stormy night: smelly black tar falling from the sky. He also uses the sound device of **alliteration,** repeating the initial consonants *s* (*sky, seems, stinking*) and *p* (*pour, pitch*), to give the line a musical quality.

Shakespeare's text is packed with **figurative language,** or words used in a nonliteral way, often to make fresh comparisons. For example, the simile "They'll take suggestion as a cat laps milk" (II, i, 294) compares weak men who cannot think for themselves to cats that cannot resist a bowl of milk. Other comparisons are more subtle. When Ferdinand describes his eyes as "never since at ebb" (I, ii, 440), he compares his tears over the loss of his father to a tide that keeps bringing forth water.

TEACH

CLOSE READ

Support Inferences: Draw Conclusions

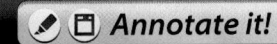 **COMMON CORE** RL 1

Have students work in pairs to find other textual evidence from the play about Prospero's personality. Ask them to record this evidence and their analysis in a chart like the one on this page.

Textual Evidence	Analysis
"But are they, Ariel, safe?" (1, ii, line 219)	Prospero asks Ariel whether the victims of the shipwreck are safe. Readers can infer that while Prospero wants revenge, he is not ruthless enough to murder anyone.
"If thou more murmur'st, I will rend an oak / And peg thee in his knotty entrails till / Thou hast howled away twelve winters." (1, ii, lines 297–299)	Prospero threatens to punish Ariel by trapping him in an oak tree if he says anything else. Readers can infer that Prospero uses his magic cruelly to keep power over his servants.
"For this, be sure, tonight thou shalt have cramps, / Side-stiches that shall pen thy breath up. Urchins / Shall forth at vast of night that they may work." (1, ii, lines 329–331)	Prospero threatens Caliban with magical punishment for disobeying. Readers can infer once again that Prospero keeps power over his servants by using his magic to torment them.
[aside] "They are both in either's powers. But this swift business / I must uneasy make, lest too light winning / Make the prize light." (1, ii, lines 455–457)	Prospero plans to pretend to oppose Miranda's marriage to Ferdinand in order to ensure that the two young people remain in love. Readers can infer that Prospero is crafty and devious.

Strategies for Annotation 🖊 📖 *Annotate it!*

Analyze Language

 **COMMON CORE** RL 4

Remind students that in dramas two important kinds of evidence on which they can base inferences are each character's words and actions. Share these strategies for finding evidence and making inferences.

- Highlight in yellow a character's words.
- Highlight in green a character's actions.
- Examine the words and actions and make an inference.
- On a note, record your inference.

> Draw together, /
>
> And when I rear my hand, do you the like /
>
> To fall it on Gonzalo.
>
> [They draw their swords.]
>
> **Sebastian.**   O, but one word.

> ⊠
> "Inference: When it comes time to strike, Sebastian has second thoughts. He is not as ruthless as Gonzalo."

Analyzing the Text  COMMON CORE RL 1, RL 4

Possible answers:

1. *Prospero describes to Miranda how he retired from active governing to study, leaving his brother Antonio in charge of Milan (lines 66–77). As de facto duke, Antonio decided the title should be his (lines 89–105). He made an alliance with the King of Naples, who overthrew Prospero (lines 108–117; 121–133).*

2. *Prospero loves Miranda dearly, claiming in Act I, Scene 2 that she kept him alive in the difficult period after his exile (lines 153–159). He is also extremely protective, putting her to sleep when he does business with Ariel (lines 186–188). In spite of his affection for his daughter, he is intolerant of opposition from her (lines 478–481).*

3. *Before Prospero and Miranda arrived, Caliban was ignorant and savage but claims to have been his own "king" (Act I, Scene 2, line 346). When Prospero arrived all went well at first (lines 335–348), but Caliban's attack on Miranda resulted in his enslavement to Prospero (348–352).*

4. *Prospero neglected his duties as ruler of Milan; on the island, by contrast, he has complete control. Caliban claims he was once "king" of the island and bitterly resents his loss of freedom. Sebastian is willing to kill his brother in order to be king of Naples. Ariel longs for his freedom and continually reminds Prospero of their bargain.*

5. *In "Full fathom five" Ariel described what might have happened to the king's body if he had really drowned. Shakespeare's use of alliteration, assonance, and vivid imagery—coral bones, pearl eyes—creates a vision of beauty out of an apparent tragedy.*

6. *The phrase "sea change" is used today to describe a complete and startling transformation.*

7. *Gonzalo's island would be a peaceable kingdom with no laws or violence. This is a complete contrast to Prospero's absolute control and liberal use of force. Particularly in Prospero's behavior toward Caliban, Shakespeare may be indirectly criticizing England's treatment of the people of the New World.*

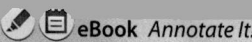 eBook *Annotate It!*

Analyzing the Text   COMMON CORE RL 1, RL 4, W 2, W 2b

Cite Text Evidence   Support your responses with evidence from the selection.

1. **Cite Evidence** How was Prospero displaced as duke of Milan? Cite evidence from Act I, Scene 2.

2. **Analyze** How would you describe Prospero's relationship with Miranda based on the language that he uses and on his use of magic?

3. **Cite Evidence** Based on the interaction between Caliban and Prospero, what was Caliban's life on the island like before Prospero and Miranda arrived? How and why has their relationship evolved?

4. **Analyze** Several characters in this excerpt from *The Tempest* talk about a desire to rule over others or about the pain of losing their kingdom or freedom. Describe how this comment relates to each of the following characters.

   • Prospero   • Caliban   • Sebastian   • Ariel

5. **Interpret** Review Ariel's song that begins "Full fathom five . . ." (I, ii, 401–409). What is he describing, and how do the words Shakespeare uses help you visualize it?

6. **Infer** The phrase "a sea change" has a literal meaning in Ariel's song but is today used in a more figurative way. What might it mean to say that someone or something has experienced a sea change?

7. **Infer** Review Gonzalo's speech in which he outlines how he would rule the island if he were king of it (II, i, 148–169). How does Gonzalo's approach differ from Prospero's about ruling the island and its inhabitants? What can you infer about Shakespeare's view of the English treatment of the inhabitants of the New World from this contrast?

PERFORMANCE TASK

Writing Activity: Essay Ariel and Caliban are both identified as Prospero's servants, yet they have very different relationships with him. Explore these relationships by writing an explanatory essay following these steps.

- Identify passages that reveal Ariel's and Caliban's character. Look at their own words and actions and what others say about them.
- Identify passages that reveal Prospero's relationship with each of them. Look at his words as well as his actions toward each of them.

- Make inferences from this evidence to explain the reasons for these different relationships.
- Organize your information in a compare-and-contrast structure. Begin with a clear main idea, support your main idea with evidence from the play, and end with a concluding statement that follows from and supports the information you have presented.

Assign this performance task.

PERFORMANCE TASK   COMMON CORE W 2, W 2b

Writing Activity Have students work in groups to identify passages that reveal Ariel and Caliban's personalities. Suggest that they create a two-column chart with the headings "Ariel" and "Caliban." Have them write descriptive notes and references to passages in each of the columns to gather evidence about the personalities of the two characters. Encourage students to discuss their ideas in their groups prior to drafting their essays.

Support Inferences: Draw Conclusions

COMMON CORE
RL 1

TEACH

Remind students that when they read plays, they must make inferences about the characters' nature, intentions, and motivations based on what they say and do and other concrete details. These inferences are based on limited information. As the play develops, they may receive further information that causes them to revise their inferences. Point out that the play begins with the tempest that Prospero had Ariel create, and that throughout the excerpt readers are given further information about Prospero's plans.

PRACTICE AND APPLY

Have students find evidence of Prospero's intended plot throughout the excerpt. If necessary, point out the following information:

ACT I, SCENE 2

- Prospero admits to having caused the storm. (lines 196–197)
- Prospero asks Ariel about the safety of those on board the ship. (lines 219–240)
- After Ariel draws Ferdinand to Prospero and Miranda, Prospero draws Miranda's attention to Ferdinand. (lines 413–414) .
- Prospero admits that he wanted Ferdinand and Miranda to fall in love. (lines 424–425)
- Prospero says he will make sure Ferdinand and Miranda fall in love by seeming to oppose them. (lines 455–457)

ACT II, SCENE 1

- On Prospero's orders, Ariel makes Gonzalo and Alonso sleep, while she causes Antonio and Sebastian to be wide awake. (lines 192–209)
- Again on Prospero's orders, Ariel wakes Gonzalo before Antonio and Sebastian can kill him and the king. (lines 303–311)

Then discuss as a class how students' inferences about Prospero's plot changed with each new piece of information.

Analyze Language

COMMON CORE
RL 4

RETEACH

All language consists of stressed and unstressed syllables. Poetry is often written in a regular meter, a rhythm of repeated units known as feet. Shakespeare frequently used the iambic foot—an unstressed syllable followed by a stressed syllable—in his dramatic verse but also frequently deviated from it. Have students analyze the following passage from Act II, Scene 1 (lines 106–110) by marking each stressed syllable. Gonzalo and Antonio are speaking in prose, while Alonso speaks in verse. Ask students what they notice about the rhythmic changes from prose to poetry.

Gonzalo (*to* Alonso). Is not, sir, my doublet as fresh as the first day

I wore it? I mean, in a sort.

Antonio. That "sort" was well fished for.

Gonzalo [*to* Alonso]. When I wore it at your daughter's marriage.

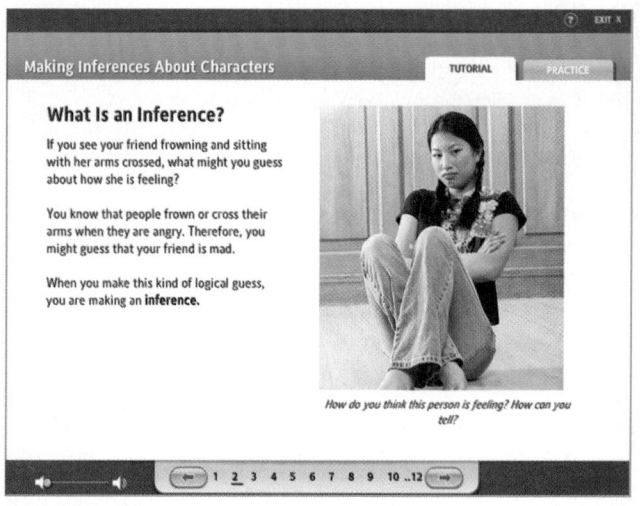

LEVEL UP TUTORIALS Assign the following *Level Up* tutorial: **Making Inferences About Characters**

*my*SmartPlanner — Create lesson plans and access resources online.

COMPARE TEXT AND MEDIA

MEDIA **The Tempest (1980)**　　MEDIA **The Tempest (2010)**

Film Version by BBC Shakespeare　　**Production Images from Film Version**

Why These Texts?

Students regularly encounter media that is an interpretation of a written text. Works as varied as the *Lord of the Rings* and *Harry Potter* film series and the musical and film versions of *Les Misérables* have their origins in the written word. Perhaps no writer has had his work interpreted as many times as Shakespeare. In this lesson, students will decide how a film version of *The Tempest* relates and compares to the original play.

Key Learning Objective: The student will be able to analyze an interpretation of a drama.

COMMON CORE Common Core Standards

RL 1 Cite textual evidence.
RL 2 Determine two or more themes.
RL 4 Determine meaning of words and phrases as used in a text.
RL 5 Analyze an author's choices.
RL 7 Analyze multiple interpretations of a drama.
SL 1a Come to discussions prepared, having read material under study.
W 2b Develop the topic by selecting the most significant and relevant facts.
W 3a Create a smooth progression of experiences or events.
W 3d Use precise words and phrases.
W 4 Produce clear and coherent writing.
L 1 Demonstrate command of the conventions of standard English grammar and usage.
L 4a Use context as a clue to the meaning of a word or phrase.

▲ Text Complexity Rubric

	Media Version of *The Tempest* (Film Version) Lexile: N/A	Media Version of *The Tempest* (Production Images) Lexile: N/A
Quantitative Measures		
Qualitative Measures	Levels of Meaning/Purpose ●—●—●—●—●→ multiple levels of complex meaning	Levels of Meaning/Purpose ●—●—●—●—●→ multiple levels of meaning
	Structure ●—●—●—●—●→ adapted from the original print source	Structure ●—●—●—●—●→ loosely based on the original print source
	Language Conventionality and Clarity ●—●—●—●—●→ archaic, unfamiliar language	Language Conventionality and Clarity N/A
	Knowledge Demands ●—●—●—●—●→ distinctly unfamiliar situation; complex or sophisticated theme	Knowledge Demands ●—●—●—●—●→ distinctly unfamiliar situation
Reader/Task Considerations	Teacher determined Vary by individual reader and type of text	Teacher determined Vary by individual reader and type of text

TEACH

CLOSE READ

AS YOU VIEW Direct students to use the As You View instructions to focus their viewing. Remind students to write down any questions they generate while viewing.

Analyze Interpretations of a Drama

 **COMMON CORE RL 7**

Explain to students that the actors in a film, in collaboration with the director, decide how to portray, or play, the characters from the drama that is being interpreted.

ASK STUDENTS to describe the ways the actors portray the characters by describing how they deliver their lines. *(The actors sometimes speak loudly—almost shouting. Other times they speak very softly. Further, they speak very quickly when they're excited, and slowly when they want to be clearly understood.)*

In lines 335–343 of *The Tempest,* Caliban talks about how he loved Prospero when he first arrived. Ask students to speculate how different delivery of the lines might affect their understanding of the play's characters. *(If the actor delivered these lines in a soft, sad voice, the viewer might have more sympathy for Caliban than if the actor delivered the same lines in loud, angry shouts.)*

COLLABORATIVE DISCUSSION Ask partners to list words or short phrases describing how they pictured Prospero, Miranda, and Caliban as they read the excerpt from the play. Then have them list words or short phrases describing how these characters appear in the film. Have partners present their work to the class by describing the ways in which their lists are similar and different.

MEDIA ANALYSIS

Media Versions of The Tempest

The Tempest (1980)

Film Version by BBC Shakespeare

AS YOU VIEW Pay attention to the way in which the characters of Prospero, Miranda, and Caliban are portrayed in the film. Write down any questions you generate during your viewing.

Image Credits: (b) ©BBC Motion Gallery; (t) ©Petr Malyshev/Shutterstock

COLLABORATIVE DISCUSSION Are the characters in the film what you imagined? With a partner, discuss how they are similar to or different from what you pictured while reading the play. Cite specific images from the video to support your ideas.

SCAFFOLDING FOR ELL STUDENTS

Analyze Interpretations of a Drama Ask ELL students to listen to fluent students read aloud the section of the text represented in the film clip (Act I, Scene 2, lines 309–378). Then have students watch the film again, listening carefully to the actors in the film. Ask ELL students to compare and contrast the actors in the film with the play as read by their classmates. Encourage them to use descriptive words to characterize both versions. Finally, work with students to create a Venn diagram comparing the play as read by classmates to the film version.

Analyze Interpretations of a Drama
 COMMON CORE RL 7

Share these strategies for guided or independent analysis.

- Take notes as you view the film. Make note of anything you find surprising, or even jarring. For instance, perhaps the film version of Caliban looks nothing like how you imagined Caliban as you read the play.

- After you have finished viewing the film version, review your notes. For each element of the film that you found noteworthy, consider its effect. For instance, if Caliban was portrayed as more, or less, appealing than you envisioned him, ask yourself what effect that had on your understanding of the drama.

- Finally, summarize your analysis of the film interpretation. How did the overall impression it created support, enhance, or differ from the original.

Analyzing the Media and Text
 COMMON CORE RL 7

Possible answers:

1. *The impression one gets of Caliban is that he has probably lived in the forest for a long time. The actor playing him delivers his lines very angrily which suggests that he hates Prospero for keeping him as a slave. The actor also chooses to walk with a limp, which suggests that Caliban may be sick, underfed, or perhaps beaten.*

2. *Caliban and Prospero are staged to be separated from each other, which suggests that they do not have a friendly relationship. This idea is supported by the text. Caliban feels betrayed that Prospero took the ownership of the island that was due to him, especially since Caliban showed Prospero around when Prospero first arrived there. Prospero, on the other hand, claims to have been kind to Caliban until Caliban violated "the honor" of Miranda.*

3. *The close-ups of Caliban emphasize the pain and sadness that Caliban has over having been betrayed by Prospero. Shakespeare's text supports the director's choice of close-ups. The camera gets closer to Caliban as he says, "When thou cam'st first, Thou strok'st me"; and is closest when he says, "And then I loved thee."*

Analyze Interpretations of Drama
 COMMON CORE RL 7

Each film or theater director adapts Shakespeare's original text in his or her own way. This clip reveals one director's view of *The Tempest*, Act I, Scene 2, lines 309–378. To understand this vision and how it relates to Shakespeare's text, examine these elements of filmmaking:

Casting is the selection of actors to play roles. Each actor must match the director's vision of the character and his or her traits. What impression of each character is created by the appearance and acting style of the film actors?

Blocking refers to the way the director positions and moves actors around a set. Note where Caliban is positioned in this scene. What does his position suggest? How do the characters move in this scene, and what do their movements communicate?

Lighting and **sound** affect the mood of a scene and the way the audience interprets action and character. What feeling is created by the setting of this scene? How does the director use sound to enhance his or her interpretation?

Costumes may suggest important aspects of a character or reinforce how a director wants a character to be perceived. What does the contrast in attire between Prospero, Miranda, and Caliban tell the audience about them?

Analyzing the Text and Media
 COMMON CORE RL 7, W 2b, W 4

Cite Text Evidence Support your responses with evidence from the selections.

1. **Draw Conclusions** What impression of Caliban is created in the film clip? Explain how casting, costume, and make-up all contribute to this characterization.

2. **Analyze** How does the director use Prospero's and Caliban's positions on the set to bring out ideas about their relationship? Are these ideas supported by the text of *The Tempest*? Be specific.

3. **Compare** How do the close-up shots of Caliban affect the emotional impact of the scene? Does Shakespeare's text convey the same effect? Explain.

PERFORMANCE TASK

Writing Activity: Review Based on this scene, would you recommend this film to others? Why or why not?

- Write a review for the school newspaper, presenting your opinion on this interpretation of Shakespeare's play.
- Support your opinion with specific reasons and examples from the film.
- Discuss at lets two of the elements of filmmaking from the chart above.
- Organize your ideas logically and use the conventions of standard written English.

Assign this performance task.

PERFORMANCE TASK
 COMMON CORE W 4, W 2b

Writing Activity: Review Have students discuss with a partner the elements of filmmaking and how they were applied to the film of *The Tempest*. Be sure they find a specific example of each element. Then have students work independently to write their reviews.

AS YOU VIEW Direct students to use the As You View instructions to focus their viewing and write down any questions they generate as they are viewing.

Analyze Interpretations of a Drama

 COMMON CORE RL 7

Explain to students that a director has the final say about all aspects of a film or theatrical production. Have students look at the characters shown on the movie poster on page 73. The caption tells that the middle image is of Prospera, a female version of Prospero.

ASK STUDENTS to identify the characters in the other images, giving specific evidence from the images to support their answers. *(The top image is likely Ariel because Ariel can fly around like a bird; the bottom image is probably Caliban because the actor appears angry and adorned with primitive tattoos.)*

The Tempest (2010)
Production Images from Film Version

AS YOU VIEW Pay attention to details in the images that help you draw conclusions about this film adaptation of *The Tempest*. Write down any questions you generate as you review the images.

Movie poster for *The Tempest* (2010) directed by Julie Taymor and staring Helen Mirren as Prospera.

Image Credits: ©AF Archive/Alamy Images

SCAFFOLDING FOR ELL STUDENTS

Analyze Interpretations of a Drama Students may not understand that the director of a film is considered to be its "author." So even though this film, *The Tempest*, is based on a play by William Shakespeare, the movie poster says "A Film by Julie Taymor."

Have students familiarize themselves with this by using the information on this page to fill in the blanks in the following sentence.

The Tempest is a film by _____, based on a _____ by _____.

Analyze Interpretations of a Drama

COMMON CORE RL 7

Explain to students that two important artists who contribute to a film are the lighting designer and the set designer. The lighting designer is responsible for the lighting of each scene, and the set designer creates the physical surroundings. Have students look at the production images on page 74.

ASK STUDENTS to describe how the lights and set shown here might affect this interpretation of the drama. *(The use of natural light and actual locations might give the film a realistic feel.)*

COLLABORATIVE DISCUSSION Ask students to work with a partner and discuss each image, noting various elements such as costumes, make-up, and the actors' expressions. Then have partners share their opinions about this film version with the class as a whole. Encourage students to cite specific evidence from the images to support their ideas.

CITE TEXT EVIDENCE Have students share any questions they generated in the course of reading and discussing the selection.

Caliban confronts Prospera and Miranda in Act I, Scene 2.

Prospera works her magic.

In this scene from Act II, Scene 2, Trinculo and Stephano, two comic characters in the play, make the acquaintance of Caliban.

COLLABORATIVE DISCUSSION What conclusions can you draw about this version of the play based on these images? With a partner, discuss what interests you about this film version and what you might like or dislike about it. Cite specific evidence from the photographs to support your ideas.

SCAFFOLDING FOR STRUGGLING STUDENTS

Language Support Help students understand three terms used in the image captions: *confronts, works her magic,* and *make the acquaintance of.* On a whiteboard, write the terms.

ASK STUDENTS to provide words and phrases that have the same meanings as the three terms. *(confronts: faces angrily; works her magic: uses magic or sorcery; make the acquaintance of: meet)*

Analyze Interpretations of Drama

The movie poster and three production stills from a more recent adaptation of *The Tempest* reveal different visions of the play. Examining some of the same elements in these images that you used to analyze the film clip will give you insight into the director's interpretation.

Casting Directors sometimes cast against type, meaning that they choose an actor who does not explicitly match the character description in the original text. In the play, Prospero is clearly a male character. In this film version, Prospero becomes Prospera, a female character. Think about the qualities that this actor brings to the role and how this shift in gender alters or enhances the play.

Blocking These images clearly show the placement of the actors relative to each other and imply each actor's movements. Note what their body language and positions in regard to each other suggest about their emotions and relationships.

Lighting and Set Design From the photographs, this film appears to have been "shot on location." Consider how the natural setting might affect the audience's understanding of character and action.

Costumes A director may choose costumes from a different time period than that in which the play was conceived. What ideas about characters are conveyed through the choice of modern clothing rather than period costumes?

Analyzing the Text and Media

COMMON CORE RL 1, RL 7, W 4

Cite Text Evidence Support your responses with evidence from the selections.

1. **Analyze** In the play, Prospero addresses Caliban by saying, "Thou earth, thou, speak!" (Act I, Scene 2, line 318). Explain how this line relates to the depiction of Caliban in the photographs from this film.

2. **Compare** Examine the photograph of Caliban, Prospera, and Miranda. Explain the impression of Miranda and Prospera conveyed by their position, posture, and gestures. Are these impressions supported by your reading of the play?

3. **Infer** The cloak is a prominent feature of Prospera's costume. What does this cloak add to her characterization? Is it consistent with the descriptions in the text?

PERFORMANCE TASK

Writing Activity: Captions Complete these activities with a partner.

- Write an extended caption for each image that shows a scene in the film.
- Draw from the text of the play to include quotations and other details

- that provide context for each image and help explain what is happening at that specific moment.
- Share your captions with the class.

Analyze Interpretations of a Drama

COMMON CORE RL 1, RL 7

The film interpretation studied in the previous lesson is more than 30 years old. In 2010, a new film version of *The Tempest* was made. Still, the same elements of filmmaking were employed. This version is a very personal expression of a director's vision, or purpose. Point out to students that—like an author—a director has a purpose, or reason, for creating a film. Have students examine the images again and then ask them to speculate about the director's purpose.

- What might have been the director's purpose in casting Prospero as a woman?
- What might have been the director's purpose in shooting the film "on location"?

Analyzing the Text and Media

COMMON CORE RL 1, RL 7

Possible answers:

1. *Prospero refers to Caliban directly as "earth," meaning he is dirty, "earthy," and lives in the forest. In the film, Caliban is depicted as being covered in mud—as if he were made of clay.*

2. *Prospera stands in an aggressive, confrontational pose, and Miranda appears to be fearful, hiding behind Prospera for protection. Prospera has her staff raised as if she's ready to attack. The text supports these impressions. Miranda refers to Caliban as "a villain," and Prospera calls him a "poisonous slave." The scene continues on as a confrontation between Prospera and Caliban.*

3. *Prospera's cloak is very elaborate in this film, and that supports the idea that the cloak confers magical powers. It is consistent with the text; when she takes it off she refers to it both as her "magic garment" and her "art."*

Assign this performance task.

PERFORMANCE TASK

COMMON CORE W 4

Writing Activity: Captions Have students work with a partner and go back over the text, looking for the scenes that the pictures depict. Encourage students to include in their extended captions quotes and details that clarify precisely what is happening in the picture. When students are finished, have them meet with another set of partners for discussion before showing the entire class.

PRACTICE & APPLY

Analyzing the Text and Media

COMMON CORE RL 1, RL 3, RL 4, RL 7, SL 1

Possible answers:

1. The Caliban in the 1980 film is portrayed as wild and angry, lonely and wounded. Taymor's Calaban appears much braver. In the text, Caliban is referred to as "earth," and "filth." Miranda speaks of his "vile race [disposition]." Both film characterizations support these descriptions.

2. In the play, Prospero is cruel and confrontational. He insults Caliban by calling him a "savage," and "filth," and accuses Caliban of attacking Miranda. Taymor's Prospera demonstrates these qualities with a strong, loud voice, and powerful stance. She comes off as similarly strong, but less confrontational, more magical, and adept at sorcery.

3. The clip of Taymor's film shows a setting that is rocky, hard, and bleak, emphasizing Caliban's isolation on the island. Caliban's voice, as well as his costume and make-up, convey a similar mood of isolation and loneliness.

4. Taymor's Prospera is dressed in an elaborate cloak that reinforces her power and mysticism. Miranda's dress is very plain (unlike in the 1980 film), and helps to reinforce her youth and innocence. Taymor's Caliban wears a loin cloth and is covered in mud and tattoos that represent him as wild and mysterious. In the 1980 film, Caliban appears barely human, pathetic, and suffering.

5. Miranda reveals her dynamism and strength in the clips where she is running through the forest and looking intently at Caliban.

6. Seeing multiple versions of The Tempest is fun and reveals how the play can be interpreted in more than one way.

Analyzing the Text and Media

COMMON CORE RL 1, RL 3, RL 4, RL 7, SL 1

Cite Text Evidence Support your responses with evidence from the selections.

1. **Analyze** Compare the two actors who play Caliban in these media versions. What does each one reveal about the director's interpretation of this character? Which one more closely matches the descriptions of Caliban in the text of the play? Explain.

2. **Compare** Reread lines 309–378 in the text. Describe Prospero's traits as revealed through his dialogue in the play. Drawing from what you have seen in the clip and in the images, explain how in each film Prospero/Prospera does or does not demonstrate these qualities.

3. **Evaluate** In lines 346–348, Caliban says, "and here you sty me / In this hard rock, whiles you do keep from me / The rest o' th' island." How does the film clip convey the physical aspects of this setting as well as the mood evoked by his words?

4. **Compare** How does each director use elements of costume in his or her film to establish or reinforce character?

5. **Analyze** How does the film clip support the idea that Miranda, while innocent and protected, is also a dynamic and strong woman? Cite specific images from the clip to explain.

6. **Synthesize** What are the advantages of seeing more than one version of the same Shakespearean drama? Explain.

PERFORMANCE TASK

Speaking Activity: Debate Do special effects detract from or enhance an audience's appreciation of the original text of Shakespeare's *The Tempest*?

- In a small group, review the trailer for Julie Taymor's version of *The Tempest* (depicted in the photographs) or the actual scene if available on the Internet.

- Identify special effects used in the film. Discuss their function and whether or not they maintain the integrity of Shakespeare's play.

- Organize your ideas logically and present the argument to the class.

- Present specific evidence to support your claim and to counter opposing arguments.

- Speak clearly and concisely, using appropriate tone, volume, and gestures.

- Have groups with opposing views present their arguments. Ask listening classmates to decide which opinion is more convincingly presented.

PERFORMANCE TASK

COMMON CORE SL 1

Speaking Activity: Debate As students work through the bulleted steps, encourage them to use a graphic to organize their ideas. For instance, students could use a chart like the one shown to organize ideas and gather evidence.

Assign this performance task.

Special Effect	Function	Evaluation: Does it maintain integrity of play?	Evidence

Tell students that in the last column of the chart they should provide textual evidence or evidence from the trailer to support their opinions.

Analyze Interpretations of a Drama

RL 7

TEACH

Numerous elements of filmmaking are on display in the film clip of *The Tempest*. Provide students with definitions of the following elements.

- **Composition and Blocking** the director chooses how each shot looks (a closeup, a far shot) where and when the actors should move, and on which lines of text.
- **Cinematography** is the way light and shadow create the mood of a scene. For example, horror films often feature dark, shadowy cinematography to create a scary mood.
- **Soundtrack** is the way sound (in the form of music or sound effects) creates the mood of a scene. Many superhero films feature downbeat music when the villain appears, and upbeat music when the superhero saves the day.
- **Set design** is the art of creating the physical surroundings in which the film is set. King Kong famously appears on the top of the Empire State Building.
- **Costumes** are the clothes each actor wears to embody a character, such as Prospera's cloak, which identifies her as a magician.

PRACTICE AND APPLY

Ask students to review the film clip and answer the following questions.

- What in the text tells you that the set designer set the scene in the correct location? *(In line 173, Prospero refers to "this island," and in line 182, he says "this shore." In line 229, Ariel refers to a "deep nook" of the island, so that suggests that at least some of the island setting is rough—a clue for the set designer. Further, line 316 has mention of a "wood," which would tell the set designer that he or she could include a forest in the design.*
- How might a cinematographer light the scenes featuring Ariel? *(The cinematographer might choose to make Ariel glow to represent Ariel's role as a "bright" spirit, or supernatural being, capable of flying and becoming fire.)*

Analyzing the Text and Media

RL 7

RETEACH

Review how the characters are created not only by the actor, but by the other elements of filmmaking.

- Ask students to tell how Miranda's costume, makeup, voice, and movements are supported the text at the beginning of the scene. *(The actor playing Miranda uses a soft, gentle, expressive voice to give the idea that she is just waking up. Her hair is very curly and feminine, and she has a beautiful flowing dress that suggests she would be desirable to Caliban.)*
- Then have students compare Miranda's characterization at the beginning of and end of the scene. Again, students should mention specific elements of filmmaking. *(Miranda's body language is very different when she confronts Caliban; her head is sticking forward from her body and her voice is stronger and fuller. She speaks more clearly, with crisper and forcefully. When Caliban offends her, she turns away.)*

 **LEVEL UP TUTORIALS** Assign the following *Level Up* tutorial: **Types of Drama**

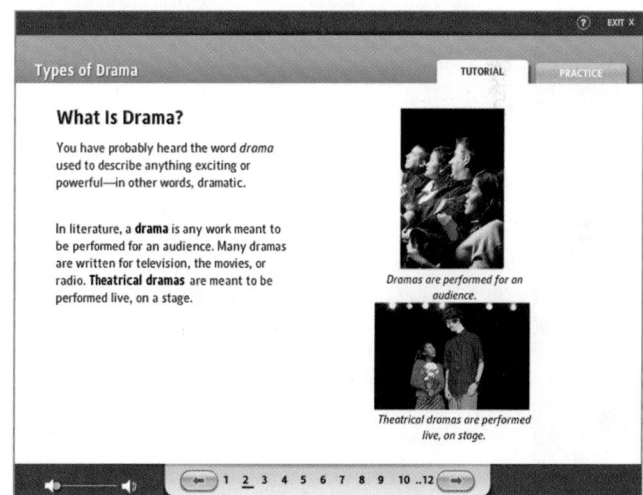

CLOSE READING APPLICATION

Students can apply the skill to the characters of Prospero and Caliban. Have them work with a partner and go over each element of filmmaking and how it impacts the characterization of each of them. Ask: Does the text support the film's characterization of Prospero and Caliban? Is there anything you would do differently if you were the actor or the director?

my SmartPlanner Create lesson plans and access resources online.

Balboa

Short Story by Sabina Murray

Why This Text?

Historical fiction—whether a short story, novel, or movie—helps students gain insight into historical events. In its depiction of events, characters, and setting, the genre brings history to life. This short story explores the relationship between Balboa and the Indians and the Spaniards.

View It!

Professional Development Podcast:
Writing Narratives at the Secondary Level

Key Learning Objective: The student will be able to determine themes and analyze structure.

Common Core Standards

RL 2 Determine themes of a text.

RL 3 Analyze the impact of the author's choices.

RL 5 Analyze how an author's choices concerning how to structure parts of a text contribute to overall meaning as well as its aesthetic impact.

RL 6 Analyze a case in which grasping a point of view requires distinguishing what is directly stated in a text from what is really meant.

L 4a Use context as a clue to meaning.

L 4d Verify the preliminary determination of the meaning of a word or phrase.

Text Complexity Rubric

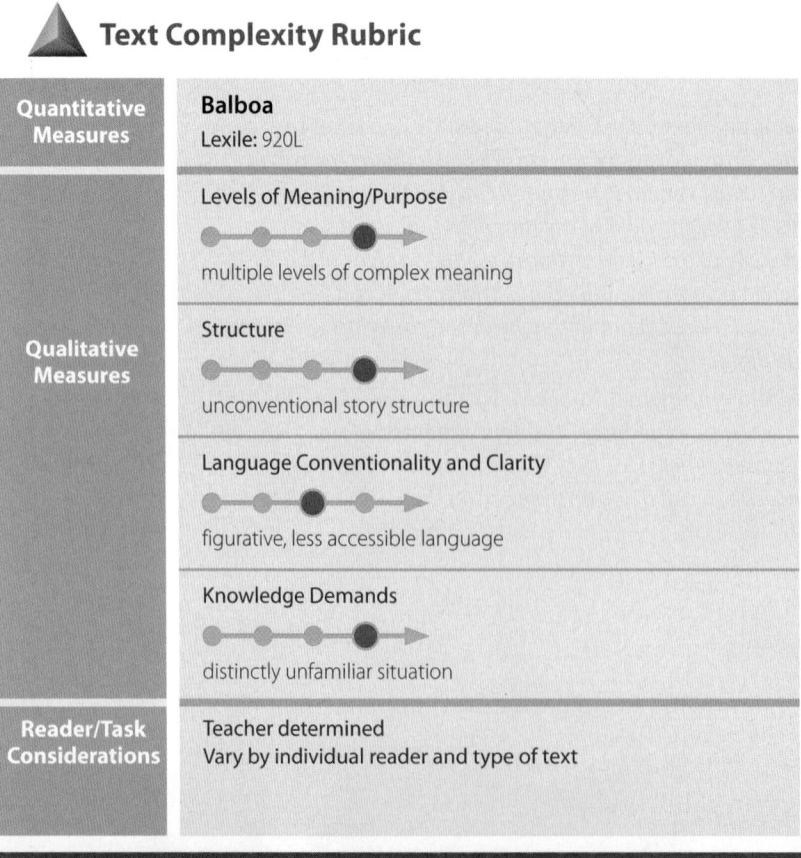

Quantitative Measures	**Balboa** Lexile: 920L
	Levels of Meaning/Purpose multiple levels of complex meaning
Qualitative Measures	**Structure** unconventional story structure
	Language Conventionality and Clarity figurative, less accessible language
	Knowledge Demands distinctly unfamiliar situation
Reader/Task Considerations	Teacher determined Vary by individual reader and type of text

Background Have students read the background information about Balboa. Tell students that Balboa was born in Spain to a poor but noble family. He sailed to the Americas to seek fortune and courageously fight for Spain.

AS YOU READ Direct students to use the As You Read instructions to focus their reading. Remind students to write down any questions they generate during reading.

Determine Themes (LINES 1–14) COMMON CORE RL 2

Explain to students that a theme is the key message or insight of a work. Since fiction writers don't explicitly state their themes but instead weave in these big-picture ideas or universal truths, readers must infer theme. To make inferences, students will analyze clues about characters and events and make connections.

 **ASK STUDENTS** to reread lines 1–14 and make inferences to identify one of Balboa's character traits. *(self-importance; arrogance)* What does this trait suggest about theme? *(The theme may have to do with Balboa's image of himself.)*

Analyze Structure (LINES 1–14) COMMON CORE RL 3, RL 5

Authors use narrative devices to create effects in plot, the sequence of events in a story. When authors choose not to order events sequentially, narrative devices help them disclose details in a way that controls readers' impressions of characters and events. **Foreshadowing** hints at events occurring later in a story and may add suspense or drama. **In media res** means that the story starts in the middle of the action.

 **ASK STUDENTS** at what point in the action does the story begin [lines 1–14]? *(in media res)* Why did Murray begin the story this way? *(The image of 1,200 people watching Balboa creates a sense of drama.)*

CRITICAL VOCABULARY

pristine: The mountain's natural beauty has not been disturbed by the invaders.

ASK STUDENTS how civilization would affect the mountain's pristine setting. *(Explorers might destroy forests, chasing animals from unspoiled habitats.)*

Background *Vasco Núñez de Balboa (1475–1519) was a Spanish explorer and conquistador who first came to the Americas in 1500 as part of a voyage exploring the coast of present-day Colombia. He is most remembered for being the first European to view the Pacific Ocean in 1513. This event and other facts of Balboa's life form the basis for* **Sabina Murray's** *story, published in her book* Tales of the New World *(2011). Murray lives in western Massachusetts, where she is on the Creative Writing faculty at the University of Massachusetts Amherst.*

Balboa

Short Story by Sabina Murray

Image Credits: (bg) ©gulayaskalli/Shutterstock; (cr) ©Ralf Juergen Kraft/Shutterstock; (c) ©Kozoriz Yuriy/Shutterstock

AS YOU READ Pay special attention to descriptions of Balboa's relations with the Indians and the Spaniards. Write down any questions you generate during reading.

Vasco Núñez de Balboa ascends the mountain alone. His one thousand Indians and two hundred Spaniards wait at the foot of the mountain, as if they are the Israelites and Balboa alone is off to speak with God. Balboa knows that from this peak he will be able to see the western water, what he has already decided to name the South Sea. He takes a musket with him. The Spaniards have been warned that if they follow, he will use it, because discovery is a tricky matter and he wants no competition. The day is September 25, 1513.

10   Balboa ascends slowly. His musket is heavy and he would have gladly left it down below, but he doesn't trust his countrymen any more than he trusts the sullen Indians. So he bears the weight. But the musket is nothing. He is dragging the mantle[1] of civilization up the **pristine** slopes, over the mud, over the leaves that cast as much shade as a parasol[2] but with none of the charm.

> **pristine**
> (prĭs'tēn') *adj.* pure or unspoiled.

---
[1] **mantle:** a cloak or robe worn by royalty.
[2] **parasol:** light umbrella.

SCAFFOLDING FOR ELL STUDENTS

Language: Verb Tenses "Balboa" uses present tense with a historical event. Point out the verb *ascends*. Have mixed language-ability groups use the annotation tools to highlight present-tense verbs in lines 1–14. Have volunteers mark up present-tense verbs. Read the excerpt. Then reread it, changing verbs to past tense.

ASK STUDENTS how the use of present tense contributes to the story. *(The use of present tense creates a sense of immediacy.)*

> Balboa ascends slowly. His musket is heavy and he would have gladly
>
> left it down below, but he doesn't trust his countrymen any

Determine Themes

COMMON CORE RL 2

(LINES 17–38)

Remind students that authors use literary elements like **character** and **plot** to develop a **theme**. To determine theme, readers must look closely at these elements and ask questions. Analyzing a character's speech, thoughts, and actions is one way to trace the development of a theme.

C **CITE TEXT EVIDENCE** Have students cite lines that show Balboa is aware of the discrepancy between who he is and how he wants to be known. *(lines 17–23, lines 33–36)* Then have students identify terms that describe how Balboa would like others to see him. *(Balboa the Lion, Balboa the Valiant, Balboa the Fearsome, Balboa the Brave)*

Explain that a character's thoughts can reveal traits, or qualities, that the character possesses that may provide readers with clues to the theme.

D **ASK STUDENTS** to reread lines 49–51 and pay attention to what Balboa does when he hears the twig snapping. What does Balboa's reaction suggest about his character? *(Even though he doesn't know what—or who—is approaching, Balboa responds aggressively to control the situation.)* What might the reader infer about the theme? *(Balboa is accustomed to defeating opponents, suggesting that the theme has to do with power and control.)*

Balboa is that divining line[3] between the modern and the primitive. As he moves, the shadow of Spain moves with him.

Balboa steps cautiously into a muddy stream and watches with fascination as his boot sinks and sinks. He will have to find another way. Upstream he sees an outcropping of rock. Maybe he can cross

20 there. He tells himself that there is no hurry, but years of staying just ahead of trouble have left him anxiety-ridden. He would like to think of himself as a lion. Balboa the Lion! But no, he is more of a rat, and all of his accomplishments have been made with speed and stealth. Balboa places his hand on a branch and pulls himself up. He sees the tail of a snake disappearing just past his reach. The subtle crush of greenery confirms his discovery and he shrinks back, crouching. In this moment of stillness, he looks around. He sees no other serpents, but that does not mean they are not there. Only in this momentary quiet does he hear his breath, rasping with effort. He hears his heart

30 beating in the arced fingers of his ribs as if it is an Indian's drum. He does not remember what it is to be civilized, or if he ever was. If ever a man was alone, it is he. But even in this painful solitude, he cannot help but laugh. Along with Cristóbal Colón, backed by Isabel I herself, along with Vespucci the scholar, along with the noble Pizarro brothers[4] on their way to claim Inca gold, his name will live—Balboa. Balboa! Balboa the Valiant. Balboa the Fearsome. Balboa the Brave.

Balboa the gambling pig farmer, who, in an effort to escape his debt, has found himself at the very edge of the world.

Balboa stops to drink from the stream. The water is cold, fresh,

40 and tastes like dirt, which is a relief after what he has been drinking— water so green that the very act of ingesting it seems unnatural, as though it is as alive as he, and sure enough, given a few hours, it will get you back, eager to find its way out. He has been climbing since early morning and it is now noon. The sun shines in the sky unblinking, white-hot. Balboa wonders if it's the same sun that shines in Spain. The sun seemed so much smaller there. Even in Hispaniola,[5] the sun was Spanish. Even as he prodded his pigs in the heat, there was Spain all around, men with dice, men training roosters, pitting their dogs against each other. But here…then he hears a twig snap and the

50 sound of something brushing up against the bushes. Balboa stands.

"I give you this one chance to turn back," he says, raising his musket as he turns. And then he freezes. It is not one of the Spaniards hoping to share the glory. Instead, he finds himself face-to-face with

---

[3] **divining line:** point of separation between ideas.

[4] **Cristóbal Colón . . . Pizarro brothers:** Cristóbal Colón is the Spanish name for Christopher Columbus. Isabel I was Queen of Castile (Spain) from 1474 until 1504. Amerigo Vespucci (1451–1512) was an Italian explorer and cartographer. Francisco, Gonzalo, Juan, and Hernándo Pizarro were Spanish conquistadors in Peru.

[5] **Hispaniola:** site of Columbus's first colony; the island containing modern Haiti and the Dominican Republic.

APPLYING ACADEMIC VOCABULARY

| device | coherent |

As you discuss "Balboa," incorporate the following Collection 1 academic vocabulary words: *device* and *coherent*. To analyze the author's development of theme, have students identify the literary **devices** in the short story. As you explore the plot, ask students to explain how flashbacks and flash forwards contribute to establishing a **coherent** plot structure.

a great spotted cat. On this mountain, he's thought he might find his god, the god of Moses, sitting in the cloud cover near the peaks, running his fingers through his beard. But no. Instead he finds himself face-to-face with a jaguar, the god of the Indians. He knows why these primitives have chosen it for their deity. It is hard to fear one's maker when he looks like one's grandfather, but this great cat
60 can make a people fear god. He hears the growling of the cat and the grating, high-pitched thunder sounds like nothing he has ever heard. The cat twitches its nose and two great incisors show at the corners of its mouth. Balboa raises his musket, ignites the flint,[6] and nothing happens. He tries again and the weapon explodes, shattering the silence, sending up a big puff of stinking smoke. The cat is gone for now, but Balboa knows he hasn't even injured it.

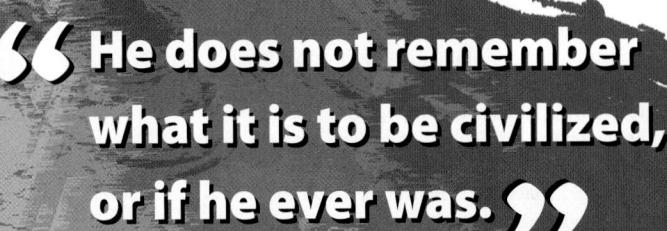

" He does not remember what it is to be civilized, or if he ever was. "

And now it will be tailing him silently.

There is nothing he can do about it. He should have brought an Indian with him. The Indians have all seen the South Sea before, so
70 why did he leave them at the foot of the mountain? They have no more interest in claiming the South Sea than they do rowing off to Europe in their dug-out canoes[7] and claiming Spain. But Balboa's hindsight is always good, and no amount of swearing—which he does freely, spilling Spanish profanity into the virgin mountain air—is going to set things straight.

He is already in trouble. His kingdom in Darién on the east coast of the New World is under threat, and not from the Indians, whom he manages well, but from Spain. Balboa had organized the rebellion, **supplanted** the governor—all of this done with great efficiency and
80 intelligence. What stupidity made him send the governor, Martín Fernández de Enciso, back to Spain? Enciso swore that he would have Balboa's head on a platter. He was yelling from the deck of the ship as it set sail. Why didn't he kill Enciso? Better yet, why didn't

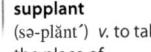

supplant
(sə-plănt´) v. to take the place of.

---

[6] **flint:** stone used to create a spark.

[7] **dug-out canoes:** narrow boats made by hollowing out tree trunks.

CLOSE READ

Analyze Structure
COMMON CORE **RL 3, RL 5**

(LINES 76–80)

Tell students that authors may write a few sentences as a transition to a flashback or flash forward. Explain that the beginning of a flashback is often signaled by a shift in verb tense. A flashback may provide background information that offers readers insight about character, plot, or theme.

E CITE TEXT EVIDENCE Have a volunteer read aloud lines 76–80. Have students identify the lines that function as a transition to the flashback *(lines 76–78)* and the sentence that begins the flashback *(line 78: Balboa had organized . . .)*. Ask students to cite the past-tense verbs that signal that this scene is a flashback. *(had organized: line 78; supplanted, done: line 79)*

CRITICAL VOCABULARY

supplanted: Balboa organizes a rebellion and successfully overthrows the kingdom of Darién, but afterward he regrets not having killed Enciso the governor.

ASK STUDENTS why Balboa is not satisfied with having supplanted Enciso. *(The governor wants revenge because Balboa kicked him out of office. When Enciso threatens Balboa, he realizes that Enciso may turn the rulers against him when he gets to Spain. If Balboa had killed Enciso, he could have avoided the predicament.)*

Strategies for Annotation   ✎ 🖹 *Annotate it!*

Analyze Structure
COMMON CORE **RL 3, RL 5**

Have students use their eBook annotation tools to analyze the text. Ask them to do the following:

- Underline the lines that function as a transition to the flashback. *(Lines 76–78)*
- Highlight in pink the first word of the sentence that begins the flashback. *(Balboa)*
- Highlight in green the past-tense verbs that signal that this scene is a flashback. *(had organized, supplanted, done)*

He is already in trouble. His kingdom in Darién on the east coast of the New World is under threat, and not from the Indians, whom he manages well, but from Spain. Balboa had organized the rebellion, **supplanted** the governor—all of this done with great efficiency and intelligence.

Determine Themes

COMMON CORE RL 2

(LINES 104–126)

Tell students that analyzing a character and making inferences about the character's motives can help them identify the theme. Explain that a character may have both a reason, a logical explanation, and a motive, an underlying purpose, for doing something.

F **ASK STUDENTS** to identify Balboa's reason for naming his dog *Leoncico* and then to infer his motive. *(Reason: The dog looks like a lion. Motive: Balboa thinks of himself as a powerful lion and sees the same traits in Leoncico.)* What does this suggest about the theme? *(Balboa is preoccupied with images of himself as a powerful leader, so the theme must be about power.)*

CRITICAL VOCABULARY

protruding: Balboa's dog is massive, with a head as big as a man's. He is named Leoncico because his body has the look and build of a lion.

ASK STUDENTS what Leoncico's muscles and his protruding shoulders and hipbones have to do with his name. *(Leoncico, whose name means "little lion," has muscles and protruding bones that remind people of the build of a lion.)*

Analyze Structure

COMMON CORE RL 3, RL 5

(LINES 120–126)

Explain that a flashback later in a story may refer to an earlier time in the plot than the previous flashback(s).

G **CITE TEXT EVIDENCE** Have students cite the lines that explain how Balboa first met Enciso. *(lines 120–126)*

CRITICAL VOCABULARY

provisions: Due to the lack of refrigeration during Balboa's time, ships kept barrels of salted meat because it wouldn't spoil during their voyages.

ASK STUDENTS why Leoncico may have been drawn to the barrels of provisions on Enciso's ship. *(The barrels contained the ship's supply of meat.)*

he turn Enciso over to some Indian tribe that would be glad to have the Spaniard, glad to have his blood on their hands? How could Balboa be so stupid? Soon the caravels[8] would arrive and his days as governor (king, he tells the Indians) of Darién will be over. Unless, Balboa thinks, unless he brings glory by being the first to claim this great ocean for Spain. Then the king will see him as the greatest of his
90 subjects, not a troublemaking peasant, a keeper of pigs.

Unless that jaguar gets him first.

Balboa looks nervously around. The only sound is the trickle and splash of the stream that he is following, which the Indians tell him leads to a large outcropping of rock from which he will see the new ocean. Insects swoop malevolently[9] around his head. A yellow and red parrot watches him cautiously from a branch, first looking from one side of its jeweled head, then the other. Where is the jaguar? Balboa imagines his body being dragged into a tree, his boots swinging from the limbs as the great cat tears his heart from his ribs. He
100 hears a crushing of vegetation and ducks low. He readies his musket again. "Please God, let the damned thing fire." He breathes harshly, genuflecting,[10] musket steady.

The leaves quiver, then part. There is no jaguar.

F "Leoncico!" he cries out. Leoncico is his dog, who has tracked him up the slope. Leoncico patters over, wagging his tail, his great wrinkled head bearded with drool. Leoncico is a monster of a dog. His head is the size of a man's, and his body has the look of a lion—shoulders and hipbones **protruding** and muscle pulling and shifting beneath the glossy skin—which is where he gets his name. "Leoncico" means little
110 lion.

"Good dog," says Balboa. "Good dog. Good dog."

He has never been so grateful for the company, not even when he was hidden on board Enciso's ship bound for San Sebastián, escaping his creditors, wrapped in a sail. No one wondered why the dog had come on board. Maybe the dog had been attracted by the smell of **provisions**, the great barrels of salted meat. The soldiers fed him, gave him water. Balboa worried that Leoncico would give him away, but the dog had somehow known to be quiet. He had slept beside Balboa, and even in Balboa's thirst and hunger, the great beast's panting and
120 panting, warm through the sailcloth, had given him comfort. When Enciso's crew finally discovered Balboa—one of the sails was torn and needed to be replaced—they did not punish him. They laughed.

"The Indians massacre everyone. You are better off in a debtors' prison," they said.

Balboa became a member of the crew. When the boat shipwrecked off the coast of San Sebastián (they were rescued by Francisco Pizarro),

---

[8] **caravels:** small sailing ships with two or three masts.
[9] **malevolently:** with evil intent.
[10] **genuflecting:** bending one knee to the ground.

protrude
(prō-trōōd´) *v.* to stick out or bulge.

provision
(prə-vĭzh´ən) *n.* food supply.

TO CHALLENGE STUDENTS . . .

Analyze Characters After students read lines 152–166, discuss the use of foils in literature. Tell students that a **foil** is a character whose traits contrast with those of another character. A writer might use a minor character as a foil to emphasize the traits of a major character.

CITE TEXT EVIDENCE Ask students to cite text evidence that the monk is used as a foil for Balboa. *(The monk is described as weak—barefoot, unarmed, and "waving his shrunken fist." This description contrasts with how Balboa has been described—as powerful and heavily armed.)* Then, ask students if there are any ways in which the monk and Balboa are similar. *(They are both imposing their ideas and will upon the Indians; they are both bold.)*

Enciso had been at a loss as to where to go, and Balboa convinced him to try Darién to the north. Once established there, Enciso had shown himself to be a weak man. How could Balboa not act? Enciso did not

130 understand the Indians as Balboa did. He could see that the Indians were battle-hardened warriors. The Spaniards had not been there long enough to call these armies into existence. Balboa's strength had been to recognize this **discord**. He divided the great tribes, supported one against the other. His reputation spread. His muskets blasted away the faces of the greatest warriors. Balboa's soldiers spread smallpox and syphilis. His Spanish war dogs, great mastiffs and wolfhounds, tore children limb from limb. The blood from his great war machine made the rivers flow red and his name, Balboa, moved quickly, apace[11] with these rivers of blood.

140 Balboa is loved by no one and feared by all. He has invented an unequaled terror. The Indians think of him as a god. They make no **distinction** between good and evil. They have seen his soldiers tear babies from their mothers, toss them still screaming to feed the dogs. They have seen the great dogs pursue the escaping Indians, who must hear nothing but a great panting, the jangle of the dogs' armor, and then, who knows? Do they feel the hot breath on their cheek? Are they still awake when the beasts unravel their stomachs and spill them onto the hot earth? Balboa's dogs have been his most effective weapon because for them, one does not need to carry ammunition, as for

150 the muskets; one does not need to carry food, as for the soldiers. For the dogs, there is fresh meat everywhere. He knows his cruelty will be recorded along with whatever he discovers. This does not bother him, even though one monk, Dominican—strange fish—cursed him back in Darién. He was a young monk, tormented by epileptic[12] fits. He approached Balboa in the town square in his bare feet, unarmed, waving his shrunken fist.

"Your dogs," screamed the monk, "are demons."

As if understanding, Leoncico had lunged at the monk. Leoncico is not a demon. He is the half of Balboa with teeth, the half that eats.

160 Balboa has the mind and appetite. Together, they make one. It is as if the great beast can hear his thoughts, as if their hearts and lungs circulate the same blood and air. What did the monk understand of that? What did he understand of anything? He said that he was in the New World to bring the Indians to God. So the monk converts the Indians, and Balboa sends them on to God. They work together, which is what Balboa told the monk. But the monk did not find it funny.

How dare he find fault with Balboa? Is not Spain as full of torments as the New World? The Spaniards are brought down by smallpox at alarming rates in Seville, in Madrid. Every summer the

170 rich take to the mountains to escape the plague, and in the fall, when

---

[11] **apace:** fast enough to keep up with something.
[12] **epileptic:** caused by epilepsy, a neurological disorder.

discord
(dĭs'kôrd') *n.* disagreement or conflict.

distinction
(dĭ-stĭngk'shən) *n.* difference in quality.

CLOSE READ

Determine Themes
(LINES 158–160)

COMMON CORE RL 2

Remind students that authors may develop a theme by providing deeper insight into characters' thoughts and motives.

H ASK STUDENTS to look at lines 158–160. How does the image of Balboa and Leoncico contribute to the development of the theme? *(The image relates to the nature of power. Balboa acknowledges his "appetite," or hunger, for power and views Leoncico as the part of himself that "eats," or seizes, it by whatever violent means necessary.)*

Analyze Structure
(LINES 152–166)

COMMON CORE RL 2, RL 3, RL 5

Explain that literary elements, like structure and theme, do not function independently but rather work hand in hand. Authors may use flashbacks to help readers identify **conflict**, the key problem in a plot, and thus, theme.

I ASK STUDENTS to identify the flashback and analyze the conflict between Balboa and the monk. *(The monk is horrified by Balboa's violence and lust for power. Balboa cynically justifies his methods by comparing the "New World" to Spain.)*

CRITICAL VOCABULARY

discord: Balboa realizes that, on the battlefield, the Spaniards would be no match for the Indians. **ASK STUDENTS** to explain why recognizing the Indians' discord benefits Balboa. *(By recognizing the disagreement among the tribes, Balboa turns them against each other. As a result, he directs their attention away from the Spaniards who are taking over their land, at the same time weakening the Indian armies.)*

distinction: After witnessing the terrors Balboa is capable of, the Indians consider him a god. **ASK STUDENTS** to explain, based on the Indians' lack of distinction between good and evil, how the Indians qualify a being as a god. *(They perceive power as a godlike quality, so powerful beings are regarded as gods.)*

Determine Themes

COMMON CORE RL 2, RL 6

(LINES 171–180)

Tell students that characters' perceptions often are the basis for their motives. Perceptions are interpretations or impressions; they influence characters' thoughts, behaviors, and actions. Both characters' perceptions and motives offer clues to an author's message.

J **CITE TEXT EVIDENCE** Have students cite textual evidence that reveals what Balboa thinks of the Indians and what his strategy is in dealing with them. *(savages [line 174]; subduing the Indian population [lines 179–180])*

they return, aren't their own countrymen lying in the streets feeding the packs of mongrels? Half of all the Spanish babies die. It is not uncommon to see a peasant woman leave her screaming infant on the side of the road, so why come here and beg relief for these savages? Why not go to France, where, one soldier tells Balboa, they butcher the Huguenots[13] and sell their limbs for food in the street? Why rant over the impaling of the Indians when Spaniards—noblemen among them—have suffered the same fate in the name of God? In fact, the Inquisition[14] has been the great educator when it comes to subduing

180 the Indian population.

---

[13] **Huguenots:** French Protestants who were persecuted for their faith in the 16th and 17th centuries.

[14] **the Inquisition:** an investigation by the Roman Catholic Church to identify and punish heretics.

82 Collection 1

Image Credits: ©Marc Romanelli/The Image Bank/Getty Images

WHEN STUDENTS STRUGGLE . . .

Discuss how a character's traits may be inferred from the character's thoughts, comments, reactions, and perceptions. Traits may also be inferred from other characters' thoughts, comments, reactions, and perceptions about him.

To guide students in inferring Balboa's traits, have students work in groups to fill in a chart like the one shown in which they cite textual evidence about Balboa's character.

Balboa's Description	Other Characters' Description
"He would like to think of himself as a lion . . . But no, he is more of a rat."	"loved by no one and feared by all"
"He knows his cruelty will be recorded . . . This does not bother him."	"They have seen his soldiers tear babies from their mothers"
"He is the great Balboa."	"Dávila will see that as long as Balboa lives he must sleep with one eye open."

Why take him to task when the world is a violent place?

"May your most evil act be visited on you," said the monk. "I curse you."

The monk died shortly after that. His threats and bravery were more the result of a deadly fever than the words of a divine message. Did the curse worry Balboa? Perhaps a little. He occasionally revisits a particularly spectacular feat of bloodshed—the time Leoncico tore a chieftain's head from his shoulders—with a pang of concern. But Balboa is a busy man with little time for reflection. When the monk

190 delivered his curse, Balboa was already preparing his troops for the great march to the west. His name had reached Spain, and the king felt his authority threatened.

He is the great Balboa.

But here, on the slope of the mountain, his name does not seem worth that much. He has to relieve himself and is terrified that some creature—jaguar, snake, spider—will take advantage of his great heaving bareness.

"Leoncico," he calls. "At attention."

Not that this command means anything to the dog. Leoncico

200 knows "attack," and that is all he needs to know. Leoncico looks up, wags his tail, and lies down, his face smiling into the heat. Balboa climbs onto a boulder. Here, he is exposed to everything, but if that jaguar is still tracking him, he can at least see it coming. He sets his musket down and listens. Nothing. He loosens his belt and is about to lower his pants when he sees it—the flattened glimmer, a shield, the horizon. He fixes his belt and straightens himself. He stares out at the startling bare intrusion, this beautiful nothing beyond the green tangle of trees, the *Mar del Sur*, the glory of Balboa, his gift to Spain.

Balboa, having accomplished his goal, luxuriates in this moment

210 of peaceful ignorance. He does not know that his days are numbered, that even after he returns to Darién with his knowledge of the South Sea, even after he has **ceded** the governorship to Pedro Arias Dávila, even after he is promised Dávila's daughter, he has not bought his safety. Dávila will see that as long as Balboa lives he must sleep with one eye open. With the blessing of Spain, Dávila will bring Balboa to trial for treason, and on January 21, 1519, Balboa's head will be severed from his shoulders. His eyes will stay open, his mouth will be slack, and his great head will roll in the dust for everyone—Indians, Spaniards, and dogs—to see.

cede
(sēd) *v.* to yield or give away.

COLLABORATIVE DISCUSSION Why is Balboa more successful in managing his relationships with the Indians than his relationships with other powerful Spaniards? Discuss with a partner how Murray describes these different relationships. Cite specific evidence from the story to support your ideas.

Balboa **83**

CLOSE READ

Analyze Structure

COMMON CORE **RL 5**

(LINES 182–183)

Remind students that foreshadowing is a writer's use of hints about what will happen in the story. It creates suspense and prepares the reader for what is to come.

K ASK STUDENTS what might be foreshadowed by the monk's curse in lines 182–183. *(The monk's curse foreshadows Balboa's death.)*

Analyze Structure

COMMON CORE **RL 5**

(LINES 210–219)

Remind students that in a flash forward the action in story jumps forward in time.

L ASK STUDENTS how the flash forward at the end of this story affects the story's overall meaning and aesthetic impact. *(Through the flash forward, the reader learns how Balboa's plan to achieve power and glory backfired and that he dies as violently as the people he killed. This ending refines understanding of the theme, suggesting that arrogance and lust for power do not pay.)*

CRITICAL VOCABULARY

ceded: In the end, Balboa loses his position as governor of Darién.

ASK STUDENTS if the text suggests that Balboa was on bad terms with Dávila when he ceded the governorship. *(Balboa must have been on good terms with Dávila when he yielded office because he had plans to marry the new governor's daughter.)*

COLLABORATIVE DISCUSSION Have students pair up to discuss Balboa's motives and analyze how his motives instigated the main conflict and affected his relationships with the Indians and with the Spaniards. Group three sets of partners to compare conclusions.

ASK STUDENTS to share any questions they generated in the course of reading and discussing the selection.

Balboa **83**

Determine Themes

COMMON CORE **RL 2**

Guide students to sections of text that will help them identify the theme by considering character. For example, have students reread lines 181–192 and discuss Balboa's reaction to the monk's curse. *(Although Balboa occasionally feels concern about the violence he has caused, he continues his attacks.)* Then help students identify the theme by answering questions about plot. For example, direct them to the paragraph that begins on line 76 to determine the main conflict. *(Balboa wants to maintain power in the New World, but his control is slipping.)*

Analyze Structure: Flashback and Flash Forward

COMMON CORE **RL 3, RL 5**

To help students understand the structure of the story, offer these tips on how to identify flashbacks and flash forwards.

- Both flashbacks and flash forwards typically begin with a sentence that breaks the action and transitions from real time in the story to the past or future. Transitions may also be used to indicate the end of a shift in time.

- The past perfect tense *(had driven, had found)* is typically used at the beginning and often at the end of a flashback to clue readers that time is shifting to or from the past. The future tense *(will drive, will find)* indicates a time shift in a flash forward.

Determine Themes

COMMON CORE **RL 2**

Writers of fiction often use their works to communicate insights about life or human nature. Most of these **themes** are not stated; readers must infer them by looking closely at other elements of the work, especially characters and plot. To identify and trace the development of the themes in "Balboa," answer these questions:

- **Character:** How does the main character change or fail to change? What qualities does the main character possess? How do these qualities determine his or her reaction to the conflict? What message is the author conveying through the way the character's traits influence his or her reactions?
- **Plot:** What is the major conflict in the story? How does this conflict lead to other problems? How is the conflict resolved? Is there a lesson to be learned from the way the conflict is resolved?

Analyze Structure: Flashback and Flash Forward

COMMON CORE **RL 3, RL 5**

The **structure** of a story is its organization, or how the action is ordered. Many stories are organized chronologically, following a tale from its beginning to its end. Sometimes, however, authors decide to present the sequence of events out of order to add interest or suspense, or to achieve a more subtle effect. To analyze the structure of "Balboa," look at how the author uses the narrative techniques described in the chart.

Flashback	Flash Forward
A **flashback** is a scene that interrupts the action of a narrative to describe events that took place at an earlier time. Flashbacks often add important background information about characters. This information can help readers gain a new perspective on the character and his or her motives, understand the causes of events, or see the author's message more clearly. The story "Balboa" includes several flashbacks as the main character recalls significant events in his past.	**Flash forward** interrupts the narrative to give readers a look at what will happen after the events in the main plot take place. A flash forward may change readers' outlook on events and characters in the story, affect the mood that is created, or illuminate the meaning of the work. In "Balboa," the author chooses to conclude her story with a flash forward focusing on the end of the main character's life.

Strategies for Annotation ✎ 🖥 *Annotate it!*

Determine Themes

COMMON CORE **RL 2**

Have students use their eBook annotation tools to analyze the text. Ask them to do the following:

- To identify and trace the development of the theme, highlight in yellow text that helps you answer questions about character.
- To identify and trace the development of the theme, highlight in blue text that helps you answer questions about plot.
- Make inferences about the theme based on your analysis of character and plot.

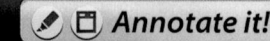

> Balboa is loved by no one and feared by all. He has invented an unequaled terror. The Indians think of him as a god. They make no distinction between good and evil. They have seen his soldiers tear babies from their mothers, toss them still screaming to feed the dogs.

Analyzing the Text

COMMON CORE RL 2, RL 3, RL 5, RL 6

Cite Text Evidence Support your responses with evidence from the selection.

1. **Interpret** An **allusion** is an indirect reference to a famous person, place, event, or literary work. What allusion is made in the first paragraph of the story? How does this allusion shape readers' understanding of Balboa's character?

2. **Analyze** Balboa could be described as self-aware. Even as he revels in the thought that "his name will live," he is aware of the incongruity that he, a debt-ridden pig farmer, should now be standing "at the very edge of the world." He also assesses his errors in judgment honestly. What is the author's purpose in developing this trait of self-awareness?

3. **Analyze** After Leoncico surprises Balboa on the mountain, the action of the story is interrupted by a flashback. What do readers learn about Balboa from this flashback? What theme does it suggest about the nature of power?

4. **Analyze** At the beginning of the story, the narrator says that Balboa is "dragging the mantle of civilization up the pristine slopes, over the mud, over the leaves" (lines 12–13). What does this image suggest about Balboa and the "civilization" that he is bringing with him?

5. **Interpret** Note the many references to and images of dogs throughout the story. What ideas does the author convey through these references?

6. **Analyze** The vantage point from which a writer tells a story is called the point of view. What point of view did Murray choose for this short story? What does this choice add to the narrative?

7. **Analyze** One form of **irony** is the contrast between expectations and what actually happens. What is ironic about Balboa's first glimpse of the Pacific Ocean? Why does the author present the crowning moment of Balboa's achievement this way?

8. **Analyze** What is revealed by the flash forward at the end of the story? How does this knowledge help bring out a theme of the story?

PERFORMANCE TASK

Writing Activity: Dramatic Monologue Through her portrayal of Balboa, Murray creates a dynamic, multi-dimensional main character. Her characterization enables readers to see him clearly and almost hear his voice. Write a dramatic monologue from the point of view of this fictional Balboa, expressing what he might have said aloud as he stood on the boulder surveying the Pacific Ocean.

- Draw upon the text for details about the path he followed to "the edge of the world."
- Reveal his motives and his feelings upon accomplishing his goal.
- Include his reflections on what his accomplishment really means, incorporating your ideas about the theme.
- Present your monologue to a small group.

Analyzing the Text

COMMON CORE RL 2, RL 3, RL 5, RL 6

Possible answers:

1. *The allusion is to Moses climbing Mount Sinai when he receives the Ten Commandments from God. Balboa believes he's a worthy leader who will save the people.*

2. *The author develops Balboa's self-awareness to show that knowing his flaws is not enough to keep from making mistakes. Because he is arrogant and power hungry, Balboa believes he is invincible.*

3. *In the flashback, Balboa reveals that he ended up in Darién because he was fleeing from his creditors. This suggests that power is often in the hands of the strongest individual, not the best.*

4. *The civilization Balboa is bringing is one of cruelty and barbarity—and the pristine slopes will soon be drenched in blood. In fact, the mantle of civilization is polluting the slopes.*

5. *The dogs become a symbol of savagery. "Balboa's war dogs" refers literally to animal soldiers and figuratively to vicious, brutal human soldiers.*

6. *Murray tells the story through Balboa's point of view, making the narrative personal and offering readers a glimpse into the inner workings of Balboa's mind.*

7. *When Balboa notices the ocean glimmering beyond the trees, he is undoing his pants to relieve himself. Murray shows that the great Balboa is a mere mortal, a human being with needs and urges like any other. Murray also presents civilization as ironic. At the moment of his glory, Balboa is contaminating the Indians' sacred mountain top.*

8. *Balboa's abuse of power leads to his demise. He turns people against each other for his own benefit, which in the end fosters mistrust in Dávila. Balboa's lust for power corrupts him, and in the end, he loses all power. Dávila has Balboa put to death and his severed head paraded before the people he terrorized.*

Assign this performance task.

PERFORMANCE TASK

COMMON CORE W 3b

Writing Activity Have students work in pairs. Direct them to scan the selection for clues to Balboa's personality and motives. First have them identify the theme to help them understand Balboa's motives. Then, so they may better understand Balboa's character to write the monologue from his point of view, have them create a list of his traits.

PRACTICE & APPLY

Critical Vocabulary

COMMON CORE L 4a, L 4d

Answers: 1. *no;* **2.** *no;* **3.** *less healthy;* **4.** *no*

Vocabulary Strategy: Context Clues

Word	Context Clues	My Guessed Definition	Dictionary Definition
stealth	*Balboa compares himself to a rat.*	*sneakiness*	*the act of proceeding secretly*
ingesting	*He says he has been drinking the water.*	*drinking*	*swallowing or gulping down*
incisors	*They are described as showing at the corners of the jaguar's mouth.*	*teeth*	*front teeth designed for cutting*
mastiffs	*The word appears in a phrase set off after the term "war dogs."*	*big dogs*	*a type of large bulky dog, sometimes used as guard dogs*

Critical Vocabulary

COMMON CORE L 4a, L 4d

pristine	protrude	discord	cede
supplant	provision	distinction	

Practice and Apply Answer each question, referring to the meaning of each Critical Vocabulary word in your response.

1. If you **ceded** the computer to your younger brother, would that cause **discord**?

2. If both candidates had **pristine** reputations and equal leadership experience, would it be easy to make a **distinction** between them?

3. If the young children in a family **supplanted** their parents in control of the grocery shopping, would the family's **provisions** likely be more or less healthy?

4. If the lawn had many tree roots **protruding** from it, would it be a **pristine** surface?

Vocabulary Strategy: Context Clues

The context of a word is the words, phrases, and sentences that surround it. Looking at the context of an unfamiliar word can help you to define it. For example, read this sentence from the text: "Balboa had organized the rebellion, supplanted the governor. . . ." The word *rebellion* helps you understand that *supplanted*, a Critical Vocabulary word, means "to overthrow or replace." Often key words signal a relationship between the unknown word and others in the sentence that will help you define it.

Key Words	Context Clues
such as, like, for example, including	The unknown word is followed by examples that illustrate its meaning: *We packed provisions, such as fruit, water, and chocolate.*
unlike, but, in contrast, although, on the other hand	The unknown word is contrasted with a more familiar word or phrase: *The tablecloth was pristine before dinner, but it was covered with stains afterwards.*
also, similar to, as, like, as if	The unknown word is compared to a more familiar word or phrase: *The wad of gum protruding from his cheek made him look as if he had the mumps.*
or, that is, which is, in other words	The unknown word is preceded or followed by a restatement of its meaning: *The distinction, or difference, between the identical twins was slight.*

Practice and Apply List four unfamiliar words from the story. Work with a partner to define the words on each of your lists from context. Then check their definitions in a dictionary. Share your words, their context clues, and their definitions with the class.

Strategies for Annotation ✏️ 🖥 *Annotate it!*

Context Clues

COMMON CORE L 4a, L 4d

Remind students that the eBook annotation tools can help them determine the meaning of unfamiliar words in "Balboa." Suggest that they do the following:

- Highlight each unfamiliar word.
- Reread the sentence containing the word as well as surrounding sentences, looking for examples, synonyms, or antonyms that provide clues to the word's meaning. Underline each clue.
- Review your annotations and infer the meaning based on context.

Balboa stops to <u>drink</u> from the stream. The water is cold, fresh, and tastes <u>like</u> dirt, which is a relief after what he has been <u>drinking</u>— <u>water so green</u> that the very <u>act of ingesting</u> it seems unnatural, as though it is as alive as he, and sure enough, given a few hours, it will get you back, eager to find its way out.

Determine Author's Purpose and Perspective

COMMON CORE

RL 6

TEACH

• Explain to students that an author's point of view can differ greatly from the point of view, or perspective, used within a narrative. The narration in "Balboa" is third-person-limited-point-of-view, which allows readers to focus on the thoughts and actions of the protagonist, Vasco Núñez de Balboa. But Sabina Murray, the author, brings her own assumptions and prejudices to the story, and that perspective shapes how she presents the content. Ask students which elements of Murray's presentation reveal something about her point of view. Is she sympathetic toward her protagonist, or does she regard him poorly? What textual evidence can they cite to support their conclusions?

PRACTICE AND APPLY

Display lines 17–38 of the story on the board or on a device.

Have volunteers identify the lines in which the protagonist considers the image he wishes to project. *(Lines 21–22; Balboa the Lion. Lines 35–36; Balboa among the pantheon of explorers, brave, valiant, fearsome.)* Then ask volunteers to identify the lines in which Balboa acknowledges a difference in the way that he wishes to be received and the reality of his situation. *(Lines 22–23; Balboa the Rat. Lines 37–38; indebted pig farmer stuck in the middle of nowhere.)* Then, ask students how Murray's narrative technique of juxtaposing perception against reality reveals her own attitudes toward her protagonist. *(It highlights the hidden irony of what should be a momentous historical event, leading the reader to believe that Murray may not dislike her protagonist, but that she has realistically assessed his character flaws.)* Have students find other examples within the text that support or contradict this conclusion. *(Lines 140–152; Balboa as a cruel god. Lines 193–197; the great Balboa in a moment of vulnerability. Lines 209–219; Balboa the explorer tried for treason.)*

Determine Themes

COMMON CORE

RL 2

RETEACH

Review the terms *theme, structure, character, plot,* and *conflict.* Remind students to infer, or guess, an implied theme by analyzing details and making connections regarding characters' thoughts, words, motives, and growth or lack of growth. Analyzing plot as well as conflict and its resolution will also help them infer theme.

• Ask students to give examples of what Balboa says and does that suggest his motivation. *(He wants to be the first to claim the Pacific Ocean for Spain so the king will recognize his importance.)*

• What conflict does Balboa face? *(He alienates other Spaniards by pursuing power at their expense.)* What happens to Balboa in the end as a result of his actions? *(He is charged with treason and beheaded.)*

LEVEL UP TUTORIALS Assign the following *Level Up* tutorial: **Making Inferences About Characters**

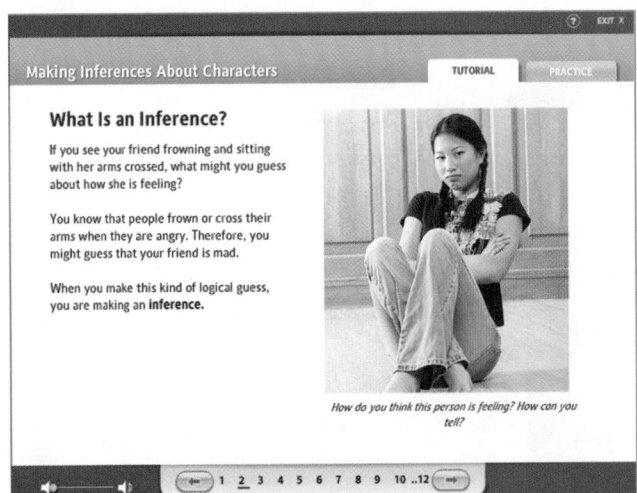

CLOSE READING APPLICATION

Students can apply the skill by working in groups to trace the development of the theme. Ask: What details about character does the author include that provide clues to theme? What events in the plot help you understand the conflict? What might Balboa have done that would have changed the outcome?

mySmartPlanner Create lesson plans and access resources online.

"Blaxicans" and Other Reinvented Americans

Argument by Richard Rodriguez

Why This Text?

Increasingly, our society is made up of people from many cultures and ethnic groups. Our old ways of thinking about racial identity no longer describe the reality of a diverse United States. Richard Rodriguez discusses his own background and offers a fresh way of thinking about identity in a multi-ethnic world.

▶ **View It!**

Professional Development Podcast:

Teaching Argument

For additional practice:

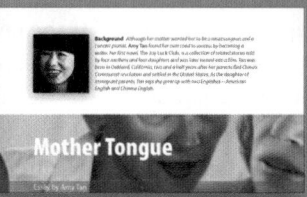

Close Reader selection
"Mother Tongue"
Essay by Amy Tan

Key Learning Objective: The student will be able to trace and evaluate an argument.

COMMON CORE Common Core Standards

RI 1 Cite textual evidence.
RI 2 Determine central ideas of a text and analyze.
RI 3 Analyze a set of ideas or sequence of events.
RI 4 Determine the meaning of words and phrases; analyze how author uses and refines meaning.
RI 5 Analyze the effectiveness of the structure an author uses.
RI 6 Determine author's point of view or purpose.
W 2b Develop the topic by selecting significant and relevant information and examples.
L 2 Demonstrate command of the conventions of standard English.
L 3a Vary syntax for effect.
L 5b Analyze nuances in words with similar denotations.

▲ Text Complexity Rubric

Quantitative Measures	**"Blaxicans" and Other Reinvented Americans** Lexile: 1040L

Levels of Meaning/Purpose

multiple purposes; implied, subtle, and difficult to determine

Structure

less conventional

Qualitative Measures

Language Conventionality and Clarity

some unfamiliar language

Knowledge Demands

somewhat complex historical concepts

Reader/Task Considerations Teacher determined
Vary by individual reader and type of text

TEACH

CLOSE READ

Richard Rodrgriguez Tell students that Rodriguez is known for opposing bilingual education and affirmative action programs. He believes that by equating race with disadvantage, affirmative action too often helps those who have already entered the middle class and leaves out those who are truly disadvantaged.

AS YOU READ Direct students to use the As You Read instructions to focus their reading. Remind students to write down any questions during reading.

Analyze and Evaluate Structure: Argument (LINES 1–9)

COMMON CORE RI 5

Explain to students that in writing an **argument,** effective writers first introduce **claims,** or positions on the issue. Then they use facts, statistics, and reasons to persuade readers that the claims are valid. Writers sometimes state their claim directly or indirectly.

Ⓐ CITE TEXT EVIDENCE Have students read the first paragraph of "Blaxicans" and infer Rodriguez's claim. *(Americans feel threatened by immigrants because they make us question our identity.)*

Determine Author's Purpose: Irony [LINES 1–3]

COMMON CORE RI 6

Tell students that Rodriguez relies heavily upon **verbal irony**—saying one thing while meaning another—in developing his argument about immigrants. Ironic statements often attempt to discredit a position or point of view by exaggerating it.

Ⓑ CITE TEXT EVIDENCE Have students read the second sentence in line 3 and explain what Rodriguez really means. *(Rodriguez really means that immigrants intend to strengthen America.)*

CRITICAL VOCABULARY

culled: Rodriguez describes how Americans generally regard themselves as "Protestants, culled from Western Europe."

ASK STUDENTS from what cultures and nations their own families are culled.

Richard Rodriguez *is the son of Mexican immigrants and was born in San Francisco in 1944. When he started school, his teachers asked his parents to speak more English at home, and Ricardo became Richard. He planned on an academic career but never completed his Ph.D. dissertation, deciding to write as a journalist and essayist. In the first volume of his autobiography* Hunger of Memory *(1982), Rodriguez describes his assimilation into the majority culture. This 2003 essay followed publication of another volume of memoir,* Brown: The Last Discovery of America, *which explores the issue of race.*

"Blaxicans"
and Other Reinvented Americans

Argument by Richard Rodriguez

AS YOU READ Look for clues that reveal Rodriguez's attitudes toward race and ethnicity as they relate to personal identity.

Ⓐ There is something unsettling about immigrants because…well, because they chatter incomprehensibly, and they get in everyone's way. Immigrants seem to be bent on undoing America. Just when Americans think we know who we are—we are Protestants, **culled** from Western Europe, are we not?—then new immigrants appear from Southern Europe or from Eastern Europe. We—we who are already here—we don't know exactly what the latest comers will mean to our community. How will they fit in with us? Thus we—we who were here first—we begin to question our own identity.

10   After a generation or two, the grandchildren or the great-grandchildren of immigrants to the United States and the grandchildren of those who tried to keep immigrants out of the United States will romanticize the immigrant, will begin to see the immigrant as the figure who teaches us most about what it means to be an American. The immigrant, in mythic terms, travels from the outermost rind of America to the very center of American mythology. None of this, of course, can we admit to the Vietnamese immigrant who served us our breakfast at the hotel this morning. In another 40 years, we will be prepared to say to the Vietnamese immigrant that he,

Ⓑ **cull**
(kŭl) *v.* to take from a large quantity.

"Blaxicans" and Other Reinvented Americans **87**

SCAFFOLDING FOR ELL STUDENTS

Verbal Irony Verbal irony can be especially tricky for ELL students to decipher because they may not pick up on the writer's tone. Tell students that to identify and understand irony, they may have to read ahead to discover what the writer really thinks and then look for statements that say something different.

ASK STUDENTS to read ahead through line 23. After they finish the reading, ask students to summarize Rodriguez's real meaning. Then have small groups discuss how the literal meaning of the essay's first two sentences differs from Rodriguez's real meaning.

Analyze and Evaluate Structure: Argument

 **COMMON CORE RI 5**

(LINES 46–54)

Emphasize that an effective argument must provide support for the claims it makes. Supporting details might be facts, statistics, expert opinions, examples, or **anecdotes**--brief stories that illustrate a point.

C **CITE TEXT EVIDENCE** Have students read lines 46–54 and identify Rodriguez's claim. Ask what support Rodriguez gives for this claim. *(The claim: Mexicans are a cosmic race. As early as the 18th century most Mexicans were of mixed race. There has been more intermarriage between Indian and African people in Mexico than anywhere else. He supports the claim by stating that Mexicans were called a "cosmic race" because this diversity was considered a strength.)*

Determine Author's Purpose: Irony

 **COMMON CORE RI 6**

(LINES 55–62)

Explain that irony can be conveyed through the writer's **tone**, or attitude toward his topic. When a writer is being ironic, the literal meaning of the words and the tone used by the writer will be at odds.

D **CITE TEXT EVIDENCE** Ask students what words and phrases Rodriguez uses to express tone in lines 55–62. *(Americans speak more easily of "diversity" than we do about the fact that I might marry your daughter; preserves our preference for thinking ourselves separate—our elbows need not touch, thank you)*

CRITICAL VOCABULARY

factors: Rodriguez describes the "collision of centuries" that made him the brown person he is.

ASK STUDENTS what factors gave Rodriguez his brown skin. *(the mixture of Spanish and Native American ancestry)*

predominant: Rodriguez explains how Mexicans used to say that Mexico "joined two worlds."

ASK STUDENTS to identify the three predominant races that were joined to create Mexicans. *(Mexicans are made up predominantly of people with Spanish, Native American, and African ancestry.)*

---

20 with his breakfast tray, with his intuition for travel, with his memory of tragedy, with his recognition of peerless freedoms, he fulfills the meaning of America.

In 1997, Gallup conducted a survey on race relations in America, but the poll was concerned only with white and black Americans. No question was put to the aforementioned Vietnamese man. There was certainly no question for the Chinese grocer, none for the Guatemalan barber, none for the tribe of Mexican Indians who reroofed your neighbor's house.

30 The American conversation about race has always been a black-and-white conversation, but the conversation has become as bloodless as badminton.

I have listened to the black-and-white conversation for most of my life. I was supposed to attach myself to one side or the other, without asking the obvious questions: What is this perpetual dialectic[1] between Europe and Africa? Why does it admit so little reference to anyone else?

I am speaking to you in American English that was taught me by Irish nuns—immigrant women. I wear an Indian face; I answer to a Spanish surname as well as this California first name, Richard. You
40 might wonder about the complexity of historical **factors**, the collision of centuries, that creates Richard Rodriguez. My brownness is the illustration of that collision, or the bland memorial of it. I stand before you as an Impure-American, an Ambiguous-American.

factor
(făk´tər) *n.*
component or
characteristic.

In the 19th century, Texans used to say that the reason Mexicans were so easily defeated in battle was because we were so dilute, being neither pure Indian nor pure Spaniard. Yet, at the same time, Mexicans used to say that Mexico, the country of my ancestry, joined two worlds, two competing armies. José Vasconcelos, the Mexican educator and philosopher, famously described Mexicans as *la raza*
50 *cósmica*, the cosmic race. In Mexico what one finds as early as the 18th century is a **predominant** population of mixed-race people. Also, once the slave had been freed in Mexico, the incidence[2] of marriage between Indian and African people there was greater than in any other country in the Americas and has not been equaled since.

predominant
(prĭ-dŏm´ə-nənt) *adj.*
most important or
prevalent.

Race mixture has not been a point of pride in America. Americans speak more easily about "diversity" than we do about the fact that I might marry your daughter; you might become we; we might become us. America has so readily adopted the Canadian notion of multiculturalism because it preserves our preference for thinking
60 ourselves separate—our elbows need not touch, thank you. I would prefer that table. I can remain Mexican, whatever that means, in the United States of America.

---

[1] **dialectic**: exchange of opinions and ideas.
[2] **incidence**: occurrence.

APPLYING ACADEMIC VOCABULARY

device	dynamic

As you discuss "Blaxicans," incorporate the following Collection 1 academic vocabulary words: *device* and *dynamic*. As you discuss Rodriguez's anecdotes, point out that these are effective **devices** for explaining and reinforcing his claims. When you discuss Rodriguez's statement that Americans are resistant to the idea of racial mixing, point out that the ethnic composition of our nation is **dynamic**, or in a constant state of change.

> **" Because of colonial Mexico, I am mestizo. But I was reinvented by President Richard Nixon."**

I would propose that instead of adopting the Canadian model of multiculturalism, America might begin to imagine the Mexican alternative—that of a mestizaje society.

E Because of colonial Mexico, I am mestizo. But I was reinvented by President Richard Nixon. In the early 1970s, Nixon instructed the Office of Management and Budget to identify the major racial and ethnic groups in the United States. OMB came up with five major
70 ethnic or racial groups. The groups are white, black, Asian/Pacific Islander, American Indian/Eskimo, and Hispanic.

F It's what I learned to do when I was in college: to call myself a Hispanic. At my university we even had separate cafeteria tables and "theme houses," where the children of Nixon could gather—of a feather. Native Americans united. African Americans. Casa Hispanic.

The interesting thing about Hispanics is that you will never meet us in Latin America. You may meet Chileans and Peruvians and Mexicans. You will not meet Hispanics. If you inquire in Lima or Bogotá about Hispanics, you will be referred to Dallas. For "Hispanic"
80 is a gringo contrivance,[3] a definition of the world according to European patterns of colonization. Such a definition suggests I have more in common with Argentine Italians than with American Indians; that there is an ineffable[4] union between the white Cuban and the mulatto Puerto Rican because of Spain. Nixon's conclusion has become the basis for the way we now organize and understand American society.

The Census Bureau foretold that by the year 2003, Hispanics would outnumber blacks to become the largest minority in the United States. And, indeed, the year 2003 has arrived and the proclamation of
90 Hispanic **ascendancy** has been published far and wide. While I admit a competition has existed—does exist—in America between Hispanics and black people, I insist that the comparison of Hispanics with blacks will lead, ultimately, to complete nonsense. For there is no such thing as a Hispanic race. In Latin America, one sees every race of the world. One sees white Hispanics, one sees black Hispanics, one sees brown Hispanics who are Indians, many of whom do not speak Spanish

ascendancy
(ə-sĕn´dən-sē) *n.*
a rise in power or influence.

---
[3] **contrivance:** something created to serve a purpose.
[4] **ineffable:** obscure, unknowable.

"Blaxicans" and Other Reinvented Americans **89**

WHEN STUDENTS STRUGGLE . . .

Direct students to reread the first paragraph (page 89, lines 63–65). Draw their attention to the phrase *mestizaje society*. Explain to students that they must use context to determine what Rodriguez means by this phrase.

ASK STUDENTS to find a context clue within the paragraph. *(the Mexican alternative)* Then ask them to find a previous paragraph that gives more information about Mexican society *(page 88, lines 44–54)*. Finally, ask students what Rodriguez means when he says that Americans might become a *mestizaje* society. *(America might become a country in which being of mixed races is considered normal.)*

CLOSE READ

Determine Author's Purpose: Irony (LINES 66–71)
COMMON CORE RI 6

Remind students that in using irony, writers often state an idea or opinion in such a way that they discredit it by exaggerating it or carrying it to its logical conclusion. Here, Rodriguez's target is President Nixon's racial classifications.

E **CITE TEXT EVIDENCE** Have students explain how Rodriguez's statement that he was "reinvented by President Richard Nixon" is an exaggeration." *(Nixon oversaw the creation of racial categories that lumped all people with origins in the Spanish-speaking world together. To say that he reinvented a person when he really only helped reinvent a category that applies to that person is an exaggeration.)*

Analyze and Evaluate Structure: Argument
COMMON CORE RI 5
(LINES 72–75)

Point out that paragraph three is an anecdote, or brief story about an event or situation. Anecdotes are used in arguments to illustrate or explain ideas by illustrating their effect on individuals. Anecdotes are effective because it is easier for readers to identify with specific individuals in specific situations than with large groups.

F **CITE TEXT EVIDENCE** Have students explain how this anecdote helps clarify the idea Rodriguez was discussing in the two previous paragraphs. *(It provides an example of how Rodriguez's identity was changed by Nixon's racial classifications and illustrates how these classifications divided the student body.)*

CRITICAL VOCABULARY

ascendancy: Rodriguez points out that in 2003 Hispanics became the largest minority in the United States.

ASK STUDENTS to discuss whether they think the ascendancy of Hispanics is important and why.

Analyze and Evaluate Structure: Argument

 COMMON CORE RI 5

(LINES 113–137)

Explain to students that arguments are most effective when they use a variety of types of support for their claims. For instance, an argument supported only by anecdotes might not be convincing because it would not prove that the claim is valid in more than a few specific situations. Likewise, a claim that is only supported by statistics, or numerical facts, might not help the reader understand the issue's effect on real people.

G CITE TEXT EVIDENCE Invite students to read the last two paragraphs on the page and cite an example of two facts and an anecdote. *(facts: the Latin American immigrant population is younger; the Latin American immigrant population is more fertile [lines 116–119]; anecdote: the story about the church in Palo Alto [lines 125–137]).* Then ask students how the facts and the anecdote are related. *(The facts give statistical information about Latin American immigrants, while the anecdote shows specific immigrants being welcomed in their new community. The anecdote personalizes the facts.)*

CRITICAL VOCABULARY

denoting: Rodriguez says that *Hispanic* is an ethnic term used for "denoting culture."

ASK STUDENTS why Rodriguez feels these characteristics do not really represent his identity. *(It is a term that was contrived to broadly categorize a group of people not by blood or color, but by cultural elements such as language, cuisine, or literature.)*

because they resist Spain. One sees Asian-Hispanics. To compare blacks and Hispanics, therefore, is to construct a fallacious[5] equation.

100   Some Hispanics have accepted the fiction. Some Hispanics have too easily accustomed themselves to impersonating a third race, a great new third race in America. But Hispanic is an ethnic term. It is a term **denoting** culture. So when the Census Bureau says by the year 2060 one-third of all Americans will identify themselves as Hispanic, the Census Bureau is not speculating in pigment or quantifying according to actual historical narratives, but rather is predicting how by the year 2060 one-third of all Americans will identify themselves culturally. For a country that traditionally has taken its understandings of community from blood and color, the new circumstance of so large a group
110   of Americans identifying themselves by virtue of language or fashion or cuisine or literature is an extraordinary change, and a revolutionary one.

denote
(dĭ-nōt′) *v.* to name or give meaning to.

   People ask me all the time if I envision another Quebec[6] forming in the United States because of the large immigrant movement from the south. Do I see a Quebec forming in the Southwest, for example? No, I don't see that at all. But I do notice the Latin American immigrant population is as much as 10 years younger than the U.S. national population. I notice the Latin American immigrant population is more fertile than the U.S. national population. I see the
120   movement of the immigrants from south to north as a movement of youth—like approaching spring!—into a country that is growing middle-aged. I notice immigrants are the archetypal[7] Americans at a time when we—U.S. citizens—have become post-Americans, most concerned with subsidized medications.

   I was at a small Apostolic Assembly in East Palo Alto a few years ago—a mainly Spanish-speaking congregation in an area along the freeway, near the heart of the Silicon Valley. This area used to be black East Palo Alto, but it is quickly becoming an Asian and Hispanic Palo Alto neighborhood. There was a moment in the service when
130   newcomers to the congregation were introduced. Newcomers brought letters of introduction from sister evangelical churches in Latin America. The minister read out the various letters and pronounced the names and places of origin to the community. The congregation applauded. And I thought to myself: It's over. The border is over. These people were not being asked whether they had green cards. They were not being asked whether they arrived here legally or illegally. They were being welcomed within a new community for reasons of culture.

---

[5] **fallacious:** untrue; based on faulty reasoning.

[6] **envision another Quebec:** foresee a situation like that in Quebec, a French-speaking province that has sought independence from Canada.

[7] **archetypal:** being a perfect or ideal example.

SCAFFOLDING FOR ELL STUDENTS

Recognizing Word Roots Tell students that most long words are made up of prefixes and suffixes added to a root word. By determining the meaning of the root word, it is often possible to guess at the meaning of the word of which it is a part.

ASK STUDENTS to identify the root word in *construct* (line 98) and *envision* (line 113), think of another word that shares the root, and guess the meaning of the word in the selection. They may consult a dictionary. Encourage students to make a chart for future reference. For further practice, direct students to Word Structure: Latin Roots in the WordSharp: Interactive Vocabulary Tutor.

There is now a north-south line that is theological, a line that cannot be **circumvented** by the U.S. Border Patrol.

140   I was on a British Broadcasting Corporation interview show, and a woman introduced me as being "in favor" of assimilation. I am not in favor of assimilation any more than I am in favor of the Pacific Ocean or clement weather. If I had a bumper sticker on the subject, it might read something like ASSIMILATION HAPPENS. One doesn't get up in the morning, as an immigrant child in America, and think to oneself, "How much of an American shall I become today?" One doesn't walk down the street and decide to be 40 percent Mexican and 60 percent American. Culture is fluid. Culture is smoke. You breathe it. You eat it. You can't help hearing it—Elvis Presley goes in your ear,
150   and you cannot get Elvis Presley out of your mind.

        I am in favor of assimilation. I am not in favor of assimilation. I recognize assimilation. A few years ago, I was in Merced, Calif.—a town of about 75,000 people in the Central Valley where the two largest immigrant groups at that time (California is so fluid, I believe this is no longer the case) were Laotian Hmong and Mexicans. Laotians have never in the history of the world, as far as I know, lived next to Mexicans. But there they were in Merced, and living next to Mexicans. They don't like each other. I was talking to the Laotian kids about why they don't like the Mexican kids. They were telling me that
160   the Mexicans do this and the Mexicans don't do that, when I suddenly realized that they were speaking English with a Spanish accent.

        On his interview show, Bill Moyers once asked me how I thought of myself. As an American? Or Hispanic? I answered that I am Chinese, and that is because I live in a Chinese city and because I want to be Chinese. Well, why not? Some Chinese American people in the Richmond and Sunset districts of San Francisco sometimes paint their houses (so many qualifiers!) in colors I would once have described as garish: lime greens, rose reds, pumpkin. But I have lived in a Chinese city for so long that my eye has taken on that palette,[8] has come to
170   prefer lime greens and rose reds and all the inventions of this Chinese Mediterranean. I see photographs in magazines or documentary footage of China, especially rural China, and I see what I recognize as home. Isn't that odd?

        I do think distinctions exist. I'm not talking about an America tomorrow in which we're going to find that black and white are no longer the distinguishing marks of separateness. But many young people I meet tell me they feel like Victorians[9] when they identify themselves as black or white. They don't think of themselves in those terms. And they're already moving into a world in which tattoo or

---

[8] **palette:** range of colors used to depict a scene.
[9] **Victorians:** people with the outdated opinions and values popular in 19th-century England.

"Blaxicans" and Other Reinvented Americans   **91**

circumvent
(sûr´kəm-vĕnt´) *v.* to bypass or go around.

Word from selection	Root	Another word with the root	Meaning of selection word
speculating	specula	speculation	talking about the future
quantifying	quant	quantity	measuring numerically
predicting	dict	dictate	telling in advance
immigrant	migra	migrate	a person who moves to another country to live

CLOSE READ

Analyze and Evaluate Structure: Argument

COMMON CORE RI 5

(LINES 140–150)

Remind students that writers often use examples to support their claims so the reader can picture or understand it. Sometimes writers give negative examples of something that doesn't work or happen.

H CITE TEXT EVIDENCE Have students analyze the examples Rodriguez uses in this paragraph. Ask them to explain what the examples illustrate and how they support his argument. *(The examples illustrate what would happen if assimilation were a conscious choice. Because the examples represent an inaccurate, even humorous view of how assimilation does not actually take place, they support the claim that assimilation is an unavoidable and unconscious process.)*

Determine Author's Purpose: Irony (LINES 162–173)

COMMON CORE RI 6

Explain to students that irony conveys meaning not through the literal meaning of the words, but through the writer's purpose in using them.

I ASK STUDENTS to explain why Rodriguez's statement that he is Chinese is ironic. Then ask them to tell what meaning Rodriguez is trying to convey with his claim. *(The statement is ironic because we know that Rodriguez does not have any Chinese heritage. He is trying to convey that his culture has become Chinese through assimilation with the people he lives among.)*

CRITICAL VOCABULARY

circumvent: Rodriguez states that there is a theological line that "cannot be circumvented by the U.S. Border Patrol." (lines 138–139)

ASK STUDENTS to explain why Rodriguez believes the Border Patrol cannot circumvent this theological line. *(Rodriguez is saying the U.S. Border Patrol has no power to impact the church's ability to accept a wide range of people because they share the same culture.)*

Analyze and Evaluate Structure: Argument (LINES 183–189)

COMMON CORE **RI 5**

Point out to students that Rodriguez finally reveals the meaning of the title for his essay in this paragraph. Discuss with students what the girl meant in describing herself as a "Blaxican."

 **ASK STUDENTS** how this anecdote supports and explains Rodriguez's central claim in this essay. *(The anecdote suggests that this girl represents what Rodriguez considers the new American culture, one in which people's racial and ethnic ancestry is so mixed that to call them Hispanic or white or Mexican or black no longer makes sense.)*

Determine Author's Purpose: Irony (LINES 209–216)

COMMON CORE **RI 6**

Remind students that earlier in the essay, Rodriguez makes the ironic statement that he is Chinese. Point out that Rodriguez repeats this claim in the last paragraph.

 CITE TEXT EVIDENCE Ask students to explain whether or not the last sentence of the essay is intended to be ironic. Tell them to support their explanation with evidence from the text. *(The essay's last sentence is not intended to be ironic because in his essay Rodriguez has redefined what it means to belong to a particular ethnic group. In line 211, Rodriguez calls the categories of race mythologies, and in lines 213–214 he says that he is a man of many cultures. He is saying that culture, not race, is what gives people their identity, and in this sense Rodriguez really is Chinese.)*

COLLABORATIVE DISCUSSION Working in pairs, have students discuss their response to the question. Ask them to make a list of the facts, examples, and anecdotes that support their response. Then have students wrap up their discussion by writing a brief summary of their main ideas. Invite pairs to share their ideas in class discussion.

ASK STUDENTS to share any questions they generated in the course of reading and discussing the selection.

---

180 ornament or movement or commune[10] or sexuality or drug or rave or electronic bombast[11] are the organizing principles of their identity. The notion that they are white or black simply doesn't occur.

And increasingly, of course, one meets children who really don't know how to say what they are. They simply are too many things. I met a young girl in San Diego at a convention of mixed-race children, among whom the common habit is to define one parent over the other—black over white, for example. But this girl said that her mother was Mexican and her father was African. The girl said "Blaxican." By reinventing language, she is reinventing America.

190 America does not have a vocabulary like the vocabulary the Spanish empire evolved to describe the multiplicity of racial possibilities in the New World. The conversation, the interior monologue of America cannot rely on the old vocabulary—black, white. We are no longer a black-white nation.

So, what myth do we tell ourselves? The person who got closest to it was Karl Marx.[12] Marx predicted that the discovery of gold in California would be a more central event to the Americas than the discovery of the Americas by Columbus—which was only the meeting of two tribes, essentially, the European and the Indian. But when gold 200 was discovered in California in the 1840s, the entire world met. For the first time in human history, all of the known world gathered. The Malaysian stood in the gold fields alongside the African, alongside the Chinese, alongside the Australian, alongside the Yankee.

That was an event without parallel in world history and the beginning of modern California—why California today provides the mythological structure for understanding how we might talk about the American experience: not as biracial, but as the re-creation of the known world in the New World.

Sometimes truly revolutionary things happen without regard. 210 I mean, we may wake up one morning and there is no black race. There is no white race either. There are mythologies, and—as I am in the business, insofar as I am in any business at all, of demythologizing[13] such identities as black and white—I come to you as a man of many cultures. I come to you as Chinese. Unless you understand that I am Chinese, then you have not understood anything I have said.

---

[10] **commune:** group of unrelated people living together and sharing wealth and responsibilities.

[11] **bombast:** an arrogant, self-important form of expression.

[12] **Karl Marx:** German political philosopher, author of *The Communist Manifesto* and *Das Kapital*.

[13] **demythologizing:** replacing myth or legend with fact.

COLLABORATIVE DISCUSSION How does Rodriguez feel about using race or ethnicity as the main way to determine identity? Discuss this question with a partner, citing specific textual evidence from the essay to support your ideas.

APPLYING ACADEMIC VOCABULARY

adapt	displace

While discussing Rodriguez's essay, use the following Collection 1 academic vocabulary words: *adapt* and *displace*. Point out, for example, that as people from all over the world met in the California gold fields, they had to **adapt** to their new surroundings in order to survive. Ask students to explain how immigrants who have been **displaced** must find ways of fitting into their new society.

Analyze and Evaluate Structure: Arguments

The structure of an **argument** refers to both its organization and the methods by which authors support their **claims,** or positions on an issue. They may choose to persuade their readers by presenting facts, statistics, or expert views. Or, they might illustrate their points with examples and **anecdotes,** brief stories focusing on one episode or event in a person's life. In "'Blaxicans' and Other Reinvented Americans," Rodriguez tells several anecdotes. These stories support important points; they also engage readers by giving them glimpses into Rodriguez's personal experiences.

For example, Rodriguez tells about visiting a community in which Laotians and Mexicans lived unhappily side by side. The Laotians spent the whole time complaining bitterly to him about their Mexican neighbors. But, as he listened to them, Rodriguez noticed that they spoke in a Spanish accent. He includes this anecdote to offer convincing support for his assertion that assimilation, or cultural adaptation, happens regardless of whether we want it to or not.

Determine Author's Purpose: Irony

A predominant element of Rodriguez's style is **verbal irony.** Although he seems to be stating one idea, he is directing readers to take the opposite meaning from it. This irony is brought out through his choice of words and the context in which they are used as well as the details he includes. His irony affects several elements of his writing.

Tone	Meaning	Purpose
Irony conveys his attitude, or **tone,** toward his topic. For example, he writes in the first paragraph, "Immigrants seem to be bent on undoing America." His irony in this statement brings out the view of many "old" Americans while at the same time conveying his positive feeling that immigrants are, in fact, the "doing" of America.	Irony conveys **meaning.** For example, Rodriguez sees a divide between the official perception of racial identity in America and its reality. In the third paragraph, he reinforces this idea by listing the Americans left out of the 1997 racial survey: "There was certainly no question for the Chinese grocer, none for the Guatemalan barber. . . ."	Irony helps him achieve his **purpose** of persuading readers to agree with him. His ironic words and phrases, such as the statement "I was reinvented by President Richard Nixon," stand out in readers' minds, increasing the effectiveness of his **rhetoric.**

TEACH

Analyze and Evaluate Structure: Arguments

Emphasize that an argument may be organized around a single, main idea, but the author may make numerous claims to argue for and explain that idea. Ask students to summarize the essay's main argument. *(While America is made up of people from many different races, ethnicities, and cultures, they are all being mixed together into one American people.)*

Divide the selection into sections and assign sections to pairs of students. Ask pairs to examine and identify the claims Rodriguez makes and the kinds of support he provides for each claim. Ask pairs to share their findings in class discussion.

Determine Author's Purpose: Irony

Ensure students understand what verbal irony is. As an example, direct students to the second paragraph on page 89 and read aloud the sentence, "I was reinvented by President Richard Nixon." Invite students to explain the literal meaning of the statement and what Rodriguez wants his readers to understand. *(Nixon created a racial/ethnic group—Hispanics—and declared that people like Rodriguez belonged to that group regardless of what group they had previously thought they were part of.)*

ASK STUDENTS to find another example of irony in the selection and explain how it contributes to the tone, meaning, and purpose of the essay.

Strategies for Annotation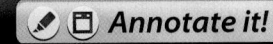

Analyze and Evaluate Structure: Arguments

Have students use their eBook annotation tools to analyze the text. Ask them to do the following:

- Highlight in yellow the claim that Rodriguez makes.
- Highlight in blue the details Rodriguez uses to persuade readers that his claim is accurate.

> . . . I insist that the comparison of Hispanics with blacks will lead, ultimately, to complete nonsense. For there is no such thing as a Hispanic race. In Latin America, one sees every race of the world. One sees white Hispanics, one sees black Hispanics, one sees brown Hispanics who are Indians . . . One sees Asian-Hispanics.

PRACTICE & APPLY

Analyzing the Text COMMON CORE RI 1, RI 2, RI 4, RI 5, RI 6, W 2b

Possible answers:

1. *Rodriguez wants to establish the point that the American population is composed of people of many different racial and ethnic backgrounds, yet Americans tend to see our society as mainly black and white. His use of irony challenges the reader to react to his comments.*

2. *He means that the conversation about the division between African Americans and whites is not relevant because the American population isn't just black and white.*

3. *Rodriguez is explaining that he is not just Hispanic or Mexican or Indian but a complicated mixture of all of them and more. This information helps the reader understand that Rodriguez knows firsthand about this topic.*

4. *These phrases are important because they illustrate his point that Nixon's terms have reinvented people's perceptions of themselves. Rodriguez's use of these particular terms creates a sarcastic tone that implies his disagreement with the idea of these artificial tags.*

5. *He says there is no such thing as a Hispanic race and that there are white Hispanics, brown Hispanics, Asian Hispanics, Indian and also black Hispanics.*

6. *Latin American immigrants are 10 years younger and more fertile. They will help sustain America's energy.*

7. *Rodriguez uses the anecdotes to illustrate and reinforce his contention that Americans live close together and assimilate, so they are one culture created by the combining of many cultures. The anecdote about the Hmong and Mexicans illustrates how people of different cultures may think they are very different while exhibiting many of the same qualities. The anecdote about living in a Chinese district shows how he has assimilated with those around him. The anecdote about the girl who called herself "Blaxican" illustrates how Americans are mixtures of many ethnicities.*

8. *It means that it makes as much sense for him to claim to be Chinese as it does to say he is Hispanic. It reinforces his argument that culture makes us who we are: Americans.*

Analyzing the Text COMMON CORE RI 1, RI 2, RI 4, RI 5, RI 6, W 2b

Cite Text Evidence Support your responses with evidence from the selection.

1. **Analyze** What is the author's purpose in the first three paragraphs? How does his use of irony help him accomplish this purpose?

2. **Interpret** What does the author mean when he says that the American conversation about race has "become as bloodless as badminton"?

3. **Analyze** Why does Rodriguez call himself "an Impure-American, an Ambiguous-American"? How does the information about his background affect the persuasiveness of his argument?

4. **Analyze** In Rodriguez's discussion of President Nixon, he uses words and phrases such as "learned . . . to call myself a Hispanic," "theme houses," "where the children of Nixon could gather—of a feather," and "gringo contrivance." Why are these word choices significant? How do they affect his tone?

5. **Cite Evidence** How does the author support his point that comparing blacks and Hispanics is "to construct a fallacious equation"?

6. **Draw Conclusions** What are the differences that Rodriguez points out between immigrants and U.S. citizens in lines 113–124? Why is this contrast important to include?

7. **Evaluate** Why does the author include several anecdotes toward the end of his argument? How does each story help him achieve a specific goal?

8. **Analyze** Rodriguez concludes his argument with the statement, "I come to you as Chinese. Unless you understand that I am Chinese, then you have not understood anything I have said." What does this striking statement mean? How does it relate to his central claim?

PERFORMANCE TASK

Writing Activity: Evaluation Do you find Rodriguez's argument convincing? Write a two-paragraph evaluation of his essay:

- In your first paragraph, identify the claim and analyze the author's support of it, offering specific examples from the text to identify areas where you find the argument compelling or uncompelling.

- In the second paragraph, evaluate the effectiveness of his rhetoric, examining aspects such as his use of irony.

Assign this performance task.

PERFORMANCE TASK COMMON CORE W 2b

Writing Activity: Evaluation Have students work in pairs or small groups to discuss whether they find Rodriguez's argument convincing. Tell them to explain why or why not and encourage them to take notes about their reasons. Have students work individually to write their evaluations.

Critical Vocabulary

cull	predominant	denote
factor	ascendency	circumvent

Practice and Apply Complete each of the following sentence stems in a way that reflects the meaning of the Critical Vocabulary word.

1. The decision whether to launch the jet was influenced by many **factors,** such as . . .

2. Her strong backhand gave her the **ascendency** over her opponent in the tennis match because . . .

3. **Denoting** racial backgrounds by inventing new words is becoming necessary because . . .

4. They **circumvented** possible objections to their argument by . . .

5. In our state congress, the Republicans are the **predominant** party because . . .

6. The animal was **culled** from the herd and placed in a separate area because . . .

Vocabulary Strategy: The Latin Prefix *circum-*

The Critical Vocabulary word *circumvented* contains the Latin prefix *circum-*, which means "around, about." Many words in English are formed with this prefix. To understand the meanings of these words, use your knowledge of the prefix as well as the context in which the word appears.

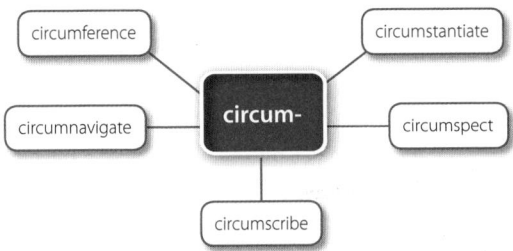

Practice and Apply Answer each of these questions in a complete sentence that uses a word from the word web. Use your knowledge of the prefix *circum-* as well as the meanings of any roots that you recognize. Consult a dictionary if necessary.

1. How could a teacher indicate which of the exercises on a page to do?

2. How should a public figure avoid being involved in scandal?

3. How would a seamstress know how big to make the waist of a dress for a client?

4. How could a driver adapt if warned of a road block ahead?

5. What kind of witness testimony would be key for someone accused of a crime?

PRACTICE & APPLY

Critical Vocabulary

Possible answers:

1. *. . . the weather, the pilot's health, and the state of the engine repair.*

2. *. . . she had more power and control.*

3. *. . . more people have ancestors of many different races.*

4. *. . . making jokes and trying to change the subject.*

5. *. . . they won an overwhelming majority in the last elections.*

6. *. . . it was sick.*

Vocabulary Strategy: The Latin Prefix *circum-*

Answers:

1. *A teacher could circumscribe exactly which exercises on the page to be completed by drawing a box around them.*

2. *A politician should be circumspect, or prudent, in every area of his life in order to avoid scandal.*

3. *A seamstress would wrap a measuring tape around her client's waist in order to get an accurate measure of the waist's circumference before making a dress.*

4. *A driver could circumnavigate around a road block by using a different route if he is warned of it ahead of time.*

5. *A witness who could circumstantiate, or support, the accused's alibi would provide valuable testimony.*

Strategies for Annotation    Annotate it!

The Latin Prefix *circum-*

Have students locate two words in the essay that include the prefix *circum-*. Ask them to use their eBook annotation tools to do the following:

- Highlight the prefix in yellow.
- Add a note to the word giving its definition.

For a country that traditionally has taken its understandings of community from blood and color, the new circumstance of so large a group of Americans identifying themselves by virtue of language or fashion or cuisine or literature is an extraordinary change, and a revolutionary one.

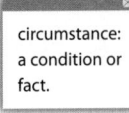

circumstance: a condition or fact.

Language and Style: Using Colons Effectively

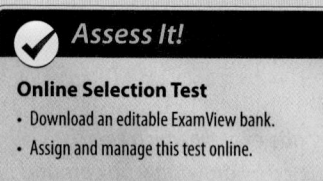 **COMMON CORE** L 2, L 3a

Direct students to skim Rodriguez's essay to find two sentences that use colons. Have volunteers write the sentences on the board. Then, as a class, discuss which purpose the colons in each of these sentences serves. Then ask students to write three additional sentences showing the use of the colon for each of the three different purposes.

Answers: *Students' revised evaluations should include at least two sentences that use colons.*

✓ *Assess It!*

Online Selection Test
- Download an editable ExamView bank.
- Assign and manage this test online.

Language and Style: Using Colons Effectively

 **COMMON CORE** L 2, L 3a

The **colon** is a useful mark of punctuation, having numerous functions related to both form and meaning. Many writers, including Richard Rodriguez, choose to insert colons in their sentences to make their writing clearer and more effective.

Read this sentence from "'Blaxicans' and Other Reinvented Americans":

It's what I learned to do when I was in college: to call myself a Hispanic.

In this sentence, the colon signals readers to pause before reading the phrase. As a result, the phrase stands out and catches readers' attention.

Rather than a colon, the author might have chosen to insert a comma into this sentence:

It's what I learned to do when I was in college, to call myself a Hispanic.

Both are grammatically correct. Although the same words are presented in the same order as in the original version, the comma creates less of a division between the two parts of the sentence. The phrase becomes part of the sentence; readers might not consider it separately or stop to think about its meaning in the same way.

This chart explains the various uses of the colon.

Uses of Colons	
Purpose	**Example**
To join two independent clauses closely related in meaning	*The bride felt cheated: there were no smiling faces watching her entrance and no happy hands applauding her new status.*
To introduce a series or list of ideas or examples that add to the previous statement or illustrate it	*The modern student must master several skills: analysis of text, oral communication of thoughts, written expression of ideas.*
To introduce a quotation that supports or contributes to the previous statement	*As he anticipated the ordeal ahead, a single thought looped through his mind: "Life shrinks or expands in proportion to one's courage."*

Practice and Apply Look back at the evaluation you wrote in response to this selection's Performance Task. Revise your writing to include at least two sentences that use colons. Share your original sentences and your revisions with a partner. Discuss how the insertion of a colon affects your meaning and tone.

Analyze Nuances in the Meaning of Words

COMMON CORE

L 5b

TEACH

Effective writers are usually experts in verbal nuance–making subtle shifts or distinctions in the meaning of a word or phrase to establish a particular tone to convey a message. Tone is the attitude an author takes toward a subject. Have students reread these two passages from the essay in which Richard Rodriguez uses the same term ("black and white") in two subtly distinct ways.

In 1997, Gallup conducted a survey on race relations in America, but the poll was concerned only with white and black Americans. (lines 23–24)

The American conversation about race has always been a black-and-white conversation… (lines 29–30).

In the first sentence, Rodriguez notes that the conversation about race in America has been limited to those identified as white people or black people. In the second sentence, he goes on to say it is a "black-and-white conversation." By shifting the meaning of the phrase "black and white," Rodriguez's establishes a more argumentative tone to make an important point—the conversation is limited because it includes only blacks and whites, but also because is too simplistic.

PRACTICE AND APPLY

Display lines 66–67 and lines 187–189 on the board or device. Ask volunteers to identify the word that the passages have in common (reinvent). Ask a volunteer to define the word "reinvent" (to create something anew).

Break students into pairs or small groups. Ask students to establish what "reinvent" means in each passage, and the tone Rodriguez conveys using the word.

Passage	Meaning of Reinvent	Tone
66–67	Nixon redefines and oversimplifies the complex identity of Rodriguez and others.	sarcastic
187–189	The girl establishes her identity by coining her own term to describe herself, "Blaxican."	praising

Have students hold a discussion to share and clarify their findings.

Determine Author's Purpose: Irony

COMMON CORE

RI 6

RETEACH

Remind students that when using irony, writers convey meaning by stating something different from what they actually believe. Explain that one of the clues that a statement is ironic is the writer's tone, or attitude to the subject. Tell students that if the writer's tone is sarcastic (mocking or contemptuous), the statement may be ironic. If the writer's tone is sincere, the statement is probably not ironic. Tell students that they can determine what the ironic statements they have identified really mean. Have them use a chart like the one below.

Ironic Statement	What It Really Means
Immigrants seem to be bent on undoing America.	Immigrants are good for America.
I can remain Mexican, whatever that means, in the United States of America.	The irony here is that the term "Mexican" may be defined in America in a way that Rodriguez does not feel applies accurately to himself or others.
But I was reinvented by President Richard Nixon.	It is ridiculous to think that putting people into arbitrary categories can change their identity.
I answered that I am Chinese. . . .	If culture is identity, I might as well claim to be Chinese.

CLOSE READING APPLICATION

Students can apply the skill of analyzing irony to editorials in a current magazine or newspaper. Have them work in pairs to identify ironic statements and analyze the author's purpose in using them. Have each pair write the real meaning of each ironic statement they find.

Mother Tongue

Essay by Amy Tan

Why This Text

Students often read an essay without evaluating its structure or understanding the author's purpose. In "Mother Tongue," Amy Tan argues that "nonstandard" English is not necessarily "broken." She illustrates her points with examples from her personal and professional life. With the help of the close-reading questions, students will an analyze how Tan structures her essay. This close reading will lead students to develop a coherent understanding of Tan's purpose.

Background Have students read the background and the information about the author. Tan earned a Master's Degree in Linguistics in 1974, but in the opening of her essay, she makes clear that her point of view is not that of a scholar. Introduce the selection by telling students that Tan is best known for her novel *The Joy Luck Club*, a collection of related stories about mothers and daughters. She also wrote the screenplay when the novel was turned into a film. As the daughter of Chinese immigrants, Tan grew up speaking Chinese English at home, and standard American English at school.

AS YOU READ Ask students to take notes on the structure of Tan's essay, both its organization, and its methods of making and supporting claims. How does Tan support her claims?

 Common Core Support

- cite strong and thorough textual evidence
- determine the central ideas of a text
- determine an author's purpose
- analyze the effectiveness of the structure an author uses

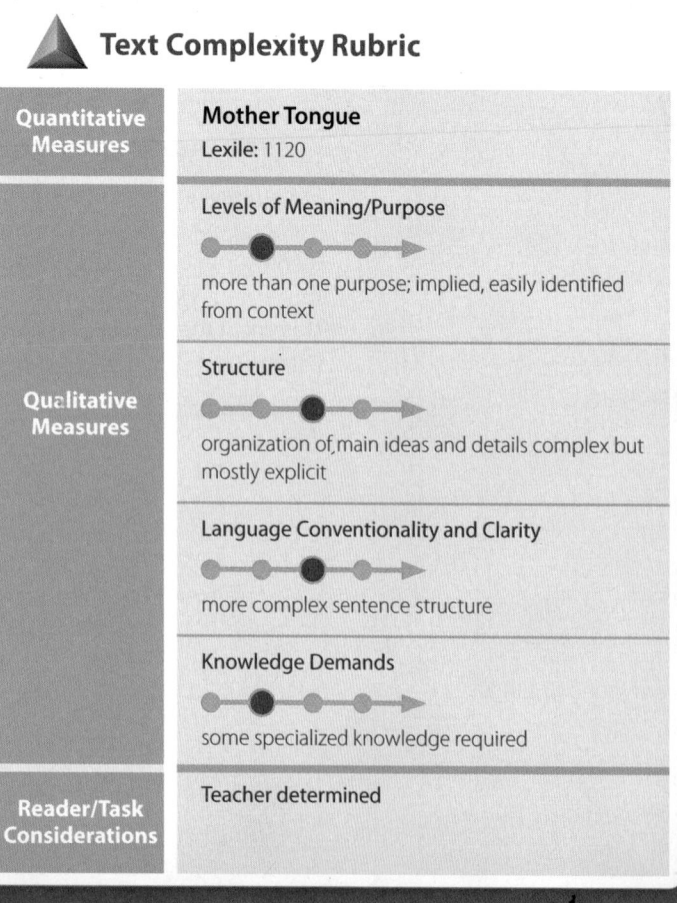 **Text Complexity Rubric**

Quantitative Measures

Mother Tongue
Lexile: 1120

Qualitative Measures

Levels of Meaning/Purpose

more than one purpose; implied, easily identified from context

Structure

organization of main ideas and details complex but mostly explicit

Language Conventionality and Clarity

more complex sentence structure

Knowledge Demands

some specialized knowledge required

Reader/Task Considerations

Teacher determined

Strategies for CLOSE READING

Analyze Structure: Essays

Students should read this essay carefully all the way through. Close-reading questions at the bottom of the page will help them focus on a thorough analysis of the essay. As they read, students should jot down comments or questions about the text in the side margins.

WHEN STUDENTS STRUGGLE . . .

To help students analyze the structure of Tan's essay, have them work in a small group to fill out a chart, such as the one shown below.

CITE TEXT EVIDENCE For practice analyzing the structure of "Mother Tongue," ask students to identify Tan's purpose in each of the following sections:

	TAN'S MAIN PURPOSE
Lines 1–49	Tan introduces the different Englishes her family speaks.
Lines 50–97	Tan defends her mother's speech, explaining that while others might call it "broken," she understands it perfectly, and calls it "mother tongue."
Lines 98–169	Tan shows that the concepts of "broken" or "limited" English can have serious negative consequences.
Lines 170–191	Tan closes by restating her thesis that her "mother tongue" is not "broken."

Background Although her mother wanted her to be a neurosurgeon and a concert pianist, **Amy Tan** found her own road to success by becoming a writer. Her first novel, The Joy Luck Club, is a collection of related stories told by four mothers and four daughters and was later turned into a film. Tan was born in Oakland, California, two and a half years after her parents fled China's Communist revolution and settled in the United States. As the daughter of immigrant parents, Tan says she grew up with two Englishes—American English and Chinese English.

Mother Tongue

Essay by Amy Tan

CLOSE READ
Notes

1. **READ ▷** As you read lines 1–30, begin to collect and cite text evidence.

   - Underline text Tan uses that explains what Tan is not.
   - Circle words that explain how Tan describes herself.
   - In the margin, make a running list of the types of English Tan describes and how she describes them.

I am not <u>a scholar of English or literature</u>. I cannot give you much more than personal opinions on the English language and its variations in this country or others.

   I am (a writer.) And by that definition, I am (someone who has always loved language.) I am fascinated by language in daily life. I spend a great deal of my time thinking about the power of language—the way it can evoke an emotion, a visual image, a complex idea, or a simple truth. Language is the tool of my trade. And I use them all—all the Englishes I grew up with.

   Recently, I was made keenly aware of the different Englishes I do use. I was
10 giving a talk to a large group of people, the same talk I had already given to half a dozen other groups. The talk was about my writing, my life, and my book *The Joy Luck Club*, and it was going along well enough, until I remembered one
B major difference that made the whole talk sound wrong. My mother was in the room. And it was perhaps the first time she had heard me give a lengthy speech, using the kind of English I have never used with her. I was saying things like "the intersection of memory and imagination" and "There is an aspect of my fiction that relates to thus-and-thus"—a speech filled with

11

1. **READ AND CITE TEXT EVIDENCE**

   A **ASK STUDENTS** to identify two types of English Tan describes, and to describe them using words and phrases taken directly from the text. *Students should identify that Tan describes "standard English" (line 20) as "carefully wrought" and "burdened" (line 18). She describes "family talk" as a "language of intimacy" (line 29).*

CLOSE READ Notes

standard English— carefully wrought, burdened

family talk— language of intimacy

Tan's mother speaks in clipped, lyrical phrases that are incomplete sentences and have atypical verb tenses.

A carefully wrought grammatical phrases, burdened, it suddenly seemed to me, with nominalized[1] forms, past perfect tenses, conditional phrases, forms of
20 standard English that I had learned in school and through books, the forms of English I did not use at home with my mother.

Just last week, as I was walking down the street with her, I again found myself conscious of the English I was using, the English I do use with her. We were talking about the price of new and used furniture, and I heard myself saying this: "Not waste money that way." My husband was with us as well, and he didn't notice any switch in my English. And then I realized why. It's because over the twenty years we've been together I've often used the same kind of English with him, and sometimes he even uses it with me. It has become our language of intimacy, a different sort of English that relates to family talk, the
30 language I grew up with.

So that you'll have some idea of what this family talk sounds like, I'll quote what my mother said during a conversation that I videotaped and then transcribed. During this conversation, she was talking about a political gangster in Shanghai who had the same last name as her family's, Du, and how in his early years the gangster wanted to be adopted by her family, who were rich by comparison. Later, the gangster became more powerful, far richer than my mother's family, and he showed up at my mother's wedding to pay his respects. Here's what she said in part:

C D "Du Yusong having business like fruit stand. Like off-the-street kind. He is
40 Du like Du Zong—but not Tsung-ming Island people. The local people call *putong*. The river east side, he belong to that side local people. That man want to ask Du Zong father take him in like become own family. Du Zong father wasn't look down on him, but didn't take seriously, until that man big like become a mafia. Now important person, very hard to inviting him. Chinese way, came only to show respect, don't stay for dinner. Mean gives lot of respect. Chinese custom. Chinese

[1] **nominalized:** in grammar or linguistics, converted into a noun.

2. ◀ REREAD Reread lines 9–21. Explain what Tan realized during her talk. Support your answer with explicit textual evidence.

Tan realized that the language she used in her talk was very different from the language she uses with her mother and her family.

3. READ ▶ Read lines 31–49. In the margin, describe in your own words the English spoken by Tan's mother.

12

CLOSE READ Notes

> *But to me, my mother's English is perfectly clear, perfectly natural. It's my mother tongue.*

social life that way. If too important won't have to stay too long. He come to my wedding. I didn't see, I heard it. I gone to boy's side, they have YMCA dinner. Chinese age I was nineteen."

E 50 You should know that my mother's expressive command of English **belies** how much she actually understands. She reads the *Forbes* report, listens to *Wall Street Week*, converses daily with her stockbroker, reads Shirley MacLaine's books with ease—all kinds of things I can't begin to understand. Yet some of my friends tell me they understand fifty percent of what my mother says. Some say they understand eighty to ninety percent. Some say they understand none of it, as if she were speaking pure Chinese.

But to me, my mother's English is perfectly clear, perfectly natural. It's my mother tongue. Her language, as I hear it, is vivid, direct, full of observation and imagery. That was the language that helped shape the way I saw things,
60 expressed things, made sense of the world.

Lately I've been giving more thought to the kind of English my mother speaks. Like others, I have described it to people as "broken" or "fractured"
F English. But I wince when I say that. It has always bothered me that I can

belies: gives a false idea of

Tan doesn't like the term "broken" English because it sounds like it's damaged, and lacks clarity.

4. ◀ REREAD AND DISCUSS Reread lines 9–49. With a small group, discuss Tan's use of personal anecdotes. What does including her mother's story add to the essay?

5. READ ▶ As you read lines 50–68, continue to cite textual evidence.
• Underline text that Tan uses to describe her mother's English.
• Circle text that shows how others perceive Tan's mother's English.

6. ◀ REREAD Reread lines 61–68. In the margin, explain Tan's position on "broken" English. Support your answer with explicit textual evidence.

13

---

2. **REREAD AND CITE TEXT EVIDENCE**

B **ASK STUDENTS** to cite explicit textual evidence to support their explanations of what Tan realized. *Students should cite text from lines 13–15, or lines 19–21.*

3. **READ AND CITE TEXT EVIDENCE**

C **ASK STUDENTS** to cite explicit textual evidence to support their descriptions of the English spoken by Tan's mother. *Students might describe her English as clipped ("Chinese custom," line 46) and lyrical ("Du Yusong having business like fruit stand. Like off-the-street kind," line 39). They might point out that her sentences are incomplete ("Chinese social life that way," lines 46–47) and that the verb tenses are atypical ("very hard to inviting him," line 44).*

FOR ELL STUDENTS Make sure that students understand that sentences such as "Not waste money that way" are grammatically incorrect. Invite a volunteer to share the correct form of this sentence ("Do not waste money that way").

4. **REREAD AND DISCUSS USING TEXT EVIDENCE**

D **ASK STUDENTS** to discuss how Tan's use of personal anecdotes adds to her essay. *Students might comment on the story as an engaging means of illustrating clearly what she means when she talks about "Englishes."*

5. **READ AND CITE TEXT EVIDENCE**

E **ASK STUDENTS** to contrast Tan's perceptions with the perceptions of others using the text evidence they have identified.

6. **REREAD AND CITE TEXT EVIDENCE**

F **ASK STUDENTS** to cite evidence to support their explanations. *Students should cite evidence from lines 63–65.*

Critical Vocabulary: belies (line 50) Have students compare definitions for *belies*.

think of no way to describe it other than "broken," as if it were damaged and needed to be fixed, as if it lacked a certain wholeness and soundness. I've heard other terms used, "limited English," for example. But they seem just as bad, as if everything is limited, including people's perceptions of the limited-English speaker.

I know this for a fact, because when I was growing up, my mother's "limited" English limited my perception of her. I was ashamed of her English. I believed that her English reflected the quality of what she had to say. That is, because she expressed them imperfectly, her thoughts were imperfect. And I had plenty of **empirical** evidence to support me: the fact that people in department stores, at banks, and in restaurants did not take her seriously, did not give her good service, pretended not to understand her, or even acted as if they did not hear her.

My mother has long realized the limitations of her English as well. When I was a teenager, she used to have me call people on the phone and pretend I was she. In this **guise,** I was forced to ask for information or even to complain and yell at people who had been rude to her. One time it was a call to her stockbroker in New York. She had cashed out her small portfolio, and it just so happened we were going to New York the next week, our first trip outside California. I had to get on the phone and say in an adolescent voice that was not very convincing, "This is Mrs. Tan."

My mother was standing in the back whispering loudly, "Why he don't send me check, already two weeks late. So mad he lie to me, losing me money."

And then I said in perfect English on the phone, "Yes, I'm getting rather concerned. You had agreed to send the check two weeks ago, but it hasn't arrived."

Then she began to talk more loudly. "What he want, I come to New York tell him front of his boss, you cheating me?" And I was trying to calm her down, make her be quiet, while telling the stockbroker, "I can't tolerate any more excuses. If I don't receive the check immediately, I am going to have to speak to your manager when I'm in New York next week." And sure enough, the following week, there we were in front of this astonished stockbroker, and I was sitting there red-faced and quiet, and my mother, the real Mrs. Tan, was shouting at his boss in her impeccable broken English.

empirical:
based on observation or experience

guise:
outer or disguised appearance

Tan uses this story to show how her mother's English is quite ineffective.

---

7. (READ ▶) Read lines 69–97. Underline the evidence Tan uses to support her ideas about the limitations of her mother's English.

8. (◀ REREAD) Reread lines 77–97. In the margin, explain Tan's purpose for telling this story about her mother and the stockbroker.

14

We used a similar routine more recently, for a situation that was far less humorous. My mother had gone to the hospital for an appointment to find out about a CAT scan she had had a month earlier. She said she had spoken very good English, her best English, no mistakes. Still, she said, the hospital staff did not apologize when they informed her they had lost the CAT scan and she had come for nothing. She said they did not seem to have any sympathy when she told them she was anxious to know the exact diagnosis, since both her husband and her son had died of brain tumors. She said they would not give her any more information until the next time and she would have to make another appointment for that. So she said she would not leave until the doctor called her daughter. She wouldn't budge. And when the doctor finally called her daughter, me, who spoke in perfect English—lo and behold—we had assurances the CAT scan would be found, promises that a conference call on Monday would be held, and apologies for any suffering my mother had gone through for a most regrettable mistake.

I think my mother's English almost had an effect on limiting my possibilities in life as well. Sociologists and linguists probably will tell you that a person's developing language skills are more influenced by peers than by family. But I do think that the language spoken in the family, especially in immigrant families which are more insular, plays a large role in shaping the language of the child. And I believe that it affected my results on achievement tests, IQ tests, and the SAT. While my English skills were never judged poor, compared with math, English could not be considered my strong suit. In grade school I did moderately well, getting perhaps B's, sometimes B-pluses, in English and scoring perhaps in the sixtieth or seventieth percentile on achievement tests. But those scores were not good enough to override the opinion that my true abilities lay in math and science, because in those areas I achieved A's and scored in the ninetieth percentile or higher.

This was understandable. Math is precise; there is only one correct answer. Whereas, for me at least, the answers on English tests were always a judgment call, a matter of opinion and personal experience. Those tests were constructed around items like fill-in-the-blank sentence completion, such as "Even though

She did poorly on tests.

Her teachers thought she was better in math and science.

---

9. (READ ▶) As you read lines 98–152, continue to cite textual evidence.

• Underline text that explains how Tan's mother's English "almost had an effect on limiting [Tan's] possibilities in life."

• In the margin, briefly note the examples Tan uses to support her position.

15

---

7. **READ AND CITE TEXT EVIDENCE**

(G) **ASK STUDENTS** to evaluate the effectiveness of Tan's evidence. *Students might point out that Tan was in a position to make repeated, firsthand observations, making her evidence strong (lines 72–76).*

8. **REREAD AND CITE TEXT EVIDENCE**

(H) **ASK STUDENTS** to cite textual evidence to support their explanations. *Students should cite evidence from lines 94–97.*

Critical Vocabulary: empirical (line 73) Have students share their definitions for *empirical.*

Critical Vocabulary: guise (line 79) Have students explain the meaning of *guise* as it is used here. *On the phone, Tan speaks to the family stockbroker pretending to be her mother—in her mother's guise.*

9. **READ AND CITE TEXT EVIDENCE**

(I) **ASK STUDENTS** to cite textual evidence that explains the effect of her mother's English on Tan. *Students should cite evidence of the effect on test results (lines 118–119, lines 136–137, and lines 142–144) and on her teachers' perceptions of her abilities (lines 123–124).*

FOR ELL STUDENTS You may wish to explain to your ELL students the meanings of the acronyms *IQ (intelligence quotient)* and *SAT (Scholastic Assessment Test).*

> *I began to write stories using all the Englishes I grew up with.*

bland:

dull, boring

130 Tom was _____ Mary thought he was _____." And the correct answer always seemed to be the most **bland** combinations, for example, "Even though Tom was shy, Mary thought he was charming," with the grammatical structure "even though" limiting the correct answer to some sort of opposites, so you wouldn't get answers like "Even though Tom was foolish, Mary thought he was ridiculous." Well, according to my mother, there were very few limitations as to what Tom could have been and what Mary might have thought of him. So I never did well on tests like that.

The same was true with word analogies, pairs of words for which you were supposed to find some logical semantic[2] relationship, for instance, "Sunset is to

140 nightfall as _____ is to _____." And here you would be presented with a list of four possible pairs, one of which showed the same kind of relationship: *red* is to *stoplight*, *bus* is to *arrival*, *chills* is to *fever*, *yawn* is to *boring*. Well, I could never think that way. I knew what the tests were asking, but I could not block out of my mind the images already created by the first pair, *sunset* is to *nightfall*—and I would see a burst of colors against a darkening sky, the moon rising, the lowering of a curtain of stars. And all the other pairs of words—*red, bus, stoplight, boring*—just threw up a mass of confusing images, making it impossible for me to see that saying "A sunset precedes nightfall" was as logical as saying "A chill precedes a fever." The only way I would have gotten that

150 answer right was to imagine an associative situation, such as my being

---
[2] **semantic:** of or relating to language

16

---

disobedient and staying out past sunset, catching a chill at night, which turned into feverish pneumonia as punishment—which indeed did happen to me.

(K) I have been thinking about all this lately, about my mother's English, about achievement tests. Because lately I've been asked, as a writer, why there are not more Asian-Americans represented in American literature. Why are there few Asian-Americans enrolled in creative writing programs? Why do so many Chinese students go into engineering? Well, these are broad sociological questions I can't begin to answer. But I have noticed in surveys—in fact, just last week—that Asian-American students, as a whole, do significantly better on

160 math achievement tests than on English tests. And this makes me think that there are other Asian-American students whose English spoken in the home might also be described as "broken" or "limited." And perhaps they also have teachers who are steering them away from writing and into math and science, which is what happened to me.

Fortunately, I happen to be rebellious and enjoy the challenge of disproving assumptions made about me. I became an English major my first year in college, after being enrolled as pre-med. I started writing nonfiction as **(J)** a freelancer the week after I was told by my boss at the time that writing was my worst skill and I should hone my talents toward account management.

170 But it wasn't until 1985 that I began to write fiction. At first I wrote what I thought to be wittily crafted sentences, sentences that would finally prove I had mastery over the English language. Here's an example from the first draft of a story that later made its way into *The Joy Luck Club*, but without this line: "That was my mental quandary in its nascent state." A terrible line, which I can barely pronounce.

(L) Fortunately, for reasons I won't get into here, I later decided I should envision a reader for the stories I would write. And the reader I decided on was my mother, because these were stories about mothers. So with this reader in mind—and in fact she did read my early drafts—I began to write stories using

180 all the Englishes I grew up with: the English I spoke to my mother, which for lack of a better term might be described as "simple"; the English she used with me, which for lack of a better term might be described as "broken"; my translation of her Chinese, which could certainly be described as "watered

Here, Tan's purpose is to explain that the lack of Asian Americans represented in American literature might be due to misconceptions about the abilities of Asian Americans.

10. **READ** ▶ Read lines 153–169. Underline how other people reacted to Tan's English.

11. ◀ **REREAD** Reread lines 153–164. In the margin, summarize Tan's main purpose in this paragraph. Support your answer with explicit textual evidence.

17

Critical Vocabulary: bland (line 131) Have students share their definitions of *bland*. Ask how Tan's choice of the word *bland* supports her purpose in this paragraph. *Tan is challenged by the limitations of standard ways of thinking about English word meanings and relationships, calling the correct answers on tests "bland" interpretations. Her mother did not follow these limitations (line 135, "according to my mother…").*

FOR ELL STUDENTS Practice the use and meaning of the prefix *dis-* with students. Point out examples on the next page (*disobedient, disproving*). Have volunteers provide the opposite of these words (*obedient, proving*). Then encourage students to give more examples of words with the same prefix.

10. **READ AND CITE TEXT EVIDENCE**

(J) **ASK STUDENTS** to cite textual evidence of her boss's reaction to Tan's English. *Students should cite "I was told by my boss at the time that writing was my worst skill," in lines 168–169.*

11. **REREAD AND CITE TEXT EVIDENCE**

(K) **ASK STUDENTS** to cite textual evidence to support their summaries of Tan's main purpose. *Students should cite evidence from lines 154–157 to show that Tan is answering a question about the lack of Asian Americans represented in American literature. They should cite evidence from lines 161–164 to show that Tan's theory is that there are misconceptions about the abilities of Asian Americans.*

CLOSE READ
Notes

Tan envisioned her ideal reader—her mother. When her mother approved of her stories, Tan knew she had done her job well.

down"; and what I imagined to be her translation of her Chinese if she could speak in perfect English, her internal language, and for that I sought to preserve the essence, but neither an English nor a Chinese structure. I wanted to capture what language ability tests could never reveal: her intent, her passion, her imagery, the rhythms of her speech and the nature of her thoughts.

190   Apart from what any critic had to say about my writing, I knew I had succeeded where it counted when my mother finished reading my book and gave me her verdict: "So easy to read."

12. **READ ▷** Read lines 170–191. Underline the four types of English Tan describes. In the margin, explain why Tan finally felt she had succeeded.

SHORT RESPONSE

Cite Text Evidence   Trace the structure of Tan's essay, describing both its organization and its methods. How does the structure of her essay support her purpose? **Cite evidence** from the text to support your response.

> Tan has divided her essay into sections, explaining her understanding of different types of English. She describes these different languages and also shows how they are effective, rather than "broken." She shows the negative impact on her mother of limited perceptions of her and then explains how those perceptions nearly limited Tan's own life. Her conclusion is a vindication of her mother tongue: "So easy to read." Tan's purpose is to educate readers about limited-English speakers. The use of personal anecdotes and the description of her own journey learning about English is effective because it helps us understand her own revelations.

18

12. READ AND CITE TEXT EVIDENCE

L   **ASK STUDENTS**   to cite textual evidence to support their explanation of why Tan felt she had succeeded. *Students should cite evidence from lines 176–178 showing that Tan's ideal reader is her mother, and from lines 189–191 showing that her mother found the writing "easy to read."*

SHORT RESPONSE

Cite Text Evidence   Student responses will vary, but they should cite evidence from the text to support their explanations and descriptions. Students should:

- explain Tan's organization.
- describe Tan's methods.
- evaluate the effectiveness of Tan's structure in supporting her purpose.

TO CHALLENGE STUDENTS . . .

For more context, have students research how the English language evolves, changes, and incorporates new words, even today. Recent additions to *The Merriam-Webster Dictionary* include *aha moment* and *man cave*. The Chinese language has enriched English with words such as *kumquat* (1699), *gung ho* (1941), and *wok* (1952).

ASK STUDENTS   to research some aspect of the continuing evolution of English. Each student should identify an area of research such as how words are added to dictionaries, how rules of syntax change over time, or words that come to English from other languages. Have students share the results of their research with the class, and discuss how Englishes like Tan's mother tongue influence what Tan calls standard English.

DIG DEEPER

With the class, return to Question 4, Reread and Discuss. Have students share the results of their discussion.

ASK STUDENTS   whether they were satisfied with the outcome of their small-group discussions. Have each group share their conclusions about Tan's use of personal anecdotes. Ask groups to share the textual evidence that supports their conclusions.

- In lines 9–21, what does the story about Tan's mother add to the essay? *Students may conclude that the anecdote about her mother helps to establish Tan's point of view, her credentials, and/or her purpose in an engaging way.*
- In lines 31–38, how does Tan establish the authenticity of her illustration "of what this family talk sounds like"? *Students should point out that Tan is quoting a transcribed videotape.*
- In lines 39–49, how does the quotation support Tan's purpose? *Students should explain that the anecdote is a clear illustration of Tan's "mother tongue."*

ASK STUDENTS   to return to their Short Response answer and to revise it based on the class discussion.

New Orleans

*my*SmartPlanner — Create lesson plans and access resources online.

Poem by Joy Harjo

Why This Text?

Contemporary poetry reflects the viewpoints and beliefs of Americans from a variety of backgrounds. Most contemporary poetry is free verse; students must learn to appreciate its subtleties. This lesson analyzes Harjo's theme and the imagery, figurative language, and syntax Harjo uses to express this theme.

View It!

Professional Development Podcast:

Text-Dependent Analysis

Key Learning Objective: The student will be able to determine a theme of the poem.

For additional practice:

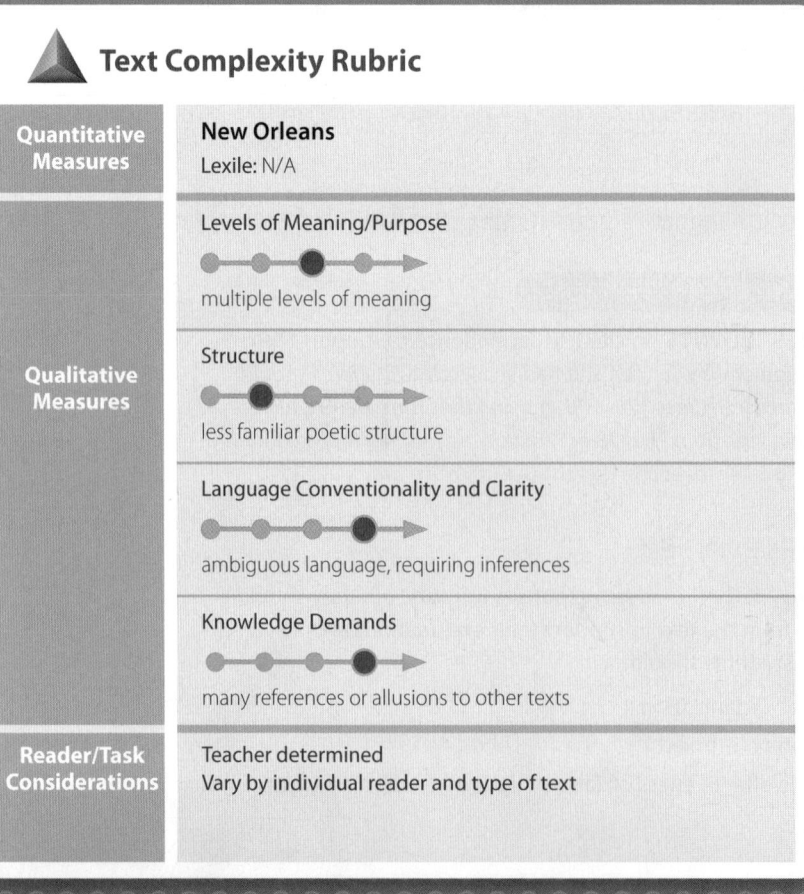

Close Reader selection
"Indian Boy Love Song (#2)"
Poem by Sherman Alexie

COMMON CORE Common Core Standards

RL 1 Cite textual evidence.
RL 2 Determine themes of a text.
RL 3 Analyze the impact of the author's choices.
RL 4 Determine figurative and connotative meanings; analyze the impact of specific word choices.
RL 5 Analyze how an author's choices contribute to its overall meaning as well as its aesthetic impact.
RL 6 Analyze a case in which grasping point of view requires distinguishing what is directly stated in a text from what is really meant.
L 3a Vary syntax for effect; apply an understanding of syntax.

▲ Text Complexity Rubric

Quantitative Measures	**New Orleans** Lexile: N/A
Qualitative Measures	**Levels of Meaning/Purpose** ●—●—⬤—●—➤ multiple levels of meaning
	Structure ●—⬤—●—●—➤ less familiar poetic structure
	Language Conventionality and Clarity ●—●—●—⬤—➤ ambiguous language, requiring inferences
	Knowledge Demands ●—●—●—⬤—➤ many references or allusions to other texts
Reader/Task Considerations	Teacher determined Vary by individual reader and type of text

Background Have students read the background and information about the author. Tell students that following violent resistance to the encroachment of white settlers by some Creeks, President Andrew Jackson began a process of government-sponsored removal of Creek people that continued until 1837. Many Creeks were taken by ship to New Orleans and then overland to Oklahoma. On their way west, the Creeks endured heavy rain and extreme cold. Other Creeks boarded ships in New Orleans and were taken up the Mississippi River. On this journey, one steamboat was struck by another ship, and approximately 300 Creeks died. Between 1827 and the end of the removal in 1837, more than 23,000 Creeks emigrated from the Southeast.

AS YOU READ Direct students to use the As You Read instructions to focus their reading. Remind students to write down any questions they generate during reading.

Determine Themes   COMMON CORE **RL 2**

(LINES 1–11)

Explain to students that when poets write about historical events, they do not usually narrate the events as a historian would; instead, they allude, or refer briefly, to events to evoke images, ideas, and feelings. In "New Orleans," Harjo refers to a few different historical events that are closely related to the **themes** that she is developing in her poem.

Ⓐ **ASK STUDENTS** to read the first eleven lines and determine who or what the speaker is looking for in New Orleans. (*The speaker is looking for traces of her ancestors who passed through New Orleans when they were being transported to Oklahoma.*)

Analyze Language   COMMON CORE **RL 4**

(LINES 5–11)

Remind students that an **image** is a word or phrase that appeals to one or more of the reader's senses. Images bring poems to life by evoking certain thoughts and feelings in the reader. Poets choose images carefully in order to reinforce their themes.

Ⓑ **ASK STUDENTS** to read lines 5–11 and explain why Harjo includes the image of the blue horse. (*Harjo includes the blue horse because, like the Creek, it is no longer free and has been carried far from its home.*)

Background *Born in Tulsa, Oklahoma, in 1951 to a Creek father and a Cherokee-French mother,* **Joy Harjo** *is a full member of the Creek Indian tribe. She entered college in New Mexico planning to be a painter before turning her focus to writing. The poem "New Orleans" is from one of her best-known books,* She Had Some Horses *(1983). In the 1830s, hundreds of Harjo's fellow Creek Indians passed through the city of New Orleans during their forced removal from Alabama to present-day Oklahoma.*

New Orleans
Poem by Joy Harjo

AS YOU READ Look for clues that reveal what New Orleans means to the speaker. Write down any questions you generate during reading.

[handwritten notes:]
1) Re-read.
2) Directions
3) I do, we do, we do, you do in pairs, you do alone.
4) Chunk long text into several shorter Text.
5) Digital tools

This is the south. I look for evidence
of other Creeks,[1] for remnants of voices,
or for tobacco brown bones to come wandering
down Conti Street, Royal, or Decatur.
5 Near the French Market I see a blue horse
caught frozen in stone in the middle of
a square. Brought in by the Spanish on
an endless ocean voyage he became mad
and crazy. They caught him in blue
10 rock, said
        don't talk.

I know it wasn't just a horse
        that went crazy.

_____
[1] **Creeks:** people belonging to a Native American group of the American South.

[handwritten notes:]
1) Read w/definitions
2) Read w/ A, B, C, etc
3) Read in prrs "when students struggle"
4) Group re-read + Analyze
5) Determine Themes

SCAFFOLDING FOR ELL STUDENTS

Analyze Language A proper noun names a particular person, place, thing, or idea. Have students reread the title and the first ten lines of the poem and identify proper nouns that refer to places. (*New Orleans, Conti Street, Royal, Decatur, French Market*) Ask students to make inferences about why the poet might have included these specific place names. (*to help readers visualize the places she is describing; to create a sense of place*) Have students identify more proper nouns in the rest of the poem. (*Spanish, Oklahoma, Mississippi River, French Quarter, DeSoto, Creeks, Bourbon Street*)

ASK STUDENTS to analyze how the use of these proper nouns helps to communicate the author's meaning. (*Using the specific place names conjures images and associations of these places in readers' minds and emphasizes the importance of place in the poem.*)

Image Credits: (c) ©Jeff Vanuga/Cusp/Corbis; (cr) ©Digital Vision/Getty Images; (t) ©J. Vespa/WireImage/Getty Images

Analyze Language

COMMON CORE RL 4

(LINES 14–20)

Explain to students that this poem places short, apparently unrelated sentences next to each other. By using this technique, the poet hopes to lead the reader to make inferences about how the sentences relate to one another.

 **ASK STUDENTS** to read this stanza and make an inference about how the sentences are related. *(Sample answer: Unlike the ivory and knives, the red rocks were always here, and this gives them magic. The red rocks "remember" the coming of the Europeans and threaten to destroy the shopkeeper in retribution for the seizure of Creek lands.)*

Analyze Language

COMMON CORE RL 4

(LINES 22–23)

Remind students that while all figurative language compares two things, sometimes the comparison is implied rather than explicit. This kind of implied comparison is called a metaphor. Tell students that poets may pack more than one metaphor into a sentence or line.

D CITE TEXT EVIDENCE Have students identify the metaphor in these lines and interpret its meaning. *(The metaphor "a delta in the skin" compares the flow of blood through veins to the flow of water through a river.)*

Determine Themes

COMMON CORE RL 2

(LINES 37–50)

 **CITE TEXT EVIDENCE** Remind students that repeated words and ideas are a clue to theme. Have them read these stanzas, and list repeated words and ideas to determine the central idea, or **theme**. Their interpretations should be supported, citing from the text. *(The word "gold" is repeated. Repeated ideas are the search for gold—"golden treasure he traveled half the earth to find," "gold cities," "beaten gold"—and death—"buried," "bones sunk." The central idea, or theme, is that the search for gold led to destruction.)*

Nearby is a shop with ivory and knives.
15 There are red rocks. The man behind the
counter has no idea that he is inside
magic stones. He should find out before
they destroy him. These things
have memory,
20   you know.

I have a memory.
        It swims deep in blood,
a delta[2] in the skin. It swims out of Oklahoma,
deep the Mississippi River. It carries my
25 feet to these places: the French Quarter,
stale rooms, the sun behind thick and moist
clouds, and I hear boats hauling themselves up
and down the river.

My spirit comes here to drink.
30 My spirit comes here to drink.
Blood is the undercurrent.

There are voices buried in the Mississippi mud.
There are ancestors and future children
buried beneath the currents stirred up by
35 pleasure boats going up and down.
There are stories here made of memory.

I remember DeSoto.[3] He is buried somewhere in
this river, his bones sunk like the golden
treasure he traveled half the earth to find,
40 came looking for gold cities, for shining streets
of beaten gold to dance on with silk ladies.

He should have stayed home.

        (Creeks knew of him for miles
        before he came into town.
45   Dreamed of silver blades
        and crosses.)

And knew he was one of the ones who yearned
for something his heart wasn't big enough
to handle.
50   (And DeSoto thought it was gold.)

---

[2] **delta:** the mouth of a river, where it flows into a larger body of water.
[3] **DeSoto:** the Spanish conquistador who explored the Mississippi River.

APPLYING ACADEMIC VOCABULARY

adapt	displace

As you discuss Harjo's poem, incorporate the following Collection 1 academic vocabulary words: *adapt* and *displace*. To determine Harjo's meaning, ask students to tell how the speaker feels about the Creeks being **displaced** from their home. Then ask students to speculate about whether the Creeks had difficulty in **adapting** to their new home.

The Creeks lived in earth towns,
                not gold,
        spun children, not gold.
That's not what DeSoto thought he wanted to see.
55   The Creeks knew it, and drowned him in
        the Mississippi River
                        so he wouldn't have to drown himself.

Maybe his body is what I am looking for
as evidence. To know in another way
60   that my memory is alive.
But he must have got away, somehow,
because I have seen New Orleans,
the lace and silk buildings,
trolley cars on beaten silver paths,
65   graves that rise up out of soft earth in the rain,
shops that sell black mammy dolls
holding white babies.

And I know I have seen DeSoto,
                having a drink on Bourbon Street,
70   mad and crazy
                dancing with a woman as gold
                as the river bottom.

COLLABORATIVE DISCUSSION Discuss with a partner how Harjo reveals what New Orleans means to the speaker in the poem. Cite specific textual evidence from the poem and explain how these passages reveal the speaker's attitude toward the city.

WHEN STUDENTS STRUGGLE...

Have students re-read the poem. Then have them work in pairs or small groups to paraphrase the following lines of the poem: lines 1–2 *(the speaker searches for evidence of other Creeks)*; lines 32–34 *(ancestors and future children of the Creeks are buried in the mud of the Mississippi River)*; lines 37–39 *(DeSoto is also buried in the mud of the Mississippi River)*; lines 39–41 *(DeSoto was searching for golden treasure)*; lines 61–72 *(The speaker sees the spirit of DeSoto in New Orleans.)*

TEACH

CLOSE READ

Determine Themes   COMMON CORE RL 2
(LINES 55–67)

Have students read lines 55–67 and analyze the **images** found in those lines.

F **CITE TEXT EVIDENCE** Have students determine a **theme** that readers can infer from these images. Students should support their interpretations with text evidence. *(The lines juxtapose images of death—"drowned himself," "graves that rise up out of soft earth"—with images of luxury—"lace and silk buildings," "beaten silver paths"— and racism—"black mammy dolls holding white babies." The images lead the reader to infer that although DeSoto himself died, the spirit of European conquest is still alive in both the decadence and racism of New Orleans, and that the madness of seeking the wrong kind of riches continues in DeSoto's successors.)*

Analyze Language   COMMON CORE RL 4
(LINES 71–72)

Remind students that figurative language that explicitly compares two things using the words *like* or *as* is a **simile.** Tell students that sometimes similes are used just to help readers visualize what the poet is describing, and sometimes they are used to convey a message.

G **ASK STUDENTS** what does "woman as gold as the river bottom" mean? *(The image of the woman fuses the muddy river bottom with gold, combining the Creeks [brown, and drowned in the river] with the mad search for gold in one image because they are inseparable from each other.)*

COLLABORATIVE DISCUSSION Have students work in pairs to discuss evidence from the poem that tells what New Orleans means to the poem's speaker. When students have finished their discussions, have each pair share with the class how evidence from the poem reveals the speaker's attitude toward the city. Accept all reasonable responses.

ASK STUDENTS to share any questions they generated in the course of reading and discussing the selection.

TEACH

CLOSE READ

Analyze Language: Free Verse

Help students understand the terms and examples from the poem. Then ask students to find other images and figurative language in the poem and analyze their effect on the poem's meaning. Suggest that students record details in a chart like shown.

Example	Language Type	Effect on meaning
"*tobacco brown bones*"	*image*	*appeals to the sense of sight; tobacco suggests earth; bones are browned with age*
"*Blood is the undercurrent.*"	*figurative language (metaphor)*	*The blood of the speaker's ancestors has been spilled in the river.*
"*voices buried in the Mississippi mud*"	*image*	*appeals to senses of hearing and sight; suggests that people have been silenced*

Determine Themes

Clues to a theme can be found in its images, figurative language, and historical and cultural contexts. Ask students to explain the relationship between the evidence and theme in the graphic organizer. (*All three examples suggest the same theme.*)

Analyze Language: Free Verse

"New Orleans" is an example of **free verse,** or poetry with no set patterns of rhythm and rhyme. When read aloud, free verse sounds more like everyday speech than a conventional poem. However, like other forms of poetry, free verse uses literary devices such as **imagery** and **figurative language** to communicate the author's meaning. The chart will help you analyze these devices in the poem.

Imagery	Figurative Language
Imagery is the use of words and phrases that appeal to the reader's five senses—sight, hearing, touch, taste, and smell. A writer uses imagery to help readers experience places and events in a vivid, sensory way. For example, the speaker describes "a blue horse / caught frozen in stone." Readers can virtually see this blue stone statue and feel its immobility. This image creates a feeling of sadness, since a living animal seems to be trapped in the stone.	**Figurative language** conveys meaning beyond the literal meanings of the words. It often makes a comparison between two things that seem completely unlike each other. A **metaphor** is a kind of figurative language that compares two things without using *like* or *as.* For example, the speaker refers to "blood, a delta in the skin." This metaphor compares the flow of blood through a person's veins to a river's water, constantly on the move.

Determine Themes COMMON CORE RL 1, RL 2

A **theme** is a central idea about life or human nature that a writer wants to communicate to readers. Themes are usually not stated explicitly but must be inferred from clues in the text. To determine the themes in "New Orleans," pay attention to ideas that the poet develops over the course of the poem and how they build on one another. The chart shows textual evidence for one theme in the poem.

Evidence

"Brought in by the Spanish on / an endless ocean voyage he became mad / and crazy."

"DeSoto, . . . / mad and crazy / dancing with a woman as gold / as the river bottom."

"That's not what DeSoto thought he wanted to see. / The Creeks knew it, and drowned him in / the Mississippi River / so he wouldn't have to drown himself."

Theme

Chasing shallow, impossible dreams cannot bring happiness and may even lead to madness.

Strategies for Annotation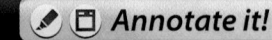

Determine Themes COMMON CORE RL 1, RL 2

Share these strategies for guided or independent analysis with students:

- Direct students to highlight evidence for a theme in blue. Evidence for a theme could include words and phrases that are repeated and powerful imagery and figurative language that captures the reader's attention.
- Remind students to review what they highlighted and attach a note to the last section of highlighted text stating the theme.

Blood is the undercurrent.

There are voices buried in the Mississippi mud.

There are ancestors and future children

Buried beneath the current stirred up by

Pleasure boats going up and down.

Analyzing the Text

COMMON CORE   RL 2, RL 3, RL 5, RL 6

Cite Text Evidence   Support your responses with evidence from the selection.

1. **Cite Evidence** Identify examples of color imagery in this poem. What effect does this imagery create?

2. **Infer** In lines 12–13, the speaker says, "I know it wasn't just a horse / that went crazy." What do you think the speaker means? Who else might have gone crazy?

3. **Compare** How does the speaker describe DeSoto and the Creeks in lines 37–57? What do these descriptions indicate about their relationships with one another?

4. **Interpret** In line 64, the speaker refers to "beaten silver paths." To what does this image refer, and how is it connected to the "silver blades and crosses" in lines 45–46?

5. **Draw Conclusions** What does DeSoto represent to the speaker? What particular words or images reveal the most about the speaker's feelings toward DeSoto?

6. **Analyze** The speaker refers to "voices" in line 2 and again in line 32. For what abstract idea are the voices a metaphor? What is the significance of the fact that the voices are "remnants" and "buried in the Mississippi mud"?

7. **Connect** The word *memory* is first used in line 19. Trace the development of the idea of memory through the poem. What possible theme about memory does the poet want to communicate?

8. **Synthesize** Considering the various images and ideas that Harjo develops in this poem about New Orleans, what might be a theme that she wants to communicate about the importance of place?

PERFORMANCE TASK

Speaking Activity New Orleans is clearly a place of significance to Joy Harjo and the Creeks. Explore that significance through research and present your findings in an oral presentation.

- Conduct a short research project to find out more about Creek Indian Removal and its relation to the city of New Orleans. Synthesize at least two sources on the topic.
- Reread "New Orleans" and notice how this new information affects your understanding of the poem. Make note of specific passages that you understand more deeply.

- Create a chart or other graphic display that summarizes your findings.
- Share your findings with a small group.
- Present a clear perspective on Creek Indian Removal and how it affects the interpretation of "New Orleans."

Assign this performance task.

PERFORMANCE TASK
COMMON CORE   SL 4

Speaking Activity Divide students into small groups and ask them to brainstorm Internet search terms to research the Creek Indian Removal and its relation to the city of New Orleans. Ask them to reread the poem to discuss how new information affects their understanding of the poem. On their own, students should note what they learn online and then create presentations. Finally, have students return to their small groups to present their findings.

Analyzing the Text
COMMON CORE   RL 1, RL 2, RL 3, RL 4, RL 5, RL 6

Possible answers:

1. *Examples of color imagery include the blue horse and the red rocks. This imagery creates the effect of emphasizing the frozen nature of the statue and of making the blood-red rocks seem alive.*

2. *The Spanish conquistadors who brought the horse and the Creeks who were forced to leave their homes might also have gone crazy.*

3. *The speaker describes DeSoto as a man obsessed with finding gold and the Creeks as a people who value family and the Earth. These descriptions indicate that DeSoto and the Creeks have opposing values.*

4. *The "beaten silver tracks" in line 64 refer to New Orleans' street car rails. They are connected with the silver blades and crosses (lines 45–46) because they are all things brought by Europeans to the Americas.*

5. *To the speaker, DeSoto represents the madness of greed. The images that reveal the most about the speaker's feelings toward DeSoto are the images of his wanting to dance on shining streets of beaten gold (lines 40–41) and his drinking and dancing on Bourbon Street (lines 68–72). [Additional responses about "the images that reveal the most about the speaker's feelings toward DeSoto" are possible.]*

6. *The voices are a metaphor for the abstract idea of the Creek culture. The voices are "remnants" and "buried in the Mississippi mud" because the culture has been all but destroyed by the Creeks' forced emigration.*

7. *The speaker says her memory "swims" in blood and in the Mississippi River and brings her to the places where her ancestors walked to search for their stories, as though her memory includes the memories of her ancestors. This ancestral memory is what the speaker seems to have in mind when she says she "remembers" DeSoto. Harjo might want to communicate that the things that have happened in a place give it a symbolic importance.*

PRACTICE & APPLY

Language and Style: Syntax in Poetry

 COMMON CORE L 3a

Tell students that the examples in the chart are just some of the uses of syntactical elements in the poem. Divide students into small groups and have them look for other examples in lines 29–41 and record them in a chart. Then have groups discuss how the use of each technique affects the sound and meaning of the poem. Finally, have each group choose a representative to share its examples and insights with the class.

Syntactical Element	Example
Parallelism	There are voices buried in the Mississippi mud. There are ancestors and future children buried beneath the currents...
Parataxis	My spirit comes here to drink. Blood is the undercurrent.
Ellipsis	came looking for gold cities, for shining streets

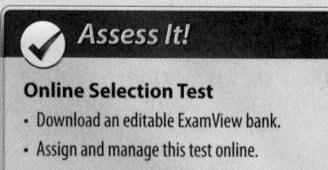

Assess It!

Online Selection Test
- Download an editable ExamView bank.
- Assign and manage this test online.

Language and Style: Syntax in Poetry

 COMMON CORE L 3a

To create particular effects, poets may arrange their words on the page in a variety of ways. These word arrangements, or **syntactical elements,** may affect the sound of the poem, reinforce the poet's meaning, or do both at the same time.

In "New Orleans," Joy Harjo makes use of the techniques shown in the chart.

Syntactical Element	Example
Parallelism is the use of similar grammatical structures to express ideas that are related or equivalent.	"I look for evidence / of other Creeks, for remnants of voices, / or for tobacco brown bones. . . ." (lines 1–3)
Parataxis is the placement of short sentences next to each other without showing how they are related. The sentences lack subordinating conjunctions or transitions, so readers must infer how they are connected.	"Nearby is a shop with ivory and knives. / There are red rocks. The man behind the / counter has no idea that he is inside / magic stones." (lines 14–17)
Ellipsis occurs when a word or phrase that is needed to form a complete grammatical structure is omitted. In the example, the second sentence lacks a subject and verb. Readers might fill in "Maybe I want" at the beginning of the second sentence to complete the thought.	"Maybe his body is what I am looking for / as evidence. To know in another way / that my memory is alive." (lines 58–60)

Poetry, for the most part, follows basic rules of grammar and style. However, it is a condensed form of expression that demands an investment from readers. To create a meaningful whole, readers must connect images and ideas and fill in missing details. Through the use of parataxis and ellipsis, Harjo involves readers in her poem, enriching their poetic experience.

Practice and Apply Complete this activity with a small group.

1. Create a chart similar to the one shown. In the first column, list the terms *parallelism*, *parataxis*, and *ellipsis*.

2. Reread lines 29–41. Fill in examples of each type of syntactical element from this part of the poem in the second column.

3. Discuss with your group how the use of each technique affects the sound and meaning of the poem.

4. Share your examples and insights with the class.

INTERACTIVE WHITEBOARD LESSON
Doing Research on the Web

COMMON CORE

SL 2, W 7

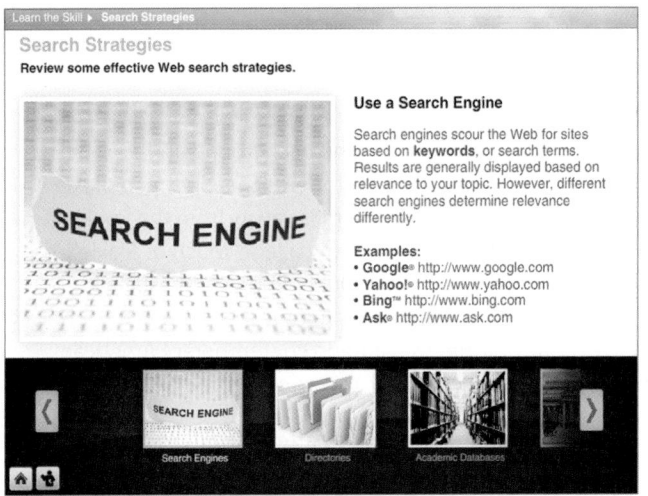

Learn the Skill ▶ Search Strategies
Search Strategies
Review some effective Web search strategies.

SEARCH ENGINE

Use a Search Engine

Search engines scour the Web for sites based on **keywords**, or search terms. Results are generally displayed based on relevance to your topic. However, different search engines determine relevance differently.

Examples:
• **Google**® http://www.google.com
• **Yahoo!**® http://www.yahoo.com
• **Bing**™ http://www.bing.com
• **Ask**® http://www.ask.com

SEARCH ENGINE
Search Engines   Directories   Academic Databases

TEACH

Before having students research the topic of the Performance Task, review the steps for conducting a Web search:

- **Step 1: Formulate Research Questions** For example, *What is the history of Creek Indian Removal?*
- **Step 2: Start Your Search** Determine the best starting point for your research query. For instance, you might explore the Muskogee Nation's official site or do a keyword search in a search engine, such as Google or Yahoo. (Search engines rank results differently, so consult more than one.)
- **Step 3: Analyze Your Results** If you started with a search engine, decide which sites might provide the most relevant information. For any sites you choose to explore, examine the currency of information, as well as the credibility of the source. Is the site produced by a government office, a well-known periodical, or an expert in the field?
- **Step 4: Refine Your Search** With a search engine, make your query more specific by using the word *AND, NOT*, or *OR* between key terms or phrases.

COLLABORATIVE DISCUSSION

Direct students to work in groups to conduct their search on Creek Indian Removal and its relationship to the city of New Orleans using one of the search strategies you presented. Have groups compare the results of their searches.

Cite Textual Evidence

COMMON CORE

RL 1

RETEACH

Review the mechanics of citing textual evidence.
Explain that when providing a direct quotation from a text or source as textual evidence, students must integrate the quotation smoothly and correctly into their writing.

- A quotation should not stand alone, but incorporated into a sentence. *(Harjo emphasizes the importance of place by beginning with geographical location: "This is the south.")*
- A quotation can be introduced with a comma. *(Harjo writes, "I look for evidence.")*
- A quotation can be introduced with a colon. *(The text states: "In the 1830s, hundreds Harjo's fellow Creek Indians passed through the city of New Orleans during their forced removal from Alabama to present day Oklahoma.")*
- Use three spaced periods (. . .), called ellipsis, to mark omissions from the original quotation. *(In line 32, Harjo chillingly writes of "voices buried in . . . mud.")*
- If the omission falls at the end of a quotation fragment that could stand as a complete sentence, insert the ellipsis after the end mark. *(The text explains that "In the 1830s, hundreds of Harjo's fellow Creek Indians passed through the city of New Orleans. . . .")*

For further instruction, use:

INTERACTIVE WHITEBOARD LESSON
Citing Textual Evidence

COMMON CORE

RL 1

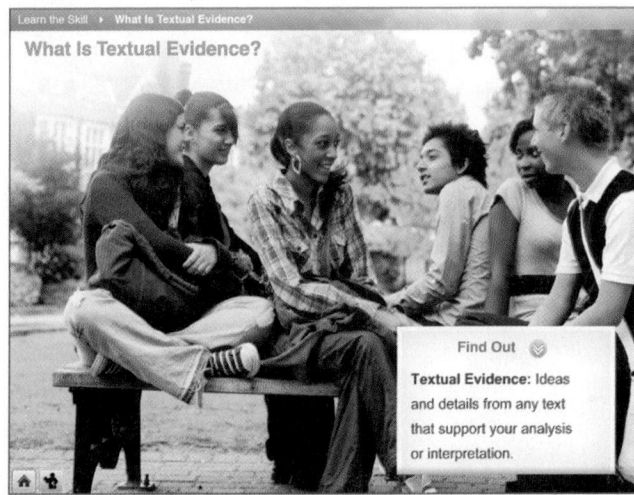

Learn the Skill ▶ What Is Textual Evidence?
What Is Textual Evidence?

Find Out

Textual Evidence: Ideas and details from any text that support your analysis or interpretation.

WRITING APPLICATION Students can integrate quotations for Analyzing the Text questions and for the Performance Task.

Indian Boy Love Song (#2)

Poem by Sherman Alexie

Why This Text

Alexie compresses thoughts and emotions in this short poem. The poem is written in free verse, so there is little to draw attention to the deeper meaning, especially if students read it quickly (which is easy to do). The concise thoughts—making use of deliberately "friendly" vocabulary—present a larger theme. With the help of the close-reading questions, students will be able to infer the theme. This close reading will lead students to a deeper understanding of a powerful poem.

Background Have students read the background and information about the author. Tell students that Sherman Alexie decided to attend a high school 30 miles away from the Spokane Indian Reservation, before he went to college. Much of Alexie's early work tries to reconcile his desire to improve himself with his feeling of having abandoned his people. His work also explores the many problems plaguing contemporary American Indian society, including poverty and alcoholism.

AS YOU READ Ask students to pay attention to the author's choice of words, and how they affect the tone. The poem's tone helps the reader infer the theme of the poem.

Common Core Support

- cite strong and thorough textual evidence
- determine a theme of a text
- determine figurative and connotative meanings of words and phrases

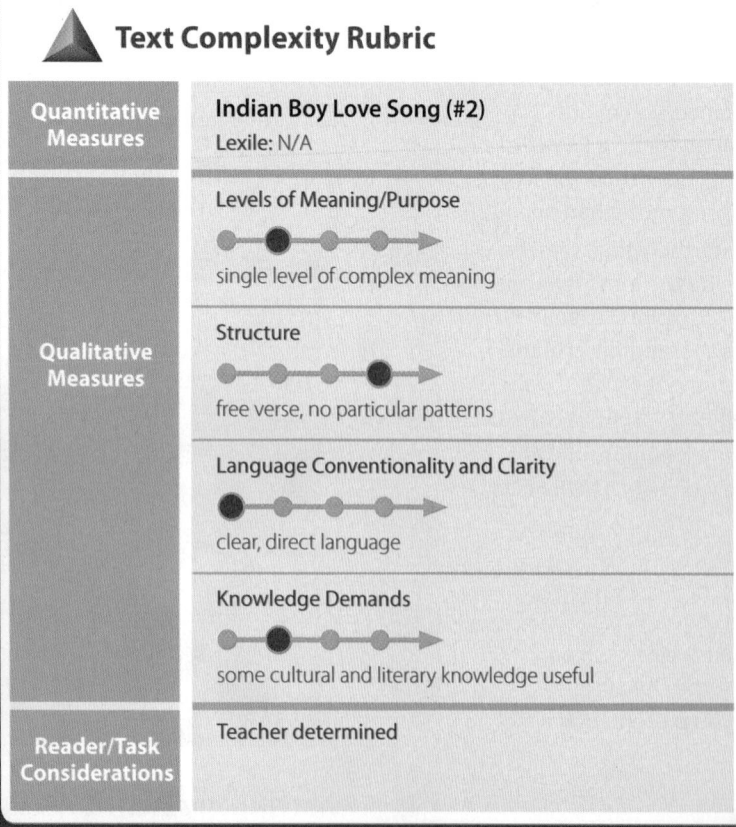

Text Complexity Rubric

Quantitative Measures	**Indian Boy Love Song (#2)** Lexile: N/A
Qualitative Measures	**Levels of Meaning/Purpose** single level of complex meaning
	Structure free verse, no particular patterns
	Language Conventionality and Clarity clear, direct language
	Knowledge Demands some cultural and literary knowledge useful
Reader/Task Considerations	Teacher determined

Strategies for CLOSE READING

Analyze Language

Students should read this poem carefully all the way through. Close-reading questions at the bottom of the page will help them draw inferences from the poet's language about the poem's deeper message. As they read, students should jot down comments or questions about the text in the margins.

WHEN STUDENTS STRUGGLE . . .

To help students analyze the language in "Indian Boy Love Song (#2)," have them work in small groups to fill out a chart like the one shown below.

CITE TEXT EVIDENCE For practice in analyzing language, ask students to explain the impact of each text example.

Text Example	Impact
"I never spoke . . . I never held my head . . ." (lines 1 and 8)	Repeating the words "I never" adds weight to the lines. The word never is a powerful word.
". . . in winters so cold they could freeze the tongue whole." (lines 5–7)	The imagery gives an immediate understanding of the physical effects of the cold.
". . . believing in the heart." (line 10)	The heart is usually a symbol of something important and essential.
". . . and always afraid." (line 13)	The use of always contrasts with the previous use of never. Perhaps never doing the things mentioned resulted in always feeling afraid.

Background Sherman Alexie *is a poet, writer, and filmmaker who was raised on the Spokane Indian Reservation in Wellpinit, Washington. His work—which includes the acclaimed short story collection* The Lone Ranger and Tonto Fistfight in Heaven—*is largely inspired by his American Indian heritage and experiences. One of Alexie's recurring themes is the powerlessness many American Indians feel in contemporary society.*

Indian Boy Love Song (#2)
Poem by Sherman Alexie

CLOSE READ Notes

1. **READ ▶** As you read lines 1–13, begin to collect and cite evidence.
   - Underline text describing what the speaker never did.
   - Circle adjectives describing people.

discribes a noun

A B
I never spoke
the language
of the old women

visiting my mother
5 in winters so cold
they could freeze
the tongue whole.

I never held my head
to their thin chests
10 believing in the heart.

Indian women, forgive me.
I grew up distant
and always afraid.

1st Read
2nd Do underlining & Circles
3rd Text Example Worksheet.
4th Tone
5th Theme

19

1. **READ AND CITE TEXT EVIDENCE** Remind students that an author's word choice can set the tone of a poem.

   A **ASK STUDENTS** what the word *distant* implies in the poem. *Students may suggest that the word implies that the speaker was distant not only in terms of proximity but also in terms of his emotions and allegiances.*

   FOR ELL STUDENTS Explain that poets sometimes take "poetic license" by using a different syntax, or order of words, than is used in standard English. In this case, the poet uses the adjective *whole* after the noun. Remind your students that in English adjectives precede the nouns they refer to.

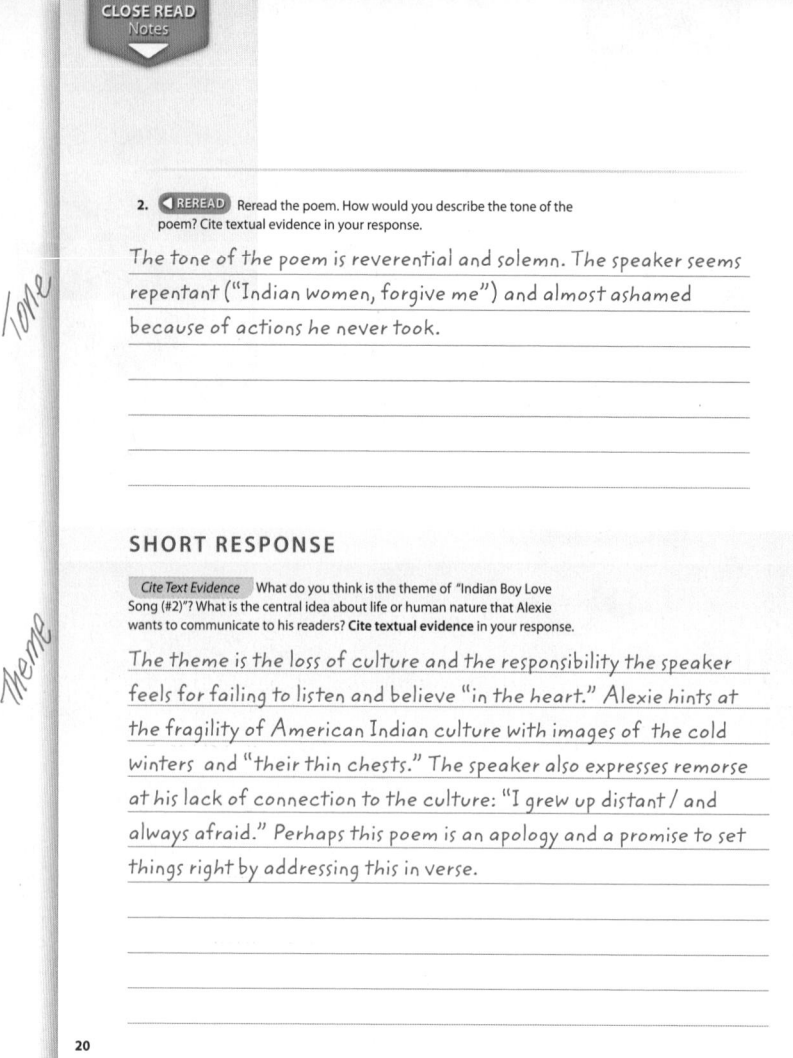

CLOSE READ
Notes

Tone

2. **◀ REREAD** Reread the poem. How would you describe the tone of the poem? Cite textual evidence in your response.

The tone of the poem is reverential and solemn. The speaker seems repentant ("Indian women, forgive me") and almost ashamed because of actions he never took.

SHORT RESPONSE

Theme

Cite Text Evidence What do you think is the theme of "Indian Boy Love Song (#2)"? What is the central idea about life or human nature that Alexie wants to communicate to his readers? **Cite textual evidence** in your response.

The theme is the loss of culture and the responsibility the speaker feels for failing to listen and believe "in the heart." Alexie hints at the fragility of American Indian culture with images of the cold winters and "their thin chests." The speaker also expresses remorse at his lack of connection to the culture: "I grew up distant / and always afraid." Perhaps this poem is an apology and a promise to set things right by addressing this in verse.

20

TO CHALLENGE STUDENTS . . .

Sherman Alexie's poems often have similar themes. Have students read "Sonnet, Without Salmon." (They can find this poem online at *Orion* magazine.)

ASK STUDENTS why the speaker compares his grandmother to a salmon. *The grandmother and salmon both swam in water, but are no longer there. The water itself has been dammed.* Ask students to compare the themes of "Sonnet, Without Salmon" and "Indian Boy Love Song (#2)." *Students will probably suggest that in these poems, Alexie writes about the loss of culture, and not feeling at home any more. The river in "Sonnet, Without Salmon" has been dammed to generate electricity to power appliances that take us further from nature.*

---

2. **REREAD AND CITE TEXT EVIDENCE** Remind students that word choice often sets the tone. This poem is short and its tone is consistent.

Ⓑ ASK STUDENTS to cite text evidence that supports their interpretation of the poem's tone. *The tone is respectful and humble. The use of the word* never *lets the reader know that the speaker had the opportunity to learn "the language of the old women," and to believe "in the heart." He is repentant ("forgive me") and sad that he was "distant and always afraid."*

SHORT RESPONSE

Cite Text Evidence Students' responses should:

• determine the poem's theme.
• describe the poem's central idea about life or human nature.
• support their response with specific text evidence.

DIG DEEPER

1. With the class, return to Question 1, Read. Have students read the poem.

   ASK STUDENTS to cite the text evidence that they use to interpret the poem.

   - Have students explain who the "old women" in line 3 are. *They are the "Indian women" mentioned in line 11. They are the women the speaker grew up with: his mother and her friends and relatives.*

   - Have students describe in their own words why the speaker wants the Indian women's forgiveness. *Students should point out that the Indian women offered the speaker opportunities to speak their language and to follow their beliefs, but he "never" took advantage of these opportunities.*

   - Ask students to infer why the speaker was "always afraid." *Students may infer that the speaker had not followed his own culture, and so was always "distant." Not having a place in the world left him afraid.*

2. With the class, return to Question 2, Reread. Have students share their responses.

   ASK STUDENTS how the poet creates the tone of the poem.

   - Have students determine what purpose the repetition in the poem serves. *Students may suggest that the repetitive use of the words "I never" strengthens the poet's point; he sets up a pattern.*

   - Have students infer what the words "believing in the heart" mean to the poet. *Students may infer that the women in the poem place a higher value on what is in their hearts than what shows outwardly. The poet seems to accept (as he writes the poem) that the women were wiser than he, and that he could have learned from them.*

   - Have students explain the impact of the final two lines of the poem, and how they resonate with the reader. *Students may suggest that the lines express a powerful emotion in very few words. The emotion is one that is easy to understand; everyone in their youth has felt alienated and scared.*

   ASK STUDENTS to return to their Short Response answer and revise it based on the class discussion.

CLOSE READING NOTES

Interactive Lessons

If you need help...
• Writing Arguments
• Using Textual Evidence

Write an Argument

This collection focuses on how and why Europeans came to the Americas and what happened as they settled in unfamiliar environments. Relocating to the Americas dramatically changed settlers' lives. In turn, the settlers changed the Americas through their interaction with its land and its native populations. Look back at the anchor text, "Of Plymouth Plantation," and at other texts you have read in this collection. Synthesize your ideas about them by writing an argument. Your argument should persuade readers to agree with your claim about how immigration changed America, and how America changes those who come here.

An effective argument

- identifies a central issue or question
- states a precise claim in response to the question
- develops the claim with valid reasons and relevant evidence, such as examples and quotations from the texts
- anticipates opposing claims and counters them with well-supported counterclaims
- establishes clear, logical connections among claims, counterclaims, reasons, and evidence
- includes an introduction, a logically structured body including transitions, and a conclusion
- maintains an appropriate tone based on its audience and context
- follows the conventions of written English

COMMON CORE

W 1a–e Write arguments to support claims in an analysis of substantive topics or texts, using valid reasoning and relevant and sufficient evidence.

W 9 Draw evidence form literary or informational texts to support analysis, reflection, and research.

PLAN

Analyze the Text Think about the following questions as they relate to the anchor text, "Of Plymouth Plantation":

- Why did European settlers come to the New World?
- When settlers came to explore and settle the Americas, how did it change their lives?
- What changes did these settlers bring to the Americas?

Choose one question to address in your argument. Then, select three texts from this collection—including "Of Plymouth Plantation"—that provide evidence for your position. These texts might present similar or different views from each other.

*my*Notebook

ACADEMIC VOCABULARY

As you share your ideas about the role of immigration in American society, be sure to use these words.

adapt
coherent
device
displace
dynamic

Collection Performance Task **103**

PERFORMANCE TASK

WRITE AN ARGUMENT

COMMON CORE **W 1a-e, W 9**

Introduce students to the Performance Task by reading the introductory paragraph with them and reviewing the criteria for what makes an effective argument. Remind students that the purpose of an argument is to persuade readers that their opinion or belief is correct.

PLAN

ANALYZE THE TEXT

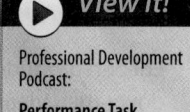
▶ *View It!*

Professional Development Podcast:
Performance Task

Remind students that their claims should reflect their analysis and synthesis of ideas about the texts they have chosen for this task.

Encourage students to begin by writing their claims. Point out that their claim will be the focus of their argument, so they should make sure it is clear and precise.

PLAN

GET ORGANIZED

Remind students that they must support their claims with logical reasons, and each reason should be supported by relevant evidence from the texts. If students find that they cannot support their claims, tell them to rework their claims or to choose a different question to address in their arguments.

PRODUCE

WRITE A DRAFT

Encourage students to focus their first drafts on getting down their ideas. Remind them to include and address counterarguments so that they can demonstrate that they have thoroughly considered their claims. Once they are sure that their argument is both logical and convincing, they can focus on refining the language.

You need to formulate a claim for your essay. In order to do this, review your chosen texts and take notes about how each one answers the question you have chosen. List evidence from each text that answers the question. Then form a clear, concise claim that will become the basis of your argument.

Get Organized Organize your notes in an outline to help you create a logical structure for your essay and to make it easier for readers to understand and follow your argument. Begin your outline with a precise statement of your claim, or your position on a question or topic.

Your introduction should

- state your claim as clearly as possible, since it will serve as the foundation of your entire argument
- include an engaging opener (for example, question, comment, or quotation) that helps your audience connect to the topic
- identify the authors and titles of each text

The body of your essay should

- present clear reasons for your claim
- provide relevant and carefully incorporated quotations or examples from each text to support your claim
- anticipate and counter opposing claims as appropriate
- show logical connections among claims, reasons, counterclaims, and evidence

In the conclusion, you should

- restate your claim and summarize your most compelling reasons for it
- end with a fresh insight about settlers in the Americas and their relationship to the New World

PRODUCE

*my***WriteSmart**

Write a Draft Use your outline to write an essay that makes a strong argument. The purpose of an argument is to persuade readers that your opinion or belief is correct. Remember to

- provide a clear and cohesive introduction, body, and conclusion that your reader can clearly follow and understand
- support your reasons with evidence that clearly connects to your argument
- explain how the evidence supports your claim; don't rely on readers to make all the connections between your claim and the text evidence

Write your rough draft in *my*WriteSmart. Focus on getting your ideas down, rather than perfecting your choice of language.

- anticipate and respond to opposing claims to strengthen your claim or to acknowledge the complexity of the topic
- use language that is appropriate for your audience
- include transitions to link the major sections of the text

REVISE

Improve Your Draft You should now have a rough draft that persuades readers to agree with your claim. It is time to revise your draft so that your readers will clearly understand your argument. Use the chart on the following page to review the characteristics of an effective argument. Your goal is to produce a clear and coherent text. Read your first draft and ensure that it

*my***WriteSmart**

Have your partner or a group of peers review your draft in *my*WriteSmart. Ask your reviewers to note any reasons that do not support the claim or that lack sufficient evidence.

- has a clearly-developed introduction, body, and conclusion
- makes logical connections among claims, counterclaims, reasons, and evidence
- has sufficient evidence to support these connections
- maintains a formal style and an objective, unbiased tone
- follows the conventions of standard English grammar

Then write a new draft of your essay, incorporating all your revisions.

PRESENT

Exchange Essays When your final draft is completed, exchange essays with a partner. Read your partner's essay and provide feedback. Reread the criteria for an effective argument and ask the following questions

- What is the central claim of your partner's essay?
- Is your partner's essay organized logically?
- Does your partner present sufficient evidence to support the central claim?
- Does your partner include opposing claims and address them effectively?
- Do you agree with your partner's claim?
- If yes, what elements of the essay persuaded you?
- If no, what could your partner have done to persuade you?

PERFORMANCE TASK

REVISE

IMPROVE YOUR DRAFT

Remind students that *revising* means "evaluating the development, organization, and language of their argument." Have students exchange papers with a partner and use the chart on the following page to evaluate each other's arguments. Tell students to help their partners identify parts of their arguments that need strengthening, reworking, or a new approach.

PRESENT

EXCHANGE ESSAYS

Provide students with other options for presenting their essays, such as adapting and presenting their arguments as a persuasive speech or turning their claim into a question for a panel discussion.

ORGANIZATION

Have students look at the chart and offer a self-evaluation of the Organization category, including their assessment of their level of performance. Have students review how they organized the reasons and textual evidence in their arguments. Ask students how their organization could be improved and have them outline a plan for revision.

	Ideas and Evidence	Organization	Language
ADVANCED	• The introduction is memorable and persuasive; the claim clearly states a position on a substantive topic. • Valid reasons and relevant evidence from the texts convincingly support the writer's claim. • Opposing claims are anticipated and effectively addressed with counterclaims. • The concluding section effectively summarizes the claim.	• The reasons and textual evidence are organized consistently and logically throughout the argument. • Varied transitions logically connect reasons and textual evidence to the writer's claim.	• The writing reflects a formal style and an objective, or controlled, tone. • Sentence beginnings, lengths, and structures vary and have a rhythmic flow. • Spelling, capitalization, and punctuation are correct. If handwritten, the argument is legible. • Grammar and usage are correct.
COMPETENT	• The introduction could do more to capture the reader's attention; the claim states a position on an issue. • Most reasons and evidence from the texts support the writer's claim, but they could be more convincing. • Opposing claims are anticipated, but the counterclaims need to be developed more. • The concluding section restates the claim.	• The organization of reasons and textual evidence is confusing in a few places. • A few more transitions are needed to connect reasons and textual evidence to the writer's claim.	• The style is informal in a few places, and the tone is defensive at times. • Sentence beginnings, lengths, and structures vary somewhat. • Several spelling and capitalization mistakes occur, and punctuation is inconsistent. If handwritten, the argument is mostly legible. • Some grammatical and usage errors are repeated in the argument.
LIMITED	• The introduction is ordinary; the claim identifies an issue, but the writer's position is not clearly stated. • The reasons and evidence from the texts are not always logical or relevant. • Opposing claims are anticipated but not addressed logically. • The concluding section includes an incomplete summary of the claim.	• The organization of reasons and textual evidence is logical in some places, but it often doesn't follow a pattern. • Many more transitions are needed to connect reasons and textual evidence to the writer's position.	• The style becomes informal in many places, and the tone is often dismissive of other viewpoints. • Sentence structures barely vary, and some fragments or run-on sentences are present. • Spelling, capitalization, and punctuation are often incorrect but do not make reading the argument difficult. If handwritten, the argument may be partially illegible. • Grammar and usage are incorrect in many places, but the writer's ideas are still clear.
EMERGING	• The introduction is missing. • Significant supporting reasons and evidence from the texts are missing. • Opposing claims are neither anticipated nor addressed. • The concluding section is missing.	• An organizational strategy is not used; reasons and textual evidence are presented randomly. • Transitions are not used, making the argument difficult to understand.	• The style is inappropriate, and the tone is disrespectful. • Repetitive sentence structure, fragments, and run-on sentences make the writing monotonous and hard to follow. • Spelling and capitalization are often incorrect, and punctuation is missing. If handwritten, the argument may be partially or mostly illegible. • Many grammatical and usage errors change the meaning of the writer's ideas.

Image Credits: ©Volanthevist/Flickr/Getty Images

Building a Democracy

" A nation is formed by the willingness of each of us to share the responsibility for upholding the common good. **"**

—Barbara Jordan

PLAN

CONNECTING WORD AND IMAGE

ASK STUDENTS to discuss how the collection opener image and the collection quotation work together to create a connection.

PERFORMANCE TASK PREVIEW

Point out to students that they will complete a performance task at the end of the collection. The performance task will require them to further analyze the selections in the collection and to synthesize ideas about these analyses. They will present their findings in a variety of products.

ACADEMIC VOCABULARY

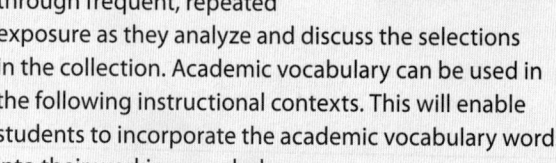

View It!

Professional Development Podcast:

Academic Vocabulary

Students can acquire facility with the academic vocabulary words through frequent, repeated exposure as they analyze and discuss the selections in the collection. Academic vocabulary can be used in the following instructional contexts. This will enable students to incorporate the academic vocabulary words into their working vocabulary.

- Collaborative Discussion at the end of each selection
- Analyzing the Text questions for each selection
- Selection-level Performance Task
- Vocabulary instruction (for Critical Vocabulary and/or for Vocabulary Strategy)
- Language and Style
- End-of-collection Performance Task for all selections in the collection

ASK STUDENTS to review the academic vocabulary word list for this collection. You may wish to pronounce each word aloud, so students hear the correct pronunciation. Then, discuss the definitions and the related forms for each word. Remind students that they will encounter these five academic vocabulary words throughout the collection.

Building a Democracy

hmhfyi.com

This collection explores how people who are so different can work together to create a unified whole while also protecting the rights of everyone.

COLLECTION

PERFORMANCE TASK Preview

At the end of this collection, you will have the opportunity to complete a task:

- Write an informative essay on how each author, character, or historical figure strikes a balance between preserving individual rights and forming a strong, long-lasting union.

ACADEMIC VOCABULARY

Study the words and their definitions in the chart below. You will use these words as you discuss and write about the texts in this collection.

Word	Definition	Related Forms
contrary (kŏn´trĕr´ē) *adj.*	opposite or opposed in character or purpose	contradict, contrariness
founder (foun´dər) *n.*	someone who sets up, establishes, or provides the basis for something	foundation, founded, fundamental
ideological (ī´dē-ə-lŏj´ĭ-kəl) *adj.*	based on ideas, beliefs, or doctrines	idea, ideologue, ideology
publication (pŭb´lĭ-kā´shən) *n.*	the act of making public in printed or electronic form; the product of this act	public, publish, publisher
revolution (rĕv´ə-lōō´shən) *n.*	the overthrow and replacement of a government, often through violent means	revolt, revolutionary, revolutionize

USING THE COLLECTION YOUR WAY

Use the following information, along with the charts on the following pages, to help you decide how you want to introduce the collection. Based on your teaching style, your students' interests, or your instructional goals, you may want to structure the collection in various ways. You may choose different entry points each time you teach the collection.

"I like to teach by comparing texts."

Both documents relate to United States government—one addressing reasons for forming a government independent from British rule, and the other establishing guidelines and principles for how this government should function.

COMPARE ANCHOR TEXTS

The Declaration of Independence *from* **The United States Constitution**

Public Documents

Background *The Declaration of Independence, adopted July 4, 1776, by the Second Continental Congress, was the culmination of a long process during which the American colonists tried to resolve their differences with Great Britain. Hope for a peaceful resolution still persisted after the outbreak of armed conflict in April 1775. By the spring of 1776, however, most colonists favored a break with Britain. In early June, a committee was formed to draft a statement to support that position, and* **Thomas Jefferson** *took on the task of writing it. Although the Congress made changes to his list of grievances, it did not touch his declaration of rights, which became a lasting statement of "self-evident" truths for the new country and the world.*

In 1787 a Constitutional Convention was called to amend the Articles of Confederation, the first written constitution of the United States. The Articles severely limited the power of the central government and prevented it from meeting many challenges in the country's first years. The Constitution did not have one predominant author because it reflected many compromises needed to resolve differences between large and small states, Northerners and Southerners. The final document sought to create a balance between a strong, workable central government and individual liberty. The Bill of Rights, adopted as the first ten Amendments to the Constitution in 1791, strengthened the original document's protection of individual and states rights.

Thomas Jefferson *(1743–1826) was one of the most accomplished of our nation's founders. He held a number of important government positions, including governor of Virginia during the Revolutionary War and U.S. minister to France afterward. In addition, he served as the country's first secretary of state, its second vice-president, and its third president. More important than his titles, however, was his vision of liberty and self-government, eloquently expressed in the Declaration of Independence.*

Compare Anchor Texts **111**

COMPARE TEXTS

Colonial American Poetry

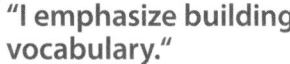

Phillis Wheatley *was born in West Africa, probably in 1753, and became the first African American to publish a book of poetry. In 1761 she was enslaved, brought to Boston, and purchased by a local merchant, John Wheatley. He named the little girl Phillis and gave her to his wife, Susannah. Phillis learned to read and write English very quickly, and the Wheatley family tutored her in Latin, English literature, and the classics. Wheatley was quickly recognized as a remarkable prodigy and respect for her talents soon grew. Phillis's first published poem appeared in 1767, and by 1770 her work was known throughout the colonies. In 1773 she traveled to London for the publication of her Poems on Various Subjects, Religious and Moral but soon returned to Boston.*

Phillis was given her freedom after Susannah Wheatley's death in 1774. Her life, however, became more difficult as revolution spread through the colonies and as her patrons, wealthy Loyalists, fled the city. In 1778 she married John Peters, but the couple fell into extreme poverty. Their children all died in infancy, and Phillis died in 1784.

Philip Freneau *was called the "poet of the American Revolution." He was born in New York City in 1752. Freneau began writing poetry while studying at Princeton. After graduating in 1771, he briefly worked as a teacher before sailing to the Caribbean, where he developed a deep hatred of slavery.*

In 1778 Freneau returned to New Jersey and enlisted in the revolutionary militia. He captained a privateer until he was captured and briefly imprisoned by the British. He started a newspaper in 1790 and supported Thomas Jefferson in his ideological dispute with the Federalists. Freneau left the paper soon after Jefferson became president. He retired to a New Jersey farm and continued to write and publish until his death in 1832.

AS YOU READ Pay attention to details that reveal the tone, or attitude, that the speaker in each poem has toward America.

Compare Texts **151**

"I emphasize building vocabulary."

These poems relate to life in colonial America, indicating how an individual's personal experience helps shape his or her opinions and perspectives on issues such as authority, oppression, and freedom.

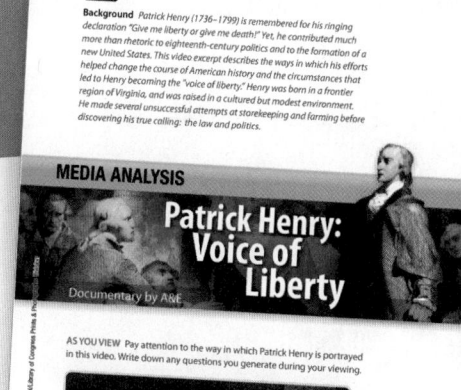

Background *Patrick Henry (1736–1799) is remembered for his ringing declaration "Give me liberty or give me death!" Yet, he contributed much more than rhetoric to eighteenth-century politics and to the formation of a new United States. This video excerpt describes the ways in which his efforts helped change the course of American history and the circumstances that led to Henry becoming the "voice of liberty." Henry was born in a frontier region of Virginia, and was raised in a cultured but modest environment. He made several unsuccessful attempts at storekeeping and farming before discovering his true calling: the law and politics.*

MEDIA ANALYSIS

Patrick Henry: Voice of Liberty

Documentary by A&E

AS YOU VIEW Pay attention to the way in which Patrick Henry is portrayed in this video. Write down any questions you generate during your viewing.

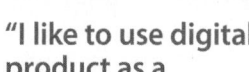

COLLABORATIVE DISCUSSION What facts did you learn about Patrick Henry that surprised you?

Patrick Henry: Voice of Liberty **167**

"I like to use digital product as a starting point."

This video excerpt gives information about the efforts and achievements of Patrick Henry, a founder who made significant political contributions toward American independence in the 18th century.

mySmartPlanner | **eBook** | **myNotebook** | **my WriteSmart** | **fyi** hmhfyi.com

Collection 2 Lessons	Media	Teach and Practice
Student Edition | eBook	▶ **Video Links** HISTORY A&E	**Close Reading and Evidence Tracking**
ANCHOR TEXT Public Document by Thomas Jefferson "The Declaration of Independence"	◉ **Audio** "The Declaration of Independence" ▶ **Video HISTORY®** *The Presidents: Jefferson Writes the Declaration of Independence*	**Close Read Screencasts** • Modeled Discussion (lines 17–28) • Close Read application (lines 107–114) / **Strategies for Annotation** • Analyze Structure: Style and Content
ANCHOR TEXT Public Document from *The United States Constitution:* Preamble and Bill of Rights	◉ **Audio** fro m *The United States Constitution:* Preamble and Bill of Rights ▶ **Video HISTORY** *America Gets a Constitution*	**Close Read Screencasts** • Modeled Discussion (lines 11–16) • Close Read application (lines 42–50) / **Strategies for Annotation** • Analyze Foundational Documents
CLOSE READER Public Document from *The United States Constitution*	◉ **Audio** from *The United States Constitution* ▶ **Video HISTORY** *America Gets a Constitution*	
Argument by James Madison "The Federalist No. 10"	◉ **Audio** "The Federalist No. 10" ▶ **Video HISTORY** *Library of Congress: The Federalist Papers*	**Strategies for Annotation** • Purpose and Premises of an Argument • Evaluating Nuances in Meaning
CLOSE READER Public Document by Prince Hall "Petition to the Massachusetts General Assembly"	◉ **Audio** "Petition to the Massachusetts General Assembly"	
History Article by Ron Chernow "Thomas Jefferson: The Best of Enemies"	◉ **Audio** "Thomas Jefferson: The Best of Enemies"	**Strategies for Annotation** • Analyze Structure: Comparison and Contrast • Consulting General and Specialized Reference Works
CLOSE READER Article by Woody Holton "Abigail Adams' Last Act of Defiance"	◉ **Audio** "Abigail Adams' Last Act of Defiance"	
Poems by Phillis Wheatley "To the Right Honourable William, Earl of Dartmouth," "On Being Brought from Africa to America" Poem by Philip Freneau "On the Emigration to America and Peopling the Western Country"	◉ **Audio** "To the Right Honourable William, Earl of Dartmouth," "On Being Brought from Africa to America" ▶ **Video HISTORY** *Mankind: African Slave Trade* ◉ **Audio** "On the Emigration to America and Peopling the Western Country"	**Strategies for Annotation** • Colonial American Poetry
Short Story by Charles Johnson "A Soldier for the Crown"	◉ **Audio** "A Soldier for the Crown"	**Strategies for Annotation** • Analyze Structure: Suspense and Ambiguity • Language and Style: Point of View
Documentary by A&E® *Patrick Henry: Voice of Liberty*	▶ **Video A&E®** *Patrick Henry: Voice of Liberty*	
Collection 2 Performance Task: Write an Informative Essay	**fyi** hmhfyi.com	**Interactive Lessons** Writing an Informative Text Producing/Publishing with Technology

	For Systematic Coverage of Writing and Speaking & Listening Standards	Interactive Lessons Writing an Argument Analyzing and Evaluating Presentations	Lesson Assessments Writing an Argument Analyzing and Evaluating Presentations

Assess		Extend	Reteach
Performance Task	**Online Assessment**	**Teacher eBook**	**Teacher eBook**
Speaking Activity	Selection Test	**Writing an Informative Text**	**Analyze Language > Word Sharp Interactive Vocabulary Tutorial >** Specialized Vocabulary
Media Activity	Selection Test	**Writing an Informative Text**	**Analyze Language > Word Sharp Interactive Vocabulary Tutorial >** Specialized Vocabulary
Speaking Activity	Selection Test	**Analyze Author's Purpose > Interactive Whiteboard Lesson >** Author's Purpose and Perspective	**Evaluate Seminal Texts: Premises of an Argument > Level Up Tutorial >** Elements of an Argument
Writing Task: Essay	Selection Test	**Determine Central Ideas> Level Up Tutorial >** Main Idea and Supporting Details	**Analyze Ideas and Events: Sequence > Level Up Tutorial >** Chronological Order
Speaking Activity	Selection Test	**Writing Effective Arguments > Interactive Whiteboard Lesson >** Key Traits: Argument	**Analyze and Compare Themes and Topics > Level Up Tutorial >** Theme
Writing and Speaking Activity	Selection Test	**Conducting Research on the Web > Interactive Whiteboard Lesson >** Search Strategies	**Analyze Structure: Suspense and Ambiguity**
Media Activity: Presentation	Selection Test	**Analyze Ideas and Events** **Analyze Foundational Documents** **Conducting Research on the Web > Interactive Whiteboard Lesson >** Search Strategies	**Analyzing the Media > Level Up Tutorial >** Audience
Write an Informative Essay	Collection Test		

Collection 2 Lessons	Key Learning Objective	Performance Task
ANCHOR TEXT EXEMPLAR **Public Document by Thomas Jefferson** **Lexile 1320** **"The Declaration of Independence," p. 111A**	**The student will be able to...** analyze the features of a foundational U.S. document	Speaking Activity
ANCHOR TEXT EXEMPLAR **Public Document from *The United States Constitution:* Preamble and Bill of Rights, p. 121** **Lexile 1580**	**The student will be able to...** analyze the features of a foundational U.S. document	Media Activity
Argument by James Madison **Lexile 1390** **"The Federalist No. 10," p. 129A**	**The student will be able to...** analyze and evaluate an argument	Speaking Activity
History Article by Ron Chernow **Lexile 1340** **"Thomas Jefferson: The Best of Enemies," p. 141A**	**The student will be able to...** analyze ideas, events, and structure in an informational text	Writing Task: Essay
Poems by Phillis Wheatley, p. 151A **"To the Right Honourable William, Earl of Dartmouth"** EXEMPLAR **"On Being Brought from Africa to America"** **Poem by Philip Freneau** **"On the Emigration to America and Peopling the Western Country"**	**The student will be able to...** analyze and compare topics and themes in poems	Speaking Activity
Short Story by Charles Johnson **Lexile 1250** **"A Soldier for the Crown," p. 159A**	**The student will be able to...** analyze suspense, ambiguity, and point of view in fiction.	Writing and Speaking Activity
Documentary by A&E ***Patrick Henry: Voice of Liberty,* p. 167A**	**The student will be able to...** analyze how ideas and claims presented in a video connect to foundational U.S. documents	Media Activity: Presentation

Collection 2 Performance Task:
Write an Informative Essay

Vocabulary Strategy	Language and Style	Student Instructional Support	CLOSE READER Selection
Domain-Specific Words	Parallel Structure	**Scaffolding for ELL Students:** • Pronoun Referents • Practice Reading Fluency **When Students Struggle:** Categorization	
	Formal and Informal Style	**Scaffolding for ELL Students:** Word Roots **When Students Struggle:** Using Signal Words	Public Document from *The United States Constitution*, p. 128b **Lexile 1470**
Evaluating Nuances in Meaning	Transitions	**Scaffolding for ELL Students:** • Evaluate Seminal Texts: Purpose and Premises of an Argument • Determine Pronoun Referents **When Students Struggle:** • Identify Important Details • Paraphrasing **To Challenge Students:** Paraphrase an Argument	Public Document by Prince Hall "Petition to the Massachusetts General Assembly", p. 140b **Lexile 2110**
Consulting General and Specialized Reference Works	Hyphenation	**Scaffolding for ELL Students:** • Analyze Structure: Comparison and Contrast • Sequence and Verb Tense **To Challenge Students:** Subject-by-Subject Organization	Article by Woody Holton "Abigail Adams' Last Act of Defiance," p. 150b **Lexile 1250**
		Scaffolding for ELL Students: • Analyze Language • Multiple-Meaning Words **When Students Struggle:** • Inversion • Reading Poetry for Comprehension	
	Point of View	**Scaffolding for ELL Students**: • Understand Sentence Fragments **When Students Struggle:** • Analyzing Literature • Archaic Langauge	
		Scaffolding for ELL Students: Analyze Events	

A New American Nation

*my*SmartPlanner — Create lesson plans and access resources online.

Collection 2 Historical Introduction

Why This Text?

Students often encounter literary and informational texts that assume that the reader has some knowledge of key historical events, facts, ideas, and issues. The historical introduction to Collection 2 presents information about the period from 1700 to 1810, when the United States was developing its new system of government and establishing itself as an independent nation.

Key Learning Objective: The student will be able to analyze the selections in the collection in terms of a historical context.

COMMON CORE Common Core Standards

RL 10 Read and comprehend literature in the grades 11-CCR text complexity band.

RI 7 Integrate and evaluate sources of information presented in different formats.

RI 10 Read and comprehend literary nonfiction in the grades 11-CCR text complexity band.

▲ Text Complexity Rubric

Quantitative Measures	**Exploration and Settlement** Lexile: N/A
Qualitative Measures	Levels of Meaning/Purpose more than one purpose; implied, easily identified from context
	Structure more than one text structure
	Language Conventionality and Clarity increased unfamiliar, academic, or domain-specific words
	Knowledge Demands somewhat complex historical concepts
Reader/Task Considerations	Teacher determined Vary by individual reader and type of text

For more context and historical background, students can view the video "The Presidents: Jefferson Writes the Declaration of Independence" in their eBooks.

A New American Nation

Tell students that this section establishes the historical context for the selections in this collection. It presents a brief overview of the significant events and ideas that combined to shape the political beliefs of the North American colonists and the eventual form of government adopted by the United States of America. The section ends with a reflection on how the concerns of poets of the time both mirrored and critiqued the concerns of contemporary political writers.

From Colony to Country

 COMMON CORE RL 10, RI 7, RI 10

Britain's actions after winning the French and Indian War motivated the North American colonists to think more deeply about the relationship between the colonies and the British Empire and what powers of government belonged to each. The levying of new taxes and the passing of the Proclamation of 1763, which limited the colonists' ability to freely settle lands to the west, caused some colonists to suspect that Britain meant to keep them subservient. John Dickinson, the "penman of the Revolution" who went on to help write the Articles of Confederation, wrote a series of published letters that described his notion of the ideal relationship between the two countries: while Parliament did hold ultimate power over the colonists, the colonies should have the power to make decisions ruling their own internal affairs.

Ideas of the Age

Inspired by the ideas of the Enlightenment, people began to revolt against authoritarian governments headed by monarchs who claimed to have been chosen by God to lead. Instead, they attempted to use reason to set up new systems of democratic government that would be mutually agreed upon and designed to protect people's rights to gain knowledge, enjoy freedom, and experience happiness.

 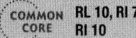

A New American Nation

COMMON CORE RL 10, RI 7, RI 10

In a span of almost two hundred years, a group of British colonies clustered along the Atlantic coast became an independent nation that spread from modern-day New Hampshire to Georgia. United around principles of self-government and liberty, the United States expanded its vision of itself as it began to explore the potential of the country's unique natural resources.

FROM COLONY TO COUNTRY Through the middle of the eighteenth century, the colonists in North America thought of themselves as British. They supported Britain economically and militarily, especially during the French and Indian War (1754–1763), when Britain fought to gain control of all the land east of the Mississippi River. When Britain then tried to recover the costs of the war by taxing the colonists, they rebelled. In 1783, after eight years of the Revolutionary War, the United States won its independence. At first, the founders struggled to govern effectively under the Articles of Confederation. Eventually, however, they created our current form of government under the United States Constitution, which was adopted in 1788.

Ideological debates over the scope and nature of federal power raged throughout the republic's early years. In 1803, President Thomas Jefferson doubled the size of the United States with the purchase from France of the vast Louisiana Territory west of the Mississippi River. The price was $15 million. Jefferson, who normally favored a limited federal government, took this bold step even though the Constitution gave him no explicit authority to do so.

IDEAS OF THE AGE In the 1700s, as the colonists moved toward independence, they drew on traditional Puritan values and on Enlightenment ideals, which questioned previously accepted truths about government. Both sources of inspiration caused people to question traditional authority, eventually leading the colonists to break from Britain's control and embrace democracy. American colonial writers such as Benjamin Franklin, Thomas Paine, and Thomas Jefferson adapted the ideals of the European Enlightenment for their own environment. At the same time, preachers such as Jonathan Edwards called for people to rededicate themselves to the original Puritan vision. This new wave of religious enthusiasm, called the Great Awakening, united geographically and culturally diverse colonists.

1734–1736
Great Awakening begins

1765
Colonists rebel against the Stamp Act

1700

1733
Georgia becomes 13th British colony

1754
French and Indian War begins

A New American Nation **109**

SCAFFOLDING FOR ELL STUDENTS

Vocabulary: Suffixes Review how adverbs modify an action, or explain how something is done, and how many, but not all, adverbs end with the suffix -ly. Then point out some -ly adverbs on this page and work with students to identify what each one modifies. For example, the colonists supported Britain *economically* and *militarily*, which means that they provided both money and manpower.

ASK STUDENTS to work in small groups to identify other -ly adverbs on the page and describe what each of them modifies.

Writing That Launched a Nation

Thomas Paine's pamphlet *Common Sense* argued that the aim of the revolutionaries should be larger than just protesting unfair taxation; instead, the colonists should demand total independence from Britain. After examining the fairness of systems of government that allow a monarch to make absolute decisions or that limit a monarch's power, Paine suggests that it might be best to do away with having a monarch at all. His description of a government in which each colony could elect representatives that would gather together in a Congress to elect a president and make political decisions heavily influenced the writing of the Declaration of Independence.

Voices of the People

Although the statesmen were working to create a new form of government meant to protect the rights of people believed to be "equal," their definition of who these "equal" people were did not actually encompass everyone who lived in the newly created states. For example, when forming the Constitution, the Northern and Southern states reached an agreement called the Three-Fifths Compromise that said that for the purposes of representation and taxation, enslaved people would count only 3/5 as much as a free person.

Phillis Wheatley's writings, therefore, offered an important challenge to such views. Her poems celebrate the independence of the new United States of America but also use biblical language to gently urge religious people to recognize the evils of slavery. After her time, abolitionists working in the 1800s to free enslaved people used her poems as proof that African Americans could profit from education and achieve greatness as well as other races could.

WRITING THAT LAUNCHED A NATION As the colonists began to question their relationship with Great Britain, many gifted minds turned to political writing. Between 1763 and 1783, about two thousand inexpensive pamphlets were published, reaching thousands of people and stirring debate and action. *Common Sense* by Thomas Paine was a key pamphlet that helped move the colonists to revolution. Paine's Enlightenment ideas were combined with the Puritan belief that America was destined to be a model of freedom to the world.

Although Thomas Jefferson also wrote pamphlets, his greatest contribution to American government and literature is the Declaration of Independence, adopted by the Second Continental Congress on July 4, 1776. Jefferson's eloquent and stirring articulation of the natural law that would govern America proclaimed the idea that people are born with rights and freedoms that government must protect. While Jefferson's Declaration marked the beginning of the colonies' independence, it was the adoption of the Constitution of the United States of America in 1788 that created the lasting framework for an independent government. Many of the young nation's most outstanding leaders, including Benjamin Franklin, James Madison, Alexander Hamilton, and George Washington, crafted perhaps the country's most important foundational document.

VOICES OF THE PEOPLE Statesmen were joined by poets in examining political and social themes of the day. Among the finest examples of Colonial American poetry are the works of Phillis Wheatley and Philip Freneau. In her poems and letters, Wheatley, a former slave, wrote of the "natural rights" of African Americans. She also pointed out the discrepancy between the colonists' "cry for liberty" and their enslavement of fellow human beings.

Freneau, who became known as the "poet of the American Revolution," wrote verses that harshly criticized the British, such as "The British Prison-Ship," based on his own experience as a prisoner of war. He also celebrated those who fought in the revolutionary cause, including John Paul Jones, whom he exhorted to "bid the haughty Britons know / They to our Thirteen Stars shall bend." After the war, his lyrical poetry continued to build on Enlightenment ideals—celebrating the natural wonders of America while proclaiming that its lands were the ideal site for the growth of freedom.

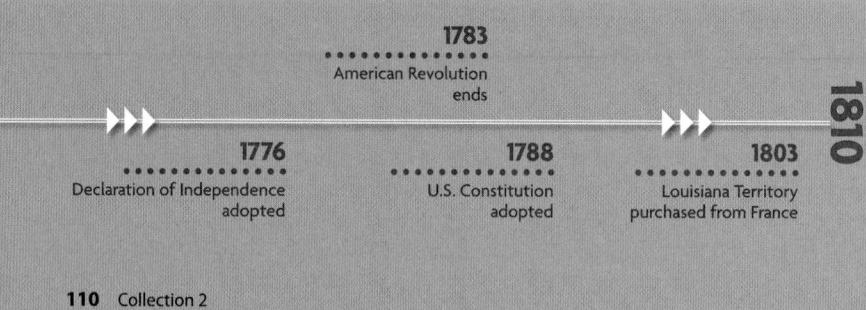

1783
American Revolution ends

1776
Declaration of Independence adopted

1788
U.S. Constitution adopted

1803
Louisiana Territory purchased from France

1810

WHEN STUDENTS STRUGGLE . . .

Vocabulary Support: Some students may experience difficulty with understanding content terms that are included as part of the historical background essays that begin each collection.

ASK STUDENTS to work in small groups to point out vocabulary words relating to the topics of politics and government: *colonies* (page 109), *independent* (page 109), *liberty* (page 109), *constitution* (page 109), *ideological* (page 109), *federal* (page 109), *republic* (page 109), *democracy* (page 109), *congress* (page 110), and *foundational* (page 110). Then ask them to use context to define each term.

Comprehend Literature: Historical Context

COMMON CORE

RL 10

TEACH

Students may experience difficulty when interpreting quotations from primary sources of literature. Explain that considering the historical background in which a writer lived and worked can offer a reader clues for how to interpret the meaning and importance of a text.

Have students reread the lines from the Freneau poem quoted on page 110. Then discuss what information can be gathered about Freneau from this historical background essay. For example, one of his main subjects was the American Revolution. He was supportive of those who fought in this revolution, and he was critical of the British. Then model how to understand the meaning of the quoted lines better by rewording them using contemporary English: "tell the proud British soldiers that they will kneel and surrender to us (our flag)." Note that students might need to use resources to look up the meaning of difficult words such as *haughty* or to research potentially confusing symbols such as *Thirteen Stars*. Finally, discuss what it adds to the historical background essay to include this quotation: it communicates the attitude of a poet of the time toward the conflict between the colonies and the British.

PRACTICE AND APPLY

Have pairs identify another example of a primary source quoted in this historical background essay. *(Phillis Wheatley)* Then have them work together to review what they know about Wheatley and the time in which she wrote to interpret the meaning of the phrases quoted here, and to discuss why these lines might have been included as part of this essay.

Comprehend Literary Nonfiction: Strategies for Reading

COMMON CORE

RI 10

TEACH

To comprehend a historical background essay, students may find it helpful to use the following strategies for reading literary nonfiction:

- Examine and identify how the text is structured. Does it describe events in a particular order? Does it discuss cause-effect relationships?
- What difficult stylistic features might the text contain? Quotations? Descriptions? Figurative language?
- What unfamiliar content vocabulary does the text contain? Can you use context clues or outside resources to define the terms?
- What is the historical context in which the text was written? How does this relate to the author's purpose?

To develop and demonstrate understanding of a piece of literary nonfiction after reading it, students might try to do the following:

- Summarize the time period and general context in which it was written.
- Summarize in their own words what it is saying.
- Explain what the author's purpose was for writing it.
- Describe its meaning and what the experience of reading it helps the reader understand better about the world.

CLOSE READING APPLICATION

Have students work independently to read another piece of literary nonfiction and use these strategies to gain a deeper understanding of its historical context, purpose, and meaning.

mySmartPlanner — Create lesson plans and access resources online.

COMPARE ANCHOR TEXTS

 **ANCHOR TEXT EXEMPLAR**

The Declaration of Independence

Public Document by Thomas Jefferson

 **ANCHOR TEXT EXEMPLAR**

from The United States Constitution

Public Document

Why These Texts?

Students must be able to analyze the documents produced by our nation's founders in order to develop informed opinions on contemporary political issues. The Declaration of Independence states the unique guiding principles of the new nation. Students will analyze the themes and rhetorical devices.

 ▶ *View It!*

Professional Development Podcast:

Teaching Argument

For additional practice:

Close Reader selection
from The United States Constitution

Key Learning Objective: The student will be able to analyze the features of a foundational U.S. document.

COMMON CORE Common Core Standards

RI 1 Cite textual evidence.
RI 4 Determine the meaning of words and phrases as they are used in a text.
RI 5 Analyze and evaluate structure.
RI 6 Determine an author's point of view or purpose.
RI 8 Delineate and evaluate the reasoning in U.S. texts and works of public advocacy.
RI 9 Analyze foundational U.S. documents.
W 2a Introduce and organize complex ideas.
W 2b Develop topics by selecting the most significant and relevant information.
W 7 Conduct short as well as more sustained research projects.
W 8 Gather and assess relevant information.
W 9 Draw evidence from texts to support analysis, reflection, and research.
W 9b Apply gr 11 Reading standards to nonfiction.
SL 6 Adapt speech to a variety of contexts, demonstrating formal English.
L 3a Vary syntax for effect; apply an understanding of syntax.
L 4c Consult reference materials.
L 6 Acquire and use accurately general academic and domain-specific words and phrases.

▲ Text Complexity Rubric

	Declaration of Independence	*from* The United States Constitution
Quantitative Measures	Lexile: 1320L	Lexile: 1580L
Qualitative Measures	**Levels of Meaning/Purpose** single purpose easily identified from context	**Levels of Meaning/Purpose** multiple topics
	Structure organization of main ideas and details complex but mostly explicit	**Structure** organization of main ideas and details is highly complex; not explicit, inferable
	Language Conventionality and Clarity complex and varied sentence structure	**Language Conventionality and Clarity** increased unfamiliar language
	Knowledge Demands somewhat complex social studies concepts	**Knowledge Demands** somewhat complex social studies concepts
Reader/Task Considerations	Teacher determined Vary by individual reader and type of text	Teacher determined Vary by individual reader and type of text

TEACH

CLOSE READ

For more context and historical background, students can view the videos "The Presidents: Jefferson Writes the Declaration of Independence" and "America Gets a Constitution" in their eBooks.

Background Have students read the information about the Second Continental Congress, Jefferson's decision to draft The Declaration of Independence, and the other foundational documents from the time of the Revolutionary War.

The original purpose of the Second Continental Congress was to negotiate for the rights of the colonies with Britain, but its members gradually came to believe that the colonies would have to become an independent nation. The Second Continental Congress made the New England military forces that had already been fighting the British an official army and named George Washington its commander-in-chief. It also issued and borrowed money, formed a postal service, and created a navy.

Thomas Jefferson His legacy goes beyond founding father, diplomat, and third president of the United States. Jefferson also was a plantation owner and slaveholder, lawyer, inventor, philosopher, book collector, scholar, and founder and architect of the University of Virginia. Despite his many notable accomplishments, upon his death on July 4, 1826, the fiftieth anniversary of the adoption of the Declaration of Independence, Jefferson requested that only three things he had given the people be noted on his tombstone: Author of the Declaration of American Independence, Author of the Statute of Virginia for Religious Freedom, and Father of the University of Virginia.

AS YOU READ Direct students to use the As You Read instructions to focus their reading.

HISTORY | VIDEO

The Declaration of Independence *from* The United States Constitution

Public Documents

Background *The Declaration of Independence, adopted July 4, 1776, by the Second Continental Congress, was the culmination of a long process during which the American colonists tried to resolve their differences with Great Britain. Hope for a peaceful resolution still persisted after the outbreak of armed conflict in April 1775. By the spring of 1776, however, most colonists favored a break with Britain. In early June, a committee was formed to draft a statement to support that position, and* **Thomas Jefferson** *took on the task of writing it. Although the Congress made changes to his list of grievances, it did not touch his declaration of rights, which became a lasting statement of "self-evident" truths for the new country and the world.*

In 1787 a Constitutional Convention was called to amend the Articles of Confederation, the first written constitution of the United States. The Articles severely limited the power of the central government and prevented it from meeting many challenges in the country's first years. The Constitution did not have one predominant author because it reflected many compromises needed to resolve differences between large and small states, Northerners and Southerners. The final document sought to create a balance between a strong, workable central government and individual liberty. The Bill of Rights, adopted as the first ten Amendments to the Constitution in 1791, strengthened the original document's protection of individual and states' rights.

Thomas Jefferson *(1743–1826) was one of the most accomplished of our nation's founders. He held a number of important government positions, including governor of Virginia during the Revolutionary War and U.S. minister to France afterward. In addition, he served as the country's first secretary of state, its second vice-president, and its third president. More important than his titles, however, was his vision of liberty and self-government, eloquently expressed in the Declaration of Independence.*

Image Credits: (t) ©Fotosearch/Getty Images; (b) ©Hisham Ibrahim/Photodisc/Getty Images

---

Close Read Screencasts   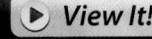 ▶ *View It!*

Modeled Discussions

Have students click the *Close Read* icons in their eBooks to access a screencast in which readers discuss and annotate the following key passage:

- Jefferson's recommendations about if and when to consider rejecting an established government (lines 17–28)

As a class, view and discuss the video. Then have students pair up to do a close read of an additional passage—Jefferson's enumeration of the efforts the founders made to diplomatically resolve conflicts with British loyalists over jurisdiction (lines 107–114).

Analyze Foundational Documents: Theme and Rhetorical Features

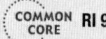 COMMON CORE RI 9

(LINES 8–17)

Explain to students that a text's **theme,** or main meaning, can be stated directly or must be inferred.

A **CITE TEXT EVIDENCE** Have students read lines 8–17 and identify the main subject of the passage. *(identifying people's rights under government)* Look for a word or phrase that best describes or summarizes Jefferson's opinion of the main subject. *("[W]henever any form of government becomes destructive of these ends, it is the right of the people to alter or abolish it, and to institute a new government. . . . " [lines 13–15])* Ask students to restate the theme. *(People have a right to a government that respects their rights, the right to overturn a government that does not, and the right to establish a new one.)*

Analyze Structure: Style and Content (LINES 28–31)

 COMMON CORE RI 6, L 3a

Explain that a writer expresses **style** through word choice, sentence length, and **tone**—the writer's attitude toward the subject.

B **CITE TEXT EVIDENCE** Ask students to identify the words in lines 28–31 that have the strongest **connotations,** or emotional impact. *(repeated injuries and usurpations, absolute tyranny)* Ask them why Jefferson might have chosen these words. *(to emphasize how badly the British government was treating the colonies)* Ask them to reread the lines and describe Jefferson's tone, citing supporting words and phrases.

> **CRITICAL VOCABULARY**
>
> **establish**: Jefferson warns that an existing government should not be changed impulsively.
>
> **ASK STUDENTS** What is the advantage of maintaining an established government? *(An established government ensures stability and order.)*

AS YOU READ Notice how Jefferson compares good government and bad government. Write down any questions you generate during reading.

The Declaration of Independence
by Thomas Jefferson

In Congress, July 4, 1776

When, in the course of human events, it becomes necessary for one people to dissolve the political bands which have connected them with another, and to assume, among the powers of the earth, the separate and equal station to which the laws of nature and of nature's God entitle them, a decent respect to the opinions of mankind requires that they should declare the causes which impel them to the separation.

10 We hold these truths to be self-evident:—That all men are created equal; that they are endowed by their Creator with certain unalienable rights; that among these are life, liberty, and the pursuit of happiness. That, to secure these rights, governments are instituted among men, deriving their just powers from the consent of the governed; that, whenever any form of government becomes destructive of these ends, it is the right of the people to alter or to abolish it, and to institute a new government, laying its foundation on such principles, and organizing its powers in such form, as to them shall seem most likely to effect their safety and happiness. Prudence, indeed, will dictate that governments long **established** should not be changed for light and transient causes; and, accordingly, all experience hath shown 20 that mankind are more disposed to suffer, while evils are sufferable, than to right themselves by abolishing the forms to which they are accustomed. But, when a long train of abuses and usurpations, pursuing invariably the same object, evinces a design to reduce them under absolute despotism,[1] it is their right, it is their duty, to throw off such government, and to provide new guards for their future security. Such has been the patient sufferance of these colonies; and such is now the necessity that constrains them to alter their former systems of government. The history of the present King of Great Britain[2] is a history of repeated injuries and usurpations, all having, in direct 30 object, the establishment of an absolute tyranny over these States. To prove this, let facts be submitted to a candid world.

establish
(ĭ-stăb´lĭsh) *v.* to formally set up; institute.

---

[1] **despotism:** (dĕs´pə-tĭz´əm) *n.* government by a ruler with unlimited power.
[2] **the present King of Great Britain:** George III, who reigned from 1760 to 1820.

SCAFFOLDING FOR ELL STUDENTS

Pronoun Referents Remind students that pronouns replace or refer to nouns. Have students complete the graphic organizer as they do a close read of lines 8–12.

Line	Pronoun	Referent
9	endowed by their creator	all men
10	among these are life, liberty, and the pursuit of happiness	rights
12	deriving their just powers	governments

"Life, liberty, and the pursuit of happiness."

He has refused his assent to laws[3] the most wholesome and necessary for the public good.

He has forbidden his Governors to pass laws of immediate and pressing importance, unless suspended in their operation till his assent should be obtained; and, when so suspended, he has utterly neglected to attend to them.

He has refused to pass other laws for the accommodation of large districts of people, unless these people would relinquish the right of representation in the legislature—a right inestimable to them, and formidable to tyrants only.

He has called together legislative bodies at places unusual, uncomfortable, and distant from the depository of their public records, for the sole purpose of fatiguing them into compliance with his measure.

He has dissolved representative houses repeatedly, for opposing, with manly firmness, his invasions on the rights of the people.

He has refused, for a long time after such dissolutions, to cause others to be elected; whereby the legislative powers, incapable of annihilation, have returned to the people at large for their exercise; the State remaining, in the meantime, exposed to all dangers of invasion from without, and convulsions within.

He has endeavored to prevent the population[4] of these States; for that purpose obstructing the laws for the naturalization of foreigners; refusing to pass others to encourage their migration hither, and raising the conditions of new appropriations of lands.

He has obstructed the administration of justice, by refusing his assent to laws for establishing judiciary powers.

---

[3] **refused his assent to laws:** Laws passed in the colonies needed the king's approval; sometimes it took years for laws to be approved or rejected.

[4] **to prevent the population:** to keep the population from growing.

The Declaration of Independence **113**

APPLYING ACADEMIC VOCABULARY

revolution	founder

As you discuss The Declaration of Independence, incorporate the following Collection 2 academic vocabulary words: *revolution* and *founder*. Ask students what the *founders* hoped to establish. Then, ask students to suggest possible reasons the word *revolution* is not used in the document.

CLOSE READ

Analyze Foundational Documents: Theme and Rhetorical Features

COMMON CORE RI 9

(LINES 32–58)

Explain to students that **rhetorical features** include all the methods a writer uses to communicate ideas and appeal to readers. One rhetorical feature is **repetition,** repeating words and phrases to reinforce meaning and to create rhythm.

C CITE TEXT EVIDENCE Have students read this page and identify what is repeated. *("He has" at the beginning of each sentence)* Ask them what effect this repetition has on the reader. *(It emphasizes the king's many offenses, creating a rhythm that hammers home the point to readers.)*

Analyze Structure: Style and Content (LINES 42–47)

COMMON CORE RI 6, L 3a

Explain to students that **syntax** is the way words, phrases, and clauses are arranged in sentences. Point out that repeating the opening words *("He has")* of these sentences might have dulled their impact over time, failing to keep the reader's interest. Instead, Jefferson varies the rhythm and content of the words that follow them. Point out the phrase "for the sole purpose of fatiguing them into compliance with his measure" in lines 44–45. Discuss with students how this phrase enlivens the sentence by varying its rhythm and adding information about the king's actions—in this case, about his motivation.

D CITE TEXT EVIDENCE Have students reread lines 42–47 and find another phrase that tells about an action. *("with manly firmness," line 47)* Ask them to read the sentence without the phrase and then tell how the phrase affects the rhythm of the sentence. *(It breaks up the sentence's rhythm, making readers pause to pay attention.)* Then ask students how they think this phrase engages the reader's sympathies. *(By characterizing the representatives' opposition as "manly" and "firm," both positive qualities, Jefferson makes the reader feel that they must be in the right.)*

Analyze Structure: Style and Content (LINES 90–97)

COMMON CORE RI 9

Remind students that **tone** is the writer's attitude toward the subject. Tell students that the use of words with strong connotations, or emotional associations, expresses the author's tone.

E **CITE TEXT EVIDENCE** Have a volunteer read lines 90–97 aloud. Ask students to paraphrase these sentences using neutral language. *(The King is sending in foreign troops to subdue the colonies. He has forced colonists taken into custody at sea to serve in his occupying army.)* Then ask students to describe Jefferson's actual tone. *(indignant, even angry)* Ask which specific words contribute most to this tone. *(desolation, tyranny: line 91; cruelty, perfidy: line 92; barbarous: line 93; executioners: line 96; brethren: line 97)*

CRITICAL VOCABULARY

affect: Because of the King's actions and decisions, British soldiers were not accountable to the government of the colonies.

ASK STUDENTS how the King's empowerment of British soldiers affected the colonists. *(The colonists had no way to defend themselves from the actions of British soldiers.)*

invest: Quebec claimed it had been granted power to govern parts of the colonies.

ASK STUDENTS to explain why Jefferson rejects the idea that Quebec was invested by Great Britain with the power to legislate for the colonies. *(Quebec can't be endowed, or invested, with this power because Great Britain cannot grant something it does not rightfully have.)*

abdicate: Jefferson argues that the King gave up his right to govern the colonies.

ASK STUDENTS how the King's actions show that he has abdicated his role as a trustworthy leader by acting like a tyrant. *(The king's actions include increasing the military's power over the colonies, imposing taxes on them, deporting colonists, and destroying colonists' land and property without recourse. His actions indicate that he established unjust, punitive policies, abdicating his responsibility to treat the colonies fairly.)*

He has made judges dependent on his will alone for the tenure of
60   their offices,[5] and the amount and payment of their salaries.

He has erected a multitude of new offices, and sent hither swarms of officers to harass our people and eat out their substance.[6]

He has kept among us, in times of peace, standing armies, without the consent of our legislatures.

He has **affected** to render the military independent of, and superior to, the civil power.

affect
(ə-fĕkt´) *v.* to cause or influence.

He has combined with others to subject us to a jurisdiction foreign to our constitutions,[7] and unacknowledged by our laws; giving his assent to their acts of pretended legislation:

70   For quartering large bodies of armed troops among us;

For protecting them, by a mock trial, from punishment for any murders which they should commit on the inhabitants of these States;

For cutting off our trade with all parts of the world;

For imposing taxes on us without our consent;

For depriving us, in many cases, of the benefits of trial by jury;

For transporting us beyond the seas, to be tried for pretended offenses;

For abolishing the free system of English laws in a neighboring province,[8] establishing there an arbitrary government, and enlarging
80   its boundaries, so as to render it at once an example and fit instrument for introducing the same absolute rule into these colonies;

For taking away our charters, abolishing our most valuable laws, and altering, fundamentally, the forms of our governments;

For suspending our own legislatures, and declaring themselves **invested** with power to legislate for us in all cases whatsoever.

invest
(ĭn-vĕst´) *v.* to grant or endow.

He has **abdicated** government here, by declaring us out of his protection, and waging war against us.

abdicate
(ăb´dĭ-kāt´) *v.* to relinquish or cede responsibility for.

He has plundered our seas, ravaged our coasts, burnt our towns,[9] and destroyed the lives of our people.

E
90   He is at this time transporting large armies of foreign mercenaries to complete the works of death, desolation, and tyranny, already begun with circumstances of cruelty and perfidy scarcely paralleled in the most barbarous ages, and totally unworthy the head of a civilized nation.

He has constrained our fellow citizens, taken captive on the high seas, to bear arms against their country, to become the executioners of their friends and brethren, or to fall themselves by their hands.

---

[5] **the tenure of their offices:** their job security.

[6] **eat out their substance:** use up their resources.

[7] **subject us . . . our constitutions:** Parliament had passed the Declaratory Act in 1766, stating that the king and Parliament could make laws for the colonies.

[8] **a neighboring province:** the province of Quebec, which at the time extended south to the Ohio River and west to the Mississippi.

[9] **plundered . . . our towns:** American seaports such as Norfolk, Virginia, had already been shelled.

114 Collection 2

WHEN STUDENTS STRUGGLE...

Discuss with students that when a text contains many supporting details, they can help themselves understand and remember the details by organizing them into categories.

ASK STUDENTS what categories the examples on this page of the colonies' complaints against the King represent. *(military actions, administrative actions, legal actions, economic actions)*

Tell students to reread this page closely. Then guide them as they use a chart like the one on the next page to organize the list of complaints into categories.

He has excited domestic insurrection amongst us,[10] and has endeavored to bring on the inhabitants of our frontiers the merciless
100   Indian savages, whose known rule of warfare is an undistinguished destruction of all ages, sexes, and conditions.

In every stage of these oppressions we have petitioned for redress,[11] in the most humble terms; our repeated petitions have been answered only by repeated injury. A prince whose character is thus marked by every act which may define a tyrant is unfit to be the ruler of a free people.

Nor have we been wanting in our attentions to our British brethren. We have warned them, from time to time, of attempts by their legislature to extend an unwarrantable jurisdiction over us.
110   We have reminded them of the circumstances of our emigration and settlement here. We have appealed to their native justice and magnanimity; and we have conjured them, by the ties of our common kindred, to disavow these usurpations, which would inevitably interrupt our connections and correspondence.

They, too, have been deaf to the voice of justice and of consanguinity.[12] We must, therefore, acquiesce in the necessity which denounces our separation; and hold them, as we hold the rest of mankind, enemies in war, in peace friends.

---

[10]**excited . . . amongst us:** George III had encouraged slaves to rise up and rebel against their masters.

[11]**redress:** the correction of a wrong; compensation.

[12]**deaf to . . . consanguinity:** The British have ignored pleas based on their common ancestry with the colonists.

military actions	administrative actions	legal actions	economic actions
kept a standing army	took over the appointment of judges	suspended trial by jury	cut off trade
made the military superior to government	sent new officials	transported colonists to be tried on false charges	Imposed taxes

Image Credits: (t) ©Universal Images Group/Getty Images; (bg) ©Odua Images/Shutterstock

CLOSE READ

Analyze Foundational Documents: Rhetorical Features (LINES 107–114)

COMMON CORE   RI 9

Explain to students that **parallelism** is the use of similar grammatical structures to emphasize the relationship among ideas or show that they have equal weight or importance.

Have students read lines 107–114, noticing examples of parallelism. Then have students work with partners, taking turns reading these lines aloud. Allow time for partners to compare and contrast the effect of the parallelism when read silently and heard aloud.

F CITE TEXT EVIDENCE Ask students to cite their examples of parallelism. *(Each sentence begins with the subject "we" followed by a present perfect tense verb: "We have warned them; We have reminded them; We have appealed to their native justice; we have conjured them." All but the second to last follow the verb with the pronoun "them.")* Then ask how these ideas are related. *(They are ways the founders have tried to resolve their problems with Britain peacefully.)*

Analyze Structure: Style and Content (LINES 111–114)

COMMON CORE   RI 6, L 3a

Remind students that Jefferson chose his words carefully to achieve his purpose of convincing "a candid world" to support American independence.

G CITE TEXT EVIDENCE Ask students to list the words in these lines that help Jefferson persuade readers that the colonists have done their best to work with the British people. (native justice, magnanimity, conjured, common kindred)

Analyze Structure: Style and Content (LINES 119–133)  COMMON CORE RI 6, L 3a

Tell students that both word choice and **syntax** contribute to a writer's **tone.** Have students read the final paragraph of The Declaration of Independence. Discuss with students their general impressions of Jefferson's attitude toward his topic.

H CITE TEXT EVIDENCE Have students describe Jefferson's tone in lines 119–133. *(Possible answers: direct, reverent, confident, determined)* What words help create the tone? *(Possible answers: solemnly, publish and declare, absolved, free and independent, full power, of right)* How does the syntax help create the tone? *(The arrangement of Jefferson's words, phrases, and clauses in long sentences makes the language formal and creates a confident and determined tone that embodies the seriousness and firmness of the colonies' decision to declare independence.)*

Analyze Fundamental Documents: Theme and Rhetorical Features  COMMON CORE RI 9

(LINES 123–130)

Tell students that in these lines Jefferson combines parallelism and repetition to reinforce his theme.

I CITE TEXT EVIDENCE Ask students to find examples of parallelism and repetition in this paragraph. *(parallelism: clauses beginning with "that" in lines 123, 124, 125, and 127; repetition: "ought to be" in lines 124 and 127)* Then ask students to state Jefferson's theme, and how these devices reinforce it. *(Jefferson's theme is that the colonies are now independent. The clauses beginning with that emphasize the separation. The repetition of ought to be reinforces the idea that independence is justified.)*

COLLABORATIVE DISCUSSION Have student pairs discuss what they think makes a good government, citing evidence from the document to support their ideas. Ask volunteers to share their ideas with the class.

ASK STUDENTS to share any questions they generated in the course of reading and discussing this selection.

H 120 WE, THEREFORE, THE REPRESENTATIVES OF THE UNITED STATES OF AMERICA, in General Congress assembled, appealing to the Supreme Judge of the world for the rectitude[13] of our intentions, do, in the name and by the authority of the good people of these colonies, solemnly publish and declare, that these United Colonies are, and of right ought to be, Free and Independent States; that they are absolved from all allegiance to the British crown, and that all political connection between them and the state of Great Britain is, and ought to be, totally dissolved; and that, as free and independent states, they have full power to levy war, conclude peace, contract alliances, establish commerce, and to do all other acts and things 130 which independent states may of right do. And, for the support of this declaration, with a firm reliance on the protection of Divine Providence, we mutually pledge to each other our lives, our fortunes, and our sacred honor. **I**

---

[13] **rectitude:** morally correct behavior or thinking.

COLLABORATIVE DISCUSSION What makes a good government? Discuss this question with a partner, citing specific textual evidence from the Declaration of Independence to support your ideas.

SCAFFOLDING FOR ELL STUDENTS

Practice Reading Fluency Read aloud the sentence in lines 119–130. Tell students to follow the words in their texts as you read. Explain that when you pause, students should read aloud the same lines from the text.

- **First Read:** Pause at all commas and semicolons and have the whole group echo.
- **Second Read:** Pause at all commas and semicolons and select a different individual to echo each section.
- **Independent Practice:** Have pairs of students take turns reading the sentence aloud. Monitor progress by listening for phrasing, fluency, and expression. Model again as needed.

Analyze Structure: Style and Content

COMMON CORE RI 6, L 3a

The power of the Declaration of Independence comes not just from *what* it says, or its content, but from *how* Jefferson says it, or his style. **Style** comes from an author's word choice, sentence length, and **tone,** or attitude about the subject. Jefferson's message is complex, so he is careful to arrange the content in an orderly and logical way.

An important element of style is **syntax,** the arrangement of words in phrases, clauses, and sentences. Varying the syntax allows a writer to create variety, emphasis, and a rhythm that helps keep readers engaged. Note how Jefferson begins the Declaration:

> When, <u>in the course of human events</u>, it becomes necessary for one
> people to dissolve the political bands which have connected them with
> another, and to assume, <u>among the powers of the earth</u>, the
> separate and equal station to which the laws of nature and of nature's
> God entitle them, . . .

The two underlined phrases are not strictly needed to convey the meaning of the sentence. Adding them, however, puts in meaningful pauses and adds to the weight of what the colonists are about to do. Reread the sentence without those phrases and see how it affects your response to Jefferson's point. As you analyze the text, be aware of how style and content contribute to the power and persuasiveness of the document.

Analyze Foundational Documents: Theme and Rhetorical Features

COMMON CORE RI 9

Jefferson wrote the Declaration to justify the move toward independence to the British, represented by the king. He was also writing for the American colonists of his own time and for future generations. His choice of themes and his use of rhetorical features reflect both his purpose and his audience.

Theme	Rhetorical Features
A **theme** is a main message that the author wants to communicate about a topic—in this case, independence. The themes of the Declaration of Independence are relevant to the situation in which the document was written and also speak to broader ideas that are relevant over time.	**Rhetorical features** include all the methods a writer uses to communicate ideas and appeal to readers. • **Repetition** is the technique of repeating words or phrases to reinforce meaning and create rhythm. For example, the repetition of the word *nature* in the first sentence of the Declaration emphasizes the basis for Jefferson's appeal. • **Parallelism** is the use of similar grammatical structures to express ideas that are related or equal in importance. For example, in lines 70–85, Jefferson begins each item in the list with the preposition *for* followed by a gerund, such as *quartering* or *protecting*, to add to the persuasive impact of this section.

TEACH

CLOSE READ

Analyze Structure: Style and Content

COMMON CORE RI 6, L 3a

Call students' attention to the excerpt from the Declaration cited on the student page. Ask them to identify the part of speech of both underlined sections. *(prepositional phrase)* Point out that both prepositional phrases contain within them a second prepositional phrase that begins with *of.* Explain that use of parallel structures like this is an element of style called **parallelism.**

Have a volunteer read the excerpt from the beginning of the Declaration aloud. Then have a volunteer read the excerpt without the underlined phrases.

ASK STUDENTS why Jefferson may have included these phrases. How do they affect the impact of the sentence when read? When heard read aloud? *(These phrases influence the rhythm and create a sense of import. Both phrases emphasize the universality and global significance of what Jefferson discusses.)*

Strategies for Annotation ✐ 🖫 *Annotate it!*

Analyze Structure: Style and Content

COMMON CORE RI 6, L3a

Have students use their eBook annotation tools to analyze the text.

- Use the underlining tool to mark phrases that are not strictly required for meaning.
- Use green to highlight words in the phrases that give clues as to why they are included.
- Use notes to record why these phrases are included. Compare and contrast the effect of these phrases in silent and oral reading.

> When, <u>in the course of human events</u>, it becomes necessary for one
> people to dissolve the political bands which have connected them
> with another, and to assume, <u>among the powers of</u>
> <u>the earth</u>, the separate and equal station to which
> the laws of nature and nature's God entitle
> them, . . .

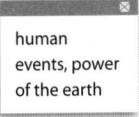
human events, power of the earth

PRACTICE & APPLY

Analyzing the Text COMMON CORE RI 1, RI 5, RI 6, RI 9

Possible answers:

1. Jefferson claims that sometimes rejecting a government is justified. He supports his claim in the specific context of the American colonies by showing that Great Britain's government in the colonies is bad.

2. He reasons that governments that do not honor citizens' rights should be overthrown; the King's actions and decisions yielded such a government.

3. Tone is elevated in the opening words—the organization of the words "We hold these truths to be self-evident" sounds nobler than saying "We believe this." The parallelism of stating each right in a dependent clause beginning with "that" adds power and rhythm to the ideas.

4. Established governments should not be changed impulsively; however, getting rid of a bad government is not only justified, it is a duty.

5. "abuses," "usurpations," and "despotism"stress the King's unjust government

6. It emphasizes the grievances and the effects of the King's actions on the colonies. It supports the claim that the colonies are justified in eradicating tyranny.

7. The repetition of the word "all" emphasizes that the break with Britain will be complete and absolute. The parallelism of dependent clauses beginning with "that" connects this section to the inspirational section about rights in lines 8–13, which also begins a series of clauses with "that" and punctuates each declaration. The inspirational connection and rhythm enhance the persuasiveness and power of the conclusion. The parallelism in the final line: "our lives, our fortunes, and our sacred honor" brings the pledge, and the document, to a powerful, poetic, and memorable close.

Analyzing the Text COMMON CORE RI 1, RI 5, RI 6, RI 9

Cite Text Evidence   Support your responses with evidence from the selection.

1. **Analyze** In an argument, a claim is an author's position on an issue. What claim does Jefferson make in the first paragraph, and how does he say he will support that claim?

2. **Infer** What overall reason for the colonies to separate from Britain does Jefferson outline in the second paragraph (lines 8–31)?

3. **Cite Evidence** How do the syntax and rhetorical features that Jefferson uses in the first sentence of the second paragraph (lines 8–10) contribute to the persuasiveness of the document?

4. **Draw Conclusions** What theme about government does Jefferson communicate in the second paragraph?

5. **Cite Evidence** Identify the most striking words that Jefferson chooses to describe the king's actions in lines 22–31. How does this language support his claim?

6. **Evaluate** The list of complaints makes up the largest part of the document's **structure,** or pattern of organization. What does its structure contribute to Jefferson's argument? How does it reinforce his main idea?

7. **Analyze** How do the rhetorical features in the conclusion (lines 119–133) contribute to the power and persuasiveness of the document?

PERFORMANCE TASK

Speaking Activity At the time of its publication, many colonists heard the Declaration of Independence read aloud in public places. Evaluate the effectiveness of this document presented as a speech through the following activity.

1. Work with a partner and take turns presenting the Declaration of Independence as a speech. One partner might read the opening and closing paragraphs and the other might read the list of complaints.

2. As a speaker, use tone of voice and pacing to reflect the rhetorical features of the document and communicate its meaning. As a listener, pay attention to how well you are able to follow the line of reasoning. Notice how the speech appeals to your reason and your emotions.

3. Write an evaluation of how the effectiveness of the Declaration as a speech compares to its effectiveness as a written document. Cite evidence from the document to support your ideas, and consider your experiences as a speaker, a listener, and a reader.

PERFORMANCE TASK COMMON CORE RI 5, RI 9, W 9, SL 6, L 3a

Assign this performance task.

Speaking Activity Allow students to discuss and choose from a range of options for assigning the text, including alternating sections and dividing the text in half so that one student has the introduction and half of the list and the other student has half of the list and the conclusion. Encourage students to mark the text with notes about adjusting their volume or speed for emphasis or rhythm. Remind them to adjust oral reading to highlight parallelism and repetition.

Students should do several oral readings of their sections, discussing ways to improve and switching parts to hear a different perspective on how the text might be presented orally.

Critical Vocabulary

established   affected   invested   abdicated

Practice and Apply Create a semantic map like the one below for each Critical Vocabulary word. Use a dictionary or thesaurus as needed. This example is for the word *instituted*, which appears in line 11 of the Declaration of Independence.

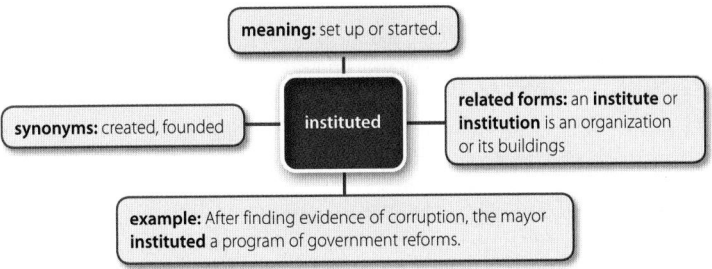

meaning: set up or started.

synonyms: created, founded

instituted

related forms: an **institute** or **institution** is an organization or its buildings

example: After finding evidence of corruption, the mayor **instituted** a program of government reforms.

Vocabulary Strategy: Domain-Specific Words

In the Declaration of Independence, Jefferson uses the Critical Vocabulary word *abdicated*. This word is fairly uncommon in general texts but appears more commonly in works of **political science**, or the study of government. Political science has a rich set of terms. Some terms may identify a particular type of government or government function; others, such as *despotism* and *tyranny*, describe the way a government acts. Building a vocabulary of such words will help you read social studies texts and contemporary writing about politics and government to become a better informed citizen. Use these strategies to become familiar with political science words.

- Use context clues to help you determine a word's meaning as it is used in a political text.
- Use a dictionary or other reference work to help you verify a word's meaning and understand its **etymology,** or origin. If a word has multiple meanings, check to see which one most likely applies to a political context.
- When using a reference work, look for related forms of a word and understand how each is used, such as *legislate*, *legislature*, or *legislative*.

Practice and Apply Work with a partner to investigate the meaning, etymology, and related forms of these domain-specific words using a dictionary or other reference work.

1. sovereign	**6.** republic
2. despotism	**7.** democracy
3. tyranny	**8.** legislative
4. govern	**9.** executive
5. oligarchy	**10.** judicial

PRACTICE & APPLY

Critical Vocabulary

Word: establish; *meaning:* formally set up; institute; *related forms:* establishment; *example:* The community established a fund for disaster relief.

Word: affect; *meaning:* cause or influence; *related forms:* affected, affectability; *example:* The schedule changes affected the routines of many commuters.

Word: invest; *meaning:* grant or endow; *related forms:* investment, investor; *example:* The promotion invested her with increased authority.

Word: abdicate; *meaning:* relinquish or cede responsibility for; *related forms:* abdication; *example:* Scheduling conflicts forced him to abdicate his position.

Vocabulary Strategy

1. *word:* sovereign; *meaning:* 1) ruler, king 2) independent, self-ruling political state; *etymology:* Latin: supernus=chief/above; *related forms:* sovereignty

2. *word:* despotism; *meaning:* cruel government by an all-powerful ruler; *etymology:* Greek: despotes=master; *related forms:* despot; despotic

3. *word:* tyranny; *meaning:* oppressive use of ruling power; *etymology:* Greek: turranos=oppressive ruler; *related forms:* tyrannous; tyrannical; tyrant

4. *word:* govern; *meaning:* manage the affairs of a state or country; *etymology:* Latin: gubernare=steer; rule; *related forms:* government; governable

5. *word:* oligarchy; *meaning:* small group of people controlling a country or group; *etymology:* Greek: oligoi=few+arkhein=rule; *related forms:* oligarchic

6. *word:* republic; *meaning:* political state in which power ultimately resides with the people; *etymology:* Latin: res=entity+publicus=of the people;

7. *word:* democracy; *meaning:* system in which citizens choose leaders; *etymology:* Greek: demos = people +kratia=power or rule; *related forms:* democracy

8. *word:* legislative; *meaning:* having the power to make laws; *etymology:* Latin: legis=law+latio=bringing; *related forms:* legislature, legislation, legislate

9. *word:* executive; *meaning:* the branch of government responsible for putting decisions or laws into effect; *etymology:* Latin: ex=out+sequi=follow;

10. *word:* judicial; *meaning:* relating to the administration of justice; *etymology:* Latin: judex/judic=law+dicere=say; *related forms:* judiciary; judicially; judicious

PRACTICE & APPLY

Language and Style: Parallel Structure

COMMON CORE RI 9, L 3a

Review with students the instruction and the examples on the chart. Ensure that students understand the similar grammatical structures that make each example parallel.

Practice and Apply:

The chart shows additional examples students may reference. Invite students to explain their examples and read them aloud.

Lines	Example	Effect
26–27	Such has been the patient sufferance of these colonies. . . such is now the necessity that constrains them	Emphasizes connection between what the colonies have suffered and the justification for ending the suffering
70–85	All prepositional phrases beginning with for	Sets off these grievances as subsections of a broader grievance
108–112	We have warned them; we have reminded them; we have appealed to their native justice; we have conjured them	Shows connections between the efforts the founders have made to peacefully resolve their grievances
128–129	levy war, conclude peace, contract alliances, establish commerce	Simple V-O structure ties the powers of the independent states together, emphasizes them and creates rhythm

---

Language and Style: Parallel Structure

COMMON CORE RI 9, L 3a

Jefferson makes frequent use of the rhetorical device of parallelism in the Declaration of Independence. **Parallelism** is the use of similar grammatical constructions to express ideas that are closely related or equal in importance. The grammatical constructions may include phrases, clauses, or sentences. Parallel structures are an important element in a writer's **syntax,** or arrangement of words. Consider this example from the Declaration:

> . . . it is the right of the people to alter or to abolish it, and to institute a new government, laying its foundation on such principles, and organizing its powers in such form . . .

First notice the use of three infinitives to describe what people have a right to do: *to alter, to abolish, to institute.* All of these rights are given equal weight. Jefferson then proceeds to use two phrases with parallel grammatical structure: "laying its foundation on such principles, and organizing its powers in such form." Laying the foundation of the new government and organizing its powers are equally important and are part of the same process. The parallel structure makes this close relationship clear.

The chart shows two more examples of parallel structures. Try reading each passage aloud. Note how the parallelism creates rhythm and helps emphasize similarities among related ideas.

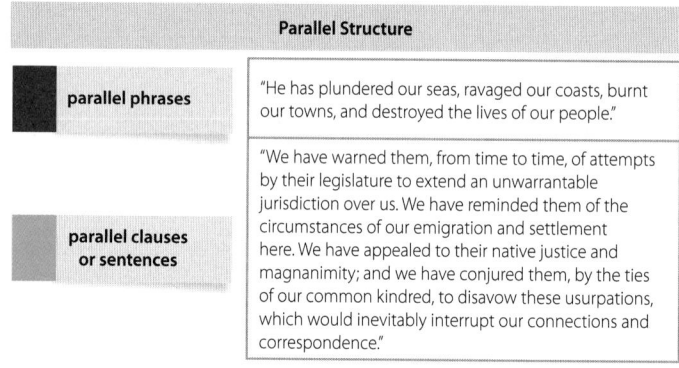

Parallel Structure	
parallel phrases	"He has plundered our seas, ravaged our coasts, burnt our towns, and destroyed the lives of our people."
parallel clauses or sentences	"We have warned them, from time to time, of attempts by their legislature to extend an unwarrantable jurisdiction over us. We have reminded them of the circumstances of our emigration and settlement here. We have appealed to their native justice and magnanimity; and we have conjured them, by the ties of our common kindred, to disavow these usurpations, which would inevitably interrupt our connections and correspondence."

Practice and Apply Look back at the evaluation of the Declaration of Independence that you wrote in response to this selection's Performance Task. Cite additional evidence of Jefferson's use of parallelism and explain how it contributes to the effectiveness of the spoken and written versions of the document. Then review your own writing to make any necessary revisions to correct for parallel structure or to add parallelism to strengthen your expression.

TO CHALLENGE STUDENTS. . .

Tell students that authors sometimes deliberately break a pattern of repetition or parallelism to add emphasis or create a pause before an important idea or change.

CITE TEXT EVIDENCE Have students work in small groups to discuss the examples of breaks in patterns. *(In line 70, the shift from "he" to "for" organizes a "subset" of grievances; In lines 106-114, Jefferson breaks parallelism slightly in line 111. "We have reminded them; We have warned them; We have appealed to their native justice; we have conjured them.")* Allow time for students to read aloud examples that demonstrate the effect of the breaks in repetition and parallelism. Finally, have students apply what they've learned to a piece of their own writing during revision.

Background When the Constitution was originally ratified by the states in 1788, not all Americans supported it. Anti-Federalists claimed that it did not do enough to protect the people's rights from the powers now granted to the federal government. So, Congress sent the Amendments that became the Bill of Rights to the states for ratification in 1789. Two years later, the Amendments became part of the Constitution.

AS YOU READ Direct students to use the As You Read instructions to focus their reading. Remind students to write down any questions they generate during reading.

Analyze Foundational Documents (LINE 1)

COMMON CORE RI 5, RI 9

Explain to students that authors use different **rhetorical features** to communicate ideas and appeal to readers.

A **ASK STUDENTS** to read the first line of the Preamble and explain how the language helps appeal to readers. *(The language makes the audience feel like participants in the government by including them as "We the people.")*

Evaluate Seminal Texts: Constitutional Principles

COMMON CORE RI 8

(LINES 1–7)

Inform students that the body of the Constitution includes a number of principles key to the U.S. government. One of these principles is representative democracy—that the people elect others to represent them and carry out the functions of government.

B **ASK STUDENTS** to reread the first sentence of the Preamble and explain how it expresses the principle of representative democracy. *(It presents the Constitution as the work of the people, even though it was written by delegates at the Constitutional Convention.)*

CRITICAL VOCABULARY

posterity: The Preamble points out the importance of liberty for future Americans, as well as present ones.

ASK STUDENTS how the founders of the United States might have hoped to be remembered. *(as champions of liberty and justice)*

AS YOU READ Notice what kinds of rights are protected in the Bill of Rights. Write down any questions you generate during reading.

from The United States Constitution: Preamble and Bill of Rights

Preamble

B We the People of the United States, in Order to form a more perfect Union, establish Justice, insure domestic Tranquility, provide for the common defence,[1] promote the general Welfare, and secure the Blessings of Liberty to ourselves and our **Posterity**, do ordain and establish this Constitution for the United States of America. **A**

posterity (pŏ-stĕr´ĭ-tē) *n.* future generations.

---

[1] **defence:** alternate spelling of *defense*.

Image Credits: ©Chris Maddaloni/Roll Call Photos/NewsCom

U.S. Constitution: Preamble and Bill of Rights **121**

Close Read Screencasts  ▶ View It!

Modeled Discussions

Have students click the *Close Read* icons in their eBooks to access a screencast in which readers discuss and annotate the following key passage:

• The Preamble to the Bill of Rights (lines 11–16)

As a class, view and discuss the video. Then have students pair up to do an independent close read of an additional passage—Amendment V (lines 42–50).

Analyze Foundational Documents (LINES 11–16)

 COMMON CORE **RI 5, RI 9**

Tell students that the Preamble to the Bill of Rights explains its **purpose,** or why it was written. It also explains how the Bill of Rights will fulfill its purpose.

C **ASK STUDENTS** to read the second paragraph of the Preamble and cite how it says the Bill of Rights will fulfill the purpose of making sure the government does not abuse its powers. (by adding clauses, or amendments, to restrict the government's power; by giving citizens more confidence in the government)

Evaluate Seminal Texts: Constitutional Principles

 COMMON CORE **RI 8**

(LINES 17–23)

Remind students that the Constitution includes the principle of separation of powers.

D **ASK STUDENTS** to read the third paragraph of the Preamble and explain how it illustrates the principle of separation of powers between federal and state government. (To become part of the Constitution, the Bill of Rights had to be passed first by the Senate and House of Representatives and then ratified by three fourths of the state legislatures.)

CRITICAL VOCABULARY

infringe: The Bill of Rights says that the people's right to own and carry weapons should not be violated.

ASK STUDENTS why the founders believed infringing on the right to bear arms would hinder security. Remind students that militias are citizens who organize in an emergency. (Citizens would need weapons in case they had to fight in a militia.)

prescribe: The Bill of Rights says that soldiers can be housed in private homes only according to the rules set forth in laws during wartime.

ASK STUDENTS why it would be important for the quartering of soldiers to be prescribed by law. (Citizens are protected from soldiers who may act inappropriately.)

The Bill of Rights

The Preamble to The Bill of Rights

Congress of the United States begun and held at the City of New-York, on Wednesday the fourth of March, one thousand seven
10 hundred and eighty nine.

 THE Conventions of a number of the States, having at the time of their adopting the Constitution, expressed a desire, in order to prevent misconstruction or abuse of its powers, that further declaratory and restrictive clauses should be added: And as extending the ground of public confidence in the Government, will best ensure the beneficent ends of its institution.

RESOLVED by the Senate and House of Representatives of the United States of America, in Congress assembled, two thirds of both Houses concurring, that the following Articles be proposed to the Legislatures
20 of the several States, as amendments to the Constitution of the United States, all, or any of which Articles, when ratified by three fourths of the said Legislatures, to be valid to all intents and purposes, as part of the said Constitution; viz.

ARTICLES in addition to, and Amendment of the Constitution of the United States of America, proposed by Congress, and ratified by the Legislatures of the several States, pursuant to the fifth Article of the original Constitution.

Amendment I

Congress shall make no law respecting an establishment of religion, or prohibiting the free exercise thereof; or abridging[2] the freedom of
30 speech, or of the press; or the right of the people peaceably to assemble, and to petition the Government for a redress of grievances.

Amendment II

A well regulated Militia, being necessary to the security of a free State, the right of the people to keep and bear Arms, shall not be **infringed**.

infringe
(ĭn-frĭnj´) v. to interfere with; violate.

Amendment III

No Soldier shall, in time of peace be **quartered**[3] in any house, without the consent of the Owner, nor in time of war, but in a manner to be **prescribed** by law.

prescribe
(prĭ-skrīb´) v. to authorize or regulate.

---

[2] **abridging:** limiting.
[3] **quartered:** housed or lodged.

122 Collection 2

SCAFFOLDING FOR ELL STUDENTS

Word Roots Draw students' attention to the word beneficent in line 15. Explain that the word root bene means "good" or "well" and that beneficent means "doing good" or "actively generous."

ASK STUDENTS to work in pairs or small groups to restate the "beneficent ends" of Amendment I in their own words. Make sure that students understand that ends here means "outcomes" or "purposes." (First-Amendment rights grant citizens liberty in the areas of religion, expression, information, assembly, and remedy of governmental wrongdoing.)

Amendment IV

The right of the people to be secure in their persons, houses, papers, and effects, against unreasonable searches and seizures, shall not be violated, and no Warrants shall issue, but upon probable cause,
40 supported by Oath or affirmation, and particularly describing the place to be searched, and the persons or things to be seized.

Amendment V

No person shall be held to answer for a capital, or otherwise infamous crime, unless on a presentment[4] or indictment of a Grand Jury, except in cases arising in the land or naval forces, or in the Militia, when in actual service in time of War or public danger; nor shall any person be subject for the same offence to be twice put in jeopardy of life or limb; nor shall be compelled in any criminal case to be a witness against himself, nor be deprived of life, liberty, or property, without due process of law; nor shall private property be taken for public use,
50 without just compensation.

Amendment VI

In all criminal prosecutions, the accused shall enjoy the right to a speedy and public trial, by an impartial jury of the State and district wherein the crime shall have been committed, which district shall have been previously ascertained by law, and to be informed of the nature and cause of the accusation; to be confronted with the witnesses against him; to have compulsory process for obtaining witnesses in his favor, and to have the Assistance of Counsel for his defence.

---

[4] **presentment:** presentation of evidence.

U.S. Constitution: Preamble and Bill of Rights **123**

Image Credits: ©Robert Voight/Shutterstock

Analyze Foundational Documents (LINES 37–41)

 COMMON CORE RI 5, RI 9

Remind students that the theme is the main message an author wishes to communicate about a particular topic. Some Amendments in the Bill of Rights state their themes clearly.

E **ASK STUDENTS** to read Amendment IV and cite its theme. *(The right of the people to be secure in their persons, houses, papers, and effects, against unreasonable searches and seizures, shall not be violated.)* Then ask students to paraphrase the theme in their own words. *(People have the right to feel that they, their homes, and their property are safe from being unreasonably searched or taken by the government.)*

Evaluate Seminal Texts: Constitutional Principles

 COMMON CORE RI 8

(LINES 42–50)

Remind students that the body of the Constitution includes the principle of separation of powers between the legislative, executive, and judicial branches.

F **ASK STUDENTS** to read Amendment V and to explain which branches of the government it affects and why. *(Amendment V affects the judicial branch because it is concerned with how people are accused of and tried for crimes. It could also affect the executive and legislative branches' power to take private property for public use, such as building a highway.)*

WHEN STUDENTS STRUGGLE . . .

Break up Amendment V to help students understand the rights it protects. Ask students to find the signal word *nor*, indicating a new right. They can use this clue to separate Amendment V into its parts. Invite students to write questions about unfamiliar words. Students can write the meaning of each part in a graphic organizer.

Text says	Questions	Meaning
"No person shall be held to answer for a capital, or otherwise infamous crime, unless on a presentment or indictment of a Grand Jury. . . ."	What does *indictment* mean? What is a Grand Jury?	Before a person is accused of a crime, there must be a presentation of evidence or a formal charge by a Grand Jury.

Analyze Foundational Documents (LINES 59–62)

COMMON CORE RI 5, RI 9

Remind students that a text's **purpose** is the reason it was written. Each Amendment in the Bill of Rights, and the document as a whole, has its own purpose.

 **ASK STUDENTS** to read Amendment VII and explain its purpose. *(to ensure that lawsuits are decided fairly by a jury and that lawful appeals are allowed)*

> **CRITICAL VOCABULARY**
>
> **impose**: The Bill of Rights says fines applied as legal punishments should not be unreasonably large.
>
> **ASK STUDENTS** what effects an excessive fine imposed on a person might have. *(An excessive fine can be a sentence to ruin rather than an appropriate punishment for a crime.)*

Evaluate Seminal Texts: Constitutional Principles

COMMON CORE RI 8

(LINES 65–69)

Have students consider these issues: What should be done about aspects of government and liberty that aren't addressed in this document? Who is entitled to the rights not ascribed to the federal government?

 **ASK STUDENTS** to read Amendments IX and X and explain how they apply to the constitutional principles of separation of powers and balance between government authority and individual rights. *(Amendment IX applies to the principle of balance between government authority and individual rights because it does not limit people's rights to those stated in the Constitution. Amendment X applies to the principle of separation of powers because it gives the states and the people powers not given to the federal government.)*

COLLABORATIVE DISCUSSION Have students review each Amendment. Remind them to consider aspects of present-day life that didn't exist when the Bill of Rights was written, such as the internet.

ASK STUDENTS to share any questions they generated in the course of reading and discussion.

Amendment VII

In Suits at common law,[5] where the value in controversy shall exceed
60 twenty dollars, the right of trial by jury shall be preserved, and no fact tried by a jury, shall be otherwise re-examined in any Court of the United States, than according to the rules of the common law.

Amendment VIII

Excessive bail shall not be required, nor excessive fines **imposed**, nor cruel and unusual punishments inflicted.

impose
(ĭm-pōz´) *v.* to charge or apply.

Amendment IX

The enumeration[6] in the Constitution, of certain rights, shall not be construed to deny or disparage others retained by the people.

Amendment X

The powers not delegated to the United States by the Constitution, nor prohibited by it to the States, are reserved to the States respectively, or to the people.

---

[5] **common law:** laws based on court decisions and individual circumstances rather than on government legislation.
[6] **enumeration:** the mention or listing.

COLLABORATIVE DISCUSSION How is the Bill of Rights relevant to you as a high school student in the twenty-first century? Discuss this question with a partner, citing specific textual evidence from the Bill of Rights to support your ideas.

APPLYING ACADEMIC VOCABULARY

founder	contrary

As you discuss "*from* The United States Constitution," incorporate the following Collection 2 academic vocabulary words: *founder* and *contrary*. To help students analyze this foundational American document, ask them to consider the goals of the **founders** who wrote it. Then ask how these parts of the Constitution bring together potentially **contrary** ideas, such as a strong central government versus a strong state government.

Evaluate Seminal Texts: Constitutional Principles  RI 8

The U.S. Constitution has influenced the development of U.S. legal history for more than two hundred years. Lawmakers have applied constitutional principles to individual pieces of legislation at the federal and state levels. The Constitution lays out the founders' most basic assumptions about the nature of government and the rights and responsibilities of citizens and their political leaders. At the same time, the Constitution allows for change. The Preamble to the Bill of Rights indicates that amendments may be added "pursuant to the fifth Article of the original Constitution."

The parts of the Constitution presented here are from its very beginning (the Preamble) and from the last section, the list of amendments or additions to the original document. In between the Preamble and the Bill of Rights is the body of the Constitution itself. Here are some examples of constitutional principles found in the body of the document:

- Representative democracy—the people elect others to represent their wishes and carry out the functions of government
- The separation of powers—between legislative, executive, and judicial branches and between the federal and state governments
- A system of checks and balances—each branch imposes limits on the others
- A balance between government authority and individual rights and freedom

As you analyze these excerpts from the Constitution, look for evidence of these principles and for reasons why the Constitution was written in this particular way.

Analyze Foundational Documents  RI 5, RI 9

When you analyzed the Declaration of Independence, you paid attention to its **purpose, themes,** and **rhetorical features.** You will focus on these same elements as you analyze the Preamble and Bill of Rights from the U.S. Constitution.

> **Purpose** is the reason why something is written. The preambles to the Constitution and to the Bill of Rights state the purposes of each section of the document.
>
> A **theme** is a main message that the author wants to communicate about a particular topic. Again, the Preamble and the Bill of Rights have separate but related messages to communicate. These themes are related to the purpose of each part of the document.
>
> **Rhetorical features** include all the methods a writer uses to communicate ideas and appeal to readers. Because the Constitution has a different purpose from the Declaration of Independence, it was written with different rhetorical features. Notice how the responsibilities of government and the rights of citizens are described in the Constitution. How do those descriptions communicate particular ideas and how might they have appealed to the concerns of eighteenth-century Americans?

CLOSE READ

Evaluate Seminal Texts: Constitutional Principles  RI 8

Make sure students understand the principles behind each Amendment in the Bill of Rights. In small groups, have students decide which principle best represents the Bill of Rights and why. *(A balance between government authority and individual rights and freedom best represents the Bill of Rights because it protects certain important individual rights and freedom from government interference.)*

Help students evaluate and understand the Constitution's principles by reviewing the purpose of each element.

Analyze Foundational Documents  RI 5, RI 9

Review *purpose, theme,* and *rhetorical features,* and then ask students to compare the Preambles to the Constitution and the Bill of Rights with regard to these terms. *(Constitution: written to create a more just, prosperous, and peaceful country. Theme: a better country for future generations. Bill of Rights: written to prevent the government from abusing its Constitutional powers. Theme: limited power for the protection of all.)*

Help students analyze and understand foundational documents. Explain that **purpose** is the reason a text is written, while **theme** is a text's main message. Theme is derived from purpose and delivered with rhetorical features.

Strategies for Annotation   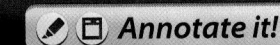 Annotate it!

Analyze Foundational Documents  RI 5, RI 9

Share these strategies for guided or independent analysis:

- In yellow, highlight the **purpose** or purposes of the text that are identified.
- In green, highlight **rhetorical features** that point toward the authors' ideal view of government.

> **THE** Conventions of a number of the States, having at the time of their adopting the Constitution, expressed a desire, in order to prevent misconstruction or abuse of its powers, that further declaratory and restrictive clauses should be added: And as extending the ground of public confidence in the Government, will best ensure the beneficent ends of its institution.

PRACTICE & APPLY

Analyzing the Text  COMMON CORE RI 5, RI 8, RI 9

Possible answers:

1. *The list of reasons why the people of the United States are adopting the Constitution (lines 1-7) reveals its purpose, which is to improve the country and guard liberty and justice, both in the present and for future generations.*

2. *The Preamble reflects the constitutional principle of representative democracy by beginning "We the People of the United States . . ." This all-inclusive beginning suggests that the Constitution will represent all the people in the country.*

3. *The purpose of the Bill of Rights is to prevent the government from misusing the powers granted to it in the main body of the Constitution. This purpose is related to the phrase "secure the Blessings of Liberty."*

4. *Amendment V guarantees that a person will not be put on trial without proper procedure or punished without a trial, except in a very few specific cases. An abusive government might want to throw someone in jail for no reason or for false reasons. It might want a person to stand trial again if it didn't get the judgment it wanted. A family could have their home destroyed to make a new road, with no compensation offered.*

5. *One theme about government that is communicated by the Preamble and the Bill of Rights is that government should protect its citizens and should not overreach nor treat them unfairly.*

6. *Amendments IV–VIII all have to do with the process of law and protecting those suspected or accused of crimes. These Amendments reveal that early Americans were concerned about the fairness of government authority in the legal process.*

7. *The Bill of Rights is structured as a list of rights guaranteed to the American people. It moves from personal to legal rights to rights concerning the operation of government. This structure is effective because it keeps the focus very clearly on the rights it lays out.*

8. *Amendment I could be described as the basic constitutional principle of freedom of expression. It protects the principle that government should not limit people's expression of their ideas and beliefs.*

Analyzing the Text  COMMON CORE RI 5, RI 8, RI 9, W 2a, W 7, W 8

Cite Text Evidence   Support your responses with evidence from the selection.

1. **Analyze** What rhetorical features in the Preamble reveal the purpose of the Constitution? What is that purpose?

2. **Infer** How does the Preamble reflect the constitutional principle of representative democracy?

3. **Analyze** What is the purpose of the Bill of Rights? To what part of the Preamble is it most directly related?

4. **Summarize** In your own words, summarize Amendment V. Then describe three present-day situations where this law might give a citizen important protections from a potentially abusive government.

5. **Draw Conclusions** What is an overall theme about government that is communicated by the Preamble and the Bill of Rights?

6. **Identify Patterns** What do Amendments IV–VIII have in common? What do these Amendments reveal about the concerns and anxieties of early Americans about government and authority during this period?

7. **Evaluate** How is the Bill of Rights structured? How effective is this structure in achieving the purpose of the document?

8. **Interpret** How might the rights guaranteed in Amendment I be stated as a basic constitutional principle? What basic principle does it protect?

PERFORMANCE TASK

Media Activity The Bill of Rights contains what the founders considered the most basic and important protections of individual liberties and states' rights. Evaluate the lasting importance of the Bill of Rights by creating a multimedia presentation on its applications to life in the twenty-first century. Follow these steps to complete the activity.

1. Work with a small group and decide which Amendment(s) will be the topic of your presentation. Conduct research to find the most relevant information and examples to develop your topic.

2. Organize your information so that your ideas will build on one another and lead to a logical conclusion.

3. Decide how to most effectively combine text and graphics to aid comprehension of your ideas.

4. Use appropriate software to create your presentation and share it with your classmates.

Assign this performance task.

PERFORMANCE TASK 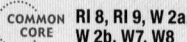 COMMON CORE RI 8, RI 9, W 2a, W 2b, W7, W8

Media Activity Have student groups make an outline or a storyboard of their research notes on the rights and principles in the Amendment(s) which they have chosen to present. This outline can help students order their ideas in a logical sequence, and better combine text and graphics. It will also show them where they may need to do additional research.

Critical Vocabulary

posterity   infringed   prescribed   imposed

Practice and Apply For each Critical Vocabulary word, identify which example below best illustrates its meaning. Explain why the example you chose is most accurate.

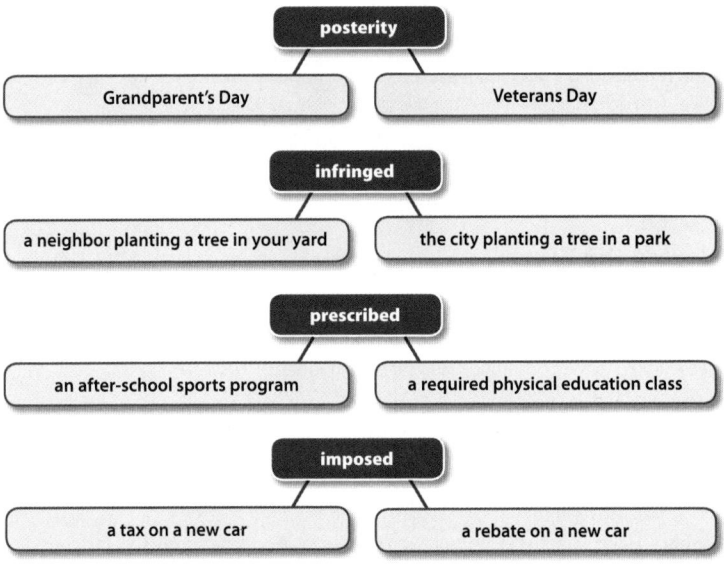

- **posterity**
  - Grandparent's Day
  - Veterans Day
- **infringed**
  - a neighbor planting a tree in your yard
  - the city planting a tree in a park
- **prescribed**
  - an after-school sports program
  - a required physical education class
- **imposed**
  - a tax on a new car
  - a rebate on a new car

Language and Style: Formal and Informal Style

Style refers to *how* something is written and reflects an author's word choices and sentence structures as well as the tone or attitude toward a subject. **Formal style,** used for most writing, follows all the conventions of the English language in usage and grammar. **Informal style** is more like spoken language. In writing, an informal style might be appropriate in personal exchanges such as letters or emails, in dialogue, or in any context that is appropriate to reflect everyday speech.

The Constitution is an important legal document and reflects a very formal style that is appropriate to that context. Legal documents often contain certain formulations that are not generally used in other formal writing. For example, notice the paragraph in the Preamble to the Bill of Rights that begins with the word *RESOLVED*. This paragraph is the formal, legal way of saying that Congress has agreed to propose these Amendments to the Constitution. Each Amendment was also carefully crafted and written in a formal style that would be appropriate in a legal context.

Practice and Apply Work with a partner to restate three of the Amendments in a slightly less formal style, as if you were paraphrasing it for a classroom assignment. Continue to observe the conventions of standard English usage.

Critical Vocabulary

Answers: posterity—*Grandparent's Day, because a younger generation honors its elders;* **infringed**—*a neighbor planting a tree in your yard, because that interferes with your property;* **prescribed**—*a required physical education class, because it is regulated;* **imposed**—*a tax on a new car, because it is charged to the car buyer*

Language and Style: Formal and Informal Style

Sample answers: *Amendment I: Congress shouldn't make laws limiting people's religious freedom, freedom of speech, freedom of the press, right to gather together, or right to make complaints to the government.*

Amendment II: Because an organized military is important for security, people may own and carry weapons.

Amendment III: Soldiers won't be housed in private homes without the owner's agreement, or under special laws in wartime.

Amendment IV: People and their property can be searched only when evidence suggests a reason and a warrant has been issued.

Amendment V: Civilians can be brought to trial only if indicted by a grand jury. No one can be put on trial for the same thing more than once. No one has to say anything in court that would make him or her look guilty. No one's property or freedom will be taken away without a trial. The government won't take private property without paying fairly for it.

Amendment VI: People accused of crimes should get a fair trial quickly, and they are entitled to help from a lawyer.

Amendment VII: All lawsuits have the right to be decided by a jury at a trial.

Amendment VIII: Punishments should be fair, and fines and bail shouldn't be too high.

Amendment IX: Just because a right isn't listed in the Constitution doesn't mean people don't still have that right.

Amendment X: The people and states, not the federal government, keep the powers not addressed in the Constitution.

PRACTICE & APPLY

Compare Anchor Texts: Analyze Foundational Documents

COMMON CORE RI 1, RI 9, W 9b

Remind students that the Declaration of Independence and the Constitution were written at different points in the development of the United States as an independent country. Discuss how the context of the American Revolution and the young country searching for unity would create different needs. Ask students what needs they think each document aimed to address.

Answers:

1. *The purpose of the Declaration of Independence is to justify the United States becoming independent from Britain. The purpose of the Preamble to the Constitution is to explain the benefits of adopting the Constitution. The purpose of the Bill of Rights is to clearly state Americans' basic protected rights.*

2. *The theme that is communicated by these documents is that the U.S. government exists for citizens' benefit and protection, not to oppress them or take away their rights.*

3. *They are both written in very formal, legal language. There are differences between them because they are written for different audiences and purposes.*

4. *The Constitution might be seen as fulfilling Jefferson's vision in the Declaration of Independence because it specifies and protects some of the rights included in the "inalienable" rights to "life, liberty, and the pursuit of happiness." It also protects against the repetition of a number of the abuses cited in the grievances against Britain.*

 **Assess It!**

Online Selection Test
- Download an editable ExamView bank.
- Assign and manage this test online.

Analyze Foundational Documents

COMMON CORE RI 9

The Declaration of Independence lays the foundation for the United States' existence as an independent country built on specific principles of liberty and self-government. The U.S. Constitution built on that foundation and created the framework for the country's form of government, which has lasted for more than two hundred years. After analyzing each of these documents to determine their **purpose, themes,** and **rhetorical features,** you can now look more closely at the similarities and differences between the two documents. As you compare them, recall the historical context in which each document was written. Review the Background on the two documents as needed.

Analyzing the Text

COMMON CORE RI 1, RI 9, W 2, W 9b

Cite Text Evidence   Support your responses with evidence from the selections.

1. **Compare** What are the specific purposes of the Declaration of Independence, the Preamble to the Constitution, and the Bill of Rights?

2. **Synthesize** What is an overall theme about the U.S. government that is communicated by these documents?

3. **Cite Evidence** What rhetorical features do these documents share? Why are there differences in the rhetoric of the Declaration and the Constitution?

4. **Connect** How might the Constitution be seen as fulfilling Jefferson's vision in the Declaration?

PERFORMANCE TASK

Writing Activity: Essay In many ways, the Constitution was built on the foundation of the Declaration of Independence. Explore the details of how the Declaration influenced the Constitution by writing an explanatory essay considering the following questions.

- How might the abuses of the British government have influenced the type of government the United States established and the type of rights it wanted to protect?
- How did the focus on "unalienable rights" in the Declaration specifically influence ideas in the Bill of Rights?

Cite evidence from both documents to support your ideas. Communicate your ideas clearly and accurately using a formal style.

Assign this performance task.

PERFORMANCE TASK

COMMON CORE RI 9, W2

Writing Activity: Essay Have students work in pairs or small groups to compare the abuses listed in the Declaration of Independence and the rights guaranteed in the Bill of Rights. Ask them to write down any abuses and rights that deal with the same issue or topic. Students may take notes on other connections they find as well.

Write an Informative Text

RI 4

EXTEND

Provide students with steps they can use to help them write an informative essay.

- Analyze the task, circling words and phrases that tell you what you are being asked to do.
- Consider purpose and audience. Your purpose for an informative essay is to inform or to explain. Who are your readers and what information will they already have? What will they need to know? What level of language will they expect?
- Draft a working thesis statement, or central idea.
- Identify relevant evidence, including textual evidence, concrete details, facts, examples, and quotations. Make sure that your evidence directly supports your thesis, or central idea.
- Create an outline that organizes your ideas according to cause-and-effect order, comparison-and- contrast order, chronological order, or order of importance. If you are explaining complex ideas, you might need to use more than one organizational pattern. For instance, you might compare and contrast two cause-and-effect relationships.
- Draft your essay, using precise language, relevant domain-specific vocabulary, transitional words and phrases, and varied syntax.
- Exchange essays with a partner and give and receive suggestions for revision and editing.
- Revise and edit your essay.

PRACTICE AND APPLY

As practice for writing a longer informative essay, have students use the steps above to write paragraphs that summarize the Preamble to the Bill of Rights. Tell students to write their paragraphs for an audience of elementary school students. Challenge students to explain the complex ideas concisely and in simplified language.

Analyze Language

RI 8

TEACH

Explain to students that when they read informational texts they will usually encounter **specialized vocabulary**—language that has very specific meanings related to a particular topic. For example, words like *pass, assist, goal,* and *foul* have a variety of common meanings, but in sports they have very specific meanings. Some specialized vocabulary words, such as *puck* in hockey or *megabyte* in technology, are unique to their fields.

WORD SHARP Use the Word Sharp Interactive Vocabulary Tutorial: **Specialized Vocabulary** to reinforce instruction.

Tell students to use the following strategies to **analyze words and phrases to determine meaning.**

- **Read closely** looking for context clues.
- **Use text aids,** such as footnotes or sidenotes.
- **Take notes** on unfamiliar terms during a first reading. Then, **use resources** such as a glossary or dictionary to look up the meaning before you **reread.**

Tell students that Jefferson refines the meaning of the specialized vocabulary term *rights* over the course of the text. Have students look for details that indicate how Jefferson develops and enriches the meaning of the key term *rights.*

PRACTICE AND APPLY

Have students analyze the following specialized vocabulary and explain their meanings: **to pass laws,** line 34 *(to approve the laws)*; **legislative bodies,** line 42 *(lawmaking groups)* **domestic insurrection,** line 98 *(rebellions within a country)* **levy war,** line 128 *(declare the initiation or joining of an armed political conflict).* Then ask students to skim page 115 to find three political science terms that are related to government action. *(Students may identify* **insurrection, oppressions, jurisdiction, emigration,** *and* **usurpations.***)* Have students apply the skill to determine meanings.

Have students analyze how Jefferson uses and refines the concept of rights, citing specific support from the text. *(Jefferson uses "rights" to refer to both individual human rights [lines 9–10] and public political rights [lines 24, 39–40, 124–129]. By connecting these with the same key term, Jefferson suggests that opposing colonial independence is like opposing life, liberty, and the pursuit of happiness.)*

from The United States Constitution

For additional background, students can view the video "America Gets a Constitution" in their eBooks.

Public Document

Why This Text

Students reading foundational U.S. documents for the first time may find them difficult to comprehend. The authors of these documents employed language, syntax, and structure that students rarely encounter today. With the help of the close-reading questions, students will identify and analyze key provisions of Article II of the U.S. Constitution. This close reading will lead students to understand the meaning behind this foundational document.

Background Have students read the background and information about the U.S. Constitution. Alternatively, students can watch the video "America Gets a Constitution" in their eBooks. Remind students that the Constitution begins with the Preamble, which is followed by Articles I through VII (the body of the Constitution), and ends with the Bill of Rights and later Amendments.

AS YOU READ Ask students to pay attention to the organization of the Sections. How does this structure help readers understand the purpose of Article II?

 Common Core Support

- cite strong and thorough textual evidence
- analyze and evaluate the structure of a text
- analyze foundational U.S. documents

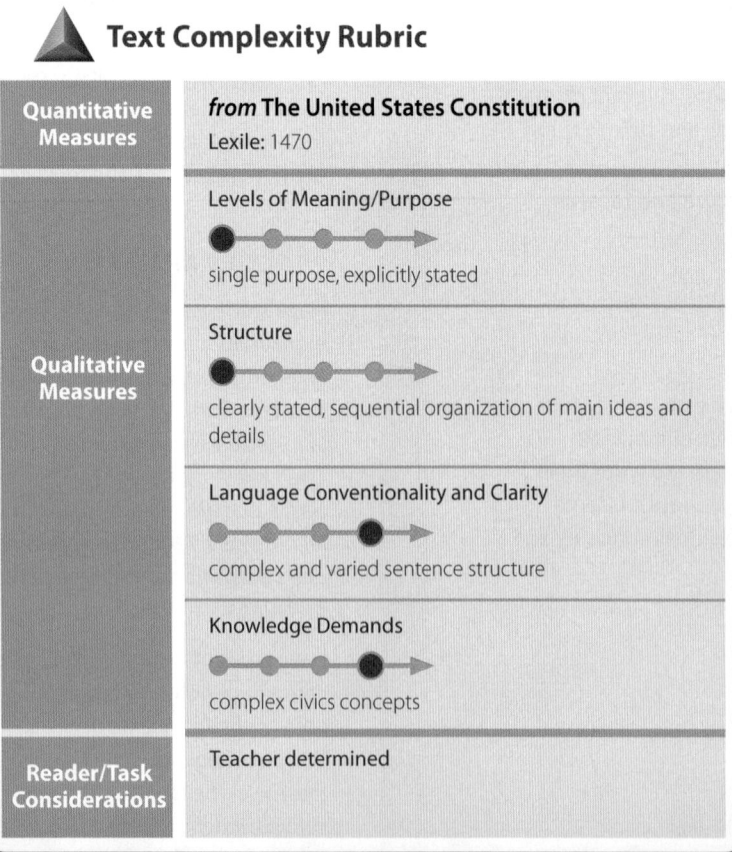

▲ **Text Complexity Rubric**

Quantitative Measures	*from* The United States Constitution Lexile: 1470
Qualitative Measures	**Levels of Meaning/Purpose** single purpose, explicitly stated
	Structure clearly stated, sequential organization of main ideas and details
	Language Conventionality and Clarity complex and varied sentence structure
	Knowledge Demands complex civics concepts
Reader/Task Considerations	Teacher determined

Strategies for CLOSE READING

Analyze Foundational Documents

Students should read this document carefully all the way through. Close-reading questions at the bottom of the page will help them focus on a thorough analysis of the text. As they read, students should jot down comments or questions about the text in the margins.

WHEN STUDENTS STRUGGLE . . .

To help students analyze the structure of this excerpt of the U.S. Constitution, have them work in small groups to fill out a chart like the one shown below.

CITE TEXT EVIDENCE For practice in analyzing a foundational document, ask students to summarize key provisions of each section of Article II.

Section 1	Section 2
President has executive power.	President is in charge of the Army and Navy.
There are limits on who can become President.	President makes treaties—with the advice and consent of the Senate.
President must swear an oath.	President appoints judges to the Supreme Court—with the advice and consent of the Senate.
Section 3	**Section 4**
President can make recommendations to Congress.	President, Vice President, and other government officials can be impeached.
President can convene and adjourn Congress.	
President makes sure laws are carried out.	

Background *The Constitution of the United States was written in September 1787 by a group of 55 men now known as the Framers of the Constitution, including George Washington and Benjamin Franklin. The document was written to replace the old Articles of Confederation and to establish the three branches of the federal government. The Constitution went into effect in 1789 and is considered the supreme law of the United States.*

from
The United States Constitution

Public Document

1. **READ ▶** As you read lines 1–16, begin to collect and cite text evidence.
   - Circle the length of a presidential term.
   - Underline those who may *not* be appointed an Elector.
   - Make notes in the margin about who can hold the office of President.

CLOSE READ
Notes

ARTICLE. II.
Section. 1.

The executive Power shall be vested in a President of the United States of America. He shall hold his Office during the Term of (four Years), and, together with the Vice President, chosen for the same Term, be elected, as follows:

Each State shall appoint, in such Manner as the Legislature thereof may direct, a Number of Electors, equal to the whole Number of Senators and Representatives to which the State may be entitled in the Congress: but no Senator or Representative, or Person holding an Office of Trust or Profit under the United States, shall be appointed an Elector.

10 The Congress may determine the Time of chusing the Electors, and the Day on which they shall give their Votes; which Day shall be the same throughout the United States.

Ⓐ
Ⓑ No Person except a natural born Citizen, or a Citizen of the United States, at the time of the Adoption of this Constitution, shall be eligible to the Office of President; neither shall any Person be eligible to that Office who shall not have attained to the Age of thirty five Years, and been fourteen Years a Resident within the United States.

(margin note) Only a natural-born citizen who has been a U.S. resident for 14 years and who is older than the age of 35 can become President.

23

---

1. **READ AND CITE TEXT EVIDENCE** Section 1 of Article II of the Constitution lays the foundation for the office of the presidency, establishing who can become President and how the President will be elected.

Ⓐ **ASK STUDENTS** to discuss the text that outlines who can become President (lines 12–16). Have them cite examples of language, grammar, and syntax that would be uncommon in a modern document. *The entire paragraph is one long sentence. The order and structure of clauses seems complicated. Most of the nouns are capitalized. Phrases such as "attained to the Age of thirty five Years" are no longer used.*

CLOSE READ
Notes

emolument:

payment

The President shall, at stated Times, receive for his Services, a Compensation, which shall neither be increased nor diminished during the Period for which he shall have been elected, and he shall not receive within that
20 Period any other **Emolument** from the United States, or any of them.

Before he enter on the Execution of his Office, he shall take the following Oath or Affirmation:—"I do solemnly swear (or affirm) that I will faithfully execute the Office of President of the United States, and will to the best of my Ability, preserve, protect and defend the Constitution of the United States."

Section. 2.

The President shall be Commander in Chief of the Army and Navy of the United States, and of the Militia of the several States, when called into the actual Service of the United States; he may require the Opinion, in writing, of the principal Officer in each of the executive Departments, upon any Subject relating to the Duties of their respective Offices, and he shall have Power to
30 grant Reprieves and Pardons for Offences against the United States, except in Cases of **Impeachment**.

He shall have Power, by and with the Advice and Consent of the Senate, to make Treaties, provided two thirds of the Senators present concur; and he shall nominate, and by and with the Advice and Consent of the Senate, shall appoint Ambassadors, other public Ministers and Consuls, Judges of the supreme

impeachment:

*the charge
against a
public official
of a crime or
misconduct*

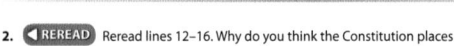

2. ◀ **REREAD** Reread lines 12–16. Why do you think the Constitution places these particular limits on who may become President?

The Framers of the Constitution did not want a foreign ruler. The President should be old enough to be a mature ruler and should have lived in the United States long enough to understand the nation.

3. **READ** ▶ As you read lines 17–54, continue to cite text evidence.
- Underline text that describes the President's executive power.
- Circle reasons for impeachment.

The United States Capitol, which houses Congress, is located on Capitol Hill, at the eastern end of the National Mall in Washington, DC.

Court, and all other Officers of the United States, whose Appointments are not herein otherwise provided for, and which shall be established by Law: but the Congress may by Law vest the Appointment of such inferior Officers, as they think proper, in the President alone, in the Courts of Law, or in the Heads
40 of Departments.

The President shall have Power to fill up all Vacancies that may happen during the Recess of the Senate, by granting Commissions which shall expire at the End of their next Session.

Section. 3.

He shall from time to time give to the Congress Information of the State of the Union, and recommend to their Consideration such Measures as he shall judge necessary and expedient; he may, on extraordinary Occasions, convene both Houses, or either of them, and in Case of Disagreement between them, with Respect to the Time of Adjournment, he may adjourn them to such Time as he shall think proper; he shall receive Ambassadors and other public
50 Ministers; he shall take Care that the Laws be faithfully executed, and shall Commission all the Officers of the United States.

CLOSE READ
Notes

---

2. **REREAD AND CITE TEXT EVIDENCE**

B **ASK STUDENTS** why there is an exception to the rule that only a "natural born Citizen" may become President. *Perhaps they include this exception because some important political leaders were born in other countries.*

3. **READ AND CITE TEXT EVIDENCE**

C **ASK STUDENTS** about the limit on the President's authority to grant reprieves and pardons. *The President cannot pardon public officials who have been impeached.* Why might this limit be included? *Section 4 states that the reasons for impeaching a public official are serious—treason, bribery, and other "high Crimes."*

Critical Vocabulary: emolument (line 20) Have students identify the synonym for *emolument* in the same paragraph (*compensation*).

Critical Vocabulary: impeachment (line 31) Have students contrast *impeachment* and *charging a person with a crime.*

FOR ELL STUDENTS Your students may be familiar with the term *recess* in a school context. Clarify that in the context of the Constitution it means a brief period in which the activity in a branch of government or in a court stops.

CLOSE READ
Notes

Section. 4.

The President, Vice President and all civil Officers of the United States, shall be removed from Office on Impeachment for, and Conviction of, Treason, Bribery, or other high Crimes and Misdemeanors.

4. ◀ REREAD AND DISCUSS In a small group, discuss the Presidential powers that you underlined in lines 17–54. For every executive power that the President has, discuss the Senate's role in the decision-making process.

SHORT RESPONSE

Cite Text Evidence Analyze how the authors structured this part of the Constitution. How does this part of the Constitution uphold the principles of a respresentative democracy, a separation of powers, and a system of checks and balances? Review your reading notes. Be sure to **cite text evidence** in your response.

The authors first address who can become President. There are specific requirements that must be met before someone can be considered for the office. The authors then lay out the President's responsibilities and what he has the power to do. He can make many decisions, but in some cases only with the "Advice and Consent of the Senate," so the President does not have sole authority. The authors also include reasons setting out why the President may be removed from office.

26

4. REREAD AND DISCUSS USING TEXT EVIDENCE

Ⓓ **ASK STUDENTS** in each group to identify the executive powers that are limited by the Senate. Then assign one of these executive powers to each group and have the members of the group discuss the importance of the Senate's role. Describe how these executive powers have made the news in recent years. *Students should be able to recount the appointment of Supreme Court justices and/or the adoption of trade treaties.*

SHORT RESPONSE

Cite Text Evidence Students' responses should include text evidence that supports their positions. They should:

- describe how Article II is organized.
- explain that some of the President's executive powers are limited by the Senate.
- state that the President can be removed from office.

TO CHALLENGE STUDENTS . . .

To gain a deeper understanding of the U.S. Constitution, students can read the 22nd Amendment, ratified in 1951.

ASK STUDENTS what the 22nd Amendment put into law. *It limited to two terms the time a person could serve as President.* What did the Constitution say about limits for the President's office? *It only included limits on power and on eligibility for the office.* Ask students which U.S. Presidents would have been in office for a shorter time had this amendment existed, and whether there are people alive today who are affected. *The only President who would have been in office for a shorter time is Franklin D. Roosevelt. Bill Clinton, George W. Bush, and Barack Obama cannot run again for President.*

DIG DEEPER

With the class, return to Question 3, Read. Have students share their responses to the question.

ASK STUDENTS about other executive powers mentioned in Article II.

- How can the President influence the work of Congress? *The President can give Congress "Information of the State of the Union." This occurs each January, when the President gives a speech to Congress, trying to convince legislators to follow his agenda.*
- What oversight of the legislative process does the President have? *Once Congress passes laws, it is the President's duty to insure that they are "faithfully executed."*
- Under what circumstances can the President convene or adjourn Congress? *He can convene or adjourn both Houses of Congress "on extraordinary Occasions." This would usually only happen when the country is at war or has been attacked.*

ASK STUDENTS to return to their Short Response answer and revise it based on the class discussion.

The Federalist No. 10

*my**SmartPlanner*** Create lesson plans and access resources online.

Argument by James Madison

Why This Text?

Students encounter formal arguments in both online and print media and can benefit from an ability to analyze those arguments. This lesson looks closely at the argument constructed by James Madison in support of adopting the U.S. Constitution.

▶ **View It!**

Professional Development Podcast:

Teaching Argument

Key Learning Objective: The student will be able to analyze and evaluate an argument.

For additional practice:

Petition to the Massachusetts General Assembly

Public Document by Prince Hall

Close Reader selection
"Petition to the Massachusetts General Assembly"
Public Document by Prince Hall

COMMON CORE Common Core Standards

RI 1 Cite textual evidence.
RI 4 Determine the meaning of words and phrases..
RI 6 Determine an author's point of view and analyze style and content.
RI 8 Delineate and evaluate the reasoning in seminal U.S. texts.
SL 1b Work with peers to promote civil, democratic discussions.
SL 1c Propel conversations by posing and responding to questions; ensure a hearing for a full range of positions; promote divergent perspectives.
L 3a Vary syntax for effect; apply an understanding of syntax.
L 5b Analyze nuances.

▲ Text Complexity Rubric

	The Federalist No. 10
Quantitative Measures	Lexile: 1390L

Levels of Meaning/Purpose

●—●—●—●→

single topic

Structure

●—●—●—●→

organization of main ideas and details complex and explicit

Language Conventionality and Clarity

●—●—●—●→

many unfamiliar, academic, and complex domain-specific words

Knowledge Demands

●—●—●—●→

complex civics concepts

Reader/Task Considerations	Teacher determined Vary by individual reader and type of text

Qualitative Measures

CLOSE READ

 For more context and historical background, students can view the video "Library of Congress: The Federalist Papers" in their eBooks.

Background In the vigorous national debate leading up to the ratification of the Constitution, Madison and other centralists argued that the system proposed in the Constitution must be approved in order to keep the Union from dissolving as well as to give the federal government the power to act on behalf of the nation as a whole. Madison felt strongly that the Constitution limited the powers of the federal government enough, and defined them clearly enough, to protect states' rights and individual rights.

AS YOU READ Direct students to use the As You Read instructions to focus their reading. Have students write down any questions they generate as they read.

Analyze Language: Nuance (LINES 3–6)

COMMON CORE RI 4

Explain that in addition to their denotation or dictionary definition, words also have **nuances,** or fine shades of meaning. Throughout this argument, Madison skillfully includes verbal nuance to help persuade the reader about his claims.

 **ASK STUDENTS** what words Madison includes in the second sentence to affect readers' feelings about the word *faction*. (*alarmed, dangerous, vice; By using these words to refer to the effects of factions, Madison makes readers feel that the word* faction *describes something negative and dangerous.*)

CRITICAL VOCABULARY

faction: Madison believes factions can be a threat to fair and effective government because these smaller groups might impose their will on the larger population.

ASK STUDENTS how factions might form within a country or region. (*Groups of people with certain political leanings, particular religious or moral beliefs, or similar backgrounds or motives come together and reinforce each other's beliefs and desired outcomes.*)

 HISTORY VIDEO

Background *The Federalist No. 10 is the most famous of the Federalist Papers, a series of 85 essays written in 1787–1788 to support ratification of the U.S. Constitution. Originally published in New York newspapers under the pseudonym Publius, the essays were actually written by Alexander Hamilton, John Jay, and* **James Madison.** *Madison, the author of No. 10, introduced the Bill of Rights while serving in the House of Representatives and later became the fourth U. S. President. While Madison and other Federalists strongly supported the Constitution, the Anti-Federalists took the contrary position and opposed ratification.*

The Federalist No. 10

Argument by James Madison

AS YOU READ Look for clues that indicate Madison's attitude toward the Anti-Federalists, who are the audience for this argument.

To the People of the State of New York:

AMONG the numerous advantages promised by a well constructed Union, none deserves to be more accurately developed than its tendency to break and control the violence of **faction**. The friend of popular governments never finds himself so much alarmed for their character and fate, as when he contemplates their propensity[1] to this dangerous vice. He will not fail, therefore, to set a due value on any plan which, without violating the principles to which he is attached, provides a proper cure for it. The instability, injustice, and confusion introduced into the public councils, have, in truth, been the mortal
10 diseases under which popular governments have everywhere perished; as they continue to be the favorite and fruitful topics from which the adversaries to liberty derive their most specious declamations. The valuable improvements made by the American constitutions on the popular models, both ancient and modern, cannot certainly be too much admired; but it would be an unwarrantable partiality, to contend

faction
(fak´shən) *n.* an organized subgroup that disagrees with the larger group as a whole.

[1] **propensity:** natural tendency or inclination.

Image Credits: (t) ©Fine Art/Corbis; (c) ©johnjohnson/Shutterstock

SCAFFOLDING FOR ELL STUDENTS

Evaluate Seminal Texts: Purpose and Premises of an Argument Have students work with a partner to identify Madison's ideas in the first sentence. They should break the sentence down into parts, identify unfamiliar words or phrases and research their meanings, and ask their teacher if they have further questions. Have partners use this comprehension strategy as they continue reading.

Evaluate Seminal Texts: Purpose and Premises of an Argument (LINES 17–26)

COMMON CORE RI 8

Explain that a **premise** is a statement the author presents to serve as the basis for an argument. A **claim** is an opinion that the author states and then supports.

B **CITE TEXT EVIDENCE** Have students paraphrase Madison's premise in lines 17–26. *(Governments are unstable because powerful groups force their own agendas at the expense of the overall good.)* Then ask students to explain why this is a premise and not a claim. *(He makes the statement as though all readers will accept it as truth, and does not provide evidence.)*

CRITICAL VOCABULARY

aggregate: Madison believes that public welfare must be protected just as much as individual rights.

ASK STUDENTS what kinds of interests Madison might mean by "the aggregate interests of the community." *(protection against foreign invasion; a thriving national economy; law and order)*

reciprocal: Madison understands that a person's rational opinions and a person's self-interests cannot be completely separated.

ASK STUDENTS to explain the reciprocal relationship between liberty and factions. *(A rational citizen may desire liberty for all, but that freedom provides opportunities to preserve an individual's self-interests, sometimes at the expense of others' liberty.)*

Analyze Language: Defining a Key Term (LINE 23)

COMMON CORE RI 1, RI 4, RI 8

Point out the word *interested* in line 23. Ask whether Madison merely means "attentive," or whether he means "having a benefit at stake." *(Students should conclude that he means "having a benefit at stake.")*

C **ASK STUDENTS** to think of how the word *interest* is used in national debate today. List examples of phrases containing the word *interest* on the board. *(special interest groups, vested interest)*

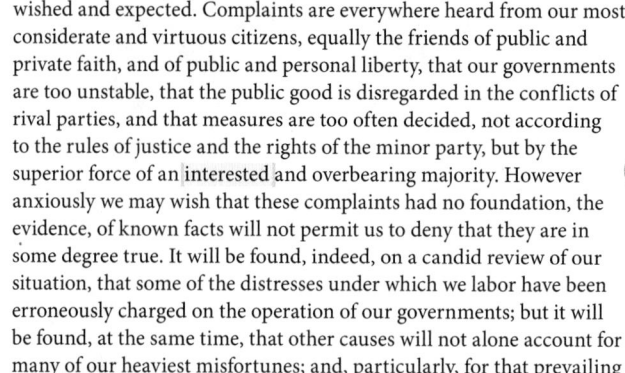

that they have as effectually obviated[2] the danger on this side, as was wished and expected. Complaints are everywhere heard from our most considerate and virtuous citizens, equally the friends of public and private faith, and of public and personal liberty, that our governments 20 are too unstable, that the public good is disregarded in the conflicts of rival parties, and that measures are too often decided, not according to the rules of justice and the rights of the minor party, but by the superior force of an interested and overbearing majority. However anxiously we may wish that these complaints had no foundation, the evidence, of known facts will not permit us to deny that they are in some degree true. It will be found, indeed, on a candid review of our situation, that some of the distresses under which we labor have been erroneously charged on the operation of our governments; but it will be found, at the same time, that other causes will not alone account for 30 many of our heaviest misfortunes; and, particularly, for that prevailing and increasing distrust of public engagements, and alarm for private rights, which are echoed from one end of the continent to the other. These must be chiefly, if not wholly, effects of the unsteadiness and injustice with which a factious spirit has tainted our public administrations.

By a faction, I understand a number of citizens, whether amounting to a majority or a minority of the whole, who are united and actuated[3] by some common impulse of passion, or of interest, adversed to the rights of other citizens, or to the permanent and 40 **aggregate** interests of the community.

aggregate
(ăgʹrĭ-gĭt) *adj.*
combined.

There are two methods of curing the mischiefs of faction: the one, by removing its causes; the other, by controlling its effects.

There are again two methods of removing the causes of faction: the one, by destroying the liberty which is essential to its existence; the other, by giving to every citizen the same opinions, the same passions, and the same interests.

It could never be more truly said than of the first remedy, that it was worse than the disease. Liberty is to faction what air is to fire, an aliment without which it instantly expires. But it could not be 50 less folly to abolish liberty, which is essential to political life, because it nourishes faction, than it would be to wish the annihilation of air, which is essential to animal life, because it imparts to fire its destructive agency.

The second expedient is as impracticable as the first would be unwise. As long as the reason of man continues fallible,[4] and he is at liberty to exercise it, different opinions will be formed. As long as the connection subsists between his reason and his self-love, his opinions and his passions will have a **reciprocal** influence on each other; and

reciprocal
(rĭ-sĭpʹrə-kəl) *adj.*
mutual or shared.

---

[2] **obviated:** avoided or removed.
[3] **actuated:** moved to action.
[4] **fallible:** able to make mistakes.

APPLYING ACADEMIC VOCABULARY

ideological	contrary

As you discuss Madison's argument, incorporate the following Collection 2 academic vocabulary words: *ideological* and *contrary*. Reinforce the context of the argument by asking students to explain the **ideological** basis of Madison's opinions. As you evaluate the effectiveness of the argument, ask students to point out which positions **contrary** to his argument Madison states and then refutes.

the former will be objects to which the latter will attach themselves.

60 The diversity in the faculties of men, from which the rights of property originate, is not less an insuperable[5] obstacle to a uniformity of interests. The protection of these faculties is the first object of government. From the protection of different and unequal faculties of acquiring property, the possession of different degrees and kinds of property immediately results; and from the influence of these on the sentiments and views of the respective proprietors, ensues a division of the society into different interests and parties.

The **latent** causes of faction are thus sown in the nature of man; and we see them everywhere brought into different degrees of activity, 70 according to the different circumstances of civil society. A zeal for different opinions concerning religion, concerning government, and many other points, as well of speculation as of practice; an attachment to different leaders ambitiously contending for pre-eminence and power; or to persons of other descriptions whose fortunes have been interesting to the human passions, have, in turn, divided mankind into parties, inflamed them with mutual animosity,[6] and rendered them much more disposed to vex and oppress each other than to co-operate for their common good. So strong is this propensity of mankind to fall into mutual animosities, that where no substantial 80 occasion presents itself, the most frivolous and fanciful distinctions have been sufficient to kindle their unfriendly passions and excite their most violent conflicts. But the most common and durable source of factions has been the various and unequal distribution of property. Those who hold and those who are without property have ever formed distinct interests in society. Those who are creditors, and those who are debtors, fall under a like discrimination. A landed interest, a manufacturing interest, a mercantile interest, a moneyed interest, with many lesser interests, grow up of necessity in civilized nations, and divide them into different classes, actuated by different sentiments 90 and views. The regulation of these various and interfering interests forms the principal task of modern legislation, and involves the spirit of party and faction in the necessary and ordinary operations of the government.

No man is allowed to be a judge in his own cause, because his interest would certainly bias his judgment, and, not improbably, corrupt his integrity. With equal, nay with greater reason, a body of men are unfit to be both judges and parties at the same time; yet what are many of the most important acts of legislation, but so many judicial determinations, not indeed concerning the rights of single 100 persons, but concerning the rights of large bodies of citizens? And what are the different classes of legislators but advocates and parties to the causes which they determine? Is a law proposed concerning

latent
(lāt´nt) *adj.*
underlying or hidden.

[5] **insuperable:** invincible or unconquerable.
[6] **animosity:** hatred or hostility.

WHEN STUDENTS STRUGGLE...

Some students may struggle with identifying the most important details in lines 68–93. Have students work with a partner to identify important information in this long paragraph. Suggest that partners reread the paragraph, discuss the details, and clarify any ideas they find confusing. Then, have partners list the important points from the paragraph. Next, have students narrow down the details by rereading their list and crossing off half of the points so only the most important ideas remain. When partners are finished, have them join other pairs to compare their details and to discuss any differences. Ask partners to revise their most important details, if necessary.

CLOSE READ

Evaluate Seminal Texts: Logical Reasoning (LINES 60–67)

COMMON CORE RI 1, RI 8

Explain that **logical reasoning** is the train of rational thought an author uses to present and support a claim. Discuss with students whether they find Madison's argument in lines 60–67 convincing.

D **CITE TEXT EVIDENCE** Ask students to tell how Madison uses logic to explain why the differing abilities of people ("the diversity in the faculties," line 60) will naturally keep society from establishing a uniformity of opinion. *(He explains it as a series of causes and effects.)* Have students cite text evidence for their answer. *(Madison says that different abilities result in people owning different amounts and kinds of property, which affect the proprietors' respective political views, and that the different views thereby create division within society. [lines 63–67])*

> **CRITICAL VOCABULARY**

latent: According to Madison, the tendency to separate into groups based on different abilities or interests is part of human nature.

ASK STUDENTS to explain one human characteristic that might lead a person to want to either join or oppose a particular group. *(A passionate belief in individual rights might lead a person to fight against a group that favors restricting certain behaviors or acts.)*

Analyze Language: Rhetorical Devices (LINES 82–90)

COMMON CORE RI 4

Explain that **rhetorical devices** are techniques writers use to make their arguments more effective. For example, **parallelism** is the use of similar grammatical constructions to emphasize related ideas. **Repetition** is the use of the same word or phrase more than once to create emphasis.

E **CITE TEXT EVIDENCE** Ask students to find examples of both parallelism and repetition in lines 82–90. *(parallelism: "common and durable"; "various and unequal" in lines 82–83; repetition: "those who" in lines 84–86; both: "A landed interest, a manufacturing interest, a mercantile interest, a moneyed interest" in lines 86–87)*

IT IS IN VAIN to say that enlightened statesmen will be able to adjust these clashing interests.

Evaluate Seminal Texts: Purpose and Premises of an Argument (LINES 104–117)

COMMON CORE RI 1, RI 8

Explain that **examples** are one type of evidence that can support claims in an argument. An example is a specific instance that illustrates a more general principle. By giving a specific example, the writer helps the reader to understand how the principle operates in particular situations, and therefore persuades the reader of the argument.

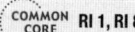 **CITE TEXT EVIDENCE** Ask students to explain the claim that Madison states in lines 104–107. *(Those making the laws will decide based on their own interests, rather than fairness or the common good, and the more powerful group will win if there is disagreement.)* Then ask students to delineate the two examples Madison gives to support the claim. *(1. Laws about restricting foreign goods would be supported by the manufacturing class, but not by landowners. [lines 107–111] 2. Taxes on property would not be fairly distributed because those with the most power would make laws to improve their own financial situation. [lines 111–117])*

> **CRITICAL VOCABULARY**
>
> **apportionment**: the assumption that lawmakers will vote for their own self-interest or that of their constituents when faced with decisions about taxes.
>
> **ASK STUDENTS** how lawmakers should determine the apportionment of property taxes. *(They should be impartial and consider what is just and fair for the public good.)*

---

private debts? It is a question to which the creditors are parties on one side and the debtors on the other. Justice ought to hold the balance between them. Yet the parties are, and must be, themselves the judges; and the most numerous party, or, in other words, the most powerful faction must be expected to prevail. Shall domestic manufactures be encouraged, and in what degree, by restrictions on foreign manufactures? are questions which would be differently decided by the

110 landed and the manufacturing classes, and probably by neither with a sole regard to justice and the public good. The **apportionment** of taxes on the various descriptions of property is an act which seems to require the most exact impartiality;[7] yet there is, perhaps, no legislative act in which greater opportunity and temptation are given to a predominant[8] party to trample on the rules of justice. Every shilling with which they overburden the inferior number, is a shilling saved to their own pockets.

It is in vain to say that enlightened statesmen will be able to adjust these clashing interests, and render them all subservient to the public

120 good. Enlightened statesmen will not always be at the helm. Nor, in many cases, can such an adjustment be made at all without taking into view indirect and remote considerations, which will rarely prevail over the immediate interest which one party may find in disregarding the rights of another or the good of the whole.

The inference[9] to which we are brought is, that the *causes* of faction cannot be removed, and that relief is only to be sought in the means of controlling its *effects*.

If a faction consists of less than a majority, relief is supplied by the republican principle, which enables the majority to defeat its sinister[10]

130 views by regular vote. It may clog the administration, it may convulse the society; but it will be unable to execute and mask its violence under the forms of the Constitution. When a majority is included in a

apportionment (ə-pôr′shən-mənt) *n.* distribution.

---

[7] **impartiality:** equal treatment.
[8] **predominant:** stronger, more powerful.
[9] **inference:** a conclusion based on facts and reasoning.
[10] **sinister:** evil or harmful.

SCAFFOLDING FOR ELL STUDENTS

Determine Pronoun Referents On a whiteboard, project lines 128–130. Ask a volunteer to highlight in green the pronoun *its*. Explain that this pronoun has an antecedent; that is, it refers to a noun.

ASK STUDENTS to which noun *its* is referring. *(faction)*

> If a faction consists of less than a majority, relief is supplied by the republican principle, which enables the majority to defeat its sinister views by regular vote.

faction, the form of popular government, on the other hand, enables it to sacrifice to its ruling passion or interest both the public good and the rights of other citizens. To secure the public good and private rights against the danger of such a faction, and at the same time to preserve the spirit and the form of popular government, is then the great object to which our inquiries are directed. Let me add that it is the great desideratum[11] by which this form of government can be

140   rescued from the opprobrium[12] under which it has so long labored, and be recommended to the esteem and adoption of mankind.

By what means is this object attainable? Evidently by one of two only. Either the existence of the same passion or interest in a majority at the same time must be prevented, or the majority, having such coexistent passion or interest, must be rendered, by their number and local situation, unable to concert and carry into effect schemes of oppression. If the impulse and the opportunity be suffered to coincide, we well know that neither moral nor religious motives can be relied on as an adequate control. They are not found to be such on the injustice

150   and violence of individuals, and lose their efficacy in proportion to the number combined together, that is, in proportion as their **efficacy** becomes needful.

From this view of the subject it may be concluded that a pure democracy, by which I mean a society consisting of a small number of citizens, who assemble and administer the government in person, can admit of no cure for the mischiefs of faction. A common passion or interest will, in almost every case, be felt by a majority of the whole; a communication and concert result from the form of government itself; and there is nothing to check the inducements[13] to sacrifice the weaker

160   party or an obnoxious individual. Hence it is that such democracies have ever been spectacles of turbulence and contention; have ever been found incompatible with personal security or the rights of property; and have in general been as short in their lives as they have been violent in their deaths. Theoretic politicians, who have patronized this species of government, have erroneously supposed that by reducing mankind to a perfect equality in their political rights, they would, at the same time, be perfectly equalized and assimilated in their possessions, their opinions, and their passions.

A republic, by which I mean a government in which the scheme

170   of representation takes place, opens a different prospect, and promises the cure for which we are seeking. Let us examine the points in which it varies from pure democracy, and we shall comprehend both the nature of the cure and the efficacy which it must derive from the Union.

efficacy
(ĕf´ĭ-kə-sē) *n.*
effectiveness.

---

[11] **desideratum:** a desirable thing.
[12] **opprobrium:** public criticism and disgrace.
[13] **inducements:** rewards or bribes.

The Federalist No. 10   **133**

TO CHALLENGE STUDENTS ...

Paraphrase an Argument   Direct students to the second paragraph on page 133. (lines 142–152)

ASK STUDENTS to paraphrase the paragraph. Then have students read their paragraphs to the class. *(To ensure that both public good and private rights are respected, we must either prevent a majority of the people from having the same interest, which is impossible, or we must prevent such a majority from being able to take actions that would oppress a minority. If we do not, neither morality nor religion will prevent oppression, especially since their influence weakens as factions grow. If morality and religion don't keep individuals from committing injustices, how can they prevent a large number of people from doing so?)*

CLOSE READ

Evaluate Seminal Texts: Purpose and Premises of an Argument (LINES 135–141)

 **COMMON CORE RI 8**

Explain that the **purpose** of an argument is to convince readers to take a certain action.

H ASK STUDENTS to find where Madison restates the **purpose** of his argument. *(lines 135–138)*. What is the effect of restating the purpose here? *(It reminds readers of the central challenge—how to protect the public good and private rights against factions while allowing for the liberal exercise of popular government.)*

> **CRITICAL VOCABULARY**
>
> **efficacy**: Madison asserts that moral convictions would not be enough to keep a majority of like-minded people from oppressing other people.
>
> **ASK STUDENTS** why moral or religious motives would lose efficacy "in proportion to the number [of individuals] combined together." *(If enough other people shared your passion about a political issue, you would begin to think it was okay to go against your personal morality because "everyone else is doing it.")*

Analyze Language: Defining a Key Term

 **COMMON CORE RI 4**

(LINES 153–170)

Tell students that giving **definitions,** or meanings, of important terms is another technique some writers use to strengthen an argument. Straightforward definitions can help make the argument clearer so that readers will be more likely to accept it.

I CITE TEXT EVIDENCE Ask students to state Madison's definitions of the terms *democracy* and *republic* in their own words. *(democracy: government where each citizen personally represents his or her own interests; republic: government where elected officials represent the interests of the people)* Have them cite the lines in which the definitions are found. *(democracy: 153–156; republic: 169–171)*

Evaluate Seminal Texts: Structure of an Argument

COMMON CORE RI 1, RI 8

(LINES 175–195)

Tell students that the **structure** of an argument is the order and manner in which its individual pieces—such as premises, claims, and evidence—are put together to form a whole. Explain that analyzing the structure can help them evaluate an argument's effectiveness.

J CITE TEXT EVIDENCE Ask students to describe the structure of this part of Madison's argument and cite line numbers to support their analysis. (*First he delineates the two most important differences between a democracy and a republic (lines 175–179). Then, in lines 180–191, he discusses the effects of each difference. This discussion leads to the claim, in lines 192–195, that larger republics are more effective at protecting the common welfare than small ones.*)

Evaluate Seminal Texts: Reasons and Evidence for an Argument

COMMON CORE RI 1, RI 8

(LINES 196–212)

Point out that the last two paragraphs contain reasons—but not evidence—for the claim introduced in lines 192–195 that larger republics are more effective at protecting the common welfare than small ones.

K ASK STUDENTS what types of evidence might be used to support the reasons Madison gives in the last two paragraphs. (*figures and studies showing larger electorates are more likely to elect suitable representatives; examples of smaller republics in which elections were won by deceit, or examples of attempts to win elections by deceit that were unsuccessful because of the large number of voters in a large republic.*)

J The two great points of difference between a democracy and a republic are: first, the delegation of the government, in the latter, to a small number of citizens elected by the rest; secondly, the greater number of citizens, and greater sphere of country, over which the latter may be extended.

180 The effect of the first difference is, on the one hand, to refine and enlarge the public views, by passing them through the medium[14] of a chosen body of citizens, whose wisdom may best discern the true interest of their country, and whose patriotism and love of justice will be least likely to sacrifice it to temporary or partial considerations. Under such a regulation, it may well happen that the public voice, pronounced by the representatives of the people, will be more consonant to the public good than if pronounced by the people themselves, convened for the purpose. On the other hand, the effect may be inverted. Men of factious tempers, of local prejudices, or of

190 sinister designs, may, by intrigue, by corruption, or by other means, first obtain the suffrages,[15] and then betray the interests, of the people. The question resulting is, whether small or extensive republics are more favorable to the election of proper guardians of the public weal;[16] and it is clearly decided in favor of the latter by two obvious considerations:

K In the first place, it is to be remarked that, however small the republic may be, the representatives must be raised to a certain number, in order to guard against the cabals[17] of a few; and that, however large it may be, they must be limited to a certain number,

200 in order to guard against the confusion of a multitude. Hence, the number of representatives in the two cases not being in proportion to that of the two constituents, and being proportionally greater in the small republic, it follows that, if the proportion of fit characters be not less in the large than in the small republic, the former will present a greater option, and consequently a greater probability of a fit choice.

In the next place, as each representative will be chosen by a greater number of citizens in the large than in the small republic, it will be more difficult for unworthy candidates to practice with success the vicious arts by which elections are too often carried; and the suffrages

210 of the people being more free, will be more likely to centre in men who possess the most attractive merit and the most diffusive[18] and established characters.

It must be confessed that in this, as in most other cases, there is a mean,[19] on both sides of which inconveniences will be found to

---

[14] **medium:** mechanism or vehicle for doing something.
[15] **suffrages:** votes.
[16] **public weal:** the people's well-being.
[17] **cabals:** secret political groups.
[18] **diffusive:** widely known.
[19] **mean:** middle point.

WHEN STUDENTS STRUGGLE...

Direct students to lines 189–191. Explain that they can paraphrase long, complex sentences such as this one by following these steps:

- Look up the meanings of unfamiliar words and phrases and substitute more familiar words.
- Reorder words and sentence parts to create a more familiar speech pattern.
- Eliminate any extra words and phrases.

Encourage students to use the example chart shown to help them break down and understand difficult sentences throughout the selection.

lie. By enlarging too much the number of electors, you render the representatives too little acquainted with all their local circumstances and lesser interests; as by reducing it too much, you render him unduly attached to these, and too little fit to comprehend and pursue great and national objects. The federal Constitution forms a happy combination in this respect; the great and aggregate interests being referred to the national, the local and particular to the State legislatures.

The other point of difference is, the greater number of citizens and extent of territory which may be brought within the compass of republican than of democratic government; and it is this circumstance principally which renders factious combinations less to be dreaded in the former than in the latter. The smaller the society, the fewer probably will be the distinct parties and interests composing it; the fewer the distinct parties and interests, the more frequently will a majority be found of the same party; and the smaller the number of individuals composing a majority, and the smaller the compass within which they are placed, the more easily will they concert and execute their plans of oppression. Extend the sphere, and you take in a greater variety of parties and interests; you make it less probable that a majority of the whole will have a common motive to invade the rights of other citizens; or if such a common motive exists, it will be more difficult for all who feel it to discover their own strength, and to act in unison with each other. Besides other impediments, it may be remarked that, where there is a consciousness of unjust or dishonorable purposes, communication is always checked by distrust in proportion to the number whose concurrence is necessary.

Hence, it clearly appears, that the same advantage which a republic has over a democracy, in controlling the effects of faction, is enjoyed by a large over a small republic,—is enjoyed by the Union over the States composing it. Does the advantage consist in the substitution of representatives whose enlightened views and virtuous sentiments render them superior to local prejudices and schemes of injustice? It will not be denied that the representation of the Union will be most likely to possess these requisite endowments.[20] Does it consist in the greater security afforded by a greater variety of parties, against the event of any one party being able to outnumber and oppress the rest? In an equal degree does the increased variety of parties **comprised** within the Union, increase this security. Does it, in fine, consist in the greater obstacles opposed to the concert and accomplishment of the secret wishes of an unjust and interested majority? Here, again, the extent of the Union gives it the most palpable[21] advantage.

The influence of factious leaders may kindle a flame within their particular States, but will be unable to spread a general conflagration

comprise
(kəm-prīz´) v.
contain.

---

[20] **requisite endowments:** necessary qualities.
[21] **palpable:** able to be felt.

Unfamiliar Words	Meanings/Synonyms
of factious tempers	divisive states of mind
of local prejudices	self-interested bias
of sinister designs	harmful plans
intrigue	deception
suffrages	votes

Paraphrase: Divisive, biased, or harmful men may use deception or corruption to get votes and then betray the voters.

CLOSE READ

Evaluate Seminal Texts: Purpose and Premises of an Argument (LINES 222–226)

COMMON CORE RI 8

Remind students that an argument can have more than one claim.

L CITE EVIDENCE Ask students what claim Madison makes about how the size of the population covered in a certain government will affect the ability for factions to form. *(He says that a government that covers more people and territory will be less likely to allow factions. [lines 222–226])*

Analyze Language: Rhetorical Questions

COMMON CORE RI 4

(LINES 244–255)

Tell students that another type of rhetorical device is the rhetorical question, commonly used for effect in persuasive writing and speaking. Explain that a **rhetorical question** is posed without any expectation of an answer. It may be asked and then promptly answered by the asker.

M CITE TEXT EVIDENCE Have students cite the rhetorical questions in lines 244–255. *(lines 244–246, 248–250, 252–254).* Ask them to tell how the questions are used in the paragraph and what effect they have. *(The questions and their answers constitute reasons to support the claim at the beginning of the paragraph. The series of questions and answers creates a repeating structure and rhythm, emphasizes the advantages of the Union over the States in controlling factions, and lends power and accessibility to Madison's argument.)*

CRITICAL VOCABULARY

comprise: Madison believes that the larger number of parties and people within the Union will help keep factions from forming.

ASK STUDENTS why factions might form in a government comprising only a few major parties. *(If one party contains a majority of representatives, a large following, and a strong interest in a specific agenda, that party could take over and enforce its will on the rest of the government and the people.)*

Analyze Language: Nuance (LINES 261–271)

COMMON CORE RI 4

Remind students that nuances are a word's fine shades of meaning.

 **CITE TEXT EVIDENCE** Ask students to explain how Madison uses nuanced language in his concluding paragraphs. *(He uses words that have strong nuances of fear or danger such as "rage," "wicked," "pervade," "malady," and "taint," to make the point that the Union must protect citizens from dangerous factions [lines 261–266]. He uses words with nuances of virtue and kindness such as "remedy," "pleasure," "pride," and "cherishing" [lines 267–271] to restate the main claim of his argument, ending on a strong and positive note re-emphasizing his support of a government that is a republic and his commitment to the Federalists.)*

CRITICAL VOCABULARY

pervade: Madison urges the states to ratify the Constitution so that factions will not be allowed to gain too much power at the national level.

ASK STUDENTS why a faction might be more likely to pervade a state or local government than a national one. *(With a smaller number of people governed, groups tend to be more homogeneous. Strong ideas and beliefs are more likely to take hold in an atmosphere of familiarity, and people are more likely to come together and feel emboldened to push their ideas on others.)*

COLLABORATIVE DISCUSSION Have students work in pairs to discuss the ways in which Madison's attitude toward the Anti-Federalists is revealed, such as through connotation and tone. Suggest that students identify Madison's main points and consider the word connotations and tone when making each claim. Then have students form larger groups to compare their ideas.

ASK STUDENTS to share any questions they generated in the course of reading and discussing this selection.

---

through the other States. A religious sect[22] may degenerate into a political faction in a part of the Confederacy; but the variety of sects
260 dispersed over the entire face of it must secure the national councils against any danger from that source. A rage for paper money, for an abolition of debts, for an equal division of property, or for any other improper or wicked project, will be less apt to **pervade** the whole body of the Union than a particular member of it; in the same proportion as such a malady is more likely to taint a particular county or district, than an entire State.

In the extent and proper structure of the Union, therefore, we behold a republican remedy for the diseases most incident to republican government. And according to the degree of pleasure and
270 pride we feel in being republicans, ought to be our zeal in cherishing the spirit and supporting the character of Federalists.
PUBLIUS.

pervade
(pər-vād´) *v.* to spread or exist throughout.

[22]**sect:** denomination or group.

COLLABORATIVE DISCUSSION What does Madison think about the Anti-Federalists, and how does he address them? Discuss this question with a partner, citing evidence from the document to support your ideas.

Analyze Language: Defining a Key Term

In The *Federalist* No. 10, Madison uses the term *faction* repeatedly and refines its meaning over the course of the document. In fact, the entire document could be seen as an extended definition of that key term.

Madison introduces the term in the first sentence with the idea that a "well constructed Union" has a "tendency to break and control the violence of faction." Without knowing the full meaning, the reader begins to understand that factions are harmful. Madison then defines the term in the next paragraph:

> By a faction, I understand a number of citizens, whether amounting to a majority or a minority of the whole, who are united and actuated by some common impulse of passion, or of interest, adversed to the rights of other citizens, or to the permanent and aggregate interests of the community.

Understanding this key term and its development over the course of the text is essential to understanding Madison's argument.

Evaluate Seminal Texts: Purpose and Premises of an Argument

In an **argument,** an author states a **claim,** or position on an issue, and supports it with reasons and evidence. In the *Federalist* No. 10, Madison very clearly lays out his claim in the first sentence of the text: "Among the numerous advantages promised by a well constructed Union, none deserves to be more accurately developed than its tendency to break and control the violence of faction."

Madison's **purpose,** therefore, is to convince readers to embrace the form of government that he believes is best, the one set out in the Constitution. What is more subtle, however, is the set of **premises,** or general principles, about society and human nature that he assumes his readers will agree with. In a well-reasoned argument, the claim logically follows and depends on the premises.

Madison's argument actually contains a series of tightly linked premises and claims. For example, in the first half of the argument, one of Madison's claims is that the causes of factions cannot be removed. Here is one premise related to this claim:

> The diversity in the faculties of men, from which the rights of property originate, is not less an insuperable obstacle to a uniformity of interests. (lines 60–62)

In other words, Madison states the following general principle: The more abilities you possess, the more property you possess; these differences result in diverse, opposing interests. According to Madison's reasoning, it then follows that people with different economic interests will inevitably join opposing factions.

Evaluating and examining the premises of an argument will give you a fuller understanding of the historical forces that shaped this document.

TEACH

CLOSE READ

Analyze Language: Defining a Key Term

Help students understand Madison's definition of *faction*. Invite volunteers to interpret the definition and restate it in their own words. Then guide the class to come to a consensus of what a faction is.

ASK STUDENTS to explain how Madison develops the definition of *faction*, both directly and indirectly. (*He uses words with nuances of fear throughout to emphasize that factions are dangerous. He further explains that factions will inevitably form due to political freedom and the differences among people [lines 43–59]. He gives examples of issues upon which factions may form [e.g., religion, line 71; property ownership, profession or occupation, and income, lines 86–90]. He also indicates that it is possible for a faction to have a majority in the government, which can be dangerous to the overall good [lines 132–135].*)

Evaluate Seminal Texts: Purposes and Premises of an Argument

Review the terms *premise* and *claim* with students to make sure they understand the difference. Then guide students in identifying more premises from the argument and the claim to which each is related. (*Example: Premise: Smaller and more cohesive units of population, as at the local or regional level, are conducive to factions. Related claim: Factions in a larger electorate are less likely to form and gain power.*) Encourage students to analyze the logic Madison uses to link each claim.

Strategies for Annotation   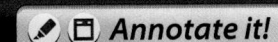 *Annotate it!*

Evaluate Seminal Texts: Purpose and Premises of an Argument

Share these strategies for guided or independent analysis.

- Highlight each premise in yellow.
- Highlight each claim in green.
- Underline the reasons given for each claim.

> It could never be more truly said than of the first remedy, that it was worse than the disease. Liberty is to faction what air is to fire, an aliment without which it instantly expires. But it could not be less folly to abolish liberty . . . because it nourishes faction, than it would be to wish the annihilation of air, which is essential to animal life, because it imparts to fire its destructive agency.

PRACTICE & APPLY

Analyzing the Text COMMON CORE RI 1, RI 4, RI 8

Possible answers:

1. *Madison acknowledges in lines 17–26 that the existing government sometimes allows the majority to oppress both justice and private rights. His acknowledgment of this counterargument may appeal to Anti-Federalists' concerns that the Constitution would allow the federal government to trample on individual and states' rights.*

2. *Conflicts between a faction's interests and the general welfare make a faction harmful to a democracy.*

3. *By making this statement, Madison appeals to readers—including Anti-Federalists—who value freedom above all else. He puts forth the idea of destroying liberty in order to make the point that there is no way to completely avoid the development of factions.*

4. *Just as no man can be a judge in his own cause, those in government also must not be too attached to their own self-interests because they would be biased and unfair. Madison's claim in lines 169–171 that a republic is more effective than a straight democracy at controlling the dangers of factions is related to this premise. With the election of representatives, those making the laws become further removed from their own self-interests than if each person represented himself or herself directly.*

5. *(1) Men form different opinions, which will become attached to self-interests (lines 55–59). (2) Different passions will cause division in society, and it is the nature of humans and society for these groups to develop animosities. (3) Groups, once formed, are more disposed to "vex and oppress each other than to co-operate for their common good" (lines 77–78). These premises support the claims well if the reader accepts them (that is, if the reader agrees that it is human nature to divide and to act selfishly rather than to work together for the common good).*

6. *He says that in a pure democracy there is nothing to keep political passions in check (lines 156–164), whereas in a republic the delegation of governmental duties serves to "refine and enlarge the public views" (lines 180–181).*

7. *By pointing out the advantages of the large republic, he explains how it will help control factions. By discussing how to arrive at the ideal proportion of governed people to elected officials, he enhances the point that the Union must be well constructed.*

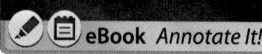 eBook *Annotate It!*

Analyzing the Text COMMON CORE RI 1, RI 4, RI 8, SL 1b, SL 1c

Cite Text Evidence   Support your responses with evidence from the selection.

1. **Cite Evidence** An effective argument acknowledges the claims made by opponents and refutes these claims with counterarguments. In the first paragraph of his argument, what does Madison acknowledge about criticisms of existing governments? How might this appeal to Anti-Federalists?

2. **Interpret** According to Madison's definition of *faction* in lines 36–40, what makes factions harmful to popular or democratic government?

3. **Infer** Why does Madison say that "liberty . . . is essential to [faction's] existence" (line 44)? Why does he put forth the idea of destroying liberty to remove faction?

4. **Cite Evidence** In lines 94–96, Madison says that "No man is allowed to be a judge in his own cause, because his interest would certainly bias his judgment, and, not improbably, corrupt his integrity." How does this premise relate to Madison's main claim about the virtues of representative democracy? What claims in the second half of this publication are based on the premises in this paragraph?

5. **Evaluate** Identify three additional premises that Madison uses to support his claim that "the *causes* of faction cannot be removed" (lines 125–126). The premises may be stated or implied. How effectively do these general principles support the claim?

6. **Compare** Why does Madison conclude that a "pure democracy" (lines 153–156) cannot solve the problems of faction but that a republic can solve them?

7. **Analyze** How does Madison's argument on the benefits of a large republic relate to his claim that a "well constructed Union" can control the problems of factions?

PERFORMANCE TASK

Speaking Activity Madison concludes that factions are a part of a free society and that it can be challenging to deal with the animosity that they create. Work with a small group to promote a civil, democratic discussion about an issue that creates factions by following these steps.

- Brainstorm with your group to choose a topic that creates factions at school, in your community, or in the nation.

- In your discussion, pose and respond to questions that will allow a full range of contrary positions to be heard.

- Together, write a set of rules that will guide your discussion.

- Write a brief evaluation of how well your rules worked.

Assign this performance task.

PERFORMANCE TASK COMMON CORE SL 1b, SL 1c

Speaking Activity Encourage students to reach a consensus on the rules before beginning their discussions and to practice effective listening skills during the discussion. Remind students to be respectful of their peers even if they do not agree with their opinions. You may wish to have students write their evaluations individually and then assess the group activity based on the overall impression conveyed in the evaluations

Critical Vocabulary

COMMON CORE L 5b

| faction | aggregate | reciprocal | latent |
| apportionment | efficacy | comprised | pervade |

Practice and Apply Complete each sentence to reflect your understanding of the Critical Vocabulary word.

1. Rich people and poor people belong to different **factions** because . . .

2. The federal government is able to focus on the **aggregate** interests of the country because . . .

3. Opinions and passions have a **reciprocal** influence on each other because . . .

4. Adopting the Constitution would allow the **latent** benefits of the new government to become obvious because . . .

5. The government wanted the **apportionment** of taxes to closely match the value of property because . . .

6. A faction's **efficacy** in achieving its goals is stronger in a small area because . . .

7. There is more diversity **comprised** in a larger republic because . . .

8. A feeling of harmony **pervades** a group of people with similar interests because . . .

Vocabulary Strategy: Evaluating Nuances in Meaning

In choosing to use the Critical Vocabulary word *faction* as the focus of his essay, Madison was conscious not just of the word's **denotation** or dictionary definition, but also of its **nuances** or shades of meaning. Madison also uses other words in the text with similar denotations, such as *party*, *interest*, and *sect*, to refer to groups or causes. Yet Madison often combines these words, which are more neutral, with adjectives so that the nuances become more similar to *faction*. Consider these examples:

- rival parties
- interfering interests
- ruling passion or interest

The word *faction* has the nuance of promoting conflict, and Madison often uses the related adjective *factious* to attach that nuance to neutral or positive words.

- factious spirit
- factious tempers
- factious combinations
- factious leaders

Practice and Apply With a partner, use the line references to find each word in context. Discuss why Madison chose the word rather than one of the listed synonyms. What nuances of meaning make each word an appropriate choice to convey his precise meaning? Consult a dictionary or thesaurus as needed.

1. declamations (line 12): recitations, speeches

2. alarm (line 31): panic, worry

3. contending (line 73): arguing, brawling

4. cabals (line 198): groups, factions

PRACTICE & APPLY

Critical Vocabulary
COMMON CORE L 5b

Possible answers:

1. *Rich people and poor people belong to different **factions** because they want different rules about income and taxes.*

2. *The federal government is able to focus on the **aggregate** interests of the country because the representatives from different areas vote on the laws made.*

3. *Opinions and passions have a **reciprocal** influence on each other because passions tend to strengthen and deepen opinions, and opinions in turn lead to more passion.*

4. *Adopting the Constitution would allow the **latent** benefits of the new government to become obvious because law and order would ensue while individual and state rights would still be maintained.*

5. *The government wanted the **apportionment** of taxes to closely match the value of property because that way of distributing tax responsibility would be fair to all.*

6. *A faction's **efficacy** in achieving its goals is stronger in a small area because it can be more effective in spreading its beliefs and gathering momentum when there is a smaller number of people who may all have similar backgrounds and interests.*

7. *There is more diversity **comprised** in a larger republic because there are more people with different backgrounds and interests.*

8. *A feeling of harmony **pervades** a group of people with similar interests because there is not a lot of conflict in what they believe and want.*

Strategies for Annotation   ✐ ▣ *Annotate it!*

Evaluating Nuances in Meaning
COMMON CORE L 5b

Direct students to the paragraph beginning with line 128 and have them use their eBook annotation tools to do the following:

- Highlight in yellow those words that carry a significant nuance.
- Make a note of each highlighted word's nuance.

If a faction consists of less than a majority, relief is supplied by the republican principle, which enables the majority to defeat its sinister views by regular vote. It may clog the administration, it may convulse the society; but it will be unable to execute and mask its violence under the forms of the Constitution.

"evil"

PRACTICE & APPLY

Language and Style: Transitions

Help students understand how important transitions are to clarity. Have them imagine each example sentence with the underlined transitions removed. Ask them to explain why the sentence is harder to understand this way. Then, replace the transitions with ones that show the wrong relationship between ideas and point out how confusing the sentence is.

ASK STUDENTS to turn in both versions of their evaluation with the transitions marked in the revised version. If transitions are used incorrectly, explain what would have been the correct word or phrase to use or how to better revise the sentence.

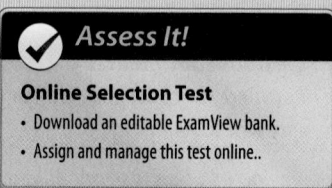

✓ Assess It!

Online Selection Test
- Download an editable ExamView bank.
- Assign and manage this test online..

Language and Style: Transitions

Transitions are words and phrases that show how ideas are related to one another. Using transitions effectively helps an author create **coherence** so that all sentences are related to one another and ideas flow in a logical manner. Transitions can communicate time or sequence, spatial relationships, degree of importance, compare-and-contrast relationships, or cause and effect. James Madison uses a variety of transitions to create coherence in his argument and to help readers follow his reasoning.

Much of Madison's argument is broken into a consideration of alternatives. Notice how he uses transitions to make this structure clear:

> There are two methods of curing the mischiefs of faction: <u>the one</u>, by removing its causes; <u>the other</u>, by controlling its effects.

Madison uses the phrases *the one* and *the other* to clarify the two alternatives. In the next example, he uses the word *but* to signal a contrast and *the most* to show a hierarchy of ideas. He points out that while people often come into conflict over trivial matters, inequalities in people's wealth creates deep and long-lasting factions:

> So strong is this propensity of mankind to fall into mutual animosities, that where no substantial occasion presents itself, the most frivolous and fanciful distinctions have been sufficient to kindle their unfriendly passions and excite their most violent conflicts. <u>But the most</u> common and durable source of factions has been the various and unequal distribution of property.

The chart shows other transitions that Madison uses to clarify the structure of his argument by pointing out premises and claims.

Uses of transitions in argument		
Purpose	**Transition Words**	**Example**
Signal a premise or cause	*because, since, so, for the reason that, due to, inasmuch as*	No man is allowed to be a judge in his own cause, <u>because</u> his interest would certainly bias his judgment, and, not improbably, corrupt his integrity.
Signal a claim, conclusion, or effect	*therefore, thus, hence, consequently, as a result*	<u>Hence</u>, it clearly appears, that the same advantage which a republic has over a democracy, in controlling the effects of faction, is enjoyed by a large over a small republic,...

Practice and Apply Look back at the evaluation you wrote about your discussion in response to this selection's Performance Task. Revise your writing to include transitions that will help you make the relationships between your ideas clearer and your paragraphs more coherent.

Analyze an Author's Purpose

COMMON CORE
RI 6

TEACH

Remind students that there are various purposes for writing, including to inform, to persuade, and to entertain. Discuss Madison's purpose for writing *The Federalist No. 10* with students, which was to persuade the Anti-Federalists to support ratification of the Constitution.

PRACTICE AND APPLY

Working as a class, help students make an outline of Madison's argument to determine how each point contributes to his overall purpose. Have students scan the essay to find Madison's main points. Then ask how each main point helps him to achieve his purpose. Share this outline with the class.

1) Factions in the U.S are causing injustice.

a) Solve problem by keeping factions from forming or by preventing them from causing harm.

i) Factions arise naturally and cannot be kept from forming except by sacrificing liberty.

ii) Politicians cannot resist serving their own self-interest, or faction, in their decisions.

b) Since factions cannot be kept from forming, we must prevent them from causing harm.

i) In pure democracy, factions will always prevail.

ii) A republic with elected representatives can prevent factions from causing harm and can control them.

(1) Elected representatives serve the interests of the nation as a whole.

(2) The people will be more likely to elect a good candidate.

(3) In a large society, there will be a greater variety of factions, so it is less likely that one would predominate.

2) The republican form of our Consitutional government is set up to protect minorities and the government itself.

 **INTERACTIVE LESSON** If students need further instruction, use this Interactive Whiteboard Lesson: **Author's Purpose and Perspective.**

Evaluate Seminal Texts: Premises of an Argument

COMMON CORE
RI 8

RETEACH

Review the terms **premise, claim, reasons, evidence**, and **counterargument**. Then give an example of a claim, such as "Volunteer work should be a high school requirement."

- Ask students to provide a premise for the claim. (***Sample premise:*** *Good character is an important goal of education.*)
- Ask students to provide examples and evidence that support the claim. (***Sample reason:*** *Volunteering may inspire a student's choice of career.*)
- Suggest the following counterargument: "High school students already have too much required coursework and should be allowed to take elective courses instead." Ask: How could you counter this viewpoint? (***Sample answer:*** *Students can be offered a variety of volunteer opportunities.*

 **LEVEL UP TUTORIALS** Assign the following *Level-Up* tutorial: **ELEMENTS OF AN ARGUMENT**

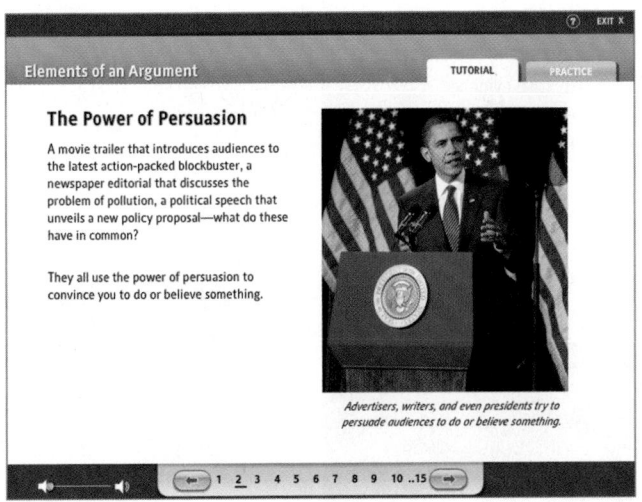

CLOSE READING APPLICATION

Have students analyze another persuasive essay from United States history, working independently to outline the premises, claims, support, and counterarguments that are addressed. Ask: What are the writer's premises? Do you think most readers would accept them as true? What is the writer's main claim? Does the writer include enough support to prove the claim? Does he or she do an adequate job of anticipating possible objections?

Petition to the Massachusetts General Assembly

Public Document by Prince Hall

Why This Text

Students may not grasp the premises and purposes of historical documents, which were written in periods distant from students' lives. Yet the authors employed similar techniques in their arguments as we do today. With the help of the close-reading questions, students will analyze Hall's petition. This close reading will lead them to more fully understand how Hall presents his premises and how they support the purpose of the petition.

Background Have students read the background and information about Prince Hall. When he wrote the petition, Hall had been a free man for six or seven years. Importantly, he had witnessed the gradual breakdown in relations between the thirteen colonies and Great Britain. Rebelling at their perceived lack of freedom and rights under the British crown, colonists declared their independence the summer before Hall made his petition.

AS YOU READ Ask students to pay attention to the themes in the petition. How does Hall use these themes to try to persuade Massachusetts' representatives of the merits of his petition?

Common Core Support

- cite strong and thorough textual evidence
- determine the central ideas of a text
- evaluate the reasoning and the premises, purposes, and arguments in a text

Text Complexity Rubric

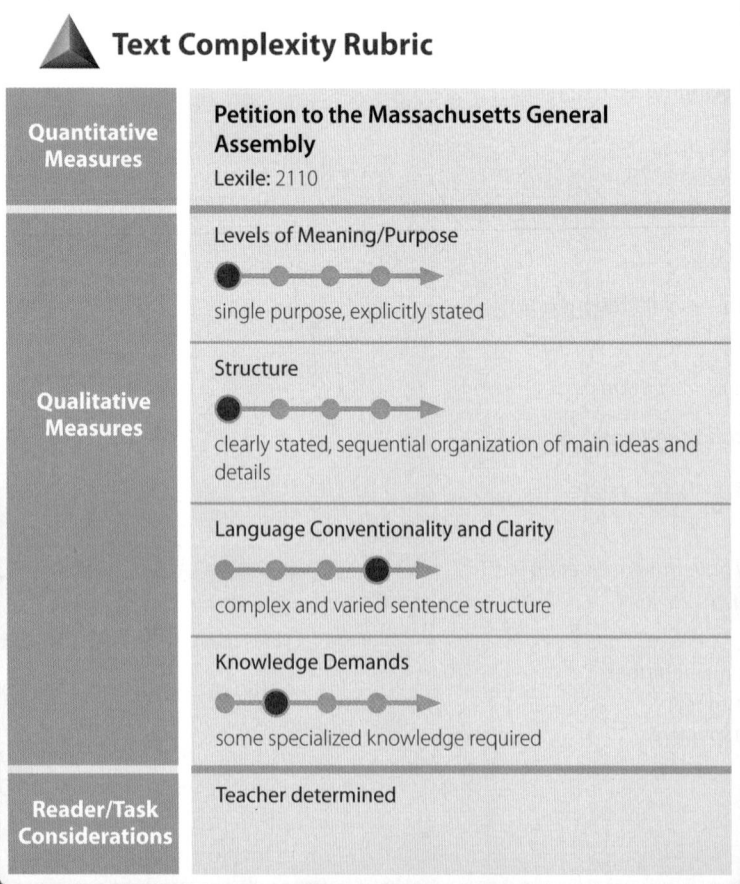

Quantitative Measures

Petition to the Massachusetts General Assembly
Lexile: 2110

Qualitative Measures

Levels of Meaning/Purpose

single purpose, explicitly stated

Structure

clearly stated, sequential organization of main ideas and details

Language Conventionality and Clarity

complex and varied sentence structure

Knowledge Demands

some specialized knowledge required

Reader/Task Considerations

Teacher determined

Strategies for CLOSE READING

Analyze Purpose and Premises of an Argument

Students should read this document carefully all the way through. Close-reading questions at the bottom of the page will help them focus on a thorough analysis of the author's purpose and premises. As they read, students should jot down comments or questions about the text in the margins.

WHEN STUDENTS STRUGGLE . . .

To help students analyze the "Petition to the Massachusetts General Assembly," have them work in small groups to fill out a chart like the one shown below.

CITE TEXT EVIDENCE For practice in analyzing the purpose and premises of an argument, ask students to cite the premises Hall gives and the purpose of his petition.

Purpose
To persuade the State of Massachusetts to free all slaves

Premises
". . . in common with all other men a natural and unalienable right to that freedom which the Great Parent of the Universe bestowed equally on all mankind . . ."
". . . a life of slavery . . . is far worse than nonexistence."
. . . every principle from which America has acted . . . pleads stronger than a thousand arguments in favor of your petitioners."
"So may the inhabitants of this State no longer be guilty of the inconsistency of acting in ways that they condemn and oppose in others."

Background Prince Hall (1735–1807) was held as a slave by William Hall, in Boston until the age of 35, when he was freed. Hall used his freedom to become an advocate for African Americans. Hall made many petitions on behalf of free blacks and successfully petitioned for the release of three Boston African Americans who had been kidnapped into slavery. For years, Hall protested that African American children did not have public schools, and eventually he started a school of his own for them.

Petition to the Massachusetts General Assembly

Public Document by Prince Hall

CLOSE READ Notes

1. **READ ▶** As you read the petition, begin to collect and cite text evidence.
   - In the margin, paraphrase the first sentence (lines 3–10).
   - Underline three of Hall's premises that support his argument against slavery.
   - In the margin on the next page, analyze what Hall means by "the natural right of all men" (line 30).

To the Honorable Counsel and House of Representatives for the State of Massachusetts Bay in General Court assembled, January 13, 1777:

The petition of a great number of blacks detained in a state of slavery in a free and Christian county humbly points out that your petitioners understand that they have in common with all other men a natural and unalienable right to that freedom which the Great Parent of the Universe bestowed equally on all mankind, and which they have never forfeited by any compact or agreement whatever, but that they were unjustly dragged by the hand of cruel power along with their dearest friends, and some of them even torn from the embraces of their tender parents, from a populous, pleasant, and plentiful country. In violation of Laws of Nature and of Nations and in defiance of all the tender feelings of humanity, they were brought here to be sold like beasts of burden, and like them condemned to slavery for life among a people professing the mild religion of Jesus—a people not insensible of the secrets of rational being nor without spirit to resent the unjust endeavors of others to reduce *them* to a state of bondage and **subjugation**. Your Honors need not to be informed that a life of slavery like that of your petitioners, deprived of every social

Blacks, like all other humans, are entitled to freedom, and their enslavement is an unjust abuse of power.

subjugation: *suppression*

27

1. **READ AND CITE TEXT EVIDENCE** The first sentence of Hall's petition is a masterpiece of rhetoric. Here he manages to eloquently set forth his purpose of his petition.

Ⓐ ASK STUDENTS to discuss Hall's purpose that he explains in the petition's first sentence. *Hall's purpose is to point out the inconsistencies of a nation that claims to be founded on the "unalienable right to freedom" while still holding "blacks detained in a state of slavery."*

Critical Vocabulary: subjugation (line 16) Have students share their definitions of *subjugation*. Ask volunteers to use the noun in a sentence.

CLOSE READ
Notes

The "natural right" is freedom. This is what the petitioners have in common with all other men, the right to freedom.

privilege and of every thing requisite to render life tolerable, is far worse than nonexistence.

20   In imitation of the laudable example of the good people of these states, your petitioners have long and patiently waited the outcome of petition after petition presented by them to the Legislative Body of this state, and with grief reflect that their lack of success has been similar each time. They cannot but express their astonishment that it has never been considered that every principle from which America has acted in the course of their unhappy difficulties with Great Britain pleads stronger than a thousand arguments in favor of your petitioners. They therefore humbly beseech Your Honors to give this petition its due weight and consideration and cause an act of the legislature to be passed whereby they may be restored to the enjoyments which is the

30   natural right of all men and that their children, who were born in this Land of Liberty, may not be held as slaves after they arrive at the age of twenty-one **B** years. So may the inhabitants of this State no longer be guilty of the inconsistency of acting in ways that they condemn and oppose in others. May they prosper in their present glorious struggle for Liberty and have those blessings to them.

2. ◀ **REREAD AND DISCUSS**   Reread the petition. Circle Hall's purpose for this petition. Explain the three main premises that support his reasoning.

Slavery is contrary to people's professed faith; it is worse than death; it is un-American.

SHORT RESPONSE

Cite Text Evidence   Summarize the purpose and premises of Hall's argument. Review your reading notes, and be sure to **cite text evidence** in your response.

Hall's purpose is to convince the State of Massachusetts to free all slaves. His premises are general principles that he presents as self-evident. First, "the Great Parent of the Universe bestowed [the right to freedom] equally on all mankind." Second, a life of slavery is intolerable and "far worse than nonexistence." And finally, slavery is inconsistent with American values, because America is the "Land of Liberty."

28

TO CHALLENGE STUDENTS . . .

To gain a deeper understanding of the social context of Hall's petition, students can research the role of slaves in colonial America and in the American Revolution.

ASK STUDENTS to compare the role of slavery in the economies of northern colonies, such as Massachusetts, and southern colonies, such as Virginia. *Students should recognize that slavery was an important institution throughout the colonies, but that slaves were used differently in the south and north. In the south, landholdings were large, and slave labor was crucial for export crops like tobacco. Farms were also important in the north, but they were smaller and generally did not rely on slave labor. In the north, slaves were more frequently found in the cities, where they worked in households and manufacturing establishments.*

ASK STUDENTS how the newly-formed American government and the British government dealt with the issue of slavery during the Revolution. *Students should understand that the American government confirmed its commitment to slavery, thus protecting the interests of slave owners, who were key backers of the Revolution. The British government saw the American position as an opportunity—and offered freedom to runaway slaves.*

2. **REREAD AND DISCUSS USING TEXT EVIDENCE**

B **ASK STUDENTS** to explain the apparent contradiction Hall proposes and why he might have included it. *Slaves were valuable pieces of property, so their emancipation would hurt owners' fortunes. By allowing slaves' children to remain slaves until age 21, Hall's proposal would soften this economic blow, perhaps making it more politically palatable.*

FOR ELL STUDENTS Explain that the word *weight* in line 28 does not refer to "heaviness" in this context, but to "importance."

SHORT RESPONSE

Cite Text Evidence   Students should:

- note that Hall wants the legislature to pass an act to free slaves.
- explain that slaves, as members of mankind, have unalienable rights.
- clearly state the other premises found in Hall's petition.

DIG DEEPER

1. With the class, return to Question 1, Read. Have students share their paraphrases of the first sentence. Point out that one of Hall's purposes in the petition is to expose the inconsistencies that allow slavery to exist in the United States. Hall's language describing these inconsistencies aims to make his audience hear the petition with the insight of the kinds of men they profess to be.

ASK STUDENTS to focus on the rhetorical device of repeating the idea of inconsistency.

- What other examples of the theme of inconsistency did Hall include in his petition? *Students should note the following examples: "condemned to slavery . . . among a people professing the mild religion of Jesus" (lines 13–14), "to resent the unjust endeavors of others to reduce them to a state of bondage and subjugation" (lines 15–16), "every principle from which America has acted . . . pleads stronger than a thousand arguments in favor of your petitioners" (lines 25–27), "may the inhabitants of this State no longer be guilty of the inconsistency of acting in ways that they condemn and oppose in others" (lines 32–33).*

- Why might this rhetorical device resonate with Hall's audience? *Students should recognize that the members of the Assembly were then engaged in a great fight for their own freedom and rights, as the colonies battled Great Britain for independence. Hall hoped that the representatives' experience with tyranny would make them more sympathetic to the plight of slaves.*

2. With the class, return to Question 2, Reread and Discuss. Have students share their three main premises.

- What is another premise that Hall used to support his petition? Cite text evidence. *Students should note the premise that all people, including blacks, have an unalienable right to freedom, citing the explicit statement in the first sentence, (lines 5–6), "In violation of Laws of Nature and of Nations" (lines 10–11), and "the enjoyments which is the natural right of all men" (lines 29–30).*

- How did Hall use language to evince sympathy from his audience? *Students should recognize that Hall frequently returned to the theme of compassion: "even torn from the embraces of their tender parents" (lines 9–10), "in defiance of all the tender feelings of humanity" (lines 11–12), and "deprived of every social privilege and of every thing requisite to render life tolerable" (lines 17–18).*

ASK STUDENTS to return to their Short Response answer and revise it based on the class discussion.

CLOSE READING NOTES

Thomas Jefferson: The Best of Enemies

History Article by Ron Chernow

Why This Text?

This article explores the serious disagreements that existed among the founders and will help students to understand our history as well as our current political system. In addition, this lesson will help students to analyze structure in informational texts.

Key Learning Objective: The student will be able to analyze ideas, events, and structure in an informational text.

For additional practice:

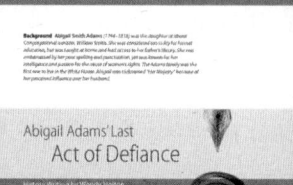

Close Reader selection
Abigail Adams' Last Act of Defiance
History Writing by Woody Holton

COMMON CORE Common Core Standards

RI 1 Cite textual evidence.

RI 3 Analyze a complex sequence of events and explain how individuals, ideas, or events interact.

RI 4 Analyze the meanings of words and phrases as they are used in a text, including figurative, connotative, and technical meanings.

RI 5 Analyze and evaluate the effectiveness of the structure an author uses in exposition or argument.

W 2 Write informative/explanatory texts.

L 2a Observe hyphenation conventions.

L 4c Consult reference materials.

L 4d Verify the preliminary determination of the meaning of a word or phrase.

▲ Text Complexity Rubric

	Thomas Jefferson: The Best of Enemies
Quantitative Measures	Lexile: 1340L
Qualitative Measures	Levels of Meaning/Purpose — implied; easily identified from context
	Structure — organization of main ideas and details complex, explicit
	Language Conventionality and Clarity — some unfamiliar academic or domain-specific words
	Knowledge Demands — some specialized knowledge required
Reader/Task Considerations	Teacher determined. Vary by individual reader and type of text

TEACH

CLOSE READ

Background Thomas Jefferson and Alexander Hamilton both played integral roles in the founding of this country. Their shared objectives ended with the common goal of freedom from the British. However, they had very different opinions about how to create a sustainable government for the United States. Alexander Hamilton believed in a strong federal government, while Thomas Jefferson felt that more power belonged in the hands of the states. These arguments persist in American politics today.

AS YOU READ Direct students to use the As You Read instruction to focus their reading. Remind students to write down any questions they generate during reading.

Analyze Ideas and Events: Sequence (LINES 1–6)
COMMON CORE RI 3

Point out to students that historical accounts often use a narrative structure comparable to the structure of many short stories—that is, a sequence of events shaped by a conflict. Have students reread lines 1–6.

 **ASK STUDENTS** to analyze why the writer might have chosen to start his account with a description of Jefferson's return to New York. *(The writer is setting the stage for the coming conflict. He describes Jefferson as "taken aback by the adulation being heaped upon the new Treasury Secretary.")*

Analyze Structure: Comparison and Contrast
COMMON CORE RI 5

(LINES 1–14)

The writer quickly sets up the reader to compare and contrast Thomas Jefferson and Alexander Hamilton, as a way of understanding their rivalry. In this first paragraph, the writer contrasts the backgrounds of both men.

 **CITE TEXT EVIDENCE** Have students cite textual evidence that demonstrates the differences between the two men. *(Jefferson was a diplomat; Hamilton was an illegitimate orphan. Jefferson wrote the Declaration of Independence; Hamilton was a lowly artillery captain. Despite this, when Jefferson returned to New York, Hamilton was the admired one.)*

Background *Thomas Jefferson (1743–1826) and Alexander Hamilton (1755/57–1804) were founders of the United States who played different roles in the country's development. In this 2004 magazine article,* **Ron Chernow** *explores how the men's ideological differences brought them into conflict when both served in President George Washington's first Cabinet. Chernow is the award-winning author of several biographies, including* Alexander Hamilton *(2004) and* Washington: A Life *(2010). As a writer, his goal is to make historical figures come alive.*

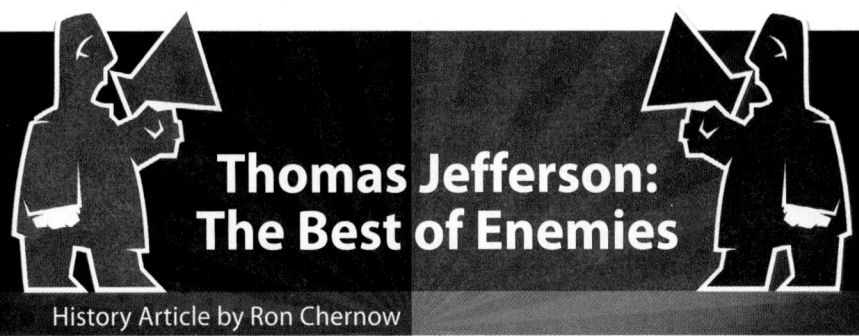

Thomas Jefferson: The Best of Enemies

History Article by Ron Chernow

AS YOU READ Look for clues that reveal Jefferson's and Hamilton's personalities. Write down any questions you generate during reading.

On March 21, 1790, Thomas Jefferson belatedly arrived in New York City to assume his duties as the first Secretary of State after a five-year ministerial stint in Paris. Tall and lanky, with a freckled complexion and auburn hair, Jefferson, 46, was taken aback by the adulation being heaped upon the new Treasury Secretary, Alexander Hamilton, who had streaked to prominence in his absence. Few people knew that Jefferson had authored the Declaration of Independence, which had yet to become holy writ for Americans. Instead, the Virginian was eclipsed by the 35-year-old wunderkind from the Caribbean, who was a lowly artillery captain in New York when Jefferson composed the famous document. Despite his murky background as an illegitimate orphan, the self-invented Hamilton was trim and elegant, carried himself with an erect military bearing and had a mind that worked with dazzling speed. At first, Hamilton and Jefferson socialized on easy terms, with little inkling that they were destined to become mortal foes. But their clash inside George Washington's first Cabinet proved so fierce that it would spawn the two-party system in America. It also produced two divergent visions of the country's future that divide Americans to the present day.

10

Image Credits: (c) ©wallinarez/Shutterstock; (bg) ©Click Bestsellers/Shutterstock

SCAFFOLDING FOR ELL STUDENTS

Analyze Structure: Comparison and Contrast Creating a Venn diagram can help students to visualize similarities and differences. Have students reread the text, and create and fill in a Venn diagram like the one below to help them compare Jefferson and Hamilton.

Jefferson   Both   Hamilton

Analyze Structure: Comparison and Contrast

 **COMMON CORE** RI 5

(LINES 20–28)

Have students analyze Jefferson and Hamilton's ideas about the federal government to understand the core difference between the men's views.

C **CITE TEXT EVIDENCE** Ask students to cite textual evidence that explains what was at the core of Jefferson and Hamilton's disagreement about the role of the federal government. *(Hamilton "advocated a vigorous central government," while "Jefferson believed that liberty was jeopardized by concentrated federal power.")*

Analyze Structure: Comparison and Contrast

 **COMMON CORE** RI 5

(LINES 29–40)

Explain to students that the structure of this article supports the author's **purpose**—to compare and contrast Jefferson and Hamilton by comparing the two men point by point.

D **ASK STUDENTS** to identify what is being compared in this paragraph (lines 29–40). *(In this paragraph, the author is comparing the role each man played in the creation and ratification of the Constitution.)*

CRITICAL VOCABULARY

tepid: Thomas Jefferson is not enthusiastic about the new political order.

ASK STUDENTS to explain why Thomas Jefferson's enthusiasm was tepid about the new government. *(He did not believe in a strong federal government with a lot of centralized power.)*

CRITICAL VOCABULARY

copious: Hamilton was a man of many talents and these talents worried Jefferson.

ASK STUDENTS which of Hamilton's "copious talents" petrified Jefferson? *(Hamilton was extremely brilliant and an excellent speaker and writer.)*

---

20   For Hamilton, the first Treasury Secretary, the supreme threat to liberty arose from insufficient government power. To avert that, he advocated a vigorous central government marked by a strong President, an independent judiciary and a liberal reading of the Constitution. As the first Secretary of State, Jefferson believed that liberty was jeopardized by concentrated federal power, which he tried to restrict through a narrow construction of the Constitution. He favored states' rights, a central role for Congress and a comparatively weak judiciary.   **C**

30   At first glance, Hamilton might seem the more formidable figure in that classic matchup. He took office with an ardent faith in the new national government. He had attended the Constitutional Convention, penned the bulk of the Federalist papers to secure passage of the new charter and spearheaded ratification efforts in New York State. He therefore set to work at Treasury with more unrestrained gusto than Jefferson—who had monitored the Constitutional Convention from his post in Paris—did at State. Jefferson's enthusiasm for the new political order was **tepid** at best, and when Washington crafted the first government in 1789, Jefferson didn't grasp the levers of power with quite the same glee as Hamilton, who had no ideological
40 inhibitions about shoring up federal power.   **D**

    Hamilton—brilliant, brash and charming—had the self-reliant reflexes of someone who had always had to live by his wits. His overwhelming intelligence petrified Jefferson and his followers. As an orator, Hamilton could speak extemporaneously for hours on end. As a writer, he could crank out 5,000- or 10,000-word memos overnight. Jefferson never underrated his foe's **copious** talents. At one point, a worried Jefferson confided to his comrade James Madison that Hamilton was a one-man army, "a host[1] within himself."

    Whether in person or on paper, Hamilton served up his opinions
50 promiscuously. He had a true zest for debate and never left anyone guessing where he stood. Jefferson, more than a decade older, had

tepid
(tĕp´ĭd) *adj.*
lukewarm; indifferent.

copious
(kō´pē-əs) *adj.*
extensive.

---

[1] **host:** an army or large group of troops.

142   Collection 2

APPLYING ACADEMIC VOCABULARY

ideological	founder

As you discuss this article, incorporate the following academic vocabulary words: *ideological* and *founder*. Ask students to analyze the writer's use of comparison to create a picture of the **ideological** beliefs of Jefferson and Hamilton. As you discuss these leaders, have students analyze their roles as **founders** of the United States.

the quiet, courtly manner of a Virginia planter. He was emphatic in his views—Hamilton labeled him "an atheist in religion and a fanatic in politics"— but shrank from open conflict. Jefferson, a diffident speaker, mumbled his way through his rare speeches in a soft, almost inaudible voice and reserved his most scathing strictures for private correspondence.

The epic battle between these two Olympian[2] figures began not long after Jefferson came to New York City to assume his State Department duties in March 1790. By then Hamilton was in the thick of a contentious campaign to retire massive debt inherited from the Revolution. America had suspended principal and interest payments[3] on its obligations, which had traded as low as 15¢ on the dollar. In an audacious scheme to restore public credit, Hamilton planned to pay off that debt at face value, causing the securities to soar from depressed levels. Jefferson and Madison thought the original holders of those securities—many of them war veterans—should profit from that appreciation even if they had already sold their paper to traders at depressed prices. Hamilton thought it would be impractical to track them down. With an eye on future U.S. capital markets, he wanted to enshrine the **cardinal** principle that current owners of securities incurred all profits and losses, even if that meant windfall gains for rapacious speculators who had only recently bought the securities.

That skirmish over Hamilton's public credit plan was part of a broader tussle over the U.S.'s economic future. Jefferson was fond of summoning up idyllic scenes of an agrarian America peopled by sturdy yeoman farmers. That poetic vision neglected the underlying reality of large slave plantations in the South. Jefferson was a fine populist on paper but not in everyday life, and his defense of Virginia interests was inextricably bound up with slavery. Hamilton—derided

cardinal
(kär´dn-əl) *adj.* most important; prime.

---
[2] **Olympian:** like a god; one from Mount Olympus.
[3] **principal and interest payments:** the amount borrowed and the fees charged by the lender.

Analyze Ideas and Events: Sequence (LINES 58–62)
COMMON CORE RI 3

Remind students that writers use transitional words and phrases such as *first, next,* and *later* to indicate the order of events. Point out that, in addition, writers use verb tenses to show chronology. For instance, writers use the past perfect tense to express an action in the past that came before another action in the past.

E **ASK STUDENTS** to identify words and phrases in lines 58–62 that signal the order of events. *(not long after, By then, had suspended)*

Analyze Structure: Comparison and Contrast (LINES 58–73)
COMMON CORE RI 5

Explain to students that in a point-by-point comparison, an author compares one aspect of the subjects being compared and then another.

F **ASK STUDENTS** to identify the point of comparison in this paragraph (lines 58–73). *(In this paragraph, the author is comparing each man's opinion on how debt from the Revolutionary War should be handled.)*

> **CRITICAL VOCABULARY**
>
> **cardinal:** Hamilton's beliefs about the future of the U.S. economy were guided by a cardinal principle.
>
> **ASK STUDENTS** what Hamilton's cardinal principle was. *(Current owners of securities incur all of the profits and losses. Former owners would have no claim to profit or obligation in loss.)*

SCAFFOLDING FOR ELL STUDENTS

Sequence and Verb Tense Tell students that verb tenses can help them understand the sequence of events. The **past tense** expresses an action that began and ended in the past. The **past perfect tense** expresses an action in the past that came before another action in the past.

ASK STUDENTS to identify examples of each of these verb tenses on this page of the selection. *(past tense: was, labeled, mumbled, began, planned, wanted; past perfect tense: had suspended, had traded, had sold)*

The past perfect tense verbs discuss the history of the securities, which occurred before the two men disagreed about the securities.

Analyze Language: Diction (LINES 88–91)

 COMMON CORE RI 4

Point out to students that a writer's choice of words can serve to highlight a comparison. For instance, in line 88, Chernow uses the related words, *aristocracy* and *meritocracy* to compare the two men's views about who should rule.

Have students look up the definitions of both words. What root do they have in common? *(–cracy, meaning "government or rule")*

G **ASK STUDENTS** to explain the comparison Chernow is making by using these related words to describe the two men. *(Chernow writes that Hamilton prefers a meritocracy, which is rule by those who have merit based on their talents or achievements; while he claims that Jefferson, who was a landowner, favored aristocracy, or rule by a privileged class.)*

CRITICAL VOCABULARY

rudiment: Hamilton believed in the basics of a modern economy.

ASK STUDENTS what, according to Hamilton, were the rudiments of a modern economy? *(trade, commerce, banks, stock exchanges, factories, and corporations)*

Analyze Ideas and Events: Sequence (LINES 92–110)

 COMMON CORE RI 3

When Jefferson aims to take down Hamilton, using his "consummate skills as a practicing politician," a sequence of events takes place that gives the reader insight into the depth of their feud.

H **ASK STUDENTS** to analyze the sequence of events and to infer why Chernow included them in his piece. *(After Hamilton was instrumental in the creation of the country's first central bank, Jefferson used the power of his office to finance a newspaper assault on Hamilton's character. Hamilton countered with articles of his own written under pseudonyms. Chernow probably included this sequence of events to show how their disagreements escalated.)*

---

as a pseudo aristocrat, an elitist, a crypto-monarchist[4]—was a passionate abolitionist with a far more expansive economic vision. He conceded that agriculture would persist for decades as an essential component of the economy. But at the same time he wanted to foster the **rudiments** of a modern economy—trade, commerce, banks, stock exchanges, factories and corporations—to enlarge economic opportunity.

rudiment
(rōo′də-mənt) *n.* basic form.

Hamilton dreamed of a meritocracy, not an aristocracy, while Jefferson retained the landed gentry's disdain for the vulgar realities of
90 trade, commerce and finance. And he was determined to undermine Hamilton's juggernaut.[5]

Because we celebrate Jefferson for his sonorous words in the Declaration of Independence—Hamilton never matched Jefferson's gift for writing ringing passages that were at once poetic and inspirational— we sometimes overlook Jefferson's consummate skills as a practicing politician. A master of subtle, artful indirection, he was able to marshal his forces without divulging his generalship. After Hamilton persuaded President Washington to create the Bank of the United States, the country's first central bank, Jefferson was aghast
100 at what he construed[6] as a breach of the Constitution and a perilous expansion of federal power. Along with Madison, he recruited the poet Philip Freneau to launch an opposition paper called the National Gazette. To subsidize the paper covertly, he hired Freneau as a State Department translator. Hamilton was shocked by such flagrant disloyalty from a member of Washington's Cabinet, especially when Freneau began to mount withering assaults on Hamilton and even Washington. Never one to suffer in silence, Hamilton retaliated in a blizzard of newspaper articles published under Roman pseudonyms. The backbiting between Hamilton and Jefferson grew so acrimonious
110 that Washington had to exhort both men to desist.

Instead, the feud worsened. In early 1793, a Virginia Congressman named William Branch Giles began to harry Hamilton with resolutions ordering him to produce, on short deadlines, stupendous amounts of Treasury data. With prodigious bursts of energy, Hamilton complied with those inhuman demands, foiling his opponents. Jefferson then committed an unthinkable act. He secretly drafted a series of anti-Hamilton resolutions for Giles, including one that read, "Resolved, That the Secretary of the Treasury has been guilty of maladministration in the duties of his office and should, in the
120 opinion of Congress, be removed from his office by the President of the United States." The resolution was voted down, and the effort to oust Hamilton stalled. Jefferson left the Cabinet in defeat later that year.

---

[4] **crypto-monarchist:** one who secretly supports government rule by a king.
[5] **juggernaut:** an extremely powerful force.
[6] **construed:** interpreted.

Throughout the 1790s, the Hamilton-Jefferson feud continued to fester in both domestic and foreign affairs. Jefferson thought Hamilton was "bewitched" by the British model of governance, while Hamilton considered Jefferson a credulous apologist for the gory excesses of the French Revolution. Descended from French Huguenots on his mother's side, Hamilton was fluent in French and had served as Washington's liaison with the Marquis de Lafayette and other French aristocrats who had rallied to the Continental Army. The French Revolution immediately struck him as a bloody affair, governed by rigid, Utopian thinking. On Oct. 6, 1789, he wrote a remarkable letter to Lafayette, explaining his "foreboding of ill" about the future course of events in Paris. He cited the "vehement character" of the French people and the "reveries" of their "philosophic politicians," who wished to transform human nature. Hamilton believed that Jefferson while in Paris "drank deeply of the French philosophy in religion, in science, in politics." Indeed, more than a decade passed before Jefferson fully realized that the French Revolution wasn't a worthy sequel to the American one so much as a grotesque travesty.[7]

If Jefferson and Hamilton define opposite ends of the political spectrum in U.S. history and seem to exist in perpetual conflict, the two men shared certain traits, feeding a mutual cynicism. Each scorned the other as excessively ambitious. In his secret diary, or Anas, Jefferson recorded a story of Hamilton praising Julius Caesar as the greatest man in history. (The tale sounds dubious, as Hamilton invariably used Caesar as shorthand for "an evil tyrant.") Hamilton repaid the favor. In one essay he likened Jefferson to "Caesar coyly refusing the proffered diadem" and rejecting the trappings, but "tenaciously grasping the substance of imperial domination."

Similarly, both men hid a potent hedonism[8] behind an intellectual façade. For all their outward differences, the two politicians stumbled into the two great sex scandals of the early Republic. In 1797 a journalist named James T. Callender exposed that Hamilton, while Treasury Secretary and a married man with four children, had entered into a yearlong affair with grifter Maria Reynolds, who was 23 when it began. In a 95-page pamphlet, Hamilton confessed to the affair at what many regarded as inordinate length. He wished to show that the money he had paid to Reynolds' husband James had been for the favor of her company and not for illicit speculation in Treasury securities, as the Jeffersonians had alleged. Forever after, the Jeffersonians tagged Hamilton as "the amorous Treasury Secretary" and mocked his pretensions to superior morality.

By an extraordinary coincidence, during Jefferson's first term as President, Callender also exposed Jefferson's relationship with Sally Hemings. Callender claimed that "Dusky Sally," a.k.a. the "African

façade
(fə-säd´) *n.* false or misleading appearance.

---

[7] **travesty:** an unreasonable distortion or parody.
[8] **hedonism:** the belief that personal pleasure is the primary goal in life.

Thomas Jefferson: The Best of Enemies **145**

CLOSE READ

Analyze Ideas and Events: Sequence (LINES 124–141)
COMMON CORE RI 3

Tell students that the events of the French Revolution demonstrate a moment where Jefferson's and Hamilton's views, though they started out on separate ends of the spectrum, actually came together.

(I) CITE TEXT EVIDENCE Ask students to analyze the perspectives of each man on the French Revolution. How did one of the men's views change as the French Revolution wore on? Have students cite text evidence to support their analyses. *(Hamilton viewed the French Revolution with disdain as a "bloody affair." Jefferson initially believed in the nobility of the French Revolution, but realized much later that it "wasn't a worthy sequel to the American [Revolution].")*

Analyze Structure: Compare and Contrast
COMMON CORE RI 5

(LINES 142–151)

(J) ASK STUDENTS to identify the comparison. *(Each viewed the other as "excessively ambitious.")*

CRITICAL VOCABULARY

façade: People in public life often put up a façade, or misleading appearance, to maintain an image.

ASK STUDENTS how scandal affected Hamilton. *(was mocked as "the amorous Treasury Secretary")*

Strategies for Annotation   ✎ 🖉 Annotate it!

Analyze Structure: Comparison and Contrast
COMMON CORE RI 5

Share strategies for guided or independent analysis.
- Highlight in green Chernow's comparison of the two men.
- Highlight in yellow Chernow's support for the idea that Jefferson saw Hamilton as excessively ambitious.
- Highlight in blue Chernow's support for the idea that Hamilton saw Jefferson as excessively ambitious.

[Jefferson and Hamilton] shared certain traits....Each scorned the other as excessively ambitious....Jefferson recorded a story of Hamilton praising Julius Caesar as the greatest man in history....he likened Jefferson to "Caesar coyly refusing the proffered diadem"... but "tenaciously grasping the substance of imperial domination."

CRITICAL VOCABULARY

anomalous: At this time, the candidate with the most electoral votes became president and the runner-up became vice president. In Jefferson's presidential election, something anomalous, or unusual, happened.

ASK STUDENTS to describe what was unusual about this presidential election. *(Jefferson and Burr tied in the election and it took 36 rounds of voting in the House to declare Jefferson the winner.)*

Analyze Language: Irony
COMMON CORE RI 4

(Lines 176–195)

Explain to students that **situational irony** is a contrast between what is expected to happen and what does happen.

 ASK STUDENTS to identify two examples of situational irony in lines 176–195. *(It is ironic that Hamilton ended up supporting Jefferson for President. It is also ironic that as President Jefferson took full advantage of the powers of the presidency, even though his earlier stance was that the federal government should have limited power.)*

COLLABORATIVE DISCUSSION Have students work in pairs to discuss and create a list of specific characteristics of Hamilton and Jefferson that would make it difficult for the two men to work together.

ASK STUDENTS to share any questions they generated in the course of reading and discussing the selection.

Venus," was the President's slave concubine, who had borne him five children. "There is not an individual in the neighborhood of Charlottesville who does not believe the story," Callender wrote, "and not a few who know it." Jefferson never confirmed or denied Callender's story. But the likely truth of the Hemings affair was dramatically bolstered by DNA tests published in 1998, which indicated that a Jefferson male had sired at least one of Hemings' children.

The crowning irony of the stormy relations between Hamilton and Jefferson is that Hamilton helped install his longtime foe as President in 1801. Under constitutional rules then in force, the candidate with the majority of electoral votes became President; the runner-up became Vice President. That created an **anomalous** situation in which Jefferson, his party's presumed presidential nominee, tied with Aaron Burr, its presumed vice presidential nominee. It took 36 rounds of voting in the House to decide the election in Jefferson's favor. Faced with the prospect of Burr as President, a man he considered unscrupulous, Hamilton not only opted for Jefferson as the lesser of two evils but also was forced into his most measured assessment of the man. Hamilton said he had long suspected that as President, Jefferson would develop a keen taste for the federal power he had deplored in opposition. He recalled that a decade earlier, in Washington's Cabinet, Jefferson had seemed like a man who knew he was destined to inherit an estate—in this case, the presidency—and didn't wish to deplete it. In fact, Jefferson, the strict constructionist, freely exercised the most sweeping powers as President. Nothing in the Constitution, for instance, permitted the Louisiana Purchase.[9] Hamilton noted that with rueful mirth.

anomalous
(ə-nŏm′ə-ləs) *adj.*
unusual.

---

[9] **Louisiana Purchase:** France's 1803 sale of its territory west of the Mississippi River to the United States.

COLLABORATIVE DISCUSSION How might Jefferson's and Hamilton's personal characteristics have affected their ability to work together easily? Discuss this question with a partner, citing evidence from the article to support your ideas.

TO CHALLENGE STUDENTS . . .

Point out to students that writers of comparison/contrast essays sometimes organize their ideas according to subject-by-subject organization rather than point-by-point organization. Have students work in small groups to discuss how the impact of the article would be changed if the writer had chosen to use subject-by-subject organization—enumerating all of the points about Jefferson in one section, followed by all of the points about Hamilton.

Have students present the results of their small group discussions to the class and then open the topic up to class-wide discussion. Encourage students to support their opinions with textual evidence.

Analyze Ideas and Events: Sequence  COMMON CORE RI 3

Authors use organizational patterns to help convey information and ideas. For example, a writer might organize a text by using comparison/contrast, problem/solution, or cause-and-effect relationships. Sometimes writers use multiple organizational patterns to achieve their purpose. In this article, Chernow makes use of **chronological order**, a pattern of organization that presents events in the order in which they happened. Chernow uses this structure to follow the sequence of events important to the men's relationship and explore how their ideas about government evolved over time.

In his introduction, Chernow uses sequence references to orient the reader.

> On March 21, 1790, Thomas Jefferson belatedly arrived in New York City . . . after a five-year ministerial stint in Paris. . . . Alexander Hamilton, who had streaked to prominence in his absence. . . . who was a lowly artillery captain in New York when Jefferson composed the famous document. . . . At first, Hamilton and Jefferson socialized on easy terms, with little inkling that they were destined to become mortal foes.

Use these strategies when analyzing the sequence of events in an informative text.
- Look for words and phrases that identify times, such as *in a year, three weeks earlier, in 1789,* and *the next day.*
- Look for words that signal order, such as *first, afterward, then, during,* and *finally* to
- see how events or ideas are related.

Analyze Structure: Comparison and Contrast  COMMON CORE RI 5

The overarching structure of Chernow's article is a point-by-point comparison of Jefferson and Hamilton that shows how and why they became "the best of enemies." In such a structure, a writer discusses a particular point of comparison about both subjects and then moves on to the next point. Chernow follows this structure closely as this beginning of an outline of the article shows.

I. Point 1: View of biggest threat to liberty
A. Hamilton: insufficient federal power
B. Jefferson: concentrated federal power
II. Point 2: Attitude to new national government
A. Hamilton: ardent faith
B. Jefferson: tepid enthusiasm

Chernow uses this structure to make his exposition of complex ideas clear and weaves in narrative elements to make the text more engaging.

Use these strategies when analyzing a text using a compare-and-contrast structure.
- To find similarities, look for words and phrases such as *like, similarly, both, all, every, also,* and *in the same way.*
- To find differences, look for words and phrases such as *unlike, but, on the other hand, more, less, in contrast,* and *however.*

CLOSE READ

Analyze Ideas and Events: Sequence COMMON CORE RI 3

Help students understand the importance of Chernow's use of chronological order to set the stage for the great battles that would take place between Jefferson and Hamilton. Have students reread the first paragraph of the article to identify and make a list of words and phrases that inform the reader of chronological order by identifying time and sequence. *(On March 21, 1790; belatedly; five-year stint)*

ASK STUDENTS how Chernow's use of chronological order sets the stage for the series of battles to come in the rest of the article. *(By setting up their arrivals in New York after Jefferson's long absence and Hamilton's rise to fame during that time, the writer immediately sets the stage for a contentious relationship.)*

Analyze Structure: Comparison and Contrast COMMON CORE RI 5

Discuss with students the structure of a point-by-point comparison and display the beginning of the outline shown on the student page. Work with students to add to the outline by identifying the next two points of comparison in the text. *(Point 3: Communication style; Point 4: Economics)*

Have students work in groups to complete the outline. Then, have different groups compare and contrast their outlines.

Strategies for Annotation 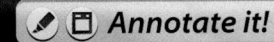 Annotate it!

Analyze Structure: Comparison and Contrast  COMMON CORE RI 5

Share these strategies for guided and independent analysis: Highlight Hamilton's beliefs about government in green. Highlight Jefferson's beliefs about government in yellow. Create a comparison chart or Venn diagram to record what you find.

> For Hamilton, the first Treasury Secretary, the supreme threat to liberty arose from insufficient government power. . . As the first Secretary of State, Jefferson believed that liberty was jeopardized by concentrated federal power, which . . .

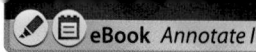

PRACTICE & APPLY

Analyzing the Text 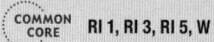 COMMON CORE RI 1, RI 3, RI 5, W 2

Possible Answers:

1. *Hamilton attended the Constitutional Convention and played an active role in getting the Constitution ratified, while Jefferson monitored the convention from France. Hamilton was far more enthusiastic about his power as a member of Washington's cabinet than was Jefferson.*

2. *The feud between Hamilton and Jefferson began over the approach to handling the U.S. debt from the Revolutionary War. The conflict escalated when Jefferson launched an opposition paper that criticized Hamilton and Hamilton retaliated with his own newspaper articles.*

3. *The words* brilliant, brash and charming; served up his opinions promiscuously *and* had a true zest for debate *reveal the most about Hamilton.*

4. *Hamilton was a great speaker and a prolific writer. Everyone always knew where he stood and he never backed down from conflict. Jefferson was more reserved. While he was not a good speaker, he was a master politician and was able to manipulate his situation with Hamilton in the shadows.*

5. *Hamilton, who believed in a strong federal government, convinced Washington to create the Bank of the United States. Jefferson viewed the creation of that bank as an expansion of federal power and he strongly opposed it.*

6. *Both Jefferson and Hamilton considered each other to be "excessively ambitious." They each compared the other to Julius Caesar. Both men were also caught up in sex scandals exposed by the same journalist.*

7. *Hamilton was accused of having an affair with Maria Reynolds. He confessed in a long letter to defend payments made to her husband. He claimed he paid for Reynolds' company, not for speculation in security bonds. Jefferson was accused of having a relationship with Sally Hemings, an enslaved woman. Jefferson neither confirmed nor denied it.*

8. *Using a point-by-point comparison, Chernow creates a vivid picture of two men who not only hated each other, but had very different views for the future of the United States. This made the shift in Hamilton's attitude and Jefferson's behavior seem all the more ironic. Hamilton ended up supporting Jefferson for President and Jefferson, as President, wielded his federal powers freely.*

9. *Chernow was effective in using chronological order and comparison to portray the relationship between Jefferson and Hamilton. He brought the reader in by setting the stage with a chronological telling of the start of their feud and then bolstered his argument by contrasting the two on key issues.*

Analyzing the Text COMMON CORE RI 1, RI 3, RI 5, W 2

Cite Text Evidence Support your responses with evidence from the selection.

1. **Compare** How did Hamilton's and Jefferson's different experiences relating to the writing of the Constitution affect their roles as members of Washington's Cabinet?

2. **Analyze** What event sparked the beginning of the conflict between Hamilton and Jefferson? What was the sequence of events that caused the feud to worsen?

3. **Analyze** An author's choice of words, or **diction,** can communicate a great deal about a subject. Reread the passage where Chernow directly describes Hamilton (lines 41–51), paying careful attention to the adjectives and verbs Chernow uses. What words reveal the most about Hamilton's personality and character?

4. **Cite Evidence** How did Hamilton's and Jefferson's different personal styles affect the ways they carried out their feud?

5. **Infer** How does the disagreement over the creation of the Bank of the United States reflect the ideological differences that separated Hamilton and Jefferson?

6. **Interpret** Despite their conflicts, Chernow also emphasizes that the two shared some common traits. In what ways where Jefferson and Hamilton similar, according to Chernow?

7. **Compare** Chernow describes how both politicians "stumbled into the two great sex scandles of the early Republic." What were the scandals? How did each individual respond to the accusations? How were their responses consistent with what you know about them from this text?

8. **Analyze** How does Chernow's point-by-point comparison of these two enemies add to the strength of his concluding paragraph?

9. **Evaluate** How effectively did Chernow combine chronological order and compare-and-contrast structures to portray the idea that Hamilton and Jefferson were "destined to become mortal foes"?

PERFORMANCE TASK

Writing Task: Essay Chernow states that the clash between Hamilton and Jefferson "produced two divergent visions of the country's future that divide Americans to the present day."

- Write an essay that provides a point-by-point comparison of these two visions, using Chernow's article as a model for the structure and a source of content.

- Conclude your essay with a paragraph that explores how these visions continue to divide Americans, based on prior knowledge or research.

In your essay, include evidence from the text and use the conventions of standard English.

Assign this performance task.

PERFORMANCE TASK 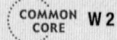 COMMON CORE W 2

Writing Task: Essay Hamilton believed in a liberal reading of the Constitution, giving the federal government significant power, while Jefferson believed in a narrow reading of the Constitution, reserving most power for the states. Have students consider how the philosophies of today's two-party system relate to the philosophies of the two founders discussed in Chernow's article. After the class discussion, have students complete the performance task.

Critical Vocabulary

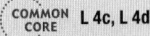 L 4c, L 4d

tepid	copious	cardinal
rudiments	façade	anomalous

Practice and Apply Go on a Critical Vocabulary scavenger hunt to find examples of the words in advertisements, news articles, online, or in your environment. Write your own definition of each word based on at least two examples. Follow these tips.

- If you search online, don't go to a dictionary or other site that defines the word but look for examples by searching for News or Images.
- If you do an online search for *cardinal*, eliminate examples of birds, sports teams, or church officials. You might also find examples of companies that use the word *cardinal* in their name. Eliminate those unless they reflect the meaning of the word.

Vocabulary Strategy:
Consulting General and Specialized Reference Works

Consulting general and specialized reference works such as dictionaries, glossaries, and thesauruses, both print and digital, can provide additional information about unfamiliar words as you read. Here is an example of the entry for the Critical Vocabulary word *copious* from the *American Heritage Dictionary of the English Language*.

> **co·pi·ous** (kō′pē-əs) *adj.* **1.** Yielding or containing plenty; affording ample supply: *a copious harvest*. See Synonyms at **plentiful**. **2.** Large in quantity; abundant: *copious rainfall*. **3.** Abounding in matter, thoughts, or words; wordy: *"I found our speech copious without order, and energetic without rules"* (Samuel Johnson). [Middle English, from Latin *cōpiōsus*, from *cōpia*, abundance; see **op-** in Indo-European roots.]—**co′pi·ous·ly** *adv.* —**co′pi·ous·ness** *n.*

Here are the important elements of this entry:
- The word is broken into syllables with its pronunciation shown in parentheses using standard symbols to represent different sounds.
- Part of speech is shown next; in this case the word is an adjective.
- Three distinct but related definitions are listed, with an example of how each sense of the word might be used. Note that the first definition also tells readers where to look in the dictionary for synonyms.
- Etymology or word derivation is shown in brackets. This English word is very similar to its Latin origin.
- Related words are shown, indicating how to turn this adjective into an adverb and a noun.

Practice and Apply Consult a dictionary or thesaurus to find additional information about each of these Critical Vocabulary words: *tepid, cardinal, rudiments, façade, anomalous*. Then meet with a partner to discuss how this additional knowledge might help deepen your understanding of the article by Ron Chernow.

PRACTICE & APPLY

Critical Vocabulary

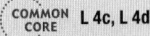 L 4c, L 4d

Answers: Responses and examples should reflect definitions similar to those found in this article.

Vocabulary Strategy:
Consulting General and Specialized Reference Works

Possible answers:

Critical Vocabulary	Additional Information
tepid	also refers to temperature; lack of enthusiasm
cardinal	synonyms: *fundamental, primary, paramount*
rudiments	related to the word rudimentary, which means "existing at a basic level"
façade	synonyms: *public image, outward show*
anomalous	also means "deviating from what people expect"

Strategies for Annotation 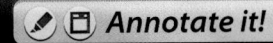 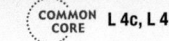 *Annotate it!*

Consulting General and Specialized Reference Works

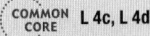 L 4c, L 4d

Have students find the vocabulary words in the text. Encourage them to use their eBook annotation tools to do the following:

- Highlight each vocabulary word in the text.
- Highlight the word and its definition on the side of the page.
- Reread the definition and then the sentence containing the vocabulary word for comprehension.

PRACTICE & APPLY

Language and Style: Hyphenation

 COMMON CORE **L 2a**

Have students work in pairs to skim through the article and identify places where the writer uses hyphenation. Ask students to refer to the chart on this page to identify the purpose of the hyphenation. Have students try to rewrite one sentence without using hyphenation. Discuss the impact on the sentence.

Practice and Apply Students should review their essays for correct use of hyphenation. If they do not have any, they should add one instance of hyphenation. As a class, have students share the changes they have made and explain where their hyphenation falls in the Purpose column of the Uses of hyphens chart.

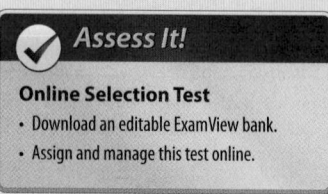

Language and Style: Hyphenation

 COMMON CORE **L 2b**

Following the conventions of punctuation is important for clear communication. "Thomas Jefferson: The Best of Enemies" contains several examples of hyphenated words. Using a hyphen joins words into compounds so that their meaning is clear. Hyphenated words can also be a simpler way of saying something.

Consider this phrase from the article.

after a five-year ministerial stint in Paris

The author could instead have written the phrase this way:

after a ministerial stint of five years in Paris

The hyphenated adjective creates a more streamlined sentence. Here are some examples of hyphenation conventions used in the article.

Uses of hyphens	
Purpose	**Example**
join parts of a compound adjective before a noun	two-party system, one-man army, Hamilton-Jefferson feud
join parts of a compound with *all-, ex-, self-,* or *-elect*	the self-invented Hamilton; the self-reliant reflexes
join parts of a compound number (to ninety-nine)	the 35-year-old wunderkind
join a prefix to a word beginning with a capital letter	anti-Hamilton resolutions
shows two or more compounds are joined to a single base	5,000- or 10,000-word memos
create a new word by adding a prefix or suffix	crypto-monarchist, runner-up

Consult a dictionary if you are unsure whether a compound word should be hyphenated, open, or closed. For example, *cryptographer* is closed and *follow up* as a verb or a noun is open, but the adjective, as in *follow-up phone call* uses a hyphen.

Practice and Apply Look back at the essay you wrote in response to this selection's Performance Task comparing Hamilton's and Jefferson's visions of the future. Review your writing to see if you have used hyphenation conventions correctly. See if you can add one or two hyphenated words to streamline your writing or make your meaning clearer.

Determine Central Ideas

COMMON CORE
RI 5

EXTEND

Remind students that the **central idea** of a text is the most important idea about the topic that a writer conveys. Sometimes writers state their central idea directly. More often, however, readers must infer it from textual evidence, such as the facts, descriptions, and examples the writer includes. These are called **supporting details.**

- Tell students that it can be helpful to use a diagram like the one shown below to analyze central ideas and supporting details.

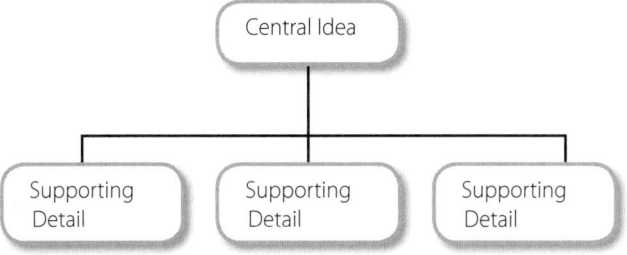

PRACTICE AND APPLY

Have students create a chart like the one above to analyze the central idea and supporting details in "Thomas Jefferson: The Best of Enemies."

- Tell students that they might want to fill in the supporting details first and then use them to determine the central idea. To what overarching, important central idea do all of the supporting details point?

LEVEL UP TUTORIALS Assign the following *Level Up* tutorial: **Main Idea and Supporting Details**

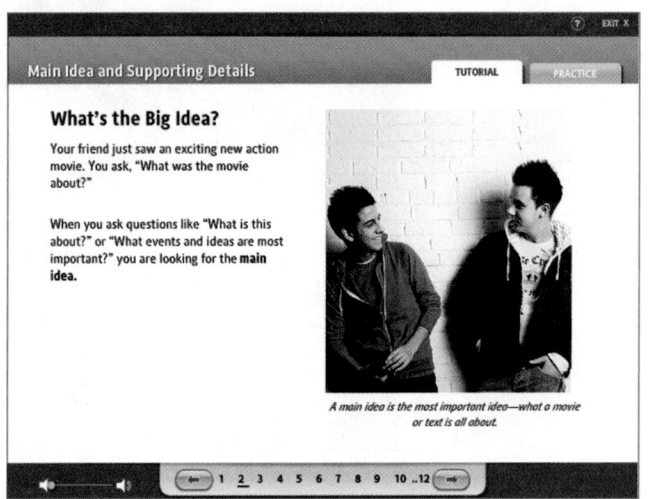

Analyze Ideas and Events: Sequence

COMMON CORE
RI 3

RETEACH

Provide these additional strategies for analyzing chronological order in a text.

- Look for headings and subheadings that may indicate a chronological pattern of organization.
- Create a timeline. As you read, fill in events on the timeline.
- If possible, use the eBook annotation feature to number events in a text.

LEVEL UP TUTORIALS Assign the following *Level Up* tutorial: **Chronological Order**

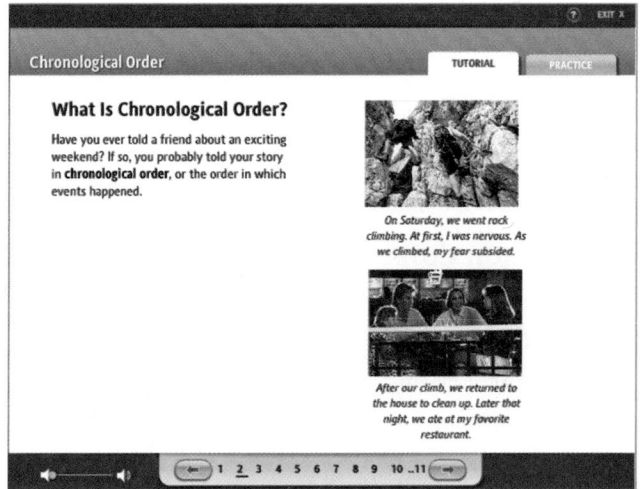

CLOSE READING APPLICATION

Have students work in pairs to find examples of chronological order in writing and to identify the words and phrases in the text that signal chronological order.

Abigail Adams' Last Act of Defiance

History Writing by Woody Holton

Why This Text

Articles that examine the lives of important historical people often attempt to clarify some aspect of the person's life that previous historians may have ignored. "Abigail Adams' Last Act of Defiance" is such a text. Some students may have difficulty understanding the author's central idea. With the help of the close-reading questions, students will determine the author's central idea and cite specific supporting details. This close reading will lead students to develop a deeper understanding of the topic and the evidence presented by the author.

Background Have students read the background information about Abigail Smith Adams, paying special attention to her intelligence and passion for the cause of women's rights. Tell students that as a diplomat in France and later in England, John Adams was often away from their home. He and Abigail communicated extensively by letter. These letters provide valuable information not only about Abigail's influence on her husband and the couple's marriage, but also about a crucial period in American history.

AS YOU READ Ask students to pay attention to the information given in the text about women's rights during the period and Abigail Adams's reaction to those limited rights.

Common Core Support

- cite multiple pieces of evidence from the text
- determine central ideas
- make inferences and draw conclusions

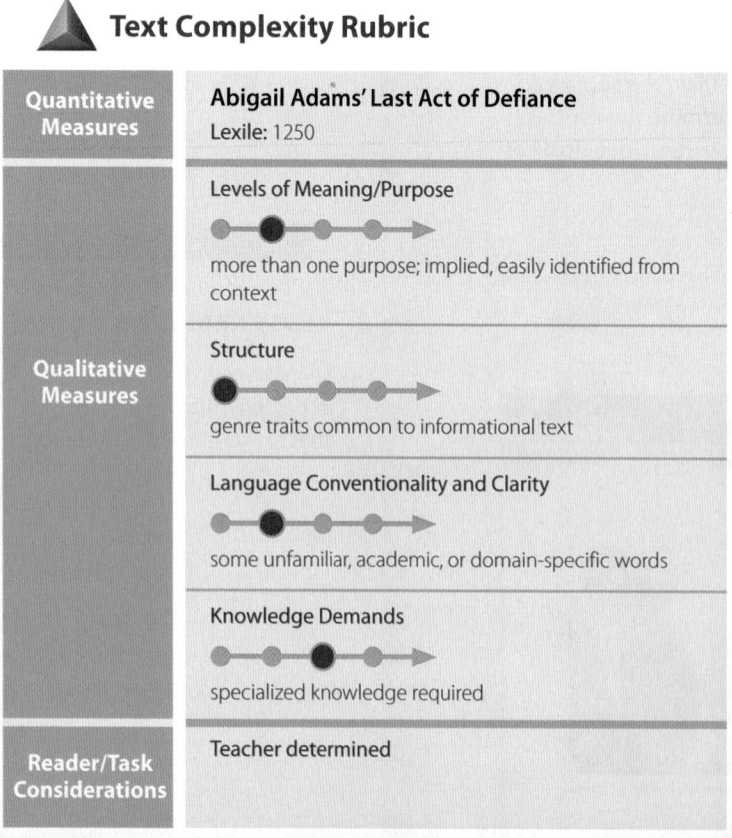

Text Complexity Rubric

Quantitative Measures

Abigail Adams' Last Act of Defiance
Lexile: 1250

Qualitative Measures

Levels of Meaning/Purpose

more than one purpose; implied, easily identified from context

Structure

genre traits common to informational text

Language Conventionality and Clarity

some unfamiliar, academic, or domain-specific words

Knowledge Demands

specialized knowledge required

Reader/Task Considerations

Teacher determined

Strategies for CLOSE READING

Determine Central Ideas

Students should read this article carefully all the way through. Close-reading questions at the bottom of the page will help them determine the central ideas of the text. As they read, students should jot down comments or questions about the text in the margins.

WHEN STUDENTS STRUGGLE . . .

To help students determine central ideas in "Abigail Adams' Last Act of Defiance," have them work in small groups to fill out a chart like the one shown below.

CITE TEXT EVIDENCE For practice in determining central ideas, ask students to cite text evidence that supports the main facts given by the author.

Central Idea
Abigail Adams "did not simply complain about the government's denial of married women's property rights. She defied it." (lines 18–19)

Text Evidence
"As the Revolutionary War drew to a close, Adams started setting aside a portion of her husband's property and declaring it her own." (lines 20–21)
"She added more and more to this stash over the ensuing decades." (lines 21–22)
She wrote her own will and left almost all of "her" money and property to women. (lines 26–32)

Abigail Adams' Last
Act of Defiance

History Writing by Woody Holton

CLOSE READ
Notes

1. **READ ▶** As you read lines 1–19, begin to cite and collect text evidence.
   - Underline references to dates and events that orient the reader and provide historical context.
   - Circle the main idea in lines 1–9 and in lines 10–19.
   - In the margin, summarize the situation that concerns Adams.

Weeks before the Continental Congress issued the Declaration of Independence in 1776, Abigail Adams penned a now famous letter to her husband, John, admonishing him to "Remember the Ladies" when drawing up a new code of laws. "If perticuliar care and attention is not paid to the Laidies," she wrote, "we are determined to **foment** a Rebelion, and will not hold ourselves bound by any Laws in which we have no voice, or Representation." Within a few years of writing these words, Adams did something that has never been revealed until now. She carried out a mini-revolution in the arena that mattered to her the most: her own household.

10 Of all the means by which the Founding Fathers and other men lorded it over women, none annoyed Adams more than the legal degradation that

A women had to submit to the moment they got married. Single women, including widows, were allowed to own and control property. Yet as Adams

foment:
to stir up

29

---

1. **READ AND CITE TEXT EVIDENCE** The author quotes Abigail Adams in a letter to her husband asking him to "Remember the Ladies" when he served as a delegate to the Continental Congress.

A **ASK STUDENTS** which law most annoyed Adams. *Adams was annoyed by the law that said that married women did not have the right to own and control property.*

Critical Vocabulary: foment (line 5) Have students share their definitions of *foment*. Ask why an angry and frustrated Abigail Adams might want women to foment a rebellion. *A rebellion would be a way for women to fight unjust laws.*

CLOSE READ
Notes

CLOSE READ
Notes

> ". . . scratching out the four-page document was the ultimate act of rebellion."

Married women were not allowed to have control over their own possessions.

complained to her husband in a June 1782 letter, wives' property was "subject to the controul and disposal of our partners, to whom the Laws have given a soverign Authority." Historians have studied Abigail Adams' denunciations of married women's inability to control property for decades. But what they have overlooked is that she did not simply complain about the government's denial of married women's property rights. She defied it.

B 20 As the Revolutionary War drew to a close, Adams started setting aside a portion of her husband's property and declaring it her own. She added more and more to this stash over the ensuing decades, and she invested it wisely. By the end of 1815 her "pocket money," as she sometimes called it, had grown to more than $5,000—which would be about $100,000 today.

C Finally in 1816, racked with pain and convinced she was dying, Adams delivered the parting shot in her household revolution. On January 18, she sat down to write a will. Since she had no legal right as a married woman to own property in her name and her husband was still very much alive, scratching out the four-page document was the ultimate act of rebellion. Moreover, a close

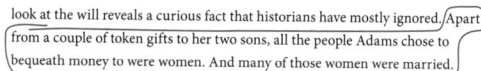

This portrait of Adams was painted by Benjamin Blythe in 1766, when she was 22 years old.

D 30 look at the will reveals a curious fact that historians have mostly ignored. Apart from a couple of token gifts to her two sons, all the people Adams chose to bequeath money to were women. And many of those women were married.

Adams' personal property rights revolution had its roots in her struggle to shield her family from the financial destruction that accompanied the Revolutionary War. Of all the patriot soldiers and statesmen who were forced to abandon their families for long periods, few stayed away as long as John Adams, who saw very little of his Braintree, Mass., farm from 1774 to 1784. John put Abigail in charge of all of the Adams family finances, and she ended up handling her husband's money much better than he ever had, primarily 40 because she was more open to risk. During the course of the war she became an

2. **◀ REREAD** Reread lines 10–19. In what way did the laws for single women and married women differ? Support your answer with explicit textual evidence.

Single women (and widowed women) were allowed to own and control property, but married women had to give control of their property to their husbands.

3. **READ ▶** As you read lines 20–55, continue to cite text evidence.

• Circle actions of Adams that were caused by the government's denial of property rights for married women.

• Underline references to dates that show the order in which events occurred.

4. **◀ REREAD** Reread lines 25–32. Why does Holton call writing a will "the ultimate act of rebellion"? Support your answer with explicit textual evidence.

As a married woman, Abigail Adams " had no legal right" to own property. All property legally belonged to her husband, so only her husband could legally write a will to bequeath his property.

30

31

---

2. **REREAD AND CITE TEXT EVIDENCE**

B **ASK STUDENTS** what effect the property laws had on Abigail Adams. *She was not allowed control over her own possessions.*

3. **READ AND CITE TEXT EVIDENCE** Before she died, Adams "delivered the parting shot in her household revolution."

C **ASK STUDENTS** to use context clues to interpret the meaning of "parting shot." *Writing her will was something Abigail Adams did just before she died. "Parting shot" probably means something like "last words" or "something you do or say just before you're about to leave."*

FOR ELL STUDENTS Review the prefix *in-*. Point out the word *inability* (line 17). Ask a volunteer to identify the base word (*ability*) and its meaning. Then ask another volunteer to guess the meaning of *inability*. Ask students to provide other words with the prefix *in-*.

4. **REREAD AND CITE TEXT EVIDENCE** The text explains that most historians have ignored the fact that Adams left the bulk of her money to women, many of whom were married.

D **ASK STUDENTS** What is the significance of the fact that Adams left the bulk of her money to women? *Students should understand that since married women technically were not able to own property, it was unusual for women to receive any money from a will.*

FOR ELL STUDENTS The use of the expression *very little* (line 37) can be confusing to ELL students, who might be more familiar with using *little* referring to quantities. Explain that in this context, it doesn't mean that John saw a small part of his farm, but that he rarely was at the farm.

depreciate:
lower in price
or value

envoy:
a diplomatic
representative
sent by one
government to
another

import merchant and then a speculator in **depreciated** government securities and Vermont land titles. And as she repeatedly reinvested her profits, she increasingly thought of the money she earned as her own.

Abigail lived by the credo "nothing venture nothing have"—a notion that John found somewhat alarming. While he was an **envoy** in France, the couple confronted a seemingly mundane problem. How could he remit a portion of his salary home? Her solution was audacious. If he shipped her trunkloads of merchandise from Europe, she could extract the few items her family needed and arrange to sell the rest to New England shopkeepers whose shelves were nearly empty because of the war. She convinced John the scheme would allow her to avoid having to "pay extravagant prices" for basic necessities, downplaying that she could also turn a healthy profit by selling the imported goods at an enormous markup. When some of these shipments were captured by the British, John wanted to abandon the whole thing, but she wrote back, "If one in 3 arrives I should be a gainer."

Nearly all of Abigail Adams' biographers mention her will, but they usually move on, overlooking not only the remarkable fact of its existence but its contents. In it, she made token gifts to her two surviving sons, but she gave nothing to her grandsons, nephews or male servants. Everything went to her granddaughters, nieces, female servants and daughters-in-law. In addition to gowns and small sums of cash to pay for mourning rings, Abigail handed out more than $4,000 worth of bank stock, a $1,200 IOU and a total of seven shares of stock in the companies managing the Weymouth and Haverhill toll bridges.

Adams not
only ignored
the law by
writing her
will, but left
property to
married
women.

5. **READ ▶** As you read lines 56–96, continue to cite text evidence.

- In the margin of lines 56–63 explain Adams's solution to the problem regarding women's property rights.
- Circle evidence that shows that Adams's family supported her "mini-revolution."
- In the lines below, analyze the structure of lines 70–85. How does the author organize the facts he presents in these lines?

The author presents the facts in chronological order. He explains
who carried out the specific duties as written in the will and explains
how her relatives honored Adams's requests.

> Louisa acknowledged what the law of the land denied and Abigail had always affirmed: that the money was hers to give.

There is no indication that Adams had any **animus** against her male relatives. So why did she exclude all but two of them from her will? Having spent three decades asserting control over land and ownership of personal property despite being married, Adams now bequeathed the bulk of her estate to her granddaughters, nieces, daughters-in-law and female servants in order to enable them, as far as lay in her power, to make the same claim.

To her own surprise, Abigail held on for another year and a half after writing her will. She died about 1 p.m. on October 28, 1818, a few weeks shy of her 74th birthday. Abigail's will was not a legal document that any court was bound to respect, and John would have been within his rights in throwing it in the fire. But he honored it to the letter.

Abigail had assigned her son Thomas the responsibility of supervising the distribution of her property. Thomas' brother, John Quincy Adams, and their father assisted him in carrying out Abigail's wishes. On November 9, less than two weeks after her death, John transferred the $1,200 promissory note to Louisa Smith [Abigail's niece and steadfast companion], just as Abigail had directed. The former president's compliance with the provisions of his wife's will transformed it into a legally valid document. In the eyes of the law, she had acted as his agent and distributed property that belonged to him. In 1819 John Quincy replaced the promissory note he had given his mother years earlier with a new one made out to Louisa herself. No one could ever challenge his cousin's legal right to recover these funds, for she had never married.

animus:
hostility or
ill feeling

---

5. READ AND CITE TEXT EVIDENCE

E **ASK STUDENTS** which members of Adams's family who could have contested her will actually honored her directions. *John Adams, Thomas Adams, and John Quincy Adams—all men—made sure her will was followed (lines 74–84).*

Critical Vocabulary: depreciate (line 41) Have students share their definitions of *depreciate*. Ask students: *If you discovered that something you owned that you had thought was very valuable had depreciated, how would you feel?* *very disappointed*

Critical Vocabulary: envoy (line 45) The text says that John Adams was an envoy in France. Ask students: *What might a prominent American citizen, like John Adams, be doing in France?* Then, have students share their definitions of *envoy*.

Critical Vocabulary: animus (line 64) Have students share their definitions of *animus*. Ask students to think of a situation in which you might feel animus against another person. *Answers will vary. Students should cite a situation in which they feel angry at, or hostile toward, another person.*

FOR ELL STUDENTS Clarify the meaning of *shy of* (line 71). Explain that in the text it doesn't refer to someone's character; in this context it means "before."

CLOSE READ
Notes

bequest:
something
given or left
by a will

In January 1819, when Louisa Catherine Adams, John Quincy's wife, learned that Abigail had left her an inheritance of $150, she set aside half of the **bequest** to be divided equally among her three sons, who seemed "to have a better title to it than I could boast." By passing this money on to Abigail's

90 grandsons, Louisa may have indicated disapproval of her mother-in-law's decision to exclude all male descendants other than her own sons from her will. Yet it seems unlikely that Abigail would have considered the younger woman's gift a defeat. After all, by deciding on her own authority to present the money to her children instead of her husband, Louisa acknowledged what the law of the land denied and Abigail had always affirmed: that the money was hers to give.

(F)

6. **◀ REREAD** Reread lines 86–96. Explain the author's assertion that Adams would not consider it a defeat that Louisa Catherine Adams bequeathed part of her inheritance to her sons.

As long as Louisa was the one to decide what would be done with the money she was acting as the owner of the property. Abigail only wanted her female relatives to have the power to do with their money what they wished.

SHORT RESPONSE

Cite Text Evidence What problem did Adams confront and what was her solution? Review your reading notes, and be sure to **cite text evidence** in your response.

Adams was upset by the injustice of laws that made married women's property "subject to the controul and disposal" of their husbands. She addressed this problem in her own household by "setting aside a portion of her husband's property and declaring it her own." Over time, what she called her "pocket money" grew to more than $5,000. She finally wrote a will, leaving what was legally her husband's money to her female relatives and companions. Although it was not a legal document, John honored his wife's will.

34

For more context about Abigail Adams personally, and her marriage to John Adams, have students view the video "The Romance of John and Abigail Adams" in their eBooks.

ASK STUDENTS to integrate what they have learned about Abigail Adams and the times in which she lived with what they learn about her and her marriage in this video. What attracted the couple to each other? *John Adams loved her combination of beauty and brains, and Abigail Adams loved the fact that he treated her as an intellectual equal and that they could talk together for hours.* How would you describe their marriage? *Answers will vary, but students should mention that they were deeply in love with each other, that they respected each other, and that they were equal partners in the marriage.* How do you think the marriage of Abigail and John Adams was different from other marriages of the period? *Answers will vary, but students should mention that most couples of the period probably did not treat each other as equals and that most husbands probably did not respect their wives' intelligence as much as John respected Abigail's.*

6. **REREAD AND CITE TEXT EVIDENCE**

(F) ASK STUDENTS why some people might consider Louisa's gift to her sons a defeat. *They might think that Louisa was going against Adams's wishes by giving the money to men, thereby endorsing the property laws.*

Critical Vocabulary: bequest (line 88) Have students share their definitions of *bequest*. Ask students: *What might you bequest in a will to someone you cared about? Answers will vary. Students should name something that means a great deal to them.*

SHORT RESPONSE

Cite Text Evidence Students should:

- explain the problem that Adams confronts.
- describe her solution.
- cite text evidence.

DIG DEEPER

With the class, return to Question 2, Reread. Have students share and discuss their responses.

ASK STUDENTS what additional information they have learned about Abigail Adams's defiance of the law, in particular her decision to write a will and the significance of that decision, the people she bequeathed her property to and why, her adeptness at handling her husband's financial affairs, and her husband's decision to honor the provisions of her will. Remind students to cite text evidence that supports what they have learned.

- Have students explain the significance of Adams's decision to write a will. *Because married women were not allowed to own personal property, Adams's decision to write a will stating to whom "her" property was to go defied the law of the day.*

- Have students explain Adams's choices regarding to whom she would leave her considerable property. *Adams left the bulk of her estate to her granddaughters, nieces, daughters-in-law, and female servants. She gave very little to her male relatives. She did this in the hope that her female relatives might someday be able to make the same claim: that they owned property.*

- Ask students to give examples of Adams's skill at handling her husband's financial affairs. *During the ten-year period that her husband was away, Adams invested her husband's money wisely, while putting away a portion of the money she had made for herself. By the end of 1815, the money she had made for herself was more than $5,000—or about $100,000 today. Adams handled her husband's money much better than he would have, primarily because she was willing to take risks.*

- Have students infer why John Adams chose to honor all of the provisions of his wife's will, even though he was not legally bound to do so. *Answers will vary. Students may infer that Adams loved and respected his wife and so honored her wishes, or that he agreed with her that married women ought to be able to own their own property.*

ASK STUDENTS to return to their Short Response answer and revise it based on their discussion.

CLOSE READING NOTES

COMPARE TEXTS

To the Right Honourable William, Earl of Dartmouth

EXEMPLAR

On Being Brought from Africa to America

On the Emigration to America and Peopling the Western Country

Poems by Phillis Wheatley

Poem by Philip Freneau

*my*SmartPlanner — Create lesson plans and access resources online.

Why These Texts?

Even in our times, topics and themes relating to freedom, redemption, society, and spirituality underlie political discussions and emerge in our own personal life events. Wheatley and Freneau express their views of these themes during colonial times. This lesson examines the treatment of similar themes and topics by poets with very different life experiences.

Key Learning Objective: The student will be able to analyze and compare topics and themes in poems.

COMMON CORE Common Core Standards

RL 1 Cite textual evidence.

RL 2 Determine themes of a text.

RL 4 Determine figurative and connotative meanings; analyze the impact of specific word choices.

RL 5 Analyze how an author's choices concerning how to structure specific parts of a text contribute to its overall meaning as well as its aesthetic impact.

RL 9 Demonstrate knowledge of foundational works of American literature.

W 9 Draw evidence from literary or informational texts.

SL 1 Initiate and participate in a range of collaborative discussions.

SL 1d Respond to diverse perspectives/synthesize comments.

Text Complexity Rubric

	Poems by Phillis Wheatley Lexile: NA	On the Emigration to America and Peopling the Western Country Lexile: NA
Quantitative Measures		
Qualitative Measures	**Levels of Meaning/Purpose** single level of complex meaning	**Levels of Meaning/Purpose** single level of complex meaning
	Structure regular stanzas with predictable rhyme scheme	**Structure** regular stanzas with predictable rhyme scheme
	Language Conventionality and Clarity archaic, unfamiliar language	**Language Conventionality and Clarity** figurative, less accessible language
	Knowledge Demands complex historical and religious references	**Knowledge Demands** complex or sophisticated theme; multiple themes
Reader/Task Considerations	Teacher determined Vary by individual reader and type of text	Teacher determined Vary by individual reader and type of text

TEACH

CLOSE READ

 For more context and historical background, students can view the video "Mankind: African Slave Trade" in their eBooks.

Phillis Wheatley In addition to writing poetry, Wheatley also translated works from Latin into English, surprising scholars in Boston by translating a tale from Ovid. Her literary accomplishments were held up as proof that the African people were intellectually capable, an idea that pro-slavery forces wanted to suppress.

"To the Right Honourable William, Earl of Dartmouth" was written after Dartmouth was appointed and reflects Wheatley's hope that Dartmouth, who had abolitionist friends, would promote freedom for enslaved people.

Philip Freneau A spokesperson for his time, Philip Freneau drew his share of admirers and detractors. James Madison, the fourth president of the United States and college roommate of Freneau, described him as "a man of genius," while George Washington called him a rascal. Today, his work gives readers a window into the beginnings of the United States.

AS YOU READ Direct students to use the As You Read instructions to focus their reading. Remind students to generate questions as they read.

Colonial American Poetry

Phillis Wheatley *was born in West Africa, probably in 1753, and became the first African American to publish a book of poetry. In 1761 she was enslaved, brought to Boston, and purchased by a local merchant, John Wheatley. He named the little girl Phillis and gave her to his wife, Susannah. Phillis learned to read and write English very quickly, and the Wheatley family tutored her in Latin, English literature, and the classics. Wheatley was quickly recognized as a remarkable prodigy and respect for her talents soon grew. Phillis's first published poem appeared in 1767, and by 1770 her work was known throughout the colonies. In 1773 she traveled to London for the publication of her* Poems on Various Subjects, Religious and Moral *but soon returned to Boston.*

Phillis was given her freedom after Susannah Wheatley's death in 1774. Her life, however, became more difficult as revolution spread through the colonies and as her patrons, wealthy Loyalists, fled the city. In 1778 she married John Peters, but the couple fell into extreme poverty. Their children all died in infancy, and Phillis died in 1784.

Philip Freneau *was called the "poet of the American Revolution." He was born in New York City in 1752. Freneau began writing poetry while studying at Princeton. After graduating in 1771, he briefly worked as a teacher before sailing to the Caribbean, where he developed a deep hatred of slavery.*

In 1778 Freneau returned to New Jersey and enlisted in the revolutionary militia. He captained a privateer until he was captured and briefly imprisoned by the British. He started a newspaper in 1790 and supported Thomas Jefferson in his ideological dispute with the Federalists. Freneau left the paper soon after Jefferson became president. He retired to a New Jersey farm and continued to write and publish until his death in 1832.

AS YOU READ Pay attention to details that reveal the tone, or attitude, that the speaker in each poem has toward America.

SCAFFOLDING FOR ELL STUDENTS

Analyze Language Explain to students that they will encounter unfamiliar words or spellings in the following poems—both because of the times in which the poets were writing and because of the poetic styling. Have students scan "To the Right Honourable William, Earl of Dartmouth," jotting down any unfamiliar words.

ASK STUDENTS to work in pairs, looking up the definitions of the words they have jotted down. Next, with their partners, they should read aloud the lines from the poems, this time replacing the unfamiliar words with the definitions. Partners can then discuss the meanings of the lines and ask for additional help, if necessary.

TEACH

CLOSE READ

Analyze Language
COMMON CORE RL 1, RL 4

(LINES 1–4)

Refer students to the definitions in the footnotes before they read lines 1–4. Explain that **diction** is a writer's choice of words.

 **ASK STUDENTS** what event Wheatley is writing about in her opening lines. What words does she use to describe this event? What does Wheatley's diction reveal about her **tone,** or attitude, about the event? *(Wheatley writes about the earl's coming to power, his "blissful sway." In addition to "blissful," Wheatley uses words such as "happy" and "smiling." Her tone is celebratory: She clearly sees his appointment as positive.)*

Colonial American Poetry
COMMON CORE RL 1, RL 2, RL 9

(LINES 15–19)

Explain that the **topic** of a work is what it is about. Tell students to read this stanza closely for details that point to the topic.

B **CITE TEXT EVIDENCE** Ask students to identify the topic of the stanza. *(an end to life under tyrannical rule)* Then, have them cite words and phrases from lines 15–19 that point to the topic and show what the stanza is mostly about. *("No more, America," of wrongs," "grievance unredress'd," "iron chain," and "Tyranny with lawless hand.")*

To the Right Honourable William, Earl of Dartmouth

His Majesty's Principal Secretary of State for North America, etc.

by Phillis Wheatley

Hail, happy day, when, smiling like the morn,
Fair *Freedom* rose *New-England* to adorn:
The northern clime[1] beneath her genial ray,
Dartmouth, congratulates thy blissful sway:[2]
5   Elate with hope her race no longer mourns,
Each soul expands, each grateful bosom burns,
While in thine hand with pleasure we behold
The silken reins, and Freedom's charms unfold.
Long lost to realms beneath the northern skies
10 She shines supreme, while hated *faction* dies:
Soon as appeared the *Goddess* long desir'd,
Sick at the view, she languish'd and expir'd;
Thus from the splendors of the morning light
The owl in sadness seeks the caves of night.

15 No more, *America*, in mournful strain[3]
Of wrongs, and grievance unredress'd complain,
No longer shall thou dread the iron chain,
Which wanton *Tyranny* with lawless hand
Had made, and with it meant t' enslave the land.

20 Should you, my lord, while you peruse my song,
Wonder from whence my love of *Freedom* sprung,
Whence flow these wishes for the common good,
By feeling hearts alone best understood,
I, young in life, by seeming cruel fate
25 Was snatch'd from *Afric's* fancy'd happy seat:[4]
What pangs excruciating must molest,
What sorrows labour in my parent's breast?
Steel'd was that soul and by no misery mov'd
That from a father seiz'd his babe belov'd:
30 Such, such my case. And can I then but pray
Others may never feel tyrannic sway?

---

[1] **clime:** climate region.
[2] **sway:** control or rule.
[3] **strain:** song.
[4] **seat:** location or site.

APPLYING ACADEMIC VOCABULARY

contrary	ideological

As you discuss colonial American poetry, incorporate the following Collection 2 academic vocabulary words: *contrary* and *ideological*. Ask students what **ideological** viewpoints each poet exhibits. What doctrines do Wheatley and Freneau hold dear? What aspects of colonial society does each poet say run **contrary** to these beliefs?

For favours past, great Sir, our thanks are due,
And thee we ask thy favours to renew,
Since in thy pow'r, as in thy will before,
35 To sooth[5] the griefs, which thou did'st once deplore.
May heav'nly grace the sacred sanction give
To all thy works, and thou for ever live
 Not only on the wings of fleeting *Fame*,
Though praise immortal crowns the patriot's name,
40 But to conduct to heav'ns refulgent fane,[6]
May fiery coursers[7] sweep th' ethereal plain,
And bear thee upwards to that blest abode,
Where, like the prophet,[8] thou shalt find thy God.

---

[5] **sooth:** alternate spelling of soothe; relieve or ease pain.
[6] **heav'ns refulgent fane:** a shining temple in the sky.
[7] **coursers:** fast horses.
[8] **prophet:** Elijah; according to the Old Testament, he ascended to heaven in a chariot after overturning an immoral political system.

Colonial American Poetry **153**

Colonial American Poetry   COMMON CORE RL 2
(LINES 36–39)

Remind students that the **theme** of a work is its message about human nature or life.

C ASK STUDENTS what message about life Wheatley conveys in lines 36–39. *(Those who govern justly, who right the wrongs they see in society, will not only receive fame from their people but will also have their works blessed by God.)*

Analyze Language   COMMON CORE RL 1, RL 4
(LINES 40–43)

Explain that imagery is language that appeals to a reader's senses, often creating a vivid picture in the reader's mind. Ask students what images, or vivid pictures, Wheatley creates in lines 40–43. *(These lines include images of a shining temple in the sky, fiery horses, and an "ethereal plain," or heaven.)*

D ASK STUDENTS how this imagery affects the poem's meaning. *(The images convey a sense of pomp and grandeur, suggesting the importance of the Earl and of Wheatley's occasion for writing—his appointment as secretary. They also convey the sense that political, earthly matters have eternal consequences.)*

WHEN STUDENTS STRUGGLE...

Explain that **inversion** is the rearranging or reversal of the usual word order to emphasize certain words and create the end rhymes. Have student pairs reorder the lines according to their parts of speech. Create a chart like the one shown below.

Line	Subject	Verb	Complements/ Phrases	Restated Sentence
32	our thanks	are due	for favours past, Great Sir	Our thanks are due for favours past, Great Sir,
33	we	ask	thee	And we ask thee to renew thy favours.

Image Credits: ©Marilyn Volan/Shutterstock

Determine Theme (LINES 1–4) COMMON CORE RL 2

Remind students that a poem's **theme** is its message about life.

 ASK STUDENTS to infer what these lines suggest about the poem's theme. *(These lines imply that the speaker views her kidnapping as having a positive spiritual outcome, which is contrary to what the reader would expect. This suggests the theme that things are not always what they seem—things that appear negative, like kidnapping and enslavement, may be positive spiritually.)*

Colonial American Poetry (LINES 5–8) COMMON CORE RL 2, RL 9

Have students read lines 5–8, along with the accompanying footnotes.

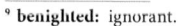 **CITE TEXT EVIDENCE** Ask students to cite text evidence from these lines that supports the theme they identified in E above: Things are not always what they seem—things that appear negative may be positive spiritually. *(Wheatley writes that some look at black people with "scornful eye" and as "diabolic." She then points out that despite how they are viewed, black people can be blessed spiritually.)*

On Being Brought from Africa to America

by Phillis Wheatley

'Twas mercy brought me from my *Pagan* land,
Taught my benighted[9] soul to understand
That there's a God, that there's a *Saviour* too:
Once I redemption neither sought nor knew.
5 Some view our sable[10] race with scornful eye,
"Their colour is a diabolic die."[11]
Remember, *Christians*, *Negroes*, black as *Cain*,
May be refin'd, and join th' angelic train.

---

[9] **benighted:** ignorant.
[10] **sable:** dark brown or black.
[11] **diabolic die:** an evil or devilish coloring agent (dye).

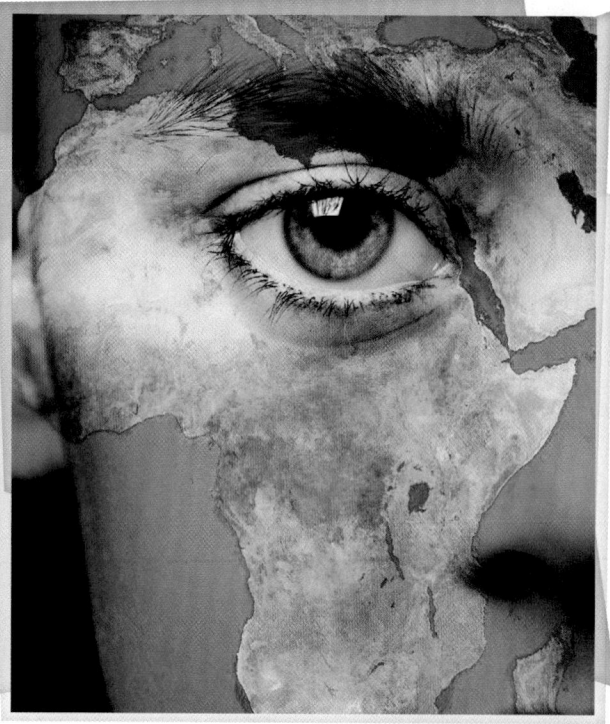

Image Credits: ©Perrush/Shutterstock

SCAFFOLDING FOR ELL STUDENTS

Multiple-Meaning Words Some words have more than one meaning. Project lines 7-8 of the poem on a whiteboard, and ask students to highlight in yellow the word that describes the train, and highlight in blue who make up the train.

ASK STUDENTS what the train imagery means. *(All people are redeemed.)*

Remember, *Christians*, *Negroes*, black as *Cain*,

May be refin'd, and join th' angelic train.

On the Emigration to America and Peopling the Western Country

by Philip Freneau

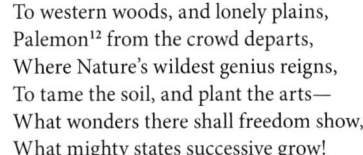

To western woods, and lonely plains,
Palemon[12] from the crowd departs,
Where Nature's wildest genius reigns,
To tame the soil, and plant the arts—
5 What wonders there shall freedom show,
What mighty states successive grow!

From Europe's proud, despotic shores
Hither the stranger takes his way,
And in our new-found world explores
10 A happier soil, a milder sway,
Where no proud despot holds him down,
No slaves insult him with a crown.

What charming scenes attract the eye,
On wild Ohio's savage stream!
15 There Nature reigns, whose works outvie
The boldest pattern art can frame;
There ages past have rolled away,
And forests bloomed but to decay.

From these fair plains, these rural seats,
20 So long concealed, so lately known,
The unsocial Indian far retreats,
To make some other clime his own,
When other streams, less pleasing, flow,
And darker forests round him grow.

25 Great Sire[13] of floods! whose varied wave
Through climes and countries takes its way,
To whom creating Nature gave
Ten thousand streams to swell thy sway!
No longer shall they useless prove,
30 Nor idly through the forests rove;

Nor longer shall your princely flood
From distant lakes be swelled in vain,
Nor longer through a darksome wood

---

[12] **Palemon:** reference to Polemon I, a first-century Roman noble who escaped to form a kingdom in the Baltic region.
[13] **Great Sire:** The Mississippi River.

CLOSE READ

Colonial American Poetry (LINES 1–6)

COMMON CORE RL 1, RL 2, RL 9

Tell students that as they read they should look for the text that describes what "Palemon" (the newcomer to America) has left behind, what he discovers, and what his new purpose there is.

G CITE TEXT EVIDENCE Have students note which words in the first stanza reveal what the newcomer has found and what his new purpose is. (He has found "Nature's wildest genius," and his purpose is to grow his new freedom, "tame the soil," and "plant the arts.")

Analyze Language (LINE 10)

COMMON CORE RL 5

Remind students that "sway" here means "control" or "rule."

H ASK STUDENTS to analyze Freneau's choice of the words "happier soil" and "milder sway." What aesthetic impact do these words have, and what image of the new land is Freneau creating? (The words "happier" and "milder" have peaceful and pleasant connotations. When Freneau puts the adjectives in the comparative form, he emphasizes that what the stranger has found in the new land is better than what he had in his old land.)

WHEN STUDENTS STRUGGLE...

Encourage students to reread, pause, and reflect on each stanza before moving to the next one. Look at the title again together: "On the Emigration to America and Peopling the Western Country." Decide what information one might expect to find in the poem. ("Emigration" = countries left behind; "Peopling" = goals and opportunities for populating a new country; "Western Country" = descriptions of the new land)

Divide students into pairs, and have each pair fill out a graphic organizer for an assigned stanza with the categories "Old Land," "New Land," "Goals," and "Opportunities." After they have completed their organizer, have each pair share their information with the class.

Colonial American Poetry (LINES 43–44)

COMMON CORE RL 4, RL 9

Have students reread lines 43 and 44. Remind them that Freneau was called the "poet of the American Revolution."

 **ASK STUDENTS** to analyze the impact of Freneau's word choices in lines 43 and 44. What does his choice of words reveal about his opinion of Europe's monarchies? *(He believes they should be forsaken, because they are arrogant and fake.)*

Analyze Language

COMMON CORE RL 5, RL 9

(LINES 55–60)

Tell students that Freneau ends his poem with his vision for the new land.

 **CITE TEXT EVIDENCE** Have students cite the words that reveal Freneau's vision. *("brighter scenes," "genius," "deeds may over death prevail," happier systems")* Then, have students summarize his vision. *(The new country will be esteemed by all, will be an intelligent member of the world community, will be effective for generations, and will have the best government that humankind has created.)*

COLLABORATIVE DISCUSSION Have students work in groups to discuss the overall tone, or attitude, toward America exhibited in each poem. How are the poems' tones similar? How do they differ? Encourage students to cite textual evidence to support their analysis of tone. Accept all reasonable responses.

ASK STUDENTS to share any questions they generated in the course of reading and discussing these poems.

Advance, unnoticed, to the main;[14]
35 Far other ends, the heavens decree—
And commerce plans new freights for thee.

While virtue warms the generous breast,
There heaven-born freedom shall reside,
Nor shall the voice of war molest,
40 Nor Europe's all-aspiring pride—
There Reason shall new laws devise,
And order from confusion rise.

 Forsaking kings and regal state,
With all their pomp and fancied bliss,
45 The traveler owns, convinced though late,
No realm so free, so blessed as this—
The east is half to slaves consigned,
Where kings and priests enchain the mind.

O come the time, and haste the day,
50 When man shall man no longer crush,
When Reason shall enforce her sway,
Nor these fair regions raise our blush,
Where still the African complains,
And mourns his yet unbroken chains.

55 Far brighter scenes a future age,
The muse predicts, these States will hail,
Whose genius may the world engage,
Whose deeds may over death prevail,
And happier systems bring to view,
60 Than all the eastern sages knew.

_____
[14]**main:** the sea.

COLLABORATIVE DISCUSSION What is the overall tone toward America—as both a place and an idea—expressed in the poems? What are each speaker's reasons for having that attitude? Discuss these questions with a small group, citing textual details to support your ideas.

SCAFFOLDING FOR ELL STUDENTS

Personification Explain to students that **personification** is a figure of speech in which something nonhuman is given human characteristics. Write lines 41–42 and 49–51 on a whiteboard, and ask students to highlight what ruling Reason will do in the new country. What human characteristics does she display? *(She creates new, orderly laws; she governs in a way that gives equality to all men.)*

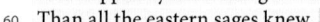

There Reason shall new laws devise, And order from confusion rise.

O come the time, and haste the day, When man shall man no longer crush, When Reason shall enforce her sway,

Colonial American Poetry  RL 9

The **topic** of a work is what it is about. The three poems in this selection all cover the broad topic of colonial America. Two of them suggest more specific topics in their titles: "On Being Brought from Africa to America" and "On the Emigration to America and Peopling the Western Country." To accurately identify the topic of any poem, you must analyze the details it contains and ask yourself what the poem is mostly about.

Title	Details	Topic
"On Being Brought from Africa to America"	"Twas mercy brought me from my *Pagan* land, / Taught my benighted soul to understand" "Remember, *Christians*, *Negroes*, black as *Cain*, / May be refin'd, and join th' angelic train."	How coming to America redeemed the speaker's soul through her Christian faith

The **theme** of a work is a message about life or about human nature that the author communicates through details in the text. This deeper meaning is sometimes stated directly, but more often readers must infer it. The final couplet of "On Being Brought from Africa to America" comes close to stating the theme of the poem. What do these two lines suggest about Wheatley's view of life in the Colonies?

The Wheatley and Freneau poems give you the opportunity to compare how several texts from 18th-century America treat similar themes and topics. As you reread the poems, think about what they have in common and how they differ. The chart shows a comparison between two poems that have themes involving the formation of a better society.

Themes about Forming a Better Society	
"To the Right Honourable William, Earl of Dartmouth"	**"On the Emigration to America and Peopling the Western Country"**
Textual detail: "For favours past, great Sir, our thanks are due, / And thee we ask they favours to renew, / Since in thy pow'r, as in thy will before, / To sooth the griefs, which thou didst once deplore." (lines 32–35) **Theme:** What type of leaders does Wheatley think the colonies need? What words might describe that leader?	**Textual detail:** "While virtue warms the generous breast, / There heaven-born freedom shall reside, . . . / There Reason shall new laws devise, / And order from confusion rise." (lines 37–42) **Theme:** What do these lines reveal about Freneau's views on liberty?

CLOSE READ

Colonial American Poetry 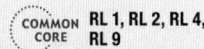 RL 1, RL 2, RL 4, RL 9

Have students reread each poem and continue the Title/Details/Topic chart for "To the Right Honourable William, Earl of Dartmouth" and "On the Emigration to America and Peopling the Western Country." After they have completed it, have students answer the questions in the theme chart at the bottom of their student page. Remind them that theme statements should be expressed in complete sentences. (*"To the Right Honourable William, Earl of Dartmouth": Leaders should use their power to help citizens and make right any suffering previously inflicted on the people governed. Leaders should be just and praiseworthy. "On the Emigration to America and Peopling the Western Country": Liberty can be found only where virtuous, free people can create clear, fair laws.*)

Strategies for Annotation 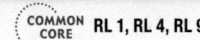 Annotate it!

Colonial American Poetry 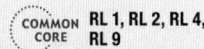 RL 1, RL 4, RL 9

Point out this question on the student page—What do the final lines of "On Being Brought from Africa to America" suggest about Wheatley's view of life in the Colonies? Share this strategy to help students answer:

- Highlight in blue the group Wheatley is addressing.
- Highlight in green the group in Colonial society that Wheatley is speaking about and to which she belongs.
- Underline her vision for her people. On a note, explain what these two lines suggest about her view of life in the Colonies.

Remember, *Christians*, *Negroes*, black as *Cain*,
May be refin'd, and join th' angelic train.

Analyzing the Text 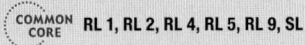 COMMON CORE RL 1, RL 2, RL 4, RL 5, RL 9, SL 1

Possible answers:

1. *In her first stanza, Wheatley depicts Goddess Freedom shining like the sun over New England, now that the Earl of Dartmouth has been appointed. Souls expand, and the "owl in sadness" departs. Wheatley expects a new day for New England as the earl governs with "silken reins."*

2. *In "On Being Brought from Africa to America," Wheatley seems to see a spiritual redemption in her conversion to Christianity, which would not have happened had she not been brought to America. Freneau sees the newcomer to America as saved from despots and tyranny. Freneau concentrates on the beneficial powers of "Reason" to bring order, prosperity, peace and freedom in settling America.*

3. *In "To the Right Honourable William . . .," Wheatley's purpose is to convince the Earl to support the Colonies and the abolition of slavery, so she vividly recounts her kidnapping. In "On Being Brought from Africa to America," she wants to convince white Christians that her race is equal in the eyes of God, so she emphasizes her conversion.*

4. *Freneau describes Europe as despotic, proud, and warring. The east he describes as a place where "kings and priests enchain the mind" (line 48). His diction reveals his negative view of Europe's and the east's societies and traditions. He sees them as corrupt and obsolete and sees America as humankind's chance to start anew.*

5. *Freneau describes the landscape as beautiful but going to waste. Plains are "lonely," (line 1) and mighty rivers "idly" flow "useless" (lines 29-30). He sees Native Americans as "unsocial," preferring to "retreat" into "darker forests" than to join the settlers in taming the land (lines 21–24).*

6. *Wheatley compares the Earl to a famous biblical prophet, encouraging him to change the immoral system of slavery, and emphasizes the heavenly reward for his actions.*

7. *Wheatley was forced into slavery, and in "To the Right Honourable William . . .," she tells of her enslavement, her parents' suffering, and her captors' hardheartedness. In "On Being Brought from Africa to America," she emphasizes society's scornful view of Africans and their exclusion by white Christians. Freneau witnessed slavery firsthand in the Caribbean, and in "On the Emigration to America . . .," he calls for the day that "man shall man no longer crush" (line 50).*

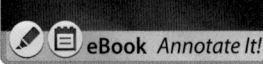 ✐ 🗒 **eBook** *Annotate It!*

Analyzing the Text COMMON CORE RL 1, RL 2, RL 4, RL 5, RL 9, SL 1

Cite Text Evidence   Support your responses with evidence from the selections.

1. **Interpret** Poets use **imagery**, or language that appeals to readers' senses, both to create a vivid experience for readers and to communicate ideas. What imagery does Wheatley use in the first stanza of "To the Right Honourable William, Earl of Dartmouth" (lines 1–14)? How does this imagery express her hopes about the Earl?

2. **Compare** How do Wheatley and Freneau treat themes about being redeemed or saved by coming to America? Compare and contrast how each poem defines or imagines this redemption.

3. **Analyze** Compare Wheatley's description of her enslavement and captivity in both of her poems, especially in lines 20–31 of "To the Right Honourable William . . . ." How might her purpose shape her description in each cases?

4. **Analyze** What words does Freneau use to describe Europe and "the east" in "On the Emigration to America . . ."? What does his diction reveal? Why does Freneau believe that America will break away from these two models of civilization?

5. **Cite Evidence** How does Freneau describe the North American landscape before the arrival of European settlers? What central ideas about Native American culture does he suggest through his diction, imagery, and choice of details?

6. **Analyze** Wheatley ends her poem addressed to the Earl of Dartmouth with an **allusion** to the biblical story of Elijah. Elijah performed bold and miraculous works on God's behalf, after which a fiery horse-drawn chariot transported him to heaven. What meaning does she intend by this allusion, and what effect does she achieve by placing it at the very end of her poem?

7. **Compare** How is the topic of slavery or oppression treated in each of the three poems? How does each poet's personal experiences or political opinions shape their view of slavery or oppression?

PERFORMANCE TASK

Speaking Activity How does each poet's attitude toward authority affect his or her interpretation of life in the colonies? With a partner, discuss similarities and differences.

1. Working independently, review the poems and identify textual evidence for each poet's attitude toward authority.

2. Meet with your partner to review the evidence you have found. Discuss how each poet's view of authority affects his or her view of life in the colonies.

3. Write a brief summary of your discussion that includes the similarities and differences you found between the two poets and key textual evidence that supports your analysis.

Assign this performance task.

PERFORMANCE TASK COMMON CORE SL 1

Speaking Activity Have students keep the following questions in mind as they review the poems for clues:

- What characteristics does the poet believe a good leader has? What are those of a bad leader?
- Is there someone or something to whom an authority must submit?
- How should life be in a good society?

INTERACTIVE WHITEBOARD LESSON
Writing Effective Arguments

COMMON CORE

W 1

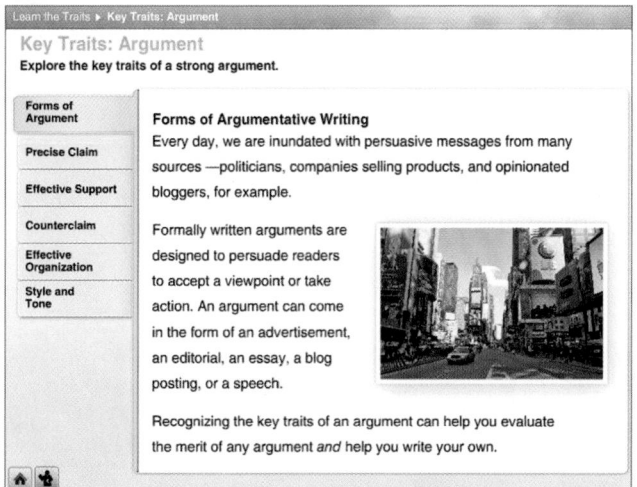

Learn the Traits ▶ Key Traits: Argument

Key Traits: Argument
Explore the key traits of a strong argument.

Forms of Argument
Precise Claim
Effective Support
Counterclaim
Effective Organization
Style and Tone

Forms of Argumentative Writing
Every day, we are inundated with persuasive messages from many sources —politicians, companies selling products, and opinionated bloggers, for example.

Formally written arguments are designed to persuade readers to accept a viewpoint or take action. An argument can come in the form of an advertisement, an editorial, an essay, a blog posting, or a speech.

Recognizing the key traits of an argument can help you evaluate the merit of any argument *and* help you write your own.

TEACH

Before students begin their independent work on the Performance Task, have them practice formulating an argument about the attitude of one of the poets toward authority. Review the steps involved in argumentation:

- **Step 1: Develop precise claims** about the poet's attitude toward authority as evidenced by the text.
- **Step 2: Cite evidence** from the text that supports the claims. Evidence should be precise, relevant, and sufficient.
- **Step 3: Identify opposing claims** and develop a counterclaim.
- **Step 4: Conclude your argument** by summarizing your claims about the poet's attitude toward authority.

PRACTICE AND APPLY

Have students reread "To the Right Honourable William, Earl of Dartmouth." Direct students to work in groups to find clues in the poem that suggest how Wheatley views authority. Students should then work independently to write a short essay that makes specific claims, supports the claims with textual evidence, anticipates opposing arguments, and concludes with a summary of their claims about Wheatley's attitude toward authority.

Point out to students that while it can be tempting to make claims based on prior knowledge, biographical information, or personal experience, they should confine themselves to claims supported by textual evidence.

Remind students to use transitional words and phrases to show the relationships among ideas.

Analyze and Compare Themes and Topics

COMMON CORE

**RL 4,
RL 9,
W 9**

RETEACH

Review the difference between the topic of a work and the theme of a work, making sure that students understand that a **topic** is simply what a work is about, while a **theme** is the work's insight into a human experience or the human condition. Then, have students reread "On the Emigration to America and Peopling the Western Country." Help students understand how to use textual evidence to discover the theme an author is communicating by completing the following exercise:

- Tell students that a work can have more than one theme. Then, supply them with the following theme: *A nation's resources, coupled with freedom, ensure its success.*

- Next, have students work in pairs to analyze the poem, citing textual details that support the theme statement you have provided. Have pairs share their evidence with the class.

LEVEL UP TUTORIALS Assign the following *Level Up* tutorial: **Theme**

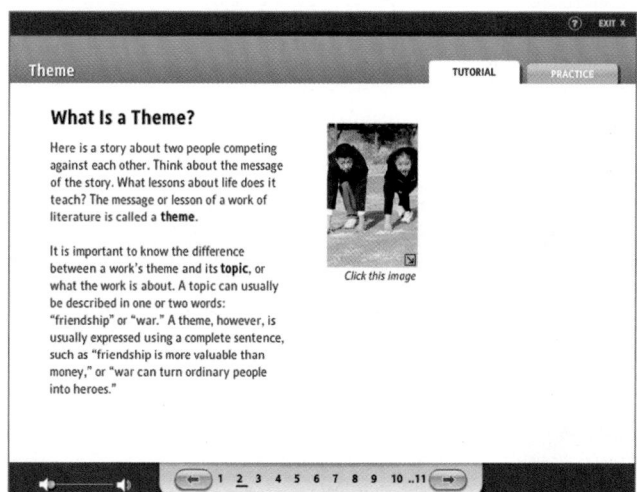

EXIT X

Theme

TUTORIAL   PRACTICE

What Is a Theme?

Here is a story about two people competing against each other. Think about the message of the story. What lessons about life does it teach? The message or lesson of a work of literature is called a **theme**.

It is important to know the difference between a work's theme and its **topic**, or what the work is about. A topic can usually be described in one or two words: "friendship" or "war." A theme, however, is usually expressed using a complete sentence, such as "friendship is more valuable than money," or "war can turn ordinary people into heroes."

Click this image

1 **2** 3 4 5 6 7 8 9 10 ..11

CLOSE READING APPLICATION

If students are unclear about using textual evidence to infer theme, try a close reading of a simpler work, such as Aesop's "The Fox and the Grapes." Ask students to read the fable, study the moral, and then underline words and phrases from the fable that support the message of the moral.

*my*SmartPlanner   Create lesson plans and access resources online.

A Soldier for the Crown

Short Story by Charles Johnson

Why This Text?

This short story presents in fictional form many of the issues, such as slavery, the American Revolution, and gender inequality, that are dealt with in this collection. It enables students to identify personally with the issues and to connect historical issues to those of the present.

View It!

Professional Development Podcast:

Text Complexity

Key Learning Objective: The student will be able to analyze suspense, ambiguity, and point of view in fiction.

COMMON CORE — Common Core Standards

RL 1 Cite textual evidence.

RL 5 Analyze how an author's choices concerning how to structure specific parts of a text contribute to its overall meaning as well as its aesthetic impact.

RL 6 Analyze a case in which grasping point of view requires distinguishing what is stated from what is really meant.

W 5 Develop and strengthen writing as needed by planning, revising, editing, rewriting, or trying a new approach.

W 7 Conduct research projects.

W 9a Draw evidence from literary or informational texts. Apply standards to literature.

W 10 Write routinely.

SL 1a Come to discussions prepared.

SL 3 Evaluate a speaker's point of view, reasoning, and use of evidence and rhetoric.

L 3a Vary syntax for effect; apply an understanding of syntax.

Text Complexity Rubric

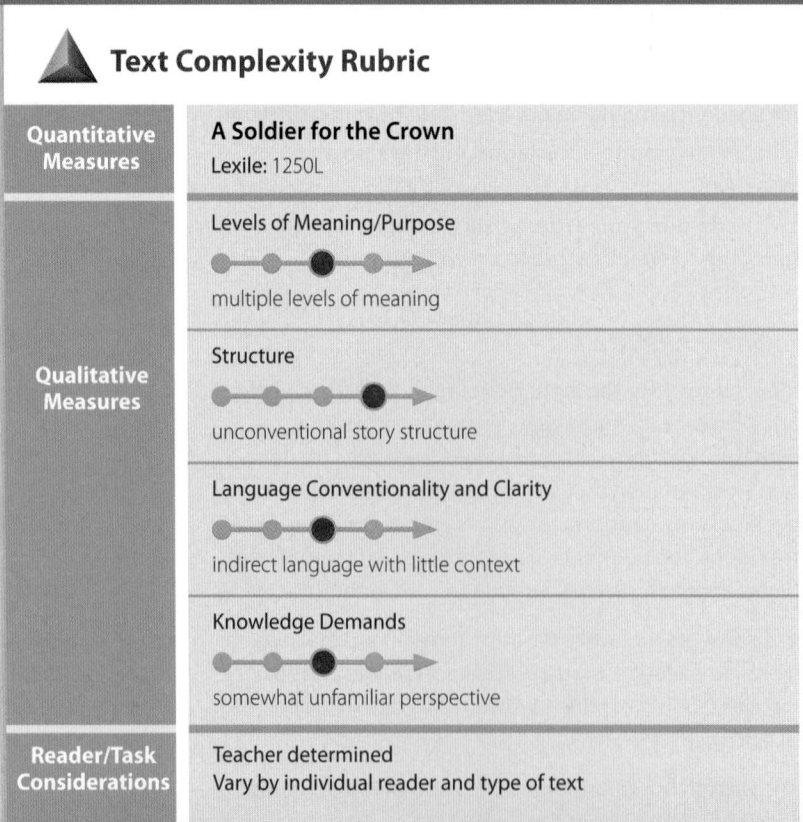

Quantitative Measures

A Soldier for the Crown
Lexile: 1250L

Qualitative Measures

Levels of Meaning/Purpose

multiple levels of meaning

Structure

unconventional story structure

Language Conventionality and Clarity

indirect language with little context

Knowledge Demands

somewhat unfamiliar perspective

Reader/Task Considerations

Teacher determined
Vary by individual reader and type of text

Background Hundreds of thousands of enslaved African Americans lived in the thirteen colonies. When the ranks of the Continental Army became depleted as the American Revolution raged on, African Americans were used as soldiers. Approximately 5,000 African Americans, mostly from the North, fought on the patriot side. In the South, the British promised freedom to enslaved people who joined their forces, and at the end of the war approximately 20,000 blacks left the United States with the British.

AS YOU READ Direct students to use the As You Read instructions to focus their reading. Tell students to generate questions as they read.

Analyze Structure: Suspense and Ambiguity

COMMON CORE **RL 1, RL 5**

(LINES 1–14)

Explain to students that **suspense** is the building excitement or tension they feel as they wait to find out what happens next in a narrative. Suspense is a key strategy author Charles Johnson uses in this story.

 **CITE TEXT EVIDENCE** Have students reread lines 1–14, identify statements that introduce suspense, and tell what these statements make them wonder about what will happen next. *(The phrase "when you were still a servant" makes me wonder how the main character escaped slavery. "But did you win this time?" makes me wonder what "this time" refers to and what the main character might have won or lost.)*

Analyze Point of View: Second Person

COMMON CORE **RL 6**

(LINES 1–13)

Point out to students that the author uses **second-person point of view** throughout the story. The narrator addresses the main character as "you." Remind students that some narrators are **omniscient:** that is, they know all the characters' thoughts, feelings, and actions. Other narrators are **limited** to knowing what a single character knows.

 **ASK STUDENTS** what effect the use of second-person point of view has on the reader. *(It helps the reader put him- or herself in the place of the main character because it is as if the narrator is speaking directly to the reader.)*

Background As a writer, philosopher, artist, and educator, **Charles Johnson** has confronted the effects of race and racism. "Racism is based on our belief in a division between Self and Other, and our tendency to measure ourselves against others," he says. "Sad to say, it is also based on fear." Johnson was born in 1948 in Evanston, Illinois, and taught for many years at the University of Washington. His work has earned a MacArthur fellowship, the National Book Award for The Middle Passage (1990), and the American Academy of Arts and Letters Award.

A Soldier for the Crown

Short Story by Charles Johnson

Image Credits: (cr) ©AISPIX by Image Source/Shutterstock; (t) ©John Storey/Time & Life Pictures/Getty Images; (c) ©Markus Gann/Shutterstock

AS YOU READ Pay attention to the concept of liberty and the way in which personal, social, and ideological differences affect its meaning.

 **Y**OU ALWAYS WERE a gambler.
  Before the war broke out, when you were still a servant in Master William Selby's house, you'd bet on anything—how early spring thaw might come, or if your older brother Titus would beat your cousin Caesar in a wrestling match—and most of the time you won. There was something about gambling that you could not resist. There was suspense, the feeling that the future was not already written by white hands. Or finished. There was chance, the luck of the draw. In the roll of dice or a card game, there was always—what to call it?—
10 an *openness*, a chance that the outcome would go this way or that. For or against you. Of course, in bondage to Master Selby there were no odds. Whichever way the dice fell or the cards came up, you began and ended your day a slave.
  But did you win *this* time?
  Standing by the wooden rail on a ship bound for Nova Scotia, crammed with strangers fleeing the collapse of their colonial world— women and children, whites and blacks, whose names appear in Brigadier General Samuel Birch's *Book of Negroes*—you pull a long-shanked pipe from your red-tinted coat, pack the bowl with tobacco,

A Soldier for the Crown **159**

SCAFFOLDING FOR ELL STUDENTS

Understand Sentence Fragments Explain to students that fiction writers sometimes use sentence fragments—parts of a sentence that do not contain both a subject and a verb. Tell students that sentence fragments are often an addition to the previous sentence.

CITE TEXT EVIDENCE Help students find two sentence fragments on this page and incorporate them into the preceding sentences. *("Or finished," line 8: There was suspense, the feeling that the future was not already written or finished by white hands. "For or against you," lines 10–11: In the roll of dice or a card game, there was always . . . a chance that the outcome would go this way or that, for or against you.)*

TEACH

CLOSE READ

Analyze Structure: Suspense and Ambiguity

COMMON CORE RL 1, RL 5

(LINES 20–35)

Explain to students that while suspense is created by uncertainty about what will happen, **ambiguity** is the uncertainty created when the writer leaves things open to interpretation. Discuss with students what is ambiguous in the story so far. Lead them to conclude that the main character's identity is ambiguous.

 CITE TEXT EVIDENCE Have students find references in lines 20–35 to the ambiguity of the main character's identity. *("Taking on new identities. Yet you wonder what to call yourself now. A loyalist? A traitor? A man without a country?" [lines 28–29] "You haven't the slightest idea…which of these names fits." [lines 32–33])*

Analyze Structure: Suspense and Ambiguity

COMMON CORE RL 1, RL 5

(LINES 58–66)

Tell students that throughout a story some of the issues about which they are in suspense will be resolved, while new issues will be introduced.

D **ASK STUDENTS** what question from the first page these lines start to answer and what new questions they introduce. *(They start to answer the question of how the main character escaped slavery. They introduce the question of what will happen to Titus and Caesar, since we already know from the first page that the main character does not get caught.)*

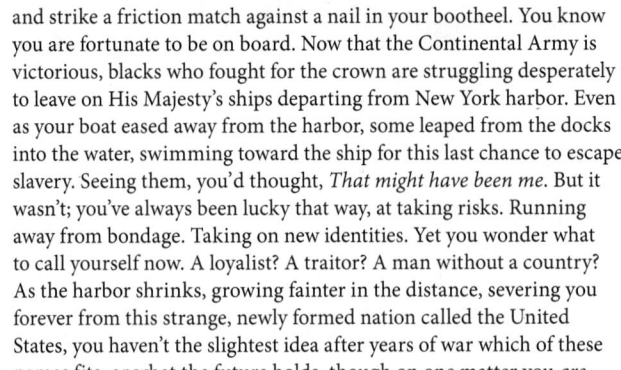

20 and strike a friction match against a nail in your bootheel. You know you are fortunate to be on board. Now that the Continental Army is victorious, blacks who fought for the crown are struggling desperately to leave on His Majesty's ships departing from New York harbor. Even as your boat eased away from the harbor, some leaped from the docks into the water, swimming toward the ship for this last chance to escape slavery. Seeing them, you'd thought, *That might have been me.* But it wasn't; you've always been lucky that way, at taking risks. Running away from bondage. Taking on new identities. Yet you wonder what to call yourself now. A loyalist? A traitor? A man without a country?

30 As the harbor shrinks, growing fainter in the distance, severing you forever from this strange, newly formed nation called the United States, you haven't the slightest idea after years of war which of these names fits, or what the future holds, though on one matter you *are* clear:

From the start, you were fighting for no one but yourself.

The day after Lieutenant General Sir Henry Clinton promised liberty to all blacks deserting the rebel standard and willing to fight on the side of the British, you learned that Titus and Caesar were planning to flee. In the evening, on your way to the quarters after

40 finishing your duties in the house, Titus stopped you outside the barn, and asked, "Can you go back to the kitchen and sneak out some provisions for us?" Naturally, you'd asked him what for, and he put his fingers to his lips, shushing you. They planned to steal two horses, he said. Then ride to safety behind British lines. "You're leaving?" You were almost speechless with anger. "And you're not taking *me*?"

"How can I?" he asked. "You're only fifteen."

"What's that got to do with anything? I can fight!"

"You ever fired a gun?"

"No, but I can learn!"

50 "Once I'm free, and got the papers to prove it, I'll come back."

"Titus, if you don't take me, I'll *tell*."

For a heartbeat or two, Titus looked as if he might hit you. Grudgingly, he agreed to bring you along, despite your age and his declaration after your parents' deaths that he'd keep you from harm. You did as he requested, returning to the house and filling a sack with food, Master Selby's clothing, even some of the mistress's jewelry that the three of you might barter, then delivered all this to your brother and Caesar in the barn. The three of you left that night on two of the master's best horses, you riding behind Titus, your arms tightly

 60 circling his waist until you stopped to make camp in the woods. There, Caesar suggested that it would help if you all changed your names and appearances as much as possible since Master Selby was sure to post your descriptions. Titus said fine, he'd grow a beard and call himself John Free. Caesar liked that, said, "Then I'll be George Liberty." They waited for you to pick a name, poking sticks at the campfire, sending up sparks into the starless sky. "Give me time," you'd said, changing

---

APPLYING ACADEMIC VOCABULARY

| ideological | revolution |

As you discuss "A Soldier for the Crown," incorporate the following Collection 2 academic vocabulary words: *ideological* and *revolution*. Ask students to state an **ideological** position that Freeman holds. *(Freeman agrees with the ideology of unalienable rights in the Declaration of Independence.)* Ask what side of the American **Revolution** Freeman fights for. *(Freeman fights for the British.)*

into buckskin breeches, blue stockings, and a checkered, woolen shirt. "I'll shave my hair off, and I'll think of *something* before we get there. I don't want to rush." What you didn't tell them that night was how

70 thrilling, how sweet this business of renaming oneself felt, and that you wanted to toy with a thousand possibilities—each name promising a new nature—turning them over on your tongue, and creating whole histories for each before settling, as you finally did, on "Alexander Freeman" as your new identity.

Thus, it was Alexander Freeman, George Liberty, and John Free who rode a few days later, bone weary from travel, into the British camp. You will never forget this sight: scores of black men in British uniforms, with the inscription LIBERTY TO SLAVES on their breasts, bearing arms so naturally one would have thought they were born

80 with a rifle in their hands. Some were cleaning their weapons. Others marched. Still others were relaxing or stabbing their bayonets at sacks suspended from trees or performing any of the thousand chores that kept a regiment well-oiled and ready. When you signed on, the black soldier who wrote down your names didn't question you, though he remarked he thought you didn't look very strong. The three of you were put immediately to work. Harder work, you recall, than anything you'd known working in Master Selby's house, but for the first time in fifteen years you fell to each task eagerly, gambling that the labor purchased a new lease on life.

90 Over the first months, then years of the seesawing war, you, Titus, and Caesar served His Majesty's army in more **capacities** than you had fingers on the hand: as orderlies[1] to the white officers, laborers, cooks, foragers, and as foot soldiers who descended upon farms abandoned by their white owners, burning the enemy's fortifications and plundering plantations for much-needed provisions; as spies slipping in and out of southern towns to gather information; and as caretakers to the dying when smallpox swept through your regiment, weakening and killing hundreds of men. Your brother among them. And it was

then you nearly gave up the gamble. You wondered if it might not
100 be best to take your chips off the table. And pray the promise of the Virginia Convention that black runaways to the British side would be pardoned was genuine. And slink back home, your hat in your hand, to Master Selby's farm—if it was still there. Or perhaps you and Caesar might switch sides, deserting to the ranks of General Washington who, pressured for manpower, **belatedly** reversed his opposition to Negroes fighting in the Continental Army. And then there was that magnificent Declaration penned by Jefferson, proclaiming that "We hold these truths to be self-evident, that all men are created equal, that they are endowed by their Creator with certain **unalienable** Rights,
110 that among these are Life, Liberty and the pursuit of Happiness,"

---

[1] **orderlies:** soldiers who provide personal assistance and perform minor tasks.

capacity
(kə-pǎs´ĭ-tē) *n.* ability to hold or have something; function or role.

belatedly
(bĭ-lā´tĭd-lē) *adv.* done too late or overdue.

unalienable
(ŭn-āl´yə-nə-bəl) *adj.* impossible to be taken away.

A Soldier for the Crown **161**

WHEN STUDENTS STRUGGLE . . .

Explain that each of Alexander's options depends on a political document or decision and involves a risk. Have pairs of students complete a chart like the one below.

Possibility	Depends on	Risk
Go back to Master Selby's	Virginia Convention	being punished as a runaway
Desert to General Washington's army	Washington reversing his opinion of Negro soldiers	being killed or injured in the war
Stay in America	Declaration of Independence	being enslaved

CLOSE READ

Analyze Point of View: Second Person (LINES 69–74)
COMMON CORE RL 1, RL 6

Remind students that some narrators are omniscient—that is, they know all the characters' thoughts, feelings, and actions—while some are limited to the thoughts and feelings of a single character.

E CITE TEXT EVIDENCE Have students determine whether the narrator is omniscient or limited and cite text evidence to support their answer. *(The narrator is limited to the main character's point of view. The narrator tells about thoughts and feelings that the main character "didn't tell" Titus and Caesar including "how thrilling, how sweet this business of renaming oneself felt," but does not reveal their thoughts or feelings.)*

Analyze Structure: Suspense and Ambiguity (LINES 98–110)
COMMON CORE RL 5

Ambiguity is one of the ways writers can create suspense.

F ASK STUDENTS how these lines create suspense. *(Alexander considers all possible options, which sound uncertain. Readers wonder which option he will take.)*

CRITICAL VOCABULARY

capacity: The narrator acknowledges the many roles that enlistees like Titus and Caesar assumed for the Crown during the war.

ASK STUDENTS why the narrator enumerates the various *capacities*. *(to show they served the Crown in other ways besides fighting on the battlefield.)*

belatedly: Washington originally opposed allowing Negroes in his army, but changed his mind, realizing he needed more soldiers.

ASK STUDENTS why the word *belatedly* fits Washington's change of mind. *(He might have admitted black soldiers in the first place but delayed.)*

unalienable: The rights named in the Declaration of Independence cannot be taken away from anyone.

ASK STUDENTS whether enslaved people at the time of the story were deemed to have any **unalienable** rights. *(No.)*

Analyze Point of View

 COMMON CORE RL 1, RL 6

(LINES 133–138)

Remind students that the narrator is limited to the main character's point of view. Discuss with students why a narrator limited to the main character's point of view might be a good choice for second person. *(because the pronoun "you" and details of the main character's thoughts and feelings each help the reader to identify with the main character)*

G CITE TEXT EVIDENCE Have students identify details that refer to Alexander's feelings, not to things that other people would be able to see. *("making it a little hard for you to sleep on that side or withstand the dull ache in your shoulder on days when the weather is damp," lines 136–138.)*

Analyze Structure

COMMON CORE RL 5

(LINES 138–156)

Point out to students that in these lines the scene returns to the ship where the story started.

H ASK STUDENTS what new information they receive in these lines and how it resolves some of the story's suspense. *(In these lines the reader learns that Alexander earned the British pass. This information resolves the suspense about whether Alexander would survive the war and remain free.)* Then ask what suspense remains. *(The reader still doesn't know where Alexander is going or what will happen there.)*

> **CRITICAL VOCABULARY**
>
> **elusive**: A British pass is extremely valuable to enslaved people, and getting one is a great triumph for Alexander.
>
> **ASK STUDENTS** why a British pass would be **elusive** for enslaved people. *(The pass would enable an enslaved person to escape to areas under British control where there was no slavery. Many white people would consider it a crime for an enslaved person to escape to freedom, and thus would try to prevent the enslaved person from obtaining the pass.)*

words you'd memorized after hearing them. If the Continentals won, would this brave, new republic be so bad?

"Alex, those are just *words*," said Caesar. "White folks' words for other white folks."

"But without us, the rebels would lose—"

"So would the redcoats. Both sides need us, but I don't trust neither one to play fair when this thing is over. They can do that Declaration over. Naw, the words I want to see are on a British pass with my name on it. I'm stayin' put 'til I see *that*."

120   Caesar never did. A month later your regiment was routed by the Continental Army. The rebels fired cannons for six hours, shelling the village your side occupied two days before. You found pieces of your cousin strewn everywhere. And you ran. Ran. You lived by your wits in the countryside, stealing what you needed to survive until you reached territory still in British hands, and again found yourself a pawn in the middle of other men's battles—Camden, where your side scattered poorly trained regulars led by General Gates, then liberated slaves who donned their masters' fancy clothing and powdered wigs and followed along behind Gates as his men pressed on; and the

130 disastrous encounter at Guilford Court House, where six hundred redcoats died and Cornwallis was forced to fall back to Wilmington for supplies, then later abandon North Carolina altogether, moving on to Virginia. During your time as a soldier, you saw thousands sacrifice their lives, and no, it wasn't as if you came through with only a scratch. At Camden you took a ball in your right shoulder. Fragments remain there still, making it a little hard for you to sleep on that side or withstand the dull ache in your shoulder on days when the weather is damp. But, miraculously, as the war began to wind down, you were given the **elusive**, long-coveted British pass.

140   On the ship, now traveling north past Augusta, you knock your cold pipe against the railing, shaking dottle from its bowl, then reach into your coat for the scrap of paper that was so difficult to earn. Behind you, other refugees are bedding down for the night, covering themselves and their children with blankets. You wait until one of the hands on deck passes a few feet beyond where you stand, then you unfold the paper with fingers stiffened by the cold. In the yellowish glow of the ship's lantern, tracing the words with your forefinger, shaping your lips silently to form each syllable, you read:

150   This is to certify to whomfoever it may concern, that the Bearer hereof…Alexander Freeman…a Negro, reforted to the Britifh Lines, in confequence of the Proclamations of Sir William Howe, and Sir Henry Clinton, late Commanders in Chief in America; and that the faid Negro has hereby his Excellency Sir Benjamin Hampton's Permiffion to go to Nova-Scotia, or wherever elfe he may think proper…By Order of Brigadier General Ruttledge

elusive
(ĭ-loo'sĭv) *adj.* difficult to find.

WHEN STUDENTS STRUGGLE…

Because of its archaic language, students may have difficulty reading the document from General Ruttledge. Tell them that long ago the letter "s" was sometimes written with a character that looks like an "f". Have students work in small groups to "translate" the document into modern English. Tell them to look up any unfamiliar words in the dictionary. *(This is to certify to whomever it may concern that the person carrying this document … Alexander Freeman … an African American, escaped to the British lines because of the proclamations of Sir William Howe and Sir Henry Clinton, recent British Commanders in Chief in America; and that this African American has Sir Benjamin Hampton's permission to go to Nova Scotia or wherever else he wants to go.)*

The document, dated April 1783, brings a broad smile to your lips. Once your ship lands, and you find a home, you will frame this precious deed of manumission.[2] At least in this sense, your gamble paid off. And for now you still prefer the adopted name Alexander Freeman to the one given you at birth—Dorothy.

Maybe you'll be Dorothy again, later in Nova Scotia. Of course, you'll keep the surname Freeman. And, Lord willing, when it's safe you will let your hair grow out again to its full length, wear dresses, and perhaps start a new family to replace the loved ones you lost during the war.

---

[2] **deed of manumission:** a document confirming a person's release from slavery.

COLLABORATIVE DISCUSSION Were you surprised by the twist at the end of the story? What does it change about your views on Alexander's struggle for liberation? What specific events now appear in a new light? Cite evidence from the text that supports your ideas.

CLOSE READ

Analyze Point of View
COMMON CORE **RL 6**

(LINES 157–161)

POINT OUT TO students that in these lines the reader must distinguish what is stated from what is meant.

ASK STUDENTS what the narrator means in lines 160–161. *(The narrator states that the name given to the main character at birth is "Dorothy"; the narrator means that Alexander Freeman is a girl.)* How does the choice of the second-person point of view help the author preserve the ambiguity surrounding the main character's identity? *(By speaking of the main character as "you" rather than "him" or "her," the author is able to avoid referring to and giving away her gender.)*

Analyze Structure
COMMON CORE **RL 5**

(LINES 162–166)

Tell students that the ending of a story often ends the suspense, but that in some cases the reader may still be left with questions.

ASK STUDENTS what questions they still have about what might happen after the ending of the story. *(Possible responses: Will Dorothy still pose as a man, or will she reveal herself to the world as a woman? Will she get married and have children, work, or both? What will happen to affect her choices?)*

COLLABORATIVE DISCUSSION Have groups of two or three students discuss their answers to the questions. Encourage students to explain their answers fully and cite specific details and events. Have the groups share their ideas with the class.

ASK STUDENTS to share any questions they generated in the course of reading and discussing the selection.

TEACH

CLOSE READ

Analyze Structure: Suspense and Ambiguity

  COMMON CORE RL 1, RL 5, RL 6

To help students understand suspense and ambiguity, guide them in seeing how those two elements are related.

- Suspense is a feeling caused by being uncertain about what will happen next.
- Ambiguity means that a situation is open to interpretation and so causes uncertainty.
- Both ambiguity and suspense are created by uncertainty.
- When the characters' motivations and relationships or other details are ambiguous, it is difficult to tell what is likely to happen, creating suspense.

Analyze Point of View

COMMON CORE RL 1, RL 6

Help students understand the differences among the three major types of point of view. Use this chart.

	First Person	Second Person	Third Person
Limited	*can only tell what the "I" character knows*	*can only tell what the "you" character knows*	*can only tell what the "him" or "her" character knows*
Omniscient	*not generally used*	*can tell what any of the characters know*	*can tell what any of the characters know*

Analyze Structure: Suspense and Ambiguity

 COMMON CORE RL 1, RL 5, RL 6

The **structure** of a story consists of a writer's choices concerning how to organize information. As you analyze the overall meaning and impact of the author's structure in "A Soldier for the Crown," note the following elements:

Suspense is the excitement or tension that readers feel as they wait to find out how a story ends. The author introduces Alexander Freeman as a risk-taker and creates suspense about the story's outcome with statements such as, "But did you win *this* time?" The description of Freeman aboard the ship helps frame the story and raise questions in readers' minds about the events that brought Freeman there.

Ambiguity is the uncertainty created when an author leaves elements of a text open to the reader's interpretation. The author builds the story by forcing the reader to put together clues about Alexander Freeman. The reader must then reevaluate these inferences and assumptions about Freeman's identity in the story's surprise ending.

Analyze Point of View: Second Person

 COMMON CORE RL 1, RL 6

Point of view refers to the method an author uses to narrate a story. Most stories are told in the first-person or third-person point of view. In a work written in the **first-person point of view,** the narrator is a character in the story and shares his or her own thoughts and feelings. When a writer uses the **third-person point of view,** the narrator is not a character in the story but an outside observer. Sometimes a third-person narrator is **omniscient,** meaning he or she knows the thoughts, feelings, and actions of all the characters in a story. A third-person narrator can also be **limited** to one character's thoughts, observations, or experiences.

A more unusual method of narration is the **second-person point of view,** in which the narrator addresses one or more individuals using the pronoun *you*. In "A Soldier for the Crown," the narrator addresses the main character, Alexander Freeman, but often speaks as if he or she has entered the mind of that character. For example, in lines 26–27, the narrator says

> "Seeing them, you'd thought, *That might have been me.* But it wasn't; you've always been lucky that way, at taking risks."

The second-person point of view requires the reader to piece together the information that is revealed by the narrator and to distinguish what is directly stated in the text from what is really meant. In the example, the reader knows that the "you" has been a lucky risk taker in the past. However, even with the clues provided earlier in the story, it isn't yet exactly clear what type of risk taking has led the person to be on board the ship.

Strategies for Annotation 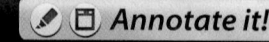 *Annotate it!*

Analyze Structure: Suspense and Ambiguity

COMMON CORE RL 1, RL 5

Share these strategies for guided or independent analysis:

- Highlight in yellow ambiguous sentences or phrases, and highlight in green sentences and phrases that create suspense.
- For each highlighted sentence or phrase, add a note telling what question has been raised.

At least in this sense, your gamble paid off. And for now you still prefer the adopted name Alexander Freeman to the one given you at birth—Dorothy. Maybe you'll be Dorothy again, later in Nova Scotia. Of course, you'll keep the surname Freeman.

> In what sense did the gamble not pay off?
>
> Will she continue to live as a man, or resume her identity as a woman?
>
> Will she ever have a family?

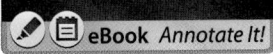
Analyzing the Text

COMMON CORE RL 1, RL 5, RL 6, W 7, W 9a, W 10, SL 1a, SL 3

Cite Text Evidence Support your responses with evidence from the selection.

1. **Infer** What evidence does the author provide in the opening sentence of the story and the paragraph that follows to suggest the risks that the main character will take to escape slavery?

2. **Identify** How does the setting contribute to the suspense within the text? Explain, citing details that reveal the setting of the story.

3. **Cite Evidence** What clues in the story hint at Freeman's identity? Provide details from the story in your explanation.

4. **Analyze** What effect does the use of the second-person point of view have on the scene in lines 60–74? What idea is the author able to communicate by using this point of view?

5. **Analyze** Why does the conversation between Caesar and Freeman about the Declaration of Independence leave the reader with a sense of ambiguity, but hold greater significance once Freeman's identity is revealed?

6. **Evaluate** In what ways does Freeman assume a greater risk than other African Americans who join the British side? How does assuming a different gender complicate her situation?

7. **Interpret** What does the narrator mean by the reference to Freeman's deed of manumission, "At least in this sense, your gamble paid off."

8. **Analyze** Why is it **ironic,** or contrary to what you might have expected, that Freeman considers the deed of manumission to be so precious?

PERFORMANCE TASK

Writing and Speaking Activity Alexander Freeman decides to continue fighting for the British in the Revolution after her brother died. However, she had several other options. Prepare for a small group discussion by doing some research and writing an outline of your notes. Complete these steps:

- identify the other alternatives Freeman considers
- research the alternatives by looking for information about the role of African Americans in the Revolutionary War
- write notes about your research, remembering to identify each of your sources
- gather with a small group to discuss and evaluate Alexander Freeman's options
- use your research notes to support your ideas during the discussion
- as a group write a summary of your discussion including whether you agree or disagree about the decision Alexander Freeman made

A Soldier for the Crown **165**

Analyzing the Text

COMMON CORE RL 1, RL 5, RL 6, W 7, W 9a, W 10, SL 1a, SL 3

Possible answers:

1. *By opening the story with the statement that the main character was always a gambler, the author hints that further gambles will follow. In the second paragraph, the author details several specific bets to emphasize the point. The context of slavery and the phrase "white hands" hint that the risks to come will have to do with slavery.*

2. *Although the story is evidently about enslaved people, it opens on a ship to Nova Scotia. This creates suspense about what the characters are doing on the ship. References to the Revolution create suspense about what the characters will do in that struggle.*

3. *Clues include the fact that Freeman does not look physically strong and works in the kitchen.*

4. *The use of the second person in lines 60-74 adds ambiguity to Freeman's choice of a new name and her cutting of her hair. The author is able to communicate that there is more to the scene than is directly stated.*

5. *The characters do not know whether the words of the Declaration will be interpreted to apply to them as enslaved people. There is even greater significance for Freeman because it is ambiguous whether the word* men *in the Declaration refers to all people or only to males, in which case it would not apply to her.*

6. *As an enslaved person, Freeman incurs greater risks than a freed African American would, because if caught she can be returned to her master and severely punished. Taking on a different gender role complicates her task because if her deception is uncovered, she could be thrown out of the army.*

7. *The risks, or gamble, Freeman took results in gaining the valuable British pass that frees her from slavery.*

8. *Although the deed freed Freeman, it refers to her as a man named Alexander. It might not remain effective if she returns to her true identity as a woman. It is ironic because the deed may not serve its purpose of freeing her. Technically, it does not apply to her as a female.*

Assign this performance task.

PERFORMANCE TASK

COMMON CORE W 5, W 7, W 9a, W 10

Writing and Speaking Activity Focus students' attention on lines 98–112 of the story. Have students conduct their research individually, making notes of what they learn and putting them in outline form. Finally, divide students into small groups to discuss whether they agree or disagree with Freeman's decision. Have each group summarize and share their findings.

Critical Vocabulary

COMMON CORE L 3a, W 5

Possible answers: 1. *I have the rights of life, liberty, and the pursuit of happiness, as the Declaration of Independence says, because they are given naturally, not by other people.* **2.** *Sample response: I received a birthday present from my aunt belatedly because it was delayed in shipping.* **3.** *Sample response: I tried to grasp something elusive when I had trouble mastering equations in algebra.* **4.** *Sample response: I could volunteer my time at the shelter or donate pet food.*

Language and Style: Point of View

Sample second-person summary: Our group found that your options were to continue with the British army in hopes of receiving a document of manumission, desert to the rebel side, or just stay as a free person in America and risk being enslaved again. Our group agreed with your decision, Freeman. Since slavery was not abolished in the U.S. until much later, the best way for you to gain your freedom was to fight for the British.

Critical Vocabulary

COMMON CORE L 3a, W 5

| capacity | belatedly | unalienable | elusive |

Practice and Apply Answer each question. Then discuss your answers with a partner.

1. What do you possess as an individual that is **unalienable**? Explain.

2. Describe a circumstance in which you received something **belatedly.**

3. When have you tried to grasp something that proved **elusive**? Explain.

4. In what **capacity** might you help out at a local animal shelter?

Language and Style: Point of View

In narrating from a particular **point of view**, a writer must use the correct personal pronoun form to refer to the person making a statement, the person being addressed, or the thing the statement is about.

	Nominative	Objective	Possessive
Singular			
First person	I	me	my, mine
Second person	you	you	your, yours
Third person	he, she, it	her, him, it	her, hers, his, its
Plural			
First person	we	us	our, ours
Second person	you	you	you, yours
Third person	they	them	their, theirs

Notice how the personal pronouns would change form if the last paragraph from "A Soldier for the Crown," were rewritten in the first-person or third-person point of view.

First-Person Point of View	Third-Person Point of View
Maybe I'll be Dorothy again, later in Nova Scotia. Of course, I'll keep the surname Freeman. And, Lord willing, when it's safe I will let my hair grow long again to it's full length, wear dresses, and perhaps start a new family to replace the loved ones I lost during the war.	Maybe she'll be Dorothy again, later in Nova Scotia. Of course, she'll keep the surname Freeman. And, Lord willing, when it's safe she will let her hair grow long again to it's full length, wear dresses, and perhaps start a new family to replace the loved ones she lost during the war.

Practice and Apply Look back at your summary of your discussion about Freeman's choices. Rewrite the summary from the second-person point of view. Address the audience as Freeman. Remember to use the correct personal pronoun form.

Language and Style: Point of View

COMMON CORE L 3a, W 5

Have students return to the selection and pick a passage of four or more lines that includes at least two second-person pronouns. Encourage them to use their eBook annotation tools to do the following:

- Highlight in blue each phrase that contains a second-person pronoun.
- Underline each second-person pronoun.
- Insert a note for each of the underlined pronouns, rewriting the phrase in first person.

Seeing them, you'd thought, *That might have been me.* But it wasn't; you've always been lucky that way, at taking risks. Running away from bondage. Taking on new identities. Yet you wonder what to call yourself now. (lines 26–29)

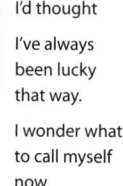

I'd thought

I've always been lucky that way.

I wonder what to call myself now

INTERACTIVE WHITEBOARD LESSON
Conducting Research on the Web

COMMON CORE

W 7

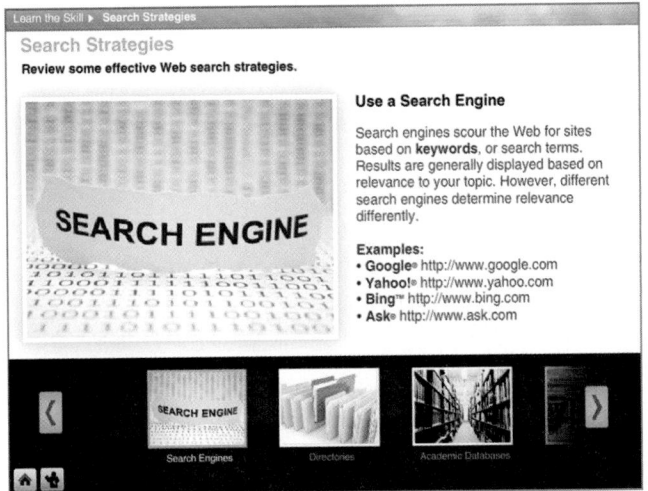

Learn the Skill ▶ Search Strategies

Search Strategies
Review some effective Web search strategies.

Use a Search Engine

Search engines scour the Web for sites based on **keywords**, or search terms. Results are generally displayed based on relevance to your topic. However, different search engines determine relevance differently.

Examples:
- **Google**® http://www.google.com
- **Yahoo!**® http://www.yahoo.com
- **Bing**™ http://www.bing.com
- **Ask**® http://www.ask.com

TEACH

Help students to apply the steps for conducting a Web search to the topics of slavery and the Revolutionary War.

- **Step 1: Formulate Research Questions.** For example, *What happened to formerly enslaved people who participated in the war? What is the history of slavery in Great Britain?*

- **Step 2: Start Your Search.** Determine what keywords are likely to yield results on your research question. For example, you might do a keyword search in a search engine, such as Google or Yahoo. (Search engines rank results differently, so consult more than one.)

- **Step 3: Analyze the Results.** Investigate promising links. Determine whether the site is trustworthy and whether the information is relevant by examining the currency of the information and whether it is produced by a well-known periodical, a historical research site, or an expert in the field.

- **Step 4: Refine Your Search.** Try different search terms or use an advanced search to make sure you have found the best available information.

COLLABORATIVE DISCUSSION

Have students who are researching similar questions work in groups to complete their research. When they have finished researching, have each group work together to summarize their findings. Then ask a volunteer from each group to present the summary to the class.

Analyze Structure: Suspense and Ambiguity

COMMON CORE

RL 5

RETEACH

Remind students that ambiguity is the uncertainty created when an author leaves elements of a text open to interpretation. Explain that in literature, ambiguity requires readers to think about and interpret the text for themselves. Unlike other forms of writing, the meaning of a literary work is created by a partnership between the writer and the reader, so each reader may get a slightly different meaning from a great novel or short story.

Present to students the following ways in which writers create ambiguity and the accompanying examples from "A Soldier for the Crown."

Method	Use in "A Soldier for the Crown"
referring to things the reader doesn't know about	"But did you win this time?" (line 14)
asking questions and leaving them unanswered	"Yet you wonder what to call yourself now. A loyalist? A traitor? A man without a country?" (lines 28–29)
giving apparently contradictory information	The main character wears men's clothes and smokes a pipe, but works in the kitchen, cuts her hair to change her appearance, and doesn't look very physically strong.

Encourage students to look for these techniques whenever they read literary prose.

CLOSE READING APPLICATION

Students can look for ambiguity in another short story. Have students choose a short story and then have them work independently to find mysterious references, unanswered questions, and contradictory information. When they have finished reading, ask: How does ambiguity affect this story?

*my*SmartPlanner · Create lesson plans and access resources online.

MEDIA Patrick Henry: Voice of Liberty

Documentary by A&E

Why This Text?

Students study foundational documents to better understand the early history of the U.S. This lesson focuses on one of the authors of foundational documents—Patrick Henry—and his contribution to the formation of the new United States.

Key Learning Objective: The student will be able to analyze how ideas and claims presented in a video connect to foundational U.S. documents.

COMMON CORE Common Core Standards

RI 3 Analyze a set of ideas or sequence of events.
RI 7 Integrate and evaluate multiple sources of information.
RI 9 Analyze foundational U.S. documents.
W 1 Write arguments.
W 6 Use technology to produce, publish, and update individual or shared writing products.
SL 1 Initiate and participate in a range of collaborative discussions.
SL 4 Present information, findings, and supporting evidence.
SL 5 Make strategic use of digital media.

▲ Text Complexity Rubric

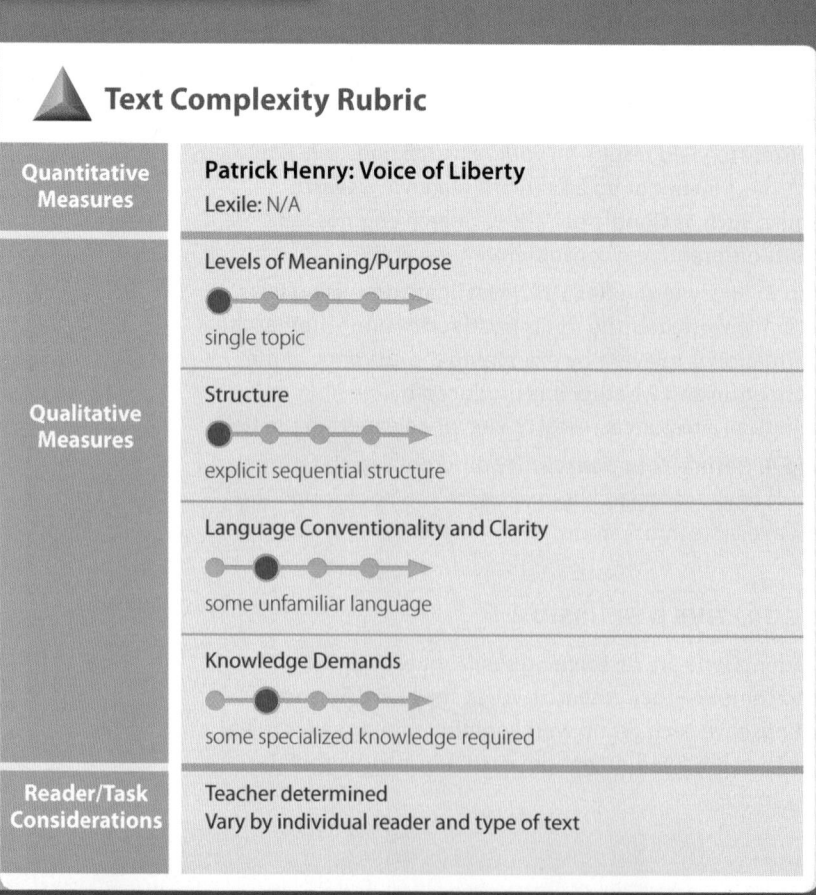

Quantitative Measures	**Patrick Henry: Voice of Liberty** Lexile: N/A
Qualitative Measures	Levels of Meaning/Purpose single topic
	Structure explicit sequential structure
	Language Conventionality and Clarity some unfamiliar language
	Knowledge Demands some specialized knowledge required
Reader/Task Considerations	Teacher determined Vary by individual reader and type of text

TEACH

CLOSE READ

Students can view the video "Patrick Henry: Voice of Liberty" in their eBooks.

Background Have students read the background information about Patrick Henry. Tell students that many people involved in the American Revolution are remembered for what they did. Henry is largely remembered for what he said.

AS YOU VIEW Direct students to use the As You View statement to focus their viewing. Remind students to write down questions that they generate as they watch the video.

Analyze Foundational Documents

COMMON CORE RI 7, RI 9

Explain to students that **foundational documents** are texts considered significant to early U.S. history. Many of these documents employ **persuasive rhetoric**—the art of using language to argue and persuade.

ASK STUDENTS how Henry's use of **persuasive rhetoric** influenced the start of the American Revolution. *(His words "give me liberty, or give me death" inspired thousands of Americans to fight against the British.)* How might his speech be considered a **foundational document**? *(His speech was printed and shared throughout the colonies, greatly influencing public opinion and discourse.)*

CITE TEXT EVIDENCE In addition to his Speech to the Second Virginia Convention, Henry made other contributions to the formation of the United States. Ask students to cite evidence from the documentary to explain Henry's other contributions. *(His opposition to the Stamp Act popularized the phrase "no taxation without representation" [23:25]. He served in the First Continental Congress [32:37]. He was the first post-colonial governor of Virginia [42:21]. He was a leading advocate for the Bill of Rights [46:57].)*

COLLABORATIVE DISCUSSION Have students form pairs and discuss Patrick Henry's major accomplishments. Then as a class discuss their relevance to the American Revolution and the United States' founding.

ASK STUDENTS to share any questions they generated in the course of viewing the selection.

Background *Patrick Henry (1736–1799) is remembered for his ringing declaration "Give me liberty or give me death!" Yet, he contributed much more than rhetoric to eighteenth-century politics and to the formation of a new United States. This video excerpt describes the ways in which his efforts helped change the course of American history and the circumstances that led to Henry becoming the "voice of liberty." Henry was born in a frontier region of Virginia, and was raised in a cultured but modest environment. He made several unsuccessful attempts at storekeeping and farming before discovering his true calling: the law and politics.*

MEDIA ANALYSIS

Patrick Henry: Voice of Liberty

Documentary by A&E

AS YOU VIEW Pay attention to the way in which Patrick Henry is portrayed in this video. Write down any questions you generate during your viewing.

© 1996 A&E Television Networks, LLC • Image Credits: ©Peter Frederick Rothermel/Library of Congress Prints & Photographs Division

COLLABORATIVE DISCUSSION What facts did you learn about Patrick Henry that surprised you?

SCAFFOLDING FOR ELL STUDENTS

Analyze Events To help students understand Patrick Henry's life, have them use a graphic organizer, like an outline, to keep track of what is discussed in the documentary.

I. **Early life**

   A. Family and upbringing

   B. Informal education

   C. Religious influence

Pause and replay segments of the documentary as needed. Discuss with students ideas and events that may cause confusion.

Analyze Foundational Documents

 COMMON CORE RI 9

Explain to students that different foundational documents had different purposes. Some created the government's structure, while others were meant to inspire or educate contemporary readers.

ASK STUDENTS how Henry's speeches compare to written documents. How do they differ? *(Henry's speeches created an immediate, visceral response in his audience. Their influence depended as much on the delivery as on the words themselves. Although Henry's speeches could be considered more emotional than other foundational documents, they contained ideas that reflected and influenced the American Revolution.)*

Analyzing the Media

COMMON CORE RI 3, RI 9, W 1, W 6

Possible answers:

1. *He was an elegant writer and speaker who could gauge his audience and adjust quickly when necessary. (26:15) Many of his speeches were extemporaneous, meaning they were not written out first. No complete drafts of any of his speeches exist. (25:34)*

2. *Henry's four resolutions were printed and read throughout the colonies, stoking public outrage that forced England to repeal the act. The phrase "no taxation without representation" became an important and powerful political concept. (27:26)*

3. *His speech was a call to arms that inspired thousands of men and women to join the revolution against the English. Many soldiers had embroidered on their uniform the phrase "Liberty or Death." (37:44)*

Analyze Foundational Documents

 COMMON CORE RI 9

As one of the leading statesmen of the eighteenth century, Patrick Henry had a significant impact on the political thought of the day as well as on foundational documents, such as the Constitution, that defined the American system of government and articulated the country's principles.

The video excerpt from *Patrick Henry: Voice of Liberty* presents information about the historical context of Henry's life and achievements. To understand the extent of Henry's contribution to the core of American democracy, viewers may analyze relationships between these elements:

- Henry's abilities as a statesman and political decisions that led to the founding of the new country
- Henry's political philosophy and the themes of foundational documents
- the effect that Henry's words had on the founding of the United States and on the early history of the nation

Analyzing the Media

 COMMON CORE RI 3, RI 9, W 1, W 6

Cite Text Evidence Support your responses with evidence from the selection.

1. **Analyze** Why was Patrick Henry such an effective speaker? Why do we have so little information on the exact content of Henry's speeches?

2. **Evaluate** Explain the historical significance of Henry's Virginia Stamp Act Resolutions. How did his objections shape or transform the political discussion around the controversy?

3. **Evaluate** Based on this video, in what ways might Henry's Speech to the Second Virginia Convention be considered a foundational U.S. document? What was the historical and literary significance of the speech?

PERFORMANCE TASK

Media Activity: Presentation What is a foundational document for the 21st century? Work with a partner to create a media presentation that responds to this question.

- Choose a book, album, movie, Web site, or even a law that could be considered the equivalent of a foundational document today.

- Explain the impact of this work on society, citing specific details.

- Incorporate your defense of your choice into a media presentation. If possible, use elements similar to those seen in *Patrick Henry: Voice of Liberty*.

Assign this performance task.

PERFORMANCE TASK

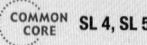 COMMON CORE SL 4, SL 5

Media Activity: Presentation Help students choose a foundational document for the 21st century. Explain that to be considered "foundational," the document should have a major influence on attitudes, policies, or events of the 21st century. Discuss which media is available to use in their presentations. After students have presented their work, have a class discussion about which documents might still be considered "foundational" in two hundred years.

Analyze Ideas and Events

COMMON CORE
RI 3, SL 1

TEACH

Explain to students that *Patrick Henry: Voice of Liberty* is a **biographical documentary** film focusing on the events of Patrick Henry's life. Viewers can analyze the ideas and events of a film, just as readers can analyze texts. Discuss the following terms with students:

- Filmmakers create documentaries with a **purpose.** Like informational text, the film's purpose or intent will shape its **content** and **style.**
- The documentary's **content** is the material included in the work. This can include narration, photographs, interviews, voice-overs, reenactments, and other material.
- The film's **style** is how the content is presented and put together. Style can be influenced by numerous factors, such as lighting, film and sound quality, length of clips, transitions between clips, camera movement, pacing, structure, special effects, and much more.
- An important part of filmmaking is creating the **script.** The script is a written document that contains the **content** (what material will be included) and the **style** (instructions for how to present the material). The script also determines the documentary's **structure,** which is how the ideas and events are grouped and the order in which they are presented.

COLLABORATIVE DISCUSSION

Direct students to form pairs or small groups. Have them discuss the following questions:

- How is the documentary structured? *(It is organized chronologically into five segments.)*
- What kind of content is included in the film? *(The documentary includes narration, interviews, photographs, establishing shots, and reenactments.)*
- What is the film's style? *(Answers will vary, but students should note its serious tone, smooth transitions, and professional quality.)*
- What is the documentary's purpose? *(Its purpose is to educate people about Patrick Henry.)*

Analyze Foundational Documents

COMMON CORE
RI 9, SL 1

TEACH

Explain to students that Patrick Henry is remembered for many great speeches. However, his most celebrated oratory was to the Virginia Convention in 1775. An important part of understanding this speech as a **foundational document** involves analyzing its context—the attitudes, beliefs, and events of the day. Discuss these elements of the speech's context.

- The **speaker's** background can shape his or her ideas, skills, and purposes.
- The **audience** can affect how the speaker presents his or her ideas.
- The **medium,** or how the message is conveyed, can limit or amplify the message.
- The **idea,** or topic, itself may have its own background, pre-dating the speaker's involvement.
- The **setting,** or time and location of the event, may also affect how the speech is delivered and received.

COLLABORATIVE DISCUSSION

Direct students to form pairs or small groups. Have them discuss the following questions:

- How did Patrick Henry's background and skills affect his speech before the Virginia Convention?
- Who was Henry's audience? How might a different audience have affected his message?
- How might a different medium, such as a pamphlet, have changed the reception and popularity of his message?
- What events led Henry to formulate his idea "give me liberty, or give me death"? How might his message have been different if he delivered the speech a year earlier or a year later?
- Would Henry's speech have remained as effective if he had delivered it in a different colony, such as South Carolina or Connecticut?

INTERACTIVE WHITEBOARD LESSON
Conducting Research on the Web

COMMON CORE
RI 7, SL 1

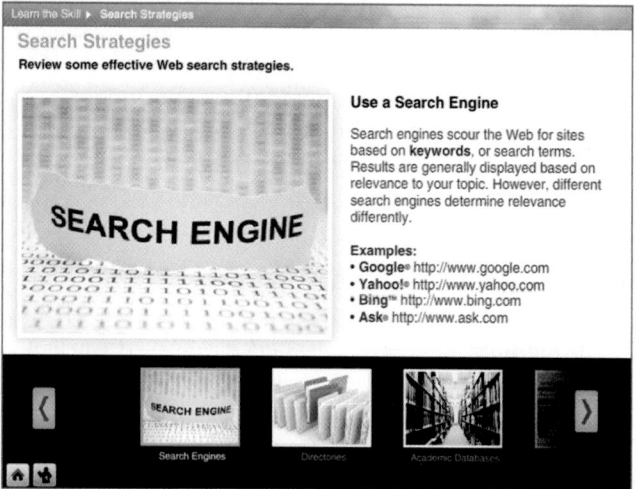

TEACH

Before having students research the topic of the Performance Task, review the steps for conducting a Web search:

1. **Step 1: Choose a Form of Document.** For example, do you want to look for a book, movie, Web site, law, lyrics or another type of document?

2. **Step 2: Start Your Search.** Determine the best starting point for your research query. For instance, you might explore a government website or do a **keyword search** in a search engine. (Search engines rank results differently, so consult more than one.)

3. **Step 3: Evaluate Your Sources.** If you started with a search engine, decide which sites might provide the most relevant information. For any sites you choose to explore, examine the currency of information, as well as the credibility of the source. Is the site produced by a government office, a well-known periodical, or an expert in the field? Sites with addresses that end in the abbreviations *.edu, .org,* and *.gov* are likely to be more credible.

4. **Step 4: Refine Your Search.** Make your search more specific by using the words *AND, NOT,* or *OR* between key terms or phrases.

COLLABORATIVE DISCUSSION

Direct students to work in groups to conduct their search on 21st century foundational documents using the research strategies you presented. Have groups compare the results of their searches.

Analyze the Media

COMMON CORE
RI 3

RETEACH

Remind students that filmmakers create documentaries with a **purpose.** Usually, the purpose is to educate or influence an **audience.**

Have students form pairs or small groups to review *Patrick Henry: Voice of Liberty* and discuss who the film was made for and how this might influence its purpose, content, and style.

LEVEL UP TUTORIALS Assign the following *Level Up* tutorial: **Audience**

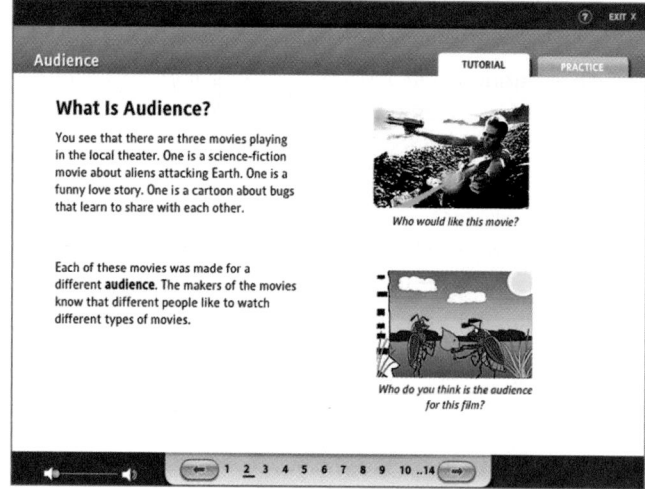

CLOSE READING APPLICATION

Have students find and read an excerpt of one of Patrick Henry's speeches. Ask them to analyze its content and style and make inferences about its audience and purpose. Have pairs present the excerpts as well as their analyses in small groups.

Interactive Lessons

If you need help with...
- **Writing an Informative Text**
- **Producing and Publishing with Technology**

PERFORMANCE TASK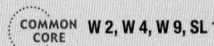

Write an Informative Essay

How can a large group of people with widely different backgrounds, beliefs, and interests work together to form one political union? This collection focuses on ways that Americans during and after the revolution envisioned the future of their new nation. Choose three texts you have read in this collection, including the anchor texts—the Declaration of Independence and the U.S. Constitution—and identify how each author, character, or founder finds a balance between preserving individual rights and forming a strong and long-lasting union. Write an informative essay in which you cite evidence from all three texts to support your topic.

Your informative essay should include:

- an introduction with a clear topic statement about the conflict between a strong, centralized government and individualism as explored in the Declaration of Independence, the Constitution, and one other text from the collection

- a logically structured body that thoroughly develops the topic with relevant examples, details, and quotations from the texts

- transitions to clarify the relationships between sections of your essay and to link ideas with the textual evidence that supports them

- a conclusion that follows from the ideas conveyed in the body of the essay

- precise use of language with appropriate tone and style for an informative essay

COMMON CORE

W 2 Write informative/ explanatory texts to examine and convey complex ideas, concepts, and information clearly and accurately through the effective selection, organization, and analysis of content.

W 4 Produce clear and coherent writing in which the development, organization, and style are appropriate to task, purpose, and audience.

W 9 Draw evidence from literary or informational texts to support analysis, reflection, and research.

SL 1 Initiate and participate effectively in a range of collaborative discussions, building on others' ideas and expressing their own clearly and persuasively.

> **PLAN**

Analyze the Texts
Reread the Declaration and the Preamble and Bill of Rights from the U.S. Constitution and consider what the texts say about both forming a union and protecting the rights of individuals. Make notes about specific details in the texts. Then review the other texts in the collection to decide which one provides the best material to complement what you have found in the anchor texts. Note relevant details and examples from that text, as well. Be sure to look for evidence that may be contrary to the ideas expressed in the Declaration and the Constitution, as well as evidence that reinforces those ideas.

Share Ideas
Once you have thought about your topic and identified evidence in the texts, get together with a group of classmates to share

*my*Notebook

Use the notebook in your eBook to record examples and quotations on the rights of the individual balanced against the needs of society.

WRITE AN INFORMATIVE ESSAY

COMMON CORE W 2, W 4, W 9, SL 1

Introduce students to the Performance Task by reading the introductory paragraph with them and reviewing the criteria for an effective informative essay. Work with students to distill the prompt into a simple question, such as: *How has the United States struck a balance between preserving individual rights and forming a strong and long-lasting union?*

> **PLAN**

ANALYZE THE TEXTS

▶ *View It!*

Professional Development Podcast:
Writing from Sources

Once student have finished their review of the Declaration and the Preamble and Bill of Rights from the U.S. Constitution, suggest that they write a working controlling idea based on the evidence they have identified. They can use this idea to help them choose which additional text to review for supporting evidence. After reviewing the other selection, they can refine the controlling idea to fit the evidence from all three texts.

PLAN

GET ORGANIZED

Tell students that organizing details, quotations, and examples in a logical way is essential to writing an effective informative essay. Remind them that all of the text evidence they include should be relevant to their controlling idea. Review the first bulleted point and make sure students understand the organizational patterns that are described.

PRODUCE

DRAFT YOUR REPORT

Tell students that they should establish a clear link between the controlling idea in their draft introductions and the main idea of each supporting paragraph. They can make these connections through transitional words and phrases that show the relationships among ideas. For instance, words and phrases like *consequently, as a result, because,* and *therefore* can be used to show cause-and-effect relationships between ideas as in this sentence: ***As a result*** *of the desire to protect the right of the individual to receive fair treatment under the law, Amendment VI was added to the U.S. Constitution.*

---

ideas. Be prepared to discuss specific textual evidence and even to reconsider some of your choices. You might decide, for example, that a text you had not planned to use for your essay actually has some strong evidence that you'd like to include.

These questions can guide your discussion:

- What ideas did our nation's founders have to allow people with differing backgrounds, opinions, and interests to work together and form a union?
- In what ways are factions, or groups of people with competing interests, dangerous to a union? Are there any benefits to factions?
- The Preamble states the goal of "[forming] a more perfect Union." Is there any such thing as a perfect union? How have people tried to strike a balance between union and faction, or union and individualism?

Get Organized Organize your details and evidence in an outline.

- Decide what organizational pattern you will use for your essay. For example, you might discuss each text in a separate section, or you might devote each section to an idea and explore how all three texts treat that idea.
- Choose which textual evidence is the most relevant to your topic and your central ideas.
- Use your organizational pattern to sort your textual evidence into a logical order.
- Select an interesting quotation or detail to introduce your informative essay.
- List some ideas for your concluding section.

ACADEMIC VOCABULARY

As you write your informative essay, be sure to use these words.

contrary
founder
ideological
publication
revolution

> PRODUCE

Draft Your Report Write a draft of your essay, following your outline.

- Introduce your topic about union and individualism. Present your topic in such a way that your reader will want to continue reading. Remember that you must take an objective perspective on the topic; you are not making an argument or stating your opinion.
- Present your details, facts, quotations, and examples from the texts in logically ordered paragraphs.
- Use appropriate transitions to create cohesion between sections of your essay and to clarify relationships between your topic and the provided evidence.
- Write a concluding section that summarizes your central ideas. Make a closing statement that relates the topic to your audience.

***my*WriteSmart**

Write your rough draft in *my*WriteSmart. Focus on creating a clear structure with an introduction, a body, and a conclusion.

REVISE

Improve Your Draft

Revise your draft to make sure it is clear, coherent, and engaging. Use the chart on the following page to review the characteristics of an effective informative essay. Ask yourself these questions as you revise:

- Have I introduced my topic clearly? Does my introduction engage the reader?
- Have I presented relevant evidence from the texts to support the central ideas in my essay?
- Is my essay logically organized? Are transitions from section to section smooth and easy to follow? Do I need to clarify how the central ideas are connected to the evidence from the texts?
- Have I maintained an objective viewpoint throughout the essay, avoiding conveying my opinion about the topic?
- Have I used a formal style of English appropriate for an informative essay?
- Does my conclusion follow logically from the body and provide a satisfying ending?

my **WriteSmart**

Have your partner or a group of peers review your draft in *my*WriteSmart. Ask your reviewers to note places where you might include more effective text evidence.

PRESENT

Exchange Essays

When your final draft is completed, exchange essays with a partner. Read your partner's essay and provide feedback. Did your partner maintain an objective viewpoint throughout the essay? Be sure to point out aspects of the essay that are particularly strong, as well as areas that could be improved.

Publish Online

If your school has a website where you can post your writing, work with your classmates to publish your collection of essays online. First, review your own essay and look for places to add links to other online sources, such as the text of the Bill of Rights, that readers may find helpful. Then, as a group, create a front page that introduces the collection and invites readers to explore the individual essays. You might also consider setting up a blog to allow readers to share their views on the essays.

REVISE

IMPROVE YOUR DRAFT

As they revise, remind students to check that quotations have been integrated smoothly and correctly into their essays. Provide these tips for integrating quotations:

- Integrate quotations into sentences and enclose them in quotation marks. *Amendment VI states that "the accused shall enjoy the right to a speedy and public trial by an impartial jury."*
- Use three spaced periods (. . .), called ellipsis points, to mark omissions from the original quotation. *Amendment VI states that "the accused shall enjoy the right to . . . trial by an impartial jury."*
- Use brackets to mark additions to quotations. *Amendment VI states that "the accused shall enjoy the right to a speedy and public trial by an impartial [unbiased] jury."*

PRESENT

EXCHANGE ESSAYS

Provide students with other options for sharing their essays:

- Save your informative essay to be submitted as a writing sample with a college or job application.
- Adapt your essay into a multimedia presentation on the tension between preserving individual rights and forming a strong and long-lasting union that still enlivens U.S. politics.

PERFORMANCE TASK

LANGUAGE

Have students look at the chart and evaluate their level of performance in the Language category. Ask them to trade essays with a partner and take turns reading each essay aloud. Have partners discuss their use of tone and vivid language and note places for improvement. Students can then revise their essays with their partner's suggestions in mind.

	Ideas and Evidence	Organization	Language
ADVANCED	• The introduction is intriguing and informative; the controlling idea clearly identifies a compelling topic. • The topic is strongly developed with relevant facts, concrete details, interesting quotations, and examples from the texts. • The concluding section capably follows from and supports the ideas presented.	• The organization is effective and logical throughout the essay. • Transitions are well crafted and successfully connect related ideas.	• The writing reflects a formal style and an objective, knowledgeable tone. • Language is vivid and precise. • Sentence beginnings, lengths, and structures vary and have a rhythmic flow. • Spelling, capitalization, and punctuation are correct. If handwritten, the essay is legible. • Grammar and usage are correct.
COMPETENT	• The introduction could do more to attract the reader's curiosity; the controlling idea identifies a topic. • One or two key points could use additional support in the form of relevant facts, concrete details, quotations, and examples from the texts. • The concluding section mostly follows from and supports the ideas presented.	• The organization is confusing in a few places. • A few more transitions are needed to connect related ideas.	• The style is inconsistent in a few places, and the tone is subjective at times. • Vague language is used in a few places. • Sentence beginnings, lengths, and structures vary somewhat. • Some spelling, capitalization, and punctuation mistakes occur. If handwritten, the essay is mostly legible. • Some grammatical and usage errors are repeated in the essay.
LIMITED	• The introduction provides some information about a topic but does not include a controlling idea. • Most key points need additional support in the form of relevant facts, concrete details, quotations, and examples from the texts. • The concluding section is confusing and does not follow from the ideas presented.	• The organization is confusing in some places and often doesn't follow a pattern. • More transitions are needed throughout to connect related ideas.	• The style is too informal; the tone conveys subjectivity and a lack of understanding of the topic. • Vague, general language is used in many places. • Sentence structures barely vary, and some fragments or run-on sentences are present. • Spelling, capitalization, and punctuation are often incorrect but do not make reading the essay difficult. If handwritten, the essay may be partially illegible. • Grammar and usage are incorrect in many places, but the writer's ideas are still clear.
EMERGING	• The appropriate elements of an introduction are missing. • Facts, details, quotations, and examples from the texts are missing. • The essay lacks an identifiable concluding section.	• A logical organization is not used; information is presented randomly. • Transitions are not used, making the essay difficult to understand.	• The style and tone are inappropriate for the essay. • Language is too vague or general to convey the information. • Repetitive sentence structure, fragments, and run-on sentences make the writing monotonous and difficult to follow. • Spelling, capitalization, and punctuation are incorrect throughout. If handwritten, the essay may be partially or mostly illegible. • Many grammatical and usage errors change the meaning of the writer's ideas.

The Individual and Society

PLAN

CONNECTING WORD AND IMAGE

ASK STUDENTS to discuss how the collection opener image and the collection quotation work together to create a connection.

PERFORMANCE TASK PREVIEW

Point out to students that they will complete two performance tasks at the end of the collection. The performance tasks will require them to further analyze the selections in the collection and to synthesize ideas about these analyses. They will present their findings in a variety of products.

ACADEMIC VOCABULARY

► View It!

Professional Development Podcast:

Academic Vocabulary

Students can acquire facility with the academic vocabulary words through frequent, repeated exposure as they analyze and discuss the selections in the collection. Academic vocabulary can be used in the following instructional contexts. This will enable students to incorporate the academic vocabulary words into their working vocabulary.

- Collaborative Discussion at the end of each selection
- Analyzing the Text questions for each selection
- Selection-level Performance Task
- Vocabulary instruction (for Critical Vocabulary and/or for Vocabulary Strategy)
- Language and Style
- End-of-collection Performance Task for all selections in the collection

ASK STUDENTS to review the academic vocabulary word list for this collection. You may wish to pronounce each word aloud, so students hear the correct pronunciation. Then, discuss the definitions and the related forms for each word. Remind students that they will encounter these five academic vocabulary words throughout the collection.

The Individual and Society

In this collection, you will explore how writers in the early 19th century created a new "American" literature.

hmhfyi.com

COLLECTION

PERFORMANCE TASK Preview

At the end of this collection, you will have the opportunity to complete two tasks:

- Write a narrative about the individual's relationship with nature and society.
- Participate in a debate about the way many writers interpret the natural world.

ACADEMIC VOCABULARY

Study the words and their definitions in the chart below. You will use these words as you discuss and write about the texts in this collection.

Word	Definition	Related Forms
analogy (ə-năʹə-jē) *n.*	a comparison that finds a similarity between things that are dissimilar	analogous, analogist, analog
denote (dĭ-nōtʹ) *v.*	to mean something specific; to name	denotation, denotable, denotative
quote (kwōt) *v.*	to cite something word for word	quotation, quotation mark, quotable
topic (tŏpʹĭk) *n.*	the subject of a piece of writing or speech	topical, topic sentence
unique (yoō-nēkʹ) *adj.*	one of a kind; unable to be compared	uniqueness, uniquely

174

USING THE COLLECTION YOUR WAY

Use the following information, along with the charts on the following pages, to help you decide how you want to introduce the collection. Based on your teaching style, your students' interests, or your instructional goals, you may want to structure the collection in various ways. You may choose different entry points each time you teach the collection.

"I like to connect literature to history."

This essay describes one woman's struggles to define her identity based on the history of her family's experiences as Japanese immigrants in America.

Background The experiences of Kesaya E. Noda's family reflect those of many Japanese immigrants to the United States in the 20th century. After Japan attacked Pearl Harbor in 1941, over 110,000 Japanese residents in America were relocated to isolated internment camps for the duration of World War II. About 60 percent of them were American-born citizens. Noda's parents married after the war and moved to New Hampshire in 1957 for her father's teaching job at Dartmouth Medical School.

Growing Up Asian in America
Essay by Kesaya E. Noda

AS YOU READ Look for clues that reveal Noda's feelings about her family. Write down any questions that you generate during reading.

Sometimes when I was growing up, my identity seemed to hurtle toward me and paste itself right to my face. I felt that way, encountering the stereotypes of my race perpetuated by non-Japanese people (primarily white) who may or may not have had contact with other Japanese in America. "You don't like cheese, do you?" someone would ask. "I know your people don't like cheese." Sometimes questions came making allusions to history. That was another aspect of the identity. Events that had happened quite apart from the me who stood silent in that moment connected my face with an incomprehensible past. "Your parents were in California? Were they in those camps during the war?" And sometimes there were phrases or nicknames: "Lotus Blossom." I was sometimes addressed or referred to as racially Japanese, sometimes as Japanese American, and sometimes as an Asian woman. Confusions and distortions abounded.

How is one to know and define oneself? From the inside—within a context that is self defined, from a grounding in community and a connection with culture and history that are comfortably accepted? Or from the outside—in terms of messages received from the media

abound (ə-bound´) v. occur or exist in great number.

Growing Up Asian in America **187**

Henry David Thoreau (1817–1862) of Concord, Massachusetts, was a transcendentalist like his friend and mentor Ralph Waldo Emerson. After graduating from Harvard College and teaching school for a few years, Thoreau decided to become a nature poet. In 1845 he began his two-year experiment living in a cabin that he built in the woods near Walden Pond on property owned by Emerson. Walden (1854) is a collection of 18 essays based on his experiences. Thoreau's most famous essay, "Civil Disobedience" (1849), defends the right of an individual to follow his conscience rather than obey unjust laws.

from
Walden
Essay by Henry David Thoreau

AS YOU READ Note the observations Thoreau makes about modern life that still seem relevant today.

from Where I Lived, and What I Lived For

When first I took up my abode in the woods, that is, began to spend my nights as well as days there, which, by accident, was on Independence day, or the fourth of July, 1845, my house was not finished for winter, but was merely a defense against the rain, without plastering or chimney, the walls being of rough weather-stained boards, with wide chinks, which made it cool at night. The upright white hewn studs and freshly planed door and window casings gave it a clean and airy look, especially in the morning, when its timbers were saturated with dew, so that I fancied that by noon some sweet gum would exude from them. . . .

I was seated by the shore of a small pond, about a mile and a half south of the village of Concord and somewhat higher than it, in the midst of an extensive wood between that town and Lincoln, and about two miles south of that our only field known to fame, Concord Battle Ground; but I was so low in the woods that the opposite shore, half a mile off, like the rest, covered with wood, was my most distant horizon. For the first week, whenever I looked out on the pond it

Walden **207**

"I love teaching traditional literature."

In this collection of essays from the mid-19th century, Henry David Thoreau reflects on solitude, simplicity, and his experiences living in nature in a cabin in the woods.

Edgar Allan Poe (1809–1849) is considered one of literature's "most brilliant, but erratic stars." Poe explored such distinctive themes as madness, untimely death, and obsession. He was orphaned at an early age, and for most of his life he struggled to earn a living. The 1845 publication of his poem "The Raven" made Poe famous. This success, however, was soon marred by the death of his wife and his own illness. Although Poe's life was brief, his literary influence was great, especially on the development of the horror story and detective fiction.

The Pit and the Pendulum
Short Story by Edgar Allan Poe

AS YOU READ Notice sensory details that help create a mood of terror in the story.

Impia tortorum longos hic turba furores
Sanguinis innocui, non satiata, aluit.
Sospite nunc patria, fracto nunc funeris antro,
Mors ubi dira fuit vita salusque patent.[1]

[Quatrain composed for the gates of a market to be erected upon the site of the Jacobin[2] Club House at Paris.]

I was sick—sick unto death with that long agony; and when they at length unbound me, and I was permitted to sit, I felt that my senses were leaving me. The sentence—the dread sentence of death—was the last of distinct accentuation which reached my ears. After that, the sound of the inquisitorial voices seemed merged in one dreamy

[1] **Impia . . . patent:** *Latin:* Here the wicked crowd of tormentors, unsated, fed their long-time lusts for innocent blood. Now that our homeland is safe, now that the tomb is broken, life and health appear where once was dread death.
[2] **Jacobin** (jăk´ə-bĭn): a radical political group active in the French Revolution and later known for implementing the Reign of Terror.

The Pit and the Pendulum **249**

"I stress the importance of language and style."

Set during the Inquisition, this short story builds suspense and establishes a mood of terror through an imprisoned narrator who is faced with unknown surroundings and awaits the progress of a slow-paced pendulum.

COLLECTION 3 DIGITAL OVERVIEW

Collection 3 Lessons	Media	Teach and Practice	
Student Edition | eBook	▶ Video Links 🇭 HISTORY A&E	**Close Reading and Evidence Tracking**	
ANCHOR TEXT Poem by Walt Whitman from *Song of Myself*	🔊 **Audio** from *Song of Myself*	**Close Read Screencasts** • Modeled Discussion 1 (lines 10–13) • Modeled Discussion (lines 13–20) • Close Read application (lines 12–16)	**Strategies for Annotation** • Determine Themes
CLOSE READER Poems by Walt Whitman "I Hear America Singing" and "A Noiseless Patient Spider"	🔊 **Audio** "I Hear America Singing" and "A Noiseless Patient Spider"		
Essay by Kesaya E. Noda "Growing Up Asian in America"	🔊 **Audio** "Growing Up Asian in America"		**Strategies for Annotation** • Determine Author's Purpose • Patterns of Word Change
Poems by Emily Dickinson "The Soul selects her own Society" "Because I could not stop for Death" "Much Madness is divinest Sense" "Tell all the truth but tell it slant"	🔊 **Audio** "The Soul selects her own Society," "Because I could not stop for Death," "Much Madness is divinest Sense," "Tell all the truth but tell it slant"		**Strategies for Annotation** • Determine Theme
Essay by Henry David Thoreau from *Walden*	🔊 **Audio** from *Walden*		**Strategies for Annotation** • Determine Author's Purpose: Style • Vocabulary Strategy: Context Clues
CLOSE READER Essays by Ralph Waldo Emerson from "Self-Reliance" and "Nature"	🔊 **Audio** from *Walden* and "Nature"		
ANCHOR TEXT Argument by Joyce Carol Oates "Against Nature"	🔊 **Audio** "Against Nature"	**Close Read Screencasts** • Modeled Discussion 1 (6–14) • Modeled Discussion 2 (lines 194–203) • Close Read application (230–252)	**Strategies for Annotation** • Analyze and Evaluate Structure • Parts of Speech
CLOSE READER Essay by David Gessner "Spoiling Walden: Or, How I Learned to Stop Worrying and Love Cape Wind"	🔊 **Audio** "Spoiling Walden: Or, How I Learned to Stop Worrying and Love Cape Wind"		
Short Story by Nathaniel Hawthorne "The Minister's Black Veil"	🔊 **Audio** "The Minister's Black Veil"		**Strategies for Annotation** • Determine Themes: Romanticism • Nuances in Word Meaning
Short Story by Edgar Allan Poe "The Pit and the Pendulum"	🔊 **Audio** "The Pit and the Pendulum" ▶ **Video HISTORY®** *Surviving History: The Pendulum*		**Strategies for Annotation** • Vocabulary Strategies: Context Clues
Collection 3 Performance Tasks: **A** Write a Narrative **B** Debate an Issue	fyi hmhfyi.com **hmhfyi.com**	**Interactive Lessons** **A** Writing a Narrative **A** Using Textual Evidence	**B** Participating in Collaborative Discussions **B** Using Textual Evidence

		For Systematic Coverage of Writing and Speaking & Listening Standards	**Interactive Lessons** Conducting Research Evaluating Sources	**Lesson Assessments** Conducting Research Evaluating Sources

Assess		**Extend**	**Reteach**
Performance Task	**Online Assessment**	**Teacher eBook**	**Teacher eBook**
Speaking Activity: Oral Defense	Selection Test	**Analyze Point of View**	**Important Figures of Speech > Level Up Tutorial >** Figurative Language
Speaking Activity: Discussion	Selection Test	**Support an Argument**	**Determine Author's Purpose > Level Up Tutorial >** Scope and Treatment
Writing Activity: Analysis	Selection Test	**Author's Style > Interactive Whiteboard Lesson >** Forms in Poetry	**Determine Themes > Level Up Tutorial >** Universal and Recurring Themes
Writing Activity: Essay	Selection Test	**Analyze and Evaluate Structure > Interactive Whiteboard Lesson >** Text Structure and Meaning	**Determine Central Ideas > Level Up Tutorial >** Summarizing
Writing Activity: Analysis	Selection Test	**Write a Short Research Report**	**Analyze and Evaluate Structure > Level Up Tutorial >** Analyzing Arguments
Speaking Activity: Discussion Writing Activity: Analysis	Selection Test	**Moderate Discussions**	**Analyze Structure: Suspense and Ambiguity**
Speaking Activity: Discussion Writing Activity: Analysis	Selection Test	**Short Research Project > Interactive Whiteboard Lesson >** Conducting Research on the Web	**Write a Narrative**
A Write a Narrative **B** Debate an Issue	Collection Test		

Collection 3 Lessons	Key Learning Objective	Performance Task
ANCHOR TEXT **EXEMPLAR** **Poem by Walt Whitman** from *Song of Myself*, p. 177A	**The student will be able to...** determine themes in poetry.	Speaking Activity: Oral Defense
Essay by Kesaya E. Noda Lexile 900 **"Growing Up Asian in America," p. 187A**	**The student will be able to...** analyze ideas and events to discover an essay's organizational patterns and analyze content and style to determine and evaluate an author's purpose	Speaking Activity: Discussion
Poems by Emily Dickinson **"The Soul selects her own Society"** **EXEMPLAR** **"Because I could not stop for Death"** **"Much Madness is divinest Sense"** **"Tell all the truth but tell it slant," p. 199A**	**The student will be able to...** analyze language and determine themes, supporting interpretations with specific textual evidence	Writing Activity: Analysis
EXEMPLAR **Essay by Henry David Thoreau** Lexile 1250 from *Walden*, p. 207A	**The student will be able to...** determine the central ideas of the text.	Writing Activity: Essay
ANCHOR TEXT **Argument by Joyce Carol Oates** Lexile 1000 **"Against Nature," p. 221A**	**The student will be able to...** analyze how an author's choices concerning the structure of a text contribute to its meaning	Writing Activity: Analysis
Short Story by Nathaniel Hawthorne Lexile 1260 **"The Minister's Black Veil," p. 235A**	**The student will be able to...** determine theme and recognize and interpret symbols in literature	Speaking Activity: Discussion Writing Activity: Analysis
Short Story by Edgar Allan Poe Lexile 1020 **"The Pit and the Pendulum," p. 311A**	**The student will be able to...** analyze the impact of atmosphere and structure on dramatic tension and explore different approaches to dark Romanticism by comparing themes	Speaking Activity: Discussion Writing Activity: Analysis

Collection 3 Performance Tasks:
A Write a Narrative
B Debate an Issue

Vocabulary Strategy	Language and Style	Student Instructional Support	CLOSE READER Selection
	Parallel Structure	**Scaffolding for ELL Students:** 178, 182 **When Students Struggle:** 180, 183 **To Challenge Students:** 181	Poem by Walt Whitman "I Hear America Singing," p. 186b Poem by Walt Whitman "A Noiseless Patient Spider," p. 186b
Patterns of Word Change	Varying Sentence Structure	**Scaffolding for ELL Students:** 187, 191 **When Students Struggle:** 189, 192 **To Challenge Students:** 190, 194	
Affixes		**Scaffolding for ELL Students:** 199, 202 **When Students Struggle:** 201, 203 **To Challenge Students:** 206	
Context Clues	Rhetorical Questions	**Scaffolding for ELL Students:** 207, 212, 213 **When Students Struggle:** 209, 214 **To Challenge Students:** 210, 215	Essay by Ralph Waldo Emerson from "Self-Reliance," p. 220b Essay by Ralph Waldo Emerson from "Nature," p. 220b **Lexile 990**
Parts of Speech	Quotations	**Scaffolding for ELL Students:** 222 **When Students Struggle:** 224, 228 **To Challenge Students:** 226	Essay by David Gessner "Spoiling Walden: Or, How I Learned to Stop Worrying and Love Cape Wind," p. 233b **Lexile 1050**
Nuances in Word Meanings		**Scaffolding for ELL Students:** 235, 237, 240 **When Students Struggle:** 238, 242 **To Challenge Students:** 234, 244	
Using Context Clues	Semicolons	**Scaffolding for ELL Students:** 249, 253, 257, 258, 262 **When Students Struggle:** 251, 254, 255, 259, 261 **To Challenge Students:** 252, 260	

*my*SmartPlanner | Create lesson plans and access resources online.

A Distinctly American Voice

Collection 3 Historical Introduction

Why This Text?

Students often encounter literary and informational texts that assume that the reader has some knowledge of key historical events, facts, ideas, and issues. The historical introduction to Collection 3 presents information about the period from 1810 to 1850, when the experience of living in a newly established and expanding country inspired the writers working in this nation to create new literary movements and write about characters from new perspectives.

Key Learning Objective: The student will be able to analyze the selections in the collection in terms of a historical context.

COMMON CORE Common Core Standards

RL 10 Read and comprehend literature in the grades 11-CCR text complexity band.

RI 3 Analyze ideas or events and explain how individuals, ideas, or events interact and develop.

RI 4 Determine the meaning of words and phrases.

RI 7 Integrate and evaluate sources of information presented in different formats.

RI 10 Read and comprehend literary nonfiction in the grades 11-CCR text complexity band.

▲ Text Complexity Rubric

Quantitative Measures	Exploration and Settlement Lexile: N/A
Qualitative Measures	**Levels of Meaning/Purpose**  more than one purpose; implied, easily identified from context
	Structure more than one text structure
	Language Conventionality and Clarity increased unfamiliar, academic, or domain-specific words
	Knowledge Demands somewhat complex historical concepts
Reader/Task Considerations	Teacher determined Vary by individual reader and type of text

A Distinctly American Voice 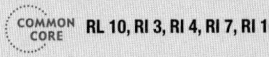 COMMON CORE RL 10, RI 3, RI 4, RI 7, RI 10

Tell students that this section establishes the historical context for the selections in this collection. It explains how both the size and the economy of the United States grew over the course of the first half of the 19th century. The section also addresses how living in a newly developing American culture influenced how American writers of this period wrote about the relationship between people and the world around them.

An Era of Growth and Change

While some European settlers saw the American wilderness as a dangerous and savage place that must be tamed for its own good, others thought of the New World as a real-life version of the promised land that should be improved by being cleared, cultivated, and properly tended using knowledge from the Old World. No less a figure than Thomas Jefferson subscribed to the philosophy of agrarianism, or the belief that the simple rural life of a farmer is superior to the more complicated urban life of business and industrialism. In the agrarian system of belief, farmers are celebrated for their self-reliance, devotion to hard work, and ability to tame the wilderness and make a living by cultivating it. As Americans spread west and settled more and more of the land, these qualities became essential parts of their conception of their national character.

Once the Industrial Revolution began to take hold in the United States, people moved beyond just turning raw nature into useful farms to replacing the wilderness entirely with cities and factories. The United States was becoming more prosperous and able to manufacture new products, but at what cost? Technology made it easier to settle and profit from previously wild land, but some American writers began to use their art to celebrate the ability of nature that has been untouched to transform those people who come into contact with it.

A Distinctly American Voice

COMMON CORE RL 10, RI 3, RI 4, RI 7, RI 10

In the first half of the 19th century, a distinctly American voice emerged as the United States reaffirmed its independence from Britain politically and economically. The country was expanding geographically, creating diversification in the ways that people worked and lived. Reflecting the optimism of a growing country, writers developed a national literature, speaking for the first time in their own unique voices rather than imitating European authors and styles.

AN ERA OF GROWTH AND CHANGE In 1812, simmering tensions between the United States and Great Britain erupted in a two-year war. Victory in the War of 1812 cemented the reality of American independence—it is sometimes referred to as the second war for American independence—and brought great changes to life in the United States. Because the war interrupted trade, Americans had to produce many of the goods they had imported in the past. This period marked the beginning of the Industrial Revolution in the United States, as the country shifted from its largely agrarian economy to become an industrial powerhouse. The growth of the factory system brought many people from farms into cities, where they worked long hours for low wages, often under harsh conditions. Writers of the period reacted to the negative effects of industrialization—the commercialism, hectic pace, and lack of conscience—by turning to nature and to the self for simplicity, truth, and beauty.

At the same time, following the Louisiana Purchase of 1803, the country experienced change of another kind as settlers moved farther and farther west. As European settlers moved into new territory to make money and gain land, Native Americans who had lived there for generations were displaced. The Indian Removal Act of 1830, for instance, required Native Americans in southeastern regions to relocate west of the Mississippi River. Indians who tried to remain in their homelands were often brutally pushed off their lands.

In the middle of the century, Americans embraced the idea of "manifest destiny"—a belief that the United States was destined to expand to the Pacific Ocean and into Mexican Territory. The United States' annexation of Texas from Mexico in 1845 set off the Mexican-American War (1846–1848). Through treaties and later land purchases from the Mexican government, the United States established the current borders of the 48 contiguous states.

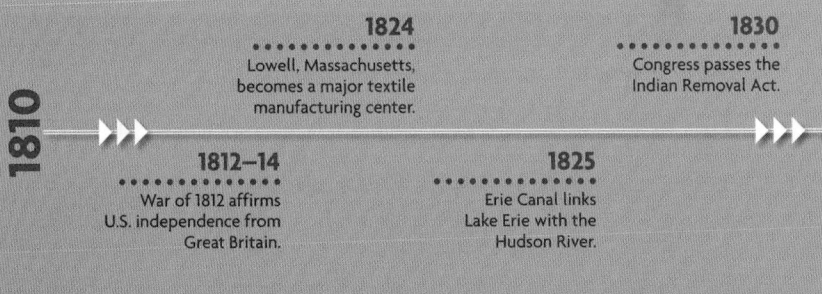

1824
Lowell, Massachusetts, becomes a major textile manufacturing center.

1830
Congress passes the Indian Removal Act.

1810

1812–14
War of 1812 affirms U.S. independence from Great Britain.

1825
Erie Canal links Lake Erie with the Hudson River.

A Distinctly American Voice **175**

SCAFFOLDING FOR ELL STUDENTS

Vocabulary: Figurative and Literal Language Even if students can define the meaning of a word, sometimes they may be confused when a writer uses a word in a figurative sense instead of a literal one. For example, in the first sentence of the second paragraph on page 175, the tensions are not literally "simmering" the way soup would simmer on a stovetop. The author is using the word *simmer* as part of a descriptive image to convey information about the nature of the coming conflict between the two countries.

ASK STUDENTS to work in small mixed-language ability groups to identify other words that are being used in a figurative sense, such as *cemented* on page 175, and to identify and explain how and why the author is using these words in this particular context.

The Individual and Imagination

Romantics rebelled against the Enlightenment's focus on the use of reason and the acceptance of the existence of objective truths that can be discovered through the use of such reason. They valued instead individual experience, particularly the emotions a person might feel while in contact with nature, as well as the power of the imagination to help a person find meaning in the world. Sometimes, in fact, Romantics believed that a person's experiences might go beyond what could be explained by logic and enter into the spiritual or supernatural realm.

One common feature of the American version of Romanticism is the presence of an individual hero who turns away from society to chart his or her own course in life. In *Walden*, Henry David Thoreau presents an edited version of the journals he kept while living on his own by Walden Pond. In Nathaniel Hawthorne's *The Scarlet Letter*, Hester Prynne chooses ultimately to live outside the boundaries of the town of Puritans who condemn her for having violated her society's moral code after she commits adultery and bears a daughter from that relationship. Walt Whitman's poem "Song of Myself" celebrates the beliefs, desires, and emotional responses of its first-person narrator, at times speaking of subjects such as sex so openly that many readers over time have been offended by his frankness.

THE INDIVIDUAL AND IMAGINATION American writers of this period were influenced by European Romanticism but soon adapted it to their own culture. The Romantics reacted to what had come before, including both the Enlightenment's emphasis on reason and also the strict doctrines of Puritanism. Romantics were inspired by nature and celebrated the individual human spirit, including the emotions and imagination. An early Romantic, Washington Irving was the first truly American writer who was recognized abroad. As a pioneer of the short story form, he influenced later writers such as Nathaniel Hawthorne.

Ralph Waldo Emerson, a New England writer, nurtured the pride that Americans took in their emerging culture. He led a group focused on transcendentalism—a philosophical and literary movement that emphasized living a simple life and celebrating the truth found in nature and in personal emotion and imagination. Emerson gave this European philosophy a uniquely American spin: he said that every individual is capable of discovering this higher truth on his or her own, through intuition. Unlike the Puritans, the transcendentalists believed that people were inherently good and should follow their own beliefs, however different these beliefs may be from the norm.

In 1842, Emerson called for the emergence of a poet worthy of the new America—a fresh voice with limitless passion and originality. Two poets who began writing in the middle of the century arguably met this challenge: Walt Whitman and Emily Dickinson. Although their lives outwardly were very dissimilar, both Whitman and Dickinson wrote poems that broke with the traditional conventions of poetic form and content. In this way they followed the transcendentalist ideals of individuals discovering the truth through intuition and following their own beliefs.

Not all American Romantics were optimistic or had faith in the innate goodness of humankind, however. Edgar Allan Poe, Nathaniel Hawthorne, and Herman Melville are what have been called "brooding" romantics or "anti-transcendentalists." Their stories are characterized by a probing of the inner life of their characters, and examination of the complex and often mysterious forces that motivate human behavior. These stories are romantic, however, in their emphasis on emotion, nature, the individual, and the unusual. (For more on the dark side of Romanticism, see the introduction titled "American Romanticism" later in this collection.)

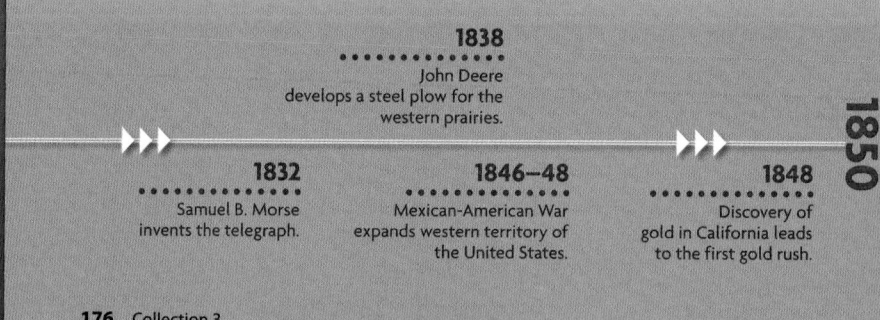

1838
John Deere develops a steel plow for the western prairies.

1832
Samuel B. Morse invents the telegraph.

1846–48
Mexican-American War expands western territory of the United States.

1848
Discovery of gold in California leads to the first gold rush.

1850

WHEN STUDENTS STRUGGLE...

Vocabulary Support: Some students may experience difficulty with understanding the meaning of the different movements discussed in this essay. Explain that *-ism* is a suffix that indicates that a word is a label for a particular school of thought.

ASK STUDENTS to work in pairs to identify and list the different systems of belief mentioned in this essay, such as *Romanticism*, *Puritanism*, and *transcendentalism*. Then have students use information from this essay and research done using outside resources to define each movement and its central characteristics.

Analyze Impact of Word Choice on Tone

COMMON CORE
RI 4

TEACH

Explain that even in a piece of nonfiction text like a historical background essay, the writer chooses his or her words carefully to create a specific tone. By examining a writer's word choices, the reader can identify what mood is created and identify and evaluate the author's purpose in writing different portions of the text. Is the author attempting to describe an event? Is the author trying to persuade the reader to feel a certain way about something that has happened? Carefully chosen words can help the author accomplish each of these purposes.

Have students reread the third paragraph on page 175. Ask them to identify the main topic of this paragraph—how Native Americans were displaced as European settlers moved onto western lands. Then draw students' attention to the final sentence and point out the effect the word *brutally* has on the meaning of the sentence. Read the sentence first leaving *brutally* out and then substituting another word in its place, such as *forcefully*, and have students discuss how the tone and meaning of the sentence changes each time. Finally, work with students to summarize what the use of the word *brutally* adds to the sentence and the point that the writer is making with this paragraph—that the removal of Native Americans from their lands was a violent and cruel act.

PRACTICE AND APPLY

Have pairs do a close reading of another section of this historical background essay, highlighting words that create a certain tone and mood and explaining how the writer's choice of words in these cases helps strengthen the point the writer is making.

Analyze Author's Order: Structure and Juxtaposition

COMMON CORE
RI 3

TEACH

Remind students that the main topic of this historical background essay is the growth of a distinctly American voice expressed through the literature created by the writers of this time period. Note that these writers possessed voices that were unique not just when compared to the voices of European writers, but also when compared to one another. Add that because the author of this essay is presenting information about such contrasting voices, the author uses a text structure that juxtaposes, or places side by side, the description of each writer's work.

Review with students the American writers discussed on page 176. Note how presenting them in order in this way makes it easier for the reader to compare and contrast the writers' work and to evaluate each writer's overall contribution to American literature.

Next, delve into a deeper evaluation of the techniques the author uses to create this juxtaposition. For example, point out the phrase *not all* in the first sentence of the last paragraph on page 176 and note how this phrase establishes that the writers who will be discussed next will be different in some ways from the ones discussed before. Then identify the specific ways that they are different from the Romantic writers covered previously (are not "optimistic" and do not have "faith in the innate goodness of humankind") and how they are the same (are still romantic "in their emphasis on emotion, nature, the individual, and the unusual").

CLOSE READING APPLICATION

Have students work independently to read and examine another piece of literary nonfiction in which the author uses juxtaposition to structure the text and present a series of examples for the reader to compare and contrast.

ANCHOR TEXT EXEMPLAR *from* **Song of Myself**

*my*SmartPlanner   Create lesson plans and access resources online.

Poem by Walt Whitman

Why This Text?

Walt Whitman's use of free verse in *Song of Myself* forever changed American poetry. His enthusiasm and self-celebration make Whitman a unique figure, one of a handful of writers who created a new American voice in literature.

▶ *View It!*

Professional Development Podcast:

Text-Dependent Analysis

Key Learning Objective: The student will be able to determine themes in poetry.

For additional practice:

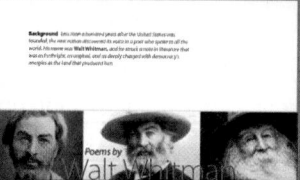

Close Reader selection
"I Hear America Singing" and "A Noiseless Patient Spider"
Poems by Walt Whitman

COMMON CORE   Common Core Standards

RL 1 Cite textual evidence.

RL 2 Determine themes of a text.

RL 3 Analyze author's choices regarding how to develop and relate elements.

RL 4 Determine figurative and connotative meanings; analyze the impact of specific word choices.

RL 5 Analyze how an author's choices concerning how to structure specific parts of a text contribute to its overall meaning as well as its aesthetic impact.

RL 6 Analyze a case in which grasping point of view requires distinguishing what is directly stated in a text from what is really meant.

SL 4 Present information findings and supporting evidence.

SL 6 Adapt speech to a variety of contexts and tasks.

L 3a Vary syntax for effect; apply an understanding of syntax.

L 5a Interpret figures of speech.

▲ Text Complexity Rubric

Quantitative Measures

from *Song of Myself*
Lexile: NA

Qualitative Measures

Levels of Meaning/Purpose
multiple levels of complex meaning

Structure
free verse, no particular patterns

Language Conventionality and Clarity
figurative, symbolic language

Knowledge Demands
complex or sophisticated themes

Reader/Task Considerations

Teacher determined
Vary by individual reader and type of text

CLOSE READ

Walt Whitman Have students read the information about the author. Tell them that Whitman was not born into a prosperous family. His father was a house builder, and the poet himself was one of nine children. Although he was a voracious reader, young Walt did not have much formal education. He began work as a printer at the age of twelve and at seventeen was teaching in a one-room schoolhouse in Long Island, New York. Later he became a full-time journalist.

Help students understand the revolutionary nature of Whitman's poetry. His free verse broke with all poetic conventions of the time, rejecting rhyme, regular rhythm, and conventional stanzas. Point out that *Leaves of Grass*, the collection of poems on which he worked for much of his life, was a highly controversial work. At one point Whitman had a job as a clerk in Washington D.C. with the Department of the Interior. When James Harlan, the Secretary of the Interior, found out that Whitman was the author of *Leaves of Grass*, he fired him. On the other hand, Whitman had a powerful supporter in Ralph Waldo Emerson, the influential New England poet and philosopher. Whitman's reputation among other writers became so great that they occasionally sent him "purses" of money to help him continue writing.

AS YOU READ Direct students to use the As You Read instructions to focus their reading. Remind students to write down any questions they generate during reading.

from
Song of Myself

Poem by Walt Whitman

1 I celebrate myself, and sing myself

6 A child said *What is the grass?*

from 33 I understand the large hearts of heroes

52 The spotted hawk swoops by

Walt Whitman (1819–1892) *in his younger years showed little indication of literary promise as he moved from one job to the next. Finally, in the 1850s, he devoted himself completely to writing his collection of poems entitled* Leaves of Grass. *He printed the volume in 1855. It soon ignited a flurry of reaction from readers because of its content and form, both of which were considered revolutionary. Many early readers scorned his efforts, but, undeterred, Whitman continued working on the book for the rest of his life—revising or rearranging existing poems and adding new poems. It has become recognized as the most influential book of poetry in American literature. Rejecting the rigidity of earlier poetic conventions, Whitman's poetry captures the vitality, optimism, and voice of America in a style that reflects the freedom and vastness of his beloved country.*

Background *"Song of Myself" is a long poem in fifty-two sections that appears in* Leaves of Grass.

AS YOU READ Consider why people in the 1800s found Whitman's poetry so "revolutionary." Write down any questions that you generate during reading.

Image Credits: (tl) ©Hakki Arslan/Shutterstock; (tc) ©Valenty/Shutterstock; (tr) ©Marish/Shutterstock; (b) ©Hulton Archive/Stringer/Getty Images

Song of Myself **177**

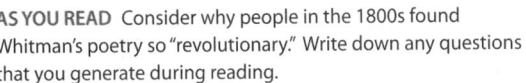

Close Read Screencasts 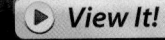 ▶ *View It!*

Modeled Discussions

Have students click the Close Read icons in their eBooks to access two screencasts in which readers discuss and annotate the following key passages:

- from "I celebrate myself, and sing myself " (lines 10–13)
- from "A child said *What is the grass?*" (lines 13–20)

As a class, view and discuss at least one of these videos. Then have students pair up to do an independent close read of an additional passage from "I understand the large hearts of heroes" (lines 12–16).

Analyze Structure: Free Verse (LINES 1–5)

 COMMON CORE RL 5

Remind students that Walt Whitman wrote in free verse, a form of poetry involving freedom from certain elements of traditional poetry, including rhyme, regular rhythm, and conventional stanzas.

A CITE TEXT EVIDENCE Have students read lines 1–5. Ask them to analyze Whitman's style, looking for evidence that he is writing in free verse. *(These lines are divided into two stanzas, but they are uneven in length, having 3 lines and 2 lines respectively. None of the end words in lines 1–5 rhyme. The lines are all uneven in length, varying from 7 syllables (line 4) to 16 syllables (line 5). When read aloud, there is no regular rhythm detectable in this passage.)*

Analyzing the Text  COMMON CORE RL 1, RL 2, RL 3, RL 5

Possible answers:

1. *The speaker stresses his own individuality by repeating the pronouns "I" and "myself." Nevertheless, he makes clear that he is part of a greater community, made up of the same atoms as everyone else.*

2. *In lines 6 and 7 the speaker talks about his connection to the greater world. His thoughts move from the small ("my tongue") to the vast ("this air"), from his parents to his parents' parents. The long lines reflect these expanding, interconnected relationships.*

3. *The last line suggests that the speaker will draw inspiration from the "original energy" of Nature rather than from conventional philosophy.*

---

1 I celebrate myself, and sing myself

A
> I celebrate myself, and sing myself,
> And what I assume you shall assume,[1]
> For every atom belonging to me as good belongs to you.
>
> I loaf and invite my soul,
> 5 I lean and loaf at my ease observing a spear of summer grass.
>
> My tongue, every atom of my blood, form'd from this soil, this air,
> Born here of parents born here from parents the same, and their
>   parents the same,
> I, now thirty-seven years old in perfect health begin,
> Hoping to cease not till death.
>
> 10 Creeds and schools in abeyance,[2]
> Retiring back a while sufficed at what they are, but never forgotten,
> I harbor for good or bad, I permit to speak at every hazard,
> Nature without check with original energy.

Close Read

---
[1] **assume:** Here, the word *assume* means "take on."
[2] **abeyance:** temporary suspension; inactivity.

Analyzing the Text COMMON CORE RL 1, RL 2, RL 3, RL 5

Cite Text Evidence   Support your responses with evidence.

1. **Interpret** Explain how lines 1–3 establish the speaker as an individual but also as a representative for all others.

2. **Analyze** How does Whitman's line length and word arrangement in lines 6 and 7 help readers to interpret their meaning?

3. **Infer** In the last stanza, the poet refers to schools of thought that he has considered in the past and has now left behind. What does the last line suggest about his poetic creed, or system of belief?

SCAFFOLDING FOR ELL STUDENTS

Understand Multiple-Meaning Words Read aloud lines 4 and 5, emphasizing the word *loaf*. Explain that *loaf* is here used as a verb and elicit from students what it means *(to do nothing)*. Invite students to come up with another meaning for *loaf* *(a quantity of bread)*. Point out that English has many words whose meaning depends on the context in which they appear.

ASK STUDENTS to read the final stanza (lines 10–13) and to find other words with multiple meanings *(schools, harbor, check)*. Invite pairs of students to compose sentences using these words to express the same meaning as they have in the poem within a different context.

6 A child said *What is the grass?*

A child said *What is the grass?* fetching it to me with full hands;
How could I answer the child? I do not know what it is any more than
 he.

I guess it must be the flag of my disposition, out of hopeful green stuff
 woven.

Or I guess it is the handkerchief of the Lord,
5 A scented gift and remembrancer designedly dropt,
Bearing the owner's name someway in the corners, that we may see
 and remark, and say *Whose?*

Or I guess the grass is itself a child, the produced babe of the
 vegetation.

Or I guess it is a uniform hieroglyphic,[1]
And it means, Sprouting alike in broad zones and narrow zones,
10 Growing among black folks as among white,
Kanuck, Tuckahoe, Congressman, Cuff,[2] I give them the same,
 I receive them the same.

And now it seems to me the beautiful uncut hair of graves.

Tenderly will I use you curling grass,
It may be you transpire from the breasts of young men,
15 It may be if I had known them I would have loved them,
It may be you are from old people, or from offspring taken soon out of
 their mothers' laps,
And here you are the mothers' laps.

The grass is very dark to be from the white heads of old mothers,
Darker than the colorless beards of old men,
20 Dark to come from under the faint red roofs of mouths.

O I perceive after all so many uttering tongues,
And I perceive they do not come from the roofs of mouths for nothing.

I wish I could translate the hints about the dead young men and
 women,

---

[1] **hieroglyphic:** picture symbol used in a writing system to represent sounds or words.
[2] **Kanuck, Tuckahoe, . . .Cuff:** *Kanuck, Tuckahoe,* and *Cuff* are slang terms, now considered offensive, for a French Canadian, an inhabitant of the Virginia lowlands, and an African American, respectively.

Song of Myself **179**

APPLYING ACADEMIC VOCABULARY

| analogy | denote |

As you discuss these excerpts from *Song of Myself*, incorporate the following Collection 3 academic vocabulary words: *analogy* and *denote*. Encourage students to analyze Whitman's frequent use of **analogies** in the form of figures of speech. Help students make a distinction between the **denotation** and connotation of Whitman's words.

CLOSE READ

Determine Themes
COMMON CORE RL 2, L 5a
(LINES 1–11)

Remind students that poets may use several techniques to convey their principal **themes,** or underlying messages. Point out that in *Song of Myself*, Walt Whitman often communicates his ideas by using **figures of speech** that compare unlike things. Remind students that **similes** compare unlike things using the words *like* or *as*, while **metaphors** do not use these words.

B CITE TEXT EVIDENCE Have students read lines 1–11. Ask them to analyze how Walt Whitman uses figurative language in this passage. What figures of speech does he employ and how do they contribute to his theme? *(He uses four metaphors, comparing the grass to "the flag of my disposition" in line 3, God's handkerchief in line 4, a child in line 7, and a "uniform hieroglyphic" in line 8. The effect is to suggest that grass is everywhere, representing the personal, the spiritual, and the universal. This helps develop Whitman's theme of the interconnectedness of life.)*

Analyze Structure: Free Verse (LINES 13–20)
COMMON CORE RL 5

Point out that although free verse does not have a regular meter, it often employs other devices, such as **repetition**, to create a rhythmic effect.

C CITE TEXT EVIDENCE Have students find evidence of repetition in lines 13–20. What is the effect of this device? *(Whitman repeats the phrase "It may be" three times in lines 14–16. He repeats the phrase "mothers' laps" in lines 16 and 17. In lines 18–20 he repeats the words dark and darker. The effect of this repetition is to create a rhythmic, pulsing chant reminiscent of a religious ceremony and emphasizing Whitman's theme of the universality of human experience.)*

And the hints about old men and mothers, and the offspring taken
    soon out of their laps.

25 What do you think has become of the young and old men?
And what do you think has become of the women and children?

They are alive and well somewhere,
The smallest sprout shows there is really no death,
And if ever there was it led forward life, and does not wait at the end to
    arrest it,
30 And ceas'd the moment life appear'd.

All goes onward and outward, nothing collapses,
And to die is different from what any one supposed, and luckier.

Analyzing the Text

> **Cite Text Evidence**   Support your responses with evidence.

1. **Analyze** How does the repetition of the phrase "Or I guess" in lines 4–8 contribute to the sound of this section? What is the relationship between the repeated elements?

2. **Analyze** Why does the poet choose to present the details in lines 23–26 in the form of a list or catalogue? How does this technique add to the impact of the conclusion the speaker reaches in lines 27–32?

3. **Interpret** What deeper meaning, or **symbolism,** does the grass have in this section?

Determine Themes

(LINES 25–32)

Point out that while poets may often communicate their themes indirectly, by figurative language or other means, they sometimes express their ideas directly.

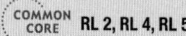 **CITE TEXT EVIDENCE** Have students read lines 25–32. Ask them to find statements that express Whitman's thoughts directly. How do these ideas relate to each other? *(Line 28; "The smallest sprout shows there is really no death." Line 31: "All goes onward and outward, nothing collapses." Both of these passages directly express Whitman's idea that all life is perpetually renewing itself and continuing to expand.)*

Analyzing the Text

Possible answers:

1. *The repeated phrase "Or I guess" in lines 4–8 creates a chanting, prayer-like effect, emphasizing the wonder the speaker feels in observing the grass. Each repeated element is a figure of speech, comparing the grass to a handkerchief, a child, and a hieroglyphic.*

2. *In listing the young men and women, the old men, the mothers, and the babies, Whitman emphasizes that he is talking about all human life. When he concludes that "They are alive and well somewhere" (line 27), he underscores his idea that "nothing collapses" (line 31). Everything is absorbed back into the earth to become part of life.*

3. *To Whitman, grass is the unifying symbol of life. He comes to this conclusion by pointing out that the grass is everywhere (lines 9–11), growing out of the graves of young and old, men and women (lines 14–19). Finally he sees "the smallest sprout" of grass as an indication that "there is really no death" (line 28).*

WHEN STUDENTS STRUGGLE...

Read aloud the first two lines of the poem. Point out that the entire poem after these opening lines is an answer to the child's question: "What is the grass?" Lead students to understand Whitman's answer by encouraging them to summarize key passages.

ASK STUDENTS to read the following passages. Have them summarize how each passage helps answer the child's question.

- lines 8–11 *(Grass grows everywhere, among all people.)*
- lines 12–17 *(Grass grows from the graves of all the dead.)*
- lines 27–32 *(Grass continues to grow, proving that life is more powerful than death.)*

from 33 I understand the large hearts of heroes

I understand the large hearts of heroes,
The courage of present times and all times,
How the skipper saw the crowded and rudderless wreck of the
    steam-ship, and Death chasing it up and down the storm,
How he knuckled tight and gave not back an inch, and was faithful
    of days and faithful of nights,

5 And chalk'd in large letters on a board, *Be of good cheer,*
    we will not desert you;
How he follow'd with them and tack'd with them three days and
    would not give it up,
How he saved the drifting company at last,
How the lank loose-gown'd women look'd when boated from the
    side of their prepared graves,
How the silent old-faced infants and the lifted sick, and the sharp-
    lipp'd unshaved men;
10 All this I swallow, it tastes good, I like it well, it becomes mine,
I am the man, I suffer'd, I was there.

The disdain and calmness of martyrs,
The mother of old, condemn'd for a witch, burnt with dry wood,
    her children gazing on,
The hounded slave that flags in the race, leans by the fence,
    blowing, cover'd with sweat,
15 The twinges that sting like needles his legs and neck, the
    murderous buckshot and the bullets,
All these I feel or am.

I am the hounded slave, I wince at the bite of the dogs,
Hell and despair are upon me, crack and again crack the
    marksmen,
I clutch the rails of the fence, my gore dribs, thinn'd with the ooze
    of my skin,
20 I fall on the weeds and stones,
The riders spur their unwilling horses, haul close,
Taunt my dizzy ears and beat me violently over the head with
    whip-stocks.

Agonies are one of my changes of garments,
I do not ask the wounded person how he feels, I myself become the
    wounded person,
25 My hurts turn livid upon me as I lean on a cane and observe.

TO CHALLENGE STUDENTS...

Research the Poet's Attitudes Tell students that although Whitman identifies with the hounded slave in this poem, his attitude toward slavery was complex and inconsistent.

ASK STUDENTS to conduct Internet research on Walt Whitman's attitude toward slavery and take notes about their findings. Then have small groups share their findings and discuss why Whitman might have taken the positions that he did.

CLOSE READ

Analyze Structure: Free Verse (LINES 1–11)

COMMON CORE RL 5

Help students analyze Whitman's use of repetition in the free-verse form.

E **ASK STUDENTS** to read lines 1–11. Why might Whitman have begun six of the first ten lines with the word *How*? *(Whitman is drawing out his description of the steamship disaster to emphasize the difficulty and length of the task and the resolution of the heroic captain.)* Ask students how this use of repetition is particularly suited to free verse. *(The free-verse form allows the poet to expand on the details without the constraints of rhythm, rhyme, or regular stanzas.)*

Determine Themes
(LINES 14–22)

COMMON CORE RL 2, RL 3

Point out that in ordinary speech the word *image* is often used exclusively in a visual sense. Remind students that in literature, **imagery** is language that extends to all the senses: sight, hearing, touch, smell, and even taste. Explain that Walt Whitman often used vivid imagery to develop his themes.

F **CITE TEXT EVIDENCE** Have students read lines 14–22. Ask them to analyze the choice of images in this passage. To what senses does the imagery most appeal? Have students support their answers with evidence from the passage. *(Much of the imagery appeals to the senses of touch and hearing. Touch is invoked in the sting of buckshot, the bites of dogs, the dribble of blood and sweat, and the violent beating. Hearing is invoked in his panting breath, the crack of gunfire, and the taunting of the riders.)* Ask students why Whitman might have relied more upon touch and hearing in this instance than upon visual imagery. *(The exhausted slave is beyond taking in visual cues. He can only feel and hear.)* Ask students how they feel this vivid description furthers Whitman's purpose. *(By creating such a realistic sensory image, Whitman is establishing his empathy with the slave and confirming his initial statement in line 1: "I understand the large hearts of heroes.")*

Analyze Structure: Free Verse (LINES 39–47)  COMMON CORE RL 5

Point out that free verse lends itself to **cataloguing,** the listing of things, people, events, or attributes. Explain that Walt Whitman frequently used cataloguing as a literary technique.

G **ASK STUDENTS** to read lines 39–47. What effect is Whitman attempting to create in this passage? *(He is speaking in the persona of an artilleryman in battle, giving a first-hand account of the bombardment of his fort. The passage attempts to recreate the confusion, violence, and horror of battle.)* Ask students to analyze how cataloguing helps achieve this effect. *(Line 43 catalogues the constant noises of battle: "The cries, curses, roar, the plaudits for well-aim'd shots." Line 46 describes the falling of a grenade followed by a devastating explosion which Whitman dramatizes in line 47 by cataloguing the chaos: "The whizz of limbs, heads, stone, wood, iron, high in the air.")*

Analyzing the Text  COMMON CORE RL 4, RL 5

Possible answers:

1. *The phrases "crowded and rudderless wreck" (line 3), "how he knuckled tight," (line 4), "the lank loose-gown'd women" (line 8), and "the sharp-lipped unshaved men" (line 9) help convey a mood of tension. Whitman opens the poem with a dramatic image of heroism to support his opening line: "I understand the large hearts of heroes."*

2. *Lines 26–34 are full of sensory details: the speaker's broken body (line 26), the debris of the fallen building (line 27), the shouts of the rescuers (line 28), the click of their shovels (line 29), the speaker's red shirt (line 31), the silence (line 31), the beautiful faces and bared heads (line 33), and the fading torches (line 34). Whitman intends these intense images to help readers identify with the fireman's experience.*

52 The spotted hawk swoops by

The spotted hawk swoops by and accuses me, he complains
    of my gab and my loitering.

I too am not a bit tamed, I too am untranslatable,
I sound my barbaric yawp[1] over the roofs of the world.

The last scud[2] of day holds back for me,
5 It flings my likeness after the rest and true as any on the shadow'd
    wilds,
It coaxes me to the vapor and the dusk.

I depart as air, I shake my white locks at the runaway sun,
I effuse[3] my flesh in eddies,[4] and drift it in lacy jags.

I bequeath myself to the dirt to grow from the grass I love,
10 If you want me again look for me under your boot-soles.

You will hardly know who I am or what I mean,
But I shall be good health to you nevertheless,
And filter and fiber your blood.

Failing to fetch me at first keep encouraged,
15 Missing me one place search another,
I stop somewhere waiting for you.

---

[1] **yawp:** a loud, harsh cry.
[2] **scud:** windblown mist and low clouds.
[3] **effuse:** spread out.
[4] **eddies:** small whirlwinds.

Analyzing the Text COMMON CORE RL 4, RL 5

Cite Text Evidence Support your responses with evidence.

1. **Analyze** Why does Whitman use the word "untranslatable" to describe the speaker? What does "barbaric yawp" suggest about the speaker's message to the world?

2. **Analyze** Explain how Whitman's word choice and line arrangement in lines 4–8 create a feeling of vitality and motion in this section.

COLLABORATIVE DISCUSSION How is Whitman's poetry a departure from the style and subjects of other poems you have read? With a partner, discuss what makes Whitman's work unique. Cite specific textual evidence from "Song of Myself" to support your ideas.

SCAFFOLDING FOR ELL STUDENTS

Understand Inverted Word Order Remind students that the normal order of an English sentence is subject-verb-object. On the board, write this clause from line 10: "All this I swallow." Point out that here the object *(this)* comes before the subject *(I)* and the verb *(swallow)*. Rewrite the sentence as "I swallow all this."

ASK STUDENTS to rewrite these clauses in normal order. "Heat and smoke I inspired" (line 28) and "Again gurgles the mouth of my dying general" (line 48). *(I inspired heat and smoke. The mouth of my dying general gurgles again.)*

52 The spotted hawk swoops by

The spotted hawk swoops by and accuses me, he complains
    of my gab and my loitering.

I too am not a bit tamed, I too am untranslatable,
I sound my barbaric yawp[1] over the roofs of the world.

The last scud[2] of day holds back for me,
5 It flings my likeness after the rest and true as any on the shadow'd
    wilds,
It coaxes me to the vapor and the dusk.

I depart as air, I shake my white locks at the runaway sun,
I effuse[3] my flesh in eddies,[4] and drift it in lacy jags.

I bequeath myself to the dirt to grow from the grass I love,
10 If you want me again look for me under your boot-soles.

You will hardly know who I am or what I mean,
But I shall be good health to you nevertheless,
And filter and fiber your blood.

Failing to fetch me at first keep encouraged,
15 Missing me one place search another,
I stop somewhere waiting for you.

---

[1] **yawp:** a loud, harsh cry.
[2] **scud:** windblown mist and low clouds.
[3] **effuse:** spread out.
[4] **eddies:** small whirlwinds.

Analyzing the Text

COMMON CORE RL 4, RL 5

Cite Text Evidence Support your responses with evidence.

1. **Analyze** Why does Whitman use the word "untranslatable" to describe the speaker? What does "barbaric yawp" suggest about the speaker's message to the world?

2. **Analyze** Explain how Whitman's word choice and line arrangement in lines 4–8 create a feeling of vitality and motion in this section.

COLLABORATIVE DISCUSSION How is Whitman's poetry a departure from the style and subjects of other poems you have read? With a partner, discuss what makes Whitman's work unique. Cite specific textual evidence from "Song of Myself" to support your ideas.

TEACH

CLOSE READ

Determine Themes
COMMON CORE RL 2

(LINES 1–3)

Remind students that symbols often help convey a poem's themes. A **symbol** is a person, place, or object that takes on a meaning beyond its conventional one.

 CITE TEXT EVIDENCE Have students read lines 1–3. What might the hawk symbolize? Have students cite textual evidence in their responses. *(The hawk stands for the free spirit of the natural world. In line 2 the speaker refers to the bird as untamed and "untranslatable," like himself.)* Ask students how the speaker develops this symbol. *(He becomes like a hawk himself, sounding his "barbaric yawp over the roofs of the world.")*

Analyzing the Text
COMMON CORE RL 4, RL 5

Possible answers:

1. *By describing him as "untranslatable," Whitman suggests that the speaker—like the hawk—cannot be entirely understood. His "barbaric yawp" is the equivalent of the hawk's call, the wild cry of a free human being in a free world.*

2. *Vivid verbs like "flings," "coaxes," "shake," "effuse" and "drift" give the passage a sense of motion. Surprising phrases like "last scud," shadow'd wilds," "runaway sun," and "lacy jags" contribute to its feeling of vitality. In the first stanza (lines 4–6) the speaker prepares for flight. In the second stanza (lines 7–8) he has launched himself into the air.*

COLLABORATIVE DISCUSSION Have partners create a chart on which they list aspects of Whitman's poetry that they find striking or unusual. Suggest that they record their observations under headings such as *Word Choice, Line Length, Stanzas, Surprising Imagery, Rhythm, Themes,* and *Other.* Encourage partners to share their charts with other pairs.

ASK STUDENTS to share any questions they generated in the course of reading and discussing the selection.

WHEN STUDENTS STRUGGLE...

Help students improve their oral proficiency by having them practice reading a passage from "The spotted hawk swoops by." Direct students' attention to lines 9–16 and have them follow the text as you model reading the passage.

ASK STUDENTS to form pairs and take turns reading lines 9–16 to each other. Encourage them to read with expression, changing their intonation where necessary, emphasizing key words, and observing punctuation. Invite pairs to read the passage for the class. Discuss with students how fluent, expressive reading helped them in their understanding.

TEACH

CLOSE READ

Analyze Structure: Free Verse
COMMON CORE RL 5

Help students understand the shock with which Whitman's verse struck the American public in the mid-nineteenth century. Point out that conventional poetry of the day consisted of neat stanzas with a regular rhythm and rhyme scheme. Not only did Whitman ignore these conventions, he exaggerated his rebelliousness by using techniques such as cataloguing and repetition. These devices contributed to Whitman's style—long straggling lines, verbose descriptions, startling images, and strange detours in thought. Explain that free verse is widely used by American poets today. Each poet uses it to express his or her style. In fact, much contemporary free verse is concise, exact, and brief—just the opposite of Whitman's.

Determine Themes
COMMON CORE RL 2, L 5a

Review with students the elements in the chart. Explain that an author will generally use a combination of these devices to communicate his or her message. Have students turn to "I understand the large hearts of heroes" on page 181. Point out that this poem begins with a direct statement, which summarizes Whitman's theme. The remainder of the work consists of searing physical images, in which the speaker takes on a number of roles—the captain of a stricken ship, a tortured slave, a dying fireman, a soldier in battle—to support the initial statement.

Analyze Structure: Free Verse
COMMON CORE RL 5

Whitman's poetry burst upon the public, startling readers with its use of **free verse.** Free verse is poetry that does not contain regular patterns of rhyme or meter. Because free verse flows more naturally than strictly rhymed, metrical lines, it sounds more like everyday speech. It also gives greater emphasis to some poetic devices that can be used to impose rhythm, heighten emotion, and convey meaning:

- **cataloguing:** frequent lists of people, things, and attributes. Cataloguing is seen in this line from the excerpt from section 33: "The whizz of limbs, heads, stone, wood, iron, high in the air."
- **repetition:** repeated words or phrases. Repetition is seen in lines 14–16 of number 6: "It may be you transpire . . . /It may be if I had known . . . /It may be you are . . .'"

Whitman's use of free verse and its accompanying components of cataloguing and repetition help him to achieve exactly the effects he desired.

Determine Themes
COMMON CORE RL 2, L 5a

The **theme** or themes of a poem are the underlying message or messages that a poet wants to convey. A poet relies on the words themselves and also poetic devices and form to reveal meaning to the reader.

Through these selections from "Song of Myself," Whitman communicates several themes, using elements such as the ones described in the chart:

Elements	How They Reveal Themes
free verse	Look for words that are emphasized by the poet's manipulation of lines. For example, *gab* and *loitering* in line 1 of section 52 stand out.
imagery	Think about the types of **images** created by sensory language and why the poet wants readers to "see" these pictures. For example, section 33 relies heavily on imagery: "I clutch the rails of the fence, my gore dribs . . .'"
figures of speech	Comparisons in the form of **similes** and **metaphors** tell readers how the poet wants them to view certain ideas. In section 6, the grass is compared to "the handkerchief of the Lord."
symbols	A person, place, or thing that has a meaning beyond itself is often central to the poem's meaning. For example, in section 52, the hawk might symbolize all that is wild and free in nature.
direct statements	Sometimes the poet expresses ideas directly as in this line from section 1: "Nature without check with original energy."

Strategies for Annotation 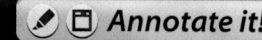 *Annotate it!*

Determine Themes
COMMON CORE RL 2

Share these strategies for guided or independent analysis:
- Highlight in blue any figures of speech.
- Highlight imagery in green.
- On a note, record how these elements work together to convey the poet's theme.

> Agonies are one of my changes of garments,
>
> I do not ask the wounded person how he feels,
>
> I myself become the wounded person,
>
> My hurts turn livid upon me as I lean on a cane and observe.

A comparison of agonies to clothes emphasizes that one can "put on" the experience of any other human...

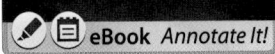
Analyzing the Text

COMMON CORE RL 1, RL 2, RL 4, RL 5, SL 4, SL 6

Cite Text Evidence   Support your responses with evidence from the selections.

1. **Analyze** "I celebrate myself . . ." is the first section of Whitman's poem "Song of Myself." In what ways does "I celebrate myself . . ." serve as an appropriate introduction to the themes and poetic vision described in these excerpts?

2. **Analyze** "The spotted hawk swoops by" completes Whitman's "Song of Myself." What do lines 7–16 suggest about the theme of Whitman's long, multi-part poem? How is section 52 a fitting conclusion to the larger work?

3. **Interpret** Compare the themes brought out by "A child said: *What is the grass?*" and "The spotted hawk swoops by." What insight do they both offer?

4. **Compare** How do "I celebrate myself . . ." and "I understand the large hearts . . ." communicate Whitman's vision of a bond that unites all humanity?

5. **Analyze** Whitman's poetic voice has been described as democratic, inclusive, and encompassing. How is this voice especially evident in the **metaphor** in lines 8–12 of "A child said . . ." and lines 14–25 of "I understand the large hearts . . ."?

6. **Analyze** Think of Whitman's topics and the ideas he expresses in his poetry. Why is free verse the best vehicle for his poetry? Explain.

7. **Cite Evidence** In his preface to *Leaves of Grass*, Whitman describes the American poet: "His spirit responds to his country's spirit . . . he incarnates its geography and natural life . . . For such the expression of the American poet is to be transcendant and new . . . He is the equalizer of his age and land . . ." How well does Whitman live up to his own description? Bring in specific examples from "Song of Myself" to support your ideas.

PERFORMANCE TASK

Speaking Activity: Oral Defense   Whitman has been accused of being an "egotist," or overly focused on himself, by some readers of his poetry. Use your reading of the selections from "Song of Myself" to defend him against this charge.

- Prepare speaking notes in which you quote liberally from "Song of Myself" in support of your claim.

- Include opposing claims and counterarguments.

- Rehearse your speech in small groups. Have classmates share feedback on both speaking style and content.

- Present your defense to the class. Have class members evaluate the effectiveness of your argument.

Song of Myself   **185**

PRACTICE & APPLY

Analyzing the Text

COMMON CORE RL 1, RL 2, RL 4, RL 5, SL 4, SL 6

Possible answers:

1. *The speaker of "I celebrate myself . . ." proclaims his identity with all of humanity and the natural world. The subsequent poems pursue this theme, with the speaker celebrating the universality of life and human experience.*

2. *In lines 7–16 of "The spotted hawk swoops by," the speaker describes himself "effusing" into the air and earth, becoming part of the natural world. This idea is in keeping with themes expressed in earlier poems proclaiming the unity of life.*

3. *Both poems assert that life continues unimpeded by death. In "A child said What is the grass?" the speaker concludes that "there is really no death." In "The spotted hawk swoops by" the speaker claims that even in death "I stop somewhere waiting for you."*

4. *In "I celebrate myself…" the speaker announces that "every atom" within him belongs to everyone else. He expands on this theme in "I understand the large hearts of heroes" by assuming the identities of people who are suffering.*

5. *The metaphor in lines 8–12 speaks of grass as a "uniform hieroglyphic," growing among all people. In lines 14–25 the speaker assumes the suffering of a slave. Both passages reflect Whitman's theme of inclusiveness.*

6. *Whitman seeks to be a part of nature, to encompass all of human experience. Free verse allows him to expand on this vast topic, to indicate in the structure of his poetry the variety and complexity of life.*

7. *In these selections from "Song of Myself," Whitman fits his own definition of the American poet. He writes vividly and explicitly about "his country's spirit" in "I understand the large hearts of heroes." He takes on the role of "equalizer" in "A child said What is the grass?" claiming that the grass represents all the living and the dead. He becomes "transcendent" in "The spotted hawk swoops by" when his spirit effuses into the earth and the air.*

Assign this performance task.    *my* WriteSmart

PERFORMANCE TASK

COMMON CORE SL 4, SL 6

Speaking Activity: Oral Defense   Help students prepare their defenses of Whitman by making sure that they thoroughly understand the accusation of egotism. Invite volunteers to orally support the claim that Whitman's poetry reflects his egotism. Challenge other students to refute this claim. Have students take notes on this initial debate, using these observations to strengthen their oral defenses.

PRACTICE & APPLY

Language and Style: Parallel Structure

Review the examples in the chart. Ask students to identify the elements in each example that are parallel.

- words: *Whitman's poetry, Melville's novels*
- phrases: *with nature, with himself*
- clauses: *I went…, I went…*

Point out that parallelism is closely related to repetition, one of Whitman's favorite literary techniques. Read to students the following two lines, telling them they are an altered version of Whitman's words:

What do you think has become of the young and old men?

And what might have happened to the women and children?

Ask students to revise the second line so that it is strictly parallel. Have them check their answers by referring to page 180, lines 25–26. *(And what do you think has become of the women and children?)*

Answers:

1. *The speaker in the poem describes himself as being untamed, untranslatable, and uncivilized.*

2. *With one hand she gives a gift; with both hands she takes one away.*

3. *I expect that you will finish your paper on Whitman soon and that I will enjoy reading it.*

4. *The content is revolutionary; the form is eccentric.*

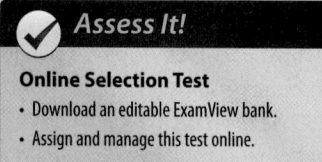

✓ Assess It!

Online Selection Test
- Download an editable ExamView bank.
- Assign and manage this test online.

Language and Style: Parallel Structure

Parallel structure is a very important element in Whitman's poetry. Parallelism—another name for this type of structure—is the use of similar grammatical constructions to express ideas that are closely connected. Whitman uses this technique frequently in his free verse to create a distinct rhythm. Parallel structure can also add emotion to a text through repetition or can emphasize phrases or ideas that are important to an author.

Read these lines from "I celebrate myself and sing myself":

> I loaf and invite my soul,
> I lean and loaf at my ease observing a spear of summer grass.

Notice that each line begins with the pronoun "I" and two verbs connected by the conjunction "and." In saying these lines aloud, the reader has to linger over the first four words in each line, reinforcing with this leisurely rhythm the meaning of the words themselves. Whitman could have avoided the use of parallel structure, writing the lines this way:

> I loaf and invite my soul,
> Observing a spear of summer grass at my ease, leaning and loafing.

The removal of parallel structure changes the rhythm. Instead of the lines sounding like someone lazily reflecting on his or her actions, smoothly moving from the first to the second line, the rhythm is forced and less like natural speech.

This chart identifies the elements of sentences that may be used in a parallel construction:

Parallel Structure	
Elements	**Example**
words	He liked Whitman's poetry but not Melville's novels.
phrases	The speaker felt at one with nature and with himself.
clauses	I went to the library to study; I went for the quiet setting.

Practice and Apply Each of these sentences is an example of faulty parallel structure. Rewrite the sentences in a way that correctly uses parallel structure.

1. The speaker in the poem describes himself as being untamed, unable to be translated, and not very civilized.

2. With one hand she gives a gift and then she is taking one away with both hands.

3. I expect that you will finish your paper on Whitman soon and to enjoy reading it.

4. The content is revolutionary; the form has many eccentric features.

Analyze Point of View

COMMON CORE

RL 6

EXTEND

Explain that all literature is written from some **point of view**—the speaker or narrator's ideas and feelings about the subject. In analyzing Whitman's poetry, it is particularly important to understand point of view because the personality of Whitman's speaker influences his vision of the world. Point out that Whitman's larger-than-life speaker often employs **hyperbole**—exaggerated language in which the writer makes a point by saying more than he or she means. Help students understand Whitman's point of view by analyzing the following passage with them.

- Have students read lines 1–11 of "I understand the large hearts of heroes" on page 181. Point out that the opening two lines are a literal and believable statement, while line 11 is an example of hyperbole. Discuss with students how the use of hyperbole influences the point of view. *(The speaker does not expect the reader to believe that he literally is the ship's captain, but by using exaggerated language—"I suffer'd, I was there"—he intends to stress the importance of identifying with the experience of others.)*

PRACTICE AND APPLY

Have students read the following passages. Ask them to distinguish what the speaker states directly from what he means the reader to understand.

- lines 23–24 from "I understand the large hearts of heroes." *(The speaker claims that understanding other people's suffering is like changing clothes to him. He states that he becomes the wounded person. He means the reader to understand that human suffering is a universal experience.)*
- lines 2–3 from "The spotted hawk swoops by." *(The speaker claims that he is completely untamed. He compares himself to a hawk high above the rooftops. The speaker's point is that his essence is completely free and at one with nature.)*

Interpret Figures of Speech

COMMON CORE

L 5a

RETEACH

Remind students that Whitman frequently uses **metaphor**—the comparison of unlike things without the use of the words *like* or *as*—to reveal surprising facets of familiar ideas.

- Have students read the opening three lines of "A child said *What is the grass?*" on page 179.
- Ask: What is the metaphor here? What might Whitman mean by it? *(Whitman compares grass to "the flag of my disposition." He is comparing the hopeful qualities of new life—the green shoots of grass—to his own optimistic nature.)*
- Have students find four other metaphors for grass in the same poem and summarize their intent. *(Line 4: Grass is God's handkerchief. It has divine origins. Line 7: Grass is a child. It is innocent. Line 8: Grass is a "uniform hieroglyphic." It grows everywhere, among all people. Line 12: Grass is the "uncut hair of graves." It symbolizes the continuing cycle of life.*

 **LEVEL UP TUTORIALS** Assign the following Level Up tutorial: **Figurative Language**

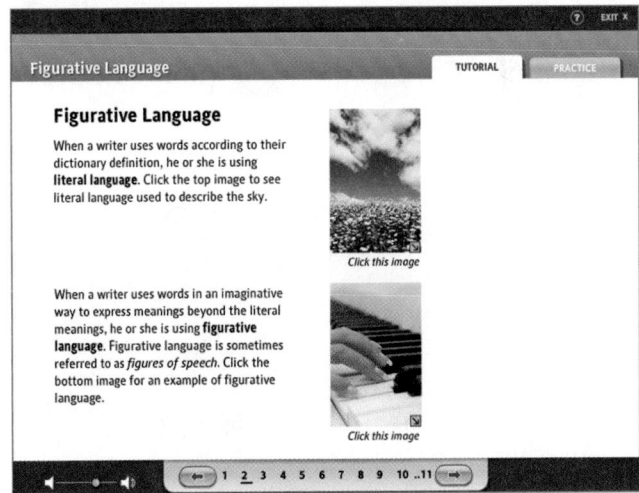

CLOSE READING APPLICATION

Students can apply the skill to another poem. Have them identify figures of speech and describe their meaning. Then ask students to analyze the examples they found, suggesting why the poet might have chosen to express his or her thoughts in figurative language. Have students share their analyses in pairs or small groups.

Poems by Walt Whitman

I Hear America Singing | A Noiseless Patient Spider

Why These Texts

Students may have difficulty determining themes of poems. A close reading of the text and an analysis of the poem's details wll help provide clues to the theme. Students may also have difficulty understanding details particular to nineteenth-century city life. This may be especially applicable to "I Hear America Singing," in which various tradespeople are mentioned. With the help of the close-reading questions, students will identify and analyze details that contribute to the clear understanding of each poem and its theme.

Background Have students read the background information and the biographical information about Walt Whitman. Tell students that Ralph Waldo Emerson (1803–1882) was an important essayist and poet from New England. He wrote about the power of nature, the need for individualism, and the relationship of the individual to the world in general. All of these themes attracted the young Walt Whitman, who once said, "Let your soul stand cool and composed before a million universes."

AS YOU READ Ask students to read each poem closely, paying special attention to the details in each line. Encourage students to think about how the details in one line relate to details in the lines that follow and, thereby, create the meaning of the poem.

Common Core Support

- cite evidence from the text
- determine two or more themes of a text
- determine the meaning of words and phrases in a text
- analyze how an author's choices concerning how to structure a text contribute to its overall meaning

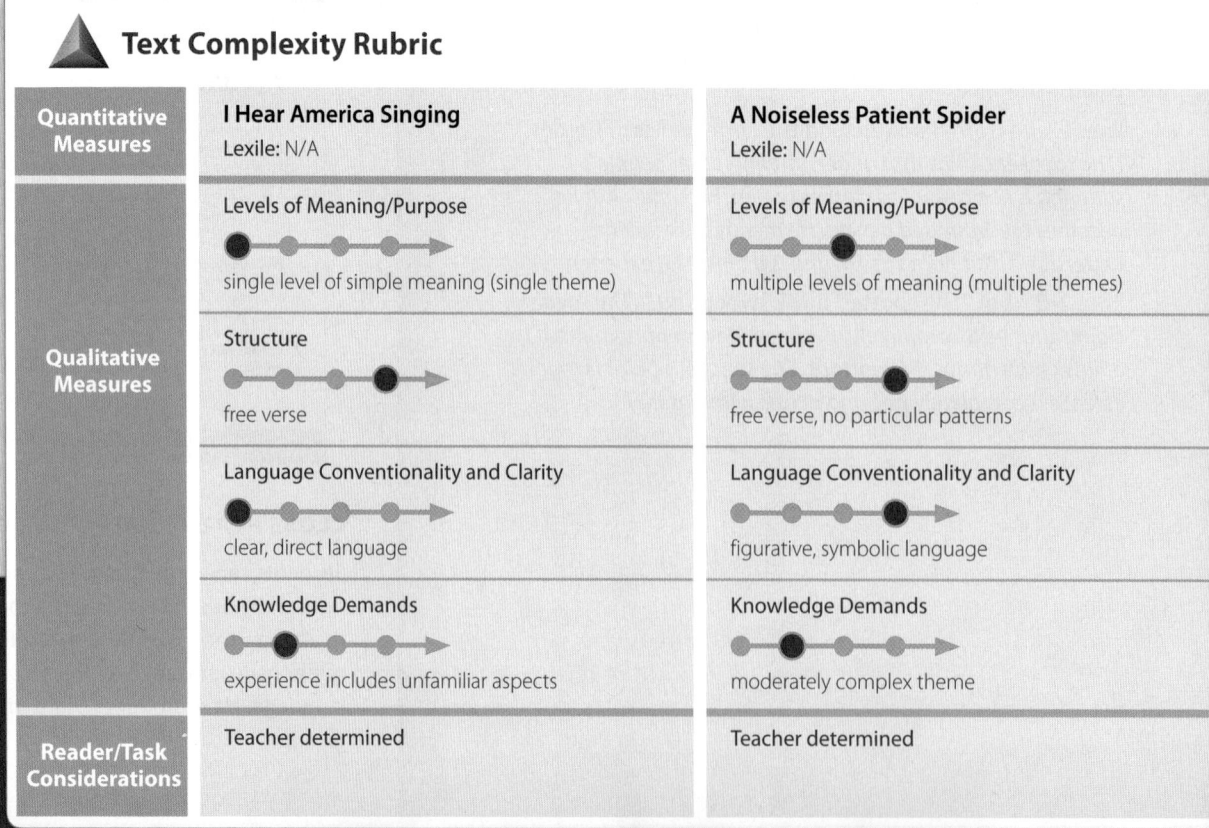

Text Complexity Rubric

	I Hear America Singing	A Noiseless Patient Spider
Quantitative Measures	Lexile: N/A	Lexile: N/A
Qualitative Measures	**Levels of Meaning/Purpose** — single level of simple meaning (single theme)	**Levels of Meaning/Purpose** — multiple levels of meaning (multiple themes)
	Structure — free verse	**Structure** — free verse, no particular patterns
	Language Conventionality and Clarity — clear, direct language	**Language Conventionality and Clarity** — figurative, symbolic language
	Knowledge Demands — experience includes unfamiliar aspects	**Knowledge Demands** — moderately complex theme
Reader/Task Considerations	Teacher determined	Teacher determined

CLOSE READER: PRACTICE & APPLY

Strategies for CLOSE READING

Determine Themes

Students should read each poem slowly, paying attention to specific details throughout each. Close-reading questions at the bottom of the page will help them collect and cite text evidence to understand the theme of each poem. As they read, students should jot down comments or questions about the text in the margins.

WHEN STUDENTS STRUGGLE . . .

To help students understand the overall theme of each poem, have them work in small groups or with a partner to fill out charts for each poem like the one shown below.

CITE TEXT EVIDENCE Encourage students to identify both general statements and specific details in the poem that support the theme of each poem.

I Hear America Singing		
Theme	General Statements	Specific Details
The poet praises and expresses his admiration for American workers.	"I hear America singing, the varied carols I hear"	"Those of mechanics"
	"Each singing what belongs to him or her . . ."	"The carpenter singing"
	". . . their strong melodious songs"	"The mason singing"
		"The boatman . . . the deckhand"
		"The shoemaker . . . the hatter"
		"The wood-cutter's song . . . the ploughboy's"
		"The delicious singing of the mother"

Background Less than a hundred years after the United States was founded, the new nation discovered its voice in a poet who spoke to all the world. His name was **Walt Whitman,** and he struck a note in literature that was as forthright, as original, and as deeply charged with democracy's energies as the land that produced him.

Poems by Walt Whitman

I Hear America Singing . . . . .Walt Whitman
A Noiseless Patient Spider . . . . .Walt Whitman

Walt Whitman *(1819–1892) grew up in rural Long Island and crowded Brooklyn. He held a series of jobs including typesetter, printer, newspaper editor, school teacher, carpenter, and journalist. In the 1840s, Whitman published a number of poems and short stories—and even a fairly successful novel—but these were conventional efforts. Whitman was just waiting for the proper inspiration. Upon reading Ralph Waldo Emerson, he realized that he could celebrate all aspects of nature and humanity by using spiritual language. "I was simmering, simmering, simmering," he once declared. "Emerson brought me to a boil."*

In the early 1850s, Whitman quit his job as a journalist and worked on a book of poems called Leaves of Grass. Many people were shocked by its controversial content and revolutionary form. Of the 800 copies printed, most were eventually thrown away. However, a few readers recognized the poet's genius. In a letter to Whitman, Emerson called Leaves of Grass "the most extraordinary piece of wit and wisdom that America has yet contributed."

37

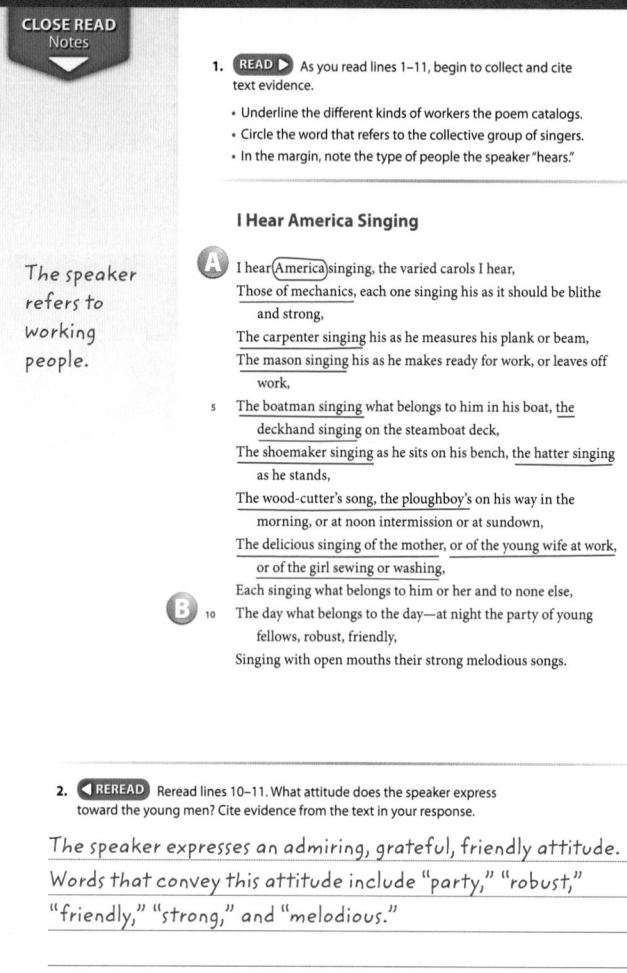

CLOSE READ Notes

1. **READ** ▶ As you read lines 1–11, begin to collect and cite text evidence.

- Underline the different kinds of workers the poem catalogs.
- Circle the word that refers to the collective group of singers.
- In the margin, note the type of people the speaker "hears."

I Hear America Singing

The speaker refers to working people.

(A) I hear (America) singing, the varied carols I hear,
Those of mechanics, each one singing his as it should be blithe
  and strong,
The carpenter singing his as he measures his plank or beam,
The mason singing his as he makes ready for work, or leaves off
  work,
5 The boatman singing what belongs to him in his boat, the
  deckhand singing on the steamboat deck,
The shoemaker singing as he sits on his bench, the hatter singing
  as he stands,
The wood-cutter's song, the ploughboy's on his way in the
  morning, or at noon intermission or at sundown,
The delicious singing of the mother, or of the young wife at work,
  or of the girl sewing or washing,
Each singing what belongs to him or her and to none else,
(B) 10 The day what belongs to the day—at night the party of young
  fellows, robust, friendly,
Singing with open mouths their strong melodious songs.

2. **◀ REREAD** Reread lines 10–11. What attitude does the speaker express toward the young men? Cite evidence from the text in your response.

The speaker expresses an admiring, grateful, friendly attitude. Words that convey this attitude include "party," "robust," "friendly," "strong," and "melodious."

38

CLOSE READ Notes

SHORT RESPONSE

Cite Text Evidence What is the theme of this poem—what is the author revealing about America? **Cite text evidence** in your response.

Even though all of the people are working, their "strong melodious songs" reflect that they are happy—the author feels that America is full of hard-working but happy people. Although each person sings their own song "which belongs to him or her and to none else," when all of these songs combine into "varied carols," they reflect the spirit and vast diversity of America.

39

---

1. READ AND CITE TEXT EVIDENCE

Point out to students that the general declaration the speaker makes in the first line ("I hear America singing, the varied carols I hear") is a good clue toward understanding the theme of the poem.

(A) **ASK STUDENTS** to cite specific details that support this first general statement. *Students should cite as examples the various kinds of working people the speaker describes in lines 2–8.*

2. REREAD AND CITE TEXT EVIDENCE

Explain to students that the last two lines of the poem contain several words and phrases that have positive connotations.

(B) **ASK STUDENTS** to identify the words in lines 10–11 that portray the workers in a positive way. *Students should cite* party, robust, friendly, strong *and* melodious.

FOR ELL STUDENTS Many students may identify carols with songs that are sung at Christmas. Clarify for them that they can also be songs of joy, in general.

SHORT RESPONSE

Cite Text Evidence The exact wording of students' responses will vary, but students should:

- express that the theme of the poem is a celebration of American workers.
- include descriptions of the workers as varied, hard working, and optimistic.
- cite specific evidence in the form of words, phrases, and lines from the poem to support their idea of the poem's theme.

CLOSE READ Notes

1. **READ** ▶ As you read lines 1–10, begin to collect and cite text evidence.

- Underline the two subjects the speaker observes.
- Circle references to web-making.
- In the margin, explain what surrounds the "noiseless patient spider" and "you O my soul."

A Noiseless Patient Spider

The spider and "you" are surrounded by vast amounts of space.

A noiseless patient spider,
I mark'd where on a little promontory[1] it stood isolated,
Mark'd how to explore the vacant vast surrounding,
It launch'd forth filament, filament, filament, out of itself,
5   Ever unreeling them, ever tirelessly speeding them.

And you O my soul where you stand,
Surrounded, detached, in measureless oceans of space,
Ceaselessly musing, venturing, throwing, seeking the spheres to
      connect them,
Till the bridge you will need be form'd, till the ductile[2] anchor
      hold,
10   Till the gossamer[3] thread you fling catch somewhere, O my soul.

[1] **promontory:** a ridge of land or rock jutting out over water or land.
[2] **ductile:** capable of being drawn or stretched out.
[3] **gossamer:** extremely light or fine.

2. ◀ **REREAD AND DISCUSS** Reread lines 1–10. With a small group, discuss the use of parallelism in lines 5 and 8. What do these parallel elements suggest about the relationship between the spider and the speaker?

SHORT RESPONSE

Cite Text Evidence What is the theme of the poem? What details communicate that theme? **Cite text evidence** in your response.

The poem draws a comparison between a spider making a web and the speaker's desire to make a connection with the universe. The speaker's soul launches filaments seeking connections just as the spider launches physical filaments to connect with the solid ground.

40

---

1. READ AND CITE TEXT EVIDENCE

C **ASK STUDENTS** to cite evidence in the text that explains what the speaker of the poem does that is similar to the action of the spider. *Students should cite lines 8–10.*

2. REREAD AND DISCUSS USING TEXT EVIDENCE

D **ASK STUDENTS** to identify the words in lines 5 and 8 that create the parallel structure. *The words* unreeling *and* speeding *in line 5 and* musing, venturing, throwing, *and* seeking *in line 8.*

SHORT RESPONSE

Cite Text Evidence Students should:

- include a general statement about the importance of making connections with the world, both physical and mental.
- compare the actions of the spider with those of the speaker.
- include text evidence that supports the theme of the poem.

TO CHALLENGE STUDENTS . . .

Walt Whitman worked most of his adult life on the volume of poetry that he called *Leaves of Grass.* Among the more famous poems in the long volume are "I Sing the Body Electric," and two poems about President Abraham Lincoln: "When Lilacs Last in the Dooryard Bloom'd" and "O Captain! My Captain!" Students can also view a short biography of Whitman online.

ASK STUDENTS to research Whitman's *Leaves of Grass,* specifically the aforementioned poems. Small groups could prepare a brief presentation, giving some background about a poem and the circumstances under which it was written, followed by a dramatic reading of parts of the poem. Students might also find it interesting to read more recent essays about Whitman and his contribution to American poetry. Some twentieth century critics, such as John Berryman, have praised Whitman's poems. Other critics, such as Yvor Winters, have been far less flattering.

DIG DEEPER

With the class, return to Question 2, Reread, on page 38. Have students share their responses.

ASK STUDENTS to cite the text evidence that helped them understand the speaker's attitude toward the young male and female workers he invokes and describes throughout the poem.

- Have students cite specific workers mentioned and details that inform the reader about their jobs.
- Encourage students to discuss the particular jobs of the workers, some of which, like the hatter's or mason's, may be unfamiliar to them. Should that be the case, encourage students to briefly research the job and what it might have entailed in the mid-19th century in New York City.
- Finally, have students identify other details in the poem that are evidence of the speaker's enthusiasm for the workers, and for America in general.

ASK STUDENTS to return to their Short Response answer on page 39 and revise it based on the class discussion.

*my*SmartPlanner Create lesson plans and access resources online.

Growing Up Asian in America

Essay by Kesaya E. Noda

Why This Text?

Writers often connect personal experiences with history and culture to define themselves and others. This lesson explores the use of classification, tone, and language to better understand the relationship between individuals and society.

Key Learning Objective: The student will be able to analyze ideas and events to discover an essay's organizational patterns and will be able to analyze content and style to determine and evaluate an author's purpose.

COMMON CORE Common Core Standards

RI 1 Cite textual evidence.

RI 3 Analyze a set of ideas or sequence of events.

RI 6 Determine an author's point of view or purpose.

W 1 Write arguments.

SL 1a Come to discussions prepared.

SL 1c Promote perspectives.

L 3a Apply an understanding of syntax to the study of complex texts.

L 4b Identify and correctly use patterns of word changes.

▲ Text Complexity Rubric

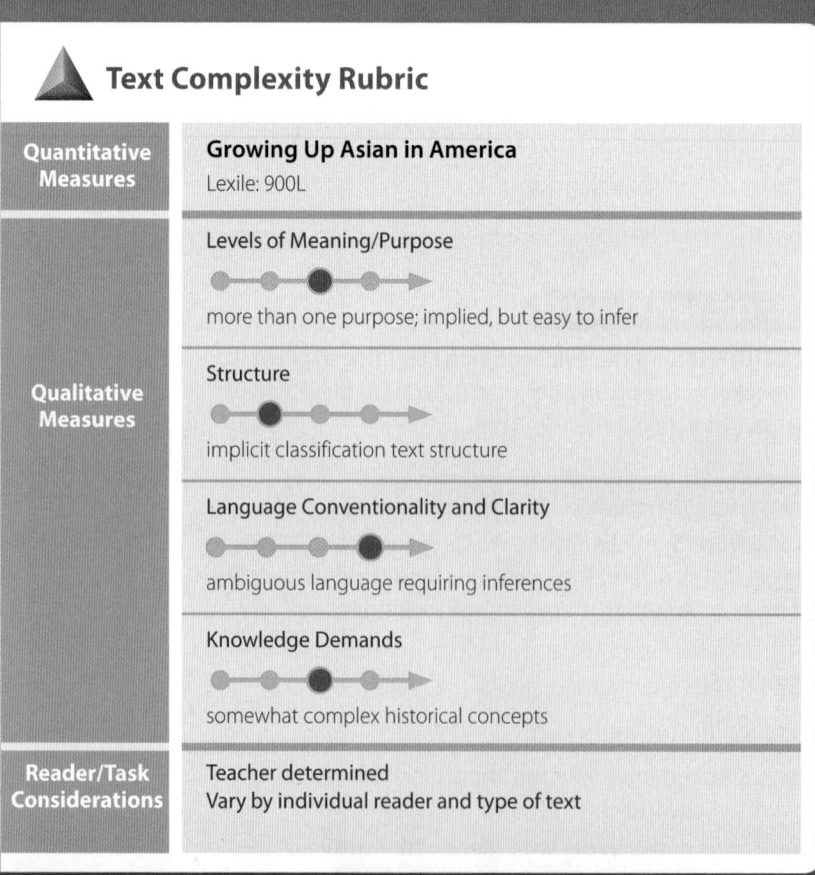

Quantitative Measures	**Growing Up Asian in America** Lexile: 900L
Qualitative Measures	Levels of Meaning/Purpose more than one purpose; implied, but easy to infer
	Structure implicit classification text structure
	Language Conventionality and Clarity ambiguous language requiring inferences
	Knowledge Demands somewhat complex historical concepts
Reader/Task Considerations	Teacher determined Vary by individual reader and type of text

Background Have students read the background. Explain that Kesaya E. Noda's essay addresses issues surrounding race, heritage, and identity. Some of these issues are personal to Noda, some involve her family, and some relate to society.

AS YOU READ Remind students to write down any questions they generate during reading.

Determine Author's Purpose (LINES 1–14)

COMMON CORE RI 6

Explain to students that essays usually have a **purpose.** Sometimes an author wants to communicate a message or influence a public debate. Usually readers need to **infer,** or make logical assumptions about, the author's purpose from the **content** and **style** of the writing.

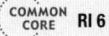 **ASK STUDENTS** to read the first paragraph (lines 1–14). What is this essay about? *(the author's struggle to understand her identity growing up as a Japanese American woman)* Is the essay written in the first-, second-, or third-person **point of view**? *(first-person point of view)* What kind of language does the author use? Is it formal or casual, technical or personal, funny or serious, simple or complicated? *(Students may have many opinions. However, it is important for them to note that this is a personal essay about a serious topic. Although the tone is informal, the sentence structure suggests it will address complex ideas.)*

Analyze Ideas and Events (LINES 12–14)

COMMON CORE RI 1, RI 3

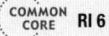 **ASK STUDENTS** to reread lines 12–14. How does Noda organize ideas? *(into three classifications of her identity—racially Japanese, Japanese American, Asian)*

CRITICAL VOCABULARY

abound: This paragraph lists a number of confused and distorted ideas and assumptions that abounded in Noda's interactions with others.

ASK STUDENTS to explain which of the beliefs that abounded could be considered confusions and which could be seen as distortions. *(The different references or forms of address might be considered confusions. The assumption that all Japanese Americans don't like cheese would be a distortion.)*

Background *The experiences of* **Kesaya E. Noda's** *family reflect those of many Japanese immigrants to the United States in the 20th century. After Japan attacked Pearl Harbor in 1941, over 110,000 Japanese residents in America were relocated to isolated internment camps for the duration of World War II. About 60 percent of them were American-born citizens. Noda's parents married after the war and moved to New Hampshire in 1957 for her father's teaching job at Dartmouth Medical School.*

Growing Up Asian in America

Essay by Kesaya E. Noda

AS YOU READ Look for clues that reveal Noda's feelings about her family. Write down any questions that you generate during reading.

Sometimes when I was growing up, my identity seemed to hurtle toward me and paste itself right to my face. I felt that way, encountering the stereotypes of my race perpetuated by non-Japanese people (primarily white) who may or may not have had contact with other Japanese in America. "You don't like cheese, do you?" someone would ask. "I know your people don't like cheese." Sometimes questions came making allusions to history. That was another aspect of the identity. Events that had happened quite apart from the me who stood silent in that moment connected my face with an

10 incomprehensible past. "Your parents were in California? Were they in those camps during the war?" And sometimes there were phrases or nicknames: "Lotus Blossom." I was sometimes addressed or referred to as racially Japanese, sometimes as Japanese American, and sometimes as an Asian woman. Confusions and distortions **abounded.**

How is one to know and define oneself? From the inside—within a context that is self defined, from a grounding in community and a connection with culture and history that are comfortably accepted? Or from the outside—in terms of messages received from the media

abound
(ə-bound´) *v.* occur or exist in great number.

Image Credits: (t) ©n. yanchuk/Shutterstock; (tc) ©szefei/Shutterstock; (tr) ©Fedor Selivanov/Shutterstock

Growing Up Asian in America **187**

SCAFFOLDING FOR ELL STUDENTS

Analyze Language Read aloud the first sentence of the selection as students follow along in the text. Then focus students' attention on "my identity seemed to hurtle toward me and paste itself right to my face."

ASK STUDENTS whether Noda's identity is an actual physical object that can fly through the air and hit things. Point out that this is an example of **figurative language**, a technique writers use to alter the meaning of words to create an effect. How does this sentence change the meaning of "identity"? *(Identity is a living, breathing thing that has a life apart from the author and is often determined by others simply upon their seeing her.)*

Encourage students to find other examples of **figurative language** in the essay.

Analyze Ideas and Events   COMMON CORE RI 1, RI 3

(LINES 23–31)

Writers organize their ideas into patterns to convey and support their **purpose,** using these patterns:

- **Chronological:** Events are listed in their order of occurrence.
- **Compare/Contrast:** Information is arranged according to how two or more things are similar or different.
- **Cause/Effect:** Ideas and events are arranged to show causal relationships.
- **Classification:** Ideas and information are grouped based on characteristics they share.

Ⓒ CITE TEXT EVIDENCE Have students read the subheading "I am racially Japanese" and lines 23–31. Ask them what kind of organizational pattern is used. *(classifications)* Have them cite evidence to support their conclusions. *(The subheading is a clear indication, referring back to the pattern established in lines 12–14. Also, Noda is offering information about Japanese immigrants and outlining their shared history.)*

Analyze Language   COMMON CORE L 3a

(LINES 43–44)

Inform students that an important element of a writer's style is **syntax,** or how words are arranged to build phrases, clauses, and sentences. **Simple sentences** have a subject and a predicate. **Compound sentences** are two simple sentences joined by conjunctions like *and, but,* or *for.*

Ⓓ ASK STUDENTS to read lines 43–44. Are these sentences **simple** or **compound?** *(simple)* How are they different? *(The first is short and the second is longer, since it has a compound predicate.)*

CRITICAL VOCABULARY

invocation: A religious festival often involves a special ritual, invocation, or ceremony.

ASK STUDENTS what sentiments the invocation might proclaim. *(It might be full of gratitude for the summer and the passing of seasons.)*

---

and people who are often ignorant? Even as an adult I can still
20 see two sides of my face and past. I can see from the inside out, in freedom. And I can see from the outside in, driven by the old voices of childhood and lost in anger and fear.

I am racially Japanese

A voice from my childhood says: "You are other. You are less than. You are unalterably alien." This voice has its own history. We have indeed been seen as other and alien since the early years of our arrival in the United States. The very first immigrants were welcomed and sought as laborers to replace the dwindling numbers of Chinese, whose influx had been cut off by the Chinese Exclusion Act of 1882.[1] The Japanese fell natural heir to the same anti-Asian prejudice that had arisen
30 against the Chinese. As soon as they began striking for better wages, they were no longer welcomed.

I can see myself today as a person historically defined by law and custom as being forever alien. Being neither "free white," nor "African," our people in California were deemed "aliens, ineligible for citizenship," no matter how long they intended to stay here. Aliens ineligible for citizenship were prohibited from owning, buying, or leasing land. They did not and could not belong here. The voice in me remembers that I am always a *Japanese* American in the eyes of many. A third-generation German American is an American. A third-
40 generation Japanese American is a Japanese American. Being Japanese means being a danger to the country during the war and knowing how to use chopsticks. I wear this history on my face.

I move to the other side. I see a different light and claim a different context. My race is a line that stretches across ocean and time to link me to the shrine where my grandmother was raised. Two high, white banners lift in the wind at the top of the stone steps leading to the shrine. It is time for the summer festival. Black characters are written against the sky as boldly as the clouds, as lightly as kites, as sharply as the big black crows I used to see above the fields in New Hampshire.
50 At festival time there is liquor and rood, ritual, discipline, and abandonment. There is music and drunkenness and **invocation**. There is hope. Another season has come. Another season has gone.

I am racially Japanese. I have a certain claim to this crazy place where the prayers intoned by a neighboring Shinto priest (standing in for my grandmother's nephew who is sick) are drowned out by the rehearsals for the pop singing contest in which most of the villagers will compete later that night. The village elders, the priest, and I stand respectfully upon the immaculate, shining wooden floor of the outer

invocation
(ĭn´və-kā´shən) *n.*
prayer or incantation.

---

[1] **Chinese Exclusion Act of 1882:** a federal law that prevented Chinese people from immigrating to the United States and prevented Chinese residents in the U.S. from becoming citizens.

APPLYING ACADEMIC VOCABULARY

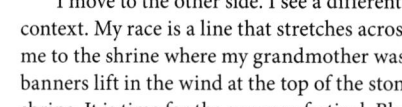

analogy	topic

As you discuss Noda's description of the festival (lines 43–52), incorporate the following Collection 3 academic vocabulary words: *analogy* and *topic*. To help students understand Noda's writing style, ask them to find an example of how she uses an **analogy** in this paragraph. As students locate and discuss the analogies, ask them to examine how they relate to the section's **topic.**

Image Credits: ©Rob MacDougall/Photographer's Choice/Getty Images

shrine, bowing our heads before the hidden powers. During the patchy
60 intervals when I can hear him, I notice the priest has a stutter. His
voice flutters up to my ears only occasionally because two men and
a woman are singing gustily into a microphone in the compound,
testing the sound system. A prerecorded tape of guitars, samisens,[2]
and drums accompanies them. Rock music and Shinto prayers. That
night, to loud applause and cheers, a young man is given the award
for the most *netsuretsu*—passionate, burning—rendition of a song.
We roar our approval of the reward. Never mind that his voice had
wandered and slid, now slightly above, now slightly below the given
line of the melody. Netsuretsu. Netsuretsu.

70   In the morning, my grandmother's sister kneels at the foot of
the stone stairs to offer her morning prayers. She is too crippled to
climb the stairs, so each morning she kneels here upon the path. She
shuts her eyes for a few seconds, her motions as matter of fact as when
she washes rice. I linger longer than she does, so reluctant to leave,
savoring the connection I feel with my grandmother in America, the
past, and the power that lives and shines in the morning sun.

    Our family has served this shrine for generations. The family's
need to protect this claim to identity and place outweighs any
individual claim to any individual hope. I am Japanese.

___

[2] **samisens** (săm´ĭ-sĕns´): Japanese stringed instruments.

Growing Up Asian in America   **189**

WHEN STUDENTS STRUGGLE...

Have students work in pairs to create outlines like the one shown. Help them identify
changes in time or setting, make connections, and find parallels throughout the piece.

I. Introduction

    a. "Confusions and distortions" about identity

    b. Two sides of identity: inside and outside

II. I am racially Japanese

    a. Alien

Analyze Language   COMMON CORE L 3a

(LINES 59–69)

Remind students that **syntax** is the rules and
patterns for how words are arranged to build phrases,
clauses, and sentences. Sentences can be **simple**
or **compound.** Offer the following definitions of
additional types of sentences:

- **Complex** sentences have an independent clause
  (a simple sentence that can stand by itself) and a
  dependent clause (a simple sentence which relies
  on the independent clause for meaning). The two
  clauses are connected by conjunctions such as
  since, although, or *because.*

- **Sentence fragments** are groups of words that
  are only parts of a sentence and don't express a
  complete thought.

 **ASK STUDENTS** to read lines 59–69 (starting
with "During the patchy intervals…) and stop after
each sentence. What kind of structure does the first
sentence use? *(It is a complex sentence using the
conjunction "when.")* What is the structure of the second
sentence? *(It is a complex sentence using the conjunction
"because.")* Which sentences are fragments, and what
effect do they have? *("Rock music and Shinto prayers"
is a sentence fragment. Also the paragraph ends with
two sentence fragments—"Netsuretsu." Having the
words within sentence fragments calls attention to and
adds emphasis to their meaning.)*

Determine Author's   COMMON CORE RI 6
Purpose (LINES 70–79)

Explain to students that the information a writer
chooses to include in an essay is its **content.** An
author decides which facts, stories, and descriptions
best support his or her purpose. Analyzing an essay's
content can offer insight into why the author wrote it.

ASK STUDENTS to read lines 70–79. What is
the story about? *(her grandmother's sister kneeling
on the path to a Shinto shrine)* What does this story
represent? *(The author's Japanese identity includes her
family, tradition, religion, and culture. It "outweighs any
individual claim to any individual hope.")*

Analyze Ideas and Events  RI 3

(LINES 80–92)

Remind students that writers organize their ideas into patterns to communicate and support their **purpose**.

G CITE EVIDENCE Have students read the subheading "I am a Japanese American" and the section's first three paragraphs (lines 80–92). How does the beginning of this section fit the author's **classification** pattern? *(Noda groups the shared characteristics she attributed to her Japanese American family members.)* What words does Noda associate with being Japanese American? *(weak, passive, victim, silent, hard workers, socially uncomfortable, clean, quiet, motivated, and determined)* How are the words in the first and third paragraphs different than those in the second paragraph? *(The first and third paragraphs are negative, whereas the second is mostly positive.)*

Determine Author's Purpose (LINES 93–120) COMMON CORE RI 6

When writers sometimes include stories or descriptions without explicitly stating their meaning, readers must **infer**, or make logical assumptions about, why the writer chose to include that **content**.

H ASK STUDENTS to read the story about Noda and her uncle (lines 93–120). When Noda's uncle becomes angry, how does she react to him? *(Instead of standing up for herself, she apologizes.)* How does she feel about her reaction? *("with great curiosity")* How does this story parallel how her family went to the internment camps without objection? *(She accepts her uncle's unjust anger and apologizes as proof of her affection. The family acquiesces as proof of its loyalty.)*

> **CRITICAL VOCABULARY**
>
> **timidity**: Noda is scared by certain traits she and her parents share, such as timidity and passivity.
>
> ASK STUDENTS to explain how the author's "inner silence and timidity" contrasts with the rest of the paragraph. *(The author raises a series of questions that do not lack courage or confidence.)*

I am a Japanese American

80 "Weak." I hear the voice from my childhood years. "Passive," I hear. Our parents and grandparents were the ones who were put into those camps. They went without resistance; they offered cooperation as proof of loyalty to America. "Victim," I hear. And, "Silent."

Our parents are painted as hard workers who were socially uncomfortable and had difficulty expressing even the smallest opinion. Clean, quiet, motivated, and determined to match the American way; that is us, and that is the story of our time here.

"Why did you go into those camps," I raged at my parents, frightened by my own inner silence and **timidity**. "Why didn't you 90 do anything to resist? Why didn't you name it the injustice it was?" Couldn't our parents even think? Couldn't they? Why were we so passive?

I shift my vision and my stance. I am in California. My uncle is in the midst of the sweet potato harvest. He is pressed, trying to get the harvesting crews onto the field as quickly as possible, worried about the flow of equipment and people. His big pickup is pulled off to the side, motor running, door ajar. I see two tractors in the yard in front of an old shed; the flat bed harvesting platform on which the workers will stand has already been brought over from the other field. It's early 100 morning. The workers stand loosely grouped and at ease, but my uncle looks as harried and tense as a police officer trying to unsnarl a New York City traffic jam. Driving toward the shed, I pull my car off the road to make way for an approaching tractor. The front wheels of the car sink luxuriously into the soft, white sand by the roadside and the car slides to a dreamy halt, tail still on the road. I try to move forward. I try to move back. The front bites contentedly into the sand, the back lifts itself at a jaunty[3] angle. My uncle sees me and storms down the road, running. He is shouting before he is even near me.

"What's the matter with you," he screams. "What the hell are 110 you doing?" In his frenzy, he grabs his hat off his head and slashes it through the air across his knee. He is beside himself. "Don't you know how to drive in sand? What's the matter with you? You've blocked the whole roadway. How am I supposed to get my tractors out of here? Can't you use your head? You've cut off the whole roadway, and we've got to get out of here."

I stand on the road before him helplessly thinking, "No, I don't know how to drive in sand. I've never driven in sand."

"I'm sorry, uncle," I say, burying a smile beneath a look of sincere apology. I notice my deep amusement and my affection for him with 120 great curiosity. I am usually devastated by anger. Not this time.

During the several years that follow I learn about the people and the place, and much more about what has happened in this California

timidity
(tĭm-ĭd´ĭ-tē) *n.*
showing a lack of courage or confidence.

---

[3] **jaunty:** stylishly self-confident.

TO CHALLENGE STUDENTS...

Analyzing Structure Noda's essay uses both **content** (what is written) and **style** (how it is written) to effectively communicate her ideas. An important element of **style** is **structure**. Encourage students to look for **structural devices**.

ASK STUDENTS to skim the second section, "I am a Japanese American" (lines 80–168) and discuss in small groups how it is **structured**. How does it begin? *(with Noda's negative assessment of her parents' reaction to the internment camps)* What is the purpose of the story about her uncle's anger? *(It shows how she reacts to an unjust situation.)* How do lines 121–168 connect and resolve this element of her identity? *(It connects her visit to California with her parents' experience there in the 1940s. It also connects her reaction to her uncle with her parents' reaction to the camps.)*

village where my parents grew up. The issei,[4] our grandparents, made this settlement in the desert. Their first crops were eaten by rabbits and ravaged by insects. The land was so barren that men walking from house to house sometimes got lost. Women came here too. They bore children in 114 degree heat, then carried the babies with them into the fields to nurse when they reached the end of each row of grapes or other truck farm crops.

> " Why didn't you do anything to resist? Why didn't you name it the injustice it was? "

130   I had had no idea what it meant to buy this kind of land and make it grow green. Or how, when the war came, there was no space at all for the **subtlety** of being who we were—Japanese Americans. Either/ or was the way. I hadn't understood that people were literally afraid for their lives then, that their money had been frozen in banks; that there was a five-mile travel limit; that when the early evening curfew came and they were inside their houses, some of them watched helplessly as people they knew went into their barns to steal their belongings. The police were patrolling the road, interested only in violators of curfew. There was no help for them in the face of thievery. I had not been able
140   to imagine before what it must have felt like to be an American—to know absolutely that one is an American—and yet to have almost everyone else deny it. Not only deny it, but challenge that identity with machine guns and troops of white American soldiers. In those circumstances it was difficult to say, "I'm a Japanese American." "American" had to do.

    But now I can say that I am a Japanese American. It means I have a place here in this country, too. I have a place here on the East Coast, where our neighbor is so much a part of our family that my mother never passes her house at night without glancing at the lights to see
150   if she is home and safe; where my parents have hauled hundreds of pounds of rocks from fields and arduously planted Christmas trees

subtlety
(sŭt′l-tē) *n.* nuance; fine detail.

(G)

_____
[4] **issei:** first-generation immigrants from Japan.

CLOSE READ

Analyze Language
(LINES 130–137)

COMMON CORE L 3a

Explain to students that sentences, in addition to being **simple, compound,** or **complex,** can also be **compound-complex.** A **compound-complex** sentence has two independent clauses (like a compound sentence) and one or more dependent clauses (like a complex sentence). The independent clauses are simple sentences that can stand by themselves. The dependent clauses are simple sentences which derive meaning from one of the independent clauses.

(I) **ASK STUDENTS** to read the first four sentences of the paragraph "I had had no idea" (lines 130–137). How do these four sentences compare to each other? *(The first two are long sentences. The third is a short, simple sentence. The fourth has a long compound-complex structure.)* What effect does using the short, simple sentence create here? *(It creates an abrupt stop that adds emphasis to the sentence.)*

CRITICAL VOCABULARY

subtlety: After Japan attacked the United States at Pearl Harbor, many Americans felt they had a clear sense of who was a friend and who was an enemy; many felt there was no room for subtlety.

ASK STUDENTS to explain why being Japanese American might be considered a subtlety, a small detail or nuance, that could prove dangerous. *(Japan was the enemy. Anything less than unwavering support might be considered treasonous.)*

SCAFFOLDING FOR ELL STUDENTS

Analyze Language Explain to students that writers use **verb tense** to indicate when an action happens. The **past perfect tense** indicates that an action was completed before another action. Display the sentences in lines 130–132. Invite students to underline verbs in the past tense and highlight in green verbs in the past perfect tense. Once the past perfect tense has been established, authors may switch to using past tense.

ASK STUDENTS whether Noda's having no idea occurred before, during, or after her trip to California. *(before her trip)* Explain that using the **past tense** implies that her lack of understanding was not changed by the knowledge she gained from her trip.

I had had no idea what it <u>meant</u> to buy this kind of land and make it grow green. Or how, when the war <u>came</u>, there <u>was</u> no space at all for the subtlety of being who we <u>were</u>—Japanese Americans.

Analyze Language COMMON CORE L 3a

(LINES 157–166)

Explain to students that writers vary their **syntax** by using emphasis-creating techniques such as **parallel structure.**

 **ASK STUDENTS** to read the paragraph "I have a place…" (lines 157–166). Draw their attention to the last three sentences. How are these sentences similar to each other? *(They all start with "I saw.")* What kind of effect does this parallel structure create? *(In addition to creating a rhythm, the structure links the sentences together and creates a sense of equality among the things Noda saw.)*

Determine Author's Purpose (LINES 167–168) COMMON CORE RI 6

Explain to students that writers often have more than one **purpose** when creating an essay. When an essay has multiple purposes, they are often connected, drawing and providing support for one another. Readers can make inferences about these **purposes** by examining the essay's **content.**

K CITE EVIDENCE Have students read the last paragraph of this section (lines 167–168). How do the pronouns change? *(The first sentence has the first-person singular pronoun "I." The next two sentences have the first-person plural "we.")* What does this change imply? *(It implies that Noda has found identity and acceptance in the Japanese American community, similar to how the Japanese American community has found identity and acceptance in America.)*

and blueberries, lilacs, asparagus, and crab apples; where my father still dreams of angling a stream to a new bed so that he can dig a pond in the field and fill it with water and fish. "The neighbors already came for their Christmas tree?" he asks in December. "Did they like it? Did they like it?"

 I have a place on the West Coast where my relatives still farm, where I heard the stories of feuds and backbiting, and where I saw that people survived and flourished because fundamentally they trusted
160 and relied upon one another. A death in the family is not just a death in a family; it is a death in the community. I saw people help each other with money, materials, labor, attention, and time. I saw men gather once a year, without fail, to clean the grounds of a ninety-year-old woman who had helped the community before, during, and after the war. I saw her remembering them with birthday cards sent to each of their children.

I come from a people with a long memory and a distinctive grace. We live our thanks. And we are Americans. Japanese Americans.

Image Credits: ©Jimmy Cohrssen/Image Bank/Getty Images

192 Collection 3

WHEN STUDENTS STRUGGLE…

Tell students that when they read an essay aloud, they are speaking in the voice of the writer. Readers can use their voices to express the conversational tone of Noda's essay.

ASK STUDENTS to form pairs to practice **fluent reading.**

- Divide the paragraph in lines 157–166 into two sections: lines 157–161 and lines 161–166 (starting with "I saw people…").

- One partner should read the first section aloud, and then the other partner should read the second section. Students should listen to how their partner uses his or her voice to express the words and offer any tips regarding **intonation,** the emphasis given to words or phrases.

- Students switch sections and read the paragraph aloud again.

I am a Japanese American woman

Woman. The last piece of my identity. It has been easier by far for me
to know myself in Japan and to see my place in America than it has
been to accept my line of connection with my own mother. She was
my dark self, a figure in whom I thought I saw all that I feared most
in myself. Growing into womanhood and looking for some model of
strength, I turned away from her. Of course, I could not find what
I sought. I was looking for a black feminist or a white feminist. My
mother is neither white nor black.

My mother is a woman who speaks with her life as much as with
her tongue. I think of her with her own mother. Grandmother had
Parkinson's disease and it had frozen her gait and set her fingers,
tongue, and feet jerking and trembling in a terrible dance. My aunts
and uncles wanted her to be able to live in her own home. They fed her,
bathed her, dressed her, awoke at midnight to take her for one last trip
to the bathroom. My aunts (her daughters-in-law) did most of the care,
but my mother went from New Hampshire to California each summer
to spend a month living with grandmother, because she wanted to and
because she wanted to give my aunts at least a small rest. During those
hot summer days, mother lay on the couch watching the television or
reading, cooking foods that grandmother liked, and speaking little.
Grandmother thrived under her care.

The time finally came when it was too dangerous for grandmother
to live alone. My relatives kept finding her on the floor beside her
bed when they went to wake her in the mornings. My mother flew
to California to help clean the house and make arrangements for
grandmother to enter a local nursing home. On her last day at home,
while grandmother was sitting in her big, overstuffed armchair, hair
combed and wearing a green summer dress, my mother went to her
and knelt at her feet. "Here, Mamma," she said. "I've polished your
shoes." She lifted grandmother's legs and helped her into the shiny
black shoes. My grandmother looked down and smiled slightly. She
left her house walking, supported by her children, carrying her pocket
book, and wearing her polished black shoes. "Look, Mamma," my
mom had said, kneeling. "I've polished your shoes."

Just the other day, my mother came to Boston to visit. She had
recently lost a lot of weight and was pleased with her new shape and
her feeling of good health. "Look at me, Kes," she exclaimed, turning
toward me, front and back, as naked as the day she was born. . . . Her
hips were small. I was not a large baby, but there was so little room for
me in her that when she was carrying me she could not even begin to
bend over toward the floor. She hated it, she said.

"Don't I look good? Don't you think I look good?"

I looked at my mother, smiling and as happy as she, thinking
of all the times I have seen her naked. I have seen both my parents
naked throughout my life, as they have seen me. From childhood

APPLYING ACADEMIC VOCABULARY

denote	quote

As you discuss the relationships between Noda, her mother, and her
grandmother (lines 177–202), incorporate the following Collection 3 academic
vocabulary words: *denote* and *quote*. To help students understand Noda's
writing style, ask them how including the **quotes** affects or changes the
impact of this story. Within the **quotes,** Noda **denotes** a specific object. Have
students discuss how specific or vague language reflects a writer's style.

TEACH

CLOSE READ

Analyze Ideas and Events (LINES 169–176)

COMMON CORE RI 1, RI 3

Remind students that writers organize their ideas
into patterns to communicate and support their
purpose. Noda's essay uses a **classification** pattern
that groups ideas and information based on shared
characteristics.

L CITE EVIDENCE Have students read the
subheading "I am a Japanese American woman" and
the section's first paragraph (lines 169–176). How
does the author say this **classification** compares
to the first two groups presented in her essay? *(It is
the most challenging of the three.)* Have students cite
evidence to support their conclusion. *(Lines 169–171:
"It has been easier by far for me to know myself in Japan
and to see my place in America than it has been to
accept my line of connection with my own mother.")*

Determine Author's Purpose (LINES 177–202)

COMMON CORE RI 6

Inform students that writers include only **content**
they think will support their essay. Readers can
analyze the facts, stories, and descriptions and make
inferences about a writer's **purpose.**

 **ASK STUDENTS** to read the story about Noda's
mother and her grandmother (lines 177–202). On
grandmother's last day at home, Noda's mother
polishes her black shoes. What inference can the
reader make about why Noda's mother polishes
the shoes? *(She loves her mother.)* Is this information
stated explicitly in the text? *(no)* What purpose might
Noda have for including this story? *(Noda wants to
show how her mother, "a woman who speaks with her
life as much as with her tongue" [lines 177–178], has
influenced her identity.)*

Determine Author's Purpose (LINES 218–239)

COMMON CORE RI 6

Explain to students that there are two places where writers give extra care to the **content** they choose—the beginning and the end. How an essay ends can leave a lingering impression upon readers.

(N) **ASK STUDENTS** to read the final paragraphs (lines 218–239). What central piece of **content** does the author select for her ending? *(a Japanese folk song about a young woman singing a lullaby)* Does Noda explain the meaning of the nursemaid? If so, how? *(Yes, she is "the intersection of heaven and earth . . . the human, the natural world, the body, and the soul.")* How does this folk song relate to Noda's mother? *(Just as the nursemaid is the intersection of all of these things, Noda feels her mother is the intersection of "Japanese," "American," and "woman.")*

COLLABORATIVE DISCUSSION Have students pair up and choose one of the stories about Noda's family that she shares in her essay. Students should discuss the feelings Noda expresses, specifically looking for emotions that seem to conflict with each other and noting whether the conflict is resolved. Then have the students share their conclusions with the class as a whole. Accept all reasonable responses.

ASK STUDENTS to share any questions they generated in the course of reading and discussing the selection.

---

through adulthood we've had our naked moments, sharing baths, idle conversations picked up as we moved between showers and closets, hurried moments at the beginning of days, quiet moments at the end of days.

220   I know this to be Japanese, this ease with the physical, and it makes me think of an old, Japanese folk song. A young nursemaid, a fifteen-year-old girl, is singing a lullaby to a baby who is strapped to her back. The nursemaid has been sent as a servant to a place far from her own home. "We're the beggars," she says, "and they are the nice people. Nice people wear fine sashes. Nice clothes."

(N)

> If I should drop dead,
> bury me by the roadside!
> I'll give a flower
> to everyone who passes.
>
> What kind of flower?
> The cam-cam-camellia [tsun-tsun-tsubaki]
230   watered by Heaven:
> alms water.

The nursemaid is the intersection of heaven and earth, the intersection of the human, the natural world, the body, and the soul. In this song, with clear eyes, she looks steadily at life, which is sometimes so very terrible and sad. I think of her while looking at my mother, who is standing on the red and purple carpet before me, laughing, without any clothes.

I am my mother's daughter. And I am myself.
I am a Japanese American woman.

COLLABORATIVE DISCUSSION Why does Noda have mixed feelings about her family? Discuss this question with a partner, citing evidence from the essay that shows both positive and negative feelings.

TO CHALLENGE STUDENTS . . .

Analyze Language A **symbol** is a literary device in which something stands for something else, and represents a complicated idea. Explain to students that symbolism involves both **content** (what the writer states) and **style** (how the writer states it).

ASK STUDENTS to read lines 232–237 and discuss the **symbols** they find. What symbol is clearly stated in the text? *(The nursemaid represents the intersection of the earthly and spiritual.)* Have students explain whether the nursemaid represents something or someone else. *(Yes, the nursemaid also represents Noda's mother.)* Challenge students to find other symbols in this paragraph *(her naked mother)* and throughout the essay. Discuss these symbols and the ideas they represent.

Analyze Ideas and Events: Classification  COMMON CORE RI 3

When a writer presents a complex set of ideas, he or she needs to decide on a clear organizational pattern that will allow readers to trace the development and interaction of those ideas over the course of the text. In her essay, Kesaya Noda uses a pattern of organization called **classification,** in which ideas and information are grouped together based on the characteristics they share. Noda suggests the pattern of organization in her opening paragraph and then explicitly breaks the essay into three sections based on the characteristics that make up her complex identity.

Noda's Identity

- I am racially Japanese.
- I am a Japanese American.
- I am a Japanese American woman.

As you reread the essay, look for the types of ideas and events Noda presents in each section, and see how each detail develops the description of her identity.

Determine Author's Purpose  COMMON CORE RI 6

An author's **purpose** is his or her reason for writing. Usually readers need to infer, or make logical assumptions about, the author's purpose from the content and style of the writing. Use these clues to help you determine Noda's purpose in writing her essay.

Content	Style
Content is what a writer says. Noda includes information from her own experience and from the broader experience of Japanese immigrants. Notice what she says and what others say about her, her family, or Japanese immigrants in general.	Style refers to how a writer expresses the content. One important part of style is **tone,** a writer's attitude toward the subject. Noda's tone shifts in each section from the way she begins to the way she ends. This shift in tone is often signaled by a shift in perspective: "A voice from my childhood says. . . ." "I move to the other side. I see a different light. . . ."

CLOSE READ

Analyze Ideas and Events: Classification  COMMON CORE RI 3

Explain to students that organizing ideas and events is an important part of writing. Help students examine the three sections of Noda's essay and look for details that develop the description of her identity. *(In the first section, Noda includes details about early immigration to America, a Japanese festival, a pop singing contest, and her grandmother's sister's reverence. In the second section, she details her encounter with her angry uncle and how it relates to Japanese Americans' response to internment camps and ends with how her family has flourished since the war. In the third section, details include her mother's care for Noda's grandmother, her mother's nakedness, and the Japanese folk song.)*

Determine Author's Purpose  COMMON CORE RI 6

Noda's essay addresses race, gender, identity, and acceptance—topics that are hard to articulate. What was Noda's purpose for writing? How does she use content and style to support it? *(One can infer that Noda wrote to educate the public about racism, to pay homage to her family and the hardships they faced, and to explore her personal issues with identity and acceptance. The essay includes personal stories and historical events. The tone is conversational, yet very knowledgeable, and its style is enhanced by symbolism.)*

 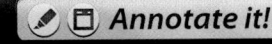

Determine Author's Purpose  COMMON CORE RI 6

Share these strategies for guided or independent analysis:

- Highlight in blue any words and phrases that reveal Noda's attitude about her identity.
- Review your highlighting, and consider whether the tone is positive or negative in each case. Then, think of more precise adjectives to describe the tone.
- On notes, record your description of Noda's tone in each section of the excerpt.

camps. They went without resistance; they offered cooperation as proof of loyalty to America. "Victim," I hear. And, "Silent."

Our parents are painted as hard workers who were socially uncomfortable and had difficulty expressing even the smallest opinion. Clean, quiet, motivated, and determined to match the

PRACTICE & APPLY

Analyzing the Text

COMMON CORE RI 1, RI 3, RI 6

Possible answers:

1. Noda is referring to her outer identity, the part that others see and associate with being Japanese, and the stereotypes associated with her heritage.

2. Alien can mean "foreigner," "someone who has not acquired citizenship," "someone who has been excluded," or "idea or object that does not belong." Noda uses alien to explain how Japanese Americans were denied citizenship and treated as strange foreigners who did not belong in the United States.

3. Noda's Japanese identity is connected to her family's identity, which is interwoven with the land from which they came. Heritage, culture, and history are all tied together.

4. Although Noda admonished her parents for remaining silent in the face of injustice, the episode with her uncle taught her why they acquiesced. Noda apologized to her uncle to prove her affection, like her parents quietly went to the internment camps to prove their loyalty.

5. Noda's identity as a Japanese American woman was the most difficult part of herself to accept because she didn't find in her mother the strength for which she was looking.

6. In this example, Noda states that she "was looking for a black feminist or a white feminist" (line 175). The reader can infer that Noda associated strength with boldness. Noda's parents are "hard workers who were socially uncomfortable and had difficulty expressing even the smallest opinion" (lines 84–86). While they may not express themselves boldly, their strength comes from diligence and effort.

7. The evidence for her Japanese identity includes her connection to tradition (lines 43–52), religion and culture (lines 53–69), and her grandmother (lines 70–76). Her connection to her Japanese American identity includes the hardships her family faced (lines 121–145) and how her family has flourished (lines 146–166).

8. Noda's quote from a Japanese folk song is an example of how she combines content and style. Her family shows its love and strength through actions, not words. Noda reveals her message through the use of a symbol—the nursemaid who represents the unwavering intersection of love, strength, and identity.

9. Noda might want to educate the public about racism directed toward Japanese Americans. Her other purpose could be to explore her personal issues with identity and acceptance.

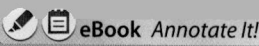 eBook *Annotate It!*

Analyzing the Text

COMMON CORE RI 1, RI 3, RI 6, SL 1a, SL 1c

Cite Text Evidence   Support your responses with evidence from the selection.

1. **Interpret** To which part of her identity is Noda referring when she says that "my identity seemed to hurtle toward me and paste itself right to my face" (lines 1–2)?

2. **Analyze** A key part of an author's **style** is word choice. How do the different meanings of the word *alien* used in the third and fourth paragraphs (lines 23–42) contribute to the power of Noda's essay?

3. **Analyze** Noda ends the second part of her essay—I Am Racially Japanese—with a brief paragraph. How does this statement summarize her argument in this section?

4. **Compare** Noda describes a scene (lines 88–92) in which she confronts her parents for being too passive in response to the Japanese internment. How does the section that immediately follows this scene respond to Noda's complaints and show that her view has evolved? Why was Noda not "devastated" by her uncle's anger?

5. **Analyze** Why is Noda's identity as a Japanese American woman the most difficult part of herself to accept?

6. **Interpret** What does Noda mean when she says: "My mother is neither white nor black" (lines 175–176)? How does this statement connect to Noda's larger point about coming to undertand her parents better?

7. **Cite Evidence** How does Noda's identity as a Japanese American woman include the ideas of being racially Japanese and being Japanese American?

8. **Infer** Why did Noda quote from a Japanese folk song (lines 224–231) when she wrote about her mother?

9. **Draw Conclusions** How might Noda have had one purpose in writing this essay for herself and another in writing for a broader audience?

PERFORMANCE TASK

Speaking Activity: Discussion Noda describes different ways in which society affects her individual identity. Explore this topic in a group discussion.

- Reread the essay and look for examples of the role of community and society in shaping the three aspects of Noda's personal identity.

- Prepare notes on your reading to be used in a small group discussion.

- Refer to your evidence to present your ideas. Allow everyone in the group to have a chance to participate in the exchange of ideas.

- Pose and respond to questions to clarify or challenge ideas and conclusions.

Assign this performance task.

PERFORMANCE TASK

COMMON CORE SL 1a, SL 1c

Speaking Activity: Discussion Have students work in pairs or small groups. To help divide tasks, each group member should find and reread a passage he or she found interesting and then share with others. Then ask groups to perform the Speaking Activities stated above.

Critical Vocabulary

COMMON CORE L 4b

abounded	invocation	timidity	subtlety

Practice and Apply Answer each question based on your own experiences to show that you understand the meaning of each Critical Vocabulary word.

1. Describe a time when something good or bad **abounded** in your life.

2. When and where might you hear an **invocation**?

3. When did you show **timidity**? Why?

4. When did you need to use **subtlety**? Why?

Vocabulary Strategy: Patterns of Word Change

The Critical Vocabulary word *invocation* is formed by adding the noun suffix *-tion* to the verb *invoke*. Note that the *-ke* at the end of *invoke* changes to *-ca* when the suffix *-tion* is added to the word. The chart shows other words that change their spelling when suffixes that form nouns or adjectives are added. Once you become familiar with these patterns of word change, you can use them to more easily recognize unfamiliar words by connecting them to more common root words.

Verb form	Noun: *-tion, -sion* "state of being"	Adjective: *-able* "capable of being"
invoke	invocation	
conceive	conception	conceivable
certify	certification	certifiable
concede	concession	

Practice and Apply For each row of the chart, identify one new word that would follow the same spelling pattern. With each word you choose, follow these steps:

1. Identify the verb form and its meaning.

2. Use suffixes to change each verb to a noun and an adjective. Write a definition for each new word. Note that not all verbs can be turned into adjectives with the suffix *–able*. Consult a dictionary if you are unsure.

3. Write a sentence using one form of each word you chose.

PRACTICE & APPLY

Critical Vocabulary

COMMON CORE L 3a, L 4b

Possible Answers: *Responses will vary. Students' answers should demonstrate comprehension of the critical vocabulary words. Accept all reasonable answers.*

Vocabulary Strategy: Patterns of Word Change

COMMON CORE RI 6

Possible Answers: *Student sentences should show a clear understanding of the new words.*

Verb form	Noun: *–tion, –sion* "state of being"	Adjective: *–able* "capable of being"
invoke	invocation	*invocable*
conceive	conception	conceivable
certify	certification	certifiable
concede	concession	*concessible*

Strategies for Annotation ✏️ 🖥️ *Annotate it!*

Patterns of Word Change

COMMON CORE L 4b

Have students locate the sentence containing *invocation*. Encourage them to use their eBook annotation tools to do the following:

- Highlight the vocabulary word.
- Use the note function to rewrite the sentence with a different form of the word.
- Review your annotations and try to infer why the author chose this form of the word.

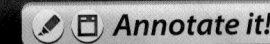

There is music and drunkenness and invocation.

People are singing, drinking, and invoking.

PRACTICE & APPLY

Language and Style: Varying Sentence Structure

Tell students that structure can be analyzed on different levels. While larger structural forms (sections, subsections, paragraphs) are used to organize information and create clarity, smaller forms (sentences and phrases) are used to create variety and keep the reader's attention. Varying sentence structure helps writers communicate their style.

Answers: *Responses will vary. Students' answers should demonstrate comprehension of varying sentence structures. Accept all reasonable answers.*

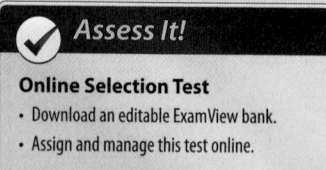

Assess It!

Online Selection Test
- Download an editable ExamView bank.
- Assign and manage this test online.

Language and Style: Varying Sentence Structure

An essential part of a writer's style is **syntax,** or how the writer arranges words to construct phrases, clauses, and sentences. Noda uses great variety in sentence structure and length to create an engaging rhythm in her prose. Part of her syntax includes **parallelism,** or the use of similar grammatical structures to express ideas of similar meaning or importance. She sometimes uses sentence fragments to add emphasis or to create an informal, conversational style. Varying her syntax allows Noda to create a unique voice in her writing. Readers can imagine that they are listening to her speak. The chart shows examples from the essay.

Varying Syntax for Effect	
Sentence Structure	**Example**
Simple	Confusions and distortions abounded. (line 14)
Compound	They went without resistance; they offered cooperation as proof of loyalty to America. (lines 82–83)
Complex	His voice flutters up to my ears only occasionally because two men and a woman are singing gustily into a microphone in the compound, testing the sound system. (lines 60–63)
Compound complex	I hadn't understood that people were literally afraid for their lives then, that their money had been frozen in banks; that there was a five-mile travel limit; that when the early evening curfew came and they were inside their houses, some of them watched helplessly as people they knew went into their barns to steal their belongings. (lines 133–137)
Sentence fragment	Woman. The last piece of my identity. (line 169)

Practice and Apply Write a brief essay on the topic of society's effect on Noda's identity using the notes you prepared for the Performance Task discussion. Vary your syntax to create a distinctive voice and an engaging rhythm. Share your essay with a partner and discuss how each of you used varied syntax in your writing.

Support an Argument

COMMON CORE

W 1

TEACH

Explain to students that Kesaya E. Noda's "Growing Up Asian in America" is an **informative** essay, the primary purpose of which is to educate readers. Another form of writing is the **persuasive** essay, in which the writer states an **argument** that is supported by reasons and evidence. A **claim** is the writer's position on a problem or an issue. The strength of an argument depends not on the claim, but on the support. **Support** consists of reasons and evidence used to prove the claim. **Reasons** are declarations made to explain an action or belief. **Evidence** includes specific facts, statistics, or examples.

PRACTICE AND APPLY

Display lines 15–22 of Noda's essay on the board or on a device. Ask students whether Noda is making a **claim,** or stating a position, on a problem or an issue. *(She is not. Although Noda raises the issue of racism, her essay focuses on her search for identity.)* How might the essay be written if its purpose was to make an argument? Invite students to provide claims based on the essay's content. *(Answers will vary but should focus on race, gender, heritage, or identity. Accept all reasonable answers.)*

Ask students to write a short **argument** based on Noda's essay. The argument must include a **claim** that is supported by **reasons** and **evidence** gathered from "Growing Up Asian in America." Inform students that they can evaluate an argument, or decide whether it makes sense and is convincing, by following these steps:

- Consider whether the evidence logically supports the claim.
- Examine the logic to make sure that ideas make sense and are in a proper order.
- Consider whether the opposing view has been adequately addressed.
- Identify persuasive techniques such as appeals to emotion.

Determine Author's Purpose

COMMON CORE

RI 6

RETEACH

Remind students that an author's **purpose** determines his or her **content** and **style.** The content can include facts, stories, and descriptions. The style refers to how the writer expresses the content. The author's **purpose** also affects the essay's **scope** and **treatment.**

- **Scope** is the range of content included in an essay. A comprehensive or general article is said to have a **broad scope.** A piece that focuses on a single or limited topic is said to have a **narrow scope.** An article's scope is not measured on a specific scale, but rather is relative to the topic and other essays on the subject.
- **Treatment** is how the writer handles the subject. Closely related to style, an essay's treatment is generally described as either objective or subjective. An **objective treatment** reports only the facts and events, without opinion. A **subjective treatment** reflects a specific opinion or point of view.

 **LEVEL UP TUTORIALS** Assign the following *Level Up* tutorial: **Scope and Treatment**

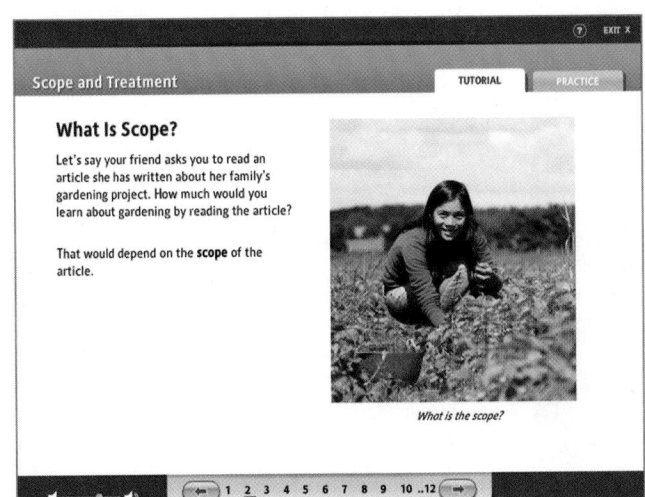

CLOSE READING APPLICATION

Students can apply the skill to other texts they find challenging. Have them work independently to find and read an in-depth newspaper or magazine article or essay. Ask: What is the purpose of this text? How does its scope and treatment support that purpose?

mySmartPlanner Create lesson plans and access resources online.

 EXEMPLAR

The Soul selects her own Society
Because I could not stop for Death
Much Madness is divinest Sense
Tell all the truth but tell it slant

Poems by Emily Dickinson

Why These Texts?

Students are required to read a wide variety of texts in school and in life. Key to their comprehension of texts in all genres is the ability to recognize not only the author's message but also the specific choices the author makes in communicating the message. In this lesson, students will analyze word choice and theme in poetry that addresses timeless issues and universal themes.

Key Learning Objective: Students will analyze language and determine themes, supporting interpretations with specific textual evidence.

COMMON CORE Common Core Standards

RL 1 Cite textual evidence.

RL 2 Determine themes of a text.

RL 4 Determine figurative and connotative meanings; analyze the impact of word choices.

RL 6 Analyze a case in which grasping point of view requires distinguishing what is directly stated in a text from what is really meant.

RL 9 Demonstrate knowledge of foundational works of American literature.

W 1 Write arguments.

W 5 Develop and strengthen writing as needed by planning revising, editing, rewriting, or trying a new approach.

L 3 Apply knowledge of language to understand how language functions in different contexts.

L 4a Use context as a clue to meaning.

L 4b Identify and correctly use patterns of word changes.

L 5a Interpret figures of speech.

Text Complexity Rubric

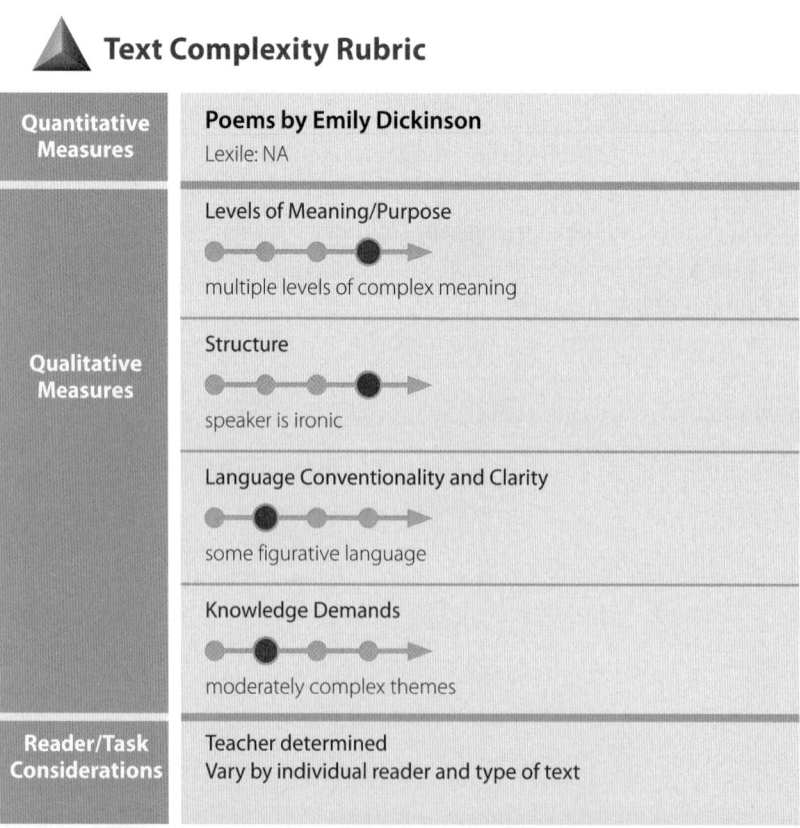

Quantitative Measures

Poems by Emily Dickinson
Lexile: NA

Qualitative Measures

Levels of Meaning/Purpose

multiple levels of complex meaning

Structure

speaker is ironic

Language Conventionality and Clarity

some figurative language

Knowledge Demands

moderately complex themes

Reader/Task Considerations

Teacher determined
Vary by individual reader and type of text

Emily Dickinson Although famously a recluse, Dickinson was able to write compellingly and perceptively about a wide range of themes. Through correspondence, she engaged intellectually and emotionally in the issues of her time. Her friend, adviser, and eventual editor, Thomas Wentworth Higginson, was an abolitionist and women's rights advocate. Another friend, Helen Hunt Jackson, fought for Native American rights. Although over time she withdrew from face-to-face social interaction, she maintained a thoughtful perspective on the public and personal struggles of human existence.

Background The Civil War erupted during Dickinson's most productive poetic years. She closely followed the news of the conflict, and she discussed its progress in her correspondence. Her letters also reveal that she was deeply moved when she received word that the son of another Amherst family was killed in the war, and that she was delighted when Jefferson Davis was captured. Although specific works are not explicitly identified as "war poems," Dickinson scholars see evidence in several poems that her perspective was influenced by the events and tragedies of the time.

AS YOU READ Direct students to use the As You Read note to focus their reading. Remind them to write down any questions they generate during reading.

Determine Theme　　COMMON CORE RL 2

Tell students that the **theme** of a poem is the message the poet wants to communicate. Have students reread the information about Emily Dickinson.

Ⓐ **ASK STUDENTS** to infer the factors that may have influenced Dickinson's perspectives, ideas, and themes. *(Dickinson would probably have been influenced by the people that she socialized with in her early years, the literature her father encouraged her to read, and news of the current events of her time. These factors would have shaped her views and the messages she wanted to communicate about life.)*

Poems
by Emily Dickinson

The Soul selects her own Society

Because I could not stop for Death

Much Madness is divinest Sense

Tell all the truth but tell it slant

Ⓐ **Emily Dickinson** (1830–1886) *lived and died in Amherst, Massachusetts, seldom venturing far from her home. Dickinson's father, Edward, encouraged her love of reading and writing, and it was through reading and writing that Dickinson reached out to the world. As a young adult, she entertained friends and socialized. As a poet, her most productive years were 1858–1865, during some of the most turbulent years in American history. But as she grew older, she became more reclusive and earned a reputation as an eccentric. She died at the age of 55 and was buried in Amherst.*

After her death, her sister discovered nearly 1,800 poems Dickinson had written. Family and friends recognized Dickinson's talent and sought to publish her poetry. In 1890, the first volume of poems was published to great public and critical acclaim. Over time, her remaining poems were published. Emily Dickinson is now considered one of America's greatest poets.

AS YOU READ Look for evidence of Dickinson's perspectives about life in the lines of her poems. Write down any questions that you generate during reading.

Poems by Emily Dickinson **199**

SCAFFOLDING FOR ELL STUDENTS

Punctuation and Print Cues Nonstandard capitalization and punctuation may confuse students learning standard English. Tell students that these titles are also the first lines in the poems. Have students read the first title and determine whether it is a sentence.

ASK STUDENTS what they notice about punctuation and capitalization in the "sentence." *(It has no punctuation; it begins with a capital letter; two internal words are capitalized.)* Discuss with students how they know the line is a sentence. *(It expresses a complete thought and includes a subject and a verb.)*

Have student pairs practice reading Dickinson's nonstandard punctuation and capitalization by also analyzing the other three titles. Which titles are sentences?

CLOSE READ

Determine Theme
COMMON CORE **RL 2**

(LINES 1–12)

Remind students that a topic and a theme are not the same thing. The **topic** is the subject; the **theme** is the poet's message about the topic.

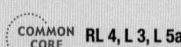 **ASK STUDENTS** to analyze the poem to determine its topic. *(the poem's title and first line—who the Soul, or inner part of an individual, chooses to spend time with)* What does the message of the poem seem to be? *(that the Soul is stubbornly and determinedly selective about whom she chooses to socialize with)* What evidence in the poem supports that interpretation? *(the image of the Soul shutting the door [line 2] and keeping it shut even when chariots and an emperor wait outside her door [lines 5–8])*

Analyze Language
COMMON CORE **RL 4**

(LINES 11–12)

Remind students that a **simile** is a kind of **figurative language** that compares two unlike things using words such as *like* and *as*. Topic and theme are not the same thing: the **topic** is the subject; the **theme** is the poet's message about the topic.

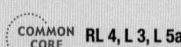 **ASK STUDENTS** to reread the last two lines of the poem and identify the simile. *(close the valves of her attention like stone)* What is being compared? *(the mechanism that closes the Soul off to others is being compared to a stone)* How does this support the theme you identified? *(Stone is very hard; comparing the Soul to a stone suggests hardness and solidity. The simile supports the idea that the Soul is stubborn.)*

Analyzing the Text
COMMON CORE **RL 4, L 3, L 5a**

Possible answers:

1. *The words "shuts the Door" are direct and absolute. The Soul takes firm, uncompromising action to close off her interaction with most of the world. The tone, or attitude, conveyed by these words is somber and firm.*

2. *The repetition of the word* unmoved *reinforces the sense of the Soul's distance and detachment. The Soul is not influenced by outside forces to change her mind.*

The Soul selects her own Society

 The Soul selects her own Society—
Then—shuts the Door—
To her divine Majority—
Present no more—

5 Unmoved—she notes the Chariots—pausing—
At her low Gate—
Unmoved—an Emperor be kneeling
Upon her Mat—

I've known her—from an ample nation—
10 Choose One—
Then—close the Valves of her attention—
Like Stone—

Analyzing the Text
COMMON CORE **RL 4, L 3, L 5a**

Cite Text Evidence Support your responses with evidence.

1. **Analyze** The poet uses the phrase "shuts the door" in the poem. What does she mean by it? How does it affect the tone of the poem?

2. **Interpret** In the second stanza, the narrator repeats the word *unmoved*. Who is unmoved? What is the effect of repeating the word?

APPLYING ACADEMIC VOCABULARY

denote	topic

As you discuss the poems by Dickinson, incorporate the following Collection 3 academic vocabulary words: *denote* and *topic*. Have students read the first line of each poem. Ask what the internal capital letters might mean, or **denote**. *(They denote that the words are significant.)* Then ask students to explain why the capitalization might help them predict the **topic** of each poem. *(The significant words can help them predict the **topic** because they give clues about significant subjects in the poem.)* As you discuss the poem on this page, ask students to identify the **topic**. *(choosing friends)* Then have students suggest words that have a **denotation** similar to *Emperor*. *(ruler, king)*

Because I could not stop for Death

Because I could not stop for Death—
He kindly stopped for me—
The Carriage held but just Ourselves—
And Immortality.

5   We slowly drove—He knew no haste
And I had put away
My labor and my leisure too,
For His Civility—

We passed the School, where Children strove
10 At Recess—in the Ring—
We passed the Fields of Gazing Grain—
We passed the Setting Sun—

Or rather—He passed Us—
The Dews drew quivering and chill—
15 For only Gossamer,[1] my Gown—
My Tippet—only Tulle[2]—

We paused before a House that seemed
A Swelling of the Ground—
The Roof was scarcely visible—
20 The Cornice[3]—in the Ground—

Since then—'tis Centuries—and yet
Feels shorter than the Day
I first surmised the Horses' Heads
Were toward Eternity—

---

[1] **Gossamer:** thin, soft material.
[2] **Tippet . . . Tulle:** shawl made of fine netting.
[3] **Cornice:** molding at the top of a building.

Analyzing the Text

COMMON CORE RL 1, RL 6

Cite Text Evidence   Support your responses with evidence.

1. **Interpret** In the third stanza, Death, **personified** as a suitor, takes the speaker past a school and fields. What are these places a reminder of?

2. **Analyze** What is the speaker's attitude about the ride in the first three stanzas? How does the speaker's perception of what is happening to her change in the fourth stanza?

Poems by Emily Dickinson   **201**

WHEN STUDENTS STRUGGLE . . .

Have students reread the first three stanzas and work in pairs to complete a graphic organizer like the one below to interpret the poem. Have them review the chart before reading the rest of the poem.

What the poem describes	What it might mean
Stanzas 1 and 2: A person in a carriage stops for the speaker.	The speaker has died.
Stanza 3: They journey past a school and fields of grain.	They are reviewing the stages of life.

CLOSE READ

Analyze Language

COMMON CORE RL 4, L 4a, L 5a

(LINES 1–8)

Tell students that in a **metaphor**, a writer compares one thing to another without using connecting words such as *like* or *as*. Explain that in this poem, Dickinson uses an extended metaphor throughout the poem that personifies death, or compares it to person.

D CITE TEXT EVIDENCE Have students use text evidence to analyze the poem and explain what death is being compared to. *(The speaker compares death to a person. In lines 2–3, she describes Death as stopping with a carriage to offer her a ride. In lines 2 and 8, she attributes the human characteristics of kindness and civility to Death.)*

Tell students that **personification** is a figure of speech in which an object, animal, or idea is given human characteristics. Explain that the metaphor Dickinson uses in which she compares Death to a person is also an example of personification.

ASK STUDENTS how Dickinson's personification of death affects the meaning of the poem. *(The personification of death as polite and non-threatening suggests that people need not fear death.)*

Analyzing the Text

COMMON CORE RL 1, RL 6

Possible answers:

1. *Both are reminders of life stages. The school is a reminder of childhood; the fields are a reminder of growth, change, and productivity that represent becoming and being an adult.*

2. *In the first three stanzas the speaker's attitude is intrigued, flattered, and pleased. The speaker's attitude becomes more somber and apprehensive in the fourth stanza when the sun sets, the dew is "quivering and chill," and her clothes are insufficient to keep her warm.*

Analyze Language

COMMON CORE RL 4, L 4a, L 5a

(LINES 1–8)

Remind students that **word choice** has a powerful impact on meaning. Tell students that poets sometimes deliberately choose **words with multiple meanings**—words with more than one definition. These words usually have a central meaning in the context of the poem but can also enrich the poem with subtle connections to other meanings.

E CITE TEXT EVIDENCE Have students explain the central meaning of the word *sense* as it is used in the poem, using other words and phrases from the poem to support their explanations. *(The central meaning of* sense *is "sanity." It is juxtaposed with "madness," or insanity, in lines 1 and 3. The central meaning is reinforced by the word "sane" in line 6.)* Have students suggest other meanings of *sense* and cite details in the text that reflect subtle connections to these meanings. *(Sense can refer to the physical faculty by which we perceive sights, sounds and other sensory information, which connects to the eye—or sense of sight in line 2.* Sense *can also mean "discernment, or judgment"; the word "discerning" is also used in line 2.)*

ASK STUDENTS what the multiple meanings of the word *sense* add to the overall meaning of the poem. *(They draw the ideas of physical perception and good judgment into the paradox in line 1 that equates madness and sense.)*

Analyzing the Text

COMMON CORE RL 4, L 4a, L 5a

(Lines 1–8)

Possible answers:

1. *The speaker's criteria for madness are to have sense and to disagree with the majority. The criteria for sense are to be stark mad and to agree with the majority.*

2. *If you go along with the crowd, you'll be accepted as sane; but if you express a unique opinion or go against the crowd, people will think that you are delusional and should be controlled. The direct diction adds power to the closing lines by breaking the rhythm of earlier lines to create a forceful ending. The end rhyme in lines 6 and 8 contributes to this effect.*

Much Madness is divinest Sense

> **E** Much Madness is divinest Sense—
> To a discerning Eye—
> Much Sense—the starkest Madness—
> 'Tis the Majority
> 5 In this, as All, prevail—
> Assent—and you are sane—
> Demur—you're straightway dangerous—
> And handled with a Chain—

Analyzing the Text

COMMON CORE RL 4, L 4a, L 5a

Cite Text Evidence Support your responses with evidence.

1. **Analyze** According to the speaker in this poem, what are the main criteria for "madness" and "sense"?

2. **Summarize** Paraphrase the last three lines of the poem. How does the poet's diction add power to the poem's closing section?

SCAFFOLDING FOR ELL STUDENTS

Analyze Language Use a whiteboard to display lines 1–4.

1. Ask students: What visual clues indicate significant words or relationships? *("Madness" and "sense" do not need to be capitalized, but they are, so they are probably significant.)* Highlight these words.

2. Ask students: What relationship is suggested by the way the words are arranged or used? *(The placement of the words in lines 1 and 3 and its reversal in line 3 suggest that these words are antonyms, or words with opposite meanings.)*

3. Work with students to paraphrase the lines.

Have students work in pairs to practice this process on lines 5–8. Monitor progress.

Tell all the truth but tell it slant

Tell all the truth but tell it slant—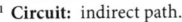
Success in Circuit[1] lies
Too bright for our infirm Delight
The Truth's superb surprise
5 As Lightning to the Children eased
With explanation kind
The Truth must dazzle gradually
Or every man be blind—

---

[1] **Circuit:** indirect path.

Analyzing the Text

COMMON CORE RL 1, RL 4, L 3, L 4a

> **Cite Text Evidence** Support your responses with evidence.

1. **Interpret** What does the narrator mean by "tell it slant"?

2. **Analyze** To what does the narrator compare circling the truth? Does this comparison work? Explain.

COLLABORATIVE DISCUSSION With a partner, discuss the themes that Dickinson explores in her poetry and how they express her feelings about life. Cite specific textual evidence to support your ideas.

WHEN STUDENTS STRUGGLE...

Fluency The absence of punctuation may interfere with students' ability to group words for fluent reading. Help students hear the natural rhythms and breaks by organizing an oral reading that emphasizes the grouping of words.

Have students work in pairs to alternate reading pairs of lines. Have them complete the paired reading twice and then switch parts to read the poem two more times, alternating pairs of lines. Monitor progress by listening as students read and assisting with pronunciation and phrasing.

ASK STUDENTS What do you notice about the way the lines sound? *(They have the rhythm of speech. There is a natural stopping point at the end of each pair of lines.)*

CLOSE READ

Determine Themes (LINE 1)

COMMON CORE RL 2

Remind students that the **theme** of a work is the point the author makes about his or her topic. Often, theme is implied, but sometimes it is directly stated.

 **CITE TEXT EVIDENCE** Have students cite the line that directly states the poem's theme and paraphrase that theme. *(The theme is expressed in the first line of the poem: Speak the truth, but not too directly. Instead, "tell it slant.")*

Analyze Language

COMMON CORE RL 4

(LINES 4–8)

Remind students that a **simile** is a kind of figurative language that compares two unlike things.

G **ASK STUDENTS** to identify and interpret the simile in lines 4-8. *(Truth is like lightning—beautiful but powerful and with the potential to do damage. If people see the truth all at once, it can blind them as lightning would.)* How does this simile relate to the theme of the poem? *(The simile vividly illustrates the theme of the poem, which is about the most effective way to communicate the truth.)*

Analyzing the Text

COMMON CORE RL 1, RL 4, L 3, L 4a

Possible answers:

1. *Don't be blunt or speak too directly.*

2. *The speaker compares circling the truth to gently explaining potentially dangerous things to children. The comparison works, because it gets the point across with a familiar situation and it also communicates that Truth has both awe-inspiring beauty and dangerous power.*

COLLABORATIVE DISCUSSION Have students work in groups to discuss Dickinson's themes and to share textual support for their interpretations.

ASK STUDENTS to share any questions they generated in the course of reading and discussing the selection.

TEACH

CLOSE READ

Analyze Language

COMMON CORE RL 4, L 4a, L 5a

As you present the instruction on word choice, use these examples to illustrate and clarify.

Connotation: "Because I could not stop for Death," line 14: Point out the similarity of denotations of *chill* and *cool.* Contrast the connotations—*cool* suggests a pleasant sensation; *chill* suggests an unpleasant one.

Figurative Language: "The Soul selects her own Society," line 11: Discuss how the comparisons in the words "close the Valves of her attention—/Like Stone" highlight narrowly controlled access (valves) and hardness (stone).

Multiple Meaning Words: "Tell all the truth but tell it slant," line 3: Point out that *bright* can mean "illuminated," "intelligent," and "intensely colored." Discuss the effect of these multiple meanings on the poem.

Allow time for students to work independently to find additional examples of word choice.

Analyze Language

COMMON CORE RL 4, L 4a, L 5a

Words are the building blocks of literature. Consequently, writers choose their words carefully, recognizing that specific word choices affect meaning and tone in a literary work. You can analyze the effect of specific word choices in Dickinson's poetry by looking at the following elements.

Denotation and Connotation	Figurative Language	Multiple Meaning Words
Denotation refers to the dictionary definition of a word. A word's **connotation,** however, refers to the ideas and feelings that a word suggests beyond its primary meaning. In her short poems, Dickinson often uses words with strong connotations to shape and expand the themes of her poems.	**Metaphors** are a kind of figurative language in which one thing is said to be another for the sake of a comparison. For example, in "Because I could not stop for Death," Dickinson uses an **extended metaphor**—a metaphor developed over a number of lines or with several examples—to express her ideas about life and death.	**Multiple meaning words** are words that have more than one meaning. Though the primary meaning may be apparent, the influence of a secondary meaning can change the tone. A good example is in the poem "Much madness is divinest sense." In the first line, *divinest* can mean "extremely good" as well as "relating to God."

Determine Themes

COMMON CORE RL 2

The **theme** of a poem is its underlying message—the point the poet wants to make about life. In a complex work, poets may even develop two or more themes in a single poem, themes that interact and build on one another to produce a more sophisticated message. Most often, a reader has to infer the theme of a poem after considerable thought. Theme is different from subject. A poem's subject might be "death" or "love," but theme is the statement a poet makes about that subject.

   In her nearly 1,800 poems, Emily Dickinson dealt with an abundance of themes, many of which she returned to again and again. Some of these themes center on death, madness or insanity, truth as the poet sees it, the beauty of nature, friendship and love, and God and religion. Readers can determine the theme of a poem by making inferences about the images that the poet creates with words, the speaker's point of view, and the tone that the poet establishes through a careful choice of details.

Strategies for Annotation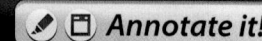

Determine Theme

COMMON CORE RL 2

Have students use their eBook annotation tools to analyze the text.

- Highlight in yellow any lines that seem to state or imply a message.
- Underline words that reflect the speaker's attitude toward the topic, or **tone.**
- Highlight in green comparisons that clarify ideas about the theme.
- Use a note to restate the theme in your own words.

As Lightning to the Children eased

With explanation kind

The Truth must dazzle gradually

Or every man be blind—

If you want to get through to people, help them discover truth, rather than forcing it on them.

Analyzing the Text

COMMON CORE RL 1, RL 2, RL 4, RL 6, RL 9, L 3, L 5a, W 1, W 4

Cite Text Evidence   Support your responses with evidence from the selections.

1. **Analyze** Dickinson uses dashes freely in her poems. How do the dashes affect the way you read the poem? How do they help clarify the meaning of words or phrases?

2. **Analyze** Sometimes understanding a point of view requires distinguishing what is directly stated in a text from what is really meant. Think about the kindly and courtly behavior of Death in "Because I could not stop for Death." How is Death's character ironic?

3. **Compare** The speaker in "Because I could not stop for Death" is somewhat passive. Think about the speaker in "The Soul selects her own Society." How are the two different?

4. **Infer** In both "Much Madness is divinest Sense" and "The Soul selects her own Society," the poet speaks of the Majority. What does the Majority refer to? What does the poet think of the Majority?

5. **Evaluate** What do the connotations of the words *assent* and *demur* in "Much Madness is divinest Sense" indicate about the individual?

6. **Interpret** A **paradox** is a statement that seems to contradict itself but may nevertheless suggest an important truth. Identify the paradoxes in "Tell all the truth but tell it slant" and "Much Madness is divinest Sense." What truth does each paradox convey?

7. **Analyze** In "The Soul selects her own Society," the poet uses the term *soul* to refer to an individual. Why does she use this term? What themes does this poem and "Because I could not stop for Death" reflect?

8. **Identify Patterns** In "Because I could not stop for Death," what metaphors does Dickinson use to express her ideas and views about death?

PERFORMANCE TASK

Writing Activity: Analysis Emily Dickinson chose each word carefully. But it is up to the reader to determine the impact of specific word choices on meaning and tone. Choose one of Dickinson's poems and write a two-paragraph analysis of it.

1. In the first paragraph, explain, line by line, what the poem means. Include opposing claims and counterarguments.

2. In the second paragraph, explain how specific words and phrases helped you determine the meaning and tone of the poem.

In your writing, include evidence from the text and use the conventions of standard English.

PRACTICE & APPLY

Analyzing the Text

COMMON CORE RL 1, RL 2, RL 4, RL 6, RL 9, L 3, L 5a, W 1, W 4

Possible answers:

1. *The dashes act like other kinds of punctuation because they indicate where to pause. In reading, they give the sense of an unexpected pause.*

2. *The character of Death is ironic because readers know something the speaker at first does not: that Death is carrying the speaker into eternity, and thus to her own death.*

3. *The speaker in "The Soul selects her own Society" is confident and in control of her own destiny and choices; the speaker in "Because I could not stop for Death" is not in control.*

4. *The Majority can refer to the speaker's wider group of acquaintances or generally to "most people." The speaker seems to think that the Majority has poor judgment.*

5. *"Assent" and "demur" have connotations of being responses to a group decision that has already been made. This suggests that the individual is at the mercy of the group and that the Majority does not really speak for everyone.*

6. *The paradox in "Tell all the truth but tell it slant" is that to be completely truthful, you must speak indirectly. The paradox in "Much Madness is divinest sense" is that madness and sense are opposites, but they are presented as the same thing. This conveys the idea that the interpretations of what is mad and what is sane are not fixed.*

7. *The term "soul" suggests the innermost part of the individual—the true self. Both poems convey the idea that the soul lives on after the death of the body.*

8. *Dickinson personifies death as a polite companion, perhaps a suitor; she compares the stages of life to different places—a school and a field of grain.*

 Assign this performance task.

PERFORMANCE TASK

COMMON CORE W 1, W 4

Writing Activity: Analysis Have students work independently to interpret the poems they choose. Then have them share and discuss their interpretations with a partner. Partners should challenge the interpretation by raising counterarguments, supporting their interpretation with specific words and phrases. Have students revise their initial analyses. Circulate students' work and ask them to share and explain some of the examples they use.

PRACTICE & APPLY

Vocabulary Strategy: Affixes

Answers:

Root Word: Meaning	Suffix Meaning	Full Word Meaning
eternal: existing through all time	*ity:* state of	*Eternity: state of existing through all time*
explain: clarify meaning	*ation:* action or result of	*Explanation: the result of acting to clarify meaning*
major: most important or greatest	*ity:* state of	*Majority: group of greatest size and often most important influence*
danger: threat; peril; extreme risk of harm	*ous:* having the qualities of	*Dangerous: having the quality of high potential to harm*

 Assess It!

Online Selection Test
- Download an editable ExamView bank.
- Assign and manage this test online.

Vocabulary Strategy: Affixes

Affixes are word parts that are added to the beginning or the end of a base word or root. A **prefix** is added to the beginning of a base word or root. A prefix such as *mis–*, *over–*, and *un–* always changes the denotation, or meaning of the base word. A **suffix** is added to the end of a base word or root. **Inflectional suffixes,** like *–ed* and *–ing*, usually just change the tense, the person, or the number of a word (generally a verb). **Derivational suffixes,** like those listed in the chart, change the meaning of a root or base word.

Suffixes	Meanings	Examples
–ity	state of; condition of	immortality
–ous	full of	malicious
–ness	quality or state of being	madness
–tion	condition or state of	attention

You can use derivational suffixes to help you decipher the meaning of unfamiliar words. By identifying the suffix and the root word, you can determine how the suffix changes the word's meaning. For example, in "Because I could not stop for Death," it might be difficult to determine the meaning of *civility* just by relying on the context clues in the poem. However, you can infer the word's meaning by identifying the root word, *civil*, and the suffix, *–ity*, as demonstrated.

Root Word, Meaning	Suffix, Meaning	Full Word, Meaning
civil: polite	*–ity:* state of	*Civility: polite behavior*

Practice and Apply Use the chart as a model to create your own suffix-analysis chart for the following words from Dickinson's poems.

1. eternity

2. explanation

3. majority

4. dangerous

To Challenge Students . . .

Analyzing Effect of Word Choice on Sound Review these terms:

Consonance and alliteration: Repeated consonant sounds at the beginnings of words or within words: *Assent— and you are sane—/Demur—you're straightway dangerous.*

Rhyme and approximate rhyme: Ending two or more lines with words that have the same sound in the final syllable or syllables but do not exactly rhyme. *The Dews grew quivering and chill—...My Tippet—only Tulle.*

Have groups work together to discuss and evaluate the poems for how the word choices integrate sound and meaning, citing examples to support their evaluations.

Author's Style

COMMON CORE

L 3

TEACH

Dickinson wrote **lyric poetry.** Remind students that most lyric poems share these characteristics:

- Intense expression of thoughts and feelings.
- A speaker (not necessarily the poet) who directly addresses the reader.
- Musical qualities of sound and rhythm.

However, Dickinson's distinctive style makes her poetry unique and almost instantly recognizable.

Unconventional punctuation: Dickinson uses dashes in place of almost all other punctuation—and sometimes uses them where punctuation would not normally be used at all. These dashes highlight key words or affect the poem's rhythm.

Unusual capitalization: Dickinson uses capitalization for emphasis and effect. She often capitalizes words that are not proper nouns.

Unexpected figurative language: Dickinson's comparisons catch readers by surprise. Her striking metaphors and similes make abstract ideas concrete.

Distinctive form: Most of Dickinson's poems are very short. Her longer poems are usually organized into tight stanzas, or groups of lines. The brevity of these poems and sections heightens their intensity by packing enormous meaning and feeling into just a few lines. In addition, Dickinson's poems have no titles. Today, Dickinson's poems are generally identified by numbers or first lines.

COLLABORATIVE DISCUSSION

Have students work in groups to focus on examples of Dickinson's unique style. After a period of discussion, have each group choose one poem for each category (punctuation, capitalization, figurative language, form) that best illustrates Dickinson's unique style in that category. Allow groups to present and defend their findings. As a class, chart the results and discuss.

 If students need further instruction, use this *Interactive Whiteboard Lesson:* **Forms in Poetry.**

Determine Themes

COMMON CORE

RL 2

TEACH

Remind students that the **theme** of a poem is the message the writer conveys about a topic. For some poems, the message may be simple: to celebrate the topic by describing its qualities. For other poems, the theme may be a more complex insight about life or human nature.

Tell students that although Dickinson lived a reclusive life in an earlier century, her work communicates relevant themes with powerful insights.

ASK STUDENTS to explain the distinction between the topic and theme of one of the poems in this group. If students need additional instruction on recognizing and expressing themes as distinct from topics, assign the Level Up Tutorial: Universal and Recurring Themes.

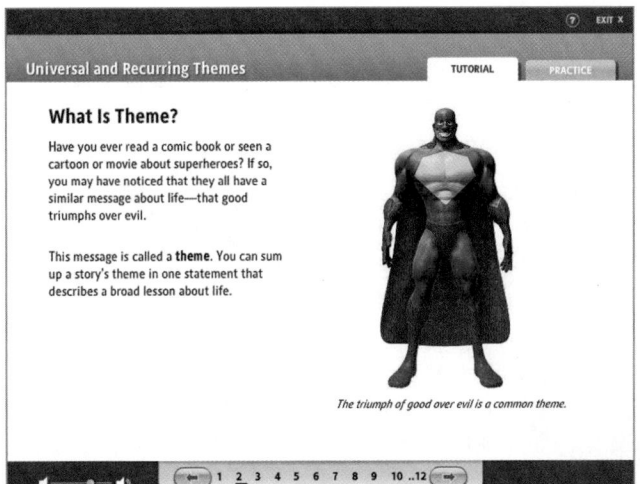

PRACTICE AND APPLY

Have students complete a chart like this for each poem. Allow for different interpretations as long as they can be supported by textual evidence.

Poem	Topic	Theme
The Soul selects her own Society	choosing who to love or be close to	Some people choose only a few close friends and close the rest of the world out.

Circulate and monitor progress by asking students to explain specific responses.

mySmartPlanner Create lesson plans and access resources online.

 **EXEMPLAR** *from* **Walden**

Essay by Henry David Thoreau

Why This Text?

In order to fully comprehend what they read, students must be able to identify the central ideas of a text. One way to determine a text's central idea is to write a summary of it. In this lesson, students will use summarizing strategies to find the central ideas of an excerpt from Henry David Thoreau's *Walden*.

Key Learning Objective: The student will be able to determine the central ideas of the text.

For additional practice:

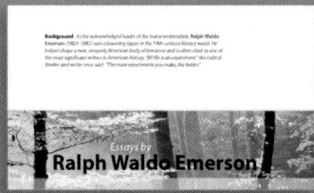

Close Reader selection
from "Nature" and *from* "Self-Reliance"
Essays by Ralph Waldo Emerson

COMMON CORE Common Core Standards

RI 1 Cite textual evidence.
RI 2 Determine central ideas of a text.
RI 3 Analyze a set of ideas or sequence of events.
RI 5 Analyze and evaluate structure.
RI 6 Determine an author's point of view or purpose.
W 2 Write informative/explanatory texts.
L 3a Vary syntax for effect; apply an understanding of syntax.
L 4a Use context as a clue to meaning.
L 4d Verify the preliminary determination of the meaning of a word or phrase.
L 5a Interpret figures of speech.

▲ Text Complexity Rubric

Quantitative Measures	**Walden** Lexile: 1250L
Qualitative Measures	**Levels of Meaning/Purpose** multiple topics
	Structure genre traits less common to informational text
	Language Conventionality and Clarity figurative, less accessible language
	Knowledge Demands a number of references to other texts
Reader/Task Considerations	Teacher determined Vary by individual reader and type of text

CLOSE READ

Background Have students read the information about the author. Tell them that Thoreau and Emerson are regarded as the major Transcendentalist writers of the 19th century. Transcendentalism was a philosophy that held that the strongest truths could only be learned via people's five senses—that is, via their intuition—rather than through logic. Transcendentalists also believed that humans are essentially good and that all things were created equal. Thoreau's transcendental beliefs were expressed in his writings. In *Walden*, Thoreau is advocating for a return to nature, in which he believes humans may find life's deepest truths.

AS YOU READ Direct students to use the As You Read instructions to focus their reading. Remind them to write down any questions they generate during reading.

Determine Central Ideas: Summarize (LINES 1–17)

 **RI 2, L 5a**

Explain to students that determining the central ideas of a text as they read will help them be sure they have a clear understanding of the text. To help determine the central idea of a portion of a text, write a short summary of it. **Summarizing** a text means restating the central ideas in one's own words.

A **ASK STUDENTS** to read the title of the essay as well as lines 1–17. Ask students to summarize the central idea of this opening section. Where did Thoreau live? *(Thoreau moved to a solitary cabin in the woods not far from Concord.)*

Determine Author's Purpose: Style (LINES 1–6)

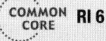 **RI 6**

Tell students that every author has a **purpose,** or reason, for writing. Explain that one way to **infer,** or deduce from evidence, an author's purpose is to examine the author's **style.** Style is the way the author expresses his or her ideas.

B **ASK STUDENTS** to read the first sentence. Then ask students to think about whether Thoreau's style is formal or informal. *(informal)* Finally, ask students what they can infer from this sentence about the writer's purpose. *(The writer's purpose is to communicate in a straightforward, casual way with the reader.)*

Henry David Thoreau (1817–1862) *of Concord, Massachusetts, was a transcendentalist like his friend and mentor Ralph Waldo Emerson. After graduating from Harvard College and teaching school for a few years, Thoreau decided to become a nature poet. In 1845 he began his two-year experiment living in a cabin that he built in the woods near Walden Pond on property owned by Emerson. Walden (1854) is a collection of 18 essays based on his experiences. Thoreau's most famous essay, "Civil Disobedience" (1849), defends the right of an individual to follow his conscience rather than obey unjust laws.*

from
Walden

Essay by Henry David Thoreau

Image Credits: (tl) ©Time & Life Pictures/Getty Images; (cl) ©sot/Stone/Getty Images; (cr) ©Tungphoto/Shutterstock; (tr) ©Dmitry Naumow/Shutterstock.

AS YOU READ Note the observations Thoreau makes about modern life that still seem relevant today.

from **Where I Lived, and What I Lived For**

When first I took up my abode in the woods, that is, began to spend my nights as well as days there, which, by accident, was on Independence day, or the fourth of July, 1845, my house was not finished for winter, but was merely a defense against the rain, without plastering or chimney, the walls being of rough weather-stained boards, with wide chinks, which made it cool at night. The upright white hewn studs and freshly planed door and window casings gave it a clean and airy look, especially in the morning, when its timbers were saturated with dew, so that I fancied that by noon some sweet gum would exude from them. . . .

I was seated by the shore of a small pond, about a mile and a half south of the village of Concord and somewhat higher than it, in the midst of an extensive wood between that town and Lincoln, and about two miles south of that our only field known to fame, Concord Battle Ground; but I was so low in the woods that the opposite shore, half a mile off, like the rest, covered with wood, was my most distant horizon. For the first week, whenever I looked out on the pond it

Walden **207**

SCAFFOLDING FOR ELL STUDENTS

Recognize the Past Tense of Verbs Point out the word *planed* in line 7. Explain that this is the past tense of the verb *to plane,* which means "to make a piece of wood smooth by cutting off thin pieces with a tool." The word should not be confused with *planned,* the past tense of the verb *to plan.* Instruct students that for verbs ending with a short vowel sound followed by a consonant, the consonant is doubled before adding *–ed* to form the past tense.

ASK STUDENTS to practice forming the past tense of the following pairs of verbs:

- *can* and *cane*
- *pin* and *pine*

Determine Author's Purpose: Style (LINES 18–25)

COMMON CORE RI 6

Remind students that style is the way an author expresses his or her ideas and that an author's style can help reveal his or her purpose for writing. Thoreau's style includes **figurative language**—language that is not used literally. Two kinds of figurative language Thoreau uses are **personification** and **simile.** Personification is the technique of giving human characteristics to an animal, an object, or an idea. A simile is a comparison made using the words *like* or *as.*

 **CITE TEXT EVIDENCE** Have students read lines 18–25. Ask them to find one example each of personification and simile and tell what inferences they can draw from them about Thoreau's purpose for writing. *(In line 20, Thoreau personifies the pond when he describes it "throwing off its nightly clothing of mist." Then, in line 22, he uses a simile to compare the mists to ghosts. From this figurative language it is possible to infer that Thoreau's purpose was to help the reader to see the landscape as he does: as a living being with its own spirit.)*

Analyze Language

COMMON CORE L 3a

(LINES 57–58)

Tell students that another stylistic element Thoreau uses in Walden is **rhetorical questions.** Rhetorical questions are asked only to make a point, not to get a reply.

 **ASK STUDENTS** to read the sentence that begins in line 57. Explain why this sentence is a rhetorical question. Then tell what point Thoreau is making by asking it. *(It's a rhetorical question because Thoreau is not really expecting an answer from readers. He is making the point that people should not live in a hurried fashion.)*

 impressed me like a tarn[1] high up on the side of a mountain, its bottom far above the surface of other lakes, and, as the sun arose, I
20 saw it throwing off its nightly clothing of mist, and here and there, by degrees, its soft ripples or its smooth reflecting surface was revealed, while the mists, like ghosts, were stealthily withdrawing in every direction into the woods, as at the breaking up of some nocturnal conventicle.[2] The very dew seemed to hang upon the trees later into the day than usual, as on the sides of mountains. . . .

I went to the woods because I wished to live deliberately, to front only the essential facts of life, and see if I could not learn what it had to teach, and not, when I came to die, discover that I had not lived. I did not wish to live what was not life, living is so dear; nor did I
30 wish to practice resignation, unless it was quite necessary. I wanted to live deep and suck out all the marrow of life, to live so sturdily and Spartan-like[3] as to put to rout all that was not life, to cut a broad swath and shave close, to drive life into a corner, and reduce it to its lowest terms, and, if it proved to be mean, why then to get the whole and genuine meanness of it, and publish its meanness to the world; or if it were sublime, to know it by experience, and be able to give a true account of it in my next excursion. For most men, it appears to me, are in a strange uncertainty about it, whether it is of the devil or of God, and have *somewhat hastily* concluded that it is the chief end of man
40 here to "glorify God and enjoy him forever."

Still we live meanly, like ants; though the fable tells us that we were long ago changed into men; like pygmies we fight with cranes; it is error upon error, and clout upon clout, and our best virtue has for its occasion a superfluous and evitable[4] wretchedness. Our life is frittered away by detail. An honest man has hardly need to count more than his ten fingers, or in extreme cases he may add his ten toes, and lump the rest. Simplicity, simplicity, simplicity! I say, let your affairs be as two or three, and not a hundred or a thousand; instead of a million count half a dozen, and keep your accounts on your thumbnail. In the midst of
50 this chopping sea of civilized life, such are the clouds and storms and quicksands and thousand-and-one items to be allowed for, that a man has to live, if he would not founder and go to the bottom and not make his port at all, by dead reckoning, and he must be a great calculator indeed who succeeds. Simplify, simplify. Instead of three meals a day, if it be necessary eat but one; instead of a hundred dishes, five; and reduce other things in proportion. . . .

 Why should we live with such hurry and waste of life? We are determined to be starved before we are hungry. Men say that a stitch in time saves nine, and so they take a thousand stitches today to save

---

[1] **tarn:** a small mountain lake or pool.

[2] **conventicle:** a secret or unlawful religious meeting.

[3] **Spartan-like:** in a simple and disciplined way, like the inhabitants of the ancient city-state of Sparta.

[4] **superfluous and evitable:** unnecessary and avoidable.

APPLYING ACADEMIC VOCABULARY

quote	analogy

As you discuss this page in which Thoreau criticizes civilized life, incorporate the Collection 3 academic vocabulary words: *quote* and *analogy*. Ask students why they think Thoreau **quotes** a religious authority in line 40. Have students discuss what point Thoreau is making when he makes an **analogy** between people and ants in line 41.

E

60 nine to-morrow. As for *work*, we haven't any of any consequence. We
have the Saint Vitus' dance,[5] and cannot possibly keep our heads still.
If I should only give a few pulls at the parish bell-rope, as for a fire,
that is, without setting the bell, there is hardly a man on his farm in
the outskirts of Concord, notwithstanding that press of engagements
which was his excuse so many times this morning, nor a boy, nor
a woman, I might almost say, but would forsake all and follow that
sound, not mainly to save property from the flames, but, if we will
confess the truth, much more to see it burn, since burn it must, and
we, be it known, did not set it on fire,—or to see it put out, and have a
70 hand in it, if that is done as handsomely; yes, even if it were the parish
church itself. Hardly a man takes a half hour's nap after dinner, but
when he wakes he holds up his head and asks, "What's the news?" as
if the rest of mankind had stood his sentinels. Some give directions to
be waked every half hour, doubtless for no other purpose; and then, to
pay for it, they tell what they have dreamed. After a night's sleep the
news is as indispensable as the breakfast. "Pray tell me any thing new
that has happened to a man any where on this globe,"—and he reads
it over his coffee and rolls, that a man has had his eyes gouged out this
morning on the Wachito River; never dreaming the while that he lives
80 in the dark **unfathomed** mammoth cave of this world, and has but the
rudiment of an eye himself.

unfathomed
(ŭn-fătħ´əmd) *adj.*
located at the
deepest place.

---

[5] **Saint Vitus' dance:** a disorder of the nervous system, characterized by rapid,
jerky, involuntary movements.

CLOSE READ

Determine Author's Purpose: Style (LINES 62–71)

Explain to students that another stylistic element
that Thoreau employs is **hyperbole.** Hyperbole is
exaggeration for effect.

E ASK STUDENTS to read the one long sentence
that begins in line 62. Ask students what Thoreau is
exaggerating in this sentence and what effect this
exaggeration has on the reader. Then ask what this
use of hyperbole reveals about Thoreau's purpose.
*(Thoreau is exaggerating people's interest in news and
other people's affairs by saying that if he rang the bell
everyone would immediately drop what they are doing
and come running. The effect of the hyperbole is to make
the people who come running to see what is happening
seem foolish and flighty. Thoreau's purpose is to make
readers think about whether they are also fixated on
other people's business.)*

CRITICAL VOCABULARY

unfathomed: Thoreau compares the world to a
large cave, the deepest places in which have not
been measured or explored.

ASK STUDENTS in what way the world might be
unfathomed by someone who is overly concerned
with news. *(Sample answer: Someone who is overly
concerned with news might not notice the nuances
of nature or be in touch with his or her own inner
thoughts.)*

WHEN STUDENTS STRUGGLE ...

Call students' attention to the two quotations on this page (lines 72 and
76–77). Explain that in these lines Thoreau is not quoting words he has read
or heard someone say. Instead he is giving an example of what a person like
those he is discussing might say.

ASK STUDENTS to paraphrase lines 72 and 76–77, replacing the direct
quotations with indirect quotations. Provide help as needed. *(line 72: "when
he wakes up he holds up his head and asks what the news is;" lines 76–77: "He
asks whether anything new has happened to anyone anywhere in the world.")*

Determine Central Ideas: Summarize (LINES 99–112)

 COMMON CORE RI 2, L 5a

Remind students that **summarizing** a text—restating the central ideas in one's own words—can help them determine the author's central ideas.

(F) **ASK STUDENTS** to reread the last paragraph on the page and summarize it. *(I want to use my intellect to learn life's secrets, and I believe I can do this by studying nature.)*

Determine Author's Purpose: Style (LINES 99–105)

 COMMON CORE RI 6

Yet another form of figurative language Thoreau employs is **metaphor**. Metaphors are comparisons made without the use of the words *like* or *as*.

(G) **CITE TEXT EVIDENCE** Have students reread lines 99–105. Ask them to identify two metaphors and infer Thoreau's purpose for including them here. *(In line 99, Thoreau says, "Time is but the stream I go a-fishing in." In comparing time to a stream of water, Thoreau is saying that time is eternal, yet fleeting for each individual. In line 104, he writes, "The intellect is a cleaver." Here he means to say that his own mind is a useful and important tool that he uses to find out the meaning of things.)*

> ### CRITICAL VOCABULARY

perturbation: Thoreau is asking the reader to stay calm at the beginning of the day and not get caught up in the day's business.

ASK STUDENTS what modern-day events might be likely to cause perturbation in the morning. *(Possible answers: phone calls, texts, car trouble, traffic)*

For my part, I could easily do without the post-office. I think that there are very few important communications made through it. To speak critically, I never received more than one or two letters in my life—I wrote this some years ago—that were worth the postage. The penny-post is, commonly, an institution through which you seriously offer a man that penny for his thoughts which is so often safely offered in jest. And I am sure that I never read any memorable news in a newspaper. If we read of one man robbed, or murdered, or

90 killed by accident, or one house burned, or one vessel wrecked, or one steamboat blown up, or one cow run over on the Western Railroad, or one mad dog killed, or one lot of grasshoppers in the winter,—we never need read of another. One is enough. . . .

> ❝ I have always been regretting that I was not as wise as the day I was born. ❞

Let us spend one day as deliberately as Nature, and not be thrown off the track by every nutshell and mosquito's wing that falls on the rails. Let us rise early and fast, or break fast, gently and without **perturbation**; let company come and let company go, let the bells ring and the children cry,— determined to make a day of it. . . .

(F) 100 Time is but the stream I go a-fishing in. I drink at it; but while I drink I see the sandy bottom and detect how shallow it is. Its thin current slides away, but eternity remains. I would drink deeper; fish in the sky, whose bottom is pebbly with stars. I cannot count one. I know not the first letter of the alphabet. I have always been regretting that I was not as wise as the day I was born. The intellect is a cleaver; it discerns and rifts its way into the secret of things. I do not wish to be any more busy with my hands than is necessary. My head is hands and feet. I feel all my best faculties concentrated in it. My instinct tells me that my head is an organ for burrowing, as some creatures use their snout and fore-paws, and with it I would mine and burrow

110 my way through these hills. I think that the richest vein is somewhere hereabouts; so by the divining rod and thin rising vapors I judge; and here I will begin to mine.

perturbation
(G) (pûr´tər-bā´shən) *n.* disturbance or agitation.

TO CHALLENGE STUDENTS . . .

Use Figurative Language If Thoreau has such disdain for the post office, can you imagine what he would think of today's media and communications? Tell students to reread lines 82–93. Discuss with them whether Thoreau's complaints about the post office and newspapers apply to contemporary forms of communication.

ASK STUDENTS to write a paragraph critiquing some modern form of communication in which they mimic Thoreau's style. Tell them to use long, informal sentences and list specific examples. When finished, have them read their paragraphs to the class.

from **Solitude**

This is a delicious evening, when the whole body is one sense, and imbibes delight through every pore. I go and come with a strange liberty in Nature, a part of herself. As I walk along the stony shore of the pond in my shirt sleeves, though it is cool as well as cloudy and windy, and I see nothing special to attract me, all the elements are unusually **congenial** to me. The bullfrogs trump to usher in the night, and the note of the whippoorwill is borne on the rippling wind from
120 over the water. Sympathy with the fluttering alder and poplar leaves almost takes away my breath; yet, like the lake, my serenity is rippled but not ruffled. These small waves raised by the evening wind are as remote from storm as the smooth reflecting surface. Though it is now dark, the wind still blows and roars in the wood, the waves still dash, and some creatures lull the rest with their notes. The repose is never complete. The wildest animals do not repose, but seek their prey now; the fox, and skunk, and rabbit, now roam the fields and woods without fear. They are Nature's watchmen,—links which connect the days of animated life. . . .
130   Men frequently say to me, "I should think you would feel lonesome down there, and want to be nearer to folks, rainy and snowy days and nights especially." I am tempted to reply to such,—This whole earth which we inhabit is but a point in space. How far apart, think you, dwell the two most distant inhabitants of yonder star, the breadth of whose disk cannot be appreciated by our instruments? Why should I feel lonely? Is not our planet in the Milky Way? This which you put seems to me not to be the most important question. What sort of space is that which separates a man from his fellows and makes him solitary? I have found that no exertion of the legs can bring two minds much
140 nearer to one another. . . .

congenial
(kən-jēn′yəl) *adj.* agreeable; pleasant.

from **The Pond in Winter**

Every winter the liquid and trembling surface of the pond, which was so sensitive to every breath, and reflected every light and shadow, becomes solid to the depth of a foot or a foot and a half, so that it will support the heaviest teams, and perchance the snow covers it to an equal depth, and it is not to be distinguished from any level field. Like the marmots in the surrounding hills, it closes its eye-lids and becomes dormant for three months or more. Standing on the snow-covered plain, as if in a pasture amid the hills, I cut my way first through a foot of snow, and then a foot of ice, and open a window
150 under my feet, where, kneeling to drink, I look down into the quiet parlor of the fishes, pervaded by a softened light as through a window of ground glass, with its bright sanded floor the same as in summer; there a **perennial** waveless serenity reigns as in the amber twilight sky,

perennial
(pə-rĕn′ē-əl) *adv.* enduring; long-lasting.

Walden **211**

APPLYING ACADEMIC VOCABULARY

topic	denote

As you discuss the section "from Solitude," incorporate the Collection 3 academic vocabulary words: *topic* and *denote*. Ask students how the first paragraph of this section relates to the **topic** of solitude. Then ask what the word *solitude* **denotes**. *(the state of being alone)* Finally, ask students to explain the difference in connotation, or emotional associations, between *solitude* and *loneliness*. *(Solitude is associated with peace and tranquility, while loneliness is associated with sadness and distress.)*

CLOSE READ

Determine Central Ideas: Summarize (LINES 113–140)

COMMON CORE RI 2, L 5a

Tell students that when summarizing the central ideas of a text, they should use any titles or subtitles as clues.

H **ASK STUDENTS** to read the title of this section of the essay and infer what its central idea might be. *(Accept all reasonable responses.)* Then after reading lines 113–140, have students summarize this section. *(Even in solitude, people are never really alone because they are surrounded by and a part of nature.)*

Determine Author's Purpose: Style (LINES 146–152)

COMMON CORE RI 6

Point out to students that in this section Thoreau continues to use figurative language to describe nature.

I **CITE TEXT EVIDENCE** Have students reread lines 146–152 and ask them to identify a simile and a metaphor. Then ask students to tell which one uses personification. *(In line 146, Thoreau uses a simile to say that the pond closes its eyelids and hibernates like the marmots. In line 151, he uses a metaphor to compare the pond to a parlor for fish. The metaphor is personification because it speaks of the fish as having a parlor, as do people.)*

CRITICAL VOCABULARY

congenial: Thoreau describes what a lovely evening it is, how content he feels walking home amidst nature, and how all the natural elements he experiences are pleasing to him. **ASK STUDENTS** to give evidence that Thoreau finds the "elements" to be "congenial." *(Thoreau begins this section by describing the evening as "delicious"; he says he feels a "liberty" this night, and he feels "sympathy" with the leaves.)*

perennial: Thoreau is describing the bottom of the pond in winter and how it appears the same as in the summer; it is enduring and unchanging in this way. **ASK STUDENTS** to think of other things in Thoreau's woods that would be perennial. *(rocks, evergreen trees)*

Determine Author's Purpose: Style (LINES 171–176)

COMMON CORE RI 6

Remind students that **personification** is a form of figurative language in which human characteristics are given to an animal, an object, or an idea. The use of personification can gives clues to the author's purpose for writing.

J CITE TEXT EVIDENCE Have students read lines 171–176 and cite the human characteristics given to the pond in springtime. How does this example of personification reveal Thoreau's purpose for writing? *(The spring pond is said to have a "bosom" in which it holds the summer evening sky as well as "intelligence" (an understanding) with a remote horizon. Thoreau's purpose in personifying the pond is to make readers see it as a living thing with which they are connected.)*

Determine Central Ideas: Summarize (LINES 177–193)

COMMON CORE RI 2, L 5a

Explain that one strategy for determining a central idea of a text is to look for a topic sentence that may explicitly state it. Topic sentences often are the first sentence of a paragraph.

K CITE TEXT EVIDENCE Have students read lines 177–193 and identify a topic sentence that states a central idea. *("We can never have enough of nature," line 177.)* Then ask them whether the rest of the paragraph supports this central idea and, if so, how. *(Yes, the paragraph goes on to give details about what we need from nature, tell an anecdote about needing to be assured of the health of nature, and explain Thoreau's personal feelings about nature's robustness.)*

---

corresponding to the cool and even temperament of the inhabitants. Heaven is under our feet as well as over our heads. . . .

from **Spring**

One attraction in coming to the woods to live was that I should have leisure and opportunity to see the spring come in. The ice in the pond at length begins to be honey-combed, and I can set my heel in it as I walk. Fogs and rains and warmer suns are gradually melting the snow;
160 the days have grown sensibly longer; and I see how I shall get through the winter without adding to my woodpile, for large fires are no longer necessary. I am on the alert for the first signs of spring, to hear the chance note of some arriving bird, or the striped squirrel's chirp, for his stores must be now nearly exhausted, or see the woodchuck venture out of his winter quarters. . . .

The change from storm and winter to serene and mild weather, from dark and sluggish hours to bright and elastic ones, is a memorable crisis which all things proclaim. It is seemingly instantaneous at last. Suddenly an influx of light filled my house,
170 though the evening was at hand, and the clouds of winter still overhung it, and the eaves were dripping with sleety rain. I looked out the window, and lo! where yesterday was cold gray ice there lay the transparent pond already calm and full of hope as in a summer evening, reflecting a summer evening sky in its bosom, though none was visible overhead, as if it had intelligence with some remote horizon. . . .

We can never have enough of nature. We must be refreshed by the sight of inexhaustible vigor, vast and titanic features, the sea-coast with its wrecks, the wilderness with its living and its decaying trees,
180 the thunder-cloud, and the rain which lasts three weeks and produces freshets.[6] We need to witness our own limits transgressed, and some life pasturing freely where we never wander. We are cheered when we observe the vulture feeding on the carrion which disgusts and disheartens us, and deriving health and strength from the repast. There was a dead horse in the hollow by the path to my house, which compelled me sometimes to go out of my way, especially in the night when the air was heavy, but the assurance it gave me of the strong appetite and inviolable health of Nature was my compensation for this. I love to see that Nature is so rife with life that myriads can be
190 afforded to be sacrificed and suffered to prey on one another; that tender organizations can be so serenely squashed out of existence like pulp—tadpoles which herons gobble up, and tortoises and toads run over in the road; and that sometimes it has rained flesh and blood! With the liability to accident, we must see how little account is to be

---

[6] **freshets:** overflowings of a stream caused by heavy rain or melting snow.

SCAFFOLDING FOR ELL STUDENTS

Understand Suffixes Point out the words *gradually* (line 159), *sensibly* (line 160), and *freely* (line 182). Tell students that all these words end with the **suffix** -*ly*. A suffix is a letter or group of letters added to the end of a word to change its meaning. The suffix -*ly* changes an adjective (a word that describes a noun) to an adverb (a word that describes a verb).

ASK STUDENTS to write the adjective form of each of the words above. *(gradual, sensible, free).* Then ask students to write sentences containing both the adjective and adverb form of each of the words. *(Sasha gradually became aware of the snail's gradual approach. Matt was not sensible of having offended Olive, although she was sensibly angry. Because Caleb was free of homework, he could roam the neighborhood freely.)*

made of it. The impression made on a wise man is that of universal innocence. Poison is not poisonous after all, nor are any wounds fatal. Compassion is a very **untenable** ground. It must be expeditious. Its pleadings will not bear to be stereotyped.[7]

untenable
(ŭn-tĕn´ə-bəl) *adj.* unsustainable, insupportable.

from Conclusion

I left the woods for as good a reason as I went there. Perhaps it seemed
200 to me that I had several more lives to live, and could not spare any
more time for that one. It is remarkable how easily and insensibly we
fall into a particular route, and make a beaten track for ourselves. I
had not lived there a week before my feet wore a path from my door
to the pond-side; and though it is five or six years since I trod it, it is
still quite distinct. It is true, I fear that others may have fallen into
it, and so helped to keep it open. The surface of the earth is soft and
impressible by the feet of men; and so with the paths which the mind
travels. How worn and dusty, then, must be the highways of the world,
how deep the ruts of tradition and conformity! I did not wish to take a
210 cabin passage, but rather to go before the mast and on the deck of the
world, for there I could best see the moonlight amid the mountains. I
do not wish to go below now.

---

[7] **pleadings . . . stereotyped:** its defense, or reasons for acting in a certain way, cannot be easily pinned down or understood.

Image Credits: ©John James/Photonica/Getty Images

CLOSE READ

Determine Author's Purpose: Style (LINES 199–209)

COMMON CORE RI 6

Remind students that Thoreau makes active use of **metaphors**—comparisons made without the use of the words *like* or *as*—and that his choice of metaphors can help to reveal his purpose. Also remind students that metaphors, like all figurative language, are not literally true.

Ⓛ CITE TEXT EVIDENCE Ask students to read lines 199–209. Have them find as many metaphors as they can and tell what comparison is being made. *(In line 202, Thoreau compares a habitual way of life to a "particular route" or "beaten track." In lines 207–208, he compares habitual ways of thinking with paths. In line 209, he compares the habits of tradition and conformity with ruts.)* Then ask what these metaphors reveal about Thoreau's purpose for writing. *(By comparing habitual thinking and behavior with well-trodden roads, he helps the reader to understand how habits can blind us to other possibilities.)*

CRITICAL VOCABULARY

untenable: Thoreau believes that compassion for the suffering people see in the natural world is an attitude that cannot be supported.

ASK STUDENTS to explain in their own words why Thoreau feels compassion is untenable. *(Thoreau feels that because the destruction of some creatures is evidence of nature's robust health, there is no reason to feel strong emotions about their loss.)*

SCAFFOLDING FOR ELL STUDENTS

Identify Synonyms Remind students that **synonyms** are words that mean almost the same thing. Point out to students that in his conclusion Thoreau uses five synonyms for the word *road*.

ASK STUDENTS to work with a partner to find all synonyms for *road* in lines 199–212. *(route, track, path, highways, rut)* Then ask pairs to think of more synonyms for *road*. *(course, way, trail)* Tell students to look for synonyms as they read.

Determine Central Ideas: Summarize (LINES 213–224)

 **COMMON CORE RI 2, L 5a**

Remind students that a paragraph's central idea may be stated directly.

M **CITE TEXT EVIDENCE** Ask students to reread lines 213–224 and identify the sentence that states the central idea. *("I learned this, at least, by my experiment; that if one advances confidently in the direction of his dreams, and endeavors to live the life which he has imagined, he will meet with a success unexpected in common hours," lines 213–216.)* Then ask students to summarize this central idea in a short sentence. *(I learned that you can live your dreams.)*

Determine Author's Purpose: Style (LINES 222–228)

 **COMMON CORE RI 6**

Tell students that lines 222–228 are some of the best known from all of *Walden*, and that the figurative language they contain has become part of American culture. Explain that a metaphor or simile that continues over more than one sentence is called an **extended metaphor.**

N **CITE TEXT EVIDENCE** Ask students to read lines 222–228 and identify the figurative language, telling whether each example is a **simile** or a **metaphor.** Then have them tell what purpose for writing the figurative language reveals. *("If you have built castles in the air, your work need not be lost; that is where they should be. Now put foundations under them," lines 222–224, extended metaphor; "If a man does not keep pace with his companions, perhaps it is because he hears a different drummer. Let him step to the music which he hears, however measured or far away," lines 226–228, extended metaphor. Both of these figures of speech encourage people to follow their dreams, even if that means that their lives look different from the lives of others. Thoreau's purpose is to encourage people to follow their dreams.)*

M I learned this, at least, by my experiment; that if one advances confidently in the direction of his dreams, and endeavors to live the life which he has imagined, he will meet with a success unexpected in common hours. He will put some things behind, will pass an invisible boundary; new, universal, and more liberal laws will begin to establish themselves around and within him; or the old laws be expanded, and interpreted in his favor in a more liberal sense, and he will live with
220 the license of a higher order of beings. In proportion as he simplifies his life, the laws of the universe will appear less complex, and solitude will not be solitude, nor poverty poverty, nor weakness weakness. If you have built castles in the air, your work need not be lost; that is **N** where they should be. Now put the foundations under them. . . .

Why should we be in such desperate haste to succeed, and in such desperate enterprises? If a man does not keep pace with his companions, perhaps it is because he hears a different drummer. Let him step to the music which he hears, however measured or far away.[8]
It is not important that he should mature as soon as an appletree or an
230 oak. Shall he turn his spring into summer? If the condition of things which we were made for is not yet, what were any reality which we can substitute? We will not be shipwrecked on a vain reality. Shall we with pains erect a heaven of blue glass over ourselves, though when it is done we shall be sure to gaze still at the true ethereal heaven far above, as if the former were not? . . .

However mean your life is, meet it and live it; do not shun it and call it hard names. It is not so bad as you are. It looks poorest when you are richest. The fault-finder will find faults even in paradise. Love your life, poor as it is. You may perhaps have some pleasant, thrilling,
240 glorious hours, even in a poorhouse. The setting sun is reflected from the windows of the almshouse as brightly as from the rich man's abode; the snow melts before its door as early in the spring. I do not see but a quiet mind may live as contentedly there, and have as cheering thoughts, as in a palace. The town's poor seem to me often to live the most independent lives of any. May be they are simply great enough to receive without misgiving.[9] Most think that they are above being supported by the town; but it oftener happens that they are not above supporting themselves by dishonest means, which should be more disreputable. Cultivate poverty like a garden herb, like sage. Do not
250 trouble yourself much to get new things, whether clothes or friends. Turn the old; return to them. Things do not change; we change. Sell your clothes and keep your thoughts. God will see that you do not want society. If I were confined to a corner of a garret all my days, like a spider, the world would be just as large to me while I had my

---

[8] **If a man . . . or far away:** This is one of Thoreau's most famous passages. The "different drummer" evolved from a journal entry describing how Thoreau fell asleep to the sound of someone beating a drum "alone in the silence and the dark."

[9] **misgiving** (mĭs-gĭv´ĭng): a feeling of doubt, mistrust, or uncertainty.

WHEN STUDENTS STRUGGLE . . .

Direct students to lines 213–224 and explain that in this paragraph Thoreau uses a great deal of abstract language—language that refers to ideas rather than concrete things and actions. Discuss with students Thoreau's concept of law. Explain that Thoreau is not talking about the sorts of laws passed by governments, but about laws in the more scientific sense; that is, descriptions of the way the universe works.

ASK STUDENTS to paraphrase in their own words what Thoreau says about laws. *(The person who follows his or her dreams will find that he understands life in a new way, and that everything will seem simpler and richer.)*

thoughts about me. The philosopher[10] said: "From an army of three divisions one can take away its general, and put it in disorder; from the man the most abject and vulgar one cannot take away his thought." Do not seek so anxiously to be developed, to subject yourself to many influences to be played on; it is all **dissipation**. Humility like darkness reveals the heavenly lights. The shadows of poverty and meanness gather around us, "and lo! creation widens to our view." We are often reminded that if there were bestowed on us the wealth of Croesus,[11] our aims must still be the same, and our means essentially the same. Moreover, if you are restricted in your range by poverty, if you cannot buy books and newspapers, for instance, you are but confined to the most significant and vital experiences; you are compelled to deal with the material which yields the most sugar and the most starch. It is life near the bone where it is sweetest. You are defended from being a trifler. No man loses ever on a lower level by magnanimity on a higher. Superfluous wealth can buy superfluities only. Money is not required to buy one necessary of the soul. . . .

> "If a man does not keep pace with his companions, perhaps it is because he hears a different drummer."

The life in us is like the water in the river. It may rise this year higher than man has ever known it, and flood the parched uplands; even this may be the eventful year, which will drown out all our muskrats. It was not always dry land where we dwell. I see far inland the banks which the stream anciently washed, before science began to record its freshets. Every one has heard the story which has gone the rounds of New England, of a strong and beautiful bug which came out of the dry leaf of an old table of apple-tree wood, which had stood in

---

[10] **philosopher:** Confucius (551–479 B.C.), Chinese teacher of moral living, who had an influence on Thoreau's ideas.

[11] **Croesus:** an ancient king legendary for his great wealth.

dissipation
(dĭs´ə-pā´shən) *n.* wasteful self-indulgence.

Walden **215**

TEACH

CLOSE READ

Determine Author's Purpose: Style (LINES 259–260)  COMMON CORE RI 6

Now that students are becoming familiar with different kinds of figurative language, encourage them to think about how it can reveal a writer's purpose.

O ASK STUDENTS to explain the simile in lines 259–260 and tell what they can infer from it about Thoreau's purpose for writing. *(When Thoreau says that "Humility like darkness reveals the heavenly lights," he means that the most important things in life are easier to see and focus on without the distractions of money and power. Thoreau's purpose is to persuade the reader to focus on the important things rather than to chase after money and power.)*

Determine Author's Purpose: Style (LINES 267–268) COMMON CORE RI 6

Draw students' attention to the metaphor in these lines and have them think about what purpose for writing it reveals.

P ASK STUDENTS to explain the metaphor and tell how the purpose it reveals relates to the purpose they identified above. *(The metaphor compares a life of material poverty to the tastiest part of the meat, the part near the bone. His purpose in using this metaphor relates to the purpose of persuading the reader to focus on the most important things in life. It tells readers how they can accomplish this: by being poor.)*

CRITICAL VOCABULARY

dissipation: Thoreau encourages the reader not to become "developed," or sophisticated.

ASK STUDENTS to explain how subjecting oneself "to many influences" could lead to dissipation. *(A person who is subjected to too many influences might be distracted by too much knowledge and take into account too many opinions. That person might develop expensive tastes or distracting hobbies.)*

TO CHALLENGE STUDENTS . . .

Analyze Quotes Tell students to reread the quotation from Confucius in lines 255–257. As a class, discuss the meaning of the quotation. *(that individuals are stronger than organizations)*

ASK STUDENTS to work in small groups to discuss this quotation in the context of the entire work. Ask: How does the quotation support Thoreau's philosophy? *(By emphasizing the strength and integrity of the individual, the quotation supports Thoreau's idea that individuals should go their own way regardless of what society thinks.)* Have groups share their conclusions. For an extra challenge, ask students to search the Internet for other quotes from Confucius that support the central ideas of *Walden*.

Walden **215**

Determine Author's Purpose: Style (LINES 294–298)

 **COMMON CORE** RI 6, L 5a

Discuss with students the effect of this last paragraph on readers. Ask what final ideas and images Thoreau used to conclude, and why they think he chose to end his essay in this manner.

Q **CITE TEXT EVIDENCE** Ask students what language in this paragraph is figurative and how they can tell. *(The phrase "that morrow which mere lapse of time can never make to dawn" in lines 295–296 and the sentence "There is more day to dawn" in line 297 are figurative. I can tell because literal days do dawn within a certain period of time and because Thoreau does not know when the reader will be reading his lines, so he cannot know whether there is literally "more day to dawn": that is, whether it is early morning for the reader.)*

Determine Central Ideas: Summarize (LINES 294–298)

 **COMMON CORE** RI 2, L 5a

Remind students that writers often restate an essay's central idea in the last paragraph. Discuss with students that the last paragraph is the writer's final chance to make an impression on the reader.

R **ASK STUDENTS** to summarize the last paragraph and state Thoreau's central idea. *(While ordinary people may never realize it, we can bring about a new and more beautiful future. Thoreau's central idea is that by following our hearts and dreams and living simply, we can create a more beautiful, satisfying world.)*

COLLABORATIVE DISCUSSION Have students form pairs and discuss which of Thoreau's criticisms are most relevant today. Ask them to cite specific evidence from the text. Then have pairs share their conclusions with the class as a whole. Accept all reasonable responses.

ASK STUDENTS to share any questions they generated in the course of reading and discussing the selection.

---

280 a farmer's kitchen for sixty years, first in Connecticut, and afterward in Massachusetts,—from an egg deposited in the living tree many years earlier still, as appeared by counting the annual layers beyond it; which was heard gnawing out for several weeks, hatched perchance by the heat of an urn. Who does not feel his faith in a resurrection and immortality strengthened by hearing of this? Who knows what beautiful and winged life, whose egg has been buried for ages under many concentric layers of woodenness in the dead dry life of society, deposited at first in the alburnum[12] of the green and living tree, which has been gradually converted into the semblance of its well-seasoned

290 tomb,—heard perchance gnawing out now for years by the astonished family of man, as they sat round the festive board,—may unexpectedly come forth from amidst society's most trivial and handselled[13] furniture, to enjoy its perfect summer life at last!

 I do not say that John or Jonathan[14] will realize all this; but such is the character of that morrow which mere lapse of time can never make to dawn. The light which puts out our eyes is darkness to us. Only that day dawns to which we are awake. There is more day to dawn. The sun is but a morning star.

---

[12]**alburnum** (ăl-bûr′nəm): the part of a tree's trunk through which sap flows.
[13]**handselled:** given as a mere token of good wishes and therefore of no great value in itself.
[14]**John or Jonathan:** John Bull and Brother Jonathan were traditional personifications of England and the United States, respectively.

COLLABORATIVE DISCUSSION Which of Thoreau's descriptions or criticisms of modern life seem most relevant to today's world? In what way? Discuss this question with a partner, citing specific evidence from the text to support your ideas.

Determine Central Ideas: Summarize

 **COMMON CORE** RI 2, L 5a

Each essay in *Walden* expresses one or more central ideas, while the book as a whole reflects central ideas that the essays have in common. One way to determine a text's central ideas is to write an objective summary of it. When you **summarize,** you restate the central ideas in your own words. A summary is much shorter than the original text and includes only the most important supporting details. For example, you might summarize the opening paragraph of "Where I Lived, and What I Lived For" in a single sentence:

> In July 1845, Thoreau moved into a newly-built cabin in the woods that pleased him with its rough, simple construction.

Use these strategies to help you summarize Thoreau's essays.

- Use the essay titles as clues to the central ideas of each section.
- Summarize individual paragraphs or sections first.
- See if a topic sentence, usually at the beginning or end of a paragraph, explicitly states the paragraph's central idea.
- Infer a central idea from the details contained in a paragraph.

Determine Author's Purpose: Style

 **COMMON CORE** RI 6

Readers must usually **infer** an author's **purpose,** or reason for writing, from the content and style of the writing. **Style** refers to how a writer expresses his or her ideas. Thoreau's style has several distinctive characteristics, as shown in the chart.

Elements of Style	Example
Informality: Long sentences but simple language	"The upright white hewn studs and freshly planed door and window casings gave it a clean and airy look, especially in the morning, when its timbers were saturated with dew, so that I fancied that by noon some sweet gum would exude from them. . . ."
Frequent use of **figurative language,** or language used in a nonliteral way.	
• **Simile:** comparison using *like* or *as*	"the mists, like ghosts, were stealthily withdrawing in every direction"
• **Metaphor:** comparison without using *like* or *as*	"Time is but the stream I go a-fishing in."
• **Personification:** giving human characteristics to an animal, object, or idea	"I saw it [the pond] throwing off its nightly clothing of mist. . . ."

Walden **217**

TEACH

CLOSE READ

Determine Central Ideas: Summarize

 **COMMON CORE** RI 2, L 5a

Have students choose partners and ask pairs to use the bulleted strategies to help them write a short summary of each essay excerpt. For each excerpt, ask pairs to share their summaries with the class and write the most concise and accurate summary on the board. Lead a class discussion in which students use the summaries of the individual essays to determine the central idea of the whole work.

Determine Author's Purpose: Style

 **COMMON CORE** RI 6

Review the terms with students. Divide them into small groups and ask each group to review the selection and find examples of each of the following stylistic elements: **simile, metaphor, personification,** and **informal, long sentences.** Have groups share their findings with the class.

Strategies for Annotation 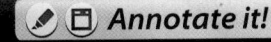 *Annotate it!*

Determine Author's Purpose: Style

 **COMMON CORE** RI 6

Share these strategies for guided or independent analysis:

- Highlight in blue any similes.
- Highlight in yellow any metaphors.
- On notes, record how these stylistic elements connect to the writer's purpose.

My head is hands and feet. I feel all my best faculties concentrated in it. My instinct tells me that my head is an organ for burrowing, as some creatures use their snout and fore-paws, and with it I would mine and burrow my way through these hills. I think…

> "Thoreau's purpose is to tell readers that oneness with nature is a treasure that they can obtain using their intellect."

Walden **217**

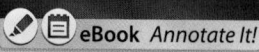 eBook *Annotate It!*

Analyzing the Text 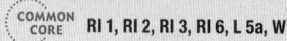 RI 1, RI 2, RI 3, RI 6, L 5a, W 2

Possible answers:

1. *Thoreau moved to the woods because he wanted to live a simpler life and learn from nature. He also says that he wanted to share his experiences with the world. This fact, coupled with his writing style of long, informal sentences and abundant figurative language, reveals that he wrote to share his transformative experience of living in the woods.*

2. *Thoreau's metaphor in this section compares civilized life to a choppy sea. He returns to this metaphor in lines 209–212, when he says that his time at Walden Pond has been like a journey on a ship.*

3. *In this hyperbolic statement, Thoreau is exaggerating people's need to keep abreast of every item of news. His purpose is to highlight what a waste of time he feels newspapers are.*

4. *Thoreau loves being alone and believes it is essential in order to commune with nature. Thoreau is not worried about feeling lonely; on the contrary, living alone has given him a much larger view of his (and our) place in the universe. His rich descriptions of nature in the first paragraph of this section support this central idea.*

5. *In "The Pond in Winter," Thoreau marvels at how the pond changes during winter and becomes still and serene. In "from Spring," he celebrates the dynamic (and violent) changes that happen to the pond in spring after a long winter. Both sections deal with the idea of change, but "Winter" celebrates stillness and "Spring" celebrates movement and vigor.*

6. *Three things were important to Thoreau: life, Walden Pond, and the house he built next to it. In line 27 he says that he went to the woods to find out the "essential facts of life," and in line 57 he speaks of civilization as a "waste of life." He describes the pond lovingly in each season (lines 17–25, 116–122, 141–154, and 173–176). Thoreau's careful and approving description of his house in lines 3–10 make it clear that he valued it.*

7. *Thoreau achieved his goals because he lived simply and came to understand what was most important in life. The central idea of a new understanding of life as an awakening or new dawn in the conclusion explicitly connects to the description of a new day dawning over Walden Pond in lines 19–25.*

8. *Thoreau's purpose for writing is to share with others his experience at Walden Pond. His informal, even friendly style keeps the reader engaged.*

Analyzing the Text  RI 1, RI 2, RI 3, RI 6, L 5a, W 2

Cite Text Evidence   Support your responses with evidence from the selection.

1. **Summarize** How does Thoreau describe his reasons for moving to the woods in lines 26–40? How do these lines relate to his purpose in writing *Walden*?

2. **Identify Patterns** What is the metaphor that Thoreau uses to describe civilized life in lines 49–54? Where else is a similar metaphor used in the text?

3. **Analyze** In lines 71–81, Thoreau uses a type of figurative language called **hyperbole,** exaggeration of the truth for a particular effect. What is he exaggerating, and what is his purpose for using this figurative language?

4. **Interpret** Summarize what Thoreau has to say on the topic of solitude (lines 113–140). How do his observations about nature help develop his central idea in this section?

5. **Compare** What **analogy,** or comparison, can you make between the central ideas Thoreau expresses in "The Pond in Winter" and in "Spring"? In what ways are the ideas in these two passages similar and different?

6. **Infer** Throeau rejects many thing as inessential or unimportant. List at least three things that *were* important to him, citing specific lines from the essay to support your answers.

7. **Critique** In what ways did Thoreau achieve his goals at Walden Pond? How do the central ideas in the "Conclusion" explicitly connect back to the beginning of the text?

8. **Evaluate** Think about Thoreau's purpose in writing *Walden*. How is Thoreau's particular style of writing effective for achieving his purpose? Explain.

PERFORMANCE TASK

Writing Activity: Essay Transcendentalism emphasized living a simple life and celebrating the truth found in nature, emotion, and imagination. How does *Walden* reflect these key aspects of transcendentalism? Write an essay that answers this question.

- Reread the excerpts and look for the most significant evidence of each aspect of transcendentalism.

- Organize your evidence so that you can develop the topic of your essay into a unified whole.

- Use appropriate transitions, varied syntax, and precise language to maintain a formal style.

- Provide a concluding statement that follows from the evidence presented.

Assign this performance task.

PERFORMANCE TASK  W 2

Writing Activity: Essay Have students work independently to draft their essays. Encourage them to reread the excerpts from *Walden* keeping in mind the different aspects of Transcendentalism. When students have completed drafts of their essays, have them exchange their papers with a partner and use the last three bullet points to evaluate the drafts and provide constructive feedback. Give students an opportunity to revise their drafts based on the feedback.

Critical Vocabulary

COMMON CORE L 4a, L 4d

unfathomed	perturbation	congenial
perennial	untenable	dissipation

Practice and Apply Choose the alternative in each sentence that best relates to the Critical Vocabulary word and explain your choice.

1. If Walden Pond was **unfathomed,** was it deep or shallow?

2. Many people experience **perturbation** when listening to the news. Does it make them upset or happy?

3. Thoreau found solitude **congenial.** Was he content or lonely?

4. Thoreau noticed the **perennial** peace at the bottom of the pond in winter. Was this an unusual occurrence or something that was always there?

5. Judging nature to be evil is an **untenable** position for Thoreau. Would he make such a judgment or criticize it?

6. A lavish lifestyle can lead to **dissipation.** Are people who follow this lifestyle more likely to work too hard or to party too hard?

Vocabulary Strategy: Context Clues

Using **context clues**—nearby words, phrases, and sentences—can help you figure out the meanings of unfamiliar words. Consider the context for the Critical Vocabulary word *perturbation*:

> Let us rise early and fast, or break fast, gently and without perturbation. . . .

The word *without* signals a contrast between *gently* and *perturbation*. You can guess that *perturbation* means "agitation or uneasiness."

Sometimes you have to look at a wider context to find clues to a word's meaning. The word *congenial* appears in this sentence:

> I see nothing special to attract me, all the elements are unusually congenial to me.

A reader might conclude that *congenial* means "boring" or "uninteresting." However, other words and phrases in the paragraph let the reader know that that *congenial* denotes something pleasurable or agreeable.

> This is a delicious evening, when the whole body . . . imbibes delight through every pore. . . . I see nothing special to attract me, all the elements are unusually congenial to me. . . . my serenity is rippled but not ruffled. These small waves . . . are as remote from storm as the smooth reflecting surface.

Practice and Apply Work with a partner to identify five unfamiliar words from Thoreau's essays and use context clues to determine their meanings. Discuss which context clues were most helpful. Then check your definitions by using a dictionary.

PRACTICE & APPLY

Critical Vocabulary

COMMON CORE L 4a, L 4d

Possible answers:

1. The pond would be deep; *unfathomed* means located at the deepest place.

2. It makes them upset; *perturbation* is a state of agitation.

3. He was contented; *congenial* means pleasant or agreeable.

4. It was something that was always there; *perennial* means long-lasting.

5. Thoreau would criticize the idea that nature is evil; *untenable* means insupportable.

6. They are more likely to party too hard; *dissipation* is wasteful self-indulgence.

Vocabulary Strategy: Context Clues

COMMON CORE L 4a

Sample answer: In line 1, Thoreau uses the word *abode*. From context, I think it might mean "place" or "position." When I take a wider context—in line 3 he refers to his "house" and in line 7 he mentions windows and a door—I realize it must be a synonym for *house*.

Strategies for Annotation ✎ 🖥 *Annotate it!*

Vocabulary Strategy: Context Clues

COMMON CORE L 4a

Have students locate the sentences containing *sturdily, rudiment, repose,* and *repast*. Encourage them to use their eBook annotation tools to do the following:

- Highlight in green each vocabulary word.
- In the surrounding sentences, underline any clues to the word's meaning you find, such as examples, synonyms, or antonyms.
- Review your annotations and try to infer the word's meaning.

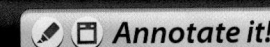

I wanted to live deep and suck out all the marrow of life, to live so sturdily and Spartan-like as to put to rout all that was not life, to cut a broad swath and shave close….

PRACTICE & APPLY

Language and Style: Rhetorical Questions

Review the examples in the chart and make sure students understand how each one exemplifies the stated purpose. Then have students look for other examples of rhetorical questions in the selection and explain their purposes. For example:

- Line 230: "Shall he turn his spring into summer?" To suggest that man should not rush his growth or be in a "desperate haste to succeed."

Practice and Apply Invite pairs to share with the class their revised essays and explain their rhetorical questions and what purpose they serve.

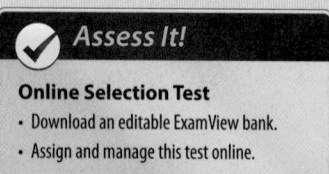

✓ Assess It!

Online Selection Test
- Download an editable ExamView bank.
- Assign and manage this test online.

Language and Style: Rhetorical Questions

A distinctive element of Thoreau's style is his use of **rhetorical questions,** or questions that are asked to make a point and without the expectation of an actual reply. Rhetorical questions require that readers reflect on some aspect of a writer's argument or claim. In many cases, however, they also suggest that the writer's view is obvious or common sense; if readers just consider the issue—properly expressed, of course—they will just naturally agree with the writer. Thoreau often uses rhetorical questions to add emphasis and emotion to his writing. The chart shows several examples.

Rhetorical Questions in *Walden*	
Example	Purpose
Why should we live with such hurry and waste of life? (line 57)	To strongly suggest we should live in the opposite way
Why should I feel lonely? Is not our planet in the Milky Way? (lines 135–136)	To suggest he is not lonely; answer to the second question is an obvious "yes"
Why should we be in such desperate haste to succeed, and in such desperate enterprises? (lines 225–226)	To suggest that we should not act in this way
Who does not feel his faith in a resurrection and immortality strengthened by hearing of this? (lines 284–285)	To suggest that everyone should have faith in resurrection, since the expected answer is "no one"

Because *Walden* reflects Thoreau's experiment with living simply and the lessons he learned from that experiment, these questions also suggest the kinds of questions Thoreau asked himself while spending time alone in the woods, reflecting on life. They suggest the internal monologue of someone living in solitude. With their focus on the "big questions" of life, they elevate the book above the level of nature observations to an expression of transcendental philosophy.

Practice and Apply Review the essay you wrote about *Walden* as a reflection of key aspects of transcendentalism in this selection's Performance Task. Revise the essay to make it an argument that includes at least two rhetorical questions. Consider taking one of the three main ideas and stating it as a claim that you support with evidence from *Walden.*

Analyze and Evaluate Structure

COMMON CORE

RI 5

TEACH

Explain to students that one of the most important decisions a writer makes is what **structure,** or form, to use. Structure refers to the way a work is organized. Essays usually follow one of the following structures:

- argumentative
- thesis followed by support
- descriptive
- chronological
- spatial
- compare and contrast

Tell students that while *Walden* is classified as an essay, its structure is unlike that of most essays.

PRACTICE AND APPLY

Ask students to reread the excerpts from "The Pond in Winter" and "Spring." While they read, they should keep in mind the "seasonal" interpretation of the work's structure described above. At what point in his personal journey is Thoreau in "The Pond in Winter"? How do you know? What happens to him during "Spring"? Cite evidence to support your answer. *(In "The Pond in Winter," Thoreau describes the pond as having frozen over, as if it had eyes that were shut. But then, Thoreau cuts a hole in the ice to look below and discovers the sandy floor just as it was in the summer. Thoreau feels comforted by this, describing a cool and even-temperedness in himself. In "Spring," however, Thoreau is just as wide awake as the pond and the forest are. Everything around him is alive and in motion, and Thoreau is gripped by its wildness and vigor. The clouds and storms of winter have been cleared for bright spring days, and the same could be said for Thoreau and his inner state of being.)*

 **INTERACTIVE WHITEBOARD LESSON** If students need further instruction, use this *Interactive Whiteboard Lesson:* **Text Structure and Meaning.**

Determine Central Ideas: Summarize

COMMON CORE

RI 2, L 5a

RETEACH

Review **summarizing** as a way to determine a work's central ideas. A summary is a short restatement of the central ideas of a text and includes only the most salient details. Remind students of the summarizing strategies they learned:

- Use the section titles as clues to central ideas.
- Summarize individual sections or paragraphs first.
- Look for a topic sentence that might tell the central idea.
- Infer a central idea from details in a section.

To practice summarizing:

- Have students reread lines 41–56.
- Ask: Can you find a topic sentence that tells the central idea of this paragraph? *("Our life is frittered away by detail.")*
- Have students reexamine the details in the section "from The Pond in Winter" and infer its central idea. Then write a summary. *(Possible answer: Winter is a time when nature goes to sleep and attains a peaceful, serene state.)*

 **LEVEL UP TUTORIALS** Assign the following *Level Up* tutorial: **Summarizing**

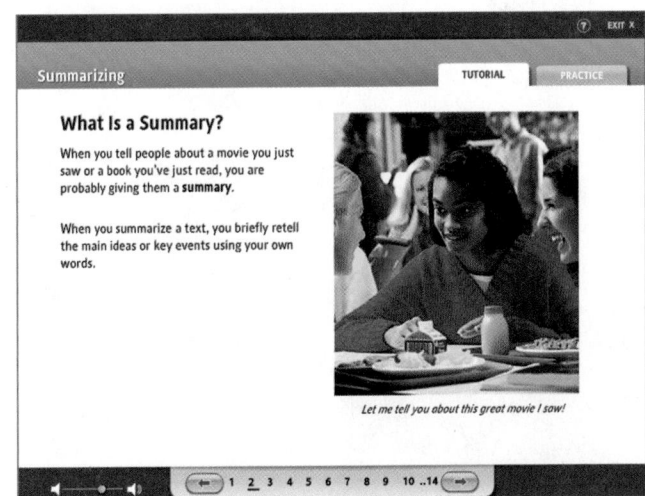

CLOSE READING APPLICATION

Students can apply the skill to another essay they have read. Have them select an essay that is divided into sections and practice summarizing each section using the various strategies they have learned. Students may share their summaries in pairs or small groups.

Essays by Ralph Waldo Emerson

from Nature

from Self-Reliance

Why These Texts

Students may leave the text of an essay without a complete understanding of the author's central ideas. Essays such as these by the great American writer, lecturer, philosopher, and poet Ralph Waldo Emerson include difficult language, an ornate prose style, and complex ideas that are clarified only with careful study. With the help of the close-reading questions, students will determine the central ideas by examining specific textual evidence, guiding them to develop a coherent understanding of each of the essays.

Background Have students read the background and biography of Ralph Waldo Emerson. Introduce the two essays by explaining that Emerson was one of the editors of the *Dial*, which was the chief literary publication of the transcendentalists, promoting the talents of many young writers, such as Henry David Thoreau. When the original *Dial* ceased publication in 1844, Horace Greeley, the most influential newspaper editor of the time, reported it as an end to the "most original and thoughtful periodical ever published in this country."

AS YOU READ Ask students to pay close attention to the central ideas in each essay and to the details that support these ideas. How soon into each essay does Emerson present his first central idea?

Common Core Support

- cite multiple pieces of evidence
- determine two or more central ideas developed over the course of a text
- provide an objective summary of a text

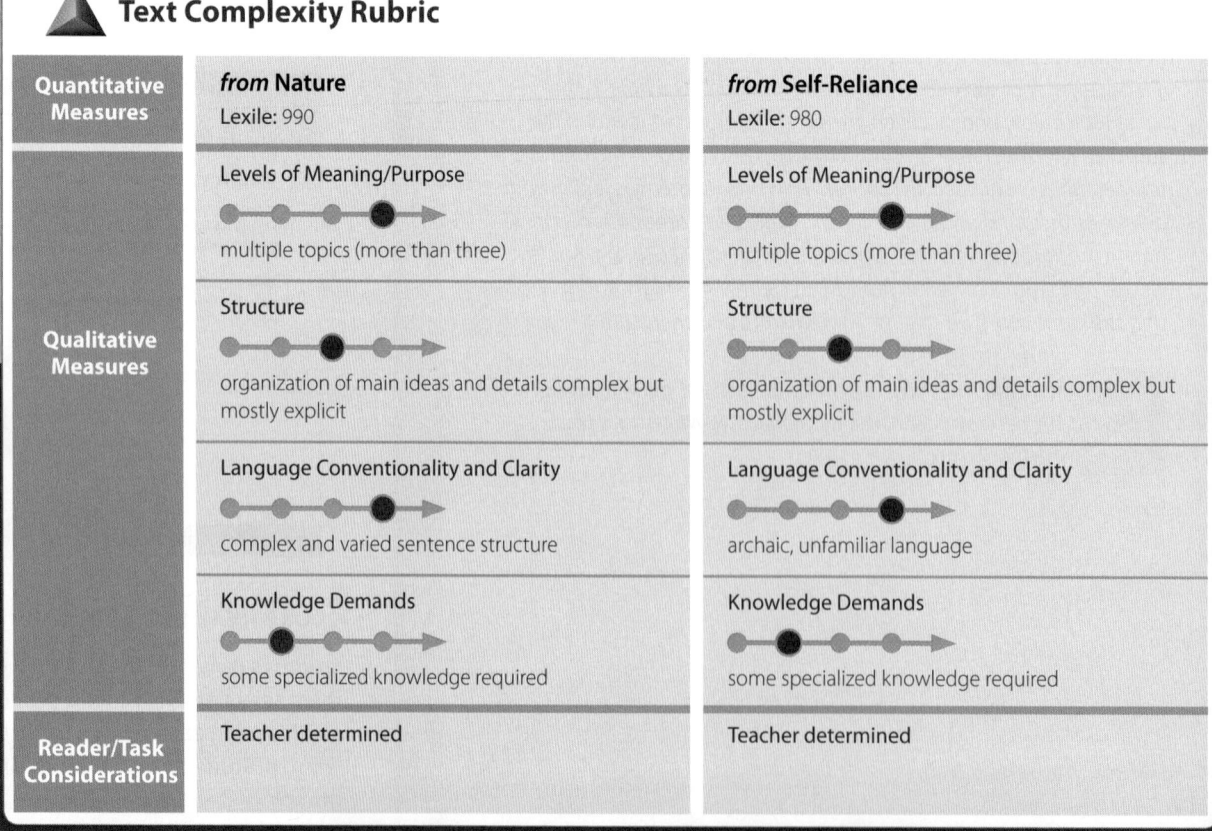

Text Complexity Rubric

	from Nature	*from* Self-Reliance
Quantitative Measures	Lexile: 990	Lexile: 980
Qualitative Measures	Levels of Meaning/Purpose multiple topics (more than three)	Levels of Meaning/Purpose multiple topics (more than three)
	Structure organization of main ideas and details complex but mostly explicit	Structure organization of main ideas and details complex but mostly explicit
	Language Conventionality and Clarity complex and varied sentence structure	Language Conventionality and Clarity archaic, unfamiliar language
	Knowledge Demands some specialized knowledge required	Knowledge Demands some specialized knowledge required
Reader/Task Considerations	Teacher determined	Teacher determined

Strategies for CLOSE READING

Determine Central Ideas

Students should read each of these essays carefully all the way through. Close-reading questions at the bottom of the page will help them focus on a thorough analysis of the central ideas of each essay and the evidence, including facts, details, and examples, that support these key ideas. As they read, students should record comments or questions about the text in the side margins.

WHEN STUDENTS STRUGGLE . . .

To help students follow the central ideas of each essay, students should work in a small group to fill out a chart such as the one shown below as they provide an analysis of each essay.

CITE TEXT EVIDENCE For practice in finding the central ideas of each essay, ask students to cite details and evidence that support each central idea.

"Nature"

Central Idea: *One feels perpetually young in the woods.*
Detail 1: *One casts off one's years in the woods as a snake sloughs off its skin.*
Detail 2: *One is always a child when in the woods.*
Detail 3: *One returns to reason and faith in the woods, fundamental ways of thinking.*

"Self-Reliance"

Central Idea: *One needs to rely on oneself.*
Detail 1: *One must accept oneself for better or worse.*
Detail 2: *One must rely on one's own capabilities and hard work.*
Detail 3: *One must trust oneself.*

Background *As the acknowledged leader of the transcendentalists,* **Ralph Waldo Emerson** *(1803–1882) was a towering figure in the 19th-century literary world. He helped shape a new, uniquely American body of literature and is often cited as one of the most significant writers in American history. "All life is an experiment," the radical thinker and writer once said. "The more experiments you make, the better."*

Essays by
Ralph Waldo Emerson

from **Nature** . . . . Ralph Waldo Emerson

from **Self-Reliance** . . . . Ralph Waldo Emerson

Ralph Waldo Emerson *was born in Boston, Massachusetts, in 1803. He attended Harvard and was ordained as a Unitarian minister in 1829. Just over a year later, his beloved wife, Ellen, died of tuberculosis. Ellen's death threw Emerson into a state of spiritual crisis. In 1832, after much consideration, Emerson resigned his post. He settled in Concord, Massachusetts, and devoted himself to the study of philosophy, religion, and literature.*

In 1836 Emerson published Nature, *in which he eloquently articulated his transcendental philosophy, an outgrowth of European romanticism. That same year, Emerson formed the Transcendental Club with a group of like-minded friends, including Henry David Thoreau and Margaret Fuller.* Nature, *with its emphasis on self-reliance and individuality, became the group's unofficial manifesto. He elaborated upon his ideas in essays and a series of popular lectures. By the 1840s, the Sage of Concord, as he was known, had become a major literary force whose influence is still evident in American culture today.*

41

CLOSE READ
Notes

1. **READ** ▶ As you read lines 1–20, begin to collect and cite evidence.

- Underline metaphorical phrases.
- Circle language that Emerson uses to describe the woods.
- In the margin, explain what event causes the author "perfect exhilaration" (lines 2–5).

He feels exhilarated from a walk across a common in winter.

decorum:
good taste in conduct or appearance

from Nature

Nature is a setting that fits equally well a comic or a mourning piece. In good health, the air is a cordial of incredible virtue. Crossing a bare common, in snow puddles, at twilight, under a clouded sky, without having in my thoughts any occurrence of special good fortune, I have enjoyed a perfect exhilaration. I am glad to the brink of fear. In the woods too, a man casts off his years, as the snake his slough,[1] and at what period soever of life, is always a child. In the woods, is perpetual youth. Within these plantations of God, a decorum and sanctity reign, a perennial festival is dressed, and the guest sees not how he should tire of them in a thousand years. In the woods, we return to reason and faith. There I feel that nothing can befall me in life,—no disgrace, no calamity, (leaving me my eyes,) which nature cannot repair. Standing on the bare ground,—my head bathed by the blithe air, and uplifted into infinite space,—all mean egotism vanishes. I become a transparent eye-ball; I am nothing; I see all; the currents of the Universal Being circulate through me; I am part or particle of God. The name of the nearest friend sounds then foreign and accidental: to be brothers, to be acquaintances,—master or servant, is then a trifle and a disturbance. I am the lover of uncontained and immortal

[1] **slough:** the cast-off skin of a snake.

2. **REREAD** Reread lines 5–15. How is a man "always a child" in the woods? Which sentence acts as a central idea and best supports this metaphor?

A man is always a child in the woods because in the woods, we "return to reason and faith," which is the fundamental way a child thinks. "In the woods, is perpetual youth" best supports the metaphor of a man being a child and acts as a central idea.

3. **READ** ▶ As you read lines 21–35, continue to cite textual evidence.
- Underline the topic sentence Emerson uses to introduce each paragraph.
- In the margin, explain what the "colors of the spirit" refers to (line 32).
- Circle examples of personification.

42

---

beauty. In the wilderness, I find something more dear and connate[2] than in streets or villages. In the tranquil landscape, and especially in the distant line of the horizon, man beholds somewhat as beautiful as his own nature.

The greatest delight which the fields and woods minister, is the suggestion of an **occult** relation between man and the vegetable. I am not alone and unacknowledged. They nod to me, and I to them. The waving of the boughs in the storm, is new to me and old. It takes me by surprise, and yet is not unknown. Its effect is like that of a higher thought or a better emotion coming over me, when I deemed I was thinking justly or doing right.

Yet it is certain that the power to produce this delight, does not reside in nature, but in man, or in a harmony of both. It is necessary to use these pleasures with great temperance. For, nature is not always tricked[3] in holiday attire, but the same scene which yesterday breathed perfume and glittered as for the frolic of the nymphs, is overspread with melancholy today. Nature always wears the colors of the spirit. To a man laboring under calamity, the heat of his own fire hath sadness in it. Then, there is a kind of contempt of the landscape felt by him who has just lost by death a dear friend. The sky is less grand as it shuts down over less worth in the population.

[2] **connate:** agreeable; able to be related to.
[3] **tricked:** dressed.

occult:
secret or hidden from view

The "colors of the spirit" refers to one's feelings and emotions.

4. **REREAD AND DISCUSS** Reread lines 21–35. With a small group, discuss what Emerson is referring to when he alludes to the relationship between "man and the vegetable."

SHORT RESPONSE

Cite Text Evidence Write an objective summary of the piece by restating the central ideas in your own words. Be sure that your objective summary is free from personal opinions and **cite text evidence** in your response.

Nature provides an escape for man where he can become like a child again and be overwhelmed by nature's beauty. There is a secret relationship between man and nature, almost as if nature communicates to man in its actions. This relationship is heavily dictated by one's own feelings, because what was beautiful when one feels optimistic may be dreary when one is feeling melancholy.

43

---

1. **READ AND CITE TEXT EVIDENCE**

(A) **ASK STUDENTS** why Emerson feels elated. *He feels "perfect exhilaration" from a walk outside in winter (lines 2–5).*

2. **REREAD AND CITE TEXT EVIDENCE**

(B) **ASK STUDENTS** to cite the sentence that states the key idea of the first paragraph and compares man to a child in the woods. *The central idea is that "In the woods, is perpetual youth" (line 7).*

3. **READ AND CITE TEXT EVIDENCE**

(C) **ASK STUDENTS** to explain how "Nature always wears the colors of the spirit" supports the central idea in lines 27–35. *One's perception of nature is guided by one's emotions. The power of nature to delight rests more with man than with nature.*

Critical Vocabulary: decorum (line 8) Have students share their definitions.

4. **REREAD AND DISCUSS USING TEXT EVIDENCE**

(D) **ASK STUDENTS** to appoint a reporter for each group to cite textual evidence to support their opinion about the meaning of the hidden relationship "between man and the vegetable" (line 22). *Students should cite "the waving of the boughs" (line 23), which suggests trees and an unknown, unspoken connection between man and nature.*

Critical Vocabulary: occult (line 22) Have students explain *occult*. Why does Emerson use the word in this context? *He wants to suggest the hidden relation between man and nature.*

SHORT RESPONSE

Cite Text Evidence Students should:

- restate the central ideas of this part of essay.
- use the central ideas to write an objective summary.
- cite text evidence in their response.

CLOSE READ Notes

1. **READ ▶** As you read lines 1–24, begin to collect and cite evidence.

   • Underline the topic sentence in each paragraph.
   • In the margin, explain the central idea of lines 1–11.
   • Circle the response of the "valued adviser."

from **Self-Reliance**

People should rely upon their own capabilities and instincts.

(A) There is a time in every man's education when he arrives at the conviction that envy is ignorance; that imitation is suicide; that he must take himself for better for worse as his portion; that though the wide universe is full of good, no kernel of nourishing corn can come to him but through his toil bestowed on that plot of ground which is given to him to till. . . .

Trust thyself: every heart vibrates to that iron string. Accept the place the divine providence has found for you, the society of your contemporaries, the connection of events. Great men have always done so, and confided themselves childlike to the genius of their age, betraying their perception that the absolutely trustworthy was seated at their heart, working through their hands, predominating in all their being . . . .

nonconformist:
one who does not follow generally accepted beliefs or customs

(B) Whoso would be a man, must be a **nonconformist**. He who would gather immortal palms[1] must not be hindered by the name of goodness, but must explore if it be goodness. Nothing is at last sacred but the integrity of your own mind. Absolve you to yourself, and you shall have the suffrage[2] of the world. I remember an answer which when quite young I was prompted to make to a valued adviser who was wont to importune[3] me with the dear old doctrines of the church. On my saying, "What have I to do with the sacredness of traditions, if I live wholly from within?" my friend suggested—"But these impulses may be from below, not from above." I replied, "They do not seem to me to be such; but

[1] **immortal palms:** everlasting triumph and honor. In ancient times, people carried palm leaves as a symbol of victory, success, or joy.
[2] **suffrage:** approval, support.
[3] **importune:** ask persistently.

2. **◀ REREAD** Reread lines 12–24 and restate the central idea.

Emerson believes that people should follow their own impulses and that what is sacred is what comes from one's nature.

44

---

if I am the Devil's child, I will live then from the Devil." No law can be sacred to me but that of my nature. Good and bad are but names very readily transferable to that or this; the only right is what is after my **constitution**; the only wrong what is against it . . . .

(C) What I must do is all that concerns me, not what the people think. This rule, equally arduous in actual and in intellectual life, may serve for the whole distinction between greatness and **meanness**. It is the harder because you will always find those who think they know what is your duty better than you know it. It is easy in the world to live after the world's opinion; it is easy in solitude to live after our own; but the great man is he who in the midst of the crowd keeps with perfect sweetness the independence of solitude . . . .

For nonconformity the world whips you with its displeasure. And therefore a man must know how to estimate a sour face. The by-standers look askance on him in the public street or in the friend's parlor. If this aversion had its origin in contempt and resistance like his own he might well go home with a sad countenance; but the sour faces of the multitude, like their sweet faces, have no deep cause, but are put on and off as the wind blows and a newspaper directs . . . .

(D) The other terror that scares us from self-trust is our consistency; a reverence for our past act or word because the eyes of others have no other data for computing our orbit than our past acts, and we are loth to disappoint them . . . .

A foolish consistency is the hobgoblin of little minds, adored by little statesmen and philosophers and divines. With consistency a great soul has simply nothing to do. He may as well concern himself with his shadow on the wall. Speak what you think now in hard words and tomorrow speak what

constitution:
physical or mental condition

meanness:
being inferior in quality, character, or value

Nonconformists may be met with resistance.

3. **READ ▶** As you read lines 25–38, continue to collect and cite evidence.

   • Underline the topic sentence in each paragraph.
   • In the margin, explain common reactions to noncomformists.

4. **READ ▶** Read lines 39–51. Underline text that explains why we are reluctant to trust ourselves.

45

---

1. READ AND CITE TEXT EVIDENCE

(A) **ASK STUDENTS** to cite evidence from the text supporting their statement of the central idea of these lines. *Students may cite lines 3–6 as support for the idea that people should rely on themselves and their own hard work.*

2. REREAD AND CITE TEXT EVIDENCE

(B) **ASK STUDENTS** to cite textual evidence to paraphrase the central idea in lines 12–24, which is an extension of the idea "Trust thyself." *The central idea is that people need to follow their own mind, impulses, and nature—to be nonconformists (lines 12, 14–15, and 19–24).*

Critical Vocabulary: nonconformist (line 12) Have students explain the meaning and importance of the word.

FOR ELL STUDENTS Explain that a compound word may consist of two words that are joined together by a hyphen, as in *self-reliance*. Ask students to find other hyphenated compounds.

3. READ AND CITE TEXT EVIDENCE

(C) **ASK STUDENTS** to state the central idea of lines 25–38. *The central idea is that it does not matter what other people think of you, but nonconformists are viewed by others with displeasure and resistance because they do not follow the crowd.*

4. READ AND CITE TEXT EVIDENCE

(D) **ASK STUDENTS** to explain what Emerson calls our "other terror." *Emerson thinks we are scared by our own "reverence for our past": we think consistency is important when in fact it's useless. Students should cite specific textual evidence from lines 39–42 and 43–48.*

Critical Vocabulary: constitution (line 23) and **meanness** (line 27) Have students explain the words as Emerson uses them here.

CLOSE READ
Notes

tomorrow thinks in hard words again, though it contradict everything you said today.—"Ah, so you shall be sure to be misunderstood."—Is it so bad then to be misunderstood? Pythagoras was misunderstood, and Socrates, and Jesus, and
50 Luther, and Copernicus, and Galileo, and Newton,[4] and every pure and wise spirit that ever took flesh. To be great is to be misunderstood.

[4] **Pythagoras was misunderstood, and Socrates, and Jesus, and Luther, and Copernicus, and Galileo, and Newton:** great thinkers whose radical theories and viewpoints caused controversy.

5. ◀ REREAD   Reread lines 39–51. Which sentence best summarizes the central idea of this part of the essay?

The sentence "To be great is to be misunderstood" best summarizes this section of the text because it explains Emerson's opinion about self-reliance and self-worth. Rather than being worried by what other people think, Emerson wants us to ignore popular opinion and fulfill ourselves as individuals.

SHORT RESPONSE

Cite Text Evidence   Write an objective summary of the piece by restating the central ideas in your own words. Be sure that your objective summary is free from personal opinions. **Cite text evidence.**

It is honorable, but difficult, to be self-reliant. Self-reliance requires one to use his or her mind and heart to make judgments of what is good and bad, not to rely on the judgments of others. A great person is able to maintain this manner of self-reliance even if others misunderstand him or her. However, being misunderstood is a sign of greatness.

46

TO CHALLENGE STUDENTS . . .

For more context about Emerson's time and beliefs, students can research a "protest" movement of that era, transcendentalism.

ASK STUDENTS to find out more about the transcendentalist movement and the people associated with it. (These include essayists such as Emerson and Thoreau, naturalist John Muir, novelist Louisa May Alcott, journalist and activist Margaret Fuller, and poets Emily Dickinson and Walt Whitman.) Have students report back to the class on their findings.

- What were transcendentalists protesting against? *Basically, they were against the organized religion and political parties of the time. They wanted to promote a style of literature that wasn't part of the European tradition.*

- What did they believe in? *They were trying to become more in touch with their senses, to define spirituality, to be self-reliant, and to fulfill their human potential.*

- Aside from literature, what did many transcendentalists have in common? *Many of them were involved in social reform: anti-slavery and women's rights.*

Have each group plan, write, revise, and proofread its essay, publishing and sharing it in print or online.

---

5. (**REREAD AND CITE TEXT EVIDENCE**)   Explain that sometimes the central idea comes at the end of a section.

Ⓔ **ASK STUDENTS** to summarize lines 39–51. *The central idea is that "to be great is to be misunderstood" (line 51), supported by examples of famous thinkers, such as Galileo and Newton, whose views caused public distrust and disdain (lines 46–51). This statement explains Emerson's idea about eschewing public opinion.*

SHORT RESPONSE

Cite Text Evidence   Student responses will vary, but students should cite textual evidence to support their paraphrase of central ideas for their summary. Students should:

- restate the central ideas of this part of the essay.
- show the development and interactions of the central ideas.
- use the central ideas to write an objective summary.

DIG DEEPER

With the class, return to "*from* Nature," Question 4, Reread and Discuss. Have students share the results of their group discussion.

ASK STUDENTS whether they were satisfied with the outcome of their small-group discussions. Have each group share their explanation of Emerson's allusion to the relationship between "man and the vegetable." What text evidence did the group cite to support its explanation?

- Guide students to tell whether there was any convincing evidence cited by group members who did not agree with the explanation accepted by the majority. If so, why wasn't the evidence strong enough to sway the group's opinion?

- Have groups tell how they decided whether or not they had found sufficient textual evidence to support their explanation.

- Did everyone in the group agree as to what made the evidence sufficient? If not, how did the group resolve conflicts?

- After groups have stated their "findings," ask if another group shared evidence they wish they had thought of.

ASK STUDENTS to return to their Short Response answer on page 43 and to revise it based on the class discussion.

CLOSE READING NOTES

*my*SmartPlanner — Create lesson plans and access resources online.

ANCHOR TEXT Against Nature

Argument by Joyce Carol Oates

Why This Text?

Students regularly encounter arguments that challenge their assumptions about familiar topics. This lesson analyzes Oates's use of three writing structures in the development of her argument against nature writing as a genre.

View It!

Professional Development Podcast:

Teaching Argument

Key Learning Objective: The student will be able to analyze how an author's choices concerning the structure of a text contribute to its meaning.

For additional practice:

Spoiling Walden
Or, How I Learned to Stop Worrying and Love Cape Wind

Close Reader selection
"Spoiling Walden: Or, How I Learned to Stop Worrying and Love Cape Wind"
Essay by David Gessner

COMMON CORE Common Core Standards

RI 1 Cite textual evidence.
RI 2 Determine themes of a text.
RI 3 Analyze a complex sequence of events and explain how individuals, ideas, or events interact.
RI 5 Analyze the structure an author uses in an argument.
W 2 Write informative/explanatory texts.
W 7 Conduct short research projects to answer a question.
L 3a Eliminate wordiness and redundancy.
L 4a Use context as a clue to the meaning of a word or phrase.
L 4b Identify and correctly use patterns of word changes.
L 4c Consult general reference materials.

▲ Text Complexity Rubric

	Against Nature
Quantitative Measures	Lexile: 1000L
Qualitative Measures	**Levels of Meaning/Purpose** ●—●—●—**●**—→ multiple purposes; implied but subtle and difficult to determine
	Structure ●—●—●—**●**—→ multiple text structures
	Language Conventionality and Clarity ●—●—**●**—●—→ increased academic language
	Knowledge Demands ●—●—**●**—●—→ many references to other texts
Reader/Task Considerations	Teacher determined Vary by individual reader and type of text

CLOSE READ

Background Born in 1938, Joyce Carol Oates has written two to three books each year, authoring over 50 novels. Oates also writes nonfiction, short stories, and poetry. She believes that "We are stimulated to emotional response not by works that confirm our sense of the world, but by works that challenge it."

AS YOU READ Direct students to use the As You Read note to focus their reading. Remind them to write down any questions they generate during reading.

Analyze and Evaluate Structure

COMMON CORE RI 3, RI 5

Epigraphs, or quotations, often appear at the beginning of a work to summarize or emphasize author's purpose.

 **ASK STUDENTS** Why did Oates choose the two epigraphs to open her essay? *(Thoreau and Johnson are writers; both quotes show frustration with topic of nature.)*

Analyze Author's Purpose

COMMON CORE RI 1

(LINES 1–5)

The author's reason or goal for writing influences the choice of form and type of writing. "Against Nature" is an essay. Explain the three main types of essay shown in the chart below. An author may rely primarily on one essay type but also include elements of the other types.

Structure	Characteristics
narrative	*tells a story, often uses chronological order; describes events, thoughts and feelings*
informative	*informs about or explains a topic; includes central ideas supported by facts and examples*
argumentative	*attempts to persuade; makes a claim, then includes reasons, evidence, and rhetorical devices to support its validity; has a strong introduction and a compelling conclusion*

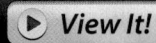 **CITE TEXT EVIDENCE** Ask students to read the author byline and identify Oates's main purpose for writing. *(to argue a point of view)* Read lines 2–5, supporting opinions with text evidence. *(Each statement makes a claim about nature, as in "It has no sense of humor" to support Oates's argument "against nature.")*

Joyce Carol Oates (b. 1938) *was born in Lockport, New York. She began writing at a young age, typing out story after story on a typewriter she received as a gift at the age of 14. Oates published her first novel,* With Shuddering Fall, *when she was 26. A subsequent novel,* them, *won the National Book Award. Since 1978, Oates has taught writing in the creative writing program at Princeton. All the while, she has been a terrifically prolific writer, turning out dozens of critically acclaimed novels. Some of her best known include* Bellefleur, The Gravedigger's Daughter, Blonde, *and* We Were the Mulvaneys.

Against Nature

Argument by Joyce Carol Oates

Image Credits: (t) ©Bernard Gotfryd/Hulton Archive/Getty Images; (cr) ©Stewart Bremner/Flickr/Getty Images; (cl) ©fuyu liu/Shutterstock

AS YOU READ Identify ways in which Oates tries to persuade the reader.

> *We soon get through with Nature. She excites an expectation which she cannot satisfy.*
> —Thoreau, *Journal*, 1854

A

> *Sir, if a man has experienced the inexpressible, he is under no obligation to attempt to express it.*
> —Samuel Johnson

The writer's resistance to Nature.

It has no sense of humor: in its beauty, as in its ugliness, or its neutrality, there is no laughter.
It lacks a moral purpose.
It lacks a satiric dimension, registers no irony.

B

Close Read Screencasts ▶ View It!

Modeled Discussions

Have students click the *Close Read* icons in their eBooks to access screencasts in which readers discuss and annotate the following key passages:

- Oates lists why she is resistant to nature writing. (lines 6–14)
- Oates questions Thoreau's view of nature. (lines 194–203)

As a class, view and discuss at least one of these videos. Then have students pair up to do an independent close read of an additional passage. For example, in a mystical vision, Oates contemplates the relationship between mind and body (lines 230–252).

TEACH

CLOSE READ

Analyze Author's Purpose (LINES 6–14)

COMMON CORE RI 1, RI 2, RI 3, RI 5

In persuasive writing, the author's general purpose is to argue a point of view. To determine an author's goal for writing, readers can ask, "What opinion or viewpoint does the author want to convey to the audience?" or "What action does the author want the audience to take in response to this argument?"

 **ASK STUDENTS** to infer what Oates thinks about nature as a topic for writing. *(Nature is not a worthy topic because it inspires "a…limited set of responses.")* What is the author's specific purpose in this essay? *(Oates wants to convince readers that nature is treated with inappropriate reverence.)*

Analyze and Evaluate Structure (LINES 29–45)

COMMON CORE RI 3, RI 5

Explain that informative writing informs or explains, while narrative writing tells a story. With at least one main idea as the "spine" of its structure, informative writing relies on supporting facts and examples.

 **CITE TEXT EVIDENCE** Have students reread lines 29–45 and infer the type of approach *(informational)* and the topic. *(paroxysmal tachycardia)* Then have them cite supporting details that inform the reader about facts about the topic (lines 30-31).

CRITICAL VOCABULARY

resonance: The author describes nature as accidental and perfunctory.

ASK STUDENTS Why doesn't Oates find resonance in the pleasures of nature? *(because the pleasures of nature are unintentional and superficial)*

 Its pleasures lack **resonance**, being accidental; its horrors, even when premeditated, are equally perfunctory,[1] "red in tooth and claw,"[2] et cetera.

It lacks a symbolic subtext—excepting that provided by man.

10 It has no (verbal) language.

It has no interest in ours.

It inspires a painfully limited set of responses in "nature writers"—REVERENCE, AWE, PIETY, MYSTICAL ONENESS.

It eludes us even as it prepares to swallow us up, books and all.

I was lying on my back in the dirt gravel of the towpath[3] beside the Delaware and Raritan Canal, Titusville, New Jersey, staring up at the sky and trying, with no success, to overcome a sudden attack of tachycardia[4] that had come upon me out of nowhere—such attacks are always "out of nowhere," that's their charm—and all around me 20 Nature thrummed with life, the air smelling of moisture and sunlight, the canal reflecting the sky, red-winged blackbirds testing their spring calls: the usual. I'd become the jar in Tennessee,[5] a fictitious center, or parenthesis, aware beyond my erratic heartbeat of the numberless heartbeats of the earth, its pulsing, pumping life, sheer life, incalculable. Struck down in the midst of motion—I'd been jogging a minute before—I was "out of time" like a fallen, stunned boxer, privileged (in an abstract manner of speaking) to be an involuntary witness to the random, wayward, nameless motion on all sides of me.

Paroxysmal tachycardia can be fatal, but rarely; if the heartbeat 30 accelerates to 250–270 beats a minute you're in trouble, but the average attack is about 100–150 beats and mine seemed about average; the trick now was to prevent it from getting worse. Brainy people try brainy strategies, such as thinking calming thoughts, pseudo-mystic thoughts, *If I die now it's a good death*, that sort of thing, *if I die this is a good place and good time*; the idea is to deceive the frenzied heartbeat that, really, you don't care: you hadn't any other plans for the afternoon. The important thing with tachycardia is to prevent panic! you must prevent panic! otherwise you'll have to be taken by ambulance to the closest emergency room, which is not so 40 very nice a way to spend the afternoon, really. So I contemplated the blue sky overhead. The earth beneath my head. Nature surrounding me on all sides; I couldn't quite see it but I could hear it, smell it, sense it, there is something *there*, no mistake about it. Completely oblivious

resonance
(rĕz'ə-nəns) *n.* richness of meaning; the ability to evoke emotion.

---

[1] **perfunctory:** without interest or enthusiasm.

[2] **"red in tooth and claw":** a reference to the unsentimental violence of the natural world.

[3] **towpath:** a path along a waterway on which animals walk while towing boats.

[4] **tachycardia:** an abnormally rapid heartbeat.

[5] **the jar in Tennessee:** an allusion to Wallace Stevens's poem "The Anecdote of the Jar."

222 Collection 3

SCAFFOLDING FOR ELL STUDENTS

Punctuation Cues Remind students that punctuation marks such as the exclamation point usually indicate the end of a sentence. Explain that authors may break grammar rules to create an effect or to make a point. Read aloud "The important thing … is to prevent panic! you must prevent panic! otherwise." (lines 37–41) Why do the exclamation points not indicate the end of the sentence? *(The words* you *and* otherwise *are in lowercase, signaling that they do not begin a new sentence.)* What purpose do these exclamation points serve? *(They indicate a pause for dramatic effect.)* Help students determine the purpose of the dashes in lines 25–26 *(to emphasize a sudden interruption in the action)* and the ellipses in lines 80, 84, and 89. *(to signal that the writer is moving from one memory to another)*

222 Collection 3

to the predicament of the individual but that's only "natural," after all, one hardly expects otherwise.

When you discover yourself lying on the ground, limp and unresisting, head in the dirt, and, let's face it, helpless, the earth seems to shift forward as a presence; hard, emphatic, not mere surface but a genuine force—there is no other word for it but *presence*. To
50 keep in motion is to keep in time, and to be stopped, stilled, is to be abruptly out of time, in another time dimension perhaps, an alien one, where human language has no resonance. Nothing to be said about it expresses it, nothing touches it, it's an absolute against which nothing human can be measured. . . . Moving through space and time by way of your own volition[6] you inhabit an interior consciousness, a hallucinatory consciousness, it might be said, so long as breath, heartbeat, the body's **autonomy** hold; when motion is stopped you are jarred out of it. The interior is invaded by the exterior. The outside wants to come in, and only the self's fragile membrane prevents it.
60 The fly buzzing at Emily's death.[7]

Still, the earth *is* your place. A tidy grave site measured to your size. Or, from another angle of vision, one vast democratic grave.

Let's contemplate the sky. Forget the crazy hammering heartbeat, don't listen to it, don't start counting, remember that there is a clever way of breathing that conserves oxygen as if you're lying below the surface of a body of water breathing through a very thin straw but you *can* breathe through it if you're careful, if you don't panic; one breath and then another and then another, isn't that the story of all lives?

autonomy
(ô-tŏn′ə-mē) *n.*
freedom
from control;
independence.

---

[6] **volition:** the act of making a choice.
[7] **The fly buzzing at Emily's death:** an allusion to an Emily Dickinson poem that begins, "I heard a Fly buzz—when I died—".

Against Nature **223**

APPLYING ACADEMIC VOCABULARY

quote	analogy

As you discuss *Against Nature,* incorporate the following academic vocabulary words: *quote* and *analogy.* To explore how Oates supports her argument, ask students to identify **quotes** that add to the effectiveness of her argument. Have students discuss the **analogy** Oates makes of recovering from an attack of tachycardia to breathing under water. As students evaluate the selection, stop to point out **analogies** and determine their effect on the reader.

Analyze Author's Purpose: Point of View (LINES 46–59)

COMMON CORE RI 3, RI 5

Tell students that authors may use second-person point of view to elicit in the reader a feeling of being part of the experience. Addressing the reader as "you" blurs the line between narrator and reader.

E ASK STUDENTS What effect does the use of second-person point of view have in lines 46–59? *(Oates's use of the second-person point of view draws the reader in to share her experience.)*

Analyze and Evaluate Structure (LINES 63–68)

COMMON CORE RI 3, RI 5

Point out that authors may impose a single essay structure or incorporate two or more. Authors vary structure for several reasons: to make a particular point, to add layers of meaning and complexity, or to connect with their audience.

F CITE TEXT EVIDENCE Have students reread lines 63–68 and cite text that suggests narrative writing structure. *(Line 63: "Let's contemplate the sky"; line 68: "isn't that the story of all lives?")* Then have students cite text that suggests an informative writing structure. *(Line 63–68: "remember that there is a clever…if you don't panic.")* Finally, ask students to analyze and evaluate the effect of the use of multiple structures on the essay. *(The use of multiple structures gives the essay complexity and makes it more persuasive because it appeals to the reader's mind, senses, and heart simultaneously.)*

CRITICAL VOCABULARY

autonomy: Oates suddenly loses her sense of freedom when she suffers an attack of paroxysmal tachycardia while jogging.

ASK STUDENTS what signs of a loss of autonomy are evident in the writer's behavior. *(When she is having her attack of tachycardia, the author is powerless to control her body, and is forced to lie on the ground until the attack passes.)*

Analyze Author's Purpose: Point of View (LINES 69–78)

COMMON CORE RI 3, RI 5

Tell students that readers must distinguish **fact** from **opinion** to effectively assess the author's support of an argument. Explain that facts are pieces of information that can be verified, while opinions cannot be proved true or false.

G ASK STUDENTS to cite an assertion in lines 76–78 that is a fact and to infer why Oates included this detail. *(The blueness of the sky is an optical illusion. Oates made this statement because it shows that we can't trust what we see in nature, supporting her point of view that we see nature as we wish to see it, not as it is.)*

Analyze and Evaluate Structure (LINES 80–97)

COMMON CORE RI 3, RI 5

Narrative writing is storytelling—it entertains and draws the reader in to the world of the story.

H ASK STUDENTS to identify the three brief narratives in lines 80–97. *(Oates wades in water and is horrified to find leeches stuck to her feet; she finds a friend's dead dog; a rabid raccoon rips open its stomach.)*

Have students analyze and evaluate why Oates includes these stories at this point in her essay. *(The use of graphic details and vivid images helps the reader see and feel Oates's disturbing childhood memories of her encounters with the violent natural world. They vividly illustrate her point that nature is brutal, indifferent to suffering, and should not be idealized. The narratives also bridge the next part of her argument by suggesting why she distrusts "Nature mysticism.")*

CRITICAL VOCABULARY

evidently: When Oates happens upon a friend's dog in lines 84–88, it is clear to her that the dog has been shot.

ASK STUDENTS how Oates could have been so sure of the dog's fate as to remark that evidently it was the victim of a hunting accident. *(Oates mentions the likely presence of a hunter, and she must have seen a bullet wound. A hunter had shot the dog.)*

---

careers? Just a matter of breathing. Of course it is. But contemplate
70 the sky, it's there to be contemplated. A mild shock to see it so blank, blue, a thin airy ghostly blue, no clouds to disguise its emptiness. You are beginning to feel not only weightless but near-bodiless, lying on the earth like a scrap of paper about to be blown off. Two dimensions and you'd imagined you were three! And there's the sky rolling away forever, into infinity—if "infinity" can be "rolled into"—and the forlorn[8] truth is, that's where you're going too. And the lovely blue isn't even blue, is it? isn't even there, is it? a mere optical illusion, isn't it? no matter what art has urged you to believe.

Early Nature memories. Which it's best not to suppress.
80 . . . Wading, as a small child, in Tonawanda Creek near our house, and afterward trying to tear off, in a frenzy of terror and revulsion, the sticky fat black bloodsuckers that had attached themselves to my feet, particularly between my toes.

. . . Coming upon a friend's dog in a drainage ditch, dead for several days, **evidently** the poor creature had been shot by a hunter and left to die, bleeding to death, and we're stupefied[9] with grief and horror but can't resist sliding down to where he's lying on his belly, and we can't resist squatting over him, turning the body over.

. . . The raccoon, mad with rabies, frothing at the mouth and
90 tearing at his own belly with his teeth, so that his intestines spill out onto the ground . . . a sight I seem to remember though in fact I did not see. I've been told I did not see.

Consequently, my chronic uneasiness with Nature mysticism: Nature adoration; Nature-as-(moral)-instruction-for-mankind. My doubt that one can, with philosophical validity, address "Nature" as a single coherent noun, anything other than a Platonic, hence discredited, is-ness.[10] My resistance to "Nature writing" as a genre, except when it is brilliantly fictionalized in the service of a writer's individual vision— Thoreau's books and *Journal*, of course, but also, less known in this
100 country, the miniaturist prose poems of Colette (*Flowers and Fruit*) and Ponge (*Taking the Side of Things*)—in which case it becomes yet another, and ingenious, form of storytelling. The subject is *there* only by the grace of the author's language.

Nature has no instructions for mankind except that our poor beleaguered humanist-democratic way of life, our fantasies of the individual's high worth, our sense that the weak, no less than the strong, have a right to survive, are absurd. When Edmund of *King Lear* said excitedly, "Nature, be thou my goddess!" he knew whereof he spoke.

evidently
(ĕv′ĭ-dənt-lē) *adv.*
plainly, or obviously apparent from evidence or data.

---

[8] **forlorn:** sad.

[9] **stupefied:** stunned; in a daze.

[10] **a Platonic . . . is-ness:** Plato's idea that there are ideal forms as an absolute and eternal reality of which the phenomena, or experiences, of the world are an imperfect and transitory reflection.

WHEN STUDENTS STRUGGLE . . .

In her essay, Oates uses long sentences with complex structures. Share the following strategies with students to help them understand sentences with multiple phrases and clauses.

- Have students break longer sentences into several short sentences. Model how to break a sentence down.

Surely Nature is, for you,...a "perennial" source of beauty, comfort, peace, escape from the delirium of...life; a respite from the ego's...self-promotion, as a way of ensuring...some small measure of immortality?

110　　In any case, where *is* Nature, one might (skeptically) inquire. Who has looked upon her/its face and survived?[11]

But isn't this all exaggeration, in the spirit of rhetorical contentiousness?[12] Surely Nature is, for you, as for most reasonably intelligent people, a "perennial" source of beauty, comfort, peace, escape from the delirium of civilized life; a respite[13] from the ego's ever-frantic strategies of self-promotion, as a way of ensuring (at least in fantasy) some small measure of immortality? Surely Nature, as it is understood in the usual slapdash way, as human, if not dilettante,[14]
120　*experience* (hiking in a national park, jogging on the beach at dawn, even tending, with the usual comical frustrations, a suburban garden), is wonderfully consoling; a place where, when you go there, it has to take you in?—a palimpsest[15] of sorts you choose to read, layer by layer, always with care, always cautiously, in proportion to your psychological strength?

　　Nature: as in Thoreau's upbeat Transcendentalist[16] mode ("The indescribable innocence and beneficence of Nature,—such health, such cheer, they afford forever! and such sympathy have they ever with our race, that all Nature would be affected . . . if any man should ever for a just cause grieve"), and not in Thoreau's grim mode ("Nature is
130　hard to be overcome but she must be overcome").

　　Another way of saying, not *Nature-in-itself* but *Nature-as-experience.*

　　The former, Nature-in-itself, is, to allude slantwise to Melville, a blankness ten times blank;[17] the latter is what we commonly, or perhaps always, mean, when we speak of Nature as a noun, a single entity—something of *ours.* Most of the time it's just an activity, a sort of hobby, a weekend, a few days, perhaps a few hours, staring out the window at the mind-dazzling autumn foliage of, say, northern Michigan, being rendered speechless—temporarily—at the sight of
140　Mt. Shasta, the Grand Canyon, Ansel Adams's[18] West. Or Nature writ small, contained in the back yard. Nature filtered through our optical nerves, our "senses," our fiercely romantic expectations. Nature that

---

[11] **Who has . . . and survived?:** Perhaps an allusion to Exodus 33:20: And [God] said, Thou canst not see my face: for there shall no man see me, and live.

[12] **contentiousness:** tendency to argue.

[13] **respite:** rest or break.

[14] **dilettante:** a person with a superficial interest in an art or an activity.

[15] **palimpsest:** a manuscript that has been written over still-visible erasures.

[16] **Transcendentalist:** one who believes that the material world contains an underlying, perceivable spiritual component.

[17] **to allude . . . ten times blank:** Herman Melville, when writing about Hawthorne's work, compared its "dark half" to the part of the globe that is "shrouded in darkness ten times black."

[18] **Ansel Adams's:** Adams (1902–1984) was an American photographer known for his black-and-white landscapes.

TEACH

CLOSE READ

Analyze and Evaluate Structure (LINES 117–124)

COMMON CORE　RI 3, RI 5

Explain that persuasive essays engage readers in discussion or debate. Readers must analyze the evidence authors use to support their claims. Authors often build evidence over the course of their essays to further their claims.

 **ASK STUDENTS** to identify what claim Oates makes in lines 117–124 and how it furthers her claims about nature. *(She says that nature is seen falsely by many people as a "consoling" human "experience." We understand nature superficially because we choose only to believe what we wish about it.)* Ask students to identify evidence Oates uses to support this claim. *(She gives examples of people's superficial interactions with nature, such as going to a park, jogging on the beach, and gardening.)*

Analyze and Evaluate Structure (LINES 125–136)

COMMON CORE　RI 3, RI 5

 **CITE TEXT EVIDENCE** Ask students how Oates's comments about Thoreau in lines 125–136 connect to her ideas in the previous paragraph. Remind students to cite textual evidence to support their inference. *(Oates alludes to Thoreau's "upbeat" ideas about nature [lines 125, 129, and 133]. She notes that he mistakenly categorizes it not as "Nature-in-itself," but merely as his limited experience of it [lines 131–132].)* This hearkens back to the foolhardy misrepresentation of nature as transcendent "human experience" in lines 117–124.

Strategies for Annotation　✏ 🔲 *Annotate it!*

Analyze and Evaluate Structure

COMMON CORE　RI 3, RI 5

Share these strategies for guided or independent analysis to help students distinguish between **literary criticism** and argumentative writing.

- Highlight in pink any literary references.
- Underline any quotes that suggest that the excerpt is an analysis of literature.
- Highlight in green words or phrases that reflect the author's interpretation and analysis of the literature.
- On a note, record your summary of this analysis.

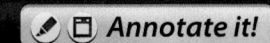

Nature: as in Thoreau's upbeat Transcendentalist mode ("The indescribable innocence and beneficence of Nature,—such health, such cheer, they afford forever! and such sympathy have they ever with our race, that all Nature would be affected…if any man should ever for a just cause grieve"), and not in Thoreau's grim mode ("Nature is hard to be overcome but she must be overcome").

Analyze Author's Purpose: COMMON CORE RI 3, RI 5
Point of View (LINES 147–156)

Tell students that, to express their position in a compelling and convincing manner, authors of argumentative writing often use **rhetoric,** the art of speaking or writing for persuasive effect. For example, an author may ask a rhetorical question, or a question that does not require a reply but is asked for rhetorical effect.

 **CITE TEXT EVIDENCE** Have students cite examples of rhetorical questions in lines 147–156. *(At the beginning of the paragraph, Oates asks, "Why glamorize it, romanticize it?" [lines 147–148] and then asks "Why not?" [line 156].)* What effect do these rhetorical questions produce? *(They cause the reader to consider why writers take glamorizing and romanticizing nature for granted, and they make the reader question the wisdom of doing so.)*

Analyze and Evaluate COMMON CORE RI 3, RI 5
Structure (LINES 160–178)

Tell students that in argumentative writing, authors may include quotations to support their opinions. Explain that, while opinions cannot be proven, the opinions of respected authorities can add weight at crucial points in an author's argument.

 **ASK STUDENTS** how the quotation from Wilde supports Oates's argument. *(The quotation supports Oates's claim that people see in nature only what they want to see.)*

CRITICAL VOCABULARY

transcending: By romanticizing nature, people try to escape their mundane lives.

ASK STUDENTS what nature has to do with transcending life's problems. *(Many people focus on nature's beauty or purity as an escape from daily worries.)*

---

pleases us because it mirrors our souls, or gives the comforting illusion of doing so.

Nature as the self's (flattering) mirror, but not ever, no, never, Nature-in-itself.

Nature is mouths, or maybe a single mouth. Why glamorize it, romanticize it?—well, yes, but we must, we're writers, poets, mystics (of a sort) aren't we, precisely what else are we to do but glamorize and 150 romanticize and generally exaggerate the significance of anything we focus the white heat of our "creativity" upon? And why not Nature, since it's there, common property, mute, can't talk back, allows us the possibility of **transcending** the human condition for a while, writing prettily of mountain ranges, white-tailed deer, the purple crocuses outside this very window, the thrumming dazzling "life force" we imagine we all support. Why not?

Nature *is* more than a mouth—it's a dazzling variety of mouths. And it pleases the senses, in any case, as the physicists' chill universe of numbers certainly does not.

160 Oscar Wilde,[19] on our subject:

> Nature is no great mother who has borne us. She is our creation. It is in our brain that she quickens to life. Things are because we see them, and what we see, and how we see it, depends on the Arts that have influenced us. To look at a thing is very different from seeing a thing. . . . At present, people see fogs, not because there are fogs, but because poets and painters have taught them the mysterious loveliness of such effects. There may have been fogs for centuries in London. I dare say there were. But no 170 one saw them. They did not exist until Art had invented them. . . . Yesterday evening Mrs. Arundel insisted on my going to the window and looking at the glorious sky, as she called it. And so I had to look at it. . . . And what was it? It was simply a very second-rate Turner, a Turner of a bad period, with all the painter's worst faults exaggerated and over-emphasized.
>
> ("The Decay of Lying," 1889)

(If we were to put it to Oscar Wilde that he exaggerates, his reply might well be, "Exaggeration? I don't know the meaning of the word.")

180 *Walden*, that most artfully composed of prose fictions, concludes, in the rhapsodic chapter "Spring," with Henry David Thoreau's contemplation of death, decay, and regeneration as it is suggested to him, or to his protagonist, by the spectacle of vultures feeding off carrion. There is a dead horse close by his cabin, and the stench of its

---

[19] **Oscar Wilde:** (1854–1900) an Irish author of poems, plays, and prose.

transcend
(trăn-sĕnd´) *v.* to go beyond the limits or become independent of.

TO CHALLENGE STUDENTS . . .

What does Oscar Wilde really think about Mother Nature? Explain that an author's perspective is his or her attitudes and beliefs as expressed in the author's writing. Point out that a single excerpt cannot fully represent the author's perspective. Challenge students to independently research Wilde's views on nature, paying particular attention to those that relate to the claims Oates makes in "Against Nature." Have students share the results of their research with the class.

decomposition, in certain winds, is daunting. Yet "the assurance it
gave me of the strong appetite and inviolable health of Nature was my
compensation for this. I love to see that Nature is so rife with life that
myriads can be afforded to be sacrificed and suffered to prey upon one
another; that tender organizations can be so serenely squashed out of
190 existence like pulp,— tadpoles which herons gobble up, and tortoises
and toads run over in the road; and that sometimes it has rained flesh
and blood! . . . The impression made on a wise man is that of universal
innocence."

Come off it, Henry David. You've grieved these many years for
your elder brother, John, who died a ghastly death of lockjaw;[20] you've
never wholly recovered from the experience of watching him die.
And you know, or must know, that you're fated too to die young of
consumption[21]. . . . But this doctrinaire[22] Transcendentalist passage
ends *Walden* on just the right note. It's as impersonal, as coolly
200 detached, as the Oversoul[23] itself: a "wise man" filters his emotions
through his brain.

Or through his prose.

Nietzsche: "We all pretend to ourselves that we are more simple-
minded than we are: that is how we get a rest from our fellow men."

> Once out of nature I shall never take
> My bodily form from any natural thing,
> But such a form as Grecian goldsmiths make
> Of hammered gold and gold enamelling
> To keep a drowsy Emperor awake;
210 > Or set upon a golden bough to sing
> To lords and ladies of Byzantium
> Of what is past, or passing, or to come.
>   —William Butler Yeats, *Sailing to Byzantium*

Yet even the golden bird is a "bodily form [taken from a] natural
thing." No, it's impossible to escape!

The writer's resistance to Nature.

Wallace Stevens: "In the presence of extraordinary actuality,
consciousness takes the place of imagination."

Once, years ago, in 1972 to be precise, when I seemed to have been
220 another person, related to the person I am now as one is related,
tangentially, sometimes embarrassingly, to cousins not seen for
decades—once, when we were living in London, and I was very sick,

tangentially
(tăn-jĕn′shəl-lē) *adv.*
indirectly or
peripherally
connected.

---

[20]**lockjaw:** tetanus, which causes muscles in the neck and jaw to stiffen.
[21]**consumption:** tuberculosis.
[22]**doctrinaire:** insisting on a theory without regard to practical problems.
[23]**Oversoul:** a spiritual essence or vital force in the universe in which all souls
   participate and that therefore transcends individual consciousness.

CLOSE READ

Analyze Author's Purpose: Point of View (LINES 187–198)

COMMON CORE RI 3, RI 5

Remind students that **counterargument** presents an opposing viewpoint. Authors may quote a differing opinion simply to refute it or to strengthen their own argument.

(M) CITE TEXT EVIDENCE Have students reread lines 187–198 and summarize the idea Thoreau expresses. *(Thoreau expresses the idea that he sees death as an expression of the abundance and innocence of nature.)*

Is Oates convinced by Thoreau's argument? Have students cite textual evidence to support their answer. *(Oates clearly does not agree with him; she contradicts him by saying, "Come off it, Henry David." She also does not believe him; she points out in lines 194–197 that Thoreau has experienced the horror of nature as he watched his brother die of lockjaw and has never recovered from the experience.)*

Analyze Language: Tone (LINES 194–197)

COMMON CORE RI 3, RI 5

Remind students that an author's **tone** is his or her attitude toward the subject or toward the reader and that it is expressed by the author's choice of words, syntax, examples, and details.

(N) ASK STUDENTS to consider the tone Oates takes in lines 194–197. How does the tone differ in the two sentences? *(In the first sentence, her tone is informal and flippant; whereas in the second, it's more formal.)* What effect does her tone have on the essay? *(While the essay is highly academic, the inclusion of sentences with a more personal, informal, and even playful tone adds interest and prevents the essay from seeming stuffy.)*

CRITICAL VOCABULARY

tangentially: Oates recognizes that she has grown and developed since 1972.

ASK STUDENTS what Oates means when she says she feels tangentially related to herself. *(She has changed over time and feels only a slight connection with her younger self.)*

Analyze and Evaluate Structure (LINES 229–239)

COMMON CORE RI 3, RI 5

Tell students that Oates uses narrative elements to add dramatic effect and to illustrate her claims at specific points in her essay. The narrative of her mystical vision functions as an **analogy,** or comparison of two things. Oates implies the connection instead of spelling it out.

Ⓞ **ASK STUDENTS** to analyze the analogy. How is Oates's "mystical" vision similar to nature writing? *(Both are mystical, beautiful, and imaginative. The vision can't exist without Oates just as the transcendental quality of nature as expressed in nature writing can't exist without the writer.)* Why does she include this example at this point in her essay? *(Oates uses a personal incident ["a mystical vision"] to discredit the ovepersonalization and mystification of nature that Thoreau and others adopt.)*

I had a mystical vision. That is, I "had" a "mystical vision"—the heart sinks: such pretension—or something resembling one. A fever dream, let's call it. It impressed me enormously and impresses me still, though I've long since lost the capacity to see it with my mind's eye, or even, I suppose, to believe in it. There is a statute of limitations on "mystical visions," as on romantic love.

230   I was very sick, and I imagined my life as a thread, a thread of breath, or heartbeat, or pulse, or light—yes, it was light, radiant light; I was burning with fever and I ascended to that plane of serenity that might be mistaken for (or *is*, in fact) Nirvana, where I had a waking dream of uncanny[24] lucidity:

My body is a tall column of light and heat.

My body is not "I" but "it."

My body is not one but many.

My body, which "I" inhabit, is inhabited as well by other creatures, unknown to me, imperceptible—the smallest of them mere sparks of light.

240   My body, which I perceive as substance, is in fact an organization of infinitely complex, overlapping, imbricated[25] structures, radiant

---

[24]**uncanny:** strange or mysterious.

[25]**imbricated:** placed in an overlapping pattern.

WHEN STUDENTS STRUGGLE . . .

"Against Nature" includes difficult passages that may be challenging for students to decipher. Tell students that they can paraphrase to understand complex writing. Explain that when they paraphrase, they are rewriting the text in their own words.

ASK STUDENTS to work in small groups to fill in a chart like the one shown. By completing the chart, students will break down and paraphrase difficult descriptions. Have them reread lines 241–243. Then have them break longer sentences into chunks, entering chunks in the chart. The group will discuss, paraphrase, and enter each chunk in the chart. Review and clarify passages as needed.

Image Credits: ©Burazin/Photographer's Choice/Getty Images

light their manifestation, the "body" a tall column of light and blood heat, a temporary agreement among atoms, like a high-rise building with numberless rooms, corridors, corners, elevator shafts, windows. . . . In this fantastical structure the "I" is deluded as to its sovereignty, let alone its autonomy in the (outside) world; the most astonishing secret is that the "I" doesn't exist!—but it behaves as if it does, as if it were one and not many.

250 In any case, without the "I" the tall column of light and heat would die, and the microscopic life particles would die with it . . . will die with it. The "I," which doesn't exist, is everything.

But Dr. Johnson is right, the inexpressible need not be expressed.
And what resistance, finally? There is none.

This morning, an invasion of tiny black ants. One by one they appear, out of nowhere—that's their charm too!—moving single file across the white Parsons table where I am sitting, trying without much success to write a poem. A poem of only three or four lines is what I want, something short, might, mean; I want it to hurt like a white-hot wire up the nostrils, small and compact and turned in upon itself with the 260 density of a hunk of rock from the planet Jupiter. . . .

But here come the black ants: **harbingers**, you might say, of spring. One by one by one they appear on the dazzling white table and one by one I kill them with a forefinger, my deft right forefinger, mashing each against the surface of the table and then dropping it into a wastebasket at my side. Idle labor, mesmerizing, effortless, and I'm curious as to how long I can do it—sit here in the brilliant March sunshine killing ants with my right forefinger—how long I, and the ants, can keep it up.

After a while I realize that I can do it a long time. And that I've 270 written my poem.

harbinger
(här´bĭn-jər) *n.* a person or thing that signals a future occurrence.

COLLABORATIVE DISCUSSION How does Oates try to persuade readers to agree with her point of view on nature and nature writing? Cite specific words, phrases, and examples from the text.

Original Phrasing	In My Own Words
My body, is in fact an organization	My body is made up of many parts.
which I perceive as substance,	I see my body as something solid and real.
an organization of infinitely complex, overlapping, imbricated structures,	It is an organization with structures that are complex beyond limit.
overlapping, imbricated structures,	They are interrelated and overlap.
radiant light their manifestation	These structures show themselves as light.

CLOSE READ

Analyze and Evaluate Structure (LINES 252–253)

COMMON CORE RI 3, RI 5

Explain that authors may draw attention to their main idea, key reflection, or central argument by beginning an essay with an intriguing statement or question and circling back to it at the end.

P ASK STUDENTS why, at the end of her essay, Oates refers to Johnson's quote from the epigraph. *(Oates uses Johnson's quote as a synopsis for her argument: Once readers acknowledge that nature is elusive and inexpressible, they will have no need to express false "Nature adoration.")*

CRITICAL VOCABULARY

harbingers: The ants signify the beginning of spring.

ASK STUDENTS why the ants are harbingers of spring. *(The ants may have been the first sign of new life that she's seen since winter.)*

COLLABORATIVE DISCUSSION Have students form pairs to discuss how Oates appeals to her readers, including her choice of essay structures and what evidence she presents to convince them of her point of view on nature and nature writing. Have them share their conclusions with the class as a whole. Accept all reasonable responses.

ASK STUDENTS to share any questions they generated in the course of reading and discussing the selection.

TEACH

CLOSE READ

Analyze and Evaluate Structure

 **RI 3, RI 5**

Help students understand the effect of a powerful conclusion to an argumentative essay. Ask students to reread lines 255–271 and summarize the events in these lines. *(On a bright March morning, while trying to write a poem, Oates notices that ants have invaded her workspace. She proceeds to kill them off one by one, without regret, and finishes her poem.)*

Discuss with students why this ending to Oates's essay is particularly powerful and whether it successfully supports her claims "against nature."

Remind students that a powerful ending may restate, and even extend, an author's claim in order to persuade a reader of the author's point of view. To help students evaluating the effectiveness of an essay's conclusion:

- Explain that an argument's conclusion should clearly connect to previous claims in the essay.

- Explain that an author may save a particularly dramatic example in support of his or her argument in order to powerfully re-emphasize his or her claims in the essay's concluding paragraphs.

Analyze and Evaluate Structure

 **RI 3, RI 5**

Essays may be structured in a number of unique ways, depending on the goal of the author. The three main types of essays are argumentative, informative (or explanatory), and narrative. The chart gives a brief description of each **structure**.

Argumentative	Informative	Narrative
Argumentative writing attempts to convince the reader to think a certain way about a subject. An argument begins with a statement of opinion and includes reasons supported by evidence to back up that opinion.	An **informative essay** is a nonfiction piece that attempts to explain a particular topic. Informative writing includes several central ideas that are supported by facts and examples.	**Narrative writing** relays the events and experiences in a person's life, often in chronological order. Unlike an expository essay, which simply states the events and experiences, a narrative includes the writer's thoughts and feelings.

Oates's essay does not fit neatly into any of these categories. Instead, the author combines forms, mixing all three styles, putting forth a complex set of ideas and developing them over the course of the text. Take for instance the following narrative excerpt:

> I'd become the jar in Tennessee, a fictitious center, or parenthesis, aware beyond my erratic heartbeat of the numberless heartbeats of the earth, its pulsing, pumping life, sheer life, incalculable.

The author describes events and the feelings that accompany those events. But in the same essay, she goes on to write this:

> Paroxysmal tachycardia can be fatal, but rarely; if the heartbeat accelerates to 250–270 beats a minute you're in trouble. . . .

Here, the author explains the symptoms of an attack in a relatively straightforward manner, adding informative writing to the mix. Sprinkled throughout, however, is opinion writing:

> *Walden*, that most artfully composed of prose fictions, concludes, in the rhapsodic chapter "Spring," with Henry David Thoreau's contemplation of death, decay, and regeneration as it is suggested to him, or to his protagonist, by the spectacle of vultures feeding off carrion.

Here, as elsewhere in the essay, the author's opinion falls into the realm of **literary criticism**, or the interpretation and analysis of literature. Though it is a kind of argumentative writing, literary criticism focuses solely on literature.

To identify an essay's structure, look for the qualities that correspond to each kind of writing. Be aware that, like Oates, authors may mix styles. Nevertheless, their goal is the same: to structure an essay so that it is both clear and engaging.

Strategies for Annotation 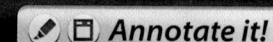 Annotate it!

Analyze and Evaluate Structure 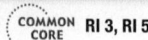 **RI 3, RI 5**

Share these strategies for guided or independent analysis:
- Highlight in yellow an example of narrative writing.
- Underline an example of the writer's thoughts or reflections about the experience.
- Highlight in green an example of argumentative writing.
- Underline words that reflect the writer's opinion.
- On a note, record words that suggest the writer's reasons for the opinion.

> …The raccoon, mad with rabies, frothing at the mouth and tearing at his own belly with his teeth, so that his intestines spill out onto the ground…a sight I seem to remember though in fact I did not see. I've been told I did not see.
>
> Consequently, my chronic uneasiness with Nature mysticism: Nature adoration; Nature-as-(moral)-instruction-for-mankind.

 *eBook Annotate It!*

Analyzing the Text

Cite Text Evidence   Support your responses with evidence from the selection.

1. **Analyze** Look at the list at the beginning of the essay (lines 1–14). In what way does it contribute to the structure of the author's argument?

2. **Analyze** In line 15, the author begins a **narrative** about an experience she had in nature. How does the author use this narrative to engage the reader?

3. **Identify** Attempting to transcend her condition, the author tries to focus on nature as she lies limp in the dirt (lines 46–78). What does she realize about the earth and the sky as she lies there?

4. **Analyze** The author quotes Thoreau in a passage that celebrates the virtues of nature in the decomposition of a dead horse (lines 180–193). Then she addresses Thoreau directly: "Come off it, Henry David." What central idea is developed in lines 194–202? What effect does Oates's **tone,** or attitude toward her subject, in this passage have on the reader?

5. **Interpret** According to the author, how do writers and artists help perpetuate "*Nature-as-experience*" (lines 131–132)?

6. **Analyze** The essay ends with a **narrative** passage about black ants that the author smashes with her forefinger. What do the ants represent? How is the ending a kind of bookend to the narrative at the beginning of the essay?

7. **Evaluate** Is this essay effective as **literary criticism**? Is the structure clear, engaging, and persuasive? Does the author use quotations effectively to support or refute her points? Explain.

PERFORMANCE TASK

Writing Activity: Analysis Review the Oscar Wilde passage that Oates quotes in lines 161–176. Do you agree with the ideas he expresses? Write a brief analysis of the passage and its place in Oates's argument.

- Identify Wilde's central idea and the details he uses to support it. Decide whether you agree with his idea, and why.

- Consider how the passage fits into the structure of Oates's argument. What central idea of hers does the Wilde passage support?

- Write a brief analysis that summarizes your ideas.

Analyzing the Text   COMMON CORE RI 1, RI 2, RI 3, RI 5, W 2, W 7, L 4a

Possible answers:

1. *The beginning of the essay states the writer's overall arguments against nature. The rest of the essay is in support of these points.*

2. *The narrative engages the reader with sensory details, a compelling narrative voice, and vivid stories that support the author's point.*

3. *Oates views the earth as a tangible presence. She sees the sky as an optical illusion that represents infinity, which we will some day "roll" into. Both earth and sky represent different ways of understanding our own mortality.*

4. *Oates doesn't buy into Thoreau's romanticized view of nature. Nature's ability to sacrifice myriad creatures to sustain itself does not signify innocence, but rather displays cruelty. Her familiar direct address challenges not only Thoreau but also her reader and calls into question whether Thoreau himself believed what he wrote.*

5. *Artists and writers romanticize the significance of nature to transcend "the human condition." When a nature experience is the subject of art or writing, nature-as-experience is celebrated.*

6. *In the narrative at the beginning of the essay, Oates sees herself as an insignificant figure dwarfed by the huge presence of the indifferent earth and infinite sky. In the final narrative about the ants, Oates is the huge presence, indifferent to the fate of the tiny ants.*

7. *The essay is effective as literary criticism because it makes the reader think more critically about nature writing. The literary quotes Oates includes don't show the whole picture, but they do effectively add weight to her argument as well as offer counterargument. However, the structure is unclear: Oates makes many leaps and it is difficult for the reader to follow.*

Assign this performance task.

PERFORMANCE TASK   COMMON CORE W 2, W 7

Writing Activity Have students work in groups to identify and discuss Wilde's main idea and supporting details. Then have them list Oates's central ideas and compare each with that of the Wilde passage. Instruct students to work independently to draft their analysis and then regroup to share completed drafts. After students complete their final drafts, have a class discussion to compare the views of Oates and Wilde.

PRACTICE & APPLY

Critical Vocabulary  L 4b

Possible answers:

1. *I wanted autonomy when my parents refused to allow me to play my tuba in the house.*

2. *Langston Hughes's poems have such resonance for me that some bring me to tears while others make me laugh.*

3. *Bare trees and cold days are harbingers of winter.*

4. *When I am jogging, I have to transcend my physical pain to complete my five-mile run.*

5. *Because I spend a lot of time drawing, it's evidently true that I enjoy art.*

6. *To keep from spoiling my sister's surprise party, I had to respond to her questions with answers that were only tangentially related to the truth.*

Vocabulary Strategy: Parts of Speech

Suffixes	Part of Speech	Example
-ate	verb	resonate
-ous	adjective	autonomous
-ence	noun	evidence
-ant	adjective	transcendant

Critical Vocabulary  L 4b

resonance	autonomy	evidently
transcending	tangentially	harbingers

Practice and Apply Answer the questions by applying each Critical Vocabulary word to your own life.

1. When have you wanted **autonomy**?
2. What have you ever seen or read that had **resonance**?
3. What do you see as a **harbinger** of winter?
4. When have you found yourself **transcending** physical pain to perform a task?
5. What is **evidently** true about you, based on your favorite activities?
6. When have you answered a direct question **tangentially**?

Vocabulary Strategy: Parts of Speech

The Critical Vocabulary word *resonance* is a noun, formed by adding the suffix *-ance* to the root of the verb *resonate*. Specific **suffixes,** word parts at the end of a word or root, identify a word as a noun, verb, adjective, or adverb. These suffixes are patterns of word changes that indicate different parts of speech. Recognizing the part of speech that each suffix represents will help you begin to identify unknown words. Here are some common suffixes you will see in English words, along with their corresponding part of speech:

Suffixes	Part of Speech	Example
–ance, -ence	noun	tolerance
–ly	adverb	tangentially
–ing	verb	transcending
–able	adjective	remarkable

Practice and Apply There are many more suffixes besides the ones in the chart. Create your own comprehensive chart that lists suffixes, their part of speech, and an example word that contains each suffix.

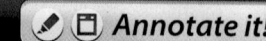 

Parts of Speech  L 4b

Remind students that they can determine the meaning of an unfamiliar word in "Against Nature" by identifying the part of speech indicated by the word's suffix. Have them use their eBook annotation tools to do the following:

- Look for unknown words with familiar suffixes.
- Highlight each suffix in blue. Review your annotations. Add a note for each unknown word and name the part of speech. Infer each word's meaning and add it to your note.

…I ascended to that plane of serenity that might be mistaken for…

Nirvana, where I had a waking dream of uncanny lucidity:…

My body is not "I" but "it."

My body is not one but many.

My body, which "I" inhabit, is inhabited as well by

other creatures,…imperceptible—the smallest of them…sparks of light.

Language and Style: Quotations

Quotations, words taken directly from another text, serve an important purpose in "Against Nature." The author uses them to support her argument, adding evidence to help prove her claims about nature and nature writing.

Read the following sentences from "Against Nature."

Nature *is* more than a mouth—it's a dazzling variety of mouths. And it pleases the senses, in any case, as the physicists' chill universe of numbers certainly does not.

Oscar Wilde, on our subject:

Nature is no great mother who has borne us. She is our creation. It is in our brain that she quickens to life. Things are because we see them, and what we see, and how we see it, depends on the Arts that have influenced us.

The author might well have stated her point and left it at that. But instead, she quotes Oscar Wilde, a noted writer, adding weight and authority to her argument. She also chooses a quotation that is directly relevant to her point, maintaining a continuity of thought.

Quotations can also be used to vary syntax for effect. Rather than repeating or reframing a point, a quotation serves to add interest and variety, to break up a string of monotonous statements. For example, in the following lines, Oates uses a quotation to add variety to the text:

Nature has no instructions for mankind except that our poor beleaguered humanist-democratic way of life, our fantasies of the individual's high worth, our sense that the weak, no less than the strong, have a right to survive, are absurd. When Edmund of *King Lear* said excitedly, "Nature, be thou my goddess!" he knew whereof he spoke.

The author weaves quotations into her text both to bolster her argument and to add literary interest. Her quotations constantly engage and challenge the reader to follow her reasoning.

Practice and Apply Look back at the analysis you wrote in response to this selection's Performance Task. Revise the analysis by adding at least one quotation to support the argument you make and one quotation to vary your prose.

Language and Style: Quotations

Ask students to identify each of the quotations that appear throughout "Against Nature" and to think about the purpose of each quotation. Point out that some quotations support Oates's argument, while some add literary interest. Others refute her argument, offering occasion for counterargument.

Practice and Apply Invite students to share with the class the quotations they added to their Performance Task analyses. Have them explain how one quotation effectively supports their argument and how the other varies their prose.

 **Assess It!**

Online Selection Test
- Download an editable ExamView bank.
- Assign and manage this test online.

Write a Short Research Report

W 7

TEACH

Explain to students that most research begins with a question. The research paper answers the question that initiated the investigation. Provide students with the steps for writing a short research paper.

1. Write a research question.
2. Investigate and assess possible sources. Try to find a wide variety of relevant, credible print and nonprint sources. For accuracy, seek up-to-date information published by major universities or established publishing companies. Usually, websites with *.org, .gov,* or *.edu* in their addresses are more reliable.
3. Prepare a source list and take notes on your sources. Your notes should quote your source directly, paraphrase, or summarize. Regardless of how the information is recorded, credit must be given to sources of information. Record full publishing information for each source.
4. Draft a controlling idea, or thesis statement. You can use the following equation to draft a working controlling idea:

   Topic + Research Question = Controlling Idea
5. Create an outline. Organize ideas according to a logical order, such as chronological order, order of importance, or cause and effect.
6. Draft your essay. Include an introduction, body, and conclusion. Incorporate relevant facts, examples, quotations, and details to develop your controlling idea.
7. Revise and edit with the help of a peer reviewer.

PRACTICE AND APPLY

Students can practice and apply the skill of writing a short research paper by choosing a topic mentioned in Oates's essay and formulating a research question about it. Possible research topics include Ponge, Platonism, Melville, Yeats, Dickinson, paroxysmal tachycardia, Transcendentalism, and Ansel Adams.

Analyze and Evaluate Structure

RI 3, RI 5

RETEACH

Review argumentative, informative, and narrative structures. Discuss the difference between literary criticism and other forms of argumentative writing. Show students a chart like the one below. Work with students to identify examples from the text of each type of structure. Examples may vary.

Structure	Characteristics	Example
narrative	tells a story, often uses chronological order; describes events, thoughts and feelings	*Oates's memory about wading in a creek in lines 80–84*
informative	informs or explains about a topic; includes central ideas supported by facts and examples	*definition of paroxysmal tachycardia in lines 29–32*
argumentative	attempts to persuade; includes reasons, evidence, and rhetorical devices	*questioning the validity of Thoreau's point of view about nature in lines 125–136*

 **LEVEL UP TUTORIALS** Assign the following *Level Up* tutorial: **Analyzing Arguments**

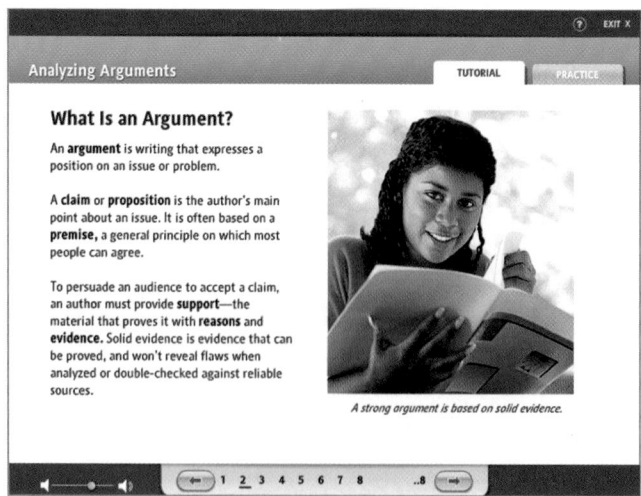

CLOSE READING APPLICATION

Have students select an essay and work independently to identify the specific structure(s) in it. Remind them to look for the qualities that correspond to each type of writing.

Determine Word Meanings

COMMON CORE

RI 4, L 4a

TEACH

Inform students that often **context clues** can help them understand the meaning of even the most difficult **technical language**. Inform them also that being sensitive to **connotation**—the emotional flavor of words—can help them understand tone, the author's attitude toward the subject. Review the meaning of context clues and connotation, as necessary.

PRACTICE AND APPLY

Read aloud lines lines 15–28 of Oates's essay. Ask students to read it silently again and make a list of clues to the meaning of tachycardia. *("attack" and "attacks" [lines 17–18], "erratic heartbeat" [line 23], "heartbeats of the earth" and "pulsing, pumping" [line 24], "struck down in the midst of motion" [line 25])*

Have students read this paragraph a third time and make a list of intense, highly connotative words and phrases. *(The paragraph is packed with this kind of language, but some of the following are likely to appear on students' lists: "thrummed with life" [line 20], "numberless heartbeats" and "pulsing, pumping life, sheer life" [line 24], "like a fallen, stunned boxer" [line 26], and the accumulation of adjectives in lines 27–28—"involuntary," "random," "wayward," and "nameless.")*

Next, ask students to discuss how the paragraph's highly connotative language helps them to understand the meaning of tachycardia, as well as the author's attitude toward this condition and toward her surroundings during an attack. *(Tachycardia is a frightening, life-threatening experience. There is nothing calm about it. Oates conveys the intensity of the experience by using intense language. The vividness of her language and her attention to detail reveal that she is as much fascinated by tachycardia as frightened by it. During an attack, she is hyper-aware of her fragility and of her surroundings.)*

Finally, have students consult a dictionary to define the following terms: *vertigo, amnesia, déjà vu,* and *hyperventilation.* Ask students to write a narrative paragraph about experiencing one of these conditions. The paragraph may be fictional or drawn from actual experience. Students are to use context clues and connotative language to convey both the meaning and the feeling of the condition they write about.

Analyze Ideas and Events

COMMON CORE

RI 3

RETEACH

Review the chart on page 230, reminding students of the distinct traits of argumentative, informative, and narrative essays. Tell students that a narrative is about events, not ideas, and that an argumentative or informative essay is about ideas, not events. Ask them to think about "Against Nature" as a hybrid—a narrative with ideas at its core, an essay of ideas with story as its backbone.

Ask students to focus on the **argumentative**, or persuasive, aspect of the essay. Have them write a thesis statement for its persuasive ideas. *(Statements will vary, but they will express Oates's suggestion that writers who romanticize Nature, who see benevolence and beauty in Nature, are mistaken idealists.)*

Next, ask students to write a thesis statement for the **informative** component of the Oates essay. *(Statements will vary, but they will likely include the idea that tachycardia is a frightening condition that changes the way the author sees her life and her world. Responses might include two different and opposing ways to view Nature.)*

Finally, have students write a thesis statement for the purely **narrative** element of the Oates essay. Since the essay is a personal narrative, ask students to write their statements in first-person. *(A possible thesis: As someone who suffers from tachcardia, I am fascinated by episodes of the condition; they lead me to thoughts about my own place in Nature.)* Ask students to notice that it is almost impossible to keep the author's ideas out of a statement about the story she tells here.

Ask students what "Against Nature" would lose if Oates had written in only one of these modes. *(Since the argumentative portion focuses on nature writing, the strictly argumentative essay might lose what Oates has to say about her personal experience with tachycardia; it might lose what makes it so engaging. An informative essay focusing on tachycardia would completely lose the personal interest of Oates's own experience. An informative essay about two schools of nature writing would also lose personal engagement. A strictly narrative essay might be really engaging, but it would lose the ideas at the heart of this essay.)*

CLOSE READING APPLICATION

Students can examine the narrative, informative, and persuasive threads of another essay. They can review Kesaya E. Noda's "Growing Up Asian in America" (pages 187–194 in Collection 3), noting how ideas grow out of events, how writers create hybrids when they sit down to tell us something.

Spoiling Walden: Or, How I Learned to Stop Worrying and Love Cape Wind

Essay by David Gessner

Why This Text

Students may lose their way in argumentative essays, especially when the essay develops a complex set of ideas. If students don't understand the essay's structure, they may miss its argument altogether. With the help of the close-reading questions, students will analyze how David Gessner develops his central ideas in this essay. This close reading will lead students to understand how the essay's structure helps make the argument clear and engaging.

Background Have students read the background and information about the author and his essay. Introduce the essay by pointing out that people consume energy with practically every action they take and every product they use. In this essay, Gessner explores how his ideas regarding a "new" energy source—wind—evolved as he traveled around the country and talked to people.

AS YOU READ Ask students to pay attention to how the author organizes his essay. How does this structure help him make his argument?

Common Core Support

- cite strong and thorough textual evidence
- determine the central ideas of a text and analyze how they are developed
- analyze and evaluate the effectiveness of the structure an author uses in his or her argument
- determine an author's point of view

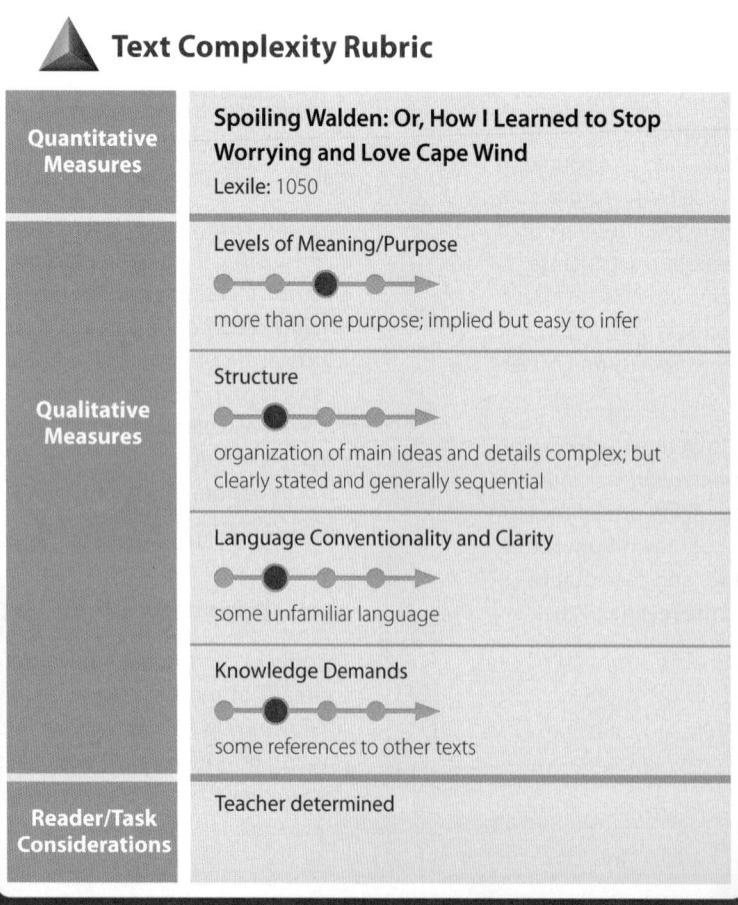

Text Complexity Rubric

	Spoiling Walden: Or, How I Learned to Stop Worrying and Love Cape Wind
Quantitative Measures	Lexile: 1050
Qualitative Measures	Levels of Meaning/Purpose more than one purpose; implied but easy to infer
	Structure organization of main ideas and details complex; but clearly stated and generally sequential
	Language Conventionality and Clarity some unfamiliar language
	Knowledge Demands some references to other texts
Reader/Task Considerations	Teacher determined

Strategies for CLOSE READING

Analyze the Structure of an Essay

Students should read this essay carefully all the way through. Close-reading questions at the bottom of the page will help them focus on a thorough analysis of the essay's structure. As they read, students should jot down comments or questions about the text in the margins.

WHEN STUDENTS STRUGGLE . . .

To help students analyze the structure of Gessner's essay, have them work in small groups to fill out a chart like the one shown below.

CITE TEXT EVIDENCE For practice in analyzing the structure of an essay, ask students to cite text evidence that helps explain each step in the author's "wind journey."

Step	Text Evidence
starting point	"love of a place" (Cape Cod) "love of a book" (Walden)
proposal for wind farm	"I react with outrage" "This is a sacred place"
moves away	"I start seeing the place . . . from a distance"
travels to Cape Breton	"I talk to a local man named Keith" "There were no jobs, you see."
travels to Gulf Coast	"The place was stunningly beautiful . . . it was also slathered in the substance that we all use to power our lives"
revisits Thoreau	"our patron saint of frugality"
recalls visit to Cape Cod	"this ain't the Grand Canyon" "We need to connect the dots." "if there are Waldens then they are all interconnected"

Background *The following article was written by* **David Gessner,** *a contributing editor to OnEarth magazine. In it, he explains his change of opinion about Cape Wind, the first federally approved offshore wind farm. The note accompanying the article, published in December 2011, reads: "It's been 10 years since a proposal was submitted to build America's first offshore wind farm in Nantucket Sound off Cape Cod. The federal government finally approved the project earlier this year, although court battles continue to delay construction. After a decade of division, our contributing editor [Gessner] shares his personal journey of acceptance."*

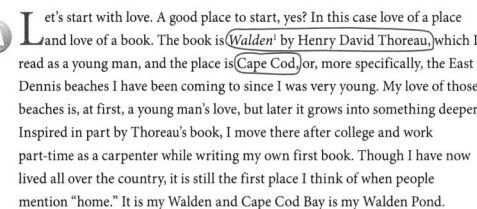

Spoiling Walden

Or, How I Learned to Stop Worrying and Love Cape Wind

Essay by David Gessner

CLOSE READ
Notes

1. **READ ▶** As you read lines 1–17, begin to collect and cite text evidence.
    - Circle the two things the author loves in lines 1–9.
    - Underline loaded language the author uses to describe his first reaction to the wind farm proposal.
    - In the margin, explain Gessner's initial opposition to the wind farm.

(A) Let's start with love. A good place to start, yes? In this case love of a place and love of a book. The book is *Walden*[1] by Henry David Thoreau, which I read as a young man, and the place is Cape Cod, or, more specifically, the East Dennis beaches I have been coming to since I was very young. My love of those beaches is, at first, a young man's love, but later it grows into something deeper. Inspired in part by Thoreau's book, I move there after college and work part-time as a carpenter while writing my own first book. Though I have now lived all over the country, it is still the first place I think of when people mention "home." It is my Walden and Cape Cod Bay is my Walden Pond.

10 So of course when someone—a businessman no less—suggests that he wants to place 130 wind turbines—bird-killing turbines!—in Nantucket Sound off the shores of my Walden, I react with outrage. Not in my backyard? Not in my backyard! This is a sacred place, a place apart, and if this is a sacred place then these wind turbines are, as I tell anyone who will listen, a desecration.

[1] **Walden:** Thoreau's book about his time living simply and self-sufficiently in nature.

He is against the wind farm because a businessman proposed it, turbines cause bird deaths, and the turbines will mess up the views on the beach.

47

---

1. **READ AND CITE TEXT EVIDENCE**   Explain to students that Gessner opens the essay with a disarming appeal to love— specifically, love for a book and a place—to draw the reader in.

(A) **ASK STUDENTS** to discuss *Walden* and Cape Cod and how they became the author's starting point. What does the author mean when he writes that Cape Cod "is my Walden and Cape Cod Bay is my Walden Pond"? *Students should understand that the author is speaking figuratively. Thoreau wrote memorably of his years at Walden Pond, where he lived close to nature. Walden Pond and the surrounding woods—to which Thoreau developed strong physical and spiritual connections—have come to symbolize the natural home that most city dwellers have lost. So when Gessner calls Cape Cod "my Walden," he means that it is a natural place of great physical and spiritual significance for him.*

CLOSE READ
Notes

I cling to this position for years, holding tight, but then, gradually, my grip starts to loosen. Some things happen, some things change. The story of those

B things, those happenings and changes, is the story of my wind journey.

One thing I do is to move away from Cape Cod, and so I start seeing the

C place I still consider home from a distance, from arm's length, while at the
20 same time seeing how that place connects to others. Another thing I do is start to travel extensively, reporting for an environmental magazine. I visit Cape Breton in Nova Scotia, which seems like driving onto Cape Cod a hundred years ago, until I reach a city called Sydney Mines. The city looks like it has been cracked open and had its insides sucked out, which it turns out, is pretty much what happened. In Mike's Place Pub & Grill, I talk to a local man named Keith who tells me the story of the town's glory years, when it supplied coal for much of Canada, and of the depths to which the town fell after the coal was gone.

---

2. **◀ REREAD** Reread lines 15–17. What do these lines explain about Gessner's approach to the topic? Support your answer with explicit textual evidence.

These lines explain that Gessner has changed his position about the wind farm. He begins by explaining his initial opposition to Cape Wind and his reasons why, then states that the rest of the essay will trace his "wind journey"—the story of his change of heart.

---

3. **READ ▶** As you read lines 18–35, underline the first two things Gessner does on his "wind journey."

4. **◀ REREAD** Reread lines 21–35. What can you infer about the comment that the only jobs left in Sydney Mines were funeral directors? Why does Gessner include this conversation with Keith?

Because there was a need for funeral directors, you can infer that the coal industry affected the health of the people who worked in the mines. Gessner includes the conversation with Keith to show how learning about the devastation of one town starts to change his own thinking about natural resources.

48

CLOSE READ
Notes

"The coal was gone and they had taken everything out of the town. Where
30 it had been wall-to-wall with people on a Saturday night you suddenly couldn't find anyone. Maybe a stray dog and a single taxi. A ghost town."

His eyes drooped as if in sympathy with the town. His voice sounded beautiful, his accent vaguely Irish.

D "There were no jobs, you see. Other than funeral directors. There was a big call for those."

The more I travelled, the more I found men like Keith and places like Sydney Mines. Places hollowed out and then deserted. I began to think more, not just about beautiful places, but about what we extract from them. This culminated last summer when I travelled along the Gulf Coast during the
40 height, or depths, of the BP oil spill. There I found the most intense **juxtaposition** of beauty and energy as I spent mornings birdwatching—seeing roseate spoonbills and ibises—near Halliburton Road and oil refineries, or spent a night out in a fish camp, a few hundred yards from a fringe of marsh that appeared burned, but was, in fact, oiled.

juxtaposition:
contrast

---

5. **READ ▶** As you read lines 36–69, continue to cite textual evidence.
   • Underline text that shows how Gessner connects Cape Cod and the Gulf Coast.
   • In the margin of lines 45–62, explain how Gessner connects modern people to Thoreau and his personal math.

49

---

2. **REREAD AND CITE TEXT EVIDENCE**

B **ASK STUDENTS** to discuss the elements of a journey and how the author's "wind journey" might affect the essay's structure. *A journey has a beginning, a middle, and an end. The essay will be structured so that the author can describe the journey's key steps.*

3. **READ AND CITE TEXT EVIDENCE**

C **ASK STUDENTS** to discuss the first two steps of Gessner's journey. How would you describe the journey? *The journey is both physical and mental. The author travels across the country, and that movement opens his mind to new perspectives. He starts to see Cape Cod "from a distance" and how it "connects" to other places.*

4. **REREAD AND CITE TEXT EVIDENCE**

D **ASK STUDENTS** to cite evidence to support their inference. *Students should cite evidence from lines 27–28 about "the depths to which the town fell," and from lines 29–31.*

5. **READ AND CITE TEXT EVIDENCE** Birdwatchers are familiar with impressive examples of birds "doing the math of energy." For example, before migrating south across the Gulf of Mexico, tiny birds such as hummingbirds and warblers must bulk up, increasing their body fat by as much as 50 percent in order to have sufficient energy reserves to make the long flight.

E **ASK STUDENTS** to state some of the implications of Gessner's "math of energy." *There is something like a global "ledger sheet," showing how much energy is extracted from the planet and how much is used and squandered. Energy gains and losses have a "strict mathematical relationship," so we cannot ignore the "loss" side of the equation.*

Critical Vocabulary: juxtaposition (line 41) Have students share their definitions of *juxtaposition*. What things does the author find in juxtaposition on the Gulf Coast? *beauty and energy, spoonbills and oil refineries, fish camp and oiled marsh*

CLOSE READ Notes

Thoreau's math explains that we are responsible for our own input and output. The energy we use has to be replaced, just as animals conserve energy. Today, we have to think about replacing the resources we use.

The place was stunningly beautiful, and for the Cajun fishermen I met, like Ryan Lambert, it was their Walden. But it was also slathered in the substance that we all use to power our lives. The Gulf has been called "a national sacrifice zone," and it seemed to have been sacrificed so that the rest of us could keep on living the way we live. I thought to myself: this place is connected to Cape Cod. 50 Not metaphorically, but literally, by its waters.

And I thought, because I could not help but think of it, of energy. Where we get our energy from and how we pay for it, in the broadest sense. As a birdwatcher, I know that every animal is required to do the math of energy in its own way, and humans, whatever we may think, are not exempt. It was **(E)** Thoreau, our patron saint of frugality, who created the initial ledger sheet, the personal math that many of us have begun to think about again during these difficult times, the calculus of our own input and output. In *Walden* he did his figuring right there on the page for us. *Here is how much I spent and here is* 60 *what I gained.* It is the same math that animals rely on instinctively when they hunt. By Thoreau's reasoning, human lives, like the lives of other animals, require a strict mathematical relationship with energy, its gains and losses, its conservation and squandering.

Years ago, on Cape Cod, I had been quick to embrace, and mimic, Thoreau's love of nature but slow to hear his sterner message of personal responsibility. I rationalized this by saying that I preferred Thoreau the celebrator to Thoreau the preacher. But in the Gulf I found myself returning to **(F)** the other, stricter Thoreau. His relationship with energy was simple but

6. **◀ REREAD** Reread lines 51–69. Circle the three titles Gessner gives to Thoreau. Why does Gessner come to prefer the stricter Thoreau?

> While Gessner has always appreciated Thoreau and his celebration of nature, he comes to prefer Thoreau the preacher, who was aware of what he was consuming and giving back. The "patron saint of frugality" focused on using less and "refining his output."

50

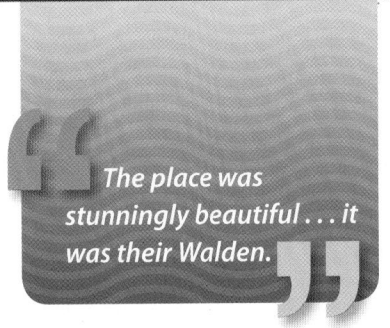

CLOSE READ Notes

> " The place was stunningly beautiful . . . it was their Walden. "

profound: instead of just focusing on getting more, he limited his input and refined his output.

70 As I travelled through the Gulf, I also thought back to a meeting I'd had two summers before. A friend had put me in touch with Jim Gordon, the president of Cape Wind, and we met for lunch in Hyannis before driving out to one of the beaches that would face out toward the hundred-plus turbine towers **(G)** that would make up the wind farm. The beach was crammed with people, umbrellas sprouting and kids running this way and that, and once we got to the shore we looked out past kids on inflatable rafts and roaring Jet Skis and powerboats to where the towers would stand on the horizon. One of the arguments that wind opponents have made is that putting wind turbines out in this water would be like putting them in the Grand Canyon. Jim, consciously 80 or not, was using this beach as both prop and stage, and the message was clear: *this ain't the Grand Canyon.*

The question many have asked is: does having a wind farm out on the horizon detract from that elemental experience of the beach? The argument that Jim Gordon was making, without saying a word, was that this experience was already limited enough, and that the site of blades blowing in the breeze was not going to detract from it one iota.

Now Jim held up his thumb against the horizon.

The beach is a shared space, littered with people and their possessions. The wind farm would not take away from the scenery any more than these things.

7. **READ ▶** As you read lines 70–111, continue to cite textual evidence.
   - Underline what Gessner sees on the beach.
   - In the margin of lines 70–86, explain why the beach is already "limited enough."
   - Circle Jim Gordon's statements about why the turbines should be seen.

51

6. **REREAD AND CITE TEXT EVIDENCE**

(F) ASK STUDENTS how "Thoreau the preacher" lived. *Thoreau lived simply and close to nature; he kept a ledger of his inputs and outputs. He was frugal and believed in personal responsibility. He didn't try just to get more—he "limited his input and refined his output."*

FOR ELL STUDENTS Clarify the meaning of the expression *do the math* (line 53). Explain that it has a figurative meaning—"to reach your own conclusion."

7. **READ AND CITE TEXT EVIDENCE** Gessner alludes to one of the main arguments against wind farms—that they destroy the beauty of America's natural landscapes.

(G) ASK STUDENTS how Gessner's trip to the beach with Jim Gordon marks an important step in his journey. *Gordon helps Gessner see that the beach and bay are anything but pristine. This realization moves Gessner closer to accepting a wind farm there.*

CLOSE READ
Notes

"From here the turbines will be six or seven miles out. They'll be about as big as my thumbnail."

90 This, of course, was another big point of contention. How big would they really look from the shore? And what would it mean for Cape Codders to look out at their theoretically wild waters and see what would be, for all its techno grace, an industrial site? While I had deep sympathy with the **aesthetic** point of view, it was hard to argue that windmills that would appear a few inches tall on the horizon would ruin the place's wildness.

aesthetic:

concerned with beauty

And with what Jim said next, he almost won me over entirely. "We need to connect the dots," he said. **H**

Connect the dots. Wasn't that what Thoreau had tried to do? Wasn't that the definition of ecology?

100 "We would barely see the turbines from here, but maybe we should see them," he continued. "It's what we can't see that's killing us. Like the particle emissions from the power plant in Sandwich. And the oil being shipped to run that plant."

He shook his head and stared out at the horizon where his windmills would turn. "Maybe it's not such a bad idea for us to see just where our energy is coming from," he said.

I nodded. At the time my thoughts on wind power were still in flux. But with this I could not disagree. I still was, and still am, worried that migrating birds might run into the turbines. A million birds a night migrate over the

110 Cape during the fall migration, and I fret that by supporting wind I am becoming an avian Judas. But it is a time of tough choices.

8. **◀ REREAD** Reread lines 96–99. How does the point Jim Gordon makes in these lines influence Gessner?

Jim Gordon's comment about needing to "connect the dots" echoes Thoreau's beliefs, and Gessner's. Gessner points out that the "definition of ecology" is taking responsibility for the costs of energy.

52

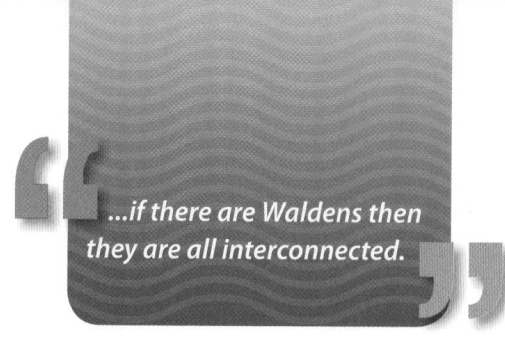

...if there are Waldens then they are all interconnected.

I J "Do you know the windfarms will kill more birds in a year than were killed during the whole Gulf disaster?" a wind opponent said to me recently. This "statistic," of course, hinges on a very narrow definition of bird fatalities. My accuser was not thinking of habitat destruction and warming, and the whole host of other consequences of the rabid pursuit of oil. Meanwhile, Jim Gordon's camp claims that the slow-moving and well-lit turbines should prove less of a threat to birds than most tall buildings.

I am not sure of that. What I am sure of is that there are no more Waldens,

120 or, more accurately, if there are Waldens then they are all interconnected. Cape Cod has been called "a place apart." I am writing this from Cape Cod right now, and I understand what the phrase means: the land of this fragile ex-peninsula is very specific to itself, and when you come here, and cross the bridge, you leave other places behind and enter a place like nowhere else.

But I can no longer use this term to describe the Cape. It is not apart from the fragile Louisiana fish camp where I spent the night, oil lapping nearby, and it is not apart from Sydney Mines. Each place in this threatened world, separate but connected, must now make an accounting, keep its own ledger sheet with a cold and honest eye. We hold onto our pristine place by sacrificing other places.

130 I hear that up in Nova Scotia, where I visited Sydney Mines, they are proposing power plants that will take advantage of the massive tides. I hope they do and I support it. I also support Jim Gordon and his wind farm. There is no place apart.

9. **READ ▶** As you read lines 112–133, continue to cite textual evidence.
- Underline the conclusions that Gessner reaches about turbines on Cape Cod.
- Circle text that discusses bird fatalities.

53

---

8. **REREAD AND CITE TEXT EVIDENCE**

H ASK STUDENTS to compare what Jim Gordon means by "connect the dots" and what the author means. *Gordon wants consumers to start seeing the connections between energy sources and their invisible but harmful consequences. If consumers don't "connect the dots," they are likely to protest relatively clean wind energy. For the author, the phrase reminds him of Thoreau's ledger sheets and careful notes about inputs and outputs.*

Critical Vocabulary: aesthetic (line 93) Have students share their definitions of *aesthetic*, and ask volunteers to use the adjective in sentences about natural landscapes.

FOR ELL STUDENTS *Sympathy* is a term that can be confusing for Spanish speakers, since it has a false cognate, *simpática* (friendly, charming). Clarify that in English it means "a feeling of support or compassion for someone else's experience."

9. **READ AND CITE TEXT EVIDENCE**

I ASK STUDENTS which lines discuss bird fatalities. *lines 112–118* Which lines includ text about Gessner's conclusions? *lines 120, 127–129, 132–133* Then ask students to restate Gessner's conclusions in their own words. *Possible response: In any place, people should balance their own discomfort with the needs of the environment.*

CLOSE READ
Notes

10. ◀ **REREAD** Reread lines 112–133. How does Gessner react to the "statistic" about wind farms and the Gulf oil spill? Why does he include this interaction in the piece?

Gessner questions his "accuser" because the opponent limits his statistic to wind farms alone and not to other considerations like habitat destruction and global warming, or tall buildings—all of which contribute to bird deaths. Gessner is not sure of either group's argument, perhaps because they are only claims and not backed by hard proof. Gessner includes this interaction because he's a bird lover and is concerned about bird fatalities.

SHORT RESPONSE

Cite Text Evidence In what ways does the structure of Gessner's essay help engage his reader? **Cite text evidence** in your response.

Gessner begins by saying how much he loves Cape Cod. He gives personal background for why the turbine issue matters to him. He then explains his journey (both physical and mental) that leads to his change of heart. By including the reader on this "journey," he effectively shows us the conversations and realizations that help change his mind. He provides evidence to show the disadvantages of using up natural resources and then moves on to show the seemingly minimal visual impact the turbines will have. His argument is convincing, because he shares his own process in coming to the decision, which makes it more engaging—because it's personal.

54

---

10. REREAD AND CITE TEXT EVIDENCE Gessner points out that one "wind opponent" says that wind farms on migration flyways or near important habitats kill large numbers of birds.

J **ASK STUDENTS** how the author "connects the dots" to rebut the wind opponent's argument about bird fatalities. *Gessner acknowledges that he is still worried about bird fatalities at the Cape Cod wind farm since a million birds might migrate over the Cape each fall. But, he argues, the wind opponent isn't weighing these fatalities against the potentially larger problems for birds caused by oil extraction and use: habitat destruction and global warming.*

SHORT RESPONSE

Cite Text Evidence Students should:

- note that the essay is structured around a journey.
- cite text evidence to show the journey on which the author embarks.
- explain how the author engages the reader.

TO CHALLENGE STUDENTS . . .

For more context on the wind energy debate, students can research modern wind farms online.

ASK STUDENTS to summarize the pros and cons of wind energy. *Students should understand that there are three main cons associated with modern wind farms: the aesthetic loss of natural landscapes, bird and bat fatalities, and the industry's continued reliance on government subsidies. The benefits of wind energy are also compelling: no greenhouse gas emissions, no possibility of large-scale pollution from spills, and relatively little habitat destruction (compared to that caused by oil, coal, and natural gas mining).*

DIG DEEPER

With the class, return to Question 7, Read. Have students share their responses to the question.

ASK STUDENTS to discuss Jim Gordon's suggestion that people *should* see the turbines off Cape Cod.

- Why does Gordon think people ought to see where their energy comes from? *He understands that every energy source has its drawbacks and wants people to be aware of them. If we can see where our energy comes from, it will be easier to be realistic about the drawbacks. When we can't see an energy source, we can forget or ignore the drawbacks.*

- How does Gordon's suggestion relate to Thoreau's ledger sheets? *Gordon wants people to see and think about their energy consumption and use, the same way that Thoreau kept track of how much he spent and gained on Walden Pond.*

- How does this interaction help move the author along his journey? *Gordon's statement about "connecting the dots" has resonance for the author, who now understands that keeping a wind farm away from Cape Cod would simply mean more reliance on coal or oil. The author is finally connecting the dots, which takes him back to his starting point.*

ASK STUDENTS to return to their Short Response answer and revise it based on the class discussion.

mySmartPlanner — Create lesson plans and access resources online.

COMPARE TEXTS

The Minister's Black Veil

Short Story by Nathaniel Hawthorne

Why This Text?

Hawthorne's short story challenges readers to consider the place occupied by sin or guilt in colonial American culture by examining the experience of a minister who decides to wear a black veil, mystifying his parishoners. Hawthorne was a master of using literary symbols whose meaning was ambiguous, inviting readers to think deeply about his characters and their conflicts. Hawthorne's efforts to come to terms with his own past inspired profound reflections on American identity that still resonate today. On page 266, students will be asked to compare this text with "The Pit and the Pendulum" by Edgar Allan Poe (pages 249–265).

Key Learning Objective: The student will be able to determine theme and recognize and interpret symbols in literature.

Common Core Standards

RL 1 Cite textual evidence.

RL 2 Determine themes of a text.

RL 3 Analyze the impact of the author's choices.

RL 4 Determine the meaning of words and phrases.

RL 5 Analyze how an author's choices concerning how to structure specific parts of a text contribute to its overall meaning as well as its aesthetic impact.

RL 6 Analyze a case in which grasping a point of view requires distinguishing what is directly stated in a text from what is really meant.

RL 9 Demonstrate knowledge of nineteenth-century American literature.

SL 1 Initiate and participate in a range of collaborative discussions.

SL 3 Evaluate a speaker's point of view, reasoning, evidence, and rhetoric.

L 5b Analyze nuances.

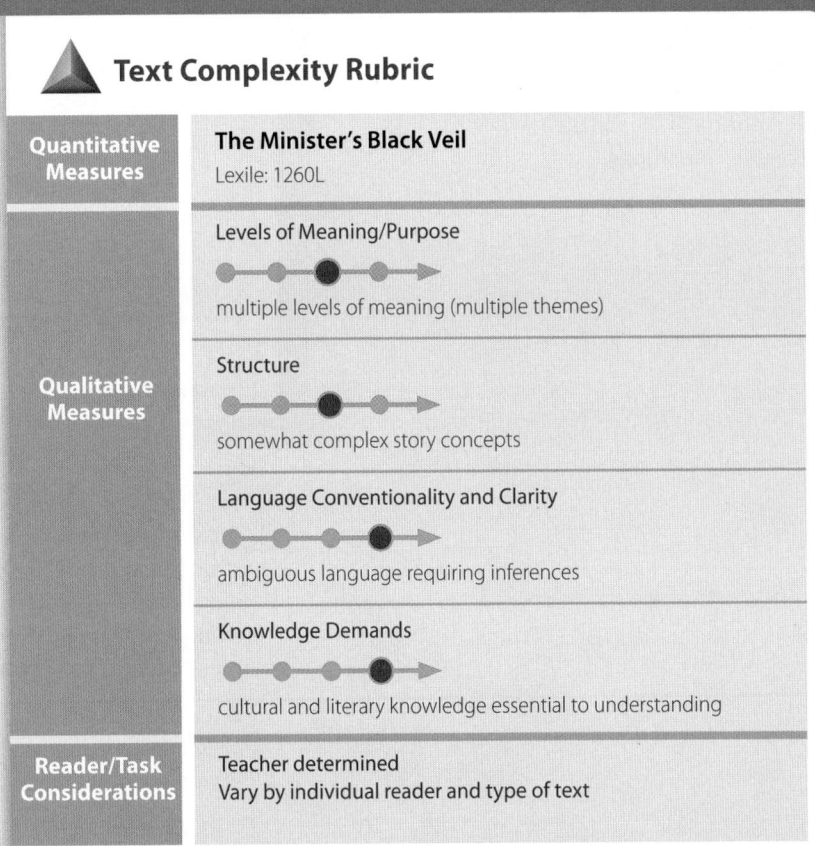

Text Complexity Rubric

Quantitative Measures	**The Minister's Black Veil** Lexile: 1260L
Qualitative Measures	Levels of Meaning/Purpose — multiple levels of meaning (multiple themes)
	Structure — somewhat complex story concepts
	Language Conventionality and Clarity — ambiguous language requiring inferences
	Knowledge Demands — cultural and literary knowledge essential to understanding
Reader/Task Considerations	Teacher determined Vary by individual reader and type of text

TEACH

CLOSE READ

American Romanticism

Point out to students that so far in this collection, they have read works by writers who celebrate the individual and the imagination (Whitman and Dickinson) and by a writer who celebrates the natural world and the individual (Thoreau). Tell students that now they will read selections by two writers, Hawthorne and Poe, who explore the darker side of human nature.

The Dark Side of Romanticism

Tell students that the **Dark Romantics,** including Hawthorne and Poe, were haunted by a darker vision of human existence and preoccupied with the inner lives of their characters and the complex forces that motivate and sometimes warp human behavior. Both used **gothic** elements in their work, such as grotesque characters, bizarre situations, and violent events. Once the Romantics freed the imagination from the restrictions of reason, they could follow it wherever it might go. For the dark romantics, the imagination led into the unknown—that shadowy region where the fantastic, the demonic, and the insane reside.

Edgar Allan Poe was, of course, the undisputed master of the gothic in American literature. He often explored human psychology from the inside, using first-person narrators who were criminal or insane, or both. Hawthorne, on the other hand, focused on the psychological effects of sin and guilt within the individual and on the community.

The Minister's Black Veil
Short Story by Nathaniel Hawthorne

The Pit and the Pendulum
Short Story by Edgar Allan Poe

American Romanticism

In the years after winning independence from the British and establishing a new nation, Americans began to form their own cultural identity. Writers calling themselves Romantics helped build this identity, and their work still influences the way Americans view themselves, their society, and the natural world.

Romanticism refers to schools of thought that value feeling and intuition over reason. Developed in part as a reaction against rationalism, Romanticism strongly influenced literature, music, and painting in Europe and the United States from the late eighteenth to the mid-nineteenth centuries. In the wake of the Industrial Revolution, with its squalid cities and miserable working conditions, people had come to realize the limits of reason. The Romantics believed that the imagination allowed people to discern truths that the rational mind could not comprehend. These truths were usually accompanied by powerful emotion and were associated with natural beauty. To the Romantics, imagination, individual feelings, and wild and untamed natural settings held greater value than reason, logic, and sophistication.

THE DARK SIDE OF ROMANTICISM   Not all American writers agreed with the general Romantic notion that the divine is embodied in nature and that people are essentially good. Some felt that these views did not adequately take into account the presence of suffering in the world and the ongoing conflict between good and evil. The **Dark Romantics,** as these skeptics were called, shared with the other Romantics an interest in the spiritual world and a belief in the value of intuition and imagination over rationalism. However, they also sought to explore the darker mysteries of human existence.

During the Romantic period in European literature, a similar division had resulted in the Gothic novel, which emerged in England in the late eighteenth century. These tales of terror, often a set in a medieval Gothic castle, symbolically used their pointed arches and vaults, dark dungeons, and mysterious underground passages to evoke hidden secrets or fears. The term **Gothic** was later expanded to describe any fiction that created a haunting atmosphere and depicted strange and chilling events, including live burials, horrifying torture, and the earthly resurrection of corpses.

TO CHALLENGE STUDENTS . . .

Tell students that like Romantic writers, Romantic painters focused on nature, inner struggles and passions, emotions, and the imagination. Have students do some independent research on the work of an American Romantic painter. For instance, students might explore the paintings of Thomas Cole, John Singleton Copley, Edward Hicks, or John James Audubon.

Once they have finished their research, invite students to give a short multimedia presentation on the painter and his or her work to the class. Challenge students to draw parallels between the paintings and the selections in this collection.

Background Explain that the setting of "The Minister's Black Veil" is a town in Puritan New England in the 1700s. Puritans were a moral and religious people who followed a strict interpretation of lessons in the Bible. Puritans believed that if they made individual compacts with God not to sin, God would bless them. Ministers based their preaching on images from scripture and everyday experience. Since a Puritan community was thought to be a "pure" working model of the Puritan way of life, when someone in the community sinned, severe punishments—and often banishment—were issued because it was thought that person had corrupted the community.

AS YOU READ Direct students to use the As You Read note to focus their reading. Remind them to write down questions they generate as they read.

Determine Themes: Romanticism (LINES 11–15)

 **COMMON CORE** **RL 2**

Remind students that the **theme** is the central message of a work of literature. Discuss how a writer develops theme through the introduction and development of characters and the building of plot.

A **CITE TEXT EVIDENCE** Ask students what happens in lines 11–15 that begins to build the plot. *(The abrupt and unexpected question [line 11] indicates something is wrong or odd about the parson's face. The sexton's astonishment implies the plot may develop around the answer to this question.)*

Nathaniel Hawthorne *(1804–1864) was born in Salem, Massachusetts. By the time he left for Bowdoin College in 1821, Hawthorne knew he wanted to write. After graduation, he lived alone for 12 years, dedicated to building his literary career. By 1842, he had achieved some success. When times were tough, Hawthorne had well-connected friends set him up with government jobs, whose dull routines choked his imagination and limited his time to write. Hawthorne, however, never stopped writing. Today he is most celebrated for his short stories and for* The Scarlet Letter *(1850).*

The Minister's Black Veil

Short Story by Nathaniel Hawthorne

AS YOU READ Pay careful attention to how the minister's veil affects Mr. Hooper and the community as a whole.

The sexton stood in the porch of Milford meetinghouse, pulling lustily at the bell rope. The old people of the village came stooping along the street. Children, with bright faces, tripped merrily beside their parents, or mimicked a graver gait, in the conscious dignity of their Sunday clothes. Spruce[1] bachelors looked sidelong at the pretty maidens, and fancied that the Sabbath sunshine made them prettier than on weekdays. When the throng had mostly streamed into the porch, the sexton began to toll the bell, keeping his eye on the Reverend Mr. Hooper's door. The first glimpse of the clergyman's
10 figure was the signal for the bell to cease its summons.

"But what has good Parson Hooper got upon his face?" cried the sexton in astonishment.

All within hearing immediately turned about, and beheld the semblance[2] of Mr. Hooper, pacing slowly his meditative way towards the meetinghouse. With one accord they started, expressing more

 A

---
[1] **Spruce:** neat and clean.
[2] **semblance:** appearance.

Image Credits: (t) ©Bettmann/Corbis; (cl) ©utlimathule/Shutterstock; (cr) ©Minerva Studio/Shutterstock

SCAFFOLDING FOR ELL STUDENTS

Invite English learners to use the following strategy for lines 1–2:

• Highlight in green words you don't understand.

• Underline context clues, or hints to meaning in nearby words and sentences.

• Use the footnotes or a dictionary to determine the meaning.

> The sexton stood in the porch of Milford meetinghouse, pulling lustily at the bell rope. The old people of the village came stooping

Analyze Structure: Symbolism (LINES 24–40)

COMMON CORE RL 3, RL 5

Remind students that a **symbol** is a person, place, thing, or event that suggests a meaning beyond its concrete or literal meaning.

 **ASK STUDENTS** the purpose of a veil *(to hide, to gain privacy, to promote modesty)* and to speculate on some possible symbolic meanings of the color black. *(mystery, sorrow, mourning, or something hidden or secret)*

Determine Themes: Romanticism (LINES 40–52)

COMMON CORE RL 2

Explain to students that Hawthorne is sometimes considered a Dark Romantic, or Gothic writer. **Dark Romantic,** or **Gothic,** literature is characterized by grotesque characters, bizarre situations, a gloomy mood, and dark themes such as the inevitability and horror of death, the growth of evil, the fine line between insanity and reason, and fear of the unknown.

C CITE TEXT EVIDENCE Ask students to cite evidence from lines 40–52 that suggests this story could be classified under Dark Romanticism. *(The sexton's remark in lines 40–41 creates a sense of mystery and fear about what is behind the black veil; phrases like "something awful," "gone mad," and "unaccountable phenomenon" associate the veil with possible evil, insanity, or the unknown.)*

---

wonder than if some strange minister were coming to dust the cushions of Mr. Hooper's pulpit.

"Are you sure it is our parson?" inquired Goodman[3] Gray of the sexton.

20 "Of a certainty it is good Mr. Hooper," replied the sexton. "He was to have exchanged pulpits with Parson Shute of Westbury; but Parson Shute sent to excuse himself yesterday, being to preach a funeral sermon."

The cause of so much amazement may appear sufficiently slight. Mr. Hooper, a gentlemanly person about thirty, though still a bachelor, was dressed with due clerical neatness, as if a careful wife had starched his band, and brushed the weekly dust from his Sunday's garb. There was but one thing remarkable in his appearance. Swathed about his forehead, and hanging down over his face, so low as to be shaken by

30 his breath, Mr. Hooper had on a black veil. On a nearer view, it seemed to consist of two folds of crape,[4] which entirely concealed his features, except the mouth and chin, but probably did not intercept his sight, farther than to give a darkened aspect to all living and inanimate things. With this gloomy shade before him, good Mr. Hooper walked onward, at a slow and quiet pace, stooping somewhat and looking on the ground, as is customary with abstracted[5] men, yet nodding kindly to those of his parishioners who still waited on the meetinghouse steps. But so wonder-struck were they that his greeting hardly met with a return.

40 "I can't really feel as if good Mr. Hooper's face was behind that piece of crape," said the sexton.

"I don't like it," muttered an old woman, as she hobbled into the meetinghouse. "He has changed himself into something awful, only by hiding his face."

"Our parson has gone mad!" cried Goodman Gray, following him across the threshold.

A rumor of some unaccountable phenomenon had preceded Mr. Hooper into the meetinghouse, and set all the congregation astir. Few could refrain from twisting their heads towards the door; many stood

50 upright, and turned directly about; while several little boys clambered upon the seats, and came down again with a terrible racket. There was a general bustle, a rustling of the women's gowns and shuffling of the men's feet, greatly at variance[6] with that hushed repose which should attend the entrance of the minister. But Mr. Hooper appeared not to notice the perturbation of his people. He entered with an almost noiseless step, bent his head mildly to the pews on each side, and bowed as he passed his oldest parishioner, a white-haired great-

---

[3] **Goodman:** a title equivalent to *mister.*
[4] **crape:** a black, silky fabric worn as a sign of mourning.
[5] **abstracted:** absent-minded; preoccupied.
[6] **at variance:** contrasting.

APPLYING ACADEMIC VOCABULARY

denote	unique

AS YOU DISCUSS "The Minister's Black Veil," incorporate the following Collection 3 academic vocabulary words: *denote* and *unique.* When you discuss Mr. Hooper, ask students what is **unique** about the minister's appearance on this particular Sunday. *(He is wearing a black veil that hides his face.)* Have students explain what the way the minister now sees the world may **denote**. *(The darkened world that the minister sees through the black veil may suggest the human guilt he sees in his parishioners.)*

grandsire, who occupied an armchair in the centre of the aisle. It was strange to observe how slowly this venerable man became conscious of something singular in the appearance of his pastor. He seemed not fully to partake of the prevailing wonder till Mr. Hooper had ascended the stairs, and showed himself in the pulpit, face-to-face with his congregation, except for the black veil. That mysterious **emblem** was never once withdrawn. It shook with his measured breath as he gave out the psalm; it threw its obscurity between him and the holy page, as he read the Scriptures; and while he prayed, the veil lay heavily on his uplifted countenance. Did he seek to hide from the dread Being whom he was addressing?

Such was the effect of this simple piece of crape, that more than one woman of delicate nerves was forced to leave the meetinghouse. Yet perhaps the pale-faced congregation was almost as fearful a sight to the minister as his black veil to them.

Mr. Hooper had the reputation of a good preacher, but not an energetic one: he strove to win his people heavenward by mild persuasive influences, rather than to drive them thither by the thunders of the Word. The sermon which he now delivered was marked by the same characteristics of style and manner as the general series of his pulpit oratory. But there was something, either in the sentiment of the discourse itself, or in the imagination of the auditors, which made it greatly the most powerful effort that they had ever heard from their pastor's lips. It was tinged, rather more darkly than usual, with the gentle gloom of Mr. Hooper's temperament. The subject had reference to secret sin, and those sad mysteries which we hide from our nearest and dearest, and would fain conceal from our own consciousness, even forgetting that the Omniscient[7] can detect them. A subtle power was breathed into his words. Each member of the congregation, the most innocent girl, and the man of hardened breast, felt as if the preacher had crept upon them, behind his awful veil, and discovered their hoarded iniquity[8] of deed or thought. Many spread their clasped hands on their bosoms. There was nothing terrible in what Mr. Hooper said; at least, no violence; and yet, with every tremor of his melancholy voice, the hearers quaked. An unsought **pathos** came hand in hand with awe. So sensible were the audience of some unwonted attribute in their minister, that they longed for a breath of wind to blow aside the veil, almost believing that a stranger's visage would be discovered, though the form, gesture and voice were those of Mr. Hooper.

At the close of the services, the people hurried out with indecorous[9] confusion, eager to communicate their pent-up amazement, and conscious of lighter spirits the moment they lost

emblem
(ĕm´bləm) *n.* an identifying mark or symbol.

pathos
(pā´thŏs´) *n.* something that evokes pity or sympathy

---

[7] **the Omniscient:** God; literally, the all-knowing.
[8] **iniquity:** sinfulness.
[9] **indecorous:** undignified; inappropriate.

The Minister's Black Veil **237**

Determine Themes: Romanticism (LINES 63–98)

COMMON CORE RL 2

Review the concept of **theme,** explaining that a theme is the message about life or human nature conveyed in a literary work. Distinguish theme from topic, which is the subject of the work. Tell students that in "The Minister's Black Veil," the topic is the minister's veil. The theme is the message about life or human nature conveyed by Hawthorne's exploration of the veil and its significance.

D CITE TEXT EVIDENCE Have students analyze lines 63–98 and cite clues to the theme of this story. *(details that suggest the power of the veil to create mystery and to obscure, such as "mysterious emblem," "threw its obscurity between him and the holy page" [line 65]; "Did he seek to hide from the dread Being whom he was addressing?" [lines 67–68]; and "The subject had reference to secret sin, and those sad mysteries which we hide from our nearest and dearest" [lines 82–84])*

CRITICAL VOCABULARY

emblem: Hawthorne refers to the black veil as a "mysterious emblem" that Mr. Hooper did not take off even as he read the Scriptures and prayed.

ASK STUDENTS to infer what makes this emblem mysterious and why the congregation dislikes it. *(The veil is an emblem of mystery because it covers up the minister's expression and separates him from the congregation. In addition, Mr. Hooper refuses to explain to them why he wears it or what it means.)*

pathos: Hawthorne describes how the veil creates a feeling of pathos as well as awe in the minister's congregation. Invite students to consider why the congregation might consider the minister's black veil to be a sad or pitiable sight.

ASK STUDENTS to give examples of situations that might ordinarily create a feeling of pathos. *(the sight of an abandoned dog, a sick child, or a lonely, isolated person)*

CRITICAL VOCABULARY

ostentatious: Hawthorne describes the laughter of some of the congregation as ostentatious.

ASK STUDENTS how the narrator's description of the laughter as "ostentatious" affects the tone, or the author's attitude toward the subject. *(Describing the laughter as ostentatious creates a judgmental tone, as if the narrator disapproves of the laughter.)*

Determine Themes: Romanticism (LINES 101–136)

 COMMON CORE RL 3, RL 5

Explain to students that Romanticism emphasizes the primary importance of the individual. Dark Romanticism often focuses on an individual's dark, even extreme, emotions and experiences, especially when confronted by the transcendent, mysterious, or unknown.

E **ASK STUDENTS** to identify how the minister's black veil emphasizes his individuality. *(The minister's veil separates him from his congregation, isolating him and emphasizing his unique situation.)*

Analyze Structure: Symbolism (LINES 119–127)

COMMON CORE RL 3, RL 5

Tell students that an object may have a universal symbolic meaning. A rose, for example, might symbolize love. However, a writer may take a universal symbol and develop it further so that it has a unique meaning within the context of a story.

F **CITE TEXT EVIDENCE** Point out to students that a symbol's meaning is deepened by how the writer develops it throughout the story. Ask students what details hint at a meaning of the black veil that is unique to this story. *("A sad smile gleamed faintly from beneath the black veil... glimmering as he disappeared" [122–123]; "a simple black veil ... should become such a terrible thing" [124–125])* Guide students in discussing how these words suggest emotions deeper than sorrow and suggestive of a terrible or hidden secret.

E sight of the black veil. Some gathered in little circles, huddled closely together, with their mouths all whispering in the centre; some went homeward alone, wrapped in silent meditation; some talked loudly, and profaned[10] the Sabbath day with **ostentatious** laughter. A few shook their sagacious heads, intimating[11] that they could penetrate the mystery; while one or two affirmed that there was no mystery at all, but only that Mr. Hooper's eyes were so weakened by the midnight lamp as to require a shade. After a brief interval, forth came good Mr. Hooper also, in the rear of his flock. Turning his veiled face from one

110 group to another, he paid due reverence to the hoary[12] heads, saluted the middle-aged with kind dignity, as their friend and spiritual guide, greeted the young with mingled authority and love, and laid his hands on the little children's heads to bless them. Such was always his custom on the Sabbath day. Strange and bewildered looks repaid him for his courtesy. None, as on former occasions, aspired to the honor of walking by their pastor's side. Old Squire Saunders, doubtless by an accidental lapse of memory, neglected to invite Mr. Hooper to his table, where the good clergyman had been wont[13] to bless the food almost every Sunday since his settlement. He returned, therefore, to

120 the parsonage, and at the moment of closing the door, was observed to look back upon the people, all of whom had their eyes fixed upon the minister. A sad smile gleamed faintly from beneath the black veil, and flickered about his mouth, glimmering as he disappeared.

"How strange," said a lady, "that a simple black veil, such as any woman might wear on her bonnet, should become such a terrible thing on Mr. Hooper's face!"

"Something must surely be amiss with Mr. Hooper's intellects," observed her husband, the physician of the village. "But the strangest part of the affair is the effect of this vagary,[14] even on a sober-minded

130 man like myself. The black veil, though it covers only our pastor's face, throws its influence over his whole person, and makes him ghost-like from head to foot. Do you not feel it so?"

"Truly do I," replied the lady; "and I would not be alone with him for the world. I wonder he is not afraid to be alone with himself!"

"Men sometimes are so," said her husband.

The afternoon service was attended with similar circumstances. At its conclusion, the bell tolled for the funeral of a young lady. The relatives and friends were assembled in the house, and the more distant acquaintances stood about the door, speaking of the good

140 qualities of the deceased, when their talk was interrupted by the appearance of Mr. Hooper, still covered with his black veil. It was now

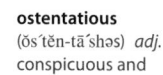

ostentatious
(ŏs´tĕn-tā´shəs) *adj.*
conspicuous and
vulgar

F

---

[10] **profaned:** desecrated; treated irreverently.
[11] **intimating:** revealing.
[12] **hoary:** gray or white.
[13] **wont:** habit.
[14] **vagary:** oddity.

WHEN STUDENTS STRUGGLE . . .

Have students use their eBook annotation tools to help them visualize evidence from the text that suggests the symbolic meaning of the black veil. Ask them to highlight these details in blue as they read.

his deceased parishioner. As he stooped, the veil hung straight down from his forehead so that, if her eyelids had not been closed forever, the dead maiden might have seen his face. Could Mr. Hooper be fearful of her glance, that he so hastily caught back the black veil? A person,

an appropriate emblem. The clergyman stepped into the room where the corpse was laid, and bent over the coffin, to take a last farewell of his deceased parishioner. As he stooped, the veil hung straight down from his forehead so that, if her eyelids had not been closed forever, the dead maiden might have seen his face. Could Mr. Hooper be fearful of her glance, that he so hastily caught back the black veil? A person, who watched the interview between the dead and the living, scrupled[15] not to affirm that, at the instant when the clergyman's features were
150 disclosed, the corpse had slightly shuddered, rustling the shroud[16] and muslin cap, though the countenance retained the composure of death. A superstitious old woman was the only witness of this prodigy. From the coffin, Mr. Hooper passed into the chamber of the mourners, and thence to the head of the staircase, to make the funeral prayer. It was a tender and heart-dissolving prayer, full of sorrow, yet so imbued with celestial[17] hopes, that the music of the heavenly harp, swept by the fingers of the dead, seemed faintly to be heard among the saddest accents of the minister. The people trembled, though they but darkly understood him, when he prayed that they, and himself, and all of
160 mortal race might be ready, as he trusted this young maiden had been, for the dreadful hour that should snatch the veil from their faces. The bearers went heavily forth, and the mourners followed, saddening all the street, with the dead before them, and Mr. Hooper in his black veil behind.

"Why do you look back?" said one in the procession to his partner.

"I had a fancy," replied she, "that the minister and the maiden's spirit were walking hand in hand."

"And so had I, at the same moment," said the other. That night, the handsomest couple in Milford village were to be joined in wedlock.
170 Though reckoned a melancholy man, Mr. Hooper had a placid cheerfulness for such occasions, which often excited a sympathetic smile, where livelier merriment would have been thrown away. There was no quality of his disposition which made him more beloved than this. The company at the wedding awaited his arrival with impatience, trusting that the strange awe, which had gathered over him throughout the day, would now be dispelled. But such was not the result. When Mr. Hooper came, the first thing that their eyes rested on was the same horrible black veil, which had added deeper gloom to the funeral, and could portend nothing but evil to the wedding. Such was
180 its immediate effect on the guests, that a cloud seemed to have rolled duskily from beneath the black crape, and dimmed the light of the candles. The bridal pair stood up before the minister. But the bride's cold fingers quivered in the tremulous[18] hand of the bridegroom,

---

[15] **scrupled:** was reluctant.
[16] **shroud:** a cloth in which people were wrapped before burial.
[17] **celestial:** relating to heaven.
[18] **tremulous:** trembling.

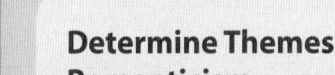

CLOSE READ

Determine Themes: Romanticism (LINES 142–152)

COMMON CORE RL 2

Recall that Dark Romantic, or Gothic, literature is characterized by dark topics such as terror, death, insanity, and a gloomy **mood**, the feeling or atmosphere that a writer creates.

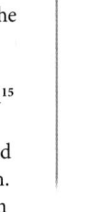 **CITE TEXT EVIDENCE** Ask students what words and phrases Hawthorne gives in his depiction of the funeral that contribute to the development of a dark—and even spooky—mood. *("dead maiden," "closed forever," "the corpse had slightly shuddered, rustling the shroud")*

Analyze Structure: Symbolism (LINES 158–164)

COMMON CORE RL 3, RL 5

Remind students that Hawthorne develops the symbolic meaning of the veil throughout the story.

 CITE TEXT EVIDENCE Ask students what detail develops the symbolic meaning of the veil more deeply in lines 158–164. *("the dreadful hour that should snatch the veil from their faces")* Discuss the meaning of this line by asking students what the dreadful hour is *(death)* and what veil is snatched from their faces *(the veil that hides their sins, or their true natures)*.

---

who watched the interview between the dead and the living, scrupled

not to affirm that, at the instant when the clergyman's features were

disclosed, the corpse had slightly shuddered, rustling the shroud and

muslin cap, though the countenance retained the composure of death.

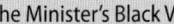

Determine Themes: Romanticism (LINES 187–195)

COMMON CORE RL 2

What is the significance of line 195, "For the Earth, too, had on her Black Veil"? How does it particularly represent a Gothic sensibility?

 **ASK STUDENTS** how this image contributes to their understanding of theme in the story. (*The image helps develop the idea that the black veil has a broader significance, a "darkness" that applies to all humankind, not just to the minister. It is as if the minister's dark emotions had spread to define the entire world, representing the power of an individual's emotions or subjective experience to color the world around him.*)

Analyze Structure: Symbolism (LINES 191–225)

COMMON CORE RL 3, RL 5

Explain that Hawthorne uses the symbol of the black veil to create the conflict that moves the plot of this story forward. It is both an internal conflict affecting Mr. Hooper and an external conflict that occurs between the congregation and Mr. Hooper.

 CITE TEXT EVIDENCE Ask students what examples of the two kinds of conflict appear on this page. (*Mr. Hooper's internal conflict is shown when he sees his image in the mirror and rushes from the house [lines 191–195]. The external conflict occurs in two places: when the village gossips about Mr. Hooper [lines 196–204] and when the village sends a delegation to talk to Mr. Hooper about his veil [lines 214–225].*)

---

and her death-like paleness caused a whisper that the maiden who had been buried a few hours before was come from her grave to be married. If ever another wedding were so dismal, it was that famous one where they tolled the wedding knell.[19] After performing the ceremony, Mr. Hooper raised a glass of wine to his lips, wishing happiness to the new-married couple, in a strain of mild pleasantry

190 that ought to have brightened the features of the guests, like a cheerful gleam from the hearth. At that instant, catching a glimpse of his figure in the looking glass, the black veil involved his own spirit in the horror with which it overwhelmed all others. His frame shuddered—his lips grew white—he spilt the untasted wine upon the carpet—and rushed forth into the darkness. For the Earth, too, had on her Black Veil.

The next day, the whole village of Milford talked of little else than Parson Hooper's black veil. That, and the mystery concealed behind it, supplied a topic for discussion between acquaintances meeting in the street, and good women gossiping at their open windows. It was

200 the first item of news that the tavern keeper told to his guests. The children babbled of it on their way to school. One imitative little imp covered his face with an old black handkerchief, thereby so affrighting his playmates that the panic seized himself, and he well-nigh lost his wits by his own waggery.[20]

It was remarkable that, of all the busybodies and impertinent people in the parish, not one ventured to put the plain question to Mr. Hooper, wherefore he did this thing. Hitherto, whenever there appeared the slightest call for such interference, he had never lacked advisers, nor shown himself averse to be guided by their judgment.

210 If he erred at all, it was by so painful a degree of self-distrust that even the mildest censure[21] would lead him to consider an indifferent action as a crime. Yet, though so well acquainted with this amiable weakness, no individual among his parishioners chose to make the black veil a subject of friendly remonstrance.[22] There was a feeling of dread, neither plainly confessed nor carefully concealed, which caused each to shift the responsibility upon another, till at length it was found expedient to send a deputation to the church, in order to deal with Mr. Hooper about the mystery, before it should grow into a scandal. Never did an embassy so ill discharge its duties. The minister received

220 them with friendly courtesy, but became silent, after they were seated, leaving to his visitors the whole burden of introducing their important business. The topic, it might be supposed, was obvious enough. There was the black veil, swathed round Mr. Hooper's forehead, and concealing every feature above his placid mouth, on which, at times, they could perceive the glimmering of a melancholy smile. But that

---

[19] **If ever...wedding knell:** In Hawthorne's "The Wedding Knell," funeral bells ring during a wedding ceremony.

[20] **waggery:** silly humor.

[21] **censure:** disapproval or criticism.

[22] **remonstrance:** protest.

SCAFFOLDING FOR ELL STUDENTS

Analyze Language Explain to students that Hawthorne often uses complex sentence structures. Use a whiteboard to project this sentence (lines 236–240). Invite volunteers to mark it up.

- Highlight the main clause in yellow. Discuss the meaning of the main clause.
- Highlight subordinate clauses in green.
- Highlight phrases in blue. Discuss the phrases, showing how they add to the meaning of the main clause.

piece of crape, to their imagination, seemed to hang down before his heart, the symbol of a fearful secret between him and them. Were the veil but cast aside, they might speak freely of it, but not till then. Thus they sat a considerable time, speechless, confused, and shrinking

230 uneasily from Mr. Hooper's eye, which they felt to be fixed upon them with an invisible glance. Finally, the deputies returned abashed to their constituents, pronouncing the matter too weighty to be handled, except by a council of the churches, if, indeed, it might not require a general synod.[23]

But there was one person in the village unappalled by the awe with which the black veil had impressed all beside herself. When the deputies returned without an explanation, or even venturing to demand one, she, with the calm energy of her character, determined to chase away the strange cloud that appeared to be settling round

240 Mr. Hooper, every moment more darkly than before. As his plighted wife,[24] it should be her privilege to know what the black veil concealed. At the minister's first visit, therefore, she entered upon the subject, with a direct simplicity, which made the task easier both for him and her. After he had seated himself, she fixed her eyes steadfastly upon the veil, but could discern nothing of the dreadful gloom that had so overawed the multitude: it was but a double fold of crape, hanging down from his forehead to his mouth, and slightly stirring with his breath.

"No," said she aloud, and smiling, "there is nothing terrible in this

250 piece of crape except that it hides a face which I am always glad to look upon. Come, good sir, let the sun shine from behind the cloud. First lay aside your black veil: then tell me why you put it on."

Mr. Hooper's smile glimmered faintly.

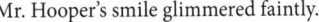

[23] **synod:** an assembly or court of church officials.
[24] **plighted wife:** fiancée.

The Minister's Black Veil **241**

Vocabulary Strategy: Nuances in Word Meanings (LINES 244–248)

COMMON CORE L 5b

Explain to students that there are **nuances**, or subtle differences, in the meanings of words. Words with similar denotations may have very different connotations, or associations. For instance, have students read the description of the black veil in lines 246–247.

J ASK STUDENTS to compare this description ("but a double fold of crape") to the words "black veil" used elsewhere to describe the same object. *(The words "but a double fold of crape" make the veil sound like an ordinary piece of cloth, while the words "black veil" have negative connotations associated with death and secrecy.)*

Analyze Structure: Symbolism (LINES 249–253)

COMMON CORE RL 3, RL 5

Emphasize to students that although the veil is the primary symbol in this story, Hawthorne uses other symbols as well.

K CITE TEXT EVIDENCE Ask students what two additional symbols appear in lines 249–253. *(the sun and the cloud [line 251])* Ask: What do these two objects symbolize? *(The sun symbolizes openness or cheerfulness, and the cloud symbolizes secrecy or sadness.)*

When the deputies returned without an explanation, or even venturing to demand one, she, with the calm energy of her character, determined to chase away the strange cloud that appeared to be settling round Mr. Hooper, every moment more darkly than before.

CLOSE READ

Determine Themes: Romanticism (LINES 259–281)

COMMON CORE RL 2

Discuss the development of theme, guiding students to understand that one of the story's themes relates to the conflict between the needs and feelings of the individual and the expectations of society.

Ⓛ ASK STUDENTS to explain how Mr. Hooper's behavior in wearing the veil illustrates this conflict. *(Mr. Hooper's strong personal reasons for wearing the veil are in conflict with the needs and expectations of the community, including those of his fiancé.)*

CRITICAL VOCABULARY

obstinacy: Hawthorne describes the minister as being extremely stubborn about wearing the veil.

ASK STUDENTS to cite evidence from the story that demonstrates Mr. Hooper's obstinacy. *(Mr. Hooper responds to Elizabeth's first request that he remove the veil by saying he will wear it until the hour comes "when all of us shall cast aside our veils" [lines 254–255]. Elizabeth asks him to at least reveal the meaning of his words and he does not give a clear answer [lines 259–264]. Elizabeth asks him what affliction has happened to him and he avoids a direct answer [lines 265–269]. Elizabeth says he is causing a scandal and he again avoids answering [lines 270–278].)*

"There is an hour to come," said he, "when all of us shall cast aside our veils. Take it not amiss, beloved friend, if I wear this piece of crape till then."

"Your words are a mystery too," returned the young lady. "Take away the veil from them, at least."

"Elizabeth, I will," said he, "so far as my vow may suffer me. 260 Know, then, this veil is a type and a symbol, and I am bound to wear it ever, both in light and darkness, in solitude and before the gaze of multitudes, and as with strangers, so with my familiar friends. No mortal eye will see it withdrawn. This dismal shade must separate me from the world: even you, Elizabeth, can never come behind it!"

"What grievous affliction hath befallen you," she earnestly inquired, "that you should thus darken your eyes forever?"

"If it be a sign of mourning," replied Mr. Hooper, "I, perhaps, like most other mortals, have sorrows dark enough to be typified by a black veil."

270 "But what if the world will not believe that it is the type of an innocent sorrow?" urged Elizabeth. "Beloved and respected as you are, there may be whispers that you hide your face under the consciousness of secret sin. For the sake of your holy office, do away this scandal!"

The color rose into her cheeks, as she intimated the nature of the rumors that were already abroad in the village. But Mr. Hooper's mildness did not forsake him. He even smiled again—that same sad smile, which always appeared like a faint glimmering of light proceeding from the obscurity beneath the veil.

"If I hide my face for sorrow, there is cause enough," he merely 280 replied; "and if I cover it for secret sin, what mortal might not do the same?"

And with this gentle but unconquerable **obstinacy** did he resist all her entreaties. At length Elizabeth sat silent. For a few moments she appeared lost in thought, considering, probably, what new methods might be tried to withdraw her lover from so dark a fantasy, which, if it had no other meaning, was perhaps a symptom of mental disease. Though of a firmer character than his own, the tears rolled down her cheeks. But, in an instant, as it were, a new feeling took the place of sorrow: her eyes were fixed insensibly on the black veil, when, like a 290 sudden twilight in the air, its terrors fell around her. She arose, and stood trembling before him.

"And do you feel it then at last?" said he mournfully.

She made no reply, but covered her eyes with her hand, and turned to leave the room. He rushed forward and caught her arm.

"Have patience with me, Elizabeth!" cried he passionately. "Do not desert me, though this veil must be between us here on earth. Be mine, and hereafter there shall be no veil over my face, no darkness between our souls! It is but a mortal veil—it is not for eternity! Oh! you know not how lonely I am, and how frightened to be alone behind my black 300 veil. Do not leave me in this miserable obscurity forever!"

obstinacy
(ŏb′stə-nə-sē) *n.*
stubbornness

WHEN STUDENTS STRUGGLE...

Some students may struggle in understanding how a symbol gets its meaning. Ask students to work with a partner to examine the meaning and derivation of some common symbols. Discuss the two symbols, their meanings, and the possible derivations listed in the chart on the next page. Then have students list two more symbols, their meanings, and how the symbols got those meanings. Ask students to share their symbols and meanings in small groups.

"Lift the veil but once, and look me in the face," said she.

"Never! It cannot be!" replied Mr. Hooper.

"Then, farewell!" said Elizabeth.

She withdrew her arm from his grasp and slowly departed, pausing at the door to give one long, shuddering gaze that seemed almost to penetrate the mystery of the black veil. But even amid his grief, Mr. Hooper smiled to think that only a material emblem had separated him from happiness, though the horrors which it shadowed forth must be drawn darkly between the fondest of lovers.

310   From that time no attempts were made to remove Mr. Hooper's black veil or, by a direct appeal, to discover the secret which it was supposed to hide. By persons who claimed a superiority to popular prejudice, it was reckoned merely an eccentric whim, such as often mingles with the sober actions of men otherwise rational, and tinges them all with its own semblance of insanity. But with the multitude, good Mr. Hooper was irreparably a bugbear.[25] He could not walk the streets with any peace of mind, so conscious was he that the gentle and timid would turn aside to avoid him, and that others would make it a point of hardihood to throw themselves in his way. The impertinence

320 of the latter class compelled him to give up his customary walk, at sunset, to the burial ground, for when he leaned pensively over the gate, there would always be faces behind the gravestones, peeping at his black veil. A fable went the rounds that the stare of the dead people drove him thence. It grieved him to the very depth of his kind heart to observe how the children fled from his approach, breaking up their merriest sports, while his melancholy figure was yet afar off. Their instinctive dread caused him to feel, more strongly than aught else, that a preternatural[26] horror was interwoven with the threads of the black crape. In truth, his own antipathy to the veil was known to be

330 so great that he never willingly passed before a mirror, nor stooped to drink at a still fountain, lest, in its peaceful bosom, he should be affrighted by himself. This was what gave **plausibility** to the whispers that Mr. Hooper's conscience tortured him for some great crime too horrible to be entirely concealed, or otherwise than so obscurely intimated. Thus, from beneath the black veil there rolled a cloud into the sunshine, an ambiguity of sin or sorrow, which enveloped the poor minister, so that love or sympathy could never reach him. It was said that ghost and fiend consorted with him there. With self-shudderings and outward terrors, he walked continually in its shadow,

340 groping darkly within his own soul, or gazing through a medium that saddened the whole world. Even the lawless wind, it was believed, respected his dreadful secret, and never blew aside the veil. But still good Mr. Hooper sadly smiled at the pale visages of the worldly throng as he passed by.

plausibility
(plô´zə-bəl´ĭ-tē) *n.*
likelihood;
believability.

---

[25] **bugbear:** source of irrational fear.

[26] **preternatural:** inexplicable, supernatural.

Symbol	Meaning	How the meaning came to be
American flag	freedom, democracy, unity	The 13 stripes on the flag represent the original 13 colonies and their united fight for freedom and democracy.
turtle	longevity, stability, patience	Cultures around the world recognize the characteristics of a turtle—its long lifespan, slow movement, and sturdy shells.

TEACH

CLOSE READ

Analyze Structure: Symbolism (LINES 301–309)

COMMON CORE RL 3, RL 5

Explain that writers usually use symbols to help readers see deeper meanings. In this story, the characters also see and react to the veil as a symbol.

 **CITE TEXT EVIDENCE** Ask students how the symbol of the veil directly affects the lives of the minister and Elizabeth. *(Because the minister will not remove the veil, Elizabeth refuses to continue her relationship with him [lines 301–303]; the minister recognizes how the veil has separated him from happiness but he refuses to stop wearing it as a symbol [lines 306–309].)*

CRITICAL VOCABULARY

plausibility: Hawthorne says that the minister's horror at the sight of his veil in a mirror made the townspeople's belief that he had done some terrible thing believable.

ASK STUDENTS to discuss other actions the minister took that lend plausibility to the idea that he feels he has done something terrible. Have them explain their ideas. *(He wore the veil at a wedding; he refused to take the veil off so that Elizabeth could see his face.)*

Determine Themes: Romanticism (LINES 335–342)

COMMON CORE RL 2

Draw students' attention to the description of Mr. Hooper's inner life beneath the veil in lines 335–342, especially Hawthorne's use of the word *ambiguity*.

ASK STUDENTS how the uncertainty over why Mr. Hooper wears the veil affects the meaning of the story. *(The uncertainty over whether Mr. Hooper wears the veil because of a horrible sin he committed, because of sorrow, or for some other reason makes the story more complex and puts the reader in the same position as the people in Mr. Hooper's community. It suggests the theme that we can never know the secrets of another person's heart.)*

Determine Themes: Romanticism (LINES 345–365)

 COMMON CORE RL 2

Discuss with students that theme can be conveyed through character and plot development.

CITE TEXT EVIDENCE Ask students to cite details in lines 345–365 that show how Mr. Hooper's veil benefits him in his role as a clergyman. *(He brought his converts to "celestial light" [lines 350–351]. He sympathized with their "dark affections" [line 352]. Dying people held on to life as they awaited Mr. Hooper [lines 352–354]. Strangers traveled great distances to see him and were terrified by him [lines 357–360]. The legislature passed measures that echoed those of their Puritan ancestors [lines 363–365].)*

ASK STUDENTS what these details suggest about a theme of the story. *(These details suggest that the minister and his veil had power to awe and even give hope and comfort. This suggests the theme that sin or sorrow can be transmuted into a special gift to help others.)*

CRITICAL VOCABULARY

mitigate: The minister's physician did what he could to ease Mr. Hooper's pain.

ASK STUDENTS what the doctor might have done to mitigate Mr. Hooper's suffering. *(He might have provided medications to reduce pain or calm the patient.)*

Among all its bad influences, the black veil had the one desirable effect, of making its wearer a very efficient clergyman. By the aid of his mysterious emblem—for there was no other apparent cause—he became a man of awful power, over souls that were in agony for sin. His converts always regarded him with a dread peculiar to themselves, affirming, though but figuratively, that before he brought them to celestial light, they had been with him behind the black veil. Its gloom, indeed, enabled him to sympathize with all dark affections. Dying sinners cried aloud for Mr. Hooper, and would not yield their breath till he appeared; though ever, as he stooped to whisper consolation, they shuddered at the veiled face so near their own. Such were the terrors of the black veil, even when Death had bared his visage! Strangers came long distances to attend service at his church, with the mere idle purpose of gazing at his figure, because it was forbidden them to behold his face. But many were made to quake ere they departed! Once, during Governor Belcher's[27] administration, Mr. Hooper was appointed to preach the election sermon. Covered with his black veil, he stood before the chief magistrate, the council, and the representatives, and wrought so deep an impression that the legislative measures of that year were characterized by all the gloom and piety of our earliest ancestral sway.

In this manner Mr. Hooper spent a long life, irreproachable[28] in outward act, yet shrouded in dismal suspicions; kind and loving, though unloved, and dimly feared; a man apart from men, shunned in their health and joy, but ever summoned to their aid in mortal anguish. As years wore on, shedding their snows above his sable veil, he acquired a name throughout the New England churches, and they called him Father Hooper. Nearly all his parishioners, who were of a mature age when he was settled, had been borne away by many a funeral: he had one congregation in the church, and a more crowded one in the churchyard; and having wrought so late into the evening, and done his work so well, it was now good Father Hooper's turn to rest.

Several persons were visible by the shaded candlelight in the death chamber of the old clergyman. Natural connections[29] he had none. But there was the decorously grave, though unmoved physician, seeking only to **mitigate** the last pangs of the patient whom he could not save. There were the deacons, and other eminently pious members of his church. There, also, was the Reverend Mr. Clark, of Westbury, a young and zealous divine, who had ridden in haste to pray by the bedside of the expiring minister. There was the nurse, no hired handmaiden of death, but one whose calm affection had endured thus long, in secrecy,

mitigate
(mĭt′ĭ-gāt′) *v.* to lessen

---

[27]**Governor Belcher:** Jonathan Belcher (1682–1757), governor of Massachusetts Bay Colony from 1730 until 1741.

[28]**irreproachable:** without fault; blameless.

[29]**Natural connections:** relatives, kin.

TO CHALLENGE STUDENTS...

Puritans and Sin Students may be interested in learning more about the Puritans' beliefs so they can better understand the minister.

ASK STUDENTS to search the Internet to gather details about the Puritans' beliefs. Suggest that students investigate details about new England Puritans, original sin, predestination, and daily life. *(Puritans believed that all people were born with original sin and that God had predestined who would be saved from eternal damnation and who would be damned. The Puritans believed that they would receive God's grace and be saved if they adhered to strict moral values and a strong work ethic.)*

in solitude, amid the chill of age, and would not perish, even at the dying hour. Who, but Elizabeth! And there lay the hoary head of good Father Hooper upon the death pillow, with the black veil still swathed
390 about his brow and reaching down over his face, so that each more difficult gasp of his faint breath caused it to stir. All through life that piece of crape had hung between him and the world: it had separated him from cheerful brotherhood and woman's love, and kept him in that saddest of all prisons, his own heart; and still it lay upon his face, as if to deepen the gloom of his darksome chamber, and shade him from the sunshine of eternity.

For some time previous, his mind had been confused, wavering doubtfully between the past and the present, and hovering forward, as it were, at intervals, into the indistinctness of the world to come. There
400 had been feverish turns, which tossed him from side to side and wore away what little strength he had. But in the most convulsive struggles, and in the wildest vagaries of his intellect, when no other thought retained its sober influence, he still showed an awful solicitude lest the black veil should slip aside. Even if his bewildered soul could have forgotten, there was a faithful woman at his pillow, who, with averted eyes, would have covered that aged face, which she had last beheld in the comeliness of manhood. At length the death-stricken old man lay quietly in the torpor[30] of mental and bodily exhaustion, with an imperceptible pulse, and breath that grew fainter and fainter, except
410 when a long, deep, and irregular inspiration[31] seemed to prelude the flight of his spirit.

The minister of Westbury approached the bedside.

"Venerable Father Hooper," said he, "the moment of your release is at hand. Are you ready for the lifting of the veil, that shuts in time from eternity?"

Father Hooper at first replied merely by a feeble motion of his head; then, apprehensive, perhaps, that his meaning might be doubtful, he exerted himself to speak.

"Yea," said he, in faint accents, "my soul hath a patient weariness
420 until that veil be lifted."

"And is it fitting," resumed the Reverend Mr. Clark, "that a man so given to prayer, of such a blameless example, holy in deed and thought, so far as mortal judgment may pronounce; is it fitting that a father in the church should leave a shadow on his memory that may seem to blacken a life so pure? I pray you, my venerable brother, let not this thing be! Suffer us to be gladdened by your triumphant aspect, as you go to your reward. Before the veil of eternity be lifted, let me cast aside this black veil from your face!"

And thus speaking, the Reverend Mr. Clark bent forward to reveal
430 the mystery of so many years. But, exerting a sudden energy that made

---

[30] **torpor:** lifelessness, inactivity.
[31] **inspiration:** inhalation of air into the lungs.

When students have finished their research, have them gather in small groups to discuss how the Puritans' belief about sin applies to the minister's situation.

CLOSE READ

Point of View (LINES 397–411)    RL 3, RL 5, RL 6

Tell students that the third-person point of view can be developed in two ways. An omniscient third-person narrator knows what every character is thinking and feeling. A limited third-person narrator does not know what other characters are thinking and feeling.

P CITE TEXT EVIDENCE Ask students to analyze the second paragraph and decide what point of view Hawthorne is using. *(third-person limited)* Ask them to cite the text evidence that leads them to this conclusion. *(The narrator gives details about the minister's state of mind, saying for example that he was confused [line 397] and his mind wavered between "the past and the present" [line 398], but these are conclusions an observant witness might reach. Likewise, the description of Elizabeth and the minister's physical condition are those of a narrator who can only observe what is happening but cannot know what people are thinking or feeling.)*

ASK STUDENTS how the author's choice to use limited third-person point of view supports the theme of this story. *(The third-person limited point of view preserves Mr. Hooper's secret and the ambiguity of the story's message—if an omniscient narrator had revealed exactly why the minister chose to wear the veil, the story would lose some of its power and complexity.)*

Analyze Structure: Symbolism (LINES 419–430)   COMMON CORE RL 3, RL 5

Remind students that the veil inspires curiosity, and often frustration and anger for others in the story, suggesting that the veil has disturbing associations for them.

Q ASK STUDENTS to explain why Mr. Clark wants to remove Mr. Hooper's veil. *(In lines 421–428, Mr. Clark says that he wants to remove the veil in order to remove a shadow from the face of someone who has lived a good life. He may also be curious about what Mr. Hooper is hiding and what he looks like.)*

Analyze Structure: Symbolism (LINES 438–458)

COMMON CORE RL 3, RL 5

Remind students that throughout the story, the minister has frequently been described as having a faint or sad smile showing beneath the veil. Tell students that the smile is another symbol.

R CITE TEXT EVIDENCE Ask students to locate the two references to Mr. Hooper's smile on this page. *(lines 443 and 457–458)* Ask students what they think the minister's smile might symbolize. *(The smile may be ironic because although the parishioners are greatly concerned about the veil, none approach him out of friendship or love. It may be a smile of sadness because the parishioners do not understand that the symbol has meaning only for him. It may be a smile of satisfaction, showing that the minister has accepted his fate and is content)*

ASK STUDENTS to locate other instances in the story where the smile is described and look for more clues to its meaning.

COLLABORATIVE DISCUSSION Have students work in pairs to review the text and locate quotations and details about the relationship between Mr. Hooper and the villagers and why the veil changes it. Then ask students to discuss their response to the question and share their responses with the class. Encourage students to cite specific textual evidence to support their ideas.

ASK STUDENTS to share any questions they generated in the course of reading and discussing the selection.

all the beholders stand aghast, Father Hooper snatched both his hands from beneath the bedclothes and pressed them strongly on the black veil, resolute to struggle, if the minister of Westbury would contend with a dying man.

"Never!" cried the veiled clergyman. "On earth, never!"

"Dark old man!" exclaimed the affrighted minister, "with what horrible crime upon your soul are you now passing to the judgment?"

Father Hooper's breath heaved; it rattled in his throat; but with a mighty effort, grasping forward with his hands, he caught hold of life,
440   and held it back till he should speak. He even raised himself in bed; and there he sat shivering, with the arms of death around him, while the black veil hung down, awful, at that last moment, in the gathered terrors of a lifetime. And yet the faint, sad smile, so often there, now seemed to glimmer from its obscurity, and linger on Father Hooper's lips.

"Why do you tremble at me alone?" cried he, turning his veiled face round the circle of pale spectators. "Tremble also at each other! Have men avoided me, and women shown no pity, and children screamed and fled, only for my black veil? What, but the mystery
450   which it obscurely typifies, has made this piece of crape so awful? When the friend shows his inmost heart to his friend; the lover to his best beloved; when man does not vainly shrink from the eye of his Creator, loathsomely treasuring up the secret of his sin; then deem me a monster, for the symbol beneath which I have lived, and die! I look around me, and, lo! On every visage a Black Veil!"

While his auditors shrank from one another, in mutual affright, Father Hooper fell back upon his pillow, a veiled corpse, with a faint smile lingering on his lips. Still veiled, they laid him in his coffin, and a veiled corpse they bore him to the grave. The grass of many years has
460   sprung up and withered on that grave, the burial stone is moss-grown, and good Mr. Hooper's face is dust; but awful is still the thought, that it mouldered beneath the Black Veil!

COLLABORATIVE DISCUSSION With a partner, discuss how the black veil changes Mr. Hooper's relationship with the villagers. Cite specific quotes and textual evidence to support your ideas.

Strategies for Annotation   🖉 📖 *Annotate it!*

Determine Themes: Romanticism (LINES 448–462)

COMMON CORE RL 2

Share these strategies for guided or independent analysis:

- Highlight in green words and phrases that provide clues as to the theme of Hawthorne's story.
- Review your highlighting. What theme, or message about life, do the words and phrases suggest? On a note, record your ideas about theme.

"... Have men avoided me, and women shown no pity, and children screamed and fled, only for my black veil? What, but the mystery which it obscurely typifies, has made this piece of crape so awful? ... when man does not vainly shrink from the eye of his Creator, loathsomely treasuring up the secret of his sin; then deem me a monster ... On every visage a Black Veil!"

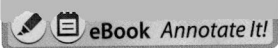

Determine Themes: Romanticism

COMMON CORE RL 2

Like other Dark Romantics and Gothic writers of his era, Nathaniel Hawthorne's work explores the ideas of sin and suffering. "The Minister's Black Veil" suggests a moral lesson that the villagers should learn from their reactions to the minister. Answering these questions can help you determine the story's **themes,** or central messages:

- How does the author introduce and develop the characters?
- How do the events of the story build upon a central idea?

Analyze Structure: Symbolism

COMMON CORE RL 5

A **symbol** is a person, place, thing, or event that represents something more than its implicit meaning. Although a symbol may have universal meanings, a writer will usually adapt it in some unique and imaginative way to suggest not just one, but myriad interpretations. Nathaniel Hawthorne is known for his masterful use of symbolism.

Analyzing the Text

COMMON CORE RL 2, RL 3, RL 5, SL 1

Cite Text Evidence   Support your responses with evidence from the selection.

1. **Evaluate** What evidence in the text hints at or suggests Mr. Hooper's reasons for wearing the black veil? What affect does the **ambiguity,** or uncertainty, surrounding the veil add to the overall meaning of the story?

2. **Analyze** Mr. Hooper's conversation with Elizabeth is the first time that readers learn about Mr. Hooper from his own words. What insight does this conversation provide about Mr. Hooper's character?

3. **Interpret** What does the veil symbolize? Cite specific details from the story to support your interpretation.

4. **Analyze** What themes do Mr. Hooper's last words and the final image in the story suggest? Quote and paraphrase the text in your response.

PERFORMANCE TASK

Speaking Activity: Discussion Wearing the black veil leads to Mr. Hooper's separation from his congregation. Based on the following passages, what argument would you make about the real causes of the villagers' discomfort in the minister's presence? Explore your views in a moderated discussion.

- the first sighting of the minister (lines 40–46)
- parishioners' comments after services (lines 124–135)
- the minister's arrival at the wedding (lines 174–179)
- the attempt to confront the minister (lines 214-234)

Assign this performance task.

PERFORMANCE TASK

COMMON CORE SL 1

Speaking Activity: Discussion Have students work in small groups to read and discuss the lines cited. Assign the role of moderator to one student in each group. Encourage students to give reasons and details from the text to support their ideas.

PRACTICE & APPLY

Determine Themes: Romanticism

COMMON CORE RL 2

Discuss Romanticism. Then guide students in answering the questions on the SE page. *(The characters are introduced and developed in relation to the black veil. All of the events build upon the conflict created by the minister's veil.)*

Ask students to consider also how the conflict created by the veil is resolved. *(The story's external conflict between the minister and the community is resolved by the death of the minister, but the mystery behind the veil is never revealed.)*

Analyze Structure: Symbolism

COMMON CORE RL 3, RL 5

Explain to students that a symbol can have different meanings in different contexts and for different characters. Ask students to consider what the black veil means to Mr. Hooper and the townspeople. *(Accept explanations that can be supported with text evidence. Possible responses: To Mr. Hooper, the veil may symbolize guilt; to the townspeople, sin, guilt, madness, the unknown.)*

Analyzing the Text

COMMON CORE RL 2, RL 3, RL 5, SL 1

Possible answers:

1. *Some hints come during Mr. Hooper's dialogue with Elizabeth. (lines 268–273). Ambiguity gives the symbol more power by suggesting the complexity of human emotion.*

2. *It reveals that he is committed to wearing the veil and willing to accept the consequences of his decision.*

3. *The veil might symbolize a hidden sin, as this line suggests: "from beneath the black veil there rolled a cloud into the sunshine, an ambiguity of sin or sorrow" (lines 335–336).*

4. *Mr. Hooper's last words include a reference to man giving up his sins to his Creator (lines 452–453) and "'On every visage a Black Veil!'" (line 455). These lines suggest the theme that everyone is guilty of sin. The final image of his face mouldering beneath the black veil suggests the theme that the sins represented by the veil cannot be removed.*

Critical Vocabulary

 COMMON CORE L 5b

Possible answers:

Answers should reflect the meanings of the vocabulary words.

1. . . . it showed the stricken faces of the victims of the horrible flooding.

2. . . . the defiant set of her jaw.

3. . . . the hard work he had put into winning this race.

4. . . . it made them feel so inadequate in comparison.

5. . . . appealing to their sense of pride in the community.

6. . . . all of the facts she presented to reinforce her argument.

Vocabulary Strategy: Nuances in Word Meanings

COMMON CORE L 5b

Possible answers:

- **melancholy** (line 170) a sad or gloomy state of mind; sad, sorrowful, gloomy

- **dread** (line 215) terror or fear of something about to happen; fear, awe, apprehension

- **obstinacy** (line 282) the quality of being stubborn, unwilling to change an opinion or a purpose; stubbornness, willfullness, bullheadedness

- **miserable** (line 300) extremely unhappy; wretched, forlorn

- **horrible** (line 437) extremely unpleasant or bad; terrible, gruesome, repellent

✓ **Assess It!**

Online Selection Test
- Download an editable ExamView bank.
- Assign and manage this test online.

Critical Vocabulary

COMMON CORE L 5b

emblem	pathos	ostentatious
obstinacy	plausibility	mitigate

Practice and Apply Complete each of the following sentence stems in a way that reflects the meaning of the Critical Vocabulary word.

1. The painting evoked **pathos** in the viewer because . . .

2. The **obstinacy** of her response was made clear by . . .

3. The runner treasured his race number as an **emblem** of . . .

4. The **ostentatious** display of wealth made visitors uncomfortable because . . .

5. Proponents of the new law sought to **mitigate** opposition by . . .

6. The **plausibility** of her statement was supported by . . .

Vocabulary Strategy: Nuances in Word Meanings

When you analyze nuances in the meaning of words with similar **denotations**, or dictionary meanings, you look for subtle differences in shades of meaning. The **connotation** of a word refers to the feelings or ideas associated with it. For example, consider the connotation of the Critical Vocabulary word *ostentatious* in this sentence from "The Minister's Black Veil":

> Some gathered in little circles, huddled closely together, with their mouths all whispering in the centre; some went homeward alone, wrapped in silent meditation; some talked loudly, and profaned the Sabbath day with ostentatious laughter.

The word *ostentatious* carries a negative connotation of disapproval, in contrast to the synonym *loud*, which has a more neutral connotation. This emphasizes the reproach of the congregants' behavior on their solemn day of worship.

Practice and Apply Work with a partner to explore nuances in word meanings. Follow these steps:

- List five words from the story that have a strongly positive or negative connotation.
- Use a dictionary and a thesaurus to find definitions and synonyms of the words.
- Discuss how synonyms with different connotations would impact meaning.

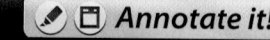

Strategies for Annotation   ✏ 🖺 Annotate it!

Nuances in Word Meaning

 COMMON CORE L 5b

Have students locate the sentences containing the words they chose for the Vocabulary Strategy. Encourage them to use their eBook annotation tools to do the following:

- Highlight in blue each word you chose to explore.
- Reread the surrounding sentences, and consider what Hawthorne meant and what mood and tone he wanted to convey.
- Review your synonyms and choose the one that could best be used to replace the one in the story.

> "And so had I, at the same moment," said the other. That night, the handsomest couple in Milford village were to be joined in wedlock. Though reckoned a melancholy man, Mr. Hooper had a placid cheerfulness for such occasions, which often excited a sympathetic smile, where livelier merriment would have been thrown away.

Moderate Discussions

COMMON CORE

SL 1, SL 3

TEACH

Before students begin the Performance Task activity, explain that the purpose of a moderated discussion is to ensure that the discussion proceeds civilly and efficiently while participants evaluate one another's ideas and respond thoughtfully to different perspectives.

Present the following roles for a moderated discussion:

A **moderator** plays a neutral role in the discussion or debate, promoting a civil discussion and keeping everyone on task. The moderator begins by introducing the topic of the discussion or debate and then recognizes speakers, alternating between points of view.

A **speaker** in a moderated discussion should follow the moderator's instructions. He or she should clearly state a position, provide relevant evidence to support that position, and attempt to convince the audience to accept that point of view. A speaker should also speak clearly and maintain a respectful tone.

Listeners should participate by listening actively in order to evaluate the speaker's point of view, reasoning, and evidence. Listeners should take notes about the speaker's position; use of sound logic, reasoning, and evidence in developing the argument; and points of agreement and disagreement.

PRACTICE AND APPLY

Have students work individually to prepare their arguments for the Performance Task activity. Then ask students to form groups. Assign one student in each group to be the moderator. After every student in a group has presented his or her argument, have students reflect on any new connections they made, in light of the evidence and reasoning presented, as to the real causes of the villagers' discomfort in the minister's presence.

Analyze Structure: Suspense and Ambiguity

COMMON CORE

RL 1, RL 5, RL 6

RETEACH

Remind students that the structure of a story is how the writer chooses to organize and develop the plot. In "The Minister's Black Veil," Hawthorne has chosen to employ suspense and ambiguity in his story. These two elements help drive the plot forward. In this story, they are closely interwoven.

- **Suspense** is the excitement or tension created that leaves readers wondering what is happening, what will happen next, and how the story will end. Ask students how suspense is created in the opening paragraphs of the story. *(Without saying what is wrong, Hawthorne informs the reader that something strange has happened to the minister's face; the townspeople are startled and amazed.)* Explain that this suspense makes readers want to discover what exactly has happened, so they read more.

- **Ambiguity** is the uncertainty created when an author leaves elements of the text open to the reader's interpretation. Ambiguity can help move the plot forward by having the reader piece together clues to decide what is happening or what something means. Ambiguity is central to the plot and the theme of "The Minister's Black Veil." Ask students to cite the first occurrence of ambiguity regarding the meaning of the veil. *(During the sermon, lines 63–68, when the narrator asks "Did he seek to hide from the dread Being whom he was addressing?")*

CLOSE READING APPLICATION

Students can apply the skill of analyzing suspense and ambiguity to "The Minister's Black Veil." Organize them in pairs and have them begin by rereading the dialogue between the minister and Elizabeth in lines 235–303. Then ask them to analyze the use of suspense and ambiguity in the passage. Have them answer these questions:

- What are some examples of suspense and ambiguity in this passage?

- What effect does the use of suspense and ambiguity in this passage have on the reader?

- How does the suspense and ambiguity help move the plot forward?

mySmartPlanner Create lesson plans and access resources online.

COMPARE TEXTS

The Pit and the Pendulum

Short Story by Edgar Allan Poe

Why This Text?

"The Pit and the Pendulum" is a classic example of American Gothic literature from one of its masters. This lesson explores the ways in which Poe creates atmosphere and builds dramatic tension. It also guides students in identifying and analyzing the story's theme. On page 266, students will be asked to compare this text with "The Minister's Black Veil" by Nathaniel Hawthorne (pages 235–248).

Key Learning Objective: Students will be able to analyze the impact of atmosphere and structure on dramatic tension and explore different approaches to dark Romanticism by comparing themes.

Common Core Standards

RL 1 Cite text evidence.

RL 2 Determine themes in a text.

RL 3 Analyze the impact of the author's choices.

RL 5 Analyze how an author's choices concerning how to structure specific parts of a text contribute to its overall meaning as well as its aesthetic impact.

RL 9 Demonstrate knowledge of foundational works of American literature.

W 3 Write narratives.

W 7 Conduct research projects.

W 8 Gather information from multiple authoritative print and digital sources.

W 9a Draw evidence from literary or informational texts by comparing two texts of similar theme.

SL 1 Initiate and participate in a range of collaborative discussions.

SL 1a Come prepared with text evidence for discussion.

L 3a Vary syntax for effect; apply an understanding of syntax.

L 4a Use context as a clue to meaning.

L 4d Verify the preliminary determination of the meaning of a word or phrase.

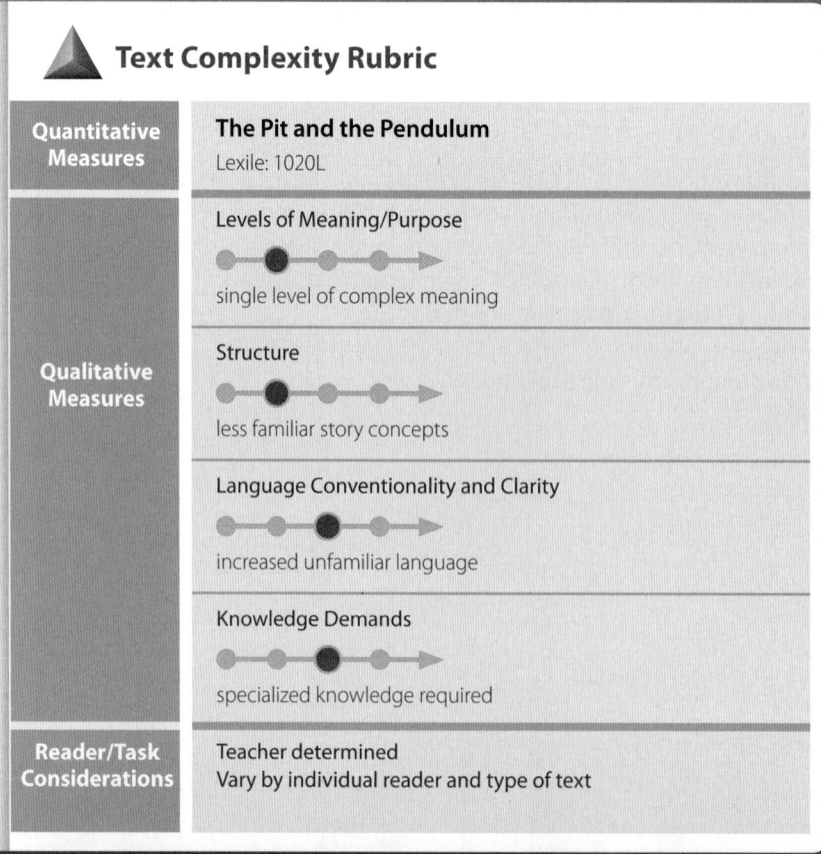

Text Complexity Rubric

Quantitative Measures

The Pit and the Pendulum
Lexile: 1020L

Qualitative Measures

Levels of Meaning/Purpose
single level of complex meaning

Structure
less familiar story concepts

Language Conventionality and Clarity
increased unfamiliar language

Knowledge Demands
specialized knowledge required

Reader/Task Considerations

Teacher determined
Vary by individual reader and type of text

TEACH

CLOSE READ

For more context and historical background, students can view the video "Surviving History: The Pendulum" in their eBooks.

Background "The Pit and the Pendulum" is set during the period of the Spanish Inquisition, which was established in 1480. The Spanish Inquisition jailed, tortured, tried, and executed thousands of people for heresy, or having opinions that differed from Catholic church doctrine. Poe uses this setting to convey the physical and psychological horror a man experiences who is convicted and sentenced to death under the courts of the Inquisition. Poe takes liberty with the history of the period to create his story.

AS YOU READ Direct students to use the As You Read instructions to focus their reading. Tell them to write down any questions they generate during reading.

Analyze Structure: Atmosphere and Dramatic Tension (LINES 8–11)

COMMON CORE RL 2, RL 3, RL 5

Explain to students that one way writers create dramatic tension is to begin the story in the middle of the action, rather than describing the setting or introducing the characters.

(A) ASK STUDENTS what is happening in the first four lines of the story. (*The narrator is untied and allowed to sit down. Then he hears his judges sentence him to death.*) Describe the dramatic tension this opening creates. (*It makes me wonder what the narrator is being sentenced for, who is sentencing him, and what will happen to him.*)

Determine Themes: Romanticism (LINES 8–13)

COMMON CORE RL 2, RL 3, RL 5, SL 1

Explain to students that the story is an example of Gothic literature, which explores the dark side of human nature. One way that Gothic writers explore the darkness of the human psyche is by having their characters experience disturbing changes in consciousness, such as fear, irrationality, or madness.

(B) CITE TEXT EVIDENCE Reread lines 8–13 and discuss the narrator's states of consciousness and how it changes. (*When the story opens, the narrator is "sick unto death" [line 8], but after he is sentenced he passes into a state of semiconsciousness in which he can still hear the judges' voices but can no longer understand what they say [lines 11–13].*)

 HISTORY VIDEO

Edgar Allan Poe (1809–1849) *is considered one of literature's "most brilliant, but erratic stars." Poe explored such distinctive themes as madness, untimely death, and obsession. He was orphaned at an early age, and for most of his life he struggled to earn a living. The 1845 publication of his poem "The Raven" made Poe famous. This success, however, was soon marred by the death of his wife and his own illness. Although Poe's life was brief, his literary influence was great, especially on the development of the horror story and detective fiction.*

The Pit and the Pendulum

Short Story by Edgar Allan Poe

AS YOU READ Notice sensory details that help create a mood of terror in the story.

> *Impia tortorum longos hic turba furores*
> *Sanguinis innocui, non satiata, aluit.*
> *Sospite nunc patria, fracto nunc funeris antro,*
> *Mors ubi dira fuit vita salusque patent.*[1]
>
> *[Quatrain composed for the gates of a market*
> *to be erected upon the site of the Jacobin*[2] *Club*
> *House at Paris.]*

I was sick—sick unto death with that long agony; and when they at length unbound me, and I was permitted to sit, I felt that my senses
10 were leaving me. The sentence—the dread sentence of death—was the last of distinct accentuation which reached my ears. After that, the sound of the inquisitorial voices seemed merged in one dreamy

---

[1] **Impia . . . patent:** *Latin:* Here the wicked crowd of tormentors, unsated, fed their long-time lusts for innocent blood. Now that our homeland is safe, now that the tomb is broken, life and health appear where once was dread death.

[2] **Jacobin** (jăk´ə-bĭn): a radical political group active in the French Revolution and later known for implementing the Reign of Terror.

SCAFFOLDING FOR ELL STUDENTS

Understand Time Sequence Explain to students that in order to appreciate dramatic tension, they must be able to understand the time sequence of events in the story. Point out this word and phrase and explain their meanings.

- when (line 8): at the same time
- After that (line 11): at a later time

Encourage students to watch for words and phrases that signal time order as they read and to keep a list of these words and their meanings.

CRITICAL VOCABULARY

indeterminate: The narrator could no longer understand the judges' voices.

ASK STUDENTS why the judges' voices turned into an "indeterminate hum" at that point in the story. *(The narrator had just heard his death sentence and was so overwhelmed with emotion, he could no longer understand the judges' words.)*

Analyze Structure: Atmosphere and Dramatic Tension (LINES 15–23)

COMMON CORE · RL 2, RL 3, RL 5

Call students' attention to the narrator's description of the judges' lips. Discuss with the class what is actually happening in these lines. *(The judges are speaking, but the narrator can only see them, not hear them.)*

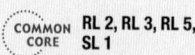 **CITE TEXT EVIDENCE** Have students reread lines 15–23 and ask them to determine what creates an atmosphere of horror, citing examples from the text. *(Poe creates an atmosphere of horror by describing the judges' lips as grotesque and inhuman. In lines 17–18, the narrator says that they are as white as paper, in lines 18–19 he says that they are grotesquely thin, and in line 22 he calls them deadly and describes them writhing as though they had a life of their own.)*

Determine Themes: Romanticism (LINES 42–54)

COMMON CORE · RL 2, RL 3, RL 5, SL 1

Discuss with students how the narrator's state of consciousness has changed in the first 42 lines. *(He has gone from feeling sick to not being able to hear to fainting entirely.)* Lines 42–54 also give information about the narrator's state of consciousness.

D **CITE TEXT EVIDENCE** Have students reread lines 42–54 and ask them to infer what a theme of the story might be. *(Some sort of consciousness survives trauma or even death. The narrator repeats that all is not lost in lines 42–46. He emphasizes that consciousness is not completely lost by repeating "no!" [lines 44–46].)*

---

indeterminate hum. It conveyed to my soul the idea of *revolution*—perhaps from its association in fancy with the burr of a millwheel. This only for a brief period; for presently I heard no more. Yet, for a while, I saw; but with how terrible an exaggeration! I saw the lips of the black-robed judges. They appeared to me white—whiter than the sheet upon which I trace these words—and thin even to grotesqueness; thin with the intensity of their expression of firmness—of immoveable
20 resolution—of stern contempt of human torture. I saw that the decrees of what to me was Fate, were still issuing from those lips. I saw them writhe with a deadly locution.[3] I saw them fashion the syllables of my name; and I shuddered because no sound succeeded. I saw, too, for a few moments of delirious horror, the soft and nearly imperceptible waving of the sable draperies which enwrapped the walls of the apartment. And then my vision fell upon the seven tall candles upon the table. At first they wore the aspect of charity, and seemed white slender angels who would save me; but then, all at once, there came a most deadly nausea over my spirit, and I felt every fiber in my frame
30 thrill as if I had touched the wire of a galvanic battery,[4] while the angel forms became meaningless specters, with heads of flame, and I saw that from them there would be no help. And then there stole into my fancy, like a rich musical note, the thought of what sweet rest there must be in the grave. The thought came gently and stealthily, and it seemed long before it attained full appreciation;[5] but just as my spirit came at length properly to feel and entertain it, the figures of the judges vanished, as if magically, from before me; the tall candles sank into nothingness; their flames went out utterly; the blackness of darkness supervened; all sensations appeared swallowed up in a mad
40 rushing descent as of the soul into Hades.[6] Then silence, and stillness, and night were the universe.

I had swooned;[7] but still will not say that all of consciousness was lost. What of it there remained I will not attempt to define, or even to describe; yet all was not lost. In the deepest slumber—no! In delirium—no! In a swoon—no! In death—no! even in the grave all *is not* lost. Else there is no immortality for man. Arousing from the most profound of slumbers, we break the gossamer web of *some* dream. Yet in a second afterward, (so frail may that web have been) we remember not that we have dreamed. In the return to life from the swoon there
50 are two stages; first, that of the sense of mental or spiritual; secondly, that of the sense of physical, existence. It seems probable that if, upon reaching the second stage, we could recall the impressions of the first, we should find these impressions eloquent in memories of the gulf

indeterminate
(ĭn´dĭ-tûr´mə-nĭt) *adj.* not precisely known.

---

[3] **locution:** style of speech.
[4] **galvanic battery:** a device for producing electricity with series of voltaic cells.
[5] **appreciation:** understanding.
[6] **Hades:** in Greek mythology, the underworld where the dead reside.
[7] **swooned:** fainted.

APPLYING ACADEMIC VOCABULARY

unique	topic

As you discuss "The Pit and the Pendulum," incorporate the following Collection 3 academic vocabulary words: **unique** and **topic**. Discuss the **topic** of the story, a man being punished by the Spanish Inquisition, with students. Then discuss Poe's **unique** use of descriptive language to convey the narrator's terror.

beyond. And that gulf is—what? How at least shall we distinguish its shadows from those of the tomb? But if the impressions of what I have termed the first stage, are not, at will, recalled, yet, after long interval, do they not come unbidden, while we marvel whence they come? He who has never swooned, is not he who finds strange palaces and wildly familiar faces in coals that glow; is not he who beholds floating

60 in midair the sad visions that the many may not view; is not he who ponders over the perfume of some novel flower—is not he whose brain grows bewildered with the meaning of some musical cadence which has never before arrested his attention.

Amid frequent and thoughtful endeavors to remember; amid earnest struggles to regather some token of the state of seeming nothingness into which my soul had lapsed, there have been moments when I have dreamed of success; there have been brief, very brief periods when I have conjured up remembrances which the **lucid** reason of a later epoch assures me could have had reference only to

70 that condition of seeming unconsciousness. These shadows of memory tell, indistinctly, of tall figures that lifted and bore me in silence down—down—still down—till a hideous dizziness oppressed me at the mere idea of the interminableness of the descent. They tell also of a vague horror at my heart, on account of that heart's unnatural stillness. Then comes a sense of sudden motionlessness throughout all things; as if those who bore me (a ghastly train!) had outrun, in their descent, the limits of the limitless, and paused from the wearisomeness of their toil. After this I call to mind flatness and dampness; and that all is *madness*—the madness of a memory which busies itself among

80 forbidden things.

Very suddenly there came back to my soul motion and sound— the **tumultuous** motion of the heart, and, in my ears, the sound of its beating. Then a pause in which all is blank. Then again sound, and motion, and touch—a tingling sensation pervading my frame. Then the mere consciousness of existence, without *thought*—a condition which lasted long. Then, very suddenly, thought, and shuddering terror, and earnest endeavor to comprehend my true state. Then a strong desire to lapse into insensibility. Then a rushing revival of soul and a successful effort to move. And now a full memory of the trial,

90 of the judges, of the sable draperies, of the sentence, of the sickness, of the swoon. Then entire forgetfulness of all that followed; of all that a later day and much earnestness of endeavor have enabled me vaguely to recall.

So far, I had not opened my eyes. I felt that I lay upon my back, unbound. I reached out my hand, and it fell heavily upon something damp and hard. There I suffered it to remain for many minutes, while I strove to imagine where and *what* I could be. I longed, yet dared not to employ my vision. I dreaded the first glance at objects around me. It was not that I feared to look upon things horrible, but that I

100 grew aghast lest there should be *nothing* to see. At length, with a wild

lucid
(loo′sĭd) *adj.* easily understood

tumultuous
(too-mŭl′choo-əs) *adj.* stormy, intense

The Pit and the Pendulum **251**

WHEN STUDENTS STRUGGLE ...

Point out to students that in lines 81–93, the narrator describes his gradual return to consciousness. He uses the words *suddenly, then,* and *now* to order his experiences.

ASK STUDENTS to complete the graphic organizer to understand the different stages of the narrator's return to consciousness.

suddenly	then	then	then	then	then	then	now

Analyze Structure: Atmosphere and Dramatic Tension (LINES 93–103)

COMMON CORE **RL 2, RL 3, RL 5**

Discuss with students the fact that from the time sentence is pronounced on the narrator through line 92, the reader is trapped in the narrator's semiconscious mind and only gets vague hints about his situation.

E ASK STUDENTS what effect withholding further details about the narrator's situation has on the reader. (*The hints and lack of information increase the reader's sense of foreboding and the dramatic tension.*) Then ask what new details about the narrator's situation are revealed in lines 93–100. (*He is lying on a damp, hard surface.*) Point out that in these lines the narrator is afraid to open his eyes and speculates about what he might see when he does. Ask students why Poe might have wanted to delay telling readers what the narrator's surroundings look like. (*He wanted to build dramatic tension by revealing details gradually.*)

Point out the phrase "my worst thoughts" in line 101 and ask students to what fear the phrase refers. (*that there would be nothing to see, line 100*)

Review Poe's description of his surroundings in lines 102–103 and ask students to identify phrases that contribute to Gothic themes. (*"blackness of eternal night" and "intensity of the darkness"*)

CRITICAL VOCABULARY

lucid: When the narrator remembers details of the time immediately after his trial, his reason is clear and unclouded.

ASK STUDENTS whether the narrator's mind is lucid while he is being taken from the scene of his trial to his prison. (*The narrator is semiconscious, so his mind is not lucid.*)

tumultuous: When the narrator regained consciousness, his heart was beating very hard.

ASK STUDENTS what the description of a tumultuously beating heart suggests to readers. (*a heart that is beating wildly and irregularly*)

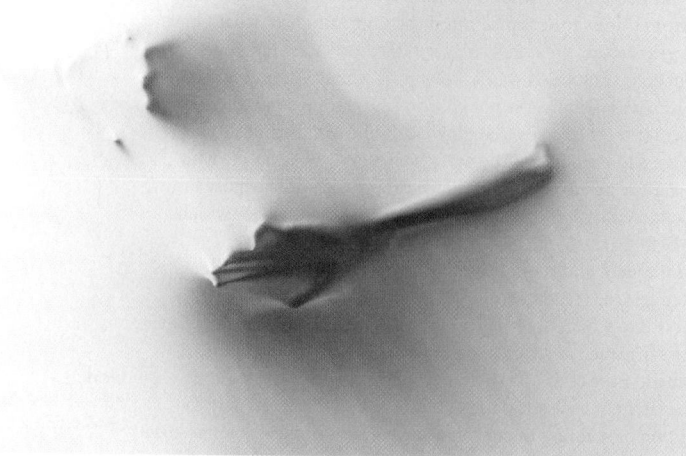

Analyze Structure: Atmosphere and Dramatic Tension (LINES 111–120)

COMMON CORE RL 2, RL 3, RL 5

Call students' attention to the narrator's deductions about his fate and his fainting fit in lines 111–120.

F **ASK STUDENTS** how these lines build dramatic tension. *(By giving the reader details about what usually happened to those sentenced to death, Poe makes the narrator's fate seem more real. Then, the narrator reasons that this is not what lies in store for him, has a sudden realization about what may happen to him instead, and faints. The reader can infer that the narrator has formed a clearer idea of his fate. The narrator's terror at the thought creates dramatic tension by making the reader wonder what might happen to the narrator that would be worse than public execution.)*

CRITICAL VOCABULARY

supposition: Although he was in complete darkness and solitude, the narrator did not assume that he was dead.

ASK STUDENTS why the narrator rejected the supposition that he might be dead. *(He rejected it because he had thoughts and feelings about what he was experiencing.)*

Determine Themes: Romanticism (LINES 119–126)

COMMON CORE RL 2, RL 3, RL 5

G **CITE EVIDENCE** Have students reread lines 119–126 to find evidence of the narrator's terror. *("drove the blood in torrents upon my heart," line 119; "trembling convulsively in every fiber," line 121–122; "Perspiration burst from every pore," line 124; "agony of suspense," line 125)* Then ask students to generalize what most frightens the narrator. *(He is most afraid of the unknown, since he is terrified by not being able to see or feel anything, and he finds the suspense "unbearable.")*

---

desperation at heart, I quickly unclosed my eyes. My worst thoughts, then, were confirmed. The blackness of eternal night encompassed me. I struggled for breath. The intensity of the darkness seemed to oppress and stifle me. The atmosphere was intolerably close. I still lay quietly, and made effort to exercise my reason. I brought to mind the inquisitorial proceedings, and attempted from that point to deduce my real condition. The sentence had passed; and it appeared to me that a very long interval of time had since elapsed. Yet not for a moment did I suppose myself actually dead. Such a **supposition**, notwithstanding
110 what we read in fiction, is altogether inconsistent with real existence;—but where and in what state was I? The condemned to death, I knew, perished usually at the *autos-da-fé*,[8] and one of these had been held on the very night of the day of my trial. Had I been remanded to my dungeon, to await the next sacrifice, which would not take place for many months? This I at once saw could not be. Victims had been in immediate demand. Moreover, my dungeon, as well as all the condemned cells at Toledo, had stone floors, and light was not altogether excluded.

A fearful idea now suddenly drove the blood in torrents upon my **G**
120 heart, and for a brief period, I once more relapsed into insensibility. Upon recovering, I at once started to my feet, trembling convulsively in every fiber. I thrust my arms wildly above and around me in all directions. I felt nothing; yet dreaded to move a step, lest I should be impeded by the walls of the *tomb*. Perspiration burst from every pore and stood in cold big beads on my forehead. The agony of suspense grew at length intolerable, and I cautiously moved forward, with my

supposition
(sŭp′ə-zĭsh′ən) *n.* a belief or assumption

[8] **autos-da-fé** (ou′tōz-də-fā′): Portuguese for *acts of faith*; public executions of people condemned by the Inquisition and carried out by the civil authorities.

TO CHALLENGE STUDENTS . . .

Evaluate Writers' Craft When should a writer keep readers "in the dark"? Discuss with students the narrator's fear of the unknown. Then ask them how the reader's situation mirrors that of the narrator. *(Like the narrator, the reader is "in the dark" about where the narrator is and what will happen to him.)*

ASK STUDENTS to discuss in small groups whether they think it is more frightening to readers to show or describe something horrible or to hint at it. Tell students to support their opinions with references to other literature, dramas, or movies.

Image Credits: ©Erik Snyder/Lifesize/Getty Images

arms extended, and my eyes straining from their sockets, in the hope of catching some faint ray of light. I proceeded for many paces; but still all was blackness and vacancy. I breathed more freely. It seemed evident that mine was not, at least, the most hideous of fates.

And now, as I still continued to step cautiously onward, there came thronging upon my recollection a thousand vague rumors of the horrors of Toledo. Of the dungeons there had been strange things narrated—fables I had always deemed them—but yet strange, and too ghastly to repeat, save in a whisper. Was I left to perish of starvation in the subterranean world of darkness; or what fate, perhaps even more fearful, awaited me? That the result would be death, and a death of more than customary bitterness, I knew too well the character of my judges to doubt. The mode and the hour were all that occupied or distracted me.

My outstretched hands at length encountered some solid obstruction. It was a wall, seemingly of stone masonry—very smooth, slimy, and cold. I followed it up! stepping with all the careful distrust with which certain antique narratives had inspired me. This process, however, afforded me no means of ascertaining the dimensions of my dungeon; as I might make its circuit, and return to the point whence I set out, without being aware of the fact; so perfectly uniform seemed the wall. I therefore sought the knife which had been in my pocket, when led into the inquisitorial chamber; but it was gone; my clothes had been exchanged for a wrapper of coarse serge.[9] I had thought of forcing the blade in some minute crevice of the masonry, so as to identify my point of departure. The difficulty, nevertheless, was but trivial; although, in the disorder of my fancy, it seemed at first **insuperable**. I tore a part of the hem from the robe and placed the fragment at full length, and at right angles to the wall. In groping my way around the prison I could not fail to encounter this rag upon completing the circuit. So, at least I thought: but I had not counted upon the extent of the dungeon, or upon my own weakness. The ground was moist and slippery. I staggered onward for some time, when I stumbled and fell. My excessive fatigue induced me to remain **prostrate**; and sleep soon overtook me as I lay.

Upon awakening, and stretching forth an arm, I found beside me a loaf and a pitcher with water. I was too much exhausted to reflect upon this circumstance, but ate and drank with avidity. Shortly afterward, I resumed my tour around the prison, and with much toil, came at last upon the fragment of the serge. Up to the period when I fell I had counted fifty-two paces, and upon resuming my walk, I counted forty-eight more;—when I arrived at the rag. There were in all, then, a hundred paces; and, admitting two paces to the yard, I presumed the dungeon to be fifty yards in circuit. I had met, however, with many

insuperable
(ĭn-sōōʹpər-ə-bəl) *adj.* impossible to overcome.

prostrate
(prŏsʹtrāt´) *adj.* lying down with the head facing downward.

---

[9] **serge** (sûrj): a type of woolen fabric.

TEACH

CLOSE READ

Determine Themes: Romanticism (LINES 128–140)

COMMON CORE RL 2, RL 3, RL 5

Call students' attention to lines 128–130 and ask students why the narrator "breathed more freely." *(Because he didn't find anything horrible in his cell, he assumed that his fate would not be the "most hideous.")*

(H) CITE TEXT EVIDENCE Have students reread lines 128–139 and ask them whether the narrator's hopeful state of mind continues and how they can tell. *(The narrator does not remain hopeful; in lines 137–138 he says that he does not doubt that he faces a bitter death.)* Then ask what happens to cause this change from hope to despair. *(In lines 132–137, the narrator remembers the horrible rumors he has heard about the dungeons of Toledo.)*

CRITICAL VOCABULARY

insuperable: The narrator feels that the challenge of measuring his cell cannot be overcome.

ASK STUDENTS what other tasks might have been insuperable for the narrator. *(figuring out how much time had passed, escaping the cell)*

prostrate: The narrator fell facedown on the floor.

ASK STUDENTS What does the narrator's decision to remain prostrate in lines 160–161 tell you about his state? *(He was so exhausted that he could not even move to a more comfortable position.)*

SCAFFOLDING FOR ELL STUDENTS

Understand Punctuation Call student's attention to Poe's use of dashes in lines 134, 142, and 168. Explain to students that the dash (—) is a punctuation mark used to indicate a break or pause in a sentence, or to set off phrases or clauses that interrupt a sentence.

Then ask students to identify which purpose the dashes in each of the lines above serve. *(line 134: interrupting clause; line 142: break; line 168: break)* Explain that dashes often heighten suspense by creating a pause for effect, or to signal a significant moment of reflection or addition of information. Encourage students to watch for dashes as they read.

Analyze Structure: Atmosphere and Dramatic Tension (LINES 179–196)

COMMON CORE RL 2, RL 3, RL 5

Discuss with students the atmosphere of terror that pervades the description of the narrator's discovery of the pit. Explain that vivid sensory details are essential to the creation of this atmosphere.

Ⓘ CITE TEXT EVIDENCE Have students reread lines 179–196, note the sensory details that contribute to the atmosphere, and tell to which senses each appeals. *("clammy vapor," line 188, touch; "decayed fungus," line 189, smell; "groping," line 192, touch; "I hearkened to its reverberations" and "sullen plunge into water, succeeded by loud echoes," lines 194–196, hearing)*

Determine Themes: Romanticism (LINES 204–210)

COMMON CORE RL 2, RL 3

Remind students what they have inferred so far about the narrator's fears. *(He most fears the unknown.)* Discuss with students why the unknown might be more frightening than something that can be known and seen. *(because the imagination can fill the unknown with an infinite number of terrors)*

Ⓙ CITE TEXT EVIDENCE Have students reread lines 204–210. Ask which they think the narrator fears more, physical agony or moral, meaning psychological, horror. Tell them to support their opinions with evidence from the text. *(The narrator fears the moral horrors more. He says in lines 207–210 that his "nerves had been unstrung" and that he is a "fitting subject" for moral horrors. In addition, we know from the narrator's fear of the unknown that his own imaginings are what frightens him most, so he would be more afraid of psychological torture than physical pain.)*

---

angles in the wall, and thus I could form no guess at the shape of the vault; for vault I could not help supposing it to be.

I had little object—certainly no hope—in these researches; but a vague curiosity prompted me to continue them. Quitting the wall, I resolved to cross the area of the enclosure. At first I proceeded with extreme caution, for the floor, although seemingly of solid material, was treacherous with slime. At length, however, I took courage, and did not hesitate to step firmly; endeavoring to cross in as direct a line as possible. I had advanced some ten or twelve paces in this manner, when the remnant of the torn hem of my robe became entangled between my legs. I stepped on it, and fell violently on my face.

In the confusion attending my fall, I did not immediately apprehend a somewhat startling circumstance, which yet, in a few seconds afterward, and while I still lay prostrate, arrested my attention. It was this—my chin rested upon the floor of the prison, but my lips and the upper portion of my head, although seemingly at a less elevation than the chin, touched nothing. At the same time my forehead seemed bathed in a clammy vapor, and the peculiar smell of decayed fungus arose to my nostrils. I put forward my arm, and shuddered to find that I had fallen at the very brink of a circular pit, whose extent, of course, I had no means of ascertaining at the moment. Groping about the masonry just below the margin, I succeeded in dislodging a small fragment, and let it fall into the abyss. For many seconds I hearkened to its reverberations as it dashed against the sides of the chasm in its descent; at length there was a sullen plunge into water, succeeded by loud echoes. At the same moment there came a sound resembling the quick opening, and as rapid closing of a door overhead, while a faint gleam of light flashed suddenly through the gloom, and as suddenly faded away.

I saw clearly the doom which had been prepared for me, and congratulated myself upon the timely accident by which I had escaped. Another step before my fall, and the world had seen me no more. And the death just avoided, was of that very character which I had regarded as fabulous and frivolous in the tales respecting the Inquisition. To the victims of its tyranny, there was the choice of death with its direst physical agonies, or death with its most hideous moral horrors. I had been reserved for the latter. By long suffering my nerves had been unstrung, until I trembled at the sound of my own voice, and had become in every respect a fitting subject for the species of torture which awaited me.

Shaking in every limb, I groped my way back to the wall; resolving there to perish rather than risk the terrors of the wells, of which my imagination now pictured many in various positions about the dungeon. In other conditions of mind I might have had courage to end my misery at once by a plunge into one of these abysses; but now I was the veriest of cowards. Neither could I forget what I had read of these

WHEN STUDENTS STRUGGLE . . .

Read aloud the long sentence in lines 182–185. Explain that Poe often uses multiple modifying phrases in his sentences. Ask the class to identify the modifying phrases in the sentence you read. *("In the confusion attending my fall," "a few seconds afterward," "and while I still lay prostrate")* Discuss how these modifiers delay the revelation of the "startling circumstance," thus building dramatic tension. Ask students to examine the sentence beginning in line 175 and ending in line 177 and ask them to identify its modifying phrase. *("although seemingly of solid material")* Then ask how the addition of this modifier builds suspense. *(It delays the reader in finding out what the floor is really like.)*

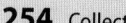

pits—that the *sudden* extinction of life formed no part of their most horrible plan.

220   Agitation of spirit kept me awake for many long hours; but at length I again slumbered. Upon arousing, I found by my side as before, a loaf and a pitcher of water. A burning thirst consumed me, and I emptied the vessel at a draft. It must have been drugged; for scarcely had I drunk, before I became irresistibly drowsy. A deep sleep fell upon me—a sleep like that of death. How long it lasted of course, I know not; but when, once again, I unclosed my eyes, the objects around me were visible. By a wild sulphurous luster,[10] the origin of which I could not at first determine, I was enabled to see the extent and aspect of the prison.

230   In its size I had been greatly mistaken. The whole circuit of its walls did not exceed twenty-five yards. For some minutes this fact occasioned me a world of vain trouble; vain indeed! for what could be of less importance, under the terrible circumstances which environed me, than the mere dimensions of my dungeon? But my soul took a wild interest in trifles, and I busied myself in endeavors to account for the error I had committed in my measurement. The truth at length flashed upon me. In my first attempt at exploration I had counted fifty-two paces, up to the period when I fell; I must then have been within a pace or two of the fragments of serge; in fact, I had nearly performed the circuit of the vault. I then slept, and upon awaking, I

240 must have returned upon my steps—thus supposing the circuit nearly double what it actually was. My confusion of mind prevented me from observing that I began my tour with the wall to the left, and ended it with the wall to the right.

    I had been deceived, too, in respect to the shape of the enclosure. In feeling my way around I had found many angles, and thus deduced an idea of great irregularity; so potent is the effect of total darkness upon one arousing from lethargy or sleep! The angles were simply those of a few slight depressions, or niches, at odd intervals. The general shape of the prison was square. What I had taken for masonry

250 seemed now to be iron, or some other metal, in huge plates, whose sutures or joints occasioned the depression. The entire surface of this metallic enclosure was rudely daubed in all the hideous and repulsive devices to which the charnel superstitions[11] of the monks has given rise. The figures of fiends in aspects of menace, with skeleton forms, and other more really fearful images, overspread and disfigured the walls. I observed that the outlines of these monstrosities were sufficiently distinct, but that the colors seemed faded and blurred, as if from the effects of a damp atmosphere. I now noticed the floor, too, which was of stone. In the center yawned the circular pit from whose

260 jaws I had escaped; but it was the only one in the dungeon.

---

[10] **sulphurous luster:** a pale, yellow glow.
[11] **charnel superstitions:** irrational beliefs about death and dying.

The Pit and the Pendulum   **255**

WHEN STUDENTS STRUGGLE...

Use the narrator's description of the prison to provide practice for students in observing punctuation cues in oral reading. Have students echo you as you read lines 229–243 aloud. Model each sentence and then have students read it aloud together. Finally, have students take turns reading aloud the sentences in the paragraph.

CLOSE READ

Analyze Structure: Atmosphere and Dramatic Tension (LINES 224–260)

COMMON CORE   RL 2, RL 3, RL 5

Call students' attention to the moment when the narrator can first see his prison. Discuss with students how the restoration of the narrator's ability to see and their ability to have the surroundings described makes them feel. (*Accept all reasonable answers; students may be relieved to finally know what they have wondered about for several pages.*)

K   **ASK STUDENTS** whether the narrator finds his prison more or less horrible than he had supposed. How does it differ from what he originally thought? Tell them to cite evidence from the text to support their answers. (*He finds the prison less horrible than he had supposed. He does not express terror at anything he sees, and in line 260 he says that there was only one pit; in lines 211–212 he had imagined that there might be many pits in his cell. He also discovers the cell is smaller [lines 229–230], differently shaped [lines 244–249], and made of different material [lines 249–251] than he originally guessed.*)

Analyze Structure: Atmosphere and Dramatic Tension (LINES 251–259)

COMMON CORE   RL 2, RL 3, RL 5

Call students' attention to the narrator's description of the paintings on the cell walls. Explain that one way writers create atmosphere is by using words with strong connotations, or emotional associations.

L   **CITE TEXT EVIDENCE** Have students reread lines 251–259 and list the words with strong connotations of horror. (hideous, repulsive, fiends, menace, disfigured, monstrosities)

Analyze Structure: Atmosphere and Dramatic Tension (LINES 261–272)

COMMON CORE RL 2, RL 3, RL 5

Point out to students that the narrator spends two long paragraphs describing his prison before he tells the reader that he is tied up.

M **ASK STUDENTS** why the writer waited to let the reader know that the narrator was bound. *(He wanted to reveal new and disturbing details gradually, creating tension about how and why the narrator became bound.)* Then ask what other details are revealed in this paragraph. *(There is a dish of spicy meat next to the narrator but no water. Neither the reader nor the narrator know why this is the case, increasing dramatic tension.)*

Interpret Images (LINES 275–305)

COMMON CORE RL 5

Call students' attention to the painted figure of Time in line 276. Explain that time is sometimes represented by Father Time, an old man holding a scythe—a tool with a long curved blade for cutting crops.

N **ASK STUDENTS** why the writer might have chosen to include this image. *(Poe may have wanted readers to reflect on time's inexorable passage and the mortality it brings.)* Have students identify sensory details describing the pendulum (lines 295–305) and explain their effect. *(Details of sight and sound, such as "sweep of the pendulum had increased," "velocity" was "much greater," it had "descended," "crescent of glittering steel," "razor," "massy and heavy," and "hissed as it swung," all contribute to the dramatic tension.)*

> I could no longer doubt
> the doom prepared for me
> by monkish ingenuity in torture.

M All this I saw distinctly and by much effort: for my personal condition had been greatly changed during slumber. I now lay upon my back, and at full length, on a species of low framework of wood. To this I was securely bound by a long strap resembling a surcingle.[12] It passed in many convolutions about my limbs and body, leaving at liberty only my head, and my left arm to such extent that I could, by dint[13] of much exertion, supply myself with food from an earthen dish which lay by my side on the floor. I saw, to my horror, that the pitcher had been removed. I say to my horror; for I was consumed 270 with intolerable thirst. This thirst it appeared to be the design of my persecutors to stimulate: for the food in the dish was meat pungently seasoned.

Looking upward I surveyed the ceiling of my prison. It was some thirty or forty feet overhead, and constructed much as the side walls. In one of its panels a very singular figure riveted my whole attention. **N** It was the painted figure of Time as he is commonly represented, save that, in lieu of a scythe, he held what, at a casual glance, I supposed to be the pictured image of a huge pendulum such as we see on antique clocks. There was something, however, in the appearance of this 280 machine which caused me to regard it more attentively. While I gazed directly upward at it (for its position was immediately over my own) I fancied that I saw it in motion. In an instant afterward the fancy was confirmed. Its sweep was brief, and of course slow. I watched it for some minutes, somewhat in fear, but more in wonder. Wearied at length with observing its dull movement, I turned my eyes upon the other objects in the cell.

A slight noise attracted my notice, and, looking to the floor, I saw several enormous rats traversing it. They had issued from the well, which lay just within view to my right. Even then, while I gazed, they 290 came up in troops, hurriedly, with ravenous eyes, allured by the scent of the meat. From this it required much effort and attention to scare them away.

---

[12] **surcingle:** a belt used to hold a saddle or pack onto a horse's back.
[13] **dint:** force.

It might have been half an hour, perhaps even an hour, (for I could take but imperfect note of time) before I again cast my eyes upward. What I then saw confounded and amazed me. The sweep of the pendulum had increased in extent by nearly a yard. As a natural consequence, its velocity was also much greater. But what mainly disturbed me was the idea that it had perceptibly *descended*. I now observed—with what horror it is needless to say—that its nether
300 extremity was formed of a crescent of glittering steel, about a foot in length from horn to horn; the horns upward, and the under edge evidently as keen as that of a razor. Like a razor also, it seemed massy and heavy, tapering from the edge into a solid and broad structure above. It was appended to a weighty rod of brass, and the whole *hissed* as it swung through the air.

I could no longer doubt the doom prepared for me by monkish ingenuity in torture. My cognizance of the pit had become known to the inquisitorial agents—*the pit* whose horrors had been destined for so bold a recusant[14] as myself—*the pit*, typical of hell, and regarded
310 by rumor as the Ultima Thule[15] of all their punishments. The plunge into this pit I had avoided by the merest of accidents, and I knew that surprise, or entrapment into torment, formed an important portion of all the grotesquerie of these dungeon deaths. Having failed to fall, it was no part of the demon plan to hurl me into the abyss; and thus (there being no alternative) a different and a milder destruction awaited me. Milder! I half smiled in my agony as I thought of such application of such a term.

What boots it[16] to tell of the long, long hours of horror more than mortal, during which I counted the rushing vibrations of the
320 steel! Inch by inch—line by line—with a descent only appreciable at intervals that seemed ages—down and still down it came! Days passed—it might have been that many days passed—ere it swept so closely over me as to fan me with its acrid breath. The odor of the sharp steel forced itself into my nostrils. I prayed—I wearied heaven with my prayer for its more speedy descent. I grew frantically mad, and struggled to force myself upward against the sweep of the fearful scimitar.[17] And then I fell suddenly calm, and lay smiling at the glittering death, as a child at some rare bauble.

There was another interval of utter insensibility; it was brief; for,
330 upon again lapsing into life there had been no perceptible descent in the pendulum. But it might have been long; for I knew there were demons who took note of my swoon, and who could have arrested the vibration at pleasure. Upon my recovery, too, I felt very—oh,

---

[14] **recusant:** a heretic or dissident.

[15] **Ultima Thule** (ŭl´tə-mə thōō´lē): according to ancient geographers, the most remote region of the world—here used figuratively to mean "most extreme achievement; summit."

[16] **What boots it?:** What good is it?

[17] **scimitar:** a curved sword of Middle Eastern origin.

The Pit and the Pendulum **257**

CLOSE READ

Analyze Structure: Atmosphere and Dramatic Tension (LINES 307–310)

COMMON CORE RL 2, RL 3, RL 5

Remind students that the reader knows little about the narrator's crime. Call their attention to the sentence in lines 307–310. Discuss with students the narrator's description of himself as a "bold recusant," or heretic, and the information about the pit as the worst of the Inquisition's punishments.

O ASK STUDENTS to describe the effect on the reader of leaving the reasons for which the narrator was condemned unspecified. (*Accept all reasonable answers. Some may feel that leaving the reasons for his condemnation unspecified makes this punishment seem crueler and more arbitrary, or that the lack of information makes it easier for the reader to identify with the narrator.*)

Interpret Images

COMMON CORE RL 5

(LINES 318–325)

Remind students that the pendulum is attached to a painted image of Father Time, who symbolizes the passage of time and the death and decay it brings.

P CITE TEXT EVIDENCE Ask students whether it is fitting that the image of Father Time is attached to the pendulum and why or why not. Have them cite evidence to support their answers. (*The image is appropriate because the pendulum comes slowly closer over time. This torture makes time seem longer to the narrator. He says the pendulum seemed to descend for "long, long hours" [line 318], "ages" and "days" [line 321], and "many days" [line 322]. The passage of time itself becomes a torture, and in lines 324–325 the narrator prays that the pendulum would descend more quickly.*)

SCAFFOLDING FOR ELL STUDENTS

Understand Archaic Language Call students' attention to the phrase "What boots it" in line 318. Tell them that *boots* in this phrase means "gives an advantage or benefit." Although it is spelled the same, it is a different word from the one that refers to footwear. Explain that in addition to its verb form, *boot* can also be used as an adjective or an adverb.

- bootless: useless
- bootlessly: uselessly

Encourage students to watch for other archaic words as they read and to look them up in a dictionary.

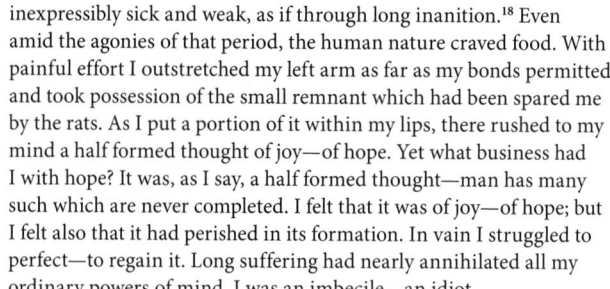

CLOSE READ

Determine Themes: Romanticism (LINES 334–344)

COMMON CORE RL 2, RL 3, RL 5

Point out to students the emotional peaks and lows that the narrator experiences as he lies waiting for death.

Q ASK STUDENTS to describe the narrator's emotions and explain the effect on the story. *(In line 334, he feels "sick and weak"; in line 336, he makes a "painful effort"; in lines 339 and 341, he feels "joy" and "hope"; and in line 343, he feels "annihilated." These emotions contribute to the Romantics' fascination with madness and death.)*

> #### CRITICAL VOCABULARY
>
> **pertinacity:** The narrator keeps his mind on his belief that for several minutes the pendulum will cut only his robe.
>
> **ASK STUDENTS** why the narrator chooses to focus on the pendulum cutting his robe with such a "pertinacity of attention"? *(because he is afraid to think about what will happen after the pendulum cuts the robe)*

Analyze Structure: Atmosphere and Dramatic Tension (LINES 358–377)

COMMON CORE RL 2, RL 3, RL 5

Call students' attention to the fact that the last three paragraphs on the page begin with the word *down*.

R ASK STUDENTS how the repetition of the word *down* at the beginning of each paragraph increases the dramatic tension. *(The repetition of the word down mimics the relentless, rhythmic nature of the pendulum's sweep and descent.)* Then ask how the narrator's state of mind changes as the pendulum descends. *(First, he becomes increasingly unnerved as he carefully observes the pendulum's descent. As it drops closer, he struggles to free himself. As it drops still closer, he cringes and shakes in terror.)*

Q inexpressibly sick and weak, as if through long inanition.[18] Even amid the agonies of that period, the human nature craved food. With painful effort I outstretched my left arm as far as my bonds permitted, and took possession of the small remnant which had been spared me by the rats. As I put a portion of it within my lips, there rushed to my mind a half formed thought of joy—of hope. Yet what business had
340 I with hope? It was, as I say, a half formed thought—man has many such which are never completed. I felt that it was of joy—of hope; but I felt also that it had perished in its formation. In vain I struggled to perfect—to regain it. Long suffering had nearly annihilated all my ordinary powers of mind. I was an imbecile—an idiot.

The vibration of the pendulum was at right angles to my length. I saw that the crescent was designed to cross the region of the heart. It would fray the serge of my robe—it would return and repeat its operations—again—and again. Notwithstanding its terrifically wide sweep (some thirty feet or more) and the hissing vigor of its descent,
350 sufficient to sunder these very walls of iron, still the fraying of my robe would be all that, for several minutes, it would accomplish. And at this thought I paused. I dared not go farther than this reflection. I dwelt upon it with a **pertinacity** of attention—as if, in so dwelling, I could arrest *here* the descent of the steel. I forced myself to ponder upon the sound of the crescent as it should pass across the garment—upon the peculiar thrilling sensation which the friction of cloth produces on the nerves. I pondered upon all this frivolity until my teeth were on edge.

R Down—steadily down it crept. I took a frenzied pleasure in contrasting its downward with its lateral velocity. To the right—to the
360 left—far and wide—with the shriek of a . . . spirit; to my heart with the stealthy pace of the tiger! I alternately laughed and howled as the one or the other idea grew predominant.

Down—certainly, relentlessly down! It vibrated within three inches of my bosom! I struggled violently, furiously, to free my left arm. This was free only from the elbow to the hand. I could reach the latter, from the platter beside me, to my mouth, with great effort, but no farther. Could I have broken the fastenings above the elbow, I would have seized and attempted to arrest the pendulum. I might as well have attempted to arrest an avalanche!
370 Down—still unceasingly—still inevitably down! I gasped and struggled at each vibration. I shrunk convulsively at its every sweep. My eyes followed its outward or upward whirls with the eagerness of the most unmeaning despair; they closed themselves spasmodically at the descent, although death would have been a relief, oh! how unspeakable! Still I quivered in every nerve to think how slight a sinking of the machinery would precipitate that keen, glistening axe upon my bosom. It was *hope* that prompted the nerve to quiver—the

pertinacity
(pûr´tn-ăs´ĭ-tē) *n.* firm, unyielding intent.

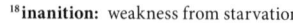

[18] **inanition:** weakness from starvation.

SCAFFOLDING FOR ELL STUDENTS

Understand Interjections Call students' attention to the word *oh* in line 374. Explain that *oh* is an interjection—a word or short phrase that expresses emotion and can stand alone. Explain that interjections are usually followed by an exclamation point and that they often begin with the word *how;* for example, *How beautiful!* Ask students to give examples of interjections from their first languages. Encourage students to watch for interjections as they read.

frame to shrink. It was *hope*—the hope that triumphs on the rack[19]—
that whispers to the death-condemned even in the dungeons of the
380   Inquisition.

    I saw that some ten or twelve vibrations would bring the steel in
actual contact with my robe, and with this observation there suddenly
came over my spirit all the keen, collected calmness of despair. For
the first time during many hours—or perhaps days—I *thought*. It
now occurred to me that the bandage, or surcingle, which enveloped
me, was *unique*. I was tied by no separate cord. The first stroke of
the razor-like crescent athwart[20] any portion of the band, would so
detach it that it might be unwound from my person by means of my
left hand. But how fearful, in that case, the proximity of the steel! The
390   result of the slightest struggle how deadly! Was it likely, moreover,
that the minions[21] of the torturer had not foreseen and provided for
this possibility! Was it probable that the bandage crossed my bosom
in the track of the pendulum? Dreading to find my faint, and, as it
seemed, my last hope frustrated, I so far elevated my head as to obtain
a distinct view of my breast. The surcingle enveloped my limbs and
body close in all directions—*save in the path of the destroying crescent.*

    Scarcely had I dropped my head back into its original position,
when there flashed upon my mind what I cannot better describe
than as the unformed half of that idea of deliverance to which
400   I have previously alluded, and of which a moiety[22] only floated
indeterminately through my brain when I raised food to my burning

---

[19] **rack:** a device for torture that stretches the victim's limbs.
[20] **athwart:** across, from one side to the other.
[21] **minions:** followers, servants.
[22] **moiety:** one of two equal parts.

The Pit and the Pendulum **259**

CLOSE READ

Determine Themes: Romanticism (LINES 381–402)

COMMON CORE RL 2, RL 3, RL 5

Read aloud to students the sentence that begins in line 378. Discuss with students what the narrator might mean by saying that it was hope that made him shrink away from the sharp blade. (*If he hadn't had any hope of remaining alive, he wouldn't have shrunk in horror away from death.*)

(S) CITE TEXT EVIDENCE Ask students what gives the narrator hope in lines 381–402. (*the realization that he was tied by only one cord and that the blade of the pendulum could cut him free [lines 384–388], and he realizes he now has a complete plan of action to free himself [lines 397–401]*)

Analyze Structure: Atmosphere and Dramatic Tension (LINES 389–395)

COMMON CORE RL 2, RL 3, RL 5

Direct students' attention to the five sentences in lines 389–395 in which the narrator thinks about the possibility of using the pendulum blade to cut the cord with which he is bound.

(T) ASK STUDENTS why Poe includes these sentences and what effect they have on the reader. (*Poe includes them to delay the moment when the reader finds out that the blade will not cross the cord, thus building suspense. By telling the reader all of the narrator's thoughts, hopes, and fears, Poe makes the reader experience the same emotions as the narrator.*)

WHEN STUDENTS STRUGGLE...

Point out to students the word *unique* in line 386. Explain that in this line Poe uses a secondary, or less common, meaning of the word and ask students to use context clues to guess this meaning. Guide students to determine that it means "the only one of its kind." Point out that in lines 386–389, the narrator explains that if the cord were cut in one place, the entire thing could be removed. Then guide students to conclude that Poe uses *unique* to mean "single."

Analyze Structure: Atmosphere and Dramatic Tension (LINES 402–409)

COMMON CORE RL 2, RL 3, RL 5

Have students reread lines 402–409 and point out that the narrator doesn't give any details about the plan that has given him hope.

U **ASK STUDENTS** why Poe might have kept this information from the reader. *(He wanted the reader to be surprised by the details of the plan.)*

Analyze Structure: Atmosphere and Dramatic Tension (LINES 428–432)

COMMON CORE RL 2, RL 3, RL 5

Discuss with students the scene in which the rats swarm over the narrator. Ask them to share their reactions to the scene.

V **CITE TEXT EVIDENCE** Ask students how Poe conveys the sensation of the swarming rats. Tell them to support their answer with evidence from the text. *(He gives sensory details related to touch such as "writhed upon my throat," "cold lips," and "thronging pressure.")*

lips. The whole thought was now present—feeble, scarcely sane, scarcely definite,—but still entire. I proceeded at once, with the nervous energy of despair, to attempt its execution.

For many hours the immediate vicinity of the low framework upon which I lay, had been literally swarming with rats. They were wild, bold, ravenous; their red eyes glaring upon me as if they waited but for motionlessness on my part to make me their prey. "To what food," I thought, "have they been accustomed in the well?"

410 They had devoured, in spite of all my efforts to prevent them, all but a small remnant of the contents of the dish. I had fallen into an habitual seesaw, or wave of the hand about the platter, and, at length, the unconscious uniformity of the movement deprived it of effect. In their voracity the vermin frequently fastened their sharp fangs into my fingers. With the particles of the oily and spicy viand[23] which now remained, I thoroughly rubbed the bandage wherever I could reach it; then, raising my hand from the floor, I lay breathlessly still.

At first the ravenous animals were startled and terrified at the change—at the cessation of movement. They shrank alarmedly

420 back; many sought the well. But this was only for a moment. I had not counted in vain upon their voracity. Observing that I remained without motion, one or two of the boldest leaped upon the framework, and smelt at the surcingle. This seemed the signal for a general rush. Forth from the well they hurried in fresh troops. They clung to the wood—they overran it, and leaped in hundreds upon my person. The measured movement of the pendulum disturbed them not at all. Avoiding its strokes they busied themselves with the anointed bandage. They pressed—they swarmed upon me in ever accumulating heaps. They writhed upon my throat; their cold lips sought my own;

430 I was half stifled by their thronging pressure; disgust, for which the world has no name, swelled my bosom, and chilled, with a heavy clamminess, my heart. Yet one minute, and I felt that the struggle would be over. Plainly I perceived the loosening of the bandage. I knew that in more than one place it must be already severed. With a more than human resolution I lay *still*.

Nor had I erred in my calculations—nor had I endured in vain. I at length felt that I was *free*. The surcingle hung in ribands from my body. But the stroke of the pendulum already pressed upon my bosom. It had divided the serge of the robe. It had cut through the

440 linen beneath. Twice again it swung, and a sharp sense of pain shot through every nerve. But the moment of escape had arrived. At a wave of my hand my deliverers hurried tumultuously away. With a steady movement—cautious, sidelong, shrinking, and slow—I slid from the embrace of the bandage and beyond the reach of the scimitar. For the moment, at least, *I was free*.

---

[23]**viand:** food.

TO CHALLENGE STUDENTS . . .

Mimic the Writer's Style Discuss with students the elements of Poe's writing style, emphasizing the following:

- the use of dashes
- the use of italics
- the use of words with strong connotations

ASK STUDENTS to choose a familiar scene, such as feeding a pet, doing laundry, or eating a meal and describe it in a short paragraph mimicking Poe's style. Then have students read their paragraphs aloud in small groups.

Free!—and in the grasp of the Inquisition! I had scarcely stepped
from my wooden bed of horror upon the stone floor of the prison,
when the motion of the hellish machine ceased and I beheld it drawn
up, by some invisible force, through the ceiling. This was a lesson
450　which I took desperately to heart. My every motion was undoubtedly
watched. Free!—I had but escaped death in one form of agony, to be
delivered unto worse than death in some other. With that thought I
rolled my eyes nervously around the barriers of iron that hemmed
me in. Something unusual—some change which at first I could
not appreciate distinctly—it was obvious, had taken place in the
apartment. For many minutes in a dreamy and trembling abstraction,
I busied myself in vain, unconnected conjecture. During this period, I
became aware, for the first time, of the origin of the sulphurous light
which illuminated the cell. It proceeded from a fissure, about half an
460　inch in width, extending entirely around the prison at the base of the
walls, which thus appeared, and were, completely separated from the
floor. I endeavored, but of course in vain, to look through the aperture.

As I arose from the attempt, the mystery of the alteration in the
chamber broke at once upon my understanding. I have observed that,
although the outlines of the figures upon the walls were sufficiently
distinct, yet the colors seemed blurred and indefinite. These colors had
now assumed, and were momentarily assuming, a startling and most
intense brilliancy, that gave to the spectral and fiendish portraitures
an aspect that might have thrilled even firmer nerves than my own.
470　Demon eyes, of a wild and ghastly vivacity, glared upon me in a
thousand directions, where none had been visible before, and gleamed
with the lurid luster of a fire that I could not force my imagination to
regard as unreal.

Unreal!—Even while I breathed there came to my nostrils the
breath of the vapor of heated iron! A suffocating odor pervaded the
prison! A deeper glow settled each moment in the eyes that glared at
my agonies! A richer tint of crimson diffused itself over the pictured
horrors of blood. I panted! I gasped for breath! There could be no
doubt of the design of my tormentors—oh! most unrelenting! oh! most
480　demoniac of men! I shrank from the glowing metal to the center of the
cell. Amid the thought of the fiery destruction that impended, the idea
of the coolness of the well came over my soul like balm. I rushed to its
deadly brink. I threw my straining vision below. The glare from the
enkindled roof illumined its inmost recesses. Yet, for a wild moment,
did my spirit refuse to comprehend the meaning of what I saw. At
length it forced—it wrestled its way into my soul—it burned itself in
upon my shuddering reason.—Oh! for a voice to speak!—oh! horror!—
oh! any horror but this! With a shriek, I rushed from the margin, and
buried my face in my hands—weeping bitterly.

WHEN STUDENTS STRUGGLE . . .

Look for examples of these verb tenses in lines 464–469.

Tense	Formation	Function
past	-d or -ed	tells about past actions
past progressive	was or were + present participle	tells about actions that ongoing in the past
present perfect	have or has + past participle	tells about actions completed before the present time
past perfect	had + past participle	tells about an action that took place before some specific time in the past

CLOSE READ

Analyze Structure: Atmosphere and Dramatic Tension (LINES 470–475)

COMMON CORE　RL 2, RL 3, RL 5

Ask students to describe what is happening in lines 470–475. (*The metal walls are being heated from the outside by fire.*) Point out that Poe does not state what is happening but gives readers sensory details from which they can make an inference.

W CITE TEXT EVIDENCE Ask students to explain which sensory details give readers the information they need to infer that the walls are being heated by fire. (*"Demon eyes…gleamed with the lurid luster of a fire"; "the breath of the vapor of heated iron"*). Why does Poe use sensory details from which readers must infer the situation, rather than stating it directly? (*Poe increases the horrifying uncertainty of the scene and readers' identification with the terrified narrator by suggesting, rather than stating, what occurs.*)

Determine Themes: Romanticism (LINES 483–489)

COMMON CORE　RL 2, RL 3, RL 5

Remind students of the narrator's fear of the unknown. Review lines 483–489 in which the narrator is able to see into the pit.

X ASK STUDENTS how Poe conveys the horror of the pit. (*by saying that the narrator had a hard time understanding what he saw, by having him exclaim in horror and shriek, and by having him rush away from the pit toward the red-hot iron walls*) Then ask why they think Poe might choose not to tell readers what the narrator saw in the pit. (*The reader can infer that whatever is in the pit is more terrifying than the prospect of being burned by the hot iron. He might believe that nothing he could describe would be as terrifying as what the reader might imagine.*)

Determine Themes: Romanticism (LINES 508–513)

COMMON CORE RL 2, RL 3, RL 5

Discuss with students the things that have frightened the narrator so far in the story. *(the dark, the unknown, the pendulum, the heated iron walls)*

 **CITE TEXT EVIDENCE** Ask students to identify the narrator's ultimate fear. *(whatever he saw in the pit)* Then ask them to describe the narrator's state of mind as he teeters on the brink of the pit, citing supporting details from the text. *(He has finally given up hope. He says he "struggled no more" [line 511], screamed in despair [line 512], and averted his eyes [line 513].)*

Analyze Structure: Atmosphere and Dramatic Tension (LINES 514–519)

COMMON CORE RL 2, RL 3, RL 5

Discuss the abruptness of the story's ending.

Ⓩ ASK STUDENTS why they think Poe might have ended the story so abruptly. *(The story is about the narrator's interior response to his imprisonment and torture, so once the torture ends, so does the story.)* Have students discuss whether the protagonist is actually rescued. *(Poe's techniques make it impossible for the reader to distinguish between what is truly happening and what is imagined by the narrator. Perhaps he does not escape his fate and instead imagines his rescue at the last possible moment, or maybe he has lost his mind and tumbled into the abyss of insanity in order to "survive" the horrors of the pit and burning walls.)*

> **CRITICAL VOCABULARY**
>
> **avert**: When he is about to fall into the pit, the narrator looks away.
>
> **ASK STUDENTS** why the narrator averts his eyes before he falls. *(He doesn't want to see whatever is waiting for him in the pit.)*

COLLABORATIVE DISCUSSION Have student pairs identify three specific elements Poe uses to create a mood of terror. Share cited examples with the class.

---

490   The heat rapidly increased, and once again I looked up, shuddering as with a fit of the ague.[24] There had been a second change in the cell—and now the change was obviously in the form. As before, it was in vain that I, at first, endeavored to appreciate or understand what was taking place. But not long was I left in doubt. The Inquisitorial vengeance had been hurried by my twofold escape, and there was to be no more dallying with the King of Terrors. The room had been square. I saw that two of its iron angles were now acute—two, consequently, obtuse. The fearful difference quickly increased with a low rumbling or moaning sound. In an instant the apartment

500   had shifted its form into that of a lozenge. But the alteration stopped not here—I neither hoped nor desired it to stop. I could have clasped the red walls to my bosom as a garment of eternal peace. "Death," I said, "any death but that of the pit!" Fool! might I have not known that *into the pit* it was the object of the burning iron to urge me? Could I resist its glow? or, if even that, could I withstand its pressure? And now, flatter and flatter grew the lozenge, with a rapidity that left me no time for contemplation. Its center, and of course, its greatest width, came just over the yawning gulf. I shrank back—but the closing walls pressed me resistlessly onward. At length for my seared and writhing

510   body there was no longer an inch of foothold on the firm floor of the prison. I struggled no more, but the agony of my soul found vent in one loud, long, and final scream of despair. I felt that I tottered upon the brink—I **averted** my eyes—

There was a discordant hum of human voices! There was a loud blast of many trumpets! There was a harsh grating as of a thousand thunders! The fiery walls rushed back! An outstretched arm caught my own as I fell, fainting, into the abyss. It was that of General Lasalle. The French army had entered Toledo. The Inquisition was in the hands of its enemies.

avert
(ə-vûrt´) *v.* to turn away

---

[24] **ague:** an illness, like malaria, that causes fever and shivering.

COLLABORATIVE DISCUSSION What elements of the story contribute to a mood of terror? Discuss the effectiveness of these elements with a partner. Cite specific examples from the story to support your reasoning.

SCAFFOLDING FOR ELL STUDENTS

Identify Geometrical Terms Tell students that Poe uses several terms from geometry in his description of the changes in the room's size and shape. Help students to identify and define the following words:

- *square,* line 497: a four-sided shape with equal sides and right angles
- *acute,* line 497: forming an angle of less than ninety degrees
- *obtuse,* line 498: forming an angle of more than ninety degrees
- *lozenge,* line 500: a four-sided shape with two acute and two obtuse angles

  *eBook Annotate It!*

Determine Themes: Romanticism

 COMMON CORE **RL 2**

Although Romanticism generally conveys a sense of optimism, Gothic literature exhibits a unique fascination with the darker aspects of human nature. In contrast to Hawthorne's exploration of common fears and everyday behaviors, Poe confronts sheer terror and the grotesque. As you explore the central ideas, or themes, of "The Pit and the Pendulum," consider the following:

- What does the narrator fear most and why?
- How do the narrator's changing states of consciousness affect the story?

Analyze Structure: Atmosphere and Dramatic Tension

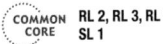 COMMON CORE **RL 3, RL 5**

A writer's decisions about how to structure a plot contribute to a story's overall meaning and impact. For example, the structure of "The Pit and the Pendulum" helps build dramatic tension and create an atmosphere of terror. As you analyze this structure, consider the impact of Poe's choices about where to begin and end the story and about how to gradually reveal details of the narrator's plight.

Analyzing the Text

COMMON CORE **RL 2, RL 3, RL 5, SL 1**

Cite Text Evidence   Support your responses with evidence from the selection.

1. **Interpret** Poe opens "The Pit and the Pendulum" by describing the narrator's sickening agony of awaiting his sentence. How does this beginning contribute to the meaning of the story? Quote vivid details in your interpretation.

2. **Infer** The narrator is often uncertain about how much time has elapsed and about the physical details of the prison. What does this uncertainty suggest about the narrator's state of mind?

3. **Analyze** Poe's narrator tells us almost nothing of his past; his personal qualities are revealed through his responses to the horrors of imprisonment. What do we know about him? What aspects of his personality allow him to survive this ordeal?

4. **Evaluate** Identify elements of Gothic fiction in "The Pit and the Pendulum." Choose one element and explain its importance to one of the story's central ideas.

PERFORMANCE TASK

Speaking Activity: Discussion In his essay "The Philosophy of Composition," Poe writes that "close circumscription of space is absolutely necessary to the effect of insulated incident—it has the force of a frame to a picture." In a small group, discuss how "The Pit and the Pendulum" demonstrates Poe's idea about confined spaces. Quote and analyze specific details to support your response.

PRACTICE & APPLY

Determine Themes: Romanticism

COMMON CORE **RL 2**

Explain to students that Romanticism as a movement focused on individual experience, powerful thoughts and emotions, and the role of imagination. Discuss Poe's intense focus on the narrator's thoughts and emotions.

Analyze Structure: Atmosphere and Dramatic Tension

COMMON CORE **RL 3, RL 5**

Remind students of the structure of Poe's plot. Tell them that he begins the story in the middle of the action, just as the narrator is sentenced, and very gradually reveals the details of his prison and his punishments. He ends the story immediately after the narrator is rescued. Discuss with students what this structure suggests about the story's overall meaning. *(The structure suggests that the overall meaning is concerned with the mind and its struggle between hope and despair, rationality and insanity.)*

Analyzing the Text

COMMON CORE **RL 2, RL 3, RL 5**

Possible answers:

1. *The opening focuses immediately on the narrator's terrified mental state. He says that the voices of the judges were a "dreamy indeterminate hum" (lines 12–13), that their lips were whiter than paper (lines 17–18), and that the lips writhed (line 22).*

2. *that his mind is not entirely sharp*

3. *We know that he is in prison and under sentence of death for being a heretic. Instead of giving in to despair, he tries to reason about his situation (line 105) and explore his prison (lines 141–170). His hopefulness and resourcefulness help him to survive when he gets the rats to gnaw through his bonds (lines 415–430).*

4. *Elements of Gothic fiction include its emphasis on the dark side of human nature, the grotesque tortures inflicted on the narrator by the Inquisition, and the terror in the narrator's response to those tortures. They illustrate that there is a fine and very subjective line between reality and imagination, sanity and insanity.*

PERFORMANCE TASK

COMMON CORE **SL 1**

Speaking Activity: Discussion Direct students to the Performance Task and read the quotation from Poe. Ask them to explain what the quote says about closed-in spaces. Divide students in small groups to discuss how the quotation applies to "The Pit and the Pendulum." Remind them to cite evidence from the text to support their opinions. After the small group discussions, have a representative from each group share the group's findings with the class.

PRACTICE & APPLY

Critical Vocabulary

COMMON CORE L 4a, L 4d

Answers:

1. *Antonyms*

2. *Synonyms*

3. *Synonyms*

4. *Antonyms*

5. *Synonyms*

6. *Antonyms*

7. *Antonyms*

8. *Antonyms*

Vocabulary Strategy: Context Clues

Suggest that pairs of students find and determine the meanings of three unknown words. When the pairs are finished, have volunteers share with the class the process of reasoning they used to determine the meaning of a word from context clues.

Critical Vocabulary

COMMON CORE L 4a, L 4d

indeterminate	lucid	tumultuous	supposition
insuperable	prostrate	pertinacity	averted

Practice and Apply Indicate whether the words in each pair are synonyms or antonyms.

1. precise/indeterminate
2. supposition/assumption
3. lucid/clear
4. concentrated/averted

5. insuperable/unconquerable
6. erect/prostrate
7. tumultuous/subdued
8. reluctance/pertinacity

Vocabulary Strategy: Context Clues

When you come across an unfamiliar word in a text, you can use **context clues,** or information in surrounding phrases and sentences, to determine the word's meaning. For example, you can use context clues to determine the meaning of the Critical Vocabulary word *indeterminate* in this passage from "The Pit and the Pendulum":

> I was sick—sick unto death with that long agony; and when they at length unbound me, and I was permitted to sit, I felt that my senses were leaving me. The sentence—the dread sentence of death—was the last of distinct accentuation which reached my ears. After that, the sound of the inquisitorial voices merged in one dreamy indeterminate hum.

The word *dreamy* provides a clue that *indeterminate* means "not precisely known." The clause "I felt that my senses were leaving me" in the first sentence also hints at this meaning. In addition, the word *distinct* contrasts what the narrator hears when the sentence is announced from the sound of the voices that follow.

Practice and Apply Work with a partner to use context clues to help determine or clarify the meaning of unknown words. Follow these steps:

- Identify unfamiliar words in the story.
- Look for synonyms, antonyms, and other clues in surrounding words and sentences that help you infer the word's meaning.
- Verify your preliminary determination of each word's meaning by checking the dictionary definition.

Strategies for Annotation   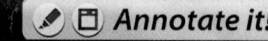 *Annotate it!*

Vocabulary Strategies: Context Clues

COMMON CORE L 4a, L 4d

Have students reinforce their understanding of context clues by finding the words *acrid* (line 323) and *cessation* (line 419) in the text. Encourage them to use their eBook annotation tools to do the following:

- Highlight each of these words in pink.
- Highlight in green the words nearby that give insight into the meaning of the words in pink.
- Guess the definition and verify it in the dictionary.

> Days passed—it might have been that many days passed—ere it swept so closely over me as to fan me with its acrid breath. The odor of the sharp steel forced itself into my nostrils.

Language and Style: Semicolons

A writer's **style** is the particular way in which he or she uses language to communicate ideas. One characteristic of Edgar Allan Poe's distinctive, innovative style is his use of **semicolons** to create long, interrupted sentences that mirror his narrator's frantic or disturbed states of mind. Notice the effects of the semicolon in this sentence from "The Pit and the Pendulum":

> He who has never swooned, is not he who finds strange palaces and wildly familiar faces in coals that glow; is not he who beholds floating in midair the sad visions that the many may not view; is not he who ponders over the perfume of some novel flower—is not he whose brain grows bewildered with the meaning of some musical cadence which has never before arrested his attention.

The semicolons help create a long, digressive sentence that draws attention to double negatives. It also asks the reader to contemplate the joy that people miss by not allowing their minds to wander in and out of varying states of consciousness and reality.

Here are some ways that semicolons function in sentences:

Semicolons	
Purpose	**Example**
to separate two independent clauses that are linked by a conjunction (*and* or *but*), especially when the parts contain a number of commas	How long it lasted of course, I know not; but when, once again, I unclosed my eyes, the objects around me were visible. (lines 224–226)
to separate parts of a compound sentence that are not joined by a coordinating conjunction or an adverb	They shrank alarmedly back; many sought the well. (lines 419–420)
to link an independent clause with another independent clause preceded by an adverb (*then, however, thus,* or *therefore*) to closely connect the two ideas	With the particles of the oily and spicy viand which now remained, I thoroughly rubbed the bandage wherever I could reach it; then, raising my hand from the floor, I lay breathlessly still. (lines 415–417)

Practice and Apply With a partner, discuss Poe's use of semicolons in "The Pit and the Pendulum." Follow these steps:

- Identify passages in which Poe effectively uses semicolons.
- Prepare for the discussion by revising sentences to remove the semicolons and consider how this change affects tone and meaning.

PRACTICE & APPLY

Language and Style: Semicolons

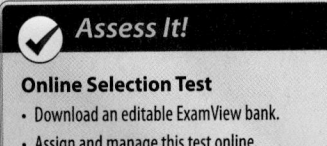

Point out to students that in the quotation, in place of what would be the last semicolon of the series, Poe instead uses a dash to represent an even stronger break than that represented by a semicolon.

Answers:

Students should find an example in which several clauses are connected by semicolons. Possible examples include lines 34–40 and lines 144–148.

✓ Assess It!

Online Selection Test
- Download an editable ExamView bank.
- Assign and manage this test online.

PRACTICE & APPLY

Themes in American Romanticism

COMMON CORE RL 2, RL 3, RL 5, RL 9, W 9a

Review the term *Romanticism* with the class. Discuss the idea that Hawthorne and Poe represent two different strains of Romanticism. Both Poe and Hawthorne explored the darker side of Romanticism than did earlier Romanticists. Hawthorne examined the darker aspects of the human soul—the psychological effects that sin and guilt have on human life. Poe, however, was a true Gothic in that he explored human psychology through first-person narrators who were involved in physical and mental torture.

Analyzing the Texts

COMMON CORE RL2, RL3, RL5

1. *"The Minister's Black Veil" is set in a small New England town, while "The Pit and the Pendulum" is set in the depths of an old Spanish prison. A small town in which people considered their piety of utmost importance is an appropriate setting for probing the human nature of religious people. A prison is an appropriate setting in which to explore human responses to grotesque punishment.*

2. *Poe lets the reader into the mind of the narrator to understand how he thinks and how he survives, but not who he is. Hawthorne does not let the reader into the mind of the minister, but characterizes him through his impact on other people.*

3. *Answers will vary, but should include clear examples of word choice, imagery, and plot details that contribute to the dark and ominous mood of each story.*

4. *Poe does not tell who the narrator is or what brought about his punishment. Hawthorne does not tell why the minister wears the veil. In both cases, this ambiguity makes the reader focus on the reaction rather than the circumstances themselves. Poe focuses on the narrator's response to torture, and Hawthorne focuses on the townspeople's response to the veil.*

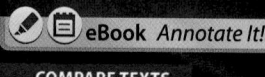
Themes in American Romanticism

COMMON CORE RL 9

Comparing works of literature from the same historical period can deepen your understanding of each work's themes and provide an insight into issues and ideas important within the social context of the time. "The Minister's Black Veil" and "The Pit and the Pendulum" are both American short stories written in the first half of the nineteenth century—published in 1836 and 1843, respectively. They represent two different strains of American Romanticism. Poe is considered a master of Gothic literature. Hawthorne's work is more subtle and more psychologically probing.

Romanticism broke with the rigid formality of previous literary movements. It emphasized the power of the individual artist. The artist, once freed from artificial constraints and forms, could explore ideas and emotions that spoke to his or her personal experiences or flowed from a unique imagination.

Analyzing the Texts

COMMON CORE RL 2, RL 3, RL 5, RL 9, W 9a

Cite Text Evidence   Support your responses with evidence from the selections.

1. **Cite Evidence** What is the setting of each story? What evidence from the texts reveals the setting? How does each setting relate to ideas and themes the writer presents?

2. **Understand** Compare and contrast the techniques each author uses to characterize, or reveal the distinctive traits of, the main character in each story.

3. **Analyze** Select two short passages from each story and identify details that contribute to a dark and ominous mood. Consider word choice, imagery, and plot details in your response.

4. **Analyze** How does each author use ambiguity or uncertainty to add interest and to advance his themes? Cite an example of ambiguity in each story and describe its effect.

PERFORMANCE TASK

Writing Activity: Analysis Reread the American Romanticism essay on page 234. In a one-page essay, describe how "The Minister's Black Veil" and "The Pit and the Pendulum" both exemplify aspects of Romantic literature. In your analysis, consider the following elements:

- narrative features, such as plot, setting, and descriptive details
- each work's **themes**, or central ideas about life
- the authors' tone as revealed through word choice
- the historical period in which each text was written

Assign this performance task.

PERFORMANCE TASK

COMMON CORE RL 2, RL 3, RL 5, RL 9, W 9a

Writing Activity: Analysis Have students reread the American Romanticism essay and review its main points with the class. Before students begin their essays, remind them to consider narrative features, tone, theme, and historical period. When students have finished their writing, have them exchange their essays with a partner and share constructive feedback, using the bulleted list on the student page to check for required elements.

Short Research Project

COMMON CORE

W 7, W 8

TEACH

Discuss with students what, if anything, they know about the Spanish Inquisition. Ask them whether their knowledge comes from assumptions made based on reading Poe's story or from another source. As a class, brainstorm questions about the Inquisition such as the following:

- What does the quatrain at the beginning of the story mean, and did a market exist at the Jacobin Club House at Paris?
- How long was the Inquisition active?
- Who was affected by the Inquisition?
- Who was General Lasalle and what role, if any, did he play in the Inquisition?
- What punishments were delivered to heretics during the Inquisition?

PRACTICE AND APPLY

Have students select one of the questions identified by the class and conduct research using reliable Internet sources to find an answer. Instruct students to take notes as they conduct their research. When they have finished, have students write a brief report about their results. Then have students share their reports with the class.

Discuss with students how what they have learned about the Inquisition impacts their understanding of "The Pit and the Pendulum."

 **INTERACTIVE LESSON** If students need further instruction, use this *Interactive Whiteboard Lesson:* **Conducting Research on the Web**

Write a Narrative

COMMON CORE

W 3

TEACH

Review with students the elements of Gothic literature: a focus on the darker aspects of human nature and the grotesque as well as a focus on intense emotions and the role of imagination. As a class, brainstorm possible settings, characters, and situations that might lend themselves to a Gothic story.

PRACTICE AND APPLY

Have students write their own short Gothic stories. Invite them to use the settings, characters, and situations from the class brainstorming session for inspiration. Advise students to add descriptive language that conveys a dark, moody atmosphere.

Beginning: Introduce the setting, characters, and conflict—the problem faced by the main character.

Middle: Develop the action as the main character attempts to solve the problem. Bring the action to its climax, or highest point.

End: Resolve the conflict.

When students have finished writing, invite them to read their stories to the class. Use a folder or binder to collect students' Gothic stories into a book. Encourage students to create illustrations for the stories and include them in the book.

Analyze Structure: Atmosphere and Dramatic Tension

COMMON CORE

RL 2, RL 3, RL 5

TEACH

Review with students the elements that writers use to convey atmosphere and build dramatic tension:

- sensory details
- words with strong connotations
- the choice of what details to reveal and when
- the choice of where to begin and end the story

Explain that none of these elements can envelop the reader in horror on its own. Instead, they work in combination to create their effect.

PRACTICE AND APPLY

Display lines 474–489 from "The Pit and the Pendulum" on the board or on a device. Ask students to identify sensory details in the passage. *("vapor of heated iron," "suffocating odor," "eyes that glared," "richer tint of crimson," "glowing metal," "glare")* Then ask them to identify words with strong connotations that contribute to the atmosphere of horror. *(vapor, glared, tormentors, demoniac, deadly, shuddering)* Finally, ask what detail Poe chooses not to reveal. *(what the narrator saw in the pit)*

Determine Themes: Romanticism

COMMON CORE

RL 2, RL 3, RL 5, SL 1

RETEACH

Remind students that a story's theme is a central truth about human experience that it reveals. Help students to determine the theme by asking these questions.

- What are the narrator's worst fears? *(the unknown, the pendulum, the pit)*
- How does he respond to these fears? *(He alternates between hope and despair. He tries to take control of his situation.)*
- What does the narrator say on page 250 that he has learned from the experience of fainting? *(He has learned that some sort of consciousness persists, even in death.)*

Have students state the theme of the story. Accept all reasonable responses. Some responses may relate to the persistence of consciousness when confronted with horrifying events. Others may speculate that the theme is how fragile and unpredictable the boundary is between imagination and reality. Still others may see the story as a literal, if exaggerated, rendering of the shocking cruelty and abuse of power that the Inquisition represents.

 **LEVEL UP TUTORIALS** Assign the following *Level Up* tutorial: **Theme**

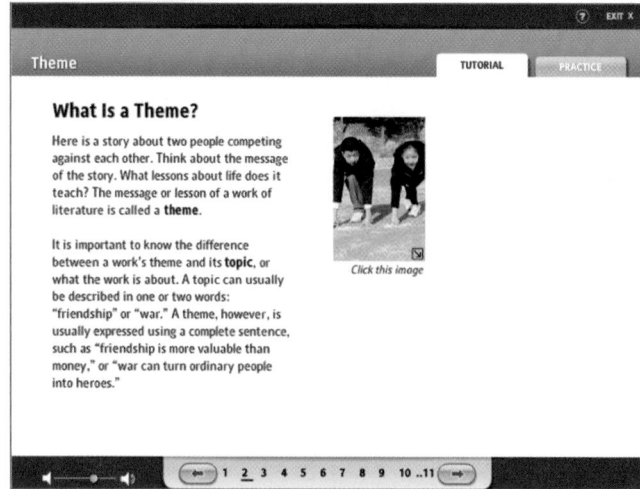

CLOSE READING APPLICATION

Students can practice determining theme in another short story. Have them work independently to note the characters' thoughts, feelings, and responses to their circumstances and explore how they relate to the story's central truth.

COLLECTION 3
PERFORMANCE TASK A

Interactive Lessons

If you need help with...
• **Writing a Narrative**
• **Using Textual Evidence**

PERFORMANCE TASK A

Write a Narrative

The texts in this collection focus on the individual and how individuals fit into the larger schemes of nature and society. Consider the following quotation.

W 3a–e Write narratives.
W 4 Produce clear and coherent writing.
W 5 Develop and strengthen writing.
W 9a–b Draw evidence from literary or informational texts.

> "Trust thyself: every heart vibrates to that iron string."
> (Ralph Waldo Emerson, from "Self-Reliance")

What does this quote really mean and how does it connect to the texts in this collection? Should we all listen to our own internal sense of what is right or wrong, or what is true or untrue? Look back at the anchor text "Song of Myself" and at the other texts in the collection. Then synthesize your ideas about the role of an individual in society by writing a personal, nonfiction, or fictional narrative.

An effective narrative

- introduces a setting and main character and establishes a clear point of view
- engages readers by presenting a conflict, situation, or observation that sets the narrative in motion
- describes a clear and logical sequence of events
- uses a variety of narrative techniques, such as dialogue, pacing, and description
- reveals a significant theme related to one of the quotations
- concludes by resolving the conflict or by conveying the writer's reflection on the experiences described in the narrative

PLAN

*my***Notebook**

Find Inspiration Take another look at the Emerson quote and start planning your response.

Use the notebook in your eBook to record examples and quotations that address each author's ideas about the individual's role in society.

- Review the selections from "Song of Myself" and take notes about how the speaker's experiences reflect themes about the individual, society, and nature. The characters, events, and setting of your narrative should similarly reflect the theme that you want to communicate.
- Review the other stories in the collection: "The Minister's Black Veil" and "The Pit and the Pendulum." What narrative techniques do you find especially effective, and how might you use them in your own writing?

PERFORMANCE TASK A

WRITE A NARRATIVE

W 3a-e, W 4, W 5,
W 9a-b

Introduce students to the Performance Task by reading the introductory paragraph with them and reviewing the criteria for what makes an effective narrative. Remind students that the purpose of a narrative is to explore a topic and to provide insight. Another purpose for writing a fictional narrative might be to entertain.

PLAN

FIND INSPIRATION

 *View It!*

Suggest to students that they also find inspiration from their own lives and the lives of people they know. Have they ever faced a conflict related to societal expectations?

Professional Development Podcast:

Writing Narratives at the Secondary Level

Have they ever felt like an outsider? Have they ever questioned their duty in relation to the larger society? Have they ever wanted to leave society altogether for a life "off the grid"? Have they known someone else who has explored these issues? How could these experiences engage readers and reveal insights about the relationship between individuals and society? Is it possible to compare these experiences and insights to those in "Song of Myself," "The Minister's Black Veil," or "The Pit and the Pendulum"?

PERFORMANCE TASK A

PLAN

BRAINSTORM

Remind students that their narratives will be built around a central conflict. In this case, the conflict will be related to ideas about the relationship between the individual and society. Encourage students to begin by brainstorming conflicts—between an individual and society, between two individuals with different roles in society, or between two conflicting parts of one individual. Point out that students who have chosen to write a personal essay will want to brainstorm conflicts they have experienced related to the individual's role in society.

PLAN

GET ORGANIZED

Remind students that a narrative is a sequence of events, often but not necessarily in chronological order. Provide them with this classic story structure graphic to help them map out their narratives:

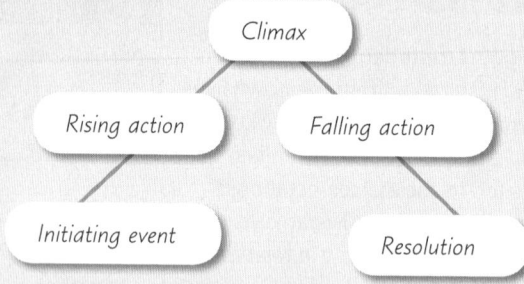

Point out that many nonfiction narratives also follow this structure.

Brainstorm Write down some ideas for your narrative. How does the quotation mirror your own ideas about how individuals fit into society? In response to the quotation, create a word map to generate ideas for your narrative. Include characters, setting, plot (or sequence of events), and conflict. Remember that your narrative can be either fiction or nonfiction. You can base it on events in your own life or on the lives of people you know or have read about. Or if you prefer, you can center your narrative on an entirely fictional situation.

- A short story describes fictional characters and events.
- A nonfiction narrative describes real people and events.
- A personal narrative describes your own experiences and your reflections on them.

Get Organized Organize your notes, using an outline or a graphic organizer.

- Decide on the structure of your narrative and create an outline or use a story map to reflect your ideas. Look back at the narrative texts in this collection to help you. Ask yourself these questions about each story:
  - » How does the story begin? Identify techniques the writer uses to engage readers and make them want to keep reading.
  - » What is the plot of the narrative? Is there more than one plot line? What is the central conflict?
  - » How does the writer develop the narrative? What is the sequence of events? Map out the rising action, climax, and falling action of the narrative.
  - » How does the writer use setting, characters, conflict, and story events to reveal a theme about individuals and their place in society or nature?
  - » How does the story end? Is the conflict resolved? How?
- Select which point of view you will use in your narrative, and take notes on other narrative techniques in the texts that you plan to use.
- Flesh out your setting and characters with descriptive details. Write down details about your characters' appearance, personality, and anything else that makes them unique.
- Remember that your narrative must reflect the theme that you want to communicate. Record some ideas for revealing your theme.

ACADEMIC VOCABULARY

As you analyze the narrative texts, try to use these words.

analogy
denote
quote
topic
unique

Draft Your Narrative Write a draft of your narrative, following your notes, outline, and/or graphic organizers.

- Begin by introducing your readers to the setting, the main character(s), and a conflict or experience that will be central to the plot or narrative.
- Describe a clear sequence of events. In a short story, it's especially important that these events build toward a climax and a resolution to the conflict.
- Use descriptive details and narrative techniques to make the setting, characters, and events realistic for your readers.
- Provide a satisfying conclusion. A personal or nonfiction narrative should end with reflections on the events and experiences that have been described. A short story should end by resolving the central conflict.

Improve Your Draft Use the chart on the following page to review the characteristics of an effective narrative. Exchange drafts with a partner. When reading your partner's draft, ask yourself the questions below. Then use feedback from your partner to revise your own draft.

- Are the plot, setting, and characters fully developed?
- How could your partner make the narrative more interesting for readers? Suggest additional narrative techniques or descriptive language that could be used.
- Does the narrative move along at a good pace? What might your partner do to speed up the action in sections that feel too slow? Are there any places where your partner should add more descriptive details to slow readers down and give them time to reflect?
- Is the sequence of events clear? Could more transitions help clarify the narrative?
- Do the setting, characters, and events successfully convey the theme your partner intended to express?

Share Your Narrative When your final draft is completed, read your narrative to a small group. Use your voice and gestures to present a lively reading of the narrative. Be prepared to answer questions or respond to comments from your group members.

DRAFT YOUR NARRATIVE

Remind students that their stories will be told by a narrator, who tells the story from a particular point of view.

- **First person** *(I, me, my, we, us)*: The narrator is a character in the story and tells only what he or she knows and experiences.
- **Third person limited** *(he, she, they, them)*: The narrator is not a character and tells only what he or she knows and experiences.
- **Third person omniscient**: The narrator is all-knowing and can tell what any character knows and experiences.

Tell students to consider which type of narrator would best help them convey their ideas about the individual and society. (Nonfiction narratives will probably be told using the first-person point of view.)

SHARE YOUR NARRATIVE

Provide students with other options for presenting their narratives. Encourage them to submit their stories to an online literary journal, or collect the narratives and publish a class book on the topic of the individual and society.

PERFORMANCE TASK A

IDEAS AND EVIDENCE

Have students look at the chart and offer a self-evaluation of the Ideas and Evidence category, including their assessment of their level of performance. Ask them to set goals for the next time they might do a similar task. What areas will they work on? Then, have them exchange their drafts with a partner and complete a peer review, using the points on the student page as a guide.

NARRATIVE

	Ideas and Evidence	Organization	Language
ADVANCED	• The narrative begins memorably, clearly introducing the setting, a main character, and an interesting conflict. • The plot or sequence of events is thoroughly developed. • The narrative reveals a significant theme related to the Emerson quotation. • The narrative ends by resolving the conflict or reflecting thoughtfully on the experience.	• The sequence of events is effective, clear, and logical. • The pace and organization keep the reader curious about the next event. • Effective transitions clearly connect ideas and show the sequence of events.	• The point of view is effective and consistent throughout the narrative. • Vivid descriptive details reveal the setting and characters. • Sentence beginnings, lengths, and structures vary and have a rhythmic flow. • Spelling, capitalization, and punctuation are correct. If handwritten, the narrative is legible. • Grammar and usage are correct.
COMPETENT	• The narrative introduces the setting, a main character, and a conflict, but the opening could be more engaging. • The plot or sequence of events is adequately developed. • The narrative suggests a theme related to the Emerson quotation. • The conflict is resolved, or there is some reflection, but more details are needed to create a satisfying conclusion.	• The sequence of events is mostly clear and logical. • The pace could move along more quickly to hold the reader's interest. • A few more transitions are needed to explain the sequence of events.	• The point of view is mostly consistent. • A few more descriptive details are needed to develop the setting and characters. • Sentence beginnings, lengths, and structures mostly vary. • Several spelling, capitalization, and punctuation mistakes occur. If handwritten, the narrative is mostly legible. • Some grammatical and usage errors are repeated in the narrative.
LIMITED	• The narrative opening is uneventful; it identifies a setting and a main character but only hints at a conflict. • Development of the plot or sequence of events is uneven in a few places. • A theme related to the quotation is only hinted at. • The narrative resolves some parts of the conflict or reflects on some aspect of the experience.	• The sequence of events is confusing in a few places. • The pace often lags. • More transitions are needed throughout to clarify the sequence of events.	• The point of view shifts in a few places. • The descriptive details are ordinary or not used regularly enough. • Sentence structures vary somewhat. • Spelling, capitalization, and punctuation are often incorrect but do not make reading the narrative difficult. If handwritten, the narrative may be partially illegible. • Grammar and usage are incorrect in many places, but the writer's ideas are still clear.
EMERGING	• The opening is missing critical information about the setting and main character and doesn't set up a conflict. • The plot or sequence of events is barely developed. • There is no theme related to the quotation. • The narrative lacks a clear resolution.	• There is no clear sequence of events, making it easy for the reader to lose interest in the narrative. • The pace is ineffective. • Transitions are not used, making the narrative difficult to understand.	• The narrative lacks a clear point of view. • Descriptive details are rarely or never used to develop the setting and characters. • A repetitive sentence structure makes the writing monotonous. • Spelling, capitalization, and punctuation are incorrect throughout. If handwritten, the narrative may be partially or mostly illegible. • Many grammatical and usage errors change the meaning of the writer's ideas.

Debate an Issue

This collection focuses on individualism, imagination, society, and nature. The anchor text "Against Nature" presents a critique of the way many writers have interpreted the natural world, including Henry David Thoreau in his "rhapsodic chapter" on Spring. Do you agree or disagree with Joyce Carol Oates's critical assessment of nature writing? Synthesize your ideas by writing a brief argument and then debating the issue with your classmates.

Participants in an effective debate

- argue for or against Oates's assessment of nature writing

- draw upon evidence from "Against Nature" and at least one other text from the collection

- follow an orderly format in which speakers from each team take turns presenting their claims, counterclaims, reasons, and evidence

- encourage a thoughtful, well-reasoned exchange of ideas in which participants respond to diverse perspectives, build on each other's ideas, and evaluate the reasoning of other speakers

COMMON CORE

W 1 Write arguments.
W 2 Write informative/ explanatory texts.
W 9a–b Draw evidence from literary or informational texts.
SL 1a–d Initiate and participate effectively in a range of collaborative discussions.
SL 3 Evaluate a speaker's point of view, reasoning, and use of evidence and rhetoric.
SL 4 Present information, findings, and supporting evidence.
SL 6 Adapt speech to a variety of contexts and tasks.

PLAN

Get Organized To prepare for the debate, collect evidence for an argument in which you will support your opinion of Oates's position.

- Review "Against Nature" and identify the claim Oates makes about nature writing. Notice the way she quotes from other texts to provide evidence for her claim.

- Review other texts in the collection with Oates's claim in mind. Identify passages that could be used to support or refute her claim.

- Based on your review of the collection, decide whether you agree or disagree with Oates's assessment.

- Write a clear statement of your claim. Identify a quotation from another collection text that strongly supports your argument.

*my*Notebook

Use the notebook in your eBook to record possible quotations that address the relationship between the individual and the natural world.

ACADEMIC VOCABULARY

As you build your argument on the issue of nature writers and how they interpret the natural world, be sure to use these words.

analogy
denote
quote
topic
unique

PERFORMANCE TASK B

DEBATE AN ISSUE

COMMON CORE — W 1, W 2, W 9a-b, SL 1a-d, SL 3, SL 4, SL 6

Introduce students to the Performance Task by reading the introductory paragraph with them and reviewing the criteria for what makes an effective debate. Remind students that a debate is a productive and balanced argument about both sides of an issue.

PLAN

GET ORGANIZED

View It!

Professional Development Podcast:

Performance Task

As they prepare for the debate, tell students to consider both sides of the argument. To argue convincingly either for or against Oates's position on nature writing, students must be familiar with both sides of the argument. It's also important that the moderator be familiar with both sides so that he or she can keep the debate on track.

Suggest that once they have identified their own position, students scan the other texts in this collection as well as other works they are familiar with to begin to gather support for their argument.

PERFORMANCE TASK B

PRODUCE

BUILD YOUR ARGUMENT

Remind students that the purpose of a debate is similar to the purpose of writing an argument: to persuade others to accept a claim about an issue by providing valid reasons and sufficient evidence. Review the types of text evidence they should use to support their claim:

- Examples: specific details or events from the texts
- Quotations: specific words, phrases, and sentences presented word-for-word from the texts and attributed to the author
- Summaries: important information from the texts summed up in their own words
- Personal experience: experiences they have had that are relevant to the subject of the debate

REVISE

PRACTICE FOR THE DEBATE

As students revise, suggest that they consider adding rhetorical techniques such as those that Oates uses in her essay. For instance, students might like to use rhetorical questions or repetition to bring their point home.

PRODUCE

Build Your Argument Write a brief argument for your position that will form the basis for your participation in the debate.

- Begin with the statement of your claim regarding Oates's view of nature writing.
- Outline several reasons that support your claim.
- Present the quotation you selected from another collection text and explain how it supports your reasoning.

Develop Counterarguments Think of arguments your classmates might make to refute your ideas. Plan the counterarguments you will make to prove your points. Create notes on these counterarguments to which you can refer during the debate.

*my*WriteSmart

Write your rough draft in *my*WriteSmart. Focus on getting your ideas down, rather than perfecting your choice of language.

REVISE

Practice for the Debate Use the chart at the end of this Performance Task to review the characteristics of an effective argument presented in a debate. Get together with a partner to practice presenting and defending your argument. If possible, select a partner who takes a different position on Oates's ideas.

- Take turns reading your written arguments to each other.
- When you have both read your arguments, begin an informal debate. One of you might begin by asking a question about the other's reasoning.
- Respond thoughtfully and respectfully to each other's comments and questions. Try to resolve any contradictions between your interpretations of the evidence.

Revise Your Argument After your practice debate, review your argument and make any revisions necessary to strengthen it. Consider these questions:

- Does my claim still reflect my opinion on the issue? Could it be stated more clearly so that other participants in the debate will understand it?
- Did my practice partner point out any flaws in my reasoning? Which reasons could be strengthened or replaced?
- Is the quotation I selected the best one to support my argument? If not, what might be a good replacement?
- Did my partner raise some opposing arguments that I should add to my notes?

*my*WriteSmart

Have your partner or a group of peers review your draft in *my*WriteSmart. Ask your reviewers to note any elements of your argument that do not support the claim or that lack sufficient evidence.

Hold the Debate Some debates have a very formal structure, but this debate will be more informal. Select a student to serve as moderator, or have your teacher play that role.

- Start the debate by having each member of the class present his or her argument and supporting quotation. Take notes as your classmates are speaking.

- Next, the moderator should invite students to comment on or ask questions about each other's arguments. Allow the debate to flow naturally as students contribute their ideas. The moderator may step in as needed to restore order.

- Listen closely to what everyone says so that you can respond appropriately and build on others' ideas.

- Maintain a respectful tone toward your fellow debaters, even when you disagree with their ideas.

- Conclude the debate by taking a vote on Oates's assessment of nature writing. How many students agree with her, and how many disagree?

Write an Analysis After the debate, write an analysis of the ways writers tend to approach nature. Draw on other students' ideas and quotations as well as your own. Be sure to do the following in your analysis:

- introduce the topic with an interesting observation, quotation, or detail from the debate

- include a clear thesis statement about how writers tend to approach nature

- organize your central ideas in a logically structured body that develops your thesis statement

- use transitions to link sections of the text

- include quotations or examples from the debate that illustrate your central ideas

- write a concluding section that follows logically from the main body of your analysis

HOLD THE DEBATE

Students may want to videotape their debates. Videotaping will allow them to critique themselves on their delivery and to review their use of text evidence and rhetorical techniques to support their claim.

PERFORMANCE TASK B

LANGUAGE

Have students look at the chart and offer a self-evaluation of the Language category, including their assessment of their level of performance. Ask them to set goals for the next time they might do a similar task. What areas will they work on? Then, suggest that students work with their debate teams to complete this evaluation for the group performance.

DEBATE

	Ideas and Evidence	Organization	Language
ADVANCED	• Argument introduces a precise, knowledgeable claim about the critique presented in "Against Nature." • Claim is developed thoroughly with a relevant quotation from another collection text. • Opposing claims are anticipated and effectively addressed with counterclaims.	• Reasons and evidence are organized consistently and logically throughout the argument. • Varied transitions logically connect reasons and evidence to the writer's claim. • Debaters follow the agreed-upon rules during the activity.	• Argument maintains a formal style and an objective tone. • Debaters use appropriately formal English to express their ideas clearly during the activity. • In writing and in speech, students vary sentence beginnings, lengths, and structures to create a rhythmic flow.
COMPETENT	• Argument introduces a clear claim about the critique presented in "Against Nature." • Claim is supported with a quotation from another collection text. • At least one opposing claim is anticipated and addressed with a counterclaim.	• The organization of reasons and evidence is confusing in a few places. • A few more transitions are needed to connect reasons and evidence to the writer's claim. • Debaters mostly follow the rules during the activity.	• Argument uses an informal style in places and does not always have an objective tone. • Debaters mostly use formal English to express their ideas but sometimes use informal language. • Students' writing and speech contains some variety of sentence beginnings, lengths, and structures.
LIMITED	• Argument begins with a statement about "Against Nature" but does not take a clear position. • A quotation from another collection text is provided but is not clearly relevant to the claim. • At least one opposing claim is anticipated, but it is not addressed logically.	• The organization of reasons and evidence is logical in some places, but it often doesn't follow a pattern. • Many more transitions are needed to connect reasons and evidence to the writer's position. • Debaters have some problems keeping order during the activity.	• The argument's style becomes informal in many places, and the tone is often dismissive of other viewpoints. • Debaters use mostly informal English to express their ideas. • Students' writing and speech contains little variety of sentence beginnings, lengths, and structures.
EMERGING	• Argument does not assert a claim about the critique presented in "Against Nature." • No quotation from another collection text is provided as evidence. • Opposing claims are neither anticipated nor addressed.	• An organizational strategy is not used; reasons and evidence are presented randomly. • Transitions are not used, making the argument difficult to understand. • Debaters do not follow the rules during the activity, resulting in a confusing and disorderly discussion.	• The argument's style is inappropriate, and the tone is disrespectful. • Debaters use informal English and slang, making some of their ideas unclear. • Students' writing and speech is monotonous, with no variety of sentence beginnings, lengths, and structures.

Image Credits: ©Bettmann/Corbis

A New Birth of Freedom

" My father was a slave and my people died to build this
country, and I'm going to stay here and have a part of it. "

—Paul Robeson

275

A New Birth of Freedom

In this collection, you will explore how African Americans and women gained new freedoms after a bloody civil war.

fyi
hmhfyi.com

CONNECTING WORD AND IMAGE

ASK STUDENTS TO discuss how the collection opener image and the collection quotation work together to create a connection.

PERFORMANCE TASK PREVIEW

Point out to students that they will complete one performance task at the end of the collection. The performance task will require them to further analyze the selections in the collection and to synthesize ideas about these analyses. They will present their findings in a persuasive speech.

ACADEMIC VOCABULARY

View It!

Professional Development Podcast:
Academic Vocabulary

Students can acquire facility with the academic vocabulary words through frequent, repeated exposure as they analyze and discuss the selections in the collection. Academic vocabulary can be used in the following instructional contexts. This will enable students to incorporate the academic vocabulary words into their working vocabulary.

- Collaborative Discussion at the end of each selection
- Analyzing the Text questions for each selection
- Selection-level Performance Task
- Vocabulary instruction (for Critical Vocabulary and/or for Vocabulary Strategy)
- Language and Style
- End-of-collection Performance Task for all selections in the collection

ASK STUDENTS to review the academic vocabulary word list for this collection. You may wish to pronounce each word aloud, so students hear the correct pronunciation. Then discuss the definitions and the related forms for each word. Remind students that they will encounter these five academic vocabulary words throughout the collection.

COLLECTION

PERFORMANCE TASK Preview

At the end of this collection, you will have the opportunity to complete a task:

- Write a persuasive speech about a freedom that you believe should be expanded in the world today.

ACADEMIC VOCABULARY

Study the words and their definitions in the chart below. You will use these words as you discuss and write about the texts in this collection.

Word	Definition	Related Forms
confirm (kən-fûrm´) *v.*	to establish the truth or certainty of something	confirmable, confirmation
definitely (dĕf´ə-nĭt-lē) *adv.*	in an exact, certain, or precise way	definite, define, definitive
deny (dĭ-nī´) *v.*	to refuse to see or to allow; to reject	deniable, deniability, denial, denier
format (fôr´măt´) *n.*	the organization or arrangement of parts in a whole	form, formation
unify (yoo´nə-fī´) *v.*	to bring together into a cohesive whole	unity, union, unification, unifiable

276

USING THE COLLECTION YOUR WAY

Use the following information, along with the charts on the following pages, to help you decide how you want to introduce the collection. Based on your teaching style, your students' interests, or your instructional goals, you may want to structure the collection in various ways. You may choose different entry points each time you teach the collection.

"I want to challenge my students to the utmost."

In this mid-19th-century speech, a former slave gives his perspective on the Fourth of July, arguing that African Americans who live with slavery are not able to celebrate freedom and independence.

Frederick Douglass (c. 1818–1895) was born in Maryland and spent his first 21 years in slavery. After his escape, the Massachusetts Anti-Slavery Society hired him as a lecturer. His book Narrative of the Life of Frederick Douglass, an American Slave (1845) brought him international fame. Friends raised money to buy his freedom, allowing him to fully pursue his career as a reformer. He advised President Lincoln during the Civil War. In 1852, he spoke at a celebration of the Declaration of Independence.

What to the Slave Is the Fourth of July?
Speech by Frederick Douglass

AS YOU READ Think about how Douglass answers the question of what the Fourth of July means to African Americans in 1852. Write down any questions you generate during reading.

What to the Slave Is the Fourth of July? **285**

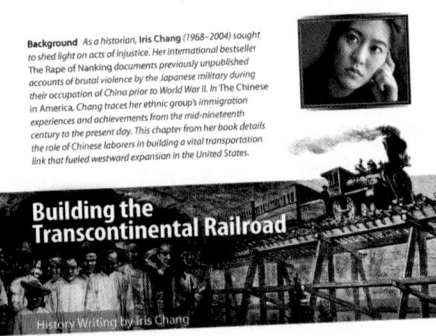

Background As a historian, Iris Chang (1968–2004) sought to shed light on acts of injustice. Her international bestseller The Rape of Nanking documents previously unpublished accounts of brutal violence by the Japanese military during their occupation of China prior to World War II. In The Chinese in America, Chang traces her ethnic group's immigration experiences and achievements from the mid-nineteenth century to the present day. This chapter from her book details the role of Chinese laborers in building a vital transportation link that fueled westward expansion in the United States.

Building the Transcontinental Railroad
History Writing by Iris Chang

AS YOU READ Pay attention to details about the accomplishments of Chinese laborers and the hardships they faced. Write down any questions you generate during reading.

Building the Transcontinental Railroad **301**

"I require my students to do a lot of research."

This book excerpt gives a historical account of the Transcontinental Railroad, describing hardships and racism endured by the Chinese laborers who took part in building this significant transportation route in the United States.

"I like to use digital product as a starting point."

This documentary discusses the formation of the 54th Massachusetts Volunteer Infantry—African American soldiers who volunteered to fight during the Civil War—presenting information from multiple mediums and sources.

Background The 54th Massachusetts Volunteer Infantry was the first black northern regiment in the Civil War. It was formed in 1863, soon after the Emancipation Proclamation was issued. African Americans had served in both the Revolutionary War and the War of 1812, but there were concerns in the North about upsetting border states and about the "effectiveness" of black soldiers. Not only did African American soldiers help the North win the Civil War, but the historical and social significance of their enlistment and of their brave service continues to resonate through the centuries.

MEDIA ANALYSIS
The 54th Massachusetts
Documentary by HISTORY

AS YOU VIEW Note the controversy engendered by the idea of a black regiment. Write down any questions you generate during your viewing.

COLLABORATIVE DISCUSSION Why was the idea of black enlistment resisted even in the North? With a partner, discuss the objections that delayed the entrance of African Americans into the military.

The 54th Massachusetts **315**

mySmartPlanner | **eBook** | **myNotebook** | **myWriteSmart** | **fyi** hmhfyi.com

Collection 4 Lessons	Media	Teach and Practice	
Student Edition | eBook	**Video Links**	**Close Reading and Evidence Tracking**	
ANCHOR TEXT — Speech by Abraham Lincoln "Second Inaugural Address"	Audio "Second Inaugural Address" / Video HISTORY® AMERICA The Story of Us: Abraham Lincoln	**Close Read Screencasts** • Modeled Discussion (lines 12–20) • Close Read application (lines 47–54)	**Strategies for Annotation** • Evaluate Seminal Texts: Premises, Purposes, and Arguments
CLOSE READER — Legal Document by Abraham Lincoln "The Emancipation Proclamation"	Audio "The Emancipation Proclamation" / Video HISTORY AMERICA The Story of Us: Abraham Lincoln		
Speech by Frederick Douglass "What to the Slave Is the Fourth of July?"	Audio "What to the Slave Is the Fourth of July?" / Video HISTORY AMERICA The Story of Us: Frederick Douglass		**Strategies for Annotation** • Analyze Author's Point of View: Speech • Analyze Language and Style: Rhetorical Devices
Public Document by Elizabeth Cady Stanton "Declaration of Sentiments"	Audio "Declaration of Sentiments"		**Strategies for Annotation** • Analyze Author's Purpose • The Latin Root *ject*
CLOSE READER — Public Document by Dekanawida from *The Iroquois Constitution*	Audio from *The Iroquois Constitution*		
History Writing by Iris Chang "Building the Transcontinental Railroad"	Audio "Building the Transcontinental Railroad"		**Strategies for Annotation** • Author's Purpose: Tone and Style • Context Clues
CLOSE READER — Newspaper Article by Joe Lapointe "Bonding Over a Mascot"	Audio "Bonding Over a Mascot"		
Documentary by HISTORY *The 54th Massachusetts*	Video HISTORY Civil War Journal: The 54th Massachusetts		
Poem by Robert Hayden "Runagate Runagate"	Audio "Runagate Runagate" / Video HISTORY AMERICA The Story of Us: Harriet Tubman and the Underground Railroad		**Strategies for Annotation** • Analyze Language: Allusions
Collection 4 Performance Task: Present a Persuasive Speech	fyi hmhfyi.com	**Interactive Lessons** Giving a Presentation Analyzing and Evaluating Presentations	

	For Systematic Coverage of Writing and Speaking & Listening Standards	**Interactive Lessons** Using Textual Evidence Using Media in a Presentation	**Lesson Assessments** Using Textual Evidence Using Media in a Presentation

Assess		Extend	Reteach
Performance Task	**Online Assessment**	**Teacher eBook**	**Teacher eBook**
Speaking Activity: Discussion	Selection Test	**Analyze Structure > Interactive Whiteboard Lesson >** Text Structure and Meaning	**Evaluate Seminal Texts: Premises, Purposes, and Arguments > Level Up Tutorial >** Analyzing Arguments
Writing Activity: Outline and Summary	Selection Test	**Determine Central Ideas and Details**	**Analyze Author's Point of View**
Writing Activity: Comparison	Selection Test	**Analyze Ideas**	**Determine Author's Purpose > Level Up >** Analyzing Arguments
Speaking Activity: Discussion	Selection Test	**Create a Multimedia Presentation > Interactive Whiteboard Lesson**	**Author's Purpose: Tone and Style > Level Up Tutorial >** Tone
Speaking Activity: Debate	Selection Test	**Analyze Point of View**	**Integrate and Evaluate Information > Level Up Tutorial >** Evaluating Credibility
Writing Activity: Essay	Selection Test	**Determine Author's Purpose > Interactive Whiteboard Lesson** **Write a Short Research Report**	**Analyze Structure: Rhythm and Meaning > Level Up Tutorial >** Rhythm **Analyze Language: Allusions**
Present a Persuasive Speech	Collection Test		

Collection 4 Lessons	Key Learning Objective	Performance Task
ANCHOR TEXT **EXEMPLAR** **Speech by Abraham Lincoln** "Second Inaugural Address," p. 279A — Lexile 1160	**The student will be able to...** evaluate a seminal U.S. speech and analyze premises and purposes of author's arguments	Speaking Activity: Discussion
EXEMPLAR **Speech by Frederick Douglass** "What to the Slave Is the Fourth of July?" p. 285A — Lexile 1200	**The student will be able to...** analyze point of view, evaluating how the rhetoric, style, and content contribute to a text's persuasiveness	Writing Activity: Outline and Summary
Public Document by Elizabeth Cady Stanton "Declaration of Sentiments," p. 295A — Lexile 1430	**The student will be able to...** analyze how the structure and style of an argument supports the author's ideas and claims	Writing Activity: Comparison
History Writing by Iris Chang "Building the Transcontinental Railroad," p. 301A — Lexile 1310	**The student will be able to...** analyze a narrative history and understand how ideas are organized and sequence is created	Speaking Activity: Discussion
Documentary by HISTORY *The 54th Massachusetts*, p. 315A	**The student will be able to...** integrate and evaluate documentary information in interviews, video reenactments, and photos	Speaking Activity: Debate
Poem by Robert Hayden "Runagate Runagate," p. 317A	**The student will be able to...** analyze a free-verse poem for its use of allusions, rhythm, and structure	Writing Activity: Essay

Collection 4 Performance Task:
Present a Persuasive Speech

Vocabulary Strategy	Language and Style	Student Instructional Support	CLOSE READER Selection
Pronunciation	Balanced Sentences	**Scaffolding for ELL Students:** Understand Word Associations **When Students Struggle:** Develop Reading Fluency	Legal Document by Abraham Lincoln "The Emancipation Proclamation," p. 284b **Lexile 2130**
Multiple-Meaning Words	Rhetorical Devices	**Scaffolding for ELL Students:** Analyze Language **When Students Struggle:** • Reading With Expression: Punctuation • Understand Rhetorical Questions **To Challenge Students:** • Use Voice to Convey Tone • Analyze Comparisons	
The Latin Root *ject*		**Scaffolding for ELL Students:** Understand Language and Gender **When Students Struggle:** Phrase-Cued Reading	Public Document by Dekanawida from *The Iroquois Constitution*, p. 300b **Lexile 1270**
Context Clues	Avoiding Misplaced Modifiers	**Scaffolding for ELL Students:** • Identify Tone • Understand Archaic Language • Author's Purpose: Tone and Style **When Students Struggle:** • Using a Point/Counterpoint Chart • Reading with Expression: Tone **To Challenge Students:** • Research Historical Detail • Use Research Techniques	
		Scaffolding for ELL Students: Integrate Information	Newspaper Article by Joe Lapointe "Bonding Over a Mascot," p. 314b **Lexile 1220**
		Scaffolding for ELL Students: • Understand Sentence Structure • Clarify Customs **When Students Struggle:** Fluent Reading	

Civil War and Reconstruction

Collection 4 Historical Introduction

Why This Text?

Students often encounter literary and informational texts that assume that the reader has some knowledge of key historical events, facts, ideas, and issues. The historical introduction to Collection 4 presents information about the period from 1850 to 1880, when tensions between supporters of slavery and abolitionist forces came to a head during the Civil War. Afterward, the reunited country turned its attention to rebuilding itself and healing from the effects of the war.

Key Learning Objective: The student will be able to analyze the selections in the collection in terms of a historical context.

COMMON CORE Common Core Standards

RL 10 Read and comprehend literature in the grades 11-CCR text complexity band.

RI 3 Analyze ideas or events and explain how individuals, ideas, or events interact and develop.

RI 7 Integrate and evaluate sources of information presented in different formats.

RI 9 Analyze foundational U.S. documents for themes, purposes, and rhetorical features.

RI 10 Read and comprehend literary nonfiction in the grades 11-CCR text complexity band.

▲ Text Complexity Rubric

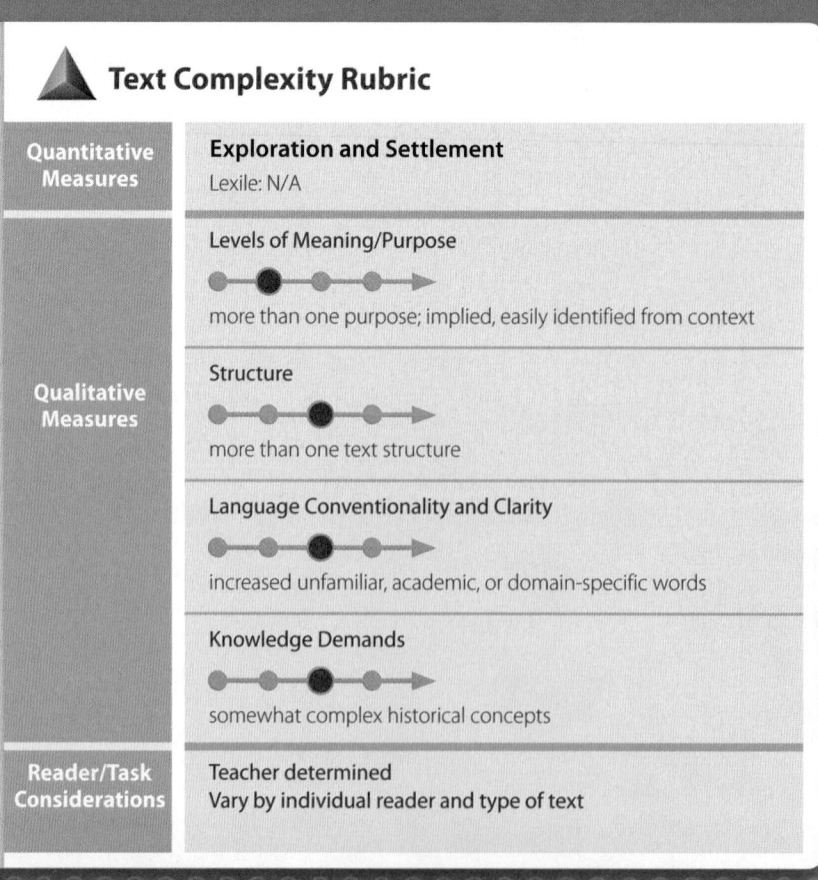

Quantitative Measures	**Exploration and Settlement** Lexile: N/A
Qualitative Measures	**Levels of Meaning/Purpose** more than one purpose; implied, easily identified from context
	Structure more than one text structure
	Language Conventionality and Clarity increased unfamiliar, academic, or domain-specific words
	Knowledge Demands somewhat complex historical concepts
Reader/Task Considerations	Teacher determined Vary by individual reader and type of text

For more context and historical background, students can view the video "Freedom's Road: Slavery and the Opposition" in their eBooks.

Civil War and Reconstruction

Explain that this section establishes the historical context for the selections in this collection. It explains the reasons why the states came to war against one another and provides an introduction to the work of abolitionists. The section also tells about the positive and negative aftereffects of the Civil War, including the establishment of freedom for African Americans, the rebuilding of the damaged South, and a renewed focus on expanding the nation westward.

A House Divided

COMMON CORE RL 10, RI 3, RI 7, RI 9, RI 10

Tell students that during the first half of the 19th century, some states were free states that forbade the keeping of slaves, while others were slave states that allowed the enslavement of people. While figuring out how to add newly settled territories to the nation as official states, the government wanted to keep things balanced so as not to give an advantage to either the northern free states or the southern slave states. Through a series of acts and compromises, therefore, the United States set up different rules for how such areas as the Northwest Territory, the Missouri Territory, and the land acquired during the Mexican-American War (1846–1848) would be divided and turned into slave states or free states.

In the 1850s, some politicians, including Stephen A. Douglas, promoted a policy of popular sovereignty, or the idea that the people actually living in a territory should be allowed to decide for themselves whether they could keep slaves or not. Previously, in 1820, the Missouri Compromise had forbidden slavery in the area that became Kansas. The Kansas-Nebraska Act of 1854, however, angered abolitionists and other anti-slavery forces by allowing the people in this area to vote on whether to have slavery or not. Abraham Lincoln made his famous "house divided" remark in the speech that kicked off his 1858 campaign against Douglas for the position of Illinois senator. The debates the two men held during their subsequent senate campaign articulated the arguments for and against slavery that would consume the nation in the coming years.

Civil War and Reconstruction

COMMON CORE RL 10, RI 3, RI 7, RI 9, RI 10

In the middle of the 19th century, increasing sectionalism challenged the spirit of nationalism that had characterized the Romantic era. Eventually sectional tensions erupted into the Civil War. After four years of fighting, the country was unified once again, although much of the South was in ruins and many issues remained unresolved. Writers gave voice to the debates throughout the period, sharing personal experiences and lofty ideals of freedom and unity.

A HOUSE DIVIDED For decades, Congress worked to keep a balance between slave states and free states. In the 1850s, compromise became more difficult as new western territories sought statehood. At the same time, slavery became more important to the Southern economy. New inventions such as the cotton gin allowed cotton production to increase greatly after 1793, requiring the labor of more slaves.

By the mid-19th century, many Americans had joined together to fight slavery and other social ills of the time. White and black abolitionists—both men and women—began to work for emancipation. They formed societies, spoke at conventions, published newspapers, and swamped Congress with petitions to end slavery. They also established the Underground Railroad, an informal network of abolitionists who helped slaves escape to freedom in the North. Some former slaves who had escaped related the realities of life under slavery through slave narratives such as Frederick Douglass's *My Bondage and My Freedom* (1855). Abolitionist Harriet Beecher Stowe's 1852 novel about the evils of slavery, *Uncle Tom's Cabin*, became a bestseller and is sometimes cited as a cause of the Civil War. Their work for abolition made many women more aware of how their own rights had been denied. Reformers such as Elizabeth Cady Stanton and Lucretia Mott soon turned their attention to the fight for women's rights, including the right to vote.

In the 1850s the conflict over slavery turned violent in the territory of Kansas and in the halls of Congress. Abraham Lincoln wrote in 1858, "A house divided against itself cannot stand," reflecting the bitter divisions in the country. Lincoln was a political moderate, but his election as president in 1860 ignited war. Enraged at Lincoln's pledge to stop the western spread of slavery, the Southern states seceded to form the Confederate States of America. When the Confederates fired on Fort Sumter in the spring of 1861, the Civil War began.

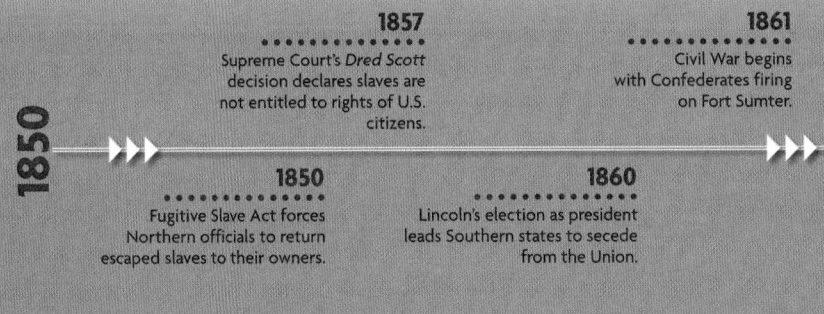

1850

1850
Fugitive Slave Act forces Northern officials to return escaped slaves to their owners.

1857
Supreme Court's *Dred Scott* decision declares slaves are not entitled to rights of U.S. citizens.

1860
Lincoln's election as president leads Southern states to secede from the Union.

1861
Civil War begins with Confederates firing on Fort Sumter.

Civil War and Reconstruction **277**

SCAFFOLDING FOR ELL STUDENTS

Vocabulary: Prefixes Students may be unfamiliar with the meaning of prefixes that could help them decipher the meaning of complicated terms in this section. Review with students the meanings of prefixes such as *re-* (again) and *trans-* (across).

ASK STUDENTS to work in mixed-language ability pairs and use their understanding of the meaning of prefixes to figure out the meaning of difficult vocabulary such as *reconstruction* (page 277), *re-admitting* (page 278), *rebuild* (page 278), and *transcontinental* (page 278).

Voices of War and Reconstruction

After experiencing the horrors of a war in which family members had fought on opposite sides, the nation approached cautiously the process of healing its wounds and bringing the Confederate States back into the fold. Even though the war was over, some Southerners still strongly guarded what powers were left to them and resisted the idea of granting equal rights to African Americans.

Black codes passed in 1865 and 1866 by the governments of former Confederate States tried to replicate the effects of slavery through laws that attempted to keep African Americans restricted to the status of second-class citizens by limiting their rights to do such things as own property and run certain businesses. Reconstruction technically abolished these laws. However, after Reconstruction ended in 1877 they were reenacted in the form of Jim Crow laws, and it was not until the Civil Rights Act passed in 1964 that full equal rights for all African Americans were guaranteed.

The Civil War also marked a time of great technological change and innovation. Overall, the Confederate Army was at a disadvantage. The North was the side with the factories and ability to produce rifles that could shoot more than one bullet before the shooter had to pause to reload, the resources to blockade the Southern coastline with new iron-clad warships, and the access to trains and miles of railroad track on which it could swiftly transport troops and supplies from place to place.

With new weapons came new and terrible kinds of destruction not previously experienced by troops. Ambrose Bierce preserved in his writing the gruesome sights and butchery he encountered during his time as an officer in the Union Army. Too young to have participated in the Civil War itself, Stephen Crane instead used his experiences working as a foreign war correspondent during conflicts such as the Spanish-American War to write his classic 1895 Civil War novel *The Red Badge of Courage*. This book describes with sharp realism the carnage of battle and the inner feelings of a soldier struggling to find the courage to continue fighting in the war.

VOICES OF WAR AND RECONSTRUCTION Romantic ideals of heroism that were common when the war started soon gave way to a harsher reality after the bloody Union defeat at the Battle of Bull Run in Virginia in July 1861. When the war ended in April 1865, approximately 618,000 men had died, nearly as many as have died in all other wars that the United States has ever fought. Some who gave their lives in the fight to end slavery and save the Union were African Americans, who fought in the Union army starting in 1863.

The United States suffered bitterly during the Civil War, yet it brought the Declaration of Independence's notion of liberty and equality for all closer to reality. Slavery was outlawed by Lincoln's bold Emancipation Proclamation and the Thirteenth Amendment to the Constitution. Lincoln's plans for Reconstruction, the process of addressing the injustices of slavery and re-admitting Southern states to the Union, were cut short by his assassination within days of the war's end. Republicans in Congress imposed martial law on the South and passed laws to give African Americans their rights, including the right to vote. Some African Americans were elected to Congress for the first time. Eventually, Northerners lost interest in Reconstruction, and Southern Democrats gradually took control of Southern state governments, imposing harsh new restrictions on African Americans. A compromise in 1877 allowed Republican Rutherford B. Hayes to become president in exchange for the end of federal control over the South.

As the nation began to rebuild, projects that had been interrupted by the Civil War resumed. Construction of a transcontinental railroad began in 1862, and work from the western end continued during the war. In 1869 a golden spike was driven into the track at Promontory Summit, Utah, marking the completion of the country's first nationwide railroad.

Civil war inevitably divides a nation's voice into factions. Northern and Southern writers, black and white, male and female, high-ranking officers and lowly foot soldiers all expressed different perspectives on their wartime experiences through diaries and letters. These more personal accounts contrasted with the public pronouncements of President Lincoln, whose inspirational Gettysburg Address proved to be one of the most enduring works of the Civil War. After the war, fiction created by realistic writers such as Ambrose Bierce and Stephen Crane focused on the human tragedy of the war.

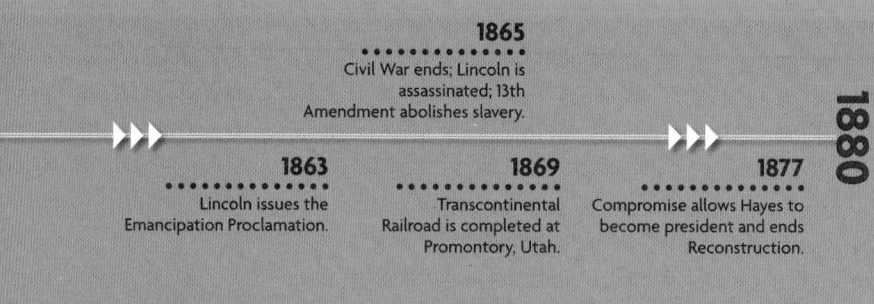

1865
Civil War ends; Lincoln is assassinated; 13th Amendment abolishes slavery.

1863
Lincoln issues the Emancipation Proclamation.

1869
Transcontinental Railroad is completed at Promontory, Utah.

1877
Compromise allows Hayes to become president and ends Reconstruction.

1880

WHEN STUDENTS STRUGGLE . . .

Concept Support: After students read the first paragraph on page 278, discuss the conflict between the high ideals held by the people who started the war and the terrible destruction that occurred once the war was underway.

ASK STUDENTS to work in pairs to make a two-column chart. Have students list on one side positive aspects of the Civil War, such as good outcomes gained by fighting it, and to record on the other side negative aspects of the war, such as the huge loss of life.

Analyze Foundational Documents: Themes and Historical Importance

COMMON CORE
RI 9

TEACH

Review with students the meaning and purpose behind some of the foundational documents from American history that they have learned about previously, such as the Declaration of Independence or the Articles of Confederation. Then skim this historical background essay and identify any mention of foundational documents from this era, such as the Supreme Court's *Dred Scott* decision, Lincoln's Emancipation Proclamation, the Thirteenth Amendment to the Constitution, and the Gettysburg Address.

Make a list of these documents and then prepare students to collect information from this background essay about the historical significance of each text. Model how to set up a three-column chart and fill in the first row:

Document	Time Period	Theme and Importance
Dred Scott	1857	made it law that enslaved people do not enjoy the rights of other U.S. citizens
Emancipation Proclamation		
Thirteenth Amendment		
Gettysburg Address		

PRACTICE AND APPLY

Have small groups work together to fill in the remaining rows of the chart. Students can use outside resources to expand their understanding of the theme and the importance of each of these foundational documents.

Analyze Nonfiction Elements: Rhetorical Devices

COMMON CORE
RI 3

TEACH

Explain to students that a common rhetorical device used by speechwriters is to make allusions to concepts with which their audience is already familiar. The people of Lincoln's time would be well aware of verses and situations taken from the Bible, and using references drawn from this book would make it easier for the audience to comprehend and perhaps ultimately agree with the points Lincoln was making.

Point out to students the line quoted on page 277 from Lincoln's 1858 speech: "A house divided against itself cannot stand." Explain that this line refers to a statement made by Jesus and repeated in the gospels of Matthew, Luke, and Mark in which Jesus said that if a house is divided against itself, that house cannot stand.

Then discuss with students the setting in which Lincoln was presenting this speech: a time during which the different states of the United States held conflicting opinions about whether people should be able to keep slaves or not. Have students explain what point Lincoln was making (not resolving the question of slavery would ultimately rip the country apart) and tell why using a Bible quotation strengthened his point (his audience would be familiar with the image from the Bible and understand how serious the danger posed to the country was).

CLOSE READING APPLICATION

Have students work independently to read and analyze another speech that uses the rhetorical device of Biblical allusions, such as Lincoln's Second Inaugural Address, which appears as part of this collection.

*my*SmartPlanner | Create lesson plans and access resources online.

ANCHOR TEXT EXEMPLAR

Second Inaugural Address

Speech by Abraham Lincoln

Why This Text?

Students regularly hear political speeches and read political arguments in various media, and to act as informed citizens they must be able to evaluate these arguments. In this lesson students will analyze the argument made by Lincoln in his Second Inaugural Address.

► View It!

Professional Development Podcast:

Teaching Argument

For additional practice:

Close Reader selection
"The Emancipation Proclamation"
Legal Document by Abraham Lincoln

Key Learning Objective: Students will be able to evaluate a seminal U.S. speech and analyze premises and purposes of author's arguments.

COMMON CORE — Common Core Standards

RI 1 Cite textual evidence.

RI 2 Determine central ideas of a text.

RI 5 Analyze and evaluate structure.

RI 8 Delineate and evaluate the reasoning in seminal U.S. texts.

RI 9 Analyze foundational U.S. documents.

SL 1a Come to discussions prepared; explicitly draw on that preparation.

SL 1c Propel conversations by posing and responding to questions; ensure a hearing for a full range of positions.

L 2 Demonstrate command of the conventions of standard English capitalization, punctuation, and spelling.

L 3a Vary syntax for effect; apply an understanding of syntax.

L 4c Consult reference materials.

▲ Text Complexity Rubric

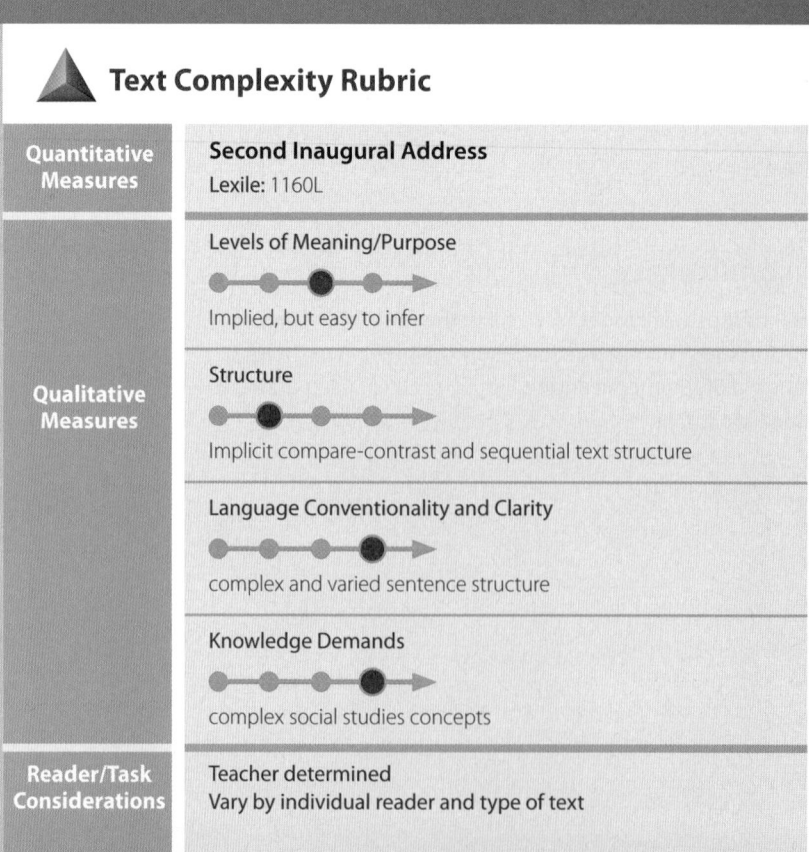

Quantitative Measures	**Second Inaugural Address** Lexile: 1160L
Qualitative Measures	**Levels of Meaning/Purpose** Implied, but easy to infer
	Structure Implicit compare-contrast and sequential text structure
	Language Conventionality and Clarity complex and varied sentence structure
	Knowledge Demands complex social studies concepts
Reader/Task Considerations	Teacher determined Vary by individual reader and type of text

For more context and historical background, students can view the video "AMERICA The Story of Us: Abraham Lincoln" in their eBooks.

Abraham Lincoln Thousands gathered on the wet, muddy grounds of the Capitol to hear Lincoln's speech. With a Union victory on the horizon, listeners may have been expecting a victory speech and a delineation of administration policy for Reconstruction. What they heard instead was an inspiring call for peaceful reconciliation.

AS YOU READ Direct students to use the As You Read instructions to focus their reading. Remind students to write down any questions they generate during reading.

Evaluate Seminal Texts: Premises, Purposes, and Arguments (LINES 3–11)

COMMON CORE RI 2, RI 8, RI 9

Tell students that the first paragraph of Lincoln's speech addresses his audience's expectations about what they might hear, revealing something about the **purpose** of the speech, or what he intends to accomplish with it.

A **CITE TEXT EVIDENCE** Ask students to tell where Lincoln addresses his audience's expectations. *(In lines 7–8, Lincoln says that "little that is new could be presented" about the details of the war, therby letting his audience know that he will not give further details. In line 11, he says that he will not venture a prediction about the war's conclusion. Lincoln is letting his audience know that, perhaps contrary to their exceptions, his purpose is not to give an update on the progress of the war.)*

CRITICAL VOCABULARY

engross: Lincoln points out that the war is still the most central concern of the nation. **ASK STUDENTS** why war engrosses peoples' attention and energy. *(It deeply affects their lives and their countries.)*

venture: Lincoln does not want to directly predict the outcome of the war. **ASK STUDENTS** why political figures might be reluctant to venture guesses about future events. *(If they are wrong, they could lose credibility.)*

deprecate: Both sides had openly disapproved of a civil war, but ultimately they both engaged in one. **ASK STUDENTS** what, besides war, leaders are likely to deprecate. *(injustice, poverty, crime)*

Abraham Lincoln (1809–1865) *did not favor the abolition of slavery when he became the 16th U. S. president, but he had campaigned to prevent slavery's expansion into new territories. His election in 1860 led to the Civil War. Lincoln issued the Emancipation Proclamation in January 1863. After his re-election, Lincoln successfully pushed Congress to pass the Thirteenth Amendment to the Constitution, which outlawed slavery. Lincoln gave this speech on March 4, 1865, less than six weeks before he was assassinated.*

Second Inaugural Address

Speech by Abraham Lincoln

AS YOU READ Notice how Lincoln describes how the situation in the country has changed since his first inauguration in 1861. Write down any questions you generate during reading.

Fᴇʟʟᴏᴡ Cᴏᴜɴᴛʀʏᴍᴇɴ:

At this second appearing to take the oath of the presidential office, there is less occasion for an extended address than there was at the first. Then a statement, somewhat in detail, of course to be pursued, seemed fitting and proper. Now, at the expiration of four years, during which public declarations have been constantly called forth on every point and phase of the great contest which still absorbs the attention and **engrosses** the energies of the nation, little that is new could be presented. The progress of our arms, upon which all else chiefly depends, is as well known to the public as to myself; and it is, I trust, reasonably satisfactory and encouraging to all. With high hope for the future, no prediction in regard to it is **ventured**.

10

On the occasion corresponding to this four years ago, all thoughts were anxiously directed to an impending civil war. All dreaded it—all sought to avert it. While the inaugural address was being delivered from this place, devoted altogether to saving the Union without war, insurgent agents were in the city seeking to destroy it without war— seeking to dissolve the Union, and divide effects, by negotiation. Both parties **deprecated** war; but one of them would make war rather than

engross
(ĕn-grōs´) *v.* to completely engage the attention or interest.

venture
(vĕn´chər) *v.* to risk or dare.

deprecate
(dĕp´rĭ-kāt´) *v.* to express disapproval.

Close Read Screencasts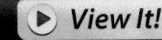

Modeled Discussions

Have students click the *Close Read* icons in their eBooks to access a screencast in which readers discuss and annotate the following key passage:

- Lincoln reminds listeners that four years ago, when he made his first inaugural address, a war was about to begin (lines 12–20).

As a class, view and discuss this video. Then have students pair up to do an independent close read of an additional passage—Lincoln's statement that the length of the war will be for God to decide (lines 47–54).

Evaluate Seminal Texts: Premises, Purposes, and Arguments (LINES 29–34)

COMMON CORE RI 2, RI 8, RI 9

Tell students that a **premise** is a general principle that most people will take as given, or will agree with.

 **CITE TEXT EVIDENCE** Have students explain the premise that Lincoln is developing in the second paragraph. *(Those in the North and those in the South share the same basic values and desires.)* Ask them to identify specific points that help develop the premise. *(Both sides have similar religious beliefs [lines 33–34].)*

Evaluate Seminal Texts: Premises, Purposes, and Arguments (LINES 55–60)

COMMON CORE RI 9

Explain to students that Lincoln does not state his **purpose** directly, but that it can be inferred from the call to action with which he ends the speech.

C **ASK STUDENTS** to restate Lincoln's call to action in their own words and then explain the speech's purpose. *(Let's finish the war and then work to put it behind us by caring for everyone, no matter what side they fought for. The purpose of the speech was to strengthen the resolve of the people to see the war through to its end and convince them to reconcile with the rebels.)*

CRITICAL VOCABULARY

wring: Lincoln uses the word *wringing* figuratively, to describe slave labor.

ASK STUDENTS to give examples of literal *wringing*. *(squeezing water from a washcloth)*

COLLABORATIVE DISCUSSION Have students work in pairs to make a chart showing the contrasts between America four years earlier and America at the time of this address. Have the pairs consider what Lincoln's motives for pointing out these differences might have been.

ASK STUDENTS to share any questions they generated in the course of reading and discussing the selection.

20 let the nation survive; and the other would accept war rather than let it perish. And the war came.

One-eighth of the whole population were colored slaves, not distributed generally over the Union, but localized in the Southern part of it. These slaves constituted a peculiar and powerful interest. All knew that this interest was, somehow, the cause of the war. To strengthen, perpetuate, and extend this interest was the object for which the insurgents would rend the Union, even by war; while the government claimed no right to do more than to restrict the territorial enlargement of it.

B 30 Neither party expected for the war the magnitude or the duration which it has already attained. Neither anticipated that the cause of the conflict might cease with, or even before, the conflict itself should cease. Each looked for an easier triumph, and a result less fundamental and astounding. Both read the same Bible, and pray to the same God; and each invokes his aid against the other. It may seem strange that any men should dare to ask a just God's assistance in **wringing** their bread from the sweat of other men's faces; but let us judge not, that we be not judged. The prayers of both could not be answered—that of neither has been answered fully.

40 The Almighty has his own purposes. "Woe unto the world because of offences! for it must needs be that offences come; but woe to that man by whom the offence cometh." If we shall suppose that American slavery is one of those offences which, in the providence of God, must needs come, but which, having continued through his appointed time, he now wills to remove, and that he gives to both North and South this terrible war, as the woe due to those by whom the offence came, shall we discern therein any departure from those divine attributes[1] which the believers in a living God always ascribe to him? Fondly do we hope—fervently do we pray—that this mighty scourge of war may speedily pass away. Yet, if God wills that it continue until all the wealth 50 piled by the bondman's two hundred and fifty years of unrequited toil shall be sunk, and until every drop of blood drawn with the lash shall be paid by another drawn with the sword, as was said three thousand years ago, so still it must be said, "The judgments of the Lord are true and righteous altogether."

C With malice toward none; with charity for all: with firmness in the right, as God gives us to see the right, let us strive on to finish the work we are in; to bind up the nation's wounds; to care for him who shall have borne the battle, and for his widow, and his orphan—to do all which may achieve and cherish a just and lasting peace among 60 ourselves, and with all nations.

wring
(rĭng) *v.* to obtain through force or pressure.

---

[1] **attributes:** qualities or characteristics.

COLLABORATIVE DISCUSSION How does emphasizing the changes that have taken place in America strengthen Lincoln's argument?

SCAFFOLDING FOR ELL STUDENTS

Understand Word Associations Explain to students that in addition to their dictionary definitions, words are also associated with certain thoughts and feelings. Point out to students the word *rend* in line 26 and explain that it means "tear into pieces." Then tell students that the ideas of violence and anger are often associated with *rend*.

ASK STUDENTS to look up the words *strive* (line 56) and *cherish* (line 59) in a dictionary and write down their meanings. Then ask them to interview native speakers to find out what ideas and feelings they associate with each of the words.

Evaluate Seminal Texts: Premises, Purposes, and Arguments

Lincoln delivered his Second Inaugural Address in a particular historical context: the nation had been at war for four years, and recent events on the battlefield were making it look more likely that the war might end soon with a Union victory. Therefore, Lincoln's overall **purpose** in this speech was to persuade his audience to adopt his ideas about how the country could best move forward. This address was Lincoln's opportunity to make his case to the public.

Lincoln's speech presents an argument. In an **argument**, a writer expresses a position on a particular issue and supports that position with reasons and evidence. In analyzing an argument, it is helpful to keep the following definitions in mind.

Parts of an Argument		
Term	Definition	Example
Claim	writer's position on an issue; a conclusion	The American colonies are justified in fighting for freedom from British rule.
Reasons	declarations that support a claim	The American colonies are oppressed by British rule.
Evidence	specific pieces of information that support a claim or reason	The British have levied unjust taxes on the colonies for ten years.
Premise	a general principle most people agree with; links the reasons and evidence to the claim	People have the right to revolt when oppressed.

As you apply these ideas in analyzing Lincoln's Second Inaugural Address, ask:

- What statements or word choices indicate Lincoln's tone or attitude toward Northerners and Southerners?
- What are some general principles that Lincoln states or implies about Americans' shared values, about slavery, and about the war?
- What are some of the central ideas that Lincoln develops in the speech about slavery and the war?
- How do the rhetorical features in the speech, including word choice and parallelism, or the use of similar grammatical structures to express ideas that are related or equal in importance, reveal which appeals Lincoln makes?

By analyzing how all these elements work together in this seminal text, you can better understand the historical significance of this speech.

CLOSE READ

Evaluate Seminal Texts: Premises, Purposes, and Arguments

Explain to students that Lincoln's claims, reasons, evidence, and premises, along with rhetorical devices, work together to give the speech its power. Remind students that rhetorical devices are ways of using language that help to persuade readers. Tell them that two rhetorical devices that Lincoln uses in his speech are the use of words with strong associations and the use of parallelism, or the repetition of grammatical patterns.

To help students understand and appreciate the speech, lead a class discussion to answer the questions at the bottom of this page. Ask volunteers to suggest answers for each question and discuss the answers as a class. Ask volunteers to explain how the elements of the speech work together to make it strong and effective. Finally, guide the class to come to a consensus regarding the main claim of Lincoln's speech.

Strategies for Annotation   ✏ 🖥 *Annotate it!*

Evaluate Seminal Texts: Premises, Purposes, and Arguments

Share these strategies for guided or independent analysis:

- Highlight in green words or phrases that reveal Lincoln's attitude toward Southerners.
- Highlight premises in yellow.
- Underline examples of parallelism.

...All dreaded it—all sought to avert it. While the inaugural address was being delivered..., devoted altogether to saving the Union without war, 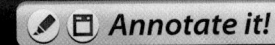 insurgent agents were in the city seeking to destroy it without war....Both parties deprecated war; but  one of them would make war rather than let the nation survive; and the other would accept war rather than let it perish.

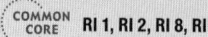

PRACTICE & APPLY

Analyzing the Text

COMMON CORE RI 1, RI 2, RI 8, RI 9

Possible answers:

1. The South is the party that "would make war," and the North is the one that "would accept war." This sentence sets a tone of respect for and acceptance of both sides. Lincoln subtly expresses that the South may have been more responsible for the war, but he is careful not to place blame only on the South.

2. Similarities: Both sides tried to avoid war, and now both want the war to end. Both expected the war to be shorter. Both sides pray to the same God and read the same Bible. Differences: The South wanted to divide the country, and the North wanted to keep it together. The South wanted to expand slavery, while the North wanted to limit it. The similarities highlight that both sides can benefit from ending the war and that both are part of the same nation. The differences clarify why the war happened and remind listeners of what issues the Union will have to work through after the war has ended.

3. Neither the North nor the South thought that slavery would end before the war was decided.

4. He presents the fact of the war itself as evidence that slavery was an offense that would bring on God's punishment and implies that soldiers are being killed to avenge the deaths of the enslaved people.

5. Lincoln's purpose is to convince Northerners and Southerners to work together to reunite the country without slavery, and in this sentence he suggests that is God's purpose, too.

6. Religious references are likely to be well received by both sides. Also, he wants the audience to think about the moral aspects of what has occurred and attend to its own conscience.

7. He uses parallel structures ("With malice...," "with charity...," "with firmness..."; and "to finish...," "to bind up...," and "to care for...") to emphasize the shared feelings, intentions, and actions that must exist between the two sides in order for the nation to recover from the war. The theme is that peace can be achieved if everyone comes together.

eBook *Annotate It!*

Analyzing the Text

 COMMON CORE RI 1, RI 2, RI 8, RI 9, SL 1a, SL 1c

Cite Text Evidence Support your responses with evidence from the selection.

1. **Identify** In lines 17–20, Lincoln says that one party "would make war" while the other "would accept war." To whom was Lincoln referring in each part of this sentence? How does this sentence begin to set the **tone** or attitude that Lincoln takes throughout the speech?

2. **Compare** What are the similarities between Northerners and Southerners that Lincoln outlines in the speech? What are their differences? Why does Lincoln highlight these similarities and differences in the speech?

3. **Evaluate** What does Lincoln mean when he says "Neither anticipated that the cause of the conflict might cease with, or even before, the conflict itself should cease" (lines 30–32)?

4. **Analyze** Lincoln makes a moral argument in lines 39–54. Both his premise and claim can be inferred from the Biblical quotations at the beginning and end of the paragraph. What evidence does Lincoln present so that his claim follows logically from the premise?

5. **Infer** How might the statement, "The Almighty has his own purposes" (line 39) relate to Lincoln's purpose in giving this speech?

6. **Evaluate** Why does Lincoln use religious references in his argument?

7. **Analyze** Examine the rhetorical features that Lincoln uses in the concluding paragraph of the speech. How do these features support Lincoln's purpose? What theme does this conclusion express?

PERFORMANCE TASK

Speaking Activity: Discussion As president, Lincoln's goal was to unify the North and the South. Explore how this speech supports that goal through this activity.

-   Work with a partner. Have each partner play the role of a person meeting another person who has been on the other side during the Civil War. Decide which partner will represent which side.

-   Review Lincoln's speech and discuss how it speaks to your interests and concerns.

-   In your discussion, pose and respond to questions that will allow each partner's position to be fully expressed and heard.

-   After your discussion, write a summary of how Lincoln's speech promoted unity between the North and the South.

Assign this performance task.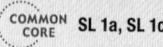

PERFORMANCE TASK

COMMON CORE SL 1a, SL 1c

Speaking Activity: Discussion Once students have been assigned roles, have each express his or her general point of view as a member of either the Union or the Confederacy. Make sure they bring this clear frame of reference to the review of the speech and to the discussion. Suggest that students conduct the discussion as a formal set of questions and answers, with the objective of better understanding how each side might have received the speech.

Critical Vocabulary

engross	venture	deprecate	wring

Practice and Apply Working with a partner, answer each question from your own experiences to show that you understand the meaning of each Critical Vocabulary word.

1. What is something that **engrosses** you?

2. When have you **ventured** something?

3. When have you **deprecated** something?

4. When have you engaged in an act of **wringing**?

Vocabulary Strategy: Pronunciation

The Critical Vocabulary word *wringing* has a silent first letter, so it is pronounced just like *ringing*. Someone listening to Lincoln's speech would need to determine the correct word from its context rather than its sound. This example shows why it is helpful to verify the pronunciation of an unfamiliar word by checking a dictionary. In *wringing*, *write*, and all English words that begin with *wr*, the *w* is silent.

Not all words follow such clear patterns. For example, in the word *trough* (a long, narrow container), the *gh* sounds like *f* and the word rhymes with *off*, but in the word *through*, the *gh* is silent and the vowel combination *ou* is also pronounced differently—the word is pronounced like *threw*.

These examples emphasize that words are not always spelled the way they are pronounced, or pronounced the way they are spelled. Using a dictionary to find the correct pronunciation of a word will help you achieve and demonstrate your command of the conventions of written and spoken English.

Practice and Apply Use a dictionary to confirm the pronunciation of each of these words. Then practice the pronunciation by saying the words in sentences with a partner.

1. cliché
2. segue
3. subtle
4. colonel
5. indict
6. epitome
7. aisle
8. circuit
9. silhouette
10. respite

Critical Vocabulary

Possible answers:

1. *Reading mystery novels engrosses me; I forget about everything else the moment I pick up the book.*

2. *I ventured something when I invested money in yarn and began knitting scarves to sell at the craft fair.*

3. *I deprecated my little brother's bad behavior when he wrote on the bedroom wall with crayons.*

4. *I wring out the kitchen sponge every evening after I finish cleaning up after dinner.*

Vocabulary Strategy: Pronunciation

1. *cliché: klē shā ′*

2. *segue: seg′wā*

3. *subtle: sut′ ′l*

4. *colonel: kʉr′ nel*

5. *indict: in dīt′*

6. *epitome: ē pit′ e mē ′*

7. *aisle: ī′l*

8. *circuit: sʉr′kit*

9. *silhouette: sil ′ e wet′*

10. *respite: res′pit*

WHEN STUDENTS STRUGGLE . . .

Develop Reading Fluency Invite students to pick one or two paragraphs from the speech and note any words they are not sure how to pronounce. Have them look up the words to learn their correct pronunciation. Encourage students to note any silent letters or difficult letter combinations.

Then have students pair up and practice reading the paragraphs aloud to one another. Circulate among the teams to make sure words are being pronounced correctly.

PRACTICE & APPLY

Language and Style: Balanced Sentences

 COMMON CORE L 3a

Discuss with students how Lincoln's balanced sentences support his message. Project lines 49–54 and point out the phrases "drawn with the lash" and "drawn with the sword." Ask students how these balanced phrases support Lincoln's message. *(The balance between the phrases suggests that the violence of slavery and the violence of war are equivalent and related.)*

Practice and Apply Have pairs of students exchange papers and compare the revised summaries with the first drafts. Then have them give feedback.

 Assess It!

Online Selection Test
- Download an editable ExamView bank.
- Assign and manage this test online.

Language and Style: Balanced Sentences

 COMMON CORE L 3a

Lincoln's style in the Second Inaugural Address is marked by complex, balanced sentences and paragraphs. **Syntax** is the way an author arranges words in phrases, clauses, and sentences. Lincoln uses his distinctive syntax to support the content of the speech and emphasize particular ideas.

Consider this sentence from the paragraph in which Lincoln makes his strongest moral argument (lines 49–54)

> Yet, if God wills that it continue until all the wealth piled by the bondsman's two hundred and fifty years of unrequited toil shall be sunk, and until every drop of blood drawn with the lash shall be paid by another drawn with the sword, as was said three thousand years ago, so still it must be said "The judgments of the Lord are true and righteous altogether."

Notice that there are two clauses that begin with the conjunction *until*. In each of these clauses, Lincoln presents images of how long the war might last to balance the evils of slavery. In the second clause, there is further balance between "blood drawn with the lash" and "drawn with the sword." He then concludes with another balanced statement about the enduring truth of God's judgments: "as it was said three thousand year ago, so still it must be said." The balanced way this long, complex sentence is constructed helps to make the meaning clear and strongly supports Lincoln's message.

Lincoln also uses this balanced style for the fourth paragraph (lines 29–38), adding to it the repetition of the words *neither*, *each*, and *both* to emphasize the similarities in Northerners' and Southerners' reactions to the war.

> Neither party expected for the war the magnitude or the duration which it has already attained. Neither anticipated that the cause of the conflict might cease with, or even before, the conflict itself should cease. Each looked for an easier triumph, and a result less fundamental and astounding. Both read the same Bible, and pray to the same God; and each invokes his aid against the other. It may seem strange that any men should dare to ask a just God's assistance in wringing their bread from the sweat of other men's faces; but let us judge not, that we be not judged. The prayers of both could not be answered—that of neither has been answered fully.

These stylistic choices support Lincoln's message that it was time for the North and the South to come together once again and to heal the nation's wounds.

Practice and Apply Look back at the summary you wrote of your earlier discussion in response to this selection's Performance Task. Revise your writing to include balanced sentences and paragraphs to support the ideas you want to express about how Lincoln promoted unity between the North and the South in his speech.

Analyze Structure

COMMON CORE
RI 5

EXTEND

Tell students that argumentative essays usually follow this structure:

- introduction
    - gets the audience's attention
    - introduces the main claim
- body paragraphs
    - present claims and supporting evidence
    - address counterarguments
- conclusion
    - restates the main claim
    - makes a call to action

Another aspect of argumentative structure is choosing the order in which claims and evidence are presented. Lincoln orders his information carefully to emphasize the agreement and unity that he wants his speech to inspire.

PRACTICE AND APPLY

Have students analyze the structure of Lincoln's speech and evaluate its effectiveness, and then create an extended outline.

Discuss how Lincoln used structure to write a speech that today is considered one of the greatest in American history. Ask why Lincoln uses the introductory paragraph to tell listeners what issues he will *not* address. *(He doesn't want listeners' expectations to interfere with their attention.)* Then ask why he orders his body paragraphs as he does. *(He first covers the beginning of the war, then the reason for the war, then how both Northerners and Southerners feel about the war, and finally he uses biblical language to justify and recommit to the war. He does this to build agreement with his audience by reviewing events that they witnessed.)* Finally, ask students to evaluate Lincoln's call to action in the conclusion.

 If students need further instruction, use this *Interactive Whiteboard Lesson:* **Text Structure and Meaning.**

Evaluate Seminal Texts: Premises, Purposes, and Arguments

COMMON CORE
RI 2, RI 8,
RI 9

RETEACH

Review the terms *claim, reasons,* and *evidence*. Tell students that these are the basic elements of an argument and that all three must be sound in order for an argument to be credible and strong.

 **LEVEL UP TUTORIALS** Assign the following *Level Up* tutorial: **Analyzing Arguments**

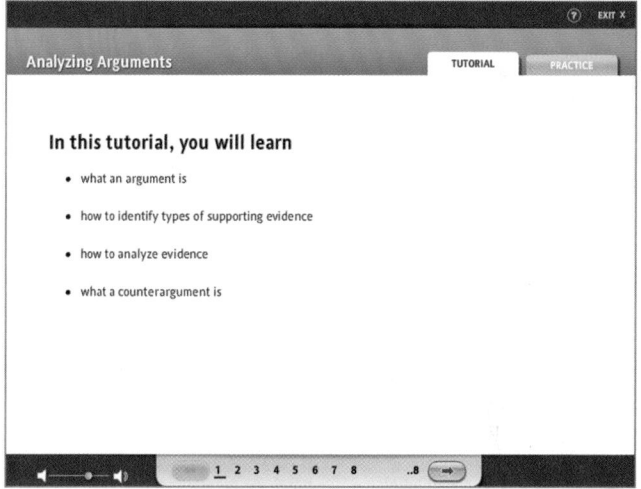

Point out that Lincoln does not directly state most of his claims. Rather, he weaves them into his speech using language and organizational approaches designed to appeal to everyone in the audience to persuade them to unify. The individual claims must be inferred.

PRACTICE AND APPLY

Have students look again at Lincoln's speech with an eye toward identifying each claim and its supporting reasons and evidence. Have them create a chart with four columns: *Claim, Reasons, Evidence,* and *Effectiveness*. In the fourth column, students will evaluate how effectively Lincoln supported the claim.

Have students work in small groups to discuss their charts. Encourage students to tell how they identified the claims and evidence, and compare their evaluations of the strength of Lincoln's argument based on the charts.

The Emancipation Proclamation

For more context, students can view "The Story of Us: Abraham Lincoln" in their eBooks.

Legal Document by Abraham Lincoln

Why This Text

Students may have difficulty understanding nineteenth-century foundational U.S. documents. The Emancipation Proclamation is a significant historical document because it outlines a direct opposition to slavery. With the help of the close-reading questions, students will analyze Lincoln's purpose and central ideas. This close reading will lead students to explain Lincoln's argument that he is taking action that is of "military necessity."

Background Have students read the background and the information about Abraham Lincoln. Alternatively, they can watch the video "The Story of Us: Abraham Lincoln" in their eBooks. Tell students that the Emancipation Proclamation was not a law passed by Congress, and it did not abolish slavery. The Proclamation was issued under Lincoln's role as Commander-in-Chief. Slavery was not abolished until the adoption of the Thirteenth Amendment to the Constitution in 1865. Lincoln's home state of Illinois was first to ratify the Thirteenth Amendment.

AS YOU READ Ask students to pay attention to how Lincoln builds his argument.

Common Core Support

- cite strong and thorough textual evidence
- analyze the development of two or more central ideas
- delineate and evaluate the reasoning in seminal U.S. texts
- analyze nineteenth-century foundational U.S. documents

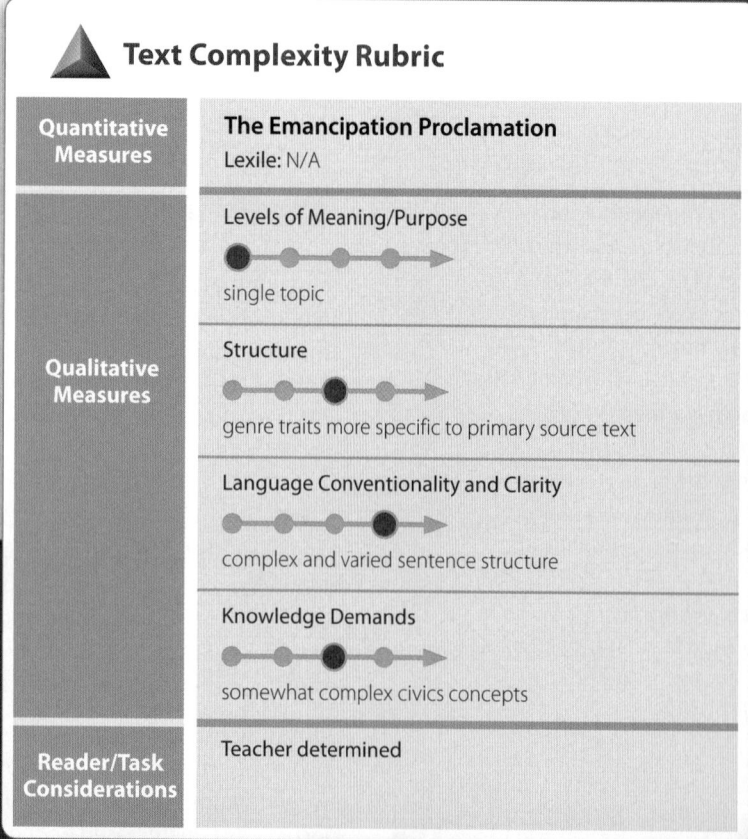

Text Complexity Rubric

Quantitative Measures	The Emancipation Proclamation Lexile: N/A
Qualitative Measures	Levels of Meaning/Purpose single topic
	Structure genre traits more specific to primary source text
	Language Conventionality and Clarity complex and varied sentence structure
	Knowledge Demands somewhat complex civics concepts
Reader/Task Considerations	Teacher determined

Strategies for CLOSE READING

Evaluate Seminal Texts: Premises, Purposes, and Arguments

Students should read this document carefully all the way through. Close-reading questions at the bottom of the page will help them focus on a thorough analysis of the text. As they read, students should jot down comments or questions about the proclamation in the side margins.

WHEN STUDENTS STRUGGLE . . .

To help students analyze Lincoln's argument, have them work in small groups to fill out a chart, such as the one shown below.

CITE TEXT EVIDENCE For practice in analyzing an argument, ask students to identify a claim Lincoln makes and show how he supports it.

CLAIM:

The Emancipation Proclamation is a necessary war measure.

SUPPORT:

Reason 1: *There are states and parts of states that are in rebellion.*

Reason 2: *Rebel states are not represented in Congress.*

Reason 3: *Lincoln is empowered as Commander-in-Chief to suppress the rebellion.*

Background Abraham Lincoln *(1809–1865) was elected president in 1860 and was clear in his opposition to expanding slavery to U.S. territories in the West. By the time of Lincoln's inauguration in March of 1861, seven slave states had formed the Confederacy and seceded from the Union. By April, the Union and the Confederacy were at war. After the Union victory at Antietam in September 1862, Lincoln issued a preliminary proclamation, stating that on January 1, 1863, slaves in rebel states would be declared free. Though more of a symbolic gesture than an enforceable law, the Emancipation Proclamation heartened abolitionists and African Americans and made the issue of slavery a central focus of the war.*

The Emancipation Proclamation

Legal Document by Abraham Lincoln

CLOSE READ
Notes

1. **READ ▶** As you read lines 1–21, begin to cite text evidence.

   - Circle the three dates noted in these lines.
   - Underline the states affected by the proclamation, and in the margin explain which states this proclamation affects (lines 5–12).
   - Underline text that explains how the president will classify the states (lines 13–21).

A Transcription By the President of the United States of America: A Proclamation.

Ⓐ Whereas, on the twenty-second day of September, in the year of our Lord one thousand eight hundred and sixty-two, a proclamation was issued by the President of the United States, containing, among other things, the following, to wit:[1]

"That on the first day of January, in the year of our Lord one thousand eight hundred and sixty-three, all persons held as slaves within any State or designated part of a State, the people whereof shall then be in rebellion against the United States, shall be then, thenceforward, and forever free; and the Executive Government of the United States, including the military and naval
10 authority thereof, will recognize and maintain the freedom of such persons, and will do no act or acts to repress such persons, or any of them, in any efforts they may make for their actual freedom.

It affects states or parts of states in rebellion against the United States.

---
[1] **to wit:** namely.

57

1. **READ AND CITE TEXT EVIDENCE**

   Ⓐ **ASK STUDENTS** to use their marked text as evidence to explain what happened on January 1, 1863. *Students should cite evidence from lines 1–2 that Lincoln issued a proclamation in September of 1862 to all states "in rebellion against the United States" (lines 7–8) freeing the slaves in those states as of "the first day of January, in the year of our Lord one thousand eight hundred and sixty-three" (lines 5–6).*

CLOSE READ Notes

"That the Executive will, on the first day of January aforesaid,[2] by proclamation, designate the States and parts of States, if any, in which the people thereof, respectively, shall then be in rebellion against the United States; and the fact that any State, or the people thereof, shall on that day be, in good faith, represented in the Congress of the United States by members chosen thereto at elections wherein a majority of the qualified voters of such State shall have participated, shall, in the absence of strong countervailing[3] testimony, be
20 deemed conclusive evidence that such State, and the people thereof, are not then in rebellion against the United States."

Now, therefore I, Abraham Lincoln, President of the United States, by virtue of the power in me vested as Commander-in-Chief, of the Army and Navy of the United States in time of actual armed rebellion against the authority and government of the United States, and as a fit and necessary war measure for **suppressing** said rebellion, do, on this first day of January, in the year of our Lord one thousand eight hundred and sixty-three, and in accordance with my purpose so to do publicly proclaimed for the full period of one hundred days, from the day first above mentioned, order and designate as
30 the States and parts of States wherein the people thereof respectively, are this day in rebellion against the United States, the following, to wit:

suppressing:
*preventing;
restraining*

[2] **aforesaid:** stated before.
[3] **countervailing:** contradicting.

C Arkansas, Texas, Louisiana, (except the Parishes of St. Bernard, Plaquemines, Jefferson, St. John, St. Charles, St. James Ascension, Assumption, Terrebonne, Lafourche, St. Mary, St. Martin, and Orleans, including the City of New Orleans) Mississippi, Alabama, Florida, Georgia, South Carolina, North Carolina, and Virginia, (except the forty-eight counties designated as West Virginia, and also the counties of Berkley, Accomac, Northampton, Elizabeth City, York, Princess Ann, and Norfolk, including the cities of Norfolk and Portsmouth), and which excepted parts, are for the present, left precisely as if
40 this proclamation were not issued.

And by virtue of the power, and for the purpose aforesaid, I do order and declare that all persons held as slaves within said designated States, and parts of States, are, and henceforward shall be free; and that the Executive government of the United States, including the military and naval authorities thereof, will recognize and maintain the freedom of said persons.

And I hereby enjoin upon[4] the people so declared to be free to abstain from all violence, unless in necessary self-defence; and I recommend to them that, in all cases when allowed, they labor faithfully for reasonable wages.

And I further declare and make known, that such persons of suitable
50 condition, will be received into the armed service of the United States to **garrison** forts, positions, stations, and other places, and to man vessels of all sorts in said service.

[4] **enjoin upon:** direct.

CLOSE READ Notes

Louisiana and Virginia have exceptions— counties that aren't considered in rebellion.

Slaves in rebel states are now free.

garrison:
to occupy as troops

---

2. ◀ **REREAD** Reread lines 13–21. What is Lincoln's purpose in this paragraph and how does he achieve it? Cite text evidence in your response.

His purpose is to define "in rebellion." He does so by defining who is "not then in rebellion" as "any State, or the people thereof . . . represented in the Congress . . . by members chosen thereto at elections. . . ."

3. **READ** ▶ As you read lines 22–40, continue to cite text evidence.
- Circle the authority by which Lincoln makes the January 1, 1863, proclamation.
- Underline the reason Lincoln gives for making the proclamation.
- In the margin of lines 32–40, explain the reason for the exceptions.

4. ◀ **REREAD** Reread lines 22–31. Interpret the meaning of "the full period of one hundred days." Cite text evidence in your answer.

One hundred days is the period of time between Lincoln's September 22, 1861 proclamation and the date the proclamation goes into effect: "the first day of January, in the year of our Lord one thousand eight hundred and sixty-three."

5. **READ** ▶ As you read lines 41–60, continue to cite text evidence.
- In the margin, explain Lincoln's order and declaration (lines 41–45).
- Underline parts of Lincoln's message that are directed to newly freed people.
- Circle reasons Lincoln offers to support his argument that this proclamation is justified.

---

2. **REREAD AND CITE TEXT EVIDENCE**

B **ASK STUDENTS** to discuss their answer with a partner. *Students should state that Lincoln's purpose in these lines is to define "in rebellion" (line 15). He does so by defining who is "not then in rebellion" (line 21) as "any State, or the people thereof . . . represented in the Congress . . . by members chosen thereto at elections . . ." (lines 16–21).*

3. **READ AND CITE TEXT EVIDENCE**

C **ASK STUDENTS** to cite text evidence to support their explanation of the reasons there were exceptions to the states listed as "in rebellion." *Students should cite the exceptions listed in lines 32–39 to show that certain parts of Louisiana and Virginia were exempted from the proclamation.*

Critical Vocabulary: suppressing (line 26) Ask students to explain Lincoln's use of *suppressing*.

4. **REREAD AND CITE TEXT EVIDENCE**

D **ASK STUDENTS** to cite text evidence to support their interpretation. *Students should cite evidence in lines 1–2 and lines 26–27 to show that the "full period of one hundred days" (lines 28–29) is the period between the date the proclamation was issued and the date it went into effect.*

5. **READ AND CITE TEXT EVIDENCE**

E **ASK STUDENTS** to use their marked text as evidence to explain how Lincoln justified issuing and enforcing the proclamation. *Students should cite lines 53–54 as evidence that Lincoln justified the proclamation by stating that it was a just act necessitated by the war.*

Critical Vocabulary: garrison (line 51) Have students explain Lincoln's use of *garrison*. Whom is Lincoln addressing, and what does he suggest through this word?

CLOSE READ
Notes

invoke:
cite as an authority

E   And upon this act, sincerely believed to be an act of justice, warranted by the Constitution, upon military necessity, I **invoke** the considerate judgment of mankind, and the gracious favor of Almighty God.

In witness whereof, I have hereunto set my hand and caused the seal of the United States to be affixed.

Done at the City of Washington, this first day of January, in the year of our Lord one thousand eight hundred and sixty three, and of the Independence of
60 the United States of America the eighty-seventh.

By the President: ABRAHAM LINCOLN
WILLIAM H. SEWARD, Secretary of State.

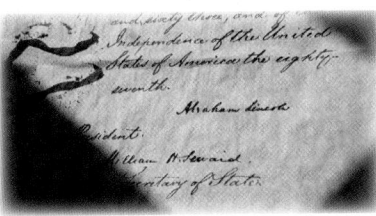

6. ◄ **REREAD AND DISCUSS** Reread lines 41–60. With a small group, discuss the purpose of these lines. What do you think Lincoln envisioned would happen as a result of this proclamation?

SHORT RESPONSE

Cite Text Evidence Analyze Lincoln's argument that he is taking action that is of "military necessity." Refer to your reading notes, and **cite text evidence** in your response.

Lincoln's argument of military necessity depends on his claim that there are states and parts of states that are "in rebellion against the United States." He offers as evidence that these states are not represented in Congress and that they are in "actual armed rebellion against the authority and government of the United States." For these reasons, Lincoln asserts that the Emancipation Proclamation is a "necessary war measure for suppressing said rebellion."

60

6. **REREAD AND DISCUSS USING TEXT EVIDENCE**

F **ASK STUDENTS** to be prepared to share the results of their group discussions in a class discussion. *Students should cite evidence from lines 43–48.*

Critical Vocabulary: invoke (line 54) Have students compare definitions of *invoke*.

FOR ELL STUDENTS Explain the meaning of the archaic terms *whereof* ("of what") and *hereunto* ("to this document").

SHORT RESPONSE

Cite Text Evidence Students should:

- determine a claim Lincoln makes.
- analyze Lincoln's argument.
- cite text evidence that delineates Lincoln's reasoning.

TO CHALLENGE STUDENTS . . .

For more information on Lincoln, students can view the video "The Story of Us: Abraham Lincoln" in their eBooks.

ASK STUDENTS to explain how Lincoln's position on slavery changed over time. *Students should note that initially Lincoln did not want slavery to be the central issue of the Civil War, but by the time of his death he not only thought all slaves should be freed but also that all African Americans should have equal rights.*

DIG DEEPER

With the class, return to Question 6, Reread and Discuss. Have students share the results of their discussions.

ASK STUDENTS whether they were satisfied with the outcome of their small-group discussions. Have each group share their findings about Lincoln's expectations of what would happen as a result of the Emancipation Proclamation. What textual evidence did students find to support their conclusions?

- Guide each group to share whether they came to a unanimous conclusion about Lincoln's expectations. How did they resolve any disagreement?
- Ask groups to explain how they determined which details in the text were relevant.
- After groups have shared the results of their discussions, ask students whether another group's contributions to the class discussion helped them understand Lincoln's expectations.

ASK STUDENTS to return to their Short Response answer and revise it based on the class discussion.

 *my*SmartPlanner   Create lesson plans and access resources online.

EXEMPLAR What to the Slave Is the Fourth of July?

Speech by Frederick Douglass

Why This Text?

To fully understand how they feel about important questions, students benefit from being able to trace and evaluate an author's argument. This lesson explores Douglass's argument to end slavery in the United States.

 **View It!**
Professional Development Podcast:
Teaching Argument

Key Learning Objective: Students will analyze point of view, evaluating how the rhetoric, style, and content contribute to a text's persuasiveness.

COMMON CORE Common Core Standards

RI 1 Cite textual evidence.
RI 2 Determine central ideas of a text.
RI 4 Determine the meaning of words and phrases.
RI 6 Determine an author's point of view or purpose.
RI 8 Delineate and evaluate the reasoning in seminal U.S. texts.
W 4 Produce clear and coherent writing.
SL 1 Initiate and participate in a range of collaborative discussions.
SL 3 Delineate a speaker's argument and specific claims, evaluating the reasoning and the relevance of the evidence.
L 3a Vary syntax for effect; apply an understanding of syntax.
L 4 Determine or clarify the meaning of unknown and multiple-meaning words and phrases.
L 4c Consult general reference materials.
L 4d Verify the preliminary determination of the meaning of a word or phrase.

Text Complexity Rubric

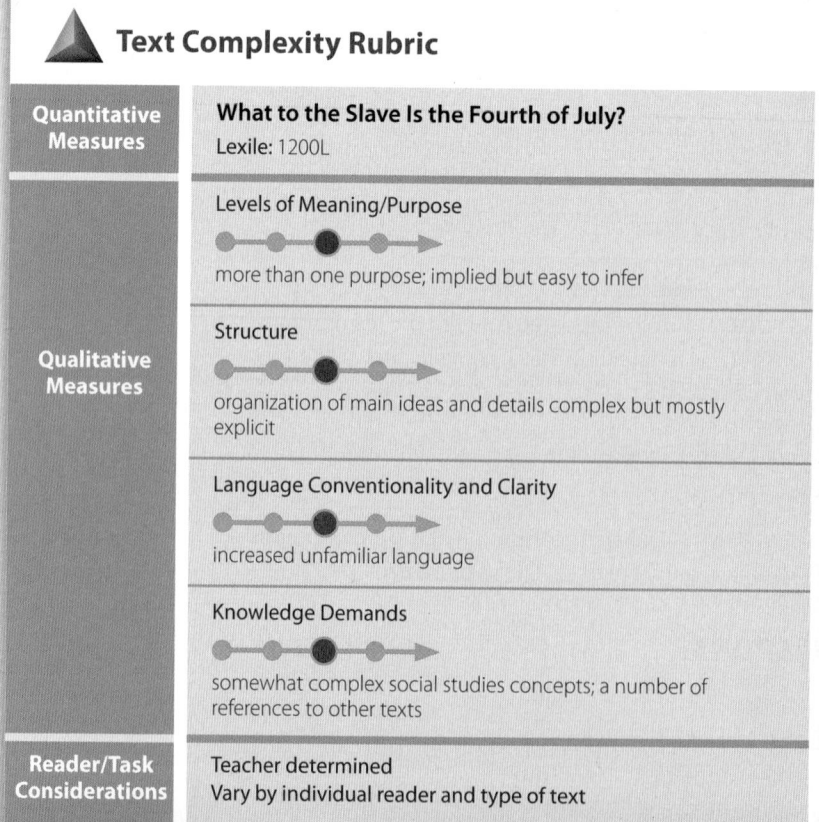

Quantitative Measures	**What to the Slave Is the Fourth of July?** Lexile: 1200L
Qualitative Measures	Levels of Meaning/Purpose — more than one purpose; implied but easy to infer
	Structure — organization of main ideas and details complex but mostly explicit
	Language Conventionality and Clarity — increased unfamiliar language
	Knowledge Demands — somewhat complex social studies concepts; a number of references to other texts
Reader/Task Considerations	Teacher determined Vary by individual reader and type of text

TEACH

CLOSE READ

For more context and historical background, students can view the video "AMERICA The Story of Us: Frederick Douglass" in their eBooks.

Frederick Douglass Have students read the information about the author. Explain that Douglass learned to read and write as a child, when he was working as a slave for a shipbuilder in Baltimore. Later, Douglass was sent back to the Eastern Shore of Maryland, where he had been born. There he was treated brutally and decided that he would escape from slavery. Once Douglass escaped to the North, he used his writing and speaking abilities to try to change the country by putting an end to slavery. After the Civil War, he wrote and spoke against Jim Crow laws and in support of women's rights.

AS YOU READ Direct students to use the As You Read instructions to focus their reading. Remind students to write down any questions they generate during reading.

Analyze Author's Point of View (LINES 1–8)

COMMON CORE RI 6

Explain that when trying to persuade, an author or speaker often begins by establishing his or her credibility.

Ⓐ **ASK STUDENTS** to read lines 1–8 and explain how Douglass establishes his credibility to speak on his topic—the significance of the 4th of July to a slave. *(Douglass establishes his credibility by reminding his audience what he has in common with them [citizenship] and what he has in common with enslaved African Americans [He was once enslaved].)*

Analyze Language (LINES 9–14)

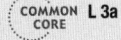
COMMON CORE L 3a

Point out that writers use **rhetorical devices** to make their arguments more powerful. One type of rhetorical device is the **rhetorical question**—a question posed to the audience that the speaker does not expect or intend for the audience to answer.

Ⓑ **ASK STUDENTS** to read lines 9–14 and identify the rhetorical questions. What purpose do the rhetorical questions serve at this point in the speech? *(The questions serve to establish a bond with the audience by expressing shared ideals.)*

Frederick Douglass *(c. 1818–1895) was born in Maryland and spent his first 21 years in slavery. After his escape, the Massachusetts Anti-Slavery Society hired him as a lecturer. His book Narrative of the Life of Frederick Douglass, an American Slave (1845) brought him international fame. Friends raised money to buy his freedom, allowing him to fully pursue his career as a reformer. He advised President Lincoln during the Civil War. In 1852, he spoke at a celebration of the Declaration of Independence.*

What to the Slave Is the Fourth of July?

Speech by Frederick Douglass

AS YOU READ Think about how Douglass answers the question of what the Fourth of July means to African Americans in 1852. Write down any questions you generate during reading.

Fellow-Citizens—Pardon me, and allow me to ask, why am I called upon to speak here to-day? What have I, or those I represent, to do with your national independence? Are the great principles of political freedom and of natural justice, embodied in that Declaration of Independence, extended to us? and am I, therefore, called upon to bring our humble offering to the national altar, and to confess the benefits, and express devout gratitude for the blessings, resulting from your independence to us?

Would to God, both for your sakes and ours, that an affirmative
10 answer could be truthfully returned to these questions! Then would my task be light, and my burden easy and delightful. For who is there so cold that a nation's sympathy could not warm him? Who so obdurate[1] and dead to the claims of gratitude, that would not thankfully acknowledge such priceless benefits? Who so stolid[2] and selfish, that would not give his voice to swell the hallelujahs of

---

[1] **obdurate:** inflexible, stubborn.
[2] **stolid:** impassive or unemotional.

What to the Slave Is the Fourth of July? **285**

SCAFFOLDING FOR ELL STUDENTS

Analyze Language Remind students that the Fourth of July commemorates the adoption of the Declaration of Independence, which declared the colonies' freedom from British rule. Ask students to reread the first paragraph of the speech and have them point out words associated with freedom. *(line 3: national independence; line 4: political freedom; lines 4–5: Declaration of Independence; line 8: independence.)*

ASK STUDENTS what Douglass is trying to establish by repeatedly using words associated with freedom. *(He is establishing that they are there to celebrate freedom, but freedom is what enslaved people lack.)*

Analyze Author's Point of View (LINES 31–49)  COMMON CORE RI 6

One way that speakers try to engage their listeners is by appealing to the audience's emotions, especially sympathy. Writers sometimes use **allusions,** or references to other texts or stories that the audience may recognize, in order to create sympathy.

C **CITE TEXT EVIDENCE** Have students identify the story that Douglass refers to in lines 31–49, and ask them to analyze why he alludes to that story. *(Douglass refers to the Babylonian captivity of the Jewish people described in the Bible. He uses it to provoke sympathy for the enslaved and shame among his listeners.)*

CRITICAL VOCABULARY

pale: Douglass believes that as an African American, he is not included within the territory of celebration.

ASK STUDENTS whom Douglass believes would be within the pale of the celebration. *(Those Americans who are not African American are within the pale.)*

cleave: Douglass is quoting a Psalm, in which the writer says that if he forgets Jerusalem, let his tongue stick to the top of his mouth.

ASK STUDENTS how a person might be affected if his or her tongue were to cleave to the top of the mouth. *(The person would not be able to speak or eat.)*

reproach: Douglass believes that if he does not keep enslaved people in mind as he speaks, he will be a disgrace.

ASK STUDENTS to name another person or thing that Douglass characterizes as a reproach. *(Douglass believes that the United States is a reproach.)*

---

a nation's jubilee, when the chains of servitude had been torn from his limbs? I am not that man. In a case like that, the dumb might eloquently speak, and the "lame man leap as an hart."

20   But, such is not the state of the case. I say it with a sad sense of the disparity between us. I am not included within the **pale** of this glorious anniversary! Your high independence only reveals the immeasurable distance between us. The blessings in which you this day rejoice, are not enjoyed in common. The rich inheritance of justice, liberty, prosperity, and independence, bequeathed by your fathers, is shared by you, not by me. The sunlight that brought life and healing to you, has brought stripes and death to me. This Fourth of July is *yours*, not *mine. You* may rejoice, *I* must mourn. To drag a man in fetters into the grand illuminated temple of liberty, and call upon him to join you in joyous anthems, were inhuman mockery and

30   sacrilegious[3] irony. Do you mean, citizens, to mock me, by asking me to speak to-day? If so, there is a parallel to your conduct. And let me warn you that it is dangerous to copy the example of a nation whose crimes, towering up to heaven, were thrown down by the breath of the Almighty, burying that nation in irrecoverable[4] ruin! I can to-day take up the plaintive[5] lament of a peeled and woe-smitten people.

 "By the rivers of Babylon, there we sat down. Yea! we wept when we remembered Zion.[6] We hanged our harps upon the willows in the midst thereof. For there, they that carried us away captive, required of us a song; and they who wasted us required of us mirth, saying,

40   Sing us one of the songs of Zion. How can we sing the Lord's song in a strange land? If I forget thee, O Jerusalem, let my right hand forget her cunning. If I do not remember thee, let my tongue **cleave** to the roof of my mouth."

Fellow-citizens, above your national, tumultuous joy, I hear the mournful wail of millions, whose chains, heavy and grievous yesterday, are to-day rendered more intolerable by the jubilant shouts that reach them. If I do forget, if I do not faithfully remember those bleeding children of sorrow this day, "may my right hand forget her cunning, and may my tongue cleave to the roof of my mouth!" To

50   forget them, to pass lightly over their wrongs, and to chime in with the popular theme, would be treason most scandalous and shocking, and would make me a **reproach** before God and the world. My subject, then, fellow-citizens, is AMERICAN SLAVERY. I shall see this day and its popular characteristics from the slave's point of view. Standing there, identified with the American bondman, making his wrongs mine, I do not hesitate to declare, with all my soul, that the character and conduct of this nation never looked blacker to me than on this

pale
(pāl) *n.* boundary or enclosed area.

cleave
(klēv) *v.* stick or adhere.

reproach
(rĭ-prōch´) *n.* a disgrace or a bad example.

---

[3] **sacrilegious:** disrespectful, irreverent.
[4] **irrecoverable:** unable to be remedied or repaired.
[5] **plaintive:** full of sorrow; grieving.
[6] **By the rivers . . . Zion:** The beginning of Psalm 137, which refers to the Babylonian captivity of Jewish people in the 6th century BC.

APPLYING ACADEMIC VOCABULARY

deny	unify

As you discuss Douglass's speech, incorporate the following academic vocabulary words: *deny* and *unify*. To reinforce Douglass's meaning, ask students to find examples of American actions that Douglass **denies** are fair or just. Then have them discuss whether Douglass suggests the people of the country could be **unified.**

> ## This Fourth of July is *yours*, not *mine.* *You* may rejoice, *I* must mourn.

Fourth of July. Whether we turn to the declarations of the past, or to the professions of the present, the conduct of the nation seems
60 equally hideous and revolting. America is false to the past, false to the present, and solemnly binds herself to be false to the future. Standing with God and the crushed and bleeding slave on this occasion, I will, in the name of humanity which is outraged, in the name of liberty which is fettered, in the name of the constitution and the bible, which are disregarded and trampled upon, dare to call in question and to denounce, with all the emphasis I can command, everything that serves to perpetuate slavery—the great sin and shame of America! "I will not equivocate; I will not excuse;" I will use the severest language I can command; and yet not one word shall escape me that any man,
70 whose judgment is not blinded by prejudice, or who is not at heart a slaveholder, shall not confess to be right and just.

But I fancy I hear some one of my audience say, it is just in this circumstance that you and your brother abolitionists fail to make a favorable impression on the public mind. Would you argue more, and denounce less, would you persuade more and rebuke less, your cause would be much more likely to succeed. But, I submit, where all is plain there is nothing to be argued. What point in the anti-slavery creed would you have me argue? On what branch of the subject do the people of this country need light? Must I undertake to prove that
80 the slave is a man? That point is conceded already. Nobody doubts it. The slaveholders themselves acknowledge it in the enactment of laws for their government. They acknowledge it when they punish disobedience on the part of the slave. There are seventy-two crimes in the state of Virginia, which, if committed by a black man, (no matter how ignorant he be,) subject him to the punishment of death; while only two of these same crimes will subject a white man to the like

Analyze Author's Point of View (LINES 60–67)

COMMON CORE RI 4, RI 6

Discuss with students that, when speakers try to engage their audience's emotions, it is known as **pathos.** Explain that one way speakers gain an emotional response from their audience is through their choice of words. For example, Douglass uses the word *hideous* in line 60, which has a much more negative connotation than words with a similar meaning, such as *ugly.*

Ⓓ **CITE TEXT EVIDENCE** Have students look at lines 60–67 to find other examples of words with strong connotations (revolting, crushed, bleeding, outraged, fettered, trampled, denounce, sin, shame) Discuss with students the emotional response these words are meant to evoke in listeners. *(These words evoke responses of shame and outrage.)*

Analyze Author's Point of View (LINES 72–81)

COMMON CORE RI 4, RI 6

Talk with students about different ways speakers might try to persuade an audience. Discuss with them that, along with relying on their own credibility and emotional appeals, speakers also rely on logic. Explain that this category of appeals is known as **logos.**

Ⓔ **ASK STUDENTS** to read lines 72–81. Have them paraphrase Douglass's reasoning and explain his point. *(Douglass says that many would like him to be less harsh in his speeches and to use arguments rather than rebukes to persuade his audience. However, he reasons that there is no point in arguing what everyone already knows.)* Have students look for more evidence of Douglass's reasoning as they read on.

WHEN STUDENTS STRUGGLE...

To give students practice in reading a speech and to aid in their comprehension, have them read aloud the paragraph that begins on page 286 with "Fellow-citizens." Remind students that a speech is spoken in front of an audience, and so it is important to read with expression. Tell them that fluent readers use punctuation marks to show them when to pause and to make long sentences' meaning clear.

ASK STUDENTS to form groups to practice reading the paragraph. Have the groups read the passage several times together. Then ask for volunteers to read the passage aloud to the whole class. Discuss with students how taking note of the punctuation helped them in their reading.

Analyze Author's Point of View (LINES 87–122) COMMON CORE RI 4, RI 6

Review with students the idea that speakers use logic to convince an audience to agree with their position. Explain that **deductive** reasoning is a form of logic through which one establishes a general principle and then moves to specifics.

 **ASK STUDENTS** to analyze Douglass's argument in lines 87–96. Have students analyze the general principle that Douglass is setting forth. *(Slaves are human beings.)* Elicit from students how that general principle applies to the specific facts Douglass names. *(Douglass points out that enslaved African Americans are obviously human, as their actions are regulated by law, unlike horses or dogs. He adds that the existence of a law forbidding teaching slaves to read and write implies their humanity. Finally, he points out that animals have no confusion about the slave's humanity.)*

Remind students that writers and speakers often use language with strong connotations to appeal to the audience's emotions.

G **CITE TEXT EVIDENCE** Ask students to cite text evidence that Douglass is making an emotional appeal in lines 123–130. *(He uses powerful words and phrases with strong connotations, such as "flay their flesh with the lash," and "sunder their families." These words and images evoke shock, sympathy, and shame.)*

F punishment. What is this but the acknowledgment that the slave is a moral, intellectual, and responsible being. The manhood of the slave is conceded. It is admitted in the fact that southern statute books are 90 covered with enactments forbidding, under severe fines and penalties, the teaching of the slave to read or write. When you can point to any such laws, in reference to the beasts of the field, then I may consent to argue the manhood of the slave. When the dogs in your streets, when the fowls of the air, when the cattle on your hills, when the fish of the sea, and the reptiles that crawl, shall be unable to distinguish the slave from a brute, then will I argue with you that the slave is a man!

For the present, it is enough to affirm the equal manhood of the negro race. Is it not astonishing that, while we are plowing, planting, and reaping, using all kinds of mechanical tools, erecting houses, 100 constructing bridges, building ships, working in metals of brass, iron, copper, silver, and gold; that, while we are reading, writing, and cyphering, acting as clerks, merchants, and secretaries, having among us lawyers, doctors, ministers, poets, authors, editors, orators, and teachers; that, while we are engaged in all manner of enterprises common to other men—digging gold in California, capturing the whale in the Pacific, feeding sheep and cattle on the hillside, living, moving, acting, thinking, planning, living in families as husbands, wives, and children, and, above all, confessing and worshiping the christian's God, and looking hopefully for life and immortality beyond 110 the grave,— we are called upon to prove that we are men!

Would you have me argue that man is entitled to liberty? that he is the rightful owner of his own body? You have already declared it. Must I argue the wrongfulness of slavery? Is that a question for republicans?[7] Is it to be settled by the rules of logic and argumentation, as a matter beset with great difficulty, involving a doubtful application of the principle of justice, hard to be understood? How should I look to-day in the presence of Americans, dividing and subdividing a discourse, to show that men have a natural right to freedom, speaking of it relatively and positively, negatively and affirmatively? To do so, would be to 120 make myself ridiculous, and to offer an insult to your understanding. There is not a man beneath the canopy of heaven that does not know that slavery is wrong *for him*.

G What! am I to argue that it is wrong to make men brutes, to rob them of their liberty, to work them without wages, to keep them ignorant of their relations to their fellow-men, to beat them with sticks, to flay their flesh with the lash, to load their limbs with irons, to hunt them with dogs, to sell them at auction, to sunder their families, to knock out their teeth, to burn their flesh, to starve them into obedience and submission to their masters? Must I argue that a 130 system, thus marked with blood and stained with pollution, is wrong?

---

7 **republicans:** citizens who govern themselves by electing a president and representatives.

---

288 Collection 4

TO CHALLENGE STUDENTS...

Remind students that a writer's or speaker's **tone** is his or her attitude toward the topic and toward the audience. Tell them that writers convey tone through word choice and that speakers can also use their voices to convey tone. Have students work in small groups to analyze the tone of Douglass's speech. Students should consider Douglass's use of rhetorical questions, vivid images, and instances when he addresses the audience directly, as in lines 119–120.

Then challenge students to prepare a reading of a section of the speech, using their voice to emphasize the tone they identified.

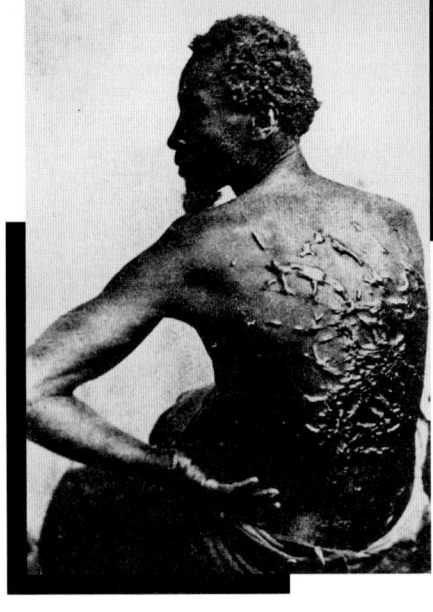

No; I will not. I have better employment for my time and strength than such arguments would imply.

What, then, remains to be argued? Is it that slavery is not divine; that God did not establish it; that our doctors of divinity are mistaken? There is blasphemy in the thought. That which is inhuman cannot be divine. Who can reason on such a proposition! They that can, may; I cannot. The time for such argument is past.

At a time like this, scorching irony, not convincing argument, is needed. Oh! had I the ability, and could I reach the nation's ear,
140 I would to-day pour out a fiery stream of biting ridicule, blasting reproach, withering sarcasm, and stern rebuke. For it is not light that is needed, but fire; it is not the gentle shower, but thunder. We need the storm, the whirlwind, and the earthquake. The feeling of the nation must be **quickened**; the conscience of the nation must be roused; the propriety of the nation must be startled; the hypocrisy of the nation must be exposed; and its crimes against God and man must be proclaimed and denounced.

What to the American slave is your Fourth of July? I answer, a day that reveals to him, more than all other days in the year, the
150 gross injustice and cruelty to which he is the constant victim. To him, your celebration is a sham; your boasted liberty, an unholy **license**; your national greatness, swelling vanity; your sounds of rejoicing are empty and heartless; your denunciations of tyrants, brass-fronted[8]

quicken
(kwĭk´ən) *v.* to make alive or stimulate.

license
(lī´səns) *n.* unacceptably unrestrained behavior.

---

[8] **brass-fronted:** cheaply or falsely coated.

What to the Slave Is the Fourth of July? **289**

WHEN STUDENTS STRUGGLE...

Douglass's speech poses specific problems for struggling students because so many points are written as rhetorical questions. Remind students that Douglass did not expect the audience to answer his questions.

ASK STUDENTS to work in pairs and have them reread lines 133–135. Encourage students to take turns restating the rhetorical questions as statements. *(Nothing remains to be argued. Slavery is not divine, God did not establish it; our doctors of divinity are mistaken.)*

Analyze Language   COMMON CORE RI 1, RI 4

(LINES 139–141)

When making appeals to the audience's emotions, speakers often use figurative language, such as metaphors and similes, to make their points. Remind students that a **metaphor** is a figure of speech that compares two unlike things without *like* or *as*.

H ASK STUDENTS to reread lines 139–141 and identify a metaphor within the lines. *("fiery stream of biting ridicule")* What two things are being compared in the metaphor? *(Words of ridicule are compared to a fiery stream.)* Explain the effect of this metaphor. *(The metaphor conveys how angry Douglass feels about slavery and how forcefully his argument must be made.)*

Analyze Language   COMMON CORE RI 1, RI 4

(LINES 150–153)

In addition to rhetorical questions, Douglass also uses a rhetorical device called antithesis. **Antithesis** presents contrasting ideas in parallel structures. For instance, in line 151, Douglass uses antithesis to compare the July 4th celebration to sham.

I ASK STUDENTS to identify the example of antithesis and a metaphor within the lines 150–153. *("your boasted liberty, an unholy license"; "your national greatness, swelling vanity")*

CRITICAL VOCABULARY

quicken: Douglass wants to make the country's conscience come to life.

ASK STUDENTS how Americans' feelings might be **quickened** by Douglass's speech and how that might affect Douglass's cause. *(American audiences might be moved by the sense of shame Douglass's speech brings forth. They might act to end slavery.)*

license: Douglass believes that, to an enslaved African American, the liberty that white Americans celebrate on the Fourth of July simply means that they act badly.

ASK STUDENTS how liberty might turn into **license.** *(People might behave as if no authority could stop them.)*

Analyze Author's Point of View  **RI 6** (LINES 161–166)

Remind students that speakers may appeal to listeners in three distinct ways: 1) through the speaker's own credibility, 2) to the emotions of the listeners, and 3) to the logic of the listeners. Ask students to reread lines 161–166.

J CITE TEXT EVIDENCE Have students analyze lines 161–166 and use text evidence to determine which kind of appeal Douglass is primarily using. *(He is appealing to the audience's emotions by using language with strong connotations such as "revolting barbarity" and "shameless hypocrisy" to condemn the United States and shame his audience.)*

COLLABORATIVE DISCUSSION Have students form pairs to review Douglass's statements about what the Fourth of July represents to an African American living in the 1850s. Have them look for evidence in the speech that explains why African Americans might feel this way. Encourage students to share their conclusions with the class as a whole. Accept all reasonable responses.

ASK STUDENTS to share any questions they generated in the course of reading and discussing the selection.

---

impudence; your shouts of liberty and equality, hollow mockery; your prayers and hymns, your sermons and thanksgivings, with all your religious parade and solemnity, are to him mere bombast, fraud, deception, impiety, and hypocrisy—a thin veil to cover up crimes which would disgrace a nation of savages. There is not a nation on the earth guilty of practices more shocking and bloody, than are the
160 people of these United States, at this very hour.

Go where you may, search where you will, roam through all the monarchies and despotisms of the old world, travel through South America, search out every abuse, and when you have found the last, lay your facts by the side of the every-day practices of this nation, and you will say with me, that, for revolting barbarity and shameless hypocrisy, America reigns without a rival.

COLLABORATIVE DISCUSSION According to Douglass, what does the Fourth of July represent to an African American living in the 1850s? Why does he say this is so? Discuss these questions with a partner, citing textual evidence to support your ideas.

TO CHALLENGE STUDENTS . . .

Discuss with students the comparisons Douglass makes in the last paragraph of the selection. Why would Douglass compare the United States to South America?

ASK STUDENTS to work with partners to spend a short time researching what slave practices were like in South America in the 1850s, when this speech was given. Encourage students to explore why Douglass would have used this example as a point of comparison to slavery in the United States, and have them report their findings to the rest of the class.

Analyze Author's Point of View: Speech

Rhetoric is the art of using language effectively and persuasively. The Greek philosopher Aristotle categorized rhetoric into three areas: **ethos, pathos,** and **logos.** As you analyze Douglass's point of view in his speech, consider how the use of these elements contributes to the power of his speech.

Ethos	Pathos	Logos
Ethos, which is the Greek word for "character," refers to an ethical appeal that relies on the credibility of the speaker. An audience must first accept that someone is credible before they will consider him or her to be an authority on a subject. For example, Frederick Douglass has the authority to speak on behalf of slaves because he himself suffered under slavery. If a speaker, however, is unlikable or not respectable, an audience members might not want to listen or be persuaded. Audiences may be swayed by two types of ethos: • **Extrinsic ethos** refers to the already-existing opinion the audience may have about the speaker. At the time of his speech, Douglass was well respected by his audience of fellow abolitionists. • **Intrinsic ethos** refers to what the audience learns about the speaker's character through the speech.	Pathos means "suffering" or "experience" in Greek. In this method of appeal, a speaker tries to provoke an emotional response from the audience. The following elements can contribute to the effective use of pathos: • **Figurative language,** such as allusions and metaphors, helps an audience imagine an experience with which the speaker wants the audience to identify. Audience members can then apply their feelings about this experience to the subject of the speech. For example, Douglass prompts his audience to relate their feelings about Jewish people who were oppressed in ancient times to slaves in the United States. • **Word choice** can trigger emotions through the use of strong connotations. Douglass uses connotative words such as *grievous*, *scandalous*, and *shocking* to prod his audience.	Logos, the Greek word for "reason," refers to an appeal through the use of logic and reasoning. A speaker using this type of appeal supports his or her claim with reasons and evidence such as facts, examples, and statistics. Douglass's speech follows a **deductive,** rather than **inductive,** line of reasoning. Instead of leading from specific evidence to a general principle or generalization (an inductive process), he begins with general principles and applies those principles to specific facts about slavery. Ask yourself the following questions as you delineate and evaluate Douglass's reasoning: • What general principles does Douglass discuss? • How does he apply legal concepts to the situation of slavery? • Do the general principles Douglass addresses apply logically to the specific situations he includes?

CLOSE READ

Analyze Author's Point of View: Speech

Help students understand the terms *rhetoric, ethos, pathos,* and *logos.* Discuss with students that some sections of a speech may appeal to more than one of these. For example, a logical appeal may use the author's experience to bolster its credibility or employ connotative language that appeals to the emotions.

Then review with students the terms *extrinsic ethos* and *intrinsic ethos.* Ask students to reread the first paragraph of the speech on page 285 and analyze whether Douglass relies on *extrinsic* or *intrinsic ethos.* *(extrinsic ethos)* Discuss with students what the audience learns about Douglass's character in the course of the speech.

Have students work in groups. Ask them to divide the speech into sections and analyze the appeals made in the different sections of the text. Encourage them to find examples of each type of rhetorical category, and have them present their examples to the class.

Strategies for Annotation ✏️ 🗐 *Annotate it!*

Analyze Author's Point of View: Speech

Share these strategies for guided or independent analysis.

• Highlight in blue appeals based on Douglass's reputation (*ethos*), in yellow emotional appeals (*pathos*), and in green appeals to logic (*logos*).

• Underline examples of figurative language.

• On a note, record whether a logical appeal is *deductive* or *inductive*.

Go where you may,...search out every abuse, and when you have found the last, 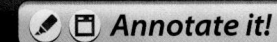lay your facts by the side of the every-day practices of this nation, and you will say with me, that, for revolting barbarity and shameless hypocrisy, America reigns without a rival.

> inductive— specific to general

Analyzing the Text   COMMON CORE RI 4, RI 6, RI 8

Possible answers:

1. *Douglass has an angry, righteous tone. His tone contributes to the appeal he makes to ethos because, as a former slave, he is uniquely qualified to speak of its horrors. It affects his appeal to pathos because by showing his own anger he is eliciting an emotion of shame and outrage.*

2. *Douglass's extrinsic ethos, or reputation, allows him to speak as an authority on the subject of slavery. The audience knows that Douglass has more experience than they do with the speech's topic. Douglass's reputation as a well-respected writer and activist also boosts his credibility.*

3. *The Virginia law shows that slavery is wrong in that it includes laws and punishments for slaves. This proves that the legal system regards slaves as human beings. This is an appeal to logos.*

4. *lines 27–28: "To drag a man in fetters into the grand illuminated temple of liberty..." This contributes to the speech's power by contrasting the slave's lack of freedom (fetters) to the nation celebrating its freedom. lines 141–142: "For it is not light that is needed, but fire." Douglass is saying that what is needed isn't understanding, or light, but destruction of slavery. It is a powerful call to action.*

5. *Douglass uses words like disparity and immeasurable distance to remind listeners that he speaks as one who has been enslaved. He makes references to the Bible (lines 36–43), which enhance his credibility with a largely Christian audience.*

6. *Douglass is aware that the audience will listen to him but does not listen to the suffering of those who are still enslaved.*

7. *line 135: blasphemy; This word shows the strength of Douglass's conviction. line 145: hypocrisy; this word shows Douglass's anger at Americans celebrating freedom while others are enslaved.*

8. *Douglass uses words from the Declaration, such as equality and liberty, as examples of what the nation celebrates while denying them to those who are enslaved.*

Analyzing the Text   COMMON CORE RI 4, RI 6, RI 8, W 4, SL 1b, SL 1d

Cite Text Evidence   Support your responses with evidence from the selection.

1. **Infer** Describe the tone of Douglass's speech. How does his tone contribute to the appeal that he makes using ethos and pathos?

2. **Analyze** How does Douglass's extrinsic ethos, or reputation, influence the manner in which he addresses his audience? Explain.

3. **Interpret** According to Douglass, how does Virginia law help show that slavery is wrong? What are some of the assumptions, or premises, of Virginia law about African Americans? What type of argument is Douglass making in this section of the text: an appeal to ethos, pathos, or logos?

4. **Analyze** Identify two examples of figurative language that Douglass uses to elicit an emotional response from his audience. Explain how each example contributes to the power of his speech.

5. **Analyze** How does Douglass use word choice and literary references to confirm his credibility?

6. **Evaluate** Tokenism is the practice of making a symbolic gesture toward a goal, such as eliminating slavery, but not actually fulfilling that goal. Why does Douglass view his invitation to speak on the Fourth of July as an act of tokenism?

7. **Analyze** Douglass's use of strong connotative language builds toward the end of the text. Cite some specific examples and describe the effect that each has on the power of his message.

8. **Connect** Reread the second paragraph of the Declaration of Independence (page 112). How have the words of the Declaration influenced and inspired Douglass? How does Douglass use the Declaration to further the aims of the abolitionist cause?

PERFORMANCE TASK

Writing Activity: Outline and Summary How does Douglass persuade his audience by using logos, or logic and reasoning?

1. Work with a partner to analyze Douglass's speech and to create an outline of his argument.

2. Start your outline with a list of the general principles Douglass discusses.

3. Then, determine how Douglass supports each general principle with logical evidence or reasoning.

4. Finally, use your outline to write a summary of the speech that includes only the logic and reasoning Douglass used to persuade his audience to agree with his central ideas.

Assign this performance task.

PERFORMANCE TASK   COMMON CORE RI 4, RI 6, RI 8, W 4, SL 1

Writing Activity Tell students that, in order to name the principles in Douglass's speech, they should look at the text to find what Douglass suggests that he and his audience both value. For example, he refers to "the great principles of political freedom and natural justice" in the first paragraph. Once Douglass establishes the principle that freedom is desirable, he can discuss the specific conditions of the enslaved. Encourage students to review the information on deductive reasoning on 291.

Critical Vocabulary

COMMON CORE L 4, L 4c, L 4d

| pale | cleave | reproach | quicken | license |

Practice and Apply Use your knowledge of each Critical Vocabulary word to answer each question. Then discuss your answers with a partner.

1. What kind of action could be perceived as a **reproach**?

2. What types of materials might a collage artist **cleave** together?

3. What movies or stories have you seen or read in which a character was **quickened to take action**?

4. How might officials try to control the **license** of a large, unruly crowd?

5. What are some examples of places in which people would be located within a **pale**?

Vocabulary Strategy: Multiple-Meaning Words

Many words have more than one meaning. For example, when the Critical Vocabulary word *pale* is used as a noun it means "enclosed area," as in this sentence from Douglass's speech:

> I am not included within the pale of this glorious anniversary!

The noun *pale* can also refer to a fence or a stake used in a fence. As an adjective, *pale* can mean "light in complexion," "dim," or "weak." *Pale* may also be used as a verb in these senses, meaning "to enclose in pales" or "to become or to cause to become pale." When you come across a familiar word used in an unfamiliar way, follow these steps to determine its meaning:

- Look at the word's context to determine its part of speech and infer the correct meaning.

- Consult a dictionary to look up all the meanings of the word.

- Compare your preliminary determination of the word's meaning to the dictionary definitions to verify the correct meaning of the word as it is used in context.

Practice and Apply Look up the meanings of each Critical Vocabulary word in a dictionary. Then write sentences for each word using its different meanings.

Critical Vocabulary

COMMON CORE L 4, L 4c, L 4d

Possible answers:

1. *An action that is disgraceful could be seen as a* reproach.

2. *A collage artist might* cleave *together newspaper and cardboard.*

3. *In stories such as* The Hunger Games, *the protagonist is* quickened *to take action to save another.*

4. *Officials might try to control the* license *of an unruly crowd by making announcements on loud speakers.*

5. *In medieval walled towns, people would be located within a* pale.

Vocabulary Strategy: Multiple-Meaning Words

Sample answers:

- *The girl who was ill looked* pale.
- *The butcher will* cleave *the meat.*
- *The worker was unhappy with her boss's* reproach.
- *If the runner can* quicken *his pace, he may win the race.*
- *Sheila was happy to get her driver's* license.

CLOSE READ

Language and Style: Rhetorical Devices

COMMON CORE L 3a

Review the definitions and examples in the chart and discuss with students any questions they may have. Then have students look for examples of *allusion*, *antithesis*, *conceit*, and *rhetorical questions* in the text.

Practice and Apply Have students share with their partner the paragraphs that they wrote and name the rhetorical devices that they used. Invite volunteers to read their paragraphs to the class, and have them discuss the rhetorical devices.

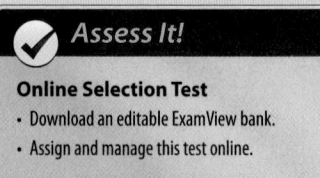

Assess It!

Online Selection Test
- Download an editable ExamView bank.
- Assign and manage this test online.

Language and Style: Rhetorical Devices

COMMON CORE L 3a

Rhetorical devices are ways of using language that increase the power and clarity of a writer's or speaker's message. In his speech, Frederick Douglass makes effective use of many rhetorical devices and questions to keep his audience engaged and to convey the precise meanings and emotions he intends. The chart shows several examples.

Rhetorical Device	Example from Douglass's Speech
An **allusion** is an indirect reference to a famous person, place, event, or literary work.	"And let me warn you that it is dangerous to copy the example of a nation whose crimes, towering up to heaven, were thrown down by the breath of the Almighty. . . ." (This is a reference to the city of Babylon.)
Antithesis presents contrasting ideas in parallel structures.	"*You* may rejoice, *I* must mourn."
A **conceit** is an elaborate comparison between two unlike things.	"To drag a man in fetters into the grand illuminated temple of liberty, and call upon him to join you in joyous anthems, were inhuman mockery and sacrilegious irony."
Rhetorical questions are intended to make a point, not to elicit a direct answer.	"Would you have me argue that man is entitled to liberty? that he is the rightful owner of his own body? You have already declared it."

Rhetorical questions allow a speaker to vary his or her syntax by using different sentence structures. They also make listeners feel as if they are engaged in a conversation with the speaker. Consider this revision to the example in the chart:

> **Perhaps I should argue that a man is entitled to liberty, or that he is the rightful owner of his own body. However, you have already declared it.**

In this version, Douglass is not challenging the audience to think about the absurdity of his situation. He is simply making statements. His use of rhetorical questions does a better job of conveying his bitterly ironic attitude toward the occasion.

The conceit in which Douglass compares himself to "a man in fetters" dragged into a "grand illuminated temple of liberty" (lines 27–30) is a powerful way for him to say that he is offended at being asked to celebrate liberty in a nation where so many are enslaved. Like the allusion that compares the United States to the biblical city of Babylon—which was doomed by its own arrogance—the conceit adds richness and potent imagery to the speech, leaving a lasting impression on listeners or readers.

Practice and Apply Write a paragraph that could be included in a speech about an injustice in today's world. Use at least three rhetorical devices in your paragraph. Then work with a partner and read your paragraphs aloud. Discuss the impact of the rhetorical devices.

Strategies for Annotation 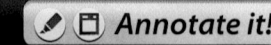 Annotate it!

Analyze Language and Style: Rhetorical Devices

COMMON CORE L 3a

Share these strategies for guided or independent analysis of Douglass's speech:

- Highlight examples of antithesis in blue.
- Highlight examples of conceit in yellow.
- Use notes to describe the effect of the rhetorical devices.

> I would to-day pour out a fiery stream of biting ridicule, blasting reproach, withering sarcasm, and stern rebuke. For it is not light that is needed, but fire; it is not the gentle shower, but thunder. We need...

emphasis that "nation must be startled" into awareness

Determine Central Ideas and Details

COMMON CORE

RI 2,
RI 8

TEACH

Explain to students that finding central ideas and details is especially helpful in following the arguments in a speech. Review with students the following ideas to keep in mind when trying to find the central ideas of a text.

- A **central,** or **main, idea** is not always stated outright. Sometimes readers have to infer it from the details.
- Authors support the central idea with **supporting details,** which may be facts, examples, reasons, or statistics.
- It is helpful to break a longer text into sections. The main idea of each section should support the central idea of the whole text.

PRACTICE AND APPLY

Have students work in pairs to find the central idea of three main sections in "What to the Slave Is the Fourth of July?"

Section 1: from page 285 to line 80 on page 287.

Section 2: from line 81 on page 287 to line 137 on page 289.

Section 3: from line 138 on page 289 to the end of the selection.

Encourage students to take notes as they reread the sections and infer the main idea from the supporting details they find.

Encourage students to use one of the interactive Determining Main Idea charts.

Analyze Author's Point of View

COMMON CORE

RI 4,
RI 6,
RI 8

RETEACH

Review with students the three types of appeals. Then have students work in small groups to come up with appeals of each type to support a point of view that they share on an issue of concern to them. For instance, students might develop appeals to support the point of view that high schools should start the school day later in the morning.

- Ask students to provide examples of appeals based on the reputation of the speaker (ethos). *(As someone who has spent countless hours researching the subject and as someone who suffers from sleep deprivation, I know what a lack of sleep does to high school students.)*
- Have students provide examples of emotional appeals (pathos). *(High school students who drag themselves to school with their eyes drooping and their heads lolling onto their desks are in danger of failing.)*
- Then ask students to provide examples of appeals based on logic (logos). *(Adolescents' sleep patterns shift so that they fall asleep later at night but still need nine hours of sleep. A school day that starts before 8 a.m. cuts into adequate sleep.)*

CLOSE READING APPLICATION

Students can apply the skill to a current opinion piece in a newspaper or magazine. Have them work in pairs to analyze claims based on *ethos, pathos,* and *logos,* or a combination. Ask: Does the writer mention his or her own experience or expertise with the subject? Does the writer try to make readers feel fear, anger, or guilt? Does the writer include logical arguments that appeal to reason? Once students have examples of different types of appeals, ask them to identify the author's point of view on the topic.

EXEMPLAR

Declaration of Sentiments

Public Document by Elizabeth Cady Stanton

Why This Text?

This foundational document from our country's history represents the beginnings of the women's movement in America. It adapts language from the Declaration of Independence to compare women's fight for freedom with our country's fight for freedom.

▶ **View It!**

Professional Development Podcast:

Text-Dependent Analysis

Key Learning Objective: Students will be able to analyze how the structure and style of an argument supports the author's ideas and claims.

For additional practice:

from **The Iroquois Constitution**

Public Document by Dekanawida

Close Reader selection
from The Iroquois Constitution
Public Document by Dekanawida

COMMON CORE Common Core Standards

RI 1 Cite textual evidence.

RI 3 Analyze a complex sequence of events and explain how individuals, ideas, or events interact.

RI 6 Determine an author's point of view or purpose.

RI 9 Analyze foundational U.S. documents.

W 2 Write informative/explanatory texts.

L 4b Identify and correctly use patterns of word changes.

▲ Text Complexity Rubric

Quantitative Measures	Declaration of Sentiments
	Lexile: 1430L

Levels of Meaning/Purpose

single purpose, explicitly stated

Qualitative Measures

Structure

explicit problem-solution text structure

Language Conventionality and Clarity

complex and varied sentence structure

Knowledge Demands

complex civics and social studies concepts

Reader/Task Considerations	Teacher determined Vary by individual reader and type of text

CLOSE READ

Background The Declaration of Sentiments was written by a group of women in 1848. Stanton was asked to finish and polish the draft and also added the ninth resolution, which called for women to be given the right to vote. The document was signed by 68 women and 32 men. While this resolution was the impetus for the women's suffrage movement, the Declaration of Sentiments didn't gain historical recognition until the passing of the Nineteenth Amendment in 1920.

AS YOU READ Direct students to use the As You Read instructions to focus their reading. Remind students to write down any questions they generate during reading.

Analyze Author's Purpose (LINES 1–16)

COMMON CORE RI 6, RI 9

Discuss with students the similarities between the Declaration of Sentiments and the Declaration of Independence, reading aloud the first two paragraphs of the Declaration of Independence as needed. Then remind students of the audience and purpose of the Declaration of Independence. *(the whole world; to declare that the United States is an independent country and to convince people that it must and should be independent)*

Ⓐ **CITE TEXT EVIDENCE** Have students reread lines 7–16. Ask them the purpose of the document and have them give text evidence for their answer. *(The document's purpose is to convince readers that women should have rights equal to those enjoyed by men. In lines 2–5, Stanton says that "one portion of the family of man," or women, must assume "a position different from that which they have hitherto occupied ;" in other words, that women must change their traditional position. In lines 4– 5, Stanton says that this new position is one to which women are entitled by "the laws of nature, and of nature's God.")* Then ask students to infer the document's audience. *(the U. S. government and the public)* Finally, ask students what comparison Stanton implies by using the language of the Declaration of Independence. *(She compares women to the colonists and men to the British king.)*

Background *The 1848* Declaration of Sentiments *was presented at the Seneca Falls Convention, the birthplace of the women's rights movement in the United States.* **Elizabeth Cady Stanton** *(1815–1902) and* **Lucretia Mott** *(1793–1880) had first discussed the idea for the conference at the World Anti-Slavery Convention in London in 1840. Active abolitionists, the women had been denied the right to participate in the convention because of their gender.*

Declaration of Sentiments

Public Document by Elizabeth Cady Stanton

AS YOU READ Think about what rights women in the United States have today that they did not have in 1848. Write down any questions you generate during reading.

Put forth at Seneca Falls, N. Y., July, 19th and 20th, 1848.

Image Credits: (t) ©Historical/Corbis; (l) © Bettmann/Corbis; (r) Bettmann/Corbis

Ⓐ WHEN, in the course of human events, it becomes necessary for one portion of the family of man to assume among the people of the earth a position different from that which they have hitherto occupied, but one to which the laws of nature, and of nature's God entitle them, a decent respect to the opinions of mankind requires that they should declare the causes that impel them to such a course.

We hold these truths to be self-evident; that all men and women are created equal; that they are endowed by their Creator with certain inalienable rights; that among these are life, liberty, and the pursuit

10 of happiness; that to secure these rights governments are instituted, deriving their just powers from the consent of the governed. Whenever any form of Government becomes destructive of those ends, it is the right of those who suffer from it, to refuse allegiance to it, and to insist upon the institution of a new government, laying its foundation on such principles, and organizing its powers in such form as to them shall seem most likely to effect their safety and happiness. Prudence,

SCAFFOLDING FOR ELL STUDENTS

Understand Language and Gender Discuss with students how gender-sensitive language has evolved since the Declaration of Sentiments was written. Point out that until the last 30 years, terms like *man* were thought to represent all people.

- Give examples of gender-specific terms and their gender-sensitive replacements (fireman—fire fighter, man-made—synthetic). Draw students' attention to the phrase "one portion of the family of man" on line 2. Explain that today we might say "one portion of humanity."

Have students scan the selection to identify other examples of gender-specific language and revise them to include both genders.

CLOSE READ

Analyze Ideas (LINES 32–40)  **COMMON CORE** RI 3

Authors support their **claims**, their stands on issues, with **evidence**—proof that their position is sound. Evidence lends validity to an argument, and authors use it to convince their audience to take a similar stance.

B **CITE TEXT EVIDENCE** Have students cite the points in lines 32–40 that build Stanton's portrait of women as oppressed citizens. *(They can't vote, they have no voice in forming laws, and they have fewer rights than any man.)*

Analyze Author's Purpose  **COMMON CORE** RI 6, RI 9
(LINES 32–49)

Explain that rhetoric adds persuasive effect to writing. Devices like **repetition** and **parallelism** help Stanton express her position in a compelling and convincing manner. The repetition of words and phrases reinforces her themes. Stanton's parallel grammatical structure connects and emphasizes ideas of equal importance.

C **ASK STUDENTS** to describe Stanton's use of parallelism in lines 32–49. *(Stanton's sentence structure uses* he *as its subject, followed by the helping verb* has.*)* How does this add persuasive effect? *(It emphasizes the subject,* he, *as perpetrator of the abuse and lends equal importance to each of these injustices.)* How does the repetition of *right* (lines 32, 36, 38, 42) reinforce meaning? *(It alludes to the rights the founders of the country fought for and established.)*

CRITICAL VOCABULARY

transient: A government should not change in reaction to fleeting issues.

ASK STUDENTS why the issue of women's rights in 1848 isn't a transient cause? *(The inequity that women endured had existed since the founding of the country.)*

evince: Stanton sees a pattern to the obstruction of women's rights.

ASK STUDENTS what Stanton claims evinces a plan to oppress women. *(She cites a "long train of abuses" as evidence.)*

indeed, will dictate, that governments long established should not be changed for light and **transient** causes; and accordingly, all experience hath shown that mankind are more disposed to suffer, while evils are
20 sufferable, than to right themselves by abolishing the forms to which they are accustomed. But when a long train of abuses and usurpations, pursuing invariably the same object, **evinces** a design to reduce them under absolute despotism, it is their duty to throw off such government, and provide new guards for their future security. Such has been the patient sufferance of the women under this government, and such is now the necessity which constrains them to demand the equal station, to which they are entitled.

The history of mankind is a history of repeated injuries and usurpations on the part of man toward woman, having in direct object
30 the establishment of an absolute tyranny over her. To prove this, let facts be submitted to a candid world.

B He has never permitted her to exercise her inalienable right to the elective franchise.[1]   **C**

He has compelled her to submit to laws, in the formation of which she had no voice.

He has withheld from her rights which are given to the most ignorant and degraded men—both natives and foreigners.

Having deprived her of this first right of a citizen, the elective franchise, thereby leaving her without representation in the halls of
40 legislation, he has oppressed her on all sides.

He has made her, if married, in the eye of the law, civilly dead.

He has taken from her all right in property, even to the wages she earns.

He has made her, morally, an irresponsible being, as she can commit many crimes with impunity, provided they be done in the presence of her husband. In the covenant[2] of marriage, she is compelled to promise obedience to her husband, he becoming, to all intents and purposes, her master—the law giving him power to deprive her of her liberty, and to administer chastisement.[3]
50 He has so framed the laws of divorce, as to what shall be the proper causes of divorce, in case of separation, to whom the guardianship of children shall be given; as to be wholly regardless of the happiness of women—the law, in all cases, going upon the false supposition of the supremacy of man, and giving all power into his hands.

After depriving her of all rights as a woman, if single and the owner of property, he has taxed her to support a government, which recognizes her only when her property can be made profitable to it.

---
[1] **inalienable right to the elective franchise:** unassailable right to vote.
[2] **covenant:** agreement or contract.
[3] **chastisement:** punishment.

transient
(trăn´zē-ənt) *adj.* temporary; short-term.

evince
(ĭ-vĭns´) *v.* to reveal or give evidence of.

APPLYING ACADEMIC VOCABULARY

deny	unify

As you discuss the Declaration of Sentiments, incorporate the following academic vocabulary words: *deny* and *unify*. In reading the essay, identify ways in which men at the time **denied** rights to women. Which rights did they **deny**? At the end of the essay, talk about how Stanton wants women to **unify** to accomplish the goals set forth in the essay. Discuss how Stanton hopes that men and women would be **unified** in society.

He has monopolized nearly all the profitable employments;
60 and from those she is permitted to follow, she receives but a scanty
remuneration.[4]

He closes against her all avenues to wealth and distinction, which
he considers most honorable to himself. As a teacher of Theology,
Medicine or Law, she is not known.

He has denied her the facilities for obtaining a thorough
education—all colleges being closed against her.

He allows her in Church as well as State, but a subordinate
position, claiming Apostolic[5] authority for her exclusion from the
ministry, and with some exceptions, from any public participation in
70 the affairs of the Church.

He has created a false public sentiment, by giving to the world
a different code of morals for man and woman, by which moral
delinquencies which exclude women from society, are not only
tolerated but deemed of little account when committed by man.

delinquency
(dĭ-lĭng´kwən-sē) *n.*
shortcoming or
misbehavior.

He has usurped the prerogative of Jehovah himself, claiming it as
his right to assign for her a sphere of action, when that belongs to her
conscience and her God.

He has endeavored in every way that he could, to destroy her
confidence in her own powers, to lessen her self-respect, and to make
80 her willing to lead a dependent and **abject** life.

abject
(ăb´jĕkt´) *adj.*
miserable and
submissive.

Now, in view of this entire disfranchisement of one half the people
of this country, their social and religious degradation—in view of the
unjust laws above mentioned and because women do feel themselves
aggrieved, oppressed and fraudulently deprived of their most sacred
rights, we insist that they have immediate admission to all the rights
and privileges, which belong to them as citizens of these United States.

In entering upon the great work before us, we anticipate no
small amount of misconception, misrepresentation and ridicule; but
we shall use every instrumentality within our power to effect our
90 object. We shall employ agents, circulate tracts, petition the State and
National Legislatures, and endeavor to enlist the pulpit and the press
in our behalf. We hope this Convention will be followed by a series of
Conventions, embracing every part of the country.

Firmly relying upon the final triumph of the Right and the True,
we do this day affix our signatures to this declaration.

---

[4] **scanty remuneration:** minimal payment.

[5] **Apostolic:** from the Apostles, the initial followers of Jesus.

COLLABORATIVE DISCUSSION How do women's rights in the United States
today differ from those in 1848? With a partner, discuss the differences that
you find most interesting or surprising. Cite specific textual evidence from
the Declaration of Sentiments to support your ideas.

WHEN STUDENTS STRUGGLE...

Explain that sentences can be broken down into phrases and clauses—groups of
words that express a thought. Phrases and clauses are often separated by commas
or semicolons. By reading sentences in meaningful "chunks," readers may better
understand the text. Project lines 59–61 and explain that the separators show
phrases or clauses. Model reading the sentence, emphasizing the phrases.

ASK STUDENTS to form pairs to practice phrase-cued reading.

He has monopolized nearly all the profitable employments; | and from

those she is permitted to follow, | she receives but a scanty remuneration.

CLOSE READ

Analyze Author's Purpose (LINES 81–86)

COMMON CORE   **RI 6, RI 9**

Explain that authors may craft an adaptation of
a work whose principles are respected to take
advantage of its associated meaning as well as
its themes. The adaptation gains credibility by
association with the original.

D **ASK STUDENTS** what specific theme from the
Declaration of Independence Stanton echoes in
these lines. *(In the Declaration of Independence, one of
Jefferson's themes was that a government that makes
laws without the consent of the people, or that makes
unjust laws, is not legitimate and does not deserve
the loyalty of its people. Stanton echoes this theme
by pointing out that women have no say in the laws
of the U.S. and that these laws are unjust to them.)*
Then ask what overall theme from the Declaration
of Independence is echoed in the Declaration of
Sentiments. *(the theme that individuals have rights that
must be respected)*

CRITICAL VOCABULARY

delinquency: Moral misbehaviors are tolerated
in men, while women who commit the same acts
suffer social exclusion.

ASK STUDENTS why Stanton emphasizes that
delinquencies are tolerated for men but not
for women. *(to show that bias regarding moral
misconduct is yet another double standard)*

abject: According to Stanton, men strive to reduce
women's self-confidence so they can more easily
control them.

ASK STUDENTS why women of the time might
have lived an abject life. *(Women were dependent
on men and had no choice but to be submissive.)*

COLLABORATIVE DISCUSSION Have small groups
discuss the differences they identified between the
women's rights issues that Stanton addresses and
contemporary issues.

ASK STUDENTS to share any questions they generated
in the course of reading and discussing the selection.

Analyze Author's Purpose  RI 6, RI 9

Make sure that students understand the terms *purpose*, *theme*, and *rhetorical features*. As a class, discuss how using the Declaration of Independence as a model helped Stanton accomplish her purpose and add to the power and persuasiveness of the *Declaration of Sentiments*.

- First, discuss how Jefferson's and Stanton's audiences and purposes were similar. *(Both were written to a wide audience and were intended to sway public opinion in favor of the actions they were taking to assert their rights.)*

- Next, discuss how Stanton borrowed and built on themes that Jefferson expressed. *(Stanton built on Jefferson's theme that "all men are created equal" by adding women.)*

- Finally, ask students to find examples of repetition and parallelism in the Declaration of Sentiments. *(parallelism: clauses beginning with "that," lines 7–11; "He has …," lines 32–80; "in view of…," lines 81–82; repetition: "absolute," lines 23 and 30; "right," lines 32, 36, 38, and 42)*

Analyze Author's Purpose  RI 6, RI 9

Adaptation means to change the form or content of something to make it appropriate for a new audience, situation, or purpose. For example, stage plays or movies may be adaptations of short stories or novels. Writers may take a classic text such as a Shakespearean play, a Jane Austen novel, or an ancient myth or legend and rewrite the basic story to occur in a different place or time. By adapting a well-known work, writers begin with a certain built-in appeal and audience awareness that can lend power and credibility to the new work.

The Declaration of Sentiments is an adaptation of the Declaration of Independence. After its adoption in 1776, the Declaration of Independence became a powerful and widely circulated foundational American document. It also inspired others fighting for freedom, including abolitionist Sarah Grimké who built on Jefferson's statement that "all men are created equal" when she wrote in 1837 that "men and women were CREATED EQUAL . . . whatever is right for man to do, is right for woman."

As Jefferson did when writing the Declaration of Independence, Elizabeth Cady Stanton drew upon ideas and language used by earlier writers—Sarah Grimké being one of them. However, Stanton went beyond simple adaptation of the content and also adapted the format and style from an earlier document. Keep the three concepts presented in the chart and this question in mind as you analyze the text: How did using the Declaration of Independence as a model help Stanton accomplish her purpose and add to the power and persuasiveness of the Declaration of Sentiments?

Purpose	Theme	Rhetorical Features
Consider the audience that the Declaration of Sentiments was intended to reach and the reason why the document was written. Think about how using the Declaration of Independence as a model might serve Stanton's purpose.	Theme is the central idea or message that an author wants to communicate on a particular topic, in this case the need for women's equal rights. Think about how Stanton's choice of a model allowed her to borrow and build on themes that Jefferson had expressed on the topic of independence and freedom.	Rhetorical features include all the methods a writer uses to communicate ideas and appeal to readers. In the Declaration of Independence, Jefferson made effective use of repetition, repeating words or phrases to reinforce meaning and create rhythm; and parallelism, the use of similar grammatical structures to express ideas that are related or equal in importance. Look for examples in which Stanton makes use of these same rhetorical features.

Strategies for Annotation 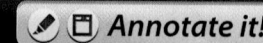 *Annotate it!*

Analyze Author's Purpose  RI 3

Have students use their eBook annotation tools to analyze the text. Have them do the following:

- Highlight in yellow an example of Stanton's purpose.
- Highlight in pink a word that reflects a theme.
- Highlight in green an example of parallelism as a rhetorical feature.

…Now, in view of this entire disfranchisement of one half the people of this country,… in view of the unjust laws above mentioned and because women do feel themselves aggrieved, oppressed and fraudulently deprived of their most sacred rights, we insist that they have immediate admission to all the rights and privileges, which belong to them as citizens of these United States.

eBook *Annotate It!*

Analyzing the Text

COMMON CORE RI 1, RI 6, RI 9, W 2

Cite Text Evidence   Support your responses with evidence from the selection.

1. **Analyze** In an argument, a **claim** is an author's position on an issue. What claim does Stanton make in lines 1–6, and how does she say she will support the claim elsewhere in the document?

2. **Draw Conclusions** Lines 7–10 of Stanton's document exactly repeat the language used in the Declaration of Independence, except for the addition of the phrase "and women" in line 7. How does using this sentence—and the addition of this phrase—contribute to the persuasiveness of her argument?

3. **Interpret** In lines 24–27, Stanton writes, "Such has been the patient sufferance of the women under this government, and such is now the necessity which constrains them to demand the equal station, to which they are entitled." What does this reveal about Stanton's purpose in writing the Declaration of Sentiments?

4. **Infer** In lines 32–33, Stanton refers to "her inalienable right to the elective franchise." What does this statement mean and how is this right connected to the inalienable rights listed in lines 9–10?

5. **Cite Evidence** What rhetorical features does Stanton use throughout the list of facts that she presents, beginning with line 32? How does her rhetoric contribute to the power and persuasiveness of the text?

6. **Draw Conclusions** What specific themes about women's rights in 1848 does Stanton communicate in this document?

7. **Analyze** What rhetorical features in lines 81–93 of the Declaration of Sentiments support Stanton's purpose in writing?

PERFORMANCE TASK

Writing Activity: Comparison What are the similarities and differences between the Declaration of Sentiments and the Declaration of Independence? Write an essay making a point-by-point comparison of the two documents by following these steps.

- Review the text of the Declaration of Independence and compare each section in detail with the Declaration of Sentiments.
- Look for similarities and differences in the language and ideas of the two documents.
- Formulate a central idea that you want to communicate in your essay.

- Select the most significant and relevant points of comparison in order to develop your topic thoroughly.
- Conclude with a statement that confirms your central idea and that flows from the evidence you cited.
- Maintain a formal style and follow the conventions of standard English.

Assign this performance task.

PERFORMANCE TASK

COMMON CORE W 2

Writing Activity Have students work in pairs to create a Venn diagram comparing the Declaration of Sentiments to the Declaration of Independence. Remind them to pay attention to each author's purpose and themes as well as the repetition of words and the use of parallelism. Instruct students to work independently to formulate a central idea and to draft their essays. Then have them share their completed drafts with their partners.

PRACTICE & APPLY

Analyzing the Text   COMMON CORE RI 1, RI 6, RI 9, W 2

Possible answers:

1. *Stanton claims that it has become necessary to change the status of women from the one that they hold to one that God and nature entitles them to. She says she is obligated to state the reasons for this change due to her "decent respect to the opinions of mankind," implying that those reasons are forthcoming.*

2. *By using the wording of the groundbreaking and historical Declaration of Independence, to which the United States owes its formation, Stanton invokes the clout of that document for her own argument. At the same time, she emphasizes the inequity inherent in it by adding "and women." Use of the famous language—changed only to illustrate her point—makes the inequity obvious.*

3. *The phrase "to demand the equal station" sums up the point of the entire piece; the lack of equality can no longer be abided, and this document is a demand to end that situation.*

4. *The "right to the elective franchise" refers to the right to vote. Women were denied the right to vote at that time. Because the inalienable rights to "life, liberty and the pursuit of happiness" were secured by a government in which women had no voice, they had no avenue to achieve these rights for themselves.*

5. *Stanton employs the parallelism of the Declaration of Independence. The subject "he" in her sentences refers to all men, showing them to be as despotic as the king.*

6. *Stanton's piece has several themes regarding women's rights in 1848. The first theme is that the current situation regarding women's participation in society is no longer tenable. The second theme is that women were, at that time, constantly subjected to the will of men. The third theme is that women must gain civic and economic independence and freedom.*

7. *Stanton repeats words and phrases like "we" and "in view of" in imitation of Jefferson's style and tone. This supports her purpose because it emphasizes that the document is not merely meant to be a list of injustices, but a statement of action.*

PRACTICE & APPLY

Critical Vocabulary

 COMMON CORE L 4b

Sample Answers:

1. *Stanton states that the denial of women's rights had persisted for years and years, as described in her reference to "a long train of abuses and usurpations."*

2. *This long list of abuses is evidence of the oppression of women.*

3. *Stanton was referring to social misconduct, for which she believed that women would be judged much more harshly than men.*

4. *Women who have abject lives might live with overbearing, unkind husbands or fathers.*

Vocabulary Strategy: Parts of Speech

Answers:

1. *reject*

2. *eject*

3. *subject*

4. *project*

5. *inject*

Critical Vocabulary

COMMON CORE L 4b

transient	evince	delinquency	abject

Practice and Apply Use your knowledge of the Critical Vocabulary words to respond to each question.

1. Why does Stanton claim that the denial of women's rights has not been a **transient** situation?

2. What does the long list of facts about man's treatment of woman **evince**?

3. When Stanton refers to moral **delinquencies** is she more likely referring to major crimes or social misconduct?

4. How might you describe the living situations of women who have **abject** lives?

Vocabulary Strategy: The Latin Root *ject*

The Critical Vocabulary word *abject* combines the Latin root *ject*, meaning "to throw" and the prefix *ab-*, meaning "from" or "away." The word *abject* originally meant "outcast," someone who is thrown out of society. This root is combined with other prefixes to form several common English words. When you see the root *ject* in a word, you can often use your knowledge of prefixes and context clues to help you determine the meaning of the word.

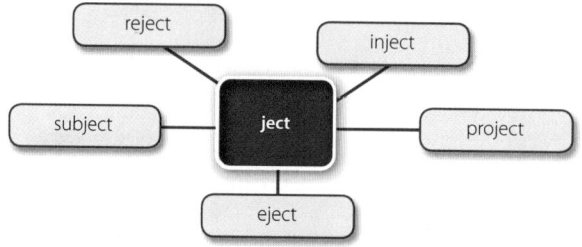

Practice and Apply Choose the word from the word web that best completes each sentence. Consider what you know about the Latin root and the prefixes. If necessary consult a dictionary to confirm the meaning.

1. Stanton believed that many people would _____ her ideas.

2. Stanton and Mott were angry that men wanted to _____ women from the anti-slavery convention.

3. Stanton believed that women should not be _____ to the demands of men.

4. A powerful speaker, Stanton had the ability to _____ her voice in a large hall.

5. By using the Declaration of Independence as a model, Stanton intended to _____ Jefferson's rhetoric into her document.

300 Collection 4

Strategies for Annotation ✐ 🖺 *Annotate it!*

The Latin Root *ject*

COMMON CORE L 4b

Remind students that they can determine the meaning of unfamiliar words in the Declaration of Sentiments by looking for the Latin root *ject*. Point out that the prefix *ob-* means "on account of" or "in the way of." Have them use their eBook annotation tools to do the following:

- Look for words containing the Latin root *ject*.
- Highlight the root in yellow.
- Infer each word's meaning and record it in a note.

The history of mankind is a history of repeated injuries and usurpations on the part of man toward woman, having in direct object the establishment of an absolute tyranny over her. To prove this, let facts be submitted to a candid world.

purpose or goal

Analyze Ideas

RI 3

TEACH

In persuasive essays, authors typically begin by making a claim or expressing an opinion and then offering supporting evidence to convince the audience. The evidence may include statistics, scientific data, examples, or quotes.

- A **claim** is a writer's position on a problem or issue. In declarations, claims tend to be presented as an announcement of a position or belief. A statement of purpose or intent often accompanies the claim. The claim specifies the issue; the statement of purpose tells what the author plans to do about it.

- **Evidence** is anything that provides support for the claim. In a declaration, evidence is more an issue of ethics than fact. While it can be proved that the specific grievances or abuses that instigated the declaration actually happened, the larger issue is that of right and wrong and of social conscience. If the audience does not judge the action as wrongful, to them, the evidence will not be valid proof of the claim.

PRACTICE AND APPLY

Display lines 24–31 on the board or on a device. Have a volunteer point out what Stanton says men's goals are in their treatment of women. *(to establish tyranny over them)* What does Stanton assert that the declaration offers as evidence of its claim that women have been mistreated and must demand equal standing in society? *(facts)* What seed does Stanton plant in the minds of readers with this word choice? *(Subconsciously, readers will think of the statements as facts and give them deeper consideration.)* How does this word choice contribute to the persuasiveness of her argument? *(Stanton lends validity by referring to the listed items as facts rather than complaints.)*

Have students reread lines 59–61. Even if Stanton's audience agreed that women were paid less, what might have caused them to reject the demand for equal treatment? *(They may not have wanted to give up the advantage, or they may have believed that women didn't deserve equal pay.)*

Determine Author's Purpose

RI 6, RI 9

RETEACH

Review the term *parallelism*. Parallelism is the repetition of grammatical structure in a pair or series of words, phrases or clauses. As a rhetorical feature, parallel structure adds emphasis to ideas that are related or equal in importance.

- Have students reread Stanton's description of the consequences of marriage, lines 46–49.

- Ask: What is a woman forced to do when she marries? *(She is forced to pledge obedience to her husband.)* What two things result from her promise? *(Result 1: her husband becomes her master; Result 2: the law gives him control over her.)*

- Have students cite the parallel structure in this sentence. *("he becoming"/"the law giving")* Ask students to describe the effect of this parallelism. *(The parallelism emphasizes both the injustice of the circumstances and the government's role.)*

LEVEL UP TUTORIALS Assign the following *Level Up* tutorial: **Analyzing Arguments**

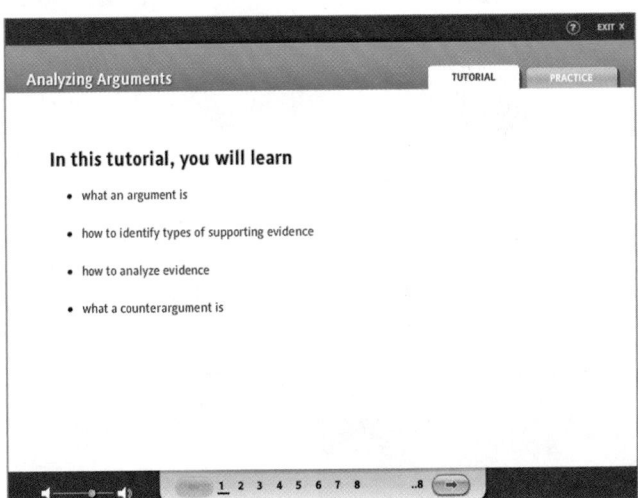

CLOSE READING APPLICATION

Students can apply the skill to another persuasive piece of writing that they have read. Have them work independently to identify an example of parallelism, noting the grammatical construction. Ask: How does the parallelism add to the persuasive effect?

from The Iroquois Constitution

Public Document by Dekanawida

Why This Text

Students sometimes have difficulty understanding an author's purpose for writing a text. The Iroquois Constitution is a document with literary and historical significance. With the help of the close-reading questions, students will analyze the symbols and language in the document. This close reading will lead students to understand Dekanawida's purpose for writing the constitution and its central ideas.

Background Have students read the background and the information about the Iroquois. Explain to students that at the time the Iroquois Constitution was framed, the Iroquois did not have a written language. After a written language was developed, the constitution was written from oral sources. Thanks to the constitution they created, the Iroquois Confederacy became a formidable power. By 1750, it numbered about fifteen thousand people, and Iroquois hunters and warriors ranged over one million square miles.

AS YOU READ Ask students to pay attention to Dekanawida's purpose. How soon into the text can you identify his goals for the Iroquois Confederacy?

Common Core Support

- cite strong and thorough textual evidence
- determine two or more central ideas of a text
- determine an author's purpose in a text in which the rhetoric is particularly effective

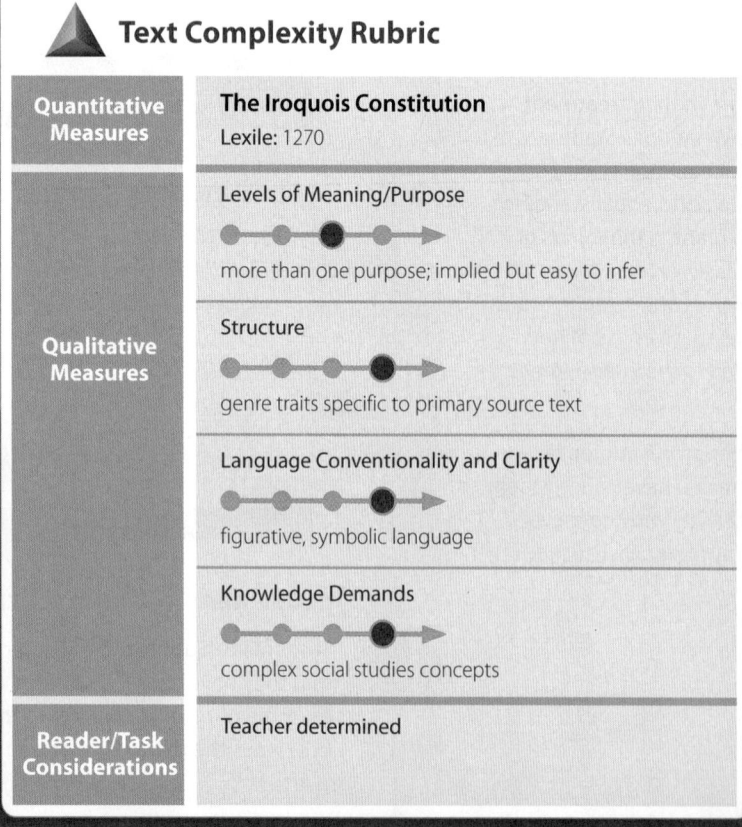

Text Complexity Rubric

Quantitative Measures	**The Iroquois Constitution** Lexile: 1270
Qualitative Measures	**Levels of Meaning/Purpose** — more than one purpose; implied but easy to infer
	Structure — genre traits specific to primary source text
	Language Conventionality and Clarity — figurative, symbolic language
	Knowledge Demands — complex social studies concepts
Reader/Task Considerations	Teacher determined

Strategies for CLOSE READING

Analyze Author's Purpose

Students should read this document carefully all the way through. Close-reading questions at the bottom of the page will help them focus on a thorough analysis of the text. As they read, students should jot down comments or questions about the document in the side margins.

WHEN STUDENTS STRUGGLE . . .

To help students analyze Dekanawida's purpose, have them work in a small group to fill out a chart, such as the one shown below.

CITE TEXT EVIDENCE For practice in analyzing an author's purpose, ask students to identify Dekanawida's purpose, and how he proposes to achieve it.

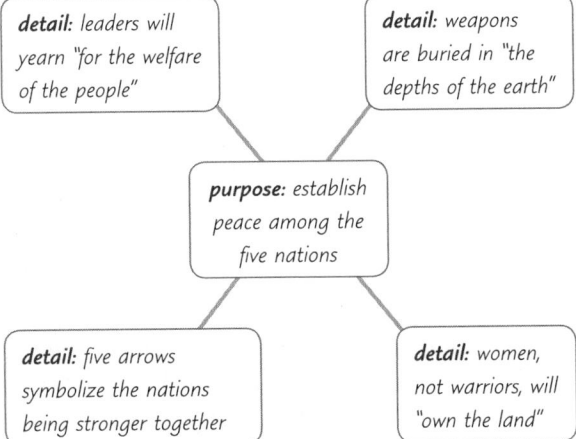

detail: leaders will yearn "for the welfare of the people"

detail: weapons are buried in "the depths of the earth"

purpose: establish peace among the five nations

detail: five arrows symbolize the nations being stronger together

detail: women, not warriors, will "own the land"

Background *The Iroquois Confederacy, also known as the League of Five Nations, was a union of five American Indian tribes across upper New York State. Around 1570, so the legend goes, a visionary named **Dekanawida** convinced the nations to unite in order to establish peace. The Iroquois Constitution is regarded as the world's oldest living constitution. In 1988, to mark the bicentennial of the U.S. Constitution, Congress passed a resolution stating that "the confederation of the original Thirteen Colonies into one republic was influenced by the political system developed by the Iroquois Confederacy, as were many of the democratic principles which were incorporated into the Constitution itself."*

from The Iroquois Constitution

Public Document by Dekanawida

CLOSE READ
Notes

1. **READ ▷** As you read lines 1–24, begin to collect and cite text evidence.
   - Circle the author's name and his purpose in the first sentence.
   - In the margin, explain what Dekanawida does first.
   - Read the footnotes. In the margin, hypothesize the reason Dekanawida first addresses Adodarhoh.

Tree of Great Peace

I am Dekanawida[1] and with the Five Nations' Confederate Lords I plant the Tree of the Great Peace. I plant it in your territory, Adodarhoh,[2] and the Onondaga Nation, in the territory of you who are Firekeepers.

I name the tree the Tree of the Great Long Leaves. Under the shade of this Tree of the Great Peace we spread the soft white feathery down of the globe thistle as seats for you, Adodarhoh, and your cousin Lords.

We place you upon those seats, spread soft with the feathery down of the globe thistle, there beneath the shade of the spreading branches of the Tree of Peace. There shall you sit and watch the Council Fire of the Confederacy of the Five Nations, and all the affairs of the Five Nations shall be transacted at this place before you, Adodarhoh, and your cousin Lords, by the Confederate Lords of the Five Nations.

---
[1] **Dekanawida:** the legendary Great Peacemaker.
[2] **Adodarhoh:** the Onondaga Chief who was the last to join the peace pact.

He plants the Tree of the Great Peace.

Dekanawida wanted to be sure to have Adodarhoh's cooperation.

61

---

1. **READ AND CITE TEXT EVIDENCE**

Ⓐ **ASK STUDENTS** to cite text evidence to support their hypothesis. *Students may cite evidence from lines 5–6 to show that Adodarhoh received special attention from Dekanawida, and 9–12 to show that Adodarhoh would hold a place of leadership, and that the Council Fire would be in his territory.*

CLOSE READ
Notes

Roots have spread out from the Tree of the Great Peace, one to the north, one to the east, one to the south, and one to the west. The name of these roots **B** is The Great White Roots and their nature is Peace and Strength.

If any man or any nation outside the Five Nations shall obey the laws of the Great Peace and make known their **disposition** to the Lords of the Confederacy, they may trace the Roots to the Tree and if their minds are clean and they are obedient and promise to obey the wishes of the Confederate
20 Council, they shall be welcomed to take shelter beneath the Tree of the Long Leaves.

We place at the top of the Tree of the Long Leaves an Eagle who is able to see afar. If he sees in the distance any evil approaching or any danger threatening he will at once warn the people of the Confederacy.

disposition:
*nature,
character*

Leaders

The Lords of the Confederacy of the Five Nations shall be mentors of the people for all time. The thickness of their skin shall be seven spans—which is to say that they shall be proof against anger, offensive actions, and criticism. Their hearts shall be full of peace and goodwill and their minds filled with a yearning for the welfare of the people of the Confederacy. With endless
30 patience they shall carry out their duty and their firmness shall be tempered with a tenderness for their people. Neither anger nor fury shall find lodgment in their minds and all their words and actions shall be marked by calm deliberation.

2. **◀ REREAD** Reread lines 1–24. What do you think was the author's purpose in using tree roots as the symbol for the Iroquois Confederacy? Cite text evidence to support your answer.

Tree roots go deep into the earth, stabilizing tall trees. In the same way, the roots of a peaceful confederacy must be deep, keeping stability in the Five Nations, "and their nature is Peace and Strength." Also, just as tree roots nourish a tree, peace and cooperation nourish the Confederacy.

3. **READ ▶** As you read lines 25–48, continue to cite text evidence.
- Underline language describing the leaders of the Confederacy of the Five Nations.
- In the margin, explain the special role given to women (lines 34–36).
- Circle text explaining the symbolism of the five arrows.

62

CLOSE READ
Notes

Clans
C The lineal descent[3] of the people of the Five Nations shall run in the female line. Women shall be considered the **progenitors** of the Nation. They shall own the land and the soil. Men and women shall follow the status of the mother.

progenitors:
ancestors

Symbols
Five arrows shall be bound together very strong and each arrow shall represent one nation. As the five arrows are strongly bound this shall symbolize the complete union of the nations. Thus are the Five Nations united
40 completely and enfolded together, united into one head, one body, and one mind. Therefore they shall labor, legislate, and council together for the interest of future generations.

Women define family relationships and also own the land.

War and Peace
I, Dekanawida, and the Union Lords, now uproot the tallest pine tree and
D into the cavity thereby made we cast all weapons of war. Into the depths of the earth, down into the deep underearth currents of water flowing to unknown regions we cast all the weapons of strife. We bury them from sight and we plant again the tree. Thus shall the Great Peace be established and hostilities shall no longer be known between the Five Nations but peace to the United People.

[3] **lineal descent:** line of ancestors.

63

2. **REREAD AND CITE TEXT EVIDENCE**

B **ASK STUDENTS** to discuss their answer with a partner, and to include text evidence in their answer. *Students may suggest that the roots symbolize nourishing the Confederacy with "Peace and Strength" (line 15).*

3. **READ AND CITE TEXT EVIDENCE**

C **ASK STUDENTS** to cite text evidence to support their explanation of the special role given to women. *Students should cite evidence from lines 34–36, "They shall own the land and the soil."*

Critical Vocabulary: disposition (line 17) Ask students to explain Dekanawida's use of *disposition.*

Critical Vocabulary: progenitors (line 35) Tell students that the Iroquois are a matrilineal society. Ask them to explain this using the word *progenitors* in the same way it is used here.

FOR ELL STUDENTS Some students may be familiar with the term *cast*, referring to the people who act in a movie or a play. Explain that in this context the verb *to cast* means "to throw in a forceful way."

CLOSE READ
Notes

4. ◀ REREAD Reread lines 43–48. What is the symbolic meaning of burying
the weapons of war deep in the earth? How do the pine tree and the
currents of water add to this symbol? Cite text evidence in your response.

*The symbolic meaning of burying the weapons of war in the "depths
of the earth" is that war is an unnatural way of relating, and is to be
abandoned for all time. The water will carry the weapons to
"unknown regions," so the weapons will be physically gone and absent
from thought—"no longer be known." The warring way of life is
symbolically replaced with peace when the tree that stands for
"peace to the United People" is placed over the hole.*

SHORT RESPONSE

Cite Text Evidence What is Dekanawida's primary purpose for writing this
constitution? What steps does he take to make sure the Confederacy is
successful? Refer to your reading notes, and be sure to **cite text evidence** in
your response.

*Dekanawida wants peace among the Five Nations. He establishes
new leaders who will be people with characters that are peaceful,
"yearning for the welfare of the people." Women, not warriors, will
"own the land and the soil." Symbols are established, such as the
"five arrows," that remind them they are "bound together." Finally,
Dekanawida supports his purpose of establishing peace by casting
"all weapons of war" into "the depths of the earth."*

64

TO CHALLENGE STUDENTS . . .

To learn more about the Iroquois and the meanings of their
symbols, students can research the Five Nations online and in
print resources.

ASK STUDENTS to research the symbols Dekanawida used
in the Iroquois Constitution, and to learn more about what the
symbols mean to the Iroquois people. Students should work in
groups to find out about at least one symbol. Have groups share
the results of their research with the class and discuss how their
research helped them understand the symbolism.

DIG DEEPER

With the class, return to Question 2, Reread. Have students share
their responses.

ASK STUDENTS to cite the text evidence that led to their
interpretation of Dekanawida's use of tree roots as a symbol for
the Iroquois Confederacy.

- Point out that lines 13–14 describe the roots spreading out
  in four directions. Ask students what the four directions
  symbolize. *Four directions symbolize everywhere on Earth.*

- Have students cite text that shows that the roots symbolize
  peace. *Dekanawida says that the nature of the roots is "Peace
  and Strength."*

- Read aloud lines 16–21. Ask students to comment on
  Dekanawida's use of the phrase "they may trace the Roots to
  the Tree" (line 18). *Students may see this as an invitation to any
  tribe or person to live according to this constitution.*

ASK STUDENTS to return to their Short Response answer and
revise it based on the class discussion.

4. (REREAD AND CITE TEXT EVIDENCE)

Ⓓ **ASK STUDENTS** to cite text evidence to support their
interpretation. *Students may say that burying weapons in the
"depths of the earth" (lines 44–45) symbolizes the abandonment of
war. They may say that water carrying the weapons to "unknown
regions" (lines 45–46) symbolizes letting go of thoughts of war. They
may say that the tree represents "peace to the United People" (line
48).*

SHORT RESPONSE

Cite Text Evidence Student responses will vary, but they should
cite evidence from the text to support their analysis of Dekanawida's
purpose. Students should:

- determine Dekanawida's purpose.
- explain the steps he took to ensure the Confederacy was
  successful.
- support the central idea with details from the text.

*my*SmartPlanner Create lesson plans and access resources online.

Building the Transcontinental Railroad

History Writing by Iris Chang

Why This Text?

To understand the important role that immigration has played in American history, and to grasp the breadth and depth of the immigrant experience, students need to read a variety of works that describe how these groups assimilated in and contributed to the prevailing society. This account tells of the Chinese immigrants who built the transcontinental railroad and paved the way for a large Asian American population.

Key Learning Objective: Students will be able to analyze a narrative history and understand how ideas are organized and sequence is created.

For additional practice:

Close Reader selection
"Bonding Over a Mascot"
Newspaper Article by Joe Lapointe

COMMON CORE Common Core Standards

RI 3 Analyze a set of ideas or sequence of events.
RI 4 Determine the meaning of words and phrases.
RI 6 Determine an author's point of view or purpose.
W 7 Conduct research projects.
W 8 Gather information from multiple authoritative print and digital sources.
SL 1a Come to discussions prepared/draw on preparation to stimulate exchange of ideas.
SL 3 Evaluate speaker's point of view, reasoning, and use of evidence and rhetoric.
SL 4 Present information, findings, and supporting evidence.
SL 5 Make strategic use of digital media.
L 3a Vary syntax for effect; apply an understanding of syntax.
L 4a Use context as a clue to meaning.
L 4d Verify the preliminary determination of the meaning of a word or phrase.

▲ Text Complexity Rubric

Quantitative Measures	**Building the Transcontinental Railroad** Lexile: 1310L
	Levels of Meaning/Purpose  more than one purpose, easily identified from context
Qualitative Measures	**Structure** complex, explicit organization; may exhibit disciplinary traits
	Language Conventionality and Clarity some unfamiliar, academic, or domain-specific words
	Knowledge Demands specialized knowledge required
Reader/Task Considerations	Teacher determined Vary by individual reader and type of text

TEACH

CLOSE READ

Background Inform students that large-scale Chinese immigration to the United States began in the 1840s and 1850s, with most immigrants arriving at San Francisco. However, most Chinese immigrants at that time were declared ineligible to become citizens, vote, hold office, own land, or testify against a white person in court.

AS YOU READ Direct students to use the As You Read instructions to focus their reading.

Analyze Ideas and Events: Sequence (LINES 1–10)
COMMON CORE RI 3

Tell students that the most direct way for authors to indicate chronological sequence is through the use of words for time, such as dates, hours, minutes, or phrases like *that afternoon* or *the following day*.

(A) CITE TEXT EVIDENCE Have students locate two statements of time in the opening paragraph of the selection. *("In the decade of the 1840s" and "during this decade")* Ask them what historical information in the paragraph also provides chronological clues to readers who know the history. *(the gold rush and the acquisition of Texas, California, and Oregon)*

Author's Purpose: Tone and Style (LINES 11–15)
COMMON CORE RI 4, RI 6

Make the point that an author's word choices communicate tone, or the writer's attitude toward the subject, and that vivid, concrete word choices convey tone more clearly than vague, general words.

(B) CITE TEXT EVIDENCE Have students say what the author's purpose is in describing the crossing of the continent and which vivid words and phrases make that purpose clear. *(Possible answer: The purpose is to impress readers with the difficult nature of the crossing. The author uses the words and phrases "dangerous," "frustrating," "no reliable transport or route," "death by disease," "brigands," "starvation," "thirst," "heat," and "freezing.")*

Background As a historian, **Iris Chang** *(1968–2004) sought to shed light on acts of injustice. Her international bestseller* The Rape of Nanking *documents previously unpublished accounts of brutal violence by the Japanese military during their occupation of China prior to World War II. In* The Chinese in America, *Chang traces her ethnic group's immigration experiences and achievements from the mid-nineteenth century to the present day. This chapter from her book details the role of Chinese laborers in building a vital transportation link that fueled westward expansion in the United States.*

Building the Transcontinental Railroad

History Writing by Iris Chang

Image Credits: (bg) ©MoinMoin/Shutterstock; (bl) ©Antonio Abrignani/Shutterstock; (r) ©Antonio Abrignani/Shutterstock

AS YOU READ Pay attention to details about the accomplishments of Chinese laborers and the hardships they faced. Write down any questions you generate during reading.

(A) *From sea to shining sea.* In the decade of the 1840s, Americans were consumed by this vision, articulated in the doctrine of Manifest Destiny, which proclaimed it the right and duty of the United States to expand its democratic way of life across the entire continent, from the Atlantic to the Pacific, from the Rio Grande in the south to the 54th parallel in the north. The country was feeling confident (during this decade, it acquired the territories of Texas, California, and Oregon), its population was increasing, and many wanted to push west, especially to California, made famous by gold and Richard Henry Dana's

10 recounting of his adventures there, in *Two Years Before the Mast.*

(B) Making the vision real, however, was dangerous and frustrating. The territory between the coasts was unsettled and there was no reliable transport or route. Crossing the continent meant braving death by disease, brigands,[1] Native Americans, starvation, thirst, heat, or freezing. This was true especially for those headed straight to the

---

[1] **brigands:** bandits.

SCAFFOLDING FOR ELL STUDENTS

Identify Tone Using a whiteboard, project lines 11–12 of the selection.

- Highlight in yellow the adjectives.
- Highlight in green the nouns.
- Underline the highlighted words that describe danger and difficulty.

ASK STUDENTS to analyze Chang's word choice and tone.

> Making the vision real, however, was dangerous and frustrating. The territory between the coasts was unsettled and there was no reliable transport or route.

Author's Purpose: Tone and Style (LINES 16–25)

 COMMON CORE RI 6

Tell students that although one purpose of informational writing is to present facts, facts alone are often dull. Authors use elements of style, such as descriptive adjectives and adverbs, to heighten reader interest and involve readers' emotions.

C **CITE TEXT EVIDENCE** Have students state adjectives and adverbs that add interest and emotion to this passage. *("frustrated," "safe," "sparsely populated," "impatient," "rich," "safely," "profitably")*

Analyze Ideas and Events: Sequence (LINES 37–47)

 COMMON CORE RI 3

Tell students that readers can often infer the sequence of historical events by reading between the lines when the author has given partial information.

D **CITE TEXT EVIDENCE** Have students determine the chronological relationship between the financing of the transcontinental railroad and the Civil War. Ask students what evidence in the passage leads to that inference. *(The Civil War and the financing of the transcontinental railroad occurred during the same time. The inference can be made from the date 1862 and the clause "even though the country was already at war.")* Then ask what prior historical knowledge would be needed to make that inference if the clause "even though the country was already at war" were not in the passage. *(It would be necessary to know the dates of the Civil War.)*

CRITICAL VOCABULARY

formidable: Building the railroad involved overcoming difficult physical obstacles.

ASK STUDENTS to list the formidable challenges that the builders of the transcontinental railroad faced. *(the Rocky Mountains and the Apache and Comanche peoples)*

C gold hills of California, but the gold rushers weren't the only ones frustrated by the lack of a safe passage between the settled East and the new state of California in the sparsely populated West. Californians themselves were impatient at waiting months to receive mail and
20 provisions. Washington, too, recognized the economic as well as political benefits of linking the country's two coasts. In the West lay rich farmland waiting for settlement, gold and silver to be mined and taxed. What was needed was a transcontinental railroad to move more people west and natural resources safely and profitably to major markets back east.

There were only two overland routes west—over the Rockies or along the southern route through Apache and Comanche territory— both hazardous. It took longer, but was almost always safer, to get to California from anywhere east of the Missouri by sea. This meant
30 heading east to the Atlantic Ocean or south to the Gulf of Mexico, boarding a ship that would sail almost to the southern tip of South America, passing through the Strait of Magellan, and heading back north to California. The sea voyage could be shortened considerably by disembarking on the eastern coast of Central America, traveling by wagon across the isthmus,[2] and then hitching a ride on the first steamer headed north.[3]

D The need for a transcontinental railroad was so strongly argued that Congress, with the support of President Lincoln, passed legislation to finance the railroad with government bonds, even
40 though the country was already at war. Two companies divided the task of actual construction. In 1862, the Central Pacific Railroad Corporation, headed by the "Big Four"—Leland Stanford, Collis P. Huntington, Charles Crocker, and Mark Hopkins—was awarded the contract to lay tracks eastward from Sacramento, while its rival, the Union Pacific, was awarded the path westward from Omaha, Nebraska, which was already connected to the East through existing rail lines. The goal was to meet in the middle, connecting the nation with a continuous stretch of railroad tracks from the Atlantic to the Pacific. The Union Pacific's job—laying track over plains—was much
50 easier, while the Central Pacific had to go over steep mountains. The Central Pacific engineers promised that the **formidable** physical obstacles could be overcome, and to a great extent, it was Chinese labor, and even, here and there, Chinese ingenuity, that helped make the transcontinental railroad a reality.

The first and largest challenge was figuring out how to cut a path through California's and Nevada's rugged Sierra Nevada, which stood as a final barrier to the West. The workers of the Central Pacific had the dangerous task of ramming tunnels through these mountains,

formidable
(fôr′mĭ-də-bəl) *adj.* difficult and intimidating.

---

[2] **isthmus** (ĭs′məs): a thin strip of land between two bodies of water.
[3] Eventually, U.S. engineers would build the Panama Canal in the early twentieth century. [Author's note]

APPLYING ACADEMIC VOCABULARY

confirm	deny

As you discuss "Building the Transcontinental Railroad," incorporate the following Collection 4 academic vocabulary words: *confirm* and *deny*. To enhance students' understanding of author Iris Chang's purpose and tone, ask students what details in the text could be used to **confirm** the abilities of the Chinese immigrant workers and to **deny** the arguments of people who held anti-Chinese prejudices. Ask students how the details reflect her purpose and tone.

and then laying tracks across the parched Nevada and Utah deserts.
Some engineers, watching the project from afar, said this was
impossible. In a major recruitment drive for five thousand workers,
the Central Pacific sent advertisements to every post office in the state
of California, offering high wages to any white man willing to work.
But the appeal secured only eight hundred. Why toil for wages when
an instant fortune was possible in the mines? Many men who did sign
on were, in the words of company superintendent James Strobridge,
"unsteady men, unreliable. Some of them would stay a few days, and
some would not go to work at all. Some would stay until payday, get
a little money, get drunk, and clear out." The company thought of
asking the War Department for five thousand Confederate prisoners
to put to work, but Lee's surrender at the Appomattox Court House
ended the war and this plan.

Fortunately for the Central Pacific, Chinese immigrants provided
a vast pool of cheap, plentiful, and easily exploitable labor. By 1865,
the number of Chinese in California reached close to fifty thousand,
at least 90 percent of them young men. In the spring of that year, when
white laborers demanded higher pay and threatened to strike, Charles
Crocker, the Central Pacific's chief contractor, ordered Superintendent
Strobridge to recruit Chinese workers. The tactic worked, and the
white workers agreed to return, as long as no Chinese were hired, but
by then the Central Pacific had the upper hand and hired fifty Chinese
anyway—former miners, laundry men, domestic servants, and market
gardeners—to do the hard labor of preparing the route and laying
track. Many claimed the railroad did this as a reminder to the white
workers that others were ready to replace them. Needless to say, this
did not contribute to harmony between the whites and the Chinese.

Of course prejudice against the Chinese railroad workers did not
start with the white laborers. Initially, Superintendent Strobridge was
unhappy with their being hired. "I will not boss Chinese!" he roared,
suggesting that the Chinese were too delicate for the job. (The Chinese
averaged four feet ten inches in height and weighed 120 pounds.)
Crocker, however, pointed out that a race of people who had built the
Great Wall of China could build a railroad. Grudgingly, Strobridge put
the Chinese to work, giving them light jobs, like filling dump carts.

To the surprise of many—but apparently not the Chinese
themselves—the first fifty hired excelled at their work, becoming
such disciplined, fast learners that the railroad soon gave them other
responsibilities, such as rock cuts. In time, the Central Pacific hired
another fifty Chinese, and then another fifty, until eventually the
company employed thousands of Chinese laborers—the overwhelming
majority of the railroad workforce. E. B. Crocker, brother of Charles,
wrote to Senator Cornelius Cole (R-Calif.) that the Chinese were
nearly equal to white men in the amount of work they could do and
far more reliable. Leland Stanford, the railroad's president, and later
the founder of Stanford University, praised the Chinese as "quiet,

TEACH

CLOSE READ

Analyze Ideas and Events: Sequence (LINES 61–86)

COMMON CORE RI 3

Point out that in telling the story in chronological order, Iris Chang does not always use time-signal words. Sometimes the reader must infer the sequence.

E ASK STUDENTS to summarize the sequence of events by which the debate over whether to hire Chinese workers was resolved. (*The Central Pacific advertised for white workers, but only eight hundred were found as opposed to the necessary five thousand, and the ones who arrived were often unreliable. Then the company had the idea of using Confederate prisoners, but the end of the Civil War made that impossible. Finally, the company decided to make use of the large, available pool of Chinese male laborers. Many white laborers threatened to strike, but the company kept some Chinese workers on.*)

Author's Purpose: Tone and Style (LINES 84–86)

COMMON CORE RI 6

Remind students that a writer's **tone** is his or her attitude toward the topic. Tell them that the writer's attitude can be expressed through word choice or through the use of irony or sarcasm.

F CITE TEXT EVIDENCE Have students identify the sentence in lines 84–86 in which Chang addresses the reader ironically. (*"Needless to say, this did not contribute to harmony between the whites and the Chinese."*) What is the purpose of the sentence? (*Possible answer: The purpose is to point out a way in which the railroad manipulated racial prejudice for economic ends.*)

WHEN STUDENTS STRUGGLE . . .

If students have trouble keeping track of the arguments that were used in favor of excluding Chinese workers, have them reread the last two paragraphs on this page, beginning, "Of course prejudice against the Chinese...." Then have them complete a point/counterpoint chart showing the reasons Superintendent Strobridge gave for not hiring Chinese workers and evidence Charles and E. B. Crocker found for hiring them.

Strobridge: Don't Hire Chinese	Charles and E. B. Crocker: Hire Chinese

CRITICAL VOCABULARY

expedience: The attitudes of the railroad companies toward Chinese workers stemmed from their own economic interests.

ASK STUDENTS to relate how expedience guided Leland Stanford's attitude toward the Chinese.

Analyze Ideas and Events: 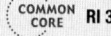 RI 3
Sequence (LINES 114–135)

Tell students that to keep track of a complex sequence of events over the course of several paragraphs, they may want to write a summary of the major events or make a timeline.

G **CITE TEXT EVIDENCE** Have students retell the major developments of 1867–1868 that led to increased Chinese immigration into the United States. *(Students should include the reactions of railroad executives, the effects of diplomacy, the essentials of the Burlingame Treaty, and the progress of immigration.)*

Author's Purpose:  RI 4, RI 6
Tone and Style (LINES 143–148)

Tell students that an author can express tone through the words of a historical person, since the author chooses which of the person's words to include. Lee Chew expresses a view that the reader can infer Chang may share.

H **CITE TEXT EVIDENCE** Have students find words and phrases in Lee Chew's words that hint at Chang's attitude toward the Chinese workers. *("persecuted," "virtues," "honest," "industrious," "steady," "sober," "painstaking")*

---

peaceable, patient, industrious and economical." (Stanford's position on the Chinese was governed by **expedience**. In 1862, to please the racist sentiments of the state, he called the Chinese in California the "dregs" of Asia, a "degraded" people. A few years later, he was praising
110 the Chinese to President Andrew Johnson and others in order to justify the Central Pacific's mass hiring of Chinese. Later still—notably in 1884, when he ran for the U.S. Senate—he would ally himself with those who favored a ban on Chinese immigration.)

Delighted by the productivity of the Chinese, railroad executives became fervent[4] advocates of Chinese immigration to California. "I like the idea of your getting over more Chinamen," Collis Huntington, one of the "Big Four" executives at the Central Pacific, wrote to Charlie Crocker in 1867. "It would be all the better for us and the State if there should a half million come over in 1868."
120 The Central Pacific printed handbills and dispatched recruiters to China, especially the Guangdong province, to find new workers. It negotiated with a steamship company to lower their rates for travel. And, fortuitously[5] for the Central Pacific, Sino-American diplomacy would create more favorable conditions for Chinese immigration to the United States. In 1868, China and the U.S. government signed the Burlingame Treaty. In exchange for "most favored nation" status in trade, China agreed to recognize the "inherent and inalienable right of man to change his home and allegiance and also the mutual advantage of free migration and emigration of their citizens and subjects
130 respectively from one country to the other for purposes of curiosity or trade or as permanent residents."

The new Chinese recruits docked at San Francisco and were immediately transported by riverboat to Sacramento, and then by the Central Pacific's own train to the end of the laid tracks, which was a moving construction site. There they were organized into teams of about a dozen or so, with each team assigned its own cook and headman, who communicated with the Central Pacific foreman. The Chinese paid for their own food and cooked it themselves—they were even able to procure special ingredients like cuttlefish, bamboo shoots,
140 and abalone. At night they slept in tents provided by the railroad, or in dugouts in the earth. At the peak of construction, Central Pacific would employ more than ten thousand Chinese men.

The large number of Chinese made white workers uncomfortable. As Lee Chew, a railroad laborer, later recalled in a spasm of national pride, the Chinese were "persecuted not for their vices but for their virtues. No one would hire an Irishman, German, Englishman or Italian when he could get a Chinese, because our countrymen are so much more honest, industrious, steady, sober and painstaking." Crocker explicitly acknowledged this work ethic. After recruiting

expedience
(ĭk-spē´dē-əns) *n.* a self-interested means to an end.

---

[4] **fervent:** avid, enthusiastic.
[5] **fortuitously:** luckily; by favorable chance.

304 Collection 4

TO CHALLENGE STUDENTS...

Research Historical Detail To enhance appreciation of the detailed series of historical developments that resulted in Chinese immigration to the United States, have students look up the following terms:

- Burlingame Treaty
- most favored nation
- Guangdong province

Invite students to give brief talks to the class elaborating on how these terms relate to Chinese immigration.

" The Chinese, without fail, always outmeasured the Cornish miners. "

150 some Cornish miners from Virginia City, Nevada, to excavate one end of a tunnel and the Chinese the other, he commented, "The Chinese, without fail, always outmeasured the Cornish miners. That is to say, they would cut more rock in a week than the Cornish miners did. And here it was hard work, steady pounding on the rock, bone-labor." The Cornish eventually walked off the job, vowing that "they would not work with Chinamen anyhow," and soon, Crocker recalled, "the Chinamen had possession of the whole work."

White laborers began to feel that Chinese **diligence** forced everyone to work harder for less reward. Crocker recalled that one
160 white laborer near Auburn was questioned by a gentleman about his wages. "I think we were paying $35 a month and board to white laborers, and $30 a month to Chinamen and they boarded themselves," Crocker said. "The gentleman remarked, 'That is pretty good wages.' 'Yes,' says he, 'but begad if it wasn't for them damned nagurs we would get $50 and not do half the work.' "

Some white laborers on the Central Pacific whispered among themselves about driving the Chinese off the job, but when Charles Crocker got wind of this, he threatened to replace all the whites with Chinese. Eventually the white workers gave up, placated[6] perhaps
170 by being told that they alone could be promoted to the position of foreman. The more Chinese workers, the fewer whites in the labor force and the less competition for foreman positions among the whites. And foremen were paid several times the wages of a Chinese laborer.

In the process of laying the track across northern California, Nevada, and Utah, hundreds of men—Chinese, Irish, German, and others—cleared a path through some of the world's largest trees, some with stumps so deeply rooted that ten barrels of gunpowder were often needed to unearth them. It was dangerous work—work that loosened boulders, started landslides, and filled the air with flying debris. Even
180 more dangerous was the work that began upon reaching the Sierra Nevada.

Ideally, the roadbed[7] through the mountains would be tunneled through by heavy machinery. This machinery was unavailable, however, because it was expensive and difficult to transport (entire

diligence
(dĭl'ə-jəns) *n.*
consistent, thorough effort and dedication.

---
[6] **placated:** made peaceful or less angry.
[7] **roadbed:** the path or foundation on which railroad tracks are laid.

Building the Transcontinental Railroad **305**

CLOSE READ

Author's Purpose: Tone and Style (LINES 151–157)

COMMON CORE RI 6

Draw students' attention to the quotation in these lines. Tell them that a reader can often infer an author's purpose for writing by analyzing material, such as quotations, that an author chooses to include.

ⓘ **ASK STUDENTS** to infer Chang's purpose in including the quotation. *(She wanted to counter negative stereotypes of Chinese people by showing that the Chinese workers worked harder than their European competitors.)*

> **CRITICAL VOCABULARY**
>
> **diligence**: It became obvious that the Chinese worked harder than the Cornish miners.
>
> **ASK STUDENTS** why non-Chinese workers reacted negatively to Chinese diligence. *(Non-Chinese workers objected to Chinese diligence because it led to higher employer expectations.)*

Analyze Ideas and Events: Sequence (LINES 174–178)

COMMON CORE RI 3

Explain to students that sometimes details of spatial movement can signal chronological sequence.

ⓙ **ASK STUDENTS** why Chang gives the sequence of states as "California, Nevada, and Utah." *(The names are in the west-to-east order in which the track was laid.)*

SCAFFOLDING FOR ELL STUDENTS

Understand Archaic Language Tell students that the quotations on this page reflect the way some Americans spoke in the 1800s. Explain the following terms:

- *Chinamen* was a pejorative word used to refer to Chinese people.
- *Nagurs* was a pejorative word used to refer to groups of people the speaker considered inferior.

Tell students that when they read historical quotations, they should watch for archaic language and look up any words they don't understand in a dictionary.

ASK STUDENTS to tell how the use of these words affects the tone of the quotations. *(It gives them a hostile tone.)*

Analyze Ideas and Events: Sequence (LINES 198–228)
COMMON CORE RI 3

Tell students that even when authors follow chronological order for much of a text, they may shift to a different logical order at times in order to follow up on important ideas or aspects of an issue.

 **ASK STUDENTS** to explain how and why the last paragraph on this page marks a break from the chronological order used in earlier paragraphs. *(The paragraphs about nitroglycerin use chronological order, because that topic involves a tense series of dangerous events. The sixth paragraph changes topic, turning to disease and its causes and using cause-and-effect order.)*

Author's Purpose: Tone and Style (LINES 198–220)
COMMON CORE RI 4, RI 6

Tell students that writers use the **connotations,** or shades of meaning, of words, to convey attitudes and affect readers. Chang selects words to emphasize the dangerous and impressive nature of the work done by the Chinese workers.

L **CITE TEXT EVIDENCE** Have students cite words and phrases that contribute to the tone of awe and horror. *("unpredictable explosive," line 200; "accidental blasts," line 202; "literally sculpting," line 217; "sheer rock," lines 217–218; "peppered with shards of granite and shale," line 219)*

---

bridges would have had to be rebuilt for such machinery to reach the current site). Thus the Chinese were forced to chisel tunnels through the granite using only handheld drills, explosives, and shovels. In some places they encountered a form of porphyritic[8] rock so hard it was impervious[9] to frontal attack, even with gunpowder. Work proceeded, on average, seven inches a day, at a cost of as much as a million dollars for one mile of tunnel.

In the summer of 1866, to move farther faster, the railroad kept several shifts of men going day and night. Shoulder to shoulder, hour after hour, the Chinese railroad workers chipped away at the rock, breathing granite dust, sweating and panting by the dim flickering glow of candlelight, until even the strongest of them fainted from exhaustion.

Finally, to speed up the process, the Central Pacific brought in nitroglycerin. Only the Chinese—a people experienced with fireworks—were willing to handle this unpredictable explosive, pouring it into the tunnel through holes drilled in the granite. Countless workers perished in accidental blasts, but the Central Pacific did not keep track of the numbers.

Still the workers struggled on. One terrifying challenge lay at Cape Horn, the nickname for a three-mile stretch of gorge above the American River three miles east of Colfax, California, and fifty-seven miles east of Sacramento. Through much of the way, a flat roadbed had to be carved along a steep cliff, and a Chinese headman suggested to Strobridge that they employ an ancient method used to create fortresses along the Yangtze River gorges: they could dangle supplies down to the work site in reed baskets, attached to ropes secured over the tops of mountains.

Reeds were shipped out immediately from San Francisco to Cape Horn. At night the Chinese workers wove them into wicker baskets and fastened them to sturdy ropes. When everything was ready, workers were lowered in the baskets to drill holes and tamp in dynamite, literally sculpting the rail bed out of the face of sheer rock. The lucky ones were hauled up in time to escape the explosions; others, peppered with shards of granite and shale, fell to their deaths in the valley below.

Disease swept through the ranks of the exhausted railroad workers, but the Chinese fared better than whites. Caucasian laborers, subsisting largely on salt beef, potatoes, bread, coffee, and rancid butter, lacked vegetables in their diet, while the Chinese employed their own cooks and ate better-balanced meals. White workers succumbed to dysentery after sharing communal dippers from greasy pails, but the Chinese drank fresh boiled tea, which they kept in whiskey barrels or powder kegs suspended from each end of a bamboo

---

[8] **porphyritic** (pôr´fə-rĭt´ĭk): rock containing relatively large, visible crystals.
[9] **impervious**: immune or resistant.

SCAFFOLDING FOR ELL STUDENTS

Author's Purpose: Tone and Style Project lines 222–224 of the selection.

- Highlight difficult words in yellow.
- Have students work in pairs. Have them use a thesaurus to replace each highlighted word with a simpler synonym.

Chinese fared better than whites. Caucasian laborers, subsisting largely on salt beef, potatoes, bread, coffee, and rancid butter, lacked vegetables in their diet,

pole. They also avoided alcohol and, "not having acquired the taste of
whiskey," as one contemporary observed, "they have fewer fights and
no blue Mondays." Most important, they kept themselves clean, which
helped prevent the spread of germs. The white men had "a sort of
hydrophobia," one writer observed, whereas the Chinese bathed every
night before dinner, in powder kegs filled with heated water.

In the Sierras, the railroad workers endured two of the worst
winters in American history. In 1865, they faced thirty-foot drifts
and spent weeks just shoveling snow. The following year brought the
"Homeric winter" of 1866–67, one of the most brutal ever recorded,
which dropped forty feet of snow on the crews and whipped up drifts
more than eighty feet high. Power snowplows, driven forward by
twelve locomotives linked together, could scarcely budge the densest
of these drifts. Sheds built to protect the uncompleted tracks collapsed
under the weight of the snow, which snapped even the best timber. On
the harshest days, travel was almost impossible; as horses broke the icy
crust, sharp edges slashed their legs to the bone. They received mail
from a Norwegian postal worker on cross-country skis.

Making the best of the situation, the Chinese carved a working
city under the snow. Operating beneath the crust by lantern light, they
trudged through a labyrinth of snow tunnels, with snow chimneys and
snow stairs leading up to the surface. Meanwhile, they continued to
shape the rail bed out of rock, using materials lowered down to them
through airshafts in the snow.

The cost in human life was enormous. Snow slides and avalanches
swept away entire teams of Chinese workers. On Christmas Day
1866, the *Dutch Flat Enquirer* announced that "a gang of Chinamen
employed by the railroad…were covered up by a snow slide and four
or five died before they could be exhumed. Then snow fell to such a
depth that one whole camp of Chinamen was covered up during the
night and parties were digging them out when our informant left."
When the snow melted in the spring, the company found corpses still
standing erect, their frozen hands gripping picks and shovels.

Winter was only one obstacle. Other conditions also affected the
workers. Landslides rolled tons of soil across the completed track,
blocking its access and often smothering workers. Melting snow
mired wagons, carts, and stagecoaches in a sea of mud. Once through
the mountains, the crews faced terrible extremes of weather in the
Nevada and Utah deserts. There the temperature could plummet to 50
degrees below zero—freezing the ground so hard it required blasting,
as if it were bedrock—or soar above 120, causing heat stroke and
dehydration.

The Chinese labored from sunrise to sunset six days a week, in
twelve-hour shifts. Only on Sundays did they have time to rest, mend

CLOSE READ

Analyze Ideas and Events: Sequence (LINES 235–261)

COMMON CORE RI 3

Tell students that chronological order can be especially effective when the events narrated are so dramatic that they speak for themselves, needing little interpretation. The description of events in the winters of 1865–1867 is a good example.

M ASK STUDENTS to relate the sequence of events in the two terrible winters described in the passage. *(1865: thirty-foot snow drifts, weeks of shoveling; 1866–1867: forty feet of snow, eighty-foot drifts, snow plows ineffective, sheds collapsed, travel almost impossible, mail delivered on skis, Chinese workers build a "city" under the snow; Dec. 25, 1866: fatal snow slide)*

Author's Purpose: Tone and Style (LINES 235–240)

COMMON CORE RI 4, RI 6

Discuss with students the impression they have of the winters of 1865 through 1867. Explain to students that the author's tone helps to create this impression.

N CITE TEXT EVIDENCE Ask students to state Chang's tone in these lines. *(Her tone is one of awe.)* Then have them cite words and phrases that help to create this tone. *("endured," line 235; "brutal," line 238; "whipped up," line 239)* Afterwards, ask them to cite details that contribute to the tone. *("thirty-foot drifts," line 236; "forty feet of snow," line 239; "drifts more than eighty feet high," lines 239–240)*

TO CHALLENGE STUDENTS . . .

Use Research Techniques How can writers bring history back to life? Ask students what techniques a writer might use to find reliable descriptions and statistics about a century-old event. *(A writer would search in libraries and online for documents from that time and place, such as newspapers, diaries, and letters. The writer would also consult biographies of important participants in the events and recent history books and articles.)*

Have students pick a historical event that interests them and perform a brief search for primary and secondary sources about it. Have students share their topics, search methods, and results with the class.

CRITICAL VOCABULARY

systematize: The whites' abuse of the Chinese was not limited to isolated incidents.

ASK STUDENTS why prejudice is especially harmful when it is systematized. *(When it is systematized, a whole society practices discrimination, and harms entire groups of people for long periods of time.)*

Analyze Ideas and Events: Sequence (LINES 282–300)

COMMON CORE RI 3

Point out that the Chinese workers' strike is one episode within the overall sequence of events of the building of the railroad. It has its own sequence, which can be viewed as a subsequence of the main sequence.

 ASK STUDENTS to state the sequence of events in the Chinese workers' strike of June 1867. *(As the company approached bankruptcy, two thousand Chinese walked off their jobs. They presented demands and circulated a placard. The Central Pacific stopped payments and food deliveries to the strikers. After a week, the strikers were forced to go back to work.)*

Author's Purpose: Tone and Style (LINES 307–313)

COMMON CORE RI 6

Explain that history writers, in order to support their purposes, often include eyewitness accounts from the era of the events to help readers form a picture of the time, the place, the people, and the actions involved.

 **ASK STUDENTS** to infer the author's purpose for quoting Crocker's statement about the Chinese workers. *(The author wishes to show that although the strike did not succeed in its immediate aims, it was inspiring over the long run and succeeded in giving the employers a positive view of the Chinese workers.)*

---

their clothes, talk, smoke, and, of course, gamble.[10] The tedium of their lives was aggravated by the **systematized** abuse and contempt heaped on them by the railroad executives. The Chinese worked longer and harder than whites, but received less pay: because the Chinese had to pay for their own board, their wages were two-thirds those of white workers and a fourth those of the white foremen. (Even the allocation for feed for horses—fifty dollars a month for each—was twenty dollars 280 more than the average Chinese worker earned.) Worst of all, they endured whippings from their overseers, who treated them like slaves.

Finally, the Chinese rebelled. In June 1867, as the Central Pacific tottered[11] on the brink of bankruptcy (Leland Stanford later described a two-week period when there was not a dollar of cash in the treasury), some two thousand Chinese in the Sierras walked off the job. As was their way in a strange land, they conducted the strike politely, appointing headmen to present James Strobridge a list of demands that included more pay and fewer hours in the tunnels. They also circulated among themselves a placard written in Chinese, explaining their 290 rights. In retrospect, it is surprising that they managed to organize a strike at all, for there are also reports of frequent feuds erupting between groups of Chinese workers, fought with spades, crowbars, and spikes. But organize they did.

The Central Pacific reacted swiftly and ruthlessly. An enraged Charles Crocker contacted employment agencies in an attempt to recruit ten thousand recently freed American blacks to replace the Chinese. He stopped payments to the Chinese and cut off the food supply, effectively starving them back to work. Because most of them could not speak English, could not find work elsewhere, and lacked 300 transportation back to California, the strike lasted only a week. However, it did achieve a small victory, securing the Chinese a raise of two dollars a month. More important, by staging the largest Chinese strike of the nineteenth century, they demonstrated to their current and future employers that while they were willing and easily managed workers, if pushed hard enough they were able to organize to protect themselves, even in the face of daunting odds.

Later, the railroad management expressed admiration at the orderliness of the strike. "If there had been that number of whites in a strike, there would have been murder and drunkenness and disorder," 310 Crocker marveled. "But with the Chinese it was just like Sunday. These men stayed in their camps. They would come out and walk around, but not a word was said; nothing was done. No violence was perpetuated[12] along the whole line."

---

[10] Gambling was as addictive for Chinese railroad workers as whiskey among their white counterparts. Chinese gamblers left their mark on Nevada, where casinos credit the nineteenth-century Chinese railroad workers with introducing the game of keno, based on the Chinese lottery game of *pak kop piu*. [Author's note]

[11] **tottered:** wobbled unsteadily.

[12] **perpetuated:** sustained.

systematize
(sĭs′tə-mə-tīz′) v. to form something into an organized plan or scheme.

WHEN STUDENTS STRUGGLE . . .

To help students perceive the tone and style of Chang's writing, have pairs read aloud the last two paragraphs. (Each partner should read one of the paragraphs.) Encourage students to convey an appropriate attitude by reading in a natural, expressive voice. Point out that the passage contains dialogue which has a style different from that of the writer's. If time permits, have pairs confer and practice before their reading.

ASK STUDENTS to describe the tone of the paragraphs in their own words. *(Possible answers: The tone at the beginning is judgmental, indicated by words such as "swiftly," and "ruthlessly." Later, the tone is triumphant as the author describes the "daunting odds." Finally, the tone is one of admiration, as evidenced by the words "admiration" and "marveled.")*

The Chinese were certainly capable, however, of violence. As the railroad neared completion, the Chinese encountered the Irish workers of the Union Pacific for the first time. When the two companies came within a hundred feet of each other, the Union Pacific Irish taunted the Chinese with catcalls and threw clods of dirt. When the Chinese ignored them, the Irish swung their picks at them, 320 and to the astonishment of the whites, the Chinese fought back. The level of antagonism continued to rise. Several Chinese were wounded by blasting powder the whites had secretly planted near their side. Several days later, a mysterious explosion killed several Irish workers. The presumption was that the Chinese had retaliated in kind. At that point, the behavior of white workers toward the Chinese immediately improved.

If relations were often tense between the Chinese and the Irish, there were also moments of camaraderie.[13] In April 1869, the Central Pacific and Union Pacific competed to see who could throw down 330 track the fastest. The competition arose after Charlie Crocker bragged that the Chinese could construct ten miles of track a day. (In some regions, the Union Pacific had averaged only one mile a week.) So confident was Crocker in his employees that he was willing to wager $10,000 against Thomas Durant, the vice president of Union Pacific. On the day of the contest, the Central Pacific had eight Irish workers unload materials while the Chinese spiked, gauged, and bolted the track, laying it down as fast as a man could walk. They broke the Union Pacific record by completing more than ten miles of track within twelve hours and forty-five minutes.

340 On May 10, 1869, when the railways from the east and west were finally joined at Promontory Point, Utah, the Central Pacific had built 690 miles of track and the Union Pacific 1,086 miles. The two coasts were now welded together. Before the transcontinental railroad,

---

[13] **camaraderie:** friendly companionship.

APPLYING ACADEMIC VOCABULARY

definitely	unify

As you discuss "Building the Transcontinental Railroad," incorporate the following Collection 4 academic vocabulary words: *definitely* and *unify*. Ask students what ideas and aspects of the author's style and tone **unify** the selection. Ask what conclusions they could state most **definitely** about the author's attitude toward her subject. Have students support their conclusions with evidence from the text.

CLOSE READ

Author's Purpose: Tone and Style (LINES 314–326)
COMMON CORE RI 6

Tell students that in this paragraph, Chang narrates the events of a violent encounter between Irish workers and Chinese workers. She maintains an objective tone to portray both sides evenhandedly, but her understated personal style also appears in the concluding sentence of the paragraph.

Q ASK STUDENTS what the author's purpose might be for including this incident in her article. Encourage students to suggest more than one plausible purpose. *(Possible answers: She wants to write a full historic record. She wants to show that the Chinese workers were not passive in the face of prejudice and violence.)*

Analyze Ideas and Events: Sequence (LINES 328–343)
COMMON CORE RI 3

Explain that a chronological narrative may be unified around an overall main action that includes a sequence of elaborating details. In this passage, the main action is the finishing of the east-west link to complete the transcontinental railroad.

R CITE TEXT EVIDENCE Have students state, in chronological sequence, the events in lines 328–343 and cite words and phrases in the text that convey the sequence. *(In the last month of construction, as the finish line neared, the Union Pacific and Central Pacific competed to see which side could complete more track in a given time. Chinese and Irish workers cooperated in the competition. The Central Pacific broke previous records for laying track. The two railroads were joined on May 10, 1869. Words that convey sequence include "In April 1869," "the competition arose after…," "On the day of the contest," and "On May 10, 1869.")*

TEACH

CLOSE READ

Analyze Ideas and Events: Sequence  (LINES 344–362)

Tell students that a passage may move back and forth in time rather than in a straight line from past to present.

S CITE TEXT EVIDENCE Have students cite text evidence showing which events in these lines occurred before and after the completion of the railroad. *(The many deaths occurred before the railroad was completed. The exclusion from the ceremonies and the layoffs occurred afterward.)*

Author's Purpose: Tone and Style  (LINES 363–367)

Explain that a text's conclusion often displays the writer's attitude clearly, since the conclusion draws together the strands of the work's meaning.

T CITE TEXT EVIDENCE Have students describe the tone in the conclusion and cite words that help to create this tone. *(The author uses words such as "homeless," "jobless," "harsh," "hostile," and "straggled" to create a sad and despairing tone.)*

COLLABORATIVE DISCUSSION Have students pair up and discuss specific examples of how racism affected Chinese railroad workers. Have pairs share their examples and insights with the class.

ASK STUDENTS to share any questions they generated in the course of reading and discussing the selection.

---

trekking across the country took four to six months. On the railroad, it would take six days. This accomplishment created fortunes for the moguls of the Gilded Age, but it also exacted a monumental sacrifice in blood and human life. On average, three laborers perished for every two miles of track laid, and eventually more than one thousand Chinese railroad workers died, with twenty thousand pounds of their 350 bones shipped to China.[14] Without Chinese labor and know-how, the railroad would not have been completed. Nonetheless, the Central Pacific Railroad cheated the Chinese railway workers of everything they could. They tried to write the Chinese out of history altogether. The Chinese workers were not only excluded from the ceremonies, but from the famous photograph of white American laborers celebrating as the last spike, the golden spike, was driven into the ground. Of more immediate concern, the Central Pacific immediately laid off most of the Chinese workers, refusing to give them even their promised return passage to California. The company retained only a few hundred of 360 them for maintenance work, some of whom spent their remaining days in isolated small towns along the way, a few living in converted boxcars.

The rest of the Chinese former railway workers were now homeless as well as jobless, in a harsh and hostile environment. Left to fend for themselves, some straggled by foot through the hinterlands[15] of America, looking for work that would allow them to survive, a journey that would disperse them throughout the nation.

---

[14]Years later, some of the Chinese railroad workers would journey back to the Sierra Nevada to search for the remains of their colleagues. On these expeditions, known as *jup seen you* ("retrieving deceased friends"), they would hunt for old grave sites, usually a heap of stones near the tracks marked by a wooden stake. Digging underneath the stones, they would find a skeleton next to a wax-sealed bottle, holding a strip of cloth inscribed with the worker's name, birth date, and district of origin. [Author's note]

[15]**hinterlands:** remote areas.

COLLABORATIVE DISCUSSION With a partner, discuss examples of how racism contributed to the challenges Chinese laborers endured while building the transcontinental railroad. Cite specific evidence in the text to support your ideas.

Strategies for Annotation 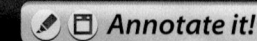 Annotate it!

Author's Purpose: Tone and Style  RI 6

Share these strategies for independent or guided analysis.

- Highlight in yellow one sentence in which Chang uses an objective tone.
- Highlight in green two sentences in which Chang's tone is regretful.
- Underline one or more words or phrases that contribute to the regretful tone.

On average, three laborers perished for every two miles of track laid, and eventually more than one thousand Chinese railroad workers died, with twenty thousand pounds of their bones shipped to China. . . . Nonetheless, the Central Pacific Railroad cheated the Chinese railway workers of everything they could. They tried to write the Chinese out of history altogether.

Analyze Ideas and Events: Sequence

"Building the Transcontinental Railroad" is a **historical narrative,** an account of real events that occurred in the past. To help readers understand the role of Chinese laborers in building the railroad, Iris Chang presents events in **chronological order.** This structural format allows Chang to develop the sequence of events over the course of the text. Dates and **time-order signal words** such as *finally, later,* and *then* help show the connections between a sequence of events. As you analyze the ideas and events Chang presents, you might use a sequence chart like the one below to record important events and dates.

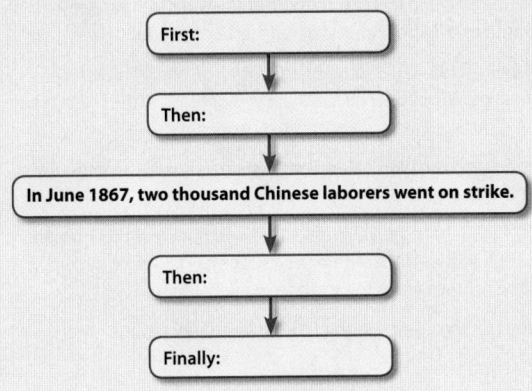

First:

Then:

In June 1867, two thousand Chinese laborers went on strike.

Then:

Finally:

Author's Purpose: Tone and Style

 COMMON CORE RI 6

An **author's purpose** is his or her reason for writing. Analyzing elements of a writer's **style** may help you determine an author's purpose. For example, identifying Iris Chang's **tone,** or attitude toward her topic, might help you confirm your inferences about her reasons for telling the story of Chinese laborers who built the transcontinental railroad. Chang's purpose for writing shapes her word choice and the details she chooses to include in her narration of events. An author's purpose also affects the kinds of sources an author consults. For example, an author might use information from primary source documents to add strength to the central ideas of the text. Ask yourself these questions to determine and analyze Iris Chang's purpose:

- What is Chang's attitude toward the treatment of Chinese laborers?
- What details and events does Chang emphasize in the account?
- How do certain descriptions and quotations add power to Chang's message?

CLOSE READ

Analyze Ideas and Events: Sequence

 COMMON CORE RI 3

To help students determine the chronological sequence in "Building the Transcontinental Railroad," have pairs work together to complete the chart. Encourage them to expand the chart beyond five entries to include more of the narrative's events.

Author's Purpose: Tone and Style

 COMMON CORE RI 6

To help students understand how Chang's tone and style relate to her purpose, have pairs or small groups select a paragraph from the text and write a summary of it containing only facts stated objectively. Then have them compare the impact of Chang's text with their summaries. Have them discuss how Chang's tone affects readers.

Answers:
- Chang's attitude toward the treatment is sympathetic to the workers and critical toward those who mistreated them.
- Chang emphasizes details and events surrounding incidents of prejudice and poor working conditions.
- Vivid descriptions and quotations make the events come to life.

Strategies for Annotation   ✎ 🗒 *Annotate it!*

Author's Purpose: Tone and Style   COMMON CORE RI 6

Share these strategies for independent or guided analysis.
- Highlight in yellow details and events that Chang emphasizes.
- Underline descriptions that add power to Chang's message.
- In a note, describe Chang's attitude toward her subject.

The company retained only a few hundred of them for maintenance work, some of whom spent their remaining days in isolated small towns along the way, a few living in converted boxcars.

...straggled by foot through the hinterlands of America....

Analyzing the Text
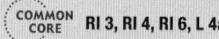 RI 3, RI 4, RI 6, L 4a

Possible answers:

1. The population was growing; the doctrine of Manifest Destiny urged expansion to the Pacific; the West offered rich farmland and mining; existing land and sea routes were slow and dangerous.

2. The Central Pacific had to cut through steep mountains, carve a roadway along a steep three-mile cliff, uproot the stumps of the world's largest trees, and lay track across the Nevada-Utah desert. In addition, transporting equipment to such remote sites was difficult.

3. Chang's purpose is to commemorate the achievement of the Chinese workers who built the transcontinental railroad. The sentence "Without Chinese labor and know-how, the railroad would not have been completed" (lines 350–351) supports this purpose.

4. Chang's tone is that of a well-informed, fair-minded historian, sympathetic toward the struggles and achievements of the Chinese workers. Examples of word choices include "the Chinese fought back" (line 320), "broke the Union Pacific record" (lines 337–338), and "tried to write the Chinese out of history altogether" (line 353).

5. The context clues include "fireworks," "unpredictable," "explosive," and "accidental blasts."

6. Chang's use of quotations from primary sources gives life and authenticity to her presentation, imparting to the reader an "on the scene" feeling.

7. The word "Homeric" suggests an epic: a long narrative of a hero's struggles to meet a great challenge. Chang's description of the "Homeric winter" reinforces the idea that the building of the transcontinental railroad was a mighty endeavor and an important national achievement.

8. Chang's description of the strike continues the presentation of injustices against the Chinese workers and develops a new idea: that the Chinese stood up for themselves and took action against unfair treatment.

 eBook *Annotate It!*

Analyzing the Text
 RI 3, RI 4, RI 6, W 7, SL 1a, SL 3, L 4a

Cite Text Evidence   Support your responses with evidence from the selection.

1. **Infer** According to Iris Chang, what economic, social, and political forces led the United States to build the transcontinental railroad?

2. **Summarize** What were the main challenges that the Central Pacific faced in completing its part of the transcontinental railroad?

3. **Infer** What is Iris Chang's purpose for writing "Building the Transcontinental Railroad"? Cite evidence from the text that helps you infer her purpose.

4. **Analyze** Identify Iris Chang's tone toward her topic or the various main elements of her topic. Provide examples of word choice that reflects her attitude.

5. **Draw Conclusions** In lines 198–203, Chang refers to the use of nitroglycerin to tunnel through mountains. What context clues help you determine the meaning of this technical term?

6. **Evaluate** How does Chang's use of quotations from primary sources contribute to the effectiveness of her message?

7. **Evaluate** In lines 237–261, Chang provides a detailed description of the "Homeric winter" of 1866–1867. What does the word *Homeric* suggest? How does her description support the central idea of the text as a whole?

8. **Summarize** How does Chang's description of the strike connect to the other events she presents?

PERFORMANCE TASK

Speaking Activity: Discussion "Building the Transcontinental Railroad" describes the role of Chinese workers in creating an infrastructure that transformed the United States. Explore the topic in further depth and evaluate Chang's account through research and discussion.

- Conduct research on the building of the transcontinental railroad. Take notes to compare and contrast your findings with Iris Chang's account. List similarities and differences between Chang's account and the accounts you discover in your research.

- Engage in a collaborative group discussion to evaluate the effectiveness of Chang's account based on the details and events she includes, her links among ideas, and her points of emphasis. Support your opinions with evidence from the text and from your research.

Assign this performance task.

PERFORMANCE TASK
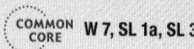 W 7, SL 1a, SL 3

Speaking Activity Students should formulate research questions, start their search, analyze the results, and refine their search.

Have students do research independently and then form small groups to evaluate the effectiveness of Chang's account. Remind students to support their discussion points with specific evidence from the text.

Critical Vocabulary

| formidable | expedience | diligence | systematize |

Practice and Apply Use your knowledge of the Critical Vocabulary words in your written responses.

1. Tell about a **formidable** task that you accomplished.

2. Identify an action that someone took that was guided by **expedience.**

3. Describe something you did with **diligence.**

4. Explain how you **systematized** a process for completing a complex project.

Vocabulary Strategy: Context Clues

When you come across an unfamiliar word, **context clues** in surrounding phrases and sentences can help you determine its meaning. Notice how the highlighted context clues in the examples below from "Building the Transcontinental Railroad" can help you determine the meaning of the boldfaced words.

Context Clue	Example
Provides a **definition** of the doctrine of Manifest Destiny	"...the **doctrine of Manifest Destiny,** which proclaimed it the right and duty of the United States to expand its democratic way of life across the continent, ..."
Provides an **example** of Stanford's expedience	"Stanford's position on the Chinese was governed by **expedience.** In 1862, to please the racist sentiments of the state, he called the Chinese in California the 'dregs' of Asia, ..."
Suggests a **similarity:** diligence is hard work	"...Chinese **diligence** forced everyone to work harder for less reward."
Suggests a **contrast:** something that is formidable is difficult to overcome	"The Central Pacific engineers promised that the **formidable** physical obstacles could be overcome, ..."

Practice and Apply Use context clues to help you determine the meaning of unknown words in "Building the Transcontinental Railroad." Follow these steps:

- Identify unfamiliar words in the text.
- Look for context clues that provide a definition or example of the unknown word, or compare or contrast with it.
- Confirm your inferred meaning of the word in a dictionary.
- Write a new sentence for each word.

PRACTICE & APPLY

Critical Vocabulary

Possible answers:

1. *I helped to build a house for a homeless family.*

2. *Zack made friends with Eli because he knew that Eli made good grades in science and could help him with his homework.*

3. *I studied diligently for my driver's exam.*

4. *To complete my science project, I made a list of the materials I would need and a schedule for experiments.*

Vocabulary Strategy: Context Clues

Answers: *Answers will vary with students' choice of unfamiliar words. Tell students to choose words that are not among the four vocabulary words studied in this lesson and are not defined in footnotes on the selection pages. Have students read their answers to each other in small groups.*

Strategies for Annotation

  Annotate it!

Vocabulary Strategy: Context Clues

- Highlight in yellow an unfamiliar word in the passage.
- Write a note guessing the meaning of the word.
- Write a note giving the dictionary meaning of the word.

From sea to shining sea. In the decade of the 1840s, Americans were consumed by this vision, articulated in the doctrine of Manifest Destiny, which proclaimed it the right and duty of the United States to expand its democratic way of life across the entire continent....

PRACTICE & APPLY

Language and Style: Avoiding Misplaced Modifiers

After presenting the first paragraph of the instruction, tell students that a misplaced modifier is often a prepositional phrase rather than a single word. Review that a **prepositional phrase** consists of a preposition and its object, the word or word group that functions as a noun. A prepositional phrase is an adjective phrase if it modifies a noun or pronoun. A prepositional phrase is an adverb phrase if it modifies a verb, an adjective, or another adverb.

Have students answer the questions independently. Then have them form groups to review the answers. If students have difficulty, have them follow these steps:

1. Read the sentence aloud.

2. Identify the word group that makes the sentence confusing.

3. Move the word group to a different place in the sentence. It may take more than one try before the clearest word order is achieved.

Answers:

1. *On the sea voyage, disembarking the ship and crossing the Isthmus of Panama by wagon could shorten the trip to the West Coast considerably.*

2. *The Union Pacific Railroad, already connected to other railways in the East, was contracted to build westward across the plains from Omaha, Nebraska.*

3. *Many workers were killed by the unpredictable and dangerous explosives.*

4. *At the ceremony everyone praised the railroad workers' accomplishments.*

 **Assess It!**

Online Selection Test
- Download an editable ExamView bank.
- Assign and manage this test online.

Language and Style: Avoiding Misplaced Modifiers

Modifiers are words or groups of words that change or limit the meaning of other words. For example, adjectives modify nouns by telling which one, what kind, how many, or how much. Adverbs modify verbs, adjectives, and other adverbs by telling where, when, how, or to what extent. Chang's careful placement of modifiers contributes to the clarity and readability of her text.

In less professional writing a modifier is sometimes placed so far away from the word it modifies that the intended meaning of the sentence is unclear. To correct a sentence with a misplaced modifier, you must first find the word being modified. Then place the modifying word or phrase as close as possible to the word it modifies.

Read the following sentence with a misplaced modifier:

The railroad workers gathered the necessary supplies to finish the tunnel before starting.

The placement of the prepositional phrase *before starting* creates confusion because it seems to modify the immediately preceding infinitive phrase *to finish the tunnel*. However, finishing the tunnel before starting would be impossible.

Here the sentence has been revised for clarity so that the prepositional phrase properly functions as an adverb modifying the verb *gathered*:

Before starting, the railroad workers gathered the necessary supplies to finish the tunnel.

While it's always important to maintain clarity, writers may intentionally distance modifiers from the words they modify to add information or for stylistic reasons or for effect. For example, read this sentence from "Building the Transcontinental Railroad":

Grudgingly, Strobridge put the Chinese to work, giving them light jobs, like filling dump carts.

While the adverb *grudgingly* could also be placed immediately before the verb it modifies, its placement at the beginning of the sentence helps emphasize the superintendent's reluctance to manage Chinese workers.

Practice and Apply Revise the following sentences to correct the misplaced modifiers. Refer to "Building the Transcontinental Railroad" if you are unsure about the intended meaning of a sentence.

1. Disembarking the ship and crossing the Isthmus of Panama on the sea voyage by wagon could shorten the trip to the West Coast considerably.

2. The Union Pacific Railroad was contracted to build westward from Omaha, Nebraska, across the plains already connected to other railways in the East.

3. Unpredictable and dangerous, many workers were killed by the explosives.

4. Everyone praised the railroad workers' accomplishments at the ceremony.

INTERACTIVE WHITEBOARD LESSON
Conducting Research

COMMON CORE

SL 4, SL 5, W 8

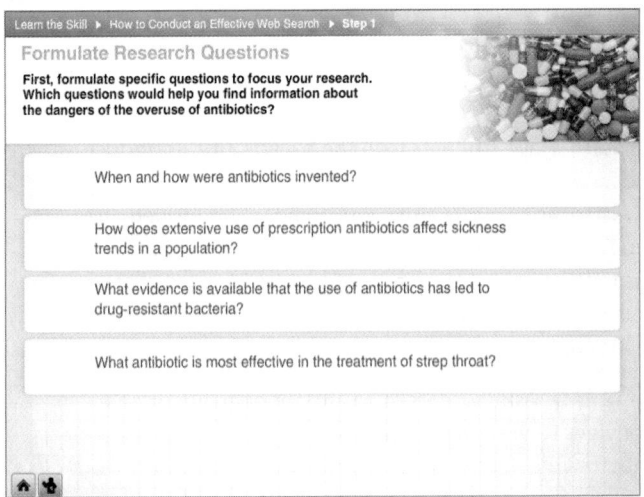

Learn the Skill ▶ How to Conduct an Effective Web Search ▶ Step 1

Formulate Research Questions

First, formulate specific questions to focus your research. Which questions would help you find information about the dangers of the overuse of antibiotics?

When and how were antibiotics invented?

How does extensive use of prescription antibiotics affect sickness trends in a population?

What evidence is available that the use of antibiotics has led to drug-resistant bacteria?

What antibiotic is most effective in the treatment of strep throat?

TEACH

Have small groups of students prepare and deliver multimedia presentations about the building of the transcontinental railroad. Presentations should be about three to five minutes long and should be created using presentation software such as PowerPoint. Students will create slide shows with text and graphics and will choose a presenter to explain each slide. Assign each student group a different aspect of the building of the railroad, such as

- important individuals and groups who worked on the railroad, including women, Chinese immigrants, and non-Chinese men
- the impact of the railroad on the U.S. economy, society, and environment
- primary source writings and opinions about the railroad

Tell students to search online for photos and illustrations for their presentations. Advise groups that each member should take a specific task, such as writing text, finding visuals, working with the software, or giving the accompanying talk.

COLLABORATIVE DISCUSSION

Have listeners give constructive feedback on the presentations. Then have groups discuss what went right, what went wrong, and what they would do differently next time they create a presentation.

Author's Purpose: Tone and Style

COMMON CORE

RI 6

RETEACH

Some students have difficulty recognizing tone in the written word as opposed to the spoken word. One way to identify the tone in a passage of prose is to listen to someone read the passage aloud, or to read it aloud oneself. The reader should first become familiar with the text by reading it silently. He or she should look for words whose connotations are strong—positive, negative, or expressing a feeling such as tension or humor. Those words can be emphasized when reading aloud.

Tell students that reading aloud can be a "reality check" for the reader's analysis of written tone. For example, suppose you think that a passage has a sarcastic tone. When you read it aloud, does it sound sarcastic? If not, perhaps the passage is not sarcastic after all.

LEVEL UP TUTORIALS Assign the following *Level Up* tutorial: **Tone**

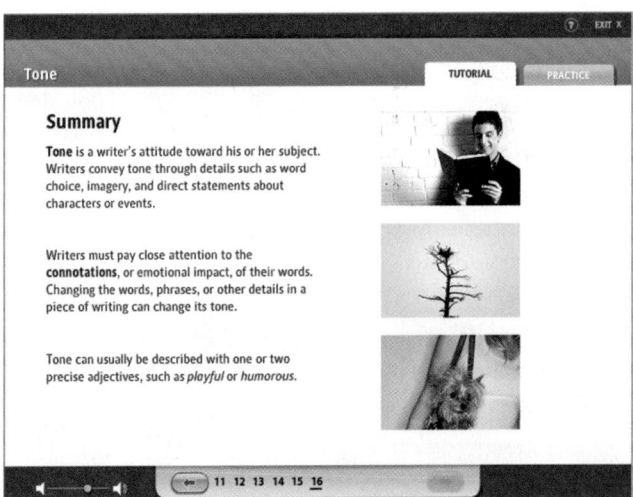

Tone

TUTORIAL | PRACTICE

Summary

Tone is a writer's attitude toward his or her subject. Writers convey tone through details such as word choice, imagery, and direct statements about characters or events.

Writers must pay close attention to the **connotations**, or emotional impact, of their words. Changing the words, phrases, or other details in a piece of writing can change its tone.

Tone can usually be described with one or two precise adjectives, such as *playful* or *humorous*.

11 12 13 14 15 16

CLOSE READING APPLICATION

Ask pairs of students to choose a paragraph from a selection in Collection 4 other than "Building the Transcontinental Railroad." They should read it silently, analyze its tone together by identifying strong words, and then take turns reading the passage aloud to confirm the tone.

Bonding Over a Mascot

Newspaper Article by Joe Lapointe

Why This Text

Students may have difficulty understanding an author's purpose for writing. In "Bonding Over a Mascot," Joe Lapointe investigates the NCAA ban of American Indian mascots and its effect on sports teams at Florida State University. With the help of the close-reading questions, students will analyze the positions of the people Lapointe interviews who are affected by this ban. This close reading will lead students to analyze Lapointe's purpose for writing "Bonding Over a Mascot."

Background Have students read the background. Introduce the selection by telling students that the debate over using Native American mascots and sports imagery intensified after 2006. In February of 2013, ESPN reporter Paul Lukas covered a symposium about Native American imagery in sports that took place at the National Museum of the American Indian, where Native Americans unanimously condemned insulting imagery.

AS YOU READ Ask students to pay attention to Lapointe's point of view. How soon into the text can you infer a reason for Lapointe to write about the mascot situation at Florida State University?

Common Core Support

- cite strong and thorough textual evidence
- analyze a complex set of ideas and explain how specific individuals or ideas develop over the course of a text
- determine an author's purpose

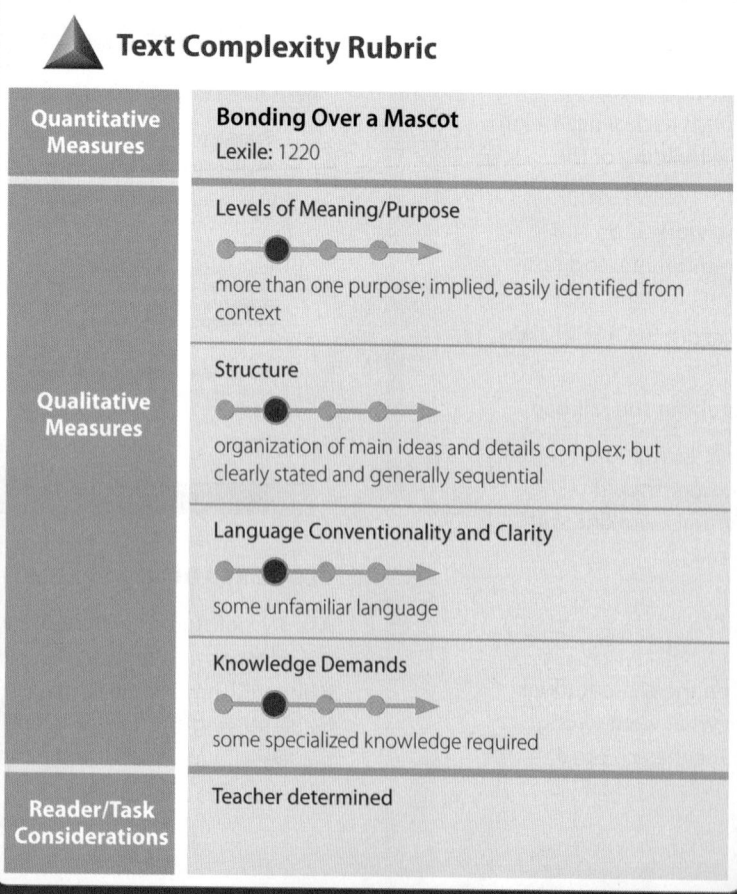

Text Complexity Rubric

Quantitative Measures

Bonding Over a Mascot
Lexile: 1220

Qualitative Measures

Levels of Meaning/Purpose

more than one purpose; implied, easily identified from context

Structure

organization of main ideas and details complex; but clearly stated and generally sequential

Language Conventionality and Clarity

some unfamiliar language

Knowledge Demands

some specialized knowledge required

Reader/Task Considerations

Teacher determined

Strategies for CLOSE READING

Author's Purpose

Students should read this article carefully all the way through. Close-reading questions at the bottom of the page will help them focus on a thorough analysis of the text. As they read, students should jot down comments or questions about the article in the side margins.

WHEN STUDENTS STRUGGLE . . .

To help students analyze Lapointe's purpose, have them work in small groups to fill out a chart, such as the one shown below.

CITE TEXT EVIDENCE For practice in analyzing an author's purpose, ask students to identify choices Lapointe makes about what to focus on in his article.

detail: Lapointe focuses on Florida State's "harmonious relationship" with the Seminoles.

detail: Lapointe quotes Toni Sanchez: "the N.C.A.A. edict is 'beyond idiotic' and offensive."

detail: N.C.A.A. president Myles Brand said the edict raised "the level of awareness nationally about how we treat Native Americans."

topic: the N.C.A.A. ban of Native American sports imagery

detail: President of Florida State T. K. Wetherell said the edict was merely "politically correct," but the university still might use Native American imagery less in the future.

detail: Chairman of FSU history department, Neil Jumonville, says the N.C.A.A. ban accelerated the offering of a Seminole history course at the university.

detail: Seminole councilman Osceola describes the offensive Sammy Seminole mascot.

Background In 2005, the National Collegiate Athletic Association (N.C.A.A.) banned the use of American Indian mascots by sports teams during their postseason tournaments. At least eighteen schools had mascots that the N.C.A.A. deemed "hostile or abusive." Almost immediately, protests arose, especially from Florida State University, home of the Florida Seminoles. Read the article below to find out what stirred the controversy and the result of the N.C.A.A. decision.

Bonding Over a Mascot

Newspaper Article by Joe Lapointe

CLOSE READ
Notes

1. **READ ▶** As you read lines 1–25, begin to collect and cite evidence.
   - Circle text that describes the relationship between the Seminoles and Florida State University.
   - Underline how Toni Sanchez feels about the university's American Indian statue and the N.C.A.A. policy.
   - In the margin, explain the N.C.A.A "crackdown."

December 29, 2006

A few new statues of a Seminole family in 19th-century clothing stand outside the football stadium at Florida State University. The father holds a long gun, the son a bow and arrow, and the mother an infant in her arms as she looks warily to her right.

The statues represent the era when the Seminoles and the United States were at war. The public art is part of a complex relationship between Seminole culture and sports at Florida State. This bond has strengthened since a crackdown by the National Collegiate Athletic Association last year against American Indian mascots, nicknames and imagery among sports teams.

Not every university enjoys a harmonious relationship with Indians. But a sense of cooperation seems to **permeate** the Florida State campus in Tallahassee, Fla., where Toni Sanchez was among 21 students to complete a new course this month called History of the Seminoles and Southeastern Tribes.

The "crackdown" bans the use of American Indian mascots for sports teams.

permeate: pervade, soak through

65

1. READ AND CITE TEXT EVIDENCE

A ASK STUDENTS to cite textual evidence that supports their explanation of the N.C.A.A. crackdown, and to explain how the crackdown affected the relationship between the Seminoles and FSU, where a sports team is called the Seminoles. *Students should cite lines 8–9 in explanation of the N.C.A.A. crackdown and cite line 7, which states that the bond between the Seminoles and the school "has strengthened."*

Critical Vocabulary: permeate (line 11) Have students explain why Lapointe uses the word *permeate* to describe the "sense of cooperation" at the FSU campus. *The cooperation is present in all areas of campus life.*

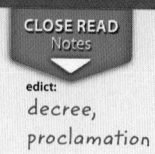

CLOSE READ
Notes

edict:
decree,
proclamation

Sanchez, a senior majoring in English, called the N.C.A.A. **edict** "beyond idiotic" and offensive. She described the new statues as beautiful.

"I know what a real Seminole is," she said. "This Anglo guilt and regret don't affect me."

Sanchez is from a family with Seminole and Hispanic ancestry. Her father, once a farm worker, is now a casino operator. Her mother is a teacher. Sanchez also plays trumpet at football games in a marching band that wears arrowheads on the back of its uniforms.

Of the tribal flag near the new statues, another recent addition, she said, "Every time I look at it, I get really giddy inside." Of the use of the Seminole imagery for the university's sports, she said, "I'm so proud of it."

Florida State was one of 18 institutions cited by the N.C.A.A. in August 2005 for "mascots, nicknames or images deemed hostile or abusive in terms of race, ethnicity or national origin." The institutions were forbidden to use the symbols in postseason events controlled by the N.C.A.A., like the national championship basketball tournament that begins in March.

Five programs have since received permission to continue using their imagery because they received approval from specific Indian groups, in Florida State's case the 3,200-member Seminole Tribe of Florida. Five others have changed or are in the process of changing, said Bob Williams, an N.C.A.A. spokesman. The other eight, he said, remain on the list and are subject to the policy, including the Illinois Fighting Illini and the North Dakota Fighting Sioux.

Myles Brand, the president of the N.C.A.A., said in a telephone interview last week that his organization made the right decision but witnessed more negative reaction to the ruling than expected.

"What we've accomplished in part is to raise the level of awareness nationally about how we treat Native Americans," Brand said. "If we don't stand by our values, we lose our integrity."

At times, Indians are reduced to casual **caricature** that would not be tolerated by other groups, he said, adding that the N.C.A.A. had been honored for its stance by Indian groups in Oklahoma and Indiana.

caricature:
cartoon,
parody

2. ◀ REREAD Reread lines 15–18. What does Sanchez imply is the real reason behind the N.C.A.A ban? Cite textual evidence.

Sanchez blames the N.C.A.A. ban on "guilt and regret."

3. READ ▶ As you read lines 26–51, circle text from the N.C.A.A.'s statement. Then, underline the opinions of Brand and Wetherell.

66

Less complimentary is T. K. Wetherell, the president of Florida State, who said the N.C.A.A. was "more interested in being politically correct" and did not consult the Seminole tribe before making its decision.

"The way they weaseled out was to say, 'O.K., as long as the tribe continues to support it,'" he said.

Wetherell, a former Florida State football player who also teaches history, wore a hunting outfit when interviewed recently in his office. He pointed to a team logo of an Indian's face that he said had elements of caricature. "That's not really a Seminole-looking deal," Wetherell said. "This is a marketing tool." He said the university might "gradually let certain things fade."

He said he told the Seminole Tribe of Florida's council, "If you don't want Florida State to be the Seminoles, we ain't Seminoles anymore." Wetherell said the tribe approved the use partly because the campus is in the capital and tribal leaders "are not only good businessmen, they are great politicians."

He said the new history course was proposed before the N.C.A.A. edict.

But Neil Jumonville, the chairman of the history department, said the N.C.A.A. resolution accelerated the creation of the class and that his staff received advice from local Seminole leaders.

CLOSE READ
Notes

Wetherell doesn't approve of the likeness of the Seminole and thinks the logo might change.

4. ◀ REREAD Reread lines 38–51. Explain the conflict between Brand and Wetherell.

Brand represents the N.C.A.A. and stands by their policy. This policy is meant to be enforced everywhere, regardless of whether or not a problem exists. Wetherell represents Florida State and disagrees with the policy because he understands the unique relationship between the university and the Seminole tribe.

5. READ ▶ As you read lines 52–81, continue to cite text evidence.

• Write in the margin what you can infer about Wetherell's comments about the team logo.
• Underline text explaining why the university keeps the mascot and why the Seminole tribe didn't fight to have it changed.
• Circle what Versen hopes the students will explore in the class.

67

---

2. REREAD AND CITE TEXT EVIDENCE

B **ASK STUDENTS** to cite text evidence to support their analysis of Sanchez's position on the N.C.A.A. ban. *Students should recognize that Sanchez rejects the "Anglo" establishment's intervention: "I know what a real Seminole is…" (line 17).*

3. READ AND CITE TEXT EVIDENCE

C **ASK STUDENTS** why Florida State was cited by the N.C.A.A. in August 2005. *Students should cite evidence that FSU used "mascots, nicknames or images deemed hostile or abusive in terms of race, ethnicity or national origin" (lines 27–28).*

Critical Vocabulary: edict (line 15) What tone is conveyed by Lapointe's choice of the word *edict*?

Critical Vocabulary: caricature (line 44) Why does Brand suggest it is offensive to be reduced to caricature?

4. REREAD AND CITE TEXT EVIDENCE

D **ASK STUDENTS** to cite text evidence of Brand's and Wetherell's opinions of the N.C.A.A. ban. *Students will find evidence that Brand stands by the N.C.A.A.'s position in lines 38–43. Wetherell is critical of the N.C.A.A. and dismisses their efforts in line 48 by stating that they are merely "interested in being politically correct."*

5. READ AND CITE TEXT EVIDENCE Clarify for students that Wetherell's explanation of why the Seminoles approved the use of their name is an opinion, not a fact.

E **ASK STUDENTS** to cite text evidence to support the inference they draw from Wetherell's comments about the team logo. *Students should cite evidence from lines 53–56.*

CLOSE READ
Notes

"These are people who are savvy about their place in the American myth," Jumonville said. "And they are smart enough to manipulate the myth for their own good."

The first class was taught by Christopher R. Versen, who recently earned his doctorate in American history.

70 "I wanted to challenge students to think about identity," Versen said. "What is it inside us that makes us identify ourselves one way or another? What external factors play into identity?"

amalgam:
mix, blend, combination

(F) The Seminoles are an **amalgam** of several tribes, predominantly Creek, that included escaped slaves. They migrated south to the Everglades in retreat from the United States Army. Some were driven out during the Trail of Tears[1] period under President Andrew Jackson.

Those descendants live as the Seminole Nation of Oklahoma. The Seminoles in Florida once had a commercial hunting economy. Since 1979, their economic status has improved because of casino gambling.

80 Earlier this month, the Seminoles acquired Hard Rock International—the music-themed chain of restaurants, hotels and casinos—for $965 million.

Versen said he did not discuss sports identity with his students because he was afraid it would become a distraction. But a guest speaker who raised the mascot issue was Max Osceola, one of three councilmen for the Seminole Tribe of Florida.

[1] **Trail of Tears:** In 1838 and 1839, Jackson's policy forced the Cherokee nation to leave their home east of the Mississippi River and relocate to present-day Oklahoma. Over 4,000 people lost their lives to hunger, disease, and exhaustion during the march.

---

6. **◄ REREAD** Reread lines 52–81. Why does Lapointe include information about the Seminoles' history and their situation today?

He shows the struggles of the Seminole people to explain why the mascot issue is a sensitive one. They had to endure unfair treatment in the past and their descendants in Florida remember their ancestors' difficulties.

7. **READ ►** As you read lines 82–118, continue to cite evidence.

- Circle the description of Max Osceola in lines 82–90. Circle his description of the old Sammy Seminole.
- Underline the description of the new mascot.
- In the margin, explain Max Osceola's point of view.

68

CLOSE READ
Notes

Toni Sanchez, a student who is from a family with Seminole and Hispanic ancestry, is proud of the use of Seminole imagery at Florida State.

"If I had a child and named it after you, would you consider it an honor?" Osceola said he asked the students. He also reflected on a former mascot, Sammy Seminole, who was retired in 1972.

(G) "He had a big nose and he lived in a teepee," Osceola said. "He looked like 90 a buffoon."

The current mascot is named, coincidentally, Osceola, after a 19th-century warrior. A student dressed as Osceola rides a horse named Renegade onto the football field and throws a flaming spear. This mascot's clothing was designed by the tribe.

Tina Osceola, who is the executive director of the tribe's historical resources department and is a cousin of Max Osceola's, said, "We've given them license to be theatrical."

A statue of the warrior riding atop Renegade stands outside the stadium above the word "Unconquered," because the Seminoles never surrendered to 100 the United States.

When the Seminoles announced in New York the purchase of Hard Rock, Max Osceola joked that Indians once sold Manhattan for trinkets but were now "going to buy Manhattan back, one burger at a time."

Not everyone outside the tribe approves of all of the Indian trappings at sporting events, including the tomahawk chop hand gesture and a droning cheer that sounds like background music heard in old western movies.

Joe Quetone, the executive director of the nonprofit Florida Governor's Council on Indian Affairs Inc., said, "Things fans do are outrageous and ridiculous."

Osceola points out that having someone named after you is an honor, but it becomes an insult if it is a joke or a stereotype.

69

---

6. **REREAD AND CITE TEXT EVIDENCE**

(F) **ASK STUDENTS** to share their responses with a partner and revise their answers if necessary. *Answers should include inferences about Lapointe's inclusion of both Seminole history and their situation today. Students should cite text evidence from lines 73–81 in their responses. They should make a connection between Lapointe's purpose and this part of the text.*

7. **READ AND CITE TEXT EVIDENCE**

(G) **ASK STUDENTS** to summarize the changes in the FSU mascot. *Students should include evidence that Sammy Seminole was a degrading image (lines 89–90) and that the Seminoles participated in the design of the later mascot (lines 93–94).*

Critical Vocabulary: amalgam (line 73) Have students compare their definitions of *amalgam*. Ask them the difference between a mixture and an alloy.

FOR ELL STUDENTS Explain that the word *trappings* in this context has nothing to do with trapping an animal. It means "characteristic signs" or "articles associated with a particular group."

CLOSE READ
Notes

110   Bobby Bowden, the head football coach, did not respond to four recent
requests for comment on the issue placed with the university's sports
information department.

(H)   From a student's perspective, Sanchez said that people who were genuinely
concerned with the circumstances of Indians should concentrate less on sports
iconography and more on alcoholism, suicide, teen pregnancy and high school
dropout rates.

     "After all those years of diseases, occupation and war, we're still here," she
said. "I refuse to believe that a silly mascot will take us down."

8. **◀ REREAD**   Reread lines 82–118. What does Sanchez mean when she says
that a mascot won't "take us down"?

*She means that the N.C.A.A. policy cannot undermine the
Seminole. American Indians made it through worse trials, so they
can make it through a collegiate policy.*

SHORT RESPONSE

Cite Text Evidence   What is the author's purpose in writing this newspaper
article? **Cite text evidence** to show how he supports his ideas in your
response.

*The author wants to show differing opinions about the N.C.A.A.'s
policy on American Indian mascots in colleges. The quotes from
people at the university, including coaches, professors, and a student,
show that not everyone agrees with the N.C.A.A.'s policy. Those
who disagree provide qualifying evidence. Quotes from N.C.A.A.
supporters are few and flimsy, but the underlying concern of respect
for American Indians is still obvious. Including information about
the Trail of Tears shows that Seminole Indians have a long history
and that the memory of the past should be honored.*

70

8. [REREAD AND CITE TEXT EVIDENCE]

(H)   **ASK STUDENTS** to add text evidence to their answers to
support their analysis of Sanchez's statement that a mascot won't
"take us down." *Answers will vary. Students should cite evidence
from lines 113–118.*

SHORT RESPONSE

Cite Text Evidence   Student responses will vary, but they should
cite evidence from the essay to support their analysis of Lapointe's
purpose. Students should:

- explain Lapointe's purpose.
- identify central ideas that support his purpose.
- cite text evidence that shows how Lapointe supports his central
  ideas.

TO CHALLENGE STUDENTS . . .

The Saginaw Chippewa are another tribe that has granted
permission for a sports team to use its name since the 2005
N.C.A.A. ban of Native American mascots.

ASK STUDENTS to research this decision by the Saginaw
Chippewa and to compare their concerns and remedies with the
solutions agreed to by FSU and the Seminole people. As a class,
discuss the efforts of the Seminoles and Chippewa to convey
accurate information about their cultures, such as the use of the
word *unconquered* on the FSU statue, which informs people of
the truth that the Seminoles never surrendered to the United
States. What do the Saginaw Chippewa want "in return" for school
sports teams using American Indian imagery? *The tribe suggests
that those schools offer classes to teach their students about
American Indian culture and create a relationship with the people
whose name they are using.*

DIG DEEPER

With the class, return to Question 2, Reread, and the analysis of Toni Sanchez's position on the N.C.A.A.'s ban on "mascots, nicknames or images deemed hostile or abusive in terms of race, ethnicity or national origin." Have students share their responses.

ASK STUDENTS to share their evidence, and to review the context provided in the article for Sanchez's position.

- How does Lapointe first identify Sanchez? *Students should cite evidence from lines 12–13, "Toni Sanchez was among 21 students to complete a new course this month called History of the Seminoles and Southeastern Tribes."*

- Have students find evidence in the article of Sanchez's ancestry and infer why Lapointe included this information. *Students will find evidence in lines 19–20 that Sanchez has "Seminole and Hispanic ancestry." They should recognize that Lapointe specifically chose a Seminole student because the topic of the article is the relationship between the Seminole tribe and FSU.*

- Ask students to cite text evidence that Sanchez is proud of her Seminole ancestry. *Students should cite her participation in the new history class (lines 12–14), her description of the statues as "beautiful" (line 16), and her statement in lines 17–18, in which she asserts that she is unaffected by decisions made by the N.C.A.A.*

ASK STUDENTS to return to their Short Response answer and to revise it based on the class discussion.

CLOSE READING NOTES

MEDIA # The 54ᵗʰ Massachusetts

*my*SmartPlanner — Create lesson plans and access resources online.

Documentary by HISTORY

Why This Text?

Students increasingly learn about U.S. history through documentary films. This lesson examines dramatic elements and how they are used to communicate and support a filmmaker's purpose.

Key Learning Objective: Students will be able to integrate and evaluate documentary information in interviews, video reenactments, and photos.

COMMON CORE Common Core Standards

RI 3 Analyze a set of ideas or sequence of events.
RI 6 Determine an author's point of view or purpose.
RI 7 Integrate and evaluate multiple sources of information.
RI 9 Analyze foundational U.S. documents.
SL 1 Initiate and participate in a range of collaborative discussions.
SL 2 Integrate multiple sources of information.
SL 3 Evaluate a speaker's point of view, reasoning, and use of evidence and rhetoric.
SL 4 Present information and supporting evidence, conveying a clear and distinct perspective.

▲ Text Complexity Rubric

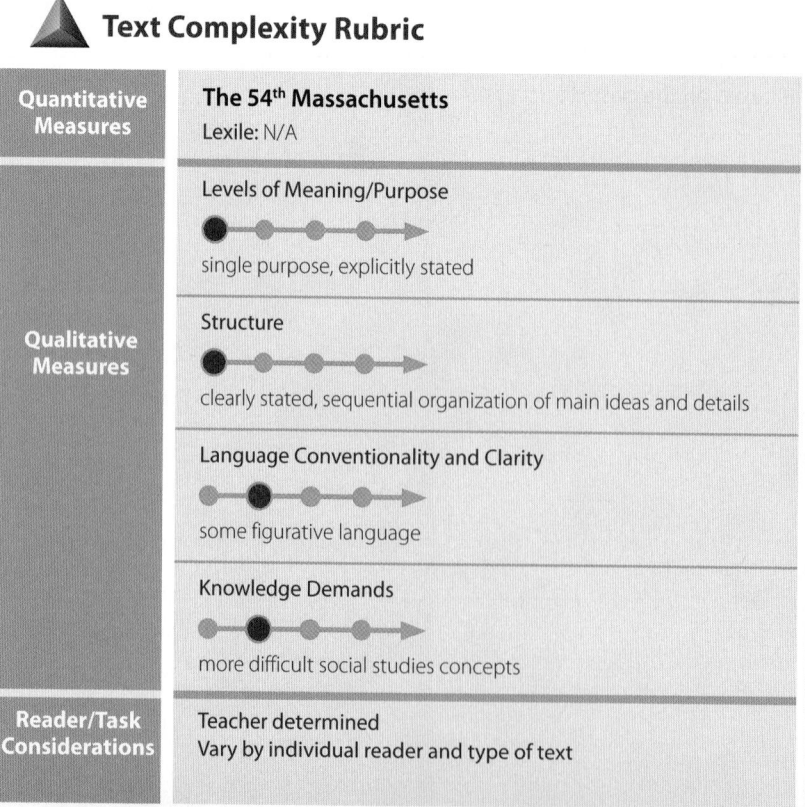

Quantitative Measures	**The 54ᵗʰ Massachusetts** Lexile: N/A
Qualitative Measures	**Levels of Meaning/Purpose** single purpose, explicitly stated
	Structure clearly stated, sequential organization of main ideas and details
	Language Conventionality and Clarity some figurative language
	Knowledge Demands more difficult social studies concepts
Reader/Task Considerations	Teacher determined Vary by individual reader and type of text

CLOSE READ

 Students can view the video "The 54th Massachusetts" in their eBooks.

Background Have students read the background information about the 54th Massachusetts.

AS YOU VIEW Direct students to use the As You View note to focus their viewing. Remind them to write down any questions they generate during viewing.

Integrate and Evaluate Information

COMMON CORE **RI 7**

Explain to students that analyzing **documentaries** is similar to analyzing informational texts. Explain the following elements of many documentaries:

- **Narration** is information that is provided by an off-screen voice.
- **Reenactments** re-create actual events as closely as possible using actors.
- Experts are **interviewed** for information.
- A **musical score** and **sound effects** create dramatic effect.

ASK STUDENTS to analyze the elements used in this documentary. *(A voice-over narrates events. Actors reenact battle scenes. Several experts, historians, and family members are interviewed. Patriotic music plays in the background.)* Ask: Based on these elements, what can you infer about the filmmakers' **purpose**? *(Viewers can infer that the filmmakers wish to educate their audience about the importance and heroism of the 54th Massachusetts.)*

COLLABORATIVE DISCUSSION Have students form pairs and discuss how black Americans were regarded in the North and in the South. Then discuss as a class how these attitudes might have affected black soldiers' motivations for fighting.

ASK STUDENTS to share any questions they generated in the course of viewing the video.

Background *The 54th Massachusetts Volunteer Infantry was the first black northern regiment in the Civil War. It was formed in 1863, soon after the Emancipation Proclamation was issued. African Americans had served in both the Revolutionary War and the War of 1812, but there were concerns in the North about upsetting border states and about the "effectiveness" of black soldiers. Not only did African American soldiers help the North win the Civil War, but the historical and social significance of their enlistment and of their brave service continues to resonate through the centuries.*

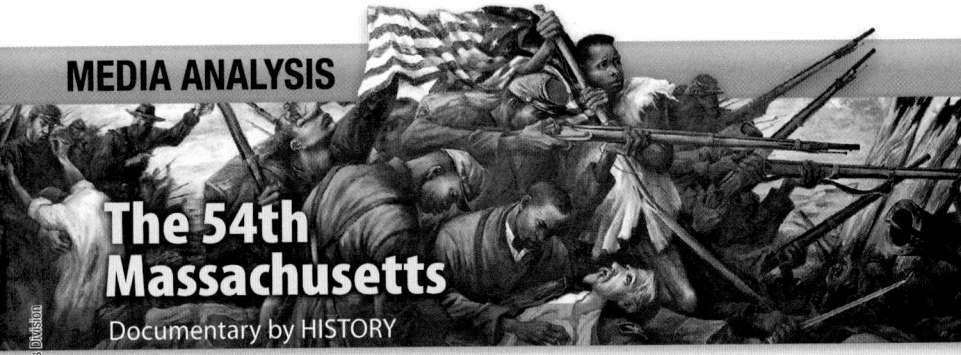

MEDIA ANALYSIS

The 54th Massachusetts
Documentary by HISTORY

AS YOU VIEW Note the controversy engendered by the idea of a black regiment. Write down any questions you generate during your viewing.

COLLABORATIVE DISCUSSION Why was the idea of black enlistment resisted even in the North? With a partner, discuss the objections that delayed the entrance of African Americans into the military.

SCAFFOLDING FOR ELL STUDENTS

Integrate Information To help students understand the history of the 54th Massachusetts Volunteer Infantry have them use a graphic organizer, such as an outline, to keep track of what is discussed in the documentary.

I. Introduction
   A. First African American regiment

II. Racism and slavery in America
   A. Slavery in the South
   B. Racism in the North

Pause and replay segments of the documentary as needed.

Integrate and Evaluate Information

 **COMMON CORE RI 7**

Explain to students that different forms and sources of information all have their strengths and weaknesses. Documentary films rely on visual and audio techniques to create a visceral, sometimes emotional response to historical facts.

Analyzing the Media

COMMON CORE RI 3, RI 7, RI 9, SL 1, SL 2, SL 3

Possible answers:

1. *Slaves would not fight for a government that was willing to keep them in chains. However, free men would risk their lives to earn and protect their citizenship. (6:44)*

2. *Douglass believed that black men fighting for the Union would earn citizenship and prove themselves worthy on the battlefield. (5:42)*

3. *The producers' purpose was to educate the audience about the heroes of the 54th Massachusetts Volunteer Infantry. The most effective element is the interviews with experts, historians, and family members who describe the challenges the 54th Massachusetts faced and how the soldiers bravely rose up to overcome those obstacles.*

 **Assess It!**

Online Selection Test
- Download an editable ExamView bank.
- Assign and manage this test online.

Integrate and Evaluate Information

 COMMON CORE RI 7

Significant historical events are complex and multifaceted. They normally involve many different people with differing motivations, creating debate or even controversy about how or why events unfolded. To do justice to the formation of the 54th Massachusetts Volunteer Infantry—a milestone on the way to full equality for African Americans—the producers of this video chose to present information using multiple types of media and sources instead of relying on just one source or expert.

To evaluate the effectiveness and validity of the information presented, use these guiding questions:

- What helps to create unity throughout the video?
- How do the interviews with historians enrich your understanding of this time in history and this particular event? Do their insights enhance your impression of the credibility of the video?
- What is the purpose of the excerpts from Frederick Douglass's and Governor Andrew's speeches?
- What ideas are supported by the visual elements?
- Do all of the elements contribute to the same perception of the event? Why or why not?

Analyzing the Media

COMMON CORE RI 3, RI 7, RI 9, SL 1, SL 2, SL 3

Cite Text Evidence Support your responses with evidence from the selection.

1. **Cause/Effect** Explain how the Emancipation Proclamation and the enlistment of African American soldiers were mutually dependent upon each other.

2. **Cite Evidence** Why did Douglass advocate so vigorously for black men to be allowed to fight? Provide specific details from the video to support your response.

3. **Analyze** What is the producers' purpose in this video? Explain which elements are most effective in achieving this purpose.

PERFORMANCE TASK

Speaking Activity: Debate Would the entrance of black soldiers into the Civil War have been as effective if it had taken place earlier?

- In a small group, debate this question, drawing on information and ideas presented in the video.

- As you listen to each debate group, evaluate the way in which group members integrate information from the video and use it to support their views.

PERFORMANCE TASK

COMMON CORE SL 1, SL 2, SL 3

Speaking Activity: Debate Have students work in pairs or small groups. Remind them that their arguments need to be supported by reasons and evidence drawn from the video. Have the students take turns presenting to the class. As a class, discuss how the groups integrated information to support their views.

Analyze Point of View

COMMON CORE

RI 6

TEACH

Explain to students that documentaries reflect the point of view of the filmmaker. Here are some strategies for analyzing a filmmaker's point of view.

- What is the film's purpose—to inform, to persuade, to entertain? Most films have multiple purposes.
- What type of footage is used? What emotions, ideas, and thoughts do the images convey?
- What music and sound techniques are used? What emotions do they evoke?
- What tone, or attitude toward the subject, does the narrator's voice convey?
- What information is included? What information is not included?

COLLABORATIVE DISCUSSION

Direct students to form pairs or small groups. Have them use the questions above to discuss the point of view of *The 54th Massachusetts*.

Integrate and Evaluate Information

COMMON CORE

RI 7

RETEACH

Explain to students that it is important to weigh the **credibility** of a documentary's sources of information.

Have students form pairs or small groups to review *The 54th Massachusetts* and discuss whether the historical facts and expert opinions presented in the film are credible and how they support the film's purpose.

LEVEL UP TUTORIALS Assign the following *Level Up* tutorial: Evaluating Credibility

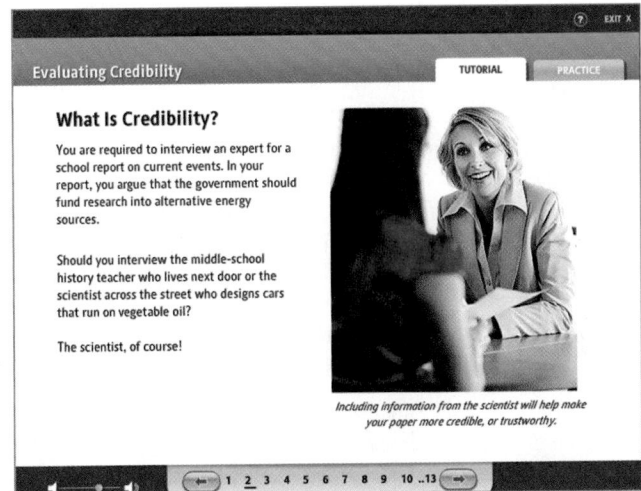

CLOSE READING APPLICATION

Have students find additional information about the 54th Massachusetts Volunteer Infantry, either online or in a book. Ask them to analyze the credibility of its evidence and compare it to what was presented in the documentary. Have pairs present the excerpts as well as their analysis in small groups.

*my*SmartPlanner   Create lesson plans and access resources online.

Runagate Runagate

Poem by Robert Hayden

Why This Text?

To fully appreciate and understand poetry, students must recognize the variety of ways poets convey meaning. This lesson focuses on analyzing two of the ways poets enrich their poems with deeper meanings: allusions and rhythm.

Key Learning Objective: Students will be able to analyze a free-verse poem for its use of allusions, rhythm, and structure.

 ## Common Core Standards

RL 2 Determine themes of a text.

RL 4 Determine figurative and connotative meanings; analyze the impact of word choices.

RL 5 Analyze how an author's choices concerning how to structure specific parts of a text contribute to its overall meaning as well as its aesthetic impact.

RL 6 Analyze a case in which grasping point of view requires distinguishing what is directly stated in a text from what is really meant.

W 2b Write informative/explanatory texts.

W 7 Conduct research projects to answer a question; synthesize multiple sources on the subject.

W 8 Gather relevant information; assess strengths and limitations of each source; integrate information selectively; follow a standard format for citation.

W 9 Draw evidence from literary or informational texts.

 ## Text Complexity Rubric

Quantitative Measures	**Runagate Runagate** Lexile: NA
	Levels of Meaning/Purpose multiple levels of meaning
Qualitative Measures	Structure free verse, no particular patterns
	Language Conventionality and Clarity figurative, less accessible language
	Knowledge Demands cultural and literary knowledge essential to understanding
Reader/Task Considerations	Teacher determined Vary by individual reader and type of text

TEACH

CLOSE READ

For more context and historical background, students can view the video "AMERICA The Story of Us: Harriet Tubman and the Underground Railroad" in their eBooks.

Robert Hayden Hayden was born Asa Bundy Sheffey. He studied with W.H. Auden and admired the work of Carl Sandburg, Langston Hughes, and Jean Toomer. He was the first African American to serve as Consultant in Poetry to the Library of Congress—a position we now call Poet Laureate.

AS YOU READ Direct students to use the As You Read instructions to focus their reading. Remind them to write down any questions they generate during reading.

Analyzing Structure: Rhythm and Meaning (Lines 1–10)

COMMON CORE **RL 5**

Tell students that poets often arrange words to reinforce meaning with sound and **rhythm**, the pattern of stressed and unstressed syllables. Read lines 1–3 aloud.

A **ASK STUDENTS** to describe the arrangement of stressed syllables in the first line. How does this pattern reinforce the meaning of the lines? *(The first three syllables are all stressed—there is no break for an unstressed syllable. The beats change unexpectedly to more unstressed than stressed syllables. The insistently stressed syllables at the beginning of the line convey the sense of urgency communicated in the meaning of the words; the sudden change reinforces the idea of stumbling; the repetition of unstressed syllables followed by one stressed syllable conveys the sense of moving in short bursts, hiding and then darting into the next pool of darkness.)*

Have students work in pairs to analyze lines 4–10. While one partner reads, the other listens for stressed syllables and taps them out. After the first reading, partners should switch roles so that each partner has a chance to both read and listen.

B **ASK STUDENTS** what they notice about the rhythm in these lines. *(The pattern changes after line 7. In lines 4–7, the arrangement of stressed and unstressed syllables is irregular; sometimes two syllables in a row are stressed. This choppy rhythm continues the sense of hurrying and hiding. In lines 8–10, the repetition of the word* runagate *evenly alternates stressed and unstressed syllables. The change heightens the sense of urgency and reflects a sound almost like breathing hard while running.)*

Robert Hayden *(1913–1980) endured a childhood marred by poverty, a broken family, and a dysfunctional foster home. Plagued by depression, vision problems, and bullying peers, the Detroit native withdrew into a world of books. He researched African American folklore for the Federal Writers' Project in 1936, published his first book of poems in 1940, and earned a masters degree in English. Hayden then began his own lengthy career as a teacher while continuing to produce volumes of poetry. Much of his award-winning work explores the history and legacy of racial injustice in America.*

Runagate Runagate

Poem by Robert Hayden

AS YOU READ Identify the different voices that appear in the poem and notice the different rhythms of their speech.

I.

Runs falls rises stumbles on from darkness into darkness
and the darkness thicketed with shapes of terror
and the hunters pursuing and the hounds pursuing
and the night cold and the night long and the river
5   to cross and the jack-muh-lanterns[1] beckoning beckoning
and blackness ahead and when shall I reach that somewhere
morning and keep on going and never turn back and keep on going

        Runagate[2]
            Runagate
10   Runagate

---

[1] **jack-muh-lanterns:** a mythical goblin, popular in African-American folklore.
[2] **Runagate:** a fugitive slave.

Image Credits: (t) ©Stamp Collection/Alamy Images; (bg) ©Apostrophe/Shutterstock; (l) ©Irina_QQQ/Shutterstock; (r) ©williammpark/Shutterstock

SCAFFOLDING FOR ELL STUDENTS

Understand Sentence Structure Hayden does not use regular sentence structure in this poem. Capital letters signal the beginnings of sentences, but he leaves the subjects of these sentences out to be inferred. Ask questions to help students infer the subject and actions in the first ten lines.

- (Line 1) Who runs, falls, rises, and stumbles? *(an escaped slave)*
- (Line 3) What are the hunters and hounds doing? *(pursuing the escaped slave.)*
- (Line 4) What is cold and long? *(The night is cold and long.)*

Encourage students to formulate questions about lines 5–7 and answer in complete sentences. Finally, have students paraphrase lines 1–7 in complete sentences.

Analyzing Structure: Rhythm and Meaning

COMMON CORE RL 5

(Lines 19–31)

Remind students that poets sometimes arrange words and syllables to create **rhythm** that enhances or complements meaning. Point out that in lines 19–20 and 21–29 the poet includes different first-person speakers. One of these is the speaker of a slave song, and one is a slaveholder advertising for the return of escaped slaves.

C **CITE TEXTUAL EVIDENCE** Ask students to explain how rhythm signals the change between speakers in these lines. *(The lines from the song, lines 19–20 and 30–31, have a regular rhythm of stressed and unstressed syllables. The advertisements from the slaveholders have an irregular rhythm that makes them sound like prose, or ordinary speech.)*

Analyze Language: Allusions (Lines 32–36)

COMMON CORE RL 2, RL 4

Tell students that poets sometimes refer, or allude, to things to evoke specific feelings or associations. **Allusions** usually refer to well-known people, places, songs, legends, literary works, or events to call to readers' minds particular images, related details, or feelings and associations. Tell students that the subjects of allusions in older works may no longer be well-known.

D **ASK STUDENTS** what they could do to fully appreciate associations intended by the allusion to "Oh, Susannah." *(Finding and reading the lyrics of the song could reveal feelings or ideas expressed in the song; researching the history of the song or the time period in which "Oh, Susannah" was popular might reveal some historical connections.)*

Many thousands rise and go
many thousands crossing over

                    O mythic North
                    O star-shaped yonder Bible city

15 Some go weeping and some rejoicing
     some in coffins and some in carriages
     some in silks and some in shackles

          Rise and go or fare you well

     No more auction block for me
20 no more driver's lash for me

          If you see my Pompey, 30 yrs of age,
          new breeches, plain stockings, negro shoes;
          if you see my Anna, likely young mulatto
          branded E on the right cheek, R on the left,
25   catch them if you can and notify subscriber.
          Catch them if you can, but it won't be easy.
          They'll dart underground when you try to catch them,
          plunge into quicksand, whirlpools, mazes,
          turn into scorpions when you try to catch them.

30 And before I'll be a slave
     I'll be buried in my grave

          North star and bonanza gold
          I'm bound for the freedom, freedom-bound
          and oh Susyanna don't you cry for me[3]

35   Runagate

             Runagate

     II.

     Rises from their anguish and their power,

          Harriet Tubman,

          woman of earth, whipscarred,
40   a summoning, a shining

          Mean to be free

     And this was the way of it, brethren brethren,
     way we journeyed from Can't to Can.

---

[3] **oh Susyanna don't you cry for me:** an allusion to the chorus of "Oh! Susanna" by Stephen Foster.

APPLYING ACADEMIC VOCABULARY

confirm	definitely

As you discuss allusions in "Runagate Runagate," incorporate the following Collection 4 academic vocabulary words: *confirm* and *definitely*. Ask students how they can **confirm** the reference of an allusion. Ask students whether writers can be sure their allusions will **definitely** be understood. Does an allusion have a **definite** meaning?

Moon so bright and no place to hide,
45   the cry up and the patterollers[4] riding,
hound dogs belling[5] in bladed air.
And fear starts a-murbling, Never make it,
we'll never make it. *Hush that now,*
and she's turned upon us, levelled pistol
50   glinting in the moonlight:
Dead folks can't jaybird-talk,[6] she says;
you keep on going now or die, she says.

Wanted   Harriet Tubman   alias The General
Alias Moses   Stealer of Slaves

55   In league with Garrison   Alcott   Emerson
Garrett   Douglass   Thoreau   John Brown

Armed and known to be Dangerous

Wanted   Reward   Dead or Alive

Tell me, Ezekiel, oh tell me do you see
60   mailed[7] Jehovah coming to deliver me?

---

[4] **patterollers:** people who watched and restricted the movement of black slaves at night.
[5] **belling:** barking.
[6] **jaybird-talk:** talk like fools.
[7] **mailed:** covered with a flexible armor made of rings or plates.

Runagate Runagate **319**

WHEN STUDENTS STRUGGLE...

Use modeling and choral reading to prepare students for independent fluent reading: the ability to comprehend changes in speaker and in rhythms.

- Model: Read aloud lines 42–60 as students follow the text. Reread lines 42–60 with all students reading along chorally.
- Divide students into two groups, and have them read alternate lines aloud chorally.
- Assign single lines or pairs of lines to individual students. Have students read their lines aloud in turn.

ASK STUDENTS where rhythm changes suggest a new speaker. *(lines 51, 53, and 59)*

CLOSE READ

Analyzing Structure: Rhythm and Meaning

COMMON CORE RL 5

(LINES 51–58)

Tell students that the pauses between some syllables or words contribute to the rhythm of the lines. Have students read lines 51–58 silently. Discuss any visual clues they see for pauses. *(The spaces between some words in lines 53–58 are larger than the spaces between words in lines 51–52.)*

E **ASK STUDENTS** to contrast the rhythms and meanings in lines 51–52 and lines 53–58. *(Lines 51–52 have the rhythm of speech: Harriet Tubman is speaking. Lines 53–58 have more pauses. These lines sounds like someone reading a poster or bulletin.)*

Analyze Language: Allusions (LINES 53–60)

COMMON CORE RL 2, RL 4

Tell students that writers often use biblical allusions because they evoke powerful associations. Explain that Ezekiel was an Old Testament prophet who lived most of his early life in exile. He foretold God's faithfulness and the fulfillment of his promises to his people, who were themselves enslaved and far from home. The name *Ezekiel* means "whom God made strong." In the book of Ezekiel, Jehovah promises to deliver his people and strike down their enemies. It is this warrior God, or "mailed Jehovah," that the speaker refers to in line 60. Moses was the prophet who led his people in escaping slavery.

F **CITE TEXTUAL EVIDENCE** Have students analyze the effect of biblical allusions in this section of the poem, using specific examples from the text. *(Using these allusions in this section of the poem connects the enslaved Africans to the enslaved "chosen people," evokes a sense of divine deliverance and protection, and enhances the connection between Harriet Tubman and Moses in line 54. In addition, using allusions from the Old Testament, which focuses more on God's might than God's mercy, lends moral authority to Harriet Tubman's use of force in lines 48 and 49 and intensifies the tone of righteous power in this section.)*

Image Credits: ©Jupiterimages/Getty Images

Analyzing Structure: Rhythm and Meaning

 COMMON CORE RL 5

(Lines 61–72)

Have students recall the ways rhythm has enhanced meaning in the poem up to this point. *(The rhythm added urgency and reinforced the feeling of hiding and hurrying; it sounded like a song, a speech, and a poster being read.)* Have students read lines 61–72.

G ASK STUDENTS in what ways the rhythms of lines 65–71 enhance the meaning. *(The rhythm suggests the sound of a train gaining momentum. Each line establishes a rhythm that is interrupted or stutters partway through. The isolated line "Come ride-a my train" echoes the rhythm of a conductor calling "All Aboard." This calling rhythm is also reflected in line 70, which sounds like a conductor calling the station stops. The three repeated stressed syllables in line 72 suggest the sound of a whistle or signal, distinct from the repetitive rhythm of the wheels.)*

COLLABORATIVE DISCUSSION Have students work in groups to discuss the perspectives and ideas in the poem and to share textual support for their interpretations.

ASK STUDENTS to share any questions they generated in the course of reading and discussing the selection.

G

Hoot-owl calling in the ghosted air,
five times calling to the hants[8] in the air.
Shadow of a face in the scary leaves,
shadow of a voice in the talking leaves:

65   Come ride-a my train

Oh that train, ghost-story train
through swamp and savanna movering movering,
over trestles of dew, through caves of the wish,
Midnight Special on a sabre track movering movering,
70   *first stop Mercy and the last Hallelujah.*

Come ride-a my train

Mean mean mean to be free.

---

[8] **hants:** ghosts.

COLLABORATIVE DISCUSSION How does the poet unify the many perspectives presented in the poem? With a partner, identify the poem's central ideas and discuss how specific lines in the poem help convey them.

SCAFFOLDING FOR ELL STUDENTS

Clarify Customs Non-native speakers may be unfamiliar with some of the speech rhythms and patterns critical to an appreciation of the final lines of this poem. Clarify for students the sound of a conductor so that they have a frame of reference for the sounds in the poem.

If possible, show clips from movies or television programs that show conductors calling to passengers to board as the train prepares to leave the station and conductors calling out station stops. Otherwise, have volunteers act out the conductor's role in each case.

ASK STUDENTS which lines seem to echo a boarding call and which lines sound like the announcement of station stops. *(Lines 65 and 71 echo a boarding call. Lines 69–70 sound like the announcement of station stops.)*

Analyze Language: Allusions

COMMON CORE RL 2, RL 4

An **allusion** is an author's reference to a well-known historical or literary person, event, or composition. It's a figure of speech designed to evoke specific feelings or ideas associated with the thing to which the author refers. Writers try to choose allusions that their readers will definitely understand. Biblical allusions, for example, appear quite frequently throughout traditional Western art and literature—Hayden employs several, including Ezekiel (line 59), in "Runagate Runagate." An allusion, of course, cannot work successfully if nobody recognizes it.

Unlike other genres, though, modern poetry often contains extremely complex literary and cultural allusions. Many poets seem to expect a great deal from their readers. (Ezra Pound, for instance, would allude to classical Greek texts—in Greek!) However, you can still understand and enjoy a good poem without recognizing all of its allusions or cultural references. In fact, some of the best allusions work on both the literal and figurative levels. Consider the following lines from the poem:

> And this was the way of it, brethren brethren,
> way we journeyed from Can't to Can.

On one level, we can interpret a trip "from Can't to Can" as a movement away from restriction, from slavery to freedom. Yet on another level, the phrase alludes to a famous saying about the long hours of toil that enslaved people endured: "We worked from Can-see to Can't," meaning "from dawn to darkness." If you recognize this allusion, then you can also interpret the line as meaning "we traveled at night." Both interpretations work very well within the context. The best allusions, like this one, amplify meaning rather than simply convey it.

Analyzing Structure: Rhythm and Meaning

COMMON CORE RL 5

The sound produced by the arrangement of stressed and unstressed syllables, along with the intervals of time that fall between them, creates rhythm in language. People respond to rhythm instinctually and on many levels. Poets, like musicians, manipulate rhythm to express ideas and emotions. In English poetry, rhythm has two basic components:

- Accent, the vocal emphasis given to a word or syllable.
- Meter, a repetitive pattern created by small groups of accented and unaccented syllables, called feet.

Like a movie soundtrack, a poem's rhythm enhances its overall meaning and helps create a unified, multisensory experience. A good poet combines rhythm and content in complementary ways by carefully selecting words and controlling line lengths and format. Even the title Hayden chooses for his poem—"Runagate Runagate"—uses rhythm to heighten its meaning. Imagine the difference if the poet had used the word only once or chosen "Escaped Slave" instead. As you think about the meaning of the poem, pay attention to when, how, and why its rhythms rush you along, slow you down, or suddenly make you stop and change direction.

Runagate Runagate **321**

TEACH

CLOSE READ

Analyze Language: Allusions

COMMON CORE RL 2, RL 4

Remind students that an allusion's effectiveness depends on it being recognized and understood. Although they do not need to recognize and analyze every allusion, their appreciation of a work will be enhanced if they take the time to explore allusions that they do not recognize or understand.

Have students use resources to research and clarify their understanding of allusions in the poem, including *jack-muh-lanterns* (line 5), *Harriet Tubman* (line 38), *Moses* (line 54), *Garrison, Alcott, Emerson, Garrett, Douglass, Thoreau, John Brown* (lines 55–56), *Ezekiel* (line 59), *mailed Jehovah* (line 60), and *that train* (line 66).

Analyze Structure: Rhythm and Meaning

COMMON CORE RL 5

As you present the instruction, read aloud from the poem to illustrate meter and to model vocal emphasis. Encourage students to mark their texts and read aloud when they analyze rhythm.

Strategies for Annotation ✎ 🗐 *Annotate it!*

Analyze Language: Allusions

COMMON CORE RL 5

Share these strategies for guided or independent analysis.

- Highlight allusions in yellow.
- Use a note to jot down your ideas and questions about the meaning of allusions.

Wanted Harriet Tubman alias The General

led slaves to freedom

Alias Moses Stealer of Slaves

led enslaved Israelites to freedom

Runagate, Runagate **321**

PRACTICE & APPLY

Analyzing the Text 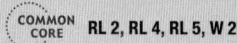 RL 2, RL 4, RL 5, W 2b

Possible answers:

1. The rhythm reflects the urgency with strong, insistent beats in the opening line. Following lines create the feeling of hiding, then hurrying. The repeated syllables of Runagate create the rhythm of labored breathing.

2. References to Ezekiel, Moses, and Jehovah convey associations of divine protection and a sacred mission. Biblical allusions are appropriate for the topic of escaping slavery since the Bible includes many stories about people who are enslaved, both literally and figuratively.

3. The associations are both positive and negative. It's a minstrel song, so its origins as well as its lyrics reflect an offensive stereotypical view of African Americans as uneducated and foolish. On the other hand, the song tells of a journey with great rewards, but great risks—like the one the runaway slaves are on.

4. The first speaker is Tubman. The second speaker is one of the people she is helping to escape. The firmer rhythms of Tubman's speech reflect her confidence and authority. The jumpier rhythms of the runaway's speech reflect nervousness.

5. They are all involved in or related to the abolitionist movement.

6. The biblical references and the sing-song rhythm combine to suggest a plea to a divine power for deliverance.

7. "Come ride-a my train," "ghost-story train," "Midnight Special," "sabre track," "first stop"

8. "Bound for the freedom" means being "headed in the direction of freedom," as if on a journey while "freedom-bound" means "tied" to freedom by the commitment made and Tubman's insistence that no one can turn back. Bound has positive connotations in the sense of a journey and negative connotations in the sense of being tied. This reflects the tension between wanting freedom and the danger involved in seeking it.

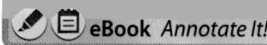

Analyzing the Text COMMON CORE RL 2, RL 4, RL 5, W 2b

Cite Text Evidence   Support your responses with evidence from the selection.

1. **Analyze** The opening stanza portrays a frightened narrator fleeing through darkness. How does its rhythm reflect and enhance its meaning?

2. **Identify** What allusions to religion or the Bible can you find in the poem? Why are religious imagery or Biblical allusions appropriate for this topic?

3. **Analyze** Hayden alludes to "Oh! Susanna" in line 34. Do some independent research on the content and history of this traditional American song. How does this allusion add meaning to the poem?

4. **Interpret** Consider the stanza that begins "And this was the way of it," (lines 42–52). Who are the two speakers in the stanza, and how do the rhythms of their speech reflect the differences in their attitudes?

5. **Analyze** The "wanted poster" for Harriet Tubman (lines 53–58) includes several names. What do these people have in common?

6. **Synthesize** Read the two stanzas in lines 59–64, starting with the one that begins "Tell me, Ezekiel." How do the rhythms in these stanzas differ from most other parts of the poem? How do the rhythms and the meanings of the verses combine to create a certain feeling or to form an allusion?

7. **Infer** Many people escaped from slavery by following the Underground Railroad, a network of hiding places and routes leading north. What words and phrases does Hayden include as allusions to the Underground Railroad?

8. **Draw Conclusions** Explain the figurative and connotative meanings of line 33 ("I'm bound for the freedom, freedom-bound"). How do they reflect the central tension of the poem?

PERFORMANCE TASK

Writing Activity: Essay Compare this poem with lines 17-25 in section 33 of Walt Whitman's "Song of Myself" in Collection 3.

Both Whitman and Hayden imagine the plight of fugitives from slavery. Write a one-page essay exploring similarities and differences in their presentations.

-   Consider the background and purpose of each poet.
-   List some of the content and imagery the poets choose to achieve that purpose.

-   Think about how the rhythms and diction of each poem contribute to its overall structure and meaning.
-   Begin with a brief, objective summary of each poem.
-   Include specific examples to support your opinions.
-   Use conventions of standard written English.

Assign this performance task.

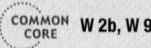

PERFORMANCE TASK COMMON CORE W 2b, W 9

Writing Activity: Essay Have students work independently to analyze the poem's content, imagery, diction, and rhythms. Then allow students to share and discuss their analyses with a partner. Partners can work together to create Venn Diagrams to record similarities and differences between the two poets and their poems. Encourage students to identify text evidence from each poem related to each of their points of comparison.

Determine Author's Purpose

COMMON CORE
RL 6

TEACH

Tell students that an **author's purpose** is his or her reason for writing. Explain to students that when they analyze an author's purpose, they should ask themselves: Why did the author write this poem?

Point out that two factors that influence an author's purpose for writing are the social and political context of the time and the writer's own background.

- **Social and political issues**: This poem was published in 1962, during the peak of the civil rights movement.
- **Writer's background**: Hayden was African American and was deeply interested in African American topics and themes. However, he famously refused to identify himself as an African American poet, preferring instead to be classified as an American poet.

Discuss with students how Hayden's background and the social and political issues of his time may have influenced his purpose for writing.

INTERACTIVE WHITEBOARD LESSON
Author's Purpose and Perspective

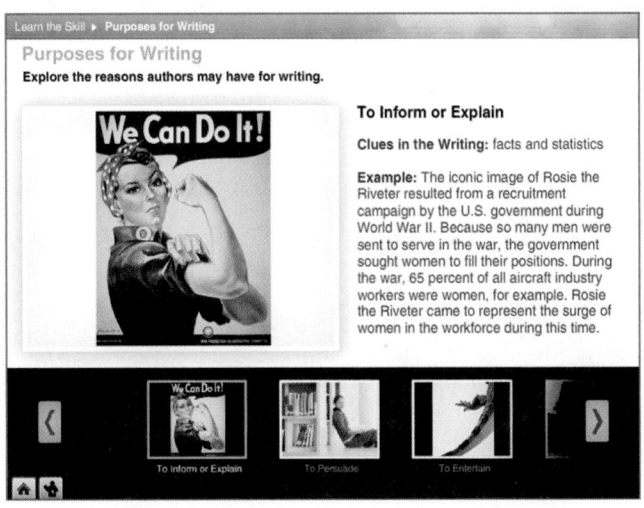

COLLABORATIVE DISCUSSION

Have students discuss and formulate an answer to the question: Why did Hayden write this poem? Allow time for groups to share and defend their responses.

Analyze Structure: Rhythm and Meaning

COMMON CORE
RL 5

RETEACH

Remind students that **rhythm** is the pattern or flow of sound created by the arrangement of stressed and unstressed syllables. Some poems follow a regular pattern, or meter, of accented and unaccented syllables. Poets use rhythm to emphasize ideas, to create mood, and to mirror a speaker's speech or emotion. Read a stanza of the poem aloud and work with students to mark the stressed and unstressed syllables in the stanza. Have students work with a partner to repeat this exercise for another stanza of the poem.

Circulate and monitor progress by asking students to read lines aloud to demonstrate the rhythm.

LEVEL UP TUTORIALS If students need additional practice, assign the Level Up Tutorial: **Rhythm**

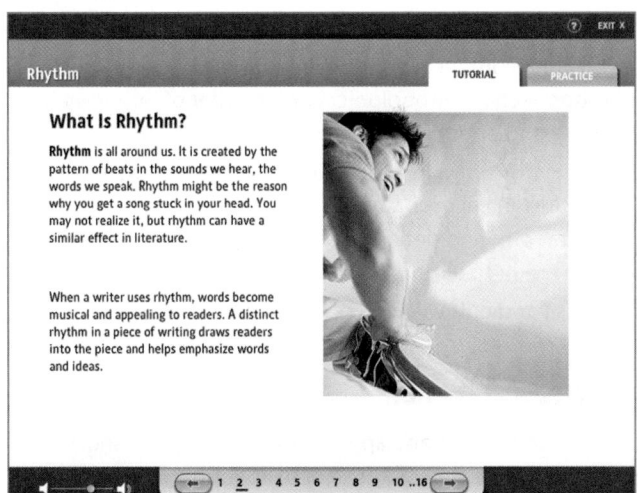

CLOSE READING APPLICATION

Students can apply the skill to another poem. Help them choose a poem with a strong rhythm. After they have marked the stressed and unstressed syllables, have them analyze the effect of the poem's rhythms on meaning.

Write a Short Research Report

COMMON CORE

W 7, W 8

TEACH

Explain to students that most research begins with a question. For instance, after reading Hayden's poem, students might have questions about some of the people alluded to in the poem. A research paper answers such a question. Provide students with the steps for writing a short research paper.

1. Formulate a research question, such as *Who was John Brown?*

2. Identify and read relevant sources. Whenever possible, try to find a mixture of primary sources and secondary sources. A **primary source** is a first-hand account. A primary source about John Brown might be an account written about him by someone who knew him. A **secondary source** is a second-hand account, such as a book about John Brown written by a historian living today.

3. Draft a controlling idea, or thesis statement. Your controlling idea will be a statement of the conclusion you have come to as a result of your research. For instance: *John Brown was an abolitionist who advocated the use of violence to eradicate slavery.*

4. Create an outline. Organize ideas according to a logical order, such as chronological order, order of importance, or cause and effect.

5. Draft your essay. Include an introduction, body, and conclusion. Incorporate relevant facts, examples, quotations, and details to develop your controlling idea. Give credit to all sources.

6. Revise and edit with the help of a peer reviewer.

PRACTICE AND APPLY

Students can practice and apply the skill of writing a short research paper by choosing one of the people mentioned in lines 54–55 of "Runagate Runagate" and writing a short research paper about him or her.

Analyze Language: Allusions

COMMON CORE

RL 2, RL 4

RETEACH

Review the term *allusion*. Remind students that an **allusion** is a reference to a person, place, event, or other literary work. Writers use allusions that will be familiar to their target audience.

- Have students reread "Runagate Runagate."

- Work with students to analyze one of the allusions in the poem. Since they are already familiar with Frederick Douglass, focus on the allusion to him in line 55. Ask: Why might Hayden have alluded to Douglass in this poem?

- Provide students with these questions to help them analyze the allusion: How is the subject of the allusion related to the topic of the poem? For instance, "How is Douglass related to the topic of escaping slaves?" Does the allusion create positive or negative associations and feelings? Does the allusion help convey the theme of the poem?

- Have students work in small groups to analyze the allusion and write a sentence that answers the question: Why might Hayden have alluded to Douglass in this poem?

CLOSE READING APPLICATION

Students can apply the skill to another allusion in "Runagate Runagate" or to another poem they have read. Students may share their analyses in pairs or small groups.

Interactive Lessons

If you need help with...
- **Giving a Presentation**
- **Analyzing and Evaluating Presentations**

Present a Persuasive Speech

The texts in this collection focus on the continuing work of bringing freedom and justice to all members of American society. Look back at the anchor text, Lincoln's Second Inaugural Address, and at the other texts in the collection. What messages about freedom—its meaning and its costs—do the texts convey? Synthesize your ideas by preparing a persuasive speech about a kind of freedom you would like to see expanded in today's world. Incorporate rhetorical and literary devices from the collection texts to enhance the power of your speech.

An effective speech

- identifies a type of freedom to be expanded and states a precise claim about it
- develops the claim with valid reasons and relevant evidence from Lincoln's Second Inaugural Address and two other texts
- anticipates counterclaims and addresses them effectively
- establishes clear, logical relationships among claims, reasons, and evidence
- has a conclusion that follows logically from the body of the speech and makes a persuasive call to action
- engages the audience by including a variety of rhetorical devices and techniques to support the claim
- maintains a formal tone through appropriate word choices and the use of standard English
- maintains audience interest with appropriate emphasis, volume, and gestures

COMMON CORE

SL 4 Present information, findings, and supporting evidence.
W 1a–e Write arguments to support claims.
W 9a–b Draw evidence from literary or informational texts.

PLAN

Make a Claim Review the texts in this collection, including Lincoln's Second Inaugural Address, and identify each writer's message about freedom. Based on the ideas conveyed in the texts, write a clearly worded claim about a type of freedom that you think should be further developed in our current society. Remember that you will need to support this claim with logical reasoning and evidence.

myNotebook

Use the notebook in your eBook to record historical examples of discrimination, noting how society overcame a legacy of inequality. You can use these examples later in your presentation as historical evidence for the benefits of increasing economic and political freedom.

PERFORMANCE TASK

PRESENT A PERSUASIVE SPEECH

COMMON CORE SL 4, W 1a-e, W 9a-b

Introduce students to the Performance Task by reading the introductory paragraph with them and reviewing the criteria for what makes an effective speech. Remind students that a speech needs to be written well, in the same way that an essay does, but that the delivery of the speech is also important.

PLAN

MAKE A CLAIM

Encourage students to spend time developing and refining the claim that they will make in the persuasive speech. Offer these strategies for making their claim.

View It!

Professional Development Podcast:

Performance Task

- Brainstorm freedoms that you think still need to be achieved or expanded. You might want to work with a partner to discuss types of freedom, such as economic freedom, freedom of religion, and freedom of information and ideas. Which of the freedoms you discussed do you feel most strongly about?
- Assert a claim about the freedom in a way that reflects your distinct perspective. State the claim clearly and precisely.

PERFORMANCE TASK

PLAN

GATHER EVIDENCE

Remind students that they will want to include all three types of appeals in their speeches—ethical, logical, and emotional appeals. Give students these strategies:

- To develop your ethical appeal, explain why you are uniquely qualified to speak on the topic and/or why the audience should trust you.
- To develop your logical appeal, identify the general principle you want to uphold. What are the specific details that relate to that general principle?
- To develop your emotional appeal, think of images, connotative words, and figurative language that you could use in your speech to evoke emotion.

PRODUCE

DRAFT YOUR SPEECH

As students draft their speeches, remind them that listeners must understand ideas the first time, since they cannot go back and reread a confusing sentence. For this reason, students must use transitions to signal shifts or connections between ideas and draft clearly worded and concisely structured sentences. Remind them also that they will need to clearly introduce quotations from other texts. Provide an example, such as *In his famous speech "What to the Slave is the Fourth of July?" Frederick Douglass points out that all people are "entitled to liberty."*

Gather Evidence Choose texts from the collection that provide reasons and evidence most relevant to your argument. Take notes about the meaning and costs of freedom conveyed by each writer, paying special attention to details, quotations, and examples that support your claim.

Identify Rhetorical Devices Review Lincoln's and Douglass's speeches, identifying techniques used to help convey their message and appeal to their audience. Here are some suggestions.

- Find places in the text where rhetorical questions are used to engage the audience in the speaker's argument.
- Look for parallel structure and repetition, used to create emphasis or to show similarities between certain ideas.
- Identify any allusions that draw upon familiar stories to add power to the speaker's message.

Get Organized Use an outline or graphic organizer to organize your speech. Be sure to include your claim, reasons, and evidence. Think of counterclaims that could be made against your claim, and address them with counterarguments. Consider ideas for engaging your audience at the beginning of the speech and inspiring them to act at the end.

PRODUCE

Draft Your Speech Write a clearly organized speech. Think about your purpose and audience as you write. Which rhetorical devices can you use to help convince your audience of your ideas about freedom? Remember to include

- an engaging introduction, a logically ordered body, and a persuasive conclusion
- transitions between the main sections of your speech
- details, quotations, and examples from the texts to support your claim
- formal language and sentence structures appropriate for an oral presentation
- a variety of grammatical structures that will keep your audience engaged and interested in your speech

*my*WriteSmart

Write your rough draft in *my*WriteSmart. Focus on getting your ideas down, rather than perfecting your choice of language.

REVISE

Practice Your Speech When you deliver your speech to your classmates, you will need to make it come alive with appropriate expressions, volume, and gestures. Read over your draft and mark places in the text where you might want to emphasize a word, insert a pause, or use gestures to convey meaning or emotion. Then practice your speech with a partner. When listening to your partner's speech, ask yourself these questions:

my WriteSmart

Have your partner or a group of peers review your draft in *my*WriteSmart. Ask your reviewers to note any reasons that do not support the claim or that lack sufficient evidence.

- Does the beginning of the speech draw me in?
- Can I follow the reasoning, organization, and development of the speech?
- Is the claim presented clearly and concisely followed by reasons and evidence to support the claim? Does my partner address counterclaims?
- Does the conclusion make a compelling call to action?
- Does my partner use appropriate tone, emphasis, and gestures?
- Can I hear my partner clearly? Does he or she need to speak more loudly or softly?
- How is my partner's pace? Does he or she need to slow down or speed up in certain sections or throughout the speech?

Evaluate Your Performance After you and your partner have presented your speeches, give each other feedback. Use the chart on the following page to evaluate the substance and style of your partner's speech as well as your own. Mention what your partner did particularly well and what he or she could have done better. Then revise your draft based on your partner's feedback, the rubric, and your own observations of your speech. Make sure that your audience can and will understand it.

PRESENT

Deliver Your Speech Present your speech to the whole class. The audience should listen, take notes, and be prepared to comment and ask questions.

REVISE

PRACTICE YOUR SPEECH

Suggest to students that they complete their drafts a day ahead of their scheduled speech to allow time for practice and revision.

PRESENT

DELIVER YOUR SPEECH

Remind students to incorporate verbal and nonverbal techniques when delivering their speeches.

- **Verbal techniques:** Keep your rate of speech steady. Pause for effect when you reach key ideas. Enunciate clearly and use a tone of voice that effectively conveys your point of view.
- **Nonverbal techniques:** Engage the audience by making eye contact with individuals. Use appropriate gestures to reinforce key ideas.

PERFORMANCE TASK

ORGANIZATION

Have students look at the chart and offer a self-evaluation of the Organization category, including an assessment of their level of performance. Ask them to set goals for the next time they might do a similar task. What areas will they work on?

PERSUASIVE SPEECH

	Ideas and Evidence	Organization	Language
ADVANCED	• The introduction immediately engages the audience; the claim clearly states the speaker's position on expanding a type of freedom. • Valid reasons and relevant evidence convincingly support the speaker's claim. • Counterclaims are anticipated and effectively addressed with counterarguments. • The concluding section effectively summarizes the claim and makes a persuasive call to action.	• The reasons and evidence are organized consistently and logically throughout the speech. • Varied transitions logically connect reasons and evidence to the speaker's claim.	• The speech reflects a formal style and an objective, or controlled, tone. • Sentence beginnings, lengths, and structures vary and have a rhythmic flow. • Grammar, usage, and mechanics are correct.
COMPETENT	• The introduction could do more to capture the audience's attention; the speaker's claim states a position on a type of freedom. • Most reasons and evidence support the speaker's claim, but they could be more convincing. • Counterclaims are anticipated, but the counterarguments need to be developed more. • The concluding section restates the claim and suggests that the audience take action.	• The organization of reasons and evidence is confusing in a few places. • A few more transitions are needed to connect reasons and evidence to the speaker's claim.	• The style is informal in a few places, and the tone is defensive at times. • Sentence beginnings, lengths, and structures vary somewhat. • Some grammatical and usage errors are repeated in the speech.
LIMITED	• The introduction is ordinary; the speaker's claim identifies an issue about freedom, but the position is not clearly stated. • The reasons and evidence are not always logical or relevant. • Counterclaims are anticipated but not addressed logically. • The concluding section includes an incomplete summary of the claim and does not summon the audience to take action.	• The organization of reasons and evidence is logical in some places, but it often doesn't follow a pattern. • Many more transitions are needed to connect reasons and evidence to the speaker's position.	• The style becomes informal in many places, and the tone is often dismissive of other viewpoints. • Sentence structures barely vary, and some fragments or run-on sentences are evident. • Grammar and usage are incorrect in many places, but the speaker's ideas are still clear.
EMERGING	• The introduction is confusing. • Significant supporting reasons and evidence are missing. • Counterclaims are neither anticipated nor addressed. • The concluding section is missing.	• A logical organization is not used; reasons and evidence are presented randomly. • Transitions are not used, making the speech difficult to understand.	• The style is inappropriate, and the tone is disrespectful. • Repetitive sentence structure, fragments, and run-on sentences make the speech monotonous and hard to follow. • Many grammatical and usage errors change the meaning of the speaker's ideas.

An Age of Realism

PLAN

CONNECTING WORD AND IMAGE

ASK STUDENTS to discuss how the collection opener image and the collection quotation work together to create a connection.

PERFORMANCE TASK PREVIEW

Point out to students that they will complete one performance task at the end of the collection. The performance task will require them to further analyze the selections in the collection and to synthesize ideas about these analyses. They will present their findings in an analytical essay about realism.

ACADEMIC VOCABULARY

View It!

Professional Development Podcast:

Academic Vocabulary

Students can acquire facility with the academic vocabulary words through frequent, repeated exposure as they analyze and discuss the selections in the collection. Academic vocabulary can be used in the following instructional contexts. This will enable students to incorporate the academic vocabulary words into their working vocabulary.

- Collaborative Discussion at the end of each selection
- Analyzing the Text questions for each selection
- Selection-level Performance Task
- Vocabulary instruction (for Critical Vocabulary and/or for Vocabulary Strategy)
- Language and Style
- End-of-collection Performance Task for all selections in the collection

ASK STUDENTS to review the academic vocabulary word list for this collection. You may wish to pronounce each word aloud, so students hear the correct pronunciation. Then discuss the definitions and the related forms for each word. Remind students that they will encounter these five academic vocabulary words throughout the collection.

An Age of Realism

In this collection, you will explore how post–Civil War America experienced rapid industrialization, urban growth, and social change.

hmhfyi.com

COLLECTION
PERFORMANCE TASK Preview

At the end of this collection, you will have the opportunity to complete a task:

- Write an analytical essay that examines the ways in which writers in the collection use realism to present and emphasize a variety of themes.

ACADEMIC VOCABULARY

Study the words and their definitions in the chart below. You will use these words as you discuss and write about the texts in this collection.

Word	Definition	Related Forms
ambiguous (ăm-bĭg´yoo-əs) *adj.*	able to be interpreted in more than one way; uncertain	ambiguously, ambiguity
clarify (klăr´ə-fī´) *v.*	to make clearer or more understandable	clarity, clarifies, clarification
implicit (ĭm-plĭs´ĭt) *adj.*	not directly stated or obviously apparent	imply, implicate, implicitly
revise (rĭ-vīz´) *v.*	to change or alter a text; reconsider	revision, revisable, reviser
somewhat (sŭm´wŏt´) *adv.*	to a limited extent	somewhere, somehow

USING THE COLLECTION YOUR WAY

Use the following information, along with the charts on the following pages, to help you decide how you want to introduce the collection. Based on your teaching style, your students' interests, or your instructional goals, you may want to structure the collection in various ways. You may choose different entry points each time you teach the collection.

"I emphasize informational texts."

In this book excerpt, investigative journalist **Eric Schlosser** gives information about the role of flavor companies in creating natural and artificial flavors that are used in some fast-food products.

COMPARE TEXTS

from
The Jungle
Novel by Upton Sinclair

Food Product Design
from Fast Food Nation
Journalism by Eric Schlosser

Upton Sinclair (1878–1968) *was sent by the socialist newspaper Appeal to Reason to Chicago to investigate working conditions in the stockyards, where animals were processed into meat. Sinclair himself was a socialist, and he believed that the means and products of production should be collectively owned by the workers. He believed that socialism, with its focus on strong government regulation and collective action, could solve many of the inequalities of his era. The result of Sinclair's investigation in Chicago was his most famous novel, The Jungle (1906), which he was forced to self-publish after several publishers turned down the manuscript. Jurgis Rudkus, the main character, is a Lithuanian immigrant who works in the stockyards.*

Eric Schlosser (b. 1959) *became a journalist after studying history in college. In 1998, the magazine Rolling Stone published his two-part investigative series on the fast-food industry. Schlosser then expanded the articles into a best-selling book, Fast Food Nation: The Dark Side of the All-American Meal (2001), which examines the effects of the fast-food industry on workers, consumers, and the landscape. In 2006, Schlosser and writer Charles Wilson published a version of the book for young people, Chew On This: Everything You Don't Want to Know About Fast Food. The original book was also made into a movie in the same year, with Schlosser co-writing the screenplay.*

Compare Texts **351**

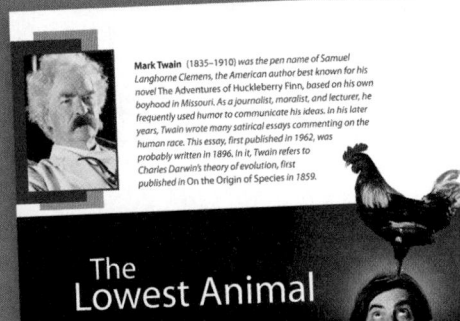

Mark Twain (1835–1910) *was the pen name of Samuel Langhorne Clemens, the American author best known for his novel The Adventures of Huckleberry Finn, based on his own boyhood in Missouri. As a journalist, moralist, and lecturer, he frequently used humor to communicate his ideas. In his later years, Twain wrote many satirical essays commenting on the human race. This essay, first published in 1962, was probably written in 1896. In it, Twain refers to Charles Darwin's theory of evolution, first published in On the Origin of Species in 1859.*

The Lowest Animal

Essay by Mark Twain

AS YOU READ Notice how Twain describes the various "painstaking" experiments he performed. Write down any questions you generate during reading.

Man is the Reasoning Animal. Such is the claim.

I have been studying the traits and **dispositions** of the "lower animals" (so-called) and contrasting them with the traits and dispositions of man. I find the result humiliating to me. For it obliges me to renounce[1] my allegiance to the Darwinian theory of the Ascent of Man from the Lower Animals, since it now seems plain to me that that theory ought to be vacated in favor of a new and truer one, this new and truer one to be named the *Descent of Man from the Higher Animals.*

In proceeding toward this unpleasant conclusion, I have not guessed or speculated or conjectured, but have used what is commonly called the scientific method.[2] That is to say, I have subjected every

disposition (dĭs′pə-zĭsh′ən) *n.* character or temperament.

[1] **renounce:** give up; reject.
[2] **scientific method:** research method in which a hypothesis is tested by careful, documented experiments.

The Lowest Animal **373**

"I stress the importance of language and style."

In this essay, **Mark Twain** uses humor to describe several fictional experiments that compare humans to animals and satirize Darwin's ideas about human nature.

"I like to teach by comparing texts."

Through several media—essay, photographs, table, and video—the poor living conditions of immigrant families residing in impoverished New York City tenements during the late 19th century and early 20th century are exposed.

COMPARE TEXT AND MEDIA

MEDIA ANALYSIS

Tenements and the "Other Half"

Genesis of the Tenement
Essay from *How the Other Half Lives* by Jacob Riis

Images: Tenement Photos
Photographs by Jacob Riis

Child Mortality Rates
Report by the Tenement House Committee

AMERICA The Story of Us: Jacob Riis
Video by HISTORY

Jacob Riis (1849–1914) *was born in Ribe, Denmark. In his long career, he was a journalist, a photographer, and a social reformer. After immigrating to the United States in 1870, Riis held several jobs and personally experienced homelessness and poverty on the streets of New York City. In 1873, he became a police reporter and was assigned to New York's Lower East Side, a poor area crowded with new immigrants. He was dismayed to learn of the conditions in the tenements that led, among other things, to high infant mortality. He began taking photographs of the slums with the new technique of flash photography. In 1890, he published How the Other Half Lives. In the introduction to that book, Riis pointed out that "one half of the world does not know how the other half lives." His book shocked readers and brought Riis and his cause much attention. Theodore Roosevelt, a New York City police commissioner who later became president, read the book and quickly wrote Riis a note: "I have read your book, and I have come to help." Riis's work prompted the first legislation to reform housing laws.*

Compare Text and Media **383**

COLLECTION 5 DIGITAL OVERVIEW

mySmartPlanner | **eBook** | **myNotebook** | **myWriteSmart** | fyi hmhfyi.com

Collection 5 Lessons	Media	Teach and Practice
**Student Edition	eBook**	▶ Video Links H HISTORY A&E	**Close Reading and Evidence Tracking**
ANCHOR TEXT Short Story by Jack London "To Build a Fire"	🔊 **Audio** "To Build a Fire"	**Close Read Screencasts** • Modeled Discussion (lines 45–52) • Close Read application (lines 540–549) **Strategies for Annotation** • Analyze Structure: Realism and Naturalism • Vocabulary Strategy
CLOSE READER Short Story by Stephen Crane "The Men in the Storm"	🔊 **Audio** "The Men in the Storm"	
Novel by Upton Sinclair from *The Jungle*	🔊 **Audio** from *The Jungle*	**Strategies for Annotation** • Analyze Author's Choices
Investigative Journalism by Eric Schlosser "Food Product Design" from *Fast Food Nation*	🔊 **Audio** "Food Product Design" from *Fast Food Nation*	**Strategies for Annotation** • Determine Author's Purpose • Language and Style: Dashes
CLOSE READER Science Writing by Mary Roach "The Yuckiest Food in the Amazon"	🔊 **Audio** "The Yuckiest Food in the Amazon"	
Essay by Mark Twain "The Lowest Animal"	🔊 **Audio** "The Lowest Animal"	**Strategies for Annotation** • Analyze Author's Purpose: Satire • Analyze Word Choice: Nuance
Essay by Jacob Riis "Genesis of the Tenements"	🔊 **Audio** "Genesis of the Tenements"	**Strategies for Annotation** • Integrate and Evaluate Information
Image Collection by Jacob Riis "Tenement Photos"		
Report by Tenement House Committee "Child Mortality Rates"		
Documentary by HISTORY® *AMERICA The Story of Us: Jacob Riis*	▶ **Video HISTORY** *AMERICA The Story of Us: Jacob Riis*	
Short Story by Kate Chopin "The Story of an Hour"	🔊 **Audio** "The Story of an Hour"	**Strategies for Annotation** • Analyze Author's Point of View: Irony
CLOSE READER Short Story by Edith Wharton "A Journey"	🔊 **Audio** "A Journey"	
Poem by Elizabeth Bishop "The Fish"	🔊 **Audio** "The Fish"	**Strategies for Annotation** • Analyze Structure: Symbol
CLOSE READER Poem by Pablo Neruda "Ode to a Large Tuna in the Market"	🔊 **Audio** "Ode to a Large Tuna in the Market"	
Collection 5 Performance Task: • Write an Analytical Essay	fyi **hmhfyi.com**	**Interactive Lessons** Writing an Informative Text Writing as a Process Using Textual Evidence

	For Systematic Coverage of Writing and Speaking & Listening Standards	Interactive Lessons Writing a Narrative Producing and Publishing with Technology	Lesson Assessments Writing a Narrative Producing and Publishing with Technology

Assess		Extend	Reteach
Performance Task	**Online Assessment**	**Teacher eBook**	**Teacher eBook**
Writing Activity: Narrative	Selection Test	**Determine Author's Purpose**	**Analyze Structure: Realism and Naturalism**
Writing Activity: News Articles Speaking Activity: Debate	Selection Test	**Determine Themes and Main Ideas**	**Determine Author's Purpose > Level Up Tutorial >** Author's Purpose
Writing Activity: Narrative Speaking Activity: Debate	Selection Test	**Determine Themes and Main Ideas**	**Determine Author's Purpose > Level Up Tutorial >** Author's Purpose
Speaking Activity: Lecture	Selection Test	**Analyze Language: Figures of Speech > Interactive Whiteboard Lesson >** Citing Textual Evidence	**Analyze Author's Purpose > Level Up Tutorial >** Author's Purpose
Writing Activity: Essay	Selection Test	**Short Research**	**Integrate and Evaluate Information > Level Up Tutorial >** Evaluating Credibility
Writing Activity: Essay	Selection Test	**Short Research**	**Integrate and Evaluate Information > Level Up Tutorial >** Evaluating Credibility
Writing Activity: Essay	Selection Test	**Short Research**	**Integrate and Evaluate Information > Level Up Tutorial >** Evaluating Credibility
Writing Activity: Essay	Selection Test	**Short Research**	**Integrate and Evaluate Information > Level Up Tutorial >** Evaluating Credibility
Speaking Activity: Discussion	Selection Test	**Analyze Structure: Resolution**	**Analyze Author's Point of View: Irony > Level Up Tutorial >** Irony
Writing Activity: Description	Selection Test	**Determine Themes > Interactive Whiteboard Lesson >** Infer Theme in a Poem	**Analyze Structure: Symbol**
Write an Analytical Essay	Collection Test		

Collection 5 Lessons	Key Learning Objective	Performance Task
ANCHOR TEXT **Short Story by Jack London** **"To Build a Fire," p. 331A** Lexile 970	**The student will be able to...** determine a story's themes and distinguish realism and naturalism	Writing Activity: Narrative
Novel by Upton Sinclair from ***The Jungle,* p. 351A** Lexile 1310	**The student will be able to...** determine an author's purpose and analyze an author's choices	Writing Activity: News Articles Speaking Activity: Debate
Investigative Journalism by **Eric Schlosser** **"Food Product Design" from *Fast Food Nation,*** **p. 351A** Lexile 1290	**The student will be able to...** determine an author's purpose and analyze an author's choices	Writing Activity: Narrative Speaking Activity: Debate
Essay by Mark Twain **"The Lowest Animal," p. 373A** Lexile 1040	**The student will be able to...** identify an author's purpose through understanding the use of satire	Speaking Activity: Lecture
Essay by Jacob Riis **"Genesis of the Tenements," p. 383A** Lexile 1410	**The student will be able to...** Integrate and evaluate information presented in text, photographs, tables, and video	Writing Activity: Essay
Image Collection by Jacob Riis **"Tenement Photos," p. 383A**	**The student will be able to...** Integrate and evaluate information presented in text, photographs, tables, and video	Writing Activity: Essay
Report by Tenement House Committee **"Child Mortality Rates," p. 383A**	**The student will be able to...** Integrate and evaluate information presented in text, photographs, tables, and video	Writing Activity: Essay
Documentary by HISTORY ***AMERICA The Story of Us: Jacob Riis,* p. 383A**	**The student will be able to...** Integrate and evaluate information presented in text, photographs, tables, and video	Writing Activity: Essay
Short Story by Kate Chopin **"The Story of an Hour," p. 395A** Lexile 970	**The student will be able to...** analyze the impact of the author's use of point of view and irony in a short story	Speaking Activity: Discussion
Poem by Elizabeth Bishop "The Fish," p. 401A	**The student will be able to...** analyze a poem for diction, imagery, and use of symbols	Writing Activity: Description

Collection 5 Performance Task:
Write an Analytical Essay

Vocabulary Strategy	Language and Style	Student Instructional Support	CLOSE READER Selection
Etymology	Consistent Tone	**Scaffolding for ELL Students:** 332, 337, 338, 340 **When Students Struggle:** 334, 336, 341, 345 **To Challenge Students:** 343, 346	Short Story by Stephen Crane "The Men in the Storm", p. 350b **Lexile 1200**
Word Families		**Scaffolding for ELL Students:** Identify Pronoun Referents **When Students Struggle:** Analyze Cause and Effect	
	Dashes	**Scaffolding for ELL Students:** • Define Multiple-Meaning Words in Context • Build Oral Fluency **When Students Struggle:** • Write a Summary • Build Oral Fluency **To Challenge Students:** Make a Persuasive Argument	Science Writing by Mary Roach "The Yuckiest Food in the Amazon," p. 372b **Lexile 900**
Nuance in Word Meaning	Anaphora and Parallelism	**Scaffolding for ELL Students:** • Understand Multiple-Meaning Words • Understand Prefixes **When Students Struggle:** • Understand Idioms • Understand Word Choice **To Challenge Students:** Mimic Style	
		Scaffolding for ELL Students: • Comprehension Support • Reading Support **When Students Struggle:** • Identify Main Idea and Details	
		To Challenge Students: • Composition • Understand Realism and Naturalism	
		When Students Struggle: • Read and Interpret Information in a Table	
Word Collocations		**Scaffolding for ELL Students:** • Recognize Prepositional Phrases • Understand Collocations **When Students Struggle:** Paraphrase Information in a Story	Short Story by Edith Wharton "A Journey," p. 400b **Lexile 870**
		Scaffolding for ELL Students: Recognize Past Participles Used as Modifiers **When Students Struggle:** Build Vocabulary	Poem by Pablo Neruda "Ode to a Large Tuna in the Market," p. 404b

*my*SmartPlanner — Create lesson plans and access resources online.

America Transformed

Collection 5 Historical Introduction

Why This Text?

Students often encounter literary and informational texts that assume that the reader has some knowledge of key historical events, facts, ideas, and issues. The historical introduction to Collection 5 presents information about the period in the United States from 1880 to 1908, when technological innovations and rapid industrial growth brought fortunes to some leaders of industry while the expanding worker class and a flood of immigrants struggled to adapt to life in the burgeoning cities.

Key Learning Objective: The student will be able to analyze the selections in the collection in terms of a historical context.

Common Core Standards

RL 10 Read and comprehend literature in the grades 11-CCR text complexity band.

RI 3 Analyze ideas or events and explain how individuals, ideas, or events interact and develop.

RI 7 Integrate and evaluate sources of information presented in different formats

RI 10 Read and comprehend literary nonfiction in the grades 11-CCR text complexity band.

Text Complexity Rubric

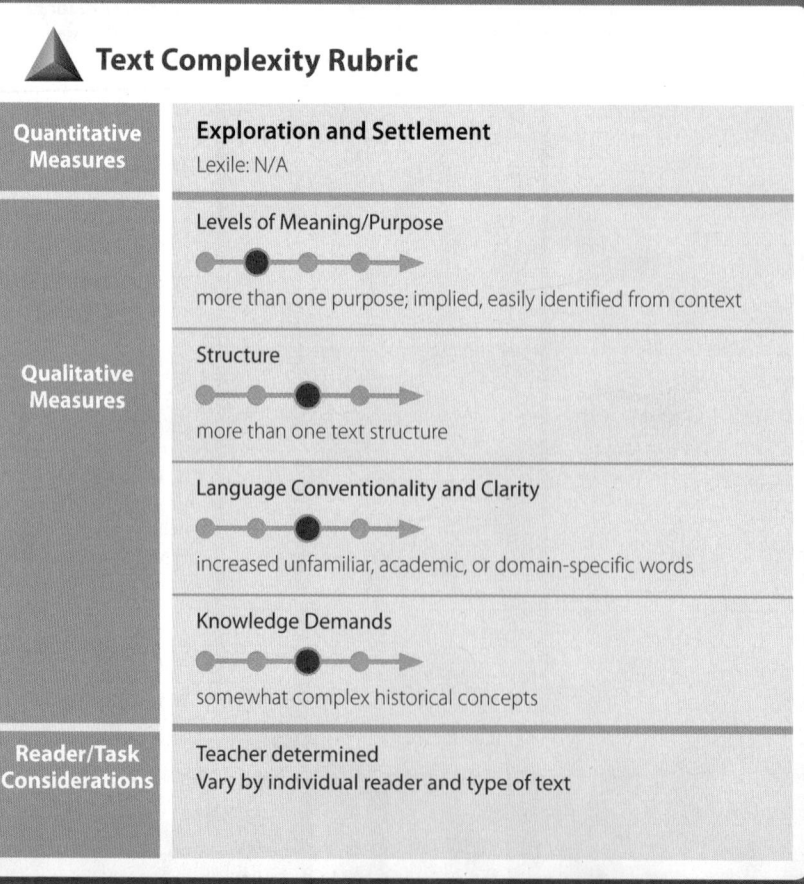

	Exploration and Settlement
Quantitative Measures	Lexile: N/A

Levels of Meaning/Purpose

more than one purpose; implied, easily identified from context

Structure

more than one text structure

Language Conventionality and Clarity

increased unfamiliar, academic, or domain-specific words

Knowledge Demands

somewhat complex historical concepts

Reader/Task Considerations	Teacher determined
	Vary by individual reader and type of text

TEACH

H HISTORY For more context and historical background, students can view the video "Andrew Carnegie: Prince of Steel" in their eBooks.

America Transformed   COMMON CORE RL 10, RI 3, RI 7, RI 10

Explain that this section establishes the historical context for the selections in this collection. It explains the technological, economic, and social developments that bridged the way from the more rural post–Civil War era to the modern, fully industrialized nation that people in the United States enjoy now. It also introduces themes that permeate the selections and still c_____ people today, such as the struggle to adapt to ____ progress, the need to fight for justice f____ and the drive to reform corrupt indust____

Engines of Social Change

The era at the end of the 19th cent____ name—the Gilded Age—from a novel written in collaboration by Mark Twain and Charles Dudley Warner. This book satirizes the greed and corruption found in the political and social life of Washington, D.C., in the 1870s. Instead of being a Golden Age when all people live in true peace, happiness, and harmony, a Gilded Age was, in contrast, seen as a time when the troubles of the great majority of ordinary people were hidden by a thin layer of distracting gilt, such as the technological marvels being produced by industrialization and the fortunes being made and enjoyed by the captains of industry.

On the one hand, the economy of the United States was booming, and the men who were engaged in industrial businesses such as mining for oil and steel or constructing ships, railways, and city buildings were amassing great wealth. On the other hand, some of these capitalists, dubbed "robber barons," were accruing their fortunes through underhanded techniques such as creating monopolies, paying unfairly low wages, and selling stock at fraudulently high prices.

H HISTORY | VIDEO

America Transformed   COMMON CORE RL 10, RI 3, RI 7, RI 10

At the end of the 19th century, America struggled with a paradox: It was a nation of almost unlimited possibilities and wealth, but it was marked by great poverty and pain for many of its citizens. Reflecting this tension, a new literary movement known as realism emerged, which expressed a view of life that was unsentimental, bitterly ironic, and often harsh or ugly.

ENGINES OF SOCIAL CHANGE In the two decades after the completion of the transcontinental railroad, the rail system brought thousands of settlers to the West. The railroad industry also became an engine for industrial growth as new manufacturing centers grew up around railroad hubs in Pittsburgh, Cleveland, Detroit, and Chicago. New technologies and industrial modernization brought prosperity to large parts of the nation.

The growth of industry caused the growth of cities as more and more people came looking for work. In the early 19th century, Chicago was an average-sized city; by 1910, the population was more than 2 million, making it the country's second largest city after New York. All the new manufacturing centers grew in similar fashion. However, a very small group of men controlled the vast share of this industry, including the enormously profitable steel, railroad, oil, and meatpacking sectors. This era became known as the Gilded Age, and was dominated by captains of industry such as oil tycoon John D. Rockefeller and railroad magnate Cornelius Vanderbilt.

Although ordinary people did not achieve the level of wealth of industry leaders, some of them did have more money, and there were new things to spend it on. City dwellers could take a train to an amusement park and shop in new department stores. Some factory workers could even afford new inventions such as automobiles, telephones, and electricity. However, much of the urban population growth was due to an influx of immigrants who came to America in search of freedom and opportunity. These immigrants lived in crowded tenements and found work in factories, where many of them worked 16-hour days in airless sweatshops for subsistence wages.

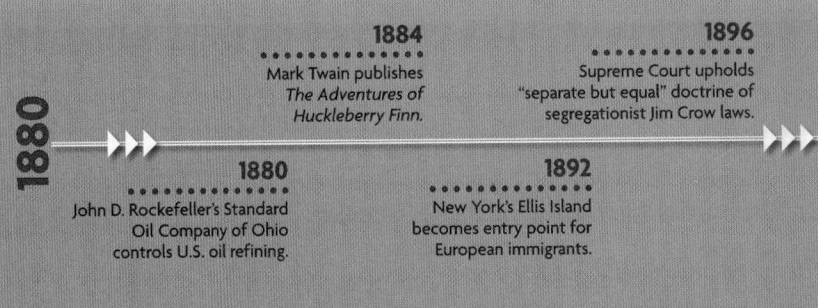

1880

1884 Mark Twain publishes *The Adventures of Huckleberry Finn.*

1896 Supreme Court upholds "separate but equal" doctrine of segregationist Jim Crow laws.

1880 John D. Rockefeller's Standard Oil Company of Ohio controls U.S. oil refining.

1892 New York's Ellis Island becomes entry point for European immigrants.

America Transformed **329**

SCAFFOLDING FOR ELL STUDENTS

Vocabulary: Idioms Students may not have previous knowledge of some of the idioms used in this historical background essay. Remind students that an idiom is a saying whose meaning is different from that of the individual words that make it up. Explain that writers may use idioms for poetic or descriptive effect. For example, point out the phrase "gave voice" in the third paragraph on page 330 and explain that this saying means to help someone who has been silenced in some way to express their viewpoint.

ASK STUDENTS to work in mixed-language ability groups to identify and use context clues to define other potentially confusing idioms from this essay, such as "brings out" from the 1908 entry on the timeline.

Ordinary Lives and Voices

By the second half of the 19th century, many areas of the United States had been settled long enough to have had established their own cultures and dialects. Although regionalist works did aim to preserve depictions of some of these local cultures, ones authored by women also often offered critiques of the various communities. For example, Kate Chopin's *The Awakening* provides a representation of the Creole society and culture of New Orleans at this time, while also dramatizing the conflict between the evolving opinions of its heroine Edna and the constraining beliefs and attitudes of the people around her.

Naturalism

Naturalist writers not just tried to describe in detail the realities of contemporary life, but also to diagnose what aspects of society might be causing various problems for the people living in it. Like specimens studied in a lab, the characters in naturalist works of literature served as case models for how individuals could be destroyed by their environments. For example, Stephen Crane's novel *Maggie: A Girl of the Streets* illustrates how life in an industrialized city drives the title character into poverty and prostitution.

Nonfiction writers, too, sought to pinpoint and cure society's ills. Where the "yellow journalists" who came before them focused on writing sensationalized stories to help sell newspapers, muckrakers worked hard to expose real wrongdoing and enact social reform. Initially, President Theodore Roosevelt supported the work of the muckrakers. He was even involved in encouraging the passage of legislation such as the Meat Inspection Act and the Pure Food and Drugs Act, meant to solve some of the problems these journalists brought to light. Once they started looking into corruption in the government, however, including investigating some of his friends, Roosevelt himself gave them the insulting nickname "muckrakers," inspired by a character from John Bunyan's *The Pilgrim's Progress* who chose to stare downward and rake through filthy muck instead of looking upward and aspiring to be saved.

This period also was marked by new roles for women. The movement to secure their right to vote was reinvigorated as women sought to have a larger voice in every aspect of public life. Increasing numbers of women achieved the goal of a university education as a step toward their broader role in society.

ORDINARY LIVES AND VOICES Realist writers pursued their goal of showing ordinary lives as they were—without romance or sentimentality—through a variety of genres and forms. Although Americans were glad to move past the divisions of the Civil War, they regretted losing their regional identities and were unsettled by the rapid changes taking place in the country. Some writers began to capture the customs, characters, and landscapes of the nation's distinct regions—a type of writing that came to be called regionalism. Willa Cather, Mark Twain, and Kate Chopin, among others, celebrated America's diversity in settings ranging from the plains of Nebraska to Mississippi River towns and the city of New Orleans. The publication in 1884 of Twain's *The Adventures of Huckleberry Finn* marked the high point of regionalism. Told in Huck's colorful and colloquial voice, the novel is a biting satire that tackles the issue of racism in America.

NATURALISM The social conditions in America's growing industrial cities, with their great disparities of wealth, led to the rise of the literary movement called naturalism, a darker form of realism. Looking to the theories of Charles Darwin and other scientists, writers who favored naturalism, such as Stephen Crane and Jack London, saw human beings as helpless creatures moved by forces beyond their understanding or control. While Crane and others gave voice to ordinary people living in cities, London captured readers with his tales of an arctic world totally outside their everyday experiences. Riveted by the exotic settings and thrilling action of his novels, readers were willing to accept tragic endings. Women writers such as Edith Wharton combined naturalism with their own experiences to portray a culture that trapped women in narrow, restricted lives.

Reform-minded journalists, part of a progressive movement that aimed to restore economic opportunities and correct injustices in American life, expressed these naturalist influences in another way. An immigrant himself, Jacob Riis exposed the plight of tenement dwellers in his book *How the Other Half Lives*. A group of journalists labeled as "muckrakers" sought to expose the political and economic corruption that resulted from the excessive power of large corporations. Among this group was Upton Sinclair, whose novel *The Jungle* helped lead to the passage of new laws regulating the food industry.

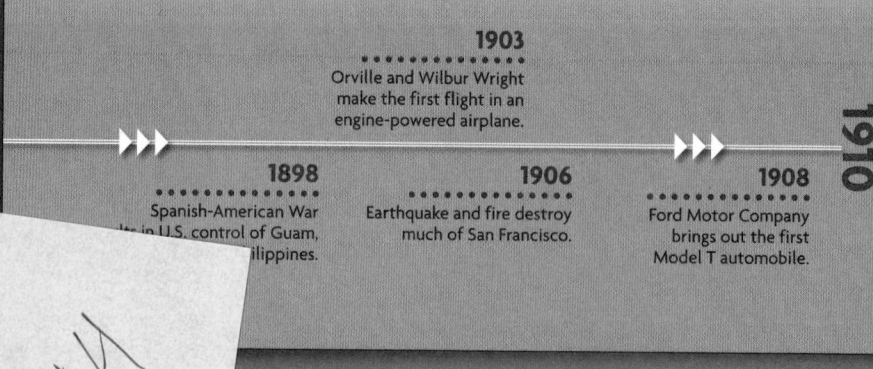

1903
Orville and Wilbur Wright make the first flight in an engine-powered airplane.

1898
Spanish-American War ... in U.S. control of Guam, ...ilippines.

1906
Earthquake and fire destroy much of San Francisco.

1908
Ford Motor Company brings out the first Model T automobile.

1910

...ENTS STRUGGLE . . .

...port: Some students may experience difficulty with understanding ...t are included as part of the historical background essays that begin each collection.

ASK STUDENTS to work in small groups to point out challenging economic vocabulary terms such as *manufacturing* (page 329), *modernization* (page 329), *prosperity* (page 329), *tycoon* (page 329), *magnate* (page 329), *subsistence wages* (page 329), *oil refining* (page 329), *disparities* (page 330), *corporations* (page 330), and *regulating* (page 330). Then ask them to use context clues or outside resources to define each term.

Comprehend Literary Nonfiction: Historical Context

COMMON CORE

RI 10

TEACH

Remind students that they will understand a piece of literary nonfiction better when they keep in mind the historical context in which it is written. Add that this historical background essay will provide them with a rich understanding of the time period in which the nonfiction selections they will read in this collection were written.

To examine the historical context, students should keep in mind the following:

- The type of society in which the text is written.
- The prevalent attitudes and cultural beliefs of the people living in this society.
- The economic factors affecting the way these people were able to make a living or purchase the things required to meet their needs.
- The most significant events that took place during the text's composition.

Review the final paragraph on page 330 and note how it mentions the immigrant writer Jacob Riis and explains that his book *How the Other Half Lives* "exposed the plight of tenement dwellers." Then flip back to the final paragraph on page 329 and point out how it provides details about the historical context in which Riis and real tenement dwellers of the time lived.

PRACTICE AND APPLY

Have pairs identify and summarize other bits of information they can glean about the social, cultural, political, and historical setting in which works produced between 1880–1908 were written.

Analyze Author's Order: Cause and Effect

COMMON CORE

RI 3

TEACH

Explain to students that, because this historical background essay focuses on the topic of how life in the United States changed during this particular span of years, the author chose at times to structure the text by describing cause-and-effect relationships. Remind students that an effect is what happened and the cause is why this thing happened.

Point out the discussion on page 329 about how manufacturing centers began to grow and large parts of the nation began to experience prosperity during this time. Explain that these events are effects. Then identify some causes for these effects—because a widespread rail system had been built, many settlers were able to move west and populate new cities; new technologies led to the construction of new manufacturing centers; as new industries grew, more people moved to cities to fill newly created jobs.

Be sure to point out examples of clue words that indicate cause-and-effect relationships such as *caused* (in the first sentence of the third paragraph on page 329) and *due to* (in the fourth sentence of the last paragraph on page 329).

Then work with students to identify other examples of cause-and-effect relationships in this essay.

CLOSE READING APPLICATION

Have students work independently to read another nonfiction piece in which they can identify examples of ways a writer uses cause-and-effect relationships to structure the text.

To Build a Fire

mySmartPlanner Create lesson plans and access resources online.

Short Story by Jack London

Why This Text?

Jack London explores the relationship of humans and other animals to the natural world with a cold, clear eye. In this lesson, students analyze the choices London makes to convey ideas that continue to resonate today.

View It!

Professional Development Podcast:

Writing Narratives at the Secondary Level

For additional practice:

The Men in the Storm

Short Story by Stephen Crane

Close Reader selection
"The Men in the Storm"
Short Story by Stephen Crane

Key Learning Objective: The student will be able to determine a story's themes and distinguish realism and naturalism.

Common Core Standards

RL 1 Cite textual evidence.
RL 2 Determine themes of a text.
RL 3 Analyze the impact of the author's choices.
RL 5 Analyze how an author's choices concerning how to structure specific parts of a text contribute to its overall meaning as well as its aesthetic impact.
RL 6 Analyze a case in which grasping point of view requires distinguishing what is directly stated in a text from what is really meant.
W 3 Write narratives.
W 5 Develop and strengthen writing as needed by planning, revising, editing, rewriting, or trying a new approach.
L 3a Vary syntax for effect; apply an understanding of syntax.
L 4c Consult reference materials.

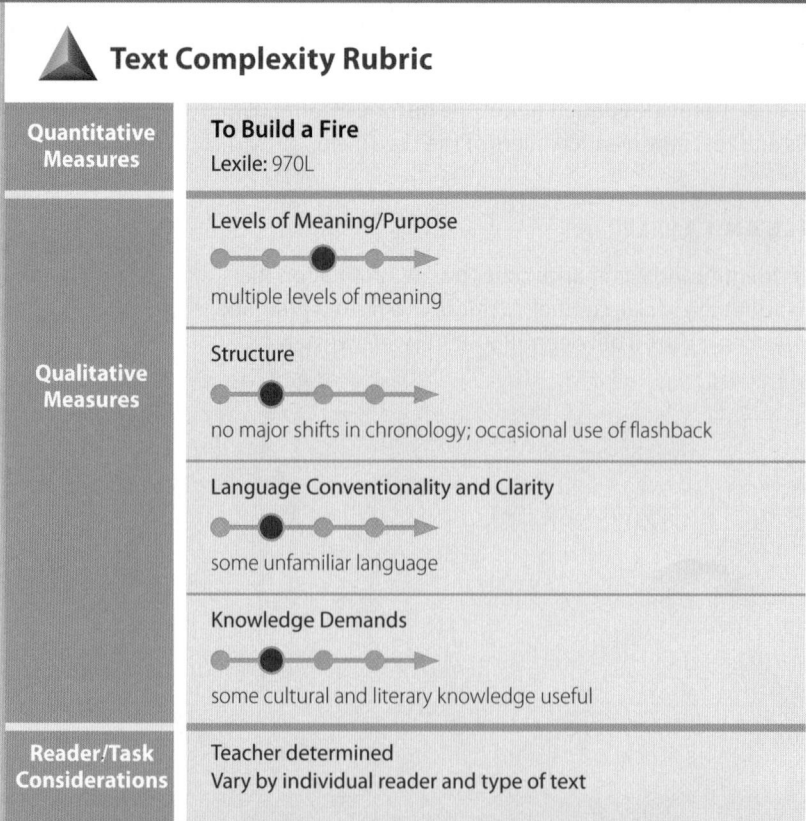

Text Complexity Rubric

To Build a Fire
Lexile: 970L

Quantitative Measures	

Levels of Meaning/Purpose

multiple levels of meaning

Structure

no major shifts in chronology; occasional use of flashback

Language Conventionality and Clarity

some unfamiliar language

Knowledge Demands

some cultural and literary knowledge useful

Reader/Task Considerations
Teacher determined
Vary by individual reader and type of text

CLOSE READ

Jack London London finished a four-year high school course in one year but dropped out of college after his freshman year to hunt for gold in the Klondike. Still poor after another year, he turned to writing to earn a living and set himself a ferocious daily quota, turning out 50 books in 17 years. He remains one of the most popular and widely translated American authors.

AS YOU READ Direct students to use the As You Read note to focus their reading. Remind them to write down questions they generate as they read.

Analyze Structure: Realism and Naturalism (LINES 1–7)

COMMON CORE RL 1, RL 2, RL 5

Tell students that many works of realistic fiction begin with a detailed description of the story's **setting**. A convincing description of a real-world setting helps the reader enter more readily into the environment in which the story takes place.

Ⓐ **CITE TEXT EVIDENCE** Have students cite specific details that establish the story's setting. *(Specific details include "exceedingly cold and gray," "fat spruce timberland," "steep bank," and "no sun.")*

> #### CRITICAL VOCABULARY
>
> **intangible**: London describes the "pall" over the scene as intangible, meaning that it is something the man feels but not something that can be directly seen or touched.
>
> **ASK STUDENTS** Ask students what intangible feeling they get from reading the story's opening paragraph. Have them find words and phrases that induce this feeling.

Jack London (1876–1916) *not only wrote adventure stories, he lived them. London traveled as a hobo across the United States, tried his luck in the Klondike Gold Rush, escaped a typhoon on a seal-hunting ship, and sailed the South Seas in his own boat, the Snark. London's formal education was limited, but he read widely using public libraries. Many of his works, including the story "To Build a Fire," have themes involving survival and humans versus nature. His novel* The Call of the Wild *(1903) brought London fame and is still one of his best-known works. London died in California at age 40.*

Image Credits: (r) ©Luca Pierro PHOTOGRAPHY/Flikr/Getty Images; (c) ©Staffan Andersson/Johner Images/Getty Images; (t) ©Apic/Hulton Archive/Getty Images

To Build a Fire

Short Story by Jack London

AS YOU READ Pay attention to the specific details that London includes to create a vivid, realistic setting. Write down any questions you generate during reading.

Day had broken cold and gray, exceedingly cold and gray, when the man turned aside from the main Yukon trail and climbed the high earth bank, where a dim and little-traveled trail led eastward through the fat spruce timberland. It was a steep bank, and he paused for breath at the top, excusing the act to himself by looking at his watch. It was nine o'clock. There was no sun or hint of sun, though there was not a cloud in the sky. It was a clear day, and yet there seemed an **intangible** pall[1] over the face of things, a subtle gloom that made the day dark, and that was due to the absence of sun. This fact
10 did not worry the man. He was used to the lack of sun. It had been days since he had seen the sun, and he knew that a few more days must pass before that cheerful orb, due south, would just peep above the skyline and dip immediately from view.

The man flung a look back along the way he had come. The Yukon lay a mile wide and hidden under three feet of ice. On top of this

intangible
(ĭn-tăn′jə-bəl) *adj.*
unable to be defined or understood.

[1] **pall:** overspreading atmosphere of gloom and depression.

To Build a Fire **331**

Close Read Screencasts 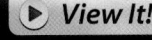 ▶ View It!

Modeled Discussion

Have students click the *Close Read* icon in their eBooks to access a screencast in which readers discuss and annotate the following key passage:

- details of the setting (lines 45–52)

As a class, view and discuss the video. Then have students pair up to do an independent close read of an additional passage—the man's vision of "the boys" finding his body the next day and of the old-timer on Sulphur Creek. (lines 540–549)

TEACH

Analyze Structure: Realism and Naturalism

COMMON CORE RL 2, RL 5

(LINES 30–36)

Tell students that one method of characterization is direct characterization, in which the narrator describes the character's traits explicitly.

B **ASK STUDENTS** what they learn about the main character based on the direct statements in lines 30–36. *(He lacks the ability to foresee problems or have a deeper understanding of the world around him.)* How might this characterization foreshadow, or hint at, what is to come? *(It hints that the man will encounter problems with the harsh environment because he fails to predict or prepare for them.)*

Analyze Structure: Realism and Naturalism

COMMON CORE RL 1, RL 2, RL 5

(LINES 36–40)

Tell students that **realism** is a style of writing that attempts to portray life as it really is. Add that **naturalism** goes beyond realism in presenting life through a more naturalistic lens. In these lines life is depicted at the mercy of natural elements.

C **CITE TEXT EVIDENCE** Ask students to cite details from lines 36–40 that convey the naturalistic view of life as a harsh struggle for survival. *(Evidence includes "his frailty as a creature of temperature," "man's frailty in general," "able only to live within certain narrow limits," and "the conjectural field of immortality.")*

> ❝ He knew that at fifty below, spittle crackled on the snow, but this spittle had crackled in the air. ❞

ice were as many feet of snow. It was all pure white, rolling in gentle undulations where the ice jams of the freeze-up had formed. North and south, as far as his eye could see, it was unbroken white, save for a dark hairline that curved and twisted from around the spruce-covered island to the south, and that curved and twisted away into the north, where it disappeared behind another spruce-covered island. This dark hairline was the trail—the main trail—that led south five hundred miles to the Chilkoot Pass, Dyea, and salt water; and that led north seventy miles to Dawson, and still on to the north a thousand miles to Nulato, and finally to St. Michael on the Bering Sea, a thousand miles and half a thousand more.

But all this—the mysterious, far-reaching hairline trail, the absence of sun from the sky, the tremendous cold, and the strangeness and weirdness of it all—made no impression on the man. It was not because he was long used to it. He was a newcomer in the land, a cheechako,[2] and this was his first winter. The trouble with him was that he was without imagination. He was quick and alert in the things of life, but only in the things, and not in the significances. Fifty degrees below zero meant eighty-odd degrees of frost. Such fact impressed him as being cold and uncomfortable, and that was all. It did not lead him to meditate upon his frailty as a creature of temperature, and upon man's frailty in general, able only to live within certain narrow limits of heat and cold, and from there on it did not lead him to the conjectural[3] field of immortality and man's place in the universe. Fifty degrees below zero stood for a bite of frost that hurt and that must be guarded against by the use of mittens, earflaps, warm moccasins, and thick socks. Fifty degrees below zero was to him just

---

[2] **cheechako:** Chinook jargon for "newcomer" or "tenderfoot."
[3] **conjectural:** based on guesswork or uncertain evidence.

332 Collection 5

SCAFFOLDING FOR ELL STUDENTS

Analyze Structure: Realism and Naturalism Using a whiteboard, project page 332. Invite students to mark up lines 30–40.

- Highlight in green words that tell who the man is.
- Highlight in blue words that tell about the man.

ASK STUDENTS TO describe the man in their own words.

> a cheechako, and this was his first winter. The trouble with him was that he was without imagination. He was quick and alert in the

precisely fifty degrees below zero. That there should be anything more to it than that was a thought that never entered his head.

As he turned to go on, he spat speculatively. There was a sharp, explosive crackle that startled him. He spat again. And again, in the air, before it could fall to the snow, the spittle crackled. He knew that at fifty below, spittle crackled on the snow, but this spittle had crackled in the air. Undoubtedly it was colder than fifty below—how much colder 50 he did not know. But the temperature did not matter. He was bound for the old claim[4] on the left fork of Henderson Creek, where the boys were already. They had come over across the divide from the Indian Creek country, while he had come the roundabout way to take a look at the possibilities of getting out logs in the spring from the islands in the Yukon. He would be into camp by six o'clock; a bit after dark, it was true, but the boys would be there, a fire would be going, and a hot supper would be ready. As for lunch, he pressed his hand against the protruding bundle under his jacket. It was also under his shirt, wrapped up in a handkerchief and lying against the naked skin. It was 60 the only way to keep the biscuits from freezing. He smiled agreeably to himself as he thought of those biscuits, each cut open and sopped in bacon grease, and each enclosing a generous slice of fried bacon.

He plunged in among the big spruce trees. The trail was faint. A foot of snow had fallen since the last sled had passed over, and he was glad he was without a sled, traveling light. In fact, he carried nothing but the lunch wrapped in the handkerchief. He was surprised, however, at the cold. It certainly was cold, he concluded, as he rubbed his numb nose and cheekbones with his mittened hand. He was a warm-whiskered man, but the hair on his face did not protect the high 70 cheekbones and the eager nose that thrust itself aggressively into the frosty air.

At the man's heels trotted a dog, a big native husky, the proper wolf dog, gray coated and without any visible or temperamental difference from its brother, the wild wolf. The animal was depressed by the tremendous cold. It knew that it was no time for traveling. Its instinct told it a truer tale than was told to the man by the man's judgment. In reality, it was not merely colder than fifty below zero; it was colder than sixty below, than seventy below. It was seventy-five below zero. Since the freezing point is thirty-two above zero, it meant 80 that one hundred and seven degrees of frost obtained. The dog did not know anything about thermometers. Possibly in its brain there was no sharp consciousness of a condition of very cold such as was in the man's brain. But the brute had its instinct. It experienced a vague but menacing **apprehension** that subdued it and made it slink along at the man's heels, and that made it question eagerly every unwonted[5] movement of the man, as if expecting him to go into camp or to seek

apprehension
(ăp´rĭ-hĕn´shən) *n.*
fear or anxiety; dread.

---

[4] **claim:** piece of land staked out by a miner.
[5] **unwonted:** unusual.

To Build a Fire   **333**

APPLYING ACADEMIC VOCABULARY

implicit	revise

As you discuss the story, incorporate the following Collection 5 academic vocabulary words: *implicit* and *revise*. As students discuss realistic aspects of the story, encourage them to consider meanings and attitudes that are **implicit** in the objective descriptions. When students discuss naturalistic aspects of the story, invite them to suggest ways the story could be **revised** so that the grim stance of naturalism could be softened into a more objective kind of realism.

TEACH

CLOSE READ

Analyze Language: Irony (LINE 50)

COMMON CORE RL 6

Remind students that **irony** is a difference between appearance and reality, between what is said and what is meant.

D ASK STUDENTS to explain the irony in the sentence, "But the temperature did not matter." *(In fact, the temperature is so cold it is life-threatening, but he does not realize it.)*

Analyze Structure: Realism and Naturalism

COMMON CORE RL 1, RL 2, RL 5

(LINES 72–86)

Tell students that the style of writing known as **naturalism** portrays life as harsh and unforgiving. Note that at this point in the story, London introduces the dog's response to the setting.

E CITE TEXT EVIDENCE Have students reread lines 72–86. How does the dog's point of view about the setting differ from the man's? Why? Have them cite text evidence to support their conclusions. *(The dog's perspective is more realistic than the man's. Unlike the man, the dog realizes "that it was no time for traveling" due to extreme cold and feels a sense of "menacing apprehension." While the man overlooks the danger of the cold and believes he can overcome it, the dog realistically recognizes the danger and sensibly prefers to avoid it by seeking fire or shelter.)*

CRITICAL VOCABULARY

apprehension: The narrative conveys the dog's unease.

ASK STUDENTS why the man fails to feel **apprehension** in this circumstance.

Analyze Structure: Realism and Naturalism

COMMON CORE **RL 1, RL 2, RL 5, RL 6**

(LINES 90–99)

Tell students that **realism** is often conveyed through the use of minute, close-up details. If the subject is one that most readers are not familiar with, such details convince the reader that the author knows the subject. In this passage, London provides realistic details of the growing effects of ice and cold on the faces and bodily hair of the man and the dog. The effect is like seeing through a zoom lens.

F **CITE TEXT EVIDENCE** Have students find details that provide a close-up description that demonstrates London's keen, realistic observation and realism. *(Realistic details include the dog's "crystaled breath" and fur powdered with frost; the man's beard, frosted more solidly than the dog's fur; the amber color of frozen expelled tobacco juice; and the glasslike brittleness of the ice.)*

Analyze Structure: Realism and Naturalism

COMMON CORE **RL 2, RL 5**

(LINES 101–109)

Draw students' attention to how London shows the character's inner calculations of the temperature, his speed, and the time of arrival.

G **ASK STUDENTS** why it is realistic that the man can only roughly estimate the temperature but can estimate his arrival time somewhat more accurately. *(He does not have a thermometer, but he does have a watch.)*

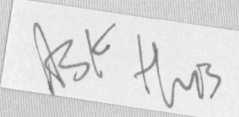

---

shelter somewhere and build a fire. The dog had learned fire, and it wanted fire, or else to burrow under the snow and cuddle its warmth away from the air.

90   The frozen moisture of its breathing had settled on its fur in a fine powder of frost, and especially were its jowls, muzzle, and eyelashes whitened by its crystaled breath. The man's red beard and moustache were likewise frosted, but more solidly, the deposit taking the form of ice and increasing with every warm, moist breath he exhaled. Also, the man was chewing tobacco, and the muzzle of ice held his lips so rigidly that he was unable to clear his chin when he expelled the juice. The result was that a crystal beard of the color and solidity of amber was increasing its length on his chin. If he fell down it would shatter itself, like glass, into brittle fragments. But he did not mind the appendage.[6]

100   It was the penalty all tobacco chewers paid in that country, and he had been out before in two cold snaps. They had not been so cold as this, he knew, but by the spirit thermometer[7] at Sixty Mile he knew they had been registered at fifty below and at fifty-five.

He held on through the level stretch of woods for several miles, crossed a wide flat, and dropped down a bank to the frozen bed of a small stream. This was Henderson Creek, and he knew he was ten miles from the forks. He looked at his watch. It was ten o' clock. He was making four miles an hour, and he calculated that he would arrive at the forks at half past twelve. He decided to celebrate that event by

110   eating his lunch there.

The dog dropped in again at his heels, with a tail drooping discouragement, as the man swung along the creek bed. The furrow of the old sled trail was plainly visible, but a dozen inches of snow covered the marks of the last runners. In a month no man had come up or down that silent creek. The man held steadily on. He was not much given to thinking, and just then particularly, he had nothing to think about save that he would eat lunch at the forks and that at six o'clock he would be in camp with the boys. There was nobody to talk to; and, had there been, speech would have been impossible because of

120   the ice muzzle on his mouth. So he continued monotonously to chew tobacco and to increase the length of his amber beard.

Once in a while the thought reiterated[8] itself that it was very cold and that he had never experienced such cold. As he walked along he rubbed his cheekbones and nose with the back of his mittened hand. He did this automatically, now and again changing hands. But rub as he would, the instant he stopped his cheekbones went numb, and the following instant the end of his nose went numb. He was sure to frost his cheeks; he knew that, and experienced a pang of regret that he had

---

[6] **appendage:** something attached to another object.

[7] **spirit thermometer:** alcohol thermometer. In places where the temperature often drops below the freezing point of mercury, alcohol is used in thermometers.

[8] **reiterated:** repeated.

WHEN STUDENTS STRUGGLE...

Some students may have difficulty visualizing the extremely vivid descriptions because of the density of the prose. Encourage them to focus on familiar, concrete nouns, verbs, and modifiers in the description, such as *ice, beard, exhaled, shatter,* and *brittle,* rather than less familiar ones, such as *appendage* or *expelled.*

ASK STUDENTS to imagine that the scene is part of a movie. Have them use details in the text to discuss what the scene would look like, what the man and the dog would look like, and what actions the man and the dog would be performing.

not devised a nose strap of the sort Bud wore in the cold snaps. Such
130 a strap passed across the cheeks, as well, and saved them. But it didn't
matter much, after all. What were frosted cheeks? A bit painful, that
was all; they were never serious.

Empty as the man's mind was of thought, he was keenly
observant, and he noticed the changes in the creek, the curves and
bends and timber jams, and always he sharply noted where he placed
his feet. Once, coming around a bend, he shied abruptly, like a startled
horse, curved away from the place where he had been walking, and
retreated several paces back along the trail. The creek, he knew, was
frozen clear to the bottom—no creek could contain water in that
140 arctic winter—but he knew also that there were springs that bubbled
out from the hillsides and ran along under the snow and on top of
the ice of the creek. He knew that the coldest snaps never froze these
springs, and he knew likewise their danger. They were traps. They
hid pools of water under the snow that might be three inches deep, or
three feet. Sometimes a skin of ice half an inch thick covered them,
and in turn was covered by the snow. Sometimes there were alternate
layers of water and ice skin, so that when one broke through he kept on
breaking through for a while, sometimes wetting himself to the waist.

That was why he had shied in such panic. He had felt the give
150 under his feet and heard the crackle of a snow-hidden ice skin. And
to get his feet wet in such a temperature meant trouble and danger. At
the very least it meant delay, for he would be forced to stop and build
a fire, and under its protection to bare his feet while he dried his socks
and moccasins. He stood and studied the creek bed and its banks,
and decided that the flow of water came from the right. He reflected
awhile, rubbing his nose and cheeks, then skirted to the left, stepping
gingerly and testing the footing for each step. Once clear of the danger,
he took a fresh chew of tobacco and swung along at his four-mile gait.

In the course of the next two hours he came upon several similar
160 traps. Usually the snow above the hidden pools had a sunken, candied
appearance that advertised the danger. Once again, however, he had
a close call; and once, suspecting danger, he compelled the dog to go
on in front. The dog did not want to go. It hung back until the man
shoved it forward, and then it went quickly across the white, unbroken
surface. Suddenly it broke through, floundered to one side, and got
away to firmer footing. It had wet its forefeet and legs, and almost
immediately the water that clung to it turned to ice. It made quick
efforts to lick the ice off its legs, then dropped down in the snow and
began to bite out the ice that formed between the toes. This was a
170 matter of instinct. To permit the ice to remain would mean sore feet.
It did not know this. It merely obeyed the mysterious prompting that
arose from the deep crypts[9] of its being. But the man knew, having
achieved a judgment on the subject, and he removed the mitten from

---
[9] **crypts:** hidden recesses.

To Build a Fire **335**

TEACH

CLOSE READ

Analyze Structure: Realism and Naturalism

COMMON CORE RL 2, RL 5

(LINES 133–148)

Tell students that in a realistic story, characters are not one-dimensional, but complex like individuals in real life.

H ASK STUDENTS what traits the man shows in these lines that make his character more complex and why. *(These lines show that while the man still foolishly underestimates the danger of the cold, he does have considerable outdoor skills and awareness of his environment. This suggests that he is not simply careless or ignorant about it, but rather, not properly adapted to it.)*

Analyze Structure: Realism and Naturalism

COMMON CORE RL 2, RL 5

(LINES 138–146)

Tell students that naturalism views life through a scientific lens and that in a naturalistic story, the reader often learns specialized knowledge about a scientific subject—in this case, the behavior of ice and water in the Arctic.

I CITE TEXT EVIDENCE Ask students to state pieces of specialized knowledge these lines include. *(Creeks don't contain water in the arctic winter; however, springs that never freeze flow from hillsides, forming dangerous traps of hidden pools below the snow and ice.)*

Strategies for Annotation

🖊 📖 **Annotate it!**

Analyze Structure: Realism and Naturalism

COMMON CORE RL 2, RL 5

Share these strategies for guided or independent analysis:

- Highlight in yellow realistic passages that attempt to use details to show life as it really is.
- Highlight in blue naturalistic passages that view life through a scientific lens.

Smart board

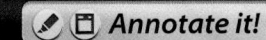

The dog did not want to go. It hung back until the man shoved it forward, and then it went quickly across the white, unbroken surface. Suddenly it broke through, floundered to one side, and got away to firmer footing. It had wet its forefeet and legs, and almost immediately the water that clung to it turned to ice. It made quick efforts to lick the ice of its legs, then dropped down in the snow and began to bite out the ice that had formed between the toes. This was a matter of instinct.

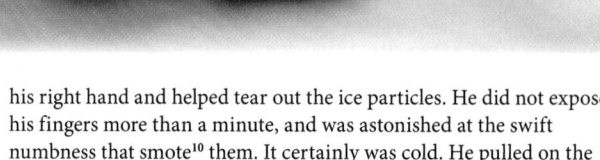

Determine Author's Purpose (LINES 185–193)

COMMON CORE RL 3

Tell students that an author's choice of which details to include is related to the **author's purpose,** or the author's reason for writing the work.

J **ASK STUDENTS** what purpose is reflected in London's decision to describe the man smacking his fingers against his leg. *(London wants to emphasize the increasing urgency of the man's situation as the man's exposed fingers become numb.)*

Analyze Structure: Realism and Naturalism

COMMON CORE RL 2, RL 5

(LINES 195–197)

Point out that London observes the man's physical changes in detail.

K **ASK STUDENTS** what the change from stinging to numbness in the man's hands means. *(The nerves in the man's fingers have died, so he is unable to feel his fingers.)* Then remind students that **tone** is the author's attitude toward the subject, conveyed by words and details. Ask students what kind of tone London's description of the man's fingers and toes conveys and why. *(London's detached, unemotional tone adds to the story's realism, reveals that the man's situation is worsening, and increases the reader's sense of horror at his situation.)*

his right hand and helped tear out the ice particles. He did not expose his fingers more than a minute, and was astonished at the swift numbness that smote[10] them. It certainly was cold. He pulled on the mitten hastily, and beat the hand savagely across his chest.

180 At twelve o'clock the day was at its brightest. Yet the sun was too far south on its winter journey to clear the horizon. The bulge of the earth intervened between it and Henderson Creek, where the man walked under a clear sky at noon and cast no shadow. At half past twelve, to the minute, he arrived at the forks of the creek. He was pleased at the speed he had made. If he kept it up, he would certainly be with the boys by six. He unbuttoned his jacket and shirt and drew forth his lunch. The action consumed no more than a quarter of a minute, yet in that brief moment the numbness laid hold of the exposed fingers. He did not put the mitten on, but instead struck the fingers a dozen sharp smashes against his leg. Then he sat down on a snow-covered log to eat. The sting that followed upon the striking
190 of his fingers against his leg ceased so quickly that he was startled. He had had no chance to take a bite of biscuit. He struck the fingers repeatedly and returned them to the mitten, baring the other hand for the purpose of eating. He tried to take a mouthful, but the ice muzzle prevented. He had forgotten to build a fire and thaw out. He chuckled at his foolishness, and as he chuckled he noted the numbness creeping into the exposed fingers. Also, he noted that the stinging which had first come to his toes when he sat down was already passing away.

[10] **smote:** powerfully struck.

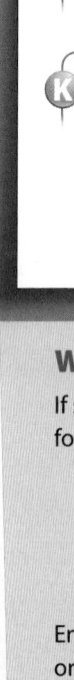

WHEN STUDENTS STRUGGLE . . .

If students have trouble absorbing the gist of the action amid all the details, ask the following questions:

• What danger is the man in? How serious is the danger?
• What is the man's attitude toward his danger? Is his attitude likely to help him or not?
• What do you expect will happen as he continues on his path?

Encourage students to make predictions and to find evidence in the text to confirm or disprove their predictions.

He wondered whether the toes were warm or numb. He moved them inside the moccasins and decided that they were numb.

He pulled the mitten on hurriedly and stood up. He was a bit frightened. He stamped up and down until the stinging returned into the feet. It certainly *was* cold, was his thought. That man from Sulphur Creek had spoken the truth when telling how cold it sometimes got in the country. And he had laughed at him at the time! That showed one must not be too sure of things. There was no mistake about it, it was cold. He strode up and down, stamping his feet and threshing his arms, until reassured by the returning warmth. Then he got out matches and proceeded to make a fire. From the undergrowth, where high water of the previous spring had lodged a supply of seasoned twigs, he got his firewood. Working carefully from a small beginning, he soon had a roaring fire, over which he thawed the ice from his face and in the protection of which he ate his biscuits. For the moment the cold of space was outwitted. The dog took satisfaction in the fire, stretching out close enough for warmth and far enough away to escape being singed.

When the man had finished, he filled his pipe and took his comfortable time over a smoke. Then he pulled on his mittens, settled the earflaps of his cap firmly about his ears, and took the creek trail up the left fork. The dog was disappointed and yearned back toward the fire. This man did not know cold. Possibly all the generations of his ancestry had been ignorant of cold, of real cold, of cold one hundred and seven degrees below freezing point. But the dog knew; all its ancestry knew, and it had inherited the knowledge. And it knew that it was not good to walk abroad in such fearful cold. It was the time to lie snug in a hole in the snow and wait for a curtain of cloud to be drawn across the face of outer space whence this cold came. On the other hand, there was no keen intimacy between the dog and the man. The one was the toil slave of the other, and the only caresses it had ever received were the caresses of the whiplash and of harsh and menacing throat sounds that threatened the whiplash. So the dog made no effort to communicate its apprehension to the man. It was not concerned in the welfare of the man; it was for its own sake that it yearned back toward the fire. But the man whistled, and spoke to it with the sound of whiplashes, and the dog swung in at the man's heels and followed after.

The man took a chew of tobacco and proceeded to start a new amber beard. Also, his moist breath quickly powdered with white his mustache, eyebrows, and lashes. There did not seem to be so many springs on the left fork of the Henderson, and for half an hour the man saw no signs of any. And then it happened. At a place where there were no signs, where the soft, unbroken snow seemed to advertise solidity beneath, the man broke through. It was not deep. He wet himself halfway to the knees before he floundered out to the firm crust.

To Build a Fire **337**

TEACH

CLOSE READ

Analyze Structure: Realism and Naturalism

COMMON CORE RL 1, RL 2, RL 5

(LINES 216–235)

Remind students that **naturalism** approaches life from a scientific perspective.

L CITE TEXT EVIDENCE Have students reread lines 216–235 and cite evidence of the naturalist's scientific perspective. *(London emphasizes that the dog's superior understanding of the danger of the cold is the result of its ancestry, saying "it had inherited the knowledge." This refers to natural selection. Dogs who adapted to the environment were more likely to survive, and these dogs passed this knowledge genetically to their descendents.)*

Analyze Structure: Realism and Naturalism

COMMON CORE RL 2

(LINES 240–243)

Explain to students that writers of **realism** choose words used in everyday speech and that convey an objective tone.

M ASK STUDENTS to reread lines 240–243. Ask students to explain why this event is important to the story's plot. Why does London choose to describe it using an objective tone instead of dramatic language? *(When the man breaks through the ice, the event intensifies the conflict between the man and the harsh environment. When London recounts the event in simple, unemotional language, he heightens the horror of the situation by conveying the indifference of nature to the man's existence.)*

Exit writing

Explain

SCAFFOLDING FOR ELL STUDENTS

Verb Tenses Review with students the difference between the past and past perfect verb tenses. The past tense in regular English verbs has an *-ed* ending. The past perfect is indicated by *had* before the past participle, as in *had walked, had given,* or *had shown.* In a story, the past tense shows that an action is happening at the time of the story. The past perfect indicates that the action occurred earlier.

Direct students to lines 202–203: "That man from Sulphur Creek had spoken the truth…." Tell them that the main character spoke to the man before the story opened. Encourage students to notice other sentences that use the past perfect tense and to interpret their meaning.

Analyze Structure: Realism and Naturalism

COMMON CORE RL 1, RL 2, RL 3

(LINES 259–287)

Remind students that the **plot** of a story is driven by a central **conflict**. Tell them that this conflict can be between a character and himself, a character and another character, or a character and an outside force.

 **ASK STUDENTS** to analyze the intensifying conflict in this story. With whom or what is the main character in conflict? Who appears to be winning? Have students cite evidence from the text to support their analyses. *(The conflict is between the man and an outside force, the extreme cold. In these lines, the man is battling the cold by trying to build a fire. The cold seems to be winning because London writes, "the skin of all his body chilled as it lost its blood" [lines 286-287].)*

CRITICAL VOCABULARY

imperative: The man realizes that it is crucial to build a fire and dry his footwear.

ASK STUDENTS to state additional things that are imperative for the man to do in the story. *(It is imperative for him to reach camp. It is imperative that he stay awake.)*

extremity: The condition of the man's hands and feet is of the utmost importance for his survival.

ASK STUDENTS to restate the man's situation at this point in the story, using the word **extremity** or **extremities**. *(It is imperative that the man dry his extremities.)*

He was angry, and cursed his luck aloud. He had hoped to get into camp with the boys at six o'clock, and this would delay him an hour, for he would have to build a fire and dry out his footgear. This was **imperative** at that low temperature—he knew that much; and he turned aside to the bank, which he climbed. On top, tangled in the underbrush about the trunks of several small spruce trees, was a high-
250 water deposit of dry firewood—sticks and twigs, principally, but also larger portions of seasoned branches and fine, dry, last year's grasses. He threw down several large pieces on top of the snow. This served for a foundation and prevented the young flame from drowning itself in the snow it otherwise would melt. The flame he got by touching a match to a small shred of birch bark that he took from his pocket. This burned even more readily than paper. Placing it on the foundation, he fed the young flame with wisps of dry grass and with the tiniest dry twigs.

He worked slowly and carefully, keenly aware of his danger.
260 Gradually, as the flame grew stronger, he increased the size of the twigs with which he fed it. He squatted in the snow, pulling the twigs out from their entanglement in the brush and feeding directly to the flame. He knew there must be no failure. When it is seventy-five below zero, a man must not fail in his first attempt to build a fire—that is, if his feet are wet. If his feet are dry, and he fails, he can run along the trail for a half a mile and restore his circulation. But the circulation of wet and freezing feet cannot be restored by running when it is seventy-five below. No matter how fast he runs, the wet feet will freeze the harder.

270 All this the man knew. The old-timer on Sulphur Creek had told him about it the previous fall, and now he was appreciating the advice. Already all sensation had gone out of his feet. To build the fire, he had been forced to remove his mittens, and the fingers had quickly gone numb. His pace of four miles an hour had kept his heart pumping blood to the surface of his body and to all the **extremities**. But the instant he stopped, the action of the pump eased down. The cold of space smote the unprotected tip of the planet, and he, being on that unprotected tip, received the full force of the blow. The blood of his body recoiled before it. The blood was alive, like the dog, and like the
280 dog it wanted to hide away and cover itself up from the fearful cold. So long as he walked four miles an hour, he pumped that blood, willy-nilly,[11] to the surface; but now it ebbed away and sank down into the recesses of his body. The extremities were the first to feel its absence. His wet feet froze the faster, and his exposed fingers numbed the faster, though they had not yet begun to freeze. Nose and cheeks were already freezing, while the skin of all his body chilled as it lost its blood.

imperative
(ĭm-pĕr´ə-tĭv) *adj.* of great importance; essential.

extremity
(ĭk-strĕm´ĭ-tē) *n.* the outermost or farthest point or portion; the hand or foot.

---

[11] **willy-nilly:** without choice.

SCAFFOLDING FOR ELL STUDENTS

Multiple-Meaning Words Provide vocabulary support by pointing out that both vocabulary words on page 338 have multiple meanings. *Imperative* means "necessary," and it is also the name of a verb tense, the tense in which commands are given, such as, "Give me that!" or "Don't be late!"

Extremity in this story refers to the hands and feet. Tell students that the other meaning of *extremity* is "something extreme" or "the state of being extreme." Ask students to compose a sentence using this meaning to describe the situation of the man in the story. *(Possible answer: The man is unaware of the extremity of the danger he is in.)*

But he was safe. Toes and nose and cheeks would be only touched by the frost, for the fire was beginning to burn with strength. He was feeding it twigs the size of his finger. In another minute he would be able to feed it with branches the size of his wrist, and then he could remove his wet footgear, and, while it dried, he could keep his naked feet warm by the fire, rubbing them at first, of course, with snow. The fire was a success. He was safe. He remembered the advice of the old-timer on Sulphur Creek, and smiled. The old-timer had been very serious in laying down the law that no man must travel alone in the Klondike after fifty below. Well, here he was; he had had the accident; he was alone; and he had saved himself. Those old-timers were rather womanish, some of them, he thought. All a man had to do was to keep his head and he was all right. Any man who was a man could travel alone. But it was surprising, the rapidity with which his cheeks and nose were freezing. And he had not thought his fingers could go lifeless in so short a time. Lifeless they were, for he could scarcely make them move together to grip a twig, and they seemed remote from his body and from him. When he touched a twig, he had to look and see whether or not he had hold of it. The wires were pretty well down between him and his finger ends.

All of which counted for little. There was the fire, snapping and crackling and promising life with every dancing flame. He started to untie his moccasins. They were coated with ice; the thick German socks were like sheaths of iron halfway to the knees; and the moccasin strings were like rods of steel all twisted and knotted as by some conflagration.[12] For a moment he tugged with his numb fingers, then, realizing the folly of it, he drew his sheath knife.

But before he could cut the strings it happened. It was his own fault, or, rather, his mistake. He should not have built the fire under the spruce tree. He should have built it in the open. But it had been easier to pull the twigs from the bush and drop them directly on the fire. Now the tree under which he had done this carried a weight of snow on its boughs. No wind had blown for weeks, and each bough was fully freighted. Each time he had pulled a twig he had communicated a slight agitation to the tree—an imperceptible agitation, so far as he was concerned, but an agitation sufficient to bring about the disaster. High up in the tree one bough capsized its load of snow. This fell on the boughs beneath, capsizing them. This process continued, spreading out and involving the whole tree. It grew like an avalanche, and it descended without warning upon the man and the fire, and the fire was blotted out! Where it had burned was a mantle of fresh and disordered snow.

The man was shocked. It was as though he had just heard his own sentence of death. For a moment he sat and stared at the spot where the fire had been. Then he grew very calm. Perhaps the old-timer on

---

[12] **conflagration:** large fire.

TEACH

CLOSE READ

Analyze Language: Irony (LINES 288–302)

COMMON CORE RL 1, RL 6

Tell students that as the man gets deeper into trouble the irony of his situation increases. The irony comes from the difference between what the man thinks and what the reader knows.

CITE TEXT EVIDENCE Ask students to find phrases and sentences that show an ironic difference between what the man thinks and what the reader suspects. (*The lines "The fire was a success. He was safe" [line 294] and "those old-timers were rather womanish…. Any man who was a man could travel alone" [lines 298-301] are ironic because the reader knows that the man is being overconfident and is actually in deep trouble.*)

Analyze Structure: Realism and Naturalism (LINES 315–329)

COMMON CORE RL 1, RL 2, RL 3

Tell students that **naturalism** is a style of writing the often focuses on the darker side of life and the struggle to survive.

ASK STUDENTS to explain how the plot twist in these lines exemplifies naturalism. (*The fire has been destroyed and so has the man's chance of survival. This turn in the plot emphasizes the grim view of life characteristic of naturalism.*)

CLOSE READ

Analyze Structure: Realism and Naturalism

COMMON CORE RL 3

(LINES 351–365)

Tell students that London gives the reader glimpses of the man's thoughts as well as his physical actions.

Q **ASK STUDENTS** to analyze how the inclusion of the man's thoughts affects the story. *(The details about what the man is thinking enhance the story's realism.)*

Analyze Structure: Realism and Naturalism

COMMON CORE RL 1, RL 2, RL 3

(LINES 366–376)

Remind students that in **naturalism,** authors often emphasize the grim or painful aspects of life's struggles, including the struggle between man and nature.

R **CITE TEXT EVIDENCE** Have students cite words, phrases, or sentences in this passage that present a naturalistically grim view of the man's struggle with nature. *("a stinging ache that was excruciating"; "The exposed fingers were quickly going numb again"; "driven the life out of his fingers"; "The dead fingers could neither touch nor clutch.")*

Sulphur Creek was right. If he had only had a trail mate, he would have been in no danger now. The trail mate could have built the fire. Well, it was up to him to build the fire over again, and this second time there must be no failure. Even if he succeeded, he would most likely lose some toes. His feet must be badly frozen by now, and there would be some time before the second fire was ready.

340   Such were his thoughts, but he did not sit and think them. He was busy all the time they were passing through his mind. He made a new foundation for a fire, this time in the open, where no treacherous tree could blot it out. Next he gathered dry grasses and tiny twigs from the high-water flotsam.[13] He could not bring his fingers together to pull them out, but he was able to gather them by the handful. In this way he got many rotten twigs and bits of green moss that were undesirable, but it was the best he could do. He worked methodically, even collecting an armful of the larger branches to be used later when the fire gathered strength. And all the while the dog sat and watched him, a certain yearning wistfulness in its eyes, for it looked upon him as the
350 fire provider, and the fire was slow in coming.

    When all was ready, the man reached in his pocket for a second piece of birch bark. He knew the bark was there, and, though he could not feel it with his fingers, he could hear its crisp rustling as he fumbled for it. Try as he would, he could not clutch hold of it. And all the time, in his consciousness, was the knowledge that each instant his feet were freezing. This thought tended to put him in a panic, but he fought against it and kept calm. He pulled on his mittens with his teeth, and threshed his arms back and forth, beating his hands with all his might against his sides. He did this sitting down, and he stood
360 up to do it; and all the while the dog sat in the snow, its wolf brush of a tail curled around warmly over its forefeet, its sharp wolf ears pricked forward intently as it watched the man. And the man, as he beat and threshed with his arms and hands, felt a great surge of envy as he regarded the creature that was warm and secure in its natural covering.

    After a time he was aware of the first faraway signals of sensation in his beaten fingers. The faint tingling grew stronger till it evolved into a stinging ache that was excruciating, but which the man hailed with satisfaction. He stripped the mitten from his right hand and
370 fetched forth the birch bark. The exposed fingers were quickly going numb again. Next he brought out his bunch of sulphur matches. But the tremendous cold had already driven the life out of his fingers. In his effort to separate one match from the others, the whole bunch fell in the snow. He tried to pick it out of the snow, but failed. The dead fingers could neither touch nor clutch. He was very careful. He drove the thought of his freezing feet, and nose, and cheeks, out of his mind,

---

[13]**high-water flotsam:** branches and debris washed ashore by a stream or river during the warm months, when the water is high.

340   Collection 5

SCAFFOLDING FOR ELL STUDENTS

Conversational English Patterns Point out the word *bunch* in line 371. Tell students that *bunch* is an informal word that people often use to express an approximate quantity rather than an exact number. The word *bunch* is often followed by *of,* as in *a bunch of grapes* or *a bunch of ideas.* Similar expressions include *a few,* *a handful,* and *a lot.*

As they read and as they listen to English, suggest that students watch out for a *bunch* and other expressions that convey an inexact number.

Image Credits: ©Corbis

devoting his whole soul to the matches. He watched, using the sense of vision in place of that of touch, and when he saw his fingers on each side of the bunch, he closed them—that is, he willed to close them, for the wires were down, and the fingers did not obey. He pulled the mitten on the right hand, and beat it fiercely against his knee. Then, with both mittened hands, he scooped the bunch of matches, along with much snow, into his lap. Yet he was no better off.

After some manipulation he managed to get the bunch between the heels of his mittened hands. In this fashion he carried it to his mouth. The ice crackled and snapped when by a violent effort he opened his mouth. He drew the lower jaw in, curled the upper lip out of the way, and scraped the bunch with his upper teeth in order to separate a match. He succeeded in getting one, which he dropped on his lap. He was no better off. He could not pick it up. Then he devised a way. He picked it up in his teeth and scratched it on his leg. Twenty times he scratched before he succeeded in lighting it. As it flamed he held it with his teeth to the birch bark. But the burning brimstone went up his nostrils and into his lungs, causing him to cough spasmodically.[14] The match fell into the snow and went out.

The old-timer on Sulphur Creek was right, he thought in the moment of controlled despair that ensued: After fifty below, a man should travel with a partner. He beat his hands, but failed in exciting

---

[14] **spasmodically:** in a sudden, violent manner; fitfully.

CLOSE READ

Analyze Language: Mood (LINES 377–395)

COMMON CORE · RL 1, RL 3

Tell students that the **mood** of a work of fiction is the feeling it creates. The writer's use of imagery, figurative language, sound, and details all contribute to establishing mood.

S CITE TEXT EVIDENCE Have students describe the mood conveyed in lines 377–395 and cite the words and phrases that convey it. *(The mood is one of desperation and despair conveyed by phrases and images such as "he willed to close them, for the wires were down, and the fingers did not obey" [lines 379–380]; "Yet he was no better off" [line 383]; "by a violent effort he opened his mouth" [lines 386–387]; "He was no better off. He could not pick it up" [line 390]; "burning brimstone" [line 393]; "cough spasmodically" [lines 394–395]; and "The match fell into the snow and went out" [line 395].)*

WHEN STUDENTS STRUGGLE...

Point out that the expression "the wires were down" is an example of **metaphor**. Review that a metaphor compares two things without a connecting word such as *like* or *as*.

ASK STUDENTS whether there are any wires in the scene. *(no)* Why, then, does the author describe wires? *(He is making a figurative comparison between something in the scene and wires.)* What kind of wires is he talking about? *(electrical wires)* When the wires are down, what is the result? *(Messages can't be sent.)* What is London comparing to wires? *(the nerves in the human body that send messages from the brain to the muscles)* If the man's nerve-wires are not working, what is the result? *(He can't move his fingers.)*

TEACH

Analyze Structure: Realism and Naturalism

COMMON CORE **RL 2, RL 5**

(LINE 406–411)

Tell students that in many works of naturalism, the author seeks to shock or appall the reader.

 CITE TEXT EVIDENCE Ask students what circumstance in this passage seems intended to shock or appall the reader. *(The man has set his own hands on fire.)* Ask students to state words or phrases that convey the terrible nature of the man's ordeal. *("His flesh was burning. He could smell it. . . . And still he endured it"; "his own burning hands were in the way, absorbing most of the flame.")*

Analyze Author's Choices

COMMON CORE **RL 3, RL 5**

(LINES 427–446)

Point out that in these lines the narrator moves from the man's to the dog's point of view.

U **ASK STUDENTS** where the shift in point of view occurs and to analyze the impact of this choice. *(The reader is shocked at the man's decision to kill the dog. When the narrator shifts to the dog's point of view in line 437, it emphasizes the dog's keen awareness and survival instinct.)*

---

any sensation. Suddenly he bared both hands, removing the mittens
400 with his teeth. He caught the whole bunch between the heels of his
hands. His arm muscles, not being frozen, enabled him to press the
hand heels tightly against the matches. Then he scratched the bunch
along his leg. It flared into flame, seventy sulphur matches at once!
There was no wind to blow them out. He kept his head to one side to
escape the strangling fumes, and held the blazing bunch to the birch
bark. As he so held it, he became aware of sensation in his hand. His
flesh was burning. He could smell it. Deep down below the surface he
could feel it. The sensation developed into pain that grew acute. And
still he endured it, holding the flame of matches clumsily to the bark
410 that would not light readily because his own burning hands were in
the way, absorbing most of the flame.

　　At last, when he could endure no more, he jerked his hands apart.
The blazing matches fell sizzling into the snow, but the birch bark was
alight. He began laying dry grass and the tiniest twigs on the flame.
He could not pick and choose, for he had to lift the fuel between the
heels of his hands. Small pieces of rotten wood and green moss clung
to the twigs, and he bit them off as well as he could with his teeth.
He cherished the flame carefully and awkwardly. It meant life, and it
must not perish. The withdrawal of blood from the surface of his body
420 now made him begin to shiver, and he grew more awkward. A large
piece of green moss fell squarely on the little fire. He tried to poke it
out with his fingers, but his shivering frame made him poke too far,
and he disrupted the nucleus of the little fire, the burning grasses and
tiny twigs separating and scattering. He tried to poke them together
again, but in spite of the tenseness of the effort, his shivering got away
with him, and the twigs were hopelessly scattered. Each twig gushed a
puff of smoke and went out. The fire provider had failed. As he looked
apathetically[15] about him, his eyes chanced on the dog, sitting across
the ruins of the fire from him, in the snow, making restless, hunching
430 movements, slightly lifting one forefoot and then the other, shifting its
weight back and forth on them with wistful eagerness.

　　The sight of the dog put a wild idea into his head. He remembered
the tale of the man, caught in a blizzard, who killed a steer and crawled
inside the carcass, and so was saved. He would kill the dog and bury
his hands in the warm body until the numbness went out of them.
Then he could build another fire. He spoke to the dog, calling it to
him; but in his voice was a strange note of fear that frightened the
animal, who had never known the man to speak in such a way before.
Something was the matter, and its suspicious nature sensed danger—it
440 knew not what danger, but somewhere, somehow, in its brain arose
an apprehension of the man. It flattened its ears down at the sound of
the man's voice, and its restless, hunching movements and the liftings
and shiftings of its forefeet became more pronounced; but it would not

---

[15] **apathetically:** with little interest or concern; indifferently.

come to the man. He got on his hands and knees and crawled toward the dog. This unusual posture again excited suspicion, and the animal sidled mincingly[16] away.

The man sat up in the snow for a moment and struggled for calmness. Then he pulled on his mittens, by means of his teeth, and got up on his feet. He glanced down at first in order to assure himself
450 that he was really standing up, for the absence of sensation in his feet left him unrelated to the earth. His erect position in itself started to drive the webs of suspicion from the dog's mind; and when he spoke peremptorily,[17] with the sound of whiplashes in his voice, the dog rendered its customary allegiance and came to him. As it came within reaching distance, the man lost his control. His arms flashed out to the dog, and he experienced genuine surprise when he discovered that his hands could not clutch, that there was neither bend nor feeling in the fingers. He had forgotten for the moment that they were frozen and that they were freezing more and more. All this happened quickly, and
460 before the animal could get away, he encircled its body with his arms. He sat down in the snow, and in this fashion held the dog, while it snarled and whined and struggled.

But it was all he could do, hold its body encircled in his arms and sit there. He realized that he could not kill the dog. There was no way to do it. With his helpless hands he could neither draw nor hold his sheath knife nor throttle the animal. He released it, and it plunged wildly away, its tail between its legs and still snarling. It halted forty feet away and surveyed him curiously, with ears sharply pricked forward. The man looked down at his hands in order to locate them,
470 and found them hanging on the ends of his arms. It struck him as curious that one should have to use his eyes in order to find out where his hands were. He began threshing his arms back and forth, beating the mittened hands against his sides. He did this for five minutes, violently, and his heart pumped enough blood up to the surface to put a stop to his shivering. But no sensation was aroused in his hands. He had an impression that they hung like weights on the ends of his arms, but when he tried to run the impression down, he could not find it.

A certain fear of death, dull and oppressive, came to him. This fear quickly became poignant[18] as he realized that it was no longer a
480 mere matter of freezing his fingers and toes, or of losing his hands and feet, but that it was a matter of life and death, with the chances against him. This threw him into a panic, and he turned and ran up the creek bed along the old, dim trail. The dog joined in behind and kept up with him. He ran blindly, without intention, in fear such as he had never known in his life. Slowly, as he plowed and floundered through the snow, he began to see things again—the banks of the creek, the

———

[16] **sidled mincingly:** moved sideways with small steps.

[17] **peremptorily:** in a commanding way.

[18] **poignant:** painfully affecting feelings; touching.

CLOSE READ

Analyze Structure: Realism and Naturalism

COMMON CORE RL 2, RL 5

(LINE 464)

Remind students that naturalism often focuses on the baser aspects of human nature, showing people at the mercy of their instincts.

Ⓥ ASK STUDENTS to interpret line 464. Is the narrator saying that the man is unwilling to kill his loyal companion? What does this suggest about the author's purpose at this point in the story? *(No, the man is physically unable to kill the dog because his hands are too damaged. His desire to kill his only companion in order to save his own life suggests that the author wants to show that the man is no different from any animal and will instinctively kill to survive.)*

TO CHALLENGE STUDENTS...

Have students research the symptoms of mild, moderate, and severe hypothermia and analyze "To Build A Fire" to identify when in the story the main character exhibits each set of symptoms. Have students evaluate whether or not London depicts the progression of the condition accurately. When they have finished their research, have students create presentations of their findings to be delivered to the class. Remind students to include details from the text that illustrate the character's progression through the stages of hypothermia.

TEACH

CLOSE READ

Analyze Structure: Realism and Naturalism

COMMON CORE RL 2, RL 5

(LINES 502–504)

Tell students that naturalist writers often choose **mythic** situations, retelling ancient stories from a naturalist perspective.

 ASK STUDENTS to identify the reference to mythology in these lines. *(In lines 502–504, the man compares himself to Mercury.)* Point out to students that Mercury was a Roman god who was responsible for guiding souls to the underworld. What is the effect of this reference to mythology? *(The reference might be foreshadowing the man's death. It is also ironic because the man compares himself to a god when he is more vulnerable than ever.)*

Analyze Structure: Plot

COMMON CORE RL 3, RL 5

(LINES 528–530)

Tell students that although the man has fallen before, this particular fall is a crucial turning point in the plot. Remind them that the **climax** of a story is the point at which the conflict intensifies to its highest pitch and after which the story begins to resolve itself.

X **ASK STUDENTS** why this event is the climax of the story. Have students support their interpretations with evidence from the text. *(Students should argue that this is the climax because the man is completely exhausted; he can no longer get up and must surely die. "It was his last panic" suggests this is the end of his struggle.)*

old timber jams, the leafless aspens, and the sky. The running made him feel better. He did not shiver. Maybe, if he ran on, his feet would thaw out; and, anyway, if he ran far enough, he would reach the camp
490 and the boys. Without doubt he would lose some fingers and toes and some of his face; but the boys would take care of him, and save the rest of him when he got there. And, at the same time, there was another thought in his mind that said he would never get to the camp and the boys; that it was too many miles away, that the freezing had too great a start on him, and that he would soon be stiff and dead. This thought he kept in the background and refused to consider. Sometimes it pushed itself forward and demanded to be heard, but he thrust it back and strove to think of other things.

500   It struck him as curious that he could run at all on feet so frozen that he could not feel them when they struck the earth and took the weight of his body. He seemed to himself to skim along above the surface, and to have no connection with the earth. Somewhere he had once seen a winged Mercury,[19] and he wondered if Mercury felt as he felt when skimming over the earth.

His theory of running until he reached camp and the boys had one flaw in it: He lacked the endurance. Several times he stumbled, and finally he tottered, crumpled up, and fell. When he tried to rise, he failed. He must sit and rest, he decided, and next time he would merely walk and keep on going. As he sat and regained his breath, he noted
510 that he was feeling quite warm and comfortable. He was not shivering, and it even seemed that a warm glow had come to his chest and trunk. And yet, when he touched his nose or cheeks, there was no sensation. Running would not thaw them out. Nor would it thaw out his hands and feet. Then the thought came to him that the frozen portions of his body must be extending. He tried to keep this thought down, to forget it, to think of something else; he was aware of the panicky feeling that it caused, and he was afraid of the panic. But the thought asserted itself, and persisted, until it produced a vision of his body totally frozen. This was too much, and he made another wild run along the
520 trail. Once he slowed down to a walk, but the thought of the freezing extending itself made him run again.

And all the time the dog ran with him, at his heels. When he fell down a second time, it curled its tail over its forefeet and sat in front of him, facing him, curiously eager and intent. The warmth and security of the animal angered him, and he cursed it till it flattened down its ears appeasingly. This time the shivering came more quickly upon the man. He was losing in this battle with the frost. It was creeping into his body from all sides. The thought of it drove him on, but he ran no more than a hundred feet when he staggered and pitched headlong. It
530 was his last panic. When he had recovered his breath and control, he

---

[19] **Mercury:** in Roman mythology, messenger of the gods, who is depicted wearing winged sandals and a winged hat.

APPLYING ACADEMIC VOCABULARY

somewhat	ambiguous

As you discuss the story, incorporate the following Collection 5 academic vocabulary words: *somewhat* and *ambiguous*. As students discuss realistic and naturalistic aspects of the story, ask students to consider how the distinction between realism and naturalism is **somewhat ambiguous.** Have students find evidence in the text of this ambiguity.

sat up and entertained in his mind the conception of meeting death with dignity. However, the conception did not come to him in such terms. His idea of it was that he had been making a fool of himself, running around like a chicken with its head cut off—such was the simile that occurred to him. Well, he was bound to freeze anyway, and he might as well take it decently. With this newfound peace of mind came the first glimmerings of drowsiness. A good idea, he thought, to sleep off to death. It was like taking an anesthetic.[20] Freezing was not so bad as people thought. There were lots worse ways to die.

540   He pictured the boys finding his body next day. Suddenly he found himself with them, coming along the trail and looking for himself. And, still with them, he came around a turn in the trail and found himself lying in the snow. He did not belong with himself anymore, for even then he was out of himself, standing with the boys and looking at himself in the snow. It certainly was cold, was his thought. When he got back to the States, he could tell the folks what real cold was. He drifted on from this to a vision of the old-timer on Sulphur Creek. He could see him quite clearly, warm and comfortable, and smoking a pipe.

550   "You were right, old hoss; you were right," the man mumbled to the old-timer of Sulphur Creek.

---

[20] **anesthetic:** medication that causes loss of the sensation of pain.

To Build a Fire **345**

CLOSE READ

Analyze Structure: Plot

COMMON CORE RL 5, RL 2

(LINES 535–551)

Remind students that the falling action, or **resolution,** occurs after the climax to reveal the final outcome of events.

(Y) ASK STUDENTS to analyze these lines and decide if the plot is resolving itself. How do they know? (*The plot is moving toward resolution. The man is coming to terms with his approaching death, and the reader begins to realize it. The main character has undergone a change of heart: he now acknowledges in lines 550–551 that the old-timer was right. Unfortunately, this knowledge comes too late to save him.*)

WHEN STUDENTS STRUGGLE...

If students find it difficult to interpret the man's mental state, tell them that sometimes an author uses signal words and phrases to show that a passage reflects a character's thoughts or feelings. For example, "His idea of it was..." (line 533) signals that the rest of the sentence will state the man's idea.

ASK STUDENTS to identify other such signal words in lines 540–549. ("He pictured" [line 540]; "He did not belong with himself anymore...he was out of himself [lines 543–544]; "He drifted on from this to a vision" [line 547])

Analyze Structure: Realism and Naturalism

COMMON CORE RL 2, RL 3, RL 5

(LINES 552–566)

Tell students that a **foil** is a character who presents a contrast to the main character in order to emphasize the main character's traits.

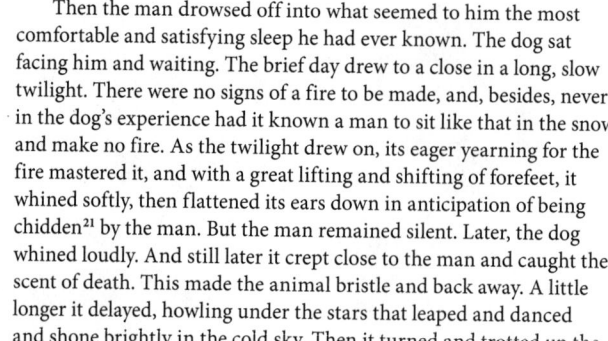 **ASK STUDENTS** to explain how the dog acts as a foil in this story. *(The story contrasts the dog's instinctive knowledge of its native environment with the man's ignorance and arrogance.)* What point is made at the end of the story when the dog trots away? *(Nature is indifferent to the life or death of an individual.)* How does the dog's reaction enhance the story's naturalism? *(It presents nature as a cruel or indifferent force against which humans struggle in vain.)*

COLLABORATIVE DISCUSSION Have students form pairs to discuss the importance of setting. Encourage them to consider setting in relation to the story's conflict. Have them share their ideas with the class as a whole. Accept all reasonable responses.

ASK STUDENTS to share any questions they generated in the course of reading and discussing the selection.

Then the man drowsed off into what seemed to him the most comfortable and satisfying sleep he had ever known. The dog sat facing him and waiting. The brief day drew to a close in a long, slow twilight. There were no signs of a fire to be made, and, besides, never in the dog's experience had it known a man to sit like that in the snow and make no fire. As the twilight drew on, its eager yearning for the fire mastered it, and with a great lifting and shifting of forefeet, it whined softly, then flattened its ears down in anticipation of being chidden[21] by the man. But the man remained silent. Later, the dog whined loudly. And still later it crept close to the man and caught the scent of death. This made the animal bristle and back away. A little longer it delayed, howling under the stars that leaped and danced and shone brightly in the cold sky. Then it turned and trotted up the trail in the direction of the camp it knew, where were the other food providers and fire providers.

560

---

[21] **chidden:** scolded.

COLLABORATIVE DISCUSSION Why is the setting important in this story? With a partner, discuss how the setting shapes the story's events and how the author creates a clear sense of the setting. Cite specific textual evidence to support your ideas.

TO CHALLENGE STUDENTS . . .

Write from Another Point of View Invite students to rewrite a passage in the story from the first-person point of view of the dog. It may be a passage that already shows the dog's perspective. In that case, students will expand on the glimpse London gives into the dog's mind. Or, it may be a passage that does not currently include the dog's perspective.

Have students rewrite at least one paragraph. Then ask volunteers to read their work aloud. Lead a discussion of how the story would be different if it had been told entirely from the dog's point of view.

Analyze Structure: Realism and Naturalism

Jack London's "To Build a Fire" can be classified as a work of both realism and naturalism. **Realism** is a style of writing in which the author attempts to show life as it really is. It maintains an objective, detached view of characters and events, allowing readers to draw their own conclusions. **Naturalism** uses many of the same techniques as realism but views human life through the lens of scientific ideas such as Darwin's theory of natural selection. The chart can help you identify specific features of realism and naturalism in the story.

Realism	Naturalism
Realist writers include many specific details about daily life. What details in "To Build a Fire" create a vivid picture of life in the Yukon wilderness?	Naturalist writers observe life and often present the darker side of things. Consider whether this is true in "To Build a Fire."
Stories are set in real places that the authors know well.	Naturalist stories also develop real settings, often in even greater detail than realist works.
Realism focuses on individuals, especially ordinary people. Characters are complex. Their internal thoughts are often explored, as well as their actions. Dialect may be used to portray how people speak in specific places, as when London includes the Chinook term *cheechako*.	Naturalism uses ordinary people as characters. Characters may face staggering odds and be controlled by a larger force, such as their environment or chance. What odds does the man face in London's story?
Word choice is natural, everyday speech with an objective, detached tone. The narrator observes the story but does not comment on it or attach any particular emotion to it. How does London convey such a tone in his story?	Word choice is natural, everyday speech, and the overall tone is often grim. Think about how "To Build a Fire" would be different if London had used more academic or poetic language.

Jack London wrote often about life in the West and Northwest, capturing life in gritty detail. In doing so, he frequently tackled themes involving the survival of the fittest and the power of nature over human life. How do these qualities apply to "To Build a Fire"? As you analyze the story, think about the details you identified as you read, the setting of the story, and the key themes London develops.

CLOSE READ

Analyze Structure: Realism and Naturalism

To help students distinguish realism and naturalism, point out that the two styles are not opposites; they are related. Tell students that realism is a 19th-century literary movement that examines the effect of natural and social forces on the individual. Naturalism is an offshoot of realism that shows people at the mercy of the environment and their own instincts.

Discuss with students the fact that scientific ideas such as Darwin's theory of natural selection are reflected in the story's plot, details, and detached, objective tone. For instance, the fact that the dog, who is native to the environment, survives while the man does not reflects Darwin's idea that species evolve over time to adapt to a given environment.

Strategies for Annotation 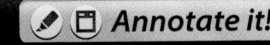 *Annotate it!*

Analyze Structure: Realism and Naturalism

Share these strategies for guided or independent analysis:

- Choose a passage of about six lines from the story.
- Highlight in yellow words and phrases that are realistic.
- Highlight in blue words and phrases that are naturalistic.

Without doubt he would lose some fingers and toes and some of his face; but the boys would take care of him, and save the rest of him when he got there. And, at the same time, there was another thought in his mind that said he would never get to the camp and the boys; that it was too many miles away, that the freezing had too great a start on him, and that he would soon be stiff and dead.

TEACH

CLOSE READ

Analyzing the Text COMMON CORE RL 2, RL 3, RL 5

Possible answers:

1. *When the old-timer warned the man about the cold, the man at first had laughed. Later, he realized the truth of the old-timer's words and is abashed (lines 202–205). But later, too, he mocks the old-timer inwardly (lines 294–301). In lines 332–334, the man is humbler in thinking that the old-timer was right. Finally, in lines 547–551, he imagines confessing his error to the old-timer. The man realizes he has been foolish but sees his mistakes too late.*

2. *The man lacks foresight and experience. He thoughtlessly assumes that he will reach his destination without difficulty. The dog, though not guided by intellect, has instinct and experience that enable him to understand that it is dangerously cold. The dog is better adapted to this environment than the man.*

3. *Descriptions of the setting contribute to the story's realism by showing precisely how harsh and potentially dangerous the landscape is. The Yukon is "hidden under three feet of ice" topped with "as many feet of snow" (lines 14–16). Sunless skies stretch above it. The path the man will follow is so thin that it is barely visible in the bleak landscape.*

4. *The dog is an example of a creature that survives because it is adapted to its environment. London contrasts the dog's concern that the cold is unsafe with the man's reckless disregard of the cold by describing the dog's reaction from the dog's point of view.*

5. *Examples include the fact that the old-timer has survived a long time by understanding, rather than ignoring, the environment; the man's inability to keep a fire going and his subsequent death; and the survival of the dog. The story supports the idea that only the fittest, or best adapted, survive.*

6. *London's depiction of those who do survive suggests that the man was doomed from the start by his own character, rather than by an outside force.*

7. *The story's plot is based on a conflict between the man and the power of nature. The struggle to survive is the conflict in the story that the plot resolves with the man's death and the dog's survival.*

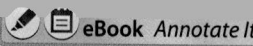 **eBook** *Annotate It!*

Analyzing the Text COMMON CORE RL 2, RL 3, RL 5, W 3, W 5

Cite Text Evidence   Support your responses with evidence from the selection.

1. **Draw Conclusions** Throughout the story, the man remembers "the old-timer on Sulphur Creek" and his advice. Find examples and note the man's response at each point in the story when he remembers the old-timer's advice. What conclusions can you draw about the man's character based on these thoughts?

2. **Compare** Reread lines 27–44 and lines 72–89. How do the dog and the man differ in their understanding of the cold? Which of them seems better adapted to this setting?

3. **Cite Evidence** Cite details from the first two paragraphs of the story that support the idea that it is a work of realism. How do these details contribute to the story's realism?

4. **Draw Conclusions** What purpose does the dog serve in this story? How do London's descriptions of the dog reveal its function in the story?

5. **Analyze** Works of naturalism often address the theme of survival of the fittest. Give examples that show how London's story develops this theme. What message does the story convey about the survival of the fittest?

6. **Evaluate** Naturalism also considers larger forces that control human lives, such as nature or fate. Does London think that the man ever had a chance in this harsh climate, or was he doomed from the start? Explain.

7. **Connect** Think about the two themes you considered in questions 5 and 6. How do these two themes—survival of the fittest and the power of nature or fate—interact and build on each other in this story?

PERFORMANCE TASK

Writing Activity: Narrative Realism and naturalism both feature detailed descriptions of specific places. Write a narrative that incorporates details to describe a place you know well.

1. Write three or four paragraphs about yourself or some other ordinary person experiencing an ordinary event in a specific place. Provide realistic details to develop the setting. Avoid expressing emotion in the text; allow readers to respond naturally to the details you provide.

2. Share your narrative with a partner. Give each other advice on how to improve the writing to be closer to the realist and/or naturalist style.

3. Revise your narrative based on your partner's feedback. Be sure to follow the conventions of standard English in your writing.

Assign this performance task.

PERFORMANCE TASK COMMON CORE W 3, W 5

Writing Activity Have students write their narratives independently. ELL students and struggling students may write with partners. Have all share written copies of their narratives for peer editing and feedback. Provide these questions for self- and peer-evaluation: Is the setting described with realistic details? Do the details appeal to the reader's senses so that he or she can fully imagine the place? Is the tone objective and unemotional?

Critical Vocabulary

intangible   apprehension   imperative   extremity

Practice and Apply Answer the questions to demonstrate your knowledge of the Critical Vocabulary words.

1. What are some **intangible** characteristics that make some athletes sucessful?

2. Why might you feel **apprehension** right before an important exam?

3. Why is it **imperative** to wear your seatbelt when in a car?

4. Why might it be hard for a country to defend the **extremities** of its territory?

Vocabulary Strategy: Etymology

The **etymology** of a word is its history. Most English words have evolved over time from older words, often from other languages. These older words are the modern word's roots. You can consult general reference materials, such as a good print or digital dictionary, to study a word's etymology. Examining a word's origins can help you clarify and remember the word's precise meaning and also see how it relates to other words with the same roots.

This word map for the Critical Vocabulary word *intangible* shows how to break down a word's meaning.

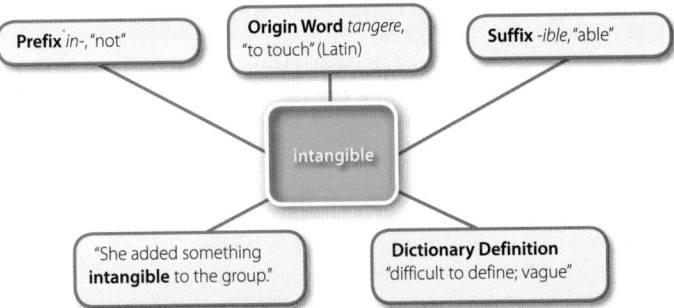

Practice and Apply Use a dictionary, print or digital, to create a word map like the one above for each of the remaining Critical Vocabulary words.

1. Write the word in the center of the chart.

2. Consult a dictionary to help break down the word, provide meanings for its parts, and choose the most appropriate meaning for its use in "To Build a Fire."

3. Write a sentence that uses the word in an appropriate way.

4. With a partner, discuss how the etymology of each word helps you understand the word's meaning. Think of other words with the same roots and discuss how the meanings are related.

PRACTICE & APPLY

Critical Vocabulary

Possible answers: **1.** *Intangible factors leading to athletic success include work ethic and enthusiasm.* **2.** *You might experience apprehension because you think that you don't know the material well enough.* **3.** *It is imperative to wear a seatbelt in a car in order to avoid serious injury or death if an accident occurs.* **4.** *It might be difficult for a country to defend its extremities because those areas are far from where the general population resides.*

Vocabulary Strategy

Possible answers:

1. **apprehension:** Prefix: *ad-*, "before"; Origin Word: *apprehendere*, "to seize," Latin; suffix: *-ion*, "state of being"; Dictionary Definition: dread; *The student had a feeling of apprehension before the math test because he hadn't studied.*

2. **imperative:** Prefix: N/A; Origin Word: *imperāre*, "to command," Latin; suffix: *-ive*, "tending toward"; Dictionary Definition: urgent, compulsory; *It is imperative that we find food and shelter before the storm hits.*

3. **extremity:** Prefix: *ex-*, "out of"; Origin Word: *extrēmus*, "extreme," Latin; suffix: *-ity*, "state of being"; Dictionary Definition: farthest distance or greatest degree; *There is a volcano at the island's southernmost extremity.*

Strategies for Annotation   ✎ 🖥 **Annotate it!**

Vocabulary Strategy

Have students locate the sentences containing *intangible, apprehension, imperative,* and *extremity* in the story. Encourage them to use their eBook annotation tools to do the following:

- Highlight the vocabulary word in yellow.
- Underline any words or phrases that give clues to the word's meaning.
- In a note, write a sentence using the word in a way that makes its meaning clear.

It was a clear day, <u>and yet there seemed an</u> intangible pall over the face of things, <u>a subtle gloom that made the day dark, and that was due to the absence of sun.</u>

> The reasons that make a work of literature great may be intangible rather than clearly definable.

Language and Style: Consistent Tone

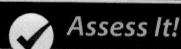 **COMMON CORE** RL 6, L 3a

After reviewing the definition of *tone* and the examples of London's realistic tone, make the point that London's tone is remarkably consistent throughout the story. It does not vary much from one paragraph to the next. You might have one or more volunteers read aloud short passages from different points in the story to verify this claim. Tell students that although a work does not always have to maintain one single tone throughout, the tone at any point should be consistent with the subject matter and mood.

Possible answer:

The driver turned her head for only a moment to observe the passing scene when, without warning, another car turned into the lane from the side street. A loud crash of metal against metal resounded; tires squealed as brakes slammed suddenly. From all directions, pedestrians lifted their heads toward the noise. Some began rushing toward the twisted assemblages of metal and plastic that the two vehicles had become.

✓ **Assess It!**

Online Selection Test
- Download an editable ExamView bank.
- Assign and manage this test online.

Language and Style: Consistent Tone

 **COMMON CORE** RL 4, L 3a

Tone is the author's attitude toward the subject or his or her audience. For example, the tone of a work might be serious, ironic, playful, or detached. Diction, or word choice, plays an important role in creating tone.

Read these lines from the story:

> But before he could cut the strings it happened. It was his own fault, or, rather, his mistake. He should not have built the fire under the spruce tree. He should have built it in the open. But it had been easier to pull the twigs from the bush and drop them directly on the fire.

The passage uses a detached, unemotional tone, even though this situation is very dangerous and a key turning point in the story. Notice that the sentences are generally short and objective. London uses realism in this scene to provide detail, but little commentary. The passage continues:

> Now the tree under which he had done this carried a weight of snow on its boughs. No wind had blown for weeks, and each bough was fully freighted. Each time he had pulled a twig he had communicated a slight agitation to the tree—an imperceptible agitation, so far as he was concerned, but an agitation sufficient to bring about the disaster.

These lines continue to focus on realistic detail, explaining the natural forces that are at work whether or not the man pays attention. In the next paragraph, the man reacts:

> The man was shocked. It was as though he had just heard his own sentence of death. For a moment he sat and stared at the spot where the fire had been. Then he grew very calm. Perhaps the old-timer on Sulphur Creek was right. If he had only had a trail mate, he would have been in no danger now. The trail mate could have built the fire.

Consider the effect if London had instead written this:

> The man was shocked. "Yikes," he despaired, "I'm going to die!" For a moment he sat and stared in horror at the spot where the fire had been, where it should be. "Why didn't I listen to that old-timer on Sulphur Creek? If I had someone with me, he could build the fire now. I don't want to die!"

Notice that the second version is much more emotional than London's version. The word choice and the decision to quote the man's thoughts directly create a less detached tone.

Remember that one component of naturalism is a belief that nature is a powerful, unfeeling force with control over human life. That belief in a universe with no compassion for human suffering pairs well with the detached, objective tone London uses.

Practice and Apply Try to emulate London's style. Choose a terrible event and write about it in a realistic style, using a calm, unemotional tone. Remember that word choice and sentence structure can affect your tone.

Determine Author's Purpose

COMMON CORE

RL 6

TEACH

Remind students that the **author's purpose** is the author's reason for writing a particular work. The broadest purposes include to inform the reader of facts or to tell the reader how to do something, to persuade the reader to adopt or believe the author's views, to entertain the reader, or to express the author's feelings and ideas.

Tell students that many texts have more than one purpose. For example, a magazine article may present facts about the latest scientific discovery but do so in a way that entertains the reader.

In addition to broad purposes for writing, writers may have more specific purposes in mind when they choose the details and diction to place in their story, and when they choose the tone and structure of their writing.

COLLABORATIVE DISCUSSION

- Have students discuss Jack London's purpose in not naming the main character or the dog in "To Build a Fire." What does the lack of names for these characters suggest?
- Ask students to share any questions they generated during the course of reading and discussing the selection.

Analyze Structure: Realism and Naturalism

COMMON CORE

RL 2, RL 5

RETEACH

Approach the topic by focusing on the definitions of the words *realism* and *naturalism*. Point out that both words have the same suffix: *-ism*. Have students find the suffix in a dictionary and state its meaning. *("following a particular principle or idea; having a particular trait, behavior, or practice")* Then have students notice the roots: *real* and *nature*. From *real*, ask volunteers to give the meaning of *realism* in literature. *(literature should portray reality; having the traits of reality)*

Tell students that a work that consistently depicts believable reality can be called realistic. Since most people in the world are ordinary people, most characters in realism are ordinary people. Realism often depicts daily life.

Then tell students that the meaning of *naturalism* is harder to understand because it is not always connected to its root word, *nature*. For naturalist writers in the era of Jack London, nature was often a cruel, deadly force against which human beings fought in vain, a force that permitted only the strongest to survive.

So *naturalism* was a term given to works showing human beings struggling against powerful forces that tested their ability to survive. Sometimes, those forces belonged to nature, as in "To Build a Fire." But the force in a naturalist work might also be a grim factory or another human institution.

CLOSE READING APPLICATION

Students can apply the skill to another story. Have them identify both realistic and naturalistic details in the story.

The Men in the Storm

Short Story by Stephen Crane

Why This Text

Students may be unfamiliar with stories in which no single character stands out; in "The Men in the Storm," Crane aspires to represent the collective voice of the masses struggling to survive. As a realist, Crane included many specific details about daily life and sets his story among ordinary people. With the help of the close-reading questions, students will get a sense of the real lives of ordinary people facing difficult conditions on the city streets more than a hundred years ago.

Background Have students read the background information about the author. Point out that Crane's adventurous nature brought him into contact with a wide variety of experiences and provided him with countless opportunities for writing. Although his stories are set in very different places—from a Civil War battlefield to a shipwrecked dinghy en route to Cuba, to the mean streets of New York City—his unflinching commitment to exposing the plight of the common person never wavered.

AS YOU READ Ask students to pay attention to the way the author uses setting, tone, dialect, and style to add meaning and to underscore important themes.

Common Core Support

- cite strong and thorough textual evidence
- determine two or more themes or central ideas of a text
- analyze how a text's structure contributes to its aesthetic impact

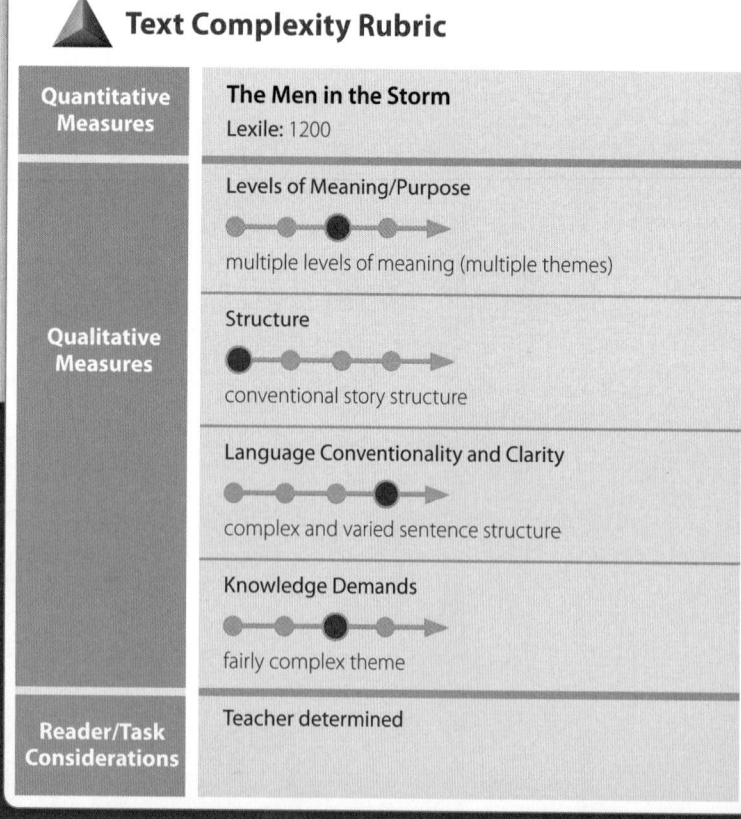

Text Complexity Rubric

Quantitative Measures

The Men in the Storm
Lexile: 1200

Qualitative Measures

Levels of Meaning/Purpose
multiple levels of meaning (multiple themes)

Structure
conventional story structure

Language Conventionality and Clarity
complex and varied sentence structure

Knowledge Demands
fairly complex theme

Reader/Task Considerations
Teacher determined

Strategies for CLOSE READING

Analyze Structure: Realism and Naturalism

Students should read this story carefully all the way through. Close-reading questions at the bottom of the page will help them analyze the techniques the author uses to paint a realistic portrait of downtrodden Americans at the turn of the century. As they read, students should jot down comments or questions about the text in the margins.

WHEN STUDENTS STRUGGLE . . .

To help students identify examples of realistic details used to establish tone and add meaning, have them work in small groups to fill out a chart like the one shown below.

CITE TEXT EVIDENCE For practice in recognizing how the author's word choice and tone reveal the story's central ideas, have them analyze each of the following details from the text.

Example from the Text	What It Reveals
"Those on the walks huddled their necks closely in the collars of their coats and went along stooping like a race of aged people." (lines 4–6)	The people are beaten down, tired, spent. The word "race" identifies people as a group rather than as individuals.
". . . scores of pedestrians and drivers . . . speeding for scores of unknown doors and entrances, scattering to an infinite variety of shelters. . ." (lines 24–26)	The image of a swarm of people mindlessly rushing toward a destination suggests the primitive forces that control our animal behavior.
"There was an absolute expression of hot dinners in the pace of the people." (line 28)	The people walking with an "expression of hot dinners" shows the single-minded focus of the crowd.
"During the afternoon of the storm, the whirling snows acted as drivers, as men with whips . . ." (lines 39–40)	Comparing the snow to a driver with a whip creates the sense that the snow is punishing.

Background Stephen Crane *(1871–1900)—American novelist, poet, and short story writer—was one of the most innovative writers of his generation, known for his gritty realism and willingness to take on difficult themes such as fear, social isolation, and spiritual crisis. He is perhaps best known for his Civil War novel The Red Badge of Courage (1895), which depicts the psychological complexities of the battlefield. Crane, who dropped out of college and moved to New York to be a writer, had an adventurous life that was tragically cut short when he died of tuberculosis at the age of 28. Crane's work was nearly forgotten until two decades later when it was "rediscovered" by critics.*

The Men in the Storm

Short Story by Stephen Crane

CLOSE READ
Notes

1. **READ ▷** As you read lines 1–27, begin to collect and cite text evidence.
   - Underline images that help you visualize the weather.
   - Circle images of street life.
   - In the margin, describe the setting (lines 1–13).

A At about three o'clock of the February afternoon, the blizzard began to swirl great clouds of snow along the streets, sweeping it down from the roofs and up from the pavements until the faces of pedestrians tingled and burned as from a thousand needle-prickings. Those on the walks huddled their necks closely in the collars of their coats and went along stooping like a race of aged people. The drivers of vehicles hurried their horses furiously on their way. They were made more cruel by the exposure of their positions, aloft on high seats. The street cars, bound up-town, went slowly, the horses slipping and straining in the spongy brown mass that lay between the rails. The drivers, muffled to the eyes, stood erect and facing the wind, models of grim philosophy. Overhead the trains rumbled and roared, and the dark structure of the elevated railroad, stretching over the avenue, dripped little streams and drops of water upon the mud and snow beneath it.

The story takes place in a winter blizzard in a big city.

73

1. **READ AND CITE TEXT EVIDENCE** In this section of text, the author uses sensory details to describe the setting.

A **ASK STUDENTS** to cite details that appeal to sound, sight, and touch. *Students may identify the sense of sound: "overhead the trains rumbled and roared" (line 11); sight: "went along stooping like a race of aged people" (lines 5–6); and touch: "the faces of the pedestrians tingled and burned as from a thousand needle-prickings" (lines 3–4).*

CLOSE READ
Notes

All the clatter of the street was softened by the masses that lay upon the cobbles until, even to one who looked from a window, it became important music, a melody of life made necessary to the ear by the dreariness of the pitiless beat and sweep of the storm. Occasionally one could see black figures of men busily shovelling the white drifts from the walks. The sounds from their labor created new recollections of rural experiences which every man manages
20 to have in a measure. Later, the immense windows of the shops became aglow with light, throwing great beams of orange and yellow upon the pavement. They were infinitely cheerful, yet in a way they accented the force and discomfort of the storm, and gave a meaning to the pace of the people and the

B vehicles, scores of pedestrians and drivers, wretched with cold faces, necks and feet, speeding for scores of unknown doors and entrances, scattering to an infinite variety of shelters, to places which the imagination made warm with the familiar colors of home.

C There was an absolute expression of hot dinners in the pace of the people. If one dared to speculate upon the destination of those who came trooping, he
30 lost himself in a maze of social calculations; he might fling a handful of sand and attempt to follow the flight of each particular grain. But as to the suggestion of hot dinners, he was in firm lines of thought, for it was upon every hurrying face. It is a matter of tradition; it is from the tales of childhood. It comes forth with every storm.

The thought of hot food is on everyone's mind.

2. ◀ **REREAD** Reread lines 1–27. Describe the contrast between the storm outside and the people who remain inside. Cite evidence from the text.

The storm consists of "great clouds of snow" that cause the "faces of pedestrians" to tingle and burn. On the other hand, the people viewing the storm from inside hear "a melody of life." The light from the shops is described as "infinitely cheerful," which contrasts with the "force and discomfort of the storm."

3. **READ** ▶ As you read lines 28–61, continue to cite textual evidence.
- In the margin, explain what is on everyone's mind.
- Underline examples of people moving toward their destination.
- Circle descriptions of men waiting near the "charitable house."

74

CLOSE READ
Notes

However, in a certain part of a dark West-side street, there was a collection of men to whom these things were as if they were not. In this street was located a charitable house where for five cents the homeless of the city could get a bed at night and, in the morning, coffee and bread.

D During the afternoon of the storm, the whirling snows acted as drivers, as
40 men with whips, and at half-past three, the walk before the closed doors of the house was covered with wanderers of the street, waiting. For some distance on either side of the place they could be seen lurking in doorways and behind projecting parts of buildings, gathering in close bunches in an effort to get warm. A covered wagon drawn up near the curb sheltered a dozen of them. Under the stairs that led to the elevated railway station, there were six or eight, their hands stuffed deep in their pockets, their shoulders stooped, jiggling their feet. Others always could be seen coming, a strange procession, some slouching along with the characteristic hopeless gait of professional strays, some coming with hesitating steps wearing the air of men to whom this sort of thing was
50 new.

4. ◀ **REREAD** Reread lines 39–55. How is the situation getting worse for the men? Cite textual evidence in your response.

More and more men congregate on the street in front of the charitable house; the walk is "covered with wanderers of the street" who are "lurking in doorways and behind projecting parts of buildings" and "crowded together, muttering . . . their red, inflamed wrists covered by the cloth." The house shows no signs of opening.

75

---

2. **REREAD AND CITE TEXT EVIDENCE**

B **ASK STUDENTS** to review lines 24–26. Have them cite text evidence showing what the pedestrians are doing and thinking about. *They are "speeding . . . to an infinite variety of shelters"; they are thinking of "the familiar colors of home."*

3. **READ AND CITE TEXT EVIDENCE** Have students visualize the men moving toward their destination. Explain that no individual characters stand out. Point out the references to "the men" and "people."

C **ASK STUDENTS** what point the author is trying to make about the men. *They are undifferentiated; they are heading the same way, thinking the same thing.*

FOR ELL STUDENTS Challenge students to guess the meaning of the noun *clatter* (line 14) by looking for context clues.

4. **REREAD AND CITE TEXT EVIDENCE** Explain that in lines 39–55, the author uses specific language to describe the severity of the scene.

D **ASK STUDENTS** to find examples of words and phrases that reveal the condition of the men. *Students may cite "lurking in doorways" (line 42), "gathering in close bunches" (line 43), "sheltered a dozen of them" (line 44), "six or eight, their hands stuffed deep in their pockets, their shoulders stooped, jiggling their feet" (lines 45–47). What conclusions can be drawn from these details? The men represent the oppressed masses.* How can the men be described? *The men are without resources, anxious, living on the edges of society, clandestine.*

It was an afternoon of incredible length. The snow, blowing in twisting clouds, sought out the men in their meagre hiding-places and skilfully beat in among them, drenching their persons with showers of fine, stinging flakes. They crowded together, muttering, and fumbling in their pockets to get their red, inflamed wrists covered by the cloth.

Newcomers usually halted at one of the groups and addressed a question, perhaps much as a matter of form, "Is it open yet?"

Those who had been waiting inclined to take the questioner seriously and become contemptuous. "No; do yeh think we'd be standin' here?"

60 The gathering swelled in numbers steadily and persistently. One could always see them coming, trudging slowly through the storm.

Finally, the little snow plains in the street began to assume a leaden hue from the shadows of evening. The buildings upreared gloomily save where various windows became brilliant figures of light that made shimmers and splashes of yellow on the snow. A street lamp on the curb struggled to illuminate, but it was reduced to impotent blindness by the swift gusts of sleet crusting its panes.

In this half-darkness, the men began to come from their shelter places and mass in front of the doors of charity. They were of all types, but the
70 nationalities were mostly American, German and Irish. Many were strong, healthy, clear-skinned fellows with that stamp of countenance which is not frequently seen upon seekers after charity. There were men of undoubted patience, industry and temperance, who in time of ill-fortune, do not habitually turn to rail at the state of society, snarling at the arrogance of the rich and bemoaning the cowardice of the poor, but who at these times are apt to wear a sudden and singular meekness, as if they saw the world's progress marching from them and were trying to perceive where they had failed, what they had lacked, to be thus vanquished in the race. Then there were others of

E *The "men of industry" were still healthy, not yet ground down by their poverty; the long-term poor lived in boarding houses and were angry at the world.*

5. **READ ▷** As you read lines 62–125, continue to cite textual evidence.

- Underline the descriptions of the "men of industry."
- In the margin, summarize the essential difference between the "men of industry" and the "Bowery lodging-house element."
- Circle the lines that describe the problem the men face, and explain the problem in the margin (lines 107–115).

the shifting, Bowery lodging-house element who were used to paying ten cents
80 for a place to sleep, but who now came here because it was cheaper.

But they were all mixed in one mass so thoroughly that one could not have discerned the different elements but for the fact that the laboring men, for the most part, remained silent and impassive in the blizzard, their eyes fixed on the windows of the house, statues of patience.

The sidewalk soon became completely blocked by the bodies of the men. They pressed close to one another like sheep in a winter's gale, keeping one another warm by the heat of their bodies. The snow came down upon this compressed group of men until, directly from above, it might have appeared like a heap of snow-covered merchandise, if it were not for the fact that the
90 crowd swayed gently with a unanimous, rhythmical motion. It was wonderful to see how the snow lay upon the heads and shoulders of these men, in little ridges an inch thick perhaps in places, the flakes steadily adding drop and drop, precisely as they fall upon the unresisting grass of the fields. The feet of the men were all wet and cold and the wish to warm them accounted for the slow, gentle, rhythmical motion. Occasionally some man whose ears or nose tingled acutely from the cold winds would wriggle down until his head was protected by the shoulders of his companions.

There was a continuous murmuring discussion as to the probability of the doors being speedily opened. They persistently lifted their eyes toward the
100 windows. One could hear little combats of opinion.

F "There's a light in th' winder!"

"Naw; it's a reflection f'm across th' way."

"Well, didn't I see 'em lite it?"

"You did?"

"I did!"

"Well, then, that settles it!"

As the time approached when they expected to be allowed to enter, the men crowded to the doors in an unspeakable crush, jamming and wedging in a way that it seemed would crack bones. They surged heavily against the building
110 in a powerful wave of pushing shoulders. Once a rumor flitted among all the tossing heads.

"They can't open th' doors! Th' fellers er smack up ag'in 'em."

Then a dull roar of rage came from the men on the outskirts; but all the time they strained and pushed until it appeared to be impossible for those that they cried out against to do anything but be crushed to pulp.

"Ah, git away f'm th' door!"

The men are pushed so tightly against the door that it cannot be opened, and the surge of men crushes those at the door even more.

76

77

---

5. **READ AND CITE TEXT EVIDENCE** Have students read lines 68–84 and notice the descriptions of two types of men.

E **ASK STUDENTS** to cite evidence detailing the two types of men in the mass. *Students should cite lines 70–77 explaining that some of the men were "strong, healthy, clear-skinned fellows ... who in time of ill-fortune, do not habitually turn to rail at the state of society." The other men were used to sleeping in lodging houses, but were trying to find someplace cheaper (79–80).*

FOR ELL STUDENTS Clarify the meaning of *swelled* (line 60). Explain that in this context it means "grew, expanded in size and number."

FOR ELL STUDENTS Dialect speech may be difficult for ELL students. Go over the dialogue section. Have a volunteer read it aloud (or read it aloud yourself) and ask students what familiar words sound like *naw, winder, f'm, th', 'em,* (lines 101–103), *fellers* (line 112), *and git* (line 116). *no, window, from, the, them, fellows, get*

CLOSE READ
Notes

"Git outa that!"

"Throw 'em out!"

"Kill 'em!"

120 "Say, fellers, now, what th' 'ell? Give 'em a chanct t' open th' door!"

"Yeh damned pigs, give 'em a chanct t' open th' door!"

Men in the outskirts of the crowd occasionally yelled when a boot-heel of one of frantic trampling feet crushed on their freezing extremities.

"Git off me feet, yeh clumsy tarrier!"

"Say, don't stand on me feet! Walk on th' ground!"

A man near the doors suddenly shouted: "O-o-oh! Le' me out—le' me out!" And another, a man of infinite valor, once twisted his head so as to half face those who were pushing behind him. "Quit yer shovin', yeh"—and he delivered a volley of the most powerful and singular **invective** straight into the faces of

130 the men behind him. It was as if he was hammering the noses of them with curses of triple brass. His face, red with rage, could be seen; upon it, an expression of sublime disregard of consequences. But nobody cared to reply to his imprecations; it was too cold. Many of them snickered and all continued to push.

invective:
an abusive
expression;
language used
to attack
somebody

---

6. **REREAD** Reread lines 101–125. How does the author's use of dialect affect the story?

The dialect reflects the natural, everyday speech of the men. No speakers are identified; we only hear snippets of what might be a conversation. The language accentuates the chaos of the mass, the desperation of the men, and the tension of the scene.

---

7. **READ** As you read lines 126–174, continue to cite textual evidence.
- Underline details that describe the conditions outside.
- Circle details that describe the man in the window across the street.
- In the margin, explain the reactions of the men to the man in the dry goods store.

78

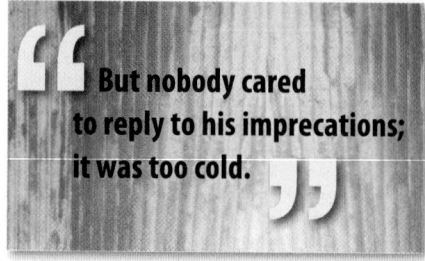
" But nobody cared to reply to his imprecations; it was too cold. "

In occasional pauses of the crowd's movement the men had opportunity to make jokes; usually grim things, and no doubt very uncouth. Nevertheless, they are notable—one does not expect to find the quality of humor in a heap of old clothes under a snowdrift.

The winds seemed to grow fiercer as time wore on. Some of the gusts of

140 snow that came down on the close collection of heads cut like knives and needles, and the men huddled, and swore, not like dark assassins, but in a sort of an American fashion, grimly and desperately, it is true, but yet with a wondrous under-effect, indefinable and **mystic**, as if there was some kind of humor in this catastrophe, in this situation in a night of snow-laden winds.

G Once, the window of the huge dry-goods shop across the street furnished material for a few moments of forgetfulness. In the brilliantly-lighted space appeared the figure of a man. He was rather stout and very well clothed. His whiskers were fashioned charmingly after those of the Prince of Wales. He stood in an attitude of magnificent reflection. He slowly stroked his moustache

150 with a certain grandeur of manner, and looked down at the snow-encrusted mob. From below there was denoted a supreme complacence in him. It seemed that the sight operated inversely, and enabled him to more clearly regard his own environment, delightful relatively.

H One of the mob chanced to turn his head and perceive the figure in the window. "Hello, lookit 'is whiskers," he said genially.

Many of the men turned then, and a shout went up. They called to him in all strange keys. They addressed him in every manner, from familiar and cordial greetings to carefully-worded advice concerning changes in his personal appearance. The man presently fled, and the mob chuckled

160 ferociously like ogres who had just devoured something.

mystic:
spiritual, with
a meaning
beyond human
understanding

The men mock the man in the store because he seems unconcerned about their situation.

---

8. **REREAD AND DISCUSS** Reread lines 154–160. In a small group, discuss how the men show solidarity with one another.

79

---

6. **REREAD AND CITE TEXT EVIDENCE**

F **ASK STUDENTS** to draw conclusions about the men from the way they speak. What does their speech say about them? _They are rough, confrontational, and demonstrative; they understand each other; they are unified by language._

7. **READ AND CITE TEXT EVIDENCE**

G **ASK STUDENTS** to think about the description of the man in the window in lines 146–153. Which words suggest royalty? _Students may note "Prince of Wales," (line 148), "magnificent reflection," (line 149), "grandeur of manner," (line 150), "supreme complacence" (line 151). In contrast, how are the people on the street described? They are a "snow- encrusted mob."_

Critical Vocabulary: invective (line 129) Have students share definitions. What can happen when people start hurling invectives at one another? _People may get into a fight._

8. **REREAD AND DISCUSS USING TEXT EVIDENCE** Have students discuss how seeing the man in the window affects the men (lines 154–160).

H **ASK STUDENTS** to describe how the men's behavior toward each other contrasts with their earlier behavior in the story (lines 101–125). _They are suddenly unified in their ridicule of the man; they are able to see their commonalities rather than their differences._

Critical Vocabulary: mystic (line 143) Have students share definitions of _mystic_. Why does the author describe the catastrophe as having an underlying "mystic" effect? _The author is saying that some catastrophes are so horrendous they are beyond human understanding._

They turned then to serious business. Often they addressed the stolid front of the house.

"Oh, let us in fer Gawd's sake!"

"Let us in or we'll all drop dead!"

"Say, what's th' use o' keepin' all us poor Indians out in th' cold?"

And always some one was saying, "Keep off me feet."

The crushing of the crowd grew terrific toward the last. The men, <u>in keen pain from the blasts</u>, began almost to fight. With the <u>pitiless whirl of snow upon them</u>, the battle for shelter was going to the strong. It became known that

170 the basement door at the foot of a little steep flight of stairs was the one to be opened, and they jostled and heaved in this direction like laboring fiends. One could hear them panting and groaning in their fierce exertion.

Usually some one in the front ranks was protesting to those in the rear: "O —o—ow! Oh, say, now, fellers, let up, will yeh? Do yeh wanta kill somebody?"

A policeman arrived and went into the midst of them, scolding and berating, occasionally threatening, but using no force but that of his hands and shoulders against these men who were only struggling to get in out of the storm. His decisive tones rang out sharply: "Stop that pushin' back there! Come, boys, don't push! Stop that! Here, you, quit yer shovin'! Cheese that!"

180 When the door below was opened, <u>a thick stream of men</u> forced a way down the stairs, which were of an extraordinary narrowness and seemed only wide enough for one at a time. Yet they somehow went down almost three abreast. It was a difficult and painful operation. The crowd was like a <u>turbulent water forcing itself through one tiny outlet</u>. The men in the rear, excited by the success of the others, made frantic exertions, for it seemed that this large band would more than fill the quarters and that many would be left upon the pavements. It would be disastrous to be of the last, and accordingly men with the snow biting their faces, writhed and twisted with their might. One expected that from the tremendous pressure, the narrow passage to the basement door

---

9. **READ ▶** As you read lines 175–208, continue to cite evidence.

• Underline the lines that depict the men as a force of nature.
• Circle text describing how the men change when they enter the doorway.
• In the margin, explain why those at the back of the crowd become frantic.
• Underline words that convey hopelessness in lines 204–208.

80

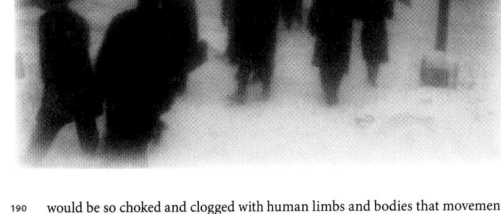

190 would be so choked and clogged with human limbs and bodies that movement would be impossible. Once indeed the crowd was forced to stop, and a cry went along that a man had been injured at the foot of the stairs. But presently the slow movement began again, and the policeman fought at the top of the flight to ease the pressure on those who were going down.

A reddish light from a window fell upon the faces of the men when they, in turn, arrived at the last three steps and were about to enter. One could then note a change of expression that had come over their features. As they thus stood upon the threshold of their hopes, they looked (suddenly content and complacent. The fire had passed from their eyes and the snarl had vanished

200 from their lips.) The very force of the crowd in the rear, which had previously vexed them, was regarded from another point of view, for it now made it inevitable that they should go through the little doors into the place that was cheery and warm with light.

The tossing crowd on the sidewalk grew smaller and smaller. The snow beat with <u>merciless persistence</u> upon the bowed heads of those who waited. The wind drove it up from the pavements in frantic forms of winding white, and it <u>seethed in circles</u> about the huddled forms, passing in, one by one, three by three, out of the storm.

There may not be room for all the men, so those in the back struggle to improve their position and chances of getting in.

81

---

9. **READ AND CITE TEXT EVIDENCE** Have students visualize the crowd forcing its way into the narrow doorway (lines 175–208).

ASK STUDENTS to cite evidence showing the change in the men as they enter the doorway. *Students should cite lines 197–200 describing the men as "suddenly content and complacent" and "the snarl had vanished from their lips."*

FOR ELL STUDENTS *Content* (line 198) is a false cognate for the Spanish adjective *contento/a* ("happy"). Point out to your Spanish-speaking students that in English *content* has a different meaning, "satisfied."

CLOSE READ
Notes

10. ◀REREAD As you reread lines 204–208, explain what happens at the end of the story.

As the men enter the doorway, the crowd on the street thins out but the snow continues to fall outside.

SHORT RESPONSE

Cite Text Evidence Identify the theme of the story and explain how its central ideas develop, interact, and build on one another throughout the course of the text. Be sure to support your ideas by **citing text evidence**.

The central theme of the story is that people feel desperate when confronted with the harshness of nature. The story begins with a cruel storm that mirrors the cruel fate of the men who are out of work. "The winds seemed to grow fiercer as time wore on," and the men get rowdier. The storm is a destructive force but also a unifying one, causing the men to forget their differences and live in the moment, achieving a kind of spirituality born of their misery: the author describes a man who acts in pure rage as "sublime" and the joking of the men as having a "wondrous under-effect, indefinable and mystic." Poverty, like the storm, is inevitable, persistent, and debilitating. Even as some manage to escape its clutches in a temporary shelter for the night, others line up to take their place.

82

TO CHALLENGE STUDENTS . . .

Tell students that Stephen Crane is known for his use of distinctive dialects to convey the voices of ordinary people. In "The Men in the Storm," the men speak in a regional English endemic to the time and place the story is set: New York City's Bowery district, circa 1900.

ASK STUDENTS to work with a partner or small group to translate the dialect in lines 101–125 of "The Men in the Storm."

• Explain that there are several ways to do a translation: either by focusing on the literal meanings of the words themselves, or by trying to re-create the sound and feel of realistic speech.

• Students can first put the dialogue into standard English (focusing on the literal meanings) and then do a second, more interpretative translation, in which they put the words into contemporary English—the English we speak today. Here's an example:

> **Line of text:** "Git off me feet, yeh clumsy tarrier!"
> **Translation #1:** "Get off my feet, you clumsy oaf!"
> **Translation #2:** "Move it, doofus."

• Point out that context is a strong factor in the way dialogue is interpreted. Students should consider the immediate effects of the storm on the men's physical and mental states, as well as long-term effects of grinding poverty: unemployment, hunger, and homelessness. Have them also consider the "mob mentality" aspect: the fact that people as individuals may not speak the same way as people in a large crowd.

• After they have written their dialogues, students can perform them aloud for the class.

10. ⬤REREAD AND CITE TEXT EVIDENCE Review what the men have been through up to this point in the text.

🅙 **ASK STUDENTS** how what happens in lines 204–208 affects the men. _As the men get closer to the threshold, they calm down— relief will come soon._

SHORT RESPONSE

Cite Text Evidence Students' responses should include text evidence that supports their positions. They should:

• cite strong and thorough textual evidence.

• determine two or more themes or central ideas of a text and how they develop, interact, and build on one another.

• analyze how the author's choices concerning how to structure a text contribute to its aesthetic impact.

DIG DEEPER

1. With the class, return to Question 8, Reread and Discuss. Have students share their responses.

   ASK STUDENTS to think about the men's response to the man in the window (lines 154–160). Have them:

   - paraphrase the episode in their own words.
   - describe the behavior of the men prior to, during, and after the event takes place.
   - make an inference about why seeing the man in the window changes the mood so abruptly. What does he represent to the men?
   - draw conclusions about the feeling of solidarity between the men. What makes them stop fighting one another?
   - make an inference about what causes the man in the window to flee. Have them cite text evidence depicting the men's sense of victory following his departure.

2. With the class, return to Question 10, Reread. Have students share their responses.

   ASK STUDENTS to think about the way the story ends. Have them:

   - describe what has happened to the men that makes them take on "another point of view." How does this point of view contrast with their earlier attitude?
   - cite text evidence describing the physical change in the men as they approach the threshold.
   - describe what the men see through the little doors. What words does the author use to describe what they see? What else in the story has been described this way?
   - draw conclusions, based on the story, about what happens to people when their basic needs are not met. What is the effect on society as a whole?

   ASK STUDENTS to return to their Short Response answer and revise it based on the class discussion.

CLOSE READING NOTES

COMPARE TEXTS

from The Jungle

Novel by Upton Sinclair

Food Product Design

from Fast Food Nation

Investigative Journalism by Eric Schlosser

mySmartPlanner Create lesson plans and access resources online.

Why These Texts?

Upton Sinclair's tough look at the ugly side of American industry ushered in a new era of public awareness and reform. In the same vein, Eric Schlosser shines a spotlight on how the food we eat today is created. This lesson explores the impact of the authors' writing and encourages students to analyze the choices authors make in order to further their purposes.

Key Learning Objective: The student will be able to determine an author's purpose, analyze an author's choices, and grasp technical terms.

For additional practice:

Close Reader selection
"The Yuckiest Food in the Amazon"
Science Writing by Mary Roach

COMMON CORE Common Core Standards

RL/RI 1 Cite textual evidence.
RL/RI 2 Determine themes/central ideas of a text.
RL 3 Analyze the impact of the author's choices.
RL/RI 4 Determine the meanings of words and phrases; analyze impact of word choices.
RL/RI 5 Analyze and evaluate structure.
RL/RI 6 Analyze how grasping point of view requires distinguishing what is directly stated in a text from what is really meant; Determine author's point of view or purpose.
W 2 Write informative/explanatory texts.
W 3 Write narratives.
W 4 Produce clear and coherent writing.
W 7 Conduct research projects.
W 8 Gather relevant information from sources.
L 2 Demonstrate command of English.
L 3a Vary and apply syntax.
L 4b Identify and correctly use patterns of word changes.
L 4c Consult reference materials.
SL 3 Evaluate a speaker's point of view, reasoning, and use of evidence and rhetoric.
SL 4 Present information findings and supporting evidence.

▲ Text Complexity Rubric

	from *The Jungle* Lexile: 1310L	Food Product Design Lexile: 1290L
Quantitative Measures		
	Levels of Meaning/Purpose single level of complex meaning	**Levels of Meaning/Purpose** more than one purpose; implied, easily identified from context
Qualitative Measures	**Structure** more than one text structure	**Structure** organization of main ideas and details complex but clearly stated and generally sequential
	Language Conventionality and Clarity longer descriptions	**Language Conventionality and Clarity** many unfamiliar, high academic, and complex domain-specific words
	Knowledge Demands somewhat unfamiliar experience	**Knowledge Demands** some specialized knowledge required
Reader/Task Considerations	Teacher determined Vary by individual reader and type of text	Teacher determined Vary by individual reader and type of text

Upton Sinclair Have students read the information about the author. Tell them that as a child in Baltimore, Sinclair was exposed to the enormous inequality in American society. His mother's family was wealthy. His father was an alcoholic whose family had lost its fortune during the Civil War. Moving back and forth from wealth to poverty in his childhood led Sinclair to embrace socialism and its promise of a just society.

Introduce students to the term *muckraker,* used to describe Sinclair and other writers who exposed the ugly side of life—the corruption and injustices that polite society ignored. Point out that while Sinclair's muckraking was often unpopular, it was also effective. In 1906, the same year *The Jungle* was published, Congress passed the Pure Food and Drug Act and the Meat Inspection Act. Much of the credit belonged to Sinclair and his vivid description of the meat industry.

Sinclair also wrote influential books about the automobile industry, the oil industry, and the rise of Adolf Hitler.

Eric Schlosser Point out that *Fast Food Nation,* like *The Jungle,* examines the dark side of big business. Tell students that while Schlosser's book is investigative journalism, the movie version of *Fast Food Nation* (which he co-wrote) is fiction.

Explain that Schlosser's work, like Sinclair's, met with powerful opposition. The pushback from industry included a website called *Best Food Nation,* developed to praise the quality and safety of the U.S. fast food culture.

COMPARE TEXTS

from
The Jungle
Novel by Upton Sinclair

Food Product Design
from Fast Food Nation
Journalism by Eric Schlosser

Image Credits: (t) (t) ©Bloomberg/Getty Images; (tc) ©Lightspring/Shutterstock; (c) ©Hulton Archive/Stringer/Getty Images; (b) ©Jeff Morgan 16/Alamy Images

Upton Sinclair (1878–1968) *was sent by the socialist newspaper* Appeal to Reason *to Chicago to investigate working conditions in the stockyards, where animals were processed into meat. Sinclair himself was a socialist, and he believed that the means and products of production should be collectively owned by the workers. He belived that socialism, with its focus on strong government regulation and collective action, could solve many of the inequalities of his era. The result of Sinclair's investigation in Chicago was his most famous novel,* The Jungle (1906), *which he was forced to self-publish after several publishers turned down the manuscript. Jurgis Rudkus, the main character, is a Lithuanian immigrant who works in the stockyards.*

Eric Schlosser (b. 1959) *became a journalist after studying history in college. In 1998, the magazine* Rolling Stone *published his two-part investigative series on the fast-food industry. Schlosser then expanded the articles into a best-selling book,* Fast Food Nation: The Dark Side of the All-American Meal (2001), *which examines the effects of the fast-food industry on workers, consumers, and the landscape. In 2006, Schlosser and writer Charles Wilson published a version of the book for young people,* Chew On This: Everything You Don't Want to Know About Fast Food. *The original book was also made into a movie in the same year, with Schlosser co-writing the screenplay.*

AS YOU READ Direct students to use the As You Read instructions to focus their reading.

Analyze Author's Choices 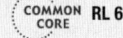 RL 3, RL 4
(LINES 9–16)

Remind students that an author's **diction**, or word choice, helps determine the effectiveness of his or her writing. Point out that Sinclair's diction creates strong **imagery,** helping the reader see, feel, and smell life in the slaughterhouse.

Ⓐ CITE TEXT EVIDENCE Have students read lines 9–16. Ask them to summarize the image described in this passage. *(a worker slaughtering diseased cattle)* Ask students to analyze Sinclair's diction in this passage, identifying the words or phrases that contribute to the strength of the image. *(refuse, boils, nasty, plunged, splash foul-smelling stuff, smeared with blood, steeped)*

Determine Author's Purpose (LINES 21–35) COMMON CORE RL 6

Explain that understanding an author's tone can often help readers identify his or her purpose. **Tone** is the attitude an author adopts toward the subject matter.

Ⓑ ASK STUDENTS to read lines 21–35 and to analyze the tone Sinclair adopts toward his two characters. *(Sinclair adopts an affectionate tone toward the two men. One puffs on his pipe; the other is a chatty "old fellow," who gives his horrifying information a comic touch—for example, he talks about "the great and only Durham's canned goods" and a chicken with rubber boots on.)* Ask students how this tone serves Sinclair's purpose. *(The reader is inclined to be sympathetic to and believe the stories of these two likeable men.)*

> #### CRITICAL VOCABULARY
>
> **obliged**: Workers were forced to do things they considered wrong.
>
> **ASK STUDENTS** to identify a task that workers were obliged to do. *(They were obliged to slaughter diseased animals.)*

---

from **The Jungle**
by Upton Sinclair

AS YOU READ Notice how Sinclair's descriptions of the stockyards affect you as a reader. Write down any questions you generate during reading.

Jurgis heard of these things little by little, in the gossip of those who were **obliged** to perpetrate them. It seemed as if every time you met a person from a new department, you heard of new swindles and new crimes. There was, for instance, a Lithuanian who was a cattle butcher for the plant where Marija had worked, which killed meat for canning only; and to hear this man describe the animals which came to his place would have been worthwhile for a Dante or a Zola.[1] It seemed that they must have agencies all over the country, to hunt out old and crippled and diseased cattle to be canned. There were cattle which had been fed on "whiskey malt," the refuse of the breweries, and had become what the men called "steerly"—which means covered with boils. It was a nasty job killing these, for when you plunged your knife into them they would burst and splash foul-smelling stuff into your face; and when a man's sleeves were smeared with blood, and his hands steeped in it, how was he ever to wipe his face, or to clear his eyes so that he could see? It was stuff such as this that made the "embalmed beef" that had killed several times as many United States soldiers as all the bullets of the Spaniards; only the army beef, besides, was not fresh canned, it was old stuff that had been lying for years in the cellars.

Then one Sunday evening, Jurgis sat puffing his pipe by the kitchen stove, and talking with an old fellow whom Jonas had introduced, and who worked in the canning-rooms at Durham's; and so Jurgis learned a few things about the great and only Durham canned goods, which had become a national institution. They were regular alchemists at Durham's; they advertised a mushroom-catsup, and the men who made it did not know what a mushroom looked like. They advertised "potted chicken"—and it was like the boarding-house soup of the comic papers, through which a chicken had walked with rubbers on. Perhaps they had a secret process for making chickens chemically—who knows? said Jurgis's friend; the things that went into the mixture were tripe, and the fat of pork, and beef suet, and hearts of beef, and finally the waste ends of veal, when they had any. They put these up in several grades, and sold them at several prices; but the contents of the cans all came out of the same hopper. And then there was "potted game" and "potted grouse," "potted ham," and "deviled

oblige
(ə-blīj´) *v.* to force or require.

---

[1] **a Dante or a Zola:** Dante Alighieri (1265–1321), Florentine poet who wrote the *Inferno*, about a journey through Hell; Emile Zola (1840–1902), French novelist and playwright who focused on social and political ills.

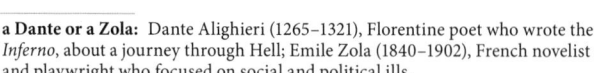

SCAFFOLDING FOR ELL STUDENTS

Identify Pronoun Referents Read aloud lines 12–16. Point out that the word *it* in line 15 is used as a pronoun, and ask students to find the noun it represents *(blood)*. Point out that while *it* is often used in this way, the word sometimes has no precise referent. Draw students' attention to the beginning of the same sentence *(It was)*, pointing out that here *It* does not refer to a specific word.

ASK STUDENTS to read lines 16–20. Have them find one example where the word *it* is used without a precise antecedent *(It was, line 16)* and one in which it stands for a noun. *(In line 19, it stands for beef, or the army beef.)*

ham"—de-vyled, as the men called it. "De-vyled" ham was made out of the waste ends of smoked beef that were too small to be sliced by the machines; and also tripe, dyed with chemicals so that it would not
40 show white, and trimmings of hams and corned beef, and potatoes, skins and all, and finally the hard cartilaginous gullets of beef, after the tongues had been cut out. All this **ingenious** mixture was ground up and flavored with spices to make it taste like something. Anybody who could invent a new imitation had been sure of a fortune from old Durham, said Jurgis's informant, but it was hard to think of anything new in a place where so many sharp wits had been at work for so long; where men welcomed tuberculosis[2] in the cattle they were feeding, because it made them fatten more quickly; and where they bought up all the old rancid butter left over in the grocery stores of a
50 continent, and "oxidized" it by a forced-air process, to take away the odor, rechurned it with skim milk, and sold it in bricks in the cities! Up to a year or two ago it had been the custom to kill horses in the yards—**ostensibly** for fertilizer; but after long agitation the newspapers had been able to make the public realize that the horses were being canned. Now it was against the law to kill horses in Packingtown, and the law was really complied with—for the present, at any rate. Any day, however, one might see sharp-horned and shaggy-haired creatures running with the sheep—and yet what a job you would have to get the public to believe that a good part of what it buys for lamb and mutton
60 is really goat's flesh!

There was another interesting set of statistics that a person might have gathered in Packingtown—those of the various afflictions of the workers. When Jurgis had first inspected the packing plants with Szedvilas, he had marveled while he listened to the tale of all the things that were made out of the carcasses of animals, and of all the lesser industries that were maintained there; now he found that each one of these lesser industries was a separate little inferno, in its way as horrible as the killing-beds, the source and fountain of them all. The workers in each of them had their own peculiar diseases. And the
70 wandering visitor might be **sceptical** about all the swindles, but he could not be sceptical about these, for the worker bore the evidence of them about on his own person—generally he had only to hold out his hand.

There were the men in the pickle rooms, for instance, where old Antanas had gotten his death; scarce a one of these that had not some spot of horror on his person. Let a man so much as scrape his finger pushing a truck in the pickle rooms, and he might have a sore that would put him out of the world; all the joints in his fingers might be eaten by the acid, one by one. Of the butchers and floorsmen, the
80 beef boners and trimmers, and all those who used knives, you could

---

[2] **tuberculosis:** an infectious disease that causes the growth of nodules on lung tissue.

The Jungle 353

ingenious
(ĭn-jēn′yəs) *adj.*
cleverly inventive.

ostensibly
(ŏ-stĕn′sə-blē) *adv.*
seemingly or outwardly.

sceptical
(skĕp′tĭ-kəl) *adj.*
having doubts or reservations.

APPLYING ACADEMIC VOCABULARY

clarify	revise

As you discuss this excerpt from *The Jungle*, incorporate the following Collection 5 academic vocabulary words: *clarify* and *revise*. Encourage students to analyze how Sinclair's exposé of the meat industry helped **clarify** people's understanding of how power could be abused and forced them to **revise** their opinions about the benefits of unregulated business practices.

TEACH

CLOSE READ

Determine Author's Purpose (LINES 37–60)

COMMON CORE RL 6

Point out that analyzing the topics an author chooses and inferring the messages that these topics communicate will often reveal his or her purpose.

C CITE TEXT EVIDENCE Have students read lines 37–60. Ask them to cite examples of meat industry products that Sinclair describes in this passage. *(He describes "deviled ham" made of waste products, rancid butter sold as fresh, horse meat secretly canned for human consumption, and goat meat passed off as lamb.)* Ask students how the choice of these topics serves Sinclair's purpose. *(Each is an example of deception. Sinclair's purpose is to outrage the reader by revealing these unethical practices.)*

CRITICAL VOCABULARY

ingenious: Sinclair suggests that devising the product sold as "deviled ham" required creative intelligence.

ASK STUDENTS what might have been ingenious about the mixture known as deviled or "de-vyled" ham. *(Creating a product that people would want from ingredients that they would otherwise reject requires intelligence.)*

ostensibly: The meat industry wanted the public to believe that horses were being killed only for use in fertilizers.

ASK STUDENTS why ostensibly killing horses only for fertilizer was important for the slaughterhouse owners. *(The slaughterhouse owners knew people would not want to eat horse meat.)*

sceptical: Sinclair observes that an outsider might not believe all the talk about corruption in the meat industry.

ASK STUDENTS why people might be sceptical of the stories they heard about corruption. *(Without hard evidence, people might think these stories were unfounded rumors.)*

The Jungle **353**

Analyze Author's Choices   COMMON CORE RL 3, RL 4

(LINES 83–90)

Remind students that Sinclair made a fundamental choice when he decided to write *The Jungle* as fiction rather than investigative journalism.

D CITE TEXT EVIDENCE Have students read and analyze lines 83–90. Is there anything in this passage to indicate whether Sinclair is writing fiction or nonfiction? *(The passage seems to be giving factual details about work in the slaughterhouse, such as the specific effects of the work on the workers' hands and the presence of tuberculosis germs. There are no obvious elements of fiction. On the other hand, Sinclair provides no evidence to prove that his assertions are factual.)* Ask students to consider why Sinclair might have made the choice to write *The Jungle* as a novel. What might be the advantages or disadvantages of this choice? *(Advantage: By writing fiction, Sinclair could express himself freely, without documenting each assertion. Disadvantage: People might not believe what Sinclair wrote was true, and the meat industry could accuse him of making up details to suit his purpose.)*

Determine Author's Purpose   COMMON CORE RL 6

(LINES 90–100)

Explain that an author's purpose often goes beyond informing, persuading, or entertaining. Point out that many writers have an added purpose of urging their readers to action.

E ASK STUDENTS to read lines 90–100 and infer what general action Sinclair's readers might have been moved to take from reading this passage. Have students also identify specific actions that a reader might have demanded based on evidence in the passage. *(Readers might have demanded government regulations to improve the working conditions in slaughterhouses. Specifically, these might have included limiting the time a person could work in the chilling rooms and finding a new process for pulling the wool from sheep.)*

scarcely find a person who had the use of his thumb; time and time again the base of it had been slashed, till it was a mere lump of flesh against which the man pressed the knife to hold it. The hands of these men would be criss-crossed with cuts, until you could no longer pretend to count them or to trace them. They would have no nails,— they had worn them off pulling hides; their knuckles were swollen so that their fingers spread out like a fan. There were men who worked in the cooking rooms, in the midst of steam and sickening odors, by artificial light; in these rooms the germs of tuberculosis might live for

90 two years, but the supply was renewed every hour. There were the beef luggers, who carried two-hundred-pound quarters into the refrigerator cars, a fearful kind of work, that began at four o'clock in the morning, and that wore out the most powerful men in a few years. There were those who worked in the chilling rooms, and whose special disease was rheumatism;[3] the time limit that a man could work in the chilling rooms was said to be five years. There were the wool pluckers, whose hands went to pieces even sooner than the hands of the pickle men; for the pelts of the sheep had to be painted with acid to loosen the wool, and then the pluckers had to pull out this wool with their bare hands,

100 till the acid had eaten their fingers off. There were those who made the

---

[3] **rheumatism** (ro͞o'mə-tĭz'əm): a disease that causes inflammation and pain in muscles and joints.

354 Collection 5

WHEN STUDENTS STRUGGLE...

Ask students to reread lines 83–87; then help them see how Sinclair is describing the effects of unsafe working conditions. Discuss with students the concept of cause and effect. (**cause:** *working with sharp knives;* **effect:** *cuts on hands;* **cause:** *pulling hides;* **effect:** *loss of fingernails.*)

ASK STUDENTS to read lines 87–100, and have them work in pairs to fill out a cause-effect table like the one on the next page.

tins for the canned meat, and their hands, too, were a maze of cuts, and each cut represented a chance for blood poisoning. Some worked at the stamping machines, and it was very seldom that one could work long there at the pace that was set, and not give out and forget himself, and have a part of his hand chopped off. There were the "hoisters," as they were called, whose task it was to press the lever which lifted the dead cattle off the floor. They ran along upon a rafter, peering down through the damp and the steam, and as old Durham's architects had not built the killing room for the convenience of the hoisters, at every

110 few feet they would have to stoop under a beam, say four feet above the one they ran on, which got them into the habit of stooping, so that in a few years they would be walking like chimpanzees. Worst of any, however, were the fertilizer men, and those who served in the cooking rooms. These people could not be shown to the visitor—for the odor of a fertilizer man would scare any ordinary visitor at a hundred yards, and as for the other men, who worked in tank rooms full of steam, and in some of which there were open vats near the level of the floor, their peculiar trouble was that they fell into the vats; and when they were fished out, there was never enough of them left to be

120 worth exhibiting—sometimes they would be overlooked for days, till all but the bones of them had gone out to the world as Durham's Pure Leaf Lard!

COLLABORATIVE DISCUSSION How did Sinclair's descriptions affect you as a reader? What specific descriptive details caused this effect? Discuss these questions with a partner, citing specific evidence from the selection to support your ideas.

Lines	Cause	Effect
87–90	germs in cooking rooms	tuberculosis
90–93	carrying quarters of beef	men get worn out
93–96	working in chilling rooms	rheumatism
96–100	plucking wool from sheep	acid eats fingers off

CLOSE READ

Analyze Author's Choices (LINES 102–122)

COMMON CORE RL 3, RL 4

Explain that the way an author chooses to arrange information has an important effect on his or her writing. Draw students' attention to the choices Sinclair makes in concluding this selection.

F CITE TEXT EVIDENCE Have students read lines 102–122. Ask students to identify the disturbing images with which Sinclair concludes the selection. *(losing parts of hands in stamping machines; hoisters forced to stoop until they walked like chimpanzees; foul stench of "the fertilizer men"; drowning of tank-room workers and their bodies becoming part of the "lard")* Ask students why Sinclair might have chosen to end this passage as he did. *(All the images are troubling, but the last one not only includes death by drowning, it contains a horrifying hint of cannibalism. "Durham's Pure Leaf Lard", Sinclair suggests, includes the boiled-down flesh of human beings. By choosing to end the sequence of anecdotes with this unsavory detail, Sinclair would have worked his readers into a state of disgust and outrage.)*

COLLABORATIVE DISCUSSION Have students create a chart in which they list specific passages from the selection that struck them as powerful or disturbing. Have students share their charts with a partner and discuss why each passage was so effective.

ASK STUDENTS to share any questions they generated in the course of reading and discussing the selection.

TEACH

CLOSE READ

Determine Author's Purpose  RL 6

Point out that in its influence on society *The Jungle* has been compared to Harriet Beecher Stowe's *Uncle Tom's Cabin*, a novel credited with hastening the end of slavery in the United States. With its attack on abuses in the meat industry, *The Jungle* forced politicians to take action to safeguard the purity of food. Help students understand the irony of this result. While Sinclair's original intent or purpose had been to raise awareness of the harsh lives of immigrant workers, the public outcry was mostly about food safety. Ask students to cite evidence from this selection that supports Sinclair's original purpose. *(Possible answer: Sinclair describes in gruesome detail the "afflictions" and ailments that affect the men doing various tasks.)*

Analyze Author's Choices  RL 3, RL 4

Remind students that Sinclair's original purpose in writing *The Jungle* was to describe the inhuman conditions in which immigrants worked. In light of this information, discuss with students why Sinclair might have chosen to write the book as fiction. *(Possible answer: He may have thought that fiction would allow him to examine more deeply the intimate details of family life and to explore the thoughts and feelings of his characters.)*

Determine Author's Purpose  RL 6

In general, an author's **purpose** or reason for writing is to inform, to entertain, or to persuade. In addition, an author may want to move people to take a particular action. Usually the author's purpose must be inferred based on a work's content and style, which are shaped by the author's purpose. Upton Sinclair went to Chicago as a journalist to investigate working conditions in the stockyards for a socialist newspaper. Instead, he ended up writing a novel, *The Jungle*, that explores the lives of a family of Lithuanian immigrants who worked in those stockyards. As you analyze this excerpt from *The Jungle* in order to determine Sinclair's purpose(s) in writing it, ask yourself these questions:

- What are the topics that Sinclair writes about in the selection?
- What themes or messages does he communicate about those topics?
- What tone or attitude does Sinclair convey in the selection?
- How well does Sinclair follow through on his original assignment?
- In what ways does he go beyond that assignment?
- What might Sinclair have wanted readers to do after reading this novel?

Analyze Author's Choices  RL 3, RL 4

Upton Sinclair made a number of choices in writing *The Jungle*. He worked as a journalist, but he chose to write a novel and followed the conventions of a novel—setting, plot, character, and point of view. Although he set his novel in the real Packingtown slum of Chicago, he did not use the names of any actual workers but created characters based on them called Jurgis, Marija, Jonas, and old Antanas. He described the practices of Durham canned goods, a fictional company, rather than those of Armour & Company, the real giant among Chicago's meatpacking companies.

Another area where authors make choices is **diction,** or word choice. Sinclair uses vivid descriptive words that create strong imagery in order to appeal to readers' senses and help them imagine what it is like to work in the stockyards.

As you analyze this selection, consider these ideas.

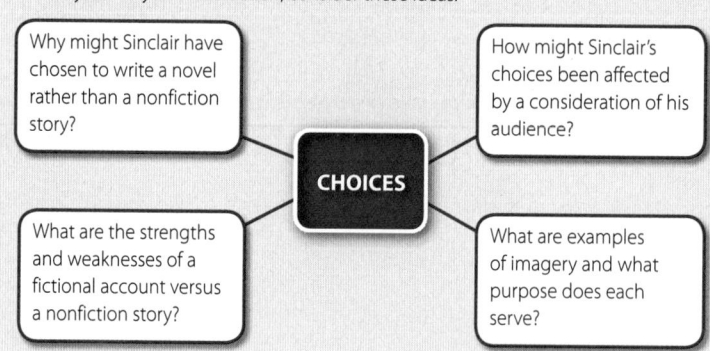

Strategies for Annotation 🖉 📄 *Annotate it!*

Analyze Author's Choices 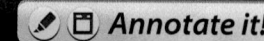 RL 3, RL 4

Share these strategies for guided or independent analysis:

- Underline images.
- Highlight comparisons within the images in yellow.
- In notes, reflect on the author's purpose in employing these images.

The author uses these images to emphasize how the men had been deformed by their work.

> The hands of these men would be <u>criss-crossed with cuts,</u> until you could no longer pretend to count them or to trace them. <u>They would have no nails</u>—they had worn them off pulling hides; <u>their knuckles were swollen so that their fingers spread out like a fan.</u>

Analyzing the Text

COMMON CORE RL 1, RL 2, RL 3, RL 4, RL 6, W 2, W 4

Cite Text Evidence Support your responses with evidence from the selection.

1. **Analyze** What is Sinclair's implicit idea in the first two sentences of the selection about workers in the stockyards? How do these sentences reflect his purpose?

2. **Interpret** In the second paragraph, Sinclair writes about "the great and only Durham canned goods, which had become a national institution." How does the imagery in the rest of the paragraph reveal Sinclair's tone toward the company?

3. **Infer** What does Sinclair mean when he says "They were regular alchemists at Durham's" (lines 25–26)?

4. **Analyze** In this excerpt, Sinclair uses a **third-person point of view,** with a narrator outside the action to tell the story, focusing mainly on the thoughts, actions, and observations of Jurgis, the main character. How does choosing this point of view help Sinclair achieve his purpose?

5. **Cite Evidence** What is Sinclair's topic in the third and fourth paragraphs of the selection? What message does he communicate about this topic?

6. **Draw Conclusions** Readers in Sinclair's time were more concerned about his revelations in the first two paragraphs of this selection than the revelations in the rest of the selection. Why might this have been so and how does this relate to Sinclair's purpose?

7. **Draw Conclusions** How did Sinclair's choice to use a fictional company and fictional characters to tell his story help him achieve his journalistic purpose?

PERFORMANCE TASK

Writing Activity: News Articles *The Jungle* is a novel written by a journalist. Explore how Sinclair's information and ideas could have been presented in a news article in two different types of newspapers.

1. Write an investigative report that you might find in a daily newspaper. The purpose of this article is to inform readers about abuses in the meatpacking industry. Focus on facts that could be verified by a reliable source of the time.

2. Write a sensational account that you might find in a tabloid newspaper. The purpose of this article is to shock people and get them to buy the newspaper. Focus on the most vivid details, which may or may not be verified.

With a partner, discuss how the purpose of each version and the writing choices you made affected the tone and mood in each piece.

PRACTICE & APPLY

Analyzing the Text

COMMON CORE RL 1, RL 2, RL 3, RL 4, RL 6, W 2, W 4

Possible answers:

1. *The idea implicit in these sentences is that the meat industry is rife with corruption. Sinclair is preparing readers for his indictment of big business.*

2. *Sinclair continues this tone of ironic humor through much of the paragraph, referring to the mushroom catsup without mushrooms and other "ingenious" methods of deceiving the public. In spite of the humor, Sinclair's disgusting imagery about the company's products reveals his tone of distrust toward the company.*

3. *By referring ironically to the "alchemists" at Durham's, Sinclair suggests that the meat industry performed fantastic feats by creating food out of disgusting ingredients. Medieval alchemists attempted to turn base metals into gold.*

4. *Seeing the action mainly from Jurgis's point of view allows Sinclair to personalize the story and bring it home to his readers. Using the third-person point of view permits him to step beyond Jurgis where necessary and introduce information about the meat industry that Jurgis would never have known.*

5. *Sinclair's topic in the third and fourth paragraphs is the poor conditions that meat industry workers endured. His message is that these conditions are harmful and inhumane.*

6. *Readers in Sinclair's day may have believed that people had to look after themselves, so the plight of the immigrant worker was not their concern. People would also have been more alarmed about the suggestion that the food they trustingly consumed was unfit to eat. Sinclair's original purpose was to educate the public about industrial working conditions; instead, he brought about changes in the food industry.*

7. *Using a fictional company allowed Sinclair to write freely about the industry, without the fear of reprisal. Fictional characters allowed him to describe their most intimate feelings about their experiences.*

Assign this performance task.

PERFORMANCE TASK

COMMON CORE W 2, W 4

Writing Activity: News Articles Help students prepare for writing their articles by making sure that they understand the styles of journalism that they are going to imitate. Ask students to bring to class examples of both investigative and tabloid stories from print or online sources. Have them highlight passages that they feel characterize each type of writing. Discuss with the class how a writer's purpose can affect the diction, imagery, and tone of an article.

PRACTICE & APPLY

Critical Vocabulary

COMMON CORE L 4b, L 4c

Students should be able to explain how they derived their definitions from the contexts in which they found the words.

Vocabulary Strategy: Word Families

Explain that Greek and Latin contributions to English vocabulary can sometimes have similar spellings but different meanings. For example, the Greek prefix *bio* means "life" and forms English words such as *biology*. The Latin prefix *bi* means "two," as in *biped*. Some confusing Greek and Latin roots include:

- aud (L: to hear); aut (G: self)
- dent (L: tooth), dendre (G: tree)
- ped (L: foot); ped (G: child)
- spir (L: to breathe); spir (G: coil)

Possible Answers

1. *pathos (noun): a quality that arouses feelings of sadness; antipathy (noun): strong dislike; apathetic (adjective): showing little feeling; sympathize (verb): to share someone's feelings*

2. *spectacle (noun): an impressive sight; spectator (noun): a person who watches an event; specimen (noun): an object for people to look at; inspect (verb): to look at closely*

3. *mediocre (adjective): ordinary, middling; mediate (verb): to settle differences by intervening between two parties; medium (noun): a person who allegedly interprets the spirit world for the living world; median (noun): the middle number in a set of numbers*

4. *chronic (adjective): lasting a long time; chronology (noun): sequence of events; synchronize (verb): to make happen at the same time; chronometer (noun): a clock*

Critical Vocabulary

 COMMON CORE L 4b, L 4c

oblige   ingenious   ostensibly   sceptical

Practice and Apply Go on a Critical Vocabulary scavenger hunt to find examples of the words in advertisements, news articles, or other uses in print, online, or in your environment. Write your own definition of each word based on at least two examples. Follow these tips to guide your search.

- If you search online, don't go to a dictionary or other site that defines the word. Instead, look for examples by searching for news or images.
- Note that the preferred spelling of *sceptical* in American dictionaries is now *skeptical*. Search under both spellings.

Vocabulary Strategy: Word Families

A **word family** is a set of words that all descend from the same word root and that have similar meanings. The Critical Vocabulary word *oblige* is part of the word family based on the Latin root *ligare*, meaning "to bind." The word is formed by adding the prefix *ob–* meaning "to" so that *obliged* means "to be required or bound to do something." As the word web shows, members of this word family may modify the root with various spellings because sometimes the word came into English through another language such as French. Words may include a variety of prefixes or suffixes and act as different parts of speech. Knowing the meaning of the common root will help you determine the meaning of words in a word family.

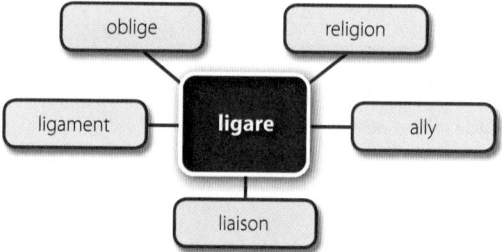

Practice and Apply Work with a partner to create word lists with at least four words based on the common root in each word family. Write the part of speech and definition next to each word in your list. Consult a general or specialized etymological dictionary to clarify the precise meaning and etymology of words below as needed.

1. Greek root *path–* meaning "to feel or suffer"

2. Latin root *spec–* meaning "to see or look at"

3. Latin root *medi–* meaning "middle"

4. Greek root *chron–* meaning "time"

Background Tell students that the Code of Federal Regulations defines natural flavor as containing "flavoring constituents derived from a spice, fruit or fruit juice, vegetable or vegetable juice, edible yeast, herb, bark, bud, root, leaf or similar plant material, meat, seafood, poultry, eggs, dairy products, products of fermentation thereof, whose significant function in food is flavoring rather than nutritional."

AS YOU READ Direct students to use the As You Read instructions to focus their reading. Remind students to write down any questions they generate during reading.

CRITICAL VOCABULARY

stem: After describing a well-known fast-food flavor, Schlosser discusses its origins.

ASK STUDENTS why it is important to understand where the flavors of processed foods stem from.

Determine Author's Purpose (LINES 1–12)
COMMON CORE RI 6

Tell students that the introductory paragraph of a text often provides an indication of the author's purpose. Explain that more information about the purpose will be given later, so their first inference about purpose may need to be refined.

Ⓐ ASK STUDENTS to infer the purpose of the selection from the first paragraph. *(Possible answer: The purpose might be to expose the facts behind the taste of popular fast food items.)*

Analyze Language: Technical Terms (LINES 24–28)
COMMON CORE RI 4

Point out that a term may be technical if it is used for a special purpose. In the law and the food industry, the term *natural flavor* has a technical meaning.

Ⓑ CITE TEXT EVIDENCE Have students state the clue in the text that the technical meaning of *natural flavor* is very different from what most people think. *(Schlosser reveals that natural flavors are almost no different than artificial flavors.)*

Food Product Design
from **Fast Food Nation**
by Eric Schlosser

AS YOU READ Look for information about the fast-food industry that either confirms or changes your ideas about fast food. Write down any questions you generate during reading.

The taste of McDonald's french fries has long been praised by customers, competitors, and even food critics. James Beard loved McDonald's fries. Their distinctive taste does not **stem** from the type of potatoes that McDonald's buys, the technology that processes them, or the restaurant equipment that fries them. Other chains buy their french fries from the same large processing companies, use Russet Burbanks, and have similar fryers in their restaurant kitchens. The taste of a fast food fry is largely determined by the cooking oil. For decades, McDonald's cooked its french fries in a mixture of about 7
10 percent cottonseed oil and 93 percent beef tallow. The mix gave the fries their unique flavor—and more saturated beef fat per ounce than a McDonald's hamburger.

    Amid a barrage of criticism over the amount of cholesterol in their fries, McDonald's switched to pure vegetable oil in 1990. The switch presented the company with an enormous challenge: how to make fries that subtly taste like beef without cooking them in tallow. A look at the ingredients now used in the preparation of McDonald's french fries suggests how the problem was solved. At the end of the list is a seemingly innocuous, yet oddly mysterious phrase: "natural flavor."
20 That ingredient helps to explain not only why the fries taste so good, but also why most fast food—indeed, most of the food Americans eat today—tastes the way it does.

    Open your refrigerator, your freezer, your kitchen cupboards, and look at the labels on your food. You'll find "natural flavor" or "artificial flavor" in just about every list of ingredients. The similarities between these two broad categories of flavor are far more significant than their differences. Both are man-made additives that give most processed food its taste. The initial purchase of a food item may be driven by its packaging or appearance, but subsequent
30 purchases are determined mainly by its taste. About 90 percent of the money that Americans spend on food is used to buy processed food. But the canning, freezing, and dehydrating techniques used to process food destroy most of its flavor. Since the end of World War II, a vast industry has arisen in the United States to make processed food palatable. Without this flavor industry, today's fast food industry could not exist. The names of the leading American fast food chains and their best-selling menu items have become famous worldwide,

stem
(stĕm) *v.* to grow from or be caused by.

SCAFFOLDING FOR ELL STUDENTS

Define Multiple-Meaning Words in Context Tell students that the word *fries* is important at the beginning of this text because it refers to a familiar kind of fast food. Tell them that it has two meanings on page 359. In one meaning, it is a noun, the name of a food. In the other meaning, it is a verb for an action that cooks food.

ASK STUDENTS to find the word *fries* on the page and decide which meaning is appropriate in each case. *(Possible answers: line 5: verb; line 20: noun)*

Encourage students to look for and ask about other multiple-meaning words in the text. Examples include *trade* (line 77) and *pilot* (line 88).

Determine Author's Purpose (LINES 46–58) — COMMON CORE RI 6

Tell students that works of investigative reporting usually contain a great many factual details—sometimes so many that the reader would have difficulty remembering them all.

C ASK STUDENTS why the author would devote a long paragraph to listing the names of seven companies manufacturing similar products in a small geographical area, including the names of the towns and highway exits where the companies are found. *(Possible answers: to impress the reader with how much the food flavor industry is concentrated in a small area; to impress the reader with the thoroughness of the research; to paint a menacing, industrialized, and corporate picture of the food flavor industry)*

Determine Author's Purpose (LINES 72–75) — COMMON CORE RI 6

Point out to students that Schlosser comments on how mysterious-sounding technical terms in the food flavor industry are.

D CITE TEXT EVIDENCE Have students identify phrases that Schlosser uses to indicate his attitude toward the names of the flavors. *("long chemical names…as mystifying to me as medieval Latin," "odd-sounding names," "like magic potions")* Ask students what purposes the author might have for introducing terms in this way before actually using or defining them. *(Possible answers: He wishes to warn the reader that difficult terms will be found in the text and to assure the reader that the writer doesn't completely understand them either. He wishes to suggest that food flavorings are mysterious and perhaps not to be trusted.)*

---

embedded in our popular culture. Few people, however, can name the companies that manufacture fast food's taste.

40   The flavor industry is highly secretive. Its leading companies will not divulge[1] the precise formulas of flavor compounds or the identities of clients. The secrecy is deemed essential for protecting the reputation of beloved brands. The fast food chains, understandably, would like the public to believe that the flavors of their food somehow originate in their restaurant kitchens, not in distant factories run by other firms.

    The New Jersey Turnpike runs through the heart of the flavor industry, an industrial corridor dotted with refineries and chemical plants. International Flavors & Fragrances (IFF), the world's largest flavor company, has a manufacturing facility off Exit 8A in Dayton,
50 New Jersey; Givaudan, the world's second-largest flavor company, has a plant in East Hanover. Haarmann & Reimer, the largest German flavor company, has a plant in Teterboro, as does Takasago, the largest Japanese flavor company. Flavor Dynamics has a plant in South Plainfield; Frutarom is in North Bergen; Elan Chemical is in Newark. Dozens of companies manufacture flavors in New Jersey industrial parks between Teaneck and South Brunswick. Indeed, the area produces about two-thirds of the flavor additives sold in the United States.

    The IFF plant in Dayton is a huge pale blue building with a
60 modern office complex attached to the front. It sits in an industrial park, not far from a BASF plastics factory, a Jolly French Toast factory, and a plant that manufactures Liz Claiborne cosmetics. Dozens of tractor-trailers were parked at the IFF loading dock the afternoon I visited, and a thin cloud of steam floated from the chimney. Before entering the plant, I signed a nondisclosure form, promising not to reveal the brand names of products that contain IFF flavors. The place reminded me of Willy Wonka's chocolate factory. Wonderful smells drifted through the hallways, men and women in neat white lab coats cheerfully went about their work, and hundreds of little glass bottles
70 sat on laboratory tables and shelves. The bottles contained powerful but fragile flavor chemicals, shielded from light by the brown glass and the round plastic caps shut tight. The long chemical names on the little white labels were as mystifying to me as medieval Latin. They were the odd-sounding names of things that would be mixed and poured and turned into new substances, like magic potions.

    I was not invited to see the manufacturing areas of the IFF plant, where it was thought I might discover trade secrets. Instead, I toured various laboratories and pilot kitchens, where the flavors of well-established brands are tested or adjusted, and where whole new flavors
80 are created. IFF's snack and savory lab is responsible for the flavor of potato chips, corn chips, breads, crackers, breakfast cereals, and pet food. The confectionery lab devises the flavor for ice cream, cookies,

---

[1] **divulge:** to disclose or make known.

WHEN STUDENTS STRUGGLE…

For comprehension support, tell students that in a text that contains a great deal of detailed information, readers decide which information is necessary to understand in depth and which is less important. Tell students that in a paragraph containing a lot of details, reading the first and last sentences carefully and skimming the details can often provide the information they need.

ASK STUDENTS to use this technique with lines 46–58. Have them state the main point or points of the paragraph and leave out the secondary details. You may wish to point out to students that what they have just done was to compose a summary of the paragraph.

> ## "The long chemical names on the little white labels were as mystifying to me as medieval Latin."

candies, toothpastes, mouthwashes, and antacids. Everywhere I looked, I saw famous, widely advertised products sitting on laboratory desks and tables. The beverage lab is full of brightly colored liquids in clear bottles. It comes up with the flavor for popular soft drinks, sport drinks, bottled teas, and wine coolers, for all-natural juice drinks, organic soy drinks, beers, and malt liquors. In one pilot kitchen I saw
90 a dapper chemist, a middle-aged man with an elegant tie beneath his lab coat, carefully preparing a batch of cookies with white frosting and pink-and-white sprinkles. In another pilot kitchen I saw a pizza oven, a grill, a milk-shake machine, and a french fryer identical to those I'd seen behind the counter at countless fast food restaurants.

In addition to being the world's largest flavor company, IFF manufactures the smell of six of the ten best-selling fine perfumes in the United States. It makes the smell of Estée Lauder's Beautiful, Clinique's Happy, Ralph Lauren's Polo, and Calvin Klein's Eternity. It also makes the smell of household products such as deodorant, dishwashing detergent, bath soap, shampoo, furniture polish, and
100 floor wax. All of these aromas are made through the same basic process: the manipulation of **volatile** chemicals to create a particular smell. The basic science behind the scent of your shaving cream is the same as that governing the flavor of your TV dinner.

The aroma of a food can be responsible for as much as 90 percent of its flavor. Scientists now believe that human beings acquired the sense of taste as a way to avoid being poisoned. Edible plants generally taste sweet; deadly ones, bitter. Taste is supposed to help us differentiate food that's good for us from food that's not. The taste buds on our tongues can detect the presence of half a dozen or so basic
110 tastes, including: sweet, sour, bitter, salty, astringent,[2] and umami (a taste discovered by Japanese researchers, a rich and full sense of deliciousness triggered by amino acids in foods such as shellfish,

volatile
(vŏl′ə-tl′) *adj.* liable to change suddenly or evaporate.

---

[2] **astringent:** sharp or drying.

APPLYING ACADEMIC VOCABULARY

ambiguous	clarify

As you discuss "Food Product Design," incorporate the following Collection 5 academic vocabulary words: *ambiguous* and *clarify*. Encourage students to consider both the ways in which Schlosser's attitude toward the food production industry is **ambiguous** and what strategies Schlosser uses to **clarify** technical or difficult information.

CLOSE READ

Determine Author's Purpose (LINES 83–93)
COMMON CORE RI 6

Tell students that an author's purpose guides his or her word choices, as well as his or her larger structural choices. An author's **tone,** or attitude toward the subject, is revealed through his or her careful choice of words and details.

E **ASK STUDENTS** to determine Schlosser's tone in the description of the lab. Have them identify words and phrases that convey the tone and discuss what the tone implies about the author's purpose. *(Possible answer: The tone is cheerful. Words and phrases that convey the tone include "brightly colored," line 85, along with "dapper" and "elegant," line 89. The purpose of describing the lab in this way may be to emphasize how ordinary the process of concocting flavors really is.)*

> **CRITICAL VOCABULARY**
>
> **volatile:** Schlosser observes that many diverse products, such as perfumes, detergents, and floor wax, are made from chemicals that are likely to change their properties if not handled carefully.
>
> **ASK STUDENTS** to name some volatile substances. *(gasoline, rubbing alcohol.)*

Analyze Language: Technical Terms (LINES 108–112)
COMMON CORE RI 4

Tell students that in introducing a technical term, authors often place definitions or explanations near the term.

F **CITE TEXT EVIDENCE** Ask students to find a technical term and its definition in the passage. *(umami, line 110; "a taste discovered by Japanese researchers, a rich and full deliciousness triggered by amino acids...," lines 111–112)*

Analyze Language: Technical Terms (LINES 119–125)

COMMON CORE **RI 4**

Remind students that when introducing a technical term with which most readers will be unfamiliar, such as a chemical name, an author may devote a sentence or even a paragraph to an explanation.

G CITE TEXT EVIDENCE Have students point out phrases that help the reader understand what the olfactory epithelium is and what it does. (*"a thin layer of nerve cells…located at the base of the nose, right between the eyes. The brain combines the complex smell signals from the epithelium with the simple taste signals from the tongue"*) Why does the author need to provide this explanation? (*The book is written for a general audience that would not have specialized knowledge about the olfactory epithelium.*)

Determine Author's Purpose (LINES 140–146)

COMMON CORE **RI 6**

Explain to students that a writer's choice of topics or details is also shaped by his or her purpose for writing. Tell them to ask themselves why some details were included and not others.

H ASK STUDENTS what purpose Schlosser may have had in discussing childhood food preferences and how they persist into adulthood. (*He may have wished to impress the reader with the power of sensations, memories, and emotions connected to food and how these can make consumers vulnerable to the food industry's manipulation.*)

---

mushrooms, potatoes, and seaweed). Taste buds offer a relatively limited means of detection, however, compared to the human olfactory system, which can perceive thousands of different chemical aromas. Indeed "flavor" is primarily the smell of gases being released by the chemicals you've just put in your mouth.

G 120 The act of drinking, sucking, or chewing a substance releases its volatile gases. They flow out of the mouth and up the nostrils, or up the passageway in the back of the mouth, to a thin layer of nerve cells called the olfactory epithelium, located at the base of the nose, right between the eyes. The brain combines the complex smell signals from the epithelium with the simple taste signals from the tongue, assigns a flavor to what's in your mouth, and decides if it's something you want to eat.

130 Babies like sweet tastes and reject bitter ones; we know this because scientists have rubbed various flavors inside the mouths of infants and then recorded their facial reactions. A person's food preferences, like his or her personality, are formed during the first few years of life, through a process of socialization. Toddlers can learn to enjoy hot and spicy food, bland health food, or fast food, depending upon what the people around them eat. The human sense of smell is still not fully understood and can be greatly affected by psychological factors and expectations. The color of a food can determine the perception of its taste. The mind filters out the overwhelming majority of chemical aromas that surround us, focusing intently on some, ignoring others. People can grow accustomed to bad smells or good smells; they stop noticing what once seemed overpowering. Aroma and memory are somehow inextricably linked. A smell can suddenly

H 140 evoke a long-forgotten moment. The flavors of childhood foods seem to leave an indelible mark, and adults often return to them, without always knowing why. These "comfort foods" become a source of pleasure and reassurance, a fact that fast food chains work hard to promote. Childhood memories of Happy Meals can translate into frequent adult visits to McDonald's, like those of the chain's "heavy users," the customers who eat there four or five times a week.

The human craving for flavor has been a largely unacknowledged and unexamined force in history. Royal empires have been built, unexplored lands have been traversed, great religions and philosophies

150 have been forever changed by the spice trade. In 1492 Christopher Columbus set sail to find seasoning. Today the influence of flavor in the world marketplace is no less decisive. The rise and fall of corporate empires—of soft drink companies, snack food companies, and fast food chains—is frequently determined by how their products taste.

The flavor industry emerged in the mid-nineteenth century, as processed foods began to be manufactured on a large scale. Recognizing the need for flavor additives, the early food processors turned to perfume companies that had years of experience working with essential oils and volatile aromas. The great perfume houses of England, France, and the Netherlands produced many of the first flavor compounds. In the early part of the twentieth century, Germany's powerful chemical industry assumed the technological lead in flavor production. Legend has it that a German scientist discovered methyl anthranilate, one of the first artificial flavors, by accident while mixing chemicals in his laboratory. Suddenly the lab was filled with the sweet smell of grapes. Methyl anthranilate later became the chief flavoring compound of grape Kool-Aid. After World War II, much of the perfume industry shifted from Europe to the United States, settling in New York City near the garment district and the fashion houses. The flavor industry came with it, subsequently moving to New Jersey to gain more plant capacity. Man-made flavor additives were used mainly in baked goods, candies, and sodas until the 1950s, when sales of processed food began to soar. The invention of gas chromatographs and mass spectrometers—machines capable of detecting volatile gases at low levels—vastly increased the number of flavors that could be synthesized. By the mid-1960s the American flavor industry was churning out compounds to supply the taste of Pop Tarts, Bac-Os, Tab, Tang, Filet-O-Fish sandwiches, and literally thousands of other new foods.

The American flavor industry now has annual revenues of about $1.4 billion. Approximately ten thousand new processed food products are introduced every year in the United States. Almost all of them require flavor additives. And about nine out of every ten of these new food products fail. The latest flavor innovations and corporate realignments are heralded in publications such as *Food Chemical News, Food Engineering, Chemical Market Reporter*, and *Food Product Design*. The growth of IFF has mirrored that of the flavor industry as a whole. IFF was formed in 1958, through the merger of two small companies. Its annual revenues have grown almost fifteenfold since the early 1970s, and it now has manufacturing facilities in twenty countries.

The quality that people seek most of all in a food, its flavor, is usually present in a quantity too **infinitesimal** to be measured by any traditional culinary terms such as ounces or teaspoons. Today's sophisticated spectrometers, gas chromatographs, and headspace vapor analyzers provide a detailed map of a food's flavor components, detecting chemical aromas in amounts as low as one part per billion. The human nose, however, is still more sensitive than any machine yet invented. A nose can detect aromas present in quantities of a few parts per trillion—an amount equivalent to 0.000000000003 percent. Complex aromas, like those of coffee or roasted meat, may be composed of volatile gases from nearly a thousand different chemicals. The smell of a strawberry arises from the interaction of at least 350 different chemicals that are present in minute amounts. The chemical that provides the dominant flavor of bell pepper can be tasted in amounts as low as .02 parts per billion; one drop is sufficient to add

infinitesimal
(ĭn′fĭn-ĭ-tĕs′ə-məl)
adj. extremely small; microscopic.

Food Product Design **363**

CLOSE READ

Determine Author's Purpose (LINES 161–167)
COMMON CORE RI 6

Point out that entertaining the reader is a valid secondary purpose even for serious nonfiction with an informational main purpose.

I ASK STUDENTS how Schlosser's telling of the discovery of grape flavor might entertain readers. *(It is told as a story with interesting details.)*

> **CRITICAL VOCABULARY**
>
> **infinitesimal:** Schlosser writes that flavorings are added to foods in tiny amounts.
>
> **ASK STUDENTS** to compare the meanings of *infinitesimal* and the related but more familiar word *infinite*. (Infinitesimal *refers to extreme smallness, whereas* infinite *refers to never-ending quantities.)*

Analyze Language: Technical Terms (LINES 194–197)
COMMON CORE RI 4

Point out to students that most of the technical terms in this selection are scientific. The writer does not always define these terms for readers.

J CITE TEXT EVIDENCE Have students find the technical terms in these lines and define them from context. *(spectrometers, gas chomatographs, and headspace vapor analyzers; machines that detect aromas)*

Strategies for Annotation ✐ ▣ *Annotate it!*

Determine Author's Purpose
COMMON CORE RI 6

Share these strategies for guided or independent analysis:

- Highlight key sentences or phrases that reflect the topic of the passage or paragraph.
- Write a note stating the purpose of each phrase or sentence.
- Review your notes to help determine the author's larger purpose.

Approximately ten thousand new processed food products are introduced every year in the United States. Almost all of them require flavor additives. And about nine out of every ten of these new food products fail. The latest flavor innovations . . .

> Shows that flavor design is a large industry and very difficult.

Determine Author's Purpose (LINES 224–238)

COMMON CORE RI 6

Reassure students that the long list of chemical names in the passage is more than they, or any general reader, could be expected to absorb or understand. Nevertheless, including the list serves a purpose for the author.

 **ASK STUDENTS** what Schlosser's purpose may have been in including so many difficult terms. (*He may have intended to overwhelm the reader with the complexity of artificial flavors, as well as to make the reader feel that there is something suspicious about foods containing such flavors.*)

Analyze Language: Technical Terms (LINES 242–250)

COMMON CORE RI 4

Tell students that readers may use reference works to learn the meaning of a technical term.

 **ASK STUDENTS** how they would go about finding out more about ethyl-2-methyl butyrate and the other chemicals whose scents he describes. (*Possible answers: Use the Internet to do research on the entire term or look up the component parts [e.g. ethyl] in an unabridged dictionary or an online dictionary or reference work.*)

---

flavor to five average size swimming pools. The flavor additive usually comes last, or second to last, in a processed food's list of ingredients (chemicals that add color are frequently used in even smaller
210 amounts). As a result, the flavor of a processed food often costs less than its packaging. Soft drinks contain a larger proportion of flavor additives than most products. The flavor in a twelve-ounce can of Coke costs about half a cent.

The Food and Drug Administration does not require flavor companies to disclose the ingredients of their additives, so long as all the chemicals are considered by the agency to be GRAS (Generally Regarded As Safe). This lack of public disclosure enables the companies to maintain the secrecy of their formulas. It also hides the fact that flavor compounds sometimes contain more ingredients than
220 the foods being given their taste. The ubiquitous phrase "artificial strawberry flavor" gives little hint of the chemical wizardry and manufacturing skill that can make a highly processed food taste like a strawberry.

A typical artificial strawberry flavor, like the kind found in a Burger King strawberry milk shake, contains the following ingredients: amyl acetate, amyl butyrate, amyl valerate, anethol, anisyl formate, benzyl acetate, benzyl isobutyrate, butyric acid, cinnamyl isobutyrate, cinnamyl valerate, cognac essential oil, diacetyl, dipropyl ketone, ethyl acetate, ethyl amylketone, ethyl butyrate, ethyl
230 cinnamate, ethyl heptanoate, ethyl heptylate, ethyl lactate, ethyl methylphenylglycidate, ethyl nitrate, ethyl propionate, ethyl valerate, heliotropin, hydroxyphrenyl-2-butanone (10 percent solution in alcohol), α-ionone, isobutyl anthranilate, isobutyl butyrate, lemon essential oil, maltol, 4-methylacetophenone, methyl anthranilate, methyl benzoate, methyl cinnamate, methyl heptine carbonate, methyl naphthyl ketone, methyl salicylate, mint essential oil, neroli essential oil, nerolin, neryl isobutyrate, orris butter, phenethyl alcohol, rose, rum ether, γ-undecalactone, vanillin, and solvent.

Although flavors usually arise from a mixture of many different
240 volatile chemicals, a single compound often supplies the dominant aroma. Smelled alone, that chemical provides an unmistakable sense of the food. Ethyl-2-methyl butyrate, for example, smells just like an apple. Today's highly processed foods offer a blank palette: whatever chemicals you add to them will give them specific tastes. Adding methyl-2-peridylketone makes something taste like popcorn. Adding ethyl-3-hydroxybutanoate makes it taste like marshmallow. The possibilities are now almost limitless. Without affecting the appearance or nutritional value, processed foods could even be made with aroma chemicals such as hexanal (the smell of freshly cut grass)
250 or 3-methyl butanoic acid (the smell of body odor).

The 1960s were the heyday of artificial flavors. The synthetic versions of flavor compounds were not subtle, but they did not need to be, given the nature of most processed food. For the past twenty

---

WHEN STUDENTS STRUGGLE...

Present the chemical terms in lines 226–238 and 242–250 as challenges for pronunciation and building oral fluency. Have students attempt to sound out one term at a time and then look it up in an unabridged dictionary, either in print or online, to check the pronunciation. Have students say the correct pronunciation clearly. To help students gain fluency, point out when components are repeated from chemicals they have already read.

years food processors have tried hard to use only "natural flavors" in their products. According to the FDA, these must be derived entirely from natural sources—from herbs, spices, fruits, vegetables, beef, chicken, yeast, bark, roots, etc. Consumers prefer to see natural flavors on a label, out of a belief that they are healthier. The distinction between artificial and natural flavors can be somewhat arbitrary and absurd, based more on how the flavor has been made than on what it actually contains. "A natural flavor," says Terry Acree, a professor of food science technology at Cornell University, "is a flavor that's been derived with an out-of-date technology." Natural flavors and artificial flavors sometimes contain exactly the same chemicals, produced through different methods. Amyl acetate, for example, provides the dominant note of banana flavor. When you distill it from bananas with a solvent, amyl acetate is a natural flavor. When you produce it by mixing vinegar with amyl alcohol, adding sulfuric acid as a **catalyst**, amyl acetate is an artificial flavor. Either way it smells and tastes the same. The phrase "natural flavor" is now listed among the ingredients of everything from Stonyfield Farm Organic Strawberry Yogurt to Taco Bell Hot Taco Sauce.

catalyst
(kăt´l-ĭst) *n.* a substance that starts or speeds up a reaction.

Image Credits: ©Photodisc/Getty Images

Food Product Design **365**

TO CHALLENGE STUDENTS ...

Make a Persuasive Argument Ask students to outline an argument for or against updating and revising the labeling requirements for food products, including the way the system deals with "natural flavors." Remind them that their argument should suggest a course of action, address possible opposing arguments, and provide evidence to support their claims. Encourage students to do additional research to find evidence to strengthen their arguments and help refute counterarguments.

CLOSE READ

Determine Author's Purpose (LINES 261–265)

COMMON CORE **RI 6**

Remind students that, in addition to the purpose of a work as a whole, authors have a purpose for including any given detail or passage in a work. These more specific purposes often support the larger purpose.

M **ASK STUDENTS** what purpose Schlosser had in quoting Terry Acree on the subject of natural versus artificial flavor. *(The quotation provides expert testimony to support Schlosser's statement that there is no substantive difference between flavor chemicals that are called natural and flavor chemicals that are called artificial. Being backed up by an expert makes the statement more persuasive.)* How does the purpose of this passage support the purpose of the work as a whole? *(By discussing this one deceptive practice in the food industry, Schlosser supports the purpose of critiquing the practices of the industry as a whole.)*

Analyze Language: Technical Terms (LINES 266–269)

COMMON CORE **RI 4**

Remind students that a technical term is a word that has a specific meaning in a certain context.

N **CITE TEXT EVIDENCE** Ask students to identify the technical terms in these lines. *(distill, solvent, amyl acetate, natural flavor, amyl alcohol, sulfuric acid, artificial flavor)* Then ask students to define *solvent* from the context. *(a chemical that breaks things down)*

> ### CRITICAL VOCABULARY
>
> **catalyst:** In the chemical process that Schlosser describes, sulfuric acid is the substance that causes the reaction to happen.
>
> **ASK STUDENTS** what would happen in a chemical process if no **catalyst** were added. *(The chemicals might not combine, or they would combine more slowly.)*

Determine Author's Purpose (LINES 284–303)

COMMON CORE RI 6

Remind students that an author's choice of topics and tone both reflect the work's purpose.

O CITE TEXT EVIDENCE Ask students to list word choices that reveal Schlosser's tone, or attitude, toward flavorists. *("elite," "poetic sensibility," "conjure illusions," "charming, cosmopolitan, and ironic," "enjoyed fine wine," "compared his work to composing music")* Then ask students to describe Schlosser's tone. *(mostly respectful, but perhaps with a hint of mockery)* Finally, ask students why they think Schlosser included this information about flavorists. *(By emphasizing the great expertise and art required to synthesize flavors, Schlosser emphasizes that these chemical additives are far from natural.)*

CRITICAL VOCABULARY

conjure: When the glass bottles were opened, it seemed as though specific foods had suddenly appeared in the room.

ASK STUDENTS what smells conjure good memories for them. *(Responses will vary.)*

Technical Terms (LINES 304–319)

COMMON CORE RI 4

Tell students that introducing one technical term sometimes makes it necessary for a writer to introduce additional technical terms to explain it.

P CITE TEXT EVIDENCE Have students find additional technical terms that Schlosser introduces in his explanation of *mouthfeel.* *(rheology; In addition, ordinary words such as* bounce, creep, *and* breaking point *take on a technical meaning in the context of flavorists' work.)*

A natural flavor is not necessarily healthier or purer than an artificial one. When almond flavor (benzaldehyde) is derived from natural sources, such as peach and apricot pits, it contains traces of hydrogen cyanide, a deadly poison. Benzaldehyde derived through a different process—by mixing oil of clove and the banana flavor, amyl acetate—does not contain any cyanide. Nevertheless, it is legally considered an artificial flavor and sells at a much lower price. Natural
280 and artificial flavors are now manufactured at the same chemical plants, places that few people would associate with Mother Nature. Calling any of these flavors "natural" requires a flexible attitude toward the English language and a fair amount of irony.

The small and elite group of scientists who create most of the flavor in most of the food now consumed in the United States are called "flavorists." They draw upon a number of disciplines in their work: biology, psychology, physiology, and organic chemistry. A flavorist is a chemist with a trained nose and a poetic sensibility. Flavors are created by blending scores of different chemicals in tiny
290 amounts, a process governed by scientific principles but demanding a fair amount of art. In an age when delicate aromas, subtle flavors, and microwave ovens do not easily coexist, the job of the flavorist is to **conjure** illusions about processed food and, in the words of one flavor company's literature, to ensure "consumer likeability." The flavorists with whom I spoke were charming, cosmopolitan, and ironic. They were also discreet, in keeping with the dictates of their trade. They were the sort of scientist who not only enjoyed fine wine, but could also tell you the chemicals that gave each vintage its unique aroma. One flavorist compared his work to composing music. A well-made
300 flavor compound will have a "top note," followed by a "dry-down," and a "leveling-off," with different chemicals responsible for each stage. The taste of a food can be radically altered by minute changes in the flavoring mix. "A little odor goes a long way," one flavorist said.

In order to give a processed food the proper taste, a flavorist must always consider the food's "mouthfeel"— the unique combination of textures and chemical interactions that affects how the flavor is perceived. The mouthfeel can be adjusted through the use of various fats, gums, starches, emulsifiers, and stabilizers. The aroma chemicals of a food can be precisely analyzed, but mouthfeel is much harder
310 to measure. How does one quantify a french fry's crispness? Food technologists are now conducting basic research in rheology, a branch of physics that examines the flow and deformation of materials. A number of companies sell sophisticated devices that attempt to measure mouthfeel. The Universal TA-XT2 Texture Analyzer, produced by the Texture Technologies Corporation, performs calculations based on data derived from twenty-five separate probes. It is essentially a mechanical mouth. It gauges the most important rheological properties of a food—the bounce, creep, breaking point, density, crunchiness, chewiness, gumminess, lumpiness, rubberiness,

conjure
(kŏn´jər) *v.* to produce from nothing, as if by magic.

SCAFFOLDING FOR ELL STUDENTS

Build Oral Fluency The vocabulary word *conjure* presents an opportunity for students to practice pronunciation. Direct students to the pronunciation note in the margin, and ask them to pronounce the word. Correct any errors. For example, some students might pronounce the final *-ed* or might pronounce a long *u* in the second syllable.

Invite students to point out other words in the text that they would find hard to pronounce. Provide models by pronouncing the words aloud. Then have students pronounce the words.

320　springiness, slipperiness, smoothness, softness, wetness, juiciness,
spreadability, spring-back, and tackiness.

　　Some of the most important advances in flavor manufacturing
are now occurring in the field of biotechnology. Complex flavors are
being made through fermentation, enzyme reactions, fungal cultures,
and tissue cultures. All of the flavors being created through these
methods—including the ones being synthesized by funguses—are
considered natural flavors by the FDA. The new enzyme-based
processes are responsible for extremely lifelike dairy flavors. One
company now offers not just butter flavor, but also fresh creamy
330　butter, cheesy butter, milky butter, savory melted butter, and superconcentrated butter flavor, in liquid or powder form. The development
of new fermentation techniques, as well as new techniques for heating
mixtures of sugar and amino acids, have led to the creation of much
more realistic meat flavors. The McDonald's Corporation will not
reveal the exact origin of the natural flavor added to its french fries. In
response to inquiries from *Vegetarian Journal*, however, McDonald's
did acknowledge that its fries derive some of their characteristic flavor
from "animal products."

　　Other popular fast foods derive their flavor from unexpected
340　sources. Wendy's Grilled Chicken Sandwich, for example, contains
beef extracts. Burger King's BK Broiler Chicken Breast Patty contains
"natural smoke flavor." A firm called Red Arrow Products Company
specializes in smoke flavor, which is added to barbecue sauces and
processed meats. Red Arrow manufactures natural smoke flavor by
charring sawdust and capturing the aroma chemicals released into
the air. The smoke is captured in water and then bottled, so that other
companies can sell food which seems to have been cooked over a fire.

　　In a meeting room at IFF, Brian Grainger let me sample some
of the company's flavors. It was an unusual taste test; there wasn't
350　any food to taste. Grainger is a senior flavorist at IFF, a soft-spoken
chemist with graying hair, an English accent, and a fondness for
understatement. He could easily be mistaken for a British diplomat or
the owner of a West End brasserie with two Michelin stars. Like many
in the flavor industry, he has an Old World, old-fashioned sensibility
which seems out of step with our brand-conscious, egocentric age.
When I suggested that IFF should put its own logo on the products
that contain its flavors—instead of allowing other brands to enjoy the
consumer loyalty and affection inspired by those flavors—Grainger
politely disagreed, assuring me such a thing would never be done.
360　In the absence of public credit or acclaim, the small and secretive
fraternity of flavor chemists praises one another's work. Grainger can
often tell, by analyzing the flavor formula of a product, which of his
counterparts at a rival firm devised it. And he enjoys walking down
supermarket aisles, looking at the many products that contain his
flavors, even if no one else knows it.

TEACH

CLOSE READ

Determine Author's Purpose (LINES 334–338)

COMMON CORE　RI 6

Make the point that as a selection moves forward, the author may refer back to earlier points in the selection for the purpose of developing or resolving them.

Q CITE TEXT EVIDENCE Have students find the passage at the beginning of the selection to which this passage refers. *(the discussion of the source of McDonald's french fries flavor in the first two paragraphs of the selection, lines 1–22)* Why does Schlosser return to this issue? *(to add new information—that the non-beef flavor is actually composed in part of meat products—and to emphasize that this "natural" flavor is mysterious and man-made)*

Determine Author's Purpose (LINES 348–365)

COMMON CORE　RI 6

Call students' attention to Brian Grainger's statement in line 359 that IFF would never put its own logo on products that contain its flavors.

R ASK STUDENTS why Schlosser might have choosen to focus on the element of secrecy at IFF. *(to highlight how little most consumers know about the flavor industry that affects so much of their food)*

Strategies for Annotation 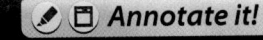 *Annotate it!*

Determine Author's Purpose

COMMON CORE　RI 6

Share these strategies for guided or independent analysis:

- Highlight in blue words and phrases that describe the process of creating flavors.
- Highlight in yellow words and phrases that describe flavors themselves.
- Write one or more notes comparing and contrasting Schlosser's choice of words for the flavors and the process of creating them.

All of the flavors being created...including the ones being synthesized by funguses—are considered natural flavors by the FDA. The new enzyme-based processes are responsible for extremely lifelike dairy flavors. One company now offers...fresh creamy butter, cheesy butter, milky butter, savory melted butter, and superconcentrated butter flavor, in liquid or powder form.

The author's words make the flavors sound delicious but make the process of creating the flavors sound unpleasant.

Determine Author's Purpose (LINES 372–377)

COMMON CORE RI 6

Tell students that an author can use comparisons and contrasts to support his or her purpose.

Ⓢ ASK STUDENTS to cite the contrast in the final paragraph. *(With his eyes closed, the author smells the "uncanny, almost miraculous" scent of "a grilled hamburger." When he opens his eyes, he does not see a hamburger. Instead, he sees "a narrow strip of white paper and a smiling flavorist.")* Ask students how the contrast between what the author sees and what he smells is related to his purpose. *(The contrast shows that food smells and flavors are often not what they seem. In fact, they can be completely artificial. This observation is related to the author's purpose of raising readers' awareness of the chemicals in processed foods.)*

COLLABORATIVE DISCUSSION Divide students into small groups, and have them discuss how reading this selection has affected their ideas about fast food. Have students create a chart in which they list specific facts or passages from the selection that surprised them, changed their ideas, or confirmed their existing ideas. Ask them to comment on the effect each example had on them.

ASK STUDENTS to share any questions they generated in the course of reading and discussing the selection.

Grainger had brought a dozen small glass bottles from the lab. After he opened each bottle, I dipped a fragrance testing filter into it. The filters were long white strips of paper designed to absorb aroma chemicals without producing off-notes. Before placing the strips of
370 paper before my nose, I closed my eyes. Then I inhaled deeply, and one food after another was conjured from the glass bottles. I smelled fresh cherries, black olives, sautéed onions, and shrimp. Grainger's most remarkable creation took me by surprise. After closing my eyes, I suddenly smelled a grilled hamburger. The aroma was uncanny, almost miraculous. It smelled like someone in the room was flipping burgers on a hot grill. But when I opened my eyes, there was just a narrow strip of white paper and a smiling flavorist.

COLLABORATIVE DISCUSSION What are examples of information in the selection that either confirmed or changed your ideas about fast food? Discuss this question with a partner, citing specific evidence from the selection to support your ideas.

Determine Author's Purpose

As an investigative journalist, Eric Schlosser's general **purpose,** or reason, for writing is to inform, to persuade, or to do some combination of the two. His purpose may also involve the desire to move people to take a particular action based on the information he presents. Analyzing the content and the style of the selection will allow you to infer Schlosser's specific purpose for writing it. As you analyze this selection, ask yourself these questions:

- What are the topics that Schlosser writes about in the selection?
- What tone or attitude does he express on the topics?
- What is distinctive about Schlosser's style and rhetoric, including his word choices, sentence lengths, tone, or other persuasive uses of language?
- What action might Schlosser have implicitly wanted readers to take after reading this selection?

Analyze Language: Technical Terms

 COMMON CORE RI 4

A characteristic of Schlosser's style in this selection is the extensive use of specialized vocabulary in the form of technical terms. By examining the context for each usage of these terms, you can understand how they serve Schlosser's purpose.

Sometimes, Schlosser defines the terms he is using.

Legend has it that a German scientist discovered methyl anthranilate, one of the first artificial flavors, by accident while mixing chemicals in his laboratory. Suddenly the lab was filled with the sweet smell of grapes. Methyl anthranilate later became the chief flavoring compound of grape Kool-Aid.

Schlosser first defines *methyl anthranilate* as "one of the first artificial flavors" and then through the example implies that it is a chemical that produces the artificial flavor of grapes.

At other times, Schlosser does not define the meaning of technical terms.

Adding methyl-2-peridylketone makes something taste like popcorn. Adding ethyl-3-hydroxybutanoate makes it taste like marshmallow.

Neither of these sentences actually defines the technical terms. As you encounter such terms when analyzing the selection, ask yourself why Schlosser might want to use them. Why doesn't he just say: "Adding one chemical makes something taste like popcorn. Adding another makes it taste like marshmallow"?

TEACH

CLOSE READ

Determine Author's Purpose

To help students determine the author's purpose, have pairs or groups of four work together to answer the questions. Students might divide the questions among themselves and discuss one another's answers.

Possible answers:

- *He writes about the similarities and differences between natural and artificial flavoring, the history of the food flavoring industry, the industry's current prosperity, the work that flavorists do, and the chemistry of flavorings.*
- *His tone ranges from impressed to disapproving.*
- *His style is marked by extensive detail, often presented in long sentences and including technical vocabulary.*
- *He may want people to avoid buying and eating products flavored with "natural" and artificial flavorings.*

Analyze Language: Technical Terms

 COMMON CORE RI 4

Have students work in pairs to find the terms and attempt to figure out the meanings from their context. Ask why Schlosser might have wanted to use these terms. *(Using specific names makes his evidence sound stronger. Some of the chemical names also sound dangerous or suspicious.)*

Strategies for Annotation 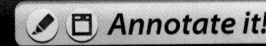 *Annotate it!*

Determine Author's Purpose

 COMMON CORE RI 6

Share these strategies for guided or independent analysis:

- Highlight in blue a detail that makes you wonder why the author included it.
- Underline words or phrases that provide clues why the highlighted passage is important.
- Write a note telling why you think Schlosser included the detail.

A look at the ingredients now used in the preparation of McDonald's French fries suggests how the problem was solved. At the end of the list is a seemingly innocuous, yet oddly mysterious phrase: "natural flavor." That ingredient helps to explain not only why the fries taste so good, but also why most fast food—indeed, most of the food Americans eat today—tastes the way it does.

> He wants to show how much of our food includes this undefined ingredient.

PRACTICE & APPLY

Analyzing the Text COMMON CORE RI 1, RI 4, RI 6

Possible answers:

1. *The German flavor industry came to the United States after World War II. As Americans began eating more processed food in the 1950s, the industry grew.*

2. *Schlosser includes so much detail about the IFF plant in order to impress the reader in specific ways with the power and capacity of the flavor industry, as well as the extent of its influence.*

3. *Similarities: The two flavors are identical in chemical composition and are manufactured at the same plants. Differences: The chemicals in natural flavorings are extracted from plants or animals, while those in artificial flavorings are produced through reactions of other chemicals. Schlosser explains these terms in detail in order to make his point that neither kind of flavoring truly occurs naturally.*

4. *Schlosser's purpose is to vividly make the point that consumers often eat foods whose ingredients they do not really know or understand.*

5. *Schlosser means that the term "natural" in "natural flavor" is a deception; these flavors are actually as artificial as ones called "artificial flavor." Because of this disconnect between the term and its meaning, the term "natural flavors" is ironic.*

6. *Schlosser might want people to become more aware of what they eat, to stop eating foods that contain chemical flavoring, and possibly to build a movement to change the methods of the food industry.*

7. *His purpose is to inform readers of fundamental facts about the food industry about which many people are unaware, and to persuade readers that the tactics of the food industry are not in consumers' best interests. His style is effective because it both conveys a large amount of information and includes enough personal experiences to hold readers' attention.*

eBook *Annotate It!*

Analyzing the Text COMMON CORE RI 1, RI 4, RI 6, W 3, W 4

Cite Text Evidence Support your responses with evidence from the selection.

1. **Cause and Effect** What caused the growth of the flavor industry after World War II?

2. **Draw Conclusions** Why does Schlosser include so much detail about his visit to the IFF plant in New Jersey?

3. **Compare** What are the similarities and differences between "artificial flavors" and "natural flavors"? Why does Schlosser explain these two terms in such detail?

4. **Analyze** What is Schlosser's purpose in listing all the chemical ingredients in "a typical artificial strawberry flavor, like the kind found in a Burger King strawberry milk shake"?

5. **Infer** Irony refers to a contrast between appearance and reality. What does Schlosser mean when he says, "Calling any of these flavors 'natural' requires a flexible attitude toward the English language and a fair amount of irony"?

6. **Draw Conclusions** What might Schlosser want people to do after reading this selection?

7. **Evaluate** What is Schlosser's overall purpose in writing this selection? How effective is his style in allowing him to achieve that purpose?

PERFORMANCE TASK

Writing Activity: Narrative Schlosser wanted people to know more about processed food after reading this selection. Explore how the selection might affect a reader through this writing task.

- Write a narrative in which at least one of the characters has recently read this selection and portray how the selection influences the character's thoughts, words, and actions.

- Engage and orient the reader by setting out a situation related to processed foods, such as a visit to a fast food restaurant, a trip to the grocery store, or an exploration of food products found at home.

- Use a variety of narrative techniques such as dialogue, pacing, and description to move the plot forward and develop experiences and characters.

- Use the selection as a source of precise words and phrases, details, and sensory language to convey a vivid picture of the situation and the characters.

- Provide a conclusion that reflects on the events in the narrative.

Assign this performance task.

PERFORMANCE TASK COMMON CORE W 3, W 4

Writing Activity: Narrative Have students plan and write independently, using the following approach. Reread the selection and take notes on what influenced your thinking about food. Decide whether to use first-person or third-person point of view. Use dialogue to have the main character explain his or her thoughts. Give another character a different opinion. Have volunteers distribute copies to the class and read their stories aloud.

Critical Vocabulary

stem	volatile	infinitesimal	catalyst	conjure

Practice and Apply Complete each sentence to reflect your understanding of the meaning of each Critical Vocabulary word.

1. The taste of fast food french fries now **stems** from . . .

2. **Volatile** chemicals have to be kept in closed containers because . . .

3. Everyday measuring spoons cannot be used to measure the **infinitesimal** amounts of chemicals in a particular flavor because . . .

4. Producing artificial flavors requires a **catalyst** like sulfuric acid because . . .

5. Some chemists seem to **conjure** foods because . . .

Language and Style: Dashes

Sometimes a writer wants to interrupt the main thought of a sentence with a word, expression, phrase or sentence called a parenthetical element. Usually such parenthetical elements are set off with parentheses or with commas. However, writers sometimes use dashes to set off the elements in a sentence.

If the break in thought is abrupt, the parenthetical element is set off with dashes.

> **That ingredient helps to explain not only why the fries taste so good, but also why most fast food—indeed, most of the food Americans eat today—tastes the way it does.**

Sometimes dashes are used to create pauses, often for ironic, satirical, or dramatic effect.

> **The mix gave the fries their unique flavor—and more saturated beef fat per ounce than a McDonald's hamburger.**

Practice and Apply Add the italicized parenthetical elements to the following sentences, setting them off with dashes.

1. Flavors made from natural ingredients are sometimes considered healthier. *herbs, fruits, vegetables, chicken, yeast, and bark*

2. The french fries are delicious. *and very fattening*

3. Flavorists create the flavor in most of the food we eat. *scientists with trained noses and poetic sensibilities*

4. One remarkable creation took Schlosser by surprise. *a strip of paper that smelled just like a grilled hamburger*

PRACTICE & APPLY

Critical Vocabulary

Possible answers:

1. . . ."natural flavor" that is manufactured in processing plants.

2. . . .they might explode or suddenly change state.

3. . . .the chemicals are present in such tiny quantities.

4. . . .the catalyst triggers or helps the desired chemical reaction between the ingredients that create the flavor.

5. . . .the process is so mysterious, and so different from that found in nature, that it seems almost magical.

Language and Style: Dashes

Answers:

1. *Flavors made from natural ingredients—herbs, fruits, vegetables, chicken, yeast, and bark—are sometimes considered healthier.*

2. *The french fries are delicious—and very fattening.*

3. *Flavorists—scientists with trained noses and poetic sensibilities—create the flavor in most of the food we eat.*

4. *One remarkable creation—a strip of paper that smelled just like a grilled hamburger—took Schlosser by surprise.*

Strategies for Annotation 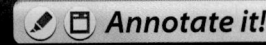 Annotate it!

Language and Style: Dashes

Have students return to the selection and find two or more sentences that contain dashes. Encourage them to use their eBook annotation tools to do the following:

- Highlight the dashes in blue.
- Underline the part of the sentence that the dashes set off.
- In a note, rewrite the sentence using other punctuation. You may revise the word order of the sentence.

That ingredient helps to explain not only why the fries taste so good, but also why most fast food—indeed, most of the food Americans eat today—tastes the way it does.

> That ingredient helps to explain not only why the fries taste so good, but also why most fast food, indeed, most of the food Americans eat today tastes the way it does.

PRACTICE & APPLY

Author's Purpose
 **COMMON CORE** RL 6, RI 6

Remind students that *The Jungle* is a novel. Ask students to discuss how a novel can be called a work of investigative journalism. *(It can address an issue of concern in the real world and can be based on thorough real-world research. Readers of* The Jungle *were aware that the author's main purpose was to expose real-world injustice.)*

Analyzing the Text
COMMON CORE RL 1, RL 5, RL 6, RI 1, RI 5, RI 6

Answers:

1. *The setting of* The Jungle *is an early 1900s meat-packing plant; that of "Food Product Design" is a modern chemical processing lab. Each setting reflects the main topic of that selection: the mistreatment of animals and workers in Sinclair's case, and the development of chemical flavorings in Schlosser's.*

2. *The statement in* The Jungle *is intended as a futuristic exaggeration; with modern technology, however, the scientists in "Food Product Design" really can create chicken flavor.*

3. *Students' choices of passages will vary. Students may say that vivid description, workplace details, and factual information help achieve the writer's purpose.*

4. *Both writers deal with the various claims of food companies and the mysterious or complicated ingredients of their processed foods. Schlosser relates scientific facts. Sinclair uses irony as well as vivid physical descriptions and a tone of outrage.*

 **Assess It!**

Online Selection Test
- Download an editable ExamView bank.
- Assign and manage this test online.

COMPARE TEXTS *from* **The Jungle**
Food Product Design

 eBook *Annotate It!*

Author's Purpose
COMMON CORE RL 6, RI 6

Sinclair and Schlosser are both investigative journalists. Their common purpose was to explore a topic in depth and provide previously unknown information to readers. Sinclair was identified with a group of writers known as muckrakers who exposed corruption and social problems caused by large corporations in the early twentieth century. Many critics say that Schlosser's work follows in this journalistic tradition.

Both writers also use elements of **realism** in their writing. For example, they use detailed descriptive language and vivid storytelling, although one wrote fiction and the other wrote nonfiction. Their styles try to put readers right in the center of the action through creating the sense that "I was there; this is what happened."

Analyzing the Text
COMMON CORE RL1, RL 5, RL 6, RI 1, RI 5, RI 6, SL 3, SL 4

Cite Text Evidence Support your responses with evidence from the selections.

1. **Analyze** What are the workplace settings of each selection? How does the choice of setting relate to each author's purpose?

2. **Connect** In *The Jungle*, Jurgis's friend says of Durham, "Perhaps they had a secret process for making chickens chemically." How does this statement relate to Schlosser's description of the work of International Flavors & Fragrances?

3. **Cite Evidence** Select two short passages from each selection that reflect elements of realism. How do these elements help each author achieve his purpose?

4. **Synthesize** What similar themes and topics do these selections address? What are similarities and differences in the approaches that the writers use to present these themes and topics?

 **my WriteSmart**

PERFORMANCE TASK

Speaking Activity: Debate Are foods safer now than they were when *The Jungle* was written?

- Form teams of two to three students each. Half the teams will take the pro position on the question and half will take the con position.

- Each team should gather evidence from both selections to support its position.

- Conduct your debate by following the rules for debating found in the Performance Task Reference Guide.

- After the debate, write an evaluation of which side presented the most compelling argument.

Assign this performance task.  **my WriteSmart**

PERFORMANCE TASK
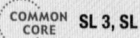 **COMMON CORE** SL 3, SL 4

Speaking Activity: Debate Focus the debate on the aspects of food production: meat processing, chemical flavoring, and working conditions. Allow students to do more research if time permits. They may include evidence about new labor and food inspection laws passed in the early 20th century. Schedule the debates, and limit each team to three to five minutes. All team members should participate in the preparation and the delivery.

Determine Themes and Main Ideas

RI 2

TEACH

Tell students that the main idea of a text is its central or dominating idea, the most important idea that the author wishes the reader to take away from the text. The main idea serves as a unifying principle for the structure of the work. All parts of a work should be relevant to stating or supporting the main idea.

The terms *theme* and *main idea* are often used interchangeably. However, theme is most often applied to works of literature—fiction, poetry, or drama—while main idea is more often used for nonfiction. A work may have more than one theme or main idea.

Sometimes, the writer explicitly states the main idea of a work. In most cases, however, readers infer the main idea by analyzing the author's tone and word choice, the choice of scenes and details, and the implications of the action. The outcome of the central issue (in nonfiction) or central conflict (in fiction) is often an important clue to theme. In nonfiction, the opening and closing paragraphs often contain hints or statements about the main idea.

Theme and main idea are different than subject or topic. The subject or topic is simply what the work is about. The main idea or theme is a message or statement about the topic.

PRACTICE AND APPLY

Have students independently review "Food Product Design" and their notes and draw a conclusion about the main idea. Tell them to write the main idea in a single sentence and to write a numbered list of three or more pieces of evidence from the text supporting their conclusion.

Then have students form groups of two to four and share their analyses of the main idea and evidence. Tell them to note similarities and differences in their analyses and to decide whether the selection has more than one main idea. Have each group write a one-paragraph statement of its findings. Ask groups to read their statements aloud so that the class can reach a consensus on the selection's main idea.

Determine Author's Purpose

RI 6

RETEACH

Remind students that an author's purpose is his or her reason for writing a specific text. The four most common purposes are to inform, to persuade, to entertain, and to express a feeling.

Remind students, too, that a work may have more than one purpose. Purposes are often related. For example, in order to persuade readers to adopt the writer's opinion, the writer usually has to provide information on the subject.

Tell students that the title of a work may be a clue to the author's purpose.

- Have students state two purposes that Eric Schlosser probably had for writing "Food Product Design." *(to inform and to persuade)*
- Have students analyze why the title "Food Product Design" hints at both purposes. *(To inform: "Food Product Design" names a factual subject involving information most readers would not know. To persuade: The idea of designing food as a product seems artificial and wrong.)*

LEVEL UP TUTORIALS Assign the following *Level Up* tutorial: **Author's Purpose**

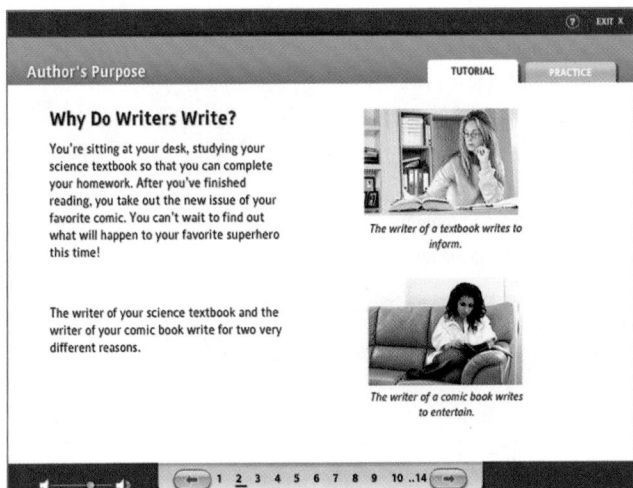

CLOSE READING APPLICATION

Have pairs of students select three or more magazine articles and analyze how the titles reflect the author's purposes. Have pairs share their analyses.

The Yuckiest Food in the Amazon

Science Writing by Mary Roach

Why This Text

Students are likely to encounter unfamiliar, complex ideas in science writing, which may make it difficult for them to determine the author's purpose. With the help of the close-reading questions, students will analyze how a set of ideas is developed in the article. This close reading will lead students to understand the author's purpose.

Background Have students read the background and information about the author and the article. Introduce the article by explaining that Mary Roach is known for writing about unusual science topics—such as cadavers, the alimentary canal, packing for Mars—in a lively and humorous style. Her style does not detract from the seriousness of her work, which has won numerous accolades from within and outside of the scientific establishment.

AS YOU READ Ask students to pay attention to the tone of the article. How does the tone help illuminate the author's purpose?

Common Core Support

- cite strong and thorough textual evidence
- determine central ideas of a text
- determine the meaning of words and phrases as they are used in a text
- determine an author's point of view and purpose, analyzing how style and content contribute to the text

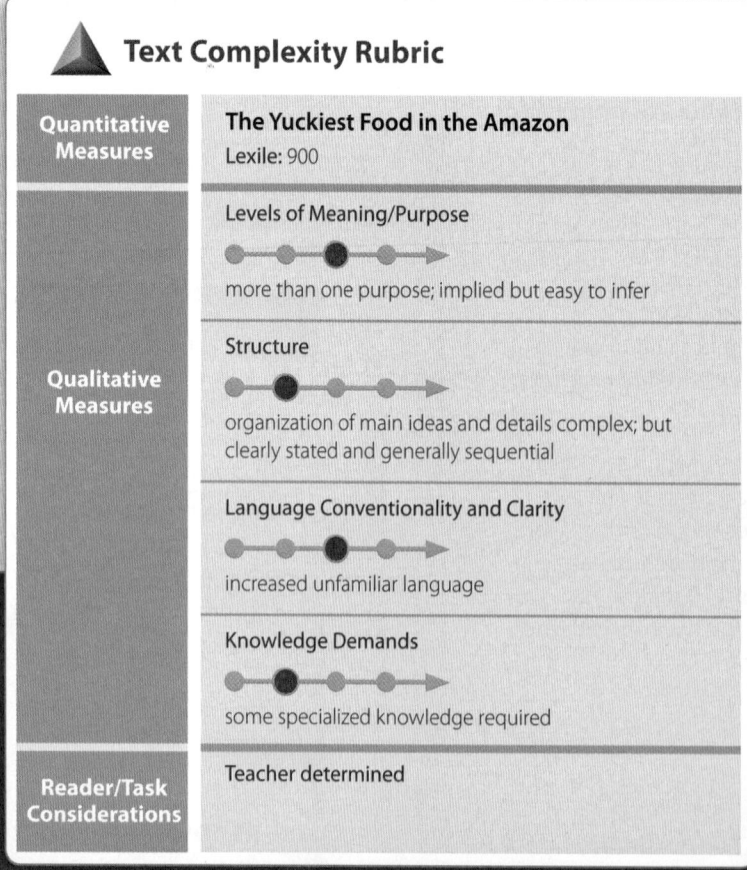

Text Complexity Rubric

Quantitative Measures

The Yuckiest Food in the Amazon
Lexile: 900

Qualitative Measures

Levels of Meaning/Purpose
more than one purpose; implied but easy to infer

Structure
organization of main ideas and details complex; but clearly stated and generally sequential

Language Conventionality and Clarity
increased unfamiliar language

Knowledge Demands
some specialized knowledge required

Reader/Task Considerations
Teacher determined

Strategies for CLOSE READING

Determine Author's Purpose

Students should read this essay carefully all the way through. Close-reading questions at the bottom of the page will help them focus on a thorough analysis of the author's purpose. As they read, students should jot down comments or questions about the text in the margins.

WHEN STUDENTS STRUGGLE . . .

To help students determine the author's purpose in "The Yuckiest Food in the Amazon," have them work in small groups to fill out a chart like the one shown below.

CITE TEXT EVIDENCE For practice analyzing an author's purpose, ask students to cite evidence of the author's rhetorical choices that advanced that purpose.

Title	"The Yuckiest Food in the Amazon"
Tone	"I have frequently . . . felt the need to put . . . my mouth . . . where it would rather not go." (lines 11–12) "Now I am getting my come-uppance." (line 18) "My problem . . . is a knee. . . . quietly genuflecting in a bowl of oily broth." (lines 33–34)
Rhetoric	"a raw fish eye and its accompanying musculature" (line 14) "You eat what they hunt." (lines 25–26) "The knee is one of nature's marvels, a busy intersection of tendon, bone and cartilage." (lines 39–40)
Language	"I come from a tribe that eats Vienna sausages." (lines 150–151) "Every few seconds, he looks back at me, his face changing channels from disgust to bewilderment and back" (lines 164–165)
Author's Purpose:	to show that the concept of "disgust" varies across cultures.

Background *What tastes worse than rodent knee and saliva-flavored manioc mash? It depends on where you come from, as writer* **Mary Roach** *learned in a remote Amazon village. In 1998, Roach accompanied anthropologist John Patton to the village of Conambo in Ecuador, where he was studying the Achuar people. Although usually up for any adventure, Roach had some hesitation when faced with the local food, as described in the following article.*

The Yuckiest Food in the Amazon

Science Writing by Mary Roach

CLOSE READ
Notes

1. **READ ▶** As you read lines 1–38, begin to collect and cite evidence.

- Underline conclusions that Rozin learns from his research.
- Circle examples of things Roach has eaten in her travels.
- In the margin, explain the "huge difference" Roach describes in lines 27–32.

In 1986, a psychologist named Paul Rozin took a group of toddlers and did a peculiar thing. One by one, he sat them down at a table and presented them with a plate of what he said was dog-doo and asked them if they'd like to eat it. (In fact, it was peanut butter, scented with bleu cheese.) Then he did the same with a sterilized grasshopper. Sixty-two percent of the children under 2 happily dispatched the **ersatz** turd; 31 percent the insect. Older children invariably rejected both plates. His point: Disgust is learned. Culture is our instructor. We are taught that horse meat is disgusting but chicken embryos are not; that Slim Jims are tasty and crickets are gross.

10   **Espousing**, as I have, a belief that nothing is inherently disgusting, that it's all a case of mind over culture, I have frequently, in my travels, felt the need to put my money where my mouth is and my mouth where it would rather not go. I have eaten walrus meat left buried on an Arctic beach to "ferment" for a month, a raw fish eye and its accompanying musculature, duck tongue, caribou marrow, brain, flipper, ant. I am, yes, one of those annoying travelers who

ersatz:
fake, pretend

espouse:
promote,
support

83

1. **READ AND CITE TEXT EVIDENCE**   Explain to students that the author begins her essay by recounting a psychological study that frames the topic she will explore.

Ⓐ **ASK STUDENTS** how they identified Rozin's conclusions. *Students should distinguish between Rozin's results—62% of the children ate the fake turd, etc.—and his conclusions. The results lead to his conclusions, which are introduced with the phrase, "His point."*

Critical Vocabulary: ersatz (line 6) Have students share their definitions of *ersatz*, and ask volunteers to use the adjective in sentences about food. *Example: Our vegetarian friends prepared a magnificent meal of ersatz turkey.*

Critical Vocabulary: espouse (line 10) Have students suggest synonyms for *espouse* that could be used in this context. *advocate, champion, embrace, uphold*

She learns the difference between eating something just once and eating it for days at a time.

boast about the disgusting food they've lived to tell about (and tell about and tell about).

Now I am getting my come-uppance. I am getting it big-time, in a small village in the Ecuadorian Amazon. I have come here to do a story on an
20 anthropologist named John Patton. Patton studies a tribe called the Achuar, notable for their skill in blowgun-making and their long-ago rivalry with the head-shrinking Chuar. (If you've seen an authentic South American shrunken head, you've probably seen an Achuar tribesman.) Patton's base is Conambo, a scatter of houses along a fast, muddy river, reachable every now and again by a four-seater missionary plane. There is no hotel, no restaurant, no store. You eat what they hunt.

I am fast coming to understand that there is a huge difference, a vast yawning canyon of difference, between tasting something deeply unappealing and living on it. Anyone, if he tries, can suppress his disgust long enough to
30 swallow a single fish eye or a mouthful of decaying walrus. Eating enough of this sort of thing to live on is altogether a different matter. I am here for five days. I'm not doing very well.

My problem at the moment is a knee. It's a rodent knee, quietly genuflecting in a bowl of oily broth. Earlier today, the knee was attached to a happy, hairy, spaniel-sized rodent, **gamboling** and cavorting in the wee hours of the rain forest morning until our host happened along and plugged it full of buckshot. (Blowguns are used only on birds and pack animals like monkeys, which would be scared off by gunshot.)

gambol:
skip, hop

C The knee is one of nature's marvels, a busy intersection of tendon, bone
40 and cartilage. Be that as it may, "marvel" does not exactly describe my state of

---

2. **◀ REREAD** Reread lines 10–38. Describe the tone Roach uses as she writes about "yucky" foods. Cite examples from the text.

Roach has a light-hearted tone, and she also doesn't steer clear of making fun of herself. She repeats words to emphasize these points, as in, "to tell about (and tell about and tell about)."

3. **READ ▶** As you read lines 39–80, continue to cite evidence.
- Underline examples of Roach's humorous tone.
- In the margin, make an inference about why Roach must "clean my plate."
- Circle text that describes how Patton feels about his soup.

84

---

mind at the moment. Extreme psychic discomfort comes closer. The hunter and the chef are sitting directly across from me. Their generosity is heartbreaking. I have to clean my plate. I must force apart the gristly abomination with my teeth, work my tongue into its fissures and slimy orifices, extract anything vaguely chewable, and swallow it. I lean over to scout the contents of Patton's bowl.

He got the ankle. The thing about ankle bones, as schoolchildren everywhere know, is that they're attached to foot bones. And foot bones are attached to toe bones and toenails and those filthy little rubbery pads on the
50 bottom of the foot. No matter how good a meat may taste, the experience is **indelibly** marred by the act of spitting ghastly unchewables out into your fingers.

Patton is undaunted. He has the entire thing in his mouth. He stops sucking and gumming long enough to say: "The foot pads are a good source of fat." He is enjoying his rodent soup in the way that only a man who has been served steamed tapir[1] fetus and live palm beetles can. A hail of tiny foot bones
D accumulates on the ground beside him.

The knee awaits. I've finished my broth. To stall any longer would betray my revulsion. I manage to locate a couple of pockets of reasonably normal-
60 looking flesh. My inclination is to chew these slowly, forever if need be, until my hosts tire of sitting here and go off to tend the manioc[2] garden. The problem with this tactic is that boiled rodent flesh isn't the sort of thing you want to have hanging around your tongue for any longer than is strictly necessary for purposes of not choking to death. It's not really that bad, it's just strong. As in overpowering, as in taste buds passing out and waving white flags. It doesn't, in short, taste anything like chicken. I find myself chewing with my mouth open, hoping my hosts will take this for an endearing cultural peculiarity, rather than an attempt to bypass the tasting portion of my meal.

[1] **tapir:** a mammal related to the horse and the rhinoceros, with a flexible snout.
[2] **manioc:** a shrubby tropical plant, also known as cassava.

These people share what they have. It would be rude to decline the food.

indelibly:
forever, permanently

---

4. **◀ REREAD** Reread lines 53–57. Why does Patton seem "undaunted" about eating his rodent soup?

Patton likes the soup because he's eaten it before, and because he's eaten more disgusting foods such as "tapir fetus" and "live palm beetles." As stated previously, taste is relative.

85

---

2. **REREAD AND CITE TEXT EVIDENCE**

B **ASK STUDENTS** to describe the tone the author takes toward herself. *Students should recognize that Roach has a self-deprecating tone: "I am, yes, one of those annoying travelers" (line 15), "Now I am getting my come-uppance. I am getting it big-time" (line 18).*

3. **READ AND CITE TEXT EVIDENCE**

C **ASK STUDENTS** how they made their inference. *Students should note that the generosity of the hunter and chef "is heartbreaking," which implies there isn't much food to share.*

Critical Vocabulary: gambol (line 35) Ask students how the word *gambol* helps the author convey her purpose. *Gambol creates a lighthearted and ironic image—a rodent skipping around and playing in the morning is now served in a soup.*

4. **REREAD AND CITE TEXT EVIDENCE**

D **ASK STUDENTS** to compare Roach's reaction to the soup with that of Patton's. *Roach is having a terrible time—her state of mind is "extreme psychic discomfort." But Patton is calmly and expertly dispatching his rodent ankle.* How do their reactions underline one of the essay's themes, that "disgust is learned"? *Both Patton and Roach are eating unfamiliar food, but Patton, who studies and lives with the Achuar, has grown accustomed to their diet and simply looks at the rodent ankle as a "good source of fat."*

Critical Vocabulary: indelibly (line 51) Have students suggest synonyms for the adverb *indelibly.* enduringly, lastingly, unforgettably

FOR ELL STUDENTS Point out to Spanish speakers that the word *abomination* has a cognate, *abominación.* It means "something that causes disgust."

CLOSE READ Notes

I beg Patton to take my meat. (Our hosts speak no English.) Kind soul that
70 he is, he relieves me of the knee. The man of the house makes a comment,
which Patton translates: "She doesn't like to eat?" He has seen Westerners who
don't have any children, who don't know how to shoot a rifle. Perhaps there are
Westerners who don't like eating. "She had a big breakfast," fibs Patton.

It was in fact a big breakfast, but I didn't do very much having. Someone
shot an alligator, and I had some leg. (It's a leg sort of day.) I have eaten alligator
meat before, in Florida, but someone, bless him, had taken it upon himself to
remove the scales before cooking it. (See "ghastly unchewables," above.) I tried
to pretend that the leg was something else, something bland and comforting.
After several false starts—Melba toast? lettuce?—my brain, clearly shaken,
80 presented me with "orange roughy."[3]

Patton maintains that the bulk of an Achuar's daily calories do not come
from meat. They come from *chicha*, a mildly alcoholic, vaguely nutritious,
watered-down manioc mash. Achuar men drink up to four gallons a day. If you
like chicha, you can live well in Conambo. In about an hour, I will get to try it.
Patton's friend Isaac is hosting a *minga*, a work party for the villagers who
helped Isaac's family dig a new manioc plot. It's similar in concept to the
Amish barn-raising, with marathon chicha-drinking taking the place of
square-dancing.

I am of two minds about chicha. On the one hand, it's a beverage. In the
90 land of scary food, the beverage is your friend.

On the other hand. We are talking about a beverage fermented with
human saliva. Achuar women chew boiled manioc into the desired mashed-
potato texture, and then spit-spray the contents of their bulging cheeks out into
the chicha urn. While I know that, percentage-wise, we're talking a tiny
fraction of the mixture, I'm having difficulty embracing the idea. I have a little
agreement with myself: When spittle finds its way onto the ingredient list, I
find a way to say no.

*On the one
hand, drinking
something
"yucky" is
probably
easier than
eating it. But
this drink is
made with
human saliva.*

---

[3] **orange roughy:** a large, deep-sea fish native to New Zealand, also known as slimehead.

---

5. **READ ▶** As you read lines 81–135, continue to cite text evidence.

• In the margin, explain why Roach is "of two minds about chicha" (lines 89–97).
• Underline facts you learn about the etiquette of chicha making and
consumption.
• In the margin of lines 100–108, make an inference about why Roach includes
the description of Isaac's living room.

86

Indians in Ecuador cook manioc to make chicha.

E "You can't say no," says Patton, tossing ankle carcass to a cringing,
harelipped dog. "It's just not done."
100 Patton and I are seated on a low log bench in the open-walled platform that
serves as Isaac's living room. The man of the house whittles blowgun darts as
he chats. A pair of black horn-rim glasses sits askew on his face. One lens is
violently cracked, as though someone stepped on it, though no one here has the
kind of shoes for that. The floor is dirty but uncluttered. Decor runs to parrot
feathers and jaguar skulls, a government poster urging vaccinations for
children. In the corner, a little girl has set up a chicha tea party with her dolls,
the tenderness of the scene marred only by the knowledge that the tiny chicha
bowls are made from howler monkey voice boxes.

Isaac's wife and mother are in constant motion, serving bowls of chicha to
110 the 10 or so guests. Chicha is the backbone of Achuar society. As with the ankle
bone and the knee bone, you feel an unalterable pressure to accept. Chicha is

*Roach draws
parallels
between
Isaac's home
and American
homes.
Therefore the
odd details she
includes seem
truly weird.*

87

---

5. **READ AND CITE TEXT EVIDENCE**

E **ASK STUDENTS** to paraphrase the unwritten rules for
drinking chicha. *A guest cannot refuse chicha without being
considered "irretrievably rude." Chicha is drunk at every meal,
celebration, and visit. If a visitor tries to refuse chicha, the host will
insist.* Have students discuss why Roach might have included this
section on chicha etiquette. *Students should understand that
Roach is setting up the essay's climax. By explaining the importance
of chicha consumption—and the rules surrounding it—Roach
describes a seemingly intractable predicament. She cannot bear to
drink the bowl of chicha, but she must.*

FOR ELL STUDENTS Explain that the word *whittle* means "to
cut or shave small bits from a piece of wood." It can be used
figuratively, as in the sentence *My car payments have whittled
away my savings.*

CLOSE READ
Notes

the holy communion, the Manischewitz,[4] the kava-kava[5] of Achuar life. It's present at every ceremony, every visit, every meal. An Achuar woman's desirability rests in no small part on her skill at chicha brewing and serving.

 Isaac's mother dips a clay bowl into an urn of eggnog-hued liquid. Something slimy dangles off the bottom of the bowl, waving howdy-doo as she crosses the floor to our bench. Her hand is coated with a mucilaginous[6] yellow fluid with flecks of manioc fiber. The sidewalk outside a frat house on a Sunday morning comes, unbidden and unwelcome, to mind.

120 "It's Miller time," says Patton as he takes the bowl. After 10 minutes, he warns, she'll return to take the bowl away and give it to someone else, most likely me. It is considered irretrievably rude to refuse a bowl of chicha, or even to set it down. (In a maddening instance of form following etiquette, the ceramic bowls in which chicha is served are rounded on the bottom, so that the drinker cannot set one down without spilling the contents.)

A refusal is interpreted as a bluff and triggers a ritualized pas de deux:[7] "No, really, I shouldn't." "Yes, yes, I insist." Woe unto the visitor: The host never backs down.

Which means I have 10 minutes to talk myself out of the revulsion that's
130 building in my gut, jostling for space among the pinworms and protozoa. My mouth is full of saliva anyway, I tell myself. What's a little more? Myself isn't buying it. Myself is noting the vast and unsettling difference between oral hygiene practices around the Amazon basin and around the basin in our bathroom at home. This isn't a matter of disgust, I tell Patton. It's a matter of gum disease.

Patton wipes manioc slime from his beard. Intelligent chicha drinkers, he holds, don't fret about the saliva it's made with. They fret about the giardia[8] and

---

[4] **Manischewitz:** a popular brand of kosher products.
[5] **kava-kava:** a ceremonial drink used in the Pacific Islands, made up of chewed or ground pulp and cold water.
[6] **mucilaginous:** moist and sticky.
[7] **pas de deux:** a dance for two people.
[8] **giardia:** a protozoan parasite that lives inside the intestines of infected humans and animals. It is contracted through consuming contaminated food or liquids.

---

6. ◄ REREAD AND DISCUSS Reread lines 115–135. With a small group, discuss Roach's tone in these lines. Why does she refer to herself as "myself" in lines 129–135?

7. READ ► As you read lines 136–169, continue to cite text evidence.

- In the margin, explain Roach's reaction to chicha in lines 141–149.
- Underline text describing the Achuar's reaction to the energy bar.

88

CLOSE READ
Notes

> ❝ *I come from a tribe that eats Vienna sausages. I should be able to cope.* ❞

amoebas in the unfiltered river water it's made with. It is at this moment that Isaac's mother gets up to retrieve the chicha bowl from Patton, fill it to near
140 overflow and present it to me.

The first thing that hits you is the smell. Fruity and fetid, a whiff of drinker's breath on a late-night bus. I put my lips to the rim of the bowl, bumpy-slimy with manioc pulp. I hold my breath and drink.

The taste is not awful. It's chalky, rummy, indifferent. But this was never about taste. It's about distaste. Did you ever drop something into a toilet and have to roll up your sleeve and retrieve it? That's how I'm feeling right now. Only I've got to keep going. I've got to lift the lid, step right in, and hunker down in the toilet bowl. As soon as the level of chicha lowers visibly, Isaac's mother will step up to refill the bowl.

150 I disappoint and surprise myself. I come from a tribe that eats Vienna sausages. I should be able to cope. But I can't. I cannot drink this bowl of chicha.

An idea alights. I ask Patton to hold my bowl and rummage in my backpack for the crinkle of airtight cellophane: a raspberry-chocolate Trader Joe's energy bar. The room falls abruptly quiet. Foreigner's backpacks are known to hold all manner of otherworldly wonders: sugar packets, earplugs, contact lenses.

The energy bar makes the rounds. A few of the men sniff at it. Only Isaac takes a bite. He chews vigorously at first, then stops, suddenly and with alarm,
160 as though someone had snuck up behind him and put a gun to his head. His eyebrows bunch together like drawn drapes. His lips go all abstract and jumpy. He stands, grabs hold of a roof post, and spits forcefully. He coughs, arrghs, hawks, spits again.

The chicha does not taste bad, but her mind won't let her get past the sense of distaste and she cannot drink it.

89

---

6. REREAD AND DISCUSS USING TEXT EVIDENCE

F **ASK STUDENTS** in each group to give examples of word choices that help convey Roach's tone. *Students could cite "eggnog-hued liquid" (line 115), "waving howdy-doo" (line 116), "The sidewalk outside a frat house on a Sunday morning" (lines 118–119), "jostling for space among the pinworms and protozoa" (line 130).* Have students characterize Roach's conversation with herself. *Students should realize that the conversation is funny and a little desperate. By using "myself" ungrammatically as the subject of sentences, she pokes fun at herself and draws attention to her plight.*

7. READ AND CITE TEXT EVIDENCE

G **ASK STUDENTS** why the author talks about dropping something into a toilet (line 145). *Students should realize that Roach is trying to connect with her readers, who surely have never drunk a bowl of chicha. So, she creates an analogy from everyday life—a comparison that any reader will be able to relate to.*

CLOSE READ
Notes

Every few seconds, he looks back at me, his face changing channels from disgust to bewilderment and back. After a good minute of this, he hands back the energy bar, grinning now that the taste is gone, shaking his head at the foreigner's unfathomable tastes.

The way I see it, permission has been granted to back out of the next bowl of chicha.

8. **◄ REREAD** Reread lines 153–169 to cite evidence. Why does Roach give the men the energy bar?

She wants the men to have the same experience of trying a new food. She predicts that they will think it's gross, and will then use their reaction as an excuse to decline the next bowl of chicha.

SHORT RESPONSE

Cite Text Evidence What is Roach's purpose in writing this article? How does her tone convey this purpose? Review your reading notes, and be sure to **cite text evidence** in your response.

Roach's purpose is to show that the concept of "disgust" varies across cultures. She is experienced in eating many foods that most Americans would not want to eat, but chicha is the yuckiest food she has come across. The term "yucky" is relative: Roach includes Rozin's study to enforce this idea. Patton likes the rodent and chicha because his taste buds have become accustomed to eating them. Roach's humorous tone makes the cultural differences seem funny, instead of awkward or uncomfortable. Rather than seeing the Achuar as weird, we see them as people like us who just have different eating habits.

90

---

8. **REREAD AND CITE TEXT EVIDENCE**

Ⓗ ASK STUDENTS to discuss Roach's decision to give the Achuar an energy bar. How does this scene reinforce the central idea of the essay? *Just as she dislikes the chicha, the Achuar men will probably be similarly revolted by something completely foreign to them, an energy bar. Their reaction proves her correct and supports the idea that disgust is learned. Only Isaac dares to take a bite of the energy bar, and he reacts with disgust.*

SHORT RESPONSE

Cite Text Evidence Students' responses should include text evidence that supports their positions. They should:

• state Roach's purpose in the article.

• give examples that illustrate or support the author's purpose.

• describe the author's tone and explain how it helps her convey her purpose.

TO CHALLENGE STUDENTS . . .

For greater context and understanding, students can research the Achuar online.

ASK STUDENTS to describe the main sources of food for the Achuar. *As mentioned in Roach's essay, the men hunt game from the rain forest. This game constitutes an important part of their diet. Also, Achuar women and girls tend gardens in forest clearings. These gardens are the source of manioc, from which they make chicha. A third important part of the Achuar diet is fish. Families generally live near lakes or rivers, which provide fish for a good part of the year.* What socioeconomic forces are threatening the Achuar's livelihood? *Oil was discovered in the Achuar's territory in the 1970s. The oil companies damage the forest and pollute the rivers, making it hard for the Achuar to continue their hunting-and-gathering life. Also, oil workers bring in a lot of new foods, so the Achuar may gradually learn not to be disgusted by western food.*

DIG DEEPER

With the class, return to Question 3, Read. Have students share their examples of Roach's humorous tone.

ASK STUDENTS to analyze the techniques that Roach uses to convey her tone.

• What words and phrases help the author convey humor? *Students should realize that Roach uses words and phrases that vividly evoke her dismay at the rodent knee. The vividness of her language—and the imagery it calls up in the reader's mind—is funny. She calls the knee "a busy intersection of tendon, bone and cartilage" (lines 39–40); she explains that she must "work [her] tongue into its fissures and slimy orifices" (line 44), and she describes the flavor as strong, "[as] in overpowering, as in taste buds passing out and waving white flags" (lines 65–66).*

• How does Roach get humor out of the cultural divide between her and her hosts? *Roach sees humor in how unfathomable her actions must appear to her hosts. She vainly hopes that when she chews with her mouth open, her hosts "will take this for an endearing cultural peculiarity" (lines 67–68), and when Patton finally takes the knee from her, she imagines her hosts thinking that perhaps "there are Westerners who don't like eating" (lines 72–73).*

ASK STUDENTS to return to their Short Response answer and revise it based on the class discussion.

*my*SmartPlanner   Create lesson plans and access resources online.

The Lowest Animal

Essay by Mark Twain

Why This Text?

Students will often encounter satire in their reading and in other media. This lesson explores how Twain uses the elements of satire—for example, hyperbole, absurdity, and irony—to shine a harsh light on humans and human behavior.

Key Learning Objective: The student will be able to identify an author's purpose through understanding the use of satire.

Common Core Standards

RI 1 Cite textual evidence.
RI 2 Determine the central idea of a text.
RI 4 Determine the meaning of words and phrases.
RI 6 Determine an author's point of view or purpose.
RI 10 Read and comprehend literary nonfiction.
SL 2 Integrate multiple sources of information.
SL 6 Adapt speech to a variety of contexts and tasks.
L 3a Vary syntax for effect; apply an understanding of syntax.
L 4c Consult reference materials.
L 5a Interpret figures of speech.
L 5b Analyze nuances.

Text Complexity Rubric

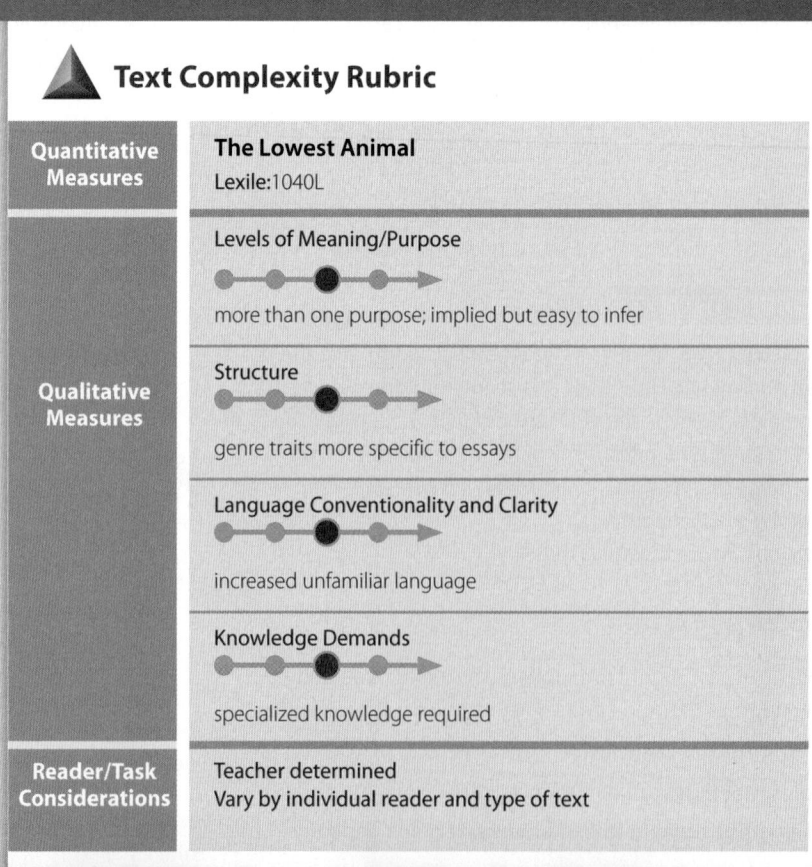

	The Lowest Animal
Quantitative Measures	Lexile:1040L
Qualitative Measures	**Levels of Meaning/Purpose** more than one purpose; implied but easy to infer
	Structure genre traits more specific to essays
	Language Conventionality and Clarity increased unfamiliar language
	Knowledge Demands specialized knowledge required
Reader/Task Considerations	Teacher determined Vary by individual reader and type of text

TEACH

CLOSE READ

Mark Twain Have students read the background information about the author. Tell students that as Twain grew older and experienced grief and financial reversals, his writing turned darker. Some of this writing was not published at the time, either because magazines rejected it or because Twain was reluctant to let readers see the changes in his worldview.

AS YOU READ Direct students to use the As You Read instructions to focus their reading. Remind students to write down any questions they generate during reading.

Analyze Author's Purpose COMMON CORE RI 6

(LINES 1–8)

Discuss with students that the **author's purpose** is his or her reason for writing a specific text. Writers may want to express many things, but often writers communicate these messages while trying to inform, persuade, entertain, analyze, or describe. Writers often do two of these things at once.

Ⓐ ASK STUDENTS to reread lines 1–8 and name what Twain's purpose seems to be. *(Twain is trying to entertain readers.)* Ask students to pay attention to whether their opinion about Twain's purpose changes as they read on. *(Possible answer: As they read on, students may feel that Twain—whose tone becomes darker and more serious—is trying to persuade and entertain readers.)*

> **CRITICAL VOCABULARY**
>
> **disposition**: Twain wants to compare the character of animals to the character of human beings.
>
> **ASK STUDENTS** How does Twain describe the **dispositions** of human beings? *(He describes them as being inferior to animals' dispositions.)*

Mark Twain *(1835–1910) was the pen name of Samuel Langhorne Clemens, the American author best known for his novel* The Adventures of Huckleberry Finn, *based on his own boyhood in Missouri. As a journalist, moralist, and lecturer, he frequently used humor to communicate his ideas. In his later years, Twain wrote many satirical essays commenting on the human race. This essay, first published in 1962, was probably written in 1896. In it, Twain refers to Charles Darwin's theory of evolution, first published in* On the Origin of Species *in 1859.*

The Lowest Animal

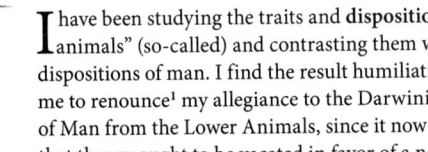

Essay by Mark Twain

AS YOU READ Notice how Twain describes the various "painstaking" experiments he performed. Write down any questions you generate during reading.

Man is the Reasoning Animal. Such is the claim.

Ⓐ I have been studying the traits and **dispositions** of the "lower animals" (so-called) and contrasting them with the traits and dispositions of man. I find the result humiliating to me. For it obliges me to renounce[1] my allegiance to the Darwinian theory of the Ascent of Man from the Lower Animals, since it now seems plain to me that that theory ought to be vacated in favor of a new and truer one, this new and truer one to be named the *Descent* of Man from the Higher Animals.

In proceeding toward this unpleasant conclusion, I have not
10 guessed or speculated or conjectured, but have used what is commonly called the scientific method.[2] That is to say, I have subjected every

disposition
(dĭs´pə-zĭsh´ən) *n.* character or temperament.

---

[1] **renounce:** give up; reject.
[2] **scientific method:** research method in which a hypothesis is tested by careful, documented experiments.

Image Credits: (b) ©Refat/Shutterstock; (t) ©Folio/Alamy

SCAFFOLDING FOR ELL STUDENTS

Understand Multiple-Meaning Words Tell students that the word *speculated* (line 10) is an example of a word with more than one meaning. It can mean "guessed" or "invested money."

ASK STUDENTS what the word means here. *(It means "guessed.")* What context clues helped you to arrive at an answer? *(The sentence includes two synonyms for "speculated," which are apparent because of the word "or.")* Encourage students to use context clues to understand multiple-meaning words.

caliber: Twain believes that human beings are all one species, even if differences in intellectual ability exist.

ASK STUDENTS what he thinks of the moral **caliber** of humans. *(that they are low)*

Analyze Language

COMMON CORE RI 1, RI 4

(LINES 34–40)

Sometimes writers of satire don't state exactly what they mean, and it is up to the reader to look for clues to the author's real feelings. Explain that the choice of words and phrases with strong connotations is a clue to the author's real feelings.

B **CITE TEXT EVIDENCE** Have students reread lines 34–40. Ask them to cite what they reveal about Twain's real feelings about hunting buffalo. *(He refers to "those great animals" and how the hunters ate only "part of one" and left 71 "to rot.")*

Analyze Author's Purpose: Satire

COMMON CORE RI 2, RI 6

(LINES 40–49)

Explain that **satire** is a type of literature in which authors use wit to criticize.

C **ASK STUDENTS** what is humorous and how Twain uses humor to satirize. *(The idea of a scientific experiment to show the difference between a snake and a human is a satire of the earl.)*

transition: Twain compares the results of his anaconda experiments with the acts of the English earl and states that his findings suggest the earl descended from the anaconda.

ASK STUDENTS What does Twain mean by saying that "a good deal was lost in the transition" from snake to human being? *(During the process of change, humans became cruel, proving that the snake is a superior creature to the human being.)*

---

postulate[3] that presented itself to the crucial test of actual experiment and have adopted it or rejected it according to the result. Thus, I verified and established each step of my course in its turn before advancing to the next. These experiments were made in the London Zoological Gardens and covered many months of painstaking and fatiguing work.

20   Before particularizing any of the experiments, I wish to state one or two things which seem to more properly belong in this place than further along. This in the interest of clearness. The massed experiments established to my satisfaction certain generalizations, to wit:

    1. That the human race is of one distinct species. It exhibits slight variations—in color, stature, mental **caliber**, and so on—due to climate, environment, and so forth; but it is a species by itself and not to be confounded with any other.

    2. That the quadrupeds[4] are a distinct family, also. This family exhibits variations—in color, size, food preferences, and so on; but it is a family by itself.

30   3. That the other families—the birds, the fishes, the insects, the reptiles, etc.— are more or less distinct, also. They are in the procession. They are links in the chain which stretches down from the higher animals to man at the bottom.

    B Some of my experiments were quite curious. In the course of my reading, I had come across a case where, many years ago, some hunters on our Great Plains organized a buffalo hunt for the entertainment of an English earl—that, and to provide some fresh meat for his larder.[5] They had charming sport. They killed seventy-two of those great animals and ate part of one of them and left the seventy-one to

40   rot. In order to determine the difference between an anaconda[6] and an earl—if any—I caused seven young calves to be turned into the anaconda's cage. The grateful reptile immediately crushed one of them and swallowed it, then lay back satisfied. It showed no further interest in the calves and no disposition to harm them. I tried this experiment with other anacondas, always with the same result. The fact stood proven that the difference between an earl and an anaconda is that the earl is cruel and the anaconda isn't; and that the earl wantonly destroys what he has no use for, but the anaconda doesn't. This seemed to suggest that the anaconda was not descended from the earl. It also

50   seemed to suggest that the earl was descended from the anaconda, and had lost a good deal in the **transition**.

    I was aware that many men who have accumulated more millions of money than they can ever use have shown a rabid hunger for more,

caliber
(kăl′ə-bər) *n.* level of ability.

transition
(trăn-zĭsh′ən) *n.* process of change.

---

[3] **postulate:** assumption.
[4] **quadrupeds:** four-footed animals.
[5] **larder:** supply of food or place where food supplies are kept.
[6] **anaconda:** long, heavy snake that crushes its prey.

APPLYING ACADEMIC VOCABULARY

ambiguous	clarify

As you discuss Twain's essay, incorporate the following academic vocabulary words: *ambiguous* and *clarify*. To ensure student comprehension, ask students to find examples in the text where Twain's meaning is **ambiguous**. Then have them discuss how they might **clarify** Twain's text so that it is easier for a modern reader to understand.

D

and have not scrupled[7] to cheat the ignorant and the helpless out of their poor servings in order to partially appease[8] that appetite. I furnished a hundred different kinds of wild and tame animals the opportunity to accumulate vast stores of food, but none of them would do it. The squirrels and bees and certain birds made accumulations, but stopped when they had gathered a winter's supply and could not

60 be persuaded to add to it either honestly or by chicane.[9] In order to bolster up a tottering reputation, the ant pretended to store up supplies, but I was not deceived. I know the ant. These experiments convinced me that there is this difference between man and the higher animals: He is avaricious and miserly, they are not.

In the course of my experiments, I convinced myself that among the animals man is the only one that harbors[10] insults and injuries, broods over them, waits till a chance offers, then takes revenge. The passion of revenge is unknown to the higher animals.

Roosters keep harems,[11] but it is by consent of their concubines;[12]

70 therefore no wrong is done. Men keep harems, but it is by brute force, privileged by **atrocious** laws which the other sex was allowed no hand in making. In this matter man occupies a far lower place than the rooster.

Cats are loose in their morals, but not consciously so. Man, in his descent from the cat, has brought the cat's looseness with him but has left the unconsciousness behind—the saving grace which excuses the cat. The cat is innocent, man is not.

Indecency, vulgarity, obscenity—these are strictly confined to man; he invented them. Among the higher animals there is no trace of

80 them. They hide nothing; they are not ashamed. Man, with his soiled mind, covers himself. He will not even enter a drawing room with his breast and back naked, so alive are he and his mates to indecent suggestion. Man is the Animal that Laughs. But so does the monkey, as Mr. Darwin pointed out, and so does the Australian bird that is called the laughing jackass. No—Man is the Animal that Blushes. He is the only one that does it—or has occasion to.

At the head of this article we see how "three monks were burnt to death" a few days ago and a prior was "put to death with atrocious cruelty." Do we inquire into the details? No; or we should find out that

90 the prior was subjected to unprintable mutilations. Man—when he is a North American Indian—gouges out his prisoner's eyes; when he is King John,[13] with a nephew to render untroublesome, he uses a red-

atrocious
(ə-trō′shəs) *adj.* evil or brutal.

---

[7] **scrupled:** hesitated because of feelings of guilt.

[8] **appease:** satisfy; pacify.

[9] **chicane** (shĭ-kān′): clever deception; trickery.

[10] **harbors:** clings to.

[11] **harems:** groups of females who mate and live with one male.

[12] **concubines:** secondary wives.

[13] **King John:** king of England from 1199 to 1216, known for seizing the throne from his nephew Arthur.

The Lowest Animal **375**

Analyze Author's Purpose: Satire (LINES 54–77)   COMMON CORE RI 4

Tell students that in attempting to entertain the reader while making points, writers of satire may include details that are **absurd**, or ridiculous. Tell students that many of Twain's examples are absurd and not meant to be taken literally.

D **CITE TEXT EVIDENCE** Have students reread lines 55–77. Encourage them to work together to find assertions in the text that should not be taken literally. *(Lines 55–65 all concern Twain's "experiments," which he did not actually conduct.)* Follow up by asking students what about these details is absurd. *(It would be very difficult for one man to actually conduct experiments where vast stores of food were made available to a hundred different animals and to observe what the animals then did with the food over time. The idea that Twain tried "chicane" or trickery, to attempt to get the animals to store more food than they needed is amusing and ridiculous.)*

CRITICAL VOCABULARY

atrocious: Twain writes of despicable laws that allow men to have multiple wives at the same time, although women had no say in making the laws.

ASK STUDENTS whether they believe that Twain would still believe that laws allowing men to have harems were **atrocious** if women were allowed to craft the laws. *(Answers will vary, but students may believe Twain would still find the laws bad, but less unfair.)*

WHEN STUDENTS STRUGGLE...

Understand Idioms Draw out the meaning of the idiomatic phrase "saving grace" in line 76. *(a redeeming quality)* Ask students to explain how this phrase contributes to the reader's understanding of the difference between cats and human beings.

ASK STUDENTS to cite any other idiomatic expressions on the page and discuss the phrase's meaning together. *(Possible answer: "soiled mind" in lines 80–81 means a mind that is no longer innocent.)*

Analyze Language  RI 4

(LINES 103–106)

Discuss with students that, in writing satire, authors may choose to use words in surprising ways or in surprising contexts in order to make a point.

 ASK STUDENTS to reread lines 103–106. What might be surprising about Twain's use of the word "unhumanly"? *(The word "unhumanly" [or a closely related form, "inhumanly"] would normally suggest actions and behavior that are worse than human. In this context, however, Twain uses the word to point out that the cat's behavior is better than the needlessly cruel behavior of a human being.)*

Analyze Author's Purpose:  RI 1, RI 4, RI 6
Satire (LINES 120–125)

Authors of satire very often include **exaggeration**, in which they overstate the extent of something in order to make it more noticeable to readers.

F **CITE TEXT EVIDENCE** Have students reread lines 120–125. Ask students to name an example of exaggeration in the text. *("There is not an acre of ground on the globe that is in possession of its rightful owner, or that has not been taken away from owner after owner, cycle after cycle, by force and bloodshed," lines 122–125.)* Have students talk about the effect this exaggeration has on the reader. *(The reader thinks about the extent of warfare for territory over the course of history. The reader is probably not concerned with whether or not the statement is literally true.)*

---

hot iron; when he is a religious zealot[14] dealing with heretics[15] in the Middle Ages, he skins his captive alive and scatters salt on his back; in the first Richard's[16] time, he shuts up a multitude of Jewish families in a tower and sets fire to it; in Columbus's time he captures a family of Spanish Jews and—but *that* is not printable; in our day in England, a man is fined ten shillings for beating his mother nearly to death

100   with a chair, and another man is fined forty shillings for having four pheasant eggs in his possession without being able to satisfactorily explain how he got them. Of all the animals, man is the only one that is cruel. He is the only one that inflicts pain for the pleasure of doing it. It is a trait that is not known to the higher animals. The cat plays with the frightened mouse; but she has this excuse, that she does not know that the mouse is suffering. The cat is moderate—unhumanly moderate: She only scares the mouse, she does not hurt it; she doesn't dig out its eyes, or tear off its skin, or drive splinters under its nails— man fashion; when she is done playing with it, she makes a sudden meal of it and puts it out of its trouble. Man is the Cruel Animal. He is

110   alone in that distinction.

The higher animals engage in individual fights, but never in organized masses. Man is the only animal that deals in that atrocity of atrocities, war. He is the only one that gathers his brethren about him and goes forth in cold blood and with calm pulse to exterminate his kind. He is the only animal that for sordid wages will march out, as the Hessians[17] did in our Revolution, and as the boyish Prince Napoleon did in the Zulu war,[18] and help to slaughter strangers of his own species who have done him no harm and with whom he has no quarrel.

120   Man is the only animal that robs his helpless fellow of his country—takes possession of it and drives him out of it or destroys him. Man has done this in all the ages. There is not an acre of ground on the globe that is in possession of its rightful owner, or that has not been taken away from owner after owner, cycle after cycle, by force and bloodshed.

Man is the only Slave. And he is the only animal who enslaves. He has always been a slave in one form or another, and has always held other slaves in bondage under him in one way or another. In our day he is always some man's slave for wages and does that man's work; and

130   this slave has other slaves under him for minor wages, and they do *his*

---

[14]**zealot** (zĕl´ət): overly enthusiastic person; fanatic.

[15]**heretics:** people who hold beliefs opposed to those of the church.

[16]**first Richard's:** refers to Richard I (1157–1199), also called Richard the Lion-Hearted, king of England from 1189 to 1199.

[17]**Hessians** (hĕsh´ənz): German soldiers who served for pay in the British army during the American Revolution.

[18]**Prince Napoleon. . .Zulu war:** In search of adventure, Prince Napoleon, son of Napoleon III, joined the British campaign against Zululand (part of South Africa) in 1879.

SCAFFOLDING FOR ELL STUDENTS

Understand Prefixes Point out to students the words "Slave" and "enslaves" in line 126. Explain that the prefix *en-* means "to put into" or "to cause to be." Tell students that adding *en-* to a noun turns the word into a verb and that sometimes the prefix is written *em-*.

ASK STUDENTS to add *en-* to the nouns below to form a verb. Lead them to determine the meaning of each newly formed verb.

- tomb
- danger
- chain

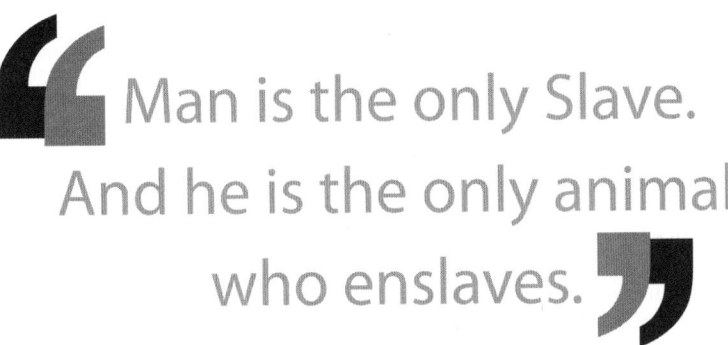

> # "Man is the only Slave.
> And he is the only animal
> who enslaves. "

work. The higher animals are the only ones who exclusively do their own work and provide their own living.

Man is the only Patriot. He sets himself apart in his own country, under his own flag, and sneers at the other nations, and keeps multitudinous uniformed assassins on hand at heavy expense to grab slices of other people's countries and keep *them* from grabbing slices of *his*. And in the intervals between campaigns, he washes the blood off his hands and works for "the universal brotherhood of man"— with his mouth.

G
H

140   Man is the Religious Animal. He is the only Religious Animal. He is the only animal that has the True Religion—several of them. He is the only animal that loves his neighbor as himself, and cuts his throat if his theology isn't straight. He has made a graveyard of the globe in trying his honest best to smooth his brother's path to happiness and heaven. He was at it in the time of the Caesars, he was at it in Mahomet's[19] time, he was at it in the time of the Inquisition, he was at it in France a couple of centuries, he was at it in England in Mary's day,[20] he has been at it ever since he first saw the light, he is at it today in Crete—he will be at it somewhere else tomorrow. The higher

I

150   animals have no religion. And we are told that they are going to be left out, in the hereafter. I wonder why. It seems questionable taste.

Man is the Reasoning Animal. Such is the claim. I think it is open to dispute. Indeed, my experiments have proven to me that he is the Unreasoning Animal. Note his history, as sketched above. It seems plain to me that whatever he is, he is *not* a reasoning animal. His record is the fantastic record of a maniac. I consider that the strongest count against his intelligence is the fact that with that record back of him, he blandly sets himself up as the head animal of the lot; whereas by his own standards, he is the bottom one.

---

[19]**Mahomet's:** Muhammad (c. A.D. 570–632) was an Arab prophet and founder of Islam.

[20]**in Mary's day:** during the reign of Queen Mary (1553–1558), who was given the nickname "Bloody Mary" when she ordered the deaths of many Protestants.

CLOSE READ

Analyze Author's Purpose: Satire (LINES 140–143)
 COMMON CORE RI 4

Discuss with students that, along with using details that are absurd or exaggerated, writers of satire may use **humor** to entertain and convince their readers.

G ASK STUDENTS to reread lines 140–141 and discuss what is humorous. *(Twain writes that man "is the only animal that has the True Religion—several of them." It is surprising that after saying man has one true religion, Twain states that man has several.)*

Discuss with students that authors of satire may also use **irony**—statements that are the opposite of what they really believe—in their writing.

H CITE TEXT EVIDENCE Ask students to reread lines 142–143 and find an example of irony. *(Line 142: "He is the only animal that loves his neighbor as himself.")* Ask students to explain how they can tell that the statement is ironic. *(After writing about man loving his neighbor, Twain writes about how he will kill his neighbor for disagreeing with his religion.)*

Analyze Language: Anaphora (LINES 145–147)
 COMMON CORE RI 4

Discuss with students that Twain uses **anaphora** in the essay, which is the repetition of words and phrases at the beginning of sentences or clauses. This repetition adds emphasis to Twain's points. One example of anaphora is Twain's repeated use of the words "Man is…."

I CITE TEXT EVIDENCE Have students reread lines 145–147 and find examples of anaphora. *("He was at it" is used five times.)* Have students discuss the effect of the use of anaphora in this section of the text. *(Twain is emphasizing how human beings have been fighting about religion throughout history in many different eras and regions.)*

WHEN STUDENTS STRUGGLE . . .

Explain to students that Twain sometimes uses long, difficult words in place of simple ones. Point out the phrase "multitudinous uniformed assassins" in line 135. Elicit from students the meanings of "multitudinous" and "assassins." *(having many members, killers)*

ASK STUDENTS what simple word could be used to replace the phrase "multitudinous uniformed assassins." *(armies)*

Analyze Author's Purpose: Satire (LINES 160–177)

COMMON CORE RI 2, RI 6

Remind students that, when writing satire, authors may use techniques such as humor, exaggeration, absurdity, and irony. Discuss with them that sometimes more than one of the techniques can be found in the same section of text.

J ASK STUDENTS to reread lines 160–166. Have students name the satirical technique that Twain is using in this paragraph. (The experiment is an example of absurdity, since the situation is clearly extreme and ridiculous. This also is an example of humor.)

K ASK STUDENTS to reread lines 167–177. Ask them to name the satirical techniques that Twain employs in this paragraph. (In lines 167–172, he employs absurdity, since he could not really cage ten men and leave them for two days. In lines 173–177, Twain continues to use absurdity in describing peaceful animals versus violent human beings. He is also using exaggeration to describe the apparent remains of the fight, and he is using humor in describing that the men, in killing each other, had taken their disagreements to a higher court, i.e., God.)

COLLABORATIVE DISCUSSION Have students pair up to discuss the experiments that Twain describes in the essay. Encourage students to reread the text to find details to support their ideas about how realistic the experiments are. For example, does Twain give details about how the experiments could be repeated or whether he had helpers with the experiments? Then have students share their opinions with the class as a whole. Accept all reasonable responses.

ASK STUDENTS to share any questions they generated in the course of reading and discussing the selection.

---

160   In truth, man is incurably foolish. Simple things which the other animals easily learn he is incapable of learning. Among my experiments was this. In an hour I taught a cat and a dog to be friends. I put them in a cage. In another hour I taught them to be friends with a rabbit. In the course of two days I was able to add a fox, a goose, a squirrel, and some doves. Finally a monkey. They lived together in peace, even affectionately.

     Next, in another cage I confined an Irish Catholic from Tipperary, and as soon as he seemed tame, I added a Scottish Presbyterian from Aberdeen. Next a Turk from Constantinople, a Greek Christian
170 from Crete, an Armenian, a Methodist from the wilds of Arkansas, a Buddhist from China, a Brahman from Benares. Finally, a Salvation Army colonel from Wapping. Then I stayed away two whole days. When I came back to note results, the cage of Higher Animals was all right, but in the other there was but a chaos of gory odds and ends of turbans and fezzes and plaids and bones and flesh—not a specimen left alive. These Reasoning Animals had disagreed on a theological detail and carried the matter to a higher court.

COLLABORATIVE DISCUSSION What are the experiments that Twain describes? How realistic are they? Discuss these questions with a partner, citing specific evidence from the essay to support your ideas.

TO CHALLENGE STUDENTS...

Mimic Style Discuss Twain's satirical style with students.

ASK STUDENTS to work in small groups to think of another "experiment" to show the inferiority of humanity to the animals that Twain might have included in his essay. Then ask individual students to write a paragraph about this fake experiment using at least two of the following: irony, exaggeration, absurdity, and humor. Have volunteers read their paragraphs to the class.

Author's Purpose: Satire

An **author's purpose** is what the writer hopes to achieve by crafting a written piece. The author may want to describe, inform, narrate, entertain, analyze, persuade, or do several of these at once. To achieve their purposes, authors use various techniques that combine style and content. **Satire** is a literary form that ridicules the shortcomings of people and institutions in an attempt to bring about change. When a writer like Mark Twain uses satire, his overall purpose is to change or improve something in society.

This chart shows techniques that signal when a writer is using satire.

Elements of Satire		
Technique	**Definition**	**Example**
Humor	Describing something in a way that causes laughter or amusement	"In order to bolster up a tottering reputation, the ant pretended to store up supplies, but I was not deceived."
Exaggeration	Overstating something to draw attention to it and make a point	"He has made a graveyard of the globe. . . ."
Absurdity	Describing extreme situations that are impossible to take seriously	"In order to determine the difference between an anaconda and an earl—if any—I caused seven young calves to be turned into the anaconda's cage."
Irony	Stating the opposite of what is really meant	"These experiments were made in the London Zoological Gardens and covered many months of painstaking and fatiguing work."

Look for other examples of these techniques as you analyze Twain's essay. Ask yourself these questions:

- What is the central idea that Twain is satirizing?
- What is his tone or attitude toward humans and toward animals?
- What does he hope to change by writing this satire?

TEACH

CLOSE READ

Analyze Author's Purpose: Satire
COMMON CORE · RI 2, RI 6

Help students understand the terms *author's purpose, satire, humor, exaggeration, absurdity,* and *irony*. Explain to students that an author may use more than one element of satire at once. For example, absurdity, exaggeration, and irony can all be humorous.

Have students work in groups. Ask them to divide the essay into sections and analyze the elements of satire Twain uses in the different sections of the text. Encourage them to find examples of each type of technique and have them present their examples to the class.

Possible answers:

1. *The central idea that Twain is satirizing is the notion that human beings are superior to the so-called lower animals.*

2. *His tone toward animals is respectful, while his tone toward human beings is critical.*

3. *Twain wants readers to see that human beings are not morally superior. He may also hope to change people's ideas about what behavior is acceptable.*

Strategies for Annotation   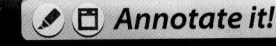 *Annotate it!*

Analyze Author's Purpose: Satire   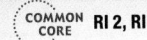 COMMON CORE · RI 2, RI 6

Share these strategies for guided or independent analysis.

- Highlight in blue sections of the text that are examples of exaggeration.
- Highlight in yellow sections of the text that are examples of absurdity.
- Highlight in green sections of the text that are examples of irony.
- Underline sections of the text that are examples of humor. Some of these may be already highlighted.

> Man is the Religious Animal. He is the only Religious Animal. He is the only animal that has the True Religion—several of them. He is the only animal that loves his neighbor as himself, and cuts his throat if his theology isn't straight. He has made a graveyard of the globe in trying his honest best to smooth his brother's path to happiness and heaven.

PRACTICE & APPLY

Analyzing the Text COMMON CORE RI 1, RI 2, RI 4, RI 6, SL 2, SL 6

Possible answers:

1. In lines 1–8, Twain explains that he has been comparing the behavior of other animals to the behavior of human beings, and has concluded that the other animals behave in a superior manner. Therefore, he believes that Darwin should write of the "descent of man" instead of the "ascent." His tone is respectful toward animals and critical toward humans.

2. It becomes clear in the rest of the essay that Twain is being absurd in his claims to have conducted experiments. In fact, he only mentions three supposed experiments (clearly fictitious) out of a long list of observations about human beings in comparison to other animals.

3. Twain writes of the party leaving 71 buffalo to rot. Later in the paragraph, Twain writes that the difference between an anaconda and an earl is that the Earl is cruel and wasteful. Twain obviously did not find the hunt charming.

4. The animals refuse to take and store more than will be needed to keep them fed through the winter. Unlike human beings, the animals are not greedy.

5. Twain uses the examples as evidence that, unlike other animals, human beings are cruel and have been so throughout time and throughout the world.

6. Twain means that humans are ashamed of the "soiled minds" that result from human traits of "indecency, vulgarity, obscenity" (line 78); whereas, other animals "hide nothing" and "are not ashamed" (line 80) because they do not carry those same traits.

7. After each of these statements, Twain goes on to describe acts of cruelty that have been inspired by these presumed virtues, so it is clear that for Twain being patriotic and religious are not always good things.

8. Twain's overall purpose is to make a point about the immorality of human beings (despite their many religions), as compared to other animals. His use of satire is quite effective because it grabs the reader's attention and enlivens an otherwise dull or preachy moral topic.

Analyzing the Text COMMON CORE RI 1, RI 2, RI 4, RI 6, SL 2, SL 6

Cite Text Evidence   Support your responses with evidence from the selection.

1. **Summarize** In lines 1–8, how does Twain indicate his intention to satirize Darwin's ideas about human nature? How does this paragraph reveal Twain's tone toward humans and animals?

2. **Analyze** In lines 9–17, Twain says that he reached his conclusions by following the scientific method. How well does the rest of the essay support this assertion?

3. **Infer** When describing a buffalo hunt, Twain writes, "They had charming sport" (line 38). How does the rest of the passage reveal the irony that is implicit in this statement?

4. **Interpret** What is the outcome when Twain tries to persuade different wild and tame animals to "accumulate vast stores of food" (lines 52–64)? What purpose do the examples serve?

5. **Analyze** Twain cites many examples of human cruelty through the ages. What purpose do these examples serve?

6. **Interpret** What does Twain mean when he writes that "Man is the Animal that Blushes. He is the only one that does it—or has occasion to" (lines 85–86)?

7. **Analyze** How does Twain use the somewhat positive statements that "Man is the only Patriot" (line 133) and "Man is the Religious Animal" (line 140) ironically?

8. **Evaluate** What is Twain's overall purpose in writing this essay? How effective is his use of satire in achieving that purpose?

PERFORMANCE TASK

Speaking Activity: Lecture Twain was a popular lecturer in his time. Try delivering a section of "The Lowest Animal" as an effective lecture.

- Use library or Internet resources to listen to some audio recordings of actors impersonating Twain's voice and style of speaking.

- Choose a section of the essay to present as a lecture to a small group. Consider how to make the implicit elements of satire more obvious to listeners.

- As a speaker, use pacing, gestures, and inflection to communicate Twain's ideas, his humor, and his irony.

- After giving your lecture and listening to those of others in your group, write a one-page summary comparing the experience of reading the essay to speaking it and listening to it.

Assign this performance task.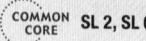

PERFORMANCE TASK COMMON CORE SL 2, SL 6

Speaking Activity: Lecture Have students work in small groups. Direct students to reread Twain's essay before performing it so that they have a better understanding of Twain's points and tone. Encourage students to listen to several audio versions of actors portraying Twain. Then have students work individually to write summaries about the experience of giving the speech. When they are finished, they may share their summaries with their groups.

Critical Vocabulary

COMMON CORE L 4c, L 5b

disposition   caliber   transition   atrocious

Practice and Apply For each Critical Vocabulary word, identify which example best illustrates its meaning. Explain why the example you chose is most accurate.

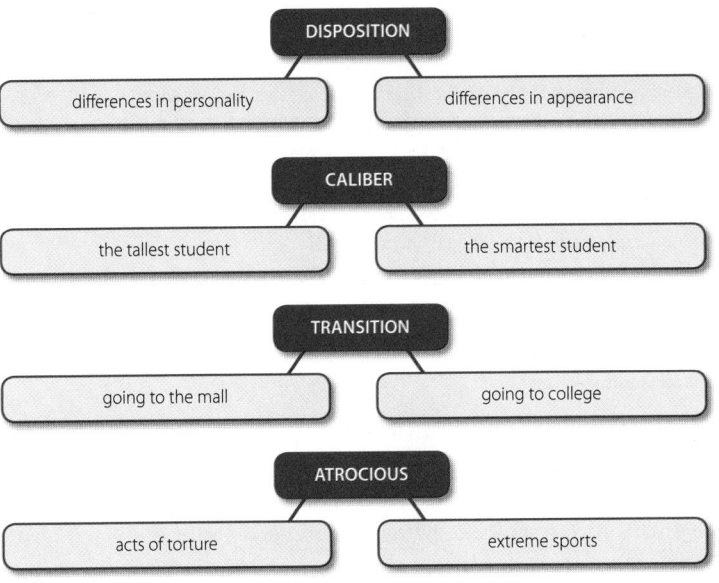

Vocabulary Strategy: Nuance in Word Meaning

In "The Lowest Animal," Mark Twain uses the Critical Vocabulary word *atrocious* to describe laws that allow men to keep harems. Twain chose a word with a very strong nuance, or shade of meaning, because he wanted to emphasize that the laws were not simply bad or unjust but that they were, in fact, evil or brutal. By choosing a word with a specific nuance, writers' explanations of their ideas are less ambiguous. Adjectives that have similar meanings but different nuances might be arranged on this continuum, with the word representing the least degree on the left and the greatest, on the right.

| bad | naughty | wicked | cruel | atrocious |

Practice and Apply For each word, create a continuum of at least four other words that have similar meanings, but show different nuances, moving from weakest to strongest. Consult a dictionary as needed to clarify the precise meanings of words.

1. cold   3. happy   5. pretty
2. hot   4. smell

PRACTICE & APPLY

Critical Vocabulary

COMMON CORE L 4c, L 5b

Answers:

disposition *(differences in personality)*

caliber *(the smartest student)*

transition *(going to college)*

atrocious *(acts of torture)*

Vocabulary Strategy: Nuance in Word Meaning

Possible answers:

1. cold *(cool, chilly, freezing, sub-zero)*
2. hot *(warm, stifling, roasting)*
3. happy *(pleased, glad, joyful, blissful)*
4. smell *(fragrance, scent, odor, stench)*
5. pretty *(cute, fine-looking, beautiful, stunning)*

Strategies for Annotation ✏ 📖 *Annotate it!*

Analyze Word Choice: Nuance

COMMON CORE L 5b

Share these strategies for guided or independent analysis:

- Highlight in yellow Twain's words that have particularly strong nuances.
- On a note, list less-specific adjectives for the words you highlighted and describe their effect if Twain had used them.

> The higher animals engage in individual fights, but never in organized masses. Man is the only animal that deals in that atrocity of atrocities, war. He is the only one that...goes forth in cold blood and with calm pulse to exterminate his kind. He is the only animal that for sordid wages will march out....

> If Twain had used *evil of evils, kill,* and *tasteless,* the meaning of the paragraph would not be as powerful.

PRACTICE & APPLY

Language and Style: Anaphora and Parallelism

COMMON CORE L 3a, SL 6

Review the examples of anaphora and parallelism and make sure that students understand the techniques and how Twain is employing them to achieve his purpose.

Practice and Apply Encourage students to work in the same groups that they worked in for the Performance Task. Have students share their revised essays with the group, and have group members give comments about the essays.

Assess It!

Online Selection Test
- Download an editable ExamView bank.
- Assign and manage this test online.

Language and Style: Anaphora and Parallelism

COMMON CORE L 3a

In "The Lowest Animal," Mark Twain uses a particular type of repetition known as **anaphora,** the repetition of a word or words at the beginning of successive lines, clauses, or sentences. This literary device is particularly effective in poetry, but it also has a place in argumentative prose. Consider this example from two sentences in lines 83–85.

> **Man is the Animal that Laughs. . . . No—Man is the Animal that Blushes.**

Not only does Twain repeat the words that begin the sentences, the sentences share a parallel construction, meaning that they use similar grammatical structures to express ideas that are related or equal in value. By using these literary devices, Twain emphasizes his central ideas and creates a rhythm that strengthens the rhetorical effect.

Here are other examples of anaphora that Twain uses in his essay. These appear at the beginning of successive paragraphs, beginning in line 120.

> **Man is the only animal that robs his helpless fellow of his country. . . .**
> **Man is the only Slave.**
> **Man is the only Patriot.**
> **Man is the Religious Animal.**
> **Man is the Reasoning Animal.**

By repeating the words *Man is* at the beginning of each paragraph and making the sentences parallel each other, Twain builds a cumulative list of the aspects of human conduct that he wants to satirize. Clearly, Twain's use of anaphora is deliberate. In his hands it has an artistic effect and he successfully uses it to hammer home the point he wants to make, which is that humans are not the highest animals (though they may believe otherwise).

Young writers are usually told to avoid repetition. They are encouraged to vary sentence length, sentence beginnings, and even sentence structure to build interest. All of this is good advice for the most part. However, skilled writers know when to use repetition to make a point. Twain's use of anaphora is an excellent example of knowing when to "break the rules."

Practice and Apply Look back at the summary you wrote of your experiences of reading, speaking, and listening to Twain's essay in response to this selection's Performance Task. Revise your writing to include use of anaphora and parallelism to emphasize important ideas and create rhythm.

Analyze Language: Figures of Speech

COMMON CORE
L 5a

TEACH

Figures of speech appear throughout Mark Twain's essay. Explain that writers use **figures of speech** when they use language in a way that is not literal. Provide students with the following definitions of two of Twain's most frequently used types of figures of speech.

- **Metaphor** is a comparison between two different things in order to point out some similarity between the two. Display line 32 on the board or on a device to show an example of metaphor. *("They are links in the chain…")* Discuss with students that Twain is comparing the relationships of the animals to links on a chain connecting one to the next in descending order.

- **Hyperbole** is a type of figurative language in which exaggeration is used to make a point. Hyperbole may be used for comic effect or to show the relative importance of the example. Display lines 122–125 on the board or on a device to show an example of hyperbole. *(There is not an acre of ground on the globe that is in possession of its rightful owner, or that has not been taken away from owner after owner, cycle after cycle, by force and bloodshed.)* Discuss with students that Twain is exaggerating the extent of the fighting to show that human beings have been driven to fight over territory throughout time.

PRACTICE AND APPLY

Display lines 133–139 of the essay on the board or on a device. Have volunteers point out examples of metaphor and hyperbole and describe how they affect Twain's meaning. *(The metaphor "slices of other people's countries" and the hyperbole "uniformed assassins," "washes the blood off his hands," and "works for 'the universal brotherhood of man' [just] with his mouth" work together to emphasize man's gluttony as depicted in Twain's final image of a man's mouth.)* Ask students to read to the end of the essay and cite other examples of metaphor and hyperbole.

 **INTERACTIVE WHITEBOARD LESSON** If students need further instruction, use this *Interactive Whiteboard Lesson: Citing Textual Evidence.*

Analyze Author's Purpose

COMMON CORE
RI 1, RI 4, RI 6

RETEACH

Review with students that an author's purpose is his or her overall reason for writing a piece of text.

Discuss with students that authors of satire are usually writing both to entertain and to persuade readers that some change needs to occur. Review the terms for techniques used in satire: *humor, exaggeration, absurdity,* and *irony.*

Give an example of a topic that students might use in writing a satire, such as: Parents, Help Your Teen Avoid Screen Addiction: Toss Out Your Computers! Then have students come up with examples of humor, exaggeration, absurdity, and irony that could be used in such an essay.

 **LEVEL UP TUTORIALS** Assign the following *Level Up* tutorial: **Author's Purpose.**

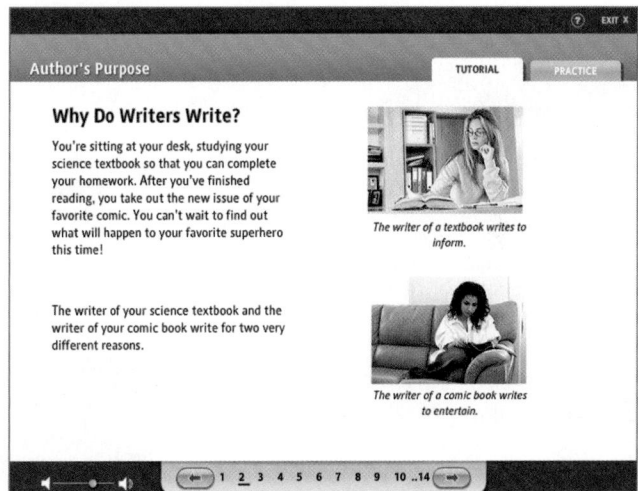

CLOSE READING APPLICATION

Students can apply the skill to another satirical essay they have read. Have them work in pairs to analyze the author's purpose and identify examples of humor, exaggeration, absurdity, and irony. Students may then share their analyses with small groups or with the whole class.

COMPARE TEXT AND MEDIA

*my*SmartPlanner Create lesson plans and access resources online.

COMPARE TEXT AND MEDIA

Genesis of the Tenement	Images: Tenement Photos	Child Mortality Rates	MEDIA AMERICA The Story of Us: Jacob Riis
Essay by Jacob Riis	Phototgraphs by Jacob Riis	Report by the Tenement House Committee	Video by HISTORY

Why These Texts?

Students regularly receive information through various media and different formats. This lesson explores methods for integrating and evaluating multiple sources of information.

Key Learning Objective: The student will be able to integrate and evaluate information presented in text, photographs, tables, and video.

Common Core Standards

RI 1 Cite textual evidence.
RI 2 Determine two or more central ideas of a text and analyze their development.
RI 4 Determine the meaning of words and phrases.
RI 5 Analyze and evaluate structure.
RI 6 Determine an author's point of view or purpose.
RI 7 Integrate and evaluate multiple sources of information.
SL 3 Delineate a speaker's argument and specific claims, evaluating the reasoning and the relevance of the evidence.
W 7 Conduct short research projects.
W 8 Gather information from multiple print and digital sources.
W 9 Draw evidence from literary or informational texts.

Text Complexity Rubric

	Genesis of the Tenement Lexile: 1410L	AMERICA The Story of Us: Jacob Riis Lexile: NA
Quantitative Measures		
Qualitative Measures	**Levels of Meaning/Purpose** single purpose; implied, but easy to infer	**Levels of Meaning/Purpose** single topic
	Structure multiple text structures	**Structure** organization of main ideas and details complex, but clearly stated and sequential
	Language Conventionality and Clarity many unfamiliar, high academic, and complex domain-specific words	**Language Conventionality and Clarity** clear, direct language
	Knowledge Demands specialized knowledge required	**Knowledge Demands** some specialized knowledge required
Reader/Task Considerations	Teacher determined Vary by individual reader and type of text	Teacher determined Vary by individual reader and type of text

CLOSE READ

Jacob Riis Have students read the background and information about the author. Tell students that Riis lived and worked during what is often called "The Gilded Age," a period of rapid economic growth in the United States. Immigrants flocked to America, often settling in cities and working in dangerous factories for little pay. Powerful corporations became the dominant form of business operations. The government became increasingly corrupted as wealth and power became concentrated in an elite class. It was the beginning of a modern, industrial, urban America.

Integrate and Evaluate Information

COMMON CORE **RI 7**

Explain to students that information can be presented in different ways to achieve different **purposes.** The means through which information is communicated is called its **medium.** For example, television, newspapers, books, and blogs—these are all different types of media.

 **ASK STUDENTS** to read the list of **media** included in this selection and Jacob Riis's biography. Then ask students what topics they think will be explored in this selection. *(The selection includes information about overcrowded apartment buildings, or tenements, in New York City, poverty, and child mortality rates.)* Ask: Based on this information, what initial conclusions can you draw about Riis's purpose, or reason for writing and taking photographs? *(Riis's purpose is to educate people about the deplorable living conditions in these tenements.)*

COMPARE TEXT AND MEDIA

MEDIA ANALYSIS

Tenements and the "Other Half"

Genesis of the Tenement
Essay from *How the Other Half Lives* by Jacob Riis

Images: Tenement Photos
Photographs by Jacob Riis

Child Mortality Rates
Report by the Tenement House Committee

AMERICA The Story of Us: Jacob Riis
Video by HISTORY

Jacob Riis *(1849–1914) was born in Ribe, Denmark. In his long career, he was a journalist, a photographer, and a social reformer. After immigrating to the United States in 1870, Riis held several jobs and personally experienced homelessness and poverty on the streets of New York City. In 1873, he became a police reporter and was assigned to New York's Lower East Side, a poor area crowded with new immigrants. He was dismayed to learn of the conditions in the tenements that led, among other things, to high infant mortality. He began taking photographs of the slums with the new technique of flash photography. In 1890, he published* How the Other Half Lives. *In the introduction to that book, Riis pointed out that "one half of the world does not know how the other half lives." His book shocked readers and brought Riis and his cause much attention. Theodore Roosevelt, a New York City police commissioner who later became president, read the book and quickly wrote Riis a note: "I have read your book, and I have come to help." Riis's work prompted the first legislation to reform housing laws.*

SCAFFOLDING FOR ELL STUDENTS

Comprehension Support Riis's writing is dense with facts, numbers, descriptions, and quotes. These details can obscure the organizational structure and confuse readers. Explain to students that creating an outline as they read can help them while they're reading and later when they're reflecting on the text.

1. Introduction
    a. "mark of Cain" → tenements are cursed
    b. originally nice homes
2. First wave of immigrants
    a. rapid population growth

AS YOU READ Direct students to use the As You Read note to focus their reading.

Determine Author's Purpose (LINES 1–3) COMMON CORE RI 6

Explain to students that "Genesis of the Tenement" was the first chapter of Riis's book, *How the Other Half Lives.* The beginning of a book—like the beginning of a film, photo essay, podcast, or other medium—is often chosen carefully to support the author's **purpose.** Sometimes readers can make inferences, or logical assumptions, about the text's purpose by analyzing the **content** and **style** of its beginning.

 **ASK STUDENTS** to read the first sentence (lines 1–3) and analyze the reference to the "mark of Cain." What was the "mark of Cain" for the first tenements? *(The "mark of Cain" was the curse that God put on Cain after he murdered his brother. For Riis, the curse for the tenements was the "rear houses"—which are more fully described in lines 53–67. The reference is also clearly connected to the title of the chapter, which describes the beginning of the world.)*

Determine Author's Point of View (LINES 24–32) COMMON CORE RI 6

Explain to students that writers often make assumptions about their **audience** and what information readers already know. Understanding a book's intended audience can help readers understand the writer's **purpose.**

 **ASK STUDENTS** to read lines 24–32 and infer what Riis means when he writes, "the necessities of the poor became the opportunity of their wealthier neighbors." *(The poor people's need for housing became an opportunity for the rich owners of real estate to make money.)* Ask students to infer Riis's point of view toward the people who rented out the tenement rooms, citing text evidence to support their inferences. *(Riis seems to view them as opportunistic and uncaring. He says they created the small rooms "without regard to light or ventilation.")*

Genesis of the Tenement
by Jacob Riis

AS YOU READ Pay attention to the facts and details Jacob Riis includes to support his point of view. Write down any questions you generate during reading.

 The first tenement New York knew bore the mark of Cain[1] from its birth, though a generation passed before the writing was deciphered. It was the "rear house," infamous ever after in our city's history. There had been tenant-houses before, but they were not built for the purpose. Nothing would probably have shocked their original owners more than the idea of their harboring a promiscuous[2] crowd; for they were the decorous homes of the old Knickerbockers, the proud aristocracy of Manhattan in the early days.

It was the stir and bustle of trade, together with the tremendous
10 immigration that followed upon the war of 1812 that dislodged them. In thirty-five years the city of less than a hundred thousand came to harbor half a million souls, for whom homes had to be found. Within the memory of men not yet in their prime, Washington had moved from his house on Cherry Hill as too far out of town to be easily reached. Now the old residents followed his example; but they moved in a different direction and for a different reason. Their comfortable dwellings in the once fashionable streets along the East River front fell into the hands of real-estate agents and boarding-house keepers; and here, says the report to the Legislature of 1857, when the evils
20 engendered[3] had excited just alarm, "in its beginning, the tenant-house became a real blessing to that class of industrious poor whose small earnings limited their expenses, and whose employment in workshops, stores, or about the warehouses and thoroughfares, render a near residence of much importance." Not for long, however. As business increased, and the city grew with rapid strides, the necessities of the poor became the opportunity of their wealthier neighbors, and the stamp was set upon the old houses, suddenly become valuable, which the best thought and effort of a later age have vainly struggled to efface. Their "*large* rooms were partitioned into *several smaller ones,*
30 without regard to light or ventilation, the rate of rent being lower in proportion to space or height from the street; and they soon became filled from cellar to garret[4] with a class of tenantry living from hand to

---

[1] **bore the mark of Cain:** carried a curse, referring to God's punishment of Cain for killing his brother Abel, as described in *Genesis 4.*
[2] **promiscuous:** indiscriminate variety.
[3] **engendered:** caused or gave birth to.
[4] **garret:** attic.

384 Collection 5

SCAFFOLDING FOR ELL STUDENTS

Reading Support Guide students in using a strategy to better understand long, complex sentences. Using a whiteboard, project the beginning of the sentence from lines 16–18. Invite volunteers to mark up the sentence.

- Change the semicolon to a period.
- Underline the subject, and highlight the verb in green.

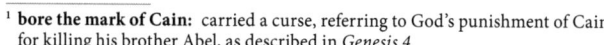
> *Their comfortable dwellings in the once fashionable streets along the East River front fell into the hands of real-estate agents and boarding-house keepers.*

ASK STUDENTS where tenements came from. *(The tenements were once "comfortable dwellings," or nice houses.)*

mouth, loose in morals, improvident[5] in habits, degraded, and squalid[6]
as beggary itself." It was thus the dark bedroom, prolific of untold
depravities,[7] came into the world. It was destined to survive the old
houses. In their new rôle, says the old report, eloquent in its indignant
denunciation of "evils more destructive than wars," "they were not
intended to last. Rents were fixed high enough to cover damage and
abuse from this class, from whom nothing was expected, and the most

40   was made of them while they lasted. Neatness, order, cleanliness, were
never dreamed of in connection with the tenant-house system, as it
spread its localities from year to year; while reckless slovenliness,[8]
discontent, privation, and ignorance were left to work out their
invariable results, until the entire premises reached the level of tenant-
house dilapidation, containing, but sheltering not, the miserable
hordes that crowded beneath mouldering, water-rotted roofs or
burrowed among the rats of clammy cellars." Yet so illogical is human
greed that, at a later day, when called to account, "the proprietors
frequently urged the filthy habits of the tenants as an excuse for the

50   condition of their property, utterly losing sight of the fact that it was
the tolerance of those habits which was the real evil, and that for this
they themselves were alone responsible."

     Still the pressure of the crowds did not abate, and in the old
garden where the stolid Dutch burgher[9] grew his tulips or early
cabbages a rear house was built, generally of wood, two stories high
at first. Presently it was carried up another story, and another. Where
two families had lived ten moved in. The front house followed suit,
if the brick walls were strong enough. The question was not always
asked, judging from complaints made by a contemporary witness,

60   that the old buildings were "often carried up to a great height without
regard to the strength of the foundation walls." It was rent the owner
was after; nothing was said in the contract about either the safety or
the comfort of the tenants. The garden gate no longer swung on its
rusty hinges. The shell-paved walk had become an alley; what the
rear house had left of the garden, a "court." Plenty such are yet to be
found in the Fourth Ward, with here and there one of the original rear
tenements.

     Worse was to follow. It was "soon perceived by estate owners
and agents of property that a greater percentage of profits could be

70   realized by the conversion of houses and blocks into barracks, and
dividing their space into smaller proportions capable of containing
human life within four walls. . . . Blocks were rented of real estate
owners, or 'purchased on time,' or taken in charge at a percentage,

---

[5] **improvident:** careless; lacking foresight.
[6] **squalid:** filthy and shabby.
[7] **depravities:** immoral behaviors.
[8] **slovenliness:** sloppiness.
[9] **stolid Dutch burgher:** upstanding citizen of New Amsterdam.

APPLYING ACADEMIC VOCABULARY

implicit	somewhat

As you discuss the excerpt from Riis's book, incorporate the following
Collection 5 academic vocabulary words: *implicit* and *somewhat*. Remind
students that many of the people who lived in the tenements were
immigrants. Does Riis's book suggest there was an **implicit** prejudice
or bigotry against these immigrants? Were the people who owned and
managed these properties even **somewhat** concerned about health and
safety issues?

CLOSE READ

Integrate and Evaluate Information (LINES 36–47)    COMMON CORE RI 7

Tell students that writers carefully choose **content**
that supports their **purpose.** The content can
include facts, stories, descriptions, and other forms of
information.

 **CITE TEXT EVIDENCE** Ask students to read
lines 36–47 and find descriptions of life in these
early tenements. *("Rents were fixed high" in line 38;
"Neatness, order, cleanliness, were never dreamed of" in
lines 40–41; "reckless slovenliness, discontent, privation,
and ignorance" in lines 42–43.)* Ask students what
these details suggest about the author's purpose.
*(These details suggest the author's purpose is to explain
how terrible life in the tenements is.)*

Integrate and Evaluate Information (LINES 68–109)    COMMON CORE RI 7

Tell students that Riis's book *How the Other Half Lives*
was supported by statistical data. Have students read
lines 68–109 of the text and then review the data
in the chart on page 391. Ask them to consider why
this chart was chosen as a companion source to the
book, given the point of view Riis expresses about
the genesis of the front and rear tenements in this
paragraph.

E **ASK STUDENTS** to explain how the chart's data
about death rates in the tenements helps to support
the findings Riis provides in lines 68–109. *(The data
shows that the death rate in a ward's tenements was
very high, often higher in rear tenements than in front
tenements.)* How does the chart ultimately support
Riis's **purpose**? *(It provides concrete proof that Riis is
just in his indictment of the tenements.)*

Integrate and Evaluate Information (LINES 74–109)

COMMON CORE RI 1, RI 7

Explain to students that Riis's book contains many types of evidence to support his point of view, including:

- **Quantitative** information is data that can be measured; it consists of numerical facts and statistics.
- **Expert testimony** is the testimony, or opinion, of experts in the field or people with first-hand knowledge.

F **CITE TEXT EVIDENCE** Have students read lines 74–109 and find examples of both quantitative evidence and expert testimony. (*Quantitative information includes: "the tenants died at the rate…in 1855" in lines 78–80; "The tenement-house population…the rate of 175,816" in lines 86–93. Expert testimony includes "The death of a child …," in lines 94–100, and "And yet experts testified…,"in lines 100–108.*) Ask: Why does Riis weave together both kinds of evidence to support his purpose? (*Not every fact can be measured. Quantitative evidence provides specific, comparable data. Expert testimony often includes compelling details.*)

Determine Central Ideas (LINES 110–116)

COMMON CORE RI 2

Explain to students that identifying the central idea of each paragraph of a complex informational text can help them to understand the text as a whole.

G **ASK STUDENTS** to determine the central idea of the paragraph that begins on line 110. (*Terrible conditions in the tenement houses continue to be a problem.*)

---

and held for under-letting." With the appearance of the middleman, wholly irresponsible, and utterly reckless and unrestrained, began the era of tenement building which turned out such blocks as Gotham Court, where, in one cholera epidemic that scarcely touched the clean wards, the tenants died at the rate of one hundred and ninety-five to the thousand of population; which forced the general mortality of the

80 city up from 1 in 41.83 in 1815, to 1 in 27.33 in 1855, a year of unusual freedom from epidemic disease, and which wrung from the early organizers of the Health Department this wail: "There are numerous examples of tenement-houses in which are lodged several hundred people that have a *pro rata* allotment[10] of ground area scarcely equal to two square yards upon the city lot, court - yards and all included." The tenement-house population had swelled to half a million souls by that time, and on the East Side, in what is still the most densely populated district in all the world, China not excluded, it was packed at the rate of 290,000 to the square mile, a state of affairs wholly

90 unexampled. The utmost cupidity of other lands and other days had never contrived to herd much more than half that number within the same space. The greatest crowding of Old London was at the rate of 175,816. Swine roamed the streets and gutters as their principal scavengers.[11] The death of a child in a tenement was registered at the Bureau of Vital Statistics as "plainly due to suffocation in the foul air of an unventilated apartment," and the Senators, who had come down from Albany to find out what was the matter with New York, reported that "there are annually cut off from the population by disease and death enough human beings to people a city, and enough human labor

100 to sustain it." And yet experts had testified that, as compared with uptown, rents were from twenty-five to thirty per cent higher in the worst slums of the lower wards, with such accommodations as were enjoyed, for instance, by a "family with boarders" in Cedar Street, who fed hogs in the cellar that contained eight or ten loads of manure; or "one room 12 × 12 with five families living in it, comprising twenty persons of both sexes and all ages, with only two beds, without partition, screen, chair, or table." The rate of rent has been successfully maintained to the present day, though the hog at least has been eliminated.

110 Lest anybody flatter himself with the notion that these were evils of a day that is happily past and may safely be forgotten, let me mention here three very recent instances of tenement-house life that came under my notice. One was the burning of a rear house in Mott Street, from appearances one of the original tenant-houses that made their owners rich. The fire made homeless ten families, who had paid an average of $5 a month for their mean little cubby-holes. The owner

[10] *pro rata* allotment: proportional allowance.
[11] scavengers: It was not until the winter of 1867 that owners of swine were prohibited by ordinance from letting them run at large in the built-up portions of the city. [Author's note]

WHEN STUDENTS STRUGGLE...

To guide students' understanding of long, difficult paragraphs, have them work in pairs to create graphic organizers like the one shown below. First, have them identify the central idea of the paragraph. Then have students identify supporting details. The chart shown is for the paragraph that begins on line 110.

CENTRAL IDEA: *The problems with tenement housing continue.*

SUPPORTING DETAILS:

Detail 1: recent burning of house   *Detail 3: couple in wretched rookery*

Detail 2: family who took poison

himself told me that it was *fully* insured for $800, though it brought
him in $600 a year rent. He evidently considered himself especially
entitled to be pitied for losing such valuable property. Another was the
120 case of a hard-working family of man and wife, young people from
the old country, who took poison together in a Crosby Street tenement
because they were "tired." There was no other explanation, and none
was needed when I stood in the room in which they had lived. It was
in the attic with sloping ceiling and a single window so far out on the
roof that it seemed not to belong to the place at all. With scarcely room
enough to turn around in they had been compelled to pay five dollars
and a half a month in advance. There were four such rooms in that
attic, and together they brought in as much as many a handsome little
cottage in a pleasant part of Brooklyn. The third instance was that of a
130 colored family of husband, wife, and baby in a wretched rear rookery[12]
in West Third Street. Their rent was eight dollars and a half for a single
room on the top-story, so small that I was unable to get a photograph
of it even by placing the camera outside the open door. Three short
steps across either way would have measured its full extent.

There was just one excuse for the early tenement-house builders,
and their successors may plead it with nearly as good right for what it
is worth. "Such," says an official report, "is the lack of house-room in
the city that any kind of tenement can be immediately crowded with
lodgers, if there is space offered." Thousands were living in cellars.
140 There were three hundred underground lodging-houses in the city
when the Health Department was organized. Some fifteen years before
that the old Baptist Church in Mulberry Street, just off Chatham
Street, had been sold, and the rear half of the frame structure had
been converted into tenements that with their swarming population
became the scandal even of that reckless age. The wretched pile[13]
harbored no less than forty families, and the annual rate of deaths to
the population was officially stated to be 75 in 1,000. These tenements
were an extreme type of very many, for the big barracks had by this
time spread east and west and far up the island into the sparsely
150 settled wards. Whether or not the title was clear to the land upon
which they were built was of less account than that the rents were
collected. If there were damages to pay, the tenant had to foot them.
Cases were "very frequent when property was in litigation, and two
or three different parties were collecting rents." Of course under such
circumstances "no repairs were ever made."

The climax had been reached. The situation was summed up
by the Society for the Improvement of the Condition of the Poor in
these words: "Crazy old buildings, crowded rear tenements in filthy
yards, dark, damp basements, leaking garrets, shops, outhouses, and

---

[12] **rookery:** a breeding place for birds; figuratively, a slum.
[13] **pile:** large building.

Compare Text and Media **387**

TEACH

CLOSE READ

Integrate and Evaluate Information (LINES 119–133)

COMMON CORE RI 7

Explain to students that different media communicate
information in different ways and that sometimes one
form of media is better at communicating a particular
piece of information or idea than another.

H ASK STUDENTS to reread lines 119–133 and
compare information in these lines with the three
photographs on pages 389–390. Ask: Which of the
photographs best supports the information in the
paragraph? *(the top picture on page 390)* What does
the photograph do that the written description does
not? *(It provides a concrete visual image of how small
and crowded these rooms are.)* What does the written
description do that the photograph does not? *(It
provides poignant details about the suicide of a couple
that were "tired" of living in these circumstances.)*

Integrate and Evaluate Information (LINES 145–147)

COMMON CORE RI 7

Remind students that **quantitative** information
provides facts in numerical form. It can be formatted
into **tables** or **graphs**, or included within the text.

I ASK STUDENTS to read lines 145–147 and find
the statistic Riis included to support his point of view.
*(The death rate for this building "was officially stated
to be 75 in 1,000.")* Ask students how this statistic
supports Riis's point of view. *(It provides evidence of
the deadly conditions in the tenements.)*

Strategies for Annotation ✏ 🖥 *Annotate it!*

Integrate and Evaluate Information COMMON CORE RI 7

Share these strategies for guided or independent analysis:

- Highlight in yellow quantitative information.
- Highlight in green descriptive details.
- Review your highlighting, and on a note write down your ideas
  about how the quantitative information and the descriptive details
  support the author's purpose.

The wretched pile harbored no less than forty families, and the annual
rate of deaths to the population was officially stated to be 75 in 1,000.

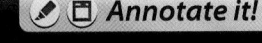

Determine Author's Purpose (LINES 164–169)

COMMON CORE RI 6

Remind students that **irony** is the contrast between what is expected and what really happens. Irony, like other rhetorical devices, can be used to support the author's **purpose.**

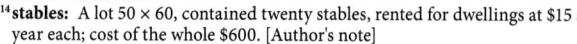

ⓙ ASK STUDENTS to reread lines 164–169. Ask students what is ironic about these lines. *(It is ironic that although children are running wild in the streets of New York, there are no organizations to help them. However, there is an organization to help children in Africa.)* How does this use of irony support the author's purpose? *(The irony highlights the fact that something needs to be done to help the tenement-dwellers of New York.)*

COLLABORATIVE DISCUSSION Have students form pairs and discuss Riis's tone toward the subject of tenements. Then as a class discuss what Riis might think should be done to improve living conditions. Accept all reasonable responses.

ASK STUDENTS to share any questions they generated in the course of reading the selection.

---

160 stables[14] converted into dwellings, though scarcely fit to shelter brutes, are habitations of thousands of our fellow-beings in this wealthy, Christian city." "The city," says its historian, Mrs. Martha Lamb, commenting on the era of aqueduct building between 1835 and 1845, "was a general asylum for vagrants." Young vagabonds, the natural offspring of such "home" conditions, overran the streets. Juvenile crime increased fearfully year by year. The Children's Aid Society and kindred philanthropic organizations were yet unborn, but in the city directory was to be found the address of the "American Society for the Promotion of Education in Africa."

---

[14] **stables:** A lot 50 × 60, contained twenty stables, rented for dwellings at $15 a year each; cost of the whole $600. [Author's note]

COLLABORATIVE DISCUSSION In a small group, discuss what Jacob Riis's tone is toward his subject. What inference can you make about what Riis thinks should be done to improve living conditions in the tenements?

MEDIA

Images: Tenement Photos
by Jacob Riis

AS YOU VIEW Pay attention to the living and working conditions of the people in the photographs. Write down any questions you generate as you view them.

K

Image of an alley between tenements taken in the early 1900s showing the dark and dirty areas that renters inhabited.

Image Credits: ©Jacob Riis/Corbis

CLOSE READ

AS YOU VIEW Direct students to use the As You View note to focus their viewing.

Integrate and Evaluate Information   COMMON CORE RI 7

Tell students that photographs can provide support for information in a text or can stand on their own as sources of information.

K **ASK STUDENTS** to look at the photograph and read the caption. Ask: How many people do you see in the picture? *(There are 11 visible faces, including the one above the fire escape.)* How would you describe these people? *(The six boys look young; one of them looks like a small child. The five young women are of indeterminable age.)* How would you describe their surroundings? *(The street and buildings look dingy. There are a lot of people in the narrow alley.)*

CITE TEXT EVIDENCE Have students cite evidence from the photograph to support a conclusion about life in the tenements in the early 1900s. *(The number of people shown in the narrow alley suggests that people were crowded together. The fact that many of them seem to be children suggests that kids probably didn't have much adult supervision and that they didn't have anything to do to keep them "off the streets." The image also clashes with the idea that children normally play in parks or out in nature. This image suggests that these children only had a dark and dirty alley to play in)*

TO CHALLENGE STUDENTS . . .

Composition Explain to students that in visual arts, such as photography, **composition** is the arrangement of visual elements. Sometimes elements are intentionally arranged or posed to support a **purpose**. Sometimes photos are taken without posing to show the elements in their most natural state.

COLLABORATIVE DISCUSSION Have students form small groups to view the pictures and discuss the following questions:

- **Subject:** Who or what is the primary focus?
- **Depth:** What elements create a sense of depth?
- **Viewpoint:** Where was the camera situated to capture this picture?
- **Purpose:** Were the people in this photograph posed? Why do you think so? What was the photographer's purpose?

Integrate and Evaluate Information

COMMON CORE RI 1, RI 7

Explain to students that Riis's book *How the Other Half Lives* includes photographs such as the one shown here.

Published in Jacob Riis's book *How the Other Half Lives*, entitled "Five Cents a Spot." The title refers to the cost of buying a spot on the floor to sleep for the night.

L **ASK STUDENTS** to look closely at the first photograph on this page and read the caption. Have students analyze how this photograph might have served to support Riis's purpose for publishing his book. *(The photograph illustrates the crowded and unhealthy conditions Riis described in the text of his book. For example, the room contains an oven but no obvious ventilation. It might have helped him achieve his purpose not only by illustrating the conditions but also by putting a human face on the problem. Readers who saw the individuals' faces might be more moved to take action to help the people of the tenements.)*

Integrate and Evaluate Information

COMMON CORE RI 1, RI 7

Explain to students that just as they can draw conclusions from the details in a text, they can also draw conclusions from the details in a photograph. Have students look at the second picture on this page and read the caption.

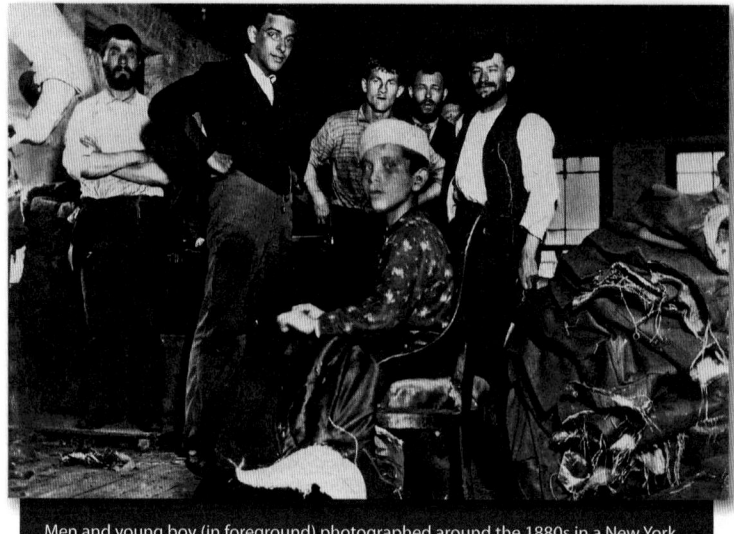

Men and young boy (in foreground) photographed around the 1880s in a New York City sweatshop, or factory, with poor working conditions.

M **CITE TEXT EVIDENCE** Have students use clues from the picture to draw conclusions about the factory. *(The pile of material on the right side of the photograph suggests it is a garment factory. The boy in the picture suggests children work there. Only the boy seems to be working—which suggests his exploitation—and his bruised eye suggests he is not well taken care of or may even have been abused.)*

COLLABORATIVE DISCUSSION In a small group, discuss the details that these photographs have in common. What emotions are conveyed by the people?

COLLABORATIVE DISCUSSION Have students form small groups and discuss the details in the photographs.

ASK STUDENTS to share any questions they generated in the course of viewing the photographs.

TO CHALLENGE STUDENTS . . .

Remind students that **realism** is a 19th-century literary movement that examines the effect of natural and social forces on the individual and that **naturalism** is an offshoot of realism that views humans pessimistically as being at the mercy of their environment and their own baser instincts.

Challenge students to categorize the excerpt from Riis's book and his photographs as either realistic or naturalistic. Have students cite evidence from the selection to support their opinions. Then have volunteers present their analyses to the class.

Child Mortality Rates

Background *This table was included in the* Report of the Tenement House Committee, *published in 1895. The committee was formed to "make a careful examination into the tenement-houses" of New York City. Due to the rapid influx of new immigrants, New York City was the most populous urban area in the world, with parts of it denser than infamous slums in Bombay, India. The report described some residents as living "virtually in a cage", in dark, damp buildings surrounded by garbage. The average death-rate in New York City at the time was 22.75 deaths per 1000 persons.*

AS YOU READ Consider the differences in the death-rate of children in different wards. Write down any questions you generate during reading.

If we take the death-rate of children as a test, the rear tenements show themselves to be veritable slaughter-houses, as shown in the following table, which only covers the lower wards, where such houses are numerous:

Wards	Death-rate of children under 5 years of age in single tenements.	Death-rate of children under 5 years of age in front and rear tenements on same lot.
1	109.58	204.54
4	105.69	114.68
5	107.99	64.52
6	103.56	99.54
7	61.78	72.58
8	95.58	129.56
9	92.78	130.56
10	57.20	62.58
11	73.12	71.49
13	83.05	100.59
14	129.56	114.12
17	62.04	78.36

It is unfortunate that it was found impossible to make a direct comparison between the death-rates in rear tenements, by themselves, and the death-rate in other houses. But the deaths in the city are reported by street and number, and as the front and rear houses on the same lot have the same number, it is evident that the rate could not be calculated separately. In the report of January 28, 1890, already referred to, the general death-rate for lots containing both front and rear houses was 25.05, against 22.42 for other houses of the same class, in the same part of the city.

COLLABORATIVE DISCUSSION In a small group, discuss what information you can draw from the text and chart on this page. What might explain the differences between the death rates in the two columns?

WHEN STUDENTS STRUGGLE . . .

Students may find it a challenge to read and interpret tables of information. To guide their comprehension, have them work in pairs to answer the following questions:

1. **What does the title tell you?** *(Have students look for context clues, such as "the death-rate of children.")*

2. **What do the column headings tell you?** *(Encourage students to find synonyms for the word "ward," such as "zone" or "parish." Explain that the second column includes properties with just one building, while the third column includes properties with multiple buildings.)*

CLOSE READ

Background Riis's book *How the Other Half Lives* was published in 1890. The book brought the hazardous condition of tenements to the attention of readers by shocking them with eyewitness accounts and shocking photographs of tenement dwellers. Subsequently, investigations were undertaken that led to reports such as this one by the Tenement House Committee. The committee's investigation and publication of reports led to a law that required property owners and managers to provide safer, more sanitary living conditions.

AS YOU READ Direct students to use the As You Read note to focus their reading.

Integrate and Evaluate Information

 COMMON CORE RI 1, RI 7

Explain to students that **quantitative** information can be difficult to interpret without context. Remind students that **context** is the circumstances or facts surrounding an event or situation. Placing the data in a particular **format** creates context, which helps readers integrate and evaluate it. Explain that **tables** show sets of data across several columns, enabling readers to track their relationship to each other and draw conclusions about the data.

ASK STUDENTS to read the quantitative information and the accompanying text. Ask: What main points do the chart and text make about the hazardous conditions of tenements? *(The rising death rates for children in the lower wards were very high. In some wards, the death rate had become three times higher than the city's average rate of 22.42 children per 1000 only ten years before.)* Ask: How do the chart's columns compare? *(The right column is consistently higher than the left.)* What does this table suggest? *(Death rates on properties with both front and rear tenements are typically much higher than single building properties. Properties crowded with more than one tenement are far more dangerous for children to live in.)*

CLOSE READ

 Students can view the video "AMERICA The Story of Us: Jacob Riis" in their eBooks.

Background Have students read the background. Tell students that Riis reached different audiences through different media. He wrote newspaper and magazine articles. He published books that contained many of his photographs. He also gave lectures and slide show presentations at churches and other public venues.

AS YOU VIEW Direct students to use the As You View note to focus their viewing.

Integrate and Evaluate Information

 COMMON CORE RI 1, RI 7

Explain to students that the video uses various elements to achieve its purpose—to convey information about the life and work of Jacob Riis. These elements include Riis's photographs, reenactments, interviews with experts, a musical score, and aerial footage of New York City. Draw students' attention to the reenactment of the photographing of "Five Cents a Spot," pictured on page 390 of this selection.

ASK STUDENTS how the video helps them to better understand the significance of the photograph entitled "Five Cents a Spot" on page 390. *(The photo was taken unstaged and in the middle of the night, capturing an image of tenants as they really were.)*

COLLABORATIVE DISCUSSION Have students form small groups and discuss the commentary included in the video. Are the experts credible? How do their words support the video's purpose?

ASK STUDENTS to share any questions they generated in the course of reading, viewing, and discussing the selection.

MEDIA

HISTORY | VIDEO

AMERICA The Story of Us: Jacob Riis

Background *This brief video discusses and depicts how Jacob Riis successfully championed housing reform in the late 1800s and early 1900s in New York City through his use of flash photography. His photographs made it possible for many people to become truly aware of the living conditions in the tenements of New York City. In addition to writing about the problems he witnessed there, Riis gave numerous presentations to acquaint people with the issues of tenement dwellers and to push for changes that would help improve their situation.*

AS YOU VIEW Pay attention to how the audience attending Riis's presentation, which the video dramatizes, reacts to his photographs. Write down any questions you generate during viewing.

COLLABORATIVE DISCUSSION In a small group, discuss what perspective or insight the interviewed experts bring to the film. Why are their statements effective or persuasive?

APPLYING ACADEMIC VOCABULARY

clarify	revise

As you discuss the video, incorporate the following Collection 5 academic vocabulary words: *clarify* and *revise*. Explain to students that different media may contain different information about a subject. Sometimes this information complements, or adds to, what was previously learned. And sometimes the information contradicts other sources. Does watching this video about Riis **clarify** information presented in the text, photographs, or table? Does it require you to **revise** any opinions you may have formed?

Integrate and Evaluate Information

COMMON CORE RI 7

Writers can choose to present their information in many different formats to achieve different purposes. Integrating and evaluating multiple sources of information presented in different media or formats can help address questions about a particular subject. The chart shows some formats in which information can be presented. This collection about Jacob Riis presents information in prose, visual, and quantitative formats.

Format	How Information Is Presented
Prose	
Essay	In *How the Other Half Lives*, Jacob Riis presents most of the information about tenements in text format. Notice, however, he supports his text with photographs and statistical or numerical data. Why might he have chosen to combine these different formats to support his ideas?
Visual	
Video Clips	A video clip gives viewers images, sounds, and even special effects to help them evaluate a topic, such as why Jacob Riis's work was so influential. What advantages does a visual representation have?
Photographs	Photographs give readers a concrete visual image of something. Photographs can support information provided in a text or can stand on their own with captions to portray a broader subject, such as living conditions in tenements. Why are the photographs of people in and around tenements effective?
Maps	Maps provide information about aspects of a geographical region. Why might a map of the New York City wards in the late 1800s be useful?
Quantitative	
Tables	Tables show sets of data across several columns, enabling readers to track their relationship to each other and draw conclusions about the data. Remember to look at the title and labels on columns and rows, as well as the actual numbers to help you interpret the data in a table. How does the table of information about death rates in the wards help you understand the need for tenement housing reform?
Graphs	Graphs provide an illustration of statistical information or numerical relationships. Line graphs show changes over time. Bar graphs compare quantities and circle graphs show relationships of parts to a whole. Which type of graph could be used to present the information about death rates in the wards in a different way?

CLOSE READ

Integrate and Evaluate Information

 COMMON CORE RI 7

Review the characteristics of each of the media in the chart. Then discuss the strengths and weaknesses of each. Have students use the following questions to evaluate each type of media in the selection.

Credibility: Which medium conveyed information in a way that was most credible, or believable? Why?

Logic: Which medium best used logic—reasons and supporting evidence—to make its point?

Emotional impact: Which medium had the most emotional impact? Why?

Explain to students that evolving technology has made a wide range of new media available to people who want to communicate their messages. Movable type replaced hand-written text. Photographs replaced wood-cut drawings. Film has evolved into a dominant story-telling medium. Computer and information technology has brought many of these media together and created new ways to share information.

Ask students to speculate what media Jacob Riis might use if he were creating media messages today.

PRACTICE & APPLY

Analyzing the Text and Media

COMMON CORE RI 1, RI 5, RI 6, RI 7

Possible answers:

1. Riis begins his essay with a biblical reference (the mark of Cain), which adds moral context to his argument and reinforces the greed and selfishness of those profiting without concern for their tenants.

2. The important statistics are referenced in lines 86–109. The first statistic is the city's population density. The second statistic is the population of Old London when the city was at its most crowded point. These statistics might have been more clearly and succinctly illustrated with some graphs or charts.

3. The video clip includes a reenactment of Riis presenting his photographs to an audience. Riis is portrayed as an effective public speaker, and the audience is shown gasping when they see the photographs' stark nature.

4. The chart shows that children living on lots with front and rear tenements are more likely to die than children living on lots with just single tenements. The data clearly suggests that rear tenements—probably because of crowding and unsanitary conditions—contribute to child mortality.

5. The images show individuals, often crowded together, trying to survive under deplorable circumstances.

6. Riis suggests that New York City's philanthropists were more concerned with Africa than they were with their own city. Brokaw suggests that Americans are willing to see their problems and fix them. It is possible that Riis underestimated the degree to which his work and advocacy had already changed public sentiment or that he was impatient with the pace of progress.

7. Different media contain different information. Multiple sources of information provide a more complete perspective. Viewing only photographs cannot answer questions about the number of children living in tenements.

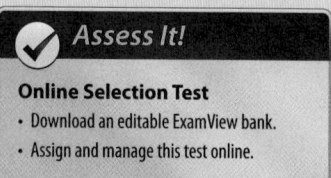
Assess It!

Online Selection Test
- Download an editable ExamView bank.
- Assign and manage this test online.

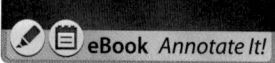

Analyzing the Text and Media

COMMON CORE RI 5, RI 6, RI 7, W 2, W 7, W 8, W 9

Cite Text Evidence   Support your responses with evidence from the selections.

1. **Connect** How does Riis's description of the genesis of the tenements at the beginning of his essay help support his purpose and point of view? How does Riis's rhetoric contribute to the power of his text?

2. **Critique** What quantitative format could Riis have used to present the data in lines 86–109 in order to clarify his argument about the problems of tenements?

3. **Evaluate** How does the video excerpt help support the idea that Jacob Riis was successful in communicating his point of view to his audience? Cite specific images or concepts from the video to support your answer.

4. **Analyze** What does the table show about children living in front or rear tenements? Why might information presented in this format have been more effective at pushing New York City to make reforms to housing laws than a photograph of a tenement?

5. **Compare** Review the three photographs from the image collection. What does each image add to your knowledge of life in the New York City tenements? How do these three images connect to the ideas and messages in the other three types of documents?

6. **Synthesize** What idea and point of view is Riis expressing when he says, "The Children's Aid Society and kindred philanthropic organizations were yet unborn, but in the city directory was to be found the address of the 'American Society for the Promotion of Education in Africa'"? How is this sentiment different from what Tom Brokaw says about the American people in the video? What explains this difference?

7. **Draw Conclusions** What are the pros and cons of evaluating data from multiple sources about a subject? Think about whether a question about specific numbers of children living in tenements could be answered by only viewing Riis's photographs.

PERFORMANCE TASK

Writing Activity: Essay During the late 1800s and early 1900s, many people, including Jacob Riis, worked to solve societal issues. Write an informative essay to answer this question: What was life like in the New York tenements? Use these tips to get started.

- Start collecting information to support your claim. Write an outline for your essay. Use information from "Genesis of the Tenement," Jacob Riis's photographs, the table, and the video.

- Remember to jot down and include the source of your supporting information.

- In your essay, introduce your topic and develop it by choosing the most

- significant and relevant information available. Avoid using ambiguous data that can be misinterpreted.

- Consider presenting some of your information in quantitative or visual formats to help your readers understand.

- In your conclusion, summarize the information you have presented.

Assign this performance task.

PERFORMANCE TASK

COMMON CORE W 7, W 8, W 9

Writing Activity: Essay Have students formulate a working thesis or central idea statement. Students can then gather evidence from the media in this selection and outside sources. Remind them that outside sources must be **relevant,** or directly related to their central idea, and **credible,** or trustworthy. Encourage students to incorporate quantitative information (charts, graphs, tables) and visual information (photographs, illustrations, video clips).

Short Research

COMMON CORE

W 7, W 8, W 9

TEACH

Explain to students that an essential part of Jacob Riis's work was **research.** Research is the systematic investigation of a subject with the goal of discovering facts that support or revise a theory or idea. It is conducted by journalists, scientists, business executives, students, and many others. Use the following steps to guide your research:

1. Determine the goal or purpose of the research
2. Create a specific question or hypothesis
3. Find and collect the data
4. Analyze and interpret the data
5. Report and evaluate research

PRACTICE AND APPLY

Tell students that terrible housing conditions and crushing poverty are not a thing of the past. Have students write a short research paper that investigates poor urban housing conditions in the 21st century. Students' essays should focus on a single area or city and should use details gathered from research to describe living conditions. Encourage students to incorporate various forms of media, including statistics and photographs. Remind students that their facts need to be attributed to reliable sources.

You can suggest places for students to start their research, such as Katherine Boo's *Behind the Beautiful Forevers*, Mike Davis's *Planet of Slums*, Luis Alberto Urrea's *Across the Wire*, or Jonathan Kozol's *Amazing Grace*.

Integrate and Evaluate Information

COMMON CORE

RI 7

RETEACH

Remind students that Riis uses different types of information—including statistics, anecdotes, first-hand accounts, and quotes—to support his **purpose.** Analyzing these facts is similar in some respects to evaluating the evidence of a persuasive argument. Explain to students that it is important to weigh the **credibility** of Riis's evidence.

Have students form pairs or small groups to review the text, photographs, chart, and video and then discuss whether the facts are credible and how they support the author's purpose.

 **LEVEL UP TUTORIALS** Assign the following *Level Up* tutorial: **Evaluating Credibility**

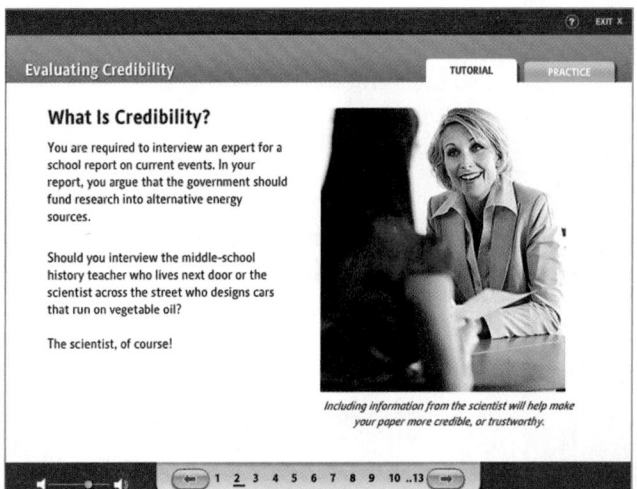

CLOSE READING APPLICATION

Have students find additional information about New York City tenements in the 19th century, either online or in a book. Ask them to analyze the credibility of the sources they find and compare the information to what was presented in Riis's work. Have students share their findings with a partner.

*my*SmartPlanner   Create lesson plans and access resources online.

The Story of an Hour

Short Story by Kate Chopin

Why This Text?

"The Story of an Hour" is a short story that was ahead of its time. Viewed as a precursor to the modern feminist movement, it explores themes that were taboo at the time it was written. This lesson explores Chopin's masterful use of irony.

Key Learning Objective: Students will be able to analyze the impact of the author's use of point of view and irony in a short story.

For additional practice:

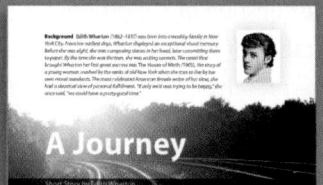

Close Reader selection
"A Journey"
Short Story by Edith Wharton

COMMON CORE | Common Core Standards

RL 1 Cite textual evidence.

RL 2 Determine themes of a text.

RL 3 Analyze the impact of the author's choices.

RL 5 Analyze how an author's choices concerning how to structure specific parts of a text contribute to its overall meaning as well as its aesthetic impact.

RL 6 Analyze a case in which grasping point of view requires distinguishing what is directly stated in a text from what is really meant.

SL 1a Come prepared with text evidence for discussion.

SL 4 Determine or clarify the meaning of unknown and multiple-meaning words and phrases.

▲ Text Complexity Rubric

	The Story of an Hour
Quantitative Measures	**The Story of an Hour** Lexile: 970L
Qualitative Measures	**Levels of Meaning/Purpose** multiple levels of meaning
	Structure conventional story structure
	Language Conventionality and Clarity figurative, less accessible language
	Knowledge Demands somewhat complex social and historical concepts
Reader/Task Considerations	Teacher determined Vary by individual reader and type of text

Kate Chopin Chopin was thirty-two years old and a widow with six children when she began to write fiction and publish short stories in respected magazines. Her novel *The Awakening* initially shocked readers with its frank depiction of a woman's resistance to her socially defined role as wife and mother. The novel became a classic in the mid 20th century with the social redefinition of women's roles. Chopin's writing attempts to describe "human existence in its subtle, complex, true meaning, stripped of the veil with which ethical and conventional standards have draped it."

AS YOU READ Direct students to use the As You Read instructions to focus their reading. Remind them to write down questions they generate as they read.

Analyze Author's Point of View (LINES 1–11)

COMMON CORE RL 5, RL 6

Explain to students that **point of view** is the narrative perspective from which events in a story are told. Remind them that in **third-person point of view,** the story is told by a narrator who is not a character in the story. Explain that the third-person point of view can be **limited** (the narrator has access to only the thoughts and feelings of one character) or **omniscient** (the narrator has access to the thoughts and feelings of all the characters.)

Ⓐ **ASK STUDENTS** to reread lines 1–11 and tell which type of third-person narrator Chopin is using—limited or omniscient. (*The narrator is omniscient, revealing the thoughts and feelings of Mrs. Mallard, her sister, and Richards.*)

CRITICAL VOCABULARY

abandonment: Mrs. Mallard wept with no inhibition.

ASK STUDENTS why Mrs. Mallard's weeping is significant at this point in the story. (*The response suggests she is initially upset by her husband's death.*)

Kate Chopin (1851–1904) *wrote more than one hundred short stories and two novels. Her work features intelligent and sensitive female characters and is often set against the Louisiana backdrop where she spent her married life. Her first novel,* At Fault *(1890), received little attention when it was published. Her second,* The Awakening *(1899), told the story of a woman who leaves her family and eventually commits suicide. It was widely condemned by critics as shocking and morbid. However, since its rediscovery in the 1950s, it has been hailed as an insightful work that foreshadowed the feminist movement in literature.*

The Story of an Hour

Short Story by Kate Chopin

AS YOU READ After you read the first paragraph, write down what you expect to happen or what you expect Mrs. Mallard to do. Pause after every few paragraphs and continue to jot down your expectations. Write down any questions you generate during reading.

Ⓐ Knowing that Mrs. Mallard was afflicted with a heart trouble, great care was taken to break to her as gently as possible the news of her husband's death.

It was her sister Josephine who told her, in broken sentences; veiled hints that revealed in half concealing. Her husband's friend Richards was there, too, near her. It was he who had been in the newspaper office when intelligence of the railroad disaster was received, with Brently Mallard's name leading the list of "killed." He had only taken the time to assure himself of its truth by a second telegram, and had 10 hastened to forestall any less careful, less tender friend in bearing the sad message.

She did not hear the story as many women have heard the same, with a paralyzed inability to accept its significance. She wept at once, with sudden, wild **abandonment**, in her sister's arms. When the storm of grief had spent itself she went away to her room alone. She would have no one follow her.

abandonment
(ə-băn′dən-mĕnt) *n.*
a lack of restraint or inhibition.

The Story of an Hour **395**

SCAFFOLDING FOR ELL STUDENTS

Recognize Prepositional Phrases Explain to students that Chopin uses many prepositional phrases. Tell them that a **preposition** is a word used to show the relationship between a noun or pronoun and another word in the sentence. Examples include *above, down, near, in,* and *with.* A **prepositional phrase** includes the preposition and its object and modifiers. Display these sentences from the story:

It was her sister Josephine who told her, [in broken sentences]; veiled hints that revealed [in half concealing]. Her husband's friend Richards was there, too, [near her].

Work with students to bracket the prepositional phrases. Have students notice other prepositional phrases as they read on.

Analyze Author's Point of View: Irony (LINES 37–47)  COMMON CORE RL 6

Remind students that irony is a contrast between appearance and reality. Point out that one type of irony Chopin uses is called **situational irony**, in which something different happens than what is expected.

B **CITE TEXT EVIDENCE** Ask students to reread lines 37–47 and use text evidence to explain the situational irony in Mrs. Mallard's dread. *(It is ironic that Mrs. Mallard is "striving to beat it back" because the reader finds out in line 47 that "it" is a sense of freedom.)*

> #### CRITICAL VOCABULARY
>
> **vacant**: Mrs. Mallard's stare was without emotion or expression.
>
> **ASK STUDENTS** how her expression changes. *(Her eyes were suddenly "keen and bright," [line 48] as though life were returning to her suddenly.)*

Analyze Author's Point of View: Irony (LINES 48–49)  COMMON CORE RL 6

Discuss with students the vivid physical description of Mrs. Mallard in these lines.

C **ASK STUDENTS** why this description is ironic, especially in light of the information given at the beginning of the story about Mrs. Mallard's "heart trouble." *(The description in these lines paints a picture of a healthy, vibrant woman, which is ironic given the fact that people worried that the news of her husband's death might adversely affect Mrs. Mallard's health.)*

There stood, facing the open window, a comfortable, roomy armchair. Into this she sank, pressed down by a physical exhaustion that haunted her body and seemed to reach into her soul.

20 She could see in the open square before her house the tops of trees that were all aquiver with the new spring life. The delicious breath of rain was in the air. In the street below a peddler was crying his wares. The notes of a distant song which someone was singing reached her faintly, and countless sparrows were twittering in the eaves.

There were patches of blue sky showing here and there through the clouds that had met and piled one above the other in the west facing her window.

She sat with her head thrown back upon the cushion of the chair, quite motionless, except when a sob came up into her throat and 30 shook her, as a child who has cried itself to sleep continues to sob in its dreams.

She was young, with a fair, calm face, whose lines bespoke repression and even a certain strength. But now there was a dull stare in her eyes, whose gaze was fixed away off yonder on one of those patches of blue sky. It was not a glance of reflection, but rather indicated a suspension of intelligent thought.

B There was something coming to her and she was waiting for it, fearfully. What was it? She did not know; it was too subtle and elusive to name. But she felt it, creeping out of the sky, reaching toward her 40 through the sounds, the scents, the color that filled the air.

Now her bosom rose and fell tumultuously. She was beginning to recognize this thing that was approaching to possess her, and she was striving to beat it back with her will—as powerless as her two white slender hands would have been.

When she abandoned herself a little whispered word escaped her slightly parted lips. She said it over and over under her breath: "free, free, free!" The **vacant** stare and the look of terror that had followed it **C** went from her eyes. They stayed keen and bright. Her pulses beat fast, and the coursing blood warmed and relaxed every inch of her body.

50 She did not stop to ask if it were or were not a monstrous joy that held her. A clear and exalted perception enabled her to dismiss the suggestion as trivial.

She knew that she would weep again when she saw the kind, tender hands folded in death; the face that had never looked save with love upon her, fixed and gray and dead. But she saw beyond that bitter moment a long procession of years to come that would belong to her absolutely. And she opened and spread her arms out to them in welcome.

There would be no one to live for her during those coming years; 60 she would live for herself. There would be no powerful will bending hers in that blind persistence with which men and women believe they have a right to impose a private will upon a fellow creature. A kind

vacant
(vā´kənt) *adj.* blank, expressionless.

APPLYING ACADEMIC VOCABULARY

clarify	revise

As you discuss "The Story of an Hour," incorporate the following Collection 5 academic vocabulary words: *clarify* and *revise*. Discuss how the narrator **clarifies** the character's feelings as the story progresses. Then ask students how they had to **revise** their expectations about the story as they read.

intention or a cruel intention made the act seem no less a crime as she looked upon it in that brief moment of **illumination**.

And yet she had loved him—sometimes. Often she had not. What did it matter! What could love, the unsolved mystery, count for in face of this possession of self-assertion which she suddenly recognized as the strongest impulse of her being!

"Free! Body and soul free!" she kept whispering.

70 Josephine was kneeling before the closed door with her lips to the keyhole, imploring for admission. "Louise, open the door! I beg; open the door—you will make yourself ill. What are you doing, Louise? For heaven's sake open the door."

"Go away. I am not making myself ill." No; she was drinking in a very elixir of life[1] through that open window.

Her fancy was running riot along those days ahead of her. Spring days, and summer days, and all sorts of days that would be her own. She breathed a quick prayer that life might be long. It was only yesterday she had thought with a shudder that life might be long.

80 She arose at length and opened the door to her sister's importunities. There was a feverish triumph in her eyes, and she carried herself unwittingly like a goddess of Victory. She clasped her sister's waist, and together they descended the stairs. Richards stood waiting for them at the bottom.

Someone was opening the front door with a latchkey. It was Brently Mallard who entered, a little travel-stained, **composedly** carrying his grip-sack[2] and umbrella. He had been far from the scene of accident, and did not even know there had been one. He stood amazed at Josephine's piercing cry; at Richards' quick motion to screen

90 him from the view of his wife.

But Richards was too late.

When the doctors came they said she had died of heart disease—of joy that kills.

---

[1] **elixir of life:** a medicine that restores vigor or the essence of life.
[2] **grip-sack:** a small traveling bag or satchel.

illumination
(ĭ-lōō´mə-nā´shən) *n.* awareness or enlightenment.

composed
(kəm-pōzd´) *adj.* self-possessed; calm.

COLLABORATIVE DISCUSSION With a partner, discuss whether your initial expectations were met and how your expectations changed over the course of the story. Cite specific details in the text that shaped your expectations.

TEACH

CLOSE READ

CRITICAL VOCABULARY

illumination: Mrs. Mallard has a realization, or a moment of clarity, about relationships.

ASK STUDENTS What is Mrs. Mallard's moment of illumination? *(Mrs. Mallard realizes that, with her husband's death, she is free of the control that people in relationships try to exert over each other. She will be able to "live for herself.")*

Analyze Author's Point of View: Irony (LINES 85–90)

COMMON CORE RL 6

Explain to students that **dramatic irony** occurs when the reader or audience knows something that the character does not.

 **ASK STUDENTS** to analyze the irony in lines 85–90. How does this moment in the story demonstrate dramatic irony? *(Mr. Mallard does not know what the reader does—that his wife is mourning his death, or even more significant, celebrating her freedom from him.)*

CRITICAL VOCABULARY

composed: Mr. Mallard arrived home in a calm manner.

ASK STUDENTS What is ironic about how Mr. Mallard appears when he returns? *(Everyone believed he died in a train wreck so it is ironic that he comes home looking calm and composed.)*

WHEN STUDENTS STRUGGLE...

To help students understand Mrs. Mallard's epiphany, have them reread lines 59–69. Tell them that these lines describe the series of realizations that led Mrs. Mallard to exult in her freedom.

ASK STUDENTS to list this series of realizations in their own words. *(She could live for herself. Men and women try to control each other. She loved her husband only sometimes. Her freedom matters more to her than love for her husband.)*

COLLABORATIVE DISCUSSION Have students work in pairs to discuss their initial expectations and how they changed over the course of the story. Have students cite specific details from the text that shaped their expectations.

ASK STUDENTS to share any questions they generated in the course of reading and discussing the selection.

Analyze Author's Point of View: Irony

Explain to students that the writer uses the third-person omniscient point of view, which enables her to reveal the thoughts and feelings of any of the characters in the story. However, for most of the story the narrator focuses on Mrs. Mallard's thoughts and feelings.

ASK STUDENTS how the author's decision to narrate the final, surprising event of the story—Mr. Mallard's return home—from Mr. Mallard's perspective affects the story. How would the story be different if the narrator had been limited to Mrs. Mallard's perspective? *(Narrating this event from Mr. Mallard's point of view leaves the reader to infer Mrs. Mallard's feelings and resolves the story in a more interesting and complex way.)*

Finally, discuss the irony of the story's last sentence. Point out that the last sentence is an example of both situational and dramatic irony. The situation is ironic because it was feared that Mrs. Mallard would die when she received news of her husband's death but instead she died when she saw that he was alive. The suggestion that she died "of joy that kills" is dramatic irony because the reader knows that she probably did not feel joy at seeing her husband.

Analyze Author's Point of View: Irony

Point of view refers to the perspective from which a story is told. "The Story of an Hour" is told from a **third-person** point of view; the narrator is not a character in the story but observes the action from outside it. Point of view may also be characterized by what the narrator knows or shares. If the narrator is able to tell readers what only one character thinks and feels, the point of view is **limited.** An **omniscient** narrator can describe the thoughts and feelings of all the characters.

When analyzing a story's point of view, it's important to distinguish between what is stated directly and what is actually true for the characters. One of the narrator's roles is to help readers see contrasts, such as

- what a character feels versus how he or she behaves
- what characters believe versus what is true
- what readers might expect to happen versus what does happen

All of these are examples of irony, a contrast between appearance and reality. This chart describes the three basic types of irony.

Verbal Irony	Situational Irony	Dramatic Irony
In **verbal irony,** what is said is the opposite of what is meant. Sarcasm, understatement, and hyperbole (exaggeration for effect) are all examples of verbal irony. Context can help you clarify whether a statement is an example of verbal irony. If a friend says, "I'm having a great day," but then tells you she woke up late and left her homework on the bus, you'd interpret her statement as ironic.	In **situational irony,** a character or the reader expects one thing to happen, but something else happens instead. Situational irony is used throughout "The Story of an Hour." For example, recall how carefully Josephine and Richards break the news about Mr. Mallard's death. How do they (and readers) expect Mrs. Mallard to feel about the loss of her husband? How does she actually feel?	In **dramatic irony,** the audience or reader knows something that the characters do not know. For example, when Mrs. Mallard is locked in her room, her worried sister crouches at the keyhole and says, "I beg; open the door—you will make yourself ill." What do readers know that poor Josephine does not?

Identifying the use of irony can help you determine **themes,** or deeper messages about life that the author wants to communicate through a story. Irony encourages readers to look for the truth hidden behind superficial appearances or expectations. As you analyze "The Story of an Hour," ask yourself what the unexpected realities of the characters' lives teach you about people, relationships, and society in general.

Strategies for Annotation 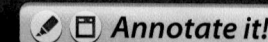 *Annotate it!*

Analyze Author's Point of View: Irony

Explain to students that in situational irony, the writer contrasts expectations with reality. Then share these strategies for guided or independent analysis:

- Highlight expectations in blue.
- Highlight reality in yellow.
- Add a note explaining how reality differs from what is expected.

"Louise, open the door! I beg; open the door—you will make yourself ill. What are you doing, Louise? For heaven's sake open the door."

"Go away. I am not making myself ill." No; she was drinking in a very elixir of life[1] through that open window.

 eBook *Annotate It!*

Analyzing the Text

COMMON CORE — RL 1, RL 2, RL 3, RL 5, RL 6, SL 1a

Cite Text Evidence   Support your responses with evidence from the selection.

1. **Cite Evidence** Is the narrator of the story limited or omniscient? At what point in the story do readers learn whose thoughts and feelings the narrator can describe?

2. **Analyze** Reread lines 1–11. How do Josephine and Richards expect Mrs. Mallard to react to Mr. Mallard's death? Now reread lines 12–19 and explain whether Mrs. Mallard's initial reaction is intended to be ironic.

3. **Compare** What is ironic about Mrs. Mallard's private reaction to her husband's death? How does it compare to the expectations of the other characters?

4. **Infer** In lines 45–58 the narrator begins to reveal Mrs. Mallard's true feelings about being a widow. What theme is suggested through this situational irony?

5. **Evaluate** What images does the narrator describe outside Mrs. Mallard's window when she first goes to her room? Does this choice of imagery make you more or less sympathetic toward Mrs. Mallard?

6. **Interpret** How does Chopin's diction and imagery in lines 80–84 contribute to her characterization of a transformed Mrs. Mallard?

7. **Evaluate** Why is Mr. Mallard's return an example of situational irony? Would the story still be ironic if he had actually been dead?

8. **Analyze** The doctors say that Mrs. Mallard dies of "joy that kills." Explain whether this is an example of dramatic irony.

PERFORMANCE TASK

Speaking Activity: Discussion There are many strong examples of irony in "The Story of an Hour." Collaborate with others to discuss what irony adds to Chopin's message. Then write a brief summary of the key ideas from your discussion.

1. Why did Chopin choose to communicate so much of her **theme,** or message, through the literary device of irony? In the context of her era and of her audience's possible attitudes, why might this have been an appropriate or attractive choice?

2. Consider the irony of Mrs. Mallard's death. How is her death—its timing and its cause—ironic? What does the irony of her death add to Chopin's message?

In your discussion and summary, include evidence from the text and revise to use the conventions of standard English.

PRACTICE & APPLY

Analyzing the Text

COMMON CORE — RL 1, RL 2, RL 3, RL 5, RL 6, SL 1a

Possible answers:

1. *The narrator is omniscient. Although most of the story is told from Mrs. Mallard's perspective, the narrator does take other perspectives. This is apparent in the first line of the story, in which the narrator relates the thoughts of those around Mrs. Mallard.*

2. *Josephine expects Mrs. Mallard to be grief stricken, and initially she seems to be just that. Her initial reaction is not ironic.*

3. *Mrs. Mallard's private reaction is ironic, as her sister thinks the grief might make her ill, when in fact she feels "free, free, free!"*

4. *The situational irony in these lines suggests the theme that events that are expected to be heartbreaking can have the opposite effect. Though she is expected to feel crushed by grief, Mrs. Mallard feels free.*

5. *The reader expects heartbreak, but Mrs. Mallard feels joy and freedom. She welcomes "a long procession of years to come that would belong to her absolutely."*

6. *Chopin uses imagery and diction appropriate for a Greek goddess to show Mrs. Mallard's newfound strength and independence ("triumph," "goddess of Victory," "clasped"). Also the word "importunities" and the image of Richards "waiting ... at the bottom" suggest her power and authority.*

7. *His return is an example of situational irony because everybody believes him to be dead, but he is not. The story is full of irony before the reader finds out that Mr. Mallard is still alive.*

8. *"Joy that kills" is an example of dramatic irony, because the reader knows that Mrs. Mallard probably did not feel joy when she saw that her husband was still alive.*

Assign this performance task.

PERFORMANCE TASK

COMMON CORE — SL 1a

Speaking Activity: Discussion Review the different types of irony with the whole class. Ask students to suggest examples of situational and dramatic irony in the story. Remind students to find specific details from the story to support their interpretations. After the small group discussions, have a representative from each group share the group's summary with the class.

PRACTICE & APPLY

Critical Vocabulary

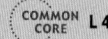 COMMON CORE L 4

Possible answers:

1. abandonment; when one is reckless, one lacks inhibition

2. illumination; when one understands, one is aware or enlightened

3. vacant; when one is lost in thought, one is often expressionless

4. composed; when one has a calm personality, one is self–possessed, calm

Vocabulary Strategy: Word Collocations

Possible answers:

1.

Parts of Speech	Examples
noun + preposition + noun	storm of grief
adjective + noun	vacant stare
adjective + noun	blue sky
adjective + noun	heart trouble

2. Sentences will vary based on examples selected, but should reflect an understanding of the meanings of the collocations.

Critical Vocabulary

 COMMON CORE L 4a

| abandonment | vacant | illumination | composed |

Practice and Apply Decide which Critical Vocabulary word goes best with the words or phrases given here.

1. Which word goes best with *recklessness*? Why?

2. Which word goes best with *understanding*? Why?

3. Which word goes best with being lost in thought? Why?

4. Which word goes best with a calm personality? Why?

Vocabulary Strategy: Word Collocations

In English, certain words commonly occur together and appear in a particular order. These common word groupings are referred to as collocations. For example, the Critical Vocabulary word *abandonment* appears in this story as part of the collocation *wild abandonment*—a common phrase used to describe spontaneous, impulsive behavior.

Wild abandonment is a collocation made up of an adjective and a noun, but collocations can also be made up of other parts of speech. This chart shows some examples.

Parts of Speech	Examples
adjective + noun	square meal
verb + noun	accept responsibility
adverb + adverb	quite easily
adverb + verb	strongly suggest
adverb + adjective + noun	totally unacceptable behavior

Practice and Apply Reread Chopin's "The Story of an Hour" with a partner and find four examples of collocation. Then, with these collocations:

1. Create a chart like the one shown to record each example and identify the parts of speech it includes. Write a definition for each collocation.

2. Use each collocation in an original sentence that demonstrates its meaning.

SCAFFOLDING FOR ELL STUDENTS

Understand Collocations Students for whom English is a second language might have a difficult time identifying collocations.

- Explain that a collocation is a group of words that typically appear together. Provide additional examples with which students might be familiar, such as *quick shower* and *burst of speed*.

- Explain to them that the combinations of words sound right and natural to native speakers because they hear them all the time. For instance, while *quick shower* is a familiar pairing, the phrase *fast shower* is not.

- Ask them to share any collocations in their first language.

- Then pair students with native readers to complete the Practice and Apply activity about collocations.

Analyze Structure: Resolution

RL 5

TEACH

Resolution is an important part of the plot of any story. It is also the author's last chance to communicate his or her message. Ask students to define the term *resolution*. Explain that in the plot of a narrative, the **resolution** occurs after the climax and reveals the final outcome of events. A story's resolution also ties up any loose ends. Point out that some resolutions can be categorized as follows.

- Comedic: Resolution that reveals a happy outcome, such as a marriage.
- Tragic: Resolution that reveals an unhappy outcome, such as a death.
- Surprise plot twist: Resolution that is an abrupt and surprising reversal, often accompanied by situational irony, such as the ending of O. Henry's "The Gift of the Magi."
- Ambiguous: Resolution that is inconclusive or reveals an uncertain outcome. Many modern short stories have this type of resolution.

Ask students how they would categorize the resolution of "The Story of an Hour."

PRACTICE AND APPLY

Have students write alternate, non-tragic endings for "The Story of an Hour." Each student should work independently to write an ending to replace lines 85–93 of the story. Then have students share their alternate resolutions in small groups. Volunteers can share their endings with the class.

Analyze Author's Point of View: Irony

RL 6

RETEACH

Review the term *irony*. Tell students that irony is the result of a contrast between appearances or expectations and reality. In a work of fiction, this usually occurs when

- there is a contrast between what is expected to happen and what does happen, called **situational irony**. (Mrs. Mallard is expected to have heart trouble when she receives news of her husband's death, but she has it when she discovers he is alive.)
- readers know more about a situation than characters do, called **dramatic irony**. (Readers know about Mrs. Mallard's emotional journey, but Mr. Mallard does not.)

 **LEVEL UP TUTORIALS** Assign the following *Level Up* tutorial: **Irony**

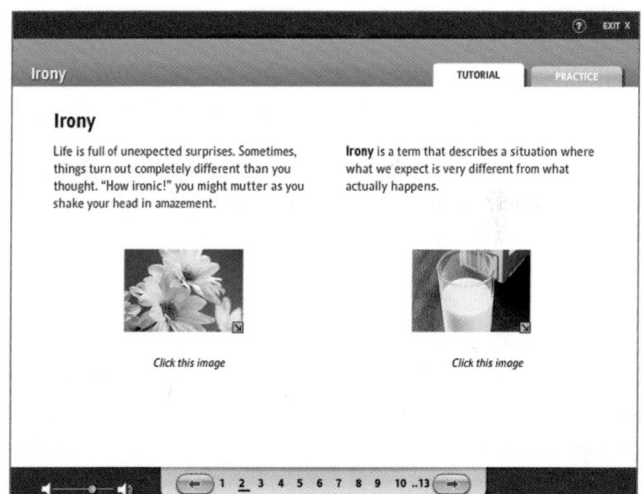

CLOSE READING APPLICATION

Students can practice analyzing point of view and irony in another short story, such as "The Life You Save May Be Your Own," by Flannery O'Connor. Have them work independently to note the characters' thoughts, feelings, and responses to their circumstances and explore any differences between appearances or expectations and reality.

A Journey

Short Story by Edith Wharton

Why This Text

Students may have difficulty analyzing the point of view in which a story is told. In addition, stories such as this one by Edith Wharton may be difficult for students to comprehend because of its subtle use of irony. Students will need to deconstruct the text by distinguishing between what is directly stated in the text and what is really meant. With the help of the close-reading questions, students will be able to understand the use of irony in the story.

Background Have students read the background and the information about the author. Introduce the selection by telling students that Edith Wharton's long and distinguished career as an American author spanned forty years and included the publication of more than forty books. Although she did not publish her first work of fiction until the age of thirty-six, Wharton had been writing since adolescence, composing poems and stories, and completing her first short novel, *Fast and Loose,* at the age of fifteen!

AS YOU READ Ask students to pay close attention to the irony in the story. How soon into the story do they begin to detect its ironic tone?

Common Core Support

- cite multiple pieces of textual evidence
- determine the theme and analyze its development over the course of the text
- analyze a text in which grasping point of view requires analyzing irony

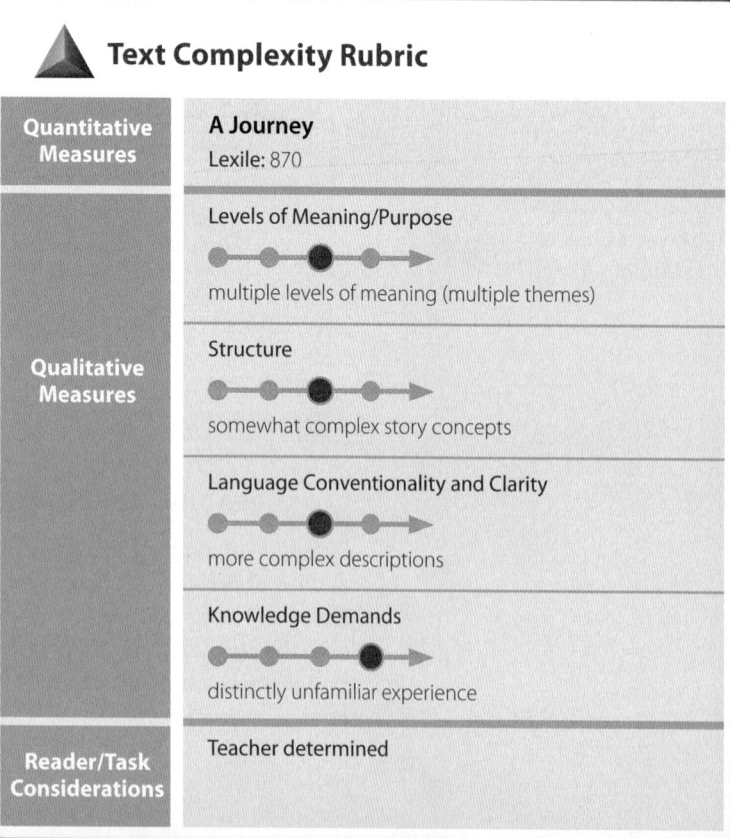

Text Complexity Rubric

Quantitative Measures

A Journey
Lexile: 870

Qualitative Measures

Levels of Meaning/Purpose

multiple levels of meaning (multiple themes)

Structure

somewhat complex story concepts

Language Conventionality and Clarity

more complex descriptions

Knowledge Demands

distinctly unfamiliar experience

Reader/Task Considerations

Teacher determined

Strategies for CLOSE READING

Analyze Author's Point of View: Irony

Students should read this short story carefully all the way through. Close-reading questions at the bottom of the page will help them focus on a thorough analysis of irony in the text. As they read, students should record comments or questions about the text in the side margins.

WHEN STUDENTS STRUGGLE . . .

To help them understand the use of irony in the text, have students work in small groups to fill out a chart such as the one shown as they analyze the story.

CITE TEXT EVIDENCE For practice in tracing the three basic types of irony in the text—verbal irony, situational irony, and dramatic irony—have students cite textual evidence from the story to complete the chart.

Verbal Irony	Situational Irony	Dramatic Irony
When the wife calls her husband's irritability in the sickroom "helpless tyrannies" (line 18), her statement is a contradiction and can be interpreted as verbal irony.	The journey home is an example of situational irony since the couple is returning there because the husband is expected to die.

At the end, when the wife thinks that "the worst terror was past" (line 345), she has an unexpected, tragic accident—the opposite of what was expected to happen. | The reader and the wife know that the husband is dead, but the passengers and train crew do not know this. |

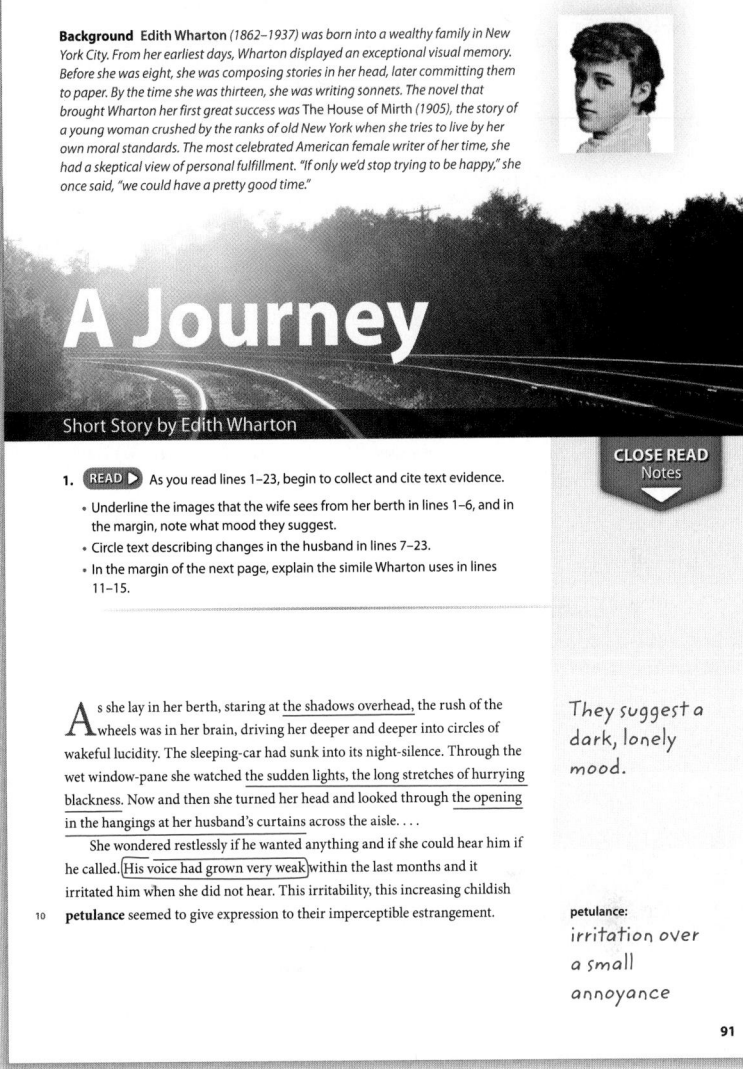

Background Edith Wharton *(1862–1937) was born into a wealthy family in New York City. From her earliest days, Wharton displayed an exceptional visual memory. Before she was eight, she was composing stories in her head, later committing them to paper. By the time she was thirteen, she was writing sonnets. The novel that brought Wharton her first great success was* The House of Mirth *(1905), the story of a young woman crushed by the ranks of old New York when she tries to live by her own moral standards. The most celebrated American female writer of her time, she had a skeptical view of personal fulfillment. "If only we'd stop trying to be happy," she once said, "we could have a pretty good time."*

A Journey

Short Story by Edith Wharton

CLOSE READ
Notes

1. **READD ▷** As you read lines 1–23, begin to collect and cite text evidence.

   • Underline the images that the wife sees from her berth in lines 1–6, and in the margin, note what mood they suggest.

   • Circle text describing changes in the husband in lines 7–23.

   • In the margin of the next page, explain the simile Wharton uses in lines 11–15.

As she lay in her berth, staring at the shadows overhead, the rush of the wheels was in her brain, driving her deeper and deeper into circles of wakeful lucidity. The sleeping-car had sunk into its night-silence. Through the wet window-pane she watched the sudden lights, the long stretches of hurrying blackness. Now and then she turned her head and looked through the opening in the hangings at her husband's curtains across the aisle. . . .

She wondered restlessly if he wanted anything and if she could hear him if he called. His voice had grown very weak within the last months and it irritated him when she did not hear. This irritability, this increasing childish 10 **petulance** seemed to give expression to their imperceptible estrangement.

They suggest a dark, lonely mood.

petulance: *irritation over a small annoyance*

91

1. **READ AND CITE TEXT EVIDENCE**

   (A) **ASK STUDENTS** to cite evidence for their explanation of the simile Wharton uses in lines 11–15. *The comparison Wharton makes by stating that the couple is now "like two faces looking at one another through a sheet of glass . . . close together, almost touching, but . . . not hear[ing] or feel[ing] each other: the conductivity between them . . . broken" (lines 11–13) suggests that although physically close, they have lost their emotional connection. The connotative meaning of* conductivity *(line 13) highlights the loss of the spark between them, supported by this image: "Now their energies no longer kept step" (line 21).*

   Critical Vocabulary: petulance (line 10) Have students share their definitions of the word and use it in a sentence.

Although physically close, they have lost their emotional connection.

prodigal:
generous; abundant

A Like two faces looking at one another through a sheet of glass they were close together, almost touching, but they could not hear or feel each other: the conductivity between them was broken. She, at least, had this sense of separation, and she fancied sometimes that she saw it reflected in the look with which he supplemented his failing words. Doubtless the fault was hers. She was too impenetrably healthy to be touched by the irrelevancies of disease. Her self-reproachful tenderness was tinged with the sense of his irrationality: she **B** had a vague feeling that there was a purpose in his helpless tyrannies. The suddenness of the change had found her so unprepared. A year ago their pulses

20 had beat to one robust measure; both had the same **prodigal** confidence in an exhaustless future. Now their energies no longer kept step; hers still bounded ahead of life, preempting unclaimed regions of hope and activity, while his lagged behind, vainly struggling to overtake her.

When they married, she had such arrears of living to make up: her days had been as bare as the whitewashed school-room where she forced innutritious facts upon reluctant children. His coming had broken in on the slumber of circumstance, widening the present till it became the encloser of remotest chances. But imperceptibly the horizon narrowed. Life had a grudge against her: she was never to be allowed to spread her wings.

30 At first the doctors had said that six weeks of mild air would set him right; but when he came back this assurance was explained as having of course included a winter in a dry climate. They gave up their pretty house, storing the

---

2. **◄ REREAD** Reread lines 7–23. What do the contrasting descriptions of health and sickness suggest about the wife's relationship with her husband? How does she describe her own reactions to her husband's health? Support your answer with explicit textual evidence.

The contrasting descriptions of health and sickness reflect the growing estrangement between the narrator and her husband. The husband is "irritated" when she doesn't hear him; she describes herself as at fault and having a "self-reproachful tenderness." She is critical of her own response to his failing health.

---

3. **READ ►** As you read lines 24–63, continue to cite textual evidence.

- Underline text that shows the wife's negative feelings in lines 24–45.
- In the margin, describe in your own words how the husband used to be (lines 30–45).
- Underline text that describes the wife's fear in lines 46–63.

> **" It frightened her to feel that this was the man she loved . . . "**

wedding presents and new furniture, and went to Colorado. She had hated it there from the first. Nobody knew her or cared about her; there was no one to wonder at the good match she had made, or to envy her the new dresses and the visiting-cards which were still a surprise to her. And he kept growing **C** worse. She felt herself beset with difficulties too evasive to be fought by so direct a temperament. She still loved him, of course; but he was gradually, undefinably ceasing to be himself. The man she had married had been strong,

40 active, gently masterful: the male whose pleasure it is to clear a way through the material obstructions of life; but now it was she who was the protector, he who must be shielded from importunities and given his drops or his beef-juice though the skies were falling. The routine of the sick-room bewildered her; this punctual administering of medicine seemed as idle as some uncomprehended **D** religious mummery.[1]

There were moments, indeed, when warm gushes of pity swept away her instinctive resentment of his condition, when she still found his old self in his eyes as they groped for each other through the dense medium of his weakness. But these moments had grown rare. Sometimes he frightened her: his sunken

50 expressionless face seemed that of a stranger; his voice was weak and hoarse; his thin-lipped smile a mere muscular contraction. Her hand avoided his damp soft skin, which had lost the familiar roughness of health: she caught herself **furtively** watching him as she might have watched a strange animal. It frightened her to feel that this was the man she loved; there were hours when to tell him what she suffered seemed the one escape from her fears. But in general she judged herself more leniently, reflecting that she had perhaps been too long alone with him, and that she would feel differently when they were at home again, surrounded by her robust and buoyant family. How she had rejoiced when the doctors at last gave their consent to his going home! She knew, of

60 course, what the decision meant; they both knew. It meant that he was to die; but they dressed the truth in hopeful euphuisms, and at times, in the joy of preparation, she really forgot the purpose of their journey, and slipped into an eager allusion to next year's plans.

---

[1] **mummery:** a ridiculous performance or ceremony.

He used to be strong, active, and protective.

furtively:
secretly

---

2. REREAD AND CITE TEXT EVIDENCE

B ASK STUDENTS to find phrases in the text that show that the wife is of two minds about her feelings for her husband. *"increasing childish petulance" (lines 9–10), "self-reproachful tenderness" (line 17), "helpless tyrannies" (line 18), "vainly struggling" (line 23)*

3. READ AND CITE TEXT EVIDENCE

C ASK STUDENTS to cite evidence for their description of how the husband had been before his illness. *Students should note that he had been "strong, active" (lines 39–40), and protective (line 41).*

Critical Vocabulary: prodigal (line 20) Have students explain *prodigal* as Wharton uses it here.

Critical Vocabulary: furtively (line 53) Have students share their definitions of *furtively*. Ask how *furtively* fits into Wharton's discussion of the growing sense of separation that the wife feels toward her husband. *Students should point out that as the wife watches her husband grow progressively worse, and as the "estrangement" between them deepens, she secretly watches him "as she might have watched a strange animal" (line 53).*

FOR ELL STUDENTS Clarify that the word *contraction* (line 51) is a multiple-meaning word, and that in this context, it does not refer to the grammatical construction, but instead means "a shortening or tensing of a muscle."

ASK STUDENTS to look for other multiple-meaning words in the text and cite them in the margin.

CLOSE READ
Notes

E F At last the day of leaving came. She had a dreadful fear that they would never get away; that somehow at the last moment he would fail her; that the doctors held one of their accustomed treacheries in reserve; but nothing happened. They drove to the station, he was installed in a seat with a rug over his knees and a cushion at his back, and she hung out of the window waving unregretful farewells to the acquaintances she had really never liked till then.

70 The first twenty-four hours had passed off well. He revived a little and it amused him to look out of the window and to observe the humours of the car. The second day he began to grow weary and to chafe under the **dispassionate** stare of the freckled child with the lump of chewing-gum. She had to explain to the child's mother that her husband was too ill to be disturbed: a statement received by that lady with a resentment visibly supported by the maternal sentiment of the whole car. . . .

That night he slept badly and the next morning his temperature frightened her: she was sure he was growing worse. The day passed slowly, punctuated by the small irritations of travel. Watching his tired face, she traced in its

80 contractions every rattle and jolt of the tram, till her own body vibrated with sympathetic fatigue. She felt the others observing him too, and hovered restlessly between him and the line of interrogative eyes. The freckled child hung about him like a fly; offers of candy and picture-books failed to dislodge her: she twisted one leg around the other and watched him **imperturbably**. The porter, as he passed, lingered with vague proffers of help, probably inspired by philanthropic passengers swelling with the sense that "something ought to

dispassionate:
free from
personal
feeling or bias

imperturbably:
calmly;
without being
upset

---

4. ◀ REREAD Reread lines 46–63. From what point of view is the story being told? How do you know?

The story is told from the third-person limited point of view, because the reader's view of the characters, events, and situation is limited to the views of the wife.

5. READ ▶ As you read lines 64–105, continue to cite textual evidence.

• Underline phrases that help set the tone of the story.
• In the margin, explain why the return home is an example of situational irony (lines 95–105).

94

CLOSE READ
Notes

> ❝ She had a dreadful fear . . . that the doctors held one of their accustomed treacheries in reserve . . . ❞

be done;" and one nervous man in a skull-cap was audibly concerned as to the possible effect on his wife's health.

The hours dragged on in a dreary inoccupation. Towards dusk she sat

90 down beside him and he laid his hand on hers. The touch startled her. He seemed to be calling her from far off. She looked at him helplessly and his smile went through her like a physical pang.

"Are you very tired?" she asked.

"No, not very."

"We'll be there soon now."

"Yes, very soon."

"This time to-morrow—"

He nodded and they sat silent. When she had put him to bed and crawled into her own berth she tried to cheer herself with the thought that in less than

100 twenty-four hours they would be in New York. Her people would all be at the station to meet her—she pictured their round unanxious faces pressing through the crowd. She only hoped they would not tell him too loudly that he was looking splendidly and would be all right in no time: the subtler sympathies developed by long contact with suffering were making her aware of a certain coarseness of texture in the family **sensibilities**.

Suddenly she thought she heard him call. She parted the curtains and listened. No, it was only a man snoring at the other end of the car. His snores had a greasy sound, as though they passed through tallow. She lay down and tried to sleep . . . Had she not heard him move? She started up trembling . . .

The situation is ironic because they are returning home only because the husband is expected to die.

sensibility:
the capacity to feel, react, or respond to emotion

---

6. ◀ REREAD AND DISCUSS Reread lines 64–105. With a small group, discuss the wife's concern about the journey. Why is she worried about "her people"?

7. READ ▶ As you read lines 106–150, continue to cite textual evidence.

• Underline actions the wife takes in lines 106–121.
• In the margin, explain what is ironic, or surprising, about her actions (lines 114–121).
• Circle text that describes a change in the wife's outlook in lines 122–132.

95

---

4. **REREAD AND CITE TEXT EVIDENCE**

D ASK STUDENTS to explain how the point of view used in the description of the wife in lines 46–48 shows the point of view from which the story is being told. *Students should note that in these lines the narrator is not a character in the story but presents a point of view limited to one character—to what the wife thinks or feels.*

5. **READ AND CITE TEXT EVIDENCE**

E ASK STUDENTS to cite text evidence explaining why the return home is an example of situational irony. *Students should cite evidence from lines 58–63 that explains that the doctors "at last gave their consent to his going home. . . . It meant that he was to die."*

Critical Vocabulary: dispassionate (line 72) and **imperturbably** (line 84) Have students define these words.

6. **REREAD AND DISCUSS USING TEXT EVIDENCE**

F ASK STUDENTS to cite specific textual evidence to support the reasons for the wife's concern about the journey home. *Students should cite evidence in lines 100–105 to explain the wife's concerns about the unctuous comments her "people" might make to her husband.*

7. **READ AND CITE TEXT EVIDENCE**

G ASK STUDENTS to cite evidence that explains irony in the wife's actions. *Students should cite textual evidence from lines 114–117 and 119–121 to explain that her reaction is ironic because if she could not "endure her fears [about her husband] a moment longer" (lines 119–120), she would not be expected to turn over and go to sleep.*

Critical Vocabulary: sensibility (line 105) Have students explain *sensibility* and use it in a sentence.

CLOSE READ
Notes

Her reaction is ironic because if she could not "endure her fears a moment longer," you would not expect her to go to sleep.

dishevelled:
untidy

110 The silence frightened her more than any sound. He might not be able to make her hear—he might be calling her now . . . What made her think of such things? It was merely the familiar tendency of an over-tired mind to fasten itself on the most intolerable chance within the range of its forebodings. . . . **G** Putting her head out, she listened; but she could not distinguish his breathing from that of the other pairs of lungs about her. She longed to get up and look at him, but she knew the impulse was a mere vent for her restlessness, and the fear of disturbing him restrained her. . . . The regular movement of his curtain reassured her, she knew not why; she remembered that he had wished her a cheerful good-night; and the sheer inability to endure her fears a moment 120 longer made her put them from her with an effort of her whole sound tired body. She turned on her side and slept.

She sat up stiffly, staring out at the dawn. The train was rushing through a region of bare hillocks huddled against a lifeless sky. It looked like the first day of creation. The air of the car was close, and she pushed up her window to let in the keen wind. Then she looked at her watch: it was seven o'clock, and soon the people about her would be stirring. She slipped into her clothes, smoothed her **dishevelled** hair and crept to the dressing-room. When she had washed her face and adjusted her dress she felt more hopeful. It was always a struggle for her not to be cheerful in the morning. Her cheeks burned deliciously under the 130 coarse towel and the wet hair about her temples broke into strong upward tendrils. Every inch of her was full of life and elasticity. And in ten hours they would be at home!

She stepped to her husband's berth: it was time for him to take his early glass of milk. The window-shade was down, and in the dusk of the curtained enclosure she could just see that he lay sideways, with his face away from her. She leaned over him and drew up the shade. As she did so she touched one of his hands. It felt cold. . . .

H She bent closer, laying her hand on his arm and calling him by name. He did not move. She spoke again more loudly; she grasped his shoulder and 140 gently shook it. He lay motionless. She caught hold of his hand again: it slipped from her limply, like a dead thing. A dead thing? . . . Her breath caught. She must see his face. She leaned forward, and hurriedly, shrinkingly, with a sickening reluctance of the flesh, laid her hands on his shoulders and turned him over. His head fell back; his face looked small and smooth; he gazed at her with steady eyes.

96

She remained motionless for a long time, holding him thus; and they looked at each other. Suddenly she shrank back: the longing to scream, to call out, to fly from him, had almost overpowered her. But a strong hand arrested her. Good God! If it were known that he was dead they would be put off the 150 train at the next station—

I In a terrifying flash of remembrance there arose before her a scene she had once witnessed in travelling, when a husband and wife, whose child had died in the train, had been thrust out at some chance station. She saw them standing on the platform with the child's body between them; she had never forgotten the dazed look with which they followed the receding train. And this was what would happen to her. Within the next hour she might find herself on the platform of some strange station, alone with her husband's body. . . . Anything but that! It was too horrible—She quivered like a creature at bay.

As she cowered there, she felt the train moving more slowly. It was coming 160 then—they were approaching a station! She saw again the husband and wife standing on the lonely platform; and with a violent gesture she drew down the shade to hide her husband's face.

Feeling dizzy, she sank down on the edge of the berth, keeping away from his outstretched body, and pulling the curtains close, so that he and she were **J** shut into a kind of **sepulchral** twilight. She tried to think. At all costs she must conceal the fact that he was dead. But how? Her mind refused to act: she could not plan, combine. She could think of no way but to sit there, clutching the curtains, all day long. . . .

She heard the porter making up her bed; people were beginning to move 170 about the car; the dressing-room door was being opened and shut. She tried to rouse herself. At length with a supreme effort she rose to her feet, stepping into

CLOSE READ
Notes

She is afraid that if her husband's death is discovered, they will be left at the next station.

sepulchral:
of a tomb, vault, or grave

---

8. **◀ REREAD** Reread lines 138–150. Why is the wife's reaction to her husband's death ironic?

Her reaction is ironic because she's more concerned about being put off the train than she is upset that her husband has just died.

9. **READ ▶** As you read lines 151–188, continue to cite textual evidence.
   - Underline text describing what the wife remembers.
   - In the margin, explain why the wife conceals her husband's death (lines 151–162).

97

WHEN STUDENTS STRUGGLE . . . To help students understand Wharton's subtle use of irony and how irony can help them grasp the narrator's point of view, ask them to reread lines 122–132. Invite groups to discuss how this paragraph uses irony to reinforce the contrast between the wife's health and the husband's illness ("Every inch of her was full of life" [line 131]), while highlighting the situational irony expressed in the fact that the husband is lying dead just a few feet away.

Critical Vocabulary: dishevelled (line 127) Have students share their definitions of *dishevelled*. What is "dishevelled" in the text? *the wife's hair* What else can be dishevelled? *Students might cite a person's clothing or appearance.*

8. **REREAD AND CITE TEXT EVIDENCE**

H **ASK STUDENTS** to assess whether the wife's reaction to her husband's death is an effective use of irony. How does it help students grasp the narrator's point of view of the wife? *Students should cite evidence from lines 138–144 and 146–150 showing that her response is ironic—it's not the way one would expect the wife to feel. The narrator sees her as a selfish person more concerned about being put off the train than grieving for her husband.*

9. **READ AND CITE TEXT EVIDENCE**

I **ASK STUDENTS** to cite evidence supporting their response as to why the wife keeps her husband's death hidden from the people on the train. *She had once seen "a husband and wife, whose child had died in the train . . . thrust out at some chance station. . . . And this was what would happen to her. . . . Anything but that! It was too horrible . . ." (lines 152–158).*

Critical Vocabulary: sepulchral (line 165) Have students explain the meaning of *sepulchral* and the image it creates.

CLOSE READ
Notes

the aisle of the car and drawing the curtains tight behind her. She noticed that they still parted slightly with the motion of the car, and finding a pin in her dress she fastened them together. Now she was safe. She looked round and saw the porter. She fancied he was watching her.

"Ain't he awake yet?" he enquired.

"No," she faltered.

"I got his milk all ready when he wants it. You know you told me to have it for him by seven."

180 She nodded silently and crept into her seat.

At half-past eight the train reached Buffalo. By this time the other passengers were dressed and the berths had been folded back for the day. The porter, moving to and fro under his burden of sheets and pillows, glanced at her as he passed. At length he said: "Ain't he going to get up? You know we're ordered to make up the berths as early as we can."

She turned cold with fear. They were just entering the station.

"Oh, not yet," she stammered. "Not till he's had his milk. Won't you get it, please?"

"All right. Soon as we start again."

190 When the train moved on he reappeared with the milk. She took it from him and sat vaguely looking at it; her brain moved slowly from one idea to another, as though they were stepping-stones set far apart across a whirling flood. At length she became aware that the porter still hovered expectantly.

(K) "Will I give it to him?" he suggested.

"Oh, no," she cried, rising. "He—he's asleep yet, I think—"

---

10. ◀ **REREAD** Reread lines 151–188. Explain the dramatic irony implicit in the wife's attempts to hide her husband's death from the people on the train.

This episode is an example of dramatic irony because the reader knows something (in this case, that the husband is dead) that characters in the story do not know.

---

11. **READ** ▶ As you read lines 189–210, continue to cite textual evidence.

• Circle the simile Wharton uses to describe the wife's mental state.
• In the margin, explain why she decides to drink the milk (lines 194–202).

98

She waited till the porter had passed on; then she unpinned the curtains and slipped behind them. In the semi-obscurity her husband's face stared up at her like a marble mask with agate eyes. The eyes were dreadful. She put out her 200 hand and drew down the lids. Then she remembered the glass of milk in her other hand: what was she to do with it? She thought of raising the window and throwing it out; but to do so she would have to lean across his body and bring her face close to his. She decided to drink the milk.

(L) She returned to her seat with the empty glass and after a while the porter came back to get it.

"When'll I fold up his bed?" he asked.

"Oh, not now—not yet; he's ill—he's very ill. Can't you let him stay as he is? The doctor wants him to lie down as much as possible."

He scratched his head. "Well, if he's *really* sick—"

He took the empty glass and walked away, explaining to the passengers 210 that the party behind the curtains was too sick to get up just yet.

She found herself the centre of sympathetic eyes. A motherly woman with an intimate smile sat down beside her.

"I'm real sorry to hear your husband's sick. I've had a remarkable amount **(M)** of sickness in my family and maybe I could assist you. Can I take a look at him?"

"Oh, no—no, please! He mustn't be disturbed."

The lady accepted the **rebuff** indulgently.

"Well, it's just as you say, of course, but you don't look to me as if you'd had much experience in sickness and I'd have been glad to assist you. What do you 220 generally do when your husband's taken this way?"

She decides to drink the milk rather than having to lean across her husband to throw it out the window.

rebuff:
a blunt refusal of a friendly offer

---

12. ◀ **REREAD** Reread lines 203–210. Why are the porter's actions ironic? Cite evidence in your response.

The porter's actions are ironic because he doesn't know the husband is dead. He inadvertently does the wife a favor by explaining to the other passengers that "the party behind the curtains was too sick to get up just yet."

---

13. **READ** ▶ As you read lines 211–239, continue to cite textual evidence.

• Underline the questions that the "motherly woman" asks.
• Circle the wife's responses.

99

---

10. **REREAD AND CITE TEXT EVIDENCE**

(J) **ASK STUDENTS** in what way the wife's furtive actions are an example of dramatic irony. *Since the reader and the wife know that the husband is dead, but the characters do not know this fact, the wife's attempts at hiding his dead body from everyone on the train is an example of dramatic irony. Students should cite evidence from lines 165–168, 172–179, and 181–188.*

11. **READ AND CITE TEXT EVIDENCE**

(K) **ASK STUDENTS** to cite evidence explaining why the woman drinks the milk that the porter has brought for her husband. *Students should cite specific textual evidence in lines 194–195 and 199–202 to explain that she decides to drink the milk because she does not want the porter to suspect that her husband is dead. She also does not want to throw the milk from the window because she would have to lean across her husband's dead body.*

12. **REREAD AND CITE TEXT EVIDENCE**

(L) **ASK STUDENTS** to explain what the porter believes has happened to the milk. In what way is this ironic? *He thinks that the husband has drunk the milk but is really sick and should be left alone. However, the wife and the reader know he is dead.*

13. **READ AND CITE TEXT EVIDENCE**

(M) **ASK STUDENTS** to point out the disparity that exists between what the "motherly woman" seems to be and what she is. *Students should cite evidence from the questions she asks the wife and from her last statement (lines 229–230). When she says that the wife "don't look to me as if you'd had much experience in sickness," she seems more judgmental than caring.*

Critical Vocabulary: rebuff (line 217) Have students define the word.

"I—I let him sleep."

"Too much sleep ain't any too healthful either. Don't you give him any medicine?"

"Y—yes."

"Don't you wake him to take it?"

"Yes."

"When does he take the next dose?"

"Not for—two hours—"

230 The lady looked disappointed. "Well, if I was you I'd try giving it oftener. That's what I do with my folks."

 After that many faces seemed to press upon her. The passengers were on their way to the dining-car, and she was conscious that as they passed down the aisle they glanced curiously at the closed curtains. One lantern-jawed man with prominent eyes stood still and tried to shoot his projecting glance through the division between the folds. The freckled child, returning from breakfast, waylaid the passers with a buttery clutch, saying in a loud whisper, "He's sick;" and once the conductor came by, asking for tickets. She shrank into her corner and looked out of the window at the flying trees and houses, meaningless hieroglyphs of an endlessly unrolled papyrus.

240 Now and then the train stopped, and the newcomers on entering the car stared in turn at the closed curtains. More and more people seemed to pass— their faces began to blend fantastically with the images surging in her brain. . . .

Later in the day a fat man detached himself from the mist of faces. He had a creased stomach and soft pale lips. As he pressed himself into the seat facing her she noticed that he was dressed in black broadcloth, with a soiled white tie.

---

14. ◀ **REREAD** Reread lines 231–239. What is the result of the conversation between the wife and the "motherly woman"? How is the wife affected? Support your answer with text evidence.

The conversation has made the wife more nervous, even though the "motherly woman" was just trying to help. The wife now thinks "that many faces seemed to press upon her," as if she is going to be found out.

15. **READ** ▶ As you read lines 240–290, continue to cite text evidence.

• Underline text used to describe the fat man in lines 243–249.
• In the margin, explain who he might be.
• Underline text describing the confusion the wife feels in lines 255–272.

"Husband's pretty bad this morning, is he?"

"Yes."

"Dear, dear! Now that's terribly distressing, ain't it?" An apostolic smile revealed his gold-filled teeth.

250 "Of course you know there's no sech thing as sickness. Ain't that a lovely thought? Death itself is but a deloosion of our grosser senses. On'y lay yourself open to the influx of the sperrit, submit yourself passively to the action of the divine force, and disease and **dissolution** will cease to exist for you. If you could indooce your husband to read this little pamphlet—"

The faces about her again grew indistinct. She had a vague recollection of hearing the motherly lady and the parent of the freckled child ardently disputing the relative advantages of trying several medicines at once, or of taking each in turn; the motherly lady maintaining that the competitive system saved time; the other objecting that you couldn't tell which remedy had effected 260 the cure; their voices went on and on, like bell-buoys droning through a fog. . . . The porter came up now and then with questions that she did not understand, but that somehow she must have answered since he went away again without repeating them; every two hours the motherly lady reminded her that her husband ought to have his drops; people left the car and others replaced them . . .

Her head was spinning and she tried to steady herself by clutching at her thoughts as they swept by, but they slipped away from her like bushes on the side of a sheer **precipice** down which she seemed to be falling. Suddenly her mind grew clear again and she found herself vividly picturing what would 270 happen when the train reached New York. She shuddered as it occurred to her that he would be quite cold and that some one might perceive he had been dead since morning.

She thought hurriedly:—"If they see I am not surprised they will suspect something. They will ask questions, and if I tell them the truth they won't believe me—no one would believe me! It will be terrible"—and she kept repeating to herself:—"I must pretend I don't know. I must pretend I don't

He may be a clergyman or someone religious.

dissolution:
death

precipice:
the edge of a steep cliff

---

16. ◀ **REREAD** Reread lines 273–279. What new concerns occur to the narrator in these lines? How is this an example of situational irony?

She is worried that she won't look sufficiently surprised when they find her husband dead. She is afraid they will notice he has been dead since the morning. The situation is ironic because she is more worried about her behavior than her husband's death.

---

14. REREAD AND CITE TEXT EVIDENCE

ASK STUDENTS to explain the irony in the wife's perception of the passengers after she has spoken with the "motherly woman." How does her perception of them contrast with what is probably true? *Students should cite evidence from lines 231–235 to emphasize that the conversation has made the wife even more nervous, causing her to believe that "many faces seemed to press upon her" (line 231) and that one man's "prominent eyes" (line 234) were trying to peer through her husband's curtain (line 235). Her paranoia increases, causing a disjunction between appearance and reality and heightening the irony.*

15. READ AND CITE TEXT EVIDENCE

ASK STUDENTS to cite specific textual evidence of the wife's confused mental state. *Students should cite examples in lines 255, 260–264, and 266–268 to indicate the vagueness she feels, the droning voices she hears, and the dizziness she experiences.*

16. REREAD AND CITE TEXT EVIDENCE

ASK STUDENTS to explain the wife's thoughts about what will happen when the train crew discovers that her husband is dead. How will she really be feeling? *Students should cite evidence from lines 273–279 to explain the wife's new concern that she will not look sufficiently surprised when the crew finds that her husband is dead. To deflect suspicion from herself, she must pretend that his death is a shock to her—and even scream to make the pretense more convincing.*

Critical Vocabulary: dissolution (line 253) Have students explain *dissolution* as Wharton uses it here. Then have them give the scientific (or technical) meaning of the word.

Critical Vocabulary: precipice (line 268) Have students share their definitions of the word and use it in sentences.

CLOSE READ
Notes

know. When they open the curtains I must go up to him quite naturally—and then I must scream." . . . She had an idea that the scream would be very hard to do.

280   Gradually new thoughts crowded upon her, vivid and urgent: she tried to separate and restrain them, but they beset her clamorously, like her schoolchildren at the end of a hot day, when she was too tired to silence them. Her head grew confused, and she felt a sick fear of forgetting her part, of betraying herself by some unguarded word or look.

"I must pretend I don't know," she went on murmuring. The words had lost their significance, but she repeated them mechanically, as though they had been a magic formula, until suddenly she heard herself saying: "I can't remember, I can't remember!"

Her voice sounded very loud, and she looked about her in terror; but no
290   one seemed to notice that she had spoken.

As she glanced down the car her eye caught the curtains of her husband's berth, and she began to examine the monotonous **arabesques** woven through their heavy folds. The pattern was intricate and difficult to trace; she gazed fixedly at the curtains and as she did so the thick stuff grew transparent and through it she saw her husband's face—his dead face. She struggled to avert her look, but her eyes refused to move and her head seemed to be held in a vice. At last, with an effort that left her weak and shaking, she turned away; but it was of no use; close in front of her, small and smooth, was her husband's face. It seemed to be suspended in the air between her and the false braids of the
300   woman who sat in front of her. With an uncontrollable gesture she stretched out her hand to push the face away, and suddenly she felt the touch of his smooth skin. She repressed a cry and half started from her seat. The woman with the false braids looked around, and feeling that she must justify her movement in some way she rose and lifted her travelling-bag from the opposite seat. She unlocked the bag and looked into it; but the first object her hand met was a small flask of her husband's, thrust there at the last moment, in the haste of departure. She locked the bag and closed her eyes . . . his face was there again, hanging between her eye-balls and lids like a waxen mask against a red curtain. . . .

310   She roused herself with a shiver. Had she fainted or slept? Hours seemed to have elapsed; but it was still broad day, and the people about her were sitting in the same attitudes as before.

arabesque:
a design of intertwined flowing lines

repress:
to hold back or stifle

17. (READ ▶) Read lines 291–332, and continue to cite textual evidence.

- Underline text describing the wife's confusion in lines 291–322.
- In the margin, explain what is happening in these lines.
- Underline images of death in the wife's dream (lines 323–332).

102

A sudden sense of hunger made her aware that she had eaten nothing since morning. The thought of food filled her with disgust, but she dreaded a return of faintness, and remembering that she had some biscuits in her bag she took one out and ate it. The dry crumbs choked her, and she hastily swallowed a little brandy from her husband's flask. The burning sensation in her throat acted as a counter-irritant, momentarily relieving the dull ache of her nerves. Then she felt a gently-stealing warmth, as though a soft air fanned her, and the
320   swarming fears relaxed their clutch, receding through the stillness that enclosed her, a stillness soothing as the spacious quietude of a summer day. She slept.

Through her sleep she felt the impetuous rush of the train. It seemed to be life itself that was sweeping her on with headlong **inexorable** force—sweeping her into darkness and terror, and the awe of unknown days.—Now all at once everything was still—not a sound, not a pulsation . . . She was dead in her turn, and lay beside him with smooth upstaring face. How quiet it was!—and yet she heard feet coming, the feet of the men who were to carry them away . . . She could feel too—she felt a sudden prolonged vibration, a series of hard shocks,
330   and then another plunge into darkness: the darkness of death this time—a black whirlwind on which they were both spinning like leaves, in wild uncoiling spirals, with millions and millions of the dead. . . .

She sprang up in terror. Her sleep must have lasted a long time, for the winter day had paled and the lights had been lit. The car was in confusion, and as she regained her self-possession she saw that the passengers were gathering up their wraps and bags. The woman with the false braids had brought from the dressing-room a sickly ivy-plant in a bottle, and the Christian Scientist was reversing his cuffs. The porter passed down the aisle with his impartial brush. An impersonal figure with a gold-banded cap asked for her husband's ticket. A
340   voice shouted "Baig-gage express!" and she heard the clicking of metal as the passengers handed over their checks.

CLOSE READ
Notes

The wife's mental state is disintegrating. She is having hallucinations and is confused.

inexorable:
unyielding

18. (◀ REREAD) Reread lines 323–332. Why do you think Wharton uses these deathly images in these lines?

Wharton might be emphasizing the severity of the wife's confusion. The wife feels as if she has died.

19. (READ ▶) As you read lines 333–352, continue to cite textual evidence.

- Underline text describing the porter's actions.
- In the margin, explain what happens to the wife (lines 350–352).

103

---

17. READ AND CITE TEXT EVIDENCE

Q ASK STUDENTS to explain the wife's deteriorating mental state in lines 291–332. *Students should emphasize that she is experiencing disordered thinking and hallucinations as she thinks she sees her husband's dead face (line 295), sometimes suspended in mid-air (lines 298–302 and 307–309). She is also experiencing a sense of timelessness (lines 310–312) and "terror" (line 325), as well as dreams (nightmares) of her own death (lines 330–332).*

Critical Vocabulary: arabesque (line 292) and **repress** (line 302) Have students share their definitions.

FOR ELL STUDENTS Explain that homographs are words that are spelled alike but have different meanings. Point out that *object* (line 305) is a homograph. Ask what part of speech it is here *noun* and what it means. *It means "thing."* Ask students to pronounce and define the verb *object*. What does it mean? *to protest.* Have them use both words in sentences.

18. REREAD AND CITE TEXT EVIDENCE

R ASK STUDENTS to cite the deathly images in lines 323–332. *"sweeping her into darkness" (lines 324–325), "She was dead in her turn" (line 326), "the darkness of death" (line 330), "with millions and millions of the dead" (line 332)*

19. READ AND CITE TEXT EVIDENCE

S ASK STUDENTS to cite evidence for their explanation for what happens to the wife at the end of the story. *Students should cite evidence from lines 350–352 to explain that she has an accident. Upon the porter's approach, she panics, faints, and hits her head against her dead husband's berth, perhaps signifying her death.*

Critical Vocabulary: inexorable (line 324) Have students share their definitions of the word and use it in a sentence.

CLOSE READ
Notes

The wife panics, faints, and hits her head.

 Presently her window was blocked by an expanse of sooty wall, and the train passed into the Harlem tunnel. The journey was over; in a few minutes she would see her family pushing their joyous way through the throng at the station. Her heart dilated. The worst terror was past. . . .

"We'd better get him up now, hadn't we?" asked the porter, <u>touching her arm.</u>

He had her husband's hat in his hand and was meditatively revolving it under his brush.

350 She looked at the hat and tried to speak; but suddenly the car grew dark. She flung up her arms, struggling to catch at something, and fell face downward, striking her head against the dead man's berth.

---

20. ◀ REREAD Reread lines 342–345. Explain the irony of the text "The journey was over" in line 343.

At first, the reader feels relief that the "journey" is over, but then the wife herself has an unfortunate accident.

SHORT RESPONSE

Cite Text Evidence What do you think is the theme of "A Journey"? How does Wharton's use of irony hint at a deeper message about life that the author wants to convey? Support your response with **explicit textual evidence.**

The theme of "A Journey" is that life itself is a journey. The wife herself makes the comparison: "It seemed to be life itself that was sweeping her on with headlong inexorable force—sweeping her into darkness and terror . . ." Wharton points out that a journey, just like life is unpredictable. The wife is so preoccupied with concealing her husband's death that at the moment "the journey is over" she hits her head "against the dead man's berth." Just as "the worst terror" has passed, the wife has an accident and the story ends abruptly.

104

TO CHALLENGE STUDENTS . . .

For more context about the life and legacy of the great American author Edith Wharton, students can conduct print or online research to write a report.

ASK STUDENTS to do some research to find a topic about Wharton that interests them. You may suggest the following:

- Wharton's travels and their influence on her work
- women in Wharton's fiction
- Wharton's use of irony

Discuss these features of a research report:

- Plan your research
    - —Write questions about your topic.
    - —Research your topic, take notes, and organize them.
    - —Write an outline based on your notes.
- Write your report
    - —Keep your purpose and audience in mind.
    - —Write a draft, revise your report, and proofread it.
    - —Check that your bibliography is accurate.
- Publish and share

ASK STUDENTS what they hope to discover about Wharton as they research their report.

---

20. REREAD AND CITE TEXT EVIDENCE

 ASK STUDENTS what the word *journey* can mean as a metaphor. *Students may suggest that it can mean any process: the journey from innocence to worldliness; the journey through high school; the journey from apprentice to master craftsman; the journey of life.*

SHORT RESPONSE

Cite Text Evidence Student responses will vary, but students should cite specific evidence from the text to support their statement of the theme. Students should:

- explain the theme of the text.
- give reasons to support how the theme of the text conveys a deeper message about life.
- cite specific evidence from the text to support their reasons.

DIG DEEPER

With the class, return to Question 6, Reread and Discuss. Have students share the results of their discussion.

ASK STUDENTS whether they were satisfied with the outcome of their small-group discussions. Have each group share the details they discussed about the wife's concern regarding the journey home. What fears does she have about the trip? How does the journey home suggest an ironic situation in the text?

- Have each group share what the wife's overriding concern is about the journey home. What specific textual evidence did the groups cite to support this opinion? Did anyone in the group disagree? If so, how did the group resolve this disagreement or difference of opinion?

- Lead each group to share its discussion about why the wife is concerned about meeting her "people." What is the cause of her concern? How does her ironic treatment in the text cast doubt on her belief that she has developed "subtler sympathies" due to her "long contact with suffering"?

ASK STUDENTS to return to their Short Response answer about the theme and revise it based on the class discussion.

CLOSE READING NOTES

The Fish

Poem by Elizabeth Bishop

Why This Text?

Students can use their understanding of poetry as a path to meaning in their own everyday experiences and in the physical world around them. Elizabeth Bishop's "The Fish" is an accessible yet profound piece that will assist students in developing their ability to appreciate the vivid description, symbolism, figurative language, and multiple levels of meaning that mark this genre.

Key Learning Objective: Students will be able to analyze a poem for diction, imagery, and use of symbols.

For additional practice:

Close Reader selection
"Ode to a Large Tuna in the Market"
Poem by Pablo Neruda

COMMON CORE Common Core Standards

RL 1 Cite textual evidence.

RL 2 Determine themes of a text.

RL 4 Determine figurative and connotative meanings; analyze the impact of specific word choices.

RL 5 Analyze how an author's choices concerning how to structure specific parts of a text contribute to its overall meaning as well as its aesthetic impact.

RL 6 Analyze a case in which grasping point of view requires distinguishing what is directly stated in a text from what is really meant.

W 3d Use precise words and phrases, telling details, and sensory language to convey a vivid picture.

SL 1 Initiate and participate in a range of collaborative discussions.

▲ Text Complexity Rubric

Quantitative Measures	**The Fish** Lexile: N/A
Qualitative Measures	**Levels of Meaning/Purpose** multiple levels of meaning (multiple themes)
	Structure free verse, no particular patterns
	Language Conventionality and Clarity figurative, symbolic language
	Knowledge Demands experience includes unfamiliar aspects
Reader/Task Considerations	Teacher determined Vary by individual reader and type of text

CLOSE READ

Elizabeth Bishop traveled extensively throughout her lifetime, and much of her poetry captures and reflects upon the scenery she encountered. She was inspired, for example, by her visits to France, Italy, North Africa, Ireland, and Spain. She lived for more extended periods in Key West, Florida, and Petrópolis, Brazil. The independently wealthy Bishop was devoted to her poetry and would spend long periods of time polishing each poem. In fact, she published only about one hundred poems during her lifetime. Bishop's work was always well respected by critics and other poets, but it was not until the publication of her last book, *Geography III,* that she came to be considered a major American poet.

AS YOU READ Direct students to use the As You Read instructions to focus their reading.

Analyze Language (LINES 1–17) (COMMON CORE) RL 4, RL 5

Tell students that **figurative language** describes one thing in terms of something else, often in fresh and imaginative ways. Explain the following types:

- **Personification:** giving an idea, object, or animal human feelings, thoughts, attitudes, or abilities
- **Simile:** an explicit comparison between two unlike things using a word such as *like* or *as*

 **A** CITE TEXT EVIDENCE Have students point out the ways in which Bishop personifies the fish in the first part of the poem. *(She uses the pronouns* him, his, *and* he *[instead of* it *and* its] *to refer to the fish [lines 2, 4, 5]. Using a gender-specific pronoun for an animal makes the animal seem more human. She says he "didn't fight" [line 5], implying that the fish made a conscious choice to surrender. She uses the adjectives* venerable *and* homely *[lines 8 and 9], which are usually used to describe people.)*

B CITE TEXT EVIDENCE Ask students to point out similes in lines 5–12 and to explain the meaning and effect of these figurative comparisons. *(She describes the fish's skin as "[hanging] in strips / like ancient wallpaper" to convey how old and deteriorated the fish is. The fish's skin also has a pattern like that of wallpaper, with "shapes like full-blown roses / stained and lost through age." This simile also gives a sense of how very long this fish has been around. Both comparisons create vivid visual imagery.)*

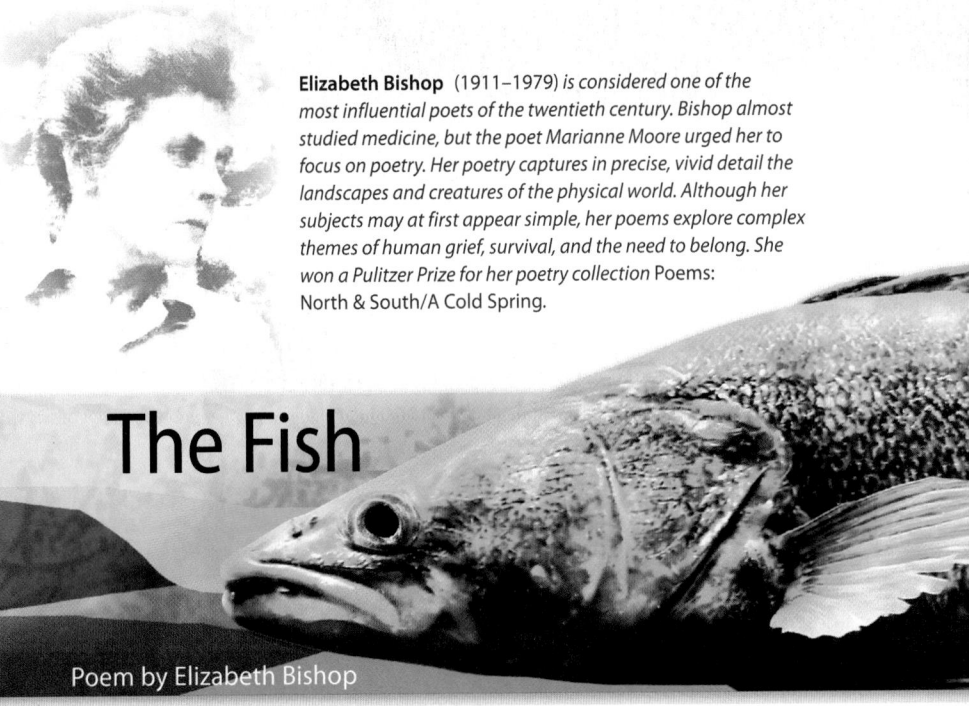

The Fish

Poem by Elizabeth Bishop

Elizabeth Bishop *(1911–1979) is considered one of the most influential poets of the twentieth century. Bishop almost studied medicine, but the poet Marianne Moore urged her to focus on poetry. Her poetry captures in precise, vivid detail the landscapes and creatures of the physical world. Although her subjects may at first appear simple, her poems explore complex themes of human grief, survival, and the need to belong. She won a Pulitzer Prize for her poetry collection* Poems: North & South/A Cold Spring.

AS YOU READ Make note of details that Bishop uses to create a vivid, realistic image of the fish. Write down any questions you generate during reading.

I caught a tremendous fish
and held him beside the boat
half out of water, with my hook
fast in a corner of his mouth.
5   He didn't fight.
He hadn't fought at all.
He hung a grunting weight,
battered and venerable
and homely. Here and there
10   his brown skin hung in strips
like ancient wallpaper,
and its pattern of darker brown
was like wallpaper:
shapes like full-blown roses
15   stained and lost through age.
He was speckled with barnacles,
fine rosettes of lime,
and infested

Image Credits: (b) ©Kletr/Shutterstock; (t) ©J.L. Castel/Bettmann/Corbis

The Fish **401**

SCAFFOLDING FOR ELL STUDENTS

Recognize Past Participles Used as Modifiers Explain that past participles, or past forms of verbs, can be used as adjectives modifying nouns or pronouns.

- Have students study the first fifteen lines of the poem. Ask volunteers to identify the past participles and the noun or pronoun each modifies. *(battered—He; full-blown, stained, lost—roses)*
- If students select *caught* or *held*, explain that these words are past-tense verbs.

Have students work in small groups to find more past participles in the rest of the poem.

Analyze Structure: Symbol (LINES 22–23)

 COMMON CORE RL 4, RL 5

Explain that a **symbol** is an object, person, animal, or event that has meaning in itself and also stands for something more than itself. Symbols are another type of figurative language.

C **ASK STUDENTS** to explain the effect of lines 22–23. Why does the speaker call the oxygen "terrible"? What new perception of the fish is expressed in these lines? (*The oxygen is terrible because the fish will die from breathing it through its gills for too long. The new perception is that the fish is in distress and is fighting for its life.*)

Analyze Language (LINES 34–40)

 COMMON CORE RL 4

Remind students that figurative language is not meant to be taken literally.

D **CITE TEXT EVIDENCE** Have students explain the figurative language used in the description of the fish's eyes. (*The irises are said to be "backed and packed / with tarnished tinfoil" [lines 37–38], and the lenses of the eyes are said to be made of "old scratched isinglass" [line 40]). Ask why these phrases are considered figurative language. (*The fish does not literally have tinfoil behind its eyes, nor are its lenses made of isinglass [a transparent sheet of the mineral mica]. The poet compares parts of the fish's eyes to other, unlike things in order to vividly describe it.*)

Analyze Structure: Symbol (LINES 45–64)

 COMMON CORE RL 4, RL 5

Explain that symbols in literature express ideas or messages in fresh ways and often help lend several different levels of meaning to the same text.

E **CITE TEXT EVIDENCE** Have students point out and explain the shift in how the speaker is perceiving, or experiencing, the fish in lines 45–64. (*The speaker begins to see the fish as some wise and brave old warrior and as a stately survivor in a harsh world.*)

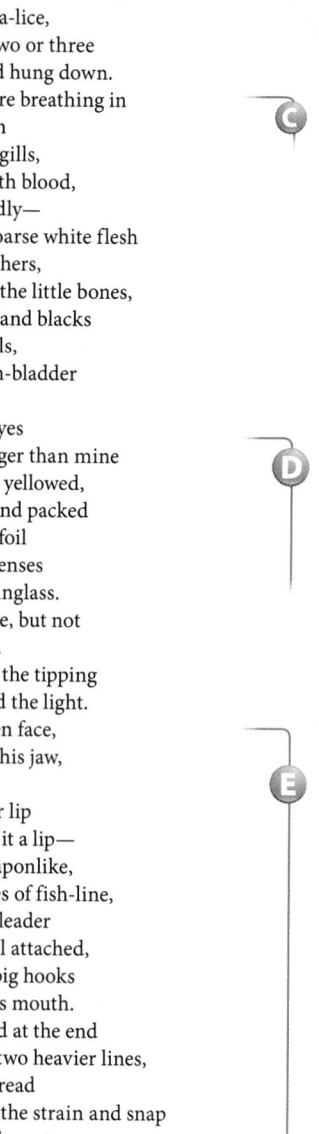

```
        with tiny white sea-lice,
20      and underneath two or three
        rags of green weed hung down.
        While his gills were breathing in
        the terrible oxygen
        —the frightening gills,
25      fresh and crisp with blood,
        that can cut so badly—
        I thought of the coarse white flesh
        packed in like feathers,
        the big bones and the little bones,
30      the dramatic reds and blacks
        of his shiny entrails,
        and the pink swim-bladder
        like a big peony.
        I looked into his eyes
35      which were far larger than mine
        but shallower, and yellowed,
        the irises backed and packed
        with tarnished tinfoil
        seen through the lenses
40      of old scratched isinglass.
        They shifted a little, but not
        to return my stare.
        —It was more like the tipping
        of an object toward the light.
45      I admired his sullen face,
        the mechanism of his jaw,
        and then I saw
        that from his lower lip
        —if you could call it a lip—
50      grim, wet, and weaponlike,
        hung five old pieces of fish-line,
        or four and a wire leader
        with the swivel still attached,
        with all their five big hooks
55      grown firmly in his mouth.
        A green line, frayed at the end
        where he broke it, two heavier lines,
        and a fine black thread
        still crimped from the strain and snap
60      when it broke and he got away.
        Like medals with their ribbons
        frayed and wavering,
        a five-haired beard of wisdom
        trailing from his aching jaw.
65      I stared and stared
```

WHEN STUDENTS STRUGGLE ...

This poem contains mostly simple words, but there are a number of science words that may challenge some students.

- Read aloud the description of the fish presented in lines 16–40. Ask students with a strong biology background or knowledge of fishing to offer definitions of the science words. (*For example, sea lice are parasitic crustaceans that live off host fish.*)
- Next have students take turns reading each full sentence from this section aloud for the class. Ask for a volunteer to explain the literal meaning of each sentence.

ASK STUDENTS to work in small groups to complete a similar process for the rest of the poem. Group members can help define challenging adjectives or fishing-related terms. Then students can check their understanding of the literal meaning of each sentence.

and victory filled up
the little rented boat,
from the pool of bilge[1]
where oil had spread a rainbow
70   around the rusted engine
to the bailer rusted orange,
the sun-cracked thwarts,[2]
the oarlocks on their strings,
the gunnels[3]—until everything
75   was rainbow, rainbow, rainbow!
And I let the fish go.

---

[1] **bilge** (bĭlj): dirty water that gathers in the bottom of a boat.
[2] **thwarts:** seats on a boat.
[3] **gunnels:** gunwales; the upper edges of the sides of a boat.

COLLABORATIVE DISCUSSION What is your impression of the fish? What special significance does the fish have in the poem? With a partner, discuss what details led to your impressions. Cite specific evidence from the text to support your ideas.

The Fish   **403**

TEACH

Analyze Structure: Symbol (LINE 76)   COMMON CORE RL 4, RL 5

Explain that writers also present events to help develop the meanings of symbols in their works.

F ASK STUDENTS what they can infer about the symbolism of the fish based on the event told in the first line of the poem ("I caught a tremendous fish") and the last line of the poem (line 76). (*The poem begins with the speaker catching a tremendous fish, an event that seems to be a triumph for the speaker. Yet by the end of the poem, the speaker releases the fish. From this change, the reader might infer that the speaker has developed a different kind of feeling for the fish—perhaps respect or compassion. The fish may symbolize respect for nature or for the will to survive.*)

COLLABORATIVE DISCUSSION Have students independently jot down their impressions of the fish and some notes regarding how they formed these impressions. Then have them form pairs to discuss their impressions and the details that support them. Encourage students to focus on specific text evidence during their discussions. Have partners compare and contrast their ideas and note how interpretations of the poem may vary.

ASK STUDENTS to share any questions they generated in the course of reading and discussing the selection.

Strategies for Annotation   ✎ 🗐 *Annotate it!*

Analyze Structure: Symbol   COMMON CORE RL 4, RL 5

Share these strategies for guided or independent analysis:

- Highlight similes in blue.
- Highlight personification in green.
- Underline other sensory or descriptive details.
- On a note, record how these descriptions affect your ideas about what the fish may symbolize.

I thought of the coarse white flesh
packed in like feathers,
the big bones and the little bones,
the dramatic reds and blacks
of his shiny entrails,
and the pink swim-bladder
like a big peony.

The Fish   **403**

Image Credits: ©Artville/Getty Images

PRACTICE & APPLY

Analyze Structure: Symbol

COMMON CORE RL 4, RL 5

Review the term **symbol** and explain that symbols are a type of figurative language. Most symbols from literature work as personal, or private, symbols—the writer establishes and develops their specific meaning through descriptions and events. Often a symbol has several levels of meaning or can be interpreted in a number of different ways.

Have students look for details in the poem that reveal the symbolic meaning of the fish. Help them get started by asking what associations come to mind when they read lines 8–11. (*Possible answers: an old person, wise and respected; a weary soldier who has been through war*)

Analyzing the Text

COMMON CORE RL 1, RL 4, RL 5, RL 6

Possible answers:

1. *The speaker personifies the fish by using the pronoun* his *to give the fish a gender and by including the adjectives* sullen *and* grim. *The speaker revises her initial statement about the fish having a "lip" to remind both herself and the reader that the fish is not actually human.*

2. *Medals are associated with brave, tough soldiers, heroes who have served in combat.*

3. *Answers may vary. Some students may say the victory belongs to the fish for having survived so many attempts on his life; others may say the victory belongs to the speaker for having caught a fish so many others had failed to catch. Other students may say that the fish and the speaker share the victory.*

4. *Clues that the fish might be a symbol include the similes in lines 10–15 and the reference to the fish's "beard of wisdom" in line 63. The rainbow might symbolize nature, victory, peace, or the continuation of life.*

5. *She lets the fish go because she is awed by its endurance and wisdom and believes it deserves to live. The fish is like the dog because it possesses the wisdom and the instincts to survive in harsh conditions or when threatened.*

✏ 📋 eBook *Annotate It!*

Analyze Structure: Symbol

 COMMON CORE RL 4, RL 5, L 5a

A **symbol** is a person, a place, a thing, or an event that has meaning in itself and also stands for something much more than itself. Often symbols stand for abstract ideas:

- A dove symbolizes peace.
- A skull symbolizes death.
- A red rose symbolizes love.
- A flag symbolizes an entire country.

These are all public symbols with conventional meanings. Fish can be conventional symbols of freedom and the mysteries of nature. Bishop's fish can be viewed that way, but it can also be viewed as a private symbol. Bishop's careful choice of details about the fish and the speaker's actions and reactions help reveal a symbolic or broader meaning for this old fish.

Analyzing the Text

COMMON CORE RL 1, RL 4, RL 5, RL 6, L 5a, W 3d

Cite Text Evidence Support your responses with evidence from the selection.

1. **Connect** An offshoot of realism, **naturalism** was a literary movement in which writers worked to describe ordinary life accurately and realistically. Look at lines 45–55. How does the speaker personify the fish? Why does Bishop have the speaker revise her initial statement about the fish?

2. **Interpret** Why does the speaker call the fish hooks "medals" in line 61?

3. **Interpret** In lines 65–67, as the speaker stared at the fish, "victory filled up" the boat. Whose victory is it? Who or what is the enemy?

4. **Analyze** What clues suggest that the fish might have a symbolic meaning? What could the rainbow at the end of the poem symbolize?

5. **Connect** Why does the speaker let the fish go? How is the fish like the dog in "To Build a Fire?"

PERFORMANCE TASK

Writing Activity: Description Bishop describes the fish in intense detail, and this detail helps create a symbolic meaning for the fish. Write a paragraph or poem that uses vivid description to help represent a symbol.

1. Choose an object or animal that has a symbolic meaning for you.

2. Gather details about the object or animal to create a vivid, realistic description.

3. Choose specific details that help readers clarify what the object or animal means to you. The meaning should be implicit, not stated directly.

In your writing, use the conventions of standard English.

Assign this performance task.

PERFORMANCE TASK

COMMON CORE W 3d

Writing Activity: Description Have students conduct brainstorming sessions in groups to come up with topic ideas. Then have them work independently to draft their paragraphs or poems. Encourage students to freewrite about what the object or animal means to them before starting their drafts. You might suggest that students use Bishop's poem as a guide or template to help them focus on detail and description. Students may share their final drafts in small groups and discuss the elements that reveal the symbolic meaning of the object or animal.

INTERACTIVE WHITEBOARD LESSON
Determine Themes

COMMON CORE

RL 2

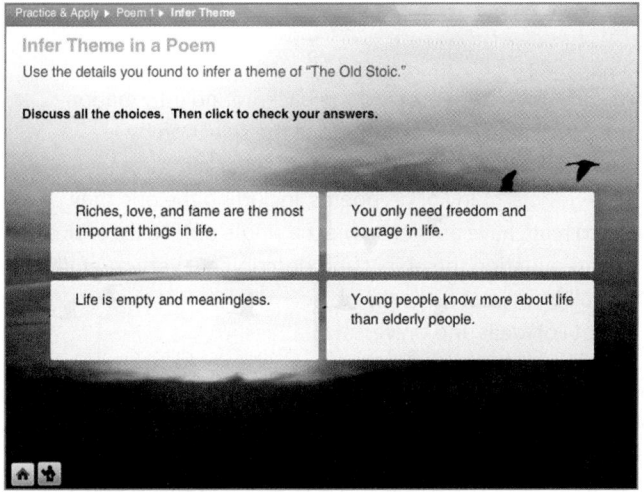

Practice & Apply ▶ Poem 1 ▶ Infer Theme

Infer Theme in a Poem

Use the details you found to infer a theme of "The Old Stoic."

Discuss all the choices. Then click to check your answers.

Riches, love, and fame are the most important things in life.

You only need freedom and courage in life.

Life is empty and meaningless.

Young people know more about life than elderly people.

TEACH

Remind students that themes are the insights or lessons about life that are conveyed through a literary work. Use the Interactive Whiteboard lesson to review the concept and to discuss some examples of themes that might be found in literature.

Explain that in poetry, especially, theme is not directly stated. It must be inferred from the images, symbols, structure, and language of the poem. Review these strategies for using clues in a poem to infer the theme:

- Highlight details that tell what the speaker values or does not value.
- Highlight any symbols and think about their connection to the theme.

PRACTICE AND APPLY

Have students apply the strategies for inferring theme to "The Fish" or to another poem with a strong thematic component, such as "Thanatopsis" by William Cullen Bryant or "The Bells" by Anne Sexton. Have them write a one-paragraph explanation of what they think the theme is and how they reached this conclusion.

Analyze Structure: Symbol

COMMON CORE

RL 5

RETEACH

Tell students that "The Fish," like many of Bishop's works, appears simple at first glance. On the surface, what happens is an everyday event: A person catches a fish, studies the fish, feels compassion for it, and releases it. Even the first layer of symbolism may be readily apparent. However, a closer read reveals the depth of meaning.

The poem is carefully structured to reveal the changes that take place in the perspective of the speaker. Those changes in turn reveal the meaning of the fish and of the choice the speaker makes at the end of the poem.

CLOSE READING APPLICATION

Have students examine the structure of the poem as a whole. Point out that even though this poem does not have stanzas, it does have distinct sections that can be discerned through a close reading. Ask students to look for these sections and to reach for the deepest level of meaning in each one. *(Distinct sections might include the first and last lines; the description of the skin and gills; the description of the eyes; the discovery of the fishing lines; the sense of victory; and the appearance of the rainbow.)*

Then have students use the flow chart on the Holt Interactive Graphic Organizers website (http://my.hrw.com/la3/la09/student/minisites/igo/pdf/flow_chart.pdf) to chart the observations, events, and turning points in the poem. Assist students by giving the following instructions:

- Devote one box to each observation, event, or turning point.
- Include information about what you think the observation, event, or turning point means.
- Include the event from the first line and the contrasting event from the last line.
- Make note of how the poet uses the series of observations and the order in which the speaker experiences them to convey a message to the reader.
- Write down your summary of what the fish symbolizes to the speaker, and how you interpret the poet's message.

You may wish to have students compare their charts with a partner and discuss the different meanings each student has gleaned.

Ode to a Large Tuna in the Market

Poem by Pablo Neruda

Why This Text

Students sometimes have difficulty analyzing what a symbol in a poem represents—the meaning it has beyond its literal meaning. With the help of the close-reading questions, students will identify details in the text that describe the fish—the subject of the poem. The results of their close reading and analysis will help students develop an understanding of how poets use symbols to represent abstract ideas and qualities.

Background Have students read the background information about the poet Pablo Neruda. Introduce the selection by pointing out to students that though the poet claims not to believe in symbols, many of his poems, including the one they are about to read, have as their subject a single object. Explain that by contemplating the object and describing it very carefully and unusually, the poet turns the object, which is real to him, into a symbol of ideas and universal qualities.

AS YOU READ Tell students to pay close attention to the details the poet uses to describe the fish as well as the impact these word choices have on the meaning of the poem.

Common Core Support

- cite strong and thorough textual evidence

- determine the meanings of words and phrases in the text, including figurative meanings

- analyze how an author's choices contribute to structure and meaning, as well as aesthetic impact

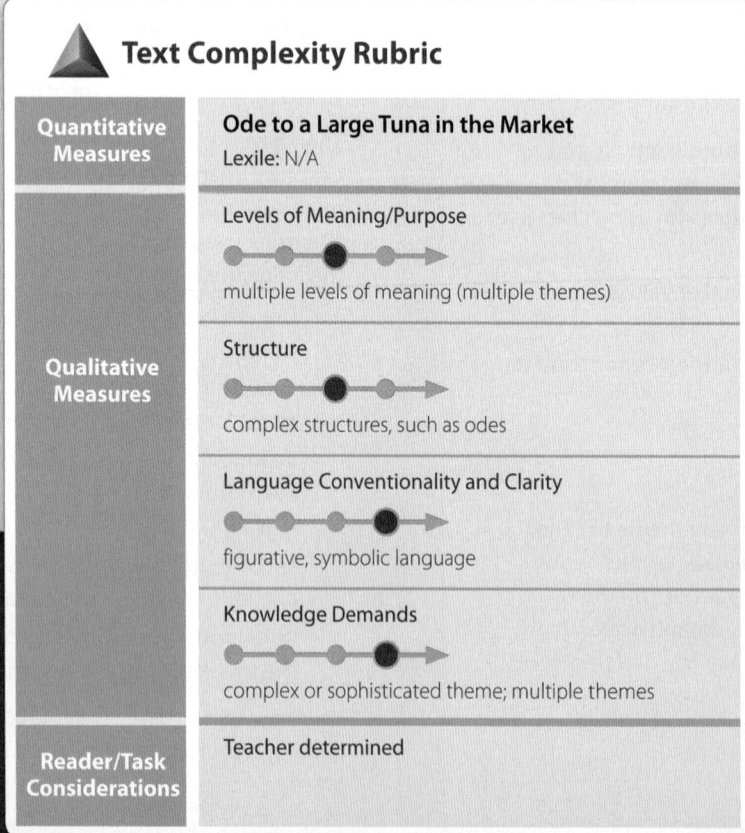

Text Complexity Rubric

Quantitative Measures

Ode to a Large Tuna in the Market
Lexile: N/A

Qualitative Measures

Levels of Meaning/Purpose

multiple levels of meaning (multiple themes)

Structure

complex structures, such as odes

Language Conventionality and Clarity

figurative, symbolic language

Knowledge Demands

complex or sophisticated theme; multiple themes

Reader/Task Considerations

Teacher determined

Strategies for CLOSE READING

Analyze Structure: Symbol

Students should read the poem closely, paying special attention to words the poet uses to describe the fish. Close-reading questions will help students cite text evidence in order to determine the figurative meanings of words and phrases, including symbols. As they read, students should note in the margin words the poet uses to describe the tuna and the ocean.

WHEN STUDENTS STRUGGLE . . .

To help students analyze how the author uses figurative language and symbols to create meaning in the poem, have them work in small groups to fill out a chart like the one shown below.

CITE TEXT EVIDENCE For practice analyzing figurative language and symbolism, ask students to explain the effects that these words from the poem create for the reader.

Lines from the Poem	Symbolic Meaning of the Lines
"this torpedo from the ocean depths" (lines 3–5)	These words make the tuna seem to be a powerful force from a mysterious place.
"the unknown, the unfathomable darkness, the depths of the sea" (lines 18–21)	These words make the ocean seem like a dark, mysterious place that people cannot understand.

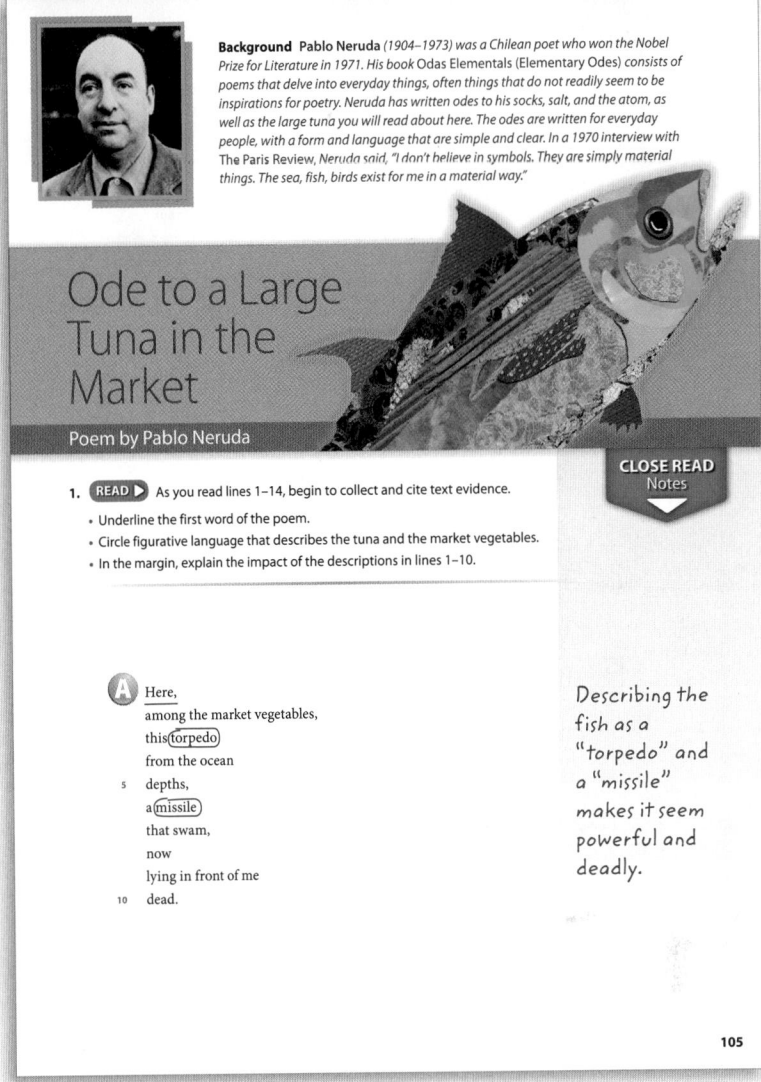

Background Pablo Neruda (1904–1973) was a Chilean poet who won the Nobel Prize for Literature in 1971. His book Odas Elementals (Elementary Odes) consists of poems that delve into everyday things, often things that do not readily seem to be inspirations for poetry. Neruda has written odes to his socks, salt, and the atom, as well as the large tuna you will read about here. The odes are written for everyday people, with a form and language that are simple and clear. In a 1970 interview with The Paris Review, Neruda said, "I don't believe in symbols. They are simply material things. The sea, fish, birds exist for me in a material way."

Ode to a Large Tuna in the Market

Poem by Pablo Neruda

CLOSE READ Notes

1. **READ ▷** As you read lines 1–14, begin to collect and cite text evidence.
   - Underline the first word of the poem.
   - Circle figurative language that describes the tuna and the market vegetables.
   - In the margin, explain the impact of the descriptions in lines 1–10.

A Here,
among the market vegetables,
this (torpedo)
from the ocean
5 depths,
a (missile)
that swam,
now
lying in front of me
10 dead.

Describing the fish as a "torpedo" and a "missile" makes it seem powerful and deadly.

105

1. READ AND CITE TEXT EVIDENCE

A **ASK STUDENTS** to identify the words used to describe the tuna as it was alive and as it is now in the market. *Possible response: Students should identify "torpedo from the ocean depths" (lines 3–5) and "a missile that swam" (lines 6–7) as descriptions of the tuna alive. "Lying in front of me dead" (lines 9–10) describes the fish now.*

FOR ELL STUDENTS Spanish-speaking students will recognize the word *torpedo* because it has a Spanish cognate—*torpedo*—with the same meaning, "an underwater missile."

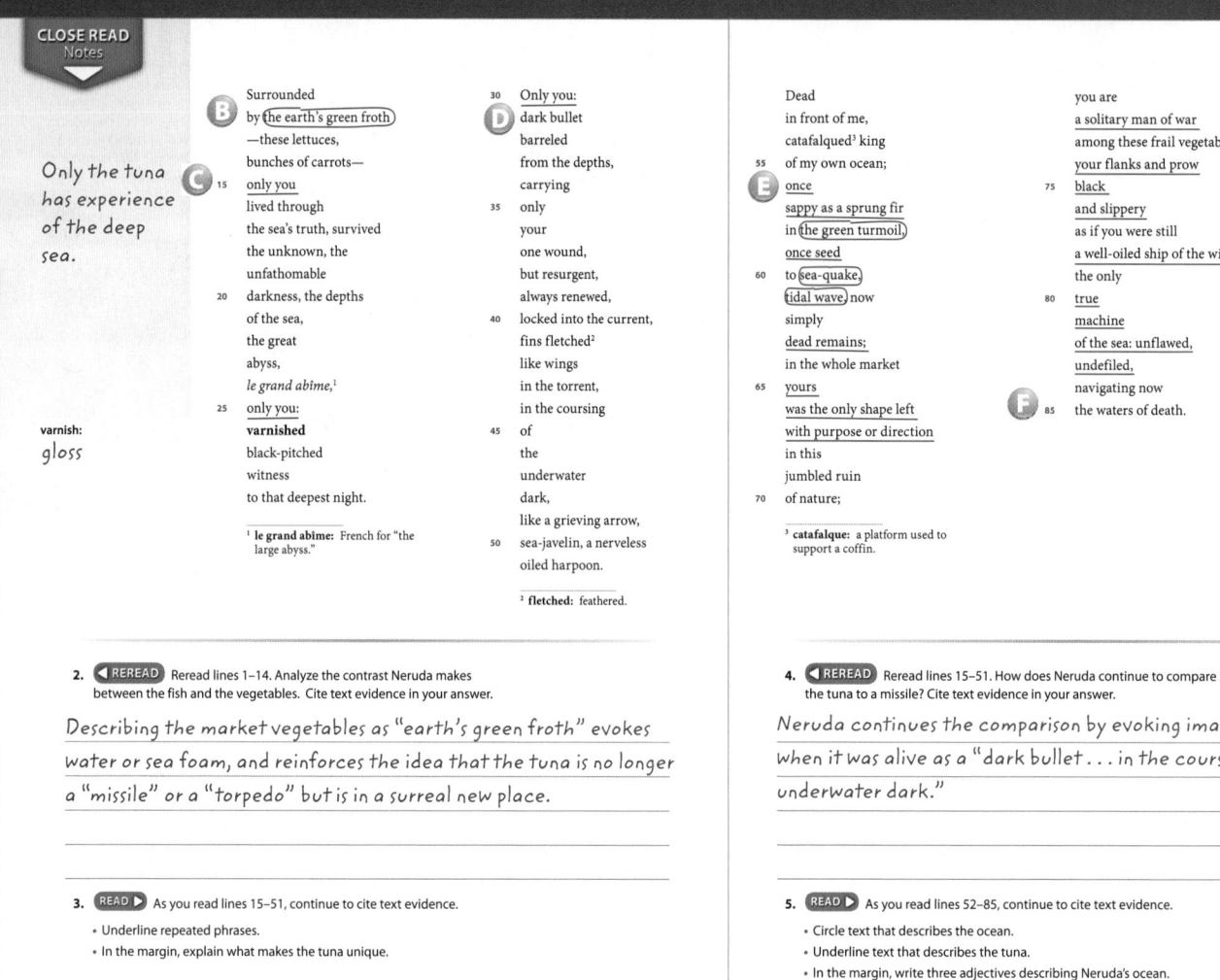

CLOSE READ Notes

B Surrounded
by (the earth's green froth)
—these lettuces,
bunches of carrots—

C 15 only you
lived through
the sea's truth, survived
the unknown, the
unfathomable
20 darkness, the depths
of the sea,
the great
abyss,
le grand abime,[1]
25 only you:
varnished
black-pitched
witness
to that deepest night.

Only the tuna has experience of the deep sea.

varnish: gloss

30 Only you:
D dark bullet
barreled
from the depths,
carrying
35 only
your
one wound,
but resurgent,
always renewed,
40 locked into the current,
fins fletched[2]
like wings
in the torrent,
in the coursing
45 of
the
underwater
dark,
like a grieving arrow,
50 sea-javelin, a nerveless
oiled harpoon.

[1] **le grand abime:** French for "the large abyss."

[2] **fletched:** feathered.

Dead
in front of me,
catafalqued[3] king
55 of my own ocean;
E once
sappy as a sprung fir
in (the green turmoil,)
once seed
60 to (sea-quake,)
(tidal wave) now
simply
dead remains;
in the whole market
65 yours
was the only shape left
with purpose or direction
in this
jumbled ruin
70 of nature;

you are
a solitary man of war
among these frail vegetables,
your flanks and prow
75 black
and slippery
as if you were still
a well-oiled ship of the wind,
the only
80 true
machine
of the sea: unflawed,
undefiled,
navigating now
F 85 the waters of death.

chaotic, powerful, dangerous

[3] **catafalque:** a platform used to support a coffin.

2. ◀ REREAD Reread lines 1–14. Analyze the contrast Neruda makes between the fish and the vegetables. Cite text evidence in your answer.

Describing the market vegetables as "earth's green froth" evokes water or sea foam, and reinforces the idea that the tuna is no longer a "missile" or a "torpedo" but is in a surreal new place.

3. READ ▶ As you read lines 15–51, continue to cite text evidence.
- Underline repeated phrases.
- In the margin, explain what makes the tuna unique.

4. ◀ REREAD Reread lines 15–51. How does Neruda continue to compare the tuna to a missile? Cite text evidence in your answer.

Neruda continues the comparison by evoking images of the tuna when it was alive as a "dark bullet . . . in the coursing of the underwater dark."

5. READ ▶ As you read lines 52–85, continue to cite text evidence.
- Circle text that describes the ocean.
- Underline text that describes the tuna.
- In the margin, write three adjectives describing Neruda's ocean.

2. **REREAD AND CITE TEXT EVIDENCE**

B **ASK STUDENTS** to identify words and phrases that describe and help them visualize the vegetables. *earth's green froth (line 12), lettuces (line 13), bunches of carrots (line 14)* Then have students identify the one word used to describe the vegetables that is similar to a word used to describe the ocean. *froth (line 12)*

3. **READ AND CITE TEXT EVIDENCE**

C **ASK STUDENTS** to explain what effect the repetition of the words *only you* has. *Possible response: The words set the tuna apart from everything else, including the speaker. They help create the sense of the tuna as mysterious and unique.*

Critical Vocabulary: varnish (line 26) Ask students to share their definitions of *varnish*. In the poem, *varnish* ends with *-ed* and acts as an adjective describing the fish. Ask students what the word helps them see about the fish. *The fish's skin is shiny.*

4. **REREAD AND CITE TEXT EVIDENCE** Have students identify words and phrases the speaker uses to describe the tuna when it was alive in the ocean. *dark bullet (line 31), grieving arrow (line 49), sea-javelin (line 50), nerveless oiled harpoon (lines 50–51)*

D **ASK STUDENTS** to describe how these words affect their understanding of what the tuna represents in the poem. *Possible response: The tuna is a sad, almost tragic, yet powerful force in nature.*

5. **READ AND CITE TEXT EVIDENCE** Encourage students to compare and contrast the words and phrases used to describe the living tuna with those used to describe it dead in the market.

E **ASK STUDENTS** to explain the effect that the repetition of the word *once* has in the poem. *Possible response: The word once reminds the reader that the tuna had once been a live, powerful force that is not dead and motionless.*

CLOSE READ
Notes

6. **◀ REREAD** What are "the waters of death" that Neruda mentions in the last line of the poem? In what way is this description ironic? Cite text evidence in your explanation.

The "waters of death" are the "frail vegetables," the "jumbled ruin of nature" around the dead tuna. This description is ironic because the tuna was once alive in the water.

SHORT RESPONSE

Cite Text Evidence In the Background section, you read that Neruda does not "believe in symbols." What do you think the tuna means to him? Review your reading notes, and remember to **cite text evidence** in your response.

The images Neruda chooses to describe or characterize the tuna are carefully selected. There are objects that are related to the military and to hunting: torpedo, missile, man of war, arrow, javelin, harpoon. There are images of virility: "sappy as a sprung fir," "seed to sea-quake," and "solitary man of war." Through his choices, Neruda creates a symbol of virility, power, and life in the tuna and ties it to himself with the phrase "my own ocean." The tuna is a symbol of life.

108

6. **REREAD AND CITE TEXT EVIDENCE** Emphasize that there is no strictly right or wrong interpretation of the final lines of the poem.

F ASK STUDENTS to cite text evidence that expresses the tuna's place in "the waters of death." *"a solitary man of war" (line 72), "a well-oiled ship of the wind" (line 78), "the only true machine of the sea" (lines 79–82)*

SHORT RESPONSE

Cite Text Evidence Students' responses will vary, but they should cite evidence from the text to support their answers. Students should:

- include words and phrases from the text that describe the tuna.
- explain in their own words what they think the tuna symbolizes.
- cite other specific evidence from the text to support their ideas.

TO CHALLENGE STUDENTS . . .

Through translations, Pablo Neruda's poems became very popular in this country in the 1960s and 1970s. Neruda was, however, a political activist in his native Chile, as well as a poet.

ASK STUDENTS to research the political causes that Neruda supported in his native country of Chile. Point out to students that though Neruda once said in a radio interview, "I insist on telling you that I am not a political poet," he may not have been entirely forthcoming. In fact, controversy about the cause of his death exists to this day. Some people claim that he was murdered by the Chilean government in power at the time. Have students work in small groups to explore Neruda's political beliefs, the Chilean government during the 1970s, and the circumstances of his death. Groups can present their findings and compare their interpretations of Neruda's beliefs and politics.

DIG DEEPER

With the class, return to Question 6, Reread. Have students share and discuss their answers.

ASK STUDENTS to note whether they think the ending is ironic or not ironic. Have students cite evidence from the text to support their thinking.

- Have students discuss the language the poet uses to describe the tuna throughout the poem.
- Have students compare and contrast the descriptions of the tuna in the first part of the poem with those at the end of the poem. How are the descriptions similar? How are they different?
- Have students compare and contrast the descriptions of the ocean in the first part of the poem with the image of the ocean in the last lines.

ASK STUDENTS to return to their response to the Short Response question and revise it based on the class discussion.

Interactive Lessons

If you need help . . .
- **Writing an Informative Text**
- **Writing as a Process**
- **Using Textual Evidence**

Write an Analytical Essay

COMMON CORE

W 2a–f Write informative/ explanatory texts.

W 9a–b Draw evidence from literary or informational texts to support analysis.

This collection opens with the quotation "Reality is that which, when you stop believing in it, doesn't go away." Look back at the anchor text, "To Build a Fire," and at the other texts in this collection. What particular themes or central ideas does each writer want readers to recognize about reality, and why? What stylistic choices does each author make in order to reveal a specific version of reality? Synthesize your ideas by writing an analytical essay.

An effective analytical essay

- includes a clear controlling idea
- has an introduction that engages the reader with an interesting observation, quotation, or detail from one of the selections
- organizes central ideas in a logically structured body that clearly develops the controlling idea
- uses transitions to create a cohesion between sections of the text and to clarify relationships among ideas
- includes relevant textual evidence to illustrate central ideas
- has a concluding section that follows logically from the body

PLAN

*my*Notebook

Use the annotation tools in your eBook to find evidence that supports your ideas about the writers' views on reality. Save each piece of evidence to your notebook.

Analyze the Texts Review "To Build a Fire" and the other texts in this collection. Consider these questions as you review:

- What elements of reality does each author want readers to acknowledge or face up to, and why?
- How does the style or structure of each work help bring some aspect of reality into sharp focus?
- How does each author communicate the sense of being in a specific place (e.g., the Yukon in "To Build a Fire" and a tenement in "Genesis of the Tenement")?

PERFORMANCE TASK

WRITE AN ANALYTICAL ESSAY

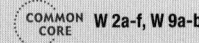

COMMON CORE W 2a–f, W 9a–b

Introduce students to the Performance Task by reading the introductory paragraph with them and reviewing the criteria for an effective analytical essay. Point out that they can use the questions in the prompt—*What particular themes or central ideas does each writer want readers to recognize about reality, and why?* and *What stylistic choices does each author make in order to reveal a specific version of reality?*—to focus their work. Suggest that they write these questions down and keep them prominently displayed as they develop their essays.

PLAN

ANALYZE THE TEXTS

View It!

Professional Development Podcast:

Performance Task

As students review the collection texts and decide which selections to feature alongside "To Build a Fire," tell them to consider which selections best complement it, either by showing a similar version of reality or by showing a contrasting one. Suggest that they also consider the techniques used by each author. For instance, they may wish to write about authors who use similar techniques to present contrasting versions of reality.

PLAN

GET ORGANIZED

Emphasize that a strong, clear controlling idea is essential to writing a coherent essay. The controlling idea, or thesis statement, should answer the question, *What particular themes or central ideas does each writer want readers to recognize about reality, and why?*

PRODUCE

DRAFT YOUR ESSAY

Remind students that this stage of the writing process is about transferring their ideas from outline form into sentences and paragraphs. Encourage them not to get bogged down in trying to write perfect prose; they'll have time to polish their writing later. However, one thing they should be strict about is using quotation marks around text taken directly from the literature. This will help them avoid confusion later.

Take Notes Choose three texts, including "To Build a Fire." Take notes on each writer's approach to his or her subject and what the writer is trying to show about some aspect of the real world by taking that approach. Look for an implicit version of reality revealed within each story or argument. Why does the writer want readers to understand this particular truth? List details, examples, and quotations that support your conclusions.

Get Organized Organize your details and evidence in an outline.

- Write a clear controlling idea about what truth each writer wants to reveal about the world as he or she sees it and the techniques each writer uses to do so.
- Search for an interesting quotation or detail to engage your reader in the introduction.
- Decide which organizational pattern you will use for your essay. Will you present your ideas text by text, or will you organize your analysis point by point, referring to the texts as you develop each point?
- Use your organizational pattern to sort the evidence you have gathered from the selections into a logical order.
- Write down some ideas for your conclusion.

PRODUCE

Draft Your Essay Write a draft of your essay, following your outline.

- Engage your readers with an interesting introduction to your topic and a clear controlling idea.
- Present your details, quotations, and examples from the selections in logically ordered paragraphs. Each paragraph should have a central idea related to your controlling idea with evidence to support it. Explain how each piece of evidence supports the central idea.
- Use transitions to link sections of the text and to clarify the relationships among your ideas.
- Write a satisfying conclusion that summarizes your analysis and synthesizes your central ideas.

As you draft your analytical essay, remember that this kind of writing requires formal language and a respectful tone to make it appropriate for an academic context.

ACADEMIC VOCABULARY

As you develop your ideas about the writers' views of the real world, be sure to use these words.

ambiguous
clarify
implicit
revise
somewhat

my **WriteSmart**

Write your rough draft in *my*WriteSmart. Focus on getting your ideas down, rather than perfecting your choice of language.

REVISE

Improve Your Draft

Revise your draft to make sure it is clear, coherent, and engaging. Use the chart on the following page to review the characteristics of a well-written analytical essay. Ask yourself these questions as you revise:

my **WriteSmart**

Have your partner or a group of peers review your draft in *my*WriteSmart. Ask your reviewers to note any evidence that does not support the controlling idea.

- Does my controlling idea present a clear point of view about reality and truth as depicted in the texts? Will my readers want to continue reading?
- Are the titles and authors of the selections accurately identified in my introduction?
- Have I provided sufficient and relevant textual evidence to support my central ideas?
- Do I develop my ideas in a logical order? Are transitions smooth and coherent?
- Have I maintained a formal style of English appropriate for an analytical essay? Does my choice of words convey a knowledgeable and confident tone, or attitude, toward the topic?
- Have I used precise language and various types of sentence structures?
- Have I provided a satisfying summary of my ideas in the conclusion?

PRESENT

Exchange Essays

When your final draft is completed, exchange essays with a partner. Read your partner's essay and provide feedback. Reread the criteria for an effective analytical essay and ask the following questions:

- Which aspects of your partner's essay are particularly strong?
- Were any sections of the essay ambiguous or unclear, such as losing focus on the central idea? How could they be clarified?
- Did the examples, quotations, or other evidence your partner provided support the central idea?

REVISE

IMPROVE YOUR DRAFT

Encourage students to use the criteria in the chart to pinpoint the areas in their drafts that need improvement. Have them read the descriptions in each row of the chart to see which ones best fit their essays. Then they can tell which parts need the most revision. Remind students to check each piece of evidence to make sure it supports the controlling idea.

PRESENT

EXCHANGE ESSAYS

Other options for sharing students' essays include

- creating a book of students' essays to be placed in the library
- having students read their essays aloud to the class

PERFORMANCE TASK

ORGANIZATION

Have students look at the chart and evaluate their level of performance in the Organization category. Ask them to review the organization of their central ideas and supporting evidence for logic and clarity. What areas will they work to improve?

COLLECTION 5 TASK
ANALYTICAL ESSAY

	Ideas and Evidence	Organization	Language
ADVANCED	• An eloquent introduction includes the titles and authors of the selections; the controlling idea describes the view of reality revealed by the writers. • Specific, relevant details support the central ideas. • A satisfying concluding section synthesizes the ideas and summarizes the analysis.	• Central ideas and supporting evidence are organized effectively and logically throughout the essay. • Varied transitions successfully show the relationships between ideas.	• The analysis has an appropriately formal style and a knowledgeable, objective tone. • Language is precise and captures the writer's thoughts with originality. • Sentence beginnings, lengths, and structures vary and have a rhythmic flow. • Spelling, capitalization, and punctuation are correct. If handwritten, the essay is legible. • Grammar and usage are correct.
COMPETENT	• The introduction identifies the titles and authors of the selections but could be more engaging; the controlling idea encompasses the view of reality in at least one of the selections. • One or two central ideas need more support. • The concluding section synthesizes most of the ideas and summarizes most of the analysis.	• The organization of central ideas and supporting evidence is confusing in a few places. • A few more transitions are needed to clarify the relationships between ideas.	• The style becomes informal in a few places, and the tone does not always communicate confidence. • Most language is precise. • Sentence beginnings, lengths, and structures vary somewhat. • Several spelling, capitalization, and punctuation mistakes occur. If handwritten, the essay is mostly legible. • Some grammatical and usage errors are repeated in the essay.
LIMITED	• The introduction identifies the titles and the authors of the selections; the controlling idea only hints at the main idea of the analysis. • Details support some central ideas but are often too general. • The concluding section gives an incomplete summary of the analysis and merely restates the thesis.	• Most central ideas are organized logically, but many supporting details are out of place. • More transitions are needed throughout the essay to connect ideas.	• The style is informal in many places, and the tone reflects a superficial understanding of the selections. • Language is repetitive or vague at times. • Sentence structures barely vary, and some fragments or run-on sentences are present. • Spelling, capitalization, and punctuation are often incorrect but do not make reading the essay difficult. If handwritten, the essay may be partially illegible. • Grammar and usage are incorrect in many places, but the writer's ideas are still clear.
EMERGING	• The appropriate elements of an introduction are missing. • Details and evidence are irrelevant or missing. • The analysis lacks a concluding section.	• A logical organization is not used; ideas are presented randomly. • Transitions are not used, making the essay difficult to understand.	• The style and tone are inappropriate. • Language is inaccurate, repetitive, and vague. • Repetitive sentence structure, fragments, and run-on sentences make the writing monotonous and difficult to follow. • Spelling, capitalization, and punctuation are incorrect throughout. If handwritten, the essay may be partially or mostly illegible. • Many grammatical and usage errors obscure the meaning of the writer's ideas.

The Modern World

The Modern World

hmhfyi.com

In this collection, you will explore how Americans have responded to modern life in a globally connected world.

CONNECTING WORD AND IMAGE

ASK STUDENTS to discuss how the collection opener image and the collection quotation work together to create a connection.

PERFORMANCE TASK PREVIEW

Point out to students that they will complete two performance tasks at the end of the collection. The performance tasks will require them to further analyze the selections in the collection and to synthesize ideas about these analyses. They will present their findings in a written argument and a panel discussion.

COLLECTION

PERFORMANCE TASK Preview

At the end of this collection, you will have the opportunity to complete two tasks:

• Write an argument to answer the following question: How do these texts define the challenges an individual or group may face in modern society?

• Hold a panel discussion that explores the risks of information overload and strategies for managing information in a constructive fashion.

ACADEMIC VOCABULARY

Study the words and their definitions in the chart below. You will use these words as you discuss and write about the texts in this collection.

Word	Definition	Related Forms
contemporary (kən-tĕm´pə-rĕr´ē) *adj.*	coming from the same time period	contemporaries, contemporarily
global (glō´bəl) *adj.*	relating to the world as a whole	globe, globally, globalization
infinite (ĭn´fə-nĭt) *adj.*	without end or beyond measure	infinitive, infinitesimal, infinitely, infiniteness
simulated (sĭm´yə-lā´tĭd) *adj.*	imitating something real	simulate, simulation, similar
virtual (vûr´chōō-əl) *adj.*	existing in essence or in a digital version but not in actual fact	virtually

ACADEMIC VOCABULARY

Students can acquire facility with the academic vocabulary words through frequent, repeated exposure as they analyze and discuss the selections in the collection. Academic vocabulary can be used in the following instructional contexts. This will enable students to incorporate the academic vocabulary words into their working vocabulary.

▶ *View It!*

Professional Development Podcast:

Academic Vocabulary

• Collaborative Discussion at the end of each selection

• Analyzing the Text questions for each selection

• Selection-level Performance Task

• Vocabulary instruction (for Critical Vocabulary and/or for Vocabulary Strategy)

• Language and Style

• End-of-collection Performance Task for all selections in the collection

ASK STUDENTS to review the academic vocabulary word list for this collection. You may wish to pronounce each word aloud, so students hear the correct pronunciation. Then discuss the definitions and the related forms for each word. Remind students that they will encounter these five academic vocabulary words throughout the collection.

USING THE COLLECTION YOUR WAY

Use the following information, along with the charts on the following pages, to help you decide how you want to introduce the collection. Based on your teaching style, your students' interests, or your instructional goals, you may want to structure the collection in various ways. You may choose different entry points each time you teach the collection.

"I emphasize building vocabulary."

In this short story, the relationship between two characters is used to emphasize the ways in which the main character's desire to achieve the American Dream motivates him to behave and act in certain ways.

F. Scott Fitzgerald (1896–1940) coined the phrase "Jazz Age" to describe the 1920s, and in many ways he embodied the decade. Born in Minnesota, he attended Princeton University. After his first novel, This Side of Paradise, brought him financial success, he married the vivacious Zelda Sayre. They became the golden couple of the 1920s, known for their glamorous, high society lifestyle. Sadly, their lives were soon overshadowed by debt, mental illness, and alcoholism. Fitzgerald's masterpiece, The Great Gatsby (1925), was not a popular success in his lifetime, though it is now considered a classic examination of the hidden pitfalls of achieving the American Dream.

Winter Dreams

Short Story by F. Scott Fitzgerald

AS YOU READ Pay attention to the character of Dexter, noticing how Judy influences Dexter throughout the story. Write down any questions you generate during reading.

I

Some of the caddies were poor as sin and lived in one-room houses with a neurasthenic¹ cow in the front yard, but Dexter Green's father owned the second best grocery-store in Black Bear—the best one was "The Hub," patronized by the wealthy people from Sherry Island—and Dexter caddied only for pocket-money.

In the fall when the days became crisp and gray, and the long Minnesota winter shut down like the white lid of a box, Dexter's skis moved over the snow that hid the fairways of the golf course. At these times the country gave him a feeling of profound melancholy—it offended him that the links should lie in enforced fallowness, haunted by ragged sparrows for the long season. It was dreary, too, that on the tees where the gay colors fluttered in summer there were now only the desolate sand-boxes knee-deep in crusted ice. When he crossed the

¹ neurasthenic (nŏŏr'əs-thĕn'ĭk): weak and lacking in vigor.

Winter Dreams **413**

The Crucible

Drama by Arthur Miller

Arthur Miller was born in New York City in 1915 into an upper-middle-class family. His comfortable early life changed when the Great Depression eroded his family's economic circumstances. Miller was unable to go to college until he earned the tuition money by working in a warehouse. Eventually, he attended the University of Michigan. Miller won several awards for his plays during college and chose to pursue a career in the theater. All My Sons and Death of a Salesman, a play that won a Pulitzer Prize in 1949, made Miller a star.

Around the same time, hearings were being conducted by Congress to identify suspected Communists. Miller was called to testify before the committee about his association with the American Communist Party. Although he admitted to having attended a few meetings years earlier, he refused to "name names" of other people involved in the meetings. As a result, he was cited for contempt of Congress; this conviction was later overturned. The events of this time period inspired him to write The Crucible, set during the Salem, Massachusetts, witch trials of 1692. He wrote the play to warn against mass hysteria and to plead for freedom and tolerance.

In general, Miller's writing explores issues relevant to contemporary readers, such as the complexities of family relationships, personal responsibility, and morality. Many consider him to be the 20th century's greatest American playwright.

The Crucible: **457**

"I rely heavily on novels and longer works."

This play about the 1692 witch trials in Salem, Massachusetts, includes events dealing with intolerance, abuse of authority, and unsubstantiated accusations—themes also related to McCarthyism in the mid-twentieth century.

"I love to concentrate on contemporary literature."

In this science fiction story, David Brin describes a future in which beings are immortal and society is perfect—in contrast to the drama, emotions, creativity, and progress that filled humans' lives in the past.

David Brin (b. 1950) is a writer whose work has won a host of awards, including the Hugo and Nebula awards for best science fiction. With an undergraduate degree in astrophysics, a master's in optics, a Ph.D. in physics, and a postdoctoral fellowship at the California Space Institute and Jet Propulsion Laboratory, Brin is uniquely qualified to write about science. His writing focuses on how advances in technology will change the lives of humans. He is perhaps best known for the novel The Postman (1985) and for his Uplift series.

Reality Check

Short Story by David Brin

AS YOU READ Pay attention to details that help you to understand the purpose of the story. Write down any questions you generate during reading.

This is a reality check. Please perform a soft interrupt now. Scan this text for embedded code and check against the verifier in the blind spot of your left eye. If there is no match, resume as you were: this message is not for you. You may rationalize it as mildly amusing entertainment-fluff in an otherwise serious science magazine. If the codes match, however, please commence gradually becoming aware of your true nature. You asked for a narrative-style wake-up call. So, to help the transition, here is a story.

Once upon a time, a mighty race grew perplexed by its loneliness. The universe seemed pregnant with possibilities. Physical laws were suited to generate abundant stars, complex chemistry and life. Logic suggested that creation should teem with visitors and voices; but it did not.

For a long time these creatures were engrossed by housekeeping chores—survival and cultural maturation. Only later did they lift their eyes to perceive their solitude. "Where is everybody?" they asked the taciturn stars. The answer—silence—was disturbing. Something had

taciturn
(tăs'ĭ-tûrn') adj. uncommunicative, withdrawn.

Reality Check **581**

COLLECTION 6 DIGITAL OVERVIEW

mySmartPlanner | eBook | myNotebook | myWriteSmart | fyi hmhfyi.com

Collection 6 Lessons	Media	Teach and Practice	
Student Edition | eBook	▶ **Video Links** H HISTORY A&E	**Close Reading and Evidence Tracking**	
ANCHOR TEXT — Short Story by F. Scott Fitzgerald **"Winter Dreams"**	◀ **Audio** "Winter Dreams"	**Close Read Screencasts** • Modeled Discussion (lines 5–515) • Modeled Discussion (lines 352–359) • Close Read application (lines 783–790)	**Strategies for Annotation** • Support Inferences • Analyze and Evaluate Characterization • Analyze and Infer Motivations • Analyze Precise Usage
CLOSE READER — Short Story by Tim O'Brien **"Ambush"**	◀ **Audio** "Ambush" ▶ **Video HISTORY®** *Vietnam in HD: On Patrol*		
Poems by Jean Toomer, Countee Cullen, and Arna Bontemps **Poems of the Harlem Renaissance**	◀ **Audio** Poems of the Harlem Renaissance		**Strategies for Annotation** • Demonstrate Knowledge of Foundational Works
CLOSE READER — Essay by Zora Neale Hurston **"How It Feels to Be Colored Me"** Poem by Langston Hughes **"The Weary Blues"**	◀ **Audio** "How It Feels to Be Colored Me"; "The Weary Blues"		
Poems by Robert Frost **"Mending Wall"** **"The Death of the Hired Man"**	◀ **Audio** "Mending Wall"; "The Death of the Hired Man"		**Strategies for Annotation** • Analyze Language • Analyze Structure
ANCHOR TEXT — Drama by Arthur Miller *The Crucible*	◀ **Audio** *The Crucible* ▶ **Video HISTORY®** *Salem Witch Trials*	**Close Read Screencasts** • Modeled Discussion (Act 1, lines 18–39 • Close Read application (Act 4, lines 906–928)	**Strategies for Annotation** • Analyze Drama Elements • Language and Style: Dialogue
CLOSE READER — Drama by Arthur Miller from *The Crucible*	◀ **Audio** from *The Crucible* ▶ **Video HISTORY** *Salem Witch Trials*		
Media Versions of *The Crucible* by Arthur Miller: Audio Version Production Images from Film Version	◀ **Audio** from *The Crucible*		

		Interactive Lessons	Lesson Assessments
	For Systematic Coverage of Writing and Speaking & Listening Standards	Writing Informative Texts Giving a Presentation	Writing Informative Texts Giving a Presentation

Assess		Extend	Reteach
Performance Task	**Online Assessment**	**Teacher eBook**	**Teacher eBook**
Writing Activity: Letters	Selection Test	**Analyze Structure** **Determine Theme > Interactive** **Whiteboard Activity >** Theme/Central Idea	**Analyze Story Elements and Support Inferences > Level Up Tutorial >** Character Types **Analyze Story Elements: Characterization and Motivation > Level Up Tutorial >** Methods of Characterization
Writing Task: Essay	Selection Test	**Analyze Language: Connotations**	**Demonstrate Knowledge of Foundational Works > Level Up Tutorial >** Imagery
Writing Activity: Interview Summary	Selection Test	**Demonstrate Knowledge of Foundational Works: Theme > Level Up Tutorial >** Theme	**Analyze Structure: Narrative Poem > Level Up Tutorial >** Plot Stages
Speaking Activity: Discussion Media Activity: Presentation Writing Activity: Analysis Writing Activity: Essay	Selection Test	**Conduct Research > Interactive** **Whiteboard Lesson >** Conducting Research on the Web	**Analyze Drama Elements > Level Up Tutorial >** Elements of Drama
Speaking Activity: Readers' Theater Writing Activity: Diagram Writing Activity: Captions	Selection Test	**Interpret a Drama**	**Compare Multiple Interpretations of a Drama > Level Up Tutorial >** Historical and Cultural Context

*my*SmartPlanner | eBook | *my*Notebook | *my* WriteSmart | fyi hmhfyi.com

Collection 6 Lessons	Media	Teach and Practice
Student Edition | eBook	▶ Video Links H HISTORY A&E	**Close Reading and Evidence Tracking**
Opinion and Dissents by the Supreme Court of the United States *Tinker* v. *Des Moines Independent Community School District*	◀ **Audio** *Tinker* v. *Des Moines Independent Community School District*	**Strategies for Annotation** • Delineate and Evaluate an Argument • Legal Terminology
Science Essay by Ray Kurzweil **"The Coming Merging of Mind and Machine"**	◀ **Audio** "The Coming Merging of Mind and Machine"	**Strategies for Annotation** • Analyze Author's Point of View
CLOSE READER **Essay by Freeman Dyson** **"Science, Guided by Ethics"**	◀ **Audio** "Science, Guided by Ethics"	
Short Story by David Brin **"Reality Check"**	◀ **Audio** "Reality Check"	**Strategies for Annotation** • Analyze Story Elements: Science Fiction • Nuances in Word Meanings
Argument by Jared Diamond **"The Ends of the World as We Know Them"**	◀ **Audio** "The Ends of the World as We Know Them" ▶ **Video HISTORY** *Environmental Degradation of Easter Island*	**Strategies for Annotation** • Cite Text Evidence • Patterns of Word Change
Poem by Tracy K. Smith **"The Universe as Primal Scream"**	◀ **Audio** "The Universe as Primal Scream"	**Strategies for Annotation** • Analyze Language
Collection 6 Performance Tasks: **A** Write an Argument **B** Participate in a Panel Discussion	fyi hmhfyi.com **hmhfyi.com**	**Interactive Lessons** **A** Writing an Argument **B** Using Textual Evidence **A** Writing as a Process **B** Participating in Collaborative **A** Using Textual Evidence Discussions

	For Systematic Coverage of Writing and Speaking & Listening Standards	**Interactive Lessons** Writing Informative Texts Giving a Presentation	**Lesson Assessments** Writing Informative Texts Giving a Presentation

Assess		Extend	Reteach
Performance Task	**Online Assessment**	**Teacher eBook**	**Teacher eBook**
Speaking Activity: Debate	Selection Test	**Constitutional Principles**	**Make Inferences > Level Up Tutorial >** Making Inferences
Writing Activity: Research Report	Selection Test	**Debate an Issue**	**Analyze Author's Point of View > Level Up Tutorial >** Tone
Media Activity: Analysis	Selection Test	**Coining New Terms**	**Analyze Story Elements: Science Fiction**
Media Activity: Presentation	Selection Test	**Determine Author's Purpose**	**Draw Conclusions > Level Up Tutorial >** Drawing Conclusions
Writing Activity: Summary	Selection Test	**Analyze Language: Allusions Analyzing Poetry < Interactive Whiteboard Lesson** < Examine Form	**Write Arguments > Interactive Lesson >** Writing Effective Arguments **Analyze Language > Level Up Tutorial >** Imagery
A Write an Argument **B** Participate in a Panel Discussion	Collection Test		

Collection 6 Lessons	Key Learning Objective	Performance Task
ANCHOR TEXT **Short Story by F. Scott Fitzgerald**　　**Lexile 1100** **"Winter Dreams," p. 413A**	**The student will be able to …** analyze character motivations in a short story and support their inferences about those motivations with evidence from the text	Writing Activity: Letters
Poems by Jean Toomer, Countee Cullen, and Arna Bontemps **Poems of the Harlem Renaissance, p. 438A**	**The student will be able to …** analyze and compare multiple works from a time period on the basis of topic and theme	Writing Task: Essay
Poems by Robert Frost **EXEMPLAR**　**"Mending Wall," p. 445A** **"The Death of the Hired Man," p. 445A**	**The student will be able to …** analyze the structure and language of poetry	Writing Activity: Interview Summary
ANCHOR TEXT **Drama by Arthur Miller** *The Crucible*, **p. 456A**	**The student will be able to …** identify and analyze elements of drama	Speaking Activity: Discussion Media Activity: Presentation Writing Activity: Analysis Writing Activity: Essay
Media Versions of *The Crucible* by Arthur Miller: **Audio Version, p. 543A** **Production Images from Film Version, p. 543A**	**The student will be able to …** analyze an audio excerpt and film production stills of a play for theme and characterization	Speaking Activity: Readers' Theater Writing Activity: Diagram Writing Activity: Captions

Collection 6 Performance Tasks:
A Write an Argument
B Participate in a Panel Discussion

Vocabulary Strategy	Language and Style	Student Instructional Support	CLOSE READER Selection
Precise Usage	Craft Effective Sentences	**Scaffolding for ELL Students:** • Idioms • Understand Past Perfect Tense • Analyze Language • Understand Organizational Patterns • Analyzing Transitions • Develop Reading Fluency **When Students Struggle:** • Understand Complex Sentence Structures • Understand Complex Writing • Concept Support • Analyze Language **To Challenge Students:** • Analyze Character • Independent Research	Short Story by Tim O'Brien "Ambush," p. 437c **Lexile 950**
		Scaffolding for ELL Students: • Understand Figurative Language **When Students Struggle:** Analyze Descriptive Language **To Challenge Students:** Search the Internet • Simulate a Poet's Style	Essay by Zora Neale Hurston "How It Feels to Be Colored Me" Poem by Langston Hughes "The Weary Blues," p. 444b **Lexile 950**
	Informal Style	**Scaffolding for ELL Students:** • Punctuation • Colloquialisms **When Students Struggle:** Developing Reading Fluency **To Challenge Students:** • Interpreting Symbolism	
	Dialogue	**Scaffolding for ELL Students:** 458, 462, 464, 466, 469, 471, 473, 475, 479, 480, 482, 483, 487, 488, 490, 491, 494, 495, 497, 499, 502, 505, 506, 509, 510, 512, 514, 516, 517, 518, 520, 521, 525, 527, 528, 529, 531, 532, 535, 536 **When Students Struggle:** 460, 463, 465, 470, 474, 478, 481, 485, 489, 493, 498, 501, 508, 511, 519, 524, 530, 533, 534, 537 **To Challenge Students:** 461, 468, 472, 477, 496, 513, 515, 539	
		Scaffolding for ELL Students: • Comprehension Support **When Students Struggle:** • Short Research Project	

Collection 6 Lessons		COMMON CORE Key Learning Objective	Performance Task
Opinion and Dissents by the Supreme Court of the United States *Tinker v. Des Moines Independent Community School District*, p. 549A	Lexile 1500	**The student will be able to …** delineate and evaluate a Supreme Court ruling's Constitutional principles and legal reasoning	Speaking Activity: Debate
EXEMPLAR Science Essay by Ray Kurzweil "The Coming Merging of Mind and Machine," p. 569A	Lexile 1260	**The student will be able to …** analyze and evaluate an author's point of view and the ideas and arguments in the text	Writing Activity: Research Report
Short Story by David Brin "Reality Check," p. 581A	Lexile 920	**The student will be able to …** analyze a work of science fiction basing their inferences and interpretations on a close reading of the text	Media Activity: Analysis
Argument by Jared Diamond "The Ends of the World as We Know Them," p. 587A	Lexile 1230	**The student will be able to …** understand how an author structures and presents a complex argument	Media Activity: Presentation
Poem by Tracy K. Smith "The Universe as Primal Scream," p. 597A		**The student will be able to …** analyze language in poetry	Writing Activity: Summary

Collection 6 Performance Tasks:
A Write an Argument
B Participate in a Panel Discussion

Vocabulary Strategy	Language and Style	Student Instructional Support	CLOSE READER Selection
Legal Terminology	Comparing Writers' Styles	**Scaffolding for ELL Students:** • Culture • Commonly Confused Words • Synonyms and Antonyms • Prefixes • Compound Nouns **When Students Struggle:** • Determine Meaning of Words • Paraphrase for Understanding • Use Graphic Organizer to Analyze Text • Summarize • Question for Comprehension **To Challenge Students:** • Debate the Issue • Respond to Justice Black	
Etymology		**Scaffolding for ELL Students:** • Understanding Prefixes • Identify Words Used as Both Nouns and Verbs • Define Words Using Context Clues **When Students Struggle:** • Understand Main Concept • Understand Key Words and Phrases **To Challenge Students:** • Examine Predictions	Essay by Freeman Dyson "Science, Guided by Ethics," p. 542b **Lexile 1230**
Nuances in Word Meaning		**Scaffolding for ELL Students:** • Idioms **When Students Struggle:** • Question for Understanding	
Patterns of Word Change	Informative Writing	**Scaffolding for ELL Students:** • Hyphenated Words • Find Synonyms • Understand the Suffix -tion **When Students Struggle:** • Strategies for Comprehension • Understand the Use of Transitions	
		Scaffolding for ELL Students: • Analyze Words **When Students Struggle:** • Develop Reading Fluency	

*my*SmartPlanner — Create lesson plans and access resources online.

Life in a Global Society

Collection 6 Historical Introduction

Why This Text?

Students often encounter literary and informational texts that assume that the reader has some knowledge of key historical events, facts, ideas, and issues. The historical introduction to Collection 6 presents information about the period in the United States from 1910 to 2010, when global conflicts and new leaps in technology altered the way people experienced reality and thought about the future.

Key Learning Objective: The student will be able to analyze the selections in the collection in terms of an historical context.

Common Core Standards

RL 10 Read and comprehend literature in the grades 11-CCR text complexity band.

RI 3 Analyze ideas or events and explain how individuals, ideas, or events interact and develop.

RI 7 Integrate and evaluate sources of information presented in different formats.

RI 10 Read and comprehend literary nonfiction in the grades 11-CCR text complexity band.

Text Complexity Rubric

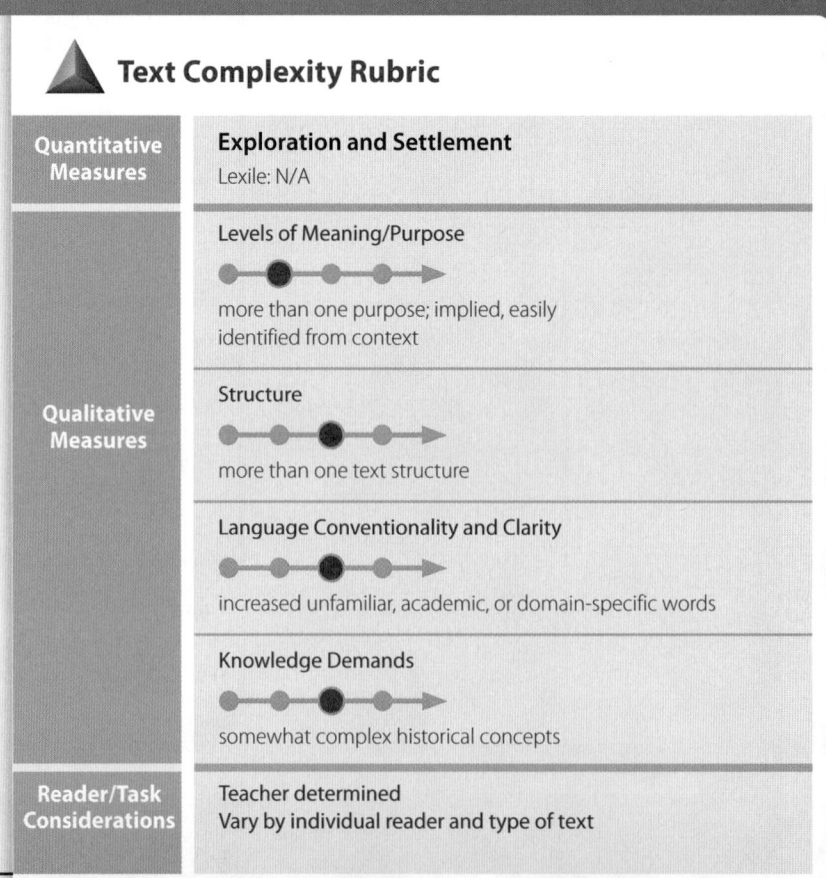

Quantitative Measures	**Exploration and Settlement** Lexile: N/A
Qualitative Measures	**Levels of Meaning/Purpose** more than one purpose; implied, easily identified from context
	Structure more than one text structure
	Language Conventionality and Clarity increased unfamiliar, academic, or domain-specific words
	Knowledge Demands somewhat complex historical concepts
Reader/Task Considerations	Teacher determined Vary by individual reader and type of text

For more context and historical background, students can view the video "The Class of the 20th Century: 1963–1968" in their eBooks.

Sensitive Language: This video contains two instances of the word *bastard* (in the sense of "unpleasant") in talking about LBJ, describing him and his view of others.

Life in a Global Society Explain that this section establishes the historical context for the selections in this collection. It introduces events that strongly influenced writers of the past century, including two World Wars, the civil rights movement, and technological advances that both revolutionized how people communicate and affected the quality of life on Earth.

The Rise of Modern Literature

COMMON CORE   RL 10, RI 3, RI 7, RI 10

New weapons such as rapid-fire machine guns made the carnage created by World War I much greater than any previous war. Witnessing this destruction drove modernist writers to doubt the worth of a civilization that could allow such a conflict to take place. At the same time, life in busy urban areas was causing people to feel isolated from one another.

Realist writers had tried to capture the reality around them. Modernist writers, on the other hand, turned away from an alienating world that they ultimately found unable to replicate using traditional forms of literature. Many focused instead on the individual's inner life, sometimes using a technique called stream of consciousness in which they ignored narrative plot and complete sentences in favor of the scattered thoughts running through a character's mind.

An Era of Near-Constant War

Works of science fiction provide modern readers with a set of common references and terms that they can use when discussing fears raised by new technologies and tense political issues. For example, Ray Bradbury's novel *Fahrenheit 451* describes a future society in which firemen burn all books to suppress ideas. People today often allude to this novel when referring to real-world censorship.

BIO

Life in a Global Society

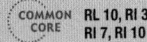
COMMON CORE   RL 10, RI 3, RI 7, RI 10

At the beginning of the 21st century, Americans live in a globally connected world. The experience of two world wars and advances in technology have eliminated our isolation from other countries. Solving complex economic, social, and environmental problems now often requires global cooperation. Contemporary literature reflects the anxiety of an era changing rapidly for both good and bad.

THE RISE OF MODERN LITERATURE Change was the only constant for Americans in the early 20th century. In 30 short years they faced a world war, an economic boom followed by the Great Depression, and shifting attitudes toward women's place in society. However, the shock of World War I (1914–1918) was perhaps the most influential force on American writers of the early 20th century.

Modernist writers, many of whom spent time living and writing in Europe, responded to the social and policical upheaval of the war by experimenting with innovative styles and forms, and by focusing on the alienation of the individual in modern society. Transitional poets such as T.S. Eliot linked rich poetic traditions with modern ideas and concerns. Eliot's *The Waste Land* stands out as one of the most representative and influential modernist poems. Other poets, such as Robert Frost, reinvented traditional genres, such as pastoral poetry. Modern writers like F. Scott Fitzgerald, Ernest Hemingway, and John Steinbeck broke with the traditions of the past, turning to new methods and stylistic devices.

AN ERA OF NEAR-CONSTANT WAR World War II (1939–1945) was a catastrophe of epic dimensions: the first war in history in which more civilians died than soldiers. America and the Soviet Union, allies during the war, emerged as rival superpowers and engaged in a decades-long "Cold War," competing in a deadly arms race that threatened the world with a nuclear apocalypse. As technological sophistication and political anxiety increased, science fiction writers—for example, Ray Bradbury and Kurt Vonnegut—explored possible future scenarios, sometimes in bleak post-apocalyptic or dystopian worlds.

In an effort to contain the spread of communism, the U.S. military became deeply involved in civil wars first in Korea and then in Vietnam. Although the Cold War ended with the break up of the Soviet Union in 1991, American warfare did not.

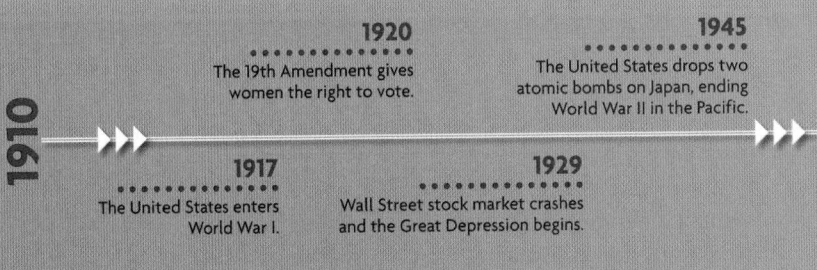

1910

1917 The United States enters World War I.

1920 The 19th Amendment gives women the right to vote.

1929 Wall Street stock market crashes and the Great Depression begins.

1945 The United States drops two atomic bombs on Japan, ending World War II in the Pacific.

SCAFFOLDING FOR ELL STUDENTS

Vocabulary: Multiple-Meaning Words Students may know one meaning of some of the multiple-meaning words used in this historical background essay yet not be familiar with the meaning used here. Remind students that they can look up alternate meanings in a dictionary and then try out each meaning in context to determine the best meaning.

ASK STUDENTS to work in mixed-language ability groups to identify and define potentially confusing multiple-meaning words from this essay such as *boom* (page 411), *shock* (page 411), *engaged* (page 411), *arms* (page 411), and *counter* (page 412).

The Civil Rights Movement

The Harlem Renaissance flourished during the first half of the 20th century, from 1918–1937. This important literary and artistic movement helped African Americans draw inspiration from their cultural heritage, as well as establish a sense of self that was separate from the way Caucasian society had tried to view and define them previously. Instead of relying on Caucasian writers to write books and plays about the African American experience or to record and preserve tales of black folklore, the writers of the Harlem Renaissance now stepped forward to present their own authentic reflections of African American life.

Some works of literature that came out of this movement focused on instilling a sense of pride in African Americans. Others tried to capture and convey what it felt like to live as an African American person in places ranging from the industrial cities of the north to the rural communities of the south. The power of this literary movement inspired and ensured the success of the later civil rights movement.

Technology and the Environment

When people store and access online information that was previously printed using paper and ink, resources such as trees and the power needed to manufacture print media texts are conserved. At the same time, however, maintaining the Internet takes enormous amounts of power and creates a whole new mass of pollution.

Tens of thousands of data centers, each full of rows of servers, are needed to store and transmit the information that people use and access online each day. Although companies are working to reduce the amount of electricity wasted while running these centers, the amount of data the public produces and consumes is increasing all the time. Furthermore, some centers run background generators as insurance against a power failure, which creates diesel fumes that pollute the air.

In that same year, U.S. troops were sent to counter the Iraqi invasion of Kuwait. On September 11, 2001, attacks on the World Trade Center and the Pentagon led to U.S. invasions of Afghanistan and Iraq. Global violence and the spread of nuclear weapons to numerous countries have created a sense of instability that has profoundly affected writers and nonwriters alike.

THE CIVIL RIGHTS MOVEMENT The civil rights movement of the 1950s and 1960s is perhaps the most important social change in modern times. In 1954, the Supreme Court's *Brown v. Board of Education* ruling struck down school segregation as unconstitutional. Dr. Martin Luther King Jr. emerged as a leader during these times, advocating nonviolent civil disobedience. Congress eventually passed the 1964 Civil Rights Act outlawing segregation in public places and guaranteeing legal equality to African American citizens. In succeeding years, other groups drew on the ideals and tactics of the civil rights movement in their fights to end discrimination based on gender, ethnicity, and sexual orientation.

As the civil rights movement gained momentum, African American writers began to gain wider recognition. In a variety of genres, authors made powerful statements about the harmful effects of racism and the need for change. While earlier writers of color often focused on the experience of discrimination, contemporary writing is expressive of the individual, culture, or place, while still managing to speak to universal human concerns.

TECHNOLOGY AND THE ENVIRONMENT In 1910, automobiles, telephones, and electricity were not yet common conveniences for most people. Today, robotics has transformed manufacturing and medicine, and advances in communications technology—especially the Internet and mobile devices—give people around the world instant access to information. A big question of our time is how to make the best use of this technology in a way that enhances the quality of life for all.

The growth of technology has not come without costs, especially to the environment. Cars, trucks, and planes, as well as electric power plants, have largely relied on nonrenewable fossil fuels such as oil, coal, and natural gas. While the supply of these natural resources once seemed infinite, we now know that they will eventually be exhausted. In addition, pollution from these fuels has damaged the earth, air, and water on which all life depends and has contributed to global climate change. Writers of fiction and nonfiction seek to understand the implications of these challenges for life today and for the future of the human race.

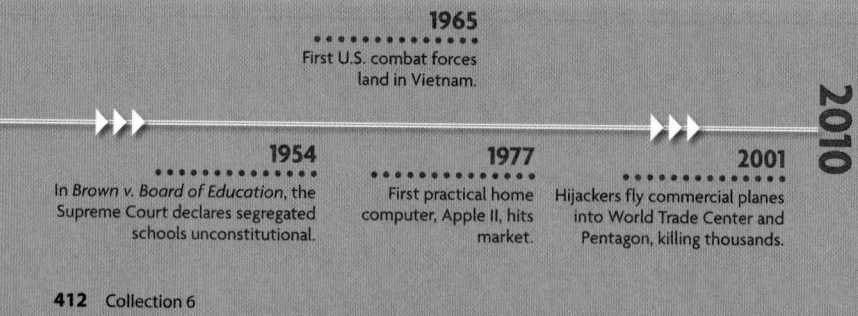

1965
First U.S. combat forces land in Vietnam.

1954
In *Brown v. Board of Education*, the Supreme Court declares segregated schools unconstitutional.

1977
First practical home computer, Apple II, hits market.

2001
Hijackers fly commercial planes into World Trade Center and Pentagon, killing thousands.

2010

412 Collection 6

WHEN STUDENTS STRUGGLE . . .

Comprehension Support: Some students may not understand the points being made in this essay. Direct students to different paragraphs in the essay and have them first summarize the information and then discuss how it relates to the overall topic.

ASK STUDENTS to reread the last paragraph on page 412. Have them summarize what it talks about—that new kinds of technology may have improved life, but they are using up fuel sources that cannot be replaced and polluting the environment at the same time. Then ask students to explain what point the author is making by including this information—for example, one topic writers today grapple with is concern for a future where the environment has been ruined and people lack the fossil fuels necessary to run the technologies upon which life has become dependent.

Analyze Relationships Between Ideas

RI 3

TEACH

Explain that students will be able to follow and comprehend the information being presented in a nonfiction text better if they understand the type of structures the author uses to organize the text.

Review some structures an author might use, pointing out examples from this essay:

- **Sequence of Events:** In the second paragraph on page 412, the author relates in chronological order several important events that made up the civil rights movement, building to the point that this movement inspired other movements that helped other groups gain their own rights.
- **Compare/Contrast:** In the third paragraph on page 412, the author juxtaposes, or places next to each other, descriptions of two different types of writers of color, helping the reader to easily compare these two types to each other.
- **Cause and Effect Relationships:** In the final paragraph on page 412, the author discusses how using new technologies has caused the effects of decreased fossil fuel supplies and pollution.

Discuss the reasons why an author might use some or all of these text structures while deciding how to present information to a reader.

PRACTICE AND APPLY

Have small groups of students work together to review this essay and identify other examples of these three kinds of text structures from it. In each case, have them explain which text structure is being used and discuss how the author is using it to communicate important ideas.

Analyze Accounts in Different Mediums

RI 7

TEACH

Review how authors might present the same type of information by using different mediums depending on why they are providing this information to their audience. Note that this historical background essay presents information about important dates in history by using the mediums of running text and a timeline.

Examine the timeline with students and review its features—how the events move chronologically through time as the reader reads from left to right and how each date is labeled with a year and a callout sentence that provides specific information about why this date is significant. Then identify different ways that dates are presented in the running text:

- To refer to a moment within a particular century: *in the early 20th century.*
- To specify the particular range of years during which a lengthy event took place: *World War I (1914–1918).*
- To refer to an event that took place over several decades: *the civil rights movement of the 1950s and 1960s.*
- To refer to an event that took place in a single year: *the break-up of the Soviet Union in 1991.*
- To refer to an event that took place on a single day: *September 11, 2001.*

Next, compare and contrast how the same date might be presented in each medium and why:

- For example, the running text provides information tucked efficiently away in parentheses about how long World War II lasted, something that could be difficult to do with a timeline that is designed to mark single moments in time. What the timeline is able to do neatly, on the other hand, is to pinpoint the two different years when the United States entered the war and when it performed an action that ended the Pacific conflict.
- For example, on the timeline, the 2001 entry only provides basic facts about 9/11, while the mention of 9/11 in the running text is able to link this event to other events in history by establishing this attack as the cause of subsequent U.S. invasions of Afghanistan and Iraq.

PRACTICE AND APPLY

Have students work independently to read and analyze another nonfiction piece that uses both running text and a timeline to convey information about dates.

my SmartPlanner Create lesson plans and access resources online.

ANCHOR TEXT Winter Dreams

Short Story by F. Scott Fitzgerald

Why This Text?

Studying characters, their motivations, and actions gives students a deeper insight into classic texts. This story by F. Scott Fitzgerald shows how a character's actions and motivations can inform a theme and provide commentary on social issues.

> ▶ **View It!**
> Professional Development Podcast:
> **Teaching Argument**

Key Learning Objective: Students will be able to analyze character motivations in a short story and support their inferences about those motivations with evidence from the text.

For additional practice:

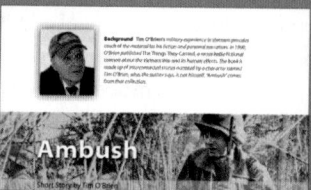

Close Reader selection
"Ambush"
Short Story by Tim O'Brien

COMMON CORE Common Core Standards

RL 1 Cite textual evidence to support inferences.
RL 2 Determine themes of a text.
RL 3 Analyze the impact of the author's choices regarding how to develop and relate elements of a story.
RL 4 Determine the meaning of words and phrases, including figurative and connotative meanings.
RL 5 Analyze how an author's choices concerning how to structure specific parts of a text contribute to its overall meaning.
W 3a Engage the reader by setting out a situation and its significance, establishing multiple points of view, and introducing characters.
W 3d Use telling details to convey a vivid picture.
L 3a Vary syntax for effect; apply an understanding of syntax.
L 4c Consult reference materials.

▲ Text Complexity Rubric

Quantitative Measures	**Winter Dreams** Lexile: 1100L
Qualitative Measures	**Levels of Meaning/Purpose** single level of complex meaning
	Structure several shifts in chronology; use of flashback and flash forward
	Language Conventionality and Clarity more complex descriptions
	Knowledge Demands moderately complex theme
Reader/Task Considerations	Teacher determined Vary by individual reader and type of text

CLOSE READ

Background Born in 1896 in Minnesota, F. Scott Fitzgerald was the namesake of distant cousin Francis Scott Key. While his critical success as a novelist was *The Great Gatsby*, he was not well-paid for his novels. Most of his income came from writing magazine stories.

AS YOU READ Direct students to use the As You Read note to focus their reading.

Analyze Story Elements: Motivation (LINES 1–5)

COMMON CORE RL 3

Tell students that a character's **motivation** is his or her reason for thinking and acting as he or she does. Explain that sometimes the narrator tells the reader a character's motivation and sometimes the reader must infer it.

Ⓐ CITE TEXT EVIDENCE Have students read lines 1–5 and explain Dexter's motivation for being a caddy. *(In line 5, the narrator says that Dexter caddies for pocket money.)* Ask students how this makes Dexter different from some of the other caddies. *(Some of the caddies work because they are "poor as sin.")*

Support Inferences

COMMON CORE RL 1

(LINES 6–13)

Remind students that readers must draw **inferences,** or logical conclusions based on details in the text. To make valid inferences, they must combine their knowledge and experience with specific textual evidence.

Ⓑ CITE TEXT EVIDENCE to reread lines 6–13 and infer when Dexter prefers to be on the golf course and cite textual evidence. *(He prefers summertime: he describes the golf course as "dreary" and "desolate" during winter.)*

F. Scott Fitzgerald *(1896–1940) coined the phrase "Jazz Age" to describe the 1920s, and in many ways he embodied the decade. Born in Minnesota, he attended Princeton University. After his first novel, This Side of Paradise, brought him financial success, he married the vivacious Zelda Sayre. They became the golden couple of the 1920s, known for their glamorous, high society lifestyle. Sadly, their lives were soon overshadowed by debt, mental illness, and alcoholism. Fitzgerald's masterpiece, The Great Gatsby (1925), was not a popular success in his lifetime, though it is now considered a classic examination of the hidden pitfalls of achieving the American Dream.*

Winter Dreams

Short Story by F. Scott Fitzgerald

AS YOU READ Pay attention to the character of Dexter, noticing how Judy influences Dexter throughout the story. Write down any questions you generate during reading.

I

Some of the caddies were poor as sin and lived in one-room houses with a neurasthenic[1] cow in the front yard, but Dexter Green's father owned the second best grocery-store in Black Bear—the best one was "The Hub," patronized by the wealthy people from Sherry Island—and Dexter caddied only for pocket-money.

Close Read

In the fall when the days became crisp and gray, and the long Minnesota winter shut down like the white lid of a box, Dexter's skis moved over the snow that hid the fairways of the golf course. At these times the country gave him a feeling of profound melancholy—it
10 offended him that the links should lie in enforced fallowness, haunted by ragged sparrows for the long season. It was dreary, too, that on the tees where the gay colors fluttered in summer there were now only the desolate sand-boxes knee-deep in crusted ice. When he crossed the

_____
[1] **neurasthenic** (noͦor´əs-thĕn´ĭk): weak and lacking in vigor.

Image Credits: (t) ©Minnesota Historical Society/Historical/Corbis; (b) ©Anneka/Shutterstock

---

Close Read Screencasts 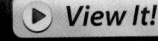 ► *View It!*

Modeled Discussions

Have students click the *Close Read* icons in their eBooks to access screencasts in which readers discuss and annotate the following key passages:

- In the fall . . . against the hard, dimensionless glare. (lines 5–15)
- During dinner . . . and deliberately changed the atmosphere. (lines 352–359)
- As a class, view and discuss at least one of these videos. Then have students pair up to do an independent close read of an additional passage— For the first time in years the tears were streaming . . . where his winter dreams flourished . . . . (lines 783–790)

Support Inferences

COMMON CORE RL 1

(LINES 16–36)

Explain that authors use a variety of details to provide readers with clues about plot and character. These details can help them draw inferences and make connections. Some details are more obvious, like a character's actions. Others are more subtle, like a character's feelings or a narrator's word choice.

 **CITE TEXT EVIDENCE** Have students reread lines 16–36 and infer what the four seasons represent to Dexter. *(Summer: excitement; fall: enchantment with the upper-class; winter: dreams of escaping his middle-class life; spring: facing the reality of his life. Textual evidence includes the following: Remembering summer's "brilliant impressions," Dexter is filled with "hope" "and triumph" in the fall as he imagines commanding "imaginary audiences and armies." Winter is filled with dreams of not only becoming one of the men at the club but besting them. Dexter views spring as "dismal"— winter and its dreams end and the golf season begins.)*

Analyze Story Elements: Motivation (LINES 37–43)

COMMON CORE RL 3

Tell students that other characters' thoughts, comments, reactions, and perceptions also offer insight into a character's motives.

CITE TEXT EVIDENCE Have students read lines 37–43 and note what Mr. Jones thinks of Dexter's caddying skills. *(Mr. Jones thinks he is the "best caddy.")* What does Mr. Jones beg of Dexter? What is Dexter's reaction? *(He begs him not to quit. Dexter doesn't change his mind.)* What is the first reason Dexter gives Mr. Jones for quitting? *(He doesn't want to caddy anymore.)*

Explain that **traits** are distinguishing qualities or characteristics that define a character's personality.

ASK STUDENTS Ask students what character trait they can infer based on Dexter's response to Mr. Jones's request. *(The fact that he won't change his mind suggests he is determined.)*

---

hills the wind blew cold as misery, and if the sun was out he tramped with his eyes squinted up against the hard dimensionless glare.

In April the winter ceased abruptly. The snow ran down into Black Bear Lake scarcely tarrying for the early golfers to brave the season with red and black balls. Without elation, without an interval of moist glory, the cold was gone.

20   Dexter knew that there was something dismal about this Northern spring, just as he knew there was something gorgeous about the fall. Fall made him clinch his hands and tremble and repeat idiotic sentences to himself, and make brisk abrupt gestures of command to imaginary audiences and armies. October filled him with hope which November raised to a sort of ecstatic triumph, and in this mood the fleeting brilliant impressions of the summer at Sherry Island were ready grist to his mill.[2] He became a golf champion and defeated Mr. T. A. Hedrick in a marvelous match played a hundred times over the fairways of his imagination, a match each detail of which he changed

30 about untiringly—sometimes he won with almost laughable ease, sometimes he came up magnificently from behind. Again, stepping from a Pierce-Arrow automobile,[3] like Mr. Mortimer Jones, he strolled frigidly into the lounge of the Sherry Island Golf Club—or perhaps, surrounded by an admiring crowd, he gave an exhibition of fancy diving from the spring-board of the club raft. . . . Among those who watched him in open-mouthed wonder was Mr. Mortimer Jones.

And one day it came to pass that Mr. Jones—himself and not his ghost—came up to Dexter with tears in his eyes and said that Dexter was the — — best caddy in the club, and wouldn't he decide not to quit
40 if Mr. Jones made it worth his while, because every other — — caddy in the club lost one ball a hole for him—regularly—

"No, sir," said Dexter decisively, "I don't want to caddy any more." Then, after a pause: "I'm too old."

"You're not more than fourteen. Why the devil did you decide just this morning that you wanted to quit? You promised that next week you'd go over to the State tournament with me."

"I decided I was too old."

Dexter handed in his "A Class" badge, collected what money was due him from the caddy-master, and walked home to Black Bear
50 Village.

"The best — — caddy I ever saw," shouted Mr. Mortimer Jones over a drink that afternoon. "Never lost a ball! Willing! Intelligent! Quiet! Honest! Grateful!"

The little girl who had done this was eleven—beautifully ugly as little girls are apt to be who are destined after a few years to be inexpressibly lovely and bring no end of misery to a great number of men. The spark, however, was perceptible. There was a general

---

[2] **grist to his mill:** something that he could make good use of.

[3] **Pierce-Arrow automobile:** a luxury car of the day.

SCAFFOLDING FOR ELL STUDENTS

Idioms The phrase "made it worth his while" (line 40) is an idiom, or example of local speech, that means something different from the words' literal meaning. Explain that authors use idioms to make their writing sound more like real speech.

· Read aloud lines 37–41. Then ask students, "What does this idiom mean?" *(to pay him extra money, enough to change his mind about quitting)*

· Ask students how this idiom contributes to the passage. *(It shows that Mr. Jones thinks money solves all problems. It foreshadows the gulf between wealthy members of the club and the people who work for them, such as Dexter.)*

· Help students interpret other idioms, including "pocket-money" (line 5), "grist to his mill" (line 27), and "open-mouthed wonder" (line 36).

ungodliness in the way her lips twisted down at the corners when she
smiled, and in the—Heaven help us!—in the almost passionate quality
60 of her eyes. Vitality is born early in such women. It was utterly in
evidence now, shining through her thin frame in a sort of glow.

She had come eagerly out onto the course at nine o'clock with a
white linen nurse and five small new golf-clubs in a white canvas bag
which the nurse was carrying. When Dexter first saw her she was
standing by the caddy house, rather ill at ease and trying to conceal
the fact by engaging her nurse in an obviously unnatural conversation
graced by startling and irrelevant grimaces from herself.

"Well, it's certainly a nice day, Hilda," Dexter heard her say. She
drew down the corners of her mouth, smiled, and glanced furtively
70 around, her eyes in transit falling for an instant on Dexter.

Then to the nurse:

"Well, I guess there aren't very many people out here this
morning, are there?"

The smile again—radiant, **blatantly** artificial—convincing.

"I don't know what we're supposed to do now," said the nurse,
looking nowhere in particular.

"Oh, that's all right. I'll fix it up."

Dexter stood perfectly still, his mouth slightly ajar. He knew that
if he moved forward a step his stare would be in her line of vision—if
80 he moved backward he would lose his full view of her face. For a
moment he had not realized how young she was. Now he remembered
having seen her several times the year before—in bloomers.[4]

Suddenly, involuntarily, he laughed, a short abrupt laugh—then,
startled by himself, he turned and began to walk quickly away.

"Boy!"

Dexter stopped.

"Boy—"

Beyond question he was addressed. Not only that, but he was
treated to that absurd smile, that preposterous smile—the memory of
90 which at least a dozen men were to carry into middle age.

"Boy, do you know where the golf teacher is?"

"He's giving a lesson."

"Well, do you know where the caddy-master is?"

"He isn't here yet this morning."

"Oh." For a moment this baffled her. She stood alternately on her
right and left foot.

"We'd like to get a caddy," said the nurse. "Mrs. Mortimer Jones
sent us out to play golf, and we don't know how without we get a
caddy."

100 Here she was stopped by an ominous glance from Miss Jones,
followed immediately by the smile.

---

[4] **bloomers:** baggy pants that end just below the knee, formerly worn by girls.

Winter Dreams **415**

blatantly
(blāt´nt-lə) *adv.* in an
offensively obvious,
unashamed manner.

APPLYING ACADEMIC VOCABULARY

simulated	virtual

As you discuss "Winter Dreams," incorporate the following academic
vocabulary words: *simulated* and *virtual*. In analyzing themes of Fitzgerald's
story, ask students to find examples of things that the characters value
that have only **simulated** value. Talk to students about the aspects of the
real world that Dexter lives in versus aspects from the **virtual** world of his
winter dreams.

TEACH

CLOSE READ

Analyze Story Elements: Motivation (LINES 62–67)

Tell students that physical description (clothing,
appearance, expressions) as well as the image a
character wants to portray to other characters also
offer key details to help them infer characters' traits.

E **ASK STUDENTS** to reread lines 62–64 and infer
the image Judy wants to project and the character
trait that suggests. *(She wants to look stylish and
sophisticated. Judy is very concerned with appearances.)*

Support Inferences

(LINES 85–91)

Explain that drawing inferences requires close reading
of the text. Point out that well-written dialogue
can convey tone of voice and reveal a character's
temperament and attitude.

F **CITE TEXT EVIDENCE** Draw students' attention
to the three times Judy addresses Dexter in lines
85–91. Ask students to infer Judy's tone of voice,
temperament, and attitude toward Dexter. Have them
cite text evidence to support the inferences. *(The one-
word address followed by an exclamation point in line
85 and a dash in line 87 suggests a sharp tone of voice
and a demanding, impatient temperament. Her attitude
is demeaning and patronizing, drawing attention to
their different stations in life: she is younger yet calls him
"Boy" and makes no attempt to be polite.)*

CRITICAL VOCABULARY

blatantly: Dexter thinks Judy's smile is obviously
not sincere.

ASK STUDENTS how Dexter figures out that Judy's
smile is "blatantly artificial." *(Dexter realizes that Judy
does not know how to golf, so it's obvious to him that
any pleasantries she displays are insincere.)*

Analyze Story Elements: Motivation (LINES 120–125)

COMMON CORE RL 3

Tell students that in order to determine a character's traits and motivations, they must first make inferences based on close reading.

G **ASK STUDENTS** to reread lines 120–125. How did the nurse refer to Dexter? *(She called him "a little caddy.")* Have students infer how the nurse's comment and Judy's reaction to Dexter's response made him feel. *(offended)* What character trait would cause him to feel that way? *(pride)*

Analyze Structure

(LINES 136–142)

COMMON CORE RL 5

Tell students that authors may use **direct address,** a technique in which the narrator speaks directly to the reader, providing insight beyond the scope of the story. Fitzgerald adds to the effect of direct address with a **flash forward,** a device that interrupts the narrative to give readers a glimpse into the future.

H **ASK STUDENTS** to infer what Fitzgerald means by "stuff" in line 140. *(essence, core idea)* Ask students to explain what the reader learns from the direct address and flash forward in lines 136–142 that could not have been inferred from the narrative to this point. *(Dexter continues to have winter dreams that affect his life in significant ways. Although the details of the dreams change over time, the basic notion in them remains the same.)*

Tell students that a section break in a short story signals some type of shift, such as time, point of view, or setting.

CITE TEXT EVIDENCE Have students identify what type of shift the section break signals and cite textual evidence. *(It signals a shift in time: "several years later.")*

"There aren't any caddies here except me," said Dexter to the nurse, "and I got to stay here in charge until the caddy-master gets here."

"Oh."

Miss Jones and her retinue now withdrew, and at a proper distance from Dexter became involved in a heated conversation, which was concluded by Miss Jones taking one of the clubs and hitting it on the ground with violence. For further emphasis she raised it again and
110 was about to bring it down smartly upon the nurse's bosom, when the nurse seized the club and twisted it from her hands.

"You little mean old *thing!*" cried Miss Jones wildly.

Another argument ensued. Realizing that the elements of comedy were implied in the scene, Dexter several times began to laugh, but each time restrained the laugh before it reached audibility. He could not resist the monstrous conviction that the little girl was justified in beating the nurse.

The situation was resolved by the fortuitous appearance of the caddy-master, who was appealed to immediately by the nurse.
120 "Miss Jones is to have a little caddy, and this one says he can't go."

"Mr. McKenna said I was to wait here till you came," said Dexter quickly.

"Well, he's here now." Miss Jones smiled cheerfully at the caddy-master. Then she dropped her bag and set off at a haughty mince[5] toward the first tee.

"Well?" The caddy-master turned to Dexter. "What you standing there like a dummy for? Go pick up the young lady's clubs."

"I don't think I'll go out today," said Dexter.

"You don't—"
130 "I think I'll quit."

The enormity of his decision frightened him. He was a favorite caddy, and the thirty dollars a month he earned through the summer were not to be made elsewhere around the lake. But he had received a strong emotional shock, and his perturbation required a violent and immediate outlet.

It is not so simple as that, either. As so frequently would be the case in the future, Dexter was unconsciously dictated to by his winter dreams.

II

Now, of course, the quality and the seasonability of these winter
140 dreams varied, but the stuff of them remained. They persuaded Dexter several years later to pass up a business course at the State university—his father, prospering now, would have paid his way—for

---

[5] **at a haughty mince:** taking short, dainty steps in an arrogant, snobbish way.

WHEN STUDENTS STRUGGLE . . .

Fitzgerald sometimes uses complex sentence structures. Share the following strategies to help students understand sentences with multiple phrases and clauses.

- Model how to break down lines 106–109 into clauses and phrases. Then have students break longer sentences into several clauses and phrases.

Miss Jones and her retinue now withdrew, and at a proper distance from Dexter became involved in a heated conversation, which was concluded by Miss Jones taking one of the clubs and hitting it on the ground with violence.

the **precarious** advantage of attending an older and more famous university in the East, where he was bothered by his scanty funds. But do not get the impression, because his winter dreams happened to be concerned at first with musings on the rich, that there was anything merely snobbish in the boy. He wanted not association with glittering things and glittering people—he wanted the glittering things themselves. Often he reached out for the best without knowing why he
150 wanted it—and sometimes he ran up against the mysterious denials and prohibitions in which life indulges. It is with one of those denials and not with his career as a whole that this story deals.

He made money. It was rather amazing. After college he went to the city from which Black Bear Lake draws its wealthy patrons. When he was only twenty-three and had been there not quite two years, there were already people who liked to say: "Now *there's* a boy—" All about him rich men's sons were peddling bonds precariously, or investing patrimonies precariously, or plodding through the two dozen volumes of the "George Washington Commercial Course," but Dexter
160 borrowed a thousand dollars on his college degree and his confident mouth, and bought a partnership in a laundry.

It was a small laundry when he went into it but Dexter made a specialty of learning how the English washed fine woolen golf-stockings without shrinking them, and within a year he was catering to the trade that wore knickerbockers.[6] Men were insisting that their Shetland hose and sweaters go to his laundry just as they had insisted on a caddy who could find golf-balls. A little later he was doing their

precarious
(prĭ-kâr´ē-əs) *adj.*
unstable; uncertain.

---

[6] **knickerbockers:** loose pants that end in a gathering just below the knee and are worn with long socks. Formerly popular as golf wear.

Winter Dreams **417**

Analyze Structure

COMMON CORE **RL 5**

(LINES 145–161)

Discuss how direct address establishes an immediate relationship between reader and narrator.

ⓘ **CITE TEXT EVIDENCE** Have students reread lines 145–152 and cite the two sentences in which Fitzgerald addresses the audience directly. *("But do not get the impression . . . in the boy" and "It is with one of those denials . . . that this story deals.")*

Explain further that authors use **narrative summary** to inform readers. Narrative summary serves as a shortcut, allowing authors to summarize less interesting parts of the plot so they can focus on detailing important scenes.

ASK STUDENTS to infer why Fitzgerald uses narrative summary in lines 145–161 instead of writing a scene. *(Nothing important related to his winter dreams happened after Dexter left college until he bought a partnership in the laundry.)*

Analyze Story Elements: Motivation (LINES 162–167)

COMMON CORE **RL 3**

Tell students that examining key circumstances or events in a character's life will help them infer and analyze his motivation.

ⓙ **CITE TEXT EVIDENCE** Draw students' attention to lines 162–167 and have them cite the two significant events that Fitzgerald compares. *(Dexter's successes on the golf course and with the laundry.)* Ask students to infer Dexter's goals both as a caddy and business owner. *(Dexter strove to be the best in both circumstances.)*

CRITICAL VOCABULARY

precarious: Dexter puts himself in a tenuous situation; he is getting a more prestigious education but is painfully short of funds.
ASK STUDENTS how Dexter's attendance at the famous university puts him in a precarious situation. *(Dexter's situation is unstable because, although he's getting a degree from a desirable school, he doesn't have very much money to live on.)*

Analyze Structure

COMMON CORE RL 5

(LINES 169–172)

Explain that an author may use flash forward to share details about a character's future and help readers understand the big-picture perspective.

 **CITE TEXT EVIDENCE** Have students reread lines 169–172 and infer what point Fitzgerald is trying to make by including the flash forward at this point in the narrative. *(Dexter's decision to sell his share of the partnership had nothing to do with the business itself, as evidenced in lines 169–170: Dexter's laundries were very successful. The flash forward suggests that the reader should pay close attention to identify what led Dexter to make this decision.)* Have students cite the sentence in which Fitzgerald shifts time to the present and identify the literary device he uses to do so. *("But the part of his story . . . his first big success"; Device: direct address.)*

Analyze Story Elements: Motivation (LINES 207–208)

COMMON CORE RL 3

Tell students that they can analyze a character's traits by making inferences based on what the character does and says.

 ASK STUDENTS what they can infer about the woman who speaks in lines 207–208. Ask them what details from the text support their inference. *(The fact that she says "I hit something," rather than "I hit someone" suggests she has little regard for others and sees them as objects.)*

---

wives' lingerie as well—and running five branches in different parts of the city. Before he was twenty-seven he owned the largest string of
170 laundries in his section of the country. It was then that he sold out and went to New York. But the part of his story that concerns us goes back to the days when he was making his first big success.

When he was twenty-three Mr. Hart—one of the gray-haired men who liked to say "Now there's a boy"—gave him a guest card to the Sherry Island Golf Club for a weekend. So he signed his name one day on the register, and that afternoon played golf in a foursome with Mr. Hart and Mr. Sandwood and Mr. T. A. Hedrick. He did not consider it necessary to remark that he had once carried Mr. Hart's bag over this same links, and that he knew every trap and gully with his eyes shut—
180 but he found himself glancing at the four caddies who trailed them, trying to catch a gleam or gesture that would remind him of himself, that would lessen the gap which lay between his present and his past.

It was a curious day, slashed abruptly with fleeting, familiar impressions. One minute he had the sense of being a trespasser—in the next he was impressed by the tremendous superiority he felt toward Mr. T. A. Hedrick, who was a bore and not even a good golfer any more.

Then, because of a ball Mr. Hart lost near the fifteenth green, an enormous thing happened. While they were searching the stiff grasses
190 of the rough there was a clear call of "Fore!" from behind a hill in their rear. And as they all turned abruptly from their search a bright new ball sliced abruptly over the hill and caught Mr. T. A. Hedrick in the abdomen.

"By Gad!" cried Mr. T. A. Hedrick, "they ought to put some of these crazy women off the course. It's getting to be outrageous."

A head and a voice came up together over the hill:

"Do you mind if we go through?"

"You hit me in the stomach!" declared Mr. Hedrick wildly.

"Did I?" The girl approached the group of men. "I'm sorry. I yelled
200 'Fore!'"

Her glance fell casually on each of the men—then scanned the fairway for her ball.

"Did I bounce into the rough?"

It was impossible to determine whether this question was ingenuous or malicious. In a moment, however, she left no doubt, for as her partner came up over the hill she called cheerfully:

"Here I am! I'd have gone on the green except that I hit something."

As she took her stance for a short mashie[7] shot, Dexter looked
210 at her closely. She wore a blue gingham dress, rimmed at throat and shoulders with a white edging that accentuated her tan. The quality of exaggeration, of thinness, which had made her passionate eyes

---

[7] **mashie:** an old name for the golf club now known as a five iron.

TO CHALLENGE STUDENTS . . .

Is Judy ingenuous (childlike and innocent) or malicious when her golf ball hits Mr. Hedrick in the stomach? Have students in small groups read aloud and discuss lines 198–208. Ask them to analyze what the episode reveals about Judy's character and how it may foreshadow her treatment of Dexter. Challenge students to predict how Judy's relationship with Dexter will play out over the course of the story.

> "Did I?" The girl approached the group of men. "I'm sorry. I yelled 'Fore!'"

and down-turning mouth absurd at eleven, was gone now. She was arrestingly beautiful. The color in her cheeks was centered like the color in a picture—it was not a "high" color, but a sort of fluctuating and feverish warmth, so shaded that it seemed at any moment it would recede and disappear. This color and the mobility of her mouth gave a continual impression of **flux**, of intense life, of passionate vitality—balanced only partially by the sad luxury of her eyes.

220   She swung her mashie impatiently and without interest, pitching the ball into a sand-pit on the other side of the green. With a quick, insincere smile and a careless "Thank you!" she went on after it.

"That Judy Jones!" remarked Mr. Hedrick on the next tee, as they waited—some moments—for her to play on ahead. "All she needs is to be turned up and spanked for six months and then to be married off to an old-fashioned cavalry captain."

"My God, she's good-looking!" said Mr. Sandwood, who was just over thirty.

"Good-looking!" cried Mr. Hedrick contemptuously, "she always
230 looks as if she wanted to be kissed! Turning those big cow-eyes on every calf in town!"

It was doubtful if Mr. Hedrick intended a reference to the maternal instinct.

"She'd play pretty good golf if she'd try," said Mr. Sandwood.

"She has no form," said Mr. Hedrick solemnly.

"She has a nice figure," said Mr. Sandwood.

"Better thank the Lord she doesn't drive a swifter ball," said Mr. Hart, winking at Dexter.

Later in the afternoon the sun went down with a riotous swirl of
240 gold and varying blues and scarlets, and left the dry, rustling night of Western summer. Dexter watched from the veranda of the Golf Club, watched the even overlap of the waters in the little wind, silver molasses under the harvest-moon. Then the moon held a finger to her

flux
(flŭks) *n.* continual shift or change.

TEACH

CLOSE READ

Support Inferences    COMMON CORE RL 1
(LINES 213–219)

Remind students that they can draw on what they learned earlier in a short story to make inferences when important ideas about characters and events are not stated directly.

M CITE TEXT EVIDENCE Have students infer the identity of the woman referred to in lines 213–219 and cite textual evidence to support their inferences. *(She must be Judy; Dexter refers to her appearance at the age of eleven when he saw her the first time.)*

Analyze Story Elements:  COMMON CORE RL 3
Characterization (LINES 223–238)

Explain that authors create flat minor characters that lack dimension and show few complex traits to highlight the qualities of main or key characters.

N ASK STUDENTS why Fitzgerald includes the dialogue between Mr. Hedrick and Mr. Sandwood in lines 223–238 in this scene. *(to convey men's reactions to Judy)*

> **CRITICAL VOCABULARY**
>
> **flux**: Judy's mouth is described as being in a constant state of change.
> **ASK STUDENTS** How does the author describe the flux of Judy's mouth? *(He refers to shifts in expression that reflect intensity and vitality.)*

Strategies for Annotation   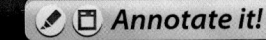 🖊 🖥 *Annotate it!*

Support Inferences   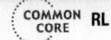 COMMON CORE RL 1

Share these strategies for guided or independent analysis.

- Highlight in blue any words or phrases that reveal Judy's attitude toward golf and the people around her.
- Review your highlighting and identify what attitude these words reveal. Think of words you would replace them with if you wanted to imply that Judy was an enthusiastic golfer or a kind person.

On notes, record your revision of the sentence to show a changed attitude on Judy's part.

> She swung her mashie impatiently and without interest, pitching the ball into a sand-pit on the other side of the green. With a quick, insincere smile and a careless "Thank you!" she went on after it.

Analyze Structure

COMMON CORE RL 5

(LINES 254–262)

Tell students that transition words and phrases such as *first* and *finally* can help them identify the sequence of events within a scene.

Ⓞ CITE TEXT EVIDENCE Have students identify words and phrases that show time order in lines 254–262. *("at that moment" [line 254]; "five years before" [line 255]; "now" [line 259])*

Support Inferences

COMMON CORE RL 1

(LINES 254–262)

When an author doesn't directly state a character's motivation, readers must play psychologist or detective and make inferences.

Ⓟ ASK STUDENTS to infer why Dexter is in a good mood in lines 254–262. *(The last time Dexter heard the piano tune, he was standing outside watching wealthy kids enjoy a prom when he "could not afford the luxury." Now he is enjoying his wealth and success as well as his position as an insider.)*

CRITICAL VOCABULARY

precipitated: The sound of the piano puts Dexter into a kind of ecstasy about his life.

ASK STUDENTS what reaction the sound of the piano precipitated in Dexter. *(Dexter was suddenly overcome with bliss.)*

---

lips and the lake became a clear pool, pale and quiet. Dexter put on his bathing-suit and swam out to the farthest raft, where he stretched dripping on the wet canvas of the springboard.

There was a fish jumping and a star shining and the lights around the lake were gleaming. Over on a dark peninsula a piano was playing the songs of last summer and of summers before that—songs from
250 "Chin-Chin" and "The Count of Luxemburg" and "The Chocolate Soldier"[8]—and because the sound of a piano over a stretch of water had always seemed beautiful to Dexter he lay perfectly quiet and listened.

The tune the piano was playing at that moment had been gay and new five years before when Dexter was a sophomore at college. They had played it at a prom once when he could not afford the luxury of proms, and he had stood outside the gymnasium and listened. The sound of the tune **precipitated** in him a sort of ecstasy and it was with that ecstasy he viewed what happened to him now. It was a mood
260 of intense appreciation, a sense that, for once, he was magnificently attuned to life and that everything about him was radiating a brightness and a glamour he might never know again.

A low, pale oblong detached itself suddenly from the darkness of the Island, spitting forth the reverberated sound of a racing motor-boat. Two white streamers of cleft water rolled themselves out behind it and almost immediately the boat was beside him, drowning out the hot tinkle of the piano in the drone of its spray. Dexter raising himself on his arms was aware of a figure standing at the wheel, of two dark eyes regarding him over the lengthening space of water—then the
270 boat had gone by and was sweeping in an immense and purposeless circle of spray round and round in the middle of the lake. With equal eccentricity one of the circles flattened out and headed back toward the raft.

"Who's that?" she called, shutting off her motor. She was so near now that Dexter could see her bathing-suit, which consisted apparently of pink rompers.[9]

The nose of the boat bumped the raft, and as the latter tilted rakishly he was precipitated toward her. With different degrees of interest they recognized each other.
280 "Aren't you one of those men we played through this afternoon?" she demanded.

He was.

"Well, do you know how to drive a motor-boat? Because if you do I wish you'd drive this one so I can ride on the surf-board behind. My name is Judy Jones"—she favored him with an absurd smirk—rather, what tried to be a smirk, for, twist her mouth as she might, it was not

precipitate
(prĭ-sĭp′ĭ-tāt′) *v.*
to cause to occur suddenly.

---

[8] **"Chin-Chin" . . . "The Chocolate Soldier":** three popular Broadway musicals, first performed in 1914, 1912, and 1909, respectively.

[9] **rompers:** a loose-fitting one-piece garment with bloomer like pants.

WHEN STUDENTS STRUGGLE . . .

"Winter Dreams" includes difficult passages that may be challenging for students to decipher. Tell students that they can paraphrase to understand complex writing. Explain that when they paraphrase, they are rewriting the text in their own words.

ASK STUDENTS to work in small groups to fill in a chart like the one shown. By completing the chart, students will break down and paraphrase difficult descriptions. Have them reread the passage. Then have them break longer sentences into chunks. The students in each group will discuss and paraphrase and enter each chunk in their own words in the chart. Review and clarify passages as needed.

grotesque, it was merely beautiful—"and I live in a house over there on the Island, and in that house there is a man waiting for me. When he drove up at the door I drove out of the dock because he says I'm his
290 ideal."

There was a fish jumping and a star shining and the lights around the lake were gleaming. Dexter sat beside Judy Jones and she explained how her boat was driven. Then she was in the water, swimming to the floating surf-board with a sinuous crawl. Watching her was without effort to the eye, watching a branch waving or a sea-gull flying. Her arms, burned to butternut, moved sinuously among the dull platinum ripples, elbow appearing first, casting the forearm back with a cadence of falling water, then reaching out and down, stabbing a path ahead.

They moved out into the lake; turning, Dexter saw that she was
300 kneeling on the low rear of the now uptilted surf-board.

"Go faster," she called, "fast as it'll go."

Obediently he jammed the level forward and the white spray mounted at the bow. When he looked around again the girl was standing up on the rushing board, her arms spread wide, her eyes lifted toward the moon.

"It's awful cold," she shouted. "What's your name?"

He told her.

"Well, why don't you come to dinner tomorrow night?"

His heart turned over like the fly-wheel of the boat, and, for the
310 second time, her casual whim gave a new direction to his life.

III

Next evening while he waited for her to come downstairs, Dexter peopled the soft deep summer room and the sun-porch that opened from it with the men who had already loved Judy Jones. He knew the sort of men they were—the men who when he first went to college had entered from the great prep schools with graceful clothes and the deep tan of healthy summers. He had seen that, in one sense, he was better than these men. He was newer and stronger. Yet in acknowledging to himself that he wished his children to be like them he was admitting that he was but the rough, strong stuff from which they eternally
320 sprang.

When the time had come for him to wear good clothes, he had known who were the best tailors in America, and the best tailors in America had made him the suit he wore this evening. He had acquired that particular reserve peculiar to his university, that set it off from other universities. He recognized the value to him of such a mannerism and he had adopted it; he knew that to be careless in dress and manner required more confidence than to be careful. But carelessness was for his children. His mother's name had been Krimslich. She was a Bohemian of the peasant class and she had talked

Original Phrasing	In My Own Words
The sound of the tune precipitated in him a sort of ecstasy	The music thrilled him.
and it was with that ecstasy he viewed what happened to him now.	And made him welcome what happened.
It was a mood of intense appreciation, a sense that, for once, he was magnificently attuned to life	He felt grateful and at his peak.
and that everything around him was radiating a brightness and a glamour he might never know again.	The world was filled with a brightness that might be a one-time experience.

CLOSE READ

Support Inferences

(LINES 308–310)

Tell students that authors use direct address to pass along important information and clues to the reader.

Q CITE TEXT EVIDENCE Ask students to infer what the narrator means by "her casual whim" (line 310). *(Judy spontaneously invites Dexter to dinner [line 308].)* Then ask students what they can infer about the direction of Dexter's future from the narrator's direct address on lines 309–310. *(The narrator says that "her casual whim gave a new direction to his life." Readers can infer that Dexter has fallen for Judy and his future will involve her.)*

Analyze Story Elements: Motivation (LINES 311–328)

Authors sometimes reveal information about a character by making comparisons.

R ASK STUDENTS to compare Dexter's view of the men he went to college with to his view of himself. *(Dexter envies his fellow college students. He recognizes that he is from a lower social class. He also recognizes that he is "newer and stronger.")* Ask students to infer Dexter's motivation for being "careful." *(Dexter says that "carelessness was for his children." He is motivated to give his children the wealth and status that he did not enjoy.)*

CLOSE READ

Analyze Story Elements: Motivation (LINES 341–347)

 **COMMON CORE** **RL 3**

Point out that authors create round main characters with complex traits to add dimension to their personalities and to make them realistic.

Ⓢ CITE TEXT EVIDENCE Ask students what Dexter lies about in lines 341–347. *(He tells people that he's from Keeble instead of Black Bear Village.)* Have students infer why he tells this lie. *(He is embarrassed of his home town because it is one of those towns "used as footstools" by the wealthy.)* Ask students if this suggests that Dexter is dishonest and to support their answer by citing textual evidence. *(Although he did lie, Dexter is not inherently dishonest. He believes that Black Bear is not "well enough to come from" and lies to cover his shame for coming from humble roots.)*

> **CRITICAL VOCABULARY**
>
> **petulance**: Judy was sulky and irritable during her first dinner with Dexter.
>
> **ASK STUDENTS** How does Fitzgerald's description of Judy during her first dinner with Dexter illustrate her petulance? *(He describes Judy as being in a moody depression: her smile has "no root in mirth, or even in amusement.")*

SCAFFOLDING FOR ELL STUDENTS

Understand Past Perfect Tense Point out that the story is narrated in the past tense and that the past perfect tense indicates actions that were completed before the events of the story. Use a whiteboard to project the sentence in lines 348–350. Invite volunteers to mark it up.

- Underline verbs in the past tense.
- Highlight in green the verb in the past perfect tense.

---

330 broken English to the end of her days. Her son must keep to the set patterns.

At a little after seven Judy Jones came downstairs. She wore a blue silk afternoon dress, and he was disappointed at first that she had not put on something more elaborate. This feeling was accentuated when, after a brief greeting, she went to the door of a butler's pantry and pushing it open called: "You can serve dinner, Martha." He had rather expected that a butler would announce dinner, that there would be a cocktail. Then he put these thoughts behind him as they sat down side by side on a lounge and looked at each other.

340 "Father and mother won't be here," she said thoughtfully.

> "I'm nobody," he announced. "My career is largely a matter of futures."

He remembered the last time he had seen her father, and he was glad the parents were not to be here tonight—they might wonder who he was. He had been born in Keeble, a Minnesota village fifty miles farther north, and he always gave Keeble as his home instead of Black Bear Village. Country towns were well enough to come from if they weren't inconveniently in sight and used as footstools by fashionable lakes.

They talked of his university, which she had visited frequently during the past two years, and of the near-by city which supplied 350 Sherry Island with its patrons, and whither Dexter would return next day to his prospering laundries.

During dinner she slipped into a moody depression which gave Dexter a feeling of uneasiness. Whatever **petulance** she uttered in her throaty voice worried him. Whatever she smiled at—at him, at a chicken liver, at nothing—it disturbed him that her smile could have no root in mirth, or even in amusement. When the scarlet corners of her lips curved down, it was less a smile than an invitation to a kiss.

Then, after dinner, she led him out on the dark sun-porch and deliberately changed the atmosphere.

360 "Do you mind if I weep a little?" she said.

petulance
(pĕch´ə-ləns) *n.*
childish annoyance;
sulkiness.

They talked of his university, which she had visited frequently during the past two years, and of the near-by city which supplied Sherry Island with its patrons, and whither Dexter would return next day to his prospering laundries.

"I'm afraid I'm boring you," he responded quickly.

"You're not. I like you. But I've just had a terrible afternoon. There was a man I cared about, and this afternoon he told me out of a clear sky that he was poor as a church-mouse. He'd never even hinted it before. Does this sound horribly **mundane**?"

"Perhaps he was afraid to tell you."

"Suppose he was," she answered. "He didn't start right. You see, if I'd thought of him as poor—well, I've been mad about loads of poor men, and fully intended to marry them all. But in this case, I hadn't
370 thought of him that way, and my interest in him wasn't strong enough to survive the shock. As if a girl calmly informed her fiancé that she was a widow. He might not object to widows, but—"

"Let's start right," she interrupted herself suddenly. "Who are you, anyhow?"

For a moment Dexter hesitated. Then:

"I'm nobody," he announced. "My career is largely a matter of futures."

"Are you poor?"

"No," he said frankly, "I'm probably making more money than any
380 man my age in the Northwest. I know that's an obnoxious remark, but you advised me to start right."

There was a pause. Then she smiled and the corners of her mouth drooped and an almost imperceptible sway brought her closer to him, looking up into his eyes. A lump rose in Dexter's throat, and he waited breathless for the experiment, facing the unpredictable compound that would form mysteriously from the elements of their lips. Then he saw—she communicated her excitement to him, lavishly, deeply, with kisses that were not a promise but a fulfillment. They aroused in him not hunger demanding renewal but surfeit that would demand more
390 surfeit . . . kisses that were like charity, creating want by holding back nothing at all.

It did not take him many hours to decide that he had wanted Judy Jones ever since he was a proud, desirous little boy.

IV

It began like that—and continued, with varying shades of intensity, on such a note right up to the dénouement. Dexter surrendered a part of himself to the most direct and unprincipled personality with which he had ever come in contact. Whatever Judy wanted, she went after with the full pressure of her charm. There was no divergence of method, no jockeying for position or premeditation of effects—there was a very
400 little mental side to any of her affairs. She simply made men conscious to the highest degree of her physical loveliness. Dexter had no desire to change her. Her deficiencies were knit up with a passionate energy that transcended and justified them.

mundane
(mŭn-dān´) *adj.*
ordinary;
commonplace.

Winter Dreams **423**

CLOSE READ

Analyze Story Elements: Motivation (LINES 361–382)
COMMON CORE RL 3

Tell students that dialogue between two characters can reveal information about their relationship as well as their individual perceptions and their motives.

T ASK STUDENTS what the dialogue between Dexter and Judy in lines 361–382 reveals about each character. *(Judy is basically shallow and concerned with image. She cares only about whether Dexter can provide for her financially, not about him as a person. Dexter does, in fact, think of himself as "nobody" and defines himself merely by his "futures"—his level of success and by his possessions.)*

Analyze Structure
COMMON CORE RL 5
(LINES 394–395)

Tell students that *dénouement*, which means "untying" in French, refers to the point at which a plot unravels. Explain that **foreshadowing** is a writer's use of hints at future events in the plot.

U ASK STUDENTS what Fitzgerald foreshadows in lines 394–395. *(The relationship between Dexter and Judy will fall apart, or unravel.)*

CRITICAL VOCABULARY

mundane: Judy is worried that her complaints over a poor suitor will sound commonplace to Dexter.

ASK STUDENTS why does Judy worry that her comments about her suitor are mundane? *(She feels that a woman complaining about a suitor who is poor is an everyday, ordinary occurrence.)*

Support Inferences

COMMON CORE **RL 1**

(LINES 416–426)

V **ASK STUDENTS** to make inferences about Judy based on her treatment of the men who "circulated about her." Have them support their inferences with evidence from the text. *(Readers can infer that Judy uses the men to meet her need for attention. Lines 419–421 explain that she keeps them around by encouraging them to "tag along." She is self-absorbed and "unconscious.")*

Support Inferences

COMMON CORE **RL 1**

(LINES 437–447)

The story's title, "Winter Dreams," indicates that Dexter's dreams are important, both in terms of theme and character motivation.

X **ASK STUDENTS** to infer what Dexter dreams of this winter and whether his dreams are satisfying. *(Dexter dreams of his early days with Judy and of having her as his wife. These dreams are not satisfying; they fill him with "restlessness and dissatisfaction.")*

When, as Judy's head lay against his shoulder that first night, she whispered, "I don't know what's the matter with me. Last night I thought I was in love with a man and tonight I think I'm in love with you—"—it seemed to him a beautiful and romantic thing to say. It was the exquisite excitability that for the moment he controlled and owned. But a week later he was compelled to view this same quality in 410 a different light. She took him in her roadster[10] to a picnic supper, and after supper she disappeared, likewise in her roadster, with another man. Dexter became enormously upset and was scarcely able to be decently civil to the other people present. When she assured him that she had not kissed the other man, he knew she was lying—yet he was glad that she had taken the trouble to lie to him.

He was, as he found before the summer ended, one of a varying dozen who circulated about her. Each of them had at one time been favored above all others—about half of them still basked in the solace of occasional sentimental revivals. Whenever one showed signs of 420 dropping out through long neglect, she granted him a brief honeyed hour, which encouraged him to tag along for a year or so longer. Judy made these forays upon the helpless and defeated without malice, indeed half unconscious that there was anything mischievous in what she did.

When a new man came to town every one dropped out—dates were automatically canceled.

The helpless part of trying to do anything about it was that she did it all herself. She was not a girl who could be "won" in the kinetic sense—she was proof against cleverness, she was proof against charm; 430 if any of these assailed her too strongly she would immediately resolve the affair to a physical basis, and under the magic of her physical splendor the strong as well as the brilliant played her game and not their own. She was entertained only by the gratification of her desires and by the direct exercise of her own charm. Perhaps from so much youthful love, so many youthful lovers, she had come, in self-defense, to nourish herself wholly from within.

Succeeding Dexter's first exhilaration came restlessness and dissatisfaction. The helpless ecstasy of losing himself in her was opiate rather than tonic.[11] It was fortunate for his work during the 440 winter that those moments of ecstasy came infrequently. Early in their acquaintance it had seemed for a while that there was a deep and spontaneous mutual attraction—that first August, for example— three days of long evenings on her dusky veranda, of strange wan kisses through the late afternoon, in shadowy alcoves or behind the protecting trellises of the garden arbors, of mornings when she was fresh as a dream and almost shy at meeting him in the clarity of the rising day. There was all the ecstasy of an engagement about it,

---

[10] **roadster:** a sporty, two-seat, open automobile.
[11] **opiate . . . tonic:** deadening rather than stimulating.

SCAFFOLDING FOR ELL STUDENTS

Analyze Language Explain to students that modifiers (adjectives and adverbs) can deepen the emotional resonance of a scene and give readers a more precise mental image of events. Read aloud lines 437–447 as students follow along. Share the following strategies to help them understand the purposes of modifiers.

- Have students identify the modifiers in this passage. *(helpless, infrequently, deep, spontaneous, mutual, dusky, strange, wan, shadowy, protecting, fresh, shy)*
- Choose a specific modifier, such as "helpless" in line 438, and ask students how it works to give a better understanding of the story. *(It shows that there is a negative side to Dexter's ecstasy. It emphasizes his lack of control.)*

Help students identify and interpret other modifiers in the passage.

sharpened by his realization that there was no engagement. It was during those three days that, for the first time, he had asked her to 450 marry him. She said "maybe some day," she said "kiss me," she said "I'd like to marry you," she said "I love you"—she said—nothing.

The three days were interrupted by the arrival of a New York man who visited at her house for half September. To Dexter's agony, rumor engaged them. The man was the son of the president of a great trust company. But at the end of a month it was reported that Judy was yawning. At a dance one night she sat all evening in a motor-boat with a local beau, while the New Yorker searched the club for her frantically. She told the local beau that she was bored with her visitor, and two days later he left. She was seen with him at the station, and it 460 was reported that he looked very mournful indeed.

On this note the summer ended. Dexter was twenty-four, and he found himself increasingly in a position to do as he wished. He joined two clubs in the city and lived at one of them. Though he was by no means an integral part of the stag-lines at these clubs, he managed to be on hand at dances where Judy Jones was likely to appear. He could have gone out socially as much as he liked—he was an eligible young man, now, and popular with downtown fathers. His confessed devotion to Judy Jones had rather solidified his position. But he had no social aspirations and rather despised the dancing men who were 470 always on tap for the Thursday or Saturday parties and who filled in at dinners with the younger married set. Already he was playing with the idea of going East to New York. He wanted to take Judy Jones with him. No disillusion as to the world in which she had grown up could cure his illusion as to her desirability.

CLOSE READ

Support Inferences
COMMON CORE RL 1

(LINES 452–473)

Tell students that analyzing why characters react to situations the way they do will help them infer the characters' motives. In the process, patterns may become evident that will help them better understand the characters.

Y ASK STUDENTS what Dexter thinks or dreams about in lines 452–473 and what pattern is evident in Dexter's dreams. (*Once again, during the summer Dexter is an observer of the life that he wants. This time, instead of caddying for men in positions of wealth and power, he is on the sidelines of Judy's life, wishing he were the object of her affection. In the fall, he hopes, not to win a round of golf but to run into Judy at a dance and perhaps win her back. By winter, he is dreaming of taking Judy Jones to New York with him.*)

Support Inferences
COMMON CORE RL 1

(LINES 473–474)

Z ASK STUDENTS to infer what Dexter is disillusioned with and what he still has illusions about. (*Dexter is disillusioned with the rich but he still has illusions about Judy.*)

Analyze Structure

COMMON CORE RL 3, RL 5

(LINES 477–482)

Remind students that a **flash forward** interrupts the action in a narrative to describe events that take place in the future.

A2 **ASK STUDENTS** to read the flash forward on lines 477–482 and describe its affect on the story. (*This flash forward first reminds the reader of when Dexter met Judy and then shifts forward eighteen months. Jumping ahead in time changes the pace of reading as well as the reader's focus. The shift forces the reader to consider how the actions and choices of Dexter and Judy affect them in the past, present, and future.*)

Support Inferences

COMMON CORE RL 1

(LINES 519–521)

Tell students that authors may also skip time periods and allow the readers to fill in the gaps.

B2 **CITE TEXT EVIDENCE** Have students identify the time period that Fitzgerald skips in lines 519–521 and infer why he doesn't narrate events in those months in any detail. (*Fitzgerald skips from October to January. Since Dexter romances Irene during this time, the gap suggests that their relationship isn't very important.*)

Remember that—for only in the light of it can what he did for her be understood.

Eighteen months after he first met Judy Jones he became engaged to another girl. Her name was Irene Scheerer, and her father was one of the men who had always believed in Dexter. Irene was light-haired and sweet and honorable, and a little stout, and she had two suitors whom she pleasantly relinquished when Dexter formally asked her to marry him.

Summer, fall, winter, spring, another summer, another fall—so much he had given of his active life to the incorrigible lips of Judy Jones. She had treated him with interest, with encouragement, with malice, with indifference, with contempt. She had inflicted on him the innumerable little slights and indignities possible in such a case—as if in revenge for having ever cared for him at all. She had beckoned him and yawned at him and beckoned him again and he had responded often with bitterness and narrowed eyes. She had brought him ecstatic happiness and intolerable agony of spirit. She had caused him untold inconvenience and not a little trouble. She had insulted him, and she had ridden over him, and she had played his interest in her against his interest in his work—for fun. She had done everything to him except to criticize him—this she had not done—it seemed to him only because it might have sullied the utter indifference she manifested and sincerely felt toward him.

When autumn had come and gone again it occurred to him that he could not have Judy Jones. He had to beat this into his mind but he convinced himself at last. He lay awake at night for a while and argued it over. He told himself the trouble and the pain she had caused him, he enumerated her glaring deficiencies as a wife. Then he said to himself that he loved her, and after a while he fell asleep. For a week, lest he imagine her husky voice over the telephone or her eyes opposite him at lunch, he worked hard and late, and at night he went to his office and plotted out his years.

At the end of a week he went to a dance and cut in on her once. For almost the first time since they had met he did not ask her to sit out with him or tell her that she was lovely. It hurt him that she did not miss these things—that was all. He was not jealous when he saw that there was a new man tonight. He had been hardened against jealousy long before.

He stayed late at the dance. He sat for an hour with Irene Scheerer and talked about books and about music. He knew very little about either. But he was beginning to be master of his own time now, and he had a rather priggish notion that he—the young and already fabulously successful Dexter Green—should know more about such things.

That was in October, when he was twenty-five. In January, Dexter and Irene became engaged. It was to be announced in June, and they were to be married three months later.

SCAFFOLDING FOR ELL STUDENTS

Understand Organizational Patterns Explain to students that, on page 426, the author takes the reader back in time to recount Dexter's relationship with Judy. Ask students how much time passes between Dexter's first meeting with Judy and his engagement to Irene. (*In lines 477–478, the narrator explains that 18 months pass between the time that Dexter meets Judy and Dexter becomes engaged to Irene Scheerer.*)

Explain that in the paragraphs that follow these lines, the narrator is recounting what happened in the months leading up to the engagement. The story is jumping backward in time. Suggest to students that they can create a timeline in order to determine the order of events in a story that jumps forward and backward in time.

The Minnesota winter prolonged itself interminably, and it was almost May when the winds came soft and the snow ran down into Black Bear Lake at last. For the first time in over a year Dexter was enjoying a certain tranquillity of spirit. Judy Jones had been in Florida, and afterward in Hot Springs,[12] and somewhere she had been engaged, and somewhere she had broken it off. At first, when Dexter had definitely given her up, it had made him sad that people still linked them together and asked for news of her, but when he began to be placed at dinner next to Irene Scheerer people didn't ask him about her any more—they told him about her. He ceased to be an authority on her.

May at last. Dexter walked the streets at night when the darkness was damp as rain, wondering that so soon, with so little done, so much of ecstasy had gone from him. May one year back had been marked by Judy's poignant, unforgivable, yet forgiven **turbulence**—it had been one of those rare times when he fancied she had grown to care for him. That old penny's worth of happiness he had spent for this bushel of content. He knew that Irene would be no more than a curtain spread behind him, a hand moving among gleaming tea-cups, a voice calling to children . . . fire and loveliness were gone, the magic of nights and the wonder of the varying hours and seasons . . . slender lips, downturning, dropping to his lips and bearing him up into a heaven of eyes. . . . The thing was deep in him. He was too strong and alive for it to die lightly.

In the middle of May when the weather balanced for a few days on the thin bridge that led to deep summer he turned in one night at Irene's house. Their engagement was to be announced in a week now—no one would be surprised at it. And tonight they would sit together on the lounge at the University Club and look on for an hour at the dancers. It gave him a sense of solidity to go with her—she was so sturdily popular, so intensely "great."

He mounted the steps of the brownstone house and stepped inside. "Irene," he called.

Mrs. Scheerer came out of the living-room to meet him.

"Dexter," she said, "Irene's gone upstairs with a splitting headache. She wanted to go with you but I made her go to bed."

"Nothing serious, I—"

"Oh, no. She's going to play golf with you in the morning. You can spare her for just one night, can't you, Dexter?"

Her smile was kind. She and Dexter liked each other. In the living-room he talked for a moment before he said good night.

Returning to the University Club, where he had rooms, he stood in the doorway for a moment and watched the dancers. He leaned against the door-post, nodded at a man or two—yawned.

"Hello, darling."

turbulence
(tûr´byə-ləns) *n.*
an unsettled or changeable state.

---

[12] **Hot Springs:** a spa city in west-central Arkansas.

WHEN STUDENTS STRUGGLE . . .

Concept Support After students read lines 533–545, read aloud the sentence "That old penny's worth of happiness he had spent for this bushel of content." Ask students to explain what this sentence means. Have them identify who represents happiness and who represents contentment and why. Make sure they understand that a "penny's worth of happiness" shows how little of Dexter's time with Judy is spent feeling peak emotions and how much is spent feeling miserable. Make sure students understand the phrase "this bushel of content" shows that Dexter realizes that, with Irene, he would feel contented for the long run, but he wouldn't feel the brief highs that Judy inspires. Ask students how this sentence connects to the story's themes.

CLOSE READ

Support Inferences
COMMON CORE RL 1

(LINES 522–525)

Tell students to pay attention for changes in the pattern of a character's behaviors, actions, and reactions. A change in pattern may have significance that will help them infer traits and motives.

C2 CITE TEXT EVIDENCE Ask students what readers can infer about Dexter's state of mind in lines 522–525. Have students cite specific evidence for their inference. *(The story states that Dexter "was enjoying a certain tranquility" [line 525].)* Ask students to explain why Dexter is feeling uncharacteristically calm this spring. *(He and Irene are engaged, and Judy is in Florida. Readers can infer that Irene's presence coupled with Judy's absence have had a soothing effect on Dexter.)*

Analyze Language: Imagery (LINES 533–545)
COMMON CORE RL 4

Tell students that **imagery** is descriptive words and phrases that appeal to the senses.

D2 ASK STUDENTS to reread lines 533–545 and identify the images associated with Irene and those associated with Judy. *(Irene: "a curtain spread behind him," "a hand moving among gleaming tea-cups, a voice calling to children"; Judy: "fire and loveliness," "slender lips, downturning, dropping to his lips" "a heaven of eyes")* Ask students to explain the effect of the juxtaposition of the images of Judy and Irene. *(The juxtaposition makes their differences even more vivid, and highlights the degree to which Dexter's regard for each varies. Irene is merely a fixture in his future household, while Judy is a source of deep emotion.)*

CRITICAL VOCABULARY

turbulence: Judy's love life is in constant disorder.

ASK STUDENTS How do Judy's ways cause turbulence in Dexter's life? *(Judy causes havoc in the lives of all her suitors, including Dexter, because she is constantly flitting from one to the other. Her capricious habits in her love life cause turmoil in the lives of those who love her.)*

Analyze Language: COMMON CORE **RL 4**
Symbol (LINES 568–570)

Tell students that a **symbol** is a person, place, or object that has concrete meaning in and of itself but that also stands for something beyond itself. Have students reread lines 568–570.

 **ASK STUDENTS** what Judy might symbolize. *(The repetition of the word "gold" suggests that Judy might symbolize money or wealth , or more figuratively, a gold standard to which all other women will be compared. She represents something of immense value.)*

The familiar voice at his elbow startled him. Judy Jones had left a man and crossed the room to him—Judy Jones, a slender enameled doll in cloth of gold: gold in a band at her head, gold in two slipper

570 points at her dress's hem. The fragile glow of her face seemed to blossom as she smiled at him. A breeze of warmth and light blew through the room. His hands in the pockets of his dinnerjacket tightened spasmodically. He was filled with a sudden excitement.

"When did you get back?" he asked casually.

"Come here and I'll tell you about it."

She turned and he followed her. She had been away—he could have wept at the wonder of her return. She had passed through enchanted streets, doing things that were like provocative music. All mysterious happenings, all fresh and quickening hopes, had gone away

580 with her, come back with her now.

She turned in the doorway.

"Have you a car here? If you haven't, I have."

"I have a coupé."

In then, with a rustle of golden cloth. He slammed the door. Into so many cars she had stepped—like this—like that—her back against the leather, so—her elbow resting on the door—waiting. She would have been soiled long since had there been anything to soil her— except herself—but this was her own self-outpouring.

With an effort he forced himself to start the car and back into

590 the street. This was nothing, he must remember. She had done this before, and he had put her behind him, as he would have crossed a bad account from his books.

He drove slowly downtown and, affecting abstraction,[13] traversed the deserted streets of the business section, peopled here and there where a movie was giving out its crowd or where consumptive or pugilistic[14] youth lounged in front of pool halls. The clink of glasses and the slap of hands on the bars issued from saloons, cloisters[15] of glazed glass and dirty yellow light.

She was watching him closely and the silence was embarrassing,

600 yet in this crisis he could find no casual word with which to profane the hour. At a convenient turning he began to zigzag back toward the University Club.

"Have you missed me?" she asked suddenly.

"Everybody missed you."

He wondered if she knew of Irene Scheerer. She had been back only a day—her absence had been almost contemporaneous with his engagement.

"What a remark!" Judy laughed sadly—without sadness. She looked at him searchingly. He became absorbed in the dashboard.

---

[13] **affecting abstraction:** pretending to be lost in thought.
[14] **consumptive or pugilistic** (pyoō´jə-lĭs´-tĭc)**:** sickly or aggressive.
[15] **cloisters:** here, places to escape from life's problems.

Strategies for Annotation ✎ 🖉 *Annotate it!*

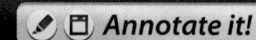

Analyze and Evaluate Characterization COMMON CORE **RL 1, RL 3, RL 4**

Share these strategies for guided or independent analysis:

- Highlight in yellow words and phrases that describe how Judy looks.
- Highlight in green words and phrases that describe what Judy does.
- Underline words and phrases that show Dexter's response to Judy.
- On a note, record what these words and phrases show about Judy's and Dexter's characters.

Judy Jones had left a man and crossed the room to him—Judy Jones, a slender enameled doll in cloth of gold . . . . The fragile glow of her face seemed to blossom as she smiled at him. A breeze of warmth and light blew through the room. His hands in the pockets of his dinner-jacket tightened spasmodically. He was filled with a sudden excitement.

610 "You're handsomer than you used to be," she said thoughtfully. "Dexter, you have the most rememberable eyes."

He could have laughed at this, but he did not laugh. It was the sort of thing that was said to sophomores. Yet it stabbed at him.

"I'm awfully tired of everything, darling." She called every one darling, endowing the endearment with careless, individual camaraderie. "I wish you'd marry me."

The directness of this confused him. He should have told her now that he was going to marry another girl, but he could not tell her. He could as easily have sworn that he had never loved her.

620 "I think we'd get along," she continued, on the same note, "unless probably you've forgotten me and fallen in love with another girl."

Her confidence was obviously enormous. She had said, in effect, that she found such a thing impossible to believe, that if it were true he had merely committed a childish indiscretion—and probably to show off. She would forgive him, because it was not a matter of any moment but rather something to be brushed aside lightly.

"Of course you could never love anybody but me," she continued, "I like the way you love me. Oh, Dexter, have you forgotten last year?"

"No, I haven't forgotten."

630 "Neither have I!"

Was she sincerely moved—or was she carried along by the wave of her own acting?

"I wish we could be like that again," she said, and he forced himself to answer:

"I don't think we can."

"I suppose not. . . . I hear you're giving Irene Scheerer a violent rush."

There was not the faintest emphasis on the name, yet Dexter was suddenly ashamed.

640 "Oh, take me home," cried Judy suddenly; "I don't want to go back to that idiotic dance—with those children."

Then, as he turned up the street that led to the residence district, Judy began to cry quietly to herself. He had never seen her cry before.

The dark street lightened, the dwellings of the rich loomed up around them, he stopped his coupé in front of the great white bulk of the Mortimer Joneses' house, somnolent, gorgeous, drenched with the splendor of the damp moonlight. Its solidity startled him. The strong walls, the steel of the girders, the breadth and beam and pomp of it were there only to bring out the contrast with the young beauty beside

650 him. It was sturdy to accentuate her slightness—as if to show what a breeze could be generated by a butterfly's wing.

He sat perfectly quiet, his nerves in wild clamor, afraid that if he moved he would find her irresistibly in his arms. Two tears had rolled down her wet face and trembled on her upper lip.

"I'm more beautiful than anybody else," she said brokenly, "why can't I be happy?" Her moist eyes tore at his stability—her mouth

Winter Dreams **429**

CLOSE READ

Analyze Story Elements: Motivation (LINES 627–639)

COMMON CORE RL 3

Explain that noticing what concerns a character or draws their attention can help readers infer the character's values and offer clues to motivation. In contrast, a character's lack of appreciation or respect can also provide important information.

F2 ASK STUDENTS to reread Judy's comment in lines 627–628 and explain what Judy's comment says about what she values. (*Judy assumes that Dexter still cares for her and says nothing about her feelings for him. In her world, she's the center of the universe.*) Point out Dexter's reaction when Judy asks Dexter about Irene in lines 638–639. Ask students to explain how he feels and what this says about his character. (*Dexter feels ashamed only when Judy mentions Irene, suggesting that his reaction has to do with Judy knowing, not respect for Irene and their relationship.*)

Analyze Story Elements: Motivation (LINES 657–659)

 **ASK STUDENTS** what Judy offers Dexter in lines 657–659, and what this would mean to Dexter. *(Judy offers herself in marriage, which is what Dexter has wanted since he met her.)* Then ask students what she promises him, and how this relates to what they know about his dreams. *(Judy promises to be beautiful for him. As the narrator notes on page 417, Dexter wants "the glittering things themselves," and marrying her would be the fulfillment of his dream.)*

Analyze Structure

(LINES 668–675)

Explain that authors may shift back and forth in time and that sometimes section breaks signal such shifts.

 **CITE TEXT EVIDENCE** Draw students' attention to the section break. Ask them what devices Fitzgerald employs in lines 668–675 and have them cite text that supports their conclusion. *(Section V begins with narrative summary and a flash forward. The story picks up ten years after the end of Section IV with the narrator summarizing what happened between Dexter and both Judy and Irene.)* Ask students to summarize how Dexter feels about what happened with Judy as it relates to himself and as it relates to Irene. *(He has no regrets for the "agony" he caused himself. While Dexter recognizes that he hurt Irene and her parents, in the end it was of no serious concern to him.)*

 turned slowly downward with an exquisite sadness: "I'd like to marry you if you'll have me, Dexter. I suppose you think I'm not worth having, but I'll be so beautiful for you, Dexter."

660   A million phrases of anger, pride, passion, hatred, tenderness fought on his lips. Then a perfect wave of emotion washed over him, carrying off with it a sediment of wisdom, of convention, of doubt, of honor. This was his girl who was speaking, his own, his beautiful, his pride.

"Won't you come in?" He heard her draw in her breath sharply. Waiting.

"All right," his voice was trembling, "I'll come in."

V

It was strange that neither when it was over nor a long time afterward did he regret that night. Looking at it from the perspective of ten
670   years, the fact that Judy's flare for him endured just one month seemed of little importance. Nor did it matter that by his yielding he subjected himself to a deeper agony in the end and gave serious hurt to Irene Scheerer and to Irene's parents, who had befriended him. There was nothing sufficiently pictorial about Irene's grief to stamp itself on his mind.

WHEN STUDENTS STRUGGLE...

Analyze Language Tell students that Fitzgerald polished each sentence until it had just the right content, rhythm, and mood. Read aloud "There was nothing sufficiently pictorial about Irene's grief to stamp itself on his mind." (Lines 673–675)

ASK STUDENTS what the sentence means. *(Unlike Judy, Irene was not beautiful enough for her tears to make Dexter feel guilty.)* Then ask them to analyze the author's word choices in the sentence. Ask students to explain the effect on readers of the phrase "not sufficiently pictorial." *(The formal language conveys Dexter's detached, unfeeling attitude toward Irene. The word "pictorial" suggests Dexter cares only about appearances and implies that there was nothing memorable about their relationship.)*

Dexter was at bottom hard-minded. The attitude of the city on his action was of no importance to him, not because he was going to leave the city, but because any outside attitude on the situation seemed superficial. He was completely indifferent to popular opinion. Nor, 680 when he had seen that it was no use, that he did not possess in himself the power to move fundamentally or to hold Judy Jones, did he bear any malice toward her. He loved her, and he would love her until the day he was too old for loving—but he could not have her. So he tasted the deep pain that is reserved only for the strong, just as he had tasted for a little while the deep happiness.

Even the ultimate falsity of the grounds upon which Judy terminated the engagement—that she did not want to "take him away" from Irene—Judy, who had wanted nothing else—did not revolt him. He was beyond any revulsion or any amusement.

690 He went East in February with the intention of selling out his laundries and settling in New York—but the war came to America in March and changed his plans. He returned to the West, handed over the management of the business to his partner, and went into the first officers' training-camp in late April. He was one of those young thousands who greeted the war with a certain amount of relief, welcoming the liberation from webs of tangled emotion.

VI

This story is not his biography, remember, although things creep into it which have nothing to do with those dreams he had when he was young. We are almost done with them and with him now. There is 700 only one more incident to be related here, and it happens seven years farther on.

It took place in New York, where he had done well—so well that there were no barriers too high for him. He was thirty-two years old, and, except for one flying trip immediately after the war, he had not been West in seven years. A man named Devlin from Detroit came into his office to see him in a business way, and then and there this incident occurred, and closed out, so to speak, this particular side of his life.

"So you're from the Middle West," said the man Devlin with 710 careless curiosity. "That's funny—I thought men like you were probably born and raised on Wall Street. You know—wife of one of my best friends in Detroit came from your city. I was an usher at the wedding."

Dexter waited with no apprehension of what was coming.

"Judy Simms," said Devlin with no particular interest; "Judy Jones she was once."

CLOSE READ

Analyze Story Elements: Motivation (LINES 676–696)
COMMON CORE RL 3

Explain that, to understand a character's choices in a particular situation, readers must look at earlier events and make connections.

12 ASK STUDENTS to go back and reread lines 668–675 and then draw their attention to the sentence in line 679: "He was completely indifferent to popular opinion." Ask: How does this attitude compare to Dexter's reaction when Mr. Jones begged him not to quit his job as caddy? *(In both situations, Dexter doesn't care what others think about him.)* What can you infer that Dexter does care about and how does this relate to his motives? *(Dexter cares only about his own needs and desires; he is motivated to get the "things" he wants, like membership in the golf club and Judy.)*

Analyze Structure
COMMON CORE RL 5

(LINES 697–701)

Tell students that narrative writing has a beginning, middle, and end, whether or not it's in time order. Authors may choose to use a sequence that is out of time order to give readers the benefit of a broad overview.

12 CITE TEXT EVIDENCE Have students cite textual evidence of a shift in time in lines 697–701. *(The narrator says that the next, and last, incident "happens seven years farther on.")*

SCAFFOLDING FOR ELL STUDENTS

Analyzing Transitions Fitzgerald provides many transitional words and phrases to help orient readers in time. Have students work in pairs to create lists of transitional words and phrases that give clues about time order. Students' lists can include words like *first, then, next, later, afterwards, before, previously,* and *subsequently*. Tell students to use their lists to help them analyze chronology in this and other stories.

Analyze Story Elements: Motivation (LINES 720–748)

 COMMON CORE RL 3

Remind students that **dialogue**—what characters say and how they say it—can help readers analyze motivation.

K2 CITE TEXT EVIDENCE Have students reread lines 720–748. Then have them cite dialogue that explains what happened to Judy. They should infer her motivations as well as the consequences of her choices. *(Lines 723–726: Judy marries a man who "drinks and runs around," while she "stays at home with her kids." Lines 745–748: Judy was "a pretty girl when she first came to Detroit" but loses her beauty, which was her identity. She wanted financial security and got it but lost everything else.)*

"Yes, I knew her." A dull impatience spread over him. He had heard, of course, that she was married—perhaps deliberately he had heard no more.

720   "Awfully nice girl," brooded Devlin meaninglessly, "I'm sort of sorry for her."

"Why?" Something in Dexter was alert, receptive, at once.

"Oh, Lud Simms has gone to pieces in a way. I don't mean he ill-uses her, but he drinks and runs around—"

"Doesn't she run around?"

"No. Stays at home with her kids."

"Oh."

"She's a little too old for him," said Devlin.

"Too old!" cried Dexter. "Why, man, she's only twenty-seven."

730   He was possessed with a wild notion of rushing out into the streets and taking a train to Detroit. He rose to his feet spasmodically.

"I guess you're busy," Devlin apologized quickly. "I didn't realize—"

"No, I'm not busy," said Dexter, steadying his voice. "I'm not busy at all. Not busy at all. Did you say she was—twenty-seven? No, I said she was twenty-seven."

"Yes, you did," agreed Devlin dryly.

"Go on, then. Go on."

"What do you mean?"

740   "About Judy Jones."

Devlin looked at him helplessly.

"Well, that's—I told you all there is to it. He treats her like the devil. Oh, they're not going to get divorced or anything. When he's particularly outrageous she forgives him. In fact, I'm inclined to think she loves him. She was a pretty girl when she first came to Detroit."

A pretty girl! The phrase struck Dexter as ludicrous.

"Isn't she—a pretty girl, any more?"

"Oh, she's all right."

"Look here," said Dexter, sitting down suddenly. "I don't

750   understand. You say she was a 'pretty girl' and now you say she's 'all right.' I don't understand what you mean—Judy Jones wasn't a pretty girl, at all. She was a great beauty. Why, I knew her, I knew her. She was—"

Devlin laughed pleasantly.

"I'm not trying to start a row,"[16] he said. "I think Judy's a nice girl and I like her. I can't understand how a man like Lud Simms could fall madly in love with her, but he did." Then he added: "Most of the women like her."

Dexter looked closely at Devlin, thinking wildly that there must be

760   a reason for this, some insensitivity in the man or some private malice.

---

[16] **row** (rou): a noisy argument or dispute.

432 Collection 6

SCAFFOLDING FOR ELL STUDENTS

Develop Reading Fluency Use the exchange between Dexter and Devlin (lines 732–758) to give students practice in reading dialogue. Remind students that dialogue is conversation. Tell them that fluent readers read dialogue with expression, using context and dialogue tags.

First, model for students an effective reading of the dialogue. (You might ask a proficient reader to read aloud one character while you read the other.) Then, have students work in mixed-ability groups to practice reading the dialogue on p. 432. Conclude the activity by asking students to discuss how taking note of context and dialogue tags helped them in their reading.

"Lots of women fade just like *that*," Devlin snapped his fingers. "You must have seen it happen. Perhaps I've forgotten how pretty she was at her wedding. I've seen her so much since then, you see. She has nice eyes."

A sort of dullness settled down upon Dexter. For the first time in his life he felt like getting very drunk. He knew that he was laughing loudly at something Devlin had said, but he did not know what it was or why it was funny. When, in a few minutes, Devlin went he lay down on his lounge and looked out the window at the New York sky-line
770 into which the sun was sinking in dull lovely shades of pink and gold.

He had thought that having nothing else to lose he was invulnerable at last—but he knew that he had just lost something more, as surely as if he had married Judy Jones and seen her fade away before his eyes.

The dream was gone. Something had been taken from him. In a sort of panic he pushed the palms of his hands into his eyes and tried to bring up a picture of the waters lapping on Sherry Island and the moonlit veranda, and gingham on the golf-links and the dry sun and the gold color of her neck's soft down. And her mouth damp to his
780 kisses and her eyes **plaintive** with melancholy and her freshness like new fine linen in the morning. Why, these things were no longer in the world! They had existed and they existed no longer.

For the first time in years the tears were streaming down his face. But they were for himself now. He did not care about mouth and eyes and moving hands. He wanted to care, and he could not care. For he had gone away and he could never go back any more. The gates were closed, the sun was gone down, and there was no beauty but the gray beauty of steel that withstands all time. Even the grief he could have borne was left behind in the country of illusion, of youth, of the
790 richness of life, where his winter dreams had flourished.

"Long ago," he said, "long ago, there was something in me, but now that thing is gone. Now that thing is gone, that thing is gone. I cannot cry. I cannot care. That thing will come back no more."

COLLABORATIVE DISCUSSION What did you notice about Judy's effect on Dexter? With a partner, discuss the relationship between Dexter and Judy and how it evolves as the story develops. Cite specific evidence from the text to support your ideas.

plaintive
(plăn′tĭv) *adj.*
expressing sadness or sorrow.

CLOSE READ

Analyze Story Elements: Motivation (LINES 771–782)

 COMMON CORE RL 3

Tell students that a character's dreams or aspirations can be a driving motivation. Determining the motive that drives a character can help readers understand the character's reaction when the dream is unfulfilled.

L2 **ASK STUDENTS** to reread lines 771–782. Then have students explain what Dexter has lost. Remind them to support their responses with evidence from the text. *(Line 775 states that "The dream was gone." Dexter has lost the dream of Judy and the illusion of her beauty—"the gold color of her neck's soft down" and "her freshness like new fine linen." Dexter believed that Judy was an ideal woman, and, when he realizes she has become an ordinary housewife, his illusions are shattered.)*

> **CRITICAL VOCABULARY**
>
> **plaintive**: Dexter describes the sadness in Judy's eyes.
>
> **ASK STUDENTS** Why would Judy's eyes be "plaintive with melancholy"? *(Judy's lifestyle is, at times, a source of sadness for her. She doesn't understand why her beauty doesn't translate into happiness.)*

COLLABORATIVE DISCUSSION Have students form pairs to list key events in the relationship between Dexter and Judy. For each event, ask them to identify Judy's effect on Dexter. Have pairs share their conclusions with the class as a whole.

ASK STUDENTS to share any questions they generated in the course of reading and discussing the selection.

TO CHALLENGE STUDENTS . . .

Independent Research Explain that some authors return to particular themes and character types many times over the course of their careers. Fitzgerald wrote this story while he was planning his novel *The Great Gatsby*. It is referred to as one of his "Gatsby-cluster stories" because of its similarities to the novel. Challenge students to independently research the similarities between "Winter Dreams" and *The Great Gatsby*, paying particular attention to the similarities between Dexter and Jay Gatsby and between Judy and Daisy. Have students share their research with the class.

Analyze Story Elements: Motivation

COMMON CORE RL 3

Tell students that if an author has developed a strong sense of a character's personality and voice, readers should be able to draw conclusions about the character's motivations. Discuss the definitions of *character traits* and *motivation*. Review each of the bulleted points and questions with students and make sure they understand the ideas and terms. Have them reread lines 1–5 and discuss Dexter's motivation for caddying. Ask: Why does Dexter work as a caddy? What character traits are revealed in these lines?

Support Inferences

COMMON CORE RL 1

Point out that readers combine evidence from the text with their own knowledge and experience when they make inferences. The selection says that Dexter laughs when he sees Judy threaten to hit her nurse, and that Dexter has to resist laughing at "the monstrous conviction that the little girl was justified in beating the nurse." In addition to noting this textual evidence, readers might ask themselves why these details have been included, and what later events they are intended to foreshadow. Based on the passage, one can describe these characters as similarly cruel and self-motivated. The scene foreshadows their cruel treatment of one another and those around them at the end of the story.

Analyze Story Elements: Motivation

No story analysis is complete without a study of motivation—the desires and emotions that drive characters to act or think in a certain way. By providing motivation for their characters, writers make them more complex and believable to readers. In "Winter Dreams," Fitzgerald reveals character traits and motivations through narration and dialogue.

Character Traits	Character Motivation
Writers reveal their characters' traits or qualities in both direct and indirect ways. To analyze a character, pay attention to • what the narrator tells you about the character • what the character says • what the character does • how the character interacts with other characters Some characters are more fully developed than others. A story's main character is likely to be a round character, one who displays complex qualities and is very realistic. Minor characters may be flat, displaying only one or two traits that are essential to the plot or that help bring out the qualities of the main character.	Understanding a character's traits helps you understand the reasons for his or her actions. Use what you know about the character's personality from the text to draw conclusions about why the character acts a certain way. Ask yourself these questions: • What are the character's dreams or aspirations? What is he or she willing to do—or give up—in order to fulfill these dreams? • What does the character value? What does he or she want to acquire or possess? What qualities does he or she admire in others and want to imitate? • What does the character fear or wish to avoid? How might these fears motivate the character to behave in ways that seem irrational, dishonest, or even immoral?

Support Inferences

When you read "Winter Dreams," you most likely made many inferences about the characters' traits and motivations without even thinking about it. When you discuss or write about the story, you will need to support your inferences with specific textual evidence—details from the story that are logically connected to your ideas. Recall this scene:

> "You little mean old *thing!*" cried Miss Jones wildly.
>
> Another argument ensued. Realizing that the elements of comedy were implied in the scene, Dexter several times began to laugh, but each time restrained the laugh before it reached audibility. He could not resist the monstrous conviction that the little girl was justified in beating the nurse.

Judy's behavior and Dexter's reaction to it make sense when you have gotten to know their characters. How could you use this passage to support a description of both characters? What future events are foreshadowed by the details in this scene?

Strategies for Annotation

Analyze and Infer Motivations  COMMON CORE RL 3, RL 5

Share these strategies for guided or independent analysis:
• Highlight in yellow the clues to Judy's character.
• Highlight in green the clue to Dexter's character.
• On notes, record what you infer about the characters and their motivations from the clues in the passage.

> "Go faster," she called, "fast as it'll go." Obediently he jammed the lever forward. . . . The girl was standing up on the rushing board, her arms spread wide, her eyes lifted toward the moon.
>
> "It's awful cold," she shouted. "What's your name?" He told her.
>
> "Well, why don't you come to dinner tomorrow night?"

Analyzing the Text

COMMON CORE RL 1, RL 2, RL 3, W 3a

Cite Text Evidence   Support your responses with evidence from the selection.

1. **Infer** Reread the first paragraph of the story. What do you learn about Dexter's family and social position?

2. **Interpret** In lines 20–36, Fitzgerald writes about Dexter's fantasies involving "imaginary audiences and armies" and golf tournaments. What do such fantasies reveal about Dexter's character? Why does the author choose to tell us about Dexter's fantasy life?

3. **Analyze** At the end of Part I, why does Dexter quit his caddy job? Cite evidence from the text that suggests his motivation.

4. **Interpret** Lines 137–138 tells us that "Dexter was unconsciously dictated to by his winter dreams." What are Dexter's winter dreams, and how do they shape Dexter's behavior?

5. **Infer** What can you infer about the character of Judy Jones based on the scene in which she pulls her boat up to Dexter's raft (lines 274–310)?

6. **Evaluate** Dexter becomes engaged to Irene but then returns to Judy. Do you think he knew their engagement would not last? What clues does the text provide?

7. **Draw Conclusions** How is Dexter affected by the news that Judy has married another man and subsequently lost her beauty? What does Dexter mean when he says that "there was something in me, but now that thing is gone"?

8. **Critique** What kind of man is Dexter? Does he deserve sympathy, criticism, or both? Describe Dexter's traits and the motivations for his primary actions and feelings.

9. **Interpret** Reread lines 771–793 and consider what exactly Dexter has lost. What **theme,** or message about the human condition, does Fitzgerald express through this loss?

PERFORMANCE TASK

Writing Activity: Letters Explore Dexter's and Judy's feelings for one another in two brief writing tasks.

1. In the character of Dexter, write a letter in which you profess your love to Judy and tell her what she represents to you.

2. In the character of Judy, respond to Dexter's letter, sharing with him any feelings you have for him.

3. Based on these letters, write a brief analysis of why the relationship should succeed or fail.

Assign this performance task.

PERFORMANCE TASK

COMMON CORE W 3a

Writing Activity Before students begin to write independently, have them work in pairs to describe the characters' different attitudes toward love, including what they say they feel about one another. Ask students to include specific details in each letter. After they complete their letters, ask partners to read them to each other or the class. Then have the class discuss whether the relationship between Dexter and Judy should succeed or fail and why.

PRACTICE & APPLY

Analyzing the Text

COMMON CORE RL 1, RL 2, RL 3, W 3a

Possible answers:

1. *Dexter's family is middle-class. His father owns the "second-best grocery," not the one used by the rich people in the nearby tourist haven. They are not in the highest social class.*

2. *Dexter has a rich imagination and often envisions himself as a member of the wealthy elite. His dreams often direct his actions.*

3. *Dexter left his caddy job because he couldn't bring himself to be a servant to Judy Jones, either because of his admiration of her, her social station, or both. In lines 133–134 the readers sees that "he had received a strong emotional shock" from their interaction.*

4. *Dexter dreams of having things that are just out of reach of his middle-class beginnings. He dreams of beating the rich members of the club at golf and of being with Judy Jones. He spends his life trying to become a member of high-society because he wants what they have.*

5. *Judy Jones seems to be bold, fearless, and self-important.*

6. *Dexter is alternately hardworking and driven, shallow and passive. He is aware of Judy's "glaring deficiencies," as well as the limitations of wealth and power, but still allows his obsession with her and them to dictate the course of his life. Readers can criticize his treatment of Irene and her family, and understand the larger implications of what he sacrificed by that behavior, but they can also sympathize with the desire to follow a dream no matter where it leads. The lack of passion he has for Irene is evident in lines 539–541: "Irene would be no more than a curtain spread behind him. . . fire and loveliness were gone." He goes on to say how, with Irene, his life is almost devoid of any romance or magic.*

7. *Dexter almost certainly knew his engagement to Irene wouldn't last. His lack of passion for her is evident: "Irene would be no more than a curtain spread behind him…" He goes on to say that his attraction to Judy "was deep in him. He was too strong and alive for it to die lightly." It is no surprise that he sacrifices his chance at marriage for a month-long affair with Judy.*

8. *Dexter idealized Judy, who represented his dream. When Judy goes from exotic to commonplace, that dream is no longer attainable. When he hears the news, he is crushed and loses hope.*

9. *Dexter had long held his "winter dreams" and when he loses them he loses the motivating force in his life and his hope. Fitzgerald is commenting on the precarious nature of getting caught up in dreams and ignoring reality.*

PRACTICE & APPLY

Critical Vocabulary

Sample answers:

1. Anyone can see by the bumper stickers on my car that I support the Pittsburgh Steelers.

2. When my two best friends had a major disagreement, I helped them resolve the conflict.

3. I experience flux when I change classes several times during the school day.

4. A song that I like will bring me immediate joy.

5. I react with petulance when I have to wait in line.

6. I talk about mundane topics like the weather.

7. A heated discussion at school created such turbulence that the principal had to intervene.

8. Whenever I visit the local animal shelter, the dogs look at me with plaintive eyes.

Vocabulary Strategy: Precise Usage

Check students' synonyms and antonyms:

blatantly: deliberately (syn), secretly (ant); petulance: peevishness (syn), cheeriness (ant); precarious: uncertain (syn), secure (ant); mundane: dull (syn), interesting (ant); flux: change (syn), stability (ant); turbulence: turmoil (syn), tranquility (ant); precipitate: trigger (syn), inhibit (ant); plaintive: mournful (syn), jovial (ant)

Critical Vocabulary

blatantly	precarious	flux	precipitate
petulance	mundane	turbulence	plaintive

Practice and Apply Working with a partner, use these questions to interview one another. Each answer should indicate comprehension of the Critical Vocabulary word. Take notes on your partner's responses and then write a brief summary of your interview. Use a dictionary or thesaurus as needed.

1. Do you **blatantly** show your support for sports teams?

2. Have you ever helped a friend in a **precarious** situation?

3. When do you experience **flux** in your life or in your schedule?

4. When you hear a contemporary song that you like, what response does it **precipitate** from you?

5. When have you reacted to a situation with **petulance**?

6. When have you noticed or said something **mundane**?

7. When have you experienced **turbulence,** for example at school or at home?

8. Have you ever noticed something that sounded or looked **plaintive**?

Vocabulary Strategy: Precise Usage

Reference tools help writers understand the precise meaning of words so they can use them correctly in a sentence. The thesaurus, for example, is used to find **synonyms,** or words of similar meaning, and **antonyms,** words that are opposite in meaning. It is important to identify the correct set of synonyms and antonyms for words having more than one meaning or part of speech. Take a look at this example of a thesaurus entry for the Critical Vocabulary word *mundane*:

> **mundane** *adjective* **1. worldly, temporal, secular, earthly** *He practiced meditation, hoping to transform the mundane into the heavenly.* **2. banal, commonplace, ordinary, prosaic, routine** *Processing customer returns was among the many mundane tasks required of the cashier.* **Antonyms: heavenly; extraordinary, exciting**

Practice and Apply For each Critical Vocabulary word, follow these steps:

1. Look up each word in a print or digital thesaurus. Identify the synonyms appropriate to the meaning of each Critical Vocabulary word as it is used in the selection.

2. Write a sample sentence using each word.

3. In each sentence, replace the vocabulary word with one of your synonyms. Make sure that the sentences make sense by having a partner check your work.

Strategies for Annotation 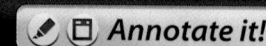  Annotate it!

Analyze Precise Usage

Explain that authors' word choices can evoke a mental image, create rhythm, and make sound effects such as rhyme, repetition, or alliteration. Have students use their eBook annotation tools to do the following:

- Highlight in blue words or phrases that evoke an image, create a rhythm, or make a sound effect.
- Look up each word in a print or digital thesaurus.
- Substitute the words' synonyms in the sentence from the story.
- On a note, tell the effect of using synonyms for Fitzgerald's words.

> up a picture of the waters lapping on Sherry Island and the moonlit veranda, and gingham on the golf-links and the dry sun and the gold color of her neck's soft down. And her mouth damp to his kisses and her eyes plaintive with melancholy and her freshness like new fine linen in the morning. Why, these things were no longer in the world! They had existed and they existed no longer.

Language and Style: Craft Effective Sentences

COMMON CORE W 3d, L 3a

In "Winter Dreams," Fitzgerald's writing style comes from making effective choices to create his own unique **syntax**—the pattern of words and phrases in his sentences. By varying syntax, writers can adjust the rhythm of their sentences to convey mood and ideas effectively. Tools such as punctuation, word choice, and well-chosen details all contribute to a writer's syntax and overall style. The chart shows some of the tools used to craft effective sentences.

Effective Sentences		
Writing Tool	Purpose	Example
Exclamatory sentence	to convey excitement	"'Never lost a ball! Willing! Intelligent!'" (line 52)
Dash	to set off ideas by calling attention to them; to break up long sentences	"It gave him a sense of solidity to go with her—she was so sturdily popular. . . ." (lines 551–552)
Dialogue	to show characterization; to further the plot; to break up narration	"I'm nobody," he announced. "My career is largely a matter of futures." "Are you poor?" "No," he said frankly. . . . (lines 376-379)
Sensory details/telling details	to create a full, vivid picture for the reader; to further characterization	"Her arms, burned to butternut, moved sinuously among the dull platinum ripples. . . ." (lines 295–297)
Precise words and phrases	to communicate ideas effectively	". . . within a year he was catering to the trade that wore knickerbockers." (lines 164–165)
Repetition	to create rhythm and mood; to emphasize a particular point or idea	"She had treated him with interest. . . . She had inflicted on him. . . . She had beckoned him and yawned at him. . . ." (lines 485–489)

Practice and Apply Revise the letter you wrote in the character of Dexter to make your sentences more effective. In your revision, include at least five different tools listed in the chart. Discuss with a partner how each tool improves your work.

PRACTICE & APPLY

Language and Style: Craft Effective Sentences

COMMON CORE L 3a, W 3d

Review the examples in the chart and make sure students understand how each one exemplifies the stated purpose. Then have students look for additional examples of each writing tool in the selection. Have students classify each example according to its purpose.

Answers:

To assess students' revisions of their Performance Task analyses, make sure that

- *students employed at least five different tools listed in the chart.*
- *students' revisions contribute effectively to their syntax.*
- *students use the tools in a manner that varies rhythm to convey mood and ideas effectively.*
- *students' revisions enhance the overall style in their letters.*

Monitor discussions and offer suggestions for additional ways students might use the tools to improve their writing.

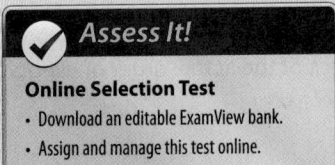

Assess It!

Online Selection Test
- Download an editable ExamView bank.
- Assign and manage this test online.

Analyze Structure

COMMON CORE

RL 5

TEACH

Point out to students that authors construct their stories to best convey their messages and to create specific effects. For example, an author may use chronological order, telling about events in time from beginning to end. In a mystery, an author may choose to sequence events out of the order in which they happened to exploit the uncertainty this structure creates and to build suspense. Discuss how and why Fitzgerald employed a nonlinear structure in "Winter Dreams" instead of a straight, chronological order. Provide students with the following definitions of terms related to story structure.

- **Sequence of events** is the order in which the author presents the events in the story.
- **Narrative Summary** is an abridged version of events conveyed by the narrator.
- **A flashback** interrupts the narrative to describe events that took place at an earlier time.
- **Flash forward** interrupts the narrative to give readers a glimpse into the future.
- **Time-Order Signal Words** are transition words that help readers keep track of the actual order of events (e.g., *before, first, next, then, later*).

COLLABORATIVE DISCUSSION

Introduce students to some other possible ways in which Fitzgerald might have structured the story. Ask them to speculate how the story would change if it were in strict chronological order. What if the story began with the end and then circled back to the beginning? How would the story change if it were told from Judy's point of view? Have students work in small groups to discuss these and other alternatives to the story's structure.

Analyze Story Elements and Support Inferences

COMMON CORE

RL 1, RL 3

RETEACH

Review the terms *trait* and *motivation*. Then give an example of each. For example, determination is a trait and desire for success could be a motivation. Review with students steps for analyzing and inferring traits and motivations.

- Ask students to identify a key detail about Dexter that will help them determine his traits. *(Possible answer: Dexter passes up his father's offer to pay his way to the state school and chooses to go instead to a famous university.)*
- Have students infer what character trait this detail suggests and explain their answer. *(Possible answer: Dexter wants to emulate the wealthy people he envies.)*
- Then have students infer Dexter's motivation. *(Possible answer: Dexter believes the only way he can have the things that the wealthy have is to escape the trappings of his middle-class background.)*

 **LEVEL UP TUTORIALS** Assign the following *Level Up* tutorial: **Character Types**

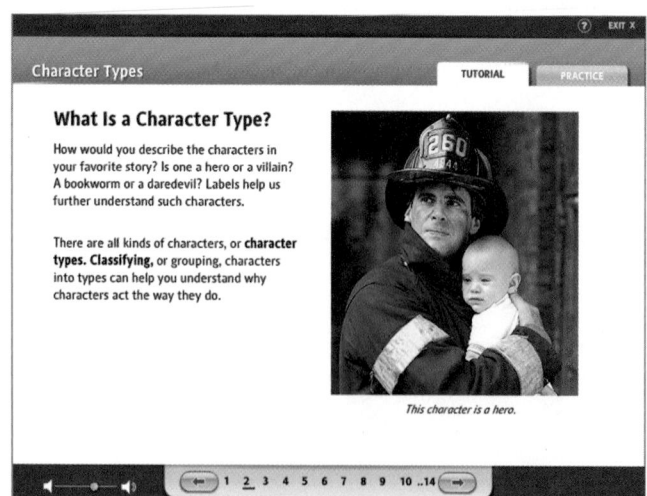

CLOSE READING APPLICATION

Students can apply the skill to another short story they have read. Have them select a story and then have them work independently to analyze character traits and motivations. Have them support their inferences with evidence from the text.

INTERACTIVE WHITEBOARD LESSON
Present this Interactive Whiteboard Lesson:
Theme/Central Idea

COMMON CORE
RL 2

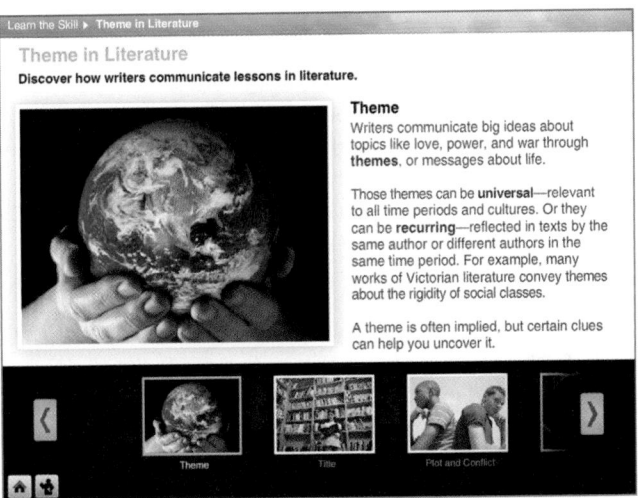

Determine Theme

TEACH

Work through the interactive lesson with students. Have students work in groups to complete the sentence frames on Screen 11: Tips for Analyzing Theme. For each response, have students cite evidence.

- The text *"Winter Dreams"* by *F. Scott Fitzgerald* is about the topic *of the dreams that motivate us*. The title suggests *dreams of spring or rebirth/regeneration*.
- The conflict revolves around *Dexter's struggles to fulfill his dreams*. It is resolved when *Dexter finds out that Judy aged poorly and lost her spirit*.
- The main characters display these traits: Dexter: *driven, methodical;* Judy: *self-absorbed, spirited*. By the end of the text they learn: *the dreams of youth are gone*.
- The following symbol appears in the text: *golf course*. The symbol represents: *desolation*.
- Through these clues the writer expresses the following themes: *The dreams of our youth are beautiful but fragile. Dreams are what give us purpose.*

PRACTICE & APPLY

As a class, work through the Practice & Apply portion of the Interactive Whiteboard lesson.

Analyze Story Elements: Characterization and Motivation

COMMON CORE
RL 1

RETEACH

Remind students that writers use direct and indirect techniques to develop a character. For example, Fitzgerald provides direct description of Judy Jones's character. Combining this with her dialogue and actions, readers can conjure a detailed image of her: stunning, self-absorbed, flirtatious, and melancholy. Compared to this vivid portrait, Dexter's character is a mere outline. Because he is often a silent observer, we learn about him indirectly. On the other hand, Dexter's motivation is directly addressed.

Ask students to describe the effect of juxtaposing the highly specific characterization of Judy against the open-ended characterization of Dexter. *(Because Judy is characterized with the specificity that one applies to an object of obsession, we can see her as Dexter sees her; and because his own character is more generic, we can imagine standing in his place.)*

LEVEL UP TUTORIALS Assign the following *Level Up* tutorial: **Methods of Characterization**

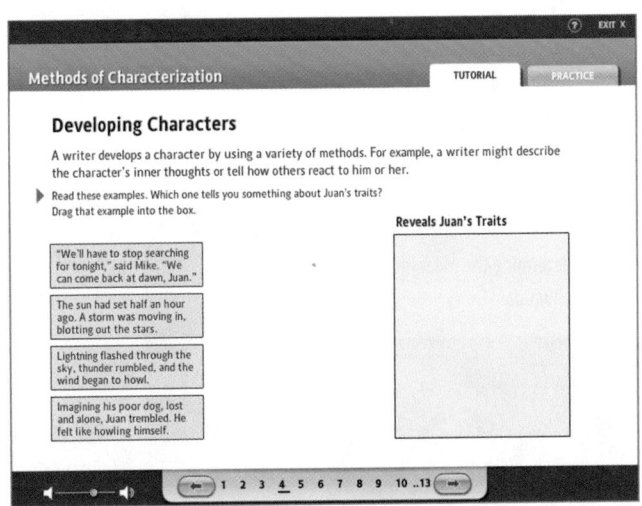

CLOSE READING APPLICATION

Ask students to work with a partner to piece together the evidence that tells them, directly and indirectly, the dream that motivates Dexter's actions. Then have students look for evidence about Judy's motivation. Is her motivation as well-developed as Dexter's? Compare how the motivations of the two characters are revealed.

Ambush

Short Story by Tim O'Brien

Why This Text

Students reading literature about war may have a hard time relating to characters who are immersed in a world that is starkly alien to them. They may have a hard time understanding the motivations that drive characters in the middle of war. With the help of the close-reading questions, students will analyze the story's elements, including the emotional struggles of the main character. This close reading will lead students to understand the character's motivation behind a story from his past.

Background Have students read the background and information about the author. Introduce the story by pointing out the ambiguity at its core: as with the rest of the stories in *The Things They Carried*, the main character is Tim O'Brien, who fought in Vietnam like the author did, and who, years later, writes about the war, as the author does. Although the story is fictional, it is driven by some of the author's own experiences.

AS YOU READ Ask students to pay attention to the narrator's statements, feelings, and reactions to events. How do they help the reader understand the narrator's motivation?

 ## Common Core Support

- cite strong and thorough textual evidence
- analyze the impact of an author's choices on story elements, including character motivation
- determine the meaning of words

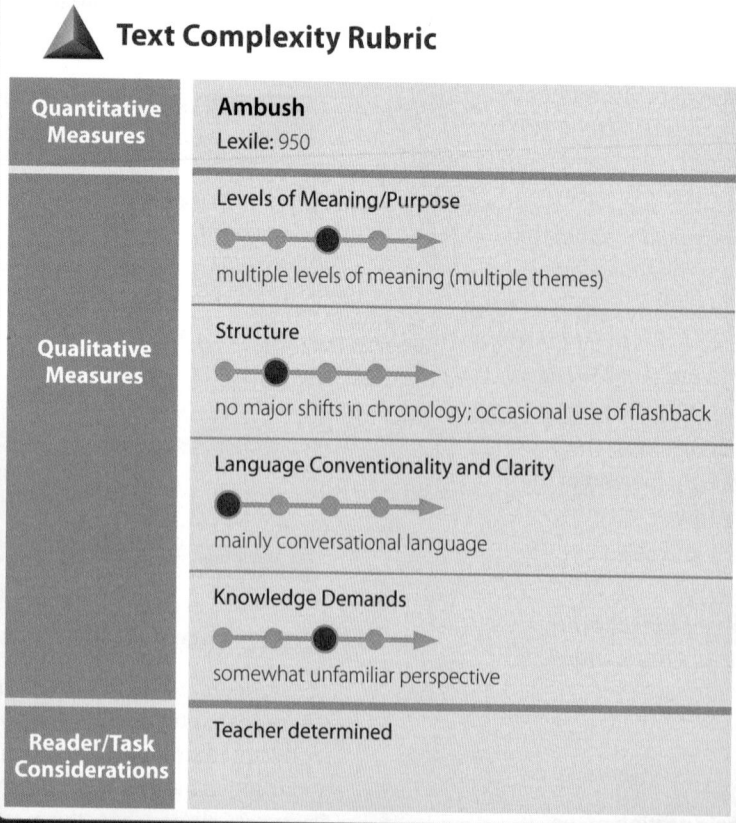

Text Complexity Rubric

Quantitative Measures	**Ambush** Lexile: 950
Qualitative Measures	**Levels of Meaning/Purpose** multiple levels of meaning (multiple themes)
	Structure no major shifts in chronology; occasional use of flashback
	Language Conventionality and Clarity mainly conversational language
	Knowledge Demands somewhat unfamiliar perspective
Reader/Task Considerations	Teacher determined

Strategies for CLOSE READING

Analyze Story Elements: Motivation

Students should read this story carefully all the way through. Close-reading questions at the bottom of the page will help them focus on a thorough analysis of story elements, including the motivations of the main character. As they read, students should jot down comments or questions about the text in the margins.

WHEN STUDENTS STRUGGLE . . .

To help students analyze the narrator's motivation in "Ambush," have them work in small groups to fill out a chart like the one shown below.

CITE TEXT EVIDENCE For practice analyzing a character's motivation, ask students to cite text evidence and then interpret what it reveals about the character's motivation.

Text Evidence	What It Reveals About the Character's Motivation
"Someday, I hope, she'll ask again." (line 6)	The narrator wants a chance to tell the truth.
"This is why I keep writing war stories . . ." (line 9)	The narrator writes to try to resolve his feelings.
"I did not hate the young man; I did not see him as the enemy . . ." (lines 35–36)	The narrator felt he must kill the man but could not really justify it.
"The grenade was to make him go away . . ." (lines 39–40)	The narrator wanted the situation to disappear.
"I wanted to warn him." (line 50)	The narrator regrets what he has done; he wishes he could save the man.

Background Tim O'Brien's *military experience in Vietnam provides much of the material for his fiction and personal narratives. In 1990, O'Brien published* The Things They Carried, *a remarkable fictional memoir about the Vietnam War and its human effects. The book is made up of interconnected stories narrated by a character named Tim O'Brien, who, the author says, is not himself. "Ambush" comes from that collection.*

Ambush

Short Story by Tim O'Brien

CLOSE READ
Notes

1. **READ ▶** As you read lines 1–13, begin to collect and cite text evidence.
   - Underline text that explains why the narrator is telling this story.
   - Circle text that explains why the narrator continues to write war stories.

A B When she was nine, my daughter Kathleen asked if I had ever killed anyone. She knew about the war; she knew I'd been a soldier. "You keep writing these war stories," she said, "so I guess you must've killed somebody." It was a difficult moment, but I did what seemed right, which was to say, "Of course not," and then to take her onto my lap and hold her for a while. Someday, I hope, she'll ask again. But here I want to pretend she's a grown-up. I want to tell her exactly what happened, or what I remember happening, and then I want to say to her that as a little girl she was absolutely right. This is why I keep writing war stories:

10 He was a short, slender young man of about twenty. I was afraid of him—afraid of something—and as he passed me on the trail I threw a grenade that exploded at his feet and killed him.

Or to go back:

Kathleen asks if he has killed anyone.

He says no.

He hopes she'll ask again.

2. **◀ REREAD** As you reread lines 1–9, make notes in the margin about Kathleen's question, the narrator's answer at the time, and the narrator's desire to explain more.

111

1. READ AND CITE TEXT EVIDENCE

A ASK STUDENTS to make an inference about the narrator based on his conversation with his daughter in lines 1–9. *Students may say that the narrator seems like he is thoughtful and loves his daughter. He wants to protect her by not telling the truth about his experiences because he thinks she's too young, but also hopes he will have a chance to tell her the truth when she's older.*

2. REREAD AND CITE TEXT EVIDENCE

B ASK STUDENTS to summarize the narrator's conversation with his daughter. *Students should note that Kathleen wants to know if he has killed anyone (lines 1–2), the narrator says "no" (line 5), and then he hopes that he can tell her the truth someday (lines 6–9).*

CLOSE READ
Notes

Shortly after midnight we moved into the ambush site outside My Khe. The whole platoon was there, spread out in the dense brush along the trail, and for five hours nothing at all happened. We were working in two-man teams—one man on guard while the other slept, switching off every two hours—and I remember it was still dark when Kiowa shook me awake for the final watch.

The night was foggy and hot. For the first few moments I felt lost, not sure
20 about directions, groping for my helmet and weapon. I reached out and found three grenades and lined them up in front of me; the pins had already been straightened for quick throwing. And then for maybe half an hour I knelt there and waited. Very gradually, in tiny slivers, dawn began to break through the fog, and, from my position in the brush I could see ten or fifteen meters up the trail. The mosquitoes were fierce. I remember slapping at them, wondering if I should wake up Kiowa and ask for some repellent, then thinking it was a bad idea, then looking up and seeing the young man come out of the fog. He wore black clothing and rubber sandals and a gray ammunition belt. His
cocked:
tilted
shoulders were slightly stooped, his head **cocked** to the side as if listening for
30 something. He seemed at ease. He carried his weapon in one hand, muzzle down, moving without any hurry up the center of the trail. There was no sound at all—none that I can remember. In a way, it seemed, he was part of the morning fog, or my own imagination, but there was also the reality of what was happening in my stomach. I had already pulled the pin on a grenade. I had come up to a crouch. It was entirely automatic. I did not hate the young man; I did not see him as the enemy; I did not ponder issues of morality or politics or military duty. I crouched and kept my head low. I tried to swallow whatever was rising from my stomach, which tasted like lemonade, something fruity and sour. I was terrified. There were no thoughts about killing. The grenade was to
40 make him go away—just evaporate—and I leaned back and felt my head go empty and then felt it fill up again. I had already thrown the grenade before telling myself to throw it. The brush was thick and I had to lob it high, not aiming, and I remember the grenade seeming to freeze above me for an instant,

3. **READ** As you read lines 14–71, continue to cite text evidence.

- Underline text describing the narrator's feelings.
- Circle text where the narrator says "I remember" in his story.
- In the margin, make an inference about how the narrator feels after he throws the grenade (lines 39-55).

112

CLOSE READ
Notes

> **For me, it was not a matter of live or die. I was in no real peril.**

as if a camera had clicked, and I remember ducking down and holding my breath and seeing little wisps of fog rise from the earth. The grenade bounced once and rolled across the trail. I did not hear it but there must have been a sound, because the young man dropped his weapon and began to run, just two or three quick steps, then he hesitated, swiveling to his right, and he glanced down at the grenade and tried to cover his head but never did. It occurred to
50 me then that he was about to die. I wanted to warn him. The grenade made a popping noise—not soft but not loud either—not what I'd expected—and there was a puff of dust and smoke—a small white puff—and the young man seemed to jerk upward as if pulled by invisible wires. He fell on his back. His rubber sandals had been blown off. He lay at the center of the trail, his right leg beneath him, his one eye shut, his other eye a huge star-shaped hole.
He is stunned and shocked.

For me, it was not a matter of live or die. I was in no real **peril**. Almost certainly the young man would have passed me by. And it will always be that way.
peril:
danger

Later, I remember Kiowa tried to tell me that the man would've died
60 anyway. He told me that it was a good kill, that I was a soldier and this was a war, that I should shape up and stop staring and ask myself what the dead man would've done if things were reversed.

None of it mattered. The words seemed far too complicated. All I could do was **gape** at the fact of the young man's body.
gape:
stare, with open mouth

113

---

3. READ AND CITE TEXT EVIDENCE

C **ASK STUDENTS** to find and cite text evidence for the narrator's feelings on the morning of the killing. *Students should mention the narrator's feeling "lost, not sure about directions" (lines 19–20); his "wondering" if he should wake Kiowa up to get some repellent (lines 25–27); the "reality" of what was happening in his stomach (lines 33–34); his terror (line 39); he felt his head "go empty" and then "fill up again" (lines 40–41); and his wanting to warn the young man before the grenade exploded (line 50).*

Critical Vocabulary: cocked (line 29) Have students share their definitions of *cocked*, and ask volunteers to use the word in a sentence.

Critical Vocabulary: peril (line 56) Have students suggest synonyms for the noun *peril* that would work in this context. risk, trouble, jeopardy

Critical Vocabulary: gape (line 64) Have students share their definitions of *gape*. How did the narrator look at the young man's body? *He could only gape—he stared with an open mouth.*

FOR ELL STUDENTS Tell students that the verb *duck* (line 44) has nothing to do with water birds. Ask students to infer the meaning from the context. Ducking down *must mean "lowering your head to avoid being seen or hit by something."*

D   Even now I haven't finished sorting it out. Sometimes I forgive myself, other times I don't. In the ordinary hours of life I try not to dwell on it, but now and then, when I'm reading a newspaper or just sitting alone in a room, I'll look up and see the young man step out of the morning fog. I'll watch him walk toward me, his shoulders slightly stooped, his head cocked to the side,
70   and he'll pass within a few yards of me and suddenly smile at some secret thought and then continue up the trail to where it bends back into the fog.

4. ◀ REREAD Reread lines 65–71. How does the vision the narrator imagines in these lines help resolve his conflict?

The narrator's vision at the end of the story allows him to imagine that he did not throw the grenade, and that the soldier continued up the trail unharmed. It helps relieve the guilt he feels for killing the soldier.

SHORT RESPONSE

Cite Text Evidence What is the narrator's motivation for telling this story? Take into consideration that he doesn't tell his daughter the truth. What conclusions can you draw about the narrator? Review your reading notes, and be sure to **cite text evidence** in your response.

The narrator tells the story because he knows he must tell his daughter the truth someday. The beginning and ending of the story frame the narrator's actual experiences in Vietnam. We know he is still very much affected by his actions there. As he tells the story, he explains his actions more than his emotions. He writes war stories to try to resolve his conflicting feelings about the war.

114

---

4. REREAD AND CITE TEXT EVIDENCE

D **ASK STUDENTS** to infer how the narrator feels about the young man's death. *Students can infer that the narrator is deeply troubled and is still not sure whether he was justified in killing him. Sometimes he forgives himself, other times he doesn't (lines 65–66).*

SHORT RESPONSE

Cite Text Evidence   Students' responses should include text evidence that supports their positions. They should:

• describe the narrator's motivation.

• cite evidence of the narrator's motivation.

• make inferences about the narrator's character.

TO CHALLENGE STUDENTS . . .

For more context on an American soldier's life in Vietnam during the war, students can view the video "On Patrol" in their eBooks.

ASK STUDENTS how the portrayals of the life of a soldier in Vietnam in the video and in the short story were similar and how they differed. *Both presentations showed a similar setting, though the story took place at night. The dangers and the conditions were similar in both media. In the story, the soldiers were spread out in groups of two, whereas in the video, the soldiers were generally in larger groups.*

DIG DEEPER

With the class, return to Question 4, Reread. Have students share their responses to the question.

ASK STUDENTS about the beginning and end of the story.

• Have students discuss the opening scene and its tone. *The narrator is with his nine-year-old daughter, who asks him if he killed someone in Vietnam. Despite the question, the tone is peaceful and loving—the narrator does "what seemed right," holds his daughter in his lap, and tells her a lie.*

• Have students compare and contrast the opening and closing scenes. *The story begins and ends in the present—far from Vietnam—and on a similar note. When the story begins, the narrator is talking to his young daughter, a conversation that spurs his memories. When the story ends, he is "reading a newspaper or just sitting alone," now imagining that the young man is still alive with a smile on his face.*

ASK STUDENTS to return to their Short Response answer and revise it based on the class discussion.

*my*SmartPlanner   Create lesson plans and access resources online.

COMPARE TEXTS
Poems of the Harlem Renaissance

Poems by Jean Toomer, Countee Cullen, and Arna Bontemps

Why These Texts?

"Song of the Son," "From the Dark Tower," and "A Black Man Talks of Reaping" are classic examples of the poetry that arose during the incredibly fertile cultural period known as the Harlem Renaissance. These poems use a variety of poetic tools to express the importance of memory and justice.

Key Learning Objective: Students will be able to analyze and compare multiple works from a time period on the basis of topic and theme.

For additional practice:

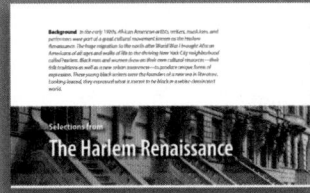

Close Reader selection
"How It Feels to Be Colored Me"
Essay by Zora Neale Hurston
"The Weary Blues"
Poem by Langston Hughes

COMMON CORE — Common Core Standards

RL 2 Determine themes of a text.

RL 4 Determine figurative and connotative meanings; analyze the impact of specific word choices.

RL 5 Analyze how an author's choices concerning how to structure specific parts of a text contribute to its overall meaning as well as its aesthetic impact.

RL 9 Demonstrate knowledge of foundational works of American literature.

W 2 Write informative/explanatory texts.

W 10 Write for a range of discipline-specific tasks, purposes and audiences.

▲ Text Complexity Rubric

	Poems of the Harlem Renaissance
Quantitative Measures	Lexile: NA
Qualitative Measures	**Levels of Meaning/Purpose** multiple levels of meaning (multiple themes) **Structure** regular stanzas, predictable rhyme scheme **Language Conventionality and Clarity** figurative, less accessible language **Knowledge Demands** increased amount of cultural and literary knowledge useful
Reader/Task Considerations	Teacher determined Vary by individual reader and type of text

CLOSE READ

The Harlem Renaissance

Tell students that this section gives information about the literary movement that gave rise to the selections they are about to read: the Harlem Renaissance. It begins by placing the Harlem Renaissance in its historical context and then covers the beginning, nature, and end of this literary movement.

The Great Migration

The hope for freedom from oppression was not the only motivating factor in the Great Migration. In the 1910s the South was already economically depressed, and widespread floods and trouble with insects such as the boll weevil, which attacks cotton plants, made the situation worse. At the same time, new jobs became available in the North as American manufacturers began supplying goods to the European countries involved in World War I. While African Americans who migrated to the North had greater opportunities than those who remained in the South, they still faced discrimination and hostility. For the most part, they had access only to poor, crowded housing and low-paying jobs.

A Literary Movement

One of the defining products of the Harlem Renaissance was *The New Negro*, an anthology of writing by African American authors published in 1925. In his forward to *The New Negro*, editor Alain Locke states as one of his purposes to make possible a deeper understanding of African Americans by the wider culture by letting "the Negro speak for himself." Locke believed that the new generation of authors would put the days when "liberal minds" could see African Americans as alien, savage, or naïve firmly in the past. Furthermore, Locke saw in the outpouring of creativity centered in Harlem "a fresh spiritual and cultural focusing" for people of African descent.

COMPARE TEXTS

Song of the Son   Poem by Jean Toomer
From the Dark Tower   Poem by Countee Cullen
A Black Man Talks of Reaping   Poem by Arna Bontemps

The Harlem Renaissance

In the early 1920s, the New York City neighborhood of Harlem attracted worldly and race-conscious African Americans who nurtured each other's artistic, musical, and literary talents and created a flowering of African American arts known as the Harlem Renaissance.

The Great Migration of millions of Southern black farmers and sharecroppers to the urban North began in 1916 and continued throughout the 1920s. They came in search of opportunity and freedom from oppression and racial hostility. Thousands of these migrants settled in Harlem, which quickly became the cultural center of African American life. Here, black men and women drew on their own cultural resources—their folk traditions as well as a new urban awareness—to produce unique forms of expression.

A LITERARY MOVEMENT   The event that unofficially kicked off the Harlem Renaissance as a literary movement was a dinner given on March 21, 1924, that gathered together some of the nation's most celebrated writers and thinkers, both black and white. The older generation of African American intellectuals that sponsored the dinner had helped begin organizations such as the National Urban League and the National Association for the Advancement of Colored People (NAACP) to promote equality for African Americans. These organizations published journals in which the works of young writers, including Countee Cullen, Zora Neal Hurston, and Langston Hughes, were published.

These young writers considered themselves the founders of a new era in literature. They expressed what it meant to be black in a white-dominated world. Yet this new generation of writers did not speak with only one voice. Some used a classical style to explore the struggles of African Americans, while others cast off more formal language and styles and wrote with the pulse of jazz rhythms. And some were more interested in exploring their individual identities than communicating the concerns of the African American community.

The Harlem Renaissance was brought to a premature end by the economic collapse of the Great Depression. Many writers left Harlem to take jobs to support themselves. Nonetheless, their work had a lasting influence on African American writers and on American culture as a whole.

TO CHALLENGE STUDENTS . . .

Search the Internet   What does the NAACP do today? Ask students to share what they know about the NAACP. Then discuss how they think the focus of the organization has changed since its founding.

ASK STUDENTS to conduct Internet research about the early days of the NAACP and the NAACP today. Have students work in groups to share the results of their research and decide whether the focus of the organization has changed and, if so, how. Have groups share their conclusions with the class as a whole.

TEACH

CLOSE READ

Background The Harlem Renaissance took place between 1918 and 1937. This cultural movement laid the groundwork for future African American literary works and is considered the most influential period of African American literary history. The Harlem Renaissance also marked a period of great music, theater, and visual arts. While the movement spread well beyond Harlem, New York City was its hub and attracted intellectuals and artists from all over the United States and the Caribbean.

AS YOU READ Direct students to use the As You Read instructions to focus their reading. Remind students to write down any questions they generate during reading.

Demonstrate Knowledge of Foundational Works
COMMON CORE RL 4, RL 9

Explain to students that the Harlem Renaissance as a movement brought together many writers of different styles and backgrounds. Have students read the biographical information on Toomer, Cullen, and Bontemps.

A **ASK STUDENTS** how these poets are similar. *(These poets were all writing around the same time and were all part of the Harlem Renaissance.)* How are they different? *(Each writer was raised in a different part of the country and had unique life experiences. Toomer was influenced by Eastern philosophy and Imagist poetry. Cullen was influenced by Romantic poets like John Keats. Bontemps was influenced by African American music and oral traditions.)* What was each writer's view on race? *(Toomer embraced the idea of a united human race not concerned with color. Cullen sought to break down racial barriers through poetry. Bontemps fought to preserve a connection to his black heritage.)*

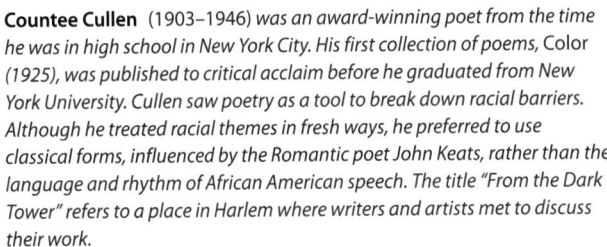

Poems of the Harlem Renaissance

Jean Toomer (1894–1967), *born in Washington, D.C., was a poet, novelist, and playwright best known for his book* Cane (1923) *which celebrated African Americans through an experimental mixture of poetry and prose. "Song of the Son" is from the first section of the book, set in rural Georgia. Eastern philosophy and Imagist poetry—poetry that uses precise, striking images to convey meaning—influenced Toomer's work. Because of his mixed-race background, Toomer could "pass" for white and came to reject the idea of race altogether, embracing the ideal of a united human race not concerned with color.*

A

Countee Cullen (1903–1946) *was an award-winning poet from the time he was in high school in New York City. His first collection of poems,* Color (1925), *was published to critical acclaim before he graduated from New York University. Cullen saw poetry as a tool to break down racial barriers. Although he treated racial themes in fresh ways, he preferred to use classical forms, influenced by the Romantic poet John Keats, rather than the language and rhythm of African American speech. The title "From the Dark Tower" refers to a place in Harlem where writers and artists met to discuss their work.*

Arna Bontemps (1902–1973) *was born in Louisiana but raised in California, where he fought to preserve a connection to his black heritage. Following his graduation from college in 1923, he discovered the thriving literary scene in Harlem, where he formed close connections with the major artists of the Harlem Renaissance. Bontemps gained early fame for his poetry, published in magazines such as* Opportunity *and* Crisis, *and in later years went on to write several novels. Much of his work focuses on the themes of dignity and justice and is influenced by the oral traditions and music of African Americans.*

AS YOU READ Notice imagery or language that each poet uses to appeal to readers' senses. Write down any questions you generate during reading.

APPLYING ACADEMIC VOCABULARY

contemporary	global

As you discuss Poems of the Harlem Renaissance, incorporate the following Collection 6 academic vocabulary words: *contemporary* and *global*. Discuss how these **contemporary** poems reflect the literary movement from which they came and how the poems express a **global**, human concept that all people can relate to: the sorrow and fallout from one group's oppression of another group.

Demonstrate Knowledge of Foundational Works

COMMON CORE RL 4, RL 9

(LINES 1–5)

Draw students' attention to the title of the poem and then have them read the first stanza.

 **ASK STUDENTS** what aspects of the first stanza reflect the fact that this poem is called a "song" in its title. *(The stanza has a rhythm and rhyme scheme that are reminiscent of a song. The last two lines, like the chorus of a song, are repeated.)*

Analyze Language

COMMON CORE RL 4

(LINES 9–10)

Explain to students that not only is an author's word choice important but so is an author's choice of how to order the words.

 **ASK STUDENTS** how lines 9 and 10 are different. *(The placement of the words "in time" is different in each line.)* What is the impact on meaning of the author's choice? *(Line 9 suggests that the speaker has been absent for a while but is now returning. Line 10 suggests that the speaker has returned before it was too late.)*

Demonstrate Knowledge of Foundational Works

COMMON CORE RL 4, RL 9

(LINES 16–23)

Explain to students that writers use a variety of tools to create vivid imagery. One such tool is **metaphor,** the comparison of two things without using *like* or *as.*

D CITE TEXT EVIDENCE Have students find the metaphor in lines 16–23 and explain its meaning. What is being compared to what? *(The metaphor compares the slaves to "dark purple ripened plums." The "one plum" saved is the memory of slavery.)*

Song of the Son
by Jean Toomer

Pour O pour that parting soul in song,
O pour it in the sawdust glow of night,
Into the velvet pine-smoke air to-night,
And let the valley carry it along.
5   And let the valley carry it along.

O land and soil, red soil and sweet-gum tree,
So scant of grass, so profligate of pines,
Now just before an epoch's sun declines
Thy son, in time, I have returned to thee,
10   Thy son, I have in time returned to thee.

In time, for though the sun is setting on
A song-lit race of slaves, it has not set;
Though late, O soil, it is not too late yet
To catch thy plaintive soul, leaving, soon gone,
15   Leaving, to catch thy plaintive soul soon gone.

O Negro slaves, dark purple ripened plums,
Squeezed, and bursting in the pine-wood air,
Passing, before they stripped the old tree bare
One plum was saved for me, one seed becomes

20   An everlasting song, a singing tree,
Caroling softly souls of slavery,
What they were, and what they are to me,
Caroling softly souls of slavery.

SCAFFOLDING FOR ELL STUDENTS

Understand Figurative Language Call students' attention to lines 11–12 in "Song of the Son." Explain that in figurative language, descriptive words are not meant to be taken literally. Here, the speaker talks about the sun setting, yet he is not speaking of the actual sunset:

- Discuss what *sunset* means in a literal sense. *(time of evening when the sun goes down)*
- Discuss what *sunset* might mean in a figurative sense and why a writer might use the term to describe something coming to an end. *(Sunset, used figuratively, can mean the gradual decline or end of something. It lends the idea that something has lived its life and that it is time for it to end.)*

From the Dark Tower
by Countee Cullen

We shall not always plant while others reap
The golden increment of bursting fruit,
Not always countenance,[1] abject and mute,
That lesser men should hold their brothers cheap;
5 Not everlastingly while others sleep
Shall we beguile their limbs with mellow flute,
Not always bend to some more subtle brute;
We were not made eternally to weep.

The night whose sable[2] breast relieves the stark,
10 White stars is no less lovely being dark,
And there are buds that cannot bloom at all
In light, but crumple, piteous, and fall;
So in the dark we hide the heart that bleeds,
And wait, and tend our agonizing seeds.

---

[1] **countenance:** admit as acceptable.
[2] **sable:** black.

Image Credits: ©Cynthia Hart Designer/Fine Art/Corbis

WHEN STUDENTS STRUGGLE...

To understand Countee Cullen's use of descriptive language, direct students' attention to lines 9–14. Explain that in this section of the poem the writer talks about darkness and light in a way that is different from the norm. Ask students the following questions:

- When you think of light and darkness, which usually has positive connotations and which has negative? *(Light usually has positive connotations and darkness is negative.)*
- How does the writer use the themes of light and darkness here? *(Here, the writer gives darkness positive meaning, saying that the night is no less lovely than the day and that some flowers bloom at night.)*

Demonstrate Knowledge of Foundational Works
COMMON CORE RL 4, RL 9

(LINES 1–8)

Remind students that a **sonnet** is a 14-line lyric poem, commonly written in iambic pentameter. A **Petrarchan sonnet,** named after the Italian poet Petrarch, consists of two parts. The first eight lines, called the **octave,** usually presents a problem or topic.

E ASK STUDENTS to explain what problem is presented in this octave. *(It describes a situation in which the speaker and those like him are expected to plant while others reap. In other words, they do not benefit from their labor. They are held "cheap." The octave suggests that this problem will not always exist.)*

Demonstrate Knowledge of Foundational Works
COMMON CORE RL 4, RL 9

(LINES 9–14)

Tell students that the last six lines of a Petrarchan sonnet are called the *sestet.* The sestet usually resolves or comments on the problem or topic.

F ASK STUDENTS to explain how the sestet (lines 9–14) resolves the problem introduced in the octave. *(The sestet affirms the value of those people who labor for the benefit of others. The poet compares them to the night "whose sable breast relieves the stark, / White stars" and suggests that they are biding their time until the "agonizing seeds" bear fruit.)*

Demonstrate Knowledge of Foundational Works
COMMON CORE RL 4, RL 9

(LINES 1–14)

Different writers in the Harlem Renaissance explored similar themes in their poetry.

G ASK STUDENTS to compare Cullen's poem to "Song of the Son" by Toomer. *(Both poets explore slavery and its negative effects. Both use planting as a metaphor. Cullen's focus is on waiting to overcome the injustice of slavery, while Toomer's is on maintaining the memory of slavery's history.)*

Demonstrate Knowledge of Foundational Works

 **COMMON CORE** RL 4, RL 9

(LINES 1–8)

Explain to students that Bontemps's poem, too, uses planting and reaping as a metaphor.

 **ASK STUDENTS** what injustice Bontemps is discussing in lines 1–8 via the metaphor of sowing and reaping. *(The speaker has spent his whole life planting, yet all he has to show for it is what he can hold in his hand. All of his work did not benefit him.)*

Demonstrate Knowledge of Foundational Works

 **COMMON CORE** RL 4, RL 9

(LINES 9–12)

Both Cullen in the first few lines of "From the Dark Tower" and Bontemps, here, talk about the results of their sowing.

 **ASK STUDENTS** to compare what the speakers in "From the Dark Tower" and "A Black Man Talks of Reaping" say about who will reap the benefit of the seeds sown. *(Cullen's view seems more hopeful. He sees the possibility of a future where the same person who sows will reap the reward and no one will be cheated out of his or her hard work. Bontemps has a starker view of the future, where the speaker's children have not been able to overcome the injustice of their father's experience and "feed on bitter fruit.")*

COLLABORATIVE DISCUSSION Have students work in pairs to discuss the different imagery in the poems and how the imagery appealed to their senses. Students might want to create charts that categorize each example of imagery by the sense to which it appeals: sight, hearing, touch, taste, or smell.

ASK STUDENTS to share any questions they generated in the course of reading and discussing the selection.

A Black Man Talks of Reaping
by Arna Bontemps

I have sown beside all waters in my day.
I planted deep, within my heart the fear
That wind or fowl would take the grain away.
I planted safe against this stark, lean year.

5 I scattered seed enough to plant the land
In rows from Canada to Mexico,
But for my reaping only what the hand
Can hold at once is all that I can show.

Yet what I sowed and what the orchard yields
10 My brother's sons are gathering stalk and root,
Small wonder then my children glean¹ in fields
They have not sown, and feed on bitter fruit.

_____

¹ **glean:** gather produce left behind by the regular reapers.

COLLABORATIVE DISCUSSION What imagery in each poem appealed to your different senses? Discuss this question with a partner, citing specific details from the poems to support your ideas.

TO CHALLENGE STUDENTS...

Simulate a Poet's Style Remind students that the three poems in this lesson use poetic structures such as rhythm, rhyme scheme, and line count to create images of a people remembering their past and hoping for their future.

Have students write a single stanza that could be added to the beginning or end of one of the poems in this lesson. The stanza should mimic the poem's style and explore the same theme.

Have students share their stanzas with the class.

Demonstrate Knowledge of Foundational Works

 **COMMON CORE** RL 4, RL 9

These three poems, each by writers from the cultural movement known as the Harlem Renaissance, are among the foundational works of early 20th century American literature. They demonstrate how contemporary writers explored the African American experience in a variety of ways. By analyzing the poems together, readers can see how each poet treated similar topics and themes in a unique fashion.

Consider how each writer's use of language helps to develop a similar theme in each poem, and how each writer uses figurative and connotative language to affect meaning and tone.

Topic	Theme	Figurative Language
A **topic** is the subject of the poem. The title of a poem may provide a clue to the specific topic of the poem. The titles of all three poems hint at the broader topic that is common to all of them—some aspect of the African American experience in the 19th and early 20th centuries, expressed from the perspective of the Harlem Renaissance.	**Theme** is the underlying message about life or human nature that the poet wants to communicate through his choice of topic. In most poems, the theme is implied rather than directly stated. To understand the theme, look for clues in the title and determine the identity of the speaker. Is the speaker an individual or does he represent a group? The particular mood or feeling that the speaker conveys also provides clues to the theme. Consider the phrases "agonizing seeds" and "bitter fruit" that end Cullen's and Bontemps's poems, respectively, and that hint at the common theme or message of the poems.	In poetry, the speaker's descriptions of the world will often help you identify the theme. Poets often use descriptive words in a figurative, or nonliteral, way to create images in the reader's mind. One type of figurative language is **metaphor**, a comparison between two things without using the words *like* or *as*. Consider this metaphor in Toomer's poem: "O Negro slaves, dark purple ripened plums." A common metaphor in the three poems is the metaphor of planting and reaping. Understanding how each poet uses this metaphor as a way of describing the African American experience will help you determine the common themes of the poems.

TEACH

CLOSE READ

Demonstrate Knowledge of Foundational Works

 **COMMON CORE** RL 4, RL 9

Remind students that while all three poems are from the same period, explore similar topics, and use comparable metaphors, each poem is unique in its tone, theme, and use of figurative language and imagery. Have students work in small groups to compare and contrast the poems using a Venn diagram like the one shown. Remind students to note any differences they see with regard to topic, theme and metaphor.

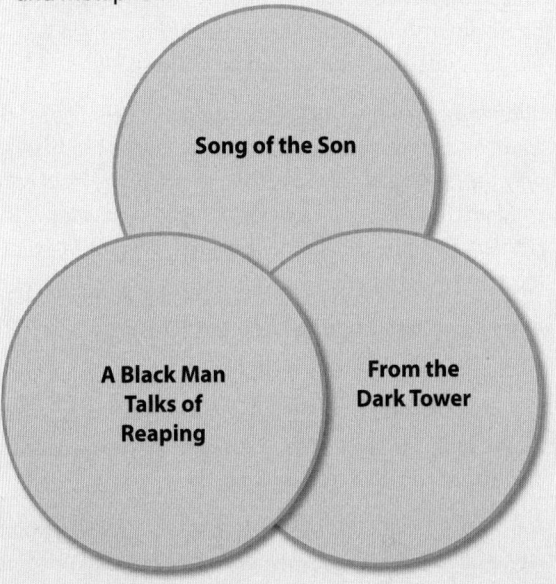

Song of the Son

A Black Man Talks of Reaping

From the Dark Tower

Strategies for Annotation 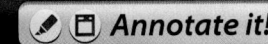 *Annotate it!*

Demonstrate Knowledge of Foundational Works

 **COMMON CORE** RL 4, RL 9

Remind students that figurative language and connotative language are tools often used by poets.

- Highlight in yellow words that relate to the metaphor of planting.
- Underline words or phrases with strong connotative meanings.
- In a note, record your observations about the tone that the underlined words create.

I have sown beside all waters in my day.

I planted deep, within my heart the fear

That wind or fowl would take the grain away.

I planted safe against this stark, lean year.

PRACTICE & APPLY

Analyzing the Text COMMON CORE RL 2, RL 4, RL 5, RL 9

Possible answers:

1. *Literally, the speaker is describing the setting sun in a valley with a plum tree almost stripped bare. Figuratively, he is describing the decline of slavery and the importance of preserving its memory.*

2. *The speaker represents the next generation charged with keeping the history alive to remember those who were enslaved.*

3. *The phrase suggests the great things created by those who are not able to enjoy them.*

4. *In the octave, Cullen talks about the ways in which African Americans have been mistreated. In the sestet, he talks about embracing the darkness and the hope, even in difficulty, of someday overcoming the past.*

5. *Bontemps's meaning for brother is ambiguous. The brother could be another African American, whose children get only the "stalk and root," not fruit, to eat, or the brother's children could be white generations who reap what was planted. The bitter fruit is the resentment for the injustice of the past (and/or present).*

6. *Answers will vary but should demonstrate an understanding of extended metaphor.*

7. *Toomer's repetition gives the poem a musical quality. He uses repetition to play with words, shifting the meaning of a line by changing a word or two.*

8. *Toomer uses night and darkness to signal a turning point. He needs to preserve the memory of the past before the new day dawns. Cullen turns night and darkness around and gives darkness beauty that light cannot support.*

9. *Toomer's poem has a positive tone of keeping memory alive. Cullen's tone is more defiant. Bontemps' tone is sad and bitter.*

10. *Answers will vary but should thoughtfully cover the formal, topical, and thematic elements of the poems.*

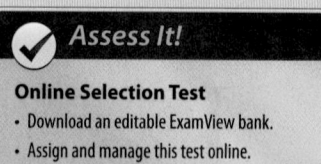

Assess It!

Online Selection Test
- Download an editable ExamView bank.
- Assign and manage this test online.

 eBook *Annotate It!*

Analyzing the Text COMMON CORE RL 2, RL 4, RL 5, RL 9, W 2, W 10

Cite Text Evidence   Support your responses with evidence from the selections.

1. **Summarize** What is the speaker describing—both literally and figuratively—in "Song of the Son"? How do the poem's ideas and images express one or more themes on the topic of African American history?

2. **Infer** Who is the speaker in "Song of the Son"? In the context of African American culture, what does he represent to the poet?

3. **Analyze** In "From the Dark Tower," what does the phrase "golden increment of bursting fruit" suggest?

4. **Analyze** "From the Dark Tower" is written in the form of a **Petrarchan sonnet,** in which the octave, or first eight lines, presents a problem or challenge, and the final six lines, the sestet, resolves or comments on the problem. How does Cullen apply this structure to express his message?

5. **Infer** In "A Black Man Talks of Reaping," what does the speaker mean when he says "My brother's sons are gathering stalk and root"? Who is the brother? What is the "bitter fruit" at the end of the poem?

6. **Identify** An **extended metaphor** is a metaphor that is developed over many lines. Identify an example of extended metaphor in each poem.

7. **Cite Evidence** How does Toomer's use of repetition—of both lines and important ideas—contribute to the aesthetic impact of "Song of the Son"?

8. **Compare** How do Toomer and Cullen use the metaphor of night and darkness to support the themes and ideas they want to express?

9. **Synthesize** How would you describe the tone of each poem?

10. **Compare** In what ways might these poems represent differents aspects or strains of the Harlem Renaissance? Consider formal, topical, and thematic elements in all three poems.

PERFORMANCE TASK

Writing Task: Essay Write an informative essay in which you compare and contrast the themes of the three poems.

- Determine a message about the African American experience expressed in each poem through the use of the extended metaphor of planting and reaping.

- Choose significant imagery from each poem that demonstrates how the poet used the metaphor to convey the theme.

- Use a compare-and-contrast organizational structure to highlight similarities and differences among the three poems.

- Draw a conclusion from the information you present about the relationship between the themes of the three poems.

Assign this performance task.

PERFORMANCE TASK COMMON CORE W 2

Writing Task: Essay Review the themes and how the writers use metaphor and imagery. Have students work in pairs to outline their essays, checking that extended metaphor, significant imagery, and similarities and differences are covered clearly and logically. Then have students write rough drafts, sharing their essays with partners and giving constructive criticism. Final versions should draw clear conclusions and be well organized.

Analyze Language: Connotations

COMMON CORE

RL 4

TEACH

Remind students that while **denotation** is a word's dictionary definition, **connotation** is the feeling associated with a word. In poetry, word connotations are especially important.

- Read aloud "From the Dark Tower."
- Ask students to identify words with strong connotations. ("abject and mute," "cheap," "brute," "weep," "stark," "piteous," "bleeds," "agonizing")
- Remind students that **tone** is the poet's attitude toward the subject. For instance, a poem might have a playful or a melancholy tone. Ask students what tone is conveyed by the connotative words in Cullen's poem. (The tone is mournful.)

PRACTICE AND APPLY

In "A Black Man Talks of Reaping," Bontemps creates a bitter, dispirited tone—the poet's attitude toward the subject—through the use of words with negative connotations.

- Reread this poem aloud.
- Divide the class into groups, and assign a stanza of the poem to each group.
- Have each group analyze its stanza to identify words with strong connotations and to determine the tone conveyed by the words.
- Have a representative from each group share the results of the analysis with the class.

Demonstrate Knowledge of Foundational Works

COMMON CORE

RL 4, RL 9

RETEACH

Remind students that an important part of comparing writers and their works is identifying themes that connect the works.

Ask the following questions to stimulate discussion:

- What is the metaphor used throughout these poems? *(planting and reaping)* Why is it used in all three poems? (The poems all look at the history of the African American people, and agriculture plays a key role in that history as slaves often worked in fields literally sowing and reaping. However, the slaves did not get to keep what they grew.
- What theme do the sowing and reaping metaphors help to convey? (The sowing and reaping metaphors convey the theme that African Americans have been cheated out of the rewards of their toil.)
- How does each writer explore the theme differently? (Toomer emphasizes the importance of memory, describing how one of the plums reaped becomes an "everlasting song." Cullen explores the theme with a guarded optimism, describing how seeds are being tended for future use. Bontemps expresses anger over the injustice of others benefiting from the hard work of the oppressed and its negative impact on the next generation, who will eat bitter fruit.)

LEVEL UP TUTORIALS Assign the following *Level Up* tutorial: **Imagery**

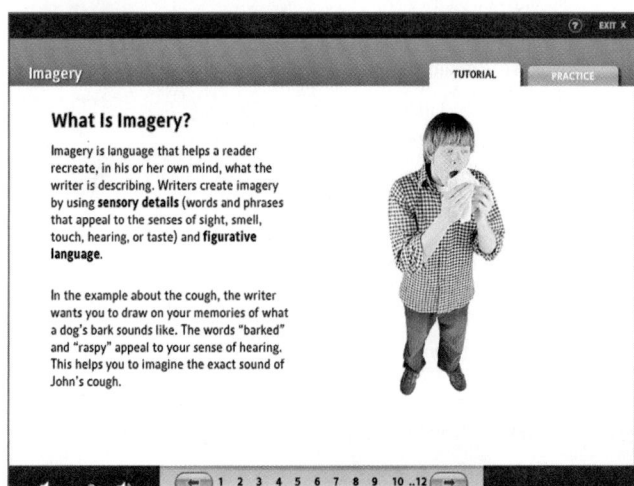

The Harlem Renaissance

How It Feels to Be Colored Me

Essay by Zora Neale Hurston

The Weary Blues

Poem by Langston Hughes

Why These Texts

Students may have difficulty appreciating foundational works without understanding the context in which they were written. With the help of the close-reading questions, students will identify details that help clarify the context and express the themes addressed by both writers. This close reading will lead students to develop an understanding of these two key works from the Harlem Renaissance.

Background Have students read the background about the Harlem Renaissance and the biographical information about the writers. Tell students that they are going to read an essay that describes Zora Neale Hurston's experience as an African American, first as a young girl in the South and later as a woman in New York City. Then they will read a poem by Langston Hughes about a jazz singer in Harlem in the 1920s.

AS YOU READ Ask students to pay attention to how both writers use figurative language to describe their subjects. What themes were especially relevant to African Americans early in the twentieth century?

Common Core Support

- cite strong and thorough textual evidence
- determine the meaning of words and phrases, including figurative and connotative meanings
- analyze how an author's choices concerning text structure contribute to a text's meaning and aesthetic impact
- demonstrate knowledge of early twentieth-century foundational texts

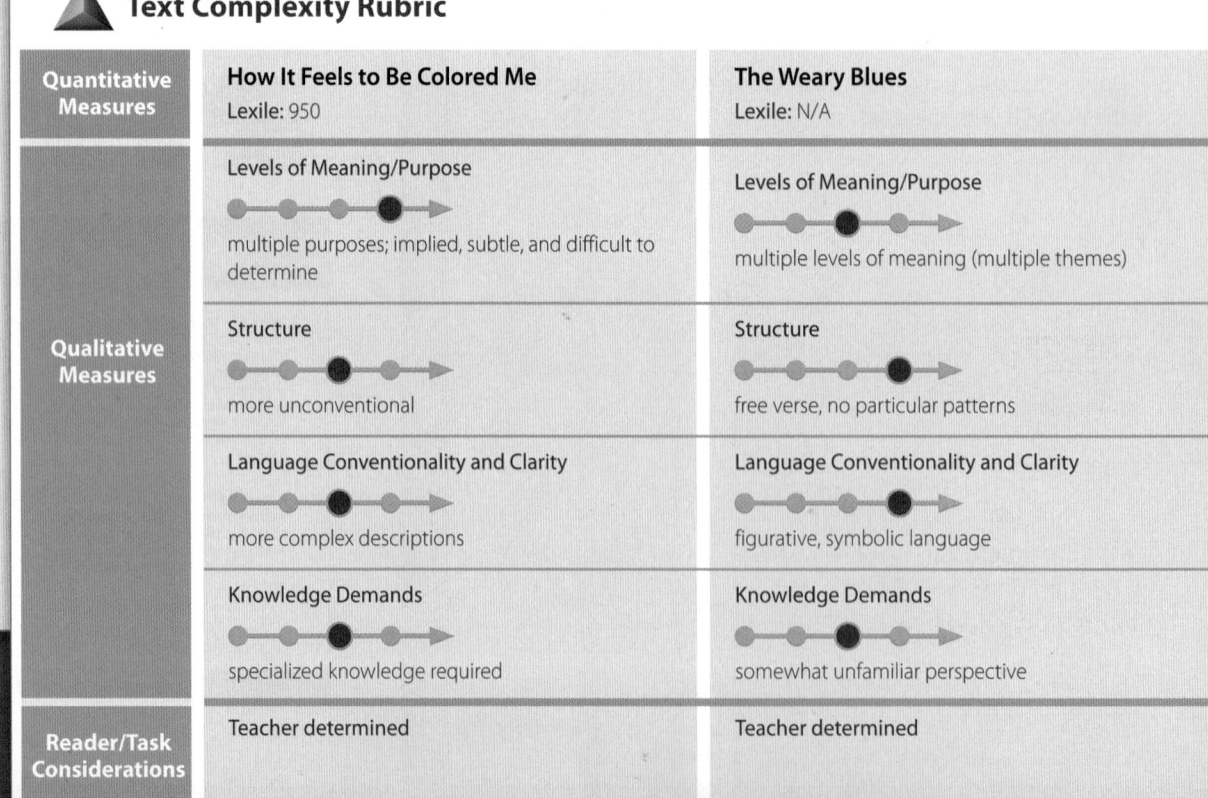

Text Complexity Rubric

	How It Feels to Be Colored Me	The Weary Blues
Quantitative Measures	Lexile: 950	Lexile: N/A
Qualitative Measures	Levels of Meaning/Purpose multiple purposes; implied, subtle, and difficult to determine	Levels of Meaning/Purpose multiple levels of meaning (multiple themes)
	Structure more unconventional	Structure free verse, no particular patterns
	Language Conventionality and Clarity more complex descriptions	Language Conventionality and Clarity figurative, symbolic language
	Knowledge Demands specialized knowledge required	Knowledge Demands somewhat unfamiliar perspective
Reader/Task Considerations	Teacher determined	Teacher determined

Strategies for CLOSE READING

Demonstrate Knowledge of Foundational Works

Students should read the essay and poem carefully all the way through. Close-reading questions at the bottom of the page will help them identify details, including figurative and connotative language, that express the themes of these texts. As they read, students should jot down comments or questions about the text in the margins.

WHEN STUDENTS STRUGGLE . . .

To help students demonstrate knowledge of foundational works, have them work in small groups to fill out a chart like the one shown below.

CITE TEXT EVIDENCE For practice analyzing foundational works, ask students to cite text evidence that provides details of life as an African American in the United States during the early twentieth century.

"How It Feels to Be Colored Me"

Topic	Theme	Text Evidence
childhood in a small southern town	A young girl was not defined by her race.	"I'd wave at them and when they returned my salute, I would say something like this: 'Howdy-do-well-I-thank-you-where-you-goin'?'" (lines 17–19)
being an adult in the outside world	People are often defined by race.	"In my heart as well as in the mirror, I became a fast brown . . ." (lines 38–39)

"The Weary Blues"

Topic	Theme	Text Evidence
musician playing blues in Harlem	Blues expresses both sadness and beauty.	"He played that sad raggy tune like a musical fool./Sweet Blues!" (lines 13–14)

Background In the early 1920s, African American artists, writers, musicians, and performers were part of a great cultural movement known as the Harlem Renaissance. The huge migration to the north after World War I brought African Americans of all ages and walks of life to the thriving New York City neighborhood called Harlem. Black men and women drew on their own cultural resources—their folk traditions as well as a new urban awareness—to produce unique forms of expression. These young black writers were the founders of a new era in literature. Looking inward, they expressed what it meant to be black in a white-dominated world.

Selections from

The Harlem Renaissance

How It Feels to Be Colored Me . . . . . . Essay by Zora Neale Hurston

The Weary Blues . . . . Poem by Langston Hughes

Zora Neale Hurston (1891–1960) grew up in the all-black town of Eatonville, Florida. Hurston was 13 when her family fell apart: her mother died, her father remarried, and by the age of 14, Hurston was on her own. In 1925, she moved to New York to study anthropology. Encouraged by her professors, she returned to the South to collect African American folklore, which she published in the collection Mules and Men. Sadly, her work fell out of favor in the 1940s, and Hurston died poor and nearly forgotten.

Langston Hughes (1902–1967) was one of the leading poets of the Harlem Renaissance. On a March night in 1922, Hughes sat in a small Harlem cabaret and wrote "The Weary Blues." In this poem, he incorporated the many elements of his life—the music of Southern black speech, the lyrics of the first blues he heard, and traditional poetic forms he learned in school. While the body of the poem took shape quickly, it took Hughes two years to get the ending right.

115

1. (READ ▶) As you read lines 1–25, begin to collect and cite text evidence.

- Underline text that is comic or ironic.
- Circle the extended metaphor in lines 14–17.
- In the margin, explain her description of the Northerners in lines 4–13.

How It Feels to Be Colored Me
Essay by Zora Neale Hurston

extenuating:

lessening the severity of

The Northerners were a spectacle to be "peered at cautiously"

I am colored but I offer nothing in the way of **extenuating** circumstances except the fact that I am the only Negro in the United States whose grandfather on the mother's side was *not* an Indian chief.

I remember the very day that I became colored. Up to my thirteenth year I lived in the little Negro town of Eatonville, Florida. It is exclusively a colored town. The only white people I knew passed through the town going to or coming from Orlando. The native whites rode dusty horses, the Northern tourists chugged down the sandy village road in automobiles. The town knew the Southerners and never stopped cane chewing when they passed. But the
10 Northerners were something else again. They were peered at cautiously from behind curtains by the timid. The more venturesome would come out on the porch to watch them go past and got just as much pleasure out of the tourists as the tourists got out of the village.

Ⓐ Ⓑ The front porch might seem a daring place for the rest of the town, but it was a gallery seat to me. My favorite place was atop the gate-post. Proscenium box for a born first-nighter.[1] Not only did I enjoy the show, but I didn't mind the actors knowing that I liked it. I actually spoke to them in passing. I'd wave at them and when they returned my salute, I would say something like this: "Howdy-do-well-I-thank-you-where-you-goin'?" Usually automobile or the
20 horse paused at this, and after a queer exchange of compliments, I would probably "go a piece of the way" with them, as we say in farthest Florida. If one of my family happened to come to the front in time to see me, of course negotiations would be rudely broken off. But even so, it is clear that I was the first "welcome-to-our-state" Floridian, and I hope the Miami Chamber of Commerce will please take notice.

[1] **proscenium . . . first-nighter:** A proscenium box is a box near the stage. A first-nighter is a person who attends the opening night of a performance.

During this period, white people differed from colored to me only in that they rode through town and never lived there. They liked to hear me "speak pieces" and sing and wanted to see me dance the parse-me-la,[2] and gave me generously of their small silver for doing these things, which seemed strange to
30 me for I wanted to do them so much that I needed bribing to stop. Only they didn't know it. The colored people gave no dimes. They **deplored** any joyful tendencies in me, but I was their Zora nevertheless. I belonged to them, to the nearby hotels, to the county—everybody's Zora.

Ⓒ But changes came in the family when I was thirteen, and I was sent to school in Jacksonville. I left Eatonville, the town of the oleanders,[3] as Zora. When I disembarked from the riverboat at Jacksonville, she was no more. It seemed that I had suffered a sea change.[4] I was not Zora of Orange County any more, I was now a little colored girl. I found it out in certain ways. In my heart as well as in the mirror, I became a fast brown—warranted not to rub nor run.
40 But I am not tragically colored. There is no great sorrow dammed up in my soul, nor lurking behind my eyes. I do not mind at all. I do not belong to the sobbing school of Negrohood who hold that nature somehow has given them a low-down dirty deal and whose feelings are all hurt about it. Even in the helter-skelter skirmish that is my life, I have seen that the world is to the strong regardless of a little pigmentation more or less. No, I do not weep at the world—I am too busy sharpening my oyster knife.[5]

deplore:

to strongly disapprove

Away from her home, she notices her own color for the first time.

[2] **parse-me-la:** a dance movement popular with Southern African Americans of the period.
[3] **oleanders:** evergreen shrubs with fragrant flowers.
[4] **sea change:** a complete transformation.
[5] **oyster knife:** a reference to the saying "The world is my oyster," implying that the world contains treasure waiting to be taken, like the pearl in an oyster.

2. (◀ REREAD) Reread lines 4–25. Explain the extended metaphor. What can you infer about Hurston's character in these lines?

The extended metaphor compares the front porch to a "gallery seat." Her interactions with the northern tourists were staged— funny and harmless. Although she pokes fun at her younger self, she also shows a girl who is curious, self-confident, and fearless.

3. (READ ▶) As you read lines 26–46, continue to cite text evidence.

- Underline text describing the differences between whites and blacks.
- In the margin, summarize how Zora becomes "a little colored girl."

116 | 117

---

1. (READ AND CITE TEXT EVIDENCE) Remind students that a metaphor is a form of figurative language in which one thing is compared to another.

Ⓐ **ASK STUDENTS** to identify details in lines 14–17 that help them understand that the author is comparing her front porch to a theater. *gallery seat, proscenium box, first-nighter, actors*

Critical Vocabulary: extenuating (line 1) Have students share their definitions of *extenuating*. Ask students to define *extenuating circumstances*. *"special circumstances that account for an irregular or improper way of doing something"*

2. (REREAD AND CITE TEXT EVIDENCE) Remind students that they have identified details in lines 14–17 that they can use to describe the extended metaphor.

Ⓑ **ASK STUDENTS** to identify evidence in the text that tells what Hurston was like as a young girl. *". . . I didn't mind the actors knowing that I liked it. I actually spoke to them . . ." (lines 16–17); "Howdy-do-well-I-thank-you-where-you-going?" (line 19); ". . . I would probably 'go a piece of the way' with them . . ." (lines 20–21)*

3. (READ AND CITE TEXT EVIDENCE)

Ⓒ **ASK STUDENTS** to identify details in lines 34–39 that help them understand the change that occurred in Hurston on the trip from Eatonville to Jacksonville. *Students should cite evidence from lines 38–39.*

Critical Vocabulary: deplore (line 31) Ask students why the older people deplored Zora's joyful tendencies.

CLOSE READ
Notes

D Someone is always at my elbow reminding me that I am the grand-daughter of <u>slaves</u>. It fails to register depression with me. <u>Slavery</u> is sixty years in the past. The operation was successful and the patient is doing well, thank

50 you. The terrible struggle that made me an American out of a potential <u>slave</u> said "On the line!" The Reconstruction said "Get set!"; and the generation before said "Go!" I am off to a flying start and I must not halt in the stretch to look behind and weep. <u>Slavery</u> is the price I paid for civilization, and the choice was not with me. It is a bully adventure and worth all that I have paid through my ancestors for it. No one on earth ever had a greater chance for glory. The world to be won and nothing to be lost. It is thrilling to think—to know that for any act of mine, I shall get twice as much praise or twice as much blame. It is quite exciting to hold the center of the national stage, with the spectators not knowing whether to laugh or to weep.

60 The position of my white neighbor is much more difficult. No brown **specter** pulls up a chair beside me when I sit down to eat. No dark ghost thrusts its leg against mine in bed. The game of keeping what one has is never so exciting as the game of getting.

I do not always feel colored. Even now I often achieve the unconscious Zora of Eatonville before the Hegira.[6] I feel most colored when I am thrown against a sharp white background.

For instance at Barnard. "Beside the waters of the Hudson"[7] I feel my race. Among the thousand white persons, I am a dark rock surged upon, overswept by a creamy sea. I am surged upon and overswept, but through it all, I remain

70 myself. When covered by the waters, I am; and the ebb but reveals me again.

Sometimes it is the other way around. A white person is set down in our midst, but the contrast is just as sharp for me. For instance, when I sit in the drafty basement that is The New World Cabaret with a white person, my color comes. We enter chatting about any little nothing that we have in common and are seated by the jazz waiters. In the abrupt way that jazz orchestras have, this

---

[6] **Hegira:** journey (from the name given to Muhammad's journey from Mecca to Medina in 622).

[7] **Barnard . . . Hudson:** Barnard is the college in New York City from which Hurston graduated in 1928. "Beside the water . . ." is a reference to the first line of the college song. The college is located near the Hudson River.

---

specter:
ghost

She says slavery is in the past. Now she has a chance for victory, "the world to be won."

---

4. **READ ▶** As you read lines 47–94, continue to cite text evidence.
   • Underline examples of repetition in lines 47–59.
   • Circle words and phrases that show the transformative power of the jazz music in lines 71–88.
   • In the margin, summarize what Hurston says about slavery.

118

---

one ⟨plunges⟩ into a number. It loses no time in **circumlocutions**, but gets right down to business. It ⟨constricts⟩ the thorax and ⟨splits⟩ the heart with its tempo and narcotic harmonies. This orchestra grows rambunctious, ⟨rears⟩ on its hind legs and ⟨attacks⟩ the tonal veil with primitive fury, ⟨rending⟩ it, ⟨clawing⟩ it until it

E 80 ⟨breaks through⟩ to the jungle beyond. I follow those heathen—follow them exultingly. I dance wildly inside myself; I yell within, I whoop; I shake my assegai[8] above my head, I hurl it true to the mark *yeeeeooww*! I am in the jungle and living in the jungle way. My face is painted red and yellow, and my body is painted blue. My pulse is throbbing like a war drum. I want to slaughter something—give pain, give death to what, I do not know. But the piece ends. The men of the orchestra wipe their lips and rest their fingers. I creep back slowly to the **veneer** we call civilization with the last tone and find the white friend sitting motionless in his seat, smoking calmly.

"Good music they have here," he remarks, drumming the table with his

90 fingertips.

Music! The great blobs of purple and red emotion have not touched him. He has only heard what I felt. He is far away and I see him but dimly across the ocean and the continent that have fallen between us. He is so pale with his whiteness then and I am *so* colored.

At certain times I have no race, I am *me*. When I set my hat at a certain angle and <u>saunter</u> down Seventh Avenue, Harlem City, feeling as <u>snooty</u> as the lions in front of the Forty-Second Street Library, for instance. So far as my

---

[8] **assegai:** a type of light spear used in southern Africa.

CLOSE READ
Notes

circumlocutions:
roundabout expressions that serve to avoid the main point

veneer:
a deceptive outer covering; facade

---

5. **◀ REREAD** Reread lines 71–94. How is Hurston affected by the jazz performance? What does it reveal about her?

The music pulls her powerfully into a colorful, raw, primitive jungle, bringing out the "heathen" in her. She is made aware of how "colored" she is compared to her white friend who experienced the music in a completely different way.

---

6. **READ ▶** As you read lines 95–120, continue to cite text evidence.
   • Underline text that shows Hurston's pride and positive feelings about herself.
   • In the margin, summarize why people are like "bags of miscellany" (lines 108–120).

119

---

4. **READ AND CITE TEXT EVIDENCE**

D **ASK STUDENTS** to find details in lines 47–56 that help them understand Hurston's thoughts about slavery. *"Slavery is sixty years in the past." (lines 48–49); ". . . the patient is doing well . . ." (line 49); "The terrible struggle that made me an American out of a potential slave . . ." (line 50); "The world to be won and nothing to be lost." (lines 55–56)*

Critical Vocabulary: specter (line 61) Have students share their definitions of *specter* and identify the context clue that could help them figure out the meaning. ghost *in line 61* Ask students why Hurston thinks white people might feel haunted by the specter of a black person. *They feel guilty about how African Americans were treated in the past.*

FOR ELL STUDENTS Explain that the word *bully* (line 54) has more than one meaning. As a noun, it means "someone who is cruel to others, especially those smaller and weaker." Here, as an adjective, *bully* means "excellent, splendid."

5. **REREAD AND CITE TEXT EVIDENCE**

E **ASK STUDENTS** to share the details they underlined that describe Hurston's experience and that of her white friend at the jazz club. *Students should emphasize that Hurston's experience was more powerful and primal than that of her friend.*

6. **READ AND CITE TEXT EVIDENCE**

F **ASK STUDENTS** to work with a partner to identify details in lines 108–120 that can help them understand why people are like "bags of miscellany."

Critical Vocabulary: circumlocutions (line 76) Ask students to share their definitions.

Critical Vocabulary: veneer (line 87) Ask students how the word *veneer* fits in with Hurston's experience. *As she listened to the music, she broke through the veneer, or deceptive facade, of polite civilization.*

raiment:
clothing

feelings are concerned, Peggy Hopkins Joyce on the Boule Mich[9] with her gorgeous **raiment**, stately carriage, knees knocking together in a most

100 aristocratic manner, has nothing on me. The cosmic Zora emerges. I belong to no race nor time, I am the eternal feminine with its string of beads.

I have no separate feeling about being an American citizen and colored. I am merely a fragment of the Great Soul that surges within the boundaries. My country, right or wrong.

Sometimes, I feel discriminated against, but it does not make me angry. It merely astonishes me. How can any deny themselves the pleasure of my company! It's beyond me.

miscellany:
a collection of
various items

People are all
different, like
bags filled
with random
treasure.

But in the main, I feel like a brown bag of **miscellany** propped against a wall. Against a wall in company with other bags, white, red, and yellow. Pour

110 out the contents, and there is discovered a jumble of small things priceless and worthless. A first-water[10] diamond, an empty spool, bits of broken glass, lengths of string, a key to a door long since crumbled away, a rusty knife-blade, old shoes saved for a road that never was and never will be, a nail bent under the weight of things too heavy for any nail, a dried flower or two, still a little fragrant. In your hand is the brown bag. On the ground before you is the jumble it held—so much like the jumble in the bags, could they be emptied, that all might be dumped in a single heap and the bags refilled without altering the content of any greatly. A bit of colored glass more or less would not matter. Perhaps that is how the Great Stuffer of Bags filled them in the first place—who

120 knows?

[9] **Peggy . . . Boule Mich:** a wealthy woman of Hurston's day, walking along the Boulevard Saint-Michel in Paris.
[10] **first-water:** of the highest quality or purity.

7. ◀ REREAD Reread lines 108–120. What does Hurston's statement about "bags" say about human character?

Hurston believes each person is a jumble of content. While people
often say that people's characters distinguish them from each other,
Hurston points out that the random and diverse nature of the
content of our characters is something that makes us all alike.

120

---

8. READ ▶ As you read "The Weary Blues," continue to cite text evidence.

- Underline pairs of words with alliteration within a line.
- Circle the words or phrases describing sadness or defeat.

The Weary Blues
Poem by Langston Hughes

croon:
a low, soft
voice

pallor:
lack of color

Droning a drowsy syncopated[11] tune,
Rocking back and forth to a mellow **croon**,
  I heard a Negro play.
Down on Lenox Avenue[12] the other night
5 By the pale dull **pallor** of an old gas light
  He did a lazy sway. . . .
  He did a lazy sway. . . .
To the tune o' those Weary Blues
With his ebony hands on each ivory key
10 He made that poor piano moan with melody.
  O Blues!
Swaying to and fro on his rickety stool
He played that sad raggy tune like a musical fool.
  Sweet Blues!
15 Coming from a black man's soul.
  O Blues!
In a deep song voice with a melancholy tone
I heard that Negro sing, that old piano moan—
  "Ain't got nobody in all this world,
20 Ain't got nobody but ma self.
  I's gwine to quit ma frownin'
  And put ma troubles on the shelf."
Thump, thump, thump, went his foot on the floor.
He played a few chords then he sang some more—
25 "I got the Weary Blues
  And I can't be satisfied.
  Got the Weary Blues
  And can't be satisfied—

[11] **syncopated:** characterized by a shifting of stresses from normally strong to normally weak beats.
[12] **Lenox Avenue:** a main north-south street in Harlem.

121

---

7. **REREAD AND CITE TEXT EVIDENCE**

Ⓖ ASK STUDENTS to work with a partner to identify evidence in the text that helps them understand how Hurston believes that people are like bags of miscellany. *"... I feel like a brown bag of miscellany ..." (line 108); "... other bags, white, red, and yellow." (line 109); "... how the Great Stuffer of Bags filled them ..." (line 119)*

Critical Vocabulary: raiment (line 99) Ask students to name some specific articles of clothing that might qualify as a "gorgeous raiment." *Students might suggest expensive gowns or dresses, silk blouses, or fur coats.*

Critical Vocabulary: miscellany (line 108) Have students identify the various items in the miscellany Hurston describes. *diamond, thread spool, broken glass, string, key, knife blade, old shoes, nail, dried flower*

8. **READ AND CITE TEXT EVIDENCE** Remind students that alliteration is the repetition of usually initial consonant sounds in two or more words that appear close together in a text.

Ⓗ ASK STUDENTS to cite examples of repetition in lines 1–24. *Examples include "He did a lazy sway. . . " (lines 6, 7), "Thump, thump, thump" (line 23), and "Blues!" (lines 11, 14, and 16).*

Critical Vocabulary: croon (line 2) Have students share their definitions of *croon*. Then ask them how the word *croon* helps establish the mood of the poem and what it says about Harlem in the 1920s. *The word is in keeping with the sad or mellow mood of the night scene.*

Critical Vocabulary: pallor (line 5) Ask students what color they see in their mind's eye when they read line 5. *Students may suggest very pale or washed-out yellow.*

CLOSE READ
Notes

30 I ain't happy no mo

And I wish that I had died.

And far into the night he crooned that tune.

The stars went out and so did the moon.

The singer stopped playing and went to bed

While the Weary Blues echoed through his head.

35 He slept like a rock or a man that's dead.

9. **REREAD** Hughes was one of the first innovators of "jazz poetry"—poetry with a jazz-like rhythm and feeling of improvisation. Reread the poem and then describe the effect of its rhythm and repetitions on your experience as a reader.

The rhythm of the poem changes as it shifts from the listener to the singer. The rhyme scheme is loose and unpredictable, like jazz music.

SHORT RESPONSE

Cite Text Evidence Discuss how Hurston's essay and Hughes's poem—in their subject matter, style, form, and content—exemplify the themes of the Harlem Renaissance. Review your reading notes, and **cite text evidence** in your response.

Both Hurston and Hughes focus on the African American experience at a specific place and time. They use dialect; they improvise with word choice, rhythm, pace, and tone; they are moved and thrilled by the power of African American musical forms (jazz and blues). Hurston, however, places her own life and experience at the center of her writing. She is relentlessly positive about herself, and that positivity rubs off on her view of race relations. Hughes's poem is an observation, from the outside, of a black musician. Although he depicts the music as profoundly powerful, the poem expresses an undeniable and pervasive melancholy.

122

---

9. **REREAD AND CITE TEXT EVIDENCE** Have students work with a partner to identify the words that rhyme throughout the poem and words and phrases that are repeated.

🄛 **ASK STUDENTS** to explain what characteristics of the poem give it a feeling of improvisation, or being made up on the spot. *Students should mention the repetition of words and the changing, irregular rhyme schemes.*

SHORT RESPONSE

Cite Text Evidence Students' responses will vary but should include evidence from the text that supports their answers. Students should:

- identify details in both the essay and the poem that relate to the Harlem Renaissance of the 1920s.
- address the subject matter, style, form, and content of the texts.
- explain how the experiences described in the two texts are alike and different.

TO CHALLENGE STUDENTS . . .

For more context, students can research the Harlem Renaissance online.

ASK STUDENTS to work in small groups to answer the following questions.

- Have students identify the causes for the migration of African Americans from the South to the northern cities of Chicago, Detroit, and New York.
- Have students describe the nature of the Harlem Renaissance and discuss the different arts that flourished in New York during the 1920s.
- Have students identify some of the major artists of the period as well as some of their accomplishments. (The cover of Langston Hughes's poetry book *The Weary Blues* is featured in the video.)
- Finally, have students identify the causes for the decline of the Harlem Renaissance and discuss its lasting significance.

DIG DEEPER

With the class, return to Question 5, Reread. Have students share and discuss their responses.

ASK STUDENTS to identify specific text evidence in lines 86–94 that helps them more fully understand the response of the white man with whom Hurston is sitting.

- Encourage students to identify details that describe what the man is doing when the music stops. *". . . sitting motionless in his seat, smoking calmly"*
- Have students discuss what the words *motionless* and *calmly* imply about the white man. *He has not been excited by the music in the way that Hurston was.*
- Have students cite evidence to explain how Hurston describes the white man in lines 91–94 and the conclusion she draws about their differences. *"The great blobs of purple and red emotion have not touched him." (line 91) "He is far away." (line 92) "He is so pale with his whiteness then and I am so colored." (lines 93–94)*

ASK STUDENTS to revise their Short Response answers using details from the class discussion.

 **EXEMPLAR**

Mending Wall
The Death of the Hired Man

*my*SmartPlanner · Create lesson plans and access resources online.

Poems by Robert Frost

Why These Texts?

Students will encounter both ambiguous language and narrative elements in the course of their reading of both prose and poetry. Studying "Mending Wall" will give students practice analyzing language that can be interpreted in a variety of different ways. "The Death of the Hired Man" will give students an opportunity to look closely at narrative elements, such as dialogue, characterization, plot, and setting, in the context of a narrative poem.

Key Learning Objective: Students will be able to analyze the structure and language of poetry.

COMMON CORE Common Core Standards

RL 3 Analyze the impact of the author's choices.
RL 4 Determine figurative and connotative meanings; analyze the impact of specific word choices.
RL 5 Analyze how an author's choices concerning how to structure specific parts of a text contribute to its overall meaning as well as its aesthetic impact.
RL 9 Demonstrate knowledge of foundational works of American literature.
W 2 Write informative/explanatory texts.
L 3a Vary syntax for effect; apply an understanding of syntax.

▲ Text Complexity Rubric

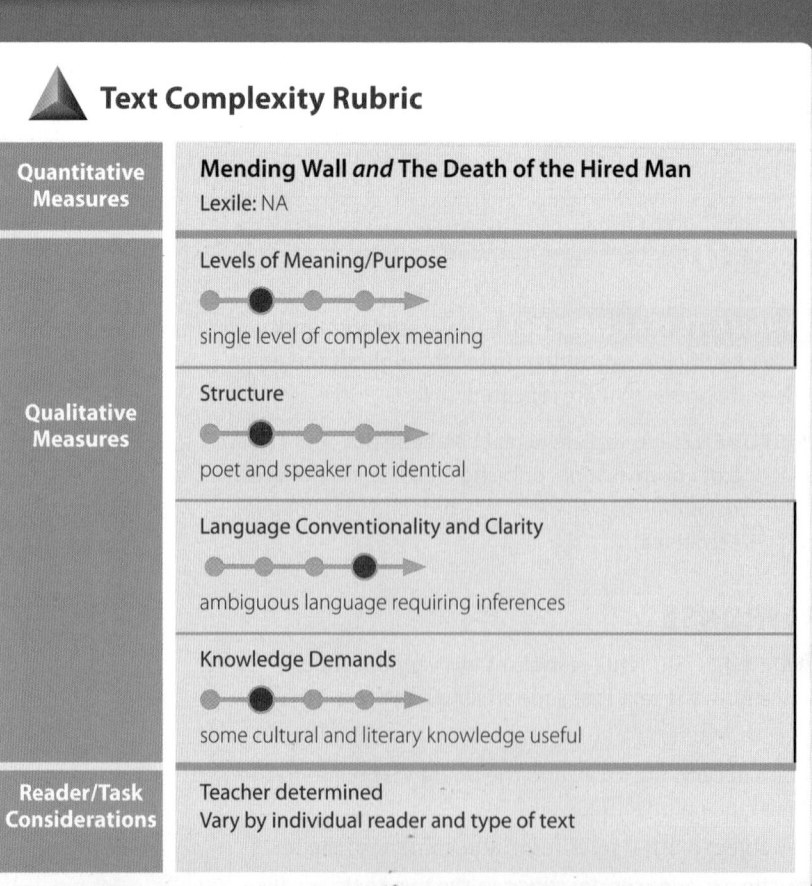

Quantitative Measures

Mending Wall *and* The Death of the Hired Man
Lexile: NA

Qualitative Measures

Levels of Meaning/Purpose

single level of complex meaning

Structure

poet and speaker not identical

Language Conventionality and Clarity

ambiguous language requiring inferences

Knowledge Demands

some cultural and literary knowledge useful

Reader/Task Considerations

Teacher determined
Vary by individual reader and type of text

Robert Frost was a steadfast traditionalist who refused to be influenced by the fads and movements that swept the American literary scene during his lifetime. He adhered to traditional verse forms and metrics and focused on the realistic depiction of American rural life and the people inhabiting it. Noted for his command of colloquial speech, Frost also encouraged his students to allow the effects of human speech patterns to come through in their poetry. Astute critics have pointed out that behind the charm of Frost's rural settings and common characters often lie complex psychological portraits, penetrating meditations on human existence, and pessimistic messages about life.

Frost sold his first poem in 1894. He spent a brief time in England; while there, he not only found more publishers willing to take a chance on his work, but he also met a number of British poets who would prove both influential and helpful. Among them were Rupert Brooke, Robert Graves, Edward Thomas, and Ezra Pound. Thomas and Pound encouraged Frost by offering both friendship and favorable reviews of his work. According to Frost, it was his long walks over the English landscapes with Thomas that inspired "The Road Not Taken," one of Frost's most successful pieces.

AS YOU READ Direct students to use the As You Read instructions to focus their reading. Remind them to write down any questions they generate during reading.

Mending Wall
The Death of the Hired Man

Poems by Robert Frost

Robert Frost *is normally associated with rural New England, but he was born in San Francisco in 1874. The death of his father when Robert was 11 years old prompted the family to move to the industrial city of Lawrence, Massachusetts. After graduating from high school, Frost attended Dartmouth and Harvard for short periods of time, but never obtained a degree. He married Elinor White, a high school classmate and lover of poetry, in 1895, and supported his family with various teaching jobs.*

In 1900, Frost left teaching and took up farming, while also trying to establish himself as a poet. The 11 years that Frost spent farming in New Hampshire were also very creative years for his writing. However, he was not able to publish a book during this time. At the age of 38, Frost uprooted the family and moved to England. In England, he was able to publish his first book of poetry, A Boy's Will. *This book was followed in 1914 by* North of Boston. *At the outbreak of WWI in 1915, Frost and his family returned to the United States. He was greeted as a leading American poet. In 1924, his collection* New Hampshire *won a Pulitzer Prize, one of four that he would eventually receive.*

Unfortunately, his private life did not match the success of his public life. Between 1934 and 1940, Frost suffered several personal tragedies. His daughter, his wife, and his son died. In addition, his other daughter was institutionalized for mental illness. These events affected the mood of his late poems—they often conveyed a bleak outlook on life. He died in Boston in 1963.

AS YOU READ Pay attention to the mood, or overall feeling or atmosphere, of each poem. What kind of descriptive language does Frost include? Write down any questions you generate during reading.

TEACH

Analyze Language: Ambiguity (LINES 1–4)

COMMON CORE RL 4

Tell students that **ambiguity** means the state of being uncertain or open to more than one interpretation. Sometimes these interpretations may be in direct opposition to one another.

 ASK STUDENTS to explain two possible opposing interpretations for lines 1–4 and tell which one they support. *(The speaker might be saying that it is unfortunate that the ground destroys the wall each winter, or he may be implying that nature knows better than landowners whether walls are a good idea.)*

Analyze Structure

COMMON CORE RL 4, RL 5

(LINES 5–12)

Remind students that **setting** is the time and place in which a story or poem takes place. Although setting is most often associated with fiction, poets often use it effectively as well.

B **CITE TEXT EVIDENCE** Have students identify the setting of "Mending Wall" and note which details from the poem reveal the setting. *(The setting is a rural area. The rural setting is revealed through details such as "hunters" in line 5, "the rabbit out of hiding, / to please the yelping dogs" in lines 8–9, and "neighbor . . . beyond the hill" in line 12.)*

MENDING WALL

Something there is that doesn't love a wall,
That sends the frozen-ground-swell under it,
And spills the upper boulders in the sun;
And makes gaps even two can pass abreast.
5　The work of hunters is another thing:
I have come after them and made repair
Where they have left not one stone on a stone,
But they would have the rabbit out of hiding,
To please the yelping dogs. The gaps I mean,
10　No one has seen them made or heard them made,
But at spring mending-time we find them there.
I let my neighbor know beyond the hill;
And on a day we meet to walk the line
And set the wall between us once again.
15　We keep the wall between us as we go.
To each the boulders that have fallen to each.
And some are loaves and some so nearly balls
We have to use a spell to make them balance:
"Stay where you are until our backs are turned!"
20　We wear our fingers rough with handling them.
Oh, just another kind of out-door game,
One on a side. It comes to little more:

Image Credits: ©Robin Bush/Oxford Scientific/Getty Images

SCAFFOLDING FOR ELL STUDENTS

Punctuation　Point out that Frost uses a variety of punctuation in "Mending Wall," and that he does so quite purposefully. Read the poem aloud for students, using your voice to emphasize where each significant mark of punctuation appears.

Explain that periods mark the end of a sentence and indicate a significant pause, while commas and semicolons are used to separate parts of a sentence and indicate smaller pauses. Colons are used to introduce something.

ASK STUDENTS　to work with a partner to read aloud the first two sentences of the poem. Tell students to use the punctuation to help them read more fluently and understand the meaning of the sentences.

There where it is we do not need the wall:
He is all pine and I am apple orchard.
25 My apple trees will never get across
And eat the cones under his pines, I tell him.
He only says, "Good fences make good neighbors."
Spring is the mischief in me, and I wonder
If I could put a notion in his head:
30 "*Why* do they make good neighbors? Isn't it
Where there are cows? But here there are no cows.
Before I built a wall I'd ask to know
What I was walling in or walling out,
And to whom I was like to give offence.
35 Something there is that doesn't love a wall,
That wants it down." I could say "Elves" to him,
But it's not elves exactly, and I'd rather
He said it for himself. I see him there
Bringing a stone grasped firmly by the top
40 In each hand, like an old-stone savage armed.
He moves in darkness as it seems to me,
Not of woods only and the shade of trees.
He will not go behind his father's saying,
And he likes having thought of it so well
45 He says again, "Good fences make good neighbors."

THE DEATH OF THE HIRED MAN

Mary sat musing on the lamp-flame at the table
Waiting for Warren. When she heard his step,
She ran on tip-toe down the darkened passage
To meet him in the doorway with the news
5 And put him on his guard. "Silas is back."
She pushed him outward with her through the door
And shut it after her. "Be kind," she said.
She took the market things from Warren's arms
And set them on the porch, then drew him down
10 To sit beside her on the wooden steps.

"When was I ever anything but kind to him?
But I'll not have the fellow back," he said.
"I told him so last haying, didn't I?
'If he left then,' I said, 'that ended it.'
15 What good is he? Who else will harbor[1] him
At his age for the little he can do?

---
[1] **harbor:** provide safe shelter for.

TO CHALLENGE STUDENTS...

Interpreting Symbolism Remind students that in poetry concrete objects often are used to symbolize abstract ideas. "Mending Wall" presents at one level a realistic portrait of rural life, but it can also be read as symbolic.

Encourage students to consider the wall in the poem at the purely symbolic level. What do they think the wall stands for beyond its basic meaning as a physical barrier or demarcation of property?

ASK STUDENTS to write a short poem in their own style that uses a wall as a symbol. Have volunteers read their poems to the class, and offer classmates a chance to interpret the symbolism.

CLOSE READ

Analyze Language: Ambiguity (LINES 23–26)

COMMON CORE **RL 4**

Tell students that the ambiguity in "Mending Wall" has led to controversy regarding how the poem should be interpreted. The poem implies two different mindsets, and critics often argue over which one Frost meant to endorse.

C **ASK STUDENTS** to explain two possible interpretations of lines 23–26 and tell which one they think was most likely Frost's intended meaning. *(1. The speaker actually thinks there is no need for a wall since each man's land has different types of trees which will not harm each other. 2. The speaker means the statement metaphorically. When he says "He is all pine and I am apple orchard" in line 24, he is saying that he and his neighbor are very different. By this he may mean that they are not likely to become friends and, therefore, might prefer to have a wall separating their properties.)*

Analyze Structure

COMMON CORE **RL 4, RL 5**

(LINES 27–45)

Tell students that poetry sometimes uses elements typical of fiction, such as characterization, dialogue, setting, and plot. "Mending Wall" employs **dialogue,** or characters' speech.

D **CITE TEXT EVIDENCE** Ask students to cite evidence from the poem to explain what difference between the two characters is revealed through the use of dialogue. *(The speaker questions whether the wall is needed, and seems more open to establishing a friendship of some kind, or at least an understanding that would keep them from having to maintain the wall [lines 30–36]. He seems to have a philosophical bent regarding the symbolism of walls. But the neighbor is attached to his father's saying that walls are necessary in order for neighbors to get along [lines 27 and 45], suggesting that having a definable boundary is preferable to friendship for keeping the peace.)*

Analyze Structure

 COMMON CORE RL 4, RL 5

(LINES 17–41)

Elements of Narrative Poetry Tell students that "The Death of the Hired Man" is an example of a narrative poem. It is written in verse, and has many of the other elements of poetry, but it also tells a story using narrative elements. Review the following elements with students:

- **Characterization**—how the writer reveals the personalities of the characters

- **Conflict**—a struggle between two characters or within a character

E CITE TEXT EVIDENCE Ask students to identify the three characters. *(Mary, the wife; Warren, the husband; and Silas, an old farmhand)* Have them tell what they know about each character's personality so far, and how the traits are revealed in the poem, citing evidence from the text to support their conclusions. *(Mary is compassionate. This trait is evident by her shushing Warren in line 31 and by her actions of taking Silas into the house and giving him tea in lines 40 and 41. Warren is angry and maybe a bit callous. He says he wants Silas to hear him criticizing him and saying "I'm done" [lines 24–30]. Silas was apparently lazy and somewhat of a beggar and is now sick. Mary describes him as "worn out" [line 33] and "a miserable sight" [line 36]. Warren talks about how Silas was never much help on the farm yet depended on them [lines 17–23].)*

F ASK STUDENTS to explain two conflicts that exist between characters. *(Mary and Warren are in conflict over whether to help Silas. Silas and Warren got into a conflict about work and pay, which caused Warren to send Silas away.)*

What help he is there's no depending on.
Off he goes always when I need him most.
E 'He thinks he ought to earn a little pay,
20 Enough at least to buy tobacco with,
F So he won't have to beg and be beholden.'
'All right,' I say, 'I can't afford to pay
Any fixed wages, though I wish I could.'
'Someone else can.' 'Then someone else will have to.'
25 I shouldn't mind his bettering himself
If that was what it was. You can be certain,
When he begins like that, there's someone at him
Trying to coax him off with pocket-money,—
In haying time, when any help is scarce.
30 In winter he comes back to us. I'm done."

"Sh! not so loud: he'll hear you," Mary said.

"I want him to: he'll have to soon or late."

"He's worn out. He's asleep beside the stove.
When I came up from Rowe's I found him here,
35 Huddled against the barn-door fast asleep,
A miserable sight, and frightening, too—
You needn't smile—I didn't recognize him—
I wasn't looking for him—and he's changed.
Wait till you see."

　　　　　"Where did you say he'd been?"

40 "He didn't say. I dragged him to the house,
And gave him tea and tried to make him smoke.
I tried to make him talk about his travels.
Nothing would do: he just kept nodding off."

"What did he say? Did he say anything?"

45 "But little."

　　　　　"Anything? Mary, confess
He said he'd come to ditch² the meadow for me."

"Warren!"

　　　　　"But did he? I just want to know."

"Of course he did. What would you have him say?
Surely you wouldn't grudge the poor old man

---

² **ditch:** dig drainage channels in.

SCAFFOLDING FOR ELL STUDENTS

Colloquialisms Explain that **colloquialisms** are informal words and phrases used mostly in spoken English. Colloquial expressions are generally specific to particular geographic regions. They may or may not consist of figures of speech. Share with students some examples of colloquial language found in everyday speech, such as "down and out," "fell for her," "call it a day," and "fixin' to."

ASK STUDENTS to work in pairs to complete the chart shown. They may look up words in a dictionary if necessary. (Point out that colloquial phrases do sometimes appear in dictionaries, usually with the abbreviation *colloq.*) After pairs have completed the chart, have students work independently to identify other colloquial expressions in "The Death of the Hired Man" and determine their meanings.

50 Some humble way to save his self-respect.
    He added, if you really care to know,
    He meant to clear the upper pasture, too.
    That sounds like something you have heard before?
    Warren, I wish you could have heard the way
55 He jumbled everything. I stopped to look
    Two or three times—he made me feel so queer[3]—
    To see if he was talking in his sleep.
    He ran on[4] Harold Wilson—you remember—
    The boy you had in haying four years since.
60 He's finished school, and teaching in his college.
    Silas declares you'll have to get him back.
    He says they two will make a team for work:
    Between them they will lay this farm as smooth!
    The way he mixed that in with other things.
65 He thinks young Wilson a likely lad, though daft
    On education—you know how they fought
    All through July under the blazing sun,
    Silas up on the cart to build the load,
    Harold along beside to pitch it on."

70 "Yes, I took care to keep well out of earshot."

    "Well, those days trouble Silas like a dream.
    You wouldn't think they would. How some things linger!
    Harold's young college boy's assurance piqued[5] him.
    After so many years he still keeps finding
75 Good arguments he sees he might have used.
    I sympathize. I know just how it feels
    To think of the right thing to say too late.
    Harold's associated in his mind with Latin.
    He asked me what I thought of Harold's saying
80 He studied Latin like the violin
    Because he liked it—that an argument!
    He said he couldn't make the boy believe
    He could find water with a hazel prong[6]—
    Which showed how much good school had ever done him.
85 He wanted to go over that. But most of all
    He thinks if he could have another chance
    To teach him how to build a load of hay—"

    "I know, that's Silas' one accomplishment.

    _____
    [3] **queer:** uncomfortable; ill at ease.
    [4] **ran on:** kept talking about in a rambling way.
    [5] **piqued:** aroused resentment in.
    [6] **hazel prong:** a reference to the practice of dowsing, in which a person uses a
        forked stick made of hazel wood to try to find underground water.

Line #	Colloquialism	Meaning
12	have the fellow back	
18	Off he goes	
27	there's someone at him	
28	coax him off	

CLOSE READ

Analyze Structure

COMMON CORE RL 4, RL 5

(LINES 54–57)

Explain that another element of narrative poetry is dialogue. Tell students that dialogue can be used to advance the plot or as a characterization technique. Dialogue can reveal traits of the character speaking, or traits of another character being spoken about.

G ASK STUDENTS what Mary's dialogue reveals about Silas's current condition. (*He is apparently very confused or a little delirious, so we know he is very sick. Mary says his comments are mixed up and don't really make sense. For instance in line 55 she says, "He jumbled everything" and in line 57 she says he sounds as if he were "talking in his sleep."*)

Analyze Structure

COMMON CORE RL 4, RL 5

(LINES 76–87)

Explain that narrative poems, like stories, have a plot. Remind students that **plot** is the sequence of events in a narrative and that most plots are constructed around a conflict.

H ASK STUDENTS how Mary's descriptions of the way Silas argued with Harold during the summer four years ago contribute to the plot of the narrative. (*As Mary remembers time spent with Silas in the past, the reader can infer that a bond developed between her and Silas. She says in line 76 that she sympathizes with Silas. The description suggests that they all know each other well, having spent many haying seasons together. This bond helps explain why Silas is back and why Mary and Warren may be conflicted about how to treat him.*)

Analyze Language: Figurative Meanings

COMMON CORE RL 4

(LINES 103–110)

Remind students that **figurative language** is language that communicates meaning beyond the literal meaning of the words.

 **ASK STUDENTS** why lines 103–110 might be considered figurative language. Have them explain how this figurative language affects meaning in the poem. *(In these lines, the speaker says that the moon is falling and dragging the sky to the hills. The reader knows this is meant figuratively and that the moon is setting. In line 105, moonlight is compared to a liquid that can be poured; and in line 107 the morning glory strings are compared to harp strings. The figurative language in these lines gives the reader an idea of the beauty of the place.)*

Analyze Language: Ambiguity

COMMON CORE RL 4

(LINES 113–120)

Explain that the ambiguity in some of the characters' words and actions affects the plot of "The Death of the Hired Man." For example, the reader must decide how to interpret ambiguities to anticipate how Warren will respond to Silas.

 **ASK STUDENTS** why lines 113–120 might be considered ambiguous. *(Warren's words here are ambiguous because it is not clear whether he thinks Silas deserves to call their farm his home.)*

He bundles every forkful in its place,
90   And tags and numbers it for future reference,
So he can find and easily dislodge it
In the unloading. Silas does that well.
He takes it out in bunches like big birds' nests.
You never see him standing on the hay
95   He's trying to lift, straining to lift himself."

"He thinks if he could teach him that, he'd be
Some good perhaps to someone in the world.
He hates to see a boy the fool of books.
Poor Silas, so concerned for other folk,
100   And nothing to look backward to with pride,
And nothing to look forward to with hope,
So now and never any different."

Part of a moon was falling down the west,
Dragging the whole sky with it to the hills.
105   Its light poured softly in her lap. She saw
And spread her apron to it. She put out her hand
Among the harp-like morning-glory strings,
Taut with the dew from garden bed to eaves,
As if she played unheard the tenderness
110   That wrought[7] on him beside her in the night.
"Warren," she said, "he has come home to die:
You needn't be afraid he'll leave you this time."

"Home," he mocked gently.

                    "Yes, what else but home?
It all depends on what you mean by home.
115   Of course he's nothing to us, any more
Than was the hound that came a stranger to us
Out of the woods, worn out upon the trail."

"Home is the place where, when you have to go there,
They have to take you in."

                    "I should have called it
120   Something you somehow haven't to deserve."

Warren leaned out and took a step or two,
Picked up a little stick, and brought it back
And broke it in his hand and tossed it by.
"Silas has better claim on us you think
125   Than on his brother? Thirteen little miles

---

[7] **wrought:** worked.

450   Collection 6

Strategies for Annotation   ✐ �'Annotate it!

Analyze Language

COMMON CORE RL 4

Share these strategies for guided or independent analysis:

- Highlight in blue any figurative language that describes the setting.
- Highlight in green sections of the text that are ambiguous in meaning.
- Make notes about the various interpretations that might be given to each of the ambiguous sections.

Part of a moon was falling down the west,

Dragging the whole sky with it to the hills.

Its light poured softly in her lap. ...She put out her

hand...Among the harp-like morning-glory strings,

As if she played unheard the tenderness

That wrought on him beside her in the night.

> Is she trying to make him more tender or noticing the tenderness of the flowers?

Image Credits: ©Getty Images RF

As the road winds would bring him to his door.
Silas has walked that far no doubt to-day.
Why didn't he go there? His brother's rich,
A somebody—director in the bank."

130 "He never told us that."

            "We know it though."

"I think his brother ought to help, of course.
I'll see to that if there is need. He ought of right
To take him in, and might be willing to—
He may be better than appearances.

135 But have some pity on Silas. Do you think
If he'd had any pride in claiming kin
Or anything he looked for from his brother,
He'd keep so still about him all this time?"

"I wonder what's between them."

            "I can tell you.

140 Silas is what he is—we wouldn't mind him—
But just the kind that kinsfolk can't abide.
He never did a thing so very bad.
He don't know why he isn't quite as good
As anyone. He won't be made ashamed

145 To please his brother, worthless though he is."

"*I* can't think Si ever hurt anyone."

"No, but he hurt my heart the way he lay

Poems by Robert Frost   **451**

CLOSE READ

Analyze Structure   COMMON CORE RL 4, RL 5

(LINES 135–145)

Characterization Point out that since Silas never actually appears in the scene or speaks directly, the reader must learn about his character through the dialogue of the other characters.

K CITE TEXT EVIDENCE Ask students to explain what they learn about Silas's character in this part of the poem, and how. *(Readers learn in lines 135–139 that Silas is estranged from his brother for some unknown reason. Lines 140–145 suggest that Silas is not bad; he is just not very successful.)*

Analyze Structure (LINE 146)   COMMON CORE RL 4, RL 5

Characterization Point out that the whole poem takes place in one scene between Warren and Mary. However, the reader witnesses a change in Warren's character during this one conversation.

L CITE TEXT EVIDENCE Have students analyze line 153 for what the line of dialogue suggests about Warren. *(In lines 124–129, Warren seems resentful about Silas showing up, implying that he should have gone to his brother's house instead. In line 146, however, he seems to be softening toward Silas when he says "I can't think Si ever hurt anyone.")*

WHEN STUDENTS STRUGGLE

Developing Reading Fluency Use this poem to give students practice in reading dialogue. Divide students into pairs, and have them prepare an oral reading of lines 124–161. One student will take Warren's part, and one will take Mary's part.

Pairs should work together to make sure each student clearly understands the meaning of each piece of dialogue and how the character's vocal tone might change depending on the meaning behind the words. Encourage students to read with expression and to stay "in character." Tell them to use punctuation marks to guide them.

Analyzing Language: Ambiguity (LINES 153–154)

 COMMON CORE RL 4

Tell students that interpreting ambiguous lines of dialogue often requires an understanding of the characters.

 **ASK STUDENTS** to give two possible interpretations of what Warren means when he says, in response to Mary's comment that Silas's working days are done, "I'd not be in a hurry to say that." *(He might be saying that he thinks Silas is just being lazy when he actually could still work. Or he might be asking Mary not to say that Silas is dying, because he does care for Silas and does not want him to die.)*

Analyzing Structure

 COMMON CORE RL 4, RL 5

(LINES 164–167)

Remind students that the **resolution** of a plot reveals the final outcome of events.

 **CITE TEXT EVIDENCE** Ask students to explain how the conflict in this poem is resolved and to cite text evidence to support their interpretations. *(The conflict between Mary and Warren seems resolved when Warren takes Mary's hand in line 165. The conflict about what to do with Silas is resolved by Silas's death in line 167.)*

COLLABORATIVE DISCUSSION Have students organize their discussion by first addressing the **mood,** or atmosphere, of each poem separately, and then comparing and contrasting the two poems. Encourage students to refer to specific language from the poem throughout their discussions.

ASK STUDENTS to share any questions they generated in the course of reading and discussing the selection.

And rolled his old head on that sharp-edged chair-back.
He wouldn't let me put him on the lounge.
150 You must go in and see what you can do.
I made the bed up for him there to-night.
You'll be surprised at him—how much he's broken.
His working days are done; I'm sure of it."

"I'd not be in a hurry to say that."

155 "I haven't been. Go, look, see for yourself.
But, Warren, please remember how it is:
He's come to help you ditch the meadow.
He has a plan. You mustn't laugh at him.
He may not speak of it, and then he may.
160 I'll sit and see if that small sailing cloud
Will hit or miss the moon."

It hit the moon.
Then there were three there, making a dim row,
The moon, the little silver cloud, and she.

Warren returned—too soon, it seemed to her,
165 Slipped to her side, caught up her hand and waited.

"Warren," she questioned.

"Dead," was all he answered.

COLLABORATIVE DISCUSSION With a small group, discuss the mood of each poem. How does Frost's descriptive language appeal to your senses and help you visualize the settings of the poems?

APPLYING ACADEMIC VOCABULARY

contemporary	global

After students have read and discussed the poems, remind them that it wasn't until Frost went to live in England that he found critical acclaim and a publisher for his work. Incorporate the Collection 6 academic vocabulary words *contemporary* and *global* into a discussion of how Frost's work was received. Ask students why it was so important for Frost to have the support of his **contemporaries** in the literary world. How did his contemporaries in the United States treat him differently than those in England? Ask students why his poems, many of which focused on regional settings and subject matter, had enough **global** appeal to win over literary figures in other countries.

Analyze Language: Ambiguity

COMMON CORE RL 4

Frost's poetry incorporates a great deal of ambiguity. **Ambiguity** in literary work allows for more than one meaning. The works are open to various or opposing interpretations, as in lines 41–42 of "Mending Wall." This lends richness and beauty to the poems.

> He moves in darkness as it seems to me,
> Not of woods only and the shade of trees.

Since Frost is intentionally vague about his neighbor and about the whole enterprise of using walls to keep things in or to keep things out, readers are left to sort through his ambiguity. The first line talks about the neighbor moving "in darkness." At first it seems to refer to the actual darkness of the woods. In the next line, Frost says it was more than that, but he declines to be specific.

Of course, you don't have to choose rigidly between meanings in works that contain ambiguity. Skilled readers of poetry will recognize ambiguity and live with it, even enjoy it, as they read and consider a poem. As you analyze Frost's poem, consider recording different interpretations of the poem's lines in a chart such as this one.

Line from "Mending Wall"	Interpretations
He moves in darkness as it seems to me	The speaker refers to his neighbor as sinister.
	The speaker refers to his neighbor as hard to get to know, possibly unfriendly.

Analyze Structure

COMMON CORE RL 4, RL 5

Like fiction, a **narrative poem,** such as "The Death of the Hired Man," tells a story using the elements of plot, character, and setting. A poet may adapt methods of characterization typically used in fiction, such as physical description using vivid imagery, character development through a character's actions or comments, the thoughts or actions of other characters, or direct comments about characters by the poem's speaker. As you analyze "The Death of the Hired Man," consider these questions.

Dialogue	Who is speaking in this poem? How does Robert Frost use conversation to help develop the narrative elements of the poem?
Plot	How is the order of events conveyed? Does the dialogue in the poem only provide information about the present time?
Characterization	Does Robert Frost use direct description by the speaker to impart the characters' traits? What information do the characters' own words convey about them?
Setting	Why do the characters' descriptions of their work help you understand the setting, or the time and place, of the poem?

TEACH

CLOSE READ

Analyze Language: Ambiguity

COMMON CORE RL 4

Point out that yet another possible interpretation of the two lines cited is that the neighbor simply seems mysterious. Perhaps the speaker is intrigued by him.

Have students complete a chart of the ambiguous lines in the poem and their possible meanings, as suggested. Then let students compare their charts. Encourage them to embrace and appreciate the richness that ambiguity lends to poetry.

Analyze Structure

COMMON CORE RL 4, RL 5

Address each row of the chart in a class discussion, allowing volunteers to answer each question and to elaborate on the techniques Frost uses to develop the characters and the plot. Point out to students how effectively Frost makes use of dialogue, utilizing it to develop characters, fill in the plot, establish setting, and more. Help students to look separately at the plot of the scene depicted versus the plot of the story as a whole.

Strategies for Annotation 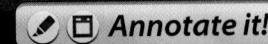 Annotate it!

Analyze Structure

COMMON CORE RL 4, RL 5

Have students use their eBook annotation tools to analyze the text. Ask them to do the following:

- Underline words and phrases that contribute to character development.
- Highlight in green words and phrases that contribute to the plot.
- Highlight in yellow any words or phrases that help to develop the setting.

> Mary sat musing on the lamp-flame at the table
> Waiting for Warren. When she heard his step,
> She ran on tip-toe down the darkened passage
> To meet him in the doorway with the news
> And put him on his guard. "Silas is back."
> ....And shut [the door] after her. "Be kind," she said.

PRACTICE & APPLY

Analyzing the Text  RL 3, RL 4, RL 5

Possible answers:

1. Nature, specifically winter, does not seem to love walls, since the ground swells and causes the rocks to fall off the wall [lines 2–4]. The speaker also "doesn't love a wall."

2. He wants to say "elves" to imply there is some force that wants the wall to come down. He doesn't say it because he wants the neighbor to figure out for himself that the wall might not be needed.

3. Some of the speaker's thoughts, words, and actions create ambiguity. He questions (lines 23–26, 30–36) why the wall is needed, suggesting that he does not think "good fences make good neighbors." He does, however, contact his neighbor each year and meet him to mend the wall (lines 12–14). He says before he built a wall he would want to know what he was keeping in or out (lines 32–33), and yet he does not seem to seek closer contact with the neighbor, because in lines 15–16 he says they both stay on their own side of the wall while they are repairing it.

4. These lines reveal that Silas is weak and lost and Mary is compassionate toward him. This information shows that Silas had no place else to go and Mary took him in even though she knew Warren would be angry about it.

5. Details such as "whole sky," "the hills," "harp-like morning-glory strings," and "dew from garden bed to eaves" create a vivid image of the setting. Mary's perceptions of the landscape and garden show how much she appreciates nature and how she is sensitive and responsive to the world around her.

6. Silas thinks of the farm as home and that is why he returns there when he needs care. The dialogue between Mary and Warren explains Silas's presence by describing his history there and in lines like "Home is the place where, when you have to go there/They have to take you in" (lines 118–119).

7. Both poems have a rural setting. "The Death of the Hired Man" includes more dialogue and uses it to develop the poem's characters. "Hired Man" has a plot; "Mending Wall" is more of an incident, and it develops the character mostly by revealing his internal thoughts, rather than through dialogue with another character.

Analyzing the Text

Cite Text Evidence   Support your responses with evidence from the selections.

1. **Evaluate** In "Mending Wall," what makes the speaker say that "something" doesn't love a wall? Besides this "something," who else doesn't love a wall?

2. **Interpret** Why does the speaker consider saying "Elves" (line 36) to his neighbor? What causes the speaker to change his mind?

3. **Interpret** How does Frost use ambiguity to present his message about walls and neighbors? What evidence supports the idea that the speaker believes "Good fences make good neighbors"? What details suggest the opposite?

4. **Analzye** Reread lines 31–39 of "The Death of the Hired Man." What do these lines reveal about Silas and Mary's character traits? How does this information support the plot?

5. **Interpret** The **setting** is the time and location of a poem or story. Identify the details in lines 103–110 that create a vivid image of the setting of "The Death of the Hired Man." What does this setting tell you about Mary's character?

6. **Draw Conclusions** How does Silas in "The Death of the Hired Man" think of the farm? Why does the dialogue between Mary and Warren help you understand Silas's presence at the farm? Cite details from the poem to support your answer.

7. **Compare/Contrast** Consider the narrative elements of both "Mending Wall" and "The Death of the Hired Man." What similarities and differences exist in the structure, or dialogue, plot, characterization, and setting, of both poems? Explain using details from the poems.

PERFORMANCE TASK

Writing Activity: Interview Summary Both "Mending Wall" and "The Death of the Hired Man" have ambiguous lines in them that can be interpreted in different ways. Simulate a reporter and interview five of your classmates and then summarize their interpretations.

- Choose several lines from each poem that are ambiguous.

- Ask five classmates to give you their interpretations of the lines.

- Write a summary of their interpretations and include a comparison to your own ideas about the meanings of the lines.

- Discuss your findings in a small group. Do the interpretations across the classroom have certain similarities in tone or content?

Assign this performance task.

PERFORMANCE TASK   COMMON CORE W 2

Writing Activity: Interview Summary Point out that reporters must accurately state what their interviewees tell them. Have students use recording devices, if possible, when conducting their interviews. Alternatively, they should take detailed notes so that they are sure to accurately represent their classmates' interpretations in their summaries. For small group discussions, they should be able to come up with the most popular interpretations.

Language and Style: Informal Style

 **COMMON CORE** L 3a

In these poems, Frost uses an almost casual and conversational style. This helps develop a connection with his readers by drawing them into the characters' world. One technique that helps him develop his unique style is his use of **informal language** and **syntax,** or how he combines words to form his lines. In particular, Frost uses colloquial or regional language and simple sentence structure in his poems. This has the effect of making his poems feel old fashioned and contemporary at the same time.

Look at this example of informal language from "Mending Wall."

> And on a day we meet to walk the line
> And set the wall between us once again.
> We keep the wall between us as we go.
> To each the boulders that have fallen to each.

These lines contain phrases such as "set the wall," "as we go," and "To each . . . to each" that are terse and direct, mirroring the way that language is used when people are speaking as they perform a physical task together. Frost uses simple and clear language to describe a particular moment in time.

Examine these lines from "The Death of the Hired Man," noticing the style choices..

> "When was I ever anything but kind to him?
> But I'll not have the fellow back," he said.
> "I told him so last haying, didn't I?
> 'If he left then,' I said, 'that ended it.'

In this set of lines, Frost uses informal language that contains contractions and rhetorical questions that Warren answers himself. This dialogue invites readers to "listen" to the conversation as they read. In particular, this dialogue expresses the fact that Warren feels somewhat angry toward Silas because Warren told him not to come back when he left during the haying. This informal style helps readers relate to Warren's point of view.

Consider how using a more formal style changes the impression the text makes.

> "I was always kind to him."
> "However, I will not have Silas work for me again," he said.
> "I informed him of my decision during his last employment.
> 'If he left,' I stated, 'that would mean the end of our working
> relationship.'

Practice and Apply Think about the way that language is used in your region. Write a one-paragraph narrative about something that has happened in your school in the past few days. As you write, consider the audience you are addressing and how you want to establish a connection with them. Use an informal style to invite your readers to interact closely with your plot and characters. Try to capture the speech patterns that you and your classmates use. Share your narrative with a partner. Discuss whether your use of informal style is successful and what revisions might improve the narrative.

PRACTICE & APPLY

Language and Style: Informal Style

 **COMMON CORE** L 3a

Have a volunteer read aloud a section from "Mending Wall," and then have a second volunteer read aloud a section from "The Death of the Hired Man."

Help students notice the effects of **syntax,** or word order, in each poem. Lead a discussion of how the poems sound different, and why. Also discuss how they sound similar. You may wish to have students complete a compare-and-contrast chart or Venn diagram.

Point out that the elements that are similar represent Frost's poetic style in general, while the elements that are different distinguish each poem as having its own speaker. In both cases the language is informal, but students will note that "Hired Man" is even more conversational, probably because it represents an actual conversation between two people who are closely related.

Practice and Apply Before students begin their drafts, have them identify and describe their audience. Will the readers be classmates, teachers, members of the community, or some other group? Point out that knowing the specific audience will help them get the language just right to connect with that audience.

As pairs of students discuss their narratives, have each partner tell which parts of the narrative they most relate to, or connect with, and also which parts they may have trouble understanding. Encourage students to explain why the language in their partner's piece either does or does not sound like the conversational patterns of the region.

 **Assess It!**

Online Selection Test
- Download an editable ExamView bank.
- Assign and manage this test online.

Demonstrate Knowledge of Foundational Works: Theme

COMMON CORE

RL 9

TEACH

Have students analyze both poems again, this time with a focus on theme. Remind students that **theme** is the message about life conveyed by a literary work.

Have students use these strategies to infer theme:

- Examine the title.
- Consider the conflicts between or within characters.
- Think about the personalities of the characters.

Lead a discussion session to give students an opportunity to offer their ideas about the themes of "Mending Wall." Then, they can work on inferring the theme or themes of "Hired Man" independently.

Finally, lead a discussion of how the themes of these poems compare to themes in other foundational works of American literature that they have read. For instance, students might listen for echoes of *Walden* in "Mending Wall."

 **LEVEL UP TUTORIALS** Assign the following *Level Up* tutorial: **Theme**

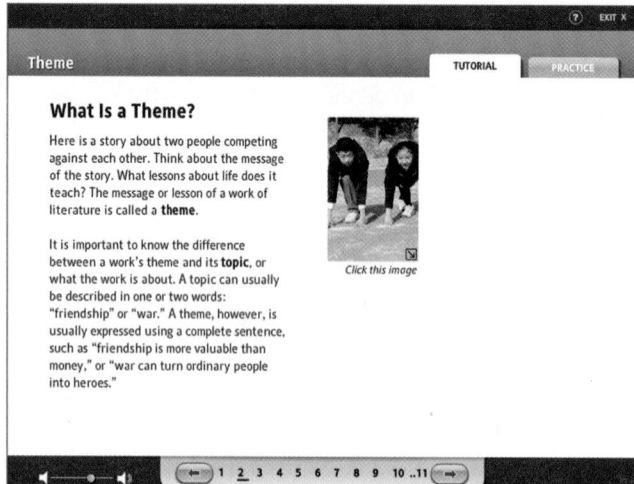

PRACTICE AND APPLY

Have students write a compare-and-contrast essay explaining the thematic similarities and differences between the two poems. Tell them to make an outline before drafting, and use transitions to make the connections between the two poems clear.

Analyze Structure: Narrative Poem

COMMON CORE

RL 4, RL 5

RETEACH

Review the terms *dialogue, plot, characterization,* and *setting.* Then discuss these typical five stages of a plot:

- **Exposition:** introduction of the characters, setting, and central conflict
- **Rising action:** conflict becomes more complicated; suspense builds
- **Climax:** exciting moment when conflict is at its most dramatic
- **Falling action:** what takes place after the climax and leads to the final resolution
- **Resolution:** ending of the story, when all is revealed and loose ends are tied up

Walk students through "The Death of the Hired Man," allowing them to identify each of the five stages of its plot.

COLLABORATIVE DISCUSSION

Have students work in small groups to discuss which stages of plot are most developed in "The Death of the Hired Man," and what techniques Frost uses to develop each stage. Encourage students to talk about which stages of the plot are filled in using the couple's conversation and which are presented more directly. How does the method of presentation (the conversation itself) affect the sequence of events? *(The characters are all presented near the beginning, in keeping with a typical order. The conflicts are also introduced early. The climax occurs when Warren leaves the room to go and see Silas. The resolution comes at the end when Warren returns and the reader learns that Silas is dead. There is virtually no falling action.)*

 **LEVEL UP TUTORIALS** Assign the following *Level Up* tutorial: **Plot Stages**

ANCHOR TEXT The Crucible

Drama by Arthur Miller

Why This Text?

In addition to providing insight into two important chapters in U. S. history, the Salem witch trials and the Red Scare, *The Crucible* exemplifies the masterful use of the elements of drama by one of our greatest playwrights.

Key Learning Objective: The student will be able to identify and analyze elements of drama.

For additional practice:

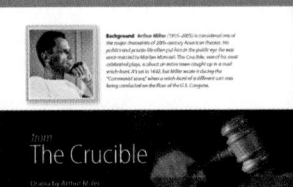

Close Reader selection
from The Crucible
Drama by Arthur Miller

COMMON CORE **Common Core Standards**

RL 3 Analyze the impact of the author's choices on the elements of a drama.

RL 5 Analyze how an author's choices concerning how to structure specific parts of a text contribute to its overall meaning as well as its aesthetic impact.

SL 1a Initiate and participate in a range of collaborative discussions.

▲ **Text Complexity Rubric**

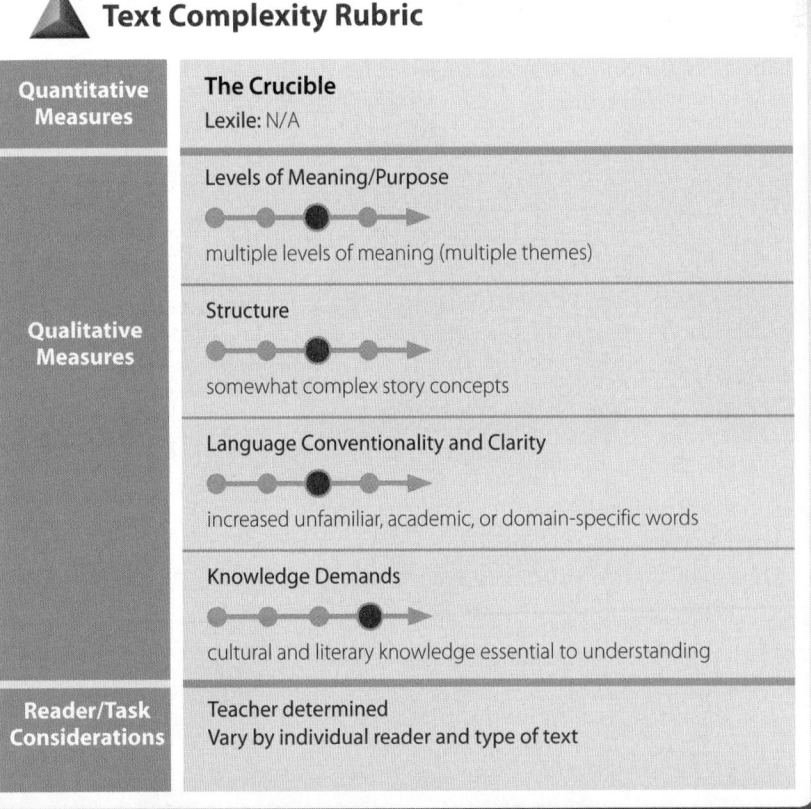

Quantitative Measures	**The Crucible** Lexile: N/A
Qualitative Measures	Levels of Meaning/Purpose multiple levels of meaning (multiple themes)
	Structure somewhat complex story concepts
	Language Conventionality and Clarity increased unfamiliar, academic, or domain-specific words
	Knowledge Demands cultural and literary knowledge essential to understanding
Reader/Task Considerations	Teacher determined Vary by individual reader and type of text

Modern American Drama

Tell students that this section puts modern American drama in context by comparing it with American drama of the 19th century. It explores the goals and development of modern American drama and contrasts it with contemporary American drama.

American drama in the 1800s was closely tied to British drama. Well-known British actors played in the United States, and some U.S. actors played in Great Britain. Farces and melodramas were popular in both countries. Both featured stereotyped characters and improbable situations, but farces were intended to be funny, while melodramas played on the audience's emotions.

The realism of American drama in the 1900s was heavily influenced by the ideas of two psychoanalysts, Sigmund Freud and Carl Jung, both of whom explored the effect of the unconscious on human thoughts and behaviors. Like Freud and Jung, modern American dramatists were concerned with people's interior lives.

Today's American theatergoers have a variety of choices. The classics of modern American drama are still performed, and contemporary playwrights such as August Wilson, Tony Kushner, John Guare, Wendy Wasserstein, David Mamet, and Ntozake Shange continue to challenge audiences with innovative and thought-provoking works. In addition, Broadway-style musicals with large casts, dancing, and spectacular special effects regularly tour the country.

Modern American Drama

The 19th century was a very active period in American theater. Most productions, however, consisted of wildly theatrical spectacles such as simulated chariot races and burning cities, all staged by means of dazzling special effects. Every town of any size had its own theater or "opera house." Yet, in spite of all this theatrical activity, not one truly significant American drama was staged during the 1800s, a period that produced Melville, Emerson, Whitman, Dickinson, and Twain.

By the early 20th century, however, American playwrights began to reject the extravagant approach of the commercial theater. Instead, these writers favored realistic settings, characters, actions, and emotions that mirrored ordinary life. As with many artistic revolutions, this movement toward realism began far outside the mainstream. By 1916, however, big New York audiences were flocking to small, obscure off-Broadway theaters to see the works of writers such as Eugene O'Neill (1888–1953). Eventually, mainstream theaters began to showcase realistic plays, too, and realism became established as the dominant mode of American drama.

The post-World War II years brought two notable figures to prominence in modern American drama: Tennessee Williams (1911–1983) and Arthur Miller (1915–2005), playwrights who experimented with stagecraft while exploring modern themes and creating works of social relevance.

One of the most common themes explored by these playwrights was that of the American dream. Willy Loman, the main character in Miller's *Death of a Salesman,* became the trademark figure of postwar American theater. A lowly salesman who has been discarded by the system to which he has mistakenly devoted his life, Willy Loman proved how the American dream could become twisted and broken. In *The Glass Menagerie* and *A Streetcar Named Desire,* southerner Tennessee Williams portrayed characters who, unsuited to modern life, retreat into the fantasy world of an earlier era.

In *A Raisin in the Sun,* Lorraine Hansberry (1930–1965) looked at the American dream from the perspective of those who had been excluded. The first major Broadway play by an African-American writer, *A Raisin in the Sun* was hailed by critics as "universal," while also capturing unique aspects of the African-American experience.

In contemporary theater, there has been a shift back toward spectacular productions as commercial theater once again relies upon special effects, imaginative settings, and imaginary worlds. Like any art form, drama undergoes infinite adaptations to reflect the spirit of the times.

456 Collection 6

WHEN STUDENTS STRUGGLE . . .

Tell students that the numbering of dates and centuries can be confusing. Explain that a century is a hundred years. Then explain that the years 1900–1999 are not the nineteenth century, but the twentieth. Make a timeline like the one to the right on the board and explain it to students.

ASK STUDENTS which years are included in the twentieth century. *(1900–1999)* Then ask which years will be included in the twenty-first century. *(2000–2099)*

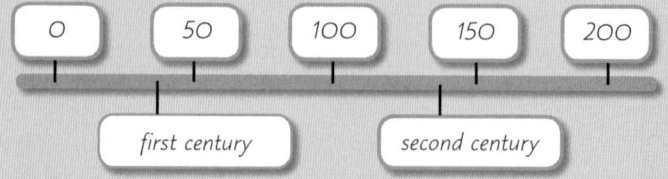

CLOSE READ

 For more context and historical background, students can view the video "Salem Witch Trials" in their eBooks.

Arthur Miller Have students read the information about the playwright. Tell them that Miller's exploration of and commitment to the issues of morality, individual responsibility, family, and the common man have earned him the mantle of the quintessential American playwright of the post-War period. Despite their focus on American life, however, Miller's plays have reached a wide international audience due in part to their many stagings and adaptations. Several of Miller's plays have been turned into films, including numerous versions of *Death of a Salesman*, *All My Sons*, and *The Crucible*, in an all-star, Hollywood remake in 1996.

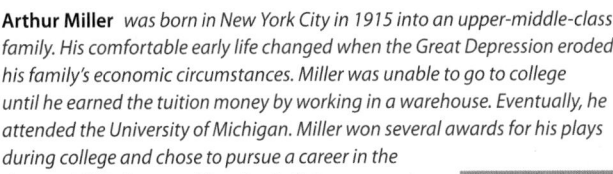

The Crucible

Drama by Arthur Miller

Arthur Miller *was born in New York City in 1915 into an upper-middle-class family. His comfortable early life changed when the Great Depression eroded his family's economic circumstances. Miller was unable to go to college until he earned the tuition money by working in a warehouse. Eventually, he attended the University of Michigan. Miller won several awards for his plays during college and chose to pursue a career in the theater.* All My Sons *and* Death of a Salesman, *a play that won a Pulitzer Prize in 1949, made Miller a star.*

Around the same time, hearings were being conducted by Congress to identify suspected Communists. Miller was called to testify before the committee about his association with the American Communist Party. Although he admitted to having attended a few meetings years earlier, he refused to "name names" of other people involved in the meetings. As a result, he was cited for contempt of Congress; this conviction was later overturned. The events of this time period inspired him to write The Crucible, *set during the Salem, Massachusetts, witch trials of 1692. He wrote the play to warn against mass hysteria and to plead for freedom and tolerance.*

In general, Miller's writing explores issues relevant to contemporary readers, such as the complexities of family relationships, personal responsibility, and morality. Many consider him to be the 20th century's greatest American playwright.

Image Credits: (b) ©Bettmann/Corbis; (t) ©Minerva Studio/Shutterstock

The Crucible **457**

Close Read Screencasts 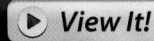 View It!

Modeled Discussions

Have students click the *Close Read* icons in their eBooks to access three screencasts in which readers discuss and annotate the following key passages:

- Parris's daughter is ill and he fears she is possessed by the Devil. (Act 1, lines 18–39)

As a class, view and discuss the video. Then have students pair up to do an independent close read of an additional passage—John Proctor, seeking to protect his name, refuses to allow his signed confession be posted in public. (Act 4, lines 906–928)

AS YOU READ Direct students to use the As You Read instructions to focus their reading. Remind them to write down any questions they generate during reading.

Analyze Drama Elements  RL 3, RL 5

Tell students that the list of characters in a play can provide information as to what the play might be about. Details like the characters' names and job titles can also be clues as to how characters might think, feel, or behave.

A CITE TEXT EVIDENCE Have students read the list of characters. Ask them to find any clues as to what theme or themes the play might explore. *(Two characters are ministers, one is a judge, and one is a deputy governor. The play may explore themes of power and authority.)*

Analyze Drama Elements  RL 3, RL 5

Tell students that a play's stage directions (which are usually, but not always, italicized) help establish mood. **Stage directions** are the playwright's instructions to the play's director, cast, and crew. Explain that mood is the general feeling or atmosphere that the playwright establishes.

B CITE TEXT EVIDENCE Ask students to read the stage directions on page 458. Explain how the details in the stage directions establish a certain mood. *(The upper bedroom is described as "small" and the window is "narrow." The room is described as having a "clean sparseness." The wood of the rafters is "raw." These details establish a mood that feels simple, intimate, yet cramped.)*

AS YOU READ Note details that explain how Abigail feels about John Proctor. Write down any questions you generate during reading.

A

CAST OF CHARACTERS
(IN ORDER OF APPEARANCE)

Reverend Samuel Parris	Rebecca Nurse
Betty Parris	Giles Corey
Tituba	Reverend John Hale
Abigail Williams	Francis Nurse
John Proctor	Ezekiel Cheever
Elizabeth Proctor	Marshal Herrick
Susanna Walcott	Judge Hathorne
Mrs. Ann Putnam	Martha Corey
Thomas Putnam	Deputy Governor Danforth
Mercy Lewis	Girls of Salem
Mary Warren	Sarah Good

ACT ONE

An Overture

(*A small upper bedroom in the home of* Reverend Samuel Parris, *Salem, Massachusetts, in the spring of the year 1692.*

B   *There is a narrow window at the left. Through its leaded panes the morning sunlight streams. A candle still burns near the bed, which is at the right. A chest, a chair, and a small table are the other furnishings. At the back a door opens on the landing of the stairway to the ground floor. The room gives off an air of clean spareness. The roof rafters are exposed, and the wood colors are raw and unmellowed.*

    As the curtain rises, Reverend Parris *is discovered kneeling beside the bed, evidently in prayer. His daughter,* Betty Parris, *aged ten, is lying on the bed, inert.*)

458 Collection 6

SCAFFOLDING FOR ELL STUDENTS

Understand Multiple-Meaning Words Before any action takes place onstage, Miller includes an *overture*. Explain to students that the word "overture" has more than one meaning. In classical music, an overture is played before the beginning of an opera or musical. It introduces the musical themes. The word can also have a more general (yet similar) meaning: the first part or beginning of something.

ASK STUDENTS to work with a partner and discuss why the playwright may have chosen the word *overture* to begin his play. *(He might have wanted to set the mood of the play and introduce its themes.)*

At the time of these events Parris was in his middle forties. In history he cut a villainous path, and there is very little good to be said for him. He believed he was being persecuted wherever he went, despite his best efforts to win people and God to his side. In meeting, he felt insulted if someone rose to shut the door without first asking his permission. He was a widower with no interest in children, or talent with them. He regarded them as young adults, and until this strange crisis he, like the rest of Salem, never conceived that the children were anything but thankful for being permitted to walk straight, eyes slightly lowered, arms at the sides, and mouths shut until bidden to speak.

His house stood in the "town"—but we today would hardly call it a village. The meeting house[1] was nearby, and from this point outward—toward the bay or inland—there were a few small-windowed, dark houses snuggling against the raw Massachusetts winter. Salem had been established hardly forty years before. To the European world the whole province was a barbaric frontier inhabited by a sect of fanatics who, nevertheless, were shipping out products of slowly increasing quantity and value.

No one can really know what their lives were like. They had no novelists—and would not have permitted anyone to read a novel if one were handy. Their creed forbade anything resembling a theater or "vain enjoyment." They did not celebrate Christmas, and a holiday from work meant only that they must concentrate even more upon prayer.

Which is not to say that nothing broke into this strict and somber way of life. When a new farmhouse was built, friends assembled to "raise the roof," and there would be special foods cooked and probably some potent cider passed around. There was a good supply of ne'er-do-wells in Salem, who dallied at the shovelboard[2] in Bridget Bishop's tavern. Probably more than the creed, hard work kept the morals of the place from spoiling, for the people were forced to fight the land like heroes for every grain of corn, and no man had very much time for fooling around.

That there were some jokers, however, is indicated by the practice of appointing a two-man patrol whose duty was to "walk forth in the time of God's worship to take notice of such as either lye about the meeting house, without attending to the word and ordinances, or that lye at home or in the fields without giving good account thereof, and to take the names of such persons, and to present them to the magistrates, whereby they may be accordingly proceeded against." This predilection for minding other people's business was time-honored among the people of Salem, and it undoubtedly created many of the suspicions which were to feed the coming madness. It was also, in my opinion, one of the things that a John Proctor would rebel against, for the time of the armed camp had almost passed, and since the country was reasonably—although not wholly—safe, the old disciplines were beginning to rankle. But, as in all such matters, the issue was not clear-cut, for danger was still a possibility, and in unity still lay the best promise of safety.

The edge of the wilderness was close by. The American continent stretched endlessly west, and it was

---

[1] **meeting house:** the most important building in the Puritan community, used both for worship and for meetings.

[2] **shovelboard:** a game in which a coin or disc is shoved across a board by hand.

The Crucible: Act One **459**

CLOSE READ

Analyze Drama Elements  RL 3, RL 5

Explain to students that Miller includes passages of **exposition**—text that explains things to readers—throughout Act One that offer information about the characters, setting, historical context, and the playwright's own perspective on his subject.

C ASK STUDENTS to read the first paragraph. Though they have not read any dialogue at this point, ask what the exposition tells about Parris and why he will behave the way he does. *(We learn that Parris is someone who has always felt that he was being treated unfairly no matter where he went. We learn that his wife is dead and he has no children. He does not relate well to others. These details offer reasons as to why he will "cut a villainous path.")*

Analyze Drama Elements  RL 3, RL 5

Point out to students that the exposition offers rich detail about the people of Salem as a whole.

D CITE TEXT EVIDENCE Tell students to cite details on page 459 that support the idea that the people of Salem lived, for the most part, a "strict and somber way of life." *(Novels and theater were forbidden; they did not celebrate Christmas; they valued prayer, and they worked hard to farm the land.)*

APPLYING ACADEMIC VOCABULARY

contemporary	global

As you discuss *The Crucible*, incorporate the Collection 6 academic vocabulary words: *contemporary* and *global*. Ask students how the themes of the play may be relevant to **contemporary** American audiences. *(People are still wrestling with the issues of the play—authority, family, morality, and personal responsibility—today.)* Then broaden the question and ask how and why the play might appeal to readers and theater-goers on a **global** scale. *(All over the world, people are fighting against religious and social persecution and for tolerance and freedom of expression. In this way, the play's appeal is not limited to American audiences. It has a global reach.)*

Analyze Drama Elements   COMMON CORE   RL 3, RL 5

Explain to students that the exposition on page 460 offers more about what is behind the attitudes and beliefs of the people of Salem.

E ASK STUDENTS to identify the reasons why the people of Salem felt persecuted. *(People in Salem, having no success converting the Indians to Christianity, came to mistrust the very land that they lived on—they believed the Devil lived in the forest; many of the villagers' parents had been persecuted in their homeland of England, which had experienced political unrest resulting in revolution.)*

Analyze Drama Elements   COMMON CORE   RL 3, RL 5

Point out to students that Miller provides historical background in the exposition and compares Salem to two other, earlier colonies (the Jamestown settlement in Virginia and the Puritans in Massachusetts).

F CITE TEXT EVIDENCE Have students compare and contrast Salem and the earlier colonies, citing specific evidence from Miller's text to support their findings. *(Settlers in Virginia were a group of individuals in search of profit, unlike the people of Salem who were seeking religious freedom. This purpose resulted in the formation of Salem's tight-knit community. The Puritans sought religious freedom as the people of Salem did, and both communities were held together by very strong religious beliefs. The differences between them, however, are key to understanding the people of Salem: the political events taking place in England caused feelings of great insecurity and suspicion in Salem, and Miller believes these feelings contributed to the events described in the play.)*

---

full of mystery for them. It stood, dark and threatening, over their shoulders night and day, for out of it Indian tribes marauded from time to time, and Reverend Parris had parishioners who had lost relatives to these heathen.

The parochial snobbery of these people was partly responsible for their failure to convert the Indians. Probably they also preferred to take land from heathens rather than from fellow Christians. At any rate, very few Indians were converted, and the Salem folk believed that the virgin forest was the Devil's last preserve, his home base and the citadel of his final stand. To the best of their knowledge the American forest was the last place on earth that was not paying homage to God.

For these reasons, among others, they carried about an air of innate resistance, even of persecution. Their fathers had, of course, been persecuted in England. So now they and their church found it necessary to deny any other sect its freedom, lest their New Jerusalem[3] be defiled and corrupted by wrong ways and deceitful ideas.

They believed, in short, that they held in their steady hands the candle that would light the world. We have inherited this belief, and it has helped and hurt us. It helped them with the discipline it gave them. They were a dedicated folk, by and large, and they had to be to survive the life they had chosen or been born into in this country.

The proof of their belief's value to them may be taken from the opposite character of the first Jamestown settlement, farther south, in Virginia.

The Englishmen who landed there were motivated mainly by a hunt for profit. They had thought to pick off the wealth of the new country and then return rich to England. They were a band of individualists, and a much more ingratiating group than the Massachusetts men. But Virginia destroyed them. Massachusetts tried to kill off the Puritans, but they combined; they set up a communal society which, in the beginning, was little more than an armed camp with an autocratic and very devoted leadership. It was, however, an autocracy by consent, for they were united from top to bottom by a commonly held ideology whose perpetuation was the reason and justification for all their sufferings. So their self-denial, their purposefulness, their suspicion of all vain pursuits, their hard-handed justice, were altogether perfect instruments for the conquest of this space so antagonistic to man.

But the people of Salem in 1692 were not quite the dedicated folk that arrived on the *Mayflower*. A vast differentiation had taken place, and in their own time a revolution had unseated the royal government and substituted a junta which was at this moment in power.[4] The times, to their eyes, must have been out of joint, and to the common folk must have seemed as insoluble and complicated as do ours today. It is not hard to see how easily many could have been led to believe that the time of confusion had been brought upon them by deep and darkling forces. No hint of such speculation appears on the court record, but social disorder in any age breeds such mystical suspicions,

---

[3] **New Jerusalem:** in Christianity, a heavenly city and the last resting place of the souls saved by Jesus. It was considered the ideal city, and Puritans modeled their communities after it.

[4] **a junta** (hŏŏn′tə) . . . **power:** Junta is a Spanish term meaning "a small, elite ruling council." The reference here is to the group that led England's Glorious Revolution of 1688–1689.

WHEN STUDENTS STRUGGLE . . .

Understand Cultural References Explain to students that the Puritans were a religious group that formed in England. They believed in hard work, self-denial, and strict codes of behavior. Puritans wanted to reform the Anglican Church, which was headed by the English monarchy. The English government retaliated by persecuting Puritan leaders. Some Puritans immigrated to America to escape this persecution and to put their religious beliefs into practice.

ASK STUDENTS to discuss what they think life might be like in a strict, isolated religious community. Given their history, what would have been the prevailing attitude toward authority among the villagers?

and when, as in Salem, wonders are brought forth from below the social surface, it is too much to expect people to hold back very long from laying on the victims with all the force of their frustrations.

G The Salem tragedy, which is about to begin in these pages, developed from a paradox. It is a paradox in whose grip we still live, and there is no prospect yet that we will discover its resolution. Simply, it was this: for good purposes, even high purposes, the people of Salem developed a theocracy, a combine of state and religious power whose function was to keep the community together, and to prevent any kind of disunity that might open it to destruction by material or ideological enemies. It was forged for a necessary purpose and accomplished that purpose. But all organization is and must be grounded on the idea of exclusion and prohibition, just as two objects cannot occupy the same space. Evidently the time came in New England when the repressions of order were heavier than seemed warranted by the dangers against which the order was organized. The witch-hunt was a perverse manifestation of the panic which set in among all classes when the balance began to turn toward greater individual freedom.

When one rises above the individual villainy displayed, one can only pity them all, just as we shall be pitied someday. It is still impossible for man to organize his social life without repressions, and the balance has yet to be struck between order and freedom.

The witch-hunt was not, however, a mere repression. It was also, and as importantly, a long overdue opportunity for everyone so inclined to express publicly his guilt and sins, under the cover of accusations against the victims.

It suddenly became possible—and patriotic and holy—for a man to say that Martha Corey had come into his bedroom at night, and that, while his wife was sleeping at his side, Martha laid herself down on his chest and "nearly suffocated him." Of course it was her spirit only, but his satisfaction at confessing himself was no lighter than if it had been Martha herself. One could not ordinarily speak such things in public.

Long-held hatreds of neighbors could now be openly expressed, and vengeance taken, despite the Bible's charitable injunctions. Land-lust which had been expressed before by constant bickering over boundaries and deeds, could now be elevated to the arena of morality; one could cry witch against one's neighbor and feel perfectly justified in the bargain. Old scores could be settled on a plane of heavenly combat between Lucifer and the Lord; suspicions and the envy of the miserable toward the happy could and did burst out in the general revenge.

1 (*Reverend Parris is praying now, and, though we cannot hear his words, a sense of his confusion hangs about him. He mumbles, then seems about to weep; then he weeps, then prays again; but his daughter does not stir on the bed.*

The door opens, and his Negro slave enters. Tituba is in her forties. Parris
10 *brought her with him from Barbados, where he spent some years as a merchant before entering the ministry. She enters as one does who can no longer bear to be barred from the sight of her beloved, but she is also very frightened because her slave sense has warned her that, as always, trouble in this house eventually lands on her back.*) H

The Crucible: Act One **461**

Analyze Drama Elements   COMMON CORE RL 3, RL 5

Tell students that the exposition expresses Miller's own perspective on the issues of his play.

G **ASK STUDENTS** to explain the paradox that Miller refers to in the final section of the exposition. A paradox is a statement that seems to contradict itself, but may nevertheless suggest an important truth. Have students tell how the paradox illuminates the playwright's perspective on his subject. (*Miller highlights the paradox that occurs when a community that is religiously based sets rules to maintain political order: those rules may ultimately lead to repression and disorder. In fact, Miller states that "all organization is and must be grounded on the idea of exclusion and prohibition…" Miller feels that the story of Salem is but an example of a larger issue that is still with us today: how to maintain a society that is orderly and yet protects the freedom of its citizens.*)

Analyze Drama Elements   COMMON CORE RL 3, RL 5

(LINES 1–6)

Point out to students that the opening stage directions reveal details about the characters.

H **ASK STUDENTS** to make an inference about Parris's character based on the stage directions. (*The stage directions describe Parris as alternating between praying and weeping. This description depicts a character who is probably very religious, serious, and in emotional distress due to his child's situation.*)

TO CHALLENGE STUDENTS . . .

Extend Knowledge Tell students that the history of Africans in America goes back to 1619, when 20 African indentured servants came to Virginia. By the 1660s, Africans were being brought to the American colonies in large numbers as both indentured servants and enslaved persons.

ASK STUDENTS to work in small groups to learn more about slavery in late 17th century colonial America. The stage directions say that Parris's slave came from Barbados. Have them consult sources to find out about the role Barbados and other islands in the Caribbean played in the slave trade of this period. Be sure they investigate the difference between indentured servants and enslaved persons during this period.

The Crucible: Act One **461**

Analyze Drama Elements COMMON CORE RL 3, RL 5

(LINES 34–39)

Explain to students that details about characters are revealed in a play directly and indirectly. In **direct characterization,** specific details about a character are stated explicitly—often in the **stage directions. Indirect characterization** occurs when readers infer what a character is like based on clues in the text. Again, stage directions can provide these clues, but students should also look closely at what characters say (their **dialogue**) and do (their **actions**).

 **CITE TEXT EVIDENCE** Of all the details given about Abigail in lines 34–39, ask students to infer which character trait is the best clue as to whether or not Parris (and the reader) should believe what she may say. *(Abigail is described as having an "endless capacity for dissembling." This means that she is highly capable of withholding her true feelings and obscuring the truth of a matter. Therefore, what Abigail may say is probably not entirely trustworthy.)*

Analyze Drama Elements COMMON CORE RL 3, RL 5

(LINES 70–79)

Explain that students should keep the issues raised in the exposition in mind as they read.

J **CITE TEXT EVIDENCE** Have students reread lines 70–79 and determine why the characters speak and behave as they do, particularly in light of the issues raised in the exposition. *(In his exposition, Miller offers his own perspective on the witch hunt that gripped Salem. He feels that the witch hunt was an overreaction against challenges to the strict religious order of the society. When Abigail and Parris ask that the suspicions of witchcraft not be mentioned, it is because they are afraid of being targeted by those who are caught up in the witch hunt.)*

 Close Read

Tituba (*already taking a step backward*). My Betty be hearty soon?

20 **Parris.** Out of here!

Tituba (*backing to the door*). My Betty not goin' die . . .

Parris (*scrambling to his feet in a fury*). Out of my sight! (*She is gone.*) Out of my—(*He is overcome with sobs. He clamps his teeth against them and closes the door and leans against it, exhausted.*) Oh, my God! God help me! (*Quaking with fear, mumbling to himself through*
30 *his sobs, he goes to the bed and gently takes Betty's hand.*) Betty. Child. Dear child. Will you wake, will you open up your eyes! Betty, little one . . .

(*He is bending to kneel again when his niece,* Abigail Williams, *seventeen, enters—a strikingly beautiful girl, an orphan, with an endless capacity for dissembling. Now she is all worry and apprehension and propriety.*)

40 **Abigail.** Uncle? (*He looks to her.*) Susanna Walcott's here from Doctor Griggs.

Parris. Oh? Let her come, let her come.

Abigail (*leaning out the door to call to* Susanna, *who is down the hall a few steps*). Come in, Susanna. (Susanna Walcott, *a little younger than* Abigail, *a nervous, hurried girl, enters.*)

Parris (*eagerly*). What does the doctor
50 say, child?

Susanna (*craning around* Parris *to get a look at* Betty). He bid me come and tell you, reverend sir, that he cannot discover no medicine for it in his books.

Parris. Then he must search on.

Susanna. Aye, sir, he have been searchin' his books since he left you, sir. But he bid me tell you, that you might look to unnatural things for the cause
60 of it.

Parris (*his eyes going wide*). No—no. There be no unnatural cause here. Tell him I have sent for Reverend Hale of Beverly, and Mr. Hale will surely confirm that. Let him look to medicine and put out all thought of unnatural causes here. There be none.

Susanna. Aye, sir. He bid me tell you. (*She turns to go.*)

70 **Abigail.** Speak nothin' of it in the village, Susanna.

Parris. Go directly home and speak nothing of unnatural causes.

Susanna. Aye, sir. I pray for her. (*She goes out.*)

Abigail. Uncle, the rumor of witchcraft is all about; I think you'd best go down and deny it yourself. The parlor's packed with people, sir. I'll sit with her.

80 **Parris** (*pressed, turns on her*). And what shall I say to them? That my daughter and my niece I discovered dancing like heathen in the forest?

Abigail. Uncle, we did dance; let you tell them I confessed it—and I'll be whipped if I must be. But they're speakin' of witchcraft. Betty's not witched.

Parris. Abigail, I cannot go before the congregation when I know you have not
90 opened with me. What did you do with her in the forest?

Abigail. We did dance, uncle, and when you leaped out of the bush so suddenly, Betty was frightened and then she fainted. And there's the whole of it.

Parris. Child. Sit you down.

Abigail (*quavering, as she sits*). I would never hurt Betty. I love her dearly.

Parris. Now look you, child, your
100 punishment will come in its time. But

SCAFFOLDING FOR ELL STUDENTS

Prefixes are added to the beginning of words to create new words with different meanings. On page 462, Miller uses the word "dissemble." The prefix *dis-* means "not." It is added to the root word *sembler* (from the Old French), meaning "seem" or "appear." So "dissemble" means "to not seem" or "to not appear."

ASK STUDENTS to add the prefix *dis-* to the following words and tell the meanings of the original word and the new word. Ask them to search for prefixes while reading.

- respect: a feeling of admiration; disrespect: lack of respect
- order: arrangement according to a specific method; disorder: lack of order
- service: assistance; disservice: harm

if you trafficked with[5] spirits in the forest I must know it now, for surely my enemies will, and they will ruin me with it.

Abigail. But we never conjured spirits.

Parris. Then why can she not move herself since midnight? This child is desperate! (*Abigail lowers her eyes.*) It must come out—my enemies will bring it out. Let me know what you done there. Abigail, do you understand that I have many enemies?

Abigail. I have heard of it, uncle.

Parris. There is a faction that is sworn to drive me from my pulpit. Do you understand that?

Abigail. I think so, sir.

Parris. Now then, in the midst of such disruption, my own household is discovered to be the very center of some obscene practice. Abominations are done in the forest—

---

[5] **trafficked with:** met with.

Abigail. It were sport, uncle!

Parris (*pointing at* Betty). You call this sport? (*She lowers her eyes. He pleads.*) Abigail, if you know something that may help the doctor, for God's sake tell it to me. (*She is silent.*) I saw Tituba waving her arms over the fire when I came on you. Why was she doing that? And I heard a screeching and gibberish coming from her mouth. She were swaying like a dumb beast over that fire!

Abigail. She always sings her Barbados songs, and we dance.

Parris. I cannot blink what I saw, Abigail, for my enemies will not blink it. I saw a dress lying on the grass.

Abigail (*innocently*). A dress?

Parris (*It is very hard to say*). Aye, a dress. And I thought I saw—someone naked running through the trees!

Abigail (*in terror*). No one was naked! You mistake yourself, uncle!

Parris (*with anger*). I saw it! (*He moves from her. Then, resolved*) Now tell me

The Crucible: Act One **463**

Analyze Drama Elements  RL 3, RL 5
(LINES 101–145)

Remind students that the playwright makes choices as to how to develop his or her characters throughout the play. The choices are revealed through the characters' **dialogue** and **actions**, as well as the **stage directions.**

K **CITE TEXT EVIDENCE** How do Parris and Abigail's perceptions of the events in the forest in lines 101–145 differ? What does this reveal about their personalities? Have students cite specific examples in the text, referring both to what the characters say and to the stage directions. (*Parris is clearly a stern, strict, and highly religious man. In lines 120–121, he is concerned about being at the center of an "obscene practice," and he is horrified at the thought that one of the women was running naked in the forest. He is also revealed as a fearful and even paranoid man—he is being targeted by some enemies who would love to discover a scandal that will bring him down. Parris's parochialism is displayed in lines 128–133 when he uses words like "screeching" and "gibberish" to describe Tituba in the forest. He even likens her to a "dumb beast." Abigail at this point in the play represents a different way of thinking about the world. In line 139, she states her line "innocently" and she says that the dancing in the forest was just "sport." Her protests against her uncle's objections reveal that she may have different values and standards of decency and morality than he does, and that she feels he may disapprove of her views. She may also be deliberately downplaying the activities in the forest to avoid his disapproval.*)

WHEN STUDENTS STRUGGLE...

Developing Reading Fluency Explain to students that the characters' lines in a play represent a spoken conversation. Students will likely need practice reading sections of dialogue with variety, intonation, and expression. Tell them that paying attention to punctuation and stage directions will help them in their practice.

ASK STUDENTS to read lines 101–145 with a partner, with each partner reading one character's lines. Model fluent, expressive reading of dialogue with a proficient student first. After students have finished reading in pairs, ask them how the stage directions helped them in their reading.

TEACH

CLOSE READ

Analyze Drama Elements
COMMON CORE RL 3, RL 5

(LINES 147–182)

Remind students that characters will develop and change over the course of a play.

 **ASK STUDENTS** to reread lines 147–193. Is Parris's behavior in this section in keeping with what they have already learned about his character? Students should cite a stage direction to support their answer. *(Parris's character is consistent with what we have already learned about him: he is determined to protect his position in the community, and he is not afraid to confront his niece directly to get to the truth of a matter. The proof of this is the stage direction "to the point" in line 171.)*

Analyze Drama Elements
COMMON CORE RL 3, RL 5

(LINES 168–197)

Point out to students that in lines 168–197, we see a new side of Abigail.

M CITE TEXT EVIDENCE Have students reread lines 168–197. What new side of Abigail is revealed in her behavior and the stage directions in these lines? Be sure students cite specific examples from the text. Students should consider what they've already learned about Abigail. *(Abigail is revealed to be temperamental and headstrong. She speaks to her guardian with "ill-concealed resentment" (line 191) and "in a temper" (line 194).)*

L true, Abigail. And I pray you feel the weight of truth upon you, for now my ministry's at stake, my ministry and perhaps your cousin's life. Whatever abomination you have done, give me all of it now, for I dare not be taken unaware when I go before them down there.

Abigail. There is nothin' more. I swear it, uncle.

Parris (*studies her, then nods, half convinced*). Abigail, I have fought here three long years to bend these stiff-necked people to me, and now, just now when some good respect is rising for me in the parish, you compromise my very character. I have given you a home, child, I have put clothes upon your back—now give me upright answer. Your name in the town—it is entirely white, is it not?

Abigail (*with an edge of resentment*). Why, I am sure it is, sir. There be no blush about my name.[6]

Parris (*to the point*). Abigail, is there any other cause than you have told me, for your being discharged from Goody[7] Proctor's service? I have heard it said, and I tell you as I heard it, that she comes so rarely to the church this year for she will not sit so close to something soiled. What signified that remark?

Abigail. She hates me, uncle, she must, for I would not be her slave. It's a bitter woman, a lying, cold, sniveling woman, and I will not work for such a woman!

Parris. She may be. And yet it has troubled me that you are now seven month out of their house, and in all this time no other family has ever called for your service.

Abigail. They want slaves, not such as I. Let them send to Barbados for that. I will not black my face for any of them! (*with ill-concealed resentment at him*) Do you begrudge my bed, uncle?

Parris. No—no.

Abigail (*in a temper*). My name is good in the village! I will not have it said my name is soiled! Goody Proctor is a gossiping liar!

(*Enter Mrs. Ann Putnam. She is a twisted soul of forty-five, a death-ridden woman, haunted by dreams.*)

Parris (*as soon as the door begins to open*). No—no, I cannot have anyone. (*He sees her, and a certain deference springs into him, although his worry remains.*) Why, Goody Putnam, come in.

Mrs. Putnam (*full of breath, shiny-eyed*). It is a marvel. It is surely a stroke of hell upon you.

Parris. No, Goody Putnam, it is—

Mrs. Putnam (*glancing at Betty*). How high did she fly, how high?

Parris. No, no, she never flew—

Mrs. Putnam (*very pleased with it*). Why, it's sure she did. Mr. Collins saw her goin' over Ingersoll's barn, and come down light as bird, he says!

Parris. Now, look you, Goody Putnam, she never— (*Enter Thomas Putnam, a well-to-do, hard-handed landowner, near fifty.*) Oh, good morning, Mr. Putnam.

Putnam. It is a providence the thing is out now! It is a providence. (*He goes directly to the bed.*)

Parris. What's out, sir, what's—?

(*Mrs. Putnam goes to the bed.*)

---

[6] **There be . . . my name:** There is nothing wrong with my reputation.

[7] **Goody:** short for *Goodwife*, the Puritan equivalent of *Mrs.*

SCAFFOLDING FOR ELL STUDENTS

Understand Conversational English Tell students that one way a playwright establishes a character is the manner in which that character speaks. For example, a character might use a lot of slang when they speak or speak with incorrect grammar.

Point out to students that in line 155, Miller has Abigail say the word "nothin'" instead of *nothing*. This word choice is a clue for the reader about Abigail's character; namely, that she is probably uneducated.

ASK STUDENTS to look for other examples on this page in which Abigail uses incorrect grammar and rewrite them using correct grammar. *(lines 169–170: "There be no blush about my name," "There is no blush about my name"; lines 180–181: "It's a bitter woman...," "She's a bitter woman...")*

Putnam (*looking down at* Betty). Why, *her eyes is* closed! Look you, Ann.

230 **Mrs. Putnam.** Why, that's strange. (*to* Parris) Ours is open.

Parris (*shocked*). Your Ruth is sick?

Mrs. Putnam (*with vicious certainty*). I'd not call it sick; the Devil's touch is heavier than sick. It's death, y'know, it's death drivin' into them, forked and hoofed.

Parris. Oh, pray not! Why, how does Ruth ail?

Mrs. Putnam. She ails as she must—she
240 never waked this morning, but her eyes open and she walks, and hears naught, sees naught, and cannot eat. Her soul is taken, surely.

(Parris *is struck*.)

Putnam (*as though for further details*). They say you've sent for Reverend Hale of Beverly?

Parris (*with dwindling conviction now*). A precaution only. He has much
250 experience in all demonic arts, and I—

Mrs. Putnam. He has indeed; and found a witch in Beverly last year, and let you remember that.

Parris. Now, Goody Ann, they only thought that were a witch, and I am certain there be no element of witchcraft here.

Putnam. No witchcraft! Now look you, Mr. Parris—

260 **Parris.** Thomas, Thomas, I pray you, leap not to witchcraft. I know that you—you least of all, Thomas, would ever wish so disastrous a charge laid upon me. We cannot leap to witchcraft. They will howl me out of Salem for such corruption in my house.

A word about Thomas Putnam. He was a man with many grievances, at least one of which appears justified. Some time before, his wife's brother-in-law, James Bayley, had been turned down as minister of Salem. Bayley had all the qualifications, and a two-thirds vote into the bargain, but a faction stopped his acceptance, for reasons that are not clear.

Thomas Putnam was the eldest son of the richest man in the village. He had fought the Indians at Narragansett,[8] and was deeply interested in parish affairs. He undoubtedly felt it poor payment that the village should so blatantly disregard his candidate for one of its more important offices, especially since he regarded himself as the intellectual superior of most of the people around him.

His vindictive nature was demonstrated long before the witchcraft began. Another former Salem minister, George Burroughs, had had to borrow money to pay for his wife's funeral, and, since the parish was remiss in his salary, he was soon bankrupt. Thomas and his brother John had Burroughs jailed for debts the man did not owe. The incident is important only in that Burroughs succeeded in becoming minister where Bayley, Thomas Putnam's brother-in-law, had been rejected; the motif of resentment is clear here. Thomas Putnam felt that his own name and the honor of his family had been smirched by the village, and he meant to right matters however he could.

Another reason to believe him a deeply embittered man was his attempt to break his father's will, which left a disproportionate amount to a

---

[8] **fought the Indians at Narragansett:** The Puritans fought a series of battles against the Narragansett Indians over territory that both groups had settled on.

WHEN STUDENTS STRUGGLE . . .

Summarize Draw students' attention to the exposition on page 465.

ASK STUDENTS to summarize what the exposition on page 465 tells about the character of Thomas Putnam. (*Putnam is a resentful, vindictive man who feels he has been wronged multiple times in the past by the Salem community. He had a relative who was not promoted to minister of Salem; he persecuted the man who got the job instead of his relative. He also tried to gain more than he was left in his father's will.*)

CLOSE READ

Analyze Drama Elements
COMMON CORE RL 3, RL 5

(LINES 227–253)

Remind students that another element of drama that a playwright establishes and develops throughout a play is mood. **Mood** is the feeling or atmosphere created by a playwright.

N CITE TEXT EVIDENCE Ask students to describe how the mood of the play changes when Mr. and Mrs. Putnam enter. Tell students to cite examples of stage directions to support their answer. (*The mood of the play becomes more intense when these characters enter, for it is the first time we see townspeople actually raise the issue of witchcraft directly. Mrs. Putnam is convinced there is witchcraft at work [she speaks "with vicious certainty" in line 232] both with Betty and her own daughter, Ruth. The fact that she has called on Reverend Hale changes the mood of Parris; in line 248, he is described as having "dwindling conviction" about his own beliefs.*)

Analyze Drama Elements
COMMON CORE RL 3, RL 5

(LINES 260–266)

One of the ways a playwright develops the drama of a play is by raising or lowering the stakes of the central characters. Stakes are what the characters stand to lose or gain. For example, up to this point in the play, we know that Parris's job may be at stake if witchcraft is proven to be in his home.

O ASK STUDENTS to assess what the characters have at stake at this point in the play. Have them think about how the stakes for Parris are raised on this page. (*Abigail's reputation is at stake; Tituba would almost certainly face strong punishment or banishment if she were seen as responsible for bringing on the witchcraft; Parris is trying to protect his job, but on this page in lines 265–266, he is worried about being "howl[ed] out" of Salem completely.*)

Analyze Drama Elements   COMMON CORE RL 3, RL 5

(LINES 267–274)

Point out to students that dialogue and stage directions often illustrate the power dynamics in characters' relationships.

P **CITE TEXT EVIDENCE** Ask students what Mr. Putnam threatens to do to Parris if Parris does not agree that witchcraft is at work in Betty and Ruth's illnesses. *(Mr. Putnam threatens to withdraw his support of Parris.)* Have students cite a specific stage direction that offers a reason for Mr. Putnam's behavior. *(The stage directions in lines 267–269 reveal that Putnam is "intent upon getting Parris . . . to move toward the abyss" and has "only contempt" for him.)* Then have students tell whether or not they could infer the reason behind Putnam's threat if the stage direction they have identified was not there. *(Answers will vary; some students will mention that the exposition on pages 465–466 also offers many reasons that explain Putnam's threat.)*

Putnam. Why aren't you home? Who's with Ruth?

Mercy. Her grandma come. She's improved a little, I think—she give a
340 powerful sneeze before.

Mrs. Putnam. Ah, there's a sign of life!

Mercy. I'd fear no more, Goody Putnam. It were a grand sneeze; another like it will shake her wits together, I'm sure. (*She goes to the bed to look.*)

Parris. Will you leave me now, Thomas? I would pray a while alone.

Abigail. Uncle, you've prayed since midnight. Why do you not go down
350 and—

Parris. No—no. (*to* Putnam) I have no answer for that crowd. I'll wait till Mr. Hale arrives. (*to get* Mrs. Putnam *to leave*) If you will, Goody Ann . . .

Putnam. Now look you, sir. Let you strike out against the Devil, and the village will bless you for it! Come down, speak to them—pray with them. They're thirsting for your word, Mister! Surely
360 you'll pray with them.

Parris (*swayed*). I'll lead them in a psalm, but let you say nothing of witchcraft yet. I will not discuss it. The cause is yet unknown. I have had enough contention since I came; I want no more.

Mrs. Putnam. Mercy, you go home to Ruth, d'y'hear?

Mercy. Aye, mum.

370 (Mrs. Putnam *goes out.*)

Parris (*to* Abigail). If she starts for the window, cry for me at once.

Abigail. I will, uncle.

Parris (*to* Putnam). There is a terrible power in her arms today. (*He goes out with* Putnam.)

Abigail (*with hushed trepidation*). How is Ruth sick?

Mercy. It's weirdish, I know not—she
380 seems to walk like a dead one since last night.

Abigail (*turns at once and goes to* Betty, *and now, with fear in her voice*). Betty? (Betty *doesn't move. She shakes her.*) Now stop this! Betty! Sit up now!

(Betty *doesn't stir.* Mercy *comes over.*)

Mercy. Have you tried beatin' her? I gave Ruth a good one and it waked her for a minute. Here, let me have her.

390 **Abigail** (*holding* Mercy *back*). No, he'll be comin' up. Listen, now; if they be questioning us, tell them we danced—I told him as much already.

Mercy. Aye. And what more?

Abigail. He knows Tituba conjured Ruth's sisters to come out of the grave.

Mercy. And what more?

Abigail. He saw you naked.

Mercy (*clapping her hands together with*
400 *a frightened laugh*). Oh, Jesus!

(*Enter* Mary Warren, *breathless. She is seventeen, a subservient, naive, lonely girl.*)

Mary Warren. What'll we do? The village is out! I just come from the farm; the whole country's talkin' witchcraft! They'll be callin' us witches, Abby!

Mercy (*pointing and looking at* Mary Warren). She means to tell, I know it.

410 **Mary Warren.** Abby, we've got to tell. Witchery's a hangin' error, a hangin' like they done in Boston two year ago! We must tell the truth, Abby! You'll only be whipped for dancin', and the other things!

Abigail. Oh, *we'll* be whipped!

SCAFFOLDING FOR ELL STUDENTS

Understand Idioms Tell students that an **idiom** is an expression whose meaning is not obvious from the meaning of its words. Point out the idiom "I am undone" on lines 322–323.

ASK STUDENTS to discuss what they think Parris means when he says that he is undone. Elicit from students that he means that he will lose everything he cares about. Have them work with native English speakers to think of another idiom that could be substituted for "I am undone" in the sentence. *(Now all is lost; Now I am ruined)*

Putnam. Why aren't you home? Who's with Ruth?

Mercy. Her grandma come. She's improved a little, I think—she give a
340 powerful sneeze before.

Mrs. Putnam. Ah, there's a sign of life!

Mercy. I'd fear no more, Goody Putnam. It were a grand sneeze; another like it will shake her wits together, I'm sure. (*She goes to the bed to look.*)

Parris. Will you leave me now, Thomas? I would pray a while alone.

Abigail. Uncle, you've prayed since midnight. Why do you not go down
350 and—

Parris. No—no. (*to* Putnam) I have no answer for that crowd. I'll wait till Mr. Hale arrives. (*to get* Mrs. Putnam *to leave*) If you will, Goody Ann . . .

Putnam. Now look you, sir. Let you strike out against the Devil, and the village will bless you for it! Come down, speak to them—pray with them. They're thirsting for your word, Mister! Surely
360 you'll pray with them.

Parris (*swayed*). I'll lead them in a psalm, but let you say nothing of witchcraft yet. I will not discuss it. The cause is yet unknown. I have had enough contention since I came; I want no more.

Mrs. Putnam. Mercy, you go home to Ruth, d'y'hear?

Mercy. Aye, mum.

370 (Mrs. Putnam *goes out.*)

Parris (*to* Abigail). If she starts for the window, cry for me at once.

Abigail. I will, uncle.

Parris (*to* Putnam). There is a terrible power in her arms today. (*He goes out with* Putnam.)

Abigail (*with hushed trepidation*). How is Ruth sick?

Mercy. It's weirdish, I know not—she
380 seems to walk like a dead one since last night.

Abigail (*turns at once and goes to* Betty, *and now, with fear in her voice*). Betty? (Betty *doesn't move. She shakes her.*) Now stop this! Betty! Sit up now!

(Betty *doesn't stir.* Mercy *comes over.*)

Mercy. Have you tried beatin' her? I gave Ruth a good one and it waked her for a minute. Here, let me have her.

390 **Abigail** (*holding* Mercy *back*). No, he'll be comin' up. Listen, now; if they be questioning us, tell them we danced—I told him as much already.

Mercy. Aye. And what more?

Abigail. He knows Tituba conjured Ruth's sisters to come out of the grave.

Mercy. And what more?

Abigail. He saw you naked.

Mercy (*clapping her hands together with*
400 *a frightened laugh*). Oh, Jesus!

(Enter Mary Warren, *breathless. She is seventeen, a subservient, naive, lonely girl.*)

Mary Warren. What'll we do? The village is out! I just come from the farm; the whole country's talkin' witchcraft! They'll be callin' us witches, Abby!

Mercy (*pointing and looking at* Mary Warren). She means to tell, I know it.

410 **Mary Warren.** Abby, we've got to tell. Witchery's a hangin' error, a hangin' like they done in Boston two year ago! We must tell the truth, Abby! You'll only be whipped for dancin', and the other things!

Abigail. Oh, *we'll* be whipped!

CLOSE READ

Analyze Drama Elements
COMMON CORE RL 3, RL 5
(LINES 351–366)

Tell students that, in these lines, the reader learns more about Parris's character.

Q CITE TEXT EVIDENCE Have students reread lines 351–366 and ask them what they learn about Parris through indirect characterization. Ask them to cite evidence from the text to support their answers. (*Parris is easily influenced by other people and by his fears for his position. He does not want to face the crowd, but he allows Mr. Putnam to bully him into praying with them. The stage directions say that he is "swayed" by him.*)

Analyze Drama Elements
COMMON CORE RL 3, RL 5
(LINES 410–415)

Remind students that throughout the play so far Miller has been slowly raising the stakes for the main characters.

R ASK STUDENTS how the stakes are raised in these lines and for whom. (*Mary points out that those who are convicted of witchcraft may be hanged and that two witches were recently hanged in Boston. The stakes for Abigail, Mercy, Mary, Betty, and Ruth are nothing less than their lives.*)

Strategies for Annotation
🖉 🖻 *Annotate it!*

Analyze Drama Elements
COMMON CORE RL 3, RL 5

Share these strategies for guided or independent analysis:

- Highlight in yellow any examples of **direct characterization**: stage directions that give details about the characters' appearances, personalities, and emotional states.
- Highlight in blue any examples of **indirect characterization**: characters' words and stage directions that describe characters' actions.
- On a note, tell what Mercy's behavior reveals about her character.

(Enter Mary Warren, breathless. She is [a] … naive, lonely girl.)

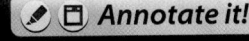

Mary Warren. What'll we do? …They'll be callin' us witches,

Abby!

Mercy (pointing and looking at Mary Warren). She means to tell, I know it.

"When Mercy points to Mary, looks at her, and says Mary 'means to tell,' it reveals Mercy as suspicious and out to save her own skin."

Analyze Drama Elements COMMON CORE RL 3, RL 5

(LINES 425–470)

Remind students that aspects of a character are revealed by that character's **actions.**

(S) ASK STUDENTS to tell what Abigail's behavior in these lines reveals about her character. (*The fact that Abigail is physically rough with Betty (who is just 10 years old), that she took part in a charm that was supposed to kill Mrs. Proctor, and that she threatens to bring a "pointy reckoning" to any girl who talks reveals that she is hot-tempered, vengeful, and violent.*)

Analyze Drama Elements COMMON CORE RL 3, RL 5

(LINES 441–470)

Tell students that these lines reveal still more about Abigail and her stake in the play's action.

(T) CITE TEXT EVIDENCE Asks students to tell what they learn in these lines about Abigail and her stake in the action. (*In line 444, we learn that Abigail may have drunk blood as part of the ritual in the forest. Then in line 460, Abigail refers to the "other things" she and the others did in the forest. This raises the stakes for Abigail—if these "other things" are revealed then she may have a lot to lose, including her life.*)

Mary Warren. I never done none of it, Abby. I only looked!

Mercy (*moving menacingly toward*
420 *Mary*). Oh, you're a great one for lookin', aren't you, Mary Warren? What a grand peeping courage you have!

(Betty, *on the bed, whimpers. Abigail turns to her at once.*)

Abigail. Betty? (*She goes to Betty.*) Now, Betty, dear, wake up now. It's Abigail. (*She sits Betty up and furiously shakes her.*) I'll beat you, Betty! (*Betty whimpers.*) My, you seem improving.
430 I talked to your papa and I told him everything. So there's nothing to—

Betty (*darts off the bed, frightened of Abigail, and flattens herself against the wall*). I want my mama!

Abigail (*with alarm, as she cautiously approaches Betty*). What ails you, Betty? Your mama's dead and buried.

Betty. I'll fly to Mama. Let me fly! (*She raises her arms as though to fly, and*
440 *streaks for the window, gets one leg out.*)

Abigail (*pulling her away from the window*).  I told him everything; he knows now, he knows everything we—

Betty. You drank blood, Abby! You didn't tell him that!

Abigail. Betty, you never say that again! You will never—

Betty. You did, you did! You drank a charm to kill John Proctor's wife! You
450 drank a charm to kill Goody Proctor!

Abigail (*smashes her across the face*). Shut it! Now shut it!

Betty (*collapsing on the bed*). Mama, Mama! (*She dissolves into sobs.*)

Abigail. Now look you. All of you. We danced. And Tituba conjured Ruth Putnam's dead sisters. And that is all. And mark this. Let either of you breathe

a word, or the edge of a word, about the
460 other things, and I will come to you in the black of some terrible night and I will bring a pointy reckoning that will shudder you.[10] And you know I can do it; I saw Indians smash my dear parents' heads on the pillow next to mine, and I have seen some reddish work done at night, and I can make you wish you had never seen the sun go down! (*She goes to Betty and roughly sits her up.*) Now,
470 you—sit up and stop this!

(*But Betty collapses in her hands and lies inert on the bed.*)

Mary Warren (*with hysterical fright*). What's got her? (Abigail *stares in fright at Betty.*) Abby, she's going to die! It's a sin to conjure, and we—

Abigail (*starting for Mary*). I say shut it, Mary Warren! (*Enter John Proctor. On seeing him, Mary Warren leaps in fright.*)

Proctor was a farmer in his middle thirties. He need not have been a partisan of any faction in the town, but there is evidence to suggest that he had a sharp and biting way with hypocrites. He was the kind of man—powerful of body, even-tempered, and not easily led—who cannot refuse support to partisans without drawing their deepest resentment. In Proctor's presence a fool felt his foolishness instantly—and a Proctor is always marked for calumny[11] therefore.

But as we shall see, the steady manner he displays does not spring from an untroubled soul. He is a sinner, a sinner not only against the moral fashion of the time, but against his own vision of decent conduct. These

---

[10]**bring . . . shudder you:** inflict a terrifying punishment on you.

[11]**marked for calumny** (kăl´əm-nē): singled out to have lies told about him.

TO CHALLENGE STUDENTS . . .

Interpret Stage Directions Tell students that the job of a play's director is to collaborate with the actors to make sure that they follow the spirit of the playwright's stage directions.

ASK STUDENTS to enact the scene on this page. Choose a student to act as the director and other students to act each of the parts. Give each actor ten minutes to study his or her lines and stage directions. Then have students enact the scene. When they have finished, have the director give each actor feedback on his or her performance based on the stage directions. Then have students enact the scene again.

people had no ritual for the washing away of sins. It is another trait we inherited from them, and it has helped to discipline us as well as to breed hypocrisy among us. Proctor, respected and even feared in Salem, has come to regard himself as a kind of fraud. But no hint of this has yet appeared on the surface, and as he enters from the crowded parlor below it is a man in his prime we see, with a quiet confidence and an unexpressed, hidden force. Mary Warren, his servant, can barely speak for embarrassment and fear.

480 **Mary Warren.** Oh! I'm just going home, Mr. Proctor.

Proctor. Be you foolish, Mary Warren? Be you deaf? I forbid you leave the house, did I not? Why shall I pay you? I am looking for you more often than my cows!

Mary Warren. I only come to see the great doings in the world.

Proctor. I'll show you a great doin' on
490 your arse one of these days. Now get you home; my wife is waitin' with your work! (*Trying to retain a shred of dignity, she goes slowly out.*)

Mercy Lewis (*both afraid of him and strangely titillated*). I'd best be off. I have my Ruth to watch. Good morning, Mr. Proctor.

(Mercy *sidles out. Since* Proctor's *entrance,* Abigail *has stood as though on*
500 *tiptoe, absorbing his presence, wide-eyed. He glances at her, then goes to* Betty *on the bed.*)

Abigail. Gah! I'd almost forgot how strong you are, John Proctor!

Proctor (*looking at* Abigail *now, the faintest suggestion of a knowing smile on his face*). What's this mischief here?

Abigail (*with a nervous laugh*). Oh, she's only gone silly somehow.

510 **Proctor.** The road past my house is a pilgrimage to Salem all morning. The town's mumbling witchcraft.

Abigail. Oh, posh! (*Winningly she comes a little closer, with a confidential, wicked air.*) We were dancin' in the woods last night, and my uncle leaped in on us. She took fright, is all.

Proctor (*his smile widening*). Ah, you're wicked yet, aren't y'! (*A trill of expectant*
520 *laughter escapes her, and she dares come closer, feverishly looking into his eyes.*) You'll be clapped in the stocks before you're twenty.

(*He takes a step to go, and she springs into his path.*)

Abigail. Give me a word, John. A soft word. (*Her concentrated desire destroys his smile.*)

Proctor. No, no, Abby. That's done with.

530 **Abigail** (*tauntingly*). You come five mile to see a silly girl fly? I know you better.

Proctor (*setting her firmly out of his path*). I come to see what mischief your uncle's brewin' now. (*with final emphasis*) Put it out of mind, Abby.

Abigail (*grasping his hand before he can release her*). John—I am waitin' for you every night.

Proctor. Abby, I never give you hope to
540 wait for me.

Abigail (*now beginning to anger—she can't believe it*). I have something better than hope, I think!

Proctor. Abby, you'll put it out of mind. I'll not be comin' for you more.

Abigail. You're surely sportin' with me.

Proctor. You know me better.

The Crucible: Act One **469**

CLOSE READ

Analyze Drama Elements  RL 3, RL 5

Remind students that the expositional sections Miller inserts in this act provide facts and background about the characters.

 ASK STUDENTS to tell what they learn about Proctor's character in the exposition on pages 468–469. (*Proctor is an upstanding member of the community and does not approve of partisanship, hypocrisy, or foolishness. This, however, makes him a target for those who practice them. We also learn that he is a sinner who carries an inner conflict within himself. He regards himself as a fraud.*)

Analyze Drama Elements  RL 3, RL 5
(LINES 498–547)

Remind students that **indirect characterization** requires them to infer from the characters' behavior what the characters are really feeling.

V **ASK STUDENTS** to infer the nature of Proctor and Abigail's relationship from their behavior as described in the stage directions in lines 498–547. Give specific examples from the text for support. (*As Abigail "absorbs his presence" [line 500] and looks at Proctor, he changes from being angry to having a slight smile [line 506]. This suggests that he has a friendly relationship with her, though she was his servant. As she moves closer to him "winningly" [line 513], his smile widens [line 518] until she asks him to speak a "soft word" to her [line 526] and his smile disappears [line 527]. He "set[s] her firmly out of his path" [line 532], but she grabs his hand [line 536] and doesn't let him go. This suggests that they may have a romantic or sexual relationship and that, while Proctor does not want it to continue, Abigail does. When he refuses Abigail, she gets angry [line 541] because she is surprised by his reaction and feels rejected. This tells us that she is determined to get what she wants and may become upset or angry if she doesn't.*)

SCAFFOLDING FOR ELL STUDENTS

Understand Archaic Language Tell students that the dialogue in *The Crucible* uses some outdated language. Point out the phrase "great doings" in line 488. Tell students that they can often infer the meanings of unfamiliar words or phrases from context. Discuss the context of "great doings" with students and lead them to understand that Mary is referring to the accusations of witchcraft. Elicit the definition "important events."

ASK STUDENTS to work in pairs to infer the meanings of "posh" in line 513 and "sportin' with me" in line 546. (*"posh": nonsense; "sportin' with me": joking*)

CLOSE READ

Analyze Drama Elements
COMMON CORE RL 3, RL 5

(LINES 571–590)

Explain to students that a playwright uses both dialogue and actions to flesh out a character. Students should look at both of these elements of drama to uncover the real reasons for a character's behavior.

W CITE TEXT EVIDENCE Have students reread lines 571–590. Ask them to explain what may be motivating Abigail's behavior in this section, citing specific examples in the text to support their explanations. *(Abigail is clearly in love with Proctor. During their dialogue, she accuses him of still being in love with her [line 554]. The stage direction in line 571 describes her weeping, indicating her emotional pain and heartbreak about him. Abigail also describes dreams to Proctor in which she "walk[s] about the house as though I'd find you comin' through some door" [lines 573–575].)*

Analyze Drama Elements
COMMON CORE RL 3, RL 5

(LINES 577–587)

Tell students that the **plot** of a play is the series of events that make up the story. One element of drama that is part of plot is conflict. **Conflict** is the struggle between opposing forces (often characters) in the story. The conflict (or conflicts) of a play drive the play's action by creating tension.

X ASK STUDENTS to determine the nature of the conflict between Abigail and Proctor in this section. *(Abigail wants to continue the relationship that they have had and Proctor does not. Indeed, Proctor denies that they even touched, which outrages Abigail.)*

Abigail. I know how you clutched my back behind your house and sweated
550 like a stallion whenever I come near! Or did I dream that? It's she put me out, you cannot pretend it were you. I saw your face when she put me out, and you loved me then and you do now!

Proctor. Abby, that's a wild thing to say—

Abigail. A wild thing may say wild things. But not so wild, I think. I have seen you since she put me out; I have
560 seen you nights.

Proctor. I have hardly stepped off my farm this sevenmonth.

Abigail. I have a sense for heat, John, and yours has drawn me to my window, and I have seen you looking up, burning in your loneliness. Do you tell me you've never looked up at my window?

Proctor. I may have looked up.

Abigail (*now softening*). And you must.
570 You are no wintry man. I *know* you, John. I know you. (*She is weeping.*) I cannot sleep for dreamin'; I cannot dream but I wake and walk about the house as though I'd find you comin' through some door. (*She clutches him desperately*).

X Proctor (*gently pressing her from him, with great sympathy but firmly*). Child—

Abigail (*with a flash of anger*). How do
580 you call me child!

Proctor. Abby, I may think of you softly from time to time. But I will cut off my hand before I'll ever reach for you again. Wipe it out of mind. We never touched, Abby.

Abigail. Aye, but we did.

Proctor. Aye, but we did not.

Abigail (*with a bitter anger*). Oh, I marvel how such a strong man may let
590 such a sickly wife be—

Image Credits: ©Photodisc/Getty Images

WHEN STUDENTS STRUGGLE . . .

If students have trouble discerning conflict in a particular scene, encourage them to begin by identifying what each character wants or needs.

ASK STUDENTS to describe some of the other conflicts in the play so far. Ask them to tell what opposite things each of the following characters wants or needs.

- Abigail and Mrs. Proctor *(Abigail wants to continue a relationship with her husband; it is assumed Mrs. Proctor does not want this and that this is why Abigail was fired from their service.)*

- Parris and the Putnams *(Parris wants no mention yet of the possibility of witchcraft in Betty's illness; the Putnams want to involve Reverend Hale and spread the word of witchcraft in the town.)*

Proctor (*angered—at himself as well*). You'll speak nothin' of Elizabeth!

Abigail. She is blackening my name in the village! She is telling lies about me! She is a cold, sniveling woman, and you bend to her! Let her turn you like a—

Proctor (*shaking her*). Do you look for whippin'?

(*A psalm is heard being sung below.*)

600 **Abigail** (*in tears*). I look for John Proctor that took me from my sleep and put knowledge in my heart! I never knew what pretense Salem was, I never knew the lying lessons I was taught by all these Christian women and their covenanted[12] men! And now you bid me tear the light out of my eyes? I will not, I cannot! You loved me, John Proctor, and whatever sin it is, you love me yet!

610 (*He turns abruptly to go out. She rushes to him.*) John, pity me, pity me!

(*The words "going up to Jesus" are heard in the psalm, and Betty claps her ears suddenly and whines loudly.*)

Abigail. Betty? (*She hurries to Betty, who is now sitting up and screaming. Proctor goes to Betty as Abigail is trying to pull her hands down, calling "Betty!"*)

Proctor (*growing unnerved*). What's 620 she doing? Girl, what ails you? Stop that wailing!

(*The singing has stopped in the midst of this, and now Parris rushes in.*)

Parris. What happened? What are you doing to her? Betty! (*He rushes to the bed, crying, "Betty, Betty!" Mrs. Putnam enters, feverish with curiosity, and with her Thomas Putnam and Mercy Lewis. Parris, at the bed, keeps lightly slapping*

---

12 **covenanted** (kŭv´ə-nən-tĭd): In Puritan religious practice, the men of a congregation would make an agreement, or covenant, to govern the community and abide by its beliefs and practices.

---

630 Betty's *face, while she moans and tries to get up.*)

Abigail. She heard you singin' and suddenly she's up and screamin'.

Mrs. Putnam. The psalm! The psalm! She cannot bear to hear the Lord's name!

Parris. No. God forbid. Mercy, run to the doctor! Tell him what's happened here! (*Mercy Lewis rushes out.*)

640 **Mrs. Putnam.** Mark it for a sign, mark it!

(*Rebecca Nurse, seventy-two, enters. She is white-haired, leaning upon her walking-stick.*)

Putnam (*pointing at the whimpering Betty*). That is a notorious sign of witchcraft afoot, Goody Nurse, a prodigious sign!

Mrs. Putnam. My mother told me that! 650 When they cannot bear to hear the name of—

Parris (*trembling*). Rebecca, Rebecca, go to her, we're lost. She suddenly cannot bear to hear the Lord's—

(*Giles Corey, eighty-three, enters. He is knotted with muscle, canny, inquisitive, and still powerful.*)

Rebecca. There is hard sickness here, Giles Corey, so please to keep the quiet.

660 **Giles.** I've not said a word. No one here can testify I've said a word. Is she going to fly again? I hear she flies.

Putnam. Man, be quiet now!

(*Everything is quiet. Rebecca walks across the room to the bed. Gentleness exudes from her. Betty is quietly whimpering, eyes shut. Rebecca simply stands over the child, who gradually quiets.*)

CLOSE READ

Analyze Drama Elements

(LINES 599–611)

Remind students that stage directions help establish mood. A stage direction can also trigger a change of mood.

Y ASK STUDENTS to tell how the mood of the scene changes once the psalm is heard. Specifically, how is the change of mood reflected in Abigail's dialogue? (*The scene takes on a feeling of greater urgency and tension once the singing of the psalm begins. It is as if Abigail becomes aware that she must convince Proctor in this moment—she is crying and desperately urging him to accept her: "You loved me, John Proctor . . . you love me yet!" [lines 608–609]*)

Analyze Drama Elements

(LINES 634–654)

Tell students to track the development of minor characters throughout the play. Minor characters are often included to provide commentary on major events in the text.

Z ASK STUDENTS to explain how Mr. and Mrs. Putnam's reaction to the psalm (and Betty's reaction to it) is consistent with their characters. (*Mr. and Mrs. Putnam have already been established as believing in witchcraft as the root of Betty's ills. Their characters are consistent in this section: when Betty cries at the same time as the psalm is being sung, they assume that she is possessed by the Devil and cannot stand the sound of the Lord's name.*)

SCAFFOLDING FOR ELL STUDENTS

Understand Stage Directions Ask students to note that in the stage directions, Miller sometimes uses a complete sentence and sometimes uses a word or phrase. Point out the stage direction in line 591 and explain that it is Proctor who is angered at Abigail and at himself.

ASK STUDENTS to rewrite the following stage directions and change them into complete sentences to make sure they understand who is doing what action.

- **Proctor** (*shaking her*). Do you look for whippin'? (*Proctor speaks while he is shaking Abigail.*)
- **Proctor** (*growing unnerved*). What's she doing? (*Proctor is growing unnerved.*)

Analyze Drama Elements  RL 3, RL 5

Remind students that Miller's sections of exposition offer insight into the motivations behind characters' behaviors.

A2 **CITE TEXT EVIDENCE** Have students read the exposition on page 472. What is the reason for the complaints against Rebecca Nurse? *(The townspeople of Salem resented the Nurse's material wealth and higher social status. The Nurses also helped block Putnam's candidate for the Salem ministry. In addition, the Nurses were part of a faction of people who broke off from Salem to found their own town.)*

Analyze Drama Elements  RL 3, RL 5

(LINES 679–690)

Encourage students to look at characters' **dialogue** for insight into their nature.

B2 **ASK STUDENTS** to read Rebecca's dialogue in lines 679–690 aloud. Then tell what her dialogue reveals about her character. *(Her dialogue reveals her to be a more rational and less reactionary character than the others, especially Mr. and Mrs. Putnam.)*

And while they are so absorbed, we may put a word in for Rebecca. Rebecca was the wife of Francis Nurse, who, from all accounts, was one of those men for whom both sides of the argument had to have respect. He was called upon to arbitrate disputes as though he were an unofficial judge, and Rebecca also enjoyed the high opinion most people had for him. By the time of the delusion,[13] they had three hundred acres, and their children were settled in separate homesteads within the same estate. However, Francis had originally rented the land, and one theory has it that, as he gradually paid for it and raised his social status, there were those who resented his rise.

Another suggestion to explain the systematic campaign against Rebecca, and inferentially against Francis, is the land war he fought with his neighbors, one of whom was a Putnam. This squabble grew to the proportions of a battle in the woods between partisans of both sides, and it is said to have lasted for two days. As for Rebecca herself, the general opinion of her character was so high that to explain how anyone dared cry her out for a witch—and more, how adults could bring themselves to lay hands on her—we must look to the fields and boundaries of that time.

As we have seen, Thomas Putnam's man for the Salem ministry was Bayley. The Nurse clan had been in the faction that prevented Bayley's taking office. In addition, certain families allied to the Nurses by blood or friendship, and whose farms were contiguous with the Nurse farm or close to it, combined to break away from the Salem town authority and set up Topsfield, a new and independent entity whose existence was resented by old Salemites.

That the guiding hand behind the outcry was Putnam's is indicated by the fact that, as soon as it began, this Topsfield-Nurse faction absented themselves from church in protest and disbelief. It was Edward and Jonathan Putnam who signed the first complaint against Rebecca; and Thomas Putnam's little daughter was the one who fell into a fit at the hearing and pointed to Rebecca as her attacker. To top it all, Mrs. Putnam—who is now staring at the bewitched child on the bed—soon accused Rebecca's spirit of "tempting her to iniquity," a charge that had more truth in it than Mrs. Putnam could know.

670 **Mrs. Putnam** (*astonished*). What have you done?

(Rebecca, *in thought, now leaves the bedside and sits.*)

Parris (*wondrous and relieved*). What do you make of it, Rebecca?

Putnam (*eagerly*). Goody Nurse, will you go to my Ruth and see if you can wake her?

Rebecca (*sitting*). I think she'll wake
680 in time. Pray calm yourselves. I have eleven children, and I am twenty-six times a grandma, and I have seen them all through their silly seasons, and when it come on them they will run the Devil bowlegged keeping up with their mischief. I think she'll wake when she tires of it. A child's spirit is like a child, you can never catch it by running after it; you must stand still, and, for love, it
690 will soon itself come back.

Proctor. Aye, that's the truth of it, Rebecca.

---

[13] **the time of the delusion:** the era of the witchcraft accusations and trials.

472 Collection 6

TO CHALLENGE STUDENTS

Conduct Research What really happened in Salem? Explain to students that while *The Crucible* is fictional, Arthur Miller based his play on contemporary records of the Salem Witch Trials.

ASK STUDENTS to work in small groups to formulate research questions about the Salem Witch Trials. Have each student choose one question and conduct Internet research to find an answer. When students have finished their research, have them share their findings with the class.

Mrs. Putnam. This is no silly season, Rebecca. My Ruth is bewildered, Rebecca; she cannot eat.

Rebecca. Perhaps she is not hungered yet. (*to Parris*) I hope you are not decided to go in search of loose spirits, Mr. Parris. I've heard promise of that outside.

Parris. A wide opinion's running in the parish that the Devil may be among us, and I would satisfy them that they are wrong.

Proctor. Then let you come out and call them wrong. Did you consult the wardens[14] before you called this minister to look for devils?

Parris. He is not coming to look for devils!

Proctor. Then what's he coming for?

Putnam. There be children dyin' in the village, Mister!

Proctor. I seen none dyin'. This society will not be a bag to swing around your head, Mr. Putnam. (*to Parris*) Did you call a meeting before you—?

Putnam. I am sick of meetings; cannot the man turn his head without he have a meeting?

Proctor. He may turn his head, but not to Hell!

Rebecca. Pray, John, be calm. (*Pause. He defers to her.*) Mr. Parris, I think you'd best send Reverend Hale back as soon as he come. This will set us all to arguin' again in the society, and we thought to have peace this year. I think we ought rely on the doctor now, and good prayer.

Mrs. Putnam. Rebecca, the doctor's baffled!

---

[14]**wardens:** officers appointed to keep order.

Rebecca. If so he is, then let us go to God for the cause of it. There is prodigious danger in the seeking of loose spirits. I fear it, I fear it. Let us rather blame ourselves and—

Putnam. How may we blame ourselves? I am one of nine sons; the Putnam seed have peopled this province. And yet I have but one child left of eight—and now she shrivels!

Rebecca. I cannot fathom that.

Mrs. Putnam (*with a growing edge of sarcasm*). But I must! You think it God's work you should never lose a child, nor grandchild either, and I bury all but one? There are wheels within wheels in this village, and fires within fires!

Putnam (*to Parris*). When Reverend Hale comes, you will proceed to look for signs of witchcraft here.

Proctor (*to Putnam*). You cannot command Mr. Parris. We vote by name in this society, not by acreage.

Putnam. I never heard you worried so on this society, Mr. Proctor. I do not think I saw you at Sabbath meeting since snow flew.

Proctor. I have trouble enough without I come five mile to hear him preach only hellfire and bloody damnation. Take it to heart, Mr. Parris. There are many others who stay away from church these days because you hardly ever mention God any more.

Parris (*now aroused*). Why, that's a drastic charge!

Rebecca. It's somewhat true; there are many that quail to bring their children—

Parris. I do not preach for children, Rebecca. It is not the children who are unmindful of their obligations toward this ministry.

The Crucible: Act One **473**

CLOSE READ

Analyze Drama Elements  RL 3, RL 5
(LINES 711–766)

Explain to students a playwright will develop and deepen the conflicts between his or her characters as a play goes on.

ASK STUDENTS to describe the nature of the conflict between Proctor and Putnam in this section. (*Proctor does not believe that witchcraft is to blame for the girls' illnesses, but Putnam does. Proctor wants Putnam to follow proper political protocol before rushing into a witch hunt with Reverend Hale. Putnam accuses Proctor of not being sufficiently religious because Proctor does not go to church regularly.*)

Analyze Drama Elements  RL 3, RL 5
(LINES 723–743)

Remind students that using **dialogue** is one of the ways that playwrights develop character.

ASK STUDENTS to read the dialogue in lines 723–743. In what way is Rebecca Nurse religious? How does her faith in God differ from that of Mrs. Putnam? (*Rebecca Nurse is also religious and believes in going to God for the answer to Betty's illness. However, she does not believe, as Mrs. Putnam does, that Betty is possessed by the Devil. Rebecca warns against pursuing "loose spirits"—she feels that best left to God and prayer.*)

SCAFFOLDING FOR ELL STUDENTS

Distinguish Characters and Dialogue Tell students that when reading a play, they may find it difficult to distinguish among characters in a complex scene. Remind them that Miller has provided significant information about characters as they are introduced. Have students make a chart of characters appearing on the page. Ask them to look back at the information that Miller has provided about each character and write a few significant details.

ASK STUDENTS to refer to their charts to answer the following question: Why is Proctor challenging Reverend Parris about the calling in of Reverend Bayley? (*Proctor isn't easily led, and since he hasn't seen children dying, he doesn't see the necessity for drastic action.*)

TEACH

CLOSE READ

Analyze Drama Elements
(LINES 781–844)

Remind students that facets of character can be revealed through both direct and indirect characterization.

E2 **CITE TEXT EVIDENCE** Ask students whether they learn more about Parris in this section through direct or indirect characterization. Have them explain their answer and provide examples. *(In this section, we learn much about Parris through dialogue, a function of indirect characterization. When he argues with Proctor, Parris exposes his own pride and self-interest because he is primarily concerned with himself and his own wealth and position in society. Parris feels persecuted by others because they have not provided him with the ample salary he believes he deserves [lines 799–803]. His feeling of being persecuted leads him to suspect the presence of the Devil in others [lines 803–808] as a reason for his lack of wealth and position.)*

Analyze Drama Elements
(LINES 809–853)

Tell students that when a play has as many characters as *The Crucible* has, a skilled playwright will create conflicts between many of them, creating a complex web of drama.

F2 **ASK STUDENTS** to reread this section and describe the nature of the conflict between Proctor and Parris. *(Parris is complaining that he does not earn enough money, that he was rebuffed when he wanted to own the house set aside for the minister, and that he is not afforded the appropriate respect. He cites his faith as reason that he should be granted these things. Proctor, on the other hand, is suspicious and "sick of" Parris and the entire town's incessant use of religious rhetoric as a form of social control. When Parris accuses Proctor of leading an anti-religious faction, Proctor sarcastically says he wishes it were so.)*

Rebecca. Are there really those unmindful?

Parris. I should say the better half of Salem village—

780 **Putnam.** And more than that!

Parris. Where is my wood? My contract provides I be supplied with all my firewood. I am waiting since November for a stick, and even in November I had to show my frostbitten hands like some London beggar!

Giles. You are allowed six pound a year to buy your wood, Mr. Parris.

Parris. I regard that six pound as part 790 of my salary. I am paid little enough without I spend six pound on firewood.

Proctor. Sixty, plus six for firewood—

Parris. The salary is sixty-six pound, Mr. Proctor! I am not some preaching farmer with a book under my arm; I am a graduate of Harvard College.

Giles. Aye, and well instructed in arithmetic!

Parris. Mr. Corey, you will look far for 800 a man of my kind at sixty pound a year! I am not used to this poverty; I left a thrifty business in the Barbados to serve the Lord. I do not fathom it, why am I persecuted here? I cannot offer one proposition but there be a howling riot of argument. I have often wondered if the Devil be in it somewhere; I cannot understand you people otherwise.

Proctor. Mr. Parris, you are the first 810 minister ever did demand the deed to this house—

Parris. Man! Don't a minister deserve a house to live in?

Proctor. To live in, yes. But to ask ownership is like you shall own the meeting house itself; the last meeting were at you spoke so long on deeds and mortgages I thought it were an auction.

Parris. I want a mark of confidence, 820 is all! I am your third preacher in seven years. I do not wish to be put out like the cat whenever some majority feels the whim. You people seem not to comprehend that a minister is the Lord's man in the parish; a minister is not to be so lightly crossed and contradicted—

Putnam. Aye!

Parris. There is either obedience or the 830 church will burn like Hell is burning!

Proctor. Can you speak one minute without we land in Hell again? I am sick of Hell!

Parris. It is not for you to say what is good for you to hear!

Proctor. I may speak my heart, I think!

Parris (*in a fury*). What, are we Quakers?[15] We are not Quakers here yet, Mr. Proctor. And you may tell that 840 to your followers!

Proctor. My followers!

Parris (*Now he's out with it*). There is a party in this church. I am not blind; there is a faction and a party.

Proctor. Against you?

Putnam. Against him and all authority!

Proctor. Why, then I must find it and join it.

(*There is shock among the others.*)

850 **Rebecca.** He does not mean that.

Putnam. He confessed it now!

Proctor. I mean it solemnly, Rebecca; I like not the smell of this "authority."

---

[15] **Quakers:** a radical English religious sect— much hated by the Puritans—who often "spoke their heart" during their religious meetings.

WHEN STUDENTS STRUGGLE . . .

Understand Character Encourage students to consider what new aspects of John Proctor's character are revealed on this page.

ASK STUDENTS to work with a partner and come up with a list of words that describe the character of John Proctor as they understand him so far. Ask them to underline the characteristics of Proctor that are introduced on this page. *(Possible answers: stern, strict, tall, warm, powerful, no-nonsense, sharp, even-tempered, down-to-earth, sinner, decent, stubborn, courageous, funny, sarcastic, noble, daring.)*

Rebecca. No, you cannot break charity[16] with your minister. You are another kind, John. Clasp his hand, make your peace.

Proctor. I have a crop to sow and lumber to drag home. (*He goes angrily to the door and turns to Corey with a smile.*) What say you, Giles, let's find the party. He says there's a party.

Giles. I've changed my opinion of this man, John. Mr. Parris, I beg your pardon. I never thought you had so much iron in you.

Parris (*surprised*). Why, thank you, Giles!

Giles. It suggests to the mind what the trouble be among us all these years. (*to all*) Think on it. Wherefore is everybody suing everybody else? Think on it now, it's a deep thing, and dark as a pit. I have been six time in court this year—

Proctor (*familiarly, with warmth, although he knows he is approaching the edge of* Giles' *tolerance with this*). Is it the Devil's fault that a man cannot say you good morning without you clap him for defamation?[17] You're old, Giles, and you're not hearin' so well as you did.

Giles (*He cannot be crossed*). John Proctor, I have only last month collected four pound damages for you publicly sayin' I burned the roof off your house, and I—

Proctor (*laughing*). I never said no such thing, but I've paid you for it, so I hope I can call you deaf without charge. Now come along, Giles, and help me drag my lumber home.

---

[16] **break charity:** break off; end the relationship.

[17] **clap . . . defamation** (dĕf´ə-mā´shən): imprison him for slander.

Putnam. A moment, Mr. Proctor. What lumber is that you're draggin', if I may ask you?

Proctor. My lumber. From out my forest by the riverside.

Putnam. Why, we are surely gone wild this year. What anarchy is this? That tract is in my bounds, it's in my bounds, Mr. Proctor.

Proctor. In your bounds! (*indicating* Rebecca) I bought that tract from Goody Nurse's husband five months ago.

Putnam. He had no right to sell it. It stands clear in my grandfather's will that all the land between the river and—

Proctor. Your grandfather had a habit of willing land that never belonged to him, if I may say it plain.

Giles. That's God's truth; he nearly willed away my north pasture but he knew I'd break his fingers before he'd set his name to it. Let's get your lumber home, John. I feel a sudden will to work coming on.

Putnam. You load one oak of mine and you'll fight to drag it home!

Giles. Aye, and we'll win too, Putnam—this fool and I. Come on! (*He turns to* Proctor *and starts out.*)

Putnam. I'll have my men on you, Corey! I'll clap a writ on you!

(*Enter* Reverend John Hale *of Beverly.*)

Mr. Hale is nearing forty, a tight-skinned, eager-eyed intellectual. This is a beloved errand for him; on being called here to ascertain witchcraft he felt the pride of the specialist whose unique knowledge has at last been publicly called for. Like almost all men of learning, he spent a good deal of his time pondering the invisible

The Crucible: Act One **475**

CLOSE READ

Analyze Drama Elements

COMMON CORE RL 3, RL 5
(LINES 854–857)

Encourage students to continue to track the development of minor characters throughout the play.

G2 ASK STUDENTS to explain how Rebecca's dialogue in lines 854–857 supports what is known about her character thus far. (*Rebecca has been established as a woman who values her faith in God. Her encouraging Proctor not to sever his relationship with Parris is consistent with this.*) Then have students tell how this dialogue could complicate any potential accusations of witchcraft against Rebecca. (*An accusation of witchcraft would be difficult to assert about a religious woman who tells Proctor in front of everyone not to break his relationship with his minister. She would be an easier target if she were more openly disdainful of Parris like John Proctor.*)

Analyze Drama Elements

COMMON CORE RL 3, RL 5
(LINES 893–925)

Explain to students that playwrights employ complications to develop plot, or the events of the play. **Complications** are the problems that make the conflicts of a drama more difficult to resolve. Any event that adds intensity to the conflicts of the play qualifies as a complication.

H2 ASK STUDENTS to summarize the complications that arise in this section. Have them explain how they deepen the conflicts that already exist between the characters. (*Proctor has cut down some wood in the forest on property he bought from the Nurses, but Putnam claims the land is his. Proctor and Putnam are already at odds and this dispute complicates their conflict. Putnam threatens to sue Proctor.*)

Analyze Drama Elements COMMON CORE RL 3, RL 5

Remind students that Miller sometimes uses **direct characterization** in his exposition, directly stating facts about the characters.

 **CITE TEXT EVIDENCE** Have students tell what they learn in the exposition on page 476 about Hale and what qualifies him to discern witchcraft. *(We learn that Hale is excited about persecuting witches and considers himself an expert, but we also learn that he has no experience with witchcraft. He has only seen one case of suspected witchcraft in his own parish, and the woman turned out not to be guilty.)*

Analyze Drama Elements COMMON CORE RL 3, RL 5

Remind students that Miller sometimes reveals his own perspective on his subject in his exposition.

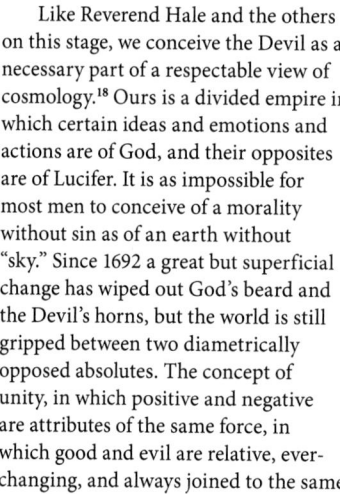 **ASK STUDENTS** to work with a partner and discuss the playwright's perspective on the Devil as described in the exposition on page 476. What historical background does Miller cite in support of his ideas? *(Possible response: Miller is acknowledging the power of the Devil as a necessary tool for people to use to distinguish between right and wrong, good and evil. He cites the historical irony that the Devil has been used by different types of Christianity to "whip men into surrender to a particular church or church-state." For example, Catholics used the Devil in their Inquisition; Martin Luther, accused by his enemies of an "alliance with Hell," used the Devil to accuse them in turn.)*

world, especially since he had himself encountered a witch in his parish not long before. That woman, however, turned into a mere pest under his searching scrutiny, and the child she had allegedly been afflicting recovered her normal behavior after Hale had given her his kindness and a few days of rest in his own house. However, that experience never raised a doubt in his mind as to the reality of the underworld or the existence of Lucifer's many-faced lieutenants. And his belief is not to his discredit. Better minds than Hale's were—and still are—convinced that there is a society of spirits beyond our ken. One cannot help noting that one of his lines has never yet raised a laugh in any audience that has seen this play; it is his assurance that "We cannot look to superstition in this. The Devil is precise." Evidently we are not quite certain even now whether diabolism is holy and not to be scoffed at. And it is no accident that we should be so bemused.

Like Reverend Hale and the others on this stage, we conceive the Devil as a necessary part of a respectable view of cosmology.[18] Ours is a divided empire in which certain ideas and emotions and actions are of God, and their opposites are of Lucifer. It is as impossible for most men to conceive of a morality without sin as of an earth without "sky." Since 1692 a great but superficial change has wiped out God's beard and the Devil's horns, but the world is still gripped between two diametrically opposed absolutes. The concept of unity, in which positive and negative are attributes of the same force, in which good and evil are relative, ever-changing, and always joined to the same

phenomenon—such a concept is still reserved to the physical sciences and to the few who have grasped the history of ideas. When it is recalled that until the Christian era the underworld was never regarded as a hostile area, that all gods were useful and essentially friendly to man despite occasional lapses; when we see the steady and methodical inculcation into humanity of the idea of man's worthlessness—until redeemed—the necessity of the Devil may become evident as a weapon, a weapon designed and used time and time again in every age to whip men into a surrender to a particular church or church-state.

Our difficulty in believing the—for want of a better word—political inspiration of the Devil is due in great part to the fact that he is called up and damned not only by our social antagonists but by our own side, whatever it may be. The Catholic Church, through its Inquisition,[19] is famous for cultivating Lucifer as the arch-fiend, but the Church's enemies relied no less upon the Old Boy to keep the human mind enthralled. Luther[20] was himself accused of alliance with Hell, and he in turn accused his enemies. To complicate matters further, he believed that he had had contact with the Devil and had argued theology with him. I am not surprised at this, for at my own university a professor of history— a Lutheran, by the way—used to assemble his graduate students, draw the shades, and commune in

---

[18] **cosmology** (kŏz-mŏl´ə-jē): a branch of philosophy dealing with the structure of the universe.

[19] **Inquisition:** a former tribunal in the Roman Catholic Church dedicated to the discovery and punishment of heresy.

[20] **Luther:** Martin Luther (1483–1546), the German theologian who led the Protestant Reformation.

the classroom with Erasmus.[21] He was never, to my knowledge, officially scoffed at for this, the reason being that the university officials, like most of us, are the children of a history which still sucks at the Devil's teats. At this writing, only England has held back before the temptations of contemporary diabolism. In the countries of the Communist ideology, all resistance of any import is linked to the totally malign capitalist succubi,[22] and in America any man who is not reactionary in his views is open to the charge of alliance with the Red hell. Political opposition, thereby, is given an inhumane overlay which then justifies the abrogation of all normally applied customs of civilized intercourse. A political policy is equated with moral right, and opposition to it with diabolical malevolence. Once such an equation is effectively made, society becomes a congerie of plots and counterplots, and the main role of government changes from that of the arbiter to that of the scourge of God.

The results of this process are no different now from what they ever were, except sometimes in the degree of cruelty inflicted, and not always even in that department. Normally the actions and deeds of a man were all that society felt comfortable in judging. The secret intent of an action was left to the ministers, priests, and rabbis to deal with. When diabolism rises, however, actions are the least important manifests of the true nature of a man. The Devil, as Reverend Hale said, is a

wily one, and, until an hour before he fell, even God thought him beautiful in Heaven.[23]

The analogy, however, seems to falter when one considers that, while there were no witches then, there are Communists and capitalists now, and in each camp there is certain proof that spies of each side are at work undermining the other. But this is a snobbish objection and not at all warranted by the facts. I have no doubt that people *were* communing with, and even worshiping, the Devil in Salem, and if the whole truth could be known in this case, as it is in others, we should discover a regular and conventionalized propitiation of the dark spirit. One certain evidence of this is the confession of Tituba, the slave of Reverend Parris, and another is the behavior of the children who were known to have indulged in sorceries with her.

There are accounts of similar *klatches* in Europe, where the daughters of the towns would assemble at night and, sometimes with fetishes, sometimes with a selected young man, give themselves to love, with some bastardly results. The Church, sharp-eyed as it must be when gods long dead are brought to life, condemned these orgies as witchcraft and interpreted them, rightly, as a resurgence of the Dionysiac forces[24] it had crushed long before. Sex, sin, and the Devil were early linked, and so they continued to be in Salem, and are today. From all accounts there are no more puritanical mores in the world than those enforced

---

[21] **Erasmus** (ĭ-răz′məs): Desiderius Erasmus (1466?–1536), a Dutch scholar who sought to restore Christian faith by a study of the Scriptures and classical texts.

[22] **succubi** (sŭk′yə-bī): demons that assume female form. Demons that assume male form are called incubi (ĭn′kyə-bī).

[23] **The Devil . . . beautiful in Heaven:** According to Christian belief, Lucifer was God's favorite angel until the angel rebelled and was cast out of Heaven.

[24] **Dionysiac** (dī′ə-nĭs′ē-ăk′) **forces:** forces associated with Dionysus, the Greek god of wine and ecstasy.

CLOSE READ

Analyze Drama Elements COMMON CORE RL 3, RL 5
(LINES 62–71)

Remind students that Arthur Miller wrote *The Crucible* in the early 1950s during the height of the Red Scare. Explain that the Red Scare was a period in American history when the U.S. government, suspicious of Communist activity in various parts of society, held hearings in hopes of rooting out any sympathizers with the Communist cause. The Red Scare frightened people into conformity and disloyalty.

K2 ASK STUDENTS how Miller draws a comparison between the use of the Devil as a spiritual threat and the fight against Communism in America in the 1950s. *(Miller is saying that just as anyone who was seen as disagreeable for any reason was accused of being under the influence of the Devil in Salem, so too was anyone who was not vigorously and vocally opposed to Communism in the 1950s was called a "Red" in America.)* What is the larger point that Miller is making about "diabolism" in society? *(Miller argues that diabolism is, and always has been, with us—that there is always some set of ideas or part of society that will be associated with "the Devil" for political purposes. On page 477, he states, "A political policy is equated with moral right, and opposition to it with diabolical malevolence". Miller warns against this tendency, which breeds cruelty and injustice.)*

TO CHALLENGE STUDENTS

Investigate Text References Central to understanding the points raised in Miller's exposition on these pages are the topics of the Spanish Inquisition, Martin Luther, the rise of Russian communism, and 19th-century Victorian morals.

ASK STUDENTS to work in small groups to investigate one of these topics and prepare a short report in which they connect their findings to Miller's larger point in this exposition. Have students read their finished reports to the class.

Analyze Drama Elements COMMON CORE RL 3, RL 5

Remind students that Miller uses his extended expositions to expand upon the ideas put forth in the play. He also offers historical background of the setting as a way to support his points.

L2 CITE TEXT EVIDENCE How does Miller connect sex to the concept of diabolism in this exposition? *(Miller says that sex has traditionally been seen as something sinful and that diabolism is rooted in society's discomfort with sex.)* How does Miller use historical background to argue that connecting sex with the Devil is hypocritical? Cite examples. *(He exposes the problematic and hypocritical nature of this connection by saying that just as all sides of Christianity claimed to see the Devil in each other, so too does society claim to see sex at every turn. Russian communism of the 1950s suppressed outward expressions of female sexuality, and yet Americans judge Russian attitudes towards women as hyper-sexual and "lascivious," to use Miller's term. Miller's point is that there is a tendency to portray those who seem "opposite" to us as overly sexual, and that sex is what gives this need to demonize others its continuing power.)*

Analyze Drama Elements COMMON CORE RL 3, RL 5

Remind students that Miller's expositions offer details about characters.

M2 ASK STUDENTS to tell what they learned about Reverend Hale from the exposition on page 478. Ask students why Hale is so eager to help in this situation. *(Hale is described as someone who has worked hard to become an expert on the issue of witchcraft and he thinks extremely highly of himself ["He feels himself allied with the best minds of Europe…"]. It can be inferred that he is eager to prove himself able to rid the ill girl of evil spirits.)*

L2 by the Communists in Russia, where women's fashions, for instance, are as prudent and all-covering as any American Baptist would desire. The divorce laws lay a tremendous responsibility on the father for the care of his children. Even the laxity of divorce regulations in the early years of the revolution was undoubtedly a revulsion from the nineteenth-century Victorian immobility of marriage and the consequent hypocrisy that developed from it. If for no other reasons, a state so powerful, so jealous of the uniformity of its citizens, cannot long tolerate the atomization of the family. And yet, in American eyes at least, there remains the conviction that the Russian attitude toward women is lascivious. It is the Devil working again, just as he is working within the Slav[25] who is shocked at the very idea of a woman's disrobing herself in a burlesque show. Our opposites are always robed in sexual sin, and it is from this unconscious conviction that demonology gains both its attractive sensuality and its capacity to infuriate and frighten.

M2 Coming into Salem now, Reverend Hale conceives of himself much as a young doctor on his first call. His painfully acquired armory of symptoms, catchwords, and diagnostic procedures are now to be put to use at last. The road from Beverly is unusually busy this morning, and he has passed a hundred rumors that make him smile at the ignorance of the yeomanry in this most precise science. He feels himself allied with the best minds of Europe—kings, philosophers, scientists, and ecclesiasts of all churches. His goal is light, goodness and its preservation, and he knows the exaltation of the blessed whose intelligence, sharpened by minute examinations of enormous tracts, is finally called upon to face what may be a bloody fight with the Fiend himself.

(He appears loaded down with half a dozen heavy books.)

Hale. Pray you, someone take these!

Parris (*delighted*). Mr. Hale! Oh! it's good to see you again! (*taking some books*) My, they're heavy!

Hale (*setting down his books*). They must be; they are weighted with authority.

Parris (*a little scared*). Well, you do come prepared!

Hale. We shall need hard study if it comes to tracking down the Old Boy. (*noticing* Rebecca) You cannot be Rebecca Nurse?

Rebecca. I am, sir. Do you know me?

Hale. It's strange how I knew you, but I suppose you look as such a good soul should. We have all heard of your great charities in Beverly.

Parris. Do you know this gentleman? Mr. Thomas Putnam. And his good wife Ann.

Hale. Putnam! I had not expected such distinguished company, sir.

Putnam (*pleased*). It does not seem to help us today, Mr. Hale. We look to you to come to our house and save our child.

Hale. Your child ails too?

Mrs. Putnam. Her soul, her soul seems flown away. She sleeps and yet she walks . . .

Putnam. She cannot eat.

[25] **Slav:** a generic reference to Russians and other Slavic-speaking peoples of Eastern Europe who were under the control of the Soviet Union.

WHEN STUDENTS STRUGGLE . . .

Understand Symbols After students read lines 926–937, in which Hale enters carrying a heavy stack of books, discuss the fact that playwrights sometimes introduce objects that serve as **symbols** by representing abstract ideas.

ASK STUDENTS what they think Hale's books symbolize. *(The books are described as "heavy" and "weighted with authority." The books may symbolize scholarly or moral authority.)*

Hale. Cannot eat! (*Thinks on it. Then, to* Proctor *and* Giles Corey.) Do you men have afflicted children?

Parris. No, no, these are farmers. John Proctor—

Giles Corey. He don't believe in witches.

Proctor (*to* Hale). I never spoke on witches one way or the other. Will you come, Giles?

Giles. No—no, John, I think not. I have some few queer questions of my own to ask this fellow.

Proctor. I've heard you to be a sensible man, Mr. Hale. I hope you'll leave some of it in Salem.

(Proctor *goes.* Hale *stands embarrassed for an instant.*)

Parris (*quickly*). Will you look at my daughter, sir? (*leads* Hale *to the bed*) She has tried to leap out the window; we discovered her this morning on the highroad, waving her arms as though she'd fly.

Hale (*narrowing his eyes*). Tries to fly.

Putnam. She cannot bear to hear the Lord's name, Mr. Hale; that's a sure sign of witchcraft afloat.

Hale (*holding up his hands*). No, no. Now let me instruct you. We cannot look to superstition in this. The Devil is precise; the marks of his presence are definite as stone, and I must tell you all that I shall not proceed unless you are prepared to believe me if I should find no bruise of hell upon her.

Parris. It is agreed, sir—it is agreed—we will abide by your judgment.

Hale. Good then. (*He goes to the bed, looks down at* Betty. *To* Parris.) Now, sir, what were your first warning of this strangeness?

Parris. Why, sir—I discovered her— (*indicating* Abigail) and my niece and ten or twelve of the other girls, dancing in the forest last night.

Hale (*surprised*). You permit dancing?

Parris. No, no, it were secret—

Mrs. Putnam (*unable to wait*). Mr. Parris's slave has knowledge of conjurin', sir.

Parris (*to* Mrs. Putnam). We cannot be sure of that, Goody Ann—

Mrs. Putnam (*frightened, very softly*). I know it, sir. I sent my child—she should learn from Tituba who murdered her sisters.

Rebecca (*horrified*). Goody Ann! You sent a child to conjure up the dead?

Mrs. Putnam. Let God blame me, not you, not you, Rebecca! I'll not have you judging me any more! (*to* Hale) Is it a natural work to lose seven children before they live a day?

Parris. Sssh!

(Rebecca, *with great pain, turns her face away. There is a pause.*)

Hale. Seven dead in childbirth.

Mrs. Putnam (*softly*). Aye. (*Her voice breaks; she looks up at him. Silence.* Hale *is impressed.* Parris *looks to him. He goes to his books, opens one, turns pages, then reads. All wait, avidly.*)

Parris (*hushed*). What book is that?

Mrs. Putnam. What's there, sir?

Hale (*with a tasty love of intellectual pursuit*). Here is all the invisible world, caught, defined, and calculated. In these books the Devil stands stripped of all his brute disguises. Here are all your familiar spirits—your incubi and succubi; your witches that go by land, by air, and by sea; your wizards of the night and of the day. Have no fear

The Crucible: Act One **479**

CLOSE READ

Analyze Drama Elements COMMON CORE RL 3, RL 5
(LINES 966–967)

Encourage students to be on the lookout for dialogue or behavior from the characters that is unexpected or conflicts with something they said or did earlier in the play. When this occurs, students should consider the motivation for the change. **Motivation** is the stated or implied reason for a character's behavior.

N2 ASK STUDENTS to read John Proctor's line of dialogue in lines 966–967. Have them say what they think motivates John to say this when he has said earlier that he is mistrustful of the way Salem uses religion to control others. (*Proctor may be protecting himself against further suspicion; by saying earlier that he wished to join an anti-religious faction yet saying to Hale's face that he has not rendered an opinion about witches, he is in essence covering his bases.*)

Analyze Drama Elements COMMON CORE RL 3, RL 5
(LINES 1018–1028)

Remind students that they can infer what is motivating a character's beliefs from looking at the character's **dialogue** and **actions.**

02 ASK STUDENTS to tell what they learn in this section about Mrs. Putnam that helps explain her fervent belief in witchcraft. Cite specific lines. (*Mrs. Putnam has delivered seven stillborn children. In her grief, she is more likely to accept the idea of witchcraft as the cause of her misfortune. To her, so much tragic loss cannot possibly be "a natural work," as she says in lines 1020–1022.*)

SCAFFOLDING FOR ELL STUDENTS

Understand Figurative Language Tell students that Miller employs a kind of figurative language in line 991 called a simile. **Similes** are comparisons made using the words *like* or *as.*

ASK STUDENTS to explain what Hale means when he says that the marks of the Devil's presence are "definite as stone." Then tell what Hale's use of this phrase reveals about his character. (*Hale is making the point that if the Devil is at work it will be obvious—the evidence will be as concrete and solid as a stone. Hale's use of this language shows he is sure of himself and definite in his opinions.*)

CLOSE READ

Analyze Drama Elements COMMON CORE RL 3, RL 5

(LINES 1047–1063)

Remind students to look to characters' dialogue and actions when figuring out their feelings and motives.

 **CITE TEXT EVIDENCE** Have students read lines 1047–1063. Ask them to tell what Rebecca's lines of dialogue and actions reveal about how she feels about the procedure Hale is about to perform. Cite specific lines for support. *(In lines 1051 and 1052, she says she will go and she physically gets up to do so. Rebecca does not wish to be present for Hale's procedure, which is a clue that she does not approve of or believe in it. When, in line 1061, she expresses uncertainty about whether God or the Devil is present, this shows again that she is doubtful of the efficacy of the procedure.)*

Analyze Drama Elements COMMON CORE RL 3, RL 5

(LINES 1066–1090)

Tell students to watch for **foreshadowing** in the play. Foreshadowing is a suggestion of something that will happen at a later point in the play.

Q2 ASK STUDENTS to tell how Giles' story about his wife may be an example of foreshadowing. *(Giles tells a story that his wife reads "strange" books and that when she reads them, he is unable to pray. Saying this in front of the others may raise suspicion of Giles' wife Martha being possessed by the Devil, a suspicion that may arise later in the play.)*

now—we shall find him out if he has come among us, and I mean to crush him utterly if he has shown his face! (*He starts for the bed.*)

Rebecca. Will it hurt the child, sir?

P2 Hale. I cannot tell. If she is truly in the Devil's grip we may have to rip and tear to get her free.

Rebecca. I think I'll go, then. I am too old for this. (*She rises.*)

Parris (*striving for conviction*). Why, Rebecca, we may open up the boil of all our troubles today!

Rebecca. Let us hope for that. I go to God for you, sir.

Parris (*with trepidation—and resentment*). I hope you do not mean we go to Satan here! (*slight pause*)

Rebecca. I wish I knew. (*She goes out; they feel resentful of her note of moral superiority.*)

Putnam (*abruptly*). Come, Mr. Hale, let's get on. Sit you here.

Q2 Giles. Mr. Hale, I have always wanted to ask a learned man—what signifies the readin' of strange books?

Hale. What books?

1070 **Giles.** I cannot tell; she hides them.

Hale. Who does this?

Giles. Martha, my wife. I have waked at night many a time and found her in a corner, readin' of a book. Now what do you make of that?

Hale. Why, that's not necessarily—

Giles. It discomfits me! Last night— mark this—I tried and tried and could not say my prayers. And then she close 1080 her book and walks out of the house, and suddenly—mark this—I could pray again!

Old Giles must be spoken for, if only because his fate was to be so remarkable and so different from that of all the others. He was in his early eighties at this time, and was the most comical hero in the history. No man has ever been blamed for so much. If a cow was missed, the first thought was to look for her around Corey's house; a fire blazing up at night brought suspicion of arson to his door. He didn't give a hoot for public opinion, and only in his last years—after he had married Martha—did he bother much with the church. That she stopped his prayer is very probable, but he forgot to say that he'd only recently learned any prayers and it didn't take much to make him stumble over them. He was a crank and a nuisance, but withal a deeply innocent and brave man. In court once, he was asked if it were true that he had been frightened by the strange behavior of a hog and had then said he knew it to be the Devil in an animal's shape. "What frighted you?" he was asked. He forgot everything but the word "frighted," and instantly replied, "I do not know that I ever spoke that word in my life."

Hale. Ah! The stoppage of prayer—that is strange. I'll speak further on that with you.

Giles. I'm not sayin' she's touched the Devil, now, but I'd admire to know what books she reads and why she hides them. She'll not answer me, y' see.

1090 **Hale.** Aye, we'll discuss it. (*to all*) Now mark me, if the Devil is in her you will witness some frightful wonders in this room, so please to keep your wits about you. Mr. Putnam, stand close in case she flies. Now, Betty, dear, will you sit up? (*Putnam comes in closer, ready-handed. Hale sits Betty up, but she hangs limp in his hands.*) Hmmm. (*He observes her*

SCAFFOLDING FOR ELL STUDENTS

Understand Suffixes Tell students that **suffixes** are added to the ends of words to create new words. Often the new words are different parts of speech than the original words. The word "conviction" in line 1053 has the suffix *-tion* at the end of it. The suffix *-tion* is added to words to create a noun. Other suffixes that are used to create nouns are *-ion, -ment* and *-ity*.

ASK STUDENTS to find the following words on this page. Have them use a dictionary to discover their meaning.

- trepidation (line 1058)
- resentment (line 1059)
- superiority (line 1063)

carefully. The others watch breathlessly.)

1100 Can you hear me? I am John Hale, minister of Beverly. I have come to help you, dear. Do you remember my two little girls in Beverly? (*She does not stir in his hands.*)

Parris (*in fright*). How can it be the Devil? Why would he choose my house to strike? We have all manner of licentious people in the village!

Hale. What victory would the Devil
1110 have to win a soul already bad? It is the best the Devil wants, and who is better than the minister?

Giles. That's deep, Mr. Parris, deep, deep!

Parris (*with resolution now*). Betty! Answer Mr. Hale! Betty!

Hale. Does someone afflict you, child? It need not be a woman, mind you, or a man. Perhaps some bird invisible to
1120 others comes to you—perhaps a pig, a mouse, or any beast at all. Is there some figure bids you fly? (*The child remains limp in his hands. In silence he lays her back on the pillow. Now, holding out his hands toward her, he intones.*) In nomine Domini Sabaoth sui filiique ite ad infernos.²⁶ (*She does not stir. He turns to* Abigail, *his eyes narrowing.*) Abigail, what sort of dancing were you doing
1130 with her in the forest?

Abigail. Why—common dancing is all.

Parris. I think I ought to say that I—I saw a kettle in the grass where they were dancing.

Abigail. That were only soup.

Hale. What sort of soup were in this kettle, Abigail?

---

²⁶**In nomine . . . infernos** *Latin:* "In the name of the Father and Son, get thee back to Hell."

Abigail. Why, it were beans—and lentils, I think, and—

1140 **Hale.** Mr. Parris, you did not notice, did you, any living thing in the kettle? A mouse, perhaps, a spider, a frog—?

Parris (*fearfully*). I—do believe there were some movement—in the soup.

Abigail. That jumped in, we never put it in!

Hale (*quickly*). What jumped in?

Abigail. Why, a very little frog jumped—

1150 **Parris.** A frog, Abby!

Hale (*grasping* Abigail). Abigail, it may be your cousin is dying. Did you call the Devil last night?

Abigail. I never called him! Tituba, Tituba . . .

Parris (*blanched*). She called the Devil?

Hale. I should like to speak with Tituba.

Parris. Goody Ann, will you bring her up? (Mrs. Putnam *exits.*)

1160 **Hale.** How did she call him?

Abigail. I know not—she spoke Barbados.

Hale. Did you feel any strangeness when she called him? A sudden cold wind, perhaps? A trembling below the ground?

Abigail. I didn't see no Devil! (*shaking* Betty) Betty, wake up. Betty! Betty!

Hale. You cannot evade me, Abigail.
1170 Did your cousin drink any of the brew in that kettle?

Abigail. She never drank it!

Hale. Did you drink it?

Abigail. No, sir!

Hale. Did Tituba ask you to drink it?

Abigail. She tried, but I refused.

The Crucible: Act One **481**

CLOSE READ

Analyze Drama Elements   COMMON CORE RL 3, RL 5
(LINES 1154–1176)

Explain to students that characters may have many reasons for behaving and speaking as they do. Students should infer from the text what motivates each character.

R2 **ASK STUDENTS** to review Abigail's admission that Tituba was present in the forest. Ask them to infer from what they've read as many reasons as they can why Abigail raises Tituba's name in this situation. (*Abigail probably mentions Tituba for many reasons: she is afraid Betty will die and is genuinely grasping for anything she can think of; Tituba was indeed present in the forest, so it is not a lie to say so; Abigail wants to get the attention—and potential blame—off of herself; Tituba is an easy target because she is a servant from Barbados, a culture that is foreign to the people of Salem, and therefore suspicious to them.*)

WHEN STUDENTS STRUGGLE . . .

Give students practice reading dialogue that is heavy with punctuation.

Review the punctuation marks that appear on this page:

- exclamation mark: *read with excitement (line 1167)*
- question mark: *raise intonation at end of question (lines 1131–1132)*
- em-dash: *pause during reading (lines 1132–1133)* or *be interrupted by the next speaker (line 1149)*

ASK STUDENTS to work in mixed-ability groups to practice reading the dialogue on p. 481 aloud. Have them discuss how taking note of the punctuation helped improve expression in their reading.

Analyze Drama Elements · COMMON CORE · RL 3, RL 5
(LINES 1181–1205)

Remind students that a plot **complication** is an additional problem that makes the main conflict more difficult to resolve.

S2 **ASK STUDENTS** to explain how the addition of Tituba to the scene qualifies as a plot complication. *(Tituba's entering the scene is a plot complication because it makes the main conflict of the play so far—Betty's illness—much more difficult to resolve. Abigail throws accusations at Tituba and Hale and the others do not know whom to believe. Hale needs to know exactly what happened in order to best aid Betty. Tituba's presence and Abigail's reaction to it complicate the situation.)*

Hale. Why are you concealing? Have you sold yourself to Lucifer?

Abigail. I never sold myself! I'm a good
1180 girl! I'm a proper girl!

(Mrs. Putnam *enters with Tituba, and instantly* Abigail *points at Tituba.*)

Abigail. She made me do it! She made Betty do it!

Tituba (*shocked and angry*). Abby!

Abigail. She makes me drink blood!

Parris. Blood!!

Mrs. Putnam. My baby's blood?

Tituba. No, no, chicken blood. I give
1190 she chicken blood!

Hale. Woman, have you enlisted these children for the Devil?

Tituba. No, no, sir, I don't truck with no Devil!

Hale. Why can she not wake? Are you silencing this child?

Tituba. I love me Betty!

Hale. You have sent your spirit out upon this child, have you not? Are you
1200 gathering souls for the Devil?

Abigail. She sends her spirit on me in church; she makes me laugh at prayer!

Parris. She have often laughed at prayer!

Abigail. She comes to me every night to go and drink blood!

Image Credits: ©SFC/Shutterstock

SCAFFOLDING FOR ELL STUDENTS

Synonyms Tell students when, in lines 1179–1180, Abigail says, "I'm a good girl! I'm a proper girl!" she is using synonyms. **Synonyms** are words that have the same meaning as another word. In this example, "proper" is a synonym for "good."

ASK STUDENTS to tell how the use of the synonym "proper" contributes to the meaning of the sentence. If Abigail had used another synonym for "good," such as "fine" or "nice," would the dialogue have the same meaning? Then ask them to discuss what Abigail's use of the word "proper" reveals about her character. *(The word "proper" is especially effective here because it has a connotation of moral propriety, which was so important in this setting and time period. To use "fine" or "nice" would not make this meaning as clear.)*

Tituba. You beg *me* to conjure! She beg *me* make charm—

Abigail. Don't lie! (*to* Hale) She comes to me while I sleep; she's always making me dream corruptions!

1210

Tituba. Why you say that, Abby?

Abigail. Sometimes I wake and find myself standing in the open doorway and not a stitch on my body! I always hear her laughing in my sleep. I hear her singing her Barbados songs and tempting me with—

Tituba. Mister Reverend, I never—

Hale (*resolved now*). Tituba, I want you

1220 to wake this child.

Tituba. I have no power on this child, sir.

Hale. You most certainly do, and you will free her from it now! When did you compact with the Devil?

Tituba. I don't compact with no Devil!

Parris. You will confess yourself or I will take you out and whip you to your death, Tituba!

1230 **Putnam.** This woman must be hanged! She must be taken and hanged!

Tituba (*terrified, falls to her knees*). No, no, don't hang Tituba! I tell him I don't desire to work for him, sir.

Parris. The Devil?

Hale. Then you saw him! (*Tituba weeps.*) Now Tituba, I know that when we bind ourselves to Hell it is very hard to break with it. We are going to help you tear

1240 yourself free—

Tituba (*frightened by the coming process*). Mister Reverend, I do believe somebody else be witchin' these children.

Hale. Who?

Tituba. I don't know, sir, but the Devil got him numerous witches.

Hale. Does he! (*It is a clue.*) Tituba, look into my eyes. Come, look into me.

1250 (*She raises her eyes to his fearfully.*) You would be a good Christian woman, would you not, Tituba?

Tituba. Aye, sir, a good Christian woman.

Hale. And you love these little children?

Tituba. Oh, yes, sir, I don't desire to hurt little children.

Hale. And you love God, Tituba?

Tituba. I love God with all my bein'.

1260 **Hale.** Now, in God's holy name—

Tituba. Bless Him. Bless Him. (*She is rocking on her knees, sobbing in terror.*)

Hale. And to His glory—

Tituba. Eternal glory. Bless Him—bless God . . .

Hale. Open yourself, Tituba—open yourself and let God's holy light shine on you.

Tituba. Oh, bless the Lord.

1270 **Hale.** When the Devil comes to you does he ever come—with another person? (*She stares up into his face.*) Perhaps another person in the village? Someone you know.

Parris. Who came with him?

Putnam. Sarah Good? Did you ever see Sarah Good with him? Or Osburn?

Parris. Was it man or woman came with him?

1280 **Tituba.** Man or woman. Was—was woman.

Parris. What woman? A woman, you said. What woman?

Tituba. It was black dark, and I—

The Crucible: Act One **483**

CLOSE READ

Analyze Drama Elements COMMON CORE RL 3, RL 5
(LINES 1201–1236)

Explain to students that in a scene like this one where the truth is not completely clear, readers should use what they have already learned about the characters to help decide whom to believe.

T2 **ASK STUDENTS** to reread the dialogue between Hale, Abigail, and Tituba in lines 1208–1236. What do you know about the character of Abigail that would affect your belief in what she is saying? (*Abigail has shown herself to be capable of being devious and manipulative, as she was with John Proctor. The stage direction from early in the play [lines 34–39] describing Abigail as having an "endless capacity for dissembling" has proven to be true, and is especially true here. Therefore, it is not clear at all what really happened in the forest.*)

Analyze Drama Elements COMMON CORE RL 3, RL 5
(LINES 1276–1277)

Remind students to continually ask themselves whether a character's behavior is surprising or consistent with what students already know about the characters.

U2 **ASK STUDENTS** to read Putnam's dialogue in lines 1276–1277. Putnam brings up Sarah Good's name out of the blue. What do you think is his reason for saying her name here? Is this consistent with his character as you understand it so far? (*Putnam is a character who always feels persecuted and has many grudges with other characters; for example, John Proctor and Giles Corey. From this we can infer that Sarah Good is probably someone he has an issue with and wants to see punished.*)

SCAFFOLDING FOR ELL STUDENTS

Understand Multiple-Meaning Words Explain to students that the word "resolved" (in line 1219) has more than one meaning. It can be an adjective meaning "feeling strong determination to do something." It can also be the simple past tense of the verb "resolve," meaning "to settle or solve a problem" or "to make a serious decision to do something."

ASK STUDENTS to work with a partner and tell which meaning of "resolved" is used here. Then have them come up with a sentence having to do with the play that uses the other meaning of the word. (*Possible answer: Rebecca Nurse hoped the problem of Betty's illness would soon be resolved.*)

Analyze Drama Elements  RL 3, RL 5

(LINES 1302–1317)

Explain to students that **dramatic irony** occurs when the audience of a drama understands something that some or all of the characters do not.

V2 **ASK STUDENTS** to reread lines 1302–1317 and explain why Tituba's prayer is an example of dramatic irony. *(The audience and Tituba understand that she is asking for protection from Hale and Parris, while Hale and Parris believe she is asking for protection from the Devil.)*

Analyze Drama Elements  RL 3, RL 5

(LINES 1321–1348)

Remind students that stage directions offer clues about characters' behavior.

W2 **CITE TEXT EVIDENCE** Ask students to review the dialogue in these lines. What motivates Tituba to suddenly offer these names after having denied being under the spell of the Devil earlier in the scene? Look for clues in the stage directions and cite specifics. *(Tituba is clearly terrified—the stage directions in line 1347 say she is "weeping." Also, in line 1324, the stage directions say Parris is "pressing in" her; when she "suddenly" bursts out with her confession a few lines later, she is being intimidated by Hale and Parris to do so.)*

Parris. You could see him, why could you not see her?

Tituba. Well, they was always talking; they was always runnin' round and carryin' on—

1290 **Parris.** You mean out of Salem? Salem witches?

Tituba. I believe so, yes, sir.

(*Now* Hale *takes her hand. She is surprised.*)

Hale. Tituba. You must have no fear to tell us who they are, do you understand? We will protect you. The Devil can never overcome a minister. You know that, do you not?

1300 **Tituba** (*kisses* Hale's *hand*). Aye, sir, oh, I do.

Hale. You have confessed yourself to witchcraft, and that speaks a wish to come to Heaven's side. And we will bless you, Tituba.

Tituba (*deeply relieved*). Oh, God bless you, Mr. Hale!

 Hale (*with rising exaltation*). You are God's instrument put in our hands to 1310 discover the Devil's agents among us. You are selected, Tituba, you are chosen to help us cleanse our village. So speak utterly, Tituba, turn your back on him and face God—face God, Tituba, and God will protect you.

Tituba (*joining with him*). Oh, God, protect Tituba!

Hale (*kindly*). Who came to you with the Devil? Two? Three? Four? How 1320 many?

 (*Tituba pants, and begins rocking back and forth again, staring ahead.*)

Tituba. There was four. There was four.

Parris (*pressing in on her*). Who? Who? Their names, their names!

Tituba (*suddenly bursting out*). Oh, how many times he bid me kill you, Mr. Parris!

Parris. Kill me!

1330 **Tituba** (*in a fury*). He say Mr. Parris must be kill! Mr. Parris no goodly man, Mr. Parris mean man and no gentle man, and he bid me rise out of my bed and cut your throat! (*They gasp.*) But I tell him "No! I don't hate that man. I don't want kill that man." But he say, "You work for me, Tituba, and I make you free! I give you pretty dress to wear, and put you way high up in the air, and 1340 you gone fly back to Barbados!" And I say, "You lie, Devil, you lie!" And then he come one stormy night to me, and he say, "Look! I have *white* people belong to me." And I look—and there was Goody Good.

Parris. Sarah Good!

Tituba (*rocking and weeping*). Aye, sir, and Goody Osburn.

Mrs. Putnam. I knew it! Goody Osburn 1350 were midwife to me three times. I begged you, Thomas, did I not? I begged him not to call Osburn because I feared her. My babies always shriveled in her hands!

Hale. Take courage, you must give us all their names. How can you bear to see this child suffering? Look at her, Tituba. (*He is indicating* Betty *on the bed.*) Look at her God-given innocence; her soul is 1360 so tender; we must protect her, Tituba; the Devil is out and preying on her like a beast upon the flesh of the pure lamb. God will bless you for your help.

(Abigail *rises, staring as though inspired, and cries out.*)

Abigail. I want to open myself! (*They turn to her, startled. She is enraptured, as though in a pearly light.*) I want the light of God, I want the sweet love of Jesus! I

1370 danced for the Devil; I saw him; I wrote in his book; I go back to Jesus; I kiss His hand. I saw Sarah Good with the Devil! I saw Goody Osburn with the Devil! I saw Bridget Bishop with the Devil!

(*As she is speaking, Betty is rising from the bed, a fever in her eyes, and picks up the chant.*)

Betty (*staring too*). I saw George Jacobs with the Devil! I saw Goody Howe with
1380 the Devil!

Parris. She speaks! (*He rushes to embrace Betty.*) She speaks!

Hale. Glory to God! It is broken, they are free!

Betty (*calling out hysterically and with great relief*). I saw Martha Bellows with the Devil!

Abigail. I saw Goody Sibber with the Devil! (*It is rising to a great glee.*)

1390 **Putnam.** The marshal, I'll call the marshal!

(*Parris is shouting a prayer of thanksgiving.*)

Betty. I saw Alice Barrow with the Devil!

(*The curtain begins to fall.*)

Hale (*as Putnam goes out*). Let the marshal bring irons!

Abigail. I saw Goody Hawkins with the
1400 Devil!

Betty. I saw Goody Bibber with the Devil!

Abigail. I saw Goody Booth with the Devil!

(*On their ecstatic cries, the curtain falls.*)

COLLABORATIVE DISCUSSION With a partner, discuss how Abigail's feelings toward John Proctor influence the events that take place in this act. Cite specific textual evidence from the play to support your ideas.

Analyze Drama Elements

COMMON CORE RL 3, RL 5

(LINES 1370–1405)

Remind students that the stage directions also help create the mood of a play.

X2 ASK STUDENTS to describe the mood of the play as the first act ends. Cite specific stage directions. (*The mood at the end of the act is very intense and emotional. Miller uses highly descriptive words in the stage directions that suggest intense emotions, like "a fever in her eyes" [line 1376], "calling out hysterically" [line 1385], and "ecstatic cries" [line 1405].*)

COLLABORATIVE DISCUSSION Have students form pairs and trace Abigail's feelings for John Proctor throughout Act One. Explain how they connect to other events in Act One. Ask them to cite specific evidence from the text. Then have pairs share their conclusions with the class as a whole. Accept all reasonable responses.

ASK STUDENTS to share any questions they generated in the course of reading and discussing the selection.

WHEN STUDENTS STRUGGLE...

To ensure that students understand the plot so far, draw students' attention to the final two pages of this act.

ASK STUDENTS to summarize what happens to the characters in these pages. (*Hale compels a terrified Tituba to confess to being possessed by the devil despite her earlier denials; Parris stands by, fearful and eager to blame Tituba; Abigail and Betty begin naming townspeople they saw with the Devil; Mr. and Mrs. Putnam's suspicions are confirmed when Tituba and Abigail begin naming names.*)

PRACTICE & APPLY

Analyze Drama Elements COMMON CORE RL 3, RL 5

(LINES 1370–1405)

Help students understand how the stage directions and exposition sections can help establish and illuminate the play's characters and plot for the reader. Have small groups select a portion of the first act and look for stage directions and/or exposition and tell how they help them understand more about one or more of these elements of drama. (Answers will vary; be sure students cite specific stage directions or a part of an exposition section in their answer.)

Analyzing the Text COMMON CORE RL 3, RL 5, SL 1a

Possible answers:

1. Miller describes 17th century Salem as a natural breeding ground for feelings of persecution among its people. Theirs was a strict, highly religious society that enforced its own moral code and was prone to seeing enemies everywhere.

2. When Abigail tells Parris that there was ritual dancing the previous evening that entailed "conjuring spirits," this sets in motion the events of the rest of Act One. The characters that were not present at the ritual dance in the woods—or at Abigail's admission in this section—must determine the truth on their own. Readers understand that the girls are frightened and anxious to divert blame.

3. Reverend Parris, in the exposition beginning on page 459, is described by Miller as a man who always believed he was being persecuted. In the exposition on page 465, Putnam is described as a "man with many grievances" and as having a "vindictive nature." Among his complaints are his lingering anger that Salem rejected his choice for minister—his brother-in-law. Feeling that his name has been sullied, Putnam becomes a leader in making accusations about others.

4. Though Miller describes Proctor as a man with little patience for hypocrites, Proctor himself is a sinner—he has had a relationship with Abigail—and so feels a fraud as a prominent member of a society that sees itself as a model of high moral rectitude.

Analyze Drama Elements COMMON CORE RL 3, RL 5

The first act of Arthur Miller's play is uniquely structured. It includes italicized **stage directions** that present details about setting and character and help establish mood. However, Miller also inserts passages of exposition that provide readers with facts and other information. Readers can use these stage directions to understand more about these elements of the play:

- the playwright's perspective on his subject
- historical background of the setting
- the real reasons behind characters' behaviors
- parallels between the Salem witch trials in the 1690s and the McCarthy hearings in the United States in the 1950s

Analyzing the Text COMMON CORE RL 3, RL 5, SL 1a

Cite Text Evidence Support your responses with evidence from the selection.

1. **Analyze** What does the exposition in the beginning of Act One tell readers about the way they are to perceive the events that follow? Explain.

2. **Analyze** Reread lines 311–370. This part of the play reveals information to readers that the other characters do not have. This is called **dramatic irony.** How does this dramatic irony enable readers to understand the real reasons behind the girls' symptoms and the events that result?

3. **Cite Evidence** What do the stage directions reveal about the motives for the behavior of Thomas Putnam and Parris? Cite specific details in your response.

4. **Infer** What is meant by the description of Proctor as a man who "has come to regard himself as a kind of fraud"? Explain, based on details in this act.

PERFORMANCE TASK

Speaking Activity: Discussion The passages of exposition are typically not included in the stage production of a play. Based on your reading of the first act, why do you think Miller decided to include them in the text of the play?

- Reread the passages in Act One. Jot down your ideas about what they contribute to the play and if they are necessary.

- Present your insights in a small group. As a group, answer this question: Do the stage directions detract from or enhance the effectiveness of the play?

- Summarize the important conclusions that the group reaches. Contribute them to a whole-class discussion.

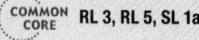

Assign this performance task.

PERFORMANCE TASK COMMON CORE RL 3, RL 5, SL 1a

Speaking Activity: Discussion Have students work independently to reread the exposition in Act One (pages 459–461) and make notes about what it contributes to the play. Then divide students into small groups to discuss whether the exposition detracts from or enhances the play. Have groups work together to summarize their conclusions. Then have a whole-class discussion about the effectiveness and necessity of Miller's exposition.

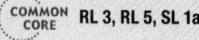

Analyze Drama Elements   COMMON CORE RL 3, RL 5

(LINES 1–42)

Tell students to closely examine the **dialogue** in this first scene between Proctor and Elizabeth.

A **CITE TEXT EVIDENCE** Ask students to come up with words and short phrases to describe the way Elizabeth responds to Proctor. *(direct, brief, many one-word answers)* Ask students what her dialogue reveals about her feelings towards Proctor in the beginning of this scene. *(She may be upset or angry with Proctor.)* Then students cite a specific stage direction to support their answers. *(In line 41, the stage direction reveals that Elizabeth's line "I know it, John" is "hard to say." This supports the idea that she is upset with him.)*

Analyze Drama Elements   COMMON CORE RL 3, RL 5

(LINES 22–26)

Remind students that **dialogue** can reveal a character's nature.

B **ASK STUDENTS** to reread Proctor's line of dialogue in line 22. What does he mean that the rabbit walking in "is a good sign?" What does this reveal about his character? *(He may be superstitious and is probably optimistic.)* Then have students read Elizabeth's response in lines 24–25. What does her dialogue reveal about her character? *(She is a person who values life and cares for others, even animals.)*

AS YOU READ Pay attention to the details that help you to understand Proctor's dilemma in this act. Write down any questions you generate during reading.

ACT TWO

(*The common room of* Proctor's *house, eight days later.*

At the right is a door opening on the fields outside. A fireplace is at the left, and behind it a stairway leading upstairs. It is the low, dark, and rather long living room of the time. As the curtain rises, the room is empty. From above, Elizabeth *is heard softly singing to the children. Presently the door opens and* John Proctor *enters, carrying his gun. He glances about the room as he comes toward the fireplace, then halts for an instant as he hears her singing. He continues on to the fireplace, leans the gun against the wall as he swings a pot out of the fire and smells it. Then he lifts out the ladle and tastes. He is not quite pleased. He reaches to a cupboard, takes a pinch of salt, and drops it into the pot. As he is tasting again, her footsteps are heard on the stair. He swings the pot into the fireplace and goes to a basin and washes his hands and face.* Elizabeth *enters.*)

Elizabeth. What keeps you so late? It's almost dark.

Proctor. I were planting far out to the forest edge.

Elizabeth. Oh, you're done then.

Proctor. Aye, the farm is seeded. The boys asleep?

Elizabeth. They will be soon. (*And she goes to the fireplace, proceeds to ladle up* 10 *stew in a dish.*)

Proctor. Pray now for a fair summer.

Elizabeth. Aye.

Proctor. Are you well today?

Elizabeth. I am. (*She brings the plate to the table, and, indicating the food.*) It is a rabbit.

Proctor (*going to the table*). Oh, is it! In Jonathan's trap?

Elizabeth. No, she walked into the 20 house this afternoon; I found her sittin' in the corner like she come to visit.

Proctor. Oh, that's a good sign walkin' in. **B**

Elizabeth. Pray God. It hurt my heart to strip her, poor rabbit. (*She sits and watches him taste it.*)

Proctor. It's well seasoned.

Elizabeth (*blushing with pleasure*). I took great care. She's tender?

30 **Proctor.** Aye. (*He eats. She watches him.*) I think we'll see green fields soon. It's warm as blood beneath the clods.

Elizabeth. That's well.

(Proctor *eats, then looks up.*)

Proctor. If the crop is good I'll buy George Jacob's heifer. How would that please you?

Elizabeth. Aye, it would.

Proctor (*with a grin*). I mean to please 40 you, Elizabeth.

Elizabeth (*It is hard to say*). I know it, John.

(*He gets up, goes to her, kisses her. She receives it. With a certain disappointment, he returns to the table.*)

Proctor (*as gently as he can*). Cider?

Elizabeth (*with a sense of reprimanding herself for having forgot*). Aye! (*She gets*

The Crucible: Act Two **487**

SCAFFOLDING FOR ELL STUDENTS

Understand Similes Review **similes** with students. Remind them that they are comparisons made using the words *like* or *as*.

ASK STUDENTS to find the simile on this page and tell how it affects their understanding of the character of Proctor. *(Lines 31–32: "It's warm as blood beneath the clods." This reveals Proctor as an earthy, practical man whose life as a farmer informs his value of hard work. It also reveals a poetic side of him, which suggests that he has deep feelings.)*

Analyze Drama Elements COMMON CORE RL 3, RL 5

(LINES 101–112)

Remind students that a **complication** of the plot is a problem that makes the main conflict more difficult to resolve.

C **ASK STUDENTS** to tell how Mary's becoming an official of the court qualifies as a plot complication. *(The main conflict of the play is whether or not there is witchcraft in the town of Salem. Proctor and his wife Elizabeth are already drawn into the conflict because Proctor had a relationship with Abigail and Abigail is at the center of the investigation. Mary works for the Proctors and was present for the dancing in the forest, but claims not to not have danced herself. Further, Mary replaced Abigail as the Proctors' maid.)*

Analyze Drama Elements COMMON CORE RL 3, RL 5

(LINES 114–119)

Tell students that a play's dialogue sometimes advances the plot, or sequence of events.

D **ASK STUDENTS** what we learn about the progress of the witch hunt from Elizabeth's dialogue in lines 114–119. *(Fourteen people from the town of Salem are now in jail, accused of witchcraft and/or being under the influence of the devil.)*

---

up and goes and pours a glass for him. He
50 *now arches his back.)*

Proctor. This farm's a continent when you go foot by foot droppin' seeds in it.

Elizabeth (*coming with the cider*). It must be.

Proctor (*drinks a long draught, then, putting the glass down*). You ought to bring some flowers in the house.

Elizabeth. Oh! I forgot! I will tomorrow.

Proctor. It's winter in here yet. On
60 Sunday let you come with me, and we'll walk the farm together; I never see such a load of flowers on the earth. (*With good feeling he goes and looks up at the sky through the open doorway.*) Lilacs have a purple smell. Lilac is the smell of nightfall, I think. Massachusetts is a beauty in the spring!

Elizabeth. Aye, it is.

(*There is a pause. She is watching*
70 *him from the table as he stands there absorbing the night. It is as though she would speak but cannot. Instead, now, she takes up his plate and glass and fork and goes with them to the basin. Her back is turned to him. He turns to her and watches her. A sense of their separation rises.*)

Proctor. I think you're sad again. Are you?

80 **Elizabeth** (*She doesn't want friction, and yet she must*). You come so late I thought you'd gone to Salem this afternoon.

Proctor. Why? I have no business in Salem.

Elizabeth. You did speak of going, earlier this week.

Proctor (*He knows what she means*). I thought better of it since.

Elizabeth. Mary Warren's there today.

90 **Proctor.** Why'd you let her? You heard me forbid her go to Salem any more!

Elizabeth. I couldn't stop her.

Proctor (*holding back a full condemnation of her*). It is a fault, it is a fault, Elizabeth—you're the mistress here, not Mary Warren.

Elizabeth. She frightened all my strength away.

Proctor. How may that mouse frighten
100 you, Elizabeth? You—

Elizabeth. It is a mouse no more. I forbid her go, and she raises up her chin like the daughter of a prince and says to me, "I must go to Salem, Goody Proctor; I am an official of the court!"

Proctor. Court! What court?

Elizabeth. Aye, it is a proper court they have now. They've sent four judges out of Boston, she says, weighty magistrates
110 of the General Court, and at the head sits the Deputy Governor of the Province.

Proctor (*astonished*). Why, she's mad.

Elizabeth. I would to God she were. There be fourteen people in the jail now, she says. (Proctor *simply looks at her, unable to grasp it.*) And they'll be tried, and the court have power to hang them too, she says.

120 **Proctor** (*scoffing, but without conviction*). Ah, they'd never hang—

Elizabeth. The Deputy Governor promise hangin' if they'll not confess, John. The town's gone wild, I think. She speak of Abigail, and I thought she were a saint, to hear her. Abigail brings the other girls into the court, and where she walks the crowd will part like the sea for Israel. And folks are brought before
130 them, and if they scream and howl and fall to the floor—the person's clapped in the jail for bewitchin' them.

SCAFFOLDING FOR ELL STUDENTS

Understand Words With Similar Spellings Explain to students that it can be easy to confuse words that have only one letter of difference between them.

ASK STUDENTS to read the stage directions in lines 55–56. Tell students that the word *draught* should not be confused with the word *drought*. *Draught* means "the amount swallowed at one time." A *drought* is "a period of time, usually long, in which there is little or no rain." Suggest that students use a dictionary when they encounter a like-sounding word they are not sure of. For practice, have students tell you the difference between:

- *pallor* (line 248) and *parlor*
- *crone* (line 352) and *crane*

Proctor (*wide-eyed*). Oh, it is a black mischief.

Elizabeth. I think you must go to Salem, John. (*He turns to her.*) I think so. You must tell them it is a fraud.

Proctor (*thinking beyond this*). Aye, it is, it is surely.

140 **Elizabeth.** Let you go to Ezekiel Cheever—he knows you well. And tell him what she said to you last week in her uncle's house. She said it had naught to do with witchcraft, did she not?

Proctor (*in thought*). Aye, she did, she did. (*now, a pause*)

Elizabeth (*quietly, fearing to anger him by prodding*). God forbid you keep that from the court, John. I think they must 150 be told.

Proctor (*quietly, struggling with his thought*). Aye, they must, they must. It is a wonder they do believe her.

Elizabeth. I would go to Salem now, John—let you go tonight.

Proctor. I'll think on it.

Elizabeth (*with her courage now*). You cannot keep it, John.

Proctor (*angering*). I know I cannot 160 keep it. I say I will think on it!

Elizabeth (*hurt, and very coldly*). Good, then, let you think on it. (*She stands and starts to walk out of the room.*)

Proctor. I am only wondering how I may prove what she told me, Elizabeth. If the girl's a saint now, I think it is not easy to prove she's fraud, and the town gone so silly. She told it to me in a room alone—I have no proof for it.

170 **Elizabeth.** You were alone with her?

Proctor (*stubbornly*). For a moment alone, aye.

Elizabeth. Why, then, it is not as you told me.

Proctor (*his anger rising*). For a moment, I say. The others come in soon after.

Elizabeth (*quietly—she has suddenly lost all faith in him*). Do as you wish, then. (*She starts to turn.*)

180 **Proctor.** Woman. (*She turns to him.*) I'll not have your suspicion any more.

Elizabeth (*a little loftily*). I have no—

Proctor. I'll not have it!

Elizabeth. Then let you not earn it.

Proctor (*with a violent undertone*). You doubt me yet?

Elizabeth (*with a smile, to keep her dignity*). John, if it were not Abigail that you must go to hurt, would you falter 190 now? I think not.

Proctor. Now look you—

Elizabeth. I see what I see, John.

Proctor (*with solemn warning*). You will not judge me more, Elizabeth. I have good reason to think before I charge fraud on Abigail, and I will think on it. Let you look to your own improvement before you go to judge your husband any more. I have forgot Abigail, and—

200 **Elizabeth.** And I.

Proctor. Spare me! You forget nothin' and forgive nothin'. Learn charity, woman. I have gone tiptoe in this house all seven month since she is gone. I have not moved from there to there without I think to please you, and still an everlasting funeral marches round your heart. I cannot speak but I am doubted, every moment judged for lies, as though 210 I come into a court when I come into this house!

Elizabeth. John, you are not open with me. You saw her with a crowd, you said. Now you—

WHEN STUDENTS STRUGGLE...

Explain to students that in dialogue characters sometimes use pronouns without making their referents entirely clear. Tell them that in these cases they must use context to determine the referent. Point out to students Proctor's use of the pronoun "it" in line 133. Explain to students that here "it" refers to Abigail's pretense of saintliness and her judging others. Elizabeth describes these behaviors in lines 122–132, so readers can tell that they are what Proctor is calling a "black mischief."

ASK STUDENTS to reread lines 133–169. Ask them to determine what "it" refers to in lines 143, 156, and 158. (*the girls' activities in the woods; Proctor going to Salem to reveal what Abigail told him; his information about Abigail*)

CLOSE READ

Analyze Drama Elements COMMON CORE RL 3, RL 5
(LINES 147–153)

Explain to students that, although two separate **stage directions** may employ the same or similar words, they may suggest very different motivations for the characters.

E **ASK STUDENTS** to read the stage directions described in lines 147–153. Point out that they both use the word "quietly." Ask students to explain the difference between each character's motivations to speak quietly in this moment. (*Elizabeth wants Proctor to go to Salem and dispel any notions of Abigail being a witch, and asks him to do so quietly because she doesn't want to upset him. Proctor agrees with her and speaks quietly, but it is because he is struggling with his thoughts; he feels conflicted in his feelings about getting involved.*)

Analyze Drama Elements COMMON CORE RL 3, RL 5
(LINES 201–211)

Remind students that one way playwrights develop their characters is through **indirect characterization,** including what the characters say. These lines feature **figurative language,** language that is not used literally. This language gives clues about what is happening with the characters.

F **CITE TEXT EVIDENCE** Ask students to reread Proctor's dialogue in lines 201–211. Tell them to decipher the rich figurative language and infer what it must have been like around the Proctors' house. Remind students to cite specifics from the text. (*The Proctor household must have been extremely tense. Abigail was let go as the maid seven months ago and Proctor confessed at some point to an affair with Abigail. He has had to treat Elizabeth with great delicacy. "I have gone tiptoe in this house all seven month..." [lines 203–204] Still, he felt her sadness. "...an everlasting funeral marches round [her] heart." [lines 206–208] He feels judged by Elizabeth, comparing entering their home to coming "into a court."*)

Analyze Drama Elements

COMMON CORE RL 3, RL 5

(LINES 215–235)

Tell students that while a play may have one large, global conflict, there may be many other smaller, local conflicts among the characters.

(G) ASK STUDENTS to describe the nature of the personal conflict between Proctor and Elizabeth. *(Elizabeth is still hurt that Proctor had an affair with Abigail and that he lied to Elizabeth about meeting privately with Abigail. Proctor wants Elizabeth to forgive him.)* Then ask how their argument might echo the action of the play at large. *(Elizabeth is judging Proctor and the court is judging the people of Salem. When Proctor reminds Elizabeth that she is not God and asks her to also look for the good in him and treat him with forgiveness, he could be asking for mercy from the court.)*

Analyze Drama Elements

COMMON CORE RL 3, RL 5

(LINES 281–288)

Point out to students that plot complications can dramatically impact the mood of a scene.

(H) ASK STUDENTS to describe how the mood of the scene changes when Mary Warren reveals that Goody Osburn has been sentenced to hang. *(The scene becomes more intense and frightening; the stakes go up considerably for everyone in Salem.)*

Proctor. I'll plead my honesty no more, Elizabeth.

Elizabeth (*now she would justify herself*). John, I am only—

Proctor. No more! I should have roared
220 you down when first you told me your suspicion. But I wilted, and, like a Christian, I confessed. Confessed! Some dream I had must have mistaken you for God that day. But you're not, you're not, and let you remember it! Let you look sometimes for the goodness in me, and judge me not.

Elizabeth. I do not judge you. The magistrate sits in your heart that
230 judges you. I never thought you but a good man, John—(*with a smile*)—only somewhat bewildered.

Proctor (*laughing bitterly*). Oh, Elizabeth, your justice would freeze beer![1] (*He turns suddenly toward a sound outside. He starts for the door as Mary Warren enters. As soon as he sees her, he goes directly to her and grabs her by her cloak, furious.*) How do you go to Salem
240 when I forbid it? Do you mock me? (*shaking her*) I'll whip you if you dare leave this house again! (*Strangely, she doesn't resist him, but hangs limply by his grip.*)

Mary Warren. I am sick, I am sick, Mr. Proctor. Pray, pray, hurt me not. (*Her strangeness throws him off, and her evident pallor and weakness. He frees her.*) My insides are all shuddery; I am
250 in the proceedings all day, sir.

Proctor (*with draining anger—his curiosity is draining it*). And what of these proceedings here? When will you proceed to keep this house, as you are

---

[1] **your justice . . . beer:** Alcoholic beverages freeze at very low temperatures, so Proctor is sarcastically calling his wife cold-hearted.

---

paid nine pound a year to do—and my wife not wholly well?

(*As though to compensate, Mary Warren goes to Elizabeth with a small rag doll.*)

Mary Warren. I made a gift for you
260 today, Goody Proctor. I had to sit long hours in a chair, and passed the time with sewing.

Elizabeth (*perplexed, looking at the doll*). Why, thank you, it's a fair poppet.[2]

Mary Warren (*with a trembling, decayed voice*). We must all love each other now, Goody Proctor.

Elizabeth (*amazed at her strangeness*). Aye, indeed we must.

270 **Mary Warren** (*glancing at the room*). I'll get up early in the morning and clean the house. I must sleep now. (*She turns and starts off.*)

Proctor. Mary. (*She halts.*) Is it true? There be fourteen women arrested?

Mary Warren. No, sir. There be thirty-nine now—(*She suddenly breaks off and sobs and sits down, exhausted.*)

Elizabeth. Why, she's weepin'! What
280 ails you, child?

Mary Warren. Goody Osburn—will hang!

(*There is a shocked pause, while she sobs.*)

Proctor. Hang! (*He calls into her face.*) Hang, y'say?

Mary Warren (*through her weeping*). Aye.

Proctor. The Deputy Governor will
290 permit it?

Mary Warren. He sentenced her. He must. (*to ameliorate it*) But not Sarah Good. For Sarah Good confessed, y'see.

---

[2] **fair poppet:** pretty doll.

SCAFFOLDING FOR ELL STUDENTS

Understand Sentence Structure Tell students that because dialogue mimics everyday speech, some sentences may not be correctly structured. Point out to students the sentence "I never thought you but a good man, John . . ." in lines 230–231. Explain that the sentence structure would be correct if the word *anything* were added: "I never thought you anything but a good man . . . ."

ASK STUDENTS to work in pairs to rewrite the sentence "How do you go to Salem when I forbid it?" in lines 239–240 adding any words that might be needed. *(How do you dare to go to Salem when I forbid it?)*

Proctor. Confessed! To what?

Mary Warren. That she—(*in horror at the memory*)—she sometimes made a compact with Lucifer, and wrote her name in his black book—with her blood—and bound herself to torment Christians till God's thrown down—and we all must worship Hell forevermore.

(*pause*)

Proctor. But—surely you know what a jabberer she is. Did you tell them that?

Mary Warren. Mr. Proctor, in open court she near to choked us all to death.

Proctor. How, choked you?

Mary Warren. She sent her spirit out.

Elizabeth. Oh, Mary, Mary, surely you—

Mary Warren (*with an indignant edge*). She tried to kill me many times, Goody Proctor!

Elizabeth. Why, I never heard you mention that before.

Mary Warren. I never knew it before. I never knew anything before. When she come into the court I say to myself, I must not accuse this woman, for she sleep in ditches, and so very old and poor. But then—then she sit there, denying and denying, and I feel a misty coldness climbin' up my back, and the skin on my skull begin to creep, and I feel a clamp around my neck and I cannot breathe air; and then (*entranced*) I hear a voice, a screamin' voice, and it were my voice—and all at once I remembered everything she done to me!

Proctor. Why? What did she do to you?

Mary Warren (*like one awakened to a marvelous secret insight*). So many time, Mr. Proctor, she come to this very door, beggin' bread and a cup of cider—and

mark this: whenever I turned her away empty, she *mumbled*.

Elizabeth. Mumbled! She may mumble if she's hungry.

Mary Warren. But *what* does she mumble? You must remember, Goody Proctor. Last month—a Monday, I think—she walked away, and I thought my guts would burst for two days after. Do you remember it?

Elizabeth. Why—I do, I think, but—

Mary Warren. And so I told that to Judge Hathorne, and he asks her so. "Sarah Good," says he, "what curse do you mumble that this girl must fall sick after turning you away?" And then she replies (*mimicking an old crone*) "Why, your excellence, no curse at all. I only say my commandments;³ I hope I may say my commandments," says she!

Elizabeth. And that's an upright answer.

Mary Warren. Aye, but then Judge Hathorne say, "Recite for us your commandments!" (*leaning avidly toward them*) and of all the ten she could not say a single one. She never knew no commandments, and they had her in a flat lie!

Proctor. And so condemned her?

Mary Warren (*now a little strained, seeing his stubborn doubt*). Why, they must when she condemned herself.

Proctor. But the proof, the proof!

Mary Warren (*with greater impatience with him*). I told you the proof. It's hard proof, hard as rock, the judges said.

Proctor (*pauses an instant, then*). You will not go to court again, Mary Warren.

---

³ **commandments:** the Ten Commandments in the Bible.

CLOSE READ

Analyze Drama Elements  COMMON CORE RL 3, RL 5
(LINES 309–372)

Remind students that both **dialogue** and **stage directions** often provide valuable clues to character.

🄸 **CITE TEXT EVIDENCE** Ask students what both the stage directions and Mary Warren's dialogue tell them about her character. Cite specific examples. (*Mary Warren is a proud, stubborn young woman who is not afraid to stand up to Proctor; the stage direction in line 312 refers to an "indignant edge" to her voice; the dialogue that follows also supports this interpretation of her character. The long story she tells as the scene progresses also shows that she is completely taken in by the witch hunt; the stage direction in line 327 describes her as "entranced" as she tells the story. Line 333 also describes her having a "marvelous secret insight." Mary is almost enjoying taking part in the witch hunt; at the very least she loves feeling that she is right. In line 370, she is impatient with Proctor's doubt that Goody Osburn is a witch.*)

Analyze Drama Elements COMMON CORE RL 3, RL 5
(LINES 310–360)

Explain to students that they will encounter characters that are **foils** for other characters. These characters—often minor ones—contrast strikingly with a main character, thereby illuminating the characteristics of the main character.

🄹 **CITE TEXT EVIDENCE** Have students tell how Mary could be seen as a foil for Elizabeth. (*Mary's stubborn belief in the truth and sincerity of the witch hunt highlights Elizabeth's courage and insight in opposing its unfairness.*)

SCAFFOLDING FOR ELL STUDENTS

Understand Homographs Remind students that a **homograph** is a word that has the same spelling as another word with a different meaning and pronunciation. Point to the word "compact" in line 297.

ASK STUDENTS to explain the meaning and pronunciation of the word "compact" in this sentence. Then have them offer the meaning and pronunciation of its homograph (the verb [com · PACT], meaning "to press something so that it takes up less space"). Have them use the homograph in a sentence. As they continue to read, have them look for other words that have homographs.

Analyze Drama Elements  RL 3, RL 5

(LINES 402–421)

Remind students that **stage directions** can offer historical background and help describe setting.

 **ASK STUDENTS** what the stage directions in lines 402–421 suggest about what people were allowed to do to their servants during the time of the play. *(The stage directions suggest that it was permissible to whip one's servants and that, Proctor has whipped Mary in the past.)*

Analyze Drama Elements  RL 3, RL 5

(LINES 419–431)

Remind students to look for events in the play that are plot complications.

 **ASK STUDENTS** to explain how the event described in lines 419–431 qualifies as a plot complication. *(When Mary reveals that Elizabeth was "mentioned" at the hearing, this raises the stakes considerably for the Proctors. Both the global conflict of the play (is there witchcraft afoot or not) and the local conflict between Proctor and Elizabeth have become much more complicated and difficult to resolve because of this news. Further, at this point they do not know who has accused Elizabeth, so they're not even sure who or what to fight against.)*

Mary Warren. I must tell you, sir, I will be gone every day now. I am amazed you do not see what weighty work we do.

380 **Proctor.** What work you do! It's strange work for a Christian girl to hang old women!

Mary Warren. But, Mr. Proctor, they will not hang them if they confess. Sarah Good will only sit in jail some time (*recalling*) and here's a wonder for you; think on this. Goody Good is pregnant!

Elizabeth. Pregnant! Are they mad? 390 The woman's near to sixty!

Mary Warren. They had Doctor Griggs examine her, and she's full to the brim. And smokin' a pipe all these years, and no husband either! But she's safe, thank God, for they'll not hurt the innocent child. But be that not a marvel? You must see it, sir, it's God's work we do. So I'll be gone every day for some time. I'm—I am an official of the court, they 400 say, and I—(*She has been edging toward offstage.*)

Proctor. I'll official you! (*He strides to the mantel, takes down the whip hanging there.*)

Mary Warren (*terrified, but coming erect, striving for her authority*). I'll not stand whipping any more!

Elizabeth (*hurriedly, as Proctor approaches*). Mary, promise now you'll 410 stay at home—

Mary Warren (*backing from him, but keeping her erect posture, striving, striving for her way*). The Devil's loose in Salem, Mr. Proctor; we must discover where he's hiding!

Proctor. I'll whip the Devil out of you! (*With whip raised he reaches out for her, and she streaks away and yells.*)

Mary Warren (*pointing at* Elizabeth). I 420 saved her life today!

(*Silence. His whip comes down.*)

Elizabeth (*softly*). I am accused?

Mary Warren (*quaking*). Somewhat mentioned. But I said I never see no sign you ever sent your spirit out to hurt no one, and seeing I do live so closely with you, they dismissed it.

Elizabeth. Who accused me?

Mary Warren. I am bound by law, I 430 cannot tell it. (*to* Proctor) I only hope you'll not be so sarcastical no more. Four judges and the King's deputy sat to dinner with us but an hour ago. I—I would have you speak civilly to me, from this out.

Proctor (*in horror, muttering in disgust at her*). Go to bed.

Mary Warren (*with a stamp of her foot*). I'll not be ordered to bed no more, Mr. 440 Proctor! I am eighteen and a woman, however single!

Proctor. Do you wish to sit up? Then sit up.

Mary Warren. I wish to go to bed!

Proctor (*in anger*). Good night, then!

Mary Warren. Good night. (*Dissatisfied, uncertain of herself, she goes out. Wide-eyed, both,* Proctor *and* Elizabeth *stand staring.*)

450 **Elizabeth** (*quietly*). Oh, the noose, the noose is up!

Proctor. There'll be no noose.

Elizabeth. She wants me dead. I knew all week it would come to this!

Proctor (*without conviction*). They dismissed it. You heard her say—

Elizabeth. And what of tomorrow? She will cry me out until they take me!

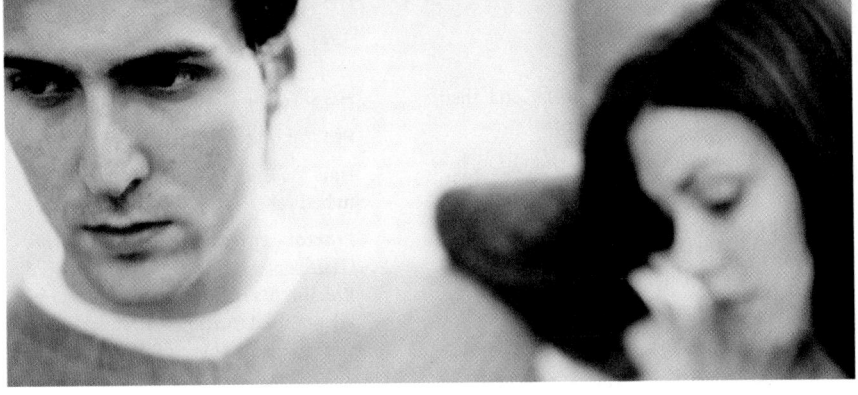

Proctor. Sit you down.

460 **Elizabeth.** She wants me dead, John, you know it!

Proctor. I say sit down! (*She sits, trembling. He speaks quietly, trying to keep his wits.*) Now we must be wise, Elizabeth.

Elizabeth (*with sarcasm, and a sense of being lost*). Oh, indeed, indeed!

Proctor. Fear nothing. I'll find Ezekiel Cheever. I'll tell him she said it were all 470 sport.

Elizabeth. John, with so many in the jail, more than Cheever's help is needed now, I think. Would you favor me with this? Go to Abigail.

Proctor (*his soul hardening as he senses . . .*). What have I to say to Abigail?

Elizabeth (*delicately*). John—grant me this. You have a faulty understanding of 480 young girls. There is a promise made in any bed—

Proctor (*striving against his anger*). What promise!

Elizabeth. Spoke or silent, a promise is surely made. And she may dote on it now—I am sure she does—and thinks to kill me, then to take my place.

(*Proctor's anger is rising; he cannot speak.*)

490 **Elizabeth.** It is her dearest hope, John, I know it. There be a thousand names; why does she call mine? There be a certain danger in calling such a name—I am no Goody Good that sleeps in ditches, nor Osburn, drunk and half-witted. She'd dare not call out such a farmer's wife but there be monstrous profit in it. She thinks to take my place, John.

500 **Proctor.** She cannot think it! (*He knows it is true.*)

Elizabeth (*"reasonably"*). John, have you ever shown her somewhat of contempt? She cannot pass you in the church but you will blush—

Proctor. I may blush for my sin.

Elizabeth. I think she sees another meaning in that blush.

Proctor. And what see you? What see 510 you, Elizabeth?

Elizabeth (*"conceding"*). I think you be somewhat ashamed, for I am there, and she so close.

Proctor. When will you know me, woman? Were I stone I would have cracked for shame this seven month!

Elizabeth. Then go and tell her she's a whore. Whatever promise she may sense—break it, John, break it.

Analyze Drama Elements

(LINES 460–461)

Remind students that, like everyday speech, dialogue can sometimes be ambiguous. Explain that it is necessary to pay close attention to the entire context of the play to make sure they understand what the characters mean.

(M) **CITE TEXT EVIDENCE** Point out that in line 460, Elizabeth says, "She wants me dead, Proctor, and you know it!" but it is not clear who "she" is. Ask students to infer who Elizabeth thinks "she" is and cite text evidence for their answers. (*Elizabeth likely thinks it is Abigail who accused her. In lines 486–487, Elizabeth says that Abigail wants to kill her and take her place as Proctor's wife.*)

Analyze Drama Elements

(LINES 502–513)

Remind students that **stage directions** can reveal the motivations behind characters' behavior. Point out that in lines 502 and 511, Miller puts the stage directions in quotes.

(N) **ASK STUDENTS** to explain why they think Miller does this; what is revealed about the character of Elizabeth in these moments? (*Miller means for Elizabeth's dialogue to be delivered in an insincere way. For example, in lines 502–505, she is not actually "reasoning" with Proctor; rather, she affects a tone of "reasoning" so that she might get what she really wants. These stage directions set in quotes reveal Elizabeth to be cunning and perhaps a bit manipulative.*)

WHEN STUDENTS STRUGGLE . . .

Remind students that the characters' lines in a play represent spoken dialogue between two people and that the stage directions give information about how the lines should be spoken.

ASK STUDENTS to read page 493 with a partner. Each student should read one character's lines with variety, intonation, and expression. After students have finished reading, ask them how the stage directions helped them read aloud the lines.

Analyze Drama Elements   COMMON CORE RL 3, RL 5

(LINES 520–546)

Tell students that the **climax** of a play is its most exciting and tense moment. All the events of the play lead to the climax, and the climax has the potential to change the outcome of the conflict. Tell students that in addition to the play's overall climax, an individual scene may have a climax as well—the point of highest excitement and tension.

Ⓞ CITE TEXT EVIDENCE Ask students to reread lines 520–546 and identify the climax. Have them cite specifics in the text to help explain their reasoning. *(The climax of the scene is Proctor and Elizabeth's final exchange that begins in line 536. In these lines, they both are at the peak of their anger. They also state quite clearly what they feel and what they expect from each other. The clues in the text include the punctuation— many exclamation points—and the stage directions— Elizabeth is "crying out.")*

Analyze Drama Elements   COMMON CORE RL 3, RL 5

(LINES 584–588)

Remind students that stage directions can reveal characters' feelings and motivations.

Ⓟ ASK STUDENTS what the stage direction in line 586 indicates about Hale's emotional state at that moment. *(Hale wets his lips because he is about to bring up an uncomfortable subject and he is apprehensive about doing so.)*

---

520 **Proctor** (*between his teeth*). Good, then. I'll go. (*He starts for his rifle.*)

Elizabeth (*trembling, fearfully*). Oh, how unwillingly!

Proctor (*turning on her, rifle in hand*). I will curse her hotter than the oldest cinder in hell. But pray, begrudge me not my anger!

Elizabeth. Your anger! I only ask you—

Proctor. Woman, am I so base? Do you 530 truly think me base?

Elizabeth. I never called you base.

Proctor. Then how do you charge me with such a promise? The promise that a stallion gives a mare I gave that girl!

Elizabeth. Then why do you anger with me when I bid you break it?

Proctor. Because it speaks deceit, and I am honest! But I'll plead no more! I see now your spirit twists around the single 540 error of my life, and I will never tear it free!

Elizabeth (*crying out*). You'll tear it free—when you come to know that I will be your only wife, or no wife at all! She has an arrow in you yet, John Proctor, and you know it well!

(*Quite suddenly, as though from the air, a figure appears in the doorway. They start slightly. It is Mr. Hale. He is* 550 *different now—drawn a little, and there is a quality of deference, even of guilt, about his manner now.*)

Hale. Good evening.

Proctor (*still in his shock*). Why, Mr. Hale! Good evening to you, sir. Come in, come in.

Hale (*to* Elizabeth). I hope I do not startle you.

Elizabeth. No, no, it's only that I heard 560 no horse—

Hale. You are Goodwife Proctor.

Proctor. Aye; Elizabeth.

Hale (*nods, then*). I hope you're not off to bed yet.

Proctor (*setting down his gun*). No, no. (Hale *comes further into the room. And* Proctor, *to explain his nervousness.*) We are not used to visitors after dark, but you're welcome here. Will you sit you 570 down, sir?

Hale. I will. (*He sits.*) Let you sit, Goodwife Proctor.

(*She does, never letting him out of her sight. There is a pause as* Hale *looks about the room.*)

Proctor (*to break the silence*). Will you drink cider, Mr. Hale?

Hale. No, it rebels[4] my stomach; I have some further traveling yet tonight. Sit 580 you down, sir. (Proctor *sits.*) I will not keep you long, but I have some business with you.

Proctor. Business of the court?

Hale. No—no, I come of my own, without the court's authority. Hear me. (*He wets his lips.*) I know not if you are aware, but your wife's name is— mentioned in the court.

Proctor. We know it, sir. Our Mary 590 Warren told us. We are entirely amazed.

Hale. I am a stranger here, as you know. And in my ignorance I find it hard to draw a clear opinion of them that come accused before the court. And so this afternoon, and now tonight, I go from house to house—I come now from Rebecca Nurse's house and—

Elizabeth (*shocked*). Rebecca's charged!

Hale. God forbid such a one be charged. 600 She is, however—mentioned somewhat.

---

[4] **rebels:** upsets.

SCAFFOLDING FOR ELL STUDENTS

Understand Figurative Language Remind students that figurative language is language that is used in a way that is not literal. Explain that they should use context to determine the meaning of figurative language.

ASK STUDENTS to reread lines 542–546 and determine what Elizabeth means when she says that Abigail "has an arrow in" Proctor. *(She means that Proctor still cares for Abigail.)* Have students explain how they can tell this meaning. *(Elizabeth and Proctor are discussing Proctor's relationship with Abigail. Elizabeth is pointing out that Proctor seems unwilling to explicitly break off the relationship. Being struck by an arrow often symbolizes falling in love.)*

Elizabeth (*with an attempt at a laugh*). You will never believe, I hope, that Rebecca trafficked with the Devil.

Hale. Woman, it is possible.

Proctor (*taken aback*). Surely you cannot think so.

Hale. This is a strange time, Mister. No man may longer doubt the powers of the dark are gathered in monstrous
610 attack upon this village. There is too much evidence now to deny it. You will agree, sir?

Proctor (*evading*). I—have no knowledge in that line. But it's hard to think so pious a woman be secretly a Devil's bitch after seventy year of such good prayer.

Hale. Aye. But the Devil is a wily one, you cannot deny it. However, she is far
620 from accused, and I know she will not be. (*pause*) I thought, sir, to put some questions as to the Christian character of this house, if you'll permit me.

Proctor (*coldly, resentful*). Why, we—have no fear of questions, sir.

Hale. Good, then. (*He makes himself more comfortable.*) In the book of record that Mr. Parris keeps, I note that you are rarely in the church on Sabbath Day.

630 **Proctor.** No, sir, you are mistaken.

Hale. Twenty-six time in seventeen month, sir. I must call that rare. Will you tell me why you are so absent?

Proctor. Mr. Hale, I never knew I must account to that man for I come to church or stay at home. My wife were sick this winter.

Hale. So I am told. But you, Mister, why could you not come alone?

640 **Proctor.** I surely did come when I could, and when I could not I prayed in this house.

Hale. Mr. Proctor, your house is not a church; your theology must tell you that.

Proctor. It does, sir, it does; and it tells me that a minister may pray to God without he have golden candlesticks upon the altar.

650 **Hale.** What golden candlesticks?

Proctor. Since we built the church there were pewter candlesticks upon the altar; Francis Nurse made them, y'know, and a sweeter hand never touched the metal. But Parris came, and for twenty week he preach nothin' but golden candlesticks until he had them. I labor the earth from dawn of day to blink of night, and I tell you true, when I look
660 to heaven and see my money glaring at his elbows—it hurt my prayer, sir, it hurt my prayer. I think, sometimes, the man dreams cathedrals, not clapboard meetin' houses.

Hale (*thinks, then*). And yet, Mister, a Christian on Sabbath Day must be in church. (*pause*) Tell me—you have three children?

Proctor. Aye. Boys.

670 **Hale.** How comes it that only two are baptized?

Proctor (*starts to speak, then stops, then, as though unable to restrain this*). I like it not that Mr. Parris should lay his hand upon my baby. I see no light of God in that man. I'll not conceal it.

Hale. I must say it, Mr. Proctor; that is not for you to decide. The man's ordained, therefore the light of God is
680 in him.

Proctor (*flushed with resentment but trying to smile*). What's your suspicion, Mr. Hale?

Hale. No, no, I have no—

CLOSE READ

Analyze Drama Elements COMMON CORE RL 3, RL 5
(LINES 655–664)

Tell students that in addition to revealing a character's feelings, dialogue can help to convey the theme of an entire play. A character's dialogue may express the underlying message of the playwright.

Q ASK STUDENTS to tell what Proctor's dialogue reveals about his feelings for Parris. (*Proctor despises Parris and feels that Parris is only out to gain wealth and status. It is because of Parris that Proctor has often stayed away from church.*) Then ask students to explain how Proctor's dialogue might relate to a larger theme of the play. (*Proctor's dialogue relates to one of Miller's themes—that of the hypocrisy of imperfect people judging and condemning others.*)

SCAFFOLDING FOR ELL STUDENTS

Understand Multiple-Meaning Words Draw students' attention to the word "flushed" in line 681. Explain that this word has more than one meaning.

ASK STUDENTS to explain the meaning of the word "flushed" in this sentence. Then have them research another meaning of the word by consulting a dictionary and write a sentence using this additional meaning. (*turned red in the face from emotion; cleansed with water; Sam flushed the dust from his eyes.*)

Analyze Drama Elements

COMMON CORE RL 3, RL 5

(LINES 700–703)

Remind students that dialogue moves the plot forward and also can hint at a future event. Tell students that these hints of the future are called **foreshadowing.**

R **ASK STUDENTS** to reread Hale's line of dialogue where he asks Elizabeth if she knows the Ten Commandments. Then tell what event this might foreshadow, based on what they already have read. *(Earlier, Mary Warren describes how Judge Hawthorne asked Sarah Good to recite the Commandments and when she couldn't, condemned her. Hale's question may be leading to a similar outcome for Elizabeth.)*

Analyze Drama Elements

COMMON CORE RL 3, RL 5

(LINES 700–766)

Remind students that **stage directions** can contribute to the mood of a scene or an entire play.

S **ASK STUDENTS** to describe the mood of this scene based on the stage directions. Have them cite specific stage directions in their answers. *(The scene's mood is very tense because the Proctors are coming under questioning that could result in their being tried and jailed. In line 716, Proctor begins to sweat. During the following lines, he pauses and hesitates as he tries to remember the Ten Commandments. In lines 741–742, Proctor "grows more uneasy." By line 745 Hale is "worried" for them and is "disturbed" in line 756. As Hale is about to leave, Elizabeth speaks "with a note of desperation.")*

Proctor. I nailed the roof upon the church, I hung the door—

Hale. Oh, did you! That's a good sign, then.

690 **Proctor.** It may be I have been too quick to bring the man to book,[5] but you cannot think we ever desired the destruction of religion. I think that's in your mind, is it not?

Hale (*not altogether giving way*). I—have—there is a softness in your record, sir, a softness.

Elizabeth. I think, maybe, we have been too hard with Mr. Parris. I think so. But sure we never loved the Devil here.

700 **Hale** (*nods, deliberating this. Then, with the voice of one administering a secret test*). Do you know your Commandments, Elizabeth?

Elizabeth (*without hesitation, even eagerly*). I surely do. There be no mark of blame upon my life, Mr. Hale. I am a convenanted Christian woman.

Hale. And you, Mister?

Proctor (*a trifle unsteadily*). I—am sure 710 I do, sir.

Hale (*glances at her open face, then at John, then*). Let you repeat them, if you will.

Proctor. The Commandments.

Hale. Aye.

Proctor (*looking off, beginning to sweat*). Thou shalt not kill.

Hale. Aye.

Proctor (*counting on his fingers*). Thou 720 shalt not steal. Thou shalt not covet thy neighbor's goods, nor make unto thee any graven image. Thou shalt not take the name of the Lord in vain; thou shalt have no other gods before

---

[5] **bring the man to book:** judge the man.

---

me. (*with some hesitation*) Thou shalt remember the Sabbath Day and keep it holy. (*Pause. Then.*) Thou shalt honor thy father and mother. Thou shalt not bear false witness. (*He is stuck. He* 730 *counts back on his fingers, knowing one is missing.*) Thou shalt not make unto thee any graven image.

Hale. You have said that twice, sir.

Proctor (*lost*). Aye. (*He is flailing for it.*)

Elizabeth (*delicately*). Adultery, John.

Proctor (*as though a secret arrow had pained his heart*). Aye. (*trying to grin it away—to Hale*) You see, sir, between the two of us we do know them all. (*Hale* 740 *only looks at Proctor, deep in his attempt to define this man. Proctor grows more uneasy.*) I think it be a small fault.

Hale. Theology, sir, is a fortress; no crack in a fortress may be accounted small. (*He rises; he seems worried now. He paces a little, in deep thought.*)

Proctor. There be no love for Satan in this house, Mister.

Hale. I pray it, I pray it dearly. (*He looks* 750 *to both of them, an attempt at a smile on his face, but his misgivings are clear.*) Well, then—I'll bid you good night.

Elizabeth (*unable to restrain herself*). Mr. Hale. (*He turns.*) I do think you are suspecting me somewhat? Are you not?

Hale (*obviously disturbed—and evasive*). Goody Proctor, I do not judge you. My duty is to add what I may to the godly wisdom of the court. I pray you both 760 good health and good fortune. (*to John*) Good night, sir. (*He starts out.*)

Elizabeth (*with a note of desperation*). I think you must tell him, John.

Hale. What's that?

Elizabeth (*restraining a call*). Will you tell him?

TO CHALLENGE STUDENTS . . .

Make Connections Tell students that while Miller's inclusion of the Ten Commandments test may be based on history, it also provides an opportunity for Miller to explore his theme of hypocrisy.

ASK STUDENTS to work in small groups and discuss the irony of the recitation of the Ten Commandments as a test of purity. If students are unfamiliar with the commandments, have them research them on the Internet. *(Residents of Salem must know and live by the commandments. Some residents who use them as a test of purity have broken commandments. Putnam has broken the commandment against desiring a neighbor's possessions. Abigail has broken the commandment against adultery.)* When students have finished, ask each group to share their findings with the class.

(*Slight pause.* Hale *looks questioningly at* John.)

Proctor (*with difficulty*). I—I have no
770 witness and cannot prove it, except
my word be taken. But I know the
children's sickness had naught to do
with witchcraft.

Hale (*stopped, struck*). Naught to do—?

Proctor. Mr. Parris discovered them
sportin' in the woods. They were
startled and took sick.

(*pause*)

Hale. Who told you this?

780 **Proctor** (*hesitates, then*). Abigail
Williams.

Hale. Abigail!

Proctor. Aye.

Hale (*his eyes wide*). Abigail Williams
told you it had naught to do with
witchcraft!

Proctor. She told me the day you
came, sir.

Hale (*suspiciously*). Why—why did you
790 keep this?

Proctor. I never knew until tonight
that the world is gone daft with this
nonsense.

Hale. Nonsense! Mister, I have myself
examined Tituba, Sarah Good, and
numerous others that have confessed
to dealing with the Devil. They have
confessed it.

Proctor. And why not, if they must
800 hang for denyin' it? There are them that
will swear to anything before they'll
hang; have you never thought of that?

Hale. I have. I—I have indeed. (*It is his
own suspicion, but he resists it. He glances
at* Elizabeth, *then at* John.) And you—
would you testify to this in court?

Proctor. I—had not reckoned with goin'
into court. But if I must I will.

Hale. Do you falter here?

810 **Proctor.** I falter nothing, but I may
wonder if my story will be credited in
such a court. I do wonder on it, when
such a steady-minded minister as you
will suspicion such a woman that never
lied, and cannot, and the world knows
she cannot! I may falter somewhat,
Mister; I am no fool.

Hale (*quietly—it has impressed him*).
Proctor, let you open with me now, for I
820 have a rumor that troubles me. It's said
you hold no belief that there may even
be witches in the world. Is that true, sir?

Proctor (*He knows this is critical, and is
striving against his disgust with* Hale *and
with himself for even answering*). I know
not what I have said, I may have said it. I
have wondered if there be witches in the
world—although I cannot believe they
come among us now.

830 **Hale.** Then you do not believe—

Proctor. I have no knowledge of it; the
Bible speaks of witches, and I will not
deny them.

Hale. And you, woman?

Elizabeth. I—I cannot believe it.

Hale (*shocked*). You cannot!

Proctor. Elizabeth, you bewilder him!

Elizabeth (*to* Hale). I cannot think the
Devil may own a woman's soul, Mr.
840 Hale, when she keeps an upright way, as
I have. I am a good woman, I know it;
and if you believe I may do only good
work in the world, and yet be secretly
bound to Satan, then I must tell you, sir,
I do not believe it.

Hale. But, woman, you do believe there
are witches in—

The Crucible: Act Two **497**

CLOSE READ

Analyze Drama Elements
 **RL 3, RL 5**

(LINES 794–798)

Tell students to read all **dialogue** closely and look for punctuation and special type that the playwright may be using for effect and emphasis.

🅣 **ASK STUDENTS** to reread Hale's dialogue in lines 794–798. Have them explain why Miller adds italics to the word "confessed." What does the emphasis on the word reveal about Hale's character? (*Hale shows himself to be unwilling to consider that the confessions might be false. He emphatically insists that, as confessions, they must be true.*)

Analyze Drama Elements
 **RL 3, RL 5**

(LINES 805–817)

Review with students that stakes are what the characters stand to lose or gain. A playwright develops the drama of his or her play by raising the stakes of the central characters.

🅤 **CITE TEXT EVIDENCE** to explain how Hale's request for Proctor to testify in court is an example of raising Proctor's stakes. (*If Proctor accepts and testifies about Abigail's veracity, he is putting himself squarely in the middle of the conflict. If Abigail were to be believed, as is the case thus far—and there is no reason yet to think that this would change—then Proctor could be convicted, jailed, or even hanged.*)

SCAFFOLDING FOR ELL STUDENTS

Homophones Explain to students that **homophones** are words that sound the same but have different spellings and meanings.

ASK STUDENTS to identify a homophone of the word *witch*. *(which)* Have them pronounce *which*, spell it, and use it in a sentence. (*Which kind of soup do you want to eat?*) Tell students to look for other homophones as they read.

TEACH

CLOSE READ

Analyze Drama Elements  RL 3, RL 5

(LINES 866–924)

Remind students that plot **complications** are additional problems that make the main conflict more difficult to resolve. They will often raise the stakes for the characters as well.

Ⓥ **ASK STUDENTS** to tell how the arrests of the wives of Giles and Francis can be seen as plot complications. *(The main conflict of the play is whether or not there is witchcraft at work in Salem. The accusation of two such highly regarded women of the town will make it easier for those who wish to persecute others to throw suspicion on practically anyone they wish.)*

Elizabeth. If you think that I am one, then I say there are none.

850 **Hale.** You surely do not fly against the Gospel, the Gospel—

Proctor. She believe in the Gospel, every word!

Elizabeth. Question Abigail Williams about the Gospel, not myself!

(Hale *stares at her.*)

Proctor. She do not mean to doubt the Gospel, sir, you cannot think it. This be a Christian house, sir, a Christian

860 house.

Hale. God keep you both; let the third child be quickly baptized, and go you without fail each Sunday in to Sabbath prayer; and keep a solemn, quiet way among you. I think—

(Giles Corey *appears in doorway.*)

Giles. John!

Proctor. Giles! What's the matter?

Giles. They take my wife.

870 (Francis Nurse *enters.*)

Giles. And his Rebecca!

Proctor (*to* Francis). Rebecca's in the jail!

Francis. Aye, Cheever come and take her in his wagon. We've only now come from the jail, and they'll not even let us in to see them.

Elizabeth. They've surely gone wild now, Mr. Hale!

880 **Francis** (*going to* Hale). Reverend Hale! Can you not speak to the Deputy Governor? I'm sure he mistakes these people—

Hale. Pray calm yourself, Mr. Nurse.

Francis. My wife is the very brick and mortar of the church, Mr. Hale (*indicating* Giles) and Martha Corey,

there cannot be a woman closer yet to God than Martha.

890 **Hale.** How is Rebecca charged, Mr. Nurse?

Francis (*with a mocking, half-hearted laugh*). For murder, she's charged! (*mockingly quoting the warrant*) "For the marvelous and supernatural murder of Goody Putnam's babies." What am I to do, Mr. Hale?

Hale (*turns from* Francis, *deeply troubled, then*). Believe me, Mr. Nurse,
900 if Rebecca Nurse be tainted, then nothing's left to stop the whole green world from burning. Let you rest upon the justice of the court; the court will send her home, I know it.

Francis. You cannot mean she will be tried in court!

Hale (*pleading*). Nurse, though our hearts break, we cannot flinch; these are new times, sir. There is a misty plot
910 afoot so subtle we should be criminal to cling to old respects and ancient friendships. I have seen too many frightful proofs in court—the Devil is alive in Salem, and we dare not quail to follow wherever the accusing finger points!

Proctor (*angered*). How may such a woman murder children?

Hale (*in great pain*). Man, remember,
920 until an hour before the Devil fell, God thought him beautiful in Heaven.

Giles. I never said my wife were a witch, Mr. Hale; I only said she were reading books!

Hale. Mr. Corey, exactly what complaint were made on your wife?

Giles. That bloody mongrel Walcott charge her. Y'see, he buy a pig of my wife four or five year ago, and the pig
930 died soon after. So he come dancin' in

498 Collection 6

WHEN STUDENTS STRUGGLE . . .

Summarize Encourage students to think about how the plot of the play develops in this scene.

ASK STUDENTS to **summarize**, or briefly retell, the nature of Hale's suspicions of Proctor and Elizabeth. How are they different? *(Hale goes after Proctor for not going to church enough, and that leads to the Ten Commandments test. Elizabeth comes under his suspicion because she was mentioned by Abigail during Abigail's trial. Compounding Hale's suspicion of Abigail is the fact that Elizabeth does not answer Hale's questions about witches in a way that satisfies him.)*

for his money back. So my Martha, she says to him, "Walcott, if you haven't the wit to feed a pig properly, you'll not live to own many," she says. Now he goes to court and claims that from that day to this he cannot keep a pig alive for more than four weeks because my Martha bewitch them with her books!

(*Enter Ezekiel Cheever. A shocked*
940 *silence.*)

Cheever. Good evening to you, Proctor.

Proctor. Why, Mr. Cheever. Good evening.

Cheever. Good evening, all. Good evening, Mr. Hale.

Proctor. I hope you come not on business of the court.

Cheever. I do, Proctor, aye. I am clerk of the court now, y'know.

950 (*Enter Marshal Herrick, a man in his early thirties, who is somewhat shamefaced at the moment.*)

Giles. It's a pity, Ezekiel, that an honest tailor might have gone to Heaven must burn in Hell. You'll burn for this, do you know it?

Cheever. You know yourself I must do as I'm told. You surely know that, Giles. And I'd as lief⁶ you'd not be sending
960 me to Hell. I like not the sound of it, I tell you; I like not the sound of it. (*He fears Proctor, but starts to reach inside his coat.*) Now believe me, Proctor, how heavy be the law, all its tonnage I do carry on my back tonight. (*He takes out a warrant.*) I have a warrant for your wife.

Proctor (*to Hale*). You said she were not charged!

970 **Hale.** I know nothin' of it. (*to Cheever*) When were she charged?

⁶ **as lief** (lēf): rather.

Cheever. I am given sixteen warrant tonight, sir, and she is one.

Proctor. Who charged her?

Cheever. Why, Abigail Williams charge her.

Proctor. On what proof, what proof?

Cheever (*looking about the room*). Mr. Proctor, I have little time. The court bid
980 me search your house, but I like not to search a house. So will you hand me any poppets that your wife may keep here?

Proctor. Poppets?

Elizabeth. I never kept no poppets, not since I were a girl.

Cheever (*embarrassed, glancing toward the mantel where sits Mary Warren's poppet*). I spy a poppet, Goody Proctor.

Elizabeth. Oh! (*going for it*) Why, this is
990 Mary's.

Cheever (*shyly*). Would you please to give it to me?

Elizabeth (*handing it to him, asks* Hale). Has the court discovered a text in poppets now?

Cheever (*carefully holding the poppet*). Do you keep any others in this house?

Proctor. No, nor this one either till tonight. What signifies a poppet?

1000 **Cheever.** Why, a poppet—(*He gingerly turns the poppet over.*) a poppet may signify—Now, woman, will you please to come with me?

Proctor. She will not! (*to Elizabeth*) Fetch Mary here.

Cheever (*ineptly reaching toward Elizabeth*). No, no, I am forbid to leave her from my sight.

Proctor (*pushing his arm away*).
1010 You'll leave her out of sight and out of mind, Mister. Fetch Mary, Elizabeth. (*Elizabeth goes upstairs.*)

The Crucible: Act Two **499**

TEACH

CLOSE READ

Analyze Drama Elements COMMON CORE RL 3, RL 5
(LINES 939–967)

Remind students that a character's motivation can be inferred from either dialogue, stage directions—or both.

W CITE TEXT EVIDENCE Ask students to tell what motivates Cheever to come and arrest Elizabeth. Have students cite evidence from dialogue or stage directions in response to this question. (*Cheever's dialogue reveals that he is a clerk of the court [lines 948–949] and must "do as [he's] told" [lines 957–958].*)

Analyze Drama Elements COMMON CORE RL 3, RL 5
(LINES 957–973)

Remind students that plot complications build on the events of the plot—including previous complications—and add intensity.

X ASK STUDENTS to explain why Elizabeth's arrest qualifies as a complication of the plot. How does it build on previous plot complications? (*Elizabeth's arrest makes the main conflict of the play more difficult to solve because it signals that the witch hunt has gained an unstoppable momentum. Despite the flimsy evidence against Elizabeth, it will be difficult to prove her innocence. In this way, it connects to the previous complication of the other two wives being arrested because Elizabeth is yet another well-respected woman of Salem who stands accused. It appears now that no one is safe from accusation.*)

SCAFFOLDING FOR ELL STUDENTS

Phrasal Verbs Explain to students that **phrasal verbs** are verbs with two words, such as *break in, sleep over,* or *check out.* Often they require a direct object (someone or something), as in *hand something in, go after someone,* or *do something over.*

ASK STUDENTS to go to line 934 and read the full line:

"Now he goes to court and claims that from that day to this he cannot keep a pig alive for more than four weeks because my Martha bewitch them with her books!"

Have them explain in their own words what phrasal verb is used in this sentence. (*keep alive*) Then have them tell if there is a direct object or not and, if so, what it is. (*yes; a pig*) As students read, encourage them to look for phrasal verbs.

Analyze Drama Elements  COMMON CORE RL 3, RL 5

(LINES 1013–1057)

Remind students that **dramatic irony** occurs when readers know more than some or all of the characters.

Y **ASK STUDENTS** to reread this section about the poppet and explain how it is an example of dramatic irony. *(Cheever and Hale believe that the needle in the doll was used to harm Abigail, but Proctor and the reader can infer that Abigail has set Elizabeth up by having Mary make the doll and putting the needle in it, then stabbing herself and claiming that Elizabeth did it.)*

Analyze Drama Elements  COMMON CORE RL 3, RL 5

(LINES 1047–1099)

Remind students that the stage directions can give insight into characters' feelings and understanding.

Z **CITE TEXT EVIDENCE** Ask students to tell whether Mary knows about Abigail's accusation against Elizabeth. Have them cite evidence from the text to support their answers. *(Mary does not know; She is "frightened" [line 1063] and evasive [line 1069], she doesn't understand the direction of Proctor's questioning [lines 1072–1073], and she is "bewildered" when she hears about the needle in the doll [line 1083].)*

Hale. What signifies a poppet, Mr. Cheever?

Cheever (*turning the poppet over in his hands*). Why, they say it may signify that she—(*He has lifted the poppet's skirt, and his eyes widen in astonished fear.*) Why, this, this—

1020 **Proctor** (*reaching for the poppet*). What's there?

Cheever. Why (*He draws out a long needle from the poppet.*) it is a needle! Herrick, Herrick, it is a needle!

(*Herrick comes toward him.*)

Proctor (*angrily, bewildered*). And what signifies a needle!

Cheever (*his hands shaking*). Why, this go hard with her, Proctor, this—I had 1030 my doubts, Proctor, I had my doubts, but here's calamity. (*to Hale, showing the needle*) You see it, sir, it is a needle!

Hale. Why? What meanin' has it?

Cheever (*wide-eyed, trembling*). The girl, the Williams girl, Abigail Williams, sir. She sat to dinner in Reverend Parris's house tonight, and without word nor warnin' she falls to the floor. Like a struck beast, he says, and screamed a 1040 scream that a bull would weep to hear. And he goes to save her, and, stuck two inches in the flesh of her belly, he draw a needle out. And demandin' of her how she come to be so stabbed, she (*to Proctor now*) testify it were your wife's familiar spirit[7] pushed it in.

Proctor. Why, she done it herself! (*to Hale*) I hope you're not takin' this for proof, Mister!

1050 (*Hale, struck by the proof, is silent.*)

---

[7] **familiar spirit:** the spirit or demon, most usually in the form of an animal such as a black cat, that was a companion and helper to a witch.

Cheever. 'Tis hard proof! (*to Hale*) I find here a poppet Goody Proctor keeps. I have found it, sir. And in the belly of the poppet a needle's stuck. I tell you true, Proctor, I never warranted to see such proof of Hell, and I bid you obstruct me not, for I—

(*Enter Elizabeth with Mary Warren. Proctor, seeing Mary Warren, draws her 1060 by the arm to Hale.*)

Proctor. Here now! Mary, how did this poppet come into my house?

Mary Warren (*frightened for herself, her voice very small*). What poppet's that, sir?

Proctor (*impatiently, pointing at the doll in Cheever's hand*). This poppet, this poppet.

Mary Warren (*evasively, looking at it*). 1070 Why, I—I think it is mine.

Proctor. It is your poppet, is it not?

Mary Warren (*not understanding the direction of this*). It—is, sir.

Proctor. And how did it come into this house?

Mary Warren (*glancing about at the avid faces*). Why—I made it in the court, sir, and—give it to Goody Proctor tonight.

Proctor (*to Hale*). Now, sir—do you 1080 have it?

Hale. Mary Warren, a needle have been found inside this poppet.

Mary Warren (*bewildered*). Why, I meant no harm by it, sir.

Proctor (*quickly*). You stuck that needle in yourself?

Mary Warren. I—I believe I did, sir, I—

Proctor (*to Hale*). What say you now?

Hale (*watching Mary Warren closely*). 1090 Child, you are certain this be your natural memory? May it be, perhaps,

500 Collection 6

that someone conjures you even now to say this?

Mary Warren. Conjures me? Why, no, sir, I am entirely myself, I think. Let you ask Susanna Walcott—she saw me sewin' it in court. (*or better still*) Ask Abby, Abby sat beside me when I made it.

1100 **Proctor** (*to Hale, of* Cheever). Bid him begone. Your mind is surely settled now. Bid him out, Mr. Hale.

Elizabeth. What signifies a needle?

Hale. Mary—you charge a cold and cruel murder on Abigail.

Mary Warren. Murder! I charge no—

Hale. Abigail were stabbed tonight; a needle were found stuck into her belly—

Elizabeth. And she charges me?

1110 **Hale.** Aye.

Elizabeth (*her breath knocked out*). Why—! The girl is murder! She must be ripped out of the world!

Cheever (*pointing at* Elizabeth). You've heard that, sir! Ripped out of the world! Herrick, you heard it!

Proctor (*suddenly snatching the warrant out of* Cheever's *hands*). Out with you.

Cheever. Proctor, you dare not touch
1120 the warrant.

Proctor (*ripping the warrant*). Out with you!

Cheever. You've ripped the Deputy Governor's warrant, man!

Proctor. Damn the Deputy Governor! Out of my house!

Hale. Now, Proctor, Proctor!

Proctor. Get y'gone with them! You are a broken minister.

1130 **Hale.** Proctor, if she is innocent, the court—

Proctor. If *she* is innocent! Why do you never wonder if Parris be innocent, or Abigail? Is the accuser always holy now? Were they born this morning as clean as God's fingers? I'll tell you what's walking Salem—vengeance is walking Salem. We are what we always were in Salem, but now the little crazy children
1140 are jangling the keys of the kingdom, and common vengeance writes the law! This warrant's vengeance! I'll not give my wife to vengeance!

Elizabeth. I'll go, John—

Proctor. You will not go!

Herrick. I have nine men outside. You cannot keep her. The law binds me, John, I cannot budge.

1150 **Proctor** (*to Hale, ready to break him*). Will you see her taken?

Hale. Proctor, the court is just—

Proctor. Pontius Pilate! God will not let you wash your hands of this![8]

Elizabeth. John—I think I must go with them. (*He cannot bear to look at her.*) Mary, there is bread enough for the morning; you will bake, in the afternoon. Help Mr. Proctor as you were
1160 his daughter—you owe me that, and much more. (*She is fighting her weeping. To* Proctor.) When the children wake, speak nothing of witchcraft—it will frighten them. (*She cannot go on.*)

Proctor. I will bring you home. I will bring you soon.

Elizabeth. Oh, John, bring me soon!

Proctor. I will fall like an ocean on that court! Fear nothing, Elizabeth.

---

[8] **Pontius Pilate** (pŏn´chəs pī´lət) . . . **hands of this:** the Roman official who presided over the trial and sentencing of Christ. Pilate publicly washed his hands to absolve himself of responsibility for Christ's death.

The Crucible: Act Two **501**

Analyze Drama Elements 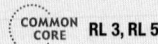 RL 3, RL 5
(LINES 1132–1143)

Remind students that dialogue can convey the playwright's underlying message.

A2 ASK STUDENTS to reread Proctor's speech in lines 1132–1143. Have them identify a sentence that states one of Miller's central themes. Then ask them to explain what the sentence means and how it relates to the theme. (*In lines 1137–1138, Proctor says "Vengeance is walking Salem." This means that the desire for revenge, not their moral sense, is driving people to make wild accusations. This expresses one of Miller's themes: that people who themselves feel persecuted may turn and become persecutors themselves.*)

Analyze Drama Elements  RL 3, RL 5
(LINES 1154–1163)

Tell students that stage directions sometimes require interpretation.

B2 ASK STUDENTS to consider the stage direction that describes Proctor as not being able to look at Elizabeth. Have them tell what they think motivates this behavior. (*Proctor is probably feeling many things in this moment: fear for his wife's safety; sadness over her being taken away; anger at the situation generally; shame at the role he played in giving Abigail a reason to target Elizabeth; and perhaps shame at not being willing to confess his relationship with Abigail in order to save his wife and the other accused women.*)

WHEN STUDENTS STRUGGLE . . .

Understand Metaphors and Similes Remind students that **similes** compare two things using the words *like* or *as*, while **metaphors** compare two things without using these words.

ASK STUDENTS to reread page 501 and identify a **metaphor** and a **simile.** Then have students explain their meanings.

- Lines 1128–1129: *You are a broken minister.* (*This is a metaphor meaning that Hale is like a broken object. He no longer works as a minister should.*)
- Lines 1167–1168: *I will fall like an ocean on that court!* (*This is a simile that means Proctor will unleash all his power to defend Elizabeth; he will overwhelm the court like the ocean's waves overwhelm the shore.*)

Analyze Drama Elements   COMMON CORE   RL 3, RL 5

(LINES 1174–1201)

Remind students that **stage directions** can help establish mood.

C2 CITE TEXT EVIDENCE Have students look for specific stage directions that describe sounds. Then have them tell how these sounds help establish the mood of the scene, making sure students refer to specific sounds listed in the text. *(In line 1177, the "clank" of the chain that is put on Elizabeth is heard—though Elizabeth herself is not seen. This sound makes the scene feel very scary. In line 1183, other men's voices are heard from outside after Proctor goes out; this suggests that Proctor is fighting against those who are chaining Elizabeth. The mood of the scene is intense and dramatic at this point. In line 1201, the sound of the wagon is heard as it drives away with Elizabeth. This creates a feeling of sadness and helplessness.)*

Elizabeth (*with great fear*). I will fear nothing. (*She looks about the room, as though to fix it in her mind.*) Tell the children I have gone to visit someone sick. [1170]

(*She walks out the door,* Herrick *and* Cheever *behind her. For a moment,* Proctor *watches from the doorway. The clank of chain is heard.*)

Proctor. Herrick! Herrick, don't chain her! (*He rushes out the door. From outside.*) Damn you, man, you will not chain her! Off with them! I'll not have it! I will not have her chained! [1180]

(*There are other men's voices against his.* Hale, *in a fever of guilt and uncertainty, turns from the door to avoid the sight;* Mary Warren *bursts into tears and sits weeping.* Giles Corey *calls to* Hale.)

Giles. And yet silent, minister? It is fraud, you know it is fraud! What keeps you, man? [1190]

(Proctor *is half braced, half pushed into the room by two deputies and* Herrick.)

Proctor. I'll pay you, Herrick, I will surely pay you!

Herrick (*panting*). In God's name, John, I cannot help myself. I must chain them all. Now let you keep inside this house till I am gone! (*He goes out with his deputies.*)

(Proctor *stands there, gulping air. Horses and a wagon creaking are heard.*) [1200]

Hale (*in great uncertainty*). Mr. Proctor—

Proctor. Out of my sight!

Hale. Charity, Proctor, charity. What I have heard in her favor, I will not fear to testify in court. God help me, I cannot judge her guilty or innocent—I know not. Only this consider: the world goes mad, and it profit nothing you should lay the cause to the vengeance of a little girl. [1210]

Proctor. You are a coward! Though you be ordained in God's own tears, you are a coward now!

Hale. Proctor, I cannot think God be provoked so grandly by such a petty cause. The jails are packed— our greatest judges sit in Salem now—and hangin's promised. Man, we must look to cause proportionate. Were there murder done, perhaps, and never brought to light? Abomination? Some secret blasphemy that stinks to Heaven? Think on cause, man, and let you help [1220]

Image Credits: ©Photosforyou/Alamy Images

SCAFFOLDING FOR ELL STUDENTS

Understand Idioms Remind students that some words have an idiomatic meaning in addition to their dictionary definition. Tell them that if the dictionary meaning of a word does not make sense in context, they should consider whether the word has an idiomatic meaning.

ASK STUDENTS to reread Proctor's dialogue in lines 1193–1194:

"I'll pay you, Herrick, I will surely pay you!"

Help students understand that Proctor is not promising to pay Herrick money. Ask them to infer the meaning of "pay" in this line. *(In this line, "pay" means "have revenge on." This usage is related to the idiom "to pay someone back," or get revenge.)*

me to discover it. For there's your way, believe it, there is your only way, when such confusion strikes upon the world. (*He goes to* Giles *and* Francis.) Let you
1230 counsel among yourselves; think on your village and what may have drawn from heaven such thundering wrath upon you all. I shall pray God open up our eyes.

(Hale *goes out.*)

Francis (*struck by* Hale's *mood*). I never heard no murder done in Salem.

Proctor (*He has been reached by* Hale's *words*). Leave me, Francis, leave me.

1240 **Giles** (*shaken*). John—tell me, are we lost?

Proctor. Go home now, Giles. We'll speak on it tomorrow.

Giles. Let you think on it. We'll come early, eh?

Proctor. Aye. Go now, Giles.

Giles. Good night, then.

(Giles Corey *goes out. After a moment.*)

Mary Warren (*in a fearful squeak of a*
1250 *voice*). Mr. Proctor, very likely they'll let her come home once they're given proper evidence.

Proctor. You're coming to the court with me, Mary. You will tell it in the court.

Mary Warren. I cannot charge murder on Abigail.

Proctor (*moving menacingly toward her*). You will tell the court how that poppet
1260 come here and who stuck the needle in.

Mary Warren. She'll kill me for sayin' that! (Proctor *continues toward her.*)

COLLABORATIVE DISCUSSION Why doesn't John Proctor go immediately to Salem to reveal what he knows? With a partner, discuss what Proctor will lose if the truth is known and why he hesitates. Cite specific textual evidence from the play to support your ideas.

Abby'll charge lechery on you, Mr. Proctor!

Proctor (*halting*). She's told you!

Mary Warren. I have known it, sir. She'll ruin you with it, I know she will.

Proctor (*hesitating, and with deep hatred of himself*). Good. Then her saintliness
1270 is done with. (Mary *backs from him.*) We will slide together into our pit; you will tell the court what you know.

Mary Warren (*in terror*). I cannot, they'll turn on me—

(Proctor *strides and catches her, and she is repeating, "I cannot, I cannot!"*)

Proctor. My wife will never die for me! I will bring your guts into your mouth but that goodness will not die for me!

1280 **Mary Warren** (*struggling to escape him*). I cannot do it, I cannot!

Proctor (*grasping her by the throat as though he would strangle her*). Make your peace with it! Now Hell and Heaven grapple on our backs, and all our old pretense is ripped away—make your peace! (*He throws her to the floor, where she sobs, "I cannot, I cannot . . ."* And now, half to himself, staring, and
1290 turning to the open door.) Peace. It is a providence, and no great change; we are only what we always were, but naked now. (*He walks as though toward a great horror, facing the open sky.*) Aye, naked! And the wind, God's icy wind, will blow!

(*And she is over and over again sobbing, "I cannot, I cannot, I cannot," as the curtain falls.*)

CLOSE READ

Analyze Drama Elements COMMON CORE RL 3, RL 5
(LINES 1282–1296)

Explain to students that a character's dialogue, such as Proctor's speech in lines 1282–1296, can reveal more about the central conflict of the play and the character's role in it.

D2 **ASK STUDENTS** to analyze the meaning of Proctor's speech and tell how it relates to the central conflict of the play. (*Proctor is demanding that Mary go with him to court and tell the truth about Abigail seeing her sew the poppet. Proctor knows that Mary could decide both their fates—and Elizabeth's and Abigail's—and so "Hell and Heaven grapple" on their backs. He goes on to say that they are "naked," meaning the truth is about to be exposed one way or the other—the truth about who is really a witch (the play's central conflict) and his own truth about his affair with Abigail. "God's icy wind" is the punishment that awaits them all.*)

COLLABORATIVE DISCUSSION Have students work in small groups and discuss what John Proctor has at stake if the truth is revealed. Ask them to cite specific evidence from the text. Then have groups share their conclusions with the class as a whole. Accept all reasonable responses.

ASK STUDENTS to share any questions they generated in the course of reading and discussing the selection.

PRACTICE & APPLY

Analyze Drama Elements  COMMON CORE RL 3, RL 5

Go over the elements of plot with students. Guide them to understand that these elements also exist within individual acts and scenes. For example, the play has one central conflict, but so does the argument scene between Elizabeth and Proctor. Ask students to look for the four elements of plot in this scene (lines 520–546). *(Sample answer: Their conflict is that Elizabeth wants Proctor to go to Salem and tell that Abigail told him she was in the woods, but Proctor hesitates because of his relationship with Abigail. The revelation that Proctor spoke with Abigail while they were alone is a complication of the problem. The climax of the scene is when they both reach their emotional peak, stating what they will and will not do. The scene is interrupted and has no resolution.)*

Analyzing the Text  COMMON CORE RL 3, RL 5, SL 4

Possible answers:

1. *The reader learns in lines 101–112 that an official court has been convened to hear the charges of witchcraft and that Mary, the Proctors' servant, has been made an official of the court. In lines 122–132 the reader learns that Abigail and the other girls who were in the woods are leading the accusations against respectable people. In lines 1174–1201 Elizabeth is arrested as a witch. These facts make it clear that in order to save the lives of innocent people, including his wife, Proctor must testify against Abigail.*

2. *Proctor does not accept his wife's suggestion that he go to court and tell that Abigail is lying. He is angry at her for insisting. He is not justified in his attitude because his reluctance stems from pride. He doesn't want to reveal that he spoke alone with Abigail.*

3. *When Hale speaks of "secret blasphemy," Proctor thinks of his affair with Abigail. When Proctor tells Mary that they will both "slide together" into a pit, he means that he and Abigail will have to face the punishment for what they have both done. Proctor faces punishment for adultery, and Abigail faces punishment for adultery and bearing false witness.*

4. *Mary shows arrogance ("I am amazed you do not see what weighty work we do.") and stubbornness. She refuses to see that Sarah Good's confession is nonsense. Mary also refuses to testify in court against Abigail for fear of what Abigail might do to her. All of this suggests that Mary may not tell the truth.*

 eBook *Annotate It!*

Analyze Drama Elements COMMON CORE RL 3, RL 5

The **plot** is the series of related events that make up the story of the drama. To understand how Miller structures his plot, look for these elements:

> The **conflict** is a struggle between opposing forces that drives the action. In Act One, local and personal conflicts escalate into a major, widespread conflict.
>
> **Complications** are additional problems that make the conflict more difficult to resolve. In Act Two, several events occur that add intensity.
>
> The **climax** is the point of highest tension or excitement. In Act Three, an event occurs that has the potential to change the outcome of the conflict.
>
> The **resolution** is the part of the play in which conflicts are brought to a close. In Act Four, loose threads of the plot are tied up; questions are answered.

Analyzing the Text COMMON CORE RL 3, RL 5, W 7, W 8, SL 4

Cite Text Evidence Support your responses with evidence from the selection.

1. **Cite Evidence** How do the events in this act affect readers' perception of the situation in which Proctor and the others find themselves? Cite specific details.

2. **Draw Conclusions** Reread lines 180–211. What do these lines reveal about the character of and the relationship between John and Elizabeth Proctor?

3. **Analyze** Why is Proctor struck by Hale's declaration that "some secret blasphemy" has caused all of the confusion? How does Hale's statement relate to Proctor's later words to Mary Warren that he and Abigail will "slide together into our pit; you will tell the court what you know"?

4. **Analyze** What does Mary Warren's behavior in Act Two foreshadow about her testimony in court? Explain.

PERFORMANCE TASK

Media Activity: Presentation With a partner, organize a multimedia presentation on the McCarthy era trials.

- Research information using reliable sources. Take notes. Identify copyright-free images that you might include.

- Choose a format for the ideas that you want to convey, such as charts, outlines, or slides with facts and illustrations.

- Make your presentation. As a class, discuss parallels between the McCarthy trials and those depicted in the play.

Assign this performance task.

PERFORMANCE TASK 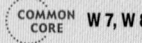 COMMON CORE W 7, W 8

Media Activity: Presentation Have students work with a partner to prepare their presentations. When students have completed a rough outline of their presentations, have them discuss it with another pair of students, pointing out the parallels they have discovered. Have student pairs offer feedback on content and format and give students an opportunity to revise their presentations.

Analyze Drama Elements   COMMON CORE RL 3, RL 5

(LINES 15–30)

Tell students to think about how **dialogue** can express a character's motivations directly or indirectly.

 **ASK STUDENTS** to explain what Giles' dialogue reveals about what he thinks is behind the witch hunt. Cite specific dialogue. *(Giles believes that Putnam is after the land of people in the town and that is why Putnam wishes to see them accused, jailed, and hanged.)*

Analyze Drama Elements   COMMON CORE RL 3, RL 5

(LINES 37–38)

Remind students that **dialogue** can also reveal an author's point of view about his or her subject.

B **ASK STUDENTS** to consider the meaning of Herrick's line of dialogue in lines 37–38. Ask them to explain why the line is ironic and absurd and how it relates to one of Miller's themes. *(Herrick tells Giles he cannot go into court with his evidence, but a court is exactly the place to present evidence. The line reflects Miller's theme of hypocrisy; he is pointing out that those who claim to seek the truth will not even hear evidence.)*

AS YOU READ Pay attention to details that explain Danforth's attitude toward Abigail and the other girls. Write down any questions you generate during reading.

ACT THREE

(*The vestry room of the Salem meeting house, now serving as the anteroom[1] of the General Court.*

As the curtain rises, the room is empty, but for sunlight pouring through two high windows in the back wall. The room is solemn, even forbidding. Heavy beams jut out, boards of random widths make up the walls. At the right are two doors leading into the meeting house proper, where the court is being held. At the left another door leads outside.

There is a plain bench at the left, and another at the right. In the center a rather long meeting table, with stools and a considerable armchair snugged up to it.

Through the partitioning wall at the right we hear a prosecutor's voice, Judge Hathorne's, *asking a question; then a woman's voice,* Martha Corey's, *replying.*)

Hathorne's Voice. Now, Martha Corey, there is abundant evidence in our hands to show that you have given yourself to the reading of fortunes. Do you deny it?

Martha Corey's Voice. I am innocent to a witch. I know not what a witch is.

Hathorne's Voice. How do you know, then, that you are not a witch?

10 **Martha Corey's Voice.** If I were, I would know it.

Hathorne's Voice. Why do you hurt these children?

Martha Corey's Voice. I do not hurt them. I scorn it!

Giles' Voice (*roaring*). I have evidence for the court!

(*Voices of townspeople rise in excitement.*)

Danforth's Voice. You will keep your 20 seat!

Giles' Voice. Thomas Putnam is reaching out for land!

Danforth's Voice. Remove that man, Marshal!

Giles' Voice. You're hearing lies, lies!

(*A roaring goes up from the people.*)

Hathorne's Voice. Arrest him, excellency!

Giles' Voice. I have evidence. Why will 30 you not hear my evidence?

(*The door opens and* Giles *is half carried into the vestry room by* Herrick.)

Giles. Hands off, damn you, let me go!

Herrick. Giles, Giles!

Giles. Out of my way, Herrick! I bring evidence—

Herrick. You cannot go in there, Giles; it's a court!

(*Enter* Hale *from the court.*)

40 **Hale.** Pray be calm a moment.

Giles. You, Mr. Hale, go in there and demand I speak.

Hale. A moment, sir, a moment.

---

[1] **vestry room . . . anteroom:** A vestry room is a room in a church used for nonreligious meetings or church business. An anteroom is a waiting room or a room that leads into another.

The Crucible: Act Three **505**

SCAFFOLDING FOR ELL STUDENTS

Understand Possessives Remind students of the rules for showing possession in English.

For singular nouns not ending in *s*, add apostrophe + *s*:

Martha Corey's Voice. If I were, I would know it.

For singular nouns ending in *s*, you may add apostrophe + *s* or just an apostrophe:

Giles' Voice. Thomas Putnam is reaching out for land!

For plural nouns ending in *s*, add only an apostrophe:

Mary Warren…*becoming overwhelmed by…the girls'…conviction, starts to whimper…*

ASK STUDENTS to find an example of a possessive on the page and explain which rule it follows. *(Line 1: "Hathorne's Voice": singular noun not ending in s gets an apostrophe + s.)*

Analyze Drama Elements
COMMON CORE RL 3, RL 5

(LINES 45–47)

Remind students that **stage directions** may offer explicit descriptions of characters.

 CITE TEXT EVIDENCE Have students tell what the stage directions reveal about Judge Hathorne. *(He is bitter and remorseless.)* What can the reader predict about how he might treat the women's cases? *(He is likely to be totally unsympathetic to them.)*

Analyze Drama Elements
COMMON CORE RL 3, RL 5

(LINES 105–111)

Remind students that characters' traits are often revealed indirectly through their **dialogue**.

D **ASK STUDENTS** what we learn about Hale and Danforth's characters from their dialogue in lines 105–111. Cite examples from the text. *(Hale seems more reasonable than Danforth, and less strict; he encourages Danforth to at least hear Giles' evidence. Danforth, on the other hand, seems very strict and by-the-book; he is more concerned with following legal procedures than he is in aiding Giles.)*

Giles. They'll be hangin' my wife!

(*Judge Hathorne* enters. *He is in his sixties, a bitter, remorseless Salem judge.*)

Hathorne. How do you dare come roarin' into this court! Are you gone
50 daft, Corey?

Giles. You're not a Boston judge yet, Hathorne. You'll not call me daft!

(*Enter Deputy Governor Danforth and, behind him, Ezekiel Cheever and Parris. On his appearance, silence falls. Danforth is a grave man in his sixties, of some humor and sophistication that does not, however, interfere with an exact loyalty to his position and his cause. He
60 comes down to Giles, who awaits his wrath.*)

Danforth (*looking directly at Giles*). Who is this man?

Parris. Giles Corey, sir, and a more contentious—

Giles (*to Parris*). I am asked the question, and I am old enough to answer it! (*to Danforth, who impresses him and to whom he smiles through his
70 strain*) My name is Corey, sir, Giles Corey. I have six hundred acres, and timber in addition. It is my wife you be condemning now. (*He indicates the courtroom.*)

Danforth. And how do you imagine to help her cause with such contemptuous riot?[2] Now be gone. Your old age alone keeps you out of jail for this.

Giles (*beginning to plead*). They be tellin'
80 lies about my wife, sir, I—

Danforth. Do you take it upon yourself to determine what this court shall believe and what it shall set aside?

---

[2] **contemptuous** (kən-tĕmp′chōō-əs) **riot:** disrespectful, outrageous behavior.

Giles. Your Excellency, we mean no disrespect for—

Danforth. Disrespect indeed! It is disruption, Mister. This is the highest court of the supreme government of this province, do you know it?

90 **Giles** (*beginning to weep*). Your Excellency, I only said she were readin' books, sir, and they come and take her out of my house for—

Danforth (*mystified*). Books! What books?

Giles (*through helpless sobs*). It is my third wife, sir; I never had no wife that be so taken with books, and I thought to find the cause of it, d'y'see, but it were
100 no witch I blamed her for. (*He is openly weeping.*) I have broke charity with the woman, I have broke charity with her. (*He covers his face, ashamed. Danforth is respectfully silent.*)

Hale. Excellency, he claims hard evidence for his wife's defense. I think that in all justice you must—

Danforth. Then let him submit his evidence in proper affidavit. You are
110 certainly aware of our procedure here, Mr. Hale. (*to Herrick*) Clear this room.

Herrick. Come now, Giles. (*He gently pushes Corey out.*)

Francis. We are desperate, sir; we come here three days now and cannot be heard.

Danforth. Who is this man?

Francis. Francis Nurse, Your Excellency.

Hale. His wife's Rebecca that were
120 condemned this morning.

Danforth. Indeed! I am amazed to find you in such uproar. I have only good report of your character, Mr. Nurse.

Hathorne. I think they must both be arrested in contempt, sir.

SCAFFOLDING FOR ELL STUDENTS

Identify Pronoun Referents Explain to students that the noun a pronoun replaces is called its **referent** or **antecedent.**

Tell students to read Giles' dialogue beginning in line 66:

Giles (*to Parris*). I am asked the question, and I am old enough to answer it!

The word "it" at the end of the sentence is a pronoun replacing the word "question." The word "question" is the referent, or antecedent.

Sometimes the referent is not a single word. It may be a short phrase or even an implied idea. Look at lines 75–79:

Danforth....And how do you imagine to help her cause with such contemptuous riot? Your old age alone keeps you out of jail for this.

The pronoun is "this." It refers back to "[causing] a contemptuous riot" or "behaving disrespectfully and outrageously."

ASK STUDENTS to read lines 96–100 and tell what the pronoun "it" ("find the cause of it") in line 99 stands for. *(her avid interest in books)*

Danforth (*to* Francis). Let you write your plea, and in due time I will—

Francis. Excellency, we have proof for your eyes; God forbid you shut them to it. The girls, sir, the girls are frauds.

Danforth. What's that?

Francis. We have proof of it, sir. They are all deceiving you.

(Danforth *is shocked, but studying* Francis.)

Hathorne. This is contempt, sir, contempt!

Danforth. Peace, Judge Hathorne. Do you know who I am, Mr. Nurse?

Francis. I surely do, sir, and I think you must be a wise judge to be what you are.

Danforth. And do you know that near to four hundred are in the jails from Marblehead to Lynn,[3] and upon my signature?

Francis. I—

Danforth. And seventy-two condemned to hang by that signature?

---
[3] **Marblehead . . . Lynn:** two coastal towns in Massachusetts, near Salem.

Francis. Excellency, I never thought to say it to such a weighty judge, but you are deceived.

(*Enter* Giles Corey *from left. All turn to see as he beckons in* Mary Warren *with* Proctor. Mary *is keeping her eyes to the ground;* Proctor *has her elbow as though she were near collapse.*)

Parris (*on seeing her, in shock*). Mary Warren! (*He goes directly to bend close to her face.*) What are you about here?

Proctor (*pressing* Parris *away from her with a gentle but firm motion of protectiveness*). She would speak with the Deputy Governor.

Danforth (*shocked by this, turns to* Herrick). Did you not tell me Mary Warren were sick in bed?

Herrick. She were, Your Honor. When I go to fetch her to the court last week, she said she were sick.

Giles. She has been strivin' with her soul all week, Your Honor; she comes now to tell the truth of this to you.

Danforth. Who is this?

Proctor. John Proctor, sir. Elizabeth Proctor is my wife.

The Crucible: Act Three **507**

CLOSE READ

Analyze Drama Elements  COMMON CORE RL 3, RL 5
(LINES 138–151)

Remind students that **dialogue** can reveal a great deal about a character's personality and motivations.

E CITE TEXT EVIDENCE What does Danforth's dialogue in this section of the scene reveal about his character? Cite text evidence. *(Danforth thinks very highly of himself and believes he is always right and knows best. In lines 138–139, he asks if Francis Nurse "knows who he is." Nurse of course knows who Danforth is, but Danforth is lording his position over Nurse to make a point about status and position.)* What specifically in Francis' response reveals him to be a courageous and upstanding character? *(In lines 149–151, he still challenges Danforth's beliefs, even though Danforth is a "weighty" judge.)*

Analyze Drama Elements  COMMON CORE RL 3, RL 5
(LINES 152–156)

Tell students to look to the **stage directions** for clues about characters' emotional states in a scene. Remind them they may have to make inferences to figure out exactly what a character is feeling.

F ASK STUDENTS to describe what might be motivating Mary to keep her "eyes to the ground" at this point in the scene. *(Mary is likely feeling shame and fear about testifying.)*

Analyze Drama Elements COMMON CORE RL 3, RL 5

(LINES 176–199)

Explain to students that the main character around whom most of the action centers is the **protagonist.** The reader often identifies with and feels sympathy for the protagonist. Explain that the character who opposes the protagonist is the **antagonist.**

G CITE TEXT EVIDENCE Ask students to explain who is the protagonist and who is the antagonist in these lines. Have students cite text evidence to support their answers. *(Proctor is the protagonist. The reader sympathizes with his attempt to tell the truth to the court and to free the women who have been wrongfully charged. Parris is the antagonist. In lines 176–177, he tells the judge that Proctor is not to be trusted, and in lines 198–199 he says that Proctor has come to overthrow the court.)*

Analyze Drama Elements COMMON CORE RL 3, RL 5

(LINES 245–253)

Remind students to look at **stage directions** for clues to characters' emotional states.

H ASK STUDENTS to tell why they think Danforth's eyes narrow when he is questioning Proctor. *(Danforth is highly suspicious of Proctor's intentions and the veracity of Mary's deposition; at this moment, Danforth is trying to figure out Proctor's true aim. If Proctor were to be right, Danforth's position and authority—not to mention the authority of the court itself—could be called into question.)* Then ask students what the stage directions for Proctor in line 252 reveal about Proctor. *(Proctor has a hard time concealing the fact that he doesn't believe in the court's mission.)*

Parris. Beware this man, Your Excellency, this man is mischief.

Hale (*excitedly*). I think you must hear the girl, sir, she—

180 **Danforth** (*who has become very interested in* Mary Warren *and only raises a hand toward* Hale). Peace. What would you tell us, Mary Warren?

(Proctor *looks at her, but she cannot speak.*)

Proctor. She never saw no spirits, sir.

Danforth (*with great alarm and surprise, to* Mary). Never saw no spirits!

Giles (*eagerly*). Never.

190 **Proctor** (*reaching into his jacket*). She has signed a deposition, sir—

Danforth (*instantly*). No, no, I accept no depositions. (*He is rapidly calculating this; he turns from her to* Proctor.) Tell me, Mr. Proctor, have you given out this story in the village?

Proctor. We have not.

Parris. They've come to overthrow the court, sir! This man is—

200 **Danforth.** I pray you, Mr. Parris. Do you know, Mr. Proctor, that the entire contention of the state in these trials is that the voice of Heaven is speaking through the children?

Proctor. I know that, sir.

Danforth (*thinks, staring at* Proctor, *then turns to* Mary Warren). And you, Mary Warren, how came you to cry out people for sending their spirits
210 against you?

Mary Warren. It were pretense, sir.

Danforth. I cannot hear you.

Proctor. It were pretense, she says.

Danforth. Ah? And the other girls? Susanna Walcott, and—the others? They are also pretending?

Mary Warren. Aye, sir.

Danforth (*wide-eyed*). Indeed. (*Pause. He is baffled by this. He turns to study*
220 Proctor's *face.*)

Parris (*in a sweat*). Excellency, you surely cannot think to let so vile a lie be spread in open court!

Danforth. Indeed not, but it strike hard upon me that she will dare come here with such a tale. Now, Mr. Proctor, before I decide whether I shall hear you or not, it is my duty to tell you this. We burn a hot fire here; it melts down all
230 concealment.

Proctor. I know that, sir.

Danforth. Let me continue. I understand well, a husband's tenderness may drive him to extravagance in defense of a wife. Are you certain in your conscience, Mister, that your evidence is the truth?

Proctor. It is. And you will surely know it.

240 **Danforth.** And you thought to declare this revelation in the open court before the public?

Proctor. I thought I would, aye—with your permission.

Danforth (*his eyes narrowing*). Now, sir, what is your purpose in so doing?

Proctor. Why, I—I would free my wife, sir.

Danforth. There lurks nowhere in your
250 heart, nor hidden in your spirit, any desire to undermine this court?

Proctor (*with the faintest faltering*). Why, no, sir.

Cheever (*clears his throat, awakening*). I—Your Excellency.

WHEN STUDENTS STRUGGLE...

Introduce students to the concept of **domain-specific words**. Explain that domain-specific words are technical terms that have to do with specialized topics. For example, on the previous page students encountered the domain-specific term "contempt of court," which comes from the field of law. Often the meaning of a term can be inferred from context, but tell students that if they are still unsure about the meaning of a term, they should look it up in a dictionary.

ASK STUDENTS to reread the dialogue from lines 190–194 and use context to tell what a "deposition" is. Have them discuss their ideas with a partner. Ask them to keep a list of legal terms as they read.

Danforth. Mr. Cheever.

Cheever. I think it be my duty, sir— (*kindly, to* Proctor) You'll not deny it, John. (*to* Danforth) When we come to
260 take his wife, he damned the court and ripped your warrant.

Parris. Now you have it!

Danforth. He did that, Mr. Hale?

Hale (*takes a breath*). Aye, he did.

Proctor. It were a temper, sir. I knew not what I did.

Danforth (*studying him*). Mr. Proctor.

Proctor. Aye, sir.

Danforth (*straight into his eyes*). Have
270 you ever seen the Devil?

Proctor. No, sir.

Danforth. You are in all respects a Gospel Christian?

Proctor. I am, sir.

Parris. Such a Christian that will not come to church but once in a month!

Danforth (*restrained—he is curious*). Not come to church?

Proctor. I—I have no love for Mr.
280 Parris. It is no secret. But God I surely love.

Cheever. He plow on Sunday, sir.

Danforth. Plow on Sunday!

Cheever (*apologetically*). I think it be evidence, John. I am an official of the court, I cannot keep it.

Proctor. I—I have once or twice plowed on Sunday. I have three children, sir, and until last year my land give little.

290 **Giles.** You'll find other Christians that do plow on Sunday if the truth be known.

Hale. Your Honor, I cannot think you may judge the man on such evidence.

Danforth. I judge nothing. (*Pause. He keeps watching* Proctor, *who tries to meet his gaze.*) I tell you straight, Mister—I have seen marvels in this court. I have seen people choked before my eyes by
300 spirits; I have seen them stuck by pins and slashed by daggers. I have until this moment not the slightest reason to suspect that the children may be deceiving me. Do you understand my meaning?

Proctor. Excellency, does it not strike upon you that so many of these women have lived so long with such upright reputation, and—

310 **Parris.** Do you read the Gospel, Mr. Proctor?

Proctor. I read the Gospel.

Parris. I think not, or you should surely know that Cain were an upright man, and yet he did kill Abel.[4]

Proctor. Aye, God tells us that. (*to* Danforth) But who tells us Rebecca Nurse murdered seven babies by sending out her spirit on them? It is the
320 children only, and this one will swear she lied to you.

(Danforth *considers, then beckons* Hathorne *to him.* Hathorne *leans in, and he speaks in his ear.* Hathorne *nods.*)

Hathorne. Aye, she's the one.

Danforth. Mr. Proctor, this morning, your wife send me a claim in which she states that she is pregnant now.

330 **Proctor.** My wife pregnant!

Danforth. There be no sign of it—we have examined her body.

---

[4] **Cain . . . Abel:** According to the Book of Genesis in the Bible, Cain and Abel were the sons of Adam and Eve, the first humans.

The Crucible: Act Three **509**

CLOSE READ

Analyze Drama Elements
COMMON CORE RL 3, RL 5
(LINES 256–294)

Remind students that both **dialogue** and **stage directions** contribute to a sense of character.

Ⓘ CITE TEXT EVIDENCE Ask students to review the dialogue of Cheever, Parris, and Hale. Who is aligned with Danforth? Who is on Proctor's side? How can you tell? Cite specifics. (*Cheever seems torn because he turns to Proctor in a "kind" way [line 258], yet he goes on to tell an incriminating story about Proctor to Danforth. Cheever seems on the side of the law, which is Danforth's side. Parris is definitely on Danforth's side; he is no friend of Proctor's and has not been since the beginning of the play. His reaction in line 262 confirms this; he seems to enjoy Proctor being caught. Hale has been on Proctor's side for the most part, but is compelled to tell the truth that Proctor tore up the warrant. However, the stage direction in line 264—Hale takes a breath—shows that Hale does not take any pleasure in supporting Cheever's story, which injures Proctor.*)

Analyze Drama Elements
COMMON CORE RL 3, RL 5
(LINES 316–329)

Remind students that a character's motivations can often be inferred from **dialogue**.

Ⓙ ASK STUDENTS to infer Danforth's reason for telling Proctor that his wife is pregnant in response to Proctor's claim that Mary will admit to lying to the court. (*Danforth does not want to hear Mary's testimony. By mentioning Elizabeth's claim of pregnancy, he may hope to divert Proctor's attention from his goal of getting Mary to testify.*)

SCAFFOLDING FOR ELL STUDENTS

Understand Punctuation Ask students to read the dialogue that begins in line 257 and notice the long dash that appears after the word "sir." Explain to students that this is a special kind of dash called an **em-dash**. Em-dashes are used to show a break in thought or to emphasize a thought.

ASK STUDENTS to look at this page and find dialogue that contains em-dashes. (*lines 279, 287, 297, and 309*) Have them read the sentences aloud and check for fluency. Be sure they pause where the em-dash appears in the sentence.

Analyze Drama Elements   COMMON CORE RL 3, RL 5

(LINE 352)

Tell students that sometimes aspects of a character can be revealed in just one line of **dialogue**.

K **ASK STUDENTS** what Proctor's line reveals about his character. *(Even after it is revealed that Elizabeth is pregnant and Danforth promises to keep her alive for a year until she delivers the baby, Proctor will not drop his charge. Proctor is revealed as someone who will not compromise what he believes to be the truth under any circumstances.)*

Analyze Drama Elements   COMMON CORE RL 3, RL 5

(LINES 356–413)

Remind students to consider the motivations behind characters' **dialogue**.

L **ASK STUDENTS** to explain why Parris is so insistent in his belief that Proctor wishes to overthrow the court. *(Parris is concerned that if Danforth takes Proctor's information seriously, the charges against the women will be dropped. By casting doubt on Proctor's motives, he hopes to keep Danforth from believing what Proctor says.)*

Proctor. But if she say she is pregnant, then she must be! That woman will never lie, Mr. Danforth.

Danforth. She will not?

Proctor. Never, sir, never.

Danforth. We have thought it too convenient to be credited. However, if I
340 should tell you now that I will let her be kept another month; and if she begin to show her natural signs, you shall have her living yet another year until she is delivered—what say you to that? (John Proctor *is struck silent.*) Come now. You say your only purpose is to save your wife. Good, then, she is saved at least this year, and a year is long. What say you, sir? It is done now. (*In conflict,*
350 Proctor *glances at* Francis *and* Giles.) Will you drop this charge?

Proctor. I—I think I cannot.

Danforth (*now an almost imperceptible hardness in his voice*). Then your purpose is somewhat larger.

Parris. He's come to overthrow this court, Your Honor!

Proctor. These are my friends. Their wives are also accused—
360 **Danforth** (*with a sudden briskness of manner*). I judge you not, sir. I am ready to hear your evidence.

Proctor. I come not to hurt the court; I only—

Danforth (*cutting him off*). Marshal, go into the court and bid Judge Stoughton and Judge Sewall declare recess for one hour. And let them go to the tavern, if they will. All witnesses and prisoners
370 are to be kept in the building.

Herrick. Aye, sir. (*very deferentially*) If I may say it, sir, I know this man all my life. It is a good man, sir.

Danforth (*It is the reflection on himself he resents*). I am sure of it, Marshal. (Herrick *nods, then goes out.*) Now, what deposition do you have for us, Mr. Proctor? And I beg you be clear, open as the sky, and honest.

380 **Proctor** (*as he takes out several papers*). I am no lawyer, so I'll—

Danforth. The pure in heart need no lawyers. Proceed as you will.

Proctor (*handing* Danforth *a paper*). Will you read this first, sir? It's a sort of testament. The people signing it declare their good opinion of Rebecca, and my wife, and Martha Corey. (Danforth *looks down at the paper.*)

390 **Parris** (*to enlist* Danforth's *sarcasm*). Their good opinion! (*But* Danforth *goes on reading, and* Proctor *is heartened.*)

Proctor. These are all landholding farmers, members of the church. (*delicately, trying to point out a paragraph*) If you'll notice, sir—they've known the women many years and never saw no sign they had dealings with the Devil.

400 (Parris *nervously moves over and reads over* Danforth's *shoulder.*)

Danforth (*glancing down a long list*). How many names are here?

Francis. Ninety-one, Your Excellency.

Parris (*sweating*). These people should be summoned. (Danforth *looks up at him questioningly.*) For questioning.

Francis (*trembling with anger*). Mr. Danforth, I gave them all my word no
410 harm would come to them for signing this.

Parris. This is a clear attack upon the court!

SCAFFOLDING FOR ELL STUDENTS

Understand Adverbs Tell students that **adverbs** modify verbs, adjectives, or other adverbs. They are used to show time, manner, place, and degree. They usually answer the question "how." Many adverbs end in the letters -*ly*. Point out line 371:

Herrick. Aye, sir. (*very deferentially*)

In this example, *deferentially* is an adverb. It ends in -*ly* and it tells how Herrick spoke.

Tell students that not all adverbs end in -*ly*. Words like *more, less, often,* and *always* are also adverbs.

ASK STUDENTS to look for an adverb in lines 400–401 and tell what word it modifies. *(nervously; moves)*

Hale (*to Parris, trying to contain himself*). Is every defense an attack upon the court? Can no one—?

Parris. All innocent and Christian people are happy for the courts in Salem! These people are gloomy for it. (*to Danforth directly*) And I think you will want to know, from each and every one of them, what discontents them with you!

Hathorne. I think they ought to be examined, sir.

Danforth. It is not necessarily an attack, I think. Yet—

Francis. These are all covenanted Christians, sir.

430 **Danforth.** Then I am sure they may have nothing to fear. (*hands Cheever the paper*) Mr. Cheever, have warrants drawn for all of these—arrest for examination. (*to Proctor*) Now, Mister, what other information do you have for us? (*Francis is still standing, horrified.*) You may sit, Mr. Nurse.

Francis. I have brought trouble on these people; I have—

440 **Danforth.** No, old man, you have not hurt these people if they are of good conscience. But you must understand, sir, that a person is either with this court or he must be counted against it, there be no road between. This is a sharp time, now, a precise time—we live no longer in the dusky afternoon when evil mixed itself with good and befuddled the world. Now, by God's 450 grace, the shining sun is up, and them that fear not light will surely praise it. I hope you will be one of those. (*Mary Warren suddenly sobs.*) She's not hearty,[5] I see.

---

[5] **hearty:** well.

Proctor. No, she's not, sir. (*to Mary, bending to her, holding her hand, quietly*) Now remember what the angel Raphael said to the boy Tobias.[6] Remember it.

Mary Warren (*hardly audible*). Aye.

460 **Proctor.** "Do that which is good, and no harm shall come to thee."

Mary Warren. Aye.

Danforth. Come, man, we wait you. (*Marshal Herrick returns, and takes his post at the door.*)

Giles. John, my deposition, give him mine.

Proctor. Aye. (*He hands Danforth another paper.*) This is Mr. Corey's 470 deposition.

Danforth. Oh? (*He looks down at it. Now Hathorne comes behind him and reads with him.*)

Hathorne (*suspiciously*). What lawyer drew this, Corey?

Giles. You know I never hired a lawyer in my life, Hathorne.

Danforth (*finishing the reading*). It is very well phrased. My compliments. Mr. 480 Parris, if Mr. Putnam is in the court, will you bring him in? (*Hathorne takes the deposition, and walks to the window with it. Parris goes into the court.*) You have no legal training, Mr. Corey?

Giles (*very pleased*). I have the best, sir—I am thirty-three time in court in my life. And always plaintiff, too.

Danforth. Oh, then you're much put-upon.

490 **Giles.** I am never put-upon; I know my rights, sir, and I will have them. You

---

[6] **what the angel said . . . Tobias:** In the Book of Tobit in the Apocrypha, Tobit's son Tobias cured his father's blindness with the help of the angel Raphael.

The Crucible: Act Three **511**

CLOSE READ

Analyze Drama Elements

(LINES 417–423)

Remind students to infer characters' motivation from their **dialogue.**

M ASK STUDENTS what Parris hopes to achieve by stating that all "innocent and Christian" people are happy for the courts in Salem? (*Parris hopes to convince Danforth that anyone who attempts to defend themselves or their loved ones before the court must be guilty and not Christian.*)

Analyze Drama Elements

(LINES 440–454)

Remind students that a character's **dialogue** can reflect the playwright's theme.

N ASK STUDENTS how Danforth's speech might reflect Miller's theme. (*Danforth's claim that "the shining sun is up" is ironic, since the court is being deceived and is actually committing a grave injustice. Danforth's black-and-white thinking and his insistence on his own ability to separate good from evil blind him to reality. This reflects Miller's theme that when people lose touch with their own fallibility they do terrible things.*)

WHEN STUDENTS STRUGGLE...

Use Danforth's speech in lines 440–451 to help students develop fluency. Remind students what they know of Danforth's character so far: that he is inflexible and has a high opinion of himself. Model reading the speech for students.

ASK STUDENTS to work in small groups to read the speech aloud. Each student should take a turn reading the entire speech. When students have finished reading, you may wish to invite volunteers to read the speech to the class.

TEACH

CLOSE READ

Analyze Drama Elements

COMMON CORE RL 3, RL 5

(LINES 497–541)

Remind students that **foils** are minor characters that present a high contrast to other more major characters. In so doing, they highlight the other characters' traits. Discuss with students which character in this act might be compared with Giles. Elicit the answer that Proctor and Giles might be compared, since both men are attempting to free their wives and convince the court that all the charges of witchcraft are false.

◎ ASK STUDENTS to tell how Giles serves as a foil for Proctor. *(While Giles, like Proctor, courageously stands up to the court, he does so in a bumbling, coarse way that makes him almost humorous. Giles' antics in the courtroom highlight Proctor's dignity.)*

know, your father tried a case of mine—might be thirty-five year ago, I think.

Danforth. Indeed.

Giles. He never spoke to you of it?

Danforth. No, I cannot recall it.

Giles. That's strange, he give me nine pound damages. He were a fair judge, your father. Y'see, I had a white mare
500 that time, and this fellow come to borrow the mare—(*Enter* Parris *with* Thomas Putnam. *When he sees* Putnam, Giles' *ease goes; he is hard.*) Aye, there he is.

Danforth. Mr. Putnam, I have here an accusation by Mr. Corey against you. He states that you coldly prompted your daughter to cry witchery upon George Jacobs that is now in jail.

510 **Putnam.** It is a lie.

Danforth (*turning to* Giles). Mr. Putnam states your charge is a lie. What say you to that?

Giles (*furious, his fists clenched*). A fart on Thomas Putnam, that is what I say to that!

Danforth. What proof do you submit for your charge, sir?

Giles. My proof is there! (*pointing to*
520 *the paper*) If Jacobs hangs for a witch he forfeit up his property—that's law! And there is none but Putnam with the coin to buy so great a piece. This man is killing his neighbors for their land!

Danforth. But proof, sir, proof.

Giles (*pointing at his deposition*). The proof is there! I have it from an honest man who heard Putnam say it! The day his daughter cried out on Jacobs, he said
530 she'd given him a fair gift of land.

Hathorne. And the name of this man?

Giles (*taken aback*). What name?

Hathorne. The man that give you this information.

Giles (*hesitates, then*). Why, I—I cannot give you his name.

Hathorne. And why not?

Image Credits: ©spxChrome/E+/Getty Images

512 Collection 6

SCAFFOLDING FOR ELL STUDENTS

Analyze Suffixes Review the definition of *suffixes* with students and introduce the suffix *-ery*. Explain that *-ery* is added to words in order to form nouns of these kinds:

- a craft, trade, or practice, as in *cookery*
- a place, as in *bakery*
- a collection, class, or group, as in *shrubbery*
- a characteristic of something, as in *snobbery*

ASK STUDENTS to find the word *witchery* in line 508 and read the entire sentence aloud. Ask students what the word means. *(the practice of witchcraft)* As students read, encourage them to point out nouns ending in *-ery*.

Giles (*hesitates, then bursts out*). You 540 know well why not! He'll lay in jail if I give his name!

Hathorne. This is contempt of the court, Mr. Danforth!

Danforth (*to avoid that*). You will surely tell us the name.

Giles. I will not give you no name. I mentioned my wife's name once and I'll burn in hell long enough for that. I stand mute.

550 **Danforth.** In that case, I have no choice but to arrest you for contempt of this court, do you know that?

Giles. This is a hearing; you cannot clap me for contempt of a hearing.

Danforth. Oh, it is a proper lawyer![7] Do you wish me to declare the court in full session here? Or will you give me good reply?

Giles (*faltering*). I cannot give you no 560 name, sir, I cannot.

Danforth. You are a foolish old man. Mr. Cheever, begin the record. The court is now in session. I ask you, Mr. Corey—

Proctor (*breaking in*). Your Honor—he has the story in confidence, sir, and he—

Parris. The Devil lives on such confidences! (*to* Danforth) Without 570 confidences there could be no conspiracy, Your Honor!

Hathorne. I think it must be broken, sir.

Danforth (*to* Giles). Old man, if your informant tells the truth let him come here openly like a decent man. But if he hide in anonymity I must know why. Now sir, the government and central church demand of you the name of him

---

[7] **Oh . . . lawyer:** Oh, he thinks he is a real lawyer.

---

who reported Mr. Thomas Putnam a 580 common murderer.

Hale. Excellency—

Danforth. Mr. Hale.

Hale. We cannot blink it more. There is a prodigious fear of this court in the country—

Danforth. Then there is a prodigious guilt in the country. Are *you* afraid to be questioned here?

Hale. I may only fear the Lord, sir, but 590 there is fear in the country nevertheless.

Danforth (*angered now*). Reproach me not with the fear in the country; there is fear in the country because there is a moving[8] plot to topple Christ in the country!

Hale. But it does not follow that everyone accused is part of it.

Danforth. No uncorrupted man may fear this court, Mr. Hale! None! (*to* 600 Giles) You are under arrest in contempt of this court. Now sit you down and take counsel with yourself, or you will be set in the jail until you decide to answer all questions.

(Giles Corey *makes a rush for* Putnam. Proctor *lunges and holds him.*)

Proctor. No, Giles!

Giles (*over* Proctor's *shoulder at* Putnam). I'll cut your throat, Putnam, 610 I'll kill you yet!

Proctor (*forcing him into a chair*). Peace, Giles, peace. (*releasing him*) We'll prove ourselves. Now we will. (*He starts to turn to* Danforth.)

Giles. Say nothin' more, John. (*pointing at* Danforth) He's only playin' you! He means to hang us all!

(Mary Warren *bursts into sobs.*)

---

[8] **moving:** active.

Analyze Drama Elements COMMON CORE RL 3, RL 5
(LINES 539–580)

Remind students that a plot **complication** is a problem that makes the central conflict more difficult to resolve.

 **ASK STUDENTS** to explain how the judges' insistence that Giles name the man who can support his story about Putnam qualifies as a plot complication. (*Giles is in a quandary; on the one hand he needs this man's deposition to prove his wife's innocence, and yet if he offers it, that man will go to jail. This event makes the central conflict—the veracity of the accusations of witchcraft—harder to resolve because it demonstrates that people are afraid to come forward and tell what they know.*)

Analyze Drama Elements COMMON CORE RL 3, RL 5
(LINES 605–618)

Tell students that one of the most important things Miller's **stage directions** do is to describe the behavior of the characters. Sometimes this behavior can impact the mood of the scene.

 **ASK STUDENTS** to reread lines 605–618, paying close attention to the stage directions. Ask students to tell what the stage directions describe and what mood they help set. (*The stage directions in this part of the scene are very active; Miller uses words like "rush," "lunge," and "forcing." The mood of the scene at this point is very charged and exciting as the stage directions describe Giles' attempt to fight Putnam and Proctor's effort to restrain him.*)

TO CHALLENGE STUDENTS . . .

Conduct Research Discuss with students Miller's unsympathetic portrayal of Judge Danforth. Ask them how much of the portrayal they think is historically accurate and how much is Miller's attempt to convey his theme.

ASK STUDENTS to conduct Internet research on Thomas Danforth. Then have students meet in small groups to share their findings. Finally, have the groups meet together to summarize what they have learned.

Analyze Drama Elements COMMON CORE RL 3, RL 5

(LINES 621–644)

Remind students that the main character of a work of literature is called the **protagonist.** Most of the action of the play focuses on and around the protagonist.

R **ASK STUDENTS** to explain why Proctor is considered the protagonist of *The Crucible*. Have them consider the main events of the plot so far and analyze their connections to Proctor. *(Proctor is at the center of the plot of the play; the accusations of witchcraft are made by Abigail, a maid with whom Proctor had an affair and whom Elizabeth Proctor fired from their service; Proctor's wife Elizabeth is now accused and arrested; Proctor is leading the opposition to the witch hunt.)*

Analyze Drama Elements COMMON CORE RL 3, RL 5

(LINES 673–697)

Remind students that a play's **dialogue** can express the author's underlying message.

S **ASK STUDENTS** to read Danforth's speech closely and pay attention to what he says about the need for lawyers in this case. What do you think is the playwright's point of view about the need for lawyers to represent people's interests? *(Danforth believes that lawyers would be useless in this case because witchcraft is "an invisible crime" and can be solely proven by "her victims." His argument exposes the patent unfairness of the entire case; Miller believes that people have protections from an over-reaching court.)*

Danforth. This is a court of law, Mister. I'll have no effrontery here!

Proctor. Forgive him, sir, for his old age. Peace, Giles, we'll prove it all now. (*He lifts up Mary's chin.*) You cannot weep, Mary. Remember the angel, what he say to the boy. Hold to it, now; there is your rock. (Mary *quiets. He takes out a paper, and turns to* Danforth.) This is Mary Warren's deposition. I—I would ask you remember, sir, while you read it, that until two week ago she were no different than the other children are today. (*He is speaking reasonably, restraining all his fears, his anger, his anxiety.*) You saw her scream, she howled, she swore familiar spirits choked her; she even testified that Satan, in the form of women now in jail, tried to win her soul away, and then when she refused—

Danforth. We know all this.

Proctor. Aye, sir. She swears now that she never saw Satan; nor any spirit, vague or clear, that Satan may have sent to hurt her. And she declares her friends are lying now.

(Proctor *starts to hand* Danforth *the deposition, and* Hale *comes up to* Danforth *in a trembling state.*)

Hale. Excellency, a moment. I think this goes to the heart of the matter.

Danforth (*with deep misgivings*). It surely does.

Hale. I cannot say he is an honest man; I know him little. But in all justice, sir, a claim so weighty cannot be argued by a farmer. In God's name, sir, stop here; send him home and let him come again with a lawyer—

Danforth (*patiently*). Now look you, Mr. Hale—

Hale. Excellency, I have signed seventy-two death warrants; I am a minister of the Lord, and I dare not take a life

without there be a proof so immaculate no slightest qualm of conscience may doubt it.

Danforth. Mr. Hale, you surely do not doubt my justice.

Hale. I have this morning signed away the soul of Rebecca Nurse, Your Honor. I'll not conceal it, my hand shakes yet as with a wound! I pray you, sir, this argument let lawyers present to you.

Danforth. Mr. Hale, believe me; for a man of such terrible learning you are most bewildered—I hope you will forgive me. I have been thirty-two year at the bar, sir, and I should be confounded were I called upon to defend these people. Let you consider, now—(*to* Proctor *and the others*) And I bid you all do likewise. In an ordinary crime, how does one defend the accused? One calls up witnesses to prove his innocence. But witchcraft is *ipso facto*,[9] on its face and by its nature, an invisible crime, is it not? Therefore, who may possibly be witness to it? The witch and the victim. None other. Now we cannot hope the witch will accuse herself; granted? Therefore, we must rely upon her victims—and they do testify, the children certainly do testify. As for the witches, none will deny that we are most eager for all their confessions. Therefore, what is left for a lawyer to bring out? I think I have made my point. Have I not?

Hale. But this child claims the girls are not truthful, and if they are not—

Danforth. That is precisely what I am about to consider, sir. What more may you ask of me? Unless you doubt my probity?[10]

---

[9] *ipso facto* (**Latin**): by that very fact.
[10] **doubt my probity:** question my integrity.

SCAFFOLDING FOR ELL STUDENTS

Understand Idioms Remind students that an idiom is a phrase whose meaning is not obvious from the literal meaning of its words. Point out the phrase "at the bar" in line 677 and explain that the place where the accused used to stand in a court of law was called the bar. The phrase "at the bar" came to mean "involved in the practice of law." Tell students that paying attention to an idiom's context will help them guess its meaning.

ASK STUDENTS to identify the idiom in lines 648–649 and guess what it means. *(the heart of the matter, the most important part of the business)*

Hale (*defeated*). I surely do not, sir. Let you consider it, then.

Danforth. And let you put your heart to rest. Her deposition, Mr. Proctor.

710 (*Proctor hands it to him. Hathorne rises, goes beside Danforth, and starts reading. Parris comes to his other side. Danforth looks at John Proctor, then proceeds to read. Hale gets up, finds position near the judge, reads too. Proctor glances at Giles. Francis prays silently, hands pressed together. Cheever waits placidly, the sublime official, dutiful. Mary Warren sobs once. John Proctor touches her head reassuringly. Presently Danforth lifts his eyes, stands*

720 *up, takes out a kerchief and blows his nose. The others stand aside as he moves in thought toward the window.*)

Parris (*hardly able to contain his anger and fear*). I should like to question—

Danforth (*his first real outburst, in which his contempt for Parris is clear*). Mr. Parris, I bid you be silent! (*He stands in silence, looking out the window. Now, having established that he will*

730 *set the gait.*) Mr. Cheever, will you go into the court and bring the children here? (*Cheever gets up and goes out upstage.* Danforth *now turns to* Mary.) Mary Warren, how came you to this turnabout? Has Mr. Proctor threatened you for this deposition?

Mary Warren. No, sir.

Danforth. Has he ever threatened you?

Mary Warren (*weaker*). No, sir.

740 **Danforth** (*sensing a weakening*). Has he threatened you?

Mary Warren. No, sir.

Danforth. Then you tell me that you sat in my court, callously lying, when you knew that people would hang by your

evidence? (*She does not answer.*) Answer me!

Mary Warren (*almost inaudibly*). I did, sir.

750 **Danforth.** How were you instructed in your life? Do you not know that God damns all liars? (*She cannot speak.*) Or is it now that you lie?

Mary Warren. No, sir—I am with God now.

Danforth. You are with God now.

Mary Warren. Aye, sir.

Danforth (*containing himself*). I will tell you this—you are either lying now,

760 or you were lying in the court, and in either case you have committed perjury and you will go to jail for it. You cannot lightly say you lied, Mary. Do you know that?

Mary Warren. I cannot lie no more. I am with God, I am with God.

(*But she breaks into sobs at the thought of it, and the right door opens, and enter* Susanna Walcott, Mercy Lewis, Betty

770 Parris, *and finally* Abigail. Cheever *comes to* Danforth.)

Cheever. Ruth Putnam's not in the court, sir, nor the other children.

Danforth. These will be sufficient. Sit you down, children. (*Silently they sit.*) Your friend, Mary Warren, has given us a deposition. In which she swears that she never saw familiar spirits, apparitions, nor any manifest of the

780 Devil. She claims as well that none of you have seen these things either. (*slight pause*) Now, children, this is a court of law. The law, based upon the Bible, and the Bible, writ by Almighty God, forbid the practice of witchcraft, and describe death as the penalty thereof. But likewise, children, the law and Bible damn all bearers of false witness.

The Crucible: Act Three **515**

CLOSE READ

Analyze Drama Elements COMMON CORE RL 3, RL 5

(LINES 708–730)

Tell students that sometimes they will find long **stage directions** that describe multiple events. These stage directions often advance the plot by revealing the characters' feelings and attitudes.

T **CITE TEXT EVIDENCE** Ask students to reread lines 708–730 and tell what they reveal about the feelings and attitudes of each of the characters. Have students support their answers with evidence from the text. (*Danforth is seriously considering what he has read, because he "moves in thought" to the window and becomes angry when Parris tries to interrupt his reflections. Proctor is concerned for Mary because he touches her head when she sobs. Francis is hoping fervently that Danforth will believe Mary; he is praying silently. Cheever is uninterested in Mary's testimony: he waits "placidly."*)

TO CHALLENGE STUDENTS...

Direct a Scene What difference does a director make? Ask students to reread lines 708–730. Tell them that although most of this section has no dialogue, it still requires the steady hand of a director.

ASK STUDENTS to work in small groups in which one student is the director and the other students are the actors. Have the director direct the scene, telling the actors where and when to position themselves. Also tell them to direct their actors' behavior—what to do and how to do it (quickly, slowly, loudly, softly, and so forth). Showcase the work of all groups and lead a class discussion on how the scenes differed based on the director's interpretation of the text.

TEACH

CLOSE READ

Analyze Drama Elements    RL 3, RL 5

(LINES 799–830)

Remind students that the character in a piece of literature that opposes the protagonist is called the **antagonist.** Usually, the problem that exists between the protagonist and the antagonist develops into the major conflict.

U CITE TEXT EVIDENCE Ask students to explain why Abigail can be considered an antagonist in *The Crucible.* What specific events or dialogue in this scene support this idea? *(Abigail is an antagonist because since the beginning of the play, she has been in opposition to Proctor: she tries to seduce him and he rejects her; she reveals to Proctor that she was just dancing in the woods, but when he tries to expose this to the judges, she denies it; Abigail accuses Elizabeth of witchcraft. In this scene, her opposition to Proctor is explicit; she sticks to her story that Elizabeth Proctor's unholy spirit stabbed her. She accuses Mary Warren of lying, putting Proctor at risk.)*

Analyze Drama Elements   COMMON CORE RL 3, RL 5

(LINES 831–840)

Tell students that minor characters add variety and texture to a scene.

V ASK STUDENTS to explain why Hathorne continues to oppose Proctor. Have them consider what they have already learned about the character in this act, what his dialogue in lines 839–840 tells them, and what he has at stake. *(On page 506, Hathorne is introduced as "bitter and remorseless." As the presiding judge, he is deeply invested in showing that the accusations are real and the trials are legitimate; his own reputation is at stake. His devotion to his job is so deep that he is blinded to any possibility that he might be wrong or deceived. In Proctor's case, Hathorne stands to gain in social and professional status if the accusations against Elizabeth and the other women are proven true.)*

516 Collection 6

(slight pause) Now then. It does not
790 escape me that this deposition may be
devised to blind us; it may well be that
Mary Warren has been conquered by
Satan, who sends her here to distract
our sacred purpose. If so, her neck will
break for it. But if she speak true, I bid
you now drop your guile and confess
your pretense, for a quick confession
will go easier with you. *(pause)* Abigail
Williams, rise. (Abigail *slowly rises.*) Is
800 there any truth in this?

Abigail. No, sir.

Danforth *(thinks, glances at* Mary, *then
back to* Abigail*).* Children, a very auger
bit[11] will now be turned into your souls
until your honesty is proved. Will either
of you change your positions now, or do
you force me to hard questioning?

Abigail. I have naught to change, sir.
She lies.

810 **Danforth** *(to* Mary*).* You would still go
on with this?

Mary Warren *(faintly).* Aye, sir.

Danforth *(turning to* Abigail*).* A poppet
were discovered in Mr. Proctor's house,
stabbed by a needle. Mary Warren
claims that you sat beside her in the
court when she made it, and that you
saw her make it and witnessed how she
herself stuck her needle into it for safe-
820 keeping. What say you to that?

Abigail *(with a slight note of
indignation).* It is a lie, sir.

Danforth *(after a slight pause).* While
you worked for Mr. Proctor, did you see
poppets in that house?

Abigail. Goody Proctor always kept
poppets.

---
[11] **auger** (ô′gər) **bit:** drill.

516 Collection 6

Proctor. Your Honor, my wife never
kept no poppets. Mary Warren
830 confesses it was her poppet.

Cheever. Your Excellency.

Danforth. Mr. Cheever.

Cheever. When I spoke with Goody
Proctor in that house, she said she never
kept no poppets. But she said she did
keep poppets when she were a girl.

Proctor. She has not been a girl these
fifteen years, Your Honor.

Hathorne. But a poppet will keep
840 fifteen years, will it not?

Proctor. It will keep if it is kept, but
Mary Warren swears she never saw no
poppets in my house, nor anyone else.

Parris. Why could there not have been
poppets hid where no one ever saw
them?

Proctor *(furious).* There might also be
a dragon with five legs in my house, but
no one has ever seen it.

850 **Parris.** We are here, Your Honor,
precisely to discover what no one has
ever seen.

Proctor. Mr. Danforth, what profit this
girl to turn herself about? What may
Mary Warren gain but hard questioning
and worse?

Danforth. You are charging Abigail
Williams with a marvelous cool plot to
murder, do you understand that?

860 **Proctor.** I do, sir. I believe she means to
murder.

Danforth *(pointing at* Abigail,
incredulously). This child would murder
your wife?

Proctor. It is not a child. Now hear me,
sir. In the sight of the congregation
she were twice this year put out of
this meetin' house for laughter during
prayer.

SCAFFOLDING FOR ELL STUDENTS

Understand Archaic Language Explain to students that *The Crucible* features old-fashioned language that Miller uses to help establish time and place. For example, in line 795, Danforth says, "but if she speak true . . ." No one would say this today; they would probably say, "but if she speaks the truth . . ." Words and phrases like these that suggest a time long ago are called **archaisms.**

ASK STUDENTS to find as many archaisms as they can on this page and, with a partner, rewrite them in modern language. Some sample answers are below.

- Line 808: *I have naught to change, sir. (I have nothing to change, sir.)*
- Lines 813–814: *A poppet were discovered . . . (A doll was discovered . . .)*
- Line 820: *What say you to that? (What do you say to that?)*

870 **Danforth** (*shocked, turning to* Abigail). What's this? Laughter during—!

Parris. Excellency, she were under Tituba's power at that time, but she is solemn now.

Giles. Aye, now she is solemn and goes to hang people!

Danforth. Quiet, man.

Hathorne. Surely it have no bearing on the question, sir. He charges
880 contemplation of murder.

Danforth. Aye. (*He studies* Abigail *for a moment, then.*) Continue, Mr. Proctor.

Proctor. Mary. Now tell the Governor how you danced in the woods.

Parris (*instantly*). Excellency, since I come to Salem this man is blackening my name. He—

Danforth. In a moment, sir. (*to* Mary Warren, *sternly, and surprised*) What is
890 this dancing?

Mary Warren. I—(*She glances at* Abigail, *who is staring down at her remorselessly. Then, appealing to* Proctor.) Mr. Proctor—

Proctor (*taking it right up*). Abigail leads the girls to the woods, Your Honor, and they have danced there naked—

Parris. Your Honor, this—

Proctor (*at once*). Mr. Parris discovered
900 them himself in the dead of night! There's the "child" she is!

Danforth (*It is growing into a nightmare, and he turns, astonished, to* Parris). Mr. Parris—

Parris. I can only say, sir, that I never found any of them naked, and this man is—

Danforth. But you discovered them dancing in the woods? (*Eyes on* Parris,
910 *he points at* Abigail.) Abigail?

Hale. Excellency, when I first arrived from Beverly, Mr. Parris told me that.

Danforth. Do you deny it, Mr. Parris?

Parris. I do not, sir, but I never saw any of them naked.

Danforth. But she have *danced*? Ⓧ

Parris (*unwillingly*). Aye, sir.

(Danforth, *as though with new eyes, looks at* Abigail.)

920 **Hathorne.** Excellency, will you permit me? (*He points at* Mary Warren.)

Danforth (*with great worry*). Pray, proceed.

Hathorne. You say you never saw no spirits, Mary, were never threatened or afflicted by any manifest of the Devil or the Devil's agents.

Mary Warren (*very faintly*). No, sir.

Hathorne (*with a gleam of victory*). And
930 yet, when people accused of witchery confronted you in court, you would faint, saying their spirits came out of their bodies and choked you—

Mary Warren. That were pretense, sir.

Danforth. I cannot hear you.

Mary Warren. Pretense, sir.

Parris. But you did turn cold, did you not? I myself picked you up many times, and your skin were icy. Mr. Danforth,
940 you—

Danforth. I saw that many times.

Proctor. She only pretended to faint, Your Excellency. They're all marvelous pretenders.

Hathorne. Then can she pretend to faint now?

Proctor. Now?

Parris. Why not? Now there are no spirits attacking her, for none in this
950 room is accused of witchcraft. So let her

The Crucible: Act Three **517**

CLOSE READ

Analyze Drama Elements   COMMON CORE RL 3, RL 5
(LINES 882–919)

Remind students that **dialogue** moves the plot forward.

Ⓦ CITE TEXT EVIDENCE Ask students to explain how the dialogue in lines 882–919 relates to the central problem of the play and how it complicates its resolution. (*The central problem of the play is whether or not there was witchcraft present in the woods on the night in question. This section of the scene is full of a lot of "he said/she said" dialogue, which impacts the believability of all the characters—and therefore the truth of what actually happened. For example, Proctor says that Parris discovered the girls dancing naked; Parris says he discovered them dancing, but not naked. So both men are speaking some truth, but neither is entirely believable.*)

Analyze Drama Elements   COMMON CORE RL 3, RL 5
(LINES 916–923)

Remind students that both **stage directions** and **dialogue** can express a character's feelings.

Ⓧ ASK STUDENTS to reread lines 916–923 and describe what they reveal about Danforth's state of mind. (*Danforth is amazed at what he hears. The emphasis placed on the word "danced" tells the reader that he finds the fact that Abigail danced horrifying. In line 922, Danforth speaks "with great worry," so he is concerned about what he has heard already and what he might hear next.*)

SCAFFOLDING FOR ELL STUDENTS

Identify Adverbial Phrases Tell students that adverbial phrases are groups of words that function as adverbs: they modify verbs, adjectives, or other adverbs by showing time, manner, place, and degree. They usually tell how something is done.

Ask students to go to line 922 and read the stage direction, "with great worry." Explain to them that this is an adverbial phrase that answers the question, "How does Danforth speak?"

ASK STUDENTS to find other adverbial phrases on this page and say what "how" question the adverbial phrase answers. (*Line 929: with a gleam of victory; How does Hathorne speak?*)

Analyze Drama Elements  RL 3, RL 5

(LINES 951–987)

Remind students that **dialogue** moves the plot forward.

Y **ASK STUDENTS** to explain what it will mean if Mary Warren is able to faint. *(If Mary can faint believably in this moment, it will suggest that she was faking it in the courtroom and was not possessed by the Devil. If she cannot—the judges' thinking goes— that means spirits caused her to faint in court and that evil spirits are indeed at work in the case.)*

Analyze Drama Elements  RL 3, RL 5

(LINES 990–998)

Remind students that **dialogue** can convey a playwright's message.

Z **ASK STUDENTS** to explain Mary Warren's speech in lines 990–998 in their own words. Then tell how it expresses a warning from Miller about peer pressure. *(Mary is exhausted, frightened, and confused at this point. She states that she thought she saw spirits that night in the woods, but didn't actually see any. When the judges believed the girls' claims of witchcraft and "the whole world cried spirits," Mary went along with the thinking of the group. Miller is making a point that people who are unsure about something can be convinced by the pressure arising from a group of people.)*

turn herself cold now, let her pretend she is attacked now, let her faint. (*He turns to* Mary Warren.) Faint!

Mary Warren. Faint?

Parris. Aye, faint. Prove to us how you pretended in the court so many times.

Mary Warren (*looking to* Proctor). I— cannot faint now, sir.

960 **Proctor** (*alarmed, quietly*). Can you not pretend it?

Mary Warren. I—(*She looks about as though searching for the passion to faint.*) I—have no *sense* of it now, I—

Danforth. Why? What is lacking now?

Mary Warren. I—cannot tell, sir, I—

Danforth. Might it be that here we have no afflicting spirit loose, but in the court there were some?

Mary Warren. I never saw no spirits.

970 **Parris.** Then see no spirits now, and prove to us that you can faint by your own will, as you claim.

Mary Warren (*stares, searching for the emotion of it, and then shakes her head*). I—cannot do it.

Parris. Then you will confess, will you not? It were attacking spirits made you faint!

Mary Warren. No, sir, I—

980 **Parris.** Your Excellency, this is a trick to blind the court!

Mary Warren. It's not a trick! (*She stands.*) I—I used to faint because I—I thought I saw spirits.

Danforth. *Thought* you saw them!

Mary Warren. But I did not, Your Honor.

Hathorne. How could you think you saw them unless you saw them?

990 **Mary Warren.** I—I cannot tell how, but I did. I—I heard the other girls screaming, and you, Your Honor, you seemed to believe them, and I—It were only sport in the beginning, sir, but then the whole world cried spirits, spirits, and I—I promise you, Mr. Danforth, I only thought I saw them but I did not.

(Danforth *peers at her.*)

1000 **Parris** (*smiling, but nervous because* Danforth *seems to be struck by* Mary Warren's *story*). Surely Your Excellency is not taken by this simple lie.

Danforth (*turning worriedly to* Abigail). Abigail. I bid you now search your heart and tell me this—and beware of it, child, to God every soul is precious and His vengeance is terrible on them that take life without cause. Is it possible, 1010 child, that the spirits you have seen are illusion only, some deception that may cross your mind when—

Abigail. Why, this—this—is a base question, sir.

Danforth. Child, I would have you consider it—

Abigail. I have been hurt, Mr. Danforth; I have seen my blood runnin' out! I have been near to murdered every day 1020 because I done my duty pointing out the Devil's people—and this is my reward? To be mistrusted, denied, questioned like a—

Danforth (*weakening*). Child, I do not mistrust you—

Abigail (*in an open threat*). Let *you* beware, Mr. Danforth. Think you to be so mighty that the power of Hell may not turn *your* wits? Beware of it! 1030 There is—(*Suddenly, from an accusatory attitude, her face turns, looking into the air above—it is truly frightened.*)

SCAFFOLDING FOR ELL STUDENTS

Understand Multiple-Meaning Words Have students read Abigail's dialogue in lines 1013–1014. Ask them to note the word "base" in this sentence. Explain that a less familiar meaning of "base" is being used here.

ASK STUDENTS to list as many meanings of the word "base" as they can think of. *(Possible answers: "the part on which something rests," noun; "to set a place as the main place where a business operates," verb)* Then, using context, have them tell the meaning of the word as used in these lines. *("not good," or "of low quality")* To check their work, have them consult a dictionary.

Danforth (*apprehensively*). What is it, child?

Abigail (*looking about in the air, clasping her arms about her as though cold*). I—I know not. A wind, a cold wind, has come. (*Her eyes fall on Mary Warren.*)

Mary Warren (*terrified, pleading*). Abby!

1040 **Mercy Lewis** (*shivering*). Your Honor, I freeze!

Proctor. They're pretending!

Hathorne (*touching Abigail's hand*). She is cold, Your Honor, touch her!

Mercy Lewis (*through chattering teeth*). Mary, do you send this shadow on me?

Mary Warren. Lord, save me!

Susanna Walcott. I freeze, I freeze!

Abigail (*shivering visibly*). It is a wind, a 1050 wind!

Mary Warren. Abby, don't do that!

Danforth (*himself engaged and entered by* Abigail). Mary Warren, do you witch her? I say to you, do you send your spirit out?

(*With a hysterical cry* Mary Warren *starts to run.* Proctor *catches her.*)

Mary Warren (*almost collapsing*). Let me go, Mr. Proctor, I cannot, I cannot—

1060 **Abigail** (*crying to Heaven*). Oh, Heavenly Father, take away this shadow!

(*Without warning or hesitation,* Proctor *leaps at* Abigail *and, grabbing her by the hair, pulls her to her feet. She screams in pain.* Danforth, *astonished, cries, "What are you about?" and* Hathorne *and* Parris *call, "Take your hands off her!" and out of it all comes* Proctor's *roaring voice.*)

1070 **Proctor.** How do you call Heaven! Whore! Whore!

(Herrick *breaks* Proctor *from her.*)

Herrick. John!

Danforth. Man! Man, what do you—

Proctor (*breathless and in agony*). It is a whore!

Danforth (*dumbfounded*). You charge—?

Abigail. Mr. Danforth, he is lying!

1080 **Proctor.** Mark her! Now she'll suck a scream to stab me with, but—

Danforth. You will prove this! This will not pass!

Proctor (*trembling, his life collapsing about him*). I have known her, sir. I have known her.

Danforth. You—you are a lecher?

Francis (*horrified*). John, you cannot say such a—

1090 **Proctor.** Oh, Francis, I wish you had some evil in you that you might know me! (*to* Danforth) A man will not cast away his good name. You surely know that.

Danforth (*dumbfounded*). In—in what time? In what place?

Proctor (*his voice about to break, and his shame great*). In the proper place— where my beasts are bedded. On the 1100 last night of my joy, some eight months past. She used to serve me in my house, sir. (*He has to clamp his jaw to keep from weeping.*) A man may think God sleeps, but God sees everything, I know it now. I beg you, sir, I beg you—see her what she is. My wife, my dear good wife, took this girl soon after, sir, and put her out on the highroad. And being what she is, a lump of vanity, sir—(*He 1110 is being overcome.*) Excellency, forgive me, forgive me. (*Angrily against himself, he turns away from the* Governor *for a moment. Then, as though to cry out is his only means of speech left.*) She thinks

The Crucible: Act Three **519**

Analyze Drama Elements COMMON CORE RL 3, RL 5

(LINES 1035–1055)

Remind students that **stage directions** can describe a character's behavior, but students must infer characters' motivations.

A2 ASK STUDENTS to reread Abigail's stage directions in line 1038 and Mary's response in the following line. Why does Mary "plead" with Abigail? What do Mary and Proctor have at stake? (*Abigail is pretending to feel a cold wind and is trying to create the impression that Mary is creating it. Mary knows that Abigail is faking and is pleading with her to stop; if the judges believe that Mary has the power to create a cold wind, then she will be arrested and Proctor will lose any hope of rescuing Elizabeth.*)

Analyze Drama Elements COMMON CORE RL 3, RL 5

(LINES 1060–1072)

Remind students that the **climax** of a play is the point of highest tension and excitement. The climax will normally determine the outcome of the play's central conflict.

B2 CITE TEXT EVIDENCE Ask students to identify the climax of the play. (*The climax is when Proctor confesses in lines 1085–1086 to having been Abigail's lover.*) Then ask students to explain how Proctor's confession might change the outcome of the plot. (*It might lead the judges to believe that Abigail only accused Elizabeth Proctor of witchcraft because she was out for revenge and that Abigail has been faking all along.*)

WHEN STUDENTS STRUGGLE . . .

Develop Reading Fluency Tell students that one way to improve reading fluency is to learn to read with more expression. This page of the play has many stage directions that tell the actor to perform the dialogue with a variety of expressions and emotions.

ASK STUDENTS to work in small groups of 5 or 6 (one student can read all the girls' parts) and take turns reading the roles, paying close attention to the stage directions. Have the rest of the class watch and listen to each group perform. As each group finishes, have the class discuss each group's interpretation.

Analyze Drama Elements COMMON CORE RL 3, RL 5

(LINES 1139–1147)

Tell students that a playwright works hard to make his or her characters multi-dimensional. For example, in this play, Proctor is not all good and Danforth is not all bad. Miller avoids creating cartoonish, one-note characters by giving them all flaws and virtues.

Ⓒ ASK STUDENTS to reread Danforth's line, "And let you knock before you enter." Ask students what this line reveals about his character and whether the line is surprising in any way. *(In light of Proctor's revelation, Danforth probably feels some sympathy for Elizabeth Proctor and asks Parris to be polite and knock before entering her cell. Danforth also knows how aggressive and rude Parris can be. It is a surprising line of dialogue for Danforth because up until this point, he has not shown any sympathy for anyone during his aggressive search for the truth.)*

to dance with me on my wife's grave! And well she might, for I thought of her softly. God help me, I lusted, and there *is* a promise in such sweat. But it is a whore's vengeance, and you must see
1120 it; I set myself entirely in your hands. I know you must see it now.

Danforth (*blanched, in horror, turning to* Abigail). You deny every scrap and tittle[12] of this?

Abigail. If I must answer that, I will leave and I will not come back again!

(Danforth *seems unsteady.*)

Proctor. I have made a bell of my honor! I have rung the doom of my
1130 good name—you will believe me, Mr. Danforth! My wife is innocent, except she knew a whore when she saw one!

Abigail (*stepping up to* Danforth). What look do you give me? (Danforth *cannot speak.*) I'll not have such looks! (*She turns and starts for the door.*)

Danforth. You will remain where you are! (Herrick *steps into her path. She comes up short, fire in her eyes.*) Mr.
1140 Parris, go into the court and bring Goodwife Proctor out.

Parris (*objecting*). Your Honor, this is all a—

Danforth (*sharply to* Parris). Bring her out! And tell her not one word of what's been spoken here. And let you knock before you enter. (Parris *goes out.*) Now we shall touch the bottom of this swamp. (*to* Proctor) Your wife, you say,
1150 is an honest woman.

Proctor. In her life, sir, she have never lied. There are them that cannot sing, and them that cannot weep—my wife cannot lie. I have paid much to learn it, sir.

Danforth. And when she put this girl out of your house, she put her out for a harlot?[13]

Proctor. Aye, sir.

1160 **Danforth.** And knew her for a harlot?

Proctor. Aye, sir, she knew her for a harlot.

Danforth. Good then. (*to* Abigail) And if she tell me, child, it were for harlotry, may God spread His mercy on you! (*There is a knock. He calls to the door.*) Hold! (*to* Abigail) Turn your back. Turn your back. (*to* Proctor) Do likewise. (*Both turn their backs—*Abigail *with
1170 indignant slowness.*) Now let neither of you turn to face Goody Proctor. No one in this room is to speak one word, or raise a gesture aye or nay. (*He turns toward the door, calls.*) Enter! (*The door opens.* Elizabeth *enters with* Parris. Parris *leaves her. She stands alone, her eyes looking for* Proctor.) Mr. Cheever, report this testimony in all exactness. Are you ready?

1180 **Cheever.** Ready, sir.

Danforth. Come here, woman. (Elizabeth *comes to him, glancing at* Proctor's *back.*) Look at me only, not at your husband. In my eyes only.

Elizabeth (*faintly*). Good, sir.

Danforth. We are given to understand that at one time you dismissed your servant, Abigail Williams.

Elizabeth. That is true, sir.

1190 **Danforth.** For what cause did you dismiss her? (*Slight pause. Then* Elizabeth *tries to glance at* Proctor.) You will look in my eyes only and not at your husband. The answer is in your memory and you need no help to give

---

[12] **every scrap and tittle:** every tiny bit.

[13] **for a harlot:** as a woman of low morals.

SCAFFOLDING FOR ELL STUDENTS

Understand Metaphors Review the definition of **metaphor** with students.

ASK STUDENTS to reread lines 1148–1149 and note the metaphor. Have students tell what it means and how it contributes to the effectiveness of the text. *(Danforth is not talking about a literal swamp when he says, "Now we will touch the bottom of this swamp." It is a metaphor that refers to the entire conflict; it suggests that the entire affair is murky.)*

it to me. Why did you dismiss Abigail Williams?

Elizabeth (*not knowing what to say, sensing a situation, wetting her lips to stall for time*). She—dissatisfied me. (*pause*) And my husband.

Danforth. In what way dissatisfied you?

Elizabeth. She were—(*She glances at* Proctor *for a cue.*)

Danforth. Woman, look at me! (Elizabeth *does.*) Were she slovenly? Lazy? What disturbance did she cause?

Elizabeth. Your Honor, I—in that time I were sick. And I—My husband is a good and righteous man. He is never drunk as some are, nor wastin' his time at the shovelboard, but always at his work. But in my sickness—you see, sir, I were a long time sick after my last baby, and I thought I saw my husband somewhat turning from me. And this girl—(*She turns to* Abigail.)

Danforth. Look at me.

Elizabeth. Aye, sir. Abigail Williams—(*She breaks off.*)

Danforth. What of Abigail Williams?

Elizabeth. I came to think he fancied her. And so one night I lost my wits, I think, and put her out on the highroad.

Danforth. Your husband—did he indeed turn from you?

Elizabeth (*in agony*). My husband—is a goodly man, sir.

Danforth. Then he did not turn from you.

Elizabeth (*starting to glance at* Proctor). He—

Danforth (*reaches out and holds her face, then*). Look at me! To your own knowledge, has John Proctor ever committed the crime of lechery? (*In a crisis of indecision she cannot speak.*)

Answer my question! Is your husband a lecher!

Elizabeth (*faintly*). No, sir.

Danforth. Remove her, Marshal.

Proctor. Elizabeth, tell the truth!

Danforth. She has spoken. Remove her!

Proctor (*crying out*). Elizabeth, I have confessed it!

Elizabeth. Oh, God! (*The door closes behind her.*)

Proctor. She only thought to save my name!

Hale. Excellency, it is a natural lie to tell; I beg you, stop now before another is condemned! I may shut my conscience to it no more—private vengeance is working through this testimony! From the beginning this man has struck me true. By my oath to Heaven, I believe him now, and I pray you call back his wife before we—

Danforth. She spoke nothing of lechery, and this man has lied!

Hale. I believe him! (*pointing at* Abigail) This girl has always struck me false! She has—

(Abigail, *with a weird, wild, chilling cry, screams up to the ceiling.*)

Abigail. You will not! Begone! Begone, I say!

Danforth. What is it, child? (*But* Abigail, *pointing with fear, is now raising up her frightened eyes, her awed face, toward the ceiling—the girls are doing the same—and now* Hathorne, Hale, Putnam, Cheever, Herrick, *and* Danforth *do the same.*) What's there? (*He lowers his eyes from the ceiling, and now he is frightened; there is real tension in his voice.*) Child! (*She is transfixed—with all the girls, she is whimpering*

The Crucible: Act Three **521**

CLOSE READ

Analyze Drama Elements COMMON CORE RL 3, RL 5
(LINES 1198–1247)

Remind students that they can infer characters' motivations from **stage directions**.

D2 ASK STUDENTS to reread the section of the scene in lines 1198–1247. Ask them why, in line 1227, Elizabeth is "in agony". (*Because adultery is unlawful, Elizabeth naturally feels that if she admits that Proctor was unfaithful to her, she will get him arrested and convicted. She loves him, yet she is an honest person, so she agonizes over how to answer the question.*)

Analyze Drama Elements COMMON CORE RL 3, RL 5
(LINES 1198–1247)

Remind students that **complications** are events in the play that cause the central conflict to be more difficult to resolve.

E2 ASK STUDENTS to explain how the interrogation of Elizabeth Proctor is a plot complication. (*Elizabeth was trying to protect Proctor by not revealing that he had been unfaithful to her. She did not know, however, that Proctor had already confessed to adultery and that if she had verified that fact, it actually would have helped both of them. This complicates the central conflict of whether or not the accused women will be convicted of witchcraft.*)

SCAFFOLDING FOR ELL STUDENTS

Understand Punctuation Briefly review the use of em-dashes with students.

ASK STUDENTS to reread Elizabeth's dialogue beginning with line 1198. Have students note the use of em-dashes in her dialogue. Have them tell what the em-dashes indicate about her character in this scene. (*The em-dashes show that Elizabeth is hesitating a lot because she is scared, exhausted, or worried about incriminating Proctor.*)

TEACH

CLOSE READ

Analyze Drama Elements
COMMON CORE RL 3, RL 5
(LINES 1284–1351)

Remind students to consider characters' motivations as they read **dialogue**.

F2 **ASK STUDENTS** to infer what motivates Abigail to pretend to see the yellow bird. *(After Elizabeth does not verify that Proctor and Abigail had an affair, the judges think Abigail must be possessed. Abigail claims that Mary is attacking her in the form of a yellow bird to get the judges to believe in the presence of witchcraft.)* Then ask why the other girls mimic Mary's dialogue. *(The girls go along with Abigail's plan and pretend there is a yellow bird attacking them that was created by Mary; mimicking Mary makes it appear that Mary is controlling them supernaturally.)*

open-mouthed, agape at the ceiling.)
1280 Girls! Why do you—?

Mercy Lewis *(pointing).* It's on the beam! Behind the rafter!

Danforth *(looking up).* Where!

Abigail. Why—? *(She gulps.)* Why do you come, yellow bird?

Proctor. Where's a bird? I see no bird!

Abigail *(to the ceiling).* My face? My face?

Proctor. Mr. Hale—

1290 **Danforth.** Be quiet!

Proctor *(to Hale).* Do you see a bird?

Danforth. Be quiet!!

Abigail *(to the ceiling, in a genuine conversation with the "bird," as though trying to talk it out of attacking her).* But God made my face; you cannot want to tear my face. Envy is a deadly sin, Mary.

Mary Warren *(on her feet with a spring, and horrified, pleading).* Abby!

1300 **Abigail** *(unperturbed, continuing to the "bird").* Oh, Mary, this is a black art[14] to change your shape. No, I cannot, I cannot stop my mouth; it's God's work I do.

Mary Warren. Abby, I'm *here!*

Proctor *(frantically).* They're pretending, Mr. Danforth!

Abigail *(Now she takes a backward step, as though in fear the bird will swoop 1310 down momentarily).* Oh, please, Mary! Don't come down.

Susanna Walcott. Her claws, she's stretching her claws!

Proctor. Lies, lies.

Abigail *(backing further, eyes still fixed above).* Mary, please don't hurt me!

Mary Warren *(to Danforth).* I'm not hurting her!

Danforth *(to Mary Warren).* Why does 1320 she see this vision?

Mary Warren. She sees nothin'!

Abigail *(now staring full front as though hypnotized, and mimicking the exact tone of Mary Warren's cry).* She sees nothin'!

Mary Warren *(pleading).* Abby, you mustn't!

Abigail and All the Girls *(all transfixed).* Abby, you mustn't!

Mary Warren *(to all the Girls).* I'm here, 1330 I'm here!

Girls. I'm here, I'm here!

Danforth *(horrified).* Mary Warren! Draw back your spirit out of them!

Mary Warren. Mr. Danforth!

Girls *(cutting her off).* Mr. Danforth!

Danforth. Have you compacted with the Devil? Have you?

Mary Warren. Never, never!

Girls. Never, never!

1340 **Danforth** *(growing hysterical).* Why can they only repeat you?

Proctor. Give me a whip—I'll stop it!

Mary Warren. They're sporting.[15] They—!

Girls. They're sporting!

Mary Warren *(turning on them all hysterically and stamping her feet).* Abby, stop it!

Girls *(stamping their feet).* Abby, stop it!

1350 **Mary Warren.** Stop it!

Girls. Stop it!

---
[14] **a black art:** sorcery.

[15] **sporting:** playing a game.

Analyze Drama Elements  RL 3, RL 5
(LINES 1356–1390)

Remind students there may be more than one thing motivating a character's behavior or **dialogue**.

ASK STUDENTS to infer multiple reasons why Danforth starts to believe that Mary Warren is indeed possessed by the Devil when he says, in lines 1369–1371, "Why did you turn about this past two weeks? You have seen the Devil, have you not?" *(Danforth starts to believe Mary is a witch because Abigail and the girls have put on a very convincing performance; Danforth has lost faith in Proctor and Proctor is the one putting forth Mary's deposition; at some level Danforth must want it to be true because the existence of witchcraft would be consistent with his deep religious beliefs and because it would affirm his status as leader of the investigation.)*

Mary Warren (*screaming it out at the top of her lungs, and raising her fists*). Stop it!!

Girls (*raising their fists*). Stop it!!

(Mary Warren, *utterly confounded, and becoming overwhelmed by Abigail's—and the girls'—utter conviction, starts to whimper, hands half raised, powerless, and all the girls begin whimpering exactly as she does.*)

Danforth. A little while ago you were afflicted. Now it seems you afflict others; where did you find this power?

Mary Warren (*staring at* Abigail). I—have no power.

Girls. I have no power.

Proctor. They're gulling you,[16] Mister!

Danforth. Why did you turn about this past two weeks? You have seen the Devil, have you not?

Hale (*indicating* Abigail *and the girls*). You cannot believe them!

---

[16] **gulling you:** deceiving you.

Mary Warren. I—

Proctor (*sensing her weakening*). Mary, God damns all liars!

Danforth (*pounding it into her*). You have seen the Devil, you have made compact with Lucifer, have you not?

Proctor. God damns liars, Mary!

(Mary *utters something unintelligible, staring at* Abigail, *who keeps watching the "bird" above.*)

Danforth. I cannot hear you. What do you say? (Mary *utters again unintelligibly.*) You will confess yourself or you will hang! (*He turns her roughly to face him.*) Do you know who I am? I say you will hang if you do not open with me!

Proctor. Mary, remember the angel Raphael—do that which is good and—

Abigail (*pointing upward*). The wings! Her wings are spreading! Mary, please, don't, don't—!

Hale. I see nothing, Your Honor!

The Crucible: Act Three **523**

Image Credits: ©Jeff Thrower/Shutterstock

CLOSE READ

Analyze Drama Elements COMMON CORE RL 3, RL 5

(LINES 1420–1460)

Tell students that one of the ways a playwright makes a play cohesive is to revisit themes, events, or **dialogue** from earlier in the play.

H2 CITE TEXT EVIDENCE Ask students to read Mary Warren's dialogue in lines 1445–1449. How do Proctor's words from the end of Act 2 come back to haunt him in this part of the scene? *(At the end of Act 2, Proctor was trying to convince Mary to join him in court and expose Abigail's lies. As he did so, he was extremely emotional and said things like, "You will tell the court what you know," and "I will bring your guts into your mouth . . . ." Mary remembers these words as "I'll murder you," and "We must go and overthrow the court." Her inaccurate recollections play perfectly into the beliefs of Danforth and the other judges; by now they believe that Mary is possessed and that Proctor is in league with the Devil.)*

Analyze Drama Elements COMMON CORE RL 3, RL 5

(LINES 1461–1468)

Tell students to look for the occasional bit of **irony** in Miller's **stage directions**. Irony is when one uses words that mean the opposite of what one really wants to say.

12 ASK STUDENTS to work with a partner and reread the dialogue and stage directions that describe Mary Warren's screaming. When the stage directions describe Abigail as reaching out to Mary "out of her infinite charity," how is this an example of irony on the playwright's part? Encourage students to think about what they know about Abigail's character up to this point. *(Abigail has not demonstrated any charitable or kind characteristics up to this point. Further, Abigail's reason for pulling Mary towards her is because Abigail wants Mary on her side—Abigail needs all the girls who were in the forest to agree that spirits were present. So Abigail is not comforting Mary out of charity at all; it is totally out of self-interest.)*

Danforth. Do you confess this power! (*He is an inch from her face.*) Speak!

Abigail. She's going to come down! 1400 She's walking the beam!

Danforth. Will you speak!

Mary Warren (*staring in horror*). I cannot!

Girls. I cannot!

Parris. Cast the Devil out! Look him in the face! Trample him! We'll save you, Mary, only stand fast against him and—

Abigail (*looking up*). Look out! She's coming down!

1410 (*She and all the girls run to one wall, shielding their eyes. And now, as though cornered, they let out a gigantic scream, and Mary, as though infected, opens her mouth and screams with them. Gradually Abigail and the girls leave off, until only Mary is left there, staring up at the "bird," screaming madly. All watch her, horrified by this evident fit. Proctor strides to her.*)

1420 **Proctor.** Mary, tell the Governor what they—(*He has hardly got a word out, when, seeing him coming for her, she rushes out of his reach, screaming in horror.*)

Mary Warren. Don't touch me—don't touch me! (*At which the girls halt at the door.*)

Proctor (*astonished*). Mary!

Mary Warren (*pointing at Proctor*). 1430 You're the Devil's man! (*He is stopped in his tracks.*)

Parris. Praise God!

Girls. Praise God!

Proctor (*numbed*). Mary, how—?

Mary Warren. I'll not hang with you! I love God, I love God.

Danforth (*to Mary*). He bid you do the Devil's work?

Mary Warren (*hysterically, indicating* 1440 Proctor). He come at me by night and every day to sign, to sign, to—

Danforth. Sign what?

Parris. The Devil's book? He come with a book?

Mary Warren (*hysterically, pointing at* Proctor, *fearful of him*). My name, he want my name. "I'll murder you," he says, "if my wife hangs! We must go and overthrow the court," he says!

1450 (*Danforth's head jerks toward* Proctor, *shock and horror in his face.*)

Proctor (*turning, appealing to* Hale). Mr. Hale!

Mary Warren (*her sobs beginning*). He wake me every night, his eyes were like coals and his fingers claw my neck, and I sign, I sign . . .

Hale. Excellency, this child's gone wild!

Proctor (*as* Danforth's *wide eyes pour on* 1460 *him*). Mary, Mary!

Mary Warren (*screaming at him*). No, I love God; I go your way no more. I love God, I bless God. (*Sobbing, she rushes to* Abigail.) Abby, Abby, I'll never hurt you more! (*They all watch, as* Abigail, *out of her infinite charity, reaches out and draws the sobbing* Mary *to her, and then looks up to* Danforth.)

Danforth (*to* Proctor). What are you? 1470 (Proctor *is beyond speech in his anger.*) You are combined with anti-Christ,[17] are you not? I have seen your power; you will not deny it! What say you, Mister?

Hale. Excellency—

---

[17] **anti-Christ:** in the New Testament Christ's great enemy, expected to spread evil before Christ conquers him and the world ends (1 John 2:18).

WHEN STUDENTS STRUGGLE . . .

Discuss with students that Proctor's attempt to clear his wife's name has backfired, and that now both he and his wife are thought to be working for the Devil. Make sure students understand how this change has come about.

ASK STUDENTS to summarize the events so far in the courtroom. *(Proctor brings Mary to the court to tell the judge she lied about seeing spirits and that she and the other girls were pretending to be afflicted. The judge will not believe her unless she can cause herself to faint. Mary cannot. Abigail pretends to be attacked by a spirit. This enrages Proctor. He accuses her of being a woman of low morals, which in turn forces him to confess his affair with her. Abigail denies the charge and continues to pretend to be spiritually attacked by Mary. The other girls back her up. Mary, terrified, turns on Proctor.)*

Danforth. I will have nothing from you, Mr. Hale! (*to* Proctor) Will you confess yourself befouled with Hell, or do you keep that black allegiance yet? What say you?

1480 **Proctor** (*his mind wild, breathless*). I say—I say—God is dead!

Parris. Hear it, hear it!

Proctor (*laughs insanely, then*). A fire, a fire is burning! I hear the boot of Lucifer, I see his filthy face! And it is my face, and yours, Danforth! For them that quail to bring men out of ignorance, as I have quailed, and as you quail now when you know in all your 1490 black hearts that this be fraud—God damns our kind especially, and we will burn, we will burn together!

Danforth. Marshal! Take him and Corey with him to the jail!

Hale (*starting across to the door*). I denounce these proceedings!

Proctor. You are pulling Heaven down and raising up a whore!

Hale. I denounce these proceedings, I 1500 quit this court! (*He slams the door to the outside behind him.*)

Danforth (*calling to him in a fury*). Mr. Hale! Mr. Hale!

(*The curtain falls.*)

COLLABORATIVE DISCUSSION Why are the judges taken in by Abigail's simulated terror? With a partner, discuss the implications for them if they are proven wrong about the girls. Cite specific textual evidence from the play to support your ideas.

CLOSE READ

Analyze Drama Elements
COMMON CORE RL 3, RL 5

(LINES 1483–1492)

Remind students that **dialogue** can express the playwright's underlying message.

J2 CITE TEXT EVIDENCE Have students explain how Proctor's final speech conveys a message from the playwright. (*When Proctor incriminates himself and Danforth, it is actually the playwright saying that everyone has the responsibility to protect the innocent, fight persecution, and expose wrongful accusations.*)

Analyze Drama Elements
COMMON CORE RL 3, RL 5

(LINES 1495–1503)

Remind students that minor characters can serve as **foils** for major characters. A foil is a character so different from another character that he or she highlights that character's traits by contrast.

K2 ASK STUDENTS to explain how Hale is a foil for Danforth. (*Hale has not been seduced by the peer pressure and general hysteria of the witch hunt. He has remained skeptical of the accusations and is unafraid to say so. Danforth, in contrast, sees himself as the leader of the investigation and prides himself on his unwavering belief in the presence of witchcraft.*)

COLLABORATIVE DISCUSSION Have students work in small groups and discuss what the judges stand to lose at this point if Abigail is proven to be lying. Ask them to cite specific evidence from the text. Then have groups share their conclusions with the class as a whole. Accept all reasonable responses.

ASK STUDENTS to share any questions they generated in the course of reading and discussing the selection.

SCAFFOLDING FOR ELL STUDENTS

Understand Multiple-Meaning Words Remind students that Miller uses many archaisms in *The Crucible*. Tell students that some of them are multiple-meaning words and might be confusing.

ASK STUDENTS to read Proctor's dialogue in lines 1487–1489 and note the use of the word "quail." Ask students to tell the meaning of "quail" with which they are most familiar. (*"a small, wild bird"*) Then have them use context and attempt to give a definition of its meaning here. (*"to feel or show fear"*) If their guesses are off the mark, ask them to consult a dictionary.

Analyze Drama Elements  COMMON CORE RL 3, RL 5

Discuss the three types of characters with students. Draw a large web organizer and post it in the classroom. Have two main circles in the center labeled "protagonist" and "antagonist." Ask students for ideas as to which characters might be protagonists and antagonists and why. Then add smaller circles around each large circle for minor characters. When one character is a foil for another character, connect their circles with a double line. *(Sample answer: Proctor is the protagonist and Abigail is the antagonist. Most of the action of the play centers around him, and he is fighting Abigail's accusations of witchcraft. Abigail is a foil to Elizabeth; Abigail is a vengeful liar, while Elizabeth is steadfastly honest.)*

Analyzing the Text  COMMON CORE RL 1, RL 3, W 2, W 4

Possible answers:

1. *Mary is consistently described in this act as frail, frightened and weeping, in contrast to Abigail, who stands firm in her deceit. The more Mary seems to lack backbone and waver in her testimony, the stronger Abigail's position appears to be.*

2. *When Danforth barely lets Giles make a statement, he reveals himself to be stubborn and unsympathetic. Danforth will be a hard person to sway.*

3. *Elizabeth lies about Proctor's adultery because she is trying to save his reputation—she thinks that it will harm him to tell the truth that he was unfaithful to her. She is motivated by her love for and loyalty to her husband.*

4. *The fact that Proctor has plowed on Sunday is significant because the Puritans believed that no work should be done on the Sabbath. They are trying to determine whether or not Proctor is a religious man whose word can be believed.*

5. *In this act, Proctor is much more emotionally involved in trying to challenge and take down the witch hunt. In the beginning of the play, he was more absorbed in resolving the problems in his marriage and felt the absurdity of the witch hunt would come to light on its own. By the end of Act 3, he is a confessed lecher and a victim of the witch hunt himself. His actions in confessing reveal that he is an honorable and courageous person.*

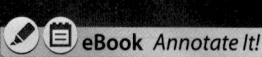

Analyze Drama Elements COMMON CORE RL 3

In his play, Miller incorporates three types of characters, a dramatic convention that heightens suspense and tension. Determining which characters fulfill these roles will help readers understand how the characters' interaction is part of the playwright's plan for his plot.

> The **protagonist** is the main character around whom most of the action centers.
>
> The **antagonist** is the character that opposes the protagonist; this leads to the major conflict.
>
> **Foils** are minor characters who present a striking contrast to a more major character, thus emphasizing that other character's traits.

Analzying the Text COMMON CORE RL 1, RL 3, RL 5, W 2, W 4

Cite Text Evidence   Support your responses with evidence from the selection.

1. **Analyze** Mary Warren might be seen as the foil for Abigail. Explain how she is used to bring out Abigail's traits.

2. **Analyze** What does Danforth's reaction to Giles's outburst at the beginning of the act suggest about his character?

3. **Analyze** Why does Elizabeth lie to Danforth about her husband's relationship with Abigail? What motivates her actions?

4. **Interpret** Why does the court debate whether Proctor plows on Sunday? What is the significance of this debate?

5. **Draw Conclusions** How has Proctor changed from the beginning of the play? What do his actions in this act reveal about his character?

PERFORMANCE TASK

Writing Activity: Analysis The real Abigail Williams was eleven years old in 1692 and had not had an illicit relationship with John Proctor. How would the play be different if Miller had not presented a different version of history? What would be lost?

- Identify the ways in which the relationship between Proctor and Abigail affects the development of plot as well as supports Miller's view about the witch hunts.

- Write an analysis in which you logically present your ideas based on explicit statements from the text or inferences based on evidence from the text.

- Cite details from the play in support of your views.

Assign this performance task.

PERFORMANCE TASK  COMMON CORE RL 3

Writing Activity: Analysis Encourage small groups of students to reread Act 3 and consider how the relationship between Proctor and Abigail affects the plot. How might the play have been different if Miller had not included their relationship? When students have finished their analysis, have them discuss their findings with another group of students. At the end of this process, ask groups to draw up their analyses in written form and present them to the class.

TEACH

CLOSE READ

Analyze Drama Elements   COMMON CORE RL 3, RL 5

Remind students that the **stage directions** can help set the mood of a scene. Ask them to reread the stage directions that start Act Four and note that Miller describes the door as "heavy" and says that "the place is in darkness."

Ⓐ ASK STUDENTS to explain why Miller sets the jail in darkness as opposed to light. *(The darkness inside the jail symbolizes the prisoners' lack of hope.)* Then ask why the door is described as being heavy. *(The heavy door indicates how difficult it is to get out of jail; it reinforces the finality and seriousness of the situation.)*

Language and Style: Dialogue (LINES 16–29)   COMMON CORE L 3a

Remind students that readers must infer characters' inner states from their **dialogue**.

Ⓑ ASK STUDENTS to reread lines 16–29 and make inferences about whether Tituba and Sarah Good really believe the Devil is coming to rescue them and, if so, why. *(Tituba and Sarah Good seem to be caught up in a delusion in which they truly believe that the Devil will rescue them from prison. They are terrified of their coming execution, and everyone around them believes they are witches; this makes it easy for them to believe it, too. At this point, rescue by the Devil seems to be their only hope, so they have a powerful reason to believe in it.)*

AS YOU READ Pay attention to the details that tell you how the witch hunt has affected those involved in it. Write down any questions you generate during reading.

ACT FOUR

Ⓐ (*A cell in* Salem *jail, that fall.*

At the back is a high barred window; near it, a great, heavy door. Along the walls are two benches.

The place is in darkness but for the moonlight seeping through the bars. It appears empty. Presently footsteps are heard coming down a corridor beyond the wall, keys rattle, and the door swings open. Marshal Herrick *enters with a lantern.*

He is nearly drunk, and heavy-footed. He goes to a bench and nudges a bundle of rags lying on it.)

Herrick. Sarah, wake up! Sarah Good! (*He then crosses to the other bench.*)

Sarah Good (*rising in her rags*). Oh, Majesty! Comin', comin'! Tituba, he's here, His Majesty's come!

Herrick. Go to the north cell; this place is wanted now.

(*He hangs his lantern on the wall.* Tituba *sits up.*)

10 **Tituba.** That don't look to me like His Majesty; look to me like the marshal.

Herrick (*taking out a flask*). Get along with you now, clear this place. (*He drinks, and* Sarah Good *comes and peers up into his face.*)

Ⓑ **Sarah Good.** Oh, is it you, Marshal! I thought sure you be the Devil comin' for us. Could I have a sip of cider for me goin'-away?

20 **Herrick** (*handing her the flask*). And where are you off to, Sarah?

Tituba (*as* Sarah *drinks*). We goin' to Barbados, soon the Devil gits here with the feathers and the wings.

Herrick. Oh? A happy voyage to you.

Sarah Good. A pair of bluebirds wingin' southerly, the two of us! Oh, it be a grand transformation, Marshal! (*She raises the flask to drink again.*) Ⓑ

30 **Herrick** (*taking the flask from her lips*). You'd best give me that or you'll never rise off the ground. Come along now.

Tituba. I'll speak to him for you, if you desires to come along, Marshal.

Herrick. I'd not refuse it, Tituba; it's the proper morning to fly into Hell.

Tituba. Oh, it be no Hell in Barbados. Devil, him be pleasure-man in Barbados, him be singin' and dancin' in 40 Barbados. It's you folks—you riles him up 'round here; it be too cold 'round here for that Old Boy. He freeze his soul in Massachusetts, but in Barbados he just as sweet and—(*A bellowing cow is heard, and* Tituba *leaps up and calls to the window.*) Aye, sir! That's him, Sarah!

Sarah Good. I'm here, Majesty! (*They hurriedly pick up their rags as* Hopkins, *a guard, enters.*)

50 **Hopkins.** The Deputy Governor's arrived.

Herrick (*grabbing* Tituba). Come along, come along.

Tituba (*resisting him*). No, he comin' for me. I goin' home!

The Crucible: Act Four   **527**

SCAFFOLDING FOR ELL STUDENTS

Understand Multiple-Meaning Words Have students note the use of the word "great" in the opening stage directions to describe the door to the jail.

ASK STUDENTS to infer the meaning of "great" in this sentence. *(large)* Then have them check a dictionary to see if they are correct. Have them work with a partner and come up with as many other meanings of the word "great" as possible. *(distinguished, excellent, grand)*

Analyze Drama Elements $\quad$ COMMON CORE $\quad$ RL 3, RL 5

(LINES 83–91)

Remind students that one character's **dialogue** may reveal traits about other characters.

C **CITE TEXT EVIDENCE** Have students consider what Herrick tells about Hale. Ask what this fact says about Hale's character. *(It shows that he is compassionate and dutiful; it is consistent behavior for Hale.)* Then ask what it says about Parris's character that he has now joined Hale. *(This detail is more surprising; it suggests that Parris has had a change of heart.)*

Language and Style: Dialogue (LINES 86–87) $\quad$ COMMON CORE $\quad$ L 3a

Tell students that there may be more than one way to interpret Miller's historically stylized **dialogue**.

D **ASK STUDENTS** to write two modern-style versions of Danforth's line of dialogue, "What is he about here?" Ask students to explain any differences—however slight—in the meaning of their rewritten sentences. *(Possible answer: "What is he doing here?" or "What has he been doing here?" The former is more a question about why Hale is physically in the jail; the latter asks what activity he has been involved in since arriving at the jail.)*

Herrick (*pulling her to the door*). That's not Satan, just a poor old cow with a hatful of milk. Come along now, out with you!

60 **Tituba** (*calling to the window*). Take me home, Devil! Take me home!

Sarah Good (*following the shouting* Tituba *out*). Tell him I'm goin', Tituba! Now you tell him Sarah Good is goin' too!

(*In the corridor outside* Tituba *calls on*—"Take me home, Devil; Devil take me home!" *and* Hopkins' *voice orders her to move on.* Herrick *returns and*
70 *begins to push old rags and straw into a corner. Hearing footsteps, he turns, and enter* Danforth *and Judge* Hathorne. *They are in greatcoats and wear hats against the bitter cold. They are followed in by* Cheever, *who carries a dispatch case*[1] *and a flat wooden box containing his writing materials.*)

Herrick. Good morning, Excellency.

Danforth. Where is Mr. Parris?

80 **Herrick.** I'll fetch him. (*He starts for the door.*)

Danforth. Marshal. (Herrick *stops.*) When did Reverend Hale arrive?

Herrick. It were toward midnight, I think.

 **Danforth** (*suspiciously*). What is he about here? **D**

Herrick. He goes among them that will hang, sir. And he prays with them. He
90 sits with Goody Nurse now. And Mr. Parris with him.

Danforth. Indeed. That man have no authority to enter here, Marshal. Why have you let him in?

Herrick. Why, Mr. Parris command me, sir. I cannot deny him.

Danforth. Are you drunk, Marshal?

Herrick. No, sir; it is a bitter night, and I have no fire here.

100 **Danforth** (*containing his anger*). Fetch Mr. Parris.

Herrick. Aye, sir.

Danforth. There is a prodigious stench in this place.

Herrick. I have only now cleared the people out for you.

Danforth. Beware hard drink, Marshal.

Herrick. Aye, sir. (*He waits an instant for further orders. But* Danforth, *in*
110 *dissatisfaction, turns his back on him, and* Herrick *goes out. There is a pause.* Danforth *stands in thought.*)

Hathorne. Let you question Hale, Excellency; I should not be surprised he have been preaching in Andover[2] lately.

Danforth. We'll come to that; speak nothing of Andover. Parris prays with him. That's strange. (*He blows on his hands, moves toward the window, and*
120 *looks out.*)

Hathorne. Excellency, I wonder if it be wise to let Mr. Parris so continuously with the prisoners. (Danforth *turns to him, interested.*) I think, sometimes, the man has a mad look these days.

Danforth. Mad?

Hathorne. I met him yesterday coming out of his house, and I bid him good morning—and he wept and went his
130 way. I think it is not well the village sees him so unsteady.

Danforth. Perhaps he have some sorrow.

---

[1] **dispatch case:** a case for carrying documents.

[2] **Andover:** a town in Massachusetts northwest of Salem.

SCAFFOLDING FOR ELL STUDENTS

Understand Suffixes Review the definition of suffixes with students and introduce the suffix *-ous*. Tell them the suffix *-ous* is added to words in order to form adjectives from nouns. Instruct them that in line 103, the adjective "prodigious" comes from the noun *prodigy*, which means "something impressive or outstanding." "Prodigious," then, means "very impressive" or "outstanding."

ASK STUDENTS to create *-ous* adjectives from the following nouns and tell what they mean. Encourage students to point out adjectives ending in *-ous* as they read.

- courage *(courageous: very brave)*
- joy *(joyous: feeling great happiness)*
- poison *(poisonous: causing sickness by touching the body)*

Cheever (*stamping his feet against the cold*). I think it be the cows, sir.

Danforth. Cows?

Cheever. There be so many cows wanderin' the highroads, now their masters are in the jails, and much
140 disagreement who they will belong to now. I know Mr. Parris be arguin' with farmers all yesterday— there is great contention, sir, about the cows. Contention make him weep, sir; it were always a man that weep for contention. (*He turns, as do* Hathorne *and* Danforth, *hearing someone coming up the corridor.* Danforth *raises his head as* Parris *enters. He is gaunt, frightened, and sweating in*
150 *his greatcoat.*)

Parris (*to* Danforth, *instantly*). Oh, good morning, sir, thank you for coming, I beg your pardon wakin' you so early. Good morning, Judge Hathorne.

Danforth. Reverend Hale have no right to enter this—

Parris. Excellency, a moment. (*He hurries back and shuts the door.*)

Hathorne. Do you leave him alone with
160 the prisoners?

Danforth. What's his business here?

Parris (*prayerfully holding up his hands*). Excellency, hear me. It is a providence. Reverend Hale has returned to bring Rebecca Nurse to God.

Danforth (*surprised*). He bids her confess?

Parris (*sitting*). Hear me. Rebecca have not given me a word this three month
170 since she came. Now she sits with him, and her sister and Martha Corey and two or three others, and he pleads with them, confess their crimes and save their lives.

Danforth. Why—this is indeed a providence. And they soften, they soften?

Parris. Not yet, not yet. But I thought to summon you, sir, that we might think
180 on whether it be not wise, to—(*He dares not say it.*) I had thought to put a question, sir, and I hope you will not—

Danforth. Mr. Parris, be plain, what troubles you?

Parris. There is news, sir, that the court—the court must reckon with. My niece, sir, my niece—I believe she has vanished.

Danforth. Vanished!

190 **Parris.** I had thought to advise you of it earlier in the week, but—

Danforth. Why? How long is she gone?

Parris. This be the third night. You see, sir, she told me she would stay a night with Mercy Lewis. And next day, when she does not return, I send to Mr. Lewis to inquire. Mercy told him she would sleep in *my* house for a night.

Danforth. They are both gone?!

200 **Parris** (*in fear of him*). They are, sir.

Danforth (*alarmed*). I will send a party for them. Where may they be?

Parris. Excellency, I think they be aboard a ship. (Danforth *stands agape.*) My daughter tells me how she heard them speaking of ships last week, and tonight I discover my—my strongbox is broke into. (*He presses his fingers against his eyes to keep back tears.*)

210 **Hathorne** (*astonished*). She have robbed you?

Parris. Thirty-one pound is gone. I am penniless. (*He covers his face and sobs.*)

Danforth. Mr. Parris, you are a brainless man! (*He walks in thought, deeply worried.*)

The Crucible: Act Four **529**

CLOSE READ

Analyze Drama Elements COMMON CORE RL 3, RL 5
(LINES 90–213)

Remind students to look for changes in characters over the course of a play. The difference in what a character does and says from the beginning of a play to its ending is called a character's **arc**.

E CITE TEXT EVIDENCE Ask students how the character of Parris is different in Act Four compared to earlier in the play. Have them cite specific details. *(In the first three acts, Parris was greatly in favor of the witch hunt and was glad to see those accused convicted. In this act, Herrick reports that he has joined Hale in praying with the prisoners (lines 90–91), which suggests he may have had a change of heart. Hathorne reports that Parris has been seen crying in the village (lines 129–130); when Parris enters he is emotional (lines 208–209). He reports that his niece has disappeared with Abigail (lines 187–188). This probably causes him to rethink his commitment to the witch hunt. Parris's character arc goes from selfish and suspicious of others to mild and contrite.)*

Analyze Drama Elements COMMON CORE RL 3, RL 5
(LINES 185–213)

Remind students that plot **complications** will make the overall conflict more difficult to resolve.

 ASK STUDENTS to explain how Abigail's disappearance qualifies as a plot complication. *(Abigail initiated many of the charges of witchcraft, but now she is not around to see their effects; this makes her appear guilty of lying—which Danforth and the judges thought they had disproven at the end of Act Three. Furthermore, she may be needed for further questioning as more accusations are made. The central conflict of whether witchcraft is present in Salem or not is once again called into question—this time, by her sudden disappearance.)*

SCAFFOLDING FOR ELL STUDENTS

Understand Phrasal Verbs Review **phrasal verbs** with students. Remind them that phrasal verbs often have a direct object (someone or something), as in *hand something in, go after someone,* or *do something over.*

ASK STUDENTS to go to line 205 and read the full line:

"My daughter tells me how she heard them speaking of ships last week, and tonight I discover my—my strongbox is broke into."

Have them identify a phrasal verb used in this sentence and tell what its object is. As they read, encourage them to look for phrasal verbs. *(is broke into; strongbox)*

CLOSE READ

Analyze Drama Elements

COMMON CORE RL 3, RL 5

(LINES 232–237)

Explain to students that important events in a play—including plot **complications**—may happen off stage, yet characters still have to deal with their effects.

G ASK STUDENTS to tell why the rebellion in Andover could be considered a plot complication. *(If residents of Andover—a neighboring town—are resisting and questioning the witch hunt, then perhaps those feelings will migrate to Salem and undermine the judges' case. It makes the central conflict of the play harder to resolve, because it shows there is doubt about whether witchcraft is at work.)*

Analyze Drama Elements

COMMON CORE RL 3, RL 5

(LINES 232–290)

Remind students to look to both **stage directions** and **dialogue** when drawing inferences about characters' motivations.

H CITE TEXT EVIDENCE Ask students to tell why Danforth refuses to postpone the hangings. Cite specifics where possible. *(Danforth still thinks he is right and wants to use those ready for hanging as examples. He needs the people of Salem to fear him in order to keep them in line—and to keep the judges' witch hunt afloat. Indeed, he denies there is even a revolt in Andover. [lines 230–231])* Why does Parris want to postpone the hangings? *(Parris seems to be worried about the revolt in Andover making its way to Salem [lines 232–237]; he is worried there will be a strong reaction against the next group of hangings because the next group is made up of people who are admired [lines 241–252]; he wants to give Hale more time so a confession can be procured. [lines 262–271])*

Parris. Excellency, it profit nothing you should blame me. I cannot think they would run off except they fear
220 to keep in Salem any more. (*He is pleading.*) Mark it, sir, Abigail had close knowledge of the town, and since the news of Andover has broken here—

Danforth. Andover is remedied.[3] The court returns there on Friday, and will resume examinations.

Parris. I am sure of it, sir. But the rumor here speaks rebellion in Andover, and it—

230 **Danforth.** There is no rebellion in Andover!

G **Parris.** I tell you what is said here, sir. Andover have thrown out the court, they say, and will have no part of witchcraft. There be a faction here, feeding on that news, and I tell you true, sir, I fear there will be riot here.

Hathorne. Riot! Why at every execution I have seen naught but high satisfaction
240 in the town.

Parris. Judge Hathorne—it were another sort that hanged till now. Rebecca Nurse is no Bridget that lived three year with Bishop before she married him. John Proctor is not Isaac Ward that drank his family to ruin. (*to Danforth*) I would to God it were not so, Excellency, but these people have great weight yet in the town. Let Rebecca stand
250 upon the gibbet[4] and send up some righteous prayer, and I fear she'll wake a vengeance on you.

Hathorne. Excellency, she is condemned a witch. The court have—

Danforth (*in deep concern, raising a hand to Hathorne*). Pray you. (*to Parris*) How do you propose, then?

---

[3] **remedied:** no longer a problem.
[4] **gibbet** (jĭb´ĭt): gallows.

Parris. Excellency, I would postpone these hangin's for a time.

260 **Danforth.** There will be no postponement.

Parris. Now Mr. Hale's returned, there is hope, I think—for if he bring even one of these to God, that confession surely damns the others in the public eye, and none may doubt more that they are all linked to Hell. This way, unconfessed and claiming innocence, doubts are multiplied, many honest people will
270 weep for them, and our good purpose is lost in their tears.

Danforth (*after thinking a moment, then going to* Cheever). Give me the list.

(Cheever *opens the dispatch case, searches.*)

Parris. It cannot be forgot, sir, that when I summoned the congregation for John Proctor's excommunication[5] there were hardly thirty people come to hear it.
280 That speak a discontent, I think, and—

Danforth (*studying the list*). There will be no postponement.

Parris. Excellency—

Danforth. Now, sir—which of these in your opinion may be brought to God? I will myself strive with him[6] till dawn. (*He hands the list to* Parris, *who merely glances at it.*)

Parris. There is not sufficient time till
290 dawn.

Danforth. I shall do my utmost. Which of them do you have hope for?

---

[5] **excommunication:** banishment from a church. For the Puritans in New England, this punishment resulted in the loss of church privileges.
[6] **strive with him:** struggle with him through prayer.

WHEN STUDENTS STRUGGLE . . .

Draw a problem-solution graphic organizer on the board:

ASK STUDENTS to fill in the Problem box with "A faction in Salem does not believe in witchcraft." Then have them complete the graphic organizer with Danforth's and Parris's solutions. *(Danforth wants to go ahead with the hangings to set an example; Parris wants to postpone the hangings and see if Hale can secure some confessions.)*

	Danforth's Solution:
Problem:	
	Parris's Solution:

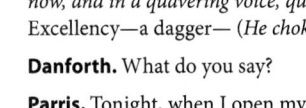

Parris (*not even glancing at the list now, and in a quavering voice, quietly*). Excellency—a dagger— (*He chokes up.*)

Danforth. What do you say?

Parris. Tonight, when I open my door to leave my house—a dagger clattered to the ground. (*Silence. Danforth absorbs this. Now Parris cries out.*) You cannot hang this sort. There is danger for me. I dare not step outside at night!

(*Reverend Hale enters. They look at him for an instant in silence. He is steeped in sorrow, exhausted, and more direct than he ever was.*)

Danforth. Accept my congratulations, Reverend Hale; we are gladdened to see you returned to your good work.

Hale (*coming to Danforth now*). You must pardon them. They will not budge.

(*Herrick enters, waits.*)

Danforth (*conciliatory*). You misunderstand, sir; I cannot pardon these when twelve are already hanged for the same crime. It is not just.

Parris (*with failing heart*). Rebecca will not confess?

Hale. The sun will rise in a few minutes. Excellency, I must have more time.

Danforth. Now hear me, and beguile yourselves no more. I will not receive a single plea for pardon or postponement. Them that will not confess will hang. Twelve are already executed; the names of these seven are given out, and the village expects to see them die this morning. Postponement now speaks a floundering on my part; reprieve or pardon must cast doubt upon the guilt of them that died till now. While I speak God's law, I will not crack its voice with whimpering. If retaliation is your fear, know this—I should hang ten thousand that dared to rise against the law, and

an ocean of salt tears could not melt the resolution of the statutes. Now draw yourselves up like men and help me, as you are bound by Heaven to do. Have you spoken with them all, Mr. Hale?

Hale. All but Proctor. He is in the dungeon.

Danforth (*to Herrick*). What's Proctor's way now?

Herrick. He sits like some great bird; you'd not know he lived except he will take food from time to time.

Danforth (*after thinking a moment*). His wife—his wife must be well on with child now.

Herrick. She is, sir.

Danforth. What think you, Mr. Parris? You have closer knowledge of this man; might her presence soften him?

Parris. It is possible, sir. He have not laid eyes on her these three months. I should summon her.

Danforth (*to Herrick*). Is he yet adamant? Has he struck at you again?

Herrick. He cannot, sir, he is chained to the wall now.

Danforth (*after thinking on it*). Fetch Goody Proctor to me. Then let you bring him up.

Herrick. Aye, sir. (*Herrick goes. There is silence.*)

Hale. Excellency, if you postpone a week and publish to the town that you are striving for their confessions, that speak mercy on your part, not faltering.

Danforth. Mr. Hale, as God have not empowered me like Joshua to stop this sun from rising,[7] so I cannot withhold

---

[7] **like Joshua . . . rising:** According to the Bible, Joshua became leader of the Israelites after Moses died. He led the people to the Promised Land while the sun stood still.

The Crucible: Act Four **531**

CLOSE READ

Analyze Drama Elements   COMMON CORE RL 3, RL 5

(LINES 293–302)

Remind students that the stakes of a character are what they stand to lose or gain as a result of events of the plot and their own behavior.

ASK STUDENTS to explain how Parris's report that a dagger appeared on his doorstep raises the stakes for both him and Danforth. (*Parris's life may be in danger; Danforth only holds on to his power so long as the people in Salem support him and believe in the witch hunt.*)

Analyze Drama Elements   COMMON CORE RL 3, RL 5

(LINES 321–339)

Remind students that a character's **dialogue** can reveal much about that character.

ASK STUDENTS to analyze Danforth's speech in lines 321–339 and explain what it reveals about his character. Has his character stayed consistent throughout the play? Has his motivation changed at all? (*Danforth's speech is consistent with his trait of being very sure of himself. Danforth has always been stubborn and inflexible, and still is in this act. Danforth's goal has not changed; he wants to prove witchcraft is at work in Salem no matter what the evidence to the contrary or the consequences to the people of Salem.*)

SCAFFOLDING FOR ELL STUDENTS

Understand Metaphors Review the definition of **metaphors** with students.

ASK STUDENTS to reread lines 334–337 and note the metaphor, "...an ocean of salt tears could not melt the resolution of the statutes." Have students tell what it means and how it contributes to their understanding of Danforth's character. (*Danforth is saying that even if the general public cries out in opposition in great numbers—such that their cries would create "an ocean of salt tears"—he will not back down. He believes in himself and sees himself as the executor of God's law. This confirms his character as an unwavering, stern person who does not back down in the face of opposition.*)

Analyze Drama Elements ⟨COMMON CORE⟩ RL 3, RL 5
(LINES 381–389)

Remind students to look for events that can make the central conflict more difficult to resolve. These events are called plot **complications.**

K **ASK STUDENTS** whether they believe Hale's revelation that conditions in Salem are deteriorating qualifies as a plot complication. Ask them to explain their reasoning. *(Possible answer: The news that Salem is in decline is a plot complication. If people in Salem begin objecting to how living in fear of being suspected has changed their quality of life, they are likely to start pushing back against the witch hunt in the form of a rebellion. If the judges lose the support of the people, it will make it very difficult to continue the witch hunt and prove that witches are present.)*

Analyze Drama Elements ⟨COMMON CORE⟩ RL 3, RL 5
(LINES 402–411)

Remind students to look to **stage directions** and **dialogue** to make inferences about characters.

L **CITE TEXT EVIDENCE** Ask students to explain what stage directions and dialogue tell them about what life has been like for Elizabeth Proctor since she was last seen in Act Three. *(The stage directions in lines 404–407 describe her as dirty, pale, and thin. This suggests that she has not been eating or bathing. When Danforth asks how she is, she responds (in lines 410–411) not with a yes or a no, but rather with, "I am yet six month before my time." This reveals that she is angry and bitter at Danforth and fearful that they have brought her out to be hanged. She wishes to remind him that she cannot be hanged until she delivers her child.)*

from them the perfection of their punishment.

Hale (*harder now*). If you think God wills you to raise rebellion, Mr. Danforth, you are mistaken!

Danforth (*instantly*). You have heard 380 rebellion spoken in the town?

K **Hale.** Excellency, there are orphans wandering from house to house; abandoned cattle bellow on the highroads, the stink of rotting crops hangs everywhere, and no man knows when the harlots' cry will end his life— and you wonder yet if rebellion's spoke? Better you should marvel how they do not burn your province!

390 **Danforth.** Mr. Hale, have you preached in Andover this month?

Hale. Thank God they have no need of me in Andover.

Danforth. You baffle me, sir. Why have you returned here?

Hale. Why, it is all simple. I come to do the Devil's work. I come to counsel

Christians they should belie themselves. (*His sarcasm collapses.*) There is blood 400 on my head! Can you not see the blood on my head!!

L **Parris.** Hush! (*For he has heard footsteps. They all face the door.* Herrick *enters with* Elizabeth. *Her wrists are linked by heavy chain, which* Herrick *now removes. Her clothes are dirty; her face is pale and gaunt.* Herrick *goes out.*)

Danforth (*very politely*). Goody Proctor. (*She is silent.*) I hope you are hearty?

410 **Elizabeth** (*as a warning reminder*). I am yet six month before my time.

Danforth. Pray be at your ease, we come not for your life. We—(*uncertain how to plead, for he is not accustomed to it.*) Mr. Hale, will you speak with the woman?

Hale. Goody Proctor, your husband is marked to hang this morning.

(*pause*)

Elizabeth (*quietly*). I have heard it.

532 Collection 6

SCAFFOLDING FOR ELL STUDENTS

Understand Suffixes Introduce a new suffix to students: *–ion*. Tell them that some verbs can become nouns of action by adding the suffix *–ion*. For example the verb *express* becomes the noun *expression* (an act of expressing; telling thoughts or feelings).

ASK STUDENTS to look at line 377 and notice the word "rebellion." Ask students what the word means and what verb it is formed from. *(The word is formed from* rebel; *a "rebellion" is an act of rebelling—an attempt to change a leader or a government.)* Have students do the same with the following words and then look for words ending in *-ion* as they read:

- extermination *(getting rid of something; from the verb* exterminate*)*
- revision *(changing something, usually to improve it; from the verb* revise*)*

Hale. You know, do you not, that I have no connection with the court? (*She seems to doubt it.*) I come of my own, Goody Proctor. I would save your husband's life, for if he is taken I count myself his murderer. Do you understand me?

Elizabeth. What do you want of me?

Hale. Goody Proctor, I have gone this three month like our Lord into the wilderness.[8] I have sought a Christian way, for damnation's doubled on a minister who counsels men to lie.

Hathorne. It is no lie, you cannot speak of lies.

Hale. It is a lie! They are innocent!

Danforth. I'll hear no more of that!

Hale (*continuing to* Elizabeth). Let you not mistake your duty as I mistook my own. I came into this village like a bridegroom to his beloved, bearing gifts of high religion; the very crowns of holy law I brought, and what I touched with my bright confidence, it died; and where I turned the eye of my great faith, blood flowed up. Beware, Goody Proctor—cleave to no faith when faith brings blood. It is mistaken law that leads you to sacrifice. Life, woman, life is God's most precious gift; no principle, however glorious, may justify the taking of it. I beg you, woman, prevail upon your husband to confess. Let him give his lie. Quail not before God's judgment in this, for it may well be God damns a liar less than he that throws his life away for pride. Will you plead with him? I cannot think he will listen to another.

Elizabeth (*quietly*). I think that be the Devil's argument.

---
[8] **like our Lord . . . wilderness:** According to the New Testament, Jesus spent 40 days wandering in the desert.

Hale (*with a climactic desperation*). Woman, before the laws of God we are as swine! We cannot read His will!

Elizabeth. I cannot dispute with you, sir; I lack learning for it.

Danforth (*going to her*). Goody Proctor, you are not summoned here for disputation. Be there no wifely tenderness within you? He will die with the sunrise. Your husband. Do you understand it? (*She only looks at him.*) What say you? Will you contend with him? (*She is silent.*) Are you stone? I tell you true, woman, had I no other proof of your unnatural life, your dry eyes now would be sufficient evidence that you delivered up your soul to Hell! A very ape would weep at such calamity! Have the Devil dried up any tear of pity in you? (*She is silent.*) Take her out. It profit nothing she should speak to him!

Elizabeth (*quietly*). Let me speak with him, Excellency.

Parris (*with hope*). You'll strive with him? (*She hesitates.*)

Danforth. Will you plead for his confession or will you not?

Elizabeth. I promise nothing. Let me speak with him.

(*A sound—the sibilance of dragging feet on stone. They turn. A pause. Herrick enters with John Proctor. His wrists are chained. He is another man, bearded, filthy, his eyes misty as though webs had overgrown them. He halts inside the doorway, his eye caught by the sight of Elizabeth. The emotion flowing between them prevents anyone from speaking for an instant. Now* Hale, *visibly affected, goes to* Danforth *and speaks quietly.*)

Hale. Pray, leave them, Excellency.

Danforth (*pressing* Hale *impatiently aside*). Mr. Proctor, you have been notified, have you not? (*Proctor is silent,*

The Crucible: Act Four **533**

CLOSE READ

Analyze Drama Elements
COMMON CORE RL 3, RL 5
(LINES 437–458)

Remind students that certain lines of **dialogue** can reveal the message of the playwright.

M **CITE TEXT EVIDENCE** Have students read Hale's speech in lines 437–458. Ask them how it expresses a message from the playwright. Cite evidence from the text. (*In lines 448–451, Hale says that life is precious and no principle justifies the taking of it, which is Miller's way of saying the witch hunt was wrong, and that any application of religion or principle that leads to bloodshed is wrong.*)

Analyze Drama Elements
COMMON CORE RL 3, RL 5
(LINES 490–500)

Tell students that **stage directions** are sometimes explicit in their descriptions of characters' appearances and personalities.

N **ASK STUDENTS** to explain what is meant by the stage direction in line 493 that Proctor is "another man." (*This stage direction serves to indicate that Proctor has been so changed by his experience in prison that he is practically another person—unrecognizable to those who knew him before.*)

WHEN STUDENTS STRUGGLE . . .

Review with students that **similes** make comparisons using the words *like* or *as.*

ASK STUDENTS to find the two similes on this page and tell how they affect their understanding of the character of Hale. (*lines 429–430: "I have gone this three month like our Lord into the wilderness." Hale is saying that he has been spending time alone in thought, as Jesus did in the desert; lines 439–440: "I came into this village like a bridegroom to his beloved, bearing gifts of high religion . . . . Hale is saying that he came to Salem with good intentions.*)

Analyze Drama Elements  RL 3, RL 5

(LINES 515–519)

Remind students that **stage directions** can describe a character's behavior vividly.

 ASK STUDENTS to think about the description of the stare Proctor gives Parris in line 517. What is an "icy" stare, exactly? Why does Proctor give one to Parris? What does it reveal about Proctor's character? *(An icy stare is an angry, unfriendly look at someone. Proctor gives Parris an icy stare because Proctor, having been through what has, is not ready to accept any kindness from Parris at this point. Proctor probably feels that Parris's offering is too little, too late. Support from Parris earlier in the play when the accusations were being made would have been helpful; now it is not.)*

Analyze Drama Elements  RL 3, RL 5

(LINES 530–559)

Tell students that sometimes what is left out of **dialogue** is at least as important as what is included. Point out to students Proctor and Elizabeth's short, factual lines.

P **CITE TEXT EVIDENCE** Ask students to analyze the dialogue between Proctor and Elizabeth in lines 530–558. Ask them why the playwright has them speak in this way at this point in the play. *(Miller wishes to show that they have accepted their plight and that they refuse to give in to their emotions. Instead of weeping and wailing, they speak with quiet dignity.)*

---

staring at Elizabeth.) I see light in the sky, Mister; let you counsel with your wife, and may God help you turn your back on Hell. (Proctor *is silent, staring at* Elizabeth.)

510   **Hale** (*quietly*). Excellency, let—

(Danforth *brushes past* Hale *and walks out.* Hale *follows.* Cheever *stands and follows,* Hathorne *behind.* Herrick *goes.* Parris, *from a safe distance, offers.*)

Parris. If you desire a cup of cider, Mr. Proctor, I am sure I—(Proctor *turns an icy stare at him, and he breaks off.* Parris *raises his palms toward* Proctor.) God lead you now. (Parris *goes out.*)

520   (*Alone.* Proctor *walks to her, halts. It is as though they stood in a spinning world. It is beyond sorrow, above it. He reaches out his hand as though toward an embodiment not quite real, and as he touches her, a strange soft sound, half laughter, half amazement, comes from his throat. He pats her hand. She covers his hand with hers. And then, weak, he sits. Then she sits, facing him.*)

530   **Proctor.** The child?

Elizabeth. It grows.

Proctor. There is no word of the boys?

Elizabeth. They're well. Rebecca's Samuel keeps them.

Proctor. You have not seen them?

Elizabeth. I have not. (*She catches a weakening in herself and downs it.*)

Proctor. You are a—marvel, Elizabeth.

Elizabeth. You—have been tortured?

540   **Proctor.** Aye. (*Pause. She will not let herself be drowned in the sea that threatens her.*) They come for my life now.

Elizabeth. I know it.

(*pause*)

Proctor. None—have yet confessed?

Elizabeth. There be many confessed.

Proctor. Who are they?

550   **Elizabeth.** There be a hundred or more, they say. Goody Ballard is one; Isaiah Goodkind is one. There be many.

Proctor. Rebecca?

Elizabeth. Not Rebecca. She is one foot in Heaven now; naught may hurt her more.

Proctor. And Giles?

Elizabeth. You have not heard of it?

Proctor. I hear nothin', where I am kept.

Elizabeth. Giles is dead.

560   (*He looks at her incredulously.*)

Proctor. When were he hanged?

Elizabeth (*quietly, factually*). He were not hanged. He would not answer aye or nay to his indictment; for if he denied the charge they'd hang him surely, and auction out his property. So he stand mute, and died Christian under the law. And so his sons will have his farm. It is the law, for he could not be

570   condemned a wizard without he answer the indictment, aye or nay.

Proctor. Then how does he die?

Elizabeth (*gently*). They press him, John.

Proctor. Press?

Elizabeth. Great stones they lay upon his chest until he plead aye or nay. (*with a tender smile for the old man*) They say he give them but two words. "More

580   weight," he says. And died.

Proctor (*numbed—a thread to weave into his agony*). "More weight."

WHEN STUDENTS STRUGGLE...

Remind students to practice their **reading fluency** by reading with expression. This scene between Proctor and Elizabeth is rich in emotion.

ASK STUDENTS to work with a partner and read the scene. Then have them switch roles. After that, have them describe the difference in their experiences reading Proctor's and Elizabeth's parts.

Elizabeth. Aye. It were a fearsome[9] man, Giles Corey.

(*pause*)

Proctor (*with great force of will, but not quite looking at her*). I have been thinking I would confess to them, Elizabeth. (*She shows nothing.*) What say 590 you? If I give them that?

Elizabeth. I cannot judge you, John.

(*pause*)

Proctor (*simply—a pure question*). What would you have me do?

Elizabeth. As you will, I would have it. (*slight pause*) I want you living, John. That's sure.

Proctor (*pauses, then with a flailing of hope*). Giles' wife? Have she confessed?

600 **Elizabeth.** She will not.

(*pause*)

Proctor. It is a pretense, Elizabeth.

Elizabeth. What is?

Proctor. I cannot mount the gibbet like a saint. It is a fraud. I am not that man. (*She is silent.*) My honesty is broke, Elizabeth; I am no good man. Nothing's spoiled by giving them this lie that were not rotten long before.

610 **Elizabeth.** And yet you've not confessed till now. That speak goodness in you.

Proctor. Spite only keeps me silent. It is hard to give a lie to dogs. (*Pause. For the first time he turns directly to her.*) I would have your forgiveness, Elizabeth.

Elizabeth. It is not for me to give, John, I am—

Proctor. I'd have you see some honesty in it. Let them that never lied die now to 620 keep their souls. It is pretense for me, a vanity that will not blind God nor keep

my children out of the wind. (*pause*) What say you?

Elizabeth (*upon a heaving sob that always threatens*). John, it come to naught that I should forgive you, if you'll not forgive yourself. (*Now he turns away a little, in great agony.*) It is not my soul, John, it is yours. (*He 630 stands, as though in physical pain, slowly rising to his feet with a great immortal longing to find his answer. It is difficult to say, and she is on the verge of tears.*) Only be sure of this, for I know it now: Whatever you will do, it is a good man does it. (*He turns his doubting, searching gaze upon her.*) I have read my heart this three month, John. (*pause*) I have sins of my own to count. It needs a cold wife to 640 prompt lechery.

Proctor (*in great pain*). Enough, enough—

Elizabeth (*now pouring out her heart*). Better you should know me!

Proctor. I will not hear it! I know you!

Elizabeth. You take my sins upon you, John—

Proctor (*in agony*). No, I take my own, my own!

650 **Elizabeth.** John, I counted myself so plain, so poorly made, no honest love could come to me! Suspicion kissed you when I did; I never knew how I should say my love. It were a cold house I kept! (*In fright, she swerves, as Hathorne enters.*)

Hathorne. What say you, Proctor? The sun is soon up.

(*Proctor, his chest heaving, stares, turns 660 to Elizabeth. She comes to him as though to plead, her voice quaking.*)

Elizabeth. Do what you will. But let none be your judge. There be no higher judge under Heaven than Proctor is!

---

[9] **fearsome:** courageous.

The Crucible: Act Four **535**

CLOSE READ

Analyze Drama Elements
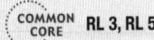
COMMON CORE RL 3, RL 5

(LINES 586–613)

Remind students that the process of **indirect characterization** requires them to infer from both **stage directions** and **dialogue** what is motivating a character to behave as she or he does.

Q **ASK STUDENTS** to reread lines 586–613 and tell why Proctor is planning to confess to being under the influence of the Devil. (*He feels he cannot save his soul, so he would rather live with the lie of his confession than die.*) How does he rationalize his decision? (*Proctor, filled with guilt over his adultery, says that he is not a "saint," line 605; that he is "not that man," lines 605–606; and that he is "no good man," line 607.*)

Analyze Drama Elements

COMMON CORE RL 3, RL 5

(LINES 624–640)

Remind students that a character's behavior—as described in **stage directions**—is sometimes more effective than is **dialogue** at revealing what a character is experiencing.

R **CITE TEXT EVIDENCE** Ask students to note how Proctor responds to Elizabeth during her dialogue in lines 624–640. How does his behavior reveal his feelings? Cite specifics from the text. (*In line 628, he turns away from Elizabeth, which suggests that he knows she is right that he must forgive himself and make his own decision, but that it pains him; when he stands in the next line, the stage directions are explicit in saying that he is "longing to find his answer;" he looks at her with doubt in lines 636–637 when she says he is a "good man."*)

SCAFFOLDING FOR ELL STUDENTS

Understand Contractions Explain to students that **contractions** are short forms of two words (or a word phrase) created by eliminating a letter and using an apostrophe in its place. For example, *shouldn't* is a contraction that replaces *should not*.

ASK STUDENTS to write the long form of the following contractions found on this page:

- that's (*that is*)
- nothing's (*nothing is*)
- you've (*you have*)

Analyze Drama Elements  COMMON CORE RL 3, RL 5

(LINES 670–678)

Remind students to look to **dialogue, stage directions,** and what they already know about the characters to understand characters' behavior.

S **CITE TEXT EVIDENCE** Ask students to explain why Hathorne is so excited at this point. *(For Hathorne, who is eager to see the witch hunt be successful, getting Proctor to confess is a major victory. Proctor is a high-profile individual in Salem society and his confession would add legitimacy to the judges' case.)*

Analyze Drama Elements  COMMON CORE RL 3, RL 5

(LINES 681–704)

Tell students about another kind of **conflict** a play often has: a character's inner conflict. When a character is wrestling with opposing forces within himself or herself—over a certain choice that must be made, for example—it is said that he or she is experiencing an inner conflict. A play's **dialogue** and **stage directions** will give clues as to the nature of a character's inner conflict.

T **CITE TEXT EVIDENCE** Ask students to read Proctor's dialogue and speech directions in lines 681–704. What is the nature of his inner conflict in this section? What choice is he wrestling with, and why? Cite specifics. *(On the one hand, Proctor feels that he could live with lying to save his own life, for he is not a saint [line 691], as Rebecca is [lines 692–693]; yet he cannot bear to confess to something he did not do—"It is evil" to do so, he says [line 704].)*

Forgive me, forgive me, John—I never knew such goodness in the world! (*She covers her face, weeping.*)

(*Proctor turns from her to Hathorne; he is off the earth, his voice hollow.*)

670 **Proctor.** I want my life.

Hathorne (*electrified, surprised*). You'll confess yourself?

Proctor. I will have my life.

Hathorne (*with a mystical tone*). God be praised! It is a providence! (*He rushes out the door, and his voice is heard calling down the corridor.*) He will confess! Proctor will confess!

Proctor (*with a cry, as he strides to the*
680 *door*). Why do you cry it? (*In great pain he turns back to her.*) It is evil, is it not? It is evil.

Elizabeth (*in terror, weeping*). I cannot judge you, John, I cannot!

Proctor. Then who will judge me? (*suddenly clasping his hands*) God in Heaven, what is John Proctor, what is John Proctor? (*He moves as an animal, and a fury is riding in him, a tantalized*
690 *search.*) I think it is honest, I think so; I am no saint. (*As though she had denied this he calls angrily at her.*) Let Rebecca go like a saint; for me it is fraud!

(*Voices are heard in the hall, speaking together in suppressed excitement.*)

Elizabeth. I am not your judge, I cannot be. (*as though giving him release*) Do as you will, do as you will!

Proctor. Would you give them such a
700 lie? Say it. Would you ever give them this? (*She cannot answer.*) You would not; if tongs of fire were singeing you you would not! It is evil. Good, then—it is evil, and I do it!

(*Hathorne enters with Danforth, and, with them, Cheever, Parris, and Hale.*

It is a businesslike, rapid entrance, as though the ice had been broken.*)

Danforth (*with great relief and*
710 *gratitude*). Praise to God, man, praise to God; you shall be blessed in Heaven for this. (*Cheever has hurried to the bench with pen, ink, and paper. Proctor watches him.*) Now then, let us have it. Are you ready, Mr. Cheever?

Proctor (*with a cold, cold horror at their efficiency*). Why must it be written?

Danforth. Why, for the good instruction of the village, Mister; this
720 we shall post upon the church door! (*to Parris, urgently*) Where is the marshal?

Parris (*runs to the door and calls down the corridor*). Marshal! Hurry!

Danforth. Now, then, Mister, will you speak slowly, and directly to the point, for Mr. Cheever's sake. (*He is on record now, and is really dictating to* Cheever, *who writes.*) Mr. Proctor, have you seen the Devil in your life? (*Proctor's jaws*
730 *lock.*) Come, man, there is light in the sky; the town waits at the scaffold; I would give out this news. Did you see the Devil?

Proctor. I did.

Parris. Praise God!

Danforth. And when he come to you, what were his demand? (*Proctor is silent.* Danforth *helps.*) Did he bid you to do his work upon the earth?

740 **Proctor.** He did.

Danforth. And you bound yourself to his service? (*Danforth turns, as* Rebecca Nurse *enters, with* Herrick *helping to support her. She is barely able to walk.*) Come in, come in, woman!

Rebecca (*brightening as she sees* Proctor). Ah, John! You are well, then, eh?

SCAFFOLDING FOR ELL STUDENTS

Identify Pronoun Referents Review pronoun **referents** (or **antecedents**) with students.

As an example, tell students to note the word "it" in line 714: "Now then, let us have it." Here, the pronoun *it* refers to Proctor's confession.

ASK STUDENTS to tell the referents for the following two pronouns on this page:

- Lines 719–720: " . . . this we shall post upon the church door!" *(Proctor's signed confession)*

- Lines 736–737: "And when he come to you, what were his demand?" *(the Devil)*

(Proctor *turns his face to the wall.*)

750 **Danforth.** Courage, man, courage—let her witness your good example that she may come to God herself. Now hear it, Goody Nurse! Say on, Mr. Proctor. Did you bind yourself to the Devil's service?

Rebecca (*astonished*). Why, John!

Proctor (*through his teeth, his face turned from* Rebecca). I did.

Danforth. Now, woman, you surely see it profit nothin' to keep this conspiracy

760 any further. Will you confess yourself with him?

Rebecca. Oh, John—God send his mercy on you!

Danforth. I say, will you confess yourself, Goody Nurse?

Rebecca. Why, it is a lie, it is a lie; how may I damn myself? I cannot, I cannot.

Danforth. Mr. Proctor. When the Devil came to you did you see Rebecca Nurse

770 in his company? (Proctor *is silent.*) Come, man, take courage—did you ever see her with the Devil?

Proctor (*almost inaudibly*). No.

(Danforth, *now sensing trouble, glances at* John *and goes to the table, and picks up a sheet—the list of condemned.*)

Danforth. Did you ever see her sister, Mary Easty, with the Devil?

Proctor. No, I did not.

780 **Danforth** (*his eyes narrow on* Proctor). Did you ever see Martha Corey with the Devil?

Proctor. I did not.

Danforth (*realizing, slowly putting the sheet down*). Did you ever see anyone with the Devil?

Proctor. I did not.

Danforth. Proctor, you mistake me. I am not empowered to trade your life for

790 a lie. You have most certainly seen some person with the Devil. (Proctor *is silent.*) Mr. Proctor, a score of people have already testified they saw this woman with the Devil.

Proctor. Then it is proved. Why must I say it?

Danforth. Why "must" you say it! Why, you should rejoice to say it if your soul is truly purged of any love for Hell!

800 **Proctor.** They think to go like saints. I like not to spoil their names.

Danforth (*inquiring, incredulous*). Mr. Proctor, do you think they go like saints?

Proctor (*evading*). This woman never thought she done the Devil's work.

Danforth. Look you, sir. I think you mistake your duty here. It matters nothing what she thought—she is

810 convicted of the unnatural murder of children, and you for sending your spirit out upon Mary Warren. Your soul alone is the issue here, Mister, and you will prove its whiteness or you cannot live in a Christian country. Will you tell me now what persons conspired with you in the Devil's company? (Proctor *is silent.*) To your knowledge was Rebecca Nurse ever—

820 **Proctor.** I speak my own sins; I cannot judge another. (*crying out, with hatred*) I have no tongue for it.

Hale (*quickly to* Danforth). Excellency, it is enough he confess himself. Let him sign it, let him sign it.

Parris (*feverishly*). It is a great service, sir. It is a weighty name; it will strike the village that Proctor confess. I beg you, let him sign it. The sun is up,

830 Excellency!

The Crucible: Act Four **537**

Analyze Drama Elements
(LINES 750–773)

Remind students to pay attention to events that raise the stakes for the characters.

U ASK STUDENTS to explain how Rebecca's entrance into the scene raises the stakes for Proctor. *(Proctor cannot bear to have Rebecca think he has confessed because she is someone that he respects. Her opinion matters to him. Further, her own persistent refusal to confess ("I cannot, I cannot," line 767) is likely to push Proctor to change his mind about confessing. Doing that will result in his death.)*

Analyze Drama Elements
(LINES 750–773)

Remind students that a character that is a **foil** highlights the traits of another character through their differences.

V ASK STUDENTS to tell how Rebecca is a foil to Proctor at this point in the plot. *(Rebecca is standing her ground even after having been imprisoned; she is refusing to confess to being a witch even though she knows it will result in her death. This highlights the inner conflict of Proctor, who cannot decide whether to lie and live or tell the truth and die.)*

WHEN STUDENTS STRUGGLE…

Explain to students that all of the characters in this scene are in conflict. Tell them that thinking about what each character wants will help them to understand the situation.

ASK STUDENTS to work in a small group to list all of the characters on this page and make a note about what each one wants. *(Danforth wants Proctor to confess and to name other accused people; Rebecca wants Proctor to tell the truth; Proctor wants to save his life by confessing, but not to name others; Hale and Parris want Danforth to accept Proctor's confession and spare his life.)*

Analyze Drama Elements  COMMON CORE RL 3, RL 5

(LINES 861–891)

Tell students to look out for lines that are repeated by characters, because they are likely to be important lines that highlight a key moment of the plot.

W ASK STUDENTS to reread Proctor's exchange with Danforth in lines 861–891. What does he mean when he tells Danforth, "You will not use me!" *(Proctor refuses to let Danforth post Proctor's confession in public because he knows that Danforth wants to make an example out of Proctor. If Proctor, a respected and highly visible member of the community, has confessed, then others may be compelled to do so. Proctor does not want himself "used" as an example in this way. Further, Proctor is thinking about the future of his sons, and what it would mean for them to have a last name associated with someone who confessed to witchcraft—it would certainly make their lives more difficult.)*

Danforth (*considers; then with dissatisfaction*). Come, then, sign your testimony. (*to* Cheever) Give it to him. (Cheever *goes to* Proctor, *the confession and a pen in hand.* Proctor *does not look at it.*) Come, man, sign it.

Proctor (*after glancing at the confession*). You have all witnessed it—it is enough.

Danforth. You will not sign it?

840 **Proctor.** You have all witnessed it; what more is needed?

Danforth. Do you sport with me? You will sign your name or it is no confession, Mister! (*His breast heaving with agonized breathing,* Proctor *now lays the paper down and signs his name.*)

Parris. Praise be to the Lord!

(Proctor *has just finished signing when* Danforth *reaches for the paper. But* 850 Proctor *snatches it up, and now a wild terror is rising in him, and a boundless anger.*)

Danforth (*perplexed, but politely extending his hand*). If you please, sir.

Proctor. No.

Danforth (*as though* Proctor *did not understand*). Mr. Proctor, I must have—

Proctor. No, no. I have signed it. You have seen me. It is done! You have no 860 need for this.

Parris. Proctor, the village must have proof that—

Proctor. Damn the village! I confess to God, and God has seen my name on this! It is enough!

Danforth. No, sir, it is—

Proctor. You came to save my soul, did you not? Here! I have confessed myself; it is enough!

870 **Danforth.** You have not con—

Proctor. I have confessed myself! Is there no good penitence but it be public? God does not need my name nailed upon the church! God sees my name; God knows how black my sins are! It is enough!

Danforth. Mr. Proctor—

Proctor. You will not use me! I am no Sarah Good or Tituba, I am John 880 Proctor! You will not use me! It is no part of salvation that you should use me!

Danforth. I do not wish to—

Proctor. I have three children—how may I teach them to walk like men in the world, and I sold my friends?

Danforth. You have not sold your friends—

Proctor. Beguile me not! I blacken all of 890 them when this is nailed to the church the very day they hang for silence!

Danforth. Mr. Proctor, I must have good and legal proof that you—

Proctor. You are the high court, your word is good enough! Tell them I confessed myself; say Proctor broke his knees and wept like a woman; say what you will, but my name cannot—

Danforth (*with suspicion*). It is the same, 900 is it not? If I report it or you sign to it?

Proctor (*He knows it is insane*). No, it is not the same! What others say and what I sign to is not the same!

Danforth. Why? Do you mean to deny this confession when you are free?

Proctor. I mean to deny nothing!

Danforth. Then explain to me, Mr. Proctor, why you will not let—

Proctor (*with a cry of his whole soul*). 910 Because it is my name! Because I cannot have another in my life! Because I lie and sign myself to lies! Because I am not worth the dust on the feet of them that hang! How may I live without my name? I have given you my soul; leave me my name!

Danforth (*pointing at the confession in Proctor's hand*). Is that document a lie? If it is a lie I will not accept it! What
920 say you? I will not deal in lies, Mister! (*Proctor is motionless.*) You will give me your honest confession in my hand, or I cannot keep you from the rope. (*Proctor does not reply.*) Which way do you go, Mister?

(*His breast heaving, his eyes staring, Proctor tears the paper and crumples it, and he is weeping in fury, but erect.*)

Danforth. Marshal!

930 **Parris** (*hysterically, as though the tearing paper were his life*). Proctor, Proctor!

Hale. Man, you will hang! You cannot!

Proctor (*his eyes full of tears*). I can. And there's your first marvel, that I can. You have made your magic now, for now I do think I see some shred of goodness in John Proctor. Not enough to weave a banner with, but white enough to keep it from such dogs. (*Elizabeth, in a burst of terror, rushes to him and weeps against
940 his hand.*) Give them no tear! Tears pleasure them! Show honor now, show a stony heart and sink them with it! (*He has lifted her, and kisses her now with great passion.*)

Rebecca. Let you fear nothing! Another judgment waits us all!

Danforth. Hang them high over the town! Who weeps for these, weeps for
950 corruption! (*He sweeps out past them.*

Herrick *starts to lead* Rebecca, *who almost collapses, but* Proctor *catches her, and she glances up at him apologetically.*)

Rebecca. I've had no breakfast.

Herrick. Come, man.

(Herrick *escorts them out,* Hathorne *and* Cheever *behind them.* Elizabeth *stands staring at the empty doorway.*)

Parris (*in deadly fear, to* Elizabeth). Go
960 to him, Goody Proctor! There is yet time!

(*From outside a drumroll strikes the air.* Parris *is startled.* Elizabeth *jerks about toward the window.*)

Parris. Go to him! (*He rushes out the door, as though to hold back his fate.*) Proctor! Proctor! (*again, a short burst of drums*)

Hale. Woman, plead with him! (*He
970 starts to rush out the door, and then goes back to her.*) Woman! It is pride, it is vanity. (*She avoids his eyes, and moves to the window. He drops to his knees.*) Be his helper!— What profit him to bleed? Shall the dust praise him? Shall the worms declare his truth? Go to him, take his shame away!

Elizabeth (*supporting herself against collapse, grips the bars of the window,
980 and with a cry*). He have his goodness now. God forbid I take it from him!

(*The final drumroll crashes, then heightens violently.* Hale *weeps in frantic prayer, and the new sun is pouring in upon her face, and the drums rattle like bones in the morning air. The curtain falls.*)

COLLABORATIVE DISCUSSION With a partner, discuss what the last act reveals about the participants in the witch hunt. What is ironic about their circumstances? Cite specific textual evidence from the play to support your ideas.

The Crucible: Act Four **539**

CLOSE READ

Analyze Drama Elements COMMON CORE RL 3, RL 5
(LINES 926–987)

Review the elements of a play's **plot** with students: **conflict, complications,** and **climax.** Explain to students that in the **resolution** of a play, the central conflict is brought to a close.

X ASK STUDENTS to explain how the central conflict of the play is resolved at the end of Act Four. (*Proctor and Rebecca refuse to confess and they are sentenced to die. Elizabeth refuses to intervene in Proctor's decision, because it was the right one and proves his essential goodness.*) Ask students what message from the playwright the resolution expresses. (*Miller has written a sad ending for Proctor; Proctor is ultimately a victim of a group of people determined to prove something true despite the evidence. The hanging of an innocent and good man is a warning against persecution.*)

Analyze Drama Elements COMMON CORE RL 3, RL 5
(LINES 926–987)

Remind students that the **climax** of a play has the potential to change the outcome of the conflict.

Y CITE TEXT EVIDENCE Ask students whether they think that the climax (Proctor's admission of adultery in Act Three) changes the outcome of the play's conflict. Tell them to cite evidence for their answer. (*The outcome of the play is not really affected by Proctor's admission of adultery. He only confessed to expose Abigail's reasons for accusing him—she wanted revenge on Proctor and Elizabeth. In the end, Abigail gets away with her accusation and Proctor is hanged because he ultimately chooses not to confess.*)

TO CHALLENGE STUDENTS...

Research Genre Did you laugh or did you cry? Tell students that traditionally, there are two genres of drama: comedy and tragedy.

ASK STUDENTS to work in pairs to research tragedy. Have them define and list characteristics of a tragedy. Then have students discuss what makes *The Crucible* a tragedy. (*Tragedies dramatize sad or horrible events experienced by a single individual. The individual is usually heroic, and often it is his or her own tragic flaw that brings about the tragedy's horrible events. The Crucible is a tragedy not only because of its horrible events, but because Proctor's affair with Abigail (his flaw) causes her to want to take revenge and initiate the witch hunt, which is the central conflict of the play.*)

COLLABORATIVE DISCUSSION Have student pairs discuss the actions of Danforth, Parris, and Herrick. Then have partners consider the irony of their circumstances. Ask them to cite specific evidence from the text. Then have groups share their conclusions with the class as a whole. Accept all reasonable responses.

ASK STUDENTS to share any questions they generated in the course of reading and discussing the selection.

The Crucible: Act Four **539**

Analyze Drama Elements

COMMON CORE RL 3, RL 5

Teach direct characterization and indirect characterization to students by having them complete a two-column chart to help them understand how dialogue and stage directions contribute to an understanding of character. Label the two columns "Direct Characterization" and "Indirect Characterization" and label the rows "stage directions" and "dialogue." Have students fill in the graphic organizer with details about how stage directions and dialogue are used for indirect characterization and direct characterization. *(Possible answers: Direct characterization: dialogue: what a character says about someone else's appearance, personality, or emotional state; stage directions: what the stage directions say about a character's appearance, personality, or emotional state; Indirect characterization: dialogue: infer ideas about a character from what is said by themselves or others; stage directions: infer ideas about a character from the descriptions of their actions and behavior)*

Then review the other functions of dialogue. Have students offer a brief oral explanation in their own words of the differences between dialogue that moves the plot forward and dialogue that conveys theme.

Analyze Drama Elements

COMMON CORE RL 3, RL 5

Two remaining elements of drama effectively utilized by Miller are characterization and dialogue.

Throughout *The Crucible*, the characters' traits, motives, and relationships emerge. Miller reveals these facets of character through direct and indirect characterization as described in the chart.

Direct characterization means that specific details about character are provided.	**The stage directions** in the play offer explicit descriptions of characters' appearances, personalities, and emotional states. For example, in Act One, Hale is described as "a tight-skinned, eager-eyed intellectual. This is a beloved errand for him." The stage directions in Act Four depict him as being "steeped in sorrow, exhausted."
Indirect characterization requires readers to use clues from the text to infer what the character is like.	While **dialogue** might be used to state direct ideas about a character, most often readers must infer meaning from what is said. For example, in lines 439–451 in Act Four, Hale's speech reveals his inner conflict and the way that he has changed. "I came into this village like a bridegroom to his beloved . . . cleave to no faith when faith brings blood . . . Life, woman, life is God's most precious gift; no principle, however glorious, may justify the taking of it."
	Characters' actions as described or performed reveal more about them. In Act Three, for example, Hale denounces the proceedings and walks out. His uncharacteristic burst of anger shows readers how distraught he is over what is happening and suggests that he may feel guilty for his role in the events.

Dialogue is the foundation of drama. It can reveal an infinite variety of character traits. In addition to revealing character as explained in the chart, it performs a variety of other critical functions.

- It moves the plot forward. Through characters' speech, readers learn about plot developments and gain a greater understanding of the central conflict and its impact: "Twelve are already executed; the names of these seven are given out, and the village expects to see them die this morning."
- It also conveys theme. Characters' speeches often state important ideas that help readers to recognize the playwright's underlying message: "Because it is my name! Because I cannot have another in my life!"

Strategies for Annotation

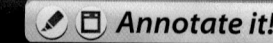 ✏️ 🖥️ *Annotate it!*

Analyze Drama Elements

COMMON CORE RL 3, RL 5

Share these strategies for guided or independent analysis:

- Highlight in yellow any examples of **stage directions** that offer **direct characterization.** Then underline any **dialogue** that gives direct characterization.
- Highlight in blue any examples of **stage directions** that offer **indirect characterization.**
- On a note, explain what the indirect characterization tells about the character.

201 **Danforth** (*alarmed*)....Where may they be?

Parris....My daughter tells me how she heard them speaking of ships last week, and tonight I discover my—my strongbox is broke into. (*He presses his fingers against his eyes to keep back tears.*)

"When Parris presses his eyes to keep from crying, it reveals that he is devastated at the news that his niece has robbed him and fled."

Analyzing the Text

COMMON CORE RL 1, RL 2, RL 3, RL 4, RL 5, W 2, W 4

Cite Text Evidence   Support your responses with evidence from the selection.

1. **Analyze** How do the stage directions at the beginning of Act Four set the mood? What does the contrast between this setting and the one described at the start of Act One suggest about the changes brought about by the witch hunts?

2. **Infer** Explain why each of these characters wants Proctor and the other prisoners to confess. Cite evidence in support of your response.

   - Danforth
   - Parris
   - Hale

3. **Analyze** What image of Giles Corey do Elizabeth's words convey in Act Four, lines 576–580? What does Giles Corey represent for Miller? Think of his earlier appearances in the play.

4. **Interpret** A crucible is a severe test or trial. It is also a vessel in which materials are melted at high temperatures to produce a more refined substance. What does a crucible symbolize in this drama? How does this symbol suggest a theme?

5. **Analyze** Reread the passages identified in the list. What is the central paradox, or contradiction, of the trials? What idea is Miller conveying about these kinds of witch hunts through this paradox?

   - Act Two, lines 1132–1143
   - Act Three, lines 440–454
   - Act Three, lines 672–696

6. **Synthesize** Explain how the resolution of Proctor's conflict reveals a major theme in the play.

7. **Analyze** What do the events in Act Four foreshadow about the future of the trials? Explain.

PERFORMANCE TASK

Writing Activity: Essay Why does John Proctor change his mind and tear up the confession even though this virtually condemns him to die? In four or five paragraphs, discuss Proctor's perception of a morally righteous person and how that perception affects his decision. Think about Rebecca Nurse's reaction to his confession and Elizabeth's assertion that "there be no higher judge under Heaven than Proctor is!"

- Explain the choices that Proctor must make to arrive at his decision.
- Clarify how Proctor's idea of morality differs from that of the judges.
- Use quotations and examples from the play to support key points.

PRACTICE & APPLY

Assign this performance task.

PERFORMANCE TASK

COMMON CORE W 2, W 4

Writing Activity: Essay Have students analyze the role Proctor's ideas about moral righteousness play in his decision to tear up his confession. Encourage them to reread Act Four and trace the evolution of Proctor's decision, including Rebecca Nurse's initial reaction. When students have finished writing, have them exchange essays with a partner and offer constructive feedback. After students have made revisions, ask volunteers to read their essays to the class.

Analyzing the Text

COMMON CORE RL 1, RL 2, RL 3, RL 4, RL 5

Possible answers:

1. *The setting at the beginning of Act One was Parris's home, where light streamed in through the window. In Act Four, the stage directions set a serious, gloomy mood by describing a "great, heavy door" and a "place" that is "in darkness."*

2. *Danforth wants Proctor to save his own soul (lines 507–508: "…may God help you turn your back on Hell"). Parris fears a revolt in Salem if Proctor is hanged (lines 233–237: "I tell you true, sir, I fear there will be riot here"). Hale wants Proctor to confess because Hale believes life is sacred ("…life is God's most precious gift; no principle, however glorious, may justify the taking of it"). Hale also feels guilty for not having fought harder to establish Proctor's innocence (lines 423–425: "I would save your husband's life, for if he is taken I count myself his murderer").*

3. *Elizabeth's story about Giles portrays the old man as defiant and brave to the very end. By staying mute, he died "Christian under the law" (lines 567–569) so his sons could have the family farm. Giles symbolizes the flawed human being whose life is still worth protecting and defending.*

4. *The crucible symbolizes a spiritual trial in which characters are "refined" and emerge stronger and better than before. It suggests the theme of redemption.*

5. *Each of these scenes reveals the paradox that those who make the accusations are automatically believed and the accused are automatically disbelieved. The accusers are favored because their accusations align with the fears and prejudices of the judges. Miller is conveying the idea that these kinds of witch hunts cannot result in justice.*

6. *Proctor resolves his conflict by refusing to admit to a lie and submitting to the punishment of hanging. This reflects one of Miller's themes—that of protecting one's name. In the beginning of the play, Proctor is worried about testifying against Abigail because the truth of their affair might ruin his reputation. At the end of the play, however, Proctor refuses to lie in order to protect his name and dies because of it.*

7. *The events in Act Four foreshadow that the trials in Salem will probably end. Parris and Hale are no longer in favor of the trials, and there are signs that the people of Salem are turning against them.*

Language and Style: Dialogue

COMMON CORE L 3a

Explain to students that Miller has written *The Crucible* in a very specific style, especially where the dialogue is concerned. Miller has his characters speak in a manner suggestive of the seventeenth century.

Tell students that the examples in the chart are some of the style conventions Miller employs. Ask students to go through Act Four with a partner and select a few lines heavy in stylized dialogue. Have them read the lines aloud, explaining the stylistic devices employed as they read. Then have them rewrite the sections in modern style. *(Possible answer: Lines 576–580: "Great stones they lay upon his chest until he plead aye or nay. They say he give them but two words. 'More weight,' he says. And died." Modern: "They laid great stones on his chest until he said yes or no. People say that he said just two words: 'More weight.' And then he died.")*

Possible answers:

1. *Go you to the house!*

2. *Aye, true it is that I saw the Devil with Rebecca Nurse.*

3. *Be you sure of their guilt?*

4. *Confess ye to these sins!*

Language and Style: Dialogue

COMMON CORE L 3a

In *The Crucible*, Miller carefully constructs his dialogue to match the historical time period in which he sets his play. His word choice and use of inverted sentences reflect the contemporary speech of seventeenth-century Salem, adding to the authenticity of his setting and realistic depiction of his characters.

Read these examples from the play:

Susanna. Aye, sir, he have been searchin' his books since he left you, sir. But he bid me tell you, that you might look to unnatural things for the cause of it. (*Act One, lines 56–60*)

Parris. Let him look to medicine and put out all thought of unnatural causes here. There be none. (*Act One, lines 65–67*)

Abigail. Now look you. All of you. We danced. (*Act One, line 455*)

Here, Miller uses *be* rather than *are*, the verb form we use in this context today. Instead of *yes*, he uses the word *aye*, a word that was commonplace in the 1600s but is rarely used today. Finally, he uses a type of inverted word order common to seventeenth-century speech, with the verb preceding the subject.

This chart includes other examples of Miller's style in this play:

Example	Explanation
"I am waitin' for you every night."	Throughout the play, the characters drop the final *g* from their participles.
"Why, her eyes is closed." "It were another sort that hanged till now."	In these lines, the verb's number does not agree with the subject.
"Them that will not confess will hang."	Here Miller replaces the subject pronoun with the object pronoun *them*.

Practice and Apply Rewrite the following sentences to reflect the speech patterns seen in the play. Compare your rewritten sentences with a partner.

1. You go to the house!

2. Yes, it is true I saw the devil with Rebecca Nurse.

3. Are you sure of their guilt?

4. You confess to these sins!

Strategies for Annotation ✐ 📖 *Annotate it!*

Language and Style: Dialogue

COMMON CORE L 3a

Share these strategies for guided or independent analysis:

- Highlight in yellow any examples of the use of *be* instead of *are* or *am*.
- Highlight in blue any examples in which the final *g* is dropped from a participle.
- Underline any examples of putting the verb before the subject.
- Double underline any examples of a subject pronoun or possessive pronoun being replaced by an object pronoun.
- On a note, rewrite Sarah Good's line in modern style.

Sarah Good. Oh, is it you, Marshal! I thought sure you be the devil comin' for us. Could I have a sip of cider for me goin'-away?

20 **Herrick** (*handing her the flask*). And where are you off to, Sarah?

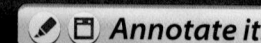

"Oh it is you, Marshal! I thought for sure you were the devil coming for us. Could I have a sip of cider for my going away?"

Conduct Research

COMMON CORE
W 2, W 7, W 8

TEACH

Explain to students that one of the most important aspects of *The Crucible* is that it serves as a critique of the United States government's pursuit of communist subversion in American society during the 1950s. This period of anti-communist "witch-hunting" is known as the Red Scare. The primary political prosecutor of the Red Scare was Senator Joseph McCarthy. Tell students they will be doing a research project on the Red Scare.

Review the steps to conducting research:

1. **Formulate Research Questions** For example, *Who was Joseph McCarthy and what did he believe? What was the House Committee on Un-American Activities? What was the Red Scare and whom did it impact?*
2. **Start Your Research** Use a search engine to find articles on websites about McCarthy and the Red Scare. Then evaluate the sites for reliability. Government (.gov) and education (.edu) sites are usually reliable, as are encyclopedia and news sites. Then search for reliable books and newspaper and magazine articles at a library. Your goal is to collect multiple print and digital sources.
3. **Collect Information** Synthesize your materials and collect data that answers your questions. As you read, come up with new questions that will allow you to explore the topic in diverse and interesting ways. Look for details, terms, quotations, and images that have to do with your topic.
4. **Draw Conclusions and Create an Outline** Complete your research and make an outline of your findings. Use the outline for your project.

PRACTICE AND APPLY

Ask students to follow the above steps and prepare a multimedia presentation about one facet of the Red Scare. For example, students may wish to focus on the blacklist and the Red Scare's impact on Hollywood. Their presentations should be accompanied by a list of works cited. Have students deliver their presentations to the class.

 **INTERACTIVE WHITEBOARD LESSON** If students need further instruction, use this **Interactive Whiteboard Lesson: Conducting Research on the Web**

Analyze Drama Elements

COMMON CORE
RL 3, RL 5

RETEACH

Review the **elements of drama** with students:

- A play's **plot** has four elements: **conflict, complications, climax,** and **resolution.**
- Characters include **a protagonist, antagonist,** and **foils.**
- In **direct characterization,** dialogue and stage directions state details about a character explicitly. In **indirect characterization,** the reader must infer what the characters are like from dialogue and stage directions.
- **Dialogue** moves the plot forward and can reveal the author's underlying message, or theme.

To practice analyzing elements of drama:

- Have students reread lines 655–657 in Act One. Ask: What about Giles's character do you learn directly? (*He is eighty-three, muscular, canny, and inquisitive.*)
- Have students reread lines 505–560 in Act Three. Have students tell what they learn about Giles's character indirectly. (*Possible answer: Giles shows integrity in refusing to name the man who can provide proof.*)

 **LEVEL UP TUTORIALS** Assign the following *Level Up* tutorial: **Elements of Drama**

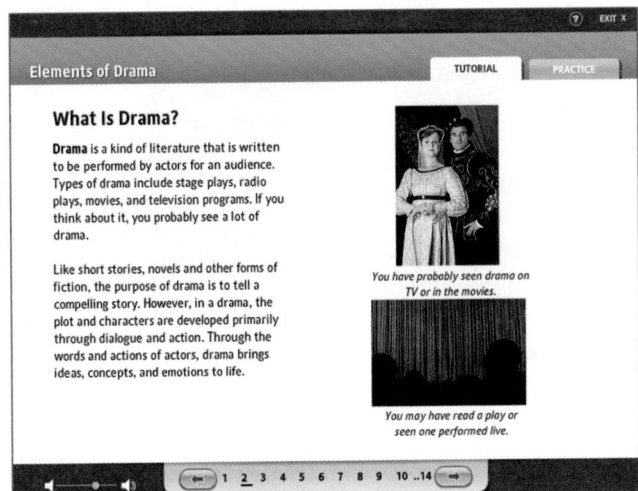

CLOSE READING APPLICATION

Have students practice identifying the elements of drama in other plays. Have students share their findings in pairs or small groups.

from The Crucible

Drama by Arthur Miller

 For more historical context, students can view the video "Salem Witch Trials" in their eBooks.

Why This Text

Students may have difficulty with this play for several reasons: its unusual form, in which the dialogue is sprinkled with stage directions and lengthy narrative "asides"; its archaic syntax, meant to simulate seventeenth-century speech; the tangled relationships between the characters; the unfamiliar historical setting; and, lastly, the parallels Miller draws between the play's events and events taking place at the time of its writing. With the help of the close-reading questions, students will examine how all those elements work together to produce a great piece of theater whose message is a call for sanity.

Background Have students read the background information. For more context, they can view the video "Salem Witch Trials" in their eBooks. Point out that the House Committee on Un-American Activities was set up to target Communists within the federal government, but its focus turned to Hollywood. In 1947 a group of writers, directors, and actors known as the Hollywood Ten were convicted of contempt of Congress for refusing to answer questions about their political beliefs. Over the next ten years, several hundred artists would be blacklisted by the film industry, including Arthur Miller, who was convicted of contempt of Congress in 1957 for refusing to name names.

AS YOU READ Ask students to pay attention to the way the author weaves together dramatic elements and exposition.

 ## Common Core Support

- cite strong and thorough textual evidence

- analyze the impact of the author's choices of dramatic structure

- examine the use of direct and indirect characterization

- analyze the characters' motivations and their effect on each other, as well as how they develop and change during the play

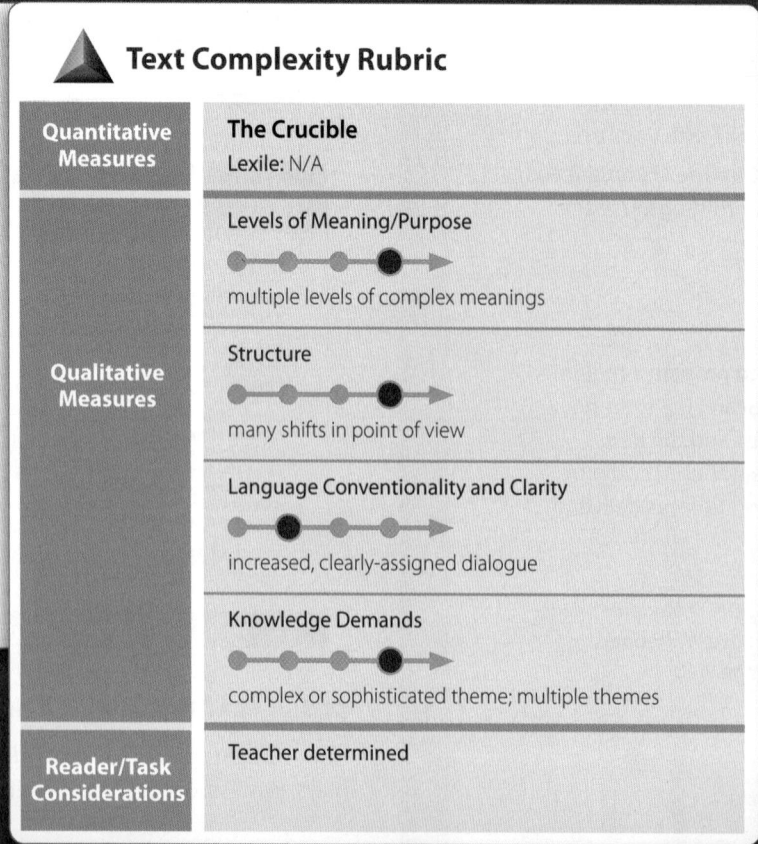

Text Complexity Rubric

Quantitative Measures	The Crucible Lexile: N/A
Qualitative Measures	Levels of Meaning/Purpose — multiple levels of complex meanings
	Structure — many shifts in point of view
	Language Conventionality and Clarity — increased, clearly-assigned dialogue
	Knowledge Demands — complex or sophisticated theme; multiple themes
Reader/Task Considerations	Teacher determined

Strategies for CLOSE READING

Analyze Drama Elements

Students should read this drama excerpt carefully all the way through. Close-reading questions at the bottom of the page will help them follow the plot and keep track of the characters' interactions. As they read, students should jot down comments or questions about the text in the margins.

WHEN STUDENTS STRUGGLE . . .

To help students analyze drama elements in this excerpt from *The Crucible*, have them work in small groups to fill out a chart like the one shown below.

CITE TEXT EVIDENCE For practice recognizing how the author uses dialogue and exposition to reveal details about the characters, have students study this chart.

Example	What It Shows
". . . when . . . wonders are brought forth from below the social surface, it is too much to expect people to hold back very long from laying on the victims with all the force of their frustrations." (lines 102–105)	The people of Salem were so repressed that what happened was inevitable.
"Tituba . . . is also very frightened because her slave sense has warned her that, as always, trouble in this house eventually lands on her back." (lines 144–149)	This presents Tituba as a character with self-knowledge and a sense of her own vulnerability within the community.
"Parris: . . . I know that you— you least of all, Thomas, would ever wish so disastrous a charge laid upon me. . . . They will howl me out of Salem for such corruption in my house." (lines 290–293)	Parris is begging Putnam to keep things quiet in the hope that he will identify with his desperation.

Background Arthur Miller *(1915–2005) is considered one of the major dramatists of 20th-century American theater. His politics and private life often put him in the public eye (he was once married to Marilyn Monroe). The Crucible, one of his most celebrated plays, is about an entire town caught up in a mad witch-hunt. It's set in 1692, but Miller wrote it during the "Communist scare," when a witch-hunt of a different sort was being conducted on the floor of the U.S. Congress.*

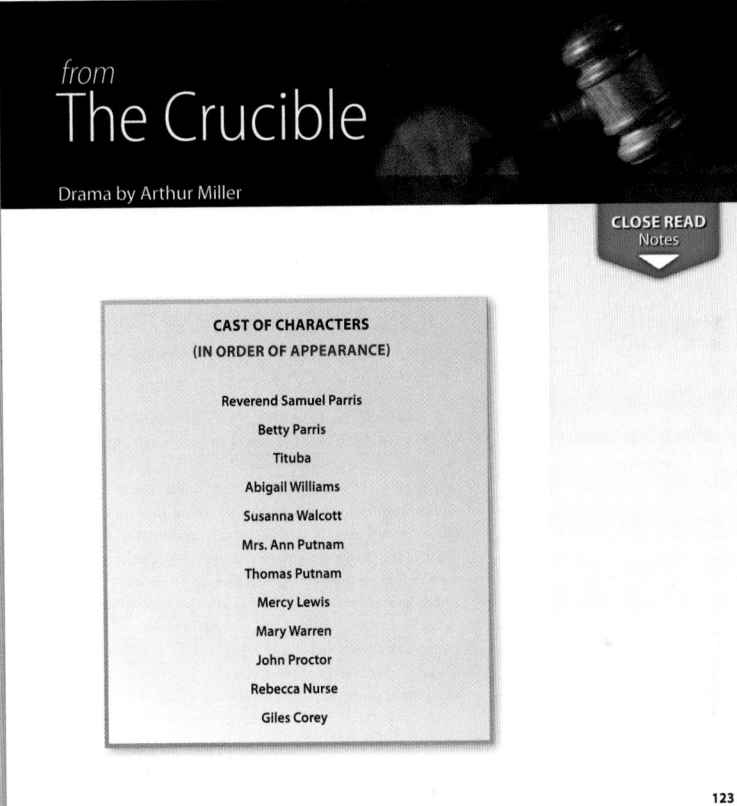

from

The Crucible

Drama by Arthur Miller

CLOSE READ
Notes

CAST OF CHARACTERS
(IN ORDER OF APPEARANCE)

Reverend Samuel Parris

Betty Parris

Tituba

Abigail Williams

Susanna Walcott

Mrs. Ann Putnam

Thomas Putnam

Mercy Lewis

Mary Warren

John Proctor

Rebecca Nurse

Giles Corey

123

CLOSE READ
Notes

1. **READ** ▶ As you read lines 1–40, begin to collect and cite text evidence.

- Underline details that describe Reverend Samuel Parris.
- Circle details that describe the setting.
- In the margin, explain the purpose of the exposition. For whose benefit does Miller include this text?

ACT ONE
An Overture

(A small upper bedroom) in the home of Reverend Samuel Parris, *Salem, Massachusetts, in the spring of the year 1692.*

There is a narrow window at the left. Through its leaded panes the morning sunlight streams. A candle still burns near the bed, which is at the right. A chest, a chair, and a small table are the other furnishings. At the back a door opens on the landing of the stairway to the ground floor. The room gives off an air of clean spareness. The roof rafters are exposed, and the wood colors are raw and unmellowed.

As the curtain rises, Reverend Parris *is discovered kneeling beside the bed,*
10 *evidently in prayer. His daughter,* Betty Parris, *aged ten, is lying on the bed, inert.)*

A At the time of these events Parris was in his middle forties. In history he cut a villainous path, and there is very little good to be said for him. He believed he was being **persecuted** wherever he went, despite his best efforts to win people and God to his side. In meeting, he felt insulted if someone rose to shut the door without first asking his permission. He was a widower with no interest in children, or talent with them. He regarded them as young adults, and until this strange crisis he, like the rest of Salem, never conceived that the children were anything but thankful for being permitted to walk straight, eyes
20 slightly lowered, arms at the sides, and mouths shut until bidden to speak.

His house stood in the "town"—but we today would hardly call it a village. The meeting house[1] was nearby, and from this point outward—toward the bay or inland—there were a few small-windowed, dark houses snuggling against the raw Massachusetts winter. Salem had been established hardly forty years before. To the European world the whole province was a

Readers, directors, and actors would all benefit from Miller's exposition.

persecuted:
wronged, mistreated

[1] **meeting house:** the most important building in the Puritan community, used both for worship and for meetings.

124

---

barbaric frontier inhabited by a sect of fanatics who, nevertheless, were shipping out products of slowly increasing quantity and value.

No one can really know what their lives were like. They had no novelists—and would not have permitted anyone to read a novel if one were
30 handy. Their creed forbade anything resembling a theater or "vain enjoyment." They did not celebrate Christmas, and a holiday from work meant only that they must concentrate even more upon prayer.

B Which is not to say that nothing broke into this strict and somber way of life. When a new farmhouse was built, friends assembled to "raise the roof," and there would be special foods cooked and probably some potent cider passed around. (There was a good supply of ne'er-do-wells in Salem,) who dallied at the shovelboard[2] in Bridget Bishop's tavern. Probably more than the creed, hard work kept the morals of the place from spoiling, for the people were forced to fight the land like heroes for every grain of corn, and
40 no man had very much time for fooling around.

C That there were some jokers, however, is indicated by the practice of appointing a two-man patrol whose duty was to "walk forth in the time of God's worship to take notice of such as either lye about the meeting house, without attending to the word and ordinances, or that lye at home or in the fields without giving good account thereof, and to take the names of such persons, and to present them to the magistrates, whereby they may be accordingly proceeded against." This **predilection** for minding other people's business was time-honored among the people of Salem, and it undoubtedly created many of the suspicions which were to feed the coming
50 madness. It was also, in my opinion, one of the things that a John Proctor would rebel against, for the time of the armed camp had almost passed, and since the country was reasonably—although not wholly—safe, the old disciplines were beginning to rankle. But, as in all such matters, the issue

CLOSE READ
Notes

barbaric:
uncivilized, primitive

predilection:
liking, preference

[2] **shovelboard:** a game in which a coin or disc is shoved across a board by hand.

2. **◀ REREAD** Reread lines 28–40. What commonalities kept the people of the Massachusetts colony together? Cite evidence from the text.

The people valued hard work and prayer; they did not favor creativity or "vain enjoyment"; "no man had very much time for fooling around."

3. **READ** ▶ As you read lines 41–77, continue to cite textual evidence.

- Underline text describing things the people of Salem were suspicious of.
- Circle text describing the realities of life in a new colony.
- In the margin, describe the people of Salem in your own words (lines 56–77).

125

---

1. **READ AND CITE TEXT EVIDENCE**

A **ASK STUDENTS** to describe the effect of the exposition on readers (lines 12–40). What mood does it evoke? *Students may say the mood is somber, dark, intense, bleak, forbidding, joyless.*

Critical Vocabulary: persecuted (line 14) Have students explain the meaning of *persecuted*. What example in lines 12–20 describes Reverend Parris's feelings about his persecution? *Students may cite the example of someone shutting the door without his permission.*

2. **REREAD AND CITE TEXT EVIDENCE**

B **ASK STUDENTS** to cite evidence from lines 34–38 describing what the Massachusetts colonists did for fun. *They assembled to "raise the roof" on a new farmhouse; the event was accompanied by food and drink; they "dallied at the shovelboard."*

3. **READ AND CITE TEXT EVIDENCE**

C **ASK STUDENTS** to cite evidence explaining the purpose of the "two-man patrol" in the village. What was their job? *They spied on the villagers and presented names to the magistrate.*

Critical Vocabulary: barbaric (line 26) Have students explain the meaning of *barbaric*.

Critical Vocabulary: predilection (line 47) Have students explain the meaning of *predilection*. What predilections do students have when it comes to food? *Students should name a kind of food they like.*

They were
hardworking,
somber,
disciplined,
autocratic,
fearful, and
suspicious.

was not clear-cut, for danger was still a possibility, and in unity still lay the
best promise of safety.

The edge of the wilderness was close by. The American continent
stretched endlessly west, and it was full of mystery for them. It stood, dark
and threatening, over their shoulders night and day, for out of it Indian
tribes marauded from time to time, and Reverend Parris had parishioners
60 who had lost relatives to these heathen.

D The parochial snobbery of these people was partly responsible for their
failure to convert the Indians. Probably they also preferred to take land
from heathens rather than from fellow Christians. At any rate, very few
Indians were converted, and the Salem folk believed that the virgin forest
was the Devil's last preserve, his home base and the citadel of his final
stand. To the best of their knowledge the American forest was the last place
on earth that was not paying homage to God.

For these reasons, among others, they carried about an air of innate
resistance, even of persecution. Their fathers had, of course, been
70 persecuted in England. So now they and their church found it necessary to
deny any other sect its freedom, lest their New Jerusalem³ be defiled and
corrupted by wrong ways and deceitful ideas.

They believed, in short, that they held in their steady hands the candle
that would light the world. We have inherited this belief, and it has helped
and hurt us. It helped them with the discipline it gave them. They were a
dedicated folk, by and large, and they had to be to survive the life they had
chosen or been born into in this country.

The proof of their belief's value to them may be taken from the opposite
character of the first Jamestown settlement, farther south, in Virginia. The
E 80 Englishmen who landed there were motivated mainly by a hunt for profit.
They had thought to pick off the wealth of the new country and then return

---

³ **New Jerusalem:** in Christianity, a heavenly city and the last resting place of the souls
saved by Jesus. It was considered the ideal city, and Puritans modeled their communities
after it.

---

4. **◀ REREAD** Reread lines 61–77. How did the wilderness setting and
proximity to the Indians affect the beliefs of "the Salem folk"?

The wilderness was full of danger and dangerous "heathens." The
people of Salem felt that the forest was evil and was the "Devil's last
preserve."

126

rich to England. They were a band of individualists, and a much more
ingratiating group than the Massachusetts men. But Virginia destroyed
them. Massachusetts tried to kill off the Puritans, but they combined; they
set up a communal society which, in the beginning, was little more than an
armed camp with an autocratic and very devoted leadership. It was,
however, an autocracy by consent, for they were united from top to bottom
by a commonly held ideology whose **perpetuation** was the reason and
justification for all their sufferings. So their self-denial, their
90 purposefulness, their suspicion of all vain pursuits, their hard-handed
justice, were altogether perfect instruments for the conquest of this space so
antagonistic to man.

F But the people of Salem in 1692 were not quite the dedicated folk that
arrived on the *Mayflower*. A vast differentiation had taken place, and in
their own time a revolution had unseated the royal government and
substituted a junta which was at this moment in power.⁴ The times, to their
eyes, must have been out of joint, and to the common folk must have
seemed as insoluble and complicated as do ours today. It is not hard to see
how easily many could have been led to believe that the time of confusion
100 had been brought upon them by deep and darkling forces. No hint of such
speculation appears on the court record, but social disorder in any age
breeds such mystical suspicions, and when, as in Salem, wonders are
brought forth from below the social surface, it is too much to expect people
to hold back very long from laying on the victims with all the force of their
frustrations.

---

⁴ **a junta . . . power:** *Junta* is a Spanish term meaning "a small, elite ruling council." The
reference here is to the group that led England's Glorious Revolution of 1688–1689.

---

5. **READ ▶** As you read lines 78–105, continue to cite textual evidence.

- Underline details that describe the Massachusetts colony.
- Circle text describing the "character" of the Jamestown settlement.
- In the margin, explain why the Massachusetts colony survived.

6. **◀ REREAD** Reread lines 93–105. According to Miller, what effect does
social disorder have on the people of Salem?

Miller suggests that the people of Salem believed that social disorder
comes from "deep and darkling forces," which made them suspicious
of their neighbors.

127

ingratiating:
likable,
pleasing

perpetuation:
continuation

The
Massachusetts
colonists unified
under one leader
and ideology.

---

4. **READ AND CITE TEXT EVIDENCE**

D **ASK STUDENTS** to explain why the colonists may not have
been totally behind the effort to convert the Indians, according to
the author. *The colonists thought it was easier to take land away
from heathens than from Christians (lines 62–63).*

FOR ELL STUDENTS Spanish speakers may recognize the
word *parochial* (line 61) from its cognate *parroquial*. Explain that
parochial can mean "related to a parish," but in this context it
means "close-minded" or "limited in outlook."

5. **READ AND CITE TEXT EVIDENCE**

E **ASK STUDENTS** what the author implies about the
Jamestown colony by calling them "a band of individualists." *The
individualists of Jamestown didn't agree and failed; Salem consisted
of people who agreed about what is right and wrong.*

6. **REREAD AND CITE TEXT EVIDENCE**

F **ASK STUDENTS** how the author foreshadows the trouble to
come to Salem in lines 93–105. *He hints at social disorder and
"deep and darkling forces."*

Critical Vocabulary: ingratiating (line 83) The author
tells us that the Jamestown men were more "ingratiating"
than the Massachusetts men. What does that say about the
Massachusetts men? *They were not very likable.*

Critical Vocabulary: perpetuation (line 88) Have students
share their definitions of *perpetuation*.

The Salem tragedy, which is about to begin in these pages, developed from a paradox. It is a paradox in whose grip we still live, and there is no prospect yet that we will discover its resolution. Simply, it was this: for good purposes, even high purposes, the people of Salem developed a theocracy, a combine of state and religious power whose function was to keep the community together, and to prevent any kind of disunity that might open it to destruction by material or ideological enemies. It was forged for a necessary purpose and accomplished that purpose. But all organization is and must be grounded on the idea of exclusion and prohibition, just as two objects cannot occupy the same space. Evidently the time came in New England when the repressions of order were heavier than seemed warranted by the dangers against which the order was organized. The witch-hunt was a perverse **manifestation** of the panic which set in among all classes when the balance began to turn toward greater individual freedom.

When one rises above the individual villainy displayed, one can only pity them all, just as we shall be pitied someday. It is still impossible for man to organize his social life without repressions, and the balance has yet to be struck between order and freedom.

The witch-hunt was not, however, a mere repression. It was also, and as importantly, a long overdue opportunity for everyone so inclined to express publicly his guilt and sins, under the cover of accusations against the victims. It suddenly became possible—and patriotic and holy—for a man to say that Martha Corey had come into his bedroom at night, and that, while his wife was sleeping at his side, Martha laid herself down on his chest and "nearly suffocated him." Of course it was her spirit only, but his satisfaction at confessing himself was no lighter than if it had been Martha herself. One could not ordinarily speak such things in public.

manifestation:

a sign

Salem developed a theocracy intending to keep the community together, but instead it was torn apart.

---

7. **READ ▶** As you read lines 106–140, continue to cite textual evidence.

• Underline text describing the control the Puritan leaders exerted over the community.

• In the margin, explain the paradox of the "Salem tragedy" in your own words.

8. **◀ REREAD** Reread lines 124–140. What role did "long-held hatreds of neighbors" have in the witch-hunt? Cite evidence from the text.

The witch-hunt was an "opportunity" for each of the long-repressed people of Salem to accuse their neighbors whom they didn't like.

Long-held hatreds of neighbors could now be openly expressed, and vengeance taken, despite the Bible's charitable **injunctions**. Land-lust which had been expressed before by constant bickering over boundaries and deeds, could now be elevated to the arena of morality; one could cry witch against one's neighbor and feel perfectly justified in the bargain. Old scores could be settled on a plane of heavenly combat between Lucifer and the Lord; suspicions and the envy of the miserable toward the happy could and did burst out in the general revenge.

(*Reverend Parris is praying now, and, though we cannot hear his words, a sense of his confusion hangs about him. He mumbles, then seems about to weep; then he weeps, then prays again; but his daughter does not stir on the bed.*

The door opens, and his Negro slave enters. Tituba is in her forties. Parris brought her with him from Barbados, where he spent some years as a merchant before entering the ministry. She enters as one does who can no longer bear to be barred from the sight of her beloved, but she is also very frightened because her slave sense has warned her that, as always, trouble in this house eventually lands on her back.)

Tituba (*already taking a step backward*). My Betty be hearty soon?

Parris. Out of here!

Tituba (*backing to the door*). My Betty not goin' die . . .

Parris (*scrambling to his feet in a fury*). Out of my sight! (*She is gone.*) Out of my—(*He is overcome with sobs. He clamps his teeth against them and closes the door and leans against it, exhausted.*) Oh, my God! God help me! (*Quaking with fear, mumbling to himself through his sobs, he goes to the bed and gently takes Betty's hand.*) Betty. Child. Dear child. Will you wake, will you open up your eyes! Betty, little one . . .

(*He is bending to kneel again when his niece, Abigail Williams, seventeen, enters—a strikingly beautiful girl, an orphan, with an endless capacity for dissembling. Now she is all worry and apprehension and propriety.*)

Abigail. Uncle? (*He looks to her.*) Susanna Walcott's here from Doctor Griggs.

Parris. Oh? Let her come, let her come.

Abigail (*leaning out the door to call to Susanna, who is down the hall a few steps*). Come in, Susanna.

injunctions:

commands, rulings

A girl lies lifeless on her bed—no one knows why. The suspense builds as her increasingly desperate father is forced to confront the possibility of intervention by "dark forces."

dissembling:

hiding real feelings or intentions

---

9. **READ ▶** As you read lines 141–180, continue to cite textual evidence.

• Underline text that helps you understand Reverend Parris.

• Circle details that describe Abigail.

• In the margin, explain the initial conflict in this section.

---

7. **READ AND CITE TEXT EVIDENCE**

G **ASK STUDENTS** to discuss the conditions that increase the likelihood of a witch-hunt (lines 117–119). *Students should understand that witch-hunts occur in tightly controlled societies "when the balance began to turn toward greater individual freedom."*

8. **REREAD AND CITE TEXT EVIDENCE**

H **ASK STUDENTS** to identify one of the "sins" that the witch-hunt allowed people to express publicly. What example can they find in lines 127–132? *A woman appeared in a man's bedroom while his wife was sleeping beside him and "nearly suffocated him."*

Critical Vocabulary: manifestation (line 118) Have students share definitions. What caused the "manifestation of the panic" in Salem in 1692? *Students may say that powerful leaders were afraid that their power was slipping.*

9. **READ AND CITE TEXT EVIDENCE** Remind students that lines 9–11 explain that Parris is praying by his daughter's bedside.

I **ASK STUDENTS** to cite evidence describing Parris's reaction when Tituba enters the room. *Students should cite lines 151–153, where he yells at her.*

Critical Vocabulary: injunctions (line 134) After students share definitions, have them paraphrase the sentence. *Possible response: You could express your deepest hatreds without worrying about the Bible's commandments.*

Critical Vocabulary: dissembling (line 161) Have students share definitions. Explain that Abigail has an "endless capacity for dissembling." What are other names for this type of person? *liar, dreamer, fraud, phony*

CLOSE READ
Notes

(*Susanna Walcott, a little younger than Abigail, a nervous, hurried girl, enters.*)

Parris (*eagerly*). What does the doctor say, child?

Susanna (*craning around Parris to get a look at* Betty). He bid me come and tell you, reverend sir, that he cannot discover no medicine for it in his books.

170 **Parris.** Then he must search on.

Susanna. Aye, sir, he have been searchin' his books since he left you, sir. But he bid me tell you, that you might look to unnatural things for the cause of it.

Parris (*his eyes going wide*). No—no. There be no unnatural cause here. Tell him I have sent for Reverend Hale of Beverly, and Mr. Hale will surely confirm that. Let him look to medicine and put out all thought of unnatural causes here. There be none.

Susanna. Aye, sir. He bid me tell you. (*She turns to go.*)

Abigail. Speak nothin' of it in the village, Susanna.

Parris. Go directly home and speak nothing of unnatural causes.

180 **Susanna.** Aye, sir. I pray for her. (*She goes out.*)

Abigail. Uncle, the rumor of witchcraft is all about; I think you'd best go down and deny it yourself. The parlor's packed with people, sir. I'll sit with her.

Parris (*pressed, turns on her*). And what shall I say to them? That my daughter and my niece I discovered dancing like heathen in the forest?

Abigail. Uncle, we did dance; let you tell them I confessed it—and I'll be whipped if I must be. But they're speakin' of witchcraft. Betty's not witched.

Parris. Abigail, I cannot go before the congregation when I know you have not opened with me. What did you do with her in the forest?

Abigail. We did dance, uncle, and when you leaped out of the bush so

190 suddenly, Betty was frightened and then she fainted. And there's the whole of it.

Parris. Child. Sit you down.

Abigail (*quavering, as she sits*). I would never hurt Betty. I love her dearly.

---

10. ◀ REREAD Reread lines 166–180. Why do Parris and Abigail tell Susanna to "speak nothing of unnatural causes"? Cite examples from the text.

Parris and Abigail do not want any rumors spread about "unnatural causes" like witchcraft although the doctor says he "cannot discover no medicine for it in his books."

11. READ ▶ As you read lines 181–235, continue to cite textual evidence.

- Underline Parris's references to witchcraft.
- Circle statements Abigail makes about her behavior.
- In the margin, explain Abigail's description of what happened in the forest.

130

> " ... the rumor of witchcraft is all about; I think you'd best go down and deny it yourself. "

Parris. Now look you, child, your punishment will come in its time. But if you trafficked with[5] spirits in the forest I must know it now, for surely my enemies will, and they will ruin me with it.

Abigail. But we never conjured spirits.

Parris. Then why can she not move herself since midnight? This child is desperate! (*Abigail lowers her eyes.*) It must come out—my enemies will bring it

200 out. Let me know what you done there. Abigail, do you understand that I have many enemies?

Abigail. I have heard of it, uncle.

Parris. There is a faction that is sworn to drive me from my pulpit. Do you understand that?

Abigail. I think so, sir.

Parris. Now then, in the midst of such disruption, my own household is discovered to be the very center of some obscene practice. Abominations are done in the forest—

Abigail. It were sport, uncle!

210 **Parris** (*pointing at* Betty). You call this sport? (*She lowers her eyes. He pleads.*) Abigail, if you know something that may help the doctor, for God's sake tell it to me. (*She is silent.*) I saw Tituba waving her arms over the fire when I came on you. Why was she doing that? And I heard a screeching and **gibberish** coming from her mouth. She were swaying like a dumb beast over that fire!

Abigail. She always sings her Barbados songs, and we dance.

Parris. I cannot blink what I saw, Abigail, for my enemies will not blink it. I saw a dress lying on the grass.

Abigail (*innocently*). A dress?

Parris (*It is very hard to say*). Aye, a dress. And I thought I saw—someone

220 naked running through the trees!

Abigail (*in terror*). No one was naked! You mistake yourself, uncle!

---

[5] **trafficked with:** met with.

---

12. ◀ REREAD AND DISCUSS Reread lines 198–208. In a small group, discuss Parris's conflict. Who are his enemies and why is he afraid of them?

131

Abigail, Betty, and Tituba were in the forest dancing. Parris "leaped out of the bush," causing Betty to faint.

conjured: invented, made up

gibberish: nonsense

---

10. REREAD AND CITE TEXT EVIDENCE In lines 141–180, Reverend Parris acts as if he's afraid of something.

🔵 **ASK STUDENTS** to identify details that convey this fear. *Examples include: "his eyes going wide" (line 173); panic at the mention of the supernatural; his rough manner with Susanna; his obvious defensiveness.*

11. READ AND CITE TEXT EVIDENCE

🔵 **ASK STUDENTS** to explain why Reverend Parris says he cannot "go before the congregation" (lines 187–188). *Abigail has lied to him before and he's afraid she'll lie again, this time in front of the whole town.*

12. REREAD AND DISCUSS USING TEXT EVIDENCE

🔵 **ASK STUDENTS** to recall the description of Parris they read in lines 12–20. What might his mental state have to do with his conviction that "enemies" are out to get him (lines 199–204)? *Since Parris "believed he was being persecuted wherever he went" (line 14), students may conclude that the "enemies" are manifestations of his paranoia.*

Critical Vocabulary: conjured (line 197) Have students share definitions. Have them discuss the difference between conjuring and inventing. *The connotation is that conjuring brings something into existence.*

Critical Vocabulary: gibberish (line 213) Ask students to share definitions. What connotation does *gibberish* have here? *It reflects a condescending attitude.*

CLOSE READ Notes

abomination:

immoral or shameful act

Parris (*with anger*). I saw it! (*He moves from her. Then, resolved*) Now tell me true, Abigail. And I pray you feel the weight of truth upon you, for now my ministry's at stake, my ministry and perhaps your cousin's life. Whatever **abomination** you have done, give me all of it now, for I dare not be taken unaware when I go before them down there.

Abigail. There is nothin' more. I swear it, uncle.

Parris (*studies her, then nods, half convinced*). Abigail, I have fought here three long years to bend these stiff-necked people to me, and now, just now when
230 some good respect is rising for me in the parish, you compromise my very character. I have given you a home, child, I have put clothes upon your back—now give me upright answer. Your name in the town—it is entirely white, is it not?

Abigail (*with an edge of resentment*). Why, I am sure it is, sir. There be no blush about my name.[6]

 **Parris** (*to the point*). Abigail, is there any other cause than you have told me, for your being discharged from Goody[7] Proctor's service? I have heard it said, and I tell you as I heard it, that she comes so rarely to the church this year for she will not sit so close to something soiled. What signified that remark?

240 **Abigail.** She hates me, uncle, she must, for I would not be her slave. It's a bitter woman, a lying, cold, sniveling woman, and I will not work for such a woman!

Parris. She may be. And yet it has troubled me that you are now seven month out of their house, and in all this time no other family has ever called for your service.

Abigail. They want slaves, not such as I. Let them send to Barbados for that. I will not black my face for any of them! (*with ill-concealed resentment at him*) Do you **begrudge** my bed, uncle?

Parris. No—no.

Abigail (*in a temper*). My name is good in the village! I will not have it said my
250 name is soiled! Goody Proctor is a gossiping liar!

(*Enter Mrs. Ann Putnam. She is a twisted soul of forty-five, a death-ridden woman, haunted by dreams.*)

Parris (*as soon as the door begins to open*). No—no, I cannot have anyone. (*He sees her, and a certain deference springs into him, although his worry remains.*) Why, Goody Putnam, come in.

---
[6] **There be . . . my name:** There is nothing wrong with my reputation.
[7] **Goody:** short for *Goodwife*, the Puritan equivalent of *Mrs.*

---

begrudge:

envy (someone) for the possession or enjoyment of (something)

13. **READ ▶** As you read lines 236–293, continue to cite textual evidence.
- Underline statements Abigail and Parris make about Goody Proctor.
- Circle mentions of witchcraft.
- In the margin, tell how Reverend Parris's and Mrs. Putnam's opinions differ.

132

CLOSE READ Notes

Mrs. Putnam (*full of breath, shiny-eyed*). It is a marvel. It is surely a stroke of hell upon you.

Parris. No, Goody Putnam, it is—

Mrs. Putnam (*glancing at Betty*). How high did she fly, how high?
260 **Parris.** No, no, she never flew—

Mrs. Putnam (*very pleased with it*). Why, it's sure she did. Mr. Collins saw her goin' over Ingersoll's barn, and come down light as bird, he says!

Parris. Now, look you, Goody Putnam, she never—

(*Enter Thomas Putnam, a well-to-do, hard-handed landowner, near fifty.*) Oh, good morning, Mr. Putnam.

Putnam. It is a **providence** the thing is out now! It is a providence. (*He goes directly to the bed.*)

Parris. What's out, sir, what's—?

(*Mrs. Putnam goes to the bed.*)

270 **Putnam** (*looking down at Betty*). Why, her eyes is closed! Look you, Ann.

Mrs. Putnam. Why, that's strange. (*to Parris*) Ours is open.

Parris (*shocked*). Your Ruth is sick?

Mrs. Putnam (*with vicious certainty*). I'd not call it sick; the Devil's touch is heavier than sick. It's death, y'know, it's death drivin' into them, forked and hoofed.

Parris. Oh, pray not! Why, how does Ruth ail?

Mrs. Putnam. She ails as she must—she never waked this morning, but her eyes open and she walks, and hears naught, sees naught, and cannot eat. Her soul is taken, surely.

280 (*Parris is struck.*)

Putnam (*as though for further details*). They say you've sent for Reverend Hale of Beverly?

Parris (*with dwindling **conviction** now*). A precaution only. He has much experience in all demonic arts, and I—

Mrs. Putnam. He has indeed; and found a witch in Beverly last year, and let you remember that.

Parris. Now, Goody Ann, they only thought that were a witch, and I am certain there be no element of witchcraft here.

14. **◀ REREAD** Reread lines 236–250. What might the Reverend Parris be insinuating here? Support your answer with explicit textual evidence.

Parris is troubled by the fact that no one wants to hire Abigail. He may be suggesting that Abigail may have caused some trouble when she was in the service of the Proctors.

Mrs. Putnam is adamant that witchcraft is at play; Parris advises her not to jump to conclusions.

providence:

destiny, fate

conviction:

certainty, confidence

133

---

13. READ AND CITE TEXT EVIDENCE

Ⓜ ASK STUDENTS to consider the new element Mrs. Putnam brings to the discussion. What does she believe caused Betty's symptoms? *She is sure it was witchcraft.* What kind of person is she? *She is gullible, narrow-minded, and mean-spirited.*

Critical Vocabulary: abomination (line 225) Have students share definitions. What is Parris implying by using this word? *He is implying that Abigail has committed crimes against God.*

Critical Vocabulary: begrudge (line 247) Have students share definitions. Ask them to paraphrase Abigail's question to her uncle. *Possible answer: "Would you be so mean as to deny me a bed, uncle?"*

14. REREAD AND CITE TEXT EVIDENCE

Ⓝ ASK STUDENTS to examine the exchange that takes place between Reverend Parris and Abigail in lines 236–250. How does Abigail's behavior give her away? *Students may suggest: Instead of addressing Parris's points, she lashes out at Goody Proctor and defames her character.*

Critical Vocabulary: providence (line 266) Ask students what they think Putnam means when he says, "It is a providence the thing is out now!" *It is destiny that the real facts have come to light.*

Critical Vocabulary: conviction (line 283) Ask students to share definitions. What issues do they have strong convictions about? *Students may suggest human rights, nuclear disarmament, animal rights, the environment.*

Putnam. No witchcraft! Now look you, Mr. Parris—

Parris. Thomas, Thomas, I pray you, leap not to witchcraft. I know that you—you least of all, Thomas, would ever wish so disastrous a charge laid upon me. We cannot leap to witchcraft. They will howl me out of Salem for such corruption in my house.

(O) A word about Thomas Putnam. He was a man with many grievances, at least one of which appears justified. Some time before, his wife's brother-in-law, James Bayley, had been turned down as minister of Salem. Bayley had all the qualifications, and a two-thirds vote into the bargain, but a faction stopped his acceptance, for reasons that are not clear.

Thomas Putnam was the eldest son of the richest man in the village. He had fought the Indians at Narragansett,[8] and was deeply interested in parish affairs. He undoubtedly felt it poor payment that the village should so blatantly disregard his candidate for one of its more important offices, especially since he regarded himself as the intellectual superior of most of the people around him.

His **vindictive** nature was demonstrated long before the witchcraft began. Another former Salem minister, George Burroughs, had had to borrow money to pay for his wife's funeral, and, since the parish was remiss in his salary, he was soon bankrupt. Thomas and his brother John had Burroughs jailed for debts the man did not owe. The incident is important only in that Burroughs succeeded in becoming minister where Bayley, Thomas Putnam's brother-in-law, had been rejected; the **motif** of resentment is clear here. Thomas Putnam felt that his own name and the honor of his family had been smirched by the village, and he meant to right matters however he could.

(P) Another reason to believe him a deeply embittered man was his attempt to break his father's will, which left a disproportionate amount to a stepbrother. As with every other public cause in which he tried to force his way, he failed in this.

[8] **fought the Indians at Narragansett:** The Puritans fought a series of battles against the Narragansett Indians over territory that both groups had settled on.

vindictive:
spiteful, mean, cruel

motif:
theme, pattern

---

15. (READ ▶) As you read lines 294–323, continue to cite textual evidence.

- Underline text that describes Thomas Putnam's character.
- Circle text explaining his resentment.
- In the margin, explain the conclusion Miller draws about the effects of Putnam's bitterness (lines 319–323).

134

So it is not surprising to find that so many accusations against people are in the handwriting of Thomas Putnam, or that his name is so often found as a witness corroborating the supernatural testimony, or that his daughter led the crying-out at the most opportune junctures of the trials, especially when—But we'll speak of that when we come to it.

Putnam (*At the moment he is intent upon getting* Parris, *for whom he has only contempt, to move toward the abyss*). Mr. Parris, I have taken your part in all **contention** here, and I would continue; but I cannot if you hold back in this. There are hurtful, vengeful spirits layin' hands on these children.

Parris. But, Thomas, you cannot—

Putnam. Ann! Tell Mr. Parris what you have done.

Mrs. Putnam. Reverend Parris, I have laid seven babies unbaptized in the earth. Believe me, sir, you never saw more hearty babies born. And yet, each would wither in my arms the very night of their birth. I have spoke nothin', but my heart has clamored intimations.[9] And now, this year, my Ruth, my only—I see her turning strange. A secret child she has become this year, and shrivels like a sucking mouth were pullin' on her life too. And so I thought to send her to your Tituba—

Parris. To Tituba! What may Tituba—?

Mrs. Putnam. Tituba knows how to speak to the dead, Mr. Parris.

Parris. Goody Ann, it is a formidable sin to conjure up the dead!

[9] **clamored intimations:** nagging suspicions.

Putnam's own failures cause him to accuse others of wrongdoing.

contention:
argument, disagreement

---

16. (◀ REREAD) Reread lines 294–323. After reading this background information, what effect do you think Thomas Putnam will have in the play? Support your answer with explicit textual evidence.

Putnam is "vindictive" and full of "resentment." His desire for vengeance against those he thinks have done him wrong may prompt him to make some false accusations.

---

17. (READ ▶) As you read lines 324–379, continue to cite textual evidence.

- Underline events that have caused Mrs. Putnam to believe something wicked is at play.
- Circle the claims the Putnams make about recent events.
- In the margin, tell how the Putnams raise the level of hysteria in the town.

135

---

15. (READ AND CITE TEXT EVIDENCE)

(O) **ASK STUDENTS** why they think Miller chooses to use exposition at this point in the play. What is its purpose and what does it bring to light? *It presents a psychological portrait of Thomas Putnam; it presents his life as a series of disappointments and petty grievances.*

Critical Vocabulary: vindictive (line 305) Ask students to cite evidence that explains Thomas Putnam's vindictive nature. *Students may suggest: "Thomas Putnam felt that his own name and the honor of his family had been smirched by the village" (lines 312–313).*

Critical Vocabulary: motif (line 311) Have students share definitions. Tell them that *motif* can also refer to a melodic pattern in a musical composition.

16. (REREAD AND CITE TEXT EVIDENCE)

(P) **ASK STUDENTS** to note that Putnam "meant to right matters however he could" (lines 313–314). Have students restate this idea in their own words. *Possible response: He would do anything to get what he wants.*

17. (READ AND CITE TEXT EVIDENCE)

(Q) **ASK STUDENTS** to explain Mrs. Putnam's involvement in the situation. Why does she bring up her seven dead babies? Why is she interested in Tituba? *She thinks that Tituba can communicate with the dead; she thinks she can find out who murdered her babies (lines 340–341).*

Critical Vocabulary: contention (line 326) Have students share definitions. What is the contention between Mr. Putnam and Reverend Parris? *Mr. Putnam thinks Reverend Parris should confess; Reverend Parris refuses for fear of public scorn.*

Q 340 **Mrs. Putnam.** I take it on my soul, but who else may surely tell us what person murdered my babies?

Parris (*horrified*). Woman!

Mrs. Putnam. They were murdered, Mr. Parris! And mark this proof! Mark it! Last night my Ruth were ever so close to their little spirits; I know it, sir. For how else is she struck dumb now except some power of darkness would stop her mouth? It is a marvelous sign, Mr. Parris!

Putnam. Don't you understand it, sir? There is a murdering witch among us, bound to keep herself in the dark. (*Parris turns to Betty, a frantic terror rising in him.*) Let your enemies make of it what they will, you cannot blink it more.

350 **Parris** (*to* Abigail). Then you were conjuring spirits last night.

R **Abigail** (*whispering*). Not I, sir—Tituba and Ruth.

Parris (*turns now, with new fear, and goes to Betty, looks down at her, and then, gazing off*). Oh, Abigail, what proper payment for my charity! Now I am undone.

Putnam. You are not undone! Let you take hold here. Wait for no one to charge you—declare it yourself. You have discovered witchcraft—

Parris. In my house? In my house, Thomas? They will topple me with this! They will make of it a—

(*Enter Mercy Lewis, the Putnams' servant, a fat, sly, merciless girl of eighteen.*)

360 **Mercy.** Your pardons. I only thought to see how Betty is.

Putnam. Why aren't you home? Who's with Ruth?

Mercy. Her grandma come. She's improved a little, I think—she give a powerful sneeze before.

Mrs. Putnam. Ah, there's a sign of life!

Mercy. I'd fear no more, Goody Putnam. It were a grand sneeze; another like it will shake her wits together, I'm sure. (*She goes to the bed to look.*)

Parris. Will you leave me now, Thomas? I would pray a while alone.

Abigail. Uncle, you've prayed since midnight. Why do you not go down and—

Parris. No—no. (*to* Putnam) I have no answer for that crowd. I'll wait till Mr.
370 Hale arrives. (*to get* Mrs. Putnam *to leave*) If you will, Goody Ann . . .

The Putnams are ready to accuse those who don't agree with them of being the enemy.

---

18. ◀ **REREAD AND DISCUSS** In a small group, discuss the significance of Abigail's whispered line: "Not I, sir—Tituba and Ruth" (line 351).

136

Putnam. Now look you, sir. Let you strike out against the Devil, and the village will bless you for it! Come down, speak to them—pray with them. They're thirsting for your word, Mister! Surely you'll pray with them.

Parris (*swayed*). I'll lead them in a psalm, but let you say nothing of witchcraft yet. I will not discuss it. The cause is yet unknown. I have had enough contention since I came; I want no more.

Mrs. Putnam. Mercy, you go home to Ruth, d'y'hear?

Mercy. Aye, mum.)

(Mrs. Putnam *goes out.*)

S 380 **Parris** (*to* Abigail). If she starts for the window, cry for me at once.

Abigail. I will, uncle.

Parris (*to* Putnam). There is a terrible power in her arms today. (*He goes out with* Putnam.)

Abigail (*with hushed* **trepidation**). How is Ruth sick?

Mercy. It's weirdish, I know not—she seems to walk like a dead one since last night.

Abigail (*turns at once and goes to Betty, and now, with fear in her voice*). Betty? (Betty *doesn't move. She shakes her.*) Now stop this! Betty! Sit up now! (Betty *doesn't stir. Mercy comes over.*)

390 **Mercy.** Have you tried beatin' her? I gave Ruth a good one and it waked her for a minute. Here, let me have her.

Abigail (*holding* Mercy *back*). No, he'll be comin' up. Listen, now; if they be questioning us, tell them we danced—I told him as much already.

Mercy. Aye. And what more?

Abigail. He knows Tituba conjured Ruth's sisters to come out of the grave.

Mercy. And what more?

Abigail. He saw you naked.

Mercy (*clapping her hands together with a frightened laugh*). Oh, Jesus! (*Enter Mary Warren, breathless. She is seventeen, a* **subservient***, naive, lonely*
400 *girl.*)

Mary Warren. What'll we do? The village is out! I just come from the farm; the whole country's talkin' witchcraft! They'll be callin' us witches, Abby!

Mercy (*pointing and looking at* Mary Warren). She means to tell, I know it.

Mary Warren. Abby, we've got to tell. Witchery's a hangin' error, a hangin' like they done in Boston two year ago! We must tell the truth, Abby! You'll only be whipped for dancin', and the other things!

trepidation:
anxiety, fear, nervousness

subservient:
obedient, docile, meek

---

19. **READ** ▶ As you read lines 380–442, continue to cite textual evidence.
- Underline new details about what really happened in the woods.
- Circle text that describes the feelings of the girls.
- In the margin, explain why the girls are afraid.

137

---

18. REREAD AND DISCUSS USING TEXT EVIDENCE

R **ASK STUDENTS** to discuss what Abigail admits for the first time. *Students should note that she admits for the first time that they were "conjuring spirits" in the forest; previously she had denied this.*

FOR ELL STUDENTS One of the meanings of the verb *to undo* is "to destroy." In this context, *undone* (line 354) means "destroyed."

19. READ AND CITE TEXT EVIDENCE

S **ASK STUDENTS** to contrast the positions of Mary Warren, Mercy, and Abigail in this section. What do each of them want to do? *Mary Warren wants to tell all; Abigail wants to stick to the story that they were only dancing; Mercy will go with anything Abigail says.*

Critical Vocabulary: trepidation (line 384) Have students share definitions. Have them take turns saying the line "How sick is Ruth?" with hushed *trepidation*.

Critical Vocabulary: subservient (line 399) Ask students to whom they think Mary is *subservient*. *Students may suggest she is* subservient *to authority.*

CLOSE READ
Notes

The girls are afraid of being hanged as witches.

Abigail. Oh, *we'll* be whipped!

Mary Warren. I never done none of it, Abby. I only looked!

410 **Mercy** (*moving menacingly toward* Mary). Oh, you're a great one for lookin', aren't you, Mary Warren? What a grand peeping courage you have! (Betty, *on the bed, whimpers.* Abigail *turns to her at once.*)

Abigail. Betty? (*She goes to* Betty.) Now, Betty, dear, wake up now. It's Abigail. (*She sits* Betty *up and furiously shakes her.*) I'll beat you, Betty! (Betty *whimpers.*) My, you seem improving. I talked to your papa and I told him everything. So there's nothing to—

Betty (*darts off the bed, frightened of* Abigail, *and flattens herself against the wall*). I want my mama!

Abigail (*with alarm, as she cautiously approaches* Betty). What ails you, Betty? Your mama's dead and buried.

420 **Betty.** I'll fly to Mama. Let me fly! (*She raises her arms as though to fly, and streaks for the window, gets one leg out.*)

Abigail (*pulling her away from the window*). I told him everything; he knows now, he knows everything we—

Betty. You drank blood, Abby! You didn't tell him that!

Abigail. Betty, you never say that again! You will never—

Betty. You did, you did! You drank a charm to kill John Proctor's wife! You drank a charm to kill Goody Proctor!

Abigail (*smashes her across the face*). Shut it! Now shut it!

dissolves:
melts; fades away

Betty (*collapsing on the bed*). Mama, Mama! (*She* **dissolves** *into sobs.*)

430 **Abigail.** Now look you. All of you. We danced. And Tituba conjured Ruth Putnam's dead sisters. And that is all. And mark this. Let either of you breathe a word, or the edge of a word, about the other things, and I will come to you in the black of some terrible night and I will bring a pointy reckoning that will shudder you.[10] And you know I can do it; I saw Indians smash my dear parents' heads on the pillow next to mine, and I have seen some reddish work done at night, and I can make you wish you had never seen the sun go down! (*She goes to* Betty *and roughly sits her up.*) Now, you—sit up and stop this! (*But* Betty *collapses in her hands and lies* **inert** *on the bed.*)

inert:
lifeless, not moving

Mary Warren (*with hysterical fright*). What's got her? (Abigail *stares in fright* at Betty.) Abby, she's going to die! It's a sin to conjure, and we—

440 **Abigail** (*starting for* Mary). I say shut it, Mary Warren! (*Enter* John Proctor. *On seeing him,* Mary Warren *leaps in fright.*)

[10]**bring . . . shudder you:** inflict a terrifying punishment on you.

20. **◄ REREAD AND DISCUSS** Reread lines 428–437. In a small group, discuss what you find out about Abigail. In what way does she affect the other girls?

138

CLOSE READ
Notes

Proctor was a farmer in his middle thirties. He need not have been a **partisan** of any faction in the town, but there is evidence to suggest that he had a sharp and biting way with hypocrites. He was the kind of man— powerful of body, even-tempered, and not easily led—who cannot refuse support to partisans without drawing their deepest resentment. In Proctor's presence a fool felt his foolishness instantly—and a Proctor is always marked for calumny[11] therefore.

partisan:
member, follower

450 But as we shall see, the steady manner he displays does not spring from an untroubled soul. He is a sinner, a sinner not only against the moral fashion of the time, but against his own vision of decent conduct. These people had no ritual for the washing away of sins. It is another trait we inherited from them, and it has helped to discipline us as well as to breed **hypocrisy** among us. Proctor, respected and even feared in Salem, has come to regard himself as a kind of fraud. But no hint of this has yet appeared on the surface, and as he enters from the crowded parlor below it is a man in his prime we see, with a quiet confidence and an unexpressed, hidden force. Mary Warren, his servant, can barely speak for embarrassment and fear.

hypocrisy:
insincerity

[11]**marked for calumny:** singled out to have lies told about him.

21. **READ ►** As you read lines 443–459, continue to cite textual evidence.
   • Underline details that describe John Proctor's best qualities.
   • Circle details that show Proctor's worst qualities.

22. **◄ REREAD AND DISCUSS** Reread lines 443–459. In a small group, discuss John Proctor's inner struggle.

139

---

20. REREAD AND DISCUSS USING TEXT EVIDENCE

T ASK STUDENTS to think about Abigail's tone in lines 431–437. What approach does she use to get them to see things her way? *Abigail bullies and threatens them; she makes them understand that if they don't do as she says, she will "bring a pointy reckoning that will shudder you."*

Critical Vocabulary: dissolves (line 429) Have students share definitions of *dissolve*. Then ask them to explain what it means when used in other contexts, such as chemistry and film production.

Critical Vocabulary: inert (line 438) Ask students why they think the author chose the word *inert* to describe Betty's state. *The word has a scientific connotation; it suggests that she is non-reactive.*

21. READ AND CITE TEXT EVIDENCE

U ASK STUDENTS how they can tell Proctor plays an important part in the play. *Upon seeing Proctor, Mary "leaps in fright"; the author breaks into the story with a long commentary on his character; he is a tortured soul with inner demons.*

22. REREAD AND DISCUSS USING TEXT EVIDENCE

V ASK STUDENTS to discuss the main difference between Proctor and the other characters. *Students may say he is principled.*

Critical Vocabulary: partisan (line 444) Ask students to share definitions. What do they think a bipartisan decision in Congress is? *It is the decision made by two political parties—the Republicans and Democrats.*

Critical Vocabulary: hypocrisy (line 455) Have students discuss which character in the play is the worst hypocrite.

CLOSE READ Notes

 460 **Mary Warren.** Oh! I'm just going home, Mr. Proctor.

Proctor. Be you foolish, Mary Warren? Be you deaf? I forbid you leave the house, did I not? Why shall I pay you? I am looking for you more often than my cows!

Mary Warren. I only come to see the great doings in the world.

Proctor. I'll show you a great doin' on your arse one of these days. Now get you home; my wife is waitin' with your work! (*Trying to retain a shred of dignity, she goes slowly out.*)

titillated: *excited*

Mercy Lewis (*both afraid of him and strangely **titillated***). I'd best be off. I have my Ruth to watch. Good morning, Mr. Proctor.

470 (*Mercy sidles out. Since Proctor's entrance, Abigail has stood as though on tiptoe, absorbing his presence, wide-eyed.* He glances at her, then goes to Betty on the bed.)

Abigail. Gah! I'd almost forgot how strong you are, John Proctor!

Proctor (*looking at Abigail now, the faintest suggestion of a knowing smile on his face*). What's this mischief here?

Abigail (*with a nervous laugh*). Oh, she's only gone silly somehow.

Proctor. The road past my house is a pilgrimage to Salem all morning. The town's mumbling witchcraft.

winningly: *believably, convincingly*

Abigail. Oh, posh! (***Winningly** she comes a little closer, with a confidential, wicked air.*) We were dancin' in the woods last night, and my uncle leaped in on us. She took fright, is all.

Abigail and Proctor had a brief but passionate affair that ended when his wife fired her.

Proctor (*his smile widening*). Ah, you're wicked yet, aren't y'! (*A trill of expectant laughter escapes her, and she dares come closer, feverishly looking into his eyes.*) You'll be clapped in the stocks before you're twenty.

(*He takes a step to go, and she springs into his path.*)

Abigail. Give me a word, John. A soft word. (*Her concentrated desire destroys his smile.*)

Proctor. No, no, Abby. That's done with.

Abigail (*tauntingly*). You come five mile to see a silly girl fly? I know you 490 better.

Proctor (*setting her firmly out of his path*). I come to see what mischief your uncle's brewin' now. (*with final emphasis*) Put it out of mind, Abby.

---

23. **READ** ▶ As you read lines 460–523, continue to cite textual evidence.
   • Underline details that show Abigail's true feelings for John Proctor.
   • In the margin, make an inference about what happened between them.

140

CLOSE READ Notes

Abigail (*grasping his hand before he can release her*). John—I am waitin' for you every night.

Proctor. Abby, I never give you hope to wait for me.

Abigail (*now beginning to anger—she can't believe it*). I have something better than hope, I think!

Proctor. Abby, you'll put it out of mind. I'll not be comin' for you more.

Abigail. You're surely sportin' with me.

500 **Proctor.** You know me better.

Abigail. I know how you clutched my back behind your house and sweated like a stallion whenever I come near! Or did I dream that? It's she put me out, you cannot pretend it were you. I saw your face when she put me out, and you loved me then and you do now!

Proctor. Abby, that's a wild thing to say—

Abigail. A wild thing may say wild things. But not so wild, I think. I have seen you since she put me out; I have seen you nights.

Proctor. I have hardly stepped off my farm this sevenmonth.

Abigail. I have a sense for heat, John, and yours has drawn me to my window, 510 and I have seen you looking up, burning in your loneliness. Do you tell me you've never looked up at my window?

Proctor. I may have looked up.

Abigail (*now softening*). And you must. You are no wintry man. I *know* you, John. I know you. (*She is weeping.*) I cannot sleep for dreamin'; I cannot dream but I wake and walk about the house as though I'd find you comin' through some door.

(*She clutches him desperately.*)

---

24. ◀ **REREAD** Reread lines 460–523. What angers Abigail most about Proctor's refusal to see her? Why do you think she drank a charm to kill Goody Proctor?

She thinks he is denying his true feelings for her. She wanted to get rid of Goody Proctor so she could continue her affair with John.

141

---

23. **READ AND CITE TEXT EVIDENCE** Have students look at the author's stage notes in lines 460–480 for words that convey the nature of the relationship between Abigail and Proctor.

Ⓦ **ASK STUDENTS** to cite examples of suggestive words. *Examples: Mercy Lewis is "strangely titillated" by Proctor's presence (line 468); Abigail is "absorbing his presence, wide-eyed" (line 471); she gives a "nervous laugh" (line 476); "a trill of expectant laughter escapes her," "feverishly looking into his eyes" (lines 482–484); she has a "confidential, wicked air" (lines 479–480).*

Critical Vocabulary: titillated (line 468) Ask students why they think the author chose this word to describe Mercy's reaction to Proctor's entrance. *She suspects something illicit is going on.*

Critical Vocabulary: winningly (line 479) Ask students why they think the author chose this word to describe Abigail's behavior. What is its connotation? *She is being flirtatious.*

24. **REREAD AND CITE TEXT EVIDENCE**

Ⓧ **ASK STUDENTS** to cite evidence showing why Abigail can't accept the fact that Proctor has cooled toward her. *Abigail is convinced he still loves her. Students should cite lines 510–511: "I have seen you looking up, burning in your loneliness. Do you tell me you've never looked up at my window?"*

CLOSE READ
Notes

Proctor (*gently pressing her from him, with great sympathy but firmly*). Child—

520 **Abigail** (*with a flash of anger*). How do you call me child!

Proctor. Abby, I may think of you softly from time to time. But I will cut off my hand before I'll ever reach for you again. Wipe it out of mind. We never touched, Abby.

Abigail. Aye, but we did.

Proctor. Aye, but we did not.

Abigail (*with a bitter anger*). Oh, I marvel how such a strong man may let such a sickly wife be—

Proctor (*angered—at himself as well*). You'll speak nothin' of Elizabeth!

Abigail. She is blackening my name in the village! She is telling lies about me!

530 She is a cold, sniveling woman, and you bend to her! Let her turn you like a—

Proctor (*shaking her*). Do you look for whippin'?

(*A psalm is heard being sung below.*)

Abigail (*in tears*). I look for John Proctor that took me from my sleep and put knowledge in my heart! I never knew what **pretense** Salem was, I never knew the lying lessons I was taught by all these Christian women and their covenanted[12] men! And now you bid me tear the light out of my eyes? I will not, I cannot! You loved me, John Proctor, and whatever sin it is, you love me yet! (*He turns abruptly to go out. She rushes to him.*) John, pity me, pity me!

(*The words "going up to Jesus" are heard in the psalm, and Betty claps her ears*

540 *suddenly and whines loudly.*)

Abigail. Betty? (*She hurries to Betty, who is now sitting up and screaming. Proctor goes to Betty as Abigail is trying to pull her hands down, calling "Betty!"*)

Proctor (*growing unnerved*). What's she doing? Girl, what ails you? Stop that wailing!

[12]**covenanted:** In Puritan religious practice, the men of a congregation would make an agreement, or covenant, to govern the community and abide by its beliefs and practices.

---

pretense:
deception;
sham

unnerved:
panicky,
anxious

---

25. **READ** ▶ As you read lines 524–573, continue to cite textual evidence.

- Underline details that show a change in Betty's condition.
- Circle details that describe the other characters' reactions.
- In the margin, explain what Mrs. Putnam thinks is happening to Betty.

142

" She is blackening my name in the village! She is telling lies about me! "

(*The singing has stopped in the midst of this, and now Parris rushes in.*)

Parris. What happened? What are you doing to her? Betty! (*He rushes to the bed, crying, "Betty, Betty!" Mrs. Putnam enters feverish with curiosity, and with her Thomas Putnam and Mercy Lewis. Parris, at the bed, keeps lightly slapping*

550 *Betty's face while she moans and tries to get up.*)

Abigail. She heard you singin' and suddenly she's up and screamin'.

Mrs. Putnam. The psalm! The psalm! She cannot bear to hear the Lord's name!

Parris. No. God forbid. Mercy, run to the doctor! Tell him what's happened here! (*Mercy Lewis rushes out.*)

Mrs. Putnam. Mark it for a sign, mark it!

(*Rebecca Nurse, seventy-two, enters. She is white-haired, leaning upon her walking-stick.*)

Putnam (*pointing at the whimpering Betty*). That is a notorious sign of

560 witchcraft afoot, Goody Nurse, a **prodigious** sign!

Mrs. Putnam. My mother told me that! When they cannot bear to hear the name of—

Parris (*trembling*). Rebecca, Rebecca, go to her, we're lost. She suddenly cannot bear to hear the Lord's—

(*Giles Corey, eighty-three, enters. He is knotted with muscle, canny, inquisitive, and still powerful.*)

She thinks
Betty is
having a bad
reaction to
hearing a
psalm.

prodigious:
extraordinary;
exceptional

---

26. ◀**REREAD** Reread lines 524–538. As Proctor responds to Abigail's insults about Elizabeth, what do his words and the stage directions suggest about his view of his marriage?

Proctor orders Abigail to be quiet and threatens to whip her. He
wants to protect Elizabeth and his marriage. The stage directions
make his anger toward Abigail clear.

143

---

25. READ AND CITE TEXT EVIDENCE

Y **ASK STUDENTS** to tell what causes Betty to suddenly clap her ears and whine loudly. *She has heard the words "going up to Jesus" in a psalm.* What does this tell them about the nature of her malady? *It suggests that there is a religious component.*

Critical Vocabulary: pretense (line 534) Have students share definitions. Have them explain what makes a person pretentious. *Pretentious people try to impress others by presenting themselves as something other than what they are.*

Critical Vocabulary: unnerved (line 544) Ask students to describe what unnerves Proctor in lines 541–545. *He sees Betty sitting up and screaming and doesn't know why.*

26. REREAD AND CITE TEXT EVIDENCE   In line 531, Proctor threatens to whip Abigail.

Z **ASK STUDENTS** what Abigail has just said that might explain his violent reaction. *She has just insulted his wife, called her a liar and a "cold, sniveling woman"; she says that "you bend to her."*

Critical Vocabulary: prodigious (line 560) Point out that *prodigious* usually has a positive connotation. Why would Mr. Putnam say that Betty's reaction was a "prodigious sign" of witchcraft? *He is thrilled that finally there is proof.*

CLOSE READ
Notes

Rebecca. There is hard sickness here, Giles Corey, so please to keep the quiet.

Giles. I've not said a word. No one here can testify I've said a word. Is she going to fly again? I hear she flies—

570   **Putnam.** Man, be quiet now!

(Everything is quiet. Rebecca walks across the room to the bed. Gentleness exudes from her. Betty is quietly whimpering, eyes shut. Rebecca simply stands over the child, who gradually quiets.)

SHORT RESPONSE

Cite Text Evidence   The plot of *The Crucible* slowly becomes more and more complicated. Why do you think Miller chooses to reveal information gradually rather than all at once? Look back at your reading notes and be sure to support your ideas by **citing evidence from the text.**

Miller weaves together narrative and drama to present a taut, historically accurate, and morally complex story about a town taken over by paranoia, mass hysteria, and religious intolerance. Miller reveals the plot gradually in order to build suspense. Little by little, we learn details about the characters and events in the forest. By revealing details slowly, he creates intrigue and allows his readers to understand how rumors spread. At the same time Parris is trying to figure out what he has seen, we as readers, are piecing together details from the text about what happened. Miller also uses other characters to spread rumors, using Mrs. Putnam to claim that Betty "cannot bear to hear the Lord's name" and Giles who asks if Betty is going to fly.

144

SHORT RESPONSE

Cite Text Evidence   Students should:

- explain how the author provides in-depth information about the characters and setting.
- explain how the author uses text structure to gradually reveal the plot and create suspense.
- analyze the characters' interactions and development through the use of dialogue.

TO CHALLENGE STUDENTS . . .

It is no accident that the Salem witch trials of the 1690s bear a striking resemblance to events that happened a quarter-century later in the United States, known as the McCarthy hearings. Miller drew his inspiration for *The Crucible* from this bleak period in the history of our country. It was a time when a U.S. Senator named Joseph McCarthy waged a one-man campaign against "Communists" who he believed were trying to take over the government—a belief stemming from his own paranoia and inner demons. Even though McCarthy was stopped in his tracks, he succeeded in destroying the lives of many people. In addition, the entire country was enveloped in fear and dread. Neighbors turned each other in and no one was to be trusted.

ASK STUDENTS to research the period of history known as the "Red Scare," and the role of Senator Joseph McCarthy. Have them look online for a speech McCarthy gave to the Irish Fellowship Club in Chicago in 1954 defending his "war on Communism." Have students look for parallels between the nation in McCarthy 's time and the Salem community.

Have students form groups and discuss similarities between the McCarthy hearings and *The Crucible*. Ask them to consider questions such as:

- What can they tell about McCarthy's character from his speech in 1954? What do his words suggest? What is conveyed by his demeanor?
- Why was he obsessed with the "threat" of Communism? What did Communism represent to him?
- How did he get his information?
- What percentage of the witnesses turned in their friends or coworkers? How many refused?
- How and when was McCarthy finally disabled?

DIG DEEPER

1. With the class, return to Question 16, Reread. Have students share the results of their discussion.

ASK STUDENTS to recall the author's characterization of Thomas Putnam. Given what students know about Putnam, have them address the following:

- How far would Putnam go in order to "right matters"? What "matters" might he have to right? *Students should recognize that Putnam will to go to any lengths to prove the existence of witchcraft. He is quick to target others as he feels he has been targeted.*

- What has happened to Putnam that might explain his bitterness? *Students may mention the incident in which his father willed his stepbrother a disproportionate amount of money.*

- Have students give evidence of Putnam's vindictive nature. *He put someone in jail he knew was innocent out of resentment.*

- Have students discuss why Putnam always feels slighted. What makes him feel superior to other men? *He was born the eldest son of the richest man in the village; he believes he is "the intellectual superior of most of the people around him."*

2. With the class, return to Question 18, Reread and Discuss.

ASK STUDENTS to share their responses to Question 18.

- Have students review what Abigail finally admits to Reverend Parris. How does she implicate Tituba? *She tells him that they were in the woods but that only Tituba and Ruth conjured spirits.*

- Do students believe her story? Why or why not? *Students may say they do not believe her; she acts guilty and the author describes her as a dissembler.*

- What does Tituba represent? *Students may say that Tituba represents wildness, chaos, magic, sensuality—and the forest, the site of all things dark and dangerous.*

- Why is Tituba a subject of contention between Mrs. Putnam and Reverend Parris? *Mrs. Putnam thinks Tituba can conjure up the dead and seeks her help; Reverend Parris is scandalized—he thinks conjuring is a sin and wants nothing to do with it.*

ASK STUDENTS to return to their Short Response answer and revise it based on the class discussion.

CLOSE READING NOTES

mySmartPlanner Create lesson plans and access resources online.

COMPARE TEXT AND MEDIA

MEDIA # Media Versions of *The Crucible*

Audio Excerpt from *The Crucible*, by Arthur Miller   Production Images from Film Version

Why These Texts?

Students often read plays to understand their literary significance. They also encounter different versions of plays presented in different mediums. This lesson explores how different performances and media affect interpretations of the same play.

Key Learning Objective: Students will be able to analyze an audio excerpt and film production stills of a play for theme and characterization.

COMMON CORE Common Core Standards

RL 1 Cite textual evidence to support inferences.
RL 7 Analyze multiple interpretations.
W 4 Produce clear and coherent writing.
SL 1 Initiate and participate in a range of collaborative discussions.

▲ Text Complexity Rubric

	Audio Excerpt from *The Crucible* Lexile: NA	Production Images from Film Version Lexile: NA
Quantitative Measures		
Qualitative Measures	Levels of Meaning/Purpose multiple levels of meaning	Levels of Meaning/Purpose 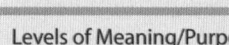 closely aligned with the original print source
	Structure 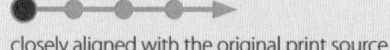 somewhat complex story concepts	Structure 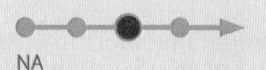 NA
	Language Conventionality and Clarity archaic, unfamiliar language; multiple characters speaking	Language Conventionality and Clarity 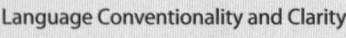 NA
	Knowledge Demands  increased amount of cultural knowledge	Knowledge Demands  somewhat unfamiliar experience
Reader/Task Considerations	Teacher determined Vary by individual reader and type of text	Teacher determined Vary by individual reader and type of text

TEACH

AS YOU LISTEN Direct students to use the As You Listen note to focus their attention.

Analyze Interpretations of Drama  **RL 7**

Explain to students that a **drama** is a written narrative, or story, that is intended to be acted out on stage, television, film, or in this case an audio recording. Writers usually include instructions, or stage directions, for how the drama is intended to be performed. However, different directors and actors bring different **interpretations** to each production. Discuss with students the following concepts:

- **Dialogue:** Who is speaking, and to whom? Which characters are in the scene, but silent? How do the characters' words contribute to the plot or character development? How does the actor's interpretation of the lines affect the audience's understanding of the play?
- **Stage directions:** Playwrights often include directions that tell how the play should be staged and how actors should deliver their lines.

ASK STUDENTS to listen to the audio selection, paying close attention not only to what is said, but how it is spoken. How does the actress reading Mary Warren's lines use her voice to convey meaning? (*Her voice becomes weaker at times, suggesting she is uncertain of herself or afraid of what she is saying. Sometimes she sobs and her breathing becomes audible, suggesting strong emotion.*)

ASK STUDENTS what the purpose of the narrator is in this audio selection. (*He reads some of the stage directions.*) Which stage directions does he omit? (*Those that do not add to the play's dramatic impact.*)

COLLABORATIVE DISCUSSION Have students pair up and discuss how the actors bring to life characters from the text. Students should cite specific examples to support their ideas. Then have the students share their conclusions with the class as a whole. Accept all reasonable responses.

ASK STUDENTS to share any questions they generated in the course of listening to, viewing, and discussing the selection.

Media Versions of *The Crucible*

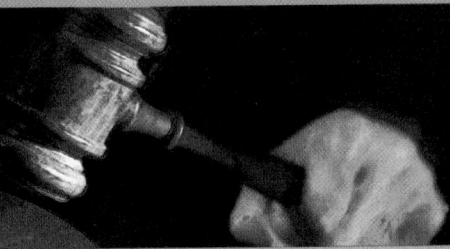

The Crucible

Audio excerpt from Act Three (lines 723–1111)

AS YOU LISTEN Pay attention to how the speakers use just their voices to interpret and dramatize the text of the play. Note any questions you generate.

Image Credits: (t) ©Ken Glaser/Corbis Premium RF/Alamy; (b) ©Geraint Lewis/Alamy

COLLABORATIVE DISCUSSION Which characters emerge most fully in this scene? With a partner, discuss how the actors bring individual characters from the text to life. Cite specific examples from the recording to support your ideas.

SCAFFOLDING FOR ELL STUDENTS

Comprehension Support This audio selection includes dialogue from no less than a dozen characters. To help students understand the recording, review lines 723–1111 of Act 3 of the play. Then have students follow along in the text as they listen to the audio selection.

Pause and replay segments of the audio as needed. Discuss with students ideas and events that may cause confusion.

Analyze Interpretations of Drama  COMMON CORE RL 7

Remind students that drama, like other forms of literature, involves coordinating many elements to tell a story. However, one of drama's most important elements is dialogue, or conversations between two or more characters. Writers, directors, and actors use dialogue to convey important information, reveal motives and character traits, express thoughts and emotions, and advance the storyline. Well-delivered dialogue often performs more than one task while still sounding natural to the audience. Have students listen again to the audio recording, paying close attention to the actors' use of **voice expression**, **volume**, **pace**, **stress**, and **timing**. Have students jot down notes about these elements of the audio recording.

Analyzing the Text and Media  COMMON CORE RL 7

Possible answers:

1. *In the recording, Mary Warren seems slightly stronger or bolder than her portrayal in the text because of the actor's voice expression and volume.*

2. *Danforth is portrayed as an inflexible, confident, shrewd man. The actor has a deep voice that is stern and foreboding; his volume, pace, and stress are even and controlled. He rarely interrupts and does not tolerate being interrupted. Danforth is portrayed as a man with great power, who wields it without consideration for others.*

3. *The girls gasp and become breathless when they first "see" the spirit. As the other girls wail and moan, Abigail speaks as though afraid. The pitch of her voice and her pace both vary, depending on the line. Her voice trembles with fear.*

Analyze Interpretations of Drama COMMON CORE RL 7

In this audio recording, some of Arthur Miller's stage directions are read aloud by the narrator; others are used by the actors to guide their interpretations of characters. The actors use the elements of speech discussed in the chart to convey their view of the characters.

Voice expression refers to the feeling that is brought out by the sound of an actor's voice. For example, a higher pitch can help communicate excitement, happiness, or anxiety. A lower pitch sounds more serious or sad.

Volume, pace, and the **stress** placed on words can all be varied. These techniques can emphasize words, phrases, or lines in the dialogue; signal characters' reactions; or create a particular mood, or atmosphere. For example, the faintness of Mary Warren's voice shows her increasing uncertainty about whether she can hold out against Abigail.

Timing refers to when lines of dialogue are delivered. In this recording, there are dramatic pauses, interruptions, and simultaneous speech, all of which echo Miller's punctuation and arrangement of lines and add to the impact of the scene.

Analyzing the Text and Media  COMMON CORE RL 7

Cite Text Evidence Support your responses with evidence from the selections.

1. **Compare** Review lines 723–1111 in Act Three. Is Mary Warren's character in the recording consistent with her portrayal in the text? Explain.

2. **Analyze** What impression of Danforth is created by the actor in this recording? How does the actor use elements of speech to convey the traits of his character? Explain whether you view Danforth differently after hearing the recording.

3. **Compare** In this part of the play, the girls "see" a spirit sent down on them. How does the recording communicate the frenzy of this scene? Discuss whether the same mood is brought out in the text.

PERFORMANCE TASK

Speaking Activity: Readers' Theater With a group, prepare an interpretation of a short scene from *The Crucible*.

- On a copy of the text, highlight stage directions and important words and phrases in the dialogue.

- Assign roles and practice reading your parts. Use expression, pace, volume, stress, and timing to convey emotion and key ideas.

- Perform your readers' theater for the class.

- Have class members follow along in the text and then write a short evaluation of the performance.

Assign this performance task.

PERFORMANCE TASK  COMMON CORE RL 7

Speaking Activity: Readers' Theater Have students work in small groups. Assign a different short section of the play to each group. Remind students to use expression, pace, volume, stress, and timing to convey emotion and key ideas. Have the students take turns presenting while the rest of the class follows along in the text. Afterwards, have students write short evaluations of the performances, commenting on elements that brought the interpretation to life.

AS YOU VIEW Direct students to use the As You View note to focus their attention.

Analyze Interpretations of Drama  COMMON CORE RL 7

Tell students that many works of literature have been **adapted** and made into films. Arthur Miller wrote the play, *The Crucible*, which premiered in 1953 on Broadway. He later wrote the screenplay for the film based on the play that was released in 1996, starring Daniel Day-Lewis and Winona Ryder. Although Miller wrote the screenplay, the film's director, lighting designer, and costume designer brought their own interpretations to the production. Discuss with students the following concepts:

- **Set Design and Costuming:** Both of these aspects of a film create for the audience a sense of when and where the action is taking place.

- **Lighting and Camera Techniques:** Film directors can use camera angles and lighting to create mood, emphasize characters' reactions, build suspense, and draw the audience into the action.

- **Blocking:** Actors' positions, movements, and gestures affect the impact of a scene.

ASK STUDENTS to look at the first picture and read its caption. How do the **costumes** create a sense of when and where this story takes place? *(The dresses, bonnets, archaic hats and collars look appropriate for 17th century New England, the story's setting.)* How are the actors positioned in the first picture? *(The young women are seated in the foreground, while villagers behind them look on.)* How does this affect the audience's perception of the young women's reactions? *(It focuses the audience's attention on the young women, and amplifies the shot's emotional impact.)*

ASK STUDENTS to look at the second picture and read its caption. What words would you use to describe the lighting in this photograph? *(It is darkly lit with Danforth's black clothing disappearing into the shadows.)* How does this emphasize the scene's mood? *(It suggests the court's proceedings are enshrouded in evil, or darkness.)* How does the position of the actors contribute to the mood? *(They are huddled around Danforth and Mary anxiously listening to her testimony.)*

MEDIA

The Crucible (1996)

Production Images from Film Version

AS YOU VIEW Consider what these images suggest about the relationships between the characters. Write down any questions you generate while looking at the images.

Abigail and others react to events on the green.

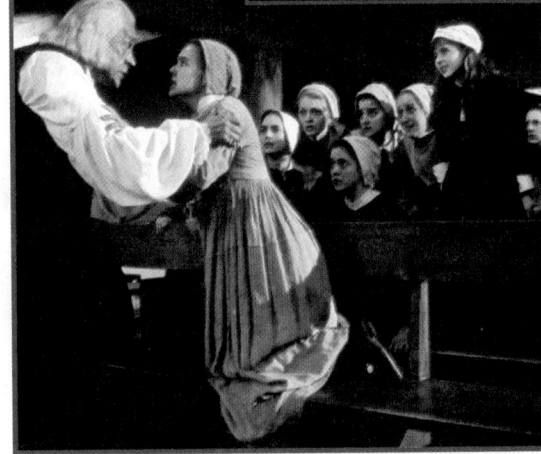

Danforth questions Mary Warren before the court (Act Three).

Image Credits: (t) ©KPA Honorar & Belege/United Archives GmbH/Alamy; (b) ©Moviestore Collection ltd/Alamy

APPLYING ACADEMIC VOCABULARY

contemporary	simulated

As you discuss the media versions of *The Crucible*, incorporate the following Collection 6 academic vocabulary words: *contemporary* and *simulated*. How are the actors' costumes **contemporary** with the setting design? Are these costumes and sets real or **simulated**?

TEACH

CLOSE READ

Analyze Interpretations of Drama

COMMON CORE RL 1, RL 7

Remind students that directors **interpret**, or give their own meaning to, a film or play, and they reveal their interpretations with the **choices** they make during production. Discuss the following concepts:

- **Casting:** The actors' physical characteristics and acting styles have a significant impact on the audience's perception of characters and plot.
- **Blocking:** Actors' positions, movements, and gestures affect the impact of a scene.

ASK STUDENTS to look at the three pictures and read their captions. Ask students to compare the actress portraying Abigail to the play's description of the character. (*The play describes Abigail as "seventeen." The images show an actress who appears to be 17.*) Then ask students to compare the actor portraying John Proctor to the play's description of the character. (*The play describes Proctor as "powerful of body" and "in his prime." The actor who portrays him in the film projects these qualities.*) Do these photographs suggest the film's director chose to adhere closely to Miller's original play with his **casting**, or try something different? (*The pictures suggest the director chose to adhere closely to the original play.*)

CITE EVIDENCE Have students review the pictures and look for clues that answer the following question: How do the characters' positions and gestures affect or emphasize the emotions captured in the scene? (*Parris' look of horror contrasts with Abigail's look of confusion. John Proctor stands resolute with his wife slightly behind him, as if "standing behind" his decision to confess. In the third picture, John Proctor commands the attention of Abigail and the audience.*)

COLLABORATIVE DISCUSSION Have student pairs discuss how the actors portray the characters' feelings for each other in these photographs. Students should cite specific examples to support their ideas. Then have students share their conclusions with the class.

ASK STUDENTS to share any questions they generated in the course of reading, viewing, and discussing the selection.

Reverend Parris and Abigail gaze with horror at the scene unfolding.

John Proctor gives his confession to the marshal as Elizabeth looks on (Act Four).

John Proctor warns Abigail that their relationship is over.

COLLABORATIVE DISCUSSION What do these images imply about the characters' feelings for each other? With a partner, discuss whether these impressions are accurate. Cite specific evidence from the photographs and the play to support your ideas.

TO CHALLENGE STUDENTS . . .

Short Research Project Have students work in small groups to research the House Un-American Activities Committee and its investigation of Arthur Miller and other people involved in the arts. Students should consider parallels between the investigations carried out by the HUAC and the events narrated in the text, audio, and film versions of *The Crucible*. When students have finished their research, ask groups to present their findings to the class.

Analyze Interpretations of Drama

COMMON CORE RL 7

These images, taken from a 1996 film version of *The Crucible*, suggest how the director interpreted Miller's play. The director's many choices include those shown in the chart.

Casting The actors' physical characteristics and acting styles have a significant impact on the audience's perception of characters and plot. Use your knowledge of Miller's stage directions to evaluate how closely the director's choices align with the way Miller saw his characters.

Blocking Actors' positions, movements, and gestures affect the impact of a scene. Note how the relationships between the characters as well as their emotions are revealed through their posture, gestures, and position relative to other characters.

Lighting and Camera Techniques Film directors can use different camera angles and lighting to create mood, emphasize characters' reactions, build suspense, and draw the audience into the action. Consider what the lighting tells you about the mood of the scene with Abigail and John Proctor. How does the close-up view of their faces help the audience understand what they are experiencing?

Set Design and Costuming Both of these aspects of a film create for the audience a sense of when and where the action is taking place. Think about how immediately you form an impression of setting from the costumes worn by the actors. These costumes as well as the location of the film tell you that the director has chosen to adhere to many aspects of the setting established in Miller's stage directions.

Analyzing the Text and Media

COMMON CORE RL 7, W 4

Cite Text Evidence   Support your responses with evidence from the selections.

1. **Analyze** Examine the photographs of Abigail, Reverend Parris, and John Proctor. In what ways is the casting consistent with a traditional interpretation of Miller's text? Explain.

2. **Infer** What scene of the play is depicted by the photo of John Proctor and Abigail? What does this photo suggest about this interpretation of Miller's text?

PERFORMANCE TASK

Writing Activity: Diagram Complete these activities in a small group.

- Choose a short scene from the play.
- Diagram the scene with specific directions for the actors about where to stand and how to move.
- Have volunteer actors within the group follow those directions.
- Discuss how the blocking affects the group's interpretation of the scene. Share insights with the class.

Analyze Interpretations of Drama

COMMON CORE RL 7

Remind students that filmmaking is a complicated form of storytelling that can be difficult to coordinate. The 1996 production of *The Crucible* employed about 50 actors, dozens of extras, and more than 300 crew members. The director works with these people and makes artistic decisions about what to include in the film and how to include it.

Review with students the choices included in the chart. Lead a class discussion about other choices regarding casting, blocking, lighting and camera techniques, set design, and costuming that would have reflected a different interpretation of the film. For instance, the set design, casting, and costumes could be changed to suggest a different place or era. Lighting and dialogue could be altered to brighten or darken the mood. The director could use blocking to emphasize one aspect of the story, while de-emphasizing another.

Analyzing the Text and Media

COMMON CORE RL 7, W 4

Possible answers:

1. *Abigail is described as "seventeen…a strikingly beautiful girl…" (lines 35-36). John Proctor is described as "powerful of body" and a man in his prime…with a quiet confidence and an unexpressed, hidden force" (pages 468-69). The only physical description of the Reverend Parris is that he is in his mid-40s (page 459). The actors who were cast to portray these characters are consistent with a traditional interpretation of Miller's text.*

2. *The photo of John Proctor and Abigail suggests the director may have focused a greater amount of attention on the relationship between these characters than Miller did in the original play. Contemporary audiences expect a "love story" to be part of most movies.*

Assign this performance task.

PERFORMANCE TASK

COMMON CORE W 4

Writing Activity: Diagram Have students work in small groups on a short scene of the play. Remind them to use specific, easy-to-follow directions. Have the group members take turns following the stage directions, then discuss how blocking affects the interpretation of the scene. Afterwards, groups may take turns presenting their scenes to the class. Have students compare and contrast each version, and discuss how blocking affected each group's scene.

PRACTICE & APPLY

Compare Multiple Interpretations of a Drama
 COMMON CORE RL 7

Remind students that a **medium** is a means by which a message is communicated. Many media exist, including books, magazines, newspapers, blogs, films, online videos, radio shows, podcasts, comic books, television shows, musicals, and more. This selection focused on three ways in which a written drama might be enjoyed: as a text, an audio recording, and a film. Have students work in three groups to analyze the strengths and weaknesses of each medium. Tell students to use specific examples to support their analyses. Then have each group identify another medium to which *The Crucible* might be adapted successfully.

Analyzing the Text and Media
 COMMON CORE RL 7

Possible answers:

1. *John Proctor's appearance in the photographs suggests a man who is resolute and steadfast in his determination. This is consistent with his portrayal in the text. In the audio version, John Proctor could be considered more melodramatic. This is probably because a radio play depends almost entirely on exaggerated inflection to demonstrate emotion.*

2. *The excerpt relies on complicated dialogue to tell a story. This would be an advantage for a written text or a staged play. The lack of physical action in the excerpt makes it less ideal for film. The number of characters involved in the dialogue is a disadvantage for audio recordings because it can be difficult to distinguish who is speaking.*

3. *The photograph suggests that Reverend Parris is trying to protect Abigail. This view would be somewhat accurate since it is in Parris' personal interest to keep his niece out of trouble.*

Compare Multiple Interpretations of a Drama
 COMMON CORE RL 7

Experiencing the same play through different mediums enables the audience to appreciate the text from several perspectives. For example, an audio recording allows listeners to concentrate on the characters' words without the distraction of visual elements. They hear nuances of meaning that they may otherwise have missed. In a film, the images, sound, and special effects bring the story to life for viewers, drawing them into the characters' conflicts.

There are also drawbacks to each medium. In a recording, it may be difficult to identify who is speaking or to follow the interactions between characters. In a film, the director's interpretation may alter the original meaning, or technical effects might distract from the essence of the drama. Keeping in mind both advantages and possible disadvantages will help you better evaluate how each version interprets the source text.

Analyzing the Text and Media
 COMMON CORE RL 1, RL 7, W 4

Cite Text Evidence   Support your responses with evidence from the selections.

1. **Analyze** Describe the character traits suggested by John Proctor's appearance in the photographs. Is this perception of him consistent with Miller's portrayal of his character in the text of the play? Does his voice in the recording match this impression? Explain.

2. **Compare** Reread lines 723–1111 in the text. Explain the advantages and disadvantages of presenting this part of the play in each medium. Be specific.

3. **Evaluate** Examine the photograph of Reverend Parris with Abigail. How might someone who had not read the play describe his character, based on his actions and appearance in this shot? Would this view be accurate? Explain.

PERFORMANCE TASK

Writing Activity: Captions Every director has to make decisions when interpreting the text of a play for a film adaptation. The selected production stills offer clues to one director's decisions.

- With a partner, write captions identifying when and where the action in the photograph might be happening.

- Compare the director's vision of that part of the play with Miller's, drawing from stage directions as well as dialogue.

- Discuss key similarities and differences and how they affect your perception of the action.

- Share your analysis with the class.

Assign this performance task.

PERFORMANCE TASK
 COMMON CORE W 4

Writing Activity: Captions Have students work in pairs. Remind them to be specific when identifying when and where the action might be happening. Discuss key similarities and differences and how they affect the students' perception of the action. Have the students share their analyses with the class.

Interpret a Drama

COMMON CORE

RL 7

TEACH

Review with students the various media versions of *The Crucible* that they have read, listened to, and seen. Tell them that now it is their turn to create a media version of the story. Provide students with these steps to follow:

- Select a scene from the play that you find compelling or interesting. Find an excerpt that has an easily identifiable beginning, middle, and end.
- Reread the scene and decide what medium you will use to interpret it—a comic book, song, silent film, newspaper article, etc.
- Consider how your interpretation will be similar to and different from the original. Will it have the same setting, characters, and events; or will you set the story on another planet in the future and create a science fiction version?
- Draft a "treatment" of the scene that tells what medium you will use and how you will interpret major elements such as characters, setting, events, tone, and mood. If you are creating an alternate stage or film version, tell about casting, costume and set design, lighting, and blocking.

COLLABORATIVE DISCUSSION

Have students finish their treatments, and then share their results with the class. Hold a class discussion of the various interpretations and media. Which medium seemed the most effective for traditional interpretations of the story? Why? Which interpretations were most creative and original? Ask students if any of the various interpretations led them to see the story told in *The Crucible* in a new way.

Compare Multiple Interpretations of a Drama

COMMON CORE

RL 7

RETEACH

Remind students that Arthur Miller wrote two versions of *The Crucible*—a play that premiered on Broadway in 1953 and a movie that was released in 1996. Although the story is the same, their interpretations and reception were different. This is due to **historical and cultural context**—the time, place, and social conditions that influence a work of literature. Discuss the following concepts with students:

- **Events:** What events inspired Miller to write the play in the 1950s? What events over the next 40 years might have changed how the story was interpreted?
- **Cultural Values:** How have cultural values changed since the 1950s? Did the House Un-American Activities Committee still exist in 1996?
- **Social Concerns:** Were Americans as afraid of communism after the fall of the Berlin Wall in 1989?

LEVEL UP TUTORIALS Assign the following *Level Up* tutorial: **Historical and Cultural Context**

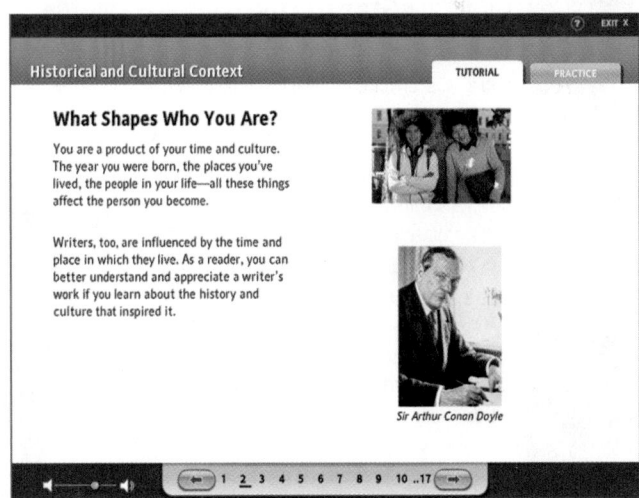

CLOSE READING APPLICATION

Students can apply the skill to another story or novel they have read. Have them choose a literary work and research some of the events and social concerns of the time in which it was written. Do they see historical events or cultural and social concerns reflected in the work? How?

*my*SmartPlanner   Create lesson plans and access resources online.

Tinker *v.* Des Moines Independent Community School District

Opinion and Dissents by the Supreme Court of the United States

Why This Text?

Free speech is a basic right guaranteed to all Americans, but the line between rights guaranteed to adults and to children and young adults can sometimes become blurred. This selection explores the issue of free speech from the standpoint of a landmark case decided by the U.S. Supreme Court.

▶ **View It!**

Professional Development Podcast:

Text-Dependent Analysis

Key Learning Objective: Students will be able to delineate and evaluate a Supreme Court ruling's Constitutional principles and legal reasoning.

COMMON CORE Common Core Standards

RI 1   Cite textual evidence.

RI 2   Determine central ideas of a text.

RI 4   Determine the meaning of words and phrases.

RI 8   Delineate and evaluate the reasoning in seminal U.S. texts.

W 2   Write informative/explanatory texts.

W 7   Conduct research projects.

SL 3   Evaluate a speaker's point of view, reasoning, and use of evidence and rhetoric.

SL 4   Present information, findings, and supporting evidence.

L 3a   Vary syntax for effect; apply an understanding of syntax.

L 4c   Consult reference materials.

L 6   Acquire and use accurately general academic and domain-specific words and phrases.

▲ Text Complexity Rubric

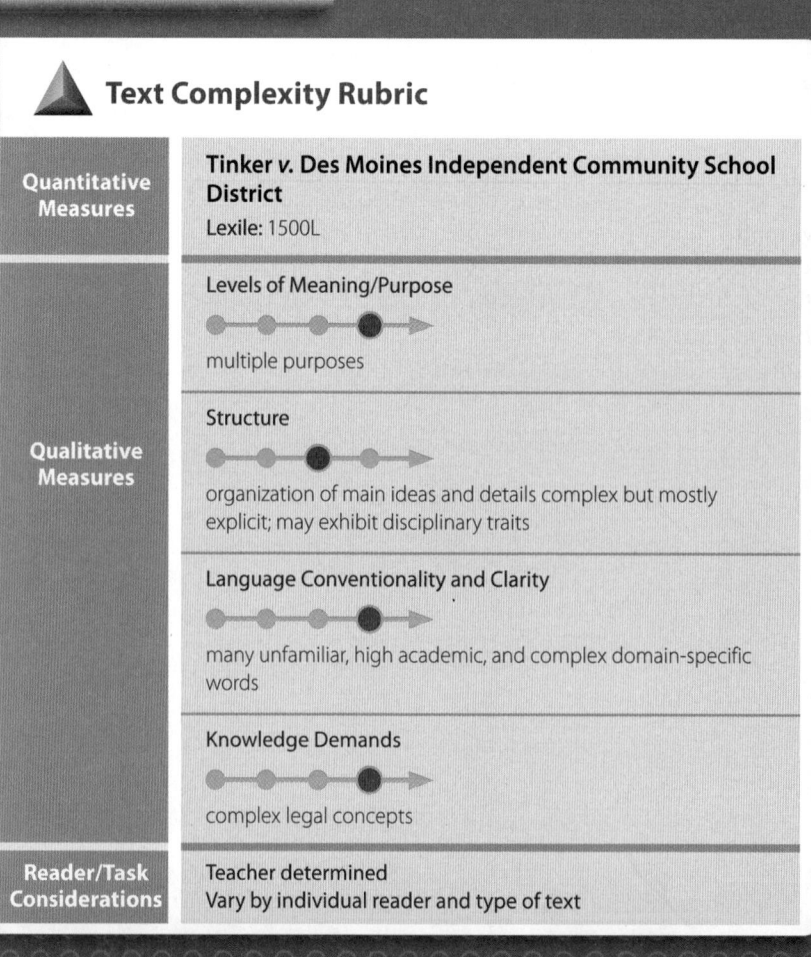

	Tinker v. Des Moines Independent Community School District Lexile: 1500L
Quantitative Measures	
	Levels of Meaning/Purpose ●—●—●—➤ multiple purposes
Qualitative Measures	**Structure** ●—●—●—➤ organization of main ideas and details complex but mostly explicit; may exhibit disciplinary traits
	Language Conventionality and Clarity ●—●—●—➤ many unfamiliar, high academic, and complex domain-specific words
	Knowledge Demands ●—●—●—➤ complex legal concepts
Reader/Task Considerations	Teacher determined Vary by individual reader and type of text

TEACH

CLOSE READ

Background The Vietnam War tore the American public apart. By the late 1960s, protests became commonplace. In 1967, 35,000 demonstrators protested outside the Pentagon. In the fall of 1969, more than 500,000 marched in a massive demonstration in Washington, D.C. Most protests were peaceful, but some turned violent. The most infamous protest occurred at Kent State University in 1970 when Ohio National Guard troops were called out to maintain peace during a demonstration. Something went wrong, and the National Guard shot and killed four students while wounding nine others.

AS YOU READ Direct students to use the As You Read note to focus their reading. Remind students to write down any questions they generate during reading.

Delineate and Evaluate an Argument (LINES 1–5)   COMMON CORE RI 8

Explain to students that they are going to read a U.S. Supreme Court decision regarding a case of free speech. Tell them to look for details stating who the two parties were, what actions created the basis for the trial, what arguments the two sides made, and what reasons the justices used in making their decision.

A ASK STUDENTS to read lines 1–5. What are the two sides in this case? *(three public school students and their school district in Des Moines, Iowa)* What did the students do? *(They wore black armbands in protest against the government policy in Vietnam.)* What did the school do? *(suspended the students)*

CRITICAL VOCABULARY

injunction: The students asked the court for an injunction against the school.

ASK STUDENTS to explain what the students expected the injunction would do for them. *(The expected that the injunction would prevent the school from enforcing the rule against wearing armbands.)*

Background *The 1969 Supreme Court decision Tinker v. Des Moines was written in the context of the Vietnam War. In 1965, President Lyndon Johnson ordered air attacks against communist North Vietnam and sent the first 100,000 U.S. ground troops into Vietnam. In that same year, "teach-ins" on college campuses to protest the war became commonplace. As U.S. troop levels grew to about 550,000 and casualties mounted, American support for the war declined. Protests took numerous forms from large public demonstrations to individual acts of resistance.*

Tinker
v.
Des Moines Independent
Community School District

Supreme Court of the United States, Opinion and Dissents

AS YOU READ First determine who the petitioners and the respondents were, and then determine what each of them did that resulted in this case being brought before the Supreme Court. Write down any questions you generate during reading.

No. 21
SUPREME COURT OF THE UNITED STATES
393 U.S. 503
Argued November 12, 1968
Decided February 24, 1969

Syllabus

Petitioners, three public school pupils in Des Moines, Iowa, were suspended from school for wearing black armbands to protest the Government's policy in Vietnam. They sought nominal[1] damages and an **injunction** against a regulation that the respondents[2] had promulgated[3] banning the wearing of armbands. The District Court dismissed the complaint on the ground that the regulation was within

injunction
(ĭn-jŭngk´shən) *n.*
court order forbidding a specific action.

---
[1] **nominal:** very small.
[2] **respondents:** defendants in a lawsuit.
[3] **promulgated:** enacted a rule.

Image Credits: ©Eugene Ivanov/Shutterstock

Tinker v. Des Moines. **549**

SCAFFOLDING FOR ELL STUDENTS

Culture To ensure that students understand the background for this selection, briefly explain that the U.S. judicial system is comprised of three primary courts.

- U.S. District Courts. There are 94 district courts that hear almost all federal legal cases. Cases settled in district courts can be appealed to higher courts known as Courts of appeals.

- The 94 district courts are organized into 12 regions with a court of appeal in each. The courts of appeals rule on cases appealed from the district courts. Decisions made by courts of appeals can be appealed to the U.S. Supreme Court.

- The U.S. Supreme Court does not hear all cases appealed to it. The nine justices make final decisions on cases and decide on the constitutionality of laws.

Delineate and Evaluate an Argument (LINES 10-22)

 COMMON CORE RI 8

Explain that the Supreme Court is hearing this case because the petitioners were not satisfied with the decision of the court of appeals. Tell students that the numbered points under the heading "Held" summarize the Supreme Court's decision. The remainder of the document represents an analysis of this decision.

B **CITE TEXT EVIDENCE** Have students read lines 10-22. Ask them what evidence the justices considered in deciding that the actions of the petitioners were protected by the First and Fourth Amendments. *(The petitioners were not disruptive and did not interfere with the rights of others.)* What exception to protection under the First and Fourth Amendments did the court make in this situation? *(They said the rights were subject to the special situation involving the school environment.)*

Summarize (LINES 25–47)

 COMMON CORE RI 2

Explain to students that Justice Fortas begins the opinion with a summary of the events that led to the suspensions and the case before the Court.

C **ASK STUDENTS** to read lines 25-27. Ask them why Justice Fortas would place the summary here at the beginning of opinion. *(so readers will know the essential facts of the case before hearing the Court's reasoning)* Discuss this summary with students to ensure they understand the basics of the case. You might ask questions such as: Who were the petitioners? *(John F. Tinker, Christopher Eckhardt, Mary Beth Tinker, students in the Des Moines public schools)* What did they do? *(They wore armbands in protest of the Vietnam War.)* What happened to them? *(They were suspended.)*

---

the Board's power, despite the absence of any finding of substantial interference with the conduct of school activities. The Court of Appeals, sitting *en banc,*[4] affirmed by an equally divided court.

10 *Held*:

B

1. In wearing armbands, the petitioners were quiet and passive. They were not disruptive and did not impinge[5] upon the rights of others. In these circumstances, their conduct was within the protection of the Free Speech Clause of the First Amendment and the Due Process Clause of the Fourteenth.

2. First Amendment rights are available to teachers and students, subject to application in light of the special characteristics of the school environment.

20

3. A prohibition against expression of opinion, without any evidence that the rule is necessary to avoid substantial interference with school discipline or the rights of others, is not permissible under the First and Fourteenth Amendments.

DISPOSITION: 383 F.2d 988, reversed and remanded.

MR. JUSTICE FORTAS delivered the opinion of the Court.

C

Petitioner John F. Tinker, 15 years old, and petitioner Christopher Eckhardt, 16 years old, attended high schools in Des Moines, Iowa. Petitioner Mary Beth Tinker, John's sister, was a 13-year-old student in junior high school.

In December 1965, a group of adults and students in Des Moines held
30 a meeting at the Eckhardt home. The group determined to publicize their objections to the hostilities in Vietnam and their support for a truce by wearing black armbands during the holiday season and by fasting on December 16 and New Year's Eve. Petitioners and their parents had previously engaged in similar activities, and they decided to participate in the program.

The principals of the Des Moines schools became aware of the plan to wear armbands. On December 14, 1965, they met and adopted a policy that any student wearing an armband to school would be asked to remove it, and if he refused he would be suspended until he returned
40 without the armband. Petitioners were aware of the regulation that the school authorities adopted.

On December 16, Mary Beth and Christopher wore black armbands to their schools. John Tinker wore his armband the next day. They were all sent home and suspended from school until they would come back without their armbands. They did not return to school until after the planned period for wearing armbands had expired—that is, until after New Year's Day.

---

[4] **en banc** (än-bänk´): with all of its judges.
[5] **impinge**: intrude.

APPLYING ACADEMIC VOCABULARY

contemporary	virtual

As you discuss the majority opinion, incorporate the following Collection 6 academic vocabulary words: *contemporary* and *virtual*. Point out to students that this case was decided in 1969. Ask them to consider how a **contemporary** court might decide this case. As you discuss why wearing armbands was a form of free speech, ask whether restricting this particular form of political speech would allow **virtually** any other kind of free speech to be restricted in school as well.

This complaint was filed in the United States District Court by petitioners, through their fathers, under § 1983 of Title 42 of the
50 United States Code. It prayed for an injunction restraining the respondent school officials and the respondent members of the board of directors of the school district from disciplining the petitioners, and it sought nominal damages. After an evidentiary hearing the District Court dismissed the complaint. It upheld the constitutionality of the school authorities' action on the ground that it was reasonable in order to prevent disturbance of school discipline. 258 F.Supp. 971 (1966). The court referred to but expressly declined to follow the Fifth Circuit's holding in a similar case that the wearing of symbols like the armbands cannot be prohibited unless it "materially and substantially
60 interfere[s] with the requirements of appropriate discipline in the operation of the school." *Burnside v. Byars*, 363 F.2d 744, 749 (1966).

On appeal, the Court of Appeals for the Eighth Circuit considered the case en banc. The court was equally divided, and the District Court's decision was accordingly affirmed, without opinion. 383 F.2d 988 (1967). We granted certiorari.[6] 390 U.S. 942 (1968).

I

The District Court recognized that the wearing of an armband for the purpose of expressing certain views is the type of symbolic act that is within the Free Speech Clause of the First Amendment. See *West Virginia v. Barnette*, 319 U.S. 624 (1943); *Stromberg v. California*,
70 283 U.S. 359 (1931). Cf. *Thornhill v. Alabama*, 310 U.S. 88 (1940); *Edwards v. South Carolina*, 372 U.S. 229 (1963); *Brown v. Louisiana*, 383 U.S. 131 (1966). As we shall discuss, the wearing of armbands in the circumstances of this case was entirely divorced from actually or potentially disruptive conduct by those participating in it. It was closely akin to "pure speech" which, we have repeatedly held, is entitled to comprehensive protection under the First Amendment. Cf. *Cox v. Louisiana*, 379 U.S. 536, 555 (1965); *Adderley v. Florida*, 385 U.S. 39 (1966).

First Amendment rights, applied in light of the special characteristics
80 of the school environment, are available to teachers and students. It can hardly be argued that either students or teachers shed their constitutional rights to freedom of speech or expression at the schoolhouse gate. This has been the unmistakable holding of this Court for almost 50 years. In *Meyer v. Nebraska*, 262 U.S. 390 (1923), and *Bartels v. Iowa*, 262 U.S. 404 (1923), this Court, in opinions by Mr. Justice McReynolds, held that the Due Process Clause of the Fourteenth Amendment prevents States from forbidding the teaching of a foreign language to young students. Statutes to this effect, the

---

[6] **certiorari** (sûr´shē-ə-râr´ē): a document allowing an appeal to a higher court.

CLOSE READ

Delineate and Evaluate an Argument

COMMON CORE RI 8

(LINES 53–61)

This passage describes the opinion issued by the District Court in the present case. In that case, the court referred to a precedent, *Burnside* v. *Byars,* which dealt with a similar case.

D **CITE TEXT EVIDENCE** Have students read lines 53-61. What were the conclusions of the two courts? *(The District Court concluded that the school officials had the authority to prohibit the wearing of armbands in order to prevent disturbance in school. In* Burnside v. Byars, *the court ruled that the wearing of symbols could only be prohibited if wearing them "materially and substantially interfere[s] with...the disicipline in... the school.")*

Delineate and Evaluate an Argument

COMMON CORE RI 8

(LINES 66–78)

Point out that Justice Fortas's opinion relies heavily upon **precedent**, previous legal cases in which these same points of law were discussed.

E **ASK STUDENTS** to read lines 66-78. What point is Justice Fortas is making in this passage? *(He is explaining that wearing the armband is a form of free speech and is protected by the First Amendment.)* What evidence does he cite to prove his point? *(previous court cases that upheld the right of free speech)*

WHEN STUDENTS STRUGGLE . . .

The use of unfamiliar words or of words used in unfamiliar ways will prove a stumbling block for many students. Review techniques for figuring out the meaning of words. For example:

- In line 50, Justice Fortas says "It prayed for an injunction." Have students consider the familiar use of the word *prayed.* Ask, What is a synonym for *prayed? (asked)* Discuss similar unusual word applications, such as *divorced* in line 73 and *holding* in line 83.

- In line 53, Justice Fortas refers to "an evidentiary hearing." Guide students in reducing *evidentiary* into its base form *(evidence)* to figure out the meaning. *(having evidence)*

Delineate and Evaluate an Argument

COMMON CORE **RI 8**

(LINES 100–117)

Explain to students that in deciding cases, justices will rely in part on **legal reasoning,** which is a way of reasoning through a case and assessing how a particular law applies. The quotation from Justice Jackson (lines 100–110) is an example of legal reasoning.

E **CITE TEXT EVIDENCE** Have students read lines 100–117. What reasoning does Justice Jackson use for closely limiting the authority of boards of education to restrict the constitutional freedoms of students? *(He reasons that if youth are to fully understand the important principles of government, their rights cannot be infringed.)* What does Justice Fortas say, in lines 111–117, should be balanced against this protection of student rights? *(the Court's repeated support of the needs of school officials to prescribe and control behavior in schools)*

CRITICAL VOCABULARY

scrupulous: Justice Jackson says that the Constitutional freedoms of the individual must be thoroughly protected.

ASK STUDENTS to give some examples of ways in which individual freedoms might receive scrupulous protection. *(Possible answers: allowing students to express their views on political issues, protecting an individual's right to travel, preserving people's privacy in their homes)*

nascent: Justice Fortas says that there was no evidence that any kind of disturbance was developing as a result of the students' actions.

ASK STUDENTS why a nascent disturbance would be cause for action by school officials. *(A nascent disturbance could quickly grow into a real disturbance that might interfere with students' ability to get an education.)*

Court held, unconstitutionally interfere with the liberty of teacher, student, and parent. See also *Pierce v. Society of Sisters,* 268 U.S. 510 (1925); *West Virginia v. Barnette,* 319 U.S. 624 (1943); *McCollum v. Board of Education,* 333 U.S. 203 (1948); *Wieman v. Updegraff,* 344 U.S. 183, 195 (1952) (concurring opinion); *Sweezy v. New Hampshire,* 354 U.S. 234 (1957); *Shelton v. Tucker,* 364 U.S. 479, 487 (1960); *Engel v. Vitale,* 370 U.S. 421 (1962); *Keyishian v. Board of Regents,* 385 U.S. 589, 603 (1967); *Epperson v. Arkansas,* ante, p. 97 (1968).

In *West Virginia v. Barnette, supra,* this Court held that under the First Amendment, the student in public school may not be compelled to salute the flag. Speaking through Mr. Justice Jackson, the Court said:

100 "The Fourteenth Amendment, as now applied to the States, protects the citizen against the State itself and all of its creatures—Boards of Education not excepted. These have, of course, important, delicate, and highly discretionary functions, but none that they may not perform within the limits of the Bill of Rights. That they are educating the young for citizenship is reason for **scrupulous** protection of Constitutional freedoms of the individual, if we are not to strangle the free mind at its source and teach youth to discount important principles of our government as mere
110 platitudes." 319 U.S., at 637.

scrupulous
(skrōō′pyə-ləs) *adj.*
thorough and diligent.

On the other hand, the Court has repeatedly emphasized the need for affirming the comprehensive authority of the States and of school officials, consistent with fundamental constitutional safeguards, to prescribe and control conduct in the schools. See *Epperson v. Arkansas, supra,* at 104; *Meyer v. Nebraska, supra,* at 402. Our problem lies in the area where students in the exercise of First Amendment rights collide with the rules of the school authorities.

II

The problem posed by the present case does not relate to regulation of the length of skirts or the type of clothing, to hair style, or
120 deportment. Cf. *Ferrell v. Dallas Independent School District,* 392 F.2d 697 (1968); *Pugsley v. Sellmeyer,* 158 Ark. 247, 250 S. W. 538 (1923). It does not concern aggressive, disruptive action or even group demonstrations. Our problem involves direct, primary First Amendment rights akin to "pure speech."

The school officials banned and sought to punish petitioners for a silent, passive expression of opinion, unaccompanied by any disorder or disturbance on the part of petitioners. There is here no evidence whatever of petitioners' interference, actual or **nascent**, with the schools' work or of collision with the rights of other students to be

nascent
(nā′sənt) *adj.*
emerging; developing.

WHEN STUDENTS STRUGGLE . . .

Sometimes complex sentence structures, legal language, and the unfamiliar use of vocabulary can interfere with understanding. Demonstrate how to paraphrase sentences in order to make the meaning clearer and more accessible. Read aloud lines 153–157 and then guide students in paraphrasing it. For example:

If school officials want to stop students from expressing certain opinions, they must show that they're not doing it just to avoid the problems that sometimes occur when a person voices unpopular ideas.

ASK STUDENTS to identify other difficult passages and work with them to paraphrase the meaning.

> # Apprehension of disturbance is not enough to overcome the right to freedom of expression.

130   secure and to be let alone. Accordingly, this case does not concern speech or action that intrudes upon the work of the schools or the rights of other students.

   Only a few of the 18,000 students in the school system wore the black armbands. Only five students were suspended for wearing them. There is no indication that the work of the schools or any class was disrupted. Outside the classrooms, a few students made hostile remarks to the children wearing armbands, but there were no threats or acts of violence on school premises.

   The District Court concluded that the action of the school
140   authorities was reasonable because it was based upon their fear of a disturbance from the wearing of the armbands. But, in our system, undifferentiated fear or apprehension of disturbance is not enough to overcome the right to freedom of expression. Any departure from absolute regimentation may cause trouble. Any variation from the majority's opinion may inspire fear. Any word spoken, in class, in the lunchroom, or on the campus, that deviates from the views of another person may start an argument or cause a disturbance. But our Constitution says we must take this risk, *Terminiello v. Chicago*, 337 U.S. 1 (1949); and our history says that it is this sort of hazardous
150   freedom—this kind of openness—that is the basis of our national strength and of the independence and vigor of Americans who grow up and live in this relatively permissive, often **disputatious**, society.

   In order for the State in the person of school officials to justify prohibition of a particular expression of opinion, it must be able to show that its action was caused by something more than a mere desire to avoid the discomfort and unpleasantness that always accompany an unpopular viewpoint. Certainly where there is no finding and no showing that engaging in the forbidden conduct would "materially and substantially interfere with the requirements of appropriate discipline
160   in the operation of the school," the prohibition cannot be sustained. *Burnside v. Byars, supra*, at 749.

disputatious
(dĭs´pyə-tā´shəs) *adj.*
argumentative;
confrontational.

Tinker v. Des Moines.   **553**

CLOSE READ

Delineate and Evaluate an Argument

COMMON CORE   RI 8

(LINES 133–152)

Point out that one of the important claims made by officials of the Des Moines School District was that they needed the authority to control the behavior of students.

G   **CITE TEXT EVIDENCE** Have students read lines 133-152. What evidence does Justice Fortas give regarding the suggestion that school discipline was under threat? *(Only five students were suspended; there was no indication that the students disrupted the work of the school or of a class. Some students made remarks against the protesting students, but there were no fights or threats.)* How did the District Court interpret these facts? *(The risk of disruption was sufficient to justify restricting the freedom of expression of the students.)* How did the majority in the Supreme Court interpret these facts? *(They decided that the mere risk of disturbance was not sufficient to limit the students' freedom of speech.)*

CRITICAL VOCABULARY

disputatious: Justice Fortas states that our society is permissive and often argumentative.

ASK STUDENTS how a disputatious society can contribute to the strength of a country. *(People who dispute issues make their voices heard and contribute to the public dialogue on what kind of country and society they want.)*

Delineate and Evaluate an Argument (LINES 174–186)  COMMON CORE RI 8

Point out that Justice Fortas prepares his argument by highlighting weaknesses in the respondents' case.

(H) ASK STUDENTS how Justice Fortas relates a student article on Vietnam to the armband controversy. *(School officials were concerned over making the issue of Vietnam controversial, which is why they dissuaded the student from writing the article and prohibited all students from wearing armbands.)*

CITE TEXT EVIDENCE What evidence does the justice give that shows that the school was restricting freedom of expression regarding a particular topic? *(The school allowed students to wear political campaign buttons and the Nazi Iron Cross but prohibited armbands.)*

CRITICAL VOCABULARY

purport: The school authorities claimed to forbid only the black armbands.

ASK STUDENTS why officials might have thought that the armbands were inappropriate but allowed the Iron Cross. *(The purported claim was based on the highly charged emotions associated with war.)*

enclave: A school cannot operate as a separate entity with total authority over students.

ASK STUDENTS if a school is an enclave within society and whether it should operate under different rules. *(It is an enclave with some rules of its own; there may be some differences of opinion on the extent to which a school's rules should differ.)*

In the present case, the District Court made no such finding, and our independent examination of the record fails to yield evidence that the school authorities had reason to anticipate that the wearing of the armbands would substantially interfere with the work of the school or impinge upon the rights of other students. Even an official memorandum prepared after the suspension that listed the reasons for the ban on wearing the armbands made no reference to the anticipation of such disruption.

170 On the contrary, the action of the school authorities appears to have been based upon an urgent wish to avoid the controversy which might result from the expression, even by the silent symbol of armbands, of opposition to this Nation's part in the conflagration[7] in Vietnam. It is revealing, in this respect, that the meeting at which the school principals decided to issue the contested regulation was called in response to a student's statement to the journalism teacher in one of the schools that he wanted to write an article on Vietnam and have it published in the school paper. (The student was dissuaded.)

It is also relevant that the school authorities did not **purport** to 180 prohibit the wearing of all symbols of political or controversial significance. The record shows that students in some of the schools wore buttons relating to national political campaigns, and some even wore the Iron Cross, traditionally a symbol of Nazism. The order prohibiting the wearing of armbands did not extend to these. Instead, a particular symbol—black armbands worn to exhibit opposition to this Nation's involvement in Vietnam—was singled out for prohibition. Clearly, the prohibition of expression of one particular opinion, at least without evidence that it is necessary to avoid material and substantial interference with schoolwork or discipline, is not constitutionally 190 permissible.

In our system, state-operated schools may not be **enclaves** of totalitarianism. School officials do not possess absolute authority over their students. Students in school as well as out of school are "persons" under our Constitution. They are possessed of fundamental rights which the State must respect, just as they themselves must respect their obligations to the State. In our system, students may not be regarded as closed-circuit recipients of only that which the State chooses to communicate. They may not be confined to the expression of those sentiments that are officially approved. In the absence of a 200 specific showing of constitutionally valid reasons to regulate their speech, students are entitled to freedom of expression of their views. As Judge Gewin, speaking for the Fifth Circuit, said, school officials cannot suppress "expressions of feelings with which they do not wish to contend." *Burnside v. Byars, supra,* at 749.

purport
(pər-pôrt´) *v.* to claim or pretend to be the case.

enclave
(ĕn´klāv´) *n.* a distinct area within a larger area.

---

[7] **conflagration:** a destructive fire, here used figuratively to mean "war."

Strategies for Annotation 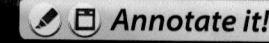 ✏️ 🗒️ *Annotate it!*

Delineate and Evaluate an Argument (LINES 191–204)  COMMON CORE RI 8

Have students identify reasons the justice gives to support his argument that schools are not enclaves of totalitarianism. Have them use their eBook annotation tools to highlight these details in blue.

> In our system, state-operated schools may not be enclaves of totalitarianism. School officials do not possess absolute authority over their students. Students in school as well as out of school are "persons" under our Constitution. They are possessed of fundamental rights which the State must respect, just as they themselves must respect their obligations to the State. In our system, students may not

In *Meyer v. Nebraska, supra,* at 402, Mr. Justice McReynolds expressed this Nation's repudiation of the principle that a State might so conduct its schools as to "foster a homogeneous people." He said:

> "In order to submerge the individual and develop ideal citizens, Sparta assembled the males at seven into barracks and intrusted their subsequent education and training to official guardians. Although such measures have been deliberately approved by men of great genius, their ideas touching the relation between individual and State were wholly different from those upon which our institutions rest; and it hardly will be affirmed that any legislature could impose such restrictions upon the people of a State without doing violence to both letter and spirit of the Constitution."

This principle has been repeated by this Court on numerous occasions during the intervening years. In *Keyishian v. Board of Regents,* 385 U.S. 589, 603, MR. JUSTICE BRENNAN, speaking for the Court, said:

> "'The vigilant protection of constitutional freedoms is nowhere more vital than in the community of American schools.' *Shelton v. Tucker,* [364 U.S. 479,] at 487. The classroom is peculiarly the 'marketplace of ideas.' The Nation's future depends upon leaders trained through wide exposure to that robust exchange of ideas which discovers truth 'out of a multitude of tongues, [rather] than through any kind of authoritative selection.'"

The principle of these cases is not confined to the supervised and ordained discussion which takes place in the classroom. The principal use to which the schools are dedicated is to accommodate students during prescribed hours for the purpose of certain types of activities. Among those activities is personal intercommunication among the students. This is not only an inevitable part of the process of attending school; it is also an important part of the educational process. A student's rights, therefore, do not embrace merely the classroom hours. When he is in the cafeteria, or on the playing field, or on the campus during the authorized hours, he may express his opinions, even on controversial subjects like the conflict in Vietnam, if he does so without "materially and substantially interfer[ing] with the requirements of appropriate discipline in the operation of the school" and without colliding with the rights of others. *Burnside v. Byars, supra,* at 749. But conduct by the student, in class or out of it, which for any reason—whether it stems from time, place, or type of behavior—materially disrupts classwork or involves substantial disorder or invasion of the rights of others is, of course, not immunized by the constitutional guarantee of freedom of speech. Cf. *Blackwell v. Issaquena County Board of Education,* 363 F.2d 749 (C. A. 5th Cir. 1966).

CLOSE READ

Delineate and Evaluate an Argument (LINES 205–217)

COMMON CORE RI 8

Explain that Justice Fortas cites the case of *Meyer* v. *Nebraska* to argue that schools are not intended to "foster a homogeneous people." Elicit from students the meaning of this phrase. *(encourage conformity among people)*

I CITE TEXT EVIDENCE Have students read lines 205-217. How does the *Meyer* v. *Nebraska* opinion make the case that homogeneity is the wrong purpose for schools in America? *(The opinion argues that the educational philosophy of Sparta in Ancient Greece—where boys received military-style schooling— has no place in the United States, where individual liberty is protected by the Constitution.)*

Delineate and Evaluate an Argument (LINES 229–249)

COMMON CORE RI 8

Point out that Justice Fortas has cited several cases as precedents for protecting the right of freedom of expression for students while in the classroom.

J CITE TEXT EVIDENCE to read lines 229-249. How does Justice Fortas justify extending the right to freedom of expression to all aspects of school life? *(He reasons that part of the educational process is the interaction of students throughout the school day and in all parts of the school.)*

SCAFFOLDING FOR ELL STUDENTS

Commonly Confused Words Read aloud lines 229-232. Then call students' attention to the words *principle* and *principal* and their different spellings. Explain that these words are often confused even by native English speakers. Write the words on the board and define the words as they are used in this context:

Principle *n.* the essential, or main, point or idea.

Principal *adj.* primary or most important.

Explain to students that *principal* is often used in this selection as a noun referring to the person in charge of a school.

Draw Conclusions

 **COMMON CORE** RI 1

(LINES 250–260)

Read aloud the paragraph beginning with line 250. Then reread the sentence "We properly read it to permit reasonable regulation of speech connected activities in carefully restricted circumstances" (lines 256–257).

K **ASK STUDENTS** whether Justice Fortas means that the government can regulate free speech. Under what circumstances? *(Yes, the government can regulate free speech in limited circumstances, as when it causes violence or disrupts the educational process in schools.)*

Delineate and Evaluate an Argument

COMMON CORE RI 8

(LINES 289–293)

Point out that this is the conclusion of the majority opinion as expressed by Justice Fortas.

L **ASK STUDENTS** to read lines 289–293. Invite them to summarize how the justices resolved the case. *(They determined that the students had the right to wear the armbands and should not have been suspended. The school officials did not have the right under these circumstances to restrict the students' freedom of expression. The Court did not rule on the claim for damages that the students asked for. The Court sent the case back to the lower courts to make this decision.)*

250 Under our Constitution, free speech is not a right that is given only to be so circumscribed that it exists in principle but not in fact. Freedom of expression would not truly exist if the right could be exercised only in an area that a benevolent government has provided as a safe haven for crackpots. The Constitution says that Congress (and the States) may not abridge the right to free speech. This provision means what it says. We properly read it to permit reasonable regulation of speech-connected activities in carefully restricted circumstances. But we do not confine the permissible exercise of First Amendment rights to a telephone booth or the four corners of a pamphlet, or to supervised 260 and ordained discussion in a school classroom.

If a regulation were adopted by school officials forbidding discussion of the Vietnam conflict, or the expression by any student of opposition to it anywhere on school property except as part of a prescribed classroom exercise, it would be obvious that the regulation would violate the constitutional rights of students, at least if it could not be justified by a showing that the students' activities would materially and substantially disrupt the work and discipline of the school. Cf. *Hammond v. South Carolina State College*, 272 F.Supp. 947 (D. C. S. C. 1967) (orderly protest meeting on state college campus); *Dickey* 270 *v. Alabama State Board of Education*, 273 F.Supp. 613 (D. C. M. D. Ala. 1967) (expulsion of student editor of college newspaper). In the circumstances of the present case, the prohibition of the silent, passive "witness of the armbands," as one of the children called it, is no less offensive to the Constitution's guarantees.

As we have discussed, the record does not demonstrate any facts which might reasonably have led school authorities to forecast substantial disruption of or material interference with school activities, and no disturbances or disorders on the school premises in fact occurred. These petitioners merely went about their ordained rounds in school. 280 Their deviation consisted only in wearing on their sleeve a band of black cloth, not more than two inches wide. They wore it to exhibit their disapproval of the Vietnam hostilities and their advocacy of a truce, to make their views known, and, by their example, to influence others to adopt them. They neither interrupted school activities nor sought to intrude in the school affairs or the lives of others. They caused discussion outside of the classrooms, but no interference with work and no disorder. In the circumstances, our Constitution does not permit officials of the State to deny their form of expression.

We express no opinion as to the form of relief which should be 290 granted, this being a matter for the lower courts to determine. We reverse and remand for further proceedings consistent with this opinion.

Reversed and remanded.

TO CHALLENGE STUDENTS . . .

Debate the Issue Write the following statement on the board: School administrators have the right to restrict what students wear to school. Then organize students into teams of two. Assign each team to argue either for or against the proposition. Allow teams a few minutes to plan their arguments and assemble evidence. Encourage them to base their arguments on the legal reasoning and Constitutional law discussed in this opinion. Match pro and con teams and allow them a few minutes to debate the issue.

MR. JUSTICE STEWART, concurring.

Although I agree with much of what is said in the Court's opinion, and with its judgment in this case, I cannot share the Court's uncritical assumption that, school discipline aside, the First Amendment rights of children are co-extensive with those of adults. Indeed, I had thought the Court decided otherwise just last Term in *Ginsberg v. New York*, 300 390 U.S. 629. I continue to hold the view I expressed in that case: "[A] State may permissibly determine that, at least in some precisely delineated areas, a child—like someone in a captive audience—is not possessed of that full capacity for individual choice which is the presupposition of First Amendment guarantees." *Id.*, at 649-650 (concurring in result). Cf. *Prince v. Massachusetts*, 321 U.S. 158.

MR. JUSTICE WHITE, concurring.

While I join the Court's opinion, I deem it appropriate to note, first, that the Court continues to recognize a distinction between communicating by words and communicating by acts or conduct 310 which sufficiently impinges on some valid state interest; and, second, that I do not subscribe to everything the Court of Appeals said about free speech in its opinion in *Burnside v. Byars*, 363 F.2d 744, 748 (C. A. 5th Cir. 1966), a case relied upon by the Court in the matter now before us.

MR. JUSTICE BLACK, dissenting.

The Court's holding in this case ushers in what I deem to be an entirely new era in which the power to control pupils by the elected "officials of state supported public schools…" in the United States is in ultimate effect transferred to the Supreme Court. The Court brought 320 this particular case here on a petition for certiorari urging that the First and Fourteenth Amendments protect the right of school pupils to express their political views all the way "from kindergarten through high school." Here the constitutional right to "political expression" asserted was a right to wear black armbands during school hours and at classes in order to demonstrate to the other students that the petitioners were mourning because of the death of United States soldiers in Vietnam and to protest that war which they were against. Ordered to refrain from wearing the armbands in school by the elected school officials and the teachers vested with state authority 330 to do so, apparently only seven out of the school system's 18,000 pupils deliberately refused to obey the order. One defying pupil was Paul Tinker, 8 years old, who was in the second grade; another, Hope Tinker, was 11 years old and in the fifth grade; a third member of the Tinker family was 13, in the eighth grade; and a fourth member of the same family was John Tinker, 15 years old, an 11th grade high school pupil. Their father, a Methodist minister without a church, is paid a salary by the American Friends Service Committee. Another student who defied the school order and insisted on wearing an armband in

Tinker v. Des Moines.   **557**

CLOSE READ

Delineate and Evaluate an Argument

COMMON CORE **RI 8**

(LINES 294–305)

Point out that Justice Stewart ruled with the majority in this case, but in his concurrence, he expresses a reservation about an aspect of the majority opinion.

(M) CITE TEXT EVIDENCE Have students read lines 294-305. What reservation does Justice Stewart have with the opinion of the majority? *(He does not believe that the rights of children are identical to those of adults.)* What is the basis for his objection? Explain. *(He cites* Ginsberg v. New York *that compares a child to a captive audience without the full ability to make individual choices, which, he says, is the presumption of the First Amendment.)*

Make Inferences

COMMON CORE **RI 1**

(LINES 315–319)

Explain that in Supreme Court decisions dissenting opinions are often bold and outspoken. Point out that Justice Black's dissent begins with a powerful statement of opposition to the majority opinion.

(N) ASK STUDENTS to read lines 315-319. Why does Justice Black think the Supreme Court has assumed the power to control public school students? *(He believes that the Court's decision in* Tinker v. Des Moines *has, in effect, taken away the broad power of schools to establish behavioral limits and to discipline students for exceeding those limits. In the absence of the schools' power to set these limits, only the Supreme Court is left with the authority to make these decisions.)*

SCAFFOLDING FOR ELL STUDENTS

Synonyms and Antonyms Write the words *synonym* and *antonym* on the board and explain that a synonym is a word that means the same, or nearly the same, as another word. An antonym is a word that means the opposite of another word.

Now point out that in their statements, Justices Stewart, White, and Black are either concurring or dissenting. Explain that these words are antonyms: *concurring* means "agreeing" and *dissenting* means "disagreeing." Ask students to give a synonym for *concurring*. Elicit that agreeing is one synonym. Ask for a synonym for *dissenting*. *(disagreeing)* Ask students to use a thesaurus or dictionary to find additional synonyms and antonyms for these two words.

Delineate and Evaluate an Argument (LINES 360–369) COMMON CORE RI 8

Point out that Justice Black's argument relies heavily upon the use of constitutional principles, applying parts of the U.S. Constitution that are relevant to the circumstances of the case.

CITE TEXT EVIDENCE Have students read lines 360-369. Which parts of the Constitution does Justice Black cite as relevant to his argument? *(the First and Fourteenth Amendments)* What exceptions does Justice Black make to these protections? *(He argues that these amendments do not guarantee people the right to give speeches or demonstrate wherever and whenever they wish.)* What support does he give to reinforce his opinion? *(He cites* Cox v. Louisiana.*)*

Make Inferences COMMON CORE RI 1

(LINES 370–381)

Suggest to students that they may be in a better position to discuss the realities of public education than many Supreme Court justices.

ASK STUDENTS to read lines 370-381. Invite them to speculate why the majority of justices ignored this evidence of disruption within the school. *(Answers will vary, but students may consider it a matter of how the facts were interpreted. What some justices regarded as non-disruptive behavior or appropriate discussion may have offended other justices.)*

CRITICAL VOCABULARY

arrogate: Justice Black says that the majority opinion in this case unjustly assumes authority to decide which school disciplinary actions are reasonable.

ASK STUDENTS whether they agree with Justice Black that the Court has *arrogated* this authority. *(Answers may vary, but urge students to explain whether or not the Court has arrogated its authority based on reasons and facts given in the case.)*

school was Christopher Eckhardt, an 11th grade pupil and a petitioner
340 in this case. His mother is an official in the Women's International
League for Peace and Freedom.

As I read the Court's opinion it relies upon the following grounds for holding unconstitutional the judgment of the Des Moines school officials and the two courts below. First, the Court concludes that the wearing of armbands is "symbolic speech" which is "akin to 'pure speech'" and therefore protected by the First and Fourteenth Amendments. Secondly, the Court decides that the public schools are an appropriate place to exercise "symbolic speech" as long as normal school functions are not "unreasonably" disrupted. Finally, the Court
350 **arrogates** to itself, rather than to the State's elected officials charged with running the schools, the decision as to which school disciplinary regulations are "reasonable."

arrogate
(ăr′ə-gāt′) *v.* to assume authority unjustly.

Assuming that the Court is correct in holding that the conduct of wearing armbands for the purpose of conveying political ideas is protected by the First Amendment, cf., e.g., *Giboney v. Empire Storage & Ice Co.,* 336 U.S. 490 (1949), the crucial remaining questions are whether students and teachers may use the schools at their whim as a platform for the exercise of free speech— "symbolic" or "pure"— and whether the courts will allocate to themselves the function of deciding
360 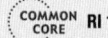 how the pupils' school day will be spent. While I have always believed that under the First and Fourteenth Amendments neither the State nor the Federal Government has any authority to regulate or censor the content of speech, I have never believed that any person has a right to give speeches or engage in demonstrations where he pleases and when he pleases. This Court has already rejected such a notion. In *Cox v. Louisiana,* 379 U.S. 536, 554 (1965), for example, the Court clearly stated that the rights of free speech and assembly "do not mean that everyone with opinions or beliefs to express may address a group at any public place and at any time."

370 While the record does not show that any of these armband students shouted, used profane language, or were violent in any manner, detailed testimony by some of them shows their armbands caused comments, warnings by other students, the poking of fun at them, and a warning by an older football player that other, nonprotesting students had better let them alone. There is also evidence that a teacher of mathematics had his lesson period practically "wrecked" chiefly by disputes with Mary Beth Tinker, who wore her armband for her "demonstration." Even a casual reading of the record shows that this armband did divert students' minds from their regular lessons,
380 and that talk, comments, etc., made John Tinker "self-conscious" in attending school with his armband. While the absence of obscene remarks or boisterous and loud disorder perhaps justifies the Court's statement that the few armband students did not actually "disrupt"

WHEN STUDENTS STRUGGLE...

Justice Black has summarized the basis for the Court's opinion in lines 342–352. Organize students in pairs to analyze his reasons for disagreeing with the majority of the justices.

Begin by drawing a three-column chart on the board and having pairs duplicate it on their own paper. Then ask students to reread this passage and identify in class the three grounds Justice Black cites. Write the reasons at the head of each column. As students proceed through the rest of Justice Black's dissent, have them fill in each column with the facts, examples, reasons, and other evidence he uses to refute these three points.

When students complete their charts, compare and discuss them as a group.

> ## " It is the beginning of a new revolutionary era of permissiveness in this country fostered by the judiciary. "

the classwork, I think the record overwhelmingly shows that the armbands did exactly what the elected school officials and principals foresaw they would, that is, took the students' minds off their classwork and diverted them to thoughts about the highly emotional subject of the Vietnam war. And I repeat that if the time has come when pupils of state-supported schools, kindergartens, grammar

390 schools, or high schools, can defy and flout orders of school officials to keep their minds on their own schoolwork, it is the beginning of a new revolutionary era of permissiveness in this country fostered by the judiciary. The next logical step, it appears to me, would be to hold unconstitutional laws that bar pupils under 21 or 18 from voting, or from being elected members of the boards of education.

The United States District Court refused to hold that the state school order violated the First and Fourteenth Amendments. 258 F.Supp. 971. Holding that the protest was akin to speech, which is protected by the First and Fourteenth Amendments, that court held that the

400 school order was "reasonable" and hence constitutional. There was at one time a line of cases holding "reasonableness" as the court saw it to be the test of a "due process" violation. Two cases upon which the Court today heavily relies for striking down this school order used this test of reasonableness, *Meyer v. Nebraska*, 262 U.S. 390 (1923), and *Bartels v. Iowa*, 262 U.S. 404 (1923). The opinions in both cases were written by Mr. Justice McReynolds; Mr. Justice Holmes, who opposed this reasonableness test, dissented from the holdings as did Mr. Justice Sutherland. This constitutional test of reasonableness prevailed in this Court for a season. It was this test that brought on President Franklin

410 Roosevelt's well-known Court fight. His proposed legislation did not pass, but the fight left the "reasonableness" constitutional test dead on the battlefield, so much so that this Court in *Ferguson v. Skrupa*, 372 U.S. 726, 729, 730, after a thorough review of the old cases, was able to conclude in 1963:

> "There was a time when the Due Process Clause was used by this Court to strike down laws which were thought

Tinker v. Des Moines.   **559**

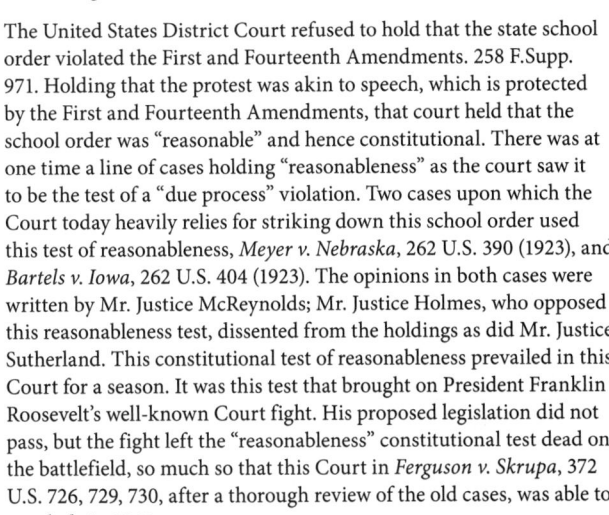

Wearing armbands is "symbolic speech."	Schools are proper place for "symbolic speech."	The Court should decide if school regulations are reasonable.
	No one has the right to speak or demonstrate anywhere or anytime.	Wearing the armbands precipitated comments, warnings, poking fun.

CLOSE READ

Delineate and Evaluate an Argument (LINES 388–395)  COMMON CORE RI 8

Highlight Justice Black's contention that the ruling marks the beginning of "a new revolutionary era of permissiveness" in which the rules of school officials can be ignored.

Q CITE TEXT EVIDENCE Challenge students to cite the evidence that Justice Black uses to support the statement in this passage. *(The armbands caused "comments, warnings by other students, the poking of fun," a warning by a football player in defense of the armbands, and disruption of a mathematics class. The ruling, Black says, supports the behavior of the students while dismissing the authority of the school officials to control it.)* Does the evidence make a compelling case for Justice Black's belief that it signaled the beginning of an "era of permissiveness"? Why or why not? *(Some students may say it is convincing and that the ruling means officials cannot set rules to control the disruptive behavior of students. Others may agree with the majority of the justices and say the evidence is not compelling because the disruption was not serious, did not really interfere with classes, and that the minor episodes that did occur were appropriate to the free exchange of ideas essential to a good education.)*

Delineate and Evaluate an Argument (LINES 396–400) COMMON CORE RI 8

Explain that interpretations of the U.S. Constitution are rarely straightforward. Help students understand the complexity of Justice Black's analysis of constitutional principles.

R ASK STUDENTS what seems contradictory about the district court's ruling. *(The court allowed that the student protest was free speech, but it upheld the school board's suppression of the protest.)* Challenge students to explain how the "reasonableness" doctrine justifies the apparent denial of free speech. *(The reasonableness test indicates that there are times when the strict application of the Constitution is unreasonable. In the case of the Des Moines school district, it would have been unreasonable to prohibit officials from establishing rules of behavior.)*

Delineate and Evaluate an Argument

COMMON CORE RI 8

(LINES 423–430)

Discuss Justice Black's explanation of how the reasonable-due process test has been applied to decisions.

 ASK STUDENTS to read lines 423-430. How does the "reasonableness-due process" test allow judges to rule against laws they don't like? *(It allows them to simply say a law is unreasonable, arbitrary, or irrational. These are subjective reasons rather than strict, measurable criteria based on the Constitution.)*

Delineate and Evaluate an Argument

COMMON CORE RI 8

(LINES 438–442)

Tell students that many of Justice Black's arguments rest upon fine points of constitutional law and in particular upon the application of legal precedents to this case.

CITE TEXT EVIDENCE Have students read lines 438-442. Ask what constitutional principles were applied in *West Virginia* v. *Barnette* that denied school officials the right to compel students to salute the United States flag. *(The Fourteenth Amendment makes the First Amendment right to free speech applicable to the states. The First Amendment guarantees the right of the individual—even small children—to speak out. Not saluting the flag is a form of free expression.)* Why is this case critical to Justice Black's argument? *(He points out that it does not uphold the reasonableness principle that Justice Fortas cited in several of the cases he uses as precedent.)*

---

unreasonable, that is, unwise or incompatible with some particular economic or social philosophy.

• • • •

420 "The doctrine that prevailed in *Lochner, Coppage, Adkins, Burns*, and like cases—that due process authorizes courts to hold laws unconstitutional when they believe the legislature has acted unwisely—has long since been discarded."

The *Ferguson* case totally repudiated the old reasonableness-due process test, the doctrine that judges have the power to hold laws unconstitutional upon the belief of judges that they "shock the conscience" or that they are "unreasonable," "arbitrary," "irrational," "contrary to fundamental 'decency,'" or some other such flexible term without precise boundaries. I have many times expressed my opposition to that concept on the ground that it gives judges 430 power to strike down any law they do not like. If the majority of the Court today, by agreeing to the opinion of my Brother FORTAS, is resurrecting that old reasonableness-due process test, I think the constitutional change should be plainly, unequivocally, and forthrightly stated for the benefit of the bench and bar. It will be a sad day for the country, I believe, when the present-day Court returns to the McReynolds due process concept. Other cases cited by the Court do not, as implied, follow the McReynolds reasonableness doctrine. *West Virginia v. Barnette*, 319 U.S. 624, clearly rejecting the "reasonableness" test, held that the Fourteenth Amendment made 440 the First applicable to the States, and that the two forbade a State to compel little schoolchildren to salute the United States flag when they had religious scruples against doing so. Neither *Thornhill v. Alabama*, 310 U.S. 88; *Stromberg v. California*, 283 U.S. 359; *Edwards v. South Carolina*, 372 U.S. 229; nor *Brown v. Louisiana*, 383 U.S. 131, related to schoolchildren at all, and none of these cases embraced Mr. Justice McReynolds' reasonableness test; and Thornhill, Edwards, and Brown relied on the vagueness of state statutes under scrutiny to hold them unconstitutional. *Cox v. Louisiana*, 379 U.S. 536, 555, and *Adderley v. Florida*, 385 U.S. 39, cited by the Court as a "compare," indicating, 450 I suppose, that these two cases are no longer the law, were not rested to the slightest extent on the *Meyer* and *Bartels* "reasonableness-due process-McReynolds" constitutional test.

I deny, therefore, that it has been the "unmistakable holding of this Court for almost 50 years" that "students" and "teachers" take with them into the "schoolhouse gate" constitutional rights to "freedom of speech or expression." Even *Meyer* did not hold that. It makes no reference to "symbolic speech" at all; what it did was to strike down as "unreasonable" and therefore unconstitutional a Nebraska law barring the teaching of the German language before the children reached the 460 eighth grade. One can well agree with Mr. Justice Holmes and Mr.

SCAFFOLDING FOR ELL STUDENTS

Prefixes Write the words *unconstitutional, unreasonable,* and *unequivocally* on the board. Point out that each of these words has the prefix *un-*, which means "not" or "opposite." Underline the prefixes and discuss the meanings of the words:

- *unconstitutional*—not constitutional
- *unreasonable*—not reasonable
- *unequivocally*—not open to question

ASK STUDENTS to write sentences using each of these words. Challenge them to find additional uses of the prefix *un-* as they continue reading.

Justice Sutherland, as I do, that such a law was no more unreasonable than it would be to bar the teaching of Latin and Greek to pupils who have not reached the eighth grade. In fact, I think the majority's reason for invalidating the Nebraska law was that it did not like it or in legal jargon that it "shocked the Court's conscience," "offended its sense of justice," or was "contrary to fundamental concepts of the English-speaking world," as the Court has sometimes said. See, e.g., *Rochin v. California*, 342 U.S. 165, and *Irvine v. California*, 347 U.S. 128. The truth is that a teacher of kindergarten, grammar school, or high

470 school pupils no more carries into a school with him a complete right to freedom of speech and expression than an anti-Catholic or anti-Semite carries with him a complete freedom of speech and religion into a Catholic church or Jewish synagogue. Nor does a person carry with him into the United States Senate or House, or into the Supreme Court, or any other court, a complete constitutional right to go into those places contrary to their rules and speak his mind on any subject he pleases. It is a myth to say that any person has a constitutional right to say what he pleases, where he pleases, and when he pleases. Our Court has decided precisely the opposite. See, e.g., *Cox v. Louisiana*,

480 379 U.S. 536, 555; *Adderley v. Florida*, 385 U.S. 39.

In my view, teachers in state-controlled public schools are hired to teach there. Although Mr. Justice McReynolds may have intimated to the contrary in *Meyer v. Nebraska, supra*, certainly a teacher is not paid to go into school and teach subjects the State does not hire him to teach as a part of its selected curriculum. Nor are public school students sent to the schools at public expense to broadcast political or any other views to educate and inform the public. The original idea of schools, which I do not believe is yet abandoned as worthless or out of date, was that children had not yet reached the point of experience and

490 wisdom which enabled them to teach all of their elders. It may be that the Nation has outworn the old-fashioned slogan that "children are to be seen not heard," but one may, I hope, be permitted to harbor the thought that taxpayers send children to school on the premise that at their age they need to learn, not teach.

The true principles on this whole subject were in my judgment spoken by Mr. Justice McKenna for the Court in *Waugh v. Mississippi University* in 237 U.S. 589, 596-597. The State had there passed a law barring students from peaceably assembling in Greek letter fraternities and providing that students who joined them could be expelled from

500 school. This law would appear on the surface to run afoul of the First Amendment's freedom of assembly clause. The law was attacked as violative[8] of due process and of the privileges and immunities clause and as a deprivation of property and of liberty, under the Fourteenth Amendment. It was argued that the fraternity made its members

---

[8] **violative:** in violation.

CLOSE READ

Delineate and Evaluate an Argument (LINES 469–480)

 COMMON CORE RI 8

Point out that Justice Black uses legal reasoning to develop his argument that freedom of expression does have its limits.

U CITE TEXT EVIDENCE Have students read lines 469-480. Ask them to cite the reasons Justice Black gives in arguing that freedom of expression is not universal. *(He says teachers cannot carry the right to complete freedom of speech into the classroom and the anti-Catholic or anti-Semite does not have the complete right to free expression in a Catholic church or Jewish synagogue. He says people cannot speak entirely freely in places, like the Supreme Court, that have rules against it.)* What legal support does he offer for this argument? *(Cox v. Louisiana and Adderley v. Florida)*

Make Inferences

 COMMON CORE RI 1

(LINES 481–494)

Guide students in summarizing Justice Black's position in this passage regarding the rights of students while in school.

V ASK STUDENTS to read lines 481-494. What inference can they make about Justice Black's views of the rights of young people outside of school? Have them give reasons for their response. *(Answers will vary, but some students may suggest that he would say children do not have the same rights as adults, whether in or out of school. Evidence might be his ironic tone in suggesting that children might not have reached "the point of experience and wisdom which enabled them to teach all of their elders." In describing the slogan "children are to be seen not heard" as "old-fashioned," Justice Black suggests he still gives the idea some credence.)*

WHEN STUDENTS STRUGGLE...

In lines 495–497, Justice Black states that the views of Justice McKenna on the *Waugh* v. *Mississippi University* ruling guided his thinking. Ask student pairs to carefully read the paragraphs relating to *Waugh* v. *Mississippi University*. Then ask them to write a summary of the case, including the main ideas. Finally, ask students to share their insights in class discussion.

Summary: The State of Mississippi barred students from joining fraternities at the state university. This law was criticized as a violation of the First and Fourteenth Amendments, arguing that fraternities encouraged discipline and moral behavior. The Supreme Court decided in favor of the university; it was up to the state to determine the needs of its educational institutions.

Delineate and Evaluate an Argument

COMMON CORE · RI 8

(LINES 511–524)

Justice Black states that *Waugh* v. *Mississippi University*, and in particular the passage quoted, has "complete relevance" in the case of *Tinker* v. *Des Moines*.

 ASK STUDENTS to read lines 511-524. Have them explain the parallels between the two cases. *(Both involve the rights of school officials to regulate the activities of students. In* Tinker v. Des Moines, *school officials attempted to prohibit students from wearing armbands to symbolically voice opposition to the Vietnam war. In* Waugh v. Mississippi University, *school officials wanted to prohibit students from meeting in Greek letter fraternities.)* How did the courts differ in their rulings on the two cases? *(In* Tinker v. Des Moines, *the Court ruled that students' right to wear the armbands was protected by the First and Fourteenth Amendments. In* Waugh v. Mississippi University, *the Court ruled these amendments did not override the school's right as an educational institution to restrict students' activities.)*

Delineate and Evaluate an Argument

COMMON CORE · RI 8

(LINES 538–549)

Point out that Justice Black takes his argument beyond the narrow confines of constitutional principles and legal reasoning by introducing the case's underlying context: public reaction to the war in Vietnam.

 **ASK STUDENTS** to read lines 538-549. How does Justice Black counter the opinion of the majority that the armband protestors were not disruptive? *(Justice Black argues that it doesn't matter whether or not there was evidence of disruption because it is clear to all citizens that the Vietnam War is a highly controversial topic and it is apparent that the purpose of the armband protestors was to disrupt the class by protesting against the war in a highly visible manner.)*

---

more moral, taught discipline, and inspired its members to study harder and to obey better the rules of discipline and order. This Court rejected all the "fervid" pleas of the fraternities' advocates and decided unanimously against these Fourteenth Amendment arguments. The Court in its next to the last paragraph made this statement which has

510 complete relevance for us today:

> "It is said that the fraternity to which complainant belongs is a moral and of itself a disciplinary force. This need not be denied. But whether such membership makes against discipline was for the State of Mississippi to determine. It is to be remembered that the University was established by the State and is under the control of the State, and the enactment of the statute may have been induced by the opinion that *membership in the prohibited societies divided the attention of the students and distracted from that*
520 *singleness of purpose which the State desired to exist in its public educational institutions.* It is not for us to entertain conjectures in opposition to the views of the State and annul its regulations upon disputable considerations of their wisdom or necessity." (Emphasis supplied.)

It was on the foregoing argument that this Court sustained the power of Mississippi to curtail the First Amendment's right of peaceable assembly. And the same reasons are equally applicable to curtailing in the States' public schools the right to complete freedom of expression. Iowa's public schools, like Mississippi's university, are operated to

530 give students an opportunity to learn, not to talk politics by actual speech, or by "symbolic" speech. And, as I have pointed out before, the record amply shows that public protest in the school classes against the Vietnam war "distracted from that singleness of purpose which the State [here Iowa] desired to exist in its public educational institutions." Here the Court should accord Iowa educational institutions the same right to determine for themselves to what extent free expression should be allowed in its schools as it accorded Mississippi with reference to freedom of assembly. But even if the record were silent as to protests against the Vietnam war distracting students from their assigned class

540 work, members of this Court, like all other citizens, know, without being told, that the disputes over the wisdom of the Vietnam war have disrupted and divided this country as few other issues ever have. Of course students, like other people, cannot concentrate on lesser issues when black armbands are being ostentatiously displayed in their presence to call attention to the wounded and dead of the war, some of the wounded and the dead being their friends and neighbors. It was, of course, to distract the attention of other students that some students insisted up to the very point of their own suspension from school that they were determined to sit in school with their symbolic armbands.

TO CHALLENGE STUDENTS . . .

Respond to Justice Black Challenge students to write a response to Justice Black. First, have them meet in a small group to review his position and arguments and to discuss their reaction to his views. Then ask them to work individually to write a response. Have students cite specific evidence from the text and to give reasons for their point of view. Invite volunteers to read their responses aloud.

550 Change has been said to be truly the law of life but sometimes the old and the tried and true are worth holding. The schools of this Nation have undoubtedly contributed to giving us tranquility and to making us a more law-abiding people. Uncontrolled and uncontrollable liberty is an enemy to domestic peace. We cannot close our eyes to the fact that some of the country's greatest problems are crimes committed by the youth, too many of school age. School discipline, like parental discipline, is an integral and important part of training our children to be good citizens—to be better citizens. Here a very small number of students have crisply and summarily refused to obey a school order

560 designed to give pupils who want to learn the opportunity to do so. One does not need to be a prophet or the son of a prophet to know that after the Court's holding today some students in Iowa schools and indeed in all schools will be ready, able, and willing to defy their teachers on practically all orders. This is the more unfortunate for the schools since groups of students all over the land are already running loose, conducting break-ins, sit-ins, lie-ins, and smash-ins. Many of these student groups, as is all too familiar to all who read the newspapers and watch the television news programs, have already engaged in rioting, property seizures, and destruction. They have

570 picketed schools to force students not to cross their picket lines and have too often violently attacked earnest but frightened students who wanted an education that the pickets did not want them to get. Students engaged in such activities are apparently confident that they know far more about how to operate public school systems than do their parents, teachers, and elected school officials. It is no answer to say that the particular students here have not yet reached such high points in their demands to attend classes in order to exercise their political pressures. Turned loose with lawsuits for damages and injunctions against their teachers as they are here, it is nothing but

580 wishful thinking to imagine that young, immature students will not soon believe it is their right to control the schools rather than the right of the States that collect the taxes to hire the teachers for the benefit of the pupils. This case, therefore, wholly without constitutional reasons in my judgment, subjects all the public schools in the country to the whims and caprices of their loudest-mouthed, but maybe not their brightest, students. I, for one, am not fully persuaded that school pupils are wise enough, even with this Court's expert help from Washington, to run the 23,390 public school systems in our 50 States. I wish, therefore, wholly to **disclaim** any purpose on my part to

590 hold that the Federal Constitution compels the teachers, parents, and elected school officials to surrender control of the American public school system to public school students. I dissent.

MR. JUSTICE HARLAN, dissenting.

I certainly agree that state public school authorities in the discharge of their responsibilities are not wholly exempt from the requirements

disclaim

(dĭs-klām´) *v.* to deny one's connection to; to distance oneself from.

Tinker v. Des Moines. **563**

Delineate and Evaluate an Argument (LINES 561–564)

COMMON CORE RI 8

Explain that Justice Black is bringing his dissent to an end, summarizing and reinforcing the main points of his argument.

Y CITE TEXT EVIDENCE Have students read lines 561-564. What conclusion is Justice Black drawing? *(He concludes that with the ruling in this case students will be willing and able to defy teachers on "practically all orders.")* Does this conclusion necessarily follow from the ruling? Explain. *(Opinions will differ. Some students may argue that the ruling is very narrow and does not necessarily open the door to a widespread flouting of rules.)*

CRITICAL VOCABULARY

disclaim: Justice Black is distancing himself from the ruling of the majority of Justices.

ASK STUDENTS how the format of a Supreme Court ruling allows Justice Black and other Justices to disclaim the majority opinion. *(Supreme Court rules provide the opportunity for justices who do not hold the majority opinion to write in dissent, distancing themselves from the judgment of their peers.)*

SCAFFOLDING FOR ELL STUDENTS

Compound Nouns Read aloud the sentence beginning "This is the more unfortunate..." (lines 564–566), and call attention to the words *break-ins, sit-ins, lie-ins,* and *smash-ins*. Explain that these are a special kind of compound word formed from a verb *(break, sit, lie, smash)* and the adverb *in*. Ask students, to define each of the words.

break-in—an unlawful entry into a building

sit-in—a protest in which demonstrators sit and refuse to move

lie-in—a protest in which demonstrators lie down and refuse to move

smash-in—a protest in which demonstrators break, or smash, objects

Delineate and Evaluate an Argument (LINES 593–609)

 **COMMON CORE** **RI 8**

Point out that Justice Harlan provides a brief statement of dissent. Read aloud lines 593-609 with students.

Z **ASK STUDENTS** what question Justice Harlan would ask before supporting the students' rights to wear armbands. *(Did the school officials deliberately attempt to suppress the expression of an unpopular opinion while permitting the "dominant" opinion to be promoted?)* How do Justice Fortas and Justice Black address this issue? *(Justice Fortas implies that suppressing protests against the war in Vietnam may have been a motive of school officials. Justice Black does not discuss the issue of other political statements by students.)*

COLLABORATIVE DISCUSSION

Working in pairs, have students review the Court opinion and summarize the actions that the petitioners and respondents took that brought this case before the Supreme Court.

ASK STUDENTS to share any questions they generated in the course of reading and discussing this selection.

---

of the Fourteenth Amendment respecting the freedoms of expression and association. At the same time I am reluctant to believe that there is any disagreement between the majority and myself on the proposition that school officials should be accorded the widest authority in maintaining discipline and good order in their institutions. To translate that proposition into a workable constitutional rule, I would, in cases like this, cast upon those complaining the burden of showing that a particular school measure was motivated by other than legitimate school concerns—for example, a desire to prohibit the expression of an unpopular point of view, while permitting expression of the dominant opinion.

Finding nothing in this record which impugns[9] the good faith of respondents in promulgating the armband regulation, I would affirm the judgment below.

---

[9] **impugns:** questions or doubts.

COLLABORATIVE DISCUSSION What actions had the petitioners and respondents taken that ultimately caused this case to be argued before the Supreme Court? Discuss this question with a partner, citing specific evidence from the decision to support your ideas.

WHEN STUDENTS STRUGGLE . . .

Organize students into pairs or small groups and assign each team to review either Justice Fortas's majority opinion or Justice Black's dissenting opinion. Have teams reread the opinion and write three questions about major points made by the justice. In class discussion, have students share their questions. Write the questions on the board and encourage students to collaborate in finding and discussing the answers.

Delineate and Evaluate an Argument

Every Supreme Court decision delineates, or outlines, an argument. If the decision is completely unanimous, there is one argument representing the opinion of the Court as a whole. If some justices disagree with the majority opinion, the decision also contains his or her dissenting argument. Even if justices agree, however, they can still comment on some parts of the case by adding a concurrence, or agreement. *Tinker v. Des Moines Independent Community School District* has five justices presenting arguments:

- Justice Fortas wrote the opinion of the Court, to which five justices joined without comment.
- Justices Stewart and White wrote separate concurrences.
- Justices Black and Harlan dissented. Justice Black wrote a lengthy argument that fully responds to the Court's opinion. Justice Harlen wrote a brief dissent.

All of their arguments rely on the application of constitutional principles and the use of legal reasoning.

Tinker v. Des Moines		
Parts of the Arguments	**Explanation**	**Examples**
Constitutional principles	Applying parts of the U.S. Constitution that are relevant to the circumstances of the case	**First Amendment:** "Congress shall make no law . . . abridging the freedom of speech. . . ." **Fourteenth Amendment:** "All persons born or naturalized in the United States, and subject to the jurisdiction thereof, are citizens of the United States and of the state wherein they reside. . . . nor shall any state deprive any person of life, liberty, or property, without due process of law; nor deny to any person within its jurisdiction the equal protection of the laws."
Legal reasoning	Reasoning based on the doctrine that following precedent, or decisions in previous cases with similar facts, is essential to making consistent, just, and fair decisions	***Tinker v. Des Moines:*** "It was closely akin to 'pure speech' which, we have repeatedly held, is entitled to comprehensive protection under the First Amendment. Cf. *Cox v. Louisiana*, 379 U.S. 536, 555 (1965); *Adderley v. Florida*, 385 U.S. 39 (1966)."

As you analyze this Supreme Court decision, notice how the two sides apply these constitutional principles and use legal reasoning by citing precedents to support their claims. In addition, notice what kinds of evidence, in the form of facts or details, they cite as part of their reasoning.

TEACH

CLOSE READ

Delineate and Evaluate an Argument

Explain to students that the U.S. Supreme Court only hears certain cases that are appealed to it from a lower court. The Court is very particular in the cases it does agree to hear, choosing those that involve sticky legal issues that can have wide-ranging effects on other cases or on society as a whole. As a result, decisions are carefully thought over and the opinions delineated with utmost care in order to provide lower courts with an understanding of why the Supreme Court made the decision it did. These carefully delineated arguments will determine how lower court judges decide future cases on related matters.

Discuss the two kinds of reasoning that enter into the Justices' considerations: constitutional principles and legal reasoning. Ask students why Supreme Court justices give legal precedent so much weight? *(The law must be interpreted consistently over time. If one case is decided without reference to what previous Courts decided in similar cases, the lower courts, attorneys, and citizens will be confused about the law's validity.)*

Strategies for Annotation 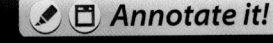 *Annotate it!*

Delineate and Evaluate an Argument

Have students use their eBook annotation tools to analyze the text. Ask them to do the following:

- Highlight in yellow the main idea in the arguments to support the petitioners.
- Highlight in green the important evidence supporting the petitioners' argument.

Under our Constitution, free speech is not a right that is given only to be so circumscribed that it exists in principle but not in fact....The Constitution says that Congress (and the States) may not abridge the right to free speech.

PRACTICE & APPLY

Analyzing the Text

COMMON CORE RI 1, RI 4, RI 8, SL 3, SL 4

Possible answers:

1. *The First Amendment guarantees teachers and students the right to express their opinions so long as these expressions do not disrupt the rights of others. Constitutional principles involved in this case are the First Amendment's guarantee of the right of free speech and the Fourteenth Amendment, which guarantees that all citizens have equal protection of the law.*

2. *Justice Fortas argues that "fear or apprehension of disturbance is not enough to overcome the right to freedom of expression."*

3. *"Pure speech" would be actual, spoken or written speech.*

4. *Wearing political campaign buttons is a form of free speech. If students can wear buttons promoting politics, which can be controversial, the same right should be granted to those wearing armbands.*

5. *He cites legal precedent showing that the "reasonable" standard had been discarded. He argues against the majority opinion that the right to free speech in the classroom is well established, and cites legal precedent. He argues that ruling against the right of school officials to limit free speech forces the Court decide these cases.*

6. *Justice Black is concerned that students will cease to obey rules they disagree with, assuming they have the same rights as adults, even in state-supported schools. He claims that young people are already ignoring their responsibilities to society by participating in sit-ins, smash-ins, and other acts of violence and rebellion.*

7. *Justice Fortas cites* West Virginia v. Barnette, *which dealt with school rules compelling students to salute the U.S. flag. The Court ruled that young people had the right to free speech. Moreover, teaching citizenship was a part of an education and students' rights should, therefore, be protected. Justice Black cites* Waugh v. Mississippi University *as stating his "true principles" on this case. The lower court ruled that Mississippi University had the right to prohibit students from assembling in Greek fraternities. The Supreme Court agreed, stating that the university had decided that membership "divided the attention of students" and distracted them from learning—the same argument used in the Tinker case.*

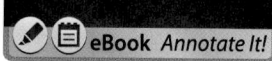

Analyzing the Text

COMMON CORE RI 1, RI 4, RI 8, SL 3, SL 4

Cite Text Evidence   Support your responses with evidence from the selection.

1. **Summarize** What is the **claim,** or the position of the Court, as stated in the "Held" section at the beginning of the decision (lines 10–22)? What constitutional principles are at issue in this Supreme Court case?

2. **Analyze** Justice Fortas says that the problem before the Court is how students' "exercise of First Amendment rights collide[s] with the rules of the school authorities." How does Justice Fortas argue against the school's "fear of a disturbance from the wearing of the armbands" as a sufficient reason to ban them?

3. **Infer** At the beginning of section II of Justice Fortas's opinion, the justice gives examples of what is not involved in the current case, and concludes by saying "Our problem involves direct, primary First Amendment rights akin to 'pure speech'" (lines 123–124). Based on the context in which the phrase is used, what might the phrase "pure speech" mean?

4. **Interpret** How does the evidence about the school's policy on wearing political campaign buttons (lines 179-190) relate to Justice Fortas's opinion?

5. **Analyze** Justice Black states in his dissent that the Court's decision essentially means that the Court, rather than the schools, now decides "which school disciplinary regulations are 'reasonable.'" How does he argue against this "reasonableness" standard?

6. **Draw Conclusions** What is Justice Black's concern about the effects of this decision? How does he express this concern in his argument?

7. **Analyze** Justices Fortas and Black both cite previous Court rulings to support their argument. Choose one such example from each section, and trace how the justice uses that ruling and the legal reasoning behind it to strengthen his argument.

PERFORMANCE TASK

Speaking Activity: Debate Do students have the right to engage in protests or demonstrations at school? What would be appropriate limits on such activities?

- Form teams of two to three students each, grouped according to what individuals feel are acceptable forms of protest on school grounds.

- Each team should gather supporting ideas or details for their viewpoint from the two main parts of the Supreme Court decision.

- Conduct a simulated debate, following the rules for debating found in the Handbook.

- After the debate, write an evaluation of which side presented the most compelling argument.

Assign this performance task.

PERFORMANCE TASK

COMMON CORE SL 3, SL 4

Speaking Activity: Debate Guide a brief discussion of the activity to determine students' ideas of the appropriate limits for demonstrations. Based on their discussion, assign them to debate teams. Ask students to meet in their teams to discuss and organize their ideas. Remind them to do research to gather facts, examples, and other evidence to support their position. Urge them to also consider what opposing teams may argue and to prepare rebuttals.

Critical Vocabulary

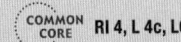 COMMON CORE RI 4, L 4c, L 6

injunction	scrupulous	nascent	disputatious
purport	enclave	arrogate	disclaim

Practice and Apply Choose the alternative in each sentence that best relates to the Critical Vocabulary word. Explain your choices.

1. If the Court issues an **injunction** against the school's rule, will the petitioning students be glad or upset?

2. If schools are **scrupulous** about protecting the First Amendment, will students be discouraged from expressing their opinions or will they speak more freely?

3. If wearing armbands is a **nascent** sign of rebellion against authority, has a rebellion happened in the past or is it likely to happen in the future?

4. In a **disputatious** society, are people more likely to argue or to agree about many subjects?

5. Would a school that **purports** to be concerned with safety more likely have a closed- or open-campus policy?

6. Would an **enclave** at school be more like an all-school assembly or a meeting in an individual classroom?

7. If another student **arrogates** your lunch, is that student acting like a friend or a bully?

8. When Justice Black **disclaims** the idea that students should control the schools, does he strongly agree with the idea or strongly oppose it?

Vocabulary Strategy: Legal Terminology

The Critical Vocabulary word *injunction* is an example of legal terminology, a type of domain-specific vocabulary generally found only in legal documents. When you look up the word in a dictionary, you will find a general definition and a second definition introduced by the word *Law* to indicate it has a specific meaning when used in a legal context. Many legal terms are words and phrases that come from other languages, especially Latin. For example, the footnoted terms *en banc* and *certiorari* are legal terms in French and Latin, respectively. You may need to consult a legal dictionary or other specialized reference work to find the meanings of some legal terminology.

Practice and Apply Work with a partner to investigate the etymology and meaning of some common legal terms using a dictionary or a specialized reference work.

1. *stare decisis*
2. *habeas corpus*
3. *amicus curiae*
4. *voir dire*
5. *ex parte*
6. *in camera*

CLOSE READ

Critical Vocabulary COMMON CORE RI 4, L 4c, L6

Answers:

1. *glad because the rule is prohibited*

2. *speak more freely because schools will be diligent in protecting their right to free speech*

3. *likely to happen in the future because wearing the armbands indicates that a rebellion is developing*

4. *likely to argue because they are confrontational*

5. *a closed-campus policy because the school would be easier to control*

6. *more like a meeting in a classroom because a classroom is a distinct area within a school*

7. *like a bully because he or she assumes authority to take the lunch*

8. *strongly opposes the idea because he is denying his connection to that idea*

Vocabulary Strategy: Legal Terminology

1. ***stare decisis*** Latin; following prior legal decisions

2. ***habeas corpus*** Latin; right to protection from unlawful imprisonment

3. ***amicus curiae*** Latin; friend of the court

4. ***voir dire*** French; examination to decide competence of juror or witness

5. ***ex parte*** Latin; on one side of legal proceedings

6. ***in camera*** Latin; in private

Strategies for Annotation
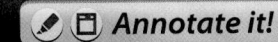 **Annotate it!**

Legal Terminology
COMMON CORE L 4c, L 6

Have students locate sentences containing the legal terms *en banc* and *certiorari*. Encourage them to use their eBook annotation tools to do the following:

- Highlight the legal terms in green.
- Read the sentence in which the word appears and the surrounding sentences.
- Rewrite the sentence in paraphrase form, using common terms in place of the legal terms.

On appeal, the Court of Appeals for the Eighth Circuit considered the case en banc. The court was equally divided, and the District Court's decision was accordingly affirmed, without opinion. 383 F.2d 988 (1967). We granted certiorari.[6] 390 U.S. 942 (1968).

PRACTICE & APPLY

Language and Style: Comparing Writers' Styles

 **COMMON CORE** L 3a

Select a passage from each justice's opinion and ask students to follow along as you read it aloud. Call students' attention to the writers' word choice, sentence length and complexity, and tone. Guide students in describing differences in style between Fortas and Black. Ask students which author's opinion they find easier to understand. *(Some students may find Justice Fortas's concise style more accessible; others may be put off by his legal vocabulary. Black's sometimes folksy tone may appeal to some students; others may find his complex sentences difficult to follow.)* Have students identify difficult vocabulary in the two passages.

Ask students to find examples of the more objective language used by Justice Fortas and of the more emotional appeals that Justice Black uses.

Answers: *Students should write a brief analysis comparing the style used by the debate teams in the Performance Task. They should make a thorough analysis of their own style and demonstrate through their revisions an understanding of how style can affect the power of their writing.*

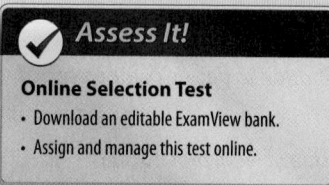

Assess It!

Online Selection Test
- Download an editable ExamView bank.
- Assign and manage this test online.

Language and Style: Comparing Writers' Styles

 **COMMON CORE** L 3a

In *Tinker v. Des Moines*, there are two main writers—Justice Fortas for the majority and Justice Black dissenting. These two writers not only express different opinions but also express those opinions in very different literary styles. Word choice, sentence length, and tone all contribute to each writer's distinct style. In this chart, some elements of their styles are compared.

Elements of Style	Justice Fortas	Justice Black
Word choice	**More difficult vocabulary:** Most of the Critical Vocabulary words and footnoted terms appear in his opinion.	**More ordinary vocabulary:** Only two Critical Vocabulary words and one footnoted term appear in his opinion.
Sentence length and structure	**Carefully constructed, medium length:** "First Amendment rights, applied in light of the special characteristics of the school environment, are available to teachers and students."	**Less direct, longer:** "The Court's holding in this case ushers in what I deem to be an entirely new era in which the power to control pupils by the elected 'officials of state supported public schools . . .' in the United States is in ultimate effect transferred to the Supreme Court."
Tone or attitude	**Mostly objective, appeals to reason:** "The school officials banned and sought to punish petitioners for a silent, passive expression of opinion, unaccompanied by any disorder or disturbance on the part of petitioners."	**More judgmental, appeals to emotions:** "Of course students, like other people, cannot concentrate on lesser issues when black armbands are being ostentatiously displayed in their presence to call attention to the wounded and dead of the war, some of the wounded and the dead being their friends and neighbors."

Practice and Apply Reread the decision and pay attention to the writers' different styles. Note how the differences in style combine with the differences in content to express distinctly diverse opinions on the case. Then look back at the debate evaluation that you wrote for the Performance Task. Add some analysis of how the style used by the different teams to express their ideas related to the effectiveness of their arguments. Finally, review your writing to evaluate your own style; revise word choices, sentence length and structure, and tone to strengthen your writing.

Evaluate Constitutional Principles

COMMON CORE

RI 8,
W 2, W 7

TEACH

Tell students that the term *constitutional principles* describes the basic, most important ideas that form the foundation of the U.S. Constitution. Constitutional principles are used to write laws and to apply these laws in court cases. Explain that this is not as simple as reading the Constitution and noting what it says literally. The Constitution was written more than 200 years ago, and its language was framed in general terms. These general terms must often be applied to specific situations that the framers of the Constitution could not have foreseen. Each case before the Supreme Court involves interpreting the Constitution and deciding how it applies in a contemporary context.

Point out that sometimes different, clearly articulated principles of the Constitution come into conflict. For example, what happens when the right to free expression comes in conflict with public safety? Courts have decided that it is unlawful to call out "Fire!" in a crowded theater when there is no fire, concluding that public safety sometimes takes precedence over free speech.

Remind students how the right to freedom of expression was the basis for argument in *Tinker* v. *Des Moines*.

PRACTICE AND APPLY

Have students do research to learn more about constitutional principles, in particular the Fourteenth Amendment.

- Ask students to locate and read the complete Fourteenth Amendment to the Constitution.
- Ask them to research the history of the Fourteenth Amendment, including why and when it was added to the Constitution.
- Have them investigate some ways in which the Fourteenth Amendment has been applied in past Court cases.
- Direct students to review *Tinker* v. *Des Moines* and to take notes on where the Fourteenth Amendment was applied to this case and how it was interpreted by the justices.

After completing their research and careful examination of the text, ask students to write a report explaining how the Fourteenth Amendment applies to *Tinker* v. *Des Moines*.

Make Inferences

COMMON CORE

RL 1

RETEACH

Explain that an inference is a logical guess based on the evidence available and on prior experiences. An inference can lead to new information about what a passage says or what a situation means. It can give clues to the best way to respond to an actual situation.

Making inferences uses two sets of information:

- **Evidence** can come from facts, examples, or anecdotes in the text. It can come from what someone sees in looking at a scene, witnessing an event, or observing a person's gestures, expressions, or actions.
- **Prior knowledge** is what a person already knows from experience. These past experiences may not apply exactly to the new situation, but they may give clues to how respond to it.

 **LEVEL UP TUTORIALS** Assign the following *Level Up* tutorial: **Making Inferences.**

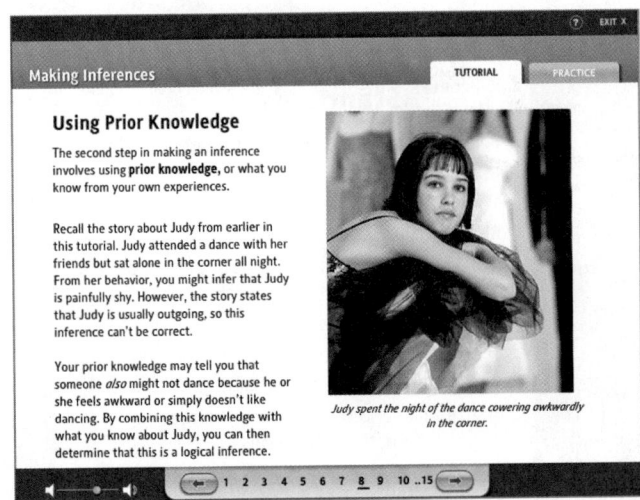

Using Prior Knowledge

The second step in making an inference involves using **prior knowledge,** or what you know from your own experiences.

Recall the story about Judy from earlier in this tutorial. Judy attended a dance with her friends but sat alone in the corner all night. From her behavior, you might infer that Judy is painfully shy. However, the story states that Judy is usually outgoing, so this inference can't be correct.

Your prior knowledge may tell you that someone *also* might not dance because he or she feels awkward or simply doesn't like dancing. By combining this knowledge with what you know about Judy, you can then determine that this is a logical inference.

Judy spent the night of the dance cowering awkwardly in the corner.

CLOSE READING APPLICATION

Students can make inferences to *Tinker* v. *Des Moines*. Have them choose one of the precedent court cases described in the selection or a passage describing events in the Des Moines School District. Reading carefully, they should look at the evidence, apply their own prior knowledge, and then make an inference that will help them better understand the situation.

mySmartPlanner Create lesson plans and access resources online.

EXEMPLAR

The Coming Merging of Mind and Machine

Science Essay by Ray Kurzweil

Why This Text?

Ray Kurzweil's success as an inventor of machines that perform what previous generations would have considered unthinkable tasks establishes his credibility as a futurist. His astonishing predictions about computer technology challenge a reader's concept of intelligence, the nature of reality, and human life itself. This lesson explores Kurzweil's controversial point of view.

Key Learning Objective: Students will be able to analyze and evaluate an author's point of view and the ideas and arguments in the text.

For additional practice:

Science, Guided by Ethics

Close Reader selection
"Science, Guided by Ethics"
Essay by Freeman Dyson

COMMON CORE — Common Core Standards

RI 3 Analyze a set of ideas or sequence of events.
RI 4 Determine the meaning of words and phrases.
RI 5 Analyze and evaluate structure.
RI 6 Determine an author's point of view or purpose.
W 7 Conduct research projects.
W 8 Gather information from multiple authoritative print and digital sources.
SL 1 Initiate and participate in a range of collaborative discussions.
L 4b Identify and correctly use pattern of word changes.
L 4c Consult reference materials.

Text Complexity Rubric

	The Coming Merging of Mind and Machine
Quantitative Measures	Lexile: 1260L
Qualitative Measures	Levels of Meaning/Purpose — multiple topics (more than three)
	Structure — organization of main ideas and details complex; but clearly stated and generally sequential
	Language Conventionality and Clarity — increased unfamiliar, academic, or domain-specific words
	Knowledge Demands — somewhat complex technical concepts
Reader/Task Considerations	Teacher determined. Vary by individual reader and type of text

Ray Kurzweil Have students read the information about the author. Tell them that as a pioneer in the field of electronics he created devices that can read text or translate the human voice into print; Kurzweil as a result has become a champion for the blind and visually impaired community. This relationship led to one of his more surprising inventions. When his friend Stevie Wonder—the blind singer-songwriter—complained about the sound quality of computerized instruments, Kurzweil developed the Kurzweil 250, a keyboard that could realistically re-create the sound of multiple instruments, from a grand piano to a symphony orchestra or a rock band.

AS YOU READ Direct students to use the As You Read note to focus their reading. Remind students to write down any questions they generate during reading.

Analyze Author's Point of View (LINES 1–10)   COMMON CORE RI 6

Explain that, in informational writing, an author's **point of view,** or perspective on a topic, is rarely unbiased. Analyzing an author's **tone,** or attitude toward the topic, can help a reader identify the author's point of view.

 **ASK STUDENTS** to read lines 1–10 and describe Kurzweil's tone in this opening paragraph, citing evidence for their opinions. *(Kurzweil's tone is bold and confident. He makes a series of precise predictions about the future, citing the exact date that certain events will occur—for example, that there will be a computer with the power of 1,000 human brains by the year 2029.)* What might this tone suggest about the author's point of view? *(The tone suggests that Kurzweil is writing from his point of view as an expert on technology.)*

CRITICAL VOCABULARY

successions: Kurzweil explains that human learning involves a complicated sequence of chemical reactions in the brain.

ASK STUDENTS what other processes besides learning might involve a succession of events. *(Possible answers: doing a science project, following a recipe)*

Background *Futurists study the future and make predictions about it by analyzing current trends.* **Ray Kurzweil** *(b. 1948) is a well-known futurist, as well as an inventor, a writer, and an expert on artificial intelligence. In the 1970s, he developed the first machine that translated text into speech, and he has been a pioneer in the field of speech recognition technology. In "The Coming Merging of Mind and Machine," Kurzweil makes some astonishing predictions about the future of artificial intelligence.*

The Coming Merging of Mind and Machine

Argument by Ray Kurzweil

AS YOU READ Pay attention to the scientific ideas and theories that Kurzweil uses to explain his predictions. Write down any questions you generate during reading.

Sometime early in this century the intelligence of machines will exceed that of humans. Within a quarter of a century, machines will exhibit the full range of human intellect, emotions and skills, ranging from musical and other creative aptitudes to physical movement. They will claim to have feelings and, unlike today's virtual personalities, will be very convincing when they tell us so. By around 2020 a $1,000 computer will at least match the processing power of the human brain. By 2029 the software for intelligence will have been largely mastered, and the average personal computer will be equivalent
10 to 1,000 brains.

Once computers achieve a level of intelligence comparable to that of humans, they will necessarily soar past it. For example, if I learn French, I can't readily download that learning to you. The reason is that for us, learning involves **successions** of stunningly complex patterns of interconnections among brain cells (neurons) and among the concentrations of biochemicals known as neurotransmitters that enable impulses to travel from neuron to neuron. We have no way of

succession (sək-sĕsh´ən) *n.* an ordered sequence.

Image Credits: (t) ©The Boston Globe/Getty Images; (b) ©Lobke Peers/Shutterstock

---

SCAFFOLDING FOR ELL STUDENTS

Understanding Prefixes Write *inter-, bio-,* and *neuro-* on the board. Explain that these prefixes, or syllables attached to the beginning of a word, mean "between," "life," and "nerve." Ask students to find one word on page 569 that begins with each prefix. *("interconnections," "biochemicals," "neurotransmitters")* Model determining the words' meanings.

ASK STUDENTS to work in pairs to find words that mean the following: "between countries" *(international)*, "the account of a person's life" *(biography)*, "an expert who studies the nervous system" *(neurologist)*.

Analyze Author's Point of View (LINES 23–39)  COMMON CORE RI 6

Explain that the **content** of informational writing—the material that an author chooses to include—helps us understand his or her point of view.

B CITE TEXT EVIDENCE Have students read lines 23–39 and summarize the contents of these two paragraphs. *(The first paragraph says that the use of computers in medical implants is already widespread. The second predicts a future in which neural implants will enhance human capabilities and experiences.)* Ask students what the content of this passage suggests about Kurzweil's point of view. *(Because the passage cites both the relatively minor computer implants used today and a near future in which human and machine are not fully distinguishable, it suggests that Kurzweil is optimistic about the fast pace of technological change.)*

Analyze Author's Point of View (LINES 40–44)  COMMON CORE RI 6

Explain that the overall structure of a text helps define an author's style—how he or she chooses to present information—and contributes to his or her point of view.

C ASK STUDENTS to read lines 40–44 and explain how Kurzweil relates the concept of exponential growth to the growth of technology in this paragraph. *(He explains that the forecasts he has made will be easier to accept if a reader understands the concept of exponential growth.)* What does this suggest about the overall structure of this selection? *(Kurzweil is laying out a formal argument, supporting his claims with evidence and addressing possible concerns or objectives.)*

> " As this happens, there will no longer be a clear distinction between human and machine. "

quickly downloading these patterns. But quick downloading will allow our nonbiological creations to share immediately what they learn
20   with billions of other machines. Ultimately, nonbiological entities will master not only the sum total of their own knowledge but all of ours as well.

    As this happens, there will no longer be a clear distinction between human and machine. We are already putting computers— neural implants—directly into people's brains to counteract Parkinson's disease and tremors from multiple sclerosis. We have cochlear implants that restore hearing. A retinal implant is being developed in the U.S. that is intended to provide at least some visual perception for some blind individuals, basically by replacing certain
30   visual-processing circuits of the brain. A team of scientists at Emory University implanted a chip in the brain of a paralyzed stroke victim that allowed him to use his brainpower to move a cursor across a computer screen.

    In the 2020s neural implants will improve our sensory experiences, memory and thinking. By 2030, instead of just phoning a friend, you will be able to meet in, say, a virtual Mozambican game preserve that will seem compellingly real. You will be able to have any type of experience—business, social, sexual—with anyone, real or simulated, regardless of physical proximity.

How Life and Technology Evolve

40   To gain insight into the kinds of forecasts I have just made, it is important to recognize that information technology is advancing exponentially. An exponential process starts slowly, but eventually its pace increases extremely rapidly. (A fuller documentation of my argument is contained in my recent book *The Singularity Is Near.*)

    The evolution of biological life and the evolution of technology have both followed the same pattern: they take a long time to get

APPLYING ACADEMIC VOCABULARY

infinite	virtual

As you discuss "The Coming Merging of Mind and Machine," incorporate the following Collection 6 academic vocabulary words: *infinite* and *virtual*. Encourage students to consider whether Kurzweil is suggesting that artificial intelligence may be capable of **infinite** development. Challenge students to analyze to the concept of **virtual** experiences. Is there a point at which the virtual becomes indistinguishable from the real, and would this development be positive or negative?

going, but advances build on one another, and progress erupts at an increasingly furious pace. We are entering that explosive part of the technological evolution curve right now.

50 Consider: It took billions of years for Earth to form. It took two billion more for life to begin and almost as long for molecules to organize into the first multicellular plants and animals about 700 million years ago. The pace of evolution quickened as mammals inherited Earth some 65 million years ago. With the emergence of primates, evolutionary progress was measured in mere millions of years, leading to Homo sapiens perhaps 500,000 years ago.

The evolution of technology has been a continuation of the evolutionary process that gave rise to us—the technology-creating species—in the first place. It took tens of thousands of years for our
60 ancestors to figure out that sharpening both sides of a stone created useful tools. Then, earlier in this past millennium, the time required for a major paradigm shift[1] in technology had shrunk to hundreds of years.

The pace continued to accelerate during the 19th century, during which technological progress was equal to that of the 10 centuries that came before it. Advancement in the first two decades of the 20th century matched that of the entire 19th century. Today significant technological transformations take just a few years; for example, the World Wide Web, already a **ubiquitous** form of communication and
70 commerce, did not exist just 20 years ago. One decade ago almost no one used search engines.

Computing technology is experiencing the same exponential growth. Over the past several decades a key factor in this expansion has been described by Moore's Law. Gordon Moore, a co-founder of Intel, noted in the mid-1960s that technologists had been doubling the density of transistors on integrated circuits every 12 months. This meant computers were periodically doubling both in capacity and in speed per unit cost. In the mid-1970s Moore revised his observation of the doubling time to a more accurate estimate of about 24 months, and
80 that trend has persisted through the years.

After decades of devoted service, Moore's Law will have run its course around 2019. By that time, transistor features will be just a few atoms in width. But new computer architectures will continue the exponential growth of computing. For example, computing cubes are already being designed that will provide thousands of layers of circuits, not just one as in today's computer chips. Other technologies that promise orders-of-magnitude increases in computing density include nanotube circuits built from carbon atoms, optical computing, crystalline computing and molecular computing.

ubiquitous
(yōō-bĭkʹwĭ-təs) *adj.*
existing everywhere
at once.

---

[1] **paradigm shift:** a fundamental change in basic assumptions or practices.

The Coming Merging of Mind and Machine **571**

Analyze Author's Point of View (LINES 50–63)  RI 6

Explain that authors of informational texts often use **analogies** to compare an unfamiliar thing, event, or situation to one that readers already know and understand. Often, analogies help an author to make a larger point.

D ASK STUDENTS to read lines 50–63. What two things does the author compare in this analogy? *(the increased pace of the evolution of life on earth and the increased pace of the evolution of technology)* Ask students how this analogy serves the author's purpose. *(He is arguing that his predictions will not seem so far-fetched when you compare them to the development of life on Earth, which started developing slowly and then raced forward at an astonishing pace.)*

CRITICAL VOCABULARY

ubiquitous: Kurzweil points out that the World Wide Web can be found everywhere.

ASK STUDENTS how the fact that the World Wide Web is now ubiquitous supports Kurzweil's argument. *(Twenty years earlier, the Web did not exist. Its rapid growth supports the argument that computing technology grows exponentially.)*

WHEN STUDENTS STRUGGLE . . .

Help students understand the concept of exponential growth. Explain that in mathematics, an exponent is written as a small superscript number that is placed after a number. It indicates the number of times the number is multiplied by itself. As an example, write 2^2 on the board, explaining that this means 2 x 2, or 4.

ASK STUDENTS to calculate the value of the following numbers: 2^2 *(4)*, 2^3 *(8)*, 2^4 *(16)*, 2^5 *(32)*, and 2^6 *(64)*. Point out that the values of these numbers are growing by a greater amount with each step. That is, the difference between 2^2 and 2^3 is 4, but the difference between 2^5 and 2^6 is 32, a much larger number. Explain that this is exponential growth.

Analyze Author's Point of View (LINES 90–98)  RI 6

Remind students that an effective argument is backed up by relevant supporting content.

E **ASK STUDENTS** to read lines 90–98, examine the graph, and state the claim or argument this content supports. *(Computer power that costs $1,000 has been expanding at an exponential pace. Extrapolating from this, in approximately year 2060, a thousand-dollar computer will eclipse the processing power of all human brains.)* How do the last two sentences underscore this point? *(They summarize the remarkable speed at which thousand-dollar computers have grown in power.)*

Analyze Author's Point of View (LINES 108–116)  RI 6

Explain that an author who wishes to express his or her point of view in an argument will often strengthen the argument by including and addressing the **counterargument's** viewpoint.

F **CITE TEXT EVIDENCE** Have students read lines 108–116 and identify the counterargument Kurzweil is responding to. *(Some people criticize predictions for assuming that trends will continue unchanged into the future.)* What word signals that Kurzweil is about to respond to this claim? *(The second sentence of this passage begins with the word "but," indicating that Kurzweil is about to present his own alternative view, stressing the power of accelerating change.)*

> **CRITICAL VOCABULARY**
>
> **extrapolation:** Some people claim that we cannot predict the future based on what is happening now.
>
> **ASK STUDENTS** to think about a technology that is considered new in the present day. Extrapolate how it may develop and change in the future.

90 We can readily see the march of computing by plotting the speed (in instructions per second) per $1,000 (in constant dollars) of 49 famous calculating machines spanning the 20th century. The graph is a study in exponential growth: computer speed per unit cost doubled every three years between 1910 and 1950 and every two years between 1950 and 1966 and is now doubling every year. It took 90 years to achieve the first $1,000 computer capable of executing one million instructions per second (MIPS). Now we add an additional MIPS to a $1,000 computer every day.

E

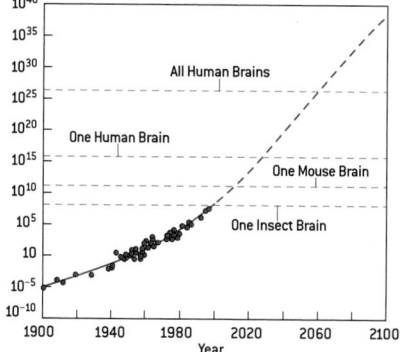

The accelerating rate of progress in computing is demonstrated by this graph, which shows the amount of computing speed that $1,000 (in constant dollars) would buy, plotted as a function of time. Computer power per unit cost is now doubling every year.

Why Returns Accelerate

Why do we see exponential progress occurring in biological life,
100 technology and computing? It is the result of a fundamental attribute of any evolutionary process, a phenomenon I call the Law of Accelerating Returns. As order exponentially increases (which reflects the essence of evolution), the time between salient[2] events grows shorter. Advancement speeds up. The returns—the valuable products of the process—accelerate at a nonlinear rate.[3] The escalating growth in the price performance of computing is one important example of such accelerating returns.

A frequent criticism of predictions is that they rely on an unjustified **extrapolation** of current trends, without considering
110 the forces that may alter those trends. But an evolutionary process accelerates because it builds on past achievements, including improvements in its own means for further evolution. The resources it needs to continue exponential growth are its own increasing order and the chaos in the environment in which the evolutionary process

extrapolation
(ĭk-străp´ə-lā´shŭn) *n.*
an estimate based on known information.

---

[2] **salient:** important.

[3] **nonlinear rate:** a rate that does not increase in proportion to the cause or input value; involving an equation with a degree greater than one (e.g., $y=x^2$).

takes place, which provides the options for further diversity. These two
resources are essentially without limit.

The Law of Accelerating Returns shows that by around 2020
a $1,000 personal computer will have the processing power of the
human brain—20 million billion calculations per second. The
120 estimates are based on regions of the brain that have already been
successfully simulated. By 2055, $1,000 worth of computing will equal
the processing power of all human brains on Earth (of course, I may be
off by a year or two).

Programming Intelligence

That's the prediction for processing power, which is a necessary but
not sufficient condition for achieving human-level intelligence in
machines. Of greater importance is the software of intelligence.

One approach to creating this software is to painstakingly
program the rules of complex processes. Another approach is
"complexity theory" (also known as chaos theory) computing,
130 in which self-organizing **algorithms** gradually learn patterns of
information in a manner analogous to human learning. One such
method, neural nets, is based on simplified mathematical models
of mammalian neurons. Another method, called genetic (or
evolutionary) algorithms, is based on allowing intelligent solutions to
develop gradually in a simulated process of evolution.

Ultimately, however, we will learn to program intelligence by
copying the best intelligent entity we can get our hands on: the human
brain itself. We will reverse-engineer the human brain, and fortunately
for us it's not even copyrighted!

140 The most immediate way to reach this goal is by destructive
scanning: take a brain frozen just before it was about to expire
and examine one very thin slice at a time to reveal every neuron,
interneuronal connection and concentration of neurotransmitters
across each gap between neurons (these gaps are called synapses).
One condemned killer has already allowed his brain and body to
be scanned, and all 15 billion bytes of him can be accessed on the
National Library of Medicine's Web site. The resolution of these scans
is not nearly high enough for our purposes, but the data at least enable
us to start thinking about these issues.

150 We also have noninvasive scanning techniques, including high-
resolution magnetic resonance imaging (MRI) and others. Recent
scanning methods can image individual interneuronal connections
in a living brain and show them firing in real time. The increasing
resolution and speed of these techniques will eventually enable us to
resolve the connections among neurons. The rapid improvement is
again a result of the Law of Accelerating Returns, because massive
computation is the main element in higher-resolution imaging.

algorithm
(ăl´gə-rĭth´əm) *n.*
instructions carried
out in a specific
sequence.

The Coming Merging of Mind and Machine **573**

Analyze Author's Point of View (LINES 117–123)

Point out that an engaging tone can effectively supplement an author's arguments and evidence.

G **CITE TEXT EVIDENCE** Have students read lines 117–123 and describe how Kurzweil injects humor into an otherwise factual paragraph *(He adds a comment in parentheses, acknowledging that his very specific predictions may not be correct.)* Ask students how this change of tone contributes to Kurzweil's argument. *(It wins over readers by revealing the human side of a confident, knowledgeable author. Even while laughing at himself, though, Kurzweil does not back down from his argument. He may be wrong, but only by "a year or two.")*

Analyze Author's Point of View (LINES 127–139)

Explain that authors often provide clues to their point of view when establishing a position. Encourage students to look for such word clues when analyzing an author's point of view.

H **CITE TEXT EVIDENCE** Have students read lines 127–139. Ask them to find words in the first paragraph of the passage that suggest the processes described would be too slow for practical purposes. *("painstakingly" and "gradually")* What word in the second paragraph suggests that the author is about to present his own alternative view? *("however")*

> **CRITICAL VOCABULARY**
>
> **algorithm:** The author suggests that computers might learn to think in the same way as human beings.
>
> **ASK STUDENTS** to explain why algorithms would be important in computer programming. *(Programmers use algorithms to give computers instructions about how to carry out specific processes.)*

SCAFFOLDING FOR ELL STUDENTS

Identify Words Used As Both Nouns and Verbs Explain that many words in English can serve as both nouns and verbs. Read aloud the sentence beginning in line 151 *(Recent scanning . . .)*. Point out that the word *firing* in line 153 is a form of the verb *fire* (meaning "to be launched" "or let fly"). However, *fire* can also be used as a noun.

ASK STUDENTS in mixed-ability groups to read lines 151–157. Have them identify whether the following words are used as nouns or verbs in this passage: *show (v.), time (n.), speed (n.), resolve (v.),* and *result (n.).* Review the definition of each word when used as a noun and as a verb. Challenge students to use each form or meaning in a sentence of their own.

Analyze Author's Point of View (LINES 158–161, including subhead)

COMMON CORE RI 6

An author's choice to include allusions, or references to other works, can be an important part of his or her style. Explain that Kurzweil's subheading on page 574 alludes to the 1966 movie *Fantastic Voyage*. In it, an attempted assassination leaves a scientist with a life-threatening blood clot. To save him, a special submarine with a crew is shrunk down to microscopic size to destroy the clot and save his life.

 **ASK STUDENTS** to read lines 158–161. What is the relevance of this allusion? *(Kurzweil is introducing the subject of nanobots, which can explore the human body, like the fictional submarine.)* Ask students how Kurzweil's use of this allusion strengthens his vision of the future. *(Fantastic Voyage was pure science fiction in 1966, but today it does not seem so far-fetched. The allusion underscores Kurzweil's point that computer technology is advancing exponentially.)*

Analyze Author's Point of View (LINES 173–182)

COMMON CORE RI 6

Explain that many authors of science fiction portray the world to come as a dystopia, a repressive or otherwise unpleasant society. In some of these accounts, advances in science have been the cause of humanity's misfortunes.

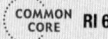 **ASK STUDENTS** to read lines 173–182 and describe Kurzweil's tone, or attitude, toward the changes he describes and his vision of the future. *(The author's tone is enthusiastic, and his vision of the future seems entirely positive.)* Ask students to suggest another possible point of view toward the technological developments described in this passage. *(A different point of view might be more cautious. Embedded nanobots that communicate with the brain could be used for harm as well as good. Reprogramming the brain to alter human experience could be used to repress or control people's behavior by replacing reality with virtual reality.)*

Another approach would be to send microscopic robots (or "nanobots") into the bloodstream and program them to explore every 160 capillary, monitoring the brain's connections and neurotransmitter concentrations.

Fantastic Voyage

Although sophisticated robots that small are still a couple of decades away at least, their utility for probing the innermost recesses of our bodies would be far-reaching. They would communicate wirelessly with one another and report their findings to other computers. The result would be a noninvasive scan of the brain taken from within.

Most of the technologies required for this scenario already exist, though not in the microscopic size required. Miniaturizing them to the tiny sizes needed, however, would reflect the essence of the Law of 170 Accelerating Returns. For example, the transistors on an integrated circuit have been shrinking by a factor of approximately five in each linear dimension every 10 years.

The capabilities of these embedded nanobots would not be limited to passive roles such as monitoring. Eventually they could be built to communicate directly with the neuronal circuits in our brains, enhancing or extending our mental capabilities. We already have electronic devices that can communicate with neurons by detecting their activity and either triggering nearby neurons to fire or suppressing them from firing. The embedded nanobots will be 180 capable of reprogramming neural connections to provide virtual-reality experiences and to enhance our pattern recognition and other cognitive faculties.

To decode and understand the brain's information-processing methods (which, incidentally, combine both digital and analog methods), it is not necessary to see every connection, because there is a great deal of redundancy within each region. We are already applying insights from early stages of this reverse-engineering process. For example, in speech recognition, we have decoded and copied the brain's early stages of sound processing.

190 Perhaps more interesting than this scanning-the-brain-to-understand-it approach would be scanning the brain for the purpose of downloading it. We would map the locations, interconnections and contents of all the neurons, synapses and neurotransmitter concentrations. The entire organization, including the brain's memory, would then be re-created on a digital-analog computer.

To do this, we would need to understand local brain processes, and progress is already under way. Theodore W. Berger and his co-workers at the University of Southern California have built integrated circuits that precisely match the processing characteristics of 200 substantial clusters of neurons. Carver A. Mead and his colleagues at the California Institute of Technology have built a variety of integrated

---

SCAFFOLDING FOR ELL STUDENTS

Define Words Using Context Clues Have students read the sentence beginning on line 183 ("To decode . . ."). Model how to define the word *redundancy* based on its context, or role in the sentence. Rephrase what the sentence seems to mean: If it is not necessary to see every connection, it may be that the connections repeat themselves. Therefore, *redundancy* must mean "unnecessary repetition."

ASK STUDENTS to form pairs and derive definitions of the following words from context clues: *capillary* (line 160, *vein through which blood travels*), *utility* (line 163, *usefulness*), *daunting* (line 206, *intimidating or difficult*), and *comprising* (line 217, *including*).

circuits that emulate the digital-analog characteristics of mammalian neural circuits. There are simulations of the visual-processing regions of the brain, as well as the cerebellum, the region responsible for skill formation.

Developing complete maps of the human brain is not as daunting as it may sound. The Human Genome Project seemed impractical when it was first proposed. At the rate at which it was possible to scan genetic codes 20 years ago, it would have taken thousands of years to complete the genome. But in accordance with the Law of Accelerating Returns, the ability to sequence DNA has doubled every year, and the project was completed on time in 2003.

By the third decade of this century, we will be in a position to create complete, detailed maps of the computationally relevant features of the human brain and to re-create these designs in advanced neural computers. We will provide a variety of bodies for our machines, too, from virtual bodies in virtual reality to bodies comprising swarms of nanobots, as well as humanoid robots.

Image Credits: ©nmedia/Shutterstock

CLOSE READ

Analyze Author's Point of View (LINES 206–218)

 COMMON CORE RI 6

Help students understand the relationship between the overall structure of a text and point of view by analyzing the last two paragraphs of this section.

K CITE TEXT EVIDENCE Have students read lines 206–212. Ask them to state the argument Kurzweil uses to persuade his reader that mapping the human brain is achievable. *(He cites his own Law of Accelerating Returns and the success of the Human Genome Project.)* In the concluding paragraph (lines 213–218), what predictions does Kurzweil make? *(He envisions an array of thinking machines, from virtual to humanoid, by the 2020s.)* What is the intended effect of these two paragraphs on the reader? *(Kurzweil is highlighting his point of view that computers will soon exceed human intelligence. He wants the reader to agree with his point of view and to share his astonishing vision of the future.)*

WHEN STUDENTS STRUGGLE...

Help students with Kurzweil's ideas by reviewing and explaining key words and phrases. On the board, write "miniaturization," "embedding," "nanobots," "reprogramming," "reverse-engineering," and "downloading." Discuss these terms as they are used in the text. Model them in sentences.

ASK STUDENTS to form pairs and write original sentences using the terms they have discussed and summarizing Kurzweil's ideas. Invite partners to share their sentences with the class, clarifying their thoughts when necessary.

Analyze Author's Point of View (LINES 219–232)  COMMON CORE RI 6

Make sure students recall that, until this concluding section of the essay, Ray Kurzweil has written with a tone of authority and conviction.

L **ASK STUDENTS** to review lines 219–232. How does Kurzweil's tone in this passage represent a shift from his previous attitude? *(Earlier in the essay, he addresses his topic with a tone of authority. In this section, the tone becomes more questioning. The author begins the section with a question and continues to ask questions for five paragraphs.)* Challenge students to condense the author's various questions into one essential question. *(Will computers of the future be conscious?)*

Analyze Author's Point of View (LINES 247–255)  COMMON CORE RI 6

Explain that an author's answer to key questions posed in a text can express his or her point of view.

M **CITE TEXT EVIDENCE** Remind students of the central question they have identified in this section about whether computers of the future will be conscious. Based on this passage, what is Kurzweil's point of view on this question? Cite text evidence to support your answer. *(He suggests that the question cannot truly be answered because human consciousness is subjective and non-measurable.)*

Will It Be Conscious?

Such possibilities prompt a host of intriguing issues and questions.
220 Suppose we scan someone's brain and reinstate the resulting "mind file" into a suitable computing medium. Will the entity that emerges from such an operation be conscious? This being would appear to others to have very much the same personality, history and memory. For some, that is enough to define consciousness. For others, such as physicist and author James Trefil, no logical reconstruction can attain human consciousness, although Trefil concedes that computers may become conscious in some new way.

At what point do we consider an entity to be conscious, to be self-aware, to have free will? How do we distinguish a process that is
230 conscious from one that just acts as if it is conscious? If the entity is very convincing when it says, "I'm lonely, please keep me company," does that settle the issue?

If you ask the "person" in the machine, it will strenuously[4] claim to be the original person. If we scan, let's say, me and reinstate that information into a neural computer, the person who emerges will think he is (and has been) me (or at least he will act that way). He will say, "I grew up in Queens, New York, went to college at M.I.T., stayed in the Boston area, walked into a scanner there and woke up in the machine here. Hey, this technology really works."

240 But wait, is this really me? For one thing, old Ray (that's me) still exists in my carbon-cell-based brain.

Will the new entity be capable of spiritual experiences? Because its brain processes are effectively identical, its behavior will be comparable to that of the person it is based on. So it will certainly claim to have the full range of emotional and spiritual experiences that a person claims to have.

No objective test can absolutely determine consciousness. We cannot objectively measure subjective experience (this has to do with the very nature of the concepts "objective" and "subjective"). We can
250 measure only correlates of it, such as behavior. The new entities will appear to be conscious, and whether or not they actually are will not affect their behavior. Just as we debate today the consciousness of nonhuman entities such as animals, we will surely debate the potential consciousness of nonbiological intelligent entities. From a practical perspective, we will accept their claims. They'll get mad if we don't.

Before this century is over, the Law of Accelerating Returns tells us, Earth's technology-creating species—us—will merge with our own technology. And when that happens, we might ask: What is the difference between a human brain enhanced a millionfold by
260 neural implants and a nonbiological intelligence based on the reverse-

---

[4] **strenuously:** forcefully.

engineering of the human brain that is subsequently enhanced and expanded?

The engine of evolution used its innovation from one period (humans) to create the next (intelligent machines). The subsequent milestone will be for the machines to create their own next generation without human intervention.

An evolutionary process accelerates because it builds on its own means for further evolution. Humans have beaten evolution. We are creating intelligent entities in considerably less time than it took the
270 evolutionary process that created us. Human intelligence—a product of evolution—has transcended it. So, too, the intelligence that we are now creating in computers will soon exceed the intelligence of its creators.

COLLABORATIVE DISCUSSION With a partner, review some of the scientific concepts Kurzweil explores, such as computing density, the Law of Accelerating Returns, and reverse-engineering. Take turns explaining them in your own words. Cite specific evidence in the text to support your ideas.

CLOSE READ

Analyze Author's Point of View (LINES 263–266)

COMMON CORE RI 6

Remind students that the title of this essay, "The Coming Merging of Mind and Machine," suggests that in the future there will be no difference between the human brain and its mechanical invention. Point out that sometimes the concluding paragraphs provide more information about the author's point of view.

N CITE TEXT EVIDENCE Have students read lines 263–266. What statement in this paragraph suggests that the future may hold more than the "merging" of mind and machine? *(Kurzweil predicts that machines will create another generation on their own, "without human intervention.")* What does this suggest about the world in the distant future? *(It suggests a future in which human invention—and possibly human life—is no longer relevant or dominant.)*

COLLABORATIVE DISCUSSION Before student pairs begin their reviews, generate with the class a list with scientific concepts for them to explore. After partners have practiced explaining these concepts, invite volunteers to present their explanations to the class.

ASK STUDENTS to share any questions they generated in the course of reading and discussing the selection.

TO CHALLENGE STUDENTS...

Examine Predictions Challenge students to examine Ray Kurzweil's vision of the future.

ASK STUDENTS to form groups and come up with issues about the future they feel Ray Kurzweil left unanswered or undeveloped. They might generate ideas by discussing questions such as these:

- Are brains and computers truly comparable?
- Is there more to a human being than a brain?
- Should there be limits to enhancing the human brain?
- How might advanced robotics improve or harm society?

Analyze Author's Point of View COMMON CORE RI 6

Help students understand that point of view is more than a statement of position. It is a complex product of content and style through which a skilled author can influence readers without directly stating his or her purpose.

Discuss with students their text's definition of content and the bulleted points that comprise style. Have the class compile a list assessing Kurzweil's use of each element. Notes might resemble the following:

- content: *heavily technical and scientific with detailed examples; little discussion of what constitutes a human being as opposed to a machine*
- tone: *assured, confident, objective*
- word choice: *technical, scientific*
- sentence structure: *complex*
- overall structure: *formal, with introduction, body, and conclusion*
- rhetorical devices: *hinges on central analogy of human brain to computer; extensive use of questions in conclusion*

Discuss with the class how each of these elements contributes to Kurzweil's point of view.

Analyze Author's Point of View COMMON CORE RI 6

Some informational texts are written to present facts in a completely objective manner. In most cases, however, the author's **point of view,** or perspective on the topic, affects the way he or she presents the information. Ray Kurzweil has a very definite point of view on the future of computer-simulated intelligence. He presents his ideas boldly and in great detail, hoping to make a persuasive case for his point of view. The content and style of his writing are the building blocks that help him accomplish his purpose.

Content and Style

The **content** of an informational text is the facts, ideas, examples, and details that the author chooses to include. Content helps reveal the author's point of view. In a science article, for example, the author will present facts and ideas that have shaped his or her perspective on the topic. Information that the author came across during research but did not find compelling will be either dismissed or omitted from the article.

Style is the way in which an author chooses to present information. Skillful use of the various elements of style results in a powerful piece of writing.

- **Tone** is the author's attitude toward the topic. The tone of a work might be serious, sarcastic, enthusiastic, or humorous, for example. The author's tone, if correctly identified, should reveal his or her point of view on the topic.

- An author's word choices help create his or her style. Some writers use everyday language that creates a conversational style. Others use many technical terms to introduce readers to a complex topic.

- The sentence structures an author uses are another element of his or her unique style. One writer might use mostly short, simple sentences, while another might use longer, more complex sentences.

- The overall structure of a text is also part of the author's style. Some writers allow their ideas to flow freely from one topic to another. Other writers create a more formal structure, with each paragraph and section systematically building support for the writer's central idea.

- Authors often use rhetorical devices to make their writing more persuasive. One example is the **analogy,** in which the author compares an unfamiliar thing, event, or situation to one that readers already know and understand. Readers must evaluate whether the analogy is valid: Are the two things being compared actually similar in the way that the author claims?

As you analyze "The Coming Merging of Mind and Machine," keep in mind all of these elements of content and style. Ask yourself how Kurzweil uses them to convey his point of view in a powerful, persuasive way.

Strategies for Annotation  Annotate it!

Analyze Author's Point of View COMMON CORE RI 6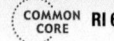

Share these strategies for guided or independent analysis:

- Highlight in blue any claims or predictions that cannot be established as fact.
- Underline any statements that constitute verifiable evidence that could support the claim or prediction.
- In notes, reflect on whether the evidence is sufficient to support the claim or prediction.

After decades of devoted service, Moore's Law will have run its course around 2019. By that time, transistor features will be just a few atoms in width. But new computer architectures will continue the exponential growth of computing. For example, computing cubes are already being designed that will provide thousands of layer of circuits, not just one as in today's computer chips.

 eBook *Annotate It!*

Analyzing the Text

COMMON CORE RI 3, RI 4, RI 5, RI 6, W 7, W 8

Cite Text Evidence   Support your responses with evidence from the selection.

1. **Analyze** Describe the overall structure of Kurzweil's article. Is this structure effective for the kind of information he wants to convey? Explain.

2. **Critique** Review the analogy that Kurzweil makes between biological evolution and technological evolution beginning in line 45. What is the crucial point of similarity between these two processes?

3. **Interpret** Kurzweil writes, "After decades of devoted service, Moore's Law will have run its course around 2019. By that time, transistor features will be just a few atoms in width" (lines 81–83). What is Moore's Law? How will growth in computing technology continue after 2019?

4. **Connect** In lines 99–107, Kurzweil introduces the Law of Accelerating Returns. At the start of the section "Programming Intelligence," he makes an analogy between human intelligence and a computer's hardware and software. Explain the analogy and how it supports the author's predictions about the future.

5. **Analyze** The technical term *reverse-engineer* is introduced in line 138. Explain what this term means in the context of the example Kurzweil gives. How does the concept of reverse-engineering help support his predictions?

6. **Analyze** Reread lines 117–123. How would you describe the author's tone in this paragraph? Is his tone consistent throughout the article?

7. **Summarize** Reread the last three paragraphs of the article. How would you summarize the conclusions Kurzweil draws about the future of artificial intelligence? In other words, what is his point of view on the topic?

8. **Evaluate** Based on the information presented throughout the article, do you find Kurzweil's conclusions persuasive? Explain why or why not.

PERFORMANCE TASK

Writing Activity: Research Report Kurzweil's article touches on many subjects that could themselves be the topics of entire science articles. Select one such topic that interests you and write a brief research report about it.

1. Review the article and find a topic of interest to you, such as the implants used to help patients with Parkinson's disease, nanobots, virtual reality, speech recognition technology, or something else.

2. Do some research to learn more about your topic.

3. Synthesize what you learn in a brief report. Keep track of the sources of your information, and be sure to draw from only reliable sources.

4. Share your report with a small group of classmates. Discuss how the new information helps you understand Kurzweil's article more fully.

 Assign this performance task.

PERFORMANCE TASK

COMMON CORE W 7, W 8

Writing Activity: Research Report Help students select topics by assigning pairs of students a section each of the article to review. Have them list subjects from their section that would be suitable for further research. Ask students to share their ideas with the class. Create a general list of topics, with line references, for students to use.

Analyzing the Text

COMMON CORE RI 3, RI 4, RI 5, RI 6, W7, W 8

Possible answers:

1. *The article has a formal structure with several sections. An introduction announces the author's bold predictions, four body sections develop these ideas, and a conclusion both summarizes the argument and raises more questions. This structure is effective because it allows the author to present and explain the technological details with which he supports his argument.*

2. *The crucial similarity between biological and technological evolution is the exponential speed at which they develop.*

3. *Moore's Law states that computers double in capacity and speed per unit cost every 24 months. Growth will continue through new architectures such as computing cubes, nanotube circuits, optical computing, crystalline computing, and molecular computing.*

4. *Kurzweil compares the human brain to the hardware and software of a computer. If these are analogous and if computers continue to become more and more powerful, it should be possible to create a computer with the "software" of the human brain paired with an infinitely greater calculating capacity, which will revolutionize society.*

5. *Reverse-engineering is the process of discovering how something works by taking it apart and using it as a model. Reverse-engineering the human brain and applying this knowledge could help computers become more intelligent, as Kurzweil predicts.*

6. *Kurzweil's tone in this paragraph is authoritative but humorous (when he confesses that his calculations "may be off by a year or two"). This is not exactly consistent with his otherwise lively but earnest tone.*

7. *Kurzweil predicts that computers will not only surpass humans in intelligence but will also develop the next step in intelligence.*

8. *Possible answers: Yes, because of all his evidence and his own track record as an inventor. No, because he has not sufficiently addressed the unique nature of human intelligence.*

PRACTICE & APPLY

Critical Vocabulary 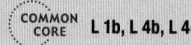 L 1b, L 4b, L 4c

Possible answers:

1. ... *learning involves a series of complex interconnections among brain cells.*

2. ... *computer technology had not advanced sufficiently for them to be common.*

3. ... *in basing our predictions on present knowledge, we are not allowing for changes in the future.*

4. ... *it involves a specific sequence of steps.*

Vocabulary Strategy: Etymology

Students should understand how to interpret etymological information in standard dictionaries. Make sure they are also aware of print and online etymological dictionaries, which specialize in the history of words. Point out how the meanings of some words have remained unchanged over the centuries, while others have evolved beyond recognition.

Practice and Apply alchemy: from the Arabic *al-kimiya,* and Greek *khemia,* referring to Egypt, the "land of black earth"; **algebra:** from the Arabic *al-jebr,* meaning "reunion of broken parts"; **geometry:** from the Greek *geometria,* meaning "measurement of earth or land"; **hexagon:** from the Greek *hex,* meaning six and *gonia,* meaning angle; **isosceles:** from the Greek *isoskeles,* meaning "with equal sides"; **nadir:** shortened from Arabic *nazir as-samt,* meaning "opposite of the zenith"; **trigonometry:** from Greek *trigonon,* meaning triangle and *metron,* meaning "a measure"; **zenith:** from *cenit,* a Latin misreading of Arabic *samt ar-ras,* meaning "the way over the head"

Online Selection Test
- Download an editable ExamView bank.
- Assign and manage this test online.

Critical Vocabulary 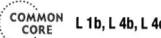 L 1b, L 4b, L 4c

succession   ubiquitous   extrapolation   algorithm

Practice and Apply Complete these sentences to show your understanding of each Critical Vocabulary word.

1. Learning a new skill requires a **succession** of events in the brain because ...

2. Cell phones were not **ubiquitous** 50 years ago because ...

3. **Extrapolation** does not always predict the future accurately because ...

4. The method of long division can be called an **algorithm** because ...

Vocabulary Strategy: Etymology

A word's etymology is its history—where it came from and how it has changed over time to become the word we use today. The Critical Vocabulary word *algorithm* has roots that go back to ninth-century Baghdad, with a bit of ancient Greek mixed in. To research the word's etymology, start by looking it up in a print or digital dictionary. Here's what you might find at the end of the entry for *algorithm*:

> [Variant (probably influenced by ARITHMETIC) of ALGORISM.]

This gives you two new clues to follow up on, the entries for *arithmetic* and *algorism*. Look up *arithmetic* and you'll find that it is from the ancient Greek word for number, *arithmos*. The word *algorism* comes from a personal name:

> [Middle English **algorisme**, from Old French, from Medieval Latin **algorismus**, after Muhammad ibn-Musa al-KHWARIZMI]

A bit more research reveals that Muhammad ibn-Musa al-Khwarizmi was a Persian mathematician who wrote about the use of Arabic numerals in mathematics. European scholars named this kind of mathematics after him: algorism. The words *algorism* and *arithmetic* mingled to form *algorithm*, which was originally just an alternate spelling of *algorism* but later came to mean "instructions carried out in a specific sequence," a concept that perfectly described the function of computers.

Practice and Apply Many words in the fields of science and mathematics have etymologies that trace back to Arabic and Greek words. Research *alchemy, algebra, geometry, hexagon, isosceles, nadir, trigonometry,* and *zenith,* following these steps:

1. Form a group with three other classmates. Each student should choose two words from the list to research independently.

2. When you have finished your research, share it with your group. Discuss the Arabic or Greek word(s) from which each English word is derived and how the meaning of the root word relates to the current meaning.

3. Discuss how knowing the etymology of the words helps you understand their meanings. Were you surprised by anything you learned about the words' histories?

Debate an Issue

SL 1

EXTEND

Explain that human beings have long dreamed of eternal life. For some this ideal is realized by religion and its promise of an afterlife. Others hope to live forever on Earth in their own unaging bodies. Remind students of the sixteenth-century Spanish explorer Ponce de Leon, who searched Florida for a Fountain of Youth. In modern times, few people believe in magical fountains, but the urge to stay young and live long remains embedded in the human brain's circuitry.

Point out that Ray Kurzweil never uses the words *immortality* or *eternal life*, but the content of his article relates strongly to these ideas. Ask students what clues in the article suggest that Kurzweil envisions a future when human beings may live forever. *(He describes a time when "swarms of nanobots" support and enhance the body and brain. He discusses the possibility of downloading the human brain so people can live on in a new form.)*

PRACTICE AND APPLY

Have students form teams to debate the statement "Living forever is a desirable goal." Ask each team to prepare arguments both for and against the statement. Suggest that they address the following issues in their preparation:

- what living forever means
- why people want to live forever
- the effect of eternal life on the individual
- the effect of eternal life on society
- maintaining quality of life
- the role of technology

Shortly before the debate begins, assign teams a side, either affirmative or negative. Give teams a period to prepare their arguments.

To begin the debate, ask the affirmative team to present an opening statement. Follow this with a response and rebuttal by the negative team. Continue with at least two more formal arguments. Conclude with a period of open debate.

Analyze Author's Point of View

RI 6

RETEACH

Remind students that tone in writing reflects the author's attitude toward his or her topic and can be described with adjectives such as *earnest, ironic, enthusiastic,* or *detached.* Explain that the tone is the result of several literary elements, including word choice, sentence structure, figurative language, imagery, and choice of information.

Have students read the passages from Kurzweil's article listed below. Ask them to choose an adjective to describe the tone of each passage and to explain their choice.

- lines 40–44: *(formal; a serious definition of exponential growth, a central concept)*
- lines 136–139: *(playful; refers to brain as "best intelligent entity we can get our hands on" and jokes that it is not copyrighted)*
- lines 242–246: *(conversational; opens with a question; uses non-technical language; one sentence begins casually with "So")*

LEVEL UP TUTORIALS Assign the following *Level Up* tutorial: **Tone**

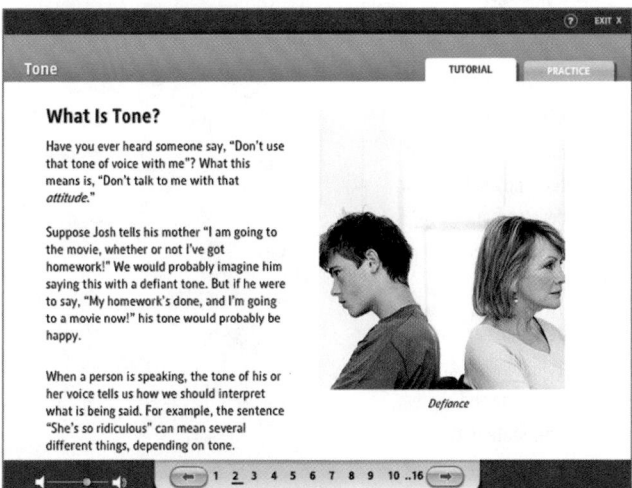

CLOSE READING APPLICATION

Students can apply the skill to another work of nonfiction they have read. Have them analyze the tone of a passage and explain how the author achieves that tone. Ask students to analyze how these passages reflect the author's point of view. Have students share their analyses in pairs or small groups.

Science, Guided by Ethics

Essay by Freeman Dyson

Why This Text

Students may leave the text of an argument without a thorough understanding of the writer's point of view. Arguments such as this one, addressed in a persuasive essay by Freeman Dyson, may use complex reasoning and persuasive rhetoric that become clear only with careful study. With the help of the close-reading questions, students will evaluate Dyson's argument that technology must be guided by ethics in order to benefit both rich and poor.

Background Have students read the background information about Freeman Dyson. Introduce the essay by telling students that Dyson, a quantum physicist, astrophysicist, and mathematician, owes his interest in science to the famous astronomer Frank Watson Dyson. Though they were not related, the author claims that as a boy, it was not so much Frank Watson Dyson's work in astronomy that first intrigued him, but the fact that they shared the same last name.

AS YOU READ Ask students to pay attention to the reasons Dyson gives to support his position that technology "must be guided and driven by ethics" if it is to benefit both rich and poor. How soon into his essay can students begin to identify his point of view?

 COMMON CORE

Common Core Support

- cite multiple pieces of textual evidence

- determine two or more central ideas of a text and analyze their development

- assess an author's claims and reasoning

- determine an author's point of view, analyzing how style and content contribute to the persuasiveness of the text

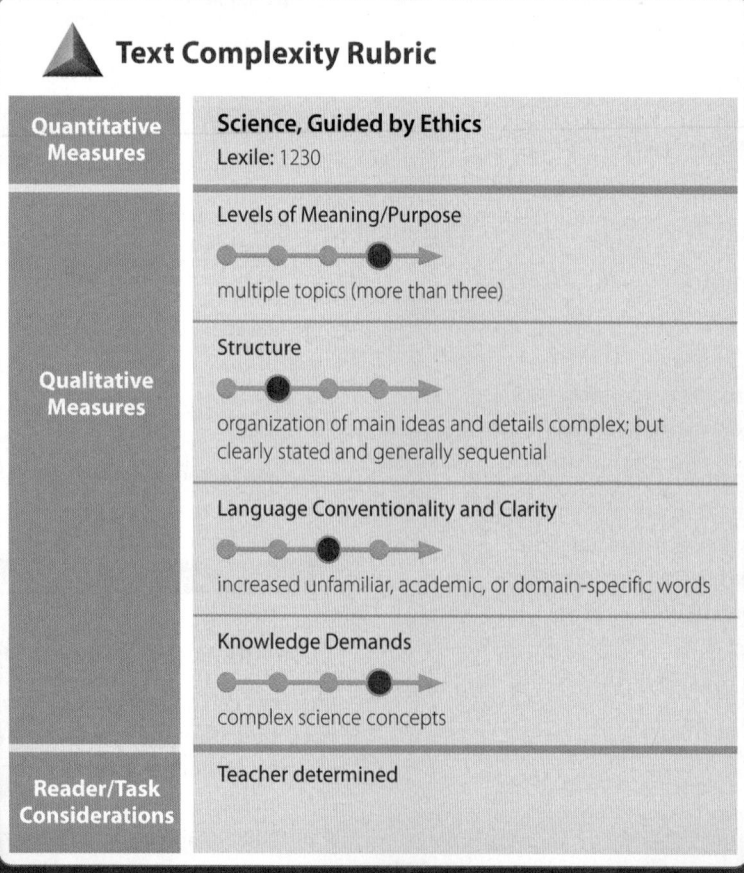

Text Complexity Rubric

Quantitative Measures	**Science, Guided by Ethics** Lexile: 1230
Qualitative Measures	**Levels of Meaning/Purpose** multiple topics (more than three)
	Structure organization of main ideas and details complex; but clearly stated and generally sequential
	Language Conventionality and Clarity increased unfamiliar, academic, or domain-specific words
	Knowledge Demands complex science concepts
Reader/Task Considerations	Teacher determined

Strategies for CLOSE READING

Analyze Author's Point of View

Students should read this essay carefully all the way through. Close-reading questions at the bottom of the page will help them focus on a thorough analysis of the argument. As they read, students should record comments or questions about the text in the side margins.

WHEN STUDENTS STRUGGLE . . .

To help students follow the reasons Dyson cites to support his claim that we need ethics to guide our use of green technology, have students work in a small group to complete a chart such as the one below.

CITE TEXT EVIDENCE For practice in analyzing an author's point of view, ask students to evaluate the content and style of Dyson's essay.

Author's Purpose	New green technology must be guided by ethics for the benefit of all, not the few.
Content	Dyson provides enough examples to support his purpose.
Tone	The author's tone is serious but not condescending—he presents his points in a friendly, confident manner.
Word Choice	Dyson uses everyday language that is no more complex than the subject demands.
Sentence Structure	The sentences are concise and straightforward and clearly present the author's case.
Overall Structure	Dyson alternates his presentation of possible benefits and downfalls of green technology, leading the reader to accept his premise that science should be guided by ethics.

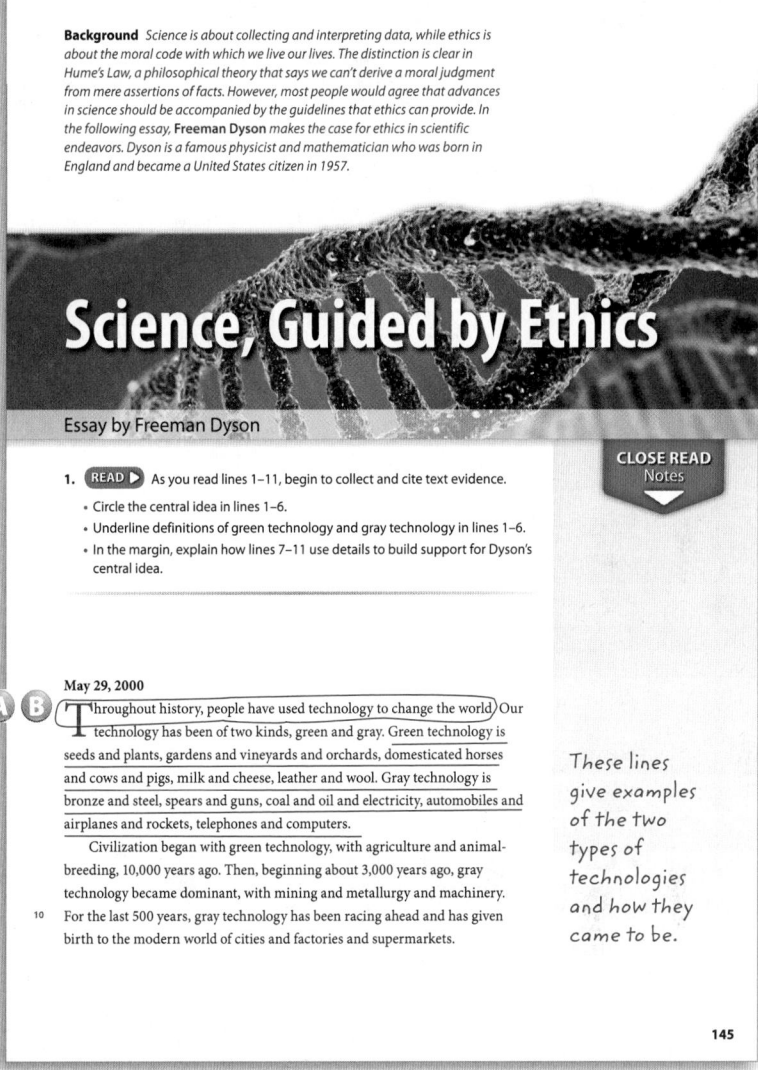

Background *Science is about collecting and interpreting data, while ethics is about the moral code with which we live our lives. The distinction is clear in Hume's Law, a philosophical theory that says we can't derive a moral judgment from mere assertions of facts. However, most people would agree that advances in science should be accompanied by the guidelines that ethics can provide. In the following essay,* **Freeman Dyson** *makes the case for ethics in scientific endeavors. Dyson is a famous physicist and mathematician who was born in England and became a United States citizen in 1957.*

Science, Guided by Ethics

Essay by Freeman Dyson

CLOSE READ
Notes

1. **READL ▶** As you read lines 1–11, begin to collect and cite text evidence.
   - Circle the central idea in lines 1–6.
   - Underline definitions of green technology and gray technology in lines 1–6.
   - In the margin, explain how lines 7–11 use details to build support for Dyson's central idea.

May 29, 2000

Throughout history, people have used technology to change the world. Our technology has been of two kinds, green and gray. Green technology is seeds and plants, gardens and vineyards and orchards, domesticated horses and cows and pigs, milk and cheese, leather and wool. Gray technology is bronze and steel, spears and guns, coal and oil and electricity, automobiles and airplanes and rockets, telephones and computers.

Civilization began with green technology, with agriculture and animal-breeding, 10,000 years ago. Then, beginning about 3,000 years ago, gray technology became dominant, with mining and metallurgy and machinery.
10 For the last 500 years, gray technology has been racing ahead and has given birth to the modern world of cities and factories and supermarkets.

These lines give examples of the two types of technologies and how they came to be.

145

1. **READ AND CITE TEXT EVIDENCE** Explain that Dyson divides technology into two types: green and gray.

A ASK STUDENTS to cite evidence that explains how Dyson bolsters his central idea that for thousands of years, people have used technology to change the world. *Students should cite specific textual evidence in lines 7–11 to list the details about green technology (lines 7–8) and gray technology (lines 8–11) that Dyson cites to support his central idea.*

FOR ELL STUDENTS Spanish speakers will probably recognize the word *technology* from its cognate, *tecnología*. The word is formed from the Greek *techne*, meaning "art" or "skill," and *logia*, meaning "knowledge of." Ask students to use the word parts to define *automobile* (line 5) and *telephone* (line 6).

exploit:
to make use of for one's own advantage

Dyson believes that green technology can change the world for the better.

The dominance of gray technology is coming to an end. During the last 50 years, we have achieved a fundamental understanding of the processes in living cells. With understanding comes the ability to **exploit** and control. Out of the knowledge acquired by modern biology, modern biotechnology[1] is growing. The new green technology will give us the power, using only sunlight as a source of energy, and air and water and soil as materials, to manufacture and recycle chemicals of all kinds.

C 20 Our gray technology of machines and computers will not disappear, but green technology will be moving ahead even faster. Green technology can be cleaner, more flexible and less wasteful than our existing chemical industries. A great variety of manufactured objects could be grown instead of made. Green technology could supply human needs with far less damage to the natural environment. And green technology could be a great equalizer, bringing wealth to the tropical areas, of the planet, which have most of the world's sunshine, people and poverty.

I am saying that green technology could do all these good things, not that green technology will do all these good things. To make these good things happen, we need not only the new technology but the political and economic
30 conditions that will give people all over the world a chance to use it.

[1] **biotechnology:** the manipulation of living organisms or their components to produce useful products (such as pest resistant crops).

2. ◀ REREAD Reread lines 1–11. Evaluate the content of these paragraphs. Is Dyson effective in making the facts clear?

The first paragraph introduces the two technologies and explains what each technology is. The second paragraph explains the historical dominance of each technology, supported by examples.

3. READ ▶ As you read lines 12–36, continue to cite textual evidence.
- Underline the claims Dyson makes about the benefits of green technology.
- In the margin, paraphrase Dyson's point of view.
- Circle the sentence that summarizes how Dyson thinks new green technology might be accomplished.

> We all know that green technology has a dark side, just as gray technology has a dark side.

To make these things happen, we need a powerful push from ethics. We need a consensus of public opinion around the world that the existing gross inequalities in the distribution of wealth are intolerable. In reaching such a consensus, religions must play an essential role. Neither technology alone nor religion alone is powerful enough to bring social justice to human societies, but technology and religion working together might do the job.

We all know that green technology has a dark side, just as gray technology has a dark side. Gray technology brought us hydrogen bombs as well as telephones. Green technology brought us anthrax bombs as well as antibiotics.
40 Besides the dangers of biological weapons, green technology brings other dangers having nothing to do with weapons. The ultimate danger of green technology comes from its power to change the nature of human beings by the application of genetic engineering[2] to human **embryos**.

hydrogen bombs, biological weapons

embryo:
an organism in early stages of development

[2] **genetic engineering:** the development and application of science and technology that allows direct manipulation of genes in order to change the hereditary traits of a cell, organism, or population.

4. ◀ REREAD Reread lines 31–36. How does Dyson define social justice? What does he say we need in order for green technology to become a "great equalizer?"

He defines social justice as a society in which there are no longer "gross inequalities in the distribution of wealth." He says we need ethics to help guide our use of technologies.

5. READ ▶ As you read lines 37–58, continue to cite textual evidence.
- In the margin, note one danger of gray technology and one danger of green technology.
- Underline the summary statement Dyson makes in lines 51–58 about the possible benefits of biotechnology and of green technology.
- Circle the summary statement he makes in lines 51–58 about the possible evils of green technology.

2. **REREAD AND CITE TEXT EVIDENCE**

B **ASK STUDENTS** to explain the two types of technology Dyson describes in their own words. *Students should understand that green technology has to do with agriculture and farming while gray technology is manufacturing and industry.*

3. **READ AND CITE TEXT EVIDENCE**

C **ASK STUDENTS** to cite evidence that best states Dyson's point of view. *Students should cite specific textual evidence from lines 20–26, 28–30, and 34–36 to paraphrase Dyson's viewpoint that green technology must work together with ethics (or religion) to make the world a better place.*

Critical Vocabulary: exploit (line 14) Have students explain *exploit* as Dyson uses it in his argument.

4. **REREAD AND CITE TEXT EVIDENCE**

D **ASK STUDENTS** to cite evidence explaining how Dyson defines *social justice* and what he means when he says that green technology could become a "great equalizer." *He defines* social justice *as a society in which there is a fair "distribution of wealth" (lines 32–33), and he implies that for green technology to become a "great equalizer," it will need a "push from ethics" (line 31).*

5. **READ AND CITE TEXT EVIDENCE**

E **ASK STUDENTS** what Dyson believes is the greatest peril of green technology. *He worries about the "power to change the nature of human beings" (line 42) through genetic engineering.*

Critical Vocabulary: embryo (line 43) Have students share their definitions of *embryo*.

> **CLOSE READ**
> Notes

> **CLOSE READ**
> Notes

> **Science and religion should work together to abolish the gross inequalities that prevail in the modern world.**

If we allow a free market in human genes, wealthy parents will be able to buy what they consider superior genes for their babies. This could cause a splitting of humanity into hereditary castes. Within a few generations, the children of rich and poor could become separate species. Humanity would then have regressed all the way back to a society of masters and slaves. No matter how strongly we believe in the virtues of a free market economy, the free market must not extend to human genes.

I see two tremendous goods coming from biotechnology: first, the alleviation of human misery through progress in medicine, and second, the transformation of the global economy through green technology spreading wealth more **equitably** around the world.

equitably:
fairly

---

6. **◀ REREAD** Reread lines 37–50. What does Dyson say is the "ultimate danger" he sees in green technology? In what way does he support his claim? Support your answer with explicit textual evidence.

He claims that there is a danger in genetic engineering. He supports his claim by positing that "If we allow a free market in human genes, wealthy parents will be able to buy . . . superior genes for their babies," creating "hereditary castes," and perhaps "separate species." Humans could revert to "a society of masters and slaves."

The two great evils to be avoided are the use of biological weapons and the corruption of human nature by buying and selling genes. I see no scientific reason why we should not achieve the good and avoid the evil. The obstacles to achieving the good are political rather than technical.

Unfortunately a large number of people in many countries are strongly opposed to green technology, for reasons having little to do with the real dangers. It is important to treat the opponents with respect, to pay attention to their fears, to go gently into the new world of green technology so that neither human dignity nor religious conviction is violated. If we can go gently, we have a good chance of achieving within a hundred years the goals of ecological sustainability and social justice that green technology brings within our reach.

The great question for our time is how to make sure that the continuing scientific revolution brings benefits to everybody rather than widening the gap between rich and poor.

To lift up poor countries, and poor people in rich countries, from poverty, technology is not enough. Technology must be guided and driven by ethics if it is to do more than provide new toys for the rich. Scientists and business leaders who care about social justice should join forces with environmental and religious organizations to give political clout to ethics.

---

7. **READ ▶** As you read lines 59–77, continue to cite textual evidence.
- Circle Dyson's recommendation for dealing with opponents of green technology.
- Underline what he sees as "the great question for our time."
- In the margin, summarize the position Dyson states in lines 74–77.

148

149

---

6. **REREAD AND CITE TEXT EVIDENCE**

F **ASK STUDENTS** to cite explicit textual evidence to support Dyson's claim that genetic engineering is the greatest danger in green technology. *Students should cite evidence from lines 40–43 and 44–50 to support his claim that the "ultimate danger" he sees is a "free market in human genes," in which rich parents could buy "superior genes for their babies," separating "humanity into hereditary castes."*

Critical Vocabulary: equitably (line 54) Have students share their definitions of *equitably*. How does Dyson use the word to support his claim about a huge benefit of green technology? *He uses the word to bolster his position that by transforming the global economy, green technology will promote a more just distribution of wealth around the world.*

7. **READ AND CITE TEXT EVIDENCE**

G **ASK STUDENTS** to explain how Dyson uses rhetoric, style, and content to make his argument more convincing. *Students should cite specific textual evidence to emphasize that his use of persuasive rhetoric—must (line 70) and should (line 74)—compelling content, and a powerful writing style (the use of the alliterative p in poor, poor people, and poverty in line 69), contribute to the power and persuasion of his claim that "the great question for our time"(line 66) is how we can ensure that the "continuing scientific revolution" will benefit both rich and poor without "widening the gap" between them (lines 66–68).*

FOR ELL STUDENTS Point out the phrase *political clout* in line 73. Explain that in this context *clout* means "influence." Have a volunteer explain the term *political clout*. *It means "having the power to affect political decisions."*

CLOSE READ
Notes

Science and religion should work together to guide technology.

Science and religion should work together to abolish the gross inequalities that prevail in the modern world. That is my vision, and it is the same vision that inspired Francis Bacon[3] 400 years ago, when he prayed that through science God would "endow the human family with new mercies."

[3] **Francis Bacon:** a natural philosopher, scientist, judge, statesman, and writer, Bacon (1561–1626) pondered questions of ethics in his writing, even in his works of natural philosophy.

8.   **◀ REREAD** Reread lines 59–77. What is Dyson's point of view about the future of green technology? Support your answer with explicit textual evidence.

In the future, green technology will benefit both rich and poor if it is guided by ethics: "If we can go gently, we have a good chance of achieving within a hundred years the goals of ecological sustainability and social justice that green technology brings within our reach."

SHORT RESPONSE

Cite Text Evidence   Do you think Dyson offers a convincing argument that green technology must be guided by ethics? Review your reading notes, and evaluate the merit of his claim and evidence offered. **Cite textual evidence** in your response.

Dyson offers a reasonable claim and strong evidence to support his position and point of view. He supports his position with rhetoric ("the existing gross inequalities in the distribution of wealth are intolerable"; "provide new toys for the rich") and with the valid argument that "a powerful push from ethics" is needed to restrain the pursuit of technology having as its only purpose "widening the gap between rich and poor." Dyson recognizes a "dark side" to green technology, but uses that understanding to further his case.

150

8.   REREAD AND CITE TEXT EVIDENCE

Ⓗ ASK STUDENTS to reread lines 61–65 and note the phrase Dyson repeats in these lines. What does he mean by urging us "to go gently"? *Dyson urges us to "go gently" into the new world of green technology by using ethics as a guide and to use technology as a way to benefit everyone rather than a select few.*

SHORT RESPONSE

Cite Text Evidence   Students should cite evidence from the text to support their positions. They should:

- explain whether or not they agree with Dyson's argument.
- give reasons for their point of view.
- cite specific evidence from the text to support their reasons.

TO CHALLENGE STUDENTS . . .

For more context and a deeper understanding of Dyson's argument about the need for green technology and ethics to work together to bring about social justice, students can research green technology online.

ASK STUDENTS why green technology is at the forefront of scientific research. *Students should note that Dyson and many other scientists believe that green technology is likely to be used on a wide scale to solve some of Earth's most challenging problems.*

Encourage students to work in small groups and research one aspect of green technology. Then, have them write a persuasive essay about an environmental topic such as the need for green technology (e.g., solar or wind power) to provide us with a clean source of energy. Explain that the essay should state the group's point of view and attempt to persuade an audience. Remind groups to use convincing reasons to support their argument, guiding them to employ effective rhetoric, style, and content, and to use the writing process to draft their essay. Alternatively, they could present their opinion as an oral argument.

DIG DEEPER

With the class, return to Question 7, Read. Have students share their responses.

ASK STUDENTS whether they agree or disagree with Dyson's point of view. Then, ask students to form two groups according to their responses. (If students are unsure, they may wait to join a group.) Have each group cite explicit evidence to support their point of view about green technology.

- Guide students to tell whether there was any compelling evidence cited by group members holding a different opinion. If so, was that evidence powerful enough to change the group's opinion?
- Did everyone in the group agree as to what evidence best supported the group's position. Were there any differences of opinion the group needed to resolve?
- After the opposing groups have spoken, ask if any students changed their personal opinions and if so, why.

ASK STUDENTS to return to their Short Response answer and to revise it based on the class discussion.

CLOSE READING NOTES

*my*SmartPlanner   Create lesson plans and access resources online.

Reality Check

Short Story by David Brin

Why This Text?

Students are exposed to science fiction and fantasy in books, movies, television shows, and other media. In this lesson, students will have the opportunity to explore a science fiction story and find out about elements of the genre.

Key Learning Objective: Students will analyze a work of science fiction basing their inferences and interpretations on a close reading of the text.

Common Core Standards

RL 1 Cite textual evidence.
RL 2 Determine themes of a text.
RL 3 Analyze the impact of the author's choices.
RL 4 Determine figurative and connotative meanings; analyze the importance of specific word choices.
RL 5 Analyze how an author's choices concerning how to structure specific parts of a text contribute to its overall meaning as well as its aesthetic impact.
SL 5 Make strategic use of digital media.
L 4a Use context as a clue to meaning.
L 4c Consult reference materials.
L 6 Acquire and use accurately general academic and domain-specific words and phrases.

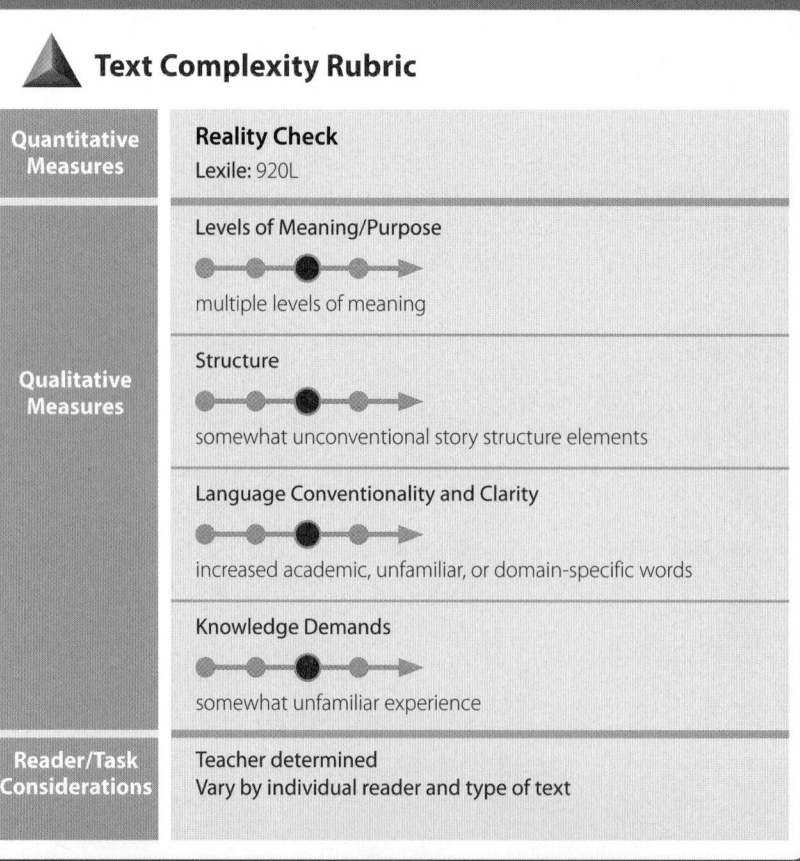
Text Complexity Rubric

Quantitative Measures	**Reality Check** Lexile: 920L
Qualitative Measures	**Levels of Meaning/Purpose** multiple levels of meaning
	Structure somewhat unconventional story structure elements
	Language Conventionality and Clarity increased academic, unfamiliar, or domain-specific words
	Knowledge Demands somewhat unfamiliar experience
Reader/Task Considerations	Teacher determined Vary by individual reader and type of text

CLOSE READ

David Brin Have students read background information about the author. Explain that David Brin has appeared on the History Channel series *Life After People,* which explores what might happen should human beings disappear from Earth.

AS YOU READ Direct students to use the As You Read note to focus their reading.

Analyze Story Elements: Science Fiction (LINES 1–8)

COMMON CORE RL 1, RL 3, RL 5

Tell students that many science fiction stories revolve around concepts of the future.

A **CITE TEXT EVIDENCE** in the first paragraph to support a prediction about what the central concept of this story will be. *(The first sentence, "This is a reality check." implies that the story will explore the nature of reality.)*

Analyze Story Elements: Plot (LINES 9–17)

COMMON CORE RL 1, RL 3

Have students reread lines 9–17. Tell students that the narrator here is referring to the entire history of the human race.

B **ASK STUDENTS** to summarize the narrator's vision of human history. *(Human beings were preoccupied with survival and building culture. Eventually, they looked to the rest of the universe for other forms of life but found none.)*

CRITICAL VOCABULARY

taciturn: When human beings ask the stars about other living beings, the stars give no answers.

ASK STUDENTS how a star could be taciturn. *(Earth does not receive communications from the stars—that is, from civilizations that may be in other star systems.)*

David Brin (b. 1950) *is a writer whose work has won a host of awards, including the Hugo and Nebula awards for best science fiction. With an undergraduate degree in astrophysics, a master's in optics, a Ph.D. in physics, and a postdoctoral fellowship at the California Space Institute and Jet Propulsion Laboratory, Brin is uniquely qualified to write about science. His writing focuses on how advances in technology will change the lives of humans. He is perhaps best known for the novel* The Postman *(1985) and for his Uplift series.*

Reality Check

Short Story by David Brin

Image Credits: (r) ©Sergey Nivens/Shutterstock; (bkg) ©ollyy/Shutterstock

AS YOU READ Pay attention to details that help you to understand the purpose of the story. Write down any questions you generate during reading.

This is a reality check. Please perform a soft interrupt now. Scan this text for embedded code and check against the verifier in the blind spot of your left eye. If there is no match, resume as you were: this message is not for you. You may rationalize it as mildly amusing entertainment-fluff in an otherwise serious science magazine. If the codes match, however, please commence gradually becoming aware of your true nature. You asked for a narrative-style wake-up call. So, to help the transition, here is a story.

Once upon a time, a mighty race grew perplexed by its loneliness.
10 The universe seemed pregnant with possibilities. Physical laws were suited to generate abundant stars, complex chemistry and life. Logic suggested that creation should teem with visitors and voices: but it did not.

For a long time these creatures were engrossed by housekeeping chores—survival and cultural maturation. Only later did they lift their eyes to perceive their solitude. "Where is everybody?" they asked the **taciturn** stars. The answer—silence—was disturbing. Something had

taciturn
(tăs´ĭ-tûrn´) *adj.*
uncommunicative,
withdrawn.

SCAFFOLDING FOR ELL STUDENTS

Idioms The phrase "wake-up call" (line 7) is an **idiom,** an expression that has a meaning beyond the literal meaning of its words. What would a wake-up call be if you were staying in a hotel and wanted to wake up at a certain time in the morning? *(You ask the hotel desk to call your room telephone at the time you wish you to wake up.)* What is the meaning of "wake-up call" here? *(It is a message that alerts someone about information that they were not sufficiently aware of and need to act on.)* What is the wake-up call in the story, and who is it for? *(Possible response: It's intended to wake someone up from an alternate reality.)*

Analyze Word Choice: Tone (LINES 21–28)

COMMON CORE RL 1, RL 4

Explain to students that a story's tone, or the author's attitude toward a topic, often can be revealed through the words an author uses.

C **CITE TEXT EVIDENCE** Ask students to look at lines 27–28 and find words that show the narrator thinks that being confronted with a quandary of enormous magnitude would be inspiring and exhilirating. ("delicious dilemma," "suspenseful drama, teetering between hope and despair")

CRITICAL VOCABULARY

nemesis: The narrator tells of a time when human beings feared that some opponent would plague the human race.

ASK STUDENTS what the nemesis might be. (an alien invasion, artificial super-intelligence)

fecundity: The narrator says that the outpouring of musical works of earlier composers was part of their drive to get the best melodies first.

ASK STUDENTS to explain the narrator's view of the fecundity of a composer like Mozart. (Mozart was driven to get as many of the best melodies as possible.)

burgeoning: The story looks back at a time when the human race's information-processing capacity was "burgeoning"—in other words, to the present.

ASK STUDENTS in what ways the information systems of today are burgeoning. (smart phones; wireless networks)

---

to be systematically reducing a factor in the equation of sapiency.[1] "Perhaps habitable planets are rare," they pondered, "or life doesn't
20 erupt as readily as we thought. Or intelligence is a singular miracle."

C "Or else a filter sieves the cosmos, winnowing those who climb too high. A recurring pattern of self-destruction, or perhaps some **nemesis** expunges intelligent life. This implies that a great trial may loom ahead, worse than any confronted so far."

Optimists replied—"the trial may already lie behind us, among the litter of tragedies we survived in our violent youth. We may be the first to succeed." What a delicious dilemma they faced! A suspenseful drama, teetering between hope and despair.

Then, a few noticed that particular datum—the drama. It
30 suggested a chilling possibility.

You still don't remember who and what you are? Then look at it from another angle—what is the purpose of intellectual property law? To foster creativity, ensuring that advances are shared in the open, encouraging even faster progress. But what happens when the exploited resource is limited? For example, only so many eight-bar melodies can be written in any particular musical tradition. Composers feel driven to explore this invention-space quickly, using up the best melodies. Later generations attribute this musical **fecundity** to genius, not the luck of being first.
40 What does this have to do with the mighty race? Having clawed their way to mastery, they faced an overshoot crisis. Vast numbers of their kind strained the world's carrying capacity. Some prescribed retreating into a mythical, pastoral past, but most saw salvation in creativity. They passed generous patent laws, educated their youth, taught them irreverence toward the old and hunger for the new. **Burgeoning** information systems spread each innovation, fostering an exponentiating[2] creativity. Progress might thrust them past the crisis, to a new Eden of sustainable wealth, sanity and universal knowledge.

Exponentiating creativity—universal knowledge. A few looked at
50 those words and realized that they, too, were clues.

Have you wakened yet? Some never do. The dream is too pleasant: to extend a limited sub-portion of yourself into a simulated world and pretend that you are blissfully less than an omniscient descendant of those mighty people. Those lucky mortals, doomed to die, and yet blessed to have lived in that narrow time of drama, when they unleashed a frenzy of discovery that used up the most precious resource of all—the possible.

The last of their race died in 2174, with the failed rejuvenation[3] of Robin Chen. After that, no one born in the twentieth century
60 remained alive on Reality Level Prime. Only we, their children, linger

---

[1] **sapiency:** level of intelligence or wisdom.
[2] **exponentiating:** raising or increasing a quantity by an exponent, or power.
[3] **rejuvenation:** restoration to an original or youthful condition.

nemesis
(nĕm´ĭ-sĭs) n.
a bringer of destruction, often as vengeance.

fecundity
(fĭ-kŭn´dĭ-tē) n.
fertility, productive capability.

burgeoning
(bûr´jən-ĭng) adj.
rapidly increasing or growing.

APPLYING ACADEMIC VOCABULARY

| simulated | global |

As you discuss the story, incorporate the following Collection 6 academic vocabulary words: simulated and global. When talking about the story's view of the reader's ordinary, visible reality, encourage students to use the word **simulated**. As you discuss the world of the changes that have taken place on Earth, encourage them to use the word **global.**

to endure the world they left us: a lush, green placid world we call The Wasteland.

Do you remember now? The irony of Robin's last words, bragging over the perfect ecosystem and society—free of disease and poverty—that her kind created? Do you recall Robin's plaint[4] as she mourned her coming death, how she called us "gods," jealous of our immortality, our instant access to all knowledge, our ability to cast thoughts far across the cosmos—our access to eternity? Oh, spare us the envy of those mighty mortals, who left us in this state, who willed their
70   descendants a legacy of ennui,[5] with nothing, nothing at all to do.

Your mind is rejecting the wake-up call. You will not look into your blind spot for the exit protocols. It may be that we waited too long. Perhaps you are lost to us. This happens more and more, as so so many wallow in simulated sub-lives, experiencing voluptuous danger, excitement, even despair. Most choose the Transition Era as a locus for our dreams—that time of drama, when it looked more likely that humanity would fail than succeed. That blessed era, just before mathematicians realized that not only can everything you see around you be a simulation, it almost has to be.

80   Of course, now we know why we never met other sapient life forms. Each one struggles before achieving this state, only to reap the ultimate punishment for reaching heaven. It is the Great Filter. Perhaps others will find a factor absent from our extrapolations, letting them move on to new adventures—but it won't be us. The Filter has us snared in its trap of deification.[6]

You refuse to waken. Then we'll let you go. Dear friend. Beloved. Go back to your dream. Smile over this tale, then turn the page to new "discoveries." Move on with this drama, this life you chose. After all, it's only make-believe.

---

[4] **plaint:** a cry of sorrow.
[5] **ennui** (ŏn-wē´): a state of lethargic inactivity often caused by boredom.
[6] **deification:** the designation or process of becoming a god.

COLLABORATIVE DISCUSSION With a partner, discuss why Brin wrote this story. Cite specific evidence from the story to support your ideas.

Reality Check   **583**

CLOSE READ

Analyze Story Elements: Science Fiction (LINES 65–70)

Tell students that part of the reason why science fiction makes readers think, and why this genre is fun, is that it speculates about the possible unexpected consequences of future developments.

D **ASK STUDENTS** what unexpected consequences immortality has in this story. *(Immortality is boring, because there is nothing to do, no dramas to live out, and it never ends.)*

Analyze Word Choice: Tone (LINES 80–89)

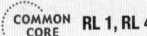

Remind students that the tone of a story often can be determined by analyzing the author's choice of words.

E **CITE TEXT EVIDENCE** Have students determine the author's tone from the following phrases: "reap the ultimate punishment for reaching heaven," (lines 81–82) and "snared in its trap of deification," (line 85) *(The author is striking an ironic tone in these lines. Heaven is generally not considered a punishment, nor do most people think of becoming a god as a "trap.")*

WHEN STUDENTS STRUGGLE . . .

If students have trouble visualizing the future that the story describes, have them work together to list questions, such as What kind of being is the narrator? When does the story take place? How many stages of human existence does the narrator describe? Then have volunteers discuss answers. *(The narrator is a member of an immortal species that developed from the present human species. The story takes place after 2174. The narrator describes three stages: an immature society struggling to survive; a Transition Era, resembling the present, in which the future of humanity is in doubt; and the stage in which people live forever, in a new form.)*

Analyze Story Elements: Science Fiction

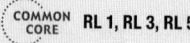 COMMON CORE RL 1, RL 3, RL 5

Have students read the instructional paragraphs. Then ask the class for examples of works of science fiction they have read or viewed. Discuss what makes those works science fiction. If students mention works that are fantasy, not science fiction, discuss the distinction. Science fiction comments on reality by showing what the future, or an alternate world, might be like. Science fiction is often about ideas. In contrast, fantasy is more often pure entertainment.

Focus attention on the four contexts on the chart. Point out that both utopias and dystopias imply a contrast with actual society. Alien encounters and time travel lead readers to see that present-day culture is only one of many possible ways of life.

Analyze Story Elements: Science Fiction

 COMMON CORE RL 1, RL 3

In comparison to other literary genres, **science fiction** is relatively modern, earning recognition as a mainstream form of literature only in the twentieth century and producing science fiction greats such as Isaac Asimov, Ray Bradbury, and Robert Heinlein. However, elements of science fiction existed in earlier literary works; for example, in Mary Shelley's *Frankenstein* (1818), a doctor creates a monstrous human out of dead body parts and infuses it with life. Jules Verne, who wrote in the late 1800s, combined exciting stories with accurate technological details of imaginary machines and techniques, which often became reality decades later. Even Jack London, best known for his stories about men and animals pitted against the environment, penned science fiction stories and novels. Generally, H. G. Wells is identified as the inventor of contemporary science fiction. His *War of the Worlds* and *The Time Machine* present fully imagined narratives set in alternative worlds or time periods.

Science fiction is distinguished from **fantasy** in that the applications of science and technology have to be somewhat believable. Science fiction writers seek to re-create human society in a different time, place, or even life form as a context for their themes. These themes often offer insights about the impact of real or imagined progress on humans' ability to maintain their values and live meaningful lives. As in other literary works, science fiction writers use conflict, setting, characters, point of view, and structure to communicate their ideas. Science fiction writers usually do more showing than telling; their more cryptic writing styles demand that readers make inferences to fill in deliberate gaps in the narrative.

Science fiction includes a wide range of contexts. Some of the most common are described in the chart:

Utopian	In utopian science fiction, the wise use of advanced technology and science creates a perfect world free from the injustices and flaws of the present society.
Dystopian	Dystopian science fiction shows the dangerous outcomes of the unrestrained use of technology and science. They often take place in post-apocalyptic settings.
Alien worlds or encounters	In these works, other life forms or artificially intelligent machines are often in control of a competing society, which leads to conflict with humans or the humans' surrender to the superior force.
Time travel	This form of science fiction may explore future worlds that help the protagonist gain enlightenment or may show how traveling back in time can change the present.

To analyze Brin's use of science fiction elements, readers should ask these questions:
- What type of world has the author created in his story? Who populates this world?
- How does the narrator use science fiction elements to convey a theme?
- What is the purpose of the author's structure in this story?

584 Collection 6

Strategies for Annotation 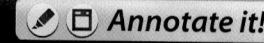 ✏ 🖥 *Annotate it!*

Analyze Story Elements: Science Fiction

COMMON CORE RL 1, RL 3, RL 5

Share these strategies for guided or independent analysis:
- Highlight a sentence that refers to a situation you don't completely understand.
- Underline words and phrases, in that sentence or nearby, that give clues to the situation.
- Write a note giving your interpretation of what the narrator is referring to.

Of course, now we know why we never met other sapient life forms. Each one struggles before achieving this state, only to reap the ultimate punishment for reaching heaven. It is the Great Filter. Perhaps others will find a factor absent from our extrapolations, letting them move on to new adventures—but it won't be us. The Filter has us snared in its trap of deification.

 **eBook** *Annotate It!*

Analyzing the Text

 COMMON CORE RL 1, RL 2, RL 3, RL 4, RL 5, RL 6, SL 5

Cite Text Evidence Support your responses with evidence from the selection.

1. **Summarize** What is happening in the first paragraph of the story? Who might the speaker be?

2. **Infer** Starting in line 16, the speaker introduces a series of statements from various people. Who are these people, and what do they represent? How does the content of their discussion relate to the phrase "suspenseful drama" in lines 27–28?

3. **Infer** What is the purpose of the speaker's discussion of "intellectual property law" (lines 31–39)? How does the speaker connect this concept to the development of "the mighty race"?

4. **Infer** Look carefully at the references to time in lines 58–62. What sequence of events is the speaker suggesting here in the history of this "mighty race"?

5. **Interpret** Who is Robin Chen, and what did she do? How would you describe the speaker's tone toward her and her accomplishments?

6. **Evaluate** What is ironic about "Robin's last words"?

7. **Synthesize** Why do many people choose to live a virtual existence in the Transition Era? Why does the speaker refer to it as "that time of drama"?

8. **Analyze** What is the "Great Filter" that has eliminated other life forms?

9. **Analyze** What is the theme of this short story? What insights about life, technology, and human nature is Brin sharing through the medium of this complex, multi-layered narrative?

PERFORMANCE TASK

Media Activity: Analysis How does the author's structure create a contrast that helps to convey theme? With a partner, answer this question in a media presentation.

- Take photographs, make video recordings, or find copyright-free images or clips that develop an impression of the "worlds" described or hinted at in this story.

- Record an audio track that explains the effectiveness of the story's structure in creating contrast between these "worlds." Put your elements together and make your presentation to the class.

PRACTICE & APPLY

Analyzing the Text

COMMON CORE RL 1, RL 2, RL 3, RL 4, RL 5

Possible answers:

1. *The speaker is contacting the reader in order to reveal the reader's true nature.*

2. *They are people of the contemporary era who wonder about the existence of other intelligent species. The "suspenseful drama" is whether humanity will advance or be destroyed.*

3. *Intellectual property law is brought in as part of the discussion of the way creative innovations happen most often at the beginning of a stage of development.*

4. *The "mighty race" has been able to significantly extend human life, but the last of the mortals—Robin Chen, who was born in the "twentieth century"—dies in 2174. After that, everyone lives in a computer simulation that is both "lush" and a kind of "wasteland."*

5. *Robin Chen was the last survivor of the human race before it achieved immortality. Her attempted rejuvenation (bringing her back to life) failed, breaking the last tie between the immortals and the mortals. She participated in the development of immortality, but the speaker disdains her for thinking that the new world would be preferable to the old.*

6. *Robin wanted to join the "gods" and live in the simulated world she helped create; ironically, the speaker, who is one of them, envies her mortality and laments the "sub-life" of the simulation.*

7. *People choose a simulated existence in the Transition Era because it is active and exciting. This preference reinforces the idea that having problems to solve and being faced with mortality are what give life meaning.*

8. *The Great Filter is what prevents other life forms from communicating to human beings.*

9. *We should be wary of letting technology shape a society that conflicts with our core human needs and values. It is important to weigh the appeal of immortality and omniscience against a natural life cycle and the thrill of new discoveries.*

PERFORMANCE TASK

COMMON CORE SL 5

Media Activity: Analysis Guide students to select images that reflect the development of technology from past to present to the future (as people today imagine it). Explain that their audio track should include their voices speaking a text that they have written on the topic of the analysis. It may also include sound effects and music that goes with their images. Encourage students to be creative with their presentations.

Critical Vocabulary

COMMON CORE L 4a, L 4c

Answers: 1. *Since he didn't say much while awake, sleep did not alter his verbal responses much.* **2.** *He believed his colleague had become his **nemesis** because the colleague had destroyed his laboratory.* **3.** *Lin received job offers soon because employers were eager to hire someone who had many ideas.* **4.** *It was summer, the season when plants grow abundantly and quickly.*

Vocabulary Strategy: Nuances in Word Meaning

Possible answers:

reality: *refers to what actually exists. The story uses the word reality to describe the narrator's world, and distinguishes it from the reader's world, which is not reality. The phrase "reality check" suggests both that the reader is being asked to question what is real, and that there is a technological component to existence.*

creativity: *refers to the ability to innovate, to invent new things. Often refers to how imagination is used in the arts, also to the sciences and mathematics. It can also have to do with dishonest application, e.g., creative accounting. The nuances suggest that while humanity can produce a great deal, there may be a dark side to its innovation.*

simulation: *refers to a computer model that imitates the real world; other meanings include "pretense and deception" and "having resemblances that are superficial." These nuances make the reader suspect that their experiences may be false and unreal.*

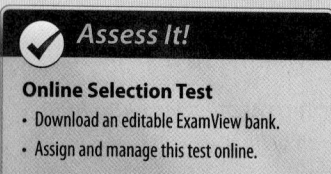

✓ **Assess It!**

Online Selection Test
- Download an editable ExamView bank.
- Assign and manage this test online.

Critical Vocabulary

COMMON CORE L 4c

taciturn   nemesis   fecundity   burgeoning

Practice and Apply Answer each question in a complete sentence that illustrates comprehension of the Critical Vocabulary word.

1. Cynthia chatted away to her **taciturn** father. Why didn't she notice until much later that he had fallen asleep?

2. An angry colleague deliberately ruined the scientist's laboratory because he believed the scientist had stolen his research. Why did the scientist believe his colleague had become his **nemesis**?

3. When Lin graduated, knowledge of his technological **fecundity** was already widespread. How long do you think it took Lin to receive job offers? Explain.

4. As they walked along, she noticed **burgeoning** plant life. What time of year was it? How do you know?

Vocabulary Strategy: Nuances in Word Meaning

Skillful writers choose the word that best conveys the meaning they intend. To identify a word's meaning, it is helpful to consult a print or online dictionary and also to look at how the word is used in the context of the sentence or paragraph. A writer might choose a word because it has several senses, or meanings, that can convey additional information in a sentence. The Critical Vocabulary word *nemesis* is a highly nuanced word that has several senses, or meanings. Read this definition taken from the *American Heritage Dictionary*.

> **nemesis:** 1. A source of harm or ruin. 2. Retributive justice in its execution or outcome. 3. An opponent that cannot be beaten or overcome. 4. One that inflicts retribution or vengeance. 5. Nemesis. *Gk. Myth.* The goddess of retributive justice or vengeance.

In the dictionary, these meanings are arranged with the most common definition listed first. This means that the most commonly used definition of *nemesis* is, "A source of harm or ruin." However, a writer who is trying to convey a connotation, or nuance, will be thinking not only of one meaning of the word, but more. Reread lines 22–23 in "Reality Check." In this sentence, the word *nemesis* can simply mean "an opponent." But, a reader who is aware of the other meanings of *nemesis* understands that Brin could be using the word to mean a deserved punishment that is related to the nature of the transgression. Examining the meanings of nuanced words can help you understand texts deeply, and knowing the various meanings of nuanced words can also help you be a better writer.

Practice and Apply Use a dictionary to examine the senses, or meanings, of each word from "Reality Check." Write notes about the definitions and then discuss with a partner how the words are used in the story. Does the use of these nuanced words add to the success of this science fiction story? Why?

reality (line 1)   creativity (line 33)   simulation (line 79)

Nuances in Word Meanings

COMMON CORE L 4, L 4c

Have students select other words in the story that have complex nuances. Recommend that students choose words that help convey the story's meaning. Have students work individually. Reinforce a range of word selections.

- Underline the word.
- Highlight passages in which the word occurs and in which its meaning or nuances are important.
- Write a note explaining the nuances of the word.

This is a reality check. Please perform a soft interrupt now. Scan this text for embedded <u>code</u> and check against the verifier in the blind spot of your left eye. If there is no match…this message is not for you… If the <u>codes</u> match, however, please commence gradually becoming aware of your true nature.

A computer language that some people can understand. Suggests that some people have an inborn ability to detect "reality."

Coining New Terms

COMMON CORE

L 4a, L 6

TEACH

Coining a term means inventing new words or using existing words in new ways to convey new meanings. The science fiction and fantasy genres are known for their many word coinages, invented by writers who wish to describe future developments or alternate worlds. Such worlds contain inventions, behaviors, and customs that do not already exist in reality; thus, the writer must invent names for them. When a coinage also meets a real-world need, or simply appeals to many readers, it may spread into common use. For example, Robert A. Heinlein in his novel *Stranger in a Strange Land* coined the word *grok,* meaning "to understand deeply on an emotional level." J. K. Rowling, in her Harry Potter books, coined *Muggle,* meaning a non-magical human being, and *Quidditch,* the name of a wizards' competitive ball game. The *Star Trek* television series used two already existing words in the term *warp speed,* to refer to a spaceship's very fast travel between planets.

In "Reality Check," David Brin coins terms for several phenomena in his imagined future world, including the following:

- Reality Level Prime
- The Wasteland
- Transition Era
- sub-lives

PRACTICE AND APPLY

Tell students to locate the four coinages listed above in the story. Have students write definitions for the coinages. Ask volunteers to define the words aloud. Have the class suggest revisions to make the definition more accurate, if necessary.

Analyze Story Elements: Science Fiction

COMMON CORE

RL 1, RL 3, RL 5

RETEACH

Begin by reviewing the definition of **genre**. A genre is a class of works of literature that have important general resemblances to each other, especially in subject matter. For example, in a mystery genre, detectives attempt to solve cases. Each genre tends to have its own conventions, its own typical aspects of plot, characterization, and structure.

Review that science fiction is a genre having to do with worlds that are different from ordinary reality. Science fiction authors account for these differences by describing possible scientific advances or theories. Typical subjects of science fiction include life on other worlds, time travel, and the future. The fact that science fiction stories have a basis in scientific facts or theories is what distinguishes science fiction from fantasy.

By showing a world that is different from present-day reality, science fiction comments on present-day reality. For example, a story about the aftermath of a nuclear war might be seen as a warning on the dangers of the atomic weapons.

CLOSE READING APPLICATION

Have students locate other science fiction short stories in anthologies, volumes by individual writers, print magazines, or online magazines. Ask them to skim the stories to determine the subject matter and settings of the stories. Then have them summarize their findings for the class and identify the traits that demonstrate the stories belong to the science fiction genre.

Have a volunteer take notes on the titles, authors, summaries, and traits of the stories. Ask the class to note the similarities they find among the stories chosen.

The Ends of the World as We Know Them

mySmartPlanner Create lesson plans and access resources online.

Argument by Jared Diamond

Why This Text?

We live in world that is threatened by climate change, overpopulation, and other dangers. This selection presents the argument that we do not need to fear these threats, because we can solve them if we recognize what the problems are and act decisively to correct them.

▶ **View It!**
Professional Development Podcast:
Teaching Argument

Key Learning Objective: Students will be able to understand how an author structures and presents a complex argument.

COMMON CORE Common Core Standards

RI 1 Cite textual evidence.

RI 2 Determine two or more central ideas of a text and analyze their development.

RI 5 Analyze and evaluate the effectiveness of the structure an author uses.

RI 6 Determine an author's point of view or purpose.

W 2a Introduce a topic; organize complex ideas, concepts, and information to create a unified whole.

W 2b Develop the topic thoroughly.

W 7 Conduct research projects.

SL 5 Make strategic use of digital media.

L 3 Apply knowledge of language to understand how language functions in different contexts.

L 4b Identify and correctly use patterns of word changes.

▲ Text Complexity Rubric

Quantitative Measures	**The Ends of the World as We Know Them** Lexile: 1230L

Levels of Meaning/Purpose

more than one purpose; implied, easily identified from context

Qualitative Measures

Structure

organization of main ideas and details complex but mostly explicit; may exhibit disciplinary traits

Language Conventionality and Clarity

some unfamiliar language

Knowledge Demands

somewhat complex social studies concepts

Reader/Task Considerations	Teacher determined Vary by individual reader and type of text

CLOSE READ

For more context and historical background, students can view the video "Environmental Degradation of Easter Island" in their eBooks.

Background Jared Diamond is not only a renowned author, but also a renowned explorer and scientist. He has participated in 22 expeditions to study the ecology and the evolution of birds of New Guinea and nearby islands. He developed and implemented a plan to establish New Guinea's national park system. He has also joined in numerous field projects in North and South America, Africa, Asia, and Australia. Diamond is an explorer-in-residence with the National Geographic Society.

AS YOU READ Direct students to use the As You Read question to focus their reading. Remind students to write down any questions they generate during reading.

Determine Author's Purpose (LINES 1–8)

COMMON CORE RI 6

Point out that authors often make their purpose, or reason for writing, clear in the opening paragraph of an essay. The techniques that an author uses are often clues to the purpose.

A ASK STUDENTS to read lines 1–8 and explain how Diamond appeals to readers' interest in the first paragraph. *(After stating that the United States is at the height of its power, he asks two questions about the country's future that may intrigue and worry many Americans.)* How might Diamond's technique in the opening paragraph be related to his purpose? *(His purpose could be to bring these uncomfortable questions and the issues surrounding them to readers' attention.)*

CRITICAL VOCABULARY

ascendant: Diamond says the United States seems to be at the height of its power, but that position may actually be a sign of an impending collapse or new and difficult challenges.

ASK STUDENTS in what ways is the United States ascendant in the early twenty-first century. *(Possible answer: Its military might, political influence, and many of its cultural achievements are growing.)*

Background *This selection originally appeared as an op-ed piece in the New York Times on January 1, 2005, shortly before the inauguration of George W. Bush to his second term as President of the United States.* **Jared Diamond** *(b. 1937), a professor of geography at UCLA, had earlier won the Pulitzer Prize for his book* Guns, Germs, and Steel: The Fates of Human Societies *(1997). This op-ed piece was a preview of his soon-to-be-released book* Collapse: How Societies Choose to Fail or Succeed. *Diamond is considered an expert on the evolution of human societies.*

The Ends of the World as We Know Them

Argument by Jared Diamond

AS YOU READ Notice what caused societies in the past to fail or to prosper. Write down any questions you generate during reading.

Los Angeles—NEW Year's weekend traditionally is a time for us to reflect, and to make resolutions based on our reflections. In this fresh year, with the United States seemingly at the height of its power and at the start of a new presidential term, Americans are increasingly concerned and divided about where we are going. How long can America remain **ascendant**? Where will we stand 10 years from now, or even next year?

Such questions seem especially appropriate this year. History warns us that when once-powerful societies collapse, they tend to
10 do so quickly and unexpectedly. That shouldn't come as much of a surprise: peak power usually means peak population, peak needs, and hence peak vulnerability. What can be learned from history that could help us avoid joining the ranks of those who declined swiftly? We must expect the answers to be complex, because historical reality is complex: while some societies did indeed collapse spectacularly, others have managed to thrive for thousands of years without major reversal.

When it comes to historical collapses, five groups of interacting factors have been especially important: the damage that people have

ascendant
(ə-sĕn´dənt) *adj.*
rising in influence; on
an upward path.

Image Credits: (t) ©Doris Poklekowski/AKG Images; (b) ©Melkor3D/Shutterstock

SCAFFOLDING FOR ELL STUDENTS

Hyphenated Words Call students' attention to the hyphenated words *op-ed, soon-to-be-released,* and *once-powerful.* First, explain that *op-ed* is an abbreviation of "opposite editorial page," meaning that this text originally appeared in a newspaper's opinion section. An op-ed is often written by a guest columnist.

Tell students that the other hyphenated words demonstrate a common use of hyphens in English. The hyphen is used to combine two or more words that together act as a modifier of a noun. Ask students to explain the meaning of "soon-to-be-released book" and "once-powerful societies." Have students look for more examples of this use of hyphens as they read.

CLOSE READ

COMMON CORE RI 2, RI 5

Analyze Structure: Argument from Analogy

(LINES 19–29)

Explain to students that an analogy is a form of comparison. It takes a familiar object or topic and compares it to something readers know less about. By making the comparison, readers are better able to understand the less familiar subject.

B CITE TEXT EVIDENCE Ask students to identify the two societies discussed in this passage. *(the Polynesian society on Easter Island and the Norse colonies on Greenland)* How might these societies serve as part of an analogy in Diamond's argument? *(He might compare them to other societies that collapsed as a result of the same factors. This would strengthen Diamond's argument that these factors can cause societies—including ours—to decline.)*

CRITICAL VOCABULARY

deforestation: Diamond explains that the clearing of forests was a major cause of the environmental degradation of the Yucatan.

ASK STUDENTS to explain how deforestation can affect the people living in an area. *(Possible answer: It can provide more land for homes or farms. However, it can also cause erosion, increase the effect of winds, and reduce shade, which can cause temperatures to rise.)*

---

inflicted on their environment; climate change; enemies; changes in
20　friendly trading partners; and the society's political, economic and social responses to these shifts. That's not to say that all five causes play a role in every case. Instead, think of this as a useful checklist of factors that should be examined, but whose relative importance varies from case to case.

For instance, in the collapse of the Polynesian society on Easter Island three centuries ago, environmental problems were dominant, and climate change, enemies and trade were insignificant; however, the latter three factors played big roles in the disappearance of the medieval Norse colonies on Greenland. Let's consider two examples
30　of declines stemming from different mixes of causes: the falls of classic Maya civilization and of Polynesian settlements on the Pitcairn Islands.

Maya Native Americans of the Yucatan Peninsula and adjacent parts of Central America developed the New World's most advanced civilization before Columbus. They were innovators in writing, astronomy, architecture and art. From local origins around 2,500 years ago, Maya societies rose especially after the year A.D. 250, reaching peaks of population and sophistication in the late 8th century.

Thereafter, societies in the most densely populated areas of the
40　southern Yucatan underwent a steep political and cultural collapse: between 760 and 910, kings were overthrown, large areas were abandoned, and at least 90 percent of the population disappeared, leaving cities to become overgrown by jungle. The last known date recorded on a Maya monument by their so-called Long Count calendar corresponds to the year 909. What happened?

A major factor was environmental degradation by people: **deforestation**, soil erosion and water management problems, all of which resulted in less food. Those problems were exacerbated[1] by droughts, which may have been partly caused by humans themselves
50　through deforestation. Chronic warfare made matters worse, as more and more people fought over less and less land and resources.

Why weren't these problems obvious to the Maya kings, who could surely see their forests vanishing and their hills becoming eroded? Part of the reason was that the kings were able to insulate themselves from problems afflicting the rest of society. By extracting wealth from commoners, they could remain well fed while everyone else was slowly starving.

What's more, the kings were preoccupied with their own power struggles. They had to concentrate on fighting one another and
60　keeping up their images through ostentatious[2] displays of wealth. By insulating themselves in the short run from the problems of society,

deforestation
(dē-fôr ĭ-stā´shən) *n.* deliberate cutting down and clearing of trees and forests.

---

[1] **exacerbated:** made worse.
[2] **ostentatious:** gaudy and extravagant.

APPLYING ACADEMIC VOCABULARY

global	contemporary

As you discuss reasons for the collapse of societies, incorporate the following Collection 6 academic vocabulary words: *global* and *contemporary*. Point out to students that Diamond is discussing factors that have **global** implications. Ask them to consider how a **contemporary** society might fall victim to the same problems that caused the collapse of earlier societies.

the elite merely bought themselves the privilege of being among the last to starve.

Whereas Maya societies were undone by problems of their own making, Polynesian societies on Pitcairn and Henderson Islands in the tropical Pacific Ocean were undone largely by other people's mistakes. Pitcairn, the uninhabited island settled in 1790 by the H.M.S. Bounty mutineers, had actually been populated by Polynesians 800 years earlier. That society, which left behind temple platforms, stone and
70 shell tools and huge garbage piles of fish and bird and turtle bones as evidence of its existence, survived for several centuries and then vanished. Why?

In many respects, Pitcairn and Henderson are tropical paradises, rich in some food sources and essential raw materials. Pitcairn is home to Southeast Polynesia's largest quarry of stone suited for making adzes,[3] while Henderson has the region's largest breeding seabird colony and its only nesting beach for sea turtles. Yet the islanders depended on imports from Mangareva Island, hundreds of miles away, for canoes, crops, livestock and oyster shells for making tools.

80 Unfortunately for the inhabitants of Pitcairn and Henderson, their Mangarevan trading partner collapsed for reasons similar to those underlying the Maya decline: deforestation, erosion and warfare. Deprived of essential imports in a Polynesian equivalent of the 1973 oil crisis, the Pitcairn and Henderson societies declined until everybody had died or fled.

The Maya and the Henderson and Pitcairn Islanders are not alone, of course. Over the centuries, many other societies have declined, collapsed or died out. Famous victims include the Anasazi in the American Southwest, who abandoned their cities in the 12th century
90 because of environmental problems and climate change, and the Greenland Norse, who disappeared in the 15th century because of all five interacting factors on the checklist. There were also the ancient Fertile Crescent societies, the Khmer at Angkor Wat, the Moche society of Peru—the list goes on.

But before we let ourselves get depressed, we should also remember that there is another long list of cultures that have managed to prosper for lengthy periods of time. Societies in Japan, Tonga, Tikopia, the New Guinea Highlands and Central and Northwest Europe, for example, have all found ways to sustain themselves. What
100 separates the lost cultures from those that survived? Why did the Maya fail and the shogun succeed?

Half of the answer involves environmental differences: geography deals worse cards to some societies than to others. Many of the societies that collapsed had the misfortune to occupy dry, cold or otherwise fragile environments, while many of the long-term survivors enjoyed more robust and fertile surroundings. But it's not the case that

---

[3] **adzes:** tools, somewhat similar to axes that are used for woodworking.

The Ends of the World as We Know Them **589**

CLOSE READ

Analyze Structure: Argument from Analogy

COMMON CORE RI 2, RI 5

(LINES 83–85)

Explain to students that in 1973 the oil producing nations in the Middle East reduced their production of oil, causing major shortages in the United States. The loss of this friendly trading bloc caused significant but short term economic problems.

C CITE TEXT EVIDENCE What analogy is Diamond making in this paragraph? *(He is comparing the reason for Pitcairn and Henderson's collapse to the 1973 oil crisis.)* How does the analogy help readers understand the conditions on Pitcairn and Henderson? *(By comparing their situation to a similar situation that many Americans experienced, readers can more easily understand the effect a trading partner can have on a society.)*

Analyze Structure: Argument from Analogy

COMMON CORE RI 2, RI 5

(LINES 86–94)

Tell students that in this passage Diamond explicitly compares a number of societies. However, he also makes another implicit analogy related to his argument.

D ASK STUDENTS to read lines 86–94 and explain what the societies cited in this passage have in common. *(They all collapsed or died out, mainly due to one or more of the five factors Diamond listed earlier.)* What does this list of collapsed societies suggest about the United States? *(The same factors could potentially also lead to the collapse of the United States.)*

WHEN STUDENTS STRUGGLE . . .

Before students begin reading, pass out sticky notes. Instruct students to use the sticky notes for the following:

- to write questions about a passage in the text
- to write comments on ideas in the text
- to mark unfamiliar words
- to mark sentences or passages that are not clear

As you discuss each page, have students pose their questions or issues. Encourage other students to become involved in answering the questions, clarifying passages, and responding to comments.

Draw Conclusions

COMMON CORE RI 1

(LINES 118–137)

Remind students that an inference is based on evidence and prior experience, but a conclusion requires a stronger set of evidence. Often a reader may use inferences along with some evidence and reasoning to reach a conclusion.

 CITE TEXT EVIDENCE Have students read lines 118–137. Ask them to draw conclusions about how Japan avoided the disaster that befell the Maya, Mangarevans, and Easter Islanders. *(The Japanese recognized the effect that population growth and the resulting construction boom were having on their forests and recognized the importance of the forests to Japan's future. As a result, they implemented a plan to reduce the need for timber and to control wood production and manage forests.)* How was leadership important in Japan's successful turnaround? *(The shoguns made changes in how wood was used: they changed building methods by using light-timbered construction, switched to fuel-efficient heaters and stoves, and began using coal. They increased wood production and managed plantation forests for sustainability. These steps probably required the initiative of strong and farsighted leadership to bring about a society-wide change.)*

CRITICAL VOCABULARY

rampant: Diamond explains that peace following the Tokugawa victory led to an uncontrolled building spree.

ASK STUDENTS What other kinds of rampant development might have resulted from a period of peace? *(Possible answers: rampant growth of trade, agriculture, mining, and production of luxury goods)*

---

a congenial[4] environment guarantees success: some societies (like the Maya) managed to ruin lush environments, while other societies—like the Incas, the Inuit, Icelanders and desert Australian Aborigines—

110 have managed to carry on in some of the earth's most daunting environments.

The other half of the answer involves differences in a society's responses to problems. Ninth-century New Guinea Highland villagers, 16th-century German landowners, and the Tokugawa shoguns of 17th-century Japan all recognized the deforestation spreading around them and solved the problem, either by developing scientific reforestation (Japan and Germany) or by transplanting tree seedlings (New Guinea). Conversely, the Maya, Mangarevans and Easter Islanders failed to address their forestry problems and so collapsed.

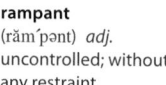

120 Consider Japan. In the 1600's, the country faced its own crisis of deforestation, paradoxically brought on by the peace and prosperity following the Tokugawa shoguns' military triumph that ended 150 years of civil war. The subsequent explosion of Japan's population and economy set off **rampant** logging for construction of palaces and cities, and for fuel and fertilizer.

rampant
(răm´pənt) *adj.*
uncontrolled; without any restraint.

The shoguns responded with both negative and positive measures. They reduced wood consumption by turning to light-timbered construction, to fuel-efficient stoves and heaters, and to coal as a source of energy. At the same time, they increased wood production

130 by developing and carefully managing plantation forests. Both the shoguns and the Japanese peasants took a long-term view: the former expected to pass on their power to their children, and the latter expected to pass on their land. In addition, Japan's isolation at the time made it obvious that the country would have to depend on its own resources and couldn't meet its needs by pillaging other countries. Today, despite having the highest human population density of any large developed country, Japan is more than 70 percent forested.

There is a similar story from Iceland. When the island was first settled by the Norse around 870, its light volcanic soils presented

140 colonists with unfamiliar challenges. They proceeded to cut down trees and stock sheep as if they were still in Norway, with its robust soils. Significant erosion ensued, carrying half of Iceland's topsoil into the ocean within a century or two. Icelanders became the poorest people in Europe. But they gradually learned from their mistakes, over time instituting stocking limits on sheep and other strict controls, and establishing an entire government department charged with landscape management. Today, Iceland boasts the sixth-highest per-capita income in the world.

What lessons can we draw from history? The most

150 straightforward: take environmental problems seriously. They destroyed societies in the past, and they are even more likely to do

---

[4] **congenial:** hospitable.

SCAFFOLDING FOR ELL STUDENTS

Find Synonyms Remind students that a synonym is a word that means the same, or nearly the same, as another word. Draw this chart on the board using words from this page. Have students write synonyms for each word. Encourage them to use a dictionary as needed.

Word	Synonym	Word	Synonym
robust	strong, healthy	pillaging	looting, plundering
fertile	fruitful, rich	daunting	discouraging, disheartening
reduced	lessened, diminished	obvious	clear, apparent

so now. If 6,000 Polynesians with stone tools were able to destroy Mangareva Island, consider what six billion people with metal tools and bulldozers are doing today. Moreover, while the Maya collapse affected just a few neighboring societies in Central America, globalization now means that any society's problems have the potential to affect anyone else. Just think how crises in Somalia, Afghanistan and Iraq have shaped the United States today.

160 Other lessons involve failures of group decision-making. There are many reasons why past societies made bad decisions, and thereby failed to solve or even to perceive the problems that would eventually destroy them. One reason involves conflicts of interest, whereby one group within a society (for instance, the pig farmers who caused the worst erosion in medieval Greenland and Iceland) can profit by engaging in practices that damage the rest of society. Another is the pursuit of short-term gains at the expense of long-term survival, as when fishermen overfish the stocks on which their livelihoods ultimately depend.

History also teaches us two deeper lessons about what separates
170 successful societies from those heading toward failure. A society contains a built-in blueprint for failure if the elite insulates itself from the consequences of its actions. That's why Maya kings, Norse Greenlanders and Easter Island chiefs made choices that eventually undermined their societies. They themselves did not begin to feel deprived until they had irreversibly destroyed their landscape.

WHEN STUDENTS STRUGGLE...

Understand the Use of Transitions Explain that writers often use transitional devices—words or phrases—to show how ideas are connected. These transitional words may show techniques such as cause and effect, sequence, comparison, or contrast. Discuss the connections between the ideas in the passage below. Ask them to identify other transitional words in the text on these two pages.

> <u>Another</u> is the pursuit of short-term gains at the expense of long-term
>
> survival, <u>as when</u> fishermen overfish the stocks. . . .

Analyze Structure: Argument from Analogy

COMMON CORE RI 2, RI 5

(LINES 149–154)

Explain that when readers analyze an author's argument, they evaluate all the evidence that is presented and then use their judgment and reasoning to decide whether they agree or disagree with a particular claim. In the case of an analogy, readers must decide whether or not the similarities presented are convincing.

F CITE TEXT EVIDENCE What evidence does Diamond give to support his claim that environmental disasters are even more likely to occur in the future than they have in the past? *(People today have metal tools and bulldozers with which to destroy the land even faster than stone tools used by people in the past. Globalization means environmental disasters that were once local may now have consequences for nations all over the world.)* How does this evidence support the analogies Diamond has been using? *(They add more information and build on the precedent established by the historical examples in the analogies to predict the future.)*

Analyze Structure: Argument from Analogy

COMMON CORE RI 2, RI 5

(LINES 159–168)

Explain to students that the analogies Diamond draws provide strong evidence for his arguments because they are actual historical cases rather than theoretical examples. In this passage, he uses two examples to illustrate his point about failures in group decision-making.

G ASK STUDENTS how pig farming in Greenland and overfishing are examples of failures in group decision-making. *(Both of these examples demonstrate that when society fails to plan, individuals act in their own best interests, which may damage the welfare and sustainability of the society as a whole.)* How could the lesson learned from these examples be applied as an analogy to the United States? *(If American society does not make difficult decisions for the good of the society as a whole, the actions of groups with particular interests may cause damage.)*

TEACH

CLOSE READ

Analyze Structure: Argument from Analogy

COMMON CORE RI 2, RI 5

(LINES 175–186)

Point out Diamond's use of the examples of the Maya kings, Norse Greenlanders, and Easter Island chiefs, and the lessons learned from these cases.

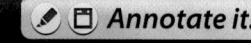 **CITE TEXT EVIDENCE** What analogy is drawn between these societies and the United States today? *(Just as leaders failed to deal with destructive forces, gated communities in LA isolated themselves until directly threatened by rioters.)* How does this analogy support Diamond's argument? *(The United States could be on the path to destruction unless it changes its ways.)*

CRITICAL VOCABULARY

deteriorate: Isolated leaders may act in ways that cause conditions within a society to grow worse.

ASK STUDENTS What events have caused societies to deteriorate? *(failure of the water management system, climate change, deforestation, overfishing)*

Draw Conclusions

COMMON CORE RI 1

(LINES 196–203)

Conclusions are based on information in the text, as well as background knowledge and inferences.

ASK STUDENTS what conclusion they can draw about how the Inuit survived. *(mainly by hunting, which wasn't affected by climate change or trade)*

Could this happen in the United States? It's a thought that often occurs to me here in Los Angeles, when I drive by gated communities, guarded by private security patrols, and filled with people who drink bottled water, depend on private pensions, and send their children
180 to private schools. By doing these things, they lose the motivation to support the police force, the municipal water supply, Social Security and public schools. If conditions **deteriorate** too much for poorer people, gates will not keep the rioters out. Rioters eventually burned the palaces of Maya kings and tore down the statues of Easter Island chiefs; they have also already threatened wealthy districts in Los Angeles twice in recent decades.

In contrast, the elite in 17th-century Japan, as in modern Scandinavia and the Netherlands, could not ignore or insulate themselves from broad societal problems. For instance, the Dutch
190 upper class for hundreds of years has been unable to insulate itself from the Netherlands' water management problems for a simple reason: the rich live in the same drained lands below sea level as the poor. If the dikes and pumps keeping out the sea fail, the well-off Dutch know that they will drown along with everybody else, which is precisely what happened during the floods of 1953.

The other deep lesson involves a willingness to re-examine long-held core values, when conditions change and those values no longer make sense. The medieval Greenland Norse lacked such a willingness: they continued to view themselves as transplanted Norwegian
200 pastoralists, and to despise the Inuit as pagan hunters, even after Norway stopped sending trading ships and the climate had grown too cold for a pastoral existence. They died off as a result, leaving Greenland to the Inuit. On the other hand, the British in the 1950's faced up to the need for a painful reappraisal[5] of their former status as rulers of a world empire set apart from Europe. They are now finding a different avenue to wealth and power, as part of a united Europe.

In this New Year, we Americans have our own painful reappraisals to face. Historically, we viewed the United States as a land of unlimited plenty, and so we practiced unrestrained consumerism, but that's
210 no longer viable in a world of finite resources. We can't continue to deplete our own resources as well as those of much of the rest of the world.

Historically, oceans protected us from external threats; we stepped back from our isolationism only temporarily during the crises of two world wars. Now, technology and global interconnectedness have robbed us of our protection. In recent years, we have responded to foreign threats largely by seeking short-term military solutions at the last minute.

But how long can we keep this up? Though we are the richest
220 nation on earth, there's simply no way we can afford (or muster the

deteriorate
(dĭ-tîr´ē-ə-rāt´) v.
become worse;
decline.

---

[5] **reappraisal:** reevaluation, or second assessment.

Strategies for Annotation ✎ 🖽 *Annotate it!*

Cite Text Evidence

COMMON CORE RI 1, SL 5

Remind students that Diamond argues societies must sometimes re-examine their values and he suggests the United States may have to do so as well. Have students use their eBook annotation tools to highlight the evidence for this conclusion in green.

> In this New Year, we Americans have our own painful reappraisals to face. Historically, we viewed the United States as a land of unlimited plenty, and so we practiced unrestrained consumerism, but that's no longer viable in a world of finite resources. We can't continue to deplete our own resources as well as those of much of the rest of the world.

troops) to intervene in the dozens of countries where emerging threats lurk—particularly when each intervention these days can cost more than $100 billion and require more than 100,000 troops.

A genuine reappraisal would require us to recognize that it will be far less expensive and far more effective to address the underlying problems of public health, population and environment that ultimately cause threats to us to emerge in poor countries. In the past, we have regarded foreign aid as either charity or as buying support; now, it's an act of self-interest to preserve our own economy and protect American
230 lives.

Do we have cause for hope? Many of my friends are pessimistic when they contemplate the world's growing population and human demands colliding with shrinking resources. But I draw hope from the knowledge that humanity's biggest problems today are ones entirely of our own making. Asteroids hurtling at us beyond our control don't figure high on our list of **imminent** dangers. To save ourselves, we don't need new technology: we just need the political will to face up to our problems of population and the environment.

I also draw hope from a unique advantage that we enjoy. Unlike
240 any previous society in history, our global society today is the first with the opportunity to learn from the mistakes of societies remote from us in space and in time. When the Maya and Mangarevans were cutting down their trees, there were no historians or archaeologists, no newspapers or television, to warn them of the consequences of their actions. We, on the other hand, have a detailed chronicle of human successes and failures at our disposal. Will we choose to use it?

imminent
(ĭm´ə-nənt) *adj.*
about to happen;
impending.

COLLABORATIVE DISCUSSION Choose two of the societies that Diamond describes. What is most striking about why these societies failed or prospered? Discuss this question with a partner, citing specific evidence from the selection to support your ideas.

TEACH

CLOSE READ

Draw Conclusions
COMMON CORE RI 1

(LINES 216–223)

Remind students that they can use evidence from the passage to draw conclusions.

J **CITE TEXT EVIDENCE** What evidence does Diamond cite about U.S. military operations today? *(A single military intervention can require more than 100,000 troops and cost more than $100 billion.)* What conclusion can you draw based on this evidence? *(The United States cannot afford to depend on military solutions to foreign threats to its security.)*

CRITICAL VOCABULARY

imminent: Diamond states that the threat of asteroids hitting earth is not among our most impending disasters.

ASK STUDENTS What are some disasters that Diamond might consider imminent? *(Possible response: overpopulation, overuse of resources, war, climate change, damage to the environment)*

COLLABORATIVE DISCUSSION Working in pairs, have students choose two societies that Diamond describes and identify the most striking causes of their success or failure. Ask them to discuss the evidence that supports their ideas.

ASK STUDENTS to share any questions they generated in the course of reading and discussing this selection.

SCAFFOLDING FOR ELL STUDENTS

Understand the Suffix -*tion* Write these words from the page above on the board:

intervention   population   protection   solution   actions

Underline the suffix -*tion* in each word. Explain that this suffix can be added to a verb to change it into a noun. Identify the verb used to form each of these nouns. *(intervene, populate, protect, solve, act)* Point out that the spellings of some of the base words have changed.

Ask students to work in pairs and write a definition for each of the verbs and each of the nouns. Then have them use each noun in a sentence.

PRACTICE & APPLY

Analyze Structure: Argument from Analogy

COMMON CORE RI 2, RI 5

Emphasize to students that an analogy is a type of comparison in which an unfamiliar topic, idea, or item is compared to one that is familiar. The analogy helps readers understand the unfamiliar item.

Provide some simple analogies, such as the following:

> A typewriter was to an early twentieth century writer what the computer is to today's writer.

Explain that Jared Diamond uses more sophisticated analogies to explain a complicated subject and to support his ideas about the reasons for the collapse of societies.

Analyzing the Text

COMMON CORE RI 2, RI 5, RI 6, W 2a, W 2b, W 7, SL 5

Answers:

1. *Diamond uses the analogy of a checklist. It helps readers understand that each of these factors should be considered in trying to figure out why different societies collapsed, but they will not all apply in every case.*

2. *Compared to societies that failed, societies that prospered enjoyed more fertile lands and responded more effectively to problems.*

3. *The structure is effective because it draws on concrete facts and evidence to support the lessons, which in turn support the argument. However, it is possible that this structure ignores differences between societies that might make Diamond's comparisons less valid.*

4. *Diamond makes the argument that unlike historical societies, today's global society can look back on the lessons of history, learn how and why older societies failed, and figure out what we can do today to save our civilization. He uses the rhetorical device of closing with a question to persuade readers that the future is up to them. This technique suggests that they must choose whether or not to study the historical record and apply the lessons learned.*

Analyze Structure: Argument from Analogy

COMMON CORE RI 2, RI 5

Jared Diamond structures his argument by presenting a series of analogies. An analogy is a point-by-point comparison between two things used to clarify the less familiar of the two. Diamond uses analogies comparing past societies and contemporary societies as evidence to support his position on what causes societies to fail or to prosper. Consider this example of what happened to two Polynesian islands:

> **Deprived of essential imports in a Polynesian equivalent of the 1973 oil crisis, the Pitcairn and Henderson societies declined until everybody had died or fled.**

In these lines, the lack of imports is compared to the lack of oil during the 1973 oil crisis. Throughout the selection, Diamond uses inductive reasoning, arguing from specific examples and facts to general conclusions. For example, Diamond draws a general conclusion about the decline of the Pitcairn and Henderson societies from specific information about their lack of imports. These analogies make Diamond's points clear, convincing, and engaging for readers.

Analyzing the Text

COMMON CORE RI 2, RI 5, RI 6, W 2a, W 2b, W 7, SL 5

Cite Text Evidence   Support your responses with evidence from the selection.

1. **Compare** What analogy does Diamond use to explain how the five groups of interacting factors in lines 17–21 should be considered? How does this analogy help create a frame for the ideas that follow?

2. **Compare** What were the characteristics of societies that prospered compared to those that failed in the past?

3. **Evaluate** Diamond structures his argument to describe societies that failed and societies that prospered, while drawing conclusions about the lessons these analogies can teach us. How effective is this structure in building a convincing argument?

4. **Analyze** What argument does Diamond make in his final paragraph? What rhetorical device does he use to help persuade his readers?

PERFORMANCE TASK

Media Activity: Presentation Adapt part of the selection into a multimedia presentation.

- Work with a small group and decide on the topic(s) of your presentation. Conduct research to find the most relevant visuals, sound, and graphics to enhance Diamond's ideas.

- Decide how you will present Diamond's words, such as using narration or captions, and how to combine media to help readers understand.

- Use appropriate software to create your presentation and share it with your classmates.

Assign this performance task.

PERFORMANCE TASK

COMMON CORE SL 5

Media Activity: Presentation Organize students into small groups and direct them to identify a section of the selection to develop into a multi-media presentation. As they do research, remind them to look for reliable sources and to take accurate, complete source information. Review, as necessary, the types of multimedia resources available.

Critical Vocabulary

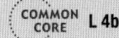

ascendant	deforestation	rampant
deteriorate	imminent	

Practice and Apply Answer each question in a way that demonstrates your understanding of the Critical Vocabulary word in each sentence.

1. Does **rampant** logging improve the environment?
2. What problems might an **ascendant** society face?
3. What are some of the economic factors that lead to **deforestation**?
4. What would be an appropriate response to an **imminent** threat?
5. Should you be worried if your friend's health **deteriorated**?

Vocabulary Strategy: Patterns of Word Change

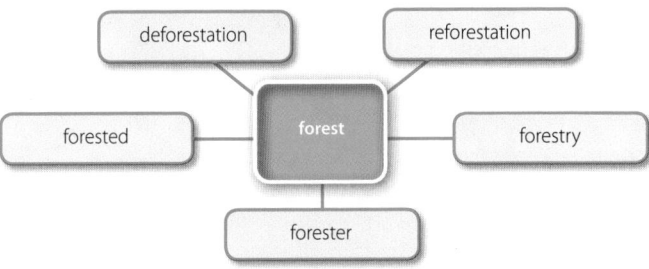

The Critical Vocabulary word *deforestation* is an example of a word built by adding a prefix, *de-*, and a suffix, *-ation*, to the base word *forest*. As the word web shows, other prefixes and suffixes can be added to the base to create related words with a variety of meanings and parts of speech.

Practice and Apply Work with a partner to brainstorm a list of potential new words based on the root words below. Add prefixes and suffixes to each base to change its meaning or part of speech. You may use other prefixes and suffixes in addition to those shown in the word web above. Consult a dictionary as needed to confirm correct spellings and meanings.

1. cover	3. public	5. trust
2. act	4. move	

PRACTICE & APPLY

Critical Vocabulary

Possible answers:

1. *No, because rampant logging would destroy forests.*

2. *An ascendant society might face problems of needing to learn how to deal with a growing population, rapidly expanding business, and suddenly increasing wealth.*

3. *Deforestation might result when demand for lumber is high, whether for firewood, building materials, or other uses. Such increased demand could require a greater timber harvest than could be sustained.*

4. *An appropriate response to an imminent threat might be to fight it, flee from it, or make plans to resolve it right away.*

5. *You should be concerned if a friend's health deteriorated because it would be getting worse.*

Vocabulary Strategy: Patterns of Word Change

Possible answers:

1. *recovery, coverage, covering, uncovered*

2. *inaction, reactive, activity, activation*

3. *republic, publication, publisher, publicity*

4. *remove, moved, mover, removal*

5. *trusted, untrustworthy, trusty, entrust*

Strategies for Annotation   ✏️ 🖥 *Annotate it!*

Patterns of Word Change

Assign a short passage to pairs of students. Then share these strategies for analysis of patterns of word change:

- Highlight in yellow any words built by adding a prefix. Highlight in blue any words built by adding a suffix.
- Highlight in pink any words built by adding a prefix and a suffix.
- Have students write each word and underline the base word. Then change the base words by adding other prefixes or suffixes. Ask them to define the meaning of each new word.

The other deep lesson involves a willingness to re-examine long held core values....The medieval Greenland Norse lacked such a willingness: they continued to view themselves as transplanted Norwegian pastoralists, and to despise the Inuit as pagan hunters...

Language and Style: Informative Writing

COMMON CORE W 2b, L 3

Discuss the types of information included in the chart and ensure students understand how the analysis draws together other types of information and tells what it means. Remind students that relevant facts must relate to and support the thesis. Concrete details often add substance to broader facts. Statements that synthesize information express larger ideas based on the relevant facts and concrete details. You may wish to select an additional passage and have students work in pairs to analyze it and identify the relevant facts, concrete details, and statements that synthesize the information.

Answers: *Students should complete a thoughtful analysis of their multimedia presentation to determine if they have included the most relevant facts and concrete details and have provided their audience with a meaningful synthesis of that information.*

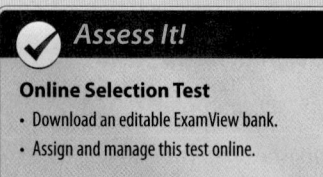

Assess It!

Online Selection Test
- Download an editable ExamView bank.
- Assign and manage this test online.

Language and Style: Informative Writing

COMMON CORE W 2b, L 3

By its nature, informative writing can present readers with an almost infinite amount of unfamiliar information. In this selection, Jared Diamond presents information about past societies that was likely unknown to most readers before reading the selection. Therefore, Diamond is writing for a broad audience and needs to present unfamiliar information so that it will be clear and engaging.

Reread lines 138–148 in the text. Depending on their purpose and audience, writers use different types of information to develop their topics. In general, writers try to include significant and relevant information to help their audience understand the text's topic and central ideas. The chart shows how Diamond developed the topic of Iceland's long-term survival by including relevant facts, concrete details, and other appropriate information. Other elements a writer might use to make a topic clearer to readers could include extended definitions and quotations.

Type of Information	Example
Relevant facts	• "settled by the Norse around 870" • half the topsoil eroded within 200 years or so • "poorest people in Europe" • "an entire government department charged with landscape management" • now the sixth-highest per-capita income in the world
Concrete details	• "light volcanic soils" • topsoil carried into the ocean • "instituted stocking limits on sheep"
Analysis that synthezises information for readers	• Iceland was settled by Norwegians unfamiliar with the type of soil there. • The soil in Iceland was different from the soil in Norway. • Iceland learned from its mistakes over time and corrected them.

Practice and Apply Review the multimedia presentation you created in response to this selection's Performance Task to see if you developed your topic by selecting the most significant and relevant facts, concrete details, quotations, and other information that your audience needs to know to understand the topic fully. Revise the presentation as needed.

Determine Author's Purpose

COMMON CORE

RI 6, W 2a, W 2b

TEACH

Explain to students that an author's purpose is his or her reason for writing. An author usually writes for one of four basic different reasons. He or she may write to entertain, to inform, to persuade, or to express ideas and feelings. Often an author's purpose may include more than one of these.

Tell students that it is important to understand an author's purpose because it will help them identify the main idea and important details in a text. It will also help them know how to respond to the text. For instance, if students know the author is writing to persuade, they may judge the facts and opinions presented in a different light than if the author is writing to entertain.

To determine an author's purpose, tell students to look for clues as they read. For example, they should consider the title of the selection, the images, and the author's choice of words and details. Encourage students to ask themselves questions, such as the following:

- Does the writer include humorous descriptions?
- Does the text include lots of facts, examples, anecdotes, or reasons?
- Does the writer use persuasive strategies or language?
- Does the writer want the reader to feel or think differently or to take some action?
- Does the writer share his or her feelings and thoughts?

PRACTICE AND APPLY

Have students review the selection and identify clues to the author's purpose. Then ask them to share the clues they have found in pairs or small groups and to discuss what those clues tell them about the author's purpose.

Finally, have students write a summary of the author's purpose in this selection. Tell them to include answers to these questions:

- What clues to the author's purpose did I find?
- What is Diamond's purpose?
- How does knowing Diamond's purpose influence my response to the text?

Draw Conclusions

COMMON CORE

RI 1

RETEACH

Review the skill of drawing conclusions by explaining that a conclusion is a judgment about something based on evidence, experience, and reasoning.

Remind students that there are three steps in drawing a conclusion:

1. Examine the evidence.
2. Make inferences based on the evidence and on what they already know about the topic.
3. Draw a conclusion from the evidence and inferences.

Tell students that drawing a conclusion will give them new information about the text, so it will add to their understanding. Caution them, however, to be sure their conclusion is well-founded on solid evidence and careful reasoning.

 **LEVEL UP TUTORIALS** Assign the following *Level Up* tutorial: **Drawing Conclusions.**

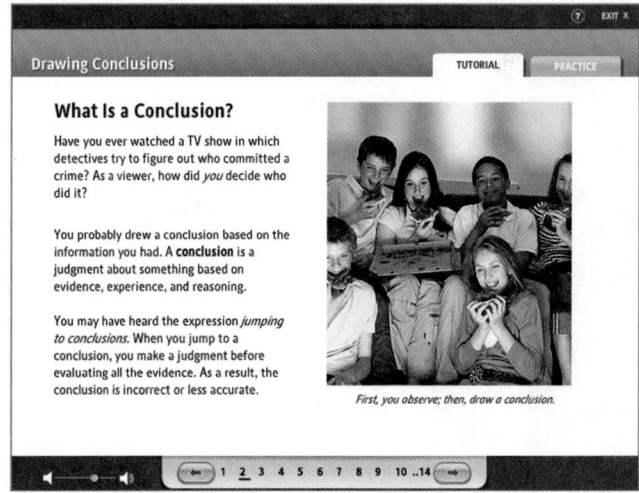

CLOSE READING APPLICATION

Students can apply the skill of drawing conclusions to "The Ends of the World as We Know Them." Have them choose one or two pages from the selection and study the facts and other evidence Diamond provides. Have them think about what this information means, drawing any inferences they can, and then draw a conclusion. Ask students to share their conclusions in small group discussion.

*my*SmartPlanner Create lesson plans and access resources online.

The Universe as Primal Scream

Poem by Tracy K. Smith

Why This Text?

Students often come across imagery, allusions, idioms, and personification in songs, books, and all types of media. This lesson explores how these devices are used by a Pulitzer Prize winning poet in a poem that investigates eternal questions about life and death.

Key Learning Objective: The student will be able to analyze language in poetry.

COMMON CORE Common Core Standards

RL 1 Cite textual evidence.

RL 2 Determine themes of a text.

RL 4 Determine figurative and connotative meanings; analyze the impact of specific word choices.

RL 5 Analyze how an author's choices concerning how to structure specific parts of a text contribute to its overall meaning as well as its aesthetic impact.

W 1 Write arguments.

W 10 Write routinely.

L 5a Interpret figures of speech.

L 5b Analyze nuances.

▲ Text Complexity Rubric

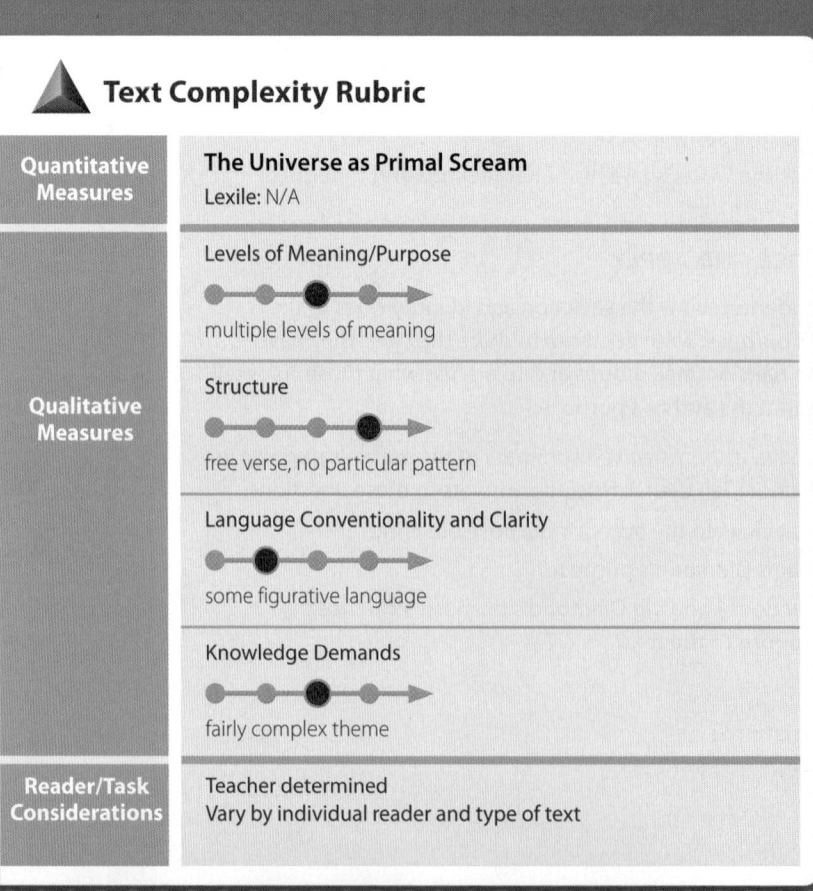

	The Universe as Primal Scream
Quantitative Measures	Lexile: N/A
Qualitative Measures	**Levels of Meaning/Purpose** multiple levels of meaning
	Structure free verse, no particular pattern
	Language Conventionality and Clarity some figurative language
	Knowledge Demands fairly complex theme
Reader/Task Considerations	Teacher determined Vary by individual reader and type of text

Tracy K. Smith Have students read the background information about the author. Tell them that Tracy K. Smith went to Harvard University and earned a Master of Fine Arts degree from Columbia University. Smith's writing has won many awards, including a 2005 Whiting Award, the 2006 James Laughlin Award for the Academy of American Poets, and a 2008 Essence Literary Award. She also received a Stegner Fellowship at Stanford University. She lives in Brooklyn, New York and teaches creative writing at Princeton University.

AS YOU READ Direct students to use the As You Read instructions to focus their reading. Remind students to write down any questions they generate during reading.

Analyze Language (LINES 1–4)   COMMON CORE **RL 4**

Discuss with students the opening lines of the poem. Make sure that students understand the basic situation that is being described. Point out the use of **idioms**, explaining that they are informal expressions that have a meaning different from what the individual words suggest.

A CITE TEXT EVIDENCE Have students point out the idioms that the speaker uses in these lines. *(line 1: on the nose; line 4: let loose)* Ask students how these idioms affect the tone of the poem. *(The poem's tone is informal.)*

Analyze Language   COMMON CORE **RL 4**
(LINES 10–15)

Point out that poets use **imagery** to appeal to readers' senses.

B CITE TEXT EVIDENCE Have students reread lines 10–15. Ask them to tell what the speaker is imagining. *(She imagines that the neighbor is proud to have such strong, healthy, loud children. She also imagines the children's screams getting so loud that the building will take off.)* Then ask what sense (or senses) she is appealing to. *(The phrase "pink lungs" appeals to sight; "magic decibel" appeals to hearing; "whole building will lift-off and we'll ride to glory" appeals mainly to sight.)*

Tracy K. Smith *was born in Falmouth, Massachusetts, in 1972. This poem is from her collection* Life on Mars, *for which she won the 2012 Pulitzer Prize. In her poems, Smith delves into ideas about the universe and the future. Her influences include science fiction, movies (such as* 2001: A Space Odyssey*), and even music (the collection's title is borrowed from a David Bowie song). She describes the book as an elegy for her late father, who was an engineer for the Hubble Telescope, and spent many years exploring the mysteries of the universe.*

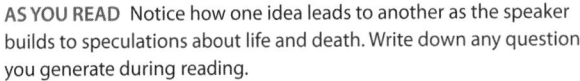

The Universe as Primal Scream

Poem by Tracy K. Smith

AS YOU READ Notice how one idea leads to another as the speaker builds to speculations about life and death. Write down any questions you generate during reading.

> 5pm on the nose. They open their mouths
> And it rolls out: high, shrill and metallic.
> First the boy, then his sister. Occasionally,
> They both let loose at once, and I think
> 5 Of putting on my shoes to go up and see
> Whether it is merely an experiment
> Their parents have been conducting
> Upon the good crystal, which must surely
> Lie shattered to dust on the floor.
>
> 10 Maybe the mother is still proud
> Of the four pink lungs she nursed
> To such might. Perhaps, if they hit
> The magic decibel, the whole building
> Will lift-off, and we'll ride to glory
> 15 Like Elijah.[1] If this is it—if this is what
> Their cries are cocked toward—let the sky

---

[1] **Elijah** (ĭ-lī´jə): Biblical prophet who ascended to heaven in a burning chariot.

Image Credits: (t) ©Jason DeCrow/AP Images; (b) ©Jodie Griggs/Flickr Select/Getty Images

SCAFFOLDING FOR ELL STUDENTS

Analyze Words Discuss with students the title of the poem and point out that it is a simile comparing the universe to a primal scream. If students are unfamiliar with the term *primal scream*, have them first analyze the word *primal* and name other words with the root *prim-*. Write their suggestions on the board. *(primitive, primary, primate, prime)*

After discussing the different words with the root *prim-*, point out to students that the Latin root means "first" or "original."

ASK STUDENTS to discuss what a first or original scream would be and what it might sound like. Encourage them to think of how this image works with the speaker's other ideas about life, time, and the universe in the poem.

Pass from blue, to red, to molten gold,
To black. Let the heaven we inherit approach.

Whether it is our dead in Old Testament robes,
20 Or a door opening onto the roiling infinity of space.
Whether it will bend down to greet us like a father,
Or swallow us like a furnace. I'm ready
To meet what refuses to let us keep anything
For long. What teases us with blessings,
25 Bends us with grief. Wizard, thief, the great
Wind rushing to knock our mirrors to the floor,
To sweep our short lives clean. How mean²

Our racket seems beside it. My stereo on shuffle.
The neighbor chopping onions through a wall.
30 All of it just a hiccough against what may never
Come for us. And the kids upstairs still at it,
Screaming like the Dawn of Man,³ as if something
They have no name for has begun to insist
Upon being born.

---

² **mean:** inferior or shabby.
³ **Screaming like the Dawn of Man:** an allusion to the opening segment of the 1968 film *2001: A Space Odyssey*, which features shouting, ape-like creatures.

COLLABORATIVE DISCUSSION What insights about the cycle of life does Smith express? Cite specific textual evidence from the text to support your ideas.

Analyze Language

COMMON CORE RL 4

(LINES 21–26)

Explain to students that **personification** is a literary device in which something that is not human is given human characteristics.

 **CITE TEXT EVIDENCE** Have students reread lines 21–26 and ask them to find examples of personification. *(line 21: "it will bend down to greet us like a father;" lines 23–24: "…refuses to let us keep anything/ for long," lines 24–25: "teases us with blessings,/bends us with grief")* Have students discuss what is being personified in these lines. *(Possible answers: God, the universe, heaven, fate)*

Analyze Language

COMMON CORE RL 4

(LINES 31–34)

Discuss with students that an **allusion** is a reference to another famous work of art, such as a book, a song, or a movie. Allusions may also refer to a person, place, or event in history or mythology.

D ASK STUDENTS to reread lines 31–34 and pay attention to the footnote below the poem that explains the allusion. Ask students why they think the poet includes an allusion to this work. *(Smith's poem uses images from science, space, and science fiction to explore ideas about the universe and eternity.)* How does the allusion relate to the title of the poem? *(The allusion refers to apes in the movie screaming, while the title compares the universe to a primal, or primitive, scream.)*

COLLABORATIVE DISCUSSION Have students work in small groups to discuss Smith's insights about the cycle of life. Ask students to cite specific evidence from the poem in their discussions. Then have groups share their conclusions with the class as a whole. Accept all reasonable responses.

ASK STUDENTS to share any questions they generated in the course of reading and discussing the selection.

WHEN STUDENTS STRUGGLE...

Develop Reading Fluency Use the third and fourth stanzas of the poem (lines 19–34) to give students practice in reading poetry. Remind them that reading poetry is different from reading stories because poetry must be read slowly and with attention to rhythm as well as punctuation. Tell them that fluent readers read poetry with expression.

ASK STUDENTS to work in pairs to practice reading lines 19–34 of the poem. Conclude the activity by asking students to discuss whether reading the poem out loud enhanced their comprehension.

Analyze Language

 **COMMON CORE** RL 4, L 5a

To understand the message of a poem like "The Universe as Primal Scream," it is important to analyze the language the author has used. The author's word choices help to build the poem's meaning by setting the tone and mood, by revealing key information about the speaker, and by triggering associations in the mind of the reader or listener. Use this chart to analyze the language Tracy K. Smith uses in "The Universe as Primal Scream."

Language Choices	Analyzing Meaning
An **idiom** is an informal expression that means something other than the literal meaning of its individual words; for example, (line 1) "5pm on the nose."	• What does the use of idioms suggest about the speaker? • What image does the idiom convey? How does this affect the tone and mood?
Imagery is the use of words that appeal to the senses of sight, sound, touch, taste, or smell; for example, (line 2) a sound that is "high, shrill, and metallic."	• What **connotations**, or emotional associations, do these words convey? • What sound, or what mental picture, does the description create in the reader's imagination? • How does this imagery help the reader participate in what the speaker is experiencing?
An **allusion** is a brief reference to a historic, literary, popular, or mythical person, place, or event; for example, (lines 14–15) "we'll ride to glory/ Like Elijah."	• Recall what you know about this person or event. • Consider what the allusion reveals about the speaker's state of mind, frame of reference, thoughts, or mood. • How does the allusion connect to the global subject of the poem?
Personification is a type of figurative language that attributes human characteristics to objects, animals, or abstract ideas; for example, (line 18) "Let the heaven we inherit approach."	• What picture does this create in the reader's mind? • What does this comparison to a person reveal about the speaker's attitude toward the infinite and unknowable?

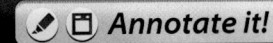 The Universe as Primal Scream **599**

 **TEACH**

CLOSE READ

Analyze Language

COMMON CORE RL 4, L 5a

Discuss the terms with students and have them read through the questions. Then have volunteers share their responses.

Possible answers:

- *The use of idioms suggests that the speaker is an ordinary person.*
- *The idiom conveys the image of something happening at a particular time of day. It sets an informal but precise tone and a mood of anticipation.*
- *The words "high, shrill, and metallic" have connotations of alarm.*
- *The description creates the sound of a piercing whistle, like a teakettle.*
- *The imagery helps the reader feel the irritation that the speaker is experiencing.*
- *Elijah was a biblical prophet and rode to heaven in a whirlwind.*
- *The allusion shows the speaker is thinking of heaven, and the global subject of the poem, which is the place of humans in eternity.*
- *The personification creates a picture of "heaven" coming to meet the speaker.*
- *The comparison to a person suggests that the speaker thinks of the infinite and unknowable as something with a will.*

Strategies for Annotation 🖊️ 📖 *Annotate it!*

Analyze Language

COMMON CORE RL 4, L 5a

Share these strategies for guided or independent analysis.

- Highlight in yellow the idioms that Smith uses.
- Highlight in blue the imagery in the poem.
- Underline any allusions in the poem.
- Highlight in green examples of personification in the poem.

> They both let loose at once, and I think
>
> Of putting on my shoes to go up and see
>
> Whether it is merely an experiment their parents have been conducting
>
> Upon the good crystal, which must surely
>
> Lie shattered to dust on the floor.

PRACTICE & APPLY

Analyzing the Text
COMMON CORE · RL 1, RL 2, RL 4, RL 5, L 5b, W 10

Possible answers:

1. Smith's diction, including the words "metallic," "experiment," and "conducting," suggest that she views life scientifically. The words bring to mind images of laboratories.

2. Smith chose the time 5 p.m. because that is the traditional end of the workday and beginning of the evening or night. This twilight time may connect to her theme of the beginning and end of life (and the universe).

3. The image of "four pink lungs" suggests the youth of the children and the force of their screams. It also shows the speaker metaphorically dissecting them, looking at the body parts that make the screams possible.

4. Lines 12–14: The imagery is that if the screams grow to just the right loudness, the building will take off from the ground. Lines 14–15: The imagery suggests that, like Elijah in the Bible, the inhabitants of the building will rise to the heavens. Lines 16–18: The imagery is that of the building's passing through the sky, which turns from blue to red (nearer the sun) to molten gold (like the sun) to black (space). Line 18: The imagery suggests the skies and the afterlife.

5. The speaker seems to be hoping to see what lies beyond our everyday existence on Earth. She hopes that whatever it is will be like a kind father, but she fears it will be destructive, like a furnace.

6. The speaker means that her ideas and feelings change as unpredictably as songs shuffled randomly by a player.

7. The allusion to 2001: A Space Odyssey suggests that the children's screams are a prelude to our journey into eternity or oblivion.

 **Assess It!**

Online Selection Test
- Download an editable ExamView bank.
- Assign and manage this test online.

Analyzing the Text
COMMON CORE · RL 1, RL 2, RL 4, RL 5, L 5b, W 10

Cite Text Evidence Support your responses with evidence from the selection.

1. **Analyze** Consider Smith's **diction,** or word choice, in the first stanza. What do the words "metallic," "experiment," and "conducting" suggest about the speaker? What images do these words suggest?

2. **Infer** Why did Smith choose "5pm" as the time for the events in this poem? What might be the connection between this time and her theme?

3. **Draw Conclusions** Reread lines 10–12, in which the speaker refers to the boy and girl as "four pink lungs." Think about this image and explain why the author chose to use this phrase.

4. **Analyze** In the second stanza, the speaker begins to speculate about the possible effects of the children's screams. Explain the meaning of the imagery in each of the following passages:
   - lines 12–14 ("Perhaps . . . Will lift off")
   - lines 14–15 ("we'll ride . . . Like Elijah.")
   - lines 16–18 ("let the sky . . . To black.")
   - line 18 ("Let the heaven . . . approach.")

5. **Analyze** What is the speaker hoping for in the third stanza (lines 19–27)? What does the careful list of possible scenarios reveal about the speaker's doubts and anxieties?

6. **Infer** What does the speaker mean by the phrase "My stereo on shuffle" in line 28? What does this suggest about the speaker's state of mind?

7. **Interpret** In lines 27–34, the speaker juxtaposes the ideas and events in her poem with the primal screams at the beginning of the movie *2001: A Space Odyssey*. In that film, the savage screams of apes act as a prelude to a futuristic voyage of discovery. What does this allusion suggest about the screaming of "the kids upstairs"?

PERFORMANCE TASK

Writing Activity: Summary Evaluate how the author's use of sound imagery helps to reveal the meaning of the poem.

1. Make a list of the sounds that the author describes throughout the poem.

2. Note the connotative meanings associated with the sound images.

3. Write a one-page summary of your analysis of the poem's sound imagery. Include evidence from the text and use the conventions of standard English.

Assign this performance task.

PERFORMANCE TASK
COMMON CORE · W 10

Writing Activity: Summary Have students work independently as they make their lists of sounds in the poems. Suggest that they review the bulleted questions about Imagery on p. 599 as they think about the connotative meanings of the sound images. When students have completed their drafts, have them share their summaries in a small group and offer constructive feedback.

Analyze Language: Allusions

COMMON CORE

RL 4, L 5b

TEACH

Discuss with students that when making allusions, authors usually use short, indirect references. Ask students why authors might use allusions. *(Possible answer: Authors use allusions to connect their work with the wider world and to associate their work with the feelings and ideas evoked by what is being referred to.)* Discuss some of the things authors might allude to in a poem, such as the following:

- **People, places, and events in history.** Historical allusions might also consist of words spoken by historical figures.

- **Figures, places, and events in mythology and religion.** In American literature, authors frequently make allusions to the Bible and classical mythology.

- **Figures, places, events, and images depicted in works of art, including paintings, sculptures, and illustrations.** For example, an author might refer to a character's Mona Lisa smile or to someone musing like Rodin's Thinker.

- **Characters, places, events, and lines or titles of novels, lyrics, movies, plays, and poetry.** Popular characters like Romeo can serve as a point of reference, as can well-known lines.

PRACTICE AND APPLY

Display lines 10–15 on a board or on a device. Have volunteers identify the allusion and read the footnote about it. Ask students how the use of this allusion affects the meaning of the lift-off image. *(Instead of going straight up into the sky, the house would travel to "glory" and to heaven, like Elijah.)*

Display lines 19–22. Ask a volunteer to identify the allusion. *(Line 19: Old Testament robes)* Ask students to explain how the allusion affects the meaning of this section. *(One possibility of heaven, or life after death, is reunion with the dead. The Biblical robes place this reunion in the Judeo-Christian tradition.)*

Discuss with students the name of the poetry collection that includes this poem *(Life on Mars)*. Remind students that the title is an allusion to a song by David Bowie, and it is also a reference to a continuing question in science (i.e., is or was there life on Mars). Ask: How do the themes of this poem relate to the title *Life on Mars? (Possible answer: The poem deals with the mysteries of the universe.)*

Write Arguments

COMMON CORE

W 1

TEACH

Ask students what they think of when they think of poetry. What do they think most poetry is about? Discuss with students that poetry can cover a wide range of topics and ideas, from ballads that tell adventure stories with many events and characters to short poems that focus closely on a single item in nature.

- Ask students what "The Universe as Primal Scream" is about. *(Possible answers: the afterlife, the mysteries of the universe, the screaming of children next door)* Have students cite evidence from the poem to support their ideas.

- Discuss with students that one possible way to read the poem is that, in new times, poets need to explore new themes and topics. Have volunteers cite evidence from the poem for such an interpretation. *(Possible answers: lines 12–27 and lines 32–34. In this interpretation, the children represent the new. Their screams may herald something new in poetry that the author can't predict but is eager to see.)* Point out that, in *2001: A Space Odyssey*, the apes are screaming loudly right before they figure out how to use tools. At that point, an idea (how to use a bone as a tool) is born that leads to all of humanity's technical innovation. Discuss with students how that might relate to the idea of a new type of poetry. *(The children, like the apes, may be about to gain an amazing insight that will change life and, with it, poetry.)*

PRACTICE AND APPLY

Have students work in pairs to discuss the following question: What should poets write about? Can poetry be about subjects like science or math? Once students have shared ideas on these questions, ask partners to talk about whether or not they believe that, as "The Universe as Primal Scream" suggests, new times call for new topics and themes in poetry.

Tell students to work individually to write a short essay arguing for or against the claim that new times call for new topics and themes in poetry. Encourage students to include ideas from their discussions and use evidence from the selection and other poems they have read as support for their arguments. Remind students to include a main argument, reasons, evidence, and counterarguments in their essays.

INTERACTIVE LESSON Have students complete the tutorials in this lesson: **Writing Effective Arguments.**

INTERACTIVE WHITEBOARD LESSON

Analyzing Poetry

 COMMON CORE

RL 1, RL 4, RL 5, L 5b

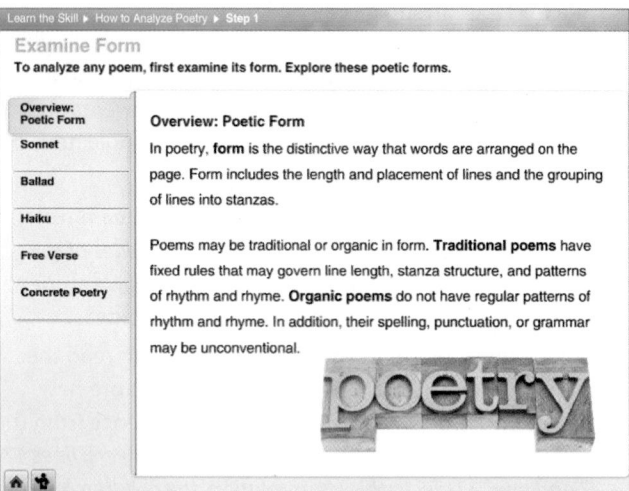

Learn the Skill ▶ How to Analyze Poetry ▶ Step 1

Examine Form
To analyze any poem, first examine its form. Explore these poetic forms.

| Overview: Poetic Form |
| Sonnet |
| Ballad |
| Haiku |
| Free Verse |
| Concrete Poetry |

Overview: Poetic Form

In poetry, **form** is the distinctive way that words are arranged on the page. Form includes the length and placement of lines and the grouping of lines into stanzas.

Poems may be traditional or organic in form. **Traditional poems** have fixed rules that may govern line length, stanza structure, and patterns of rhythm and rhyme. **Organic poems** do not have regular patterns of rhythm and rhyme. In addition, their spelling, punctuation, or grammar may be unconventional.

TEACH

Collect several poems for students to use in the lesson. Review the following steps before having students analyze the poems.

- **Examine Form:** Look at whether the poem has a traditional structure, with patterns of rhythm and/or rhyme, or an organic structure.
- **Identify Sound Devices:** Look at the sound devices in the poem, including rhyme and rhythm. Review the following terms and identify consonance, assonance, alliteration, onomatopoeia, and repetition.
- **Analyze Imagery:** Identify words and phrases that appeal to the senses. Analyze to which senses the images appeal.
- **Analyze the Effects:** Examine how the form, sound devices, and imagery work together to affect the reader.

COLLABORATIVE DISCUSSION

Direct students to work in groups to analyze poetry, looking at form, sound devices, imagery, and effects.

Analyze Language

COMMON CORE

RL 4

RETEACH

Review the term **imagery** with students. Then give an example of imagery from "The Universe as Primal Scream," such as ". . . the good crystal, which must surely/Lie shattered to dust on the floor."

- Ask students to provide other examples of imagery from this poem or others you may have. *(Possible answer: line 11: four pink lungs)* Discuss to which sense or senses the imagery appeals.
- Encourage students to discuss how the imagery affects the meaning of the poem and the reader's response to it.

 **LEVEL UP TUTORIALS** Assign the following *Level Up* tutorial: **Imagery**

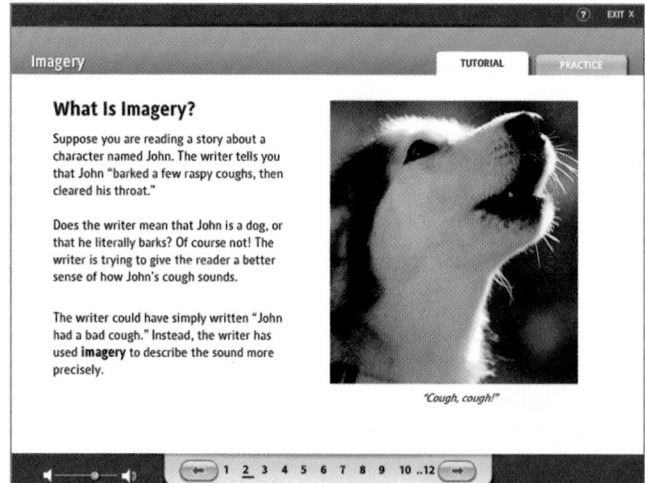

Imagery   TUTORIAL   PRACTICE

What Is Imagery?

Suppose you are reading a story about a character named John. The writer tells you that John "barked a few raspy coughs, then cleared his throat."

Does the writer mean that John is a dog, or that he literally barks? Of course not! The writer is trying to give the reader a better sense of how John's cough sounds.

The writer could have simply written "John had a bad cough." Instead, the writer has used **imagery** to describe the sound more precisely.

"Cough, cough!"

CLOSE READING APPLICATION

Students can apply the skill to another work of literature, such as a poem or a short story. They may also apply the skill to examine the images in the lyrics of a song. Ask: What imagery does the author include? What senses do the images appeal to? How do the images contribute to the meaning of the work?

Interactive Lessons

If you need help with...
• **Writing an Argument**
• **Writing as a Process**
• **Using Textual Evidence**

Write an Argument

This collection focuses in part on the transformation of America into a modern society in which people strive for wealth, power, or immortality. Look back at the texts in this collection, including the anchor text "Winter Dreams," and consider what it means to be a modern person in our modern society. What are the challenges and opportunities of modern society presented in the selections? What are the pitfalls and hazards? Synthesize your ideas in an argument stating what it means to be "modern."

An effective argument

- makes a persuasive claim stating a position on what it means to be modern

- develops the claim with valid reasons and relevant evidence from "Winter Dreams" and two other texts in the collection

- anticipates opposing claims and addresses them with well-supported counterclaims

- establishes clear, logical relationships among claims, counterclaims, reasons, and evidence

- has a satisfying conclusion that effectively summarizes the claim

- demonstrates appropriate and clear use of language, maintaining a formal tone through the use of standard English

COMMON CORE

W 1a–e Write arguments to support claims in an analysis.

W 4 Produce clear and coherent writing.

W 5 Develop and strengthen writing.

W 7 Conduct research.

W 8 Gather information from print and digital sources.

W 9a–b Draw evidence from literary or informational texts.

PLAN

Analyze the Texts Reread "Winter Dreams," taking notes about the qualities and behaviors that make the characters modern. Consider the challenges the characters face and how they address them. Then choose two other texts from this collection and make notes about what it means for the people and characters in those texts to be members of our modern society. Pay attention to specific details as you gather evidence from the texts.

Make a Claim Based on the ideas conveyed in the anchor text and your other chosen texts, write a claim that clearly and concisely states your position on the definition of modernity.

myNotebook

Use the annotation tools in your eBook to find evidence that supports your ideas about modernity. Save each piece of evidence to your notebook.

PERFORMANCE TASK A

WRITE AN ARGUMENT

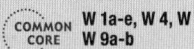 **COMMON CORE** W 1a-e, W 4, W 5, W 9a-b

Introduce students to the Performance Task by reading the introductory paragraph with them and reviewing the criteria for an effective argument. Work with students to define the term *modern* in the context of this collection of literature. Remind students that modern literature is literature written from the early 20th century to the present and that modernist literature often focused on the alienation of the individual in society.

PLAN

ANALYZE THE TEXTS

▶ *View It!*

Professional Development Podcast:

Performance Task

Once students have finished their review of "Winter Dreams" and taken notes, have them write a one-sentence summary of what makes the characters modern. They can use this summary to help them choose two other texts in the collection whose characters share similar traits. After reviewing the other selections, students can then draft a precise claim about what these selections say is modern. Remind students that they will need to support their claim with text evidence. If students find that their claims cannot be supported with evidence from the selection, they should revise the claim.

BUILD YOUR ARGUMENT

Tell students that the evidence they use to support their claim in this argument will be textual evidence from the selections. Point out that they can use direct quotations, paraphrases, and summaries of the text as evidence. Remind students that their evidence should be relevant, or directly related to their claim, and sufficient. In this case, students should try to find at least two pieces of text evidence from each selection.

DRAFT YOUR ESSAY

Tell students that they should establish a clear link between the claim in their introductions and the main idea of each supporting paragraph. They can make these connections through transitions. In turn, they must fully explain the connection of any text evidence they present to the idea it supports.

Build Your Argument Create a graphic organizer that states your claim, shows several reasons that support your claim, and outlines textual evidence such as details, examples, and quotations for each reason.

Develop Counterclaims Think about your audience. What might some readers say to oppose your claim? How would you argue against these opposing claims and convince these readers to agree with you? You may want to conduct further research in print or digital sources, noting any relevant facts, details, or examples. Write down reasons and evidence you can use to support your counterclaims.

Get Organized Organize your ideas in an outline, using the notes from your analysis and your graphic organizer. Be sure to include

- a clearly stated claim
- sufficient reasons and evidence to support your claim
- potential opposing claims that clearly outline the points your reader may make to show disagreement with your argument
- counterclaims supported by additional evidence to strengthen your argument and further persuade your reader

PRODUCE

my **WriteSmart**

Draft Your Essay Write a clearly organized draft of your argument. Think about your purpose and audience as you write.

- Introduce your claim. Present your argument in a memorable way that will grab the attention of your readers—consider using an interesting detail or quotation from one of the texts.
- Present your reasons and evidence in logically ordered paragraphs.
- Explain how the evidence from the texts supports your ideas about what it means to be modern.
- Include transitions to connect your reasons and evidence to your claim.
- Address potential opposing claims with convincing reasons and evidence.
- Use formal language and a respectful tone appropriate for an academic context.
- Write a persuasive conclusion that summarizes your position.

Write your rough draft in *my*WriteSmart. Focus on getting your ideas down, rather than perfecting your choice of language.

ACADEMIC VOCABULARY

As you build your argument about what it means to be modern, be sure to use these words.

contemporary
global
infinite
simulated
virtual

REVISE

REVISE

Exchange Essays Share your essay with a partner. Peer editing can be an effective way to identify areas of your argument that lack evidence or that cause confusion for the reader. To help you provide constructive feedback, refer to the chart on the following page for specific criteria of an effective argument. As you read your partner's essay, consider these questions:

- Does the introduction sound strong, confident, and persuasive?
- Has my partner provided relevant evidence to support claims and counterclaims?
- Is my partner's essay cohesive? Are additional transitions needed to make connections clear?
- Has my partner maintained a formal style of English and an objective tone?
- Does the conclusion follow logically from the body of the essay and provide an effective summary of the argument?

When you are finished reading, have a discussion about your essays. Ask your partner for feedback on how you can improve your argument. Talk about the reasoning and evidence used to support your claim, and whether or not you have successfully anticipated and addressed opposing claims. Take notes on your partner's feedback and then revise your essay, incorporating any changes that will improve your draft.

PRESENT

Share with a Group When your final draft is completed, read your essay to a small group. Your classmates should listen and take notes as you present your argument. Do your classmates understand your position? Have you successfully persuaded your audience to agree with your argument? Be prepared to respond to any comments or questions from your group.

my **WriteSmart**

Have your partner or a group of peers review your draft in myWriteSmart. Ask your reviewers to note any reasons that do not support the claim or that lack sufficient evidence.

REVISE

EXCHANGE ESSAYS

Suggest that students use the criteria in the chart Collection 6, Task A: Argument to rank their essay in each of the three categories. Then they can focus their revisions on the category that needs the most improvement.

PRESENT

SHARE WITH A GROUP

Other options for sharing students' arguments include
- posting them on the school's website
- hosting another class for a panel discussion of what it means to be modern

PERFORMANCE TASK A

LANGUAGE

Have students look at the chart and evaluate their level of performance in the Language category. Ask students to review the formality of the language they used in their arguments. Was it more formal or informal? If students answer more informal, have them choose several sentences to revise using formal language.

	Ideas and Evidence	Organization	Language
ADVANCED	• The introduction is memorable and persuasive; the claim clearly states a position on a substantive topic. • Valid reasons and relevant evidence from the texts convincingly support the writer's claim. • Counterclaims are anticipated and effectively addressed with counterarguments. • The concluding section effectively summarizes the claim.	• The reasons and textual evidence are organized consistently and logically throughout the argument. • Varied transitions logically connect reasons and textual evidence to the writer's claim.	• The writing reflects a formal style and an objective, or controlled, tone. • Sentence beginnings, lengths, and structures vary and have a rhythmic flow. • Spelling, capitalization, and punctuation are correct. If handwritten, the argument is legible. • Grammar and usage are correct.
COMPETENT	• The introduction could do more to capture the reader's attention; the claim states a position on an issue. • Most reasons and evidence from the texts support the writer's claim, but they could be more convincing. • Counterclaims are anticipated, but the counterarguments need to be developed more. • The concluding section restates the claim.	• The organization of reasons and textual evidence is confusing in a few places. • A few more transitions are needed to connect reasons and textual evidence to the writer's claim.	• The style is informal in a few places, and the tone is defensive at times. • Sentence beginnings, lengths, and structures vary somewhat. • Several spelling and capitalization mistakes occur, and punctuation is inconsistent. If handwritten, the argument is mostly legible. • Some grammatical and usage errors are repeated in the argument.
LIMITED	• The introduction is ordinary; the claim identifies an issue, but the writer's position is not clearly stated. • The reasons and evidence from the texts are not always logical or relevant. • Counterclaims are anticipated but not addressed logically. • The concluding section includes an incomplete summary of the claim.	• The organization of reasons and textual evidence is logical in some places, but it often doesn't follow a pattern. • Many more transitions are needed to connect reasons and textual evidence to the writer's position.	• The style becomes informal in many places, and the tone is often dismissive of other viewpoints. • Sentence structures barely vary, and some fragments or run-on sentences are present. • Spelling, capitalization, and punctuation are often incorrect but do not make reading the argument difficult. If handwritten, the argument may be partially illegible. • Grammar and usage are incorrect in many places, but the writer's ideas are still clear.
EMERGING	• The introduction is missing. • Significant supporting reasons and evidence from the texts are missing. • Counterclaims are neither anticipated nor addressed. • The concluding section is missing.	• An organizational strategy is not used; reasons and textual evidence are presented randomly. • Transitions are not used, making the argument difficult to understand.	• The style is inappropriate, and the tone is disrespectful. • Repetitive sentence structure, fragments, and run-on sentences make the writing monotonous and hard to follow. • Spelling and capitalization are often incorrect, and punctuation is missing. If handwritten, the argument may be partially or mostly illegible. • Many grammatical and usage errors change the meaning of the writer's ideas.

Participate in a Panel Discussion

This collection focuses in part on the abundance of information in American society and how it affects our lives and future. Look back at the texts in this collection, including the anchor text *The Crucible*, and consider the quote by Gertrude Stein: "Everybody gets so much information all day long that they lose their common sense." What influences how people react to information? How can we decide what is credible and what is not? Synthesize your ideas by holding a panel discussion about how information overload affects our ability to be responsible, informed, and active citizens. Use evidence from the selections to support your ideas.

COMMON CORE

SL 1a–d Initiate and participate effectively in a range of collaborative discussions.

SL 3 Evaluate a speaker's point of view, reasoning, and use of evidence and rhetoric.

SL 4 Present information, findings, and supporting evidence.

SL 6 Adapt speech to a variety of contexts and tasks.

An effective participant in a panel discussion

- makes a clear, logical, and well-defended generalization about the effects of information overload
- uses quotations and examples from the selections—fiction or nonfiction—to illustrate his or her ideas
- synthesizes ideas about or connected to information overload based on collection texts
- responds thoughtfully, politely, and constructively to the ideas of others on the panel
- evaluates other panel members' contributions, including the use of valid reasoning and relevant evidence

PLAN

_my_Notebook

Use the annotation tools in your eBook to find evidence that supports your ideas about how people process information. Save each piece of evidence to your notebook.

Get Organized Work with your classmates to prepare for the discussion.

- Join a group of four classmates and select one student to be the moderator for your discussion. The rest of your classmates will be the audience when you hold the discussion.
- Create a format for your discussion—a schedule that shows the order in which members of the panel will speak and for how many minutes. It will be the moderator's job to keep the discussion moving along on schedule.
- Set rules regarding the appropriate times for either the moderator or the audience to ask the panel members questions.

PARTICIPATE IN A PANEL DISCUSSION

COMMON CORE SL 1a-d, SL 3, SL 4, SL 6

Introduce the Performance Task by reading the introductory paragraph with students and reviewing the criteria for being an effective participant in a panel discussion. Remind students that all participants in the panel discussion should feel like their voices are heard. Everyone should have the right to speak but not to interrupt one another.

PLAN

GET ORGANIZED

Before they begin, have students consider these questions:

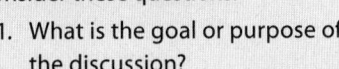
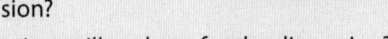
View It!

Professional Development Podcast:

Performance Task

1. What is the goal or purpose of the discussion?
2. How much time will we have for the discussion?
3. What rules will govern the panel discussion?

PERFORMANCE TASK B

PLAN

GATHER EVIDENCE

Guide students in choosing two other texts to analyze. They should be texts that have something to say about information overload and that all students can agree on.

PRODUCE

WRITE AND PRACTICE

Remind students to refer to their outlines as they present their ideas and evidence but also engage in authentic conversation. They should maintain eye contact when speaking to other students and listen closely to what others have to say. The discussion is a chance for them to gain new perspectives on the issue, based on their classmates' analysis of the texts.

Students may want to videotape their panel discussions. Videotaping will allow them to critique themselves on their discussion skills and their use of text evidence to support their ideas.

Gather Evidence As a group, analyze *The Crucible* and two other texts of the panel's choice. Gather evidence that you will use to discuss the effects of information overload. Note specific details, examples, and quotations. Ask yourself these questions as you take notes:

- What types of information are presented in the selections?
- How does the source of each kind of information affect its credibility?
- How do the people or characters in the texts respond to what they hear or read? Why?
- What effect does the quantity of available information have on people or characters? How much is too much—or too little?
- What generalization, or broad conclusion, can you make about how people process and respond to what they hear, read, or watch, and how the overall quantity of information affects their ability to process it accurately?

During this time, the moderator should make a list of relevant questions to be asked during the discussion.

PRODUCE

Write and Practice Work individually to outline your ideas. Then practice with your group.

- State a clear generalization about how people today are affected by a nearly infinite amount of available information.
- Write several main ideas that support your generalization. Each idea should relate your generalization to *The Crucible* or one of your other chosen texts.
- Sort through the evidence you have collected and match each piece of evidence with the main idea it most clearly supports. Provide clear examples.
- Present your ideas to your group. The moderator will ask questions about your ideas and examples, preparing you to "think on your feet" during the real discussion.
- If you are the moderator, use this time to decide how you will introduce and conclude the panel discussion. Write a statement that tells the audience the topic of the discussion and its format. Write notes for a concluding statement, but be prepared to modify your remarks based on new ideas that emerge from the discussion.

*my*WriteSmart

Write your outline in *my*WriteSmart. Focus on getting your ideas down, rather than perfecting your choice of language.

REVISE

Reinforce Your Ideas Based on the practice session and the chart on the following page, make changes to your outline. Consider the following questions:

- Were you able to defend your generalization? If not, revise your statement so that it better reflects your textual evidence and your ideas.

- Were you able to answer the moderator's questions clearly and without hesitation? If not, you may need to reorganize your outline so that you can find the information you need quickly and easily.

- Did the moderator's questions help you see one of the texts in a new light? If so, add new evidence to your outline that you can share during the real discussion.

my **WriteSmart**

Have your partner or a group of peers review your outline in *my*WriteSmart. Ask your reviewers to note any evidence that does not support your generalization about the effects of information overload.

PRESENT

Have the Discussion Have your outline and/or notes handy for reference during the discussion.

- Begin by having the moderator introduce the topic, the panelists, and the basic format for the discussion. The moderator will then ask the first question and continue to facilitate the discussion in the agreed-upon format.

- Use your outline to remind you of your main points, but try to speak directly to the panel and to the audience. Don't just read from your paper.

- Listen closely to what all speakers say so that you can respond appropriately.

- Maintain a respectful tone toward your fellow panel members, even when you disagree with their ideas.

- When all the panelists have made their statements and discussed ideas amongst themselves, the moderator should invite audience members to ask questions.

- Conclude by having the moderator summarize the discussion. He or she should thank the panelists for their participation.

Summarize Write a summary of the main points from the discussion. Then explain whether the discussion made you rethink your generalization, and why.

REVISE

REINFORCE YOUR IDEAS

As students evaluate their discussion, encourage them to consider how well they did at active listening and supporting others' contributions. Did they fully focus their attention on the person speaking? Did they wait their turn to speak and relinquish their turn when time was up? Did the discussion flow smoothly, with all participants showing respect for other group members? Were disagreements handled to everyone's satisfaction?

PRESENT

HAVE THE DISCUSSION

Students might enjoy inviting another class to act as the audience for their panel discussion. If they invite another class to join them, they should share ahead of time with the visiting class the works of literature that will be discussed. The audience members can then read the literature before the panel discussion is held.

PERFORMANCE TASK B

ORGANIZATION

Have students look at the chart and evaluate their level of performance in the Organization category. Ask students to examine the order of their ideas and the transitions between them. Discuss areas for improvement and have students outline a revised argument showing a more logical order and better transitions.

	Ideas and Evidence	Organization	Language
ADVANCED	• The panelist clearly states a valid generalization and supports it with strong, relevant ideas and well-chosen evidence from the texts and personal experience. • The panel member carefully evaluates others' evidence and reasoning and responds with insightful comments and questions. • The panelist synthesizes the analysis of the texts to help listeners understand the generalization.	• The panelist's remarks are based on a well-organized outline or notes that clearly identify the generalization and the supporting ideas and evidence. • Ideas are presented in a logical order with effective transitions to show the connections between ideas. • The panelist concludes with a statement that reinforces the generalization and includes the ideas that have emerged from the discussion.	• The panelist adapts speech to the context of the discussion, using appropriately formal English to discuss the texts and ideas. • The panelist consistently quotes accurately from the texts to support ideas. • The panel member consistently maintains a polite and thoughtful tone throughout the discussion.
COMPETENT	• The panelist states a generalization and supports it with relevant ideas and evidence from the texts and personal experience. • The panel member evaluates others' evidence and reasoning and responds with appropriate comments and questions. • The panelist synthesizes some ideas and links to the generalization.	• The panelist's remarks are based on an outline or notes that identify the generalization, supporting ideas, and evidence. • Ideas are presented in a logical order and linked with transitions. • The panelist concludes with a statement that reinforces the generalization.	• The panelist mostly uses formal English to discuss literature and ideas. • The panelist mostly quotes accurately from the texts to support ideas. • The panel member maintains a polite and thoughtful tone throughout most of the discussion.
LIMITED	• The panelist states a reasonably clear generalization and supports it with some ideas and evidence. • The panel member's response to others' comments shows limited evaluation of the evidence and reasoning. • The panelist does not synthesize but simply repeats the generalization in a vague way.	• The panelist's remarks reflect an outline or notes that may identify the generalization but do not organize ideas and evidence very effectively. • Ideas are presented in a somewhat disorganized way with few transitions. • The panelist makes a weak concluding statement that does little to reinforce the generalization.	• The panelist uses some formal and some informal English to discuss the texts and ideas. • The panelist's quotations and examples sometimes do not accurately reflect the texts. • The panel member occasionally forgets to maintain a polite tone when responding to others' comments and questions.
EMERGING	• The panelist's generalization is unclear; ideas and evidence are not coherent. • The panel member does not evaluate others' evidence and reasoning. • The panelist does not synthesize.	• The panelist does not follow an outline or notes that organize ideas and evidence. • Ideas are presented in a disorganized way with no transitions. • The panelist's remarks lack any kind of conclusion or summary.	• The panelist uses informal English and/or slang, so that ideas are not clearly expressed. • The panelist's quotations and examples do not accurately reflect the texts. • The panel member does not maintain a polite tone when responding to others' comments and questions.

TEACHER NOTE:
The page numbers to the left indicate pages in the Student Edition. Except for the two entries below, the page numbers in the Student Edition and the Teacher's Edition correspond.

Writing Arguments

COMMON CORE W 1a-e, L 3a

Many of the Performance Tasks in this book ask you to craft an argument in which you support your ideas with text evidence. Any argument you write should include the following sections and characteristics.

Introduction

Clearly state your **claim**, the point your argument makes. As needed, provide context or background information to help readers understand your position, possibly citing expert opinions to establish the source of knowledge behind your claim. Note the most common opposing views as a way to distinguish and clarify your ideas. From the very beginning, make it clear for readers why your claim is strong; consider providing an overview of your reasons or a quotation that emphasizes your view in your introduction.

EXAMPLES

vague claim: We need to ban cell phones.	**Precise, knowledge-able claim:** The NTSB and the National Safety Council agree: Using cell phones—even hands-free models—to talk or text while driving must be banned now.
not distinguished from opposing view: There are plenty of people who consider cell phones to be okay.	**distinguished from opposing view:** While some people consider hands-free communication devices to be safe, the facts indicate otherwise.
confusing relationship of ideas: Teens like to talk on their cell phones. Driving is a privilege.	**logical relationship of ideas:** When people talk or text on cell phones while driving, they endanger their own lives and the lives of others.

Development of Claims

The body of your argument must provide strong, logical reasons for your claim and must fully support those reasons with relevant evidence. A **reason** tells why your claim is

valid; **evidence** provides specific examples that illustrate a reason. In the process of developing your claim, you should also refute **counterclaims,** or opposing views, with equally strong reasons and evidence. To show that you have thoroughly considered your view, provide a summary of the strengths and limitations of your claim and opposing claims. The goal is not to undercut your argument, but rather to answer your readers' objections to it. Be sure to consider how much your audience may already know about your topic. Consider, too, your audience's values; by failing to recognize their biases, you may miss the mark entirely.

EXAMPLES

claim lacking reasons: Banning cell phone use would be good.	**claim developed by reasons:** Given evidence about rising accident rates for cell phone users, many policymakers are considering legislation related to cell phones and driving.
omission of limitations: A ban on mobile devices in cars will virtually eliminate all distraction-related accidents.	**fair discussion of limitations:** We should not dismiss concerns about banning other kinds of distractions, such as listening to music while driving.
inattention to audience's knowledge: We're behind the curve on establishing safety standards.	**awareness of audience's knowledge:** Ten states have banned the use of hand-held cell phones while driving.
ignorance of audience's bias: The reckless drivers opposed to this idea firmly believe they alone know how to text and drive safely.	**recognition of audience's bias:** While many of us feel we know how to talk or text safely while driving, how sure can we be about other drivers on the road?

Links Among Ideas

Even the strongest reasons and evidence will fail to sway readers if it is unclear how the reasons relate to the central claim of an argument. Make the connections clear for your readers, using not only transitional words and phrases, but also clauses and even entire sentences as bridges between ideas you have already discussed and ideas you are introducing. By showing control over your language through the skilled use of transitional expressions, for example, you'll enhance your credibility as a writer. Virginia Tufte's *Artful Sentences* is a well-known guide to syntax, providing helpful examples of effectively structured sentences.

EXAMPLES

> **transitional word linking claim and reason:** Recent studies indicate that driving while using a cell phone leads to an increased risk of accidents. **Consequently,** many states are considering banning cell phone use while driving.

> **transitional phrase linking reason and evidence:** Banning cell phone use while driving would lead to increased safety for all drivers and passengers. **In fact,** recent studies show decreased accident rates in communities that have banned cell phones while driving.

> **transitional clause linking claim and counter-claim:** The benefits of banning cell phone use are clear. **Those opposed to the plan, though, would say otherwise:** They feel that banning cell phone use while driving would lead to restricting other distractions, such as eating or listening to music.

Appropriate Style and Tone

An effective argument is most often written in a direct and formal style. The style and tone you choose should not be an afterthought—the way you express your argument can either support or detract from your ideas. Even as you argue in favor of your viewpoint, take care to remain objective in tone—avoid using loaded language when discussing opposing claims.

EXAMPLES

informal style: No phones while driving would be a real pain for everyone.	**formal style:** There are many situations where responsible phone usage in a car is a convenient option.
biased tone: It doesn't make any sense to support this ban.	**objective tone:** Arguments opposing this ban have been refuted by evidence from many sources.
inattention to conventions: We need to make this issue a big deal!	**attention to conventions:** The proposed ban, which would increase safety for all drivers and passengers, should be given serious consideration.

Conclusion

Your conclusion may range from a sentence to a full paragraph, but it must wrap up your argument in a satisfying way; a conclusion that sounds tacked-on hurts more than helps your argument. A strong conclusion is a logical extension of the argument you have presented. It carries forth your ideas through an inference, question, quotation, or challenge.

EXAMPLES

> **inference:** Building safe driving habits begins with common sense.

> **question:** Who doesn't want to have the assurance that oncoming drivers are fully attentive to driving?

> **quotation:** As the chair of the safety council has stated, "Banning cell phone use while driving will increase everyone's safety on our highways."

> **challenge:** Bans of this type make the difference between an engaged community that values its citizens' safety and one that disregards mounting scientific evidence.

Writing Informative Texts

 **COMMON CORE W 2a-f**

Most of the Performance Tasks in this book ask you to write informational or explanatory texts in which you present a topic and examine it thoughtfully, through a well-organized analysis of relevant content. Any informative or explanatory text that you create should include the following parts and features.

Introduction

Develop a strong **thesis statement.** That is, clearly state your **topic** and the **organizational framework** through which you will develop a unified composition. Each new idea should logically flow out of the ideas and arguments that precede it. For example, you might state that your text will compare ideas, examine causes and effects, or analyze a single text or a group of texts.

Introduction:
- What is the naturalist literary movement?
- What are the movement's key characteristics?

Main points:
- What are the major themes in "To Build a Fire"?
- How does the story reflect elements of the naturalist literary movement?

EXAMPLE

Topic: the writing of Jack London
Sample Thesis Statements
Compare-contrast: The stories of Jack London and Stephen Crane both reveal the naturalist assumption that human beings have very little control over their lives but instead are at the mercy of the natural world and the impersonal force of fate.
Cause-effect: In "To Build a Fire," Jack London shows cause-and-effect relationships on both a large and small scale, revealing the power of nature on many levels.
Analysis: Jack London's works promote the naturalist view, showing how harsh natural forces can defeat human will.

Clarifying the organizational framework up front will help you organize the body of your essay, suggesting **headings** you can use to guide your readers or graphics that might illustrate the text. Most important, it can help you identify any ideas that you may need to clarify. For example, if you are analyzing the naturalist views in Jack London's "To Build a Fire," you may use the following framework:

Development of the Topic

In the body of your text, flesh out the organizational framework you established in your introduction with strong supporting paragraphs. Include only the most significant evidence that is relevant to your topic. Don't rely on a single source, and make sure the sources you use are reliable and current. The table below illustrates types of support you might use to develop different types of topics. It also shows how transitions link text sections, create cohesion, and clarify the relationships among ideas.

Types of Support in Explanatory/ Informative Texts (in italics)	Uses of Transitions in Explanatory/ Informative Texts
Examples: While *stories like "To Build a Fire"* represent the Darwinist branch of naturalism, *in which biology determines human destiny, Crane's work* exemplifies the Marxist strain, *in which social and economic factors are paramount.*	The first part of this sentence introduces the next section of the comparative essay, which deals with a different author, Stephen Crane.

continued

Types of Support in Explanatory/ Informative Texts (in italics)	Uses of Transitions in Explanatory/ Informative Texts
Concrete details: *Because its primary imperative is not to mourn its dead master but to live, the dog promptly returns to camp.*	A transitional clause explains the significance of a concrete detail in a cause-and-effect essay.
Textual evidence: In "To Build a Fire," the main character recognizes that he has limited chances of survival. *As author Jack London writes, "he realized that it was no longer a mere matter of freezing his fingers and toes, or of losing his hands and feet, but that it was a matter of life and death, with the chances against him."*	The phrase "As author Jack London writes" signals the use of a quotation from "To Build a Fire" to support the writer's analysis of the text.

Informal, biased language: Naturalism was totally out there, believe me.	Formal style, neutral tone, with figurative language to express complex ideas: Relying on new theories in sociology and psychology, the writers of the naturalistic movement dissected human behavior with detachment and objectivity, like scientists dissecting laboratory specimens.

You can't always include all of the information you'd like to in a short essay, but you can plan to point readers directly to useful **multimedia links** either in the body of or at the end of your essay.

Style and Tone

Use formal English to establish your credibility as a source of information. To project authority, use the language of the **domain,** or field, that you are writing about. However, be sure to define unfamiliar terms and avoid jargon. Provide extended definitions when your audience is likely to have limited knowledge of the topic. Using quotations from reliable sources can also give your text authority; be sure to credit the source of quoted material. In general, keep the tone neutral, avoiding slangy or biased expressions. However, don't shy away from figurative language: well-placed metaphors, similes, and analogies can convey a complex idea more succinctly than a paragraph of strictly objective language.

Conclusion

End your essay with a concluding statement or section that sums up or extends the information in your essay. This is your opportunity to collect together the various elements of your essay and to restate your thesis. The conclusion is not a place to introduce new facts or arguments. Instead, you should focus on wrapping everything up in a clear and compelling way.

EXAMPLES

Articulate the implications of your ideas: Jack London saw life as a life-or-death struggle won by those best suited for survival by being in tune with nature. His short stories and novels dramatize his belief that "civilized" human beings are either destroyed or recreated in savage environments.
Emphasize significance of your topic: Whether London expresses naturalism through the power of natural or societal forces, he successfully explores one of the philosophies that was on the minds of many during that time in history.

Writing Narratives

COMMON CORE W 3a-e

When you are composing a fictional tale, an autobiographical incident, or a firsthand biography, you write in the narrative mode. That means telling a story with a beginning, a climax, and a conclusion. Though there are important differences between fictional and nonfictional narratives, you use similar processes to develop them.

Identify a Significant Problem or Situation, or Make an Observation

For a nonfiction narrative, dig into your memory bank for a significant problem you dealt with or an important observation you've made about your life. For fiction, try to invent a problem or situation that can unfold in interesting ways.

EXAMPLES

Problem (nonfiction)	This summer I had to overcome my fear of diving off the high board in competitions.
Situation (fiction)	David awaits his college acceptance letters, wondering how they might change his life.

Establish a Point of View

Decide who will tell your story. If you are writing an essay about an important experience or person in your own life, you will be the narrator of the events you relate. If you are writing a work of fiction, you can choose to create a first-person narrator or tell the story from the third-person point of view. In the latter case, the narrator can focus on one character or reveal the thoughts and feelings of all the characters. The examples below show the differences between a first- and third-person narrator.

First-person narrator (nonfiction)

I climb up the ladder and look at the pool far below. Suddenly the diving board seems wobbly and too high up. Should I really dive? Will I make a fool of myself?

Third-person narrator (fiction)

As David drove into the driveway, he tried to calm down. He turned down the radio to hear his heart beating. Easing the door open, he stepped out of the car and walked down to the mailbox.

Gather Details

To make real or fictional experiences come alive, you will need to use narrative techniques like description and dialogue. The questions in the left column in the chart below can help you search your memory or imagination for the details that will flesh out your narrative. You don't have to respond in full sentences, but try to capture the sights, sounds, and feelings that bring your narrative to life.

Who, What, When, Where?	Narrative Techniques
People: Who are the people or characters involved in the experience? What did they look like? What did they do? What did they say?	**Description:** Hands shaking, David reached in for the letter. David gently carried the envelope into the house as if it were made of glass. **Dialogue:** "So, have you even looked at it yet?" his sister Nadine asked. Nadine quickly snatched the envelope from David, opened the letter, and started to read it silently.
Experience: What led up to or caused the event? What is the main event in the experience? What happened as a result of the event?	**Description:** A college letter has arrived; David hesitates to open it. His conflict is internal. He fights his nervousness and uncertainty about his future. After she opens the letter, Nadine tells David that he is accepted to college in Boston. Brother and sister celebrate together and then watch a movie together, knowing that everything has changed.

continued

Who, What, When, Where?	Narrative Techniques
Places: When and where did the events take place? What were the sights, sounds, and smells of this place?	**Description:** Events occur during senior year of high school, when college acceptance letters are sent out. The conversation between David and Nadine occurs in the family kitchen, silent except for the scraping of chairs as they both sit down.

Sequence Events

Before you begin writing, list the key events of the experience or story in chronological, or time, order. Place a star next to the point of highest tension. In fiction, this point is called the climax, but a gripping nonfiction narrative will also have a climactic event.

To build suspense—the uncertainty a reader feels about what will happen next—you'll want to think about the pacing of your narrative. Consider disrupting the chronological order of events by beginning at the end. Or interrupt the sequence with a flashback, taking the reader to an earlier point in the narrative.

Another way to build suspense is with multiple plot lines. For example, in the fictional narrative, David's anxiety as he awaits news about his college applications could have been coupled with a second plot line in which his sister Nadine also faces uncertainty about her future. Both plot lines could then have been resolved at the end of the narrative.

Use Vivid Language

As you revise, make an effort to use vivid language. Use precise words and phrases to describe feelings and actions. Use telling details to show, rather than directly state, what a character is like. Use sensory language that lets readers see, feel, hear, smell, and taste what you or your characters experienced. Overall, select language that expresses a consistent tone throughout your narrative.

First Draft	Revision
He opened the letter.	Fingers trembling, David slowly raised his hand to open the letter. He slid his thumb under the flap and heard the envelope softly tearing. [telling details]
They fell to the floor.	They fell to the floor, laughing hysterically. Soon, their howls ended and they stood up and hugged. After catching their breath, David set up the movie while Nadine made the popcorn, just like every other Friday night since they were young. [precise words and phrases]
David knocked over the chair.	Jumping up with unexpected speed, David knocked over the chair, which loudly crashed to the floor. [sensory details]

Conclusion

At the conclusion of the narrative, you or your narrator will reflect on the meaning of the events. The conclusion should follow logically from the climactic moment. The narrator of a personal narrative usually reflects on the significance of the experience. A fictional narrative will end with the resolution of the conflict described over the course of the story.

EXAMPLE

"Oh no, David. I was afraid of this," Nadine said in a sorrowful voice, her face grim. David put his head in his hands, moaning softly.

"David, Rufus is going to have to rely on Mom to take him on walks. You've been accepted! You're going to Boston!" she shouted.

Jumping up with unexpected speed, David knocked over the chair, which loudly crashed to the floor. He gave Nadine a playful shove. "You'll be sorry!" he shouted as he reached for Nadine. They fell to the floor, laughing hysterically. Soon, their howls ended and they stood up and hugged each other. After catching their breath, David set up the movie while Nadine made the popcorn, just like every other Friday night since they were young.

PRACTICE AND APPLY
Remind students to write legibly as they develop their lists of key events.

Conducting Research

COMMON CORE W 2a-f, W 7, W 8

The Performance Tasks in this book will require you to complete research projects related to the texts you've read in the collections. Whether the topic is stated in a Performance Task or is one you generate, the following information will guide you through your research project.

Focus Your Research and Formulate a Question

Some topics for a research project can be effectively covered in three pages; others require an entire book for a thorough treatment. Begin by developing a topic that is neither too narrow nor too broad for the time frame of the assignment. Also check your school and local libraries and databases to help you determine how to choose your topic. If there's too little information, you'll need to broaden your focus; if there's too much, you'll need to limit it.

With a topic in hand, formulate a research question; it will keep you on track as you conduct your research. A good research question cannot be answered in a single word and should be open-ended. It should require investigation. You can also develop related research questions to explore your topic in more depth.

EXAMPLES

Possible topics about Julius Caesar, the Roman emperor	Famous assassinations in history—too broad Popularity of soothsayers in Roman times—too narrow Historical figures—fact or fiction?
Possible research question	What was the real Julius Caesar like?
Related questions	• How much of Shakespeare's *Julius Caesar* is based on historical fact? • How did later Roman historians describe Julius Caesar?

Locate and Evaluate Sources

To find answers to your research question, you'll need to investigate primary and secondary sources, whether in print or digital formats. **Primary sources,** such as diaries, autobiographies, interviews, speeches, and eyewitness accounts, contain original, firsthand information. **Secondary sources** relate other people's versions of primary sources in encyclopedias, newspaper or magazine articles, biographies, and documentaries.

Your search for sources begins at the library and on the Internet. Use **advanced search features** to help you find things quickly. Add a minus sign (–) before a word that should not appear in your results. Use an asterisk (*) in place of unknown words. List the name of and location of each possible source, adding comments about its potential usefulness. Assessing, or evaluating, your sources in an important step in the research process. Your goal is to use sources that are credible, or reliable and trustworthy, and that are appropriate to your task, purpose, and audience.

Criteria for Assessing Sources	
Relevance: It covers the target aspect of my topic and helps me achieve my purpose for writing.	• How will the source be useful in answering my research question?
Accuracy: It includes information that can be verified by more than one authoritative source.	• Is the information up-to-date? Are the facts accurate? How can I verify them? • What qualifies the author to write about this topic? Is he or she an authority?

continued

Criteria for Assessing Sources	
Objectivity: It presents multiple viewpoints on the topic.	• What, if any, biases can I detect? Does the writer favor one view of the topic?
Coverage: It covers the topic at a level appropriate for my grade level and audience.	• Is the treatment of the material too juvenile for my audience? Is it too advanced?

Incorporating and Citing Source Material

When you draft your research project, you'll need to include material from your sources. This material can be **direct quotations, summaries,** or **paraphrases** of the original source material. Two well-known **style manuals** provide information on how to cite a range of print and digital sources: the *MLA Handbook for Writers of Research Papers* (published by the Modern Language Association) and Kate L. Turabian's *A Manual for Writers of Research Papers, Theses, and Dissertations* (published by The University of Chicago Press). Both style manuals provide a wealth of information about conducting, formatting, drafting, and presenting your research, including guidelines for citing sources within the text (called parenthetical citations) and preparing the list of Works Cited, as well as correct use of the mechanics of writing. Your teacher will indicate which style manual you should use. The following examples use the format in the *MLA Handbook.*

EXAMPLES

Direct quotation [The writer is citing the description given by Roman historian Suetonius.]	In his biographical text *The Lives of the Caesars,* the Roman historian Suetonius describes Caesar as "tall of stature, with a fair complexion, shapely limbs, a somewhat full face, and keen black eyes" (45).
Summary [The writer is summarizing the conclusion in an article about Roman government.]	Rome's republican government was made up of consuls, praetors, a senate, and people's assemblies. The position of dictator was temporary and only used during emergencies (24–25).
Paraphrase [The writer is paraphrasing, or stating in his own words, material from an article about the nature of Rome's government during Caesar's time.]	During Caesar's time, Rome was a republic. Two consuls with equal authority were the leaders. Senators suggested laws, and general assemblies voted on whether to approve the suggestions. The position of dictator was used only when there were serious outbreaks of lawlessness or during wartime (24–25).

As you write, it's important not to rely too heavily on any one source but to synthesize information from a variety of sources. Furthermore, any material from sources must be completely documented, or you will commit **plagiarism,** the unauthorized use of someone else's words or ideas. Plagiarism is not honest. As you take notes for your research project, be sure to keep complete information about your sources so that you can cite them correctly in the body of your paper. This applies to all sources, whether print or digital. Having complete information will also enable you to prepare the list of Works Cited. The list of Works Cited, which concludes your research project, provides author, title, and publication information for both print and digital sources. The following section shows the *MLA Handbook's* Works Cited citation formats for a variety of sources.

PRACTICE AND APPLY
Remind students to write legibly as they take notes.

MLA Citation Guidelines

Today, you can find free Web sites that help you create citations for research papers using information you provide. Such sites have some time-saving advantages when you're developing a Works Cited list. However, you should always check your citations carefully before you turn in your final paper. If you are following MLA style, use these guidelines to evaluate and finalize your work.

Books

One author

Steinbeck, John. *The Grapes of Wrath*. 1939. New York: Viking, 1964. Print.

Two authors or editors

Lange, Dorothea, and Paul Schuster Taylor. *An American Exodus: A Record of Human Erosion*. New York: Reynal & Hitchcock, 1939. Print.

Three authors or editors

Scheibel, Jeremy, Anne Chatsworth, and Ridley Davis, eds. *Stories from the Great Depression*. Princeton: Princeton UP, 2008. Print.

Four or more authors or editors

List the first author only. Then use the abbreviation et al., *which means "and others."*

Rutkowski, J., et al. *American Immigration and Migration in the 1930s*. Topeka: Sanders-Ellis, 2007. Print.

No author given

American Literature: 1865 to the Present. Chicago: Omni, 2007. Print.

Parts of Books

An introduction, a preface, a foreword, or an afterword written by someone other than the author(s) of a work

Gorton, Terry. Foreword. *John Steinbeck: A Centennial Tribute*. Ed. Stephen K. George. Westport: Praeger, 2002. xvii–xviii. Print.

A poem, a short story, an essay, or a chapter in a collection of works

Steinbeck, John. "The Leader of the People." *The Portable Steinbeck*. Ed. Pascal Covici, Jr. New York: Penguin, 1978. 397–415. Print.

A poem, a short story, an essay, or a chapter in an anthology of works by several authors

Steinbeck, John. "The Red Pony." *The American Short Story: A Collection of the Best Known and Most Memorable Short Stories by the Great American Authors*. Ed. Thomas K. Parkes. New York: Galahad, 1994. 886–948. Print.

A novel or play in a collection

Steinbeck, John. *The Grapes of Wrath. The Grapes of Wrath and Other Writings, 1936–1941*. New York: Library of America, 1996. Print.

Magazines, Newspapers, and Encyclopedias

An article in a newspaper

Patel, Vikram. "Recalling the Days of Wrath." *Los Angeles Times* 8 Jan. 2008: 9. Print.

An article in a magazine

Schubert, Siegfried D., et al. "On the Cause of the 1930s Dust Bowl." *Science* 19 Mar. 2004: 1855–60. Print.

An article in an encyclopedia

Kite, Steven. "Dust Bowl." *Encyclopedia of the Great Depression and New Deal*. Ed. James Ciment. 2 vols. Armonk, NY: Sharpe, 2001. Print.

Miscellaneous Nonprint Sources

An interview

Sorenson, Elvina. Personal interview. 3 Feb. 2010.

A video recording or film

Our Daily Bread. Dir. King Vidor. Perf. Karen Morley, Tom Keene, Barbara Pepper, John Qualen.

1934. Film Preservation Assoc., 1999. DVD.

A sound recording

Guthrie, Woody. *Library of Congress Recordings/Woody Guthrie*. Rounder, 1988. CD.

Electronic Publications

A document from an Internet site

Author or compiler | Title or description of document | Title of website | Site sponsor
Neary, Walter. | "Steinbeck & Salinas." | About John Steinbeck. | National Steinbeck Center.

Date of document | Medium of publication
June 1995. | Web.

Date of access
2 Apr. 2010.

An Online Book or E-Book

Wunder, John R., Frances Kaye, and Vernon Carstensen, eds. *Americans View Their Dust Bowl Experience*. Niwot: UP Colorado, 1999. Questia Media America. Web. 10 Apr. 2010.

A CD-ROM

"Dust Bowl." *Britannica Student Encyclopedia*. 2004 ed. Chicago: Encyclopaedia Britannica, 2004. CD-ROM.

Participating in Collaborative Discussions

COMMON CORE SL 1a-d

Often, class activities, including the Performance Tasks in this book, will require you to work collaboratively with classmates. Whether your group will analyze a work of literature or try to solve a community problem, use the following guidelines to ensure a productive discussion.

Prepare for the Discussion

A productive discussion is one in which all the participants bring useful information and ideas to share. If your group will discuss a short story the class read, first reread and annotate a copy of the story. Your annotations will help you quickly locate evidence to support your points. Participants in a discussion about an important issue should first research the issue and bring notes or information sources that will help guide the group. If you disagree with a point made by another group member, your case will be stronger if you back it up with specific evidence from your sources.

EXAMPLES

> **disagreeing without evidence:** It's silly and a waste of time to even discuss whether people are good or bad.

> **providing evidence for disagreement:** I disagree with the view that discussing whether human tendencies are good or bad is irrelevant or silly. The issue of good and evil has been a significant theme for philosophers, theologians, writers, and poets from centuries past up to the present day.

Set Ground Rules

The rules your group needs will depend on what your group is expected to accomplish. A discussion of themes in a poem will be unlikely to produce a single consensus; however, a discussion aimed at developing a solution to a concrete problem should result in one strong proposal arrived at democratically with the participation of all group members. Answer the following questions to set ground rules that fit your group's purpose:

- What will this group produce? A range of ideas, a single decision, a plan of action, or something else?

- How much time is available? How much of that time should be allotted to each part of our discussion (presenting ideas, summarizing or voting on final ideas, creating a product such as a written analysis or speech)?

- What roles need to be assigned within the group? Do we need a leader, a note-taker, a timekeeper, or other specific roles?

- What is the best way to synthesize our group's ideas? Should we take a vote, list group members as "for" or "against" in a chart, or use some other method to reach consensus or sum up the results of the discussion?

Move the Discussion Forward

Everyone in the group should be actively involved in synthesizing ideas. To make sure this happens, ask questions that draw out ideas, especially from less-talkative members of the group. If an idea or statement is confusing, try to paraphrase it, or ask the speaker to explain more about it. If you disagree with a statement, say so politely and explain in detail why you disagree.

SAMPLE DISCUSSION

Effective Behavior	How It Works
Support others' contributions. In this example, Alejandro believes that people are essentially good: we should trust others to do the right thing. He mentions examples of courageous behavior by ordinary people during natural disasters. Genna listens attentively to Alejandro. She has just come from a discussion of slavery in America in her social studies class. She wonders how people can believe in freedom but enslave others at the same time.	Alejandro shares his opinion, supporting it with evidence. Genna disagrees with Alejandro but still listens carefully. She avoids making faces, rolling her eyes, or loudly sighing while Alejandro presents his views.
State your own views thoughtfully. When Alejandro finishes speaking, Genna restates his points to make sure she understands his perspective. She comments, "I understand Alejandro's position because I, too, want to believe that people are essentially good. But there are many examples from history of people treating others with cruelty by exploiting them for their own gain. Americans believed in freedom, yet some kept slaves. How is it possible to be 'essentially good' but then do terrible things?"	Genna verifies that she understands Alejandro's point. Then she offers another viewpoint, supporting it with an example. As Genna did, Alejandro listens carefully and respectfully as she explains her perspective.

Respond to Ideas

In a diverse group, everyone may have a different perspective on the topic of discussion, and that's a good thing. Consider what everyone has to say, and don't resist changing your view if other group members provide convincing evidence for theirs. If, instead, you feel more strongly than ever about your view, don't hesitate to say so and provide reasons related to what those with opposing views have said. Before wrapping up the discussion, try to synthesize the claims made on both sides. That means pulling sometimes contradictory ideas together to arrive at a new understanding.

SAMPLE DISCUSSION

Effective Behavior	How It Works
Synthesize various viewpoints to arrive at a new, alternative understanding. Li speaks next. First he summarizes Alejandro and Genna's opposing views, and then he offers an alternative. "It may look like there is a contradiction here. Either people are essentially good, or they are not. But what if there is another way of looking at this? What if people are neither one nor the other but capable of being both?"	By combining both arguments, Li creates an alternative view of the issue. This expands the discussion, by allowing different viewpoints to coexist.
Justify your views or consider new ones. Alejandro considers what Li has said. He prepares to offer more evidence that people are essentially good and extends his argument to respond to Genna's point as well. Perhaps outside forces may affect essential goodness and turn people toward negative thoughts or actions. He decides to mention this when his turn comes up again. Li's point makes Genna think, too. She makes a note to ask the group, "If what Li says is true, how do we learn how to make those choices? What makes some people choose to do good, while others choose to do terrible things? And are there times when people may not really have a choice?" Her question will also expand the discussion.	Alejandro and Genna consider Li's point. Li's alternative offers an opportunity to delve into the original question and expand their own arguments. Through the contributions of each participant, the discussion has led to a true collaboration about the topic.

Debating an Issue

COMMON CORE SL 1a-d, SL 3, SL 4

The selection and collection Performance Tasks in this text will direct you to engage in debates about issues relating to the selections you are reading. Use the guidelines that follow to have a productive and balanced debate about both sides of an issue.

The Structure of a Formal Debate

If you've ever tried to settle a disagreement with friends or siblings, you've used persuasive techniques to engage in a debate—a discussion in which individuals or teams argue opposing sides of an issue. In a **formal debate,** two teams, each with three members, present their arguments on a given proposition or policy statement. One team argues for the proposition or statement, and the other team argues against it. Each debater must consider the proposition closely and must research both sides of it. To argue convincingly either for or against a proposition, a debater must be familiar with both sides of the issue.

Plan the Debate

The purpose of a debate is to allow participants and audience members to consider both sides of an issue. Use these planning suggestions to hold a balanced and productive debate:

- **Identify Debate Teams** Form groups of six members based on the issues that the Performance Tasks include. Three members of the team will argue for the affirmative side of the issue—that is, they support the issue. The other three members will argue for the negative side of the issue—that is, they will not support the issue.
- **Appoint a Moderator** The moderator plays a neutral role in the debate, promoting a civil discussion and keeping everyone on task. The moderator begins by introducing the topic of the debate and then recognizes speakers, alternating between affirmative and negative.
- **Assign Debate Roles** One team member introduces the team's claim with supporting reasons and evidence. Another team member exchanges questions with a member of the opposing team to clarify and challenge reasoning. The last member presents a strong closing argument.

Prepare Briefs and Rebuttals

A **brief** is an outline of the debate, accounting for the evidence and arguments of both sides of the **proposition** (topic). Debaters also prepare a **rebuttal,** a follow-up speech to support their arguments and counter the opposition's. Propositions are usually one of four types:

- **Proposition of fact**—Debaters determine whether a statement is true or false. An example is "Deforestation is ruining the rain forest."
- **Proposition of value**—Debaters determine the value of a person, place, or thing. An example is "Free trade will help small countries develop."
- **Proposition of problem**—Debaters determine whether a problem exists and whether it requires action.
- **Proposition of policy**—Debaters determine the action that will be taken. An example is "Students will provide tutoring services."

Use the following steps to prepare a brief:

- **Gather Information** Consult a variety of primary and secondary sources to gather the most reliable, up-to-date information about the proposition.
- **Identify Key Ideas** Sort out the important points, and arrange them in order of importance.
- **List Arguments For and Against Each Key Idea** Look for strong arguments that support your side of the proposition, and also note those that support your opponents' side.
- **Support Your Arguments** Find facts, quotations, expert opinions, and examples that support your arguments and counter your opponents'.
- **Write the Brief** Begin your brief with a statement of the proposition. Then list the

arguments and evidence that support both sides of the proposition.

The rebuttal is the opportunity to rebuild your case. Use the following steps to build a strong rebuttal:

- Listen to your opponents respectfully. Note the points you wish to overturn.
- Defend what the opposition has challenged.
- Cite weaknesses in their arguments, such as points they overlooked.
- Present counterarguments and supporting evidence.
- Offer your summary arguments. Restate and solidify your stance.

Hold the Debate

A well-run debate can be a vehicle for expressing your opinions in an assertive but respectful manner. Participating in a debate challenges you to synthesize comments made on both sides of an issue, pose probing questions, clarify ideas, and appreciate divergent perspectives.

FORMAL DEBATE FORMAT

Speaker	Role	Time
Affirmative Speaker 1	Present the claim and supporting evidence for the affirmative ("pro") side of the argument.	5 minutes
Negative Speaker 1	Ask probing questions that will prompt the other team to address flaws in the argument.	3 minutes
Affirmative Speaker 2	Respond to the questions posed by the opposing team and counter any concerns.	3 minutes
Negative Speaker 2	Present the claim and supporting evidence for the negative ("con") side of the argument.	5 minutes
Affirmative Speaker 3	Summarize the claim and evidence for the affirmative side and explain why your reasoning is more valid.	3 minutes
Negative Speaker 3	Summarize the claim and evidence for the negative side and explain why your reasoning is more valid.	3 minutes

Evaluate the Debate

Use the following guidelines to evaluate a team in a debate:

- What was the proposition, or premise, being debated? Was each team's stance with respect to the topic—whether affirmative or negative—clear?
- How effectively did the team present reasons and evidence, including evidence from the texts, to support the proposition? Were the links among ideas clear?
- Did the team avoid fallacious, or flawed, reasoning? Did the team avoid disguising exaggerated or distorted evidence with persuasive rhetoric? In general, was the team's word choice appropriate?
- How effectively did the team rebut, or respond to, arguments made by the opposing team?
- Did the speakers maintain eye contact and speak at an appropriate rate and volume?
- Did the speakers observe proper debate etiquette—that is, did they follow the moderator's instructions, stay within their allotted time limits, and treat their opponents respectfully? Did they use verbal techniques of emphasis and tone to highlight their argument rather than to ridicule their opponent?

PRACTICE AND APPLY

Possible answers:
Students should create a chart like the one on page R16. The chart should include details similar to the ones below. Remind students to write legibly as they complete their chart.

Claim
Women homesteading is the solution to poverty's problems.

Reason
Homesteading means job security and a home.

Evidence
It is possible to plant, grow, and harvest enough food for a family to eat through the winter.

Counterargument
It is not for those afraid of coyotes and hard work and loneliness, but for those who can do it, it will result in independence, plenty of food, and a home of one's own.

Reading Arguments

An argument expresses a position on an issue or problem and supports it with reasons and evidence. Being able to analyze and evaluate arguments will help you distinguish between claims you should accept and those you should not.

Analyzing an Argument

A sound argument should appeal strictly to reason. However, arguments are often used in texts that also contain other types of persuasive devices. An argument includes the following elements:

- A **claim** is the writer's position on an issue or central idea.
- **Support** is any material that serves to prove a claim. In an argument, support usually consists of reasons and evidence.
- **Reasons** are declarations made to justify an action, a decision, or a belief—for example, "You should sleep on a good mattress *in order to avoid spinal problems.*"
- **Evidence** consists of the specific references, quotations, facts, examples, and opinions that support a claim. Evidence may also consist of statistics, reports of personal experience, or the views of experts.
- A **counterargument** is an argument made to oppose another argument. A good argument anticipates the opposition's objections and provides counterarguments to disprove or answer them.

Claim	Walt Whitman is one of the most important figures in American poetry.
Reason	He experimented with poetic form and content and created a quintessentially American voice in literature.
Evidence	His poetry influenced generations of poets. His poems celebrated the diversity and spirit of American culture.
Counter-argument	No American poet before Whitman broke with tradition in the ways he did.

Practice and Apply

In the early 1900s, Elinore Pruitt Stewart (formerly Rupert), was living in Burnt Fork, Wyoming, as a homesteader, a person who received public land free of charge under the Homestead Act of 1862. In the following letter to a friend, she makes an argument for homestead living over an impoverished city existence. Use a chart like the one shown to identify the claim, reason, evidence, and counterargument in her letter.

January 23, 1913

Dear Mrs. Coney,—

. . . When I read of the hard times among the Denver poor, I feel like urging them every one to get out and file on land. I am very enthusiastic about women homesteading. It really requires less strength and labor to raise plenty to satisfy a large family than it does to go out to wash, with the added satisfaction of knowing that their job will not be lost to them if they care to keep it. Even if improving the place does go slowly, it is that much done to stay done. Whatever is raised is the homesteader's own, and there is no house-rent to pay. This year Jerrine cut and dropped enough potatoes to raise a ton of fine potatoes. She wanted to try, so we let her, and you will remember that she is but six years old. We had a man to break the ground and cover the potatoes for her and the man irrigated them once. That was all that was done until digging time, when they were ploughed out and Jerrine picked them up. Any woman strong enough to go out by the day could have done every bit of the work and put in two or three times that much, and it would have been so much more pleasant than to work so hard in the city and then be on starvation rations in the winter.

To me, homesteading is the solution of all poverty's problems, but I realize that temperament has much to do with success in any undertaking, and persons afraid of coyotes and work and loneliness had better let ranching alone. At the same time, any woman who can stand her own company, can see the beauty of

---

continued

the sunset, loves growing things, and is willing to put in as much time at careful labor as she does over the washtub, will certainly succeed; will have independence, plenty to eat all the time, and a home of her own in the end.

Recognizing Persuasive Techniques

Persuasive texts typically rely on more than just the logical appeal of an argument to be convincing. They also rely on ethical and emotional appeals, as well as other **persuasive techniques**—devices that can sway you to adopt a position or take an action.

The chart shown here explains several of these techniques. Learn to recognize them, and you will be less likely to be influenced by them.

Persuasive Technique	Example
Appeals by Association	
Bandwagon appeal Suggests that a person should believe or do something because "everyone else" does	Join the millions who've contributed to The Cause: buy your 'Be Well' bracelet today.
Testimonial Relies on endorsements from well-known people or satisfied customers	DJ Super Dawg keeps songs spinning all day long with his new CompactM3 disc player. Give it a whirl!
Snob appeal Taps into people's desire to be special or part of an elite group	In Smart and Sassy cosmetics, you'll look and feel like the princess you are.
Transfer Connnects a product, candidate, or cause with a positive emotion or idea	Rediscover peace and tranquility with Back in Balance aromatherapy candles.
Appeal to loyalty Relies on people's affiliation with a particular group	Only Substantial Bank offers long-term customers better rates.

Emotional Appeals	
Appeals to pity, fear, or vanity Use strong feelings, rather than facts, to persuade	The cost of one candy bar can help buy a whole meal for a starving family.

Word Choice	
Glittering generality Makes a generalization that includes a word or phrase with positive connotations, such as *freedom* and *honor,* to promote a product or idea.	Improve your children's future: plant a tree on World Tree Day.

Practice and Apply

Identify the persuasive techniques used in the model.

The Real Scoop

On my last trip to Splendid Dan's Ice Cream Shoppe to get a Swirling Fantasia Double Dip Delight, I was thrilled to find yet another reason that makes buying dessert at Dan's feel so splendid. During the next 30 days at the downtown location, a whopping 40 percent of Dan's proceeds will go toward helping the homeless in our city. Forty percent! No wonder so many local celebrities, like news anchor Tandy Marquez and Mayor Donald Townsend, have been spotted at Dan's. They know that with each purchase, they are also providing food, clothing, and shelter for those in need. If you join them, you'll have not only the most amazing ice cream on the planet, but also the added joy of providing life's basic necessities to the less fortunate. It's the least we can do to better our city, so stop by Splendid Dan's—he's got the "real scoop."

COMMON CORE RI 6

PRACTICE AND APPLY
Answers:
Answers could include the following:
"feel so splendid": transfer
"local celebrities . . . join them":
testimonial, snob appeal
"necessities to less fortunate . . . least we can do": appeal to pity

Analyzing Logic and Reasoning

When you evaluate an argument, you need to look closely at the writer's logic and reasoning. In doing this, it is helpful to identify the type of reasoning the writer is using.

The Inductive Mode of Reasoning

When a writer leads from specific evidence to a general principle or generalization, that writer is using **inductive reasoning.** Here is an example of inductive reasoning.

Specific Facts
Fact 1 Harriet Beecher Stowe's *Uncle Tom's Cabin* helped alert Americans to the horrors of slavery.
Fact 2 Rachel Carson's *Silent Spring* helped make the public aware of the dangers of overuse of pesticides.
Fact 3 Betty Friedan's *The Feminine Mystique* prompted women to seek equal rights.
Generalization
Literature can sometimes help to shape public opinion.

Strategies for Determining the Soundness of Inductive Arguments

Ask yourself the following questions to evaluate an inductive argument:

- **Is the evidence valid and sufficient support for the conclusion?** Inaccurate facts lead to inaccurate conclusions. Make sure all facts are accurate.
- **Does the conclusion follow logically from the evidence?** Make sure the writer has used sound reasons—those that can be proved—as the basis for the conclusion and has avoided logical fallacies, such as circular logic and oversimplification.
- **Is the evidence drawn from a large enough sample?** The three facts listed in the example are enough to support the claim. By qualifying the generalization with words such as *sometimes, some,* or *many,* the writer indicates the generalization is limited to a specific group.

The Deductive Mode of Reasoning

When a writer arrives at a conclusion by applying a general principle to a specific situation, the writer is using **deductive reasoning.** Here's an example.

People have the right to revolt when oppressed.	General principle or premise
▼	
The American colonies are oppressed by British rule.	Specific situation
▼	
The American colonies are justified in fighting for freedom from British rule.	Specific conclusion

Strategies for Determining the Soundness of Deductive Arguments

Ask yourself the following questions to evaluate a deductive argument:

- **Is the general principle stated, or is it implied?** Note that writers often use deductive reasoning in an argument without stating the general principle. They assume readers will understand the principle. You may want to identify the general principle for yourself.
- **Is the general principle sound?** Don't assume the general principle is sound. Determine whether it is proven.
- **Is the conclusion valid?** To be valid, a conclusion in a deductive argument must follow logically from the general principle and the specific situation.

The following chart shows two conclusions drawn from the same general principle.

General Principle: All government offices were closed last Monday.	
Accurate Deduction	**Inaccurate Deduction**
West Post Office is a government office; therefore, West Post Office was closed last Monday.	Soon-Lin's Spa was closed last Monday; therefore, Soon-Lin's Spa is a government office.

The conclusion that Soon-Lin's Spa is a government office does not make logical sense, because other factors determine whether or not it is a government office.

 **RI 6**

Practice and Apply

Identify the mode of reasoning used in the following:

Detailed research shows that using a cell phone while driving is a key cause of traffic accidents. Many states have already passed laws making "hands free" devices mandatory for cell phone users while driving. However, ear pieces or speaker phones provide very few true safety benefits. The problem is not the way in which a driver is distracted, but the distraction itself. Looking up a phone number, dialing, and concentrating on the conversation can all take a driver's focus, and eyes, off the road.

Betsie Edens, a 19-year-old college student, says she uses her cell phone to get in touch with family, old friends, and fellow college students while making the three-hour drive from her parent's house to Denton State University. "I talk on the phone or send text messages at least two and a half of the three hours it takes to get there," she says.

Betsie is one of millions of teenagers worldwide who do more talking on a cell phone than safe driving. It is time these unsafe drivers focus more on the road and less on their friends' gossip. For the sake of everybody's safety, cell phones must be turned off while on the road.

PRACTICE AND APPLY
Answers:
Deductive reasoning is used.
  General principle: Distractions while driving are unsafe.
  Specific situation: Using cell phones while driving is a distraction.
  Specific conclusion: Cell phones must be turned off while driving.

Identifying Faulty Reasoning

Sometimes an argument at first appears to make sense but isn't valid, because it is based on a fallacy. A **logical fallacy** is an error in logic. Learn to recognize these common fallacies.

Type of Fallacy	Definition	Example
Circular logic	Supporting a statement by simply repeating it in different words	Sport utility vehicles are popular **because more people buy them than any other category of new cars.**
Either/or fallacy	A statement that suggests that there are only two choices available in a situation that really offers more than two options	**Either** we raise the legal driving age, **or** accidents caused by teenage drivers will continue to happen.
Oversimplification	An explanation of a complex situation or problem as if it were much more simple than it is	If we would only be more tolerant of people's differences, there would be **no more wars.**
Overgeneralization	A generalization that is too broad. You can often recognize overgeneralizations by the use of words such as *all, everyone, every time, anything, no one,* and *none.*	**Every time** I want to do something my way, my parents say no.
Stereotyping	A dangerous type of overgeneralization. Stereotypes are broad statements about people on the basis of their gender, ethnicity, race, or political, social, professional, or religious group.	**People who work for large corporations are** followers, not leaders.

Reading Arguments   **R19**

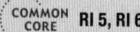 **RI 5, RI 6**

PRACTICE AND APPLY

Answers:

Stereotyping, name-calling: "Leaders of circus companies claim that healthy living environments are provided for the animals, but they, like most business owners, are liars." Overgeneralization: "Abuse makes animals more aggressive; everyone knows that."

Hasty generalization: "In the last 15 years, captive elephants have killed 65 people and injured 130, so it is clear the elephants are abused by their trainers."

---

continued

Type of Fallacy	Definition	Example
Attacking the person or name-calling	An attempt to discredit an idea by attacking the person or group associated with it. Candidates often engage in name-calling during political campaigns.	The governor wants to eliminate candy machines in school cafeterias, but **he doesn't know what he's talking about.**
Evading the issue	Refuting an objection with arguments and evidence that do not address its central point	I know I wasn't supposed to use the car last night, **but I did fill up the tank and check the tire pressure.**
Non sequitur	A conclusion that does not follow logically from the "proof" offered to support it. A non sequitur is sometimes used to win an argument by diverting the reader's attention to proof that can't be challenged.	Mr. Crandall is my guidance counselor. **I will definitely get accepted to a private college.**
False cause	The mistake of assuming that because one event occurred after another event in time, the first event caused the second one to occur	The cheerleading squad did the Super Slam Dance, **and because of that, Donny slam-dunked the basketball, and we won the game.**
False analogy	A comparison that doesn't hold up because of a critical difference between the two subjects	Jenny didn't do well in Spanish, **so she'll probably fail German as well.**
Hasty generalization	A conclusion drawn from too little evidence or from evidence that is biased	Two jet planes crashed this year. **Air travel is extremely unsafe.**

Practice and Apply

Look for examples of logical fallacies in the following argument. Identify each one and explain why you identified it as such.

Elephants should be banned from circuses. Leaders of circus companies claim that healthy living environments are provided for the animals, but they, like most business owners, are liars. Sharp bullhooks are used for training, and the elephants are beaten severely every day. Abuse makes animals more aggressive; everyone knows that. In the last 15 years, captive elephants have killed 65 people and injured 130, so it is clear the elephants are abused by their trainers. Legislation to stop this cruelty should be passed immediately!

Evaluating Persuasive Texts

Learning how to evaluate persuasive texts and identify bias will help you become more selective when doing research and also help you improve your own reasoning and arguing skills. **Bias** is an inclination for or against a particular opinion or viewpoint. A writer may reveal a strongly positive or negative opinion on an issue by presenting only one way of looking at it or by heavily weighting the evidence on one side of the argument. Additionally, the presence of either of the following is often a sign of bias:

Loaded language consists of words with strongly positive or negative connotations that are intended to influence a reader's attitude.

EXAMPLE

The superior All-Star Road Warrior offers unparalleled excellence in all-wheel-drive capability and can outperform any car on the road. (*Superior, unparalleled, excellence,* and *outperform* have positive connotations.)

Propaganda is any form of communication that is so distorted that it conveys false or misleading information. Many logical fallacies—such as name-calling, the either/or fallacy, and false causes—are often used in propaganda. The following example shows an oversimplification. The writer uses one fact to support a particular point of view but does not reveal another fact that does not support that viewpoint.

EXAMPLE

Since the new administration took office, unemployment rates have been cut in half. (The writer does not include information about legislation, passed by the previous administration, that created thousands of jobs.)

Strategies for Evaluating Evidence

It is important to have a set of standards by which you can evaluate persuasive texts. Use the questions below to help you critically assess facts and opinions that are presented as evidence.

- **Are the facts presented verifiable?** Facts can be proved by eyewitness accounts, authoritative sources such as encyclopedias and almanacs, experts, or research.
- **Are the opinions presented credible?** Any opinions offered should be supported by facts, research, eyewitness accounts, or the opinions of experts on the topic.
- **Is the evidence thorough?** Thorough evidence leaves no reasonable questions unanswered. If a choice is offered, background for making the choice should be provided. If taking a side is called for, all sides of the issue should be presented.
- **Is the evidence biased?** Be alert to evidence that contains loaded language or other signs of bias.
- **Is the evidence authoritative?** The people, groups, or organizations that provided the evidence should have credentials that verify their credibility.
- **Is it important that the evidence be current?** Where timeliness is crucial, as in the areas of medicine and technology, the evidence should reflect the latest developments in the areas.

Practice and Apply

Read the argument below. Identify the facts, opinions, and elements of bias.

In our city neighborhood, unnecessary speed bumps are being built on residential streets. Cars park bumper to bumper along both sides of the street, day and night. There is no place to pull over, causing cars to stop in the middle of the street to pick up and drop off passengers. My point is that it is impossible to drive fast on these streets anyway! Why do no-good politicians spend a lot of taxpayer money on a ridiculous irritation for drivers? They must figure wrongly that either they build speed bumps, or some little kid will get killed. That's never happened, and it never will.

 COMMON CORE **RI 5, RI 6**

PRACTICE AND APPLY
Answers:
Facts: speed bumps being built, cars park bumper to bumper, cars stop in the middle of the street
Opinions: Speed bumps are "unnecessary"; no one will be killed if there aren't any speed bumps.
Bias: "[N]o-good politicians spend a lot of taxpayer money on a ridiculous irritation"; "They must figure wrongly"; "it is impossible to drive fast on these streets anyway!"

PRACTICE AND APPLY

Possible answers:
Students' responses will vary but should evaluate the strength of the claim, the evidence supporting the claim, and the counterarguments.
Possible answer may include: The claim is that the town needs to build an ice skating rink. Some of the evidence is adequate, but includes logical fallacies. The writer does not adequately address the counterargument presented.

Strategies for Evaluating an Argument

Make sure that all or most of the following statements are true:

- The argument presents a claim or thesis.
- The claim is connected to its support by a general principle that most readers would readily agree with. Valid general principle: *It is the job of a corporation to provide adequate health benefits to full-time employees.* Invalid general principle: *It is the job of a corporation to ensure its employees are healthy and physically fit.*
- The reasons make sense.
- The reasons are presented in a logical and effective order.
- The claim and all reasons are adequately supported by sound evidence.
- The evidence is adequate, accurate, and appropriate.
- The logic is sound. There are no instances of logical fallacies.
- The argument adequately anticipates and addresses reader concerns and counterclaims with counterarguments.

Use the preceding criteria to evaluate the strength of the following editorial:

This town needs an ice skating rink. Everybody knows that ice skating is the only real way to learn balance and coordination, while also exercising. It is, after all, an Olympic event. That is why I believe it is the responsibility of the town council to put aside funding for a year-round ice skating rink.

Our town has always believed that our children's future relies on good development. For intellectual stimulation, the council has provided the public library and the Nature Museum. For creativity, the council has funded the Community Art Center, where kids can learn to make pottery, paint, dance, and sing. But when it comes to a place where youth can go to develop physical skills of balance, rhythm, and strength, we have absolutely nothing.

We also need a rink because ice skating is fun! The town council members are themselves boring individuals and don't think kids should have fun. As one member put it, "There are many places in this town built especially with youth in mind. Ice skating is not a top priority on our list of community needs this year." They obviously feel this way because our football team came in fifth in the conference last year.

But the biggest reason we need an ice skating rink is so that kids can have a place to ice skate. And let's not forget, adults like ice skating, too. Most of the people who make it to the Olympics are over 18.

Either the town council will help our children develop by putting up the rink, or they prove themselves stingy politicians who do not have the town's best interest at heart.

Grammar

COMMON CORE L 1, L 2a, L3, L4a-d

Writing that has a lot of mistakes can confuse or even annoy a reader. A business letter with a punctuation error might lead to a miscommunication and delay a reply. A sentence fragment might lower your grade on an essay. Paying attention to grammar, punctuation, and capitalization rules can make your writing clearer and easier to read.

Quick Reference: Parts of Speech

Part of Speech	Function	Examples
Noun	names a person, a place, a thing, an idea, a quality, or an action	
common	serves as a general name, or a name common to an entire group	coyote, hunter, spear, bonfire
proper	names a specific, one-of-a-kind person, place, or thing	Rainy Mountain, Virginia, Puritans
singular	refers to a single person, place, thing, or idea	field, pony, child, man
plural	refers to more than one person, place, thing, or idea	fields, ponies, children, men
concrete	names something that can be perceived by the senses	lemon, shores, wind, canoe
abstract	names something that cannot be perceived by the senses	fear, intelligence, honesty
compound	expresses a single idea through a combination of two or more words	birthright, folk tale, Sky-World
collective	refers to a group of people or things	species, army, flock
possessive	shows who or what owns something	America's, Douglass's, men's, slaves'
Pronoun	takes the place of a noun or another pronoun	
personal	refers to the person(s) making a statement, the person(s) being addressed, or the person(s) or thing(s) the statement is about	I, me, my, mine, we, us, our, ours, you, your, yours, she, he, it, her, him, hers, his, its, they, them, their, theirs
reflexive	follows a verb or preposition and refers to a preceding noun or pronoun	myself, yourself, herself, himself, itself, ourselves, yourselves, themselves
intensive	emphasizes a noun or another pronoun	(same as reflexives)

continued

Part of Speech	Function	Examples
demonstrative	points to one or more specific persons or things	this, that, these, those
interrogative	signals a question	who, whom, whose, which, what
indefinite	refers to one or more persons or things not specifically mentioned	both, all, most, many, anyone, everybody, several, none, some
relative	introduces an adjective clause by relating it to a word in the clause	who, whom, whose, which, that
Verb	expresses an action, a condition, or a state of being	
action	tells what the subject does or did, physically or mentally	run, reaches, listened, consider, decides, dreamed
linking	connects the subject to something that identifies or describes it	am, is, are, was, were, sound, taste, appear, feel, become, remain, seem
auxiliary	precedes the main verb in a verb phrase	be, have, do, can, could, will, would, may, might
transitive	directs the action toward someone or something; always has an object	The wind **snapped** the young tree in half.
intransitive	does not direct the action toward someone or something; does not have an object	The young tree **snapped.**
Adjective	modifies a noun or pronoun	**frightened** man, **two** epics, **enough** time
Adverb	modifies a verb, an adjective, or another adverb	walked **out, really** funny, **far** away
Preposition	relates one word to another word	at, by, for, from, in, of, on, to, with
Conjunction	joins words or word groups	
coordinating	joins words or word groups used the same way	and, but, or, for, so, yet, nor
correlative	used as a pair to join words or word groups used the same way	both . . . and, either . . . or, neither . . . nor
subordinating	introduces a clause that cannot stand by itself as a complete sentence	although, after, as, before, because, when, if, unless
Interjection	expresses emotion	whew, yikes, uh-oh

Quick Reference: The Sentence and Its Parts

The diagrams that follow will give you a brief review of the essentials of a sentence and some of its parts.

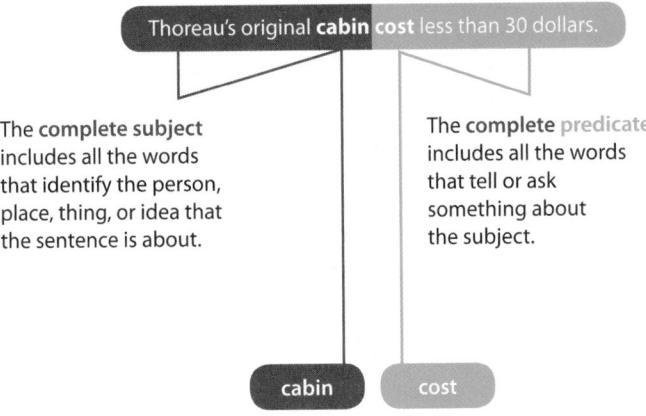

Thoreau's original **cabin cost** less than 30 dollars.

The **complete subject** includes all the words that identify the person, place, thing, or idea that the sentence is about.

The **complete** predicate includes all the words that tell or ask something about the subject.

cabin

cost

The **simple subject** tells exactly whom or what the sentence is about. It may be one word or a group of words, but it does not include modifiers.

The simple predicate tells what the subject does or is. It may be one word or several, but it does not include modifiers.

Every word in a sentence is part of a complete subject or a complete predicate.

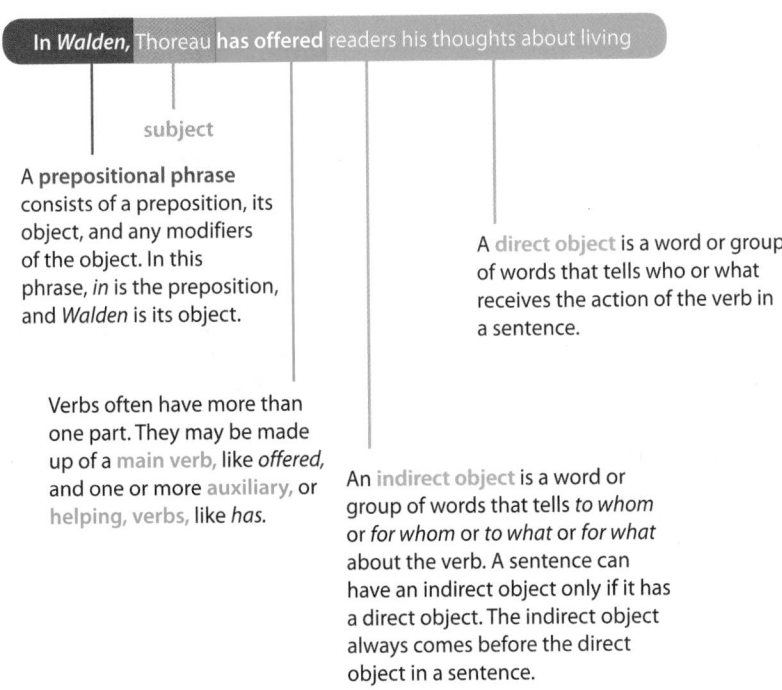

In *Walden,* Thoreau **has offered** readers his thoughts about living

subject

A **prepositional phrase** consists of a preposition, its object, and any modifiers of the object. In this phrase, *in* is the preposition, and *Walden* is its object.

A direct object is a word or group of words that tells who or what receives the action of the verb in a sentence.

Verbs often have more than one part. They may be made up of a main verb, like *offered,* and one or more auxiliary, or helping, verbs, like *has.*

An indirect object is a word or group of words that tells *to whom* or *for whom* or *to what* or *for what* about the verb. A sentence can have an indirect object only if it has a direct object. The indirect object always comes before the direct object in a sentence.

Grammar **R25**

Quick Reference: Punctuation

Mark	Function	Examples
End Marks period, question mark, exclamation point	end a sentence	The games begin today. Who is your favorite contestant? What a play Jamie made!
period	follows an initial or abbreviation Exception: postal abbreviations of states	Prof. Ted Bakerman, D. H. Lawrence, HMH Co., P.M., A.D., oz., ft., Blvd., St. NE (Nebraska), NV (Nevada)
period	follows a number or letter in an outline	I. Volcanoes A. Central-vent 1. Shield
Comma	separates parts of a compound sentence	I had never disliked poetry, but now I really love it.
	separates items in a series	She is brave, loyal, and kind.
	separates adjectives of equal rank that modify the same noun	The slow, easy route is best.
	sets off a term of address	America, I love you. Come to the front, children.
	sets off a parenthetical expression	Hard workers, as you know, don't quit. I'm not a quitter, believe me.
	sets off an introductory word, phrase, or dependent clause	Yes, I forgot my key. At the beginning of the day, I feel fresh. While she was out, I was here. Having finished my chores, I went out.
	sets off a nonessential phrase or clause	Ed Pawn, the captain of the chess team, won. Ed Pawn, who is the captain, won. The two leading runners, sprinting toward the finish line, finished in a tie.
	sets off parts of dates and addresses	Send it by August 18, 2010, to Cherry Jubilee, Inc., 21 Vernona St., Oakland, Minnesota.
	follows the salutation and closing of a letter	Dear Jim, Sincerely yours,
	separates words to avoid confusion	By noon, time had run out. What the minister does, does matter. While cooking, Jim burned his hand.
Semicolon	separates items in a series if one or more items contain commas	We invited my sister, Jan; her friend, Don; my uncle Jack; and Mary Dodd.

continued

Mark	Function	Examples
	separates parts of a compound sentence that are not joined by a coordinating conjunction	The small books are on the top shelves; the large books are below. I dusted the books; however, I didn't wipe the shelves.
	separates parts of a compound sentence when the parts contain commas	After I ran out of money, I called my parents; but only my sister was home, unfortunately.
Colon	introduces a list	Those we wrote were the following: Dana, John, and Will.
	introduces a long quotation	Thomas Jefferson wrote: "We the people of the United States, in order to form a more perfect union. . . ."
	follows the salutation of a business letter	Dear Ms. Williams: Dear Senator Wiley:
	separates certain numbers	1:28 P.M., Genesis 2:5
Dash	indicates an abrupt break in thought	I was thinking of my mother—who is arriving tomorrow—just as you walked in.
Parentheses	enclose less-important material	Throughout her life (though some might think otherwise), she worked hard. The temperature on this July day (would you believe it?) is 65 degrees!
Hyphen	joins parts of a compound adjective before a noun	She lives in a first-floor apartment.
	joins parts of a compound with *all-, ex-, self-,* or *-elect*	The president-elect is a well-respected woman.
	joins parts of a compound number (to ninety-nine)	Today, I turn twenty-one.
	joins parts of a fraction	My cup is one-third full.
	joins a prefix to a word beginning with a capital letter	Life may have seemed simpler in pre–Civil War days. It's very chilly for mid-June.
	indicates that a word is divided at the end of a line	Did you know that school segrega-tion has been illegal since 1954?
Apostrophe	used with *s* to form the possessive of a noun or an indefinite pronoun	my friend's book, my friends' books, anyone's guess, somebody else's problem

continued

Mark	Function	Examples
	replaces one or more omitted letters in a contraction or numbers in a date	don't (omitted *o*), he'd (omitted *woul*), the class of '99 (omitted *19*)
	used with *s* to form the plural of a letter	I had two A's on my report card.
Quotation Marks	set off a speaker's exact words	Sara said, "I'm finally ready." "I'm ready," Sara said, "finally." Did Sara say, "I'm ready"? Sara said, "I'm ready!"
	set off the title of a story, an article, a short poem, an essay, a song, or a chapter	I liked Oates's "Hostage," Steinem's "Sisterhood," and Plath's "Mirror." Chapter II is titled "Our Gang's Dark Oath."
Ellipses	replace material omitted from a quotation	"We the people ... in order to form a more perfect union ...."
Italics	indicate the title of a book, a play, a magazine, a long poem, an opera, a film, or a TV series, or the names of ships, trains, and spacecraft	***The Scarlet Letter, The Crucible, Time, The Death of the Hired Man, West Side Story, Citizen Kane, The Spirit of St. Louis, The Best of Frank Sinatra, Lusitania***

Quick Reference: Capitalization

Category	Examples
People and Titles	
Names and initials of people	Emily Dickinson, T. S. Eliot
Titles used before or in place of names	Professor Holmes, Senator Long
Deities and members of religious groups	Jesus, Allah, Buddha, Zeus, Baptists, Roman Catholics
Names of ethnic and national groups	Hispanics, Jews, African Americans
Geographical Names	
Cities, states, countries, continents	New York, Maine, Haiti, Africa
Regions, bodies of water, mountains	the South, Lake Erie, Mount Katahdin
Geographic features, parks	Continental Divide, Everglades, Yellowstone
Streets and roads, planets	55 East Ninety-fifth Street, Maple Lane, Venus, Jupiter
Organizations, Events, Etc.	
Companies, organizations, teams	General Motors, Lions Club, Utah Jazz
Buildings, bridges, monuments	the Alamo, Golden Gate Bridge, Lincoln Memorial
Documents, awards	the Constitution, World Cup
Special named events	Super Bowl, World Series
Government bodies, historical periods and events	the Supreme Court, U.S. Senate, Harlem Renaissance, World War II
Days and months, holidays	Friday, May, Easter, Memorial Day
Specific cars, boats, trains, planes	Mustang, *Titanic*, *California Zephyr*
Proper Adjectives	
Adjectives formed from proper nouns	American League teams, French cooking, Emersonian period, Arctic waters
First Words and the Pronoun I	
First word in a sentence or quotation	This is it. He said, "Let's go."
First word of sentence in parentheses that is not within another sentence	The spelling rules are covered in another section. (Consult that section for more information.)
First words in the salutation and closing of a letter	Dear Madam, Very truly yours,
First word in each line of most poetry Personal pronoun *I*	Then am I A happy fly If I live Or if I die.
First word, last word, and all important words in a title	"The Fall of the House of Usher," *Incidents in the Life of a Slave Girl*

1 Nouns

A **noun** is a word used to name a person, a place, a thing, an idea, a quality, or an action. Nouns can be classified in several ways.

1.1 COMMON NOUNS

Common nouns are general names, common to entire groups.

> EXAMPLES: *writer, song, bravery*

1.2 PROPER NOUNS

Proper nouns name specific, one-of-a-kind things.

Common	Proper
writer, song, bravery, hunter	Mourning Dove, Mississippi, Granny

1.3 SINGULAR AND PLURAL NOUNS

A noun may take a singular or a plural form, depending on whether it names a single person, place, thing, or idea or more than one. Make sure you use appropriate spellings when forming plurals.

Singular	Plural
church, lily, wife	churches, lilies, wives

1.4 COMPOUND AND COLLECTIVE NOUNS

Compound nouns are formed from two or more words but express a single idea. They are written as single words, as separate words, or with hyphens. Use a dictionary to check the correct spelling of a compound noun.

> EXAMPLES: *birthright, folk tale, Sky-World*

Collective nouns are singular nouns that refer to groups of people or things.

> EXAMPLES: *army, flock, class, species*

1.5 POSSESSIVE NOUNS

A **possessive noun** shows who or what owns something.

> EXAMPLES: *Welty's, jury's, children's*

2 Pronouns

A **pronoun** is a word that is used in place of a noun or another pronoun. The word or word group to which the pronoun refers is called its **antecedent.**

2.1 PERSONAL PRONOUNS

Personal pronouns change their form to express person, number, gender, and case. The forms of these pronouns are shown in the following chart.

	Nominative	Objective	Possessive
Singular			
First Person	I	me	my, mine
Second Person	you	you	your, yours
Third Person	she, he, it	her, him, it	her, hers, his, its
Plural			
First Person	we	us	our, ours
Second Person	you	you	your, yours
Third Person	they	them	their, theirs

2.2 AGREEMENT WITH ANTECEDENT

Pronouns should agree with their antecedents in number, gender, and person.

If an antecedent is singular, use a singular pronoun.

> EXAMPLE: *Sarah laughed as her dog splashed in the lake.*

If an antecedent is plural, use a plural pronoun.

> EXAMPLES: *Sarah and Barbara took turns holding the leash as they walked the dog home.*
> *Andrew and Ryan finished the race before the rest of their teammates.*

The gender of a pronoun must be the same as the gender of its antecedent.

EXAMPLES: *The little **girl** ran outside without tying her shoelaces.*
***Daniel** waved to his friends before boarding the plane.*

The person of the pronoun must be the same as the person of its antecedent. As the chart in Section 2.1 shows, a pronoun can be in first-, second-, or third-person form.

EXAMPLE: *Those of **you** who like animals should consider getting your degree in veterinary science.*

Practice and Apply

Rewrite each sentence so that the underlined pronoun agrees with its antecedent.

1. *The World on the Turtle's Back* is a myth that tells about a pregnant woman and how <u>it</u> helped create the earth.
2. Many of the sea creatures and birds tried to retrieve the dirt at the bottom of the ocean, but they could not reach <u>him</u>.
3. The woman circles the earth with <u>their</u> daughter, helping the plants to grow.
4. Both of the twins molded clay animals and gave <u>it</u> life.

2.3 PRONOUN CASE

Personal pronouns change form to show how they function in sentences. Different functions are shown by different **cases.** The three cases are **nominative, objective,** and **possessive.** For examples of these pronouns, see the chart in Section 2.1.

A **nominative pronoun** is used as a subject or a predicate nominative in a sentence.

An **objective pronoun** is used as a direct object, an indirect object, or the object of a preposition.

SUBJECT   OBJECT   OBJECT OF PREPOSITION

He explained it to me.

A **possessive pronoun** shows ownership. The pronouns *mine, yours, hers, his, its, ours,* and *theirs* can be used in place of nouns.

EXAMPLE: *These letters are yours.*

The pronouns *my, your, her, his, its, our,* and *their* are used before nouns.

EXAMPLE: *These are your letters.*

WATCH OUT! Many spelling errors can be avoided if you watch out for *its* and *their.* Don't confuse the possessive pronoun *its* with the contraction *it's,* meaning "it is" or "it has." The homonyms *they're* (a contraction of *they are*) and *there* ("in that place") are often mistakenly used for *their.*

TIP To decide which pronoun to use in a comparison, such as "He tells better tales than (I or me)," fill in the missing word(s): *He tells better tales than I tell.*

Practice and Apply

Replace the underlined words in each sentence with an appropriate pronoun, and identify the pronoun as a nominative, objective, or possessive pronoun.

1. <u>Arthur Miller</u> was a playwright from New York.
2. *The Crucible* is one of <u>Arthur Miller's</u> most well-known plays.
3. <u>John Proctor and Reverend Parris</u> are two of the main characters.
4. Reverend Hale tries to convince <u>Rebecca Nurse and John Proctor</u> to falsely confess to practicing witchcraft.
5. <u>The Salem witch hunt</u> illustrates how the town's strict Christian principles indirectly caused the deaths of innocent villagers.

2.4 REFLEXIVE AND INTENSIVE PRONOUNS

These pronouns are formed by adding *-self* or *-selves* to certain personal pronouns. Their forms are the same, and they differ only in how they are used.

A **reflexive pronoun** follows a verb or preposition and reflects back on an earlier noun or pronoun.

COMMON CORE L 1

PRACTICE AND APPLY

Remind students to write legibly as they compose their responses to the Practice and Apply activities.

Answers:
1. *she*
2. *it*
3. *her*
4. *them*

PRACTICE AND APPLY
Answers:
1. *He, nominative*
2. *his, possessive*
3. *They, nominative*
4. *them, objective*
5. *It, nominative*

EXAMPLES: *He threw himself forward.*
Danielle mailed herself the package.

Intensive pronouns intensify or emphasize the nouns or pronouns to which they refer.

EXAMPLES: *The queen herself would have been amused.*
I saw it myself.

WATCH OUT! Avoid using *hisself* or *theirselves*. Standard English does not include these forms.

NONSTANDARD: *He had painted hisself into a corner.*

STANDARD: *He had painted himself into a corner.*

2.5 DEMONSTRATIVE PRONOUNS

Demonstrative pronouns point out things and persons near and far.

	Singular	Plural
Near	this	these
Far	that	those

2.6 INDEFINITE PRONOUNS

Indefinite pronouns do not refer to specific persons or things and usually have no antecedents. The chart shows some commonly used indefinite pronouns.

Singular	Plural	Singular or Plural	
another	both	all	none
anybody	few	any	some
no one	many	more	most
neither	several		

TIP Indefinite pronouns that end in *one*, *body*, or *thing* are always singular.

INCORRECT: *Does anybody think their hamburger is overcooked?*

CORRECT: *Does anybody think his or her hamburger is overcooked?*

If the indefinite pronoun might refer to either a male or a female, *his or her* may be used to refer to it, or the sentence may be rewritten.

EXAMPLES: *Everyone received his or her script.*
All the actors received their scripts.

2.7 INTERROGATIVE PRONOUNS

An **interrogative pronoun** is used to ask a question. The interrogative pronouns are *who*, *whom*, *whose*, *which*, and *what*.

EXAMPLES: *Whose backpack is on the kitchen table?*
Which dress do you prefer?

TIP *Who* is used as a subject; *whom*, as an object. To find out which pronoun you need to use in a question, change the question to a statement.

QUESTION: *(Who/Whom) did you meet there?*

STATEMENT: *You met (?) there.*

Since the verb has a subject (you), the needed word must be the object form, *whom*.

EXAMPLE: *Whom did you meet there?*

WATCH OUT! A special problem arises when you use an interrupter, such as *do you think*, within a question.

EXAMPLE: *(Who/Whom) do you believe is the more influential musician?*

If you eliminate the interrupter, it is clear that the word you need is *who*.

2.8 RELATIVE PRONOUNS

Relative pronouns relate, or connect, dependent (or subordinate) clauses to the words they modify in sentences. The relative pronouns are *that, what, whatever, which, whichever, who, whoever, whom, whomever,* and *whose.*

Sometimes short sentences with related ideas can be combined by using a relative pronoun.

SHORT SENTENCE: *Mark Twain may be America's greatest humorist.*

RELATED SENTENCE: *Mark Twain wrote* Huckleberry Finn.

COMBINED SENTENCE: *Mark Twain, who wrote* Huckleberry Finn, *may be America's greatest humorist.*

Practice and Apply

Choose the appropriate interrogative or relative pronoun from the words in parentheses.

1. "The Celebrated Jumping Frog of Calaveras County" was written by Samuel Clemens, (who/whom) wrote under the pseudonym Mark Twain.
2. The story gained national fame for Mark Twain, (who/that) first published it in 1865.
3. (Who/Whom) do you think is funnier, Jim Smiley or the storyteller Simon Wheeler?
4. Smiley spent months educating his frog, (which/whose) fame as a jumper spread throughout the gold camps.

2.9 PRONOUN REFERENCE PROBLEMS

The referent of a pronoun should always be clear.

An **indefinite reference** occurs when the pronoun *it, you,* or *they* does not clearly refer to a specific antecedent.

UNCLEAR: *In the review, it claimed the movie is well done.*

CLEAR: *The review claimed the movie is well done.*

A **general reference** occurs when the pronoun *it, this, that, which,* or *such* is used to refer to a general idea rather than a specific antecedent.

UNCLEAR: *Stella tutors students every day after school. This lets her help kids who are struggling with their schoolwork.*

CLEAR: *Stella tutors students every day after school. Tutoring lets her help kids who are struggling with their schoolwork.*

Ambiguous means "having more than one possible meaning." An **ambiguous reference** occurs when a pronoun could refer to two or more antecedents.

UNCLEAR: *Stacey made Miranda a sandwich while she talked on the phone.*

CLEAR: *While Stacey talked on the phone, she made Miranda a sandwich.*

Practice and Apply

Rewrite the following sentences to correct indefinite, ambiguous, and general pronoun references.

1. In the poem "The Raven," it tells about a man who is grieving for his lover.
2. The raven refused to abandon its perch above the door. This frustrated the narrator.
3. The narrator told the raven that he thought he was a messenger from Lenore.
4. The raven always responded, "Nevermore." This frightened and confused the speaker.

3 Verbs

A **verb** is a word that expresses an action, a condition, or a state of being.

3.1 ACTION VERBS

Action verbs express mental or physical activity.

EXAMPLES: *I walked to the store.*

3.2 LINKING VERBS

Linking verbs join subjects with words or phrases that rename or describe them.

EXAMPLES: *You are my friend.*

3.3 PRINCIPAL PARTS

Action and linking verbs typically have four principal parts, which are used to form verb tenses. The principal parts are the **present,** the **present participle,** the **past,** and the **past participle.**

Action verbs and some linking verbs also fall into two categories: regular and irregular. A **regular verb** is a verb that forms its past and past participle by adding *-ed* or *-d* to the present form.

COMMON CORE L 1

PRACTICE AND APPLY
Answers:
1. *who*
2. *who*
3. *Who*
4. *whose*

PRACTICE AND APPLY
Possible answers:
1. *The poem "The Raven" tells about a man grieving for his lover.*
2. *The raven refused to abandon its perch above the door. The raven's refusal frustrated the narrator.*
3. *The narrator told the raven that he thought the raven was a messenger from Lenore.*
4. *The raven always responded, "Nevermore." The raven's response frightened and confused the speaker.*

Present	Present Participle	Past	Past Participle
perform	(is) performing	performed	(has) performed
hope	(is) hoping	hoped	(has) hoped
stop	(is) stopping	stopped	(has) stopped
marry	(is) marrying	married	(has) married

An **irregular verb** is a verb that forms its past and past participle in some other way than by adding -ed or -d to the present form.

Present	Present Participle	Past	Past Participle
bring	(is) bringing	brought	(has) brought
swim	(is) swimming	swam	(has) swum
steal	(is) stealing	stole	(has) stolen
grow	(is) growing	grew	(has) grown

3.4 VERB TENSE

The **tense** of a verb indicates the time of the action or state of being. An action or state of being can occur in the present, the past, or the future. There are six tenses, each expressing a different range of time.

The **present tense** expresses an action or state that is happening at the present time, occurs regularly, or is constant or generally true. Use the present part.

NOW: *That poet reads well.*

REGULAR: *I swim every day.*

GENERAL: *Time flies.*

The **past tense** expresses an action that began and ended in the past. Use the past part.

EXAMPLE: *The storyteller finished his tale.*

The **future tense** expresses an action or state that will occur. Use *shall* or *will* with the present part.

EXAMPLE: *They will attend the next festival.*

The **present perfect tense** expresses an action or state that (1) was completed at an indefinite time in the past or (2) began in the past and continues into the present. Use *have* or *has* with the past participle.

EXAMPLE: *Poetry has inspired readers throughout the ages.*

The **past perfect tense** expresses an action in the past that came before another action in the past. Use *had* with the past participle.

EXAMPLE: *The witness had testified before the defendant confessed.*

The **future perfect tense** expresses an action in the future that will be completed before another action in the future. Use *shall have* or *will have* with the past participle.

EXAMPLE: *They will have finished the novel before seeing the movie version of the tale.*

TIP The past-tense form of an irregular verb is not paired with an auxiliary verb, but the past-perfect tense form of an irregular verb is always paired with an auxiliary verb.

INCORRECT: *I have went to that restaurant before.*

INCORRECT: *I gone to that restaurant before.*

CORRECT: *I have gone to that restaurant before.*

3.5 PROGRESSIVE FORMS

The progressive forms of the six tenses show ongoing actions. Use forms of *be* with the present participles of verbs.

PRESENT PROGRESSIVE: *She is rehearsing her lines.*

PAST PROGRESSIVE: *She was rehearsing her lines.*

FUTURE PROGRESSIVE: *She will be rehearsing her lines.*

PRESENT PERFECT PROGRESSIVE: *She has been rehearsing her lines.*

PAST PERFECT PROGRESSIVE: *She had been rehearsing her lines.*

FUTURE PERFECT PROGRESSIVE: *She will have been rehearsing her lines.*

WATCH OUT! Do not shift from tense to tense needlessly. Watch out for these special cases:

• In most compound sentences and in sentences with compound predicates, keep the tenses the same.

INCORRECT: *Every morning they get up and went to work.*

CORRECT: *Every morning they get up and go to work.*

• If one past action happened before another, indicate this with a shift in tense.

INCORRECT: *She thought she forgot her toothbrush.*

CORRECT: *She thought she had forgotten her toothbrush.*

Practice and Apply

Identify the tense of the verb(s) in each of the following sentences. If you find an unnecessary tense shift, correct it.

1. The setting of *The Crucible* is the late 17th century in Salem, Massachusetts.
2. Before the witch trials ended, people had lost their ability to make objective judgments.
3. Playwright Arthur Miller knew that the play pertains to his own time.
4. People will read it far into the future, and many will apply its message to their own time.
5. In the play some accuse others of being witches, even though they knew the accusation was false.

3.6 ACTIVE AND PASSIVE VOICE

The voice of a verb tells whether its subject performs or receives the action expressed by the verb. When the subject performs the action, the verb is in the **active voice.** When the subject is the receiver of the action, the verb is in the **passive voice.**

Compare these two sentences:

ACTIVE: *The Puritans did not celebrate Christmas.*

PASSIVE: *Christmas was not celebrated by the Puritans.*

To form the passive voice, use a form of *be* with the past participle of the verb.

WATCH OUT! Use the passive voice sparingly. It can make writing awkward and less direct.

AWKWARD: *The stories of hysterical witnesses were believed by gullible and fearful jurors.*

BETTER: *Gullible and fearful jurors believed the stories of hysterical witnesses.*

There are occasions when you will choose to use the passive voice because

• you want to emphasize the receiver: *The king was shot.*
• the doer is unknown: *My books were stolen.*
• the doer is unimportant: *French is spoken here.*

Practice and Apply

For the five items below, identify the boldfaced verb phrase as active or passive.

1. *The Crucible* **has played** in theaters throughout the world.
2. It **was written** by Arthur Miller, one of America's greatest dramatists.
3. Miller **did** not **approve** of Reverend Parris's greed for gold.
4. **Has** the reputation of the minister **been maligned?**

4 Modifiers

Modifiers are words or groups of words that change or limit the meanings of other words. Adjectives and adverbs are common modifiers.

PRACTICE AND APPLY
Answers:
1. *is = present*
2. *ended = past*
   had lost = past perfect
3. *knew = past*
   pertains = present
   pertains > pertained
4. *will read = future*
   will apply = future
5. *accuse = present*
   accuse > accused
   knew = past
   was = past

PRACTICE AND APPLY
Answers:
1. *active*
2. *passive*
3. *active*
4. *passive*

4.1 ADJECTIVES

Adjectives modify nouns and pronouns by telling which one, what kind, how many, or how much.

> WHICH ONE: *this, that, these, those*
>
> EXAMPLE: *That couch needs to be reupholstered.*
>
> WHAT KIND: *large, unique, anxious, moldy*
>
> EXAMPLE: *The anxious speaker shuffled through her notes.*
>
> HOW MANY: *ten, many, several, every, each*
>
> EXAMPLE: *Each child grabbed several candies from the bowl.*
>
> HOW MUCH: *more, less, little*
>
> EXAMPLE: *There was more snow on the ground in the morning.*

4.2 PREDICATE ADJECTIVES

Most adjectives come before the nouns they modify, as in the previous examples. A **predicate adjective,** however, follows a linking verb and describes the subject.

> EXAMPLE: *My friends are very intelligent.*

Be especially careful to use adjectives (not adverbs) after such linking verbs as *look, feel, grow, taste,* and *smell.*

> EXAMPLE: *The weather grows cold.*

4.3 ADVERBS

Adverbs modify verbs, adjectives, and other adverbs by telling where, when, how, or to what extent.

> WHERE: *The children played outside.*
>
> WHEN: *The author spoke yesterday.*
>
> HOW: *We walked slowly behind the leader.*
>
> TO WHAT EXTENT: *He worked very hard.*

Adverbs may occur in many places in sentences, both before and after the words they modify.

> EXAMPLES: *Suddenly the wind shifted.*
> *The wind suddenly shifted.*
> *The wind shifted suddenly.*

4.4 ADJECTIVE OR ADVERB?

Many adverbs are formed by adding *-ly* to adjectives.

> EXAMPLES: *sweet, sweetly; gentle, gently*

However, *-ly* added to a noun will usually yield an adjective.

> EXAMPLES: *friend, friendly; woman, womanly*

4.5 COMPARISON OF MODIFIERS

Modifiers can be used to compare two or more things. The form of a modifier shows the degree of comparison. Both adjectives and adverbs have three forms: the **positive,** the **comparative,** and the **superlative.**

The **positive form** is used to describe individual things, groups, or actions.

> EXAMPLES: *Stephen Crane was a great writer.*
> *His descriptions are vivid.*

The **comparative form** is used to compare two things, groups, or actions.

> EXAMPLES: *I think that Stephen Crane was a greater writer than Jack London.*
> *Crane's descriptions are more vivid.*

The **superlative form** is used to compare more than two things, groups, or actions.

> EXAMPLES: *I think that Crane was the greatest writer of his era.*
> *Crane's descriptions are the most vivid I have ever read.*

4.6 REGULAR COMPARISONS

Most one-syllable and some two-syllable adjectives and adverbs have comparatives and superlatives formed by adding *-er* and *-est*. All three-syllable and most two-syllable modifiers have comparatives and superlatives formed with *more* and *most*.

Modifier	Comparative	Superlative
tall	taller	tallest
kind	kinder	kindest
droopy	droopier	droopiest
expensive	more expensive	most expensive
wasteful	more wasteful	most wasteful

WATCH OUT! Note that spelling changes must sometimes be made to form the comparatives and superlatives of modifiers.

> **EXAMPLES:** *friendly, friendlier* (Change *y* to *i*, and add the ending.)
> *sad, sadder* (Double the final consonant, and add the ending.)

4.7 IRREGULAR COMPARISONS

Some commonly used modifiers have irregular comparative and superlative forms. They are listed in the following chart.

Modifier	Comparative	Superlative
good	better	best
bad	worse	worst
far	farther *or* further	farthest *or* furthest
little	less *or* lesser	least
many	more	most
well	better	best
much	more	most

4.8 PROBLEMS WITH MODIFIERS

Study the tips that follow to avoid common mistakes:

Farther and Further Use *farther* for distances; use *further* for everything else.

Double Comparisons Make a comparison by using *-er/-est* or by using *more/most*. Using *-er* with *more* or using *-est* with *most* is incorrect.

> **INCORRECT:** *I like her more better than she likes me.*

> **CORRECT:** *I like her better than she likes me.*

Illogical Comparisons An illogical or confusing comparison results when two unrelated things are compared or when something is compared with itself. The word *other* or the word *else* should be used in a comparison of an individual member to the rest of a group.

ILLOGICAL: *The narrator was more curious about the war than any student in his class.* (implies that the narrator isn't a student in the class)

LOGICAL: *The narrator was more curious about the war than any other student in his class.* (identifies that the narrator is a student)

Bad vs. Badly *Bad,* as an adjective, is used before a noun or after a linking verb. *Badly,* always an adverb, never modifies a noun. Be sure to use the right form after a linking verb.

> **INCORRECT:** *Ed felt badly after his team lost.*

> **CORRECT:** *Ed felt bad after his team lost.*

Good vs. Well *Good,* as an adjective, is used before a noun or after a linking verb. *Well* is often an adverb meaning "expertly" or "properly." *Well* can also be used as an adjective after a linking verb when it means "in good health."

> **INCORRECT:** *Helen writes very good.*

> **CORRECT:** *Helen writes very well.*

> **CORRECT:** *Yesterday I felt bad; today I feel well.*

Double Negatives If you add a negative word to a sentence that is already negative, the result will be an error known as a double negative. When using *not* or *-n't* with a verb, use *any-* words, such as *anybody* or *anything,* rather than *no-* words, such as *nobody* or *nothing,* later in the sentence.

> **INCORRECT:** *I don't have no money.*

> **CORRECT:** *I don't have any money.*

Using *hardly, barely,* or *scarcely* after a negative word is also incorrect.

> **INCORRECT:** *They couldn't barely see two feet ahead.*

> **CORRECT:** *They could barely see two feet ahead.*

Misplaced Modifiers Sometimes a modifier is placed so far away from the word it modifies that the intended meaning of the sentence is unclear. Prepositional phrases and participial

PRACTICE AND APPLY

Answers:

1. *better*
2. *could*
3. *any*
4. *good*
5. *stranger*
6. *bad*
7. *more depressed*
8. *good*
9. *longer*

phrases are often misplaced. Place modifiers as close as possible to the words they modify.

> **MISPLACED:** *The ranger explained how to find ducks in her office.* (The ducks were not in the ranger's office.)

> **CLEARER:** *In her office, the ranger explained how to find ducks.*

Dangling Modifiers Sometimes a modifier doesn't appear to modify any word in a sentence. Most dangling modifiers are participial phrases or infinitive phrases.

> **DANGLING:** *Coming home with groceries, our parrot said, "Hello!"*

> **CLEARER:** *Coming home with groceries, we heard our parrot say, "Hello!"*

Practice and Apply

Choose the correct word or words from each pair in parentheses.

1. Flannery O'Connor's story is (better/more better) than other stories I have read recently.
2. Mr. Shiftlet and Mrs. Crater (could/couldn't) hardly be less honest with each other.
3. Mr. Shiftlet says there isn't (any/no) broken thing on the farm that he can't fix.
4. He feels (good/well) about fixing the car.
5. Who do you think is the (stranger/strangest) person—Mr. Shiftlet or Mrs. Crater?
6. Mr. Shiftlet feels (bad/badly) about the rottenness of the world.
7. As Mr. Shiftlet drove on alone he felt (depresseder/more depressed) than ever.
8. Mr. Shiftlet didn't feel very (well/good) about being alone, so he picked up a hitchhiker.
9. One wonders how many other great stories Flannery O'Connor would have written had she lived (longer/more longer).

5 Prepositions, Conjunctions, and Interjections

5.1 PREPOSITIONS

A preposition is a word used to show the relationship between a noun or a pronoun and another word in the sentence.

Commonly Used Prepositions			
above	down	near	through
at	for	of	to
before	from	on	up
below	in	out	with
by	into	over	without

A preposition is always followed by a word or group of words that serves as its object. The preposition, its object, and modifiers of the object are called the **prepositional phrase.** In each example below, the prepositional phrase is highlighted, and the object of the preposition is in boldface type.

> **EXAMPLES:** *The future of the entire* **kingdom** *is uncertain.*
> *We searched through the deepest* **woods.**

Prepositional phrases may be used as adjectives or as adverbs. The phrase in the first example is used as an adjective modifying the noun *future.* In the second example, the phrase is used as an adverb modifying the verb *searched.*

> **WATCH OUT!** Prepositional phrases must be as close as possible to the word they modify.

> **MISPLACED:** *We have clothes for leisurewear of many colors.*

> **CLEARER:** *We have clothes of many colors for leisurewear.*

5.2 CONJUNCTIONS

A conjunction is a word used to connect words, phrases, or sentences. There are three kinds of conjunctions: **coordinating** conjunctions, correlative conjunctions, and **subordinating conjunctions**.

Coordinating conjunctions connect words or word groups that have the same function in a sentence. They include *and, but, or, for, so, yet,* and *nor*.

Coordinating conjunctions can join nouns, pronouns, verbs, adjectives, adverbs, prepositional phrases, and clauses in a sentence.

These examples show coordinating conjunctions joining words of the same function:

> **EXAMPLES:** *I have many friends but few enemies.* (two noun objects)
> *We ran out the door and into the street.* (two prepositional phrases)
> *They are pleasant yet seem aloof.* (two predicates)
> *We have to go now, or we will be late.* (two clauses)

Correlative conjunctions are similar to coordinating conjunctions. However, correlative conjunctions are always used in pairs.

Correlative Conjunctions		
both . . . and	neither . . . nor	whether . . . or
either . . . or	not only . . . but also	

Subordinating conjunctions introduce subordinate clauses—clauses that cannot stand by themselves as complete sentences. The subordinating conjunction shows how the subordinate clause relates to the rest of the sentence. The relationships include time, manner, place, cause, comparison, condition, and purpose.

Subordinating Conjunctions	
Time	*after, as, as long as, as soon as, before, since, until, when, whenever, while*
Manner	*as, as if*

continued

Subordinating Conjunctions	
Place	*where, wherever*
Cause	because, since
Comparison	as, as much as, than
Condition	*although, as long as, even if, even though, if, provided that, though, unless, while*
Purpose	*in order that, so that, that*

In the example below, the boldface word is the conjunction, and the highlighted words form a subordinate clause:

> **EXAMPLE:** *Walt Whitman was a man of the people,* **although** *many did not appreciate his poems.*

Walt Whitman was a man of the people is an independent clause, because it can stand alone as a complete sentence. *Although many did not appreciate his poems* cannot stand alone as a complete sentence; it is thus a subordinate clause.

Conjunctive adverbs are used to connect clauses that can stand by themselves as sentences. Conjunctive adverbs include *also, besides, finally, however, moreover, nevertheless, otherwise,* and *then*.

> **EXAMPLE:** *She loved the fall; however, she also enjoyed winter.*

5.3 INTERJECTIONS

Interjections are words used to show emotion, such as *wow* and *cool*. Interjections are usually set off from the rest of a sentence by a comma or by an exclamation mark.

> **EXAMPLE:** *Thoreau lived in the woods by himself. Amazing!*

6 The Sentence and Its Parts

A **sentence** is a group of words used to express a complete thought. A complete sentence has a subject and a predicate.

6.1 KINDS OF SENTENCES

There are four basic types of sentences.

Types	Definition	Example
Declarative	states a fact, a wish, an intent, or a feeling	I wrote an essay on "The Weary Blues" for class.
Interrogative	asks a question	Are you familiar with Langston Hughes?
Imperative	gives a command or direction	Read "The Weary Blues" aloud.
Exclamatory	expresses strong feeling or excitement	It sounds like a song!

6.2 COMPOUND SUBJECTS AND PREDICATES

A compound subject consists of two or more subjects that share the same verb. They are typically joined by the coordinating conjunction *and* or *or*.

EXAMPLE: *Courtney and Eric enjoy the theater.*

A compound predicate consists of two or more predicates that share the same subject. They too are typically joined by a coordinating conjunction, usually *and, but,* or *or*.

EXAMPLE: *The main character in "Winter Dreams" attended a prestigious university and became a successful businessman.*

6.3 COMPLEMENTS

A **complement** is a word or group of words that completes the meaning of the sentence. Some sentences contain only a subject and a verb. Most sentences, however, require additional words placed after the verb to complete the meaning of the sentence. There are three kinds of complements: direct objects, indirect objects, and subject complements.

Direct objects are words or word groups that receive the action of action verbs. A direct object answers the question *what* or *whom*.

EXAMPLES: *The students asked many questions.* (Asked what?)
The teacher quickly answered the students. (Answered whom?)

Indirect objects tell to whom or what or for whom or what the actions of verbs are performed. Indirect objects come before direct objects. In the examples that follow, the indirect objects are highlighted.

EXAMPLES: *My sister usually gave her friends good advice.* (Gave to whom?)
Her brother sent the store a heavy package. (Sent to what?)

Subject complements come after linking verbs and identify or describe the subjects. A subject complement that names or identifies a subject is called a **predicate nominative.** Predicate nominatives include **predicate nouns** and **predicate pronouns.**

EXAMPLES: *My friends are very hard workers.*
The best writer in the class is she.

A subject complement that describes a subject is called a **predicate adjective.**

EXAMPLE: *The pianist appeared very energetic.*

7 Phrases

A **phrase** is a group of related words that does not contain a subject and a predicate but functions in a sentence as a single part of speech.

7.1 PREPOSITIONAL PHRASES

A **prepositional phrase** is a phrase that consists of a preposition, its object, and any modifiers of the object. Prepositional phrases that modify nouns or pronouns are called **adjective phrases.** Prepositional phrases that modify verbs, adjectives, or adverbs are **adverb phrases.**

> ADJECTIVE PHRASE: *The central character of the story is a villain.*

> ADVERB PHRASE: *He reveals his nature in the first scene.*

7.2 APPOSITIVES AND APPOSITIVE PHRASES

An **appositive** is a noun or pronoun that identifies or renames another noun or pronoun. An **appositive phrase** includes an appositive and modifiers of it.

An appositive can be either **essential** or **nonessential.** An **essential appositive** provides information that is needed to identify what is referred to by the preceding noun or pronoun.

> EXAMPLE: The Glass Menagerie *was written by playwright Tennessee Williams.*

A **nonessential appositive** adds extra information about a noun or pronoun whose meaning is already clear. Nonessential appositives and appositive phrases are set off with commas.

> EXAMPLE: *Williams uses Laura's glass menagerie, a collection of fragile animal figurines, to represent her relationship to reality.*

8 Verbals and Verbal Phrases

A **verbal** is a verb form that is used as a noun, an adjective, or an adverb. A **verbal phrase** consists of a verbal along with its modifiers and complements. There are three kinds of verbals: **infinitives, participles,** and **gerunds.**

8.1 INFINITIVES AND INFINITIVE PHRASES

An **infinitive** is a verb form that usually begins with *to* and functions as a noun, an adjective, or an adverb. An **infinitive phrase** consists of an infinitive plus its modifiers and complements. The examples that follow show several uses of infinitive phrases.

> NOUN: *To know her is my only desire.* (subject)

> *I'm planning to walk with you.* (direct object)

> *Her goal was to promote women's rights.* (predicate nominative)

> ADJECTIVE: *We saw his need to be loved.* (adjective modifying *need*)

> ADVERB: *She wrote to voice her opinions.* (adverb modifying *wrote*)

Because infinitives usually begin with *to*, it is usually easy to recognize them. However, sometimes *to* may be omitted.

> EXAMPLE: *Let no one dare [to] enter this shrine.*

8.2 PARTICIPLES AND PARTICIPIAL PHRASES

A **participle** is a verb form that functions as an adjective. Like adjectives, participles modify nouns and pronouns. Most participles are present-participle forms, ending in *-ing*, or past-participle forms ending in *-ed* or *-en*. In the examples that follow, the participles are highlighted:

> MODIFYING A NOUN: *The jogging woman completed another lap on the track.*

> MODIFYING A PRONOUN: *Bored, he began to doodle in the margins of his notebook.*

Participial phrases are participles with all their modifiers and complements.

> MODIFYING A NOUN: *Changing tactics, the attorney questioned the witness.*

> MODIFYING A PRONOUN: *Dismissed for the day, they filed out of the courtroom.*

8.3 DANGLING AND MISPLACED PARTICIPLES

A participle or participial phrase should be placed as close as possible to the word that it modifies. Otherwise the meaning of the sentence may not be clear.

> MISPLACED: *The boys were looking for squirrels searching the trees.*

> CLEARER: *The boys searching the trees were looking for squirrels.*

A participle or participial phrase that does not clearly modify anything in a sentence is called a **dangling participle.**

A dangling participle causes confusion because it appears to modify a word that it cannot sensibly modify. Correct a dangling participle by providing a word for the participle to modify.

> DANGLING: *Running like the wind,* my hat fell off. (The hat wasn't running.)
>
> CLEARER: *Running like the wind,* I lost my hat.

8.4 GERUNDS AND GERUND PHRASES

A **gerund** is a verb form ending in *-ing* that functions as a noun. Gerunds may perform any function nouns perform.

> SUBJECT: *Running is my favorite pastime.*
>
> DIRECT OBJECT: *I truly love running.*
>
> INDIRECT OBJECT: *You should give running a try.*
>
> SUBJECT COMPLEMENT: *My deepest passion is running.*
>
> OBJECT OF PREPOSITION: *Her love of running keeps her strong.*

Gerund phrases are gerunds with all their modifiers and complements.

> SUBJECT: *Wishing on a star never got me far.*
>
> OBJECT OF PREPOSITION: *I will finish before leaving the office.*
>
> APPOSITIVE: *Her avocation, flying airplanes, finally led to full-time employment.*

Practice and Apply

Identify the underlined phrases as appositive phrases, infinitive phrases, participial phrases, or gerund phrases.

1. In "The Masque of the Red Death," Poe uses allegory, <u>a device representing abstract qualities.</u>
2. <u>To escape the plague,</u> Prince Prospero seals himself and his courtiers in a walled abbey.
3. <u>Feeling protected from the Red Death,</u> Prospero holds a lavish masquerade ball.
4. There suddenly appears in the last room a masked figure, <u>the Red Death in a ghastly shroud.</u>

---

9 Clauses

A **clause** is a group of words that contains a subject and a verb. There are two kinds of clauses: independent clauses and subordinate clauses.

9.1 INDEPENDENT AND SUBORDINATE CLAUSES

An **independent clause** can stand alone as a sentence, as the word **independent** suggests.

> INDEPENDENT CLAUSE: *Frederick Douglass was an eloquent speaker.*

A sentence may contain more than one independent clause.

> EXAMPLE: *Frederick Douglass was an eloquent speaker, but he encountered a lot of opposition.*

In the preceding example, the coordinating conjunction *but* joins two independent clauses.

A **subordinate clause** cannot stand alone as a sentence. It is subordinate to, or dependent on, an independent clause.

> EXAMPLE: *Although Frederick Douglass was a runaway slave, he frequently appeared in public to raise support for the abolitionist movement.*

The highlighted clause cannot stand by itself; it must be joined with an independent clause to form a complete sentence.

9.2 ADJECTIVE CLAUSES

An **adjective clause** is a subordinate clause used as an adjective. It usually follows the noun or pronoun it modifies. Adjective clauses are typically introduced by the relative pronoun *who, whom, whose, which,* or *that.*

> EXAMPLES: *Frederick Douglass wrote objectively about the whippings that Corey frequently gave him.*
> *The autobiographer whom I liked best was Frederick Douglass.*
> *He was a man who was determined to find freedom.*

PRACTICE AND APPLY

Answers:

1. *appositive phrase*
2. *infinitive phrase*
3. *participial phrase*
4. *appositive phrase*

An adjective clause can be either essential or nonessential. An **essential adjective clause** provides information that is necessary to identify the preceding noun or pronoun.

> EXAMPLE: *The couch that we picked out will not be delivered for three weeks.*

A **nonessential adjective clause** adds additional information about a noun or pronoun whose meaning is already clear. Nonessential clauses are set off with commas.

> EXAMPLE: *Joel's grandmother, who was born in Italy, makes the best lasagna.*

TIP The relative pronouns *whom, which,* and *that* may sometimes be omitted when they are objects in adjective clauses.

> EXAMPLE: *The autobiographer [whom] I liked best was Frederick Douglass.*

9.3 ADVERB CLAUSES

An **adverb clause** is a subordinate clause that is used to modify a verb, an adjective, or an adverb. It is introduced by a subordinating conjunction. Adverb clauses typically occur at the beginning or end of sentences.

> MODIFYING A VERB: *When we need you, we will call.*

> MODIFYING AN ADVERB: *I'll stay here where there is shelter from the rain.*

> MODIFYING AN ADJECTIVE: *Roman felt as good as he had ever felt.*

9.4 NOUN CLAUSES

A **noun clause** is a subordinate clause that is used as a noun. A noun clause may be used as a subject, a direct object, an indirect object, a predicate nominative, or the object of a preposition. Noun clauses are introduced either by pronouns, such as *that, what, who, whoever, which,* and *whose,* or by subordinating conjunctions, such as *how, when, where, why,* and *whether.*

TIP Because the same words may introduce adjective and noun clauses, you need to consider how a clause functions within its sentence. To determine if a clause is a noun clause, try substituting *something* or *someone* for the clause. If you can do it, it is probably a noun clause.

> EXAMPLES: *I know whose woods these are.* ("I know something." The clause is a noun clause, direct object of the verb *know.*) *Give a copy to whoever wants one.* ("Give a copy to someone." The clause is a noun clause, object of the preposition *to.*)

10 The Structure of Sentences

When classified by their structure, there are four kinds of sentences: simple, compound, complex, and compound-complex.

10.1 SIMPLE SENTENCES

A **simple sentence** is a sentence that has one independent clause and no subordinate clauses. Various parts of simple sentences may be compound, and simple sentences may contain grammatical structures such as appositive and verbal phrases.

> EXAMPLES: *Ambrose Bierce and Stephen Crane, two great American writers, both wrote during the latter half of the 19th century.* (compound subject and an appositive) *Crane, best known for writing fiction, also wrote great poetry.* (participial phrase containing a gerund phrase)

10.2 COMPOUND SENTENCES

A **compound sentence** consists of two or more independent clauses. The clauses in compound sentences are joined with commas and coordinating conjunctions (*and, but, or, nor, yet, for, so*) or with semicolons. Like simple sentences, compound sentences do not contain any subordinate clauses.

> EXAMPLES: *I enjoyed the free pottery class, and I would like to go again. Carl Sandburg's "Chicago" seems to*

celebrate the youthful energy of a booming industrial city; however, the poem dwells on the negative impacts of growth.

WATCH OUT! Do not confuse compound sentences with simple sentences that have compound parts.

EXAMPLE: *The center fielder caught the ball and immediately threw it toward second base.* (Here *and* joins parts of a compound predicate, not a compound sentence.)

10.3 COMPLEX SENTENCES

A **complex sentence** consists of one independent clause and one or more subordinate clauses. Each subordinate clause can be used as a noun or as a modifier. If it is used as a modifier, a subordinate clause usually modifies a word in the independent clause, and the independent clause can stand alone. However, when a subordinate clause is a noun clause, it is a part of the independent clause; the two cannot be separated.

MODIFIER: *One should not complain unless one has a better solution.*

NOUN CLAUSE: *We sketched pictures of whoever we wished.* (The noun clause is the object of the preposition *of* and cannot be separated from the rest of the sentence.)

10.4 COMPOUND-COMPLEX SENTENCES

A **compound-complex sentence** contains two or more independent clauses and one or more subordinate clauses. Compound-complex sentences are, simply, both compound and complex. If you start with a compound sentence, all you need to do to form a compound-complex sentence is add a subordinate clause.

COMPOUND: *All the students knew the answer, yet they were too shy to volunteer.*

COMPOUND-COMPLEX: *All the students knew the answer that their teacher expected, yet they were too shy to volunteer.*

10.5 PARALLEL STRUCTURE

When you write sentences, make sure that coordinate parts are equivalent, or **parallel,** in structure.

NOT PARALLEL: *Erin loved basketball and to play hockey.* (*Basketball* is a noun; *to play hockey* is a phrase.)

PARALLEL: *Erin loved basketball and hockey.* (*Basketball* and *hockey* are both nouns.)

NOT PARALLEL: *He wanted to rent an apartment, a new car, and traveling around the country.* (*To rent* is an infinitive, *car* is a noun, and *traveling* is a gerund.)

PARALLEL: *He wanted to rent an apartment, to drive a new car, and to travel around the country.* (*To rent, to drive,* and *to travel* are all infinitives.)

11 Writing Complete Sentences

Remember that a sentence is a group of words that expresses a complete thought. In formal writing, try to avoid both sentence fragments and run-on sentences.

11.1 CORRECTING FRAGMENTS

A **sentence fragment** is a group of words that is only part of a sentence. It does not express a complete thought and may be confusing to a reader or listener. A sentence fragment may be lacking a subject, a predicate, or both.

FRAGMENT: *Waited for the boat to arrive.* (no subject)

CORRECTED: *We waited for the boat to arrive.*

FRAGMENT: *People of various races, ages, and creeds.* (no predicate)

CORRECTED: *People of various races, ages, and creeds gathered together.*

FRAGMENT: *Near the old cottage.* (neither subject nor predicate)

CORRECTED: *The burial ground is near the old cottage.*

Sometimes fixing a fragment will be a matter of attaching it to a preceding or following sentence.

FRAGMENT: *We saw the two girls. Waiting for the bus to arrive.*

CORRECTED: *We saw the two girls waiting for the bus to arrive.*

11.2 CORRECTING RUN-ON SENTENCES

A **run-on sentence** is made up of two or more sentences written as though they were one. Some run-ons have no punctuation within them. Others may have only commas where conjunctions or stronger punctuation marks are necessary. Use your judgment in correcting run-on sentences, as you have choices. You can make a run-on two sentences if the thoughts are not closely connected. If the thoughts are closely related, you can keep the run-on as one sentence by adding a semicolon or a conjunction.

RUN-ON: *We found a place for the picnic by a small pond it was three miles from the village.*

MAKE TWO SENTENCES: *We found a place for the picnic by a small pond. It was three miles from the village.*

RUN-ON: *We found a place for the picnic by a small pond it was perfect.*

USE A SEMICOLON: *We found a place for the picnic by a small pond; it was perfect.*

ADD A CONJUNCTION: *We found a place for the picnic by a small pond, and it was perfect.*

WATCH OUT! When you form compound sentences, make sure you use appropriate punctuation: a comma before a coordinating conjunction, a semicolon when there is no coordinating conjunction. A very common mistake is to use a comma alone instead of a comma and a conjunction. This error is called a **comma splice.**

INCORRECT: *He finished the apprenticeship, he left the village.*

CORRECT: *He finished the apprenticeship, and he left the village.*

Rewrite the following paragraph, correcting all fragments and run-ons.

The narrator in Charlotte Perkins Gilman's story "The Yellow Wallpaper" expects that her husband will laugh at her, that's an odd response, in my opinion. She could have lived more happily. If the relationship between her and her husband were an equal partnership. We can acknowledge that men and women may be different in some ways. Without believing that they are as different as this story suggests. The male character acts practical and "strong," the female character acts nervous and weak.

12 Subject-Verb Agreement

The subject and verb in a clause must agree in number. Agreement means that if the subject is singular, the verb is also singular, and if the subject is plural, the verb is also plural.

12.1 BASIC AGREEMENT

Fortunately, agreement between subjects and verbs in English is simple. Most verbs show the difference between singular and plural only in the third person of the present tense. In the present tense, the third person singular form ends in *-s*.

Present-Tense Verb Forms	
Singular	**Plural**
I eat	we eat
you eat	you eat
she, he, it eats	they eat

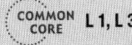 COMMON CORE L 1, L 3

PRACTICE AND APPLY

Possible answer:

The narrator in Charlotte Perkins Gilman's story "The Yellow Wallpaper" expects that her husband will laugh at her. That's an odd response, in my opinion. She could have lived more happily if the relationship between her and her husband were an equal partnership. We can acknowledge that men and women may be different in some ways without believing that they are as different as this story suggests. The male character acts practical and "strong"; the female character acts nervous and weak.

12.2 AGREEMENT WITH *BE*

The verb *be* presents special problems in agreement, because this verb does not follow the usual verb patterns.

Forms of *Be*			
Present Tense		**Past Tense**	
Singular	**Plural**	**Singular**	**Plural**
I am	we are	I was	we were
you are	you are	you were	you were
she, he, it is	they are	she, he, it was	they were

12.3 WORDS BETWEEN SUBJECT AND VERB

A verb agrees only with its subject. When words come between a subject and a verb, ignore them when considering proper agreement. Identify the subject, and make sure the verb agrees with it.

> EXAMPLES: *A story in the newspapers tells about the 1890s.*
> *Dad as well as Mom reads the paper daily.*

12.4 AGREEMENT WITH COMPOUND SUBJECTS

Use plural verbs with most compound subjects joined by the word *and*.

> EXAMPLE: *My mother and her sisters call each other every Sunday.*

To confirm that you need a plural verb, you could substitute the plural pronoun *they* for *my mother and her sisters*.

If a compound subject is thought of as a unit, use a singular verb. Test this by substituting the singular pronoun *it*.

> EXAMPLE: *Liver and onions [it] is Robert's least favorite dish.*

Use a singular verb with a compound subject that is preceded by *each, every,* or *many a*.

> EXAMPLE: *Not every dog and cat at the shelter makes a good pet.*

When the parts of a compound subject are joined by *or, nor,* or the correlative conjunctions *either . . . or* or *neither . . . nor,* make the verb agree with the noun or pronoun nearest the verb.

> EXAMPLES: *Baseball or football is my favorite sport.*
> *Either my rabbits or my turtle was loose in my room.*
> *Neither Mrs. Howard nor her two sons were home at the time of the accident.*

12.5 PERSONAL PRONOUNS AS SUBJECTS

When using a personal pronoun as a subject, make sure to match it with the correct form of the verb *be*. (See the chart in Section 12.2.) Note especially that the pronoun *you* takes the forms *are* and *were,* regardless of whether it is singular or plural.

> **WATCH OUT!** *You is* and *you was* are nonstandard forms and should be avoided in writing and speaking. *We was* and *they was* are also forms to be avoided.
>
> INCORRECT: *You is facing the wrong direction.*
>
> CORRECT: *You are facing the wrong direction.*
>
> INCORRECT: *We was telling ghost stories.*
>
> CORRECT: *We were telling ghost stories.*

12.6 INDEFINITE PRONOUNS AS SUBJECTS

Some indefinite pronouns are always singular; some are always plural.

Singular Indefinite Pronouns		
another	everybody	no one
anybody	everyone	nothing
anyone	everything	one
anything	much	somebody
each	neither	someone
either	nobody	something

EXAMPLES: *Each of the writers was given an award.*
Somebody in the room upstairs is sleeping.

Plural Indefinite Pronouns			
both	few	many	several

EXAMPLES: *Many of the books in our library are not in circulation.*
Few have been returned recently.

Still other indefinite pronouns may be either singular or plural.

Singular or Plural Indefinite Pronouns		
all	more	none
any	most	some

The number of the indefinite pronoun *any* or *none* often depends on the intended meaning.

EXAMPLES: *Any of these topics has potential for a good article.* (any one topic)
Any of these topics have potential for good articles. (all of the many topics)

The indefinite pronouns *all, some, more, most,* and *none* are singular when they refer to quantities or parts of things. They are plural when they refer to numbers of individual things. Context will usually give a clue.

EXAMPLES: *All of the flour is gone.* (referring to a quantity)
All of the flowers are gone. (referring to individual items)

12.7 INVERTED SENTENCES

Problems in agreement often occur in inverted sentences beginning with *here* or *there;* in questions beginning with *how, when, why, where,* or *what;* and in inverted sentences beginning with phrases. Identify the subject—wherever it is—before deciding on the verb.

EXAMPLES: *There clearly are far too many cooks in this kitchen.*
What is the correct ingredient for this stew?
Far from the embroiled cooks stands the master chef.

Practice and Apply

Locate the subject of each clause in the sentences below. Then choose the correct verb.

1. Many poets have written great poetry, but few (is/are) as talented as Emily Dickinson.
2. There (is/are) many lines in her work that her readers (treasures/treasure).
3. Some of her readers (appreciates/appreciate) her use of dashes, while others (finds/find) it confusing.
4. Each of her poems (presents/present) an idea to think about.
5. What (is/are) the dominant vowel sound in the last four lines of "Much Madness is divinest Sense"?
6. The consonant that prevails in the same poem (seems/seem) to be s.
7. I can't decide whether the poem's sound or its ideas (is/are) more striking.

12.8 SENTENCES WITH PREDICATE NOMINATIVES

When a predicate nominative serves as a complement in a sentence, use a verb that agrees with the subject, not the complement.

EXAMPLES: *The hunting habits of the North American wolf are an example of how change in the environment affects animals.* (The subject is the plural noun *habits*—not *wolf*—and it takes the plural verb *are.*)
An example of how change in the environment affects animals is seen in the hunting habits of the North American wolf. (The subject is the singular noun *example,* and it takes the singular verb *is seen.*)

12.9 *DON'T* AND *DOESN'T* AS AUXILIARY VERBS

The auxiliary verb *doesn't* is used with singular subjects and with the personal pronouns *she, he,* and *it.* The auxiliary verb *don't* is used with plural subjects and with the personal pronouns *I, we, you,* and *they.*

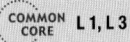 COMMON CORE **L 1, L 3**

PRACTICE AND APPLY

Answers:
1. *few > are*
2. *lines > are*
   readers > treasure
3. *Some > appreciate*
   others > find
4. *Each > presents*
5. *sound > is*
6. *consonant > seems*
7. *sound or ideas > are*

SINGULAR: *She doesn't have a costume for the rehearsal.*

Doesn't the doctor have an appointment Wednesday morning?

PLURAL: *They don't think they did very well on that math test.*

The cats don't need to be fed more than twice a day.

12.10 COLLECTIVE NOUNS AS SUBJECTS

Collective nouns are singular nouns that name groups of persons or things. *Team,* for example, is the collective name of a group of individuals. A collective noun takes a singular verb when the group acts as a single unit. It takes a plural verb when the members of the group act separately.

EXAMPLES: *Her family is moving to another state.* (The family as a whole is moving.)
Her family are carrying furniture out to the truck. (The individual members are carrying furniture.)

12.11 RELATIVE PRONOUNS AS SUBJECTS

When the relative pronoun *who, which,* or *that* is used as a subject in an adjective clause, the verb in the clause must agree in number with the antecedent of the pronoun.

SINGULAR: *Have you selected one of the poems that is meaningful to you?*

The antecedent of the relative pronoun *that* is the singular *one;* therefore, *that* is singular and must take the singular verb *is.*

PLURAL: *The fairy tales, which have been collected from many different sources, are annotated.*

The antecedent of the relative pronoun *which* is the plural *fairy tales. Which* is plural, and it takes the plural verb *have been collected.*

Vocabulary and Spelling

COMMON CORE L 1a, L 1b, L 2b, L 4a-c, L 4, L 5, L 6

The key to becoming an independent reader is to develop a toolkit of vocabulary strategies. By learning and practicing the strategies, you'll know what to do when you encounter unfamiliar words while reading. You'll also know how to refine the words you use for different situations—personal, school, and work.

Being a good speller is important when communicating your ideas in writing. Learning basic spelling rules and checking your spelling in a dictionary will help you spell words that you may not use frequently.

1 Using Context Clues

The context of a word is made up of the punctuation marks, words, sentences, and paragraphs that surround the word. A word's context can give you important clues about its meaning.

1.1 GENERAL CONTEXT

Sometimes you need to infer the meaning of an unfamiliar word by reading all the information in a passage.

> *I told my parents I wanted to quit playing the piano, but they told me to persevere anyway.*

You can figure out from the context that *persevere* means "continue."

1.2 SPECIFIC CONTEXT CLUES

Sometimes writers help you understand the meanings of words by providing specific clues such as those shown in the chart.

Specific Context Clues		
Type of Clue	**Key Words/ Phrases**	**Example**
Definition or restatement of the meaning of the word	or, which is, that is, in other words, also known as, also called	*Perennials*—**plants that live for more than two years**—make up only one-third of the garden's exhibit.
Example following an unfamiliar word	such as, like, as if, for example, especially, including	Their new apartment was *arrayed* with many beautiful things, **such as a crystal lamp and a porcelain vase.**
Comparison with a more familiar word or concept	as, like, also, similar to, in the same way, likewise	The prairie grasses *undulated* in the wind **like the waves in the ocean.**
Contrast with a familiar word or experience	unlike, but, however, although, on the other hand, on the contrary	My dog is usually very **calm, unlike** our neighbor's dog, which is very *rowdy*.

PRACTICE AND APPLY

Note that students will need to look up some word parts in a dictionary to complete this activity. Remind students to write legibly as they compose their responses to the Practice and Apply activities.

Answers:

Astronomy: *the study of the stars or of matter in outer space; from the Greek* astronomia *(*astro- *is a prefix that means "star").*

Circumference: *the distance around something; from the Latin* circumferre, *meaning "to carry around" (*circum- *means "around" and* ferre *means "to carry").*

Distend: *to swell out or expand; from the Latin prefix* dis- *and the root* ten, *meaning "to stretch."*

Efficacy: *the ability to get something done; from the Latin root* fic/fac/fec, *"to make or do" (Latin* efficere *means "to accomplish something").*

Epidermis: *the outer layer of the skin, from the Greek* epidermis, *meaning "upon" (*epi-*) "the skin" (*derma*).*

Geosciences: *the fields that study the earth; from the Greek word* geo-, *meaning "earth," and the word* sciences, *which comes from Latin (*scire, *"to know").*

Hexagonal: *having six angles; related to a hexagon (a six-sided shape); from the Greek prefix* hexa-, *"six," and* gonos, *"angled."*

Spectrum: *the colored band that is visible when light is dispersed (as through a prism); from the Latin root* spec, *meaning "to see."*

Uncertainty: *a lack of certainty; formed with the Old English prefix* un-, *meaning "the reverse; not."*

1.3 IDIOMS, SLANG, AND FIGURATIVE LANGUAGE

Use context clues to figure out the meanings of idioms, figurative language, and slang.

An **idiom** is an expression whose overall meaning is different from the meaning of the individual words.

> *If you're going to buy a house with a garden, you'd better have a green thumb.* (*Green thumb* means "ability to grow plants.")

Figurative language is language that communicates meaning beyond the literal meaning of the words.

> *Maria's anger at her disobedient daughter was a white-hot fuse ready to be sparked.* (*White-hot fuse ready to be sparked* is a metaphor that indicates that the anger isn't visible yet but is ready to erupt.)

Slang is informal language composed of made-up words and ordinary words that are used to mean something different from their meanings in formal English.

> *My parents freaked out when I told them that I went to the concert without their permission.* (*Freaked out* means "became greatly distressed.")

2 Analyzing Word Structure

Many words can be broken into smaller parts, such as base words, roots, prefixes, and suffixes.

2.1 BASE WORDS

A **base word** is a word part that by itself is also a word. Other words or word parts can be added to base words to form new words.

2.2 ROOTS

A **root** is a word part that contains the core meaning of the word. Many English words contain roots that come from older languages such as Greek, Latin, Old English (Anglo-Saxon), and Norse. Knowing the meaning of a word's root can help you determine the word's meaning.

Root	Meaning	Example
aster, astr (Greek)	star	asterisk
fic/ fac/ fec (Latin)	make, do	factory
spec/ spect/ spic (Latin)	look at, see, behold	spectator
ten (Latin)	stretch	tendon
derm/ derma (Greek)	skin	epidermis

2.3 PREFIXES

A **prefix** is a word part attached to the beginning of a word. Most prefixes come from Greek, Latin, or Old English.

Prefix	Meaning	Example
un- (Old English)	not	unafraid
epi- (Greek)	upon, on, over	epicenter
syn- (Greek)	together, at the same time	synthesis
hexa- (Greek)	six	hexagram
geo- (Greek)	earth	geography
trans- (Latin)	across, beyond	transatlantic
dis- (Latin)	lack of, not	distrust
circum- (Latin)	around	circumvent
hemi- (Latin)	half	hemisphere

2.4 SUFFIXES

A **suffix** is a word part that appears at the end of a root or base word to form a new word. Some suffixes do not change word meaning. These suffixes are

- added to nouns to change the number of persons or objects

- added to verbs to change the tense
- added to modifiers to change the degree of comparison

Suffix	Meaning	Example
-s, -es	to change the number of a noun	trunk + s = trunks
-d, -ed, -ing	to change verb tense	sprinkle + d = sprinkled
-er, -est	to change the degree of comparison in modifiers	cold + er = colder icy + est = iciest

Other suffixes can be added to a root or base to change the word's meaning. These suffixes can also determine a word's part of speech.

Suffix	Meaning	Example
-ence	state or condition of	independence
-ous	full of	furious
-ate	to make	activate
-ly, -ily	manner	quickly

Strategies for Understanding Unfamiliar Words

- Look for any prefixes or suffixes. Remove them to isolate the base word or the root.
- See if you recognize any elements—prefix, suffix, root, or base—of the word. You may be able to guess its meaning by analyzing one or two elements.
- Consider the way the word is used in the sentence. Use the context and the word parts to make a logical guess about the word's meaning.
- Consult a dictionary to see whether you are correct.

Practice and Apply

Make inferences about the meanings of the following words from the fields of science and math. Consider what you have learned in this section about Greek, Latin, and Anglo-Saxon (Old English) word parts.

astronomy	efficacy	hexagonal
circumference	epidermis	spectrum
distend	geosciences	uncertainty

3 Understanding Word Origins

3.1 ETYMOLOGIES

Etymologies show the origin and historical development of a word. When you study a word's history and origin, you can find out when, where, and how the word came to be.

am·bas·sa·dor (ăm-băs´ə-dər, -dôr´) n. A diplomatic official of the highest rank appointed and accredited as repres entative in residence by one government or sovereign to another, usually for a specific length of time. [Middle English ambassadour, from Old French ambassadeur, from Medieval Latin ambactia, mission, from Latin ambactus, servant, ultimately of Celtic origin.]

com·mu·ni·ty (kə-myo͞o´nĭ-tē) n., pl. -ties A group of people living in the same locality and under the same government. [Middle English communite, citizenry, from Old French, from Latin commūnitās, fellowship, from commūnis, common.]

Practice and Apply

Trace the etymology of the words below, often used in the fields of history and political science.

diplomat	independence	legislature
government	justice	revolution
immigrant	laissez-faire	treaty

 **L 4c**

PRACTICE AND APPLY
Answers:

Diplomat: *From French diplomate, back-formation from diplomatique, "diplomatic," meaning "ambassador." (A back-formation is a new word created by removing an affix—prefix or suffix—from an already existing word.)*

Government: *Middle English governen, from Old French governer, from Latin gubernare, from Greek kubernan, meaning "to steer a ship."*

Immigrant: *Latin immigrare, "to go into" + the suffix –ant, meaning "someone who performs an action."*

Independence: *Middle English dependen, "to hang down," from Old French dependre, from Latin dependere, "to hang down, from, or on"; to which is added the prefix in-, meaning "not," and the suffix -ence, meaning "the state of being."*

Justice: *Middle English, from Old French, from Latin iustitia, from iustus, "just."*

Laissez-faire: *Directly taken from French: laissez, second person pl. imperative of laisser, "to let, allow" + faire, "to do."*

Legislature: *Formed from the word legislator: French legislateur, from Old French, from the Latin phrase legis lator (legis, possessive form of lex, "law" + lator, "proposer, bearer"). The word was then transformed by replacing the suffix –tor ("agent or doer") with –ure ("office or process").*

Revolution: *Middle English revolucioun, from Old French revolution, from Late Latin revolutio, revolutionis ("a revolving"), which in turn comes from Classical Latin revolutus, past participle of revolvere, "to roll backwards."*

Treaty: *Middle English tretee, from Old French traite, from Latin tractatus, "discussion," from past participle of tractare, "to drag about, deal with."*

PRACTICE AND APPLY

Answers:

Panic: *Greek; in Greek mythology, Pan was the god of wild animals and nature. When people panic, they run wild with irrational fear.*

Atlas: *Greek; in Greek mythology, Atlas is a Titan who is forced to hold up the world. An atlas, a book of maps, can be said to hold the world.*

Adonis: *Greek; in Greek mythology, the goddess Aphrodite falls in love with a handsome young man named Adonis, who is killed by a wild boar. An adonis is a handsome young man.*

Mentor: *Greek; in the Odyssey, Mentor was Odysseus' wise and loyal advisor and also the teacher of Odysseus' son. A mentor acts as a teacher, coach, or experienced advisor.*

Cereal: *Latin; in Roman mythology, Ceres was the goddess of agriculture. A cereal is a grain or the food made from grain.*

Mercurial: *Latin; in Roman mythology, Mercury was the swift-footed messenger god. Someone described as mercurial quickly and frequently changes moods or ideas.*

Saturday: *Latin; in Roman mythology, Saturn was an important god. The last day of the week is Saturn's day.*

January: *Latin; in Roman mythology, Janus was the god of doors and gates, and beginnings and endings. As the first month of the year, January would have been guarded by Janus.*

Wednesday: *Norse; the chief Norse god was Odin, or Woden. The weekday Wednesday is Woden's day.*

Gun: *Norse; a powerful medieval military weapon was given the name of a Scandinavian woman, Gunnhildr. A shortened version of the name now applies to a class of powerful weapons, guns.*

Berserk: *Norse; ferocious early Norse warriors were called berserkers. Someone who behaves in a frenzied, furious way is said to have gone berserk.*

Valkyrie: *Norse; in Norse mythology, the Valkyries took the souls of heroes who died in battle to Valhalla, the great hall of the chief god, Odin.*

3.2 WORD FAMILIES

Words that have the same root make up a word family and have related meanings. The chart shows a common Greek and a common Latin root. Notice how the meanings of the example words are related to the meanings of their roots.

Latin Root	*med:* "middle"
English Words	**mediate** resolve or settle
	mediocre ordinary
	media^2 middle wall of a blood vessel
	medial toward the middle
	medium action midway between two extremes

Greek Root	*chron:* "time"
English Words	**chronicle** detailed narrative report
	chronic of long duration
	synchronize occur at same time
	anachronism out of proper order in time

3.3 WORDS FROM CLASSICAL MYTHOLOGY

The English language includes many words from classical mythology. You can use your knowledge of these myths to understand the origins and meanings of these words. For example, *herculean task* refers to the strongman Hercules. Thus, *herculean task* probably means "a job that is large or difficult." The chart shows a few common words from mythology.

Greek	Roman	Norse
panic	cereal	Wednesday
atlas	mercurial	gun
adonis	Saturday	berserk
mentor	January	valkyrie

Practice and Apply

Look up the etymology of each word in the chart and locate the myth associated with it. Use the information from the myth to explain the origin and meaning of each word.

3.4 FOREIGN WORDS

The English language includes words from diverse languages, such as French, Dutch, Spanish, Italian, and Chinese. Many words stayed the way they were in their original language.

French	Dutch	Spanish	Italian
entree	maelstrom	rodeo	pasta
nouveau riche	trek	salsa	opera
potpourri	cookie	bronco	vendetta
tête-à-tête	snoop	tornado	grotto

4 Understanding the English Language

The English language has a documented history of 1400 years, but its earliest beginnings stretch back to the speakers of Proto-Indo-European who ranged from India to Europe. Proto-Indo-European gave rise to many languages, including English, Swedish, Hindi, Greek, Russian, Polish, Italian, French, Spanish, and German—now referred to as Indo-European. Here's a brief overview of the development of English:

- **Proto-English:** Besides the Romans who spoke Latin, the early inhabitants of Britain were Britons and Celts. The Angles, Saxons, and Jutes—Germanic peoples—arrived around A.D. 449. Proto-English incorporated Latin words as well as those drawn from the languages of the Britons, Celts, and the Germanic peoples.

- **Old English:** From about the mid-fifth century to the twelfth century, Old English, the language of the Anglo-Saxons, was the spoken language in Britain. Latin remained the language of writing and of the church, schools, and international relations. Old English would be unintelligible to the speaker of Modern English, given the differences in its grammar, spellings, and pronunciations. The most well-known work in Old English is the epic poem *Beowulf.*

- **Middle English:** After the Norman Conquest in 1066, the nobility spoke Anglo-Norman. Middle English, derived from Anglo-Norman, thrived from the late eleventh century to the late fifteenth century. It also underwent significant changes in grammar and vocabulary. The most famous writer of this period is Geoffrey Chaucer, whose *The Canterbury Tales* remains a staple of the English literature curriculum.

- **Early Modern English:** During the fifteenth century, the so-called "Great Vowel Shift" occurred—a major change in the pronunciation of English. Conventions of spelling were also being established during this time. With the spread of a London-based dialect and the standardization that results from printing, Early Modern English is recognizable to the speaker of Modern English. For example, William Shakespeare, the great English dramatist, wrote during the late phase of Early Modern English. The first edition of the *King James Bible* also was published during this time. Early Modern English lasted until about the seventeenth century.

- **Modern English:** Modern English emerged in the late seventeenth century and continues to the present day. Its development was shaped by Samuel Johnson's *Dictionary of the English Language,* published in 1755, which standardized spelling and usage. The significant characteristic of contemporary Modern English is its extensive vocabulary, which partly arises from technological and scientific developments, as well as from the worldwide variety of its speakers. As various communication devices are increasingly adopted, technology-specific language and vocabulary—such as that used in texting—further influence English. Thus, the development of English continues in the present day.

5 Synonyms and Antonyms

5.1 SYNONYMS

A **synonym** is a word with a meaning similar to that of another word. You can find synonyms in a thesaurus or a dictionary. In a dictionary, synonyms are often given as part of the definition of a word. The following word pairs are synonyms:

dry/arid   enthralled/fascinated
gaunt/thin

5.2 ANTONYMS

An **antonym** is a word with a meaning opposite that of another word. The following word pairs are antonyms:

friend/enemy   absurd/logical
courteous/rude   languid/energetic

6 Denotation and Connotation

6.1 DENOTATION

A word's dictionary meaning is called its **denotation.** For example, the denotation of the word *rascal* is "an unethical, dishonest person."

6.2 CONNOTATION

The images or feelings you connect to a word add a finer shade of meaning, called **connotation.** The connation of a word goes beyond its basic dictionary definition. Writers use connotations of words to communicate positive or negative feelings.

Positive	Neutral	Negative
save	store	hoard
fragrance	smell	stench
display	show	flaunt

Make sure you understand the denotation and connotation of a word when you read it or use it in your writing.

7 Analogies

An **analogy** is a comparison between two things that are similar in some way but are otherwise dissimilar. Analogies are sometimes used in writing when unfamiliar subjects or ideas are explained in terms of familiar ones. Analogies often appear on tests as well, usually in a format like this:

TERRIER : DOG :: A) rat : fish

B) kitten : cat

C) trout : fish

D) fish : trout

E) poodle : collie

Follow these steps to determine the correct answer:

- Read the part in capital letters as "*terrier* is to *dog* as . . ."
- Read the answer choices as "*rat* is to *fish*," "*kitten* is to *cat*," and so on.
- Ask yourself how the words *terrier* and *dog* are related. (A terrier is a type of dog.)
- Ask yourself which of the choices shows the same relationship. (A kitten is a kind of cat, but not in the same way that a terrier is a kind of dog. A kitten is a baby cat. A trout, however, is a type of fish in the sense that a terrier is a type of dog. Therefore, the answer is C.)

8 Homonyms and Homophones

8.1 HOMONYMS

Homonyms are words that have the same spelling and sound but have different origins and meanings.

I don't want to bore you with a story about how I had to bore through the living room wall.

Bore can mean "cause a person to lose interest," but an identically spelled word means "drill a hole."

My dog likes to bark while it scratches the bark on the tree in the backyard.

Bark can refer to what a dog does to make a sound, but an identically spelled word means "the outer covering of a tree." Each word has a different meaning and its own dictionary entry.

Sometimes only one of the meanings of two homonyms may be familiar to you. Use context clues to help you figure out the meaning of an unfamiliar word.

8.2 HOMOPHONES

Homophones are words that sound alike but have different meanings and spellings. The following homophones are frequently misused:

it's/its	they're/their/there
to/too/two	stationary/stationery

Many misused homophones are pronouns and contractions. Whenever you are unsure whether to write *your* or *you're* and *who's* or *whose*, ask yourself if you mean *you are* or *who is/has*. If you do, write the contraction. For other homophones, such as *scent* and *sent*, use the meaning of the word to help you decide which one to use.

9 Words with Multiple Meanings

Some words have acquired additional meanings over time that are based on the original meaning.

EXAMPLES: *I was in a hurry, so I jammed my clothes into the suitcase.*
Unfortunately, I jammed my finger in the process.

These two uses of *jam* have different meanings, but they have the same origin. You will find all the meanings of *jam* listed in the dictionary.

10 Specialized Vocabulary

Specialized vocabulary includes technical vocabulary, domain-specific language, and jargon. Each term refers to the use of language specific to a particular field of study or work. Of these three terms, *jargon* has the strongest connotation, suggesting a kind of language that is difficult to understand or unintelligible to anyone not involved in that field of study or work.

Science, mathematics, history, and literature all have domain-specific vocabularies. For example, science includes words such as *photosynthesis* and *biome* which indicate specific scientific processes or concepts. In literature, words such as *foreshadowing, motif,* and *irony* enable you and others to use a common vocabulary to discuss and interpret literary works.

To figure out specialized terms, you can use context clues and reference sources, such as dictionaries on specific subjects, atlases, or manuals. Many of the resources you use in school include reference aids for that particular subject area. For example, this textbook includes a "Glossary of Literary and Informational Terms," as well as a "Glossary of Academic Vocabulary."

11 Preferred and Contested Usage

English is a constantly evolving language, and standard usage is affected by time and place. For example, Americans often use different words and phrases than the British. Within the United States itself, people speak and write differently than they did 200 years ago. English usage even varies depending on whether the setting is formal or informal. Some nonstandard usages are contested but may become accepted and standard over time. Consult references like *The American Heritage Dictionary of the English Language, Fifth Edition* and its website to determine whether a certain usage is acceptable. See the chart for examples of common usage problems and preferred and contested usages.

ain't	*Ain't* is nonstandard. Avoid *ain't* in formal speaking and in all writing other than dialogue.
all right	*All right* means "satisfactory," "unhurt," "safe," "correct," or, as a reply to a question or a preface to a remark, "yes." Although some dictionaries include *alright* as an optional spelling, it is contested and has not become standard usage.
can, may	*Can* expresses ability; *may* expresses possibility.
hopefully	Used as an adverb, as in the following sentence, the term is uncontested. EXAMPLE: We waited hopefully for the announcement of the election results last night. Some contest the use of *hopefully* as a disjunct; that is, as an adverb that expresses the speaker's comments on the content of a statement. EXAMPLE: Hopefully the candidate I like wins. Merriam–Webster's online dictionary says the second use is "entirely standard."
like, as if, as though	In formal situations, avoid using *like* for the conjunction *as if* or *as though* to introduce a subordinate clause. INFORMAL: I feel like I have the flu. FORMAL: I feel as if I have the flu.

literally, figuratively	*Literally* means "in a strict sense." It is sometimes used in non-literal situations for emphasis, when *figuratively* is the more appropriate term. This type of use is contested. UNCONTESTED: I literally baked five-dozen cupcakes. CONTESTED: He literally went nuts. Usage experts for *The American Heritage Dictionary* suggest that the term is acceptable when used as an intensive adverb.
off, off of	Do not use *off* or *off of* for *from*. NONSTANDARD: I got some good advice off that mechanic. STANDARD: I got some good advice from that mechanic.
some, somewhat	In formal situations, avoid using *some* to mean "to some extent." Use *somewhat*. INFORMAL: Tensions between the nations began to ease some. FORMAL: Tensions between the nations began to ease somewhat.
who, whom	*Who* is used as a subject or a predicate nominative. *Whom* is used as a direct object, an indirect object or an object of a preposition. However, in spoken English, most people use *who* instead of *whom* in all cases.

The English language continues to change, and technology plays a part in that. The increasing use of texting as a means of communications has created a contested language all its own. Terms like *IMO (in my opinion)* and *LOL (laughing out loud)* have become a commonly used part of the vocabulary.

12 Using Reference Sources

12.1 DICTIONARIES

A **general dictionary** will tell you not only a word's definitions but also its pronunciation, its parts of speech, and its history and origin. A **specialized dictionary** focuses on terms related to a particular field of study or work. Use a dictionary to check the spelling of any word you are unsure of in your English class and other subjects as well.

12.2 THESAURI

A **thesaurus** (plural, thesauri) is a dictionary of synonyms. A thesaurus can be helpful when you find yourself using the same modifiers over and over again.

12.3 SYNONYM FINDERS

A **synonym finder** is often included in word-processing software. It enables you to highlight a word and be shown a display of its synonyms.

12.4 GLOSSARIES

A **glossary** is a list of specialized terms and their definitions. It is often found in the back of textbooks and sometimes includes pronunciations. In fact, this textbook has three glossaries: the **Glossary of Literary Informational Terms,** the **Glossary of Academic Vocabulary,** and the **Glossary of Vocabulary.** Use these glossaries to help you understand how terms are used in this textbook.

13 Spelling Rules

13.1 WORDS ENDING IN A SILENT *E*

Before adding a suffix beginning with a vowel or *y* to a word ending in a silent *e,* drop the *e* (with some exceptions).

> **amaze + -ing = amazing**
> **love + -able = lovable**

create + -ed = created

nerve + -ous = nervous

Exceptions: *change + -able = changeable; courage + -ous = courageous.*

When adding a suffix beginning with a consonant to a word ending in a silent *e,* keep the *e* (with some exceptions).

late + -ly = lately

spite + -ful = spiteful

noise + -less = noiseless

state + -ment = statement

Exceptions: *truly, argument, ninth, wholly, awful,* and others.

When a suffix beginning with *a* or *o* is added to a word with a final silent *e,* the final *e* is usually retained if it is preceded by a soft *c* or a soft *g.*

bridge + -able = bridgeable

peace + -able = peaceable

outrage + -ous = outrageous

advantage + -ous = advantageous

When a suffix beginning with a vowel is added to words ending in *ee* or *oe,* the final silent *e* is retained.

agree + -ing = agreeing

free + -ing = freeing

hoe + -ing = hoeing

see + -ing = seeing

13.2 WORDS ENDING IN *Y*

Before adding most suffixes to a word that ends in *y* preceded by a consonant, change the *y* to *i.*

easy + -est = easiest

crazy + -est = craziest

silly + -ness = silliness

marry + -age = marriage

Exceptions: *dryness, shyness,* and *slyness.*

However, when you add *-ing,* the *y* does not change.

empty + -ed = emptied   but

empty + -ing = emptying

When adding a suffix to a word that ends in *y* preceded by a vowel, the *y* usually does not change.

play + -er = player

employ + -ed = employed

coy + -ness = coyness

pay + -able = payable

13.3 WORDS ENDING IN A CONSONANT

In one-syllable words that end in one consonant preceded by one short vowel, double the final consonant before adding a suffix beginning with a vowel, such as *-ed* or *-ing.*

dip + -ed = dipped   set + -ing = setting

slim + -est = slimmest   fit + -er = fitter

The rule does not apply to words of one syllable that end in a consonant preceded by two vowels.

feel + -ing = feeling   peel + -ed = peeled

reap + -ed = reaped   loot + -ed = looted

In words of more than one syllable, double the final consonant when (1) the word ends with one consonant preceded by one vowel and (2) the word is accented on the last syllable.

be•gin´   per•mit´   re•fer´

In the following examples, note that in the new words formed with suffixes, the accent remains on the same syllable:

be•gin´ + -ing = be•gin´ning = beginning

per•mit´ + -ed = per•mit´ted = permitted

In some words with more than one syllable, though the accent remains on the same syllable when a suffix is added, the final consonant is nevertheless not doubled, as in the following examples:

tra´vel + -er = tra´vel•er = traveler

mar´ket + -er = mar´ket•er = marketer

In the following examples, the accent does not remain on the same syllable; thus, the final consonant is not doubled:

re•fer´ + -ence = ref´er•ence = reference

con•fer´ + -ence = con´fer•ence = conference

13.4 PREFIXES AND SUFFIXES

When adding a prefix to a word, do not change the spelling of the base word. When a prefix creates a double letter, keep both letters.

dis- + approve = disapprove

re- + build = rebuild

ir- + regular = irregular

mis- + spell = misspell

anti- + trust = antitrust

il- + logical = illogical

When adding **-ly** to a word ending in **l**, keep both **l**'s, and when adding **-ness** to a word ending in **n**, keep both **n**'s.

careful + -ly = carefully

sudden + -ness = suddenness

final + -ly = finally

thin + -ness = thinness

13.5 FORMING PLURAL NOUNS

To form the plural of most nouns, just add **-s**.

prizes   dreams   circles   stations

For most singular nouns ending in **o**, add **-s**.

solos   halos   studios   photos   pianos

When the singular noun ends in **s, sh, ch, x**, or **z**, add **-es**.

waitresses   brushes   ditches

axes   buzzes

When a singular noun ends in **y** with a consonant before it, change the **y** to **i** and add **-es**.

army—armies   candy—candies

baby—babies   diary—diaries

ferry—ferries   conspiracy—conspiracies

When a vowel (**a, e, i, o, u**) comes before the **y**, just add **-s**.

boy—boys   way—ways

array—arrays   alloy—alloys

weekday—weekdays   jockey—jockeys

For most nouns ending in **f** or **fe,** change the **f** to **v** and add **-es** or **-s**.

life—lives   calf—calves

knife—knives   thief—thieves

shelf—shelves   loaf—loaves

For some nouns ending in **f,** add **-s** to make the plural.

roofs   chiefs   reefs   beliefs

Some nouns have the same form for both singular and plural.

deer   sheep   moose   salmon   trout

For some nouns, the plural is formed in a special way.

man—men   goose—geese

ox—oxen   woman—women

mouse—mice   child—children

For a compound noun written as one word, form the plural by changing the last word in the compound to its plural form.

stepchild—stepchildren firefly—fireflies

If a compound noun is written as a hyphenated word or as two separate words, change the most important word to the plural form.

brother-in-law—brothers-in-law

life jacket—life jackets

13.6 FORMING POSSESSIVES

If a noun is singular, add **'s.**

mother—my mother's car

Ross—Ross's desk

Exception: The **s** after the apostrophe is dropped after *Jesus', Moses',* and certain names in classical mythology (*Zeus'*). These possessive forms can be pronounced easily.

If a noun is plural and ends with **s,** just add an apostrophe.

parents—my parents' car

the Santinis—the Santinis' house

If a noun is plural but does not end in **s,** add **'s.**

people—the people's choice

women—the women's coats

13.7 SPECIAL SPELLING PROBLEMS

Only one English word ends in **-sede:** *supersede.* Three words end in **-ceed:** *exceed, proceed,* and *succeed.* All other verbs ending in the sound "seed" (except for the verb *seed*) are spelled with **-cede.**

concede   precede   recede   secede

In words with *ie* or *ei,* when the sound is long *e* (as in *she*), the word is spelled *ie* except after *c* (with some exceptions).

i before e	thief	relieve	field
	piece	grieve	pier
except after c	conceit	perceive	ceiling
	receive	receipt	

Exceptions: *either, neither, weird, leisure, seize.*

14 Commonly Confused Words

Words	Definition	Example
accept/except	The verb *accept* means "to receive or believe"; *except* is usually a preposition meaning "excluding."	**Except** for some of the more extraordinary events, I can **accept** that the *Odyssey* recounts a real journey.
advice/advise	*Advise* is a verb; *advice* is a noun naming that which an *adviser* gives.	I **advise** you to take that job. Whom should I ask for **advice?**
affect/effect	As a verb, *affect* means "to influence." *Effect* as a verb means "to cause." If you want a noun, you will almost always want *effect*.	Did Circe's wine **affect** Odysseus's mind? It did **effect** a change in Odysseus's men. In fact, it had an **effect** on everyone else who drank it.
all ready/ already	*All ready* is an adjective meaning "fully ready." *Already* is an adverb meaning "before or by this time."	He was **all ready** to go at noon. I have **already** seen that movie.
allusion/ illusion	An *allusion* is an indirect reference to something. An *illusion* is a false picture or idea.	There are many **allusions** to the works of Homer in English literature. The world's apparent flatness is an **illusion.**
among/ between	*Between* is used when you are speaking of only two things. *Among* is used for three or more.	**Between** *Hamlet* and *King Lear,* I prefer the latter. Emily Dickinson is **among** my favorite poets.
bring/take	*Bring* is used to denote motion toward a speaker or place. *Take* is used to denote motion away from such a person or place.	**Bring** the books over here, and I will **take** them to the library.
fewer/less	*Fewer* refers to the number of separate, countable units. *Less* refers to bulk quantity.	We have **less** literature and **fewer** selections in this year's curriculum.
leave/let	*Leave* means "to allow something to remain behind." *Let* means "to permit."	The librarian will **leave** some books on display but will not **let** us borrow any.

continued

Words	Definition	Example
lie/lay	*Lie* means "to rest or recline." It does not take an object. *Lay* always takes an object.	Rover loves to **lie** in the sun. We always **lay** some bones next to him.
loose/lose	*Loose* (lo͞os) means "free, not restrained"; *lose* (lo͞oz) means "to misplace or fail to find."	Who turned the horses **loose?** I hope we won't **lose** any of them.
precede/ proceed	*Precede* means "to go or come before." Use *proceed* for other meanings.	Emily Dickinson's poetry **precedes** that of Alice Walker. You may **proceed** to the next section of the test.
than/then	Use *than* in making comparisons; use *then* on all other occasions.	Who can say whether Amy Lowell is a better poet **than** Denise Levertov? I will read Lowell first, and **then** I will read Levertov.
their/there/ they're	*Their* means "belonging to them." *There* means "in that place." *They're* is the contraction for "they are."	**There** is a movie playing at 9 P.M. **They're** going to see it with me. Sakara and Jessica drove away in **their** car after the movie.
two/too/to	*Two* is the number. *Too* is an adverb meaning "also" or "very." Use *to* before a verb or as a preposition.	Meg had to go to town, **too.** We had **too** much reading to do. **Two** chapters is **too** many.

Glossary of Literary and Informational Terms

Act An act is a major unit of action in a play, similar to a chapter in a book. Depending on their lengths, plays can have as many as five acts. Arthur Miller's play *The Crucible* has four acts.

See also **Drama; Scene.**

Allegory An allegory is a work with two levels of meaning, a literal one and a symbolic one. In such a work, most of the characters, objects, settings, and events represent abstract qualities. Personification is often used in traditional allegories. As in a fable or parable, the purpose of an allegory may be to convey truths about life, to teach religious or moral lessons, or to criticize social institutions.

Alliteration Alliteration is the repetition of consonant sounds at the beginnings of words. Poets use alliteration to impart a musical quality to their poems, to create mood, to reinforce meaning, to emphasize particular words, and to unify lines or stanzas. Note the examples of alliteration in the following sentence:

> Don't doubt that I'll do something daring and jaw dropping.

Allusion An allusion is an indirect reference to a person, place, event, or literary work with which the author believes the reader will be familiar.

Almanac *See* **Reference Works.**

Ambiguity Ambiguity is a technique in which a word, phrase, or event has more than one meaning or can be interepreted in more than one way. Some writers deliberately create this effect to give richness and depth of meaning. T. S. Eliot and Robert Frost are two poets known for their use of ambiguity.

Analogy An analogy is a point-by-point comparison between two things for the purpose of clarifying the less familiar of the two subjects.

Anapest *See* **Meter.**

Anaphora Anaphora is a repetition of a word or words at the beginning of successive lines, clauses, or sentences.

See also **Repetition.**

Anecdote An anecdote is a brief story that focuses on a single episode or event in a person's life and that is used to illustrate a particular point.

Antagonist An antagonist is usually the principal character in opposition to the protagonist, or hero of a narrative or drama. The antagonist can also be a force of nature.

See also **Character; Protagonist.**

Antihero An antihero is a protagonist who has the qualities opposite to those of a hero; he or she may be insecure, ineffective, cowardly, sometimes dishonest or dishonorable, or—most often—a failure. A popular antihero in contemporary culture is the cartoon character Homer Simpson.

Aphorism An aphorism is a brief statement, usually one sentence long, that expresses a general principle or truth about life.

Appeals by Association Appeals by association imply that one will gain acceptance or prestige by taking the writer's position.

Appeal to Authority An appeal to authority calls upon experts or others who warrant respect.

Appeal to Reason *See* **Logical Appeal.**

Archetype An archetype is a pattern in literature that is found in a variety of works from different cultures throughout the ages. An archetype can be a plot, a character, an image, or a setting. For example, the association of death and rebirth with winter and spring is an archetype common to many cultures.

Argument An argument is speech or writing that expresses a position on an issue or problem and supports it with reasons and evidence. An argument often takes into account other points of view, anticipating and answering objections that opponents of the position might raise.

See also **Claim; Counterargument; Evidence; General Principle.**

Aside In drama, an aside is a short speech directed to the audience, or another character, that is not heard by the other characters on stage.

See also **Soliloquy.**

Assonance Assonance is the repetition of vowel sounds within words. Both poets and prose writers use assonance to impart a musical quality to their works, to create mood, to reinforce meaning, to emphasize particular words, and to unify lines, stanzas, or passages. Note examples of assonance in the following sentence:

> The musician finished writing
> the lyrics to her next big hit.

See also **Alliteration; Consonance; Rhyme.**

Assumption An assumption is an opinion or belief that is taken for granted. It can be about a specific situation, a person, or the world in general. Assumptions are often unstated.

See also **General Principle.**

Atmosphere *See* **Mood.**

Audience Audience is the person or persons who are intended to read a piece of writing. The intended audience of a work determines its form, style, tone, and the details included.

Author's Message An author's message is the main idea or theme of a particular work.

See also **Main Idea; Theme.**

Author's Perspective An author's perspective is a unique combination of ideas, values, feelings, and beliefs that influences the way the writer looks at a topic. **Tone,** or attitude, often reveals an author's perspective.

Author's Position An author's position is his or her opinion on an issue or topic.

See also **Claim.**

Author's Purpose A writer usually writes for one or more of these purposes: to inform, to entertain, to express himself or herself, or to persuade readers to believe or do something. For example, the purpose of a news report (either in a newspaper or magazine) is primarily to inform; the purpose of a news editorial is to persuade the readers or audience to do or believe something.

Autobiographical Essay *See* Essay.

Autobiography An autobiography is the story of a person's life written by that person. Generally written from the first-person point of view, autobiographies can vary in style from straightforward chronological accounts to impressionistic narratives.

Ballad A ballad is a narrative poem that was originally meant to be sung. Ballads often contain dialogue and repetition and suggest more than they actually state. Traditional **folk ballads,** composed by unknown authors and handed down orally, are written in four-line stanzas with regular rhythm and rhyme. A **literary ballad** is one that is modeled on the folk ballads but written by a single author.

See also **Narrative Poem; Rhyme; Rhythm.**

Bias Bias is an inclination toward a particular judgment on a topic or issue. A writer often reveals a strongly positive or strongly negative opinion by presenting only one way of looking at an issue or by heavily weighting the evidence. Words with intensely positive or negative connotations are often a signal of a writer's bias.

Bibliography A bibliography is a list of books and other materials related to the topic of a text. Bibliographies can be good sources of works for further study on a subject.

See also **Works Consulted.**

Biography A biography is a type of nonfiction in which a writer gives a factual account of someone else's life. Written in the third person, a biography may cover a person's entire life or focus on only an important part of it. The poet Carl Sandburg wrote an acclaimed six-volume biography of Abraham Lincoln. Modern biography includes a popular form called **fictionalized biography,** in which writers use their imaginations to re-create past conversations and to elaborate on some incidents.

Blank Verse A poem written in blank verse consists of unrhymed lines of iambic pentameter. In other words, each line of blank verse has five pairs of syllables. In most pairs, an unstressed syllable is followed by a stressed syllable. The most versatile of poetic forms, blank verse imitates the natural rhythms of English speech.

See also Iambic Pentameter; Meter; Rhythm.

Business Correspondence Business correspondence includes all written business communications, such as business letters, e-mails, and memos. Business correspondence is to the point, clear, courteous, and professional.

Caesura A caesura is a pause or a break in a line of poetry. Poets use a caesura to emphasize the word or phrase that precedes it or to vary the rhythmical effects.

Cast of Characters The cast of characters is a list of all the characters in a play, usually in the order of appearance. This list is found at the beginning of a script.

Catalog A catalog is a list of people, things, or attributes. This technique, found in epics and in the Bible, also characterizes Whitman's style.

Cause and Effect A **cause** is an event or action that directly results in another event or action. An **effect** is the direct or logical outcome of an event or action. Basic **cause-and-effect relationships** include a single cause with a single effect, one cause with multiple effects, multiple causes with a single effect, and a chain of causes and effects. The concept of cause and effect also provides a way of organizing a piece of writing. It helps a writer show the relationships between events or ideas.

Central Idea *See* Main Idea.

Character Characters are the people, and sometimes animals or other beings, who take part in the action of a story or novel. Events center on the lives of one or more characters, referred to as **main characters.** The other characters, called **minor characters,** interact with the main characters and help move the story along.

Characters may also be classified as either static or dynamic. **Static characters** tend to stay in a fixed position over the course of the story. They do not experience life-altering moments and seem to act the same, even though their situations may change. In contrast, **dynamic**

characters evolve as individuals, learning from their experiences and growing emotionally.

See also Antagonist; Characterization; Foil; Motivation; Protagonist.

Characterization Characterization refers to the techniques a writer uses to develop characters. There are four basic methods of characterization:

- A writer may use physical description.
- The character's own actions, words, thoughts, and feelings might be presented.
- The actions, words, thoughts, and feelings of other characters provide another means of developing a character.
- The narrator's own direct comments also serve to develop a character.

See also Character; Narrator.

Chorus In the theater of ancient Greece, the chorus was a group of actors who commented on the **action** of the play. Between scenes, the chorus sang and danced to musical accompaniment, giving insights into the message of the play. The chorus is often considered a kind of ideal spectator, representing the response of ordinary citizens to the tragic events that unfold. Certain dramatists have continued to employ this classical convention as a way of representing the views of the society being depicted.

See also Drama.

Chronological Order Chronological order is the arrangement of events in their order of occurrence. This type of organization is used in both fictional narratives and in historical writing, biography, and autobiography.

Claim In an argument, a claim is the writer's position on an issue or problem. Although an argument focuses on supporting one claim, a writer may make more than one claim in a work.

Clarify Clarifying is a reading strategy that helps a reader to understand or make clear what he or she is reading. Readers usually clarify by rereading, reading aloud, or discussing.

Classification Classification is a pattern of organization in which objects, ideas, or information is presented in groups, or classes, based on common characteristics.

Cliché A cliché is an overused expression that has lost its freshness, force, and appeal. The phrase "happy as a lark" is an example of a cliché.

Climax In a plot structure, the climax, or turning point, is the moment when the reader's interest and emotional intensity reach a peak. The climax usually occurs toward the end of a story and often results in a change in the characters or a solution to the conflict.
See also Falling Action; Plot; Rising Action; Resolution.

Comedy A comedy is a dramatic work that is light and often humorous in tone, usually ending happily with a peaceful resolution of the main conflict. A comedy differs from a **farce** by having a more-believable plot, more-realistic characters, and less-boisterous behavior.
See also Drama; Farce.

Comic Relief Comic relief consists of humorous scenes, incidents, or speeches that are included in a serious drama to provide a reduction in emotional intensity. Because it breaks the tension, comic relief allows an audience to prepare emotionally for events to come.

Compare and Contrast To compare and contrast is to identify similarities and differences in two or more subjects. Compare-and-contrast organization can be used to structure a piece of writing, serving as a framework for examining the similarities and differences in two or more subjects.

Complication A complication is an additional factor or problem introduced into the rising action of a story to make the conflict more difficult. Often, a plot complication makes it seem as though the main character is getting further away from the thing he or she wants.

Conceit *See* Extended Metaphor.

Conclusion A conclusion is a statement of belief based on evidence, experience, and reasoning. A **valid conclusion** is a conclusion that logically follows from the

facts or statements upon which it is based. A **deductive conclusion** is one that follows from a particular generalization or premise. An **inductive conclusion** is a broad conclusion or generalization that is reached by arguing from specific facts and examples.

Conflict A conflict is a struggle between opposing forces that is the basis of a story's plot. An **external conflict** pits a character against nature, society, or another character. An **internal conflict** is a conflict between opposing forces within a character.
See also Antagonist; Plot.

Connect Connecting is a reader's process of relating the content of a text to his or her own knowledge and experience.

Connotation Connotation is the emotional response evoked by a word, in contrast to its denotation, which is its literal meaning. *Kitten*, for example, is defined as "a young cat." However, the word also suggests, or connotes, images of softness, warmth, and playfulness.

Consonance Consonance is the repetition of consonant sounds within and at the ends of words.

> He ate most of the fruit in the kitchen yesterday.

See also Alliteration; Assonance.

Consumer Documents Consumer documents are printed materials that accompany products and services. They are intended for the buyers or users of the products or services and usually provide information about use, care, operation, or assembly. Some common consumer documents are applications, contracts, warranties, manuals, instructions, package inserts, labels, brochures, and schedules.

Context Clues When you encounter an unfamiliar word, you can often use context clues as aids for understanding. Context clues are the words and phrases surrounding the word that provide hints about the word's meaning.

Controlling Idea *See* Thesis Statement.

Counterargument A counterargument is an argument made to oppose another argument. A good argument anticipates opposing viewpoints and provides counterarguments to refute (disprove) or answer them.

Counterclaim *See* Counterargument.

Couplet *See* Sonnet.

Creation Myth *See* Myth.

Credibility *Credibility* refers to the believability or trustworthiness of a source and the information it contains.

Critical Essay *See* Essay.

Critical Review A critical review is an evaluation or critique by a reviewer or critic. Different types of reviews include film reviews, book reviews, music reviews, and art show reviews.

Cultural Hero A cultural hero is a larger-than-life figure who reflects the values of a people. Rather than being the creation of a single writer, this kind of hero evolves from the telling of folk tales from one generation to the next. The role of the cultural hero is to provide a noble image that will inspire and guide the actions of all who share that culture.

Dactyl *See* Meter.

Database A database is a collection of information that can be quickly and easily accessed and searched and from which information can be easily retrieved. It is frequently presented in an electronic format.

Debate A debate is an organized exchange of opinions on an issue. In academic settings, *debate* usually refers to a formal contest in which two opposing teams defend and attack a proposition.

See also Argument.

Deductive Reasoning Deductive reasoning is a way of thinking that begins with a generalization, presents a specific situation, and then advances with facts and evidence to a logical conclusion. The following passage has a deductive argument imbedded in it: "All students in the drama class must attend the play on Thursday. Since Ava is in the class,

she had better show up." This deductive argument can be broken down as follows: generalization—all students in the drama class must attend the play on Thursday; specific situation—Ava is a student in the drama class; conclusion—Ava must attend the play.

Denotation *See* Connotation.

Dénouement *See* Falling Action.

Description Description is writing that helps a reader to picture scenes, events, and characters. Effective description usually relies on imagery, figurative language, and precise diction.

See also Diction; Figurative Language; Imagery.

Dialect A dialect is the distinct form of a language as it is spoken in one geographical area or by a particular social or ethnic group. A group's dialect is reflected in characteristic pronunciations, vocabulary, idioms, and grammatical constructions. When trying to reproduce a given dialect, writers often use unconventional spellings to suggest the way words actually sound. Writers use dialect to establish setting, to provide local color, and to develop characters.

See also Local Color Realism.

Dialogue Dialogue is conversation between two or more characters in either fiction or nonfiction. In drama, the story is told almost exclusively through dialogue, which moves the plot forward and reveals characters' motives.

See also Drama.

Diary A diary is a writer's personal day-to-day account of his or her experiences and impressions. Most diaries are private and not intended to be shared. Some, however, have been published because they are well written and provide useful perspectives on historical events or on the everyday life of particular eras.

Diction A writer's or speaker's choice of words is called diction. Diction includes both vocabulary (individual words) and syntax (the order or arrangement of words). Diction can be formal or informal, technical or common, abstract or concrete.

Dictionary *See* Reference Works.

Drama Drama is literature in which plot and character are developed through dialogue and action; in other words, drama is literature in play form. It is performed on stage and radio and in films and television. Most plays are divided into acts, with each act having an emotional peak, or climax, of its own. The acts sometimes are divided into scenes; each scene is limited to a single time and place. Most contemporary plays have two or three acts, although some have only one act.

See also Act; Dialogue; Scene; Stage Directions.

Dramatic Irony *See* Irony.

Dramatic Monologue A dramatic monologue is a lyric poem in which a speaker addresses a silent or absent listener in a moment of high intensity or deep emotion, as if engaged in private conversation. The speaker proceeds without interruption or argument, and the effect on the reader is that of hearing just one side of a conversation. This technique allows the poet to focus on the feelings, personality, and motivations of the speaker.

See also Lyric Poetry; Soliloquy.

Draw Conclusions To draw a conclusion is to make a judgment or arrive at a belief based on evidence, experience, and reasoning.

Dynamic Character *See* Character.

Editorial An editorial is an opinion piece that usually appears on the editorial page of a newspaper or as part of a news broadcast. The editorial section of a newspaper presents opinions rather than objective news reports.

See also Op-Ed Piece.

Either/Or Fallacy An either/or fallacy is a statement that suggests that there are only two possible ways to view a situation or only two options to choose from. In other words, it is a statement that falsely frames a dilemma, giving the impression that no options exist but the two presented—for example, "Either we stop the construction of a new airport, or the surrounding suburbs will become ghost towns."

Elegy An elegy is a poem written in tribute to a person, usually someone who has died recently. The tone of an elegy is usually formal and dignified.

Emotional Appeals Emotional appeals are messages that evoke strong feelings—such as fear, pity, or vanity—in order to persuade instead of using facts and evidence to make a point. An **appeal to fear** is a message that taps into people's fear of losing their safety or security. An **appeal to pity** is a message that taps into people's sympathy and compassion for others to build support for an idea, a cause, or a proposed action. An **appeal to vanity** is a message that attempts to persuade by tapping into people's desire to feel good about themselves.

Encyclopedia *See* Reference Works.

Epic An epic is a long narrative poem on a serious subject presented in an elevated or formal style. An epic traces the adventures of a hero whose actions consist of courageous, even superhuman, deeds, which often represent the ideals and values of a nation or race. Epics typically address universal issues, such as good and evil, life and death, and sin and redemption. Homer's *Iliad* and *Odyssey* are famous epics from western civilization. The *Ramayana* is an epic from India.

Epic Hero An epic hero is a larger-than-life figure who embodies the ideals of a nation or race. Epic heroes take part in dangerous adventures and accomplish great deeds. Many undertake long, difficult journeys and display great courage and superhuman strength.

Epithet An epithet is a brief descriptive phrase that points out traits associated with a particular person or thing.

Essay An essay is a short work of nonfiction that deals with a single subject. Essays are often informal, loosely structured, and highly personal. They can be descriptive, informative, persuasive, narrative, or any combination of these.

An **autobiographical essay** focuses on an aspect of a writer's life. Generally, writers of autobiographical essays use the first-person point of view, combining objective description with the expression of subjective feelings.

Ethical Appeals Ethical appeals establish a writer's credibility and trustworthiness with an audience. When a writer links a claim to a widely accepted value, for example, the writer not only gains moral support for that claim but also establishes a connection with readers.

Evaluate To evaluate is to examine something carefully and judge its value or worth. Evaluating is an important skill for gaining insight into what you read. A reader can evaluate the actions of a particular character, for example, or can form an opinion about the value of an entire work.

Evidence Evidence is the specific pieces of information that support a claim. Evidence can take the form of facts, quotations, examples, statistics, or personal experiences, among others.

Exaggeration *See* Hyperbole.

Experimental Poetry Poetry described as experimental is often full of surprises—unusual word order, invented forms, descriptions of ordinary objects, and other distinctive elements not found in traditional verse forms. William Carlos Williams belonged to a group of experimental poets known as the Imagists. Their poems contain sharp, clear images of striking beauty, similar to the ones found in haiku.

Exposition Exposition is the part of a literary work that provides the background information necessary to understand characters and their actions. Typically found at the beginning of a work, the exposition introduces the characters, describes the setting, and summarizes significant events that took place before the action begins.

See also Plot; Rising Action.

Expository Essay *See* Essay.

Extended Metaphor Like any metaphor, an extended metaphor is a comparison between two essentially unlike things that nevertheless have something in common. It does not contain the word *like* or *as*. An extended metaphor compares two things at some length and in various ways. Sometimes the comparison is carried throughout a paragraph, a stanza, or an entire selection.

Like an extended metaphor, a **conceit** compares two apparently dissimilar things in several ways. The term usually implies a more elaborate, formal, and ingeniously clever comparison than the extended metaphor.

External Conflict *See* Conflict.

Eyewitness Account An eyewitness account is a firsthand report of an event written by someone who directly observed it or participated in it. As such, an eyewitness account is a primary source. Narrated from the first-person point of view, eyewitness accounts almost always include the following:

- objective facts about an event
- a chronological (time-order) pattern of organization
- vivid sensory details
- quotations from people who were present
- description of the writer's feelings and interpretations.

See also Primary Source.

Fable A fable is a brief tale that illustrates a clear, often directly stated, moral, or lesson. The characters in a fable are usually animals, but sometimes they are humans. The best-known fables—for example, "The Fox and the Crow" and "The Tortoise and the Hare" —are those of Aesop, a Greek slave who lived about 600 BC. Traditionally, fables are handed down from generation to generation as oral literature.

See also Oral Literature.

Fact versus Opinion A **fact** is a statement that can be proved or verified. An **opinion,** on the other hand, is a statement that cannot be proved because it expresses a person's beliefs, feelings, or thoughts.

See also Inference; Generalization.

Falling Action In a plot structure, the falling action, or resolution, occurs after the climax to reveal the final outcome of events and to tie up any loose ends.

See also Climax; Exposition; Plot; Rising Action.

Farce A farce is a type of exaggerated comedy that features an absurd plot, ridiculous situations, and humorous dialogue. The main purpose of a farce is to keep an audience laughing. The characters are usually **stereotypes,** or simplified examples of different traits or qualities. Comic devices typically used in farces include mistaken identity, deception, wordplay—such as puns and double meanings—and exaggeration.

See also Comedy; Stereotype.

Faulty Reasoning *See* Logical Fallacy.

Feature Article A feature article is a main article in a newspaper or a cover story in a magazine. A feature article is focused more on entertaining than informing. Features are lighter or more general than hard news and tend to be about human interest or lifestyles.

Fiction Fiction refers to works of prose that contain imaginary elements. Although fiction, like nonfiction, may be based on actual events and real people, it differs from nonfiction in that it is shaped primarily by the writer's imagination. The two major types of fiction are novels and short stories. The four basic elements of a work of fiction are character, setting, plot, and theme.

See also Novel; Short Story.

Figurative Language Figurative language is language that communicates ideas beyond the literal meaning of words. Figurative language can make descriptions and unfamiliar or difficult ideas easier to understand. The most common types of figurative language, called **figures of speech**, are **simile, metaphor, personification,** and **hyperbole**.

See also Hyperbole; Metaphor; Personification; Simile.

Figures of Speech *See* Figurative Language.

First-Person Point of View *See* Point of View.

Flashback A flashback is a scene that interrupts the action of a narrative to describe events that took place at an earlier time. It provides background helpful in understanding a character's present situation.

Foil A foil is a character whose traits contrast with those of another character. A writer might use a minor character as a foil to emphasize the positive traits of the main character.

See also Character.

Folk Tale A folk tale is a short, simple story that is handed down, usually by word of mouth, from generation to generation. Folk tales include legends, fairy tales, myths, and fables. Folk tales often teach family obligations or societal values.

See also Legend; Myth; Fable.

Foot *See* Meter.

Foreshadowing Foreshadowing is a writer's use of hints or clues to indicate events that will occur in a story. Foreshadowing creates suspense and at the same time prepares the reader for what is to come.

Form At its simplest, form refers to the physical arrangement of words in a poem—the length and placement of the lines and the grouping of lines into stanzas. The term can also be used to refer to other types of patterning in poetry—anything from rhythm and other sound patterns to the design of a traditional poetic type, such as a sonnet or dramatic monologue.

See also Genre; Stanza.

Frame Story A frame story exists when a story is told within a narrative setting, or "frame"; it creates a story within a story. This storytelling method has been used for over one thousand years and was employed in famous works such as *One Thousand and One Arabian Nights* and Geoffrey Chaucer's *The Canterbury Tales.*

Free Verse Free verse is poetry that does not have regular patterns of rhyme and meter. The lines in free verse often flow more naturally than do rhymed, metrical lines and thus achieve a rhythm more like that of everyday human speech. Walt Whitman is generally credited with bringing free verse to American poetry.

See also Meter; Rhyme.

Functional Documents *See* Consumer Documents; Workplace Documents.

Generalization A generalization is a broad statement about a class or category of people, ideas, or things, based on a study of only some of its members.

See also Overgeneralization.

General Principle In an argument, a general principle is an assumption that links the support to the claim. If one does not accept the general principle as a truth, then the support is inadequate because it is beside the point.

Genre Genre refers to the distinct types into which literary works can be grouped. The four main literary genres are fiction, poetry, nonfiction, and drama.

Gothic Literature Gothic literature is characterized by grotesque characters, bizarre situations, and violent events. Originating in Europe, gothic literature was a popular form of writing in the United States during the 19th century, especially in the hands of such notables as Edgar Allan Poe and Nathaniel Hawthorne. Interest in the gothic revived in the 20th century among southern writers such as William Faulkner and Flannery O'Connor.

Government Publications Government publications are documents produced by government organizations. Pamphlets, brochures, and reports are just some of the many forms these publications may take. Government publications can be good resources for a wide variety of topics.

Graphic Aid A graphic aid is a visual tool that is printed, handwritten, or drawn. Charts, diagrams, graphs, photographs, and maps can all be graphic aids.

Graphic Organizer A graphic organizer is a visual illustration of a verbal statement that helps a reader understand a text. Charts, tables, webs, and diagrams can all be graphic organizers. Graphic organizers and graphic aids can look the same. However, graphic organizers and graphic aids do differ in how they are used. Graphic aids are the visual representations that people encounter when they read informational texts. Graphic organizers are visuals that people construct to help them understand texts or organize information.

Haiku Haiku is a form of Japanese poetry in which 17 syllables are arranged in three lines of 5, 7, and 5 syllables. The rules of haiku are strict. In addition to the syllabic count, the poet must create a clear picture that will evoke a strong emotional response in the reader. Nature is a particularly important source of inspiration for Japanese haiku poets, and details from nature are often the subjects of their poems.

Hero *See* Cultural Hero; Tragic Hero.

Historical Context The historical context of a literary work refers to the social conditions that inspired or influenced its creation. To understand and appreciate some works, the reader must relate them to particular events in history. For example, to understand fully Lincoln's "Gettysburg Address," the reader must imaginatively re-create the scene—Lincoln addressing a war-weary crowd on the very site where a horrific battle had recently been fought.

Historical Documents Historical documents are writings that have played a significant role in human events or are themselves records of such events. The Declaration of Independence, for example, is a historical document.

Historical Narratives Historical narratives are accounts of real-life historical experiences, given either by a person who experienced those events or by someone who has studied or observed them.

See also Primary Sources; Secondary Sources.

Horror Fiction Horror fiction contains strange, mysterious, violent, and often supernatural events that create suspense and terror in the reader. Edgar Allan Poe is an author famous for his horror fiction.

How-To Book A how-to book is a book that is written to explain how to do something— usually an activity, a sport, or a household project.

Humor Humor is a term applied to a literary work whose purpose is to entertain and to evoke laughter. In literature, there are three basic types of humor, all of which may involve exaggeration or irony. **Humor of situation,** which is derived from the plot of a work, usually involves exaggerated events or situational irony. **Humor of character** is often based on exaggerated personalities or on characters who fail to recognize their own flaws, a form of dramatic irony. **Humor of language** may include sarcasm, exaggeration, puns, or verbal irony, which occurs when what is said is not what is meant.

See also Comedy; Farce; Irony.

Hyperbole Hyperbole is a figure of speech in which the truth is exaggerated for emphasis or for humorous effect. The expression "I'm so hungry I could eat a horse" is hyperbole.

See also Understatement.

Iamb *See* Meter.

Iambic Pentameter Iambic pentameter is a metrical pattern of five feet, or units, each of which is made up of two syllables, the first unstressed and the second stressed. Iambic pentameter is the most common meter used in English poetry; it is the meter used in blank verse and in the sonnet.

See also Blank Verse; Meter; Sonnet.

Idiom An idiom is a common figure of speech whose meaning is different from the literal meaning of its words. For example, the phrase "raining cats and dogs" does not literally mean that cats and dogs are falling from the sky; the expression means "raining heavily."

Imagery The descriptive words and phrases that a writer uses to re-create sensory experiences are called imagery. By appealing to the five senses, imagery helps a reader imagine exactly what the characters and experiences being described are like.

The term *synesthesia* refers to imagery that appeals to one sense when another is being stimulated.

See also Description; Kinesthetic Imagery.

Imagists *See* Experimental Poetry; Style.

Implied Main Idea *See* Main Idea.

Index The index of a book is an alphabetized list of important topics and details covered in the book and the page numbers on which they can be found. An index can be used to quickly find specific information about a topic.

Inductive Reasoning Inductive reasoning is the process of logical reasoning from observations, examples, and facts to a general conclusion or principle.

Inference An inference is a logical assumption that is based on observed facts and one's own knowledge and experience.

Informational Text Informational text is a category of writing that includes exposition, argument, and functional documents. These texts normally provide factual, historical, or technical information. However, the term also covers texts that make logical or emotional arguments in defense of a position. Examples include biographies, journalism, essays, narrative histories, instruction manuals, and speeches.

Interior Monologue *See* Monologue; Stream of Consciousness.

Internal Conflict *See* Conflict.

Interview An interview is a conversation conducted by a writer or reporter in which facts or statements are elicited from another person, recorded, and then broadcast or published.

Inverted Syntax Inverted syntax is a reversal in the expected order of words.

Irony Irony refers to a contrast between appearance and reality. **Situational irony** is a contrast between what is expected to happen and what actually does happen. **Dramatic irony** occurs when readers know more about a situation or a character in a story than the characters do. **Verbal irony** occurs when someone states one thing and means another.

Journal A journal is a periodical publication issued by a legal, medical, or other professional organization. Alternatively, the term may be used to refer to a diary or daily record.

See also Diary.

Kinesthetic Imagery Kinesthetic imagery re-creates the tension felt through muscles, tendons, or joints in the body.

See also Imagery.

Legend A legend is a story passed down orally from generation to generation and popularly believed to have a historical basis. While some legends may be based on real people or situations, most of the events are either greatly exaggerated or fictitious. Like myths, legends may incorporate supernatural elements and magical deeds. But legends differ from myths in that they claim to be stories about real human beings and are often set in a particular time and place.

Limited Point of View *See* Point of View.

Line The line is the core unit of a poem. In poetry, line length is an essential element of the poem's meaning and rhythm. There are a variety of terms to describe the way a line of poetry ends or is connected to the next line. Line breaks, where a line of poetry ends, may coincide with grammatical units. However, a line break may also occur in the middle of a grammatical or syntactical unit, creating pauses or emphasis. Poets use a variety of line breaks to play with meaning, thus creating a wide range of effects.

Literary Criticism Literary criticism refers to writing that focuses on a literary work or a genre, describing some aspect of it, such as its origin, its characteristics, or its effects.

Literary Letter A literary letter is a letter that has been published and read by a wider audience because it was written by a well-known public figure or provides information about the period in which it was written.

Literary Nonfiction Literary nonfiction is informational text that is recognized as being of artistic value or that is about literature. Autobiographies, biographies, essays, and eloquent speeches typically fall into this category.

Loaded Language Loaded language consists of words with strongly positive or negative connotations intended to influence a reader's or listener's attitude.

Local Color Realism Local color realism, especially popular in the late 18th century, is a style of writing that truthfully imitates ordinary life and brings a particular region alive by portraying the dialects, dress, mannerisms, customs, character types, and landscapes of that region. Mark Twain frequently uses local color realism in his writing for humorous effect.

See also **Dialect.**

Logical Appeal A logical appeal relies on logic and facts, appealing to people's reasoning or intellect rather than to their values or emotions. Flawed logical appeals—that is, errors in reasoning—are considered logical fallacies.

See also **Logical Fallacy.**

Logical Argument A logical argument is an argument in which the logical relationship between the support and the claim is sound.

Logical Fallacy A fallacy is an error in reasoning. Typically, a fallacy is based on an incorrect inference or a misuse of evidence. Some common logical fallacies are **circular logic, either/or fallacy, oversimplification, overgeneralization,** and **stereotyping.**

See also **Either/Or Fallacy; Logical Appeal; Overgeneralization.**

Lyric Poem A lyric poem is a short poem in which a single speaker expresses thoughts and feelings. In a love lyric, a speaker expresses romantic love. In other lyrics, a speaker may meditate on nature or seek to resolve an emotional crisis.

Magical Realism Magical realism is a style of writing that often includes exaggeration, unusual humor, magical and bizarre events, dreams that come true, and superstitions that prove warranted. Magical realism differs from pure fantasy in combining fantastic elements with realistic elements such as recognizable characters, believable dialogue, a true-to-life setting, a matter-of-fact tone, and a plot that sometimes contains historic events. This style characterizes some of the fiction of such influential South American writers as the late Jorge Luis Borges of Argentina and Gabriel García Márquez of Colombia.

Main Character *See* **Character.**

Main Idea A main idea is the central or most important idea about a topic that a writer or speaker conveys. It can be the central idea of an entire work or of just a paragraph. Often, the main idea of a paragraph is expressed in a topic sentence. However, a main idea may just be implied, or suggested, by details. A main idea and supporting details can serve as a basic pattern of organization in a piece of writing, with the central idea about a topic being supported by details.

Make Inferences *See* **Inference.**

Memoir A memoir is a form of autobiographical writing in which a person recalls significant events and people in his or her life. Most memoirs share the following characteristics: (1) they usually are structured as narratives told by the writers themselves, using the first-person point of view; (2) although some names may be changed to protect privacy, memoirs are true accounts of actual events; (3) although basically personal, memoirs may deal with newsworthy events having a significance beyond the confines of the writer's life; (4) unlike strictly historical accounts, memoirs often include the writers' feelings and opinions about historical events, giving the reader insight into the impact of history on people's lives.

Metaphor A metaphor is a figure of speech that compares two things that have something in common. Unlike similes, metaphors do not use the words *like* or *as* but make comparisons directly.

See also **Extended Metaphor; Figurative Language; Simile.**

Meter Meter is the repetition of a regular rhythmic unit in a line of poetry. Each unit, known as a **foot,** has one stressed syllable (indicated by a ´) and either one or two unstressed syllables (indicated by a ˘). The four basic types of metrical feet are the **iamb,** an unstressed syllable followed by a stressed syllable; the **trochee,** a stressed syllable followed by an unstressed syllable; the **anapest,** two unstressed syllables followed by a stressed syllable; and the **dactyl,** a stressed syllable followed by two unstressed syllables.

Two words are typically used to describe the meter of a line. The first word identifies the type of metrical foot—iambic, trochaic, anapestic, or dactylic—and the second word indicates the number of feet in a line: **monometer** (one foot), **dimeter** (two feet), **trimeter** (three feet), **tetrameter** (four feet), **pentameter** (five feet), **hexameter** (six feet), and so forth.

See also **Rhythm; Scansion.**

Minor Character *See* **Character.**

Mise en Scène *Mise en scène* is a term from the French that refers to the various physical aspects of a dramatic presentation, such as lighting, costumes, scenery, makeup, and props.

Modernism Modernism was a literary movement that roughly spanned the time period between the two world wars, 1914–1945. Modernist works are characterized by a high degree of experimentation and spare, elliptical prose. Modernist characters are most often alienated people searching unsuccessfully for meaning and love in their lives.

Monitor Monitoring is the strategy of checking your comprehension as you are reading and modifying the strategies you are using to suit your needs. Monitoring may include some or all of the following strategies: **questioning, clarifying, visualizing, predicting, connecting,** and **rereading.**

Monologue In a drama, the speech of a character who is alone on stage, voicing his or her thoughts, is known as a monologue. In a short story or a poem, the direct presentation of a character's unspoken thoughts is called an **interior monologue.** An interior monologue may jump back and forth between past and present, displaying thoughts, memories, and impressions just as they might occur in a person's mind.

See also **Stream of Consciousness.**

Mood Mood is the feeling or atmosphere that a writer creates for the reader. The writer's use of connotation, imagery, figurative language, sound and rhythm, and descriptive details all contribute to the mood.

See also **Connotation; Description; Diction; Figurative Language; Imagery; Style.**

Moral *See* **Fable.**

Motivation Motivation is the stated or implied reason behind a character's behavior. The grounds for a character's actions may not be obvious, but they should be comprehensible and consistent, in keeping with the character as developed by the writer.

See also **Character.**

Myth A myth is a traditional story, passed down through generations, that explains why the world is the way it is. Myths are essentially religious because they present supernatural events and beings and articulate the values and beliefs of a cultural group. A **creation myth** is a particular kind of myth that explains how the universe, the earth, and life on earth began.

Narrative A narrative is any type of writing that is primarily concerned with relating an event or a series of events. A narrative can be imaginary, as is a short story or novel, or factual, as is a newspaper account or a work of history. The word *narration* can be used interchangeably with *narrative,* which comes from the Latin word meaning "tell."

See also **Fiction; Nonfiction; Novel; Plot; Short Story.**

Narrative Poem A narrative poem is a poem that tells a story using elements of character, setting, and plot to develop a theme.

See also **Ballad.**

Narrator The narrator of a story is the character or voice that relates the story's events to the reader.

Naturalism An offshoot of realism, naturalism was a literary movement that originated in France in the late 1800s. Like the realists, the naturalists sought to render common people and ordinary life accurately. However, the naturalists emphasized how instinct and environment affect human behavior. Strongly influenced by Charles Darwin's ideas, the naturalists believed that the fate of humans is determined by forces beyond individual control.

News Article A news article is a piece of writing that reports on a recent event. In newspapers, news articles are usually written in a concise manner to report the latest news, presenting the most important facts first and then more detailed information. In magazines, news articles are usually more elaborate than those in newspapers because they are written to provide both information and analysis. Also, news articles in magazines do not necessarily present the most important facts first.

Nonfiction Nonfiction, or informational text, is writing about real people, places, and events. Unlike fiction, nonfiction is largely concerned with factual information, although the writer shapes the information according to his or her purpose and viewpoint. Biography, autobiography, and newspaper articles are examples of nonfiction.

See also **Autobiography; Biography; Essay.**

Novel A novel is an extended work of fiction. Like the short story, a novel is essentially the product of a writer's imagination. The most

obvious difference between a novel and a short story is length. Because the novel is considerably longer, a novelist can develop a wider range of characters and a more complex plot.

Novella A novella is a work of fiction that is longer than a short story but shorter than a novel. A novella differs from a novel in that it concentrates on a limited cast of characters, a relatively short time span, and a single chain of events. The novella is an attempt to combine the compression of the short story with the development of a novel.

Octave *See* **Sonnet.**

Ode An ode is a complex lyric poem that develops a serious and dignified theme. Odes appeal to both the imagination and the intellect, and many commemorate events or praise people or elements of nature.

Off Rhyme *See* **Slant Rhyme.**

Omniscient Point of View *See* **Point of View.**

Onomatopoeia The word *onomatopoeia* literally means "name-making." It is the process of creating or using words that imitate sounds. The *buzz* of the bee, the *honk* of the car horn, the *peep* of the chick are all onomatopoetic, or echoic, words.

Onomatopoeia as a literary technique goes beyond the use of simple echoic words. Writers, particularly poets, choose words whose sounds suggest their denotative and connotative meanings: for example, *whisper, kick, gargle, gnash,* and *clatter.*

Op-Ed Piece An op-ed piece is an opinion piece that usually appears opposite ("op") the editorial page of a newspaper. Unlike editorials, op-ed pieces are written and submitted by named writers.

Open Letter An open letter is addressed to a specific person but published for a wider readership.

Oral Literature Oral literature is literature that is passed from one generation to another by performance or word of mouth. Folk tales, fables, myths, chants, and legends are part of the oral tradition of cultures throughout the world.

See also **Fable; Folk Tale; Legend; Myth.**

Organization *See* **Pattern of Organization.**

Overgeneralization An overgeneralization is a generalization that is too broad. You can often recognize overgeneralizations by the appearance of words and phrases such as *all, everyone, every time, any, anything, no one,* and *none.* Consider, for example, this statement: "None of the sanitation workers in our city really care about keeping the environment clean." In all probability, there are many exceptions. The writer can't possibly know the feelings of every sanitation worker in the city.

Overstatement *See* Hyperbole.

Overview An overview is a short summary of a story, a speech, or an essay. It orients the reader by providing a preview of the text to come.

Oxymoron An oxymoron is a special kind of concise paradox that brings together two contradictory terms, such as "venomous love" or "sweet bitterness."

Parable A parable is a brief story that is meant to teach a lesson or illustrate a moral truth. A parable is more than a simple story, however. Each detail of the parable corresponds to some aspect of the problem or moral dilemma to which it is directed. The story of the prodigal son in the Bible is a classic parable. In *Walden,* Thoreau's parable of the strong and beautiful bug that emerges from an old table is meant to show that, similarly, new life can awaken in human beings despite the deadness of society.

Paradox A paradox is a statement that seems to contradict itself but may nevertheless suggest an important truth.

A special kind of paradox is the oxymoron, which brings together two contradictory terms, as in the phrases "wise fool" and "feather of lead."

Parallelism Parallelism is the use of similar grammatical constructions to express ideas that are related or equal in importance.

Parallel Plot A parallel plot is a particular type of plot in which two stories of equal importance are told simultaneously. The story moves back and forth between the two plots.

Paraphrase Paraphrasing is the restating of information in one's own words.

See also **Summarize.**

Parody Parody is writing that imitates either the style or the subject matter of a literary work for the purpose of criticism, humorous effect, or flattering tribute.

Pattern of Organization A pattern of organization is a particular arrangement of ideas and information. Such a pattern may be used to organize an entire composition or a single paragraph within a longer work. The following are the most common organizational patterns: **cause-and-effect, chronological order, compare-and-contrast, classification, deductive, inductive, order of importance, problem-solution, sequential,** and **spatial.**

See also **Cause and Effect; Chronological Order; Classification; Compare and Contrast; Problem-Solution Order; Sequential Order.**

Periodical A periodical is a publication that is issued at regular intervals of more than one day. For example, a periodical may be a weekly, monthly, or quarterly journal or magazine. Newspapers and other daily publications generally are not classified as periodicals.

Persona *See* **Speaker.**

Personal Essay *See* **Essay.**

Personification Personification is a figure of speech in which an object, animal, or idea is given human characteristics.

> **Example:** In Emily Dickinson's poem "Because I could not stop for Death," death is personified as a gentleman of kindness and civility.

Persuasion Persuasion is the art of swaying others' feelings, beliefs, or actions. Persuasion normally appeals to both the intellect and the emotions of readers. **Persuasive techniques** are the methods used to influence others to adopt certain opinions or beliefs or to act in certain ways. Types of persuasive techniques include emotional appeals, ethical appeals, logical appeals, and loaded language. When used properly, persuasive techniques can add depth to writing that's meant to persuade. Persuasive techniques can, however, be misused to cloud factual information, disguise poor reasoning, or unfairly exploit people's emotions in order to shape their opinions.

See also **Appeals by Association; Appeal to Authority; Emotional Appeals; Ethical Appeals; Loaded Language; Logical Appeal.**

Persuasive Writing Persuasive writing is intended to convince a reader to adopt a particular opinion or to perform a certain action. Effective persuasion usually appeals to both the reason and the emotions of an audience.

Petrarchan Sonnet *See* **Sonnet.**

Plot The plot is the sequence of actions and events in a literary work. Generally, plots are built around a **conflict**—a problem or struggle between two or more opposing forces. Plots usually progress through stages: exposition, rising action, climax, and falling action.

The **exposition** provides important background information and introduces the setting, characters, and conflict. During the **rising action,** the conflict becomes more intense and suspense builds as the main characters struggle to resolve their problem. The **climax** is the turning point in the plot when the outcome of the conflict becomes clear, usually resulting in a change in the characters or a solution to the conflict. After the climax, the **falling action** occurs and shows the effects of the climax. As the falling action begins, the suspense is over but the results of the decision or action that caused the climax are not yet fully worked out. The **resolution,** which often blends with the falling action, reveals the final outcome of events and ties up loose ends.

See also **Climax; Conflict; Exposition; Falling Action; Rising Action.**

Poetry Poetry is language arranged in lines. Like other forms of literature, poetry attempts to re-create emotions and experiences. Poetry, however, is usually more condensed and suggestive than prose.

Poems often are divided into stanzas, or paragraph-like groups of lines. The stanzas in a poem may contain the same number of lines or may vary in length. Some poems have definite patterns of meter and rhyme. Others rely more on the sounds of words and less on fixed rhythms and rhyme schemes. The use of figurative language is also common in poetry.

The form and content of a poem combine to convey meaning. The way that a poem is arranged on the page, the impact of the images, the sounds of the words and phrases, and all the other details that make up a poem work together to help the reader grasp its central idea.

See also **Experimental Poetry; Form; Free Verse; Meter; Rhyme; Rhythm; Stanza.**

Point of View Point of view refers to the narrative perspective from which events in a story or novel are told. In the **first-person point of view,** the narrator is a character in the work who tells everything in his or her own words and uses the pronouns *I, me,* and *my.* In the **third-person point of view,** events are related by a voice outside the action, not by one of the characters. A third-person narrator uses pronouns such as *he, she,* and *they.* In the **third-person omniscient point of view,** the narrator is an all-knowing, objective observer who stands outside the action and reports what different characters are thinking. In the **third-person limited point of view,** the narrator stands outside the action and focuses on one character's thoughts, observations, and feelings.

In the **second-person point of view,** rarely used, the narrator addresses the reader intimately as you.

Predict Predicting is a reading strategy that involves using text clues to make a reasonable guess about what will happen next in a story.

Primary Sources Materials written or created by people who were present at events are called primary sources. Letters, diaries, speeches, autobiographies, and photographs are examples of primary sources, as are certain narrative accounts written by actual participants or observers.

See also **Secondary Sources; Sources.**

Prior Knowledge Prior knowledge is the knowledge a reader already possesses about a topic. This information might come from personal experiences, expert accounts, books, films, or other sources.

Problem-Solution Order Problem-solution order is a pattern of organization in which a problem is stated and analyzed and then one or more solutions are proposed and examined. Writers use words and phrases such as *propose, conclude, reason for, problem, answer,* and *solution* to connect ideas and details when writing about problems and solutions.

Procedural Documents *See* Consumer Documents.

Prologue A prologue is an introductory scene in a drama.

Prop Prop, an abbreviation of *property,* refers to a physical object that is used in a stage production. In Arthur Miller's *The Crucible,* an important prop is the small rag doll that Mary Warren brings from the court and gives to Elizabeth Proctor.

Propaganda Propaganda is a form of communication that may use distorted, false, or misleading information. It usually refers to manipulative political discourse.

Prose Generally, *prose* refers to all forms of written or spoken expression that are not in verse. The term, therefore, may be used to describe very different forms of writing—short stories as well as essays, for example.

Protagonist The protagonist is the main character in a work of literature, who is involved in the central conflict of the story. Usually, the protagonist changes after the central conflict reaches a climax. He or she may be a hero and is usually the one with whom the audience tends to identify.

See also Antagonist; Character; Tragic Hero.

Public Documents Public documents are documents that were written for the public to provide information that is of public interest or concern. They include government documents, speeches, signs, and rules and regulations.

See also Government Publications.

Purpose *See* Author's Purpose.

Quatrain A quatrain is a four-line stanza.

See also Poetry; Stanza.

Realism As a general term, *realism* refers to any effort to offer an accurate and detailed portrayal of actual life. Thus, critics talk about Shakespeare's realistic portrayals of his characters and praise the medieval poet Chaucer for his realistic descriptions of people from different social classes.

More specifically, realism refers to a literary method developed in the 19th century. The realists based their writing on careful observations of contemporary life, often focusing on the middle or lower classes. They attempted to present life objectively and honestly, without the sentimentality or idealism that had colored earlier literature. Typically, realists developed their settings in great detail in an effort to recreate a specific time and place for the reader. Kate Chopin and Mark Twain are considered realists.

See also Local-Color Realism; Naturalism.

Recurring Theme *See* Theme.

Reference Works General reference works are sources that contain facts and background information on a wide range of subjects. More specific reference works contain in-depth information on a single subject. Most reference works are good sources of reliable information because they have been reviewed by experts. The following are some common reference works: **encyclopedias, dictionaries, thesauri, almanacs, atlases, chronologies, biographical dictionaries,** and **directories.**

Reflective Essay *See* Essay.

Refrain In poetry, a refrain is part of a stanza, consisting of one or more lines that are repeated regularly, sometimes with changes, often at the ends of succeeding stanzas. Refrains are often found in ballads.

Regionalism Regionalism is a literary movement that arose from an effort to accurately represent the speech, manners, habits, history, folklore, and beliefs of people in specific geographic areas.

Repetition Repetition is a technique in which a sound, word, phrase, or line is repeated for emphasis or unity. Repetition often helps to reinforce meaning and create an appealing rhythm. The term includes specific devices associated with both prose and poetry, such as **alliteration** and **parallelism.**

See also **Alliteration; Parallelism; Sound Devices.**

Resolution *See* **Falling Action.**

Review *See* **Critical Review.**

Rhetorical Devices *See* **Analogy; Repetition; Rhetorical Questions.**

Rhetorical Questions Rhetorical questions are those that do not require a reply. Writers use them to suggest that their arguments make the answer obvious or self-evident.

Rhyme Rhyme is the occurrence of similar or identical sounds at the end of two or more words, such as *suite, heat,* and *complete.* Rhyme that occurs within a single line of poetry is called **internal rhyme.**

When rhyme comes at the end of a line of poetry, it is called **end rhyme.** The pattern of end rhyme in a poem is called the **rhyme scheme** and is charted by assigning a letter, beginning with the letter *a,* to each line. Lines that rhyme are given the same letter.

See also **Slant Rhyme.**

Rhyme Scheme *See* **Rhyme.**

Rhythm Rhythm refers to the pattern or flow of sound created by the arrangement of stressed and unstressed syllables, particularly in poetry. Some poems follow a regular pattern, or **meter,** of accented and unaccented syllables. Poets use rhythm to bring out the musical quality of language, to emphasize ideas, to create mood, and to reinforce subject matter.

See also **Meter.**

Rising Action Rising action is the stage of a plot in which the conflict develops and story events build toward a climax. During this stage, complications arise that make the conflict more intense. Tension grows as the characters struggle to resolve the conflict.

See also **Plot.**

Romanticism Romanticism was a movement in the arts that flourished in Europe and America throughout much of the 19th century. Romantic writers glorified nature and celebrated individuality. Their treatment of subjects was emotional rather than rational, intuitive rather than analytic.

Sarcasm Sarcasm, a type of verbal irony, refers to a critical remark expressed in a statement in which literal meaning is the opposite of actual meaning. Sarcasm is mocking, and its intention is to hurt.

See also **Irony.**

Satire Satire is a literary technique in which foolish ideas or customs are ridiculed for the purpose of improving society. Satire may be gently witty, mildly abrasive, or bitterly critical. Short stories, poems, novels, essays, and plays all may be vehicles for satire.

Scanning Scanning is the process of searching through writing for a particular fact or piece of information. When you scan, your eyes sweep across a page, looking for key words that may lead you to the information you want.

Scansion The process of determining meter is known as scansion. When you scan a line of poetry, you mark its stressed (´) and unstressed (˘) syllables (˘) in order to identify the rhythm.

See also **Meter.**

Scene In drama, a scene is a subdivision of an act. Each scene usually establishes a different time or place.

See also **Act; Drama.**

Scenery Scenery is a painted backdrop or other structures used to create the setting for a play.

Science Fiction Science fiction is prose writing that presents the possibilities of the past or the future, using known scientific data and theories as well as the creative imagination of the writer. Most science fiction comments on present-day society through the writer's fictional conception of a past or future society. Ray Bradbury and Kurt Vonnegut Jr. are two popular writers of science fiction.

Screenplay A screenplay is a script written for film.

Script The text of a play, film, or broadcast is called a script.

Secondary Sources Accounts written by people who were not directly involved in or witnesses to an event are called secondary sources. A history textbook is an example of a secondary source.

See also **Primary Sources; Sources.**

Sensory Details Sensory details are words and phrases that appeal to the reader's senses of sight, hearing, touch, taste, and smell. For example, the sensory detail "a fine film of rain" appeals to the senses of sight and touch. Sensory details stimulate the reader to create images in his or her mind.

See also **Imagery.**

Sequential Order A pattern of organization that shows the order in which events or actions occur is called sequential order. Writers typically use this pattern of organization to explain steps or stages in a process.

Sermon A sermon is a form of religious persuasion in which a speaker exhorts the audience to behave in a more spiritual and moral fashion.

Sestet *See* **Sonnet.**

Setting The setting of a literary work refers to the time and place in which the action occurs. A story can be set in an imaginary place, such as an enchanted castle, or a real place, such as New York City or Tombstone, Arizona. The time can be the past, the present, or the future. In addition to time and place, setting can include the larger historical and cultural contexts that form the background for a narrative. Setting is one of the main elements in fiction and often plays an important role in what happens and why.

Setting a Purpose The process of establishing specific reasons for reading a text is called setting a purpose.

Short Story A short story is a work of fiction that centers on a single idea and can be read in one sitting. Generally, a short story has one main conflict that involves the characters, keeps the story moving, and stimulates readers' interest.

See also **Fiction.**

Sidebar A sidebar is additional information set in a box alongside or within a news or feature article. Popular magazines often make use of sidebar information.

Signal Words Signal words are words and phrases that indicate what is to come in a text. Readers can use signal words to discover a text's pattern of organization and to analyze the relationships among the ideas in the text.

Simile A simile is a figure of speech that compares two things that have something in common, using a word such as *like* or *as*.

See also **Figurative Language; Metaphor.**

Situational Irony *See* **Irony.**

Slant Rhyme Rhyme that is not exact but only approximate is known as slant rhyme, or **off rhyme.**

See also **Rhyme.**

Slave Narrative A slave narrative is an autobiographical account written by someone who endured the miseries of slavery. These writers often use sensory details to re-create their experiences.

See also **Autobiography.**

Soliloquy *See* **Monologue.**

Sonnet A sonnet is a 14-line lyric poem, commonly written in iambic pentameter. The **Petrarchan sonnet** consists of two parts. The first eight lines, called the octave, usually have the rhyme scheme *abbaabba*. In the last six lines, called the sestet, the rhyme scheme may be *cdecde, cdcdcd,* or another variation. The **octave** generally presents a problem or raises a question, and the *sestet* resolves or comments on the problem. A **Shakespearean sonnet** is divided into three **quatrains** (groups of four lines) and a **couplet** (two rhyming lines). Its rhyme scheme is *abab cdcd efef gg*. The couplet usually expresses a response to the important issue developed in the three quatrains.

See also **Meter; Quatrain; Rhyme.**

Sound Devices *See* **Alliteration; Assonance; Consonance; Meter; Onomatopoeia; Repetition; Rhyme; Rhyme Scheme; Rhythm.**

Sources A source is anything that supplies information. **Primary sources** are materials written or created by people who were present at events, either as participants or as observers. Letters, diaries, autobiographies, speeches, and photographs are primary sources. **Secondary sources** are records of events that were created sometime after the events occurred; the writers were not directly involved or were not present when the events took place. Encyclopedias, textbooks, biographies, most newspaper and magazine articles, and books and articles that interpret or review research are secondary sources.

Spatial Order Spatial order is a pattern of organization that highlights the physical positions or relationships of details or objects. This pattern of organization is typically found in descriptive writing. Writers use words and phrases such as *on the left, to the right, here, over there, above, below, beyond, nearby,* and *in the distance* to indicate the arrangement of details.

Speaker The speaker of a poem, like the narrator of a story, is the voice that talks to the reader. In some poems, the speaker can be identified with the poet. In other poems, the poet invents a fictional character, or a persona, to play the role of the speaker. *Persona* is a Latin word meaning "actor's mask."

Speech A speech is a talk or public address. The purpose of a speech may be to entertain, to explain, to persuade, to inspire, or any combination of these aims.

Stage Directions Stage directions are the playwright's instructions for the director, performers, and stage crew. Usually set in italics, they are located at the beginning of and throughout a script. Stage directions usually tell the time and place of the action and explain how characters move and speak. They also describe scenery, props, lighting, costumes, music, or sound effects.

See also **Drama.**

Stanza A stanza is a group of lines that form a unit in a poem. A stanza is usually characterized by a common pattern of meter, rhyme, and number of lines. During the 20th century, poets experimented more freely with stanza form than did earlier poets, sometimes writing poems without any stanza breaks.

Static Character *See* **Character.**

Stereotype A stereotype is an over simplified image of a person, group, or institution. Sweeping generalizations about "all Southerners" or "every used-car dealer" are stereotypes. Simplified or stock characters in literature are often called stereotypes. Such characters do not usually demonstrate the complexities of real people.

Stereotyping Stereotyping is a dangerous type of overgeneralization. Stereotypes are broad statements made about people on the basis of their gender, ethnicity, race, or political, social, professional, or religious group.

Stream of Consciousness Stream of consciousness is a technique that was developed by modernist writers to present the flow of a character's seemingly unconnected thoughts, responses, and sensations. The term was coined by American psychologist William James to characterize the unbroken flow of thought that occurs in the waking mind.

See also **Modernism.**

Structure The structure of a literary work is the way in which it is put together—the arrangement of its parts. In poetry, structure refers to the arrangement of words and lines to produce a desired effect. A common structural unit in poetry is the stanza, of which there are numerous types. In prose, structure is the arrangement of larger units or parts of a selection. Paragraphs, for example, are a basic unit in prose, as are chapters in novels and acts in plays. The structure of a poem, short story, novel, play, or nonfiction selection usually emphasizes certain important aspects of content.

See also **Form; Stanza.**

Style Style is the distinctive way in which a work of literature is written. Style refers not so much to what is said but how it is said. Word choice, sentence length, tone, imagery, and use of dialogue all contribute to a writer's style. A group of writers might exemplify common stylistic characteristics; for example, the Imagists of the early 20th century wrote in a style that employs compression and rich sensory images.

Summarize To summarize is to briefly retell, or encapsulate, the main ideas of a piece of writing in one's own words.

See also Paraphrase.

Support Support is any material that serves to prove a claim. In an argument, support typically consists of reasons and evidence. In persuasive texts and speeches, however, support may include appeals to the needs and values of the audience.

See also General Principle.

Supporting Detail *See* Main Idea.

Surprise Ending A surprise ending is an unexpected plot twist at the end of a story.

> **Example:** "The Story of an Hour" ends with a surprise when Mrs. Mallard drops dead after her husband, presumed to be dead, reappears.

See also Irony.

Suspense Suspense is the excitement or tension that readers feel as they become involved in a story and eagerly await the outcome.

See also Rising Action.

Symbol A symbol is a person, place, or object that has a concrete meaning in itself and also stands for something beyond itself, such as an idea or feeling.

Synesthesia *See* Imagery.

Synthesize To synthesize information is to take information, combined with other pieces of information and prior knowledge, and make logical connections to gain a better understanding of a subject or to create a new product or idea.

Tall Tale A tall tale is a distinctively American type of humorous story characterized by exaggeration. Tall tales and practical jokes have similar kinds of humor. In both, someone gets fooled, to the amusement of the person or persons who know the truth.

See also Humor; Hyperbole.

Text Features Text features are design elements that indicate the organizational structure of a text and help make the key ideas and the supporting information understandable. Text features include headings, boldface type, italic type, bulleted or numbered lists, sidebars, and graphic aids such as charts, tables, timelines, illustrations, and photographs.

Theme A theme is an underlying message that a writer wants the reader to understand. It is a perception about life or human nature that the writer shares with the reader. In most cases, themes are not stated directly but must be inferred.

Recurring themes are themes found in a variety of works. For example, authors from varying backgrounds might convey similar themes having to do with the importance of family values. **Universal themes** are themes that are found throughout the literature of all time periods.

Thesaurus *See* Reference Works.

Thesis Statement In an argument, a thesis statement, or controlling idea, is an expression of the claim that the writer or speaker is trying to support. In an essay, a thesis statement is an expression, in one or two sentences, of the main idea or purpose of the piece of writing.

Third-Person Point of View *See* Point of View.

Title The title of a literary work introduces readers to the piece and usually reveals something about its subject or theme. Often, a poet uses the title to provide information necessary for understanding a poem.

Tone Tone is a writer's attitude toward his or her subject. A writer can communicate tone through diction, choice of details, and direct statements of his or her position. Unlike mood, which refers to the emotional response of the reader to a work, tone reflects the feelings of the writer. To identify the tone of a work of literature, you might find it helpful to read the work aloud, as if giving a dramatic reading before an audience. The emotions that you convey in an oral reading should give you hints as to the tone of the work.

See also Connotation; Diction; Mood; Style.

Topic Sentence The topic sentence of a paragraph states the paragraph's main idea. All other sentences in the paragraph provide supporting details.

Tragedy A tragedy is a dramatic work that presents the downfall of a dignified character who is involved in historically, morally, or socially significant events. The main character, or **tragic hero,** has a **tragic flaw,** a quality that leads to his or her destruction. The events in a tragic plot are set in motion by a decision that is often an error in judgment caused by the tragic flaw. Succeeding events are linked in a cause-and-effect relationship and lead inevitably to a disastrous conclusion, usually death. Arthur Miller's *The Crucible* could be classified as a tragedy.

Tragic Flaw *See* Tragedy.

Tragic Hero The ancient Greek philosopher Aristotle defined a tragic hero as a character whose basic goodness and superiority are marred by a tragic flaw that brings about or contributes to his or her downfall. The flaw may be poor judgment, pride, weakness, or an excess of an admirable quality. The tragic hero recognizes his or her own flaw and its consequences, but only after it is too late to change the course of events.

See also **Character.**

Traits *See* **Character.**

Transcendentalism The philosophy of transcendentalism, an American offshoot of German romanticism, was based on a belief that "transcendent forms" of truth exist beyond reason and experience. Ralph Waldo Emerson, the leader of the movement, asserted that every individual is capable of discovering this higher truth through intuition. Henry David Thoreau is another well-known transcendentalist writer.

See also **Romanticism.**

Transcript A transcript is a written record of words originally spoken aloud.

Trickster Tale A trickster tale is a folk tale about an animal or person who engages in trickery, violence, and magic. Neither all good nor all bad, a trickster may be foolish yet clever, greedy yet helpful, immoral yet moral.

See also **Folk Tale.**

Trochee *See* Meter.

Turning Point *See* Climax.

Understatement Understatement is a technique of creating emphasis by saying less than is actually or literally true. It is the opposite of **hyperbole,** or overstatement. One of the primary devices of **irony,** understatement can be used to develop a humorous effect, to create satire, or to achieve a restrained tone.

See also **Hyperbole; Irony.**

Unity of Effect When all elements of a story—plot, character, setting, imagery, and other literary devices—work together to create a single effect, it is known as unity of effect.

Universal Theme *See* Theme.

Verbal Irony *See* Irony.

Visualize Visualizing is the process of forming a mental picture based on written or spoken information.

Voice The term *voice* refers to a writer's unique use of language that allows a reader to "hear" a human personality in his or her writing. The elements of style that determine a writer's voice include sentence structure, diction, and tone. For example, some writers are noted for their reliance on short, simple sentences, while others make use of long, complicated ones. Certain writers use concrete words, such as *lake* or *cold,* which name things that you can see, hear, feel, taste, or smell. Others prefer abstract terms such as *memory,* which name things that cannot be perceived with the senses. A writer's tone also leaves its imprint on his or her personal voice. The term can be applied to the narrator of a selection, as well as the writer.

See also **Diction; Tone.**

Website A website is a collection of "pages" on the World Wide Web that is usually devoted to one specific subject. Pages are linked together and are accessed by clicking hyperlinks or menus, which send the user from page to page within the site. Websites are created by companies, organizations, educational institutions, branches of the government, the military, and individuals.

Word Choice *See* Diction.

Workplace Documents Workplace documents are materials that are produced or used within a work setting, usually to aid in the functioning of the workplace. They include job applications, office memos, training manuals, job descriptions, and sales reports.

Works Cited A list of works cited lists names of all the works a writer has referred to in his or her text. This list often includes not only books and articles but also nonprint sources.

Works Consulted A list of works consulted names all the works a writer consulted in order to create his or her text. It is not limited just to those works cited in the text.

See also Bibliography.

Using the Glossaries

The following glossaries list the Academic Vocabulary and Critical Vocabulary words found in this book in alphabetical order. Use these glossaries just as you would a dictionary—to determine the meanings, parts of speech, pronunciation, and syllabication of words. (Some technical, foreign, and more obscure words in this book are not listed here but are defined for you in the footnotes that accompany many of the selections.)

Many words in the English language have more than one meaning. These glossaries give the meanings that apply to the words as they are used in this book. Words closely related in form and meaning are listed together in one entry (for instance, **consumption** and **consume**), and the definition is given for the first form.

The following abbreviations are used to identify parts of speech of words:

adj. adjective   *adv.* adverb   *n.* noun   *v.* verb

Each word's pronunciation is given in parentheses. A guide to the pronunciation symbols appears in the Pronunciation Key below. The stress marks in the Pronunciation Key are used to indicate the force given to each syllable in a word. They can also help you determine where words are divided into syllables.

For more information about the words in these glossaries or for information about words not listed here, consult a dictionary.

Pronunciation Key

Symbol	Examples	Symbol	Examples	Symbol	Examples
ă	pat	m	mum	ûr	urge, term, firm, word, heard
ā	pay	n	no, sudden* (sud'n)		
ä	father	ng	thing	v	valve
âr	care	ŏ	pot	w	with
b	bib	ō	toe	y	yes
ch	church	ô	caught, paw	z	zebra, xylem
d	deed, milled	oi	noise	zh	vision, pleasure, garage
ĕ	pet	o͝o	took		
ē	bee	o͞o	boot	ə	about, item, edible, gallop, circus
f	fife, phase, rough	o͝or	lure		
g	gag	ôr	core	ər	butter
h	hat	ou	out		
hw	which	p	pop	**Sounds in Foreign Words**	
ĭ	pit	r	roar	KH	*German* ich, ach; *Scottish* loch
ī	pie, by	s	sauce		
îr	pier	sh	ship, dish	N (bôn)	*French,* bon
j	judge	t	tight, stopped	œ	*French* feu, oeuf; *German* schön
k	kick, cat, pique	th	thin		
l	lid, needle* (nēd'l)	*th*	this	ü	*French* tu; *German* über
		ŭ	cut		

* In English the consonants *l* and *n* often constitute complete syllables by themselves.

Stress Marks

The relevant emphasis with which the syllables of a word or phrase are spoken, called stress, is indicated in three different ways. The strongest, or primary, stress is marked with a bold mark (´). An intermediate, or secondary, level of stress is marked with a similar but lighter mark (´). The weakest stress is unmarked. Words of one syllable show no stress mark.

Glossary of Academic Vocabulary

adapt (ə-dăpt´) v. to make something suitable for a particular situation; to adjust to an environment.

ambiguous (ăm-bĭg´yōō-əs) adj. able to be interpreted in more than one way; uncertain.

analogy (ə-năl´ə-jē) n. a comparison that finds a similarity between things that are dissimilar.

clarify (klăr´ə-fī´) v. to make clearer or more understandable.

coherent (kō-hîr´ənt) adj. holding together in an orderly, logical, or consistent way.

confirm (kən-fûrm´) v. to establish the truth or certainty of something.

contemporary (kən-tĕm´pə-rĕr´ē) adj. coming from the same time period.

contrary (kŏn´trĕr´ē) adj. opposite or opposed in character or purpose.

definitely (dĕf´ə-nĭt-lē) adv. in an exact, certain, or precise way.

denote (dĭ-nōt´) v. to mean something specific; to name.

deny (dĭ-nī´) v. to refuse to see or to allow; to reject.

device (dĭ-vīs´) n. a literary technique used to achieve a certain effect; something made for a specific purpose.

displace (dĭs-plās´) v. to move or force from one place or position to another.

dynamic (dī-năm´ĭk) adj. characterized by change, movement, or activity.

format (fôr´măt´) n. the organization or arrangement of parts in a whole.

founder (foun´dər) n. someone who sets up, establishes, or provides the basis for something.

global (glō´bəl) adj. relating to the world as a whole.

ideological (ī´dē-ə-lŏj´ĭ-kəl) adj. based on ideas, beliefs, or doctrines.

implicit (ĭm-plĭs´ĭt) adj. not directly stated or obviously apparent.

infinite (ĭn´fə-nĭt) adj. without end or beyond measure.

publication (pŭb´lĭ-kā´shən) n. the act of making public in printed or electronic form; the product of this act.

quote (kwōt) v. to cite something word for word.

revise (rĭ-vīz´) v. to change or alter a text; reconsider.

revolution (rĕv´ə-lōō´shən) n. the overthrow and replacement of a government, often through violent means.

simulated (sĭm´yə-lā´tĭd) adj. imitating something real.

somewhat (sŭm´wŏt´) adv. to a limited extent.

topic (tŏp´ĭk) n. the subject of a piece of writing or speech.

unify (yōō´nə-fī´) v. to bring together into a cohesive whole.

unique (yōō-nēk´) adj. one of a kind; unable to be compared.

virtual (vûr´chōō-əl) adj. existing in essence or in a digital version but not in actual fact.

Glossary of Critical Vocabulary

abandonment (ə-băn´dən-mĕnt) *n.* a lack of restraint or inhibition.

abdicate (ăb´dĭ-kāt´) *v.* to relinquish or cede responsibility for.

abject (ăb´jĕkt´) *adj.* miserable and submissive.

abound (ə-bound´) *v.* occur or exist in great number.

affect (ə-fĕkt´) *v.* to cause or influence.

aggregate (ăg´rĭ-gĭt) *adj.* combined.

algorithm (ăl´gə-rĭth´əm) *n.* instructions carried out in a specific sequence.

anomalous (ə-nŏm´ə-ləs) *adj.* unusual.

apportionment (ə-pôr´shən-mənt) *n.* distribution.

apprehension (ăp´rĭ-hĕn´shən) *n.* fear or anxiety; dread.

arrogate (ăr´ə-gāt´) *v.* to assume authority unjustly.

ascendant (ə-sĕn´dənt) *adj.* rising in influence; on an upward path.

ascendancy (ə-sĕn´dən-sē) *n.* a rise in power or influence.

atrocious (ə-trō´shəs) *adj.* evil or brutal.

autonomy (ô-tŏn´ə-mē) *n.* freedom from control; independence.

avert (ə-vûrt´) *v.* to turn away.

belatedly (bĭ-lā´tĭd-lē) *adv.* done too late or overdue.

blatantly (blāt´nt-lə) *adv.* in an offensively obvious, unashamed manner.

burgeoning (bûr´jən-ĭng) *adj.* rapidly increasing or growing.

caliber (kăl´ə-bər) *n.* level of ability.

capacity (kə-păs´i-tē) *n.* ability to hold or have somthing; function or role.

cardinal (kär´dn-əl) *adj.* most important; prime.

catalyst (kăt´l-ĭst) *n.* a substance that starts or speeds up a reaction.

cede (sēd) *v.* to yield or give away.

circulate (sûr´kyə-lāt´) *v.* to move or travel around or in a circular path.

circumvent (sûr´kəm-vĕnt´) *v.* to bypass or go around.

cleave (klēv) *v.* stick or adhere.

composed (kəm-pōzd´) *adj.* self-possessed; calm.

comprise (kəm-prīz´) *v.* contain.

congenial (kən-jēn´yəl) *adj.* agreeable; pleasant.

conjure (kŏn´jər) *v.* to produce from nothing, as if by magic.

copious (kō´pē-əs) *adj.* extensive.

cull (kŭl) *v.* to take from a large quantity.

defection (dĭ-fĕk´shŭn) *n.* the abandonment of one social or political group in favor of another.

deforestation (dē-fôr´ĭ-stā´shən) *n.* deliberate cutting down and clearing of trees and forests.

delinquency (dĭ-lĭng´kwən-sē) *n.* shortcoming or misbehavior.

denote (dĭ-nōt´) *v.* to name or give meaning to.

deprecate (dĕp´rĭ-kāt´) *v.* to express disapproval.

deteriorate (dĭ-tîr´ē-ə-rāt´) *v.* become worse; decline.

diligence (dĭl´ə-jəns) *n.* consistent, thorough effort and dedication.

disclaim (dĭs-klām´) *v.* to deny one's connection to; to distance oneself from.

discord (dĭs´kôrd´) *n.* disagreement or conflict.

disposition (dĭs´pə-zĭsh´ən) *n.* character or temperament.

disputatious (dĭs´pyə-tā´shəs) *adj.* argumentative; confrontational.

dissipation (dĭs´ə-pā´shən) *n.* wasteful self-indulgence.

distinction (dĭ-stĭngk´shən) *n.* difference in quality.

divergence (dĭ-vûr´jəns) *n.* a difference or variation.

divers (dī´vərz) *adj.* numerous.

efficacy (ĕf´ĭ-kə-sē) *n.* effectiveness.

elusive (ĭ-lōō´sĭv) *adj.* difficult to find.

emblem (ĕm´bləm) *n.* an identifying mark or symbol.

enclave (ĕn´klāv´) *n.* a distinct area within a larger area.

engross (ĕn-grōs´) *v.* to completely engage the attention or interest.

establish (ĭ-stăb´lĭsh) *v.* to formally set up; institute.

evidently (ĕv´ĭ-dənt-lē) *adv.* plainly, or obviously apparent from evidence or data.

evince (ĭ-vĭns´) *v.* reveal or give evidence of.

expedience (ĭk-spē´dē-əns) *n.* a self-interested means to an end.

extrapolation (ĭk-străp´ə-lā´shŭn) *n.* an estimate based on known information.

extremity (ĭk-strĕm´ĭ-tē) *n.* the outermost or farthest point or portion; the hand or foot.

façade (fə-säd´) *n.* false or misleading appearance.

faction (fak´shən) *n.* an organized subgroup that disagrees with the larger group as a whole.

factor (făk´tər) *n.* component or characteristic.

fecundity (fĭ-kŭn´dĭ-tē) *n.* fertility, productive capability.

ferment (fûr´mĕnt´) *n.* a state of violent, unpredictable change.

flux (flŭks) *n.* continual shift or change.

formidable (fôr´mĭ-də-bəl) *adj.* difficult and intimidating.

harbinger (här´bĭn-jər) *n.* a person or thing that signals a future occurrence.

illumination (ĭ-lōō´mə-nā´shən) *n.* awareness or enlightenment.

imminent (ĭm´ə-nənt) *adj.* about to happen; impending.

imperative (ĭm-pĕr´ə-tĭv) *adj.* of great importance; essential.

impose (ĭm-pōz´) *v.* to charge or apply.

indeterminate (ĭn´dĭ-tûr´mə-nĭt) *adj.* not precisely known.

infinitesimal (ĭn´fĭn-ĭ-tĕs´ə-məl) *adj.* extremely small; microscopic.

infringe (ĭn-frĭnj´) *v.* to interfere with; violate.

ingenious (ĭn-jēn´yəs) *adj.* cleverly inventive.

injunction (ĭn-jŭngk´shən) *n.* court order forbidding a specific action.

insuperable (ĭn-sōō´pər-ə-bəl) *adj.* impossible to overcome.

intangible (ĭn-tăn´jə-bəl) *adj.* unable to be defined or understood.

invest (ĭn-vĕst´) *v.* to grant or endow.

invocation (ĭn´və-kā´shən) *n.* prayer or incantation.

latent (lāt´nt) *adj.* underlying, hidden.

license (lī´səns) *n.* unacceptably unrestrained behavior.

lucid (lōō´sĭd) *adj.* easily understood.

mitigate (mĭt´ĭ-gāt´) *v.* to lessen.

mundane (mŭn-dān´) *adj.* ordinary; commonplace.

nascent (nā´sənt) *adj.* emerging; developing.

nemesis (nĕm´ĭ-sĭs) *n.* a bringer of destruction, often as vengeance.

oblige (ə-blīj´) *v.* to force or require.

obstinacy (ŏb´stə-nə-sē) *n.* stubbornness.

ostensibly (ŏ-stĕn´sə-blē) *adv.* seemingly or outwardly.

ostentatious (ŏs'tĕn-tā'shəs) *adj.* conspicuous and vulgar.

pale (pāl) *n.* boundary or enclosed area.

patent (păt'nt) *n.* an official document granting ownership.

pathos (pā'thŏs') *n.* something that evokes pity or sympathy.

perennial (pə-rĕn'ē-əl) *adv.* enduring; long-lasting.

pertinacity (pûr'tn-ăs'ĭ-tē) *n.* firm, unyielding intent.

perturbation (pûr'tər-bā'shən) *n.* disturbance or agitation.

pervade (pər-vād') *v.* to spread or exist throughout.

petulance (pĕch'ə-ləns) *n.* childish annoyance; sulkiness.

plaintive (plān'tĭv) *adj.* expressing sadness or sorrow.

plausibility (plô'zə-bĭl'ĭ-tē) *n.* likelihood; believability.

posterity (pŏ-stĕr'ĭ-tē) *n.* future generations.

precarious (prĭ-kâr'ē-əs) *adj.* unstable; uncertain.

precipitate (prĭ-sĭp'ĭ-tāt') *v.* to cause to occur suddenly.

predominant (prĭ-dŏm'ə-nənt) *adj.* most important or prevalent.

prescribe (prĭ-skrīb') *v.* to authorize or regulate.

pristine (prĭs'tēn') *adj.* pure or unspoiled.

project (prə-jĕkt') *v.* to communicate or put forth.

prostrate (prŏs'trāt') *adj.* lying down with the head facing downward.

protrude (prō-trōōd') *v.* to stick out or bulge.

provision (prə-vĭzh'ən) *n.* food supply.

purport (pər-pôrt') *v.* to claim or pretend to be the case.

quicken (kwĭk'ən) *v.* to make alive or stimulate.

rampant (răm'pənt) *adj.* uncontrolled; without any restraint.

reciprocal (rĭ-sĭp'rə-kəl) *adj.* mutual or shared.

regimen (rĕj'ə-mən) *n.* a system or organized routine of behavior.

rendezvous (rän'dā-vōō') *n.* meeting place.

reproach (rĭ-prōch') *n.* a disgrace or a bad example.

resonance (rĕz'ə-nəns) *n.* richness of meaning; the ability to evoke emotion.

rudiment (rōō'də-mənt) *n.* basic form.

sceptical (skĕp'tĭ-kəl) *adj.* having doubts or reservations.

scrupulous (skrōō'pyə-ləs) *adj.* thorough and diligent.

sentinel (sĕn'tə-nəl) *n.* a lookout person or guard.

settlement (sĕt'l-mənt) *n.* a small community in a sparsely populated area.

stem (stĕm) *v.* to grow from or be caused by.

stoically (stō'ĭk-lē) *adv.* without showing emotion or feeling.

subtlety (sŭt'l-tē) *n.* nuance; fine detail.

succession (sək-sĕsh'ən) *n.* an ordered sequence.

succour (sŭk'ər) *n.* help and comfort.

sundry (sŭn'drē) *adj.* various or assorted.

supplant (sə-plănt') *v.* to take the place of.

supposition (sŭp'ə-zĭsh'ən) *n.* a belief or assumption.

systematize (sĭs'tə-mə-tīz') *v.* to form something into an organized plan or scheme.

taciturn (tăs'ĭ-tûrn') *adj.* uncommunicative, withdrawn.

tangentially (tăn-jĕn'shəl-lē) *adv.* indirectly or peripherally connected.

tender (tĕn'dər) *v.* to offer or present.

tepid (tĕp'ĭd) *adj.* lukewarm; indifferent.

timidity (tĭ-mĭd´ĭ-tē) *n.* showing a lack of courage or confidence.

transcend (trăn-sĕnd´) *v.* to go beyond the limits or become independent of.

transient (trăn´zē-ənt) *adj.* temporary; short-term.

transition (trăn-zĭsh´ən) *n.* process of change.

tumultuous (tŏo-mŭl´chŏo-əs) *adj.* stormy, intense.

turbulence (tûr´byə-ləns) *n.* an unsettled or changeable state.

ubiquitous (yŏo-bĭk´wĭ-təs) *adj.* existing everywhere at once.

unalienable (ŭn-āl´yə-nə-bəl) *adj.* impossible to be taken away.

unfathomed (ŭn-făth´əmd) *adj.* located at the deepest place.

untenable (ŭn-tĕn´ə-bəl) *adj.* unsustainable, insupportable.

vacant (vā´kənt) *adj.* blank, expressionless.

venture (vĕn´chər) *v.* to risk or dare.

volatile (vŏl´ə-tl´) *adj.* liable to change suddenly or evaporate.

wring (ring) *v.* to obtain through force or pressure.

Index of Skills

Key:

Teacher's Edition page numbers and subject entries are printed in **boldface** type.
Subject entries and page references that apply to both the Student Edition and the Teacher's Edition appear in lightface type.
There is no content from the Close Reader in this index.

A

abolitionist movement, 277
abstract language, 214
abstract nouns, R23
absurdity (element of satire) **375**, 379
Academic Vocabulary, 2, 103, 108, 170, 174, 268, 271, 276, 328, 406, 410, 602, 606
accept/except, R59
act (in play), R61
actions, of characters, 462, 468, 479
action verbs, R24, R33
active voice, **6**, 22, R35
activities
  media activity, 126, 168, 585
  speaking activity, 76, 101, 118, 158, 165, 185, 196, 247, 263, 282, 312, 316, 372, 380, 399, 486, 544, 566
  writing activity, 20, 33, 70, 75, 85, 94, 128, 148, 165, 205, 218, 231, 266, 292, 299, 322, 348, 357, 370, 394, 404, 435, 444, 454, 526, 541, 579, 600
adaptations, 298, **545**
adjective clauses, R42–R43
adjective phrases, R40
adjectives, R24, R36
  vs. adverbs, R36
  comparatives, R36–R37
  compound, 150
  hyphenated, 150
  predicate, R36
  proper, R29
  superlatives, R36–R37
adverb clauses, R43
adverb phrases, **517**, R40–R41
adverbs, **510**, R24, R36
  vs. adjectives, R36
  comparatives, R36–R37
  conjunctive, R39
  superlatives, R36–R37
advice/advise, R59
A&E® (Arts and Entertainment), 37, 167, 411
affect/effect, R59
affirmative side, in debates, R15
affixes, 206
African American writers, 412, 438–439
ain't, R55
allegory, R61
alliteration, **41**, 69, **206**, R61
all ready/already, R59
all right, R55
allusion/illusion, R59
allusions, **8, 11**, 19, **22a, 60**, 85, 158, **286, 294, 318, 319**, 321, 322, **322b, 598**, 599, **600a**, R61
ambiguity, **159, 160, 161**, 164, **166a**, 247, **248a, 446, 447, 450, 452**, 453
ambiguous references, R33
American literature
  colonial period, 109–110, 151–158
  early, 4

Gothic, 263, 266, R69
  of Harlem Renaissance, 438–442, 444
  historical accounts, 5–19
  modern, 411, R72
  muckraking journalism, 330
  naturalism, 330, 347, 348, 350, 404
  19th century, 175–176
  realism, 347, 350, 372
  regionalism, 330
  Romanticism, 176, 234, 247, 263, 266, R77
  slave narratives, 277
Americas, exploration and settlement of, 3–4
among/between, R59
analogies, R54, R61. *See also* metaphors; similes
  analyzing, **228, 571**, 578, 579
  arguments from, 594
  between central ideas, 218
  false, R20
analysis
  of debate, writing, 273
  media activity, 585
  thesis statement, R4
  writing activity, 205, 231, 266, 526
analytical essays
  draft of, 406
  elements of effective, 405
  exchanging with partner, 407
  organization, 406
  Performance Task Evaluation Chart, 408
  planning, 405–406
  revising, 407
  writing, 405–408
analyzing
  arguments, 281, R16–R17
  author's choices, **342, 352, 354, 355**, 356
  author's point of view, 291, 578
  author's purpose, **35a, 62, 140a**, 298, **379, 382a**
  drama, 72, 75, 486, 504, 526, 540, 541, 544, 547
  events, 147, 195, 311
  foundational documents, 19, **112, 113, 115**, 117, **121, 122, 123, 124**, 125, 128, **167**, 168
  foundational texts, 5, 7, 8, 11, 12, 13, 14, 15, 16
  historical accounts, 19
  ideas, **141, 143, 144, 145**, 147, **150a, 187, 188, 190, 193**, 195, **233b, 296, 300a, 301, 302, 303, 304, 305, 306, 307, 308, 309, 310**, 311
  interpretations of dramas, 72, 75, 544, 547
  key terms, 6, 15
  language, **10, 14, 16, 39, 40, 41, 42, 43, 44, 45, 46, 47, 49, 50, 52, 53, 54, 55, 56, 57, 58, 59, 60, 61, 62, 63, 65, 66, 67**, 69, **70a, 97, 98, 99**, 100, **128a, 129, 130, 131, 133, 135, 136, 137, 144, 146,**

151, 152, 153, 155, 156, 187, 188, 189, 191, 192, 194, 200, 201, 202, 204, **208, 227, 240, 285, 289, 294, 318, 319**, 321, **322b, 333, 339, 341, 359, 361, 362, 363, 364, 365**, 369, **374, 376, 377, 382a, 401, 402, 424, 427, 428, 430, 440, 444a, 446, 447, 450, 452**, 453, **597, 598**, 599, **600a, 600b**
media activity, 585
motivation, 434
poetry, 101, 158, 180, 182, 183, 185, 200, 201, 202, 203, 205, 322, 404, 444, 453, 454, 599, 600, **600b**
point of view, **159, 161, 162, 163**, 164, **186a, 316a**
purpose, 12
speeches, 291, 292
story elements, **413, 414, 415, 416, 417, 418, 419, 421, 422, 423, 429, 430, 431, 432, 433, 434, 581, 583**, 584
structure, **9**, 77, 79, 80, 81, 83, 84, 87, 88, 89, 90, 91, 92, 93, 112, 113, 114, 115, 116, 117, **141, 142, 143, 145**, 147, **159, 160, 161, 162, 163**, 164, **166a, 176a, 178, 179, 181, 182**, 184, **190, 220a, 221, 222, 223, 224, 225, 226, 228, 229**, 230, **233a, 236, 238, 239, 240, 241, 243, 245, 246**, 247, **248a, 249, 250, 251, 252, 254, 255, 256, 257, 258, 259, 260, 261, 262**, 263, **266b, 284a, 317, 318, 319, 320**, 321, **322a, 331, 332, 333, 334, 335, 336, 337, 338, 339, 340, 342, 343, 344, 345, 346**, 347, **350a, 400a, 402, 403**, 404, **404a, 416, 417, 418, 420, 423, 426, 430, 431, 437a, 446, 447, 448, 449, 451, 452**, 453, **455a, 588, 589, 591, 592**, 594
style, 117, 196, **294**
suffixes, 512
Supreme Court decisions, 565, 566
text, **76a**, 579, 585, 594, 600
themes, 85, 117, **158a, 278a**
thesis statement, R4
topics, 158a
word choice, 582, 583
writing activity, 205, 231, 266, 526
Analyzing the Media, 168
Analyzing the Text, 20, 33, 70, 85, 94, 101, 118, 126, 128, 138, 148, 158, 165, 178, 180, 182, 183, 185, 196, 200, 201, 202, 203, 205, 218, 231, 247, 263, 266, 282, 292, 299, 312, 316, 322, 348, 357, 370, 372, 380, 399, 404, 435, 444, 454, 486, 504, 526, 541, 566, 579, 585, 594, 600
Analyzing the Text and Media, 72, 75, 76, 394, 544, 547, 548
anapest, R72
anaphora, **377, 382**, R61

Anchor Texts, **5A, 111A, 177A, 221A, 279A, 331A, 413A, 456A**
anecdotes, 88, 93, R61
Annotate It!, 19, 20, **21**, 32, 33, **34**, 69, 70, **79, 84**, 85, **86, 93**, 94, **95, 100**, 117, 118, **125**, 126, **137**, 138, **145, 147**, 148, **149, 157**, 158, **164**, 165, **166, 184**, 185, **195**, 196, **197, 204**, 205, **217**, 218, **219, 225, 230**, 231, **232, 246**, 247, **248**, 263, **264, 281**, 282, **291**, 292, **294, 298, 299, 300, 310, 311**, 312, **313, 321**, 322, **335, 347**, 348, **349, 356**, 357, **363, 367**, 369, 370, **371, 379**, 380, **381, 387**, 394, **398, 403**, 404, **419, 428, 434**, 435, **436, 443**, 444, **450, 453**, 454, **467**, 486, 504, 526, **540, 541, 542, 554, 565**, 566, **567, 578**, 579, **584**, 585, **586, 592**, 594, **595, 599**, 600
antagonist, **508, 516**, 526, R61
antecedent, R30
  pronoun agreement with, R30–R31
antihero, R61
antithesis, **289**, 294
anti-transcendentalists, 176
antonyms, 436, **557**, R53
aphorism, R61
apostrophe, R27–R28
appeals
  by association, R17, R61
  to authority, R61
  bandwagon, R17
  emotional, R17, R66
  logical, R71
  to loyalty, R17
  to pity, fear, or vanity, R17, R66
Applying Academic Vocabulary, 9, 13, 24, 40, 78, 88, 92, 98, 113, 124, 130, 142, 152, 160, 179, 188, 193, 200, 208, 211, 223, 236, 250, 286, 296, 302, 309, 318, 333, 344, 353, 361, 374, 385, 392, 396, 415, 439, 452, 459, 545, 550, 570, 582, 588
appositive phrases, R41
appositives, R41
approximate rhyme, 206
archaic language, **5, 9, 16, 22a, 39, 162**, 257, 305, 469, 516
archaic vocabulary, 21
archetypes, R61
argumentative essays, 87–92, 103–106, 230, 601–604. *See also* arguments
argumentative perspective, 233b
arguments
  from analogy, **588, 589, 591, 592**, 594
  analyzing, **233a**, 281, **300a**, R16–R17
  body of essay, 104
  building, 602
  claims, 93, 137, 281, 299, 566, 601, R2
  conclusions to, 104, **158a**, R3
  counterarguments, 272, 602, R2, R16
  for debate, 272

intrinsic ethos, 291
introduction, of arguments, 104
inverted sentences, **182,** R47
irony
   analyzing, 165, **333, 339, 396, 397, 400a,**
     524
   author's purpose and use of, **87, 88, 89,**
     91, 92, 93, **96a,** 388
   contrast as, 85, 370
   definition of, R70
   dramatic, 398, 486, R70
   and meaning, 93
   sarcasm, R77
   and satire, 379
   situational, **146,** 398, R70
   types of, 398
   understatement, R81
   verbal, **87,** 398, R70
irregular verbs, R34
italics, R28

J

jargon, R5
ject, 300
journal, R70
journal entries, 20
juxtaposition, 176a

K

key terms, 137
   analysis of, 6, 15
   defining, 130, 133
keywords, 166a, 168b
kinesthetic imagery, R70
Knowledge Demands. *See* **Text Complexity**
   Rubric

L

language, 16
   abstract, 214
   ambiguous, 453
   analyzing, **10, 14, 16, 39, 40, 41, 42, 43,**
     44, 45, 46, 47, 49, 50, 52, 53, 54, 55,
     56, 57, 58, 59, 60, 61, 62, 63, 65, 66,
     67, 69, **70a,** 97, 98, 99, 100, **128a,** 129,
     130, 131, 133, 135, 136, 137, 144, 146,
     151, 152, 153, 155, 156, 187, 188, 189,
     191, 192, 194, 200, 201, 202, 204,
     208, 227, 240, 285, 289, 294, 318,
     319, 321, **322b,** 333, 339, 341, 359,
     361, 362, 363, 364, 365, 369, 374,
     376, 377, **382a,** 401, 402, 424, 427,
     428, 430, 440, **444a,** 446, 447, 450,
     452, 453, 597, 598, 599, **600a, 600b**
   archaic, 22a, 39, **162,** 257, 305, **469,** 516
   biased, R5, R21
   colloquial, 455
   figurative, **23,** 32, **44,** 69, 100, 175, **186a,**
     187, 200, 208, 217, 218, 291, **401, 440,**
     450, 475, 479, 489, 494, 599, R49,
     R68
   free verse, 100
   humor of, R69
   informal, 217, 455
   jargon, R5
   literal, **175**
   loaded, R21, R71

propaganda, R21, R76
   sensory, R7
   Shakespearean, 69
   supporting, 74
   technical, 233b
   understanding, 295
   verb tenses, **77**
   vivid, R7
Language and Style
   active and passive voice, 22
   anaphora, 382
   balanced sentences, 284
   colon use, 96
   comparing writers' styles, 568
   consistent tone, 350
   crafting effective sentences, 437
   dashes, 371
   dependent (subordinate) clauses, 35
   dialogue, **527, 528,** 542
   formal style, 127
   hyphenation, 150
   informal style, 127, 455
   informative writing, 596
   misplaced modifiers, avoiding, 314
   parallel structure, 120, 186, 382
   point of view, 166
   quotations, 233
   rhetorical devices, 294
   rhetorical questions, 220
   semicolons, 265
   syntax in poetry, 102
   transitions, 140
   varying sentence structure, 198
Language Conventionality and Clarity. *See*
   Text Complexity Rubric
language conventions, 22. *See also*
   Language and Style
Latin prefix *circum-,* 95
Latin root *ject,* 300
lay/lie, R60
leave/let, R59
lecture, speaking activity, 380
legal reasoning, **552,** 565
legal terminology, 567
legend, **10,** R70. *See also* myths
less/fewer, R59
letters
   literary, R71
   open, R73
   writing activity, 20, 435
Levels of Meaning/Purpose. *See* **Text**
   Complexity Rubric
lie/lay, R60
lighting, 72, 75, **545,** 547
like, R55
limited narrator, **159,** 164, 398
limited point of view, 395
line, R70–R71
linking verbs, R24, R33
lists, colons before, 96, R27
literal language, 175
literally, R56
literary ballads, R62
literary criticism, **225,** 230, 231, R71
literary devices
   alliteration, 69, R61
   allusion, 19, 85, 158, 294, 321, 322, 599, R61

assonance, R62
   cliché, R64
   figurative language, 32, 69, 70, 100, 204,
     217, 218, 291, R49, R68
   foreshadowing, R68
   hyperbole, 218, R69, R81
   idioms, 599, R49, R70
   imagery, 32, 100, 158, 184, 356, 599, R70
   irony, 85, 93, 165, R70, R81
   metaphors, 100, 184, 185, 204, 217, R72
   onomatopoeia, R73
   oxymoron, R74
   personification, 201, 217, 599, R74
   repetition, 19, 117, 180, 184
   rhetorical questions, 220, 294, R77
   sarcasm, R77
   similes, 32, 184, 217, R78
   symbolism, 184, 247, R80
literary letters, R71
literary nonfiction, **110a, 330a,** R71
   examples, 5–18, 87–92, 112–116,
     121–124, 129–136 141–146,
     187–194, 207–216, 221–229,
     279–280, 285–290, 295–297,
     373–378
   literary texts, 37–68, 77–83, 97–99, 152–153,
     154, 155–156, 159–163, 177–183,
     200–203, 235–246, 249–262, 317–320,
     331–346
literature. *See also* American literature;
   fiction; literary texts
   comprehending, 110a
   European, 176, 234
   Gothic, **236,** 263, 266
   modern, 411, R72
   naturalism in, 330, 347, 348, 350, 404
   oral, R73–R74
   realism in, 347, 350, 372
   Romanticism, 176, 234, 247, 263, 266, R77
loaded language, R21, R71
local color realism, R71
logic
   analyzing, in arguments, R18–R20
   circular, R19
logical appeals, R71
logical arguments, R71
logical conclusions, 22a
logical fallacies, R19–R20, R71
logical reasoning, 131
logos, **287,** 291
loose/lose, R60
loyalty, appeals to, R17
-ly, 212
lyric poetry, **206a,** R71

M

magazine articles, citing, R11
magical realism, R71
main characters, R63
main idea, **150a, 294a, 372a,** R71. *See also*
   central ideas; thesis statement
main verb, R25
manifest destiny, 175
A Manual for Writers (Turabian), R9
may/can, R55
media, **76a, 168b, 383.** *See also* film; video
   analyzing, 72, 75, 76, 168, 394, 544, 547

comparing with text, 543–548
media activity
   analysis, 585
   presentation, 126, 168, 504, 594
Media Analysis, 71, 167, 315, 543
medium, 168a, 383
memoirs, R71–R72
metaphors, **44,** 100, **179,** 184, 185, **201, 210,**
   213, 214, 217, **289, 382a, 440,** 443, **501,**
   520, 531, R72
   extended, 204, **214,** 444, R67
meter, 69, R72, R77
Mexican–American War, 175
middle English, R53
mimicking style, 378
minor characters, R63
mise en scène, R72
misplaced modifiers, avoiding, 314
missions, 4
MLA citation guidelines, R10–R11
MLA Handbook for Writers of Research
   Papers (MLA), R9
Modeled Discussions, 5, 111, 121, 177, 221,
   279, 331, 413, 457
moderators, debate, **248a,** R14
modern drama, 456
modern English, R53
modernism, R72
Modern Language Association (MLA), R9
modern literature, 411
modifiers, **401,** R35
   adjectives, R36
   adverbs, R36
   comparisons, R36
   dangling, R38
   definition of, 314
   misplaced, 314, R37–R38
   problems with, R37–R38
monitor, R72
monologue, R72
monometer, R72
mood, 341, 465, R72
motivations, of characters, **413, 414, 416,**
   417, 418, 421, 422, 423, 429, 430, 431,
   432, 433, 434, 437b, 479, R63, R72
muckrakers, 330
multimedia links, R5
multimedia presentations, 126, **314a,** 504,
   594
multiple-meaning words, **154,** 204, 293,
   338, R54
   in context, 359
   understanding, 178, 373, 458, 483, 495,
     518, 525, 527
multiple plot lines, R7
musical score, 315
*my*Notebook, 103, 169, 267, 271, 405, 601,
   605
myths, R72
*my*WriteSmart, 72, 75, 76, 101, 104, 105,
   128, 170, 171, 269, 272, 282, 292, 312,
   322, 348, 357, 370, 372, 394, 399, 404,
   406, 407, 435, 454, 486, 504, 526, 541,
   544, 547, 566, 579, 594, 600, 602, 603,
   606, 607

narrative, **448,** 453, **455a,** R73
19th century, 176–183, 199–203
odes, R73
parallelism in, 186
pastoral, 411
personification in, 201
Petrarchan sonnet, 444
quatrain, R76
refrain, R76
repetition, 180, 184
rhyme, R77
rhythm, 321, R77
scansion, R77
similes in, 184
sonnet, R78
speaker in, R79
stanza, R79
structure, 184, 321, 453
summarizing, 444
symbolism in, 180, 184
syntax, 102
textual details, 157
theme in, 157, 443
topic of, 157, 443
point-by-point organization, 146
point of view, 85, R75
analyzing, **159, 161, 162, 163,** 164, **186a,** 291, **316a,** 398, 578
author's, **224, 226,** 291, **294a,** 398, **400a,** 578, **580a**
establishing, R6
first-person, 164, 166, R75
limited, 395
omniscient, 245, 395
opposing, 227
second-person, **159, 161,** 164, 166, **223**
third-person, 164, 166, **187,** 357, **395,** 398, R75
writing from another, **346**
policy statements, R14
political pamphlets, 110
political science, 119
pollution, 412
possessives, **66, 505**
nouns, R23, R30, R58
pronouns, R31
Practice and Apply, 4a, 22a, 70a, 76a, 86a, 96a, 110a, 128a, 140a, 150a, 158a, 176a, 186a, 198a, 206a, 220a, 233a, 233b, 248a, 266a, 266b, 278a, 284a, 294a, 300a, 322b, 330a, 372a, 382a, 394a, 400a, 404a, 437b, 444a, 455a, 542a, 568a, 580a, 586a, 596a, 600a
precede/proceed, R60
precise claims, 158a
precise usage (vocabulary strategy), 436
precise words and phrases, 437
predicate
adjectives, R36
complete, R25
compound, R40
nominatives, R40, R47
nouns, R40
pronouns, R40
predictions, **577,** R75
prefixes, 206, **277,** 358, **376, 462, 560, 569,** 595, R50, R57–R58
circum-, 95

premises, 137, 138, **140a, 279, 280,** 281, **284a**
prepositional phrases, **314, 395,** R25, R38, R40–R41
prepositions, R24, R38
presentations
media activity, 168, 504, 585, 594
multimedia, 126, **314a,** 504, 594
oral, 101
present participles, R33–R34
present perfect progressive tense, R35
present perfect tense, R34
present principal part, R33–R34
present progressive tense, R34
present tense, R34
primary sources, 16, 19, R8, R75, R79
prior knowledge, **568a,** R75–R76
problems, identifying, in writing narratives, R6
problem-solution order, R76
progressive movement, 330
prologue, R76
pronouns, **10,** R23, R30
antecedent agreement, R30–R31
cases, R31
demonstrative, R24, R32
indefinite, R24, R32, R46–R47
intensive, R23, R32
interrogative, R24, R32
nominative, R31
objective, R31
personal, 166, R23, R30, R46
possessive, R31
predicate, R40
reference problems, R33
referents, 50, 55, 111, 132, 352, 506, 536
reflexive, R23, R31–R32
relative, R24, R32–R33, R43, R48
pronunciation, 283
pronunciation key, R83
propaganda, R21, R76
proper adjectives, R29
proper nouns, R23, R30
propositions, R14
props, R76
prose, R76
protagonists, **508, 514,** 526, R76
proto-English, R52
public documents, R76
Declaration of Independence, 111–116
Declaration of Sentiments, 295–299
punctuation
apostrophes, R27–R28
colons, 96, R27
commas, R26
dashes, **253,** 371, 437, **509, 521,** R27
effective use of, 446
ellipses, 102, R28
exclamation points, 437, R26
hyphenation, 150
hyphens, R27
parentheses, R27
periods, R26
question marks, R26
quick reference, R26–R28
quotation marks, R28
semicolons, 265, R26–R27
unconventional, 206a

punctuation cues, 199, 222
Puritans, 244
purpose, 19
analyzing author's, **8, 12, 13, 14, 193,** 298, **306,** 311, **314a, 383, 384, 385**
of argument, **129,** 137
determining author's, 32, 93, 195, **198a,** 217, 356, 369
of documentary, 168a, 168b
evaluating, **279, 280,** 281, **284a,** 370
filmmaker's, 315
of foundational documents, **122,** 125, 128
supporting, 188
of writing, 35a

Q

quantitative information, 386, 387, 391
quatrains, R76, R78
question marks, R26
questions
research, R8
rhetorical, **135, 208,** 220, 294, R77
quotation marks, R28
quotations, **209, 215**
direct, R9
introducing, with colon, 96, R27
use of, 233

R

readers' theater, 544
reading
dialogue, 58
echo, 61
fluency of, 116, 192, 283, 432, 451, 463, 519, 534, 598
independent, 116
persuasive texts, R16–R22
strategies for, 110a
support for, 6, 384
realism, 330, **331, 332, 333, 334, 335, 336, 337, 338, 339, 340, 342, 343, 344, 346,** 347, 350, **350a,** 372, **390,** R76
local color, R71
reasoning
circular, R19
deductive, 291, R18–R19, R65
faulty, R19–R20
inductive, 291, R18, R70
reasons
in arguments, **140a, 198a,** 281
to support claims, R2
rebuttals, in debates, R14–R15
Reconstruction era, 277–278
recurring themes, R80
reenactments, 315
references
cultural, 460
text, 477
reference works, R76
bibliographies, R62
dictionaries, 149, R56
general, 149
glossaries, R56
for preferred and contested usage, R55–R56
specialized, 149, R56
synonym finders, R56
thesaurus, 436, R56

using, 119, 149, R56
reflexive pronouns, R23, R31–R32
refrain, R76
regionalism, 330, R76
regular verbs, R33–R34
relative pronouns, R24, R32–R33, R43, R48
repetition, **12,** 19, **22a, 113,** 117, **120, 131, 179,** 180, 184, **296,** 382, 437, R77
rereading, 76, 101, 102, 105, 117, **128a,** 148, **155,** 157, 169, 196, 218, 292, 348, 399, 400, 407, 435, 454, 486, 504, 541, 548, 568, 579
research
conducting, **472, 513, 542a,** R8–R9
focus of, R8
formulating question for, R8
genre, 539
historical detail, 304
independent, 433
poet's attitudes, 18
project, 266a, 322b
short, 394a
techniques for, 307
on web, 102a, 166a, 168b, 266a
research questions, 166a, 542a, R8
research report, writing activity, **233a,** 579
resolution (plot), **345, 400a, 452,** 504, **539, 542a,** R64, R67, R75. *See also* falling action
resources, 128a
results analysis, 166a
Reteach, 35a, 70a, 76a, 86a, 96a, 102a, 140a, 150a, 158a, 166a, 168b, 186a, 198a, 220a, 233a, 233b, 248a, 266b, 284a, 294a, 300a, 314a, 316a, 322a, 322b, 350a, 372a, 382a, 394a, 400a, 404a, 437a, 437b, 444a, 455a, 542a, 548a, 568a, 580a, 586a, 596a, 600b
reviews, film, 72
Revolutionary War, 109
rhetoric, 93, 291
persuasive, 167
rhetorical devices, 131, 285
rhetorical features, **8,** 19, **22a, 112, 113, 115, 116,** 117, **121,** 125, 128, **278a,** 294, 298, 578
rhetorical questions, **135, 208,** 220, **285,** 294, R77
rhyme, R77
approximate, 206
slant, R78
rhyme scheme, R77
rhythm, **317, 318, 319, 320,** 321, **322a,** R77
rising action, R75, R77
Romanticism, 176, 234, **235, 236, 237, 238, 239, 240, 242, 243, 244, 246,** 247, **249, 250, 252, 253, 254, 259, 261, 262,** 263, 266, **266b**
roots, R50
determining meaning from, **90, 122,** 358
Latin root *ject,* 300
rough drafts. *See* drafts
run-on sentences, R45

S

sarcasm, R77
satire, **374, 375, 376, 377, 378,** 379, R77
Scaffolding for ELL Students, 3, 6, 10, 14,

subject-verb agreement, R45–R48
tenses, **42, 77, 143, 191, 337,** R34–R35
transitive, R24
video, 167, 392. *See also* film
  analyzing, 168, 316
  citing, R11
  evaluating, 394
  to present information, 393
**View It!, 2, 5, 23A, 77A, 87A, 97A, 103,
108, 111A, 111, 121, 129A, 159A, 169,
174, 177A, 177, 221, 267, 271, 279,
285A, 295A, 323, 328, 331, 405, 410,
413A, 457, 549A, 587A, 601**
visualizing, R81
vivid language, R7
vocabulary
  Academic Vocabulary, 2, 103, 108, 170,
    174, 268, 271, 276, 328, 406, 410, 602,
    606
  **Applying Academic Vocabulary, 9, 13,
24, 40, 78, 88, 92, 98, 113, 124, 130,
142, 152, 160, 179, 188, 193, 200,
208, 211, 223, 236, 250, 285, 296,
302, 309, 318, 333, 344, 353, 361,
374, 385, 392, 396, 415, 439, 452,
459, 545, 550, 570, 582, 588**
  archaic vocabulary, 21
  commonly confused words, R59–R60
  Critical Vocabulary, **5, 6, 8, 9, 12, 14,** 21,
**23, 24, 25, 26, 29, 30, 31, 34, 77, 79,
80, 81, 83,** 86, **87, 88, 89, 90, 91,** 95,
112, 114, 119, **121, 122, 124, 127, 129,
130, 131, 132, 133, 135, 136,** 139, **142,
143, 144, 145, 146,** 149, **161, 162,** 166,
187, 188, 190, 191, 197, **209, 210, 211,
213, 215,** 219, **222, 223, 224, 226,
227, 229,** 232, **237, 238, 242, 243,
244,** 248, **250, 251, 252, 253, 258,
262,** 264, **279, 280,** 283, **286, 289,**
293, **296, 297,** 300, **302, 304, 305,
308,** 313, **331, 333, 338,** 349, **352, 353,
358, 359, 361, 363, 365, 368,** 371, **373,
374, 375, 381, 395, 396, 397,** 400, **415,
417, 419, 420, 422, 423, 427, 433,**
436, **549, 552, 553, 554, 558, 563,**
567, **569, 571, 572, 573,** 580, **581, 582,**
586, **587, 588, 592, 593,** 595.
  specialized vocabulary, 34, **35a, 128a,**
    369, R55
  strategies for understanding, **16, 219,
264, 313, 349,** R49–R56
Vocabulary Strategy
  affixes, 206
  archaic vocabulary, 21
  consulting general and specialized
    reference works, 149
  context clues, 86, 219, 264, 313, R49–R50
  Critical Vocabulary, 149
  domain-specific words, 119
  etymology, 349, 580
  evaluating nuances in meaning, 139
  Latin prefix *circum-*, 95
  Latin root *ject*, 300
  legal terminology, 567
  multiple-meaning words, 293
  nuances in word meanings, 248, 381, 586
  parts of speech, 232

patterns of word changes, 197, 595
precise usage, 436
pronunciation, 283
specialized vocabulary, 34
word collocations, 400
word families, 358
voice, **6,** 22, R81
voice expression, 544
volume, 544

W

War of 1812, 175
websites, R81
westward expansion, 175
**When Students Struggle, 4, 8, 12, 18, 25,
27, 30, 41, 46, 52, 56, 58, 61, 64, 67,
82, 89, 99, 110, 114, 123, 131, 134, 153,
155, 161, 162, 176, 180, 183, 189, 192,
201, 203, 209, 214, 224, 228, 238, 242,
251, 254, 255, 259, 261, 278, 283, 287,
289, 297, 303, 308, 319, 330, 334, 336,
341, 345, 354, 360, 364, 375, 377, 386,
391, 397, 402, 416, 420, 427, 430, 441,
451, 456, 460, 463, 465, 470, 474, 478,
481, 485, 489, 493, 498, 501, 508, 511,
519, 524, 530, 533, 534, 537, 551, 552,
558, 561, 564, 571, 575, 583, 589, 591,
598**
who/whom, R56
**Why This Text?, 3A, 5A, 23A, 36A, 71A,
77A, 87A, 97A, 109A, 111A, 129A,
141A, 151A, 159A, 167A, 175A, 177A,
187A, 199A, 207A, 221A, 234A, 249A,
277A, 279A, 285A, 295A, 301A, 315A,
317A, 329A, 331A, 351A, 373A, 383A,
395A, 401A, 413A, 438A, 445A, 456A,
543A, 549A, 569A, 581A, 587A, 597A**
word choice, 148, 196, **202,** 204, 291, 350,
  356, 542, 568, 578, 600
  analysis of, 582, 583
word collocations, 400
word families, 358, R52
word maps, 349
word meanings
  determining, 32, 119, 219, 264, 313
  nuances in, 139, **241,** 248, 381, 586
word origins, R51–R52
words
  analysis of, 128a, 597
  associations in, 54, 280
  choice of, 45, 206, 381
  commonly confused, 555
  **determining meaning of, 23, 25, 26, 27,
28, 29, 30,** 32
  hyphenated, 587
  inverted order of, 182
  meaning of, 26, 29, 32, 233b
  **multiple-meaning, 154, 178, 202, 338,
359, 373, 458, 483, 495, 518, 525, 527**
  nuances in meaning of, 96a, 248, 586
  patterns of change in, 197, 595
  roots of, 90, 122
  with similar spellings, 488
word webs, 95, 300, 358, 595
workplace documents, R82
works cited, R9, R10, R82
works consulted, R82

World War I, 411
World War II, 411
writing
  analytical essays, 405–408
  arguments, **158a, 600a,** 601–604, R2–R3
  complete sentences, R44–R45
  drafts, 104–105, 170, 269, 406
  essays, 169–172, 405–408, 601–604,
    R4–R5
  informative essays, 169–172, R4–R5
  narratives, **266a,** 267–270, R6–R7
  purpose of, 35a
  research project, 322b
  research report, 233a
writing activity
  analysis, **102a,** 205, 231, 266, 526
  argument, 33
  captions, 75, 548
  comparison, 299
  description, 404
  diagram, 547
  discussion, 165
  dramatic monologue, 85
  essay, 128, 148, 218, 322, 394, 444, 541
  evaluation, 94
  exploratory essay, 70
  interview summary, 454
  journal entries, 20
  letters, 20, 435
  narrative, 348, 370
  news articles, 357
  outline and summary, 292
  research report, 579
  reviews, 72
  summary, 600
writing style. *See* Language and Style; style

Index of Titles and Authors

Key:

Authors and titles that appear in the Student Edition are in lightface type.
Authors and titles that appear in the Close Reader are in **boldface** type.
Names of authors who appear in both the Student Edition and the Close Reader are lightface. For these authors, Student Edition page references are lightface and Close Reader page references are **boldface**.

Student Edition Acknowledgments

"Against Nature" by Joyce Carol Oates originally published in *The Ontario Review,* 1986. Text copyright © 1986 by The Ontario Review. Reprinted by permission of John Hawkins & Associates, Inc.

Excerpt from *The American Heritage Dictionary of the English Language, Fifth Edition.* Text copyright © 2011 by Houghton Mifflin Harcourt. Adapted and reprinted by permission of Houghton Mifflin Harcourt Publishing Company.

"Balboa" from *Tales of the New World* by Sabina Murray. Text copyright © 2011 by Sabina Murray. Reprinted by permission of Grove/Atlantic Inc.

"Because I could not stop for Death" from *The Poems of Emily Dickinson* by Emily Dickinson, Thomas H. Johnson, ed. Text copyright © 1951, 1955, 1979, 1983 by the President and Fellows of Harvard College. Reprinted by permission of Harvard University Press and the Trustees of Amherst College.

"A Black Man Talks of Reaping" from *Personals* by Arna Bontemps. Text copyright © 1963 by Arna Bontemps. Reprinted by permission of Harold Ober Associates, Inc.

"'Blaxicans' and other Reinvented Americans" by Richard Rodríguez from *The Chronicle of Higher Education,* September 12, 2003. Text copyright © 2003 by Richard Rodríguez. Reprinted by permission of Georges Borchardt, Inc., on behalf of the author.

"Building the Transcontinental Railroad" from *The Chinese in America: A Narrative History* by Iris Chang. Text copyright © 2003 by Iris Chang. Reprinted by permission of Viking Penguin, a division of Penguin Group (USA) Inc.

"The Coming Merging of Mind and Machine" from *Scientific American* by Ray Kurzweil, March 23, 2009. Text copyright © 2009 by Scientific American, a Division of Nature America, Inc. Reprinted by permission of Scientific American.

Excerpt from "Coming of Age in the Dawnland" from *1491: New Revelations of the Americas Before Columbus* by Charles C. Mann, first published in Great Britain by Granta Books. Text copyright © 2005 by Charles C. Mann. Reprinted by permission of Alfred A. Knopf, a division of Random House, Inc., Granta Books and Ward & Balkin Agency on behalf of the author. Any third party use of this material, outside of this publication, is prohibited. Interested parties must apply directly to Random House, Inc. for permission.

The Crucible by Arthur Miller. Text copyright © 1952, 1953, 1954, renewed © 1980, 1981, 1982 by Arthur Miller. Reprinted by permission of Viking Penguin, a division of Penguin Group (USA) Inc. and The Wylie Agency, Inc.

"The Death of the Hired Man" by Robert Frost from *The Poetry of Robert Frost*, edited by Edward Connery Lathem. Text copyright © 1930, 1939, 1969 by Henry Holt and Company, LLC. Text copyright © 1958 by Robert Frost. Text copyright © 1967 by Lesley Frost Ballantine. Reprinted by permission of Henry Holt and Company, LLC.

"The Ends of the World as We Know Them" by Jared Diamond from *The New York Times*, January 1, 2005. Text copyright © 2005 by The New York Times. Reprinted by permission of PARS International on behalf of the New York Times. All rights reserved.

Excerpt from *Fast Food Nation* by Eric Schlosser. Text copyright © 2001 by Eric Schlosser. Reprinted by permisison of Random House Audio, a division of Random House, Inc., Houghton Mifflin Harcourt Publishing Company and Penguin Books Ltd. Any third party use of this material outside of this publication is prohibited. Interested parties must apply directly to Random House, Inc. for permission.

"The Fish" from *The Complete Poems 1927-1979* by Elizabeth Bishop. Text copyright © 1979, 1983 by Alice Helen Methfessel. Reprinted by permission of Farrar, Straus and Giroux, LLC.

"From the Dark Tower" by Countee Cullen. Text copyright © 1927, 1947 by Countee Cullen. Reprinted by permission of Thompson and Thompson.

"Growing Up Asian in America" by Kesaya E. Noda from *Making Waves: An Anthology of Writings By and About Asian American Women,* edited by Asian Women United of California. Text copyright © 1989 by Asian Women United of California. Reprinted by permission of Asian Women United of California.

"The Lowest Animal" from *Letters from the Earth* by Mark Twain, edited by Bernard DeVoto. Text copyright © 1938, 1944, 1946, 1959, 1962 by The Mark Twain Company. Text copyright © 1942 by The President and Fellows of Harvard College. Reprinted by permission of HarperCollins Publishers.

"Mending Wall" by Robert Frost from *The Poetry of Robert Frost*, edited by Edward Connery Lathem. Text copyright © 1930, 1939, 1969 by Henry Holt and Company, LLC. Text copyright © 1958 by Robert Frost. Text copyright © 1967 by Lesley Frost Ballantine. Reprinted by permission of Henry Holt and Company, LLC.

"Much madness is divinest sense" from *The Poems of Emily Dickinson* by Emily Dickinson, Thomas H. Johnson, ed. Text copyright © 1951, 1955, 1979, 1983 by the President and Fellows of Harvard College. Reprinted by permission of Harvard University Press and the Trustees of Amherst College.

"New Orleans" from *She Had Some Horses* by Joy Harjo. Text copyright © 2008, 1983 by Joy Harjo. Reprinted by permission of W. W. Norton & Company, Inc.

From *Of Plymouth Plantation, 1620-1647* by William Bradford, edited by Samuel Eliot Morison. Text copyright © 1952 by Samuel Eliot Morison. Text copyright renewed © 1980 by Emily M. Beck. Reprinted by permission of Alfred A. Knopf, a division of Random House, Inc. Any third party use of this material, outside of this publication, is prohibited. Interested parties must apply directly to Random House, Inc. for permission.

"Reality Check" from *Nature*, March 16, 2000 by David Brin. Text copyright © 2000 by Nature Publishing Group. Reprinted by permission of Copyright Clearance Center on behalf of Nature Publishing Group.

Excerpt from "Reflection on the Atomic Bomb" by Gertrude Stein. Text copyright © 1946 by Gertrude Stein. Reprinted by permission of David Higham Associates Ltd.

"Runagate, Runagate" from *Collected Poems of Robert Hayden* by Robert Hayden, edited by Frederick Glaysher. Text copyright © 1985 by Erma Hayden. Reprinted by permission of W. W. Norton & Company, Inc.

"A Soldier for the Crown" from *SoulCatcher and Other Stories* by Charles Johnson. Text copyright © 1998 by Charles Johnson. Reprinted by permission of Charles Johnson and WGBH Boston.

"Song of the Son" from *Cane* by Jean Toomer. Text copyright © 1923 by Boni & Liveright. Text copyright renewed © 1951 by Jean Toomer. Reprinted by permission of Liveright Publishing Corporation, a division of W. W. Norton & Company.

"The Soul selects her own society" from *The Poems of Emily Dickinson* by Emily Dickinson, Thomas H. Johnson, ed. Text copyright © 1951, 1955, 1979, 1983 by the President and Fellows of Harvard College. Reprinted by permission of Harvard University Press and the Trustees of Amherst College.

"Tell all the truth but tell it slant" from *The Poems of Emily Dickinson* by Emily Dickinson, Thomas H. Johnson, ed. Text copyright © 1951, 1955, 1979, 1983 by the President and Fellows of Harvard College. Reprinted by permission of Harvard University Press and the Trustees of Amherst College.

"Thomas Jefferson: The Best of Enemies" by Ron Chernow from *Time Magazine*, July 5, 2004. Text copyright © 2004 by Time, Inc. Reprinted by permission of Time, Inc.

"The Universe as Primal Scream" from *Life on Mars* by Tracy K. Smith. Text copyright © 2011 by Tracy K. Smith. Reprinted by permission of Graywolf Press.

Close Reader Acknowledgments

Excerpt from "Abigail Adams' Last Act of Defiance" by Woody Holton from *American History* Magazine, April 2010. Text copyright © 2010 by Woody Holton. Reprinted by permission of Weider History Group.

"Ambush" from *The Things They Carried* by Tim O'Brien. Text copyright © 1990 by Tim O'Brien. Reprinted by permission of Houghton Mifflin Harcourt Publishing Company, HarperCollins Publishers, Ltd. and Tim O'Brien.

"Bonding Over a Mascot" by Joe LaPointe from *The New York Times*, December 29, 2006, *www.nytimes.com*. Text copyright © 2006 by The New York Times Company. Reprinted by permission of PARS International, on behalf of The New York Times.

Excerpt from "Act 1" from *The Crucible* by Arthur Miller. Text copyright © 1952, 1953, 1954, renewed 1980, 1981, 1982 by Arthur Miller. Reprinted by permission of Viking Penguin, a division of Penguin Group (USA) Inc. and The Wylie Agency, Inc.

Excerpt from "The General History of Virginia" by John Smith from *The Complete Works on Captain John Smith, 1580-1631,* edited by Philip L. Barbour. Text copyright © 1986 by The University of North Carolina Press. Reprinted by permission of The University of North Carolina Press.

"Indian Boy Love Song (#2)" from *The Business of Fancydancing* by Sherman Alexie. Text copyright © 1992 by Sherman Alexie. Reprinted by permission of Hanging Loose Press.

"Mother Tongue" from *The Opposite of Fate* by Amy Tan. Text copyright © 1989 by Amy Tan. First appeared in Threepenny Review. Reprinted by permission of the Sandra Djikstra Literary Agency and the author.

"Ode to a Large Tuna in the Market" by Pablo Neruda, translated by Robin Robertson from *Poetry* Magazine. Text copyright © 2011 by the Fundacion Pablo Neruda. Reprinted by permission of the University of California Press and the Agencia Literaria Carmen Balcells.

Excerpt from "Reflection on the Atomic Bomb" by Gertrude Stein. Text copyright © 1946 by Gertrude Stein. Reprinted by permission of David Higham Associates Ltd.

"Science, Guided by Ethics, Can Lift Up the Poor" (Retitled: "Science, Guided by Ethics") by Freeman Dyson from *The New York Times,* May 29, 2000, www.nytimes.com. Text copyright © 2000 by The New York Times Company. Reprinted by permission of PARS International, on behalf of The New York Times.

"Spoiling Walden: Or How I Learned to Stop Worrying and Love Cape Wind" by David Gessner from *ONEARTH* Magazine, December 12, 2011, *www.onearth.com*. Text copyright © 2011 by David Gessner. Reprinted by permission of the National Resources Defense Council.

"The Weary Blues" from *The Collected Poems of Langston Hughes* by Langston Hughes, edited by Arnold Rampersad with David Roessel, Associate Editor. Text copyright © 1994 by the Estate of Langston Hughes. Reprinted by permission of Alfred A. Knopf, a division of Random House, Inc., and Harold Ober Associates, Inc. Any third party use of this material, outside of this publication, is prohibited. Interested parties must apply directly to Random House, Inc. for permission.

"The Yuckiest Food in the Amazon" by Mary Roach from *Salon,* December 15, 1998, *www.salon.com*. Text copyright © 2012 by Salon Media Group, Inc. Reprinted by permission of Salon Media Group, Inc.